NAXAL AND MAOIST TERROR IN INDIA

NAXAL AND MAOIST TERROR IN INDIA

VOLUME - I

EXPANDING RED CORRIDOR

Col. Ved Prakash

KALPAZ

ISBN : 978-93-5324-031-8 (Vol - I)
978-93-5128-212-9 (Set)

First Published, 2019

Published by

Kalpaz Publications
C-30, Satyawati Nagar,
Delhi – 110052
Ph.: 011-47034999, 9811692060
www.kalpazpublications.com
E-mail: kalpaz@hotmail.com

Printed at: G. Print Process, Delhi

Cataloging in Publication Data—DK
Courtesy: D.K. Agencies (P) Ltd. <docinfo@dkagencies.com>

Prakash, Ved, *Col.*, author.
Naxal and Maoist terror in India / Col. Ved Prakash.
volumes cm
Contents: volume I. Expanding red corridor — volume II. Combating Maoism — volume III. Development of Naxal infected regions — volume IV. Chhattisgarh and Jharkhand — volume V. Odisha and West Bengal.
ISBN 9789351282129 (set)

1. Naxalite movement—India. 2. Communism—India. 3. Communist Party of India-Maoist. 4. India—Politics and government—1947- I. Title.

LCC HX393.5.P73 2019 | DDC 320.532093 23

Contents

Volume - IV

Chhattisgarh and Jharkhand

(*Series Page No. 915-1408 See Below*)

Volume - V

Odisha and West Bengal

(*Series Page No. 1409-1808 See Below*)

Introduction

As far as the Left-Wing Extremism (LWE) goes, Naxalbari, a non-descript village in the Darjeeling district of West Bengal, can be deemed to be the first letter of its script. Of course, there was some violence in Hyderabad and its surrounding areas saw certain anti-landlord agitation, but that was too momentary to be called a movement. In that sense, Naxalism, the term derived from the Naxalbari, is the original. LWE flowed from it.

The Naxalism had its Holy Trico: Charu Mozumdar, Kanu Sanyal and Jangal Santhal. Before describing their personalities, a brief look at their creation, the baby called 'Naxalism'. The trio had been creating consciousness among the poor peasantry and tribal population about their explotation by the landlords and the rich moneyed class. The Three were indeed sure that they were working to bring revolution in their area, defined by the region that fell under the jurisdiction of three police stations: Naxalbari, Kharibari and Phansidewa. Some 65 per cent poplation of the region was SC and ST, working as agriculture labour or in mines, forests and plantations. A small percentage owned small holdings, the vast majority cultivating under the agency system (bagh Chash). Expectedly, the Bagh Chashis were exploited by *the Joteders*. The practice and Conditions, produced large-scale grievances and frustration, over the long time—waiting for a spark. The Holy Trinity mentioned above proved the agents of the spark. The preiri fire was lit on 24 May 1967, the day police were informed about some leaders of the Naxalbari (the term 'Naxal' had not yet been brought in use till then) movement hiding in Boro Jhorojote Village. Infact, there were no leaders there, only a gathering of peasants and tea garden workers. One police officer was killed in the violence that followed the police action. Kanu Sanyal explains in the 20 May 2007 interview that "it is 24 May 1967 they celebrate as a victory of our ideas" as that day indicated that the peasantry and workers understood "understood and accepted our politics and took up arms on their own". On the other hand, the other groups observe 25 May (1967) as the Martyrs day since 11 persons were killed in the police firing that day.

It is important to emphasise the intellectual perception about the very first important day in the history of their movements. Two different commemorations of the Naxalbari day (24 and 25 May) is as good an indicator as any about the ideological thinking among the leadership at that very early stage of their movement. Individually and intellectually strong minds find it so very difficult to accept even a mutually-agreed date to commemorate their victory day! It is no surprise, therefore, that within a couple of years of the May 1967 'Revolution', thre were a half-a-dozen groups among the Naxals. And the trend has continued till date in the annals of LW movement.

The two-years long struggle was led by a radical group of CPI (M) Siliguri unit. Charu Mozumdar was the key ideologue, Kanu Sanyal was among the leading organisers, and Jangal Santhal mobilized the Adivasis. By 1969, this group had split from the CPI (M) and formed the CPI (ML). It needs to be said that this merging and splitting has continued throughout. Incidentally, there are more Marxist-Leninist Parties (New Democracy, Liberation, Janashakti, Kanu Sanyal Group, Mahadadeb Mukherjee Group, to name some among them) than the Cadre.

Now, a sad story. They had created CPI (ML) but it did not make much headway during Charu's lifetime, and for that matter, even after his demise in sep. 1971. Ironically, Kanu Sanyal did not find any leadership position in CPI (ML), their very own creation.

Charu was a Chrismatic, but mercurial genius. But some critics hold he lacked vision. In May 2007 interview, Kanu said "Charu's annihilation of class enemy line" was a historical mistake. He went beyond that: "It was a fundamental deviation from Marxism-Leninism and thoughts of Mao"

Sanyal's biggest regret was that he did not speak up on certain issues that he felt could harm the movement, at the right time. There were several reasons: one, he was a fugitive and speaking out would mean compromising his security and place and direction of the movement. He also feared that some of Charu's blind supporters would harm him physically. So it is obvious that during the Naxal struggle, there were differences within the Party.

A significant event for them was the meeting of a Naxal delegation lead by Sanyal with Mao in Peking on 2 Oct. 1967. It was a 45 minute meeting. He advised them: "whatever you learn in China, try to forget it. Go to your own country, try to understand the specific situation and carry the revolution forward.

It should be noted in 1967, the Naxalbari insurrection made China's People's Daily go ballistic, one analyst prefers the adjective 'Orgiastic' in its 5 Jul editorial: "A peal of spring thunder has crashed over the land of India....under the leadership of a revolutionary group of the Indian Communist Party red arc of rural revolutionary armed struggle has been established in India. The spark in Darjeeling will start a prairie fire and will certainly set the vast expanses of India ablaze."

In May 2007, Kanu Sanyal was the only surviving member of the Trinity, and he was ailing and frail. But the 78-years old General Secretary of the Original CPI (ML) living in one-room party office in Hatigisha and sleeping on floor, still remained committed to the revolution through mass struggle.

After persistent persuasion, he agreed to an authorized biography, something no communist leader from Namboodripad, through Jyoti Basu to Harkishan Singh Surjeet ever allowed. But unfortunately, he did not live to see the final draft. Seven days before he committed suicide (on 23 Mar 2010), Sanyal Called the author Bappaditya Paul to ask about the progress of the book. When told that he was doing the last chapter, he asked him twice whether "I needed anything more."

The Naxalite movement might have been suppressed in four years, but it had its longterm effect. It resulted in the re-distribution of land among the peasantry. In political terms, the formation of the CPI (ML) was an important land mark. After all, this was the event, an important milestone, on way to the ultimate emergence of the CPI (Maost), the Scourge India is still grappling with. Its spread has been discussed in detail in this book, as also counter-measures to control and subsequently eliminate it.

A personal note is called for at this stage. The author, a soldier, felt duty-bound to visit the house of Charu Mozumdar in Naxalbari. It was nothing short of a pilgrimage. One may not agree with his methods, but he felt strongly for the poor masses and went all out to alleviate their sufferings A salute was due to him. The details are to be found in the text.

The counter-Maoist endeavour has been fought by the UPA II and NDA II governments, with varying degree of commitment and persistence. Prime Minister Manmohan Singh called it "the most serious threat to the internal security of the country". Cynics are prone to say that is his only contribution to the fight against Maoists! This may not be far off the mark for the simple reason that he failed to guide his ministers to frame a coherent counter-Maoist policy. Various Home Ministers had their own fancy ideas about dealing with these "killers". If one was a "root cause" man, other was more practical. But the latter was thwarted by loud if foolish politicos like Digvijay Singh. The NDA II has a more effective approach: Development with security. Its Home Minister Rajnath Singh declared in 2014: "Maoists menace will be eradicated in five years". It has achieved fair measure of success, but still no where near the target after 4 years period of their 5-year term!

This book's contents are a little different than is usually the case! A lot of material has been included on a single event from various published sources. It should be of some help and relevance to future scholars for their research on the subject in question. A good number of analytical pieces have also been added to its pages as further help to researchers on the subject they are working on.

Ironically, this book is dedicated to Kishenji, a daredevil Maoist leader, but not to Mupalla Lakshman Rao, 63 Years in 2013, the top gun of the Maoists, their General Secretory, popularly known as Ganapathy. He carries an award of Rs. 2.52 Cr on his head.

Now, why Kishenji? For whatever reasons, this author has certain high admiration for this dare devil Maoist leader, dedicating an entire Chapter (8) to him (and his comrade).

His name is Mollojula Koteshwar Rao. Like so many other senior Maoist leaders, he too has many aliases Most commonly used, and the popularly one, was kishenji, besides Prahalad and Baswaraj Ramji. The 55 year old, yet again, like (Ganapathy) belongs to Karimnagar district of AP, played a major role in merger of PWG and MCC to create CPI (Maoist). He was looking after West Bengal, and is part now, as he was killed on 25 Nov. 2011.

He was most Charismatic of the Maoist leader. May be, he played with fire too aften in the past, and on 25 Nov. 2011, it was one too many.

It was not surprising that some one in the strategic community of India dubbed him as the 'Bin Laden' of India.

One can only imagine what people like him, and that Maoist mastermind behind the manufacturing of their weaponry Tech Madhu, could achieve in this country had they remained in the mainstream! Sky would have been the limit in their case! For such genius, ideological convictions outweigh all other options!

Let us admit that India did not produce its own Mao Tse Tung or Ernesto Che Guevara, nor an equivalent of 'Diaries of a Bike Rider' and thank God for that.

India has faced threats, external and internal, to its integrity and sovereignty from its very birth on 15 Aug. 1947. In fact, to put the record straight, Phizo Angami, The Naga leader, declared independence for Nagas on 14 Aug. 1947. The country faced rebellion from the Mizos too in India North-East. Then there was Pakistan aggression in Oct 1947 in Jammu and Kashmir. Last came threat to the internal integrity of India with the LWE. While the troubles in the North-East are nearly over, the LWE is under control and its expanse has been reduced to 60 districts in the country from 165 at its worst. As for the J and K, ambers are still hot, being fanned, vigorously, by Pakistan and its army, with religious fanaticism. One thing ought to be stressed, India is too big an too powerful to go under with such 'pinpricks'!

This book would have served its purpose if it helps some people to understand the meaning of threat posed to India by the Maoists and some academics in their research.

1

Left-Wing Extremism: International Scene

Violence is the essential and main tool of the Left-Wing Extremism (LWE) if not the only one. In other words, it is terrorism of a different strain. It is obvious that a brief understanding and hence a discussion is called for on the subject of terrorism.

Terrorism and Guerrilla Warfare

The encyclopedia explains terrorism as the systematic use of terror (read violence) such as bombings, killings and kidnappings, as a means of forcing some political objectives. "When used by a government, it may signal efforts to stifle dissent; used by insurrectionists or guerrillas, it may be part of an overall efforts to effect desired political change."

Terrorists can't fight the government forces on equal footing. So, they resort to guerrilla warfare, which is a type of warfare characterised by irregular forces, fighting small scale limited actions against orthodox military forces. Guerrillas are usually non-descript in dress, un-conventional in weapons and equipment, lack formal supply lines and employ highly unorthodox tactics. In addition to extremely mobile, aggressive operations, these tactics embrace all aspects of psychological warfare, including the use of sabotage and terrorism.

Although this type of warfare occurs throughout history, the word guerrilla (the diminutive of Spanish ***guerra***, "war") stems from the Duke of Wellington's Iberian Campaigns (1809-13), during which Spanish-Portuguese irregulars or ***guerrilleros*** (also referred to at the time as partisans and insurgents), helped drive the French from the Peninsula. In World War II, the word partisan became synonymous with guerrilla; later, the word insurgent came into vogue. Guerrilla Warfare is by tradition a weapon of protest employed to rectify real or imagined wrongs levied on a people in the context of the subject of this book, by the ruling government.

Guerrilla Warfare: A History

The importance of guerrilla warfare has varied considerably through history. After World War II, it came to play a significant role in what has been termed revolutionary or insurgency warfare or what Communists call people's wars and wars of national liberation.

Since World War II, guerrilla warfare has been employed by non-Communist insurgencies in countries such as Indonesia, Cyprus and Algeria where it was successful and by communist insurgencies in Malaya and the Philippines, where it ultimately failed. In a complementary role, in which the guerrilla force first fights independently and later evolves into an orthodox insurgent army, it has been successfully employed by Communist insurgencies in China, Indonesia and Cuba.

One can go farther back into history. The genesis of guerrilla warfare, however is found in the American Revolution, during which the colonists, many of them veterans of Indian fighting, formed loosely-knit bands of riflemen that practiced highly unorthodox tactics against the formally trained British Redcoats. In 1780-81, one of the former Indian fighters, Francis ("the Swamp Fox") Marion, organised a ragtag group of guerrillas that complemented orthodox warfare in South Carolina by continual devastating raids in the rear of British General Charles Cornwallis/Lines.

A far more important role was played by effectively commanded guerrilla bands in the long war fought by Wellington on the Iberian Peninsula against Spanish and Portuguese guerrilla: They made life miserable for the French armies by completely disrupting their lines of communication- ("by blocking the roads, or Interrupting couriers and convoys and even waging regular war.") A book on the campaign goes further: "Numbering no more than 20,000 and despites their weakness in the open field, their intestine quarrels, their frequent oppression of the countryside and their ferocity, they rendered good service, by pinning down twice their own numbers of good French troops".[1]

Another examples is of Napoleon suffering heavily from guerrilla strikes during the long retreat from Moscow. Bands of Russian peasants, working with mounted Cossacks, harassed the French until they have been driven out.

Guerrilla warfare, in both its independent and complimentary roles, has been employed extensively since the time of Napoleon. A striking example of the protest role of guerilla warfare is the Taiping Rebellion

(1850-64) in China. Begun by impoverished peasants and by jobless coolie porters, opium, smugglers and pirates, the unsuccessful rebellion against the Manchu dynasty cost an estimated 20,000,000 lives and, in the opinion of some sinologists, constituted one of the great social upheavals of modern times.

There are also instances of guerilla actions during independence struggle/movements of various countries. Lesser but nonetheless significant guerilla actions were fought against the British in India and Africa, the French and Spanish in Morocco, the Turks and Austro-Hungarians in the Balkans and the Americans during the opening of the West.[2] Some names in the pantheons of Indian guerrilla fighters are: Khudi Ram Bose, Chandra Shekhar Azad, Bhagat Singh, Raj Guru, Sukhdev and Ashfaqullah.

In 1899-1900, the Boxer Rebellion in China constituted a protest action against a foreign invader (in the form of the Western powers whose influence, ironically has grown as a result of the Taiping Rebellion), as did both the Philippine insurrection (1890-1902), in which the guerillas ultimately lost to America regulars, and the South African War (1899-1902), in which the Afrikaners quickly abandoned orthodox tactics in favour of highly mobile, irregular operations undertaken by mounted groups called Commandos, which the British regulars defeated only with the greatest difficulty.

The most successful guerilla leader in the American Civil War was a confederate cavalry officer John Mosley, who leading a small band of mounted volunteers, effectively disrupted Union operations by his constant, dashing raids in Northern Virginia. Mexican guerillas led by Emiliano Zapata and Pancho Villa played a leading role in the Mexican Revolution.

Due to static nature of the World War I, there was no scope for guerilla warfare on the Western front but subsidiary theaters offered scope for it. In the Middle East, a British officer, TE Lawrence, led a revolt of Arab tribesmen in a prolonged guerilla action that claimed the lives of some 35000 Turkish soldiers and resulted in another 35,000 captured and wounded. The guerillas finished the War in control of some 1,00,000 Sq miles, a significant contribution to the British victory in Palestine. In German East Africa (modern Tanzania), a German officer, Lt Col Lettow Vorbeck, led a small force of German regulars supplemented by a few hundred tribesmen in a holding operation against much larger British forces, which could have been used on the Western front. Although bereft of supplies and physically exhausted, the group had still not surrendered when the war ended.

A guerrilla war, characterised by the most brutal terroristic killings and ambushes, lasted till 1921. Five years of this war paved the way for Irish Independence, less the Northern Ireland. The latter saw a lot of violence by the Irish Republican Army (IRA) in the recent decades. It was working for the reunifications of Ireland. In 1993 the Irish and British Governments worked out a peace plan to resolve the issue. After some hiccups, the IRA too, on 20 July 1997, declared an "unequivocal" ceasefire.

During the interwar period, the Communist Party in China (CPC) and its army under Mao Tse-tung fought the invading Japanese and after World War II, wrested control of the country from Chiang Kai Sheik's Nationalist Government. In some countries the Communist guerrilla forces formed in World War II facilitated the quick establishment of Communist regimes. In Yugoslavia the take over of the Government by Marshal Tito was simple and direct, while in some other cases, such as Czechoslovakia and China, it was complicated and delayed. In Vietnam; the party under Ho Chi Minh took years to unite the country. He was the President (1954-69). In Malaya and the Philippines; it was foiled "with strong-hand tactics".

In Latin America, failure of several attempts to emulate the guerrilla campaign that resulted in the overthrow of the Batista regime in Cuba in 1959 led to the concentration on revolutionary activity within the cities, or urban guerrilla warfare, as it came to be termed. "The extent to which the intermittent bombings and kidnappings in such countries as Brazil, Argentina, Guatemala and Venezuela indicate the discipline, organisation and overall strategy that are the hallmark of guerrilla warfare ramain uncertain." This was the situation in 1980s and 1990s. But presently, there are a number of countries like Venezuela which are flaunting the success of their socialist regimes.

Iconic Guerrilla Leaders

As of today, two names come to mind when we think of iconic figures in the field of guerrilla warfare: Mao Tse-tung and Ernesto Chi Guevara. Equally importantly, both are well known for not only waging successful guerrilla war in their respective regions, but also being thinkers and theoreticians of this "art"!

Somewhere along the line Guevara seems to have stolen a march on the equally venerable Mao. Somehow, the former has became a more 'romantic' figure in this particular art of war. It will be discussed a little later.

Mao Tse-tung (1893-1976)

Mao has a doctrine coined from his name which composed of the ideology and methodology developed by Mao, leader of the Chinese Communists from the 1920s and of the People's Republic of China (PRC) from its inception in 1949. Maoism has clearly represented a revolutionary method based on distinct revolutionary outlook not necessarily dependent on a Chinese or Marxist-Leninist context.

Principal Chinese Marxist theorist, soldier and statesman, Mao led the revolution that established his nation as one of the twentieth century's foremost Communist's states.

As a student, Mao was attracted to Western revolutionary leaders and the nationalistic ideas of Sun Yatsen. He enlisted in the revolutionary army in Hunan (1911) during the first rebellion against the Manchu dynasty. At Peaking University (1919) he participated in the May Fourth Movement of students. Disillusionment with Western liberalism led him to espouse the Leninist-Marxist thought of the Chinese Communist Party. He organised Communist guerrilla army units, mainly peasants enlisted as the core of the revolutionary forces (1924-25), while publicly promoting a united front with Gen Chiang Kai- Shek's Nationalist Party. He later broke with Chiang and in 1934-35 led an army of 200,000 from south-eastern China (Kiangsi) to the north-western mountain in a strategic retreat known as the Long March. During the period (1936-40) he wrote the *Strategic Problem of China's Revolutionary War* and *On New Democracy*. He instituted (1942) the Rectification Campaign, adapting Marxism to Chinese culture. His victory over Nationalists at Nanking (April 1949) was decisive and Communist PRC was established. Mao became the Chairman of the Communists party and of the Republic.

The Great Leap forward, begun in the autumn of 1957, attempted to decentralize the economy. He retired (1959) as Chairman of the Republic but remained Chairman of the party and reasserted his control in the upheavel known as Cultural Revolution, which began in 1966 and did not officially end until 1976.

Although the cult of Chairman Mao and the Mao's thought continued, Mao's final years were spent in declining health and virtual seclusion. A word on "Mao Tse-tung Thought Propaganda Teams".

> These communist teams were established during the early years of the cultural Revolution (1966-76) to manage educational institutions and influence the political education of students and teachers. The teams intended to inculcate the Chinese people with the ideology of

Mao Tse-tung (known as Mao's thought, particularly as compiled in *Quotations from Chairman Mao Tse-tung* (1966)).

While on Mao, it needs to be stated that China under him did everything to export revolution to neighbouring countries, especially to India, aimed at destabilising a potential rival. China not only supplied weapons to Indian rebels like Nagas and Mizos, but also invited them to China to be trained and equipped by Mao's guerrillas. Yet again, Naxal leaders visited China in 1967 via Kathmandu, and they were granted an audience with Chairman Mao.

Before moving on to Guevara, a word is in order to talk about their respective theatres of operations. If Mao, understandably, brought revolution to China, Guevara's canvass was much broader; after Cuba, he wanted to spread his revolution to all the countries in the South American Continent. He became a legend after his killing by the Bolivian army!

Ernesto Che Guevara

A prominent figure in the Cuban revolution of the 1950's and 1960's and an important official in Fidel Castro's first Communist government in Cuba, Che Guevara exerted an important influence on the theory and tactics of guerrilla warfare.

Ernesto Guevara de la Serna was born in Rosario, Argentina on 14 June 1928. The eldest of five children in the middle class family of Spanish-Irish descent and leftist leanings, he was known for his dynamic and radical views even as a boy. Though suffering from the attacks of asthma that were to handicap him throughout his life, he excelled as an athlete and a scholar completing his medical studies in record time in March 1953. He spent his holidays travelling in Latin American Countries. The great poverty he observed during these travels convinced him that the only solution lay in violent revolution. He was also convinced that Latin America was not a collection of separate nations but a cultural and economic entity, the liberation of which would require inter-continental strategy.

During 1953, Guevara visited Guatemala where Jacobo Arbenz headed progressive regime. He was attempting a social revolution through land reforms. The overthrow of Arbenz regime in a coup supported by the CIA in 1954 persuaded him that the USA would always oppose progressive leftist governments in Latin America and in other developing countries of the world. This conviction, which he later expressed in many speeches and writings, became the cornerstone of his plans to bring about Socialism through a world revolution.

It was in Guatemala (1953) that Guevara acquired his nickname, from a verabal mannerism of Argentineans who punctuate their speech with the interjection *che.*

From Guatemala he went to Mexico (1954) where he met Cuban brothers Fidel and Raul Castro, political exiles who were preparing to return to Cuba with an expeditionary force aiming to overthrow the dictatorship of Fulgencio Batista. Guevara joined Castro's force and began to train for guerrilla warfare. On 25 November 1956, he and 81 other young men left Mexico on the yacht "Gran ma" and landed in the Cuban Province of Oriente a few days later.

Immediately detected by Batista's army, they were nearly wiped out in the first encounter. The few survivors, including the wounded Guevara, were able to reach the mountain, Sierra Maestra, where they set-up the nucleus of guerrilla army. The rebels set slowly gained in strength, seizing weapons from Batista's Forces. They were winning support and new recruits from the local peasantry, the intellectual and workers in the cities.

Guevara exhibited great courage and skill in combat and soon became one of the Castro's ablest and most trusted aides. In July 1957, he was made a major and appointed leader of the rebel army's second column. He recorded his experience of two years spent in overthrowing Batista Government in a book entitled *Pasajes de la* ***Guerra Revolucionaria***, 1963. Its English translation ***(Reminiscences of the Cuban Revolutionary War)*** was published in 1968.

After Castro's victorious troops entered Havana on 2 January 1959 and established a Marxist Government, Guevara became a Cuban Citizen, divorced his Peruvian wife, Hilda Cadea, by whom he had one daughter, and married a member of Castro's army, Aleida March, by whom he had four children.

He became as prominent in the new government as he had been in the revolutionary army, representing Cuba on many commercial missions and delegations to African, Asian and Communist countries. He also became well-known in the West for his opposition to all form of imperialism and neocolonialism and for his attacks on US foreign policy in Asia, Africa and especially Latin America. He was an active participants in the social and economic changes brought about in Cuba by the Castro Government. He occupied such important posts in his adopted country as Chief of the Industrial Department of the National Institute of Agrarian Reform, President of the National Bank of Cuba and also as Minister of Industry.

During this period, he defined Cuba's policies and his own views in many speeches, articles, letters and essays. More important among these are:

- "El socialismo y el bombre en Cuba", 1965
- "Man and Socialism in Cuba", 1967, an examination of Cuba's new brand of Communism.
- "Guerrilla Warfare", 1961, a highly influential manual on guerrilla strategy and tactics.

After April 1965, Guevara dropped out of public life and then vanished altogether. His disappearance was varyingly attributed to the relative failure of the industrialisation scheme he had advocated while Minister of the Industry, to pressure exerted on Castro by Soviet officials disapproving of Guevara's pro-Chinese Communist outlook, and to serious differences between Guevara and Cuban leadership regarding Cuba's economic development and ideological line. In October of that year (1965), Castro revealed a Letter written to him by Guevara some months ago in which the latter reaffirmed his enduring solidarity with Cuban Revolution but explained that "other nations are calling for the help of my modest efforts and that, having "always identified with the world outcome of our Revolution", he had decided to go and fight as a guerrilla in some other liberation struggles being waged in different parts of the world.

Guevara's movement and whereabouts remained secrets for the next two years (1965-67). But he sent a letter that was read aloud at the first conference of the Tricontinental Solidarity Organisation held in Havana in April 1967. In this Letter, known as the "Message to the Tricontinental", Guevara analyzed the World situation and called for an all out war against imperialism and forces of reaction. During this period, he may have gone to North Vietnam and to several countries in Latin America. It is also probable he secretly returned to Cuba in 1966. But the facts have never been established positively. It was later learnt that he had spent some time in the Congo with other Cuban guerrillas, helping to organise the Patrice Lumumba Battalion, which fought in the civil war there.

In the autumn of 1966, Guevara went to Bolivia, incognito, to create and lead a guerrilla group in the region of Santa Cruz. He spent the next eleven months training the Bolivian guerrillas and fighting with them, meticulously recording their progress and setbacks in a diary that was found and published after his death'. On 8 October 1967, the group was encircled by a special detachment of the Bolivian army and almost annihilated. Guevara was captured after being wounded and shot soon afterwarld.

While the pictures of the dead guerrilla chief were being circulated and the circumstances of his death were debated, Guevara's legend began to spread. Demonstrations in protest against his death occurred in many parts of the world. Articles, tributes and poem's were written about his adventurous life and tragic death. Even those liberal elements that felt little sympathy with militantly Communist ideals during his life time, expressed regreat for his death and admiration for his integrity and spirit of sacrifice. He was singled out from other revolutionaries by many young people in the West because he rejected a comfortable middle class background to fight for those who were deprived of political power and economic stability.

An intellectual and a thinker he believed in putting his theories into action. He was called "the most complete human being of our age" by no less a person than French philosopher Jean Paul Sartre.[3]

Diaries of a Bike Rider

23 years old Ernesto—he would get typical Argentinean name *Che* later, as explained above—and older out-of-work leprosy doctor Alberto Grenado decided on a tour of Latin American countries in early 1950s. They were to ride Grenado's 1939500 CC Norton bike dubbed La Poderosa II (The Mighty One). Guevara maintained a meticulous record of his daily travels. These notes of an early journey across Latin America by the young medical student were not meant for publication. It would have been a pity if these notes had remained a sheaf of type-written pages as they indeed were till 1980s. It was a happenstance these were published as *The Motorcycle Diaries of Ernesto Che Guevara.* "It is needless to say these Diaries is a fundamental text that provides not only a lyrical, entertaining and insightful account of Latin America in the early 1950s but is also a record of the inward journey of arguably the most romantic of 20th century icons, the guerrilla doctor whose trademark beret, long hair, beard and leather jacket have become synonymous with revolution".[4]

The journey begins innocently enough for Guevara: Jaded with medical schools, hospitals and exams, Che's parents' worry was understandable as he is yet to get his medical degree and he is asthmatic. The *Diaries* has sentences like: "The next day was uneventful but asthmatic". But there was no stopping the young man, out searching for his guiding star in life. Here, are his sentiments in early part of the Diaries: "The rush of the roads, the dusty miles flying by the thoughtful quiet evenings in strange places, the exchange of confidences, the magic of the unpredictable encounter". Che's words capture typical youthful yearnings of the footloose: "Distant countries, heroic deeds and beautiful women spun around and around in our turbulent imaginations."

When he and Alberto stareout at the "immense sea, full of white-flecked and green reflections", each far away with his own dreams, two stow slow aways between places as evocative as Valparaiso and Antofagasta, it is only natural that he writes: "There we understood that our vocation, our true vocation, was to move for eternity along the roads and seas of the world. Always curious, looking into everything that came before our eyes, sniffing out each corner but only ever faintly — not setting down roots in any land or staying long enough to see the substratum of things; the outer limits would suffice."

The journey takes the two travellers from Argentina to Chile and then up to Peru, Venezuela and Columbia through mountains, deserts and rain forests. There are various shades to the narrative: Racy at times, intense often, sometimes light hearted, and even politically incorrect. "Che alternates between being a political thinker and a poet, and when he is neither, he is just a young man having been on the road. The two hitch-hikers are not above playing confidence tricks on strangers, for a free meal, drinks and rooms."

As Alberto, who died in 2012 in Cuba, would recall later, it was fortuitous that La Poderosa did not prove mighty enough. After a series of accidents and mechanical collapses, the bike had to be left in Chile and knights of the road suddenly became two grimy, hungry hitch-hikers, who continued their journey by truck, bus, steamship and raft. This brought them into close contact with the people, their poverty and deprivation. What could have been just another "coming of age" journey before the inevitable retreat into bourgeois comfort turned into a political awakening of the man who was to play a critical role in Cuba's revolution, as already detailed earlier as also in the Congo. By then, he had become an iconic figure for the revolutionary pantheon for the world.

He had left Cuba incognito, and ultimately died trying to bring about a revolution in Bolivia, dreaming about unchaining of all Latin America.

It should be the interest to reproduce some except from his Diary to indicate Che's values, his basic philosophy based upon Communism and his deep concern for the poor and deprived. As the duo talk to the swarms of beggars huddling under the dark staircases in the Valparaiso, he writes: We plumb the cities depths, the miasmas draw us in. Our distended nostrils inhale the poverty with sadistic intensity". In the dying eyes of an asthmatic, poor old woman who can no longer earn her living with dignity as a waitress, Che employs Communist jargon: "...Comprehending the profound tragedy circumscribing the life of the proletariat the world over".

Then, he is on his way to the massive, exploitative copper mine at Chuquicamata, a symbol of "gringo" imperialism, when his conscience is jolted by the sight of persecuted Chilean Communist couple. "The couple numb with cold, huddling against each other in the desert night, were a living representation of the proletariat in any part of the world".

He is a true Left-Wing-Extremist and his deep concern was not a put on! He was ready to lay his life on line to practice his convictions. He indeed was killed while attempting to bring revolution into Bolivia. That is why his name and his dress, as mentioned above, became a universal by word and symbol respectively, for revolution. In india, we have many bleeding hearts for the poor and the exploited, but their passion is exhausted in TV studios and pages of newspapers! None has taken cudgels on their behalf and joined them a la Guevara! Indians have not produced and possibly will not do a Che Guevara!

The Indians of Peru evoked another strong if political reaction from this born Revolutionary: "...These people who walk us walk through the streets of the town are a defeated race. Their stares are tame, almost fearful and completely indifferent to the outside world. Some give the impression that they go on living only because it is a habit they cannot shake". He is making acute observations of men and their situation, and then assign them to his Diaries using apt words and terminology, mostly Communistic, but at times poetic and lyrical! And, imagine the Diaries were not meant for publication! It would have, indeed, been a loss to humanity if these indeed were not published!

Che is expansive on his 24th birthday: "The cusp of that transcendental quarter century silver wedding of a life". He finds himself on this important day in an Amazonian leper colony. Drunk, or as he puts it, "poiscoed" on the Peruvian drink 'pisco', he dilates his views/vision of Latin America divided into "unstable and illusory nations." This division is completely fictional and he is convinced that "all the people from Mexico to the Magellan Straits Constitutes a Single Mestizo race".

That the duo have earned the respect and affection of the people they have been in close contact with during these 'wanderings' is oblivious from the farewell scene the legend describes in his Diaries and he indeed was not that well known celebrity then that he became in his later life. Still people he came in brief contact during this journey could see his empathy and compassion for them, their poverty and deprivation. When the two doctors finally leave on a raft down the river, Che's entry reads: "...The leprosy patients serenade us in a ghostly scene against the jungle, lamps reflecting in the river, and accordion player without fingers plays the instrument with little sticks tied to his wrist as he accompanies a blind singer". Could there be another person as empathetic as Guevara? Could anyone else get a farewell by as impressive and talented an orchestra as the two doctors did?

Che already had certain views on life, and they got further crystallised when he actually saw and felt the poverty of the masses which he feelingly expressed in his Diaries. It is no surprise that he exudes such passionate and fervent belief in the philosophy and intensity of revolution as a solution of mankind's ills. For him, it has to be a bloody battles. Read on: "...When the great guiding spirit cleaves humanity into two antagonistic halves, I would be with the people. I know this, I see it printed in the night sky that I, eclectic dissembler of doctrine and psychoanalyst of dogma, howling like one possessed, will assault the barricades or the trenches, will take my blood-stained weapon, and consumed with fury, slaughter any enemy that falls into my hands.....I feel my nostrils dilate savouring the acrid smell of gunpowder and blood, the enemy's death; I steel my body, ready to do battle and prepare myself to be a sacred space within which the bestial howl of the triumphant proletariat can resound with new energy and new hope".

What passion and certainty of belief and victory for his cause. So he wrote, so he lived and eventually so he died. He was not an armchair revolutionary! He gave up his life while practicing his thought and ideals. As someone wrote, blessed he was that life did not permit enough time for his ideals to corrode!

Fellow Travellers

Before closing on Che's times and his operations in various countries, it should be of interest to say a word on some of his colleagues and fellow travellers like Ciro Bustos, Jorge Ricardo Masetti, and the more famous French Marxist theoretician Regis Debray.

Bustos was 26 and at his in-law's house for a barbecue one spring Sunday in 1958 when he first heard the voice. It belonged to a fellow Argentinean, a doctor four year his senior who was fighting along-side Fidel Castro in the mountainous south-eastern Cuba. As he listened to the radio, the young artist was struck by the contrast between the grandiloquence of the Cuban and the quiet tones of the Argentinean. Busto's recollection of that broadcast has not been blunted by the intervening half century. "There was no bombast, no prime donna attitude. It was like talking to your brother, so normal, and so calm. That was what moved me so much".

The interview Radio El Mundo carried that Sunday proved a siren call. Che Guevara's voice and the political struggles he embodied would urge him to join that voice. He went to Cuba and then the two were inseparable, going to Czechoslovakia, Algeria and back to Argentina before the disastrous Bolivian expedition of 1967 that would cost Che his life and blacken Bustos' name for four decades. Until 2007, when his memoirs, "Che wants to see you", appeared in Spanish, Bustos had been seen by many as the man who betrayed Guevara and his brothers-in-arms by sketching their faces for his interrogator— to prove that he, indeed, was an artist and not a guerrilla fighters—who caught him after he marched out of the Bolivian jungle on Guevara's orders.

The book, which has just been published in English last year (2013), is prefaced by a quote from another figure that looms large in the Argentinean psyche, Jorg Luis Borges: "Moreover, we do not know if the universe belongs to the real world or the fantasy". In the context of this quote, Bustos makes an interesting observation. Given the number of accounts written by outsiders about Guevara, the accumulation of claim and counter- claim, not to mention extraordinary experiences he and Che shared, the line felt more than a little apt, says Bustos. "All the things that happened, all the good things as well as all the mistakes, seem almost imaginary, almost made up", he says in his deep, sing- song Spanish.[5]

"Bustos shares Borges obsession with the duality of heroism and betrayal and the book, he says, is his attempt to kill the myth that he sold out Guevara". He laments that no journalist contacted him to hear his side of story until the US reporter Jon Lee Anderson tracked him down to Malmo in 1995. "I can't explain why the press did this but it is like the Argentinean writer Tomas Eloy Martinez said: 'Whenever there is a hero, there is a traitor'. So that is what the press created".

It is a version for which he has paid dearly. "This story", he says with wet eyes, "has cost me 40 years; 40 years of bad faith. That is why I wrote the book. As the title suggests, Bustos book is the record of a youngman's political vocation. Although it often reads like a hagiography of Guevara, Bustos marvels at his leader's strength of character and compares him to Alexander the Great and the young Napoleon.

From their first meeting in Guevara's office in the Ministry of Industry in Havana, Bustos says Che was startlingly down to earth. Bustos and several others were trained in insurgency in Cuba and Algeria and then sent to northern Argentina to establish a guerrilla network. Their mission, which was overseen by Jeorge Lee Masetti, the journalist turned fighter who had interviewed Guevara in the Sierra Maestra five years ago, was dogged by disaster and terrible morale. As the situation in jungle worsened, Masetti was growing more and more authoritarian, ordering the weakest members of the groups to be executed. This time, it was Pupi.

Bustos writes: "I still think about Pupi, but there was a problem that needed to be dealt with. In a struggle, where you are risking your life, the worst that can happen is for morale to break down. That is what happened". Yes, Pupi was a casualty, he adds, but he was not the only one. Everyone who had volunteered for the struggle had been told the same thing: "None of us will make it to the end of it alive".

The jungle eventually claimed the life of Masetti, who emerges from the book as a tyrant to rival Kurtz in the Heart of Darkness. Despite his methods, Bustos can't help admiring his former commander's extraordinary dedication and force of will.

And now, to the sad end of the legend. Bustos emerged from the jungle to carry on building a revolutionary network in Argentina. Three years later, in 1967, Che asked him to join his guerrilla band in Bolivia, where he hoped to detonate a "Continental revolution". But like the Argentinean operation, this mission was doomed to failure: Bolivian army soon got a wind of their presence and began closing in. Bustos and the French Marxist theoretician Regis Debray, who was in the country to meet Guevara, left the guerrilla force with Che's blessings, but were soon captured by the Bolivian army.

Bustos kept his interrogators at bay for three weeks, telling them he had been on his way to a conference on political prisoners when he had run across the guerrillas. But when it became clear that the CIA and the Bolivian army already knew everything—including who many of the guerillas were—he changed tack. Bustos confirmed that he was an Argentinean artist and agreed to sketch some of the fighters to prove that he was not lying. Hence the charge of the betrayal, Bustos becoming Che's Judas, with this book, Bustos is sure that he "kills the myth that he sold out Argentinean rebel".

Star, Cigar and the Revolutionary

We end this part with a brief summary of this iconic guerrilla leader's journey in quest of spreading revolution in the entire continent of Latin America.

Ernesto Che Guevara

- Ernesto "Che" Guevara was an Argentinean Marxist revolutionary, physician, author, guerrilla leader, diplomat and military theorist.

- A major figure of the Cuban Revolution, his stylised visage has become a ubiquitous counter-cultural symbol of rebellion and global insignia within popular culture.
- Guevara was born to Celia de la Serna Llosa and Ernesto Guevara Lynch on 14 June 1928, Rosario, Argentina, eldest of five children in an Argentine family of Basque and Irish.
- Very early in life, Ernestito (as he was then called) developed an "affinity for the poor".
- Growing up in a family with Leftists leanings, Guevara was introduced to a wide spectrum of political perspectives even as a boy. His father, a staunch supporter of Republicans from the Spanish Civil War, often hosted many veterans.

Maoists going International

Maoists possibly have been facing all round reverses in West Bengal ever since Mamta Banerjee took over the reins in the State in 2011. To counter this decline, the Maoists forged a deadly alliances with Pakistan's spy agency ISI through over-ground radicals and the remnants of the banned outfit SIMI during the recent years.[6]

The revelation was made by the State's DGP Naparajit Mukherjee on 18 October 2012 while he was addressing the conference convened by the Union Home Ministry, of the Chief Secretaries and DGPs of India's Naxal-affected states in New Delhi. He said this nexus has been growing in the State's four districts, *viz* Murshidabad, West Midnapur, Purulia and Bankura. The nexus has been reported after the arrests of some Maoists who elaborated as to how the over ground sympathesisers of the Red ultras (dubbed as "Closet Maoists" by this author in this book) acted as a 'link' for them. This link has been found in these four districts. This link is believed to be helping the Maoists in getting arms and ammunition through the existing network of the North-East insurgents.

Mukherjee's disclosure assumes importance because Bengal has seen a remarkable change in the situation where it effectively controlled the Red menance in the past one year through consistent intelligence-based operations against the Maoists. The Home Ministry's latest figure on Naxal violence show that Bengal—once a hotbed of Maoist activities—has in fact "moved closer to what Andhra Pradesh had achieved" by reporting zero casualty in the past so many years. The Home Ministry statistics, based on the State's report, show that none of the three highly Maoist-affected districts—West Midnapur, Purulia and Bankura—reported any killings in the past ten months (Jan-Oct 2012).

The period which coincides with Banerjee's rule in the State, has also seen the elimination of senior Naxal leaders, including the top CPI (Maoist) politburo member Kishenji and arrest of several others during the joint operations of the state police and paramilitary forces.

West Midnapur district, whish witnessed as many as 360 deaths of civilians and security personnel during the period 2009-11, had reported zero casualty this year (2012). Purulia, Bankura, Birbhum, Murshidabad and Malda have also not reported any casualities.

Chavez, Che get fragrant Tributes

If one remembers the glory days of socialist revolutions one might like a whiff of The Che or, if one prefers more contemporary variants, one could splash on some eau de Chavez. After spending more than one year working with French perfumer Robertel, Cuban company Labiofan has created "The Che" and "The Chavez".

The company describes "The Che" as "Woodsy and refreshing", while it says, "The Chavez" is "Softer and Fruitier". Mario Valdes, design team leader, says: "We didn't want to create propaganda, but rather pay homage to them (revolutionary Ernesto 'Che' Guevara and former Venezuelan' president Hugo Chavez) and help their names endure"...

It is a form of tribute Che would probably least expect, given that, according to many reports, he rarely ever bathed.

This practice is surely something that will popularize international spirit the two Marxists would approve of!

Notes

1. Omen, Charles, A History of the peninsular War (1809-13), 6 Vol, 1902.
2. These instances are taken from Encyclopedia Britannica 1984.
3. *Source:* Encyclopedia Britannica, 1984.
4. Navtej Saran, The Hindu, 2.6.13.
5. These facts and account is sourced to the interview The Guardian (UK) conducted with Bustos in June 2013 and the article of the Guardians reproduced in the Hindustan Times, 3.7.13.
6. Vishwa Mohan, Times of India, 19.10.12.

2

The Naxalbari: The Origins and its Holy Trinity

December 1957: A newly-Commissioned Officer is on his way to the Naga Hills (presently Nagaland) to join his unit, deployed in the hotspot of the Naga insurgency, the first and the longest-running in the annals of the nation. [As of today (July 2015), the Central Government is still negotiating with a faction of the NSCN, known as (I and M) and the other faction, (K), inflicted heavy casualties, 20 fatal, on 6 Dogra troops on 4th July 2015 in Manipur's Chandel District]. At that stage, one did not know that a decade later, non-descript village, Naxalbari, figuring on the railway line in the Siliguri area of the North Bengal's Darjeeling District, would become a celebrated name!

Soon after the train left Jalpaiguri Railway Station, the officer did get a fleeting glimpse of the large upright board, bearing the words, Naxalbari. Like most Indians, he too had never heard the name. Expectedly, the name did not ring a bell.

But things changed in 1967. An insurrection was born here. The village lent its name to it and violent movement got dubbed as 'Naxalism'. Charu Mazumdar was its ideological father. Certain romanticism came to be attached to the term, Naxalism. Naxalbari and Naxalism became well-known terms to the analysts, to scholars the world over and household names in India. Its delegation was received by no less a person than Mao Tse-Tung, the great Helmsman. The Left Wing Extremism had been born in India. The iconic movement lasted only a couple of years but its progeny, Maoism, presently presents most serious threat to India's internal security, declared so a decade back by the then Prime Minister, Manmohan Singh. This chapter delineates the story of Naxalism and Naxalites, in all its ramifications.

The Origins

It all started in 1967. The area of revolt is defined by the region that falls under the jurisdiction of three police stations, *viz.* Naxalbari, Kharibari and Phansidewa. Some 65 per cent of population in the region was Scheduled Caste (SC) and tribal, working as agriculture labour or in mines, forests and plantations. A small percentage owned small holdings, the vast majority cultivating under the agency system (*bagh chash*). The *Baghchashis* were exploited by the *Jotedars.*

When the land reforms act came into force in 1955, the *jotedars' malafide* transfers of the land deprived the peasants and *Baghchashis* of their expected shares. This egregious injustice could not have gone on for long. Subsequently, the Santhals, armed with bows and arrows, forcibly occupied the lands of the Jotedars and Kulaks and lifted stocks of hoarded rice. In the consequent free-for–all, a police inspector was killed. It was on 24th May 1967 and thereby hangs the tale!

The Naxalbari Day: 24th May 1967

In an interview published on 20th May 2007, Kanu Sanyal, the only surviving member of the original/founding trinity of Naxalism, was asked about his memories of that fateful day of 25 May 1967. Here, is his reply:

> "For us, 24 May 1967 is the Naxalbari day. That day, the police were informed about some leaders of the Naxalbari (the term 'Naxal' had not been minted at that point of time) movement hiding in Boro Jhorojote village. In fact there were no leaders there, only a gathering of peasants and tea garden workers. One police officer was killed (in the violence consequent to the police action). Since the peasants understood and accepted our politics and took up arms on their own, we celebrate that day as a victory of our political ideas".[1]

Incidentally, other groups observe 25th May as the Martyrs Day since 11 persons were killed in the police firing that day. Incidentally, it—the different commemoration dates of the Naxalbari day—is as good an indicator as any about the ideological thinking among the leadership at that early stage of their movement. It is no surprise, therefore, that within a couple of years of May 1967 'revolution', there were half a dozen groups amongst the Naxals. And this trend has continued throughout the history of Left-Wing movement. Even after the two major groups joined to create CPI (Maoist). The splitting and splintering has continued.

After the 25 May 1967 firing, there were a number of such incidents. Consequently, there was a major deployment of police forces by the

West Bengal CPM Government. After several operations, the Naxal movement was effectively squashed with a heavy hand.

What all Happened

The "Naxalism," drawing its name from the non-descript village of Naxalbari, has assumed an iconic status amongst the comity of armed revolutions/insurrections in the country's annals. It is a watershed event: The armed movements in India can simply be divided into two taxonomical eras, *viz* the pre-Naxal and Post Naxal!

The Charu Mazumdar-led Naxal uprising may not have lasted long compared to others in the genre or made spectacular gains, even then the scholars and analysts are sanguine in their belief that any such movement that followed the 1967 icon, can and should be deemed to be inspired by it. Even the long-running and the current rage in this genre, Maoism, has drawn its fire from the Naxalism spark. This chapter has a somewhat comprehensive account of Naxalism: its origin, its spread and a variety of clones spawned by it.

Legacy of Naxalism

Whenever the Left intellectuals unite to create a proper entity, Naxal movement/Revolutions in this case, the seed of fission is already there. Charu Mazumdar was a brilliant ideologue but also an impulsive man at the same time. Kanu Sanyal, in the latter years, post Charu's death, has often expressed differences with the latter and regretted that he did not express his views often and strongly, such dissent is only expected when three strong willed individuals come together to achieve their common goal of helping the poor and deprived, to get their due from the powerful opponents landlords and jotedars in the instant case. Suffice it to say here that ideological differences in the leadership resulted in the split of the movement, which culminated in the formation of the CPI (ML) on 22nd April 1969. It was a sad denouement within 23 months from the birth of the movement that had a great promise!

Even though not more than a score of people were killed in this uprising, it left a far-reaching impact on the entire agrarian scene throughout the country. This impact can be compared to the several ripples a single pebble creates in a pond.

It needs recording that Jyoti Basu was West Bengal's Home Minister during the relevant period. So it was a Communist Regime and its Minister who crushed a pro-poor agrarian Revolution! Ironic, that the same Basu rose to serve Bengal as its longest-serving Chief Minister, a record for India.

Naxal Leadership

Who led this essentially brief but intense two-year long struggle? It was a radical group from the CPI (M)'s Siliguri unit. It was trinity of Charu Mazumdar, the ideologue, Kanu Sanyal, the vigorous leading organiser and Jangal Santhal, the mobiliser of the Adivasis. As stated above, this group had split from the parent party CPI (M) to form the CPI (ML) by April 1969.

What were the long-term effects of the Naxals uprising? It resulted in the redistribution of land amongst the peasantry, the avowed aim of the Naxal Movement. On the larger scale, CPI (M) learnt a good lesson from the Naxal insurrection. They carried out large scale redistribution of the land in the state, a major factor in endearing the party among the masses. Consequently, Jyoti Basu ruled for 23 years in the state and his successor for another term. Finally, they were uprooted by the mercurial Mamta Banerji, using their own high-handed and often violent ways.

On the political side, the result of Naxal Movement was formation of the CPI (ML), which was not an asset or an unalloyed achievement. The splitting was an unremitting process as far as the Left-Wing parties were concerned, as will be seen in this book.

Between 1969 and 1971, the Naxal movement spread to other parts of India, taking on a more violent, and in places, urban character. Shades of it remain in present-day CPI (ML) and the Maoists.

We leave Naxalism proper here, to return to it at a later stage. Here after are discussed some other revolutionary groups, rather briefly (detailed examination of these groups will be found in Chapter 11). Some of these groups later joined to emerge as the CPI (Maoist). These groups are discussed, as the Naxalites had some interaction with these.

Srikakulam: 1968

This district of Andhra Pradesh had a special place in the Left-Wing movements in the country.

The Girijans (hill dwellers; tribal's) form 70 per cent population of this district. They were living in the agency areas of the Eastern Ghats. Majority of them were plying agriculture and the rest were involved in collecting and dealing in minor forest produce.

The British decreed that the plains people could not buy lands in the hill/tribal areas. The traders and plains men found the way around the relevant Act to exploit the poor Girijans, their lands passing into the hands of exploiting outsiders. It goes without saying that the poverty has always been exploited by the rich. The tillers and the lease-holders were living at the mercy of the landlords, getting only subsistence wages. The Lease-holders had to give two-thirds of their produce to their landlords.

In this dismal situation redeemer appeared on the scene, Vempatapu Satyanarayana, who had started working among the Girijans in 1967, a happy coincidence as the year rings a bell as it resonates with the events in Naxalbari. He had secured substantial gains for the Girijans: wages of farm servants rose; the landlord's share of the harvest was reduced to one-third from the two-third; 2000 acres of lands was wrested from the landlords; and 5000 acres went in the possession of the Girijans.

The landlords could not accept this situation with equanimity. On 31st October 1967, occurred a clash between a large group of tribals marching for a meeting of the Marxist Party and the landlords, armed with guns. In the ensuring clash, two tribal's were killed. The incensed Girijans resorted to violence, giving birth to an agrarian armed struggle. Their leaders, Satyanarayana, organised them into guerrilla squads, called ***DALAMS***.

It was at this stage during the year 1969 that the Srikakulam leadership, which had earlier joined the CPI (M) faction of the Indian Communists, broke away from it and joined another group which had split from the CPI (M) earlier, to form a new entity, called the All India Co-ordinating Committee of Communist Revolutionaries (AICC of CR). The new entity in due course transformed itself into CPI (ML), one of whose progenitors was Charu Mazumdar, as we already know.

Meanwhile, the raids on the landlords and moneylenders continued—their houses burnt and the cash looted. Expectedly, the clash with the police occurred. Between December 1968 and January 1969, 29 policemen were killed by the *dalams*. Obviously, the level of motivation among the cadres was high.

Charu Mazumdar, the high priest of the (Naxalism) and CPI (ML), visited Srikaklam, a morale booster for the local leadership and its fighters. It gave a filip to the movement.[2]

During 1969, the Naxalites committed 23 murders and 40 dacoities.[2] Some of the murders were committed in gruesome manner. Here, is one example of a landlord, P. Jammu Naidu of the Ethamanuguda, killed on 11th May 1969. The ***DALAM*** cadre that killed him, painted slogans on the walls in his blood. He was notorious for the land of poor tribal's and taking their daughters for his wives. After his murder, it turned out that he had seven wives, two among them being little girls he had grabbed from the hapless victims of his avarice and lust. This reflects the level of the exploitation of the poor by the upper classes.

The drawing room intellectuals might wince and even condemn, gruesomeness of the murder described above. There is always other side of the picture, a counter narrative. What will they say to a tribal seeing his children dying a slow death in his presence, just because someone has illegally deprived him of his land! Can these elites understand the agony of parents whose little girl child is spending her time in the harem of a rich landlord!

West Bengal (Midnapur and Birbhum): 1967-71

The Midnapur District witnessed a well organised Naxal movement in the areas of Debra and Gopibhallavpur Police Stations.

Post-Naxalbari uprising of 1967, a section of CPI (M) workers started propagating the Naxal line. They supported the peasantry and launched struggle against jotedars. Santosh Rana and Ashim Mukherjee, both first a class graduates from the Calcutta University, were the leaders. They and a host of students from well-to-do upper class/caste families of Calcutta lived and worked among the tribals, setting personal example of identifying with the deprived.

Alarmed at the spate of killings, several companies of the CRPF and the State Police were sent to the area. By March 1970, the short-lived armed struggle was put to an end.

The Naxalites uprising in the Birbhum District was similarly masterminded from the Calcutta (Kolkata) University. Police forces were sent into the area. Some 150 CPI (ML) cadres were arrested, and consequently the movement petered out.

Bihar and Uttar Pradesh: 1968-70

The Mushahari block of Bihar's Muzzaffarpur District has 12 villages, with a total population of 10,000. Here, too were present oppressive practices, exploiting the poor. Possibly inspired by the Naxalbari saga, the peasants of Gangapur harvested in broad day light, the arhar crop of a landlord, Bijli Singh, in April 1968. This Zamindar (Landlord) of Narsingpur, incensed by the audacity of the peasants, marshalled a force of 300 men armed with lathis, swords and firearms. He led his 'army', seated on an elephant. In the battle that ensued, the landlord and his "hoodlums" were routed. The public humbling of this powerful landlord by the harijan peasants was something unheard of in the area, even in the state. There were several other cases of peasants forcibly harvesting landlord's crops. After several combing operations, the 'desperados' were on the run. Consequently, the movement died down.

The Mushahari produced ripples that spread into Darbhanga, Champaran and Chotanagpur. In May 1970, 54 adivasis were arrested in Jaduguda forests during a police operation. Mary Tyler, a British national, was among the 54. Later, she penned her thoughts in a poignant prose:

> "The Naxalite's crime was the crime of all those who cannot remain unmoved in an India where a child crawls in the dust with a begging bowl, where a poor girl can be sold as a rich man's plaything, where many are hungry while food is hoarded for profit".[3]

The Naxalites violence that erupted in Singhbhum and Ranchi assumed more serious dimensions. As an analyst put it, Jamshedpur became a mini Kolkata, with schools, government offices and police piequets coming under attacks. There were large scale attacks in Ranchi also.

Pallia area in Uttar Pradesh forms a part of the Lakhimpur District in Terai region. It is inhabited by the Tharu tribals. The State Government had encouraged the poor, landless peasants to move into Pallia area, allotting 10-12 acres of land to each migrant family. Employing their traditional exploitative practices, the landlords succeeded in ejecting the peasants from their land and forcibly occupying large chunks of it. "This offered a fertile ground to the Naxalites to help the deprived and the dispossessed. Their object was to clear the area of big farmers, thugs, corrupt political leaders and money lenders."[4]

They launched a series of attacks on the landlords, snatching a good number of their fire arms. Deployment of the armed police in the area brought the situation under control.

Above are a couple of areas outsides Naxalbari region/ West Bengal where uprisings were initiated by Naxal ideology and/or by some cadres from Naxalbari. The spark came from Naxalbari. That is why it has been stated earlier that any Left-Wing Extremism that came up anywhere in the country, Andhra Pradesh, Maharashtra, Tamil Nadu, Kerala *et. al.,* owed its parentage/origin to the Naxal spark.

It is surprising in this context that while the concept and ideology of Naxalism spread throughout the country, more specifically in the North-South corridor, extending from Bihar's border to Tamil Nadu and Kerala, it did not survive/revive in the area of its origin, Siliguri/Naxalbari, after it was crushed by communist-ruled state within two years of its inception/birth. This very ironic situation is discussed in the following pages.

Failure of Naxalism in the area of its origin

It bears re-emphasis that all the armed uprisings discussed briefly above were essentially spawned by the Naxalbari 1967. These can rightly be called

Naxalite movements, organised by different CPI (ML) groups in their states. Charu Mazumdar, the ideologue of the Naxalbari revolt, no doubt was an original thinker. But unhappily, pragmatism was not his forte. He failed to transform his initial success into some bigger, something more tangible and something long lasting. He failed to convert the spark he had produced into the prairie fires. He certainly ignited or caused to be ignited several fires in different states, but these were extinguished by their police forces.

May be, Charu was a bit of a romantic, not a hard headed realist. Perhaps, he lacked vision, as a critic put it. He was a mercurial genius, but a loner. He and his colleagues were on cloud nine, just because Chairman Mao had granted them an audience. We cannot blame them if they thought this audience and their initial successes at home would create mass uprisings, enabling them to create an Indian equivalent of Chinese PLA. In their enthusiasm and optimism, they forgot that the PLA was created by Mao after long years of struggle, relentless persistence and a leadership that had gone through fire! Then, the Indians were too diverse to be Chinese. To put it more logically, the rag-tag band of peasants who had revolted against the repression of the landlords and the money lenders, not only in North Bengal's Siliguri area, but also in some other states of the Union, did not have Mao at the apex. More importantly, if unfortunately, Charu could not take his two colleagues with him, even when they were part of the original trinity of the Naxalbari. As stated above, was he a loner? May be, he did not have all those long years as did Mao, to build and mould his flock into a Coherent leadership. After all, he died in September 1971, four years into his revolution. A counter argument can be that the things had fallen apart for him by April 1968!

Be that as it may, it may be too harsh to blame him for all the failure. May be the masses were not ready for his revolution! Or, yet again, he had no precedence to build on his initial success. Was he before his times? Possibly same can, more or less be said, about Satyanarayan Singh of Bihar: A prophet that failed.

It needs to be admitted that there are a lot of positives to his personality and work. Besides lighting the fire in Siliguri area, he also succeeded in arousing and inspiring the students in Kolkata and its universities. They abandoned their studies to live in the forest villages to identify themselves with their tribulations. Of course, the vital elements to build up a guerrilla force were missing, *viz.,* resources, equipments and training. But for these, no movements can face the might of modern state. One by one, the movements fizzled out in the affected states of the country, as the central paramilitary forces were called in and deployed in their interior areas.

They carried out well-planned raids and search operations to capture or eliminate the cadres. It is rather ironic that it was the police of a Communist Home Minister, Jyoti Basu that ruthlessly crushed Charu's baby.

It is only to repeat a cliché when the critics assert that Naxalite leadership "lacked the vision to organise the poor peasants against the might of the states, even if the cause was just".

At the other end, one must mention that in such situations, lumpen elements spy an opportunity to serve their own selfish ends. It is a case of high mindedness being vitiated by the baser elements of human nature. The lumpens, infiltrating the ranks of ideologically- inspired cadres, degrade the discipline and morale of the latter.

At the end of the line, the iconic stature of Charu Mazumdar cannot be questioned, neither can the contribution of his creation, Naxalism, towards the latter day success of Maoism as it is but a linear descendant of the former.

Looking at the larger picture

A rough estimate says there were some 4000 incidents of Naxalite violence between mid-1970 to mid-1971: 3,500 in West Bengal, 220 in Bihar and 70 in Andhra Pradesh. The Central Government planned a joint anti-Naxal operation in West Bengal, Bihar and Odisha, deploying the Army, paramilitary forces and the Central Police Forces. The operation Steeplechase lasted from 1 July to 15 August 1971. Its broad strategy was to surround an area known to be a Naxal stronghold with an outer cordon of Army troops, an inner cordon of CRPF men and the local Police operating inside. The operation disrupted the network of the Naxal Cadres and consequently, the movement stalled.

Meantime, internal dissensions between the CPI (ML) factions additionally disrupted and weakened the movement. A number of top leaders, including Charu Mazumdar were arrested, depriving the Cadres of their leadership at various levels. When Charu died shortly after this operation was over in September 1971, it marked the end of a phase of the Naxalite Movement in India. It was just a lull. This movements was to surface again, since the governments at New Delhi and in the states had failed to address the issues that had caused the fires at Naxalbari, *viz.,* lack of development in the tribal areas and the adivasis, the poor and the deprived still exposed to the exploitation by the landlords, the moneylenders and the 'dirty' rich.

The (military) forces alone cannot end such insurrections. The root causes of the problem must be addressed: Oppression and injustice inflicted on the poor, dispossessed and the downtrodden by the rich and powerful. An unequal society where extreme misery exists with luxury is certain to blow up one day. A revolt can be suppressed by brute forces, but unless it is accompanied, or at the very least, followed by, the socio-economic development of the deprived and poor majority, it would remain a temporary solution. One should not overlook the warning, and an unalloyed truth, contained in the Tupamaro manifesto: "If the country does not belong to every-one, it belongs to no one".

A Comprehensive Look at Naxalbari around 25 May 1967

Charu Mazumdar and the leadership of the Siliguri CPI (M) had been working with the deprived and the dispossessed of the region to ensure that they do get their fair share from the jotedars. They were aware that they were an exploited lot. The peasantry must resist the exploiters. Progressively, they were building the resistance by working with them and some cadres staying in their villages. All this was aimed at identifying themselves with the grievances and plight of the helpless, oppressed and exploited peasantry. They seemed to be winning the game and gaining the confidence of the peasants.

For the Naxal leaders; 24 May 1967 was the Naxalbari day because it was on this day at Boro Jhorojote Village that a police inspector was killed by bows and arrows in a clash with the peasants and tea garden workers. They had gathered there on the bidding of their leaders. These peasants had understood and accepted the politics of their leaders and taken up arms to defend their rights. They were agitating for their land ownership rights. Bora Jhorojate is seven kilometers from Naxalbari.

The Police were obviously keen to avenge the death of their inspector killed on 24 May. The events of the 25th are recounted by Paban Singh of Benguijote village, just a kilometers away from Prasodojote village where 11 people were killed. The eye witness Paban is poetic: "Some memories are like fire flies gently twinkling in the dark". But for Paban, memories of that sunny (25th) May afternoon are like pieces of a broken mirror. The shards each telling their own story; about police killing the 'original' martyrs of the cause.[5]

The quotes are Paban's words. "The next day (25 May), women activists had organised a secret meeting by the Mechi river on the Nepal border. Some informer must have told the police because when they came back to Prasadojote village, the police was waiting." Paban was at this time in his village, Benguijote, just a kilometer away. To this day, Paban can hear the sound of those gunshots. "I immediately picked up my bow arrows and ran towards the twin oak trees in Prasadjote. On my way, I saw Gaudran shaibani and a child being hit". Manoj Saha, whose shop is hardly 100 yards from the spot, recalls his father, a migrant from Bihar's Maodhapur District, telling him that he hid under the bed on hearing the gun shots." This is Palean speaking in 2007.

By the time Paban reached the spot, most of the agitators had fled, but the injured and the dead were lying on the ground. "I saw Ishwara Boudi lying on the ground and screaming. She was struck on the lower part of her leg. I could see the bullet and tried to pull it out. It was not easy, as she was screaming...I just wanted to know who was hit and who had died. My mother was lying by the muddy pathway off the road a few yards from the twin oak trees. She was dead. I went round the village looking for a piece of cloth to cover her body. Finally, I found a sack cloth and covered her body. That is all I did. There was a warrant against my name. I left the spot".

Those were painful days, overlaid with personal tragedies. Even the memories of those days must be traumatic for people like Paban. He continues, talking to the pressmen: "Much later, I learnt that the police had returned the next day, arrested every injured person and taken away the bodies. I don't know what they did with the body of my mother: Did they cremate it or just dumped it in the river".

In all, 11 people were killed, including six women and two children. In the book, *In the wake of Naxalbari,* Sumanta Banerjee writes: "while the police version of the incidents was that the rebels had attacked them from behind a wall of women and children, forcing the police to open fire, the dissident Marxist leaders alleged that the police deliberately killed women and children". Kanu Sanyal says: "It was a revenge killing".

The names of the 11 dead are inscribed on a marble slab next to the Benguijote Primary School.

Who led the two-year-long struggle? It was a radical group from CPI (M), Siliguri Unit. Charu Mazumdar was the key ideologue, Kanu Sanyal was among the leading organisers and Jangal Santhal mobilised the adivasis. By 1969, this group had split from the CPI (M) and formed CPI (ML).

The other important question is about the long-term impact the Naxalbari uprising had on the country's polity and its socio-economic scene. It resulted in the redistribution of land among the peasantry. In political terms the formation of the CPI (ML) was an important land mark. After all, this was an event, an important milestone on the way to the emergence of the CPI (Maoist), the consequences of which the nation is still grappling with, in 2015. Between 1969 and 1971, the Naxal movement had spread to various parts/states of the country, taking on a more violent and in places, an urban character. "Shades of that remain in today's CPI (ML) and the Maoists", an analyst was to write in 2007.[6] It bears repetition that by April 1969, Naxal movement had been crushed in area—Siliguri region- of its origin, even if its ideology spread beyond the confines of its region. It should be of interest to examine the situation presently (2015) in Naxalbari region.

Naxalbari Today

The situation in Naxalbari region and its impact post-1969 will be examined in two parts: The situation by 2007 and post-2007 till date (2015).

Situation about 2007: May 2007 Appraisal

This part of analysis pertains to the period when the Naxal movement- (25 May 1967 firing in specific-) had completed forty years. The subject was given a detailed treatment in this authors book, "Terrorism in India", Volume III, Kalpaz Publication, 2009. To understand it in its context, the analysis is reproduced verbatim from that book in the following text:

> "The term Naxalbari symbolises the revolutionary fervor of the 1960's. But the area where it all was born, no longer, resonates with that spirit.
>
> "It is 40 years since the police firing on 25 May 1967, that killed 11 people, including six women and two children and lit the prairie fire. Paradoxically, that event is but a fading memory in and around Naxalbari, even if it produced several Red outfits which are active in the wide swathe of India Running North-South, engaged in generating a Maoist heaven in the area under its 'Control'. It is obvious that 40 years of Naxalbari deserves a detailed look.
>
> "The 25 May1967 police firing killing of the peasantry might popularly and almost universally have become the starting point of the revolution, but the old timers insist that the Naxalbari peasant uprising was not an event but a process that had started back in the early 1950s. But that day, Naxalbari exploded into the national consciousness. Within a few years, Naxal became synonymous with any Red extremist evoking fear among landlords and policemen alike.
>
> "That was then, now as the Peasant insurrection completes its 40 years, on 25 May 2007, Naxalbari still evokes images of peasants and tea garden workers up in rebellion. For the radicals Red groups of different shades, including the Maoists, it is still an emblem and an idea that inspires. But this inspiring image in wider India is in sharp contrast to

the realities one finds during visits to the villages around Naxalbari, once the heart beat of the insurrection and the revolutionary fervor. In Naxalbari, revolution is a yesterday word, as a reporter indeed found during his visit just before 25 May 2007.[7]

"Some introductory words on the Naxalbari village. The iconic village is surrounded by picture postcard villages. The Naxalbari block is located in the Darjeeling district of West Bengal. Naxalbari railway station is barely 5 Km from the Nepal Border.

"As hinted above, Naxalbari movement was the outcome of the mobilisation carried out by the Communists at the ground level since the early 1950s. By the mid-1960s though, a group of radicals led by Charu Mazumdar within the Darjeeling District Committee of the CPI (M) wanted to carry out an armed struggle. The slogan was , 'Land to the tillers'. But the movement was not just about seizing land from the *Jotedars*. 'We believe that to take the land permanently, you also must take state power, country', says Veteran activist Shanti Munda, 64, of Shebdella village.

"The movement's social base came from *adivasis* (Mundas, Oraons and Santhals) and Rajbongshis, a schedule caste. "Even now, these groups have a lot going for them," says Abhijit Mazumdar, 45, General Secretary, CPI (ML) (Liberation), Darjeeling District. But these groups are a minority now.

"It should be of interest that in 1967, the Naxalbari insurrection made China's *People's Daily* go ballistic (one analyst prefers the adjective to be 'orgiastic') in its 5 July editorial: "A peal of spring thunder has crashed over the land of India...under the leadership of a revolutionary group of the Indian Communist Party, a Red arc of rural revolutionary armed struggle has been established in India. The spark in Darjeeling will start a prairie fire and will certainly set the vast expanses of India ablaze."

"But the Chinese mouth piece was obviously off the mark. Presently, radical mass politics appears comatose in Naxalbari. We cannot blame the children of Benguijote Primary School for not knowing who Charu Mazumdar was.

"To restate (a harsh truth), in Naxalbari, revolution is a yesterday word. There are new realities at play.

"Most radical Reds are septugenarian. A young CPI (ML) worker is a rarity. Incidentally, if surprisingly, there are more Marxist Leninist Parties (New democracy, Liberation, Janashakti, Kanu Sanyal Group,

Mahadadeb Mukherjee Group, to name only some)—than the cadre. Posters with the Charu Mazumdar photo still adorn these parts. But as veteran CPI (ML) Janashakti Group activist Khokhan Mazumdar points out, there is not even a book on the 1967 rural uprising in the local Subroti Sana library, although dozens were written in Bengali.

"Is it any surprise if a reporter says that 'barring old activitists like him who spearheaded the uprising, there is no real battle between memory and forgetting'. Youngsters admit the uprising rarely figures in their conversations. They remember it primarily because 25 May is celebrated as an annual ritual with politicians paradropping from Kolkata. Consequently for the young today, Naxalbari uprising is a story, not a way of life.

"A telling fact of Naxalbari uprising not being even a story came to light when a reporter visited the local Benguijote primary school. The teacher asks, his student: 'Who is Charu Mozumdar'? The latter shakes his head sadly and says: 'Sir, I don't Know.' The teacher calls six more students from class IV and repeats the question. He gets the same negative answer. He then being helpful, throws a broad hint through a leading question: 'Don't you remember the 'function' we had once'? Boys and girls grope for an answer, but to no avail. One of them finally gets up to say: 'jani na, who is Charu Mozumdar ke (= do not know, sir, who is Charu Mozumdar)".

"It was rather ironical. Barely ten yards from their classroom and just outside the low boundary wall of their school, is the bust of Charu Mazumdar, along with those of comrades Lenin, Stalin and Mao. Besides them is a plaque in memory of 11 martyrs, mentioned earlier.

"What could be the reason for this indifference towards an iconic figure of his time on his own turf? A major, if not the only, reason for this could be changed demographic picture of the area. Over the years, Naxalbari and its surrounding villages have been flooded by an influx of migrants from Bangladesh, men and women with no historical memory of the event. As a result of this influx, mostly illegal, the adivasis who had migrated to these parts from Bihar now Jharkhand and the Rajbangsis, who provided insurrections spine, have been reduced to a minority. The migrants, who have been gradually legalised through political patronage, serve as a vote bank for the CPI (M) and are averse to radical politics. Over the past three decades, the CPI (M) has always retained the Phansidewa assembly seat of which the Naxalbari block is a part.

"So, Naxalbari is a secret trinket tucked away on the edge of Darjeeling District. Nepal is just 5 km away. Back in the 1960s, it acted as a sanctuary for 'underground' Communist leaders. Furlongs of tea estates, paddy fields, bamboo forest and banana garden, the villages appear born to lead a green, not a Red, revolution.

"One enters Naxalbari to be welcomed by a statue of Kargil martyr Suresh Chhetri and a Lion's Club sign board, not by a statue of the Charu Mazumdar. Sitting in his tin-roofed house are sons of former CPI (M) workers who have joined CPI (M) "They are the new prosperous political elite", he says In Benguijote village, Arti Sarkar, a former CPI (ML) (Janashakti) workers' son, was picked up by police for allegedly being a Maoist. In jail for two months, he has joined CPI (M). As Abhijit Mazumdar, Charu's son and district secretary CPI (ML) (Liberation), says: 'over the years, there has been systematic witch hunt against anybody who opposes the CPI(M).

"Sources insist that CPI (M) and Congress politicians do not even fight each other because they share a common financial interest: Border smuggling of mainly clothes and electronic goods.

"Returning to the demographic realities of the area, here, is shopkeeper Manoj Saha of Prosadojote village, giving a rough estimate of ethnic and communal breakdown of the families in his village:

Biharis 2 Rajbangsis 20

Bengalis 2 Bangladeshis 50

Nepalese 10

"These are telling statistics. Bangladeshis are already having overall majority and the influx into West Bengal, as into Assam, is still continuing. It must be understood that in the totality of circumstances, Bangladeshis help the local CPI (M) in West Bengal in their political battles against the CPI (ML). This gets confirmed by the locals when they interact with the visiting journalists. Says villager Pusha Oraon: 'The Bangladeshis, mostly lower caste *Namasudra's,* have been coming in over the past few decades'. Being migrants the Bangladeshis are keen to be accepted and coopted. Opting for radical politics would mean going against the ruling coalition and consequently could invite trouble for them. A villager, talking to a reporter makes the point simply, matter-of-facilty but honest to the bone, manner: 'The CPI (M) leader takes them under his wings because it helps him gain bulk votes. They get land and ration cards in return. It is a relationship of convenience'.

"In the circumstances explained above, rebuilding radical movement is not easy.

"The process is slow and painstaking', says Abhijit Mazumdar. More so, with CPI (ML) is splintered into several factions. Without unity the radical Left is unable to offer (and function as) genuine opposition. For instance, CPI (ML) (Liberation) is marginally present in nearby Kharinari block but kanu sanyal CPI (ML) is there in Hatighasha arc. Some factions such as the Mahadev Mukherjee Group has just one or two members in the entire block.

"Notwithstanding all this, the spirit of Naxalbari survives. Shanti Munda says that when government officials recently came asking for this land for an irrigation project, the entire village rose in revolt. "We still love our land. And just like the Naxalbari day, we will die for it, '*Jaan doongi Zamin na doongi*', she says. In Nandigram the radical Reds see hope. The killing of 14 anti-SEZ protesters on 14th March 2007 by the police has ignited the spark again.

"Says the teenagers Shefali Biswakarma, whose uncle Babulal was one of the first martyrs of the movement: 'Earlier, no one wanted to listen when we spoke of Naxalbari. Now students say we must have another Naxalbari to stop Nandigram from recurring'.

"One tends to believe Shefali even when primary school children at Benguijote Primary School says they are unaware of Charu Mazumdar, the icon of Naxalbari".

Kanu Sanyal speaks: May 2007

"An inconsequential leader today"

Kanu sanyal was the leading figure of the Naxalbari movement, next only to the Charismatic Charu Mazumdar. In the 1960s, this slogan echoed through the bylanes of Calcutta and paddy fields of Naxalbari: Jail ka tala tootega! Kanu, Jangal Chhootega [the locks of prison will break! Kanu Sanyal and Jangal (Santhal) will be released]. These two were members of the iconic trinity which led the Movement. Charu had died in September 1971. Hence the slogan in 1960s. In May 2007, Kanu was the only surviving members of the trinity and he was ailing and frail. But the 78 years old General Secretary of the original CPI(ML) living in a one room party office in Hatigisha and sleeping on the floor, still remained committed to the revolution through mass struggle.

What follows are the excerpts from an interview by a reporter published in a daily in its issue of 20 May 2007.[8]

It is of interest to note that what the old and frail revolutionary says about the 1960s revolution has a ring of authenticity. Moreover, what he says on Nandigram had contemporary resonance (in 2007). Let it be put this way to do justice to the old Lion: Even 40 years after the conflagration at 78, the romantic still has fire in his stomach.

Q. Your memories of that fateful day of 25 May 1967?

A. For us, 24 May is Naxalbari Day. That day the police was informed that some leaders of the Naxalbari movements were holding in the village Boro Jhorojote. There were no leaders there but a huge gathering of peasants and tea garden workers. One police officer was killed. Since the peasants understood and accepted our politics and took up arms on their own, we celebrate that day as a victory of our political ideas.

Q. Why did the Naxalbari movement fail?

A. We had a strong base among peasants and tea garden workers. But the movements lacked a proper party structure. That was the main shortcoming.

Q. Did you meet Mao Secretly in 1967?

A. Yes, during our Naxalbari struggle, there were differences within the party. We thought the Chinese leader could help us understand what was right or wrong. It was a 45-minuts meeting. We went by road to Kathmandu. From there, the Chinese comrades took us by road to Peking. We reached China on 30 September. The Next day, we saw them celebrate 1 October as National Day. I could see people weeping at the sight of Mao. We met Mao, Chou En-lai and C-in-C. Mao's advice was: Whatever you learn in China, try to forget it. Go to your own country, try to understand the specific situation and carry the revolution forward.

Q. In retrospect, do you think that Charu Mazumdar's annihilation of class enemy line was a historical mistake?

A. It was not only a historical error but a fundamental deviation from Marxism-Lennism and thoughts of Mao. But remember, we did not follow the annihilation line (forming small squads and killing landlords, policeman and other class enemies) in Naxalbari only one landlord was killed (in Naxalbari) during the struggle. In practice, annihilation line was first followed in Srikakulam area of Andhra Pradesh in late 1969.

Q. What are the movement's long-term gains?

A. There was no protection to sharecroppers earlier. We captured land in Naxalbari and peasants are still in control of the land. After 1977, West Bengal Government was forced to bring the Bargadari Act, through which some hereditary rights were given to sharecroppers

Largely unknown outsides his village

Now a word on: "The Naxals have learnt their lessons. Today, the position is far different". Though they have formed CPI (ML), but it did not make much headway during Charu's life and for that matter, even after his demise. Likewise, Sanyal did not find any leadership position in CPI (ML) their own creation. No doubt, Charu was given a hero's welcome when he visited Andhra Pradesh in 1971, but nothing more than that. It is not a cynical statement to say that Charu's death enabled him to retain his Charismatic status in the Left Wing circle. Otherwise, he too would have been another Kanu Sanyal, spending his lonely days in some corner of Naxalbari, unknown beyond its boundaries. In this case, death was kind to him.

But it was not kind to Jawaharlal Nehru. He would have been a greater leader had he expired before the 1962 humiliation. With that single event, his life's work stood decimated before his own eyes. He died a disgraced man yet again, Mahatma Gandhi died at the right time.

Nehru and Patel could not have been able to accede to his 'idealistic and heartfelt desires' based on dictates of his righteous conscience! Nehru and Patel were running a country and not a charitable institution or an Ashram. They were facing a variety of political, economic and social problems. They could do without moral or ethical pressures the Great Mahatma would have subjected them to! His compelling the duo to pay huge amount of cash to Pakistan as demanded by his conscience proved one act too many for a "Nationalist" Indian, who felt called upon to kill him. The conscience and kindness are fine human traits but may not be appropriate values when two nations are involved in an active war! This was a digression, if unavoidable. Let us return to Kanu Sanyal, the sole survivor of the "Holy Trinity", if one can be pardoned to use this term for three human beings, however full of revolutionary fervour!

KANU SANYAL

The Last Phase

Kanu Sanyal was 78 when he gave the interview recorded earlier. It was in 2007. That was possibly his last interview. At one place, he says,

"Maoists have not learnt their lessons". He may be right in that observations, but he possibly has not realised that "today the position is far different. The movement has undergone a change both in policy and strategy. It has been strengthening itself since 1990s. A major change for the better came in 2004 when two major Left-Wing groups (MCC and PWG) came together to form a unified outfit, called CPI (Maoists).

CPI (Maoists), and MCC and PWG before it, are operating at a much wider screen, in different areas of various states. The Naxals could hardly operate beyond the confines of Siliguri region. Sanyal can hardly appreciate the logistic and scale of their operations, but it is not to take the credit away from the original revolutionarises, who were sons of the soil and had firsthand experience of deprivations suffered by the poor peasants and tea garden workers. One is fairly certain that none among the top leaders of the Maoist uprising has such an experience of poverty and deprivation. It may sound a bit uncharitable but is largely true that compared to the Naxalbari Trio, present Maoist leaders can be dubbed as "5 star leaders". It is a pity that the 2007 interviewer did not ask Kanu Sanyal a question about the quality of Maoist leaders and their life style, even while living and operating in the jungles.

But to put the things in perspectives, the Maoist leaders are deemed to be linear descendants of the Naxal leadership. Even today, decades after the Naxalbari Revolution, the term "Naxalism" and "Maoism" are used interchangeably, but for people like this author the term "Naxalism" is preferable, for the simple reason that it is Indian, and not an import like the latter. Still, this book is on "Maoist uprising", barring this chapter which deals with "original uprising" in Naxalbari area, in Siliguri sub-division of West Bengal's Darjeeling District.

The Interview

It has been mentioned earlier that no book has been written on Naxalbari uprising in any local language, even if some are available in Bengali. More regretably, it seems Indian intellectual class has no time to do a biography on any of the leading lights of the Naxal movements. Possibly, no full length biography is available even on that charismatic figure, Charu Mazumdar.

Finally, that injustice has been undone by Bappaditya Paul. Or more appropriately, he has filled the yawning gap in this field, by writing a biography of Kanu Sanyal: "The first Naxal, an authorised biography of Kanu Sanyal", by Bappaditya Paul, Cage, ₹ 550, p. 249.

The bigger tragedy is that Sanyal Committed suicide when Paul was doing the last Chapter of his biography.

What follows is the interview of Paul by Kumkum Dasgupta, which appeared in the Hindustan Times of 8 November 2014. The interview is a three column piece, with one column showing a 1996 photo of Kanu Sanyal, standing with a bag in his right hand, possibly returning from a market with some vegetables or grocery items. This piece is tilled "The Rebel who never Returned, which is followed by four lines in large font:

> "Bappaditya Paul's biography of Kanu Sanyal presents the evolution of the Communist rebel while also highlighting the stages of the Naxalites Movements in India".
>
> Now the interview's preface".
>
> "Bappaditya's *The First Naxal* is the first authorised biography of Kanu Sanyal, one of the key leaders of the Naxalbari movements that began as a peasant uprising in the spring of 1967 in West Bengal. The informative books narrates the making of Sanyal, right from his childhood to the days of the Naxalbari uprising and beyond. It goes deep into the evolution of Sanyal as a Communist rebel and throws light on the various stages of the Naxalite movement in India".

Q. When and how did you meet Kanu Sanyal?

A. In 2005, I was posted in Siliguri as a staff reporter *Statesman.* Naxalbari is just 2 Km away from Siliguri. I started reading about the movement and would visit the place once a while. It was only in 2007, when the Nandigram anti-land acquisition protests were at its peak, a colleague suggested that I interview Kanu Sanyal on the topic. But when I met Sanyal, he refused to be interviewed, saying that journalists have always 'twisted' his comment to suit their story. He relented when I promised to show him the draft of the interview.

Q. How did the book come about?

A. He was happy with the Nandigram interview and over the next few months, a kind of trust developed between us. Before I met Sanyal, like many others, I thought it was Charu Mazumdar who had waged the Naxalite movement and Sanyal was his follower lieutenant. But after I started interacting with him, I realised Sanyal was a political star in his own right. Then I started searching for books on his life, his journey to China and his contribution to the Naxal movement but could not find even one.

Q. Did the authorised you to write the book?

A. I was not the first journalist to approach him. He had turned down the earlier offers saying there was nothing spectacular about his life. But he accepted my proposal when I told him his story is also the story of the Naxalite Movement and after him there would be no one to throw light on his origin, its evolution, disintegration and the subsequent revival. This clicked with him because several misconceptions about Naxalism had made their way into public perception and Sanyal wanted to clean the air.

There is no written authorisation that I am his biographer. However, during the course of the interview, he introduced me to his family and friends. By doing so, he created a connection between them and me. They also understood that the book had Sanyal's consent.

Q. Beginning 2007, over the next three years, you met Sanyal at regular intervals. You have 121 recorded interviews with him. How did he come across as a person?

A. After he gave his consent for the book, he became very interested in the project. He had a sharp memory but sometimes he would go back to his comrades to cross-check events and information. He collected books and documents for me to read and would often call me to know about the progress of the book. Sanyal was the great listener though not very talkative. His answer would always be straight and forthright, and he was always open to critical assessments. In fact, it was he who told me about his two alleged 'affairs'. It was a collaborative effort. I think people like him are one in million; he lived as he preached and not many Indian leaders are known to do that. Sanyal was a rebel who never returned home.

Q. It is unfortunate that he did not see the final product?

A. Yes, that is a pity. Seven days before he committed suicide (23 March 2010), Sanyal called me to ask about the progress of the book. When I told him I was doing my last chapter, he asked me twice whether I needed anything more.

Q. The book very skilfully brings out some unknown facets about Naxal Movement: The ideological differences between Sanyal and

Mazumdar and its impact on the movement; Sanyal's adventurous journey to China and his meeting with Mao and Chau En-Lai and the fact that Mao told the Indian Naxalites not to blindly copy the tactics that brought him to power. Was Sanyal upset that the Chinese did not support the movement?

A. When I asked him this question, Sanyal said he did not go to China for funds or to learn military training. All he wanted to see was how they implemented the theoretical aspect of Communism in daily life. When the Maoist issue became big news in Nepal, Sanyal told me Communists of one country should not replicate what the communists of other country do because the ground situations are different.

Q. Did he have any regrets?

A. Sanyal's biggest regret was that he did not speak up on certain issues that he felt could harm the movement at the right term. He could not do so for several reasons: One, he was a fugitive and speaking out would mean compromising with his security and the place and direction of the revolution. He also feared that some of Charu Mazumdar's blind supporters would harm him physically.

Comments on the interview

Undoubtedly, this interview is an important document. Making some adverse comment on it should not detract from its value.

"I thought it was Charu Mazumdar who had waged the Naxalite movement and Sanyal was his follower lieutenant,…Sanyal was a political star in his own right". There are three parts of this statement. The first one implies Charu did not conduct this movement. To put the issue in perspective; it was the trio that conducted the movement. But in the final analysis, it is the leader who has a final say on issue and leader in this, without doubt, was Charu. Paul had made an effort to create a little doubt on this aspect, which has no basis. Charu was the leader. How his going to Andhra and visiting rebels there boosted the morale of the latter. Charu had charisma which Sanyal or Jangal did not! It can be accepted Sanyal was a star in his own right, but so was Jangal Santhal. In this respect, Sanyal was a mere follower of the Charismatic Mazumdar.

His reluctance to have a biography done for his life by someone is quite understandable for a Communist leader. It is history that no Indian leaders of the Communist Party had either written autobiography or have an authorised biography on his life. It is true of leaders starting with

Namboodripad through SA Dange, Jyoti Basu to Harkishan Singh Surjit. In Sanyal's case, he may not have given written authorisation to Paul, still he cooperated with him in its completion.

But what is more surprising is his fears that he may be physically eliminated by Mazumdar's more rabid followers. It has happened in the Communist World of Russia and China, one is not sure if it could be so in India's! Any leadership is bound to have differences within its ranks, but they usually are not aired in the open. There are examples at lower level, like that in Kerala where its General Secretary has/had difference with its seniormost octogenarian leader.

Finally, a major disappointment in the interview that issue of Sanyal's suicide is not even touched upon. One cannot easily see a leader like Sanyal ending his life this way, when he and his follower have lived by the bullet. Even this is not clarified as to how did he kill himself, though it is known that he hanged himself in the room he lived in. He was 81. What were his fears? One can only guess or imagine. He rang up to inquire about the book when its last Chapter was being written. Was he apprehensive of critics pouncing on the book? May be, some of his friends or foes still around might express serious differences about his interpretations of certain issues, events or personalities.

Is it that the author purposely did not discuss the issue of his suicide to maintain secrecy about it? Curiosity about the issue should add to the sales of the book, as disclosure in this interview would dip the sale. It is clear that one is only imagining about the reasons or possibilities!

Some other flaws or lack of information on some issues are also noteworthy. Sanyal rang up the author to inquire about this project. When it was in its last chapter. This was a week before his suicide. Author does not disclose when did he actually complete book. At the most, let us assumed, he did so by the end of 2010. What was the interregnum between Sanyal's last call and completion, rather publication of the book?

If the book is published, say by end 2010/ beginning 2011, why its review as late as in November 2014? Believing that author took time to locate a publisher for the book ('Sage' in this case), it could have been published by early 2012. Still, it's so late is not understandable. May be the press did not find the subject important enough for an immediate or early review! Equally, only one daily reviewed the book, of the six one subscribes to! Reviewing books is not considered important and a daily has large number of books it receives for reviewing, say ten, or even twenty. Possibility of a book getting reviewed is one in ten or twenty. All this will remain a matter of speculation till one goes through the book. Before finishing this part, one can think of one more reason for Sanyal's suicide: Some serious illness, which was either too painful or long running one, and he did not have the money for its treatment! Either way, it is a sad end to a great life!

Nostalgic, if emotional, trip to Naxalbari

The newly-minted commissioned officer on his first trip to the North-East (to Nagaland, then the Naga Hills) had fleeting glimpse of railway board, carrying the name the station, Naxalbari. It was 1957 and the name did not ring a bell. It was not known beyond the confines of a sub-division of Darjeeling District.

This officer (the author) had multiple postings in the North-East (Nagaland, Mizoram and Guwahati). During his second tenure there, in the 1970's Naxalbari became a household name, especially among the uniformed community. This officer was naturally inclined to visit this iconic village but could do so only in the third stint in the 1980s by then the Naxalbari Saga was long past; in fact it was all over by 1979. But Naxalbari was still an iconic village; may sacred to this officer because Charu Mazumdar, the Charismatic leader was born here. For him visiting his house was akin to a pilgrimage.

A solider respects a fighter, even if he is on the other side. He saluted the house wherein was born Charu and in and around which there must have been his numerous foot-prints even if not visible then. He had demitted the world over a decade ago, still his spirit could be felt hovering over his house and around it! (He had similar feeling when he visited Phizo's house in Nagaland's Khonoma village, some 30 Km from Kohima, in 1958. Phizo of course was underground then. Nagas are great fighters and so was Phizo).

Of course, in the 1980's Charu's was a forelorn house. Every one in the Naxalbari village know his house. So reaching it was not a problem. More than that, nothing much was known to the youngsters. But some elderly did know who Charu was. More surprisingly, very few knew who was Kanu Sanyal. Only one person knew the name of his village, a few kilometers away from Naxalbari. Due to shortage of time the officer had no time to go beyond Naxalbari. But if one has visited the house of the icon of the Naxalism, his pilgrimage should be deemed to be complete!

Now came the time for departure. By then a lot of people had gathered around the Army jeep the officer has travelled in- urchins young boys and girls and some elderly. There couldn't be much conversation, as only one elder could speak (or understand) broken Hindi.

He was moved by the respect his fellow villagers had for Charu. When the officer gave a final salute to the Charu house and left, he could see scores walking behind the moving vehicle till it went out of sight. The pilgrimage was over.

It was that day the officer decided to do a book on Naxalbari and subsequently, on its linear successor, Maoists. The Naxalism has been dealt with in the author's earlier book, a three-volume treatise, *Terrorism in India,* Kalpaz Publications, 2009. The Maoist insurrection is the subject of the present multi volume book, likely to be published by the end of this (2018) year. For obvious reasons, a Chapter (2) on Naxalism has been included in this work also. After all, Naxalism and Maoism are inseparable twins in the Indian context.

Notes

1. Avijit Ghosh, Times of India, 20.5.2007.
2. EN Rammohan,"Rise of Naxalism: Its implications for National Security and the way forward", in VR Raghavan, Ed, 2011, *Ibid.*
3. Mary Tyler, "My years in an Indian prison" (London: Gollanez, 1997) p. 91.
4. Prakash Singh, The Naxalite Movement in India, (New Delhi; Rupa, 2006), p. 72.
5. The account is based on Col Ved Prakash, Terrorism in India, Kalpaz Publications, 2009; pp. 826-832.
6. *Ibid.*, p. 829.
7. These observation are based on the article penned by Avijit Ghosh after visiting the area that appeared in the Time of India, 20.5.2007.
8. Avijit Ghosh, times of India, 20 May 2007.

3

Generally Speaking

The heading of this Chapter, 'Generally Speaking', has been purposely worded so. A variety of subjects are to be accommodated and dealt with in this chapter. Hence, the heading.

The following subjects are discussed in this Chapter:

- Are the Maoists Terrorists and should they be treated as such?
- Opinion-leaders put under a scanner.
- Press on Maoist Insurrection.
- Judiciary and Maoists.
- Common man on Maoists.

Are the Maoists Terrorists?

Of late, there has been some debate on the genre of the Maoism. Essentially, it is a slotting problem. Various views on the issue are discussed here.

Centre versus the State Wrangle: The Pioneer

In India, the Centre and the States often do not see eye to eye on certain issues of national importance. The worst instance of this dissonance is failure of the two entities to finalise the draft resolution on the National Centre for Counter Terrorism (NCCT), a legislation which would have been even more helpful in tackling Maoist insurrection in the country. It is natural and understandable in a federal polity that the constituent States will jealously guard their autonomous status and not cede any space to the Centre. In this case, the Centre should have appreciated the states' concerns and walked an extra mile to accommodate them. Same way, anti-Maoist joint operations also do not yield desired result.

The following excerpts are culled from an editorial, headed "Maoists are enemies: War on Red terror must continue", in the Pioneer of 19.9.2011. This daily has no doubt that the Maoists are terrorists and should be dealt with and fought as such.

- "Union Minister for Home Affairs admission that joint anti-Maoist operations have not yielded desired results is a signal for all stakeholders...to push ahead with even greater determination to counter Red terror.
- "This would mean a more effective coordination between the Union Government and the six States most affected by the Maoists violence.
- "It is not enough for Mr P. C. Chidambaram to say that the UPA Government has done its bit by deploying additional Central Forces and enhancing the budget allocations for security and infrastructure related sectors. The Centre must provide political support to the States, irrespective of the political parties in power there, to enable them to crush Maoism, as also to implement the development schemes there.
- "Unfortunately, such efforts take a beating when party politics takes over, the Centre and some Congress leaders blame the States not ruled by the UPA allies for their failure to contain the Maoist menace. This is not the time for blame game, because the States' enemy is also the nation's enemy. Maoists are nation's enemies, the Centre must ensure effective coordination between the States, as also between the former and the latter.
- "The Union Government might claim it is doing all it can, some of its recent actions have actually dented that effort. Induction of Binayak Sen as a member of the Planning Commission's committee on health is a case in point. Sen is facing trial on charges of colluding with the Maoists. A local court held him guilty on a host of serious charges. What sort of signal the Union Government is sending by conferring respect on such an accused? (What will be its effect on the security forces? This very Government's Prime Minister spoke of Maoists insurrection as the most serious threat to the nation!)
- "What is worse is that senior Congress leaders make contradictory statements vis-à-vis the government's stance. Mr. Chidambaram has said that the Red terror is even/more serious issue for the country than Jihadi terror. Yet we see senior Congress leaders Digvijay Singh ridiculing their own government's campaign against

the Maoists by demanding a softer approach. This internal bickering undermines nation's will to crush the Maoist ultras.

- "Romantic notions that hardcore Maoists will turn over a new leaf if they are shown compassion should not come in the way of a continued crackdown".

These Congress leaders are obviously oblivious of the serious threat posed to the country by those Maoist desperados, which was so singularly enunciated by Prime Minister Manmohan Singh and quoted ad nauseam by analysts expiating on the subject. The Prime Minister is too weak to check such irresponsible statements from his party's senior leaders, especially someone like Digvijay Singh, who ridiculed Chidambram for his high falutin English!!

This daily, the Pioneer, takes a strong stand on issues of National security, India's strategic interests, nation's integrity and sovereignty. In one word, someone on other side would dub it as ultra nationalist.

From this editorial it is obvious that the daily considers the Maoists not only terrorists but outright enemies of the country, who should be crushed with all the might at its command.

"Maoists are terrorists, don't spare them"

This is the heading of an article by Kanchan Gupta in the Pioneer dated 22.4.2012. Main points from this article are paraphrased here%

- "I was invited to a debate on Maoist violence in a TV studio and I was stunned to hear some people making asinine statements in the mistaken belief that they were being profoundly wise.
- "One of them was Professor Hargopal who refused to criticise Maoists for being what they are: Plunderers, extortionists and mass murderers. He insisted that instead of decimating these enemies of Indian State, "We should bring about the moral pressure on the Maoists and legal pressure on the Government. He also made the fantastic claim that Maoists are not in the business of kidnapping. Obviously, he is either ignorant of the facts or want to suppress them lest those he wants to protect are exposed as being no better than terrorists of other hues.
- "A third point was made by a second panelist and enthusiastically endorsed by many others: The Maoists cannot be equated with *jihadis*—such assertions are no different from the bunkum paddled by Hargopal and his Jholawallah ilk who take an indulgent view of hideous crimes committed by Maoists or terrorists (Whose ideological persuation is immaterial). It is absurd to draw a

distinction between Maoists and *jihadis,* not the least because, as my friend Ajai Sahni, an expert on security issues, put it, 'Getting killed by a Maoists bullet is as bad as getting killed by a *jihadi* bullet'. But such specificities are wasted on those who refuse to read the writing on the wall and are determined to portray ruthless killers as 'Gandhians with guns'. Debating an issue with them is as meaningless as trying to patently explain to likes of Teesta Seetalvad why a break at Kanker would do them a world of good.

- "Prof Hargopal, who has in the past been the preferred choice of the Maoists to negotiate deals with an irresolute State Government, (most notably the Government of Odisha) for reasons that do not merit elaboration, needs to be told that his claims are not founded on reality. Kidnapping civilians, officials and public servants is now a routine affair with Maoists, as routine as terrorising tribals, destroying schools and health centres, blowing up communication towers, killing security forces personnel, using women comrades as sex slaves who are subjected to unimaginable perversity to satiate the filthy desires of those who pose as revolutionaries and killing innocent people to enforce their diktat.
- "The Union Ministry of Home Affairs, which alone seems to be deeply concerned wih the threat posed by the Red terriorists to the nation's internal security, Maoists have kidnapped 1554 people in the past four years (2008-11). Some of the kidnapped were released in exchange of Maoists facing trial; others swapped for cash. As many as 328 were killed in cold blood, many of them after being tried in Kangaroo courts called "*Janadalats*" or people's courts. R.Vineel Sheel, the then DC of Malkagiri in Odisha was kidnapped in 2011, and was released after its Chief Minister Naveen Patnik agreed to free Maoists who were in jail facing trials for their crimes.
- "With each passing day, the Maoists are getting increasingly emboldened as a pusillanimous Indian state wrings its hands in despair. Instead of declaring an all out war on these ultras, we continue to twiddle our thumbs and calculate potential losses. The cautionary voices keep urging restraint lest more security forces personnel are killed in counter-insurgency operations. That is hog wash. Security forces are mandated to fight and thwart the evil forces threatening the country's integrity and sovereignty. In the process, lives will be lost and blood will flow. It does not mean lives of our security forces are expendable or that they can be sacrificed without any concern on the altar of belligerent

extremism. It simply means a nation pays a cost to fight those who threaten our Republic, our democracy and our freedom. Such fights in the past have not been without loss of life—of security forces personnel, of civilians and of those waging war on the state.

- "Public memory being short, few would recall the terrible price that had to be paid to put down the insurgency in the North East, or restore peace in Punjab. Young officers and jawans in the prime of their lives are routinely killed while fighting terrorists in the Jammu and Kashmir or while preventing *jihadis* from crossing Line of Control into India. If we must shed tears we should do so for all our men in uniform who had laid down their lives for their country and their people and steel our resolve to avenge their deaths by exterminating the practitioners of violence, no matter what the shade of their evil ideology or their purported cause".

This article by Kanchan Gupta, has been quoted en extenso by this author for reason given here:

1. Gupta has strong feelings against the Maoists' violence as their authors and the former leaves no doubts that the Maoists are no different from the Jihadi terrorist. As a matter of fact, they are more dangerous than the terrorist as they are able to garner certain support from a section of gullible Indian's masquerading as idealists who are moved by the plight of poor tribals exploited by the State who according to them, work only for the rich and the exploitative classes like the industrialists and businessmen.
2. Gupta is very harsh on people like Hargopal, who work like the overground arm of the underground Maoists. Yet again, it is like this author who has coined a self-explanatory term for such individuals, viz. the 'closet' Maoists, who have been listed and discussed in detail in the last two chapters of this book.
3. Once again, like this author, Gupta has warned the Central Government to wage a war to the finish to exterminate these Maoists, and not go soft in their approach because these jholawallahs are passionate in defending their ideological soul mates".

Can there be a more ugly coinage for these blood thirsty murderers than the "Gandhians with guns". The Mahatma and his followers, believing in *Ahimsa* (non-violence) suffered lathi blows on their bodies without a modicum of resistance, and often they got killed by the British bullets. Gandhiji firmly believed that the *Ahimsa* was the weapons of strong, not of the weak. Their strength lay in accepting and bearing suffering, be it *lathi* blows or the bullets. In contrast, these "Gandhians with guns" (a smart if detestable term) know only the use of guns, merciless murdering, killing innocent civilians, officials and security men who are doing their duty by the nation!

After reading Gupta, one will have no problem about slotting the Maoist murderes as terrorists, barring the likes of Hargopal.

"Maoists, Naxalites or Terrorists? The media seemed confused about the heartland movement" By Pratik Kanjilal.

This piece by Kanjilal appeared in the Indian Express of 1.6.2013. He notes the quibble in the media over the specific term to be applied whenever an act of violence takes place: should it be Naxalites, Maoists or terrorists. He gives some examples of terrorist violence in foreign countries when the media had a problem of slotting them as an act of terrorism or otherwise. He also mentions an instance of queasiness between two Central Ministers over the use of term terrorists vis-à-vis the Maoists. Now, to the specifics.

- "Jairam Ramesh suffered an unusual paroxyism of free speech when he referred to Maoists as terrorists, but fortunately Tribal Affairs Minister K. C. Deo was at hand with the NDTV to ask with pacific calm: how the new classification helped.
- "Indeed, invoking terrorism often confuses the issue. A gruesome killing in London was given a terrorism slant by the UK media, perhaps on the ground that David Cameron had reacted with a 'never buckle to terrorism' speech and the inquiry was being led by the Counter Terrorism Command of the Metropolitans Police. However, the case failed the most basic test of terrorism. A military man was targeted while civilians who were equally vulnerable were not attacked.
- "Governments draw a distinction with terrorists by pointing out that unlike the latter, they do not willfully harm civilians.
- "By 'terrorist', perhaps Ramesh meant 'illegitimate'. The various Maoists movements across the heartland do seem to lack the legitimacy that is conferred by ideology. But further down that route is the strange and terribly simple idyll presently populated by Praveen Swami. An incredible tweet from him: 'The cause of Maoists violence is violent Maoists". Not just dreadful thinking, but dreadful grammar too.
- "One does find a generational divide between the reporting of the original Naxalite rising and its extended presence in Bihar and

that of the present movements. The term Naxalites and the Maoist are interchanged indiscriminately and the reporters and editors do not seem to know the far left consists of multiple movements with different beliefs and strategies. Some even find electoral politics legitimate.

- "Partly, the Maoists themselves are to blame for illiterate coverage. In the absence of well-argued ideology, a militant movement to reduce to a tactical project fit for warlords. You don't care to understand it because it looks likes there is nothing to understand and uncaring reporting follows. In fact, there is media attention only after an attack. Otherwise, we are very happy to follow the latest scam on the telly.
- "Two things appear to have changed in the last four decades. The original rising had attracted the children of the best homes in what are still the Maoists-dense regions. In the West Bengal, some were killed during the movement while many more were bailed out by their families. Of them, some went on to become influential media persons, cultural figures, teachers and thinkers. Their movement generated a huge volume of publicly available literature.
- "The present movement clubbed loosely under the heads of Naxalite and Maoists do not seem to have a literature capable of explaining their position or winning hearts and minds. Naturally, urban elites are cold to them. And so are the media which cannot place these movements in any political context, but must present them in the format of war reporting. Which means that they have nothing much to say in peace time.

Now a critique of the Kanjilal excerpts, reproduced above, accompanied by this author's views and comments there on.

To begin with, Jairam Ramesh's comments are looked into, in two parts. It is rare that any Central Minister dubs the Maoists as terrorists. That is the reason Kanjilal avers it was a fit of paroxyism (of free speech) that Ramesh called the Maoists as Terrorists. One is not surprised that he was immediately questioned by one of his cabinet colleagues "with a pacific calm as to how the new classification helped". The Tribal Affairs Minister possibly had his reasons. Tribals being his constituency as their minister, maybe he did not want to antagonise the Maoists.

Kanjilal feels Ramesh, when he dubbed them as terrorists, was alluding to their, illegitimacy, essentially flowing from the fact that they do not have an ideology. It is the ideology alone that confers legitimacy on such violent movement.

Kanjilal is perplexed by Swami's tweet: "The cause of Maoist violence are violent Maoists". But on deeper level, Swami seems to have meaning. May be he feels it is Maoist's violence that invites proportionate crackdown from the Government. Swami is too well-read, knowledgeable and experienced a journalist to display a "dreadful thinking" and on second thoughts, one may concede a point to Kanjilal, because Swami seems to be preaching non-violence to the 'violent Maoists'.

Kanjilal's averment on the Maoist's lack of ideology seems to be apt. The original Naxalism was driven by ideology nurtured by that charismatic leader; Charu Mazumdar. Best minds joined him. The movement was crushed with a heavy-hand by the Jyoti Basu-Home Ministry of West Bengal. The ones who survived the ordeal rose to great heights in various fields. Secondly, that movement in the 1960's produced literature that won wide spread respectability and legitimacy for it. It is this lack of publicly-available literature which has proved a factor in their inability to win the hearts and minds of the middle classes. This very factor has caused the illiterate coverage. Consequently, the Maoists today get into the news only after some major incident of violence perpetrated by them. This media, which cannot place these movements into any political context, must present them in the form of war reporting. The fact of the Maoists destroying the existing infrastructure concerning schools, health facilities and transportation is widely reported by the 24×7 TV media. They are also seen as those coming in the way of the state trying to create development projects to ameliorate the lot of much-neglected tribal areas.

Given all this, it is not surprising that the general perception of the Maoists is no better than that of terrorists. In fact, some even perceive them as worse than the *jihadi* terrorists.

Opinion leaders put under a scanner

This section deals with some articles/opinion pieces penned by certain retired officials/IPS officers/Army officers and security specialists. A politician as also two common men also appears. These will be critiqued by this author, at times harshly if deemed necessary. All articles will be excerpted and paraphrased briefly to cover essential point.

Fragile State, Timid police, 9.6.2007 by KPS Gill

Some important parts are excerpted here

- "The institutional collapse and fragility of the State in India have once again been demonstrated by the rogue agitation by the Gujjars in Rajasthan, Haryana and Delhi.

- Throughout this agitation, the police generally stood passively, apparently under patently illegal 'directives' from the political leadership.' Taking *suo motu* notice of breakdown of the law and order, the Supreme Court has demanded that the Police Chiefs of these states explain their failure to contain the violent agitation, which it termed a 'national shame'. It reminded the police that it was bound to act by law and could not take the plea that political directives required otherwise, or were lacking.
- "By calling for explanations from the police chiefs, the top court has to put the State Governments, and indeed the entire political class, on notice.
- "Violent agitations involving mass mobilisation have invariably been accompanied by damage to public and private property and other acts of violence against the general public and this has been a regular feature since our independence, often masquerading under the rubric of *Satyagraha*, peaceful protests and 'just grievances'.
- Political violence seems to have become a routine for articulation of grievances and training ground for future 'leaders'. Public property—which is looked upon, not as a national resource, but as nobody's property—is the first target of this violence. This has become a hoary tradition in Indian politics and there are many who have achieved national leadership status through petty acts of vandalism, and a few months spent in jail or by blowing up railway lines and evading arrest by going 'underground' for a few months to emerge as heroes. It is immaterial whether they actually possess any attributes of heroism.
- "The Supreme Court's orders and registrations of cases against Gujjar leaders who provoked the recent violence exposed this faux heroism. But the use of mass violence as a political tool will not be dented or delegitimised by this single initiative.
- "I recall a conference at which a former President of the country, who had also served one time as its Home Minister, not a very successful at that (which regretfully, has been the case with all Home Ministers with the notable exception of Sardar Vallabhbhai Patel), spoke after I had made a presentation emphasising the rule of law and the need to maintain security of life and property. The eminent gentle man said I had "spoken like a policeman" and his observation was greeted with much applause and laughter by what passes for intelligentsia in this countrys unfortunate capital.

He boasted further that he had met AASU leadership at the height of agitation and thought that this was to be displayed as mark of distinction.

- "I did not, on that occasion, see it fit to embarrass him in public by telling him that we police officers in Assam- would fight the AASU on the street all day long and then meets their leaders during night to tell them to moderate their agitation, but that we would continue to maintain the law and order in the street will all the force at our command".

K.P.S. Gill is a well known figure in India. Nation will ever be beholden to him for retrieving Punjab for India during the 1980s insurrection. Chief Minister Beant Singh too deserves credit to the extent that he gave him a free hand to handle a very difficult and critical situation.

Most of his observations are unsavoury but starkly true. Crowds burning buses, houses and other public property are a common sight even today; under whatever pretext. Some young leaders using violent agitations as a training ground to build their career is again a stark truth. There are photos in the Indira Gandhi Memorial showing Sanjay Gandhi defiantly fighting police, which only proves what Mr. Gill says.

The Delhi intelligentsia applauding a former President's boast about his meeting with the AASU leaders does not reflect well for themselves. But Mr. Gills averment on country's Home Minister is over wrought. Besides the great Sardar, L.K. Advani too was an effective Home Minister, even if not of the same stature. But it is also a fact that most Prime Ministers do not want to have a powerful Home Ministers for understandable reasons. A defeated Shivraj Patil being appointed Home Minister is an apt example of this truth. He would always be beholden to Sonia Gandhi, even if Manmohan Singh was the Prime Minister.

The Author takes a liberty of expressing his long-held belief about yeoman's service rendered by this outstanding policeman to the country in dispelling and defeating Khalistani insurrection in Punjab. He deserves nothing less than the Bharat Ratna for these services for the country, his subsequent act of an indiscretion with an IAS female officer notwithstanding.

Mr. Gill's article does not exclusively deal with the issue of Maoists insurrection. Still, its critique is apposite to it, since it deals with the classes which are involved with combating and controlling it, *viz.,* the politicians, the bureaucracy and the police. There is a glimpse of disposition and conduct of the nation's intelligentsia.

An important point he makes is about the Supreme Court intervening when the police fail to act to stop the destruction of property during violent Jat agitation. We shall see the same top court ordering a State Government to disband Salwa Judum outfit, which had effectively countered the Maoist outrages. There will be more on it in a later part.

Caught between Robbers and killers: 25.7.11 (India Today) by Prakash Singh

Prakash Singh was once DGP of a State and later retired as DG, BSF. He had a reputation as an honest and outspoken officer. He wrote an interesting article in 2011 on the issue of Maoists, which is critiqued here. His piece is excerpted here.

- "The Maoists threat to internal security of the country is degenerating as a battle between robbers in the establishment and the killers amongst the Naxalites. Both swear by the ideology. Government spokespersons show their concern for the Aam Admi but the truth is that the heart of the ruling elite beats for the corporates. On the other hand, the Maoists pretend to Champion the cause of the poor but their actions have brought only sufferings to the tribals. Both, tragically, indulge in exortion-one in the garb of development and other to sustain its 'protracted people's war' against a government it finds semi-colonial and semi-faudal.
- "The Government under P. Chidambaram's policy of 'clear, hold and develop', launched a massive operation beginning 2010 to quell the Maoists rebellion. Forces were deployed in significant numbers in Naxalite-hit states of Chhattisgarh, Bihar, Jharkhand, Odisha, Maharashtra and West Bengal. The Minister asserted that Maoists scourge would be contained in a couple of years. But barely had the operations begun when discordant voices began to be heard. Jharkhand was the first to express its opposition to the use of force, its Chief Minister apprehending that such action would lead to further alienation of the people. Mamta Banerjee has consistently shown a soft corner for the Maoists. Maximum dampener to the Home Minister's campaign was the Congress General Secretary Digvijay Singh's criticism of the minister, presumably with Sonia Gandhi's blessings emphasising 'hearts and minds approach; undoubtedly, development gets high priority in counter-insurgency/Maoists areas, but it can only supplement and not substitute the security approach. There can be no state within a state, an irregular army alongside regular troops.

- "There are no overall strategic plans and the state satraps are pursuing their own ad hoc policies. There is lack of seriousness/ commitment at all levels, reflected at ground level in the slow pace of modernisation and expansion of the police forces...lack-adaisical operations by field commanders and tardy works on development front by bureaucracy which thinks it is not their battle.
- Taking advantage of those short-comings the Maoists have established their presence over a huge territorial area: 223 districts in 20 states of the Union.
- "They continue to expand, urban centres being their latest thrust areas. They have already penetrated Delhi and sneaked into the metropolitan's cities of Mumbai, Kolkata and Bangalore.
- "The schemes launched by the Government stay on the paper... and there is no intended impact essentially because the bulk of the funds are either siphoned off or embezzled.
- "Monsters of corruption are exposed but they continue to hold high office. Politicians with links to Dawood Ibrahim manage to get away; those who destroyed the national carrier remain unscathed.

Most of the points made by Prakash Singh are valid and need to be well-taken. But occasionally, he indulges in rhetorical flourish and sometimes he tends to be cynical; both are specified in this paragraph. Dubbing the Government as robbers is being downrightly cynical, too clever by half. Saying that ruling elites are all for corporates, he speaks the childish if political language of the Congress, Leftists, Samajwadi Party and Janta Dal (μ) on the NDA's land acquisition bill. Building schools and hospitals is to help the corporates. Construction and repairing of roads is to the help the corporates, as if no road can connect the villages, transport the agricultural produce from there to the market, all hospitals will admit only the rich and corporates, and communication towers for the mobile phones, with which today 82 per cent of Indians are connected, are meant only for the corporates. "There is no serious commitment to fight Maoist violence among the politicians, bureaucrats and security forces" is pure hog wash, harsh terminology is needed here. The CRPF, state police forces, and at times the BSF, are indifferent, if not happy, towards the losses suffered by them is wild generalisation, not worthy of even a Prakash Singh. The politicians are convenient whipping boys today but which community of Indians is free from the taint of corruption? The judiciary, the police, the army, officialdom or professionals? There are many J. S. Verma's, Prakash Singh's, Gen VK Singh's among these classes. Even politics has its Antony's,

Karpoori Thakurs, Jyoti Basu's, MS Namboodripads *et. al.* No system is perfect but all concerned are out doing their best. No polity has been able to eradicate corruption in the history, human's beings what they are. Forget about democracies, even the dictatorships, like China's or Russia's, have failed this test. Yes, corruption can be controlled to an extent, which some countries in the West, say Scandinavians, have done so. Even India might achieve this desideratum under a Modi or a Kejriwal.

Tentacles of Red Menace: Joginder Singh

Joginder Singh is a retired IPS officer, who headed CBI once. He has written a couple of books, and regularly contributes to the newspapers. Extracts from the first of two articles he penned for the Pioneer daily. This one was in the issue dated 12.12.11.

- "Maoists politburo member Mallujula Koteshwar Rao, alias Kishenji, wanted for various horrendous crimes was killed in a police encounter on 24 November 2011. The killing led his supporters and some political parties to allege he was killed in a fake encounter. The officials denied the charge. The CPI (Maoists) and its various front organisations called for a two-days bandh to protest Kishenji's killing.
- "Maoists neither respect citizen's rights nor believe in India's Constitution. But they are overly mindful of these murderers' rights. West Bengal Chief Minister Mamta Banerjee's response to these allegation, 27 November: "They fired 1000 rounds, did not pay heed after the police gave them three day's time....When a common man is killed, the Maoists never take out a rally or call a bandh. Does a common man have no human rights?
- "In some 1600 violent incidents by the Maoists in 2010, 669 people were killed. There have been several attacks, ambushes and explosions over the last five years...It is amazing that a crescendo of protest is raised only when a killer, be a Maoists or a terrorists, is gunned down. Obviously for these protesting groups, the killing of killers is a greater crime than killing of innocent citizens or security personnel.
- "Maoists are exploiting the dire poverty in tribal and other backward regions. Planning has failed these deprived people. November 2011 Transparency International Report indicates highest level of corruption in India. Corruption comes in the way of development of Maoism-infected area.

These are appropriate observations, keeping in mind the realities of ground situation. No comments from the Author are deemed necessary.

"Your deed is your Destiny": 2.4.12: Joginder Singh

This Article appeared in the Pioneer daily. Some important excerpts are given here.

- "In a recent trip to Chhattisgarh, Home Minister P. Chidambaram said it was condemnable that big business houses were funding the Maoists...The Essar Group has a huge plant at Bailadila in Dantewada to ferry iron dust to Vishakhapatnam through an underground pipeline which passes through Maoists-infested area...The police charge sheeted an official of the company with serious offences, including sedition, for providing 'financial support' to the insurgents. In his defence, he said he was not supplying money to the Maoists in his personal capacity, he was working on behalf of the Essar.
- "This is the first time that a corporate House is being investigated for paying off Maoists.
- "Against the background of string of Maoist attacks including the 6 April 2010 Chintagufa one in Chhattisgarh which claimed the lives of 75 CRPF men and police man, Prime Minister Manmohan Singh singled out Left-wing extremism as 'the biggest internal security threat ever faced by the Country'. Since this clarion call by him, the country has suffered umpteen attacks, but the Government has failed to come up with an effective counter-Maoists strategy due to several reasons.
- "The world knows only two ways of dealing with the Maoists: Either force or peace talks. The Home Minister had asked for the mandate but the states refused to do that. The former could not get the Chief Ministers to agree to a National Centre for Counter-Terrorism (NCCT).
- "To deal with the Maoists, the Government will do well to follow what the ***Brihadaranyanka Upanishad*** says:

  Your are what your deep, driving desire is.

  As your deep, driving desire is, so is your will.

  As your will is, so is your deed.

  As your deed is, so is your destiny.

Some points are commented upon from Joginder Singh's observations. This might be the first time that a corporate house is investigated for paying off the Maoists. But corporates are known to pay off large number of insurgent groups in the North-East who are capable of hampering or destroying their projects, assets or functioning. Then the politicians in power, Chidambaram in the instant case and AGP's Mohanta in Assam when the Tata's were found giving some financial help to the ULFA insurgents, take political mileage out of such compulsions of the corporates. If the concerned corporates offer not to pay the insurgents, can the Government can ensure the safety and security of their plants/equipments and their functioning? The ruling class will never accept the Challenge!

"A Red Corridor paved with corruption" 9.2.11

This article by Asha Shukla appeared in the Pioneer. Excerpts follow:

- "A charming drive through Keshkal Valley on the National Highway 43, from Raipur to Jagdalpur in Bastar, a visitor sees many picturesque waterfalls and forests. Nothing seems to be amiss in this rural belt in India's hinterland, conveying a sense of prosperity and development.
- "Turning off this tourist circuit, one faces a contrasting picture, forcing a question: Why are few roads in Bastar well constructed and others are at their unbelievable worst? Why does this problem still exist despite the availability of ample resources and repeated Five Year Plan budget?
- "The answer seems rather evident in its simplicity: Maoists presence. Bastar region, labeled the stronghold of the Maoists guerrillas, has always had the development process lagging, with roads being the first target. Rural Development Minister Jairam Ramesh, who, visiting the region last month (November 2011), called for a speedy completion of welfare projects, primarily rural roads, within three to four years with a sense of urgency and his characteristic 'Get-it-done' attitude, would certainly believe so.
- "But there is more to situation that meets the eye: Corruption. It exists in other parts of the country, but it has far greater disastrous consequences here. On the pretext of road construction, several contractors, bureaucracts and politicians, over the years, have garnered massive benefits for themselves. This however, does not take away the sufferings caused to the region due to Maoist violence, for the road leading to this level of corruption was laid down by this extremist violence itself.
- **"Some examples of this corruption are cited here:** (1) NH-43 has two partial bridges whose construction had started several years ago. Over the years, accidents, traffic jams etc., are the only 'benefits' the locals have received from such development efforts.

(2) The road from Kanker to Bhanupratapur in Kanker District is another road similarly scattered with such bridges. (3) poor maintenance of roads between Dantewada and Bijapur districts tell a similar tale. (4) The road from Bhairamgarh to Nimedh is dotted with several CRPF camps. It would be a lot easier to repair these roads if the labour was allowed shelter in these camps.

- "Dealing with such rampant corruption behind the pretext of Maoists fear needs streamlined planning.

Only one point needs comment on this piece. That the labour should be provided shelter in the CRPF camps is a workable suggestion. The writer should have discussed this issue with the CRPF officers which she obviously did not. It is convenient to position the labour near the construction sites. If placed away in CRPF camps, their transportation to the construction sites may be a logistical problem, besides the possibility of their being ambushed en route.

"Pity the Nation that can't fight Maoists": 15.4.12

This piece is by Kanchan Gupta that appeared in the Pioneer daily. The excerpts follow:

- "Why is it that whenever the issue of whether or not the Government should set free people accused or found guilty of ghastly crimes to secure the release of hostages held by terrorists comes up for public debate, the Kandhar swap is cited as an example. Undoubtedly the decision to set free three terrorists was a low point in India's long running battle against terrorism.
- "But should that be used as a standard? But the decision, which continues to be criticised for showing India as a soft state in fighting terrorists, was not entirely prompted by Atal Behari Vajpayee's NDA Government running out of options or reacting in panic. There was relentless pressure on the Government brought about by the families of the passengers on board IC-814 and an utterly irresponsible media discussing on weeping women and children in such a manner that a selective representation of the popular reaction to the high jacking came to be viewed as the mood of the nation, which of course it was not. The Congress, the main opposition, cynically exploited the situation to score brownie points even while telling the Government that it would support whatever decision was taken in the national interest. With hindsight, had the Government decided not to negotiate and dared the terrorists to do their worst, the Congress would have refused to approve of it.

- "All that, however, is really inconsequential. No one situation can be treated as a standard while dealing with similar situations that may vary in detail but are essentially about hostage-taking by terrorists irrespective of their ideological persuasion. If we are to look for what should be response of a state that is loath to surrender before terrorists, if an example from the past is to be held up as a lesson for those who govern India and its states today, then we should recall the firmness with which Prime Minister Indira Gandhi dealt with hostage takers in her time.
- "True, events of a quarter century ago are rarely remembered especially in a country like India where masses have a poor sense of history and the classes have a loathing for the past. Yet, at times it is necessary to recall the events if only to highlight how our national resolve has weakened in direct proportion to the strengthening of our economy.
- "Politically convenient and socially fashionable bunkum about India as soft power has left the Indian state looking vulnerable as never before. This is most evident from the response of both society and authority on terrorism. Instead of standing up and daring those who use bombs and guns to terrorise us, we meekly surrender, thus, exposing ourselves to further violence in all its burid hues.
- "Yet, it was not always like this. In February 1984, an Indian diplomat, Ravinder Mhatre, posted at Birmingham, was kidnapped by the members of the then UK-based Jammu and Kashmir Liberation Front (JKLF). Within hours of kidnapping, the abductors issued their list of demand which included one million pounds in cash and the release of Maqbool Butt, the JKLF founder, then lodged in Delhi's Tihar Jail after being sentenced to death for killing personnel of Indian security forces in Kashmir.
- "There were hectic efforts to persuade Mrs. Gandhi to agree to negotiate a deal with the abductors. She remained unmoved. Her message was unambiguous: No talks, no deal. On 6th February, Mhatre's body was found in a lane. He had been shot dead after the JKLF realised it was futile to expect a swap. A grim-faced Mrs. Gandhi struck back. Butt was executed five days later on 11th February after the then President Zail Singh was told to dismiss his mercy petition. The JKLF leaders in Birmingham panicked and fled Britain; it is another matter that British Courts failed to fetch justice to Mhatre.

- "Critics would say Mrs. Gandhi's tit-for-tat policy did not yield long-term results. This is a fallacious arguments, not the least because it overlooks certain crucial facts. Between 1984 and 1989, the JKFL cadre was on the run, with their leaders in jail. It is only when the Government in New Delhi began to falter and appeared enfeebled and emaciated that the JKLF reared its head once again: (1) Rajiv Gandhi lacked his mother's gumption as was clear in the closing days of his stint in power. (2) V.P. Singh may have been crafty but was a weakling when it came to demonstrating political courage. His appointing Mufti Mohd Sayeed as his Home Minister was a disastrous decision.
- "Mrs. Gandhi had based her decision not to negotiate a deal with Mhatre's kidnappers on the simple principle that a country as large as India could absorb the loss of one official but it could not countenance the threat posed by terrorists. It worked till VP Singh came to power and gave the Ministry of Home Affairs to the Mufti. On 8 December 1989, Rubaiya Saeed, the Mufti's daughter was kidnapped in Kashmir by JKLF terrorists. They demanded release five senior commanders from the prison. V.P. Singh capitulated and Jammu and Kashmir has never been the same again; nor has the Government been able to stand firm against terrorist demands. It irreparably broke the national spirit and the will of the Government, as was witnessed during the week-long saga of shame that followed the hijacking of IC-814 to Kandahar.
- "Tragically, since then the Indian state's capitulation at Kandahar has become a convenient cover for the pusillanimous politicians to justify their meek and timid response to terrorism. For evidence, look at how the Chief Minister of Odisha has conceded the demands of the Maoists, not once but twice in the past couple of years, leaving those waging a brutal war on the Indian State in no doubt as to whose banner flies higher. If that is a shame, then it is a pity that this nation is not enraged.

Kanchan Gupta has already appeared once earlier in this Chapter, where he left no one in doubt that he positively considers Maoists as terrorists. Here, he has extended his belief by giving a brief account of how the Indian States has capitulated before the terrorists barring a singular exception, where Mrs. Gandhi, often described as 'the only man in her cabinet' refused to strike a deal with the kidnappers of Mhatre.

The worst example was V.P. Singh's surrender to the terrorists, agreeing to swap five terrorist 'commanders' with the release of his Kashmiri Home

Minister Sayeed's daughter in December 1989. Is it a surprise that the kidnappers in this case again were the JKLF terrorists? More importantly, was it a coincidence that militancy in Jammu and Kashmir reared its vicious head in that very year?

At the end, Gupta condemns Odisha Chief Minister for conceding the demands of the Maoists twice in two years. To extend the point further, we can say he is no exception. So many other Chief Minister have talked to the Maoists, through the interlocutors appointed by them. For a change since the release of Deputy Collector Menon of a Chhattisgarh district, no occasion has risen for any negotiations or deals with the Maoists.

The UPA was unable to frame any coherent policy to combat the Maoists, though certain states had formulated guidelines to deal with the Maoists who surrendered. UPA Home Minister Chidambaram failed to finalise draft of the National Centre for Counter-terrorism Bill because some states refused to let the Centre encroach on their autonomy. The Modi Government has not as yet said anything on reviving the NCDC, which if passed, could be helpful in fighting the Maoists. We are yet far off a coordinated effort to counter Maoism where two State Governments are involved. There have been serious spats between the CRPF and a state when engaged in a joint anti-Maoists operation, as also between the IAF and a state.

NDA Home Minister Rajnath Singh has made a couple of statements in the recent past, indicating somewhat tougher policy on combating Maoist violence. But no coherent, well-thought out bill has come before the public on the issue. One hopes they do not take too long to come up with one.

"Let us not romanticize Maoists, or, demonise security forces: 16.7.12: Jairam Ramesh

What follows ar extracts from an interview, published in the Times of India on 16th July 2012. Ramesh is the only politicians to appear in this section of the Chapter. It should be of interest to examine his views on the Maoist insurrection, he being one of the most articulate ministers in the UPA Ministry/ Cabinet. Excerpts from the story are reproduced here.

- "Jairam Ramesh, Union Minister for Rural Development, is known for his contrarian views. Currently, the Maoist insurgency occupies his attention as he is visiting 31 Maoists-affected districts and exploring the issue up close. Speaking with Mono Bina Gupta, Ramesh discussed Maoists politics, tribal development and the land acquisition bill.

Q. How would you characterise the Maoists movement?

A. Of the 82 districts classified as Left-wing extremist districts, the core of the problem lies in 25-30 forest rich, tribal–dominated, mineral-rich and remote districts. So far, we have dealt with Maoists violence largely as a security issue. True, there can be no development in the absence of security, but it is a limited perspective.

On thinking about these issues, I came to believe in a two-pronged strategy of security and development. Then I realised political mobilisation was missing. In the absence of this, young men and women were being forced to join Maoists organisations. As I got more involved and looked at rural development, housing and water issues, I found the fourth missing elements of rights, dignity and justice.

I have seen how tribals have been displaced multiple times since the 1950's and 1960's, without proper relief and rehabilitation. According to Walter Fernandes, the number of the displaced is between two and five crores. Land has been taken without adequate compensation. Development alone, building bridges and schools would not work. It is about rights and justice, implementing constitutional safeguards.

It has taken Andhra Pradesh decades to deal with the Maoists problems, combining security, development, politics and justice issues. Despite my serious differences with Mamta Banerjee, I have seen the difference she and Shubhendu Adhikari have made on the ground. Mamta's action of going to the Jangal Mahal, picking up and kissing a baby has been far better than sending thousands of forces. Political cadres are active today in Jangal Mahal.

- **Q. Speaking of forces, what is your opinion on the recent Bijapur Killings?**

  A. A judicial inquiry has been ordered. I have read the report prepared by activists and had long discussion with the CRPF. As always, truth on the ground is incredibly complex, genuine mistakes may have been committed just as innocents may have been used as shields.

- **Q. What about killing human shields including many children?**

  A. I have a PS who was abducted by the Maoists in Feb 2011 in Malkangiri, kept in custody for ten days. His abductors included 14 years old. What are these activists talking about?

  Let us not romanticize Maoists—there is a certain tendency on the part of intellectuals and activists to domonise the security forces and romanticize the Maoists. I do neither. You have to be realistic.

- **Q. What is your position on the land acquisition bill?**

  A. We are giving flexibility to states. If Mamata wants the Centre to have no role and to deindustrialise Bengal—Who are we to protest? The State must play an important role in land acquisition under well-defined rules. Land and information markets are imperfect with an asymmetry of power and information. If you allow private investors to buy land, they would strike deals with large land owners bamboozling small land owners. The state has to protect the interest of the land owners and livelihood losers. This is what Singur taught us. Differing with the earlier Bill, the present Bill implicitly recognises the rights of both land and livelihood-losers.

- **Q. How do you view Centre-State relations?**

  A. We are not leaving everything to states. Why then have a Central Law? It is a bad idea to have the pendulum swing from a strong Centre to a withered away Centre. We need a strong Centre as well as strong States, nagar polikas and panchayats. Decentralisation should not mean abdication of the Central Government's role—Central Government is absolutely essential in the Indian Context.

The daily in the blurb says "Ramesh is known for his contrarian views". In this interview, he often resorts to rhetorical indulgence and speaks the language of an all-knowing politician. His interview is reproduced verbatim and will be critiqued/discussed extensively.

"So far, we have dealt with Maoist violence largely as a security issue". Knowing well that this averment is wholly true, he covers his flanks: "True, here can be no development in the absence of security". No polity can be so ignorant or foolish to treat any insurgency as law and order problem. It is also equally true that force alone cannot solve the insurgency violence. But greater truism is stated here: only forces can convince the extremists like the Maoists that their violence cannot be allowed to conquer a country and replace the democratically elected government with their extremist creed. Armed forces are in the ultimate weapon in the hand of a democracy. Development of tribal and other backward areas is a must, but that is only possibly if the Maoists are pushed in a corner. It is only then that the state can start construction of roads and building schools and hospitals. Politicians and *Jholawallas* can keep talking and mouthing clichés like "Maoists are our brethren gone astray" or "Force is not the answer". But the experience the world over tells a different story. It is only force that will convince the Maoists to come to the negotiations table, or mend their ways. As it is stated somewhere in this book, if a member of a family goes astray or become violent, he has to be retrained or even eliminated.

Ramesh knows India has not dealt with the Maoist violence as security issue. Force is the initial dose of a medicine. Same was the case when India post-independence dealt with the Phizo insurrection or Laldenga's Mizo rebels. The latter had to be even bombed for a day before ground forces could move in.

Ramesh is talking about two pronged strategy of security and development (he gets his priorities right, 'Security' and 'development') and then political mobilisation. It is good that he understands that political moblisation is possible only after the situation has been stabilised by the security forces. Even then, Ramesh cannot visit these areas without a large contingent of security force which ensures his personal safety. Additional forces have to be deployed to ensure that the Maoists do not infiltrate the areas he is visiting.

Ramesh applauds Mamata Banerjee for going to Jangal Mahal and kissing a baby, which he says is "far better than sending thousands of forces". He is not only indulging in political rhetoric, but is also trying to please- (or is it appeare) his political opponent! If kissing a baby can make thousands of forces redundant, then a daily visit to kiss tribal babies in different districts is sure to bring peace in Chhattisgarh and Jharkhand! Even naivety should have some limits. Kissing babies is an old gimmick, practiced down the line, starting with India's first Prime Minister, Nehru (only one exception seem to be that of Vallabhbhai Patel, India's Iron Man).

Political cadres are active today in Jangal Mahal, says Ramesh. If so, it is courtesy security forces. The politicians tend to forget this basic truth- the real fact of life.

Happily, Ramesh has spoken honestly on two aspects of Maoist violence. To the question about security forces killing human shields, many children. Reiterating that many abductors are 14-years-old, he adds a telling question: "What are these activists talking about"? To this Author's relief and satisfaction, it was heartening to read a Central Minister uttering ground realities truthfully, which is reproduced here: "Let us not romanticize Maoists- there is a certain tendency on the part of intellectuals and activists to demonise the security forces and romanticize the Maoists. I do neither. You have to be realistic".

In anti-Naxal war, beware turning State into a destructive power: 13.5.2012

This article, penned by Pupul Datta Prasad. He is senior superintendent of police, serving with the National Human Rights Commission, New Delhi. Excerpts follow:

- "Amid the continuing saga of abduction and killing of state functionaries by the Maoists, the country is agonizing over the ways of eliminating the Maoists problem. While all the legal and legitimate options should be on the table of the policy makers, an out-and-out bellicose and militaristic response to such crises would be ill–advised.
- "It is difficult to articulate a seemingly restrained approach to counter Maoists depredations in public discourse smacking of the either-or fallacy the George Bush variety. So, point out the risks, ethical, moral and legal issues and strategic issues which are arrayed against a purely militaristic approach and be ready to be dubbed a closet Naxalite sympathizer. One must stick one's neck out and assert that a self-destructive war against the Maoists is simply not an option. This will put the credibility of our democracy at stake.
- "First, the enthusiasm to promote armed conflict with the Maoists to the status of war seems to stem from misunderstanding that once it is 'declared' as a war, the state is free to deal with the menace unfettered by human rights considerations. This is not so even in war, where international humanitarian law prohibits causing unnecessary sufferings to the combatants and enjoins on the state to safeguards certain fundamental human rights of its enemies.

  "Secondly, there are practical and ethical considerations that weigh against any sort of War Jingoism. A democracy must ensure that it is not pushed into a situation where it is proved to commit excesses against its own people. Carpet bombing all the Naxali bastions would be ill-advised. That would cause civilian casualties, something which the Naxalites always welcome, as it enables them to have new recruits in their ranks and to claim that the Indian democracy is a mere pretence. Moreover, India is not Sri Lanka. A state has responsibilities towards its citizens, which the Maoists do not have.

"Third, hailing KPS Gill's no-holds barred offensive against extremism in Punjab as the only effective way, papers over a few home truths. No doubt, Gill's leadership was an important factor in ending militancy, but it is good to remember that a populace tired of incessant violence had voted with its feet against militants. It needs to the remembered that had the militants not lost all the sympathies of state's people, the situation may have been very different today. Add to this the alleged flagrant violations of the human rights, on the mass scale during security operation in Punjab; it becomes obvious that a brutal approach to the Naxal problem can easily prove to be its own undoing.

- "A prudent, holistic approach bereft of Chauvinism of any kind has to be followed to deal with the problem. The peculiar socio-economic, administrative and governance exploited by the Naxalites to entrench themselves has to be assiduously improved, if that entails deference to imperatives of security in the short run, then so be it. When innocent lives are being lost, the state should not convert the confrontation into a full-scale war. The remedy should not be worse than the disease."

It is an amazing piece penned by a senior serving police officer, but is quite understandable that he is doing so for and on behalf of the National Human Rights Commission (NHRC). He has been effectively 'deployed' by the latter to push its human rights agenda, even if it is at the cost of national interest. This officer has gone to the extent of advocating that national security may be compromised for a short run ("so be it") in the process. This is an act of egregious irresponsibility by this police officer to put it honestly. At a personal level, one may harshly say that he is angling for an extension of his tenure with the NHRC.

For the rest, he has used usual clichés that closet Maoists normally do to support the ultras. Interestingly, he has himself realised in the early part of his article that the type of arguments he is offering to soft-pedal the menace to national security, he is likely to be dubbed a closet variety of the Maoists. He seems to be 'preaching' to the policy-makers of India, who are unlikely to be taken in by his sermons.

With this sort of thinking, he deserves to be included in the list of closet Maoists—not merely a "Closet Naxalite sympathizer", as he himself avers!

Maoists are in business: 16.4.2012

Kidnapping civilians is better proposition

This article in the Pioneer is penned by Joginder Singh, a former Director, CBI. Some excerpts follow.

- "Blackmail has become a paying industry for terrorists of all hues, Maoists included. The Red terrorists are emboldened in their ways by the fact that both in the past and even now they have succeeded in bringing the Government to its knees by abducting innocent people. They have discovered that evenin killing the security personnel does not produce the same impact as kidnapping.
- "Recent abduction of an Italian foreigner and an Odisha MLA yielded them rich reward as the State Government agreed to release two dozen Maoists prisoners in exchange. But it is unfair to single out the Odisha Government. Naveen Patnaik's decision reflects the national policy on the issue that was adopted by the Government of India way back in 1989. The daughter of the then Union Home Minster, abducted in Srinagar on 8th February that year, was released after five days as a result of prolonged negotiations, in exchange of five terrorist captives. The event proved a turning point in the history of Kashmir; the ultras realising that kidnapping was an easy way to bend the Government to accede to their demands.
- "The result was that terrorists nearly took Srinagar and the Kashmir Valley soon after that incident. I should know since I was then IGP (CRPF) in Srinagar. The situation thence on started going downhill. It gave an aura of invincibility to the jihadists, as it has now given to Maoists. Needless to say that one incident sparked an abduction spree in Jammu and Kashmir. Some of the incidents that followed are listed here:
    - Terrorists abducted a French engineer working on a power project in Kishtwar in 1992.
    - In August 1993, five JKLF militants were released in exchange for release of a DIG, Police.
    - In 1994, two British Nationals were kidnapped from Pahalgam by Harkat-ul-Ansar but were safely released after two weeks.
- "Both terrorists and Maoists have one objective: Cow down States. Anyone nurturing the thought that either outfit is driven

solely by concern for the poor, should perish the thought! In fact, there is hardly any difference left between the common criminals and the Maoists or the *jihadists.*

- "Maharashtra's Home Minister has alleged that corporates fund the Maoists, but no action can be taken against them as there is no evidence that will stand in a court.
- "The Home Minister report puts the extoration racket of the Maoists at ₹ 1,400 crore annually. What are the sources of these collections? The sale of *Tendu* leaves, cut from the contractors, mobile service operators, protection money from the corporates and the rich, and the ransom money from the abductee's relatives. The Ministry's figure is a mere estimate and actual amount could be much larger, since neither the Maoists pay income tax, nor the payees reflect the sums in their returns. Undoubtedly, the amount collected by the Maoists in each region is substantial enough to keep them in the business.
- "Odisha succumbing to the Maoists blackmail can buy them a temporary relief, but the latter would stage more such incidents. There is already evidence of this. Police records show that Odisha logged third highest number of cases of abduction by the Maoists after Chhattisgarh and Jharkhand. In the last fours, Maoists have abducted some 140 people and killed 15 of them.

  But the trend to kidnap high-profile people in recent times began only in Feb 2011 when the Maoists abducted at gunpoint the then Collector of Malkangiri. This enabled them to exchange half a dozen of their people under police custody for release of the Collector.
- "The moists had done a similar abduction of 11 government officials including seven IAS officers in 1987 in Andhra Pradesh. They were released only after they get some hardened criminals freed (one can add the case of our national surrender before the terrorists at Qandahar in 2000). We may be in for bigger trouble ahead, as appeasement still seems to be our national policy. This will continue to compromise our national security, till we devise a coherent and purposeful national policy on countering and defeating the Maoist violence. After every Maoist excess, our politicians keep issuing bold and meaningless statements, which are seldom followed up by any concrete action. The Union Home Minister has admitted that our police is ill-equipped for the present: 'Police system is outdated. Police are ill-equipped, ill-trained and ill-

paid….Police constables who work for 12 to 14 hours a day through out the year are the most abused.' This is P. Chidambaram!

- "Interestingly, politicians get increased security after every attack. If I were to be taken a hostage, I would neither expect nor plead with the Government to accept the demands of the terrorists. I would rather be sacrificed for the sake of our national interest. This approach should be followed by the politicos, government officials and other celebrities. This is the only way to deny the bargaining powers to the terrorists, as also to rouse the common man against them."
- Joginder Singh has expressed himself honestly, even bluntly. He feels India's week-kneed policy of appeasement vis-à-vis the terrorists began in 1989. He clearly holds that the Maoists are terrorist and presently reduced to the common criminals. In the concluding part, he pleads for a national policy to fight the Maoists, which has no place for negotiations in case of abductions.

"Maoists are neither down nor out:" 20.4.2012

This article appeared in the Pioneer and is written by Ajai Sahni, Executive Director, Institute for Conflict Management, New Delhi here are excerpts.

- **The blurb of the article reads:** 'A dip in fatalities should not be interpreted as Indian State winning the war on left-wing extremism. Evidence shows the State is as vulnerable as before.'
- Three disruptive incidents, in quick succession, have shocked India out of the complacency that had set in, as the policy establishment celebrated sharp decline in violence and fatalities engineered by the Maoists over the past year.
- The worst of these incidents, of course, was the IED attack on the CRPF transport at Pustola in Gadchiroli District, Maharashtra, on 27 March, which killed 12 and injured 28. In their enthusiasm during CRPF DG Vijay Kumar's visit to Fulbodi Gatta to inspect a community outreach programme, the men had ignored the SOP, driving over a road that had not been sanitised in advance. The Maoists were quick to take a bloody advantage.
- A loss of life among the security forces personnel, however, is easily ignored and quickly forgotten by the Indian State. The abduction of foreigners and the inevitable media carnival, tends to be far more embarrassing, for much longer, especially when the 'hostage drama' extends over weeks. The 'arrest', as the Maoists

chose to describe it, of two Italians–a tourist and a tour operator–on 14th March in the Daringbadi block of Kandhmal District Odisha, has consequently, shattered the illusion of an 'improved internal security situation' to a far greater extent. The abduction took place when the Italians were moving in areas of Maoist influence, officials claim, against the advice of the administration. They have since been released.

- Even as the Italian hostage drama was played out, an MLA, tribal leader Jhina Hikaka of the ruling Biju Janata Dal, was abducted on 24th March in Koraput district, Odisha. This was when he chose to ignore security procedures while travelling in Maoist-dominated areas from Semilguda to his constituency Lakshmipur. Hikaka's vechicle was stopped near Toyaput and he was abducted after he identified himself.
- Crucially, all three actions were incidents of opportunity, reflecting Maoist capacities, rather than strategic intent and planning and demonstrating quite clearly that a decline in fatalities is not synonymous with a decline in rebel capacities or an improvement in the security situation.
- Despite many claims of cumulative 'improvement' in the capacities of Central and State security forces, the State's vulnerabilities remain largely unaddressed. At least, some claims of such 'improvement' are falsified or fabricated–including the Ministry of Home Affair's 30th November 2011 claim that the police-population ratio had been raised to 176 per 100,000, from a national crime records bureau figure of 133 her 100,000 as on 31st December 2010. Same is true of the Home Ministry's claim that 'number of Central Armed Police Force' battalions deployed in the Maoist-affected states increased from 37 in 2008 to 73 in November 2011', because it glossed over the fact that this has roughly been the level of deployment since the disastrous 'massive and coordinated operations' were launched by the Union government in end 2009. That these forces have, alongwith State police special forces, largely been frozen in a passive defensive posture since the Chintalnad massacre of April 2010, and offensive operations against the Maoists have become more and more the exception among demoralised security forces contingents, remain unsaid.
- On the other hand, anecdotal evidence of state vulnerability and disarray is mounting. In one devastating disclosure, the Home

Ministry conceded that as many as 46000 officers and men took voluntary retirement from the Central Forces between 2007 and September 2011, while another 5220 officers and me resigned from the service during the same period. As many as 461 suicides and 64 instances of fractricides were also recorded. Worse, the rate of increase of cases of resignation in the CRPF and BSF was 'alarming' –at more than 70 per cent in 2011.

- If this dry data was not sufficiently disconcerting, Rahul Sharma an IPS officer serving as SP in the Maoist–afflicted Bilaspur District in the country's worst–affected State, Chhattisgarh, committed suicide on 12th March (2012), blaming his seniors and political leadership for his decision. Sharma had reportedly confided to a friend that he was frustrated because police officers were required to do what he called 'forced labour' (=*begaar*) and 'extortion' (=*ugahi*) and that 'targets for the election expenses' for the scheduled 2013 Assembly polls had 'already been set'. This incident provides extraordinary insight into the use and morale of the police leadership in the State worst affected by the Maoist insurgency.
- Nor is Chhattisgarh an exception. In the wake of the 27th March (2012) incident in Gadchiroli, Maharashtra Home Minister R. R. Patil complained that police officers were unwilling to work in Gadchiroli and Chandrapur Districts, citing the recent example of four Sub-Inspector who resigned from the force after completing training when they were posted to the former districts he had many complaints after the Gadchiroli incident, even blaming the Centre for its failure to give advance information of Maoist attacks. Unsurprisingly, Maharashtra saw an increase in Maoist-related fatalities to 69 in 2011, over the 2010 figure of 40, even as the all-India fatalities almost halved.
- The other major Maoist-affected states–Odisha, Jharkhand, West Bengal and Bihar–suffer from equal and endemic deficiencies in their security structures, as well as from both ambivalence and infirmity in their political leaderships.
- "Some augmentation of capacities–recruitment, arming, fortification and modernisation–has no doubt occurred across the board, both in Central and State forces, but this had limited impact on their capacities and operations on the ground as a result of an incoherence of approach and strategy as well as gross deficits and deficiencies in leadership."

Ajai Sahni is a security specialist, running a think tank on the related subject. He has spoken honestly and bluntly on the Maoist threat to the country and the way top leadership, of both security forces and political class, are not showing resolute intent to control and eliminate the Maoist insurgency.

He has written about demoralisation setting in the counter-Maoist forces. The worst case is of a police officer committing suicide as he is forced by his seniors and politicos to collect funds for their personal purpose. This is obviously one of the best, if not the best, in this section.

"The bleeding heartless": 1.06.2013: Shekhar Gupta

This article appeared in the Indian Express. Gupta is a senior/leading journalist of the country. The blurbs and excerpts from article are here.

Blurbs

- On Maoists, UPA's headless chickens are coming home to roost.
- The UPA has kept mum as its embedded 'liberals' have popped up with conspiracy theories and 'root causes'. From the PM to those considered close to Sonia, from NAC members to Home Ministers, all spoke in different voices. One called them a grave threat, a bunch of bandits and so on, another romanticised them as misguided people fighting for the tribal victims of extractive industries.
- How are we to explain the indifference to the loss of police and paramilitary life in East-Central India? Could it be that we put a different value to the life of an Indian soldier, depending upon the colour of his uniform? How many OB Vans follow the coffins of CRPF men? Which ministers visit their families? Why does the Air Chief get away with his dismissal of the demand for an inquiry into how his crew fled from their downed helicopter, leaving an injured comrade in it?

Excerpts

- How do we justify using a Bushism as the UPA finally displays some clarity of vision in dealing with violent Maoists? And a Bushism like, you are either with us or against us. Because, so far, for all these nine ridiculous years, the UPA has not been able to decide whether it is with itself or against itself, on this insurgency in India's East-Central heartlands. Every few months, usually at some high-level security conference, the PM describes it as greatest threat to India. Then a Chidambram takes the cue and builds a more robust response to the armed insurrection. And both are cut down by a Digvijay Singh coming up with his own 'root causes' theory.

- Operation Green Hunt may still be a mythical codename, but the Home Ministry does launch an audacious campaign to move into the so-called 'liberated zones'. The forces make some progress and also suffer some reverses–the 76 killed in Dantewada is by far the highest single-day loss for India's security forces in counter-insurgency after the first night of Operation Blue Star (149). The third highest of a day has also been in this confused war (38, when a police boat was attacked on 29 June 2008 in Orissa). You need to put these figures in perspective. India's armed forces rarely suffer such high single-battle or single-operation casualties in counter-insurgency. They did not lose these many lives in a single day of fighting even in Kargil, even of the night Tololing or Tiger Hill were assaulted.
- And how has the UPA responded? It has kept mum as its embedded 'liberals' have popped up routinely with conspiracy theories and 'root causes'. And equally so, when the successive chiefs of the army and IAF have made unsolicited statements that their forces can't be used in fighting the Naxals, with poorly concealed delight that the paramilitary forces were getting their 'comeuppance'. No chief was questioned, countered or counselled to also stay out of the debate as much as they want to stay away from the action. On the Naxal issue, the UPA's response would confuse George Bush himself. How would he deal with a situation where a government is against an enemy, but also with it? How would you?
- For nine years, the UPA and its various elements–Prime Minister, these close to Sonia and speaking for her, the Home Ministers (there were three who ran that Ministry, Shivraj Patil, P. Chidambram and Shinde, spoke in different voices, with the first being a pure root-causes man) and NAC members spoke at cross purposes, as detailed above. For nine long years, the leadership of the Congress bought this unquestioningly. It even allowed, even welcomed, the embedding of the Maoist middle ground and sympathisers within its establishment, notably the NAC and Planning Commission. (Two examples of this are cited here). One, A Padma, wife of top Maoist Akkiraju Hargopal alias Ramakrishna. Remember, she was one of the eight Maoists released in exchange for the abducted Malkangiri collector Vineel

Krishna. More importantly, she managed NGO Aman Vedika, an orphanage run by activist and then NAC member Harsh Mander. At this NGO, they welcomed Padma (details in 'at NAC member's NGO, they wait for Padma, wife of top Maoist, Indian Express, 24 Feb 2011). Two, Dr Binayak Sen. Many way sympathised with Sen for being charged and convicted under the sedition. He may also be a likeable and soft-spoken paediatrician. But must the government appoint him in a key Planning Commission Committee (steering committee on health, drafting their 12th Five-Year Plan)? Gentle, children's doctor, yes. But he is a convicted Maoist sympathiser. Bringing him inside the tent like this, what message are you sending out ot the security forces, to the police and intelligence agencies, and people of India? Or, to twist the knife and twist a popular Hindi heartland slogan as well, *sainiko tum sangharsh karo, hamein pata nahin ham kis ke saath hain* (fight on soldiers, just that we are not sure whose side we are on). And finally, what message are you sending out to the Maoists? They only let you know last week how they read your confused minds, by wiping out the entire leadership of your party (Congress).

- It was reassuring earlier this week to see the Rural Development Minister (Jairam Ramesh) speak out on TV channels, finally using the correct and fitting description for the Maoists. But the same Minister was saying smugly until the other day that Maoism only prospered in States not governed by the Congress.

No comments are being offered on this article by Shekhar Gupta, as it is one of the best, as was the previous one by Ajai Sahni.

"Withering away of a revolution": 16.09.14 cadres are leaving Maoists in greater number than those joining them. The state has an opportunity

This article by R.K. Vij, additional DGP, Chhattisgarh, appeared in the Indian Express. Here are the excerpts:

- The recent surge in surrender of Maoist cadres, particularly in Dandakaranya, seems the reality check for the protagonists of Maoist ideology, who claims that only a protracted armed struggle can bring about social transformation in a class ridden society. Maoists of all hues–members of military formations or PLGA, political formations and the Janatana Sarkar (people's government)– are leaving the so-called 'revolutionary' path they had pledged to tread when joining the movement against the feudal and semi-colonial ruling class. The romance of the armed struggle for capturing power is, perhaps, waning.

- There are three reasons for surrender of Maoist cadres. First, the realisation of futility of the (people's) war. Three decades of violence have not produced any convincing results. Whatever existed in the name of development has been vandalised by the Maoists. Three cadres, on surrender, expressed their disillusionment with the claims of the Maoist leaders vis-à-vis the realities on the ground, especially in the Dandakaranya special zone. Second, the police's continuous persuation has resulted in a change of heart in many cadres, who had been brain washed by the maoists. The police have been approaching Maoists, family members with the Government's Surrender and Rehabilitation (S and R) schemes. A 'back-home' programme initiated by the former SP of Gadchiroli, Suvez Haque, and followed by many others have proved efficacious. This has also helped Maoist cadres to shun violence and join the mainstream by surrendering to authorities. Often, pamphlets are also distributed for the same aim in mind. The pervasive media has also played its part in spreading awareness of such schemes. Many cadres are deserting because of personal reasons: after marrying in forests, couples not allowed to enjoy conjugal life; the killing of a family member, in one case since a cadre's brother had joined police; killing a kin as an alleged police informer; and exploitation of junior cadres.
- At their 2013 Central Committee meeting, the leaders admitted that their cadres were deserting in large numbers and new recruits were not coming forward. At the last Dandakarany Special Zone Committee meeting in February 2014, the Maoists expressed serious concern about this trend and also worried about the increased movement and deployment of security forces in their strongholds.
- Meanwhile, LWE-affected states are revising their S and R policies to render them more attractive. Until recently, Andhra Pradesh policy of reward of ₹ 25 lakh on the head of the top leader, CPI (Maoist) General Secretary Ganapathy, was the maximum among the states. But presently, other states have considerably increased the surrender amount for their top leaders: Maharashtra to ₹ 1 Crore; Chhattisgarh to ₹ 60 lakh. The Chhattisgarh policy is also attractive for the cadres surrendering with weapons. The S and R scheme of the Central Government is

aimed at vocational training, so that the surrenderees can be self-employed in the course of rehabilitation. The objective of all these schemes is to enable the former cadres to shun the violence and join the mainstream.

- "But the surrender of senior cadres should be dealt with carefully. The people who have murdered people for decades or ordered and supervised such murders/killings for a long time cannot be believed to have a change of mind overnight, abandoning their dearly-held, ideological beliefs. Although S and R policies cannot set temporal limits for surrender, they intend to persuade cadres who show their willingness to change. But if surrender takes place after decades of murdering the innocent, the surrenderee might be actuated by motives not necessarily percuniary. Two instances of such surrenders are cited here. A DKSZC member, Arjun, who was incharge of the first military company when it was raised in Maad in 2004 and was throughout involved in numerous brutal killings, surrendered recently in Andhra Pradesh. He did this after spending his entire youth spreading terror. More surprisingly, his surrender did not evoke any criticism from the Maoists Yet again, G.V.K. Prasad, alias Gudsa Usendi, a spokes-person and member of the DKSZC, surrendered, saying he was against the killing of innocent people. How can such an averment from a person who oversaw ruthless killings for nearly three decades, justifying the same on ideological grounds, can be given the benefit of a change of heart? Such senior cadres must be intellectually sifted and their cost-benefit analysis to assess the impact of their surrender on the Maoist outfit. Unless their surrender causes considerable damage to the latter, directly or even indirectly, the State should be wary of rewarding post-retirement-like benefits to them, since it could be a well-considered tactical move in disguise.
- People's support is crucial to the survival of any movement. If this trend of Maoist surrender continues and the State seizes this opportunity to showcase its responsibilities in rehabilitating the surrenderees properly while pushing development into such areas to remove structural socio-economic disparities, the Maoist movement is sure to lose its revolutionary zeal.

A very generous comment on this article can be: "it is a self-serving piece by a senior serving police officer (ADGP, Chhattisgarh) charged with the responsibility combating the Maoist violence." He has painted a rosy picture, in seeing the "withering away of a revolution". And worse still, he had woven this tapestry around a single issue of trend of surrenders by the Maoist ultras and that too, pertaining essentially and limited to a specific region, Dandakaranya and not even a state.

Within months of penning this piece and with benefit of hindsight, the writer R.K. Vij would have understood that he had been day-dreaming! He was obviously indulging in self-publicity, or may be, PR jobe for his own police force! To be harsher, he was trying to tom tom his achievements to impress his political masters.

Today (April 2015), situation is worse for the country. There have been four Maoist attacks in three days (12-14 April).

Press on Maoists

Press plays an important part in a democratic polity. It should be no surprise that it is dubbed as Fourth Estate after the Executive, Legislature and Judiciary. Opinion of some leading journalists like Shekhar Gupta and Kanchan Gupta have already been examined in the preceding section, 'opinion leaders under seanner'. Now on to journalists and the Maoists.

"Fallen Heroes Forgotten"

This is the title of the editorial of *The Pioneer* dated 20 September 2011. Excerpts are reproduced here. There is one telling line below the title:

"Men Fighting Maoists are Ignored"

- "On 18th September 2009, when assistant comdts N. Manoranjan Singh and Rakesh Kumar Chaurasia of the 201 Combat Battalion for Resolute Action (COBRA) lead their elite team of six security personnel into the heart of Dantewada in Chhattisgarh where they eliminated at least 30 Maoists and destroyed a vital illicit arms factory, their brave expedition marked the successful initiation of the Union Government's five-state paramilitary counter-offensive against Red insurgents. Generally understood to be a part of what has been loosely termed as 'Operation Green Hunt', the massive two-day offensive was one of the earliest successes registered by the Government in its ongoing battle against Maoists.
- "It proved that it indeed was feasible for paramilitary forces to infiltrate Maoist-hold territory in large numbers and launch a stellar attack on the insurgents. For the first time, the Maoist were worried about their losses. They were forced to retreat",

Chhattisgarh's former DGP Vishma Ranjan had observed at the time. Two years later, as efforts continue to neutralise Maoists, the six COBRA fighters who had instilled fear in the minds of the Red terrorists have already been forgotten – not just by the people and media, but also by the government that ideally should have been grateful to brave men in uniform who sacrificed their lives to protect those of their fellow citizens. It may be recalled how members of the 201 COBRA were ambushed by a second group of heavily armed Maoists while the team was returning from the forest after successfully raiding the insurgent's hide-out and weapons depot. A court of inquiry report filed in December 2009 notes that in the violent gun battle that ensued Manoranjan Singh and Rakesh Chaurasia led their men wisely and bravely as the sadly outnumbered team caved under maoist attack.

- "The violent death meted out to 201 COBRA was no doubt tragic; what renders the episode shameful is the manner in which the team comprising sub-inspector Sushil Kumar Verma, head Constable Lalit Kumar and constables Uday Kumar Yadav and Manohar Lal has been ignored by the Union Government. These martyrs have not even been awarded a gallantry medal. Yet officers 'supervising' anti-terrors operations in Jammu and Kashmir have been duely acknowledged for their contribution. While this newspaper does not begrudge the five IPS officers who have been decorated with six gallantry medals in the past few years for monitoring anti-terror operations in Jammu and Kashmir, it does regret the manner in which foot soldiers fighting India's most significant threat to internal security threat have been wholly ignored–not just by the Government but by the people of this country too".

A brief comment is offered on the above editorial of the Pioneer. One can safely say that this is the only daily which can be called 'nationalist' in its stance on such issues of national security. This editorial is especially apposite as it shows serious concern for the brave men who lays their life on the line for security of the nation. Further it condemns the Government for not rewarding them for their supreme sacrifice.

Most English newspapers have namley pamby attitude on such issues of national security and the braves out there to secure it. If at all they tackle such issues in their editorials, there are too many 'ifs and buts' thrown in. One must congratulate a daily like the Pioneer to take a nationalist view on issue of national security.

"The bleeding heartless"

This is Shekhar Gupta's article in the Indian Express of 1 June 2013. It has been included in the previous section. Here, only some more relevant extracts will be included to reflect on his views on Maoists violence and Government's handling of it.

- For all the nine years, UPA could not decide on its policy to counter Maoists insurrection. Usually, every few months at some high-level security conference, the Prime Minister describes it as greatest threat to India. Then a Chidambaram takes the cue and builds a more robust response to the armed insurrection. And both are cut down by a Digvijay Singh coming up with his own 'root causes' theory. The Home Ministry launches an audacious campaign to move into so called liberated areas. The forces make some progress and also suffer some reverses, the 76 killed in Dantewada is by far the highest single day loss for India's security forces in counter-insurgency after the first night of operation Blue-Star (149). The third highest of the day also been in this confused war (38, when a police boat was attacked on 29 June 2008 in Odisha).
- "You need to put these figures in perspective. Indian armed forces rarely suffer such high single battle or single operation. Casualties in counter-insurgency. They did not lose these many lives in a single day of fighting even in Kargil, even on the night's Tololing and Tiger Hill were assaulted and how has the UPA responded. It has kept mum as its embedded liberals have popped up routinely with conspiracy theories and 'root causes'.
- "And equally so (i.e., kept mum) when successive chief's of Army and air forces have made unsolicited statements that their forces can't be used in fighting the Naxals. No chief has been questioned, countered or counseled to also stay out of the debate as much as they want to stay away from action.
- "UPA response to the threat of Maoism is confusing. It is a situation where the Government is against the enemy and also with it. For nine years, the UPA and its various elements were speaking at cross purposes: this being applicable to Prime Minister, to those considered close to Sonia Gandhi and speaking for her, from the Home Ministers (Shivraj Patil, Chidambaram and Shinde) to NAC members! Patil was a pure root causes man; Chidambaram was a more clear for appropriate action against the Maoists. One set of NAC member called them a grave threat, a

bunch of bandits while the others romanticized them as merely misguided, well-meaning people fighting for the tribal victims of 'extractive' industries. For full nine years, the Congress leadership bought this unquestioningly. It allowed, even welcomed, the embedding of the Maoist middle ground and sympathisers within its establishment, notably in the NAC and the Planning Commission. (Here, is one telling example). One of the eight Maoists released in exchange for the abducted Malkangiri Collector Vinod Krishna was A. Padma, wife of top Maoist Akkiraju Hargopal alias Ramkrishna and she managed Aman Vedika, an orphanage run by activist and then NAC member Harsh Mander. [At this NGO run by a NAC member, they all waited keenly for the wife of a top Maoist, and expectedly she was given a rousing welcome on arrival]. It was Feb 2011. Dr Binayak Sen may be a good paediatrician, but he is a convicted Maoist Sympathiser. Then, must he be appointed to a key Planning Commission Committee/ what message are you sending to the security forces, to the police and intelligence agencies and people of India? The message to soldiery is contained in this Hindi song, tweaked a bit for the purpose. '***Sainiko tum sangharsh Karo, Hamein pata nahin ham kis ke saath hain***'. And finally what message are you sending out to the Maoists. They only let you know last week how they read your confused mind, by wiping out the entire leadership of your party!

- "This schizophrenic approach is best represented by pronouncements of the Rural Development Minister Jairam Ramesh. It was reassuring to see him speak out on TV channels, finally using the correct and fitting description, for the Maoists. But the same Jairam was smugly saying until the other day that Maoism only prospered in states not governed by the Congress. Sadly, politicians are not the only guilty party here. Your heads and hearts should burn with fury every time an armed forces Chief says he wouldn't send his forces to fight the Maoists, because his troops can't be seen fighting their own countrymen. Own country? Then, who are the Kashmiri's you have been fighting with pride and what about the Nagas, the Manipuri's and the other tribal insurrectionists of the North-East? Are not they Indians? Have not the Indian Troops been dealing with them since the 1947?

Brief Comments. Gupta is a senior journalist and in this article, he has summed up all the problems faced by the country in dealing with the serious threat posed to the national security. He has explicitly explained the negative part played by the politicians, intellectuals embedded in the NAC, uncalled statements by the Army and IAF Chiefs and lack of sufficient respect to the sacrifices made by the Para-military forces in fighting the Naxals.

"Small and Sure–Footed"

This is the title of an article by B. Vijay Murty in the Hindustan Times of 29th January 2014. Its blurb is reproduced here.

"**Fire Power.** Larger and stronger police forces are yielding ground to ultras in Chhattisgarh and Jharkhand".

Excerpts from the article

"Judging by the current patterns, the fight with the Maoists rebels has a historical ring to it.

"Whether it is the first battle of Panipat in 1526, when a small army of Babar defeated the huge contingent of Ibrahim Lodhi or Shivaji Combats with the mighty Bijapur Kingdom in the nineteenth century, all speak of how the smaller outfits outclasses the bigger ones.

"The police in the Maoist-affected states, especially in Jharkhand and Chhattisgarh, appear to be modern-day equivalents of the larger forces. Despite being 'larger' and 'stronger', the forces are yielding ground to the comparatively weak Red Brigade.

"27.1.14 incident in Jharkhand's Giridih District, where the rebels decoyed the forces into their trap and carried out a series of explosions, killing one CRPF man and injuring 17, had once again proved the Maoists operational efficiency in areas under their control.

"DIG, Police, Jharkhand, Suman Gupta, recently said despite specific information, Senior police officers in at least five Maoists affected districts in the Hazaribagh range desisted from taking against the rebels.

"The Jharkhand, Chhattisgarh Governments have doubled their police strength to nearly 50,000 and 60,000 respectively over the last five years, but there have been no let up in violence.

In Chhattisgarh, Maoist militia, numbering 5000, influences 130 of the 392 police station in the State, while in Jharkhand, 2500 armed rebels are giving sleepless nights to the police in 18 out of 24 districts.

"CPI (M) Commander Ashokji alias Karamchand explains what gives them an edge over the police: 'our honesty, dedication and selflessness, coupled with public support, have kept us firm and strong over the years'.

He further added, 'we are down in Andhra Pradesh and other plain areas, but have gone stronger in Chhattisgarh and Jharkhand'.

Comments on the above article

The article by Murty is fatuous and cynical write up on the Maiosts rebellion in India! To put it more charitably, it is an eulogy on their murderous shenanigans!

Comparing classical, set-piece battle of Panipat and Shivaji's battles against Bijapur Kingdom is an amateurish act, to say the least and an over-clever and childish one to be more honest. Even a layman knows that a small number of well trainsed and motivated guerrillas in World War II were able to hold up large units, but that was in conjunction with the support of large formations at their back.

In the instant case, security forces are required to patrol in areas running into thousands of square miles. Often, patrols are required to move on roads, more than a hundred miles in jungles and hilly areas. It is so easy to spring an ambush at any of appropriate, suitable areas en route. Any successful ambush is neither indicative of great operational expertise of Maoists, nor inefficiency of security forces. Such things do happen in such situations. To be fair to the security forces, they are operating in these areas susceptible to ambushes and attacks, without bullet- proof jackets and anti-mine vehicles.

It seems Murty has done a paid job for the Maoists!

Judiciary and Maoists

Naxal convictions: A case (again) to revisit Act

This is an article's title appeared in the Indian Express of 12th July 2013, by Ashutosh Bhardwaj. Excerpts/text follows.

- "The recent conviction of eight persons for spreading Naxalism in the urban areas in Chhattisgarh again underlines a paradox in functioning of investigation and prosecution wings of the police. Though the state has consistently topped the chart of Maoists violence across the country it is yet to share a single conviction in assault cases. In fact, all the accused in a high profile like the Todmetla ambush in which 76 cops were killed, were acquitted "However in cases where charge is merely of being a 'Maoist supporter', the conviction records stands tall, including several activists, businessmen and writers. Is it because such cases are easier to prosecute as the nature of evidence here is relaxed, courtesy the Chhattisgarh Public Security Act that was enacted to Check Maoists but has been misused against ordinary citizens?

- "The Act makes any activity that 'interferes or tends to interfere with the maintenance of public order' unlawful, makes any outfit that indulges in such activities 'unlawful' and declares that anyone even without being its member, contributes to or aids such an outfit, can be punished. A person who may be completely unaware that he is 'contributing' to such an outfit can be punished as the onus to prove his innocence lies on him. On the contrary, the Act does not make intention or Knowledge an ingredient of crime.
- "While some of the convicts in the recent cases have substantial evidence against them, the evidence falls short in at least three cases–that of two Bilaspur-based cloth merchants, Naresh and Ramesh Khubwani and a tailor, Dayaram Sahu. The Khubwanis, says the prosecution, took orders from a top Maoists to stitch uniforms for the security guards. Sahu was then hired by the merchants to stitch the clothes. The three have been convicted despite the police admitting that this top Maoist had hidden his identity while placing the order, claiming a person who hires security guards. Their logic is that any merchant who took such large scale order for stitching 'military uniforms' must have known the identity of his clients.
- "As the State police celebrates its success in securing eight convictions, maximum in any Maoists case so far in Chhattisgarh, it should perhaps be reviewing the law that tramples over the rights the constitution mandates for its citizens".

Comments

It is always easy to blame any logislation for misuse. Application of its provisions is strictly and duly examined by a judicial officers. In the instant case, the judge must have weighed in other factors too, like the circumstantial evidence. The judges are trained for this job.

But what is an issue of greater concern is that not a single case of assault by the Maoists in Chhattisgarh, including the worst which resulted in the death of 76 policemen, has resulted in the conviction. This certainly is worrisome situation for which police alone can't be hold responsible. The judiciary must share the blame for this unhappy situation. Some authorities feel most judges are not satisfied with 100 per cent evidence, they want it to be 200 per cent to convict an accused, particularly so when they are dealing with persons involved in anti-national activities like insurrection and terrorism. Is it because they are worried about their personal security? If 76 policemen are killed by the Maoist, setting all the accuse free beats one's imagination. There is a certain possibility that some innocents may too be among the accused, but to believe that the police has rounded up the villagers just to make their numbers is also not credible.

The situation is more difficult in such cases. There are no independent witnesses in such cases. The police and the Maoists are the only ones. No villagers will come forward to identify a Maoist, even if the former knows it for certain.

The reluctance of judges to convict the accused during the days of Khalistani insurrection in the Punjab during the 1980s is well-Known. Being only humans, the judges too were worried about their lives. It was safer to declare a terrorist innocent, than to buy trouble for oneself and risk one's life. Something similar, rather worse is happening in Pakistan today. The draconian blasphemy law itself is a terror for the judges trying the cases. If a courageous judge declares a blasphemy accused innocent, he generally flees the country. Most judges are not bold enough to give justice to the blasphemy accused when thousands of frenzied Pakistanis are laying for his blood outside the court room! A classic case is citied here when an illiterate women was awarded death for writing anti-Prophet Slogan on the wall of her house! Obviously, some fanatic has done the writing on her wall out of personal enemity.

Should one ascribe such mortal fear to the judges in Chhattisgarh trying the murderous Maoists? It is difficult to be sanguine in such cases. But the Government and judiciary must put their heads together to find a way out of this situation, which will only, encourages the Maoists in their murderous ways!

"Being a Maoist is no Crime"

This is the verdict of Kerala High Court, delivered on 22 May 2015. Some excerpts follow as they appeared in a daily dated 23.5.2015.

- "The Kerala High Court 22th May 2015 said that being a Maoist is not a crime and a person cannot be arrested merely because he is one.

  The bench of Justice Mohd Mustaque, acting on a writ petition filed by Shyam Bala Krishnan, who alleged he was illegally picked by the Kerala police last year on suspicious of being a Maoist, said a person can be arrested only if he is involved in unlawful activities.

- "Being a Maoist is no crime. Freedom of thought and liberty of conscience is a natural right. Freedom becomes unlawful only when it concerns the physical law of the state', said the judge.
- "The Court asked the State Government to pay Balakrishnan ₹ 1 Lakh compensation and ₹ 10,000 as litigation cost.
- "Balakrishnan, a native of Wayanad, was taken into custody by the Thunderbolt, a special wing of the Kerala police meant to be tackle Maoists, on 20th May 2014, when he was riding a two wheeler, citing intelligence reports.
- "Balakrishnan alleged he was taken to police station, later his house were raided and police seized his laptop and mobile phone.
- Balakrishnan, who was released nine hours later, also alleged he was tortured by the police who wanted information about the identities of some of his friends.
- "Balakrishnan later moved the High Court against the police, claiming that the police action infringed on Article 21 of the Constitution. A student of philosophy, who does organic farming in his villager; he is son of retired judge Balakrishnan Nair.
- "Claiming that he is not a Maoist, 'I had moved the Court mainly against human rights violations. But the Maoists are using the Court verdict to their advantage. My only concern is violation of rights'. He claimed that some people from his village suspected his friend and his wife to be Maoists and alerted the police. It could have verified their identity. 'Instead, they kept me in custody for several hours, and raided my house. There should be procedure for the police to deal with such situations', he said.
- "Kerala Police routinely arrests people with suspected Maoist Links. Last month, three activists of the Revolutionary Democratic Front, a suspected pro-Maoist outfit, were arrested while distributing pamphlets supporting ultra-left ideology."

Comments on the above News Item

As a soldier, who had fought against the Naga rebels in 1950s, Mizo insurrectionists in the 1970s—when the two movements were at their violent worst—and Kashmiri Jihadis in the early 1960s, and 1980s, this author finds it extremely hard and difficult to reconcile his practical experience in the field of reality and idealistic pronouncements by the judiciary based on the Constitutional mandates and theoretical niceties advocated by the loud-mouthed human-rights activists who are more of publicity hounds than the genuine species. To demand the same quality of evidence in a case involving a hardened criminal—be it is a dacoit it or a Maoist—and another one dealing with a law-abiding citizen is a matter of living in an unreal world, and more accurately, an imagined world! To an extent, same applies to Balakrishnan mentioned in the news story above. Being a friend of a Maoist couple, he does not want to be arrested or questioned. Still, he insists that the police could have verified their identity. "Instead, they kept me in custody for several hours and raided my house."

Obviously, it is a clever lawyer speaking through Balakrishnan. What he says needs to be examined carefully. How does police verify the identity of the Maoist couple without talking to their friends and relatives? He says "there should be some procedure for the police to deal with such situations", but is shy of explaining it. Does he suggest the police should indulge in mind reading. His detention was essential for the police to see if his lap-top or mobile has any clues about his being an active accomplice of the Maoists couple. Lack of evidence need not mean that Balakrishman is innocent! He might have been intelligent enough to destroy all the incriminating evidence in time. This author is only trying to show the other side of the story to the world. It is so easy to find fault with the police all the time. All political parties, all criminals, and worse the judges, do it all the time. It is not that the police is peopled by the angels. Still, it is unfair to believe that they all are demons!

Balakrishnan is balanced enough to admit that "Maoists are using the court verdict to their advantage", then adds innocently, if superciliously, "my only concern is the violation of human rights". How touching! Unfortunately, too many people in India are working for the human rights of too many people, but almost none for the human rights of policemen, paramilitary people and armed forces personnel!

The last paragraph of the news story is rather surprising, even more accurately, intriguing. It starts with an innocuous, if damaging, sentence as far as the police is concerned: "Kerala police routinely arrest people with suspected Maoist links". The word 'routinely' suggest, 'without due process or adequate thought. Consequently, the very next sentence confirms this averment clearly and unambiguously that "Last month, three activists of the Revolutionary Democratic Front, a suspected pro-Maoists outfit, were arrested after they were found distributing pamphlets supporting ultra-left ideology". Is Shaju Philip, who is scribe of this news story, suggesting that the police arrested these 'activists' 'routinely'? Or, is he certain that these arrests were more than justified? These activists were not directly involved in killing people or destroying nation's assists, but only distributing pamphlets supporting ultra-leftist ideology! Do they deserve to be punished harshly, for distributing subversive pamphlets?

This story, particularly, its last paragraph, is indicative of facetious and irresponsible journalism. The contents of the story should be balanced and intent clear. Maoists are posing the most serious threat to national security and this type of namby-pamby journalism can't help the nation in any way. But it doesn't surprise this Author, as he knows that this paper, The Hindu, was once edited by N. Ram, once a card-holding Communist and he wields his evil influence on this daily even after he retired from editorship, because he still is heading the administration of this daily.

Finally, we come to the Judge who declared that being Maoist is not a crime. One cannot critique his judgment as detailed text is not available. Still some questions can be asked of the judge and some comments offered on his judgment. Did he realise that the Maoists could take undue advantage of his judgment? Did he lay some parameters or conditions to define Maoist who is not a danger to our nation's security, and the one who is? The text in this news item has a term which does not clarify things, in fact, it confuses a lay man as also a soldier who has also dealt with a variety of insurrections in his active tenure in the Army and also is well-aware of the serious threat Maoists pose to India's sovereignty and integrity: "...Freedom becomes unlawful only when it concerns the 'Physical law' of the state". The dictionary does not explain the phrase. The term physicalism is defined: "The theory that all referential terms in scientific or meaningful statements are reducible to terms connected with physical objects or events or with their properties". Is the Judge saying that unless a Maoist is caught killing people, he cannot be charged for criminal act! What about a Maoist who sits at home, help recruit cadre for CPI (Maoist), distributes literature about Maoists and justifying their murderous acts and destructive way?

Freedom of thought and liberty of conscience are fine values to talk about, but is it an unfettered right? There is also a truism that your freedom end just before it hits my nose. Maoists aim is to defeat Indian polity through violent means. Are we going to give them freedom? What will this Judge say about the arrest of these activists who were distributing pamphlets supporting ultra-Left ideology? After all, they were not killing any one! We have enough 'liberals' and 'intellectuals' supporting the violent Maoists. Is the judge wanting to join the ranks of these 'closet Maoists'? One is certain he does not want to. But must he give a ruling that can be misused, exploited and misinterupted by these blood-thirsty Maoists to add to their ranks more killers and help them commit more crimes in the name of helping the poor tribals who they claim are being exploited by the contractors and mining lobbies? Freedom of thought and expressions are fine values to talk about, but let us not forget Hitler ascended to power using his democratic freedom!

Such rulings adds to the difficulties of the security forces who are in the field to counter the depredations committed by the Maoists. Such pronouncements that Maoists are not criminals will not only hamper their fights against the Maoists ultras, it will also affect their morale.

Keeping the above in mind, one would urge the Government of India to file an appeal against the single judge ruling. This Author certainly feel that such rulings do not increase the national security parameters, these in fact, may add to government woes and worries in this field.

Common man on Maoists

"Left-wing Extremism must not be tolerated by Government"

This is the heading of a letter to the editor by Navin Aggarwal published in the Pioneer dated 15th April 2012. Excerpts follow:

"This has relevance to Chandan Mitra column, Maoists are enemies of the people (18 April). The author has correctly observed that the Maoists want to overthrow state rule by force. It is here that the Maoists err. Even China has unceremonially dumped Mao. Only by adopting free-market economy…had lifted million out of poverty. By adopting selective capitalist policies, China has become an economic gaint…will be a superpower of the future.

"Look in our neighbourhood…what is the Maoist legacy to the once peaceful kingdom of Nepal. The Maoist rebellion there has crushed the tourism industry, the mainstay of Nepal's economy Maoist may terrorise the people but they will not win popular support.

"Admittedly, India's economic and social progress had not percolated to every section of the society. Tribals in particular remain poor, and worse, even exploited. This has helped the Maoists in spreading their wings among tribal population of various states….

"Mr Mitra should remember that Maoists are the Children gone astray…Like doting parents, the state should not eliminate them, but bring them back to the mainstream through all 'legal means.' The Government should find a political solution, not a 'military' solution.

Comments on the letter

Agrawal could not resist the temptation of resorting to certain usual clichés. No nation aims at elimination of its Children gone astray. An occasional spanking is resorted to in the child's own interest. What are the legal means' have not been clarified. A nation resorts to 'military means' only as an initial step to bring the ultras to the negotiations table. Unless the Maoists are convinced that their violence, kidnapping, murders et.al., will not succeed against a nation like India, they will continue in their wild ways. A little spanking will put some sense in their brain. No political solution would work until they give up their violence. Similarly, development like building of roads, schools and hospitals will not take place if they continue killing the workers, labourers and contractors. Hence the need for employing force in the initial stages. Until they are chastised enough and convinced that India is too big and too powerful to bow before some recalcitrant elements, they will not give up arms. The nation has gone through a variety of uprisings and insurrections, starting from Naga rebellion through Mizo, Manipuri and ULFA unrest to khalistan uprising Maoism is only the last one on the list. This too will be dealt with in due course of timing.

No one need to nurture any doubts about India's resolve to maintain its integrity, sovereignty and freedom of action to face and defeat all adversaries.

'Fight the war like a war'

This is the heading of a letter by H.S. Mehta published in the Organiser of 30.06.2013.

Some excerpts follow

This is with reference to the editorial 'Fight the war like a war' in your weekly. After gruesome killing of 27 Congress persons by the Maoists on 25th May at Dantewada, VVIPs of Delhi rushed to Raipur by air with their bullet proof cars to visit the spot where this ghastly incident happened and to console the bereaved families.

"Sonia Gandhi looked very worried and nervous. Rahul Gandhi in the speech avoided the word 'Maoists'. Sonia Gandhi's NAC and Manmohan Singh always have difference of opinion in approach towards this serious problem. Her NAC members and other associates like Aruna Roy, Harsh Mander, Fr John Dayal, Swami Agnivesh and other Leftists being groomed in JNU, Jadavpur and Kolkata Universities, are sympathisers of Maoists.

"Top Congress leaders like Digvijay Singh and Manishankar Aiyar have been very vocal in favour of Maoists. After this incident, they have no words to speak. It seems they are still obsessed with imaginary saffron terror. The most shocking is that the Congress in election rallies in Dantewada has been bluntly propagating about the police excesses. It even withdrew from the all-party meeting called by CM Raman Singh. How long we can ignore this monster-like problem? When will UPA be serious?

"Modi must stop Maoists menace"

This is the heading of an article by Manjula Pal in the Pioneer of 4.6.2014. Excerpts follow:

- "In the country's Red Corridor, victims are looking to the new Prime Minister for relief. They want firm action that brings the region lasting peace.
- "While everyone in my household was rejoicing Prime Minister Narendra Modi's decisive victory, my barely-educated but politically-conscious maid, hailing from Jharkhand, was complaining. She drew attention to ever-growing wide-spread Maoist problem, rampant in her own state as also in other neighbouring states. She narrates her own experience of the atrocities committed by the Maoists on hapless villagers, mostly tribals, as well as on the jawans.
- "She says the Maoist problem is roughly a decade old. It started with stray incidents of murder but now Maoists have multiplied in numbers, spreading terror all over and behaving like the rulers of the area. They kill senselessly, mostly to punish police informants but without ever verifying the facts.
- "Wailing families is a daily affair as the Maoists claim the lives of innocent civilians and jawans. They behave like dacoits, claiming forest areas and their produce as their own. Anybody venturing into the area is killed and body hung by a tree as a message to others.
- "The worrisome part is that neither the Centre nor the State has so far done very little to curb the menace. They seem to have an edge over the bona fide leaders. The will to curb the Maoists seems to be missing. The requirements of the ill-equipped police and the CRPF are being ignored. The apathy from the establishment is frustrating. Even during the recent general elections, the Maoist problem found only a limited traction in the campaigning.
- "Official estimates hold some 50,000 people, 50 per cent among them being civilians, have been killed by the Maoists in the last decade alone across the Eastern Red Corridor. The issue has become more than just a simple retaliatory exercise by exploited-tribals-turned-Maoists, as human rights activists would like to maintain. Maoism has now become a terrorists' profession, a way of life; it is driven by the lust for power and has become a movement somewhat like the LTTE's.

- "Maoists shun development, education and democracy because those jeopradise their evil designs. The Government's offer of liberal terms for surrender too has boomranged many times. It has assumed dimensions of a full-fledged war!.... A new strategy is needed to esure prosperity of the local tribals.
- "The kind of mandate Prime Minister Modi has, seems to have put him on a pedestal, where he is seen almost like god. He is likened to Lord Krishna by many and is expected to descend from his juggernaut and rid Indians of their miseries. People's expectations have reached a record high.
- "Those living in the Red Corridor consisting of nine Maoist-inflected states of eastern India, are looking up to Modi with great expectations. They are optimistic that in due course of time, the Prime Minister will be able to find a permanent solution to this menace, because it is only then that good days for those people will begin.

There is only one appropriate comment: As in other fields—political, economic, social etc—Mr Modi has raised people's aspirations and expectations in Maoists-ravaged states also. He has to deliver and he must!

4

A History of Left–Wing Extremism in India

Till the formation of the PWG

This chapter deals with the phenomenon commonly known as Maoism (Naxalism in its earlier *avtar*), its motivation, its origin and causes of spread. From its beginning, it functioned under a variety of names. Various organisations, working towards its ideological denouement, functioned separately, then merged to achieve their common objectives and at times split due to ideological and/or personality-related causes. In a manner of speaking, these so-called revolutionary parties, too, undergo the pangs of processes of fission and fusions as do any of the political formations. This will be clear as we discuss the origin of this "armed agrarian revolution" and the transmogrification into different appellations, shapes and sizes.

Beginning of it all

Naxalism was the popular appellation for the armed insurrection launched and sustained by India's Leftist forces. Of late, it is more commonly known as Maoism. At the ideological level, the Naxalism and Maoism are known as Left-Wing Extremism (LWE).

Ancestry

Ancestry of India's LWE is popularly traced to the 1946-51 Telangana Insurrection. But factually, it needs a second look. Before India's independence, there were armed resistance and insurrection against the ruling British. One instantance that comes instantly to mind is the Naga warriors fighting bravely to thwart the British advance into their lands in India's North-East every mile of the way. They bravely fought the British arms during the sieges of Khonoma and Kohima, But it was an unequal fight. Rifles against their *dahs* (= machete) and bombs against their stones/

bricks. But more germane to our subject is tribal revolts during the British rule when their cultural belief systems and traditional ways of life associated with nature–jal, jungle, jameen (water, forest, land)–were interfered with and threatened.

Tribal revolts

Rampachodavaram rebellion of 1879. The Dorla and Koya tribals rose in revolt agsinst the British and the non-tribals when the colonial rulers imposed restrictions on access to forest resources and started penalizing liquor brewing. It was followed again by the Bastar rebellion of 1910 led by Gunda Dhur, that legendary Dhurua tribal leader who was revered as god in Bastar. It was against the British Government's attempt at banning and penalizing *podu* (= shifting cultivation), against the practice of *begar* (= free bonded labour) for landlords and against eviction from and access to forests.

The Paderu Rebellion of 1922-23

This revolt by the Koyas, the Parajas and the Kandha tribals was let by the legendary non–tribal revolutionary Alluri Sitaram Raju "Sitaram Raju, who dons the walls of every rural home and urban street in the Northern Andhra Pradesh,"[1] valiantly led these tribal communities in revolt against the colonial government's banning and penalizing of *Podu* and eviction of tribal settlements from inside the dense forests. This revolt was noteworthy for the fact that Raju led a guerilla warfare against the British–a first for the tribals to be introduced to this genre of combat. It will be only appropriate if Sitaram Raja is designated as an ancestor of Naxal leaders like Charu Mazumdar, Kanu Sanyal and Jangal Santhal.

The list of tribal revolts given above is merely illustrative. To put the issue in perspective, it is worth a note that some 70 tribal revolts took place during the 70-year periods of pre-independence India's history, that is, between 1878 and 1948. These revolts had a lot to do with the restrictions placed on access and control over forests by the criminal rulers of India with the enactment of Indian Forest Acts of 1867, 1878 and 1927 and the Madras Forest Act of 1882 that provided the legal basis for reservation of forests and 'settlements' and notification of forest rights.[2]

It later turned out that these acts had an adverse effect on the economic situation of the tribal communities. These will be looked into in another chapter.

Pre-Naxalbari Movements

Before the iconic Naxalism appeared on the scene, there were two events in the similar vein, but not related to the tribals. They belonged to the different genres, viz, the Telangana Movement and the Telangana insurrection.

The Tebhaga Movement in Undivided Bengal: 1946

In a manner of speaking, it was a protest movement by the peasantry– the tillers of the land, to be more accurate. They demanded that the share of the landlords be reduced from one-half to one-third. Starting from Rangpur to Dinajpur in the north, it spread to the 24 Parganas in the south.

With the landlords refusing to yield, the Kisan Sabhas, dominated by the Communist Party, goaded peasants to forcibly take two-thirds of the harvested crop from the granaries. Expectedly, this led to the bloody clashes between the peasants and the landlords, and local administration helped the latter. The movement could not last long against the repression on the peasantry.

The Telangana Insurrection: 1946-51

It was, once again, a movement of the peasantry, directed by the Communists. The peasants launched the struggle on the economic issues: Forced labour, illegal exactions and arbitrary evictions. This movement soon transformed into an uprising against the feudal rule of the Nizam of Hyderabad. More than 4,000 lives were lost before the Communist Party withdrew the struggle.

Nothing like this had ever been seen in any princely state of India. Going beyond the peasantry struggle, it had assumed wider configuration, embracing a variety of anti-Nizam forces when he was also embroiled with India to secure independence for his State.

It should not come as a surprise of some scholars assert that this bloody insurrection had no parallel in the Indian history since the 1857 Sepoy Mutiny, which stands rechristened, of late, as the First War of Independence.

The Saga of Naxalbari

The Naxalism, taking its name from the non-decrepit village of Naxalbari, has assumed iconic status among the comity of armed revoltions/ insurrections in the annals of India. It is a watershed : the armed movements in the country can simply be divided into two taxnomical eras–pre-Naxal and post-Naxal. The Charu Mazumdar-led Naxal uprising may not have lasted long or made spectacular gains, even then, the scholars and analysts are sanguine in their belief that any such movement that followed the 1967 icon can and should be deemed to be inspired by it. Even the long-lasting and the current rage in this genre, Maoism, has drawn its fire from the Naxalism spark. What follows is the comprehensive account of Naxalism: Its origin, its spread and a variety of clones spawned by it.

Naxalbari: 1967

The area of revolt is constituted by the region that falls under the jurisdiction of three police stations–Naxalbari, Kharibari and Phansidema. Some 65 per cent of the population in this region was scheduled castes and tribals; working as agricultural labourers or in mines, forest and platations. A small percentage owned small holdings, the vast majority cultivating under agency system (*baghchashis*). The *baghchashis* were exploited by the jotedars. When the land reforms act was passed in 1955, the jotedars' malafide transfers of land deprived the peasants and *baghchashis* of their expected shares. This could not have continued for long. Subsequently, the Santhals armed with bows and arrows forcibly occupied the lands of the kulaks, lifted stocks of hoarded rice. In this free-for-all, a police inspector was killed. It was on 24th May 1967. Thereby hangs a tale.

The Naxalbari Day: 24 May 1967

In an interview published on 20th May 2007,[3] Kanu Sanyal, the only living member of the founding trio of Naxalism, was asked about his memories of that fateful day of 25th May 1967. Here is his reply:

> "For us, 24th May (1967) is Naxalbari day. That day, the police were informed some leaders of the Naxalbari movement were hiding in Boro Jhorojote village. There were no leaders there, only a gathering of peasantry and tea garden workers. One police officer were killed. Since the peasants understood and accepted our politics and took up arms on their own, we celebrate that day as a victory of our political ideas."

Incidentally, other groups observe 25th May as Martyrs Day when 11 persons were killed in police firing.

After this firing, there were a number of such incidents. Consequently, there was a major deployment of police forces by the CPM Government. After several operations, the movement was squashed with a heavy hand.

At this stage, suffice it to say that ideological differences in the leadership resulted in the split of the movement, which culminated in the formation of the CPI (ML) on 22th April 1969.

Even though not more than a score of people were killed in this uprising, it left a far-reaching impact on the entire agrarian scene through out the country. This effect can be compared to the several ripples a single pebble creates in a pond.

It bears recording that Jyoti Basu was the Home Minister of West Bengal during this relevant period.

Who led this essentially brief but intense two-year-long struggle? A radical group from the CPI (M)'siliguri unit: Charu Mazumdar was the ideologue, Kanu Sanyal among the leading organisers and Jangal Santhal mobilised the adivasis. As stated above, by April 1969, this group had split from the CPI (M) to form CPI (ML).

What were the long-term effects of the naxalbari uprising? It resulted in the redistribution of land amongst the peasantry and formation of the CPI (ML). Between 1969 and 1971, the Naxalite movement spread to various parts of the country, taking on a more violent and in places, an urban character. Shades of it remains in today's CPI (ML) groups and the Maoists.

We rest Naxalism proper here, to revisit it at a later stage. Hereafter are examined some other groups, some of which later joined to emerge as CPI (Maoists).

Srikakulam: 1968

Seventy per cent population of this district was of Girijans (= hill dwellers; tribals), who were living in the agency areas of the Eastern Ghats. Majority of them were plying agriculture, and the rest were involved in collecting and dealing in minor forest produce.

Conscious that they may be harassed and even exploited, by the plains men, the British decreed that no land could be sold/transferrmed to a plains man without an express permission from the District Collector. (They had laid down a similar policy for the tribal communities inhabiting the forests and hills in the interior areas of India's North-East). But this Act, through devious and clever ways of manipulation, was observed more in breach. The traders and plainsmen, in Shylockean manner, exploited the poverty of the hapless Girijans. They supplied their day to day requirements of tobacco, kerosene, salt and cloth on credit and lent money for purchase of seeds. When a tribal was unable to pay back the dues beyond a certain accumulated amount of debt, he was forced to part-with his land or a part of it to square the transaction. Thus, progressively, fertile lands would keep passing into the hands of the devious plains men, traders and moneylenders.

Poverty has always been exploited by the rich. It is so even today, notwithstanding the plethora of rules and laws passed against such malpractices. In those early days, the situation lent itself for easy exploitation. The tillers and leaseholders lived at the mercy of the landlords. The latter squeezed them to the utmost limits, paying only subsistence wages and remunerations.

Leaseholder had to give two-thirds of their produce to the landlords. It was in this sad situation that a redeemer appeared among them. Vempatapu Satyanarayana started working among the Girijans in 1967. The movement he led resulted in substantial gains for the Girijans–poor and exploited lot till then. Some specifics are enumerated here: wages of farm servants rose; the landlord's wages of share of harvest was reduced from two-thirds to one-third; 2,000 acres of land was wrested from the landlords; and more than 5,000 acres of land went under the possession of the Girijans.

The exploiters could not have accepted this adverse situation with equanimity. On 31st October 1967 occurred a clash between a large group of tribals marching for a meeting of the Marxist Party and a group of landlords. The latter had guns and they shot and killed two tribals in the ensuing clash. The incensed Girijans resorted to violence, giving birth to an agrarian armed struggle. Their leader, *Satyanarayana,* organised them into guerrilla squads, called Dalams.

It was at this stage during 1969 that Srikakulam leadership, which had joined the CP (M) faction of India's Communist Party broke away from it also and joined a group which had earlier followed the same path [of breaking away from CP (M) to form a new entity, called the All India Coordination Committee of Communist Revolutionaries (AICC of CR). The AICC of CR in due course transformed itself into the Communist Party of India (Marxist–Leninist), CPI (ML). As stated above, Charu Mazumdar was one of the progenitors of the CPI (ML).

Meanwhile, the raids on the houses of landlords and moneylenders continued. The houses were burnt down and cash looted. Expectedly, there came clashes with the police. From December 1968 to January 1969, 29 policeman were killed by the Dalams. The level of motivation among the cadres was obviously high.

Charu Mazumdar, the high priest of the CPI (ML) visited Srikakulam, a morale booster for the local leadership and its fighters. It gave a fillip to the movement.

During 1969, the Naxaltes committed 23 murders and 40 *dacoities.*[4] Some of the murders were committed in a gruesome manner. Here, is an example of a landlord, P. Jammu Naidu of Ethamanuguda, who was killed on 11th May 1969. The Dalam Cadre which killed him painted slogans on the walls with his blood. He was notorious for grabbing land of the poor tribal and taking their daughters for his wives. When he was killed, it turned out that he had seven wives, two of them being little girls he had grabbed from the helpless victims of his *avarice.* This should suffice to show the extent of exploitation by the upper class landlords inflicted on their victims–the poor tribals.

The drawing room intellectuals might wince and even condemn, the gruesomeness of the murder described above. But there is a counter narrative also. What will they say of a tribal seeing his children dying in his presence, daily by inches, literally—if such a phrase can be used — just because some one has illegally deprived him of his land, pushing his children into slow death, as a result. Again, can these richer classes understand the agony of parents whose little girl child is spending her time in the harem of a rich landlord.

Here, is another instance of exploitative practices by the upper caste landlords against the poor tribals who collect minor forest produce to eke out a subsistence. It will be evident from the account of a trial of a *Sahukar* by a Peoples Court. This *Sahukar*, a habitual usurer, used to go into the agency area to collect tamarind from the forest Girijans. The list of the borrowers which he produced before the Court showed that he had lent a sum of ₹ 280.00 to the peasants in four villages. Against this amount, he proposed to collect from them 40 bundles of tamarind which at the prevailing market price was worth ₹ 1600.00. It works out to the peasants paying back ₹ 6 for every rupee they had borrowed! The usurer was arrested and tried before a Peoples Court. He repented and promised not to indulge in such usurious practices in future. In a word, he would fleece the peasants no more.

West Bengal (Midnapur and Birbhum): 1967-71

The Midnapur District of West Bengal, bordering Bihar and Orissa witnessed a well-planned and well-organised Naxal movement in the areas of Debra and Gopibhallavpur police stations. The district has a sizeable population of Santhal, Oraon and Lodha tribes, majority of them being landless labourers. A small proportion among them owned small plots of land or cultivated the jotedar's land under the *barga* system.

Gopilb hallavpur shares a long forested border with Orissa and Bihar. Post-Naxalbari uprising (in 1967), a section of CPI (M) workers in Midnapur started propagating the Naxal line, namely, the extremist line. They supported the peasantry and bargadars and launched a struggle against the jotedars. Santosh Rana and Ashim Mukherjee, both first class graduates from Calcutta University, were the leaders. They and a host of student from well-to-do upper caste families of Culcutta lived and worked among the tribals. They were setting personal example to identify themselves whole heartedly with these deprived populace.

September 1969 onwards, large tribal groups armed with spears, bows and arrows attacked the houses of jotedars–killing some of them, looting cash and burning/destroying all available land deeds. Alarmed at the spate of killings, the State Government despatched several companies of the CRPF and State police. By March 1970, the short-lived armed struggle was put to an end, bringing the area under the Government control.

The Naxalite uprising in the Birbhum district was also masterminded by the students from the Calcutta (Kolkata) University. "The State Government countered by dispatching some companies of CRPF and State Armed Police and an infantry company of army"[5] for cordon and search operation in the area. Nearly 150 CPI (M) cadres were arrested and the movement petered out.

Bihar and Uttar Pradesh: 1968-70

The Mushahari block of Bihar's Muzaffarpur District has 12 villages, with a total population of some 10,000 people. As is usual in such cases, the peasantry was subjected to a variety of opperessive practice by the upper classes. Possibly inspired by the Naxalbari *Saga,* the peasants of Gangapur harvested in April 1968 the Arhar crop of the landlord in broad daylight. Retaliation was quick in coming. Incensed by the audacity of the peasants, Bijli Singh, the Zamindar of Narsingpur, marshalled a force of 300 men armed with lathis, swords and firearms. He led his 'army', seated on an elephant. In the fight that ensued, the landlord and "his hoodlums" were routed. The public humbling of this powerful landlord by the Harijan peasants was something unheard of in the area perhaps, even the State. It had a magical, more than that, a librating effect in the surrounding villages of the area. The event inspired more such incidents/happenings.

To organise the peasantry, a number of Kisan Sangram Samitis came into existence. There were a number of incidents of peasants seizing the lands of landlords, and harvesting them. For instance in April 1969, landless peasants forcibly harvested the crop on 14 acres of a landlord's land. In the ensuing clash, the retainer of the landlord was killed Similarly, in June 1969, an attack was launched on the village of Paharchat. The landlord and his two associates were killed. Hundreds of peasants gathered subsequent to the raid. In their presence, all the land deeds and concerned documents were put to the flame and the pawned ornaments returned to their owners. This was followed by a series of similar violent events.

The State Government was alarmed enough to induct police force in the area in question. Several combing operations were mounted and the "desperados" were on the run. Consequently, the movement died down.

The Mushahari produced ripples that spread into Darbhanga, Champaran and Chota Nagpur. In May 1970, 54 adivasis were arrested in the Jaduguda forests during the police operations. Mary Tyler, a British national, was among those 54. Later, she penned her thoughts in poignant prose:

> "The Naxalites' crime was the crime of all those who cannot remain unmoved and inactive in an India where a child crawls in the dust with a begging bowl, where a poor girl can be sold as a richman's plaything, where an old woman must half starve herself in order to buy social acceptance from the powers that be in her village; where countless people die of shear neglect, where many are hungry while food is hoarded for profit, where usurers and tricksters extort the fruits of labour from those who do the work, where the honest suffer, while the villainous prosper, where justice is the exception and injustice the rule and where the total physical and mental energy of millions of people is spent on the struggle for mere survival."[6]

The Naxalite violence that erupted in Singhbhum and Ranchi assumed more serious dimensions. As an analyst put it, Jamshedpur became a mini Kolkata, with schools, government offices and police picquets coming under attacks. There were also large scale attacks in Ranchi.

In Uttar Pradesh, the Pallia area is a part of the Lakhimpur district in the Terai region and is inhabited by the Tharu tribals. The State Government had encouraged the poor, landless peasants to move to the Palia area, allotting 10-12 acres of land to each family of migrants. Ejecting the peasants, the landlords had forcibly occupied large chunks of land.

"This offered a fertile ground to the Naxalites to help the deprived and the dispossessed. Their object was to clear the area of big farmers, thugs, corrupt political leaders and money lenders."[7] They launched a series of attacks and raids on the landlords, snatching a good number of their firearms. Deployment of the armed police in the area brought the situation under control.

Failure of Naxalism in the Area of its Origin?

All the armed uprisings discussed above were essentially spawned by the Naxalbari 1967. These can be called Naxalite movements, organised by different CPI (ML) groups in their states. Charu Mazumdar, the ideologue of the Naxalbari revolt, no doubt was an original thinker but pragmatism was not his forte. He failed to transform his initial successes into something bigger. He was not able to convert the spark he produced into the prairie fires. He certainly ignited fires in several states, but these were extinguished by their police forces.

May be, Charu was a bit of a romantic. But he lacked vision, as a critic saw it. He and his colleagues were on cloud nine just because Chairmen Mao had granted them an audience! They thought this audience and their initial successes at home would create mass uprisings, and that would enable them to create an Indian equivalent of Chinese PLA. The rag-tag band of peasants who had revolted against the atrocities and repression of the landlords and the money lenders, not only in North (West) Bengal but also in some other states of the Union lacked coherent leadership. But that was not all. Charu had ideological differences even within the founding trio of Naxalbari. Was he a loner? It may be too harsh to blame him for all this failure. May be, masses were not ready for his revolution! Again, he had no precedence to build on his initial success. Or, was he before his time? Possibly, same can, more or less, be said about Satyanarain Singh of Bihar– a prophet that failed.

But there are, indeed, a lot of positives to his personality and work. Besides lighting the fires in Siliguri area, he also succeeded in arousing the student in Calcutta and its Universities. They abandoned their studies to live in the forest villages to identity with their tribulations. Of course, the vital elements for building up a guerrilla force, training and equipping its cadres to take up the might of a state were lacking. One by one, the movements fizzled out as the central paramilitary forces with the State Police forces were deployed in the interior areas. They carried out well-planned raids and search operations to capture or eliminate the cadres. It is ironic that it was the police of a communist home minister (Jyoti Basu) that ruthlessly crushed Charu's baby.

Critics aver that Naxalite leadership "lacked the vision to organise the poor peasants against the might of the state, even if the cause was just."

Yet again, as can be expected in such situations, certain lumpen elements infiltrated the ranks of these leflist groups for their selfish ends and consequently, affected their discipline and morale.

At the end of the line, the iconic stature of Charu Mazumdar cannot be questioned, neither can the contribution of his creation, Naxalism, towards the success of Maoism, as the latter is bent a linear descendant of the former.

End Notes: Initial Phase of Naxalism

A rough estimate says there were some 4,000 incident of Naxalite Violence between mid–1970 to mid–1971. Of these, 3500 were in West Bengal, 220 in Bihar and 70 in Andhra Pradesh. The Central Government planned a joint operation in West Bengal, Bihar and Orissa with the army, paramilitary forces and the State Police forces. The Operation Steeplechase lasted from 1st July to 15th August 1971. Its broad strategy was to surround an area known to be a Naxal stronghold with an outer cordon of army troops, an inner cordon of CRPF personnel, and the local police operating inside. The operation disrupted the network of the Naxal cadres and consequently, the movement stalled.

Meanwhile, internal dissensions between the CPI (ML) factions additionally disrupted and weakened the movement. A number of top leaders, including Charu Mazumdar, were arrested. When he died shortly after this, it marked the end of a phase of the Naxalite movement in India. But it was merely a lull. The movement was to surface again, since the Governments at New Delhi and in the states had failed to address the issues that had caused the fires at Naxalbari.

Pure force cannot end such insurrections. The root causes of the problem must be addressed: Oppression and injustice inflicted on the poor, dispossessed and the downtrodden by the rich and powerful. An unequal society, when the extreme misery coexists with luxury, is sure to blow up one day. A revolt can be suppressed by brute force, but unless it is accompanied or at least followed, by the socio-economic development of deprived and poor majority, it will remain a temporary solution. We should not overlook the warning and an unambiguous truth, contained in the Tupamaro Manifesto: "If the country does not belong to everyone, it will belong to no one."

Moving Towards the CPI (Maoist)

The Naxalism might have failed in the area of its origin, still its basic ideological moorings are strong. But basic tenets of its mission, working for the deprived and the dispossessed, will always be relevant till oppression and injustice prevail in an unequal world. No wonder there has been strong urge among the Leftists and others following the course of evolving revolutionary trends to continue the work started by the Naxal leadership of the 1960s. We move on to the 1980's to examine the current trends and revolutionary movements in various parts of the country.

Peoples War Group (PWG) Andhra Pradesh, Madhya Pradesh and Maharashtra: 1980

Andhra Pradesh has a radical tradition dating back to the 1946-51 Telangana movement. The Girijan awakening in Srikakulam had, in fact, preceded the Naxalite movement. The might of the State squelched the uprising by 1970. The movement however continued to simmer. After the death of Charu Mazumdar, his associates like Kondapalli Seetharamiah, K G Satyamurthy and Suniti Kumar Ghosh formed a Central Organising Committee (COC) of the CPI (ML) in December 1972, concentrating on organising and mobilising the masses. They decided to eschew militancy till the time the party was strong enough to resume the course of violence. Seetharamiah encouraged his cadres to "commit money action", an euphemism for dacoity and robbery. He was arrested on 26th April 1977, but jumped the bail. Thereafter, he involved himself in underground activities on a large scale. He broke away from the COC CPI (ML) on 20th April 1980, and formed the CPI (ML) Peoples War Group (PWG). For the next ten years, he moved from strength to strength, and PWG emerged as the most formidable Naxalite outfit in the country.[8]

What were the reasons behind the resurgence of Naxalism (the term used is still Naxalism) in the Telangana region? The major reason was the continued economic exploitation of the tribals by the landlords, traders and government officials, particularly those of the Forest Department. P. S. Sundaram explains:

> "The tribals owning small pieces of land are expropriated and sharecroppers impoverished. They all are kept under perpetual bondage towards repayment of a small debt supposedly taken generation ago. The forest wealth is freely smuggled out by contractors in connivance with the forest *staff*. The tribals get neither a remunerative price for their produce nor a fair wage for their labour."[9]

The social dimensions of exploitation are even more repulsive. The landlords of the region are commonly known as Dora (= lord) and their high-handedness and tyranny in Telangana is unmatched. C. Lokeswara Rao illustrates the same in lurid detail: "Tribal girls working on the Dora's land are forcibly taken in his household and remain at the disposal of the master and his guests. She is forced to undergo an abortion if and when she gets pregnant. She subsists on the left-overs passed on by the cook, but is obliged to satisfy the carnal appetite of just about any mail in her master's household." Naxalite songs are replete with references to rape by the landlords and to the girls growing up with the knowledge of inevitability of the rape that awaits them. Can anything be more demeaning and inhuman? Unfortunately, some of these indignites still persist!

Here is an important milestone in the annals of the PWG, dated 20th May 1981. More than 30,000 tribals had turned up for a meeting called by the Naxalites that day at Indraveli in Adilabad District. Fearing violence, the administration had refused permission. Determined to hold the meeting, the tribals converged on the venue and consequently there was police firing, following the lathi charge. 13 Gond tribals were killed. The PWG skillfully exploiting the anger of the tribals, consolidated their position in the area. Kondapalli Sitaramiah was arrested for the second time on 2nd January 1982, but yet again escaped from the hospital on 4th January 1984. He then concentrated on the proper organisation of the PWG cadres, constituting Forest Committees for the forest areas and Regional Committees for the plains areas. Armed squads (=dalams) comprising 6-10 cadres were formed. Some 50 dalams were soon active in Telangana.

Here are some measures taken by the PWG that made it popular among the hitherto dispossessed and poor peasantry. "The PWG is believed to have redistributed nearly half a million acres of land across Andhra Pradesh." Their modus operandi was simple: forcibly occupy the excess land of big/rich landlords and distribute it among the landless/labourers working on that land. By way of proof of this methodology of the Naxalites, counter-affidavit 68/82 filed by the State Government is an admission by it of the pro-poor measures of the PWG! This affidavit says in so many words that "the radicals have forcibly redistributed 80,000 acres of agricultural land and 20,000 acres of forest-land."

This affidavit permits a very terse if honest query: "What the Government had been doing all this time since the land ceiling act came into being years back?" Was it unwilling or unable to act? was it commandeered by the landlords to stay passive? Or, was it complicit in their malfeasance?

It is worthwhile to stay with the issue for a while. Inability or unwillingness of the governments to enforce the provisions of the Land Ceiling Acts was the major cause behind the rise and spread of the Naxalism in the country. It was not only Andhra Pradesh that was amiss on this all important legislation. The same was the situation in so many other states. The West Bengal Government under Jyoti Basu of the CP (M) was the only one that implemented this Act sincerely and honestly and reaped its fruits for some three and a half decades! They still could have continued their rule if the party had not allowed its self-indulgent cadres to run riot in the state, and thus giving a chance to that feisty lady, Mamta Bannerji, to push them off the chair! Before we return to the main narrative, PWG in Andhra Pradesh, it is worthwhile to emphasise that CP (M) Government in West Bengal was a quick learner: The violence launched by Charu Mazumdar's Naxals taught them a lesson and they picked up its meaning, even if for their self-preservation!

Returning to Andhra Pradesh, PWG activists got a hike in the daily minimum wages from ₹ 15 to ₹ 25 and the annual fee for *Jeetagadu* (year long labour) from ₹ 2,000 to ₹ 4,000.[10]

The poorer sections were particularly happy at these two measures but realised that it could be turned into reality only with the (violent) intervention of the Naxalites. Was it any surprise that the Naxalites came to known as "Gorakala Doras" (Lords of the Bushes) in the interiors of the forest areas.

Revolutionary writers and poets helped in furthering the Naxalite ideology. The Jana Natya Mandali is the cultural front of the PWG or the "overground arm" of the underground outfit, as some activists on the anti-Naxalite front prefer to call them! The moving spirit of this Mandali is Gummadi Vittal Rao, more popularly known as Gaddar. This wandering minstrel's ballads inspired the simple tribal, goading some into more activist mode. He became a legend in Andhra Pradesh and today he is a popular figure beyond its borders. In the national capital during a recent visit, he was a huge draw.

The PWG had fought successive battles with the Telugu Desam Party Government. When the Congress came to power in 1989, for political reasons, that is, just to prove that the TDP approach to the Naxal problem was flawed, they went soft on them and freed many of them under detention and in prison. But they did hardly anything to stop or reduce the exploitation of the tribals by the landlords or the moneylenders, the root causes behind the Naxal insurrection. The Congress Government neither took measures to enforce the land ceiling or to check the venal practices of the avaricious money lenders. Under the changed situation, when there was neither government pressure on them nor there was any let up of the exploitation of the poor tribals, the Naxalites restarted their struggle with renewed vigour, reorganising the cadres, extorting money and running peoples courts. They were running a parallel government. Alarmed by the adverse impression the public was likely to have of the Congress Government, it per force had to return to the hardline against the Naxalites, which they had criticized while in the opposition and followed in the initial months of their coming to power!

It needs to be asserted here clearly: This is the bane of politics in India. The political parties cannot agree on a common platform even when the country is facing a serious danger to its national security. And to wit, country's Prime Minister is on record averring that "Naxalism poses the greatest threat to country's security." But have his own ministers, and other run-of-the-mill politician understood this threat? Most of them are guilty of playing with the nation's security–issuing one irresponsible statement after another. They (most of them) give the impression that they do not know, or even care to know, that nation is at war today against the Naxalites/ Maoists. In this respect, they are no better than the passionate human rights activists who keep blaming the government and its security forces who are presently engaged in fighting the menace, rather scourge, of Maoism. These activists, whom the author prefer to call Human Rights Wallahs (H. R. Wallahs, for short), have been dubbed, by the harassed and frustrated security analysts as the "overground arm" of the Maoists. The issue will be dealt with in greater detail in a subsequent chapter.

PWG in Maharashtra and Madhya Pradesh

From Andhra Pradesh, the PWG spreads into the adjoining areas of Maharashtra, Madhya Pradesh and Orissa; and even into Tamil Nadu and Karnataka. They also acquired 50-60 AK 47 riffles, probably from the LTTE.

Naxalite violence gradually stepped up and peaked in 1991, with several attacks on railway and electrical installations, Police Stations, and patrols. The PWG was banned on 8th May 1992, and consequently coordinated operations were launched against them by the paramilitary forces and the State Police units. The operation was declared a success, with 3500 cadres arrested and 8500 surrendering. But they bounced back by mid-1993 with rising violence. Their increased activities need a look in two particular areas:

- Baster District of Madhya Pradesh (later in Chhattisgarh).
- Gadchiroli of Maharashtra.

Bastar Region

They made good gains in Bastar, an erstwhile princely state, nothing more than a sleepy forest outpost. The tribals there were used to a life of deprivation. With their advent into the district, the Naxalites made the truant teacher to take classes regularly and the absentee doctors started reporting for duty and attending their patients. It was something unheard of, and earned great respect, tinged with awe, for the Naxalite cadres from the tribals. The Peoples Union of Civil Liberties (PUCL) explain the phenomenon: "A lopsided socio-economic development of the district caused by exploitation through cheating and duping was an ideal setting for the Naxalites to take roots in the area. With their idealism free of corruption or other vested interests, they could win the confidence of the tibals. They even punished corrupt officials and forced the tendu leaf contractors to increase the wages."[11] The Naxalite movement spread to Balaghat and Rajnandgaon.

Gadchiroli District

The district is largely inhabited by the tribals. Of the total area of 15,434 square kilometers of the district, forest covers 10,495 square kilometer.

The life of a tribal revolves around his jungle, yet he was denied access to his forest due to an obtuse interpretation of the Forest Act and rules. When the Naxals arrived, the forest officials abandoned their posts. The best testimonial of the activities of the Naxalites–called Dadas here– in the areas and their effect on the tribal life comes from an innocent tribal who got a lift in the car of the Commissioner of Scheduled Castes and Scheduled Tribes during his visit to the district. When asked about the Naxalites, the tribal replied: "There is at least one change since the Dadas have arrived. The government atrocities are over and the police cannot harass us."[12]

Now some statistics, in 1990, there were 113 incidents of Naxalite violence in the district, with 16 fatalites. On 12 November 1991, ten CPRF personnel were killed and 13 injured in a landmine explosion under their vehicle.

The PWG has attained a high degree of expertise in making and detonating Improvised Explosive Devices (IED).

The New Left in Bihar

The best description of pre-Nitish Kumar's Bihar's dismal state of affairs comes up from Arvind N. Das: "Bihar's economy has been at a standstill for decades. The discriminatory nature of public and private investments, the green revolution bypassing the State, principally on account of non-implementation of land reforms, the willful subversion of whatever social security system existed, all these have pushed the people into poverty, the economy into backwardness and the society into violence."[13]

The resentment of the oppressed sections of the population in this environment found an outlet in the emergence of a "New Left", the term coined by the said Das. He goes further: "The New Left manifested in the form of three Naxalite groups in the beginning of 1980: The Moist Communist Centre (MCC), CPI-ML (Anti Lin Biao Group), and the CPI-ML (Party Unity). In May 1982, the Bihar Government reported that 47 out of 857 blocks were affected by the Naxalite movement. Subsequently, the movement has grown enormously in the face of a corrupt, casteist and incompetent administration".[14]

When the CPI (ML) was formed initially, one Naxalite group, Dakshin Desh, has remained aloof, its leaders being Amulya Sen and Kanai Chatterjee. They considered mass mobilisation as a precursor to armed action. As a result, their group chose Jangal Mahal area of Burdwan, with a sizeable population of Scheduled Castes and Scheduled Tribels, for its operations. Agricultural land was inadequate, irrigation virtually non-existent and the wage rates dismally low, all conditions tailor-made for a Naxalite uprising. The landlords generally belonged to the upper castes while the share croppers and landless labour belonged to the Scheduled Castes or Tribals–an ideal mix that invites the entry of the Naxalites. By 1973, the Party had 37 militias who organised actions like looting of food grains, killing of class enemy and snatching of arms.

In 1975, the group was renamed as the Maoist Communist Centre (MCC). The MCC gradually spread over central Bihar. Its cadres exceeded 10,000 and they had stockpiled some 700 weapons including some A K rifles. There were gruesome slaughters of Rajputs by Yadavs in the MCC. These were more in the form of feuds between the two communities, essentially flowing from the way the Rajput treated the Yadavs. Two instances are illustrative of this blood feud. On 29th May 1987, the Yadav cadres of the MCC slaughtered 42 Rajputs of Baghaura and Dalelchak villages of Aurangabad district.

On 12th February 1992, 37 members of the landowning Bhumihar Caste were hacked to death by the MCC cadres in Bara village of Gaya district.

Vinod Mishra formed the CPI-ML (Anti Lin Biao) faction in December 1973. It struck roots in Bhojpur district and spread to Rohtas, Jehanabad, Patna and Nalanda districts. They had 50 underground armed squads, and weapons, mostly country-made guns, a few rifles and sten guns. The Indian Peoples Front (IPF) was the political front of the Anti Lin Biao faction.

The CPI-ML (Party Unity) was formed in 1982 by the merger of the COC CPI (ML) of Andhra Pradesh and the Unity Organisation of the CPI (ML) of West Bengal. The Party Unity has about 30,000 members. It has 25 armed squads holding some 150 weapons, including a few sten guns.

The third phase of the Naxalite violence commenced with the holding of the 9th Congress of the PWG in 2001 wherein it was decided to arm the Peoples Guerrilla Army with more sophisticated weapons. This phase extended the Naxalite war to nine states of the Union.

A Brief Review

In the wide theatre of Naxalite revolt, West Bengal is the only state which has afforded a diagnostic response to the threat. It has been earlier mentioned that they learnt right lessons from Charu Mazumdar's Naxalbari uprising. The CPM Government undertook Operation Barga under which sharecropper were registered and given permanent and inheritable rights on cultivations of their plots. The exercise covered a total area of 11 lakh acres. Besides this, 1.37 lakh acres of ceiling surplus and benami lands were acquired by the State Government and distributed among 25 lakh landless and marginal cultivators. These land reforms saw the emergence of a new class, loosely termed 'rural rich' which weakened the social and political power enjoyed by the landlords in the countryside.

"In Andhra Pradesh or Bihar, Land Ceiling Act has not been enforced even after 50 years of its legislation"[15] More than this, these two states suffered from the flawed thinking on the subject of the Naxalite resurrection. "The law enforcing agencies in these two states nurtured the idea of Naxalites, being a band of criminals and thugs, just have to be wiped out." They simply treated it as law and order problem, ignoring the issues of socio-economic explotation of the poor and deprived. Only force cannot be the solution to this serious movement, even if it is sine qua non to force them to the negotiations table. It has to be a combination of the both. With such thinking of these officials, the question of enforcement of the Land Ceiling Act's provisions to improve the lot of the poor and the dispossessed does not arise. What is left unstated in this kind of thinking is that it is the birth right of the upper castes/classes to own hundreds of acres of land and the Scheduled Castes and Tribals merely exist to supply cheap labour for their lands to further enhance their riches. In this scenario, the poor have no rights, only obligation to serve!

But it is the (undivided) CPI of Kerala that should take the cake for being the first in India to put in practice their creed and ideology when they came to power in Kerala in the 1950s.

The upper classes in Kerala were generally landlords with medium holdings. A majority of these landlords had tenant farmers on their lands who deposited half of the yield to these landlords. But the landlords themselves and their progeny were educated and took up white collar jobs in the metropolises of the country. In a manner of speaking they were the absentee landlords. When the CPI came to power in the late fifties, they enacted the land tenancy laws which accorded the ownership of land to those tenants who held, tenancy for 12 or more years. With a single stroke of the law, hundreds of upper caste landlords lost their lands to their tenant farmers who had tilled them over the years. This enactment and its consequences explain the reasons for the Naxalite movement not taking roots in Kerala.

The nature of exploitation of the tribals in the forest lands of Andhra Pradesh, Maharashtra, Madhya Pradesh, Chhattishgarh and Jharkhand is of another kind. Traditionally, the forests have been the home to the tribals– living in it, using its produce for sustenance and maintaining it. Consequent to modernisation, industrialisation, and particularly the globalisation, outsiders–be they government/forest officials, contractors, mining companies, public or private, and even the local *bania* (= money lender), or minor trader–seem to be threatening his jungle, and even the means of his livelihood.

For majority of tribals, *bania* is the villain of the piece and he represent the exploitation of the poor by the upper castes. It is the Vaishya who is the trader and he also doubles as a money lender. In some forest areas of certain Naxalite-affected states, "the *bania*/Vaishya has achieved a vice-like grip on the tribals and their economy. He lends money to them and collects minor forest produce against the loans, taking care that the tribals are perpetually indebted!"

Nature of War: Mass Struggle or Armed Struggle

There are different ways to solve a problem. India's freedom struggle too was not Gandhi Ji's monolith mantra of peaceful agitation. There were other engaging in violent/armed way of achieving the same objective. Tribals' struggle to fight against injustice and for coming out of poverty-ridden existence too was/is being fought on parallel roads.

Bulk of the Maoist cadres are tribal and Maoists do enjoy certain degree of support among the tribals. But armed struggle is not the way the majority among the tribals would like to wage the war to achieve their objective. Armed struggle is not the way in which tribals are protesting their conditions. For several decades now, they have been articulating their frustration through non-violent mass protests. Since the 1970s, hundreds of tribal organisations have emerged to protest their displacement by mining projects and dams, press for better and speedy rehabilitation measures and demand access to forest resources. These organisations sit on *dharnas* (= sit-ins), go on road/long marches and block roads to focus attention on their grievances, hoping to change the ways of their class enemy. The Bahuguna-led Chipko Movement is an apt example of a non-violent agitation. Some examples of the mass organisations involved in various protests are mentioned here:

- The 1993-grant of lease to Utkal Alumina International Ltd (UAIL) for extraction of bauxite from the Baphilimali hills in Kashipur gave birth to the Prakrutik Sampad Suraksya Parishad (PSSP). This organisation has been protesting the bauxite mining and refining plant over two decades.
- In Koraput, the Chasi Mulia Adivasi Saugh (CMAS) has been active, esserting rights over the tribal land that was grabbed by non-tribal landlords. They have been campaigning for over two decades against this usurpation and consumption and sale of

liquor in the area, major causes for land alienation and tribal inebledness.

Niyamagiri Suraksha Samiti is another mass organisation active in the eponymous area, protesting against Vedanta's proposed mining project at Niyamgiri. Its success in sustaining its campaign drew attention to Vedanta's violation of environmental norms, persuading the Orissa Government to refuse permission to the company for mining at Niyamagiri.[16] (Further/latest details on the issue will be found in a separate chapter on Orissa.

If the tribals prefer mass organisational agitation over ballot box approach to redress their grievances, they have their reasons. Given their demographic distribution–they are concentrated in a few pockets across the country, their capacity to influence the outcome of the election even in states is limited, not to speak of India as a whole. Guha notes that in parliamentary polls, the tribal vote matters in 50–60 constituencies in a total of 548. Compared to this small figure, Dalits matter in some 300 constituencies.[17] (It is rather inexplicable that given the respective number of tribals and Dalits in India–7.5 and 15 per cent of the population–there is such a vide disparity in the number of constituencies their respective votes matter). Since their votes do not matter much to the governments, as numbers matter in a democratic polity, they choose alternative option of mass mobilisation and agitation to achieve their objectives.

It seems the circumstances and the governments are in league to push and even force the tribals into adopting armed struggle to reach their goals. What are these government's measures? They are: Use of force to counter the mass struggle and peaceful forms of protest; banning of several mass organisations for their "alleged" links with Maoists. Such harsh measures are denying tribals the democratic avenues of protest and leaving the space open for violent waging of conflict. Further arguments in the same vein are mentioned below:

- "We want the villagers to be aware of their rights and protest peacefully if their rights are violated, not become extreme or adopt violence. But the Government treats anyone who protests peacefully like an insurgent and this only pushes people towards extremism"
- In Orissa, Shanti Committees have been set-up by landlords and mining companies and they are "unleashing" violence on tribals asserting their rights over land.[18]
- Local police support such vigilantism. This has prompted tribal youth to counter violence with violence. In these circumstances, it

is not surprising that tribals are drawn to Maoist ideology and praxis and are turning to the gun to usher in a just order.

Comments on the Contents of the above Paragraph

Earlier also, this Author has given his comments on certain tendentious averments and contents by an academic/analyst. This is the reason that at times certain texts from some other book/writer are produced/included in this book in almost the original words. The comments follow:

1. The term "alleged" links is rather suggestive. It is more often than not that the so-called alleged links is reality. We have the over-ground Maoist who go all out to help their underground brethren.
2. The government and its security agencies are often compelled to use force against violent protestors and even insurrectionists and that is exploited by the Limo Liberals (to borrow a phrase from a columnist in a daily) as the government compelling the tribal youth "to counter violence with violence". That is not all. These 'liberals' and Maoist sympathizers assert that "in these circumstances…tribal's are drawn to Maoist ideology… and are turning to the gun to usher in a just order." It is for note that these very facetious reasoning are offered by the Maoist literature!
3. The way the arguments above are marshalled conveys a simple impression that the governing apparatus in India (ministers, administrators, police men *et.al.,*) are hell bent to use force in season or out against the "innocent" agitators! Surely, aim of all this is to produce Maoists who will unleash violence on the civilians and oust that very mindlessly incompetent polity! Some method in the madness here!
4. Shanti committees are set up to "unleash" violence on tribals. And to wit, local police "support this vigilantism". Nothing could be more self-serving than such inane, one-sided and unrestrained bilge. Anyone can see that all this is produced under an "agenda" already set by the author him/her self or by someone else for him/her! Such lack of balance and objectivity bring no credit to any analyst/academic/author.

The harsh criticism in the preceding para is honestly made, sincerely felt and is meant to be taken seriously by the readers because there are too many arm-chair critics wanting to prove their 'liberal' credentials. A mention has already been made of Limo Liberals. What can, at the best, be said about the views of the academic quoted above in extenso is that there is a semblance of truth somewhere in that text, but it has been distorted and perverted to an absurdity. One side of the starkly unbalanced, dark-hued picture has been drawn by the academic in question. To restore the balance to the Author's harsh review of the academic's text, the following para is deemed important.

The governance deficiency quotient is one of the major factors that produces conditions for birth of Maoism and its subsequent spread. The failure of the government, the powers, that–be, at various levels to deliver is indeed responsible for adding to the woes of the poor and deprive. That grievance makes this section of the poor Dalits vulnerable to the propaganda armoury of the Maoits. Human weaknesses and the greed of the flesh are important reasons for the governance failures. Then there are systemic failures. It affects all sections of the society, but the poor and the deprived suffer the most. The destitution makes the existence itself unbearable. But the concerted efforts of various governments have moved the things in the right direction. The journey may be long, but it has definitely started. Along with the eliminating of the Maoist leadership and cadres, a tremendous developmental activities are in place in the relevant areas/states! The battle is certainly winnable.

The Maoist Ways

The guerrilla warfare concept is fairly old and has its attractions for the Che Guevaras and their acolytes. In India, its most celebrated icon is Charu Mazumdar of Naxalite insurrection. Its current *avatar* is Maoism.

The ultimate objective of the Maoists, declared publicly, is the capture of political power through protracted People's War, an armed insurrection by another name. They have no faith in parliamentary politics as practiced in India, since they are convinced it is a sham and is incapable of addressing people's problems and grievances. Further they resort to the usual rhetoric of the Communists, employing the usual clichés and facile jargon: overthrow the current bourgeois order and establish a genuine people's democracy; only systemic change can end poverty and exploitation of the poor and dispossessed; peaceful movement through mass protests can usher in regime change, it cannot bring systemic change; and systemic change being their goal, they believe this necessitates armed struggle.[19]

Besides the armed struggle, the Maoists also engage in political work among the tribals: indoctrinating them into Maoist ideology and strategy (Chinese term it as political re-education) as also development work in the villages. They are known to run *Janta Sarkar* or "parallel government" in the area under their control: They take up development activities like digging wells and canals; local functionaries are put under pressure to perform better and people/tribals are coerced into clearing certain passages to facilitate their speedy exit in the face of security forces reaching the area during their anti–Naxal operations. But they do not build any roads or even dirt tracks leading to the area under their control. This enables them to guard against anti-Naxal security men making it fast into their camps. Not only that, they do not let the government agencies build roads into their areas for the same reasons! They not only forbid the locals from working on such roads, they even kidnap contractors and their men labouring hard on such a work. Any such work is carried out with the CRPF/local police contingent providing security to the construction workers. It is ironic that the same Maoists loudly condemn the ruling classes for not developing the under—developed tribal areas and their intellectual kins and overground sympathisers make even louder noise castigating the rulers for this sin.

Again, in such areas, the Maoists hold *Jan Adalats* (people's courts) that dispense quick and often ruthless justice, which occasionally results in public beheadings. The alleged "informers" often fall victims to this fatal justice.

The Maoist justice is mostly based on misinformation or even contrived facts. The Maoists initially identify the local grievances–genuine or perceived–and then work on the locals to convince them that the government is responsible for the policies that result in their grievances and problems. The next step is easy: People must work with the Maoist to end their exploitation, and consequenct deprivation. Once they get the local support, they focus on undermining the structures of civil governance in the area. Through a sustained campaign of vilification and threat to their personal safety, civilian officials and other government employees start deserting their posts. There have been press reports even police men avoiding postings in certain Naxal-infected areas of Jharkhand and Chhattisgarh. To make the matters worse, and if a retired celebrated police chief is to be believed, some police personnel buy out their postings to such areas, obviously bribing their seniors.

Maoists claim that they have taken up arms to overthrow the government/state, and to replace it with an egalitarian system. Their professed aim is to ensure for the poorest and the marginalisad sections a distributive justice. It should then come as no surprise that such a call to arms strike a chord with tribals and other such dispossessed communities.

It needs to be emphasised that the choice of the armed route to protest exploitation is not of recent origin. There were many examples of communities revolting against oppressive and unjust laws and some of the struggles and movements have been enumerated in this chapter earlier.

Colonial expansions into tribal lands triggered armed uprisings against the British from the 18th century onwards. The Nagas rose against the British for the same reasons. The colonial rulers deployed extreme force to quell such uprisings, using the kondh practice of Mariah sacrifice as moral justification for their ruthless methods to put down the incensed tribals.[20]

While the first decade after India's independence was relatively quiet in the Adivasi areas, things changed from 1960s onwards. There was a powerful uprising in the Bastar region of Chhattisgarh (then under the Madhya Pradesh State) in 1966. The subsequent Naxalbari uprising gave a strong impetus to armed struggle in tribal areas of in Andhra Pradesh and Bihar (covered, in part, in the earlier pages of this chapter).

Notes

1. Sharanya Nayak and Malini Subramaniam, "The tribal way of life: Security over Justice", in Raghavan, VR, "The Naxal threat: Causes, state responses and consequences" 2011, New Delhi, Vij Books.
2. O. Springate-Baginski *at.al.*, "redressing 'historical injustice' through the Indian Forest Rights Act, 2006: A Historical Institutional analysis of Contemporary Forest Rights Reforms", IPPG discussion paper no. 27, August 2009.
3. Avijit Ghosh, *Times of India*, 20th May 2007.
4. These figures are from E. N. Ram Mohan, "Rise of Naxalism, its implications for National Security and the way forward", in V. R. Raghavan, Ed, 2011, *ibid.*
5. *Ibid.*
6. Mary Tyler, My years in an Indian Prison, (London: Gollancz, 1977), p. 91
7. Prakash Singh, The Naxalite Movement in India (New Delhi: Rupa, 2006), p. 72.
8. *Ibid.,* p. 130.
9. Causes of spurt in Naxalite violence, Indian express, 1st September 1987.
10. Chidananda Rajghatta, "Madiga Malliah inherits the earth", *The Times of India*, 9th December 1990.
11. The illustrated weekly of India, 3rd September, 1989.
12. Commissioner for Scheduled castes and Scheduled Tribals, 29th report, 1987-89, Government of India, p. 171.
13. Arvind N. Das, The Republic of Bihar. (New Delhi, Penguin, 1992), p. 14.
14. *Ibid.,* p. 107.
15. E.N. Rammohan, Note 4, p. 109.
16. Latha Jishnu, "Clampdown on Vedanta", *Down to Earth,* 15-09-10.
17. Guha, Ramachandra, Adivasis, Naxalites and Indian Democracy", 330.
18. Sudha Ramachandran, "India Drives tribals into Maoist arms", *Asia Times online,* 16-01.10.
19. Comrade Ganapathi, "Interview with Comrade Ganapathy", *Revolution in South Asia: An internationalist Information Project.*
20. Jaganath Pathy, "Colonial Ethnography of the Kandha: 'White Man's Burdern or Political Expediency? *Economic and Political Weekly* (28-01-1995): 200-8.

5

Spread of Maoism its Roots and Causes

Inequality is built in the world order, between the nation-states, among the communities and social groupings within a nation. So, it is no surprise that there are developed countries and under-developed (now called, 'developing', may be to soothen some nerves) countries. The gap between these two groups are sought to be lessened/removed through international arrangements under the auspices of the UNO, IMF, UNESCO *et al.*

It is the social, economic and even political disparity among different sections within a country that gives rise to conflict. Then rise some committed individuals and groups/entities that take up the cudglest on behalf of the poor, the deprived and the dispossessed. In India, various such groups/ movements have been covered in the previous pages. The most successful of them is Maoist movement, subject of this book.

There are always roots and causes for any conflict. Several authors and movie-makers have given their thinking on the issue through articles, books and films. These are discussed/detailed in the chapter.

Roots and Causes of the Conflict

The Maoist conflicts has persisted for several decades, going through various escalation and de-escalation phases. Every re-escalation happens with a greater intensity. It is widely admitted that this left-wing uprising is not a law and order problem only. It has its roots in socio-economic and political grievances arising out of unmet demands and frustrated inspirations of people, especially the poor and deprived sections-represented by the tribals.

Home Ministry reveals the basic truth—the cause

After Naxalbari uprising, Ministry of Home Affairs of India compiled a report, "The Causes and Nature of Current Agrarian Tensions". It acknowledged: "The basic cause of unrest, namely, the defective implementation of laws enacted to protect this interests of the tribals, remains; unless this is attended to, it would not be possible to win the confidence of the tribals whose leadership has been taken over by the extremists".

The officials can identify the causes of a problem, but they cannot provide the solutions because vested interests come in the way. It is only the political leaders who can act effectively against the obstructionist ways of the vested interest and find solutions to the intractable problem. To wit, it was the influence of powerful landloards that hold up the implementation of the land reforms for decades after the law was enacted. It was the Communist regimes in Kerala and West Bengal that enforced the land reform. Of course, it was done in West Bengal after Naxalbari uprising. No wonder Naxalites failed to make an impact in Kerala and West Bengal, even though the Red Corridor has extended from Karnataka to Bihar.

If the country's Maoists are expanding their movement every year, it is obvious that the cause flagged by the Home Ministry officials in the early 1970s remains unaddressed. An analyst points out thus: If several decades after that report was compiled the officials are repeating the same issues at meetings, i.e. that the conflict is not a law and order problem but a socio-economic issue, "it is because the Indian a socio-economic issue, "it is because the Indian State has progressed little, and learnt still less from past experiences".[1]

Human Needs Theory

Human needs theorists have pointed to the central role the unmet human needs play in triggering conflict. This theory adumberates that conflict is generated when people feel that their basic needs for security, identity, self-determination and so on are being denied or are under threat. When social, political and economic structures, institutions and policies prevent people from meeting these needs, they are being subjected to structural violence, writes peace psychologist Daniel Christie.[2]

Structural violence provokes resistance, "violent resistance if necessary", points out human needs theorist John Burton.[3] Drawing attention to the link between unmet human needs, structural violence and violent conflict, he observes that "individuals are prepared to go to extreme length to defy system in order to pursue their deeply felt needs, even death by suicide bombing or hunger strikes".[4]

Thus, structured violence has deprived the tribals of their material and non-material resources necessary for humans to reach their potentials. India's adoption of neo-liberal policies, especially since the 1991 economic reforms has accelerated the economic growth but it has worsened the condition of rural poor. Particularly devastating has been the impact of neo-liberal policies on tribals living in mineral-rich areas of Chhattisgarh, Odisha and Jharkhand. The tribals have been expropropriated from there in large numbers. Besides suffering economic deprivation, they also have suffered displacement.

Displacement

India has large populace of internally displaced people (IDP). The tribals account for disproportionately large number among them. While they constitute only 8.08 per cent of Indian population, they account for 40 per cent of the 60 million persons displaced or affected by the development projects between 1947 and 2000[5]. Here, is one more statistic on the plight of the tribals. "A tribal is five times as likely as a non-tribal to be forced to sacrifice his home and hearth by the claims and demands of development and/or conservation".[6]

Different ways of Exploitation

Across the tribal area, exploitation and poverty may be common themes, but there are different manners of exploitation in various states. In Odisha, public and private industrial and development projects have caused wide-spread displacement of the tribals. In consequence, they have been pushed into poverty. (The point will be illustrated in greater detail in chapter on "Naxalism in Odisha".) on the other hand, in Andhra Pradesh the feudal exploitation of the landless has impoverished the tribals. In Gadchiroli, Maharashtra, the issue has a different dimension. Some tribals own land, but others engaging in picking *tendu* leaves, cutting bamboo or collecting minor forest produce, are paid low wages by the contractors, and/or are harassed by the forest officials. In short, poor are suffering or are being harassed at the hands of different authorities or powers that be!

Poverty is acute in Dantewada, epicentre of conflict in Dandakaranya.

Poverty and Harassment Produce Maoists

Tribals are victims of atrocities and rarely get justice. The police are generally reluctant to register their complaints. Data compiled by the National Dalit Movement for Justice is instructive. From 2002 to 2008, some 20,000 cases of atrocities against Dalits reached the Court, out of which only 30 per cent were registered under the stringent provisions of Atrocities Act, the rest being pursued under the milder privisions of the

Indian Penal Code or protection of Civil Rights Act. Around 81 Per cent of the cases filed by tribals are still pending.[7]

Police harassment creates Maoists, as it forces sympathizers to go underground. Further, frustration with poor governance and failure of the police and judiciary to deliver justice has deepened tribal alienation from the Indian State. It has encouraged tribal protest, "largely democratic and peaceful but increasingly violent".

This land is their land

Gaurav Gupta, in the Indian Express of 28th July 2006, discusses the importance of forests and land for the tribal societies living there in. He is a former Deputy Director, Cape York Institute, an aboriginal-led organisation which advises the Australian Government on aboriginal policy.

He is unhappy that a tribal bill is sought to be enacted in India, when he has seen a similar bill failing to achieved desired results in Australia. The aborigines then held 15 per cent of the Australian landmass but practically earned next to nothing from this. *The reason*: Granting of the land did not come with the transfer of knowledge and skills necessary to sustainably use these assets. What the Australians failed to realise was that acquisition of "land" was neither a mean nor an end in itself for today's indigenous people. The Indian bill too has the same flaw.

The Australian experience stands as a dire warning not only to the Conservationists who are up in arms against this bill but also to the Indian adivasis themselves. Mere transfer of land neither leads to reattainment of lost culture nor economic gains. The real problem has been lack of education, training and support for the tribals. So priority is education and jobs. Mere grant of land plays no role in this.

Australian Government and people have wasted tens of billions of dollars in trying to make up for the disastrous historical treatment to the aboriginal Australian through monetary hand outs and land rights. These policies failed. At a time when Australia has risen to be one of the richest countries in the world, aboriginal development indicators have steadily declined. Male life expectancy in some communities has fallen to 55. Surely, there some lessons here for India.

A non-farming community in Australia found a way to make better use of the land allotted to them. They sold the land to a farmer and got amount of money. They used it to educate their children, and bulk of it invested in the trust funds. The deal with the farmer included the right of access for hunting and fishing so that the current and future generations could maintain any cultural practices they desired.

The lessons are clear: Reversing a past wrong is not always the best way to achieve justice because the world around us has changed. Our first aim should be to understand what the adivasis of India want today. One can be sure that like all humans, their first priority is a secure livelihood and for their children to have even better opportunities than they did. "The tribal bill achieves none of this". Deforestation of the land is no solution, it will only result in the permanent desecration of the land. The solution is to allow unhindered access to the tribals, but without they owning it. Like Australian aborigines, Indian tribals too should look to engaging with the modern economy.

In short, the author suggests the tribals are no longer interested to go back to their ancient ways. They like the rest of Indians, are looking for education, health facilities for their children.

Adivasis branded as Maoists languish in prison

This is an unfortunate fact of life in the Maoists-infected areas, especially of Bastar where some innocent tribals are arrested on suspicions of being Maoists. Some of them spend long years in the prison, without any trial, and a few even die there.

It is such situations that are readily and skilfully exploited by the Maosits. Some members of their families are ready to join the Maoist ranks to avenge the injustice their families had to suffer.

Three such cases of innocent tribals are detailed in the Hindustan Times (HT), of 26th April 2015, under the title "The curse of Bastar". It adds pithily that violence in the Red Corridor between security forces and rebels has ensured that the adivasis branded as Maoists languish in prison for years. The article is penned by Dainsh Raza.

How and why it happens? Sad, but true, pattern

On the night of 25th November 2014, adivasis of Dantewada's Jangampal village (some 400 km south of Chhattisgarh's capital Raipur) noticed a battalion of security forces appearing on the hillock overlooking their village. By dawn their worst fears had come true, with 150 armed security personnel descending on their village; and during the next 30 minutes, hauled up the men and beat up the women and children. At the end of their operation, they had picked up 26 men from Jangampal and neighbouring villages of Chhota Tongpal and Chuleras. They were told they would be released after being questioned. Fellow villagers feared they would be taken away, branded Maoists and killed.

Madka Ram Sodi, former village head of Jangampal narrates what happened at the Kukamar politce station, where he and 25 others were taken. "They made me sign a document stating that I was a witness to the seizure and had seen the men participating in Maoist activities", he says. Out of 26 men, 11 were released after questioning. Charges were framed against 15, who got acquitted only in April 2015, after spending five months in jail.

Jangampal incident is not an exception. It is typical example of how every time the Maoists stage ambushes and raids on security forces in Bastar division of Chhattisgarh, adivasis are picked up and framed as Maoists or sympathisers who aid them in anti-national activities. While some of the villagers are released, several waste away in prisons for years unaware even of charges against them.

Prisons in Bastar are most overcrowded in the country with occupancy rates exceeding 400 per cent in jails in the Kanker and Dantewada districts in 2012. The high acquittal rate (96 per cent between 2005 and 2012 in Dantewada's District and Session Court) suggest that most of the accused are set free. But acquittal comes only after the accused have been subjected to long trials. It is, obviously, a case of justice delayed is justice denied.

Documents relating to four cases (three others are detailed below) were secured by the daily. They show flimsy charges, forced confessions. The villagers held in jails face other problems, says Shalini Gera who provides voluntary legal aid to adivasis in Bastar. Sometimes, the policemen who are to give evidence in the court are transferred out. Then, when the judgement is ready to the pronounced for acquittal, the accused is not produced in the Court since the jail was unable to bring him there due to shortage of security guards.

This situation raises question of efficacy of state's policy of weaning adivasis away from the Maoists. "Arresting innocent people will work against the state. The case against anyone who is arrested under such charges should be strongly built, for which investigations should be robust", says P. V. Ramana, Research Fellow, Institute for Defence Studies and Analysis.

As the Hindustan Times team left Sukma, seven security men were killed there in an encounter with the Maoists. In the next three days, nine more security men were killed in two attacks in Dantewada. Expectedly, the police is bound to intensify search operations after every Maoist killings, and more random arrests of tribals from the relevant villages will be made. "Sadly war continues". Undoubtedly, more innocents will land in jail, some even would die there, as the following there cases indicate.

"Accused No. 53"

Kawasi Hidme

Charge: Attack on a police patrol

party in Bastar, Killing 23 Policemen

Status: Acquitted

The Ramaram fair in January 2008 in etched in Hidme's memory. "With a detatchment that only increases the listener's sense of unease, the adivasi girl from Borguda village in Sukma District recalls how CRPF men picked her at the fair. "I was applying *mehndi* on the palm of my younger sister when they surrounded me", she says in her Gondi language. She was 17 then. It would be seven years before she was seen in public again. Named in the attack on a police patrol party in Bastar's Errabore village in July 2007 in which 23 policemen were killed, she was kept under detention for 15 days across the three police stations. She narrates her plight during detention: "I was brutally assaulted…They would tie me to a chair and break logs of wood on my body. I was blindfolded every time male policemen beat me…They said they would stop beating me if I accepted that I used to work for *andar-waley* (Maoists)".

The detention was followed by 15 days of treatment in a hospital in Sukma. Thereafter she was presented before a court and remanded to judicial custody. During her incarceration, she suffered cholecystitis (swelling of the gall bladder) and a prolapsed uterus which is consistent with her allegations of police torture. She is reluctant to talk any more on her torture.

Hidme was arrested on the basis of a statement given by two Special Police Officers (SPOs), three months after the Errabore incident.

It was a long list of accused, her name was 53rd. The only other testimony against her is by two sisters-in-law, who claimed she was friends with Maoists.

30 months after appearance of the witnesses, a fast track Court in Dante made set Hidme free for want of evidenece.

"The Absconder who was not"

Barse Manjhi

Crime: Attack on Congress leader

Avdhesh Gautam's House in July 2010

Stauts: Facing Trial

Soni, the bare-foot, frail woman with hollow cheeks was perturbed when Hindustan Times team reached her home in Maharakadka, a remote village in Dantewada District. Shouting loudly, she wanted the journalists to leave her house, thinking they were from police on CRPF. She calmed down only when fellow villagers came over.

Barse Manjhi, her husband of two years, is facing trial for the 8th July 2010 attack on the house of Avdhesh Singh Gautam, senior Congress leader in Dantewada. He named 67 people, including Manjhi, as attackers.

There was a catch here: Manjhi and two other tribal men mentioned in the list of 67 were already in jail on the day of the attack. Court was told the FIR was unreliable for this reason. That did not help. Manjhi was declared absconder by the court even when he was still in jail. Moreover, Gautam admitted he had not seen these 67 persons and the police had given him those names.

In 2012, Manjhi was acquitted in all the other cases for which he was facing trial. But his freedom would not last long. In November 2014, a joint team of CRPF and police claimed major breakthrough in the Gautam with the arrest of "three Moist cadres" from the forests of the Kuakonda police station range. Manjhi was one of there three arrested. Once again, he found himself behind the bears. Now, he can expect to be released only if Gautam specially tells the court that he was not involved in the attack on his house.

This the quality of justice our tribal brethren get from our judiciary !

"Curious case of the Secret Informers"

Bhima Kadti

Charge : 12 cases including explosion of passenger buses and burning trucks.

Status : Died as an undertrial

By the time he reached Raipur's Dr Bhim Rao Ambedkar Memorial Hospital in August 2012, Bhima Kadti, an alleged Maoist from Dantewada's Phulpad village, had been severely ill for 15 days. His bowels were inflamed, he had high fever and was diagnosed with a fatal form of malaria. After surgery, he suffered a cardio-respiratory arrest. Two days later, he was dead.

"I could count his ribs. He had turned into a skeleton", says his father, 48 years old Sannakadti, as he describes receiving the corpse of his only son.

Bhima was 19 when he was arrested in October 2010. The 12 Moist-related cases slapped on him included destruction of the Kuakonda Tehsil

Office, causing explosion of a passenger bus in Gaadiraas and burning trucks in the Nerla valley in Bacheli. But a close look at the case files reveals holes in the police theory. For example, take the two cases of rail derailment in which Bhima was a co-accused: In both the cases, the same two witnesses (villagers) gave their statements, eight months after the first incident and three months after second one!

They claim to have learnt from the two villagers that the people from the "Kaukonda Region"-a Tehsil in Dantewada with several dozen villages in its jurisdiction were involved in the incidents. How did such vague information lead the police to zero in on Bhima ? Here, is what the police stated in the chargesheet: "Based on the information provided by our trusted secret source and the interrogation of the arrested accused we came to know who were involved in the unlawful assembly".

It is this line alone that incriminates Bhima. There is no mention in the chargesheet or confession or witness statement about who the sources were or what kind of information they gave. "Secret information" tipped off the police in two more cases in which Bhima was named.

In March, 2015, the NHRC awarded ₹ 2 lacs in compensation to Bhima's family on the grounds that there was an unexplained five-day delay in his medical treatment.

In the 22 months that Bhima survived in the Dantewada prison, he was acquitted in five cases. His acquittal in other six cases came after his death.

"So what if he was proved innocent? He is dead," says Sanna Kadti, wrapping his son's death certificate in a plastic bag.

"Violence and the State"

"Armed struggle is not the only way to respond to State violence. There are other ways of democratic dissent," says Harsh Mander in his article in the Hindu of 28th August, 2011. Reasons for putting this article under the scanner will be explained at the end, under 'Comments from the Author'. First two paragraphs of this are interesting as they sum up two alternative viewpoints of State violence verses the violence perpetrated by the Left-Wing Extremist. The two para's are excerpted below:

> "Those who defend violent resistance believe that it is justified because of the unremitting scale and hopelessness of the oppression to which impoverished masses are subject. They argue that opponents of the Maoists violence ignore the 'Structural Violence' of the State and, by implication, equate it with the emancipatory violence of the oppressed. The CPI (ML) People's War wrote to the Sankaran Committee, which

> attempted to end and mediate Maoist Violence and State repression in Andhra Pradesh, that 'extremism (democratic struggle of the people) is inevitable in a situation of inadequately addressed social and economic problems' and felt that the Committee made 'wrong assessments' only by 'isolating the cruelty and violence from people's struggle and wrongly equating police violence with Naxalite violence.'
>
> "But in fact, on the contrary, in their report and communications, the Committee headed by a humanist S. R. Sankaran did repeatedly acknowledge the structural violence built into the societal system, such as inequality, exploitation and lack of freedom or democratic space. Like the Naxalites, it also identified the root causes to include land, human dignity, wages and employment and repression of dissent. It called upon the government to distribute to poor dalit and tribal families thousands of acres of cultivable land lying fallow in the districts. However, while acknowledging the structural violence of the State, the Committee refused to accept that this justifies politically or morally retributive or retaliatory violence by the people or by radical organisations which fight in their name. It was convinced that these injustices can be overcome best through democratic, non-violent, mass actions".

Harsh Mander has acted as a spokesman for Marxist and advocated their case so convincingly in this article that the top Marxist leader Ganapati himself could not have done that. He would lose certain credibility as all his arguments will be dubbed as self-serving! Mander is a fit candidate to be included in the list of 'Closet Maoists.' So let him be read in his own words. So excerpts follow:

> "I too have no doubt that ethically the most condemnable violence is by the State when it acts unjustly and lawlessly, because the modern democratic State assumes monoply of the legitimate exercise of violence with the pledge that is will protect all citizens with fairness and justice. As the 'licensed' dispenser of violence, its duty is to be just, and indeed non-violent, is the highest. Especially when confronted with both violent and non-violent dissent, the State's practice is often abysmal.
>
> "The Committee condemned the killing of alleged Naxalites by the police in encounters, which it described as 'targeted extra legal executions'. 'These indiscriminate killings termed as encounters introduce terror as a component of governance and erode its very democratic essence.

"CPI (ML) General Secretary Ganapati claims that five times as many people have died of hunger and disease in the past decade as those who died in revolutionary wars world wide in the last two centuries. Arundhati Roy often cites hunger and humiliation in her defence of Maoists: 'Right now, in Central India, the Maoist guerrilla army is made up entirely of desperately poor tribal living in conditions of such chronic hunger that it verges on famine of the kind we only associate sub-Saharan Africa. They are people who even after 60 years of India's so-called independence have not had access to education, healthcare and legal redress.

These are people.......Exploited for decades........Cheated by money-lenders......"There is no doubt that tribal people in India are among its most oppressed and dispossessed. But I find erroneous and indeed perilous the claim that recourse to arms is the inevitable result of such exploitation or even moral justification for violence. Less than 25 per cent of India's tribal regions are affected by Moist violence even today and even in those districts, there is no evidence of mass support of all or most tribal people for the 'dadas' or 'dadis' in military fatigues who fight in their name.

"This does not mean that those who are not fighting with weapons or conspiratorial guerrilla warfare are passively submitting to their subjugation. On the contrary, large tracts of these regions are rife with diverse and creative forms of democratic dissent. The binary opposition between violent resistance on the one hand and surrender and complicity on the other, posited by Maoist ideologues like Ganapathi, is spurious and dangerous. 'Either you were with slaves', he declares in which case Spartacus and the rebels represented a just cause, and spoke the truth, or you were with the slave-owners'. Curiously, a Bushism.

"Violent killing of civilians by Maoists occasionally is followed by explanations that such deaths are inevitable as a kind of 'Collateral damage' and expression of regret. Even such rare regret is missing when those killed by Maoists are men in uniform. Most commentators sympathetic to Maoists struggles regard these men to be agents of an oppressive State; therefore, their deaths (even by mines or guerrilla attacks rather than conventional face-to-face battle) are deemed to be fully legitimate.

"Those who justify killing of security personnel ignore the fact that most of these are just poor, working class men, often of peasant stock, who join the police or security forces as one of the few sources of livelihood available to them. The local police and Special Police Officers (SPOs) are often young tribal men from the same communities as the Maoists. One brother could be a policeman and his sister could have joined a war against the State. Brijesh Pande of *Tehelka* spent a week with the CRPF soldiers in the epicentre of Maoist territory in Dantewada and brought to us their rarely-heard voices: 'It is not death per se we are afraid of, but ignominy after death, which hurts us. A Naxal's death is covered properly and people want no Naxal to be killed. But what about us? We are the expendables, like 25 or 50 paise coins. We count for nothing? Another describes themselves as 'unwanted children of India'. A third says, 'I know I earn my livelihood from the force and I should not talk like this, but tell me, what should I tell my wife who has become paranoid after the Dante made massacre? Everytime she knows I am going for a patrol or an area-domination exercise, she goes hysterical?

"After killing of 76 CRPF men on 5th April 2010 in one of the worst Maoist attacks in Dantewada District, a loose coalition called 'Citizens Institute for Peace', tried to mobilize signatures from rights activists and writers who usually denounce State violence, to condemn this particular attack. One writer who refused to sign explained in an open email that, 'Frankly speaking' I don't feel any anguish. Let us be honest. What happened at CRPF camp on 6th April was a part of a civil war—a battle between two opposing forces. In such a battle, combatants get killed. While as human rights activists, I surely condemn the Maoists for killing non-combatants—ordinary villagers, panchayat heads, school teachers or blowing up trains killing common people—I cannot condemn them for targeting the CRPF which is the most notorious arm of the Indian State.

"I felt constrained to respond to him: 'I do mourn the loss of the CRPF *jawans.* I mourn the loss of innocent unarmed citizen lives which have been killed in the conflict. I mourn the loss of life of those who have picked up guns. Human life is precious and I cannot endorse a hierarchy of more or less legitimate killings".

Comments on the above article

A correction is called for at very outset here. Knowing him from his past writings, I thought Mander is going to be rabidly anti-security forces, particularly after he extensively quoted the so called humanist S. R. Sankaran–headed Committee Report. He had quoted this Report only to make his point that 'armed struggle is not the only way to respond to the State violence. So, Sankaran is the villain of piece here. But first let us critique some remarks by Mander himself. Mander says, 'ethically condemnable violence is by the State when it acts unjustly and lawlessly…' Pray, who will decide if the State's acts are lawless? The murderous Maoists or the Government elected in a democratic may?

Yet again, Mander seems to be approving of the Committee Report condemning all encounters killing of the alleged Maoists as 'targeted extralegal executions'. This is egregious murder of the truth. Moreover, the Committee uses the term 'alleged' for Maoists. It is an ironic situation where every Maoist killed is innocent. One hopes Mander is not in agreement with the committee and neither approving of its diabolical observations.

The Committee's sheltering behind the 'structural violence built into the societal system, such as inequality, exploitation and lack of freedom or democratic space' is laughable. Such structural flaws must be removed and that is why the Indians elect governments to do this job. Again, it is ridiculous that the Maoists are talking about democratic space when they use violent means to destroy democracy. If they are sincere, they should seek this space through fighting Indian elections and shunning their blood-thirsty ways. They are attacking the government for the deprivation suffered by the poor tribals, but if the latter plan and execute some development projects, the very Maoists would use violent means to thwart all such development—killing contractors, kidnapping workers (mostly the poor dalits and tribals), destroying villages, hospitals and schools *et al.* This excessive semantic cleverness does not convince anyone.

Mander makes a valid point: "I find erroneous and indeed perilous the claim that recourse to arms in inevitable results of such exploitation or even moral justification for violence. To put the things in perspective: It is Maoists crude and excessive violence that compels the government to use force to restore the order.

Maoists must follow their parent outfit, CPI (ML), who has taken to electoral politics, but one is reasonably certain that they would not! After all, they are lusting for State power and that too through murder and mayhem. After all, peace is neither their target or desideratum. It will create an existential problem. It would put them out of job. Violence is raison d'etre for the Maoism!

Now, on to Arundhati Roy's fulminations. It is not worth wasting too much time on her. As far as this Author is concerned, she is not Indian. Long back, she declared so. She is making a living out of the miseries of tribals. She uses her Booker to churn out and occasional anti-India tracts (=a propagandizing pamphlet) on many things including a justification for Maoist violence. I go alongwith a former Home Secretary of India, who said 'Arundhati is a fraud'. Recently, the Outlook carried a ususal 'tract' from her about a Maoist Professor held in jail. This Author wrote a letter on the issue to the Editor of the weekly, which was duly published in its issue of June 2015, and is reproduced here. The heading assigned to the letter by the Editor was: "Biting the Bullet of Words".

> "Congratulations to the editor for following in the footsteps of his illustrious pre-decessor Vinod Mehta by publishing Arundhati Roy's usual, cliche-ridden, pueril shenanigans titled *Professor P.O.W* (May 18) in your issue of the 18th instant. Years back, when she had criticised India's nuclear tests in your Weekly, I had advised her to leave such weighty and geo-strategic issues to the likes of K. Subrahmanyam and Jasjit Singh and concentrate on her writing as that may bring her a second Booker or even a literature Nobel to India.
>
> I repeat my earlier advice to her as there are enough pseudo-liberals, whom I would dub not just as Maoist sympathisers but overground Maoists and they are doing a better job of defending their kinsmen on daily basis. I do not expect her to understand, leave alone follow advice from someone who faced bullets from the Naga rebels in the '50s, Mizo rebels in the '80s and insurgents in the Kashmir Valley in 1980-85. I consider myself a nationalist for this reason, a concept she is not familiar with, given that, shunning her Indianness, she had announced herself as a 'mobile republic'. *Outllook* could have surely devoted these five pages to a nobler, much more worthwhile cause.
>
> **Col Ved Prakash,**
> Noida

Indian intellectuals are paper tigers. We have not produced a single one like Albert Camus, who fought alongside the rebels for his ideological convictions. Will a female (Roy) set an example for her male counterparts?

"More to Naxal problem than meets the eye"

This news item appeared in the *Hindu* of 14th October 2011. It is based on the Sardar Patel Memorial Lecture in New Delhi delivered by Jairam Ramesh, on "Tirupati to Pashupati: Some reflections on the Maoist issue".

Admitting that the growth of Naxalism was as much because of the failure of the Central Government as for a variety of other reason. Union Rural Development Minister underlined the need for a renewed sense of urgency to address problems afflicting the masses through a stratagem hinged on the synergy of security forces and implementing agencies.

He called for a speedy completion of public welfare project, primary rural roads within three to four years with a get-it-done attitude. Other points made by him:

- Expedite road construction by good security to the contractors, as Maoists target them to block or hamper it.
- In 25 Naxal-intense districts, the expenditure was lower than the national average and in 10 of these less than in the 60 LWE-affected district of the country.
- As the Naxals were exploiting the tribals and their region tactically for guerrilla warfare and through terror obstructed development activities, he favoured a two-track approach: deal with the Naxal leadership and addressing the concerns of the people.
- He justified Home Minister P. Chindambram's reiteration that the Centre was ready for unconditional talks with the Maoists. At the same time, he conceded that tribals were victims of State apathy and provisions like reservations had little impact on their welfare.

Some other information culled from this lecture are mentioned hereafter. The media imagery of a "liberated" Red Corridor extending from Andhra Pradesh, cutting across the heart of India, all the way to Nepal, is the most vivid representation of the threat that Maoists pose to our country, with the Prime Minister describing it as the most serious threat to India's internal security and Home Minister rating it as a "problem graver than the terrorism".

Various Committees have studied the problem from time to time. Early 1980s, Prime Minister sent a team headed by Member Secretary, Planning Commission to conduct field studies in the Naxal-affected areas of Bihar and Andhra Pradesh and recommend solutions. The Report's author is, incidentally, the present Prime Minister. Among the many recommendations, the thrust was on urgent and long-festering socio-economic concerns of weaker sections of society, if Naxal influence was to be encountered.

Three years ago (in 2008), the Planning Commission published a report by its 17-member expert group, including Debu Bandopadhyoy, S. R. Sankaran, K. Balagopal, B.D. Sharma, K. B. Saxena, Ram Dayal Munda, Dileep Singh Bhuria and Sukhdeo Thorat—all the people one would want for such an exercise. It was an extraordinary detailed report. It provided the historical, political, social and economic context to the issues, reviewed governments' efforts to deal with the problem and recommended policy and programme changes to vastly reduce, if not eradicate, the effects of the LWE.

Now, we are mentioning more details from the Ramesh lecture, summary of which has been given above. Ramesh says: “My own engagement with the issue has grown—from an intellectual interest as a student of India’s political dynamics to a more direct involvement since becoming a MP from Andhra Pradesh.....It has become clear to me that Maoists are exploiting tribals, and that tribals themselves want peace, not war”.

Two-track approach has been mentioned above. He is suggesting a complete revamp of administration in tribal areas of central and eastern India. Andhra Pradesh attempted to do it through its Integrated Tribal Development Agency....It is a sad fact that affirmative action through reservation programmes have had only marginal effect on the welfare of the Central and Eastern Indian tribal communities.

In devising our approach, we must recognize the unique characteristics that define the 60 districts across the seven States, identified by the Union Government as affected by the LWE. When you look at these districts—15 in Odisha, 14 in Jharkhand, 10 in Chhattisgarch, 8 in Madhya Pradesh, 7 in Bihar, 2 each in Maharashtra and Andhra Pradesh and one each in West Bengal and Uttar Pradesh—on a map of India, five characteristics stand out, each calling for a policy response. One, an overwhelming majority of these districts have a substantial population of tribal communities. Two, an overwhelming majority of districts have a significant area under good quality forest cover. Three, a large number of these districts are rich in minerals like coal and iron ore. Four, in a number of States, these districts are remote from the seat of power, and have large administrative units. Fifth, a large number of districts are located in tri-junction areas of different States.

Here is an interesting paragraph in his lecture, where he is almost mouthing the language of Maoists and their sympathisers. With this Ramesh-speak, he is a changed man. This aspect will be clarified in a later chapter where ‘politics’ of combating the Maoist threat will be discussed. But here, it is enough to reproduce new Ramesh-speak:

> “In some cases, the administrative response is being taken but the real challenge comes next. How do you transform administration in tribal areas so as to give people a sense of participation and involvement but, more fundamentally, to preserve and protect their dignity. How do you address their continued victimisation, first by the State and now by Naxals? Empowering tribal, who are essentially victims, by giving them access to basics by giving them what is theirs by right and by securing their livelihood, is to my mind, an absolute, undiluted must.

Then he talks about an important step of the Central Government's administrative innovation providing untied funds to troika comprising the Collector/District Magistrate, the Superintendent of Police and the District Forest Officer in these districts. The triumvirate, representing the face of the Indian State, is better-placed to identify critical developmental works that can be completed quickly so that the people begin to see the government in a new light. In 2010-11, ₹ 25 crore was released to each district and in 2011-12 another ₹ 30 crore will be released. The initiative has spurred unprecedented development work. The challenge now will be to give elected representatives and local elected institutions a role in selection and execution of works without sacrificing the flexibility and speed of execution.

The rural roads programme under the Pradhan Mantri Gram Sadak Yojna (PMGSY) is the single-most important rural development intervention that can significantly transform the ground level situation in these districts. The Maoists understand this and so they first target the roads. This explains why the PMGSY is severely lagging behind in the LWE-affected districts. So, a level of security cover is required to be provided by forces like the CRPF. The government must ensure speedy settlement of land-related disputes. In some cases, the ability of Naxal cadres to resolve land disputes in favour of the tribals and mete out what appears "instant justice" has given them a foothold and acceptance among the people at large.

The might of the Indian State in Naxal-affected areas—71 battalions of Central paramilitary forces, nearly 71,000 personnel—have been deployed. They have a vital role in backing the State police and developmental activities. "But paramilitary and police action cannot/should not be the driving force; that has necessarily to be development and addressing the daily concerns of people, who has every reason to feel alienated". Massive reforms of the police and the forest administration at the cutting edge is the need of the hour. A more humane land acquisition policy with focus on effective Rehabilitation and Resettlement (R and R) is urgently needed. It was sociologist Walter Fernandes who estimated that over 30 million people in Central and Eastern India have been displaced over the past five decades due to development projects. R and R for large number of people has yet to be completed. Worse, there are large numbers of tribals who have been subjected to repeated displacements. The last two paragraphs of Ramesh's speech are reproduced word for word.

> "It is not the Naxal who have created the ground conditions ripe for the acceptance of their ideology rather it is the failure of the successive governments in both States concerned and at the Centre to protect the dignity and the Constitutional rights of the poor and the disadvantaged

that has created a fertile breeding ground for violence and given the Maoists the space to speak the language of social welfare, which in reality is a cloak to build their guerrilla bases and recruit, most tragically, women and children".

"Where do we go from here? Let us not underestimate the seriousness of the threat. I, for one, do not believe that a 'developmentalist' strategy alone will do. Nor do I believe that a strategy based on the primacy of paramilitary and police action will yield long-term results. The two must go hand-in-hand driving strength from each other (Sorry, the Author needs to intervene. It is a pity that an intelligent politician can't restrain himself from indulging in chiche-mongering and mouthing inanities. Even a child reading about Maoist insurgency knows that it is not a question of either/or, between development and use of force to defect the murderous Maoists. It has to be both. An obtuse politician like Digvijay Singh might tell Home Minister Chidambaram that "force alone cannot solve the Maoist problem", bringing in 'root cause' bunkum, but his aim is to show to the latter and wider Congress his standing in the organisation being a Rahul Gandhi man, in fact believed to be his mentor! Even he knows that when push comes a shove, the force will take pole position. If the Maoists feel they can block the development in the tribal areas forever so that they can get more deprived tribals in their ranks, the force is the only language that will convince them that India is too large and too powerful a nation to go under. Once they get this message clear, then the two can go hand-in-hand. It is a truism today. Ramesh must understand this. He need not add unnecessary verbiage to his talk by saying that force alone or development alone cannot solve the Maoists problem. Now back to narrative of Ramesh's lecture). We are combating not just a destructive ideology but are also confronted with the wages of our own insensitivity and neglect. We need to rise above partisan political considerations and set aside old Centre versus State arguments and work concertedly to resort people's faith in the administration to be fair and just, to be prompt and caring, to be prepared to redress the injustices of the past, and to be both responsible and responsive in future. Only then will the tide of Naxalsim be stemmed.

"Growing Footprints" by Presley Thomas and Aloke Tikku

This news story on Maoism was published in the Hindustan Times of 13th April 2012. It says rampant inequality provides fertile ground for the spread of Maoism in the country. Their influence is no longer confined to the countryside. Urban India is also under threat.

The authors say that from the nine states which were LWE-affected earlier, the Maoist have, of late, setup bases in Assam, Manipur, Gujarat, Tamil Nadu, Kerala, Haryana, Uttar Pradesh, and Uttarakhand, quoting sources in the IB.

But the last two years (2010-11, 2011-12) have not been for the Maoist. Their top leaders—several of them—have been killed by the security forces, including Cherukuri Azad and Kishenji. But the forces cannot shut down in these areas, vacated by Maoist. A CRPF officer in Jharkhand says: "It is a futile war…The Maoists return the moment we shut down a camp".

A Jharkhand police officer adds another angle to story: "The problem is that forces who can enter these areas don't have powers to develop and the authorities who have the power to develop the areas do not step out of their offices". This averment may be only partly true. This police officer may be scoring points against the civilian officers—IAS and those down the lines. But it was a complaint that echoed in the power corridors of Delhi. Worries were rife that Jharkhand and Bihar could be the next hotspots of the Maoist violence due to their inability to deliver on the development promise.

Besides the lack of development, political instability also helps the Maoists. Bihar had started governance reforms on a promising note under Nitish Kumar, but it "appears to be floundering", says a government official in Delhi. It could indeed be partisan statement, or may be there is some truth in it.

Given the loopholes in the system, the Maoists are regaining lost ground—hitting back in Odisha "last month (March 2012) with three abductions that shook the establishment."

The Maoist (LWE) movement is good at staging comebacks. It was nearly down and out in the early years of this century, but revived itself with a Union between its two powerful factions, the MCC and PWG and created CPI (Maoist). Subsequent developments in the field will be found in the next chapter.

"Forest Rights Act forgotten": Anuradha Dutt

"This Act had crowned a hard struggle to protect rights of Adivasis and forest dwellers". Dutt's piece appeared in the *Pioneer* of 11th January 2013. The Cabinet was scheduled to meet on 15th January to expedite clearance of investment worth US $13.5 billion in the oil sector. There is a growing fear that such mega projects has ominous implications for the nation's security and ecology.

Union Tribal Affairs Minister Kishore Chandra Deo fears that Forest Rights Act (FRA) might be modified to accommodate these mega projects. The Act came into force from 1st January 2008. The Minister warns that any dilution of the FRA could adversely affect the UPA Government case in the Supreme Court where Vedanta had challenged Government's decision to cancel the Bauxite mining rights of the MNC in Odisha's Niyamgiri Hills. Mr Deo wrote to Minister of State for Environment and Forests (E and F) Jayanthi Natarajan, demanding that there be no dilution in the Ministry of E and F order of August 2009 that makes forest clearance conform to the FRA.

Now, to important part. The Ministry of E and F cited by Mr Deo disallows development projects that impact forests until rights to the tribals and forest dwellers are settled. Gram Sabhas have to agree to transferring land for such projects. Jairam Ramesh, the then Minister of E and F had cancelled the Vedanta mining permit since it violated this assent (or 'consent,' the term used today, in 2015) proviso.

Besides dilution of FRA, he also objected to any violation of the Panchayat (Extension to Scheduled Areas) [PESA] Act, 1996. The main provision of PESA was that the land in a V Schedule area could not be transferred to the industry as this would be in contravention of PESA. The Schedule V in the Constitution is particularly meant to safeguard the land of the tribal people.

The FRA recognises the tribals' rights over forest produce, fishing, grazing and other community work. It empowers gram sabhas to govern their forests. They are also authorised to stop projects that threaten their natural and cultural heritage.

The FRA and PESA, if implemented and interpreted correctly, will eliminate the exploitation of the tribals. The Naxals will, then, not find easy to draw the tribals into their ranks.

"The War of Winning hearts": Rahul Pandita

This article appeared in *The Hindu* of 14.4.14. It is about Chhattisgarh's first Maoist recruit and "the lessons that Indian State need to drive from his story".

It is the story of a couple—Bandranna and Latakka—who surrendered in 2000. Presently in his late 40s, he was among the first batch of men to be recruited in Chhattishgarh. He is from Dorla tribe and comes from Bijapur District's Pamed village, close to Andhra Pradesh. Presently, the former Maoist commander tends the plants in State's public park in Jagdalpur.

"In 1980, after the formation of the CPI-ML (War Group), its Andhra-based leader Kondapalli Seetharamiah sent Maoist squads to four areas in State's Telengana region: Khammam, Karimnagar, Warangal and Adilabad. Three other squads went across the Godavari River, one of them to Godchiroli in Maharashtra, while two of them went to Chhattishgarh's Bastar region (then a part of Madhya Pradesh). The idea was to create a rear base where safe guerrilla zones could be created".

One of these two reached Badranna's village. Then 13, he calls how the villagers would run away seeing the guerrillas, as the elders had told the youngsters that the latter carried a potion that could make people follow them. After failing to approach the youngsters, the Maoist, changing their track, started meeting the elders, prominents in the villages—Sarpanch or the Patel, a police informer of sorts. Once the Maoists befriended the elders, the youngsters too got over their reluctance and became comfortable with them.

The Maoist (by now, Badranna was amongst them) would buy food from villagers and also request for an old meal. Badranna says: "sometimes, to test us, they would give us stale food, almost on the verge of decay. But we ate it with a smile". By then, the Maoist cultural troupe, Jana Natya Mandali, began extensive tours in the area. The troup adapted local folk forms to revolutionary themes "that galvanised the youth".

Badranna was the first one to join the Maoist fold, along with two other men, Bimanna and Deva. The Maoists were keen to recruit women too but decided to go slow and not approach them directly. First, they chose to fight for better wages. Those days, the Maoist guerrillas had some rudimentary fire arms like the *Bharma* (muzzle-loading gun). But they were enough to scare *tendu* contractors and forest guards who often exploited tribals, threatening to jail them under archaic laws, looting their chicken and goats. The Maoists began confronting them, catching many and beating them. The contractors were forced to pay better wages.

Next, they targeted landlords and distributed their land among the landless peasants. By that time, the Maoists had won the trust of the people. They no longer needed the help of a Sarpanch or a Patel.

Once entrenched, the Maoist found a cause that would resonate among the women. In tribal societies, menstruation was deemed to be some kind of curse. Once their menstrual cycle commenced, they were forced to stay in a separate house on the outskirts of the village. They were required to hide and not show their face to men in case they happened to pass by her house. Another custom was to marry the women to much younger men. This was to ensure an extra hand for work. Once the women grow old, the man, still young would remarry. The Maoists convinced the elders to discontinue these practices. They were seen as reformers. This made them extremely popular among the women, many joining to escape the patriarchal and feudal set-ups.

In 1987, the Maoists burnt down over a dozen houses belonging to upper-caste Thakurs in Chintalnar, who had settled down in this area from the western UP. Badranna says they were believed to have ill-treated some tribals. This led to another surge of recruitment, especially of women. It was thence that Badranna's future wife joined the Maoists.

By the 1990s, the Maoists had intensified their movement in the entire Dandakaranya forest. The entire Bastar region and Godchiroli had become their strongholds. "Today (2014) this area forms the main guerrilla zone of the Maoists, the Dandakaranya Special Zone Committee" (DKSZC).

Then came the first operation by Badranna in 1995. He led a group of 30 Maoists to attack the Thalagudda police station in Bhopalpatnam block. The attack was a failure since Badranna could not properly study the map made by the local Maoist squad. The policemen retaliated and Badranna had to retreat. One policeman and five Maoists died in this attack, including Badranna's old friend, Bimanna, and a woman guerrilla called Kamalakka.

Soon thereafter, Badranna's squad was launching many audacious attacks on the police. In Golapalli, Badranna laid an ambush on a police party, killing 19 of them. In 2000, another ambush executed by Badranna in Basaguda block's Tarem village killed 16 policemen.

It is Basaguda that remained Badranna's operational area from mid-1990s till his surrender in 2000. It was here that the Maoists undertook many developmental works in villages. Under his guidances, people from nine villages worked together to dig a large pond and construct a check dam. "I am extremely popular in Basaguda area", says a smiling Badranna.

In 1999, Badranna says he met a fair-complexioned woman who had come from the city and spoke in English to a few other senior Maoist leaders. Her party name was Jankiakka. "She was extremely brave but suffered from some illness". While travelling once along with her, Badranna's squad came under the police fire. "I provided cover fire, enabling all of them to flee to safety.

Jankiakka was a senior Maoist leader, Anuradha Ghandy, who later died of Malaria in April 2008.

Fourteen years after his surrender, Pandita decides to check Badranna's claims of his popularity. He lands up in Sarkeguda (2014), under Basaguda police station. It was here in May 2012 that the COBRA troops (of CRPF) opened fire on the gathering of villagers, killing 17 of them. "There is CRPF camp right the beginning of the village".

Pandita spoke with many about the events of the night in May. The killings had taken place in a clearing outside the village. An old man stops there, on seeing this journalist. Scratching deep marks on his thigh that are bleeding now, he says "I hate the force. They have beaten so many of us; we are unable to go to the forest anymore". He was referring to the CRPF men. Pointing with his hand, Pandita asked him to stop scratching. He did not; he looked at the former puzzlingly.

"Badranna, do you know him?" The scratching stops. "I know him," he says excitedly. *"Idhar bahot aata tha"* (he used to come here often)". He recounts how Badranna and his men built that pond. "I worked in that project, too… Mere ko jaanta hai, Badranna (Badranna knows me)", he says loudly, still excited.

In 2000, Badranna decided to surrender, with his wife. "I was almost illiterate and it was causing an impediment in my way up in the party ranks", he says. He got his vasectomy reversed to become a father. He has 10-years old daughter Manisha.

After his surrender, the police will occasionally call Badranna over to acquaint themselves with the Maoist strategy. "I always told them: Do not study Maoists. Study yourselves first. Study your weaknesses".

"They do not call me any longer".

Comments on Pandita's article

It is a well-written story, but it tells only half the truth. What follows are honest comments from the Author, who knows the ways of *The Hindu* daily, once edited by a card holder Communist N. Ram. Even after giving up editorship, he still wields almost total control over the daily, since he is heading the Kasturi Ranga and Company, the publishers of the Hindu. The comments are comprehensive, covering both sides the story, warts and all.

- It is a good article which tells the readers how exploitation of the poor, the deprived and the dispossessed tribals provides the root causes for the spread of LWE. Hence, its inclusion in this chapter.
- It also tells us about the winning ways of the Maoists. They look eager to help, sincerity personified, eating even the stale food, nearly decaying, with a smile of gratitude. They have identified the rich who are the cause of the misery of the poor tribals. They win over them by distributing land of the Kulaks among exploited poor. Likewise, they help the discriminated tribal women, suffering

from age-old anti-woman practices. They are, consequently, ready to swell the Maoist rank.

- We are also told that the Maoists know how to win hearts of the tribals.
- In some cases, the CRPF men are guilty of excesses against the innocent, poor tribals. But to the fair, it will be wrong to single out the CRPF for such 'oppressive' behaviour. In such situations the world over—be it the US troops in Vietnam; Pak Armymen in Federally Administrated Tribal Areas (FATA); Indian troops in J&K and Peace Keeping Forces functioning under the UN Command in several countries—there have been reports of excesses committed by the troops. It needs telling in so many words, that despite legislations like the FRI and PESA, some reports of the tribals being denied access to their forest or their forests being taken over without due course/procedure are still coming to light.
- Undoubtedly, there are lessons for the governments at the Centre and in States, as also for paramilitary forces like BSF, CRPF etc.
- Now to the omissions of Rahul Pandita; whether these were his own failings or due to the pressure from N Ram and his *Hindu,* one can never point finger at either or both of them. Why did he surrender? Is Badranna telling the whole story, or has Pandita suppressed part of it? His getting ignored by the Maoist senior in the matter of promotion may only be partly true. There could be other reasons!
- Do the Maoists permit such 'commanders' at middle or lower middle to leave the outfit so easily, without questions? Do they impose some conditions on his conduct when he starts life as a surrendered Maoist?
- Badranna is indeed a loyal Maoist—loyal to his erstwhile comrades, loyal to the outfit, loyal to his wife—even post-surrender! Or, is he? Did he get some cash award for surrendering? Conversely, is he and his wife still loyal to their ideological beliefs and acting as spies of the Maoists and feeding them information useful to them to plan attacks on the policemen/ CRPF men still engaged in anti-Maoist operations? Is he helping them to spring ambushes on the forces moving/operating in the Maosit-infected areas?
- Is he a compromised man, supplying information to the government/forces, not only about their tactics, about their camps and about their strengths and weapons in various locations but

also, more importantly, about their leadership and factional groups within it?

- Is he under threat from the Maoists, and living under some government protection on the sly?

Some of these are valid questions, which Rahul Pandita has failed to cover in this informative article. Only he knows the reasons!

"Jharkhand encounter: 6 of 7 identified had no police case"

This news item by Santosh Singh appeared in the *Indian Express* of 11.6.15. "None of the four children killed has been identified," says the blurb of the story. It begins with, "nearly two days after 12 alleged Maoists were killed by the CRPF and Jharkhand police in a joint operation, only seven have been identified. Of them, six have no police case against them". It is datelined 10 June, from Satwarwa.

Significantly, the only one with known Maoist connections was Anurag alias R. K. 'ji' alias Doctor, said to be a top zonal commander and wanted in the January 2013 Latehar case where explosive were stitched inside a slain CRPF man's body. The others who stand identified are: Anurag's son Santosh Yadav (25), his nephew Yogesh Yadav (25), the driver of the vehicle Mohd Izaz Ahmad, a contract teacher Uday Yadav (35). Uday's cousins Neeraj Yadav (25) and Amlesh Yadav (35)

None of the four children killed has been identified.

The families of the deceased are threatening to file a case or approach the High Court over the "cold-blooded murders".

While Anurag, Santosh and Yogesh hail from Majhgava village in Chatra, Izaz lives in nearby village Nima. Izaz used to work in Madhya Pradesh and returned home and took up a job with a local electronics goods shop owner at ₹ 3000 per month.

Uday, a contract teacher who worked in Manika in Latehar, had reportedly been facing threats for the past four years.

Anurag's elder brother Lakhan Yadav, whose son Yogesh was among the killed says there were not in a touch "with Anurag for some time now". Lakhan adds further, "We made R. K. surrender in 1995. We had not spoken to him for four years. Yogesh ran a mobile phone shop in Pratapur and had gone with Santosh to an acquaintance's place. I have no idea how he landed in R.K.'s Company". Lakhan, a petty farmer, adds ruefully that his son has paid the price for being Anurag's nephew.

Similar wails and complaints come from relatives of some other deceased. Santosh's father-in-law Siteshwar Yadav, also claiming his family disowning Anurags, said Santosh was happy working as a driver and had no links with Maoists. "I met him on Monday. He left that day saying he would return by the evening", Siteshwar says. Is it a crime being Anurag's relative, he asks. "The way 12 people were killed shows they were killed from close quarters. How can a vehicle be hit multiple times and there is no blood stains?"

Same story of questions and surprise go on! Izaz's father-in-law Islam Mian, also a small farmer, says the former left home Monday following a call from his employer. The alleged shootout took place when they were travelling in employer's vehicle. Izaz could hardly have known who were the passengers in his employer's Mahendra Scorpio, Islam says.

Uday's younger brother, Hriday, claims the former had been tense lately. Uday worked as a contract teacher at Manika block town, away from their village of Newar, earning ₹ 8000 per month. Hriday continues, "He had been facing Maoist threat for four years. He did not tell anything to his wife before leaving Manika Monday morning (8.6.14)", Hariday says.

Amlesh hails from Hedu village under Panki police station in Palamau and he too had no case against him.

District SP Mayur Patel said, "We have sent a detailed report of the incident to the National Human Rights Commission (NHRC). The post-mortem report will come in a couple of days".

Comments on the above

There are, as in any such case, two sides to the incident, rather killing of 12 persons in police firing. One is as mouthed by most relatives of the deceased. They all dub it as case of murders. Barring one person, Anurag, who is a known Maoist leader, all the rest are believed innocent by their relatives. It is also possible that these relatives were unaware of the activities of their kin. They also admit that some of them were under pressure and facing Maoist threat.

The other side is that most of them were either related to a Maoist, Anurag, or were friends or known to him. Relatives might not be aware, but a good number could be accomplices of Anurag. Hence, their elimination by the police. It needs to be remembered that we are told only one side of the story. We have heard nothing from the police or other concerned officials.

But the most disconcerting fact is that four children were killed in the police firing. They have not as yet been identified. We do not even know their ages. What if they were in their teens and capable if violent attacks!

Such violent killings is not a good advertisement for the government or the country. Such incidents cause frustration among the tribals, compelling or persuading them to join the Maoist. It is the root cause, this disaffection towards the government or even the nation. Such a perception is dangerous. The facts must come out and the people informed of the truth. Any uncertainty or lack of clarity is unfortunate and can be misconstrued by interested parties to their advantage!

Such a situation is negation of the law, negation of justice, and at the very limit, negation of idea of India!

Maoist through the eyes of the Intelligentsia

This is the best section of this Chapter. It discusses certain books and films, aimed at examining as to how the authors and the directors see the Maoist insurrection. What are the positives and negatives in their view of this violent ideology? Do they see it as a redeeming idea for the polity? Do they think it will ameliorate the social adversities of the disadvantaged? Are the Maoists the modern messias? For such advocates, the jury is still out!

On the other side, many think of the Maoist as marauders and looters, exploiting the 'deprivation' of the tribal communities for their personal and outfits' benefit! They are rebels in the name of the tribals, who they claim have not been given their due by way of development of roads, schools and hospital in their areas. So they lust for power, but wrap it in the ideological blanket and aim at displacing the democratically-elected government through violent means. To note the contradiction, they will not let the government/agencies start/complete development projects like building of roads or schools by killing the contractors, threatening the labour or ambushing the troops deployed for the protection of the former. It is obvious, if the government succeeds in providing development to their areas and consequently the 'deprived' communities of yesterday become a satisfied lot, it will put these Maoists out of job. It is as simple a logic!

Now to some of the books and films made on the subject.

"When the State fails, Maoists succeed"

The author of this book is Rahul Pandita, which is reviewed by Prakash Singh, in the *Pioneer* issue dated 11.9.11. The reviewer is a retired DG, BSF and himself has authored a book on the same subject. *The Naxalite Movement in India.*

The reviewer sums up his view of the book in these words: "Pandita's book is both sympathetic and biased towards the rebels". What follows are the excerpts from the review. This practice of using the reviewers words to assess the book will be followed throughout this section.

"The book *Hellow Bastar* is a valuable addition to the Naxal literature available in the country. The author Rahul Pandita has travelled extensively in the Naxal-affected regions and interacted with the Maoist cadres and their leaders. It is a first-hand account. It has information on party's organisational structure, fundings and weapons".

"Presentation of facts show an undercurrent of sympathy and even bias towards the Maoist. Sympathy for the tribals is natural while bias is understandable....because of close association the author had with the Maoists. There are repeated references to the excesses committed by security forces, but the barbarities of the Maoists are given a sketchy mention. There is no reference to the massacre committed by the Maoists in Errabore, for example".

Actually, in the kind of situation that prevails in the Naxal-affected areas, the *Lakshman Rekha* of human rights is bound to be crossed here and there. This is not to justify those violations but only to explain their inevitability in the conflict zone. People who criticise the security forces should remember that their record is better than those of the Chinese forces in Tibet or Xinjiang".

"The Maoist movement in India has expanded not so much because of the soundness of their ideology, but more because of the incompetence and corruption of the administration. Abhujmad, figuring prominently in the book, is a classic example. An area some 4000 sqkm, the State (Chhattishgarh) Government had left its tribal inhabitants to the care of the God. There was no sign of governance, leave aside any development project".

"Corruption has become cancerous in the society, neutralising all development efforts, particularly so in the remote tribal areas".

"The tribals are attracted to the Maoist because as the author rightly says, "the uniform offers them a sense of who they are, makes them one large group, gives them some purpose in life".

"The book is written in a racy style....Factual errors are few and far between. It is said the trouble in Srikakulam broke around the same time as in Naxalbari. Actually the former predates the latter, starting respectively in 1961 and 1967, by 1967 the former had achieved a fair measure of success."

"The future of the Maoist movement in India would depend on two factors: The ability of the State to improve governance and, second, the

Maoists adapting their ideology and strategy to the prevailing socio-economic condition in India and taking cognisance of country's armed strength. Pandita's book brings into focus the weaknesses of the Indian State and to that extent, help the policy-makers to fill these gaps."

"It is a pity the government has no policy to deal with the problem, described by the Prime Minister himself as the biggest threat to the internal security of the country. Consequently, Home Minister P. Chidambaram came up with a simplistic, through pragmatic, policy of 'clear, hold and develop' but it ran into rough weather with that maverick of a politician, Digvijay Singh, opposing it.

The paramilitary forces seem content with the area-domination exercises. Development at the ground level is hardly visible, with the bureaucracy lacking commitment. The Maoists are taking full advantage of the administrative inertia and the government's hesitant response to a serious challenge."

"My role is based on Kobad Ghandy"

This is Om Puri, a leading Indian actor, speaking about his role in Prakash Jha's upcoming film "Chakravyuh." The news item was written by Madhur Tankha after speaking to the actor and appeared in the *Hindu* of 9.7.12. Excerpts follow:

- "Vetran actor Puri is playing a senior Naxalite leader, Kobad Gandhi, in Jha's film. To do justice to his character, it was important for him to understand the root cause of Naxalism. He read up a few books, including Rahul Pandita's 2011 book "Hellow Bastar": The untold story of India's Maoist Movement Puri explains: 'I wanted to know everything related to Naxalism….Jha has raised different and pertinent questions through this film. I am playing a senior Naxal leader who is not active, but is seen as an inspiration by the cadres.' "
- "As Naxals are underground and little is known about them, Puri had CPI (Maoist) leader Kobad Ghandy as a reference point. He is currently in Delhi's Tihar Central Jail. He studied at the Doon School, St. Xavier College and did his Charter accountancy from London. He returned to India and got married to Anuradha. The couple went to the jungles and lived with the Adivasis for 30 years. He was caught by the police when he visited Delhi for medical treatment. Puri wanted to meet his real life character in Tihar Jail but was denied permission."

"He is way off the mark"

Prakash Jha sends out an anti-social message with his movie *Chakravyuh,* says Ashwani Kulkarni, in the *Hindu* of 3rd November 2012. This is his review of Jha's film. Kulkarni heads a Nashik-based non-profit group Pragati Abhyan, which works for the transparency in government schemes. Excerpts from Kulkarni review are given hereafter.

> "Film Maker Prakash Jha is known for highlighting socio-economic problems through the medium of cinema. His *Chakravyuh* focuses on Naxalism, a serious and complex problem the nation is grappling with today. But Jha has failed to meet the high expectations of the people.
>
> "In the movie, the government support big corporations and turns blind eye to the poor tribal people. It breaks rules to help the rich and uses police for that purpose. We are aware of these issues and the movie brings out these aspects quite well. Then there is Mahanta, a steel company, intent to lay its hands on the natural resources in the tribal areas. It is only interested in its profits even if it is at the cost of the poor tribals and their livelihood. The Naxals are supported by the professors. They have their own laws and methods of meting out justice to the villagers. The Naxal commanders approve of their violent struggle and face no dilemma about raising funds through extortion. And the policemen are downright cruel."
>
> "The film highlights how the government, the businessman and police are unfair to the adivasis. But does it mean the Naxalism is the solution?...The Naxals can take revenge, but can they provide development? The movie does not answer that all-important question. It does not touch on the issue the effect of the Naxal movement."
>
> "There is a scene in the movie where an upright police officer, during his first visit to an adivasi, asks them to put an end to violence since it will not give them schools, hospitals and livelihood. But this point is not made again in the rest of the movie. It is disheartening that a sensitive and intelligent director like Jha has conveyed an anti-social message by making a villain out of government and heroes out of Naxals."
>
> "I wonder if Jha believes that the adivasis can change the situation with just guns in their hands. Can our society resolve our problems or bring about a meaningful change without the help of the government? I agree that it is not a simple problem, but if Jha decided to take up the Challenge making a movie on a complex issue, then he should have dealt with the complexity in a more responsible manner.

"Peace and other illusions in the time of War"

Review of the book, *"War and Peace in Junglemahal: People, State and Maoists";* edited by Biswajit Roy; Setu Prakshani, Kolkata. The review by Aman Sethi, appeared in the *Hindu* of 17.7.12. Excerpts follow:

> "The collected letters of correspondence between the CPI (Maoist) and the Indian State is an archive of Corpses: Policemen and guerrillas, commanders and comrades, police informers and Maoist sympathisers. The body count racked up by each serves as a signalling mechanism for the other."
>
> "Except for the police and Maoist commanders, the dead do not usually get to choose sides; their identities are written in reverse, a ideological narration that details seemingly insignificant decisions that end in death."
>
> "In June 2012, 19 people were killed in a joint operation by CRPF's COBRA battalion and State police, who claimed they were hardened Maoists. When newspaper reported they were villagers holding a meeting, the police pointed to six troopers in the encounter and asked why the villagers were holding a meeting at middle of the night. Maoists too have reasons for their violence…."
>
> "The notion of just principle in a normal situation is different from that in a ware situation, wrote Maoist commander Kishenji in a letter to the Bengali daily, *Dainik Statesman*, in which he explained his party's policy on killing of police informers, 'During war, freedom of thought, consciousness, initiative and innovation is much limited in scope.' "

Peace initiative

> "Kishenji's letter is just one of the several texts in the book under reviewing; it has a collection of essays that begin with the abortive peace initialtive between the Maoists and the Mamata Banerjee government. The talks began in the backdrop of Ms. Banerjee's stunning electoral victory and ended with Mr. Kishenji's corpse laid out on tiled slab in a hospital morgue."
>
> *"The primary occupation of the texts is the question of peace*: The first section attempts to understand the failure of the Bengal peace talks, section two details the experiences of similar failure elsewhere in the country and it is only in the penultimate—and possibly most interesting—section that contributors tackle the most important question of all: Can a nation-state (like India) and a proto-state (like the Maoists) peacefully negotiate the demise of the other?"

"Nivedita Menon in 'Maoist Proto-state', writes, 'the modern state has monopoly over legitimate means of coercion, thus establishing a visible horizon of violence within which we live.' "

"Approaching the CPI (Maoist) as a proto-state with its own political and military structures is crucial to understanding the nature of the violence that engulfs central and eastern India. The battle in Chhattisgarh and Bengal is not just a war for improving the human development indices of a section of the population; rather it is a battle between two well-armed, political forces for control of the adivasi constituency."

"For the Maoists, reaching out to the adivasis is part of larger project that shall end with the Red flag at the Red Fort. This, in itself, is a reason enough for the State to claim the adivasis as State's own. But as the Maoists rightly point out, there is enough poverty and deprivation in this country without the State focusing its energies on conflict-affected areas."

"This may prompt some to wonder if the State or the Maoists actually care about the adivasis; but that is the wrong question to ask. Abstract political constructs are incapable of caring, and those who inhabit these structures are consumed by the need to keep the edifice intact. So where does this leave the question of peace."

Strategy

"In his essay, 'People's War as Strategy and Peace Talks as Tactics', Gautam Navlakha writes, 'peace talks are a matter of tactics, while waging people's war is a strategy for a successful consummation of revolution.' After all, what can be the outcome of a negotiation where each party cannot countenance a rival power?"

"One of the most interesting pieces in the collection is an old Economic and Political Weekly piece by K. Balagopal in which he makes several cogent arguments about the talks between the Maoists and the Andhra Pradesh Government in 2004; 'Many among the public seem to have thought that the ultimate agenda was the establishment of peace....an expectation that has no basis in fact. Balagopal then details how the talks collapsed when Chief Minister Y. S. Rajasekhra Reddy, much like Mamata Banerjee in West Bengal, stepped away from negotiations and authorised his police force to hunt down the guerrillas. Apparently, Maoists are not the only ones who view talks as tactics."

"In his book, 'The Art of Not Being Governed: An Anarchist History of upland Southeast Asia', James Scot writes how, for most of human history, the State that pushed its subjects too far found that it had none. The possibilities of escape have diminished in tandem with the expansion of the State's horizon of control. Perhaps, the truly radical project is not the creation of a better, more perfect, state but a lesser, more porous one."

"History in pink jacket": The *Hindu*: 14.1.13

This is the heading of an article by Pheroze L. Vincent, which is essentially based on his conversation with Shubranshu Choudhary, the author of a book on the Maoists, title "Let us call him Vasu: with the Maoists in Chhattisgarh." In a manner of speaking, it is also a review of or a commentary on the book "Let us call him Vasu", published simultaneously in Hindi as "Us ka naam Vasu Nahin"(=His name is not Vasu). After working for the BBC for more than ten years, Shubhranshu returned to his home state Chhattisgarh in 2004 to start CGNet, an internet platform to exchange news. The excerpts follow:

"Journalistically speaking, life has been good for Shubhranshu Choudhary, founder of the CGNet Swara Mobile news and author of "Let us call him Vasu. In the past month (December 2012), he has been derided as Maoist and an IB agent, by people on both sides of the ideological spectrum. He confesses that his look is 'a Maoist point of view, with the camera placed on their shoulders.'"

"The book is about the Maoist movement in Chhattisgarh and starts off with his search for an old Maoist friend, described only by his nomde guerre 'vasu'. The book breaks new ground as a first draft of the history of the Maoists in Chhattisgarh since their entry from Andhra Pradesh in the early 1980s. It has interviews with several top guerrilla leaders like Mupalla Lakshman Rao alias Ganapathy, Kosa, Sonu alias Bhupathi, Sabyasachi Panda and Rajanna and also young Adivasi leaders like Venkitesh."

"The book itself reads like fiction. With a pink back cover and brush stroke fonts, it does not look like a serious treatise on the insurgency. Series of interviews have been condensed into single conversation for lucidity. Shubhranshu says this is intentional as the book is targeted at the common reader rather than the academics, though the text has gone through the rigours of fact checking."

"Shubhranshu says, 'it is not normal journalism.' He spent seven years researching for the book, says he, 'Ganpathy (General Secretary of the Maoist party) is considered the bin Laden of India. I was the first to interview him in a decade, but I finish it in two paragraphs."

"He further explains that the last batches of Naxalites from Andhra Pradesh crossed over to Chhattisgarh the early 1990s. He says, 'Now we are seeing the rise of an adivasi intellectual (within the Maoist party). People like Venkitesh are more important for me than Ganapathy because solution will come from them."

"On his interview with Venkitesh, the party's South Bastar Secretary and its highest ranking tribal leader in the State, Shubhranshu writes: 'It seems bizarre even to think that sometime in the future, the Indian Government may have to negotiate with leader who has never boarded a train, and never travelled to the capital of his State, leave alone the Capital of his country'."

"He says, 'Adivasis are very timid. I was astonished to see them coming out on to the streets to protest the rape of girls in Kanker, a few days ago. While the Maoists never claim that they came to Dandakaranya for tribal uplift—the reasons were purely strategic—people like Ganapathi have turned adivasis into fighters. But whether this will lead to tribal self-rule or whether they will be able to hold on to the land they have gained, remains to be seen'."

"Shubhranshu has come under flak from civil rights activists for quoting Maoists saying that health activists Binayak Sen was a courier for the party. In his defence, he says he cross-checked this information with Kosa and Panda, both senior leaders who are not in contact with each other. The book also has a quote from Hyderabad-based activist K. Balagopal, who says: 'I tried to start a peace process in Chhattisgarh like in Andhra, but Binayak Sen opposed it. Our entire initiative was scuttled by his opposition'."

"Shubhranshu says he wrote so knowing fully well the cost he would have to bear. 'I have lost friends. No one wanted to write about my book. I respect Sen hugely but if I don't write what I have learnt, it is disservice to my profession'."

Here, ends the excerpts from the article by Vincent. Addition of CGNet Swara to this section is considered useful as it concerns larger Gondwana region and also talks about some other relevant information on Adivasis. It is also written by Vincent and is reproduced below in full.

CGNet Swara

"After 10 years with BBC, Shubhranshu returned to his home state Chhattisgarh in 2004 to start CGNet, an internet platform to exchange news. Soon he realised that as internet penetration was negligible, they would have to move to more widely used medium like the mobile phones.

"Thus CGNet Swara came into being. People from all over the Gondwana region that in addition to Chhattisgarh, includes parts of Odisha, Andhra Pradesh, Maharashtra and Madhya Pradesh call in to give or listen to news. 'We get 200 to 300 listeners every day and 10 to 15 recordings per day. After being translated from Gondi by journalists we have trained, they are vetted, and three to five news are released on our phone service every day.

"While the Census lists some 27 lakh speakers of Gondi (unofficial estimates put it higher at 40 lakh), there are no news broadcast on Akashvani in Gondi. Although, there are news bulletins in Sanskrit, which has 14,000 speakers as per the Census.

"One of the ironies of modern India is that while we have a free press, many communities are invisible as there are hardly any journalists from their community. 'The first trained journalist from the State, Lingaram Kodopi, who worked with us, is now in jail. Most journalists only know Hindi. How will they report on adivasis if they do not know the language? he asks. 'Adivasis are now talking to Adivasis. Also, the Chief Secretary listens to it every day, so do many collectors. We have made enemies but problems are getting solved. There now exists a platform for dialogue."

"Ground realities": Swati Daftuar: The Hindu

This is the review of a book "Red Revolution 2020 and beyond: Strategic Challenges to Resolve Naxalism" by Lt Gen V K Ahluwalia, published in the Hindu of 19.12.13. The reviewer, Daftuar remarks at the outset that "despite being an Army man, he has not looked at Naxalism through just a security prism!

Some, if not most, civilian academics and analysts think that most, if not all, Army men believe that use of force is the only way to combat the recalcitrant Maoists! Nothing could be farther from this misconceived notion. Army men know better. It is a much misused and much-flaunted cliche by most politicians, led by mavericks like Digvijay Singh that "force is not the answer to Maoist violence and murderous mayhem". Let anyone quote such an assertion from any senior Army man that 'force alone' is the solution to the Maoist rebellion. Undoubtedly, development is the final answer to Maoist ideology, because it is the lack of it that leads to the deprivation, poverty and dispossession among the tribal communities, which are ideal conditions for Maoists to ingratiate themselves with the tribals.

But what is not understood by such analysts is the at can a government, any government, undertake development works — road construction, building schools, hospitals and civil works — in the regions dominated by the Murderous Maoists? Will they permit any such works? This is where the Army/Paramilitary/Police forces come in as a kind of panecia!

It is only force that will allow these development activities to proceed in the tribal areas. Unless the lawless elements like Maoists are convinced that India is too strong to go under, and it will not start cowering before their murderous, inhuman and egregious violence perpetrated on the security forces men and the tribals alike, they would not change their ways. It is the force that will put some sense in their heads. They have to be controlled, and finally eliminated. Only then can development take place. Prakash Singh, former DGP, UP and DG, BSF, who should know better, has said it all in, rather briefly: "There is no doubt that development has to be given very high priority in any counter-insurgency plan: However it can only supplement and not substitute the security approach.[8]

Finally, after they have been chastened or partially subdued, development can start. The two must go hand-in-hand, till the Maoists have been eliminated. In the given situation security approach is paramount. Then the development enters the field. Even if it is a fact that the tribals have been deprived of their due and injustice has been done to them, to undo that development must reach their doorsteps. That the ultras would not allow. Hence the paramountcy of security approach as explained above.

Now, some parts/excerpts of the review

> "The seeds of Lt Gen Ahluwalia's book were sown when he was the Army Commander (Goc-in-C, in Army parlance) of the Central Command, from 2010-12. This Command had in its area four Naxal-affected States — Chhattisgarh, Jharkhand, Odisha and Bihar — and part of his duty was to tour these states extensively. Maoism started progressively increasing from 2001 onwards. And it reached its bloodiest peak, with maximum casualties in 2009-10. The General was in command there, retiring in Feb 2012."
>
> "A book with extensive, empirical research as also an analysis of the various socio-economic factors that spur Naxalism, fulfils the need of the hour — to inform readers about the greatest internal threats nations faces today. "I travelled extensively, saw the ground realities, and that increased my interest to study the issue, to read and get statistical data concerning the socio-economic conditions, human development indices and relative deprivation of these areas', says the author. He feels the thought process even of soldiers and paramilitary forces changes once

they know the reasons behind the crisis they were handling. Even in the book, he says the Maoists are not our enemies".

"These areas are rich in minerals, forest, water and land resources, so it is a case of rich land poor people. The tribals are perhaps the worst-affected. 'This has lot to do with Indian Forest Act of 1927 and Forest Conservation Act of 1980,' he says. The tribals have been displaced not once but many times over. The problem has a huge impact on not just the affected states but on the whole nation. It has negative affect on not just the security but the economic growth of the country. 'These areas also have sensitive rail and road communications going into the North-East. It needs urgent attention'. He feels the crises can be tackled better when the country and its people realise that they have a personal stake in the problem".

"*Red Revolution 2020* is an essential read for anyone trying to understand the history and spread of the Maoist uprising in the country. After studying the spread and impact of the Maoism, the book crystal gazes into the scenario 2020 and beyond, and analyses the strategic challenges and urban perspective plan of Maoists".

Maoist Insurrection in India: The initial stages

Naxalbari uprising can indeed be acknowledge as the beginning of LWE in India. This mid-1960s uprising, though limited to a few villages in the Darjeeling district of north West Bengal, hogged headlines beyond the borders of India. After all, a Chinese daily chose to see it as a "spring thunder" over India.

Its leader, Charu Mazumdar, a charismatie leader, became a recognised name in the LWE world, even though a similar movement arose in Andhra Pradesh also, about the same period. It is accepted that MCC in Bihar and PW in Andhra Pradesh were the other names for Naxalbari movement, later becoming popular as Naxalite insurrection. After merger of MCC and PWG to become CPI(Maoist), the LWE is known as Naxalite or Maoist insurrections—the two appellations being inter-changeable.

This section deals with initial phase of LWE spread in India, with a variety of facts and figures, for the period essentially of the first decade of the 21st century.

Naxalism in India: A Broad Picture

Naxalism or Naxalite violence/armed insurrection has come to denote the LWE in India. After the merger of two left factions, as stated above, it has assumed a new if more glamorous rubric of Maoism. More significantly, the Left-wing elites prefer the term, some analysts believe, because of recent victory of their cousins in Nepal, Prachanda-led Maoists. In this work, the term Naxalism will be found used more often than its "imported" version, 'Maoism.' The following pages will have fairly extensive data and charts concerning the first half of the first decade of the 21st century.

The MHA Report: April 2006

The report confirmed an increase in the number of attacks by the Left ultras. The police casualties have gone up by 53 per cent and civilian by 11 per cent.

Tabular information on 9 LWE-hit states

The table below shows the number of attacks and relevant casualty data for the nine worst-hit states: Chhattisgarh, Jharkhand, Bihar, Odisha, AP, Maharashtra, UP, MP and West Bengal.

Naxalite Violence: 2002-2006

Year	*Maoist Attacks*	*Killed*		
		Civilians	*Police Personnel*	*Maoist*
2002	1465	382	100	141
2003	1597	410	105	216
2004	1533		100	87
2005	1594		153	223
2006 (Till 30 April)	550		62	93

Source: MHA Report: April 2006.

Naxalite activities during 2006

ACHR Report: Jan 2007

After the MHA Report, we have one by Asian Centre for Human Rights (ACHR) for the year 2006, released on 10 Jan 2007 at New Delhi.[9]

As many as 749 people were killed in the Naxalite violence in 2006, says this report. Statistical Details: Break down of the figure '749'

749 Fatalities

Civilian	285
Security Forces	135
Naxalites (alleged)	329
Total	**749**

749 Fatalities : Statewise Figures

Chattisgharh	363
Andhra Pradesh	135
Jharkhand	95
Maharashtra	60
Bihar	45
Odisha	25
West Bengal	22
UP	2
Karnataka	1
MP	1

ACHR Report: Pro-LWE bias is Obvious

Compared to 2005, when 892 people lost their lives, there was decrease in killings during 2006, i.e. 749. Now comes the bias :

"But the Salwa Judum campaign and its disastrous consequences, such as the Rights violations by the Naxalites, the security forces and Salwa Judum activists, captured centre stage during the year (2006).

Yet again, the ACHR Report says, "The (salwa Judum) campaign led to the forcible displacement of 43,740 persons as of Dec 2006 in Dantewada district, the spread of conflict to 1,427 police station, and an increase in the strike capability of the Naxalite".

Here some comments on the above observations of the Report:

- As for the rights violations, the ACHR places the illegal CPI (Maoist) at equal footing with the security forces and the civil society campaign, Salwa Judum.
- The entire displacement of 43,740 persons is caused by the Salwa Judum campaign, and the Maoists are innocent of any blame! A good example of 'objectivity' shown by the ACHR!

There is more to come. As an apparent gesture of even-handedness, the Director says: "These acts of Maoists constitute serious violations of the Genev a Comentions and Rome Statute of International Criminal Court". The Director, Suhas Chakma, says "these acts..." The CPI (Maoists) is an outlaw, and only "these acts", and by implication, all "other acts" of this illegal outfit are not "violation". To put it simply, all acts of this illegal outfit are illegal. The outfit is waging armed struggle against the democratically elected Government of India.

The Report of the ACHR is outrightly harsh on the security forces.

ACHR is harsh on the security forces

1. The claims of the forces that all persons killed were the 'Naxalites' are far from the truth. "There have been credible reports of torture, rape and extra judicial executions by the Salwa Judum activists and the security forces, especially in the process of forcibly bringing the villagers under the Salwa Judum fold," Chakma said.
2. The Report further says, "The Centre is supporting wrong policies.....The Salwa Judum campaign, which was responsible for 48.50 per cent of the total killings in Chhattisgarh, had more to do with local, political considerations than resolving the Naxalite conflict".
3. The ACHR expressed concern over the continued 'Law and Order' approach of the Government in dealing with the crisis as reflected by the creation of a division within the MHA to address the Naxalite conflict.
4. The report recommended the creation of a separate Ministry for speedy development of the Naxal-hit areas, similar to the Development of the North-Eastern Region.
5. The ACHR also wants the Centre to intervene and ask the Chhattisgarh government to end the Salwa Judum campaign, not to bring civilians in conflict with the Naxals, and investigate all complaints of human rights violations' allegations.

Comments on the Report's observations and 'pious' suggestions: Parawise

1. "Rape, torture and extra judicial killings by security forces and Salwa Judum activists." Obviously, ACHR says Naxals are the milky white angles! What and where is the evidence of "rape......" by security forces? Obviously, the report was drafted by the "overground Maoists", leading Left Commielobby of the Naxals and signed by Suhas Chakma. The Maoists have committed no crimes!
2. "The centre is supporting wrong policies". Pray, what are right policies? How impressive the exact figure of "48.50 per cent of total killings...........by Salwa Judum". What is left unsaid is that the remaining 51.50 per cent were committed by the security forces! So, it has nothing to do "with resolving the Naxalite conflict". The ACHR is silent on the "ways to resolve Naxalite conflict"! To be blunt, the organisations and NGOs like the ACHR

are 'dishonest', and 'toothless tigers'. Like the elitist supporters of the Maoists, the ACHR dare not condemn the Maoists. They can condemn, criticise and *rant* against the security forces and governments, because they are certain that no harm will come their way. As for resolving the Naxal conflict, can they persuade or force CPI (Maoist) to end their insurrection? They cannot! All they can do is: rave and rant against lawful and democratic entities and their instruments like the police and other security forces. How one wishes that one of these 'sympathisers and supporters' of the Maoists would join their ranks, flight with them and if need be, get killed. That will be conviction and sincerity. Some intellectuals did so in France. Indian intellectuals? They are the paper tigers, roaring from their air-conditioned rooms and TV studios. I am still waiting for Arundhati Roys and loud-months like Gautam Navlakha to come forward and join their beloved comrades (Maoists)!!

3. "........Concern over the law and order approach..." Again, it is dishonestly written all over! Are they suggesting "Gandhian approach" against these hardcore criminals and murderous Maoists? They suggest no alternative approach! May be, they want a free hand for these murderers, by withdrawing security forces. They are not unaware, the likes of Suhas Chakma, that until the armed rebels are convinced that the might of India will defeat them, they will never give up.
4. It recommends a Ministry for development of Naxal-hit areas." The ACHR is being facile and facetious in making this inane suggestion. Without creating a Ministry, the governments at the Centre and States have undertaken some development projects—building roads, schools, hospitals, bridges. Does not ACHR know the Maoists are thwarting all such efforts by kidnapping and killing the labour, kidnapping contractors and extracting percentage levy on total contract value, destroying the construction material, and pilfering the cordex and explosives for making the IELs. May be they honestly feel a Ministry is better: It will yield greater amount of money through looting and extractions!
5. It wants the Centre......to ask the Chhattisgarh Government to end the Salwa Judum.....not to bring civilians in conflict with Naxals.....investigate.......human rights violation by......".
   (i) "End Salwa Judum.....not to bring civilians in conflict with Naxals". It is a plea to give a free hand to Naxals to kill

unarmed civilians. Armed civilians, Salwa Judum, can give equal fight to Naxal, which is not acceptable to ACHR.

(ii) Investigate security forces, but not the Naxals, never! This disingenuousness will be so touching if it wasn't apparently so clever and incredulous! Is it within the power of ACHR to suggest investigation against Maoists? Will they ever do it?

P.S.

ACHR wrote this Report in Jan 2007. Possibly, even it was not aware that Maoist sympathisers, supporters and Left commielobby would work so vigorously that the Supreme Court would order disbandment of Salwa Judum within five years of its plea, and more surprisingly, giving same reasons—not to bring civilians in conflict with Naxals! They should all feel happy that some so-called intellectuals like R C Guha joined the 'band wagon of 'disband the Salwa Judum' brigade!

Naxalite-inflicted fatalities : 2004-2006

Governement Figures

Naxalites have killed as many as 129 people's representatives and 411 government officials, mostly policemen, between 2004 and 2006.

Almost all people's representatives, except JMM leader Sunil Mahato, killed by the Maoists during the period represented village, block and district-level ones. Mahato was incidentally, the lone MP who fell to the Maoist bullets.

These facts were placed on the table of the Rajya Sabha on 5 Sep 2007 by MOS Home Sri Prakash Jaiswal. Some other details from the Minister's reply are tabulated here.

Fatalities caused by the Naxalites (2004-2006)

Year	*People's Representatives*		*Govt officials mainly security men*
	No. of Attacks	*No. killed*	
2004	114	45	100
2005	111	64	153
2006	31	20	158

Physical spread of Naxalism

2005 A total of 1608 incidents of Naxalite violence were reported from 460 police stations in 11 states.

2006 The figure for 2006 dipped slightly to 1509 incidents which were reported from 395 police stations that constituted 4.65 per cent of the total 8,488 in the 11 states.

Districts affected by Naxalism which receive financial assistance from the Centre

	Districts which received Financial Assistance	*Naxalism-infested District*
Andhra Pradesh	8	19
Bihar	8	25
Chhattisgarh	7	10
Jharkhand	13	20
MP	2	6
Maharashtra	4	6
Odisha	7	14
UP	3	6
West Bengal	3	9
	55	
Karnataka		5
Kerala		2
Uttarakhand		2
Tamil Nadu		1
		122

It needs to be noted that 55 is the numbers of districts which are receiving financial assistance from the Central Government while 122 are the number of Naxalism-infested districts recognised by the Planning Commission as such. The latter figure of 122 is as published in the Times of India in its issue dated 22 September 2007.

Nine Naxalism-infested States receiving financial assistance from the Centre: September 2007

Rashtriya Sam Vikas Yojana Funds to 9 States

States	*No. of Naxal hit districts*	*Amount to be released by Centre Rs (CR)*	*Amount Released upto 2006-07*	*Emulative expenditure reported by the States*
Andhra Pradesh	8	360	195	126
Jharkhand	13	585	495	369
Bihar	8	360	195	155
Odisha*	3	135	98	81
Chhattisgarh	7	315	278	181
West Bengal	3	135	75	48
MP	2	90	90	64
Maharashtra	4	180	113	69
UP	3	135	120	70

* Excludes the four KBK districts of Malkangiri, Koraput, Rayagada and Nawrangpur which are covered under the Special Plan.

Source: Ministry of Panchayat Raj Website.

Is the Maoist threat overblown? June 2006

It is a valid question to ask mid 2006! As is expected in such cases, different analysts will have different views. If some would think the answer is yes, others will say no, it is not. The latter would suggest the former are over-blowing the issue. But this analysis essentially wants to see the view as propounded by a Weekly in its issue of 11 Jun 2006.[10]

Of the 28 states in India, 12 are affected by the Maoist insurgency. It should seem an alarming picture as the Maoists have their presence in the area stretching from Amlekhganj (Nepal) in the north to Adilabad (Andhra Pradesh) in the south and from Kathmandu to Karimganj in the east. "Colour these Red states in red on the map and you get a quadrilateral in the middle of the Indian state, more than one-third of its total expanse. As of today, the Red Corridor from north to south cuts the east of India from its west".

The weekly continues in the same pessimistic vein. The corridor, analysts fear, would one day become a compact revolutionary zone, where the writ of the Indian state would not run. The concept of the zone is said to have originated at a Siliguri meeting in September 2001 of Maoists from India, Nepal and Bangladesh.[11]

"If the Maoists controls this zone, trains would not run from East to West". It has serious implications for India's economy and security.

Of the 550 incidents of Naxalite violence reported in 2006 (till 30 April), 26 were attacks on public transports, including the railways.

If train services are disrupted, it would directly impact the inflow of FDI into the zone, and consequently, there would be problems of minerals from Jharkhand and Chhattisgarh making it to the industries of Maharashtra and Gujarat. So it is logical to believe that the finished goods, in whatever quantities these are manufactured, from these industries would not be allowed to be transported to reach the ports at Kolkata, Haldia, Paradip and Visakhapatnam for export to the East Asian countries.

If the Maoist threat can be, or indeed is, so debilitating to India's economy, stability and security, why is the government not acting against the Naxal in as determined a manner as it did against the insurgents in the North-East, separatists in Jammu and Kashmir and terrorists in Punjab?

The answer possibly is that the picture is not as grim as painted by this Weekly. In a democratic country of India's size, certain dissent and consequent disorder would always be there. Perhaps that is inevitable. In the instant case, the 'impressive' statistics are being distorted to make it a "seriously threatening" scenario for India's polity and security.

Twelve states, indeed have a Maoist presence, but as a MHA official asked, how much territory do the insurgents really control even in the red-crayoned districts, forget the states?

Another statistic given out by the MHA, gives a more accurate picture. In 2003, as many as 518 police stations in these 12 states reported some sort of Maoist activity within their jurisdiction, 517 in 2004 and 509 in 2005. These police stations reported this activity in some corner of their areas. Put together, these states have 8,695 police stations. That works out to six per cent of the police stations witnessed Maoist activity. Is that alarming?

Most security experts believe the Maoist threat is more of a hype than reality. An analyst who has studied Maoist insurgency in Nepal, points, "the threat of Maoists creating a compact revolutionary zone from Amlekhganj in Nepal to Adilabad in India is somewhat far-fetched".[12]

This realistic assessment is not meant to foment complacency among the security agencies, nor to belittle the dangers posed by the Maoists. In fact, after the success of their counterparts in Nepal, the Indian Maoists might start dreaming of replicating Nepal in India. But then India is not Nepal, nor its security structure so brittle. The Naxal violence in India is certainly manageable but then politics enters the scene which comes in the way of it being handled more effectively, and in a coordinated manner, which will be seen here. There are other factors also which delay the adoption of a little more effective anti-Naxal approach, perhaps a little harsher. Democracy has its compulsions!

The Maoists cannot challenge the might of the Indian state, whatever weaponry and strategy they might adopt. Prakash Singh, a former DGP MP and author of a recent book on the subject, *The Naxalite Movement in India*, points out two hurdles in the way of the Naxals realising a compact revolutionary zone: "One, the discontinuities in the areas under the influence of the Maoist, and two, the fragmentation and factionalism within the movement".

A member of the National Security Advisory Board has another but more important take on the LWE: "Their striking power is extremely limited. But they are of more than nuisance value. They can politically influence the inhabitants of these (affected) districts". Now this is the language any political class understands instantly, and the Indian politicos do the fastest. That should explain why more effective, coordinated, if harsher, anti-Naxal policy has not been institutionalised in all the affected states till now. All such things in India unfortunately fall prey to party politics, where party interest is placed above the national interest. Its popular appellation is 'vote bank' politics! The Prime Minister may characterise Naxalism as "the most serious internal security threat" to the country, but his government would not initiate effective anti-Naxal policy and strategy lest his party accuses him of damaging the party's poll prospects with his sincerity and enthusiasm!

Not to speak of Naxal threat which is still not as potent as terrorism, the country has failed to craft a no-nonsense, tough and purposeful policy on the latter. Consequently, we are perceived to be a 'soft state' against terrorist depredations. After every terrorist act—be it Mumbai 1993, Mumbai 2006 or Malegaon 2006 outrages—all we get to hear are the cliches mouthed by the government leaders, including the Prime Minister: "We will bring the perpetrators to justice,...zero tolerance to terrorism...". Even on 25 Nov 2006, Prime Minister Singh refused to institute any hasher laws to curb terrorism "but asserted all the same about zero tolerance towards it but acting within the existing laws". But having rescinded the anti-terror POTA within weaks of its coming to powre, to aphease a particular community, the UPA seems nothing more than an idle spectator while country is coming under repeated terror attacks. The UPA is under double disability: the 'vote bank' politics and the ever demanding Left, its major coalition partner, breathing down its neck every day.

The above distraction was necessary to show the political realities of Indian polity in mid-2006, and consequently, its inability to put its act together against the terrorism, and by extension, against Naxalism.

So, reverting to Naxal threat, the political considerations of ruling party's interest explains the reluctance of the Union Government to act tough against the Naxals. Even at the recent meeting of the Standing Committee of the Chief Ministers of Naxal-affected states (April 2006), the thrust was on the need for building up security and intelligence capabilities at the state level and preparations of the action plans to address the development concerns of the regions, rather than sending in Para Commandos or armed helicopters which some states had demanded. It is imperative that the centre must adopt a pro-active stance on the issue.

A researcher asserts insurgency has spread to more districts in the recent years because of launching of the large mining and other resource-based industries in the 'forested areas'. Such projects have displaced a lot of people who are not adequately compensated, and even worse, the pie is not shared with them. Such are the disillusioned tribals who fall easy prey to the recruiting agents of the Naxal 'Army'.

Understandably, the Maoist leaders talking about/against the big corporations and foreign investors get patient listeners among the affected tribals and even beyond them in the country's Left sympathisers and elite groups.

A critique of the Centre's stance

It is difficult to understand/appreciate the Centre's stance that Maoist menace is not a national problem. What are the parameters to classify a situation as a 'national problem'? Before we proceed further on the definition, let us know what Union Home Seceratary VK Duggal says on the Naxal problem.

On 28 Dec 2006, he expressed satisfaction over the decline in Naxal activities and said focus on development would go a long way in containing the menace. The states witnessing displacement in the wake of industrialisation should have better rehabilitation and resettlement policies Cynics feel these sermons, clichés and homilies make good copy for the newspapers but do not provide succour to the sufferings of the displaced.

Addressing the press at the end of two-day 22nd meeting of the National Coordination Centre on Naxalism (NCCN), at Bangalore, he said "The Naxal-affected states should make the optimum utilisation of funds under various central schemes for development and improvement of connectivity in rural areas".

Home secretaries and DGPs of the 13 Naxal-affected states attended the meeting. Some other points made by Duggal are summed up here:

- The government's approach was to bring LWE back into social mainstream. But firm action would be taken if they attacked police personnel or innocent civilians.
- Naxal menace was now limited to Bihar, Jharkhand, Odisha, Chhattisgarh, Andhra Pradesh, Eastern Maharashtra and West Bengal.
- While of a total of 510 police stations faced Naxal violence in 2005, the number came down to 372 in 2006.
- Different states making various demands for central assistance were assured of additional support to help strengthen their police forces by improving the intelligence set up and by imparting training to the policemen.
- He reiterated the government was ready to hold talks with the Maoists if they gave up arms.
- He urged other Naxal-hit states to adopt policy on surrender on the lines of one in Andhra Pradesh.

When the Home Secretary says the Naxalite threat is not a national problem, needless to say, he is voicing the views of the MHA. It is interesting to note like a generous overlord, the MHA is assuring all help to states to deal with 'their' problem of Naxalism. But this repeated but misplaced munificence is jarring and grating to the national sensibility.

This stance needs close examination and objective analysis. The MHA records show over 900 people, mere killed in Maoist volence in 2005, while 420 people have already fallen to this violence in 2006 (till October). Shouldn't this level of fatalities qualify it to be classified as a national problem.

In April 2006, the PM, speaking at the Naxal-hit states conference of Chief Ministers, describes the problem as "the biggest internal security challenge", it is beyond one's comprehension as to why his Home Secretary in Dec 2006 is baulking at calling it a national problem.

It is difficult to understand Duggal logic that Naxalism is on the wane because no. of police stations witnessing it came down from 510 in 2005 to 372 in 2006. The earlier pages of this very chapter had official data speaking about 225 districts affected by the LWE, with 8,695 police stations in its grip. There are some 9,500 Maoist cadres spread across these 13 states still it is not a national problem.

Against Centre's insistence on not calling Naxalite threat as national problem, what does one say when the same MHA in its 2006-07 Report released early April 2007 expresses serious concern about the outlawed CPI (Maoist) spreading its tentacles into southern states of Tamil Nadu, Kerala and Karnataka—the states which were not so threatened by this scourge so far?

Reasons for spread of Naxalism and problems of combating it : An expert speaks : May 2006

Before this topic of Expert-speak is examined, it should be useful to have a look at the Centre's action plan to deal with Maoist insurgency.

Centre stitches up an action plan

The Centre has of late realised that the LWE is not a mere law and order problem.

The Maoist are executing a well thought-through strategy. The decisions were taken at the 9th Congress of the CPI(Maoist) in Jan-Feb 2007 and how they are being put in practice methodically is an object lesson for security establish of the country.

The success achieved by Naxalite insurrection in its spread across the states and scale of terror unleashed by it, has finally persuaded the MHA under Shivraj Patil to draw up a strategy, encompassing security issues and other aspects germane to the Maoist problem. Its main contours are delineated here:

- Acknowledge it as more than a law and order problem. Pursue a holistic approach, simultaneously focusing on development, providing employment and land distribution.
- Provide funds to affected areas to modernise the police, viz. improve infrastructure, acquire weapons and communication equipment.
- Other states should follow the Andhra Pradesh model where the State has succeeded in checking the Maoists by raising special forces.
- Start peoples movements, like the Salwa Judum (SJ) in Chhattisgarh, to fight the Maoists.
- Deploy security forces in worst-hit areas. Centre bears cost for three years.
- Increase employment opportunities by earmarking 40 per cent recruitment in CPMF for areas affected by Naxalism.
- Allocate Rs 2,475 crore for 55 worst-hit districts under the backward districts initiative.
- Ensure a collective and coordinated approach and response from the states.

On paper, the government seems to have got it right. In any case, making a plan of action, be it on economic development or on anti-Naxal combat, is never a problem, and it is mere first baby step. To paraphrase a cliché, the devil lies in its execution. In the instant care also, security experts feel that most of its provisions will be difficult to implement, not only until the state governments display a political will to act but also, and even more significantly, the Centre also does the same, unmindful of the compulsions of coalition government, and its own MHA functions more purposefully and determinedly in leading the states in their anti-Naxalite drive.

After knowing the contours of the MHA action plan for anti-Naxal strategy, it is time to revert to the problems that come in the way of this drive.

As the law and order is decidedly a state subject, the Centre wisely tried to keep its minimum, stepping in only to supervise and help with additional forces and finances. Finally, the Centre/MHA has concluded that LWE and its control and then the defeat goes beyond tackling it at law and order level. Consequently, it has worked out an anti-Naxal plan of action, as detailed above.

Beyond administrative and law and order machinery, political will is of utmost importance. Lack of this will pose a problem.

Before we come to the importance of the political will, other issues like extent of the spread of the Naxalism and threat it poses to India's integrity and sovereignty are mentioned briefly below:

- As already discussed above, India has failed to effectively tackle Maoist threat, as was the case of tackling terrorism.
- Extent of spread of Naxalism. It has been mentioned that "Indian state's writ does not run in the Quadrilateral delineated above". This quadrilateral, from Godchiroli in Maharashtra to Abujhmaad in Chhattishgarh, has been calculated by an analyst to be measuring 92,000 sq. km. "The state and its mechanisms are simply off the radar in these parts of India", says a weekly.[13]
- If the above is not disturbing enough, read what Ajay Sahni of the KPS Gill-led Institute for Conflict Management, New Delhi, says : "While a huge chunk has already been lost, if the government does not wake up, there is a serious danger of losing more. Large parts of Chhattisgarh, Odisha, Jharkhand and West Bengal are already under the influence of Maoists, and close to being completely over run".
- The Red Corridor has been characterised by the MHA as "badly affected by the Maoist violence. Official estimates peg the strength of the Maoist cadre at 10,000 and of overground workers and sympathizers around 45,000. However, security experts believe these numbers, in both categories, are much higher.
- What lends the Maoists a deadly edge is the fact that they are armed with modern weaponry : AK-47 rifles; IEDs; INSAS and SLRs.
- They have used these weapons effectively. Just see the casualty figures and their claims on the Indian territory : In 2005 and 2006, they claimed 677 and 678 lives respectively, and in either year, the fatalities are more than the deaths in Jammu and Kashmir and the North-East put together; and 160 districts are designated 'most affected' by Maoist extremism. This is 27 per cent of total number of districts in India.
- It bears repetition that official recognition that India has full-blown crisis at hand came in mid-2006 when Prime Minister Manmohan

Singh admitted that 160 districts across the country are slipping out of government control. He reiterated that Maoist problem has assumed proportions bigger than terrorism in J and K and militancy in the North-East due to its sheer spread and organised linkages.

- Maoist threat needs to be taken seriously in view of their plans to expand their influence over the next five years. Documents of the Central Military Commission (CMC) of the CPI (Maoist) seized by the intelligence officials in Feb 2006, revealed plans to set up military commands in these unchartered territories: Delhi, Haryana, Punjab, UP, Uttarakhand and to extend the violence to urban areas and targeting industries. Finally, they have ambitious plans to control 30 per cent of the country in the next five years.

State-wise spread of the Naxalism

This spread has been outlined more than once in earlier pages and by different entities. This is from a weekly dated 15 May 2016.[14]

- *Jharkhand (10 districts)*

  Garwa, Palamu, Chatra, Hazaribagh, Bokaro, Dhanbad, Latehar, Gumla, Simdega, Lohardagga.
- *Chhattisgarh (5 districts)*

  All Five districts of the Bastar Region.
- *Odisha (5 districts)*

  Koraput, Malkangiri, Gajapati, Rayagada, Mayurbhanj
- *Andhra Pradesh*

  North Telengana and surrounding areas.
- *Bihar (5 districts)*

  Patna, Aurangabad, Gaya, Jehanabad, Nawda
- *Maharashtra (Two districts)*

  Godchiroli and Chandrapur
- *Nepal*

  14 of its 75 districts severely affected.

Questions of Political Will

Having examined the extent and strength of the Maoist insurgency in the country, we revert to examine the importance of political will in dealing with the Naxalism. Problems caused by lack of political will and related issued are mentioned by Ajay Sahni:

> "It is well-known secret that politicians have used Naxalites for their vested interests. The example of Andhra Pradesh is good one to see how its politicians have hobnobbed with the Maoists. NT Rama Rao did it. He even described them as 'desbhaktalu' (=patriots). Subsequently, the Congress under Chenna Reddy did it. In the recent times, Congress ally TRS has been accused of having struck a deal with the Maoists before the 2004 General Elections. In Bihar, politicians are known to have used both the rivals/enemies, viz, the MCC and Ranvir Sena, towards the political ends.

Another example of the above phenomenon is the fate of Salwa Judum. This anti-Naxal civil society movement/initiative, which was proving fairly successful in the initial years, become subsequently controversial, essentially become Lefty- commie, liberal-intellectual elites and some NGOs joined hands to criticise the Salwa Judum for "pitting the tribals against the Naxals as cannon foder", a catchy and an emotionally-appealing phrase which caught on when authors like RC Guha criticised it, the opposition even got louder and vociferous!

Union Home Secretary Duggal told a weekly in May 2006 : The Chhattisgarh Government has been asked to stop the Salwa Judum till it can consolidate the group and arm them better. That State is being treated as a testing ground by the (Central) Government. If the Salwa Judum experiment succeeds there, then it will be replicated elsewhere".[15]

Strength of State police forces

Even more surprising is the fact that the states facing the most intense Naxal violence do not have their police forces at the level of authorised figure. This lacuna is inexplicable, knowing as we do that the security experts assert that the police even with the full authorised strength will not be able to fight the Maoists. The states like Chhattisgarh and Jharkhand, for that reason, must be sanctioned additional police, for over and above their authorised strengths. It is only then that they can mount an effective anti-Naxal drive. Against this requirement of police forces above their authorised strength, what are the ground realities? Some of these states, fighting the more intense Naxal onslaught, are not only not having their police forces at authorized strength, they are in fact below their authorised strength. To wit, the shortage is 4,000 in case of Chhattisgarh police, and even worse, 20,000 for the Bihar police. Not to be in doubt, these figures come from Union Home Secretary Duggal.

Some other flaws and deficiencies

Some experts have their doubts about so many affected states achieving a certain, desired measure of coordination in their anti-Naxal operations. The solution, they suggest, rests with the Centre assuming a larger role in the anti-Naxal operations. Former Director IB Ajit Doval suggests the way out: "The right strategy will be for the Centre to move into the worst-affected pockets, take over the administration and make roads, setup schools and other infrastructure. Each state has a different problem. Just giving extra money and security forces will not help. Tough decision and tough measures are required. Once the state establishes its presence in the affected districts, then the development work can be taken up."

There is nothing revolutionary or unexceptionable in this suggestion from Doval, except the Centre taking over district administration and doing the things which lies within the jurisdiction of the State. There are problems even in this solution: what exactly does he mean by taking over district administration? Will the entire administration come from Delhi? What happens to the existing apparatus? Where do they go and what do they do? If it means putting some senior IAS officer from the Centre to supervise the district administration, the question will be how is former any better than the latter? Effectively, it would add one more cog to the wheel. Even more importantly, in a federal set up, will a CM accept the centre intervening in the state's jurisdiction? In the end, it needs to be emphasised that the local (state) officers are better placed to achieve the results the Director IB has in mind than one imposed from the Centre, since the former has a better understanding of the local problems as also knows the area better. What is required is that the Centre and State set the targets to be achieved in all relevant fields in each of the districts and the state ensures their implementation.

As for the development, the only way the Centre can help and ensure it is for it to give adequate CPMF strength to the states so that the latter can proceed with the development projects—construction of roads, schools, hospitals etc.—in the face of the Naxalite threats of violence. Presently, it is a vicious circle for some of the worst-affected states: Government agencies and civilian contractors cannot move because there is no security or adequate security. And consequently, the Maoists are having a field day: inching forward towards their ambitious plan of controlling 30 per cent of India's territory under their control. Obviously, the state cannot sit back and let it happen. The development work cannot wait till it establishes full control on the disturbed areas. The development and security must proceed simultaneously, the latter getting an edge over the former for understandable reasons.

CPI (Maoist) 9th Congress: Jan-Feb 2007 and the aftermath

It was an important and significant event in the history of the CPI (Maoist). It has been examined earlier in this book, but briefly. It needs a detailed look and analysis, which are afforded in this chapter.

A month-long 9th Congress was held during Jan-Feb 2007 in secured liberated zone (*Muktanchal,* in their Jargon) astride the Jharkhand-Odisha border after an interregnum of over three decades. Attended by top leaders, it mulled over the long-term strategic goals as also a list of what they plan to do over the next for coming months.

A daily says, six months down the line, the Maoist cadres are going about their assigned tasks in a manner that is chilling and seems to be as good an indicator as any about the manner of its functioning/operating. The message emanating from that Jan-Feb 2007 conclave was loud and clear : "while they would continue with their tried and tested methods of armed struggles, the major new decision was to offer all-round resistance to mega projects including steel and bauxite projects in Odisha, Chhattisgarh and AP, as also the SEZs planned in other regions". Their reason: They were leading to "massive displacements and marginalisation" of the Adivasis and farmers.[16]

The clarion call translates into: (1) a major mobilisation exercise to augment the strength of Naxalite cadre, which would enable them to extend their presence to areas they had not reached till now; (2) sourcing of arms, and (3) a 48-hour economic blockade in June (2007) that paralysed life in many parts of Chhattisgarh, Jharkhand, Bihar and West Bengal.

The latest intelligence inputs have indicated "the ultras have managed foot-holds around cities and industrial hubs in Haryana, Punjab and Delhi". That they were planning to extend their presence to those areas was also mentioned in their CMC documents seized in 2006. Besides this, parts of UP, particularly Sonebhadra and Mirzapur, and Uttarakhand have also reported the presence of the Naxalites. As for the South, their presence does not end at the borders of Andhra; Karnataka and Kerala are also waking up to their threat.

The result of the latest mobilisation is that 185 districts across six states of the Union have now Red footprints. This is something to be concerned about.

The result of the decisions taken at the 9th Congress are there for all to see. A senior police officer involved in tracking the Maoists confirms: "They are now present wherever an industrial or development project is coming up. After all, their strength lies in exploiting the sentiments of the people in the areas that are underdeveloped, so they want to resist all kinds of development".

It is not that the Centre is unaware of such developments in the field of Naxal activism. Surely, they are kept informed about such happenings by its intelligence sources. An April 2007 meeting in New Delhi saw senior officials from these states being 'sensitised' to the threat. Additional Secretary (Naxalite Movement) in the MHA, Vinay Kumar said, "We asked them to be watchful and be prepared in view of the pattern seen in the Naxal-hit states in the past".

These officials also seem to be aware of the new Naxalite strategy of targeting communication, transportation, railways and other essential services. But as the said 48-hour economic blockade showed, the security forces could find it tough to counter their new tactics. After all, it is well-nigh impossible to guard every yard of power or communication lines.

Analysts believe when the Maoists are not engaged in major attacks, they are busy consolidating. Chhattisgarh has been, in the recent months, at the receiving end of the Naxal violence. The state government sees this increased attention as sign of success of their Salwa Judum campaign which obviously has unnerved the Maoist leadership. That success of Salwa Judum and consequent nervousness of their leadership should explain their brutal reaction at Rani Bodla camp of the Salwa Judum activists. To wit, 37 of the 68 killed there were the SPOs, the brave soldiers of Salwa Judum. Its founder and that brave tribal leader Mahendra Karma offers this interpretation of the intensified Naxalite attacks in his State. Even the Centre is believed to share Karma's thoughts on this issue.

In Odisha, where Naxal have their presence for many years by now, the state government wants to raise the Naxalite-infested districts from the nine identified as such in 2003, to 14. More significantly, the new areas facing Maoist violence include Devgarh, Sambalpur, Kandhamal, Jajpur, and Dhenkanal, essentially the regions that are either seeing development or fall within the so-called Red Corridor that reputedly extends from Pashupati (temple in Nepal) to Tirupati (temple in South India)— the two holy temples of Hindus, the inexplicable landmarks for the godless Naxalites!

DGP Odisha, A Patnaik, is not all that pessimistic: "The situation is under control. The number of incidents have gone up this year (2007) but the instances of violence have not. Figures are low compared to those obtaining in the neighbouring states, particularly in Chhattisgarh". The DGP ought to know that a little 'better' than the worst should not and cannot be a cause for complacency.

In fact, the warning bells could have been heard well before the 9th Congress. Figures put out by the MHA should tell the story:

- The total number of security forces men killed in Naxalite violence in the past two years was more than the fatalities in Jammu and Kashmir, or for that matter, in the North-East, during the same two-year period.
- The number of civilians killed in Naxalite violence is for more than those killed in the separatism-hit Jammu and Kashmir. The fatalites in the North-East marginally up till 31 March 2017.
- Yet, the total number of Naxalites killed by the security men is far less than the number of terrorists killed in J and K, or the militants killed in the North-East.

Multiplicity of Coordination Mechanism

There are a number, perhaps a plethora, of coordination mechanisms at the Centre to ensure certain degree of joint and cooperative inputs into anti-Naxal drive and operations. This very multiplicity might by coming in the way of efficient and effective coordination among the affected states in their counter-Maoist operations! Ironic that mechanisms created to help a cause end up hampering it! At least, the results so far suggest this contradiction! Notwithstanding all this, these mechanisms are listed here.

1. Empowered Group of Ministers (EGoM), headed by Union Home Minister Shivraj Patil.
2. A Standing Committee of the CM, of the Naxalism-hit states, again headed by Home Minister Patil.
3. National Coordination Centre on Naxalism (NCCN). It is headed by the Union Home Secretary and comprising of Chief Secretaries and the DGPs of all the 13 Naxal-hit states.
4. A task force headed by the Special Secretary (internal security) in the MHA.
5. An Inter-Ministerial Group (IMG) headed by Additional Secretary (Naxal Management), again in the MHA.

Some comments are called for on these committees. Most such committees are frozen into life-less formalities, wasteful entities. How do these committees function: Formal, periodic meetings, inane discussions, minutes prepared by a conscientious officer, typed and filed till the whole process is repeated at the next meeting. All these, rather such committees, tend to end into fossils after a while.

First, about the ministerial groups. At one look, the two can be merged into one, headed by the Home Minister. A couple of Chief Ministers from Naxal-hit states can be coopted into the EGoM, and that committee should be good enough to do the work of the both. The minutes can be circulated to concerned ministries at the Centre and all the CMs of Naxal-hit states. There is one more and major advantage of merging the two. The state CMs would hear the Central ministers' views on the issues concerning their states, and vice-versa. A strict compartmentalisation of the two is unnecessary, available superfluity.

One doesn't even know if a strong Home Minister would need these committees. If needed and necessary, he can pick up the phone and talk to his colleagues on the issue, and vice-versa. Can you imagine Sardar Patel working through such committees!

As for the three official-level committees, it is an unavoidable evil, called empire-building. If the Home Secretary heads a committee, why should his Additional Secretary and Special Secretary? To end it all, one committee under the Union Home Secretary should suffice! One is aware that all hell will break loose at such a suggestion, with weighty reasons for their separate existence and visions of catastrophe, if merged.

Purse strings

The Centre (read MHA) also has its hand on the purse strings, for certain specific funds. The MHA operates a Security Related Expenditure (SRE) scheme, under which the Centre reimburses the expenses incurred by the states on security measures/matters, including those on anti-Naxal operations. Strengthening and modernising police and its equipment is also covered under SRE. Over Rs 100 crore have been under this head in 2007 (this June), but "there is a concern over its improper utilisation, particularly, in states like Jharkhand and Chhattisgarh". That, if true, is indeed unfortunate, as these two states are worst-hit by Naxal violence. The Centre has also been helping the states in raising India Reserve Battalions (IRBs).

On the development front, there are two schemes: The Backward Districts Initiative (BDI) and the Backward Regions Grant Fund programme. Under the BDI, Rs 1,700 have been spent.

Finally, to the same old debate! "The Centre maintains it is up to the states to deal with situation on the ground. "Law and order, after all, is a state subject and we are providing all the assistance we can". This is a senior MHA official. It is, indeed, time they, at the Centre and in the MHA, give up this paternalistic mindset. In fact, it is worse: Feudalism, at its worst.

But to abandon such attitudes will be a long haul, and all agree on this one!

Progressive expanse of LWE and counter-measures by the states: An assessment: End 2006

This is the last item in this section of this chapter. It will discuss various related issues from various stock holders.

Are the States beating the Red terror: Oct 2006

Towards the last quarter of 2006, analysts were opining that the Ultra Left extremists of the CPI (Maoists) "are down but certainly not out". After the massacre of tribals in a relief camp at Errabore in Chhattisgarh in July 2006, the ultras have suffered a series of setbacks. In Andhra, the state police scored "a victory of sorts" when it killed Burra Chinnaiah, State Committee Secretary of the CPI (Maoist) and seven others in the Nallamalla jungles. Then it seized a cache of 42 rocket launchers, rockets and IEDs in Mahboobnagar and Prakasam districts.[17]

This is also a pointer to how the Maoists in different states after uniting under the rubric of CPI (Maoist), are working on a more ambitious strategy. Gone are the days when they targeted and gunned down landowners. Now, they are executing more audacious attacks on those opposing them, viz, the police generally, and jails occasionally, to free their comrades. Ironically, and significantly, most of these attacks, including the Giridih weapons loot and the Jehanabad jail break in 2005, were launched outside the State of Andhra Pradesh, the very State that remained a nursery of insurgency for nearly three decades.

The (Andhra) state police, having gained upper hand, helped essentially by more credible information about their movement with an exclusive intelligence gathering machinery and better combat tactics employed by the specialist anti-Maoist commando force, forced the ultras to shift base from North Telangana to other parts of Andhra and Chhattisgarh, besides the under-developed districts across the other neighbouring states.

Post-Andhra Pradesh Success

The Maoists have been particularly successful in Chhattisgarh, where the state-backed counter-insurgency formation, Salwa Judum, has suffered heavy casualties in Bastar Region. The innocent tribals, mostly Murias, have become easy targets ever-since they supported the movement that had pitted tribals against the Naxalites. With the ultras enjoying the support of the Gutti Koya Tribe in parts of the state, the conflict has turned into sectarian strife between the two tribes. "Most of the hardcore militants in Chhattisgarh are Andhra migrants", says CM Raman Singh, architect of the Salwa Judum movement. (Only partly true. The real founder and architect was a brave man Mahendra Karma, a Congressman. When CM Raman Singh assumed power, he took over the task of nurturing Judum from Karma). Andhra Pradesh CM YSR Rajasekhra Reddy says, "what is needed urgently is a common strategy that is implemented by all states".

Claims of the MHA; Counter-terror measures

After launching an inter-state coordinated offensive in the Naxal-hit areas in 2005, the MHA says that number of the 'affected' districts is down from 126 to only 50 and 509 police station areas. It is also raising a special combat forces comprising personnel from CPM forces and policemen from 13 affected states. Of the 14,000 to be enlisted, some 5000 will be ex-servicemen trained in combating terrorism and dealing with the IEDs and mines. Some 52 companies of the Provincial Armed Constabulary (PAC) and IRBs are being trained to carry out anti-Naxal tasks at the Army-run Kanker anti-insurgency school in Chhattisgarh. The Army is also providing inputs on explosive detection equipment and sophisticated jammers to the Naxalite-affected states.

Maoist claims and statistical data

The Maoists understandably would want to counter the changing perception about their strength by demonstrating their strike capabilities. They claim they wield influence in 165 districts of the countrys 602. They are avowdly planning to increase their areas of influence, particularly in Karnataka, Tamil Nadu and Uttaranchal. In states like Chhattisgarh, Jharkhand, MP, Odisha and Bihar, the focus of Naxalites are the backwoods and the tribal pockets where they whip up support citing neglect of the poor by the state.

Over 930 incidents claiming 486 lives occurred in 2006 (till mid-October) compared to 1,608 incidents in 2005.

Situation in Chhattisgarh

Critics have already dubbed Salwa Judum a failure. Repeated attacks by Naxals have forced 55,000 tribals to move into camps along a highway that runs through Bastar, vacating some 600 villages which have consequently fallen under the control of Naxalites. Worse still, those in the police are opting for posting in Bhilai, Bilaspur and Raipur. More than 50 per cent of the *thanas* in the Naxalite hit areas are without Station House Officers (SHOs). "The Salwa Judum has failed, the government has no alternative plan and poor tribals are left to be slaughtered", says former CM Ajit Jogi (obviously a subjective, even biased opinion). The police response seems to be knee-jerk. "Our main Challenges are the IEDs and the land-mines. We have now requisitioned trained dogs from the Army to detect mines", says DGP OP Rathore.

Situation in Bihar

Situation is no different in Bihar, the ultras has presence in 30 of the 38 districts. The absence of trained personnel and modern weapons is a major problem. DGP Ashish Ranjan Sinha has recalled 12 IPS officers on deputation to the Centre. "We are not short of funds but we do not have sufficient infrastructure", says Bihar's ADGP GS Rath.

MHA: Correctives and Counter measures

Concerned about the ability of the militants to garner support in the backward districts, the MHA has suggested intensive and rapid economic development of such areas. Unfortunately, the states have failed to use the funds under the Backward Districts Initiative. "Only Rs 990 crore of the Rs 2,295 crore made available in the past three years for 55 districts in nine states have been spent". The political changes in Nepal have emboldened the Maoists to go in for an upgrade to match up to the Rs 1,800 crore investment in modernisation of the state police forces by the MHA.

The regular interaction the MHA has with the police chiefs of the affected states have led to the launch of joint cross-border operations and the greater funding to contain the militants. Security and development are the elements of a holistic plan that is part of the changed strategy to deal with the ultras. The counter-insurgency operations, especially in Chhattisgarh, are to gain a new dimension with the deployment of a UAV to gather ground data on the movement of the militants. The IAF is to provide air support for taking up combing operations and to transport and evacuate security forces, air dropping of food and medicines.

Empowered Group of Minister (EGoM) setup

In his recent meeting (August 2006) with the CMs, PM Manmohan Singh announced his decision for the formation of an EGoM on the Naxalite issue and emphasised New Delhi's resolve to contain the Maoists: He said, "The states will now have to take up joint operations against them and

Central funding would not be wanting. When the inputs become available, it was for the states to get their act together".

How one wishes the insurgency situations were so simple and amenable to such routinely expressed resolve. It is again feudalistic mind set of the Centre, which was earlier on full flow when the Union Home Secretary spoke, and now finding expression from the nation's Prime Minister: "States must get their act together, the Centre will provide all the funds!" Does one see the Centre's concern to get involved to "contain" Maoists beyond giving funds?

Select Statistical Data: Maoist Violence

The text from time to time provides data on progressive expanse of the Maoist area, the weapons held by them, both from the official sources as well as Maoists. The two obviously would differ.

1.	Naxal-hit districts : MHA claims	50
2.	Naxal-hit districts : Maoist claim	165
3.	Naxal violence incidents in 2006 (till mid-Oct)	930
4.	Civilian fatalities in 2006 (till mid-Oct)	486
5.	Incidents in 2005,	1608
6.	Police fatalities in 2006 (till mid-Oct)	130
7.	Naxalites killed in 2006 (till mid-Oct)	454
8.	Total people killed in 2006 (till mid-Oct)	1070

(*Source:* India Today, 23 Oct 2006)

Countering Naxalism: Some select measures

Development

Fast-paced economic development in the Naxal-affected areas is seen as the main counter-dote to the Maoist insurrection. Special packages have been announced. Linking 12 violence-hit districts of Odisha by a two-lane state-of-the-art highway is seen as an effective way to bring development to these areas.

Coordinated operations

Coordinated effort at various levels has been set in motion to achieve better results. These are mentioned here:

1. EGoM, setup by the Prime Minister.
2. Anti-terrorist cell planned in the MHA.
3. Joint task force of Naxal-hit states, already functioning.
4. NCCN, under the Union Home Secretary.

5. Counter-Maoist cross-border operations to be jointly undertaken by more than one state as envisaged by the PM to become a practice.

Police modernisation

The MHA is investing Rs 1,800 crore for modernisation of the state police forces.

Tech Support

Some states like Chhattisgarh have requested the Centre for the (Unmanned) UAV to support combing and monitoring operations. Chhattisgarh is believed to have already got one.

Comments on counter-Naxal measures

There is nothing revolutionary or even unexpected in these measures. In fact, it will be an extreme simplification of a complex problem if the authorities believe these measures will suffice to contain—much less, defeat—the LWE in India. It is utterly unrealistic solution.

These measures even do not even mention 'political will' which is sine quo non to control and then defeat this—or, for that matter, any insurrection. Besides this huge omission, there are other factors that come in the way of resolving this complex problem facing India. It is briefly and pointedly mentioned here: "Given India's lackadaisical administration, corruption in public services and development projects, and personal attitude of *sab chalta hai* (it is difficult to translate this Indianness in English), defeating home-grown LWE will be much tougher and time-consuming than the terrorism sponsored from across the borders".

A patient, brick-by-brick approach, well thought-through and balanced and painstakingly executed, is the answer to this cancerous growth on the body politic of India, that is Bharat. High-sounding, verbose resolutions and pompous proclamations are the usual stuff bureaucrats and politicians take shelter behind when a purposeful and resolute action is required.

More importantly, India has historic responsibility to succeed. A few thousand Maoists and terrorists cannot break the edifice built with an iron will by the Great Sardar. Do we need another Patel today? Will it be Rajnath Singh? Only time will tell. It is a personal conviction of this author: "India cannot go under. Succeed it will".

An early resolution of these two problems will denote early end of the sufferings of the Common Man. Let us not forget: it is he who is at the receiving end, all the time!

(The above few lines is a personal note from the Author).

"Naxalism is States' problem" MHA Status Paper

It has been said earlier that the Centre (read, Government of India) thinks Maoist insurrection is State's problem, now it has been said through an official "Status paper" from the MHA.

> "The government has ruled out Centre's intervention in anti-Naxal operations, as law and order is a State subject. Instead, the Centre will help the affected States with equipment, weaponry, logistical support and intelligence inputs, to curb the menace".

This is what a recent status paper from the MHA tells the states, as reported by a daily of 23 December 2006. The Centre is not short of advice, nor of sermons, "Naxalism being on inter-state problem, the states will adopt a collective approach and pursue a coordinated response to counter it. The states will need to improve police response and pursue effective and sustained police action against the Naxalites and their infrastructure individually and jointly".

The status paper says the government has three-pronged strategy to tackle the Naxal menace. First, it will deal strictly with Naxals indulging in mindless violence. Secondly, since Naxalism is not merely a law and order issue, efforts would simultaneously be launched on the political, security, development and public perception management fronts. Thirdly, the government will focus on socio-economic development of the backward regions, which are prone to Naxal influence.

This paper makes it clear that government will not enter into dialogue unless the Maoists lay down arms. At a parallel level, government wants the political parties to strengthen their cadre base in Naxal-infested areas, so that the youth can be weaned away from the path of Naxal ideology.

Special focus is on accelerated socio-economic development of the backward areas and regular interaction with the NGOs, intelligentsia and civil liberties groups, in order to minimise the overground support for the Maoist ideology and activity.

Significantly, the status paper approves of the Salwa Judum approach to build up people's resistance against the Maoists and their violence it adds: "Efforts will continue to be made to promote voluntary local resistance groups against the Maoists, but in a manner that the villagers are provided adequate security cover and the area is effectively dominated by the security forces."[18]

It further adds: "The states should announce a suitable transfer policy for the Naxal-hit districts. Willing, committed and competent officers will need to be posted with a stable tenure in these districts. These officers will also need to be given greater delegation and flexibility to deliver better and step up government presence and above all improve governance in these areas."

Will the Naxals join mainstream?

A senior operative of CPI (Maoist) contested the 29 March 2007 Palamu Parliamentary by-polls on the BSP ticket while lodged in the Garhwa Jail.

Kameshwar Baitha is the first senior leader of the outlawed party to take party in the democratic polls. Baitha, a former Area Commander of CPI (Maoists), finished a close second, 22,327 votes behind the winner, Ghuran Ram of the RJD. Incidentally, Baitha joined the BSP (in Jharkhand) just before these polls, held on 29 March 2007.

The fact of a former senior leader/cadre fighting elections made news, giving rise to the questions like the one contained in the headline of this news story. Analysts are already speculating: "With the Maoists in Nepal laying down their arms and entering the electoral arena, could the same be happening in Jharkhand after a Maoist, fighting polls from a jail, came a close second in the 29 March elections? Is its any sign of the Party edging towards the mainstream politics?

These seems to be no longer theoretical questions or possibilities. Nor could it be dismissed as mere kite flying. The reasoning behind such analytical story is simple: Baitha could not have joined the electoral fray without a nod from the Party leadership.

A glance at his active past is rather frightening, literally. During those days, Baitha's depredations spread across the border regions of Bihar, Jharkhand and UP for 24 long years. As a scribe puts it: "His name would send a chill down the spine of any police officer in the region". As the records show, soon after his arrest, several additional cases of murder, ammunition looting, forcible collection of money and other crimes were registered against him. Therefore, it should come as no surprise that presently, Baitha is being tried by the courts for the 78 such cases against him. With all these cases against him, Baitha would have spent the rest of his life in jail, almost anonymously, like so many other rebels spending their days in various jails, unknown unsung! All this stands changed for Baitha. His debut in the Parliamentary democracy has brought the limelight back on him!

More interesting and even surprising is the fact of so many people voting for him! It needs serious examination by analysts and academics.

Speaking to the daily from the Garhwa Jail where he is presently serving his term, Baitha sounded confident to clinch the Parliamentary seat if another chance comes his way. In fact, he is already speaking like a seasoned politician:

> "Yes, I was an extremist, even little kids know that. But, so what? The day I joined BSP, I left everything behind. I have documented my feelings in my brochure, which I wrote from this cell, and have circulated among the electorate of Palamu. Today, I strongly feel that to voice one's demands or to speak out for justice and development, one has to go through laid down systems. The tomorrow of Palamu is BSP and people of this area know me and my ways of dealing with things".[19]

Can one imagine it is an ex-Maoist speaking? In fact, he is a Maoist, speaking from Jail. He is so confident of what all he says. "To work the system, all that matters is how best you can serve your constituency and the people at large. Out there, they know that I can deliver", the bespectacled leader added, pointing towards the gate of the jail, May be, he has reasons for speaking in such a self-assured manner.

Now a word on the voting pattern in various Assembly segments of the Parliamentary Constituency of Palamu. He led by comfortable margins from Vishrampur and Bhavnathpur Assembly segments and was close on the heels of the RJD candidate after the votes from Garhwa, Husseinabad and Chhattarpur Assembly segments were counted.

Here is a political observer speaking from Ranchi: "Mr Baitha's contesting of Palamu by-elections is a significant thing in the history of the Maoist extremism. Until now, no senior operative, other than Kameshwar Baitha, has contested any form of elections. It is clear indication that there is tacit support from the Maoist leadership behind the entire process".

For the State and Central security and intelligence agencies, there is nothing to do except wait in the wings. Presently, there is no straw in the wind to indicate any trend. Till date (August 2007), there has been no development on this front. May be, the analysts will have to wait till early 2009 when the next parliamentary polls are due in the country to know if the Indian Maoists will go the Nepal way.

Post-9th Congress Situation Spread of the LWE Areas June 2007

The Congress was held for a month in Jan-Feb 2007. The latest situation as assessed by the analysts mid-2007 is depicted below.

Affected States (in the order given)

Chhattisgarh

Jharkhand

Odisha

Bihar

West Bengal

Andhra Pradesh

Karnataka

Maharashtra

MP

New Presence

Kerala Tamil Nadu UP Uttarakhand Delhi Haryana Punjab	Naxalites are learnt to have set up regional Committees in these states, a departure from their earlier practice of operating through legitimate over-ground organisations. It could be the result of decision taken at the Jan-Feb 2007, 9th congress of the CPI (Maoists).

Maoist Armed Cadre Mid-2007 and Worst-affected areas

Some 13,000-14,000 Left extremists are believed to be active in 185 districts across 16 states. Their strength was placed at 9,000 two years ago.

Some worst-affected areas, of late, as indicated by various sources are indicated hereafter.

Chhattisgarh	Rani Bodla, Bijapur district in Bastar Region.
Jharkhand	East Singhbhum district
Uttar Pradesh	Sonbhadra and Mirzapur districts
Karnataka	Western Ghats, Shimoga, Chikmagalur, Dakshina Kannada, and Udupic
Odisha	Deogarh, Sambalpur, Kandhamal, Jajpur and Dhenkenal.

Miscellaneous Information: Statistics

Fatalities: Naxalite violence

Sr.No.	*Category*	*2005*	*2006*	*2007 (till June)*
1.	Civilians	524	521	118
2.	Security Forces	153	157	91
3.	Total (1+2)	677	678	209
4.	Maoists	225	272	52
5.	Grand Total (3+4)	902	950	261

Fatalities: Jammu and Kashmir

Sr.No.	*Category*	*2005*	*2006*	*2007 (till June)*
1.	Civilians	557	389	37
2.	Security Forces	189	151	30
3.	Total (1+2)	746	540	67
4.	Militants	917	593	70
5.	Grand Total (3+4)	1663	1133	137

Fatalities: North-East

Sr.No.	*Category*	*2005*	*2006*	*2007 (till June)*
1.	Civilians	393	309	148
2.	Security Forces	70	76	30
3.	Total (1+2)	463	385	178
4.	Militants	406	395	114
5.	Grand Total (3+4)	869	780	292

Fatalities: Security Forces

Sr. No.	*Category*	*2005*	*2006*	*2007 (till June)*	*Total*
1.	Naxalite Violence	153	157	91	401
2.	Jammu and Kashmir	189	151	30	370
3.	North-East	70	76	30	176

Fatalites: Civilians

Sr. No.	*Category*	*2005*	*2006*	*2007 (till June)*	*Total*
1.	Naxalite Violence	524	521	118	1163
2.	Jammu and Kashmir	557	389	37	983
3.	North East	393	309	148	850

Fatalites: Naxalites/Militants

Sr. No.	*Category*	*2005*	*2006*	*2007 (till June)*	*Total*
1.	Naxalite	225	272	52	549
2.	Militants Jammu and Kashmir	917	593	70	1580
3.	Militants North East	406	395	114	915

(*Source:* These six tables above: Sunday Express, 22 July 2007).

Notes

1. Sumanta Banerje, "Naxalbari: Between past and Future", *Economic and Political Weekly,* 37, No. 22, (1-7 June, 2002): 2115-16.
2. Daniel J. Christie, "Reducing Direct and Structural Violence: The Human Needs Theory.
3. John W. Burton, *Violence Explained* (New York: StMartin's Press, 1997), 33.
4. *Ibid.*
5. Sudha Ramachandra, VR Raghavan Ed, p. 34.
6. Ramchandra Guha, "Adivasis Naxalites and Indian Democracy", Economic and Political Weekly, 11-17 Aug. 2007.
7. VR Raghavan, Ed, "The Naxal Threat" (Vij Books India, New Delhi) p. 37.
8. India Today, caught between Robbers and killers; 25.7.11.
9. The Hindu, 12 Jan 2007.
10. R Prasannan, The week, 11 Jun 2006.
11. Maj Gen Ashok Mehta, cited *ibid.*
12. *Ibid.*
13. Bhavna Vij Aurora, The Outlook, 15 May 2006.
14. *Ibid.*
15. The Outlook, 26 May 2006.
16. Vinay Jha, Indian Express, 22 Jul 200
17. Amarnath K. Menon and Neeraj Mishra, Indi Today 23 Oct, 2006.
18. Venkat Parsa, Asian Age, 23 Dec 2006.
19. Dipankar Bose, The Statesman, 6 April 2007.

6

The Expanding Red Corridor Maoist Tactics and Policies

Maoist aim is clear and claimed loudly: To take over the State power by displacing the democratically elected government through means of murderous act and violent. Undoubtedly, the tribal areas in the Central and Eastern India have not been beneficiaries of economic and social advancement since 1947 as have been the rest of the country. There is poverty and deprivation in these regions, the conditions favourable for LWE to make inroads there. And Maoists have skillfully and successfully exploited in the field that provided them the opportunity. As for the tactics, strategies and policies of the ultras, that enabled them to create a Red corridor in India from Tirupati to Pashupati Nath, to use a popular and highly symbolic phrase; these will be discussed in the succeeding pages.

To put it briefly, the Maoists started gaining progressively in their influence and territory by 2001 onwards. The merger of the PWG and MCC in September 2004 to create CPI (Maoist) was a major game changer in their fortunes. They never saw back after that denoument, post which they made great gains in expanding the Red Corridor. It reached its bloodiest peak with maximum casualties in 2009-10. Since then the blood sport has continued. If the government has been trying to deliver development to the tribal regions, the Maoist continues to obstruct and hamper the process. Besides the usual cat and mouse games that go on, they have succeeded in staging headlines grabbing events occasionally, like the one when they decimated entire leadership of the Chhattisgarh and another when they eliminated 76 Policemen in a single attack.

There are still problems and hurdles in the way of stemming and rolling back the Red Zone, which will be discussed in the latter chapters.

This chapter will also show the progressive expansion of the Red areas in the country. Explained below are the basic tenets of the CPI (Maoists).

Basics of the CPI (Maoists)

Here are the essential information and facts about the CPI (Maoist) in the brief.

CPI (Maoist). Founded on 21st September 2004 through the merger of the People's War Group (PWG) and the Maoist Communist Centre (MCC) are explained above.

Philosophy. It rejects parliamentary democracy and aims to capture political power through protracted armed struggle.

Goal. Seizure of political power and the settlement of the issue through protracted people's war.

Tactics. Organise an army, establish own state.

- Build bases in rural areas and transform them into "Liberated Zones".
- Military strategies include guerrilla war, mobile war and positional war.

Trends and weapons

Maoists have graduated to mobile warfare stage; moving in military formations supported by 300 members of Jan militia (village-level rebel body).

A Maoist military company will have a minimum of three light machine guns (LMGs), 15 automatic rifles, an assortment of self-loading rifles, 0.315 and 0.303 rifles, mortars, rockets and grenades.

The Expanding Red Corridor: statistically speaking

This section will indicate statistically the spread of the Maoist-infected areas at progressive stages in territorial terms and time schedules.

A snapshot

In 1967, one wing of the Indian Communism gave up the path of democracy, initiated by the veteran Namboodripad in Kerala, and took to armed struggle to achieve its goal of revolution. It needs to be mentioned and emphasised here itself that this communist group Naxals, CPI (M), was aligned to the Chinese Communist Party (CCP). Expectedly, after the formation of this ultra-Left group and its initial violent inception, its leaders went all the way to China to pay obeisance to the great oarsman and to ask for some lessons for their future course of action in Indian Conditions. It must be understood that post-1962 Chinese attack on India, the communists had split on the issue whether China was an aggressor in the event. It split into the CPI and CPI (M), the latter always pro-China ever since, following the CCP line in national and international affairs.

Here are important events and dates from the very inception of the Naxal movement, through its transformation into the Maoist Revolution, to the present days.

- **May 1967.** Police firing kills 11 at Naxalbari in Darjeeling district of West Bengal. Internal struggle intensifies in CPI (M) over land rights movement.
- **1968.** Following the Burdwan conference of the CPI (M), one faction splits and establishes all India Coordination Committee of the Communist Revolutionaries (AICC-CR).
- **April 1969.** CPI (Marxist-Leninist) formed, with Charu Mazumdar as General Secretary. Ultra-Left movement, taking Mao Zedong as guru, starts spreading. To put it in perspective, Kondapalli Sitharamaiah had been leading a leftist agitation in Andhra's Srikakulam district since 1961, and by the time Charu formed CPI (ML), the two of them obviously had come closer.
- **October 1969.** Dakshin Desh Group formed by Kanai Chatterjee and Amulya Sen.
- **July 1972.** Charu Mazumdar dies, CPI (ML) splits into many factions.
- **1975.** Dakshin Desh renamed Maoists Communist Centre (MCC).
- **April 1980.** CPI (ML) (people's war) formed with Kondapalli Sitharamaiah as General Secretary.
- **1982.** CPI (ML) (party unity-pu) formed with N Prasad as General Secretary
- **September 1993.** CPI (ML) (PW), MCC and CPI (ML) (pu) join hands to form all India people's Resistance forum.
- **April 1998.** CPI (ML) (Pu) merged with CPI (ML) (PW).
- **2003.** MCC merges with Revolutionary Communist Party of India (Maoist) and CPI (ML) (CC) to form MCC of India (MCCI).
- **21 September 2004.** CPI (ML) (PW) and MCCI merge to form the CPI (Maoist).
- **2011 (November).** Politburo member Kishenji killed in an encounter in West Midnapur, West Bengal.[1]

Spread of LWE

Ways and methods till 2007

The progressive spread of LWE its latest avatar or version being Naxalism followed by Maoism—is important to be noted and studied. Let us start with the MHA Report.

MHA report of April 2006

The report confirmed an increase in the number of attacks by the LWE. The police casualty has gone up by 53 per cent and civilian by 11 per cent.

9 Worst-hit States

The table below shows the attacks and relevant casualty data for the Nine worst–hit states: Chhattisgarh, Jharkhand, Bihar, AP, Maharashtra, West Bengal, Odisha, MP and UP.

Nine S: Maoist Violence : 2002-2006

Year	*Maoists attacks*	*Killed*		
		Civilians	*Policemen*	*Maoist*
2002	1,465	382	100	141
2003	1,597	410	105	216
2004	1,533	466	100	87
2005	1,594	516	153	223
2006 Till 30 Apr	**550**	**219**	**62**	**93**

Source: MHA Report, April 2006.

Naxalite Violence: 2006: AC HR Report

As many as 749 people were killed in the Naxalite violence during the 2006, says the Asian Centre for Human Rights (ACHR) Report (for 2006) released on 10 January 2007 in New Delhi.[2]

The Report, "Naxal Conflict in 2006", gives the break down of these 749 fatalities:

Civilian	285
Security Persons	135
Naxalites (alleged)	329
Total	**749**

State-wise Killings

Chhattisgarh	363
AP	135
Jharkhand	95
Maharashtra	60
Bihar	45
Odisha	25
West Bengal	22
UP	2
Karnataka	1
MP	1
Total	**749**

Yearly Figures

2005 A total of 1608 incidents of Naxal violence were reported from 460 police stations in 11 states.

2006 The figure for 2006 dipped slightly to 1509 incidents that were reported from 395 police station which is 4.65 per cent of the total number of 8,488 police stations in the affected 11 states.

Compared to 2005 when 892 people lost their lives, there was a decrease in killings during 2006 (749). "But the Salwa Judum campaign and its disastrous consequences, such as the riths violations by the Naxalites, the security forces and salwa Judum activists, captured centre stage" during the year (2006).

The Report said the Campaign led to the forcible displacent of 43,470 persons as of Dec 2006 in Dantewada district, the spread of conflict to 1,427 police station, and an increase in the striking capability of the Naxalites.

"These acts of Maoists Constitute serious violations of the Geneva Conventions and the Rome Statute of the International Criminal Court," says Suhas Chakma, Director ACHR.

Ironically, the Naxalite who frown at the lack of development in the tribal areas, are blocking several development initiatives and projects in these very areas, where they exercise control by targeting labourers, officials, contractors and companies. They were systematically targeting all government buildings that could provide shelter to security persons.

125 Naxal-Hit Districts

September 2007

Bihar	25
Jharkhand	20
AP	19
Odisha	14
Chhattisgarh	10
West Bengal	9
MP	6
Maharashtra	6
UP	6
Karnataka	5
Kerala	2
Uttarakhand	2
Tamil Nadu	1

Source: Recognised by the Planning Commission as such; Times of India, 22 September 2007.

March of the 'Red Army': Status Report: 2006

India is not known to have dealt effectively with the terrorism within its territory. The Same can more or less, be said about LWE in India. Till recently, the Central Government was not serious about LWE, dismissing it as law and order problem. Of late, it is more than simple law and order issue, with PM Manmohan Singh declaring it most serious threat to India's internal security.[3]

Extent of Spread of Maoist Influence

"A big chunk of Central India is fully under control of the Naxalites, Maoists or whatever they may be called locally. It is their writ—and not that of the Indian State—that runs in 92,000 sq km from Gadchiroli in Maharashtra to Abujh Maad in Chhattigarh. They make the laws and implement them. The State and its mechanisms are simply off the radar in these parts of India".

The above is truth, disturbing and unpalatable but truth all the same; it is stark even if a bit exaggerated and padded up!

That is not all. Here is what Ajay Sahni of the KPS Gilled Institute for Conflict Management, New Delhi, says: "while a huge chunk has already been lost, if the government does not wake up, there is further danger of losing more. Large parts of Chhattisgarh, Odisha, Jharkhand and West Bengal are already under the influnce of Maoists and close to being completely over run".

The Red Corridor, extending from Nepal down to Andhra Pradesh, encompassing nine states, has been categorised by the MHA as "badly affected" by Maoists Violence.

Strength and Weaponry

Official estimates peg the armed strength of Maoist cadre at some 10,000 and overground sympathisers and workers around 45,000. Security experts put the number at much higher level.

What lends the Maoist a deadly edge is the fact that they are armed with deadly weaponry. Here is some factual information, rather disturbing.

They are equipped with

- AK-47s
- IEDs
- INSAS and SLRs.
- In 2005 and 2006, they claimed 677 and 678 lives respectively. In either year, the fatalites are higher than those in J and K and the North-East put together.
- In the first four months of 2006, they had killed 130 persons, including the security men and civilians.
- 160 districts designated "most affected" by LWE. It is 27 per cent of the total number of districts in India

Official recognition that India has a full blown crisis at hand came mid-June 2006 when PM Manmohan Singh admitted that 160 districts across the country are slipping out of government control. He admitted that Maoists problem has assumed proportions larger than militancy in J and K and insurgency in the North-East due its sheer spread and organised linkages.

Maoists threat must be taken seriously, particularly so in view of their plans to expand their influence in the next five years. Documents of the Central Military Commission (CMC) of the CPI (Maoists) seized by the intelligence agencies in February 2006, revealed plans to set up their military commands in the following unchartered territories:

- Delhi
- Haryana

- Punjab
- UP
- Uttaranchal, and to extend the violence to urban areas and to target industries. Finally, they have ambitious plans to control 30 per cent of the country in next five years.

Reasons for spread and problems of combating Naxalism

As law and order is a state subject, the centre all along tried to keep its role minimal, stepping in only to supervise and help with additional forces and finances. But of late the union MHA has realised that it is more than a mere law and order problems. Consequently, it has worked out an anti-Maoist strategy, as it is summed up here:

- Acknowledge it to be more than a law and order problem, decided to pursue a holistic approach, simultaneously focusing on development, employment and land distribution.
- Provide funds to affected areas to modernise the police, improve infrastructure, acquire weapons and communication equipments.
- States must follow the Andhra Pradesh model where the states succeeded in checking the Maoists by raising Special Forces.
- Start people's movements like the Salwa Judum in Chhattisgarh, to counter the Maoists.
- Deploy security forces in worst hit areas. Centre bears cost for three years.
- Increase employment opportunities by earmarking 40 per cent recruitment in CPMF for Naxal affected areas.
- Allocated ₹ 2,475 cr for 55 worst hit districts under the Backward District Initiative.
- Ensure a collective and co-ordinated approach and response from the States.

Question of political will takes centre stage. Lack of political will to act poses problems. Sahni writes: "It is a well known secret that politicians have used Maoists for their vested interests". He cites the example of Andhra Pradesh which has a long history of politicians hobnobbing with the Maoists. "NT Rama Rao did it. He even described the Maoists as 'Deshbhaktalu' (=Patriots). Subsequently, the Congress, under Chenna Reddy, did it. In recent years, Congress ally TRS has been accused of having struck a deal with Maoists before the 2004 General Election", he says. In Bihar, politicians are known to have used both—the MCC and the Ranvir Sena of upper caste Bhumihars – for political ends.

Likewise, the Salwa Judum seen by many as a successful anti-Naxal civil society initiative has become controvertial essentially because Liberal Intellectual Elite and some NGOs have started criticising the Salwa Judum for Pitting tribals against the Naxal as 'cannon fodder'.

In fact, the Union Home Secretary told a weekly in May 2006 that "the Chhattisgarh Government has been asked to stop the Salwa Judum till it can consolidate the group and arm them better, adding, "The state of Chhatisgarh is being treated as a testing ground by the government. If the Salwa Judum experiment succeed there then it will be replicated elsewhere."

Even more surprising is the fact that the states facing the most Naxal violence do not have the police forces even up to their authorised strength. The lacuna is inexplicable, knowing as we do that the security experts believe that even the present authorised police strength is not good enough to combat the Naxal violence. The states like Chhattisgarh and Jharkhand must be sanctioned additional police far over and above their currently authorised strength to mount an effective anti-Naxal drive. Against the advice and argument for additional police strength, some such states are, in fact, short of their authorised strengths; and this shortage, for example, is 4,000 in case of Chhattisgarh and 20,000 in case of Bihar! And to wit, these figures come from Union Home Secretary Duggal.

Some experts have expressed doubts about so many affected states achieving any credible measure of co-ordination in their anti-Naxal operations. The solution, they suggest lies in the Centre assuming a greater role ensuring this co-ordination to tackle this problem. Here is a suggestion, unusual and difficult in a federal set up of the Indian polity, from the former IB Director AK Doval: "The right strategy will be for the Centre to move into the Worst-affected Pockets, take over the administration and make roads, set up schools and other infrastructure. Each state has a different problem. Just giving extra forces and funds will not help, tough decisions and tough measures are required. Once the state establishes its presence in the affected districts, then the development work can be taken up.

There is something difficult in accepting Doval's views! How does the Centre supplant a state in district administration? How and why should the Centre undertake this chore? How is the Central bureaucracy better qualified to do it than the state officials? The latter knows the area better, know the problems better and consequently can even do that job better.

The only way the centre can help is to give requisite forces to the states so that the states can not only proceed with the construction and development projects under their protection but also engage the Maoists against their violent attacks on their targets, civilians or police forces. So the development and anti-Naxal fight must proceed simultaneously.

CPI (Maiost) 9th Congress and its aftermath

Before the details of deliberations of the 9th Maoists congress are criticiqued, it is intresting to note that some analysts have credited the success achieved by the CPI (Maoist) and the scale of terror unleashed by its cadres to this Congress. It has compelled the Central Government to formulate a cohesive anti-Naxal strategy detailed above. Now to the 9th congress.

A month long 9th CPI (Maoist) congress Jan-Feb 2007 was held in a secured liberated zone ('Muktanchal' in their parlance) along the Jharkhand-Odisha border after a long interregnum of over three decades. Attended by top leaders, it mulled over long-term strategic goals as also a list of what all they planned over the next few months.

Some six months down the line, the militant cadre is going about their assigned tasks in a manner at once methodical and chilling, convincing the power that be and also security forces that the Maoists means business. The message from the conclave was loud and clear: While they would continue with their tried and tested methods of armed struggle, the major new decision was to offer all out resistance to the mega projects including steel and bauxite projects in Odisha, Chhattisgarh and Andhra Pradesh as also the SEZs planned in other regions. Their reason: They were leading to "Massive displacement and marginalisation" of the Adivasis and farmers.[5]

The clarion call from the 9th Congress translated into: A major mobilisation exercise to augment the strength of the Naxalite cadre, to enable them to establish a presence in the areas they had been absent or inactive from; sourcing of arms and a 49- hour economic blockade in June (2007) that paralysed life in parts of Chhattisgarh, Jharkhand, Bihar and West Bengal.

The latest intelligence inputs indicate that Maoists "have managed footholds around cities and industrial hubs in Haryana, Punjab and Delhi". That they were planning to extend their activities to these areas was also clear from their Central military commission documents seized in 2006. Besides these newer areas, parts of UP, particularly Sonebhadra and Mirzapur, and Uttarakhand have also reported the presence of Maoists. As for the south the Maoist activities do not end at the borders of Andhra Pradesh, having across in to Karnataka and Tamil Nadu.

The result of the latest mobilizations:

- 185 districts across the nine states of the union have now Red footprints.
- When the Maoists are not engaged in major attacks, they are busy consolidating, Chhattisgarh being an example of this.

The state Government sees this increased attention as a sign of success of their Salwa Judum campaign as also an indication of frustration in the Naxal camp as a result. Hence, the brutal reaction as at Rani Bodla. They claim to be teaching a lesson to the State and Salwa Judum activists. To wit, 37 of the 68 killed there were the SPOs. Even Mahendra Karma founder of the Judum, himself offer this interoperation of the intensified Naxal attacks in his state. Even the Centre is known to accept this view on this issue.

- In Odisha, where the Maoists have had their presence for several years by now the State Government wants to raise the number of Maoist hit districts from nine identified as such in 2003 to 14. Significantly new areas facing the Naxal heat include Devgarh, Sambalpur, Kandhamal, Jajpur and Dhenkanal, essentially the regions that are presently witnessing development or fall within the so called Red Corridor, reputedly extending from Pashupati to Tirupati, inexplicable landmarks both being highly venerated Hindu temples, to the Godless Maoists.

Statistical and miscellaneous Information

Relevant information on the Naxalite movement is given here

Fatalities: Naxalite Violence

Category	*2005*	*2006*	*2007 (till June)*
Civilians	524	521	118
Security Forces	153	157	91
Total (1+2)	677	678	209
Naxalite	225	272	52
Grand Total (3+4)	902	950	261

Fatalities: Jammu and Kashmir

Category	*2005*	*2006*	*2007 (till June)*
Civilians	557	389	37
Security Forces	189	151	30
Total (1+2)	746	540	67
Militants	917	593	70
Grand Total (3+4)	1663	1133	137

Fatalities: North –East

Category	*2005*	*2006*	*2007 (till June)*
Civilians	393	309	148
Security Forces	70	76	30
Total (1+2)	463	385	178
Militants	406	395	114
Grand Total (3+4)	869	780	292

Fatalities: Security Forces

Category	*2005*	*2006*	*2007 (till June)*	*Total*
Naxalite Violence	153	157	91	401
Jammu and Kashmir	189	151	30	370
North-East	70	76	30	176

Fatalities: Civilians

Category	*2005*	*2006*	*2007 (till June)*	*Total*
Naxalite Violence	524	521	118	1163
Jammu and Kashmir	557	389	37	983
North-East	393	309	148	850

Fatalities: Naxalites/Militants

Category	*2005*	*2006*	*2007 (till June)*	*Total*
Naxalites	225	272	52	549
Militants Jammu and Kashmir	917	593	70	1580
Militants North-East	406	395	114	915

Source: Six tables above: Sunday Express, 22 July 2007.

Maoist Moblisation consequent to their 9th Congress: Jan-Feb 2007

Nine states were already affected by the Maoist insurgency, namely: Chhattisgarh, Jharkhand, Odisha, Bihar, West Bengal, Andhra Pradesh, Karnataka, Maharashtra and MP. This is more or less in the descending order of intensity of the Maoist violence

New Presence

The Extension of their influence to the newer areas is always an ongoing process. It should not be understood to have started with the decisions taken at their 9th congress. At this Congress, they possibly decided to add greater emphasis and vigour to impell and extend this influence in the newer areas. This is summed up there.

New presence

Kerala	Naxalites are learnt to have
Tamil Nadu	set up regional committees in
UP	these states, a departure
Uttrakhand	from their earlier practices of
Delhi	operating through legitimate overground
Haryana	organisation. It could be the result of decision
Punjab	taken at the 9th congress Jan-Feb 2007

Report on their Strength : Mid 2007

Affected districts and cadre strength

Some 13,000 to 14,000 Maoist cadres are believed to be active in 125 districts across the 13 states named above.

Two years back, their cadre strength was pegged at some 9,000 by the intelligence agencies.

Some of the Worst affected areas/Districts in States

Chhattisgarh	Rani Bodli, Bijapur district in Bastar region
Jharkhand	East Singhbhun district.
UP	Sonebhadra and Mirzapur districts.
Karnataka	Western Ghats, Shimoga, Chikamagalur, Dakshina Kannada and Udupi
Odisha	Deogarh, Sambalpur, Kandhamal, Jaipur and Dhenkanal

Select Statitical Data October 2006

1.	Naxal-affected districts as claimed by MHA	50
2.	Districts under their control as claimed by CPI (Maoist)	165
3.	Incidents of Maoist violence in 2006 (till mid-Oct)	930
4.	Incidents of Maoist violence in 2005	1608
5.	Civilians lives lost in 2006 (till mid-Oct)	486
6.	Security forces lives lost in 2006 (till mid-Oct)	130

7. Naxalite killed in 2006 (till mid-Oct) 454
8. Total People Killed in Naxalite violence in 2006 (till mid-Oct) 1070

Source: India Today, 23 October 2006

Augmented strength and Strike Power Mid 2007

Their military strength estimated at 25,000 cadre, well trained and highly motivated. Unlike earlier times, a good percentage of their cadre is well educated including those holding professional skills and post graduate degree. The sophistication has added immensely to the striking power of the Naxalites.

The increased strength and its effective and efficient use was on the display in the recent years. Some of the recent incidents are recounted here at random to highlight this aspect of their strength and efficient organisation:

- **6 Feb 2004:** A group of 200 Maoists swooped upon the district armoury at Koraput and made away with 500 weapons.
- **11 Feb 2005:** Some 250 males and 50 females cadres of CPI (Maoist) suddenly descended on a Karnataka police camp killing Six Policeman and looting 10 rifles. In the same manner, some 300 Maoists attacked Madhubani, Bihar, shot dead five policemen and plundered arms as well as the nationalised bank.
- **13 Nov 2005:** Some 1,000 disciplined Maoist cadres staged a well-planned and well-executed night attack on Jehanabad, some 50 Km from Bihar's capital of Patna. They were in virtual control of the city for several hours. They freed 340 prisoners from the jail including their comrades and their leader Ajay Kanu; and killed two leaders of the Ranveer Sena Lodged in the same jail. The attacks on the Jail, police lines and offices of the district headquarters were carried out simultaneously.

Some analyst concluded that the mass support of the rural hinterland of Jehanabad was obvious for the raiders, since there was hardly any resistance. This averment and conclusion beg a question, are inane and facetious. They expect unarmed tribal's to come and oppose the murderous Maoists, well-armed and motivated.

- In another raid on the Home Guards Training Centre, Giridih, Jharkhand, some 200 weapons were looted.
- 3 Dec 2006. 14 Policemen of the Special Task Force were killed in a landmine explosion.

- 15 March 2007: This is the last serious crime to be included in the list here.
- Some 400-450 Maoists attacked a base camp at Rani Bodli, Bastar and systematically killed 68, effectively making use of petrol bombs. 38 civilians SPOs killed in the attack belonged to the Salwa Judum Campaign of Chhattisgarh.

These murderous incidents—(attacks is the right word) are recorded to show the deadly intent and military precision the Maoists marauders are capable of bearing upon their operational forays against the security forces and civilians alike. They are not only indicative of their increased numerical strength but also the enhanced sophistication of their weaponry and tactics and overall strategic planning.

The new strategy obviously is to incite and exploit people's resentment against the police. Some analysts go beyond that averment and assert that "the new strategy is to pit the police against the masses, who have rightly or wrongly been made to believe that they are victims of injustice and inequity". Besides this, the brutality of attacks and rough and ready justice is meant to convey a message to the people targeted in their attacks. Sunil Mahato and Salwa Judum activists were killed because they were 'guilty' of taking a public stand against it. The message and logic is simple: How dare you oppose the Maoist movement?

Enlarging the Red Corridor, Menacingly

Is it because of people's empathy with their movement, or because of their murderous and violent ways, that the area of Red Corridor is expanding rather fast? The following figures tell the story of this expansion, and one can draw ones own conclusion on the said question.

1. From 156 districts in 13 states in September 2004, the Maoist violence spread to 170 districts in 15 states by February 2005.
2. The above are official figures. The informed analysts assert that as of now–August 2007–186 districts in 16 states have certain presence of Maoists.
3. Yet again, here are government's IB figures: At present, some 40 per cent of the geographical area of the country and 35 per cent of its population is affected by the Maoist violence.

The Red Corridor, extending from the jungles of North Bihar to Jharkhand, odisha, Chhattisgarh, Andhra Pradesh, Maharashtra and Karnataka is fast emerging. The MHA Annual Report 2004-05 admits as much: "Despite strenuous efforts by security forces, there has been no let up in the effectuation of Compact Revolutionary Zone (CRZ) with the gaps in North Bihar and North Chhattisgarh being steadily plugged by the Naxalite outfits to link up with their strong holds in AP- Dandakaranya with those in Bihar–Jharkhand. Coupled with the Steadily increasing Naxalite influence in North odisha- South east Jharkhand, it is apparent that the Naxalite groups remain steadfast in their efforts to realise the CRZ.

The objective is to establish a CRZ in the heart of India and use this Zone and the Red Corridor for extending the Naxalite movement to the cities and ultimately to seize the power structure of the states. The ultimate goal, of course, remains the establishment of the Maoist state, no matter how many bones are broken and how much blood is spilled on the way.

As of now, the said MHA report is two years old. In the interregnum, the CPI (Maoist) seems to have not only filled the gaps as mentioned above, it has also chartered its further advances. One needs not look far and wide for the evidence to see the advance made by the ultra left outfits since the said MHA report. A brief look at the deliberations and decisions taken at the two landmark events planned and staged by the CPI (Maoist) should suffice to convince the scholars, analysts and even the skeptics about the success of their planned course.

The two are: the 9th Congress of the CPI (Maoists) held during the Jan-Feb 2007 conclave held in the Muktanchal (= Liberated Zone) along the Jharkhand-Bihar border at a 'secured site', and the Central Military commission (CMC) session of 2006. These are:

1. They will advance further into the south beyond the current limit of Andhra Pradesh, into the States of Karnataka and Tamil Nadu.
2. The CPI (Maoist) decided to extend their activities to urban areas and industrial areas, going against the teaching of Mao who laid down consolidation and occupation of rural area (villages) and countryside before focusing on the cities and urban areas.
3. The CMC resolved to set up zonal committees in the new areas like Delhi, Punjab and Haryana.
4. The CMC also decided to convert the People's Guerrilla Liberation Army (PGLA) in to the People's Liberation Army (PLA).

What is important is that State and Central Governments must keep pace with the ever advancing plans of the CPI (Maoist) to expand their influence beyond the areas currently under their influence.The anti-Naxal stretagy must match, if not outmatch, the rebel's strategy.

Maoist Strategies and Plans: 9th Congress of CPI (Maoist)

Ninth Congress of the CPI (Maoist) is an important landmark in the annals of the LWE. The Unity Congress was held after an interregnum of 36 years, since the 8th was convened in 1970. It was the first to be held after the merger of the MCC and PWG in 2004.

The venue of the Congress—a month long event held in the Muktanchal (=Liberated zone) along the Jharkhand-Bihar border—was named after Chandra Mouli, who was allegedly killed by security forces, and Karam Singh who died in October 2005.

That the Congress was held at all should be a news as much to the public as to the security and intelligence agencies of the country. "Whether the event should be attributed to the laxity of India's Security minders or to the single minded determination of the Maoist leadership" is the real question, a daily asks in Feb. 2007. —Shafi Rehman, Indian Express, 22 February 2007.

The congress was attended by 100 delegates from 16 states, and activists of the fraternal Maoist parties from Nepal, Philippines and Bangladesh. It concluded on 3rd February 2007.

The Maoist succeeded in holding the congress deep in the forests, despite the area being encircled by the security forces.

"Its focus was on strengthening unity between the two streams of CPI (ML) and MCC, whose merger took place subsequently on 21st September 2007…The Maoist conclave assumes significance as it is one of its kinds since 1970".

Outgoing CPI (Maoist) secretary Ganapathy inaugurated the 9th congress, where a new central committee was elected, signifying culmination of the two-year-long process where the documents were discussed in depth and the conferences held at the area, district, regional, and the state level. As mentioned above some days before this congress chandramouli alias Naveen was arrested along with Karna, and two others. These arrests framed a long shadow under which these discussions were held which in turn" Would affect the Indian political scene."[6]

The convening of this congress by the CPI (Maoist) must have come as a jolt to the MHA, as the outfit is waging an armed insurgency against the Indian State. Even more worrying should be the fact that the so called "unity congress" ended with a call to extend support for the secessionist struggles ranging from Kashmir to the Manipur.

Before proceeding with recording of other decisions taken at the congress, it needs to be clearly understood that sole source of all informations about the congress is the hand-outs issued by the CPI (Maoist). The facts about the duration, venue and number of delegates who attended the congress from India and abroad could be highly imaginative, self serving and may be partially true, if not totally untrue. The same goes for the decisions taken at the congress. All this could have been written by Ganapathy and his loyal coterie, sitting at his 'headquarters' in a jungle hide-out, with a fertile and fervent imagination they undoubtedly possess. To sum this "imaginative production" of all these factual information, let us end up with a simple suggestion: treat it with caution.

The deliberations and decision taken consequently are briefly mentioned below. To repeat, all these are from the two dailies, named in the two preceding footnotes, dated 22 and 26 February 2007, which in turn are based on the handouts from the Maoists.

The conclave adopted five documents of the unified party-

1. Hold high the Bright Red Banner of Marxism-Leninism Maoism.
2. Programme of the party.
3. Constitution.
4. Strategy and tactics of the Indian revolution.
5. Political Resolution.
    - Reviewed the past practice of two erstwhile Maoist parties since their formation in 1969, the People's War Group from 2001-2004 and also the issues of the day.
    - The Maoist conclave targeted the WTO-World Bank-led policies, resulting in the sanctioning of nearly 300 SEZs, contractualisation of labour, wage freeze, voluntary retirement schemes, curbs on recruitment, and rural labour floating around urban pockets.
    - The Maoists took the position that the present set of policies led to marginalisation of tribal and all forest dwellers, with huge projects causing displacement. Such projects listed by the congress are:
        - Mining and dam projects like POSCO, Kalinganagar and bauxite mines in Odisha.
        - Chargaon and Raoghat in Chhattisgarh

– Bauxite mining and Polavaram in Andhra Pradesh.
– Uranium mining in Jharkhand.

The 300 planned SEZs are all set to create de facto foreign enclaves within the country by grabbing prime cultural land. Together with this, it charges that this was a move to turn urban centres into elite enclaves and pave the way for big business retail chains into India, while demolition of slums and even permanent housing are going on.

Another daily gives another list of issues discussed and decisions taken at the congress.

- While vowing to fight the SEZs coming up in various parts of the country, the congress supported the demand for pardon of Afzal Guru, convicted in the parliament attack case as also the formation of separate states of Telangana and Vidarbha.
- It also exhausted its cadres to use all possible means to free their detained activists even through organised jail breaks.
- Ganapathi re-elected General Secretary told the delegates: "We should support the 'just struggles' of nationalities and sub-nationalities that demand separate states for their development. Kashmiris and various nationalities of the North-east, such as the Assamese, Manipuris, Nagas and Tripuris have long been waging an armed struggles against the Indian government for their right to self-determination, including the right to secede from the so called Union of India.
- Focusing on the Kashmir problem Ganapathi said: "The conflict between the Indian forces and Kashmiris has generated fresh mass resentment in the wake of the centre's design to hang Afzal Guru. The Kashmiri people, along with the enlightened democratic sections all over India, have raised the just demand to desist from hanging the innocent Afzal Guru.
- The congress decided to form organisations like "committee to release prisoners", comprising intellectuals, democracy lovers and members of the families of the imprisoned comrades. The efforts are already on the way. The credentials committee report of the Unity congress reveals that top six activists in AP and 26 in Tamil Nadu are detained under POTA, while 16 in Karnataka and some 25 in North Chhattisgarh have been languishing in jails.
- Upbeat about its "Success" in organising Dalit protest and demonstrations against the SEZs, the congress also resolved to

further strengthen people's army, and deepen the mass bases of the party.

- Recognising the role of the caste in class revolution, the Congress made significant additions to party documents by pin-pointing the specific characters of Indian feudalism and semi-feudalism as being "deeply interwoven with the caste system and Brahminical ideology".
- The Congress re-affirmed the general line of the new democratic revolution as its axis and protracted people's war as the path of Indian revolution.

Some additional details and Ganapathi's interview

This being a landmark event, all available information on the 9th congress must be recorded in this account. Some details from another daily are also examined to be included here. Then this daily also carries an all important interview. —K Srinivas Reddy, The Hindu, 2 Feb 2007.

- The congress was intended to fine-tune the course of armed revolution.
- The congress was held in one of the guerrilla zones, amid what it called the government's all out efforts disrupt it.
- Congress which re-affirmed the line of revolution with agrarian revolution as its axis and protracted people's war as its path resolved to developed guerrilla zones into base areas; strengthen the mass base; transform the PLGA into PLA and advance guerrilla war into mobile war.
- A press release signed by Ganapathi said government policies were leading to further marginalisation of Dalits, students, youth, women and tribals. It called upon the people to revolt and oppose the government programmes.

Ganapathi's first interview since taking over the top job of CPI (Maoists)

The General secretary has been elusive, wanted in several cases across the states. In his first interview since taking over as party chief, the "Naxal Commander-Chief "dealt with host of issues: his party plans for armed struggle, killing of MP Sunil Mahato, opposition to SEZs and endorsed much-talked about thesis of Hezbollah Chief Nasrallah that the Left join hands with the Islamists to fight globalisation.

The daily had approached him for the interview just after his re-election as the General Secretary at the outfit's January 2007 congress, the first since the death of the legendary Charu Mazumdar in September 1971.

The interview was published in the 15 May 2007 issue of the daily. — Mohua chatterjee, Times of india, 15 May 2007.

Text of the Interview

Q. Where was the congress held?

A. Let the intelligence agencies keep guessing on that. As for the media, we can take you people to the place sometime later. These places will assume great historical importance for future generation. Everyone will come to know.

Q. Major decisions at the congress?

A. The General direction: to intensify people's war, taking it to all fronts. In particular, the congress decided to take guerrilla war to a higher level of mobile war in areas where it is in advanced stage, and expand it to more states. Destruction of enemy forces is on the immediate agenda. Likewise, there is an immediate need to transform a vast area into war zone so that there is enough room for manoeuverability for our guerrilla forces. Police and Central Forces will be taught how dangerous it is to enter our areas.

Q. What about issues like Singur and Nandigram? Are your people involved in inciting violence in Nandigram as claimed by CPM? What are your views on SEZs?

A. One should only be surprised if we are not involved in such life and death issues of the masses. We intend to mobilise masses against conspiracies and treacherous policies of the rulers to snatch land from the people and hand it over to MNCs and big business houses in the name of the development through creation of hundreds of SEZs.

SEZs are aimed at creating neo-colonial enclaves within our country where no laws of land can be applied. Struggles against SEZs acquiring fertile farmlands and huge projects are turning out more and more militants as witnessed in Kalinga Nagar, Singur, Nandigram, Lohandiguda and Polavarm. These will go on.

As far Maoists inciting violence in Nandigram, the world will laugh at temerity of these "Left" Front rulers. Even Goebbles will turn in his grave seeing how much his art of lying has been improved by "Marxist" like the Buddhas, Karats and Yechuris.

Q. JMM MP from Jamshedpur Sunil Mahatao was gunned down by your guerrillas along with five others. According to reports, Deputy Chief Minister Sudhir Mahatao was also warned. Your take on it?

A. We do not kill just because s/he is an MP or a minister. Though all legislators are responsible for government policies, it is mainly a coterie of leaders that plays a crucial role in finalising policies. Such leaders are singled out for attacks. We had to eliminate Mahatao because he was involved in unleashing repression on the revolutionary movement in Jharkhand. He was associated with the Nagrik Suraksha Samiti (= Citizen Security Committee) in the murder of eleven of our party cadres in Longo village in East Singhhun district in 2001. Of late, he was organising armed campaign against Maoist movement to divide and pit a section of Adivasis against revolutionary movement in the name of Salwa Judum. But annihilation of Mahatao should not be interpreted as our antagonism to JMM. We are not against JMM as long as it desists from anti-people activities and attacks against the revolutionary movement.

Q. your opinion on Islamic upsurge?

A. There is people's upsurge against globalisation all over the world and Islamic upsurge is part of the world-wide people's upsurge against imperialism, imperialist globalisation, and war. In essence, we see Islamic upsurge as a progressive anti-imperialist force in the contemporary world. It is wrong to describe this struggle that is going on in Iraq, Afghanistan, Palestinian territory, Kashmir, Chechniya as a struggle by Islamic fundamentalists or as a "clash of Civilisation".

Q. Hezbollah leader Nasrallah has said Left should come close to Islamists. Your view on it?

A. I basically agree with what Nasrallah has said. One must understand he is referring to struggles for national liberation from imperialism in Islamic countries.

[*Source:* Mohua-Chatterjee@timesgroup.com]

Maoists spread to southern states, says MHA Report 2006: quoted April 2007

Maoists, biggest threat to India's national security, are now trying to expand their influence and presence into Kerala and Tamil Nadu where they were not known to have any stronghold till now. Tamil Nadu has been a threshold state but now the Naxalite are believed to be expanding into southern states. These are the observations made in the MHA report for the year 2006, quoted by a daily in April 2007.

Some of the findings from this Report are summed here:

- The new areas are in Karnataka, Kerala and Tamil Nadu, where Naxal presence has been on fringes.
- Andhra Pradesh was the epicentre of Maoist violence in the recent past. It has now shifted to Chhattisgarh. The attacks on railways and other property had been more marked in AP, Bihar and Jharkhand. The ultras were also targeting mines and mining related activities in these three states.
- They have also been intensifying their effort at social mobilisation. The Revolutionary Democratic Front (RDF) has enlarged into People's Democratic Front of India (PDFI).
- Jan Adalats (=Kangaroo Courts) are being convened by them to dispense rough (crude) and ready justice, to supplant the state apparatus and assert their hegemony over rural tracts.
- The Centre has deployed 33 battalions of CPMF for anti-Naxal action, sanctioned 291 RBs and assisted states in the task of police modernisation in terms of modern weaponry, latest telecom equipments. Besides ₹ 219 cr has been reimbursed under the SRE head.
- Naxal violence has been reported from 395 police stations out as total of 12,467. The corresponding figure for 2005 was 460.
- The worst Naxal strike was at the Salwa Judum camp at Rani Bodli, Bastar Region on 15 March 2007, where 68 were killed, including 29 SPOs.
- The pattern of attack during the year was to target police stations, railway stations, forest check posts and other government and private property.
- A total of 157 policemen were killed in 2006 in 210 attacks on security men and in 335 encounters with police. The fatalities were the result of frequent use of IEDs and landmines to blow up the vehicles of the forces.
- Weapons recovered from various naxal outfits: 854 arms and weapons such as SLRs, sten guns, 303 Rifles, DBBL guns and also grenades, landmines and detonators.

Maoists are raising an Army now Mar 2007

"The Maoists are now planning to upgrade its Revolutionary Army from the level of 'Company' to 'battalion' in order to form an 'army' by rapidly including more armed cadres in its ranks and enhance its tactical and combat capability and expertise". The expansion and improved tactical training by the outlawed outfit is aimed at achieving a capacity to destroy the police stations and camps in the area of strategic importance to convert them into "liberation zones", that is Muktanchal, as the Maoist call them in their parlance.

The improved training Charter involves countering possible air raids on their hideout by the troops and better co-ordination and mutual understanding between different naxal groups operating on various interstate borders.

All this information is culled from the CMC of the CPI (Maoists) annual report 2006, copy of which is claimed to be held by a daily in its 26 March 2007 issue. —Rakesh K Singh, Asian Age, 26 March 2007.

The Report says the Maoist will convert guerrilla tactics into mobile warfare against the security forces for "better result" and also intensify "psychological warfare" operations through political propaganda.

They plan to intensify their operations against the security during 2007 adopting twin agenda: Central attacks on them and decentralised propaganda mechanism against the State Governments. How do they want to achieve all this? By strongly implementing Maoist doctrine of people's resistance and by developing advance "Military Commissions and commands". They plan to Convert PLGA to PLA after they completed raising of the Battalions as mentioned earlier here.

The Report also advocates that Maoists attack and cut off the supply lines of the security forces by all means at their commands if they enter the "13 Naxal-dominated Zones". It further wants the Maoists to launch concentrated attacks on police camps and especially attacks the foot-soldiers of the police engaged in anti-Naxal operations.

Some other points from the Report:

- They must maintain extreme secrecy about their plans and operation in order to foil the success of counter-guerrilla war launched against them by forces as soon as they come to know of Maoist plans.
- The Report notes with concerns the loss of 300 Maoist cadres while fighting the forces in 2006, and vows to finish off the

campaign with improved tactics, training and increased Naxalites units.

- A Naxalite company usually comprises 125 personnel while a battalion has 1150 in it. The intelligence inputs inform the MHA that Maoists have already formed six armed company for carrying out strikes at the police camps. It is for note that Maoists Company (125) and battalion (1150) are a bit larger than regularly Army's company (105) and battalion (850).

An important point needs to be made on this Report. The Maoist does not seem to be running short of manpower. In the recent past, they are known to have mustered a strength ranging from 500 to 1,000 for their major strikes. 15 March 2007 Rani Bodla strike involved close to 1500 cadres. The Reports tells us that they (Maoists) are formally allotting these militants to raise new sub-units (companies) and units (battalion). A company and battalion of the Naxalites will have designated manpower on permanent basis to be launched into operations under their own commander consequently; it will streamline their operating procedures and cut down their preparatory time to launch strikes against their targets: police stations, police camps, Salwa Judum bases and marching columns of the forces.

One should be reasonably certain that given the intelligence inputs available with them, the security establishments at various levels—district, states and centre have factored in the improved capabilities of the Maoist fighting machines in their counter-Naxalites strategies and tactical plans.

Naxals Create R and D cells with experts March 2007

The Maoists might have hundreds of weapons in their armoury, almost all looted from the police and they form the backbone of their fire power. But their far-sighted leadership looked far beyond this impressive treasure. They are planning to establish their own R and D, to take a high tech route, Lapping into a growing network among scientists, extending up to sensitive institutions like Bhabha Atomic Research Centre (BARC)".

The last name may sound incredible but this bit and other information to follow was revealed by the government that Maoists used an improved version of the petrol bombs against the policemen at Rani Bodla massacring 55 of them.

Now to the BARC Connection. A married couple working at the BARC was found by the intelligence to have ultra–Red background recently. When confronted by the authorities, the two have left the facility since but the incident has left the security establishment shaken over the network of activists and sympathisers that Naxals might have built up among the scientists.

Security agency "recently unearthed an R and D unit of the Maoists near Bhopal and found that a number of such wings were running in different parts of India. —Vishwa Mohan, Times of India, 16 March 2007.

Although Naxals are known to have used such (petrol) bombs earlier, the preliminary reports of the 15 March 2007 Rani Bodla attack revealed their more potent use, suggesting even proving Maoists Expertise in improving and making the conventional weapons/bombs more lethal and deadly.

Maoists adopt "Mobile Warfare" Tactics (MHA Report: April 2007)

The attacks on the Rani Bodla (Chhattisgarh) camp, in which 68 policemen were killed and some fifty arms looted, confirms the 'Mobile warfare' tactics adopted by the Maoists' of late and more such instances are/can be expected in the near future. That incident/attack also confirms the well known plan of the Maoists to transform their guerrilla army into army by fine tuning its war efforts and upgrading its fighting formations.

The above is from the assessment Report of the MHA, a copy of which is held by a daily, as it claims in its issue of 20 April 2007. —Rakesh K. Singh, Asian Age, 20 April 2007.

Mobile warfare is conducted by using "Fluid battle fronts and deployments", changing locations and having a capability to attack the enemy on its most vulnerable spots even outside established guerrilla zones and withdraw quickly.

Besides the above, Maoists have resorted to a periodic practice they call "tactical counter-offensive campaign" in its zone, by attacking security forces as they seek to check the Naxals in their stronghold.

Some other observations from the said MHA assessment Report are mentioned below in brief:

- The prevailing situation in the LWE-hit states is grim and there is no immediate solution unless the core issues are addressed.
- New warfare strategies and techniques are being adopted by the Naxalites on the day-to-day basis with a wide networking base and improved armory and finances.
- Ultra Left extremism is advancing steadily towards its goal in a systematic, methodical and well deliberated fashion and better results can be seen in the future.

- It is imperative to quickly assess the ground situation by duly recognising the sign and symptoms and take appropriate measures by putting in place a proper response mechanism and strategy on a sustained and long-term basis at the earliest. They can and should no longer be ignored.
- The mobile warfare strategy aims at eliminating troops by launching military style attacks on police establishment with the twin objectives of looting weapons to equip its own army and demoralising the security forces. However, the strategy does not aim at retaining and capturing territory. The Central Military Commission of the outfit has succeeded in military upgradation and operating in Bihar, Jharkhand, Chhattisgarh, Odisha, Maharashtra and AP.

The MHA report cites some instances of the mobile warfare undertaken by the CPI (Maoist) in the recent years in various states. Some of the attacks are mentioned here.

- **6 February 2004.** Koraput, Odisha 506 weapons looted and three policemen killed.
- **23 June 2005.** Madhubani, Bihar, 9 weapons looted and one policeman killed.
- **11 November 2005.** Giridih, Jharkhand, 185 weapons looted and six policemen killed.
- **24 March 2006.** Udaigiri, Gajapati district, Odisha, 27 weapons looted and three policemen killed.
- **15 March 2007.** Rani Bodli, Chhattisgarh, 49 weapons looted and 68 policemen killed.

CPI (Maoist) Annual Report October 2005-September 2006 Reveals their future strike targets April 2007

The Naxal onslaught at Riga, Sitamarhi District, Bihar, has been seen as the first of series of such attacks planned by the Maoists in areas where large mining, irrigation or industrial projects are planned to be set up. This is suggested by the fact that the Annual Report of the Maoist, Oct 2005-Sep 2006, seized by the security forces recently had listed several upcoming projects in Bihar, Chhattisgarh, Jharkhand and AP for attacks as Reported by a daily in its issue of 2 April 2007.

The Riga attack may just be a symbolic call for battle to create a Red terror in the neighbouring region, where the proposed Kosi irrigation project is to come up. Incidentally, the Kosi project is on the top of the Maoist hitlist, with the Annual Report saying the region needed attention for not only repulsing the government machinery but also for mobilising the mass support.

The CPI (Maoists) met on 8 october 2006 to celebrate the sixth anniversary of their armed wing, PLGA. They reviewed the contents of the said Annual Report, which had listed in specific the following sites:

- Areas embracing proposed bauxite mines of the Jindal's near Vishakhapatnam.
- Palvaram irrigation projects in AP.
- The projects of the Tata's, Essar and Jindal are in Chhattisgarh.
- Rajghara, Raoghat, Jagdalpur rail line.
- The Steel Plants of the POSCO and Tatas in Odisha.
- Power plants of Reliance and ongoing Narmada projects in MP.

The Maoists in this 8- page report asked their cadres to put up a brave front against these projects and initiate a Kalinga Nagar- type agitation. The Kalinga Nagar incident had witnessed killing of 12 tribals during a protest against Tata Steel's proposed project in Jajpur district in Odisha in January 2006. Thousands of tribals, backed by Maoists, had opposed the plant fearing the displacements. —Vishwa Mohan, Times of India, 2 April 2007.

Besides touching upon their future plans Maoists also listed their successful operations which included the following:

- Jehanabad jail break in Bihar
- Killing of 11 Naga jawans and attack on Salwa Judum camps in Chhattisgarh.
- Killing of 14 policemen in west Singhbhum district in Jharkhand.
- An attack on Malkangiri-Udaigiri jail in Odisha.

It seems clear from the Contents of the Report that "they had been successful in such attacks despite the government putting up a large contingent of security personnel in place". It also indicates Maoist's intention to encourage their cadre by highlighting such incidents.

A caveat needs to be added to one observation in the preceding paragraph about the "large contingent in place". The government may put any number of troops on ground in such situation, the Maoist can always launch a strike on a target with a requisite cadre strength and time of its own choosing. The forces cannot cover every Sq Km of the area, especially in jungle and hilly terrain, and that gives a chance to Maoists in their guerrilla warfare tactics. It is erroneous to believe that forces deployed on the ground, in huge numbers, can prevent a guerrilla strike by the Maoists.

The correspondent restores the balance by adding that "self-congratulatory narration is understandable, at least for the morale of their cadres at the lower rung". But not to take away any credit due to them, they have achieved a degree of success.

Naxalites plan October 2007 Rally in Delhi: May 2007 Report

"Naxalite groups are planning a massive show of strength in the capital in October 2007". The decision for such a rally was taken in March 2007 when the top brass of various LWE outfits met to plan the non-violent' campaign. Even if the rally has been apparently called to protest upcoming SEZs on agricultural land all over the country, its basic agenda is to invite media attention and display its strength at the national level. Documents seized by the security forces during various raids in Jharkhand and Chhattisgarh and studied by senior officers revealed these facts.

It is a three tier strategy as explained by an intelligence officer on 28 May 2007:

- They will launch and intensify their operations in the areas where the SEZs are coming up, through their frontal organisations, which will recruit locals for their violent activities.
- The Maoists groups will set up an over ground workers network in the Hindi belt, mainly Rajasthan, Haryana, Punjab, UP, Chhattisgarh and Uttarakhand so that they can grab headlines in Delhi.
- Most importantly, they essentially aim to make their presence felt in the capital in a big way.

Women in Naxal Movement 2001-2006

If Ajitha was the female icon in the Naxalite movement of the 1960s, Nirmala Akka is the Current person doing the honours. Women were always there in the Naxal Movement, but today they have a battalion exclusively for themselves.

The story of Munni Devi is as good as any other to tell the circumstances that propelled the women into tough, men's world of guerrilla warfare. It was essentially callous society denying them social justice that brought about the drastic metamorphosis in their ordinary penury-ridden lives.

Munni Devi, 26, wife of a soldier guarding the sacred border in Jammu and Kashmir is presently serving a life sentence in the Ranchi jail after she was convicted of killing three policemen at the Chiro valley in her village

Latehaar. Her ‘crime’? She sought to release her village from tyrannical clutches of ‘oppressors’. Regret of course, she neither knows nor feel. “No Jail on earth can keep me for 20 years”, she is sure.

“Introduced to Naxalism some five years ago (2001), Munni with six cases against her, is an archetype of hundreds of women who have joined their male compatriots in the CPI (Maoist) which emerged consequent to the sep 2004 merger between the MCC and PWG, to become an inseparable part of the attack squads of Naxals signifying terror to some state governments. Munni and other women of her ilk are doing precisely what the party manifesto emphasizes: women asserting their power in the outfit and fighting gender-based discrimination.

Chhattisgarh is one of the states having sizeable women cadres in the Maoist ranks, 700 in all by 2007.

The Naxal Movement considered dead in Tamil Nadu is still active in Dharmapuri, once the cradle of LWE. The farmers Liberation Front claims the Naxals here are more concerned with social and economic issues of the people. Reena one of the Woman arrested under POTA for “undertaking arms training” near Dharmapuri in 2002, says. “We believe in Naxalleari ideology though we are not that”. She took to ‘alternative politics’ because of her mother’s plight. “I was disgusted by the way society treated my mother after she became a widow. Only social change can put an end to such an inequality”. After a long fight, Reena and other women were released on bail”.[8]

IGP Bastar Mohd Wazir Ansari says: “Women Naxals are more ruthless than their male comrades. Each Lal Dasta (= Red squad) has at least three women adept in guerrilla warfare”. ADGP Sant Kumar Paswan, Madhya Pradesh, give more information on Naxalite women:” In Dandakaranya, 30 per cent of the 70 guerrilla outfits and 30 military Dalams (=squads) have women commanders”. Paswan is in charge of controlling Maoist operations in his state.

The women, between the ages of 16 and 35, are enrolled through special recruitment drives and are subsequently trained at camps in West Champaran (Bihar). Bokaro, Chatra and Hazaribagh (Jharkhand) and some other parts of the country too. Many of them are tribal and from lower classes. Yet they are well educated and some even can speak English. Aim of these women: To wipe out economic disparity and social injustice with the help of ***Utpidan Mukti Vahini*** (= Anti-oppression Army). So today women do not join Naxals because they and their families are exploited and oppressed by the ‘class enemies’, as was the case in the initial stages. Today, they are joining for ideological reasons.

Paswan supplies additional information: "A special battalion, National Park dalam, exclusively for women Maoists, has been raised in Narayanpur. Nirmala *Akka*, a doctor heads it. Sujatha, a wife of politburo member M. Koteshwar Rao, and Nirmala, head (their Respective) outfits in Bastar. Nirmala is also a member of the Central Committee of the CPI (Maoist)".

The Women Maoists of Jharkhand first grabbed the headlines on 31 October 2001, when they attacked the Topchanchi Police station, Dhanbad, killing 13 Policemen. Decamping with the 18 SLRs, they set the station on fire. Here are some other incidents involving women Maoists.

- 3 March 2006: Dressed up as marriage revellers, they opened fire at CISF men at Chandrapur, Bokaro. Five of them and a woman Naxalite were killed.
- February 2006: Maoists decamped with weapons and explosives after blowing up a depot at National Mineral Development Corporation in Dantewada, Chhattisgarh, killing eight jawans and injuring other nine.
- 16 April 2006: They are blamed by the police for killing of 11 policemen in Bastar.
- The Maoist women cadres also played a role in coercing over 160 sarpanches, secretaries and janpad chairmen to resign from their positions in Dandakaranya.

To step up Maoist campaign against the governments' ***Jan Rapat and Gaon- Shahar Chalo***' Schmes, the male commanders of Kondagaon, Kochibara and Maad dalams have been replaced by the women Naxals.

They fight their ideological battles at several planes "Working zealously to create a classless society, they masquerade as vegetable vendors, mix with village folk and sing songs in praise of Naxalism and its struggle for an egalitarian society". These revolutionaries are often seen exhorting villagers to fight untouchability and encouraging them for inter-caste marriages. The villagers are urged to fight the higher castes and the police, seen as oppressors and committing atrocities on them. The hapless, abused women are pressed/compelled to fight their tormentors.

The police do not seem to know much about these naxal women and their activities. Obviously, the latter are well versed in the art of hiding their tracks. The police, as of now, have a few on their watch/hitlist. Barke, 19, tops the list. Hailing from West Bengal, she is involved in Maoists attacks in Jharkhand, Bihar, Odisha and Chhattisgarh besides of course her own state of West Bengal, over the past two years.

The analysts rue the fact that police efforts to stem the Maoists depredations and nab the perpetrators have been lamentable. "In Bihar, hardly a dozen women Maoists have been arrested; Veenita, accused of murdering Rohtas forest officer Sanjay Singh in February 2000 being the most prominent. She carries a bounty of ₹ 50,000 on her head, perhaps the only solace police can have is from the fact that some of the arrested cadres subsequently turn informers.

Perhaps as a clever move to create a Chasm between male and female Maoist cadres, the Jharkhand police screened a documentary Badrang Hota Lal Salaam (=fading colour of the Red salute) showing female cadres being sexually exploited by their male superiors (if we are to believe their personal histories, the women Maoists claim to be to imbued with Chairmen Mao's philosophy to fall for physical temptations. Of course, these puritans would be benumbed into deep silence if they are told about their Icon's weakness and lust for the young nubile virgins right into his old age!)

The state also announced the "Kanyadaan scheme" for women Maoists; a grant for marriage and subsequent rehabilitation. A journalist poses a pertinent question: Will marriage take them away from the armed revolution aimed at creation of a classless society? May be, he should be advised to visit Munni Devi in a Ranchi jail for the answer.

Here is news flash from their counterpart in Kathmandu. Guerrillas are demanding at least 40 per cent reservation for women in the interim government to ensure gender equality in the Himalayan nation. Members of the All Nepal Women's Organisation (Revolutionary), ANWO-R of Nepal (Maoists), "are getting ready for a brain storming session on 1 Dec 2006, focus of which is gender equality in Nepal's future political scenario. Jaypuri Gharti Magar, Chief of the ANWO-R was quite emphatic: "Having played a decisive role in the decade-old War, women cannot be marginalised when it comes to a role in nation building We want them to be ministers as well". Coming from Magar, a senior leader in the Nepal's Maoist hierarchy, this should be an inviting morsel for her Indian acolytes to chew upon!

Spread of LWE post – 2007

Maoist-infected States and Districts

A number of authorities keep making public statements about the number of states, regions (like Dandakaranya) and districts that have come under the Maoists influence at different times. This section has the information about such areas that is deemed to constitute the Red Zone, running rhetorically from Pashupati to Tirupati. But in reality the Zone has gone beyond Tirupati (which means/implies Andhra Pradesh) to reach Kerala.

Spread and strength: October 2009

This is based on the interrogation of a Senior Naxal leader Narla Rabi Sharma, arrested in Hazaribagh on 13 October 2009.

The CPI (Maoist) is well entrenched in West Bengal, Bihar, Jharkhand, Odisha, Chhattisgarh, Andhra Pradesh and Maharashtra. Naxal cadres usually start working in areas with large tribal's population and backward classes. As their strength and influence increase, they set up bases in these areas and establish Area Committees and Zonal Committees.

The party cadres in these committees in Bihar and Jharkhand are well armed and have dozen of INSAS, AK-47, Carbines, 9 mm pistols, rifles and improvised guns. A lot of weapons were snatched from police stations and barracks and improvised fire arms were acqired from local arms dealers and smugglers. Sharma himself is an expert in arms training and is believed to have trained 30-40 youths from Bihar and Jharkhand for 15 days in the jungles of Gotag and elsewhere. He also reportedly admitted to violent strikes in Latehar and Mouka in Jharkhand.

It is 60 districts: October 2011

Jairam Ramesh, in an article in the Hindu of 14.10.11, titled Tirupati to Pashupati writes that in devising our approach, we must recognise the unique characteristics that define the 60 districts, across seven states, identified by the Union Government as affected by LWE.

These 60 districts fall in nine different states as indicated below:

- Odisha, 15
- Jharkhand, 14
- Chhattisgarh, 10
- MP, 8
- Bihar, 7
- Maharashtra, 2
- Andhra Pradesh, 2
- West Bengal, 1
- UP, 1

'In the Heart of Darkness'

This is the heading of report in a daily dated 22.4.12 by two journalists who visited four LWE affected states – Chhatisgarh, Maharashtra, Jharkhand and Odisha—in March-April 2012.[9]

An Illustrated Map

The report on a full page of the daily carries a colour map, which depicts the Red Corridor in four colours:

- Blue: New areas of Maoist expansion; Deep Red: highly affected areas; Light Red: Moderately affected and Light Yellow: least affected.

A blurb next to the map is headed: "The thin Line Gets thicker". The reporters say that the Naxal movement, already strong in many states is expanding despite the "massive co-ordinated operations" launched as counter offensives".

The Naxal presence in the states concerned are transcribed hereafter. It will be useful to compare the situation painted in the map to the table described above, on the authority of Central Government. The states are dealt with north to south—a total of fourteen including two in the Northeast viz, Assam and Manipur.

Assam: Least

- The LWE movement seems to be expanding despite military intervention.

Manipur: Least

- Maoists are forming links with terror groups in the North-Easte.

Bihar

- **High:** Area along the Jharkhand border
- **Moderate:** A patch in Central Bihar and another one Contiguous to the Nepal border.
- **Least:** A patch contiguous to North West Bengal border; to be more particular, it is contiguo to the Naxalbari region.

U.P

- **Moderate:-** A patch contiguous to the Bihar-Jharkhand border.
- **Least:-**A patch contiguous to Bihar border.

Jharkhand

- **High:-**Practically, the entire state, barring a small area in its south-east contiguous to West Bengal border.

West Bengal

- **Moderate:-**An area in the south-west of the state, contiguous to Jharkhand border in part and Odisha border in part.
- **Moderate:-**A patch contiguous to the Bangladesh border.

A point to be noted here is that there are more than one district affected by LWE in 2012, while it was just one in 2011. Likewise, in 2012 there are more than one district LWE-affected, while it was one in 2011.

MP

- **Least:-**An area contiguous to Chhattisgarh border.
- **Least:-**A patch contiguous to Maharashtra border in particular contiguous to Gadchirauli area.

Maharashtra

- High:-An area in the East of State and contiguous to Chhattisgarh border. It is Godchirauli.
- Moderate:-A patch in the east central area of state.

Chhattisgarh: High

The entire state is LWE affected.

Odisha

- **Least:-**The entire north of the State barring a small area each in the east and its west.
- **High:-**Entire south of the state.

As per the table above Odisha, has largest number of districts, 15, affected by LWE.

Andhra Pradesh

- High:-The entire belt in the north of the state, running from the East to the West and contiguous to the borders of Maharashtra, Chhattisgarh and Odisha.
- Moderate:-The entire area of the State in the south and its centre. In fact, the map shows that the only area free from LWE is a narrow strip of land in the middle of the state, running east to west.

Karnataka

- **Moderate**:-A narrow strip of land, running north to south along the border of Andhra Pradesh.

- **Moderate**:- A patch in the south-west of State.
- **Least**:-A larger patch contiguous to the one mentioned above.

Surprisingly, there is no LWE-affected district in the 2011 table. So, the Maoists have made entry in Karnataka too, Post-2011!

Now, we move on the two states beyond the Tirupati, viz. Tamil Nadu and Kerala, the latest entrants into the LWE Empire, i.e., the Red corridor or Red Zone.

Tamil Nadu: Moderate

- A patch, north to south, along the Kerala border.
- Another patch, smaller in size, to the south of the one mentioned above, again along the Kerala border.

Kerala: Least

- A patch along the Tamil Nadu border, south and closer to the Tamil Nadu- Kerala- Karnataka Borders trijunction.

Now, a brief description/discussion about what the two reporters saw and experienced on their visit to examine the ground situation in the four Maoist-infected states.

Chhattisgarh: "The heart of darkness"

The blurb of this visit reads: "Even as the Naxals expand their base, the two reporters visit Chhattisgarh, the heart of the Mao land, to bring us this ground report".

It is useful to remember that this report was filed in April 2012. Again, it should be added right here that this daily and its report is biased in favour of the Maoists; it is pessimistic about the Indian State's ability to overcome the challenge posed by the Maoists; often it is cynical and consequently lack balance and objectively one is entitled to expect from an established national daily, as the Hindustan Times is (it is worth emphasising that the daily was launched by the national patriotic, Birla patriarch, hence it has a great lineage!). So, in the text, many parts/sentences which this author feels are over the top or are deemed to be lacking balance, these will be in Italics.

The very first paragraph of this article is indicative of the mind-set of the reporters as also of the CRPF commandant who spokes the way he did. For this reason the entire Para is reproduced below.

"Nisar Mohammad, commandant, 170 Battalion CRPF, runs what he calls a 24/7 air traffic control, deep in the jungles of Bijapur,

Chhattisgarh, where the CRPF and Naxals are locked in an intense game of hide and seek. This game results in death more often than it does in a catch, and so Mohammad is constantly on the wireless, enquiring if his jawans are dead or alive. Stepping out of the camp, on patrols and cordon and search operations, is laden with risk and the troops can get ambushed or blown up in a landmine explosion. Even within the confines of a camp danger lurks. The camp can be run over any minute, so the troops have to sleep with the loaded automatic rifles, within handy reach on their beds. They also have been trained to assemble and load their weapons, blind folded. The rifles are their anthem, and borrowed from an American soldier in Vietnam, they are told, "This is my rifle. There are many like it but this one is mine. My rifle is my best friend. It is my life."

"Mohammad could have been in any of the Naxal hot spots with his men and rifles. In Jharkhand or Odisha or Maharashtra or West Bengal. The jungles across ten states are swamped with uniformed men, wielding state of the art automatic rifles, mortars and rockets launchers but despite the 'massive and co-ordinated operations', launched over two years ago, the red-corridor is only expanding. Early this year, the security establishment celebrated the dip in the violence graph—142 security personnel killed in 2011 as compared to 285 in 2010; 216 police informers killed in 2011 against 323 in 2010; and 131 attacks on the police against 230.

The reporters say that the celebrations were shortlived as in the first three months of 2012 saw abduction of two Italians and an MLA in Odisha and death of 12 CRPF men in Godchiraurali in Maharashtra, Home minister Chidambaram, understanding that decline in fatalities is not synonyms with decline in rebel capacities, noticed that Maoists too had taken less hits—99 killed in 2011 compared to 172 in the previous year. So he cautioned the Chief Ministers this week (18 April 2012) at the internal security meet: decline in the overall numbers of a casualilties among civilians and security forces in the LWE affected districts may give a false sense of assurance but that is not the true picture" .

"New milestones at ground zero"

This paragraph again shows the cynicism of the reporters. "In Bijapur, we are driving along a thin metallied road; ostensibly National Highway 16, but the 21 km has only just been constructed, under the supervision of gun wielding security personnel, and it has its own mile stones. 'Ma'am this what we call ambush point. This is where we lost seven men, says a voice in the dark as we drive down the road, where turning on the headlights is inadvisable. A little further is where 12 were killed in an explosion and just ahead another mile stone: the place where a jawans died of a heart stroke. The temperature soars and here in the thick jungles of Bijapur. (One of the worst Naxal affected districts which is 70 per cent forest) there is no guarantee that you would die a martyr. A bullet or blast kill instantly, but cerebral malaria, easy to contract, is slow and painful."

One cannot resist the temptation to offer a comment or two on this report. Instead of appreciating and praising the boldness of jawans and officers, these reporters are cynical. They are not only to be blamed. They have a CRPF commandant who seems to be so scared and is always on the wireless to know if his men are alive or dead but not to know about the Maoists seen, condition of their camp, and their welfare. "Leaving the camp is risky and they are not safe inside their camp either". One wonders if this commandant was pulled over the coals. In fact, he should have been court matialed. Instead of motivating his men, such CRPF officers would lower their morale. It is no wonder if there are reports of the CRPF shying away from confrontations with the Maosts. It is disgraceful if true. And if so, action must follow against the top rung of its leadership. One has said enough about the reporters. One more, and possibly, the last instance of non-serious and even flippant approach of the two reporters: In the above paragraph they make fun of road construction under gun wielding jawans and in the succeeding paragraph, they seem to be blaming the State of ignoring the development. They have the temerity to use 'ostensibly' for the NH 16! It is clever and irresponsible journalism, not expected from a national daily. Playing to the gallery is harmful and detrimental to our fight against the Maoists. There are a lot of Left Liberal Overground Sympathesisers (nay they are intellectual Maoist) doing enough damage to the war against Maoists. We do not need more like these reporters. "CRPF has the state-of-the-art rifles, mortars". It is laughable. They do not have bullet proof vests. They do not have anti-mine vehicles. Even then they are doing a reasonably good job. Someone like the commandant Nisar Mohammad detract from their achievements. He is a scared man, possibly cowering in his bed, worrying whether he would be alive next morning!

Another foolish averment they make in the next paragraph should be nailed here itself. They say ".... Men drawn from Tamil Nadu…neither know the terrain nor the language." Nothing could be more foolish! They are not aware that there is a system of acclimatisation and terrain familiarisation for the newly inducted troops. Then, they are not operating alone. They will always get intelligence from the local police. They often have joint operations, with local Police helping them on issue of terrain local population and the Maoist presence".

It seems the aim of reporters is not a balanced and well informed judgements and explaining the realities of situation the security forces face in fighting the Maoists. Its aim is an all round smear campaign! Next paragraphs throw the dirt on that brave police officer, KPS Gill, who saved Punjab for India. It is so easy to be arm chair critics today and tragedy is that their banality is lapped up by so many!

Here is some more banality from the reporters: "Is military the solution or is it only a part of solution that must go hand in hand with development and land rights to stem the expanding influence of Naxals. The bitter truth…in an ample display in ground zero—is that well trained Paramilitary battalions are being pumped in but these men drawn from far away Haryana, UP and Tamil Nadu, neither know the terrain nor the language. As one officer said, "we are doing what local police should be doin and we have the hard task of motivating men who we are literally throwing at death's door".

Yet again two brief paragraphs follow that show the smart banality of the journalists.

> "Veteran policeman KPS Gill, acknowledged to be the man who brought peace to Punjab while earning the dubious reputation of being a killer cop, is not surprised that more swathes of territory are being ceded to the Maoists. The same man, who presided over a reign of dubious fake encounters in Punjab, believes that while operations are necessary there, in the Red Corridor the strategy has to be multi-facted and development lies at the heart of any solution, provided the tribals are viewed as its principal stake holder".

> "The troops are lucky to have malaria kits for timely detection, but what of the tribals, the dalits. Nearly half a billion live in the worst affected states and they lie at the heart of Naxal Conundrum; of what the Prime Minister often referred to as the biggest internal security threat".

The daily discusses three other states which will be taken up with the individual's states later in the book.

A Look at the Naxal-affected states, again

In this section earlier Central Minister Ramesh mentioned nine States which had 60 Naxal-affected districts distributed among them in 2011, as per the Union Home Ministry Information.

In the daily referred above, a map gives details of presence of Maoist Pockets in five additional states. These are enumerated below.

Nine states mentioned above, infected by maoist insurrection are listed here (reference, The Hindu, of 14 Oct 2011.)

1. Odisha
2. Jharkhand
3. Chhattisgarh
4. MP
5. Bihar
6. Maharashtra
7. Andhra Pradesh
8. West Bengal
9. UP

   Five additional states, which are mentioned in the daily dated 22 April 2012 are listed below, raising the total to 14 States.

10. Assam
11. Manipur
12. Karnataka
13. Tamil Nadu
14. Kerala

"Red Network Spreading South: Government"

This is the headlines of a news story, filed by the 1 MES News Network, published in the Hindu of 10 May 2012. It says after making their presence felt in Assam, the Maoists are spreading their network in the southern states of Karnataka, Kerala and Tamil Nadu as well by gradually expanding their activities beyond their traditional strongholds.

Here is what the MoS Home Affairs Jitendra Singh told the Rajya Sabha on 9 May 2012: "The CPI (Maoist) is making forays into Karnataka, Kerala and Tamil Nadu under the supervision of its south-west Regional Bureau and is planning to link the Western Ghats and the Eastern Ghats through these states". In response to a question, Singh in his written reply said, "Their (Maoists) plan includes creating a base on the border of Kerala and Karnataka".

Government agencies "have recently found that CPI (Maoist) cadres are engaged in efforts to establish a forest route from Wayanad district in Kerala to Mysore district of Karnataka".

Singh said the Central Government had sensitised the governments of Kerala, Karnataka and Tamil Nadu in this regard and had advised them to take "Necessary preventive and pre-emptive measures to foil the efforts of the CPI (Maoist)"—which is the most powerful Naxal group in the country.

CPI (Maoist) and other Naxal outfits "are active in seven states—Chhattisgarh, Bihar, Jharkhand, Odisha, West Bengal, Maharashtra and Andhra Pradesh—and have marginal presence in UP and MP. It is believed that the Red Outfits "have started moving into the new states after security agencies stepped up operations against them in their traditional strongholds in the past one year".

Ramesh:- "2 Assam districts may be declared as LWE hit"

This is the heading of news story by Anup Sharma in the Hindu of 2 December 2012. Rural Development minister Jairam Ramesh, addressing a press conference at Guwahati on 1 Dec 2012 that two districts of Assam—Tinsukia and Dibrugarh might soon be included in the list of Maoist insurgency or the LWE hit districts of the country. His ministry had moved a proposal to the Planning Commission recently to this effect, and a formal announcement from the commission was expected soon.

The two districts if included in the list of LWE hit districts, will receive a special packages of ₹ 30 crores each annually for development activities. At present there are 82 such districts included in the list under the integrated action plan (IAP), which is implemented by the Planning Commission.

Earlier, the Assam Government had taken up the issue several times with the Prime Minister's Office (PMO). During Prime Minister Manmohan Singh's visit to State this April (2012), Chief Minister Tarun Gogoi had appealed to him to include seven districts of Assam under the IAP.

The Assam Government had already marked these seven districts of the state where the Maoist activities were growing and asked the deputy commissioners of the concerned districts to expedite the development schemes in the areas.

"New Fronts in the War against the state"

India's Naxal map is changing and expanding. So says an article in a daily dated 13 April 2012.[10]

Sources in the IB holds that the Maoists writ ran large in nine states, West Bengal, Bihar, Jharkhand, Chhattisgarh, Odisha, Andhra Pradesh, MP, Maharashtra and Karnataka. But now Maoists have also set up bases in Assam, Manipur, Gujarat, Tamil Nadu, Kerala, Haryana, UP and Uttarakhand.

The scribes put the issue in perspectives when they say, " A skirmish with bows and arrows that began in West Bangal's Naxalbari in 1967 has become a pan-India insurgency. Over the last years, it has left 2,604 people—1,829 of them civilians—dead.

In September 2009, Prime Minister Manmohan Singh identified Maoist terrorism as the biggest threat to internal security. Later that year, his Home Minister P. Chidambaram, while drawing up a blue print for a grand offensive, warned it would be a "long haul".

But the last two years "have not been good for the Maoists". The security forces have killed or captured several top red leaders. The deaths of Cherukuri Azad and Kishenji have been heavy blows.

For the government, the ideas of a co-ordinated offensive involves moving in forces to wrest control from Maoists, injecting a generous doze of development and moving out the forces to repeat the process elsewhere. "But it hardly ever goes according to Script", said a CRPF officer in Jharkhand. "We are waging a futile war… The Maoists' return the moment we shut down a camp".

This CRPF officer has made this remark to more than one interlocutor over a period of time, and feels it is a great truism. Nothing could be more foolish than this thinking. It is surprising that he has been not checked or advised by some of his seniors in the CRPF hierarchy. Unfortunately there are many such loose cannons in its ranks. As for this remark it is neither well thought out nor wise. To call your serious operations, which might have cost your force some lives, as futile is a reflection on your senior's competence and professional conduct. From this camp, before abondoning it, you patrol vigorously and chase those Maoists lurking in the neighbourhood and compel them to move their camps or you destroy them. Even after vacating your camps, keep patrolling them to see Maoists don't return Such smart-alecky remarks are idiotic, to say the least!

A Jharkhand police officer says, "The problem is that the forces that can enter these areas do not have powers to develop and the authorities who have power to develop the areas do not step out of their offices". ***(This is an observation that is even cleverer and smart alecky than the one dealt with earlier. Both will be commented upon in a later chapter.)***

It was a complaint that echoed in Delhi's security corridor as well. Worries were rife that Jharkhand and Bihar could be the next hot spots of Naxal violence due to their inability to deliver on the development promise. Bihar started governance reform on a promising note, but is appears to be floundering", said a government official in Delhi.

And given the loopholes in the system, the Maoists are regaining lost grounds – "hitting back in Odisha last month (march 2012) with three abductions that have shaken the establishments".

The Maoists movement which was down and out in the early years of this century received a boost in March 2004 when two factions of Naxals, the PWG and MCC, joined hands to form the CPI (Maoist). The upheavals thereafter were engineered in tribal areas and forest lands that the government had neglected for decades. There was also Nandigram of 2007, the demonstrations against the Nanoplant in Singur in 2007 and 2008, statehood protests in Vidharbha and Telangana.... the list goes on. The blood baths had gone on hand in hand: In Bengal's Lalgarh and Chhattisgarh's Dantewada. "It is these struggles that are shaking the system", said Ram Anna alias Narendra, a member of the Maoist Central Committee, who had taken part in the 2010 massacre of the CRPF men in Chhattisgarh.

Now, the Maoist are looking to expand in new directions, said intelligence sources. Its leadership believes the movement which started from the city and is restricted to the jungle, must be taken back to the cities.

In January 2010, a release from Ganapathi, General Secretary, CPI (Maoist), asked Maoist cadre to turn urban areas into support centres to make up for losses in its rural strongholds. But it is not easy to head back to the cities because of the intense security. There are no foolproof methods yet to recruit urban youth.

"We will have to build fast and secretly", said Ram Anna.

Influence of the Maoists July 2013

They wield influence in nearly 203 of India's 708 police districts, routinely kill people and policemen in 90 districts, often have the last word in 27 of them, hope to lead a revolution and (by 2050, according to one account) overthrow the Indian States.

Source:-Aloke Tinku, Hindustan Times, 9 July 2013.

Maoist Tactics and Methods

Maoists' policy, philosophy and tactics have been mentioned rather briefly perhaps too briefly, in the opening pages of this chapter. It needs to be emphasised that those have been described and explained in terms of theory and ideology and in language generally agreeable and non-offensive. The LWE presently is fighting democratic forces in Asia, Africa and America.

The Maoists and the acolytes of the Guevara have same ideology, aims and goals. They all want to displace democratic governments through means violent, murderous and egregiously abominable. The democracy may be imperfect in some countries, but it still is the best among all the available political options.

Maoists, in the recent years have succeeded only in the one Hindu country Nepal and that too partly. The clever traditional politicians have co-opered the Maoists, and all of them have, as a collective, failed to give a constitution to that unfortunate country. Why the Maoists never try their hands in any Muslims country is too obvious: they will be gun-fodder for the rulers and assigned to their graves without unnecessary human rights brouhaha!

A Hindu nation, be it Nepal or India, will not treat these murderous elements in the fashion of a Muslims country, because of inherent values and belief systems of Hinduism. All these raucous and boisterous and overzealous activists, the so called humans rights wallah—do not seem to understand, much less appreciate the kid gloves treatment the murderous Maoists receive from Government in India.

In so many Muslims countries it is Islamist terrorists who like to be called jihadists—who are playing havoc with the current political administrations, killing and kidnapping civilians, as also the soldiers in uniforms. Their methods are cruel and in human.

And in India, unfortunately, the Maoists are coming close to duplicating the methods of those lawless Islamist terriorists viz. cruel ways of murdering their victims, assassinating them, and the most abominable of it all was the recent act of brutality they perpetrated on one of their victims. The Maoists slit open the stomach of a slain CRPF man, put IED inside and re-stitched it.

They may describe their tactics, policies and aims in grandios sounding ideological terms, but their murderous methods to achieve these are barbarity personified and ironically cruel, given their high mindedness, flaunted brazenly, so often!

This section will layout their murderous ways and inhuman methods, in some details and the cost the nation is paying for their misplaced, ideological passion.

Maoist tactics and policy: fighting the State

20 June 2009. Koteshwar Rao@kishanji, brain behind the Lalgarh operation, gave an interesting call to the CPI (M) Government of West Bengal, publicly declaring the existence of two Left's in India. He said in a statement: "If the Left people's Government wants discussion with the Left of Lalgarh (obviously meaning Maoists), the operations by the police and the security forces against them should end by this afternoon". This call came in the wake of Lalgarh operation by WB police and the security forces.

Maoists and their overground associates had formed 'police Santrosh Birodhi Janasadharaner Committee (PSBJC) and people's committee Against Police atrocities (PCAPA).

CPI (Maoist) spread their activities in the Kudremukh National Forest in Western Ghats of Karnataka State. They not only had their hide-outs, but also established their training centre (The New Indian Express, Bengaluru, 23.6.2009)

In June 2009, the politburo issued a memorandum ordering their cadres to extend the guerrilla warfare of Odisha.

Ahead of Union Home Minister P Chidambaram's visit to Jharkhand, the State police in a statement of 28 June 2009 said, "They have information about some of the Maoist leaders having amassed huge properties over the years". The police asserted CPI (Maoists) politburo member Pramod Mishra owned a palatial building in Dhanbad (The Deccan Herald, 30.6.2009)

Maoist Use children in their armed struggle

The Pioneer of 18 September 2009 disclosed that "Maoists are using children in armed struggle against the State, taking cue from the Taliban and Khmer Rouge.

Maoists are cold-blooded murders

The Times of India of 20 September 2009 quoted the Ministry of Home Affairs, Government of India, as saying, "Naxals are nothing but cold-blooded murderers".

They decapitate a policeman: 6 October 2009

Francis Induwar, Special Branch Police inspector, posted in Khunti district of Jharkhand was kidnapped on 30 September 2009. Police found his decapitated body on 6 October on Jamshedpur Ranchi Highway. A note found on the body, warning that "you should expect more of same/similar treatment if our demands are not met. Some dailies reported on 6 October 2009,"Police Inspector Induwar was executed in Taliban-style murder with his head chopped off".

Plan and the Target: October 2009

This is the information obtained from a senior Maoist leader during his interrogation. Narla Rabi Sharma was arrested at Hazaribagh in Jharkhand in October 2009.

Sharma disclosed that the Maoist intended to set up an eduction propaganda wing. In fact, he had been inducted into the outfit to indoctrinate the youth cadres as also to translate books and magazines from Telegu to English. He is said to have translated Marxist-Leninist books from English into Hindi and Urdu.

He revealed that Maoists usually relied on locals for intelligence gathering. It could be a Chaiwallah outside a police station or the driver of a private vehicles hired by the police or it could even be a local tribal youth.

The Central Committee also planned to infiltrate into political parties to keep abreast of political developments and forge a student's unions. Sharma admitted to knowing noted writer Mahasweta Devi and human rights activist Sujatha Bhadra well. He told the police that on the day of his arrest, he was leaving for West Bengal on instructions from Maoist Leader Kishanji to study the tribal areas of Bankura and Purulia.

In retaliation the Maoists had planned to kidnap police officers and government officials. The Party also plan to set up Regional Military Commission (RMC). In fact, it has already formed the Jharkhand-Chaatisgarh RMC, and also plans to form action teams in Bihar and Jharkhand.

The party, he said, would "Continue fighting oppression" and would try and get Maoists Prisoners freed. He disclosed that the Maoists had whole heartedly backed the TMC in Nandigram and even now, some of their members were in Nandigram to help TMC strengthen its position.

On the outfit's violent means, he said since it was a "protracted people's war through the barrel of the gun", they would continue to eliminate their enemies. At the local level he says, it is usually the Zonal Committee that fixes the target after consultation with the Area Committee. At the present, the target is Babulal Marandi in Jharkhand. He said they would also fight the industrialisation policy of the Mittals in Jharkhand.

Informers killed again: 7 November 2009

Maoists killed former CP (M) MLA Subhas Soren at Gopi Ballabhpur in Lalgarh region, West Mednipore. Along with his body were two more, and these were of Lakshman Das Manoranjan Mahali and Jayram Hansde. Posters of CPI (Maoist) were found near the bodies, lying on the road connecting Jhargram and Belapahari. Kishanji said they were given the ultimate punishment for being police informers. "They (the three) were extorting funds totaling ₹ 15 Lakh. Our Binapur Area Committee arrested them on 5 November and after a long trial they decided to eliminate them.

Arrested on the 5th and 'murdered' on the 7th, is a 'long' trial in the Maoist lexicon! 3 days is indeed a 'long' time in their justice system!

Informer' killed again in front of his family

14 Dec 2009. Maoists chopped off the arm/s and slit the throat of a police chowkidar in a Jharkhand village in front of his family, accusing him of being a police informer.

"Maoists in India are misusing Mao's Name"

Mao Zedong's only living grandson has suggested that the ideas of China's Great helmsman were being misused by groups such as the Maoists in India, who were invoking his image to wage violence against the State.

This was reported in a daily dated 11 March 2012.[11] Mao Xinyu, the Grandson was interacting with the Journalist in Beijing. The greater relevance of Mao's philosophy in today's world was "to help maintain peace, stability and development" and create a more equitable global order, he said, suggesting that the former chairman's ideas of "People's War" and violent struggle were less applicable in the post colonial world.

Mao Xinyou, who is a Major General in the PLA, is known in China as a scholar on Mao Zedong Thought. His father, Mao Anging, was the second son from Mao's marriage to Yang Kaihui.

The younger Mao said he did not see the Connection between the India's Maoists and his grandfather's teaching, talking to the press on the sidelines of the annual session of China's top political advisory body, the Chinese people's political consultative conference, on whose national committee he serves. He was, however, aware of the Maoist movement in Nepal, but believed that "people's war" ideas that Mao made famous were particularly applicable in the fight against the colonialism, suggesting they were not so relevant in today's world.

"Touched by cop's Kindness, Maoists abjure violence"

A Police officer, SP Rohtas, Western Bihar, has won over the hardened Maoists spending time in Sasaram jail in his district, by simply embracing their families.

Dreaded Maoist Sudama Oraon and 21 fellow rebels "have turned their backs on violence after being deeply affected by the kindness of this officer".[12]

In a recent letter to authorities, Oraon and his comrades acknowledged that they were overwhelmed by the kindness by which this IPS officer, Manu Maharaj, treated them in prison and their families outside. The rebels also expressed their desire to abjure violence and join the Mainstream, disenchanted with "double standards" of top Maoist leaders.

So consequently, Oraon and his fellow rebels "have had a transformation in jail, touched by the gesture of this IPS officer. The power of kindness to reform—the kind shown in Director V Shantaram's celebrated 1957 movie 'Do Aankhen Barah Haath'—has played out in this Sasaram jail, Rohtas district of Western Bihar bordering Uttar Pradesh.

Oraon, a Maoist Sub zonal commander of the Sone-Ganga-Vindhyachal zone, had earned notoriety for his participation in numerous Maoist strikes including his alleged role in the 2002 murder of Rohtas District Forest Officer Sanjay Singh.

Oraon, in jail since 2006, said Maharaj, a 2005 batch IPS officer, offered financial help to the jailed Maoists' families and helped them lead a decent life. "He even took pains to sort out land disputes. He also sent our children to schools and colleges. The physically challenged ones have got tricycles, which have given them new life".

Maharaj, who hails from Himachal Pradesh, said he did what he thought was right. He added, "The family members are being imparted driving lessons so that they can eke out a living. We have even provided books, Laptops and even computers".

"Maoist leaders exploit women"

Sudama Oraon and 2, other hardened Maoists, including state-level leaders Rajendra Oraon, Jagdish Chhero and Sitaram Chhero formed the Adivasis Chetna Manch (ACM) in Sasaram jail last September (2011). Oraon took this step as he was disenchanted with the "High-flying" lifestyle of top Maoist leaders.

He hinted at a caste war within the CPI (Maoist), between dominant Yadavs and cadre belonging to the depressed classes. He accused the Maoist Leadership of sexually exploiting women. He said, "The Naxal ideology has been sacrificed. Naxal leader use branded soaps and send their kids to top-end schools".

"Is the Maoist rebellion on the decline"?

The Maoists had two lean years in 2011 and 2012. So it was natural to examine, observe and analyse their standing and status in the early 2012.

In the recent years, tribal Abujhmad had a halo of a Maoist liberated zone, to use a favourite's phrase of the rebels."The 4000 sq kms of these forests in southern Chhattisgarh (a large patch extends to eastern Maharashtra) is where the CPI (Maoist) have for years sought sanctuary and laboratory".[13]

The tribal Abujhmad, a deemed fortress or a secure sanctuary of the Maoists, seems to have been breached! The ingress in mid March (2012) began with a sortie by security forces. In this case, these were the local police units working with COBRA, the "giddily named anti-Maoist arm of the CRPF". With this single success/operation, it is tempting to sound a requirem for the LWE in the State, but that might be premature. It is even more tempting to do so as it has come after a rash of arrests, deaths and surrenders of senior- and mid-level leaders of the Maoists.

Now comes a very apt truism from the scribe: "Abujhmad has never been out of bound for government or its forces. A simpler explanation is that administrations do not bother with a place unless there is commercial or political capital in it". Security forces are entering it to try and clear Maoist rebels from an entrenched refuge earned more of India's administrative abdication than seduction by Mao Dezong's overbearing spirit. "South Bastar—now better known as mineral rich Dantewada—has faced similar attention since 2005 with the formation of brutal vigilante groups by Chhattisgarh government. Vast stretches of Andhra Pradesh experienced it in the early to mid-2000s with greater efficiency of the greyhound force, that state's specialised anti-Naxal' outfit. Jharkhand, Bihar, Odisha, West Bengal, Karnataka....The list is depressingly long".

Then the scribe looks into the intra-party quarrels and problems faced by the Maoists. "It wouldn't come as a surprise were the CPI (Maoist) to break along its lines of formation. In late 2004, even as the peace talks floundered in Andhra Pradesh with the CPI(ML) People's War and its allies—and a parallel overture from Naveen Patnaik - led Odisha led no where — this group came together with the MCC to form CPI(Maoist). Whatever the assertions of the teamwork and sharing of positions in politburo, it has never been a seamless union. The Andhra centric leadership continues to call the Shots, co-ordinate work in other areas of southern India, and reinforce the rebel presence in southern Chhattisgarh. Northern Chhattisgarh, Jharkhand, Bihar, some of Odisha and West Bengal largely remained the patch of the erstwhile MCC. Control of territory and funds have led to disagreements. A truer picture of the intra-party realities was naver explained this clearly and unambiguously. No question of laymen, even large part of intelligentsia may not be aware of this reality!

Rest of the article is reproduced verbatim.

"Factional pressures remain even within territories. Jharkhand has multiple armed Left wing formations. Bihar has de-facto rebel satrapies. In Odisha, the government is negotiating with two separate, and evidently divergent, CPI (Maoist) groups over the ongoing hostage crisis. But, were it to come to the worst from the rebel point of view- and more break aways occur as a result of the repeated battle, arrests and fragile revolutionary egos, the rebellion won't disappear.

This has always remained a guerrilla war. Rebel leaders are actually aware of the fact that they are outnumbered—indeed, have always been outnumbered. So unless local guerrilla squads are set up by security forces, the rebel play book has remained focused on precise attacks. Hitting armoury to loot weapons and ammunition; the stores or trucks of a mining company for explosives; a jail to free comrades. Luring police and paramilitary forces. Taking advantage of errors, like when 36 Greyhound personal died in June 2008, as they packed into a boat on a reservoir on odisha and travelled close to a vantage point where the rebels were perched or, as it happened in Dantewada in April 2010, when 76 CRPF personal were killed as they rested in the open without any fear of being ambushed or, in Maharashtra on 27 Mar (2012), when rebels triggered a land mine explosion that tore apart a bus carrying CRPF personal. The instance are numerous. When the tide has turned, the rebels have licked their wounds, and waited.

"They know how to wait. The Naxalbari conflagration of 1967 has never really died, in spite of arrest, torture, staged encounters, amnesty, surrender and splits. From three villages, LWE has its emphatic foot prints over six states; in eight others, activity ranges from propaganda and recruitment to logistical support.

"Even with the current phase of rebellion in decline, there will be other, future, phases. Under-developed regions reclaimed by security forces have largely not been seeded with solid development and administration. More places, in Chattisgarh, Jharkhand, Odisha and Andra Pradesh, among others, are now treated to aggressive, state-aided displacement of people on account of projects: more negative energy. Unless governance is delivered, rebel groups will take on new names, leadership and Cadres, re-emerge in old places and spread to newer ones; as history has shown, always better organized, more determined.

"And Abujhmad? What will the Government of India do, once it is in its hands? Merely add this geography to long list of places diminished by administrative apathy and arrogance, warped development and corruption"

A Note on the author of this article

Sudeep Chakravarti is the author of "Red Sun: Travels in Naxalite Country and the soon-to-be-published

"Highway 39: Journeys through a Fractured Land."

The author of this book has, often, been critical of so many academics, scribes and contributor whose works, articles and news items have been included and discussed in this work of his. Most of these works lacks balance, because it is one sided, mostly Critical of the Government and official line in dealing with the Maoist uprising. It is not that the government plans are flawless in dealing with the Maist murderous violence, but it would be diabolic to think and convey that the government perversely plan and execute their counter-Moist schemes, purposely and intentionally. Some balance is called for while critiquing government's action in this respect. To convey in one's essays, articles and books that every encounter with Maoists is staged or fake is over-doing the criticsm,or one can say, it is an act of perversity, or going to extremes, it is perversity personified!

In earlier Chapters, this work has quoted or included parts of some contributors' writing in the book edited by it Gen VR Raghavan (a distinguished and senior retired officer of the Indian Army). It is a sad commentary on this general's sense of fairness and sense of balance that every contribution in the book edited by him seems to be from sympathisers, and some even overground Maoists, whom this author dubs as "Closet Maoist". All the contributors seem to be belonging to the Leftist-Liberal Brigade of India, Some of whose members even succeeded in getting entrenched in Sonia Gandhi's NAC! It is the result of influence of such "Liberals" that a convicted pro-Maoist Binayak Sen, as a senior journalist Shekhar Gupta writes earlier in this work, got appointed to an important health-related committee of the planning commission, which was to provide inputs for the Governments' health and pharmacological schemes for the next five years! He may be a soft-spoken pediatrician, but is that enough qualification the appointed to such an important committee of the planning Commission? Even if he is, for sake of argument, what message is being sent to the police and other security forces and paramilitary forces who are fighting these so-called ideologically-driven murderers at a heavy cost to their men and materials? This is where I fault Gen Raghavan, whom I hold in highest regard. Frankly speaking, this author does not have that kind of regard and respect for too many retired Maj/It Generals of the Indian Army.

General Raghavan could have retrieved himself by mentioning in his foreword, how-so-ever briefly that contributors to the book edited by him belong to a particular type of thinking, which has excessive respect for the ideology of the Maoists, which may not necessarily be right, or some words of his own choice to convey his reservations to the oneseded, biased and unduly-condemnatory-of-the-security forces and the Government contributions to the book edited by him.

This author has strong feeling on any writings which are utterly one-sided, and marked by prejudices. It is for this balanced approach displayed by Sandeep Chakravarti that large parts of his article have been reproduced verbatim in this work. If he is critical of the Government and the security forces, he is also mindful of intra-CPI (Maost) factional fights, and mentioned it in so many words. He has also written a book, 'Red Sun', on the subject, and one can be reasonably certain of it being a balanced work. More importantly, one hopes the governments at the centre and State level keep track of such writings and initiate corrective measures as adumbrated by authors like Chakravarti. It is not that the Government is not aware of the constructive measures suggested by so many author's like Chakravarti. But the government has it own inbuilt flaws, viz., the bureaucracy used to its own lethargic way of working, the courts at times delaying the execution of good schemes, powerful vested interest coming in the way, and yet again democracy (rather too much of it) coming in the way. Yet again, sometimes, lack of commitment on the part of political leadership itself plays a spoilsport!

One more point must be made about Binayak Sen's standing as a 'Closet-Maoist'! It is a tragedy of this nation that too many Indians try to be "statesmen" among the sun-of-the mill Politians, and "liberals" among the commentarial. That barring some on the right, like BJP and one daily. The Patriot, every one else have given a clean chit to Sen, which is unfortunate and sad, if not an anti-national act. One can understand the compulsions of the Congress, which has given a place to someone in the NAC, whose NGO is run by a convicted Maoist, and wife of a senior Maoist leader. Not only this! This Congress (Party) has always turned a blind eye to the influx of illegal Bangladeshi migrants into India, who have lilted the population balance in the State of Assam. For what? Because, those illegal migrants have enabled the Congress to rule over that state for long years! Even today, it is ruling that State (2015). Next, supporters of Sen are the leftist. This Author will not say much on them, since this Author has never deemed them good Indians, nay, even, Indian! They follow a foreign ideology, even foreign gods! Should any one be surprised that the 'Venerable Communist leader Jyoti Basu ruled West Bengal with the help of the same illegal Migrants, which enabled the Congress to rule in Assam! Will some one, who says the personal and party interest are paramount for such individuals (who became Prime Ministers an Chief Ministers) and party/parties who would rather retain power then lose it for sake of principles and national interest, be dubbed as overly biased against the politicians? Even more, if he feels all these parties who ruled with the help of the illegal migrants, viz. the Congress and the CPI (M), are anti-national? The subject it too serious for a short examination here. It will be dealt, in detail, in some other book.

The Sham about Binayak Sen

Reverting to Binayak Sen, the Leftist 'Clique' and Liberal 'mafia' (both terms are used, rather, advisedly) will never allow the facts about this soft-spoken 'Doctor' come to public knowledge. They will paint him as a milky-white do-gooder, and among the effusive praise heaped on him, never allow his murky side and antinational actions come out in the open. Besides these two supporting lobbies of white washers for Sen, there is third lobby of Sen – *Bhakta's* who are even more passionate physically on the TV screen. If you ever see Gautam Navlakha (and his ilk) defending these Maoists, you would be nearly convinced that the LWE, particularly of the Maist strand, has been created by India's perverse and naughty security forces. One whises they could utilize this misspent passion for a national cause!

The three entities mentioned above – the leftist, liberal (in the two are included congress party also) and vociferous supporters of the likes of Navlakha –would like the Indians to believe that Sen is the best ever that is to happen to India. He is treating India's Children selflessly and leading India's fight against ill-health and poverty throught the planning commission's committee mentioned above. But nothing could be farther from the truth! He is not only helping the Maoists through subterfuge and underhand activities, but in a more direct way. People like Navlakha and Contributors to the Raghavan-edited book may be called sympathizers, nay, over ground arm of the Maists, but Sen beats them all. He is (or was) doing more then being an ordinary cadre or a leader of the CPI (Maoist). For long years, he was a courier for them.

It is not that this role is not known to his passionate supporters. They would rather like to push it – rather, sweep it – under the carpet. Every leader or senior cadre in the CPI (Maist) must be aware of it, but obviously they would not tom tom about it. Without doing so themselves, they would want it to be kept under the carpet by the loud-mouthed Navlakhas! And his role as a Courier for the Maoists has been, yet again, confirmed in black and white, by Shubhranshu Choudhary in a recent book, already discussed earlier in this section itself. Not to repeat at length, it is summed up brifly: "Choudhuri says he learnt about Sen's role as a Maoist Courier from two senior Maoist leaders, located for away from each but also not on contact with each other; this disclosure Cost him many friends and earned him their opprobrium; they refused to do anything with his book for this one single mention of Sen being a Maoist Courier –none come forward even to review it!" One can understand the pain of Chandhary, possibly a Bengali.

But he himself has expressed his compulsion, reasons and possibly, even, call of his conscience: Having come to know of it and not putting it in the book, would be an injustice to his profession (of Journalism)! Undoubtedly a true professional, unlike so many journalists who know the fact but will not talk about it lest they lose some patrons, Clients, or even earn hostility of Maoists, their sympathizes and 'Closet Maoists'.

Now to one more fact about Binayak Sen which shows he was not only a courier, but much more than that innocuous-sounding assignment. He certainly wielded more influence than a mere courier, a rather passive appointment. He was, or certainly he seemed to be an important leader, when one proceeds to narrate another fact about his influence in the Maoist hierarchy. Choudhary gives a quote in his book from a Bangluru based activist which not only gives a lie to the passionate fulminations of the Navlakhas but also proves that Binayak Sen was more than a courier in the CPI (Maoist) set-up. Here is the quote from Balagopal, already mentioned in the earlier pages in this section: "I had initiated a move to start peace talks in Odisha, on the lines of the one already in progress between the Central Government and the Maoists (to bring peace in Chhattisgarh and Jharkhand). Binayak Sen opposed it. My proposal was destroyed by Sen!" Will all those supporters and 'closet Maoists' still have the gumption to deny that Binayak Sen was not a mere courier, he held an important position in the Maoist leadership?

This Author is conscious that the Binayak Sen topic have been given a lot of space in this chapter, but he feels this was unavoidable seeing the importance of the topic and subject. Too many people are mouthing untruth about Binayak Sen and the public is entitled to know the banality of their stand.

Maoists organisations backing Maruti agitation"

The Centre said 22 Aug 2012 several Maoist frontal organisations and their sympathisers "have been supporting the Maruti Suzuki workers' agitation and have even organised demonstrations aimed at influencing labour unions in Delhi and its adjoining industrial belts." The other front organisations, joining the banned CPI(Maoist) are Mehnatkash Mazdoor Morcha, Democratic Students Union, People's Democratic Front of India, and Committee for Release of Political Prisoners. Their objective, essentially, is to exploit the situation and gain a foot hold among the working class in the National Capital Region (NCR). This was told to the Rajya Sabha by MoS for Home Jitendra Singh.

The Minister, however, said that were no intelligence reports to suggest that the violence in the Maruti factory in Gurgaon was instigated by the

Maoists. Notably, the brutal killing of Maruti Suzuki top executive and the attack on other managers by the agitating workers at its Manesar plant, prompted the MHA to ask the Haryana police and intelligence agencies to probe into the possibility of Maoists' hand in the entire agitation.

Mr. Singh added: "The Maoists have a plan of action which integrates their activities into a pan-India framework. However, till now they have failed to make any significant headway in the urban areas of India, primarily on account of the revulsion of the urban population towards the mindless violence and atrocities perpetrated by the Maoists in their strongholds in central India[14]."

In reply to another question, the Minister made the following points/ revelations:

- Maoists had adopted new strategies, which include using women and children as human shields during exchange of fire with the security forces.
- They are using terrorist tactics like kidnappings to get their cadres released, and are attempting to link up with North-East insurgents outfits for supply of arms and ammunition.
- Naxals are increasingly using area weapons such as mortars, Molotov Cocktails through country-made launchers and better communication equipment smuggled from abroad.
- They are also deploying small "action teams" for select assassinations and Jan Militia members for IED-based operations/ warfare.
- Raising funds by encouraging opium/ganja cultivation.
- Resorting to brutalities like beheading while killing police informers and class enemies.

"CRPF recovers 'list of minors' lodged in Maoist camps"

A day after two girls, who alleged sexual assault, were rescued from a Maoist camp in Chhattisgarh, the security forces on Monday stumbled upon a 'list of children' maintained by the Maoists and were apparently made to forcibly stay in the camps[15]. This is from a daily of 6 Nov 2012.

The list in Gondi had the names under various heads such as 'women, girls and little girls.' Officials say the victims were being sexually abused by Maoist leaders. Zulfiqar Ali Hasan, 1 G (operation) CRPF, Chhattisgarh, says: "The fact that children as young as 12 were being trained by Maoists for attacks against the security forces was already known. But this disturbing trend of many young girls, some also below 10, being sexually exploited is something we have come across now."

Officials claimed these girls were being snatched away from their villages and made to work as 'sex slaves'. The two girls aged around 11-12 years who were rescued on Sunday from Madded area in Bijapur told the police that "there were many other girls who are being sexually exploited by the Naxals. Their parents were threatened when they opposed and most of the girls were forbidden from attending schools in villages."

An officer says the list did not mention the age of the girls. The CRPF, which conducted a joint operation with the state police in Nilamadu area of Bijapur on 16 September, had recovered a similar list of "Bal Sangham" containing details of 40 children.

"Reds use brutal tactics to create fear psychosis"

Maoists are not only murderous outlaws, but they also use inhuman and extremely cruel methods to create fear psychosis not only among the civilians but also among their uniformed rivals in the battle for India—this is exactly what the Maoists deem it to be! This is what is meant to be conveyed in this news item in a daily dated 19 Jan 2013[16].

After the encounter of security forces with the Maoist on 7 Jan 2013, in Karmatiya forests of Latehar, Jharkhand, the bodies of some slain CRPF men were found to be booby trapped with the IED. Four locals were killed in the IED explosions when the CRPF were trying to recover the bodies of their comrades with their help. This is not enough of a cruelty on the part of the Maoists. They are capable of going beyond the limits of cruel behavioural pattern, as they proved it "recently" when they tore apart the stomach of a slain CRPF Jawan and stitched it after placing 2.5 kg of explosives in it." For them, it is a human IED!

The condemnation of the CRPF men must be placed on record here and now for their despicable act of using local civilians as guinea pigs. (More on it in another chapter, dealing with the subject of countering and combating Maoist ultras).

Latehar district, understandably, is one of the worse Maoist-infected areas as it is extremely rich in coal, bauxite and other minerals. With secure bases in difficult forested areas, it has on its perimeter other rebel strongholds like Chatra, Palamu, Garhwa, Gumla, and Lohardaga. It is a revenue mine for the Maoists and regularly witnesses incidents of violence like kidnappings, explosions, encounters and disruption of rail traffic. They understand the value of revenue centres like Latehar and would want to do anything to gain and retain control over them, viz. stepping up violence to spread fear psychosis in the area; inflicting casualities on the security forces in attacks at time of their choosing; and such tactics are aimed at creating an aura of invincibility in the region. The 7 January encounter and inhuman practice of planting explosive material in the stomach of a slain jawan are perhaps their ways of projecting their aura.

Then the scribe discusses the tactics of the Maoists that have caused a fairly fast-spread of their "empire", termed more popularly as the Red Corridor in the country. It is obvious that they keep changing, modifying and evolving their tactics to take advantage of the structural weaknesses and operational drawbacks of the security forces deployed in the counter-insurgency operations. Some examples of the Maoists inflicting serious damages on the security forces when the latter make tactical errors in the field, namely: the CRPF troops, 76 of them, resting in the open; and 16 Greyhounds, Andhra's famed anti-Maoist arm, getting packed in a boat and possibly taking a joy ride, going round the reservoir, when they reached vantage point for the Maoist cadres hiding in the trees and getting killed without a fight!

2009 and 2010 were the bloodiest years for the security force fighting the ultras, but with a little more planning and understanding the operational tactics of their opponents, the things improved, as the following figures illustrate:

- Casualties of Civilians and security forces in 2009 and 2010 1913
- Comparative figures for 2011 and 2012 1020

It is obvious that if they can get their act together and have effective leadership, the counter-Maoist forces can get better of the insurgents. But an odd success, or even a series of them, must not induce a sense of complacence among them. A single moment of complacence or of lowering their guards can cost them dear. They must constantly study the tactics of the Maoist to offer them an appropriate counter. Maoists have displayed in the past that even after a major reversal, they can patiently wait for days, and even for weeks, and then strike after regrouping and even re-equipping to achieve maximum gains. In such a situation in the past, security forces suffered heavy casualty, including fatal.

We have already seen they are capable of inflicting egregiously inhuman brutalities on their opponents, and some of these are cited above. Even if these are the consequences of extreme frustration their leadership might be going through, but that is no cause for ignoring the possibility of such a perversity. Some facts about their tactical thinking and practices need to be noted. Their main tool against the security forces is the IED. It yields immediate and disproportionately large gains for them. One, just one Maoist, can trigger the IED, which might blow up a large vehicle carrying tens of jawans. In the process, they have avoided confrontation with the forces. The IED, and an effective intelligence system are deadly combination against the far superior security forces. The Maoists seem to have real time intelligence on troop movement when they attacked them in the Karmatiya forests.

Another tactical practice they employ so effectively against our forces need to be studied seriously. How is it that the Maoist are able to gather for an operation, upto 300 cadres, a couple of times even 500 of them, over a period of time, stretching, may be, from a week to a month? Many of them are, obviously, reaching there after covering considerable distances! Where is the intelligence? How does it miss such large movements, even if it be in the forest? Where are the drones one keeps hearing about? If the Maoists can get information through local villagers, why not the police and CRPF? Obviously, something is amiss! Knowing well that in the past, the mass attack by the Maoist cadres has often inflicted heavy damage on the security forces, why have n't the latter not developed the necessary counter? It is time the leadership thinks over it seriously. There can be many reasons, one can enumerate for this inability, but this is not the time and place for that exercise. What is required is an effective counter, earlier, the better.

As mentioned above, intelligence gather and real time one, preferably, is the most effective tool in the hands of security forces. And the Maoists know it, only two well. So, they have found effective measures to thwart this mean. To break this backbone of the anti-Maoist operations, the Maoists adopted and implemented, "kill one, terrorise ten thousand" policy. Well, the outlaws like the Maoists can practice this policy, but certainly not India's security forces.

They also know how to remain in the news and gain publicity. This was the obvious reason for their abduction of high-profile personages like the two Italians, an MLA and the District Collector of Sukma in Chhattisgarh in early 2012. They have often used civilians as human shields in their fight against the security forces, and thereafter, cleverly blaming the latter for their deaths. This adds another serious headache, rather serious problem for India's security forces. To put it more acutely, it adds sensitivity to the situation. Civilian deaths enrage the local population, civil activists make the matters worse—inflaming the situation through intense campaign to malign the forces, and in the process, lowering their morale—and create grounds for further recruitment to the ranks of the ultras.

"More women members in Red attacks"

Some interesting details about women cadre in the CPI (Maoist) has been given by a daily, quoting a source[17], in its issue of 19 Aug 2013.

Women constitute about 30 per cent of the CPI (Maoist). About one-third (23) if the 65 Maoists killed in encounters with security forces this year (2013) (till July) were women. It is understandable that the number of women involved in attacks on and encounter with the security forces has perceptibly increased.

Replying to question in the Lok Sabha on 13 Aug, MOS, Home Affairs said: "In recent incidents of Naxal attacks, participation of a substantial number of female cadre has been observed. Alarge number of female cadres have also died in exchange of fire with security forces." Proof of their larger participation came from an attack which a Maoist unit launched on a train in Bihar, killing three persons, and a large number of women were involved in it.

MOS RPN Singh made another observation in his reply: "The women cadres are tactically placed in armed units of the rebels to protect male cadres and leaders during the exchange of fire with security forces." Maoists have been using local women as human shields and it has been discussed in detail in the preceding paras—the Maoists milking their death to their advantage. That they could make use of their own female cadres for similar propaganda value is rather inexplicable! How are the well-armed women cadres accepting or acquiescing in this iniquitous practice? It is not easy to understand, much less, to accept this exploitative situation vis-à-vis women cadres of the CPI (Maoist).

More worrying is the situation for the Maoists since they are " finding it a tad difficult to recruit male cadres. A source said, "Parents send their boys away from home to keep them away from the Maoists."

"Reds to kill rather than hold hostages for long"

This is as clear a policy statement as any, announcing their policy on waging a war against the nation. This is akin to some dictatorial nations in the past embracing 'taking no prisoners' policy during the wars.

"Maoists plan the use of abduction as tactic to mount pressure on the government to extract political benefits as well as the release of their comrades. The targets for abduction will be carefully chosen, for bringing the government to its knees. The target will not be held hostage for too longor released if the government does not give into the LWE's demands. Instead, the hostage will be killed shortly after abduction."[19]

This was decided at the recent Fourth Central Committee (CC) meeting held after a gap of two years. The last Maoist CC was held in 2011, a source told the daily.

The Maoists said, in this CC meeting, "when we want to get important leaders released, we choose the target (class enemies) that would get the government to surrender. We must not give lot of time to the government to fulfil the demand. When we understand the government is taking an adamant stand, we must annihilate the people's enemy in our custody and withdraw from our area of struggle."

The change in the strategy is consequent to the assessment of Maoist leaders that abduction of senior government officials and political leaders in the last few years have not yielded results. The Maoists had to release high value hostages like Malkangiri Collector Vineel Krishna, Sukma Collector Alex Paul Menon, Odisha MLA Jhina Hikaka or Italian tourists after holding them hostages for weeks. But the Maoists suffered more losses than political gains from these abductions.[20]

The Maoists have also resolved not to appoint mediators to negotiate with the government on their behalf. The CC meeting resolution said, "If we felt it is necessary, it would be better not to appoint liberal democrats." The Maoists believe the mediators who work for them get branded and "they would face some limitations in working with other intellectual and democratic sections." Besides, these mediators would be vulnerable to harassment by police and security agencies.

CC meeting documents reveal Maoists admitted the abductions have dented their image and turned many against them. On the contrary, the government gained advantage by portraying that the abducted collectors, for instance, were bureaucrats serving the people. "This propaganda has an impact on the middle classes, too—we must punish the important government officials when they are caught as prisoners or otherwise", said the CC resolution.

The Maoists have also decided that senior party leaders must be involved in all abductions and take responsibility.

"Naxals hope to cash in on weak economy"

Trust the Maoists to make use of any situation— political, economic or social—for furtherance of their cause. Even weak economy of India can be converted into a weapon in their armoury! This tactic is as good as any for their ideological war against India. It also speaks for their fertile imagination and their intellectual prowess that no situation is without its relevance to their intellectual will! And there are reasons for their desperation to pounce on any opportunity that come their way!

"Worried over erosion of their support base, area of operation, and difficulty in making fresh recruits, the Maoists hope to utilize the growing unrest in the country due to neo-liberal policies and a weak economy to revive the flagging fortunes of their people's war[21]."

In what could be good news for the government and security forces, Maoists admitted at their 4th Central Committee CC meeting held recently that Indian State damaged their Central weapon manufacturing and supply departments, political and military intelligence units, central magazine department and their international department between 2009 and 2012. This was when the Centre had launched joint forces operations simultaneously across Maoist-hit states.

It is a given that Maoists feed on popular grievances to strengthen their protracted armed struggle against the national Government. While admitting their movement was facing crisis, the Maoist leadership resolved to exploit the grievances among the people and rally them against the government.

Employing their well-worn clichés and over-used Communists jargon, the Maoist CC "believed outdated, semi-feudal, semi-colonial production relations in our country are making peoples lives unbearable." Maoist leaders are following "the manner which people all over the world are waging movements in various forms as major contradictions in the world and are intensifying due to economic crisis of capitalist imperialist countries."

The above paragraph deserves a comment. One does n't know which world India's Maoists are living in? They certainly are not living in the 21st Century. Whether the capitalist economy is failing or succeeding, can be a matter of argument. That the Communist economy has been damaged beyond repair is a given fact today. Indian Maoists do n't seem to be aware that their idyll, the USSR, disappeared in 1991 without a trace. Even more unfortunate, their father land, Mao's China, is practicing capitalist economy. Ironically, India's Maoist still are hoping to exploit "outdated semi-feudal, semi-colonial production relations" in india! One can only pity the Maoists of India! It is time they came out of the long dead Communism slumber!

Returning to their hoped for "unbearable lives of the (exploited) Indians", the leadership plans to use this "favourable material condition" to revive the Maoist movement. In rural and urban areas, they seek to rally people on their daily issues and against the imperialists, especially the US and Indian ruling class. Besides, the Maoists movement would focus on *jal-jungle-zameen* issues and displacement.

While stressing on agrarian revolutionary programmes, the CC noted, "We should not confine to secret and illegal activities in this class struggle."

It is useful to add one sentence by way of a comment: Long last, in a conscious moment, or was it an inadvertent moment, the Indian Maoists themselves have realised, and admitted, that they have been running an illegal movement! As for the rest of India, they always know it so!

Finances of the CPI (Maoist)

Any organisation—political, social, economic, an NGO even terrorist or Maoist- needs funds to run it. So Maoists are no exception. Only means of collecting the funds would differ. To come straight to the point, the subject of this section is to examine the funding of the CPI(Maoist). It is obvious they could not be funding their nefarious, murderous activities through means fair and open. They do so mainly through violent means, namely, extortions and kidnappings—the other names for blackmailing the victims and their kin.

Blackmail has clearly become a paying industry for terrorist of all hues, Maoists included. Thus, says Joginder Singh, former director, CBI, and should know[22] he in a daily of 16 Apr 2012.

The Maoists are emboldened in their ways by the fact that both in the past and even presently, they have succeeded in bringing the government to its knees by abducting innocent people. They found out that even killing does not yield them the gains the abductions do. Killing security persons involves some risks, and killing innocent creates a wave if revulsion against them. Either way, it gives them no financial rewards.

With their abduction of two Italians and an Odisha MLA, in 2012, the Maoist struck gold. After all, the State Government agreed to release two dozen Maoist prisoners on 'humanitarian grounds' in exchange for the freedom of the hostages. It is unfair to single out the Odisha Government. It, in fact, reflect the national policy of bowing down to the blackmail. It started in Dec 1989 when New Delhi released five terrorists to secure the release of Union Home Minister's daughter who was abducted in Srinagar on the 8th of that month.

There are allegations that the corporate fund the Maoists, but obviously, it can't be proved! It has an ancestry: There were similar allegations of Assam's tea plantations funding the North-East secessionist groups like the ULFA in 1980s and 1990s.

There are some specific figures. A Union Home Ministry report puts the extortion racket of the Maoists at Rs 1,400 Crore annually. Maoists are an adept lot as far as collecting funds are concerned: It could be sale of tendu leaves, or a cut from the road contractors at the pain of death. Apart from these and kidnapping, other high income category targeted by the Maoists include mobile service operators. The Home Ministry figures are mere estimates. After all, the Maoist do not file their income tax returns, nor do the persons paying them 'protection money' report the figures.

The Home Ministry figure mentioned above seems to be different from the Institute of Defence Studies and Analysis (DSA). "Though an exact quantification is not possible, a study conducted by IDSA, Delhi has assessed that the CPI (Maoist) party has been collecting not less than Rs 1,400 Crore annually from a variety of sources like the industrialists, businessmen and contractors in the LWE-hit states", MOS for Home Ministry Kiren Rijiju told the Lok Sabha (Indian Express, 23 July 2014).

Odisha recorded third highest number of cases of abduction by Maoist after Chhattisgarh and Jharkhand. In the four years 2008 to 2011, Moaists abducted nearly 140 people and killed 15 of them. But the trend to kidnap high-profile people began essentially in Feb 2011, when the Maoists abducted the then District Collector of Malkangiri at gun point (Vineel Sheel). That abduction yielded them the release of half a dozen of their comrades from the police custody.

There is a history to the subject. In 1987 in Andhra Pradesh, the Maoists (they were still PWG at that time) abducted 11 government officials, including seven IAS officers. They were released only when some hard core cadres were freed. We have, even today no policy at national level to deal with such contingencies. In its absence, governments capitulate in the face of terror—be it the Vajpayee Government in 1999 when an aeroplane was hijacked to Kandahar, or the Home Minister Mufti's daughter in 1989, mentioned above, or the state government of Odisha in face of the Maoists' kidnapping.

The following pages examine some ways the Maoists fund their outfit and its operations.

Budget: Feb 2008: Rs 60 Crores

CPI (Maoist) had a budget of no less than Rs 60 crores for carrying out its armed struggle during 2007-09. It was revealed by Misir Besra to Vishwa Mohan of the Times of India of 18 Feb 2008. Rs 42 crores of this Rs 60 crore total was earmarked for arms, ammunition and explosives, and Rs 2 crores for intelligence gathering. The remaining (Rs 16-crore) amount was allocated for transportation, computer training, propaganda and documentation.

Funds of Maoists: Oct 2009

The information on the issue that follows comes from Senior Maoist leader Narla Rabi Sharma during his interrogation following his arrest, Oct 2009, in Hazaribag, Jharkhand.

The annual expenditure for Jharkhand and Bihar amounts to some Rs 70-80 lakh every year. The Central Committee gives the lion's share to the State Committees. About two-thirds of the State Committees' annual expenditure is taken care of by the Central Committee, and the former arrange the remaining one-third through levies and fines. Sharma reportedly disclosed that the Hindalco company in Jharkhand, the Mittals in Jharkhand and Bihar, the Tatas, Reliance and other firms pay levies to the Maoist in the two States.

He tells his interrogators that for every Rs 100 collected, Rs 30 goes to Zonal Committee, Rs 30 to Regional Committee, Rs 20 to the state Committee and Rs 20 to the Central Committtee.

Funds for revolutionaries: Extortions mainly

Maoists may like to designate it in less pejorative terms, there is no other way than to call it the extortion, all the way! Some other 'names' will be found mentioned, but it all boils down to 'extortion' expressed in different terminologies! In one word, extortion is their main source of funding their life-styles, operations, and even supporting the families of their cadres/ leaders. Looting and dacoity/robbery are other means to supplement their funding.

Interestingly, like any of us or any community, Maoists also suffer the pangs of inflation. In Dec 2009, because of inflation, they hiked the 'Protection Money' from two to five per cent of project costs to five to ten per cent in mineral-rich belt. Almost every business house or contractor pays this extortion money. The new 'Taxes', as seen from a rate chart seized from the Maoists in Dec 2009 are as follows:[23]

1. Annual extortion business placed at Rs 2,000 crore.
2. Rates from construction/maintenance work of Pakka roads doubled from 5 to 10 per cent.
3. For Kaccha roads under block development schemes hiked from 5 to 7 per cent.
4. Charges for construction of bridges and dams upped from 3 to 5 per cent.
5. For Govt buildings, "levy" increased from 5 to 7 per cent.
6. For laying tracks and repair works: 5 per cent.
7. Auction of railway scraps, 10 per cent in terms of value.
8. From manual stone crusher rate hike from Rs 5,000 to Rs 6,000.

   [They obviously do not spare even a poor labourer, a class they claim to be working/committing murders for!]

9. From mechanised Crushers Rs 8,000 hiked to Rs 16,000 annually.
10. Brick kiln owners to shell out Rs 15,000 a year per Chimney.
11. Petrol pump owner will now be charged Rs 25,000 per annum.
12. Bauxite mines owned by big industrial houses will be required to shell out Rs 10 per tonne but medium-sized mining firms will pay Rs 8 per tonne, and Rs 6 per tonne from small-time companies.

The rate chart adds the rates for coal and iron ore mines would remain unchanged till the same is revised by the Maoists.

Zonal Committee of the CPI (Maoist) would continue to remain the basic unit for collecting 'levy' and will be responsible for printing of cash receipts for the purpose, besides sending the share to outfit's politburo. The Central Committee of the terror group is responsible for fixing the shares between its various committees[24].

"The Taxman in the Red Lands"

It is the evocative heading of a news story in a daily of 9 Jul 2013, dealing with the Maoists' ways of collecting money to fund their outfit and its operations[25].

Its opening para is rather informative: "They wield influence in nearly 203 of India's 708 police districts, routinely kill people and policemen in 90 districts, often have the last word in 27 of them, hope to lead a revolution and—by 2050, according to one account —overthrow the Indian State."

The more important question is: How does the CPI (Maoist) find the money to keep the fire burning for the revolution? It has already been mentioned the IDSA study concluded that the Maoists have an annual income of Rs 1400 crores from various entities detailed in the preceding paras. The largest and principal sources of income, the Study reveals, are the mining industry, public works and collection of tendu leaves.

ML Meena, 1GP, Bokaro Range, Jharkhand, found out that in one case, local policemen were involved in brazen collusion with the coal mafia (Jan 2013).

There are various figures for the Maoist yearly budget. In 2010, the IB came up with a much larger all-India estimate of Rs 1,500 crore. A year earlier, former DGP Chhattisgarh Vishwaranjan guesstimated the figure closer to Rs 2,000 crore, but the Chief Minister Raman Singh recently put it at Rs 1,000 –Rs 1,200 crore.

A senior government official associated with anti-Maoist operations suggested much of it was an exaggeration, and actual amount could hover between Rs 140 and Rs 250 crore—It is close to IDSA figure of Rs 140 crore.

Researchers at the IDSA tried to unravel some of the mystery surrounding the Maoist finances. The Central Committee of the CPI (Maoist) fixes the annual amount to be collected at an all-India level in consultation with various levels. The Zonal Committee then conveys the decision on the amount to be collected from each source.

In mineral rich Jharkhand——one of the biggest sources of funds for the rebels—police officers have noticed that Maoists generally collected 7 per cent as levy from all development works from contractors in the areas under their dominance. A similar figure—7 per cent to 10 per cent levy—is cited as the rate for the industrial and mining companies.

Often, the armed guerrillas do not need to come into the picture, at all.

"Usually an overground member of the outfit is deputed to collect the money", the study says. Each level retains some amount for its expenses, before sending its collections to the next higher level.

Home Ministry officials in Delhi—that has been struggling to come up with ways to block the flow of funds to the Maoists—concede that choking the Maoist extortion industry is a big challenge for the security establishment.

So, it was no surprise that when the Chief Ministers of Maoist-hit states met in June (2013), this was one of the key points of discussion.

"It may be difficult to completely cut off their supply of funds, but is possible to curb the flow", said IDSA's PV Ramana. This will be a very important element in the counter-Maoist action plan.

A Quick look at three worst-hit States

Chhattisgarh

Jharkhand

Bihar

Chhattisgarh

Target: Smugglers of forest produce, illegal mine operators pay huge protection money. Even legitimate construction firms pay up.

Method: Local commanders, squads collect revenue, maintain accounts.

The booty: Cannot be estimated accurately.

Jharkhand

Target: Public, private sector mine operators have to pay a huge levy for protection. Levies on development projects.

Method: Levies collected by lower rung cadres from contractors/ proprietors and sent to regional, zonal bodies and Central Committee.

Booty: Rs 100 crore a year.

Bihar

Target: Road, bridge-building firms have to pay 30 per cent of project costs. Smaller businesses also contribute.

Method: Levies collected through local unit chiefs and zonal commanders.

Booty: More than Rs 12.45 crore collected from 16 worst-hit districts in 2012-13.

Maoist-mining firm nexus: Jan 2014

Shocking, but not unexpected revelations, emerged about a nexus among businesses, politicians and Maoists in Chhattisgarh, reported a daily in Jan 2014[26]. Arrested trader Dharmendra Chopra and his nephew, Neeraj Chopra reportedly revealed during interrogation that they were acting as conduit between a mid-size company, Jayasawal Neco Industries, and Maoists. The allegations included extortion of protection money, facilitating entry of supplies into Maoist-controlled areas and hospitality to Maoist leaders.

The company had its executives in touch with Dharmendra to initiate Corporate Social Responsibility (CSR) schemes in Kanker district and to open two mines in the area. The company executives told the daily that they were working with Dharmendra on the basis of his "reputation". Susanta Kumar Moitra offered further explanation in an e-mailed statement. Moitra, President, Corporate Affairs of the company, said: "He was appointed as our contractor in one of the mines, Laindongri. We await mining lease execution with the State government to start the mine, as all other clearances have been obtained. In other mine, Metabodli, at Chargaon village, Dharmendra approached us for starting the mine, as we could not open it, after acquiring it in 2002 due to local resistance... we decided to appoint him as contractor as he claimed to have worked with other reputed companies." The company had tried in vain to open the Metabodli mine "using various" over the past 11 years.

Moitra clarified that they had no knowledge of any other activity of Dharmendra, and their intention was to operate the mine to supply ore to the steel plant at Siltara, 15 km north of Raipur. During the meetings with Dharmendra, the company sought to build consensus among the villagers in favour of mining operations. Moitra further added: "Our aim was to ensure that the promises made to the villagers on jobs, medical facilities and education, as part of CSR programme, were honoured before we could initiate the projects. But as none of the tasks were executed by Dharmendra, the company could not execute the final contract; nor did it pay any money to him or any other concern." He continued: "However, officials at Bhanupratpur had met many villagers at different occasions to ensure starting of mining for supply of iron ore..We never knew the villagers we met and had no idea of their activities elsewhere."

The mining companies claim that they have put their agenda before the Maoists through the Chopras. An executive of another firm said: "They claimed to be close to the rebels in the villages and in the capital (Raipur). We could often see them in ministers' bungalows."

Interestingly, another daily in its interview with Dharmendra seems to have got a lot of information from Dharmendra. The latter is more forthcoming, direct in his revelations here, going to the extent of naming names. The information hereafter is from this daily[26].

The report open up with assertions: "Aided by local contractors, a bond is flourishing between Maoists of Kanker district, Bastar, and politicians and top mining firms—Dharmendra has named some key players in politics and mining, and claimed he helped the latter forge deals with Maoists" Dharmendra, who claims a friendship with Maoists, noted that no one working in interior Bastar can do without their help, and that they oblige companies and contractors in lieu of monetary and logistic support. He claimed of having close links with three political leaders. Sohan Potai, Vikram Usendi and Mohan Mandavi, and "they know I have contacts with senior Maoists."

Explaining as to what help he provided them and why the three politicos continued their friendship without informing the police, he said, "I have funded their election campaigns, managed things, you can imagine." All three are elected leaders from Kanker district. Potai is a BJP MP, Usendi BJP MLA, and Mandavi a Congress MLA, a good mix of two national parties' representatives. Mandavi was a minister in the Ajit Jogi government, while Usendi, forest minister in Raman Singh's second tenure, "is expected to get a berth in an upcoming Cabinet expansion (as of Jan 2014)." All three conceded "they know Dharmendra" but claimed they knew nothing about his Maoist links.

Dharmendra was arrested on 16 January near the Raipur airport when he was trying to escape in Potai vehicle. The three tried to stress their clean image! Potai said, "As soon as my driver learnt that he was running from police, he asked him to get down." Usendi says, "I have no idea about his personal life. I have faced attacks (from Maoists). Had I known them, I wouldn't have been attacked."

This contractor has amassed property that includes a palatial bungalow in Raipur. He was the eighth person from Kanker to be arrested in 3 days (14-16 January), as the State's top police officers at a press conference claimed to have busted a major urban network, and mentioned the Criss-crossing paths of politicians, companies and Maoists. Dharmendra Chopra described his relationship with Maoists, in some detail: "I first met them in the late 1990s. I know Prabhakar and Gopanna (both senior Maoists) well. They sought my help and I bought and carried mobiles, tablets and medicines for them, arranged vehicles. Sometimes they paid me." He named two mining companies, Jayaswal Neco and Godawari Power, and Ispat Ltd, which he claims to have helped negotiate deals with Maoists. Both have leases in Kanker, where Maoists have declared a mining ban. He says Neco had made him their contractor to facilitate a deal and claims he introduced its officials to Maoists. He also claimed that Godawari's contractor Manik Chand Jain provided him a 30 per cent share of profits for his services. "I introduced these companies to Maoists. No one can work in interior Bastar without their help."

Godawari Power, which has started mining operations, refused to comment on these claims, "But last week, ADG (Intel) Mukesh Gupta said a contractor of Godawari paid Rs 1.5 crore to Neeraj Chopra, arrested nephew of Dharmendra, who in turn made it over to Maoists for purchase of arms."

Jaiswal Neco accepted its officials were in touch with Dharmendra to initiate CSR in Kanker and to open two mines in the area. They were working with him on the basis of his experience with other companies he had claimed. Like the politicians, they denied any knowledge about his Maoist links. His interaction with this companies activities has been discussed earlier here.

Such a nexus between the industry and rebels should not surprise scholars who have studied the insurgency in India in its various parts. The Tatas were accused of collusion with the ULFA in Assam during Mohanta's AGP Government. Having put huge money into a project in such situations, the industrialists can't be expected to calmly see their fortunes sink into dust. This is not to justify the industry-insurrection collusion, but to point at governments' failure to defeat militancy which flourishes because of their callous inefficiency and banal hunger for power and pelf. Even in the instant case, only the contractor has been arrested, not the politicians involved in the nefarious nexus!

"Extortion thrives in wild, wild east"

This is another investigative piece of journalism that appeared in a daily of 12 Mar 2015 on the subject of extortion by the Maoists[27]. This supplements the information in the preceding pages.

Some important observations must be put on record at the very outset. The article leads with a fairly large photo showing four Maoist cadres walking in a jungle area, over the caption: "A CPI (M) platoon after a meeting with HT (Hindustan Time) at an undisclosed location on the Jharkhand-Chhattisgarh border on 19 Mar 2015." The blurb of the article says "In the hinterlands of Jharkhand, self-styled Left-Wing Extremist outfits do not spare even the poor from levy. Not to forget, the photo mentioned above, has its mission described in bold, big letters: OUTFITS ENGAGED IN THE BUSINESS.

The HT team has filed this report from Simdega, Jharkhand.

The two opening paragraphs of this report are reproduced below, verbatim:

> "Six months ago, a para-teacher in Simdega, South-West district of Jharkhand, was kidnapped by a group of armed criminals called Pahadi Cheetah. His family got him back after paying Rs 5,000 to the gang. Just when his shock and numbness began wearing off, they came back again demanding Rs 5,000 from the teaching assistant who earns a monthly salary of Rs 6000. And he paid up, firmly controlling his urge for bravado.
>
> "The assistant teacher had learnt the importance of discretion from his neighbour Mohd Azhar, who had brushed aside the crimimal gang's demand for Rs 10,000 three times, only to pay with his life."

This sums up the cruel ways of the Maoist thugs or their cousin outfits and helplessness of an ordinary Indian against their excess. Slain Azhar's brother Mohd Akhtar informed the reporters that his brother ran a small hardware shop at Kudek village. Pahadi Cheeta members called him thrice but Azhar "innocently" refused to oblige and one morning they saw him dead near their brick kiln. Akhtar has since shifted his brick business to a safer place in Lohardagga.

Obviously, Jharkhand extortion industry spares none. Almost every citizen living in the Countryside who has a government job, runs a business, no matter how big or small or is a contractor engaged in executing modest government project has to pay a share of his earnings to these armed outfits operating under the garb of LWE crusaders.

The paper talks about-Ravi (name changed), a mobile shop owner, was approached by a People's Liberation Front of India (PLFI) leader for 10 cell phone. Finally, they settled for Rs 5,000. Incidentally, PLFI is a breakaway group of CPI (Maoist).

Kidnappings and murders for ransom as little as Rs 2000 to Rs 5000 by the LWE group are common in Simdega. In the last four years (2011,12,13,14), the police has registered 74 murders by these outfits, maximum being 23 in 2012. As is true in such cases, the number should be much higher, as many people do not lodge complaint fearing consequences.

In the neighbouring Bolba village, PLFI and Pahadi Cheetah have killed around 12 people in the last 5 years, half of the victims being para-teachers, for refusing to pay levy.

Pahadi Cheetah is one of the 17 splinter LWE groups active in Jharkhand. "Many of the outfits that call themselves Maoists or Naxalite, are no more than hired guns and thugs patronised by the police and political parties for sniping at the CPI (Maoist), the main rebel outfit in the State."

Like the Maoists, these outfits too camp in the jungles, dress up in battle fatigues and carry sophisticated arms and ammunition. The main difference is that these splinter groups carry no ideological baggage.

Now an unfortunate, if true fact: In the last ten years, Simdega and neighbouring districts of Khunti and Gumla, have seen a rapid rise in the number of these splinter outfits, partly fuelled by the lack of job opportunities, and possibly to a greater extent, the lure of easy lucre. More than 70 per cent of the population of Simdega is tribal, living on an average per capita income of Rs 75.

With the big brother Maoists in Jharkhand pocketing more than Rs 200 crore as levy from various mining companies and government contractors in the mineral rich state, the jobless youth from the parts of the State, especially Simdega, smelt a bounty. They ganged up, grabbed guns and rode to the wild hinterlands to take a bite at the 'easy money'. Some of them joined the existing extremist groups. Police, too, give cover to some of these group to, as mentioned, to take on their main enemy—CPI (Maoist).

These outfits have marked out their territories and go hunting with a rate card. The rates are fixed, a police officer informs the HT team: Rs 2000 to Rs 5000 for ad hoc and Group IV government staff living in villages; Rs 10,000 from shop owners; some amount between Rs 12,000 and Rs 1 lakh for government contractors. Yet again, there is another nugget of information about levy imposed by the Pahadi Cheetha: Every government scheme below Rs 1 Crore, the levy is 5 per cent, and they reduce it to 3.5 per cent if it is above that amount. Things could not be neater, and simpler, than this!

Occasionally, an awkward, perhaps 'bold' and 'maverick', police officer upset the symbiosis between the politicians and the extremists. SP Rajiv Ranjan Singh turned heads in the political and administrative circles when he arrested Koloibera MLA and ex-minister Enos Ekka for conniving with LWE outfit PLFI in the abduction and murder of a para-teacher in 2014. Singh says, "I was surprised when I heard they were demanding money from *anganwari sevikas* and para teachers who get so less wages. Most of the (extremist) leaders have fled to Odisha after the MLA's arrest."

The bold Rajiv Ranjan speaks out

'The problem exists because there are no means of employment in Simdega other than government schemes. Worse: there is no source of entertainment for the youth–sports infrastructure, arts and culture centres. Higher education is missing and there is no provision for skill development. The lone ITI building inaugurated four years ago is yet to become operational. Exotic tourist sites remain untapped. In association with Chhattisgarh and Odisha, we carried out several successful raids against these outfits, arrested top members, busted their hideouts and gun factories."

Chief of Pahadi Cheetah Lele Sahu Speaks

"Police might call us criminals, but we are a Naxalite group. We do not harm innocents, but yes, we extort levy to run the outfit, and meet miscellaneous expenses. We save the jungle. We prefer peaceful co-existence with other LWE outfits and the police (It is an interesting, rather amazing statement: Author), but if confronted, we have the strength to take them head on. Barring AK 47, we have all kind of sophisticated weapons: SLRs, Insas and Rifles....We kill those who oppose our group and work against it."

Some of the LWE groups in Jharkhand

Name	*Area of operations*	*Strength*
CPI (Maoist)	Palkot, Simdega border Koleibera, Jaldega	Around 40 member platoon, led by Zonal Commandar Khudi Munda and Sub Zonal Commandar Deepak
People's Liberation Front of India	Bano, parts of Jaldega, Koleibera, Orga, Tatanagar.	40 armed cadre led by Dinesh Gope

(Contd...)

Pahadi Cheetah	Kurdeg, Kersai, Bolba Basai and Koleibera	15-20 armed members led by Lele Sahu
Bablu Paswan Group	No specific area, attacks specific targets.	8-10 armed cadres
Virat Singh Group	No specific area, attacks specific targets	Operates gang from Bokara jail
Anil Singh Group	Focuses on extracting ransom from government contractors.	Operates gang from Ranchi jail

"Maoists milk emerald mine in Jharkhand

This is another investigative story in daily of 31 Mar 2013, informing us how the Maoists fill their coffers, with means invariably foul and illegal[27].

The story is headed by a fairly large picture showing three men on motor cycles, and the caption under it reads: "Miners carry their tools on bikes for another day of illegal mining in Gudabanda." We are also told that at Gudabanda, the stones are mined in some 65 open pits.

The story has an equally telling blurb:

> UNHOLY NEXUS Authorities mum, Maoists make nearly Rs 35 lakh a month though illegal quarrying in Gudabanda.

The two journalists have filed their report from Gudabanda (East Singhbhum).

It should be useful to read two opening paras of this report verbatim.

> "Hoe and hammer in hand, Ramdhun Murmu (name Changed), 25, risks his life every day, deep inside pits of the scraggly mountain ridges of Gudabanda in Jharkhand, with hundred of tribal youngsters.
>
> "By evening, these farmers-turned labourers hand over rough green stones that they have dug up to an armed group of self-styled 'mine supervisor'. Murmu and others get a little more than the minimum wage of about Rs 100."

They have no idea of the value of the emeralds they mine in the East Singhbhum. But in the jewellery markets of Gujarat, Maharashtra and Rajasthan, these stone fetch Rs 3,500 per carat after being cleaned and polished. Now to the larger picture. These farmers are working in the new hub of emerald mining at Gudabanda, Jharkhand. But unlike India's only other emerald mine at Udaipur, Rajasthan, mining in Gudabanda is controlled by nexus of smugglers patronised by the Maoists. This is the exploitation of the poor by the Maoists by another name. The exploiters are the Maoists themselves, whose whole ideology is based upon preventing the rich, the powerful, the capitalists and the government from exploiting the deprived and poor tribals! They themselves are committing the sin, in nexus with the rich smugglers and jewellers –exploiting the very tribals.

The total picture about their earnings is mind boggling. We already have some estimates of their earnings. Here is another one. The CPI (Maoist) are believed to be earning more than Rs 200 crore annually from illegal levy on the nine owners and contractors implementing government projects. This does not include figures about earnings from extortions, protection money and abductions. Over and above this all, the special branch of the police estimated that the proceeds from illegal emerald mining are adding Rs 25 lakh to Rs 35 lakh to the coffers of the Maoist rebels every month!

That is not the entire story. Local residents allege the enforcement agencies are hand in glove with the smugger-cum-Maoist mafia. They get a huge cut, by merely looking the other way!

Now to a bit of history and other details on the mining. The mining began in 2010 and presently some 400 labourers are doing the digging job on a 9-km stretch of Gudabanda. A gang of smugglers transports the precious stones to polishing hubs and markets in other states. The emeralds are extracted from open pits, dug with hoes and shovels. There are some 65 pits, going as deep as 100 to 150 ft, which are in operation under the watchful eyes of the rebels at Parwah Pahar in Barunmuthi village, located close to the border with Odisha——a location and situation always favoured by and favourable to the rebels. In the face of any lurking danger from the security agencies, they can always cross over to other side.

Here is a double-speak by a politician, typical of the class. Local MLA Kunal Sarangi, speaking in the Assembly, refrained from blaming the Maoists ultras but said a very powerful group of people is involved in smuggling the stones and wanted the government to act swiftly to ensure that mining doesn't lead to anarchy! It is a typical case of a crafty politician mouthing a lie.

Now the more pertinent if sad part. "HT (Hindustan Times) travelled to the area where the emeralds are mined but was stopped in the foothills by purported members of 'local viglante groups.' "Police does not dare come here. How could you take the risk?" asked one of them. Gudabanda police pretended ignorance about the goings on! Arjun Purti, the officer incharge, trying to soft-pedal the issue, claimed. "The illegal mining happens at a very small scale and detecting it was too difficult."

Arjun Purty may or may not be right, but one of his predecessors, Sanjay Kumar was suspended in 2013 for allegedly conniving with Maoists and stone smugglers. He was also accused of negligence, leading to the death of a worker in a land mine blast.

As the illegal mining fills the war chests of the Maoists, workers like Murmu, who help them with these riches, can only dream of striking it rich. Murmu, knowing the facts of life, says wistfully with a touch of sadness, "We hear that our Sahabs (the Maoists) earn a lot. We are at the bottom of the ladder and earn Rs 150 a day."

Maoists are intelligent enough to take responsibility for illegal emerald mining and has plausible reason for that —claiming the activity is aimed at generating employment for the local (tribal) population. Deputy Commissioner Amitabh Kaushal, too, seems to be planning some future course:

> "We are getting an assessment of the emerald reserves done. Once it is over, we will implement the new ordinance amending the Mine and Minerals Development and Regulation Act of 1957."

The Emerald Bank

- In India, emeralds are officially mined only at Udaipur in Rajasthan.
- The emeralds in Gudabanda are of medium quality.
- India imports emeralds mostly from Columbia and Brazil, which produce superior stones.
- A carat, equal to 0.2 milligram, of high-quality Columbian emerald costs Rs 20,000 to Rs 30,000.
- Per carat value of Gudabanda emerals is Rs 3,000 to Rs 3,500.
- A survey said the emeralds are spread over 6,000 hectares, with half the area in Odisha.

Weaponry of the Maoists

There are several ways as to how the ultras come to acquire weapons and ammunition. The simplest way is to make away with the weapons of the security personnel killed in the encounters with them, or those blown up in the IED explosions, planned and executed by them. They also stage attacks on the armouries of the forces, their camps, and on the police stations/ posts. The majo gains in this respect were when 75 CRPF men were killed; the Congress convoy was ambushed in May 2013, or in 11 Mar 2014 attack in Sukma districts. These gains have been listed in various Maoist attacks over the last few years in different States affected by the red terror.

More impressively, the Maoists have among their ranks cadres and leaders with technological skills who can manufacture a variety of arms in their own arms manufacturing units. Some details are given in some next pages.

A daily gave some interesting, if alarming details[29]. The first big arms manufacturing unit was busted by the Andhra Pradesh police in 2006 when they recovered a huge stock of rocket shells and launchers in the state. Subsequent probe revealed that the Maoist technical wing designed the launchers and initially made them at a foundry in Chennai.

It is obvious the Naxalites had developed the expertise even to clone sophisticated weapons, including assault rifles of the AK series. In Jan 2010, the CRPF team busted an arms manufacturing unit in forests close to Gobardaha village in Chatra district, Jharkhand. They recovered a number of duplicate AK-47 and AK-57 rifles of fairly good standard.

Poppy Cultivation helps fund Maoist weapons

Union Home Ministry was reported to be considering a concept note on pilot project for alternative crop development in 10 states affected by illicit poppy cultivation as part of its ongoing efforts at curbing the menace. The Narcotics Control Bureau (NCB) has destroyed 14,365.17 acres of illicit poppy in States like West Bengal, Jharkhand, Bihar, Uttarkhand, Himachal Pradesh, Odisha, Karnataka, Arunachal Pradesh and Manipur. (From a daily of 8 Oct 2011.)[30]

The concept note on the pilot project for launching "alternative Development Programme" drawn up by MS Swaminathan Research Foundation (MSSRF), Chennai, along with the budget requirements is under consideration of Union Home Ministry.

The agencies suspect that there is a nexus between existing drug trafficking syndicates and terrorist/LWE network.

Inputs suggest a large part of the funding of the banned CPI (Maoist) comes from poppy cultivation and revenue generated help in militarisation of its armed wing, People's Liberation Guerrilla Army (PLGA)

"Maoists master skill of making weapons"

Technical wizards among the Maoist rebels have apparently mastered the art of reverse engineering, says a daily of 2 Apr 2012[31].

Working in the non-descript workshop in industrial areas of various cities, Maoist techies made grenades, rifle, booby traps, rockets, rockets launchers, pressure activated mines, and even carbon sub-machine guns using volumes of technical dragrams. These weapons were made using commonly available mechanical equipment such as lathe machines.

They provided tactical advantage to Maoists in successfully preventing the advance of security forces into their areas such as Bastar or Saranda forests in Jharkhand.

It is believed that such units have been set up in Tamil Nadu, Karnataka, Bihar, Jharkhand, Chhattisgarh, Odisha, Maharashtra and Andhra Pradesh.

The article carries two large photos showing the Maoists weaponry. One photo has a constable displaying a rocket launcher made by Maoists, in Guntur. The second shows a large number of rockets seized from Maoists in Mahabubnagar.

The recent arrest of a top Maoist leader, Sadanala Ramakrishna alias Dokra, has thrown more light on the vast network of these units. Dokra, who holds a mechanical engineering degree from the Regional Engineering College (renamed as National Institute of Technology) in Warrangal, was the Chief of the Technical Research and Arms Manufacturing (TRAM) units. He is said to be an exceptionally intelligent engineer.

Eluded intelligence

The methods adopted by the TRAM units were so ingenious that they escaped the attention of the intelligence agencies as well as local police. Parts of these weapons were made in cities such as Bhopal, Rourkela, Chennai, Kolkata, Bangalore and Mumbai and sent to Bastar where "mobile assembly units" assembled them to make weapons.

Sources say Maoists started such units way back in 1989. They set up a 'technical unit' led by Dokra in Basavanagudi in Bangalore, and later shifted to Sholapur and to Pune for a variety of reasons. At that time, their focus was on making double barrel weapons. But soon, they laid emphasis on producing weapons and bombs such as rocket launchers and rockets. This came to light only in 2006 when the police seized a huge contingent of rocket launchers in Mahabubnagar and Prakasam districts of Andhra Pradesh.

Within a fortnight, Maoist techie Thota Kumara Swamy alias 'Tech Madhu' was arrested. His interrogation led to the busting of weapon part making units in Ambattur industrial area of Chennai, and in Bhopal and Rourkela. Tech Madhu told police that he had manufactured 1550 rockets and 40 shoulder-fired rocket launchers.

Police believe that Dokra manufactured thousands of rockets and hundreds of rocket launchers in addition to thousands of pressure-activated mines.

Jharkhand's stunning seizure: US Army rifle being sold to Maoists

Stunning indeed, as a daily claims in its issue of 1 Sep 2012[32].

Opening paras of this news items are being reproduced verbatim, for effect:

- "The seizure of a US Army-issue assault-rifle from two men in a jungle bordering Bihar has created a flutter in Jharkhand, with police saying they would investigate if a network of suppliers of foreign-made weapons was reaching out to Maoist. An NIA team has already reached the State.
- "A M16 rifle, with markings which identify it as US Army property, was seized on Wednesday by Hazaribagh district police from Praful Malakkar and Anil Yadav, who were held in Chouparan.
- "Manufactured by Colt Defense, the M16 is the first American-made weapon confiscated in Jharkhand where security men have been battling Maoist cadres."

The M16 family, with 80 lakh manufactured pieces, has been the primary service rifle of the US armed forces since the Vietnam War. Efforts are on to phase it out.

Hazaribagh SP Manoj Kaushik said Malakkar and Yadav, both residents of Bihar, were arrested when a transaction was taking place. "Apart from M16, we found a bullet-proof jacket, Rs 28 lakh in cash, live cartridges for AK 56s and 47s, mobile phones and imported pistols. Yadav was to receive the supply and was carrying Rs 9 lakh. All, except lakh, was payment for the M16", Kaushik said.

It is not yet clear how the riffle reached the suppliers. "It could be someone hoarding a few pieces and selling them at a premium", said SN Pradhan, 1G (Operations and Intelligence), who is also the state police spokes-person. Pradhan says further: "Maoists are always looking for weapons that stay true and do not malfunction at critical times. There is an uninterrupted supply of crude weapons to them, but maintenance of locally-made weapons is a big issue." He continues: "Therefore, care is taken to ensure that at least 20 per cent of weapons in a Maoist platoon are always good arms. The M16 per se is not a huge threat. An AK-47 will always be preferred by a Maoist. But we have to look into the supply of these weapons."

"MHA concerned over Maoists acquiring modern weapons

Recovery of M16 US rifle has already been covered by a daily (The Hindu) and the same daily has come back with the same rifle, but a different angle, viz, the MHA's deep concern and its worry that the Maoists might have established links with the North-East militants[33]. It is in its issue of 6 Sep 2012.

"The recovery of a sophisticated M16...has set the alarm bells ringing in the Ministry....as it indicates the opening 'the North-East arms supply route' to the LW extremists."

Stating that soon a full-fledged inquiry would be initiated by the NIA into the inter-state nexus, and the international links, a senior MHA official said there were reports of Maoists approaching the Manipur-based PLA (People's Liberation Army) for sourcing sophisticated arms and ammunition to take on the security forces that have been acquiring modern arms themselves.

"In 2009, an agreement was signed between top Maoist commanders and leaders of the PLA (the armed wing of the Revolutionary People's Party) where it was decided that the latter would supply arms and ammunition to Maoists...it seem that this North-East route has now been activated", the official noted.

Apart from the M16 rifle, the recent seizure from the Silodar forest along the Jharkhand-Bihar border includes AK 56 rifle (a first from Maoists), four pistols and one heavy-duty UK-made bullet-proof vest. The M16 rifle, manufactured by Colt Defense, carried the 'US Army property' mark on it and is the first US-made weapon confiscated by the Jharkhand police.

Elaborating how this development was of serious concern for the Centre, the State governments and the para-military forces fighting the Maoists, the officials said: "In recent years, Maoists have not been able to snatch arms and ammunition from State police and para-military personnel. With their armoury drying up and country-made weapons not sufficient to fight the security forces, the Maoists have been approaching the North-East-based insurgent groups for supply of arms, ammunition and other item besides communication equipment."

The official said the LW extremists have also sought area weapons like rocket launchers and mortar from the North-East insurgent groups to add to their fire-power.

"These weapons are mainly source from Pakistan, Afghanistan and China and are supplied through the porous Myanmar border", the official added. Another area of concern for the security forces is the recovery of modern China-made wireless sets, which cannot be procured without licence, from Maoists in Odisha, Jharkhand and West Bengal."

"The DIY Maoist Manual"

This 'Do it yourself' 3-page article was carried by a prominent weekly on the subject of Maoist weaponry in its issue of 10 Sep 2012[34]. It is an extremely informative and has a lot of factual details . It will be extensively quoted and covered in this section of the book. The article also has names of six important and top ranking Maoists leaders, which will be included in the next Chapter on "Leadership". The subject of Maoist weaponry has, in some detail, been earlier covered in this chapter, but as this weekly's article has comparatively much more details, it deserve to be taken notice of for that reason, yet again.

The article has a photo of armed Maoists undergoing training. Its caption reads: "To the teeth—Above, at a Maoist training camp in Chhattisgarh."

Then there is a box spread nearly on half a page of the issue. It has extensive details that would be included hereafter word for word.

The blurb reads: "How they made their own rockets, rocket launchers, mortars and other weapons. And how they kept improving and improvising."

> "Being a mechanical engineer, I am well-versed with technical aspects.....I have mastered the skill of manufacturing rockets and rocket launchers. It is like a passion for me."

So said Sadanada Rama Krishna alias Techie Anna, a Maoist weapons specialist, in a statement to his interrogators. Techie Anna and Thota Kumaraswami, alias Tech Madhu, were the brains behind the arsenal of the Maoists: Techie Anna was the head of the Maoist' technical wing; Tech Madhu was the logistics, production and supply manager. Last week, the NIA charge sheeted Rama Krishna and four others for waging war against the state as members of the CPI (Maoists) and for the illegal manufacture of arms and ammunition. The NIA claims as evidence cash, ammunition and explosives, Maoist literature, diagrams and parts of rocket launchers and other weapons seized from them. Among the big seizures were 69 crates full of weapons from a Raipur godown and some material from a workshop in Kolkata.

Tech Madhu, now lodged in Mahabubnagar district jail as an under trial in many cases, is one of the key witnesses. From their interrogation reports, accessed by *Outlook,* the agency is piecing together a frightening and instructive picture of how Maoist cadres get their weapons—from rifles to sten guns, grenades to anti-personnel mines, mortars to rocket launchers. It is a supply chain that runs on make-do, improvisation and above all, stealth.

Let us consider the Maoists' development of rockets and rocket launchers, perhaps the most ambitious project they undertook—with some success. The rebels have been known to be working on it since 2001, when a cadre member is believe to have died making one in the Dandakaranya forests. Sleuths believe the Maoists have come a long way since that. The strategy is simple enough: snatch or seize a piece or two from the security forces, field-strip it, diagram its working, fashion the parts using available material and workshop machinery, assemble a piece for testing, and finally, pass on the know-how to production units. Some Telgu books, such as *Rocket Katha* and *Vishwaparignanamu,* provided information of sorts, while the Internet has been the biggest ally in their growing expertise.

In 2003, the Andhra Pradesh police, acting on a tip-off, raided a Maoist camp in Malkangiri, where 2-inch mortar shells and five rockets were to be developed and tested. The cadres escaped, but the blueprints found there left the security agencies worried. The two weapons experts have now revealed that, after the raid, some 25 rockets were made in Chennai—costing as low as Rs 950 each. Twenty were distributed to various *dalams,* five retained for testing. By 2004, before peace talks between Andhra government and the rebels, they were test-firing them. Two cadres sustained burns in the exercise, in which the rockets were tied to trees and set off.

All this time, their technical experts—Rama Krishna and Madhu, of course, but also some others like Seenu and Vishwanath—worked their brains on the project. Tech Madhu said very few in the party could mix chemicals properly to form the propellant in the right proportion, so he created a "propellant casting device" for the purpose. The team also improvised a T-shaped nozzle when they found that copying the sort fitted on security forces' weapons would prove expensive. Of the launchers, Tech Madhu's statement says, "The idea of (making) a rocket launcher with a tube was to operate them, to the maximum extent possible, parallel to the ground. We wanted to attack from elevated place with a shoulder-based launcher tube."

Satisfied with achievements so far, the Maoists bosses mandated Tech Madhu to oversee the manufacture and distribution of 1600 rockets and 40 rocket launchers to nine *dalams* in selected districts. He was given Rs 25 lakh for the purpose, in instalments. By 2006, Tech Madhu had more or less, met the production targets, but much of it was seized by Andhra Pradesh police. Some of the work was outsourced. A police officer from an anti-Maoist unit, who had served in Gadchiroli, says: "Tech unit members would make blueprints of various parts and place orders with separate industrial units. After this, they would get the parts moved by local transporters and assembled for eventual distribution by mobile assembly units."

Dr PV Ramana of the IDSA draws the time-line: "you can trace the journey of rocket launchers in Maoist camps from 2003 to 2007. In 2003, police recovered blueprints in a raid; in 2004, the launchers were test-fired;

in 2005, Maoists improved them further; in 2006, a large consignment was ordered but a good part of it was seized by police; in 2007, the Bhopal police busted a key Maoist research and development unit where both the new and old blueprints were found. If you join the dots, you will get the larger picture."

From the late 1980s, the Maoist have been working on building self-sufficiency with regards to weapons. Their technical capabilities have only grown and evolved since then. According to Techie Anna, one of the first technical units was set up in Bangalore in 1989 by him with some comrades. The aim then was humbler: To manufacture and supply .12 bore guns and ammunition, butts and barrels for .303 rifles, grenades and similar weaponry for the dalams in the forests. He told sleuths that similar units operated in urban and semi-urban centres, passing off as ordinary workshops. They would often change addresses—Basavagudi for a while, Sholapur then, and Wada-gaon in Pune around 1992.

Around that time, the Maoists were not focusing on manufacture—they would usually procure arms from local arms dealers. But after a key member, Puli Anjaiah, was trapped by police with the help of an arms dealer, the Maoists decided to stop buying and made a foray into manufacturing. So in 1994, Techie Anna set up a technical development Committee (TDC) to coordinate the work of production units. But this committee failed to live up to expectation of top Maoist leaders, so it was disbanded and a central technical Committee (CTC) was created in Jul 2001, to work directly under the Maoists' Central Military Commission (CMC) headed by Nawbala Kesava Rao alias Ganganna. This unit in 2005 rechristened the Technical Research Arms Manufacturing unit or TRAM, mandated to not only to manufacture and supply weaponry, but also acquire and develop skills and technology.

The TRAM comprises five members, with an elected secretary. Three members concentrate on development while the secretary coordinates and strategies the supply of weapons. Members are expected to visit production units twice a year, while TRAM itself convenes a meeting every 3 months. Once a year, a CMC representative attends TRAM meetings, which are held usually in Jharkhand, and once a year in Dandakaranya.

Production units (earlier referred to as S1, S2.....) are designated R-1, R-22 etc. Currently, some 15 cadres, including women, are at work, producing rocket launchers, pressure mines, grenades, booby traps, rifle parts and so on. They are also expected to overhaul weapons and conduct repair workshops for the *dalams*. There are threemembers repairing units under each Maoist district committee, with members having to assimilate a full-fledged syllabus during training. Weapon makers and their unit keep changing positions.

Today the manufacture-and-supply chain created over two-decades provide the Maoists' stock-in-trade weaponry—rifles and hand guns. Their need for ammunition and weapons is such that they still have to procure them. But they no longer buy from local arms dealers; they source them from smugglers, who bring it in from Bangladesh and other routes in North-East. Some weaponry, including LMGs and automatics, and 90 per cent of ammo is obtained from smugglers, according to the confession. But the extent and spread of Maoists' arms network has left security agencies astounded and worried.

Says an NIA officer, "The arrest of these two men have dealt a significant blow to TRAM. But it does not end there. They had several projects planned out. But now, vacancies created by these arrests must already have been filled."

Techi Anna and Tech Madhu: They created it all

These two specialists are the fountain-heads of all the weaponry and its expertise the Maoists have at their command. It is good that these two Maoist 'geniuses' are no longer with them—they are presently spending time in Indian jails (Sep 2012). And thank God for that! If they were still with them, one can only guess what all destructive power they would have bestowed to the Maoist armoury. Some of the riches they have already given to the Maoists are enumerated here[35].

Their Whole arsenal

Here are the full details of their capabilities in this field in three categories.

Weapons manufactured by the Maoists

Rockets, rocket launchers, .12 bore guns, grenades, barrels and butts for the .303 rifles, booby traps, pressure mines, IEDs, and directional mines.

Weapons serviced by their repair units

LMG (INSAS), LMG, AK-47, .303 rifles, sten guns, 30 mm carbines, carbines, SBBL, DBBL, tamanchas, grenades, grenade launchers, 2-inch mortars, Springfield rifles, pistols, revolvers, mines, booby traps, and pressure bombs.

Weapons for which spare parts are made

SBBL, DBBL, 8 mm rifles, tamancha, grenade launchers, 2-inch mortars, rocket launchers, SLR magazines, directional mines and Claymore mines.

'Tech' units

- In cites, they are located in areas with little activity. Communally sensitive areas are avoided.
- Workshop operators maintain strict timings, use only bicycles.
- Usually there are three operators, who avoid local friendships. Their relatives are not allowed to visit.
- Operators must have worked as dalam members for at least three years and have basic technical knowledge.
- They must be able to stay away from Maoist areas up to five years, women cadres must agree to live as "wives" for the period.

Safe Houses

- Usually in cities or large towns.
- Those assigned a safe house are to have no contacts whatsoever with local party affiliates.
- Everyone in safe house sticks to the same prepared story, should they be picked up by the police.

"Cheap Munger guns call the shots"

Handmade firearms of Munger district in South-east Bihar have found their way to various terror groups and criminal gangs across the country as well as Bangladesh, the police says[36].

Easy accessibility and low cost—as low as Rs 2,500 for a *Katta* (Country-made pistol)—are the unique selling points of Munger's weapons. Buyers placing bulk orders are know to get discounts.

Delhi Police are tracking the clandestine gun trade from Munger, 178 km east of Patna, on the orders of police commissioner Neeraj Kumar. After the Delhi Police cracked the botched-up Pune blasts of 1 Aug 2012 with the arrest of four persons, the recovery of Munger pistols caught Kumar's eyes. He asked his Special Commissioner (Special Cell) SN Srivastava to conduct a study and plug the supply of these weapons.

Srivastava said, "I asked an inspector who diol the study, on the source of weapons, with the help of Munger police." Since the last year (2012), police have recovered 74 pistols in and around the National Capital from criminals and terror groups. More surprisingly, during the interrogation of Feroz, an Indian Mujahideen (IM) terrorist, it was revealed that the outfit had also purchased Munger weapons from Aurangabad in Maharashtra.

The study found that in most of the cases, illicit fire arms manufactured in Munger were smuggled into Delhi by criminal gangs based in Meerut, Kanpur, Allahabad.

As to why terror outfits go for Munger's "desi" guns, the police explained that a Munger pistol is as good as a sophisticated one. Moreover, the cheap pricing is the clincher, as can be seen from the (relevant) entry below. "Cheap and dangerous."

The Munger weapons have market far beyond the borders of Bihar, where in it is manufactured! The Delhi Police found out that these weapons are in demand in Karnataka, Maharashtra, MP, UP, West Bengal, the National Capital Region and adjoining areas, and Bangladesh.

There are some interesting observations that need to be made in connection with the study on the Munger weapons. It is the Delhi Police, placed some 800 KM from Munger, that is by chance forced into this study because an 1M terror group too had the Munger weapons. There are no reports about any other state taking any action to control Munger's illicit murderous trade.

At the end, this report says "Bihar has shut down Munger's gun units, but failed to rehabilitate the 'Karigars' (specialists, the gun smiths in the instant case). One such case is of Abdullah, a gun smith who started selling pistols in 2005.

Cheap and Dangerous: Gun-runners of Bihar

- Munger is famous for replicas of SLRs, Kalashnikovs, Carbines, 9 mm pistols and 6-round revolvers, said an intelligence agency official.
- While an ordinary Munger pistol costs Rs 8,000 to 10,000, an SLR comes at Rs 45,000 and a Kalashnikov sells at Rs 2 lakh.
- There is always room to bargain
- Kattas ('desi' or country-made pistols) costs only Rs 2,500 to Rs 5,000 a piece.
- Weapons are made with specialised lathe machines located on the outskirts of Munger city, with the first set of gun smiths making various parts of the pistols.

Maoists loot 30 firearms

"The Maoist attack in Aurangabad has proved costly. While a sixth man was found to have died—a bus driver, whose death was later confirmed—the rebels have looted 30 fire-arms belonging to the force."

It is the first para of story filed from Patna in a daily (Hindustan Times) of 19 Jul 2013.

On 17 July, a day after the attack, the Maoists accepted responsibility for it. Their spokesman said it was in retaliation to the State Government's "Operation Greenhunt". He claimed they have managed to take away 3 AK-47s, 11 SLRs and 16 INSAS rifles.

Two private security personnel and three jawans of Special Auxiliary Police (SAP) had been killed in the attack.

"Rs 140 Cr is Maoists' yearly terror spend"

It was the result of a study carried out by the IDSA that the figure was pegged at Rs 140 crore. This has been examined in this chapter earlier. Another daily[37] covers the same subject in its issue of 19 July 2013. This story, too, needs examination as it has given some additional points not mentioned earlier by other publications. It needs emphasis that all such news stories and articles are essentially based on the Government hand-outs on the subject. It is to be noted this analysis does not name the IDSA, merely saying "a Security think tank." Now to the daily's news story on the finances of the Maoists. Now to the news story itself.

"The Maoists spend nearly Rs 140 crore annually to fight their bloody wars across eight states, the first government-commissioned study on the Maoists' finances has estimated." This is the opening para of the news story.

The estimate, result of extensive analysis of Maoist documents and interrogation reports, is much lower than earlier estimates of the Maoist extortion industry, ranging from Rs 200 crore to Rs 2,000 crore.

"The Maoists have been collecting not less than Rs 140 crore annually, from a variety of sources", said the draft report prepared for the Government, counting the mining report, public works and collecting tendu leaves as the main sources of their income.

This is the first time an attempt has been made to closely study how the guerrillas fund their insurgency spend the money and keep track of its expenditure. Now, an important aspect of Maoist ways of spending—— careful, watchful and avoiding wastage. They are aware of the value of money, even if it is the consequence of high-handed extortions and violent ways/means.

"The Maoists have a meticulous system of accounting and are very good at book-keeping....(They) have also issued guidelines on financial discipline and how to avoid wasteful (non-proletarian) expenditure", the document prepared by a security think-tank said.

A police officer said this could explain how the Maoists were able to run their war machinery on a shoe-string budged. As it does need to spend a considerable amount on acquiring weapons because it is not easy to rob the police any more.

Strength: CPI (Maoist): Feb 2008

Misir Besra, awaiting for court hearing in Ranchi, talked on the subject on 11 Mar 2008, to a daily[38]. He said Naxal organisation has spread to at least 15 states, though armed fighters were present in fewer. There would be 15,000-20,000 armed guerrillas in the Naxalite movement –with upto 40 per cent of them being women. "Guerrilla days, Naxals ready for a new war", was the headline of the story, a significant pointer to the Naxalite tactics for the future as also to their level of confidence, even if one discounts certain degree of exaggeration, coming as it does from the interested party.

The total strength of armed cadres of CPI (Maoist) in Chhattisgarh, speak the records of District Administrations, is 8,900.

Maoist Casualties: Chief is worried

CPI (Maoist) Chief Ganapathy 22 Dec 2009 expressed serious concern at the loss of senior leaders/cadres through arrest or demise at the hands of the security forces.

He shared these concerns with senior colleagues in a letter, pointing out "at the unfailing regularity with which the Party is losing its senior cadres. Deeply worried over the reach of the intelligence agencies, he cautioned the senior leaders not to come into contact with anyone, suggesting that they meet their couriers just once a month. The devastating effect of the series of arrests was evident when the Party's Central Committee postponed the Politburo meeting, as mentioned by Ganapathi. He concluded with: "I strongly feel that the remaining CC SMs did not learn even a small lesson for our losses at the top." (The Hindu, 10.4.2012),

A ward about the Indian media, especially the print, should be in order here. As there are overground soul-mates of the Maoists amongst the individuals (the Liberals, Leftists, minus the CPM and CPI Communists, and left-leaning authors/academia, a la Arundhati Roys, and NGOs, like PUCL), so are there in the newspaper world. *The Hindu* of Chennai tops the list of such soulmates. Other dailies too go overboard while giving the news about an encounter, or arrest of Maoists, going out of the way to tell their readers that the Government version was far from the truth. *The Hindu* goes miles beyond this proclivity of other dailies, it gives an unvarnished version of Maoist side of story, often proving—or trying proving—even its ideological underpinning. The Hindu's affiliation to Maoist shenanigans may be traced to the fact that its long-serving editor was once a card-carrying Communist! And even, N Ram, after giving up its editorship, continues to be the reigning deity of the daily.

Ganapati's worries/concerns were justified.

7 Jan 2010: Three confidants of Maoist leader Kishanji are arrested with 17 others in Salboni near Lalgarh in a raid at Lakhanpur village. This, despite a prophetic warning issued by Ganapathi a mere fortnight ago, as described in the preceding paragraphs. The arrested three are Gopal Mahato, Haripal Mahato alias Bhuwaneshwar and Malik Mahato alias Joker.

Why this wrecklessness in ignoring CPI (Maoist) Chiefs' caution? Is it intra-party one-up-manship? Is such a dare-devilry an indication of an effort to make a point for the High Command, viz. the Politburo! Or, was Kishanji naturally given to such dare-devilry? This averment could not be too far off the mark, if we know that Kishanji was indeed felled by one such act of dare-devilry in later years! To be a little more presumptuous, was Kishanji trying too hard to displace Ganapati? Such adumberations and thoughts are only natural and expected when we know that these two leaders were the Chiefs of the two respective parties, PW and MCC, when the parties merged to create CPI(Maoist). Did it rankle when kishanji became no 2 to Ganapathi at the time of merger? The debated is open to conjectures and hypotheses, depending upon one's own proclivities and prejudices!

"Seized Naxal letters reveal tales of distress, desertions"

The letters recovered by the security forces from slain Maoists and encounter sites reveal a lot about the distress conditions that the ultra Leftists are operating in. This is the news analysis in a daily of 30 May 2013[39].

Most of the Letters are written in Telgu and signed off by one "Gangur', believed to be Katakan Sudarshan alias Anand, and meant for one 'Shyam'. They were recovered from an encounter site on 18 May, near Ganglur in Bijapur district of Chhattisgarh, a day after eight civilians were killed—including three minors and a CoBRA commando—in the area.

Politburo member Sudershan is also Secretary, Central Regional buro, CPI (Maoist). The letter, accessed by the daily revealed how the enemy (government forces) "is attacking from all sides and this going on everywhere." Talking about the losses the CPI (Maoist) had incurred in March (2013), its missives said: "In March, TPC of Jharkhand attacked our Party, resulting in the loss of ten comrades. One of them was Gopal, the one who used to Communicate with BBC. His death was great loss to us. The plan of attack was jointly planned in a meeting of TPC and enemy."

It is interesting to note here that while talking about intra-party factional warfare, the victim does not fail to drag in the security forces! The Maoists behave exactly like the politicians here! It is ridiculous to suggest that security forces "jointly planned" an attack with a faction to attack the other faction! But then, it is easy to explain the loss this way to their cadres, than admit that the rival faction succeeded in Cornering them through clever, if not better, tactics!

"The same month, another attack by the enemy resulted in the death of nine, including comrade Sudhakar (Ravi) and Comrade Pushpa. They all were the members of Khammam-Karimnagar-Warrangal Divisional Committee. This was a great loss." These two entries are from the same letter.

Another Letter reveals 4 March (2013) incident in Potebatpa in south Gadchiroli which cost them five comrades, including Laxman from Gamphur, West Bastar. "He was a great leader."

Still another letter talks of desertions by CPI (Maoist) Cadres for various reasons, including romance. "One Dev Singh ran away with a woman. Also in Gadchiroli, 10 members—including Sekhar and Vijaya, a married couple –left the party." The letter than gives reasons: "Those who left are not able to face hardship of the party policy. Some of them have joined the enemy and are attacking us. This may be the failure of the party."

"Get jailed Maoists out by hook or by Crook: Ganpathy

The blurb on this Maoist story is informative: "DESPERATE: Diktat on Letter comes as 25,000 cadres are in jail across country"

This is the diktat from the top Maosits boss Mupalla Lakshman Rao, alias Ganapathy, in a 17-page top-secret letter, published in a daily[40]. of 17 Sep 2013.

All routes, legal and illegal, must be explored to get jailed Maoist leaders out, insists General Secretary, CPI(Maoists). With around 25,000 leaders and cadres in jails across the country, the letter, addressed to "all the leading comrades in jails" and accessed by the daily, strikes a note of menace and demands utmost vigilance by his leadership at various levels.

The Maoist ranks have been steadily depleting over the last three years, thanks to Operation Greenhunt. The top rung has practically been decimated through capture or killing. Central Committee leaders (read 'members') Kishanji and Azad have been killed in encounter and Kobad Ghandy, Amitabh Bagchi, and Saheb Chatterjee have landed behind the bars.

As an example of 'illegal' means, Ganpathy believed to be hiding in Chhattisgarh's Dantewada, cited the Chaibasa jail break of Jan 2011. Three senior leaders of the Jharkhand unit—Motilal Soren, Raghunath Hembram and Mangru Mahato—had managed to escape by cutting open the ventilator of their cells.

This particular para implies, may be conveys, the menacing tone! Is he suggesting inaction or lack of aggressive enough action/effort on the part of the jailed leaders, at the minimum? Surely, with his experience and knowledge, he must realise that jail authorities would not let succeed a modus operandi—the ventilator route—twice over! On the other hand, he surely knows that many cadres and at least some leaders may not be keen to come out at all in a hurry, and they may even be planning surrender. Perhaps, the menacing tone is aimed at them.

Reverting to the letter, it is a densely type set document, he tasks the jailed leaders with "fighting in the jails and trying every possibility to come out." Some other points emphasised in the latter are: "This is the main task at this historical juncture and the outside party and the comrades in the jails must put effort to fulfil this task; the jails must be turned into centres of political training and struggle; jailed leaders must keep their revolutionary spirit intact."

Then he emphasises a pious hope: "We hope all comrades would try to carry on with a long-term view, improving physical fitness, preserve health, write and send articles to party magazines, do literary work, write experiences and send it to the party and well utilise the time."

The above single para shows how tough job it is for a cadre, and even more so, for a leader, to lead a purposeful life as demanded by their General Secretary, and possibly by his party, CPI (Maoist), in its manifesto!

Finally the letter also suggests how the Maoists outside the jails can help those inside them: "The Party must pay attention to sending money and material and ensure they reach the comrades in jails in time. Party, PLGA and all mass organisations must reduce some of their daily needs and contribute the money thus saved for political prisoners."

"Maoists admit biggest set back since 2005: Lost 200 cadres last year".

Beginning their annual "martyrs week" in Dandakaranya on Monday (25 Jul 2005), the CPI (Maoist) admitted having lost 200 cadres including a Central Committee member, in the last one year.

The Maoists hold the "martyrs' week" in the memory of Charu Mazumdar who spear headed the Naxal movement in Naxalbari in West Bengal in the mid-1960s—the father figure of the LWE in India, so to say.

A press release by the CPI (Maoist), South Regional Committee, Dandakaranya, says: "In the last one year, we have lost over 200 of our leaders, members, PLGA commanders and guerrilla fighters, leaders and members of people's organisations, members of Jan Militia and revolutionary masses."

"They died for their dream to establish Socialism and Communism in the country." It also disclosed that many died of natural causes, including CC member Barun Dada and Shaheeda Didi.

Numerically, this is among the biggest losses the Maoists have suffered in the recent years, probably since the Salwa Judum years 2005-2006. At a CC meeting, 2013, Ganapathi and other senior leaders had admitted to their depleted weaponry and strength.

Security was stepped up in the region in view of the Maoist event.

Justice: The Maoist ways: cruel and Barbaric

The Maoists have devised and established their own ways of dispensing justice, "rough and ready". But their methods have gone beyond certain limits, beyond the borderland of humanity.

They hold the so-called *Jan Adalats,* or Janata Adalats in a village, or group of villages, in the presence of all the residents. The guilty is called up, and punishment announced. Earlier it could be shooting the guilty dead in presence of his fellow villagers for quick, demonstrative effect. But no more so. The beheading, and possibly more barbaric ways, is the norm presently, which will be found detailed in the coming pages.

"Parallel Governments" by the Maoists

Maoist ways of dispensing Justice

A daily (Indian Express) of 16 Mar 2009 reported that a group of some 20 Maoists killed Gitabai Topo, suspecting her to be a police informer. They slit her throat open.

The Maoists have devised and imposed their own rules on a variety of 'offences' as deemed by them. Being police informer tops the list of 'heinous' crimes in their lexicon, and death sentence is the only punishment condign enough for this crime! Delivery of death sentence and implementing it in most brutal manner in their "liberated zones" is their way to ensure that it has demonstrative effect, immediately and in widest areas possible! It is for this reason that they execute such death sentence in most cruel, obnoxious and savage ways.

So-called 'informers' were, in fact, CPI (M) Cadres, who were dragged out of their schools, or even within schools, and killed "to cleanse the territory of dissenters to the Maoist 'regime' in those liberated zone. The weak of 14 Dec 2009 probably saw the highest number of such killings, averaging between 2 and 3 daily[41].

"For them, the Maoists are the government"

This is the article in a daily, analysing 6000 sqkm thick forest of Abujhmadh straddling the Chhattisgarh-Maharashtra border, in its issue of 22 Apr 2012, filed from Bijapur, Chhattisgarh.[42]

For a broad understanding of the issues, it is considered important that first three paras of this information story is reproduced verbatim.

- "Helicopters were kept at standby for casualty evacuation; targets were chosen with care after studying satellite images and the troops were warned—the encounters could be fierce and Naxals could be in hundreds, even thousands.
- "After weeks of planning, security forces armed with automatic rifles, satellite phones and Swedish Carl Gustav rocket launchers, made their very first foray into the dense Abujhmad jungle, straddling the two states of Maharashtra and Chhattisgarh. Abujhmad, or unknown hill, 6000 sqkm of thick forest, has not been surveyed since the British (left).
- "As part of operation, security forces had zoomed in on a map of the area with the help of the Google Earth, on to a Couple of structures they identified as a 'Naxal camp'. A plan was prepared to go in and take out the Naxalites. The mission had second aim—the strong hold had to be psychologically breached since it is as much home to the Naxals as it is a zone liberated of all government control."

Primed for a fierce fight, weapons ready, the troops marched 70 km to the "Naxal camp'. On the contrary, what they found was a village with 15 to 20 thatched huts. The cluster of buildings the forces saw for the first time on Google Earth were homes of Muria tribals, themselves startled at the sight of battle ready troops in uniform!

More startlingly, the troops discovered for the first time since the Independence that there was a village here named Bodiguda. "Nobody had heard or seen this village till now", says S Elango, CRPF DIG (operations), who led the contingent into the jungle.

Now comes even more startling things: "The nameless, faceless tribals —who have never seen or heard of electricity or water taps, schools or dispensary, men or machines—have grown up believing the Naxals are the government. The rebels bring them rice and medicines and take care of their daily needs. They have never seen transport or ration through PDS; what they are familiar with is the Red Army."

The closest to civilisation, as we understand the term, is a larger village——or town —called Beharamgarh, 29 km away, which also has a police station but tribals of Bodiguda have no use for it, seldom venturing there!

P Chidambram, Union Home Minister, had adumbrated the grand strategy of "clear, hold and develop," to fight and eliminate the scourge called Maoist insurrection. Last month (Mar 2012), it was the first stage of the strategy, 'clear', that was operationalised in Abujhmad forest. What was the end result of this operation that took weeks of planning? "It ended with a one-hour exchange of fire in the jungles. Two injured jawans, no Naxal arrests, and yes, the discovery of a village (Bodiguda) for the Maoist-hit State of Chhattisgarh!"

Ironically, the same Chidambram, the author of "clear, hold and develop", speaking of the Red threat at the Chief Minister's Conference said on 20 Apr 2012. "They did not have the upper hand because there are not enough men, weapons and vehicles, not enough roads, and not enough …Civil administration." The scribe who penned the article, added cynically: The Minister could have added another line—"some states don't know of villages where our own live." Then he adds a post script: *nobody knows how many Bodigudas lie nestled in the unknown hill.*

Before, we finish with the analysis of this article, it is deemed necessary to reproduce here its telling blurb.

INSIDE RED TERRITORY HT finds main Challenge to fighting the threat: vast stretches the State has ceded to rebels.

Maoists celebrate in Style

The CPI (Maoist) deserve credit for the meticulous way they prepare for some events connected with their history, for instance, the tenth anniversary of their birth, which is covered in the following pages.

Even more deliberated are the proceedings of their party Congress and meetings of the Central Committee. They hold these events in 'liberated areas' with a huge security cover for such meets, and even more stringently, for their top leaders.

Maoist: Celebrations of important events

2-8 Dec 2008. Maoists celebrated PLGA's foundation week at Raipur. And observed 26/11 by soluting victims of 26/11 Mumbai terror attack by a gun salute to them in the dense forest of Latehar in Jharkhand.

Were the Maoists on the backfoot in 2013

As the CPI (Maoist) begins preparing to celebrate the 10th year of its formation in early 2014, the happenings of the past 12 months are bound to haunt them. Though they launched their biggest attack on a convoy of political leaders, even that turned out to be one of their major embarrassments. The other two happenings that troubled them were: one, killing of two journalists, and two, the splinter groups showing the Maoist their place, in Chhattisgarh.

The killings of PCC chief Nand Kumar Patel, his son Dinesh Patel, Mahendra Karma, the hero of Salwa Judum, SC Shukla, an old Congressmen and many others, totalling 27, brought them wide-spread criticism. So much so that weeks later, they regretted the mindless killings, particularly of father-son due. The murder of two journalists also brought them opprobrium. The twin killings, of Nemichand Jain and Sai Reddy in Bastar, brought them criticism even from their sympathisers, PUDR, even if couched in most inoffensive language. The secretariat of the PUDR referred to the CPI (Maoist) constitution, a document deemed sacrosanct by the rebels, and noted: "The two killings (of the journalists) were carried by the Maoists without even complying with the provisions of their own constitution. It raises a question if they take their own constitution seriously." They consequently apologised for the murder of Jain, blaming the junior cadres for it.

In the two months preceding 25 May Darbha massacre of 27, including the Congress leaders, the Maoists suffered huge losses across its various zones. On 28 March, the Jharkhand-based splinter of the Maoists, the Triteeya Sammelan Prastuti Committee (TSPC), an ultra-leftist outfit, killed ten Maoists in Chatra, Even worse, the TSPC held 25 Maoists hostage, and released them only on a written undertaking that they would immediately leave the CPI (Maoist) outfit. In April, the Gadchiroli police eliminated nine Maoists in two encounters. In April again, a joint team of Andhra Greyhounds, Chhattisgarh police and CRPF killed nine Maoists in Sukma.

In July, Gadchiroli police killed six women Maoists and in September, the Malkangiri police killed 14 Maoists.

The Ultras, however, did earn some psychological battles against the forces. One was when they implanted IEDs in the bodies of two CRPF men in January. But they also earned a wide-spread condemnation for such a heinous act. Then in April, a bunch of Maoists 'trapped' some 250 Jharkhand policemen on a hill in Gumla, and blocked around 1,000 cops for over 24 hours from reaching them and rescuing them. The rescue operation was personally led by the DGP, Rajiv Kumar. They looted two important weapons from the forces: in January, two "generation-X" Israel-make X-95 rifles from CRPF; and in November, a grenade launcher in Bijapur.

The year 2013 also brought heavy casualties to the Maoist ranks. Including the ones in battle, nearly 100 ultras of various ranks died, a few of them of malaria, snakebites and drowning. Yearly losses as per the MHA data are:

2009	172
2010	220
2011	99
2012	74
2013	100

The gap between the losses in the last two years (74 and 100), wide enough as it is, will be even wider if one takes into account the fact that the MHA data include victims of alleged fake encounters until they are proven innocent by an inquiry commission. (Few such queries get completed and the Ministry data continue to include such deaths). The count also includes the slain members of other banned outfits such as People's Liberation Front of India and Jharkhand Jan Mukti Parishad. The CPI (Maoist) itself have admitted 100 losses in 2013 among its cadres.

CPI (Maoist) documents describes these as major losses. They make some rather interesting revelations, summed up here:

- The Chatra incident almost wiped out the top leadership of Bihar-Jharkhand Special Regional Committee.
- The Sukma encounter virtually eliminated the Karimnagar-Warangal-Khammam (KWK) Special Committee. The KWK blow was crucial as the Maoist had been trying to regroup in the Telengana region for years.
- The Gadchiroli encounter caused them a major setback in the Maharashtra Division.

The year 2013 also saw the arrest of two members of the Central Committee, the top most decision-making unit of the outfit. Aklanta Rabha alias Mahesh was arrested from Guwahati in April. Gajanand Bhaskar alias Pareshda from Silchar in May. Maoists also lost some senior cadres to encounters in Assam.

Most importantly and significantly, there is certain degree of disillusionment among the senior cadre about the aims and functional integrity of the leadership. Once, in the initial phases, the movement had grown following support from urban areas as the leadership promised a fight against inequality. In one word, it was a promise for class struggle, the underpinning of Leftist ideology, be it in Russia, China or Cuba for that matter. Idealism gets highjacked or subverted at a certain subsequent stage. So is the case with Indian Maoism presently. The last few years saw more emphasis on violence—for reasons of abduction, extortion, revenge, funds, intra-outfit rivalries, e.g. Maoist versus TSPC——hence certain veterans are disillusioned. One of them is speaking his mind here.

"Ours was a class struggle, but it has now fizzled out", says Palamu-based Satish Kumar, a former Maoist and presently an All Jharkhand Students Union leader. "The party could not lead the peasants to the desired goal. It no longer remains a peasant movement, only armed attacks with little mass participation."

Kumar joined the PWG in 1982 and subsequently became a senior leader with the CPI (Maoists) before deciding to quit and contest 2009 Legislative Assembly poll on JMM ticket. Despite quitting, he retains his analytical faculties to warn his interlocutors against presumption that the movement would disappear. "The Party is still strong but it needs to reorganise the masses, something it did in the 1970s and 1980s in Andhra. Inequality still persists, armed groups still attract the disillusioned youth. It may not lead to revolution but unless the administration addresses the needs of the people, violence will linger longer than one can imagine[43]."

Summary of losses and strikes: 2013

Losses

- Marri Ravi @ Sudhakar, wife Pushpa. He was North-Telangana Special Zone Committee member. She was KWK Divisional Committee member. Both killed in Sukma in April.
- Lalesh Yadav@Prashant. Jharkhand Regional Committee member. killed in Chatra in March.
- Gaddam Lakshmi@Mahita. A veteran of over three decades, a teacher with CPI (Maoist)'s Central Regional Political school, Died in April.
- Nohari Bai@Samita. Veteran woman commander of over two decades. Died February.

- Karam Somli@Indira. In North Gadchiroli Division Committee. Died of snake bite in May.
- Mainu. In Barsur Squad in East Bastar. Drowned in Indravati.

Strikes

- January M1-17 shot down in Sukma.
- January. 10 cops killed in Latehar, IEDs implanted in bodies of two of these.
- April. Over 250 Jharkhand policemen trapped on a hilltop in Gumla; a 1000 strong rescue party held off for over 24 hours.
- April. Doordarshan Kendra attacked, three cops killed.
- May. Nand Kumar Patel, his son, Mahendra Karma, and other Congress leaders killed in Darbha.
- February and December. One journalist each killed in these two months.
- January and November. CRPF looted arms in Latehar (Jharkhand) and Bijapur (Chhattisgarh).

Finally, the question: were the Maoists on the back foot in the year 2014? Discussing the issue in mid-May 2014, it may be too early to come to a definitive conclusion.

Wait and watch should be the advice for analyst in a hurry to cremate the Maoism in India. As Kumar has said above, they may take longer to disappear than analysts believe. Here is a warning signal: KWK Committee, in fact, may succeed in reviving Maoism in Telengana when it is born after 2014 poll.

"CoBRA scans Abujmaad forest for key Maoist meet"

It is the story of the CPI (Maoist) holding its 10th Congress in Sep 2014 in the dense forest of Abujmaad and security forces trying to zero in on the venue. It is datelined 24 Sep 2014, and filed from Nagpur. It appeared in the 25 Sep 2014 issue of this daily[44].

"The CRPF has sent a large unit of its specialised anti-Naxal force CoBRA into the dense forests of Abujhmaad in South Chhattisgarh searching for the rebels, following intelligence inputs that the banned CPI (Maoist) was holding its much-delayed 10th Congress near Orchha in their so-called "liberated zone".

The 10th Congress was scheduled from 10 to 21 Sep 2014, if these reports are to be believed. Sources reported that security forces had strong intelligence inputs about the organisation of the event and movement of the Maoists from across the country as well as abroad to the designated place.

The operation had been planned to trap the participant as the suspected gathering was seen as a big opportunity to strike a major below to the Reds. It is learnt that the idea was to allow the delegate to converge at their venue and then encircle the location to prevent them from escaping.

CoBRA was chosen for the operation as it was one of the few units of the CRPF which was specifically trained in guerrilla warfare. "The security personnel have moved in from different directions and penetrated deep into the forests in a carefully planned manoeuvre. Till Wednesday (23 Sep), no report of any major action have come, barring a skirmish with a group of Naxals somewhere in Narayanpur along the border with Maharashtra".

"It has also been learnt that the security forces were equipped with sophisticated gadgets, including drones, and had carefully zeroed in on the places where they had planned to make advances."

"With no action reported for the last three days after the possible conclusion of the Maoist Congress, there was doubts that the event had taken place. The last Congress was held in 2007 and the 10th had been waiting due to security operations launched in 2009 under Operation Green Hunt."

"ADG (anti-Naxal operations), Chhattisgarh, RK Vij, while talking to the Indian Express confirmed that they had inputs about a large gathering following which an operation was launched from three sides, but nothing substantial has happened. The operation is likely to end in two-three days."

A film depicts the 'unreal' Naxals: 2012

Director Prakash Jha release a film, 'Chakravyuh', which aims to depict the Maoists in their labyrinth, the ways they combat the security forces and huge pile of weaponry they possess. Jha is known for realistic film on current political issues, the genre to which 'Chakravyuh' belongs, and historical subjects. Undoubtedly, he is among the few political animals in the film industry. To wit, he has contested polls in the past. But somehow, he seems to have failed to come up to critics' expectation with this movie released in Oct 2012.

Presently, Chhattisgarh is the State worst-affected by the ravages by Naxals, Bastar being its epicentre, bearing their dance of death and destruction. The film shows one encounter in jungle where the ultras flee the site. The police seize 25 AK-47s and 110 SLRs, besides plenty of other arms meant for the Naxals. This is exactly where Jha has gone over the top. The Naxals operating in just one camp of a district carrying so many weapons, and sophisticated at that, is rather unrealistic. No more than two AK-47s and 10 Kalashnikovs have been seized in the last five years.

Besides going overboard with the seized arms, Jha has also depicted Naxals almost engaged in a Conventional Warfare. The Ultras as of the present are essentially practicing guerrilla tactics against the security forces. Throughout their history, the Maoists have engaged the forces in direct gunfights only a couple of times, that too en massing a huge number at times up to 700 to 800. Their normal tactics so far have been to lay ambush on the marching columns, blowing them and their vehicles with IEDs, and then shooting at them from a nearby hill top, well selected in advance. Best example of such ambush was wiping out 27 political figures, including the entire Congress leadership of the State on 25 May 2013. One of the few instances of straight gunfights was the 16 Apr 2010 at Tadmetla, where 75 CRPF men were killed. Critics are harsh on Jha for this flaw. "Situating the entire Naxal-police on this majestic plan may lend an epic scope to the movie, but it betrays little understanding of the battle[44]."

Such an approach can't be excused as artistic licence, especially when the Director himself claims to be realistic. Mode and method of the conflict is crucial for the viewers, and general public beyond, to understand the nuances of the conflict. Glamourising a bloody conflict is least one expect from Jha, even if he aims to ensure a commercial success for his creation. Such a treatment will perpetuate a 'romantic' myth in urban India, Leftist 'intellectual', has woven around the term "Maoist"! Undoubtedly, the movement began with an honest cause decades ago, but since then it has mutated, even deteriorated. Jha may claim that the battle field he presents is the Naxal movement in a microcosm but he ignores that the movement today is layered, comprising several ethnicities and causes —— sublime here and ridiculous there. If there are committed rebels, there are plain thugs, too. Even if we ignore the differences between the Maoists of the distant lands, like Gadchiroli and Lalgarh, there is tittle similarity between the ultras of Khammam and Sukma, the two bordering districts of Andhra and Chhattisgarh. "Some comrades have ideology and total revolution wired into their DNA, while some only seek revenge against local chieftains" or upper caste leaders, such as in Bihar, and many others are disillusioned, like Kumar we have met earlier in the text and oppressed youngmen.

Here is an illustrative case of, 35, who emerged as a major Maoist Commander of the Sarguja district in north Chhattisgarh. A farmer, he was alleged framed by the police at the behest of the local trader. He escaped from jail to the neighbouring Jharkhand and returned with a *gamcha* and a gun. Soon becoming a prominent Maoist, he raised a small Red Army, aimed at looting and extortion. Expectedly, in Jun 2011, he was killed by his protégée and acolytes over the division of loot worth a few lakh. When a journalist visited his village, Balangi, his second wife and relatives related his emergence and subsequent murder or classic "badle ki aag (fire of revenge) stuff[45]. Yadav may have been wronged by the system, but he exploited the same system for personal pecuniary gains, even after avenging the said wrong. Reverting to films, Yadav served as stereotype inspirational figure for countless characters in Hindi Cinema since Sunil Dutt in *Mother India*.

If some critics have panned the movie, others have called it honest and bold.

Notes

1. Source: Strategy and tactics of Indian Revolution, Published by Central Committee CPI (Maoist.
2. The Hindu, 12 January 2007.
3. Bhavna Vij Aurora, the Outlook, 15 May 2006.
4. The Outlook, 26 May 2006.
5. Vinay Jha, Indian Express, 22 July 2007.
6. Venkat Parsa, Asian age, 26 February 2007.
7. Asian Age, 4 April 2007.
8. Rajeev PI, Indian Express, 16 June 2007.
9. The reporters are Harinder Baweja and photographer Ajay Aggarwal, in the Hindustan Times dated 22.4.12.
10. Presley Thomas and Aloke Tikku, The Hindu, 13.4.2012.
11. Anant Krishnan, the Hindu, 11.3.2012.
12. Avinash Kumar, The Hindustan Times, 16 April 2012.
13. Sudeep Chakravarti, the Hindu, 13 April 2012.
14. Sandeep Joshi, The Hindu, 23 Aug 2012.
15. Vijaita Singh, Indian Express, 6 Nov 2012.
16. Lt Gen VK Ahluwalia, Times of India, 19.1.13. He was the former Army Commander, Central Command.
17. Rakhi Chakrabarty, Times of India, 19 Aug 2013.
18. Rakhi Charkabarty, Times of India, 20 Sep 2013.
19. Rakhi Chakrabarty, Times of India, 19 Sep 2013.
20. Joginder Singh, The Pioneer, 16 Apr 2012.
21. Naxalism; Joshi, PC; Kalpaz, 2012, P. 141.
22. Rakesh K Singh, Sunday Pioneer, 27.12.2009.
23. Alok Tikku, Hindustan Times, 9 Jul 2013.
24. Bagchi, Suvojit, The Hindu, 23.1.14.

25. Bhardwaj, Ashutoh, Indian Express, 24.1.14.
26. B Vijay Murty, Hindustan Times, 12 Mar 2015.
27. Ambvesh Choudhury and Probal Sanatani, Hindustan Times, 31 Mar 2015.
28. Times of India, 18 Jan 2010.
29. Rakesh. Singh, The Hindu, 8 Oct 2011.
30. K.Srinivas Reddy, The Hindu, 2 Apr 2012.
31. Deepu Sebastian Edmond, The Hindu, 1 Sep 2012.
32. Sandeep Joshi, The Hindu, 6 Sep 2012.
33. Toral Varia Deshpande, The Outlook, 10 Sep 2012.
34. Toral Varia Deshpande, The Outlook, 10 Sep 2012.
35. Avinash Kumar and PTI, Hindustan Times, 3 June 2013.
36. Rajeev Mullick, Hindustan Times, 19 Jul 2013.
37. Neelesh Mishra, Hindustan Times, 12 Mar 2008.
38. Sanjib Kr Baruah, Hindustan Times, 30 May 2013.
39. Snigdhendu Bhattacharya, Hindustan Times, 17 Sep 2013.
40. Shikha Mukherjee, "CPM admits to misrule," The Pioneer, 22.12.2009.
41. Harinder Baweja, Hindustan Times, 22 Apr 2012.
42. Bhardwaj, Ashutosh, Indian Express, 1.1.14.
43. Vivek Deshpande, Indian Express, 25 Sep 2014.
44. Bhardwaj, Ashutosh, Indian Express, 3.11.12.
45. op cit.

Index

C

D

O

S

NAXAL AND MAOIST TERROR IN INDIA

NAXAL AND MAOIST TERROR IN INDIA

VOLUME - II

COMBATING MAOISM

Col. Ved Prakash

KALPAZ

ISBN : 978-93-5324-032-5 (Vol - II)
978-93-5128-212-9 (Set)

First Published, 2019

Published by

Kalpaz Publications
C-30, Satyawati Nagar,
Delhi – 110052
Ph.: 011-47034999, 9811692060
www.kalpazpublications.com
E-mail: kalpaz@hotmail.com

Printed at: G. Print Process, Delhi

Cataloging in Publication Data—DK

Courtesy: D.K. Agencies (P) Ltd. <docinfo@dkagencies.com>

Prakash, Ved, *Col.*, author.

Naxal and Maoist terror in India / Col. Ved Prakash.

volumes cm

Contents: volume I. Expanding red corridor — volume II. Combating Maoism — volume III. Development of Naxal infected regions — volume IV. Chhattisgarh and Jharkhand — volume V. Odisha and West Bengal.

ISBN 9789351282129 (set)

1. Naxalite movement—India. 2. Communism—India. 3. Communist Party of India-Maoist. 4. India—Politics and government—1947- I. Title.

LCC HX393.5.P73 2019 | DDC 320.532093 23

316

Contents

Volume - IV

Chhattisgarh and Jharkhand

(*Series Page No. 915-1408 See Below*)

Volume - V

Odisha and West Bengal

(*Series Page No. 1409-1808 See Below*)

7

Maoist Leadership

This is an important Chapter in this work. Leftist ideology has a hold on Indian population—al be it, a section of it—for a considerable period. In India's history, the peasants and tribal's have been rising in revolt against the ruling classes—be it in pre-mughal period, British time or Post-independence.

There is a history of peasants revolt against their exploitations. Then the tribal's rose in protest/revolt in Central and East India when their forests and lands were being forcibly taken by authorities. The Nagas fought valiantly against the British when they were advancing in their land/areas.

Left-wing extremism/(Extremists) is informed and driven by communist ideology. They are siding with the deprived and exploited and are indulging armed struggle to displace the present exploitative class and wrest the country from their clutches". The present LWE is the 1960s phenomenon, when Seetharamaioh rose in Andhra srikakulam in 1961 and Charu Mazumdar took to armed struggle in Naxalbari in 1967. The latter one is better known and gave birth to the well-known terms Naxal, Naxalite and Naxalism. Interestingly, Naxal Uprising did not last long. In fact it was crushed in two years. But its Charismatic leader Charu Mazumdar, with his counter-parts in Andhra Pradesh has established CPI (ML) by 1971. But Unfortunately Charu died in 1972. But through a process of splits of CPI (ML), and factions from north and factions from Andhra Pradesh, joining in 2004 produced CPI (Maoist). Today, Maoists are the leading LWE formation that is waging armed struggle in the country.

'Significantly, the terms Naxalism and Maoism are interchangeable even today but even more significantly, it is essentially Maoists who are conducting the struggle presently even then the popular public imagination is stuck up with the Term "Naxalism" for the Left-Wing Extremism. Be that as it may, this chapter on Maoists Leadership" is set out in four parts:

- Left ideology: Its status presently.
- Organizational set up of CPI (Maoist)
- Factionalism in the CPI (Maoist)
- Maoist leaders: Biographical sketches.

Left Ideology: Its Status presently

First, a word on communism. It was an effective and functional force for some seven decades of the twentieth century, till its collapse in 1991. With the breakup of the USSR, it proved a failed god. China is a communist country in name, but following tenets of capitalist economy. Communism as a philosophy has lost its intrinsic strength even if a shell exists.

It has been replaced, as a Leftist ideology by the Maoist thought. There are some countries in South America, which have Leftist governments during the last two decades. The latest to join the band wagon is Greece.

As for the Maoists phenomenon, it seems to be having an appeal in Asia. A decade–old Maoist armed struggle in Nepal succeeded in overthrowing the monarchy in that only Hindu nation. Presently, the Maoists are functioning in a republican, secular Nepal, in coalition with other democratic parties. The only other nation where the Maoists are making some success is India. If we regard Naxal uprising in 1960s as start of the LWE, the Maoists struggle is some five decade phenomenon in India. They aim to take over the country by 2050.

The Maoists have made considerable advances, particularly since 2004, when the MCC and PWG joined hands to form CPI (Maoists) but they have set backs twice when they lost large number of leaders and cadres. This was during the successful salwa Judum compaign of the Chhattisgarh Government. The next one was during the operation Green hunt launched jointly by the centre and state Governments in 2009-2011. But the Maoists have in the past, shown resilience and come back with greater vigour. They have shown in the past that they can wait patiently, regroup and then revive their fighting. In the last two years, they have been putting up good fight and causing considerable casuality to men and material. It is time India gets its acts together and control, and then defeat the Maoists violence.

Finally, a subject of study: Why such LWE movements are launched and succeed in Hindu nations only? First Nepal, and then India—with 85 percent Hindus in its population! Why not in even one of the 46 Muslims countries? Is a study of their phenomenon called for or not?

Is love defeating Maoists fervours?

This should be an interesting question, framed in the context of the preceding narrative. Call it love or lust, no species of human beings has ever remained untouched by this impulse—be they politicians, the scientist, professionals , or the ordinary humans! Then, why should the 'blood thirsty' Maoists be an exception to the 'universal truth' or call it universal temptations. The Maoists too are made of flesh and blood.

If the Maoists are annoyed with the desertions of comrades with their women cadres, they will do well to read up what Karl Marx wrote:" The relation of man to woman is the most genuine relation of human being to human being". The great German ideologue refused to police a couple. Then Chairman Mao, another icon of the guerrilla's world over, was hardly a puritan! But some insiders were crude enough to disclose the Helms man's hunger for "nubile beauties and virgins". Now to Pablo Neruda, "the unswerbing Communist who perhaps wrote the greatest love poetry of the last century , is treasured by the revolutionaries across the globe."[1]

Precisely for these reasons, the recent surrender of Senior Maoist Prasad with a women is significant for both what is reveals and conceals. Prasad conceded that the woman was not his wife but asserts that he plans to spend the rest of his life with her. He accused his former bosses of not telling the public that a year earlier he had informed them of his plans to divorce his wife due to serious problems with her. The CPI (Maoist) accused him of "leaving the party for wealth and woman".

Prasad's case is similar to that of Central Committee member Lanke Papi Reddy who surrounded in Andhra Pradesh in 2008. Maoists disowned him, apparently suddenly discovering that he had committed serious mistakes" and "misbehaved" with woman cadres. Prasad had left the party in the 1990s, then came back and was later punished for "misbehaving" with woman cadres. Inspite of this all, the party went on to promote him, till his surrender in January.

But these are not the only instances of such 'misbehavior'. Several commanders have recently left the party with their loves, including the one who led the team who abducted the then Sukma collector Alexpaul Menon.

It might be necessary for a guerrilla army, largely located and functioning in forests, to avoid relations and families. But by condemning the transgressors, who had served for long years as loyal soldiers as "traitors" to the cause, they may be decrying their own ideology. This is particularly inexplicable when top leaders are guilty of similar/same "misbehaviour towards woman cadres" and "serious mistakes" are never denounced. Kishenji is one well known example of such an exception.

A politburo member, Kishenji was killed in an encounter in Nov 2011, "Following a 'booby trap' helped by his aide Suchitra Mahato. Interestingly, Suchitra came close to Kishenji after her husband Sasadhar, also senior commanders, was killed in March 2011. Equally interestingly, after Kishenji's death, Suchitra married another comrade before the couple surrendered in Mar 2012.

However despite the fact that Kishenji's had been guilty of committing a grave error in allowing himself to be misled into a relationship, he was not only never denounced by the leadership, but he also continued to hold a pre-eminent position and exalted status as if nothing untoward had happened. Was it because he was too powerful to be quizzed and confronted by the hierarchy?

Another change needs to be noted about the way the surrenders are dealt with by the Maoists. Till a decade or so back, the cadres who surrendered were eliminated by their erst while comrades but there seem to be no threat of elimination to surrenderees like Lanka Papi Reddy who left in 2008 and Prasad who left recently, in Jan 2014. May be there are double standards here too. As in cases of "serious misbehavior towards the woman cadres", senior leaders do not face any censure, in surrender cases too, senior commanders are not condemned. But junior cadres in either of such cases may not be as lucky—may be, they are denounced or eliminated!

"Most Wanted: Maoists Pip Terrorists in Bounty Stakes"

This Was an intresting article that appeared in daily of 21 Sep 2014. It Compared the bounty amounts on the heads of five top Maoists and three top terrorists.[2]

Top 5 Maoists	**Bounty**
Ganpathy	Rs. 2.52 crore
Nambala Kesava Rao	Rs.1.57 crore
Kishan da alias Prashant Bose	Rs.1.47 crore
Katakam Sudershan	Rs. 1.47 crore
Deo Kumar singh alias Arvindi	Rs. 1.32 crore
Top 3 Terrorists	
Riaz Bhatkal	Rs 25 lakh
Iqbal Bhatkal	Rs. 25 Lakh
Amir Razakhan	Rs 25 Lakh

Not the top Dog

Dawood Ibrahim, With Rs 15 Lakh on his head is no more the top dog, among India's "most wanted" Information on Maharashtra Police reward on him is not in public domain.

The role of Informer

- Encounter killing of Bengal's top Maosits Kishanji in 2011 was credited to tip off from an informer
- 40 Lakh bounty was shared by cops and CRPF. The Informer was understood to have been paid from Cop's share of reward money.

Details on these issues

Dawood Ibrahim is no longer India's most wanted man, Maoists leader Ganpathy having replaced him in that slot! The Red Army of the latter is spread across the 10 states, and is virtual government unto itself in the Red corridor, from Pashupatinath to Tirupati, as it is popularly defined.

The Maoists General Secretary carries 17 times the amount offered—Rs.15 Lakh—for the 1993 Mumbai blast accused.

The Distinction does not end with the two. The Maoists, considered biggest threat to India's internal security, are miles ahead of gangsters like Dawood, and even wanted terrorists when it comes to bounty's as the table above Shows. CPI (Maoist) Pollitburio members Nambala Kesava Rao and Kishan da alias Prashant Bose are worth ₹ 1.5 D crore and ₹ 1.47 Crore, respectively, while their colleague Deo Kumar Singh alias Arvind, who holds Sway over Jharkhand-Bihar Region is Worth ₹ 1.32 crore.

On the other hand, the Indian Mujahideen's fugitive founder Riyaz Bhalkal—Whose group carries out deadly terror attacks with alarming alacrity across the country—carries a prize of Rs. 25 Lakh. Ramchandra kalasangra and Sandeep Dange, most wanted accused in the 'Hindutva terror cases', carry rewards of ₹ 20 Lakh each offered by the CBI and NIA.

Interestingly, not everyone was enthusiastic when the idea of increasing the bounty for the top Maoists was mooted by a CRPF officer at a meeting of the Maoists—hit states, after the NDA government took over. But reportedly, Home Secretary Anil Goswami backed it and asked the States to work on it since the police was a state Subject.

Acting on the proposal Maharashtra and Chhattisgarh were the first to announce ₹ 1 Crore bounty each on Ganpathi (the commulative now stands as ₹ 2.52 Crore. They also enhanced the offers for politburo members from ₹ 7-10 Lakh to ₹ 50-60 Lakh each, while the information leading to the arrest of a Central Committee member would now fetch ₹ 40-50 Lakh.

The decision to enhance the bounty was partly influenced by the Andhra Pradesh experience. Andhra's Maximum reward money had persuaded several Maoists there to surrender as they got to keep the money to start their lives afresh. They subsequently, became a useful source of information for the intelligence agencies on their Erst while comrades still in the jungles.

The MHA official reasoned that if the new reward plicy worked, the government would end up spending far less on operations launched to catch the rebels.

Odisha DGP Sanjiv Marik tells this daily that the States continually keep reviewing the bounty on individuals Maoists Leaders depending on their status, Potential for their damaging activities etc. He citied the example of Sabyaschi Panda, now arrested (sep 2014), who was worth ₹ 20 Lakh when he headed the CPI (Maoists) odisha organizing committee that looted police armouries in Nayagarh and abducted two Italian tourists. But the bounty was reduced to ₹ 5 Lakh once he was dismissed by his outfit. In contrast, the bounty on Dawood has stayed almost constant. A Former CBI official tells the daily they "received several inputs about his movements out of Pakistan but lack of international cooperation failed all attempts at action. "Even now, we keep getting inputs, which are invariably incorrect, but we still keep checking".

There were no procedures—clearly laid out and well thought out— till late for making the "wanted" Lists in India. There was no centralized data on rewards announced by states' police on top criminals and terror suspects. With the formation in 2009 of NIA, a federal agency to probe terror cases, the situation has improved. The NIA has announced substantially higher rewards (₹ 10-15 Lakh) and the information is now available on its website.

Organisational Set-up of CPI (Maoist)

Starting from the bottom, the 'dalam' is the fighting unit of the Maoists. It is the basic unit, somewhere between an infantry Section (11 Soldiers led by a NCO) and infantry Platoon (35 soldiers led by a JCO).

It needs to be noted that the NCOs and JCOs are lowest ring of the leadership levels in an infantry battalion, and they mostly function/Fight under close supervision of a company commanders usually a major.

But there can be occasions when a Section Commander and a platoon Commander find themselves fighting the enemy, without direct or an indirect supervision of the company commanders.

But opposed to what has been said about section/Platoon Commanders in the proceeding paragraphs, a dalam commander is invariably fighting his battles independently, operating in a fairly large area.

In a manner of speaking, the Dalam commander is the cutting edge of Maoists fighting Machine. The dalam might have 15 to 30 fighters in it, depending upon the area it is operating in it.

To understand the overall structure of Maoists Combat hierarchy, let us now bring in the politburo. It is the top most group of Maoists leaders, comprised of the most important ones. It is exact equivalent of a politburo of any communist party. It is equivalent of a cabinet at the centre, in a democratic country like India. As the Prime Minister is the leader in the democracy, General Secretary of the CPI (ML) is the Supremo, and he heads the Politburo.

Next to the politburo is the Central Committee (CC) of the CPI (ML). It is the national Committee of the party. To compare it with the political parties in Indian democracies, the politburo and the CC are equivalent of a political party's Parliamentary Board and National Executives Council.

Under the Central Units, Politburo and the CC, The CPI (ML) has its organizational structures at the state the level. In the State, there is an organizing committee at the top. A state is divided into Regions, and the latter into zones. A zonal Commander controls the dalams, operating in its territorial limits. Depending on the operational situation, a zone may have sub-zones in it. In that case, Dalams may operate under a Sub-zonal commander. But that is not the case often.

Organisational Structures of CPI (Maoists)

The following pages will now contain information on the composition of the two main structures of the CPI (ML), where ever necessary details are in public domain.

It should be added here that the Politburo will generally have 10 to 15 members; where as the Central Committee could have 30 to 40 members. There obviously cannot be an all time fixed membership of such bodies.

Central Military commission is another important organ of the CPI (Maoist), a plain copy of the Chinese communist Party's CMC, expectedly enough.

They also have, besides the Combat units like Dalams, Tech units and safe houses, already covered in the earlier pages.

CPI (Maoist) Politburo as on 18 Feb 2008

A 14-member CPI (Maoist) Politburo is the main decision-making body of the ultras. Seven out of these 14 top leaders were from Andhra Pradesh—four of them from Karimnagar District alone. These names were disclosed by a Politburo member Misir Besra @ Bhaskar @ Sunirmal after his arrest in Jharkhand

Politburo members

1. Muppala Laxman Rao (15 aliases including Ganapathi, Ramana, Srinivas and Malanna) was party Chief. The 58-year old is science graduate from Karimnagar district (AP).
2. Prashanth Bose (aliases Nirbhay, Mahesh and kajal) is No2 in the politburo, belongs to west Bengal. Represents the outfit at meetings with international and Indian revolutionary organizations.
3. Cherukuri Raj Kumar (aliases Uday, Parimal, Azad) aged 55, belongs to Krishna District (AP).
4. Mallojula Koteshwara Rao (aliases Kishenji, Prahalad, Baswaraj Ramji), 55. Again, belongs to Karimnagar District (AP). Responsible for merger of PWG with MCC. Currently, looks after Bengal.
5. Nambala Keshava rao (aliases Ganganna, Basavraj) aged 53, belongs to Sri kulam district (AP).
6. Kobbad Ghandhi (aliases Saleem, Rajan Kishor). Incharge of the Central propaganda Bureau, Looking after Party documentation.
7. Promod Mishra (aliases Ban Bihari, Janardhan). Belongs to Aurangabad Bihar. Incharge of Delhi, Punjab, Haryana and J and K.
8. Malla Raji Reddy (aliases mesa lanna, Sayanna, Sathenna), 55. Comes from Karimnagar (AP).
9. Sumanand Singh (alias Sujith Da, Suman), 55. Native of Bihar. In charge of 'military' activities in West-Bengal. Has reputation for planning armed operations.
10. Mallajula Venugopal (aiases Bhupathi sonu). From Karimnagar (AP).
11. Katakam Sudershan (aliases Anand, Mohan, Birender), 50. From Adilabad district (AP).
12. Akhilesh Yadav (aliases Ramanji, Prabodh, Bhupesh),65. Former school teacher. Is oldest politburo member from Gaya (Bihar), his son too is a Maoist.

13. Balraj (alias BR), 50. Looks after publication, is in-charge of north Bihar.
14. Ashutosh (aliases Bipul, Ashok), 45. From Jharkhand, elevated to the top Group after Besra's arrest.

(The Times of India, 18.2.2008)

Organisational Structure: Oct 2009

Certain information on the CPI (Maoist) organizational Structures has been given in the preceding as also in the succeeding pages. This information that follows is obtained from interrogation of the Maoist Senior leader Narla Rabi Sharma who was arrested in Oct 2009 at Hazaribag in Jharkhand.

- Politburo: The Top decision-making, it has between 12 to 14 members. M. Lakshman Rao@ Ganapathy, is the General Secretary and
- Central Committee: The most powerful body, it has 30 to 35 members. The Politburo is consisted from the members of the CC.
- Central Military Commission: The CMC is the top most armed wing of the CPI (maoist). It has its own elaborate hierarchy comprising of State or area Military Commission, below which are Regional Military Commissions. The fighting force typically has companies and platoons which are the primary armed units, with the most advanced weapons in their possession. At the lowest level are Special Regular Guerrilla Squads, and Local Regular Guerrilla Squads. At the village level, there are Gram Raksha Dals and self-defence Squads armed with sticks and other traditional weapons like bows and arrows.
- Regional Bureaus: Working under the CC are the five Regional Bureaus, detailed here after.
    1. Central Regional Bureau. Chhattisgarh, MP and Andhra Pradesh- Odisha border.
    2. South-Western Regional Bureau. Maharashtra, Karnataka, Tamil Nadu and Kerela.
    3. Northern Regional Bureau. Punjab, Haryana, North and East Bihar, Uttarakhand, Uttar Pradesh and Delhi.
    4. Eastern Regional Bureau Assam, West Bengal, South Bihar and Jharkhand.
    5. Central-Eastern Regional Bureau. Odisha.

- State Committee or Area Committee: These are set up under each Regional Bureau. Next Come Regional Committees and District or Zonal Committees, followed by Area Committees and village Committees.
- Frontal organizations. The frontal organizations are the ones that operate in Public, ostensibly espousing social causes, but which provide ideological support to the Naxalites. A number of such organizations operate in all Maoist- affected states.

CPI (Maoists): Central Committee Members: NOV 2011

Following are the members of the Central Committee as published in The Hindu, 26 Nov 2011.

1. Muppala Laxman Rao@gGanapathy (Secretary)
2. Prashanth Bose@kishanda
3. Namballa Keshava Rao@Baswa raj
4. Mallojula Venugopal@Abhay
5. Katakam Sudershan@Anand.
6. Malla Raji Reddy@Sathenna
7. Tippiri Tirupati@Deoji
8. Misir Besra@Sunirmal
9. DevKumar Singh@Nishanth
10. Jiniugu Narshimha Reddy@Jampana
11. Akkiraju Hargopal@Ramakrishna
12. Kuppuswamy Devraj@Ramesh
13. Kadari Satnarayana Reddy@Kosa
14. Gajanand@Parush
15. Chanderi Yadav@Payag
16. Mohan@Mahesh
17. Ranjith Bose@Kanchan
18. Manoj@Rajesh
19. Pulluri Prasad Rao@Chandranna
20. Ramchandra Reddy Pratap Reddy@Chalapathi
21. Moden Balakrishna@Bhaskar

Politburo (Leading Members): Sep 2012

This Information about Six members of the Politburo is from a weekly dated 10 Sep 2012.[3]

It should be of interest to compare the positions of these six members in the Feb 2008 list, in the immediate, preceding entry. It should be added here that the two most important maoist Leaders missing in the current list are Kishanji (ser 4 of the 2008 list) and Azad (ser 3 of that List) who have been killed in the encounters Since, Kobbad Ghandhi (No. 6 on the last list) and Misir Besra (new entrant in this list are in jail)

Kishen Da and Misir Besra are not on the last letter, but for the other four, it should be useful refer to it.

Ganapathi: General Secretary, CPI (Maoist)

Rank: Mentioned above. He is the Suprem

Arms Holdings: Sten Carbine. Has 5 Guards.

Reward: ₹ 12 Lakh each set by the governments of Andhra Pradesh, Chhattisgarh and Jharkhand.

It is to be noted that by Sep 2014, bounty on Ganpathi had climbed to be total of ₹ 2.52 crore, as seen in the earlier pages of this chapter

It is also be noted that Ganapathi has 15 aliases—Some record this.

Katakam Sudershan

Rank: Secretary, Central Regional Bureau.

Arms Holding: AK-47.

Rewards: ₹ 12 Lakh each announced by the governments of Andhra Pradesh, Chhattisgarh and Jharkhand.

His bounty in Sep 2014 was Rs 1.47 crore. He was N011 on the Previous list.

Misir Besra

Rank: Politburo member, and members Central Military Commission.

Arms Holding: 9 mm pistol and AK-47

Rewards: ₹ 7 Lakh set by Chhatisgarh, and Rs 12 Lakh by Jharkhand.

Nambala Kesava Rao

Rank: Secretary, Central Military Commission.

Arms Holding: AK-47

Rewards: ₹ 12 Lakh each set by Governments of Andhra Pradesh. Chhattisgarh, and Jharkhand.

The Bounty on Kesava Rao in Sep 2014 was a total of ₹ 1.57 Crore. He is No. 5 on the previous list.

Mallojula Venugopal

Rank: Incharge of Dandakaranya Special Zone Committee (DKSZC).

Arms Holding: AK-47

Rewards: ₹ 12 Lakh set be AP and Jharkhand governments and ₹ 7 Lakh by Chhattisgarh.

He is N010 on the Previous list.

Prashant Bose alias Kishan Da: N02 on Previous List.

Rank: Secretary, Eastern Regional Bureau.

Arms Holding: 9 mm Pistol.

Rewards: ₹ 7 Lakh by Chhattisgarh and ₹ 12 Lakh by Jharkhand. It was ₹ 1.47 Crore in Sep 2014.

Factionalism in the CPI (Maoist)

Any organization—Social, Political, economic or even ideological—is bound to have dissent within it. The dissenters, if they feel ignored, or not being listened too, are bound to weigh their option: To continue with the status quo, organize a faction within and fight it out with the reigning majority, or as last choice, walk out and form their own outfit.

The differences may be because of ideological reasons, or due to personal egos of the leading figures, and even, possibly due to matters of lucre.

The CPI (ML) ever since its birth in 1971 has seen many splits and then factions uniting to create different outfits, and then again spilitting. The formation finally of CPI (Maoists) by merger of MCC and PWG has been detailed earlier. Ever since then, it has been the main Left ideologically and has swathes of territory under its influence and carried out armed struggle ever since.

Not withstanding the above, Maoists too have not been able to keep themselves free of factionalism in its ranks. CPI (Maoists) might have been able to remain the major LWE formation, it has periodically suffered intra-party factional fights. The subject is covered in the next few pages of this section.

Differences in CPI (Maoists) Leadership

Differences among the leaders of any organization are rather a normal, and expected, phenomenon. It is more so in ideology-driven outfits like CPI (Maoists). Starting with the mother outfit of the Maoists, the Naxalites of the 1960s, there have been a number of splits, followed by mergers, and demergers and the present outfits, CPI (Maoist), is the result of two LWE entities merging to create it. This has been discussed in the earlier pages. Even subsequent to its formation, there are large number of the extremist Left-wing outfits, spawned by individual egos and ideological differences, which again would be discussed in a different place later in this text.

Her e is an instance of differences in the west Bengal, based upon tribal –non tribal tags as also local versus outsider labels. It was mentioned in 2010 [January].[4] It was aptly headlined "Bengal Maoist ranks spilt vide open".

It all started with a Zonal Leader Marshall, responsible for many violent incidents in Jangal Mahal area of West Bengal. He came out openly against Koteshwar Rao alias Kishanji, branding him a non tribunal leader and outsider at that! Obviously, there are others like Marshall who thinks the movements in West Bengal Should be led by Local tribals, and not by other non tribals from outside. So for them, Kishenji, a well known guerrilla fighter and leading light of the CPI (Maoists), has no locus standing to lead the tribal struggle in West Bengal.

Marshall alleged that the sons of the soil who man the front lines for dangerous tasks and loyally carry out the Maoists leadership's orders, are being side-lined by the outsiders like Kishanji. It seems Marshall intends to float a new (his own) armed outfit to fight for the tribal cause and claims to have some 150 armed men with him for his purpose.

He hails from the Purulia village of west Bengal.

"Naxal faction teases Government"

This is the news story in a daily of 26 March 2012.[5] Its blurb is significantly apt. It reads: "one Italian let off; we will release the rest if 'demands met'".

The story is datelined 25 March, and is filed from Bhubaneswar/ Jeypore, Odisha. Maoists on the 25th had released one of the two Italian tourists, Claudio Colangelo, Kept hostage by them since 14 March 2012. Sabyasachi Panda, Secretary, CPI (Maoist) state organizing Committee, handed over Colangelo to group of media persons at a place in Kandhmal district from where the two Italian nationals had been abducted 12 days ago. The media team later handed over the Italian to the SP, Ganjam District.

Panda told the media, at the release 'Ceremony' the other Italian, Paolo Bosuco would the freed after the 13-point Charter of demands is met or if they (Maoists) believe the Government is taking adequate steps in the direction. We will watch the situation and take the decision on releasing

Bosuco accordingly. This release must send some positive signals to the Governments to continue dialogue with their negotiatiors. Then, he took a high road to morality, or may be, played to the gallery on the tribal issue: "The two foreigners were abducted to warn the Government that tribals are not objects of exhibition to fill its coffers.... It was also, in part, an attempt to make public the real face of the Government as regards the Tribals."

It was an amusing, if not ridiculous statement coming from a Maoist leader, whose entire movement was sustained by adopting anti-tribal policies! In his high-mindedness, he failed to conceal the facts that they do not only kill the tribals so ruthlessly and often in a barbaric manner, dubbing them 'Government informers', but also indulge in all kinds of murderous violence to block the very development of their areas! It is rather ironic that it was the very lack of this very development that they had built their entire movement on. They exploited the deprivation and poverty of the tribal populations caused by the lack of development to initiate and then sustains it by means, fair and foul!

The ideological purity and convictions are fine to start a movement. But being only humans, even the Maoists, like their predecessors,the communists of various hues, could not maintain the ideological purity that impelled them on the revolutionary path initially, to sustain it. They fell victims not only to the weaknesses of the flesh but also to the flaws and shortcomings all organizations develop in due course! If the former led to the sexual exploitations of the women cadres and comfortable, if not luxurious, high life of leadership , the latter resulted in factionalism within the CPI (Maoist)—almost like in any political party. Hence the factional fighting, reflecting in the next part of Panda's statement.

This is where the misleading heading of this news story comes! The heading worded either by the scribe of the story on the editor of the daily, is based on the misreading of the specifics of the situation! Here, the Naxal fiction is not 'teasing' the Government, it in fact is teasing perhaps, more meaningfully, it is challenging, the rival faction! It is clear as day light from the next part of his statement to the media contingent.

Admitting that differences existed between the Koraput-Srikakulam Division Zonal Committee and the State Organizing Committee, he assured that his cadres would not commit violence in the areas under their jurisdiction till the negotiations were satisfactorily over.

The release of one hostage prompted a beaming Chief Minister Naveen Patnaik, who only one day before the release (Saturday) had asked the Maoists to name fresh negotiators following suspensions of talks and a review meeting at the secretariat, to request the current negotiatiors—Dandapani Mohanty and Dr. BD Sharma, to come forward for resuming talks.

Patnaik appealed to the Maiost leadership of the said Division to let Government know about the health of the Laxmipur MLA Jhina Hikaka and name their negotiations for talks on his release also.

The talks on the release of the Italian were suspended on the 24th after the abduction of the MLA.

The MLA was reportedly safe in the dense forest of Narayanpatna area and was in the custody of Koraput-Srikalkulam Zonal committee Deputy Commandant Sarita who is No2 hardcore Maoist in the committee. Day is the Commandant, in charge of the Division.

The zonal Committee office bearers were reportedly to hold a meeting on 26 March somewhere in the border areas of Narayanpatna, Parbatipuram, Rayagada and Koraput to finalise the list of demands to present to the Government for negotiations.

LWE Factions in Chhattisgarh

Here are some of the factions of CPI (maoist) operating in Chhattisgarh, presently, arguably, the worst Maoist-hit State in the country. This pertains to period Sep 2012.

CPI (Maoists)

It is the mother outfit, operating in areas defined by Palkot-Simdege border and Koleibera and Jaldega regions.

The rest of them are break-away factions, the major among them being people's Liberation Front of India (PLFI)

The Strength of the CPI (maoist) contingent in this State is around 40 member platoon, Led by Zonal Commander Khudi Munda and Sub-Zonal Commander Deepak.

PLFA

It operates in areas of Bano, Parts of Jaldega, Koleibera, Orga and Tatanagar. It has 40 armed cadres led by Dinesh Gope.

Pahadi Cheetah

It operates in areas in and outside Kurdog, Kersai, Bolba, Basia and Koleibera.

It has 15-20 armed members led by lele Sahu.

Bablu Paswan Group

It has no specific area, attacks specific targets. It has 8-10 armed cadres.

Virat Singh Group

It too, has no specific area and attacks Specific targets. Suprisingly, it operates the gang from Bokaro Jail.

Anil Singh Group

It focuses exclusively on extracting ransoms from government contractors. Like the above-mentioned group, it also operates from Ranchi Jail.

Is factionalism fuelled by love and money?

All revolutions are generated by ideology and nurtured with passionate idealism. As the time goes by, it is affected by weaknesses and temptations human beings are prone to. Sustaining idealism is an up hill task. With the passage of time, any movement will come to be inhabited by some ideological conviction and steadfast belief in original impulses and also by thuggery and banal urge for power and pelf. In the case of a recent 7 January 2014 surrender of a Maoist, these were clear indications of 'Love' lurking in the distant landscape!

On 7 January, Gumudavelli Venkatakrishna Prasad alias Gudsa Usendi, Spokesman for the CPI (Maoists) Dandakaranya Special Zonal Committee (DKSZC), surrendered in Andhra Pradesh with a woman. It sparked a huge reaction unprecedented in the party which has largely ignored such surrenders so far. In this case, a woman and cash took the centre stage in the Subsquent controversy.

It is the identity of the woman who surrendered on the 7th with Usendi that generated the controversy. The woman was reported to be his wife, Raji. DKSZC Secretary B Ramana, in a statement, claimed that the woman "Prasad was trying to pass off as his wife Raji.... was actually Santoshi Markami, Prasad's live-in partner". CPI (Maoist) also accused Prasad of running away with ₹ 27 Lakh of the party Fund's.[6]

While conceding that the woman indeed was Markami, Prasad denied the allegation about making away with the party funds.

He explained his position about Raji, who he married in 2001, two years after the death of his first wife. He claimed to have had serious problems with Raji from the start. He further added: "There is no ground in Ramana's allegation that I had deserted Raji and run away mith another women. The entire Party Knew about the problems in my marriage.

We separated in July 2011. In a 2012 meeting, I informed the party that I had decided to get divorce. It was included in the records of the meeting. In Jan 2013, Markami and I decided together. She has been my friend and Colleague for a longtime. We wanted to get formal approval. But due to our illness and disillusionment with party's policies,decisions and tactics, we decided to leave the party. I wrote to the leadership about my decision. Santoshi wrote a separate letter".

Prasad called the party's statement cheap that reveals its feudal mind set. A part from the differences with leaders, they also had health issues: his spinal problem and santoshi's heart condition that needs immediate surgery. All this led to surrender. He cited reason for it: " The truth is they are unable to digest that I have left. Instead of accepting that some policies were flawed, they started attacking my personal life". He gave examples of flawed decisions: destruction of school buildings since 2008; indiscriminate and excessive killings of Adivasis in the name of destroying an informer network; his opposition in 2007 to destruction of some electricity tower, resulting in a power failure throughout Bastar region.

Ramana's assertion that Prasad never raised these issues/objections in the party, the latter said his views are well-documented and known to the leaders, adding: "they always brushed away my arguments, indirectly attributing them to this 'ism' and that 'ism'. They are trying to demoralize me with baseless allegations, and particularly targeting my personal life".

He dismissed party's allegations of "wrong trends' such as bureaucracy, individualism, patriarchy, a luxurious life and misbehaving with women, questioning why these were discovered only on his surrender after nearly three decades with the party. "We feel these kinds of cheap statements will only reflect their feudal mindset".

The above development can be viewed in different ways. Are the cadres and leaders reaching the end of the ideological tether? Are they getting disillusioned? Are they feeling the fatigue of long years of jungle life, its hardship and vigorous anti-Maoist campaign by the security forces? Are the weaknesses of the human beings overtaking the intrepid Maiost fighters? India is neither Nepal nor some odd country in South America to succumb to Maoist violence. It is too big a country and too civilisationally advanced to be defeated by the ideologically-motivated rag tag 'Army' of Maoists, mouthing slogans once made attractive in Mao's China. India has shown capacity to tame the monsters in the North East from Aug 1947 onwards and those of 1980s Punjab and still engaged with jihadis in J&K. Countrymen must rest assured: India will never go under!

"Forces struggle to contain splinter Maoist groups"

This is both indicative and instructive heading of a news analysis in a weekly dated 13 July 2014.[7]

It is indicative of splintering trends or inclinations in all ideology-informed outfits, also instructive in the sense that mushrooming factions pose greater difficulties for the security forces because of the number involved of such violent, anti-national formations.

The blurb of the article is also informative: "These groups have mushroomed in Jharkhand, and are dominant in Gumla, Simdega, Lohardagga, among other areas.

It may be useful to put it right here that such mushrooming has not taken place in Jharkhand only. It is equally true of Chhattisgarh as well, as has been detailed in this very section of the Chapter.

Now to analyse the contents of this news story. Here is its very first Para: "The security forces which have successfully contained the CPI (Maoist) activities to some extents are having sleepless nights dealing with the splinter groups, which have mushroomed in Jharkhand".

Problems of such mushrooming have been hinted above. Not only security forces get divided in various areas, most of these groups are not driven by the ideology, but have their own motivations. The plintering results in more abductions, more violent attacks,and greater restrictions on the normal, day to day life of the population in the area concerned. This article cites one recent example.

The Khunti area of the State, represented by the former Lok Sabha Deput Speaker Karia Munda, witnessed a Shut-Down of over 400 schools, consequent to a call given by one such splinter group clled people's Liberation fromnt of India (PLFI). As a result of the Bandh over 4000 students were deprived of their regular studies and also their mid-day meals for some ten days.

The PLFI is possibly the largest faction of the CPI (maosit), though the epicenter of its activities is Khunti, it has of late, spread its tentacles in its neighbouring districts also, Viz Gumla, Simdega, Lohardagga and more menacingly, even in the outskirts of the State Capital Ranchi. "This has sent the police hierarchy in a tizzy" – to paint the situation in more impressive lingo. The situation was serious to compel the intervention of the State Chief Secretary Sajal Chakravarty. It was this step by the State Administration which saw the PLFI withdrawing its 10-day old mayhem.

Consequently, the Jharkhand police, in coordination with the CRPF, Jharkhand armed police (JAP) and State's own anti-Maoist forces—Like the CRPF's COBRA and Andhra Pradesh's Greyhounds—Jharkhand jaguar, launched a massive combing operations to flush out PLFI cadres and their leaders.

A senior police officer, involved in this operation, talking to this weekly, gave reasons for the birth of so many splinters: " These groups have grown in numbers over the last few months following a major offensive against the Maoists, especially in their den, Saranda forest. That offensive created a vacuum, which was filled up by several newly-born groups".

This, of course, is simplistic explanation of growth of so many splinters, all claiming to be LW extremists, as the main outfit CPI (Maoist), the mother of them all. This explanation could in fact, he self serving! It is such a tall claim—that State Police achieved total decimation of Maoists in Jharkhand—that lacks credibility. The fact is that Chhattisgarh and Jharkhand remain the two worst Maoists hit states in India. There are other reasons for so many factions in CPI (Maoist), which has already been mentioned, viz, ideological differences, personality clash, lure of lucre and unemployed youth forming groups to make easy money. Reading the LWE factions in Chhattisgarh in the earlier pages explain this phenomenon.

But Shashi Bhushan Pathak has his own take—'Spin' may even be better term—on this mushrooming of the splinters. Pathak, General Secretary, people's Union for Civil liberty (PUCL), says not just the PLFI, but a number of such splinter group had "mushroomed" in the recent past and they were all "criminal" organizations. He is emphatic: "organizations like Jharkhand Prastuti Committee, Jharkhand Liberation Tigers, Jharkhand Jan Mukti Parishad and PLFI are all run by those who were turned out by the Maoists over instances of indiscipline or falling foul of the party's ideology. All they do is collecting levy from locals".

One can understand the vehement fulmination of Pathak against these splinters. What he forgets is that all these tricks of looting and levying taxes these splinters have learnt from the original Maoists. Undoubtedly, these groups, at least some of them, are criminal organizations, but some of these split on ideological differences. To paint them all with broad black brush is being too clever and also indicative of bias in favour of the CPI (Maoist)! More importantly, no one is so ignorant as to not know that the PUCL is absolutely a PRO-Maoist organization—Some calling it over ground arm of the Maoist. It is organizations like the PUCL that provide intellectual support for the destructive ways of the murderous Maoists! Yet again, to remind Pathak, are not the Maoists still in abductions, killing people, levying taxes, extractions to collect hundred crore and more ? They are exploiting tribals in the name of ideology. Are not the senior Maoist leaders living a life of Luxury? How are they any different than the groups Pathak is roundly condemning?

Be that as it may, let Pathak continue with his self-righteous tone. Now he comes to a familiar ploy often employed by the politicians against their rivals. Pathak has learnt it too! He says "the splinter groups have had the covert backing of the police during different periods of their existence. His further averments/allegations are summed up here:

- CPI (Maoists) is different in character than the splinter groups by dint of heir social work among villagers on various issues and they should not all be clubbed together.
- "A couple of years ago, Prashant, a Maoist who was later Killed in Chatra, had given a call to all such splinter groups to work together with/Maoists for the benefit of the people. But they never took it up.
- "CPI (Maoists) continued to have small encounters with the splinter groups".

To each his own, Let Pathak be happy with his approbation of Maoists and condemnation of everyone else.

"Maoists Kill 16 of Splinter group considered close to Jharkhand Police"

This news analysis under this tell–all title appeared in a daily of 10 August 2014.[8]

It openly discloses an inter-faction fight among the Maoists. Another paper (Indian Express) covered the story same day, but rather briefly, in fact too briefly. This possibly is the fiercest fight between the Maosits and a splinter.

CPI (Maoist) cadres in Jharkhand allegedly murdered 16 members of the break away faction Tritiya Sammelan Prastuti Committee (TSPC) in cold blood on Friday night (other daily says, "We hours of Saturday). It is better to say the clash took place 8/9 Aug 2014 night. This is the highest number of Fatalities involving a splinter group in the State.

The clash took place near Kauriya village under Bishrampur Police station in Palamau district. The clash is an attempt by each of the two rival outfits to establish itself in the region by wiping out the other. No body has been recovered from the site. Jharkhand Police says bodies of the dead extremists were taken by their friends. The battle was reported to the police about 2.30AM, which rushed to the spot inside the forest. By the time cops reached there, fighters of both outfits had disappeared into the dense forest

Reports suggested that the CPI (Maoists) cadres ran away with arms of dead members of the TPC (=TSPC).

The spokesperson for the Bihar-Jharkhand-North Chhattisgarh Special Area Committee of the CPI (Maoists) said the attack was in retaliation to the murder of ten of their members in March 2013, allegedly by the TSPC cadres in Chatra's Lakramanda hamlet. At least six of the 10 had been shot at point blank range after they had surrendered.

More accurate detail says attack took place in Palamau district's Vishrampur block. "We have killed Zonal commander Anand ji and area commander Vijay Paswan", spokes person Manasji said over the Phone. Manasji was also the name used by Lalesh Yadav, the group's spokesperson killed in Lokramanda.

The Maoist claim that they had killed senior TSPC leaders in Kaurya Village's Chhoti Kauriya hamlet could not be independently verified by the daily as the TSPC cadre arrived at the village by 6 AM on the 9th and took away the bodies in tractors by 9 A.M. They did not allow an journalist to click any Photographs. The first police party arrived by 11:30 AM.

The incident seems to bring out the first fissures in the relationship between the Security forces and TSPC. The breakdown in communication—Police were in the dark about the identities of the deceased – comes after the Chief Minister indicated he was not happy with the TSPc's closeness to the police. The Chief minister Patnik had told the State Assembly on Monday (4 Aug 2014) that former DGP VD Ram had facilated the formation of Splinter groups TSPC, PLFI and JLT in 2004, effectively confirming longstanding allegation that the police had formed the TSPC and continue to enjoy good relations with it.

Residents of Chhoti Kauriya, speaking on the condition of anonymity, said that 22 uniformed cadres of the TSPC came to the village around 7;30 PM, 8 August. They went to the house of one Ramachandra Sao, who was detained by the police on 9 August. "They walked in and asked us to go to a different house, This was the second time they had come to our house; the other time was two years ago—one of them pressed a gun against my stomach when I showed reluctance", said an individual who was in the house, the largest in the hamlet.

The Maoists arrived about 11:30PM, and started going house to house. "Four of them came in front of the house, fired a round and asked me to get out. They asked me if I was hiding any TSPC men. I asked them to look for themselves," said a villager. Witnesses said that some 150-200 Maoists surrounded the village.

Villagers said there were the two children in TSPC squad who looked about 12-13 years old. They were spared by the Maoists.

Rajesh, TSPC area Commander, was apparently part of the group but was not killed because he halted at a different house. All the dead were found in their under-wear, indicating they were resting. Eight bodies were found in the courtyard, while four were found inside. Another four were found in four different directions, some 50 mtrs away from the hamlet, indicating they were shot while trying to escape. Some of the bodies had their hands tied. There were no sign of TSPC cadre putting up any resistance.

The Maoist sources said that local guerrilla squads of two sub-zonal commanders—Niteshji alias Suraj yadav and Manohar of the North Koel Sankh Zone –had led the attack. The Source also claimed that the Maoists have taken five TSPC men hostage.

After Chatra encounter, the TSPC had taken 25 Maoists hostage but released them later on the guarantee that they would leave the Maoist outfit.

The TSPC is active in the Latehar, Chatra and Palamau districts of Jharkahand.

"Red Faction Shadow over elections"

This news story about the 25 Nov 2014 Assembly polls being disrupted by a Maoist faction appeared in a daily of 5 Nov 2014.[9]

It opens with: "There are fresh concerns over the ability of Maoists or their splinter groups to disrupt Assembly elections, following 3 November killing of seven villagers of Gumla District by activists of PLFI".

The polls begin on 25 November, and these killings came a mere three weeks ahead of that date. That the PLF is behind these killings is a cause of serious concern since this outfit is Known to throw its weight behind candidates of their choice. PLFI is dominant in at least 10 of Jharkhand's 81 Assembly Constituencies: Khunti Torpa, Koliebera, Gumla, Lohardagga sisai, Tamar, Mandar, Bishnupur and simdega.

DGP Rajiv Kumar said:" Forces are combing parts of Gumla district. The entire area will be sanitized before polls. The rebels are frustrated because of repeated police action against them. Chief Secretary Sajal Chakravarty and other senior police officers visited Gumla on 4 November. "Two of the seven killed were SPOs and working to halt PLFI activities", said Gumla SP Bheem Sentuti

The PLFI is the second biggest threat to Jharkhand's internal security, after the CPI (Maoist). Police say that unlike the Maoists PLFI does not stick to any ideology, and that fact makes their attacks deadlier. They target policemen, businessmen, civilians and almost any one.

During the Apr-May Lok Sabha polls, PLFI Stopped several candidates from campaigning in their constituencies and asked villagers to vote for certain candidates. FIRs, were lodged against militants who had ordered villagers of Khunti District not to vote for anyone other than Jharkhand party's Enosh EKKa.

Those who oppose PLFI diktats are threatened. "PLFI use the 3 November massacre to create an environment of terror and force villagers to vote for certain candidates." The incident has sparked panic. said a Congress leader from Gumla.

Several candidates in PLFI strongholds are Known to be hand in glove with the rebels. In May (2014), police filed on FIR against EKKA for travelling in a car that belonged to a wanted PLFI rebel.

Maoist put up anti-poll posters

Maoists stepped up their anti-25 November polls campaign in the states, by putting up posters on 4 November asking people to boycott the elections.

Factions in Jharkhand

- CPI (Maoist). Main party. Leader: khudi Munda.
- People's Liberation Guerrilla Army (PLGA). It is guerrilla arm of PLFA. Leader: Dinesh Gope
- Pahadi Cheetah. Leader: Lele Sahu
- Bablu paswan Group
- Virat Singh Group: The two operate from jail,
- Anil Singh Group: as their leaders are in different jails.

Maoist Leaders

This section deals with the leadership of the CPI (Maoists). Career and standing of some of the leaders in the party hierarchy will be discussed, bared on the available information.

The individual leaders will appear in the alphabetical order, along with whatever biographical details are available.

Some lower level cadres too will appear here, since they have some interesting profile or some unusual story about their career in the CPI (Maoist).

Chamballa Ravinder alias Arjun

Chamballa Ravinder alias Arjun, Chief of the Abhujmaad battalion of CPI (Maoist), with his wife Wetti Adime alias Ranitha, surrendered in

Hyderabad on 1 Aug 2014. A resident of Warrangal inTelengana, Arjun was a Close lieutenant of the party's General Secretary Muppala Laxman Rao alias Ganapathy for long years.

It is for that association and linkage that Arjun's surrender is deemed a major loss to the Maoists. Is it indicative of a certain disenchantment with an ideology on the part of Arjun and his wife, which they have passionately believed in for long years? Besides, he was commanding Abhujmaad forest area, an important Shelter for the rebels, and more importantly, it is a "Liberated Zone" for them. Its location and extent adds to its strategic value for the Maoists: a 6000 SQ KM thick forest, straddling the Maharashtra-Chhattisgarh border.

Arjun participated in some of the biggest attacks on security personnel in Maoist history, including the one at Rani Bodli in Bijapur district. As many as 55 Chhatisgarh policemen were killed then, when Maoists raided a police camp in March 2007. Of late Arjun largely operated in Abujhmaad region of Bastar. This is quite understandable, after all he is commanding the Abujhmaad battalion.[10]

Arjun joined PWG in the 1990s and got the command of the first company raised by Maoists in Abujhmaad. He was subsequently, elevated as a member of the influential Dandakaranya Special Zone Committee (DKSZC). It was only recently that he replaced Ramdher as commander of the Abujhmaad battalion. While Maoists formed a battalion in South Baster in 2008, the Abujhmaad battalion was raised four year later in 2012.

"During a recent visit to Dandakaranya, this daily interacted with these (two) battalion Chiefs, and learnt that Arjun was well-versed in Hindi, English Telegu, and Gondi. He was well respected among cadres and had the image of a committed ideologue and a fierce guerrilla. None if his fellow comrades betrayed the feeling that he could surrender so soon".

These observations by the scribe after meeting Arjun are informative. Being a polyglot, a committed ideologue and fierce guerrilla. Arjun's standing in party and his value/importance to it are obvious. Does it hint at disenchantment mentioned earlier? The last sentence in the above Para could have been more directly worded: The scribe could have simply said that this fellow comrades were really surprised at this sudden decision of Arjun. Why is this scribe pulling his punches? He has been covering Maoist movement for this daily (Indian Express) and he could not venture into reasons for the surrender and the Indian Express claims to be practicising a journalism of courage. It keeps commenting on all varieties of issues, in season and otherwise, and here it is tongue tied! Or, is it that the scribe and the daily know the reasons behind the surrender but have been told by the police to keep off it? There could be various reasons on either side of the fence, not being examined here!

Politburo member: Amitabh Bagchi

Amitabh Bagchi,55@ Anil@ smit-da, was arrested 24 August 2009 by Ranchi Police , along with a Central Committee Member, Karthik, 25, alias Tauhid Mula. Both were produced in the Court of Chief Judicial Magistrate in Ranchi, who remanded them to Central Jail there. As it happens in so many of such cases, Maoist Spokesman Claimed the two leaders had been in police custody since 19 August. Later, both were granted bail by the Jharkhand High court. Both are believed to have well –established criminal antecedents Bagchi was arrested with incriminating documents, totaling 19, containing details of levies and plans for future savage attacks on government properties and machinery across the country.

Badranna: Chhattisgarh's first Maoist recruit

Badranna's career in Maoist ranks has an interesting profile, even if he did not climb very high. His life tells the story of the Maoists from the very beginning and their spread in Chattisgarh—even though the term for LWE was PW (People's War), a splinter of the CPI (ML), viz CPI-ML(PW).

Badranna hails from tribe Dorla and comes from Bijapur district's Pamed village, close to Andhra Pradesh border.

Now the history attached to his career as a Maoist. In 1980's after the formation of the CPI-ML (PW), its Andhra-baed leader Kondapalli Seetharamaiah sent Maoist squads to four areas of states Telengana region: Khammam, Karimnagar Warrangal and Adilabad. Three other Squads went across the Godavari River: One to Gadchiroli in Maharashtra and two to the Baster region of Chhattisgarh, then a part of MP. The idea was to create a rear base where safe guerrilla zones could be created.[11]

One of the latter two squads reached Badranna village. Badranna a teenager then, recalls how the villagers would run away the moment they spotted the guerrillas. Badranna's family and others lived a difficult life, collecting tendu leaves and earning a pittance from their sales. For a pack of 100 Leaves, the contractor paid them a few paise. He tells:" We would put the leaves in a string and the contractor used his head's circumference to measure it".

A change in Strategy

After their inability to reach the young, the Maoist befriended the prominent people from village— Sarpanch and its Patel, a police informer of sorts. Gradually, the young became comfortable around them as well Around the same time, Moist cultural troupe, Jana Natya Mandal began touring the area. The troupe adopted local folk forms to revolutionary themes, which galvanized the youth.

Badrana was the first one to join the Maoist fold, along with two other men, Bimanna and Deva . First they decided for better wages for the tendu leaves. During those days, Maoist guerrillas had rudimentary fire arms like Bharma (muzzle-loading guns). But they were enough to scare tendu contractors and their guards, who were exploiting the poor tribal, often looting their chickens and goats. Maoists began confronting them. Many were caught and beaten up. They were forced to pay better wages.

In the next stage, landlords were targeted; their land was distributed among the landless Peasants. The Maoists had become very popular by then. In 1987, they burnt down over a dozen houses belonging to upper caste Thakurs in Chintalnar, who had settled down in this area from Westen UP; there being many cases of ill-treatment of tribals at their hands. This led to another surge of recruitment, especially of women. It was here that Badranna's future wife Latakka joined the Maoists.

By 1990's the Maoists had intensified their movement in the whole of Dandakaranya forest. The entire Baster region and Gadchiroli in Maharastra had become their stronghold. Presently (written in Apr 2014), this area froms the main guerrilb Zone of the Maoists, the Dandakaranya Special Zonal Committee (DKSZC).

In 1995, Badranna led a group of 30 Maoists to attack the Thalagudda police station in Bhopalpatnam block. The attack was failure as he could not study the map made by local Maoist Squad. The policemen retaliated and Badranna had to retreat. One policeman and five Maoists died in this attack, including Badranna's old friend Bimanna and women guerrilla called Kamalakka.

But soon enough, Badranna's Squad was launching many audacious attacks against the police. In Golapalli, Badranna laid an ambush for a police party, that resulted in the death of 19 policeman. In 2000, another ambush executed by Badranna in Basaguda block's Tarem village killed 16 Policemen.

It is Basaguda that remained Badranna's operational area from the mid 1990s till his surrender in 2000. It is here that Maoists undertook many developemental works in villages under Badranna's guidance, people from nine villages worked together to dig a large pond and construct a checkdam. "I am extremely popular in Basaguda area", says Badranna, smilling. A scribe decided to check if he was still popular in Basaguda area, 14 years after he laid down arms, and he found he indeed was!

How is he spending his time, presently (APR 2014)? "When former Maoist commander Badranna is not tending to plants at the public park in chhatisgarh's Jagdalpur town, he likes to spend time with his 10 years old daughter Manisha and her pet parrot at their small house. His wife, Latakka, once a Maoist guerrilla herself, works with the state police after the couple surrendered in 2000". This is the scribe on his life 14 years after he laid down his gun!

Reasons for his Surrender

The scribe who interacted with Badranna in 2014, writes simply: "In 2000, Badrana decided to surrender along with his wife". He lets the moaist speak his reasons:" I am almost illiterate and it was causing an impediments in my way up in the party ranks".

Again, the scribe says ," After his surrender, the police would call Badranna over sometimes to aequaint themselves with the Maoist Strategy". Again, Badranna is allowed to speak: "I always told them: 'do'nt study Maoists. Study yourself first. Study your weakness".

Difficult to believe the reasons for surrenders

This author is intrigued at the reluctance of the two scribes to probe deep into the reasons for surrender of two fairly senior Maoist leaders – Bhardwaj in case of Arjun and Pandita in case of Badranna. Is this reluctance genvine in both cases, or have two been told not to cross the red lines drawn either by the police or by the Maoist bosses. We wouldn't know either way!

There are certain similarities inboth the cases. Badranna and Arjun both had something to do with the DKSZC during their days with the Maoists. Both surrendered after some 20 years with the rebels. Both surrendered with their Maoist wives.

Now, some differences. Badranna offered some reasons—believe able or not is not important. Arjun stays num on it, and is allowed to remain so. Badranna's wife is doing service in State police, but no word on Arjun's—may be she is not. Badranna says grandly he doesn't help police with any information on Maoists: Their methods of operations, locations of their units, personnel etc, and their leadership. All this, when his wife is in police. On the other hand, Arjun is sagely quiet on his post surrender life!

Venture into the realm of the Known

Being an army man, this author cannot but wade into deep waters. Is it that the Maoist leadership has a policy to let mid-level commanders leave the outfit when they have outlived their usefulness to it? In this case; both are leaving after serving some 20 years. This allows them to live a peaceful life among their kith and kin, and among the civilians. Or, they are serving as their eyes and ears, giving them useful information about the security forces, their operational locations, their future plans etc. So after the "use by date" within active ranks, these surrenderees are useful to the Maoists for the varieties of roles they are capable of playing!

On the other side of the fence, these surrenderees might be rendering useful services to the security forces, police and their intelligence agencies.

Finally, is it the lucre that surrender fetches which helped Arjun and Badranna to make up their minds? Finally, a mischievous possibility: are they servicing both sides of the fence?

The arguments must rest here!

A Maoists founder who never wore uniform: Badri Rai

It is an interesting, even surprising, story carried by a daily in its issue of 5 July 2013.

"Badri Rai is possibly one of the humblest men around. Dumka and Pakur police say he was one of the founding members of the CPI (Maoists) in the Santhal Pargana Zone and was a Sub Zonal commander".

This is how this incredible story opens in a daily mentioned above. The 57-years old man sitting outside his house in Dumka's Sahrupani village merely smiles and shrugs. Having been in jail from 2007 to Apr 2012, Rai, whose village is within the Kathikund block, now calls himself a farmer.

His sons have moved up to replace their father zonal commander Ram Lal Rai, 30 is now in jail, having been arrested in Feb (2013). Shahdev Rai, 35, is commander of one of the three sub Zones that comprise Santhal Pargana Zone.

It is being widely speculated that Shahdev along with Zonal commander Praveerda, planned the 2 July attack on Pakur SP Amarjit Balihar, to avenge his brother's arrest.

Badri says his sons were forced to join CPI (Maoist), since the police troubled my sons constantly when I was in jail for 5 years on trumped up charges. This was the only time he got emotional during a 45-minutes interview.

He says he joined what was then the Maoists communist centre (MCC) in 2003-2004, and never went underground, nor got any arms training. He was active only in the Maoist frontal organization Kisan Committee involved in mobilizing farmers against money lenders.

He gives more information; "The party was started in 2001 by people who came from Giridih district and Bihar's Bhagalpur. Most of my time was spent doing ground work. I never wore a uniform".

He laughs heartily when asked about his being sub-zonal commander: "The party was too small back then to be divided into sub zones; police says armed squads were formed in 2005, but Badri says arms training and levy collection began during his time in jail (2007-2012)

Badri refuses to talk about the party after his incarceration, but accepts that the Santhal Pargana Zone has entered into a new phase after the killing of Pakur SP Balihar. He says there cannot be anymore grassroots work to grow the party any further now, as most workers will have to go underground.

He has a long political background, and has vivid memories of times gone by! He was with the CPI in 1980s and was a member of its Dumka district committee. He left when Jharkhand Mukti Morcha (JMM) swallowed most of their organization: "we supported Shibu Soren for one election and he left with most of our cadres".

Badri might have left the (Maoist) party, but is excited by its growth. He talks about how Shibu Soren came to the region as Chief Minister to inauguarate an industrial project and was talking of he growing Maoists influence.

In his parting shot, he is optimist about his party: "The State had just been created,and he talked about Jharkhand turning into Lalkhand . Soon, in 2004-05, we were growing rapidly as the JMM betrayed the people by supporting huge industrial projects. What they don't seem to realize is that where ever there are mines, Maoism will grow".

The old fire is still burning bright Mines and Maoists are interconnected, indeed. It must be clear why Badri is an 'important' Maoists leader

Ganapathy: General Secretary: CPI (Maoists)

Real Name: Mupalla Lakshman Rao 63 years (in 2013)

From: Karimnagar District, Andhra Pradesh

Education: BSC, B.ed

Current Position: General Secretary, CPI (Maoists)

Ganapathy is the tallest leader among the Maoists outside jail. Apart from Ganapathy, only a few leaders are operating under ground, viz prashanta Bose, alias Kishan da (Secon-in-command), Vasav Raj(military chief), Venugopal Rao (possibly he is Abhay, present spokesperson), Kathakam Sudershan, Malla Raji Reddy and Misir Besra.

Ganapathi's 17-page Letter to his Commanders

Natural question was: "What rattled Maoist boss? What prompted him to send an SOS to the leaders of his party?

The past four years haven't been good for the Maoists. It all started with Prime Minister Manmohan Singh calling them "the greatest intern Security threat", followed by a ban on the party and massive anti-Maoist campaigns by the Central Security Forces.

"After five years of an almost free run since its formation in 2004 through the merger of the CPI-ML (PW) and the Maoist communist Centre of India, the Maoists suddenly found themselves outnumbered and leaderless as most of their top ranking leaders were picked up the Security forces". Ganapathy's 17-page Letter hinted that the arrests had been possible probably because a secion of the key operatives of the Party (had) cut deals with the government too easily. He asked his men to explore all legal or illegal ways" to get the jailed leaders out—either by breaking in or by obtaining bail.

The intelligence data accessed by this daily is extremely worrisome: 17 of the 48 members of the party's Central Committee (CC) and all powerful politburo are new behind the bars; nine have been killed by the security forces; and three top leaders died of illness, three are now inactive and one surrendered to the authorities.

Such an alarming situation is bound to rattle any supremo, even if he is the reclusive boss of Ganapathy's stature and standing. Under the situation, he had to address his fighting men.

The gap in the leadership could not be bridged even after bringing in 11 new faces to the original 37-member CC. He said since 2010 the preservation of the existing leadership had become the most important task before the party. More importantly the 17-page letter—this daily claims to have first broken the story on 17 sep 2013—admits that the party has lost considerable ground in West Bengal, Jharkhand and North Bihar, and the Dandakarnya forest area that covers vast swathes in Chhattisgarh, Odisha, Maharashtra and Andhra Pradesh.

Even though the Maoist leadership hopes to strengthen its network in Karnataka, Kerala, Tamil Nadu, North India and North-eastern states, its clout—and naturally revenues— is fast dwindling with no signs of turning around.

The crisis has been so unnerving for Ganapathy that he has made a terrible tactical mistake, which security experts, knowing his ways as the top Maoist strategist for long years, feel was totally unexpected from him: sending the letter to too many people down the line and unable to prevent its leakage.

Ganapathy has attributed this crisis essentially to two factors: the "unprecedented level of offences unleashed by security forces at a time when the party was not prepared" and weakness within the party. He identified weaknesses as "failure in maintaining a high level of secrecy" and non-proletarian trends. He felt this alienated the Maoists from their support base.

Among the major set backs is the failure of the movement in West Bengal's Lalgarh, some 180KM west of Kolkata, where unnecessary killings and continuous shut downs finally forced the locals to cooperate with the forces, although the rebels had managed to turn the area into a red fortress.

His solution to the problem is a typical text-book strategy:"If necessary, we must take a step backward where we suffered severe losses or lost initiative due to other reasons and work patiently".

Here are two important notings from the letter.

The rebel's ideological moorings

"The CPI(Maoist) was born of the merger between the people's War and the Maoist Communist Centre, both of which agreed that the Indian State was being run by a collaboration of "Imperialists the comprador bourgeoisie and feudal lords". "The revolution will be carried out and completed through armed agrarian revolutionary war".

Why does he want Maoists out of jail?

"This shows the crisis of leadership among the Maoists. Kobad Ghandy, Narayan Snayal, Pramod Misra, Ashutosh kumar singh, Amitabh Bagchi, Purendu Mukherjee— all Pulitburo members past or present—are in jail. Azad and Kishanji have been killed.

The preceding Pages mainly summarize the contents of the 17-page letter written by Ganapathi in a desperate situation. It was important to analyses its contents as it indicates a serious crisis in the history of CPI (Maoists) and also the solution of these crisis a seen by Ganapathi. Besides this letter, only a few, very few, biographical details are given in these pages. The lacuna is filled up in the paragraphs that follow.

Arms he carries: Sten carbine. Five guards for his personal security

Aliases: Has 15 alias including Ganapathy(also spelt Ganapathi, and is popularly used alias, most used), Ramana, Srinivas and Malanna.

Education: The 58-year old is a science graduate from Karimnagar district, Andhra Pradesh.

Bounty: ₹ 2.52 crore (details later).

Most wanted Indian

The issue of bounty on several Maoists has already been discussed in some detail. Some additional information is mentioned here. Ganapathy carries largest bounty on his head, ten times more offered for "India's most wanted "fugitive and Mumbai blasts accused Dawood Ibrahim.

The rewards offered for Ganpathy total a whopping ₹ 2.52 crore. The bounty has gone up from the ₹ 49 Lakh total after the Governments of Maharashtra and Chhattisgarh offered ₹ 1 crore each to anybody who provides information leading to the Maoist leader's arrest .Apart from these two states, some others too have announced rewards: Andhra Pradesh Rs. 25 Lakh; Jharkhand, ₹ 12 Lakh and the NIA, ₹ 15 Lakh.

There are some intresting, comparative details vis-a-via the IM (Indian Mujahideen) trio, the founders of two jihadi terrorist group in India, namely, Iqbal Bhatkal, Riyaz Bhatkal and Amir Reza Khan. A bounty of only ₹ 25 Lakh has been offered for these founding members of IM, responsible for a series of attacks across the country now believed to be in hiding in Pakistan. While Delhi police has offered ₹ 15 Lakh, NIA's cash rewards for the trio is Rs 10 Lakh.

Opposed to the bounty for Ganapathy's head, the rewards for India's most wanted terrorist, Dawood Ibrahim is ₹ 25 Lakh only, and that has not been revised for years. The reward was announced by the CBI and Maharashtra government after the 1993 bomb attacks in Mumbai, after which Dawood fled to Dubai and finally to Pakistan—his "safe house" ever since.

Yet again, the USA has announced the bounty of $10 million for Lashkar-e-Taiba founder Hafiz Saeed, but India has offered no reward for the alleged master mind of the 26/11 attacks. This decision of India is in explicable, unless New Delhi has doubts about Saeed being the real mastermind for those murderous attacks in Mumbai in November that year!

Rewards for others Maoists Leaders

Besides Ganapathy, other senior Maoist leaders too have attracted large rewards. Sources say, all 21 members of the Central Committee of the CPI(Maoist) carry a bounty of over ₹ 1 crore each as some states have hiked the rewards on offer. It is learnt till recently, the total amount offered on any information on the top leadership used to be between ₹ 15 Lakh and ₹ 20 Lakh each. The total amount on offer for information on the top leadership of the Maoists movement is ₹ 25 crore presently.

Increase in reward money also seems to be a part of policy to counter the Maoist depredations and violent attacks. It is better option to increase the amount for their surrenders to an extent that entice them to come overland and lead a peaceful life in some level of security and comfort, than letting them continue with their wild and violent ways! It is in this context and background that this Author sees the surrenders of two mid-level Maoist leaders—Arjun and Badranna, discussed in some detail in the earlier pages. Whatever reasons these two surrenderees might or might not have offered, are irrelevant and at the very best, half truths!

To put it simply and perhaps more honestly, the increase in rewards is also part of strategy to give an added incentive to the Maoists to quit the movement. "If they surrender, they will get the entire amount that has been announced for their arrest….. In addition, they will also get the amount laid down in the Government's Surrender policy", explains a Home ministry official.

Specific policy amounts on the surrenders

While every state has different economic incentives, the centre in 2013 put in place a policy offering enhanced packages to surrendered Maoists from a range of ₹ 10, 000 to ₹ 20.000 to up to ₹ 25,000 for handing in sophisticated weapons. In addition to this all, a monthly stipend of ₹ 4,000 is also on offer for a period of three years.

The number of surrenders has "gone up this year (2014), matching last (2013) year's figures of 283 till the end of august itself—that is in 8 months only! Perhaps this , rising surrender figures every years, was one of the concerns that Ganapathi addressed in his 17-page epistle!

Bounty count: A summary

Ganapathi: Rs 2.52 crore: total

Breakdown

- Maharashtra : ₹ 1 crore
- Chhattisgarh: ₹ 1 crore

- Andhra Pradesh : ₹ 25 Lakh
- Jharkhand: ₹ 12 Lakh
- NIA: Rs 15 Lakh.

All the 21 members of the Central Committee of the CPI (Maoist) have a bounty of our ₹ 1 crore each.

Wanted for terror activities

- Iqbal Bhatkal, Riyaz Bhatkal and Amir Reza Khan, the IM founder members: ₹ 25 Lakh
- Dawood Ibrahim (accused mastermind of the 1993 Mumbai terror attacks): ₹ 25 Lakh (not revised for years).
- Hafiz saeed (LeT founder): USA has announced a bounty of $10 million. No bounty announced by India

Some other information

General Secretary of the CPI (Maoist), the 65-years old, is considered the top leader of the armed rebel group whose publicly professed aim is the violent overthrows of the Indian government—nothing short! Intelligence inputs indicate the Andhra Pradesh-born rebel is presently hiding in the thick forests of the Abujhmaad region, a Maoists bastion in Chhattisgarh, considered the headquarters of the movement/rebels.

Besides a brief sketch on his life, the subjects of bounty on the heads of various Maoist leaders, including Ganapathi, and a brief note on government's surrender policy, have been added to the life story of the reclusive chief of the Maoists, for their relevance to counter-Maoists strategy.

Politburo member: Kobar Ghandy

Kobar Ghandty, politburo member of CPI (Maoists), who is in charge of spreading Naxalism in urban areas, was, appropriately, arrested 24 August 2009 from New Delhi, the most suitable city for his assigned mission. Two other Maoist sumpathisers, too more arrested that day, 24 August 2009, with Ghandy, Viz Chatradhar Mahato and Bhushan Yadav.

3 oct 2009, Maoists demanded release of these—Ghandy, Mahato and Bhushan yadav.

Kobbad Ghandi was member of the politburo as on 18 feb 2008, at No. 6. His aliases include Saleem, Rajan and kishor. He was/is in charge of Central Propaganda Bureau, and looks after Party documentation.

Intrestingly, even surprisingly, his name does not appear as member of the CPI (Maoist) Central Committee, in the list comprising 21 names as in

Nov 2011. One always understood that all Politburo members, ipso facto, are members of the Central committee.

Kobad Ghandy had married Anuradha Shanbag on 5 Nov 1977, and in the respective write ups on them, the two would be referred to as Kobad and Anuradha, even Anu. The two are genuine individuals, with deep conviction in Maoist—rather, communist—ideology. Both find extensive mention in Rahul Pandita Book, "Hello, Bastar", On Maoists movement, published in 2011. Interestingly the book has no foreword but it has "Afterword, titled "comrade Anuradha Ghandy and the idea of India", by kobad ghandy, written from Tihar jail, New Delhi, in Apr 2011.

To emphasise, all direct quotes on the two kobad and Anu, are from Rahul pandita's book. Direct quotes, ascribed to Kobad are from his after word. This author has no respect for Maoists of any hue but will make a distinction for kobad and Anu, both from rich families, both had genuine feelings for the poor and the deprived, both worked with deep conviction for the Maoists. But having said this all, he wishes the two had not joined the violent Maoists. There were other ways available….But let us leave that as it may.

Pandita's book is dedicated to Anuradha: "To Anu, and her imagined "biscuits"

> "The Spasm had been troubling him again. In fact, amoebic dysentery has been his constant companion, a result of a harsh life of more than three decades and an enlarged prostate too. He was more comfortable with the pain these afflictions caused than the feel of the cold metal of gun in his hands whenever he had to hold it. But that was an rare occasions, deep inside the forest along the eastern Ghats: memorial meetings for the fallen comrades, Ceremonial parades or military drills. Presently though, he was hundreds of miles away from the jungle of Central India."

> "He was in Delhi…. Living along the impoverished in…. south Delhi's Badarpur area for years, they worked in factories… out of their meager incomes, the men struggled to send as much money as possible to their families"

> "The city ran on a very complex arithmetic. It was a city drunk on power, a city from where a handful of people decided the fate of over a billion others, from Kashmir to Kanyakumari….. Those few people were India's political leaders. Their abode was the parliament in the heart of new Delhi, a place referred to as 'pigsty' by the man and his comrades"

"There were two things Delhi did not want: monkeys and poor people.... There were negotiations with the other states to take their beggars back. A few years earlier, the capital city has tried, in a similar way, sending monkeys to the wilderness of other states... And now for the games, hundreds of thousands of people will be displaced in all. In 2001, sealing of small scale factories in residential areas had rendered thousands of workers jobless. It was the ensuing unrest the comrades wanted to take up as a cause and motivate young labourers and workers to channel their anger into something 'meaningful' to be close. To such workers and win them over, the man had been living in the Molarband extension colony (Badarpur)."

"Over the last few weeks, the man had also been getting treated for his ailments at city hospitals. He was using a voter identity card, bearing the name of Dilip Patel, for all official purposes. His contacts in the city had made these arrangements"

"For purposes of communication, he shunned modern devices such as the mobile phone. Most of the communication was done through a human courier. He had one trusted courier who had been with him for some five years. Oblivious of what his trusted lieutenant had been up to, the man went about doing his work. On 20 sep 2009, he arrived at the Bhikaji Cama office Complex".

"Unknown to him, a few men sat in a car, waiting for him. It was a Sunday...The regular crowd was missing. Inside the car, a Deputy Superintendent of the Special Intelligence Branch of the Andhra Pradesh Police was getting restless. It was hot inside the car... Wiping his sweat from his brow, he looked at the man sandwiched between him and his colleague, 'Are you sure he will come? The man nodded quickly. He looked at his watch and then looked outside, and he was the only one who could identify the man they were waiting for, the man he had served as courier for years".

"At about 1 PM, the tall, thin-moustached man appeared and stopped at the bus stop next to the complex. A jute bag was slung across his shoulder. The courier now signaled. In a moment or two, the operation was over. The man was bundled inside the car and taken to special cell Branch of the Delhi police, near Delhi famous cultural hub, India Habitat Centre".

"Two days later, the police made an announcement. They had arrested Kobad Ghandy, they said, one of the senior most leaders of the Maoists movement in India. A day later, as he was produced in court, Kobad Ghandy raised slogans as feverishly as he could while struggling to overcome the exhaustion of sustained interrogation. 'Bhagat Singh Zindabad' and Anuradha Ghandy amar rahe'. No one had ever heard earlier slogans in praise of India most popular revolutionary.... And Anuradha Ghandy.... who was Anuradha Ghandy?".

Anuradha Ghandy: A committed Soul

An article on Badranna, who surrendered in 2000 written by Rahul Pandita, had a mention of Anuradha Ghandy. It is reproduced here in full.

"In 1999, Badranna says he met a fair-complexioned woman who had come from the city and spoke in English to a few other Senior Maoists leaders. Her party name was Jankiakka. 'She was extremely brave but suffered immensely because of some illnesses', says badranna. While travelling once along with her, Badranna's squad came under fire from the police. 'I provided cover fire, enabling all of them to flee to safety' says badranna. "Jankiakka was a senior Maoist leader Anuradha Ghandi, who later died of Malaria in April 2008".

All that follows are quotes from Rahul pandita's book on Anuradha and Kobad.

"She had the best hand writing among her group. On a humid Bombay night, she would sit cross legged at the floor in somebody's house and write political slogans on old newspapers. Yes, the world had to be changed; the world order had to be changed, the world order had to be changed—she was sure about it. So, ignoring the sweat gathering on her brow, she would create posters in her neat handwriting in English Hindi and Marathi. Then she and her friends would sneak out in the middle of the night. Someone would carry pot of glue made of flour. At some intersection, or in some lane, the group would stick the posters on walls and electric poles".

"It was a job fraught with danger in the early 1970s, the police were on the lookout for adventurous youth—the Naxalite types—who would talk of revolution and the plight of the poor. Tucking he pollu in at her waist, Anuradha Shanbagh would address curious on lookers and talk to them about issues they had not even thought of'.

"Though petite in appearance, Anu as Anuradha was fondly called by her friends, was the most active and vivacious among them. She was very attractive as well and had many admirers. Among her admirers was a tall, lanky bespectacled man, who had returned from London, after serving a two month sentence in a prison there. Kobad Ghandy had gone to London to pursue charter accountancy, but had instead, found him one day in the thick of a violent attack on an anti-racism meeting. The meeting, held by left-leaning students and activists, to protest against the racism faced by Indians in the UK was attacked by a white fascist gang. The police had encouraged them and ultimately arrested three of the protestors including Kobad and a pregnant White woman. Inside the police station, Kobad was further beaten up".

"After his release, Kobad happened to see a picture in a newspaper of Naxals rebels marching in single file through a vast field in Singhbhum in east India. He decided to return to India, wearing an overcoat that had 24 secret pockets, all stuffed with Maoist literature… It was then Kobad came in contact with PROYOM (Progressive youth Movement), a student organization inspired by the Naxal movement. PROYOM ran an alternative university, essentially a series of lectures that offered an alternate view (Marxist) of the subjects taught in colleges. The organization was also quite active in the slums and other areas inhabitated by the poor of Bombay. This is where he met Anuradha For the first time".

"Young people like Anuradha were inspired by the headlines of those times. A year before Charu Mazumdar had died in Kolkata. The Naxal rebels were being hunted like mad dogs. Anuradha and kobad came from different backgrounds. Anuradha was born to Ganesh and Kumud Shanbag both of them activists who choose to marry in the office of the CPI. As a young boy, Ganesh had run away from his home in COORG to join Subhash Chandra Bose's army, and later, as a lawyer, he would fight the cases of communists arrested in the Telangana struggle.While his brief case would be full of petitions filed on behalf of the arrested comrades, Kumud would be busy Knitting and collecting sweaters to be sent for soldiers fighting the war with China".

"Kobad's father Adi Ghandy was the finance director of the pharmaceutical giant Glaxo while his mother Nargis played bridge and golf and was a regular at the elite Willingdon Club. The family stayed in a 4000-sq feet Worli seaface house. Even as child, Kobad felt deeply for the poor and a family friend describes an incident to illustrate this. Adi Ghandy's gold watch disappeared one day. Later, Kobad revealed that he had gifted it to a servant who he said needed it more than his father".

"Anuradha's brother Sunil Shanbag, who is a progressive playwright, recalls her being good at studies as well as extra-curricular activities like dancing. But she was extremely aware of what was happening around her. Says sunil: 'When I was in boarding school. She would send me letters, writings about issues like the nationalization of the banks. And she was only twelve then'. Anuradha was like any other girl when she joined Bombay prestigious Elphinstone College in 1972.... She went on to do her M.A in sociology and later an M.Phil."

"Bothe kobad and Anu took an instant liking to each other. Around that time, Kobad's parents had retired and shifted to Mahabaleshwar, a small hill station some 100km from Pune. Kobad and his brother stayed on in Bombay in the Worli mansion. Kobad's brother was into making ice cream, and loved to experiment with new flavours. Kobad, Anuradha and their whole group would often assemble at the worli house for discussions. Kobad's brother would often seek group's opinion on his experiments. Anuradha simply loved his ice cream. But he improved the quality to such an extent that, eventually, the cost of making it exceeded its selling price and he went bankrupt".

"It is not clear whether Anu inspired Kobad more or the other way round Anu inspired Kobad more or the other way round but soon, as a friend puts it, both had turned into 'staunch activists'. In fact, Kobad organized the youth of Mayanagar slum near his house, and they stopped paying for water to the slumlord, linked to the Congress and had connections in the municipality and the police. By the mid-70s, the two were at the Centre of Dalit Panther movement that organized groups to retaliate against any Caste oppression. During those months, there were regular clashes with the militant Shiv Sena".

"..... Around this time, Kobad and Anuradha fell in love , and Kumud vividly remembers the day Kobad came visiting their house. 'My husband was here on this Chair', She points out, 'and kobad came and fell on his Knees and said, "can I marry your daughter"? The two got married on 5 Nov 1977 at Adi Ghandy's retreat in Mahabaleshwar. On the morning of their marriage Adi Ghandy drove down to neighboring Satara to fetch the registrar of marriages. He would not agree to come, and relented only after money and two bottles of whiskey were passed on to him".

"..... The emergency had just been lifted (on the eve of their marriage), all political prisoners including most Naxalites were released. The two were very busy and only got a week off to celebrate their marriage .... Anu and Kobad stayed on in Mahabaleshwar for another five days after the wedding (ceremonies),often taking long walks in the forest adjoining the house. It was the last time that they could enjoy such simple pleasures of life..... In Bombay , both Anu and Kobad became the shining lights of the Civil liberties movement. Anuradha played a very important role in the formation of the Committee for the protection of Democratic Rights (CPDR)".

"Meanwhile, by 1980, the naxal Squads had entered Gadchiroli. Some of the Senior Naxal leaders who were active during the Telangana struggle came in contact with Kobad and Anuradha and their group in Mumbai. These leaders finally arranged a meeting between Kondapalli Seetharamaiah (KS) and Kobad during a conference of the Radical Students Union in 1981 in Guntur, Andhra Pradesh. After the session was inaugurated, Ks sent a messenger to Kobad. But Kobad was not to be found there. Apparently, he had slipped out briefly with a friend. Varavara Rao remembers approaching Anuradha inquiring about Kobad. In a memoir written after her death VV describes those moments: 'Her (Anu's) anxiety was quite visible that Kobad was not present at a time when a great opportunity came searching for them. There were no cell phones at that time. Her lips were quivering, her face reddened and her eyes were filled with tears. She apologized several times. Meanwhile Kobad turned up. She pounced on him with anger like a child. Tears rolled down her face.... She shouted at him, revealing her love, friendship and intimacy towards him". Varavara Rao says the meeting between KS and Kobad paved the way for the foundation of the People War group in Maharashtra".

"..... Both shifted to Nagpur which has the second largest slum population in Maharashtra, and is also home to a significant number of dalits (it was in Nagpur in Oct 1956 that BR Ambedkar accepted Buddhism). Kobad would be gone for long periods for party work and often Anu would be left alone. She first stayed in a barsati in the Lakshminagar area. Kumud remembers visiting her there with her husband. 'When we saw where she stayed, we could not believe our eyes', says kumud. The roof leaked from many places. And it rained that night, 'Our helper who was with us, Crept under a table and slept there, recalls Kumud."

"By 1986, Anuradha had shifted to north Nagpur's Indore locality, the epicenter of Dalit politics. It is from here that an agitation broke out after the infamious Khairlanji case of 2006, the background being that four members of the Dalit family were lynched in Maharastra's Bhandara district, bordering Nagpur, She used to commute on a run down cycle.... Later at the insistence of other activists that Kobad bought a TVS Champ moped".

"Anuradha was a fiercely independent person and the couple had frequent fights on many issues. She would also be left fuming at Kobad's clumsiness while driving and later with his slow typing speed. A close associate rembers how she quarreled with Kobad after she fell off the moped at a speed breaker as Kobad had not applied the brakes and did not even realised that she had toppled down! But these fights apart, the two had immense respect for each other. When ever Kobad visited her, he would do most of the cleaning and washing to enable Anuradha to rest a bit".

It is obvious that a lot of space has been given to Kobad and Anuradha, and there are reasons for it: Their lives are symbolic of some other Communists and Maoists as to how they came to enter the "haloed" ranks; Some entries were taken to show certain aspects of the Maoists movements; Some entries depict their human and humane sides and some just to depict how two persons from different backgrounds came to develop such huge respect and love for each other under the canopy of a share shared ideology.

One wonders if there were any other couples among the ranks of the Maoists who rose to such eminent heights like the Ghandy's – Kobad entering politburo and Anuradha getting membership of the Central Committee of the CPI(Maoist).

Finally, for the reason mentioned above, what follows are some excerpts from Kobad's Afterword, already explained above.

> "Rahul Pandita's Hello,Bastar coincides with the third death anniversary of Anuradha Ghandy. It is an occasion to remember her monumental contribution to the understanding of the caste/Dalit question in India and significance of its resolution for the democratisation of the individuals and with it, the society".
>
> "Anuradha's pure simplicity, her total lack of any ego or arrogance and her innate attitude to see all others as her equal drew her to the issue of caste in her early college days itself. The outbreak of the Dalit panther movement in Mumbai (1974) further helped fuel thought on this question. She began studying the caste/Dalit question at a time when the issue was an anathema to most shades of Communists. And by 1980 itself, she had presented extensive analytical articles on the issue. The Dalit question and Ambedkar's role in taking it up was not in fashion amongst the Left then, and Anuradha's writings resulted in hostile reactions from many of these circles but she stood her ground Even as a lacturer in Nagpur, she lived in a Dalit basti and worked among them, there by getting a practical experience of their lives—the horrific humiliation they face, and their struggle for self respect, much before their desperate struggle for livelihood".

"She was modesty personified. Her childlike simplicity with no elements of pretence, trickery or cunning allowed her to focus fully on whatever issues she took up. Her mind was not dissipated in varied futile directions to create impressions, appearances and images. As a result, her mental sharpness and intellectual capacity continued to flower and grow even towards the last years of her life, even after she was afflicted with the deadly disease, systematic sclerosis".

"In the 35 years that I knew her—from a simple student leader to a mass leader—She never lost her straight forwardness and pristine honesty. I never saw her struggle to achieve this; it all came very naturally to her. One tends to see these values among the simple tribal folk who live with nature and have not as yet been corrupted by the system and are also outside the caste framework……Her fierce independent thinking acted as a great help to rational understanding of events, issues and people. There was no other person with whom I have had as vehement debates. This normally brought a balance to my often one sided views".

Final word on Anuradha Ghandi

- She was inducted in the Central Committiee CC) of the CPI (Maoist) at the 2007 congress of the party
- Like any member of the CC, She also carried a bounty of ₹ 1 Crore on her head
- She succumbed to sclerosis.

Updating Kobad Ghandy

Some additional information available of the Ghandy is put into these pages.

"Gujarat cops seek Ghandy's custody for interrogation": 6 April 2012

Suspecting the role of Maoist leader Kobad Ghandy in guiding Naxal activities in their state, the Gujarat Police sought his custody for interrogation from a city court in Delhi, reports a daily in Apr 2012.[14]

"The Gujarat police are suspecting Ghandy of being behind formation of an armed force and guerrilla zone in Surat, North Maharashtra, South Gujarat and other adjoining areas. The development comes following disclosure of some two dozen Naxalites arrested by the Gujarat police where in Ghandy's name figured out as their 'mentor'. The custody of Ghandy, as the Gujarat police contended, was necessary to confront him with other arrested persons and corraborate their statements to establish the case".

The Gujarat police approached the court of Chief Metropolitian Magistrate (CMM) Vinod Yadav seeking Ghandy's custody, alleging that he was involved in naxal movement in urban areas and a case was registered against him and 20 other co-accussed in Feb 2010. The Surat police have registered a case against him and others under the IPC for waging war against the country, sedition, promoting enmity, criminal conspiracy and various provisions of the UAPA.

Notably this is the second plea by that state police seeking Ghandy's custody. An earlier plea by them for custody in June 2010 was rejected by the court as the Delhi Government has put a ban on his movement till the case against him finished.

The fresh application was moved in the light of a session court order where in Ghandy was discharged of the stringent terror Charges for want of proper sanction. Ghandy has been charged for criminal conspiracy, cheating, forgery and impersonation under IPC, to undergo trial by a court of Magistrate. The Gujarat police in its application have said that on 25 Feb. 2010, a complaint was registered at Kamraj police station against unnamed CPI (Maoist) organisers and members for preparing an armed force and guerrilla zone in Surat, North Maharashtra and South Gujarat and other areas.

The application said the accused were creating "internal war between religious minorities in these areas in order to obtain militant cadres for guerrilla Zone". Police have already arrested 20 persons from various regions in Surat, Maharashtra and Gujarat. The application further said: "During the course of investigation of this crime, it is revealed that accused Kobad Ghandy, alias Salim, started CPI (M-L) PWG in Maharashtra. He was also incharge of south West Regional Bureau, and has been providing his guidance and help, and coordinating activities of Maharashtra State Committee and Surat Area Committee, a body of CPI (Maoist)."

It added that Ghandy "sent his wife late Anuradha Ghandy for spreading CPI (M-L) PWG work in Surat city and Knows about the activities undertaken by her". It also accused Ghandy of authoring, 'The Urban Plan' of CPI (Maoist) which emphasized "initiating a strong Maoist movement in Urban area for supplementing ongoing Maoist fight in rural areas". The agency said Ghandy studied problems, controversial issues of major cities and collected vital data regarding their demography, geography, economy and social structures, besides being responsible for monitoring the progress of urban plan in Pune-Ahmadabad "Golden corridor", of which Surat city is a part.

"He has been lodged in Tihar Central Jail since his arrest in Sep 2009, while allegedly trying to set up a base for the banned CPI (Maoist) in Delhi". This was in a report of another daily on the same day as the one just critiqued above.

On 28 March, a session's court framed charges of Criminal conspiracy, cheating, forgery and impersonation against Ghandy while discharging him of the UAPA Charges. Consequently, the Gujarat police decided to make a second plea in Delhi Court seeking Ghandy's Custody.

"Charges against Ghandy to be framed under anti-terror law" New-Delhi: 17 July 2012

Kobad Ghandy is back to square one. He was earlier discharged of charger under the UAPA. Now, he has been again charged with offences under the same Act, according to a fresh Charge sheet. A daily reports in its issue referred to above.[16]

The Court of Additional Session Judge Pawan Kumar Jain on Monday (16 July) ordered framing of Charges against Maoist Sympathiser Kobad Ghandy under the UAPA and the IPC. He will now be tried under the UAPA for membership of a terrorist outfit and under the IPC for forgery. Cheating and Criminal Conspiracy.

The Charges under the IPC were framed for possession of a false voter's ID card. Charges were also framed against his associate Rajender Kumar alias Arvind Joshi for forgery, use of forged document, and Criminal Conspiracy.

The trial of the Case will start on 4 September. Rebecca John, the Counsel for Ghandy, however, called the Charges a "victory over the prosecution". John explained: "The prosecution had earlier tried to charge him as a terrorist but now has only been able to frame charge against him for membership of an unlawful association. Particularly in the light of a recent SC judgements that said that mere membership of an organisation is not punishable, we are confident that the prosecution will not be able to prove any case against my client".

The police charge sheet filed against Ghandy in April (2012) had booked him under several sections of UAPA, including section 10 (penalty for being a member of an unlawful association), Section 18 (conspiracy to commit a terrorist act), and section 20 (punishment for being a member of terrorist gang). Ghandi has been accused of being a "Maoist ideologue" and of helping in the spread of Maoists activity. He was accused of living in Delhi using false documents to propagate the activities of the CPI (Maoist).

The Special Cell of Delhi Police had filed fresh charges against him after a sessions court had dropped all charges against him under the anti-terror law for want of proper sanction. The court had observed in its order on 30 April:" There is sufficient material on record to make out a prima facie case of offences under sections 20 and 30 of the UAPA against accused Kobad Ghandy".

"Dosco boys push for Kobad's Release" New Delhi: 19 Feb 2014

"Maoist ideologiue Kobad Ghandy, battling heart condition and in jail for four years without a single conviction, has not been shunned by the world as many would believe. He has found support from a band of boys he grew up with in the elite Doon School".[17]

A daily carries this story in Feb 2014 about his friends remembering him in Rose Bowl, news letter of the Doon School Old Boys Society. Ghandy, belonging to the Class Of 1963, finds more than a mention in the January issue of the news letter. His Classmate Gautam Vohra, writing on the class of 1963 that included Appan Menon, Sanjay Ghandhi and Tejeshwar Singh, says when the batchmates met in Dehradun, the "Kobad issue came to the fore".

"A few thought that as an avowed Naxalite advocating violence against the State, he would have to pay the price for his conviction", he writes. But the majority view, Vohra says, was that "since the State has not been able to sustain a single charge against him during the last four years, Kobad should be released, especially since his health is failing; under considerations of age he is entitled to special dispensation".

The Doon School friends got together and paid for Ghandy's eye operation and provide him books. Vohra says he and Ghandy keep in regular touch. "I have been campaigning for his release. It has been four years and nothing has been proved against him. Kobad admits he is a Maoist But even the Supreme Court has said being a member of a banned outfit does not mean you will put him behind bars", vohra told the daily.

The only way, Vohra says, Kobad can be convicted is if his involvement is proved in any violence. "But so far, nothing has been found. I have canvassed for his release before everyone – from Kapil Sibal to Mani Shankar Aiyar and many Human rights organisations. I am told under Unlawful Activities (prevention) Act, if he is released, many other Maoists would have to be set free", he says.

Notes

1. Bhardwaj, Ashutosh, Indian Express, 24.1.14.
2. Rajesh Ahuja, Hindustan Times, 21 sep 2014.
3. Toral Varia Deshpande, The Outlook, 10 September 2012.
4. Times of India, 8.2.2010.
5. Lal Mohan Pattanaik, The Pioneer, 26 March 2012.
6. Janyala, Sreenivas, Indian Express, 24.1.14.
7. Navtan Kumar and Abhimanyu Singh, Sunday Guardians 13 July 2014.
8. Deepu Sebestian Edmond, The Hindu, 10 August 2014.
9. Alok Mishra, Times of India, 5 Nov 2014.
10. Ashotosh Bhardwaj, Indian Express, 4 August 2014.
11. Rahul Pandita, the Hindu, 14 April 2014.
12. Deepu Sebestian Edmond, Indian Express, 5 July 2013.
13. Snigdhendu Bhallacharya, Hindustan Times, 19 Sep 2013.
14. Staff Reporter, The pioneer, 6 April, 2012.
15. Jiby Kallakayam, the Hindu, 6 April 2012.
16. Aneesha Mathur, Indian Express, 17 July 2012.
17. Akshaya Mukul, Times of India, 19 Feb 2014.

8

Kishenji: Dare devilry Personified

Name:- Mollojula Koteshwar Rao.

Aliases:- Like so many other senior Maoist leaders, he too had may aliases. Most commonly used, and the popular one was Kishenji, besides Prahalad and Baswaraj Ramji.

Brief details:- The 55-years-old, yet again (like Ganapathy) belongs to Karimnagar district, AP, played major role in the merger of PWG and MCC currently looks after West-Bengal.

He is past now, was killed in an encounter on 25 Nov 2011.

He was the most charismatic of the Maoist leaders . May be, he played with fire too often in the past and on 25 Nov 2011, it was one too many.

It was not surprising that recently someone in the strategic community of India described him "Bin Laden" of India. After a couple of entries, the encounter in which he was killed will be described, with analysis of relevant events and issues.

Koteshwar Rao@Kishanji. No. 2 of CPI (Maoist)

He is/was a Charismatic leader of the party, CPI (Maoist). It should be apt to start the sketch of his life with a dramatic incident.

A gang of 30 Maoists attacked Sank rail police station on 20 oct 2009. They abducted Atindra Nath Dutta, officer in charge, after killing his two colleagues (Dibakar Bhattacharya and Swapan Roy) inside the police station. They made away with a good number of weapons and ammunities and also looted ₹ 9.23 Lakh from the local branch of SBI. Succumbing to the Maoist pressures, the government freed 23 Maoist prisoners for release of Atindra Nath Dutta on 22 Oct 2009.

But now the important part of the story: among these 23 Maoist prisoners freed on 22 October, was Kishanji, No. 2 in their hierarchy. West Bengal PWD Minister Kshiti Goswami admitted his speaking to Kishanji on 21 October, when he had been surrounded by the State Police on all four sides, near puranpani. The ruling party of the State, CPI (M), chose Atindra Nath's Life over Kishanji Arrest.

Kishanji was known to indulge in such adventures at his 'whim and fancy', as some of his close friends would put it. One such dare devilry that cost him his life at the end, a story that will be narrated later in these pages.

Three confidents of kishanji (Gopal mahatao, Haripal Mahatao and Malik Mahato) were arrested on 7 Jan 2010 with 17 others in Salboni near Lalgarh in a raid at Lakhanpur village. This a fortnight after Ganapathi had expressed deep concern at the loss of Senior cadres through arrest or demise at the hands of the security forces. Why didi Kishanji's men undertake such adventures, notwithstanding the warning from CPI (Maoists) General Secretary? Is it some kind of rivalry between Kishanji and his leader Ganapathi, aimed at one up manship? Why this wreckless stance by Kishanji and his confidents? Why this adventurist obsession? It indeed was sad as we know that later on, it was one adventure too many that cost him his life!

Jyoti Basu is main Culprit: Kishan ji

1st Jan 2010. Kishanji brands Jyoti Basu, former Chief Minister of West Bengal as the main culprit and a negative mode of communist movement in the whole country. With such statements was Kishanji trying to upstage his party Chief Ganapathi, at ideological level. This theme has been briefly discussed above.

May be Kishanji based this observation on certain empirical evidence. After all, Jyoti Basu was the Home Minister of West Bengal when he ruthlessly dealt with Naxalites in Darjeeling area! And yet again, in the Final Year of his Chief Ministership, he was equally tough in dealing with the new avatar of Naxalism, that is, Maoist depredations! Ironically it was a 'moderate', democrative version of the Basu's Communism pitted against its extremist step-brother Communist (Maoists)!

As for the equation between Ganapathy and Kishanji, it will be an interesting and instructive exercise to go through and interview (excerpts only) at the end of this chapter, the two gave to the Magazine Peoples March, Nov –Dec 2004.

23rd Jan 2010 West Bengal police raided a hideout of Kishanji located in the forests near Tumurkota village under Kotwali Thana area. A laptop, his diary and cell phone were recovered besides a large cache of arms. But he himself escapes. It was a close run. In the past too the police came close to capturing him four times but he succeeded in giving them a slip each time.

Mamta Banerjee on 18th Jan 2010 had given 7 days to the Maoists to come forward for talks in response to an open letter to the chief minister. Kishanji said, displaying certain Chutzpah, "If you want to come to Jangal Mahal for talks without bringing in the police, you are always welcome. If the Central Government or a political party want us to lay down arms and sit for talks, then it is not possible; giving up arms is not on our agenda".

The fierce shoot-out and surroundings events

Kishenji and his guerrillas were definitely surprised and out-maneuvered. The question that still remains unanswered and unexplained is: Why did he come to Bengal at this time when things are not going well for the Maoists? He was unpredictable most of the time, but this time around, this trait cost him his life.

There are various theories doing the rounds and these will be looked into. Was he making a point with the Maoist leadership (read, Ganapathy)?

Was he indulging in one upmanship? Were there deeper games? No one known's for sure. Everyone is guessing. At the best it, can be loud thinking.

Sources held that Kishanji slipped into Bengal on Tuesday, 22nd November. Before this he had a meeting with party colleague Sabyasachi Panda in Odisha, discussing the latter's entry into the politburo. Panda seldom sees eyes to eye with the State leadership.

Even the security forces are not able to assess his re-entry into the State where the Maoists are on the receiving end. It is losing support among the people. PCPA leader Nemai Mahato feels he was on a peace mission but his military commanders sabotaged his plans: Jayanta and Ranjit Pal bumped off several TMC workers. Second story—call it a theory –goes that he took the "great risk to tone up the sagging organisational network in the state. A third explanation blames his towering ambition of retain his supremacy in the party hierarchy. [Saugar Sengupta , the Pioneer, 26 November 2011].

He seemed to be under pressure to explains the loss of support in Bengal. The series of mindless killings in the Jangal Mahal over the past few years proved counterproductive. The central committee could not see any raison d'être behind his plans!

A CRPF official is honest enough to say one day after his killings: "It is still not sinking in. That finally we have the man dead who led the security forces to merry dance in the region for the past half a decade, he could as well have repeated his feat had it not been for a chance attention to a call purportedly made by Kishenji to his Jharkhand comrades demanding 'urgent reinforcement", to break through the corridor thrown around by the CRPF".

The call led to the house of one Dharmendra Mahato alias Chandan, a college student at Gosainbandh. "We recovered a laptop, some letters dated as late as Tuesday (22nd November) making us sure of his presence".

"He was a man possessed"

"It could be Psychological, yet one could feel a nauseating reef of blood and gun powder. More than 20 hours have lapsed but the ground beneath is still soaked in blood, dried up and darkened; flies hovering around".

This is a reporter speaking from the ground zero, so to say. It is precise if cold, realistic if off-putting! He is yet describing a more horrendous scene: "By a mound lay the blown up body of Kishenji". A prize fish had been hooked! Here was the body of a guerrilla who terrorised Jangal Mahal and neighbouring Jharkhand—nay, the security forces for his uncanny ability to slip in and out of the wooded villages at will—for more than half a decade, before dying by the gun as he lived by!

He was known to be a dare-devil, a fierce fighter, always ready to take risk. He proved it even in his dying moments. A CRPF officer, who saw it first hand, testifies: "He was firing with venom, from behind this mound. He refused to give up, even when asked to surrender." Surrender and Kishenji's! It is an impossible demand, nay unthinkable! The calm in Jangal Mahal. Officer continues:" Then we charged mortar that perhaps neutralised him..... Then our boys picture last moments of Kishenji's life: was trying to guard a hand disc, some documents and a lady purse reportedly belonging to Suchitra Mahato, a close accomplice of Kishenji which were recovered from the site.

The area is comparatively clear: about a few hundred square-meter, some 500 meter away from the main road. "It is still not clear why a master strategist like him entered Bengal at a time when CPI (Maoists) are losing the organisational set-up as recovery of hundreds of Kgs of explosives and arms from the forests would indicate", wondered a senior police officer.

Uneasy Calm in Jangal Mahal

"About 500 meters away from a dense lines of trees where a bloody splattered patch on the ground is a grim reminder of the encounter in which the security forces killed Maoists politburo member Kishenji, lies the sleepy village Burisole. None dared venture out of their houses there on Friday, 25 Nov 2011, a day after the violent incident". [Shiv Sahay Singh, The Hindu, 26th November 2011.]

This is opening para of a report filed from village Burisole, district Paschim Medinipur after deafening sound of the gunfire the previous evening, an panic prevailed in the villages around the area. To put it more expressively," Tension was palpable, dread haunted the faces of the villagers, and fear stalked the dusty paths".

"None in the family could sleep throughout the last night, even my 80-years-old mother, who despite being hard of hearing, was so terrified by the sound of gunshots that she spent a restless night", said Buddheswar Mahato, whose house borders the forest.

By 10 AM, Friday security force personnel had gathered in large numbers in the village. With some holding on to the leashes of the sniffer dogs, they went into each of the thatched 60 houses in the village and asked if they have any outsider hidden in their houses. Women were asked to come out and grilled: Have you seen anyone, have you seen a women?

Search for Suchitra Mahato

They are on the lookout for Suchitra Mahato, Maoists leader and widow of slain Maoists Sasadhar Mahato, who was suspected to have been with Kishenji's when he died.

None of the children in village went to school on Friday. Some of the children played carom, casting glances at the Security personnel striding into their homes.

As in the Burisole village, residents of adjoining Sarkata and Barsole villages, too, had to put up with various rounds of searches of their homes by the security forces. Lakhan Rana of Sarkata village said he was talking to his brother who works at Kharagpur, on telephone, "When the security men took away his phone, promising to return it when they come back in the morning but they have not come yet".

The villagers admitted that the Jungle Party (Maoists) had visited the villages ahead of the Assembly polls, but had not returned since

"It is a blood Curdling calm"

Another reporter on the ground Zero paints equally eerie silence, but in more frightening term: "Curiously, a day after security forces gunned down the top Maoist military strategist inside the Burisole (another reporter spelt the village name differently as Burisol) forests, a blood curdling calm prevails over a dozen villages and hamlets nestled in 10 Km radius", even as CPI (Maoist) state Secretary called a 48 hour Bengal bandh from Saturday (the 26th) protesting the Thursday's " fake encounter" which was summarily rejected by the security forces.

Amid all this controversy, the Jangal Mahal would, however, not utter a word. "Not a bird, not a bird, would chatter, let alone a man". Though quiet descends fast in winter over the woody land of Jungal Mahal, "we have seldom seen a deadly calm as this", asserts Sona Tudu, a retired teacher who regularly shuttle between Gidhni and Jhumuria.

"It was a fake encounter"

A day after the Maoist strategist Kishenji (also spelt a Kishanji) was gunned down in the Burisole forest (on 24th Nov 2011). Maoist Sympathisers and Security forces on Friday (the 25th) traded allegations and came out with claims and counter-claims on whether he was killed in a "fake encounter". [Ananya Dutta and Shiv Shay Singh, The Hindu, 26 Nov 2011]

Expectedly, the first to declare it as a "fake" encounter was that doughty warrior, the Leftist and presently a Maoists ideologue, Varavara Rao, the revolutionary poet. He alleged in Kolkata that Kishenji's was killed in a fake encounter; "it was staged to hood wink the people and divert attention from the incident". He was addressing a rally in the city. Kishenji's niece, Deepa Rao, who was in West Bengal to claim his body, also alleged that he had been killed in a fake encounter.

This rally was called by the activists of the Association for Protection of Democratic Rights (APDR) in Kolkata, to protest against the "fake encounter". The APDR activists marched to the State Secretariat, during the protest.

On the other hand, the DG, CRPF, K Vijay Kumar, told the Journalists at Burisole that it was "an absolutely clean operation". Mr Kumar was however was not upset with all such allegations flying around, and said:" I was not surprised that the allegations have been raised. It is the habit of such people to accuse (the security forces of fake encounters)… It is custom to accuse the police, but that is part of our job".

DG, CRPF, was even pained at the double standards of those who accuse the forces of fake encounters. Rejecting all such allegation empathically, Mr. Kumar said, "When our men are killed in large numbers by the Maoists, no question is raised but when we take them on, the encounter is called fake. I am not surprised by the remarks…. The information that I have with me, I can say that I am ninety nine per cent confident that the encounter is genuine".

Now to the Varavara Rao-Speak

Given his reputation as a Maoists spokesman a Leftist ideologue and revolutionary poet, VV can be expected to build a case with his multifarious skills and powers of oratory, where none exists. This author makes this cynical observation on the great Telgu worrier, the well-Known VV, after taking into account all sides of the arguments, or even all sides of allegations. In fact, in all deaths of the ultras, called Maoists, you would expect Varavara Rao's of this world and all the Leftist/ Maoists Sympathisers/Supporters of the murderous Killers of Maoist variety, to come immediately on the roads and hold rallies to condemn security forces, even when they are doing an honest job, often costing them their lives. In fact, it would be a real surprise if you do not have VV's and APDR, coming out in droves to declare any killing of their darling Maoists as a result of "fake" encounters. How often these worthies made similar cacophonous noises when a uniformed man is killed by these 'illicit' Maoists? May be, this is the greatness of India's democratic traditions: all anti-India, anti security force, anti-Government Cacophony get immediately applause! May be, this is the Strength of the Civil Rights Activists and NGO's in India, even when we know that some of these entities get illegal, unauthorised foreign aid in American Dollars! Still, all strength to our democracy which seems to be doing good by the people, not with standing all the Shenanigans and exertions by the likes of VVs and APDRs.

Before we give free reigns to the VV and his verbosity, let us comment on another allied subject. The two dailies—The Hindu and The Pioneer—which has been used extensively by this Author, carry a very evocative and emotional photo, exactly same in both daily, of a grieving and crying Deepa Rao, mourning the violent loss of his Uncle, Kishenji, in Kolkata on 25th Nov 2011. Emotion on the death of a near and dear one is natural, only human but should one be carried over by such public display of emotion on occasion like this? The following Para is a comment on the issue.

This comment may not be liked, or approved of, by many people even beyond the hypocritical coterie of VVs and APDRs. In usual circumstances, it is in bad taste, and in fact be deemed so. But then, these comments are not being offered in usual circumstances. There are specific circumstances about this public display of grief by Deepa. This Author, being an Army man, cannot but help being honest, even blunt in commenting on Deepa's grief. The Uncle, Deepa is mourning for is not a private individual. He was one among the leading Maoists, who have played havoc with the national security and killed thousands of Indians, including civilians, uniformed personnel and even innocent tribal's, for whose cause they are indulging in an armed uprising, over the last three-and a half decades. And their outfit, CPI (Maoists), had been declared illegal. All Maoists are outlaws! Now specifically about Deepa's Uncle Kishenji: He has been indulging in murderous mayhem in the Jangal Mahal areas of West Bengal, killing and maiming hundreds of his so-called class enemy over the last half-a-decade period. He and his cadres are responsible for that widespread misery!

Now a question for Deepa: Has she ever, in public or private, expressed grief or uttered a single word of sympathy for the unfortunate relatives of those killed by his uncle in Jangal Mahal and by his party (CPI-Maoist) guerrillas all over the so-called Red Zone over all these years? Never, as is the common knowledge! Is she, given the reasons by this Author, justified in earning public sympathy by this public display of her personal grief?

The above may be dubbed as "Politically incorrect", but a soldier must speak his mind and be truthful, even if it does not fit in with this currently popular aphorism!

After expressing personal views on certain emotional issues, this author leaves the field free for the great VV's (Rao) peroration, unchecked and uncensored:

- His suspicion was that Kishenji's had been taken into police custody in Wednesday (23 November) itself, tortured and later killed.
- He claimed that the first media reports on Wednesday suggested that Kishenji and his comrades had been encircled by the thousands paramilitary forces, but they announced that he had managed to escape "If he managed to escape to Jharkhand, how did the West Bengal Government kill him? How did the Joint security forces kill him in Paschim Medinipur district", Mr. Rao asked.
- He also alleged that signs to torture were visible on Kishenji's body.
- Let DG CRPF too be quoted here: "when we die in large numbers, it is always a very fair deal and when we are able to take them on (the Maoists). This is what they say.... The security forces have been very tactical and it was an absolutely clean operation. They have acted on time and not lost even one minute".
- Mr Rao said Kishenji's death signaled that the TMC-led Mamta Government was not serious about the dialogue process and urged the interlocutors to step down.

- Mr. Rao lashed out the West Bengal government and the Centre, saying, "on the one hand you are offering talks and on the other hands you are killing the man who had offered talks long ago. Ganapathy has offered talks, Azad has offered talks and Kishanji has offered talks. They only wanted that a congenial atmosphere be created....Maoists had asked for a simultaneous ceasefire, but the outfit's West Bengal unit had even offered a unilateral ceasefire, which was violated by the state.
- "What is the development that the Left Government and TMC have given to the Jangal Mahal region? Have they given Jal, Jangal, Jamin (water, forest and land) to the people? They have only given 5,000 acres of land to the Jindal's" he said.

Varavara Rao and Deepa Rao do their bit

Stating that 85-years old mother of Kishenji's "waiting to see her son's body". His niece Deepa Rao appealed to the West Bengal Government here (at Kolkata) on the 25th to arrange his body being taken to Andhra Pradesh. [Ananya Dutta, the Hindu, 26 Nov 2011].

"My grandmother has not seen her son for 30 years.... Our family is waiting, people are waiting to see him", said Deepa, praying that the process is expedited as the body would start decomposing. She requested that the body be airlifted to Hyderabad after which it could be taken to Peddapalli, Kishenji's home town in Karimnagar district. Asked by newsmen if the body would be sent there, Chief Minister Banerjee's response was a Cryptic "yes".

Alleging that Kishenji was killed in a "fake encounter", Deepa claimed it was the responsibility of the West Bengal Government to at least ensure that his body was returned to his family.

Revolutionary poet Varavara Rao, who accompanied Deepa to Kolkata, demanded that all the stipulations of the NHRC regarding the post-mortem should be adhered to. He demanded that a case of culpable homicide be registered against the police; and condemned the Killing of Kishenji in "fake encounter" and demanded a judicial inquiry into the incident. "We will approach the high court for a fresh post-mortem in Kolkata and bring the body to his hometown Peddapalli...for last rites", said VV; lashing out at West Bengal Chief Minister Banerjee, he said the incident has exposed her real face. "After asking the Maoists to join the so-called mainstream, and making them declare a cease fire, her government has now resorted to this heinous act", he said.

In Andhra Pradesh, where Kishenji had 14 cases booked against him; he carried a remand of ₹ 12 Lakh. He was also an accused in the murder of the former speaker of AP assembly D Sripada Rao, in Karimnagar district in 1999.

APDR to file writ in HC for encounter probe

The Association for Protection of Democratic Rights has been assigned by slain Maoist leader Kishenji's mother to file a writ in Kolkata HC, demanding a probe into "fake encounter" in which the rebel top gun was killed on Thursday.

APDR secretary, DP Roy, who walked in a rally against alleged fake killing alongside VV and Deepa, said a case under Sec 302 should be lodged as per the direction of the NHRC.

"The body of Kishanji should be brought to Kolkata for an autopsy to know the real reason/cause of the death", Roy said, even as Rao claimed "Kishanji had come to Bengal to arrange for peace talks and was killed by the police in cold blood as they did to Azad when he was talking peace". [PNS, Kolkata, The Pioneer, 26 Nov 2011].

Mother Madhuramma writes to CJ

Kishanji's mother Mallojula Madhuramma has written to the Chief Justice of Kolkata HC, expressing the apprehension that her son has been killed in "fake encounter" and praying for a judicial inquiry into the incident. The letter was sent to the CJ of the Kolkata HC and a copy has been sent to the Supreme Court. We hope that human rights here will take up the matter further", Mr Rao told the Hindu. [Ananya Dutta and Shiv Sahay Singh, The Hindu, 26 Nov 2011.]

In 2010, the mother of CPI(Maoist) politburo member Cherukuri Rajkumar alias Azad who was also killed in an encounter, filed a petition in the Andhra Pradesh HC. The Court had directed the police to conduct the post-mortem at the government hospital at Mancherial in Adilabad district and to show her the body.

"Be on guard against retaliation": DG, CRPF

Calling the operation that eliminated Kishanji a "significant success", DG, CRPF K Vijay Kumar said 25th November Security forces "have none the less been cautioned against the possibility of a retaliatory attack".

After visiting the Burisole forest, the site of Thursday operation, 15 Km from Jhargram in Paschim Medinipur district, Mr Kumar confirmed that it was indeed Kishanji who was gunned down. [Staff Reporter, The Hindu, 26 Nov 2011.]

Hunt still on

The massive hunt was still on for any of Kishanji's aides who might still be holed up or hiding in the forest and its vicinity, said Alok Rajoria, Additional SP (operations), Jhargram.

Suchitra Mahato, wife of Maoist leader Sasadhar Mahato, who was killed earlier this year (2011), and who is believed to have been with Kishanji during the Thursday operation, is still at large.

There are four or five armed Maoist cadres still hiding in the area and combing operations, being conducted by the CRPF along with the State's Counter-Insurgency Force in the nearby villages of Burisole, Sarkala and Barsole under the Jamboni Police Station, could continue for the next few days.

Dismissing allegations from certain quarters that the operation was a "fake encounter". Mr Kumar said the intelligence gathered played a significant role in the operation.

The forces recovered some ₹ 90,000 along with a computer hard disk, a few letters found from a bag and 60 rounds of empty cartridges of automatic weapons. Police officials revealed that the letters found confirmed the presence of Suchitra Mahato.

Did the security forces upper hand in 2011?

One view the security experts have is that it was rash on the part of senior Maoists commander and acknowledged strategist Kishanji to have ventured in to West Bengal in Nov 2011, knowing well as he did, the adverses suffered by the LWE in 2011. They are not sure what impelled him to undertake this obviously risky and ill-advised adventures: a sense of bravado; an adventure; his past successes in getting out of seemingly dangerous and difficult operational situations; one-up manship to maintain his standing in the hierarchy and finally to retrieve some losses suffered recently, especially in 2011.

His meeting with Sabyasachi Panda just before his entry in to West Bengal is another intriguing aspect, knowing as we do that he was on rebellious path, and Kishanji helping him—rather a promise of help in his efforts to enter politburo! Was Kishanji planning to challenge the leadership of his reclusive loss at some future date? This all is some kind of loud thinking about the reasons behind entering West Bengal or, maybe he tested his luck once too many! Now to examine the situation in 2011, preceding Kishanji's venturing into West Bengal in Nov 2011.

"The top rung Maoist leadership has every reason to be worried now as intelligence agencies in different LWE- affected States have been striking gold in either arresting or killing the top leadership". [K Srinivas Reddy, The Hindu, 26 Nov 2011.]

The Maoists movement faced a series of setbacks in 2011 as the security forces succeeded in arresting four Central Committee (CC) members earlier, and to beat it all, fell the fifth blow, the killing of Kishanji on 24th Nov 2011. And not to forget, he was the man who single handedly nurtured the Marxist-Leninist- Maoist movement in West Bengal, Jharkhand and Bihar.

The series of killings or arrests of members of the CPI (Maoist) CC, the all powerful body of the most secretive organisation, is an indication that the core principle of counter-insurgency strategy is to hit the leadership. The arrest of four CC members was due to highly accurate inputs provided by the intelligence agencies of different states.

Those arrested this year include Jhantu Mukherjee alias Sahebda, Vijay Arora alias Jaspalji, and Varanasi Subramanian and Akhillesh Yadav alias Bhupesh. The fifth and the latest Strike by the security forces in West Bengal was again backed by actionable intelligence inputs.

Arguably, the Maoists succeeded in pulling off some spectacular attacks on security forces in different states, but they too began bleeding in all states, save for Chhattisgarh. In a way, the security forces, backed by fully functional intelligence units in Bihar, Jharkhand, West Bengal and Odisha, managed to turn the tide even though these States continue to face intensified rebel activity.

However, the qualitative change is that concerted effort in these States led the counter insurgency operations from a stage of 'Strategic defensive' to 'Strategic equilibrium'. The only exception in that change is Chhattisgarh, where the Maoist movement is in a 'Strategic offensive' stage.

If one were to look at the arrests or killings of top leaders, a pattern indeed is visible. The CCMs/PBM, killed included: Patel Sudhakar Reddy, Chief of the Maoists intelligence wing (May 2009); and Cherukuri Raj Kumar alias Azad, CCM/PBM and Spokesperson (July 2010)

"Kishanji died in real encounter?"

Maoists have finally admitted that their top leader Koleshware Rao alias Kishaji, was killed in real encounter and not in fake one as they as well as their over ground supporters have been saying since his death two and half years ago, said a daily dated 24 July 2014. [Snigdhendu Bhattacharya, The Hindustan Times, 24 July 2014.]

Kishenji died in an encounter in Burishole forest in West Midnapore (read Paschim Mednipur) district on 24 Nov 2011.

"Comrade Kishanji was injured in an encounter and was caught by the enemy and matyred", the CPI (Maoist) Central Committee had said in a letter to the party's rank and file issued sometimes in 2013. However, the letter only reached West Bengal Maoists recently.

But the wording of their communiqué is interesting, nay it is clever: .... "Injured..... Caught by the enemy and martyred". Obviously, he was caught injured and then "martyred", that is , done to death. They will not simply say,... "He was martyred (=killed) in the encounter.".... As the Varavara Rao's of This Left world and APDRs are convinced. They did want to convince not only the mortals like us but also the courts of India, including the Supreme Court.

Indian Politics would not let the controversy die

Even if the Maoists want to put the lid on this controversy, in howsoever mischievous manner through cleverly worded communiqué as explained above, the Indian politicians would not let it happen. In the first week of July 2015, Chief Minister Mamta Banerjee's nephew publicly asserted that Kishenji was indeed, killed in a "fake encounter."

There is no need to offer comments, yet again. Let the case rest here!!

Thimbu Oraon:Maoist-turned-educationist

The heading could read "Thimbu Oraon: Maoist-turned-educationist-cum-Mukhiya", as well.

This Maoist, Thimbu Oraon, 35, has been an inspiration for young boys to leave armed outfits and return to the mainstream. He is about to turn a new page in his life: " Set to make his political debut in the Assembly Polls this December (2014) [Anbwesh Roy Chaudhary, Hindustan Times, 3rd Sep 2014.]

He is a former Maoist, who was acquitted of all maoist cases in 2008. Thimbu won the panchayat election in 2009 and started a school in his home panchayt, Badri in Gumla, Jharkhand.

His transformation from a law-offender to a law-abider impressed Congress Vice president Rahul Gandhi, and his work has also been acclaimed by State Congress president Sukdeo Bhagat.

So, he is planning to contest the Bishnupur seat in Gumla District on Congress ticket. More importantly, he is hopeful: "young men here either join the Indian Army or the Maoists for livelihood as farming earns very little..... If I clear the polls, my primary agenda would be bringing back youngsters to the mainstream. If I am in the Fray... The Modi wave will have very little effort as villagers have an affinity towards me due to my education campaign."

Sabyasachi Panda: A Maoist Dissenter Aug-Sep 2008

CPI (Maiost) expelled its best-known leader in Odisha, Sabyasachi Panda, for his alleged role in fuelling riots in Kandhamal district in Aug-Sep 2008. [Hindustan Times,17.9.2008.]

14 Jan 2010. Milli Panda alias Subharree Dass wife of Sabyasachi Panda, secretary of Odisha State Organising Committee of CPI (Maoist), was arrested and ledged in Bhubaneshwar Jail. Subsequently, Maoists demanded her release as a pre-condition for setting free Malkangiri Collector Vineet Krishna.

He was the Maoist leader dealing with the State Government of Odisha about the release of two Italians and one MLA. He was trying to be difficult when he released one Italians, and then putting tough conditions for release of the remaining two. He was not as much "teasing" the State Government as his bosses at the State Organising Committee of the Maoists. This all has been discussed earlier Kishanji meeting him before his adventure into West Bengal too has been dealt with earlier.

The Odisha Maoist were merely waiting for some excuse for his expulsion and the Kandhamal riots served that purpose.

Patel Sudhankar Reddy: Killed 24 May 2009

Sudhankar Reddy, heading the intelligence unit of the Party, was neutralised in Prakasham District of AP. Sudhankar Reddy alias Sagar was a member of the two most important organs of the CPI (Maoist): Central Committee and Central Military Commission. Hailing from Kurti Ravulu district, he went underground in 1982 while studying Law at the Osmania, as he was wanted in Several serious cases: Attempted assassination of former CM Chandra Babu Naidu at Alipiri near Tirumala in 2003; Assassination attempt on N. Janardhan Reddy in Nellore in 2007; assassination of Former Home Minister A Madhava Reddy in Nalgonda district in 2007.

That is not all. Sudhankar Reddy was also allegedly involved in the murder of Senior IPS officers KS Vyas and Umesh Chandra in Hyderabad. He was also involved in 2008 Balimala attack in which 36 Grey-Hound Commanders died when the Maoists sank a boat on the Andhra Odisha border. (The New Indian Express, Bengaluru, 25 May 2009)

Senior leaders. Arrest of 7 Feb 2010.

UP Police STF arrested 8 activists of CPI (Maoist) in Kanpur, with half a truckload of printed material, CDs, pen drives, and ₹ 8-16 Lakh in cash. The details.......

1. Blraj@BR Arivind@Baccha Prasad, head of Northern Regional Bureau of CPI (Maoist). Close associate of Kobad Ghandy.
2. Bansidhar alias Chitanda, politburo member. M Phil degree from JL Nehru University, Delhi was in jail for three years. Hails from Champaran district, Bihar.
3. Naveen Prasad Singh.
4. Ambrish.
5. Deepak Ram.
6. Shiv Raj Singh alias Arjun.
7. Rajinder Kumar Phulara alias Arvind.
8. Kripa Shankar alias Mano (The Pioneer, 2 Feb 2010).

Sushil Roy: Politburo member seeks MERCY

A daily reported on 28 Oct 2012 that an ailing top Maoist leader and a member of their politburo, at that Sushil Roy, has applied for mercy from the Government of India [bhinandan Mishra, The Sunday Guardian, 28 Oct 2012.]

The 78-years old Roy is facing trial in 18 different cases of violence, arson and murder in Jharkhand, West Bengal and Odisha. If the officials are to be believed, the government will release the jailed Maoist.

Roy was arrested from Midnapore (West Bengal) on 21 May 2005 and lodged in Chaibasa jail and later shifted and admitted in the All India Institute of Medical Science (AIIMS) in New Delhi for treatment.

Taking cognizance of Roy's plea, the Rashtrapati Bhavan asked for a report from the Ministry of Home Affair on his Clemency petition. The MHA has written to Jharkhand government, asking for a detailed report on Roy's past record. IG (prison) Jharkhand Shivshankar Tiwari told the daily that the government will give its opinion after it receives the letter from the Centre. "He is a senior member and is over 70. I cannot say anything else". Roy was sent to the AIIMS because of his failing health.

Jharkhand state officials say that the State government is going to send a favourable report to the Centre. An official said: "The matter is pending with the State Home Department and will decide soon. Roy has been diagnosed with cancer and in the all probability he will be released soon".

The daily says its questionnaire to the MHA on the matter remain unanswered.

Central Committee member: Narla Ravi Sharma

10 Oct 2009, Ravi Sharma@Arjun @ Mahesh and his wife B. Anuradha @ Ranjitha were arrested by Hazaribagh Police. Both hail from Mehboobnagar, Andhra Pradesh, and had been running the Maoist outfit in Bihar and Jharkhand.

As reported by The Times of India of 16 Oct 2009, Narla Ravi was expert in military tactics. He had enrolled for Ph.D in Agriculture in Delhi University. He had joined the outfit in 1997, while his wife Anuradha, an Employee of a public sector Bank, joined her husband in the People's war (PW) in 2004 (The Hindustan Times, 16 Oct 2009).

A word on Sharma's Arrest

As seen in some earlier cases, it is always a problem to know or fix a date of arrest of a Maoist prisoner. To an extent, it is understandable since the police may not announce the date of arrest of a Maoist on the very first day. Yet again, the information of arrest of a Maoist comes through the press sources and not any official announcement from the Police or any other paramilitary force that might have arrested him. Even in the instant case, about Sharma's arrest, the Times of india of 16th Oct 2009 says he was arrested on the 10th, while the Indian Express of 1st November says he was arrested on the 13th. Both dailies give other details: He was arrested with his wife, and it was Hazaribagh the two were arrested in.

It is important to record the blurb of this important 'The Sunday Story', in the Indian Express of 1 Nov 2009. The Blurb reads:" During his police Interrogation, Senior Naxal leader Narla Rabi Sharma is said to have talked about the organisational structure of the CPI (Maoist), its plans and how money moves within the outfit. The Sunday Express Pieces together details of his interrogation after extensive interviews with the investigators". [Subrata Nagchaudhary, Indian Express, 1st Nov 2009.]

The details about his biographical information and his standing in the outfit are given here. But information disclosed by him on strength, finances and plans would be included in relevant section of Chapter 6 and 7.

Sharma's Biographical

Narla Ravi Sharma's luck ran out three days after he gave the Andhra Police the Slip near Patna Junction. Then on 13 October, the Jharkhand Police arrested Sharma and his Wife Bellapu Anuradha alias Ranjitha at Hazaribagh for alleged Naxal links. Sharma is wanted in several cases, including the killing of Jharkhand Special Branch Intelligence Officer PS Induwar.

An erudite face. The agricultural scientist is the latest erudite face to emerge after Doon School-educated Kobad Ghandy. Sharma was born in 1965 in Tirumalapuram village in Andhra's Mahaboobnagar district. He was the eldest of the four children born to the school teacher Sudhakar Sharma and Sulochana Devi. After his post graduation from Rajendranagar Agriculture College in Andhra Pradesh, he studied for his Ph.D at the Indian Agricultural Research institute (IARI) Delhi, from 1995 to 1993. In police records, his occupation is listed as translator-cum-teacher at the CPI (Maoist)'s Eastern Regional Bureau in Jharkhand and Bihar.

In 1985, while in his last year at the Agriculture College he joined the student's movement under the banner of Radical/Students Union, and was later elected 'City Secretary'. It marked the beginning of his shift to Naxal ideology. He told the Police he dreamt of a classless society as a youth and toured several parts of Andhra Pradesh; during these tours, the "severe exploitation, inequality, imperialism and fascism" he saw, moved him to take up arms. He joined the CPI –ML (PW) in 1998 and subsequently, when CPI –ML (PW) and the MCC merged to form CPI (Maoist), he became its member. In 1998, it he was arrested by the Andhra Pradesh Police for his alleged Naxal links but was released a year later.

That was the only time he was arrested, till his arrest last month, Oct 2009, days after the Naxals struck in Jharkhand, killing Induwar, an intelligence officer, with the State Special Branch.

Sharma and the outfit's structure

Sharma reportedly joined the Bihar cadre of the CPI –ML (PU) in 1998, and two years later became member of the Area Committee. In 2002, after being selected as State Committee member, Sharma was assigned the responsibility of party operations in Jharkhand and Bihar, a Post he held till 2006—the year he came in touch with Amit Bagchi and joined the party's State Military Commission.

Though not a member of the CC or the Politburo, Sharma seemed to know a lot about the structure of the outfit. As State Committee Member working under the Eastern Regional Bureau, he told that the party also had Special Zonal Committees and sub-Committees—he himself was a Special Area Commander in the Koyel-Sankha Zone.

He divulged details about local guerrill squads, village defences squads and two Regional Military commissions. Sharma mentioned two companies working under the Eastern Regional Bureau: the Jharkhand-Odisha/ Company and the Jharkhand Bihar Company.

Sharma is learnt to have known and interacted with members of the CC, PB and Central Military Commission (CMC), including General Secretary Ganapathy, CMC in-charge Basale Raj, West Bengal in-Charge Kishanji, Kobad Ghandy and Amit Bagchi.

The Eastern Regional Bureau operates in Bihar, Jharkhand, Odisha, West Bengal and Assam; Central Regional Bureau in Andhra Pradesh and Dandakaranya (the Bastar Region); the Northern Regional Bureau in Haryana, Punjab, Delhi and Rajasthan; and the South West Regional Bureau in Maharashtra, Karnataka, Tamil Nadu and Kerala. The party has a Research and Development wing known as Central Technical Committee, formed in 2007. The committees and units in Bhopal and Rourkela are not functional after the arrest of their members. Twelve to Thirteen platoons of CPI (Maoist) are now working in Jharkhand–Bihar–Odisha areas and the total strength of the Party is around 2,500.

Central Committee member: Mullah Tauhid

Karthik, 25, alias Mullah Tauhid, a central committee member, was arrested on 24th August 2009, by the Ranchi Police, along with Amitabh Bagchi, 55 alias Anil, alias Sumitda, a Politburo member.

As expected, CPI (Maoist) spokesman claimed the two leaders had been in police custody since 19 August.

Ravula Srinivas: A graying guerrilla commander

He may not be a Maoist leader as well known as a member of the Central Committee or of the Central Military Commission might be, but still he represents a class of leaders/Commanders who have indeed Contributed a lot to the Maoist movement.

A well known Journalist call him one of the breed of graying guerillas, and has given a brief sketch of his life in a daily in March 2014. [Praveen Swami, The Hindu, 12 March 2014.]

His life as a revolutionary starts three decades ago when "a slight young man called Ravula Srinivas left the village of Bekkal near Warangal in Andhra Pradesh, hoping to make a revolution", as all young idealists do at his age. Now from inside the Maoiats citadel in Chattisgarh's vast and remote Bastar region, he is at the head of an inner circle of graying guerrilla commanders "Who hope dramatic acts of violence may staunch of the death of their dreams". Here is an irony here what they failed to achieve in their youthful days, they want to achieve in the closing years of their not so active life presently. It is rough if ironic equivalent of the last dice of a losing player.

Srinivas, the head of the insurgent unit that carried out the 11th march 2014 massacre of State and Central police officers in Chhattisgarh, leads the insurgency in the State at a crucial time: "Corruption, disillusionment and war-fatigue are corroding a movement that once seemed perched on the edge of nation wide success". These words coming from a journalist known for his objectivity, must be a source of simultaneous elation and frustration.

In 2013, the Central Committee of the CPI (Maoist) admitted that the "intensity and expanse of the resistance of the PLGA and people decreased and non-proletarian trends increased in party and the PLGA ; recruitment decreased; [the] number of people leaving the party and PLGA increased".

It is a grim picture not only for the Central Committee Secretary Ganapathi, but also — and more so — for the graying guerrilla Srinivas. The son of a family of traditional toddy-tappers and agricultural workers, Srinivas , 53, dropped out of the village school in Grade 8. Andhra Pradesh police records show he joined the Maoist outfit, People's War in 1982, married party colleague, Savitri in 1987. He was assigned to the Bastar Region in 1995 and rose to the national prominence in 2010 after an ambush he organised claimed 40 lives, mainly civilians.

But he showed little remorse: "our aim was precise and correct", Said he in an interview to CNN-IBN, "[but] the administration is using civilians as a human shield, so they got killed". A simple as that!

In April 2010, by now, Secretary of the CPI (Maoist) DKSZC, Srinivas led an ambush that killed 75 CRPF men at Chintalnar. He followed this up in summer 2013 with a massacre of congress leaders, including the former CM Vidya Charan Shukla and the controversial vigilante leader, Mahendra Karma.

Srinivas suffered intimate losses of his own. Parshuraman, his mentor and brother killed by the police in 1994; his sister, Kanukamma, was killed fighting by his side. His son, whose name the Hindu is with holding, studied at a border school in Sukma, as his parents fought the police in the forests around it.

The Lieutenants

Srinivas' key military lieutenant, Ganesh Ueike, was an accidental Maoist in 1982, the police records show; he was studying for a Bachelor of Science degree in Nalagonda. Faced with a prospect of arrest in a case involving the murder of a rival, Ueike fled. He resurfaced in the mid 2000s, as commander of Maoist operations in Vidarbha region of Maharashtra. Kottakam Sudarshan, a key politburo member, rated by intelligence officers as the Maoist's best insurgent tactician, heads the newly formed Chhattisgarh-Odisha command of the CPI (Maoist). Born 1959-60, he grew up in the mining town of Belampalli, where his parents worked in the Singareni Coalmines.

Sudarshan studied for a BSC degree but dropped out in the 1978 to work full time with the Radical Students Union—a far left grouping that was also the nursery for five of the seven CPI (Maoist) politburo leaders still active.

In 1981, he participated in a famous strike at Singareni, which the People's War hoped would spearhead a working class revolution. Following the marginalisation of the radicals in Singareni, Sudarshan went underground—and headed for the Dandakaranya forests.

The graying revolutionaries in the Dantewada forests probably know they are not going to live to see their dreams realised: 9 of the 16 members of politburo appointed in 2007 have been either killed or imprisoned.

Soni Sori: Accused of being a Maoist by police

This indeed should be an interesting case of police charging a person to be a Maoist, and she attracting a large number of human rights activists and even a renowned professor at MIT to her defence. A number of headlines in the press will be examined on the issue, starting with the one that appeared in May 2012.

- "Chomsky and others seek justice for Soni Sori": 2 May 2012
- "Chhattisgarh woman allegedly tortured by the police on the charge that she was a Maoists"

Report in a daily is datelined Washington Narayan Lakshman, The Hindu, 2 May 2012

Nom Chomsky, liberal philosopher and institute professor at Massachusets Institute of Technology (MIT), has joined a list of close to 250 Indians and foreign intellectuals in an open letters to PM Manmohan Singh, protesting the "brutal treatment meted out to Soni Sori", a Chhattisgarh woman, said to have been tortured by police on unproven allegations that she was a Maoist.

In a letter signed by Professor Chomsky and others, including Jean Dreze, Harsh Mander, Anand Patwardhan, Aruna Roy, and Arundhati Raoy, the they called for "immediate medical attention" to Sori, 43, who was allegedly stipped, electrocuted and tortured, physically and sexually.

After the Supreme Court ordered an independent medical examination of Ms Sori at NRS Medical College, Kolkata, doctors found stones lodged in her vagina and rectum.

Fear for Life

"We fear for Soni's life and are a outraged and ashamed at the inhuman treatment of a woman in India", the authors of the letter said Sori is still under arrest in Chhattisgarh.

Pointing out that she has received virtually no follow up medical treatment for the injuries she sustained in police custody and the inflictions that have developed as a consequence", Chomsky and others said two individuals, who had met Soni last week, reported that her face was visibly swollen and her hands and feet appeared abnormally thin, indicating severe weight loss".

They urged that with six months passing since the time Sori was said to have been tortured, her attempts to communicate with Civil Society had also been stifled, and in the January (2012), a team from women's groups attempts to meet her in the Raipur jail "were prevented from doing so by the administration".

In the letter, also addressed to Home Minister P Chidambaram, the intellectuals expressed "grave concern" at Sori's medical condition and demanded immediate access for facts-finding groups to meet her.

Gallantry Medal

In a message to the daily from the Association for India's Developement (AID), a-non profit organisation, pressing for Sori's case to be heard, a member noted that contray to any notion that an investigation has been initiated against the police officers involved, SP Amit Garg, named in Sori's Letters, was awarded a gallantry Medal on Republic Day this year (2012).

"Activists demand immediate release of Soni Sori"

"Has been subjected to barbaric sexual abuse in Police Custody" New Delhi: 3rd January 2013.

"Locating the alleged sexual torture of the young tribal teacher Soni Sori in Police custody at Raipur Central Jail in the context of the ongoing debate and the agitation against violence against women activists, the intellectuals held a silent protest march from Jantar Mantar to the Supreme Court on 2 January 2013. Ahead of her case expected to be heard by a sessions court shortly, they demanded her immediate release and punishment to the SP Dantewada". [Mohammad Ali, The Hindu, 3rd January 2013.]

Chhattisgarh-based human rights activist Himanshu Kumar who has been in touch with Sori through letters, argued that Sori's human rights were being grossly violated as she was being repeatedly subjected to the most barbaric and repulsive sexual abuse for more than a year now in Police custody in Raipur Central Jail. "At least two separate medical reports have shown evidence of stones in her vaginas despite repeated protests, no action has been taken till now", he said.

Former president of then students Union Suchita De alleged that despite Sori's repeated requests for safety and protection from the "torture" of Chhattisgarh police, she has not been transferred out of the State. "She has been in jail for more than a year on spurious, trumped up charges. Finally, her case will be heard on 3rd January at the SC and we demand justice for her".

Mahatab Alam from coalition for the Protection of Human Rights Defenders (CP HRD) specifically highlighted that the SP who was accused of torturing Sori was awarded by the government. "It is a matter of great regret that instead of being punished, he was awarded the presidential police medal on 26th January 2012".

The speakers also highlighted that in reaction to the outrage across the country, the activists had demanded fast track courts to deal with rape cases. They have been ignoring the protester's demand of fast tracking the over one lakh pending cases.

The silent protest march, which, saw the participation among others by activist and lawyer Prashant Bhushan, activist Swami Agnivesh and Academician Uma Chakravarty, started from Jantar Mantar which has been seeing ongoing protest against cases of violence against women and gang rape to 23 years-old medical student. The march was stopped a few metres away from the Supreme Court.

The daily has an editorial that reads under the picture of Soni Sori:

" National Shame": a Protest by all Indian Students Association in New Delhi on 2nd Jan 2013 demanding release of tribal teacher Soni Sori Who has been languishing in a Chhattisgarh jail for over a year . They also condemned the Centre's move to award the police officer who was accussed of Physically torturing her.

A Poster along the picture of Soni Sori reads:

SHAME ON UPA GOVERNMENT FOR GIVING GALLANTRY, AWARD TO THE PERPETRATOP OF SEXUAL ASSAULT ON TRIBAL WOMAN SONI SORI IN Chhattisgarh!

"Suprenme Court allows Sori plea to shift her to Jagdalpur jail New Delhi: 9 Jan 2013

The Supreme Court on 8th January 2013 allowed a request by Soni sori, who have been arrested on alleged Maoist links, to direct the

Chhattisgarh Government for shifting her from a jail in Raipur to the Central Jail, Jagdalpur.

A Bench led by CJI Altmash Kabir accepted Sori application after senior advocate Mukul Rohatagi, who appeared for the State Government, told the court that the authorities had no objection if she was again shifted to Jagdalpur jail.

The bench also asked the State Government to ensure that Sori is provided required medical facilities after transfer.

"Sori has been lodged at the Raipur Central Jail since Oct 2011",. She had sought the transfer as it would be easier for her relatives to visit her there. The frail teacher was jailed on Charges of helping Naxals. "She is accused of receiving "protection money" from the Essar Group.

"Soni Sori, Lingaram Kopadi denied bail by Chhattisgarh High Court"

Tribal school teacher Soni Sori and her relatives Lingaram Kodopi have been denied bail by the Chhattisgarh High Court (HC) in the Essar Steel case on 8th July 2013. Rejecting the bail petition, Justice Prashant Kumar Mishra of the HC said that on the "basis of the Seriousness of the evidence", the bail petition was rejected. Activists associated with campaign to free Sori, were perhaps expecting positive order, especially after her acquittal in all other major cases in recent months. [Subojit Bagchi, the Hindu, 9 July 2013.]

One of the campaigners felt "it is extremely disappointing". Sori's lawyer in the HC Shishir Dixit was more honest with the daily:" Crime is of heinous nature and on the basis of seriousness of evidence, the bail was rejected".

Kodopi, a relative of Sori, is a professionally trained tribal journalist from Dantewada and is also linked with Sori in the Essar Steel case. Other than one minor case of allegedly torching vehicles where Sori got bail last month (June), both of them have been acquitted in all other cases. Sori has been acquitted in six other cases in the last 18 months, while Kodopi has been acquitted in the only other case of planning an attack on local Congress leader Avdesh Gautam.

The remaining case is the one of Essar Steel, where "both of them have been accused of arranging "protection money" on behalf of the company to Maoists. The main accussed DVCS Verma, GM of an Essar Steel Plant, and BK Lala, an Essar contractor, were arrested for allegedly by disbursing the money. Both Verma and Lala got bail within first few months of their arrests.

One of the lawyers of Kodopi, Amarnath Pandey, said that While court's should be "observed with utter reverence", the developments in Chhattisgarh are "deeply disturbing". Pandey explains with "clever foolishness" his Silly resoning: "The co-accussed of Sori and Kodopi are manager and contractor with Essar Steel. Manager Varma got bail on ground of ill-health and the police did not file a charge against contractor Lala within 90 days and thus facilitated his bail. Are we to conclude that if one is with Essar, he can get bail, and if one is not an employees of Essar, he or she can rot in jail".

Pandey continues his clever reasoning trail:"While police allegedly seized ₹ 15 Lakh from Lala, his "Client (Kodopi) was not carrying any money.... Yet Kodopi is in jail and Lala is out on bail".

Refusing to comment on the order on granting bail in an allegedly discriminating manner, an Essar spokesman told the daily "the granting of bail was purely the Jurisdiction before the Court".

The bail plea of Sori and Kodopi was moved to HC in Bilaspur [in June (2013)] last month amid bail to almost all the tribal people who were arrested on charge related to Naxalite activists. "The very low rate of bail to tribal people arrested for allegedly supporting the Naxalites fuels the Speculation", said a lawyer. Moreover, the fact that Sori has always been acquitted in previous cases, yet never granted bail has also keep her lawyers in two minds. This prompted all her lawyers to move the bail petition.

"This is not bail, we are still living in jail, says Soni Sori, 'exiled' in Delhi"- New delhi: 26th December 2013.

Away from their forested home in Dantewada, two alleged Maoists are living in exile in a crowded lane in Delhi, barred from entering their motherland Chhattisgarh. [Ashotosh Bhardwaj, Indian Express, 26th December 2013.]

The two are tribal teacher Sori and her nephew Kodopi, accused in the Essar-Maoist pay off case, spending their days meeting activists, students and reading Marx among other things.

Here is Sori indulging in clever if foolish play of words, the only things the Commies and their acolytes are good at: "If you say Lal Salaam or use the word Marx in Chhattisgarh you will be termed a naxal and arrested immediately. In Delhi, many people say Lal Salaam.... I am surprised Marx is taught in colleges here. Arrest all these students" Adds Kodopi, 25. 'In Chhattisgarh, Marxism is considered to constitute Maoists literature—Sufficient evidence for arrest under the Stringent Chhattisgarh Special Public Security Act (CSPSA)'.

After spending over two years in jail, the duo was released after being granted interim bail by the SC in November 2013. But they were prohibited from entering Chhattisgarh.

Sori say: "My tragedy is not the jail term. I could have lived with that. Tribals in my region (Bastar) are usually put in jail for no reason. Puri Duniya mein badnam hogayi mein (I have felt dishonoured in the wide World)".

Her two daughters and son live with her brother in Dantewada. She adds: "I cannot go back to my children, their Childhood has been ruined." On release (on bail), Sori was given little time to even meet her children, as she and Kodopi had to leave Chhattisgarh within 24 hours.

They now live in the office of their lawyer, Colin Gonsalves. Always accompanied by a guard, they are required to report to the nearest police station every week.

Kodopi speaks:" Policemen in Delhi don't know our case, they taunt us, saying that we are notorious Naxals. They say ***'tumhein Chorna Nahi Chahiye tha'***. ***Supreme Court ne tum par meharbani kar di*** (you should not have been released. The SC did you a favour)".

Sori adds:" It is no bail. We are still living in jail".

These days Kodopi is watching Seven Soderbergh's Che, a gift from a British friend. He reads English books and quotes Nelson Mandela. He asserts: "The Government of India has not done justice to tribals. We never asked for anything. We only want liberation, not reservations. My Constitution gives me the right to equalty".

This all is typical Maoist speak! It does not need any brain! It is all uttered mechanically by rote!

Now a detail about their case. The duo have been acquitted in all other cases except the Essar-Maoist payoffs case. Sori were in jail when her mother died last year (2012). Her husband and co-accused Anil Futane reportedly succumbed to injuries he sustained in jail days after he was acquitted in August 2013.

Sori makes an emotional Point:" They granted bail to Essar GM and Contractor Lala but denied it to us. If the HC had given me bail, I could have gone back to live in my village but now I have been evicted, without a home".

Essar is alleged to have paid "protection money" to Maoists, and Sori and Kodopi are alleged to have acted as conduits.

Kodopi now makes an apparently plausible if clever point: "He blames both the security forces and the Maoists. If the former wanted him to become a SPO, the latter desired he join their ranks. I refused both the offers". He continues in the same vein:" Maoists force tribal youth to join them. Several asked me to fight against the police. I refused. Now Badru is police's man! The tribal has steeled his resolve and faith in the constitution and non-violence. They have pitted me against myself. When they arrested me, I asked them to kill me, or else, I will defeat them. Even if you keep me in jail for 20 years, I will come out and defeat you". Brave words, but only words, which every Maoist is taught to mouth on such occasion!

"Innocent persons held for attack on my father": Soni Sori [Raipur : 10 November 2014]

Tribal activist and AAP leader Soni Sori "has accused the Bastar Police of implicating 'innocent' people in connection with the attack on her father by suspected Maoists in 2011". Some 35 Maoists attacked Mundararam Sori at his home in Badeledema village of Dantewada district on 14 June 2011 for "Spying for Police" and had also looted ₹ 42 Lakh.

On 6 November 2014, the Bastar Police arrested Sodi Baman and Sodi Payake from Koyanlera Fulpad village, claiming they were named by Mundararam in his FIR. But Sori told his own version to the daily:" The two arrested are innocent tribals. Badru a former Maoist who surrendered to the Police last year (2013) was the main conspirator. Badru had shot my father in the leg. But the police rewarded Badru by giving him a job in the Police Department".

"Bhushan , Arundhati share dais for arrested journalist New Delhi: 15 September 2011

This news story pertains to the time before the letter was written to PM Man Mohan Singh by those 250 activists and intellectuals. But this only pertains to Kodopi, hence its placements at the end of the section devoted to Soni Sori [HTS, Hindustan Time, and 15 September 2011.]

Supreme Court lawyer Prashant Bhushan, a Key member of team Anna, on 14 September 2011 shared the dais with writer and activist Arundhati Roy, less than a month after she had attacked the Gandhian's anti-graft movement. Bhushan addressed a press conference to demand the release of a Chhattisgarh-based journalist, Lingaram Kodopi, arrested on charges of collecting funds for the Maoist.

Roy was seated on the dais with lawyer Vrinda Grover and social worker Himanshu Kumar, when Bhushan slammed the Chhattisgarh government for targeting a tribal youth and trying to frame him on false charges.

Lingaram was arrested on 9 September (2011). "It is a classic case of witch hunt by Chhattisgarh government of a tribal youth who managed to empower himself".

Roy criticised the Centre for its approach in dealing with the tribal's living in Naxal- infested areas.

Neither Roy nor Bhushan mentioned their difference on the Anna Hazare movement. "The issue of the Press Conference was the release of the tribal youth", Bhushan later said.

Personal histories of some women leaders

Biographical sketches of four Maoist women leaders are detailed hereafter, belonging to different periods, hailing from different backgrounds and having different prospective.

K Ajitha: Early Woman Naxalite

She made the headlines in the 1960s. 56 today (2007), she was jailed for nine years from 1968 for a Naxalite attack on a police station, and is president Anweshi, a voluntary organisation. She married Yaqub, a colleague. They have a daughter Gargi, who is in College.

Her story of youthful idealism and Naxalite life of that long past is told mostly in the first person.

- "I was not adventurous by nature, but my circumstances made me take a risky path to fight for the ideals and I developed faith in rebellion. Revolution was blowing all over the world in the sixties. My parents Kunnickal Narayanan and Mandakini being firm believers of Marxism and later in doctrines of Chinese statesman Mao Tse Tung, to me revolution was only natural.
- "Used to reading Mao literature regularly and listening to Radio Peking (Now China Radio International), I became aware that everyone has a duty to perform for the progress of mankind and that each person should contribute in all possible ways to fight oppressive and capitalist forces".
- "Mao's teachings inspired me and instilled in me a sense of courage to face any difficulty in the path of revolution. When I quit studies during the pre-degree, I was fully fired up with the communist ideals Mao had been preaching—permanent revolution and the importance of the peasantry and of small scale industry and of agricultural collectivisation. I became a committed Naxalite through Mao".

- "Kerala those days was witnessing immense social inequities… Poor farmers and tribal's of Wayanad district in North Kerala faced a lot of oppression from feudal lords and the Police".
- "As revolutionary movement sprang up in Naxalbari in Darjeeling (in May 1967) and Sreekakulam, we were encouraged to take up arms against the oppressors. Through my dedication to the cause of revolution was total, many fellow Naxalites were apprehensive about teenager taking part in an armed struggle from inaccessible jungles of Wayanad. My determination soon overcame their apprehensions".
- "Being the only Woman in the group, I did face discrimination from male colleagues when they excluded me from major meetings. The revolutionary fervour enabled me to hang on".
- "The high-level thinking among Naxalites prevented the occurrence of physical temptations which could develop in a girl during teenage".
- Always guided by Mao's teachings, I never veered from the revolution path all through the long stays in the forest, the bloody attack on the Malabar Special Police Camp in Pulpaly (Wayanad) in 1968 and later one in the Jail in 1968 end" [K Srinivas Reddy, The Hindu, 22 June 2007.]

Nirmala Akka, MBBS

Born into a family of farmers in Sreekakulam, AP, Nirmala *akka* has been associated with the Naxal movement since her childhood. It was her brother's association with the movement that drew her into its fold.

She fully devoted herself to the movement after completing her medical degree from Hyderabad in 1988. Her identification with it was sealed when she married a CPI (Maoist) activist Mukiri Somaiya. The couple decided against having any children as "they do not have the time to look after anything other than the Naxalite movement". [As told to Vinu Abraham, the Week, 11 June 2006.]

Being a qualified doctor, Nirmala trained many teams to administer preliminary medical treatment to the injured comrades. Sources reveal one team has an ambulance to carry the injured to Dr Naxalite. A senior Bihar Naxal leader informs Nirmala "has visited my state and Jharkhand women Naxalites in first aid". She was in Nepal in March 2004 "To train the women Maoists. The Bihar leader continues: "Before she returned to Chhattisgarh, Nirmala spent three nights at a village in East Champaran , a border district in India". He claimed she was a great fighter, who has carried out 17 daring actions against the police and other class 'enemies'.

Nirmala now heads the National Park dalams, exclusively raised for the women Naxalites. On joining the Naxals, she was made a member of the Bhavanasi Dalam and the Tiger Reserve dalam, and stayed commander. She has also commanded Palavanka dalam in Prakasam district.

She was reportedly involved in the murder of P Srinivascharya in January 2000, and led the armed squad that killed Paturu, Ramaswamy at Nirmala Padu village, Piduguralla.

Sabita Kumari: "I have killed five, will kill 100"

Naxal leader, Sabita Kumari, 22 displays no remorse about the five murders she has committed. She promises to "murder at least a 100 if I am alive for another 10 years".

As with most of her naxal comrades, Sabita was forced to take up arms after her oppressors—money lenders from her own village Paleria in Jharkhand—murdered her two younger sisters and then seized their ancestral land with the help of police. Worst, when she sought justice from the officer-in-charge police station, he demanded sex in return. "So I decided to seek justice on my own", she recalls.

A hard-core naxal, she has a hand in some well – known cases: hacking to death 13 policemen at Chanchi Police station, Dhanbad on 13th October 2001; in 2005, she was a part of the large squad that broke into Jehanabad jail, killing 12 and freeing 340 comrades.

A member of the 12-strong armed squad, commanded by a one-eyed man, Sabita is a graduate from a college in Daltonganj and speaks a bit of English. Sabita is not her real name, it is a party name. "There are three women in our squad. We sleep together, we eat together. We do not have physical relations because we do not have time to think about that", says Sabita. Her parents wanted her to be a teacher but fate decided otherwise. Questioned about her marriage, she says: "why would I marry? My mission is to establish the rule of people in India". This is the title of the Mews story on Sabita Kumari in the Week, 11 June 2006.

Comrade Bharti: The Sarpanch

Today, Bharati is the Sarpanch of her village, Gummalakshmipuram. 'Comrade Bharati' was a teenager whom Naxalism took root in Andhra Pradesh in the late 1960s.

"We learnt to make country-made bombs and carried pistols for personal safety", recalls a Bharati, who had gone underground back then. The

Sreekakulam-Vizianagram forest "was abuzz with LWE activities then as it is even today".

Bharati, who has a case pending against her, speaks nostalgically about those (her Naxal) days: "People were attracted by anti-government songs. We understood the cause a lot better. Today, there is not much idealism left. Government schemes have diverted the people's minds, but I will not say that Naxalism is dead" cited, Lalita Iyer, the Week, 11 June 2006.

9

Dandakaranya A Case Study

The constitution of the CPI(Maoists) lays down : "The ultimate aim or maximum programme of the party is the establishment of communist society. This New Democratic Revolution will be carried out and completed through armed agrarian revolutionary war i.e. the Protracted People's War with area-wise seizure of power remaining as its central task."[1] This goal is seen to be incompatible with, nay, inimical to, the provisions of the Constitution of India, which mandates the country will be a parliamentary democracy. Several senior minister's statements and government reports stress that the Maoists goal is unacceptable and call for the need to curb their armed struggle "at any cost."[2]

The Dandakaranya Region is believed to be the first where the Maoists claim to have establised their rule. They call it a Liberated Zone. It was an intelligent choice for launching Maoist attacks as it lies on the junction of four states—Maharashtra, Chhattisgarh, Orissa, and Andhra Pradesh. Modus operandi of the Maoist operation was simple but effective: When the cadres came under pressure in one state, they will just move to the adjoining territory of another state.

Dandakaranya is thickly-forested and hilly area. It includes the following districts of the said four states:

- Gadchiroli and Chandra of Maharashtra.
- Bastar, Dantewada, and Kanker of Chhattisgarh.
- Koraput and Malkangiri in Orissa.
- Adilabad, Karimnagar, Khammam and East Godavari in Andhra Pradesh.

The Dandakaranya region is mineral-rich but its people—predominantly from tribal communitees—live in conditions of abject poverty.

The Maoist literature refers to it as the Dandakaranya Special Zone. It has been the focus of Operation Green Hunt launched by the government to eliminate the Maoists in 2011.

Participants in the Maoists Insurgency

The active participating actors in this conflict are the Maoist rebels and the state. But tribals play a central role in the conflict in Dandakarayna. It is the structural violence they experience that is driving the conflict. It is among them and on their soil that much of the confrontation is unfolding.

Tribals are Caught in A Vicious Situation

It is on their behalf that the Maoists claim to be waging a war against the state, and they are wearing the brunt of the violence. It is equally true to say that the Central and State Governments are fighting the Maoists to safeguard the interests of the tribals—their homes and hearths against the depredations of these ultras.

Maoist cadres are predominantly tribal, but obviously all tribals are not Maoist. Many of them prefer mass politics while some of them would want to keep their distance from the Maoists. Still some see them as useful allies. Again, there are tribals who are openly anti-Maoist and work with the State. The Salwa Judum comes to mind immediately. But there are differing views on the issue of Salwa Judum.

Nature of Maoist Conflict

India's Maoist conflict is often described as the one between the Maoists and the state, in which, it is strongly believed, the former aims to defeat and replace the latter. But beyond these two main actors, there are several other actors who are influencing and are also being influenced by this conflict. Some other entities are mentioned below:

1. Tribals play a central role in this conflict, moreover, the actual battles are being fought on their land and among them.
2. There are other parties like mining companies, landlords, liquor mafias etc. Their interests are self-obvious.
3. There are civil society activists and organisations, whose work is affecting and being affected by the conflict. While some are neutral, others are passionately working for the Maoists, often dubbed as their overground arm. Then there are public intellectuals who are drawing attention to the human rights violation by both sides but

more passionately against the government. It is believed their intervention have served to put pressure on the Maoists, militias and the State to refrain from targeting civilians. There is the Corporate media too, which has endorsed the government's position and strategy, prejudicing the public against the Maoists.[3]

Evolution of the Maoist Conflict

It is necessary to examine the beginning of this conflict and its subsequent spread to various parts of the country, especially in the Dandakaranya region. It is equally important to see how the scourge spread to the four states, whose peripheries constitute this region.[4]

Phases

Scholars have found that conflicts of this kind pass through various phases. Its broad phases are: the latent phase, conflict emergence, escalation, stalemate, de-escalation, settlement/ resolution, post-conflict phase building and reconciliation. But seldom these conflicts move in a linear fashion, moving neatly from one phase to the next. Phases may be skipped; an escalating conflict de-escalates without passing through a stalemate; and at times, de-escalation may not lead to peace-making/resolution of the conflict. Yet again, reversions to an earlier phase/s are not unknown. A period of de-escalation, when the parties come to the negotiations table, may end up in renewed violence. It is a known tactics of the revolutionaries, when weakened, to resort to the ploy of ceasefire and negotiations, and to use the interregnum to re-train, re-equip and reorganise their cadres. When they are ready for the War, they can create/invent any excuses to blame the government for the breakdown of the negotiations, to restart their operations.

Origin and Escalation of the Maoist Movement

This Left-Wing extremist movement has persisted for several decades, escalating/waxing and de-escalating/waning over this period. Present escalation period is the most intense so far and has lasted the longest. The origin of the Indian Maoism, in the post-Independence period, can be traced back to the 1946-51 armed struggle inspired by the Chairman Mao's "People's War" and led by the CPI. It was an armed struggle in rural Telangana for the emancipation of the peasants from the feudal rule. The agrarian uprising, initially organised around simple demands against eviction of the peasants from the lands they had tilled for years. When faced with the combined repression by landlords and the Nizam's administration, it quickly escalated into a wider struggle for overthrow of the Nizam's autocratic rule.[5] This movement coincided, initially, with Nizam's determined endeavour to gain independence from India and his *Razakars*' brazen anti-Hindu killings. When India took Police action against this princely state (of Hyderabad), Nizam's rule ended and his state passed into India's control. The movement then went underground and the fighting cadres of the CPI found a refuge in the thick forests of northern Andhra areas. It was during this periods that the revolutionaries by force of circumstances, found themselves working with the tribals. They saw the exploitation of the tribals by the landlords, and their consequent deprivation and poverty. The communist theories about exploitation of the peasantry by the 'Kulaks' they had read widely, but they were seeing it first time at close quarters only then. It was this experience that laid the foundations for their subsequent focus on the tribal deprivation.[6] In a manner of speaking, this was on the job training for their future struggle and 'wars'.

Meanwhile, Government of India under Jawahar Lal Nehru abolished the zamindari system and promised to pass laws for a series of land reforms to ameliorate the condition of farmers/peasants and to eliminate the vice-like grip of the landlords over their lives. With the onset of the hopeful and happy developments, the CPI decided to join the mainstream of parliamentary politics in 1951.[7] Consequently, the armed conflict de-escalated, even if the issues underlying it remained unresolved.

Now comes the iconic Naxalbari: 1967

It all started with a single incident. The henchmen of a local landlord assaulted a tribal sharecropper. It was something that had happened routinely in the past. But what followed was un-usual, nay unprecedented. The tribal's retaliated by attacking the landlords, and their armed bands occupied their lands. This was the eruption of armed uprising in Naxalbari in West Bengal's northern areas near Siliguri. Charu Mazumdar was the ideologue and the driving force behind this agrarian eruption, along with Kanu Sanyal and Jangal Santhal. It was 1967. It is the village of Naxalbari that has spawned the appellations Naxalites, Naxalism and Naxals. The terms 'Maoist' and 'Maoism' came into use much later (2004). The terms 'Naxalites' (even 'Naxals') and 'Maoists' are interchangeable—the former being more common and popular. The same way, the terms 'tribal', 'Adivasi' and 'scheduled tribe' are interchangble.

The uprising in Naxalbari was crushed rather quickly through use of force, but even then it spread to other parts of West Bengal, Bihar and Andhra Pradesh.

In 1969, the CPI (Marxist Leninist), CPI (ML), was set up, giving the insurgency a command structure. It made rapid gains in the initial stages but began weakening in the face of the intensive counter-insurgency operations, as also, in part, due to tactical errors by its leadership. Some analysts held it was brutal force that did it in!

But a question needs to be posed to these analysts: How do they define 'brutal force?" Are the Maoists not guilty of using brutal force against the security force, and even against the unarmed, innocent civilians, including the women and children? Will these analysts be satisfied only if the police was to fight these hardened criminals with Gandhian ways and even more appropriate, with folded hands! Such analysts obviously have not realised that the nation is at war.[8] Surely, no one, not even the bleeding hearts, should expect a kid-gloves treatment from the State, which the Maoists avowedly fight to destroy.

So by 1975, it had all but collapsed. "Most of its leaders were killed or in jail and thousands of sympathizers–many of them students and intellectuals—were in custody."[9] The remnants were scattered around the country. The setback prompted the surviving leaders to rethink and review their strategy. While some advocated mass politics and participation in parliamentary democracy, as the two major (CPI and CPM) and two minor (Forward Block and) Left political parties have already been doing, others still wanted to persist with the armed struggle.[10]

Present Phase: 1980 Onwards

After its collapse in 1975, the Maoist movement witnessed yet again another escalation period a few years later. It grew from strength to strength, starting with 1980, when Kondapalli Seetharamaiah (also spelt, Seetaramaiah) formed the People's War Group (PWG) in Andhra Pradesh. Some years later, the Maoist Communist Centre (MCC) emerged in Bihar. The two groups dominated the armed struggle in the decades that followed. In its early years, the PWG built mass organisations among the youth, peasants and women. But soon thereafter it moved exclusively to the armed struggle and expanded its operation to reach beyond Andhra into parts of northern Karnataka, Maharashtra, southern Chhattisgarh and Orissa[11] — the region collectively can be called Dandakaranya.

The PWG started Dandakaranya Adivasi Kisan Mazdoor Sangathan (DAKMS) and the Krantikari Adivasi Mahila Sangathan (KAMS) in Dantewada in the early 1980. The DAKMS raised issues like access to land and forests, fair wages for tendu[12] leaf pickers and enhanced prices for non-timber forest products. These issues, close to their hearts, did strike a chord with the tribals.[13] This enabled the PWG to create and build a support base across Dandakaranya. With this structure in place, they proceeded to create a parallel administrative set-up in the rural areas to dispense justice and settle disputes among the tribals. Sanghams were set up to displace the traditional structures of authority at the village level. *Gramrajya* committees were set up to settle village disputes and delegate developmental work. Armed guerrilla squads, called DALAMS (the lowest fighting sub-units of the operations launched by the PWG), also emerged on the scene during this period.[14] It is obvious, even self-evident from these actions that the PWG under Seetaramiah was not only preparing to launch a parallel civil administration in socio-economic sphere but also to fight more vigorously and determinedly through well-armed and well-trained cadres formed into DALAMS. Consequently, the PWG's influence (and presence) in the Dandakaranya forest was getting consolidated. But unfortunately, and almost side by side, the movement was getting weakened due to fratricidal warfare. The situation was dire by mid-1990s.

Re-escalation: The Last Phase in the Late 1990s

Starting in the late 1990s the Naxals, having learnt their lessons, were not to repeat their old errors of judgement and operational flaws. This trend at self-correction and consequent improvement in their operational achivement continued progressing along the expected lines. It was obviously not an happenstance. The acme of this fine planning and determined action was reached when the PWG and MCC merged to form the CPI(Maoist). It was a tremendous boost for all the Naxalite outfits working towards a common goal of ameliorating the lot of the deprived and the dispossessed—majority of whom were Dalit.

A brief recount of the landmarks on the way to the culmination of their efforts with the 2004 merger should bear re-emphasis. It should be noted at the outset this morale-boosting development was not an overnight happening. It had long gestation, taking years to reach fruition. To wit, the PWG had long been working on bringing various Naxalite groups under its own umbrella right from the early 1980s. But it was not till the late 1990s that its perseverance started paying off. Here are some landmarks en route:

- 1998. The CPI-ML (Party Unity) merged with the PWG, affording the latter an opportunity to spread its wings in Bihar. Its presence in Bihar, consequently enabled the PWG to link up with fraternal Maoists of Nepal.

PWG was thus the major left-wing formation in India.

- 2001. Nine South-Asian Maoist groups including the PWG, the MCC and the Communist Party of Nepal (Maoist) formed a new conglomerate: Coordinating Commttee of Maoist Parties of South Asia (CCOMPO SA)

This Conglomerate enabled them to create a "Compact Revolutionary Zone (CRZ)", or so they claim, which extends from Andhra to Nepal, passing through Chhattisgarh, Jharkhand, Orissa and Bihar. In the present day popular parlance, it is known as the Red Corridor. The CRZ has enabled the Maoists to ensure logistical cooperation and tactical Coordination among them in this large swath of land.

It is not known as to the degree of influence this Conglomerate, in particular, the PWG (its leading group), has wielded in Nepal. May be, it did have some limited influence in the Terai area, contiguous to the borderlands of North Bihar.

Present Phase of Maiost Uprising in Dandakaranya

The above was progressive spread of Maoist revolt in the country—its escalation, so to say. But what was the situation specifically in Dandakaranya, the subject matter of this chapter. An analyst (K. Srinivas Reddy) supplies the requisite information for us (in his "The Maoist challenge", SEMINAR, No. 569, January 2007).

He holds there are three stages in the revolutionary movement, as described here:

- FIRST, Organisational phase: During it, the focus is on conducting struggle on pepole's issues and violence is selective, even as they are on a defensive mode vis-à-vis the state.
- SECOND, Guerrilla Phase: The rebels here have graduated themselves to a position where they perceive themselves to be on an equal footing vis-à-vis the State and violence reaches a crescendo.
- THIRD, Mobile warfare phase: The rebels in this stage enjoy an upper hand vis-à-vis the State and are on a stategic offensive. Presently, the Maoists are in the mobile warfare phase in the Dandakaranya region of Chhattisgarh.

Spread of Maoist Insurrection

Cabinet secetary BK Chaturvedi, speaking at the annual Conference of Chief Secretaries, in New Delhi, had said on 20 April 2007 that a total of 182 districts in 16 States were Maoist-affected.

Interestingly, Moists have their own figures. Mallojula Venugopal alias Sonu alias Bhupathi, incharge of the Dandakaranya Special Zone Committee

(DK SZC) in the Central Committee of the Maoists, told *People's March*, a Maoist mouthpiece in july 2007: ".....our party has presence in 17 States."

The lates figures available peg the number much higher: 223 districts in 20 States. This was disclosed by Union Home Minister P Chidambaram on 14 september 2009 while addressing the Confrence of DGPs in New Delhi.

Situation Post-2004 Merger

As stated above the 2004 PWG-MCC merger was a great morale booster for the erstwhile Naxalites, who assumed an internationally known appellation-Maoist! The merger gave the hitherto divided Indian Maoist movement a semblance of unity, so essential for the kind of "war" they were engaged in. They put in place a unified command structure. Even though they are spread in so many states, this unity of command affords them an all India character and perspective. Consequently, they have achieved for greater degree of cooperation and coordination in planning and carrying out violent/ armed operations in different part of the country than ever before. In the past, much of their energy was consumed in fratrical fighting and in turf wars post merger, they are now able to focus and concentrate all their firepower against the State and its security agencies. The coming together of the PWG and MCC, which until their merger accounted for 88 per cent of the country-wide Maoists violence and 89 per cent of the resultant deaths, created a formidable threat and challenge [to the Government]."[15]

The merger and consequent heft it provided to the cadres and their morale improved the Maoist logistics and their operational capabilities. It translated into faster and more efficient movement of fighting cadres, weapons and funds along the stretch of large territory, called Red Corridor, which had by then extended to and embraced the Karnataka region and eastern areas of Maharashtra around Gadchiroli.

It was no surprise that it was the year 2004—the year of the merger—in which Prime Minister Manmohan Singh admitted to the Left-Wing Extremism as being the greatest threat to the national security.

The merger has contributed to the sharp increase in the Maoist capacity in the latter half of the 1900s decade. The number of the Maoist cadres has increased manifold as has the sophistication of their meaponry. As a natural consequences, the Maoist attacks have increased in frequency and magnitude. It is reflected in the following table.

Number of Maoist-related Incidents 2002-2009

Year	2002	2003	2004	2005	2006	2007	2008	2009
Number of Incidents	1465	1597	1533	1608	1509	1565	1591	2258

Source: Government of India, Ministry of Home Affairs, **Annual Report,** 2005-06: **Annual Report** 2008-09: **Annual Report** 2009-10.

Reasons Behind Dandakarayna Trouble

The unmet human needs plays major role in triggering a conflict. When social, political, and economic structures, institutions and policies come in the way of people realising their needs, they are being subjected to structural violence. So says the peace psychologist Danial Christie.[16] This structural violence is the main reason behind the uprising in Dandakarayna.

Rapid Industrialisation: Deprivation of the Tribals

Once tribals lose their land, they lose almost everything— their homes, livelihood and the very means of survival. The consequent deprivation and grievances fuelled the conflict. The Nehruvian development model, envisaging rapid industrialisation of the country, called for building of heavy industries and big dams, which to Nehru were "the temples of modern India."[17] These industrial projects and public sector mining activity resulted in large scale displacement of tribals. To make matters worse for them, new legislation restricted their access to forests and common property resources. India's neo-liberal economic policies post-1991, led by Narasimha-Manmohan duo has acclerated India's growth rate, increased the number of millionaires and expanded its middle class. This all has been at the cost of rural poor, and especially the tribals living in mineral-rich areas.

Prior to liberalisation, extraction of minerals was largely undertaken by the government. This changed with the National Mineral Policy of March 1993, which opened the doors to FDI in mineral sector. The process for FDI was further eased in 1997 and since 2006, 100 per cent FDI is being permitted in mining. It opened the floodgates to mining companies, especially in mineral-rich Chhattisgarh, Orissa and Jharkhand. All this results in inalienation of the tribal land.

Alienation of Land

With investment pouring in, permits were/are being issued for mineral extraction on tribal land in violation of legislation and court judgements that forbid sale of tribal land to non-tribals.[18] Since the opening up of mining sector to FDI, thousands of acres of forest land have been diverted to non-forest use. Such diversion shot up from 789 hectares at the end of 1993-94 to 28,769 hectares a decade later, an annual increase of 43 per cent. As much as one- third of this diversion was for mining activity.

Much of the mineral-rich land in Chhattisgarh, Orissa and Jharkhand is tribal land, land guaranteed to them under the Fifth Schedule of Indian Constitution. It is of interest to note the details of the areas in various states (nine in total) which is covered under the Fifth Schedul. The table below makes it clear.

Fifth Schedule Areas

State	*Areas*
Andhra Pradesh	Vishakhapatnam, East Godavari, West Godavari, Adilabad, Srikakulam, Vizianagaram Mahboobnagar, Prakasam (only some Mandals are scheduled Mandals)
Jharkhand	Dumka, Godda, Devgarh, Sahabganj, Ranchi, Singhbhum (East and West), Gumla, Simdega, Lohardaga. Palamu, Garwa(some districts are only partly tribal blocks)
Chhattisgarh	Sarbhuja, Bastar, Raigad, Raipur, Rajnand gaon, Durg, Bilaspur, Sehdol, Chindmara, Kanker
Himachal Pradesh	Lahaul and Spiti districts, Kinnaur, Pangi tehsil and Bharmaur sub-tehsil in Chamba district.
Madhya Pradesh	Jhabua, Mandla, Dhar, Khargone, East Nimer (Khandwa DWA) Silana tehsil in Ratlam district, Betul, Seoni, Balaghat, Morena
Gujarat	Surat, Bharauch, Dangs, Valsad, Panchmahal, Sadodara, Sabarkanta (Parts of these districts only)
Maharashtra	Thane, Nasik, Dhule, Ahmednagar, Pune, Nanded, Amravati, Yavatmal, Gadchiroli, chandrapur (parts of these districts).
Orissa	Mayurbhanj, Sundargarh, Koraput (fully scheduled are in these three districts), Raigada, Keonjhar, Sambalpur, Boudhkondmals, Ganjam, Kalahandi, Bolangir, Balasor, (parts of these districts only).
Rajasthan	Banswara, Dungarpur (fully tribal districts) Udaipur, Chittaurgarh, Sirohi (partly tribal areas)

One fact is evident from the preceding table on Fifth Schedule Areas. Most, of the land in the districts that fall under the Dandakaranya Region are Fifth Schedule areas. This Schdule guarantees tribal rights over the land they live in, with all its implications which have been delineated, in Details in Chapter 3. This Schdule insures, provided its provisions are properly implemented, that the wealth of the scheduled areas is utilised for the common good of the local community and of the country as a whole beyond that locality.

One aspect of the developmental activity in the tribal areas, discussed in detail in the preceding chapter, bears re-emphasis and Repetition albeit in brief. The government's approach to develop tribal areas in Dandakaranya is to encourage investment in the extraction and refining of its immense mineral wealth. It will not only generate jobs for the local tribals, but also result in country's economic growth.

Tribal Land Grabb Inspite of the Laws

Several thousands of acres of tribal lands were/are being handed over to mining companies. It is in violation of the Fifth Schedule and of a historic Supreme Court judgement of 1997, popularly referred to as the Samata Judgement.[19] It declared null and void the transfer of land in Scheduled Areas for private mining and upheld the Forest Protection Act of 1980. This transfer of land to the mining companies is also in violation of the Panchayat (Extension to Scheduled Areas) Act (PESA), 1996, which as a landmark legislation that mandates consultation with *Gram Sabha* before development projects in these areas can be undertaken. (It is the kind of provision which the Anna-Kejriwal team has been demanding of late. They want panchayats to be the starting point of all developmental planning).

Critics assert that often a potentially effective piece of legislation is not allowed to come into public debate. Various interest lobbies block the way. A report was Commissioned by the government and researched by Institute of Rural Management, Anand (IRMA). A full Chapter from this report was excuded from its final publication. Here is the title of this chapter:

"PESA, left wing Extremism and Governance: Concerns and Challenges in India's tribal Districts". This chapter provides details of how PESA was being violated in Fifth Schedule areas, which consequently creates room for the growth of Left-wing Extremism.

There are several instances of tribal land being taken over by the State and handed over to mining companies. In Lohandiguda in Bastar, some 2002 hectares of Fifth Schedule Area belonging to 10 villages was acquired by the government on behalf of Tata Group's Rs 1,000 Crore steel plant. Tribal land in Dhurli and Bhansi villages in Dantewada district too were acquired for the Essar Group's steel plant.

These acquisitions were in the past-2008 and 2009. Presntly (2012) a huge agitation is on against the POSCO project in Orissa.

All such violent rumblings have forced rethinking in the government circles. Presently, a bill on the acquisition of land is in the cabinet. It may be passed in the winter session (2012) of the Parliament.

Conflicting Interests of Parties Involved in the Area

The Maoist uprising is essentially a conflict between them, the rebals, and the State. But tribals are the ones who stand between the two, and are being wooed by both. But there are others who have vested interests in this conflict: like the industries and businesses involved in mining operations, dam building, transporting timber etc; landlords and small merchants; liquor mafias et al. If mining companies would wish for peace in the area, liquor mafias would profit by disturbed conditions. Worried that the growing clout of the Maoists would hamper their business ambitions, they are believed to be funding anti-Maoist militias on the quiet. The actions of Salwa Jndum outfit have already been discussed in some details as has been the stand of civil society activists.

Carpet Baggers

An economist has summed up the neo-liberal economic reforms by dubbing it as "carpet bagger capitalism" which is devastating tribal areas. 'Outsiders' are coming into tribal areas and reaping the profits of mining activity even as the areas indigenous inhabitants are bearing enormous environmental, social and human costs".[20]

Displacement

The Sardar Sarovar Project has caused large scale displacment in western India. Routledge describes multiple erasures—economic, cultral and ecological—that tribals in Gujarat, Madhya Pradesh, and Maharashtra have suffered.[21] In Dandakaranya too, people are suffering similar erasures. One apt example of NALCO should be illustrative.

NALCO set up its bauxite extraction and refinery unit in 1982 in Damanjodi in Koraput. As a result, 26 villages were affected directly and some 690 villages indirectly. Most of these were tribal villages. Compensation provided by NALCO is contested by the analysts and the locals who were displaced. Several families were provided rehablitation packages; some got financial compensation, others got land of the 600 families displaced, 597 were provided with housing in rehabilatation colonies at Analabadi and Kontaguda. Then, one able person from each displaced family was provided employment at NALCO.

Most of the above are contested. 60 per cent of land acquired by NALCO at Damanjodi was tribal common property resouces and no compensation was paid for it. For the little private land they owned, tribal famlies were paid a paltry some of Rs 6,700 per hectare, "a totally imadequate sum to start a new life." Damoder Jani, a NALCO displacee and former sarpanch of Littiguda, says the land given as compensation "was uncultivable"[22] Yet again, it is claimed the employment promised by NALCO benefitted mostly non-tribals as the Adivasis lacked skills the company required. Only one member per family was given the job, but if he died, the family was on the road.

NALCO's dynamiting of the Panchapatmalli hills has destroyed the forest. Bauxite extraction dries streams and turns the land into a near desert, making agriculture impossible, "Although the NALCO factory has an ash pond and a red-mud pond, toxic effluents are being discharged into the Kolala River regularly, polluting and poisoning the water available to villages down stream". Yet again, Jani says their crops and cattle are dying and the air, which is thick with flyash, is afflicting tribals with respiratory diseases."

The Author feels some comments and observations are called for to restore some semblance of credibility to the text:

General Observation

- It is sad, and may be harsh to say that this analyst finds nothing positive about all the activity she has observed all around her. She feels almost convinced that purpose of all the mining and allied industry in these hills is exploitation of the tribals, and developmental gains if any, are incidental. If someone says the analyst has an agenda of her own, or has been given one by some one, he may not be wide off the mark.
- Certain factual information may be exaggerated, but not to the level that it becomes suspect. Certain balance, if not the entire truth, should be hallmark of any writing.
- In a number of places, this scholars text has been left intact, just to show how baised she is on certain aspects of her research or some issues.
- It must be height of perversity for NALCO officials to insist on discharging toxic effluents into a living river, not into two ponds that are available for the purpose. Why this analyst is determined to show the NALCO officials as ghouls, is beyond one's ken. To impart some balance to her writing, all she needed to do was to interview an official of the NALCO. But she would not, because that will destroy her aim! Again there are any number of NGOs and government functionaries in the area, will they let such a

preposterous thing happen? Or allow it to continue if brought to their notice.

- Then she interviews just one displacee from the area and accepts uncritically all he he says as Gospel truth.
- The whole thing is in poor taste.
- One is compelled to return to an observation made in this book else where: why did an Indian think tank, under a reputed, well regarded retired Indian General accept foreign funds on an issue of great relevance to the Indian polity? Did the donor of the fund, Mac Arther Foundation have an agenda, or even certain conditionalities attached to the grant?
- In such a situation, even if some observations are not biased, or are even fair, still such observations are taken with certain dubiety!
- What a travesty of real life situation! The analyst could not find even one person to talk to besides the convenient Damodar Jani! It may not be uncharitable to say that Jani was not a serendiptous occurrence! It was a matter of Choice, a convenient one, at that!

It must be accepted that besides economic and ecological erasures, mining activity and dispacement can and do cause erasure of tribal culture. The Dongria Kondh tribals nurture a fear about Niyam Dongar Hill being dynamited to facilitate bauxite extraction. The Dongria Kondhs consider the Niyam Dongar Hill to be the abode their presiding deity, Niyam Raja (literally, the King of Law or the Universal Lawgiver). The dynamiting of their mountain will destroy their culture, their way of life, perhaps their very survival as a distinct people, feel these tribals.

The Bleeding Hearts/Leftists Have Point

This Author has criticised certain tendentious analysts who only feel for the Maoists, and not for their victims, nor for the governments or their security agencies. They take things too far in their prejudices and short-sighted approach to issues of national importance. In this connection, Arundhati Ray and Gautam Navlakha come to mind instantly. The others might sometimes follow these two, but occasionally do express themselves to the issues and their concerns are genuine and on the side of the truth. Some of their averments are given here in their own words. One can't disagree with what they have say:

- Dongria Kondhs have expressed their concern's if their sacred hill, Niyam Dongar, is dynamited out of existence. The UK mining giant, Vedanta Resources has the contract to extract the Bauxite in this area.

- It must be admitted that it is the poor who pay the price for a country's development. And they suffer repeatedly. And the rich classes, sitting in their opulent drawing rooms or in passionate television debates, rationalize their plight — losing homes and hearth, eviction from their small land holdings, displacement to distant lands—without even seriously thinking that this deprivation can be fatal in some cases. Here is the tragic experience of tribals living in the Chitrakonda in Malkangiri. It also provides insights on the link between displacement, development and Maoism. Displaced by Machkund Hydel Project in Koraput back in the late 1940s, the tribals moved to Chitrakonda, but only to be displaced yet again when the Balimela Hydel Project came in 1964. Since, then their villages have remained waterlocked by the Chitrakonda reservoir and are accessible only by boats. No rehabilitation or socio-economic development has taken place here for decades! There are no roads, water supply or electricity. No official visits these villages. Only the Maoists bother to come to there villages and listen to the people's grievances. It is not surprising then that this hilly, forested region, which the rest of India has forgotten, has been a Maoist hotbed for decades.[23]

In contrast what is the response of the high and mighty when they merely have to suffer minor inconveniences—mind you no loss of their homes and hearth, or of any fertile land! And to refreshen their stance when the poor and deprived are required to give their homestead or agricultural land: They must do so in the national interest! They should do so for the common good of the Community. See the contrast in the following two cases, mentioned here.

- **Lata Mangeshkar:** She protested when an overbridge was planned that skirted her bungalow, in Mumbai. She protested loudly against this project as it obstructed the view from her house, and more menacing, the passing traffic would create nuisance. She threatened to quit Mumbai, or some such threat. She relented only when her stance drew public outrage.
- **A Project to Mitigate the Traffic Jam in Vasant Vihar Objected to.** It is an interesting care of how the high and mightly are self-centred – and even selfish. Four VIP homes vehemently opposed a planned overbridge since it would reduce the width of a service road that runs by their locality. It was an essential project to reduce the traffic chaos on part of the Palam road that led to the airport. The protest was led by Karan Thapar, a well-known

television journalist. One of the reasons proffered was that the reduced width of the road would hinder the easy movement of fire tenders in case there was fire break-out in their locality. The possibility of this danger was negatived by the concerned authority.

The above-mentioned two cases only show that how the rich, the mighty and the influential offer the self-serving propositions against the common good! This aside is meant to expose the double face of such people.

Parallel Governments: The Maoist Way

Besides waging armed struggle against the State, Maoists are known to be setting up their governments in the areas under their control—liberated areas' as they like to call them. After all, if their ultimate mission is to take over India, they must have the practical experience of governance at the grass roots level. They set up such local Maoist government models in Dandakaranya.

NGO activists hold that in parts of rural Dandakaranya the civil administration—read rule of law—has been missing for years (said in 2006). Consequently, the Maoist dispensation there is not the "parallel government" but in fact the only one.[24]

A large number of schools and health centres are non-functional in many villages due to the teachers and staff not posted or absent due to the fear of Maoists. In some eases, the Maoists force them to work, as the fear of the gun they wield, work in such situations. The gun again succeeded in forcing the tendu trade contractors to pay higher wages to the tribals who pick tendu leaves and cut bamboo culms for them. A civil liberties activist says it is the enhanced earnings "that now go into their pockets that has made the gun-toting Maoists more popular with the local tribals in the entire forest region abutting the Godavari River in Telangana, Vidharbha and Chhattisgarh. Consequently, oppressive domination.....This has also put an end to the oppressive domination of the headmen and Patwaris."[25] This very same admirer of the Maoists further gushes over the do-gooders he deems the maoists to be: "The Maoists have done much rural development work too. They have helped tribals with construction of tanks, rain water harvesting and land conservation works.Villagers testify these works have improved their food security situation."

Maoists 'commitment' to the well-being of the tribals is oxymoron—even ridiculous. More authentic reality is offered by the following averments. " The government accuses Maoists of Obstructing development in tribal areas and standing in the way of several initiatives that would inprove the livelihood security of tribals. Besides they are said to be destroying the already limited infrastructure in Dandakaranya. Indeed, Maoists have destroyed railway infrastructure, telecom towers and power stations.[26] Here is country's Home Minister dubbing the Maoists as anti-development. "They have targetted the very instruments of development—school building, roads, telephone towers etc. They know that development will wean the masses away, especially poor tribals, from their grip." Chidambaram was speaking at the Chief Ministers' Conference on Internal Security in August 2009."[27]

Here is two more apologists like the one at Note 25, giving a certificate of good conduct to the Maoists even if qualified in his own words. In their study of impact of MGNREGA, two researchers points to a more complex picture. "They argue that MGNREGA is doing well in the districts that are among the worst hit by the Maoist conflict, such as Baster. Of all the permissible works under the MGNREGA, only road construction is being blocked by the Maoists as better roads facilitate movements of the security personnel. They are not obstructing other works such as afforestation, minor irrigation, land development, etc.[29]

Gautam Navlakha, a human rights activist who spent a fortnight early 2010 in the Dandakarayna forests, says: "The Maoists encourage education. The 'people's government' has prepared books that are being used to teach mathematics, social science, Politics and Hindi, and books on the history of Dandakaranya, culture, biology and general science are under preparation. Books are written in the local Gondi language".[30] Another one says the Maoists consciously promote Gondi language and literature.[31] Journalist Shubhranshu Choudhary tells Dasgupta[32] : Books prepared by the Maoists empharsise the history of the tribal people with pictures of leaders like Birsa Munda. There is also the predictable familiarisation with icons like Mao, Marx and Indian leaders like Charu Mazumdar and Kanai Chatterjee. Besides ideological indoctrination, the books provide practical information on measures to improve basic health and hygiene. The books advise on the need of washing hands before eating, boiling water before drinking it and sleeping under a mosquito net." Their civilian supporters claim Maoists have filled the deficient system in the fields of education and health, which can be attributed to laggard government officials and staff.

Here is one more supprter, a celebrity in her own right, eulogizing the Comrades. To paraphrase her: "The Maoists appear to be tackling the tribal traditions and customs that undermine women but treading carefully. The KAMS has campaigned against forced marriage, bigamy, and the custom of making menstruating women live in a separate hut in the forests. Its achivements have been mixed. Women are not allowed to sow seeds. Maoists tried to change this custom. Even if the menfolk agreed that the change is desirable, they do not let it happen in practice... So the Maoist allow women to sow seeds on common land belonging to the Janatana Sarkar. (This is from a longish 16-page article in Outlook, 29 March 2010). Like the mainline politicians, it seems they too are rather reluctant to force social change lest it cost them public support. So this celebrity rationalizes: "...Hence they prefer to move slowly on these matters."

Navlakha notes the "prominent role of women in the movement," and the sharing of all work by both sexes. Women constitute 40 per cent of those in administrative jobs, and the Maoists aim to make this 50 per cent.[34]

While there are a significant number of women in political and military wings of the Maoist movement, but their presence and role in the top decision-making bodies is still marginal. This is obvious from the fact that so far only one women – Anuradha Ghandy—has been part of the politburo. Kannabiron draws attention to the "stereotypical and hierarchal masculinities and femininities that inform the [Maoist] movement even at highest levels.[35]

Maoist justice system in their parallel government is a matter of deep concern. It is swift but crude and brute, raising the question if it can be treated as justice at all. Class enemies are summarily executed as are tribals who are loud enough of their actions or the ones suspected to be informers. Anyone can be dubbed as such to be executed, with no question asked. Here are the words of a former Maoist, Subba Atish:

> The Jan adalat is organised by the commander or deputy commander of the DALAM (armed squard). They get some 15 villages together and pass a sentence. Members of the area committee, range committee head, and divisional committee will pass the sentence. They are usually supposed to be given a chance to defend themselves...But this is how it worns: first they are brought and beaten. Beating over, they are so scared that they admit to the crime. Villagers and relatives who come to their defence are threatened into silence. It is a farce – these trials.
>
> If a relative says something in defence, the commander will say, "so you are with him? You too want the same thing to happen to you.?"

Whgat ever way they have made up their mind, they will act—opinion of the villagers do not matter.[36]

Atish describes the manner the death sentence is carried out. He witnessed the execution of four pepole in two *Jan Adalats*. Of the four, two were found guilty of conspiring against Maoist commanders and the other two of providing the police with information about a Maoist ambush. The 'guilty' had no opportunity to appeal the punishments, which were meted out soon after the verdict was pronounced publicly. Here is the manner of execution: Maoists tie a rope round the neck of the guilty. Two persons stand on either side and pull the rope-ends till the person dies. All four were killed in the same manner.[37]

Here is some truth about the real face of the Maoists, as given out by a foreign/outside agency, HRW.[38] It is unfortunate that the Indian supporters find nothing wrong with the murderous excesses of the Maoists and their exactions. It is all well-known to the security agencies and the people at large. But the partisans want to pull the wool on their eyes. Here is briefly what the HRW says on the subject:

> "The Maoists Committment to prevent tribal exploitation is open to question. It is true that it was their efforts that successfully raised the wages of tendu leaf pickers in Andhra and Chhattisgarh. It is true too that they have backed tribals in their opposition to mining activity on their land. Yet, the Maoists have also acted to protect the exploiting classes. In 2005, for instance, they enforced a strike in tendu collection to thwart the government's attempts to do away with Contractors and start cooperatives. Surely, the cooperatives would have contributed to reducing exploitation of tribals. Why then did they oppose the setting up of Cooperatives? It is well known that Maoist 'taxes' on the tendu trade amounts to millions of rupees annually and is an important source of funding their activities.
>
> It is believed that the Maoists opposed cooperatives in the tendu trade as this would cut out the contractors –their 'taxpayers'—and into their sizeable revenue. Doing away with 'exploitative contractors', therefore, is not in the Maoist agenda. There is similar relationship with the mining companies. The latter are reported to be paying the Maoists massive sums 'protection money'. The Maoists might denounce the mining activity as the 'loot of Adivasi resources', but it is unlikely that they would want the mining companies to shut down operations and leave Dandakaranya. After all, mining companies are paying them millions of rupees, which fund their military operations.

This should suffice to expose the do-gooders the Maoists are painted by their overground supporters and the fellow travellers, as described in the preceding pages.

Detrimental Impact on India's Economic Growth (of Extortion)

What is the impact of extortion by the Maoists and violence in Dandakaranya on investment and economic climate, not only within its areas but beyond it? A 2009 report by the Federation of Indian Chambers of Commerce and Industry (FICCI) warns that Maoist insurgency could "soon hurt some industrial investment plans." It laments: "At a time when India needs to ramp up its industrial machine to lock in growth and just when foreign companies are joining the party, the Naxalites are clashing with the mining and steel companies essential for india's long-term suceess."[39]

The then Finance Minister P Chidambaram told his audience at Harvard University: "Extraction of iron ore, coal, bauxite and other minerals are regarded as important for India to maintain its 8 per cent economic growth rate."[40]

FICCI's apprehessions are jusified. Tribals protests, spontaneous or orchestrated, and Maoist violence are certainly coming in the way of these plans and projects. The issues have been widely discussed in the press over the last couple of years. Some prominent cases are examined here:

- **Singur Imberoglio:** The Tata Group came under pressure to alter its production plans for its small Car project: political tug of war between CPM and Mamta Banerjee's TMC forced it out of Singur, West Bengal—to be immediately lapped up by Chief Mininster Narendra Modi of Gujarat. One wonders if Banerjee regrets her volatile enthusiasm to vanuish the CPM, her arch rivals, and losing a prestigeous Tata venture to Modi. She lost considerable employment opportunities in the State she rules.
- Vedanta's projects in Niyamgiri have run aground because of local opposition. Niyamgiri is their sacred hill, the abode of their deity. If it is razed down and disappears, the local tribals fear their very existence will be in peril.
- Other mining Projects like Arcelor Mittal's $ 9 billion steel enterprises in Jharkhand and Orissa are caught in the fierce opposition/agitation by the local tribals, incited by the Maoists.
- **POSCO Steel Preoject:** Much bigger, in fact the biggest project, the South Koroan steel giant Pohang Iron and Steel Company (POSCO)'s $32 billion steel project at Jagatsinghpur in Orissa, is stalled in the face of violent opposition from the local tribals and the Maoists.
- Jindal Steel Work's $7 billion plant at Salboni in West Bengal is also stuck up in similar whirlpool.
- Maoist attack have affected production too. Bauxite production at NALCO, for instance, has fallen by 20 per cent since the time Maoists attacked their mines in Aril 2009. Such attacks on mining companies have hit their export. Coal Minister Shriprakash Jaiswal

provided us another estimate of loss to the national exchequer: The coal production has the potential to increase by 25 per cent if Maoist violence ceased.

- It is widely known that the Maoists have damaged telecom and power infrastructure. They have repeatedly target railway infrastructure, including freight trains.
- **Bands** imposed under threat of violence have caused the paralysis of economic activity – some claim even policy paralysis is – and resulted in loss of business running into thousands of crores of rupees.[41]

Governement Sees Light of the Day, Says the Hindu (to Counter Maoists)

The Hindu is a highly respected daily, even if its left learning boss—N Ram— may not be entirely unbaised in certain ideological fields. It says (August 2010) the Government has finally decided to embark on a development course for the benefit of the poor tribals, the deprived and the marginalised. What persuaded it to this conclusion is detailed here after.[42]

The multiple costs inflicted by the Maoist violence, especially its impact on India's economic growth, has forced the government to take the Maoist problem more seriously. "Under criticism for its excessively militaristic approach and realising the importance of addressing tribal grievances for successful tackling of the Maoist problem, the government has begun giving attention to socio-economic development of the areas worst hit by the (Maoist) violence." It is considering an Integrated Action plan (IAP) for 60 districts worst affected by the conflict. The plan covers the areas not only in the armed conflict zone but also those where the Maoist insurrection is in incipient stages. Before the government starts implementation of the IAP, it will take steps to improve governance in these districts to ensure that massive funds being pumped here do reach the intended beneficiaries. This will include measures to ensure full implementation of PESA and FRA, as well as scheme like the PDS and MGNREGA.

Then the Daily says that "the government has finally woken up to the fact that enacting legislation, drawing up elaborate poverty-fighting schemes and allocating funds is not enough. These have to be implemented in letter and spirit to ensure that the benefits reach the poorest and the most marginalised sections in this country. The first steps in this direction seem to have been taken."

An analyst says (August 2010) the costs of the Maoist conflict have also forced the government to review its mining policy. "A new legislation under consideration seeks to make tribals stake-holders in mining activities. The draft Mines and Minerals (Development and Regulations) Bill 2010 provides for 26 per cent partnership in the company to people living in an area over which a mining lease is granted. While this is a step in the right direction, whether the powerful mining lobby will allow it to be enacted remains to be seen."[43]

The Way Forward: A Blinkered View

Here is an obviously pro-Maoist view of things as seen by one of their partisans. At every step, the academic puts on equal footing the Maoists and the government. His analysis on the way forward is reproduced below in extensive excerpts:

> " The Maoist conflict in Dandakaranya has drawn attention to immense injustices suffered by the rural poor. It has forced the government to address the tribal governance underlying it. Laws have beeen passed for greater tribal autonomy. Socio-economic programmes too have been put in place to reduce the crushing impact of poverty. " The Maoists too have sought to bring positive socio-economic change in the areas they control."[44]
>
> "However, the predominantly violent "waging of conflict by the two main adversaries is wiping out what ever positive impact the State or Maoists have done to address poverty."[45] This academic put the Government measures to improve the socio-economic condition of tribals at the same pedestal as the so-called socio-economic steps taken by the Maoists in the area they contro," as mentioned in the preceding para. This academic goes on in the same vein as can be seen from the following text;
>
> - It has unleashed human suffering on a far greater scale than existed before.
> - It is accentuating poverty and triggering new poverty and grievances.
>
> "The Moaits use of arms to secure justice for the tribals is resulting in new injustices. It is attracting more violence by the State. As for the State, its use of force to quel the conflict is worsening it. It has taken the violence to a new, higher level.[46]
>
> "Its adoption of economic policies and development paradigms that bring benefit to a few at the cost of others is worsening the distress underlying the conflict.
>
> "The use of force by the State and the Maoists is deepening the intractability of the conflict.

"If six decades ago, the conflict was one primarily over poverty generated by feudals, today there are 'issues such as Corporate geed, rampant vigilantism, proliferation of weapons and militarisation of society,[47] 'that have added to the conflict's complexity.

"It is only through halting violence and engaging in dialogue that the spiral of violence can begin to be broken.

Notes

1. Central Committee (P), CPI(Maoist), "Party Constitution", available online.
2. Government of India, Ministry of Home Affairs, Annual Report, 2009-10, p. 17.
3. Sevant Niman, "Media Matters: Assembly-line news", THE HINDU, 11.10.2009.
4. Some of the landmarks in the spread of the Naxalite/Maoist Movement has also been mentioned in Chapter 2.
5. Mohan Ram, "The Telangana Peasant Armed Struggle, 1946-51." *Economic and Political Weekly,* 8, no. 2 3, 9, 6.1973: 1025-32.
6. For a detailed and a ringside view of the warn and struggle of the revolutionaries in this period, SEE the Communist leader P. Sundarayya's *Telengana Pepole's Struggle and its Lessons* (New Delhi Foundation Books, 2006).
7. For a detailed account of circumstances that led to the withdrawal of the armed struggle, SEE Note.
8. Sumanta Banerjee, *India's Simmering Revolution: The Naxalite Uprising* (London; Zed Books,1984) and Biplab Dasgupta, *The Naxalite Movement* (Bombay; Allied Publishers, 1974). For an account of the impact of Naxalites' armed campaign in rural areas, SEE Biplab Dasgupta, "Naxalite Armed Struggle and the Annihilation Campaigning Rural Areas," Economic and Political Weekly, 8, No. 4/6 (Feb 1973): 173-75, 183,/85-88.
9. Sudha Ramachandran, "The Maoist Conflict in Dandakaranya", in VR Raghavan, Ed. *The Naxal Threat*, 2011. The tone of this analyst is overly sympathetic towards the Maoists—almost (seemingly) feeling sad that they collapsed.
10. Sumanta Banerjee, "Beyond Naxalbari", *Economic and Political Weekly* (22-28.07.2006): 3159-63.
11. Venkitesh Ramakrishna, "The Road from Naxalbari," Frontline, 22, No. 21, 8-21 October, 2005.
12. Its leaf is used in rolling *bidis*, or hand-made cigarettes', smoked widely in India and beyond.
13. Sudha Ramachandran, *op.cit,* Note 9.
14. Nandini Sundar, "Baster, Maoism and Salwa Judum," Economic and Political Weekly, 41. No. 29; 22 July 2006: 3189.
15. Government of India, Ministry of Home Affairs, Annual *Report* 2008-09,16.
16. Note 9, Sudha Ramachandran, VR Raghavan, Ed; p. 31.
17. Ramachandra Guha, *India after Gandhi*: The History of *The World's Largest Democracy* (New Delhi: Pan Macmillan, Picador, 2008), 212-13.

18. Front line: Prafulla Das, 19 Nov - 02 Dec 2005; Aman Sethi, 5-18 May 2007; Venkitesh Ramakrishnan, 3-16 July 2010; Ajoy Ashirwad 3-16 July 2010.
19. Asha Krishnakumar, "The Samata Judgement" Frontline 921, No 19 (11-24 september 2004).
20. CP Chandrasheker, "Liberalising loot" Frontline, 3-16 July 2010.
21. P Routledge, "Voices of the Dammed: Discursive Resistance amidst Erasure in the Narmada Valley, India," Political Geography, 22(2003): 247-70.
22. Damodar Jani said it an interview to Sudha Ramachandran, see Note 3.
23. Observations by Sudha Ramachandran, of Note 3, during her December 2009 visit.
24. A told by an NGO worker to a researcher in Khammam in Andhra Pradesh in June 2006. VR Raghavan, Ed, 2011, p. 62.
25. K. Balagopal, "Chhattisgarh: physiogonomy of violence", Economic and Political Weekly, 3-9 June 2006.
26. Kanchan Gupta, "Two eyes for an eye, the jaw for a tooth", The Pioneer, 21.02.10.
27. The Hindu, 17.08.09.
28. It is interesting, and instructive to note that this academic seldom use to term Maoist "Violence" and assiduously and consciously replaces it with "conflict" This only shows his/her tendentious thinking on Maoist insurrection in a huge swath of land. Using an innocent, innocuous term for their depradations and murderous sprees is painful to this at least.
29. Kaustav Banerjee and Partha Saha, People are getting better wages in these districts because of Maoist pressure. "The Nrega, the Maoists and the Developmental Woes of the Indian State," Economic and Political Weekly, 10 July 2010.
30. Gautam Navlakha, "Days and Nights in the Heartland of Rebellion", Economics and Political Weekly, 17.4.10.
31. People's March, Jan 2006, 7, cited in Nandini Sundar, Bastar, Maoists and Salwa Judum", 3190.
32. Debarshi Dasgupta, "My Book is Red, Outlook, 17 May 2010.
33. Arundhati Roy, "Walking with the Comrades," outlook, 29 March 2010. (She spent a weak with the Maoists in their hide –outs in the Dandakaranya forests.
34. See Note 30 above.
35. Vasanth Kannabiran, "Scattered truth, bitter seeds", Seminar, 607, March 2010.
36. *Human Rights Watch being Neutral is Our Biggest Crime:* Government Vigilante, and Naxalite Abuses in India's Chhattisgarh State, (New york: HRW, 2008), 98-99.
37. Ibid.
38. See note 36.
39. Ashish kothari, "Behind the concern", *Frontline*, 13-26 Feb 2010.
40. Chidambaram, see his speech at the Havard University's South Asia Initiative, The Harish C. Mahindra 2007 Lecture on "Poor Rich Challenges of Development." He wants that "India should mine these resources quickly and efficiently.

41. Ajit kumar Singh, "Maoists: Targeting the Economy", South Asia Intelligence Review (SAIR), 8, No. 51, 28 June 2010; cited Sudha Ramachandran, "The Maoist Conflict in Danda-karanya," in *The Naxal Threat, VR Raghavan* Ed, (Vij Books New Delhi): p. 68.
42. The Hindu, 8 August 2010.
43. Sudha Ramachandran, "India digs deep to outflank Maoists." Asia Times Outline, 4.08.10.
44. It is painful to see an intelligent academic to compare the socio-economic programmes of the Government and the Maoists—one well planned reality and other imaginary. It is an ideological chicanery at its worst!
45. *Ibid.*
46. Readers must note that this academic feels "it is the state that has taken the Violence to a new, higher level."
47. It is exclusively the State which have added to the complexity of the conflict, asserts this academic.

10

Security Forces: Combating Maoists

This section deals with the details of Central Armed Forces (CAPF) and other types of forces that are presently fighting the Maoist armed cadres. Generally, among the CAPF, it is essentially the CRPF which is leading the charge. It generally operates with the help of the police of the concerned State.

In addition, certain states have raised their specialist anti-Maoist units, like the Greyhounds of Andhra Pradesh and CRPF: Commando Battalion for Resolute Action (CoBRA).

Force level at certain specific time that is, boots on the ground, will also be reflected at appropriate places.

It is only natural that casualty data too is given in this section itself.

The CAPF are also abbreviated to Central Paramilitary Forces (CPMF), and both the terms stand for the same entity.

"Naxalites as seen through the eyes of the police" Mar 2007

This is the title of a book, edited by Ashok Kumar Mukhopadhyay and published recently. This entry is based upon the review of this book in a daily in its issue of the 17 Mar 2007.[1]

It must be clarified that it is an unusual book, whose title is given at the top above:" The Naxalites: Through the eyes of the police". This book is essentially a compilation of entries made in the Calcutta Police Gazette, (CPG), published daily as a tool of internal communication among police personnel at all levels. It is not a "Secret document". But importantly, the extracts in the book concern a particular event in the history of West Bengal, viz the Naxalbari uprising. These extracts in the book, from Jan 1967—four months prior to the first violent confrontation that took place between the State Police and organised peasants on 24 May 1967—to Dec 1975 afford us a valuable narrative on how the State represented by its police, decided to comprehend and then tackle the armed insurrection by the Naxal led by their mercurial but an inspired leader Charu Mazumdar.

But before proceeding any further on the book, it is to note that the reviewer of this book opens with a reference to Kurosawa master piece Rashomon, and how historians smile each time they see it. It shows how historiography works. The film's unusual narrative structure, with its conflicting witness accounts, points to the impossibility of obtaining the truth about a single event: Case of Rashomon, a rape and murder.

Apply the film's theme to the more recent 'event' of Naxalbari armed insurrection that engulfed the rural and urban West Bengal in the 1970s: the conflict of perspectives of this event has not its sharp edges. Even when the intervening period—of some forty years has afforded us some distance, the peasant uprising of 1967 in that North (West) Bengal village has its various narratives and versions and consequently interpretation and inferences. In this valuable collection edited by Mukhopadhyay, one sees the swirling violence that descended on the landscape of early mid -1970s Calcutta through the eyes of the police.

Now, returning to the fact as to how the police viewed the Naxal violence. Initially, the approach was largely defensive. 3 Oct 1970 CPG entry reads: "The Durga Pooja starts from the 7th instant. In this national festival of Bengalese, it is very natural that our officers and men on duty and their families will be eager to enjoy the festival.... But unfortunately, the life of a policeman today in view of the activities of certain groups and anti-socials in the city, particularly the Naxalites, need specially to be looked after".

By 1971, the CPG is giving policemen advice on how to open fire on a riotous mob ("one shall aim low at the time of firing....") as well as hinting at retribution ("our men and officers shall not forget that loss of life of any individual officer and man is not only a big loss to himself, to his family and the co-workers they leave behind but also a very great loss in many ways to the police force as such".)

Understandably, a lot of what makes up the internal communication of the CPG is sheer propaganda. The statement of arrested Naxal Leader Charu Mazumdar (reprinted as an appendix in the book), for instance, mentions how he became "addicted to wine in his College days", and later to *"ganja, bhang, opium, charas and Siddhi*". Why would he want to talk about substance abuse to his *jailors* at a time when even the writing of such a statement is doubtful, considering the state of his health?

Also, the fact gleaned from Mazumdar's Confession and revelations regarding Naxal strategy and methods of carrying out the "annihilation of the class enemy" prior to his death in police custody seem suspiciously like material that the police had already gathered and put it in the mouth of Naxal leader.

In another appendix, fellow Naxal and editor of the Naxal publications, *Liberation,* carefully points out the many discrepancies between the facts that would have been known to the brilliant Naxal leader Mazumdar and what is made evident in his 'unsigned' statement.

But the CPG notifications were not only about demonizing the Naxal leaders but also about presenting police brutalities as acts of exemplary courage. To wit, here is a notification from the CPG issue of 29 Nov 1973: "On Sep 1971, Sh Ranajit Guha Niyogi arranged a pre-dawn raid on the hideouts of extremists of Muraripukur in Eastern Calcutta. As the police party surrounded the *Bastee.* The extremists opened fire on the police. He then opened fire and hit two of the extremists and killed one of them. He also captured some arms and ammunition".

Mukhopadhyay points out this version (straight out of Hollywood action movies) sounds dodgy. He goes on to points out that as per eye witness, the armed police would raid Naxalite hideouts, selects, some young boys suspected to be Naxalites, "make them stand in a single file and then riddle them with bullets".

One thing even the Editor of the book does not explain as to why an incident/ Police action of Sep 1971 should be notified as late as in Nov 1973. What was the reason, occasion or even provocation behind recording the incident more than two years after it took place. More probably,'1973' is typo for 1971. It may be that the incident of Sep 1971 has been notified in the CPG in November 1971. If both the dates as published are correct, only explanation can be that Niyogi was retiring around Nov 1973, and the notification was a kind of eulogy for him, a parting gift so to say.

There are CPG entries pertaining to measures and methods advised to the policemen to be able to confront the Maoists. "The Commissioner of Police commands to all ranks the following excerpts from the book on Communist Insurgency by Robert Thompson [British Counter-insurgency expert]" goes a 3 Dec 1970 entry, while some others restrict and prohibit the import of seditious publications like *Mao Tse Tung: Taveel Jang ke Barre mein* (Urdu), Columbus Plastic Globes, and the magazine, *China Pictorial.* Notices announcing the "brave acts" of constables are regular features. The CGO may no be a literary masterpiece, but this genre of books should be welcome to the general to public, as a source of information, even if on occassions it reads like a self serving treatise. This important collection, at the very least, bring a new Kaleidoscope of trivia to the story of the urban battle raging in a 1970s metropolis. One should not miss humour even if it is in Kafkaesque lines like, "Avoidable places are to be avoided".

One entry reads: "This attack will increase in intensity". So, the police were there when the Naxals waged war in 1960s and 1970s Calcutta. This book tells us how they saw them. The narrative is a contemporary account of those times. It is obviously written by junior level officials and is often self serving. Nothwithstanding all this, it is valuable as a source of information. It gives us a historical perspective of events of those two decades.

Extent of Spread of Naxalism Mid-2008

By this time, large parts (majority of districts) of Andhra Pradesh and Jharkhand had been "highly-affected" by the Maoists scourge. In the rest of Andhra Pradesh, two regions in the remaining part, along the coast, in State's north-east and south-east were "Moderately affected", as shown in the map of the Red Corridor running from Bihar-Nepal border to Kerala in the country's south-west (The Week, 1.6.2008). In the remaining part of Jharkhand, the region in its south-east contiguous to the West Bengal border is "moderately-affected". As for Chhattisgarh, North and its South were affected by Maoism: districts Bastar, "highly" and Kanker and Dantewada, both "moderately". Bihar's south, contiguous to Jharkhand border was "highly affected", the rest of it "moderately". The following were "moderately affected": West Bengal, UP, small eastern area touching Jharkhand and Bihar south; Odisha, small northern areas, touching West Bengal and Jharkhand borders; Karnataka, two smaller regions, one in the east contiguous to Andhra Pradesh and the other in the south-west; Maharashtra, Gadchiroli district of the state in the east contiguous to Andhra Pradesh; and small areas of Tamil Nadu and Kerala.

Naxal-hit states to form Greyhound-type of Force to confront the Naxals

Andhra Pradesh remains the only State in India that faced and defeated the LW extremists in the period 1970-1990. The State had raised a specialist force for this purpose, the well-known, reputed Greyhounds. That in the later years especially after the creation of the CPI (Maoist) through the merger of PWG and MCC in 2005, the LWE got revived, is not any reflection on the state's success in eliminating the LWE in that earlier period.

A daily reported 7 Feb. 2009 that six Maoist-hit states (Chhattisgarh, Jharkhand, Odisha, MP, Bihar and Maharashtra) are developing special forces on the lines of Greyhounds of Andhra Pradesh to tackle Red terrors.[2]

DGP Chhattisgarh Vishwa Ranjan Tiwari told the daily that his state would be first to raise 13,000- strong crack commando forces, among these six to deal with the Maoist. The existing Chhattisgarh 'Armed Forces', headquartered at Amleshwar in Durg, has been converted into commando 'Battalion'. The battalion would be deployed in rural and forested areas to check the Maoists.

A comment needs to be made here it on two terms used in the news item. One, a state in the Union of India cannot have 'Armed forces'. The Constitution only permits the Central Government only to have its armed forces. Two, a 13,000 strong entity cannot be termed a battalion as a unit called so (be it in Army, BSF or CRPF) generally has a strength of one thousand. The two terms are used due to ignorance of matters constitutional and matters military respectively. The latter entity could be called a wing, with certain number of battalions in it, or even a range on police analogy or even 'commando force', divided into certain number of battalions. That the news story is attributed to a DGP level officer, is suprising, to say the least, for reasons explained above.

The State will also raise Anti-Terror squads (ATSs) on the lines of those raised in Maharashtra and UP to counter the terror attacks in Urban areas.

These changes were considered after Union Home Minister P Chidambaram visited Raipur to review the preparedness of the Chhattisgarh police. "He stressed on the need to have separate forces to tackle the Maoists and the terrorists. A senior police officer told the daily: "young and active boys will be recruited for the new force and trained by the experts on the lines of the training imparted to the commandos of the NSG and the similarly placed personnel of the BSF and ITBP."

Some further details about manpower was given out. A final decision on the "office for the new unit will be made soon". While 400 personnel were to be picked up from the third battalion of the Chhattisgarh Armed Forces, another 600 were to be recruited. These figures suggest that the total strength of the commando battalion would be around 1,300. Then the term battalion is appropriate. So, the figure of 13,000 is an obvious typo!

The DGP said the first batch of the Chhattisgarh ATS would be in place after a rigorous 90-day training cycle. "About 700 especially-trained commandos would remain as standby to face any terror attacks."

"Ministry fast-tracks fortification of police stations in Maoist-hit areas": Sep 2012

If there are reports of the Maoist ultras augmenting their military capabilities, the MHA has put on fast track the fortifications of 400 police stations identified for the purpose in nine Maoist-hit states. The States have been asked to step up construction and renovation work on these police stations under this project.

The pace of work has not been satisfactory so far, so the States must complete the civil works in these police stations at the earliest, particularly in Odisha, Chhattisgarh, Jharkhand and West Bengal because it is in these states that Maoists are acquiring modern weapons and consolidating their position for further strikes.

A senior MHA official told the daily that "this has been conveyed to the police chiefs of these states at a recent conference of the DGPs.[3]

It was over two years back that the Cabinet Committee on Security had okayed the project. Subsequently, the MHA identified stations in the 83 worst Maoist-hit districts spread across nine States: Andhra Pradesh, Bihar, Chhattisgarh, Jharkhand, MP, Maharashtra, Odisha, UP and West Bengal. A sum of Rs 2 Crore was to be spent on each of the station, with Rs 1.60 crore being the Share of the MHA and State governments' Rs 40 Lakh. In the last two financial years, the MHA has released Rs 200 crore, Rs 55 Lakh per police station, while for 2012-2013, Rs 210 crore has been allocated.

Out of the 400 identified police stations, 85 are in Bihar, 70 each in Chhattisgarh, Jharkhand and Odisha, 40 in Andhra Pradesh, 18 in West Bengal, 15 in UP, 12 in MP and 10 in Maharashtra.

The police stations with no proper infrastructure are easy targets for the Maoist, looting their arms and ammunition. A fortified station, with a minimum strength of 40 personnel and modern communication tools will not be an easy target. And now. even the states are equipping their police forces with modern arms.

SSB for Naxal areas and J & K: Dec 2012

With greater thrust on anti-Naxal operations in the next few years, the government may soon deploy the Sashastra Seema Bal in the LWE areas and Jammu and Kashmir. CRPF, BSF and ITBP are already deployed in various Naxal-affected districts in the country.

This was reported by the Times of India, in its issue dated 18 Dec 2012.

CRPF: The main anti-Maoist arm

Presently, the CRPF, one of the Central Armed Police forces, is the main fighting arm of the Central Government against the Maoist uprising.

Besides having adequate strength for the job in hand, the CRPF is also getting modern weapons in its armoury. This section will cover the following aspects of the CRPF operating in Naxal-affected areas:

- Operations and operational matters
- Weapons and equipment
- Casualties in the force
- Allowances and perks.
- Negatives seen and reported
- Civic action

"DG, CRPF make news": Sep 2012

DG, CRPF gets extension

In an unusual move the government is all set to give a six-month extension to CRPF DG K Vijay Kumar who is due to retire on 30 Sep 2012. It was reported in a daily dated 1 Sep 2012. It gave its reasons too: "A 1975 - batch IPS officer of Tamil Nadu cadre, Kumar is credited with revamping the force involved in Naxal operations and taking some welfare measures for his men".

The daily goes on to add: "Extensions to heads of police forces is not common practice but the government seems to be willing to make an exception in this case".

Retiring DG, CRPF has advice for his force

"Emphasising the need for the Government to 'win over' the hearts of the people in the LWE-hit districts, the outgoing DG said there has been a "turn-around" in Bihar, West Bengal and UP in tackling the situation, though Gadchiroli and Abujhmaad, Dantewada, Chhattisgarh remain areas of concern. Other areas of concern listed by him: 23 districts in Jharkhand; Malkangiri in odisha.

Mr Kumar's 2 year tenure which "ends on 30 September" is seen "highly successful" in government circles as he lifted the morale of his force, which saw 75 of its personnel gunned down by the Maosits at Dantewada in Apr 2010. Asked about the killings of the innocent in an encounter at Bijapur (Chhattisgarh) in June this year (2012) he said it was planned operation and the movement of the troops had been scientifically recorded. Refusing to comment further on the issue as a judicial inquiry is on into the encounter, he said he had not sent a "hara-kiri" (suicide) team to patrol Maoist-affected areas.

Then he commented on the situation in J and K where his CRPF took over from his BSF to deal with militancy in civilian areas after the Kargil war, while the latter 'retreated' to border areas. He said there had been a "Positive change" in the overall scenario. Successful completion of panchayat polls in the State and peaceful Amarnath yatra were major achievements.

At the end, he did not get the extension as 'revealed' by a daily on 1 Sep 2012.

While a certain pat-on-the-back self-indulgence is expected from a retiring head of a force, he should avoid over doing the act. More importantly, he should have avoided giving advice to the Government on winning the hearts of people. But what is more troubling is some unhealthy happenings in the CRPF which have drawn attention from knowledgeable quarters. Of late, this force has invited a lot of negative comments from the press, which of course, will be recorded in this section.

"CRPF sounds alarm on depleting strength"

The issue of alarming deficiency of sanctioned strength at sector/range/unit of the CRPF that is adversely affecting the smooth functioning of these formations was discussed threadbare at a senior officers conference on Wednesday (31 Oct 2012)", reported a daily in Nov. 2012.[4]

Let it be stated here and now that this news story is obviously based on close interaction of the reporter with senior CRPF officers at their HO at Delhi.

The deficiencies are occurring owing to non-creation of posts and relying instead on attachment for carrying on the necessary works. The vacancies have further been compounded due to temporary attachment/deputation/training without any ceiling on such a practice.

As per existing policy, officers/personnel having outstanding performance in the younger age band and professional excellence are borrowed by SPG/NSG/CBI/IB/NCB.

"When such a lot of officers is sent out on deputation, the force is left to compromise its excellence and efficiency in all fields. This is an established fact that all formations of CRPF are having lesser strength than the sanctioned one. Even then, there is a constant and unending demand for providing the fittest and capable strength only on temporary transfer/

attachment to MHA/ Directorate due to which it is becoming impossible for sectors/ranges/group centers/units to run their establishments smoothly", reads the agenda points of the senior officers' conference, adding there is a sudden increase in court cases against transfers which further aggravates the problem.

These factors also lead the units to compromise the operational strength, timely leave to the troops, rotational training and conduct of courses, consequently a demand has been made within the paramilitary to formulate a complete policy to deal with the situation.

Most of the group centres are made to function with only 40 to 60 per cent of the ministerial staff for months together. There should be a fixed quota for pooling out the strength from lower formations so that quality and efficiency is not made to suffer at any level. It should also be given an active consideration that how the lower formations are expected to perform efficiently and effectively while professionally sound, younger and capable lot of officers and men is pooled out and sent on deputation/attachment with higher formations, officials are learnt to have said at the conference.

In Naxal-affected States like Jharkhand, where new zones/sectors have been created, they do not have the required ministerial staff. The requirements is being made up by stop gap arrangement of pooling in officers from Group Centres that already are facing staff crunch due to deputations.

Insiders said the need of the hour is to create new posts in keeping with the growing number of personnel owing to raising of new battalions. But the creation of posts is being withheld both due to lack of a clear cut policy as well as the ongoing austerity drive under way in view of the fiscal difficulties facing the Government.

It needs to be added here that it is a well-argued case for the CRPF strength crunch to be set right. The reporter obviously have got a good briefing by the CRPF officers. It is so well-written analytical story that this Author, as in case of some other such stories, did not feel the need to change too much of the text in the daily.

"No bullet proof jackets for jawans in the Red zone": Jan 2013

"Security forces carrying out anti-Maoist operations deep inside the jungle of Jharkhand do not have bullet proof jackets, even though the State Government has ample funds to buy them".[5]

Subsequent to the 26/11 Mumbai attack the MHA in 2010 issued a circular to all states asking them not to buy bullet proof jackets below NIJ (IV) standard. But the ministry's Bureau of Police Research and

Development (BRRD) "has not framed the guidelines for buying these jackets yet".

To put the issue in perspective; this disclosure about lethargic ways of government's institutions came more than two-and-a-half years after the MHA's circular.

It is useful to know that the NIJ (National Institute of Justice) is a research, development and evaluation agency under the US Department of Justice and Standard set by it for bullet proof jackets is a benchmark specification followed by security forces Worldwide.

Even NIJ (III) standard jackets cannot stop a bullet of 7.62 caliber used in AK-47 and INSAS Rifle.

Jharkhand Police spokesman IGSN Pradhan said the 40,000- odd personnel in anti-Maoist operations in the State have just 5,000 bullet proof jackets, none of them NIJ(IV).

It is a sad reflection on the way a country can be so indifferent to the avoidable loss of life, that too for the men who are engaged in conuntering the "most serious internal security threat" to the nation, posed by the murderous Maoists. It is time India follows the example of the US and European countries that care for a single loss of a foot soldier that lay down his life in the battle fields far away from the homeland.

"50,000 paramilitary troops to be hired in two years": Mid -2014

Reeling under the acute shortage in manpower, the Central Armed Police Forces (CAPF) plan to hire 50,000 additional strength in two years. "This addition, an equivalent of 50 battalions, is expected to meet the current shortfall of some 26,000 men in the sanctioned strength of some 9 Lakh".[6]

Official sources explained the expansion of the CAPF in terms of "heightened demands", as well as "rising expectations" from them since the last one. Of the 50, about 38 battalions are proposed to be raised by the CRPF, the rest being divided among the SSB (Sashastra Seema Bal), ITBP, and the BSF.

Presently, the CRPF, with 207 battalions is the largest among the CAPF. Besides the three mentioned in the preceding paragraph, the CAPF also include Assam Rifles (AR), Central Industrial Security Force (CISF) and the National Security Guard (NSG). Functioning under the MHA, all these constituents have distinct mandates ranging from counter-insurgency, combating Maoists to guarding the border or protecting vital installations and undertaking surgical operations.

The LWE- affected States remain the main battle grounds for India's paramilitary forces, some 38 per cent of these deployed there. The other two main regions of their deployment are the North East with 26 per cent battling insurgencies of several hues and Jammu and Kashmir with 21 per cent battling the Jihadist terror. Thus, it is only 15 per cent that is left to do duty in the other states of the nation.

The functional unit of the most CAPF forces is a company. Of the total 2862 companies about 1100 paramilitary companies operate in the Red Zone.

In the next four years, the Government plans to spend Rs 11,000 crore on the upgrade of the Seven CAPFs, enumerated above.

Centre wants Chhattisgarh Police to take lead role in anti-Red ops": Aug 2014

As the NDA Government works on a revised counter Maoist blueprint Union Home secretary Anil Goswami has convened a meeting with Chhattisgarh top officials and its DGP on 29 Aug 2014, says a daily of the 28th.[7]

Mr. Goswami plans to discuss tightening of the State's response against the LWE including a dedicated action plan for fighting Maoists in the State. He reportedly plans to ask the DGP of the Chhattisgarh to focus on leading role in planning pro-active counter-operations, particularly in Bastar region, involving CRPF in their execution.

The MHA assessment holds Chhattisgarh second only to Jharkhand in the list of worst LWE-hit states in the country. However, it seems the operation launched by the State police have been on the lower side this year (2014). In fact, the slightly improved Indices of counter-Maoist activity (in the State are largely attributed to operations planned and executed by the CRPF, with the State police playing a poor second fiddle and, in some cases, even declining to come on board.

The ministry sources believe the Home Secretary is likely to impress upon the State Government to improve its counter-Naxal response by getting the ground level policing in order, stepping up intelligence gathering on Maoist activities and movements, and finally taking the lead in planning counter-operations, with the CRPF providing the boots on the ground.

A senior MHA official said: "The police stations in the Naxal –infested Bastar must be made fully functional and the local policemen must be involved more in the surgical strikes against the Reds".

"Govt to raise 31 additional IRBs, in J & K, North-East and Maoist hit states": Aug 2014

To ease pressure on Central paramilitary forces (CPF) deployed in Jammu and Kashmir, North East and Red Zone, the Centre will provide funds for raising 31 India Reserve Battalions (IRBs) there, a daily reported on 20 Aug 2014.[8]

"It will be a huge boost for the states battling terrorism and insurgency. The CPM are already stretched to their limit for being involved in static as well as temporary deployment in these states. Once the states raise their own IRBs, we will be able to move the Central forces from there and deploy them more in line with their original mandate", said a government official, 'requesting anonymity'.

The IRBs are raised by the states with the initial funds provided by the Centre. Presently, there are 145 IRBs with the states across the Country. The Centre had got requests for 50 fresh IRBs from the states, but it agreed for 31 battalions (some 31,000 personel), that too only for the three regions mentioned above. The decision has huge financial implications for the Centre as raising a new IRBs costs Rs 50 crore. The Centre agreed on this number after consulting all stake holders, including the Financel Ministry that has to approve the spending.

It is reported that five IRBs battalions have been approved for Jammu and Kashmir and the rest 26 to be shared between the North East and LWE states. Presently, there are 37 IRB battalions with the ten Maoist hit states.

"Centre to deploy more forces in red zone" Oct 2014.

"The Centre is planning more paramilitary forces to intensify the operations against the rebels in the Red Zone meaning Maoist-affected states."[9]

As a part of the new strategy, the MHA plans to provide additional battalions of Central Paramilitary Forces (CPF) to deal with the scourge, especially in the worst-affected 23 districts, most of them in Central and eastern India. The new induction of the units will be in addition to 90 battalions (90,000 total) deployed in the nine Naxal-hit states—Chhattisgarh, Odisha, Bihar, Jharkhand, MP, Andhra, UP, West Bengal and Maharashtra.

The MHA will also help reconstruction and fortification of 250 Police stations located in the Red zone. Besides the strengthening of the infrastructure of these 250, the Centre will also provide additional manpower and sophisticated weapons to the personnel of these stations.

This is in addition to the 400 police stations, the MHA is currently fortifying (Oct 2014) under a similar plan.

The MHA is also mulling over a proposal to create 4-5 development hubs in the 23 worst-hit districts with modern amenities including construction of modern medical facilities, good academic institutes, build communication infrastructure and a proper security apparatus.

The MHA will also upgrade the existing jungle warfare training institutes with expanded facilities for advanced training of the troops.

Another change is inevitable. The Integrated Action Plan (IAP) presently being implemented by the Planning Commission in 88 selected tribal and backward districts for their accelerated development will have to be taken over by the MHA as the Centre has decided to disband the Commission. This initiative is aimed, at providing public infrastructure and services in these 88 affected or contiguous districts to wean away the youth there from the enticements offered by the Maoists.

Another matter of the important detail under the IAP, Rs 25 crore were released for the 60 district during the financial years 2010-11 and 2011-12 respectively for infrastructure upgradations. The scheme has now been extended to 88 such districts. The nature of major works/projects taken up by the districts under the IAP include construction of school buildings, school furniture, anganwadi centres, drinking water facilities, rural roads, panchayat bhavans, livelihood activities, skill developments and irrigation works.

Another daily[10] has covered the issues discussed above, possibly, given in a Government hand out to the press, and some additional facts are added here from the second daily, to make this analysis more comprehensive. The second daily employs rhetoric to make a point: "If you thought one Lakh paramilitary troops were a massive number to police the Naxal grid, There would be far more boots on the ground in the days to come, particularly in Bastar." The new anti-LWE policy being finalized by the NDA Union Home Minister Rajnath Singh proposes to enhance the deployments of the Central forces like CRPF from the current level of 92,000 troops and 9,000 CoBRA battalions' personnel to a higher number by inducting newly-raised battalions into the counter-Maoist operations.

Around 60 per cent of the one Lakh Central Armed Police Forces (CAPF) manning the Red Zone are stationed in Bastar (Chhattisgarh) and adjoining areas of Malkagari (Odisha) and Gadchiroli (Maharashtra) among others. The lion's share of newly-raised battalions of the CAPF, sources in the MHA told this daily on 13 Oct 2014, too will be deployed in the same stronghold.

A senior MHA official paints an optimistic picture of the ground situation: "Maoist activity has been on the downtrend after peaking in 2010.

On the other hand, the deployment of troops in the counter-Naxal grid has grown from some 30,000 in 2004, the landmark year in the history of LWE when the PWG and MCC merged to create a new entity designated CPI (Maoist), to nearly 100,000 at present (Oct 2014). He also explained "the new strategy of the Government: Push back the Maoists further by enhancing Central Force deployment in their strongholds. This will run parallel to stepped up efforts to effect Maoist surrenders, particularly in Bastar where 221 Maoists laid down their arms until May end (2014).

One is constrained at this usual effort of the MHA officials to paint an overly optimistic picture of the Government's operations against the Maoists. May be, it is the same set of officials who were managing government's counter-Maoist policy under the UPA . Now they want to tell you that the NDA has turned the things around after a year's stint in power. May be, they are convinced that they can beguile if not fool, their new political masters. It is a sad commentary on the gullibility of these officials, perhaps even, their Ministers if they do not know the capability of the Maoist to strike back vigorously after regrouping, post any discomfiture suffered by them at the hands of security forces. But to be honest, they really have not suffered any major losses in the recent times.

Yet again, these officials are unaware about the realities behind some of the surrenders, induced fraudulently, when some local villagers were persuaded to pose as Maoists and claim the surrender money/benefits. Be that as it may, these silly claims must be taken with a shovelful of salt, to put it crudely!

This daily has mentioned five aspects of the so-called new strategy, which are reproduced below merely for information.

"New Strategy to Counter Red Terror"

"..1: Enhanced deployment of Central forces.

"..2: Stepped up coordination among States. Persuasive dialogue with States where political leadership has divergent views on tackling Naxals, particularly Bihar and Jharkhand.

"..3: Creation of block- level social sector services hubs (already detailed above).

"..4: Passing on administration of IAP to the MHA as Planning Commission is a history.

"..5: Fortification of 25 additional police station in affected areas, over and above the 400, presently being covered under the scheme".

Police forces in india: comparing the Strength with that of other countries: Oct 2014

"In the past few days, there have been a series of attacks on policemen in Delhi. A study by the Rajasthan Police and MIT shows that four out of every ten law-abiding citizens fear the police but policemen complain of disrespect from the public and long working hours.[11]

Experts have linked the force's negative image partly to high workloads. Data shows that Indian policemen are more overworked than their counterparts in most other countries.

Before giving the data,, it is more important to mention the role of policemen on the issue that concerns us here, Maoist insurrection. Popular belief links the police to the law and order subject. But that, of course, is true in normal situations. But in India, we do not have "normal" situation. We are facing largest internal security threat in the form of Maoist uprising. Police has a very important part to play in dealing with the LWE.

Undoubtedly it is the CAPF that are combating Maoists violence. But they can never succeed there without the help and active participation of the State's Police forces in the respective states. It should be useful here to refer to Punjab police's role in the Khalistan rebellion. Its morale was in its boots till that intrepid police officer KPS Gill took over as its Chief. Policemen's families had been threatened and often even killed. They were scared of the terrorist. Situation changed when Gill appeared on the scene. He boosted his men's morale step by step, built up the intelligence system, local level upwards. Consequently they led the Army to right places, had the terror merchants arrested or killed. After a long haul, the great Gill got Punjab out of the clutches of the Khalistan with the help of his proud police. Army had always been there. It was this active help and support of Panjab Police that made all the difference!

Same level of morale and active support are required today from the police of each Maoist-hit state to enable the CAPF there to defeat the murderous Maoists.

Our biggest cause of concern here is that the states do not have enough police strength to do their normal job, forget about helping fight the LWE. Its inadequate strength is further sapped by extraneous calls it get for duties like providing security to the VIPs. Finally, the political leaders have shown least interest to introduce frequently recommended police reforms that will not only ensure increased police efficiency but also independent function, uninfluenced by political interference. Now the statistics.

Police-population ratio

Police per Lakh population

Countries similarly placed as India

• Sierra Leone	175
• Lesotho	177
• India	**182**
• Argentina	196
• Canada	200
Other major countries	
• Japan	205
• US	211
• Brazil	245
• England and Wales	257
• Australia	262
• France	290
• Germany	295
• Scotland	331
• Spain	383
• North Ireland	402
• Italy	459
• Russian Federation	521
Countries with highest ratio	
• Saint Vincent and Grenadines	802
• Mauritius	867
• Grenada	920
• Brunei Darussalam	1094
• Bahrain	1619

'Fresh strategy for Maoists': Nov 2014

Here we have Intelligence Bureau Chief Syed Asif Ibrahim, giving his views on the Maoists issue on 29 Nov 2014. He was speaking at the conference of the DGPs and IGPs[12] at New Delhi.

He said although the number of killings by LWE groups has gone down in the recent months, especially because of shrinkage of their areas of operation, the security forces need to draw up a fresh strategy to deal with the Maoist more effectively.

He felt that increasing number of deserters, shortage of arms and ammunition and a crisis of leadership have collectively contributed to the reduction in Maoist activities.

And, finally he came to most important observation of his speech: Role of the State police in tackling LWE.... Something referred to the previous entry. He identified giving a bigger role to the state police forces as a key component in tackling the Maoist insurrection, war on India, nothing less.

Kin relief may be equalised for the Forces: Dec 2014

"Paramilitary forces personnel who die in battle may soon get the same compensation as those in the Army".[13] This was a report in a daily of 2 Dec 2014.

They might also be given allowances at par with the Army for deployment in "hard" areas. Home Minister Rajnath Singh wrote to the Finance Ministry, asking it to bridge the compensation gap between armed forces and paramilitary personnel.

Compensation for armed forces (army, navy and air force) personnel who fall in the battle is higher by about Rs 10 to 15 Lakh as compared to the one for paramilitary personnel (CRPF, ITBP, BSF and CISF). While paramilitary personnel's families get paid amount Rs 35 Lakh after their death, kin of Armymen get Rs 45-50 Lakh. This includes insurance money and payments from the Centre. Moreover, paramilitary personnel are not even recognized as "martyrs" when they die, unlike armed forces personnel.

The government is also trying to bring allowances for posting of paramilitary personnel in difficult areas at par with those of the army. There is currently a difference of about 30 per cent in allowances.

These benefits and incentives are good for the morale of the CAPF, who are doing a tough job in J&K, North East and the Red Zone. These little considerations go a long way in improving their operational and administrative performances.

Why CRPF gets bad press?

Occasionally in the past, and in particular, of late, CRPF has been getting a bad press. It should not be too suprising. After all, the fourth estate claims to be jealous guardian of the public interest as it sees it!

During India's struggle for independence if some papers went along the British Indian Government, so many spoke for the congress party and the country as the former was believed to be speaking for the latter. Even if the independent press suffered at the hands of the government, it was deemed to be for the national cause. There was idealism in the air.

Post-independence scene changed. Some entrepreneurs entered the field and commercial and business interests were seen to be dictating their policies in running their dailies/periodicals. Besides the Editors, senior journalists had their own strong views on matters of public interests.

Left Wing Extremism waging an armed uprising against the democratically elected government of the country has many sympathies in the press ranks.

Presently, the CRPF is the single paramilitary forces waging the nation's war against this LWE, often seen as a national scourge by so many Indians. Even then, it is not so easy to see so many negative articles and features that appear in the press, at times one can say, far too many for the liking of the CRPF!

All these cannot be dismissed as supercilious rantings of armchair critics spewing venom from their air conditioned chambers. There indeed is some merit in certain criticism of the ways certain anti-Naxal operations have been conducted. At times even the conduct and attitude of CRPF officers have come under the lens.

This chapter looks at the tone and tenor of some of the articles that are critical and mostly negative in their comments.

"How not to fight an invisible enemy": Apr 2012

This article appeared in a daily, with an even more telling blurb: "Though the CRPF has acquired army style arms, in large parts of Chhattisgarh, it is Maoists who wear fatigues and call the shots". The contents of this critical, at times cynical, article are reflected here briefly, for the readers to judge about their objectivity, without any editorial intervention from this Author. So views expressed hereafter are those of the scribe and his editor. Same will be the pattern concerning other (critical) articles included in this part.[14]

"They talk of the *Jung* (war) where the other side is the *dushman* (enemy). Army lingo is gradually entering the lexicon of the force that is fighting the Maoist menace. So are the weapons so far preferred by the infantry. Latest additions to the CRPF's arsenal: night vision enabled sniper rifles (X-95), under barrel grenade launches (UBGL), that can be attached to a gun like AK-47 to fire grenades, Glock pistols which are lighter with lesser recoil, and light weight automatic MP5A rifles. And the CRPF brass, pushing for further militarization, claims the men's morale is sky-high".

"At the ground, though the reality is a bit different. In south Chhattisgarh, Maoist heartland, the police apparently move around in civies while Maoist cadres wear olive green fatigues. Travelling from Raipur to Sukma and beyond it is difficult to spot a policeman, except in police stations fenced in by walls and barbed wire or fortified CRPF camps. Locals hardly ever enter these premises to seek help".

Between 2007 and 2011, 590 security troops were killed in Chhattisgarh. Compare this to J&K where 366 security troops were killed during the same period. Of late; an unwritten instruction has been circulated across the police stations in the region south of Bastar. "Policemen have been told not to venture out of police stations", says an officer in Jagdalpur.

Among the Maoist-infected States, Chhattisgarh has the highest number of CRPF battalions— 17 regular and two CoBRA. The main job of the CRPF men in these areas is to secure their camps. Provisions and supplies are ferried in heavily armoured vehicles or choppers. Long range patrols are usually avoided, says an officer.

TJ Longkumar tells the scribe: "The CRPF has been deployed as a defensive force. These would be the harbor areas when there is an offensive operation". He is the IG, Bastar.

A CRPF commandant tells about the men's problems connecting to their near and dear ones back homes: "They fix their mobile phones on a tall pole and keep waiting for some signal. As soon as there is a flicker of connectivity, they frantically call home just to hear the voices of their loved ones". An invisible "enemy" is not their only problem!

The scribe talks about grave disconnect between perception and reality. "The joint operations are hamstring by lack of quality intelligence, especially human intelligence". Then an activist is brought in to say his peace, "But when the forces have alienated the people, how can they expect villagers to come to them". This para has been written to show how a scribe can "hire" an activist to write what he has already decided about-here it is about failure of intelligence!

From here on, the excerpts and summary will convey whatever the scribe has written in the article.

"The stench of fake encounters hangs heavy in the areas. Villagers and activists in Sukma and Dantewada rattle off names of people branded Maoists and killed in encounters. Markam Masa of Sukma's Chhikpal village was allegedly whisked away to CRPF camp and given electric shocks. His death stirred a ground swell of protests. A joint forces team picked up Midium Bandi from his home in Sukma's Etpal village. Two years later, he was shot dead by the police, who said he was escaping from the police station."

Former CPI MLA and Adivasi Mahasabha President Manish Kunjam says: "The more police tortures villagers, the more they will lean towards Maoists". The result is almost zero intelligence flow from the Maoist heartland "Every day, the security forces are conceding ground to the Maoists", admits an intelligence officer in Raipur.

Maoists on the other hand have a strong intelligence network comprising villagers who are not even party members. "As soon as we near a village in the core area, villagers blow trumpets and burst crackers to alert the Maoists", says a CRPF officer posted in Bastar.

The CRPF is much-touted civic action programme is out of sync with the ground situation. A veteran of counter-insurgency operations explains why: "Such a programme works only if security forces have established their dominance in the area. But in Maoist strongholds of Bastar where security forces are scared to venture out of their camps, such initiatives back fire as the risk of casualities increase".

A CRPF commandant tells the story of medical camp which the forces ran 24×7 in a south Sukma village. As there was no hospital for miles in this area, the villagers flocked to it for treatment. Maoists did not like it. They stopped coming once the Maoists threatened them with dire consequences. Subsequently, they marched 20 Kms to a clinic run by Maoists near Burklanka.

As one moves deeper into south Chhattisgarh, signs of government presence recedes. For instance, the nearest hospital from Tadmetla in Sukma is in Dornapal, some 50 Kms by road that has become dirt track. Though the government has appointed rural medical assistants, people largely depend on quacks. The state of education too is abysmal. A senior district official concedes "These areas are like black holes".

It seems the government has abdicated its role and responsibility in these troubled belts and conceded large swathes of land to the Maoists. For villagers in these areas, the Maoists are the government they know and go to when in trouble.

A senior police officer puts it in perspective when he says, "Maoists run a parallel government from Burklanka, south of Sukma", There is no sign yet that Union Home Minister P Chidambaram is right when he says that the two pronged strategy of police action and development to tackle the Maoist scourge has been a success.

At the end, a note need to be put that this article is or at least seems to be a "paid job". The scribe's manner of writing, use of terms like "much-touted" and general tone and tenor of the entire article prove that it is so! Her trip to "badlands" was approved, if not sponsored, by the Maoists. She sees a lot of Maoists in fatigues. She has activists at hand to prove her anti-government and anti-CRPF stance. This pro-Maoist article must have warmed the cockles of their hearts! She (the scribe) finds nothing right with CRPF operations. They are hiding like the rats in their camps. The Maoists could not have asked for more from this scribe. They would rather more such reporters visit Naxal areas to show their success to the nation and the World beyond! One wonders if the CRPF ever felt necessary to issue rebuttal to this article. And if they did, may be the daily refused to oblige, rejecting the counter.

"2 months on, CRPF revises slain Maoist list"

This troubling headline for the CRPF's ways of conducting its affairs in its anti-Maoists operations is not a happy augury for the forces. Its blurb makes things even more clear: "BIJAPUR ENCOUNTER: Had said 7 of 17 killed in ambush were rebels, now claims 2 more had 'Naxal links".[15]

More than two months after the encounter in Chhattisgarh's Basuguda area of Bijapur district on night 28/29 June 2012, the security agencies have established that two more persons among those killed had Naxal links. Earlier, the police had said that 7 of the 17 killed in the ambush had Naxal records, asserting that not all those killed were innocent villagers.

Amid allegations of human rights violations, the State government has ordered a judicial inquiry into the case.

The CRPF, which conducted the joint operation with the Chhattisgarh police said after the incident they have changed their standard operating procedure. From now on the force will enage "more and more trackers" before undertaking any operation. It has also asked the government to provide it with night vision devices with the higher resolution. More trackers will enable them to have clearer picture of the ground reality. The area affected by Maoist activity are quite complex in nature in terms of terrain and climate.

An officer spoke in anguish: "There is a lot of anguish and resentment when adolescents and children are killed. We suspect they could have been used as human shields. A judicial inquiry is on, so we cannot give more details".

Reacting to reports about a study conducted by the Indian Institute of Management, Ahmedabad that a lot of CRPF men were leaving the Force due to stress, DG K Vijay Kumar said, "That is true. There is a lot stress among troops because of continuous deployments. WE will have to give them rest and recuperation".

"CRPF Jawan shoots four mates"

A CRPF trooper, 34 , Deep Kumar Tiwari, posted with 111 Battalian of CRPF in Aranpur, flew into a rage when challenged by his camp mates.

He grabbed a gun and sprayed a head constable and three other constables with bullets. One trooper was injured in the firing, said Dantewada SP Narendra Khare.

It is possible that the jawans were sleeping when Tiwari barged in, woke them up, and got into a fight before riddling his colleagues with bullets, said a police source.

The incident took place mid-night Monday 23/24 Dec 2012. CRPF IG Zulfiquar Hassan said an inquiry has been ordered.

Preliminary investigations suggest Tiwari was under stress. Khare said Tiwari may even have had "mental problems".

Tiwari hails from Lucknow and has been arrested. The injured trooper is Head constable Sunil Sawant from Maharashtra, who is under treatment at Jagdalpur Medical College.

The dead were identified as: Head constable Chandan Singh, 45, from Gujarat; Constable Ramesh Kumar (29), from Haryana, Purushottam Lal Sahu, 29, from Raipur, Chhattisgarh and Anirudh Ramprasad, 24, from UP.

Aranpur camp, some 60 Kms from district headquarters Dantewada town is in heavily forested area where the Maoists have been enjoying monopoly since the late 1980s.

The proceeding piece of this news item refers to the stress that affects CRPF troops serving in LWE areas. This story is about its effects. Fragging, killing of one's own fraternity, a soldier or a policeman killing soldiers or police men of the same unit, has of late rared its ugly head among the paramilitary and armed forces. It has been attributed to increasing stress and pressure building up on the soldiers/ paramilitary troopers who are frequently denied holidays, personal time and often even sleep due to reason avoidable/ unavoidable.

Experts advocate psychological help for forces deployed in locations of difficult terrain and high danger. They also press for rotation of personnel in such areas to allow them to let off steam and relax with family.

Here is an important piece of information on the issue. At least 11 instances of fragging (=killing another member of the same fighting squad/ company/battalions/ unit) have been reported from Paramilitary and Army units in various insurgency affected areas or even in distant isolated locations of inclement weather, difficult terrain or incongenial harsh conditions, in the country over the last one year.

"23 CRPF men, cops 'left without a fight as Maoists ambushed colleagues": Sep 2014

It is very disturbing news, and its headline tells the truth as bluntly as required. The blurb supplies even plainer, unfortunate details: "Sukma Attack: CRPF probe finds most survivors guilty of 'lack of satisfactory counter-action'.

The sad story about conduct of so many CRPF troops related to an ambush sprung by the Maoists on 11 Mar 2014. 43 persons-31 CRPF and 12 Chhattisgarh police—had left Tongpal police station on 11 March morning when they were caught in an ambush on National Highway with open fields on both sides. 15 security men, who formed the first lines of the party, died on the spot. Subsequent inquiry found that most of those (28) that followed those fallen 15, deserted their embattled colleagues.

The probe was ordered by 1G CRPF (Chhattisgarh) HS Sandhu. It found that the Maoist attack which took place at Tahakwada in Sukma district had killed 15 troopers on the spot— 11 of CRPF and four from the State police- and most of the survivors who followed the first line that was ambushed, instead of helping their trapped colleagues, stayed behind and later deserted them.[17]

The probe found 23 of the 28 survivor's prima facie guilty of "inaction and lack of satisfactory counter-action". The CRPF has already suspended 17 of its men and suggested the police act against its six men for dereliction of duty.

The inquiry report also said the deceased men fought bravely and has recommended gallantry awards to 10 of the 11 CRPF troopers killed in the encounter.

Of the five survivors, let off in the probe, three could have been charged with "non-action" but they had suffered injuries in the gun battle.

It is probably the first instances when over half a police team involved in an anti-Naxal operation has been found guilty of "lack of satisfactory counter action".

The inquiry also noted the "delay in sending reinforcement". Though the Tongpal police station was only 4-5 minute drive from the spot, the reinforcement party did not arrive in time. "These comprised about 25 personnel (both CRPF and police) who were present in the camp. "They have not been suspended now, but will face a separate departmental inquiry", said a CRPF officer. "The role of Thana in charge Tongpal is also under scanner".

Bastar IGP SRP Kalluri said: We are yet to receive CRPF report.

Surprisingly, while 15 security men were killed in the ambush, the Maoists made away with 18 rifles, indicating those who survived could not even hold on to their weapons.

The Maoist looted six AK-47s, some of which were fitted with UBGL (under barrel grenade launchers), 18 magazines of the same rifles, one LMG with 10 magazines, nine INSAS rifles with 30 magazines, two SLRs with six magazines and two wireless sets and as the daily put it, sufficient to raise a company of the Maoists.

"CRPF men got separated from team, became easy targets": Dec 2014

The 14 CRPF troops who died in the ambush by Maoists on 1 Dec 2014 were part of a unit that got separated/isolated, for reasons still unknown from the main columns at the outskirts of Kasalpad village in Sukma district.

The joint column of CRPF and district police (Sukma) forces were out on an operation led by CRPF 1G HS Sindhu since 29 November and had comped near Tondamarka village on night 30 November. On 1 December, as the Siddhu-led column moved towards Chintagufa base camp, one unit got isolated near an open field in Kasalpad, and was quickly surrounded by Maoists around 10 AM. Siddhu told the daily they did not know how this party got separated from the main column; that will have to be enquired into.

Trying to reclaim areas where the state administration had not entered over the last few years, the security forces were moving into an unknown terrain.

The eye witnesses hold that the Maoists, taking cover behind elevated farmlands and inside a few vacant huts nearby, opened fire on the security men, killing 14 CRPF troops, the biggest lethality suffered by the Force on the Maoist front in the last four years.

The Maoists also looted/made away with 10 AK-47s, one 1NSAS rifle, one SLR, communication devices, bullet/proof jackets and other items.

Some security men felt the Maoist were following the movement of the column for two days and found an easy opportunity to hit them at Kasalpad village. Some auxiliary constables, who were part of the operation, stated the obvious: "It was such a large operation in the forests, much easier for the Naxals to track them".

Some villagers complained they were beaten up by the CRPF at Kasalpad when it returned from Chintagufa after completing their operation. Podiyamiunga, who had suffered eye injuries in the beating stated: "They were asking us where are the Naxals (=bata naxali Kahan hain)?"[18]

Then there was question as why the IAF choppers had not landed to evacuate the CRPF casualities. It was stated that the IAF had adhered to their SOPs, and decision to not take off at 4:42 PM on the 1st, when they received the call for evacuating the casualities, was taken by the local IAF and CRPF authorities. An official explained the ground had not been sanitized and thus unsafe for chopper landing. The IAF Task Force commander in the area cleared choppers take off at 9:28 AM on the 2nd after the area was sanitised.

Kasalpad is among the villages where residents get no PDS rations, as the nearest ration shop is 40 kms away. Barse Mada explains it is such a long journey, and we have stopped going there for the last two years.

Now comes something that is even more sad and disgraceful: "A few months back, the CRPF deployed 1,500 troops to help the local administration carry several truckloads of rations to Chintatnar. The rations, however, turned out to be rotten".

For the record, this is the third major incident of the force suffering casualties at the hands of the Maoists. In March; it lost 11 of its men on the National Highway surrounded by plain, open fields near Tongpal village in Sukma district. In April, five CRPF men were killed when they violated all procedural guidelines, and took a lift in an ambulance which was subsequently blown up in a landmine blast.

"The Central Reserve Police Mess": Dec 2014

This is rather condemnatory if unflattering headline of an article in a daily.[19] It needs to be clarified here itself that the scribe is Rahul Pandita, who had some years back authored a book on the Maoists, titled "Hello Bastar". He made it clear that he had not only sympathies for the armed rebels, but also had hardly a word of praise for the anti-Naxal forces and nor for their operations against the ultras in the entire book. He went beyond even that inherent bias in his writing of that book. He did not have a foreword for his book but an afterword by a famous, Senior Maoist leader and a politburo member at that, who was then spending his time in Delhi's Tihar jail. Notwithstanding all this respect shown to a Maoist leader, his name incidentally, is Kobad Gandhi and the Contents of his book, his views in this article must be fully reflected in this book, without any editorial intervention, or even critical comments. What follows is mostly in the words of Rahul Pandita, or in a summarized form.

T he opening Para is here in full: "For 15 days, since 15 Nov (2014), more than 2000 troops from six battalions of the CRPF have been venturing out to conduct SADO—Search and Destroy Pperation (s) –in the Sukma district of Chhattisgarh. The troops roughly divided into ten groups, would traverse villages considered Maoist strongholds: Pollampalli, Kankeslanka, Puswada, Jaggawaram Korapam, Kanrajgubbal, Rangaiguda, Degalmetta, Ramaram, Pidmel and Chintagufa. Since they had no intelligence inputs, the troops were asked to engage Maoists if they ever came in contact".

There is a very little possibility of such encounters if the Maoists themselves want to engage the Force. In their strongholds, the Maoists have large number of sympathizers acting as their intelligence sources. They can avoid conflict with the CRPF looking for them as long as they want through this human intelligence. In fact several arrested Maoist cadres had revealed to the security agencies that how their squads had passed within a 100 meter of the CRPF troops without being betrayed by any villagers. The CRPF tried to win over the local populations through civic action programmes—distributing items like transistor, cycle, saris among them. But in many strongholds of Maoists, some refused to accept those goodies.

On the Independence Day this year (2014), such items were forced on them. But some of them throw away these gifts on the outskirts of their village. A CRPF officer explains: "The people here are angry because they see their near and dear ones dying of Malaria, or diarrhea, or complications during pregnancy. The government has not diagnosed the problems and is behaving like a quack".

Before proceeding any further on this article, it is even more important to read the blurb of this article, below the headline:

> "The CRPF is so ill prepared to fight the Maoist, it is a miracle its troops are not deserting en masse". Without being too critical of this scribe, whatever views he may have on the CRPF and their ways of conducting counter-Maoist operations, one thing that can be said about him is that he lacks objectivity on the issue under his scanner. He may not be wearing Maoist fatigues, but he is doing the same job more effectively by remaining in the chivvy street. Closet Maoists have been mentioned in the book earlier, but he is miles ahead of them in fighting for the cause of a Maoists. In fact he sounds and act like an anti-national when he is literally inciting the CRPF troops to desert the Service en masse!
>
> Now we revert to his article.

Gorillas, not guerrillas: Lack of discipline

The operation that ultimately led to the death of 14 CRPF men on 1 Dec (2014) was to end a day before, but was at the last hour extended by one day. On the night of 30 November, about 800 troops were asked by their commanders to "take harbor" on a hillock designated Hill 406, south of Kasalpad a village. The illagers knew about the presence of such large number of troops. By the evening, a soldier, who was present there, says the gathering has turned into a *mela* (fair). The troops lit fire and chatted loudly in groups. "Had the Maoists attacked during the night, there would have been mayhem", the soldier said.

At 6:30 the next morning (1 December), about 200 troops among the group were asked to move towards Kasalpada village and stay put on the outskirts of the village. It is the heart of the Maoist territory, and the troops halted in the open field. A CRPF officer himself makes a telling statement to the scribe: "We are told that we need to fight the guerrillas (Maoists) like the guerrillas…….. But by the time they halted (in the open field) outside kasalpada village, our troops had turned into gorillas". This officer continues: "The basic requirements of guerrilla warfare are surprise, mobility small team formations, quick action, closely-knit group, specific task, training and motivation and effective command".

It was obvious that none of these requisites were met by these 200 strong team. The Maoists were closely watching this troop movement, so there was no surprise. Then, there was restricted mobility so the troops were moving a few miles every day.

The troops were from six different battalions and were not acting on any specific inputs. Several of them had already contracted malaria and longed to go on leave.

Just before 9 AM, the commandant of the 223 battalions CRPF, Sanad Kamal, who was also the acting commander of the group, received a radio message from CRPF's IG (operations) in Chhattisgarh, HS Sindhu, asking him to join him for a meeting at a spot 400 meters away. Before he left with nine men reveal eye witnesses, his juniors asked him if they could secure Kasalpada. But Kamal just asked them to wait.

After Kamal was gone for an hour his deputy commandant BS Verma asked him on radio if they could leave the area. "No, just hold ground", he was told. Meanwhile, the troops had broken into small groups. Some took out utensils and began preparing Maggi noodles under a tree, some smoked in another corner. A few veered towards the village.

Shock and awe

The Maoists numbering 50-60 attacked the group at 10:30. Oblivious to the CRPF troops, the Maoists had positioned their snipers on top of large tamarind trees (may be tree). They led the attack with such accuracy that two officers and several others among the 223 Battalion died very early on. The rest of the troops without any command and control began firing indiscriminately in all directions, leading to complete chaos. As a result, CoBRA commandos who took position on one side could not even pinpoint locations from where Maoists were firing. The CRPF troops fired about 7,000 rounds of bullets in response to a few hundred fired by the Maoists.

"They were so agile", recounts an injured soldier, "I saw one of them taking off his chappals, climbing on a tree, fire a few shots, got down stealthily and then immediately change location". They shot with precision while the CRPF troops exhausted all their ammunition. Later, some of them just stood in daze, almost ready to surrender to the Maoists if they had come closer, said a COBRA commando.

The attack lasted one hour, and subsequently, the Maoists looted whatever weapons they could lay their hands on. The COBRA troops recovered six bodies of the soldiers beneath a tree. The Maoists had lured them one by one, showing them a glimpse of themselves, and as they took aim, the Maoists snipers took them on with precision. "And also I would be surprised if some CRPF men died of bullets fired by their own colleagues", said a COBRA commando.

The IG finally arrived at 2:30 PM; four hours after the attack had begun. The Commando recalls that he just came, shouted, *"Bharat Mata ki jai"*, and then told his men: *Jo hua so hua"*.

Then began long walk to the camp. The troops took away string cots from the villagers to carry the injured and the dead. It took them seven hours to cover a distance of seven kms through the dense jungles. "We were so scared that the Maoists might attack again", said a CRPF soldier.

They made it to the camp at 9:30 PM. Two injured troopers could not make it. They died on the way. The other injured personnel are now being treated at the civil hospital in Jagdalpur. More than 70 other CRPF men, suffering from malaria, are also admitted there. But the hospital is in a very bad shape. Succumbing to media pressure, the hospital authorities removed civilian patients from their beds offering them to the soldiers.

"It is like living in a latrine, if you ask me", said a CRPF soldiers undergoing treatments there. "One thing I tell you he said, "It is better to be a Maoist in Chhattisgarh than be a CRPF jawans."

Even if this author wishes to avoid commenting on this article by Pandita, he cannot but help some odd remarks. Pandita has written more like a fan of the stars called Maoist! The details, comprehensive and precise he has given here indicates he saw the entire operation with his own eyes. Was he an embedded correspondent to use an Americanism?

Then he so easily gets CRPF men, and even COBRA commandos, to say things that are so adulatory of the Maoists, and hugely damaging and disgraceful for the CRPF troops!

Even more significantly, Pandita account of the same event is different in many respects from the one penned by Ashutosh Bhardwaj in the Indian Express of 3 Dec 2014, covered in the Earlier pages here! Has Pandita gone overboard in his idolatry harangue for his ideological heroes? It is deemed discreet to let the issue rest here with this question!

"Postings in conflict zone traumatizing CRPF men": Jan 2015

From the look of it, the press could not have been more derogatory than the headline of an article, in a daily[20] suggests. Counter-insurgency operations are seldom an easy cup of tea, more so if you are confronted with ultra Left Maoists! Even then, one is not sure if the CRPF, sole central paramilitary assigned to combat Maoist violence, really deserve such a bad, nay, scathing, press criticism, dripping in negativity.

Be that it may, here is the contents of the article, which from its opening paragraph, seems to be indicating unfortunate impressions about the CRPF. It opens this way: "Continuous deployment in 'high intensity conflict areas' is forcing the jawans and officers of country's largest para military force, CRPF, to suffer from 'social ostracization', a report on the state of affairs of the force said

As per report, prepared on the courrent status of this three-lakh strong force, they also undergo trauma in marital and family issues and are unable to ensure good education or their children.

The report puts forth some damning facts about the "pathetic" living and work conditions as well as poor emotional and physical well-being of its men and women.

It states that while 80-89 per cent of the force remains on deployment at any given time, 80-85 per cent of them are continuously deployed to fight Maoists in 10 attected states (37 %), militancy in J&K (28%) and insurgency in the North-East (16%).

"Owing to extremely difficult and sub-human working conditions, the CRPF members are not able to fulfil their social obligations like attending marriages, deaths and other ceremonies in the immediated family and society. This creates a sense of isolation, hampers proper matrimonial alliances and they are ostracized from the society," the report, submitted to the government for redressal, said.

Within the extented family too the report said since a CRPF jawan is "most of the time absent during social functions and ceremonies on account of his official commitments; he continues to be socially isolated even within his own family".

The report goes on to state those CRPF personnel even "have problems in findings suitable life partners for themselves and their children............ Children are mostly deprived of adequate parental control. Understandably very few parents prefer their sons and daughters to marry the wards of the force personnel".

"CRPF women taste the jungle life" They broke a barrier

35 CRPF personnel recently became the first women to be engaged in combat operations in the Force's history. It is even more than that: In fact women personnel of any armed forces in the country are never sent for combat operations. Even the Indian Army does not send its women members for field operations. So the claim of the Force for something unique by way of success seems to be well-placed! After all it deployed 35 of them——recruited from Naxal hit States of Chhattisgarh, Jharkhand and Odisha—— for a 90 day stint in the jungles of Chhattisgarh, starting Jan 2013. Enthused by the success of this experiment it is quite understandable that the Force is planning a repeat.

Before their 90-day stay in jungles, they were imparted pre-induction training in jungle warfare. Currently they all are posted in Delhi for law and order duties after they returned from the jungles in Apr 2013.

IG coperations, CRPF Zulfiquar Hasan talks about this experiment: "We believe the women personnel are as capable as their male counterparts. Most of them gave a positive feedback on their return and now we will be deploying more of them in these areas".[21]

It is an interesting human interest story, unique of course as it is. The humans are nothing if not emotional. It is even more so as we have women involved in this experiment.

Four of the 35 speak their mind here. The 22-year old, who wants to be unnamed, has not told anyone in her Chhattisgarh village what she does. Bella Minj, a mother of two is still nursing the thrill of cradling an ass- ault rifle. Milbred Ekka went in with thoughts of concern only for her nine- year old son in a hostel in Ranchi. Banita Mahana had a harder time convincing her sobbing older brother that all would be fine.

The 22-year old says till 2009, she did not even know what the CRPF stood for. She joined it when her friend brought over an enrolment from. Initially she thought it was for state police. "While I got the job, my benefactor, my friend could not", she chuckles.

Her last posting was in Srinagar. A class XII dropout who is now pursuing graduation through correspondence, the 22-year old is proud of what she has achieved but knows better than to celebrate the fact back home. Her father, a farmer, who owns a small patch of land, does not discuss her daughter's occupation with anybody. If the Maoists come to know that she is with a Central Police Force, the family will have to pay a heavy price for it, says she.

"When I told my father that I was being sent to Jagdalpur, he was opposed to it, but later relented, feeling a sense of pride that I was going to my state", she adds.

For ASI Bela Minj, 45, the thrill was being trained on an X-95—an assault rifle of Israeli make, used so far only by elite COBRA commandos. The mother of two teenage daughters was one of the platoon leaders, leading the team in patrolling and reconnaissance duties. From Gumla district of Jharkhand, Minj has been in the Force for 25 years but nothing ever came close to this assignment.

They were shown video clips of women Naxal fighters to give them an idea of the kind of attack they could face. "The video clips showed how ferocious a Maoist woman was. The message was clear, we had to put up a fight on the same lines, says Minj. An estimate by the MHA has it that more women cadres are joining the Maoists than ever and constitute 60 per cent of the group now.

Milbred Ekka, 40, says she suddenly feels new vigor, the same as her colleagues half her age. Admitting that there were problems initially, she says: "My husband is a Naik with the Indian military and currently posted with the Bihar Regiment in Poonch. He was surprised when told that I was being sent for such an operation. He initially was himself reluctant, but being in Army himself, he understood I had to go. He then gave me tips on how to be safe in those areas. Our only concern was our nine-year old son".

She is also from Gumla district, Jharkhand.

The elder brother of Banita Mahana, 23, broke down on the phone when told about her assignment as dangerous as this. Both her parents died when she was young. He is like a father to me. I said, "Don't worry, even if I get killed, you will get around Rs 57 Lakh as compensation. He was furious". A resident of Mayurbhanj, Odisha, Mahana joined the Force in

2010. "We came out safe but given a chance, I will go back again", she said.

Now, let us hear some others speak of their exciting assignment.

Manjula Dubey, 26, agrees with Minj that handling X-95 was an experience of a life time. Coming from a small village in Chhattisgarh, his father is a farmer. "To get an opportunity to use X-95 was a great experience. *EK umang si thi* (it was desire fulfilled)", says Dubey.

Suneela Hansdah, 42, says they could not let their guard down even for a second inside the jungle. "We used to walk 10-15 Kms at a stretch with danger lurking around. We were not supposed to make any noise, so we learnt to communicate in sign language. The roads are rigged with/ IEDs and we were trained in detecting them".

A senior CRPF official explained sending women for such operations also had other advantages, like lesser number of complaints of human rights violations. He continued: "When a woman goes to a village, they are more receptive towards her and share their problems. There is this sense of security and the villagers don't feel threatened".

That is what Rashmi Jatwar, 25, a resident of Bilaspur in Chhattisgarh, feels the happiest about. "During our short stint there, we interacted with the villagers. Though language was a barrier, I could see a lot of them opening up to us. They were under the impression that all security forces are evil. We had to change this perception and I think we succeeded", she says.

CRPF's special perks for Naxal areas

In a much-needed boost to the Central Paramilitary Forces engaged in fighting LW extremism in the country, Home Minister Rajnath Singh announced that personnel deployed in difficult areas will be provided special area allowance on the lineds of the one given to the Army personnel, informed a news story in a daily in Sep 2014.[22]

The Home Minister was on his maiden visit, after taking over in May this year (2014), to the Naxal-hit Jharkhand on 23 September, when he announced that the risk allowance will be admissible to the CRPF troops working in the difficult areas even during their leave period.

More significantly, he also announced that CRPF troops, engaged in flushing out the Maists from the LWE-hit areas, will be equipped with new modern hi-tech arms to fight the rebels. They will receive AK-47 rifles instead of the present INSAS (Indian Small Arms System)

Singh, on his first visit to Jharkhand as part of his pre-announced programme to tour all Maoist-hit states went to a CRPF camp at Thalkobad of West Singh bhum District in Saranda forest ares, some 120 kms from Jamshedpur. At the camp, he lauded the work of the troops in extreme conditions, and also for establishing a good rapport with the local residents and working for community development apart from providing them security. On his return from the camp, and after a high-level meet with the CM, he made a statement which is simultaveously politically correct and also a must for a Union Home Minister, given the cacaphony often saised by activist pro-Maoist lobby about huma rights issues in the Naxal-hit tribal areas:

> "I have instructed the CRPF to understand the difference between the locals and Maoists, though, they are discharging their duties responsibly."

He stressed there was no place for violence in a democratic system, appealing to the Maoists to give up violence and enter into a dialogue in order to find a solution to the problem.

On his return from the camp, the Home Minister Chaired a meeting with the CM, Hemant Soren, attanded by administrative and police and CRPF officers and Chif Advisor K Vijay Kumar, the former DG CRPF. He discussed issues related to law and order, especially LWE in the State. Subsequently talking to the media at the Raj Bhawan, Ranchi, he said the CRPF troops were working in hostile conditions in their camps but they have been able to establish a good rapport with the locals.

"CRPF plans a slew of sops for jawans posted in Naxal dens": Feb 2015

Ahead of launching a major offensive against Maoists, the CRPF planned a slew of measures to motivate jawans and officers. Besides improving service conditions, the force is likely to grant out-of-turn promotions to Non-gazetted officers for exceptional performances in the Naxal theatres.

With all out operations planned against the ultras in the core areas of the Naxals, the Force has already taken certain decision on deployment issues in such areas:limiting the numbers of years a jawan has to serve in these areas; to be offered choice postings after such a stint there; plans to set up Centre for limited Departmental Competitive Examinations (LDCE) in Bastar area in Chhattisgarh, so that the troops deployed there can be easily access the Centre without any difficulty and a proposal to grant a weightage of five marks to the troops from Naxal areas appearing for LDCE, which will be applicable once the recruitment rules are amended.

The troops who had served requisite tenure in Naxal areas, will give three areas of their choice postings and will get the one decided by the authorities and also get preferential treatment in deputation and detailing on courses in other organizations.[23]

Those deployed in the Naxal areas or the ones who had completed their stint there will not be detailed for any training courses and other promotional courses and skill enhancement courses related to the Naxal theatres.

The duration of tenures as approved is given here

- DIG 2 years
- Constable to commandant Maximum of 3 years

While DIG and commandant/second-in-command will be chosen and handpicked by the CRPF Directorate at Delhi, Deputy commandant to constables will be below 45 years of age to maintain a young profile of the force in such areas.

However, postings in these areas will not be the sole criteria for availing these incentives. These will be granted on an objective system of assessment of operational performance, to be judged on the basis of GPS logs, number of operations participated in, recoveries made in these activities and other such tangible achievements.

The CRPF has classified Narayanpur, Sukma, Bastar, Bijapur, Dantewada and Kondagaon districts of Chhattisgarh as "Core area" of Naxalism. The areas falling under these districts will be treated as Special Operational Zone for launching coordination offensive against the ultra Left Maoists.

CRPF to leave Maharashtra Red districts for Chhattisgarh: Oct 2014

To ensure seamless coordination between forces across state borders, and maintain a single command chain in any given area in the Naxal-hit zones, the government has begun the process to completely remove CRPF from Maharashtra's Maoist districts. CRPF battalions presently posted in Gadchiroli are now being moved to Bastar in Chhattisgarh to bolster force presence in the Naxal heartland. The Maharashtra district will now be manned by ITBP personnel, who are already present in the contiguous district of Rajnandgaon. The idea is to put pressure on the CPI (Maoist) which is on the backfoot owing to series of surrenders and also captures, in the recent past, say some sources.[24]

In the present arrangements, both CRPF and ITBP are present in Bastar, performing anti-LWE role. It means that two chains of command are operating in the same theatre, creating avoidable problems. The conduct of coordinated operation present unnecessary difficulties, particularly because of personality clashes, as also different functional norms of two forces of CAPF.

So, the decision to convert Gadchiroli and Bastar into a single force theatres should be welcomed.

"Rape used as a weapons against the security forces in LWE areas": Mar 2013

Of the six women of Shamsetti village in Sukma district who in 2009 gave statements in the court that they have been gang raped by Salwa Judum functionaries, three have now withdrawn their charges. Three key witnesses, family members of the women, have also retracted their statements. This was reported by a daily in March 2013.[25]

Some lawyers in Dantewada, familiar with the case, say that the women are withdrawing (the case) due to serve pressures from several quarters. "Many Salwa Judum members have now been inducted into the regular police forces as constables". The lawyers say that the remaining victims and witnesses too may appear in Court soon and retract their statements. Mamta Sharma, the chief public prosecutor at Dantewada Court, who is defending the Women, says: "It is difficult to say whether their complaints were made under pressure or the withdrawal. But the way they are turning hostile, it is a matter of time before the accused that are on bail, are set free".

The case has reached an interesting stage. The public prosecutor has made an innocuously neutral averment: she said both possibilities are there— the rape case was registered under pressure or maybe it is being withdrawn under pressure. Now the activists will make statements that the latter possibility is the truth. Conversely, the security forces would like to believe that the cases were instituted falsely, and there was a reason and an easy explanation for that! The Salwa Judum movement had been subjected to so much adverse criticism, and its members— the Special Police Officers, SPOs— so defamed tarnished and demolished, that any allegations against them would stick and be believed by the media and public.

As in most such situations, the truth lies somewhere in the middle of the two extremes. Given the situation of anti-Naxal operations and the SPOs placed and operating among the village folks, there is always chances of some of the SPOs going astray and committing offences including rape. But to paint the entire Salwa Judum force members with a broad brush of rape is patently unfair, and erring on the extreme.

When a High Court decided against the Salma Judum movement and ordered its disbandment and the Supreme Court concurred, any charged against the hapless SPOs would stick.

There are statements coming from the either side, and there is no point recording them in this text. Both sides are making set piece statements. But one thing is reasonable to say. The SPOs may not be angeles, but neither were they demons. Undoubtedly, the movement had played its part in counter-Maoist operations and one wishes they should have been allowed to continue their compaign. But the security forces are helpless against the rulings of the apex court, even if they feel that ruling will help the anti-national forces in the nation. This Author holds strong views on the subject and against the practice of the Courts intervening freely even in matters military where they may not be in a position to understand the implications of their rulings on nation's strategic interests. At least they are not most qualified to rule on the matters military! Let us leave it, at this!

Casualities in Maoist-infested states

This section will give statistics about number of casualities in India due to the Maoist insurrection, at different times in its history. All this information is from open sources.

The information on recovery of explosives and IEDs etc too will be added at an appropriate space.

Combating the Maoists: casualities 2004-2008

The Maoist's declared aim is to capture state power through violence and armed struggle. By 2008, fatalities had started climbing up, as the table shows.

"Is if indeed a crucial phase"?

"With the fight against the Naxals entering a crucial phase, the MHA announced the settings up of ten battalions (10,000 personnel) of Special Action Force under the CRPF to Combat Left Wing ultras. There are reports that the Maoists are facing a shortage of manpower. Recently the ultras had asked the tribal's to spare a son or a daughter from each family for the cause".

The above was written in May 2008. Some of factual information given there- in is correct. The CRPF was sanctioned ten additional battalions for counter-Naxal operations, which were later christened COBRA battalions. Shortage of manpower with the Maoists fighting units might have only been notionally true. As for asking a son and a daughter from each family, it is routinely done to add to their numbers, to raise new teams.

The figures of casualities in the table hereafter would not show that the counter- Naxal operations were gaining upper hand. The fatal casualties suffered by the security forces were on the rise annually starting with the year 2004. Low figures for the year 2008 (but only till 20 April) seems to have led the analyst to misinterpretation about "the fight against Naxals entering a crucial phase". Moreover, the analyst's optimism seems to have been heightened by what the DGP Vishwa Ranjan told her: "Naxalism will be finished. There is no reason why it should not when the problems in the Northeast and Punjab have ended".

Without casting any aspersions on this analyst's capabilities, one can honestly say that the DGP assertion should have been taken with certain caution, if not scepticism; all such statements are not and can't be accepted as gospel truth. This is the ultimate wish and hope of every thinking Indian. In any case, the DGP cannot state otherwise. He is heading all of the counter-Naxal forces of his State. He cannot display pessimism on the issue to a visiting journalist. And to take the point further, this DGPs successor removed by five year, said on taking over last year (2013), "I shall do everything to control and reduce Naxal menace in the State".

Death toll:J&K, NE and Real Corridor

Zone	*Year*	*Civilian*	*Security Personnel*	*Extremists*	*Total*
J and K	2004	534	325	951	1810
	2005	520	216	996	1732
	2006	349	168	599	1116
	2007	162	121	492	775
	2008 (till 20 Apr)	18	20	107	145
	Total	**1583**	**850**	**3145**	**5578**
North East	2004	352	109	371	832
	2005	332	69	314	715
	2006	218	92	317	627
	2007	453	65	488	1006
	2008 (till Apr)	130	7	145	282
	Total	**1485**	**342**	**1635**	**3462**
Naxal Corridor	2004	101	89	69	259
	2005	233	113	201	547
	2006	266	128	348	742
	2007	240	218	192	650
	2008 (Till Apr)	72	42	115	229
	Total	**912**	**590**	**926**	**2427**
Chhattisgarh	2006-08 (till Apr)	291	254	236	781

Courtsy: Counter Terrorism and Jungle Warfare College.

457

Maoist Situation: First Half of 2012: Official Assessment of Casualty Figure: Jan-Jun. 2012

In the first six months of 2012, Naxals have gunned down 82 security forces, while losing only 48 of their cadres in bloody battle, between Maoist groups and security forces, that continues unabated in the Central and eastern parts of India.[26]

Naxal violence claimed a total of 244 lives, including 162 civilians, who get dubbed as police informers. The total fatalities are a little than 301, for the same period in 2011.

While Chhattisgarh remains the main battle field, Naxal groups are enhancing their presence and influence in Odisha and Jharkhand an official assessment says. The figures for fatalities in Chhattisgarh dropped from 243 for Jan-June 2011 to 211 in same period in 2012.

The assessment says that CPI (Maoist)—the main Naxalite group that is officially banned ———has retained its core battle capabilities and its large armed contigents are able to move freely across the different zones of their influence. It acknowledge that the attacks on security forces have continued while casualties inflicted on the Maoists by the police have declined sharply.

The bright spot during this period has been the neutralisatian of Technical Research and Arms Manufacturing (TRAM) nodes of CPI(Maoist) in Kolkata and Mumbai.

It (Assessment) Says While the Security forces had been able to make major inroads into a number of previously Naxal-dominated area, the over all results in neutralizing the cadres has been less than satisfactory.

Summary

Lethal casualties: Jan to Jun 2012

Total	244
Civilians	162
Security forces	82
Maoist	48

Chhattisgarh Figures: Jan- Jun 2012/2011

2012	211
2011	243

Naxal Violence Claimed More Lives than Insurgency and Terrorism: Report Dated 22.8.12

For the third consecutive year, Naxal Violence continues to claim more lives than terrorists and insurgency incident in Jammu and Kashmir and North East.[27]

Till July 2012, LWE claimed the lives of 183 civilians and 84 security men. The corresponding figures for Jammu and Kashmir stood at 7 civilians and 6 troops respectively and in the North-East it was reported at 49 and 7 lives for same seven months. This information was given by MOS Home Jitendra Singh in a written reply to the Lok Sabha.

The maximum violent incidents, 911, were reported in Naxal- affected areas while the figures for the same were 133 for J and K and 666 for the N-E.

The similar was the case for lethalities in the year 2011 as well. If the lives lost, as per official figures, in Red Zone were at 606 (464 civilians and 142 security men) respective figures for other two areas were: J and K 64 (31 and 33) and N-E 102 (70 and 32).

In fact, 2010 was the bloodiest year in terms of lethalities in LWE areas, with 1003 lives lost.

These figures are given here in a tabular illustration for effect

Period	*Naxal-affected Areas*			*Jammu and Kashmir*			*North-East*		
	Total	*Civilians*	*Security Men*	*Total*	*Civ*	*Troops*	*Total*	*Civ*	*Troops*
Jan-Jul 2012	267	183	84	13	7	6	56	49	7
2011	606	464	142	64	31	33	102	70	32
Violent incidents Jan-Jul 2012	911	-	-	133	-	-	666	-	-

Infact, 2010 was the bloodiest year in terms of lethal casualties in LWE areas, with 1,003 lives lost.

DATA 2007 TO 2012

WEAPONS SNATCHED	
2007	233
2008	1,219
2009	217
2010	256
2011	67
2012	38

WEAPONS RECOVERED	
2007	352
2008	1,511
2009	572
2010	642
2011	636
2012	373
ARRESTS	
2007	1,456
2008	1,746
2009	1,981
2010	2,916
2011	2,030
2012	1,109

Source: The Outlook, 10 Sep 2012.

Maoist Violence Registers a New Low in 2012

Relentless Counter-insurgency operations taken up in all Naxal-hit States seem to have had a desired impact, as the Maoist violence registered a record low in 2012 in the last 6-year period.

The downward trend in violence is indicative of how the security forces have succeeded in pushing the Maoists revolution into a strategic equilibrium stage. Another possibility for this could be an unannounced tactical retreat from some areas by Maiosts themselves to protect their cadre from the military operations.

This success put tremendous responsibility on civil administration in the Maoist-affected States to speed up the development works, though security experts caution that forces must not slip into complacency.

The success or failure of counter-insurgency operations is gauged in terms of rise or fall in number of violence incidents perpetrated by Maoists.

In 2012, there were 1,365 incidents of violence by Maoists in nine States. Maoists guerrillas killed 409 persons (296 civilians and 113 security personnel).

This is a record low in the last seven years with the death toll standing at 611 in 2011, 1,005 in 2010, 908 in 2009, 721 in 2008, 696 in 2007, according to the MHA statistics.

Interestingly, Jharkhand has overtaken Chhattisgarh in Maoists killing in 2012. Out of total of 409 killings in 2012, Jharkhand accounted for 160 deaths followed by Chhattisgarh (107), Odessa (45), Bihar (43), Maharashtra (41), and Andhra Pradesh (13).

A possible reason for this surge of violence in Jharkhand could be the decision of the Maoist leadership to strengthen base, while maintaining low profile in Chhattisgarh, where security forces are making inroads into the otherwise impregnable Bastar forests.

"This could mean Maoists are heightening the violence in various other States in a sustained and determined bid to spread security forces thin" said PV Ramana, senior fellow at the IDSA.

Intelligence inputs culled from various sources indicate that there is an element of despondency among Maoist strategists with their States units unable to recuit youth into the revolutionary movement.

The inputs also speak of the Maoist urban network being disrupted.

Current scenario reflects a situation where the security forces are establishing their stronghold in plain areas, while making gradual inroads in Maoist bastions in Bihar, Jharkhand, Odisha, Chhattisgarh and Maharashtra, says a senior intelligence officer.

Security Personnnel Casualties 2008-june 2014[29]

Total toll across 9 LWE states	1,267
Killed in IED blasts	447
Killed in gun battles	256

BIHAR

Seized: 7,500 kg of explosives and 228 IEDs

JHARKHAND

Seized: Highest seizure if 1,200 kg of explosives from Jharkhand.

TOTAL RECOVERY IN 2013

Explosives	9,500 kg
IEDs	900

TILL JUNE 2014

CRPF has recovered more than 2,000 kg of explosives

Casualty Figures: First Decade of 21st Century

Civilian Fatalities	4,918
Security men fatalities	1,905

Source: MHA Figures, Quoted in Terms of India 27.6.14.

No of Casualties upto 15 Sep 2014

• No. of incidents	786
• No. of civilians killed	163
• No. of security forces killed	68
• No. of Maoists killed	49

Source: The Patriot, 18 Oct 2014.

Anti-maoist Operations by CRPF: Data Till Mid- Nov 2014

• Force killed (Maoists)	23
• Apprehended	835
• Surrenders	126

Losses Suffered by CRPF: Till Mid Nov 2014

• Lives lost	35
• Injured	93
• Weapons	17
• Ammunition rounds	1,610

The Above Losses Suffered in

- 824 Operations Conducted in LWE-hit States
- These operations include 152 encounters

  Four Ambushes

  28 IED Blasts

  13 attacks on camps/posts

Recoveries Made by CRPF in the Same Period (Till Mid- November 2014) in Lwe Theatre

• Arms	475
• Ammunition rounds	11,000
• Explosives	11,224 kg
• Grenades	175
• Bombs	283
• IEDs	371
• Detonators	4,400
• Gelantine sticks	800
• Narcotics	7,600 kg
• Cash	Rs 51.67 lakh

Civilians Face Maximum Brunt: Official Figures

This very informative article appeared in a daily[30] and it was the MHA that provided all the data in response to an application under the Right to Information Act, 2005. Effort will be to give the data in tabular form, and any important observations or conclusions will be found in the words of the article, as far as possible.

Civilians have been the biggest casualty due to the Naxal violence, during the last three decades, 1980-June 2013. As many as 11,742 civilians have been killed in Naxal violence, followed by 4,638 fatalities suffered by the rebels and 2,947 by the security forces in this period.

Attrition of security forces has been maximum during the UPA I and UPA II regimes, with almost two-thirds of the deaths being recorded from 2004 to mid 2013. A substantial 1,797 security men were killed by the Naxals during this period.

Likewise, 40 per cent of the casualties suffered by the civilians were recorded during the UPA period (2004-mid 2013). But only one- third of the Naxals killed from 1980-June 2013 were recorded during the UPA regimes.

Casualties suffered by the security forces have registered an upward spiral from 2005 onwards, as can be seen from the table here.

Security Forces: Fatalities Suffered: 2005 Onwards

2005	153
2006	157
2007	236
2008	231
2009	317
2010	285
[Partially Contained after 2010]	
2011	142
2012	114
2013 (Till June)	62

UPA regime also registered the maximum number of civilian casualties in 2010 with 720 deaths. Between 2004 and 2012, an average of about 500 people were killed every year.

Maximum number of Naxalites were killed in 1998 with 296 deaths Significant liquidation was also recorded in some other years, as is seen in the table here.

Maoists Killed 1992 Onwards

1992	285
1996	187
1997	187
1998	296 (Highest)
1999	261
2000	254
2001	182
2003	214
2005	225
2006	274
2009	220

Comments by the author on a misplaced averment

"A senior official suggest that core capabilities of the Maoists have not only remained intact but have 'improvised' their lethality over the years by inflicting more and more casualties on security force personnel, trained in counter-insurgency"

This para seems to be a favourite with this reporter (Rakesh K Singh) to end his articles with. Comments follow on this SILLY fixation and other negative aspects Reporter Singh and boss of the daily he reports for.

- The Hindu is a great daily but for its biases in favour India's Left Liberal Lobby. But that is understandable! Knowing well that the Hindu's effective boss still is N. Ram, its editor till some years back. After all, once he was a card holder Communist. Even though, he is no more its editor, Hindu's Left-leanings are there for everyone to see.
- "Core capabilities have remained imtact." This inspite of the evidence to the contrary. Security forces lethalities have been shown till June 2013, but Maoist fatalities end up with year 2009. Why? Obviously, these figure will go against his pet averment. Being a sympathiser, he can bear to see Maoists losing their erst-while success.
- What is the meaning of the term " improvised" (their lethality..... by inflicting more and more casualties on the security forces...." As the table shows, figure for 2012 is 114 ! Why this self- serving untruth, Mr. Ram?

- Where and how are the 'core capabilities' remaining intact, in view of the facts given below:
  1. Maoist supremo has written a desperate letter to his commanders to get the Maoists, languishing in jail, out of them.
  2. Mid-level leaders are surrendering in large number.
  3. Recruitment is not keeping pace with attrition in its ranks.
  4. Several senior leaders and mid-level leaders have been arrested and consigned to the jails.
  5. Maoist technical experts have been arrested, ammunition factories decimated and research teams disappeared.
- The reporter invariably quotes a "senior official" to attribute this baloney to!
- N. Ram cannot bear to see his favourites(the Maoists) losing the battle!

Fatal Casualties in Naxal Violence: 1980 to June 2013

Civilians killed	11,742
Maoist rebels killed	4,638
Security men killed	2,947

Some Facts Pertaining to the UPA (I&II) Years 2004-2013

- Attrition of security forces was maximum during the UPA regimes period, with almost two-third of the deaths recorded thence 1,797 of a total of 2,947 (1980-mid 2013) were killed by the Naxals during the period.
- Likewise, 40 per cent of the civilian lethalities were recorded during UPA regimes period.
- But of the total of 4,638 Naxals killed from 1980 to mid 2013, only one-third were recorded during the UPA years.

Comparative Figures: Internal Security; Terrorism, Naxalism and North-east Rebels 2004-2005

India presently faces internal security challenges from three quarters. It is considered useful that all three are presented to the reader in comparative terms. The figures are taken from a daily[31] of 23 Apr 2014. It is given under the headline:

"The India Index: 2004-14." The data will follow in one table after brief description of each of the there types of challenges the nation faces. These figures are from the MHA.

Terrorism

Deaths due to terrorism peaked in 2005-06 with the emergence of Indian Mujahideen in 2005 leading to a string of terror attacks and subsequent emergence of Hindu terror groups that carried out retaliatory attacks. The period 2008-09 too saw high casualties, largely accounted for by 26/11 attacks in Mumbai orchestrated by Lashkar-e-Toiba, besides blasts in Delhi, Ahmedabad, Surat and Malegaon. The last four years have seen a steady decline in terrorism-related deaths.

Naxal Violence

This surged in 2009-10, when CPI(Maoist) was banned. The Prime Minister described Naxals as the biggest internal security. In 2011-13, the government deployed a large number of security forces in Naxal hit States but the violence continued. Naxals carried out one of their most audacious attacks in 2013 when they ambushed a Congress Convoy and decimated most of their leadership, including the bravest of them all, Mahendra Karma, considered the progenitor of Salma Judum movement.

THE NORTH EAST

This is one area where the government has scored, with violence in the region gradually decreasing, with more and more insurgent groups having given up arms and come to talks. Security forces have arrested large number of leaders while the NIA has attached the properties of terror groups, breaking their backs.

THE INDIA INDEX: 2004-14

LETHAL COUNT

YEAR	*Civilians*			*Forces*			*Terrorist/Naxals/Rebels*		
	Terrorism	*Naxal*	*NE*	*Terrorism*	*Naxal*	*NE*	*Terrorism*	*Naxal*	*NE*
2004	884	-	-	433	-	-	1321	-	-
2005	1,213	280	336	438	152	68	1,609	284	315
2006	1,115	267	233	390	129	94	1,263	344	315
2007	1,012	245	458	405	215	69	1,194	190	512
2008	1,032	221	404	374	215	42	1,219	216	605
2009	723	390	272	432	311	42	1,082	296	543
2010	760	627	78	370	278	23	774	279	225
2011	428	274	80	195	130	37	452	200	135
2012	252	145	92	139	108	19	410	119	210
2013	304	160	99	193	111	24	389	152	138

Source: All figures are from Ministry of Home Affairs as reported in the Indian express of 23 Apr 2014.

"Maoist Violence on the Decline: Jul 2014

"West Bengal, Bihar, Jharkhand and Andhra Pradesh Show Sharp Decline in Violence."

This seems to be an optimistic analytical story on Maoists in a weekly of 27 July 2014.[32] The blurb gives broad details.

It opens up with a claim that the Centre's fight against Maoists have started paying dividend's, with a substantial decline in ultra left violence during the last two to three years, particularly in the States named in the blurb.

The figures provided by the LWE Division of the MHA shows incidents related to Maoist violence has come down to almost half during the last five years. If there were 2,258 incidents in 2009, claiming 908 lives (including those of security forces), the number came down to 1,136 in 2013, claiming 397 lives. MOS Home Kiran Rijiju informed the Rajya Sabha that till 11 July 2014, 188 people have lost their lives in Maoist related violence.

West Bengal is a success story. It witnessed just one Maoist incident with no casualt, against 255 incidents in 2009 which cost 158 lives. D Suba Chandra, dirtector, Institute of Peace and Conflict Studies (IPCS), made balanced observations: "This is a positive trend which indicates that the fight against LWE is paying off. But we will have to wait for some more time to see if this trend is sustained."

A senior police officer involved in anti-LWE operations in Jharkhand also made some realistic comment to the weekly: "There has been substantical decline in Maoist activity. Though there is still a long way to go, but the recent trends are quite encouraging. Unlike earlier years, the morale of security forces is quite high. But we know, however, that the Maoists are down but not out."

Encouraged by this partial success, Home Minister Rajnath Singh clarified recently that there was "no question of talks with the Maoists" and Government would take a balanced approach and forces will give a befitting reply if they launch attacks." Experts see three reasons behind this decline: massive and sustained security operations; growing disenchantment with Maoist ideology and development works in Maoist-infested areas. An officer explains, "The new officers in the CRPF, the main force leading the counter-Maoist battle, are mentally very strong and fast learners."

A MP from Maoist-infested area of Jharkhand, Ghatshila, explains: "Maoists support among people is also waning. So far they thrived on the anti-State sentiment. But now there are feelings that the Maoists are not the alternatives. People may be anti-government, but they are not pro-Maoists. Thus the Maoists are losing local support." He added further that "holding panchayat elections too has empowered the people at the grassroots. Special funds for the development of Maoist-infested areas are reaching the people, who can see the change."

Under the Saranda Action Plan, the government has been able to start development work in Saranda forest on the borders of West Bengal, Odisha and Jharkhand with an investment of Rs 429 crore.

Factionalism within CPI (maoist)

Factionalism within the party can be one major reason behind the weakening of their movement. The Commitment level of the cadre does not seem to be high. Add personal ambitions of some mid-level leaders to these factors, and you have an easy explanation for creation of so many factions within the Maoist ranks, e.g., People's Liberation Front of India (PLFI), Jharkhand Prastuti Committee (JPC) and Jharkhand Liberation Tigers (JLT).

The Remaining Problem

However, Chhattisgarh, Jharkhand and Bihar still remains a Challenge for the Country. Chandra of the IPCS has a word of advice on the issue: "There is a need to maintain consistency as far as operations and development works are concerned. The government has to occupy the space which was taken over by the Maoists over the years. The Centre must also ensure that the States do not divert the funds, meant for tackling problems created by the Maoists, to other works, which generally happens."

Comment on this Articles

This author has included a variety of analytical articles for discussion in this book. Some of these are anti-government, some are balanced and this one obviously is optimistic in viewing the counter-Maoist operations launched by the Central forces. But the fact remains that Maoists are certainly not out, there is a lot of work yet to be done to gain upper hand in the three remaining States, and More Impotantly, the Government of India and the CRPF must not permit any sense of complacency in their, minds, well aware as we are about the Maoists capacity to wait and watch, lie low, rearm and regroup and return with vigour to regain lost ground.

Having said the above, it is only wise to add a note of caution: inspite of all the losses suffered by them, large scale surrenders and many senior leaders in the jail, India is nowhere near any effective solution to this LWE movement! It is a long haul yet and there is no reason to lower their guards.

TABLE RELATED TO MAOIST VIOLENCE

Below is reproduced a table from this article in the weekly.

Maoist violence : 5 years apart				
	2009		***2013***	
States	***Incidents***	***Deaths***	***Incidents***	***Deaths***
AP	66	18	36	11
Bihar	232	72	177	69
Chhattisgarh	529	290	355	111
Jharkhand	742	208	387	152
MP	1	0	1	0
Maharashtra	154	93	71	19
Odisha	266	67	101	35
UP	8	2	0	0
WB	255	158	1	0

Source: LWE Division, MHA.

"12,062 Have Been Killed In Naxal Violence Since 1980": RTI

Here is yet again, some fresh information received in reply to a question filed under RTI rules by a Meerut based activist Lokesh Khurana, as reported in a daily of 22 Jan 2015.[33]

The MHA revealed in its reply that a total of 12,062 civilians have been killed in Naxal violence since 1980. Interestingly, when the Naxalite movement began in India, only three States were affected—Andhra Pradesh, Bihar and West Bengal. But by 2014, eight States had been dragged into it.

While in 1980, 70 people had died in the violence, the number, 720, was far higher in 2010. The reply also mentions that 3,078 security men were injured in the Naxal-related violence in the last 34 years (1980-2014), the MHA did not disclose the number of lethalities in the security forces during these 34 years.

Khurana, who had filed the RTI querry on 4 Dec 2014, had asked information on the ten points: the number of citizens killed in these 34 years; number of security personnel killed; administrative efforts to contain Naxalities; reasons for the rise and spread of the naxalite movement and the annual expenditure incurred on security measures and operations in Naxalite-affected areas. The MHA only gave details of number of civilian deaths and security personnel injured."

Let it be, at the end, stated that the daily Hindu got much more detailed information on Maoist rebellion, particularly on the data on year-wise lethalities. One cannot understand the query by Khurana about reasons for the Maoist uprising, which can be varied and never precise. The MHA cannot be expected to tread in that speculative field.

"Has Cobra Lost its Bite?": June 2014

A weekly carried an article on COBRA battalions in June 2014, under the headline, "CoBRA loses bite." This assertive headline has equally negative blurb: "The elite force formed to eliminate Naxals has become a victim of its own failings."[34]

Its contents needs to be studied seriously. What follows are excerpts and summary of its Contents as found in the article.

The MHAs approves a proposal Friday, 12 Sep 2008 to set up a new commando force to fight Naxals. The Plan was to recruit and raise 10,000 strong elite force that could infiltrate the Naxal areas in small groups, in the manner of guerrilla fighters for counter-Maoist operations. Home Minister P Chidambaram handpicks K Durga Prasad, the man credited with success of the Greyhounds, the commando force that crushed Naxals in Andhra Pradesh, to head the force, Christened COBRA (Commando Battalion for Resolute Action). It was to be raised as part of the CRPF.

The Commando are trained in the art of camouflage and jungle warfare, they feel comfortable in jungle, they learn how to catch and eat snakes.

The nerve centre of the COBRA force is set up in Delhi, where Prasad and his team studiously monitor the role and operations of every COBRA battalion posted in Naxal areas. For reasons understandable, the raising of this special force was greeted with great fanfare and high hopes.

Six years later, the MHA's own assessment says COBRA is making little progress in its mission. An officer from MHA who was member of the founding team, is candid : "The elite force was our best hope....But, somehow, the whole idea behind raising a special force is not working."

COBRA has become ineffective largely because of lack of cooperation from the States, and the over all failure of its parent force, the CRPF, in its counter-Maoist combat role, in the Red Corridor, which covers one-fourth of India's landmass. The worst Naxal-hit states, Chhattisgarh and Jharkhand, suffer frequent attacks from the Maoists, and COBRA units are of no help. Despite their munitions and numbers, the COBRA's have failed to curb Maoist violence. Every COBRA battalion has 35 men in its intelligence wing, still their record of creating intelligence inputs is poor. The number of arrests and weapon recoveries has declined. "Worse, there has been a steady weakening in the will of the commandos to tackle the Naxal problem."

The MHA data shows at least one security troop loses his life to Maoists every three days since 2008, Maoists have killed 1,204 security men and 1,109 so-called police informers.

The COBRAs themselves have lost 27 commandos in different operations. Some key reforms, including plans for auxiliary training schools, conceived by DGCRPF Vijay Kumar himself, have been abandoned. At least eight of 16 such schools in the country were shut down last years (2013).

Even as Naxals became more lethal in Chhattisgarh, the MHA data shows Naxal activities in Jharkhand at an all-time high. Today more lives are lost in Naxal violence in Jharkhand than in Chhattisgarh. In the past two years alone, there have been 863 Naxal attacks in Jharkhand, accounting for 254 civilians, 59 security men and 19 Naxals.

"The elite force is not up to the mark" reads an internal assessment report of the MHA.

IG V S Yadav, who heads the force, refused any comment. What has complicated COBRA operations is the lack of something as basic as telecommunication facilities. The MHA is miffed with the Department of Telecommunications and Bharat Sanchar Nigam Ltd for going slow on a crucial communication project of constructing 2,199 mobile towers in Chhattisgarh, Jharkhand and Odisha. Commandos complain that a major operation in Chhattisgarh had to be cancelled since they were unable to communicate with the HQ from deep forest positions.

Many COBRA commandos have complaints about the poor quality of their infra-red monoculars, so essential for night visions. Then, the MHA officials admit the Commandos are over stretched. The first two battalions were raised in 2008. Four more were raised in 2009, and another four in 2010. Instead of focusing on one area or one States, these 10,000 personnel were deployed across vast areas in seven states. As if that was not enough, a battalion was deployed in Assam to fight militants.

Dr Bibhu Prasad Routray, once Dy Director in the NSC Secretariat, says: "There is little doubt that the COBRA is a well-trained commando force. However, commandos do not come with a God-given gift to succeed. They need an enabling environment to be successful—its key components being clear headed policy, intelligence and leadership. On most occasions, there is an acute lack of all three."

He compared COBRA commandos with the Greyhounds of Andhra Pradesh Police: "The latter had done exceedingly well in Andhra but received setbacks in States like Odisha, where intelligence network of the police is comparatively poor."

To crush the Naxals, Andhra adopted a well-coordinated model where-in the men on the ground, such as the Superintendent of police, had operational freedom. The State's 1B, which has acquired sophisticated communication interception technology, gathers information about Naxal leaders and their activities, which is swiftly passed on to the cops. Such command structure and coordination is missing with the COBRAs.

"Neither the Cobra nor the CRPF has interception capability," said K. Srinivasan, former IG of BSF who was hired by the CRPF in 2009 as consultant to raise its intelligence wing . "In other words, the success of our operations is completely dependent on the inputs we receive from other agencies." According to him, building of an intelligence network remains a top priority of the paramilitary forces to deal with internal security challenges. "Without precise and actionable intelligence, no commando operation can be successful", said Srinivasan.

The initial plan was to set up cobra headquarters in Andhra Prasad. Durga Prasad, who now heads the special Protection Group, was keen to have the elite force stationed in the State, said a MHA official, who was part of the founding team. An anti- insurgency expert, Prasad had a reputation as an operations man. The idea of having the force stationed in Andhra Pradesh was to facilitate better supervision and monitoring. But the headquarters was finally set up in Delhi. Soon, the commandos were deployed across the states, in places far from district headquarters. Coordination with the Cobra headquarters in Delhi became impossible. Deep inside Naxal areas, the commandos had to realise that they had to spend more time and energy to protect their own camps.

"After we raised first two battalions and deployed them in Chhatisgarh and Odisha, our immediate challenge was to protect our base camps.... It would have been a big embarrassment if our camps were attacked and looted by Naxals," explained former IGP KV Madhusudhanan who served as the first DIG of the Cobra. Despite all the challenges, CRPF raised a formidable special force. "The Cobras went to areas which were claimed by Naxals as liberated Zones. We made some very good breakthroughs," said Madhusudhanan.

But as the Maoist insurgency grew, so did the divisions in the government how to confront it. The differences between states and the central government was so visible that in the early 2010, the so-called Operation Green Hunt against Naxals became a media spectacle.

The problem has also been that Naxals are distinct from other insurgent groups. As many as 80 per cent of Naxals are tribals and farmers. Armed Naxals form only 20 per cent and are not easy to identify. Even when the enemy is identified, the Cobra faces serious command structure problems. Through a Delhi-based officer of the rank of IG heads the Cobra, operations in each state is often led by the I G of the CRPF, who does not function under the Cobra chief. The Cobra chief, therefore, remains primarily an administrator. Another difficulty is that, under the Constitution, law and order is the responsibility of state governments. So the national policy of dealing with the Naxals has been inconsistent.

The lack of coordination often results in terrible losses, such as one on March (2014), when Naxals ambushed a security patrol in a daring day time attack in Sukma district in Chhattisgarh, killing 16 people, including 11 CRPF troopers. After the attack, HS Sidhu, CRPF IG in Chhattisgarh, blamed the police for blocking a "massive operation" in Bastar that could have prevented it.

By 2011, it was clear that command and control of the Cobra had to be revised to make it more effective. The guidelines of the then D G CRPF Vijay Kumar were clear: the Cobras will not conduct traditional police activities. Instead their focus will be on gathering intelligence and conducting swift catch-and-kill operations. Kumar also instructed each company commander that instead of a 100- man-team, the commandos should move in smaller groups.

To give boost to his men, Kumar joined the Cobras in a major operation in Abujhmaad in Chhattisgarh, a 4000 sqkm area which the Naxals had dubbed a liberated zone. He trekked the tough terrain and stayed with the men. A commando recalls about this opeartion: "when we entered (the area), we were told that the last official who visited Abujh Maad did so some 25 years ago….. we broke the myth that nobody can challenge Naxals in Abujh Maad. It was the great operation."

The challenges of carrying out deep forest operations are many. For instance, in a major operation in Saranda region in Jharkhand, nearly 400 CRPF and Cobra personnel contracted malaria. Said an officer: "It was like the plague. Every second person in the battalion had malaria."

The Cobras, however, were able to push out the Naxals from Saranda and many other areas of Jharkhand and Chhattisgarh. But the things were virtually reversed in the past two years. With the security forces unable to hold captured areas, the Naxals re-emerged and spread out. So, the second rung of Chidambram edict "clear, hold and develop" was not stuck to!

According to the latest assessment report by the joint intelligence Committee (JIC), trouble is now brewing in Bihar. In a hurried response, some 200 cobra commandos were despatched early this year (2014). " They would now have to decide whether to go after the Naxals or to protect politicians. If the past experiences are anything to go buy, it is not an easy decision."

Cobras: The Problems they Face

The Cobra is a commando force formed in 2008 to tackle Naxal insurgency. Presently, 10 battalions comprising 10,000 men are deployed across Naxal-hit areas in seven states. The Cobra has struggled to combat for several reasons. Some issues are explained here.

Intelligence Void

Despite having 35 intelligence personnel in every battalion, the Cobra has no intelligence network in place.

No Cellphone

A crucial communication project to install 2,199 mobile towers in Naxal-hit states by June 2014 is hanging fire. Only 363 towers have been installed so far.

No Interceptors

The Cobra wanted telecom interceptor capability to listen to Naxal communication. The MHA, however, said 'No' saying Central intelligence agencies can share information with the Force.

Parallel Command

The Cobra chief functions primarily as an administrator. Operations are led by CRPF IG.

Overstretched

With 10,000 commandos deployed in seven States, the Cobra is spread too thin.

Ill-used

Cobras were trained to fight Naxals, but many of them are doing traditional cop duties like patrolling streets.

Night Blind

More than half of the infrared monoculars issued to the commados do not work.

"THE TRAITOR INSIDE" : Apr 2007

This is the title of an article carried by a weekly in Apr 2007. If the headline is damning, the blurb clarifies the reasons: "It is clear—somebody is passing counter-insurgency plans to ultras".[35]

The opening paragraph is explicit: "How did the Maoist operating from the hills and dense forests of Chhattisgarh, Bihar and Andhra Pradesh access the minutes of the two crucial and secret meetings last year (2006) – one held by the Prime Minister at his residence and the other chaired by the Home Secretary at North Block? Both were focused on tackling the Maoist problem. The first was attended by Chief Ministers of Naxal- hit states and by senior intelligence and security officials. The second, which involved members of the Joint operations Command of the security forces, dealt with strategy and deployment of forces."

The shocking truth surfaced during a recent operation when intelligence officials stumbled upon an eight page annual report (Oct 2005-06) of the MCC. An explosive part of its contents, yet to be revealed to the media, relates to the outfit's precise and detailed knowledge about what was discussed in these two high-profile and closed-door meetings.

Here is what their annual report says about the secret meeting of Apr 2006, held at 7, Race Coarse Road, Chaired by PM Manmohan singh: " It is clear from the minutes of the 13 April meeting that the government is planning to infiltrate our ranks and use air power in otherwise difficult and inaccessible terrains. The decisions at the meeting include penetration by intelligence agencies into Maoist leadership, use of heliborne operations against the Naxalites hiding in the forests of Kaimur hills, and training of the select paramilitary personnel in jungle warfare."

The second meeting, held on 29 Aug 2006, was chaired by the then Home Secretary VK Duggal. It discussed : details of deployment of security forces; steps to improve intelligence gathering and sharing it among various states; ways to curb Maoist operations in border areas and disrupt their coordination across inter-state borders. All these details were passed on to the Maoists. The conclusion of the report shows at all these decisions were factored there-in: "We have to be careful, Don't stay at one place for too long. Keep moving. Do not forget your tasks and do not forget your aim."

That the Maoist could lay their hands on two top secret meetings of Government of India should be matter of serious concern for the MHA and the counter-intelligence agencies of the nation. That they could get the minutes within a few months should be even more alarming. The security officials feel this could be one of the main reasons for not very successful counter-Maoist operations!

Even if only main points from the two meetings are found reflected in the annual report, Indian officials fear that finer details too might have reached the Maoists. Officials say it does not help the Naxals reveal all they know, but a subtle message has been conveyed to India that they know what all transpired at the two secret meetings.

The annual report brought out in Sep 2006 was updated till the 29 Aug meeting. A meeting, held next, was on 5 Sep 2006, again chaired by the PM. So, intelligence officers believe "we should proceed on the assumption that the details of that meeting too are with the Maoists".

As for the source of the leakage, there three are possibilities: from the Centre itself; the officials of the participating states; and the security and intelligence agencies. One can take one's pick, till the culprits are identified. Expectedly, the MHA wrote to those states " to ensure there is no leakage of the confidential information at their end."

The MCC report also lists the mining, irrigation and industrial projects it plans to target in Bihar, Chhattisgarh, Jharkhand, MP and Andhra Pradesh. Maoist have plans to create "Red terror" in Sitamarhi district of Bihar where the Kosi irrigation project is coming up. "The region needs attention not only for opposing government machinery but also for mobilising mass support."

The other sites on the Naxal hit list are: proposed bauxite mines of Jindals near Visakhapatnam; Polavaram irrigation project in Andhra Pradesh; projects of Tata's, Jindals and Essar in Chhattisgarh; the Rajghara Raoghat-Jagdalpur rail line; steel plants of Posco and Tatas in Odisha; power plants of Reliance; and ongoing Narmada projects in MP.

The rest of the report list several successful operations, latest weapons acquired by them like AK-47$_s$ and SLR launchers, in recent times. There is a mention of expanding operations to urban areas in Haryana, Uttrakhand, UP and Delhi of course, the intelligencies already know these plans. What is vital are the details of the two meetings. It is obvious "the Maoists are one step ahead of the government."

The weekly feels the MHA is so embarrassed that no inquiry has been ordered in the leak. But intelligencies are looking into this issue to determine the likely source/s. Many in the MHA feel it is important to identify them if counter-Naxal operations are to succeed.

Central Forces Find it tough to Battle Attrition, Suicides: Nov 2011

This alarming headline appeared in a daily in Nov 2011. Besides the Maoists, the forces are fighting the battles within.[36]

It is an alarming situation the Central Paramilitary Forces (CPMFs) are confronted with. They are not only witnessing an alarming attrition rate—over 850 persons are leaving the forces every month on an average so far this year (till Oct 2011)— but also suicides by its personnel, with 10 cases being reported every month.

As many as 8,550 CPMF troops opted for Voluntary Retirement Scheme (VRS), with maximum from the BSF (4,852), followed by CRPF (2,128). Regarding suicides, CRPF tops the list among six CPMFs , with 38 of its troops committing it so far, followed by BSF (36).

VRS Cases in other Forces: Assam Rifles,758; Sashastra Seemebal (SSB), 329; ITBP, 253 and CISF, 231.

In a written reply to a Lok Sabha question on 21 November, MOS Home Jitendra Singh, however said: " only few Central Armed Police Force personnel took VRS. Generally, CAPF troops have cited personal/domestic problems for seeking voluntary retirement." CAPF is another term for CPMF.

Singh sought to assert that certain measures have been taken to deal with the situation: a transparent leave policy; revamping of grievances redressal machinery; and increased risk, hardship and other allowances.

Other measures to check growing attrition include Yoga classes for better stress management; recreational and sports facilities; provision of STD telephone facilities; and medical and canteen facilities.

The cases of VRS, suicide and fratricide (=killing colleagues in one's own unit) are tabulated here.

Data for 2011: Jan to Oct			
Force	***VRS***	***Suicide***	***Fratricide***
CRPF	2,128	38	3
BSF	4,852	36	2
SSB	329	11	2
CISF	231	10	1
AR	758	8	1
ITBP	252	4	-
NSG	-	2	-

The MOS said "the causative factors in most cases were personal and domestic problems like marital discord, personal enmity, mental illness and depression among others and were not related to the force as such".

"Attrition in CPMF Dropped Below 10,000": Mar 2015

It obviously is a bit of good news for CPMF, reported a daily, in Mar 2015. The blurb explains the reasons behind the good story: "slew of steps for anti-Red Forces stops resignations."[37] The source, for the data is MHA, source tells the daily.

It be noted the news story immediately preceding this one is also on the subject of attrition, as also on suicide, though separated by four year's span.

The daily tells us thanks to a host of measures taken by the government to ease pressure on security forces battling the Maoist and also positive expectations from the 7th Pay Commission, lesser number of members of these CPMFs are hanging up their boots. For the first time in the last five years, the Cumulative annual attrition from the CPMF has dropped below 10,000.

The latest MHA figures say, in 2014, only 7,700 odd personnel quit various CAPF as against over 11,000 in 2013 and 13,000 in 2012.

Sources attribute these positive changes to measures taken by the government (both UPA and NDA) to ease the hardship of these forces combating the Maoists, as also because of expectations of better remunerations from the 7th Pay Commission, whose report is due in 2016. In simple terms, some who were planning VRS have postponed till report is out.

Between 2009 and 2012, over 44,000 personnel had quit these forces either through resignations or by opting for VRS. During this period, more CPMF troops committed suicide (398) than those who died fighting the Maoists (328). The government got so alarmed that it hired the services of 11M- Ahmedabad to study the issue and come up with remedies.

Attrition from CRPF and BSF, which face tough working conditions has dropped significantly.

The relevant data is tabulated here.

Forces	*Attrition through VRS and Resignations*				
	2010	***2011***	***2012***	***2013***	***2014***
CRPF	3,134	2,739	5,943	4,492	2788
BSF	5,625	5,081	3,966	4,020	2,583
CISF	1,418	1,088	1,653	1,626	1,043
ITBP	553	351	468	493	404
SSB	616	464	568	470	364
AR	755	624	406	551	523
Total	**12,101**	**10,347**	**13,004**	**11,652**	**7,705**

Source: The MHA, New Delhi.

"Borrowing from more Efficient Minister beyond India Borders": Dec 2014

This Author was reading an article in Dec 2014 in an Indian daily,[38] reproduced here from the Economist. It does not have much to do with India, as it was on America's Next Defence Secretary Ashton Carter, who would replace Chuck Hagel.

Here follow some excerpts, chosen at random for their intrinsic value for any country that wants an effective, assertive, and a bit-of-an-intellectual executive to head their Defence Ministry:

> "He will replace Chuck Hagel, a decorated veteran with a profound aversion to the ill-considered use of force. Mr Hagel, a Republican, was inarticulate, flummoxed by detail and floundered in the job, particularly when faced with the complex challenge of taking on the Islamic State in Syria and Iraq.
>
> "Insiders praise Carter's competence and experience. A physicist by training, he was Deputy Defence Secretary under Leon Panetta, responsible for controlling a $600 billion annual defence budget. Such was his in-dispensability that Mr. Obama asked him to continue in the job for a year after Mr. Panetta left in 2013, to help Mr. Hagel—an uncomfortable period for both men.
>
> "Before that Mr Carter was the head of acquisitions, restructuring the bloated Joint Strike Fighter (JSF) programme and cancelling costly, under performing or outdated programmes.
>
> "Soldiers in the field called him "the deliverer," for his ability to cut through the Pentagon's copious red tape and get urgently needed kit to

the front line, SUCH AS MRAPs (mine-resist ambush-protected vehicles) to protect TROOPS FROM ROAD SIDE BOMBS.

"In Bill Clinton's first administration, Mr Carter was incharge of America's Vast nuclear arsenal and led the effort to dismantle and remove more than 8,000 nuclear weapons from the states that had been part of the old soviet Union.

"Some complain that Mr Carter's intellectual confidence and command of the most esoteric technical details can make him appear arrogant or aloof, but his confirmation hearings on the Capitol Hill should be much easier than the grilling Mr Hagel received.

"Ashton Carton once urged the pre-emptive bombing of North Korea's nuclear facilities. (it was in an article he wrote in 2006, while out of office). He also wanted American troops to stay on in Iraq after 2011. Yet Obama, who is hardly known for his hawkishness, has nominated him as Defence Secretary.

Many may not see the relevance of the above excerpts from the said articles in the Indian context. There are just two aspects which are emphasized here to explain the inclusion of the same.

- Mainly, it was to give the glimpse here the way US polity works, how their ministers are appointed. How a Democratic President can have a Republican as his Defence Secretary.
- Yet again, the aim was to show how a live-wire Minister can deliver. An intellectually-gifted minister need not be a misfit in the system.
- The sole aim for this Author, an Iufantry officer of the Indian Army, is to show how an American cares for the lives of soldiers and get them MRAPs! How one yearns for a go-getter of Carter's Indian counter part to equip the Indian Army, in particular its infantry arm, with anti-mine equipment so that the foot soldiers do not lose their lives on the cheap. The equipment also includes bullet proof vests. Coming to counter-Naxal operations, which we are dealing with presently, how one wishes CAPFs/CPMFs also get their Indian Carter so that they can not only achieve better results but also do not lose precious lives of their fighting comrades, just because their commanders and the Nation did not equip them adequately against the pressure mines of many variety!

"Malaria Outbreak Hits Anti-Naxal Ops" : NOV 2013

An outbreak of malaria in Bastar was reported in a daily in Nov 2014, "which has seriously impacted the security forces on the counter-Naxal front. During the last 10 days of Nov 2014, at least one policeman Govind Tamga died and another 400 were affected by the disease. Beside the troops, huge number of civilians were also hit.[39]

The situation is compounded due to lack of medicare in the Bastar region, and it has only one major hospital. The male ward of the hospital is brimming over and some "50 men of the state police and the CRPF have to lie on the floor." Bastar IGP SRP killuri asked the state government for immediate help to the patients.

Such was the impact of this disease that at least two counter-Naxal operations in the region "had to be aborted last week," as the troops were hit by the disease in forests, forcing the commandant to order immediate retreat.

Bastar's Malaria officer Sanjay Basak said the sudden outbreak is a serious issue, adding: "So far we are giving them chloroquine and primaquine for the malaria, but these have proved ineffective. Some other medicines are being administered on the advice of the WHO."

Some policemen in acute condition were evacuated to Raipur, but 200 are still in police camps in the interiors, still to receive adequate medicare."

Expectedly as is usual in the given situation, some troops admitted to hospital, complained to the TV reporters: "We were not given proper care……we were forced to spend from our own pockets."

"156 Professionals Set to Join P M Scheme in LWE Districts". Apr 2012

In the first large scale entry of professionals in government activity, the union government was all set to enroll as many as 156 postgraduates under the prestigious PM's Rural Development Fellows Scheme (RDF) in Hyderabad on 5 Apr 2012.[40]

Union Minister for Rural Development Jairam Ramesh "Will hand over the appointment letters at a function to be attended by Deputy Chairperson of the Planning Commission Montek Singh Ahluwalia."

Besides their bearing the mantle of being the PMs Fellows, an interesting aspect of their service is that all of them —and they include IIT and IIM graduates— "have accepted the challenge of spending the entire two year's tenure of their fellowship in the tough environment of 78 Maoist-hit districts of the country."

Equally significant is the fact that as many 40 young women came forward to work with district administrations to usher in development with responsive governance in the Maoist-hit regions where the Integrated Action Plan (IAP) was under implementation. Two RDFs are to be posted in each of the 78 IAP districts. They would coordinate and evaluate the programmes being implemented in their districts.

The selection process was tough, with as many as 8,560 apirants for the fellowship. They were shortlisted on the basis of their academic qualification and three essays written by each of them. Subsequently, 816 candidates were called for rigorous interview and group discussion conducted by panels that included State government officials.

156 youths included 59 engineering graduates and seven medical graduates. Others are from streams such as literatures, linguistics, science, law, commerce, social and economic and agriculture, computers and journalism.

"Training of Troops ahead of Poll duties in Maoist Areas:" Mar 2014

The CRPF is organizing a week long special training camps for its personnel who are due to be deployed on poll-related duties, reported a daily in Mar 2014.[41] The troops are reaching Raipur for such duties. "The deployment will start next week."

CRPF DG Dilip Trivedi "is reaching Raipur 21 Mar 2014 to supervise this training and deployment." He said, "we will update our troops in Raipur about the situation in Chhattisgarh before they are sent to the Red areas."

In the wake of Maoist attack on road opening parties in Sukma that left 15 security men dead 11 Mar, the Center is rushing in 6,000 additional troops to the violence prone areas of the state.

Trivedi said, "Through, we had more companies for the Assembly polls in the state, but that consisted of forces that never had any idea of being deployed in a Maoist – affected areas ; but now all our personnel have prior experience of serving in Maoist areas. So it will make the difference."

Then the DG said something that was neither called for nor appropriate for an officer who is leading nation's anti – Naxal fight: "The Sukma attack has no doubt dented the morale of the force, but his men are capable of recovering from it." One single incident of Maoist attack, that cost it 15 lives, should not affect the morale of 3 lakh-strong paramilitary force. And its chief admitting it openly, does not speak well of his own leadership, besides that of commanders at various rungs below him. In our system there is no one to pull up such a 'silly' chief for his indiscreet admission like the one mentioned above. The Home Minister and his deputies are too innocent of implications of such simplistic-sounding statements, and the union Home Secretary, C-in –C of all CPMFs, is too engaged in day-to-day routine that he does not even know about such a statement.

The government has employed two-pronged strategy to deal with the 11 March attack and its aftermath: Have more boots on the ground and carry on precision attacks on these ultras.

Mobile Towers in Naxal- Hit States

Mobile connectivity in the states with Maoist presence is an essential instrument too tackle this LWE menace. The funds seem to be coming in the way of improving this instrument, as will be seen in detail in this section of the book.

"it has been two years since the MHA started pushing to improve this connectivity" wrote a daily in September 2012.[42] Subsequently, the MHA approached the department of telecommunications (DOT), which prepared a Rs 5,800-crore plan for setting almost 2,200 towers in nine states by the state-owned Bharat Sanchar Nigam Ltd. (BSNL). But the Cabinet returned the proposal mid-2012 after objections by the Finance Ministry, then under Pranab Mukherjee, mainly on two counts : nomination of the BSNL for executing the project without the tender process, and the large amount of subsidy sought from the government.

With P. Chidambram back in the Finance Ministry, earlier hopelessness on the issue has turned into optimism, for reasons well-understood.

The MHA officials are now hopeful that this proposal would soon get clearance from the Cabinet. Understandably MHA sources "now say a revised proposal is likely to be forwarded soon to the cabinet."

A senior MHA official confides to this daily: "We are expecting early revival of the project as Mr Chidambram, who has been the Home Minister, clearly understands the importance of the project. We do not want to get into the technicalities and financial implications of this project. It is for the DOT and Finance Ministry to decide on these matters. We wants this project completed earliest as it will be a boost to our fight against Maoists in some 80 districts spread across nine states. It will allow our security men to stay connected in remote areas and also help them track Maoists."

The DOT had 'nominated' the BSNL due to disinterest shown by private players to operate in a remote an Naxal areas, since the revenue generated is low. But the Ministry of Finance's Expenditure Finance Committee (EFC) objected to it, arguing that "any assumptions on the (lack of) revenue generating potential in the LWE areas should be backed with evidence in the form of field trials or sample surveys." While lambasting the DOT for not "providing adequate justification for assigning the work to the BSNL, on nomination basis," the EFC also criticized the BSNL for its reputation for "large delays in execution and shoddy performance" in major projects. But the MHA officials allege that some private players might have played spoilsport as there were some revenue generating towns under the projects which these companies were eyeing, without touching remote and rural areas.

The Finance Ministry was also not pleased over high costs for installation and maintenance of the towers. It objected to the DOT proposal seeking a Rs 809.38-crore subsidy for the BSNL from the Universal service Obligation Fund (USOF) created for increasing mobile penetration in rural areas for commissioning and maintaining 2,199 sites (towers) in the LWE areas for five years.

The Finance Ministry also noted that the subsidy being sought was "very large" compared to the total subsidy of Rs 211.84-crore disbursed till 2011-end from the USOF for creation and maintenance of 7,296 towers and 15,407 base transceiver stations (BTS). It further noted:

"This huge difference in costs cannot be accepted solely on the basis of estimates provided by the BSNL." Another important objection by the Finance Ministry was to the plea that the services should be free of cost if the towers are utilized by the armed forces or the police. "Such expenditure should be booked to the accounts of the MHA or to States government rather than being debited to the USOF," it had noted. But, the MHA official claim that they never sought free usage for security personnel. "We never asked for any free bies for our personnel…… we want early installation of mobile towers to aid our troops in their operations. These towers will also help the economy of rural and remote areas."

Before this analysis is closed, it should of some interest to reproduce both the headline of this story—"Home Ministry looks to Chidambram for push to mobile towers project"—and also its blurb—"Finance Minister clearly understands its importance in fighting Maoists."

It may sound parochial for a well-respected daily like the Hindu to say this: It has highlighted Chidambam's name and importance because, after all, he is the leading light of the Congress Party in South India, and more significantly, he hails from Tamil Nadu, the home base of this daily! To put the issue more upfront, if not bluntly, here is a question for the Hindu : "will it have given same headline if the political personage involved were a North Indian? After all, a newspaper caters to its home constituency! The North Indian name would not have same traction for the Hindu's readership down South as of Chidambram's! This was just an aside!

"Mobile Tower Project in 9 Maoist- Hit States Stuck Over Cost Issues": Jan 2013

Another news story on the same issue appeared in the same daily after a couple of months later,[43] suggesting zero movement on the issue of installation of the mobile towers for over two years since the MHA initiated the proposal on the project. These towers help the security forces in achieving better results in their operations against the Maoist uprising. That shows (lack of) seriousness in dealing with a problem that the then Prime Minister, Manmohan Singh himself, described as the biggest threat to the nation's internal security and its integrity.

The very first paragraph of this analysis tells the whole story: "An ambitious project of the MHA to provide seamless mobile connectivity in nine Maoist-affected States has been caught in a tussle between BSNL and the USOF, a body under the Central DOT, over cost estimates of installing mobile towers." And this delay is unexplicable, "even when the Union Home Minister Sushil Kumar Shinde has urged Communications and Information Technology Minister Kapil Sibal to speed up the case on an urgent basis in view of the growing clashes between Maoists and Security forces.

While BSNL has sought Rs 5,809 crore for installing and operating 2,199 mobile towers, the USOF has pegged the figure of Rs 3,792 crore—a difference of whopping Rs 2,015 crore.

Private Operators Reluctant

BSNL is supposed to execute the project in all the nine States – Andhra Pradesh, Bihar, Chhattisgarh, Jharkhand, MP, Maharashtra, Odisha, UP and West Bengal–as no private operator has shown interest in the project/showed inclination to start this service.

The Government has decided to finance the project from the USOF, a fund under the DOT created from contributions made by telecom operators to finance projects to boost connectivity in rural and backward areas as part of their social obligations.

With BSNL and USOF sparring over its cost estimates, the project is unlikely to see the light of the day soon. This even when Shinde has written to Sibal to expedite the issue as it is affecting the anti- Naxal operations of the forces, particularly when the Maoists are well connected than the security forces in some areas. Significantly, these towers in remote areas and villages will enable the forces to stay connected with their commands, district administration and locals for operational purposes.

First Hurdle

The project hit its first hurdle when Finance Ministry then under Pranab Mukherjee, objected to the costs, besides some other procedural drawbacks, though it had full support of Home Minister Chidambaram and Kapil Sibal. When Chidambaram took over the Finance Ministry, the proposal was expected to get early clearance. This time around it got mired into controversy over Cost estimates. Even a high-level Committee formed to resolve the costing issue seems to have failed to come out with a solution.

Chinese Towers?

Significantly, BSNL and some DOT officials feel that cost issues can be managed if the Chinese telecom equipment manufacturing companies are allowed to set up their towers, but the MHA, particularly the intelligence and security agencies, are strongly against the idea.

Will Indian Manufacturers Show the Way?

Government sources say some Indian manufacturers "have show-cased their innovative low-cost towers to the DOT officials, and proto-type of one such Indian company was highly appreciated for its cost-effectiveness and functionality.

Air Support for Counter Naxal Ops

Certain air support is essential for the security forces engaged in counter-insurgency operations, particularly so when the area of operations is forested, hilly and lacks road connectivity.

More significantly the LWE is normally rampant in under developed areas, inhabited by the poor, deprived tribal communities. These are ideal conditions where the LWE would spread its tentacles. The mobility of the troops is hampered by the obsence of good road connectivity. This is where Air Support, primarily in the shape helicopter availability, comes handy.

Choppers are generally employed for casualty evacuation from remote areas, airlifting of supplies and troops in emergency situations. The quantity and type of choppers will depend on the operational requirements of the forces deployed in Counter-Naxal operations, as also on the availability of the required type with the IAF.

Deployment of more Choppers Was Envisaged in May 2010: Clearance by CCS

The need for air support had been felt for a long time, but the deployment of 23 IAF helicopters for anti-Naxal operations got final approval by the Cabinet Committee on Security (CCS) on 29 May 2010.

The CCS note, based on this decision was moved by the MHA, seeking enhanced air support for anti-Naxal operations.

This MHA note failed to yield results for nearly two years, may be, due to government's procedural waywardness/rigmarole. "The Cabinet Secretariat has now directed the MOD for expeditiously committing two squadrons (12 operational helicopters) to the MHA,"[44]

These two squadron to be at the disposal of the MHA, would be in addition to the four MI 17 helicopters already with the CRPF and one chopper with the BSF for anti-Naxal operations.

In the latest move Cabinet Secretary Ajit Seth "has also directed the MHA to address the issue of upgrading the infrastructure at Ranchi airport for meeting the operational requirement of the airlift facilities for anti-Naxal operations.

The decisions were taken at a recent high-level meeting, chaired by Seth, and attended by the secretaries of Home, Defence, Expenditure and Director IB, DG, CRF, IT secretary, NSC secretariat. The meeting was held to resolve the differences between MHA and MOD on the issue of LWE.

Home Secretary RK Singh emphasised that the requirement of additional choppers stems from the need of the CAPFs, deployed in remote areas not connected by roads in the 9 Naxal-hit states, operational needs of the State Armed Police as well as immediate movements of reinforcements and casualty evacuation in view of the mobile and guerrilla warfare- based modus operandi of the Naxals.

Singh also underscored the need for positioning helicopters at more than one locations in some of the States due to geographically extended deployment of security forces. This, he outlined, was for timely air support at critical junctures and to reach areas highly prone to IED threat requiring airlifting of troops. Presently, only four helicopters are deployed and another two are expected to be made available later this year (2012) for anti-Naxal operations. Of the present four helicopters, each can do only 20 hours of flying per month, which limits the over all availability of helicopter support to security forces.

Now comes the Defence Secretary to put his angle before the gathering: "Only seven per cent of flying hours were used for actual anti-Naxal operations and the rest of the utilization was for troop movement." He clarified that for six operational helicopters, a full squadron of 10-11 machines was required to be engaged as per the SOP of the IAF, and the Armed Force's airlift capacity is fully booked.

On query by cabinet secretary about actual and immediate state-wise requirement of the helicopters, DG, CRPF explained: "A minimum of 10 additional helicopters are required at this juncture, making a total of 17. Of this number, four each are needed in Chhattisgarh and Jharkhand, three in Odisha and two each in Bihar, Maharashtra and West Bengal".

"NTRO IS DOING A FINE JOB OF MAPPING MAOIST AREAS:" NOV 2012

The nation's premier scientific intelligence agency, National Technical Research Organisation (NTRO), is routinely processing data generated by UAV's from Maoist-controlled areas and sending these to CRPF at Raipur. This was conveyed to a daily by both police and paramilitary sources.[45]

"NTRO's main station in Hyderabad is receiving the satellite images and other data, including audio, and sending these to CRPF over the past few months." Field level commanders of the CRPF were instructed on the basis of the information gathered from UAVs.

While the process "to regularise" the gathering of information using UAVs, parallel to human intelligence, "started about a year back, the killing of tribals in Bijapur in late June (2012) has expedited the process". A senior officer says: "Now we can get a very clear picture of the training centres, movement of insurgents and camp's location." But expectedly at the ground level, "there is a skepticism at the local level over the NTRO's information gathering system."

About a dozen UAVs based on the flying stations in Hyderabad are now operating in south Chhattisgarh's Bastar area. "The UAVs capture the movement of the rebels on ground and pass the satellite data to the NTRO". These images were passed almost in real time to the field commanders of the CRPF. Some of the signal officers of the CRPF were trained by the NTRO to read the satellite-generated data, some sources told the daily.

The previous DGP of Chhattisgarh Viswaranjan explained: "During my tenure a few years ago, 10 UAVs of the IAF were used to monitor the area. We get good inputs even from Abujh Marh but the ground force was not equipped enough for operation on the basis of available data. Eventually, the IAF withdrew the UAVs. Now the ground force is better equipped to act on the basis of the satellite images."

The officers did not divulge if any particular operation was carried out, based upon the data generated by the UAVs , till date. Now, there is also GPS in place to track the movement of the CRPF/security forces men in the forest.

But the Chhattisgarh Police are sceptical about the 'effectiveness' of the UAV generated information. One of the top officials shared his views with the daily: "It is difficult to act on basis of the satellite images. Receiving images does not mean we can act. We have to check the logistics at the ground level. The system is still not capable of replacing the human intelligence at the ground level.... However, the human intelligence and the UAV-generated images can slowly be integrated to get the best results".

"A Poor Image of IAF Pilots and Commandos": Jan 2013

An IAF chopper was brought down in an incident in Jan 2013. The Indian Air Force did not lose just an aircraft, a helicopter, that it – and the nation—can replace, it lost much more than this material asset! It lost its reputation the way the crew of the chapper and two IAF Special Force Commandos behaved in a combat situation!

The incident points to the increasing capabilities of the Naxal fighters. "More worryingly, it raises question about how the Air Force handled itself."[46] The manner in which the crew and two commandos left behind an injured police man to his own devices and made their way to a security camp, is disgraceful, and more significantly, it is against the ethos and spirit of the nation's Armed Forces who are primarily responsible for nation's security and integrity.

Leaving behind an injured comrade, even if he did not belong to your arm among the country's Armed Forces, is an act that is indicative of "Cowardness in battle field", and an offence demanding serious punishment, preferably through a court martial. It should be appropriate if these derelict IAF airmen are informed that even the Maoists do not leave their comrades behind even when they are dead, not to speak of when they are injured.

This cowardly behavior of the IAF men has bigger implications and "repercussions for a force that is looking forward to developing capabilities for a role beyond national borders."

"The policeman is now critical, with the doctors having removed his small intestines."

Besides shocking many in the military who live by the ethos of not abandoning a man behind in battle, the commandoes, by crawlling their way to safety, have raised more than one questions: it generated doubts about their professional capabilities; and even more seriously, their conduct might have emboldened the Maoists who till now stayed away from specifically targeting armed forces. Significantly, Naxal intercepts analysed after the crash reveal instructions by its commanders not to approach the chopper as it was heavily armed and had special forces on board.

"It can only be guessed how the rebels will react if such an incident occurs again." This is a legitimate concern raised by this daily.

The Response of the IAF

But the reaction of the IAF brass and their stance on the behavior of their men is neither elevating nor acceptable or appropriate. Instead of objective assessment of their derelict airmen, the IAF has gone all out to defend their actions! They failed to ask some basic questions: Did the crew display the much flaunted and fabled or treasured officer-like-qualities? Did the commandos make any efforts to dissuade the crew from abandoning an injured comrade? Instead, the IAF produced a ridiculous certificate from the victim's organization: "They cited that the police have commended them." It was mature gesture by police, which the IAF anthorities need not have tom-tomed about. After all, even after this incident too, the armed police and state police forces would have to depend upon the IAF for critical medical evacuation and urgent reinforcements in emergencies. Obviously, they decided to be discreet rather than truthful in the interest of their future operations in the LWE areas!

The daily cites the example of disconnect between the IAF and the police by quoting from the press note issued in Delhi by the IAF in defence of their derelict men: It mentions the injured policeman as a CRPF jawan, where as he belongs to the Chhattisgarh Armed Police.

Powers-that-be in Delhi are not clear about the entire incident, since Defence Minister AK Antony admitted to asking for information from "other sources."

Would the IAF honestly answer the Question: If the injured man was an airman, would they have left him behind? Its own chief a few months ago floated the motto: Not to leave "your men and machines behind." The worst was the IAF chief personally defending his derelict men!!

"Air Chief Promises Latest Choppers for Anti-naxal Operations": May 2013

A year after the MOD was ordered to earmark a minimum of 10 choppers for anti-Naxal operations, as discussed in the preceding entry of Apr 2012, IAF chief, Air Chief Marshal N A K Brown announces a bonanza for the security forces combating Maoist, in May 2013.[47]

ACM Brown said 23 May 2013 the IAF "will raise a unit of its latest Russia-built Mi-17V5 choppers in Nagpur next month to support anti-Naxal operations in Chhattisgarh's Bastar division."

So, the IAF would deploy its latest transport helicopters to bolster the capabilities of security forces battling Maoists, "at a time when rebels have mounted some of their most audacious attacks."

Four days after Naxal attack nearly wiped out the Chhattisgarh Congress leadership in the Bastar division, Brown stated technology was the key to dealing with the Naxal problem. The Mi-17V5 has the capability to carry out night operations. Presently, the IFA has assigned six Mi-17 choppers to support the Central and state police forces engaged in anti-Naxal operations. These choppers are used for ferrying security men, carrying out reconnaissance and casualty evacuation.

These choppers operate from three locations: Ranchi in Jharkhand; Raipur and Jagdalpur in Chhattisgarh. Brown explained the new squadron with 12 choppers located closer to Jagdalpur, would cut down on response time if some incident occurred there.

He also clarified that decision to raise new squadron in Nagpur was taken well before the 25 May attack on the Congress leaders.

These choppers (Mi-17) have frequently drawn hostile fire—the latest incident being of 18 January when an IAF chopper was fired upon and brought down by the Maoist cadres in Chhattisgarh.

"Chhattisgarh CM Raman Singh Wants Air Mobility to Tackle Naxals:" June 2014

The CM asked the MHA to provide "air mobility" to the security forces for anti-Maoist operations in his State. During his meeting with Home Minister Rajnath Singh on 9 June 2014, he sought at least 21 choppers. "At present there are only four choppers which are mainly used by the state and central police forces for rescue operation.[48]

Outlining its plans in a presentation to the MHA, the state government made some points : It would first locate the Maoist camps in the jungle, and then carry out operations by air dropping security men at the nearest possible location; the district administration has revenue maps, showing areas where there is habitation, and air drops will commence after collecting all information, through technology and through human intelligence, to ensure that there was no collateral damage; the state also asked for augmentation of UAVs for simultaneous surveillance of cluster of areas.

Among other measure to check LWE, the State has asked the Centre to redeploy Naga battalions, develop Gondi and Halbi dialects, pay monthly stipends to the youth, distribute transistors, solar powered TV sets and mobile phones, and open 'ashram shalas' (residential schools).

Seeking to check recruitment by Maoist groups, the State Government plans: A graded stipend of Rs 1,500-4,000 would be provided; in phase 1, around 1 lakh youth would be covered at an estimated cost of Rs 200 crore; it hopes to cover a total of 4.75 lakh youth and a total assistance of Rs 10,000 crore has been requested from the Centre for all this.

After the meeting, the CM told the press: "Two technical battalions (some 2,000 people) comprising engineers have been sought for construction projects in Chhattisgarh. We have sought MHA's help in skill development of youth living there. we want to improve schools and have a network of roads there. We have been assured of all help.

The CM was accompanied by a team which included his DGP, AN Upadhay. Saying it could convert 500 existing schools into ashram shalas, the State government said, "A tribal university, an Ayurved University, and an Armed Forces Recruitment Training School are also required.

The State Government, seeking relaxation of norms under the forest Conversation Act, demanded an amendment to it: "General approval for diversion of forest land in LWE areas up to 5 hectares is inadequate; complex and time consuming. It should be increased to 40 hectares."

Presently, only 25 per cent of Bastar has telecom coverage, that affects the intelligence gathering process and timely response by Central forces. Yet again, due to local topography, large parts of Dantewada, Bijapur, Narayanpur and Sukma districts are outside the range of Akashwani. Hence the need for the Centre to plan and provide regional language satellite services.

"Some Role for the Army in Naxal Theatre After all these Years:" Apr 2012

For years there were questions about Army not joining the fight against Maoist insurgency. It was an expected question because Army has been involved in J and K terrorism situation control since 1947, as also in insurgency situation in the North-East since long years. The news finally came that such a decision was taken on 10 Feb 2012, reported by a daily in Apr 2012.[49]

Rashtriya Rifles (RR) Army is all set for a greater role in counter-Maoist operation as the Cabinet Secretariat cleared a proposal to post them in Maoist-affected States for static/defensive roles so that the paramilitary forces could concentrate on and play a more proactive role against the ultras. A decision to this effect was taken at a meeting of the Committee of Secretaries (COS) held on 10 Feb (2012), consequent to a direction from the PMO to discuss a background note of the MHA titled "Left Wing Extremism Scenario: Current Trends," and to resolve the significant differences between the MHA and the MOD. The PMO direction had asked them to arrive at an agreed formulation with regard to the proposals contained in the background note, including the ones on deployment of the RR, 23 additional MI-17 choppers for anti-Naxal operations and Army Mine Detection Team (AMDT).

Consequent to the decision of the COS, Cabinet Secretary Ajit Seth noted that the Home Secretary could take up the matter of concurrence of the State Governments concerned on the proposal to locate Army/RR Battalions for training purposes in other LWE-hit areas. The MOD was advised to convey the availability of requisite number of Army/RR Bns for location in training ranges in Maoist-hit areas to the MHA.

The COS meet also decided and authorized the MHA to examine the possibility of recourse to some of the measures identified by the United States Joint Task Force to deal with the IED menace in Afghanistan, including successful use of ASTA MIDS (Airborne stand-off Minefield Detection system) sensors for Naxal areas.

The COS had further decided that the MHA might seek the assistance of the Armed Forces in procurement of demining equipment and training of personnel for counter-IED operations and also seek services of ex-service men and experts in such operations. DG, CRPF said there were serious problems in tackling use of IEDs embedded 12-feet below the surface by Maoist and training of paramilitary men at the IED School at Pune was not adequate. Director, IB Nehchal Sandhu suggested that with every battalion of the Army that would undergo training at any given time, another battalion should be deployed for its protection in LWE areas. Some additional areas could be further identified for such training camps in order to dominate the LWE areas, said Sandhu.

The COS also directed the MOD to commit two squadrons (12 operational helicopters) to the MHA for air support to the paramilitary and State armed police forces for combating the Red Brigade.

Union Home Secretary RK Singh said at the meet that by deploying RR, the Army would get a first hand experience of Naxal theatre, and ensured their better preparedness should there be a requirement to deploy Army/

RR at a later stage. He further added: "As has been done in the case of insurgencies in countries like Indonesia and Malaysia, all the resources at the command of the State, including Armed Forces, need to be used to tackle and to confront the growing menace (of Naxalism) in india."

Home Secretary was not done with his "wise" observations and prescriptions. Here are some more:

- "Coercive power of the States need to be used as and when required, including to protect against insurgencies.
- "Concept of national security is not static. Experience around the world suggest that threat of the conventional war is slowly being replaced by unconventional/asymmetric warfare, and therefore, the role of armed forces also needs to be dynamic, and cater to the changed/futuristic scenario.
- "Since the Army/RR have reservations regarding deployment to undertake anti-Naxal operations, it has been recommended to employ RR, which counted beyond the over all strength of the Army, for static/defensive role, as it would assist in relieving the CAPFs for more pro-active role in Naxal strongholds.
- "The positive outcome of earmarking of areas in the Bastar region and Narayanpur Range for training camps for Army has already been felt."

The daily has quoted these observations and remarks of the Home Secretary from the six-page classified minutes of the COS meeting.

The Defence Secretary make a weak attempt to counter self-serving observations of the Home Secretary, as he has been briefed rather primed, by the chiefs of the CAPFs! While six paragraphs have been devoted to RK Singh's 'peroration', a measly one could be spared for the Defence Secretary's. These are reproduced here: "The Defence Secretary stated that apart from their non-availability, deployment of the Army in the hinterland may not be advisable given the sensitivity of deploying the Army in such areas which are not declared as disturbed. However, without deployment, location of Army/RR for training purposes in LWE areas could be considered".

For Record

This meeting chaired by the seniormost IAS officer was attended by important secretaries and chiefs of the CAPFs. These are listed here:

1. Cabinet Secretary Ajit seth in the chair.
2. Secretary (Coordination), Cabinet Secretariat Alok Rawat.

3. Home Secretary RK Singh.
4. Defence Secretary Shashi Kant Sharma.
5. Director, IB Nehchal Sandhu.
6. DG, CRPF K Vijay Kumar.
7. Advisor, Cabinet Secretariat Vandana Aggarwal.
8. Joint Secretary National Security Council Secretariat Naveen Varma.
9. Additional Secretary, Department of Expenditure AC Duggal.

Accommodations for Para-military Forces Fighting Maoists

The CRPF and other paramilitary forces engaged in countering the Maoist rebels, generally do so far away from their permanent locations. Consequently, one cannot expect any accommodation available for them in the jungles and their peripherial areas, which are selected by the ultras to attack or ambush them.

For the security personnel engaged in anti-Naxal operations, billeting is a tough problem. Generally located away from population centre, and mostly in forest areas, it is generally ramshacle huts they have to do with. The security forces often set up posts in abandoned buildings, which often became easy targets for the ultras. The men posted at such buildings are replaced at short intervals—once a month, in some cases. The helicopters are deployed for their transportation. The choppers are also used to identify Naxal camps/movements in the jungle. But as a policy, they are never used to attack such camps. The reasoning: They are our own people, even if misguided. Besides, a democracy can't accept death of the innocents as a collatesal damage (The only time the independent India resorted to this extreme measure was in 1960s when the Mizo rebels were bombed in Lungleh after they declared insurrection and secession from the country. Extreme situations require extreme measures!)

At times, there are happy happenstance. During the 1980s some 200 housing quarters were built in Barsur, on the foothills of Abhujmarh for the employees of Bodhghat hydel power project. Environment concerns ensured the abandonment of the project. Later, these quarters came in handy for the security forces, which converted them into their citadel.

The composition of 25,000 strong counter-Naxal force is a microcosm of India. There are people from all over the country, including men from as far apart as J and K, Manipur and Tamil Nadu. As anywhere else among the defence units, when not involved in active combat operations, the personnel of these counter-Naxal subunits spend time in playing games and watching 24 hour television (thanks to the DTH service). They are also allowed to keep cell phones, even if not in the active operations. Locals and personnel presently deployed in the area are full of stories about the time when the Naga and Mizo units were on duty here: Street dogs and snakes became scarce because their meat was a favourite dish for their men; the men had a nice time hunting for them; and a black dog was a particularly sought after luxury and it ended up on the table soon after it was caught by them.

Steel Plant Building Barracks For Five Para-military Battalions: Dec 2012

"The public sector Bhilai Steel Plant (BSP) is going to great lengths to ensure that its Rs 5,000 crore plan to extract quality iron ore from mines located in the Maoist hinterland in the Rowghat Hills in south-central Chhattisgarh goes without a hitch."[50]

The news story filed from Raipur says the BSP will spend Rs 250 crore on setting up 22 barracks in Bhanupratappur and Rowghat. Sources said BSP is funding construction of 22 barracks for five or more paramilitary battalions along a 95-km stretch between Dalli and Rajhara and Rowghat. Six of these will be placed around Block F, allotted to BSP. A SAIL official said "one para-military battalion has started constructing barracks between Rajhara and Rowghat." The CEO of the BSP said, "a planned rail link would benefit local resident also and BSP was supporting its completion."

The steps are aimed at improving the quality of life of the people of the region, and not at fuelling conflict, the CEO said.

"We are creating a win-win situation, winning the hearts of the people."

A senior officer of the BSF said its 24 batallion had been moved to Korar in Kanker district exclusively to facilitate ore extraction at Rowghat. Six BSF battalions have already been deployed in Kanker, where Rowghat is situated.

Sources in the CRPF told this daily a few weeks ago that they were also gearing up for operations at Rowghat.

Seemingly choosing not to discuss the issue of barrack funding, BSP CEO S. Chandrasekharam said, "The top priority will be development of the Dalli-Rajhara-Rowghat rail link. It will not only ease civil transportation in the region but will also be used to transport ore from Rowghat to Rajhara." BSP was allotted Block F spread over 500 hectares some two decades ago.

Rowghat has two hills. One has Block F, and the other north-west of it, has five blocks—A, B, C, D and E. Block F, with a total deposits of

511 million tonnes of good quality ore, is getting ready for phase-wise extraction. By current rates, Block F's raw ore can fetch Rs 30,000 crore in the global market.

Notes

1. Pardeep Thakur, Times of India. 17 Mar 2007.
2. Amitabh Tiwari, Times of India, 7 Feb 2009.
3. Sandeep Joshi, The Hindu, 24 Sep 2012.
4. Rakesh K Singh. The Pioneer, 4 Nov 2012.
5. Sanjay ojha, Times of India, 13 Jan 2013.
6. Sanjib Kr Baruah, Hindustan times, June 2014.
7. Bharti Jain, times of India, 28 Aug 2014.
8. Rajesh Ahuja, Hindustan Times, 20 Aug 2014.
9. Pioneer News service, the pioneer, 14 Oct 2014.
10. Bharti Jain, Times of India, 14 Oct. 2014.
11. An illustration in Times of India of 18 Oct 2014.
12. Express News Service, Indian Express, 30 Nov 2014.
13. Deeptiman Tiwari, Times of India, 2 Dec 2014.
14. Rakhi /Chakravarti, Times of India, 29 Apr 2012.
15. Vijaita Singh, Indian Express, 11 Sep 2012.
16. Times News Service, Times of India and Pioneer News Service, The pioneer both 26 Dec 2012.
17. Ahsutosh Bhardwaj, Indian Express, 8 Sep 2014.
18. Ashutosh Bhardwaj, Indian Express, 3 Dec 2014.
19. Rahul Pandita, The Hindu, 13 Dec 2014.
20. PTI, Times of India, 12 Jan 2015.
21. Vijitha Singh, Indian Express, 11 Aug 2013.
22. Parnav Pratyush/Parvinder Bhatia, The Pioneer 24 Sep 2014.
23. Rakesh Singh, The Pioneer, 16 Feb 2015.
24. Deeptiman Tiwari, Times of India, 31 Oct 2014.
25. Suvojit Bagchi, The Hindu, 6 Mar. 2013.
26. Amitabh Sinha, Indian Express, 13 Jul 2012.
27. Pioneer News Service, The Pioneer, 22 Aug 2012.
28. K Srinivas Reddy, The Hindu, 3 Jan 2013.
29. Source: Times Of India, 3 Sep 2014; Www.times Of India.com
30. Rakesh K. Singh, The Hindu, 16 Mar 2014
31. Rahul Tripathi, Indian Express, 23.4.2014
32. Navtan Kumar, Sunday Guardian, 27 Jul 2014.
33. Sandeep Rai, times of india, 22 Jan 2015.
34. Syed Nazakat, the week, 29 June 2014.

35. Bhavna Vij-Aurora, The Outlook, 23 Apr 2007.
36. Pioneer News Service, The pioneer, 23 Nov 2011.
37. Deeptiman Tiwari, Times of india, 6 Mar 2015.
38. Indian Express, 8 Dec 2014.
39. Express News Service, Indian Express, 1 Dec 2014.
40. K. Balchand, The Hindu, 6 Apr 2012.
41. HT correspondent, Hindustan Times, 22 Mar 2014.
42. Sandeep Joshi, The Hindu, 3 Sep 2012.
43. Sandeep Joshi, The Hindu, 18 Jan 2013.
44. Rakesh K Singh, The Pioneer, 6 Apr 2012 reported a daily in Apr 2012.
45. Suvojit Bagchi, The Hindu, 3 Nov 2012.
46. Manu Pubby, Indian Expresses, 31 Jan 2013.
47. Rahul Singh, Hindustan Times, 30 May 2013.
48. Vijaita Singh, Indian Express, 10 June 2014.
49. Rakesh K Singh, The Pioneer, 7 Apr 2012.
50. Suvojit Bagchi, The Hindu, 2 Dec 2012.

11

Combating Naxalism/Maoism Policy and Related Issues

This chapter deals with policy, plans and strategy to combat the marauding Maoists and their sympathisers.

Certain other aspects of policy of dealing with the problem are also dealt with in this chapter:

- Policy on surrender.
- Policy on talks with the maoists.
- Select individuals on policy and strategy.
- Incentives policy for security forces.

Combating Maoist Uprising Policy, Plans and Strategy

As a nation, we somehow feel shy or short of laying out clear cut and unambiguous policies on important subjects. If it was the defence first, now it is Naxalism/Maoism. If most western and even some Asian nations bring out updated versions of their defence plans and strategic thought almost every year, India has not completed page 1 of a similar book. We have never enunciated our defence policy or strategic choices in so many words. Same applies to our presently most serious internal security threat, namely, Naxalism. The list can be extended to the most serious external threat India faces, viz, jihadist terrorism.

So what is the reason behind our policy, rather non-policy, of shying away from enunciating our non-negotiable and fundamental principles or ideas on such subjects of national importance? May be, we need intellectuals or experts more qualified than this Author. So, for the time being, let us take shelter behind our scriptural wisdome Neti, Neti (-not this, not this).

Because there is no official scripture on the issue of combating Naxalism, the best way is to compile it from occasional handouts that come out from some relevant ministries, or from interviews some dailies obtain from certain well-placed officials. So this chapter will examine and discuss some such documents or interviews/interactions in the succeeding pages.

Combating Maoists: Narration Till 2007

There are 66 districts affected by Naxalism which are receiving financial assistance from the Centre.

55 District Receiving Financial Assistance from the Centre to Combat Naxalism Andhra Pradesh (8): Adilabads Karimnagar, Medak, Nalgonda, Nizamabad and Warangal.

Bihar (8): Aurangabad, Bhojpur, Gaya, Jehanabad, Kaimur (Bhabua), Nalanda, Patna and Rohtas.

Chhattisgarh (7): Bastar, Dantewada, Jashpur, Kanker, Kawardha, Rajnandgaon, and Surguja.

Jharkhand (13): Bokaro, Chatra, Dhanbad, Garhwa, Giridih, Gumla, Hazaribagh, Koderma, Latehar, Lohardaga, Palamu, Ranchi and Simdega.

MP (2): Balaghat and Dindori.

Maharashtra (4): Bhandara, Chandrapur, Gadchiroli and Gondia.

Odisha (7): Gajapati, Ganjam, Mayurbhanj, Malkangiri, Koraput, Nayagada and Nawrangpur.

UP (3): Chandauli, Mirzapur, Sonbhadra

West Bengal (3): Bankura, Purulia, Midnapur.

Rashtriya, Sam Vikas Yojana Funds to the States

States	*No. of Naxal-hit districts*	*Amount to ba released by the centre*	*Amount released upto 2006-07*	*Cumulative expenditure reported by the states*
AP	8	360	195	126
Bihar	8	360	195	155
Chhattisgarh	7	315	278	182
Jharkhand	13	585	495	369
MP	2	90	90	64
Maharashtra	4	180	113	70
Odisha*	3	135	98	80
UP	3	135	120	70
West Bengal	3	135	75	48

* Excludes the four (earlier three) KBK districts of Malkangiri, Koraput, Rayagada and Nawrangpur which are covered under the special plan.

Source: Ministry of Panchayat Raj website.

Anti-Naxal Operations: Multiplicity of Coordinating Mechanism Early 2007

There several coordination mechanism at the Centre to ensure certain degree of joint and cooperative inputs in anti-Naxal operations. These multiple mechanisms must be making coordination between Maoism-hit states a little difficult. The results so far would seem to suggest this reality.

The mechanism are named here:

1. Empowered Group of Ministers (EGoM) headed by Union Home Minister Shivraj Patil.
2. A Standing Committee of Chief Minsiters of Naxal-hit states, headed again by Mr Patil.
3. National Coordination Centre on Naxalism (NCCN), headed by Union Home Secretary, comprising the Chief Secretaries and DGPs of 13 Naxal-hit states.
4. A task force headed by the Special Secretary (Internal Security) in the MHA.
5. An inter-Ministerial Group (IMG), headed by Additional Secretary (Naxal Management), again in the MHA.

This multiplicity is not only avoidable, but also unnecessary. The three official level mechanisms is indicative of 'empire building', syndrome.

Financial help to Naxalism-hit States

The Centre also has its hands on the purse strings, rendering funds to these states through certain schemes.

The Union MHA operates a Security Related Expenditure (SRE) scheme, under which it re-imburses expenses incurred by the states on security matters, including anti-Naxal operations. Strengthening and modernising the police and its equipment is also covered under 'Security expenses' head. Over Rs 100 crore have been spent under this head till June 2007 but "there was concern over improper utilization, particularly in states like Jharkhand and Chhattisgarh." That indeed is unfortunate as these are also the ones worst-hit by the Maoist violence. The Centre has also been helping the states in raising India Reserve Battalions (IRBs).

On the development front, there are two schemes: the Backward Districts Initiative and the Backward. Regions Grant Fund Programme. Under the former, Rs 1,700 has been spent so far this year.

Combating Naxalism: Some Measures and Actions during the Year 2006-07

MHA to set up Anti-Naxal Cell: May 2006

Rattled by unabated Naxal violence and its own inability to come up with a containment strategy, a concerned MHA decide to set up a dedicated anti-Naxal Cell to coordinate intelligence, development outreach and implementation of policies to check the Red menace.[1]

The MHA plans to ask for the Cell a new post of Additional Secretary (AS), one Joint Secretary (IS), and four Deputy Secretaries (DS) besides 16 secretarial staff, which in financial terms adds up to an additional expenditure of Rs 52 lakh a year. What the MHA has asked the government in terms of human resource is indicative of its intention of creating a gigantic task force to wage the anti-Naxal war, as also an acknowledgement of the stark fact that the Centre has so far failed in its anti-Naxal strategies, and consequent exertions.

One of the two posts will be tenable by an IPS officer of IG rank, mandated to tour the Naxal-hit areas to monitor the implementation of anti-Naxal plans through consultations with the DGPs and Chief Secretaries of the states concerned. Of the four DS posts, two will be tenable by DIG rank police officers.

Creating a Special Cell: Cabinet is a Divided House

That the Maoists are creating havoc in the country is a known fact. But when the Union Home Minister proposed a special Cell to tackle the menace, his own cabinet colleagues came in his way. It was reported by a daily on 15 May. Parliamentary Affairs Minister Priya Ranja, Dasmunshi intervened, saying this was a political issue and the Cell should devise a strategy against all LWE. As if this was not bad enough, the senior minister Arjun Singh (Human Resource Development - HRD) said bluntly: "The Home Ministry is unable to handle the problem!"

A riled Home Minister told the HRD Minister that he had not only handled the Naxalite problem but could also provide details about the situation in Kashmir and in other troubled spots to prove how well his Ministry fared on the internal security front.

Leaving aside these ministerial brickerings, here is an important question: Have the Maoists succedeed in dividing the Union Cabinet or are the senior ministers induling in one-up-manship at the cost of the national interest?

Fighting the Maoists

In 2005, the MHA directed the security men deployed in LWE areas to use plain clothes and travel in unmarked vehicles. It was meant to obfuscate easy identification that makes them coveted targets without any difficulty.

The Union Government is reported to have formulated a strategy to contain and defeat the Naxal violence. It includes:

- Sharing of intelligence.
- Intensified development effort in LWE areas.
- Speeding up the land reforms.
- Modernisation of police force.
- Adoption of a collective/coordinated approach by the affected states in planning and conducting anti-Maoist operations.

Bal Thackeray-speak Jun 2006 (Naxal tit for Islamic tat)

One can count on Bal Theackeray, a maverick Maharashtra politician, to come up with weird theories and amusing postulations.

To wit, examine what he said on 19 Jun 2006 at a public meeting on Mumbai convened to mark the 40th anniversary of his creation, the Shiv Sena.

> "I am ready to seek coopration of the Naxalites to fight Islamic terrorism in the country. They are Hindus. They have some social-economic issues for which they have taken to arms. When separatists are invited for talks in Delhi, why do the government ignore Naxalites? the country faces biggest threat from Islamic separatists not only in Jammu and Kashmir, but also elsewhere in India, also."[2]

In his ten-minute speech, he also addressed his pet aversions and issues: the UPA Government taking diktats from Sonia Gandhi, political parties, double speak on reservations, his inability to check (he meant 'arrest') his age which is catching on with him in spite of his famed remote control. But these inane observations has nothing to do with the subject of this book.

These have been included here to show how slipshod and clumsy some of our politicians are while commenting on a serious security issue. In fact, his observations are worse than weird. Some editorial comments are called for to show how absured and irresponsible some of our politicians can be.

- He must understand that the aims of the Islamist terrorists and the Maoists are exactly same: destabilisation, displacement and finally destruction of India as it is today.

- Both practice extremist and radical ideology: one in the field of religion and the other in the field of politics and economy.
- The governments in the past have offered talks to the Maoists if they abjure violence. They accepted the offer only to gain political and military gains from the interregnum. They will never allow quick development of the tribal areas, the cause they assert to be behind their armed insurrection, because if that goes well, they will have lost the cause celebre of their violent movement!
- Forget their central leadership, why does not this great Hindu leader contact a Maoist leader nearer home, CPI (Maoist) secretary of the Maharashtra State Committee, spreading death and destruction in the eastern part of his State and seek his cooperation to fight Islamist terror.

Private Copters to Fight Maoists: October 2006

It is not unoften that the analysts and security experts get irked with Centre's stance on fighting the Maoist insurgency that is threatening country's integrity and sovereignty. Union Government's constant refrain hasbeen: LWE is a problem concerning the individual states, hence the inadvisability of raising it to a "national" problem! Simultaneously, the MHA keep making proforma assurances to the affected states to "extend all necessary assistance — additional security forces, funds, intelligence inputs *et. al.,* — to fight the menace. It is like a recorded message repeated by the Home Minister every time a state faces a major Maoist strike! This repitition mouthed ad nauseam has become an annoying cliche!

Fortunataly, the MHA has gone beyond these robotized assurances by going in for purchase of helicopters from private firms that will enhance the anti-Naxal capability of the Naxalism-hit states. To be more specific, the MHA has signed an agreement with M/s Vertex Ltd., of Hyderabad for the supply of two helicopters on lease for none-military purposes to security forces, deployed in LWE states of Chhattisgarh, Jharkhand, Odisha and Andhra Pradesh.[3]

It is believed the "CRPF has already used the choppers on two occasions during the last couple of mouths in Chhattisgarh to air-drop personnel in remote areas for specific operations".

Andhra Government is to be the nodal agency to coordinate the use of the two machines among different states. An expense of Rs. 8 crore would be borne by the MHA from the SRE.

The decision to rope in the private players reflects government's determination to gain an upper hand against the ultras in a situation that reveals a rising trend of casualties suffered by the forces in Naxal depredations.

The comparative figures for two years are given in the table here to show the rising casts in human lives in Naxalite strikes.

Comparative Costs in Human Lives

Period	***Fatalities Suffered***	
	Security forces	***Civilians***
2005	94	364
2006 (till August)	115	401

This deal to deploy copters in the said role has a particular significance, as it comes close on the heels of private firms refusing to enter into such a deal as they mere apprehensive about the safety of their machines in the Naxal-hit areas. The discovery that the Maoists had developed rockets with a potential range of 400 mtrs had only added to their apprehensions.

These apprehensions are not unfounded. "850 rockets mere seized recently (early 2006) in Prakasam and Mahboobnagar districts, Andhra Pradesh." It has a range of 400 mtrs. More worryingly, not only the private companies, even the security force were deeply concerned since part of this stock (of 850-odd rockets) "have already fallen into the hands of the Maoists". It was understandable DG CRPF JK Sinha talling the press on 24 Oct 2006: "They only have to fill the rockets with explosives and use them against our forces."

CRPF can Operate on its own Oct 2006

Another important development, vis-a-vis anti-Naxal operations, was the launching of operations by the CRPF on its own against the ultras in Chhattisgarh. Earlier, the role of the CPMF like the CRPF was essentially to supplement the efforts of the state police.

The change for the better is the fall-out of a proposal mooted by security adviser to the state government KPS Gill, that was supported by the MHA. A senior official elucidated the issue: "The G Branch for intelligence that was inaugurated (only) five months ago for the CRPF has started yielding results. Enough information was pouring in on the Maoists that is supplemented by the State Police."

Brushing aisde the controversy on the Salwa Judum movement in Chhattisgarh, DG CRPF JK Sinha sait is was people's movement" that needed to be supported. Asked about the possibility of infiltration by the ISI into the CRPF, he was categorical: "Jawans did not have access to sensitive information and that an efficient surveillance system was in place to monitor the activities of senior officers."

Another Counter-insurgency School 2006

The MHA has given in-principle approval for setting up a specialised school where CPMF will be trained in subjects concerning the internal security issues: Commando operations; counter-guerrilla tactics; detection and disposal of explosives; jungle warfacr and anti-sabotage operations. The BSF has been entrusted with the task of setting-up this counter-insurgency (CI) institution.

The BSF, essentially and mainly engaged in guarding nations borders in peace-time, will establish a world-class institute to train para-military forces and state police personnel for the said subjects. DG BSF AK Mitra says: "The contours of anti-insurgency operations are fast changing. We need to update our personnel to familiarise them with the latest techniques and to sharpen their skills."[4]

The DG disclosed the Centre wanted the school to come up in Hazaribagh, Jharkhand, but the BSF suggested Bangaluru for the purpose as the jungle land was available there, an essential requirement for the school. The formal approval for the proposal is awaited from the MHA.

The institute will be third of its kind in the country, as two are already functioning, viz, the Army has its counter-insurgency and Jungle warfare school at Warangle, Mizoram and the NSG Training Centre at Manesar, Gurgaon, Haryana.

Some Counter-LWE Measures

Some of the measures deemed effective to counter the onslaught of the Maoism are discussed in this section.

Coordination among states for counter-Maoist operations

The states which are Naxalism - affected and are covered by the CRZ and through which the Red Corridor passes must strive for institutional arrangements for coordinated policy action against the Maoists who are operating across several such states. The coordination and cooperation between the two neighbouring states are even more necessary against the common enemy. Beyond such bilateral cooperation, collectivity of more than two such affected states too would have to plan cooperative and coordinated anti-Maoist joint operations. In this case, not only more hard work is required, but certain over-arching role of the Central agencies too is a must. Intelligence sharing is important for such action, especially the real time one.

Special Forces

Special anti-Naxal task forces, trained and equippad for counter-insurgency and jungle warfare against the ultras, will be required. The Grayhounds of Andhra Pradesh is a well-known success story in the genre. Some other states too have experimented in this field with their own versions of such forces. The CRPF, country's main anti-Maoist force, too has its COBRA for the purpose. More importantly, all such forces needs to be trained rigorously at specialised schools. If Indian Army has its well-known, well reputed CIJWS, Jharkhand, one of the two worst-hit states, has its counter-terriorism and Jungle warfare school (CTJWS) at Kanker for similar training.

National Interest and Bane of Politics

An analyst wants political considerations to be kept apart from the national interests. Is he aksing for too much, especially in the Indian context? It would seem so if we look how the Maoists were dealt with in Andhra Pradesh under two CMs. The excellent result achieved by the special units during the tenure of CM Chandra Babu Naidu's TDP Government were frittered way by the YSR Reddy Congress Government that came to power after the 1994 polls. How and why did this come to happen?

On the eve of the Assembly elections 1994 and during the run up to these polls, Opposition Congress party, looking and vying for the support of the Maoists and their overground supporters promised to declare a 'ceasefire' and hold talks with them. After coming to power in the State (Congress was in power at the Centre since 1991), prolonged negotiations were held with the Maoist leaders. Expectedly, they made a great show of it all: they insisted and were allowed to come armed with their weapons; at one stage, they insisted on dismissing the personal security provided to them by the state government and the latter gave in and finally made sure they achieved an equality of status with the chief minister and his ministers, which not only added to their respectability but also raised their stature in the eyes of their cadre. All this infused new life in their movement. They had extended these negotiations delibrately, knowing well that the interregnum was being well utilised by the Maoist leaders in the jungle to retrain, re-group and re-equip their fighting cadres. Consequently, when the negotiations ended, expectedly, sans any result, the Maoist cadres were ready to take the field with renewed vigour and enhanced confidence. The round had gone, undoubtedly, to the calculating Maoists, and not to the driven-by-vote-bank, and inane, politicians.

It was, of course, not the first time that the politics of vote bank vis-à-vis the Naxalites had been played by a CM in Andhra. NT Rama Rao had played it with consummate skill in 1982, calling the Naxalites true patriots (deshbhaktalu' was the term used by him) who had been misunderstood by the ruling classes. Honeymoon did not last long, and thank God for that! By 1985, he was forced to take action against them.

M Channa Reddy, Congress CM, acted no differently. In 1989, during assembly polls, he too declared that Naxalites were patriots. N Chandrababu Naidu, for a change, adopted a firm stand against the Maoist outlaws. He defeated them with his Greyhounds. But it was YSR Reddy's turn now, post coming to power in 1994, as narrated earlier, to appease the Maoists.

In some other states too, political parties and individual leaders have not shied away from striking an understanding of mutual help with the Maoists. An analyst says, "This has enabled the latter to have an unhindered space for their activities while the former have been getting an electoral support of the Maoist cadres at the time of elections. This mutual understanding has been widely noticed in Bihar and Jharkhand."

Politics indeed has been the bane in the field of adopting effective anti-terrorism policies of India. More specifically, vote-bank politics has hobbled these policies at various stages, which has been discussed earlier. The same flaw marks the anti-Naxal policies of various states in India. It is unfortunate that short-term political gains takes precedence over the long-term national interest. The Centre and states must craft an anti-Naxal policy, above the interests of party politics, and then deploy their available resources-- state police, paramilitary forces including specialist units - - to gain an upper hand against the rebels. Otherwise, the Maoists cannot be faulted for believing that they are facing a compromised, indecisive and even a 'tottering foe? The country has a right to expect its political leaders at the national and state levels to rise above their narrow party and personal considerations and devise an effective, united strategy and a national policy to fight against the enemy gnawing at its vitals single mindedly. Tomorrow may be too late.

It is a given that this battle will be fought and won on the political front.

Rs 23,000 crore Spent on Paramilitary Forces: Aug. 2007

The cost of fighting terrorism, Naxalism and maintaining law and order situation by the CPMF alone stands a little over Rs 23,000 cr. The amount was paid by the Centre to the CPMF and excludes the expenses incurred by the states on their police forces engaged in anti-Naxal operations. The actual cost of fighting insurgency, ultra-Left violence and terrorism could be more as the figure does not include the loss of public infrastructure and civilian lives.

In reply to a parliamentary question, the Centre admitted giving large amount to paramilitary forces for their upkeep and to the families of the men who were killed in anti-Naxal or other operations.

The amount spent on a company of a paramilitary unit of 120 strength cost some Rs 40,000 a month, that translates into Rs 333 per person per month. The salaries and training expenses are over and above this amount of Rs 333 (per man) per month. Over Rs 31 crore was paid to the families of the men killed in action against the insurgents and Maoists during the last two years.

Realising the extent of expenses incurred on fighting these insurgents, the Centre is now believed to have directed the LWE states to raise 29 (additional) India Reserve battlions (IRBs) on their own to counter the ultras and maintain law and order in their areas.

If only the expenditure by the Centre is calculated in raising the additional manpower for IRBs of the states, the figure stands at Rs 1,555 cr in the last three years.

The Centre has also allotted Rs 2,475 cr to the backward districts for their social and infrastructure development. Some of these backward districts are heavily affected by prolonged violence perpetrated by the Maoists and other insurgent groups.

Naxalites becoming Internet (Cyberspace) Warriors: April 2007

The intelligence agencies have asked the centre to prevent spread of the Maoist idealogy in cyber space and initiate action against all web-sites which are engaged in spreading this idealogy. The was reported by a daily on 28 April 2007. A rather concerned intelligence officer explained the developing worrisome situation to the daily in Question.[5]

> "Most of these networks are run by Naxalite outfits in the name of social organisations to spread their ideology and also to communicate among themselves in coded language. On the face of it, these websites and blogs do not contain anything illegal and do not promote violence directly, but the use of the Internet by the Red Army Cadre would prove more dangerous than a direct attack by Naxalites".

The Central intelligence agencies are already keeping a watch on these websites and monitoring all blogs, emails and groups which may even be slightly pro-Maoist. The officer continues: "Whatever information we have received during the monitoring of such networks has been passed on to the Centre as also the states concerned."

The 23rd meeting of the National Coordination Centre on Naxalism asked the states to share information and keep a constant watch on the movement of Naxalite groups, their weaponry, training camps, hideouts, sources of weapons and funds, areas of current activity and areas in which they plan to spread their violence and activity. States have also been asked to strenghen their security structures and intelligence gathering machinery and raise more India Reserve Battalions (IRBs).

Security forces emphasised the need for police to adhere to the field craft and SOPs during anti-Naxal operations.

On the development front, states were advised to review their resettlement and rehabilitation policies on priority basis. The need to put special focus on implementation of Backward Regions Grant Fund (BRGF), Panchayat (Extension to Scheduled Areas) Act, 1996 (PESA), NRGEP and Scheduled Tribes and other traditional forest (Reorganization of Forest Rights) Act, 2006, was emphasised, said a MHA officer.

State governemnt were urged to fill vacancies at the bottom level of the district administration, especially in rural and tribal areas, through special recuitment drives to ensure that the development agenda was not neglacted due to absence of grass roots machinery.

Some of the points adumbrated in the proceedings paragraphs are contained in the Report of the Parliamentary Standing Committee on Home Affairs (PSC-HA) tabled in the parliament on 26 Apr 2007; and other flowed from the meeting of the National Coordination Centre on Naxalism (NCCN) convered by the MHA under the chairmanship of Union Home Secretary Madhukar Gupta, after the PSA-HA report was received by it, to deliberate on its contents and recommendations.

The PSC Report said the Maoist problem has assumed a national dimension. The Report recommends: "Besieds the CPMF, State Police Forces may also contribute to the unified command structure."

The PSC headed by BJP MP Sushma Swaraj clearly mentioned that it was no longer a problem of few states, and also expressed strong displeasure over the lack of initiative by the states. The Report rued the fact that there was no perceptable change on the Socio-Economic Front.[6]

The NCCN meet, chaired by the Home Secretary was attended by the Chief Secretaries and the DGPs of the Maoist-hit states. The latter presented their state's plans of action as to how they were proceeding on the agenda, mentioned above.

They also detailed their plans of increasing the strength of their states police forces and ensuring their share in the IR(B) forces as suggested by the Centre.

Merger of Maoist Outfits: Combating the Combined Entity

The MCC merges with PWG in September, 2004 to create CPI (Maoist), which has extensive reach into the country's hinterland, especially rural and adivasi areas, and has massive armed cadre. Strength of this cadre has been covered extensively at various stages in its history.

Subsequently, post-merger, the CPI (Maoist) declared a unilateral ceasefire with the CPI(ML) in Jan 2005. "Presently, the CPI (Maoist) controlls a quarter of the country's 602 districts. It has presence in more than 12 states. Its core area is co-extensive with Bihar, Jharkhand, AP and Chhattisgarh."

The above is the assessment of the Naxal influence, perhaps a little overdone, by a weekly in its 11 Jun 2006 issue.[7]

The weekly quotes PM Manmohan Singh, addressing a meeting of the Standing Committee of Chief ministers to discuss Naxal violence on 13 Apr 2006, as saying:

"Naxals are India's biggest internal security challenge. It has gained in strength and spread to over 160 of the country's 602 districts..... Maoists are controlling administration, policing and justice in certain 'liberated' gones."

The Union Government has not under estimated and can't afford to do so, the threat of LWE in the country, as the PM has already defined it as "India's biggest internal security challenge."

A meeting of top officials from 13 Naxal-hit states held in Delhi on 31 Mar 2006 concluded that Naxals "have been spreading their tentacles across the country. In comparative terms, the MHA says: "76 districts in AP, Jharkhand, Chhattisgarh, Bihar, Maharashtra, Odisha, MP, UP and West Bengal are 'badly' affected by Maoism." (other affected states are Tamil Nadu and Karnataka).

Army's Role in Counter-Naxal Combat

Significantly and importantly, it was for the first time that the Army Commanders Conference discussed the Maoist issue on 6-7 April 2005. Army Chief Gen Joginder Jaswant Singh said: "We will try to nip the evil in the bud." He promised all Army support to police and CPMF to counter the spread of the Maoists.

There were reports that the Army was exercised over the prospects of being called out to combat Maoists. It seem the CIJW school in Varange, Mizoram, examined the issue at a theoretical level and "We found that the situation in these states is different than the areas where we have our counter-insurgency operations."

To wit, the Amry cannot operate on a long term basis in counter-Naxal role without the Armed Forces Special Powers Act (AF-SPA) being enforced in the region/state. Counter-Naxal operations are not like holding a flag-march through a riot - hit city. Not many states would be willing to impose AF - SPA, which grants certain special powers to the troops, over large number of districts, or over entire state, "you would and up alienating even those sections of the population who were till now loyal and sympathetic to the state," was the fear expressed.

That perhaps was the reason why the Army helped the Jharkhand Governement/Police to set up a Jungle Warfare School at Kanker, "before it was asked to get involved. A better way would be for the Army to set up a Jungle Warfare School in Kanker for itself." This tongue-in-cheek suggestion comes either from the ignorance of the Army role in country's defence or an attempt to be too clever by half!

Army should not be frivously asked to take on police duties, and that is what Naxal violence is all about. If police is unable to do that job, employ paramilitary forces. Asking Army to step in whenever police or paramulitary fail to do their job is not doing right thing. The solution is to improve their functional and operational efficiency by way of funds, training and professionalism. Army should be the instrument of last resort. If the Army is called out too aften to do police job, it will not only lose its sheen, but also its professionalism. The police and paramilitary force should not be allowed to keep falling by the wayside due to lethargy, inefficiency and ill-discipline. They must be pushed to deliver. Otherwise, we would be encouraging do-gooders and busybodies to keep demanding Army deployment at the drop of a hat, as they did when police repeatedly failed to nab and ferret that sandal wood bringand Veerappan out of his jungle hideout. Otherwise, Army would be too stretched on the ground and consequently reduced to a glorified, heavily-armed police force, which would not be able to defend the nation's borders as and when required. The do-gooders too aften forget that Army's primary role is to defend the nation against external aggression.

The above is an attempt to refute repeated calls made on Army to take police's chestnuts out of fire. It is not suggested that the Army cannot be called if there are natural calamitie like the floods or earthquakes.

Maoist Response to Government's Counter-Naxalite Plans

The Centre formulated certain measures to fight and control the Naxal violence in March 2006: intelligence sharing, speeding up land reforms, anti-Naxal coordinated strategy among the affected states and modernization of police forces.

Obviously not impressed with this anti-Naxal strategy, CPI (Maoist) Secretary, Dandakaranya Special Zone Committee, Kosa said rather self-assuredly: Given the growing base in Bihar, Jharkhand, AP, Chhattisgarh, Maharashtra, West Bengal, Odish, UP, Tamil Nadu, Karnataka and MP, the Maoists would be able to capture about 35 per cent of India by 2010.

28 May 2007 Explosions and Consequences: An Assessment: May 2007

Chhattisgarh continues to engage MHA with occasional Maoist violence happening there. Recent efforts to hem-in that violence were disrupted by the killings of the nine policemen in the Bastar forests on 28 May 2007.

The attack came a fortnight after the Union Home Secretary's letter of 17 May, advising the state government to strengthen the intelligence machinery to effectively tackle the Maoism, and offering all help on the issue.

The nine deaths was the result of a trap the policeman 'reportedly' walked into unsuspectedly. After the attack, the MHA placed a helicopter at the disposal of the state government for the rescue and relief operations.[8]

The situation in Chhattisa has been particularly worrisome in the past few months, the most disturbing being the attack on a Salwa jndum Camp in Bijapur's Rani Bodli on 15 Mar, 2007. 500 Maoist cadres swooped on the (police) camp at night, killing 55 security men (the figure rising to 68 subsequently) most of them SPOs of the Judum, the state supported civilian movement against the Maoists.

The daily asks if the 28 May has dampened the efforts and resolve to fight Naxalism:? That will be a rash conclusion. The security experts have been suggesting the state police make a greater use of the CPMF for more effective anti-Naxal operations.

KPS Gill Made a Scapegoat? He Speaks Out: May 2007

A weekly has an interesting question on KPS Gill in its issue of 19 May 2007: "Is Gill being made a scapegoat for police failure"? The question is fuelled by the fact that this outstanding police officer, who had been appointed Security Adviser to the Chhattisgarh Government in

April 2006, did not have his tenure extended/renewed at the end of a year in the appointment.

Along this fact came the news, as yet unconfirmed, the State Government was considering to appoint former DGP AP Swarna Singh Sen as Gill's successor.

Andhra is widely credited as the State– and only one in the country, at that– to have best handled Naxalism and even nearly decimated it. And this achievement with Sen at the helm. Sources in the State Government are keenly highlighting Sen's record to buttress their stance that appointing Gill was an error in the first place. The move to replace Gill is also seen as Chhattisgarh Government's desperate attempt to find a scapegoat for its failure illustrated by the Maoist attack on Rani Bodli camp that resulted in the massacre of 68 policeman, mostly SPOs, on 15 March 2007. It is for note the SPOs are locally recruited tribal youth for Salwa Judum Campaign which is backed by the State.

The above Maoist attack is not the only embarrasment, even if of egregious proportion, the government is saddled with. Of the 749 people killed (2006) by the Maoists in India, 48 per cent were from Chhattisgarh alone! To cap it all, then came a statement in Parliament by Union Home Minister Shivraj Patil in March 2007 that while the Naxalite violence had declined in all other states, it had increased manifold in Chhattisgarh.

Perhaps the real reason for appropriium coming Gill's way was his blunt and outspoken ways. Even while handling the toughest job of his career as DGP Punjab – when he retrieved Punjab for India from beyond even the proverbial brink – he was frank, if no-nonsense man, while dealing with the politicians and bureaucrats. Not unsurprisingly, senior officials in Chhattisgarh were rattled by this outspoken man's allegatious, nay assertions, that it was corruption in the state police that was responsible for the 'success' of Maoist violence and consequent death and destruction, in the State: Constables and junior rank were able to avoid postings to worst affected Bastar plateau or get early transfer from there by simply paying cash to their seniors at various levels.

Sources in the State police told the weekly that Gill repeatelly requested for massive recruitement in the police,[9] "even as a particular police officer was collecting bribes to transfer constables out of the Dantewada district."

Yet again, Gill had been asking for a new post, DIG (Special), whose sole responsibility would be to ensure protection of (distant and isolated) police posts and Salwa Judum camps.

Ironically, if tragically, a source in Raipur disclosed to the weekly that it was only after the 15 March 2007 Rani Bodli massacre that the State Government finally acted on Gill's recommendation!

Meanwhile, the State Government has now appointed a three-member committee, comprising the following, to recommend ways and means to deal with the Maoist insurrection:

1. A retired DG, CRPF.
2. Brig BK Pawar, Commandant, CIJW School (Jungle Warfare College).
3. Girdhar Nayak/IGP (Anti-Naxal operations), Chhattisgarh.

The KPS Gill Interview: Mid May 2007

To get other side of the story, or to get facts from no-nonsense KPS Gill, the said weekly interviewed him and published the text in its issue of 19 May 2007.

Q. What is wrong with national strategy on Naxalism?

A. You don't tackle a problem like this by having meetings. Eversince the PM said so, there has been a succession of very diffused meetings that lacked a focus. The other thing is that these states have government run by different parties and they have different strategies.

Q. So parties should have a consensus?

A. Even in Punjab consensus lasted a short while, and then we got Beant Singh as CM who had a focus. In Chhattisgarh, the DGP can't transfer a constable.

Q. Isn't the Naxalism different from terrorism you tackled in Punjab?

A. There is no difference. No state learnrs from the experience of others. Now, Chhattisgarh officials have made some visits to AP and are trying to learn from them.

Q. Do we need a joint Special Task Force for this?

A. I do not support STFs. The thana is the basic unit of the police. West Bengal overcame the Naxalites by strengthening the thanas. So it was in Punjab. The police strength of Bastar is abysmal.

Q. Has the Salwa Judum been successful considering the Rani Bodli massacre that killed, 68 policemen?

A. The Salwa Jadum has shaken up the Naxalites, but now there is a stalemate. The two major massacres by the Naxalites were actually defeats for them. This is a foolish movement where Naxalites kill tribals, who are their own support group.

Q. After the Rani Bodli massacre, there were reports in Raipur that the State's top police brass does not know what exactly has been your contribution?

A. If I am there and they do not take my advice, whose loss is it? I do not lose anything. The loss is that of the State, of the people.

Q. The Home Minister said the Maoist violence has declined in all the other states but it has increased in Chhattisgarh.

A. Depends on how you use figures. In Chhattisgarh, they are in an aggressive mode. We die, they die.

Q. So it is a civil war we are up for?

A. There is no civil war, it is a creation of journalists. Political parties tie up with Naxalites before elections. Look at Nandigram. It is totally supported by Naxalites. Advani supports it because he wants to score points against the CPM.

Q. You have said the corruption in the police has hurt the anti-Naxal efforts.

A. You don't find corruption in the police?

Q. Why does Naxalism thrive?

A. Like the mafia in Bombay, Naxalism in Chhattisgarh is an extortion operation. It runs between the *beedi* manufacturers, Naxals and the governments.

Q. Will the Army have to step in?

A. I don't agree that the situation is so serious. When Istudied the police deaths in Chhattisgarh for a few months, I found that only three or four policemen had died. The rest were all from CRPF or Naga battalion or the SPOs. So, what is the contribution of Chhattisgarh police? Policemen don't want to be posted in Bastar. They bribe and get a transfer. I submitted a proposal: Give out-of-turn promotions and provide the leaders. Insurgencies are small (junior) commanders' wars. They are not generals' wars.

Q. Is the CM an effective leader?

A. How can I comment on the leadership qualities of a CM? But I told you that the type of administrative support the police is getting is not adequate. I am sorry to say that.

Q. Don't you think fake encounters are the last thing government needs to win the trust of the tribals?

A. Bastar tribals are to be won over in 101 different ways. It starts with what bribals think is development and what we think is development. The tribal says "leave me alone and stop my exploitation by middlemen". The State makes crores out of the tribal produce and is unable to give it back to them. Improve their villages. Give them land rights. The problem in Chhattisgarh is not Naxalism. It is the administration.

Q. You wanted dogs sent for training at the cost of a few crore rupees?

A. The police dogs were totally incapable of detecting bombs. I sent a proposal to the State Government but they did not accept it. The loss is theirs. Similarly, I asked them to set up a control room, they are still doing that.

Q. There were reports that money from the police welfare was spent on your helicopter rides and Rs 25 lakh was spent on your house in Jagdalpur.

A. The helicopter belongs to the state. I used it twice: Once with the Home Minister and once with the Chief Secretary. There was one room of a mess that they built in Jagdalpur. They took a long time, otherwise, I would have gone and stayed there.

Ghosts Haunt the Anti-terrorist Fighters 37 Years after the Battle: June 2007

This is the sad story ghosts of Naxalite terrorism haunting a retired DGP of a State, 37 years after he fought it.

"The CBI court will read out the charge sheet to a former Kerala DGP P. Vijayan and 1 GP G Lakshmana for killing a Naxalite leader in contrived encounter 37 years ago." A daily has this story datelined Kochi 15 June 2007. The two have been ordered to appear before the court for killing Varghese.

Varghese had led the Spring Thunder campaigns of Kerala's fledgling Naxalite movement in the 1970s, when K Karunakaran was its Home Minister Varghese and his Cadres mostly operated in the Wayanad belt of the North Malabar, annihilating the "class enemy" and were alleged to have killed a couple of local landlords accused of oppressing their workers.[10]

The special team of Kerala police stalking Varghese announced his death on 18 Feb 1970. Claiming that he was killed in an armed encounter in the Tirunelli forest of Wayanad, the police got photograph of the slain rebel, with a country rifle near his body, printed in the newspapers.

Though Naxalites and other activist organisations in the State raised a din and moved a court alleging that it was a staged killing, the case and its investigations dragged on for several years, until the 1990s. That was when Ramachandran Nair, a former Head Constable declared that he had shot Varghese point blank on the orders of his superiors after the police had nabbed and tortured him in custody.

Nair, who died in 2006, had confessed that he was making the revelation only to clear his own conscience, and was willing to take any punishment the court found fit for his crime. He said it was Lakshmana, then a DIG, who had ordered him to shoot Varghese, threatening to kill him (Nair) if he did not obey.

Vijayan, Lakshmana, and a couple of other policemen, who are no more, were made the co-accused. CBI, having taken over the investigations post-Nair admission, had filed charge sheet with Nair as the first accused. The said accused persons had managed to get a stay on the proceedings. The case got a fillip after the High Court pulled up the accused for trying to delay the case and scrapped the stay.

Centre to Rework Strategy with the DCs": Naxal Menacc: Sep 2011

Realising that its development initiatives so far have failed to reduce the "trust deficit" among the people in the LWE - infested areas and thereby contain Naxalism, the Centre has now decided to sit across the table with the collectors of 60 Maoist-hit districts to rework its counter-Maoist strategy. It was reported by a daily in Sep 2011.[11]

The Centre will listen to these DC, from the nine relevant States to get a reality check of the existing ground scenario. Subsequent to this brain-storming, the Rural Development (RD) Ministry "is likely to make a strong case for a special package to these districts to ensure fast implementation of the reworked developmental schemes."

RD Minister Jairam Ramesh said: "Lack of governance and infrastructure is a breeding ground for Naxalism. The main concern is to push developmental strategy in the Maoist-hit areas where youth are getting influenced by the Naxals".

A national workshop on "appropriate development strategies for effective implementation of rural development schemes in Integrated Action Plan (IAP) districts," is thus being organised by his Ministry. While PM Manmohan Singh will chair the concluding session of the day-long conference, the workshop will be inaugurated by Home Minister P. Chidambram. CP Joshi, Tribal Affairs Minister and Panchayat Raj Minister V Kishore Chandra Deo, too, would attend.

It is believed that the Centre is likely to agree with the Collectors' suggestions: increase in six per cent ceiling on administrative costs in LWE districts; and allowing cement concrete roads throughout, which presently are allowed only in the areas having human habitation. The DCs, have also been seeking benefits of Indira Awas Yojana for the families affected by the LWE, besides hiring of locals for implementation of developmental schemes.

Then there are basic governance issues like non-availability of banking infrastructure, post offices, lack of security and delayed payments to the wage earners in the affected districts.

Many tribals too feel the "trust deficit" and its ill effects. Ramesh says: "We plan to provide legal help to such tribals before they fall in the trap of the illegal help from the Maoists."

The Government plans a long-term strategy to deal with Maoists as the Integrated Action Plan (IAP) being pursued as a short-term plan to push infrastructure projects for the past two years, will end in March 2012. The 60 districts received Rs 55 cr each in the past two years under the IAP to push infrastructure projects in the short-term time frame.

"Centre to Revamp Flagship Plan against Maoist": April 2012

The Centre has taken development to Maoist strongholds through the IAP, but opinion is divided on whether the three-year-old programme has bridged the trust deficit– the objective outlined by PM Manmohan Singh.[12]

Official statistics have it that some 90 per cent of the projects under the IAP for 78 Naxal-hit districts across the country has been completed. Despite its apparent success, a revamped IAP is likely to be implemented from April 2013.

Locals have no Say

Planning Commission member Mihir Shah, a critic of the present system adopted to implement the Rs 35,00 crore plan, says the flagship programme inalienate the intended beneficiaries because locals have no say in decision-making. He wants to involve the beneficiaries and the civil society to be involved in the decision-making. Involving locals in the plan would help identify area-specific needs, generate employment, and win them over. Under the IAP, villages in the Naxal-hit districts are provided high quality roads, anganwadi centres, schools, health centres and drinking water. So far, 64,000 projects have been undertaken in 378,058 habitations.

Manpower Issues

The IAP, described as success by Home Minister Chidambaram, is also grappling with lack of skilled manpower.

Some 25 per cent posts of medical staff in newly created public health centres are vacant. Many new schools have only ad hoc and untrained teachers.

The Planning Commission aims to overcome some of these issues by narrowing down the focus area from districts to blocks.

A New Approach

The new approach, which will see higher participation of civil society and locals in decision-making, has the backing of RD Minister Jairam Ramesh and Planning Commission Dy Chairman Montek Singh Ahluwalia.

The fresh approach will be built upon the work already done. Sudha Pillai, who implemented the programme till her retirement in March 2012, believes the IAP has presented a new model for implementation of programmes. "Focused approach and dedicated monitoring has worked".

IAP: Some useful Information: What is Integrated Action Plan?

Launched in 2010, this is a Central Government initiative for areas affected by LWE. Its aim is to bridge the development deficit through infrastructure ereation.

Districts Covered

Total of 78: Andra (8); Bihar (9); Chhattisgarh (10); Jharkhand (17); MP (9); Maharashtra (2); Odisha (18); UP (3); West Bengal (3).

Who is in Charge?

A committee comprising the district magistrate, superintendent of police and district forest officer.

Funds Disturbed

For 2010-11, a sum of Rs 25 crore per district and for 2011-2012, Rs 30 crore per district was allocated. A total of Rs 3,300 crore has been sanctioned by the government till date.

Achievements till Date

Building roads, anganwadi centres, schools, providing drinking water supply.

"Meet to Formulate Naxal SOP on 13 July 2012"

Faced with the flak over suspected civililyan deaths "in the anti-Maoist operations last week in Chhattisgarh, CRPF defended its action, saying it had identified seven of those killed in the Bijapur encounter as Naxals, against whom many criminal cases had been lodged in the State.

Union Home Minister Chidambaram too expressed confidence that the operation was "genuine," while reiterating he was sorry if any innocent was killed. If CM Raman Singh wanted an inquiry, it was entirely his call. DG CRPF claimed there was nothing to hide, and they suffered six casualties. Responding to questions, Chidambaram made a talling point: "In a case where recurity forces return fire and they inflict casualties, I am surprised you call it a fake encounter. And when they don't fire back, you call them incompetent."

CRPF identified seven dead as Madkam Suresh, Madkam Nagesh, Madvi Ayatu, Kaka Nagesh, Korsa Bijje, Madkam Dilip, and Irpa Narjayan as Maoists who were killed on the night 28/29 June 2012, when security forces jointly retaliated after they were 'fired upon'.

The MHA has called a meeting on 13 July (2012) to formulate SOP for future action against Maoists. The meet will take stock of the ongoing anti-Naxal offensives and emphasise on taking maximum precautions to avoid any civilian casualty. The meet will be attended by the DGPs, of all Moist-hit states, chiefs of CAPF and senior MHA officials.

A clear directive is expected to be issued to the forces to abandon the exercise if civilians are being used by Maoists as human shields during the day time.

Claiming that encounter was "bona fide", sources claimed that forensic report "has suggested the forces were indeed attacked by adversaries, buttressing force's assertion that they were forced to retaliate on being attacked."

"Four-pronged Policy Needed to Tackle Maoism": Jairam Rakesh: September 2012

RD Minister, one of our more cerebral minister, said on 23 Sep 2012: "Until now, the government has been implementing a two-pronged strategy of development and security operations.[13]

I feel we should also focus on strenghtening the political process and justice to the tribal communities." Ramesh was addressing a meeting called by Gandhian activists at the Gandhi Ashram in Sewagram, Wardha. The topic was, as given by the Gandhians: The situation in the Moist-dominated areas and to find solutions to it." His detailed observations are here.

- "It has been noted that the areas in which the political process is strong, the Maoists are weak there, and the areas where political processes are weak, the Maoists are strong. We also need to look into the justice to the tribals. We have to see if false cases are being filed against the tribals and if projects in these areas are being properly implemented or not. Until tribals think the law will provide them justice, we can't bring them in main stream."

- "The government has declared 82 districts as Maoist dominated. I have visited Tinsukia and think it should also be included in this list. Some areas have been freed from Maoist domination by the government, but there are some areas which are out of government control and are being ruled by the Maoists.
- On the Forest Rights Act, he said: "When I implemented it in Mendha Lekha in Gadchiroli, every one opposed me but it turned out to be a historic step. The Mendha Lekha Gram Panchayat has earned around Rs 1 crore. We have 3,000 potential Mendha Lekhas but the sad part is that we have not been able to have another one.
- On the peace process he said: "Our former Home Minister had said in Parliament that there is no need to abandon movement, giving up arms or disband militia but come for the dialogue. But Ganapati had put up conditions that the ban on the CPI (Maoist) should be lifted and all the political prisoners 'should be released' who would then take part in the dialogue with the government. This shows that the Maoists do not want dialogue and elections."

Centre for all-Party Meet for Consensus on Anti-Naxal Strategy June 2013

"The government will convene an all-party meeting, possibly this week, to elicit views of the political spectrum in an attempt to forge a political consensus on the anti-Maoist strategy." This was reported by a daily in a story datelined 3 June 2013 from New Delhi.[14]

The UPA leadership, which discussed the issue in a 3-hour meeting on 3 June, felt all political parties should be engaged and involved to work out the response to the Maoist threat.

The urgency to look at the strategy to tackle Maoists afresh arose after last months' deadly attack in Chhattisgarh. The UPA coordination meeting mentioned above, which was attended by Congress President Sonia Gandhi, NCP Chief Sharad Pawar, NCs Farooq Abdullah and IUML's E Ahmed, felt the issue required broad-based discussions. The meet was chaired by PM Manmohan Singh.

Parliamentary Affairs Minister Kamal Nath said: "This is an attack on the very foundation of the democracy. It is an attack on the system. It needs to be addressed by all parties."

The UPA meeting came at a time when divergent views on the strategy to be adopted to tackle the Maoists have emerged from within the UPA. The BJP has charged the government with pursuing a soft and inconsistent strategy to deal with the rebels. On 1 June, Sharad Pawar had argued that the challenge posed by the LWE cannot be tackled by treating it only as law and order problem. He advanced "development should go hand in hand with security operations" theory at a time when several of Congress ministers felt that insurgency should be dealt with an iron hand. To wit, RD Minister Jairam Ramesh had dubbed the Maoists 'terrorists' and argued that operations be stepped up!

"No Plans for Aerial attacks on Maoists": Says Chief Minister Raman Singh: June 2014

Stressing that "an integrated approach with focus on holistic development of Bastar is the only way to tackle Maoist problem". This was the response of the Chhattisgarh Government, Chief Minister Raman Singh downwards,[15] on 11 June 2014.

This was in response to the speculation that the State was preparing for aerial attacks on the rebels, consequent to a meeting Union Home Minister Rajnath Singh had with Chief Minister and his senior officials at Raipur on the 11th. Such a speculation was even justified with the chest-thumping image of the new Narendra Modi fresh in the public mind! After all, this important meeting in the capital of worst Maoist-hit state's capital took place a mere fortnight after the new government took over in New Delhi.

So, when the daily asked about the aerial bombing, the Chief Minister told it: "No. Not at all I categorically deny this. He conveyed that "if the country is to fight the LWE, then the biggest battle to be fought will be in Bastar. And this battle is possible only through the holistic development of Bastar."

Explaining the reasons behind the demand for Choppers, ADG (Naxal ops) RK Vij told the daily: "More choppers were asked for improving mobility of forces and response time in crisis situation, not for aerial attacks or dropping bombs". About the need for additional battalions he said security vacuum still existed in many areas of Bastar. So forces were needed to make inroads in such zones and for providing protection to road construction programmes.

Officers clarified that while the Centre "has approved 10 regular and two technical battalions, it has not promised even a single chopper so far, and at the most they expect only two aircraft, which will be used for ferrying forces. Many police stations and posts and CRPF camps are located in remote areas of Bastar where troops and ration is airlifted as roads do not exist."

Finally Vij: "The purpose of meeting was not to seek more battalions or choppers but to draw attention of the policy makers to the need for an integrated plan for tackling the crisis... Maoists are not the problem of Chhattisgarh alone... not just a law and order problem or a security issue. Hence the need for an integrated plan, involving all stake holders and agencies in Naxal management. Our concerns and proposals were appreciated well".

"States need to Lead in Fight against Maoists," MHA Officials on New Policy: June 2014

In its first official interaction with the top officials of the 10 LWE-hit states, on 27 June 2014, Modi Government is going to put across a nuanced message that although it is there with all its support and resources, the time has come for the states to own up the Reds as their problem and lead the charge against them. These are the first inklings of the new government's thinking on the subject, a daily quoted sources for.[16]

The MHA data for the last decade (2000s) shows some 4,918 civilians and 1905 security personnel have been killed by Maoists in different parts of the world.

A MHA official speaks on condition of anonymity: "In the last few years Odisha, West Bengal and Maharashtra have made considerable gains against Maoists. Now it is time for Bihar, Jharkhand and Chhattisgarh to show similar resolve to deal with the Reds. The Centre will back them up but the states will have to emulate Andhra Pradesh example where the outlaws were crushed by the local police."

The meeting is to be chaired by Union Home Minister Rajnath Singh. Besides the Chief Secretaries and DGPs of the 10 LWE-hit States---Bihar, Chhattisgarh, Odisha, Jharkhand, Maharashtra, Andhra Pradesh, Telangana, MP, UP and West Bengal – Chiefs of paramilitary forces involved in anti-Maoist operations will also participate.

The official further added: "The Centre is ready to send 10,000 paramilitary men for anti-Maoist operations, especially in Chhattisgarh where Bastar division is considered an epicentre of Naxals. But such a troop surge will now have a limited usefulness. The onus is now on state police to shoulder the responsibility through effective leadership which is critically lacking in Chhattisgarh."

"Centre Drawing up new Plans to take on Maoists": August 2014

As MHA officials go back to the drawing boards to reshape contours of the anit-naxal policy, there are indications of a tweaking of all existing schemes and initiatives in LWE areas. A daily claims to have been told by its sources.[17]

Whenever a new Government takes over at the Centre, such news of tweaking or even formulating new policies are only to be expected. And, we have a change at New Delhi after 10 long years of UPA rule.

Certain key proposals on the table seem to allow greater flexibility to the MHA to revise guidelines and update list of LWE-hit districts and items covered under the Security Related Expenditure (SRE) reimbursement scheme. The revised draft anti-Naxal doctrine, "which will be circulated to the affected states for their comments before being put up for cabinet approval," would also propose raising of the monetary incentives for surrender by Naxal cadres, as also higher bounty by NIA on top Maoist leaders. As of now, a surrendered higher-ranking Naxal leader gets Rs 2.5 lakh as an inmediate grant and Rs 4,000 per month for 36 months.

Importantly, the Centre, as part of its revised anti-Naxal policy, "will bat for restructuring of CRPF to suit the requirements of the LWE grid." This may entail autonomy for the CRPF to workout its own dynamics, rather than to turn to the MHA for approval of the slightest change.

If the above autonomy-related change is true, it would be a refreshing change of stancea on the part of any ministry. The Indian mentality is to grab power as and when possible, and not to let it slip out of your fist. In any case, it is too early to dish out kudos, let us wait it happening on ground, in reality.

Earlier in 2014, CRPF had proposed a restructuring plan, envisaging a single command system in conjunction with the area of responsibility. The force felt this was called for, since the concentration of its troops in the Naxal areas, J & K and North-East had resulted in its Group Centres and Range offices being far away from the battalions.

The revised counter-Naxal doctrine might propose a standing mechanism comprising the Union Home Minister and Chief Ministers of the affected states to periodically review the relevance of the anti-Naxal policy.

The other initiatives that might go through some overhaul are the scheme for Special Infrastructure (SIS) in LWE districts, under which funds are released to create infrastructure to raise special forces on the lines of the famed Greyhounds of Andhra Pradesh. This is obviously a flawed proposal, or may be, a misinterpreted one. The infrastructure should not be created at district level. It should be at the State level, and funds should be released accordingly. The Greyhound type special force should be controlled and deployed by the DGP of the State, prefereably in consultation with the seniormost CRPF officer in that state.

The utilisation of additional funds provided in this (2014-15) years' budget for police modernisation and implementation of schemes for construction of police stations will also be improved upon.

A central counter-Naxal plan had, recently, suggested an advanced mine-detection system, in use in Afghanistan, to deal with the IED threats posed by the Maoists. Another idea on the table is to focus 30-40 worst-hit districts and reward the IAS/IPS officers who deliver results.

Taking a leaf out of Punjab's success in beating Sikh militancy, the action plan suggest a single IG/DIG exercise command over both the State police and central forces lodged there-in, to ensure better coordination.

Projecting road connectivity as a game changer, the Centre's Action Plan suggests insurance subsidy for contractors and workers, and incentivising timely completion of projects.

These are the contours of the anti-Naxal policy, which might take long time for finalisation.

Steps to Counter Red Threat

There is a summary of eight steps given by this daily. It obviously is the result of a hand out from some official— called a 'source' by the newspapers in their parlance— of the MHA.

1. **Standing mechanism:** Comprising Home Minister and CMs of Naxal-hit states for a periodic review of policy.
2. **State level monitoring committees:** Officers of state government state police, central forces and Home Ministry, to review operations every month.
3. **Flexibility to central forces like CRPF:** To restructure dynamics to suit requirements of LWE areas.
4. Higher monetary incentives for surrender and rehabilitation of the Naxal leaders.

5. NIA may be asked to raise the bounty on the heads of top Maoist leaders.
6. Autonomy to the MHA to effect changes to the list of items covered under SRE scheme, in consultation with the states (changes in SRE currently require Cabinet approval).
7. Updation of technological solutions to beat the IED threat. CRPF's Institute for IED Management, Pune, may be tasked to study advanced mine detection equipment already in use in Afghanistan.
8. Quantum jump in Central funding for community policing from existing Rs 10 lakh limit.

"Rajnath to Discuss Security issues in Maoist-hit States on Friday (27 June 2014)

"Union Home Minister Rajnath Singh will hold a meeting of chief secretaries and police chiefs of Maoist-hit states on 27 June (2014) to take stock of the situation and to draw up strategy to deal with the challenge". So reported a daily dated 24 June 2014.[18]

Top officials from 10 Maoist-hit states will participate in the meeting. The states are: Chhattisgarh, Jharkhand, Odisha, Bihar, Andhra Pradesh, Maharashtra, West Bengal, UP and MP.

The meeting is an annual affair. But being the first meeting of the NDA Government after assuming power on 26 May, it assumes added importance.

Discussions on operational performance of CAPF, gaps in coordination between State and Central security agencies, performance of state government on security related schemes like fortified police stations, roads and other infrastructure projects are likely to take place during these important deliberations.

"Rajnath Singh lays down NDA Policy on Combating Maoists: No talks: June 2014

Spelling out the government's tough stand against the Maoists for the first time, Union Home Minister Rajnath Singh on 27 June 2014 ruled out any talks with the rebels, saying, "the government will adopt a balanced approach in its fight against the releals, but if attacked, the security forces will give a befitting reply."[19]

The daily feels Singh's statement is a massive shift from the stand taken by the previous UPA government, which was ready to talk to the Maoists if they abjured violence. In line with the tough stand, the government is planning to deploy young IPS officers who would lead assault teams against the armed rebels in the affected states. Again, the Centre would micro-manage road construction work so that the forces– as also development– reach the remote affected areas.

Home Secretary Anil Goswami, who briefed PM Narander Modi 27th evening, also echoed this stand during his presentation. He is believed to have said that reducing Naxals to insignificant levels" was one of the top priorities of the government.

Earlier on the 27th morning, during his meeting chief secretaries, state police chiefs and heads of the CAPFs in all the LWE-infested states, Singh said enough funds will be provided to equip and modernise their forces, and asked them to give a befitting reply if the Maoists try to challenge their authority.

The Home Minister was briefed by each of the states on the Maoist situation in their respective areas.

The IB, which also made a presentation during the meeting informed that although there was a decline in the presence of the Maoists in the past one decade in all the 10 affected states, their armed cadre strength stood at 4,000, while the overground workers strength was 36,000. Putting up a realistic scenario before the Home Minister, the IB told him that barring Assam, which has been declared free of Maoist presence in the past decade, much needs to be done in the remaining states.

A MHA official clarified that the talks with the Maoists will be held only when they shun violence and come forward for dialogue. Singh said his Ministry will fully fund formation of special forces on the lines of the elite anti-Naxal force Greyhounds of Andhra Pradesh. To start with, such forces would come up in the four states of Chhattisgarh, Odisha, Jharkhand and Bihar.

The Minister wanted road construction to be taken up on priority by the states. Chhattisgarh informed that due to the fear of the Maoists, no contractor was coming forward for the work.

The MHA and the States, during the meet, also unanimously decided to adopt a four-pronged approach to deal with the Maoists... security, development, entitlement to social welfare schemes like providing land authorisations and right to avail benefits of the government policies by the tribals and locals.

The Minister sought to enhance the incentives and allowances for CAPF men deloyed in these areas, getting them at par with those deployed in J &

K. At present, a jawan deployed in anti-Naxal operations grid gets Rs 4,000 less than his colleague deployed in J & K.

MHA Mulls soft approach to tackle Maoism, September 2014

The MHA, under the new (Modi) dispensation, is thinking of adopting a development oriented and more humane approach compared to the "bullet strategy" of the previous UPA Government, to tackle LWE. The change is based on intelligence reports from various resources that the "bullet strategy" is not working. Home Minister Rajnath Singh, IB chief Asif Ibrahim and RAW chief Alok Joshi delibrated on the issue mid September 2014 and were of the view that a "softer and development oriented" approach would yield better results. It was reported by a weekly dated 21 Sep 2014.[20]

An MHA official told the weekly: "Aggressive operations have in-alienated the population on the ground... it has proved counter productive... This excessive use of force against the locals enabled the Maoists to win them over. They have now more unarmed sympathisers than they had earlier". Another argument on similar grounds: "We need to win over the hearts of villagers... It is disgruntled villagers that fall easy prey to Maoists for filling their ranks. Previous government failed to do any development work in areas like Bastar's vast swathes and in Abujhmaar... It is surprising to learn that even today it takes two days to reach some villages in Bastar... The then Home Minister P Chidambaram announced in 2009 that the government would reclaim all areas under Maoist control in three years. More than five years later, that still remains a distant dream".

"Centre draws up growth-oriented plans to tackle Maoists Menace:" 8 October 2014

"The Centre has formulated a comprehensive policy for the Naxal-hit states for focusing on development-oriented measures as well as strengthening the operations of security agencies". This was reported by a daily of 18 Oct 2014.[21]

The policy, approved by Home Minister Rajnath Singh, set out a financial package and stipulated specific time line for its implementation for State Governments for development of tribal areas under Maoist influence. The new policy also envisages setting up a new counter-insurgency division in the CRPF to tackle the Maoist menace, said senior MHA officials.

Some of the more important points from this newly-approved counter-Maoist policy are enumerated in the succeeding paras:

- The blueprint of the new policy has already been handed out to the concerned States.

- The focus will be more on the development of neglected regions in the Naxal-hit districts in these States. Infrastructure development like the communication, roads, electricity and the water supply will be the thrust areas. There will be a coordination mechanism in the Centre with concerned ministries including Finance, Telecom, Tribal, Road transport, Panchayat Raj, and environment to monitor the implementation of the new policy.
- As for as ongoing operations by security agencies, the new policy envisages stregthening and creating of units for counter-insurgency in CRPF.
- Talks with Maoists only if they renounce violence.
- Increase in financial packages for encouraging surrenders.
- In development part, the Centre will be responsible for strengthening communication system and rapid installation of telecom towers.
- Highways will have high priority.
- Delays and disputes in settlement of title deeds of land must be rectified, as these cause public anger.
- States must declare and increase Minimum Support Price (MSP) of the forest produces. Any discontentment on this issue gives a chance to Maoists to turn the people against the government.
- New policy envisages posting of "most competend officers" and fixed tenure of three years for them in the worst-affected 22 districts in the country. These posts include DC, SP, SDO/SDM etc.
- Rebuilding of police stations in several areas as also setting up new police stations.
- The policy moots building of roads in the 10 Maoist-hit states in two phases: 15,700 km in phase 1 and 25,600 in Phase 2.

Violence by Maoists: Figures Upto 15 September 2014

- No. of incidents 786
- No. of civilians killed 163
- No. of security men killed 68
- No. of Naxals killed 49

Policy on Maoists also focuses on Welfare of Tribals": 18 Octtober 2014

The new policy of the NDA Government, analysed above, has also been covered by another daily, on the same day, as the earlier one, that is on 18 Oct 2014. Some additional points from the second daily are mentioned here after.[22]

The most significant aspect of the Centre's first cut of the policy dealing with Maoist challenge gives it the right to use all necessary forces against the Maoists but it balances the hardline approach by focusing on tribal welfare.

The new policy is the first attempt to, coherently and comprehensively, spell out the national policy to deal with the Maoists while in the opposition, the present ruling (BJP) party had often targeted the then ruling UPA government for the absence of a central policy. A source conceded the new policy was a much a strategy vision as a political document. The draft policy asks states and district SPs to take the lead in the counter-insurgency campaign with support from the CAPF. Some other points are mentioned briefly.

- The CAPF have the responsibility to hold the counter-insurgency grid together, operating seamlessly across the state borders in coordination with the state police forces.
- The policy caters for governemnt intervention in four areas: Security, development, ensuring rights and entitlements of local communities, and public perception management.
- In the new format, the Centre intends to extensively focus on 23 (most Maoist-hit) districts that accounts for 80 per cent of Maoist violence. The primary response in these districts will be a security approach.
- In the moderately-affected districts, understandably enough, the security and development responses will go on the parallel lines, literally.
- The Government sources believe many elements of new policy were already under implementation, e.g., the policy recognises that the first steps towards checking Maoist violence was reviving, strengthening/rebuilding and building additional police stations.

"State Police forces to lead anti-Naxal Operations:" A third daily looks at the issue: 18.10.15 "New Doctrine says Maoists will have to Renounce Violene for Peace Talks"

A third daily covers the new Government's policy on the Naxals. It has mentioned a couple of points not discussed by other daililes. So, this too will the looked into.[23]

A senior MHA official made an interesting claim and a candid admission: "This was the first time that a comprehensive anti-LWE policy was being put down in black and white... It largely borrowed from minutes and circulars taken out over the last 45 years while adding some new interventions."

In the less affected (worst-affected and moderately-affected have been mentioned above) areas, development interventions will take precedence.

The policy proposes oversight committee at national and state levels. The former will comprise Home Minister, Finance Minister, Tribal Affairs Minister, Environment Minister, Rural Development Minister, Panchayati Raj Minister and Road and Transport Minister, besides CMs of all Naxal-hit States, and will meet biannually. On same lines, there will be State Committee each in these 10 states.

Apart from this, there will be an interministerial group, a coordinating committee to oversee strategies, comprising Centrel and State level officers for coordinated response by State agencies.

"Appealing to Naxals to Shun violence is new Strategy"

This is the headline of an article in a daily of 17 Nov 2014.[24] This is among the series of analytical articles that appeared in the press following the circulation of NDA's draft policy on Naxals, sometime in September 2014.

The first three paras of this analysis are reproduced:

> "The Modi Government's recent emphasis on appealing to Maoists to shun violence is part of new strategy aimed at providing the extremists a way out to join the societal mainstream, especially against the backdrop of inputs that the middle rung of Maoist leadership stands wiped out and the outfit facing arms and annunition crunch.
>
> "The policy has taken into account the fact that the top leadership of the Maoists is age-ing and the 'demoralised' cadres are surrendering in large numbers after being targeted by the security forces.
>
> "However, since Maoism continues to be the biggest (internal) security challenge, the Centre would continue with its four-pronged strategy related to security-related intervention, development, entitlement of the tribals and perception management. Not taking any chance, the Centre has continued the deployment of almost 40 per cent of the CRPF in the Naxal-affected areas."

This article was occassioned by Home Minister Rajnath Singh's visit to the Diamond Jubilee celebrations of CRPF at Kadarpur Group Centre in

Gurgaon, near Delhi, where he appealed to the Maoists to shun violence, join the mainstream and help in developing India into a superpower, saying violence has no place in democracy. Some other points made by him: Mao Zedong's ideology, being followed by Indian Maoists, has been forgotten even in China, the very country where he had founded the Communist state that has become now one of the most powerful states in the world, but here in India, you are killing your innocent countrymen by following that ideology, and our democratic values are very strong and I would ask you to change the power through democratic means and not by gun.

Later at a Consultation comittee meeting, Singh said, "The security establishment is encouraged since the LWE is on the decline. But he cautioned that this should not lull us into a sense of complacency. Singh said Maoist extremism remains the biggest threat to our internal security and nation-bulding process and it has remained on top of the agenda for interventions by the Government.

At this meeting, the CRPF released some relevant and important information on the subject.

"1. Apart from other development-related projects, nearly 5,500 km of road length is being laid out in 34 severely Maoist-hit districts and over 12 lakh title deeds have been distributed to the tribals in such areas.

2. The CRPF has killed 23 Maoists, apprehended 835 and another 126 have surrendered before its troops so far this (2014) this year. In 2014, CRPF troops killed one sub-zoned commander carrying a bounty Rs 2 lakh, two area commanders, apprehended five zonal commanders and 24 area commanders.

3. The above is besides the recoveries made by its troops. Seizures in LWE theatre include over 475 arms, some 11,000 rounds of ammunition, 11,224 kg of explosives, 175 grenades, 283 bombs, 371 IEDs, 4,400 detonators, about 800 gelatine sticks, some 7,600 kg narcotics and over Rs 51,67 lakh.

4. During the year 2014, CRPF apprehended and was involved in the apprehension/surrender of Krishna Ahir alias Prasad Ji, political commissionar of CPI(M), carrying a bounty of Rs 3 lakh in Jharkhand, Jagarbatti Nagalias alias Sita, Member, Coy 2nd (carrying a reward of Rs 8 lakh, surrendered in Chhattisgarh) and Krishna Yadav alias Badal Ji of South Zonal Committee, surrendered in Jharkhand. He carried a reward of Rs 3 lakh.

5. CRPF data reveals against these achievements, its own costs were loss of lives of 35 personnal, injuries to another 93, and loss of 17

weapons and 1,610 rounds of ammunition in 824 operations conducted in the Maoist-hit states, including 152 encounters with the ultras, four ambushes, 28 IED blasts and 13 attacks on camps/ posts.

6. CRPF says large scale desertion of the Maoists had been reported due to the pressure mounted by the security forces through sustained operations. The CRPF has busted training infrastructure and arms making factories of the Maoists in Jharkhand and Chhattisgarh.

Let this analysis end with an aside. This article carries a picture of Home Minister Rajhnath with his eyes set at its foresight and his finger on the trigger of the Light Machine Gun (LMG). He was at the diamond jubilee celebrations of the CRPF, on 16 Nov 2014. It is an ambiguous posture of the C-in-C, engaged in a serious battle with the Maoists: Is his right eye seeing (at the prospects of) a distant peace, or is he ready to pull the trigger for a security operation against the Maoists? It seems a valid question as the MHA under this C-in-C has just given final touches to the counter-Naxal policy and Strategy! From another angle, is the C-in-C conveying his policy choices to the CRPF, his main combat force against the obstreperous Maoists?

No Let up in Operations to Uproot Maoists": Home Minister: 3 December 2014

So far, all documents and analytical articles that have been examined earlier in this section were drawing the information from the draft of new policy under finalisation by the (new NDA) Government. This article in a daily of 4 Dec 2014[25] is based on the suo motu statement by Rajnath Singh on 3 December in both Houses of the Parliament, Lok Sabha and Rajya Sabha.

The Minister asserted in the Lok Sabha on the 3rd "there will be no let up on operations to eliminate Maoist menace" and promised all support to the security forces to deal with it firmly. He was speaking on the killing of 14 CRPF men on 1 December. He gave details of the incident, saying Maoists attacked the forces who have been engaged in operations in the Chintagufa area of Sukma district since 16 November, which resulted in reported killing of 12 Naxals.

On the basis of intellegence inputs about the movement of CPI (Maoist) cadre, CRPF had launched a multi-phase massive operative on 16 November this area. In the operation, 2,253 CRPF and 224 State Police personnel participated.

The Minister reiterated the commitment and determination of his government to continue the operations till the problem is fully eradicated.

The Home Minister, who had visited Raipur on the 2nd to take stock of the situation, said as a result of the implementation of the multi-pronged strategy (explained/detailed earlier), the morale of the Maoists has weakened. The number of surrenders of Maoist cadres has risen substantially in the current (2014) year. "The LWE violence has also been declining since 2011, and this trend continues in the current year."

"Governments new anti-Maoists policy to recognise tribal icons and leaders:" December 2014

As a part of its multi-pronged new draft policy on Maoists, the Government plans to win tribal hearts by giving due recognition to their icons and leaders by celebrating their anniversaries and naming airports, buildings or roads after them.[26]

Multi-pronged intervention in four areas has already been well-understood. Since the Maoists' propaganda is focused on alleged exploitation of tribals, "the Government plan to deal by winning their hearts by series of measures", said a MHA official, requesting anonymity. Some of the measures envisaged in the new policy on this aspect are: Better distribution of pattas, or right to their homes under the Forest Rights Act, increase in MSP (minimum support price) for their forest produces, and making tendu leaves a good source of their income.

Besides, as part of perception-management initiatives, the government also plans to provide state patronage for celebration of the tribal festivals and cultural programmes, setting up museums and cultural centres dedicated to tribal themes, using mass media to integrate tribals in the mainstream, and highlighting atrocities committed by Maoists and destruction of development infrastructure by them, have also been flagged in the new policy. Then there are also plans to use social media platforms for this desired end.

"Forces to have say in anti-Maoist Spend: January 2015

This was an important headline reported by a daily[27] in Jan 2015. The blurb was even more explicit: "Niti Ayog: Representatives of central para-military forces CPMF, to be part of block-level spending panel". After all, it is the first time that spending panel deciding priorities in Maoist-hit areas will have representatives at regional and district level from the CRPF/BSF.

As the Planning Commission has made way for the Niti Ayog, the IAP, a Central scheme for development of the LWE districts will now be under the control of the MHA. More significantly, as stated above, the CPMF, deployed in the LWE areas, will also get a say in the IAP spending with their representatives sitting with the block-level spending committee, said an official familiar with the plan.

A CPMF official, requesting anonymity, told the daily: "The CPMF had been asking for a say in the IAP spending since 2010 when it came into force. Earlier, the district administrations, was allocating funds for the projects, which suited their political requirement rather than where it was required most. In the most-affected areas, there is no civil administration and only CPMF have ground presence and they interact with the people. Therefore, it is only they who know where spending is required for the people as also what is also necessary operationally. Having a say in the spending of the IAP will help in its better implementation."

The IAP is being implemented in 88 selected LWE districts in different states and various development schemes like construction of roads, bridges, schools, providing drinking water facilities to rural population are being executed through it. Under the IAP, each district is allocated Rs 30 cr per year.

A MHA official, again requesting anonymity, said: "The cabinet proposal has been circulated and the issue will soon come up in the cabinet for approval."

Earlier, a three-member committee comprising DC, SP and District Forest Officer used to allocate funds for the IAP. Earlier the funds were allocated at the district level, now they would be disbursed at the block level.

"Plan to end Naxal-belt Isolation" February 2015

"The consensus at a high-level meeting on Maoism, chaired by Union Home Minister Rajnath Singh, here on 9 February 2015, evolved around better coordination and multi-pronged connectivity to affected areas through a web of mobile, rail and road network."[28]

A comprehensive plan was laid out for building new roads and bridges, upgrade schools and erect over 2,000 telecom towers in the Maoist-hit areas.

The meeting chaired by the Home Minister revieved the development projects in Chhattisgarh, Telngana, Odisha and Maharashtra and Maoism-affected areas in and around the Bastar region. Singh said Bastar requires early attention for early completion of development projects and a coordinated action for dealing with the LWE. He assured the States of necessary Central assisstance.

Chhattisgarh CM Raman Singh and his Maharashtra counter-part Devendra Fadnavis attended the meeting while Telengana and Odisha were represented by their Chief secretaries and DGPs.

Union Ministers Nitin Gadkari, Ravi Shankar Prasad, Smriti Irani, Suresh Prabhu, Haribhai Parathi Bhai Chaudhary and Rajya Vardhan Singh Rathore represented the Centre along with Mr Singh and top officials of respective ministries and CPMF.

CM Raman Singh stressed the need for installing higher capacity TV and radio stations including FM radio stations for better connectivity in the Bastar region. Mr Fadnavis raised the issue of pending road works of some 150 km and work of Indirawati bridge awarded in Jan. 2014. He also stressed the need for early completion of laying a railway track in the Naxal-hit areas.

The Chief Secretaries and Directors General of Police, Odisha and Telengana pitched for necessary Central assistance for early clearances and completion of developmental projects pending in their States.

MHA officials said 500 mobile phone towers would be completed by 31 March (2015) and 1700 more towers would be constructed by August (2015).

Mr Raman Singh said, "over 280 schools in my State were damaged badly. They were replaced with portable structures for teaching upto class VIII. Those will be upgraded till class X now". He had requested the Centre to provide 10 extra battalious of CPMF for Bastar. "Four battalions have been given. I hope the remaining six will be given soon," he told the journalists. He also demanded that environment clearance should be increased from 5 hectares to 40 hectares for carrying out development projects in the Naxal-hit regions.

The Home Minister instructed senior railway officials to ensure commencement of construction work of railway track from Rowghat to Jagdalpur and expedlite laying of tracks from Dillirajhara to Rowaghat.

Policy on Surrender and Abduction

Surrender is an important issue and plays an important part in policy on dealing with the Maoists and their leaders.

Surrenders played their role during New Delhi's conflict with the Nagas and other rebel groups in the North-East. Likewise, all countries fighting terrorism have to fine tune their surrender policies.

This part will discuss various aspects of the subject vis-à-vis the Maoist insurrection. It will include some policy statements on the subject issued by the ministers or by the governments from time to time.

MHA— Convened Meeting discusses the issue of surrender: July 2012

This high-level meeting was convened by the MHA on 13 July 2012. It was attended by the police chiefs of the nine Maoist-hit States and the DGs of the Central Para-military forces. The two main issues discussed were: the SOPs for operations in the Maoist-hit states (already discussed elsewhere) and surrender policy, to be discussed in the following pages.

The meeting was told that the government was planning a major shift in its rehabilitation policy for Maoists where by all LWE-affected States would have a new uniform surrender policy offering financial incentives as high as Rs 3 lakh: Rs 1.5 lakh for surrender and a similar amount for an automatic rifle. Besides the money, a stipend of Rs 2000 per month for three years to surrendered Naxals.

Presently, these nine states follow different rehabilitation policies for surrendered Maoists, including financial incentives ranging from Rs 1 lakh to Rs 5 lakh for each unit of arms surrendered, depending on its make and fire-power.[29]

Last year (2011), the MHA had announced a policy offering differential incentives for the weapen brought by the surrenderees: Rs 15,000 for each deposited AK-Rifle, Rs 25000 for a rocket-propelled grenade/sniper rifle and Rs 3,000 for a pistol or a revolver.

A senior MHA official explained: "There is a need to review the existing surrender policy for including bigger financial incentives. States have been asked to enhance the money, while the Centre will also provide funds. We want uniformity for all states." The possibility of offering Rs 5 lakh to any one laying down a light Machine Gun (LMG) and Rs 3 lakh for an AK-47 rifle, was also discussed.

Draft Policy on Hostages: 18 October 2012

At long last, the Centre has moved to remedy a glaring gap in its security architecture, a standard, formalised policy for dealing with hostage situations caused by Maoists, "In a country beset by insurgencies and targeted by terrorists both external and internal, this is absolutely essential."[30]

The absence of such a policy has placed the state in a bind from time to time. Some instances: the kidnapping of the then Home Minister Mufti Mohd Sayeed's daughter Rubaiya Saeed in 1989: hijacking of IC 814; and Sukma district collector Alex Paul Menon. The thrust of the draft policy, that hard-core Maoists will not be released under any circumstances, "is exactly the right stand to take." But there are different views possible on this.

Those who look at this as callousness on the part of government, are viewing the issue from a skewed perspective. For one, the draft policy does not rule out swap deals altogether; it allows for the exchange of minor Maoist prisoners. More importantly, freeing major prisoners incentivises hostage taking and ensures that more such situations will occur. The next time Maoists need a captured leader freed, they will know exactly what to do. Conversely, by holding firm, it is protecting innocent civilians in a most effective way, reducing the likelihood of such situations occuring at all.

Time and again, India has paid the price for bowing to terrorists demands. For example, of those released in the IC 814 case, Maulana Masood Azahar went on to found the Jaish-e-Muhammad which has not only killed any number of innocent civilians, it also masterminded the December 2001 attack on parliament which brought India and Pakistan to the brink of war. Surely, no humanitarian purposes are served this way. It is time the Centre stood up and said no more... for the sake of citizens of this country.

But then the same daily offers a counter-view on the issue. "The burdon of unjust wars usually fall on the people who have nothing to do with creating them."[31]

That is the prism for viewing the harsh reality of any hostage policy. No civilised and humane nation can afford to take a hawkish stand, which risks the lives of its innocent citizens. "But our policy-makers in the North Block seem to believe otherwise." The hostage policy presently under the consideration of government skewer the essential principles of fairness and justice that define a civilised nation. A strict no release policy for the high-ranking terrorists or Maoists, even if that loads to deaths of innocents, smacks of rank indifference.

“A lot of hue and cry is raised about the 'soft' Indian state succumbing to hostage pressures, paving the way for more such actions. The propenents of an unyielding strong state hark back to 1999, when a Pakistan-based terrorist group hijacked IC 814 and forced the then NDA government at the end of a harrowing week, to release the three dangerous terrorists in exchange of passangers. True, such swap deals are fraught with danger. But should the IC 814 passengers have paid the price of the battles that they hadn't participated in?”

“No government would willingly set free terrorists who, in all likelihood, would go out and wreak more havoc. But what other options does it have in such situations? The argument that a tough hostage policy would secure the lives of many more people is unacceptable. Asking innocent people to sacrifice their lives for the sake of nation, which mostly is responsible for having created the situation in the first place, is hardly fair. Nations are at war with each other not because their citizens have mandated all the bloodshed but because of their skewed policies and idealogies of political violence that are on the rise."

The above are two contrary views on the draft policy of the government on hostages carried in a daily, given here in its own words.

"Against 'excessive violence', Top Maoist and his wife surrender": A major Development 9 January 2014

"In an ideological set back for the Maoists, Gudsa Usendi, their spokesman in Dandakaranya Special Zone Committee (DKSZC) surrendered before the Andhra Pradesh Police, with his-wife Raji."[32] An event of considerable importance, it has been published by most of the dailies. The coverage of three of the dailies is included here.

The DKSZC comprises border areas of Chhattisgarh, Andhra Pradesh and Odisha, and it is one of the most important zones for the Maoists. Usendi, its spokesman, had taken responsibility for the ambush of the Congress leaders convoy in Bastar in May 2013, in which VC Shukla, Mahandra Karma and Nand Kumar Patel were killed.

An MHA official, requesting anonymity, said: "Surrender of a top Maoist leader is more demoralising for their cadre in comparison of any death during counter-Naxal operations. On top of that, Usendi has surrendered due to ideological differences with top Maoist leadership over excessive use of violence".

'Usendi became a name to be Cherished

Security men involved in counter-Maoist operation reveal Gudsa Usendi was the non de guerre of Gumudavelli Venkatakrishna Prasad who hailed from Kadivendi village of Warangal district of Andhra Pradesh. Gudsa Usendi was a 17-year-old tribal youth allegedly killed by security forces during an anti-Maoist operation in 2000 in Chhattisgarh.

To keep his memory alive, the spokespersons of the DK SZC have been taking his name since then. Prasad was appointed to the DK SZC post almost five years back.

Prasad alias Gudsa Usendi was among top leaders

The MHA official further revealed: "Prasad carried Rs 20 lakh reward on his head. Post-surrender, he is likely to keep this amount besides getting additional benefits due to him under governments surrender policy. The

Andhra Pradesh DGP will conduct a press conference on 8 January to shed light on future course of action after his surrender."

Prasad was one of the top leaders among the second rung of the Maoists. Though he claimed to have ordered attack on the Congress convoy, but internally he was being sidelined as he was opposed to the excessive violence on the orders of the top leadership.

Surrender not Officially Confirmed

Gudsa Usendi, 53, and his wife Raji surrendered before the Special Intelligence Branch (SIB) on 8 January, but the SIB did not officially confirm his surrender or arrest.[33]

After holding various positions in Chhattisgarh, Prasad was appointerd to DK SZC post some five years back.

Nicknamed 'Phantom' for his stealth, he carried Rs 15 lakh on his head. Like Azad, Gudsa Usendi is a pseudonym given to all DK SZC spokespersons, as explained earlier. Original Usendi was killed in operations in Abujh Maad in Jun, 2000. A Face book page says, "Gudsa Usendi never dies, Phatom of Dantewada." More information on Prasad: "Well-regarded amongst leaders."

He left home after graduation at 20, to join the former PWG. He went underground, spending the past 30 years in the forests of Chhattisgarh and Maharashtra. Well-read and intelligent, he is known for his ingenious methods of delivering messages, statements and press releases to the media and political leaders... emails from ghost, 1 Paddresses, notes struck on doors, propaganda CDs appearing in chambers of MLAs.

Highly regarded for his soft skills, Prasad was also a part of the CPI (Maoist) think tank, writing analysis on party performance and articles on strategy, tactics and reforms. He has been critical of excessive violence by Maoists and advocated killing as last resort.

He became more prominent after Mallojula Koteswara Rao alias Kishenji was killed in an encounter with the police in West Bengal in November 2011.

It is believed he fell out with the CPI (Maoist) leadership after he severly criticised the Bastar ambush of Congress convoy. He had claimed that he ordered the ambush but regretted the results. He regretted innocent people were killed when the target was only the political leaders.

Prasad was "sidelined in the recent months as differences developed among members of the DK SZC and the CPI (Maoist) Central Committee... all important decision-making body of the Maoists.

"Blow to the Reds: Topleader surrenders"

This is the thrid article on the surrender of Prasad. It is policy of this book to include all aspects of an important event/issue from various sources which will be helpful to the future authors who want to research or write a book on the Maoist uprising.

This daily says Prasad's capitulation could "help NIA get crucial details on the Jiram Ghati massacre of the Congress leaders on 25 May 2013, in which 27 people were killed."[34]

Official sources claim NIA and Chhattisgarh police were on Usendi's trail and he fled to Andhra Pradesh under pressure. Officials revealed that since many Maoists hail from Andhra Pradesh though they had been operating in Chhattisgarh, they opt to surrender (in Andhra) rather than get caught in Chhattisgarh.

One MHA spokesperson told the daily: "This is an extremely important development. Key elements in the top Maoist leadership have realised the futility of armed struggle. We hope more leaders follow suit and join the mainstream. They will be treated well as per the existing surrender and rehabilitation policy."

The surrender, likely to be announced by Andhra Pradesh policy on 9 January, was welcomed by the MHA as a positive development in the fight against the LWE.

Prasad chose to surrender before the police of his own State which offers better incentives and rehabilitation benefits to the surrenderees.

"Usendi was also allegedly involved in the killing of 29 policemen, including SP Vinod Kumar Choubey, in an ambush in Rajnandgaon in 2009. As DK SZC spokesman, Usendi's last major statement was days after the killing of Congress leaders, attributing the attack to his zonal committee, the most powerful zonal wing of the Maoists. His strongly-worded statement had congratulated the PLGA for the successful attack, and justified the killing of VC Shukla, Mahendra Karma and Nand Kumar Patel, while regretting the killing of innocent people and junior level Congress activists.

A team of senior NIA and intelligence officials from Chhattisgarh have left for Hyderabad to interrogate Usendi.

"Maoists on Wane, as Cadres and Tribals Desert Camps:" Bhubaneswar: 21 January 2013

"Three separate groups of tribals from Nachika Linga's village last week reached the Narayan Patna police station and expressed their solidarity with the administration. They made it clear that they should not be considered as sympathisers of Maoists any more."[35]

Narayan Patna, considered the second Lalgarh by the administration, has marked the fall of an empire built brick-by-brick by the Red rebels. While Nachika Linga was taking shelter in the dense jungles of Koraput district, his erstwhile supporters faced tough time. The innocent, poor tribals have now realised that they suffer in the tussle between the police and the Maoists. Top Maoists leader Ramakrishna, incharge Maoist operations in the district, has too been feeling isolated, security experts suggest.

Both Nachika Linga and Ramakrishna used tribals as their shields to protect themselves. "Laxmipur MLA Jhina Hikaka was abducted last year (2012) reportedly by Nachika's men and later handed over to the Ramakrishna group, obviously with some help from local villagers."

The State Government, overly worried about the Maoist violence, has chosen to remain silent in this 'hopeful' developing situation. Obviously, the State administration has no specific plant to deal with such situations, and consequently reap some benefits. Since there has been a sea change in the mindset of the people, who used to shelter/protect a number of armed Maoists, the Governemnt must act purposefully, taking people into confidence and take appropriate steps to liberate Narayanpatna completely.

It is believed "that the Maoist menace as a whole has certainly declined in the State (Odisha) after reaching a peak recently." Odisha's top Maoist Sabyasachi Panda has been rendered all but defunct after his expulsion from the CPI (Maoist). Consequently, his supporters has started deserting him. With the massive presence of security forces, the ultras have been forced to retreat. They are on the backfoot.

Obviously, this is the time for administration to get its act together, swing into action and undertake fast-track development activities in these areas to win over the people to its side. This is one and only way to win the confidence of the tribals and retake the areas earlier lost to the Reds. Intelligence sources hold "there are only 400 plus ultras in the State, with their morale at low level due to situation described above. Majority of the rebels has been restricted to their hideouts. They operate under various regional outfits: Andhra-Odisha Border Special Zonal Committee (SZC), AOBSZC; Bihar-Jharkhand-North Chhattisgarh Special Area Committee (BJNCSAC); Odisha State Unit (OSU); Chhattisgarh-Odisha Border State Committee (COBSC); Dandakaranya Zonal Committee (DZC) and Bengal-Jharkhand-Odisha Border Committee (BJOBC).

Intra-Party Operational Areas

While three divisions of AOB SZC are active in Malkangiri and Koraput districts, the operational area of BJNC SAC is the districts of Sambalpur, Deogarh and Sundargarh.

With Sabyasachi Panda neutralised, the OSU's operational area has remained largely free of violence while the Kalinga Nagar Division is nearly non-existent these days. The COBSC, the most powerful unit, is active in Nuapada and Balangir areas. The BJOD too has not been seen in action for a long time now.

However, the rebels are still active in Koraput, Malkangiri, Bargarh, Balangir and Naupada districts. "These are cerrainly a cause for concern for the police," a top police officer engaged in counter-Naxal operations told the daily.

The police administration has reasons to be happy as there had been no Maoist violence in 2012 in five districts: Nayagarh, Mayurbhanj, Dhenkanal, Jajpur and Sambalpur. The years 2011 and 2012 witnessed the surrender of good number of rebels: 50 in 2011 and reduced number of 34 in 2012. The police also arrested 167 rebels in 2012, compared to 146 in 2011.

Looking at the statistics, the number of "badly-affected districts has come down to just two, Koraput and Malkangiri, while seven districts are "highly-affeted" and six others "moderately-affected."

But even if there has been no Maoist violence in five districts during 2012, the rebels are found to be consolidating their base in districts like Nabarangpur, Nuapada, Balangir, Bargarh and Kalahandi on the Odisha-Chhattisgarh border. "A special action plan is needed to deal with the Chhattisgarh Maoists," say a senior police officer. He adds under the changed circumstances, the police and the administration must focus on districts like Koraput, Nabarangpur, Malkangiri, Juapada, Balangir, Bargarh and Kalahandi. A redeployment of central forces in these areas is the need of the hour. The Government also must keep a close watch on the districts like Rayagada, Kandhamal and Gajapati where the Panda group is active, besides the minerals-rich Keonjhar district.

"We are planning to withdraw forces from certain pockets," DGP Prakash Mishra had recently told the media. But the police is yet to take any such step even as the Centre has suggested similar action to concentrate on areas heavily infested by the Maoists.

The State presently has some 14 battalions of CPMF, comprising BSF and CRPF units, besides the State's own Special Operations Group (GOG) to counter the Maoists.

The MHA has issued advisory to all affected states to beef up security preparedness and response in view of an anticipated escalation in Maoist activities in the coming summer months (of 2013). The advisory has been issued in the light of the Tactical Counter Offensive Campaign (TCOC) carried out by the Maoists during summers in which security forces witness a lot of movement of these groups and an increased risk of attacks. The TCOC is undertaken till the month of June while Maoists begin their preparations around the February.

Meanwhile, Union Rural Development (RD) Minister Jairam Ramesh has also categorically said that the Dongria Kandhas of Kalahandi Rayagada region are the new targets of the Maoists. He has suggested several development projects to win the confidence of the people in underdeveloped places. The people there fall prey to the Maoist evil designs. Ramesh has also identified the Sonabeda sanctuary in the Nuapada district as the hot-bed of the Maoist. The Maoist outlaws operate in Kalahandi, Nuapada, Balangir and other nearby districts out of their base in this wildlife sanctuary.

"Naxal surrender down: Only 143 so far this year" New Delhi: 18 July 2013

"Surrender by CPI (Maoist) leaders has taken a beating this year, indicating that security forces have not been able to exert enough pressure on the banned outfit. Against 195 Maoist leaders and cadres surrendering before security forces uptil July last year (2012), this year only 143 surrenders have taken place, the lowest reported from Bihar."[36]

The corresponding figures for 2012 and 2013 (till 17 July) for busting of the Maoist training camps are 26 and 13, respectively. The number of arrested Maoists too has dipped this year, 741, against 919 last year.

The latest MHA figures show that only three Naxalites surrendered in Bihar against 25 in Maharashtra and over a dozen in Chhattisgarh.

A senior MHA official amplifies: "The indicators show that the outfit is not on the backfoot and much more pressure needs to be built up by the anti-naxal forces in various affected states." The year 2012 had maximum number of suffenderees in five years, the figure peaking to 440. Another official added: "This year the outfit is attempting to hit back. The deadly attack on the Congress convey in May 2013 seems to have given a major boost to the outfit which had been formulating strategies to motivate its cadres for a long time. There had been a growing discontentment within the outfit with several of them choosing to surrender and join the mainstream. But their success in executing a major strike seems to have re-energised their cadres."

Allegations of fake surrenders by Maoists

There have been reports about some surrenders by the Maoists as 'staged' or 'stage-managed'. There could be a variety of reasons possible for such events: lure of money on offer for the surrendees; inducement and encouragement by the policemen for the ture of the quicker promotion prospects; and finally, some surrenders may not even be the fakes, as alleged.

Two reports appeared in the press on two successive days in July 2014. The two are included here.

"Fake surrenders: As Ranchi Police drags its feet, Express traces acused:" Khunti (Jharkhand): 21 July 2014

The daily pats itself on the back in the opening paragraphs of the report: "The Ranchi police that is yet to arrest two of the four people accused of making at least 150 people, most of them tribals, pose as members of LWE outfits and surrender here, said they could not find the two, as they live in interior villages. The FIR naming the four was registered on 28 March 2014. On 20 July, the daily traced them down in a day."[37]

"This is just one of the many glaring omissions on the part of officials investigating the case, which is believed to involve one former military intelligence officer and CRPF men. The state government has now called for a CBI inquiry."

The charge sheet framed by the Ranchi police shows reluctance to expand the scope of investigations to include more witnesses and accused, that could expose a larger conspiracy. The former MI officer, Ravi Bodra, was involved in the so-called surrenders, dating back to 2011-12, as part of a MHA plan, that now appears botched. While one of the two accused whom the Ranchi police could not arrest so far claims to have a proof of his innocence, the other is central to the case.

Caroline Kerketta, 50, has been listed as the second accused in the charge sheet filed on 27 May. She allegedly acted as an agent for Digadarshan Defence and Civil Service Zone, an institution run by the first accused Dinesh Prajapati, and brought students to him for a commission. Prajapati turned them over to Ravi alias Ramesh Bodra, who made the youngsters “surrender” before the officers of the 203 Battalion of the CRPF’s COBRA unit at the old jail in Ranchi. Bodra told the youths this would make them eligible for the Army, paramilitary and Jharkhand police jobs intended for surrended LWE.

Kerkatta lives with her duaghters in Nichitpur village in Khunti's Torpa block. She said she was introduced to Prajapati when a girl in her village who wanted to enroll for school-level tuitions at his institute, took her along in 2011. Prajapati told her that he could get government jobs for youngsters if she could introduce them to him. She took some 12 children, and was paid Rs 500 for each.

Those taken by Kerketta, such as Vijay Topno, 24, of Nichitpur, say she would point out that Prajapati was successful in getting her own sons into the Army. Ranjit and Roshan Kerkette are posted in Bangalore and Jabalpur currently.

After some probing, Kerketta admits Prajapati had helped her sons: "He took Rs 40,000 each for my sons. When there was a delay, he took us to a Pathak in (Ranchi's) Numkum and arrange for the appointment of my sons."

Among the youngsters Kerketta took to Prajapati were three girls. Prajapati took money from them, but never made them surrender.

Masi Kerketta, the third accused, is an ex-serviceman who is presently a constable with the Khunti police. He had met Prajapati only once, and had not even heard about Bodra till the news about the scam appeared in the press. Masi, who lives in Khunti town's Pahantoli, says his name was included in the FIR by mistake. Masi claims he is in good term with family of Pamesh, the victim who registered the FIR. Pamesh's father had asked Masi to tell him when any announcement on recruitment in the Army appeared in the press. When Prajapati placed an advertisement in a newspaper, guaranteeing a job in the Army in six months, Masi informed Pamesh family of it.

When Pamesh registered the FIR, he mentioned that Masi was the one who had told him of Prajapati. Masi clarifies: "After Pamesh's family forced me, I even took him along when I went to Army canteen the next time and dropped into Prajapati's office. But I was told they would talk only to parents." He has a letter from Pamesh's father, submitted to the office of the Ranchi SP, admitting that naming Masi was a mistake, only to prove his claim. Masi has moved for anticipatory bail to get the case against him quashed.

Ravi Bodra appears only as the 4th accused in the first charge sheet. The document does not even mention the fact that boys were kept on the old Ranchi jail premises for upto a year in some cases, with the help of CRPF officers.

The charges against Bodra, arrested on 7 April, and Prajapati, who surrendered on 13 May, are non-descript. They are accused of "conspiring to fraudulently offering (sic) their victims out of money," and charged under sections 406, 419, 420 and 120 (b) of the IPC.

While the police has listed only 19 youths as witnesses, at least 90 victims, including girls, had turned up for a meeting with CM Hemant Soren on 4 July.

All the victims the daily spoke to, said that at its peak, the old jail housed 450 youths. They know the exact figure as there were roll calls at night, with inmates assigned numbers.

Even though the State Police's Special Branch facilitated the CM's meeting with the victims, no attempt was apparently made to record their statements. One of those named by them, Vijar Bara of Khunti district, who allegedly recruited the 13 boys of Gutia Jamgari village, in Ranchi's Namkum block, does not find mention in the charge-sheet.

"Ex-CRPF IG wrote to DGP in 2012, raising doubts over 514 at Ranchi jail:" July 2014

The then IG (operations) of the CRPF had written to the then Jharkhand DGP GS Rath in Oct 2012 about his suspicions over the fact that 514 individuals were being held at the old Ranchi jail. But it was not before March 2014, when an FIR was filed, that they began looking into the issue.[38]

It also turns out that the alleged kingpin of the scam, in which youngsters were lured with the promise of jobs in the Army, paramilitary and the state police and made to pose as LWE extremists and surrender, had met senior officers as a military intelligence officer, promising to facilitate the surrender of CPI (Maoist) Zonal Commander Prasad Ji. A source close to Prasad Ji confirmed that Ravi Bodra was indeed in touch with him.

The letter written by the then IG MV Rao to then DGP, accessed by the daily, opens by saying that he had been informed of the 514 men shortly after taking charge and had met them in the jail premises. Rao went on to share his concerns with the DGP, calling for urgent action as the surrender policy falls in the domain of the state government, and not in that of the CPMF like the CRPF.

Rao noted in the letter that a company of the 203 Battalion of the COBRA, stationed at the jail, which was empty as a new facility has been constructed at the outskirts of Ranchi, was being tasked with looking after the men in custody. He went on to point out that the COBRA was a specialised operations unit tasked with taking on the LWE outfits. He also noted that most of the 514 men had no police record against them and this would amount to illegal confinement. He was worried that the men were free to move around and that the CRPF would be held responsible if any of them were to move out and commit crimes.

The government action against Bodra began with a 26 March report from the police's Special Branch, culminating in a 8 May request for a CBI inquiry. "I called for a report after hearing about the illegal surrenders. These boys and girls had to sell their land and become paupers as a result of this", said NN Pandey, the state's Home Secretary.

The Special Branch report notes that in 2012, the Screening Committee on surrenders had found only 56 of the 514 inmates of the old jail fit for surrender. Of the 56, five were cancelled and only six actually surrendered.

The six surrenders on 18 Feb 2013 was a major climbed own for senior officers in the CRPF and state police.

"Maharashtra First to Roll out red carpet for surrendering Maoists" Mumbai: 19 August 2014

It is the title of a news story, about the state encouraging the Maoists to lay down their arms and join the main stream. The blurb names the things: "Proposes many fold jump in cash incentives, better rehab and legal aid."[39]

Becoming the first state to act on the guidelines evolved by the Centre, the Prithviraj Chavan-led Maharashtra government is set to revise its surrender-cum-Rehabilitation policy for Naxals.

The government has decided to sweeten the deal for those laying down arms, by proposing a sharp increase in monetary incentives and formulating a rehab package catering to housing, education, employment and protection for the surrendering Naxals. Statistics reveal that some 451 Naxals have surrendered in Maharashtra since August 2005 and in 2013 alone, some 48 Naxals laid down arms.

Earlier, the Union Government, which formulated new guidelines for such surrenders in Apr 2013, had directed all Naxal-hit states to design their own policies depending on the scenario on ground. The Maharashtra government keen to beat the model code of conduct ahead of the upcoming Assembly polls, the state could be the first to act on this directive.

The new policy proposes a two to three-fold increase in monetary incentives for those who lay down arms. This would vary on the basis of their seniority in the Naxal movement. For group surrenders, the state government has proposed much higher incentives than the one proposed in the Central guideline. Stakes have also been substantially raised for the surrender of Naxals who form a part of regional, state and national committees. Additional cash rewards for those opting to surrender with weapons have also been substantially increased.

Acknowledging the threat the surrenderees face, the policy makes special DG (Nagpur) accountable for providing them protection and considering request for rehabilitation outside the influence zone.

Those without a shelter would be guaranteed one with the revenue department responsible for allotting them land and Rs 1 lakh towards construction to those who are not eligible for the benefit under existing government welfare schemes. The government has also proposed to extend free education for children and access to self-employment for mainstream Naxals.

Following Centre's guidelines to consider withdrawal or ensure speedy trial of cases against surrendering Naxals, the state government has also proposed to a DM-headed panel to review such proposals. Such people will gain access to free legal aid. To ensure that only genuine Naxal elements benefit from the policy, a watch committee, also headed by the DM, will be appointed. Their movement will be kept under watch for at least a year after surrender.

The government has, however, proposed that these benefits will be withdrawn if the person is found to have re-joined the Naxal movement. It has also been clarified that the policy would n't be applicable for sympathisers of Naxal movement, and government informers, for whom the government recently revisited its reward policy.

"Centre may double dole for quitting Reds" New Delhi: 14 September 2014

After the new NDA Government took over in May 2014, it has been acting on twin tracks to win the fight against the Maoists. If, on the one hand, it has adopted tougher anti-Naxal operational option, it is also offering better monetary and other benefits in the field of education and employment to the surrendering Maoists. Its aim seems to be to make the surrender benefits too attractive, even lucrative, to be brushed aside easily. This news item specifies one aspect of this policy, in particular, viz, financial doleouts. Other aspects too are mentioned.

"Union Home Minister Rajnath Singh is set to lend a healing touch to Centre's counter-Naxal strategy, with a new comprehensive policy on LWE approved by him, seeking to make Maoist surrenders more attractive and widen the reach of social sector services in the affected areas."[40]

The new counter-Naxal doctrine, "approved by Singh at a high-level meeting on 13 September and set to be placed before the cabinet soon, proposes a minimum two-fold rise in monetary incentives for surrendering Maoists." This would cover the one-time grant (presently Rs 2.5 lakh for higher-ranked Maoists leaders and Rs 1.5 lakh for the middle and lower level leaders), incentives for arms surrendered as will as Rs 4,000 monthly stipend a Maoist get for 36 months after surrender.

Significantly, surrenders peaked at 132 under the Modi regime (between 26 May and 15 August, from 44 in the corresponding period last year (2013).

Another fresh initiative encourages setting up of facilities like schools and hospitals in block-level clusters, rather than the current practice of distributing such centres across remote villages in Naxal-hit areas. It was noted that many such village-level schools and health centres were not functioning due to shortage of teachers, doctors, health workers and other staff, who seemed unwilling to travel to these remote facilities for security and other reasons.

As government tells the daily: "The villagers thus failed to benefit from these services, which only encouraged Naxals to build their anti-government propaganda. The new policy proposes to focus on expansion of social sector infrastructure around the block headquarters. These facilities, given their accessible locations, are more likely to attract staff. An official, who was part of the brainstorming that preceded framing of the new policy, explains: "The local tribals can travel to these clusters from villages across the block, ensuring better penetration and coverage of these services in the Naxal-hit areas."

The Ministries of Rural Development and Tribal Affairs have already been taken on board by the MHA on the contours of the new policy.

"Former Maoists join Police ranks" Dantewada (Bastar): 21 September 2014

"Carrying an AK-47 rifle is nothing new for 27-year-old Sanjay Potam alias Badru who was with the banned CPI (Maoist) in Bastar for eight years before surrendering a few months ago."[41]

The story of Badru has earlier been covered in some detail. Only some additional facts and information will be culled from this analysis. "Earlier it was more out of compulsion, but now it is a responsibility," says Badru who is presently a Jawan with the state anxiliary force.

Badru had joined the Maoists after his house and village were ransacked by a Salwa Judum mob in 2005. But after some years, he had differences with some leaders in the party and he complained to some senior party leaders about it.

"They (party leadership) agreed to the points raised by me and reprimanded those Andhra leaders. But those leaders kept the grudge against me and started conspiring against me," said Badru, who was involved in many violent activities against the security forces, and worked as the Divisional Committee member in Darbha area.

"The police received me well and gave me a job, quarters to stay and security," claimed Badru whose wife, Sukki, 24, a member of Maoist medical team, also surrendered along with him.

Hemla Sanu alias Kolha, a former Maoist who now works as a "Gopaniya Sainik" (Secret Soldier) for Dantewada police, also reiterates the same story.

"I joined the Maoists willingly and worked for them for over six year's," says Kolha who was involved in the killing of 76 CRPF men near Tadmatla village in 2010.

"I got to know about my mother's death six months late. My party leaders did not allow me to attend the funeral of my brother as well, so I decided to surrender", claimed Kolha.

Both Badru and Kolha are convinced that they will be targeted by the Maoists. "We are safe here in headquarters, but when me go to our village or go on operation with forces, there is always a chance of them (Maoists) targeting us deliberately," said Badru but added that he was happy now because he was getting paid for risking his life.

"There is no personal life or future in the forest life", said Badru, claiming to have persouaded two of his colleagues also to surrender.

"Naxals who surrender to get better deal": New Delhi: 13 October 2014

The subject has just been covered in some broad tentative details. This news story covers some specifics, which will be taken note of here. Its blurb gives us some specific information: "New Policy: MHA proposes Rs 5 lakh to those who give up arms, Rs 6,000 as stipend."

"The NDA government's proposed anti-Naxal policy includes a robust surrender and rehabilitation plan for Maoists and intends to double the amount paid to the rebels who want to surrender."[42] The respective figures during the UPA regimes and now proposed by the NDA are:

- One time payment to surrenderee from Rs 2.5 lakh to Rs 5 lakh.
- Monthly stipend for a period of 36 months post-surrender from Rs 3,000 to Rs 6000 per month.

It is to be noted the proposals are yet to be placed before the Cabinet for approval. Other changes in the new policy are mentioned in the succeeding pages.

The draft policy also proposes more "pro-active" role of the Maoist-hit states and intends to increase their power to limit their dependence on the Centre to tackle the menace. This could mean raising of additional state auxiliary forces and consequent less dependence on CPMF for operations in their areas.

Besides the above, the new policy envisages increasing the number of fortified police stations from 400 to 650 in the LWE-hit states. The MHA will allot Rs 2 crore to construct each such police station, which is to have high walls and bullet-proof gates.

Under this plan, the government will take on the second phase of Road Requirement Plan (RRP-II) to improve connectivity of such areas. Details are rather sombre, far from pleasing. RRP-I had aimed at constructing 5,477 km of the SHs and NHs in the affected district of these, only 2,750 km of roads are complete, just 50 per cent of the target. The total cost of the project is Rs 7,200 cr.

A senior MHA official explains the problems: "The most common problem we face is that the road contractors do not come forward to take up these projects when a tender is floated, and even if they do, sometimes they are rejected because of high bids they place. We have decided to give maximum security for such projects, and if nobody comes forward or does not meet the criteria, even, then any contractor can be selected and awarded the work."

Soon after taking charge, Home Minister Singh held a meeting with the chief secretaries and DGPs of all 10 Naxal-hit states and had announced the policy on the Naxal issue. "The policy will focus on the 23 worst Naxal-hit districts, which have reported 80 per cent of the violence and incidents so far.

The official said, "The states have to be self-sufficient to deal with the Maoists and it is ultimately they who have to give answers. We will step up support to the states under the Security Related Expenditure (SRE)."

"MHA tells states to fund reverse vasectomies for former Naxals: New Delhi: 27 October 2014

The MHA on 26 Oct 2014 issued an advisory to the 9 Naxal-hit states to use Central rehabilitation funds to carry out reverse vasectomies for Maoists wanting to return to the mainstream. It explained no rehabilitation can be complete if Maoist cadres can not return to normal married life and have children. "The process will also reduce the temptation of cadres to return to the Maoists fold."[43]

So state governments should consider facilitating vasectomy reversal operations of willing Maoists. The daily claims the move comes days after it reported on two Maoists in Chhattisgarh who had undergone vasectomy recently.

The advisory also told the states to use government machinery and NGOs, to spread awareness among Maoist cadres that vasectomy was reversible, in the hope that this may motivate them to leave the Naxal fold. "It is suggested that the names and addresses of Maoists who avail of this option should not be disclosed."

The government has offered to bear the cost of the operation, considering that most such surgeries are conducted in a crude manner by local quacks.

Those joining Maoists are compelled to undergo vascectomies to prevent them from having children and getting tied down to a family life.

Many of the cadres are known to have surrendered when forced to undergo this procedure.

"Abused in outfit, women Maoists surrender" Ranchi: 2 December 2014

"Two top Maoist women commanders surrendered before Zonal IG MS Batia on 1 Dec 2014 after being subjected to sexual harassment in the outlawed outfit."[44]

The two women, aged 20 and 19, decided to quit the Maoist group after they suffered sexual abuse by male rebels.

Intelligence reports reveal women cadres in the Maoist outfit have led several attacks on police men in the past. But almost every female Maoist "who has surrendered has complained of sexual harrassment", says Ranchi DIG Praveen Kumar.

"One of the woman who surrendered on the 1st was the first Section Commander of the Nari Mukti Sangh, a special armed wing for women cadres," said Ranchi Zone IG MS Bhatia, who handed her a cheque for Rs 50,000 as compensation under Jharkhand's Naxal surrender and Rehabilitation policy.

She disclosed to the Media that Kundan Pahan, a top Maoist leader, had exploited several women comrades, "He always moves around with 10 to 12 women comrades."

The second woman added: "We were unable to bear the physical and mental torture. Most women cadres suffer sexual exploitation."

"70 per cent Chhattisgarh Naxal surrenderees are not 'Naxal' on 'Surrender:'" Bastar, Raipur: 8 December 2014

Two stories on 'fake' surrenders have already been included on the subject in this part. This is the third one on the issue, with a slightly different context. Its opening para introduces the reader to the shape of things to come: "Chitu Sori of Kodenar village in Kondagaon district is a farmer. On 26 June, police declared that the 25-year-old had 'surrendered' with several fellow villagers. This was the beginning of an unprecedented run of 'surrenders' by Maoists in Chhattisgarh this year (2014). In his records, however, Sori is merely shown to have provided occasional help to Maoists. He returned to his village after the 'surrender' and continues living there."

The daily cites one more similar case. "Among the residents of Atulpara village in Sukma, who 'surrendered' on 19 August, was Barse Deva, Madkam Deva and Podiyam Deva. Like many tribals of Baster, they had long pending warrants against them, with police aften booking villagers in bulk on any suspicion. These warrants were never executed, but this year, the three say the police proposed that if they 'surrender', the warrants would be withdrawn."

The daily cites a third case. "A resident of Chingnar village of Narayanpur, Dayaram Nagar provided rations occasionally to Maoists. On 14 September, he was among those who 'surrendered'. Chaitram Salam had worked with the Maoists for some years but for a while now had been living in Narayanpur, when police asked him to 'surrender' on 25 August in lieu fo some benefits."

Going by the Chhattisgarh police's records, none of the above persons from Bastar is eligible to be called a "surrendered Maoist". And they are not alone!

Between 1 June and 28 November (2014), a total of 377 alleged Maoists are reported to have surrendered in the Maoist-dominated Bastar Division, 155 in November alone. A scrutiny of police records and meetings with these "surrendered" Maoists show that at least 270 of the 377 are actually ordinary villagers or routine criminals not eligible to be termed "surrendered Maoists."

Not one of them surrendered with a weapon, no one had got the post-surrender relief or rehabilitation, over 80 per cent of those who surrendered continue living in their villages, the remaining ones in police camps.

In sheer contrast, in the two and a half years from Jan 2012 to May 2014, the seven districts of Bastar saw only 29 Maoists surrenders.

A week before the deadliest attack on the CRPF in four years by Naxals, in Chhattisgarh's Sukma district, the MHA cited record surrenders in the state as a measure of its succeessful anti-Maoist policy. On 26 Nov (2014), the state saw the surrender of 63 more alleged Maoists, the biggest ever in one go!

Bastar IG SR Kalluri, whose tenure beginning 10 June (2014 has seen a surge in surrenders, says "he is not concerned about the eligibility criteria of the surrender policy." It is a "new strategy for winning an ideological war against Maoists", he asserts. By wooing tribals through surrenders, police can break the first line of Maoist defence, argues Kalluri.

He clarifies: "Earlier, anti-Maoism meant to mark area and go for police operations.. I have dispatched hundreds of letters in the interior villages urging people to join us. People are coming from across rivers. If they want to embrace democracy, should I embrace them or insult them by saying you are not eligible for surrender?"

On why police let them to return to their villages where Maoists could target them, Kalluri says: "We give them a choice. Bastar tribal is a free-spirited person, he enjoys forests and rivers and is not interested in your surrender policy."

Significantly, even the Home Department of Chhattisgarh doesn't appear comfortable with these numbers. A letter sent to DGP AN Upaddyaya and all SP, on 20 August cautioned that "the police should focus on the surrender of important cadres instead of lower-rung cadres."

Earlier, on 10 January, then Chhattisgarh DGP Ram Niwas had witten to all IGs and SPs asking them to avoid the hype around non-deserving surrenders, saying it "confused our ground police personnel to bear wrong priorities" and "disorients" them from their focus.

While the district police can present anyone as surrendered Naxal, a committee at the Raipur police headquarters headed by the ADG (Special Intelligence Bureau, SIB) is meant to scrutinise every case and to decide the rehabilitation package.

ADG (SIB) RK Vij elucidates: "We can take action against Maoist supporters, depending on the nature of support they provided but only a person who was an active member of any banned outfit at the time of surrender should be considered eligible for surrender. We are scrutinising the cases."

The 377 surrendered personnel fall under four broad categories:

1. "Naxal sahayogis" or the people who have occasionally helped the rebels, by choice or under force, with rations or shelter. So far,

the police would detain such villagers and release them after interrogation. IG Kalluri defends: "Imagine a boy of an interior village who has performed an occasional task of courier or sentry for the Maoists. If this boy wants to surrender, should I say that you are not a cadre or should I appreciate that he is impressed by democracy."

2. People with warrants, who are pressurised to surrender as a quid pro quo for withdrawal of cases. Only courts have the authority to withdraw criminal cases but, says Kalluri, "I tell them I am duty bound to send you before court and put you in jail. If I have to let you free, the only alternative is to show you as surrendered Maoist. I use my judgement."

   Admits ADG Vij, "It is not within the jurisdiction of a police officer to withdraw warrants."
3. Former Maoists, who left the rebel camp long ago and are now leading a family life.
4. Active Maoists or those belonging to banned front outfits. Under the policy, only they are eligible for surrender, and they make up the smallest number among all the four categories.

Argues Kalluri, "By surrenders, Maoists develop a sense of belonging with police. Others will follow their example, we will get bigger cadres."

However, contrary to what the IG says, branding ordinary villagers as Naxal may neither benefit them nor may be necessary. While it leaves them open to future harassment, there are several schemes for tribal welfare that can also help bring them into the "mainstream."

A surrendered Naxal is entitled to an "immediate grant" of at least Rs 1.5 lakh by the Centre and Rs 1 lakh by the state, "a monthly stipend Rs 4,000 for a maximum of 36 months", besides cash award between Rs 1 lakh and Rs 1 crore, depending on his or her designation. However, only 100 persons have received relief so far, that too, just Rs 2,000-5,000 as "Protsahan Rashi (encourgement amount)". Less than 10 have got class IV jobs.

Kalluri argues this could discourage other Maoists seeking to surrender: "It is up to the government to take 10 steps. Maoists go to Andhra Pradesh after surrender as they are treated there like kings." None of the 136 Maoists to have surrendered in Chhattisgarh from Jan 2009 to May 2014 has received any benefits either.

In a statement last week, the spokesperson of DK SZC, Gudsa Usendi, accused the Chhattisgarh police of "big fraud" in the name of Naxal surrenders, saying they pocketed the entire amount.

Salwa Judum: 'Fears' of Revival: Is it a bogey or otherwise

The following two stories deal with the 'fears' of revival of Salwa Judum in two South Indian publication: The week, as the name suggests, a weekly and The Hindu, a daily.... published from Kochi and Chennai, respectively.

To this Author, Salwa Judum was a great concept, unduly defamed by certain 'Liberal-Left-Intellectual' Lobly! For him, Mahendra Karma, its conceptualiser and founder, was a great Indian and a personal hero! He not only lived the life of a hero, he also died as a hero. The nation owes him a debt of gratitude. He deserves some national award/honour and not ridicule or condemnation from certain venal quarters. This Author will write on Salwa Judum elsewhere later in detail. But here, the texts and contents of the two articles only will be reflected.

"Play by the Rules" The week: 26 April 2015

The title of this article in the weekly is rather mischievous, clever, suggestive of certain malevolence by the authorities! Its blurb is even more explicit, even direct: "With the police redeploying Maoists they had lured into surrendering, Chhattisgarh is witnessing the rebirth of the controversial Salwa Judum."

This 3-page article is written by Deepak Tiwari. The following pages will carry its contents in excepts or in summarised form, without any editorial comments whatsoever.

It opens up with a clear assertion. "It is Salwa Judum redux in Chhattisgarh." A militia formed in 2005, comprising tribals armed by the government to counter Maoists in the Bastar region, Salwa Judum was disbanded in 2011 after the Supreme Court declared it illegal and unconstitutional. But now the State is witnessing its clandestine rebirth, though in a different name and manner. Though its cash-rich rehabilitation package, the government has been buring low-ranking members of the CPI (Maoist) into relinquishing arms. Many of those surrendered are now working for the same people whom they have been fighting for the last few years.

Between June 2014 and March 2015, more than 451 Maoists laid down their arms. It proved a shot in the arm for the police, which was starved of field support. The surrendered militants are now guiding and supporting security forces in operations against their former comrades. Many of them have been appointed as assistant constables... a new name for the "Special Police Officers" (SPOs), who were attached to Salwa Judum. IGP, Bastar Range SRP Kalluri says, "We have 300 to 400 such constables in each of seven districts of Bastar region... a big asset for us, as they constantly support us.

During a surrender ceremony in February (2015) in Dantewada district, the epicentre of Maoist violence in the Bastar region, Kalluri was asked whether the series of surrenders signified the revival of Salwa Judum. He sidestepped the query, saying: "This is a war of *Dhoka* (deceit) who ever has an upper hand will win it. Maoists have spun a strong web of propaganda to threaten and influence ordinary adivasis, and we are trying to counter it.

He believes the police, who were fighting a psychological war, had succeeded in putting pressure on the Maoists leadership. It is obvious that the new strategy has put the Maoists on the backfoot. The series of surrenders and the lure of rehabilitation package have upset the ideological resolve of its cadres. The fact that the proposed National Congress of the CPI (Maoist), which has been long overdue, has still not been held, shows that the Maoists leadership is under pressure. With the number of volunteers having gone down drastically, Maoists have once again started kidnapping villagers to ensure that their fiefdom stays intact.

The Maoists leaders' worry is that their secrets are now out in the open. With the surrenderees providing the police valuable intake, like the location of hideouts and sympathisers who provide shelter and food to Maoists, the anti-Maoists operations have intensified. Inspector Ajay Sharma said: "Maoists now fear eating at the homes of villagers. They live under constant fear of being poisoned. They have started forcing the food provider to first eat the meal himself."

The surrendered militants are helping the police much like Salwa Judum did. Sanjay Potam, alias Badru, of Purusnar village in south Bastar, was just 14 when he joined the Maoists' Darbha Division in the Dandakaranya Zone. His dare-devilry, sharp-shooting skills and ability to remember names and places earned him quick promotion as Malangir Area Committee Secretary of the party. Armed with Ak-47, he was part of many Maoist operations, including the 2010 Tadmetla attack, in which 76 troopers of the CRPF were killed.

But today, Badru is an important asset of the police in Dantewada. SP Dantewada Kamallochan Kashyap said: "He had become very important for us. He gave us good inputs, based on which we were able to nab many Maoists". Every morning, Badru goes to the special Naxal cell of the district police. As Assistant Constable in the state police, his sole job is to help analyse intelligence data. His wife, a former Maoists, Sudha, is employed helper at the hostel of the Government Girls, School, nearby. The couple not only assists police in processing intel but also accompanies security forces to the field.

Suresh Mahapatra, Editor, *Bastar* Impact, a newspaper in Dantewada, says: "We have noticed a greater level of precision and confidence in the police force after it started receiving help from surrenderees like Badru. He knows whom to contact and speak to if Naxals are reported staying near a village." With his razor-sharp memory, Badru is believed to be "like a wikipedia of his area."

Some 167 km north of Dantewada is Kondagaon district, carved out of Bastar in 2012. In the office of the SP, Subhash Baduram does what Badru has been doing in Dantewada. Subhash was Divisional Area Committee member of CPI (Maoist) in the North Dandakaranya Zone. Hailing from Rajguda village in Gondia in Maharashtra he joined the party when he was 14. He changed his original name, Ramdayal, and was entrusted to recruit people to spread Maoist ideology, as he was good at making speeches. "I don't remember the exact figure, but more than 200 boys must have been recruited by me." Many surrenderees have recognised him as their recruiter.

In 2002, Subhash married one of his recruites, Sanwati of Chinari village of Narayanpur. The couple was allowed to live together, but Subhash was made to undergo vasectomy in accordance with the Maoist practice. He said: "I heard on radio about the surrender drive of the government and decided to lead a calm and peaceful life. I want to have children and wish to get my vasectomy undone some day." Kondagaon SP Abhishek Meena terms Subhash a "big catch," adding, "we were flooded with surrender requests of many Maoists who heard of his surrender.

One of Subhash's former recruits, Sampat Usaru Koram, alias Suttee, is working with him in Kondagaon. Sampat was handpicked by Subhash from Padeli village in Kondagaon for his talent to sing. He joined the Chetna Natya Manch, the Cultural Wing of CPI (Maoists), and graduated to become a platoon commander in 2004. He was wanted for the murder of SP Rajnandgaon Vinod Kumar Choubey and the killing of 28 CRPF jawans in Maharabeda. Sampat was also accused of killing the security guard of the former minister Lata Usendi.

Many surrenderees have been allowed to go back to their villages and live in peace. Others like Badru, Subhash and Sampat, continue to actively support the police, because they face death threats. Sampat says, matter-of-factly, "There is no looking back. Either we kill them, or get killed by them."

Kamallochan Kashyap said the safety of the surrenderees was a concern: "We have slowed down the surrender process, because low-ranking Naxals were coming in hordes to surrender." Abhishek Meena lays it all on table: "The widespread surrender of cadres has instilled confidence in villagers, who have borne the brunt of Maoist violence. Earlier, no villager used to come to police. But now they are speaking to us. Surrendered Maoists have been instrumental in locating landmine."

The police have been offering incentives to the surrenderees. Earlier, when a Maoist with a reward on his head was arrested or killed, the money was distributed among security men. Now, surrendered militants who help nab the Maoists also a share of reward. Kalluri speaks to the weekly: "These young men know the places and people who support and form the supply chain. They are the people who matter in this war. I am focusing on the last line, like the Antyodaya scheme of the government, which is aimed at the poorest of the poor."

The police has reason to focus on the bottom rung of the Maoist hierarchy. Kalluri explains: "The top and middle-ranking Maoist leaders are of no use to us if they surrender. They barely move out for operations. The actual field knowledge and tactical know-how are with new and young cadres. The surrendered men have taken us to the hideouts of the Maoists and helped us during operations. Earlier, these men were our biggest hurdle. Now, they are our torchbearers."

The strategy, apparently, has made the Maoist top brass vulnerable. Kalluri continues: "These boys form the outer rings that keep hardcore Naxals safe inside several layers (of security). Since the outer layers are being targeted by us, there is panic among them (Maoist leaders). Now, many of these tribals are realising that only they are killed during gunfire, while the leaders remian safe. The depletion of foot soldiers would force Maoist top brass to confront the police directly. It is just like a hotel where there are no waiters, cooks or accountants, while the management is intact. With the surrenders, we have created an environment where the fence-sitters are coming to us. The police is giving them not only security, but also support in terms of giving them employment.

There are now more than 4,000 Assistant Constables in the Bastar region, each of them getting Rs 15,000 a month. Many of them were SPOs who lost their jobs when the Salwa Judum was disbanded (under the Supreme Court order). Kalluri again explains: "All these boys who are coming to us are influencing their families. For the first time since 2011, when we were forced to retreat, we have started to make a dent in the Maoist camp."

Information on Matters of Surrender and Booty Amount: The week: 26 April 2015

Number of Maoist surrenders in the Bastar region

District	*2013*	*2014*	*2015*
Kondagaon	0	99	5
Bijapur	14	48	38
Kanker	2	61	14
Dantewada	2	73	01
Narayanpur	12	65	0
Sukma	-	49	5
Bastar	1	4	0
Total			

Incentives (Cash amount) for surrendering weapons

	Rs
Light machine gun	4,50,000
AK-47	3,00,000
Self-boading rifle	1,50,000
303 Rifle	75,000
12 bore shot gun	30,000

Reward for surrender or arrest of CPI (Maoist) members

	Reward amount *Rs*
Central Committe, Secretary	1,00,00,000
Politburo Member	50,00,000
Central Military Commission, Chief	50,00,000
Central Committee, member or equivalent rank	40,00,000
State military commission, chief or equivalent rank	25,00,000
Regional committee, secretary/equivalent rank	20,00,000
Regional committee, member or equivalent rank	10,00,000
Platoon Commander or equivalent rank	8,00,000
Area committee, commander or equivalent rank	5,00,000
In-charge, Chetna Natya Manch/equivalent rank	3,00,000
In-charge, Intelligence unit or equivalent rank	2,00,000
Jan Militia, Member	1,00,000

Number of Assistant constables deployed in Bastar region

Bastar	222
Kanker	257
Bijapur	1,593
Dantewada	487
Narayanpur	444
Sukma	972
Kondagaon	130

"Once again, walking into a minefield by Kumkum Dasgupta: The Hindu: 5 Jun 2015

The daily is cautioning, nay, warning, the authorities to not re-start the defunct... rather, disbanded by a fiat of the Supreme Court... Salwa Judum. If the title is indicative of the contents of the article in cautionary language, the blurb is using a harsher language by way of warning. It reads: "Chhattisgarh must stop supporting attempts to restart campaigns that are inspired by the banned and discredited Salwa Judum."

So, for this daily, headed by a once card-holder leftist, Salwa Judum *ipso* facto is 'discredited'. Be that as it may, the contents of this article too, like the preceding one, will be reproduced with little editorial comment. The text is loaded throughout with self-serving jargon and leftist venality, without giving/showing any proof. The article follows in toto.

- "In 2009, while travelling in Chhattisgarh on an assignment, I visited a Salwa Judum camp in Maoist-hit Sukma district. The Dornapal camp... there were several across the Maoist-hit Bastar region... was set up during the heyday of Salwa Judum, the compaign that started on 5 June 2005, and used tribals as its foot soldiers (and cannon fodder) against the Red Army.
- "While Salwa Judum, brain-child of the late Mahendra Karma, a Congressman, was sold to the world outside the beautiful Bastar region as a spontaneous, self-initated movement of local tribals, having its immediate trigger in some Maoist policies such as the ban on collecting tendu leaves and participating in Assembly polls, the real story was different.
- "Salwa Judum was led by an interest group of local elites, contractors and traders for their own gains (political and economic) with active support of the state machinery. Karma, who became a minister in Congress CM Ajit Jogi's cabinet, was killed in a Maoist ambush in 2013.

- "The BJP government of Raman Singh, that took over from the Congress, also saw in Salwa Judum an opportunity to tackle the Maoists and so provided funds to set up roadside camps, like the one in Dornapal. The Salwa Judum activists then coaxed or forced the tribals to leave their villages and settle in such camps.
- "The aim was to keep a watch on the tribals to ensure that they do not aid the Maoists in any manner. For two years, the State government even gave those who stayed in the camps free rations and medical facilities and set up schools for children, although the quality of such facilities was pretty awful, even by the standards of rural India. But after years of bloodshed and human rights violations by Salwa Judum's Special Police Officiers (SPOs), the Supreme Court Banned the SPOs and Salwa Judum in 2011. It ordered the government to investigate all instances of alleged criminal activities of Salwa Judum.
- "According to a report by the Asian Centre for Human Rights (ACHR), the tribals were... and still are... the pawns of both the parties to the conflict. They were also the perpetrators (as SPOs) as well as the victims of the undeclared civil war.
- "To say that the visit to Dornapal camp, which once had over 25,000 uprooted tribals from 72 villages, was a nightmarish experience is an understatement. The camp was filthy and most of its residents seemed on the edge. Young girls and boys had arms and outsiders like me were viewed with suspicion and routinely questioned... and sometimes attacked... about their motives behind visiting the camp. All entries were monitored by gun-toting young men in military fatigues. I could sense fear... and anger-in the air.
- "Salwa Judum has pitted one tribal brother against another. We do not believe anyone any more. It was a mistake to join this. I can't go back to my village because the Mioists would kill me. I will never see my family again," a young Judum activist told me. He was almost in tears. "I know I'll die in the battle. There is no escape.
- "Despite the Salwa Judum experiment being a disaster, 10 years, after it surfaced, attempts are being made again to start a movement inspired by it.
- "I was appalled to read recent reports that said Mahendra Karma's son Chhavindra, is trying to start another Salwa Judum-inspired movement and is looking for police and government support for it. He has a different name for it, though: Vikash Sangharsh

Samiti, Chhavindra, the reports said, is planning *padayatras* with the former Judum supporters. In an interview to HT, however, he said he had no plans to restart Salwa Judum and that, the Samiti meeting was intended to discuss 'development' in the region. However, in another press interview, he said that tribals in Bastar would have to fight the Maoists to bring peace and development... almost restating what his father had said in 2005.

- "Chhavindra then clearly pointed out what his goals are: 'My aim is to take forward my father's work. The accusations of Judum being an armed movement were created because of the SPOs who walked with Judum members for protection.
- "The Congress has distanced itself from this effort, though Raman Singh led BJP government seems interested in it. IG Bastar SR Kalluri asserted recently the Salwa Judum was not properly defended in the court, and should any one challenge the legality of the new front, he will defend it. The CM is also known to believe that it was a 'people's movement' and there is nothing wrong in supporting it. Several locals believe that Chhavindra is trying to build a political career and re-establish the hold his family had in the region during his father's time.
- "The Maoists responded to such plans with a stinging press release accusing the Karma family of being an organised 'killer goonda gang in the protection of the Hindutva fascist BJP', adding actual motive is to open up resource-rich areas to multinationals in the name of development (a contested term in this region) and growth.
- "The battle lines are clearly being drawn in Bastar once again. Instead of fanning such moves... even they may look full of political and economic gains... the State government should stop these dodgy attempts. Violence perpetrated against tribals has not... and will not lead to... any gains. It will only push them further into the arms of the Maoists."

Talking to the Maoist Rebels: Prospects and Possibilities

Talks is historical instrument for resolving differences between the two rivals, or even enemies. The success of negotiations will depend upon the sincerity of the two sides involved in a dispute. Yet again, the outcome would depend on the strength of each of the two negotiating sides. Post-World War II talks between Japan and USA were between the vanquished and the victor. The same was true of the talks between Germany and the victorious US and her allies.

But in case of talks between the Maoists and the state, it will solely depend upon the sincerity of both sides. If the Maoists doubt the intention of the Central Government the latter feel the Maoists utilise the period of talks to rearm, regroup and reorient their strategy to return to the field with greater strength and determination for better results.

In this section, some propositions, based on some analytical articles, are looked into.

Impossible Conditions for Negotiations

Union Home Minister talked 5 Nov 2009 about a comprehensive offensive against Maoists. Maoist top gun 'Kicheg' in response to rising pressure from the government said they "are ready for the talks provided the former concedes the demands made by them." The major demands are:

1. The Centre must pull out paramilitary forces from Andhra Pradesh, Maharashtra, Chhattisgarh, Odisha, Bihar, Jharkhand and West Bengal.
2. Government must deal with the tribal's problems in a sympathetic manner.
3. Repeal of special Acts like Unlawful Activities Prevention Act (UAPA), Armed Forces Special Powers Act (APSPA), and vigilante and anti-Naxal groups like Salwa Judum be disbanded.

After making these exorbitant, hugely unreasonable demands, the Maoists refused to lay down their arms. This is just being too clever by half. Instead of honestly saying "We are not interested in talks," they would say they are ready talks but "only on our terms"! By this foolish stance, they reduce other side, their opponents, in this case a mighty entity called India, to a big Dummy! This is either being too smart, too foolish or too arrogant!

No government will find it possible to enter into negotiations on such brazen conditions.

"Can peace with Maoists be achieved?"

The above is the headline of an article that appeared in Nov 2011 in a daily[45] about the peace talks between the Maoists and the West Bengal government. Its contents are being examined in the pages that follow:

In (early) Nov 2011, the State-appointed interlocuters wrote to the state-Government to be relieved of their responsibilities. Chief Minister Mamata Banerjee promptly responding to their letter, called them to a meeting on Saturday, 20 November (2011). But this does not seem to be clearing the clouds gathering over the peace talks (with the Maoists).

While both the sides insist that it is in their mutual interest to sit at the negotiation table, the ground realities tell a different story, "even as Ms. Banerjee maintains that search for peace in the Maoist-hit Jangal-mahal region is a continuous process. But the moot question is: Will the glimmer of hope, that was obvious when these interlocuters were assigned their job, "survive the recent posturing of the government as also of the Maoists?"

Much, of course, will depend on the Saturday's meeting. A gridlock, Ms Banerjee is well aware of, would be difficult to unscramble. The interlocuters will expect an assurance from the government that it will exercise "restraint" in the security operations that would help them persuade the Maoists to do the same. But are not these interlocuters being unfair to the Chief Minister, expecting her to accept "restraint" by her security forces, knowing well that the Maoists have, over the recent weeks, gone back to their violent ways, unilaterally? "They were responsible for killing of four men over the past fortnight alone (4-16 November)". The state police had shown restraint for five months after the new (Banerjee-led) Government took over in Kolkata. But the daily put the same factual situation differently:

> "A for the security forces, they appear to have been galvanised into launching a fresh offensive against the Maoist after, by Ms Banerjee's own admission, lying low for 5 months since her government assumed power. What has been going on all the while are "intelligence-based operation", say security officials.

Then, the daily poses a question on the Banerjee-led Government: "Whether the decision to, as she claims, 'suspend' security operations during that period was strategically flawed... providing the Maoists to regroup and consolidate base after having been forced into retreat since the central forces were drafted to supplement the local police in June 2009... continue to be a matter of debate, particularly in political circles." The daily goes on to give its own interpretation to this decision: "But but if was the Chief Minsiter's idea of giving peace a chance in the the region, it obviously has not yielded the desired result so far."

One can't fault Ms Banerjee for giving peace a chance. After taking over she wanted to think through her policy and also give a break to the old policies. If the Reds did not reciprocate her good gesture, you can't blame Ms Banerjee for Maoists betraying bad faith. Obviously, they were not interested in the path of peace!

Disappointed at Civilian Casualties

"The developments earlier in the weak in Balrampur area of Purulia district in which four persons... two belonging to the family of a TMC activist and two Maoist rebels... were killed could well be ominous, an indication of things to come.

Whether or not Jangal Mahal becomes a war zone that it was, the casualty has been the peace process which lies severely bruised. The interlocuters seem to have read the writing on the wall. "Neither have they concealed their disappointment over the failure of both the government and the Maoists to take any tangible initiative to create, what they have been asserting, the 'mutual trust' which, they have pointed out, is a pre-requisite for any future dialogue."

Even before the interlocuters formally sought to be relieved of their responsibilities on 17 November, a perception was being circulated among them that the peace process they had initiated, which is still finding its feet, is on very shaky ground indeed. "The developments in Purulia district got them finally to ask whether not just the Maoists but also the State government are in any 'mood' to take a more conciliatory posture."

Two members of the team had even put their signatures alongside CPI (Maoist) State Secretary Akash to a joint statement stating the Maoist offer of a month-long truce, beginning 30 September was on the condition that security operations are suspended for that period. Eyebrows were raised in various government circles on this issue.

Then came the letter from the Maoist leadership to the interlocuters on 31 October, pointing out that the truce period was over as no commitment was forthcoming from either them or the State government.

Now came the most important part of this analytical article: an adverse comment on Ms Banerjee's handling of a difficult political situation. "While the immediate issue before the State government is to salvage the peace process even as it clamps down on violence and aims at restoring a semblance of normality in the strife-torn region, Ms Banerjee's rhetoric continues to spew venom against the CPI (M)". Earlier she accused the party of using the security operations against the Maoists as just another pretext for retrieving its lost political ground, she now sees the same CPI (M) as a colluder with the ultras... "against her", which is meant but left unsaid.

The daily ends with a conviction that is not easy to fault with: "Engaging in such gamesmanship is very unlikely to serve the cause of the peace process."

It is a good analysis dealing with the subject of negotiations between the State and Maoists. Though it deals with a specific state government, the problems faced by any LWE-affected state dealing with the Maoists will be of similar nature. Negotiations are bound to long-stretched, intricate and very slow moving, and more importantly, each side will blame the other for their slow speed, or even their ultimate failure. This is the nature of the game, more accurately, of the gamesmanship. This truism will be seen in some articles/ news stories that follow hereafter.

"PC justifies talks to free captives but is ready for hostage policy"

This is the sum total of the statement made by Home Minister P Chidambram on the issue in the Rajya Sabha on 9 May 2012, as reported by a daily.[46]

Days after release of two Italians, one MLA and an IAS officer from Maoist captivity through negotiations, the centre (read Home Minister) on 9 May 2012 justified mediation/talks for freeing hostages. However, the government expressed its readiness to hold consultations with states to evolve a uniform hostage policy.

Mr Chidambram, replying to a question by BJP member Prakash Javadekar, said: "We must take a practical view of having mediation and negotiations... mediation is a part of every government... Even Israel does it as it released 1000 prisoners to get one soldier... but one should know where and how to draw a line."

Mr Javadekar had arlier said there should be no swap deal in hostage situations. He had quoted CM Raman Singh, Chhattisgarh as saying that if he (Raman) were taken hostage, there should be no swap deal.

Referring to release of Sukma collector Alex Paul Menon, Chidambram said Chhattisgarh government had appointed mediators and considered it practical to do so. On the need to have a uniform hostage policy, he said, "I have advised MHA officials to have consultations with the states on whether we can have a uniform hostage policy... but I cannot say how this hostage policy evolves.

He said the Centre has been playing a crucial role in helping states resolve hostage crisis as it was a shared responsibility. "My view has been, my view is and my view will be that dealing with terrorism, Naxalism and insurgency is a shared responsibility," added the Minister.

Guha on Adivasi dilemma and tribal issues

Recorded here are some observations made by historian and author Ramchandra Guha on the issues relevant to the subject matter of this took, in Sep 2012, while addressing hundred-odd young Indian fellows and as reported in a weekly/[47]

"About 30 per cent of all Dalits (SC) are literate in the country compared to just 23 per cent Adivasis (ST). In terms of poverty too, they lag behind, with 49 per cent below the poverty line, as opposed to 41 per cent for the

Dalits. Walter Fernandes' study on displacement shows that 40 per cent of all displaced people in the country are Adivasis, who just form 8 per cent of its population." These are historian Guha's words, who was addressing young India Fellows at the Sri Aurobindo Centre for Arts and Communication.

These Young India Fellows are earmarked for posting to various tribal areas of India. The plan was conceptualised by the Man Mohan Singh Government. The aim was to spread wider India consciousness to its tribal population. These young Indians will mix with the contry's tribal people, learn about their customs and inform them of similar customs beyond their areas. It is not only a question of mutual learning and mutual respect for the two sides, but it is also about creating a wider India fraternity. Guha spoke in two distinct session, the latter of which dealt will the problems faced by tribals in the central region of the country. These lectures are meant to prepare these Young India fellows for their future assignments among the tribal populations of the country.

The observations made by Guha are so germane to our subject that large parts of his lecture deserves inclusion in this chapter.

According to Guha, there are eight tragedies concurrently happening to these tribals:

> **Adivasis** sleep on some of the richest resources of the country. They live in some of our biggest forests, next to some of our biggest forests and in areas which house some of the most bountiful mineral reserves.
>
> Historically, they have been neglected by the national movement, including Gandhi, Nehru and Ambedkar.
>
> They have been concentrated in small, isolated upland areas. This means their votes are important only in a small percentage of constituencies, nationally speaking. In contrast, the Delits are rather more dispersed throughout the country, so they will have a say in may be 400 out of 550- Odd constituencies.
>
> The *adivasis* have lacked a charismatic leader like Ambedkar, who is still admired across India. Jaipal Singh was the closest thing in this respect but his influence was limited to Jharkhand.
>
> The apathy of public officials is nothing new for the *Adivasis*. A majority of civil servants posted in tribal-dominated areas start angling for a transfer from the day they assume office. Alex Paul Menon, the Sukma DC, who was kidnapped and later released by the Maoist rebels, is a rare example of a public official who actually wanted to serve in a tribal area.

The Maoists, their presumed liberators, only want to use them as cannon fardder, in order to create a new political order through armed struggle. They are neither liberators nor friends of the *Adivasis.*

Responding to a question related to Maoist crisis, Guha said, "Perhaps the most profound remark, I have even heard about the Maoists situation came from a Muri tribal boy in Chhattisgarh, who said, "We are arguing about this situation every day. But this discussion will not be possible in a Naxalite state. They do not have the guts to leave their guns behind and come to the village to discuss things."

"Learning to talk outside gunpoint"

'In order to be effective, mechanisms for talks with Maoists must aim to address much more than the release of hostages'

This is the title of an article, with its blurb that appeared in a daily on 8 Jan 2013[48] on the subject of talks with the Maoists.

Its opening paragraph is interesting and instructive: "When Roger Fisher, negotiation guru and former director of the Harvard Negotiation Project, was asked in an interview if he could really negotiate with a terrorist, he said, 'I would much rather listen to them than fight. A lot of times, they have got legitimate grievances packed as extreme political positions."

Near the end of 2012, government decided on negotiations with the Maoists, promising to put in place Crisis Management Groups (CMG), which are essentially teams to negotiate hostage situations in the LWE States. Clearly two high file Maoist kidnaps of last year (2012), Collector Alex Paul Menon in Chhattisgarh and two Italians in Odisha... had created much national distress. But as we embark on combating a new year of conflict, there is need to reflect on the issue.

Maoists believe capturing hostages is the only way they can bring the State to listen to them. So by agreeing to talk when kidnapped, are we not asking to be held at gun point?

Getting the parties to table is not a problem, however. There is a success story from the past. We are aware of the Committee for Concerned Citizens... a group of former bureaucrats, journalists, intellectuals, and fellow citizens (CCC)... who converned the 1994 Andhra Peace talks. The CCC had earned enormous legitimacy as a result of the records of the victims of violence they built over the course of five years, and their careful taking-to-task of both sides in an impartial manner. But where they failed was in designing a realistic agenda and an effective process for parties that lacked the willingness and capacity to implement their promises.

So how can the CMG be made to develope that capacity? First, the panel must be prepared for the two sets of issues the Naxalites are known to raise. The first set of demands is tangible and easier to evaluate, namely, the release of imprisoned Maoists or return of tribal land occupied by non-tribals. These can be decided by the government, weighing their costs and benefits.

The second set of demands involves underlying needs and perceived injustices that drive their movement. These are filled with historical baggage larger in impact and potential cost and "thus harder to weigh against the value of a particular life." To work through these intricate demands requires formidable skills... which the CMGs can develop in the Naxalite and government negotiators.

Homing in on negotiation skills and techniques

Such skills need to be taught based on principled negotiation techniques: Never start with the demands, start with the needs and wants underlying them. This is done through sharing information and active listening that does not come naturally to conflicting parties.

Being trained in communication and relationship-building techniques is essential for creating necessary psychological safety at the table for frank and path-breaking discussions, especially given the harsh rhetoric in public speeches.

Physical safety is another factor. Naxalites have never been allowed to negotiate directly because of this dilemma. How to negotiate with a banned party, without lifting the ban? Naxalite negotiator and trade union leader Dandapani Mohanty suggests imprisoned Maoists be brought under police escort to negotiate on behalf of the party, rather than roping in members of civil society who are far removed from the realities of the parties' interests.

The MHA recently declared that the year 2012 had seen the lowest number of incidents of violence involving Maoist under UPA rule, with the "lowest" amounting to 1365 recorded incidents. The government has repeatedly refused to talk to the Maoists "until the violence stop." And now that the violence is at bay... lowest in the last eight years... it is propagated as a counter-insurgency success that overrides any talk for talks! If at all the talks have to happen, that is not possible with the well-meaning but fragmented mediation efforts of BD sharma, Swami Agnivesh or Professor Hargopal. The year 2013 calls for another CCC, this time with nationwide ambit, to demand talks that deal with more than just the release of hostages.

Captures of hostages unplanned

"Do you know that all (episodes of capturing) hostages are unplanned? The Italian tourists and the Collector just happened to be there when the Maoists were looking for a hostage to communicate their demands to the government," smiles Mohanty. The setting up of CMGs, is a big step forward. The question is whether they will pave the way, creating platforms to address the root causes of the movement or only produce themselves at gunpoints.

"Congress pledges dialogue with Maoists"

The Congress manifesto for Jharkhand polls promises to initiate a dialogue with Maoists, reported a daily[49] in Nov 2014.

The Congress's stance during its UPA governments has been that talks can happen with the Maoists only if they stop violence and lay down arms. But the nuanced change in manifesto says: "Alongwith taking strong action, we will keep the option of talks open."

"We will decide the details (on whether they should lay down arms first) once we come power. But the Congress Party's preference is that dialogue should take place alongwith firm action and development", said Subodh Kant Sahay, the party's campaign committee chairperson for the State.

Select Individuals on Policy and Strategy

This section records the views of some individuals who have held, or presently hold, positions dealing with security of the country, or related to it in some manner.

Their views and observations are quoted directly, and at times, just, summarised. The officers/politicians who appear in these pages are listed here:

- **KPS Gill:** Former DGP, Punjab
- **Ajit Doval:** Former Director, IB and at present, NSA
- **K Vijay Kumar:** Former DG, CRPF and at present, Adviser to Jharkhand Governor
- **Mahendra Karma:** Former Home Minister of Chhattisgarh, and founder of Salwa Judum
- **RK Vij:** Additional DGP Chhattisgarh

Righting the basic wrongs: 3 June 2013; The war against the Maoists can be won if all the affected states take lessons from Andhra Pradesh's experience

KPS Gill

KPS Gill is a former DGP, Punjab. To him goes the credit for defeating the Khalistani terrorism in the State. India owes him a debt of gratitude for retrieving the state from the brink of the abyss. President of the Institute for Conflict Management, currently, he commands an enviable reputation in the country and abroad.

The heading at the top is of the article he penned for the Times of India.

Excerpts

As details of the Darbha massacre filter into the media, one thing is obvious: there was a comprehensive failure at every level to adhere even to the most basic security norms in the prevailing situation. There has, thereafter and much before, been a great deal of talk on strategy and tactics on 'holistic' and 'multi-pronged' approaches. But the ground reality is that we have not even got a basic grip on day to day tasks, the most rudimentary processes, the a b c of policing itself.

Darbha was not an exception. How many times have errors by district police officers led to security debacles and acute political embarrassments in different states... It is time that the service stands up, stops making excuses, and takes responsibility.

There were evident and tremendous disregard for the basic necessities of policing... However, those who are painting the incident as a great 'strategic' achievement by the 'heroic Maoists' appear to have missed some details. A relatively small and poorly armed security contingent was attacked by a well-armed force of at least 250 Maoists cadres. Despite their superiority in weapons and numbers, the shock of the initial IED attack on the convoy and relative disadvantage of terrain against their ambushers, the security personnel held off the attackers for some two hours and were over run only when they ran out of their ammunition.

The enormity of this achievement is even more remarkable, since the security personnel were armed, variously, with pistols, sten guns and even .12 bore weapons, while the Maoists had SLR, and AK rifles. When the shooting ended, Mahendra Kurma... much reviled by the press... is said to have stood up and declared himself, asking the Maoists to spare others. The Congress State committee chief, Nand Kumar Patel... begged only for his son's life, something any father would do. These were acts of courage that speak highly of these men, and are at odds with the picture of scam-tainted politicians. These are images of grassroot politicians fighting extraordinary odds.

The Moist response was to strike down the son with an axe to the head before his father's eyes and shoot him repeatedly. Patel was himself shot and stabbed again and again. As for Karma, his body bore 78 stab and over 50 bullet wounds, and after he was killed, Maoists danced over his body. This gratuitous and perverse violence is not the action of revolutionary warriors, but the hate-consumed butchers. There are many in the Indian establishment who have long sympathised with the Maoist cause and constructed elaborate apologetics for their violence. It would be interseting to discover what justification they have for these acts of appalling and wanton brutality. We must not return to business as usual. At every level... district, state and national leadership... improvements are necessary... The delays, the prevarication, the bureaucratic inertia and the political incoherence and mischief that undermined effective response and the strengthening of the security apparatus in the past must be forced to an end.

States whine constantly about the Centre not doing enough. But what have the states done? Promising (and failing to deliver, in more cases than not) rice at Rs 2 per kg may win elections, but will not defeat the Maoists. Where is the steel in the administrative framework? Chief Ministers of all Maoist-hit States must be called to account for what they have done or failed to do.

If Andhra Pradesh, with little outside help, can inflict total defeat on a movement that, at one point, gravely afflicted all its 23 districts, there is no reason why other states, with a lesser problem and with increasingly generous support from the centre, should fail so spectacularly in dealing with the Maoists. The truth is that political and police establishments 'in Andhra were willing, and even eager to learn.

In several poblic speaches, HL Dora, who played a crucial role in turning the Andhra police around to effectively confront the Maoists, had declared that he had studied the Punjab experience, and applied it to that state. Why can't other state administrations and police officers study what has been done in Andhra and apply it to their circumatance? Why have the experiences of Punjab and Tripura, where vicious insurgencies were comprehensively defeated in police-led campaigns, with enormous support from Centre, been neglected in the training and orientation of the police leadership, and in the design of appropriate counter-insurgency strategies?

It bears repitition that it is not that the Maoists or their ideology are particularly strong; it is the State that has grown weak and abandoned its people and its territories to the depradations of lawless armed factions. Such a situation is particularly intolerable in a democracy, where the state's primary duty is to guarantee the security and welfare of its people. It is time to take back India from those who want to destroy it; and to restore to her people the freedom to live outside the shadow of fear.

The game is not over yet: 30 May 2013

Token gestures after every Naxal attacks will not help address larger issues. Clarity on the fundamentals and will to converts plans into reality is required: Ajit Doval

Ajit Doval is a former Director, Intelligence Bureau. He was, at the time he penned this article, Director, Vivekanand International Foundation. Presently (Aug 2015), he is the National Security Advisor, India. His credentials are impeccable. So, his views on the Maoist problem should be of interest.

At the top is the heading (with its blurb) of the article he wrote for the Hindustan Times.

Excerpts

When India is hit by depredations like the 25 May extremist (Maoist) attack, they are tragic. But more tragic is what follows... delayed tactical response, leadership confusion helpless, scripted statements carrying no conviction, and even ministers looking for opportunities to drive political mileage. In the world of security, what hapens is important, but what decides the end game is how the governments respond to them.

There is a predictable pattern of discourse that follows major attacks. Political statements and counter-statements, Centre vs State blame game, accusations of intelligence and security failure, all relevant but leading nowhere. There is no clear and unequivocal message to the predators, enunciation of a new national policy and strategy, initiatives towards capacity-building and pressing into action innovative tactical plans.

Prevention of this obfuscated discourse necessitates clarity on fundamentals. Left wing extremists are enemies of the nation... their ideology, political goals, transnational linkages, strategic plans all make it amply clear. Their history of siding with Chinese during the 1962 war supporting the Pakistan Army's genocide in East Pakistan and dubbing Indian intervention as imperialist, aligning with Kashmiri separatists and supporting the North-east insurgents, leave no doubt about their intentions. Their putting in place 18,000 plus guerrilla force, nearly 16,000 sophisticated arms, weapon procuring and manufacturing infrastructure, fund raising abilities and effective propaganda apparatus, clearly indicate their burgeoning capacities.

Misled by the rhetoric of them being social activists or crusaders for the poor, we should not underestimate their intentions and capabilities. There is no room to treat them as anything other than being enemies of the State who have to be fought, vanquished and neutralised.

Second point that obfuscates the discourse is its political dimension. The message that goes out to Naxalistes is that the government seems confused and weak, and lack the gumption to take the battle to its logical end, and welts under the pressure of media, local level political workers, extremist-linked NGOs, etc. The political crossfire between Centre and states only gladdens their hearts. There is a need to make the message to the extremists loud and clear that the state will use all its power to protect its sovereign rights. In the instant case, the Congress leaders were wrong to give it a political colour and advance possible conspiracy theories. There is ambiguity whatsoever about the role and responsibility of the Centre and the states. Article 355 of the Constitution unequivocally affirms that "It shall be the duty of the Union to protect every State against the external aggression and internal disturbances." Justice Hidayatullah in the Supreme Court Judgement of 1966 asserted that, when a threat transcends limits of public order and threatens internal security, the over- riding responsibility lies with the Union Government. However, to make it happen, the Prime Minister needs to take a strong stand both at the Centre and in the states.

The next requirement is strong laws with an efficient criminal administration system. The internal and external threats to the unity, integrity and sovereignty of India, require a different jurisprudence from the ordinary criminal laws and must empower the state to deter and neutralise its enemies. The front organisations, masquerading as NGOs and think-tanks, who skilfully assist the extremists in exploiting discontent and subvert them to take recourse to the gun must be made accountable. Those who provide them intellectual and ideological space by projecting them as social revolutionaries are as guilty as gullible people who take to arms... To bring down the crisis of legitimacy, any illegal police action or efforts to frame the innocents should be dealt with an iron hand.

The state police forces due to their superior knowledge of terrain, language and customs of the local people are best suited for counter-LWE operations. There is an urgent need to increase their strength, provide them better leadership, training, weapons and equipment. It is pertinent to note that Naxalism has taken deeproots in states where the number of policemen per one lakh population is among the lowest and much below the national average of 123. The situation should be corrected immediately and a minimum of 150 policemen per lakh population must be made available to the Naxal-hit states.

K Vijay Kumar: Now Jharkhand Governor's Adviser: January 2013

"In a move, which may work as a force multiplier for security agencies in their war against Maoists in Jharkhand, the Centre has appointed the former DG, CRPF K Vijay Kumar... a retired IPS officer who was instrumental in eliminating forest brigand Veerappan... as one of the two advisors of Governor Syed Ahmad on 18 Jan 2013, with President's rule coming into force in the state." That is how the Times of India of 19 Jan 2013 put it. This shows the standing of this ex-CRPF chief as an efficient and effective professional (Incidentally former Union. Home Secretary Madhukar Gupta... retired, IAS officer of UP cadre... will be the other advisor to the Governor. Gupta will advise the Governror on civil matters). Kumar will be responsible for security and law and order issues.

"An office order to this effect was issued after formal proclamation of the central rule in Jharkhand by President Pranab Mukherjee," an official said.

Presence of Kumar, who as the then CRPF chief had been instrumental in chalking out strategies for various successful operations against Naxals in Jharkhand. Chhattisgarh, Odisha and West Bengal during 2011-12, will give an edge to the security forces in the State against the Maoists during the central rule when they will not have to face any interference from the sympathetic Jharkhand Mukti Morcha (JMM).

JMM's, soft spot for Maoists had at times acted as a stumbling block in operations against Red ultras in the State. Security officials believe that Naxalites had turned Jharkhand as their main hideout during the JMM-BJP rule. Since the JMM was the main ally of the BJP-led coalition Government, the police had to factor in several political consideration before launching operation against Maoists.

All this is expected to change with Mr Kumar becoming an advisor to the Governor. His association with the Government of Jharkhand is believed to result in a degree of success in the operations against the Maoists.

Let us remember Mr Kumar is an old hand at the game, and to reemphasise what has been said in the beginning: The Kumar presence should prove a game changer in Jharkhand.

Observations made by Kumar

Some of the obervations by him while he was still serving as DG, CRPF are summed up here. He was interacting with a daily in Apr 2012[50]

- On the edge of losing conventional tactics like "armed struggle", Maoists in the Red Corridor are resorting to acts of terrorism like causing explosions and abducting high value assets.
- Under constant pressure from security agencies, Maoists feel highly disturbed and dislocated from their strongholds. They are on the verge of losing protracted war... They are resorting to terrorist activities to get wide publicity, and that is what they want now.
- Talking about the last week's abduction of DC Alex Paul Menon, he said efforts are on to secure the safe release of this 'popular' Collector of Sukma. Maoists want to show that they are in command... They are doing this consistently, but this kind of propaganda will not work.
- Agreeing that there was a spurt in Maoist activities in the recent past, he said CRPF was working in close coordination with the State governments. Under pressure, they are causing IEDs against the forces as they can't fight in their strong-holds. This is their way of retaliation. 75 per cent of the fatalities are by the IEDs.
- On the reports about Maoists trying to establish a base in the southern states, including Tamil Nadu, he said their attempts to gain a foothold and create a South-West Command had failed. They have not been successful in Tamil Nadu though they did try something in Karnataka. Repeated attempts to penetrate the grassroots in these states have not yielded any result owing to high level of surveillance by the law enforcing agencies.

Mahendra Karma

He was the founder of the Salwa Judum movement in 2005. He was the Congress MLA, but his initiative was supported by the BJP government in the state. It was started in Karkeli village in Farsegarh block. It was launched in Bastar, as an answer to the Naxal menace in Chhattisgarh.

It did achieve a fair success "as it brought down Naxal violence in the area to a certain extent."[51] Things started going wrong for the outfit when Human Rights Organisations accused the Judum of torturing innocent tribals who did not join them.

During its peak, thousands of armed tribals, mainly from Maria tribe, went from village to village cleansing them of Naxals. "Those who were not with Salwa Judum were considered Naxal sympathisers."

Karma holds that Salwa Judum is successor of a similar movement called Janjagaran Abhyan, which was launched in Dantewada in 1991. He claims: "That was hugely successful. The Naxals ran away and peace returned. But successive governments did not do anything to contain them later... Now the Naxals are very powerful and have become more violent... He is certain that Salwa Judum has so far yielded good results."

Despite the negative publicity, Salwa Judum has the full backing of the government. Says State's Forest and Tourism Minister Brijmohan Agarwal: "Salwa Judum will continue in Bastar as it has given the desired leverage to security forces."

Meanwhile, the battle between th Salwa Judum and Maoists continues. Some 40,000 tribals living in 23 relief camps in south Bastar are under the constant threat of Maoists for having supported the Salwa Judum. So far, 70 tribals have been killed in Maoist hits on these camps.

Salwa Judum leads from the front

Here is a weekly reporting on certain aspects of Salwa Judum.[52]

It says "the Naxals blasted many bridges to signal their dislike of the Salwa Judum, which was formed in 2005. The police are helping rebuild many of them". It is a strange averment! What is the connection between dislike of Salwa Judum and Maoists destroying bridges? Maoists did not destroy bridges before 2005? Do they have unbounden love for CRPF and police forces? It should be understood by this scribe and others that Maoists destroy bridges to impede the movement of security forces deployed in counter-Maoist role in the area.

A CRPF commandant, RK Sharma, says: "Naxals are smart and deceptive, which make the task all the more difficult. The CRPF relies on the local police and Salwa Judum members for operational support. In fact, Salwa Judum members lead from the front as they have good knowledge of the area and topography.

The Brave Karma is Killed: May 2013

Some people may have different views on Salwa Judum, but its founder was a brave man. He was among the Congress leaders of Chhattisgarh who were killed in a Maoist ambush in Bastar distruct in May 2013.

When ambushed, he stood up and disclosed his identity: "I am Mahendra Karma you can take me and let the rest go." Blood thirsty Maoists would have none of it. Karma had been stabbed 78 times and his head smashed with rock. The State Congress President Nand Kumar too had stood up and said, "Kill me but spare my son, Dinesh." Any father would do that. But what did the Maoists murderers do? They put cigerette stubs and gutka pouches inside Dinesh's skull.

Later investigations showed that former Chhattisgarh Home Minister Mahendra Karma was accompanied by only six guards instead of the sixteen assigned to him, when his convoy was attacked. Other 10 guards did not accompany Karma on his instructions, government sources said, pointing out that there was evidence that other protected persons in the convoy too were not accompanied by the full complement of their security detail.

The Union MHA is believed to have advised state government to issue instructions that all assigned policemen travel with the protectees. "Action should be taken against the police officer heading the security team". A junior police officer, Mayank Srivastava, was suspended for the security lapse night 28/29 May 2013.

Srivastava, who had served in the Naxal-infected districts for a large part of his seven years in the IPS, "has led several operations from the front, including the one in Abujh maad jungles last year."

MHA sources said this time, however, the Bastar SP appeared to have erred in not issuing detailed orders to the policeman on the precautions to be taken when the convoy of the Congress leaders passed through the district.

The son on Gandhian Model April 2014

Deepak Karma, son of Mahendra, is on election trail. He is a Congress candidate for the Bastar Lok Sabha seat. He is in his bullet proof car. He is talking about what he would like to do for Bastar. This is an aside to the main topic, that concerns his father.

He is on his way to Narayanpur on 1 Apr 2014, in Chhattisgarh, that is a Maoist stronghold... "super sensitive", as a police officer guarding Karma says. Though the route had been sensitised by security forces, the threat of a Maoist ambush looms large. Karma family has been on the hit-list for years since his father and Congress leader Mahendra Karma turned against Maoists, creating a civil militia against them... which in its last avatar came to be known as Salwa Judum.

During lunch break, he talks about Naxal causes: "Lack of development creates terrorism... The Salwa Judum phase is over, and now I am here to follow the Gandhivaadi model." Now comes an emotional moment.

In the Narayanpur market, he is received by a group of supporters. In a makeshift office, he lights up incense in front of Mahatma Gandhi's portrait and then puts a flower each in front of the portraits of Lal Bahadur Shastri, Indira and Rajiv Gandhi. There is a picture of his father as well. He stops there for an extra moment and offers two flowers.

Before we end this account of the Karmas one minor detail needs a mention. All photos of Mahendra and Deepak has one common prominent feature: Both, father and son, wear a red *tilak* on their foreheads.

RK Vij: ADGP, Chhattisgarh

He is a senior police officer, Additional DGP in Chhattisgarh, the state facing most serious Naxal threat in India. He is an articulate officer, who keeps appearing in the press occasionally and dilates upon the Naxal issue and how the security forces are dealing with it. Excerpts from his two articles are given in the succeeding pages.

"Withering away of a revolution: September 2014"

It appeared in a daily in Sep 2014,[53] with an interesting blurb: "Cadres are leaving Maoists in greater numbers than those joining them. The State has an opportunity. Excerpts follow.

- The recent surge in surrender of Maoist cadres, particularly in Danda-karanya, seems to be a reality check for the protagonists of Maoists ideology, who claim that only protracted armed struggle can bring about a social transformation in a class-ridden society. Maoists of all hues... members of military formations (PLGA), political formation and the Janatana Sarkar (People's Government) ... are leaving the so-called "revolutionary" path they had pledged to tread upon when joining the movement against the feudal and semi-colonial ruling class. The romance of the armed struggle for capturing power is, perhaps, waning.
- There are three main reasons for these surrenders. The first is the realisation of the futility of the (people's) war. More than three decades of violence have not produced any connvincing results. An ex-president of the Janatana Sarkar in the Indravati (Maad) area, venting his frustration during surrender, said he was fed up with the Maoists' lofty claims and false promises of realising collective party goals. There is little to show in terms of these achievements. Another cadre said he had joined Maoists because he had seen only Naxalites in the jungles of Maad once he saw the world outside, he decided to join the mainstream.

- Second, the police's continuous persuation has caused the change of mind and hearts in many cadres, who had earlier been brainwashed by the Maoists. The police has been explaining government's surrender and rehabilitation schemes. A "back-home" programme initiated by then SP Gadchero, Suvez Haque, and followed by others, has proved efficacious. One *dalam* commander on surrender revealed that he decided to surrender with his weapon, after reading a pamphlet distributed by villagers. A weapon carried a huge reward.
- Third, many cadres are deserting because of personal reasons: Having married in jungles, they are not allowed to enjoy conjugal life; the killing of a family member by the Maoists, allegations of being a police informer, and exploitation of junior cadres, expecially female. A divisional-level Maoist, said on his surrender: "Despite my protests, they killed my younger brother, just because he had joined the police department." He had, because of his influence, recruited many *dalam* members. Post-surrender, he ensured that those he had recruited, surrendered before the police.
- At their 4th Central Committee meeting in 2013, the Maoists admitted their cadres are deserting in large numbers and are unable to recruit new ones. At the last DKSZC meeting in Feb 2014, the Maoists not only expressed serious concern about this trend but also pondered over the shrinking size of their formations. They were worried over the increased deployment and movement of the security forces in their stronghold.
- Meanwhile, the LWE-infested states are revising their S and R policies, to make them more attractive, rather lucrative. Booty on the heads of the senior leaders runs into crores. Next rung's booty goes into lakhs.
- However, the surrender of the senior cadres, who spend most of their youths pursuing the Maoists violent ideology, needs to be viewed more crtically. Even if the S and R policies cannot set temporal limits for surrender, they intend to persuade cadres who show their willingness to change. A DK SZC member, Arjun, who was incharge of the first military company when it was constituted in 2004 and was throughout involved in numerous brutal killings, surrrendered recently in Andhra after spending his entire youth spreading terror. Surprisingly his surrender did not evoke any criticism from the Maoists.

- In the same vein, the claim made by GVK Prasad, alias Gudsa Usendi, a surrendered spokesman and member of the DK SZC, that he was against the killing of innocent people, is difficult to believe. How can a person, whoever saw ruthless killings for nearly three decades, justifying the same on the whims of ideology, can be given the benefit of change of heart? Such cadres must be intellectually sifted and cost-benefit analysis made to assess the impact of their surrender. Unless their surrender causes sufficient damage to the Maoist outfit, the state should be wary of bestowing S and R benefits to them under surrender policy, because that could be well-planned tactical move in disguise!
- People's support is crucial for survival of such movements. If the present trend of Maoist surrender continues, and the state seizes the opportunity to show-case its responsibility in rehabilitating erstwhile cadres properly, while pushing development into such areas to remove structural socio-economic disparities, the Maoist movement is sure to lose its revolutionary zeal.

Old New War: RK Vij: Dec 2014

This article appeared in a daily in Dec 2014. Its blurb reads: "Maoist hold is shaken in former bastions. For security forces, question is: What next?" The exerpts follow:[54]

- 14 CRPF men laid down their lives while fighting Maoists on 1 Dec (2014) in Sukma district, the hub of Maoist activity in Chhattisgarh. Maoists claim to have transited from guerilla warfare to mobile warfare in this area. According to Maoists tactical commandment, in guerrilla warfare: "When the enemy... read security forces, advances we retreat, when the enemy camps, we harass; when the enemy tires, we attack; when the enemy retreats, we pursue."
- The above is mere rthetor. In this attack, security forces had ventured into one such base area. Though this was a slight departure from their earlier trend of ambushing road-opening parties and convoys, Maoist tactics broadly remained the same.
- Despite a few serious setbacks, the security forces have continued to make advances into Maoist strongholds. New security camps and police stations have been established and Maoist movement restricted. Due to continuous attrition in their cadres, Maoist formation have fragmented. Their expansion into new areas in order to extend "the Red carridor" has also been checked to a large

extent. Passenger buses now ply on roads that had once been blocked to disrupt the movement of security forces. People's support for Maoists has weakened, and more security camps are being demanded. It can definitely be claimed that the Maoist hold has shaken.

- But the question that looms large is: What Next? How do we intend to defeat this insurgency, which thrives on the premise of socio-economic-political deficit, but ultimately wants to capture power through armed struggle? Recently, the Union Home Minister said it was a challenge and we accept it with the ultimater objective of dislodging the Maoists. As an insider, I can appreciate the efforts made by the governments so far to tackle the insurgecy. But till their base areas and guerrilla zones are totally dismantled, no one can guarantee that such attacks will not be repeated.
- Some three decades back, before the Maoists forced their way through Andhra Pradesh, under the banner of the CPI (ML) PWG, into the peaceful district of Bastar, spread over an area of 40,000 sq km, with more thatn 70 per cent of its population being tribal, not much of policing was required in the area. A single police station was considered sufficient to control more than 2500 sq km of jurisdiction... some having as few as 13 personnel. But the hilly terrain with dense forsets, provided Maoists cover suitable for guerrilla warfare. During the 1980s, they formed a couple of *dalams* (training camps) and gained people's confidence. In the 1990s, they enhanced their military strength, forming special guerrilla squads and then platoons to carry out attacks on police force.
- During this period, the brunt of Naxal attacks was borne essentially by Andhra Pradesh, which created a special guerrilla forces, the Greyhounds, along with the Special Intelligence Branch (SIB).
- The State of Chhattisgarh, created in 2000, adopted an aggressive policy only in the third decade of the insurgency. On 21 Sep 2004, not long into the peace talks with the Andhra Pradesh governments, CPI-ML (PWG) and MCC announced their merger to create CPI (Maoists) and started strengthening PLGA. By the time local populace of West Bastar, organised as Salwa Judum (formed in 2005), revolted against Maoists, the latter had raised only one military company. This too was consequence of well-planned attacks in the Koraput district in Odisha in 2004, during which more than 500 weapons were robbled from various police units.

Their second military company was formed in 2005 to crush the Salwa Judum. By 2010, there were ten such military companies.

- To combat the rising insurgency, the Central government rushed in CAPF battalions to assist the state and liberally sanctioned India Reserve Battalions. Initially, thrust was on securing relief camps created next to police stations to provide security to those who had been forced to leave their villages. The State responded by raising its own SIB and Special Task Force (STF), largely on the lines of the Andhra Pradesh model. But in the meantime, the Maoists had managed to form two military battalions by merging two companies each in 2010 and 2012, to scale up the level of attacks on security forces.
- Though still in their infancy, the specialised off-shoots of the state police have gained sufficient experience to set their house in order. But still there are many security vacuums, each no less than 2,000 sq km in size in South and West Bastar. The forces are deploying only along the fringes of Abujhmaad, which sprawls across an area of 4,000 sq km. May more camps are needed to move into such vacuums and restrict Maoist movement. The setting up of mobile towers over the next year may improve telecom connectivety around the security camps but the construction of roads remains a major challenge. Approch roads to security camps are essential to maintain their supply lines and other administrative need. Efforts are needed to devise improved technologies to detect IEDs, which remain the most potent weapon deployed by Maoists.
- The PLGA pyramid consists of main forces, viz, companies and battalions, at the lop; secondary forces, or local platoons and guerilla squads, in the middle; and base forces, or militia, at the bottom. The main forces, capable of waging mobile warfare, move in their base areas, and the secondary forces operate in guerrilla zones. The base forces act not only as their eyes and ears, providing information about the movement of security forces, but also join the other two forces in all operations.
- The PLGA pyramid needs security forces organised in a similar fashion... a strengthened STF to tackle Maoist base areas, district forces to dislodge them from guerrilla zones and the police stations to disarm their Jan-militia.
- More than a thousand security men have already made supreme sacrifice in Chhattisgarh since the state was formed. The road

ahead may be full of risks and challenges. More set-backs and sacrifices may be lying in wait, but we have to move forward with determination. The nation must honour its martyrs. It is at their cost that a long lasting peace will be achieved.

Incentives and Benefits for Security forces in LWE-hit areas: Policy on

It is a common practice in many countries to offer incentives and benefits to the members of their armed forces serving in difficult and in-congenial areas. Post-1962, India instituted high-altitude allowance and special rations for the troops serving in the higher regions of the Himalayas. Presently, special allowances and more nutritious rations are authorised to the units serving in Siachen Glacier region.

These benefits and privileges, like comparatively shorter tenures, in such inhospitable areas, also serve as incentives to draw good and dedicated personnel to such areas.

Same policy seems to be thought of for drawing capable, dedicated and bold leadership of security forces for the Maoist-hit districts and regions, as will be seen in the succeeding pages.

"Centre Plans special benefits for armed forces in Naxal Areas:" June 2014

The new NDA Government is planning a blueprints for Maoist-affected areas with incentives for bureaucrats and personnel belonging to the Central Armed Police Forces (CAPF) who serve in these areas.

An important decision of the new Government is "that any developmental and infrastructure activities in the LWE-hit areas would be taken up only after the area has been cleared of rebels."[55] Union Home Minister Rajnath Singh, who convened the meeting with all the senior officials, includcing MoS Home Kiren Rijiju, also decided to rename the Naxal Management Division of the MHA as LWE Division, a term coined by former Home Minister P Chidambram.

The Government may offer the officials special monetary benefit, out-of-turn promotions and choice posting after completing their tenure successfully in Maoists-affected areas.

Defining Maoist area as the "most dangerous zone" in the country, the Government also enhance hardship allowances for CAPF personnel deployed in these areas to more thatn what they get while serving in Jammu and Kashmir and the North-Eastern region.

It needs to be noted that no specific details of the planned new blueprint were announced. That should be quite understandable as the new Government is in office for less than a fortnight. That they thought of deliberating on this serious issue so early in the day is a healthy and meaningful trend in their thought process.

Notes

1. Subodh Ghildiyal, Times of India, 9 May 2006.
2. Times of India, 15 June 2006.
3. Asian Age, 26 Oct 2006.
4. Rajeev Bhattacharyya, Indian Express, 25 Oct 2006.
5. Vyay Thakur, The statesman, 28 Apr 2007.
6. Akhlesh Suman, The Pioneer, 27 Apr 2007.
7. The Week, 11 Jun 2006.
8. Shivam vij, The Tehelka Weekly, 19 May 2017.
9. A Daily 15 June 2007.
10. Cited, Editorial, The Pioneer, 30 May 2007.
11. Arehana Jyoti, The Pioneer, 13 Sep 2011.
12. Chetan Chauhan, Hindustan Times, 13 Apr 2012.
13. Staff Reporter, The Hindu, 24 Sep 2012.
14. Express News service, Indian Express, 4 Jun 2013.
15. Ashutosh Bhardwaj, Indian Express, 22 June 2014.
16. Rajesh Ahuja, Hindustan Times, 27 June 2014.
17. Bharti Jain, Times of India, 23 Aug 2014.
18. HT Correspondent, Hindustan Times, 24 Jun 2014.
19. Vijaita Singh, Indian Express, 28 Jun 2014.
20. Abhinandan Mishra, Sunday Guardian, 21 Sep 2014.
21. Pioneer News service, The Pioneer, 18 Oct 2014 .
22. HT correspondent, Hindustan Times, 18 Oct 2014.
23. Bharti Jain, Times India, 18 Oct 2014
24. Rakesh K Singh, The Hindu, 17 Nov 2014
25. Pioneer News service, The Pioneer, 4 Dec 2014
26. Rajesh Ahuja, Hindustan Times, 11 Dec 2014
27. Rajesh Ahuja, Hindustan Times, 9 Jan 2015
28. National Burw, The Hindu, 10 Feb 2015.
29. Sandeep Joshi, The Hindu, 14 Jul 2012.
30. Times of India, 18 Oct 2012.
31. Monobina Gupta, Times of India, 18 Oct 2012.
32. Rajesh Ahuja, Hindustan Times, 9 Jan 2014.
33. Sreenivas Janyala, Indian express, 9 Jan 2014, datelined Hyderabad.

34. Bharti Jain and Ahuja Jaiswal, Times of India, 9 Jan 2014, datelined New Delhi and Raipur, respectively.
35. PNS, The Pioneer, 21 Jan 2013.
36. Namrata Biji Ahuja, The Hindu, 18 Jul 2013.
37. Deepu sebestian then Edmond, Indian Express, 21 Jul 2014.
38. Ibid.
39. Sandeep Ashar, Indian Express, 19 Aug 2014.
40. Bharti Jain, Times of India, 14 Sep 2014.
41. Pavan Dahat, The Hindu, 21 Sep 2014.
42. Vijaita Singh, Indian Express, 13 Oct 2014.
43. ENS, The Indian Express, 27 Oct 2014.
44. Alok N Mishra, Times of India, 2 Dec 2014.
45. Marcus Dam, The Hindu, 18 Nov 2011.
46. Times News Network, Times of India, 10 May 2012.
47. Aditya Mani Jha, Sunday Guardian, 23 Sep 2012.
48. Boyd Fuller, teaches Negotiation at The Lee Kuan Yew School of public policy, Natinol university of Singapore. Shriya Mohan is an independent fournalist, the Hindu.
49. Deepu Sebestian Edmond, Indian Express, 20 Nov 2014.
50. S Vijay Kumar, The Hindu, 23 Apr 2012.
51. The week, 1 Jun 2008.
52. Deepak Tiwari, The week, 1 Jun 2008.
53. RK Vij, Indian Express, 16 Sep 2014.
54. RK Vij, ADGP, Chhattisgarh, Indian Express, 6 Dec 2014.
55. Express News Service, Indian Express, 7 June 2014.

Index

D

L

M

N

O

NAXAL AND MAOIST TERROR IN INDIA

NAXAL AND MAOIST TERROR IN INDIA

VOLUME - III

DEVELOPMENT OF NAXAL INFECTED REGIONS

Col. Ved Prakash

KALPAZ

ISBN : 978-93-5324-033-2 (Vol - III)
978-93-5128-212-9 (Set)

First Published, 2019

Published by

Kalpaz Publications
C-30, Satyawati Nagar,
Delhi – 110052
Ph.: 011-47034999, 9811692060
www.kalpazpublications.com
E-mail: kalpaz@hotmail.com

Printed at: G. Print Process, Delhi

Cataloging in Publication Data—DK
Courtesy: D.K. Agencies (P) Ltd. <docinfo@dkagencies.com>

Prakash, Ved, *Col.*, author.
Naxal and Maoist terror in India / Col. Ved Prakash.
volumes cm
Contents: volume I. Expanding red corridor — volume II. Combating Maoism — volume III. Development of Naxal infected regions — volume IV. Chhattisgarh and Jharkhand — volume V. Odisha and West Bengal.
ISBN 9789351282129 (set)

1. Naxalite movement—India. 2. Communism—India. 3. Communist Party of India-Maoist. 4. India—Politics and government—1947- I. Title.

LCC HX393.5.P73 2019 | DDC 320.532093 23

Contents

Volume - IV

Chhattisgarh and Jharkhand

(*Series Page No. 915-1408 See Below*)

Volume - V

Odisha and West Bengal

(*Series Page No. 1409-1808 See Below*)

12

Maoist Problem: Causes and Solutions

This chapter deals with the main causes of Maoist problem: Land, Forests and Mines. If the Government wants to use these national resources for creating wealth for the welfare of the needy, left-Liberal Lobby and Maoist are convinced that the Government is doing it for the benefits of the industrialists and rich capitalist classes. This is the conandrum faced by almost all nations endowed with the rich resources.

The chapter will also deal with some related issues.

Battle For land, forest and Mines

These are the three resources that are the cause of problems that arise between the State Government, which want to exploit them in the "national" interest and the locals/tribals who not only own these three but literally sit on them. The situation becomes worse when the private parties, industrialists and contractors enter the field. The LWE are convinced that they 'loot' the wealth of the tribal populations, and deprive them of their due share. That gives them the chance to enter the field, and prepare the 'fertile' ground to harvest rich crop of recruits who join the 'pro-tribal' outfits like Maoists.

The Maoists convince the tribals that the armed uprising is the only solution to their problems. Once they displace the present elected government and take over the powers, all their problems will be solved.

Now a look at these three resources.

Forest: The most Important asset

Forests are the most valuable asset for the nation, as also for the tribals. Both needs it for equally valid reasons the former to add to its GDP by exploiting its timber, and more importantly, the mines below it, and the latter for his day-to-day requirements.

The Government may utilise this resource, but only after ensuring that the local population is not deprived of its legitimate rights over it.

The succeeding pages look at the subject of forests in all its aspects.

"Bamboo Trade may open up for tribals": Sep 2012

In an important decision, Environment Minister Jayanti Natarajan over ruled objections from her officials to break the forest bureau cracy's monopoly over the annual Rs 10,000 crore bamboo trade and declared it a 'minor forest produce', instead of a 'tree', under forest laws. Consequently this will allow tribals, instead of forset departments, to harvest and auction bamboo, which is one of the major raw materials for the paper, pulp and board industry, from their community and private lands.[1]

The Forest Ministry had for long classified bamboo as a tree despite its scientific description as a grass. Under the Indian Forest Act, 1927, fallen bamboo got classified as timber and remained under the firm control of the forest bureaucracy which harvested and sold it to the industry. The tribals got a pittance on some occasions even as the industry got bamboo at low rate over a long lease periods.

With the introduction of UPA's flagship Forest Rights Act, the Tribal Affairs Ministery pushed to get the fast-growing species of grass out of the control of the forest officials, with the law providing that right to harvest minor forest produce (product not classified as timber) grown on traditional forest lands would lie with the tribals.

But the forest bureaucracy refused to alter its regulations and classification of the species and put up hurdles in various states based on the Indian Forest Act and its existing rules. Previous Environment Minister Jairam Ramesh too pushed the case for relaxing the archaic and incorrect classification of bamboo and easing the norms to ensure that the tribals got their rights under FRA but met with only partial success.

Earlier this year (2012), the Tribal Affairs Ministry securred Cabinet nod to offer minimum support price for minor forest produce, including bamboo, to tribals through a new scheme along the lines of the support prices provided to farmers for major crops. The PM announced the scheme in this August 15 speech (2012) as a part of UPA's pro-tribal measures.

But the Tribal Affairs Ministry, in the last stages of transferring control of bamboo to tribals and finalising the scheme, got a jolt when senior environment ministry officials stuck to the line that bamboo was a 'tree' under the Indian Forest Act, 1927, and could not be harvested, transported or sold by the tribals. Natarajan then stepped in and over ruled her officials and put on record that bamboo would be classified as 'minor forest produce' under the Indian Forest Act, 1927, as well.

The decision will pave the way for the Tribal Affairs Ministry to launch the scheme though officials still expect a lot of resistance from state forest officials in handing over real control to the tribals. In some states, forest officials have blocked tribals from selling bamboos by using other regulations like working plans for forest lands being amended to permit harvest.

Deo firm Over Tribals' Rights over Forest Land: Jan 2013

"Differing from the PMO, Union Tribal Affairs Minister V Kishore Chandra Deo has stood firm on tribal rights granted over forest land through the Forest Rights Act (FRA) as the government sought more time from the Supreme Court to finalise its position." It was reported by a daily in Jan 2013.[2]

The government's plea in the Vedanta case comes in the backdrop of differences on the consent clauses involving gram sabhas. The Minister told the daily: "I have previously stood in favour of the Aug 2009 order (of the Environment Ministry) and I am against any dilution in the order. The core of the order and this issue lies in the constitutional provisions safeguarding tribal rights."

The Minister was referring to the order of the Environment Ministry, which was the key reason for UPA's decision to deny Vedanta's project to mine bauxite in the Niyamgiri Hills... a Schedule 5 area in Odisha. The order mandates consent from affected gram sabhas, in tribal areas where project proponent require forest lands. Such consent was made mandatory in 2009 by the UPA in order to bring the forest clearance process in compliance with its flagship FRA.

But the order has recently turned into a bone of contention within the government. The PMO has asked the two nodal ministries to dilute it, advocating that the need for consent from gram sabhas in tribal areas be done away with for most projects requiring forest land. At the other end, the appellants in the Vedant case have opposed the order in the apex court.

Deo reiterated that Vedanta's mining in the Schedule 5 area fell foul not only of the FRA, but also of the constitutional provisions that regulate alienation of land from tribals. "The government cannot agree to handing over or leasing out tribal land in the Schedule 5 area, through any route to a corporate house or private entity which is not owned by scheduled tribes," he told the daily.

Sources in the green ministry said it had sought two weeks' time to ensure a joint position after consultations with the Tribal Affairs Ministry.

"PMO wants new rules to speed up linear projects in forest lands": Jan 2013

In a bid to speed up infrastructure projects, the PMO is believed to have asked the Ministry of Tribal Affairs (MTA) and the Ministry of Environment and Forests (MOEF) to issue fresh directions to facilitate 'unconditional forest clearance', waiving off the requirement for gram sabha nod for linear projects, small public utility projects and projects that do not 'substantially' affect quality of life of people.[3]

While the PMO has been asking the MOEF for the last few months to examine ways to expedite the method to grant forest and environment clearance, in a meeting held on. 12 Dec 2012, it was decided that the MTA would have to relax it guidelines. "Both ministries are yet to issue any fresh circular."

As per the FRA, a resotution of the gram sabha of the area and a public hearing endorsing that the project is in the interest of the people living there is necessary for the projects that traverse the forest land. The PMO order has undone this requirement. Its directions that were to be implemented by 31 Dec 2012, say that the gram sabha resolution should not be mandatory for linear projcts like roads, canals, laying pipelines, optical fibre cables and transmission lines. It stipulates that statutorily mandated consultation should have been carried out earlier and communicated to the state in cases where gram sabha nod has been proposed to be waived off.

Unconditional forest clearance would require a certificate from the state government stating that complete process of recognition and vesting of rights under FRA has been carried out in the forest areas proposed for diversion for a project where the vesting of forest rights is yet to begin, states will have to confirm that they will do so before giving a final nod to project proposal.

However, for mining projects, those residing in the forest areas, a gram sabha resolution and a public hearing endorsing the projects will be necessary, the PMO has clarified.

"Ministry of Tribal Affairs (MTA) schemes for the welfare of STs:" Jan 2013

These are taken out from a one-page Republic Day 2013 advertisement[4] inserted by the MTA.

Highlights of the Schemes of MTA for the welfare and development of scheduled Tribes

1. Implementation of the STs and other Traditional Forest Dwellers (Recognition of Forest Rights) Act, 2006:
   - The occupation of forest land up to an area of 4 hectares (maximum) can be recognised.
   - Rights are heritable but not alienable or transferable.
   - Persons living in and dependent on forests for livelihood shall be eligible.
   - Responsibility of protection of wild life, forest and biodiversity has been assigned to right-holders.

Right man long last in the Ministry of Tribal Affairs (MTA): Jan 2013

This is not the headline of an analytical article that appeared in a daily in Jan 2003. But this is what the scribe meant to convey. The headline the daily chose is "Finally, a step in the right direction." Its blurb is even more explicit: "For decades, actual and meaningful empowerment of *Adivasis* has suffered due to preconceived notions and schemes of patronage and charity initiated by the MTA and the State tribal departments. All that may change for the better."

The scribe starts, by saying that ever since it was created, the Union MTA has hardly done justice to about 85 million people whose interests it is charged to safeguard. Its attitude towards the country's *Adivasis* has largely been one of charity, doling out scholarships and managing do-good schemes. It has done little to either protect the economic, ecological and cultural rights of Adivasis (STs) in the face of their systematic violation by both governments and corporations, or to activate the usually moribund State-level Tribal Advisory Councils.[5]

Even laws that the MTA has the primary responsibility to implement, such as the Forest Rights Act, have been largely neglected by it. Yet again, being way down in the pecking order, many other ministries routinely bypass or overrule it!

Now the daily says, "however, current Union MTA V Kishore Chandra Deo is trying to change this perception. Hence, the right man, Over the last few months, "he has taken some decisions to show that he means business. Some instances of that:

- In a letter to the MOS Forests, Deo objected to the continued diversion of forest lands in violation of the Forest Rights Act (FRA).

The FRA recognises traditional or customary community rights to forest lands for use, protection, and management.

- Civil society groups have been pointing out that such forest lands, where communities have claimed their rights, are being given for mining, dams, roads, industries, ports and tourist resorts. Since the FRA was promulgated over 2 lakh hectares of forest lands have been diverted.
- In 2009, the then MOEF, Jairam Ramesh had issued a circular to states requiring that proposals for forest land diversion need to be accompanied by proof that (a) FRA process has been completed for that land, and (b) that the relevant gram sabhas had consented to the proposal. Ironically, that MOEF itself has been violating this by clearing proposals without ascertaining that these conditions were met.
- Mr Deo has objected to the fact that the Forest Advisory Committee (FAC) which screens proposals for forest land diversion and advises MOEF for accepting or rejecting them, has mostly not asked for proof that the 2009 circular has been complied with. In Sep 2011, non-government members of the FAC exposed this as one of several flaws in the way clearances were given.
- In Feb and May 2012, he advised the MP Chief Minister to halt a proposed dam in Sheopur district, since the FRA process has not been gone through.
- In Sep 2012, he directed the Andhra Pradesh Government to cancel several bauxite mining lease on tribal lands, to safeguard the livelihoods of *Adivasis.*
- Another matter crucial to the livelihood of tens of millions of forest dwellers is the collection and sale of non-timber forest produce. So far the primary beneficiaries of this have been State corporations and private traders,with the Adivasis getting a small share. The Tribal Affairs Minister has sought to remove State monopolies in a blid to provide minimum support prices. These actions, linked to steps that build Adivasi-capacity for managing sustainable harvesting and marketing, aim to provide immediate benefits to a huge population.

Much of these initiatives are as much a Deo's own experience as an *Adivasi* leader, as in response to civil society calls and inputs. For decades, actual and meaningful empowerment of *Adivasis* has suffered due to preconceived notions and schemes of patronage and charity initiated both by the MTA and State tribal departments.

Again, the MTA and tribal departments are themselves small players in the system where the State looks at Adivasis as an anachronism or objects of tourism interest.

There is no formal procedure now, by which the MTA can say 'no' to a development project that threatens to alienate tribal lands or displace *Adivasis.* Mr Deo had to invoke the Constitution to stop the Andhra Pradesh mines projects, but it is highly unlikely he will be able to have his way all the time. Even if he does, higher powers can ride over him. Even if the latter is an occasional possibility, it must be given to Deo that he has put in place systems under which even his officials are in a position to say 'no' to projects they deem to be against the interests of the tribals.

Already the objections from the MTA and MOEF to the proposed National Investment Board (NIB), which will have powers to over rule individual ministers to clear mega projects, have reportedly been dismissed by the PM. And the move to have a strong and coherent tribal policy to guide the government's actions, mooted long ago, is yet to see the light of the day.

Nevertheless, even these small steps are crucial. It provides Adivasis and civil society groups with more space to manoeuvre and also provides hope that politicians can act out of social conscience.

It needs to be admitted entry of Deo as a Minister here has made a difference. So finally a right man is there!

"Tribals finally get land rights using GPS Technology:" Jul 2013

The scribe opens up this article with, "Last week I visited tribal areas in Gujarat to see how technology and an activist NGO could empower once powerless tribals to get their full land rights under the Forest Rights Act (FRA), 2006."[6]

The Act provided for land titles to be given plots in Cultivation in Dec 2005. Earlier, government take over of forest had converted forest dwellers into encroachers on land they had occupied for centuries. Their villages and farms were always at risk of demolition by forest departments. The Act was supposed to end this inequity. Many state governments soon claimed, falsely, that they had implemented the Act, empowering lakhs. In fact, impelementation was terrible. No proper maps or land records existed in most areas. Semi-literate villagers were required to fill long forms and file claims. Forest Departments contemptuously veoted most claims.

Under the Act, gram Sabha certified which plots were cultivated by individual families in 2005, and forwarded the documents to the state government. But 128,000 of the 182,000 claims filed in Gujarat were fully or partly rejected. Even in the accepted cases, only part of the claimed area was approved. ARCH (Action Research in Community Health and Development) and other NGOs appealed to the High Court. The Court pulled up the state government and decreed a review of claims, allowing many sorts of evidence (including panchnamas, case records, official receipts and satellite images from Google Earth as well as the National Remote Sensing Agency) to establish ownership.

This opened the path for redress. Yet the traditional survey method of triangulation to establish the boundaries and area of each farm plot was onerous. The ARCH came up with the idea of using GPS (Global Positioning System) hand held devices, costing Rs 12,000 a piece. Holding a GPS device, a tribal simply walked around the perimeter of his plot and pressed some buttons. The device automatically sketched a map of his farm with the right latitude and longitude and exact area.

This enabled every family to produce a map of its holding, and get it verified by the gram sabha. All individual maps were then superimposed on a satallite image of the village dating from 2005, the dead line under the Act. This produced a detailed map showing the exact size and ownership of every plot. Land disputes arose if two villagers walked over the same area, and disputes were settled by the gram sabha before certification. Any encroachment on forest land after 2005 showed up clearly after superimposing today's maps on the 2005 satellite image. This assuaged the Forest Department's fears.

Thus a simple technology promoted by activist NGO provided a quick elegant solution. The overall village map was than uploaded on to the internet, empowering any villager to go to an internet cafe in a neraly town and print out a copy. This ended tribal dependance for land documentation on government departments or NGOs. Tribals are willing to pay Rs 60 to ARCH for this service, roughly enough to cover all costs. So, the project can be expanded without limit with no subsidy or donations.

The new approach yielded for better outcomes. When tribals refiled the claims using these maps and additional evidence... panchnamas and receipts... government acceptance of claims went up to 61 out of 63 in one village, and 96 out of 112 in another. ARCH hopes to average 90% success. Early project villages are training their neighbours in using GPS, speeding up tribal capacity. The project has so far covered 150 tribal villages, just one-tenth of the total. It may take 18 months to cover all villages.

The Gujarat tribals say formal ownership makes a huge difference. They are no longer treated as encroachers, and so are entitled to all government schemes for agriculture, including land levelling and well digging on their lands under MNREGA. Earlier, the forest department banned the entry of tractors into forest lands. But after getting ownership recognition, tribals use tractors 90% of plots, since they are faster and cheaper than bullock ploughing. They want to modernise fast.

There is an urgent need to spread this approach to all forested states. The liberty Institute and ARCH are trying to do so by contacting NGOs every where (see www.fra.righttoproperty.org). Some Marxists and "romantic pastoralist" oppose the very notion of individual plots, or of modernising tribals. But less ideological NGOs are cooperating. A massive countrywide effort is needed to empower millions of tribals, making them masters of their own plots and community land.

The same GPS technology could be used to help update land records across India. This may require prior work on dispute settlement, since disputes are furious and widespread. Still, the methodology has much potential.

Problems of Vanvasis (STs) and Violence of the Communists (read Maoists)

These are the two sides to the issue being dealt with in this book. Everything else flow from them.

To put the things simply, there are two issues that demand study in regard to handling tribals living in jungles, literally over mines rich in precious ores.

One: In the matter of ores, is it right for the government to drive tribals out of their ancestral and ancient homes so that the forest can be taken over not just for accessing ores but for making profits as well? What is more important: the lives of the tribals, or meeting the needs of the industry?

Two: What is morally right: letting tribals live their lives as they have for centuries or destroy their culture, drive them into urban areas to make a living so that the country at large can benefit?[7]

The same problem had once arisen in the USA when the white man was attempting to drive the Red Indians out of their homelands to the great sufferings of the natives, way back in the 18th century and after. This is being replicated today in India in a different context.

The author feels the Communists (M-L) were long pushed out of urban centre with strikes getting out-of-date and labour unions a thing of the past. So, they discovered in the trials and tribulations of the tribal populations a golden opportunity to make their presence felt. The way the tribals were being unceremoniously eased out of their homes gave the Communists a moral cause to uphold and an equal chance to resurrect a dying ideology.

Out of this was born Naxalism, more accurately described as Maoism, rooted in ruthless violence at all costs. Mao, like Stalin before him, was guilty of killing millions of his own countrymen in promoting an evil ideology. The one way of solving problems of the tribals could have been the Gandhian teachings of **Satya graha** that had proved fairly successful in the 1930s in Bihar, as well as in Gujarat. "But try and tell that to the communists and our proudo-intellectuals. To them Gandhi is a huge joke and Gandhism, an outmoded means to achieve a noble end." Violence has its attraction, with wholesale murders giving the Communists a sense of glory. "Non-violent pleas for justice have no place in their muddled thinking."

Naxalism had a beginning way back in 1967, and since then has spread like wild fire in the tribal majority areas. In 2009, Naxalites were active in some 180 districts across 10 States. After first full year of implementation of National Tribal Policy (NTP), by Aug 2010, the number of Naxal-affected districts came down to 83 across the nine States. Maoists are strongest in Chhattisgarh, where in 2006, some 114 of them were killed. Andhra Pradesh came second, with 108 killed.

Salma Judum is the Villain

Ramchandra Guha, a well-known human rights activist, blames the Chhattisgarh Government for the influence wielded by the Maoists. He says, on the one side it granted a slew of leases to industriaists, over-riding the protests of gram panchayats and handing over "large tracts" of tribal lands to mining companies. On the other side, it promoted says Guha, a 'vigilant army'... Salwa Judum... which distributed guns to young men owing albgiance to Mahandra Karma. Guha calls them "goons" who roamed the countryside looking for Naxalites, real or fictitious, burning homes, sometimes entire village, raping women and looting granaries, driving an estimated 1,50,000 adivasis out of their native villages, and in the process, giving an ideological excuse to Naxalites to resort to more violence in revenge.

Karma had set up Salma Judum which in 2006 killed 114 Maoists in Chhattisgarh and 108 in Andhra Pradesh.

The Maoists are well-equipped with arms. The MHA figures say in 2004, there were 9,300 hard-core Maoists, holding some 6,500 regular weapons, and lots of unlicensed ones. Two years later, in 2006, their strength rose to 15,000 cadres, controlling some one-fifth of Indian forests and being active in 160 of the country's 604 districts. That this number has come down by 2011 is another matter.

Maoists are opposed to development schemes, as that directly undo their cause. What they reportedly have in mind,... stupid as it may sound!... is to 'conquer' all of India!

To fight them in 2006, the Central Government deployed 37,000 CAPF in Chhattisgarh alone, and 30 companies (30,000 troops) in Jharkhand, two of the worst-hit states. The MHA allocated an annual budget of Rs 23,000 cr to address the Naxal conflict.

The author demands a serious effort to find their leaders and get them publicly hanged, as the British did in their fight with thugs. And Maoists are no better than thugs. But the UPA, after a year in power, is unclear as to how to handle the Maoists. True, in July 2006, the Planning Commission had set up a 16-member expert group headed by D. Bandopadhyay, Chairman of the Council for social development to study the causes of Naxalism and suggest remedial measures. The draft policy had suggested that "the solution lies in giving rights to the ST communities over natural and financial resources and addressing the issues of economic deprivation in a prompt and time-bound manner."

The scribe wants governments to seek help from the RSS, shedding its ideological prejudices. But he does not expect the UPA government to do much on the issue, after all after 9 years in power, it has failed to meet the authorised strength of 6,217 IAS officers, running a short fall of 1500.

"Maoists play a lead role in forest cover loss:" Feb 2012

India's forest cover has shrunk by 367 sq km in the last two years, says the latest report of the Environment Ministry.

The report released by the Environment Ministry Secretary T Chatterjee on 6 Feb 2012, "has accused the Maoists for indiscriminate destrruction of forests in Andhra Pradesh to the extent of 182 sq km.

Regarded as the most authentic assessment of the country's forest resources, the report, prepared by Forest Survey of India (FSI), said the area of forest cover in the country is 78.29 million hectare, which is 23.81 per cent of its geographical area. This includes 2.76 per cent of tree cover. This is the twelfth report in the series. The assessment has been made on the basis of the satellite imagery.[8]

Of the total decrease of 367 sq km of forest area in the country, Andhra Pradesh has contributed the largest chunk of 281 sq km. The report holds "while, the Maoists took a major toll of the forest cover in the State, the harvesting of mature eucalyptus trees and other species, has further added to its deforestation."

Chatterjee adds: "Naxals have cut trees in hundreds of acres in the two districts of Warangal and Khammam during the last two years. They cut trees to get people involved... The wood was auctioned later."

"MP tribals defend their gods with bows and arrows"

This was the headline of a news story in a daily in Apr 2012. Its blurb is even more significant: "Take on forest officials to protect forest." Here follow two opening paragraphs:

> "Bamboo bows drawn taut and lethal arrow heads catching the sun's glint, the Baigas... a dwindling tribe in the remote jungles of Ranjara in MP's Dindori district... are standing guard for their gods against whom they consider state had sponsoreWd marauders."
>
> These lush jungles have been their homes for generations and Baigas worship trees as gods. Tribal men, women and children now stand guard, armed with axes and saws... ironically, taking on forest officials who they think are facilitating the slaughter."

The local village panchayat held frequent meetings to protest the forest department's policy of felling trees. Running out of patience, the panchayat in its latest meeting asked every able man, woman and child to take up their traditional arms to ensure not a single tree is cut.

Dindori Conservator of Forest LP Tiwari offers a plausible reasoning: "We have only been cutting dead wood to provide fire wood to locals, under a sustainable yield-based working plan. The department strictly follows regulations." A total ban on tree-felling could lead to illegal logging on a massive scale, he said, adding, "This was the experience in Uttarkhand."

But for now, the Baigas are in no mood to buy this argument. Tiwari is hopeful: "We are in talks with the tribe to at least facilitate the marking of the trees that are dying or are dead there. I am hopeful an agreement will be reached." The report is filed from Bhopal.[9]

A senior forest officer feels the Maoists from the neighbouring villages of Chhattisgarh may be fuelling the tribal resistance.

The officer said, "We believe some ultra-left groups are behind this disturbing development in Ranjara. Most of its inhabitants are illiterate and poor."

The Baigas, being nature worshippers, say trees are their gods and felling them would devastate the ecology. They have vowed to die or be jailed to save them. Forest officials were stunned by the sudden and stiff resistance and are now trying hard to "thaw the differences" over tree falling.

The article has an accompanying picture with men, women and children standing in a jungle next to a tree, with their bows and arrows at the ready, to use an Army term.

"Tribals hack forest ranger to death in Andhra Pradesh": Sep 2013

Such scenes of an occasional violence are only to be expected under the circumstances explained in the earlier pages. Let the opening para of this news story datelined Nizamabad, 15 Sep 2013 speak for itself: "In an act of horrific violence, a group of tribals who had allegedly encroached on forest land, hacked a forest ranger to death at KK Tanda, a tribal village in Andhra Pradesh's Nizamabad district late on Sunday (12 September) night, apart from maiming seven forest officials who are now being treated in a hospital."[10]

The police said the villages in the tribal area attacked the staff when they went to arrest those who had illegally occupied forest land and started tilling it with tractors. Gangaiah had gone to the village on the 12th midnight along with a nine-member team, including five beat officers. They were acting on information that mechanised tilling was taking place illegally in KK Tanda under Nellavelli gram panchayat. Tragically, their vehicle got stuck in mud outside the village, which was surrounded by the tribals who threw chilli powder into their eyes and attacked them with boulders-and axes. Gangaiah, who was atached to the Dichpally forest range, was surrounded and set upon. Wounded severaly, he died on the spot.

Forest department sources said villages had planned to eliminated Gangiah. So he was lured to the spot by giving fake information of tilling the forest land and smuggling of teakwood. The attack was pre-planned, explaining the fact of tribals had chilli powder with them and they were armed with axes. Although they caught hold of four forest officials, only Gangaiah was killed. He was targeted since he had registered cases against some of them for occupying forest land. The assailants were believed to be the people who had secured bail recently.

Forest officials suspect the role of villagers Ramulu, Sailu, Jamuna, Bhaskar and Gopi in the attack. On the 13th, the officials sat on dharna, demanding their arrest. Police registered a case and "has launched a serach mission." Sub-divisional police officer S Anil kumar said they would arrest the accused soon. Divisional Forest Officer D Bheema Naik said lower-level forest officials were facing threats from Left leaders.

Land: Valuable asset in any Society

Land is the second item in the trinity of assets... Forest. Land and Mines...in this part of this chapter. Having discussed forest in the preceding pages, now we come to the land.

If the forest standing on the land is valuable, the land sans the forest is even more valuable, since it is utilised to produce a variety of crops, source of food, nutrition and wealth for the human kind, and particularly for those who own it. Besides farming, the land also comes handy for raising assets like residential houses, hospitals, schools, and more importantly, the industries of regional, national and international importance.

So land is the basic asset of any society. Its importance, especially for tribal areas, was specifically recognised by the founding Fathers of the nation by inserting two Schules, viz V and VI, in India's Constitution, dealing with the subject of such areas.

"Tribals should be the Frontline Warriors against the Maoists": May 2012

The fact that the tribals should constitute the first line of defence against the left ultras seems to be a given. Even then, when a daily makes this point with due reasoning, it deserves examination.[11]

In the last 14 months, the Maoists have conducted five high profile abduction: Feb 2011, it was DC of Malkangiri, Odisha, P Vineel Krishna; Mar 2012, it were two Italians and a BJD MLA, again from the forests of Odisha; and in Apr 2012, it was Sukma DC Alex Paul Menon (Chhattisgarh). Five abductions in three incidents.

Odisha agreed to facilitate the release of 27 under trials for the two Italinas and the MLA. The former came under criticism for agreeing to the release of the 27 hardened criminals. In the neighbouring Chhattisgarh the government agreed to set up a high-powered committee to review the cases of all prisoners languishing in the State jails, including the cases demanded by the Maoists.

It should be interesting to examine the conduct of the two sides involved in the agreement. Odisha, to its credit,, refused to free the jailed Eastern Military commander of the Red Army as well as another rebel, accused of killing 55 policement. Despite repeated demands by the ultras for the release of more people and their threat to decide the fate of the hostages in kangroo courts, the government stood its ground till the hostages were released.

On its part, the government is yet to release "most" of the '27 hardened criminals.' Whether they indeed are hardened criminals or otherwise, one can't be certain. But one thing is certain: they are impoverished tribals. The daily adds further. "Hundreds like them get caught in the crossfire between the Maoists and security forces and end up staying in jails for years since they are too poor to afford a lawyer or bail.

Certain comments should be in order on the preceding paragraph. One, the daily has not defined "most". How many of these were in jail when this report went to the press on 2 May? As the government had its reasons for not releasing at least two of the detained Maoists, it may have valid grounds for not setting free some of the 27 tribal detainees. The daily could have helped its readers to determine the reasonableness of the government if it had given the number not freed by the 2nd! It was not difficult to find out that number. Notwithstanding all this, it is a known fact that some innocents do languish in jails. But given the nature of the conflict such an unfortunate situation is unavoidable. It should also be stated to even out the record that all Maoists and their staunch/active supporters are not found out and arrested for long years. One recent example is that of a chairborne professor of Delhi University. Even beyond that, if an alleged Maoist is released by a district court, or even High Court, it does not mean he is certainly innocent! It simply means the court did not find the police evidence against him adequate. A recent case is that of an orthopaedic surgeon, and who subsequently, was given an assignment by India's Planning Commission. It is rather sad and unfortunate. Such a thing can impinge upon the nation's security. This doctor, incidentally, was known to have worked for the Maoists murderers as a loyal courier. (Now, back to the daily's analysis).

The daily believes the tribals get arrested as they can only converse in their own dialect, thus failing to give proper answers to their interrogators. Again, the daily believes-quite erroneously... the security men engaged in counter Naxal operations often arrest tribals because of their frustration due to mounting work pressure.

Both the above averments are highly unlikely, if not totally unconvincing!

The daily again makes interesting points: "This reality... of many tribals languishing in jails as they had been booked under false and fabricated cases... dawned on the Odisha government while it was negotiating for Krishna's release last year (2011). But after Krishna release, the list was buried under labyrinths of bureaucracy. It surfaced again after this (2012) years hostage crisis."

It could be a matter of debate whether the government has given in to Maoists or not, there is no doubt that the media-savvy rebels managed to score a political point by triggering a debate in media on the State's neglect of the tribals. The Maoists have exploited these issues to consolidate their base and Challenge the State's authority and bring in a sizeable chunk... definitely not the majority... of tribals to their fold.

it does not need any serious effort to make media debate on any anti-Government issues. If the powers that be makes for readers and TV matchers interest. Let us throw a counter at the Press: why were they not able to sustain a debate on the egregious and disgustingly inhuman act of Maoists stitching an IED in the belly of slain recurity man? Media does not need any Maoists to create such a debate... media itself finds and at times creates issues for their own pecuniary gains. Yet again, there are enough intellectual pretenders/over ground Maoists/Maoist sympathisers to give anti-State/ Government 'masala' to the Press for sustained debate which benefit both of them!

In the last two years, the security forces have decimated the top Maoist leadership and inflicted heavy casualties on them. This has been possible because the forces now have better fire power and Maoists have lost tribal support... a periodic cycle of loss that the rebels aften encounter... in several areas due to excesses by their reckless cadres. But the same tribals may be forced to back the Maoists (again) if the excesses by the forces continue and if there is no long-term solution to their problems.

The country's tribal areas are governed by the finest laws. But these have mostly not been implemented in letter and spirit. These must be implemented alongwith various amendments and recommendations by various commissions that have repeatedly proposed that "the tribals' concept of development and community ownership must be weaved into the planning process of these areas."

"A patch to call their Own:" Editorial in Hindu: Oct 2012

This daily has summed up those issues succinctly that directly affect the deprived of the country.[12] Its opening lines are apt, indicating the major issues involved in this long-running imbroglio:

> "The frustration behind the Jan Satyagraha, the long march of the landless to Delhi, was justified. Reforms meant to help the poor access land have been on the policy agenda since Independence, but the ground situation has hardly changed. Against the potential ceiling surplus of 21 million hectares, only about 2.7 million hectares have so for been taken possession of and distributed to the needy. As a result, number of landless poor in rural India is still as high as about 18 million and half among them live without a home of their own. Frequent evictions and forced land acquisition have added to the numbers, especially the adivasis."

It was in this context that Ekta Parishad, a federation of about 11,000 community organisations, proposed the march to high light the persisting apathy. The swelling number had forced a rethink. It was to his credit that Jairam Ramesh, initially reluctant, accepted that there were valid reasons behind the march. The 10-point agreement, the Rural Development Minister signed with Ekta Parishad, could lead to a comprehensive new policy that would reduce the number of the landless and enhance the protection of the land rights of the marginalised.

For that to happen, the promises made must translate into concrete action. They should not degenerate into mere tokenism as it happened in 2007 when a similar march was held. The government then promised to set up a National Council for Land Reforms under the chairmanship of the PM. But this has done nothing since 2008.

Land is central to alleviating rural poverty. "Whenever reforms have been implemented and plots even as small as 10 cents (one-tenth of an acre) alloted, they have enhanced the food intake and income of the poor and facilitated construction of dwellings. For these reasons, the Eleventh Five Year Plan had recommended that 10 to 15 cents of land be given to each landless family with priority given to "female-headed families." The plan envisioned that this process be completed by 2012, but that goal remains a distant dream.

Land is a State subject and much will depend on the commitment of the local governments. Barring a few States, like West Bengal and Kerala, others have not done enough. Of the 53.98 lakh beneficiaries who gained from land distribution, West Bengal alone accounts for half the number. Proteecting tenancy rights and preventing forced displacement are the other two critical aspects that need attention. Inclusive growth is impossible without an equitable and just distribution of land and it is imperative to achieve it through well thought out reforms.

This daily has examined the issues involved and given out a solution as seen right by it. In any case, there is never a problem of finding solutions to any problems including the ones deemed intraclable, but the devil lives in details. While executing these well thoughts out plans/schemes, human frailties, bureaucratic tangles and material considerations take over and spoil the show?

The above was written in Oct 2012. After years of contention, the UPA II passed the Land Bill in 2013, with the support of the main opposition/ BJP. But same BJP, after coming to power, wants a New Land Bill, which is opposed by practically every parties in opposition. Today 30 Aug 2015, PM Modi announced he would not renew the contentious Land Ordinance expiring tomorrow, the 31st. With the Congress still on war path, no one knows if the Winter session of the Parliament would be any different than the Monsoon one-just washed away! The plans of men and mouse...

"Land Bill Row: Minister Deo wants 80 per cent consent from farm hands:" Nov 2012

The ruling UPA II government's long-delayed Land Acquisition, Rehabilitation and Resettlement Bill has been facing hurdles from within as also from outside. The latest to muddy the waters further is no less a man than Minister for Tribal Affairs and Panchayat Raj V Kishore Chandre Deo.

Throwing the spanner in its plans, Deo went beyond the suggestions of Congress President Sonia Gandhi, declaring that the government must acquire the consent of 80 per cent livelihood losers to acquire land for PPP projects.[13]

This is beyond the position publicly expressed by Sonia... asking the government to impose 80 per cent consent from land owners... (not livelihood losers...) to buy land for purpose of setting up private industries. She had not objected to the Sharad Pawar led GOM's suggestion that consent clause should be kept at 67 per cent for the PPP projects because the ownership of the land in such projects remains with the government.

Deo's demands came in a note to Pawar as part of inter-ministerial consultations prior to preparing the final draft for the cabinet.

In a move that could lead to a tussle between Panchayat Raj ministry and the Commerce and Industries ministry headed by Anand Sharma, because Deo also suggestged that logistics parks and national manufacturing zones could be treated as 'infrastructure', and should be kept outside the purview of public purposes. Sharma is keen on keeping them under the public purpose head because it would make land acquisition a lot easier.

The new Land Bill aims to define public purpose, and allows the government to acquire land only for projects under the public purpose head. Deo's demands may upset current equations and make the concensus-building process more complicated.

The government, however, is determined to introduce the Bill in Parliament" during the oncoming winter session (end-2012)".

"Consent for projects diluted to 70 per cent under Land Acquisition Bill:" Dec 2012

Land Bill is an important legislation under discussion presently (end 2012). It is under pressure from various stake holders.... the industry, government and land owning/tilling class... with contrarian views/ recommendations. The latest was reported by a daily in Dec 2012: "In the latest flip-flop on the Land Acquisition Bill, due to be discussed by the Union Cabinet on 13 Dec 2012, the Rural Development (RD) Ministry has diluted the consent provisions... 70 per cent of land owners when the government acquires land for PPP projects and for all other types, it will be 80 per cent... reportedly against the wishes of Sonia Gandhi, UPA chairperson.

RD Minister Jairam Ramesh would only confirm that the version going to the Cabinet mandated consent of "something between 67 and 80 per cent" in the case of PPP projects. He expects to introduce this bill in parliament before the winter session ends on 20 December.

In its original version, the legislation... now officially titled "The Right to Fair Compensation, Resettlement, Rehabilitation and Transparency in Land Acquisition Bill... had required 80 per cent consent not just from land owners, but also the farm workers who may not own any land themselves but depend on it for their livelihood. This provision was removed after protests from industry and infrastructure lobby, and a ministerial panel headed by Agriculture Minister Sharad Pawar had further diluted consent requirements to just two-thirds (67 percent) of land owners for private and PPP projects.

Mrs Gandhi's objections... on the grounds that a farmer-friendly Bill was a key plank in the Congress' election agenda... had taken that figure back upto 80 percent.

However, pressures from within the UPA "have reportedly forced the RD Ministry to settle for the compromise figure of 70 per cent."[14]

"Land Bill: Centre puts onus on States": Jan 2013

Land Acquisition Bill, which the UPA government put forth as a remedy to curb forceful acquisitions and consequent agitations throughout the country, has proved too volatile to be formulated centrally. In its latest version, the Bill has allowed the State governments to decide on important factors, mainly compensation paid to the farmers. This way the States would have to deal with the repercussions, if any, at the ground level.

The shift is in the wake of concerns from industry, farmers, state governments and several Central ministries... each wanting its interests protected.[15]

The Bill initially introduced in Sep 2011 said the compensation to land losers shuld be four times the market value, including the solatium in rural areas. The amount... based on the distance of the acquired areas from the nearest towns... would be decided by the states now.

In another shift, the states would prescribe the limit on purchase of land by private parties, and breach of this rule would kick in rehabalitation benefits that the purchaser should extend to those losing their land.

The 2011 Bill also says that private companies that buy more than 100 acres of land in the rural areas and 50 acres in the urban areas, should comply with resettlement and rehabilitation norms.

The RD Ministry was uable to introduce the Land Bill in the 2012 Winter Session of Parliament as Minister Ramesh had announced due to a variety of amendments proposed by several stake-holders. "The Ministry now plans to introduce the related amendmants to the Land Bill in the Budget Session, 2013.

The states would now, also, set the threshold area on farmland that could be acquired for industry in a district. They would also decide the fate of any unutilised acquired land.

As per the constitution, land is a State subject but its acquisition falls under concurrent list.

An official told the daily: "The changes are based on standing Committee suggestions that states understand their regions and conditions better."

A new Land Acquisition Bill to replace the 1894 Act has been a contentious issue. "Some of the acquisition provisions are best left to the states," Shared Pawar, Chairman of the GOM set up by the PM to resolve differences within the government on the Bill, had said earlier.

"Right place, Wrong arrangement:" Jun 2013

This is an interesting headline for an article in a daily, discussing the comparative merits of schedule V and schedule VI of India's Constitution.[16]

Its blurb makes the essence of this article clear. "Moving governance of tribal areas in Central India from the Fifth to the Sixth Schedule will help address the demand for autonomy."

The summary and excerpts from the article are reproduced here.

The article opens up about the targeted attack by Maoists in Chhattisgarh against the State Congress leadership in which VC Shukla and Mahendra Karma and the party's other top leaders were killed, has rekindled a familiar debate on the military aspects of counter-insurgency. But continuing cycle of violence in the State underscores the need for closer examination of the social and political impact of the Fifth Schedule of the Constitution through which the tribal areas of peninsular India, are governed.

India's tribal population is 100 million which has constitutionally been addressed via two distinct avenues.

The Fifth Schedule applies to an overwhelining majority of India's tribals in nine States while the Sixth Schedule covers areas that are settled in the North-Eastern States bordering China and Myanmar.

Bastar District in Chhattisgarh is governed by the Fifth Schedule but it wants to shift into the Sixth Schedule.

The Sixth Schedule gives tribal communities considerable autonomy; the States of Assam, Tripura, Meghalaya and Mizoram are autonomous regions under the Sixth Schedule. The role of the Governor and the State are subject to significant limitations, with greater powers devolved locally. The District Council and the Regional Council under Sixth Schedule have real powers to make laws, possibly on the various legislative subjects, receiving grants in aids from the Consolidate Fund of India to meet the costs of schemes for development, healthcare, education, roads and regulatory powers to state control. The mandate towards devolution, deconcentration and divestment determines the protection of their customs, better economic development and most importantly, ethmic security.

The Fifth Schedule on the other hand fails because it has never been applied. The recent parliamentary moves to provide greater autonomy within the Fifth Schedule have not "had the desired results. The 1996 PESA or Panchayats (Extension of the Scheduled Areas) Act, should have been a land mark for the tribal communities. It mandates the state to devolve certain political, administrative and fiscal powers to local governments elected by the communities. This became exclusive to the Fifth Schedule areas, to promote tribal self-government. PESA was meant to benefit not only the majority of tribals but also extended to cover minority non-tribal communities. It guarantees tribes half of the seats in the elected local governments and the seat of the chairperson at all hierarchical levels of the punchayat system.

Samatha Judgement

PESA was considered the most logical step in the Fifth Schedule areas to ensure tribal welfare and accountability. But, alas, it has not been properly implemented. Tribal communities have progressively been denied self-government and rights to their communities natural resources that should have been provided under the legislation. In its 1997 Samatha decision, the

Supreme Court ruled that the Fifth Schedule enjoins governor to bar purchase of tribal land for mining activity by any entity that was not state-owned. This judgement however, led to an opposite reaction from the ministry of mines, and subsequent appeals from the Andhra Pradesh government claiming that Samatha would have an adverse effect not only on the mining sector but also on non-agricultural activities especially industrial activity and hence would impact the economic development throughout the country. In response, the Governors were then given unfettered authority in the transfer of scheduled tribe land to the government and allotment to non-tribals, altering the balance of power and undermining the stated goal of tribal autonomy.

Other examples abound, including the Scheduled Tribes and Other Traditional Forest Rights Act of Dec 2006, which ostensibly recognises the right of communities to protect and manage their forests (as does PESA), but only if the state decides whether a certain region is denoted as Village Forest and Reserved Forest. In this process, many communities are evicted without a proper channel of rehabilitation.

For these reasons, it is evident that PESA and Fifth Schedule have been counter-productive, inconsistent in addressing issues regarding tribal rights and the propensity of failure justifies serious debates on the existing endeavours.

Many tribal voices are therefore demanding introduction of the Sixth Schedule in Chhattisgarh's Bastar district, which will give them special status to participate directly in governance as in the North-East States currently under the Sixth Schedule. Moreover, the Sixth Schedule has certain features that can be implanted in any governance models for tribal areas, particularly concepts of constitutional and legislative subjects that are exclusive to local governments. An autonomous district council will get greater role in directing administrative requirements without depending on Central and State structure.

However, the working of a system is always different from the idea of it. The Sixth Schedule that embodies autonomy has its own shortcomings, breakdown of laws, elections not being conducted, rather than empowerment there is exclusion that fails to provide much-needed protection to tribes in the absence of political will, and live by the mercy of government funds.

But inspite of the negatives underlying the Sixth Schedule, Bastar district envisages a true form of local bodies like the District Council and Regional Council that have provided a fair degree of autonomy (Scribe Malhotra is with the Centre for Policy Research, New Delhi).

"Governor has discretionary powers in Schedule V areas: Government: Jul 2013

What should settle the debate on the role of governor in Schedule V areas, the Law Ministry has issued circulars to all officers, laying down that Attorney General's view that the Governor has discretionary powers in such areas will now be the government position.[17]

The circular is in response to a letter Minister for Tribal Affairs (MTA) V Kishore Chandra Deo asking Law Minister Kapil Sibal to consider the matter in the light of an affidavit filed by Assistant Solicitor General, Fouzia Mirza in the Bilaspur High Court, Chhattisgarh. Mirza had stated that the Governor had "no discretionary powers" over the formulation of rules, laws and general administration under the Schedule V of the Constitution. Deo in his letter to Sibal wrote "the ASG took a contradictory position without any substantive basis and it is an act of professional impropriety". Law Ministry officials disclosed the Government was unhappy with Mirza's actions.

Deo on 4 April had written to governors of Schedule V areas, clarifying that governor's powers in such areas are "unbridled and unfettered." "The governor may repeal or amend any act of Parliament or legislature of the state or any existing law which is for the first time being applicable to the area in question, when good governance or the peace is disturbed due to issues related either with land or money lending."

He based his argument on the opinion of Attorney General GE Vahanvati expressed in 2010: "In performance of functions and exercise of powers under the Schedule V, the governor is not bound by the aid and advice of the Council of Ministers."

Sibal on 23 May had said the A-G opinion "prima facie" appeared to be "correct." But issue needed to be examined, he said, based on the circumstances under which Mirza had filed her submission. The circular to all law officers was issued in Jun 2013. "But the MTA is yet to hear from Kapil Sibal, any official response." Is he more loyal to ASG Mirza than his responsibility as the Union Law Minister?"

Deo, who has brought a positive change in the MTA after taking it over, has been urging governors of Schedule V areas to use their powers to protect tribal rights by preventing mining activities in such areas. He recently wrote to Odisha Governor SC Jamir on the issue following the Supreme Court judgement over bauxite mining in Niyam giri.

Acquisition of Land: Problems and more problems: A detailed look at the issues: Jul 2013

Acquisition of land is assuming complex dimensions, with passage of time. Acquiring land is posing greater problems due to a variety of reasons. A daily[18] looked into a few aspects of the issue. It also interviewed two individuals on the subject. The succeeding pages see the discussion on these relevant aspects.

Wanted: Law that is fair to every one

The blurb clarifies things: "MESSY AFFAIR. Existing law on land acquisition is loaded against land owners. Critics say new law will make it unviable for industry to acquire land. Can government find the right balance?"

The daily opens up with a punch line: "The costs are rising by the day... 400,000-500,000 potential new Jobs are held up and almost eight lakh crore of corporate expenditure is getting shelved."

The main culprit: land acquisition law. There are other issues... like environmental clearances, rad tape, and corruption... that make India a difficult place to do business in, but land is arguably the biggest issue hloding up investment. The stalled projects could have added 0.1 per cent to India's GDP growth rate.

"Investors are beginning to lose patience." Within days of the Centre announcing liberalised norms to attract FDI, two of the world's largest steel companies Arcelor Mittal and POSCO, pulled out of the two steel projects in Odisha and Karnataka, respectively. The combined investments in these projects: Rs 72,000 crore. The main problem: land.

The existing Land Acquisition Act of 1894 is loaded against the land owner. To make it more equitable, the government has drawn up a new law, which, critics say will make the land prohibitively expensive and, thus, unviable for industry.

"Compensation for land, resettlement and rehabilitation should leave affected families better off, while also balancing the viability of projects," said an official, even-handedly.

Rana kapoor, President, Assocham says: "State governments must play an important role in the whole thing... we must sep up cabinet committee on investments at the state level to expedite the whole process. The new law does not address this issue."

The frustration among the investors is showing. Here is an illustrative statement from Vijay Bhatnagar, CEO, India and China, Arcelor Mittal:

"Over the last seven years, we have invested considerable resources in this (Karnataka) project. However, the delays relating to land acquisition and allocation of captive iron ore blocks mean this project is no longer viable."

Such statements create a negative international sentiment about India.

Naina Lal Kidwai, FICCI President adds her disappointment: "It is a pity that big projects should suffer because of land acquisition problems. One can not wait for so many years."

There is still hope: foreign investors are not writing India off totally. POSCO says in an e-mail to the daily: "Given India's huge potential it remains an attractive investment destination. But the government must speed up the tedious procedures for setting up industries."

The new law, when it is passed by the parliament, will, hopefully, address these concerns and balance the competing demands of industry and land owners.

Land Acquisition: A drag on economy

India's plans to create millions of jobs has been hit by massive delays relating to land acquisition and other reasons.

The numbers are telling

- 92: Number of large projects that are behind schedule.
- Rs 7,62,451 crore. Total investment in these projects that are delayed.
- 18.1 per cent overall rise in costs compared to original estimates.
- Rs 3,60,000 cr

  Estimated value of steel projects stalled because of delays in approvals for land and mines.
- 400,000-500,000

  Estimated number of jobs that this investment could have created.
- 0.1 per cent: Estimated addition to India's GDP growth rate once these projects go on stream.
- 132: India's rank among 185 countries in case of doing business, compared to China's rank at 91.

Some facts on land

- 48 per cent of land in India is devoted to agriculture. So, it may not be possible to avoid acquiring farm land for industry.
- 15 per cent of land in China is devoted to agriculture.
- 3-4 per cent: The financial return on land as an asset in India.

Land as a Holy cow

- One of the hardest political decisions the government has to make is to frame a land acquisition policy.
- Many large proposals are stymied by ambiguous titles of ownership, environmental issues, poor compensation and social concerns.

The tape is still Deep Red

The large number of government approvals and cumbersome administrative procedures related to land acquisition delay the start of business operations and push up costs, thus deterring serious investors.

Key Features of New Bill

1. To acquire land for private projects, consent of 80 per cent of landowners needed. Consent of 70 per cent of landowners needed for PPP projects.
   Counrter point: Land acquisition will become difficult for private sector industries.
2. The threshold for applying rehabilitation and resettlement provisions for private purchases may be notified by each state government.
   Counter point: No uniform rules for rehabilitation of land losers, thus, increasing uncertainty for industry and potential for disputes and delays.
3. Compensation for land owners at 4 times the market price in rural areas and two times in urban areas.
   Counter point: Will jack up land prices and make many projects unviable.
4. "Urgency clause" for taking overland can be applied only for defence, national security or "any other emergency" with approval of parliament.
   Logic: Misuse of this clause will be prevented, thus, removing a major source of litigation.

Four Case Studies

Company: POSCO

Rs 32,000 cr steel plant

Halligudi, Karnataka

By Naveen Ammembala, 22, 7.13

Fact: Farmers donot want to give up land

Bangaluru: South Korean griant POSCO has abandoned its plan for a Rs 32,000 cr steel plant in Karnataka. It had announced the project in 2010.

Land acquistion hit a road block in 2011 when about 2,500 farmers... who owned the 3,382 acres planned to be acquired... launched an agitation under the guidance of prominent lingayat seer Tontadarya Smami. The state government, then headed by another Lingayat, CM, BS Yeddyurappa, paid heed to the protests and halted land acquisition in Jul 2011.

The CM said in 2011, "There is no necessity for strikes, protests and dharnas in connection with land acquistion. Our government is not interested in establishing industries by neglecting the interests of farmers. No land will be acquired forcibly. MN Vidyashankar, Principal Secretary, Industries Department, said, "We cannot give them (POSCO) land as hundreds of farmers are protesting.

Company POSCO

Rs 47,000 cr steel plant

Jagat Singhpur, Odisha

By: Priya Ranjan Sahu, 22.7.13

Fact: Project on track, But trouble looms.

Bhubaneswar: POSCO signed a deal with the Odisha government in 2005 to set up a $12 billion (50,000 cr then; Rs 70,000 cr now) in a coastal patch of Jagatsingh pur district, known for betel vine farming.

Land acquisitoning problem led to a strong anti-POSCO movement which has delayed project though the state government says it is on track.

It was initially supposed to be a 12-million-tonne-per-annum steel mill, which was to come up in a plot of 4,004 acres, but the capacity was scaled down to 8 million tonnes (investment Rs 47,000 cr and area was reduced to 2,700 acres.

Odisha Industry Minister Niranjan Pujari says: "The problem of land acquisition for POSCO is nearly over." But reports from the ground suggest there could be more trouble ahead. The administration is finding it difficult to build a boundary wall around the area.

Company: Arcelor Mittal

Rs 40,000 Cr Steel Plant

Keonjhar, Odisha

By: Priya Ranjan Sahu, 22.7.15

Fact: Govt took no steps on land, says company.

Bhubaneswar: The Odisha government had signed a deal with the world's leading steel maker, Arcelor Mittal, in 2006 to set up a Rs 40,000 cr plant in the State.

Seven years later, the Lakshmi Mittal run company withdrew from the project in Keonjhar district. Arcelor Mittal blamed the state government for alleged inaction on land acquisition and on granting a mining lease. Odisha Steel and Mines Minister Rajanikant Singh, in a retort, said, "The company failed to do many things it had agreed to do?"

Experts hold both, government and the Arcelor Mittal, responsible for the impasse.

A source said: "Land acquisition is a problem for all industrialists, be it Arcelor Mittal, POSCO or Tata. Arcelor Mittal wanted a mining lease, which was not possible, as it did not submit a detailed project report to the government."

Arcelor Mittal did not respond to a detailed questionnaire sent by the daily.

Company: Tata Motors

Rs 2,000 cr car Plant

Singur, West Bengal

By: Snigdhendu Bhattacharya

Fact: Mamata's agitation derailed project.

Kolkata: Tata Motors Nano project in Singur had to be scrapped in 2008 when Trinamool congress (TMC) Chief (and now State CM) Mamata Banerjee led an agitation by a section of unwilling landlosers. The project eventually went to Gujarat.

The Left Front-run state government had acquired 997.11 acres of land for the project by Mar 2007 and handed it over to Tata Motors. By Oct 2008, the company had almost completed building the factory. Employees were being trained in assembling the car with parts munufactured at the Pantnagar plant in Uttrakhand.

But the plant still needed the regular protection of over 200 policemen.

The movement against land acquisition was politically beneficial for the TMC, which swept to power in 2011 on the strength of having taken up the farmer's cause. However, the land losers have not yet got their land back because the matter is sub-judice.

"Why Odisha could not deliver?" By Priya Ranjan Sahu: 22.7.13

Bhubaneswar: South Korean steel maker POSCO's $12 billion (Rs 70,000 cr) project (later scaled down to Res 47,000 cr) in Odisha is almost a case study of how not to go about acquiring land.

The state government signed an Mou with POSCO in 2005 to set up a steel mill, which was scheduled to start production by 2011. After signing the Mou, the government decided to displace locals occupying over 4,000 acres in a rich agrarian area, leading to anti-industry agitation and inordinate delays.

The correct way forward, say expert, would have been to acquire land before hand, pay compensation to displaced people, develop infrastructure and then sign Mous with companies keen on investing in the State.

"There is no point in signing Mous with 50 steel companies when you cannot provide land," said an official in a big steel company that is still struggling to get land.

"Gujarat shows the way" By Mahesh Langa: 22.7.13

Ahmedabad: Under the new policy on land acquisition unveiled in 2011, the Gujarat government acquires agricultural land, not in piecemeal manner for individual projects, but for the Gujarat Industrial Development Corporation (GIDC). The land losers/sellers are made a part of the industrialisation process by giving them a share of the resources generated.

The compensation is based on actual market prices. Besides, the seller gets 10 per cent of the differential amount the GIDC gets from the sale. The seller also has the option of buying back 1 per cent of his land after it is developed, at a token price.

Then, the GIDC sponsors one person per family for an ITI training course and provides employment to one member of each project-hit family.

So far, the GIDC has developed and sold 26,000 hectars. But recently, the state had to abandon the acquisition process across 44 villages near Ahmedabad due to farmers' agitation.

Interview: Jairam Ramesh By Sambhadra Chatterji Jul 2013

Union Rural Development (RD) Minister Ramesh has drawn up a new Land Acquisition Bill to replace the Land Acquisition Act of 1894.

Q. Two international steel giants, Arcelor Mittal and POSCO, have scrapped projects worth Rs 72,000 cr because of land Acquisition problems, your reaction.

A. The problems these companies faced were issues related to state governments. They had nothing to do with the policies of the Central government.

Q. If the new Land Act were in place, could these problems have been avoided?

A. Certainly! The incidents prove that the new Act is all the more required now to make the land buying process transparent. A transparent mechanism would have been in place and ensure land owners got their due.

Q. Some industry lobbies think the proposed law would lead to steep hike of land prices.

A. If the bill leads to more direct land purchases by private players, so be it. Land acquisition has been too easy or too long for many private industries. But that can't go on for ever. The current law, enacted way back in 1824, has not been in the interest of livelihood earners.

Q. It is feared that this bill may actually dissuade companies from investing in India, your opinion?

A. Investments and industries are most welcome. But if they want the government to buy land for them, it must be done in equitable arrangement where the land owners do not suffer. I am aware of the resentment in some quarters. But I expected this reaction. It is natural for those people who are reaping benefits of the current law to oppose the new law.

Q. What is your agenda now?

A. My job is to ensure that the process of land acquisition is made transparent. For the first time, we are trying to do justice to the land owners, tribals and other vulnerable groups. We aim to redefine two most-abused provision... the "public purpose" and the "emergency clause" in the land dealings. The 1894 Act was bad in design and worse in implementation. We will plug the loop holes.

Interview: Sanjoy Chakravorty By Varghese K George: Jul 2013

Chakravorty is a professor of geography and urban studies at Temple University, UUA, and author of a recent book, 'The Price of Land: Acquisition, Conflict, Consequence' (OUP). He talks to the daily on the unique land questions that India faces.

Before this interview is reproduced, an interesting information on the two. If Ramesh's interview is headlined, "Land acquisition has been too eary", this one is, "New law will make land unaffordable." Here goes Chakravorty interview.

Q. You say that it is in the last decade that landowners have the power to say "no" to acquisition. What will it take to make them say "yes"?

A. The new law will significantly overpay landowners. Near urban areas, it wall make acquisition difficult. The average land cost in Mumbai is higher than in New York. If you take the example of Singur, the plan was to acquire land at Rs 9 lakh an acre. After the new law is passed, the effective price per acre would be Rs 78 lakh. It would not be affordable for anyone to buy land after the new law comes into force.

Q. How have we reached this situation?

A. For decades, land owners were being arbitrarily dispossessed of their land by the state. Then, suddenly, you have a situation where the earlier information asymmetry has been resolved. Farmers who routinely faced wipeouts from their land now expect windfalls. This has created an unsustainable game situation... the smart ones wouldn't sell unless they get a particular price which they think will not go up further. But prices may never reach that level. As a result, the market will completely be distorted.

Q. Is the Indian situation a unique one?

A. Yes US and Brazil have abundant land, Russia has abundant land and an authoritarian government; In China there is no democracy; in Europe the population is declining. In India, we have democracy, growing population and economy and extremely fragmented land ownership. So we are facing unique situation.

Q. Are you suggesting that we give up hope of development?

A. The Land Bill has the best of intentions and the worst of understanding. The one way to make land available for industrial development and urbanisation is leasing it. I think that could be the way forward.

"Land Acquisition Bill will reduce infuence of Naxalites": Jairam Ramesh: 16 Sep 2013

This is the final act of the play. The Land Bill has been passed by the parliament in Sep 2013. The RD Minister, who framed and then piloted the Bill in the parliament, spoke to the media on the 15th. He described the new Land Bill as the "historic piece of legislation" and affirmed that it would reduce the influence of Naxalites in the tribal-dominated regions, through its provisions for rehabilitation and resettlement of families displaced by land acquisition. He made some important observations that are summed up here.[19]

- RD Ministry was presently engaged in framing of rules under the statute, and the Act will be notified only next year (2014).

- The States that would benefit the most from the "landmark law" are Chhattisgarh, Jharkhand and Odisha where a strong Maoist influence is visible. The new Law would enable the State Governments to solve the problems of the rural populace regarding their forest and land rights and eliminate the Naxal problem in the next five to six years.
- Paying fealty to the Congress Vice President Rahul Gandhi, Ramesh said: 'His important suggestions have been incorporated in the bill to make land acquisition process transparent and pay adequate compensation to those whose land was acquired."
- Farmers, Dalits and tribals would get the biggest benefit from the Bill.
- Land title deeds were given to 13 lakh tribals under the Forest Rights Act, 2006, The new legislations on right to Information, Right to work, Right to Education, Food Security, and NREGA enacted in the UPA II term, had established "milestones of legal rights" for the public.
- Farmers would get 40 per cent of compensation from the government for the land acquired from a middleman who bought it privately. Similarly, land title holders would get four times compensation of the actual land price in rural areas and two times in Urban areas.
- In tribal regions of southern Rajasthan, the Gram Sabha's permission would be required for executing the orders for land acquisition, while the Gram Sabha's advisory would be needed in the non-tribal districts. The tribal dominated districts in the State are Udaipur, Banswara, Dungarpur, Pratapgarh, Chhittorgarh and Bhilwara.
- He did not comment on the controversies surrounding the illegal land deals of Congress President Sonia Gandhi's son-in-law Robert Vadra in Bikaner district and the selection of land for the upcoming oil refinery in Barmer district.

Mines: Mineral Wealth

The 'mines' are the last element of the trio (of forest, land and mines) under discussion in this part of the chapter. That the tribal populations are sitting on a variety of mineral wealth is a given. The relevant question is how to make use of this resource for the benefit of the local tribal population, and for the entire nation, in a larger context.

To extract minerals from the land, the pre-requisite is that the company must have the land in its possession. The problems come up at its very inception. We have seen how the POSCO had to pull out of Karnataka as the farmers were unwilling to give land for its plant. The same goes for the Tatas at Singur in West Bengal. All that is part of a political lore.

This part deals with issues related to mining in the relevant areas.

Ramesh bats for agriculture over mines

This was reported on 14 Jan 2013. Union Rural Development Minister Jairam Ramesh on 13 January urged the governments in the mineral-rich Naxal-affected States to focus on development of agriculture and implementaiton of rural development programmes instead of focusing on mining to create employment.[20]

Addressing a gathering of Dongaria and Kutia Kandha tribal groups "on the foot hills of Niyamgiri Hills in this tribal dominated block of Kalahandi district, he underlined the need for prioritising agriculture and rural development, saying that mining in the country's mineral-rich States such as Odisha, Chhattisgarh and Jharkhand had only added to the people's miscries. Mining had only resulted in displacement of lakhs of tribal families instead of proving to be beneficial to them.

Initiative launched: "Vedanta Murdabad"

The Minister, who launched an initiative for distribution of Rs 75,000 each among 2100 families belonging to the particularly Vulnerable Tribal Groups (VTG) in villages in and around Niyamgiri for building Indira Awas housing, was welcomed with slogan, "Jairam Ramesh Zindabad, Vedanta Murdabad", as he reached the venue of the meeting.

He however, clarified that he had nothing to say about the recent closure of the 1 million tonne per annum capacity alumina refinery of Vedanta Aluminium Ltd., situated in the locality as the matter was pending before the Supreme Court. As the Union Environment and Forest Minister, Mr Ramesh had on 24 Aug 2010, rejected the forest clearnace for bauxite mining in Niyamgiri for sourcing ore for Vedanta's refinery and also halted the company's refinery expansion work.

Mr Ramesh said his visit to Kalahandi was part of his initiative to visit all 82 Maoist-hit districts spread over 9 States by the end of March this year (2013) to expedite implementation of rural development schemes.

While opposing bauxite mining in Niyamgiri Mr Ramesh said he was not opposed to Vedanta's sourcing bauxite from alternative sources. "Why is the company so keen to mine Niyamgiri, just about 4 per cent of its total requirement for its refinery?" he asked.

Mr Ramesh came down heavily on the Maoists over the incident in Latehar in which they had implanted explosives in the body of a Jawan slain by them.

Barbaric act

The Maoists, who had lost their humanity by their barbaric act at Latehar, were spreading their activities in newer areas of the country by falsely advocating the cause of the tribals, said Ramesh, while stressing the need for making development process tribal-centric in order to prevent tribal youths from joining the Maoist ranks.

"Rs 1 cr seized from arrested scientist": Jan 2013

Where ever the humans have discretionary powers, venality and greed enter the field. It is an unavoidable evil, in most cases, if not all. This is one such story of malfeasance.

A daily reports that the CBI seized Rs 1 crore from the premises of a scientist, Neeraj Kumar Khatri, with the Union Ministry of Enviornment, along with a middle man on (wednesday) 15 Jan 2013, for accepting a bribe... for environmental clearance to a lime stone mining project of a private firm in Odisha.[21] The accused scientist owns four properties.

Khatri earlier worked with this Ministry on contract, but was later confirmed. He had been working with the Ministry for the past seven years, and is presently a Deputy Director at Paryavarna Bhavan in the CGO Complex on Lodhi Road, New Delhi.

Acting on a tip-off, the CBI had laid a trap near a hotel in Mehrauli and arrested him along with the alleged middleman Chinmaya Srichandan, of Bhubaneswar-based SS Environics Pvt Ltd consultancy firm, when he was allegadly accepting a bribe of Rs 7 lakh on the 15th night.

CBI says the money was being paid to the scientist on behalf of Chariot Steel and Power Pvt Ltd, besides others, for securing environmental clearance for a lime stone mining project in Sundergarh, Odisha. "The matter was scheduled for consideration for clearance by the reconstituted Exper Appraisal Committee (Non-Coal Mining) on the 16th (Thursday) and was enlisted as the first case," said a CBI official, adding that Mr Khatri was not a part of the committee.

Based on the findings, the Agency registered a graft case against the scientist, Srichandan, and his father Achutananda Srichandan, who works as a consultant along with his son.

Following the arrest, CBI teams searched the premises of the scientist in neighbouring Gurgaon and Rohtak in Haryana, besides his office in Delhi and residential premises of the consultant in Bhubaneswar.

They seized Rs 82.5 lakh in cash from the Gurgaon house and rest of the amount from the Rohtak house of the scientist. He owns properties in Gurgaon, Rohtak, Sonepat and Chandigarh, said the CBI.

"Formula to identify 'inviolate' forest areas where mining will be banned: Jan 2013

Is it a revival of "no-go-zone" approach conceptualised by Jairam Ramesh? It was earlier vetoed due to pressure from the industrial houses.

A daily writes: "In what seems to be a successor to the controversial 'no-go-zone' concept, mining and other harmful non-forestry activities could soon be completely banned, from forest areas identified as "inviolate" using a formula created by a high-level environment ministry panel."[22]

Wildlife sanctuaries, tiger reserves, national parks... as well as a buffer zone of 1 km around such protected areas... compact patches of very dense forest, the last remnant of a forest type or forests very near perennial rivers, will all be automactically placed within the inviolate zone, according to a report of the committee to formulate objective parameters for identification of inviolate forest areas.

The panel was formed in the wake of the demise of the "no-go-zone" approach conceptualised by Ramesh, which identified dense forest areas in nine major coal fields, where forest clearance would be denied. Following intense pressure from mining industry and Coal Ministry, a ministeral group headed by then Finance Minister Pranab Mukherjee Vetoed the idea. But in Sep 2011, the group of ministers suggested that "identified pristine forest areas, where any mining industry would lead to irreversible damage, should be barred from any non-forest activity." Consequently, the Environment Ministry now headed by Jayanthi Natarajan, formed a panel to formulate parameters to identify such "inviolate" forest areas.

The panel submitted its report in Jul 2012, but the Ministry only made it public on 24 Jan 2013. The next step is to actually prepare geo-referenced maps of inviolate areas using this formula. Apart from the automatic exclusions mentioned earlier, the formula calls for scoring of forest areas based on six principles: forest type, biological richness, wildlife value, forest cover, landscape integrity and hydrological value. The country would be divided into grids of one sq km each, which will be scored, mostly using existing data. An average seore above 70, out of possible hundred, will also be declared inviolable.

As far as the fate of mining blocks are concerned, the report says that a block would be "considered inviolate if a majority of grids falling within a block have been labelled as inviolate."

Now a committee headed by DG, Forest Survey of India and comprising representatives of Wildlife Institute of India. National Biodiversity Authority, National Tiger Conservation Authority, State Forest Departments and State Remote Sensing Application Centres will help identify the "inviolate" areas. Geo-referenced maps of such areas will then be posted on the Ministry's website.

"Mining project divided Jharkhand village along caste lines:" June 2013

This is an interesting, educative and even ironic investigative analysis of caste realities of India's rural areas, as discovered and put together by a daily, well known and reputed for such type of bold journalism.[23]

Its blurb has an irony: "While tribals refuse to give up land, yadavs claim to be pro-development. Meanwhile, SC-dominated Left Wing group supports coal mining." Imagine Left Wing supporting mining!

Unusual Turn

Here was an unusual turn to the process of land acquisition for industrial projects. Jala village of Latehar district split along caste lines, with one group demanding that the Gram Sabha be convened a second time to overturn an earlier rejection of a mining project. On the other hand, a group of villagers opposing the project claim that the Tritya Sammelan Prastuti Committee (TSPC), a Left-Wing extremist group is, in favour of mining, and has even threatened to kill one of them if he does not relent.

Jala, located in Balumath block, forms almost the entire proposed site for a coal mine that will feed power projects in the region.

Jala is a part of the Ganeshpur coal block, which has been allotted to a joint venture (JV) of Tata Steel and Adhunik power and Natural Resources Ltd. The JV has been named Ganeshpur Coal Project.

A section of the villagers allege that an "illegal" Gram Sabha was converned on 15 March by those who support the project to ratify the land acquisition proposal. A Gram Sabha of 18 Aug 2012 had opposed the project.

Jala brings to the fore a major loophole in the law... that the rules do not specify as to how many times can a Gram Sabha vote on a land acquisition question. When villagers voted in Aug 2012, its residents overwhelmingly were against the project. A number of people has since changed their minds, which had led to an impasse, and, worse, communal tension.

Latehar DC Aradhana Patnaik says: "The first Gram Sabha opposed the project. However, a group of people approached me, claiming that there were illegalities. Hence, a second meeting was called recently. The other group is now claiming that the second meeting was illegal. The village was clearly split on the issue. I have told them to sit down and work out a consensus."

Jala is made up of three tolas (hamlets)... Harijala and Barwatoli have an Oraon majority, while Yadav tola's majority population comprises the Yadavs. As per the state's Primary Census data, Jala has a population of 859; 471 of them tribal, living in 169 households. Most of the tribals have opposed the project, while Yadavs have supported it.

At an important meeting under a mahua tree in Harijala, its Pradhan Ramchandra Bhagat voiced his opposition: "At the first Gram Sabha, the company representative did not turn up. At the second, there was massive police presence. I did not attend the second one, and the person who presided over it was not a tribal, which invalidates the meeting."

'Company' is the generic term used by villagers to describe either Tata Steel or Adhunik PNRL, as most of them do not know the JV.

The Jul 2009 guidelines of the MoEF specify that rights under the Forest Rights Act should be conferred before diversion of forest land for non-forestry purpose. So, in order to streng then their negotiating position, the tribals have applied for community **pattas** of 923 acres, alongwith 47 **pattas** for individual households. The total area under the Ganeshpur Coal Project is 983 acres, which include three other villages.

Bhagat said, "The company is offering to compensate for the land we own individually. What about our community forest rights? Our village has traditionally existed within these 923 acres that we now claim **patta** for."

Land acquisition is also difficult because 415 acres of 983 acres is forest land, and stage-I forest clearance is pending.

The corporates have understood the weakness in the system. "If a company wants to mine an area, it will be done. There may be a delay, but a mine will come up there. If the Gram Sabha resists, we will call another Gram Sabha. If the Pradhan refuses to support, people will find a new Pradhan," said a top official associated with the project.

The villagers have a history of resistance, having asked the Central Coalfields Ltd., (CCL) to stay away in the 1990s. "The CCL started mining in adjoining areas in 1990, but we firmly told them that we would not give our land," said Baldev Oraon.

Oraon says the TSPC has threatened him: "I was returning from the market one evening when they accosted me and took me away about 100 m inside the forest. A man about 35 years... my fellow residents insist that it was area commander Karthik Ji... told me that I should support mining here, else I will be killed."

The TSPC also tried to pull down one of the sign boards put up at the village boundary. "After company officers tried to survey our village land without permission, we installed sign boards saying that no one should enter the area without our permission. It was our way of asserting our right over this land. Some 15 TSPC cadres, most of them children in fatigues with arms, came one morning and destroyed one of the boards. We women got together and opposed it; they had to apologise and leave," said Lacho Devi.

The TSPC was reportedly established with the support of the police's Special Branch. Balumath reportedly remains largely free of CPI (Maoist) Cadres because of its (TSPC's) presence. The TSPC's cadre is drawn almost exclusively from among the SC Ganjhus. Yadav's oppression of the Ganjhus in the erstwhile MCC is the stated reasons why the TSPC's founders broke away from the parent party. In Jala though, extreneous reasons seemed to have caused the organisations alignment with a cause supported largely by the Yadavs.

"The mob gheraoed this reportor as he was leaving Jala." They claimed to be members of the Displacement Agitation Group. "We are for development. We want to talk to the company before saying an outright 'NO', unlike the others," said Kuldeep Yadav, who claimed to be the group's president. He continued: "We were in two minds when Aug 2012 Gram Sabha was held, but we have since come to the conclusion that mining will be beneficial for us."

As it turned out, four men in the crowd were from the companies involved in the project. "This is our project area; we are from the Corporate Social Responsibility team," said one of them, without identifying his organisation. The villagers calmed down only after the police talked to them.

Adhunik has started feeling the pinch of the villager's resilience. The company has commissioned a 270 MW unit of its 540 MW thermal power plant at Seraikela-kharsawan district in Oct 2012. This plant which is to get its coal from Ganeshpur block, is now dependent for coal from other areas. "We plan to raise a total of four million tonnes each annually, with each company taking half. We have tried talking to the villagers; a good number of them have agreed to listen to our proposal," said Sanjay Kumar Jain, Executive Vice President, Mines (Coal), APNRL.

APNRL claims that it has launched CSR schemes, which includes technical training for the village youth. "We have proposed a rehabilitation package. Among others, it involves Rs 9 lakh per acre, a job for an adult member of the family, a house within a 10 decimal (1/100 of an acre) plot. We took some villagers on a trip to the colony we have constructed for those displaced due to the Saraikela project, and they were impressed by what they saw," claimed Jain.

Battle for Minds and Hearts

In counter-insurgency combat, battle against the insurgents... Maoists in the instant case... is important whether through security operations or through developmental strategy. But equally important is another battle fought among the tribal population, namely, it is the battle for minds and hearts of the people whose loyalty to the nation is sought to be subverted by the insurgents.

It is not merely propaganda war or instrument of psychological war to win over the minds and hearts of the people. It should be genuine effort to educate the affected people/pouplation against the designs of the insurgents. Simultaneously, it is necessary to launch certain civic actions in various fields to win over the people.

Some of these will be discussed in the following pages.

"In Chhattisgarh, Central forces don new mantle": Apr 2011

The mandate of 28 battalions of CPMF... BSF and CRPF... deployed in the state is to counter the violence of the Maoists and instil a sense of security through security counter operations. While doing this, they help the civil administration to undertake developmental activities to improve the economic condition of the area.

The two paramilitary forces are shifting their focus to understanding the problems of the local population and the culture and traditions of tribals, knowing that security operations alone are not enough to defeat the Naxals, the forces have embarked upon "civic action" programmes in their areas of deployment.

They are conducting free computer education, organising health camps, distributing seeds and fertiliser and taking up the problem of tribals with the local administrations.

Five BSF battalions were deployed in Uttar Bastar's Kanker district only late last year (2010) but they claim their personnel "have struck rapport with the tribal population, consisting mostly of Gonds and their sub-tribles. BSF DIG Ram Avtar told the visiting journalists at 31 Battalion's camp at Lohattar, 170 km from Raipur: "When we came here, we found there was no administrative presence in the hinterland, and pockets of liberated zones were existing. Apart from the fear of Naxals, there are extreme poverty and illiteracy, and lack of basic facilities such as health, transport and electricity."

The border guards were seen in a different role at the camp. There were men who had returned from an early morning patrol. Local tribal men and women and members of the panchayats of surrounding villages were called to the camp, and they interacted with the press men and mingled with the jawans. Many tribal leaders appeared happy with the effort of the BSF in helping to establish the writ of the local administration in the hinterland, to start construction of culverts, school buildings and ponds. But others appeared concerned at the lack of facilities for farming.

"The water level here is going down. We have to depend on rains and we can just grow one crop here," complained a villager. What about the fear of Naxals? "We live in a state of uncertainty. There is a fear of unknown, we may be branded police informers", says another villager, without elaborating. Now comes 31 Bn commandant RC Sharma, "We have been able to reduce the gap between the Central Forces and the local people who want security, peace and development. At Irekgutta, we were able to organise the local market after eight years. It is gradual process, but slowly with our initiative, we are striking a rapport with the villagers." The BSF has spent Rs 60 lakh on organising a civic action programme and health camp. In the recent past, the BSF men detected 47 IEDs, lost three of their men in two ambushes laid by Maoists and claimed to have killed 15 rebels.

At keshkal, a town 35 km from Kanker, men of 188 Bn CRPF were busy conducting free computer classes for school children in a newly-constructed building that also houses the local police station.

"About 160 students have been trained in basic computer skills since Dec 2010. We have begun with just two computers, but will soon have more work stations," said Commanding Officer AK Dhyani.

"Govt goes AIR borne: Uses radio jingles to take on Maoists": Oct 2012

As a part of its plan to wean villagers and tribals away from the Maoist ideology, the government has taken to airing radio 'jingles' to reach out to people in the Naxal heart land.[24]

For this purpose, the government has roped in All India Radio (AIR) to air specially prepared audio clips in the morning and evening. The jingles, meant to counter Maoism, were produced in different local dialects including Nagpuri, Gondi, Chhattisgarhi, Odia Gondi, Maghdi, Bhojpuri, Halbi and Hindi.

The jingles, exposing Maoists obstructing the development in the tribal areas are aired through regional transmission networks in the four Naxal-hit States of Chhattisgarh, Jharkhand, Bihar and Odisha. The aim is to inform the villagers in their dialects how they have been deprived of their being part of the mainstream. These jingles also focus on the importance of education and importance. The AIR has been airing them since mid September (2012).

The programme is to cost the government some Rs 1.65 crore for two months. "The plan will be reviewed by 20 November." The government may, at a later stage, engage private individuals to counter Maoist propaganda on a much bigger scale. Use of jingles is, but, a small part of government overall counter propaganda strategy. The idea is to reach out to the villagers also through posters, short films and advertisements to inform people of what the Maoists are upto.

"Centre targets hearts in anti-Naxal SOP:" Jul 2013

The MHA wants Central Armed Police Forces (CAPF) deployed in Naxal areas to go beyond operations and win the hearts of the people, mostly tribals.[25] During a recent press conference. Home Minister Sushil Kumar Shinde said they "have formulated a standard operating procedure (SOP) on interaction with the common people and sent it to the CAPF, 1 lakh of which are deployed in Maoist-hit states." The guidelines circulated recently include instructions such as "not staring at tribal women who generally bathe in a pond, lake or canal in their village" and "not staring at tribal women who generally cover their upper body with a **dupatta** and do not wear a blouse. Some other points from the SOP/guidelines issued to the CAPF are summed up below:

- You must remember to say :"inconveniecnce regratted" after searching tribal property.
- Suspects must, preferably, be interrogated in front of village headman.
- The personnel should not go out of the camp area under the influence of alcohal.
- The troops must be aware of and respect local customs and traditions.

- Gaining faith of the local population was essential, so that attempts to defame the security forces can be reduced."
- Offices/officers should maintain a list of (tribal) festivals and acquire knowledge of traditions and symbols considered pious. Decorative hangings outside the houses of tribals should not disturbed.
- Senior citizens and prominent locals should be invited to regimental functions and may be felicitated with gifts.
- During area domination exercise, do interact with common people and take note of their dissatisfaction.

"Community Policing to fox jamshadpur Naxals" Dec 2012

Concenred over the rising cases of Maoist menace, the administration has embarked on an ambitious two-point strategy, says a daily in Dec 2012,[26] to tackle Naxalism in the state (Jharkhand). The report is filed from Jamshedpur.

If on one hand, the forces are engaged in combating the Maoists in the Naxal-infested areas, on the other, they have launched a series of initiatives under the banner of community policing to woo the villagers.

East Singhbhum district police, under community policing programme, organised a debate on "Relevance of Naxal violence in today's context" at Maubhandar in Ghatshila. A total of 30 students from Ghatshila College, Ghalshila Mahila College and Mosebani mines Inter-College, Mosabani, took part in the debate. Again, those who attended the debate included faculty members of these colleges, and members of various political outfits as also representatives of Panchayat Committees.

SSP Akhilesh Kumar Jha was the chief guest and SP (Rural) Rajiv Ranjan Singh conducted the proceedings. The SP noted that "we are addressing the issues. If the youth start to speak and are made aware of their rights, even the ultras too would see logic behind our campaign, which seeks to encourage them to give up arms and join mainstream."

A student who opposed the Naxal violence made a pertinent point. "India has produced men like Gautam Buddha and Mahatma Gandhi who brought revolutionary changes in society but they never supported violence."

Singh who conducted the debate, observed Naxalism was not a bad philosophy, but those who are active in the movement now-a-days have deviated from its path, adding: "you can describe it as our reputation building exercise of police, but it is necessary to win hearts of the people and foil the designs of the ultras." He further clarified: "We also held cultural activities and had interaction with the people. The main motive is to remove their sense of insecurity."

Apart from interaction with the villagers, the police are holding sporting events to motivate the youth and encourage them to take sports as an option for career building. In majority of the Maoist-hit blocks in three districts of Kolhan community, policing exercise will continue for next two months.

Singh concluded, "our idea is to change mindset of the villagers about police and civil administration. We are addressing their grivances and clearing their misconceptions. We will play much more active role in Naxal infested areas."

"Singing for change in Chhattisgarh" Sep 2014

Abjuring the usual hardline to combat LWE, the Chhattisgarh police has resorted to dance-drama to campaign against Maoist activities and earn the local tribals' support says this daily in Sep 2014.[27]

Police Natya Chetna March (PNCM), comprising 23 police persons from Sukma district, "has for the last month (Aug 2014) been giving performaces, set to the tunes of songs in the local Gondi, urging the tribal people to stop supporting the Maoists and come over to the government's side." Significantly, among the PNCM personal are erst while members of the CPI (Maoist) who had worked for its propaganda wing, the Natya Chetna Manch. Raj kumar kara, head of the PNCM group in Dornapal, explains: "We are singing and dancing in the market places in a few towns and villages of Sukma. The aim is to create awareness among tribals over the futility of Maoist violence."

Now comes Bheema, another member of the group, who had lost four fingers manufacturing a bomb for the Maoists some years back. He claims: "Maoists are exploiting Bastar tribals for political gains and not allowing them to benefit from development carried out by the government. Through the PNCM, we are making an effort to bring them on to our (government's) side." Bheema's colleague, Malkam Kalla says: "We want to convey to the tribals that Maoists violence is doing no good to them and how they are being ruled by a handful of "Mini Seths' (rich people) from Andhra".

According to Dornapal Senior Divisional Police Officer (SDPO) Sanjay Dhruv, the PNCM propaganda has had "visible effect". He claims: "More than 24 Maoists have surrendered after the launch of PNCM in Sukma."

Sukma district ASP Santosh Singh talked to the daily: "Police is the most visible face of the administration in Bastar. We (the police) have been reaching out to the deep interior parts where no other arm of the administration has been able to reach. So far no administration has been able to counter the Maoist propaganda. But now, the PNCM is bridging that gap." He concluded by saying, "The initiative for the PNCM came from the higher authorities of the Chhattisgarh police."

Employment necessary to wean the youth away from Maoist enticement

As a former Maoist-turned-teacher remarked: "The youth here either join the Army or they are olured by the Maoist." To ensure that they do not fall prey to the Maoist recruiters, it is necessary that other suitable avenues are made available to the vulnerable youth in the Maoist-hit states.

Some of the schemes and plans to create such jobs in these states are briefly mentioned on these pages.

"Jobes for three-lakh youths in Naxal-hit areas": Oct 2011

Apart from ensuring the immediate appointment of 18,000 panchayat development officers and as many junior engineers, the Centre has deawn up a blueprint to provide jobs for three lakh youths in 60 Maoist-hit districts in the country.

Union Minister of Rural Development Jairma Ramesh, in his consolidated note for the approval of the Empowered Group of Secretaries for the integrated action plan (IAP) under planning Commission member Sudha Pllai, dovetails a number of rural development schemes for better impact in the LWE-hit districts.

For beter implementation of the Mahatma Gandhi National Rural Employment Guarantee Scheme (MGNREGS), Mr Jairam ordered that each panchayat appoint one panchayat development officer (PDO) and a junior enginer (JE) for a period of ten years from within the district. Non-residents are ineligible for these posts.[28]

Apart from proposing that the cost be shared in the ratio of 75:25 between the Centre and States, his decision will ensure the appointment of about 18,000 graduates as PDO's and as many JE as some districts have more than 300 panchayats. All these districts will be covered under the National Rural Livelihood Mission (NRLM) by Mar 2013 with the objective of training and providing jobs to 3 lakh youths over the next five years.

To ensure better return to the tribals, a public-private-partnership (PPP) pilot project in non-timber forest produce will be launched in one district each of Odisha, Jharkhand, Chhattisgarh, Maharashtra, MP and Andhra Pradesh.

Training: Private companies will add value by training self-help groups (SHGs) and marketing the non-timber produce. Ramesh made the following points:

- The tribals were not getting the real value of their produce, and hoped that the current arrangement would help them realise the full value of their produce. He was holding talks with companies such as ITC, Ballarpur, Dabur, wipro and Emami.
- Aimed at identifying the destitute, each district administration has been ordered to construct houses under the Indira Aawas Yojana (IAY) for the disabled, windowed and old age pensioners as mere financial help did not serve the purpose unable as they were to handle the job.
- It was decided to extend support to those who have been the victims of the Maoists violence.
- Irrespective of their socio-economic standing, houses would be provided to those whose abodes bad been damaged in a Maoist attack.

It is not known how many jobs have been created in the last 2 and a half years of the UPA regime till May 2014.

"Ease job criteria for the tribal youth": Sep 2012

The Centre will urge the Maoist-hit states to lower the norms of securitment in government jobs to open up employment opportunities for greater number of local youth in tribal areas to prevent them from succumbing to Maoist propaganda, said Union Home Minister Sushil kumar Shinde at a press conference at New Delhi.[29]

A similar skill developement programme was under way in Jammu and Kashmir with satisfactory results. The success there persuaded his Ministry to launch it in Naxal-hit states. As of now, rigid administrative norms make many people ineligible for government jobs. Minimum qualification standards will be relaxed to provide more jobs to the local youth, pasrticularly in police.

"The Centre is implementing a training-cum placement programme called 'Himayat' in J and K in partnership with industry with the aim of making one lakh people, in the next five years, employable in government and private sector.

He expects similar results in Maoist-hit states. He has spent only six weeks in the MHA. His predecessor held a monthly press conference in the first week. Mr Shinde was fallowing in Mr Chidambram's foot steps.

"Public banks asked to start coaching in J and K and Maoist-hit areas:" Oct 2012

The Finance Ministry has asked public sector banks to launch special coaching programmes in Maoist-hit areas and J and K as it wants greater representation of people from such states in the country's banking system, said a daily dated 12 Oct 2012.[30] The ministry said in a recent missive to the Indian Banks Association: "It is felt the residents of such areas need to be supported for appearing in competitive examinations. Greater participation of people from such areas would also help the bank in getting over the problem of finding personnel in such areas."

The Ministry has asked the IBA to ensure that all its public sector members organise special coaching in these regions to prepare for the Common Written Examination (CWE), the recruitment test for joining public sector banks.

If there are more people from these areas in the banking cadres, that will solve the problem of not finding enough people to handle bank branches in these disturbed areas, said a senior official. Public sector banks hire over 35,000 people annually and over 7.5 lakh aspirants took the probationary officers exam in June (2012).

1,698 tribal youth absorbed in Odisha Anxiliary Police Force

In a move to supplement the efforts of the district authorities in combating the Maoist menace, as many as 1,698 tribal youth, who had been recruited as Special Police Officers (SPOs), have been absorbed in the newly-created Odisha Auxiliary Police Force (OAPF).

In 2008, the State Government had decided to recruit tribal youth as SPO, by creating 5,600 such posts in 19 police districts. At that time, it was felt "that certain groups of tribal youth are not adequately represented in police forces despite reservation in jobs." So the youth was recruited with some relaxed criteria, through absorb an open and competetive recruitement process.

Besides, at that time, the Government had agreed to absorbe them in police force after completion of three years in a contractual service. In the first phase, 2,100 SPOs were recruited in the Maoists' hot beds of Malkangiri, Rayagada, Koraput, Gajapati and Kandhamal districts. Later, other Maoist-hit districts recruited SPOs to supplement the anti-Maoist operations.

Out of 4,700 SPO, 1,698 have completed the stipulated period of three years: therefore, they have been absorbed as constables in the OAPF. They have been given police training and specialised arms training for effectiveness in aiding the anti-Maoist operations.

These tribal youth have the knowledge and familiarity with topography and were given anti-Maoist training. Meanwhile, they acquired experience of anti-Maoist operations, as also of intelligence collection and of providing logistic and operational support to the State Police and Central Armed Police Forces (CAPF).

With the SC ordering disbanding of Salwan Judum outfit and ordering the Chhattisgarh Government not to use the SPO's services in fighting the Maoist uprising, Odisha did well in taking the lead in creating the OAPF.

All the sanctioned posts of 5,600 SPOs would be filled up and as they complete three year's period, they would be absorbed as constables in the OAPF, said an official. More over, they would have the same duties and responsibilities as their counterparts in the regular police force, and similar promotion avenues as well.[31]

"Education can wean youth off Naxalism:" Shashi Tharoor: Nov 2012

Soon after taking over as Union Minister of State for Human Resource Development on 2 Nov 2012, Shashi Tharoor underscored the need for universalisation of education, with emphasis on quality.

Education, and the opportunity it threw up, could prevent the youth from taking to Naxalism and other violent activities, the Minister said.

"If you get the education and training part right, we will be able to equip the youth to take advantage of what the 21st century has to offer. But if we don't get it right, the danger is something like what we have seen with the Maoists: frustrated unemployed young men picking up the gun.[32]

"National Skill Development Corporation to train Maoist-hit States now": Nov 2012

The Home Ministry has roped in the NSDC to impart skill development training to youth from the Maoist-hit States in vocational courses. The courses are planned to facilitate employment in corporate sector like practical training in computer and mobile phone repairing, motor mechanic, catering, hospitality, carpentry, nursing assistant and driving etc.

A total of 1,500 youths will be enrolled in the three-month training course begining next month (Dec 2012), while 2000 more will be trained in the next fiscal, official sources said. The MHA will bear the expenses upto Rs 30,000 for each youth and the NSDC will ensure their placement in corporate sectors after the training.

The Nehru Yuva Kendra will select youth from Maoist-hit areas in Chhattisgarh, Jharkhand, Odisha, Bihar, West Bengal, Andhra Pradesh, Maharashtra, UP, and MP for the course.[33]

NSDC is one-of-its-kind public-private partnership in India. It aims to promote skill development by encouraging creation of quality vocational institutions.

"NSDC has tie up with corporates and they will ensure that the youths get jobs," said an official. Earlier this year (2012), a similar 5-year programme was started in Jammu and Kashmir, in which every year, 8,000 graduates, post graduates and professional degree holders would be given technical training under Udaan; which is being implemented by the NSDC and corporate sector in PPP mode and is targeted at providing well-paid jobs to trained manpower. Similar gains are expected for candidates from the Maoist-hit states.

"Defence job camps for youth in Maoist Zone soon"

As a measure to tackle Red menace, the MOD could soon start recruiting jawans from the Maoist-hit areas of the country, say MOS Defence Jitendra Singh, at Kolkata, 6 June 2013. This recruitment exercise is aimed at weaning away the local tribal youth from the clutches of the Maoists.

The MoS said there was no point setting up recruitment camps in bigger town, insisting that "the Ministry would set up special recruitement camps in the remotest areas for the youth... in the interior most areas".

Singh said the forces would not play any role in handling the Maoist problem as there were already "specialised units of the CRPF to tackle it." He was reminded that "Naxalite management needed a multi-faceted approach" in which job creation and poverty eradication should go in tandem with other means of tackling the issue.

He avoided answering that question, because it was directly related to the development of Bengal's Maoist-hit zones, and that would be breach of "Electoral Code of Conduct", just ahead of the State panchayat elections.

"Will Indian Maoists follow their Nepalese Counter-parts?" Aug 2014

Prime Minister Narandra Modi on 15 Aug 2014, in his first Independence Day speech from the ramparts of the Red Fort in Delhi, invoked the example of Nepal, where Maoists have renounced the path of violence to join the maintream, to exhort all misguided youth of the country to shun terrorism and opt for peace and brotherhood instead. His passionate appeal ran: "I want to say to those youngsters... that whatever they are and wherever they are it is all because of Mother India... I want ot ask you to think how green, how beautiful and how beneficial this earth can become if you shoulder the plough instead of the gun which spells blood on this earth." He said all this, while holding out an olive branch.[34]

During the course of his speech, the Prime Minister suggested that parents of young ultras drawn to terrorism or LWE must take the responsibility for assessing the underlying causes for the same.

Commenting on the Prime Minister's Red Fort speech, a Nepalese senior analyst, Yubaraj Ghemiri, expressed somewhat of a little sad feeling: "Prime Minister's hope that Nepal's Maoists would leave their history of violence behind and help deliver the constitution, mirrors the collective wish of Nepalese people, which is now fading." He felt Mr Modi's mention of the issue would send a strong massage across the border. Mr Ghimire made some other pertinent observations on the subject:

- "Mr Modi issued no appeal to Indian Maoists to come forward for dialogue and shun violence, but he gave enough indication that success of the Nepal's example would influence the course of Indian Maoists.
- "Indian Maoists have called their Nepalese comrades... once part of the larger campaign in South Asia under the common banner of CCOMPOSAS (Coordination Committe of Maoist Parties and Organisation of South Asia)... 'revisionists' and 'betrayers.'"

Notes

1. Nitin Sethi, Times of India, 3 Sep. 2012.
2. Nitin Sethi, Times of India, 22 Jan. 2013.
3. Ambhuti Vishnoi, Indian Express, 22 Jan. 2013.
4. The Pioneer, 26 Jan. 2013.
5. Ashish Kothari, The Pioneer, 29 Jan. 2013.
6. Swaminathan S. Anklesaria Aiyar, Times of India, 21 July 2013.
7. MV Kamath, The Organiser, 7 July 2013.
8. Pioneer News Service, The Pioneer, 8 Feb 2012.
9. Lemuel Lall, Times of India, 12 Apr. 2012.
10. TNN, Times of India, 16 Sep. 2013.
11. Priya Ranjan Rahu, Hindustan Times, 3 May 2012.
12. Editorial, The Hindu, 13 Oct, 2012.
13. Saubhadra Chatterjee, Hindustan Times, 21 Nov. 2012.
14. Atul Aneja, The Hindu, 13 Dec. 2012.
15. Prasad Nichenametla, Hindustan Times, 7 Jan. 2013.
16. Sonum Gayatri Malhotra, The Hindu, 18 Jan. 2013.

17. Ruhi Tewari, The Pioneer, 15 Jul. 2013.
18. Hindustan Times, 23 Jul. 2013.
19. The Hindu, 16 Sep. 2013.
20. Prafulla Das, The Hindu, 18 Jan. 2013.
21. Devesh K. Pandey, The Hindu, 18 Jan. 2013.
22. Priscilla Jebaraj, The Hindu, 26 Jan. 2013.
23. Deepu Sebestian Edmond, Indian Express, 28 Jun. 2013.
24. Vishwa Mohan, Times of India, 26 Oct. 2012.
25. Vijaita Singh, Indian Express, 22 Jul. 2013.
26. Parvinder Bhatia, The Pioneer, 10 Dec. 2012.
27. Pavan dahat, The Hindu, 29 Sep. 2014.
28. Special Correspondent, The Hindu, 25 Oct. 2011.
29. ENS, Indian Express, 11 Sep. 2012.
30. Surabhi, Indian Express, 12 Oct. 2012.
31. PNS, The Pioneer, 30 Oct. 2012.
32. Staff Correspondent, The Hindu, 3 Nov. 2012.
33. PNS, the Pioneer, 5 Nov. 2012.
34. TNS, Times of India, 16 Aug. 2014.

13

Polls, Politics and Maoists

This should be an interesting chapter, dealing as it is with a mix of contrarian elements.

It deals with politics of LWE, politicians' take on it and polls as seen through the eyes of Maoists.

If electioneearing is the very basis of democracy, it is also the raison d'etre for the politicians, but more surprisingly, the Maoists are no babes in the woods in this game. Often they fox even the past-masters of this game, viz professional politicians, during the polls at national, state and local levels. They seldom come upfront during polls and achieve their aims, getting candidates of their choice elected, by pulling strings from behind the stage, but never occupying it.

It is all these in this chapter.

"Polls Political Parties and Maoists"

This indeed is an important issue for study: The stance of Maoists towards the polls and electoral politics. They have taken ambivalent positions on the elections. Obviously they can't be expected to endorse or even indirectly acquiese in the poll process.

But in various states, they have indeed taken certain stances on the issue. If in one area, they sent SMS messages warning people against taking part in the polls, in another area, they have openly told people which candidates to vote for! If in an odd case, they resorted to violence to disrupt polls, in other cases, they stayed away and did not interfere at all.

They have been accused by parties of favouring and helping their rivals. The following pages have news story culled from published sources to highlight facets of Maoists' attitude to the electoral polls, and position of certain parties on this issue.

"This Red Line" Aug 2011

This news story in a weekly talks about... 'reveals' may be a better word... easy relationship between Jharkhand politicians and Maoists. Its blurb explains it: "Phone intercepts blow the lid off the cosy relationship between Jharkhand politics and Maoists."[1]

It starts with a dramatic dialogue on phone between a politician and a Maoist.

Ajoy Kumar: Samarji namaskar.

Samar: Namaskar, namaskar. What is happening?

AK: On the job samarji; *lage hue hain.*

Samar: Any hitches, worries?

AK: Not at all, with your blessings. You people wield so much influence that nobody can dare stop us.

Samar: Are you seeing a response?

AK: Yes, absolutely. Only your signal will prevail on 1 July.

The Ajoy Kumar in the conversation is the recently elected Jharkhand Vikas Morch (JVM) MP from the Jamshedpur Lok Sabha seat in Jharkhand, while Samarji is said to be Gen Secretary of the Jharkhand-Bihar-Odisha Border Regional Committee of the banned CPI (Maoist).

An audio CD, the outcome of the police intercepts and mobile surveillance in the run-up to the by-elections, was recorded on 26 June. Jharkhand BJP leader Saryu Rai made it public hours before polling for the Jamshedpur seat, vacated by the State CM, Arjun Munda, on 1 July. BJP State unit President, Dineshanand Goswami, who lost his deposit in the by-elections, lodged a complaint with Election Commission at whose behest the police registered a case against Kumar.

When Kumar, who had quit the IPS in 1996, confirmed that the voice on the CD was his, it was clear that the mainstream parties, at least some of them, were colluding with banned extremist outfits for electoral gains. Now comes the twist, or the spin, when politicians caught in an embarrassing situation give to an obvious fact Kumar, however, insists that "person impersonating Samarji must be investigated", adding, "I am a clean person. I never asked any one or the said Samarji to influence the polls. It was a trap set by the BJP." But the Weekly claims to have a copy of the CD, which also has conversation between JVM leader Prabhat Bhuiyan and Samarji.

The timing of the CD's leak a day before polling gave the JVM a handle against the ruling BJP: It was misusing official machinery to settle political scores. Kumar filed a counter-case against Goswami and Rai, alleging that the two were trying to malign him. Rai insisted the issue was alarming, as a farmer IPS officer was involved. The BJP leader was vehement in his arguments: "How can you explain a former IPS officer seeking Naxalite help for an election? You arrest a villager for letting a Maoist eat at his place, even if under duress. Here, you have an MP caught clandestinely soliciting their support, yet the police are quiet. You can't have two sets of rules."

JVM President and former CM Babulal Marandi admitted to the Weekly that he too had spoken to Samarji, but said no deals were made, explaining: "How can I stop someone from speaking to me on the phone, that too during an election? I have to protect my workers as well. But I never asked him for any support." (What an innocent justification this politician offers) But Kumar apparently had asked for support, if the transcripts are to be believed. At one point during the conversation, Samarji even talks about protecting his electoral interests despite the Maoists' boycott call.

Cornered, Marandi takes the offence-is-the-best defence option: "How can you allow hacking of the phones without following procedures? Has the Jharkhand Home Secretary ordered the taping? The goverment owes us an answer. We demand a judicial probe." Despite his best efforts to distance his party from the Maoists, the shift in Marandi's politics is now clear. From being staunchly anti-Naxalite-he has survived attempts on his life, Marandi has softened his stand and taken the middle path. Just a week before polling in Jamshedpur, Marandi even made an appeal seeking pardon for four Naxalites convicted for 2007 Chilkhari massacre in which 20 villagers, including his 22-year-old son Anup, were killed. His opponents see it as clear sign of JVM chief wooing Maoists before the Jamshedpur polls. "Kumar's subsequent conversation was only a logical extension of Marandi's mollification of the Maoists," says Rai.

Marandi is not alone in cosying up to the Maoists. There are police inputs to suggest that pliant politicians across the spectrum have been also used by the Maoists to hijack the political system in Jharkhand. With Naxalites controlling large parts of the State and several politicians such as JMM MP Sunil Mahato, CPI (ML) MLA Mahendra Singh and former JD-U minister Ramesh Singh Munda falling to their bullets, leaders across parties have found it prudent to make friends with the outlaws.

The police hide behind the argument that they have the "intelligence inputs but no hard evidence" to nail the politicians. Says Jharkhand DGP GS Rath: "Yes we have intelligence inputs suggesting a section of politicians, bureaucrats, police, businessmen and even journalists in cahoots with Maoists but we need direct evidence to act."

Former speaker of the Jharkhand Assembly and MP Inder Singh Namdhari agrees that the state politicians, across affiliations, are inclined to accede to Maoist influence. He asserts: "I lost a Lok Sabha polls when I refused to pay the rebels who, in turn, did not allow my workers to campaign. Former MLA Khiru Mahto goes a step further: "The Maoists force Jharkhand legislators to ask 'suitable questions' in the Assembly. They have to follow their diktat."

A senior IPS officer in the State confides to the Weekly under the garb of anonymity: "The Maoists are known to help select politicians during polls. They certainly have an impact on the outcome. (Playing games), they enforce boycott in select pockets, besides targeting rivals of their candidate. And there is always a quid pro quo."

A recent survey titled "Social, Economic and Political Dynamics in Extremist-Affected Areas" was conducted by the Bureau of Police Research and Development, a department under the MHA. It suggests that there is nexus between politicians and extremists. 61 per cent commoners and 86 per cent professionals of those surveyed in Jharkhand believe that extremism has had a serious impact on politics.

So confident are Maoists about influencing polls that some from their ranks such as Kameshwar Baitha, who faced 46 cases, have joined politics... he had joined JMM and presently is its MP from Palamu. "With more extremists waiting in the wings the line between politicians and the outlaws in Jharkhand is expected to blur."

The scribe of this article is unduly, or perhaps cynically, harsh on the Jharkhand politicians! He perhaps does not know that a one time militant, nay insurgent, became the CM of Mizoram and ruled it for years. These realities of life which some people like this scribe do not want to acknowledge, or understand. It is good for this scribe to know that some journalists too are in cahoots with Maoists, with much less at stake than these politicians!

Finally, the result of survey about nexus between politicians and outlaws is not confined to Jharkhand only. It is so in any state facing similar situation: be it Nagaland, Assam, J&K, Punjab, to name just four.

"Seized letters indicate Maoists in Touch with BJD and Congress Leader" Jan 2013

An article with this tell-tale title appeared in a daily in Jan 2013.

It talks about letters seized from Maoist 'commander' Ghasi alias Chenda Bhushanam, arrested in Apr 2011. They reveal that Maoists were in touch with at least one MLA Raghuram Padal of Koraput and Koraput MP Jayram Pang, both BJD and Congress MLA Ramachandra Kadam of Pottangi.

The letters seized from Ghasi were produced in the trial as part of seizure list. A top commander of Andhra-Odisha Border Special Zonal Committee, who carried a reward of Rs 10 lakh on his head, Ghasi, 46, has over 100 cases against his name. The article speaks about three photos (of one MP and two MLAs). The two letters revealing their involvement are in Oriya. This is the first documentary evidence of correspondence between Maoists and elected Odisha leaders.

In the letter written in Feb 2011, on a CPI (Maoist) letter head, Daya, Secretary, Koraput-Srikakulam Divisional Committee of the CPI (Maoist), asked MP Pang, MLA Padal, Laxmipur MLA Jhina Hikaka and a BJD leader from Pattangi, Prafulla Pangi, to attend their meeting in the Narayanpatna block. Since 2009, the block, that sits at the trijunction of Odisha Andhra Pradesh and Chhattisgarh, has been a Maoist stronghold, with rebels crossing over to bordering states after ambushing the police. The letter sent by Daya reads: "You BJD people have to attend the meeting. Please go and listen to what people are saying about the government. If you think us as your people, then please come, or else don't. The district administration and politicians should think of land problems, Dalits and tribals lodged in jails and difficulties faced by villagers in areas around police camps. Please go, see, listen and understand and try to solve the problem after discussions with local people. If you go to Narayanpatna, your future would be bright."

He also mentioned that separate letters had been issued to Congress leaders to attend the meeting.

The letter, sent by a Maoist courier, was acknowledged by Koraput MP Pangi at 6.10 PM on 6 Feb 2011, over his signatures. The letter also bears purportedly the signature of Koraput MLA Padal, acknowledging receiving it at 5.30 PM same day.

The second letter seized by police was purportedly written by Pottangi MLA Kadam of the Congress to Ghasi, acknowledging receipt of his previous letter. Addressing Ghasi as "Priya Ghasi bhai (Dear brother Ghasi)", Kadam said he wanted the people of Kanti and Narayanpatna lodged in jail to be released. Kadam writes in the letter, bearing what is purportedly his signature in Oriya: "I have raised questions about this in the Assembly. You have to wait for sometime. I have welcomed the steps taken by the government for you. I think it is a good thing if the government works for you. I don't oppose it. I am opposing Hindalco since beginning. I am with the people on this matter. I have no truck with Hindalco. All the propaganda about me having relations with Hindalco is false."

Sources believe this letter was possibly written after 29 Aug 2010, when Ghasi killed Congressman Anand Kirsani, a Zila Parishad member of Dhusura village under Semiliguda block in Koraput.

When the daily contacted BJD MP Pangi, he said he had never got the letter directly from Maoists, saying "that particular letter was shown to me by Koraput MLA Padal. He asked me to sign it. But I never went to the meeting in Narayanpatna. Some days later, some one from their side called me up over the phone asking why I did not attend the meeting. I told them I had prior engagements. The area where I live is teeming with Maoists. I can neither agree to whatever they say nor can we show defiance."

Koraput MLA Padal and Pattangi MLA Kadam flatly denied ever having received any letter from Maoists.[2]

Sources said Ghasi collected Rs 50-60 lakh a month from local politicians, traders and officials. Such was his terror that youths were known to extort money in his name without his knowledge. Involved in almost all the major operations in Odisha and Andhra, Ghasi had 63 cases lodged against him between 1991 and 1996 in Vishakhapatnam district alone. Now lodged in Koraput jail, Ghasi's strength lay in ambushing police parties, setting landmine and shooting down informers or policemen.

Incidentally, in Mar 2012 koraput-based, Chasi Mulia Adivasi Sangh (CMAS) helped the ruling BJD clinch the post of the Koraput Zila Parishad president with both the Congress and BJD tied at 14 seats each in the 29-member Parishad in the Panchayat Polls, the CMAS backed Zuro Mouka, who in turn, supported the BJD. Mouka, incidentally, was acquitted in a case of Maoist violence in 2010.

At the time, three BJD MLAs and Koraput MP Pangi had appealed to CM Naveen Patnaik to withdraw cases against CMAS activitists and stop operation Greenhunt in the Narayanpatna block.

But soon after Mouka's election, the Maoists, allegedly aided by the CMAS, had abducted Laxmipur MLA Jhina Hikaka. He was released only after one month.

"Sensitive Bastar booths may alter poll results this time:" Oct 2013: Assembly Poll

"80 per cent of polling booths in the interiors of South Bastar are considered sensitive, and ensuring smooth polling in these areas will be a tough task not only for the administration but contestants and political parties too will find it tough to make contact with the electorate. In that scenario, sensitive booths might affect the outcome to a great extent." So reported a daily in Oct 2013.[3]

Election Commission has delcared 75 per cent of the 266 polling booths in the district as "sensitive", while the remaining 25 per cent are "most sensitive."

On the basis of extent of Maoist insurgency, the "most sensitive" booths are no more accessible to the political parties in the present scenario. Though during the last elections, some of these "most sensitive" polling stations were easily approachable, but the 25 May (2013) Jeeram Valley massacre (of most Congress leaders) altered the situation drastically, forcing even field workers to restrict themselves to urbanised pockets only.

So reaching such booths will be hard, if not impossible, for the political parties. On the other hand, the administration is prepared to shift sensitive booths to safer places. Therefore, the administration has decided to shift 41 such booths to safer places and the proposals are with the Election Commission. Those booths include Pahurnar, Bhatpal, Karkoti, Munder, Kohchepal, Pondum, Gudse, Telam, Handemada, Hitawada, Cherpal, Gumalnar.

Interestingly, during the last Assembly poll (2008) it was not felt necessary to shift any booth of the Dantewada Assembly constituency because of insurgency situation, and in 2009 parliamentary poll, just one booth was identified as sensitive which witnessed zero per cent voting.

Considering these facts, Election Commission has been requested to shift 41 sensitive booths to safer places to ensure normal voting in those areas.

"Poll tickets and Ajit Jogi, not Maoists, are top of the mind in Chhattisgarh: Oct 2013

This is an interesting if significant headline of an article on situation in a run-up to the Assembly polls, in a daily in Oct 2013.[4]

In a state that saw a big Maoist attack on a Congress Convoy on 25 May (2013), wiping out its entire state leadership, the insurgency was expected to be a major issue in the run-up to the polls. But in Chhattisgarh,

Maoists are not a poll issue either for the ruling BJP or the Congress which lost its two leading stalwarts... the state chief Nand Kumar Patel and doughty Salwa Judum founder Mahendra Karma.

The attack did shake the two parties initially, with both blaming each other for being in Cahoots with the ultras. Now, the usual clamour for ticket distribution having pushed the pushed the Maoists off the Centre stage, it is (political) business as usual!

But the events in the wake of the attack dominate the polls, particularly for the Congress. After the killing of Patel, there was a battle of succession for the top job. The new PCC president, CD Mahant has to struggle to keep the party united. Ajit Jogi, a former CM is not reconciled to Mahant getting top slot.

Until 25 May, BJP had been on the backfoot because of anti-incumbency and because Patel had succeeded in uniting all congress factions. The attack initially appeared to tilt the scales farther towards the Congress amid a massive sympathy wave and charges of negligence against Raman Singh government for its faiture to ensure adequate security for the Congress convoy.

But it did not stay that way for the Congress. A month after the attack, a rebel backed by Jogi defeated the Congress nominee in a Bastarnagar panchayat poll. The Congress Yatra carrying the ashes of its slain leaders failed to evoke a public response. The BJP is bound to exploy the disarray.

"Jogi is bonus for us. He can swing at least 10-15 seats in the plains," says an elated aide of Raman Singh, who is eyeing a third term.

The BJP has launched a massive campaign, and CM Singh has resumed his Vikas Yatra, with his ministers and officials, announcing populist schemes. "Congress leaders, meanwhile, have either camped outside 10 Janpath or hosted Iftar and dinner parties at home... Hardly andy attempts have been made to energise campaign, meet people or draft manifestoe." It was not surprising, therefore, that the CM told the daily, with tongue in Cheek, "It is a strange party. Elections are ahead, but they are busy at dinner and breakfast parties. Is this the team of Rahul Gandhi?"

It is still a close fight. In a 90-seat Assembly, a margin of five seats can be decisive. The BJP won the last two polls, thanks to Bastar: 9 of 12 seats in 2003 and 11 in 2008. Even the latest surveys have put the BJP only marginally ahead, with 44-plus seats to the Congress's 40-plus. The BJP got 50 seats in the last (2008) poll but several ministers and MLAs now face public discontent.

Smaller porties such as CPI, Chhattisgarh Swabhiman Manch and the BSP are keen to register a presence.

The polls are significant for Maoists, too. Even though they have boycotted the polls, the local comrades still do not rule out covert tie-ups with favourite politicians. Maoist Podiyam Linga, recently arrested for murder of powerful BJP leader Shivdayal Tomar in Dantewada, told media in the presence of the SP and CRPF officers that he had campaigned for the party last time. He claimed close relations with Dantewada BJP MLA Bheema Mandavi, who, of course, denied it.

There are intaligence reports about possible attack on BJP leaders, during these polls. Jagdalpur BJP MLA Santosh Bafna has introduced an insurance cover of Rs 5 lakh for partymen who will campaign in sensitive areas. While the Congress has demanded CCTV cameras at all pooling booths in Bastar, it had been silent on the Maoist insurgency that almost decimated it in Chhattisgarh.

Hours after Darbha attack, Rahul Gandhi had flown down to Raipur and addressed his colleagues. "Last week, he addressed a rally in Jagdalpur. On both occasions, he brought up the death of his party men but did not mention the Maoists, or an elaborate strategy to tackle them. On the other end, CM Singh has not spoken on the Maoists either.

"What counts for the MP voter in Maoist zone and outside?: Survey: 2013

A survey commissioned by Election Commission and conducted by the Directorate of Economics and Statistics, Madhya Pradesh, in all 230 constituencies, including those in the 10 districts affected by LWE, brought out some interesting findings." It was published in a daily in Nov 2013.[5]

One finding that catches the eye is: "When it comes to casting votes, religion apparently plays a more decisive role in areas affected by LWE than in those not affected by it."

While most voters in both LWE-affected and non-LWE-affected areas chose "candidate" as the main factor (78.9 per cent and 79.5 per cent, respectively), their replies on "religion" differed more widely. In LWE-affected areas, 5.6 per cent voters said religion was the main factor that decide their votes; in non-LWE-affected areas, only 3.8 per cent voters cited religion as the main reason.

When it came to caste, there was not much to separate the two gorups: 4.3 per cent in LWE-affected and 4 per cent voters in other areas.

The survey also came up with the conclusion that though a "good candidate" ensures a higher turn-out, as opined by a majority of voters, "muscle power", "money power" and "both money and muscle power", too, were very much on display. At 8.1 per cent, money power worked much more in LWE-affected areas than at 6.5 per cent in unaffected areas. Muscle power worked less in LWE-affected (1.3 per cent) than in unaffected areas (2.1 per cent). Combined, muscle and money power, worked more (12.6 per cent) in non-LWE areas than in affected areas (10.2 per cent) in ensuring high turn-out.

The survey, called "Baseline Survey of knowledge, Attitude, Behaviour, Belief and Practices (KABBP) of Madhya Pradesh" was carried out in May-June (2013). "The results became public only recently." Activist Ajay Dubey, who used RTI to get the report, says he had been denied it initially on the ground that it was confidential.

Dubey believes the most worrying aspect of the report was that as many as 56.1 per cent voters in LWE-areas had no knowledge of the campaigns run by the Election Commission. In non-LWE areas, 44.7 per cent voters said they had no knowledge of the campaigns.

Also, most people were unaware about campaigns involving icon celebrities. In LWE areas, 64.5 per cent voters said they had not come across such campaigns.

Interestingly, at 81.3 per cent, voters in LWE-areas turned out in higher numbers than in non-LWE areas where 80.5 per cent voted in the last Assembly and General elections. Apathy as a reason for not voting more in unaffected areas (27.8 per cent) than in affected areas (24.7 per cent). Similarly, more voters in non-affected areas (11.8 per cent) than in affected areas (10.5 per cent) cited anger as the reason.

However, the overall experience of a majority of voters was "good" and some "very good" about the last elections (2008). As many as 11.3 per cent voters in affected areas replied "very good" to the 10.9 per cent in not-affected areas.

Summary of Findings

What decides the vote

Reason	*LWE-Hit*	*Other areas*
Candidate	78.9	79.5
Religion	5.6	3.8
Caste	4.3	4.0

What Brings the Voter

The Draw	*LWE-hit*	*Other areas*
Money power	8.1	6.5
Muscle power	1.3	2.1
Muscle + Money	12.6	10.2

What keeps Him/Her Away

Cause	*LWE-hit*	*Other Areas*
Apathy	24.7	27.8
Anger	10.5	11.8

No knowledge of EC campaigns

56.1 in LWE-Hit Areas

44.7 In other areas

Turn-out in last Assembly and General Elections

81.3 LWe-hit Areas

80.5 In other areas

"General Elections 2014 and Maoists

The topic is self-explanatory. This part will deal with landmark General Elections of 2014, as its results proved, bringing Narendra Modi to power at the Centre. But the treatment of the topic, General Elections 2014, will be limited to its aspects concerning the Maoists, their stance on it and the part they played in it. On the other hand, a look at the extent of the influence these polls had on the LWE and some of its practitioners, viz., the Maoists.

"Maoists Send bulk SMSes for poll boycott"

True to their poblic stance on the subject, "Maoists are sending out bulk SMSes, Apr 2014, calling for the boycott of the Lok Sabha (LS) elections in six constituencies going to the polls in the first phase in Bihar, while also threatening policemen and polling personnel".* This is the PTI report datelined Patna, 2 Apr 2014.[6] DGP, Bihar Abhyanand explained the change in their stance: "Though they have always been against elections, this is a new method they have adopted. They are now using bulk SMSes while earlier they used posters and pamphlets."

The DGP continued, "But then there is no check on anybody sending such messages. We are trying to trace the root of the SMSes. We are doing whatever is needed for smooth polling."

Police sources revealed, the SMSes are sent in the name of Maoist spokesman Avinash. They address workers, farmers, intellectuals, besides "patriots and revolutionaries."

It is not that they have completely forgotten their earlier ways and practices. "They put up posters and banners at various places across Maoist-hit areas of the State (Bihar), asking voters to boycott polls or face dire consequences."[7]

Some banners and posters were also pasted at different places in Jamui, Lakhisaria, Gaya, and Aurangabad districts, through which India-Maoist Border Zonal Committe of CPI (Maoist) spokesperson Avinash urged voters against the polls.

This daily also reported the posters apparently caused panic among political parties. A political leader of Jamui, who chose anonymity, said: "We may not risk venturing into Maoist strongholds for compaigninng. A final decision will be taken in two to three days after assessing the situation."

Reacting to the Maoists threats, Jamui SP Jitendra Rana said the police were on an alert and expressed confidence that the general elections would take place peacefully. Jamui is counted among the worst Moist-hit districts.

"Does he have a Maoist-link?" Apr 2014

A day after reports came in that a Central Intelligence Agency has sent specific inputs about JD (U) candiate from Jamui Reserved Lok Sabha constituency Uday Narayan Chaudhury seeking Maoist support to win the poll, Bihar CM Nitish Kumar 4 Apr 2014 gave a clean chit to Chaudhury, while raising doubts over such reports.[8]

The opposition BJP, expectedly, took the intelligence report as a 'serious issue.' The CM was emphatic, while addressing a poll rally at Jhajha in Jamui: *"Hai koi mai ka lal jo prove kar de... main Chaudhury Ji Ka abhinandan karta hun ki unhon ne challenge kiya hai kih koi prove kar de report ko."* He also said that such Intelligence reports are made to be leaked, to target a particular political party. The party candidate and State Assembly Speaker Chaudhury too was present on the occasion.

Chaudhury is pitted against BJP-LJP candidate Chirag Paswan, son of Ram Vilas Paswan, and Sudhanshu Shekhar Bhaskar of the RJD from Jamui Parliamentary constituency.

However earlier, another Intelligence report had allegedly charged a Minister of the Natish Cabinet and now party candidate from Sheohar Lok Sabha constituency Shahid Ali Khan for links with people associated with terrorist outfit Indian Mujahideen.

"1.5 Lakh Jawans to secure two dozen seats in Red Belt": going to polls 10.4.2014

This is an interesting if educative and informative story on implications of holding polls in Maoist-hit constituencies, and their financial and logistics costs, in a daily in Apr 2014.

"Naxal areas in six States vote together today (10 Apr 2014)", says the blurb. With over two dozen Naxal-hit constituencies across six states going to polls on the 10th, "the Election Commission and security agencies are sparing no efforts to meet the 'security challenge."[9]

Some 1.5 lakh troopers of CPMF have carpeted Maoist strong holds with 25,000 men guarding the worst-hit Bastar seat in Chhattisgarh, which saw another attack on the 9th. "Polling parties were safely escorted to spots in close vicinity of polling stations by the 9th afternoon and covered the last mile only after darkness fell to minimise the chances of an ambush."

The first major step in securing polls in Red areas was the preparation of the election schedule itself. Acting on the advice of the MHA, which sought polls to be hold together in adjoining Naxal-hit seats and that too in the initial phase to maximise force deployment, EC ensured that nearly two dozen constituencies across Bihar, Chhattisgarh, Jharkhand, Odisha, Maharashtra and MP were clubbed in one phase. Also 10 April was chosen as it was the first major polling day, covering 91 seats unlike the first two phases that covered six and seven seats, respectively.

The Maoists gave their usual boycott call and launched a couple of big ambush attacks in Bastar to instil fear in minds of locals. Though they extensively mined their strongholds to target security forces as they moved in for poll duty, the forces have been extra vigilant and pains-takingly mine-swept roads and approach routes.

EC and MHA also have some "surprise elements" in store to pre-empt Naxal attacks–like last minute relocation of polling stations to derail any Maoist plan, EC has already instructed the presiding officers to stop polling in the event of a Naxal attack and request a repoll. "A repoll will help us concentrate forces, and they will no longer be spread over large area," said an MHA official.

Politically, Congress hopes to repeat its good performance in Chhattisgarh's Red areas as in the recent state polls. while the BJP is expecting to turn the tide in its favour.

"3 CRPF Jawans killed in two Naxal attacks": 9.4.2014

As was only expected, the Maoist struck on the eve of the polls. More than 100 Maoist rebels ambushed a team of security forces, killing three CRPF men and injuring five others in the twin attacks in the tribal Bastar region on 9 Apr 2014.

The first attack took place in the Maoist-dominated Chintagufa in Sukma district when a joint team of 50 belonging to CRPF's elite COBRA battalion and Sukma district force, was returning to their base after escorting a polling team to a booth at Buranklanka.

In the second attack, Maoists triggered two powerful blasts in Bijapur district, targeting a road-opening party near Gangaloor that injured two CRPF men. (The rest of the casualities occurred during the first attack).

"Most of Naxal-affected Constituencies go to polls on 10.4.2014"

Polling in Phase III will be held in 92 constituencies in total, including some two dozen in Naxal-hit seats. These will be held across 14 states and Union Territories.

Despite a truce offer from the CPI (Maoist), the MHA has apprehensions that the outfit would indulge in violence during the first major round of general elections.[10]

The EC has also issued instructions to the MHA to ensure free, fair and peaceful conduct of polls, directing that the Central Forces "must not be deployed in less than one-section strength in insurgency/militancy/ Maoist-hit areas." Now some details on seats in LWE-hit states:

- Jharkhand: Chatra, Kodarma, Lohardaga and Palamu.
- Bihar: Gaya, (Nawada), Jamui , Aurangabad, (Karakat) and Sasaram.
- Chhattisgarh: (Maoist strong hold) Bastar.
- Odisha: Koraput, Bolongir and Kalahandi. (Behrampur) (Sundargarh, Kandhamal)
- Maharashtra: (Increased Naxal activities have been reported from) Gadchiroli-Chumar
- MP: Balaght (A "retreat and recuperation Centre" for the Maoists)

The MHA records held that a total of 109 Naxal-related incidents of violence were reported in the 2004 Lok Sabha (LS) polls. This increased to 125 incidents, causing 24 deaths in the 2009 LS polls. The worst-affected states during both the elections were Bihar, Chhattisgarh and Jharkhand.

"Will the voters breach the Red line and press the button." Phase III in Naxal area, Some additional details

This is third news story on the Phase III due on 10 Apr 2014. This daily has given poll prospects in four individual states. These are included in this part here after.[11]

Bihar: Seats 6 and canditates 80.

"Threat to chop inked fingers may keep electors away."

More thatn 9.5 milliion voters in six South Bihar constituencies will vote at 8,265 polling stations on the 10th in Phase III (but state's Phase I). Fear of Maoist violence stalks most constituencies, particularly Jamui, Sasaram, Gaya and Aurangabad. The other two constituencies voting are Karakat and Nawada. The voting on the 10th will be under heavy para-military protection. Three helicopters will keep vigil and an air ambulance will be on stand by at Patna airport. The Maoists have given a poll boycott call and threatened to chop off ink-marked fingers. Recently, they triggered a blast in Aurangabad, killing three policemen (as already mentioned).

Among the heavy weights whose fate will be decided on the 10th is Meera Kumar of Congress who is contesting from Sasaram and is on a hat-trick. Former Delhi Police Commissioner is in the fray from Aurangabad on a Congress ticket. In Naxal-hit Jamui, Ram Vilas's son Chirag Paswn is debuting. He is facing Bihar Speaker Uday Naryana Chaudhury (allegedly seeking Maoist support) of JD (U).

Jharkhand

"Villages plastered with poll-boycott posters."

Maoist scare looms in all four LS constituencies voting on the 10th. Naxalists have pointed the villages Red with poll boycott posters. Since Maoists in the past have retaliated whenever the villagers have defied them and voted, they are worried this time.

In 2009, four polling officers were abducted from Chatra constituency, while six BSF men and two civilian were killed in a land mine blast at Chandwa in the same seat. Police on the 8th and 9th ferried polling staff and security men on helicopters to the 7,058 booths, of which 2,134 are 'highly sensitive' and 2,312 'sensitive.'

Former DGP VD Ram is pitted against Maoist-turned-Trinamool MP Kameshwar Baitha in Palamu (SC reserved) constituency. In Lohardaga, Trinamool's Chamra Linda is fighting sitting BJP MP Sudershan Bhagat and Rameshwar Oraon of the Congress.

Chhattisgarh : seat 1

"Security blanket over tribal Bastar." Tribal Bastar is lone constituency in Chhattisgarh going to polls on the 10th, in the State's first phase, and it is under a tight security blanket. One of the most impoverished regions of the country and a Maoist stronghold, the major political factors here are security and development. Both BJP and Congress have talked about the need to fight the Naxalites while AAP, which has fielded tribal school teacher Soni Sori, has raised alleged issues of police and security force excesses. CPI has fielded Vimla Sori and she has been talking of tribal rights.

BJP, in power in the state, has promised large scale development initiatives, such as construction of roads, with the help of the Centre if Narendra Modi became the PM. Congress candidate Deepak Karma, son of the slain Congress leader Mahendra Karma, is banking on the sympathy factor and local level anti-incumbency against sitting BJP MP Dinesh Kashyap.

Odisha: Seats 10, Candidates 98

"10 districts on guard after 1 April blast." Large parts of West and South Odisha going to polls on the 10th have a substantial Naxal presence. Security is tight in these ten districts. In the run-up to the polls, Maoists triggered a landmine in Malkangiri on 1 April, seriously injuring two BSF Jawans.

With the stage set for the first of the two-phase polls in Odisha, stakes are high for CM Patnaik. He is spear-heading his party's challenge not just to retain his job for the fourth term, but also to try and increase his (BJD) party's LS tally. Going it alone for the first time since its formation in 1997, BJD is in contest against Congress and BJP.

Among the 70 Assembly seats, spread over 19 districts, going to the polls, is Hinjili, the CM's seat.

"Amid Maoist call for boycott Bastar goes to the Polls"

Two reports in as many dailies have been included in this chapter about whether the Maoists have indeed called for the poll boycott or not, each contradicting the other on the issue. This daily is clear on the issue: "Some 40,000 security men have been deployed in the Bastar constituency to ensure a peaceful vote on Thursday (10 April) amid the looming threat from the Maoist and a renewed call for boycott of the polls," datelined Jagdalpur (Bastar), 9 Apr 2014.[12]

Due to the Maoist threat, just one of Chhattisgarh’s, 11 constituencies go to the polls on the 10th. Chief Election Officer of the State Sunil Kunjur says "238 polling booths have already been shifted from one location to the other due to the Maoist threat." he continues: "Some 153 polling parties will be airlifted and two air ambulances will be kept ready in Raipur and

Jagdalpur in case of any untoward incident... 1,407 booths have already been identified as 'critical polling centres.'

IGP Bastar Range Arun Dev Gautam told the daily: "Security men will be deployed in every booth and the surrounding area will also be covered. Special arrangements have been made to rescue the polling parties safely."

Now comes the statement from Gudsa Usendi, spokeman, Dandakaranya Special Zone Committe, CPI (Maoist): "The parliamentary democracy prevailing in our country is a fake one. The Congress, the BJP, the CPI, the CPI(M), the BSP, the SP, the Swabhiman Manch, newly entered Aam Admi Party are to serve and protect the interests of the ruling classes." Period!

Deepak Karma (Congress), Dinesh Kashyap (BJP) and tribal activist Soni Sori (AAP) are in the fray in the Scheduled Tribes (ST) reserved seat.

Jharkhand votes in state's Phase I on 10 Apr 2014

This section has a brief look on the 10 April voting in Jharkhand. The detailed result are yet in the distance. Here we will see only some general trends through the eyes of two scribes covering the polls.[13]

"Have Maoists let ballot rule in Jharkhand?" By B Vijay Murty

The scribe has posed a question. The blurb makes a judgemental statement:

"Fixed Match: Reds allegedly put up their own candidates to gain access to system."

The scribe observes: "The first phase of polling held in Maoist-hit Chatra, Palamu and Lohardagga constituencies of Jharkhand... among the 24 most sensitive parliamentary constituencies in India... went smoothly on the 10th".

The turn out went up to 51 per cent in the three sensitive constituencies (Kodarma is the fourth constituency that went to the polls the 10th) as the rebels this time did not threaten to chop off fingers of those who defied their boycott call (The Times India of 10 Apr 2014 says the Maoists indeed issued such a threat. It is mentioned in the preceding pages). This daily says: "Ahead of the polls, they took a soft line, appealing for poll boycott in a peaceful manner. The state police says it was a sign of defeat and insecurity.

But the rumours have it that the Maoists had put up shadow candidates this time. But on the other, in a recent interview with this daily, three top Maoist leaders of Bihar, Jharkhand and North Chhattisgarh Regional

Committee... Deenbandhu, Sanjay Ganjhu and Sylvester... vehemently denied it. Deenbandhu made a self-serving statement: "We denounce this current voting system. Gullible villagers are affraid to boycott polls because next day they would be branded as Maoists by the oppressive police."

Jharkhand DGP Rajiv Kumar claimed: "Our strategy has given us good dividends so far." But he kept his fingers crossed on the security of poll officers, who were supposed to return by late evening (on 10th) to safer places.

Some 40,000 security men, comprising the CRPF and state police, were deployed in four constituencies (Koderma is the fourth). Besides, eight choppers, six Russian-made Mi-17s and two HAL-made Dhruv helicopter were pressed into service to carry poll staff and the EVMs.

"In Odisha's Maoist stronghold, 55 per cent come out to Vote" By Priya Ranjan Sahu

Malkangiri, the main Maoist stronghold in Odisha, had a relatively peaceful polling on the 10th, barring some incidents of snatching of EVM, allegedly by the ultras. This district, part of the Nabarangpur LS constituency, had a voter turn out of 55 per cent said, IGP Yashwant Jethwa. He continued: "Despite the Maoist appeal for the poll boycott, people came out in large numbers to cast their vote in this Phase 1. It indicates declines in rebels impact in the district."

As many as 165 booths in a total of 525 were identified as "sensitive" in Malkangiri, which borders Chhattisgarh and Andhra Pradesh.

34 companies of the BSF, eight-units of Odisha's elite anti-Maoist Special Operations Group (SOG) and two units of the COBRA force were deployed in the district to ward off any Maoist violence. Two choppers also provided aerial support to the polling staff.

All that the Maoists could do was to snatch eight EVMs in the district. Odisha Chief Electoral Officier (CEO) Mona Sharma gives detail: "Four EVMs were forcibly taken away on the 9th night while another four snatched when polling staff was returning after the polls (on the 10th)."

"Bengal records 79 per cent turnout; in Naxal belt, it is 63 per cent: on 17 Apr 2014

First a broader picture. "As voter enthusiasm continued to push up turn-outs, 121 Parliamentary constituencies across 12 states that went to polls on Thursady, the 17th, witnessed yet another round of brisk polling with almost all states recording a jump in poll percentages compared to the 2009 General Elections." It was reported in a daily.[14]

While there were a few incidents of violence and poll disruptions in Bihar, Jharkhand, Odisha and UP, the turn-outs here too far surpassed the 2009 figures.

Data put out by the EC at its post-poll briefing: the turn out in the three Naxal-hit seats of Chhattisgarh was 63.44 per cent (up from 57.6 per cent in 2009); 62 per cent (up from 39.3 per cent in 2009) in Bihar's seven seats; and 62.52 per cent (up from 55.09 per cent in 2009) in UP's 10 seats.

Kudos to the brave tribals who voted with zeal in the face of fatal threats from Maoists. Brave of them, indeed. Contrast this to three Bangalore seats seeing only 52-55 per cent voting.

"Target Red after saffron surge" BJP versus Maoists: In Cahoots? Analysis: Jun 2014

An interesting analysis appeared in a daily in Jun 2014, that has many strands to it. It deserves attention and a closer look.[15]

Its blurb reads: "A look at where the offensive against Naxals stands in Chhattisgarh, which has sought more fire power."

The daily speaks about Chhattisgarh's demand for additional fire power against Maoists and assurance it got from the Centre. This comes at a time when the Maoists have consolidated in key pockets, and BJP leaders are facing allegations of an understanding with the rebels, and when the party won most of the Lok Sabha seats in Naxal-dominated districts across states.

The things are obviously not jelling. The demand for additional forces, this scribe feel, does not go well with the set of facts/ground realities depicted in the latter part. There is certain dissonance somewhere!

After CM Raman Singh presented Union Home Ministger Rajnath Singh with a list of demands 9 Jun 2014, the state government issued a statement expressing satisfaction with the Centre for approving 12 battalions and promising additional helicopters.

Now, the daily highlights certain events not exactly related and certain other details which paints a picture of indifference about the Centre's handling of Chhattisgarh's insurgency situation. Here goes, the new government at the Centre was sworn in, coincidentally, a year almost to the date after the attack on Congress convoy in Darbha on 25 May 2013. Since then there has been little progress in the offensive against Naxals. The NIA is yet to file a charge sheet on the attack, while Darbha saw two more attacks during the recent polls, leading to 23 deaths.

The Centre had sanctioned Rs 150 crore for 75 police stations in Maoist-hit areas of Chhattisgarh years ago, but not one has been completed.

"56 are under construction and a proposal for a change of place for 15 is pending with the Centre," says a police officer. For some existing police stations, such as Bhadranali in Bijapur, one needs to boat across a river. Others, like the one in Farsegarh, look like hutments.

Gains and Losses of the Maoists

Last month (May 2014), the CPI (Maoist) brought on board the group CPI (ML) Naxalbari, which operates in Kerala and Karnataka. "The recent expansion in the southern part of the Western Ghats is proof that the flames of revolution will continue...," read the merger statement by CPI (Maoist) General Secretary Ganapathy and CPI (M) Naxalbari Secretary Ajith.

In a 22 January (2014) letter to the top police officers of the Maoist-hit states, the MHA had noted that Ganapathy has managed various factions well in difficult times. The acknowledgement came after the Maoists too had been admitting setbacks.

Last year (2013), this daily had reported a resolution from a CPI (Maoist) Central Committee meeting in which top leaders admitted having lost their base, weaponry and cadres across zones. In 2014 the Maoists have noted some recovery amid the set backs. "The recruitment target was achieved in south region (Sukma, Bijapur and Dantewada). Tactical counter offensive campaign (TCOC) was also achieved in south region," reads a resolution, again accessed by this daily from the DK SZC's annual meeting in Feb 2014.

It goes on to describe the setbacks: "TCOC failed in the north and West regions. We failed to stop deserters..." The resolution attributes desertions to "enhanced low-intensity conflict of the enemy, our lack of confidence, non-proletariat inclinations and our moral mistakes, the degradation of Communist ideals... no-resolution of issues of cadres." It notes that several cadres promoted too quickly later deserted.

The Maoists had set up unified commands (Unicom) in all three regions of Dandakaranya in 2013. The resolution noted that the southern Unicom worked well and northern and western ones did not.

It acknowledged as a mistake the killing of journalists Sai Reddy and Nemichand Jain. "If media persons are found to be involved in anti-party activity, then it should be thoroughly probed... They should be given a warning more than once, and elimination should be only the last resort."

BJP in Red Zone

Of the 19 LS seats in the 26 districts nationwide that the MHA identified as severely hit by Maoists, the BJP has won 13 and its ally the LJP one.

"If the police investigation have often hinted at a BJP understanding with Maoists, the electoral performance has revived such allegations (It may be a far-fetched averment). "Curiously enough again, during elections, your party never targeted BJP candidates in Chhattisgarh, who have continued to get elected all these years... even from the constituencies which are your base areas. Can you please explain this intriguing phenomenon?" Wrote veteran journalist Sumanta Banerjee, once associated with the Naxal movement in Bengal, in an open letter to Ganapathy.

"Curiously enough, your landmines have never targeted any top brass of the Sangh Parivar and its gangsters. Why? Is there any tacit understanding between your armed squads and the local BJP politicians, and corporate houses in your areas of control. He ended his letter by urging Ganapathy: "Can you please ask your cadres to preserve their firepower and keep dry what even little gunpowder is still left in your armoury, to be able to fight the agents of Hindu FASCISM.

Polls 2014

How BJP performed in the 26 severely LWE-affected districts

State	***Seats***	***BJP won***
Chhattisgarh	3	3
Jharkhand	6	6
Bihar	3	2 + 1(LJP)
Odisha	3	0
AP (Undivided)	2	1
Maharashtra	1	1
West Bengal	1	0
Total	**19**	**13 + 1**

"From the Jungle to Parliament"

This should be an apt head line for the section of this chapter that looks into an interesting if surprising transformation of two established senior Maoists: They chose to enter politics of debate and discussion, discarding that of the gun shots and murders.

They entered the electoral fray. Both fought to become "honourable Member of Parliament". But one succeedeed and the other is still trying. The two former Maoists are Kameshwar Baitha and Ranjan Yadav.

"The Maoists politics made inffective:" Kameshwar Baitha

This was a very in-your-face realistic story on Kameshwar Baitha in a daily[16] dated 31 Mar 2014. It showed that after becoming an MP, Baitha was not as effective a do-gooder for his people as he was while operating from the jungles! Reason: As an MP, he has to act within the confines of the law as laid down by the Parliament of which he was now an Honourable Member! The blurb of the article explains: "Palamu remembers what Kameshwar Baitha did for it–until he became an MP."

Yes, this is what he did before becoming an MP: "As a Maoist, he killed thieves, and severed their heads, freed his people and returned their land, and organised intercaste marriages." Since he went into politics, he has never been the same man.

He knows the difference, sitting outside a paan shop at the Pandu market in Jharkhands Palamu districts, as he tells the daily and chuckles, "Yes, he was more effective when part of the outfit [CPI (Maoist)]. Now, he is bound by all these rules; he cannot do as he wishes."

Parameshmar is the younger brother of Palamu's out going MP Kameshwar Baitha, 59. Kameshwar who won in 2009 on JMM ticket, is instantly recognised as sitting MP with the most number of criminal cases in his name. In his latest affidavit, filed as Trinamool Congress (TMC) candidate, Kameshwar has declared 51 cases, after 46 in 2009.

Even those closest to him agree the former CPI (Maoist) Central Committee member faces an up-hill task, winning this battle in 2014. Parameshwar explains: "When we go to people campaigning, they ask what he had done in these (5) years. I tell them he was in jail till 2011, since then he has been fighting his cases."

Kameshwar was ditched by the JMM, which passed on the reserved seat to RJD. He tried joining BJP, which favoured former DGP VD Ram, during whose tenure Kameshwar was in jail. The TMC is his third party... he had unsuccessfully contested a 2007 LS by-poll on a BSP ticket.

It does not matter which party he contests from. “People only see Kameshwar Baitha says Parameshwar.”

At Dhachabar village in Pandu block, Ashok Baitha squats and rubs his palm on the dirt road. He says: "Is this the road that should lead to an MP's house?" Ashok is a cousin of Kameshwar, still living in the ancestral house/village. The MP does not; he owns multiple houses but is mostly in his residence in Bishrampur.

This time, the enthusiasm is missing in the village. "No one could give us Dalits what he gave us as a rebel. The zamindars never let us sit on chairs; in fact, we always had to stand," says Devlal Baitha, husband of panchayat mukhiya Anju Devi. Ashok completes what Devlal had left aside: "He silenced zamindars. He even encouraged inter-caste couples to get married. But when he became a leader, he helped himself."

So, confines of the law are not the only obstacles that comes in the way of leader/MP wanting to do good by his people. His own 'interests' also come in the way!

Ashok narrates an incident: "Once, he caught four thieves in Basdiah. He ordered that they be killed, then cut off their heads. When the police found the thieves, their heads were kept neatly together while rest of their bodies were piled beside."

This is independently narrated by senior police officer, who also adds an anecdote villagers claim not to know about "There was an upper casteman who tried to molest one of Kameshwar's sisters. The man's goons assaulted Kameshwar's mother. When Kameshwar heard of this, he extracted his reverge", says the officer, without clarifying what the revenge was.

The road from Dhachabar to Pandu was built on Kameshwar's orders... but during his 26 years as a rebel. "We were losing in litigation with the zamindar over six acres of our land. Kameshwar may have been active in Bihar, but his influence and his outfit's goodwill meant the zamindar was forced to return it," says Bindu Ram, who is not rooting for Kameshwar this time.

In the neighbourhood of Dhachabar where Baitha's kin live, they believe he deserves one more chance. "He came overground after so many years in the jungle. Two of these five years, he was in jail," says "mukhiyapati" Devlal.

"Wait and see. The TMC will form the government and Baitha Ji will become a minister. He is the messiah of the poor," says a youngster. It turnout he is a relative of the MP as well as a police constable who is his bodyguard.

Is he Hanuman?

In Haidar Nagar market in Palamu district in Jharkhand, an area with a significant presence of Maoists, the roads are lined with red flags with images of Hanuman stitched over them. At the cross roads in the market, Bhojpuri songs blare out of the loudspeakers kept in a mini truck. These are also used to announce that Kameshwar Baitha, the sitting MP from Palamu will be holding a *nukkad* Sabha.

In 2009, Baitha, a former Maoist commander, won the LS seat from Palamu while serving a prison term in Bihar. He had commanded the Koel-Sankh Zone of the CPI (Maoist) along the Jharkhand-Chhattisgarh border. He won after defeating political heavyweights like the RJD's Ghuran Ram. After being elected to Parliament, Baitha spent another two years and 7 months in jail, getting bail only towards the end of 2011.

In March (2014), Baitha switched from the JMM to TMC after it become known that the RJD and its ruling coalition partners, the JMM and the Congress would field a common candidate. It is a reserved SC constituency. Among Baitha's rivals this time is former DGP VD Ram, who is known for his term as SP of Bhagalpur (in Bihar) when the infamous jail blinding incident took place there.

Baitha arrives dressed in a white kurta-pajama for nukkad meeting. He makes a brisk round of the market, shaking hands of the shopkeepers and the customers. "He is stocky, with matted hair and bushy moustache." Climbing atop a jeep, he then goes on to address a gathering:[17] "When I walked with a gun as a Maoist, I realised three things ail Palamu: unemployment, **akaal** (drought), and **Naxalvaad** (Naxalism). Mothers send their children to wash dishes in hotels, or to carry dung at landlord's farms. Adults here migrate in distress to work in more developed States. Unemployment, hunger, oppression and destruction of our culture is what causes Naxalivaad."

"By electing me last time, you made a social revolution possible. But I ask for your vote again to make an economic revolution this time," he concludes. He offered sattu (gram flour) water to those assembled.

Land Wars, Caste Disputes

Back in his white SUV, Baitha explains what he means by an economic revolution: "Palamu is an agricultural area. For the poor people's lives to improve, the farmers need more watershed projects to irregate their fields. Palamu's farmer need effective land re-distribution."

A word on his security arrangements. Baitha's nephew Mukesh Baitha sit at the back of his car armed with a gun. A jeep full of armed policemen is at the head of his 10-car cavalcade, passing through the broken road crisscrossing wheat fields.

In Palamu, as in entire Bihar, feudalism and the subsequent marginalisation of the lower castes, who were also landless, created a fertile ground for unrest. In the 1970s, many low caste tillers who got no relief from land reform movements joined the Maoists.

Baitha, born in a mine worker's family in a village in undivided Bihar's Bishrampur, recollects he had joined the Maoist groups Party Unity in the late 1980s after the Arwal massacre in which 21 supporters of the left-wing Mazdoor kisan Sangharsh Samiti (MKSS) were killed in police firing.

From the 1990s until now, Palamu has repeatedly figured among India's poorest districts. Splinter groups such as Tritiya Sammelan Prastuti Committee (TSPC) have prolifered here since the early 2000s, which Maoists allege receive police aid. In this conplex milieu came Kameshwar Baitha's unprecedented win in 2009.

At Devrikhurd village, when he stops at paan shop, Vijay Mehta, a farmer, complains that this is Baitha's first tour of the village after being elected. Baitha askes for forgiveness: "I only got two years and five months of my term (of five years) to work". He points to a Sheesham tree nearly: "If you plant a seed and it does not sprout to become a tall tree at first, will you not give it a second chance."

At a Gayabheega tola, there are several concrete houses, but people from the Ravidas SC community lived in the thatched huts outside the main village. An old woman in a red saree, Sarda Devi, scolds Baitha for having failed to ensure that she received her widow pension. Baitha talks to her and her family and asks them to allow him to screen a CD inside their house. "This CD has recordings of the 258 questions I raised in the Parliament on the Japla cement factory near here, on minerals use, on inflation", he says, as the group watches a recording of him taking Oath in Parliament.

Many youngsters here have migrated to cities in search of livelihood. But several families still depend on NREGA that they say is riddled with corruption. "You have been our old leader since the time we were young, but see what you can do for livelihood," the villagers tell Baitha as they affectionataly bid him farewell in the night.

"The other outlaw vying for MP honours" Ranjan Yadav: Still trying

Now comes the turn of Ranjan Yadav, the second outlaw who wants to become India's law maker, hence his entering the electoral fray. He is second of the "two former Maoists who are attempting to lift villagers out of poverty and provide electricity and education... not through an armed revolution but by contesting elections."

In the neighbouring constituency of Chatra, former Maoists commander Ranjan Yadav is contesting on a SP ticket. In 2009, while serving a prison term, Yadav had unsuccessfully contested the LS polls on a CPI (ML) ticket. Later he joined the RJD and tried lobying with the party Supremo Lalu Yadav while the latter was in Ranchi jail after his conviction in the fodder scam. After the RJD gave up the claim to field a candidate from Chatra, allowing its coalition partner Congress to field Dheeraj Sahu, Ranjan Yadav switched to the SP. The constituency consists of the tribal dominated forested Latehar district and the plains region of Chatra that has a significant population of SCs and backward castes.

Yadav says: "In Mahuadan in Latehar, and in many parts of Chatra, there is no electricity even after 60 years of Independence. Big corporations mine coal and iron ore but children in villages cannot even attend a good school. These are the issues I want to raise through politics." He is sitting in a white dhoti in his sparsely-furnished house, still under construction in Namkum on the Ranchi border.

Since Yadav joined mainstream politics, the CPI(Maoists) has issued public statements dubbing him a traitor. In Sep 2013, the local Maoist leader Sudhir issued a 6-page statement against Yadav and two others: Yugal Pal, a former member of the Maoists Zonal Committee who had announced that he plans to join the All Jharkhand Students Union and former Sub-Zonal Commander Vinod Sharma, threatening that anyone supporting them or their candidature will be tried by a **Janadalat** (People's court). Yadav says he fears for his life after the fatwa which he finds unjust. Yugal Pal has since withdrawn his announcement.

Yadav recounts he had joined the Party Unity in 1990 at 23 while working as a petty contractor in Palamu. He explains: "The party did a lot of good work for the ordinary villagers... building checkdams, schools in Garhwa. During marriages, we would distribute utensils. But I have stopped believing we will come to power through armed revolution".

Yadav feels the Maoists have weakened because some opportunists have joined them, and also because of the increased police pressure. "There have been instances where relatives of party members have become contractors. The contractors would try to bribe commanders saying they keep a cut for theselves instead of collecting funds for the party alone."

The Maoists have accused Yadav of collaborating with the police in paramilitary operations against the Maoists. He refutes the allegations: "The CPI (Maoist) have lost their hold in Chatra because of the TSPC. The police is exploiting cracks within the party by supporting such splinter groups. I have not asked TSPC for their support but I have told them not to disturb my workers and that we won't disturb theirs."

"Jharkhand Assembly Polls and Maoists Nov - Dec 2014

In this part, the role of the Maoists in the Nov-Dec 2014 polls for Legislative Assembly will be examined in detail keeping in mind, its various aspects.

It needs to be noted that Jharkhand is one of the two States (other being Chhattisgarh) which are highly affected by the LWE. To put it simply, these two are on the top of the pile as far as the Maoist violence is concerned. In Jharkhand specificially, the Maoists have their presence in 18 of its 24 districts.

"Maoist's wife contesting assembly poll"

A weekly carried this interesting and detailed story in its issue of 16 Nov 2014. Its blurb gave more clear picture: "Social worker and JMM candidate Manoroma Devi has been separated from husband for years, and wants Maoists to lay down arms and 'Work through the system.' "[18] The report is filed from a town, named distinctly: Hunterganj (Chatra).

A JMM election office was to be inaugurated mid-day 12 November at the Main Road. The journalists waited for two hours.

At 2 PM, JMM candidate Manorama Devi and her supporters arrive in a fleet of Scorpios and Boleros. Devi is the wife of Gautam Ji, a Maoist area commanders. "Call the journalists from Hunterganj," she says. Consquently, after another half hour's frantic phoning, some media persons turn up. She inaugurates the election office. As is traditional, *laddoos* are distributed.

"I apologise for your having to wait for a long time. I realise you have come from Delhi to meet me," she tells the weekly's correspondent before making her pitch: "This is the first time a woman is contesting from Chatra. There are basic issues of electricity, roads and water, and I will try to address them".

Asked about her husband, she is candid: "I have had no links with him ever since he joined Maoists some ten years ago. He is my husband in name only. I have been into social work since then. Sometime ago, some JMM leaders asked me whether I would like to contest polls, and I agreed." Devi could not communicate properly, and his brother Khedu Yadav helped her out.

Devi's replies are summed up here: "After Gautam ji joined Maoist cadre, he never came back to see the family. I cared for our children. We have three sons: one is pursuing B Tech at a college in Ranchi, another one is studying in class VIII; and the third one is at home, being differently abled. I also have one daughter who is married...I feel I can solve the problems society is facing by becoming MP or MLA. I don't know where my husband is at the moment, but would like to tell him through you (the media), that he should give up arms and join the mainstrem. Contest polls and work through the system. I would also advise other Maoist cadres to do so."

Devi's rivals are Jaiprakash Singh Bhokta (BJP), Janardan Paswan (RJD) and Satyanand Bhokta (JVM).

The JMM, believed to have links with the Maoists, "has given tickets to many former Maoists or their kin."

In the neighbouring Latehar, another Naxal hotspot, the party is fielding, Mohan Ganjhu, whose brother is the area commander of the Tritya Prastuti Committee (TPC), a Maoist splinter group.

The party is also likely to field Poulis Surin and Masi Charan Purti, both former Maoists.

Locals feel Manorama Devi is not in the fight in Chatra, and the contest is likely to be between Jarpraksh Bhokta and incumbent Janardan Paswan.

But her candidacy itself is seen as important, as a local businessman says: "Irrespective of whether she wins or loses, democracy has already won in Chatra."

"Poll officials to rent two-wheelers in Maoist Zone": 19 Nov 2014

A daily report: "officials in the polt-bound Jharkhand have decided to use rented motor bikes and bicycles to ensure smooth and fair elections, especially in remote and tough terrain of the State where Maoists are strong."[19]

Naxals have a presence in 18 of the State's 24 districts. The returning officiers in the districts have even released the rate charts for renting bikes and bicycles for movement of security forces in their constituencies.

Motor cycles can be rented for Rs 200 a day and bicycles for Rs 50 per day.

Minimise Risks

"In the rural areas where it will tough to travel on four-wheelers, it would be better to ride on bikes and bicycles. It will also minimise security risks for the patrolling personnel," said a police officer. Ranchi District Commissioner and District Election officer Vinay Chaubey also confirmed: "Motorcycles and bicycles would be used for election purposes in remote and tough terrain."

Another police officer said that in case of Maoist attack, patrol officers would be able to get faster to secure positions than had they been on four-wheelers.

Bicycles could also be used for transport of logistics comfortably to polling booths in remote rural areas.

Security Measures

"We have taken all security measures for the smooth and fair polling in the Naxal-hit areas and for this we have taken services of all kind of vehicles for safe and smoother movement of security forces."

Thousands of security forces men "from CPMF will be deployed in the state to ensure a smooth poll. The first phase, for 13 seats, is scheduled for 25 November, with the poles concluding on 20 December. The counting will be three days later."

"In Jharkhand, LWEs decide who locals should vote for:" A daily of 24 Nov 2014

This is an interesting if surprising, some may feel, 'unbelievebale,' story in a daily. The blurb is even more direct: "RED TERROR: villagers follow diktats fearing for their lives, say orders are issued two to three days before polling."[20]

First a look at the contents of this news story. The daily opens up with startling if cynical note: "In the villagers dominated by LWE in Jharkhand, the right to vote freely and without fear has no meaning. Till date, the ultras in state's hinterlands decide whom the villagers will vote for. The daily quotes two villagers to make its point:

> **One:** "command jis ko adesh dega us ko vote denge (we will vote for that candidate for whom we get the command)," said a villager who identified himself as Mangra Munda from Murhu block of Khunti district, some 75 km from Raipur.
>
> **Two:** "We cannot vote at will, if we do so, they (LWE) will kill us," said a villager from Beerbanki villate in Khunti district agains. The village is regularly visited by cadres of CPI (Maoist) and People's Liberation Front of India (PLFI).

In Jharkhand, more than 25 splinter outfits are active in the 22 LWE-affected districts. The state government has banned 17 outfits including CPI (Maoist), TPC, PLFI, TPC-2, Jharkhand Prastuti Committee, Jharkhand Jan Mukti Party (JJMP).

Despite heavy deployment of security forces in the state, "banned Maoist outfits are managing to conduct meetings with the villagers directing them to boycott polls or cast theit vote in favour of a particular party leader.

There are reports of several banned outfits holding meetings and giving diktats about whom to vote for in the villages of 13 constituencies... in Latehar, Chatra, Palamu, Garhwa, and Gumla districts... that will go to polls in the first phase on 25 November.

For instance, the TPC ordered villages under its dominance to vote for a regional party, and consequently, RJD leader and a candidate filed a complaint to the Election Commission (EC). Similarly, PLFI too issued a diktat in Khunti, Simdega and Chatra.

Villagers explained that the 'Jungle Party' (Ultras) issue diktats a few days before the polling. The daily quotes a journalist "based out of Gumla," without naming him, 'to support the thesis,' to put it this way.

Sources disclose that the political parties also seek support of the rebels to demotivate other candidates. The splinter outfits, in their area of dominance, bar the opponents' compaign vehicles from entering it. During the LS polls, activist Dayamani Birla, who had contested from Khunti, had complained that her campaign was being target by PLFI to promote another political party.

When contacted by the daily, Jharkhand's Chief Electoral Officer PK Jajoria said "We will take strict action against contestants and political parties forcing people to caste votes in their favour with the help of ultras," and added: "Programmes are being held to motivate voters to cast their ballots without the fear of ultras."

Bara Vikash, senior leader of the CPI (Maoist) said "they are not favouring any particular party. We are against the system. We are asking people to boycott polls."

"LWE outfit with stakes in politics"

This is an extremely meaningpur news story carried by a daily of 26 Nov 2014. It analyses the stance of Tritiya Sammelan Prastuti Committee (TSPC) in politics of Jharkhand and its relationship with CPI (Maoist).[21] The story is datelined Latehar.

The daily paints a picture of Hempur, on the 22 km stretch of NH-99 between Chandma and Balumath towns in Latehar district, as "looking cheerful on the 25th morning, voting day. It found: villagers "hung around polling booth No 101, Chatting and asking one another whom they had voted for." But when the daily asked villagers about the role of the TSPC in how Hempur will vote, they smiled awkwardly and walked away.

TSPC, founded in the adjoining Chatra district, is a LWE outfit banned by the state. CM Hemant Soren has alleged that the then DGP VD Ram helped form the outfit. This newspaper had reported earlier about the TSPC's good relations with security forces.

A source who lives in an adjacent village, invited the daily to Hempur. It told the latter that a TSPC armed squad of some 50 had arrived at the village at 8 AM on the 23rd. "Sunil Ji was leading it. They went around telling people to vote for Prakash Ram", the source said. Sunil is a TSPC area commander. Hailing from a nearby village, he has built the largest house in Hempur, a yellow mansion.

Prakash Ram is a former RJD MLA, "now contesting on a ticket on Babu Lal Marandi's JVM-P. Latehar is an SC constituency, Hempur has a majority of Ganjhus, who are Dalits. TSPC is led by a Ganjhu leader and Sunil too belongs to the caste. Ganesh Ganjhu, elder brother of TSPC Chief Brajesh Ganjhu, recently joined the JVM-P, and is the party's candidate from Simaria, in Chatra district.

Hempur is important also because of its proximity to Makaiyatand, it was where BJP's Latehar candidate Brijmohan Ram had an accident on 14 November. Speaking at Chandma in the constituency on 21 November, PM Narendra Modi alleged that his opponents had tried to kill Ram. Ram had been awarded the ticket only on the last day of filing nominations. This was because BJP had cancelled the ticket awarded to Naraya Bhokta, who turned out to be a Deputy Zonal Commander of TSPC.

"Voters defy terror": 3 Dec 2014

This is the first of the three reports that will be included here to see the analysis of the second phase of polling in Jharkhand on 2 Dec 2014, by different dailies.

This daily publisher the results of the polling on the 2nd under a heartening title, depicting the brave tribals voting in large numbers to defy the Maoist ban.[22]

It covers polling in J & K, against the threats by the separatists and in Jharkhand, subject of this book, against the threat by the Maoists. The opening paragraph depicts an in-your-face truthful situation: "Inclement weather and boycott call by separatists and Maoists did not deter the voters from turning out in large numbers for the second phase of polling in J & K and Jharkhand respectively."

If polling for 18 Assembly segments in J&K saw over 71 per cent voter turn out, nearly 66 per cent voters exercised their franchise for 20 constituencies in Jharkhand.

Reports from Ranchi said that phase two of the Assembly polls in 20 constituencies, including 16 reserved for the ST, spread across Kolhan and South Chota Nagpur registered higher turnout of 65.65 per cent with impressive figures for Jamshedpur (East) and Jamshedpur (West) compared to the polls conducted in 2009: 58 per cent (45.14 in 2009) and 60 per cent (42.15 per cent in 2009) respectively.

The Jharkhand CEC office signalled at the voter awareness drive and continued efforts to update voters' list to eliminate 'ghost voters', besides a host of other measures to be the reason for higher polling percentage in two constituencies of Jamshedpur, as indicated above.

Nontheless, encouraging aspect of the polls has been about no report of violence, despite 262 extremely sensitive and 196 sensitive booths in 20 constituencies that went to polls on the 2nd. Heavy deployment was made at booths in dense forests in Arki, Tamar, Khunti, Kolebira, and ultra-dominated Lapung under Mandar constituency.

"Jharkhand voters defy Maoists"

It is another (second) report in a different daily which coincidentally, if significantly, is selecting nearly same wordings for its title, implying 'defiance' in both cases.

This daily opens with: "Defying boycott calls given by Maoists some 65 per cent of the electorate cast their vote in the second phase on Tuesday." Of the 20 constituencies that went to the polls, 70 per cent are in the Maoist-affected areas.

Long queues of voters were seen at various polling stations, "especially in Maoist-hit constituencies."

In the first phase of polling on 25 November too, the State witnessed an impressive turn out of 62 per cent voters.

Over 44 lakh voters decided the fate of 223 candidates in the fray, including former CMs Arjun Munda and Madhu Koda.

Barring a few cases of defective EVM, at some places, polling was by and large incident free.

Tuesday's turn out was an improvement from the 58.26 per cent recorded in 2009. The EC seized Rs 1,12,83,479 in cash, 1.27 lakh litre liquor worth Rs 1.03 cr and drugs worth Rs 10.24 lakh.

"Maoist Strategy: From bullets to ballots through proxies:" 3 Dec 2014

This is the third and last news report on the voting on 2 Dec 2014, and with an entirely differing title. Its contents also treat different issues, in contrast to the first two.[23]

Its opening is also interesting if high-pitched: "This poll season, the Maoists and other rebel groups in Jharkhand have come out all guns blazing– not to scuttle polls but to prop up candidates of their choice."

This daily claims "there was no call from the top rebel groups to boycott polls, which, otherwise, is the stage for fierce battle with the security forces."

The CPI (Maoist) and some half-a-dozen other 'rebel' outfits are suspected of backing certain candidates. Officials in the Police HQ at Ranchi talks about intelligence reports that point to this covert relationship. "Some of the candidates are blood relatives of Maoist leaders who have either surrendered or are active," says a senior IPS officer.

Some examples of relatives are cited. In Maoist-hit Chatras the candidate of a national party is alleged to have links with rebels. It refers to Phase I on 25 Nov 2014. The TSPC, believed to be partronised by the state police, canvassed for particular candidates in Latehar and Chatra districts. One of the candidates in Chatra is the wife of a Naxal commander. The constituency saw a contest between Girija Singh and Vinod Sharma, both former rebels.

The daily is rather shy of naming names, forgetting or ignoring that most of such candidates have been identified by some dailies and mentioned in the earlier pages here.

Jharkhand Police HQ also has reports about Maoists and other splinters supporting candidates in Ghatshila, Torpa, and Kolebira Assembly constituencies that went to polls on 3 December. In Tamar, JMM candidate Salomi Turi, wife of a jailed Maoist, took on the notorious CPI (Maoist) Sub-Zonal commnander Kundan Pahan's Cousin, Ravinath, a JVM candidate.

West Singhbhum SP Narander Kumar Singh claims insurgents have given the customary boycott calls in some pockets of Saranda forest, but are not in a position to enforce the call.

"The one big reason is that they have been flushed out of most parts of the forest," Singh claims. Incidentally, Indicentally, polling percentage in Saranda forest in the recent LS polls jumped to 70 per cent, almost double the 2009 figures.

"LWE gamble: Marandi fields a Chief's brother, and JMM a Chief's wife: 9 Dec 2014

Both the names have already been covered in brief. It is worth a look as to what new angle this daily brings to the subject.[24]

First the two opening paragraphs of the article. "Babu Lal Marandi's JVM(P), depleted by the flight of 8 of its 11 MLAs, is carrying out a risky experiment in Chatra distruct's Simariya by promoting a candidate whose nomination has effectively been furthering the cause of a banned outfit he has links to." Now to para two. "The candidate is Ganesh Ganjhu, elder brother of Brajesh Ganjhu, chief of the Maoist/LWE outfit TSPC."

The TSPC threw its weight behind Ganesh, especially in Lawalong block where its top leaders live: no other party managed to open campaign office there. Reports from the ground that the TSPC, whose chief Brajesh is widely expected to become a politician eventually, has used its clout to support JVM(P) candidates in adjoining Chatra and Latehar, which voted on 25 November.

Former CM Marandi had lost his son Anup in 2007, killed by the alleged Maoists. Yet, cornered after most of his MLAs defected to the BJP, Marandi seems to have prioritised survival over everything else. His party has also given its Tamar ticket to Mahadev Ravinath Pahan, related to Kundan Pahan, the states' second-most-wanted Maoist leader.

By giving the TSPC the opportunity to win three seats, Marandi risks being beholden to the Ganjhu brothers, if they succeed. It is also a measure of the TSPC's growth over the past five years that it aspires to win three seats.

The JMM is not far behind either: it has given tickets to the wives of former Maoists in Tamar and Chatra: its Simariya candidate Rajkumari Devi is the wife of banned outfit Jharkhand Prastuti Committee (JPC) Chief Guddu Ganjhu.

"Babu Lal Marandi is a good leader but he has spoilt his party's name by giving ticket to Ganesh here," said Binod Bihari Paswan, the CPI's Simariya candidate, who was fired upon by unidentified assailant on the 6 December night. "I am sure it was the TSPC. Before I filed my nomination, two boys on a bike had threatened me saying only Ganesh Ganjhu will contest from here," said Binod, whom the bullets missed and who now moves around with seven bodyguards.

In the 2010 polls to local bodies, the TSPC had ensured that most of Lawalong should be represented by its nominees, elected unopposed. Brajesh Ganjhu is himself the Deputy Panchayat President of Lawalong. Sources in Lawalong told this daily that on 8 December, Ganesh distributed blankets among voters. These blankets are believed to have been supplied by the state government to the panchayats.

Earlier in 2014, CM Hemant Soren had told the Assembly that former DGP VD Ram had formed the TSPC. Ram is currently the LS member of the BJP; and there were allegations that the outfit had helped/supported his LS campaign. The TSPC had supported the BJP's LS campaign in Chatra too... Ganesh was then a BJP member. He had moved over from the JMM, which gave him a ticket in 2009; he came second.

This Assembly polls, Chatra's outgoing MLA and RJD candidate Janardhan Paswan has alleged the JSPC supported JVM (P) candidate Satyanand Bhokta by holding Jan adalats (people's court). This daily had reported from Latehar about how a TSPC squad threatened villagers, demanding votes for the JVM(P)'s Prakash Ram. And the JVM(P)'s LS candidate Neelam Devi... a Prakash Ram choice... was reportedly supported by the CPI (Maoist).

"Phase 3: 9 Dec 2014: 58 per cent turn out in Kashmir and 61 per cent in Jharkhand": Maoists are defied this time, too

First a brief account of voting in Kashmir, because there, too, people are defying terrorists to come out to vote. "Millions of voters defied a saparist call to boycott Assembly polls in Kashmir and exercised their franchise amid tight security in the third phase on 9 Dec 2014. The turnout was lower than the first two rounds with the voters in separatist strongholds staying away."[25]

The EC said 58 per cent of voters turned up to cast their ballot, less than 70 per cent numbers in the phases one and two, when Kashmiris battled bone-chilling winter temperatures in a bid to keep the BJP from gaining in the Muslim majority state.

Now to Jharkhand, which too defied a Maoist call to boycott the polls, with 61.35 per cent voter turnout in 17 constituencies in a bid to end years of political instability in the state that has seen 9 CMs and been under Presedent's Rule three times since its creation 14 years ago.

Barring a few cases of exchange of gun-fire between security forces and Maoists in Girdih district and clashes between two political parties in Ichagarh before polling began, the third round passed off peacefully.

A total of 289 candidates are contesting 17 out of the state's 81 Assembly seats, including former Deputy CM Sudesh Mahato and three cabinet ministers.

Results Jharkhand Assembly Polls: 23 Dec 2014

For a proper perspective, results are mentioned very briefly, as declared on 23 Dec 2014.[26]

2014 Poll Results

Total Assembly seats 81

Seats won

BJP	37
Congress	6
JMM	19
JVM (P)	8
Others	11

Performance of JMM

The party won 11 new seats but lost eight seats, including four from its political stronghold, Santhal Parganas.

The JMM emerged as the second-largest party in the Assembly polls, defying poll predictions of a wash-out and establishing itself it as the strongest regional party in Jharkhand. No wonder that for this very reason, the news story is titled, "JMM emerges as biggest satrap in Jharkhand."

The party won 19 seats, one more than the last polls in 2009. While that was far less than the BJP-led combine that won 42 seats, it was still ahead of the other regional parties... the JVM(P) and All-Jharkhand students Union Party that won 8 and 5 seats respectively.

"Bullet-less ballot: Maoists keep their guns down"

This was a happy situation for all concerned. Maoist gun went silent and played no role in the poll process. As a daily puts it: "Call it their changed strategy or dwindling influence, the CPI(Maoists) have failed to play a spoil sport during the third Assembly poll in Jharkhand."[27]

Experts call it a good sign for democracy in a state where 22 of the districts are Maoist-affected. There are no less than 17 outfits enlisted as outlaw Left Wing Extremists (LWE). "But, unlike previous years, there have not been major statements on disrupting 5-stage polls," which concluded on 23 Dec 2014.

"Even their martyr's week in the first week of December did not have any poll thwarting calls in their leaders' speeches."

IG CRPF RK Mishra said, "Yes, in fact, they (Maoists) are on the route of extinction here... Perhaps, the rebels have realised that the path of violence is not going to take them further." Jharkhand IGP (Operations) LM Meena gave the credit to COBRA and Jaguar fighters for thwarting Maoist mission.

In fact, in a handout released among villagers during the poll, the Maoists too have conceded that their organisation has weakened in Jharkhand with better intelligence within the security forces and splinter groups working as spies for the forces. As already covered in the earlier pages, CPI (Maoist) Central Committee General Secretary Ganapathi, in a 7000-word letter to his commanders has confessed to a crisis within the Party "due to lack of leaders at the top".

But political observers believe participation of Maoist leaders in the election process is another reason for the decline.

"Rs 1,000 cr in hands of Naxal-backed panch: officials fear misuse: 2 Mar 2015

This possibly is the last entry on the subject of 'Elections and the Maoists' that appeared in a daily in Mar 2015, with a startling, if breath-taking, head line! Its blurb clarifies the things further: "Candidates with 'Maoist links' sweep Bastar poll."[28]

This is about the local polls, to panchayats. "Voters in Bastar villages have elected their reprentatives, Maoist-supported panch and sarpanch." The figures are startling of the 22,416 panch elected by the villagers recently in seven districts of Bastar Region, nearly 50 per cent or 11,098 candidates won unopposed. Besides, 212 sarpanch also won unopposed.

At least 90 per cent of them, the Chhattisgarh police said, either have links with Maoists or were supported by the rebels. Several among 1,628 gram panchayats in Bastar would now witness these panch directing and monitoring the various government schemes costing at least Rs 1,000 cr annually. Maoists have always acknowledged receiving funds through commissions from the schemes in Bastar.

The Police Speaks

Concerned over the verdict, Sukma SP D Shravan and ASP Santosh Singh visited interior areas immediately after the results to meet the newly-elected representatives. Singh spoke to the daily: "We spent a week inside and met some of them. We know that they have links (with Maoists); we know that they were backed by those people (Maoists), but we told that now you have chosen the path of democracy, you have a responsibility towards the government." On the possibility of misuse of funds, he added: "We will watch them carefully. The administration will have to ensure that funds do not reach Maoists. All works will now have to be properly audited. If they (panch) show that they have done some work, they will have to produce some photographs and other details."

Maximum Presence

The maximum presence of Maoists- backed representatives is in the three southern and western districts of Bastar, where of total 6,963 panch, 5,186 or 75 per cent have won unopposed. Almost all of them are in the interior areas with little administrative presence.

Of the 1,107 panch in Naranpur, the seat of Abujhmaad, 938 were elected unopposed; of the 2,169 panch in Bijapur, 1,785 were elected unopposed; the corresponding figures for Dantewada are 1,709 and 1,335 and for Sukma 1,978 and 1,128.

The results mirror 2010, when 10,980 of 21,194 panch and 181 of the 1,438 sarpanch were elected unopposed in Bastar. ADG (Naxal ops) RK Vij "welcomed the move as people are joining democracy", but cautioned "we will have to ensure that there is no misuse of funds." Panchayats, as constitutional bodies, hold immense financial powers.

Recently, CM Raman Singh had released Rs 150 cr for gram panchayats. A gram sabha comprised a sarpanch and around 10 panch.

Underlining the significance of panchayats, Chhattisgarh CEO PC Dalai told the daily: "Many of the social security schemes like rural employment generation programmes, old age pension are implemented directly through panchayats. They constitute the real democracy at the grass roots."

Who will check and monitor?

Various studies suggest that a little or no work takes place in interior Baster, but funds are mostly shown spent. "The most recent case is of Dantewada, which won the award for best implenmentation of MNREGA, incidentally when panchayat polls were on.

An officer who has worked in the area explains: "Collectors are strictly asked to not travel beyond a point. Who will monitor the schemes? We are to rely on these panches only." (One does not understand why this scribe is shy of using a plural term "panches" for a panch? He has throughout used the term 'panch' in singular and plural forms!)

Another officer shared his experience of a decade ago when he tried to visit some interior areas for inspecting schemes in Sukma, but was stopped by others citing the Maoist threat. He said, "years later, the local MLA told me that I was fooled as they did not want me to visit the site."

Politics and Politicians on Maoist Problem

If Maoist insurrection is a serious challenge to country's security, politics and politician must enter the field, at times to clarify the issues but more after than not, to muddy the waters. To put it differently, politicisation of issues of national importance by political parties for their sectarian/political ends is an expected thing in Indian polity. Where it is question of power, political parties can do anyting to gain it, and then to retain it. The Congress and Communist parties can take a soft stand on a serious issue of East-Pakistan, and post-1971, of Bangladeshi migration into India, even if it causes serious danger to Assam's integrity and identity. Same way, the Congress Party can let Indian Muslim League join a coalition led by it, and other times, dub it a communal party.

It was a slight digration, to return to the Naxalism, parties can change their stance on it to suite their interests at a given time. This section examines the statements and stance of some parties and politicians to this serious national problem.

"PM speeches on Maoist issue: From tough talk to muted stand" 2005-2013 period

Before we examine the statements of others, it should be useful and instructive to note the stance of India's Prime Minister Manmohan Singh over the years.

Prime Minister Manmohan Singh's changing stance

A daily went to its archives and examined PM's statements, over the years. He has, expectedly made these statements at the annual CMs conferences which he usually inugurates and then presides over.

15 Apr 2005

It was his first speech on the issue at the CMs meet, the first year of UPA-1. He advocated "walk on two legs" strategy that included implementing development programmes and ensuring "effective policing."

13 Apr 2006: "Most quoted, definitive remarks"

This was his second speech on Maoist violence, and he described Naxalim as the "single biggest internal security challenge" for the nation, apprehending that "Naxal movement is now characterised by growing militarisation... and possible external links."[29]

This remark of the PM "biggest internal security challenge" remain most quoted by the analysts and commentariat, even if he never repeated this definitive phrase himself in any subequent year. Some wags are vicious enough to pronounce that this phrase was his only contribution to India's/country's counter-Naxal fight.

5 Sep 2006

He, however, revised the above 'definitive'; characterisation of Naxalism with a "blend of firm but sophisticated handling of Naxalite violence, with sensitive handling of developmental aspects" during his address to CMs this day.

20 Dec 2007 and 2009 (6 Jan)

These were his last two speeches of the UPA-1 tenure. In these editions, Singh's "walk on two legs" had given way to a suggestion to "establish specialised, dedicated forces to fight LWE" and "to choke their support infrastructure," (2007).

2009's was his last speech of UPA-1. He highlighted how the "military ethos has become dominant" among Naxals who possessed "guerrilla army" with "rudimentary capabilities to manufacture arms" and managed to "garner support from among members of civil society."

This was the last speech of the UPA-1 and it maintained somewhat tought stance of that tenure. What ever the reasons, the PM mellowed down his anti-Naxal stance post UPA-1 period, as was indicated by his very first speech of UPA-II, in Feb 2010. The analysts feel Apr 2010 massacre of 76 CRPF men caused this softening of stance towards the Naxal problem. But to be factually correct, this softening was appearent even before this traumatic incident. The records show that two speeches of the PM–on 17 Aug 2009 and 7 Feb 2010–delivered before this incident and post-inception of UPA-II in May 2009, were indicative of this softening.

UPA-II: May 2009 to May 2014

The Dantewada Apr 2010 could - or May-have been a reason for this softening after this incident. But we have seen this softened stance immediately after UPA-II period as commented above. What were, or can be, the reasons for this changed stance? One could be re-assessment of this comparatively tougher stance on the Naxalism during the UPA-I regime. Then there could be some pressure from maveriks like Digvijay Singh, unfortunately a senior Congressman, who is believed to be Rahul Gandhi's mentor and also have his ear. Their logic is simple: "The Maoists are misguided youth... They are our brethren and should not be treated as our enemies." Knowing their declared aim and intent, there could not be a more foolish and misconceived thinking on the Maoist insurrection. Be that as it may, the reason or assumption can be summed up here: "Tougher policy has not yielded expected results, a change in counter-Naxal policy is called for. Hence a softened stance.

PMs speeches on 17 Aug 2009, 7 Feb 2010, 1 Feb 2011 and 16 Apr 2012

All these speeches during UPA-II period, the daily observes, "lacked aggression." The PM called for "holistic approach" with emphasis on development in the form of "Integrated Action Plan" (IAP), with a rider that "our response to LWE must be calibrated to avoid alienating our people."

In the remarks during UPA-II, he told CMs that "LWE is another serious challenge" and called for a "balanced and nuanced strategy." Now it is "another serious challenge", in UPA-II contrasted to the "biggest internal security challenge" of Apr 2006!

Need for a tough stance again during UPA-II

The PM's moderate language in his five previous speeches in CMs conferences during UPA-II reflect a break from his aggressive stance in the last two speeches of UP A-I, as the daily puts it.

So, analysis of these speeches on Naxal threat during the UPA-II demand that the PM revert to his UPA-I tough stance, during the remaining period of his second tenure, roughly one year. The daily comments that the tough stance of UPA-I "had given way to a middle-path strategy during UPA-II after the Dentewada 2010 massacre of 76 CRPF men." This softening, possibly, was the result of the Congress pressure on the Government to go slow against the Maoists.

This go-slow stance might change post-May 2013 massacre of Chhattisgarh Congress leadership. "It may prompt the PM to up the ante, given the fact that Congress President Sonia Gandhi has also taken a tough stand against the rebels."

There is a need to put this entire situation as in June 2013 in perspective. There was less than a year left for the UPA-II Government. In fact, it was a mere 6-month period left for this Government, as due to the coming General elections poll schedule announcement, it would be a lame-duck by Jan 2014.

But by happenstance, a fresh breeze blew through the rancid MHA. It was when P Chidambaram (PC) took charge. He put in place a vigorous Counter-Maoist policy in 2012. But it did not yield expected results due to two reasons: A majority of Congress Party led by Digvijay Singh opposed new policy and PC was not a heavy-weight Congress man in MHA... even though he had established a great reputation as a Union Finance Minister. May be, the Finance was his first love and went back to it after a year in the MHA. The MHA went to another light-weight Minister, Shinde, who was not known to be overly competent, either!

The brief stint of PC in the MHA has been covered in the earlier chapters.

"Tackle Maoism block-wise": Jairam Ramesh: Aug 2011

Ramesh is one of the more voluble Ministers (Union Rural Development), and possibly, a cerebral one. So, it is only apt that his observations and suggestions are considered in the first place.

He was on a two-day visit to Odisha (13-14 Aug) to check on the progress of work under his ministry. He hold a meeting with the Collectors of six Maoist-hit district–Ganjam, Gajapati, Koraput, Rayagada, Malkangiri, Kandha and Nayagarh–to review the progress of implementation of the Mahatma Gandhi National Rural Employment Guarantee Scheme (MGNREG) in the Maoist-hit areas.

Out of 60 districts identified as LWE-affected, 15 are in Odisha.

His suggestions/remarks are summed up here:

- Blocks rather than districts should be considered the standard unit for an integrated approach to tackle the Maoist menace. He had suggested it to the Planning Commission to move away from district-based approach to tackle the problem as it was impractical to equate two districts that had a different number of blocks each, and also varying in size. In a majority of affected districts, blocks were very large in size, a major stumbling block to providing better governance. Smaller blocks were a means to provide better governance.
- The Odisha government had already made a proposal in this regard.
- Along with the deployment of security forces, rural development can be a primary instrument to combat LWE.
- The State government should form a para-legal system in the affected districts to enable tribal persons to reclaim their land. For, Maoists have long been exploiting long-standing, land-related issues in the tribal areas, by adopting "instant justice" mechanism created by themselves.
- LWE in Odisha was not as alarming as it was in adjoining Chhattisgary.[30]

He was to visit Kandhamal district on the 14th to review rehabilitation of the victims of the 2008 communal riots.

He had held the review meeting Behrampur.

"Politicisation of an unfortunate incident": June 2012

Referring to the 'hullabaloo' over the recent CRPF attack against the Maoists in Chhattisgarh, an editorial in the Organiser[31] weekly used statement from the DGP of the CRPF, leading nation's fight against the Maoists, to dispel any apprehensions that innocent tribals were killed in the BJP ruled states (which Chhattisgarh is), as "claimed by some".

Attacking the Congress, the Weekly alleges that Union Tribal Affairs Minister KC Deo's statement that those killed in the encounter were innocent villagers is part of the Congress Party's "true characteristic style" of speaking with "forked tongue(s)", pointing to the Home Minister's statement that operation was genuine.

The weekly defends CM Raman Singh's assertion that the Naxals use innocent tribals as human shields, reasoning that there could be casualties in a "pitched fight in darkness." It makes clear, however, it cannot be equated with "the cold-blooded murders the Naxals indulge in."

The editorial wants security forces to be allowed to function without "political interference."

"Let us not romanticise Maoists and demonise security forces:" Ramesh again: Jul 2012

Union Rural Development Minister is known for his contrarian views. Presently, the Maoist insurgency is occupying his mind. He is visiting 31 Maoistg-hit districts to explore the issue up close. In an interview with a daily,[32] he discussed Maoist politics, tribal displacement, and the land acquisition Bill. Points from his interview:

Q. How do you characterise Maoist movement?

Ans. Of 82 LWE-hit districts, core of the problem lies in 25-30 forest-rich, tribal-dominated, mineral-rich and remote districts. So far we have dealt with the Maoist-violence largely as a security issue... It has to be a two-pronged strategy of security and development. I found political mobilisation was missing. In its absence, young men and women were being forced to join Maoist outfits.

As I looked at rural development, housing and water issues, I found the fourth missing element of rights, dignity and justice.

The tribals have been displaced multiple times since the 1950s and 1960s, without proper relief and rehabilitation. Walter Fernande's study says the number of displaced is between 2 and 5 crores. Land was taken sans compensation. Development alone, building bridges and schools would't work. It is about rights and justice, implementing constitutional safeguards.

It has taken Andhra Pradesh decades to deal with the Maoist problem, combining security, development, politics, and justice issues. Despite my serious differences with Mamata Banerjee, I have seen the difference she and Shubhendu Adhikari have made on the ground. Mamata's action of going into Jangalmahal, picking up and kissing a baby has been for better than sending thousands of forces. Political cadres are active today in Jangalmahal.

Q. Your opinion on the recent Bijapur killing.

Ans. A judicial inquiry has been ordered. I have read the report prepared by the activists, and had a long discussion with the CRPF. As always, truth on the ground is incredibly comple... genuine mistakes may have been made, just as innocents may have been used as shields.

Q. What about killing human shields, many children?

Ans. I have a PS who was abducted by Maoists in Feb 2011 in Malkangiri, kept in captivity for 10 days. His abductors included 14-year-olds. What are these activists talking about?

Let us not romanticise Maoists. There is a certain tendency among the intellectuals and activists to demonise the security forces and romanticise the Maoists. I do neither. You have to be realistic.

Q. What is your position on land acquisition Bill?

Ans. We are giving flexibility to states. If Mamata wants the Centre to have no role and to de-industrialise Bengal... who are we to protest. The state must play an important role in land acquisition under well-defined rules. Land and information market are imperfect with an asymmetry of power and information. If you allow private investors to buy land, they would strike deals with large land-owners, bamboozling small land-owners. The state has to protect the interests of the land owners and livelihood-losers. This is what Singur taught us. Differing with the earlier bill, the present one explicitly recognises the rights of both land and livelihood-losers.

"Scam beyond parallel" in missing Bhoodan Land: Says Jairam Ramesh: Sep 2012

"Land mafias are looting land donated during the Bhoodan Movement (land gift) launched by Acharya Vinoba Bhave 60 years ago as has been now found by the Centre. It has noted that half of the total 5 million acres of Bhoodan land is "missing" in a "scam beyond parallel."[33]

Jairam Ramesh sounded the alarm bells, 20 Sep 2012: "Records of around 2.4 million acres of Bhoodan land in various States are missing and only half of the total of 4.8 million acres of Bhoodan has been distributed to the landless poor so far."

Government would soon order a survey to take stock of the land distribution process under the Movement.

Ramesh made these observations on the sidelines of the State Revenue Ministers' Conference on Modernisation of Land Records in New Delhi on 20 September, adding, "Bhoodan land is not being used by Bhoodan beneficiaries. It is being used by somebody else!"

Bhave, who launched the Movement, went all across the country, asking people with land to consider him as one of their sons and give him one-seventh of their land which he then distributed to the landless poor. But the officials in the Rural Development (RD) Ministry say that "the worst culprits" in the case of distribution of Bhoodan land are Rajasthan, MP, Jharkhand, Bihar and Andhra Pradesh.

For instance, in two blocks of Kishanganj district in Bihar, 52 people have been found to be illegally possessing over 800 acres of land, as per recent survey by the State Government.

RD Minister Ramesh wants to find out the exact status of Bhoodan Land through a countrywide survey, and thence proceed to initiated the corrective action.

In Odisha too, Bhoodan activists have alleged that the land mafias are looting the agricultural lands every day by displacing the poor in the State in the name of industrialisation and business. Some of them have also looted Bhoodan land by influencing political leaders and bureaucrats, they alleged.

Gandhian professor Ramjee Singh said the land problems have led to the Maoist activities in various states.

"Politics at its best, nay, worst": Dec 2012

Leader of Opposition in the Assembly Bhupinder Singh and Chief Whip Prasad Harichandan on 16 Dec 2012 demanded resignation of CM Naveen Patnaik for the alleged nexus between the State government and the Maoists, and demanded a probe in this case by the National Investigation Agency (NIA).[34]

Talking to the media, Singh said the CAG has revealed serious irregularities: The extended favours to companies developing five minor port projects at Astaranga, Chudamani, Dhamara, Gopalpur and

Subarnarekha under Public Private Partnership (PPP), in the Dal scam under the Supplementary Nutrition Programme (SNP) and the Mid-day Meal (MDM) scheme, incurring a loss of Rs 65 cr, procuring Dal at Rs 75 per kg against wholesale market price of Rs 46 per kg; the State failed to utilise the Central funds worth Rs 27,920 cr; and the Utilisation Certificate (UCs) were not submitted to the Centre in respact of spendings of funds since, 2003-04.

More importantly, the State spent only Rs 562 cr against the Centre's allocation of Rs 915 cr under the Integrated Action Plan (IAP), meant for the development of the tribal areas in 15 Maoist-hit districts. It doesn't speak well of the State's sincerity or determination to improve the lot of the tribal in the grip of Maoist violence.

Now, these Congress leaders speak about the Government understanding with the Maoists. Harichandan said: "We have submitted the facts and figures in the Assembly much earlier on the nexus between the State Government and the Maoists. Now the Maoist interlocuter Dandapani Mohanty and Rajya Sabha Member Pyarimohan Mohapatra told the press conference that the Government had paid Rs 6 cr to the Maoists for the release of the then DC of Malkangiri Vineel Krishna and MLA Jhina Kikaka."

Alleging that the CM is hand in glove with the Maoists, he demanded the NIA probe on the issue.

"Political mobilisation will weaken Naxals" Jairam Ramesh: Dec 2012

The Union Minister on 30 Dec 2012 suggested stepping up political mobilisation of people in remote areas to weaken naxals in their strongholds. He reasoned: "Political mobilisation is necessary. If political mobilisation is weak, Naxals can become strong. Wherever the mobilisation is strong, Naxals are weak."

Ramesh on a three-day visit to Jharkhand's Naxal-hit districts to monitor rural development works, advised political workers to spread all over the districts, even in the forest areas. "The tribals must feel that they are part of the development by implementing laws."

Asking Jharkhand to utilise maximum funds in the demand-driven MGNREGA this fiscal, he said States like Jharkhand, Odisha and Bihar should utilise more funds. He made further points: Latehar and West Singhbhum districts have done a reasonable job in construction of 79,000 dug-wells under MGNREGA; security operations against Naxals and sustained development in the rural areas could also weed out LWE; referring to the Saranda Action Plan in West Singhbhum and the Saryu Action Plan in Latehar, he said, "People did not earlier come up with their grievances. But now they are more vocal and opening up."

Later, Latehar DC Aradhana Patnaik presented the Saryu Area Development Action Plan to the Minister. He announced: funds would be released this weak for building 5,000 houses under the Indira Awas Yojana; 26 roads under the Pradhan Mantri Gram Sadak Yojana; and watershad programmes under the plan covering Bendi, Nawagarh, and Tarwadi panchayats of the districts.

25 May 2013 Darbha attack on Congress Convoy and Politics Over it: May-June 2013

The Maoist attack killed 27 people, including almost the entire Congress leadership of Chhattisgarh.

29 May 2013: New Delhi

Alleging the nexus between the ruling BJP and the Maoists in the State, the Congress said both are "hand in glove" to protect each other's interests. The party also kept up its offensive against CM Raman Singh by seeking his resignation over his failure to protect its leaders.

Party spokesman Bhakta Charan Das said: "There is substance in our charges, and we are making them forcefully." He dismissed suggestions that the attack occurred due to collusion of some party leaders with Maoists. He reitrated the charge that no proper security was arranged along the "Parivartan Yatra" route despite prior information given to the government. The party blamed the failure of the State intelligence for this tragedy, and asked "why no action has been taken against the State intelligence Chief, who is a trusted officer of the CM?"

30 May 2013: Raipur

The Congress Party boycotted the all-party meet convened by the State government to rework the strategies against Maoists following the Darbha valley attack in Jagdalpur.

The Congress spokesman Shailesh Nitin Trivedi saw no point in attending the meet when the government "has failed to provide security to our Parivartan Yatra."

Reacting to the Congress stand, the CM said: "They should attend the meet. There has to be a joint effort to fight the Naxal threat. It is a national problem."

"Ramesh fans political conspiracy theory:" 25 June 2013

Exactly a month after the ghastly Darbha Valley attack killing several Congress leaders, Rural Development Minister Jairam Ramesh said the assult was a 'Raajnaitik Saazish' (political conspiracy) as some forces do not want the Congress government in Chhattisgarh.[35]

He was addressing the condolence meeting convened by his Party in Jagdalpur to give Central government relief... Rs 5 lakh for the deceaseds' relatives and Rs 50,000 for those of the injured... to the Darbha victims. Those present included Parliamentary Affairs Minister V Narayansamy. AICC in-charge BK Hariprasad and acting PCC Chief Charan Das Mahant.

Ramesh expectedly indulged the Party: "The Naxal attack in Jeeram Ghati was a political conspiracy by the forces that don't want Congress government in the State. It needs to be noted that while the NIA has clarified that it is yet to find any conspiracy angle in the attack, Maoists too have refuted the conspiracy charges. Continuing speaking as a good Congressman, he said:

- The Centre and the Congress are effectively performing their duty towards Maoist problem.
- Naxalism has increased in non-Congress states.
- 82 districts in 9 states are Maoist-hit and 100,000 paramilitary forces are stationed there. The Centre has provided sufficient funds and forces to end terrorism, but it is the duty of the state governments to ensure security and law and order.
- He slammed the Raman Singh government for Maoist problem and taking away the credit for the state's development that actually goes to the Centre. Reinforcing this line, he said "South Bastar is the worst Maoist-hit area in the country. In 2013-14, the Centre gave Rs 2,400 cr to the State for MGNREGA, while in the last two years Rs 1,600 cr was given for PMGSY. All this development is due to Central funds."

He did not stop there. He added that contractors have links with the Maoists and commission reaches everyone involved in the work.

It is a pity Ramesh spoke like a good Congressman, but a poor Central Minister! His peroration leaves a bad taste in the mouth! He is too intelligent to come up with such a partisan performance!

"Jairam and others to spread Congress word at tribal meet"

"Looking to make a mark in a State (Jharkhand) where the party is rolling backward with every passing election, the Congress is eyeing the sizeable tribal voters," reported a daily dated 3 June 2013.[36]

Party top brass, including Ramesh, would take part in a tribal meet organised by Kendriya Pahada Jatra Samiti at Bedo, 35 km from Ranchi on the 3rd. Congress leaders due to attend: MP Subodh Kant Sahay, Legislative Party leader Rajendra Singh, and former Congress MP and NCST Chairman Rameshwar Oraon.

The Samiti, established way back in 1967, is holding 47th Jatra mahotsav that show cases tribal culture, tradition and unity.

Significantly, impressed by Ramesh's frequent visits to Jharkhand–officially linked with various development programmes–the Congress leadership has given him an added responsibility to resurrect the party.

"Maoists fighting their last battle in Chhattisgarh": CM: June 2013

"Over the days, since last month's (25 May) Maoist attack in Bastar, several senior politicians in Chhattisgarh and Delhi, have suggested the involvement of Congress insiders. Now CM Raman Singh has joined the Chorus." It was written by a daily of 4 Jun 2013.[37]

His interview is summed up here:

- "Kuch na kuch baaten beeck mein hain. Sui alag alag dish mein ghum rahi hai. Kai saare prashan uchhal rahe hain. Therefore, we have ordered a probe in the entire matter.
- He admitted Chhattigarh had become ground zero of the war against Maoist but rejected the demand for Army into the fight.
- "The state is going through a critical phase. Maoists have targeted Chhattisgarh but they are fighting their last battle... Army should not be deployed in Bastar. Situation is different than in Kashmir. Maoists are hidden among tribals. Police and CRPF are adequate for this task. We need a unified force, better trained and equipped.
- "His government was focused on development. Naxals don't want development. They committed this major incident to bring the focus back on violence and Naxalism. Chhattisgarh is the nucleus of the battle. This is a decisive geography where Maoists can be finally defeated... The roots of democracy are much deeper. We will emerge stronger.
- He was reminded of the row sporked by former DGP Punjab KPS Gill's claim that when he was the security advisor to the State, the CM told him to take his salary and sit back. CM gave a very sober

and mature reply to this jibe: "We invited Gill Sahab as an advisor. He had meetings with forces and gave suggestions. The situation of Punjab is different from Bastar as it has a different terrain. How many of his suggestions were accepted, only our police can tell. He was an expert, came here for a few days, then left."

One does not know in what context Gill made this rather 'uncomplementary remark' about the CM. Knowing Gill's ways, one can say he would have tried to take over as DGP of the state (forgetting he was just an advisor), which the then incumbent wouldn't have liked. Hence Gill's early exit!

"Law, society can together eradicate Naxalism: Guv: Jul 2013 Governor has his say, too

Jharkhand Governor Syed Ahmad had been in the job for nearly two years: A daily intervewed him. Here are excerpts from the interview on this subject of this book.[38]

Q. The State is living dangerously with Naxals. What is the solution of the menace, in your mind?

Ans. Naxalism is not a new phenomenon. It is an age-old issue. It is not there at one place, but is spread across the country, and the world. Where there are no Naxals, something else prevails.

We have tried to open one school in every area to educate people and their kids. Kids should get education and jobs to convince their parents that Naxalism is not the proper way to demand their rights. Laws are there and they are being enforced also but when law and society put efforts together, then only these problems can be eradicate. Here law is trying but society is not able to curb the Naxal menace because people are not educated.

We are trying, especially in tribal areas to set up schools, colleges and universities so that tribal people get access to education. They should understand that they would be getting more money from jobs after getting educated than they were getting by putting their lives at risk in the hands of the Maoists. We are also trying our best to make the benefits of social development schemes reach the last person in the remote villages of the State.

The Governor-speak, so to put it, is rather simplistic, verging on the innocent. Still, it is worthwhile to record his views. His sincerity and conviction seem to be beyond doubt!

"Weakness of Centre is emboldening Maoists: CM Banerjee: Jul 2013

The weakness of the government at the Centre is emboldening the Maoists, the CM of West Bengal told a rural poll rally at Lalgarh in Jangalmahal on 8 Jul 2013. "Why should Maoists be entering West Bengal from Bihar, Jharkhand, Assam and Odisha? The Centre needs to be more responsible in curbing Maoist infiltration into the State," M. Banerjee said.

Other points and observations made by her are mentioned below:

- Her life was under threat from the extremists. "Whenever I come to Jangalmahal, I gets threats that Maoists are planning to kill me. If the Centre was strong, they (the extremists) could not have spoken in such a manner."
- The Trinamoal Congress Chairperson also accused the CPI(M) of joining hands with the Maoists, alleging that they, alongwith the Congress and BJP, had formed a pact against her party.
- "We will bring peace in Jangalmahal. Those who have disrupted peace here have now come together. The politics of terror and murder cannot win people's hearts," said Ms Banerjee.
- She appealed to the people of Lalgarh not to cast a single vote to any of the independents, as "they are taking money from both the CPI(M) and the Congress," she alleged.
- Without mentioning her name, she also criticised State Election Commissioner Mira Pande for her role in deciding the panchayat election scheudle. "It has been changed thrice and now it is going to be held in the Ramzan month." This would not have happened if her term had not been extended when the Left Front was in power, she charged.

"Amarinder dares AAP to deny its two MPs were Naxalites:" Jun 2014

Amritsar MP Capt Amarinder Singh on 30 May 2014 called two of the four AAP (Aam Admi Party) MPs as Naxalites. These MPs are Dr Dharamvir Gandhi, Patiala and Prof. Sadhu Singh, Faridkot.

The very next day, 1 June, the captain challenged the AAP to deny that these two MPs were involved in the movement, and added: "He will soon come up with more details about the other Naxalites, who have actively associated themselves with the AAP."[39]

"These people were trying to exploit the alienation among the educated unemployed youth of the State in a dangerous way," Amarinder said.

Meanwhile in a rebuttal the Amritsar District Committee of AAP condemned Amarinder for terming AAP as party of Naxalites. AAP Chief of Amritsar Ashok Talwar said: "Instead of accepting people's mandate in Punjab gracefully, the Captain is resorting to defaming party members through sham propaganda. Actually, the Congress was responsible for spreading terrorism in Punjab...?

Gandhi speaks

When contacted about the allegations Patiala MP Dr Gandhi said the question of having any link with the Naxalite movement was his "personal matter", and nobody should interfere in it.

Without commenting in detail on Gandhi's reply, One should dismiss it as bizarre and untenable. Public representatives cannot have personal belief, for which other Indians are questioned by the intellingence agencies and security organisations investigating Naxal activities. One hopes this MP knows that the declared aim of the Naxalites/Maoists is to overthrow the elected government of India through armed warfare, and subsequently take over the power.

The Captain had also said, at the end that "Dr Balbir Singh, who is believed to be keen on contesting the Patiala (City) bypoll on the AAP ticket, had been associated with the Communist Party of India (Marxist-Leninist), (which in a manner can be perceived to be a progenitor of the CPI (Maoist), popularly known as Naxalites).

"CPI urges Maoists to join democratic process" Jun 2014

In the wake of Union Home Minister Rajnath Singh's statement suggesting the end of the road for dialogue with the Maoists, the Communist Party of India (CPI) on 28 Jun 2014 urged the LWE xtremists to give up violence and join the democratic process.[40]

In a statement, may be, by way of an counteract, the Centeral Secretariat of the CPI expressed disappointment over the Home Minister's remarks on no further talks with the Maoists, saying: "The CPI is disappointed with the directive of the Minister that they will be dealt with in a sterner manner... The LWE should be dealt with a socio-economic perspective which needs a political solution. Earlier attempts to treat it as a law and order problem has failed miserably... It was government's responsibility to save lives and properties... So long as poverty, indiscriminate exploitation of tribals, loot of mineral wealth continued and policy of land denial to tillers existed, this issue will continue to crop up again and again".

The statement further continued: "The root cause should be properly identified, and all attempts to solve the problem, including dialogue with Naxals to bring them to mainstream, should be tried."

The CPI asked Maoists and other armed extremist groups to "come out of the concept of individual annihilation and violence and participate in democrate struggles in the country."

"Army can solve Naxal issue in four hours, but my heart won't allow it": CM Raman Singh: May 2015: An Interview

Amid talks about possible revival of the controversial Salwa Judum movement in Chhattisgarh, CM said the issue–of local villagers being brought to the fore-front in the fight against Naxals... was a "highly sensitive" one. If villagers, alongside the security forces, were to tackle Naxals head-on in the open, the government would have to ensure their protection, Singh told the daily, reacting to suggestion made by some local leaders about the revival of the anti-Naxal force, al be it under a different **avatar**.

Days before PM Narendra Modi visited the Naxal-hit Bastar region on 5 May 2015, Chhavindra Karma, sone of the late Congress leader and Salwa Judum founder Mahendra Karma, had issued a public statement about launching a public awareness campaign or "Jan Jagaran abhiyan" against Naxals.

As is known, Mahendra Karma was killed along with other Congress leaders and party workers, in a Naxal attack in Bastar on 25 May 2013.

Naxals have threatened violent reprisals to any attempt at reviving the Salwa Judum, an armed force of villagers set up by the state government in 2005 to combat Naxals. Terming it illegal and unconstitutional, the Supreme Court had in 2011 ordered its immediate disbandment.

Some other important points and observations from the interview:[41]

- The CM claimed Salwa Judum was a people's movement, a 'Jan andolan,' for garnering consent among people, making them ready and creating a certain atmosphere–awareness have to be generated among people. "If we stand up against Naxals on the streets and bring the villagers along, I have to ensure they are protected. How far we should bring villagers–to the forefront of our fight against the Naxals is a highly sensitive issue. Creating awareness among people and educating them is a major solution."
- He never had any doubt resolving the Naxal issue... The government is working slowly but steadily to counter it.

- "It took 40,000 jawans as long as 12 years to hunt down (sandal wood smuggler) Veerappan. Here, there 1,000 Veerappans."
- He was against Army being deployed against Maoists. "The Constitution does not allow deployment against our own people, and neither does my heart. For the sake of an argument, if deployed, issue can be solved in four hours. But that should never happen."
- His most pressing demand to the Centre is for the state-of-the-art equipment to detect the IEDs, which caused 90 per cent of the casualties.
- He has urged the Centre for deployment of the Nagaland Armed Police Force, since they were most familiar with the terrain here.
- The CM slammed the previous governments at the Centre allegedly citing environmental concerns and preservation of tribal culture as (lame) excuses for stalling development in Naxal-hit areas. "The UPA had taken policy decisions that ignored the '*ameer dharti ke gareeb log*" (poor people of a rich land).
- Finally, he put it emphatically: "Abujhmaad (in Bastar) was cut off from the rest of the world. Not a single survey was conducted there. To keep tribal culture alive, you have to first keep these tribals alive."

Notes

1. Amitabh Srivastava, India Today, 15 Aug. 2011.
2. Debalirata Mohanty, Indian Express, 7 Jan. 2013.
3. PNS, The Pioneer, 8 Oct. 2013.
4. Ashulosh Bhardwaj, Indian Express, 8 Oct. 2013.
5. Milind Ghatwal, Indian Express, 8 Nov 2013.
6. PTI, Indian Express, 3 Apr. 2014.
7. Avish Kumar and PTI, Hindustan Times, 3 Apr. 2014.
8. Amarnath Tewari, The Pioneer, 5 apr. 2014.
9. Bharti Jain, Times of India, 10 Apr. 2014.
10. Devesh K Pandey, The Hindu, 10 Apr. 2014
11. Times of India, 10 Apr. 2014.
12. Pavan Dohat, The Hindu, 10 Apr. 2014.
13. Pavan Dohat, The Hindu, 10 Apr. 2014.
14. Hindustan Times, 11 Apr. 2014.
15. TNS, Times of India, 18 Apr. 2014.
16. Ashutosh Bhardwaj, Indian Express, 11 Jun. 2014.
17. Deepu Sebestian Edmond, The Hindu, 31 Mar. 2014.
18. Anumoha Yadav, The Hindu, 10 Apr. 2014.

19. Navtan Kumar, Sunday Guardian, 16 Nov. 2014.
20. Deepak Mahto, Hindustan Times, 24 Nov. 2014.
21. Deepu Sebestian Edmond, Indian Express, 26 Nov. 2014.
22. PNS, The Pioneer, 3 Dec. 2014.
23. Kumar Uttam, Hindustan Times, 3 Dec. 2014.
24. Deepu Sebestian Edmond, Indian Express, 9 Dec. 2014.
25. Taufiq Rashid in Srinagar and Sanjay Dey in Ranchi, Hindustan Times, 10 Dec. 2014.
26. Gautam Mazumdar, Hindustan Times, 24 Dec. 2014.
27. B Vijay Murty, Hindustan Times, 24 Dec. 2014.
28. Ashutosh Mhardwaj, Indian Express, 2 Mar. 2015.
29. Ravish Tiwari, Indian Express, 5 June, 2013.
30. Sib Kumar Das, The Hindu, 14 Aug. 2014.
31. The 'Organiser' is an RSS Weekly, quoted in Indian Express, 12 Jul. 2012.
32. Monobina Gupta, The Hindu, 16 Jul. 2012.
33. Pioneer News Service, The Pioneer, 21 Sep. 2012.
34. Pioneer News Service, The Pioneer, 17 Dec. 2012.
35. Express News Service, Indian Express, 26 June 2013.
36. Santosh Narayan, The Pioneer, 3 June 2013.
37. Ashutosh Bhardwaj, Indian Express, 4 Jun. 2013.
38. Pranav Pratyush an Santosh Narayan, The Patriot, 7 Jul. 2013.
39. Indian Express, 1 Jun. 2014.
40. Pioneer News Service, The Pioneer, 29 Jun. 2014.
41. Sagnik Chowdhury, Indian Express, 12 May 2015.

14

Counter-Naxal Operations

This chapter deals with the counter-Naxal operations by the CRPF and other issues that relate to these operations or impinge upon them.

The issues like availability of arms, loss of weapons to the Maoists, tracking the movements of the Maoists, incentives to troops deployed in the LWE areas, tenures there-in of various ranks, worries about the depleting strength, CRPF ranks falling to malaria and other sicknesses and the Force getting modern weapons, figure in this part:

"Joint ops a must to tackle Naxalites" New Delhi: 6 Feb 2009

The MHA on 5 Feb 2009 asked police forces of Maharashtra, Chhattisgarh, Andhra Pradesh and Orissa to pull up their socks when it comes to tackling Naxalites.[1]

The Ministry advised the forces to keep one another informed and jointly take on Naxalites on their borders. It also asked them to ensure that policemen sent on anti-Naxal operations are properly trained, have proper communication equipment and enough ammunition to take on the Maoists. At the high-level meeting in North Block on the 5th in the light of the incident on 1 Feb 2009 in Maharashtra's Gadchiroli–where the Naxalites killed 15 policemen, MHA Special Secretary (Internal Security) Raman Srivastava told DGPs of the four neighbouring Naxalite-hit states that "only well-coordinated joint police operations by them can tackle Gadchiroli-like attacks."

A senior MHA official, stressing the point made by Srivastava, says: "The spot of attack was just 8 km from Chhattisgarh border, yet the state police was not asked to join the operation."

An analysis of the Gadchiroli strike showed that the team of 15 policemen... who proceeded on the operation on being tipped off by an informer was not carrying any wireless equipment to communicate with their pears and had limited ammunition for their AK-47, and rifles. "The 15 men were out-numbered by 150 Maoists, and in the end, they ran out of ammunition."

The MHA official put the facts straight: "The Chhattisgarh police were only asked for a helicopter by the Maharashtra police... that too at a late stage when they did not hear from their police team. Eventually, when the chopper did take off from Dantewada, all the 15 policemen were dead." It also turned up that the 15 dead policemen, who joined the Maharashtra police in 2006, had not received specialist guerrilla warfare training to fight the Naxalites. Another team of the Maharashtra police sent as reinforcement, was ambushed by the ultras before reaching the spot.

The Centre believes the Gadchiroli attack to be the handiwork of the Tipagarh Dalam, headed by a couple, Diwakar and Jyoti. They entered Gadchiroli from Chhattisgarh to launch the attack. If the two states had mounted a joined operation such high casualties could have been avoided.

Maharashtra, sharing its borders with Chhattisgarh and Andhra Pradhesh, has been asked to ensure joint operations with them in future and ask for Andhra's specialist anti-Naxal force Grey hounds as also the CRPF.

"Joint anti-Naxal ops lose sting: IB Report: 7 Nov 2011[2]

It is ironic indeed that the last article has advised two states to launch joint operations against the Maoists, and this one says such joint operations have lost their sting, even if the two articles are separated by two and a half years. Even then, it should be worth our while to examine IB's reasons for their averment.

"A year after the launch of a much-touted joint operations against the Maoists, the Int reports paint a grim picture about the state of affairs. It shows the Red Brigade's plan "to intensify and consolidate" its violent movement by taking new areas in its strides.

Intelligence believes security forces have not been able to achieve enough attrition in the Maoist ranks, even as the ultras are looking at the North-East insurgent groups to get supplies in terms of arms and ammunitions. As many as 95 districts have registered incidents of Naxal violence of which 80 per cent are from 24 districts in six states.

The IB has expressed concern over the spread of Naxal violence to newer areas and accretion to military capabilities of the CPI (Maoist), that has significantly impacted the security situation in several states. The CPMF, meanwhile, have revisited the strategies, including retraining their men in jungle warfare, which have enabled them to strike at the Naxal strongholds.

A report on the assessment of Naxal violence in the country says: "of late, there has been an overall decrease in the level of Naxal violence but there appears no respite from casualties afflicted on security forces. Acquisition of additional weaponry and other war material also remained a prime focus of CPI (Maoist). These develoments indicate the future remains quite challenging as far as the dealing with Maoists violence is concerned."

Jharkhand remained the worst-affected State, followed by Chhattisgarh, Bihar and Odisha. But a significant fall in this violence was observed in West Bengal but new areas in Odisha, Chhattisgarh and Assam showed incipient ultra-Left extremism. The report further warns that the recent efforts by CPI (Maoist) to make forays into upper Assam areas "has been a worrying development."

New Developments: PFI enters the fray

The People's Front of India (PFI), a conglomeration of militant outfits from South India, is also trying to develop links with the banned CPI (Maoist) that is spearheading Naxal violence across the States. The report continues: "Although there was no sign of support by the Maoist Government of Nepal to Maoist movement in India, such a possibility can not be ruled out, which could, consequently, create a problem for India. Maoists were looking at the North-East insurgents to get support in terms of arms, ammunition etc. But the situation could turn dangerous for India if China decided to get involved in Nepal."

Failed Missions: Summaries of the above

- An intelligence report shows Red Brigade's plan to "intensify and consolate" its violent movement by adding new areas to its strongholds.
- The security forces have not been able to cause adequate attrition in the Maoist ranks.
- The ultras are looking up to the North-East insurgent groups to get supply of arms and ammunition for their operations against the Indian State.
- Jharkhand remained the worst-affected State followed by Chhattisgarh, Bihar and Odisha.

- The situation could turn dangerous for India if China decided to get involved in Nepal.

Intelligence wing sanctioned for CRPF

Finally, the government has accorded formal sanction for the creation of the CRPF Integrated Intelligence wing, reported a daily mid Jan 2012.[3] Among others, it will included an intelligence school that will train the officers and men of the CRPF in collecting intelligence in Naxal affected areas. The proposal was hanging fire for the last few years owing to various reasons.

The MHA has approved creation of 468 posts for the Intelligence School to be located at the CRPF Group Centre at Kadarpur, Gurgaon. It will be headed by a principal, a commandant rank officer.

The faculty will comprise CRPF officers who had been trained with IB, RAW and Military Intelligence. "Complete 'Training of Trainers Course' and guest faculties will be drawn from the Central Intelligence School" of the CRPF.

The School will offer five courses: Basic Intelligence Course for officers and subordinate officers; Intelligence Orientation Course for DIGs and commandants; Interrogation Course for officers and subordinate officers; Workshop on intelligence for Sector intelligence officers; and refresher course.

An official said, "The Intelligence School is first of its kind in CRPF and will train the personnel in collecting, collating and assimilating intelligence and converting the same into actionable inputs." That should go long way in countering Maoists.

Till date, the CRPF had to depend upon the local police forces of the Naxal-hit states for intelligence on the Maoists, and that was believed to be the main reason for set-backs suffered by the CRPF, and consequent domination of the area by the Maoists.

It sholuld be apt to point out here itself that the CRPF is shifting blame for their operational failures on to the shoulders of the State police forces. They are forgetting that even after they got their own intelligence wing, the best source for any intelligence is and will always be the local police, and more specifically the 'beat constable'. It was essentially with the help of Punjab Police and intelligence provided by it that KPS Gill was able to get better of the Khalistani terrorists.

Anyway, one would and should wait for a year or two to see if the CRPF's own intelligence would make any difference to their success in dealing with the Maoists!

The Naxal (Intelligence) wing will be headquartered at the CRPF Directorate at the CGO Complex and will be supplemented by Sector and COBRA headquarters in the operational areas. The Wing will initially be headed by a commandant rank officer and sector and COBRA headquarters to be headed by a deputy-commandant rank official.

The Force had earlier created an intelligence unit out of its own resources by deputing officials and staffers on an ad-hoc basis.

Its Intelligence Wing would create a data base of the Naxal masterminds/ leaders in different State and the Force would target the top rung of the banned CPI (Maoist).

CRPF insiders believe the sanctioned strength of its Intelligence Wing is sufficient for the time being, and the number might be raised if there was a need in the future.

For the present, the break up of the planned Intelligence Wing is, post-wise:

Commandants	9
Deputy Commandants	28
Inspectors and Sub-Inspesctors	57 each
Head constables	140
Constables	132
Administrative staff	The remaining numbers

"Maoist payoff case: Essar's contractor to turn approver": Dantewada: 9 Jul 2012

"Essar's former contractor in Dantewada, BK Lala, has decided to turn police approver in the alleged Maoist payoff case and disclose 'evidence' against company's alleged illegal activities in the Naxal-hit areas."[4]

The case hit the headlines in 2011 after Dantewada police booked the company and its officials for providing financial help to Maoists. A special Investigation Team (SIT) is investigating the case and a trial is on in the Dantewada court. Lala's advocate Rahul Tyagi told the daily: "We got a hint from the prosecution that if he (Lala) becomes an approver, he will be pardoned. So we decided accordingly."

Lala, the then chief contractor of the Essar in the region, was arrested in Sep 2011 when he was allegedly handing over Rs 15 lakh on behalf of company to Maoists through "Conduits" Soni Sori and Limgaram Kodapi. As the company was accused of paying extortion money to Maoists, Essar GM DVCS Verma was arrested and slapped with sedition charges. Sori and Kodapi are still in jail, while Verma and Lala are out on bail. Essar washed its handsoff Lala after the case came to light.

In a recent application before a Dantewada court, Lala claimed to have evidence against top officers of Essar against whom investigation is pending. "The applicant is willing to make a true and full disclosure of the whole circumtances and every other person concerned... owners of Essar company, Sunil Bajaj, Dilip Oomen, AK Banerjee, Babu, Srinivas Rao Chapa." These names are among the top Essar officials facing investigations. Former Dantewada SP Ankit Garg had earlier described Srinivas Rao as an "absconder".

Seeking pardon in the case, Lala's said: "Such disclosures and evidence will bring to light the modus operandi and activities of Essar, its owners and employees and their criminal activities in the Naxal-hit areas."

Essar has a big plant in Baildadila in Dantewada to supply iron ore fines through its pipeline to Vishakhapatnam. The second largest slurry pipeline on earth was blasted by Maoists a few years ago and remained damaged for over a year until Lala was appointed a contractor. He got it repaired soon, among allegations that the company paid money to the Maoists. While the company refuted the charges, Garg filed a case against Essar for supporting the Maoists.

On Lala's roll in paying the extotion money to Maoists, Tyagi said: "I am not saying he did not commit any crime... I am only saying what he did was on the instructions of the Essar. But all their officials are out, Lala is made an accused. If he is given pardon, we will reveal everything about the case and Essar's connections."

In his application, Lala also claimed to have evidence against NGO Jai Johar Sema Sansthan and its owner Paswan Dubey. Essar was allegedly routing its money under Corporate Social Responsibility (CSR) policy in Dantewada region through the NGO. The then SP, had said Dubey was also acting as a conduit between the Maoists and Essar, which has strongly refuted the charges as BASELESS.

"Panel blocks MHA plans for cell towers in Naxal areas: New Delhi: 26 Nov 2012

The MHA's push for mobile connectivity to counter Naxal insurgency is back to the drawing board as the Telecom Commission (TC) has turned down the Rs 5,800 cr proposal to set up mobile towers in the nine Maoist-hit state.[5]

The Department of Telecom (DOT) is preparing a fresh feasibility report after a 2-member panel of the TC said in Oct 2012 that the government should provide satellite phones to the CPMF rather than set up towers for mobile connectivity in the Naxal-hit regions. The TC argument: "The cost of setting up each tower works out to Rs 1 cr. Further, due to insurgency in these areas, these towers are always under threat. The possibility may be explored to use other technology, e.g., provisioning of satellite phones which addresses both connectivity and security concerns."

"Satellite technology may be better option in these circumstances because satellite communication facilities work in remote, inaccessible and hilly areas... At the same time, this technology option may be more economic in comparison to the current proposal," said the TC panel, comprising member (technical) and member (finance).

In Apr 2012, DOT moved a Cabinet proposal for Rs 1,896 cr as subsidy from the Universal Service Obligation Fund (USOF) to instal 1,836 towers and equipment through state-run Bharat Sanchar Nigam Ltd. (BSNL) in the nine states. It sought another Rs 3,911 cr for running the new towers and the existing 363 towers in these states for five years. But the proposal was returned for review after objections by the Finance Ministry, then under Pranab Mukherjee, that a large subsidy was being sought from the USOF while BSNL was being nominated for executing the project without the USOF's mandatory tender process.

BSNL subsequently "recalculated" the projec cost and the subsidy at Rs 3,792 cr, but even this is considered high by the TC panel, which supports satellite telephony.

Using the TC's input, the DOT has now proposed that in the short run, a global mobile personal communication gateway be set up with DOT funding for providing satellite-based communication services to meet the immediate requirements of the security forces. "However, the cost of user terminals and tariff will not be funded by the doT", it said. The new feasibility report would work out the money required from the USOF for switching to satelllite telephony.

As for providing mobile services to the general public in these areas, DOT plans to set up a committee under the chairmanship of its advisor (technical) to examine all technology options and suggest a "suitable solution" within a month of its formation.

Twice in the past, DOT nominated BSNL to carry out the work considering its urgency, sensitive nature and lack of commercial viability in the Naxal-hit areas but had to re-visit its proposals.

The dilly-dallying has resulted in a two-year delay since the MHA first sought improved reach in the 80 districts to track and tackle the Naxals through better connectivity among the para paramilitary forces.

"Keep track of Naxal under trials:" CRPF Chief tells the State DsGP

CRP has urges Maoist-hit States to keep a track of Naxal undertrials who furnish false sureties and jump the bail to merge into local population, as reported in a daily in Dec 2012.[6]

In a separate letters to police chiefs of Chhattisgarh, Jharkhand, Odisha and Bihar in Nov 2012, DG CRPF Pranay Sahay urged them to keep a track of the trials being conducted in important Naxal cases where-in they have inflicted huge losses on security forces.

Sahay further urged the DGs to impress upon the courts that the sureties must be well verified and at times the State can insist that only Government servants stand sureties when the case involves a senior Naxal leader. Sahay said in his letter: "It is absolutely essential to keep a track of such Naxal cadres whenever they are released on bail so that the security forces can keep a track of their accomplices, their hide-outs and their modus operandi by keeping a covert watch and ensuring appropriate surveillance."

Sahay suggested setting up a Special Court Monitoring Team at the State level so that the objective of bringing the Naxal cadres under the ambit of law is successful.

"It should also be thought of whether two or three different charge sheets can be filed under different sections of the law, so that as a matter of strategy, conviction can be obtained early in a particular chagesheet and the sentence period starts. This can go a long way to demotivate the Naxal cadres and also dissuade the fence setters from joining the Naxal movement," the CRPF DG said in his letter.

In another letter to the police chiefs, Sahay advised the DsGP to review the security arrangements of the Naxal undertrials. He expressed concern over a recent incident in Giridih wherein Maoists ambushed a jail van in broad daylight and freed six of their senior leaders. 33 other prisoners also escaped from the jail van in what was a major set back to the concerted anti-Naxal efforts put in by the security forces in the last two years.

It is necessary to ensure that the undertrial prisoners being taken from jail to courts are escorted by a competent and strong police escort.

"CRPF cautions about fresh attacks from Maoists"

There has been a lull in the Maoist violence over the last few months. Lest this induce a sense of complacency, CRPF has issued orders cautioning their formation against this possibility. In specific terms, its field commanders have been ordered to keep conducting anti-Naxal operations/ offensives on regular intervals with or without success so that they are not only familiar with the terrain but also remain active in the ultras' strongholds.

It was reported by a daily in Dec 2012. Intelligence inputs suggest the Maoists, of late, are active on the Gadchiroli-Andhra Pradesh axis and are planning to step up their offensive in the trijunction area of the Chhattisgarh-Andhra Pradesh-Odisha borders. Sources said while the deployment of the CRPF and the State police forces in this tri-junction area is nearly adequate to counter the Maoists, but lack of presence of the State police components in Gadchiroli, Maharashtra is a cause of concern.

In conduct of anti-Naxal operations by the CRPF, the presence of State police is a must, not only because the police has a better knowledge about geography of the area and its inhabitants but also because policing is a State subject under the Indian Constitution.

The anti-Naxal operations being conducted by the Central security forces/CRPF are also not resulting in good success because even IB "is not coming up with solid actionable inputs about the Maoists, particularly about their leadership positions. In specific terms, the IB has not been able to come up with any information on the replacement of Kishanji, who was eliminated in West Bengal in 2001, nor of Sabyasachi Panda, who was expelled from the CPI (Maoist) over the power tussle in the party.

One indication of shifting tactics of the Maoists is recovery of new types of weapons like one grenade launcher, two pistols, one M16 rifle, one carbine and one SBBL gun of foreign origin from the Maoists during operations in Jharkhand since 2011, "This is an indication of the fact that they (Maoists) are procuring weapons from different sources," the MHA had told the Parliament in early Dec 2012.

Even more significantly, the intelligence inputs indicated that some senior cadres of the Communist Party of Philippines had imparted training to the cadres of CPI (Maoist) in 2005 and 2011, and the "Centre is monitoring the evolving situation."[7]

"Security forces lag behind Maoists in human intelligence" New Delhi: 14 Jan 2013

This is an interesting, if surprising inference by a daily, giving low grades to the security forces compared to the Maoists, in the field of human intelligence.

"In the Latehar encounter, while Maoists got real time (intelligence) information on troop movement in the Karmatiya forests leading to Monday's ambush that killed 10 security men, anti-Naxal forces learnt of the movement of ultras only after they left a village."[8]

The daily then goes into the specifics. A contingent of CRPF and Jharkhand Jaguars was on the trail of senior Maoist leader Arvindji since 10 Dec 2012 when they learnt of his movement in the Karmatiya forests. "We always received information on his location late. He stayed in a certain village for a fortnight but we received information about it only after he left," said a CRPF officer, privy to operational details.

Maoists, however learnt of CRPF planning to raid Katoya village and had positioned themselves on the hills abutting the village, leading to an ambush. Sources in the force said there was not only a need for better human intelligence but better technical intelligence, phone interceptions and coordination within the IB.

Meanwhile, a reinforcement of 1000 CRPF men "is being sent to continue operations in Latehar and to extend it to Garhwa. The MHA has asked CRPF to launch a similar operation in Sukma. CRPF is on a recruiting spree for offensives this year and the next (2014) with 12,000 men expected to join the force through centralised exams. The force is also awaiting the MHA nod to launch special recruitment drives in Naxal-hit, border and tribal areas which have vacancies running upto 90 per cent.

"200 Maoists took part in 3-day training" Bhubaneswar: 26 Jun 2013

Two alleged Maoists arrested in connection with 25 May 2013 attack on congress convoy have told the NIA that they took part in the attack on the direction of senior Andhra Pradesh cadre Uday.[9]

Identified as Kosa Kunjam and Ura Madhi from Katmateru village, they carried arms used in the attack. Their village is 1 km from the Chhattisgarh-Odisha border. They revealed details of the "planning" of the Naxal attack that killed 28 people, including senior Congress leaders.

The NIA plan to seek custody of the two to show them photographs of top Naxal leaders who might have taken part in the attack. Some suspects from Chhattisgarh too are being questioned.

Malkangiri SP Akhileshwar Singh revealed the details as gethered from the two: Some 200 Maoists took part in the 3-day training at Kirtipalli village; on completion of training, they were divided into four groups, who walked to the Tulsi Dongar area separately, thence the groups met at a particular point where 12-13 from Odisha stayed back; and the rest walked for two days to reach the ambush site. Post-ambush, they returned and met the Odisha Maoists. Thene, they dispersed. But Kunjam and Madhi could not see clearly how the Congressmen were killed. They recalled seeing the blasts and hearing 'firing'.

Odisha DGP Prakash Mishra told the daily that they informed the NIA about the arrest of the two Naxals. He said initial questioning revealed that of the 200 Maoists who took part in the attack, 30 were from Odisha and the rest from Chhattisgarh.

The Malkangiri police were on the look out for Kunjam and Madhi in connection with an IED haul.

"Fine village if a villager helps Naxals:" says Mumbai Police Commissioner: 19 Aug 2013

"Holding entire village responsible in case a village is found to be supporting Naxals as well as slapping collective fine and curfew on all its residents."

These are some of the measures neither original nor very practical and advisable to deal with the Naxalites suggested by Mumbai Police Commissioner Satyapal Singh, in his article in the latest issue of the Indian Police Journal, a quarterly publication of the Bureau for Police Research and Development.[10]

The title of the article was "Fire in Forest: Tackling Maoist Menace"; it was published in the Jan-Mar issue. He refers to Maoists as "snakes". In a section titled "Population Control Measures," Singh talks about restricting movement of Maoist cadres and separating them from general population. His prescriptions follow.

"Extremist and public movement should be regulated through the institution of collective responsibility. The entire village should be held responsible if one among them hosts extremists, attends a Maoists meeting, or helps them by blocking roads."

"A collective fine for all the village residents or curfew for two days may be thought of. Alternatively, the village sarpanch, police patil and other village elders should be punished.

His three point formula for police: "Snakes should be driven out or neutralised, this principle may sound to some as violative of animal or human right, but... almost every one, except the sickly or coward, believe in it."

The section ends with: "Should security agency wait for their attack or should it go all out in search of them? When there is question of killing or being killed, who would prefer to be killed, instead of taking the other's life?"

Then he makes two inane and foolish averments. "Pumping of lakh of rupees has not lessened the Maoist problem or helped the administration win over locals."

"The locals are not with the administration and we should admit it. Even their passive neutrality is advantageous to Maoist militants and an obstacle for security agencies. Building roads, bridges and electrification of villages where our 70-80 per cent of Budget is being spent, has shown little improvement in the quality of life of locals."

Among his suggestions to tackle Naxalism, Singh offers recruitment to the surrendered Maoists in the district police. "If an offer is made by the government that all the cadres who surrender will be recruited in the district police, I am sure half the Naxals will come forward."

The daily records that despite repeated attempts, Singh could not be reached for comment.

Boycotting the Polls: Maoist Strategy, New Delhi: 12 Mar 2014, Lok Sabha Elections: 2014

The title of this news story reads: "Sukma Naxal ambush a 2-pronged strategy." The daily has a more direct blurb on the story: "'Chunao Bahishkar' details outfits' designs for poll boycott."[11]

The daily sees the Maoist game in its opening para: "The Naxal onslaught on the security forces on 11 Mar 2014 is part of an evolved 2-pronged strategy–to target political leaders and forces and conduct boycott campaign–to distrupt the incoming Parliamentary polls."

This analysis came to the daily's notice after it was able to lay its hands on a recently-recovered document of the banned CPI (Maoist) titled **Chunao Bahishkar** detailing the outfit's design for poll boycott through targeted attacks against security forces and political leaders.

The document was recovered by the forces on 2 Feb 2014 at Gaibathan forest area of Jamui district of Bihar.

While the political agenda entails an election boycott campaign, military designs include selective elimination and abduction of political leaders and targeting vehicles engaged in polling duties, besides ambushing police and CAPF. Surrendered Maoist leader and spokesman of the Dandakaranya zone Gudsa Usendi had earlier revealed Maoists' plans to take advantage of rather thin and dispersed deployment of the security forces during the polls.

The poll boycott campaign will be sustained by issuing press releases and distributing/pasting anti-poll pamphlets, posters and banners. They have also formed a "Vote Bahishkar Committee" to raise emotive issues like setting up of security forces camps, displacement, inflation, unemployment, arrest of Maoists and "Operation Green Hunt."

The document, issued by Jharkhand Regional Committee of CPI (Maoist), reveals plans to disrupt the polls especially in Banka, Lakhisarai, Munger, Jamui, and Bhagalpur districts of Bihar, and Dumka, Pakur, Hazaribagh, Giridih, Koderma, Dhanbad, Bokaro, Chatra, Ranchi, Sahebganj, Deogarh, Jamtara, Godda, East and West Singhbhum of Jharkhand. Similar plans exist for areas in South Bastar of Chhattisgarh, parts of Andhra Pradesh, and extensive landmine planting in Narayanpatna, Bandhugaon and Laxmipur blocks of Koraput district in Odisha.

As part of political tactice, to disrupt the polls, the outfit plans to organise meetings, rallies, torchlight processions and cultural programmes to spread the poll boycott message, besides taking disciplinary action against its own cadres found indulging in electioneering.

A note from the MHA to the Naxal-hit states informs them that an updated "Chunao Bahishkar Ghoshna Patra" prepared by the Eastern Regional Bureau of the CPI (Maoist) "would also be distributed soon". The note continues: "The CPI (Maoist) will be making a whole-hearted effort with a well laid-out strategy to subvert the poll process. The outfit will create an atmosphere of fear and vigorous poll boycott campaign."

The Centre also advised the states to conduct a thorugh review of polling stations witnessing violence in the earlier Lok Sabha and Assembly elections.

Besides advising the states to step up anti-Naxal operations, the Centre also suggested to implement a rigorous propaganda campaign at the grass roots level to enthuse the masses on the importance of democratic process and futility of (Naxal) violence, and encourage them to support election machinery in conducting fair and peaceful elections.

"India to get mine-resistant vehicles" New Delhi: 31 Mar 2014

New Delhi made an interesting if difficult-to-say-no proposals to Washington, as reported in a daily: "In a bid to avoid Sukma-type disaster... where 16 CPMF men were killed in a Maoist ambush in Chhattisgarh... the government has decided to approach the USA to purchase the state-of-the-art mine resistant ambush protected (MRAP) vehicles, which the US forces will leave behind in Afghanistan after they pull out of the country this year (2014)."

The spade work for the acquisition has already begun through the foreign military sales route with the Pentagon inclined to sell "excess defence articles" to India rather than be captured by the Taliban forces after the draw down. While the South Block has asked its officials to prepare the specifications of the MRAPs, there are five categories of some 3,800 vehicles currently in Afghanistan. Called Cougar or Buffalo, these over 14-tonne vehicles with V-shaped hulls, have minimised the US forces casualties, in IED blasts and ambush, both in Afghanistan and Iraq.

US gave some 20 such vehicles to Pakistan under the coalition support programme. The V-shaped hulls that can deflect blasts from more than 150 kg IEDs... routinely used by Indian Maoists... have a 6-inch thick bullet-proof glass, can run on flat tyres and have a maximum speed of up to 100 kmph.

A senior MEA official told the daily: "The Americans first offered the MRAPs to MOD some years ago without avail. This time the request has come from the MHA as these vehicles will help in transportation of troops as well as improve partrolling on the main highways in Sough Chhattisgarh."

Although the casualties in Tongpal ambush were partly due to violation of SOPs by the security forces and in spite of actionable intelligence, it was decided at a high-level meeting chaired by Union Home Minister Sushil Kumar Shinde that troopers needed extra protection with Maoists using planned attacks and area weapons. It was then that the MEA was alerted to approach Pentagon for sale of MRAPs under the bilateral Homeland Security programme.

Strong views on Maoists and their violent streak: New Delhi: 24 Jul 2014

The aim of this book is to give views of different persons and entities on the same subject. This is done with a view to enable future researchers to make use of this book as reference work. It is with this very aim that sometimes reports from two to three dailies are included on the same incident/ambush/attack/issue. The future researcher will have multiple viewpoints available to him.

This news story on the Maoists is from a weekly, the Organiser, generally believed to be a mouth piece of the Rashtriya Swayamsewak Sangh (RSS) and the BJP. The material was published in the Organiser, and subsequently reproduced by the Indian Express in its issue of 24 Jun 2014. The contents below are from the editorial in the Organiser.

"Maoists are the nation's enemies, crush them." This is the clarion call of the Organiser editorial. The provocation was the killing of 20 Naxalites by the CRPF in an operation in Chhattisgarh on the night 28/29 June (2014), and the consequent criticism that the action targeted a peaceful gathering of villagers.

The Organiser says: "It would be for the good of the country if the security forces are allowed to function without political interference. There are bound to be casualties of innocent people in a pitched fight in darkness. It is not a cold-blooded murder, as the Naxals indulge in. And such victims should be adequately compensated and helped by the state government. Politicians and pro-Maoist activists cannot be allowed to be the certifiers for the men in uniform. Those who are out in the jungle, fighting with their lives at stake are the best judge of their actions, in the given circumstance. Let us not demoralise them, after every small victory."

The Organiser refers to the injuries sustained by some CRPF men also in the encounter and observes that it was indicative of the fact that it was not a peaceful gathering of villagers. The journal refers to the remarks of DG CRPF K Vijay Kumar about the "peaceful gathering" claim: "The villagers do not gather at the dead of the night in the middle of the forest to dicuss forthcoming festival arrangements." Kumar had maintained that people from four villages were present and they were part of the "Jan Militia" the Maoists were organising to launch a major offensive against the CRPF, which was at the forefront of the anti-Maoist operations. He added the first firing came from the Naxal gathering, after that CRPF men could not but retaliate. At least six personnel were injured and four of them received bullet injuries.

Kuma said the Maoist sympathisers had earlier claimed that the men in uniform were injured in friendly fire indulged in deliberately to create evidence of the encounter.

The Organiser's reaction to the operation: "The very fact that the so-called human rights activists and the Left desperadoes have condemned the killings gives credence to the police version that it was a genuine operation.

For, going by the past track record, these arm-chair bourgeois-anarchists, stationed in their costy air-conditioned rooms, venture out to voice their concerns only when Maoists are injured or killed. They unfailingly keep quiet when convoys of security forces are blown up or when the poor tribals are tortured, maimed or killed by the terrorists on suspicion of being informers. The names that have issued a statement this time round, asking for a judicial probe, are the same as before, their number limited to half a dozen."

"Maoist operative killed in Pune slum", Pune: 3 Sep 2014

Are the Maoists expanding their base into Urban settlements/areas? This report in a daily would seem to suggest so. The opening paragraphs are quite explicit.

- "The Maharashtra Anti-Terrorism Squad (ATS) city unit nabbed an alleged urban operative of the banned CPI (Maoist) from the Kasewadi slums in the Bhavani Peth area here on Monday (2 Sep 2014).
- "Arun Bhanudas Bhelke, 38, of Ballarpur in Chandrapur district is said to have been in charge of recruiting youths for the banned outfit, senior ATS Inspector Bhanupratap Barge said. "Our investigations reveal that Bhelke had been active in Pune for a year. He had been absconding since Aug 2008 from Chandrapur after being released on bail by the District and Sessions Judge Court there. He was in touch with youths aged between 18 and 22 and was associated with an outfit called 'Mass Movement', which acted as his front. The ATS was investigating if he was attempting to indoctrinate Pune youth with Maoist ideology."

'Excellent organiser'

Sources said Bhelke, known to be an excellent organiser within the outfit, was fire-brand youth activist in Chandrapur who was active in Dr Babasaheb Ambedkar College in the district.

He formed an outfit called the Deshbhakti Yuva Manch, alleged to be a Maoist front for recruiting underprivileged youth. He was booked under Unlawful Activities Prevention Act (UAPA) in an arms case in Chandrapur in Jan 2008.

Granted bail, he went underground along with his wife, Bhoomi, alias Kanchan, who hails from the same area.

Bhelke, who used various aliases, lived in different places in the city, never using cell phone. He allegedly changed his appearance during the period. Meanwhile, the ATS is questioning members associated with 'Mass is Movement'. The outfit, comprising 20 youths, mostly school dropouts, purported to take an Ambedkarite line in combating oppression. The police allege that such outfits were a front to lure Dalit youths into the CPI (Maoist) cadre.

The ATS said it would hand over Bhelke to the Chandrapur police for further questioning.

"Some states want Maoism to continue:" Says CRPF Chief: 28 Nov 2014

This was a startling assertion made by outgoing CRPF DG Dilip Trivedi in a free-wheeling conversation with the journalists, as reported in daily.[12]

Coming from a DG, retiring on 30 Nov 2014, it should be deserving of a serious attention. It was given just three days before he retired, and it will be reported largely in his own words.

It was on the 27th that Trivedi made "serious allegations of Maoism benefitting Naxal-hit states." His words: "Certain states have vested interests in letting Maoist violence continue as it helped them get massive Central funds. The government is not serious about regulating sale of explosives whose easy availability to Maoists had led to increasing deaths of forces personnel."

At one stage, this retiring DG made statements beyond his call of duty, verging on to irresponsible comments: "Even blamed government policies and systemic problems for non-resolution of Jammu and Kashmir and North-East problems... Without talking about Army, he even said there was no need for Armed Forces Special Powers Act (AFSPA) and that the simple Criminal Procedure Code (CrPC) had enough protection for forces."

The above statements by this retiring IPS officer is perfect example "of irresponsible individual" venturing opinions on issues beyond his ken. His facetious and shallow comments should be dismissed with contempt.

But he does not stop here. He continues in his cavalier, even supercilious ways: He even hinted at various committees and studies conducted by the government for welfare of forces as waste of public money. Trivedi said: "Government could have just asked us. But the problem is we are not consulted. Consultants are hired who charge lakhs of rupees."

It was a question and answer session with the press. Asked about lack of participation from states in fighting Naxals, Trivedi said: "For some states, continuing Naxal violence is beneficial. It helps them get Central funds. But then, it is not their men who die but those from outside the state

(CPMF personnel)." Sources said the DG was hinting at Chhattisgarb, Jharkhand and Odisha.

As to how the Force was dealing with IED blast, Trivedi says: "The easier way of fighting IEDs is to ensure Maoists do not get the explosives easily. But the government is not serious about regulation of explosives' sail. State governments have to stop explosives from reaching Maoists."

Asked whether he thought even CRPF needed a special law, like AFSPA, given that it was working in a fairly hostile and tough conditions. Reply: "We don't need AFSPA. The CRPC provides enough protection to its forces fighting militants. India already has too many laws."

"In redrawing Red corridor, Centre faces a few red flags:" New Delhi: 26 Dec 2014

A daily draws attention to the NDA's plans "to redraw the Naxal corridor in the country... striking off several existing districts from the list of Naxal-hit ones and adding new ones on their 'potential of becoming a new hub for Maoists."[13]

Sources said nine districts in the Tamil Nadu-Kerala-Karnataka Trijunction; one in Bihar; and two in Odisha would be added to the list of LWE-hit districts. "The MHA will soon circulate a Cabinet note to redraw the Red corridor as the move also has financial implications.

The new districts would be:

- Kerala: Malappuram, Wayanad, and Kannur.
- Karnataka: Mysore, Kodagoo, Udupi, Chikmagalur and Shimoga.
- Tamil Nadu: Erode
- Bihar: Saran
- Odisha: Boudh and Sonepur

Presently, there are 106 LWE-affected districts, which get financial and Secutiry-related expenditure (SRE) from the Centre. For example, each district gets Rs 30 Cr under the SRE scheme of the MHA. Other schemes such as the Special Infrastructure Scheme, Integrated Action Plan (IAP) and civic action programme also add to the state's coffers.

Officials reveal the Centre wants to keep the number of districts intact at 106. Thus, to include new districts to the list, they will have to strike off (same number) from existing ones. This is where the Centre is facing resistance, since none of the ten states hit by the problem wants to give up the LWE tag from even one district, given the financial implications.

For instance, in the past three years, none of the three LWE-hit districts in UP has reported any major Maoist activity. "But when we go to the state with a proposal that these districts will no longer be eligible to be called LWE affected, we get a lot of resistance, said a senior MHA official.

Sources reveal "West Bengal too has been putting up tough resistance" when it comes to declaring districts 'Naxal-free.'

From 2012-14, only seven minor incidents were reported, whereas 697 were reported from the state between 2009-11. "Now it is a tricky situation as the state government tells us that any lull cannot be used to imply that the violence will not erupt again," said the official.

"HQ to clear anti-Naxal ops": DG, CRPF

"All Big operations in the LWE-hit states, which requires large scale mobilisation of security forces, will be cleared after approvals from the CRPF headquarters," said the new DG of the Force, as reported in a daily in mid-Jan 2015.[14]

CRPF DG Prakash Mishra "has taken the decision to monitor first hand important security forces offensives in the Naxal grid after he recently visited some of the worst Maoist violence-affected states of Chhattisgarh, Jharkhand and Odisha."

The decision of the new CRPF Chief is also understood to have been made in the wake of 1 December (2014) encounter in Sukma in Chhattisgarh where 14 Force personnel were killed during an operation where a large contingent of over 2,000 personnel of joint security forces were mobilised to strike the Red ultras.

Mishra, who took over the reins of country's largest para military less than a month ago, told PTI: "The large operations will be cleared by the headquarters here (New Delhi). I, including my operations team, will be involved with the ground operations during the planning and execution stages."

When asked if this "vetting" from the headquarters would lead to some crucial time-loss in launching operations, the DG said that with the advent of modern gadgets and tools, all such exercises can be followed on a virtually real-time basis.

"CRPF to hit at core of Chhattisgarh Red Terror:" Feb 2015

"CRPF has classified six districts of Chhattisgarh... Narayanpur, Sukma, Bastar, Bijapur, Dantewada and Kodagaon... as 'core areas' of Naxalism where it has suffered 67 per cent of its casualties in the last ten years. It is evolving a fresh strategy to counter the Naxals in these six districts."[15]

Out of the 482 CRPF personnel martyred since 2005 in the Maoist theatre, it suffered the maximum loss of 320 lives in these districts between 2005 and 2014.

The updated offensive planning has the CRPF treating these districts as 'Special Operational Zone' and it plans "to launch coordinated operations with focused approach in terms of strategies, tactics and training to raise the operational momentum in these areas."

Bastar Task Force: MHA takes contral

A Bastar Task Force comprising nodal-officers from various branches of this Force is being created at the CRPF Directorate in New Delhi for effective and fast disposal of various issues relating to the units deployed in these areas. A senior MHA official said: "Anti-Maoist operations in the core area will be precise, swift and avoid unnecessary holdings by the troops. Every operation will have an integral, pre-defined evacuation and reinforcement plan to avoid any counter Naxal ambush."

The Centre accorded sanction for special provisions to the CRPF for augmenting its infrastructure needs, motivational aspects, and compensation of its personnel deployed in these districts, now designated 'core areas of Naxalism.'

Presently, 19 battalions are deployed in the area, four more are planned to be deployed there to enable the force to launch fresh offensives against the Maoists. The MHA official continues: "Because of diverse geographical features, one area within South Chhattisgarh (read Bastar) itself is vastly different from other area, so is the Naxal tactics and so has to be the response of our forces. There is a need for clear cut and codified operational strategies for each of these districts." The offensive plan will be firmed up after careful analysis of the CRPF's own strengths and capability and Naxals' strategies on the basis of institutionalised data evolved over the last few years."

This whole new creation is going to become a part of the MHA, as one sees it. So, it is better to stick to the verbiage flowing out from that "wise" source:

> "The range headquarters under the DIG (operations) will function as Primary Operational Strategy Centre (POSC) and will act as focal point for operations with short, medium and long term objective. Each unit deployed in the area will have defined role to play in the formulation of operational strategies.
>
> "The elite COBRA battalions of the CRPF will now onwards be exclusively utilised for long duration and deep penetration operations,

with clarity of purpose, defined retreat plans and offensives designed to be of 'lightening strike and retreat' from core areas instead of 'come and hug me' approach.

"The role/participation of civil police in planning and execution will be clearly spelt out as an organisation policy.

"The personnel deployed in these districts will have a time-bound posting and profile of those posted will be young in order to avoid fatigue. After completion of tenure in the core areas, the personnel will be entitiled to choice postings. The incentives will be linked to operational performance like participation in operations, recoveries and other such achievements.

"The battalions deployed in the core areas will be provided sufficient special equipment and arms, optical devices and explosives besides deployment of mobile signal boosters to aid effective communication between different formations. Apart from other arms, the units will be armed with sophisticated Dragunov Sniper rifles to hit moving targets and demolition sets to destroy large number of pressure mines deployed by the ultras."

This is a hand-out from the MHA, which has divested the DG, CRPF of his legitimate duties and responsibilities. May be, this has even been done at his promptings. One has been reading press reports about the CRPF not faring well against the Maoists and it was planning to reserve the final approval of any major operation in the field with its headquarters at Delhi. That might have faced some strong opposition from certain strong field commanders in the Naxal grid... not that too many of that breed are present in its ranks! But every organisation, possibly even the CRPF, can have some mavericks who can suddenly behave "awkwardly" on cretain occassions!

So what do you do? Create a "Bastar Task Force" as a wing of the MHA, with all branches of the CRPF HQ at New Delhi represented there! So final word for an operation, in Naxal-hit Bastar would come from that 'elevated' task force! What a farce! That should be the proud privilege of the DG, CPRF! Why has that gentleman abdicated his responsibilities? Only he can answer that question. But he has given respectable garb to that abdication! And who will have last word in that Task Force? Possibly, some obscure deputy secretary of the MHA!

This Handout is a verbiage, too clever to conceal its aim. Imagine a short, medium and long term roles allotted to a CRPF battalion! Yet again, if a fleeting opportunity comes for battalion commander, he will have to seek the prior approval of the Task Force at the MHA. It has no sense from any angle!

Let the critique rest here... detailed one to wait some other time, some other place!

"Maoist Chief admits to loss of leaders, weakening base, asks cadres to open fronts:" Nagpur: 19 Apr 2015

Acknowledging "loss of considerable number of party leaders," the CPI (Maoist) has listed protection of its "Subjective leadership" as top priority and decided to intensify its campaign to strengthen cadres in view of the "weakened movement in the rural plains and urban areas." This is a daily, telling its readers that in his internally-circulated interview for the Maoist Information Bulletin, CPI (Maoist) General Secretary Muppala Lakshman Rao alias Ganapathi, listed challenges before the party: "We have lost considerable number of party leaders at all levels starting from the Central Committee to the village level party committees. Therefore, we have identified the preservation of existing subjective forces from enemy attacks as one of the foremost tasks before the party..."[16]

Stressing the importance of preserving "subjective leadership," Ganapathi called for "preparing new leadership and raising consciousness for a strong party with the continuation of leadership as a condition for success of the revolution." Admitting to mass surrender by active cadres, Ganapathi refused to attributed it to the "improved surrender policy" of the government. "More than three-fourth of the mass surrenders are due to targeting of the active cadres by means such as severe torture, rape, destruction of property, psychological warfare, threat to kill or maim etc."

Further points made by him are mentioned here:

- "Some individuals, PLGA and mass organisations are kneeling before the enemy. Yes, there is an increase in such numbers recently and a few from state, district and area committee levels have also surrendered."
- "The solution for all these is in raising the political consciousness and commitment of the cadres at all levels. The present Bolshevisation campaign is dealing with this."
- Ganapathi acknowledged that the Maoist party has weakened in the areas it existed for long. "We need to expand the movement to newer areas and open new battle fronts."
- Calling for sacrifice, including "supreme sacrifice" at all levels, he said there was need to intensify Bolshevisation (revolutionary commitment) campaign. "The reasons are intensified enemy

offensive, severe losses to the party and difficult situation faced by the movement, need to increase Proletarian trends in view of increasing non-Proletarian trends."

- He urged cadres to carry out "wide propaganda against the Modi government and Sangh Parivar's pro-imperialist and pro-feudal agenda," because these could lead to "oppression of Dalits, Muslims, and working classes due to new liberal and fascist Hindutva policies."
- He said there was "good potential for building and strengthening civil rights movements."
- Asked how the party proposed to face the "third phase of Operation Green Hunt (OGH)", he said: "We will have to resolutely unite all sections of people affected by Modi government's anti-people agenda. For this, our policies and tactics should be such that all democratic, progressive, secular and patriotic forces rally to gather, in favour of the people and oppose and fight back Modi's reactionary policies, and particularly the third phase OGH. The Parliamentary "Left will also be forced to take up people's issue. We call upon all forces to fight on all fronts against this multi-pronged enemy offensive."

It should also be noted that a couple of years back Ganapathi had addressed a letter to all his senior leaders on the same issues. That letter too had reached the press, which discussed it thread bare, bringing it to public knowledge.

"How, Why and What Next of the Maoist Story"

A significant analysis appeared in a daily that seems to be gazing at the future of the CPI (Maoist). Its blurb makes things more clear: "Five Maoists were arrested in the southern peninsula this month, and Home Minister Rajnath Singh said last week that the incidents of Maoist violence were on the decline.

How relevant is that claim? Ashutosh Bhardwaj answers key questions on the activities of the CPI (Maoist), both in its forest strongholds and clandestine urban bases, and gives a status report on its operations."

This analysis is in the form of question and answers. It is reproduced here in toto.

Q. Is the CPI (Maoist) on the decline?

Ans. Compared to the 2006-2010 period, attacks have been fewer in the last two-three years. But they remained entrenched in the forest zone across Central India, and dominate a far wider territory in Dandakaranya now than they did in 2004, when the MCC and CPI (Maoist) merged. In Chhattisgarh, over 50,000 CRPF, BSF, ITBP and state police personnel are fighting the Maoists, but politicians and officials still cannot enter many areas. 2014 is considered among the calmest years in a decade, but it was also the year in which the CRPF suffered its second highest casualty in a calendar year in Chhattisgarh.

As per the MHA figure, during 2008-14, 992 LWE cadres were killed, 13,657 were arrested, and 2,608 surrendered. But the data does not distinguish between CPI (Maoist) and other groups, several of which are active in Jharkhand. It neither distinguish between Maoists and suspected Maoists, and women and children killed in alleged encounters, and tribals sent to jail on flimsy evidence inflate the figures. Again, the MHA figures show 671 LWE cadres surrendered last year (2014), the most in the last seven years. Except in 2012, the number of annual surrenders has never crossed 400. Chhattisgarh claimed 421 in 2014, but as this daily has reported, 70 per cent of those individuals did not qualify as Maoists, and thus were ineligible to surrender. In a way, the data contradicts itself. There are not more than 20,000 armed cadres, and if over 16,000 were accounted for in the last seven years, the insurrection ought to have nearly disappeared by now.

Q. What is the Maoists' urban network?

Ans. Underground cadres who operate from the cities, sympathisers and supporters. Maoist documents stress on building a strong base in cities, and mention three kinds of urban mass organisations: secret, open and semi-open, and legal, the last including cover organisations and affiliated activists. The forest-based rebellion survives monstly on what Maoist ideologue Varavara Rao calls the "movement in urban area". From the urban network come logistics, moral and intellectual support, and the ideological argument for violence. The network is in several cities, and sympathisers occupy prominent positions. Central Committee member Malla Raji Reddy's daughter Snehlata and son-in-law C Kasim live on the Osmania University campus in Hyderabad. Kasim teaches Telegu and Snehalata edits a journal on revolutionary politics. "We support the Maoist movement, the only path available for the poor and oppressed. There have been setbacks but the movement will go on," says Kasim.

Q. How does the CPI (Maoist) operate?

Ans. A mammoth hierarchical structure operates on a 'need-to-know' basis. At the top is a 20-member Central Committee, headed by Muppala

Laxman Rao or Ganapathy. Other CC members include Nambla Keshava Rao or Ganganna who heads the Central Military Commission (CMC); military expert and Giridih resident Misir Besara; and Dalit Maharasthrian Milind Teltumlide whose brother is married to the sister of Prakash Ambedkar, the grandson of BR Ambedkar.

Under the CC are four regional bureaus, the most significant and active of which, the Central Regional Bureau (CRB), is headed by Katakam Sudarshan alias Anand. The CRB has three units: Dandakaranya Special Zonal Committee (SZC); North Telangana SZC; and Andhra-Odisha Border SZC. Slain leader Kishanji's younger brother and CC member Mallojula Venugopal Rao or Bhupathi is incharge of the DK SZC, the headquarters of the CPI (Maoist), and home to some of the top leadership. CC member Akkiraju Haragopal, who led the talks with the VSR Government in 2004, is incharge of AOB SZC. Its secretary is Modem Bala Krishna, also a CC member Pulluri Prasad Rao alias Chandanna heads the NTSZC. The North Regional Bureau comprises units in Delhi, Punjab, J & K, Himachal, Uttarakhand and UP, and is mostly defunct.

Zonal or State Committees are divided into area committees, which form the Revolutionary People's Council in villages. These have successfully replaced panchayats in many areas of Dandakaranya.

Q. What is their military capacity?

Ans. Bastar has two major battalions, Jharkhand has a fledgling one. The South Bastar Battalion, formed in 2009 and headed by Hidma, has the finest guerillas and has carried out nearly all major attacks in recent years. The Abujhmaad Battalion, headed by Ramdher, was formed in 2012, primarily to protect the top leadership soon after CRPF entered the area. Each battalion has formations like company, platoon and squad, but their numbers vary.

Bomb making capacity was hit after the head of the Technical Research Arms Manufacturing Unit Sadanala Ramkrishna was arrested in 2012. His aide Deepak Parghania, an award-winning technician from SAIL's Bhilai plant, was arrested, too. Units in Karnataka, Tamil Nadu, Bihar, Jharkhand and Andhra manufacture artillery, rifle parts, pressure mines, rocket launchers.

Q. Are there any fissures within?

Ans. Over the last decade, several senior cadres have questioned preeminent focus on violence, to the exclusion of mass awakening, building bases in the universities. Public executions in *Jan Adalats* have earned the wrath of tribals in many cases. "They are leading a necessary movement, but they need to review their violence," surrendered CC member Lanka Papi Reddy has said. Formed DK SZC spokesman Gudsa Usendi alias Sukhdev have voiced reservations against high-handedness by cadres. Of late, the Maoists have issued several apologies for attacks.

Q. Where has the state failed?

Ans. A democratic state functioning within the Constitution and law has a fundamental handicap in dealing with the challenge. There have been no killings in Andhra and Telengana, of late, but teachers, writers and journalists in cities from Warrangal to Guntur feed the movement many ways. Seminars in Hyderabad celebrated the 10th anniversary of the CPI (Maoist) last year. Spokesperson Azad lived in Delhi for years with his wife. There are enough disillusioned youth, who are attracted to their ideology, and to the lure of the gun, and romance of the forest life. In the end, the state must be able to demonstrate that the political system is not just for the moneyed, manipulative and powerful.

"Ultimately it is the local police's will that turns the tide to deal with Maoists" New Delhi: 14 Sep 2015

The country's largest CPMF, CRPF, has a strength of around 300,000 personnel. It is at the forefront of counter-Maoist operations. DG CRPF Prakash Mishra spoke to a daily[17] on the status of the fight against the CPI (Maoist). Excerpts:

Q. What are the new strategies adopted by the CRPF to deal with the Maoists?

Ans. Law and order is a state subject, and the CRPF has been supporting the police in Maoist-hit states to respond to the challenges on the ground. Central forces like the CRPF can provide the fire power and hold the ground as well in the hostile territories. However, based on my experience as the DGP Odisha, I can state with conviction that ultimately it is the will of the local police that turns the tide.

Q. Is the policy of having more boots on ground showing better results, especially in Chhattisgarh?

Ans. It is well-known and admitted by various quarters that situation has definitely improved in all affected states in general, and in West Bengal and Odisha in particular. Needless to mention, south Bastar continues to pose a serious challenge. The fact that 11,000 sq km area in Chhatisgarh has no presence of security forces gives Maoists their much-needed maneuverability. However, it would not be long before these unchartered teritories are manned.

Q. Do you think some states lack the will to effectively deal with Maoists?

Ans. I don't think the states lack the will power rather it is the need of the hour to look at the issue holistically and develop an appropriate response mechanism for the problem.

Q. Security forces have not suffered any major loss but haven't been able to catch high-ranking Maoist operative. Is it risk-aversion policy at work here?

Ans. It is true we have not been able to nab many big shots. But in 2015 alone, we have neutralised a states committee level member, three regional committee members, and a large number of zonal and divisional level leadership. All these losses have indeed dented their capabilities and fresh recruitments are not easily forthcoming. Slowly but steadily, there is erosion at the ground level which can also be gauged from the spate of surrenders, especially in Chhattisgarh and Odisha. Therefore, there are no reasons to lose hope and it would not be long before the force achieves something significant. It was only two days ago that we had an encounter with the strongest military formation of the CPI (Maosit) in Sukma, where in as per preliminary information we have been able to cause some dent to their armed cadre.

Q. What do you have to say on "one rank one pension" for paramilitary personnel?

Ans. I have no comments to offer.

National Counter-Terrorism Centre (NCTC): States adamant and refuse to bend

The NCTC has become a contentions subject between the States and Centre. The MHA has been trying to put this anti-terrorism measure on the statute book, but has failed over the past few years, to achieve this end.

Mainly it was an issue between the Congress-ruled Centre and the non-Congress governments in some states. But to make the things worse, even some Congress-ruled states have opposed it, as will be seen in the succeeding pages.

It is also a battle between the BJP and the Congress at political level, ever since the UPI-I repealed the anti-terror law, called POTA, which had been enacted by the BJP-led Vajpayee Government, claiming it to have been misused against "a particular community" (code-word for Muslim community in India). The battle goes on.

NCTC battles during 2012

The events of this year were set off by the Centre's (MHA) 3 Feb 2012 order, notifying the NCTC.

Chief Ministers write to PM to cancel the Order

The Centre's ambitious plan to create a NCTC appears to have run into rough weather with several non-Congress Chief Ministers attacking the move on the ground that it infringed upon the powers and rights of State governments.[18]

Nine Chief Ministers and a former Chief Minister, N Chandrababu Naidu of Andhra Pradesh opposed the NCTC. It is criticism of West Bengal Chief Minister Mamata Banerjee "that has hurt the UPA Government most. She and her Odisha counter-part Naveen Patnaik, in separate letters to Prime Minister Man Mohan Singh, urged him to "review and withdraw" the 3 February order. They say Centre counter-terror blue-print violates principles of federalism and encroaches upon the turf of the States.

Tamil Nadu Chief Minister Jayalalithaa said the proposed anti-terror body suffered from deficiencies and include provisions that tantamount to usurping the legitimate rights of the States. Ms Banerjee called it "arbitrary exercise of power by the Central government/Central agencies, which have a bearing on the rights and privileges of the State as enshrined in the Constitution."

Interestingly, Ms Banerjee's letter was released by Mr Patnaik's office in Bhubaneswar.

Gujarat Chief Minister Narendra Modi said in the name of fighting terrorism and Naxalism, the Centre was out to violate the federal structure of the country. MP Chief Minister Shivraj Singh Chouhan termed the notification a serious set back to the federal structure. Himachal Pradesh Chief Minister Prem Kumar Dhumal and his Bihar counter-part Nitish Kumar expressed similar sentiments. So did Chhattisgarh CM Raman Singh. Punjab CM Prakash Singh Badal said it "was a measure to usurp whatever was left of the States' authority in governance".

Amid the development, Union Home Secretary RK Singh defended the government move, saying the counter-terror body was in the national interest. It was being set up under the existing Unlawful Activities (Prevention) Act (UAPA), which have been in force for the past many years.

Congress and BJP spokespersons spoke on expected lines.

Counter-terrorn expert B. Raman said the NCTC, set up in the US after 1/11, had no power to arrest, interrogate, investigation and prosecute.

Till now, in India, these powers belonged to only the NIA and CBI and State police forces. By giving these powers to the NCTC, we are bound to create confusion in the investigation prosecution of terror-related causes. Mr Raman termed the move an "unwise step" that could further politicise the handling of counter-terrorism.

The NCTC will become functional from 1 March 2012.

Some additional remarks culled from the letter written by various Chief Ministers and quoted by another daily[19] reproduced hereafter:

1. "Why sweeping powers for the NCTC", asks TDP Chief Naidu.
2. Mr Dhumal told the PTI, "Whenever an incident of terrorism takes place, the Centre comes up with another investigating agency to divert the attention of the people and infringes on the rights of the State, weakening the federal structure."
3. Mr Jayalalithaa referred essentially to broad provisions concerning the NCTC-- the power to arest, the power to search, the power to set up the Inter-State Intelligence Support Teams and the power to seek information from any agency. Her letter was in response to an office memorandum of the MHA of 3 Feb (2012), referring to the setting up of NCTC under the Intelligence Bureau from 1 March. She said the power to arrest and seize, vested with the Joint Secretary in the MHA and the State Home Secretary, was now sought to be transferred to IB officers in the NCTC. She added: "This is highly, objectionable and can be misused to suit ends that are motivated by reasons other than fighting terror." She adverted to her "strong commitment" to supporting all measures and efforts taken to strengthen the unity and integrity of the country and for upholding its sovereignty. "I share the concerns of other Stae Chief Ministers who have expressed reservations against the attitude of certain Ministries of the Government of India acting in a high handed manner without due consultation with the States."

"Decibels rise in war cries on NCTC"

One day after, several dailies came up with more stories of strident opposition to the NCTC. The Union Home Minister P. Chidambaram was in Kolkata on 18 February for inauguration of the Regional Hub of the National Security Guard at Badu in North 24 Parganas district, West Bengal. The UPA ally TMC supremo and Chief Minister of West Bengal Mamata Banerjee was expected to attend the event, and her name was initially included in the brochure, but was subsequently dropped. It was construed as a snub from the Chief Minister for the visiting Home Minister. It was consequent to her letter to the PM, opposing the NCTC.

As the number of Chief Ministers opposing Chidambaram's pet project NCTC swelled to 10... Karnataka's Sadananda Gowda being the latest... the Centre (read Chidambaram) on the 18th sought to remind States that fighting terrorism was a shared responsibility. The States quickly retaliated questioning the Centre's responsibility by not sharing vital information about NCTC with the Chief Ministers.

The BJP upped the ante by demanding a meeting of the Inter-State Council. The Party said the proposed NCTC was not in line with that promised by the UPA and that the States should have been consulted on the issue.

Inaugurating the NSG hub, some 50 kms from Kolkata, Mr Chidambaram turned to the Constitution to assert that it "made national security, internal security a shared responsibility", adding, "I have a responsibility to work with the States to quell terror, any militancy or rebellion."

Although, Mr Chidambaram made no direct reference to the NCTC, he said the Centre, as part of its constiutional obligation, was responsible for protecting all parts of the country from external aggression as well as internal disturbances.

Communist-ruled Tripura CM Manik Sarkar on the 18th wrote to the PM, opposing the "National Counter Terrorism Centre (Organisation, Functions, Powers and Duties) Order 2012" issued by the MHA. He wrote that the order amounted to "an encroachment upon the powers of the States" and requested Dr Singh to advise Mr Chidambaram to withdraw the NCTC order and initiate a process of wider consultations with all States to evolve an appropriate mechanism for effectively dealing with the menace of terrorism in the country.

CMs conference on Internal Security: 16 Apr 2012

This event afforded the next battle field on the NCTC imbroglio between the Centre and the States.

Speaking there, Mr Chidambaram said, "As many as 21 terror modules have been neutralised and 64 terrorists arrested since the beginning of the 2011. Highlighting the continual trend of home-grown jihadis with no criminal backgrounds carrying out terror attacks, he noted that principal suspects in two major strikes... the Mumbai serial blasts and Delhi High Court blast... were Indian.

Significantly, without referring to the recent acrimony on the creation of a NCTC, the Home Minister stressed on the need for joint efforts by Central as well as state anti-terrorism mechanism. "I wish to underline the fact that one-half of the cases were cracked through the joint efforts of the Central agencies and state police concerned. This is the reality. At the operational level, there is no conflict between the Central agencies and the state police forces," he said.

PM Man Mohan Singh touched upon another aspect of the Challenge, emphasising on the need for a combination of sensitivity and firmness while dealing with the threats from terrorists, LWE, religious fundamentalists and propagation of ethnic strife, during his address.

CM Dhumal of Himachal Pradesh raised the issue of deployment of civil and military infrastructure by China along the Indo-Tibet border in the State and urged the Centre to broad gauge the Pathankot-Joginder- nagar railway line "I do hope nation gets its act together to counter any challenge posed by China".

Punjab Deputy CM Sukhbir Singh Badal sought a special security package for his State to tackle narco-terrorism and the LWE.

Though the Centre had stated in the agenda papers that it would keep the States in the loop while carrying out raids or arrests, and given even his opening speech, the dissenting CMs were not impressed. In her speech, Jayalalithaa warned against an "emerging pattern" of the Centre "abrogating" the states' powers through passage of bills. Modi said the UPA Government was pursuing a "non-consultative" approach with the state governments on key security issues. Patnaik sought urgent consultations between the Centre and States on NCTC, saying any further delay would affect law and order.

A side-show of non-Congress CMs at the Tamil Nadu House in Delhi's Chanakyapuri over-shadowed the UPA government's attempt over-shadowed the UPA government's attempt to reach out to the State heads on the proposed NCTC. Jayalalithaa hosted her counter-parts from Odisha (Patnaik) and Gujarat (Modi), at Tamil Nadu House apparently to discuss ways to mount pressure on the centre to drop the idea. It should be interesting to put this unsheduled meeting in some sort of historical perspective. "Though the outcome of these meetings is not expected to be anywhere as drastic as a similar one held by Jayalalithaa in 1999 to topple the Vajpayee government, the fact that she hosted the indignant Chief Ministers of Odisha and Gujarat has led to a speculation that they could be discussing more than just the creation of the NCTC."[20]

Tamil Nadu House sources said a similar event was likely to be held again on 4 May, on the eve of another CMs meet on the NCTC issue. Punjab CM Prakash Singh Badal may host that meeting at Punjab Bhavan.

Patnaik was first to (arrive and) meet Jayalalithaa, and two were closeted for over 25 minutes. Soon after Modi spent around 40 minutes talking to the AIADMK supremo. All the three refused to talk on what had transpired at meetings. Though Dy CM, Punjab was also scheduled to meet Jayalalithaa, he could not make it.

On the Centre-state issues, the three CMs are likely to find common grounds with Bihar's Nitish Kumar, West Bengal's Mamata Banerjee and Punjab's Prakash Singh Badal. These CMs launched a blistering attack on the Congress-led UPA government at an internal security meeting, accusing the Centre of meddling in the States' affairs by seeking to arm the NCTC with police powers and proposing intrusive changes in the BSF Act.

Ironically, the attack came on a day when bath the PM and Home Minister sought to avoid stepping on corns by emphasising and accepting the need for the Centre to work with the states. But the diplomatic approach did not prevent non-UPA CMs from hitting out at the Centre.

Home Minister tells CMs: "Don't let numbers fool you."

With Maoist attacks against security forces becoming increasingly systematic by the day, Home Minister Chidambram has scaled up the level of threat posed by the rebels... dubbing them as "the most formidable internal security challenge."

Prime Minister Man Mohan Singh, who spoke after the Home Minister at the CMs conference, said 2011 was a better year than 2010 in terms of number of people killed by LWE. But Chidambram had earlier cautioned the State heads against letting the figure give them "a false sense of assurance." He said the decline in casualty figures in LWE districts may give a false sense of assurance, "but that is not the true picture."

He stated that Assam was emerging as the new theatre of Maoist activity, and there were reports of Maoists linking up with the insurgent groups in Manipur and Arunachal Pradesh. He did not quote specific statistics as they had been circulated ahead of the meeting. The Minister made two significant admissions/disclosures; one: Acknowledging that the outcome of the bold forays into Red territory by security forces had been sub-optimal, he conceded that the government's "capacity to execute development plans is not commensurate with the nature of the challange and two: the Minister-who was instrumental in devising the Integrated Action Plan (IAP) that provides additional funds for development in Naxal-hit districts... said: "Still, we do not have the upper hand because there are not enough police stations, not enough men, weapons and vehicles; not enough infrastructure for the CAPFs; not enough roads; not enough presence of the civil administration."

CMs meet on NCTC: A stinging repeat, 5 May 2012: Non-UPA CMs were unyielding

If the PM and Home Minister repeated their set pieces before the CMs, the latter, far from being impressed, were even more scathing on the proposed NCTC.

The Prime Minister said: the UPA government was committed to working with them (CMs) and providing them all possible help to combat terrorism; the establishment of NCTC was not a "State versus Centre issue," not our government's intention... to affect the distribution of power between the States and the Union that our constitution provides for; NCTC would supplement, and, not supplant the States' counter-terrorism capabilities; the primary purpose of setting up the NCTC "is to coordinate counter-terrorism efforts throughout the country as the IB has been doing so far; the NCTC should be a vehicle of our combined efforts to reach the shared goal of curbing terrorism and eradicating militancy; drawing the attention of the CMs to the drafts of the Standard Operating Procedures circulated by the MHA, he said they reflected the detailed provisions for Centre-State Coordination in both the organisational set-up of the NCTC and in its powers and functions; terrorism was today one of the most potent threats to the national security... so counter-terrorism regimes at States and national levels are a must... Neither the States nor the Centre can fulfil this task alone; we have done a lot to strengthen our counter-terrorism capabilities both in States and at the Centre since 26/11... on the whole, there is a broad agreement on strategy and measures... to counter terrorism in its multifarious dimensions in India, including crossborder terrorism, LWE, terrorism in J & K, insurgency in the North-East and religion based terrorism... However much remained to be done."

In his opening statement, Chidambram said: advocated setting up of an anti-terror hub, like the NCTC; terrorists did not recognise boundaries and the Centre and States must work together to make the country safe and secure; explaining the rationale behind NCTC, he said it would be an important pillar of a new security architecture, given that under the constitution, countering terrorism is a shared responsibility of the Central and State governments; many terrorist organisations have capacity to commit terrorist acts across borders; human resources alone are not sufficient to counter terrorist threats and technology is the key weapon in this conflict.

Highlighting a new dimension of cyberspace in terrorist threats, Chidambram said it was the fifth domain after land, sea, air and space.

Now some observations made by some of the CMs.

Mamta Banerjee, West Bengal

She led a host of CMs in opposing setting up of NCTC: urged the union government to withdraw the 3 Feb 2012 order for setting up the body; she arged there was no need for it; police functions should remain the prerogative of the State as enshrined in the constitution; and the well-conceived equilibrium of powers and responsibilities between the Centre and the States should not be disturbed under any circumstances.

Jayalalithaa, Tamil Nadu

She demanded a sub-committee of CMs to look into the issue; the NCTC, as has now been notified, should be kept in abeyance as already demanded by her in a letter to the PM, till this sub-committee submitted its report, and any discussion on the NCTC is infructuous as long as notification is in force.

Naveen Patnaik, Odisha

He supported Jayalalitha on sub-committee of CMs, and suggested that she heads it; NCTC should not be part of IB and all actions should be part of joint operations; he apprehended that the NCTC would assume command in case of a crisis and act unilaterally without any concern for local sentiments.

Tarun Gogoi, Assam

Even he, a Congress CM, expressed certain reservations about the plan and extended support to the NCTC proposal with specific conditions.

Prakash Singh Badal, Punjab

He said the proposal went against the country's federal structure, Punjab had suffered huge financial losses owing to terrorism; and State Police played a key role in dealing with the problem.

Only Maharashtra and Rajasthan say ‘aye’

Congress-ruled Rajasthan and Maharashtra were lonely voice in favour of the NCTC, and thus were saving grace for the centre.

North-East States say 'yes' to NCTC

North-Eastern States barring Tripura ratified the Centre's move on

NCTC, but with some riders to control misuse of powers. Assam CM, as stated earlier, laid down certain conditions for his support to the NCTC.

Omar Abdullah, Jammu and Kashmir

Another UPA ally, the National Conference expressed its reservations over NCTC, by likening its provisions to the controversial Armed Forces Special Powers Act (AFSPA). He suggested NCTC assume the role of a coordinating agency, instead of controlling or prescribing counter- terrorism priorities for each stake-holder. He warned that independent operation without involving state police can cause serious law and order problems. He suggested NCTC have prior consultation with an officer designated, for this purpose by the State Government before launching its operation or undertaking arrests.

His final comment: NCTC as bad as the AFSPA.

Raman Singh, Chhattisgarh

Since terrorism directly affects national security, unity and integrity of the nation, there is need for both the Parliament and State Legislative Assemblies to make counter-terrorism laws.

Nitish Kumar, Bihar

He said the proposed NCTC reminds him of the Emergency days... He demanded its immediate withdrawal, because if such powers are given to a secret intelligence agency of the Central Government, they will remain prone to misuse against political rivals... "It has been an established practice and sacrosanct principle the world over that the secret intelligence agencies are not given power to arrest. None of the post-Independence Governments did so till date."

Manik Sarkar, Tripura

Even the NCTC of the USA, which is model for the Indian NCTC, does not have such legal powers of seizure, arrest... Arming an intelligence body, which is not accountable to Parliament or courts, with such powers, will have undesired consequences which must be considered dispassionately... He also expressed concenrs over proposed amendments to RPF and BSF Acts, which have serious implications on federalism and are tantamount to encroachment upon the rights of the States.

Narendra Modi, Gujarat

His critique of the NCTC was, perhaps, most scathing of all, and also had flashes of acerbic humour. It deserves to be quoted in full, as carried by a daily,[21] generally sympathetic to the BJP:

> "Coming along expected lines, Gujarat CM led the attack against the Government on the issue of NCTC from the front. His strongly-worded speech was acerbic in tenor and, at the same time, also laced with numerous tongue-in-cheek remarks.
>
> "While tearing into the Centre's bid to set up the anti-terror body, Modi raked up the issue of UPA Government's decision of repealing POTA in 2004. He said the Centre may be drawing a parallel between NCTC with similar bodies in the US and UK, but it failed to take into account the strong legal mechanisms adopted by them to tackle terrorism post-9/11. "Instead, he pointed out, the UPA I repealed POTA, depriving the country of the legal shield to fight terror. "And today, it seeks to use the Unlawful Activities (Prevention) Act to create NCTC through backdoor, thereby depriving States their rightful role." Modi said.
>
> "The BJP stalwart minced no words in launching a scathing attack against the ruling dispensation, whom he advised 'to come to terms with current political realities and change its mindset' of seeking to capture political space through devious executive mechanisms.
>
> "Accusing the Centre of behaving like 'viceroys of yore', he said NCTC constitution is a conscious strategy to cast the Centre as an 'omni-present' ruler with states portrayed as dependent vassals.
>
> "Apprehending that NCTC might bring covert workings of the Intelligence Bureau into the open, Modi took a dig at the Centre's move. He spoke of *guptchar's* connotation and essential quality being secrecy... The IB being such a *'guptchar vibagh'* has been a premier and nodal intelligence agency. 'Does the Union Government break this system and make intelligence an 'open char vibhag', which will be on display at every junction like a police Chowki'? Modi asked.
>
> "As the Gujarat CM charged the government with changing the 'well-defined and constitutionally mandated' boundaries of Centre-State relations, he pointed out there was a disturbing sequence of events in the recent past which revealed centralist and autocratic mindset that militates against all cancerns of federalism.
>
> "Be it proposed amendments to the RPF Act, the BSF Act, and the Limited Competitive Examination issue, the Union Government has behaved in a manner which reminds us of the Viceroys of yore.
>
> "He termed the proposed SOP giving powers of the 'designated authority' to the local ATS as another misleading move. 'It is another backdoor move to subsume even the ATS of the State Government in NCTC'."

"Jaya warns PM against NCTC bid" National Development Council Meet 27 Dec 2012

The NDC meet on 27 Dec 2012 (Thursday) was the last act of the NCTC play for the year, with expected results. This news item in a daily dated 29 Dec 2012. The NCTC must have been an important issue at this NDC meet, where all the CMs of the States are present, as it members.

All the non-UPA CMs repeated their strong 'no no' to their "pet dislike," the NCTC. But the prima donna of the show obviously was J Jayalalithaa, Tamil Nadu CM, for reasons not much to do with the NCTC, even if she shot off another strong letter to the PM, Man Mohan Singh, on the perennial issue over the past some years.

Each speaker was allotted 10 minutes of time to express their views. When the allotted time was over, the Chair rang the bell, and all hell broke out. She felt she had been humiliated, and stormed out of the meeting 'imperiously,' accusing the Centre of treating the CMs as "school children."

The day after walking out of the NDC meeting, Jayalalithaa cautioned the PM against setting up the NCTC through the backdoor. The MHA, the prime mover behind the anti-terror body, maintained that it was not rushing through it, and certainly would take into account the States' concern.

Summarily rejecting the concept of NCTC having operational powers of arrest, search and seizue in terror-related cases anywhere in the country, she wrote yet another letter to the PM, questioning him on the renewed move to set up central anti-terror body when several CMs were still opposed to it.

"Though Jayalalithaa in her letter to the PM merely reiterated her previous stand on/against the NCTC, the timing indicates upping the ante on her anti-Congress and anti-Centre stand.

Expanding on her Thursday's remarks after walking out of the NDC meeting when she alleged that the Centre's "arrogance and intolerance" had grown to "exceedingly extreme limit", the TN CM said any move on the anti-terror body was "another instance of Centre failing in its own commitment to consult states before taking a decision on the NCTC."

She said, "It is akin to the treatment meted out to me at the NDC on Thursday." The AIADMK supremo referred to "reliable resources," while pointing out that the MHA has again made a bid to set-up the anti-terror body. The MHA officials said there was no progress in this ever since Sushil Kumar Shinde took over the Ministry, as he first wanted to consult all the CMs individually before giving his nod for its operationalisation.

The Ministry, which had issued its notification on NCTC in February (2012), put its operationalisation on hold after almost all the non-Congress CMs objected to the anti-terror body at the CMs meeting on the NCTC in May. The CMs had clarified that a central body with wide powers of arrest, interrogation and seizure would hurt the federal structure of the country enshrined in the Constitution.

It seems Jayalalitha was still smarting under the humiliation she felt the day before when she wrote this letter to the PM on Friday, even if she had nothing new to say. She found the peg of "reliable resources" to hang this letter on! The Lady obviously has strong ego and too much self-esteem!

CMs meet on Internal Security, Its 2013 Edition: 5 June 2013

The 2012 Internal Security meeting has been covered in extensive detail. Nothing new of any substantial nature has been said during the 2013 session. But, as the event has been covered widely by the national dailies, a brief coverage of this important annual event should be in order, at least for the record.

PM and Home Minister stay mum on the NCTC

Significantly, Dr Man Mohan Singh and Sushil Kumar Shinde chose not to mention the controversial NCTC in their addresses, though they called for better coordination between the Centre and States on issues of internal security.

Two Congress CMs too voice their concern on NCTC

In a major set-back to the Centre's ambitious plans to set up NCTC based on a diluted draft, at least two Congress CMs... Maharashtra's Prithviraj Chavan and Karnataka's K Siddaramaiah... voiced their concerns over certain provisions of the anti-terror agency at the CMs conference on Internal Security on 5 June 2013. The heading of this news story in a daily was appropriate: "Even Congress CMs demur at NCTC."

This was the first time that Congress CMs "have openly spoken on their reservations about the NCTC, despite the fact that Mr Shinde has toned down the original version of the draft for setting up the federal agency, an idea mooted by his predecessor P. Chidambram, following stiff opposition from non-Congress States.

The major changes to the original draft include keeping the NCTC out of the purview of the Intelligence Bureau, and taking States into confidence before carrying out any operation in their territories.

Mr Chavan sought further examination of certain provisions dealing with operations against terrorist groups in the States. Some portions of the proposed draft that deal with operations against terror groups require further examination to understand the implications of these provisions for operational efficacy and clarity on roles in joint operations, he said.

Mr Siddaramaiah, who has been in the job only weeks, even argued that "some safeguards" were necessary to ensure that the proposed agency is not granted "unbridled powers" to encroach upon states' domain.

For their part, the non-Congress CMs stepped up their opposition to the proposed NCTC, which will be specified in the succeeding pages.

Prime Minister Man Mohan Singh

He chose not to touch upon the contentious issue of NCTC, though he called for "... coordinated effort by Central and State agencies to deal with terrorism and other security challenges."

In his inaugural address, he included various issues that impinge upon internal security: termed LWE a "very grave threat" to the nation; it is time to deal with challenges of terrorism, communal violence and LWE in a holistic manner; about killing of Congress leaders by Maoists in Chhattisgarh, he said such violence has no place in a democracy and urged for a national consensus on the strategy to tackle Naxalism; a meeting being convened on 10 January to discuss this crucial issue; security situation in the Kashmir Valley has improved significantly as terror incidents last year were the lowest in the past 20 years... the decline was one-third in 2012, compared to 2011; security situation in the North-East continues to be complex, but there has been considerable progress in dialogue with several insurgents and ethnic separatist groups; MoU has been signed with both factions of Dima Halam Daogah of Dima Hasao in Assam; three Meitei insurgent groups have signed a Mou in Feb 2013; talks with NSCN (1-M) are continuing; the Gorkhaland Territorial Administration has been set up as an autonomous body in Aug 2012 to administer the Gorakhaland region.

It needs a mention that erstwhile Home Minister and now Finance Minister, P. Chidambram was present at the 5 June meeting of the CMs.

Even the new Home Minister Shinde refrained from commenting on the contentious issue of NCTC. It was Finance Minister Chidambram, the NCTC architect, who took on the opponents, saying the country would have to pay heavy price if the anti-terror hub (read NCTC, a 'lead' word) does not come into existence. He deeply regretted that a few CMs opposed even the modified version of the NCTC. He told reporters: "I am afraid the kind of seriousness we should give to NCTC is lost. I regret that a couple of CMs opposed NCTC even in its present modified version. If this NCTC is opposed, I am afraid, as I said, the country will pay price from time to time.

Mr Chidambram, who was present at the meet, said had the Central Government brought the NCTC alongwith amendment to the UAPA, National Investigation Agency Act and with the Multi Agency Centre in Dec 2008 after the 26/11 terror attack, it would have got approval of the states.

Home Minister Shinde on Sikh Militancy

He blamed Pakistan for trying to revive Sikh militancy and said youth are being trained in ISI factories to carry out terror attacks in the country. He said: "There have been significant developments on the Sikh militancy front and its commanders based in Pakistan are under pressure from the ISI to further Pakistani intelligence agency's terror plans not only in Punjab but also in other parts of India... From mobile phones, terrorists today have moved on to use of satellite phones. Thuraya sets, use of spoofed IDs and coded transactions over e-mail and chat sessions, besides Voice over Internet Protocal to communicate across the border.

J Jayalalithaa, Tamil Nadu

"I fail to understand why the Centre persists in dealing with such a sensitive matter in such an insiduous manner, treating States as though they are adversaries to be suspected rather than partners, and continues trying to establish NCTC through stealth."

She did not attend the CMs meet. Her speech was read out by her minister KP Munusami.

Mamata Banerjee, West Bengal

My State is also of the opinion that the proposed version of NCTC upsets the federal structure of the country.

Shivraj Singh Chouhan, MP

I regret to say that despite all-round opposition, the Centre is bent upon setting up the NCTC, Amendments have been made, but they do not resolve practical difficulties. The Centre should limit its role to intelligence collection, analysis and its exchange and all other actions pertaining to operations should be left to States. Does the Centre not trust the State police?

Narendra Modi, Gujarat

It is not clear how big it is going to be, what forces are going to comprise it, how exactly it is going to function and which statue it will drive its powers from. I think such poorly conceived ideas that tinker with age-old existing systems rather than strengthen them, will do irreparable loss to our internal security apparatus.

Nitish Kumar, Bihar

What is the use of an operations division within the NCTC and giving it powers of conducting operations if these are going to the conducted either through or in conjunction with state police. This will create operational problems as it is not clear which of the two organisations will have the leading role and control over operations. Secondly, the draft report still retains the absolute and arbitrary provision regarding mandate to civil authorities within the states.

Raman Singh, Chhattisgarh: “Don't politicise Naxal attack, warns Raman, Slams NCTC"

With 25 May Maoist attack that wiped out almost the entire leadership of State Congress in Chhattisgarh acquiring political hue and leading to conspiracy theories, CM Raman Singh coutioned against politicing the matter.

"Given the background, it would be pertinent that no one says anything that leads to demoralisation of locals who are on the ground, facing the Naxal bullets. No one should say anything that discourages our people. I would like to state unequivocally that Chhattisgarh is fighting the biggest battle for internal security in the entire nation.

Singh called for a single national policy. "For long, people believed Naxalism was somehow different from terrorism, but even they have come round to our belief that they are two sides of the same coin," he said, even as he made a veiled attack on it defenders by terming sympathy shown to Naxals as a "cruel joke."

At the same time, he came out strongly against NCTC in its present form saying it violates the federal structure of the country/constitution. He called for its ratification by Parliament to make it responsible and answerable to people.

Maintaining that NCTC should not get powers similar to those envisaged in the NIA Act among others by allowing it to probe terror related cases without States' consent, Singh said.

His further observations: Opposed to NCTC in its present form; if it, comes into existence, it should respect the federal structure of our Constitution, participation of States in NCTC should not get reflected only on paper; States' roll should be ratified by the Parliament in order to make it effective and useful; in the proposed NCTC, an executive order may lead to duplication at the state level.

Finally, Singh stressed that his Government was not thinking contrary to national consensus that there should be coordination in gethering intelligence so the benefit of the State's experience and Centre's expertise is merged.

Naveen Patnaik, Odisha

Strongly opposing the NCTC, he said no direct or indirect interference in the State's autonomy will be tolerated, and federal rights should be respected and protected.

Pointing out that the heavy deployment of security forces in neighbouring Chhattisgarh was driving Maoists to his State, he demanded two additional CRPF battalions and a M-17 military chopper to effectively tackle the extremists in Naupada, Baragarh, and Bolangir districts.

Besides, he demanded a one-time help from the Centre for strengthening the security infrastructure in the western parts of his state in view of the present level of Maoist build-up in these places.

He asked the Centre for early re-imbursement under Security Related Expenditure (SRE) scheme under which Rs 135.41 crore has been spent between 2005-06 to 2011-12 in 19 earmarked districts.

Akhilesh Yadav, UP

He chose to remain ambivalent on his Government stand on NCDC, even as he asserted that anti-terror squad (ATS) in UP is already doing a good job in tackling terrorism.

He demanded that in view of the rising prices of land, the Centre should change its policy of states providing it free of costs for stationing central paramilitary forces there.

As for UP's view on NCTC, as a paper put it: "For Akhilesh, it remains a toss."

Omar Abdullah, Jammu and Kashmir

As on earlier occasions, he used CMs meet to make a strong pitch for phased removal of APSFA. "We cannot wait for last gun to fall silent." His logic: If AFSPA is not imposed in Maoist-hit areas, why should it continue in areas of J & K which has become by and large peaceful?

Omar also chose to raise issue of arrest of Liyaqat Shah by Delhi Police and warned that such incidents would derail the entire process of bringing back youths from POK who wanted to join the national mainstream.

Kiran Kumar Reddy, Andhra Pradesh

Even as he supported NCTC, he raised the issue of foreign web-based firms not cooperating with security agencies in monitoring anti-national activities of terrorist outfits. He asked the Centre to find a solution to this issue.

"Security agencies are facing serious problems in monitoring of communication on Internet, importantly G-mail, Yahoo mail, Nimbuzz, Skype and other VOIP Channels, because of non-cooperation from these agencies, which have their headquarters outside India," he said.

Bhupinder Singh Hooda, Haryana

He was perhaps the most vocal supporter of NCTC from among the CMs of the Congress-ruled states, and said: "It is necessary as the Maoists attack in Chhattisgarh recently had demonstrated, the "nefarious designs of terrorists... The issue needed urgent attention... Revised draft of the MHA has taken care of the States' cancerous on NCTC."

He was more explicit: "The States have been envisaged as equal functional partners in this battle against terrorism of all types."

Modi-Chidambram fire works at the meet

"A meeting of CMs on internal security triggered a fierce verbal battle between top generals of India's two biggest political parties."[22]

Gujarat CM Modi attacked the Centre, terming the meeting a 'ritual' and UPA's plan to set up NCTC "a poorly-conceived idea." "There is a law on match-fixing but no law against terrorism," he said.

The Centre's counter-attack was swift. Finance Minister Chidambram and IB Minister Manish Tiwari took on the Gujarat CM.

"Modi is asking for anti-terror law. Why does not he just say, he wants POTA and TADA," said Chidambram, referring to two highly controversial anti-terror legislations which provide for long and often arbitrary detentions without bail. He warned country will pay a price if even the diluted NCTC is not approved.

While other opposition CMs too opposed the NCTC, Nitish Kumar said it was not required at all it was Modi's no-holds-barred assult on the Centre "that made any possibility of common ground impossible."

Seen by many as BJP's potential Prime Ministerial candidate for next years general elections, Modi became the face of the opposition ruled states against the anti-terror NCTC.

NCTC bore the collateral damage of a political tussle which goverment wanted to avoid but Modi made it a point to latch on to it.

First at the conference and then in front of the TV cameras, Modi ran down the UPA Government for pushing the NCTC and even came up with his own version of what a conference of CMs should be discussing.

The Government had sensed that the issue could become a sticking point and tried to play it down, with the Prime Minister and Home Minister skipping any reference to the NCC in their opening speeches.

"The BJP's upcoming National Executive in Goa–which will see sections of the party clamour for Modi as the party's face in the general elections (in 2014)–is expected to focus on national security and corruption as the party's poll plank.

'Modi dares them to arrest him'

Here are two snippets on CM Modi, both from one daily. First a serious one, followed by a lighter one.

"The CBI's spreading net in the Ishrat Jahan fake encounter case has rattled the Narandra Modi government... so much so that on 5 June... during the CMs meet... the Chief Minister dared the UPA government to arrest him."

The Government should not misuse Central agencies and could arrest him if it wanted, Modi remarked in Delhi on the 5th. A day earlier BJP's Arun Jaitley had slammed the UPA Government, saying, "the myopic political regime in Delhi has not realised the significance of destroying institutions."

Eight years after the teenage girl from Mumbra and three others were killed... ostensibly because they were LeT terrorists on a mission to kill Modi... the investigation is moving on a fast track. The SIT established that the four were killed in cold blood by Gujarat police.

Now, the course of CBI inquiry... which involves Chief public prosecutor Sudhir Brahmbhatt and senior IB official Rajinder Kumar... may prove that Modi and his former junior Home Minister Amit Shah were in the know about the murders.

Brahmbhatt is close to Amit Shah, whose role is under scrutiny in the Sadiq Jamal fake encounter case, allegedly planted fake inputs about Lashkar targetting Modi, to facilitate the murders.

The other snippet is about "Modi, Nitish fail to see eye to eye." The daily says CM Modi ignored his Bihar counterpart Nitish Kumar at the CMs meet, with Modi walking past Nitish and not obliging lensmen waiting for the picture of two together. Tensions were high as results of by-polls in both states gave Modi a boost and Nitish a shock.

The daily is obviously biased against Modi, blaming him for not giving a chance to clique a photo of the duo together. The daily is giving the impression of Nitish being overly keen for a joint photo. If that were the case, he could said 'hello' to Modi, which he would never do. Such journalism is inanity personified!

Affected States agree on strategy to fight the common scourge, Maoists

Only one daily spared a thought for the States fighting the murderous Maoists.

After the passionate discussions on the NCTC during the CMs conference on internal security, the CMs of nine Naxal-hit states got together to discuss the common infliction they all are victims to, Maoist violence.

Meeting for the first time after the Maoists attacked that killed top Congress leaders of Chhattigarh on 25 May, the nine states agreed that each one of them need to follow the Andhra Pradesh model of anti-Naxal operations and build and strengthen the capabilities of their police forces.

The Chief Ministers of Chhattisgarh, Andhra Pradesh, Maharashtra, Bihar and Odisha, Governor of Jharkhand and representatives of MP, West Bengal, UP, met at the end of CMs conference on internal security and promised to help each other in their anti-Naxal operations.

The meeting threw up the idea of making collective effort to curb financing of Maoists by intervening in the tendu leaves business, believed to be the major source of funds, through extortions, for the rebels. The states agreed to procure the leaves instead of leaving it to the private contractors who are forced to pay Maoists... at the pain of death... to continue their business.

The states also agreed to crack down on illegal mining which is another major source of funds for the ultras.

The MHA made a 20-minute presentation on the way forward and suggested the states adopt the Andhra Pradesh model of policing. The leaders agreed and urged their police chiefs to take immediate steps to recruit, train and arm more policemen and build more police stations to establish the presence of the state in Naxal-dominated areas. The MHA told the states that until the police vacuum was filled, development and political activities could not be resumed in these areas. To fill this vacuum, police will have to take the lead... the paramilitary forces complementing the effort.

The State leaders on their part feel the central forces should aim at eliminating the top leadership of the Maoists instead of getting involved in too may skirmishes with lower level functionaries.

The state leaders also wanted Centre to be more flexible as for utilisation of the funds allotted to the states for road building projects in the Naxal-hit areas. Since roads provide connectivity, and they facilitate efficient execution of anti-Naxal operations, the states should be allowed the freedom to select the areas and regions for road construction, depending upon their comparative value towards that end. The centre should not tie the states to specifics as far as road projects are concerned, leaving some leeway to the officials and commanders on the spot.

Notes

1. Aman Sharma, Mail Today, 6 Feb. 2009.
2. Rakesh K. Singh, The Pioneer, 7 Nov. 2011.
3. Rakesh K Singh, The Pioneer, 17 Jan. 2012.
4. Ashutosh Bhardwaj, Indian Express, 9 Jul. 2012.
5. Amitav Ranjan, Indian Express, 26 Nov. 2012.
6. Rakesh K Singh, The Pioneer, 9 Dec. 2012.
7. Rakesh K Singh, The Pioneer, 27 Dec. 2012.
8. Deeptiman Tiwari, Times of India, 14 Jan. 2013.
9. Rahul Tripathi and Debabrata Mohanty, The Indian Express, 26 Jun. 2013.
10. ENS, indian Express, 19 Aug. 2013.
11. Rakesh K. Singh, The Pioneer, 12 Mar 2014.
12. Deeptinan, Tiwari, Times of India, 28 Nov. 2014.
13. Vijaita Singh, Indian Express, 26 Dec. 2014.
14. PTI, Indian Express, 19 Jan. 2015.
15. Rakesh K Singh, The Hindu, 12 Feb. 2015.
16. Vivek Deshpande, Indian Express, 19 Apr. 2015.
17. Rajesh Ahuja, Hindustan Times, 14 Sep. 2015.
18. Vinay Kumar, Indian Express, 18 Feb. 2012.
19. Manas Dasgupta, The Hindu, 18 Feb. 2012.
20. Shekhar Iyer, Hindustan Times, 17 Apr. 2012.
21. Pioneer News Service, The Pioneer, 6 May 2012.
22. Express News Service, Indian Express, 6 June, 2013.

15

Training for war Against Naxals

It was rightly assessed that police forces in India were not trained to tackle counter-insurgency threats afflicting the country... the latest being the Naxal insurrection. A complete reorientation of the police obviously became paramount to address the internal security syndrome in the country, with Naxalism seen as the greatest threat. The Chhattisgarh government-took the initiative to set up a counter-terrorism and Jungle Warfare College (CTJW) at Kanker in North Bastar, conceived, spear-headed and operated by Brig BK Panwar, AVSM, VM (Retd).[1]

Setting up the college for anti-Maoist training

A pace setting initiative had come from the erstwhile Governor of Chhattisgarh Lt Gen KM Seth who saw value in training the police for the new armed conflict. He had the first batch of 120 police personnel from Chhattisgarh trained at Indian Army Counter Insurgency and Jungle Warfare (CIJW) School at Vairangte, Mizoram in 2004. It was at his behest that a similar training institute (CTJW) was setup (2005) to train the State police in guerrilla warfare. For this pupose, Brig BK Ponwar was invited to start this school. He had been the commandant of the CIJW school, and a sector commander in the Assam Rifles.

Ponwar took up the task of setting up the CTJW Chhattisgarh the very next day he retired from the Indian Army. Within months, a batch of police men was trained. They went on to shoot down the three of the Naxalite cadres in the jungles, ten days after the termination of their course. The combat training had indeed paid off.

Thematically, curriculum was perceived to be conducted at battle field, so the trainees were addressed as 'commandos' and lived in tents in jungle openings, with minimum water and no electricity. These were the conditions quite akin to those of the Maoists. The motto was "Fight the Guerrilla, like a Guerrilla."

Endurance standards were same for men and women, as Naxals too have women who fight from front ranks. Over 180 women constables, sub-Inspectors and officers undertook the course living in similar conditions as did the men. It was a transformation in the making.

The Commandos recognised that "the Human Body is capable of withstanding tremendous stress and strain, it is often not realised till it is put to test." They did speed marches of upto 30 km at a speed of 5 to 8 minutes to a km, continuously. "No training ever stopped due to weather conditions, rain, hail, heat, cold, thick jungles, difficult terrain, rivers and gorges. Animals and reptiles were learnt to be friends with. It was stressed throughout the course that "the soldier is the weapon," as such all his senses and mental and physical fitness level should always be of highest order to be ready for combat.

At the end of 45 days, of rigorous regimen, the Commands had learnt to be self-contained in small teams, capable of operating in jungles, to disembark from helicopters by slithering, carry out people friendly operations, and an endurance levels to operate 100 kms over hilly jungle terrain in 72-96 hours. The age-old attitudes changed, and the commandos saw themselves as the protectors of the people.

College has good reputation

The college received formidable reputation and recognition. Country, wide requests were received. Personnel from Jharkhand, Odisha, Maharashtra, Bihar, UP, Kerala, Karnataka, West Bengal, Uttarakhand, in addition to Chhattisgarh undertook the indoctrination training here. The BSF, ITBP, CISF and SSB also received special reorientation. Even the CRPF, whose 76 men were 'slaughtered' by the Maoists on 6 Apr 2010 in Dantewada, came in for training to the CTJW. The entire 62 CRPF Battalion, which lost 114 troops in the counter-Naxal operations, undertook the full course. The feedback from that unit says that had they come here earlier then these lives would not have been lost.

Over 15,000 personnel have now undergone the courses since 22 Aug 2005, without any major casualties among the trainees at the college. Out of the 12 IPS officers who completed the training there, five have already been awarded the President's Police Medals for bravery. "No commando has lost his life over the last 18 months."

Brig Basant Kumar Ponwar, AVSM, VSM

The services of the Brigadier were requisitioned by Chhattisgarh Government in the rank of Inspector General of Police, IGP (Maj General). He set up the CTJW college in Kanker, a facility similar to the Army's CIJW School in Mizoram, of which he was the Commandant in his last posting of his Army career.

Even today, he is an advisor to the Chhattisgarh Government, on matters relating to force deployment, equipment profile and conduct of counter-Maoist operations.

Widely experienced in this field, he was recently invited by the International Institute of Strategic Studies, London to speak on the Naxal Challenge. He has spoken on this subject in China and Germany and on Counter Insurgency and Counter Terrorism Operations in Austalia. As Commandant, CIJW School in Mizoram, he conducted Indo-US Defence Cooperation Expercise, 'Yudh Abhyas', coordinated CI/CT training of all the Corps Battle Schools in the Army and has travelled widely in the LWE-hit States. He has delivered lectures at several Indian institutions on CI/CT operations, and of late, specifically on 'Naxal Challenge'.

He has also been speaking to the young entrepreneur's organisations in Kolkata, Bangaluru and Hyderabad.

CRPF: Weapons and Equipment

The CRPF is the main central paramilitary force assigned the responsibility of counter-Maoist operations throughout the Naxal-affected theatre, the so-called Red Zone or Red Corridor, running South from Bihar-Nepal border in the North to Karnataka, and of late, even to Tamil Nadu and Kerala.

It is only natural and expected that this Force, fighting most serious internal threat to nation's integrity and sovereignty is provided with where-withal to do the job/responsibility assigned to it.

This section will carry the news about weapons and equipment the Force has, or will get in future, as also related issues.

"CRPF seeks DRDO help to trace lost weapons"

This was an interesting and significant story about the Force concerned about the loss of its weapons to the Maoists, and the efforts to undo the consequent damage. It appeared in Sep 2011.[2]

It is first-of-its-kind measure by the CRPF to safeguard its weapons against attacks by the Maoists and their consequent loss to the ultras. The

Force has asked the DRDO to install location location finder and biometric secret code to disable and locate its weapons lost in major fights with the ultras. The move comes following loss of sophisticated weapons to the Maoists. They have, of late, inflicted major casualties on the CRPF and State police forces of the Naxal-hit States, and later making away with the arms and ammunition of the dead.

The Defence Research and Development Organisation is developing a "secret code" for the weapon so that the arms lost in operations are disabled and retrieved subsequently through path-finder based on GPS (Global Positioning System). The secret code will be based on biometric detailing like thumb impression of the weapon user and will also include an alphanumerical identification number as a measure to double the safety of the fitted arms. The weapons fitted with those devices will operate only when the relevant codes are fed into such devices.

The GPS-based location finder will help on tracking the movement of weapons and help in their retrieval besides locating the hide-outs of the ultras. A master centre at some CRPF location will help in tracking the lost weapons.

The CRPF is using a significant number and type of sophisticated weapons with cyclic rate of fire (rounds per minute), including firearms that can fire upto 1,000 rounds per minute. Loss of such high fire-power weapons to the Maoists pose a serious threat to the CRPF troops who have to operate against them in thick forest areas of the Maoist-affected States and these areas are heavily mined by these ultra-Left extremists.

A senior official involved with the CRPF operations makes an interesting claim: "This probably is the first exercise in the world towards recovering the weapons by a paramilitary force". Such claims need not be taken too seriously, since such counter-insurgency operations in its present *avatar* are going on in the world since the end of the World War II. Some one, some where must have initiated such a move decades back!

The PLGA of the banned CPI (Maoist) has been looting the weapons of the security forces over the years, after every ambush, and as a consequence, the very sophistication of these looted weapons pose a serious threat to the counter-Naxal forces like the CRPF troops, and in the ultimate analysis, to the country's integrity and sovereignty.

Some 95 per cent of the weapons lost in action are reported from the LWE-hit areas and the remaining are from Jammu and Kashmir. The weapons likely to be fitted with these (secret) devices are/include SLR 7.62 mm, AK-47, LMG 7.62 mm, INSAS LMG 5.56 mm and other sophisticated firearms like the Israeli X-95.

"CRPF gets Rs 1,200-cr anti-Naxal aid:" Jul 2012

The MHA granted sanction for acquisition of sophisticated weapons and combat vehicles worth Rs 6200 crore for the CRPF to enable it sharpen its anti-Naxal and counter-insurgency (in fact two terms in India today essentially mean one and same thing, since these weapons are to be used in the Red Zone) offensive across the country. The expenditure sanction followed a meeting between Union Home Secretary RK Singh and CRPF DGK Vijay Kumar on 4 Jul 2012, reports a daily.[3]

The big-ticket acquisition lined up include purchase of 1,050 automatic grenade launcher (Rs 176.5 crore), 84 mm rocket launchers, 1,205 (Rs 272.46 crore), 1380 hand held thermal imagers and LCD (Rs 204.30 crore), 6,777 portable night vision monocular (Rs 132.83 crore), 1,915 multiple grenade launcher and matching ammunition (Rs 99.90 crore) and 1,208 mm Gs (Rs 58.77 crore).

Some other purchases are listed below:

	Rs (crore)
• Equipment for bomb disposal squads	32.79
• 15,599 GPS	31.20
• 169 water trucks	24.26
• 75 all-terrain vehicles	15.34
• 2.4 lakh pair jungle shoes	21.07
• Combat dress for recruits	46.95
• Special riot drill equipment	14.5
• Running shoes in lieu of PT shoes, sleeping bags, and 31 JCB back hoe loaders	6.28

The issue of ban on procurement of vehicles against condemned vehicles came under review in the meeting. It was earmarked for further discussion with the financial advisor, at a later date. In a letter written to RK Singh on 8 May 2012, Kumar had raised the issue of waver of a condition that authorizes the DG of Central Paramilitary Forces to procure vehicles against condemnation only for the station from where the vehicles are junked.

The procurement of all-terrain vehicles, water trucks, back hoe loaders, portable night vision monocular, GPS, 84 mm rocket launchers and other weaponry mentioned above, will help boost "big sweep" anti-Naxal operations across the States affected by the LWE. The proposal for acquisition of these weapons and equipments were pending for the last two years.

Modern technological gadgets and equipments coupled with sophisticated weapons act as catalyst for carrying large offensives against the ultras. Maoists in the past target the security forces camps and ambush the security troops through their guerrilla warfare tactics, which involve significant number of cadres.

Senior CRPF officials explained that the Maoists take advantage of the monsoons to target security forces during which medium to large offensives are required to establish area domination.

"CRPF uses GPS, UAVs to fight Maoists:" Oct 2012

"The CRPF is deploying the latest technology to ensure the safety and security of its troops in field operations, particularly in Maoist-hit areas. It had already been monitoring the movements of its personnel in remote areas and deep jungles through Global Positioning system, (GPS), while using Unmanned Aerial Vehicles (UAV) to track the location and movements of Maoists."[4]

The CRPF, India's largest para-military force is also in the process of acquiring the latest equipment and machinery to detect the IEDs that cause maximum casualties in the force. Initially the personnel was not happy with "their position and movement being tracked by us, but we managed to convince them that it was for their own good," said a senior CRPF officer. He further noted: "Through GPS monitoring, we know their exact location and can them in case of an emergency if they are incommunicado. It helps us to alert them, giving us tactical advantage over our enemy... If they face any attack, we can rush the reinforcements, besides medical aid and rations."

Though it is presently using GPS in select areas in Chhattisgarh and Jharkhand, the CRPF wants to deploy this technology in all its fields operations, particularly in all the nine LWE-hit states where it is engaged in tough battle with the ultras. Its main advantage is that the units/ commanders can plan their operations effectively and precisely, sitting in their headquarters.

Likewise, the UAVs deployed in the Maoist-hit states have started yielding results, as they are able to pickup ground conversations and movements of Maoists. "Our personnel are now able to comb areas and carry out operations more effectively in Maoist strongholds, particularly in Chhattisgarh and Jharkhand. UAVs flash real-time imagery of Maoist movements and conversation, the data is immediately passed on to our COBRA commandos for necessary action. In our future operations, the UAVs are going to play an important role in strategising our plan," said the officer.

More significantly, the force is also scouting for the latest devices that help detecting the IEDs. The latest data shows two-thirds of the CRPF jawans are killed in IED explosions during operations. This year so far (Oct 2012), 30 jawans have died in IED blasts. The officer continues: "Efforts are on to acquire modern devices that detect IEDs even from long distances. IEDs have always been a big challenge not only for us but also for all security forces as their nature keeps changing. So there is an urgent need to have better equipment to meet this threat."

One doesn't wish to be a spoilt sport here, but this officer quoted here seems to be exulting over the operational advantages gained by his force with its acquisition of the GPS and UAVs a bit too much, like a child who get some new toys. He is just being simplistic, unreal about the "great" advantages these two latets "toys" gave to his para military force. Even when the latest such devices and equipments have been inducted in our security force, "the boots on the ground" matter, even though, these/such "toys" do give some advantages and might hasten the final results.

To give some specific advice to this officer, has the CRPF gained an upper hand vis-à-vis the Maoists? It is nearly three years by now (Sep 2015) since these two devices were received by the CRPF, has there been any improvement in the casualty levels suffered by this force? It is doubtful! More than that, things seems to be worse over these three years for the force as some quarters have reported frustration levels going up, more men/ officers wanting to quit, and increased number of fraternal shoot-outs within units. One is not singling out the CRPF, any force, including the Army, will have similar problems while fighting insurrectionary forces like the Maoists. A difference may be of degree. What is 'not done' is this officer's over-excitement after acquiring the two equipments, and his continuous exulting over it.

How far things have changed for the better after the CRPF got these two, one is not sure. But to impart some realism to the actual situation on the ground, and put the things in perspective, some of the major strikes by the Maoist and resultant casualties suffered by the force after it got the two devices, say mid-2012, are numerated here:

- 28 June 2012, 17 killed in Sarkeguda, Bijapur.
- 10 Jan 2013, 14 security forces killed in an encounter in Latehar. In a first, they implanted an IED in the abdomen of a slain CRPF braveheart... an egregious atrocity and an inhuman monstrosity.
- 9 Mar 2013, Maoists, kill six villagers in West Singhbhum district.
- 25 Mar 2013, Darbha attack in Sukma, Chhattisgarh. 27 Congress leaders killed, including VC Shukla, possibly senior most Congressman in India.

- 2 Jul 2013, Pakur district's SP Amarjit Balihar, with five of his men, gunned down by Maoists in Dumka.
- Blood count 2013.
  1. Maoist violence-related cases 1129
  2. Fatalities 394
  3. State lopping the Red depredations Jharkhand
- Dec 2014, 14 CRPF troops killed, Chhattisgarh.
- 11 Mar 2014, 16 killed: 11 CRPF personnel,
  4 Chhattisgarh police,
  1 civilian in Sukma.

"CRPF goes all out to scale up its armoury:" Nov 2012

Acquisition of weaponry and some other equipments has been covered earlier, based on a news story in Jul 2012. This is another daily covering the same subject, which appeared in Nov 2012.[5]

Weapons mentioned in this news analysis are different, though the sources in the two stories are from CRPF. It should be of interest to have a brief look at this news item also.

The story opens up this way: "The CRPF is all set to procure hand held laser range finders (HHLRF) and Belgium-made FN Minimi LMGs in a bid to add more teeth to its fight against Maoists." The MHA having already sanctioned this procurement, the CRPF officials claim the process to buy the weapons are in the final stage.

The Force will be equipped with more than 600 HHLRF and around 2,500 passive night vision weapons (PNV). The demand for PNVs was expedited after the CRPF troops came under fire in its Bijapur encounter in Chhattisgarh in Jul 2012. In the operation, 19 people including nine 'alleged' Maoists were killed. The operation was executed during might, leading to allegations that the troops opened fire on innocent villagers, a claim strongly refuted by the Force.

"The MHA has sanctioned Rs 70 crore to purchase these devices."

The new breed of Belgian Shepherd Malinois, which were raised by the CRPF last year (2011) and used in operations against the Maoists, have been trained with HHLRFs. The dogs are capable of attacking any suspect who has been identified with the help of the laser beam. These devices will in handy during situations when the suspect is trying to hide in a crowd. The MHA has sanctioned Rs 2 crore to buy quality jungle shoes. To detect the presence of IEDs, the CRPF also plans to buy fresh sets of wire locators.

"CRPF mulls fitting guns with GPS to track Maoist moves:" Jan 2012

We have already covered a news story of Sep 2011, where in CRPF had asked DRDO to install location finder and biometric secret code to disable and locate its weapons lost in major fights with the ultras. The present story in a daily[6] of 28 Jan 2013 seems to be similar in broad details but discloses its emphasis on intelligence available to CRPF. So it is advisable to cover this story also, as the sources here too are the CRPF officials.

This story on the CRPF opens up with a negative note on the Force: "Call it an out of the box idea or absolute desperation. Due to repeated intelligence failures leading anti-Naxal force walking into ambushes, the CRPF is resorting to technology to fit their guns with GPS systems. The idea is that if the Maoists loot them, it will reveal their location and movements."

But there is a problem: No GPS device available in India has a battery life of more than a day. A CRPF official explains: "We are exploring this idea. But we donot have that kind of technology at our desposal at present. If some company can provide a device with long battery life that can last for a few days, then it can be of some consequence operationally."

In the recent Latehar encounter, that claimed lives of 10 security troops, there was a clear intelligence lag which meant Maoists were always a step ahead.

CRPF sources claimed they had been tracing senior Maoist leader Arivnd Ji since 10 Dec (2012). But every time they got information on his location, he had already moved on. "In one particular village, he had stayed for over 10 days, but got to know about it only after he had left the village," said a CRPF official.

Contrary to this, Maoists got real-time information on troop movements and were waiting on the hills for the CRPF contingent when it reached Katiya village in Amwatikar jungles (in Latehar) where the ambush took place.

If the technology is available, the Force is mulling redesigning their guns to fit the GPS device innocenously. "But the batkery life should be at least 10 days to yield any operational benefit to us. Maoists move in the jungles on foot. So the movement is not very rapid. To ascertain pattern one needs tracking over a few days", said the official.

CRPF's intelligence network is still at a nascent stage. It largely depends upon the intelligence provided by State police and IB. While the IB has been providing the bulk of technical intelligence, state police has its human intelligence network that assists the forces. But there has been constant issue of lack of coordination between the three arms... one of the reasons for the CRPF setting up its own intelligence wing.

Lack of state penetration in tribal areas has led to a poor human intelligence network adding to the problem of conducting operations in Maoist-infested areas.

Nature of Casualties in CRPF ranks

In the combat zone, IED explosions claim maximum casualties. In the non-combat categories, certain diseases claim fatalities in the CRPF ranks.

These are discussed in the pages that follow.

CRPF Cell to study Naxal IED threats

The CRPF engaged in a major way in anti-Naxal operations, will establish a Research and Development Cell to study and analyse the IED threats-in LWE areas. It was reported by a daily in Jan 2013.[7]

This decision followed an interaction between the DG, CRPF Pranay Sahay and Union Home Secretary RK Singh.

The Cell will be developed in consultation with agencies having expertise on the subject and work on strategies/measures to deal with the menace of IEDs effectively as major casualties suffered by the force in LWE areas are due to explosions of such devices. The study will help reduce the challenges faced by the forces due to such explosions.

This R and D Cell will comprise "bright and experienced" officers who will carryout IED blast experiments with different types and quantities of explosives, normally used by Naxals in real situations on a set of condemned 5-tonne trucks by putting layers of sand bags to determine the absorption capacity of the vehicles.

CRPF reworks strategy to defuse IED threat: Sep 2014

Official figures reveal that more security force personnel were killed in IED blasts in the Maoist areas than by bullets. Consequently, the CRPF has decided to re-orient its combat strategy to counter the IEDs, used so effectively by the Left ultras to inflict heavy damage on the security personnel.

A senior CRPF officer said, after a recently-concluded operations conference: "Though our force has susperior fire power and fighting skills, the rebel-planted IEDs in the Red areas sometimes pose a lethal surprise. We lost our men while detecting or defusing IEDs."

There are reasons for the Maoists preferring IEDs to direct shoot outs/ confrontation with the forces. It is essentially because the latter will be too costly for them. In case of ambushes sprung by them, they hardly lose any cadres, and in a one-sided affair, inflict considerable lethalities on their opponents. Besides these favourable calculations, what weighs heavily for their preference for ambushes and use of IEDs against the forces is the easy availability of explosive from a variety of sources. CRPF DG Dilip Trivedi explains: "The Maoists operate in areas rich in minerals and mines. Leakage of explosives used in mining activity land up with Maoists." It is not that simple as the DG is trying to put it as mere 'leakage'. Sometimes the ultras hijack the entire vehicle carrying a load of them. Then they take a cut from the contractors, at gun point. At times, they even attack the work site and make away with the explosives there.

"Mosquitoes, not Maoists, kill most CRPF men in Red Zone"

This was the headline in a daily, which tells an unfortunate truth of an enemy called mosquito! The blurb was even more unfortunate, "malaria, heart attacks throw light on inhuman work conditions." But who had heard of insurgencies and LW armed struggles being conducted in benign, human and conducive work conditions! The way these scribes paint gloomy pictures create an impression among the common readers that some commander sitting some where is to blame for these "unhuman" conditions! The story appeared in a daily in Mar 2015.[8]

As an aside, it is worth mentioning that in World War II, more Allied Troops, including Indians, fell to malaria in the jungles of Burma (then called so) much before even the Japanese soldiers appeared in shooting range! Things of course, changed with the discovery and issue of the quinine tablets to troops. To remove any misconception or misinformation/ignorance, work conditions still remained "inhuman" for soldiers in those inhospitable Burmese jungles!

For the largest security force fighting Naxalites in the jungles of Chhattisgarh, Jharkhand, Bihar, the biggest enemy is not gun-toting Maoist but a mosquito. Latest government data shows that more CRPF men have died due to malaria and heart attacks than have fallen to Maoist attacks in the 106 Naxal-hit districts in the country. Table below is self explanatory.

Fatal Fight

Cause of death	*2012*	*2013*	*2014*	*2015 (till 2 March)*
Malaria	12	02	27	01
Heart attack	24	20	35	07
Other diseases	39	36	33	07
Maoist attack	37	20	50	02
Total	**112**	**78**	**145**	**17**

A worrying fact must be mentioned: There is an increasing gap in number of deaths due to malaria and heart attacks and those due to Maoist attacks, over the years. While in 2012, 36 CRPF fell to two diseases, 37 to Maoist bullets, the respective figure for 2013 are 22 and 20.

"Heart attacks kill more CRPF men than Naxals"

This story appeared in a different daily in May 2015, giving figures for various diseases compared to deaths in Maoist attacks.

Data relating to the death of CRPF personnel serving the Naxal areas had thrown up a disturbing trend: Heart attacks have killed more Jawans (642) than the Maoists have (323) in the last five years. At 228, even suicides account for a substantial number of deaths.

Number of deaths between 2009-2014

- Heart attack 642
- Naxal strike 323
- Depression (suicide cases) 228
- Malaria 108

Congress politician Motilal Vora had sought information on the number of CRPF personnel killed in Naxal areas between Jan 2009 and Dec 2014 and the measures the government plans to boost the morale of Jawans working in such conditions.

MOS Home Haribhai Chaudhary supplied the information tabulated above. He listed the measures taken to bloster the self-confidence of security personnel: leave applications from security personnel disposed of within stipulated period; field officers were instructed to encourage their men to open up about their problems and grievances; infrastructure created to provide recreational avenues; welfare and rehabilitation board was also established; condition of 10 years' qualifying service was removed for award of pension and lumpsum exgratia compensation was extended to disabled personnel besides the regular exgratia compensation given to families of martyred personnel.

CRPF woos tribals with civic action programme: June 2013

Security actions alone are not the solution to any insurrection in a country, particularly so when it is facing an ideology-driven LWE! Realising this truism, "the CRPF has gone on an overdrive to wean away alienated tribals from Maoists' clutches by undertaking a number of projects under its civic action programmes."[9]

It spent Rs 3.26 crore Jan-Mar 2013: organised pre-recruitment training for 15 days to 5,582 potential candidates in 26 severely affected districts in seven States and organised football tournaments in the Maoist hotbed, viz, Bastar, Bijapur, Kondgaon and Narayanpur, of Chhattisgarh. Such public programmes create goodwill among the tribals inhabiting the Maoist-hit areas, and also provided opportunitites to bring the public closer to the administration and consequently strengthen its intelligence network by making inroads into the otherwise alienated life of people. Consequently, the Force claims to have improved its operational efficiency against the Maoists. They quote figures to back their claims with.

In April (2013), the CRPF killed 12 ultras, apprehended 59 and led to surrender of four. They also recovered 49 arms, 348 rounds of ammunition. But these achievements came with cost... martyrdom of two CRPF personnel and injury to six Jawans. The list in March included elimination of 10 ultras in an encounter on the 13th at Saksari in Gumla district of Jharkhand besides apprehension of 111 extremists. Two Maoists surrendered but the ultras also injured two CRPF personnel during the operations. The Force also recovered 158 arms and 322 rounds of ammunition.

Inter-groups clashes on 28 March in Chatra between the Maoist factions also led to the recovery of bodies of 10 ultras, including one regional commander of Bihar Regional panel and Secretary Madhya Zone Committee. Likewise, the CRPF killed four Maoists in February and apprehended 123 extremists with injury to just one of its men. In January, the CRPF captured 91 Maoists without inflicting any casualties on the ultras. The Force however, sustained 10 casualties (fatilities?) and injury to 23 personnel during an operation at Barwadih in Lateher district of Jharkhand. The Naxals had planted IED inside the stomach of a slain jowan, leading to casualty of three other men.

DG, CRPF Pranay Sahay has asked his field commanders to continuously revisit tactics and strategies against the Maoists. Buoyed by the successes against the Maoists, Sahay has told the field commanders that it is the right time to strike at the Maoists with full potential. "I exhort you and your troops to take full advantage of the situation and to conduct more and more planned operations so that Naxals are not able to regroups", the DG told the commanders of various Maoist-hit States.

A brief comment is called for on this news item, obviously based on the daily's reporter's access to the CRPF Headquarters. The paramilitary forces like the CRPF make full use of such occassions, giving a pat-on-the-back interviews. The picture painted is rosier than demanded by the ground realities. The daily and its reporters show excessive gratitude for the favour shown by granting such opportunity and interview. They do not ask honest, if not blunt, questions, from the CRPF and its spokespersons and commanders. It is not that the dailies, particularly a paper like The Hindu, and their reporters are unaware of the other side of the coin, it is just that they want to be polite, to ensure that the door is opened next time around. There is no need to repeat the comments on an earlier occasion when a CRPF officer was exulting over the gains his force made after equipping itself with a GPS and UAVs. This over-the-top list of achievement is rather mundane, and calling them all some kind of "great achievements" is itself delusionary; avoiding a harsher term is deemed appropriate!

"AP Model to counter Maoists"

Andhra Pradesh was the only State in India that got rid of the Left Extremists in an effective manner. One can discuss reasons for that singular distinction it achieved in the early days of that insurrection. May be, they were as yet not that well-established in their dens. May be, they lacked experience of facting a concerted counter-attack by the States forces, in a sustained way. May be, Andhra's much-acclaimed 'Grey hounds'... the specialised anti-LWE force raised by that State... were too good for the Left guerrillas.

There can also be another argument to detract a little from Andhra Pradesh's success! Possibly, the neighbouring States were not taken on board when the State lauched its all-out campaign against the Left anarchists. For that reason, when faced with difficult and hopeless situation, the ultras simply fled to the neighbouring States and melted away into their favourites haunts, the forest. They recruited, rested and regrouped for another day. Had the neighbouring States too put effective blockade, most, if not all the fleeing ultras would have been decimated in that nut-cracker. Be that as it may, let the credit stay with Andhra Pradesh Government and its security forces.

This section deals with the subsequent news about some states trying to replicate the Andhra Model by raising special forces on the lines of the Grey hounds. The news on this issue keep filtering out from different sources. These are looked upon in the succeeding pages.

"Four States to follow AP Model to hound Maoists:" Jan 2013

This interesting, even aggressive heading appeared in a daily dated 16 Jan 2013. It says "alarmed at the growing firepower of the Maoists, the MHA has cleared a proposal whereby the worst-affected states of Chhattisgarh, Jharkhand, Odisha and Bihar will raise specialised police forces trained in guerilla warfare and equipped with modern weaponry to take on the rebels."[10]

These forces are to be raised on the model much-acclaimed 'Greyhounds' of Andhra Pradesh, which neutralised Maoists in that State. The project has the support of the Centre, which has termed the LWE as India's biggest internal security threat, particularly so today as the Maoists possess modern weapons and communication equipment to take on even well-equipped para-military forces.

The MHA would fund the scheme in all four States to enable their police to raise new specialised units and acquire modern arms. The proposed outlay during the Twelfth Plan is Rs 280 crore from the Centre and Rs 55 crore from the State governments. The MHA was to release funds through its Scheme for Special Infrastructure.

Knowing the success of Greyhounds, the MHA believes this strategy would deliver similar results in the other LWE-hit states. But the MHA, in its internal note, did put some conditions for the States to follow: The Special Force of the State has to be upgraded as per approved guidelines of Greyhounds; even if a Special Force has been raised in some form, it has to be re-oriented through the process mentioned in the guidelines.

"Maoists clean-up high on the Government list": Jul 2013

A similar story, as the one discussed above, apeared a few months later in another daily of 14 Jul 2013.[11] Yet again, it is based upon an interview given to this daily by the MHA officials. "Granting" (favour through such) interviews to different dailies on the same subject but at an interval is nice way of these officials ingratiating–even a very limited way–such dailies and their reporters. The latter can, as always, claim an exclusive. Giving such stories, containing some decisions taken by the government, in a press conference is better way of disseminating official news. But that is not the way preferred by the bureaucrats. It gives chance to so many press men to ask questions. Announcements at such conference assume the form of official policies, which usually is not the case. In individual interviews, the officials can divulge what they want to. It serves the purpose for both sides of the line–the interviewer and the interviewee!

The story opens with this para: "with Maoists on the warpath across the four States, the government is mulling to use the 'best practices model' successfully used in Maoist stronghold states such as Andhra Pradesh and West Midnapore district of West Bengal to counter ultra Left radicals. The daily is told for emphasis that "all the best practices that have paid dividends, operational or otherwise, in countering Maoists will be put into practice in all the 26 worst-affected districts of the countery." As is well known, in Andhra Pradesh, once a stronghold of Maoists, "operations by 2,000 Greyhound commandos and a robust intelligence network providing actionable inputs, resulted in forcing the ultra left radicals to shift base to the jungled tracts of the neighbouring states."

The MHA is planning a brain storming session by first week of August (2013), summoning the police chiefs of these 26 districts along with the DGs of the CRPF and other para military forces, to kickstart the process. An important change will be to focus on all-out pre-emptive incisive offensives in core Maoist areas. Some 8,000 specially-trained commandos will undertake surgical operations, based on actionable inputs, provided by an efficient data base and by over-hauling the present intelligence-gathering apparatus.

Now comes what was not mentioned in the earlier news item. The forceful thrust will be followed by a speedy developmental activity in the 'cleared' areas, for which other ministries will also have to assume key roles. There has been criticism of delay in ushering development in the Saranda jungles of Jharkhand, once a key camping area under the Maoists but was subsequently cleared by the security forces.

It was Chidambram, the then Union Home Minister, who had famously laid out the guidelines for fighting the Maoists in their strongholds: clear, hold and develop. But he not only faced opposition within his own (Congress) Party from the likes of Digvijay Singh, a failed Chief Minister in his own state, MP, but he also chose not to stay the course by throwing in the towel when it was time to execute the policy laid out by him and opted to return to his favourite, previous (Finance) Ministry. All the same, a greater pity since India had got an effective Home Minister after the likes of Shivraj Patil, Sushil Kumar Shinde *et al.* May be, he realised that he was not, being from the South, a heavy weight in the Sonia set up, where a member of her NAC had a greater say in counter-Maoist policy than the Union Home Minister. One need not be unduly harsh with Chidambram for throwing in the towel, being too intelligent not to understand the realities of Delhi Durbar!

A total of 106 districts have been declared as Maoist-affected in the country. Official sources put the number of hard-core Maoist cadres at 8000 or so.

Training and equipping police for counter-Maoist operations (Intelligence)

State police has often been blamed by the CPMF for their not achieving desired results in the counter-Naxal operations. While this may not be the fair criticism in all cases, but police does have a shortcoming in one specific field, namely, intelligence. Police inability or failure to provide intelligence inputs to the security forces before or during the operations, has rightly invited criticism.

This section deals with this aspect of the police functioning. Not only police reforms are overdue; and sadly, the states, even the centre/MHA, seem to be dragging their feet over the issue. What follows are some ideas/ suggestions on improving the state police forces.

What are the IB plans for Police? Sep 2012

The Intelligence Bureau is scheduled to convene a meeting of DsGP/ 1s GP on 4 Sep 2012, reports a daily on its eve.[12]

What are the issues that will figure prominently during the three-dry meet of the country's top police brass convened by the IB? The daily's list: over all insurgency situation in the North-East, Jammu and Kashmir and Naxal-affected states, besides cyber threats to critical infrastructure; radicalisation of the educated youth from a 'particular community' (code word for the Muslim community); actions to improve police to population ratio; and strengthening of the special forces.

What are the specifics as they apply to the state police forces? These are issues like police recruitment, addition of personnel from 2010 onwards; percentage of vacancies in police ranks still remaining; number of police personnel trained in post-blast investigation; and transparency in recruitment process.

The meet will, among other things, also discuss establishment of new police training facilities, training in special skills like countering IEDs, and airborne operations and progress in probe and prosecution of terror related cases.

The annual conference will also take stock of the new anti-terrorist squads (ATS) and anti-terrorist task forces setup in various states, creation of counter-insurgency and anti-terrorist schools and training in non-lethal weapons.

Creation of infrastructure of training for special forces, establishment of new jungle warfare schools, creation of new marine police stations, fortification of police stations in the Naxil-hit states and introduction of new weaponry like X-75 rifles will also figure prominently during the meeting. Other issue to be discussed are: enhancement in forensic capabilities of the police forces, computerisation of the police stations and progress achieved in strengthening of the SSB, ITBP, and the BSF in border policing.

A session on containing the ever-growing menace of Maoist violence and increasing volumes of Fake Indian Currency Notes (FICN) in the economic system and measures to counter and control the evil will also be discussed.

While the PM will inaugurate the conference, the Director IB is its chairperson. Those who will take part are Union Home Minister, NSA, Chiefs of the CPMFs, police chiefs of the states and UTs.

Disappointed with state police forces, performance: Centre to talk tough

This is the sum total of a news story that appeared in a daily in June 2013, apparently prompted by the MHA sources.[13]

To put it simply, this news analysis simply paints a dismal picture of state police forces, particularly those facing Maoist insurrection!

The opening paragraph of the news story from New Delhi, datelined 3 June 2013, is as candid as it could be: "With states continuing to rely heavily on Central forces for the fight against the Naxals, the Centre is preparing to do some tough talk at the meeting of CMs later this week, warning them that until they strengthen their police forces, the attacks like the one Chhattisgarh cannot be prevented."

The MHA is ruing the fact that despite giving thousands of crores to the states over the years as assistance to strengthen their police forces, there has been little change on the ground. The state police forces are woefully short of manpower, training, ammunition, and low on morale... hardly the kind of condition to be in to take on the Naxals not surprisingly, therefore, they are almost completely dependent on the paramilitary forces for the anti-Naxal combat.

The MHA has prepared a detailed presentation on the way forward in the anti-Naxal fight in which it has stressed that there is no alternative to a strong and fully capable state police force, working in close cooperation with the Centre and other states. The presentation is likely to emphasise on the Andhra Pradesh model of anti-naxal strategy. A MHA official said the

Andhra experience was not all about specialised Greyhounds force only. "The State had over the years, invested a lot on building its police force, which ultimately helped it in chasing the Naxals away."

The Ministry is likely to tell the CMs that while it would continue to provide money and resources, the dependence on the Centre was becoming counter-productive. During the last four years, the Centre has disbursed Rs 6,500 crore to the states under various schemes to build police infrastructure. Under the scheme for modernisation of police forces, the MHA has been allocating money to the states for construction and maintenance of secure police stations, set up communication lines, buy weapons, improve mobility, develop forensic capabilities, and upgrade training. Each of the Naxal-affected districts are given additional Rs 2 crore per year to upgrade their policing capabilities. Besides, under the SRE (scheme for reimbursement of expenditure) the MHA reimburses the expensed incurred by the state governments on security matters that are not covered by the modernisation secheme.

All this, the Centre feels, has not produced the desired result, and a more focused approach was required.

"States failed to deliver police reforms": MHA

This news story is again based on a MHA note, and reported by a daily in June 2013.[14] "After seven years and four committees on police reforms, the Centre has said the states have failed to deliver on the issue." It also claimed that UT Governments have made "significant and substantial" progress on these reforms. Its note said only 15 states have amended their existing police Acts in line with the suggestions of various panels. An MHA penal had drafted a model Police Act for the states.

In 2006, the Supreme Court had called for setting up State/UT security commission, separate investigation from law and order, minimum two-year tenure for DGs, constitute a police complaints authority and put in place police establishment boards. Acknowledging the delay in police reforms, the MHA said, "The police is seen as selectively efficient, unsympathetic to the under-priviledged and accused of politicisation and criminalisation."

The MHA has decided upon a new police Act for the UTs as their administrators are under its overall control. Patting its own back, the MHA claimed a security commission each has been formed in all the UTs barring Delhi and orders were issued in 2010 for a police complaint authority.

Similarly, a decision was taken by the MHA to fix a two-year tenure for a DGP, IGS, DIG, SP and SHO. All UTs have also successfully set up a police establishment board, the MHA noted.

Earlier on, a committee formed by the MHA had made 49 recommendations to improve policing.

"Maoists set to gain ground if like CRPF, police too go into retreat mode:" Apr 2015[15]

The very headline of this news analysis that appeared in a daily in Apr 2015 is rather unfortunate, if not alarming. Press has accepted that the CRPF, the main counter-Maoist force of the country, has already been in retreat mode. Obviously, it is the para-military force itself which must have conveyed this impression, even if it had not said so in so many words. The press does not create such a conclusion without any basis whatsoever! There must have been certain actions, certain statements, or even certain indirect hints that gave a chance to the press to have this "retreat mode" image of the CRPF in its mind. Now, this article should clarify what are the reasons that compelled this daily to conclude that the police too is following the CRPF into "retreat mode."

The scribe has built his case on the state (Chhattisgarh) suffering loss of seven STF troopeers to Maoists. His first paragraph reads: "Numerically, Saturday's (4 Apr 2015) loss of seven STF personnel in Sukma might not count for much in the battle against Maoists in a State that has seen over 1,050 troops killed in the last 14 years. However, this attack has a strategic and operational significance that goes far beyond the numbers and might just give the space the rebels needed to regain their ground in interior villages."

While in the last two years the Maoists successfully launched a few major attacks in Bastar, they also faced a general depletion of ammunition and eroding of popular base in their capital. Though the absence of civic services in Bastar continues to provide a sufficient base for the rebels among tribals, it is generally believed that the enhanced deployment of forces and operations in interior areas led to the decline of Maoist activity.

But the trend has seen a quiet reversal since Dec 2014 incident when the CRPF lost 14 men near Chintagufa in Sukma. Rattled by its biggest casualty since Tadmetla of Apr 2010, the CRPF bosses in Delhi issued strict instructions to its field commanders not to undertake any major operation without the headquarters' approval. Stressing on the personnel safety, DG CRPF Prakash Mishra even stated that the forces "don't need to do Rambo-style operations.

The CRPF has some 30,000 troops posted in Chhattisgarh, and provide crucial support to the State police. "Following the diktat from Delhi, the

Chhattisgarh CRPF has mostly remained in its barracks over the last few months."

Consequently, the state force, which has much lesser personnel earmarked for Naxal operations, is left all by itself. Chhattisgarh dedicated anti-Naxal force STF has just two battalions comprising less than 2000 men that are deployed over an area of larger than Kerala. As a result of this development, intelligence inputs and local reports of the last few months confirm that the Maoists have made a significant recruitment in South Bastar, and are attempting to recover the territory ceded to forces.

Now, coming to the attack on STF on 4 April, which inflicted the biggest casualty in a day in the recent years, "its already weekened force will come under greater pressure," feels the daily.

For the Maoists, the best period for launching the offensive is before monsoons begin. During rains, police operations decrease as the troops are mainly confined to the barracks, as the movements through streams and bushes become difficult for the trudging troops.

Keeping the above in mind, the Maoists observe Tactical Counter-Offensive Campign (TCOC) during the period Feb-June each year, when the trees are bare of leaves, sky is clear, ground dry and consequently, it is easier, perhaps convenient, to trace, track and chase the forces. It is understandable, wherefore, that all major attacks in bastar have come during this five-month window of the year.

So, it was their ability to utilise this specific period that the Maoists attacked a smaller contingent of 60 STF men this 4 Apr (2015), killing seven out of these 60. This ambush goes to prove that they have retained their ability, agility, and certain control of interior areas of the state... in southern Bastar.

The analysts fear that like the CRPF after the Dec 2014 Chintagufa loss going into "retreat mode", the State Police STF may repeat the syndrome after the 4 April (2015) loss! If so, consequences will be the decreased foot falls of the STF in the interior areas, an ideal tactical opportunity for the Maoists to recover lost ground in the year 2015... which also marks the 10th summer after the Salwa Judum.

Selecting officers for service in Red Zone

Development of the tribal areas play an important role in combating the Maoist menace. If the physical battle against the Maoists is waged by the security forces of the nation, its administrative machinery plays an equally important part in winning the battle of minds and hearts, in the tribal population. It is here that District Magistrates and Sub-Divisional officer come in the picture.

This section will discuss the importance of selecting DMs and SDOs for their right qualities, their suitability for the task, and their mental make up to face the harsh realities of service in Maoist-hit districts and areas.

"Once abducted, now strategists" Oct 2011

This is the story of how two abductees are proving useful to the Centre in its counter-Maoist campaign. The two IAS officers... R. Vineel Krishnan, DC Malkangiri district of Odisha and Vijay Kumar, were one among seven IAS officers kidnapped in 1987 in Rampochodavaram in East Godavari district of Andhra Pradesh and released after 4-day hostage drama... have both served in the Maoist-hit areas and also share commonality in the fact that they were abducted by the Maoists.

It is the experiences and the close encounters of the two IAS officers with the Naxals that are coming in good stead for Union RD Minister Jairam Ramesh, especially in implementing development strategies in the affected areas across the country.[16]

Impressed with Krishnan's track record as DC Malkangiri where his administrative measures for the welfare of the tribals have been appreciated, Ramesh brought him to Delhi as his personal secretary. In fact, during his last 16-month tenure as the Collector, he was effective in getting the tribals turn away from Maoists. Krishnan was held hostage by the Maoists for nine days in Feb (2011) and later released.

Kumar, Joint Secretary in the Ministry heads the National Rural Livelihood Mission. Acknowledging their inputs, Ramesh on 11 October, at a seminar 'From Tirupati to Pashupati: Some reflection on the Maoist issue', said: "Both the officers are very strong advocates of the SR Sankar-an approach of development and sensitive governance in tribal areas. But in my continuous conversations with them, two things have emerged. One, the Naxals are exploiting the tribals. Two, the tribals themselves want peace, not war. The Naxals are using the tribal areas and issues for their tactical purposes. The terrain and forests suit them for guerrilla warfare. They have spread their terror and ensured that the developmental activities are obstructed."

He maintained that the tribal cause, that the Naxals espouse, is only a mask to advance their own agenda. The Malkan giri incident was a clear message from the tribals of the region that they want development and not Naxal terror.

He believes two-pronged strategy was needed to tackle the menace: "One that deals with the leadership of the Naxals, who aim to overthrow the Indian State, and other, which focuses on the concerns of the people they pretend/claim to serve."

He expressed his firm belief "that a complete revamp of administration and governance in tribal areas, especially in Central and Eastern India, is the pressing need of the hour. Andhra Pradesh has attempted to do this through its Integrated Tribal Development Agency (ITDA) model, but much more needed to be done."

Drafted to Red Country: Apr 2012 (Dedicated Officers)

This news story in a daily of 29 Apr 2012 opens out with a courageous officer's non-challance towards his near-death attack by the Maoists.[17] "It is an irony that Rajat Kumar, the DM of Bijapur in Chhattisgarh, finds excruciating. The IAS officer, whose convoy was blown up on 20 Apr (2012), and who escaped certain and bloody death by inches, is aghast at what Alex Paul Menon (another DM in the State) is going through. 'It is amazing,' he says, 'Those who have kidnapped him have to realise that we are working for the same cause... the development of the tribal areas. Shoudn't we be on the same side.' "

Kumar has no mind to ask for transfer. "I'll continue working for people here... The satisfaction it gives you is worth the danger it comes with...", he says. Incidentally, he was on his way to supervise the construction of a road that had remained untouched and cut off for 15 years.

But if "unfairness" of the situation hurts some of India's bravest IAS and IPS officers working in what is clearly now one of the world's most dangerous belts, most are neither giving in nor giving up. Like Rahul Bhagat, SP of North Bastar, who has spent the last six years in Red belt and is determined to carry on. The 2005 batch IPS officer from Jharkhand was only recently joined by his family, after five lonely years.

In fact, the whole process of protecting life... your own and your men's... from a threat that is constant and relentless consumes a lot of their time. They keep planning to outwit the enemy: changing their vehicles, routes, number plates, and even tour plans. Some use bullet proof cars, others travel in private vehicles, buses, motor cycles and autos... "It is like guerrilla warfare. One wrong move may cause huge manpower loss," says Navin Gulati, the Punjab-born SP of Nalgonda, Andhra Pradesh, which falls in Red Corridor. Earlier posted on the dreaded Andhra-Odisha border, Gulati says "it is real fun to challenge them and defeat them."

It has not dampened their spirits, the challenge seems to have inspired them, encouraging many of them to opt for work in Red areas, given half a chance. In just last few years, there has been a clutch of officers from Tamil Nadu who have seen action in Chhattisgarh, Odisha, Jharkhand, Maharashtra and parts of North-East.

Interestingly, of the 10 Maoist-hit districts in Chhattisgarh, six are under the charge of officers from Tamil Nadu, most of them under 35. Sukma's kidnapped DM Paul Menon is one of them. So is the DM of Bastar, P. Anbalagan. He says the offiers with commitment who work for the development of the area they serve, putting their personal safety at risk, are on top of the Maoist hit list."

Shubhranshu Choudhary, founder of the C G net Swara, who launched a community radio service in trouble-prone areas of Chhattisgarh, says Maoist-hit areas were earlier considered punishment postings. "But the things have changed now, with idealistic officers making a big difference." He got a call from Menon's office to set up a radio service for villagers in Sukma.

In Manipur too, three out of nine districts are headed by collectors from Tamil Nadu. Jacintha Lazarus, district collector of Churachandpur and Menon's batch mate, says many young officers posted in danger zones prefer to stay on to help develop the region over a period of time.

Bhagat says lack of roads not only restricts their movement and communication with the locals, but also affects normal policing. That is one reason why 30 per cent of Bastar is practically under Maoists. Lack of intelligence also is a major hurdle.

Some cite "false cases" registered by Maoists that leave the 'babus' battling on a different front. Surprisingly, though, Maoists do not target the judiciary. Many say this helps them in obvious ways. "One is left to fight the court battles alone," laments an officer. "And that is hugely demoralizing."

Paul Menon's kidnapping highlights the amazing odds India's bureaucrats are up against in the Maoist belt. But undeterred, a new generation of braveheart babus continues to court tough assignments.

"Call the Maoist bluff, take them out" By Srivatsa Krishna: An IAS Officer

This is an article by a serving IAS officer, that appeared in May 2012, in a weekly, Sunday Guardian. He is calling for tough dealing with them. First three paras of this article are reproduced below as it tells us why for his feelings:

"Dashrath Prasad, LV Reddy, G Krishnaiah, Narendra Kumar, Surendra Babu: All outstanding IAS/IPS officers who laid down their lives while doing an honest day's work. Now, a young IAS officer (Paul Menon) is abducted in Chhattisgarh, ironically, while addressing a development meeting.

"There is virtually no other country on the planet where one-third of the nation's districts are in grip of the Naxalism. Unarguably, some of it may be in response to misgovernance, but a large part of it is a serious law and order problem.

"There is an irony here that couldn't be starker. Public perception of the IAS is at an all time low, thanks to various corruption scandals. There is enormous demand for reforms in the civil services... and rightly so... for one can't run a twenty-first century economy with a nineteenth century bureacracy administering eighteenth century laws often with a fourteenth century mindset. But, that said, it should not take away from the courageous work being done, away from the glare of media and in extremely difficult circumstances, by countless young officers like Paul Menon."

Some other important observations made by this officer are briefly summed up:

- Maoists butchered 76 CRPF men in Chhattisgarh not very long ago, when they are not killing cops, they are busy abducting officers and sending interlocuters to the government.
- Amazingly, hearing the interlocuters speak, one wonders if this is some kind of perpetual Jawahar Rozgar Yojana for them. The interlocuters could actually be mistaken for Maoist spokespersons. And if they are the latter, there is a case for the government to take action against them.
- Importantly, if the interlocuters and TV cameras can reach their hideouts so easily, then the State with all its might and Army is more than competent to do so.
- The task of combing 40,000 sq km is by no means easy. But if a bunch of determined officers with strong political backing could root out extremism in Punjab... the dreaded Tamil Tigers were defeated by the armed forces in Sri Lanka... our forces can surely take on the Maoist... why can't the success of the Grey hounds in Andhra be replicated in Chhattisgarh?
- It is time we stop whining that "these are our own people..." "they are misguided youth who need to be brought to the mainstream," or it is all about tribal disaffection with the State."

- Maoists do not allow government to construct roads or administer some of its welfare programmes.
- Time has come for the state to take on the challenge of rooting out the Naxalism head on with all its might.
- Development must accompany such efforts but food, jobs and roads may just not be enough to fight guns and bullets.

"IAS, IPS-Army talks to nip the conflict" Nov 2012

This is an apt if overdue subject that needs certain discussion for better results that should accrue from the government plans and projects launched for the good of the common man. The blurb of this story in a daily makes its intent and aim clear: "Mid-career interaction aims for bridging gap, boosting synergy."[18]

Aim of this interaction is explained this way: "In an effort to bridge the communication gap between civilian officers of the IAS and IPS and Army offiers, the Army proposes to have mid-career interaction." That should enable the bureaucrats and service officers to appreciate working ethos and conditions/constraints of each other's circumstances and work cultures. It will also help two arms of the government to effectively deal with the issues like Naxalism, terrorism and natural disasters.

The need for such an interaction has come up as the IAS and IPS officers get little exposure to the military and mid-career interaction would go a long way in synergising the function the Army and civil administration to meet unforeseen situations at a short notice.

The government in principle has given nod to proposal for a structured joint programmes between the IAS/IPS and military officers in two stages of their career: First when these officers have six to right years of service; and second after putting in 12 to 14 years. This was disclosed by the officials on 25 Nov 2012, at New Delhi.

The first interaction is expected in Dec 2012, with special focus on issues like internal security, including Naxalism and insurgency, preparedness for nuclear, biological and chemical warfare and cross-border terrorism.

Elaborating upon the objectives behind such an interaction, officials explained that the ethnic violence in Assam in July 2012 was an apt example of lack of communication... better still, perhaps, lack of understanding when to communicate... between the armed forces and civil administration over the timing and urgency to deploy the Army to control and curb the violence. This incident invited wide-spread criticism and consequent effort to shift the blame to each other for late deployment of Army in Assam. The Government realised such issues can be tackled by having better rapport between the two sides, i.e., the services and bureaucracy.

Besides this instance, the so-called turf war among various stake-holders in insurgency-hit regions like J & K and the North-East is another reason cited for need for such an interaction. Even though the Unified Command system, where senior officers of the Army, CPMF, and state police take decision in meetings chaired by the Chief Ministers, has been functioning for the last two decades, the officials feel the synergy at the cutting-edge of the ground level leaves much to desire. Hence the need for rapport between the mid-level officers of the two sides.

This will ensure that pro-active action against the terrorists is launched in real time after getting specific intelligence inputs, as time is of essence in nabbing or neutralising a threat, be it in J & K or in the North-East. [Same should apply to real time information passed to the CPMF in counter-Naxal operations, even if it is not covered by the topic under discussion here!]

The interaction will take place once a year. This decision was taken after intense discussions at the highest level of bureaucracy and military leadership. The training capsule was jointly framed by the DG Military Training (DGMT) and Department of Personnel and Training (DoPT).

Various Army Commands were also directed to conduct such interactions lasting five to ten days in their respective areas to provide an opportunity to a large number of officers to interact with each other and discuss region-specific issues in greater detail.

"A young politician has blueprint for getting government officers in Maoist belt": Feb 2013 (A mit Jogi)

Here is a young politician who seems to have taken his job seriously. A daily reports in Feb 2013: "For the seven weeks he has been an MLA, former CM Ajit Jogi's son Amit has plunged into his role with enthusiasm. In the Assembly, he has made two fiery speeches that have lasted possibly the longest for any opposition legislator. In his constituency, he has introduced a helpline, Hello Marwahi, for redressing complaints."[19]

The above is about his pedigree and his energy levels. On to the point relevant to our subject. He plans to introduce a bill... "Removal of vacancies and Absenteeism in Public Offices of Backward and LWE-Affected Areas Bill... to check absenteeism of government employees in Maosit-hit areas, which affects basic services. Those who do go there stay for years, with the government reluctant to transfer them, leading to resentment.

Jogi's bill prescribes a maximum period 1,000 working days for a posting in such regions. As the duration is marked by "working days", it means the employee has to work that long in a Maoist area. After that, even if the government fails to transfer him, the bill proposes "the employee shall be deemed to have been relieved." And if the employee fails to join within five working days of the order "without reasonable cause", he will be "removed with immediate effect."

To ensure those who have worked in such zones get a substantial break, the bill proposes that after completing one tenure in such a zone, an employee cannot be posted back before he competes "1,000 working days" in a non-scheduled zone (an area outside the Maoist belt).

Jogi told the daily: "The major issue affecting governance in Maoist areas today is the non-serious approach of the government. The CM and others are not keen to provide the basic services and hence allow vacancies and absenteeism to continue." He, of course, does not explain why the government should not be keen to provide basic services!

He accuses the government of an understanding with the Maoists. During his speech on the first day of the budget session on 3 February? he equated "Raman" (Singh CM) with "Ramanna", Secretary of the CPI (Maoists)'s DK SZC. Referring to the recent arrest of BJP men, he demanded a CBI inquiry the government would scuttle the probe as "they did in the Essar Case". He explained that the SP Dantewada had arrested an Essar GM and charged the company with funding the Maoists, but the SP was transferred. He was at his eloquent best in the Assembly and continued in the same vein: "Earlier I thought there was a conflict between the two (Maoists and government), but now it seems there is no difference between Raman and Ramannal."

The opposition was obviously enjoying the government's discomfiture over the Jogi peroration. So, when he was interrupted by the speaker on the ground that his time was up, the leader of the opposition TS Sinhadev stood up to say: "He has prepared very well. We will surrender two or three other speakers. Please give him their time." Interestingly, the Jogi camp had staunchly opposed Sinhadev's appointment as leader of the opposition? This is politics at its best!

At the end, a word on the younger Jogi. It remains to be seen how Congressmen, many of whom still complain about his family's efforts to divide the party, will take the younger Jogi. Says Amit Jogi: "There is no camp any more in the Congress; we all belong to the Rahul camp."

"Specialised training to officials in tackling Maoists:" Sep 2014[20]

All-India Services officers in eight Naxal-hit States... Chhattisgarh, MP, West-Bengal, Odisha, Andhra Pradesh, Telengana, Maharashtra, and Jharkhand... will undergo specialised training at the Chhattisgarh Academy of Administration on tackling LWE.

As a part of mid-career interaction with armed forces, conducted in coordination with the MOD, Department of Personnel and Training (DoPT) has asked the State governments to nominate at least three officers... one each from IAS, IPS and Indian Forest Service... for the 3-day training from 15 to 17 Oct (2014).

The programme intends to bring together civilian and armed forces officers from these eight states to a common discussion forum on the theme subject, "Left wing Extremism".

The DoPT directive said: "The mid-career interaction courses are conducted at the tactical and operational level and they are expected to benefit both the armed forces and civil services officers through mutual learning from each others' strengths and also by imbibing the best points of each others work culture, ethos and coutoms. This is expected to help them combat future challenges to national security in an organised manner."

"Pick DMs and SPs with anti-Naxal zeal:" Jan 2015

Describing Naxal problem as the gravest threat facing India, Home Minister Rajnath Singh on 16 Jan 2015 asked all States facing Maoist menace to appoint as DMs and SPs such officers who have the 'zeal' to fight the rebals.[21] He was addressing the Eastern Zonal Council (EZC) at Patna.

His audience included member states of the EZC, at the level of Chief Ministers: Jitan Ram Manjhi (Bihar), Raghubar Das (Jharkhand). Odisha and West Bengal were represented by their Home Ministers.

Civil Populations in the Crossfire

Where ever the security forces are engaged in anti-terrorist war, as in Jammu and Kashmir, or anti-LWE one, as in the Red Zone, innocent civilians often get entrapped in the crossfire. Not withstanding all the efforts by the security forces, the civilians suffer sometime because of unavoidable situations, and more often than not, because of machinations of the terrorists or the Maoists.

As the book is essentially concerns the Maoist rebelion, it shall deal with the situations arising out of security forces' counter-Maoist operations. Often as a strategic considerations, the Maoist make the civilians, especially the children and women, sacrificial goats in their fight against the security forces. It is done specificially to inflame the anti-Government and-security forces passions among the civil population. One easy way of doing it is their practice of using civilians as human shields in their battle against the government forces.

"Hazards of being on the right side of the law": Nov 2011

This is an attention-grabbing title of an article that appear in a daily in Nov 2011. Its blurb clarifies the things in no uncertain manner: "Many villagers in Chhattisgarh have abandoned their homes and moved into new settlements after Maoists identified them as 'police informers."[22]

First two paragraphs of this article expresses the issue in a very poignant way, so the need to reproduce them in to-to.

"An eerie silence welcome me as I walk down the row of houses. There is not a soul in sight. I know that from every tiny window in these little brick-walled units watchful, suspicious eyes follow my every move. They are assessing me, wondering if I am friend or foe. But then, in these thickly forested parts, the lines of distinction blurred many years ago. And their life could depend on the accuracy of the conclusion they draw about every visitor."

"This is life as usual in this part of the Narayanpur block of the Bastar region in Chhattisgarh, in a settlement locally referred to as *Mukhbiron ki basti*, the 'village of informers.' The residents have long stopped fighting the label. If being called an informer helps them escape the wretched life they led in their forest dwellings, so be it. It is also by choice that these wise and ancient people, traditional custodians of the forest wealth, have chosen to walk away from their forest homes to live in these tiny isolated dwellings, away from their lands: their only source of sustenance, willing to brave a life of hunger and uncertainty."

These families do not hail from Nayaranpur block. They have travelled from Abujhmaad... the other block in the newly-created/craved Narayanpur district in south Chhattisgarh, believed to be the stronghold of Maoists. Some families are there for decades while others arrived as recently as two moths back. Why would anyone leave home and lead a life of destitution in these marked areas, vulnerable to attacks for taking a stand to not support the Maoists, or worse, being called police informers?

Some families moved out of compulsion, says a villager, "Once they accept my presence as safe, they will come out to meet me."

If a family number is picked up by police for questioning, the entire family become suspect, and always at risk. Many have never been informers, but the label has stuck.

The residents recall a defining moment when the necessity to move out became evident to the villagers at large. This was some years ago when the ultras were on 'recruitment drive,' but that event sends a shiver through the silent, listening group. Some families in some remote villages collectively decided to oppose the recruitment exercise, and said so! Shortly after the event, 26 boys between 18 and 25 were executed publicly, and the rest of the village was forced to witness the macabre sight. The villagers believe that at least 10 to 15 youths and/or persons were abducted "from each village (of no sayers) and subsequently killed by the ultras, asserting that they had passed information to the police."

Here is a tribal woman in tattered saree speaking to the scribe: "Life in the village was worsening every day. There were constant threats. People would be roughed up. Hunger is easier to live with than fear and constant dissent." At this point, a man listening quietly so far burst out: "Back home, we were simply not allowed to be, to get on with our daily chores, work in our fields. They would call a meeting and it was compulsory to attend in silence. Asking questions was forbidden. We did not even have rights over our fields produce. It would be taken away by the Maoists. When we obtained PDS rations from the government, they took away half of it. After some time, even that source of food grains dried up. What were we to eat? There was no choice but to move out."

The villages in the forest lament that the resident of the settlement, no longer have schools and health services. Gradually, families began to move out. Those who stayed back are either Maoist supporters, they asserted, or some who were forced by circumstances to stay back, however, reluctantly. As violence escalated, more families started trickling out of the forests, moving to places that seemed safer. Over the last decade (2000-2010), many such settlements have come up behind Narayanpur town, in the open spaces like the hills in the vicinity. Bereft of agricultural land, the people sit idle during the harvesting season.

One of the settlement is, ironically named Shanti Nagar (= the town of peace). It has electricity, school, access roads, even drainage. Several families have settled there. One factor that unites them is desolation and loss, and often, antagonism and grief. Their lives may be safer here than in their forest homes, but what does the future have in store for them, landless and, unschooled as they are? Who is to blame? Most important, will they be able to return home?

The villagers hesitate to answer about Abujhmaad (also, Abujhwarh), a vast expanse of dense forest never surveyed during an Indian census, has no functional government presence, limited as they are to Orcha Block and Sonapur village. Maoist camps are scattered across the forest, some surrounded by landmines and inaccessible even to the tribal groups who have known these forests as their own home for several decades.

Close to the unsecured settlements of alleged informers is a heavily guarded group of 30 to 40 houses where 'special informers', recognised as Special Police Officers by the State, reside. Also locals, they accompany police during their treks, acting as guides in the thick forests. They earn a monthly salary, are trained in the use of weapons, and are protected. "The distinction between the two settlements is stark."

Political will is essential if more such settlements are to be prevented from coming up, so they matter more than mere vote banks. Till then, the harsh tales of these invisible displaced communities are likely to continue.

"Abandon operations if Maoists use human shields:" Security forces told: Jul 2012

Facing flak for the alleged killings of villagers last month (June 2012) in an encounter between the CRPF and the Maoists in Chhattisgarh, the Centre on 13 Jul 2012 asked all the security forces deployed in the LWE-hit States not to engage with the rebels if they were found to be using innocent civilians as human shields.[23]

This was one of the two crucial points discussed at a high-level meeting convened by the MHA on 13 Jul 2012 where representations of nine Maoist-hit States participated along with senior officials of security forces. (Surrender policy was the other issue discussed, which will be examined in an appropriate section of this book).

Apart from changes required in the Standard Operating Procedures (SOPs) for the security forces in the affected States/areas, the meeting discussed strengthening of the security paraphernalia in these States.

A senior official said: "The main emphasis of the SOPs is how to check the Maoists tactic of using human shields and minimise collateral damage in action... The security forces have been asked to abandon the operation if they find that civilians, particularly women and children, are being used as human shields."

Security forces conducting operations at night had been asked to carry night-vision equipment and resources to illuminate the area of operations to ensure that no civilians are present when they are engaging with the

Maoists Forces have even been asked that if necessary, they should just cordon off the area during night and conduct the operation only after dawn.

Fresh recruits and personnel going to the violence-affected area for the first time will be given special training in jungle warfare and sensitised about local environment, besides being briefed on how to engage with Naxals by avoiding collateral damage.

Now come the turn of the LWE-hit states to receive orders: Reviewed the security situation in these State and discussed ways to deal with the large build up of military wing of the CPI (Maoist) in Chhattisgarh: the MHA asked the States to deploy adequate personnel and provide arms and ammunition, in police stations falling under Naxal areas; the states were also asked to fill vacancies in middle level... from sub-inspectors to Deputy Superintendent.

This MHA-convened meeting was attended by the DGs of police from the nine States and the DGs of the Central Para-military forces.

Another daily covering the same meeting had a slightly different version of an important subject: "The MHA directed the forces to finalise the SOPs after consulting with the officers working on the ground."[24]

"MHA order on non-lethal arms irks anti-Naxal forces" Sep 2012

The Baseguda encounter had led to 17 civilian deaths. Subsrequently, only nine of them were found to be Maoists. The civilian deaths caused hue and cry in the area and anger among the civil society.

To ensure prevention of such an occurrence, the MHA issued new SOPs which suggest use of non-lethal weapons like rubber bullets and tear gas in the initial stages. If that did not work, the next step would be use of sniper attacks employing modern equipment.

There were some other recommendations also: Engaging Naxals in uninhabited areas; illuminating a place before an encounter, and a database of photographs of all women and children living in the Naxal areas. These suggestions were prompted by the revelations that Maoists had used villagers as human shields during the encounter.[25]

The new SOP reportedly divided the leadership of the CPMFs. The field officers at the junior level are not happy with these while the MHA claims to have consulted senior officers on the issue.

Field sources in the forces believe the new SOPs are impractical and were designed without keeping in mind the operational difficulties of Naxal-affected areas. Isn't it surprising then that the SOPs were formulated on the suggestions of senior officers in the forces?

The SOPs sent to the CRPF, BSF, and ITBP "are currently being studied by them." These will be sent back with suggestions, which might include certain crucial changes after consutations with the field officers.

Sources conveyed while some suggestions, such as "always going on operations with local police", could be accepted, several others were "nearly impossible." A BSF officer who has served in Bengal's Jungal Mahal, says realistically. "In jungles, you can't see anything at a distance of even 20 mtrs. If the firing starts from the other side' most of the times, we do not know where it is coming from. Where are we going to fire tear gas shells? And how will snipers spot anything in such areas?

A BSF officer spoke with a degree of incredulity at the sugestion of making a data base of photographs: "That would be a massive task who would do that? We do not even properly know where and how many villages may be there in a certain Naxal area. And even if we manage to make a data base, will it help avoid civilian casualties in the kind of encounters we face."

"In Maoist land, children bear the brunt of police operations": Dec 2012

A daily, in a story datelined 19 Dec 2012, Bala (kanker district), tells how children in these tribal areas are victims of a situation not of their making.[26]

On 12 Dec 2012, in Abujhwaad... a 4,000 sq km forest area mostly in Chhattisgarh... police fired on tribal children attending on Maoist camp, and killed a teenager, Chainu Mandawi and arrested nine others. Police say they were unaware of children attending the camp when they opened fire. The few Maoists cadre in the camp escaped and the police rounded up children and sent them to a remand house.

In another part of Abujhmaad, which lies in Maoist-controlled areas of Chhattisgarh, a security operation in March (2012) resulted in the deatlh of another teenager and several arrest. In June (2012), several children were killed in a CRPF operation in Bijapur, outside Abujhmaad area.

A word on 12 December incident. Some 240 policemen raided the day-long camp being attended by over 20 tribal children between the villages Sitram and Bala in Paralkot Reserve Forest area, 10 km inside the Maad. The night before, a few Maoist cadres arrived in the villages to select boys and girls, mostly below 14 years of age, for the camp.

The Maoists control the area, which has little police presence otherwise, and villagers would have no choice but to send their children if the Maoists asked. "They (Maoists) said there would not be any arms training but my son to carry his Bharmar (a country-made gun), which he uses for killing wild boar," said Munglee Mandawi, Chainu's mother. After the post-mortem, Mr Mandawi was given Rs 1,200 by 'some one' in Pakhanjore civil hospital, for the last rites of Chainu, the bread winner of the family of six: The Kanker SP, Rahul Bhagat, in charge of the operation... acknoweledged that the trainees in the camp were "children and teengers." Mr Bhagat said: "We showed sufficient restraint when we realised that most of them were unarmed children or teenagers." About Chainu, the SP said, "He was a gun carrying member of the party and a militia commander of Bala village... He was killed in the encounter."

The camp set up in a rectangular space about 30 by 40 ft in size... closed from all sides by thick bamboo trees, wore a deserted look four days after the operation. Two severely underweight girls presumably in their early teens, who were in the camp, said about 25 children had completed their morning drill when the firing started. Dipika Metami said: "Around 8 AM, we heard the sound of gun fire. There was lot of smoke. We heard someone shouting for help but we ran."

Family members of the teenagers picked up by the police said their children had never visited a Maoist camp earlier. The parents were shocked 'when their children were lined up in the police station. "My son was wearing a tee shirt when he was picked up, but in the police station he was wearing Maoist battle fatigue," said Sunita Mandawi of Satram village whose son Sachin was arrested by the police.

Masuram Usendi said her daughter went to meet her friends in the camp when she was picked up by the police. Another girl, Raje, had come to meet her parents from her uncle's place. The exact age of these children and teenagers is difficult to ascertain as the villagers keep no record of the age of their children.

The Kanker SP refused to comment on some local newspaper reports that the arrested girls were sexually abused by the Maoists cadres in the camp. The family members of the girls, in presence of other villagers categorically said that their children were never sexually exploited by the Maoists. Judu Koache, Raje's father, said: "My daughter went to a camp for the first time last week... how can she be sexually exploited for years?"

Villagers are angry that the police had fired on children. An angry villager who refused to be identified, said, "If the police were unaware (of the children), it is an intelligence failure and they should not have been firing." DGP Ram Niwas told the daily he will "verify" the facts.

"Children will not interact with police or Maoists:" Villagers: Dec 2012

"The residents of four villages inside Abujhmaad in South Chhattisgarh on Friday (21 Dec 2012) passed a unique resolution, resisting both the Maoists and the police," reported a daily dated 23 Dec 2012.[27]

The resolution says: "The children will not 'interact' with the Maoists or the police."

The villagers said children of "our villages will remain in their respective villages and the elders will interact with the Maoists and the Police." The resolution was passed unanimously and came nine days after the police raided a Maoist camp, arresting nine children and teenagers of Sitram and Bala villages. One boy, Chainu Mandawi, was shot dead by the police.

One of the convenors from local panchayat (of village Sitram) said on condition of anonymity: "The villagers have decided that they will continue giving food to the Maoists as they raise our issue of protecting land and forest. But we will not send the children to camp to give the food." The villagers, however, said the children were not given any 'military training' in the camp.

In the meeting, attended by some 300 villagers, the father of one of the girls arrested by the police, Masuram Usendi, said he was surprised by lack of security in the Maoist camp, adding: "Maoists put sentries around any camp to watch out for the police. But in this case, it was surprisingly absent." About 25 boys and girls were in the camp, when police opened fire last week.

Later, one of the senior leaders of south Chhattisgarh, Rajmon, Secretary, United North Bastar-Maad Division, met the scribe in Orchha block of Abujh Maad to categorically deny the allegations made by the villagers. Rajmon said the camp between Sitram and Bala was not a "training camp" and children were not "forcibly brought" in the camp, and added: "The children came to deliver some food. It was an over-night camp for cadres to stay. The food was given 'Willingly' by the villagers." On the allegation of lack of adequate 'sentry' in the camp, Rajmon said it was a 'sad lapse' on the part of the squad commander as the sentries assembled to have break fast 'together', and "that was when the police opened fire."

He (Rajmon) acknowledged that two of the nine arrested people were in Maoist militia... the peripheral ring of cadres selected from the civilians... who joined recently. Chainu Mandawi was a member of mass front of peasants, he said.

The daily says "the villagers were appalled by the fact that the police fired indiscriminately on the children." Kanker SP Rahul Bhagat earlier said the police had shown 'sufficient restraint' while firing, while acknowledging that there were children and teenagers in the group." The villagers have decided to complain against the police to 'appropriate authority' if they get an apportunity in the meeting.

The villagers are quite in the dark regarding the release of the boys as well. Masuram Usendi, who has never been to a big city, says," getting them released is our primary concern, but we do not know how to go about it." The mother of the boy, Muanglee Mandawi, did not attend the public meeting, as she said, "Now it is pointless."

"Tribals get it from both sides" Jan 2013

The title of this news story is both expressive, explicit and illustrative, as a daily has shown in the text,[28] of its 13 Jan 2013 issue

A similar, rather same, subject has been covered/dealt with in the innmediately preceding pages. It must also be understood, even if not accepted, by the lay reader that some civilians getting caught in situations of insurgencey, secessionism and terrorism is inevitable, be it in the Red Corridor, as in the instant case, in India's North-East or in Jammu and Kashmir. What is important is as to how the security forces handle this sensitive issue, to ensure the so called collateral damage... injury and fatality... to civilians are minimalised. It must also be understood that the insurgents/secessionists/terrorists would go all out to defame the State's forces by forcing some civilian casualties in various situation by their deliberate actions, namely, employing civilians... women and children, in particular–as human shields.

Before proceeding any further, the blurb of the story is reproduced: "AT RECEIVING END-villagers usually get caught in the crossfire between Maoists and security men."

The daily starts out with an interesting point: "Ranchi: This week's killing of 10 security men has again demonstrated that the Maoists' beligerence goes up sharply in January, the birth time of their armed unit, PLGA."

These celebrations, often assuming brutal form, continue for seven days. It is a well-planned annual event. Thousands of Maoists and their sympathisers participate in the celebrations and exhibit their strength. It has been the rebels tradition to execute some big-bang event... an ambush, an attack on a police station/convoy... before they disperse.

Here are some instances. On 3 Dec 2011, the rebels attacked the convoy of Chatra MP Inder Singh Namdhari in Palamu, killing 11 people, including one civilian. On 4 Jan 2008, they blew up a police jeep in Latehar, killing five, including a sub-inspector.

Jharkhand's hilly terrain and dense forests have served as ideal locations for their periodic congregations. Some 700 civilians, 448 security men and 500 rebels have been killed in the Red depredations in the State, over the past 12 years. At the Ambatikar forests on Tuesday (10 Jan 2013), the security forces had encountered a strong contingent of Maoists headed towards the Odisha border. Led by their commanders Deo Kumar Singh and Vikash Ji, both members of the CPI (Maoist), the rebels 'tried inflicting maximum damage, but they also suffered major losses in the battle. The injured CRPF and Jharkhand Jaguar Jawans claimed they had shot at no fewer than 20 Maoists, killing at least 10 of them, mostly women.

But the bodies could not be recovered, since the Maoists always take them away from the site, and often deny casualties on their side to maintain the morale of their Red Brigade at a high. Any admission of the casualties would add to the frustration of the rebel cadres, as their leadership is already facing a large-scale exodus of cadres and also confronting challenges from splinters/factions.

SP Latehar Kanti Kumar Gadideshi claimed Singh and Vikashji were explosives experts and were prone to cruelty. The duo implanted the IEDs in the bodies of some slain jawans' bodies/stomachs, aimed at blowing up the chopper in which the bodies would subsequently be flown to district headquarters. What diabolic and macabre planners, these Maoists!

Maoists are masters at propaganda! Their spokesman, named appropriately Toofan, released a CD condemning the security forces for using villagers as human shields and warned the civilians not to do such things again! He was, of course, referring to four villagers who had allegedly died while rescuing the bodies when the forces had reported asked them to do so.

In such a situation, the closet Maoists can't lag behind the official spokesman of the Maoists. Gautam Navlakha, a loud, self-oppointed supporter and fighter for the cause of the Maoists, and a member of People's Union for Democratic Rights, shouts from his house top: "Using innocent as human shields has been the practice of our forces for years. Any commission of war which does not conform to the Geneva protocol is highly condemnable. What the Maoists have done in Latehar is deplorable. But the number of cases of violation by the forces is far greater."

Collateral damage incurred in anti-Maoist Operations: MHA:" 20 May 2013

About seven people killed during an encounter between security men and Moists in Chhattisgarh on 17 may 2013 were innocent, the MHA and police sources confirmed on the 20th, reports a daily dated 21 May 2013.[29]

The State Government has ordered a judicial probe, but the MHA appears to have come around to the view that the forces might not have done a good job of implementing plans announced last year (2012) to minimise "collateral" loss of life. After 17 tribals were killed in Chhattisgarh's Bijapur district in June (last year) 2012, the MHA had issued an advisory to the security force not to engage or even abandon an operation, in case the Maoists were found using civilians as human shields.

A word on the instant case. It happened a year after that advisory was issued. Based on the intelligence inputs, the CRPF and police men targeted what was reported to be a meeting of the rebels, about 1.5 km from a village on the 17th. The Maoists who were on an elevated piece of land fired at the troops. The villagers, who were in between, got killed in the cross firing.

Let it be stated here unambiguously that notwithstanding all such advisories by authorities sitting in their distant offices in New Delhi, such collateral damage can, at times happen. The commander on the spot might come to learn about 'human shields' to late, or, might never learn about their presence, at all. Still worse, often after the unfortunate tragedy, even if the Maoists had used such shields, the fact will be denied vociferously not only by the Maoists, but also by those very villagers. They have more reasons to be scared of the outlaws, than the forces. In the final analysis, it is the man on the spot, the commander, in the thick of it all, who has to take the call on the issue, and in the heat of the moment, it is impossible to take right decisions all the times! All these factors must be understood by people who subsequently sit on judgement when things go wrong, be they the people in the MHA at Delhi or the judicial officials and not be too prompt or too officious in their judgemental fervour!

As for the instant case, besides the Rs 5 lakh compensation amount per head announced by the State Government, the MHA decided to give Rs 3 lakh, in addition, to each victim.

"Security concerns behind Chhattisgarh move on Red Cross:" Jun 2013

A daily says, "behind Chhattisgarh government's sudden directive to the International Committee of the Red Cross (LCRC) to suspend its operations in Maoist-hit district of Bijapur in Bastar region is a possible security concern."[30]

What are, or could be, the possible reasons behind this directive? If the State Government's official stand claims that the ICRC had not signed an MoU, a prerequisite for its medicare operations, and was therefore sent the notice, highly placed sources told the daily that a possibility of the agency providing health facilities to the Maoists prompted the decision.

In fact, ICRC had been working in Kutru village of Bijapur for two years without the MoU, but the "State government asked it to suspend operations only last week." Yet again, ICRC had a similar medicare centre in Chintalnar area of Sukma, another Maoist-hit district of South Bastar, but the government order pertains only to Bijapur. Chintalnar is a comparatively remotely located than Kutru, which is well-connected by a motorable road.

A senior officer told the daily: "NGOs operating in such insurgency-hit areas mostly tend to favour extremists. They support them, provide them humanitarian aid. In an area where government doctors cannot visit, how do they manage to work? Sometimes, we ignore it, but at times, we have to step in."

The matter "came to light last week when the ICRC got a letter from Bijapur Collector Mohd Qaiser Abdul Haque asking them to suspend operations. Haque claimed that while the ICRC has not yet signed an MoU with the State Government, it also needed to sort out some diplomatic issues with the Centre.

Now the daily notes some flaws in the governments handling of the issue. "The issue of non-signing of the MoU regarding medicare services in some of the remotest areas emerged in a state that often boasts of implementing maximum number of business-related MoUs. ICRC sources said they were asked to vacate the premises within a few hours." This when they are operating from a government primary health centre, and send weekly report to the Collector. The ICRC submitted a draft MoU to the Centre more than two years ago but things have not moved.

Speaking to the daily, ICRC communication coordinator Marek Resich refused to comment on the nature of MoUs, required to be signed with the state and central governments. He said, "We have got a letter (from the Bijapur administration) and we are seeking clarifications from the governments."

Principal secretary to CM N Baijendra Kumar, echoed the official stand, denied any security concerns and instisted that the "non-formation of the MoU was the only reason" for the government action.

In fact, some years ago, the then SSP Dantewada SRP Kalluri had accused the ICRC of providing medicare facilities to the Maoists, and even claimed that some rebels were arrested with its medicines. The humanitarian agency has refuted the charges.

The Judiciary and fight against Maoists

The Indian judiciary in the past has given certain verdicts on matters related to operations of army against the terrorists in Jammu and Kashmir and an anti-Maoist formation in Chhattisgarh. The respective details follow.

In Jammu and Kashmir, the Army was engaged in a prolonged operation against a number of terrorists holed inside a large house. In this nation there are good number of people who are in the field of human rights, particularly active to help to persons who are actively engaged in anti-national activities. So, some busy-body human rights wallah approached the State High Court (HC) requesting it to order the Army unit besieging the house to be considerate towards the terrorists besieged inside. To the Army's surprise, even consternation, the HC not only ordered it to give food to the terrorists holed inside the house, but also laid down its quantity and quality, including 'baryani'. In such situations, the Army would like to starve these terrorists compelling them to come out and surrender, or, they had the option to starve themselves to death inside the house, instead of either of the two options, the HC gives them life line through 'baryani' *et al,* and prolonging the operation, consequently, resulting in killing of some more Army men, laying their life on the line in the interest of the nation.

This is not the place to offer an objective critique on this judgement of the Jammu and Kashmir High Court, which this Anthor reserves the right to do some other time, some other place. Here, it is sufficient to say: one wishes the HC desists from operational matters of the nation's Armed Forces and concentrate on more important judicial issues.

The second case of courts interfering in matters that should be within the operational parametres of the Armed Forces pertain to the Supreme Court ordering Chhattisgarh Government to disband the Salwa Jadum mechanism, a part of the States anti-Maoist policy and operational perquisites, and the SC also ordered abolition of the institution of SPOs, an integral part of the Salwa Judum.

Here again, this Author would desist from offering a critique on the SC's verdict for reasons explained above. Still, it must be said that an Army man would not like the highest court to interfere in matters operational that lie within the competence and operational sphere of the Union's Armed Forces. Even then, one would say that this decision of the SC, like the one of the Jammu and Kashmir HC, could, and perhaps already has, prolonged the Maoist armed uprising against the nation... raising the costs, in men and material, to the nation in its anti-Maoist 'war'!

"FIR mandatory in encounter cases:" HC

In a landmark judgement, the Andhra Pradesh HC ruled 6 Feb 2009 that it would be mandatory for the police to register an FIR under the relevant sections of the law when an encounter death took place.[31]

Thereafter, the HC added, it would be the magistrate and not the police who would have power to decide whether to continue the trial or close the case, accepting the police argument that it was done in self defence.

This ruling pertains specifically to the police encounters. But we can be reasonably certain that some human rights busy bodies would go to the courts, demanding that this compulsory registration of the FIR be extended to all encounters, including the ones where Army personnel are involved. They would quote the principle of 'equality before the law'. Yet again, such activists, in the past, have proved they are more concerned with the death of outlaws like the Maoists at the hands of the security forces, but not vice versa! One has never seen a human rights activist registering a case against any Maoists even when a large number of security men are killed by these ultras. Some sense and principle of "equality before the law", this!

Andhra Pradesh High Court asks for details of detained tribal women Raipur: 23 Jan 2013

"The Andhra Pradesh High Court has asked the State police to produce details of two young tribal women who were picked up from Nimmalagudem village, Sukma district, Chhattisgarh, on 12 January 2013 on the charge of being Maoist militias [villagers who work for the CPI (Maosit)."[32]]

A two-judge bench of Justices MV Ramana and P Durga Prasad passed the order while hearing a habeaus corpus petition filed by Human Rights Forum (HRM).

SP Khammam, AV Ranganath, said the women arrested on 14 January, were produced in a Khammam court two days later. But IG Warangal Range, AB Venkateswara Rao told the daily that the women were picked up on the 20th: "A multilateral operation was on in the forest of Nammalagudem since the 10th in which the AP and Chhattisgarh police and the CRPF took part. These arrested women militias were involved in burning several constructions earlier. There are several charges against them. They were produced in a local court and are lodged in the Khammam sub-jail."

The disappearance of the women came to light when a HRF member by Nimmalagadum villagers was told that Madvi Parvathi, 21 and Kovasi Somidi, 15, "were partially disrobed and taken away "about 7 AM on the 12th." Parvathi was pregnant, as per her family members.

The HRF report said every time a Maoist movement was apprehended around the areas bordering Sukma and Khammam, the villagers of Nimmalagudem bore the brunt. On the 12th, a huge police party from AP, comprising over 100 men, including the anti-Naxal force Greyhounds, came to the village at day break. The report says "policemen began abusing and beating up residents, including several women and children."

The report adds: "They picked up a farmer Podium Chukklah and his minor son P Bhimaiah, 11, besides Parvathi, Somidi and one Madkam Saramma. Their hands were tied and they we taken to a spot some 500 yards from the village below a hillock where there were remnants of a camp earlier set up by the Maoists. They beat the villagers with hands and sticks."

Mr Rangnath however, denied any human rights violation. "Nimmalagudem is a notorious village and the people work as militias. On 14 January, after arresting the militias, we were bringing them to Chintoor in Khammam when we were fired upon. The police retaliated, but there were no rights violations."

"Open school:" A picture: Garu village in Latehar: 3 Sep 2014

A daily publishes a photo of school children sitting in an open school "under the sky." The caption under the picture says it all.

> "Children attend class outside a school building at Garu village in Latehar, Jharkhand. Jaguar Force personnel have occupied classrooms, disregarding a Supreme Court ruling that prohibits security forces from occupying schools."

"Notice to centre, nine states over anti-Naxal Plan:" 10 Sep 2013: New Delhi

The Supreme Court on Monday (9 Sep 2013) issued notice to the Centre and nine states on a petition for a policy to curb Naxal activities which threaten internal security. The bench of Chief Justice P Salhasivam and Justice Ms Ranjana Desai asked governments of Chhattisgarh, Odisha, West Bengal, Bihar, Jharkhand, UP, Maharashtra, Andhra Pradesh and Karnataka to respond in four weeks.[33]

In his petition, Kishore Samrite, a former SP MLA says: "In 2006, the RAW had estimated that 20,000 armed Naxalites were operating in various States. In 2007, they were thought to be active in half of India's States.

In Feb 2009, the Union government announced an integrated action plan (IAP) for broad, coordinated operations nationwide to tackle the problem. However, the plan was yet to be implemented. Undercoring various incidents in which Naxals have killed security forces and innocent persons, Samrite said that whenever such incidents happened, Union and State ministers concerned would call for urgent steps to end the menace, but no effective steps were taken.

In the absence of any regulation by the Centre the militants grew in strength and spread terror, disturbing peace, he said.

Since the plan was conceived, the MHA and Ministry of Rural Development had differed over how to carry it through, he said, pleading for a directive to the Centre for proper and effective execution of the plan.

Notes

1. Prashant Dikshit, Salute the Indian Soldier, May-June 2014.
2. Rakesh K. Singh, The Pioneer, 3 Sep 2011.
3. Rakesh K Singh, The Pioneer, 10 Jul. 2012.
4. Sandeep Joshi, The Hindu, 31 Oct. 2012.
5. Vijaita Singh, Indian Express, 26 Nov. 2012.
6. Deeptimaan Tiwari, Times of India, 28 Jan. 2013.
7. Rakesh K Singh, The Hindu, 19 Jan. 2013.
8. Deeptimaan Tiwari, The Hindu, 12 Mar. 2015.
9. Rakesh K. Singh, The Hindu, 18 June 2013.
10. Sandeep Joshi, The Hindu, 16 Jan. 2013.
11. Sanjib Baruah, Hindustan Times, 14 Jul. 2013.
12. Rakesh K. Singh, The Pioneer, 5 Sep. 2012.
13. Amitabh Sinha, Indian Express, 4 June, 2013.
14. Rahul Tripathi, Indian Express, 17 June, 2013.
15. Ashutosh Bhardwaj, Indian Express, 12 Apr. 2015.
16. Archana Jyoti, The Pioneer, 13 Oct. 2011.
17. Pooja Kashyap and Arun Janardhanan, Times of India, 29 Apr. 2012.
18. PNS, The Pioneer, 26 Nov 2012.
19. Ashutosh Bhardwaj, Indian Express, 5 Feb. 2013.
20. Devesh K. Pandey, The Hindu, 16 Sep. 2014.
21. Faizan Ahmad, The Hindu, 17 Jan. 2015.
22. Asha Shukla, Indian Express, 29 Nov. 2011.
23. Sandeep Joshi, The Hindu, 14 Jul. 2012.
24. Pioneer News Service, The Pioneer, 14 Jul 2012.
25. Deeptiman Tiwari, Times of India, 15 Sep. 2012.
26. Survojit Bagchi, The Hindu, 20 Dec. 2012.

27. Survojit Bagchi, The Hindu, 23 Dec. 2012.
28. B. Vijay Murty, Hindustan Times, 13 Jan. 2013.
29. Alok Tikku, Hindustan Times, 21 May, 2013.
30. Express News Service, Indian Express, 17 Jun. 2013.
31. Survojit Bagchi, The Hindu, 23 Jan. 2013.
32. The Hindu, 3 Sep. 2014.
33. I. Venkatesan, The Hindu, 10 Sep. 2013.

16

Development of Naxal-infected Regions

Maoist problem, like any other insurrection, is a ticklish issue for any nation. Ideologically fuelled and maintained, it cannot be purely and simply treated as a security issue, as a nation is dealing with its own nationals who are convinced that replacing a democratically-elected government through violence and taking over its reins in their own hands is the ultimate solution. With this aim, they resort to murderous mayhem to achieve it, unmindful of the human costit involves.

The debate usually is whether the Naxalism can be sorted out through development alone, or combining it with security measures to control and defeat the Left ultras, is the solution. It is certain that no political formation or analyst considers it a law and order problems. But if is also a fact that the State has to convince the Maoists that cannot have their ways against its might. It is only after showing them its might and clearing certain regions of its violent presence that the state can start development works in those regions with the help of its security forces. What follows are various facets of the issue e.g. development versus security approach.

Maoists indeed want Development: A cruel Irony

Maoists have built their entire empire on the theme of injustice meted out to the poor tribals by successive governments in India. Their heart bleeds, or so they claim, at the pitiable living conditions they are forced to live in. No roads, no water and no electricity in their jungle abodes. Worst, no schools for their children. In one word. They have no hopes even for their future generations, too!

Now, there are bleeding-heart 'liberals', Leftists, celebrity authors and sundry soulmates of this variety who are overground ideological fellow travelers of these underground 'do-gooders', called Maoists in today's India!

These overground soulmates are more dangerous than the Maoists, who openly work for destruction of democratic polity of India, its institutional framework, and replace the duly-elected government by a Mao-style dispensation - - which is despotic, autocratic and a times destructive ala 'let hundred flowers bloom' and 'Cultural Revolution' nightmares! The overground soulmates, whom I have just dubbed as more dangerous than the Maoists, want to achieve the same goals but without coming in the open, may be because of ideological dishonesty or physical timidity, or mental pusillanimity! It could be any one of the three, or all three! They go hammer and tongs at the Police and the Government whenever on ultra (Maoist) is killed in an encounter. It is always a fake-encounter! They are ever more upset, exponentially so, when a senior leader like Kishanji or Azad is killed.

These overground soulmates – more honestly, they admit being overground arm of the Maoists – appear on TV screens in full force, denouncing the treacherous government and condemnable policemen, and screaming at the co-panelists who might differ with them! The former will give the latter as much freedom of right to expression as Mao and his cohorts would give to their opponents! The worst, when an Azad or Kishanji is killed after a long, arduous fight, the "overground arm" will paint a picture of vicious murderers as angels sincerely interested in peace talks with the Government! Azad was painted by that publicity hand in saffron clothes, Swami Aqnivesh! The other zealot who easily comes to mind is Gautam Navlakha who is a screaming/ shouting madmen, who, if he had a pistol in his hand, could shoot down his co-panelists for opposing his viewpoint, and/ or his idols like Ganapati, Kishanji, Azad, *et al!* They see nothing wrong with the Maoists – murdering their opponents, slitting their throats in front of their children and wives, killing the so-called informers as if they were flies or insects spoiling their party - - and conversely, nothing right with the policemen, who are only doing their duty by the nation, or officials who are only obeying the rightful orders of the political executive, or the democratically elected Government, who have been mandates to run the country as per law, ensure its prosperity through economic policy and ensure its place in the comity of the nations. All three are wrong all the way because they are coming in the way of their darlings to achieve their goal of introducing anarchic dispensation in India ala Communist China.

Now to specific point of the Maoists thwarting all attempts of the Government to ensure some development in the tribal areas, the absence of which is the main plank of the Maoist for their ideologically murderous movement. They blame the authorities for neglecting the welfare of the tribal communities. And what do Maoists do when the authorities want to undo the past mistakes/ omissions by building the roads, bridges, schools, and hospitals in the tribal areas? They destroy the works under development, kill the labourers eeking out their sustenance from such works, kidnap/ kill the contractors doing those works, kill/ kidnap the officials supervising these projects! And not a whimper, from the loud mouths named above, against the obnoxious perpetrators of these despicable excesses! How could these overground soulmates condemn their idols! A matter of shame indeed!

Having painted a true pictures of these dastardly destructive entities, both anti-national and anti-poor tribals, here follow some instances of their anti-development record. In one word, the soulmates and the Maoists have a reason to ensure that no development takes place: That will destroy their very raison d'être.

School buildings blown up: Dec 2009

About a dozen Maoists attacked a power generation plant at Balimela Hydro-electric Project in Malkangiri on 20 Dec 2009.

Yet again, some 100 Maoists below up a double – storey school building in Dev Block under Dhibra Police Station, on 20 Dec 2009.

In fact, Maoist leadership seems to be bent upon ensuring that tribal children do not get modern education. There seems to be a vile and vicious thought behind this action: Uneducated children and Youth will make easy supply for recruitment plans of the Maoists! Poor parents, in any case, are too scared of the Maoist gun, hanging over their very existence. Maoists are a lawless lot, not answerable to any one! No one can question their pernicious designs.

Here is one example of their anti-education plans. In December 2009, Maoists targeted more than 20 school buildings in Bihar and Jharkhand in which at least 10 were blown up through dynamite in Gaya, Aurangabad, Jehanabad, Jamui, Munger and Rohtas districts. In those areas, government often used the school buildings to station para-military forces for operations against the ultras (The Pioneer, 22 Dec 2009).

School children made emotional appeals to Maoists of Bihar, to desist attacking their schools which, consequently, deprive them of education. Judging from the subsequent incidents, the appeal from the eager, if innocent children fell on the deaf ears.

Tata Steel Project: 5.5 MT and Rs 19500 Cr : A test case

The Chhattisgarh Government signed a Memorandum of Understanding (MoU) with Tata Steel in 2005 for the Greenfield project with a capacity to produce 5.5 million tonnes (MT) steel a year, on an investment of Rs 19,500 crore. The project envisages the acquisition of some 2,000 hectare (ha) of land, of which steel plant will be on 650 ha, and the rest of the land will be used for residential quarters, ancillary units, roads, schools, hospitals, and a 625 MW captive power plant. About 585 ha earmarked for the project is held by individuals, called "account holders" or "Khatadharaks" in Hindi. The rest is under the government, which can he directly allotted to the Tatas on lease. (Purnima Tripathi, in Battle of Bastar, Frontline, 4 May 2012).

This Tata Project is studied as a test case in this book for the simplest of reasons: MoU signed in 2005, a major share of cost paid to the State Government, majority of individual landholders have given their consent, all technical and legal clearances given to the Tatas, and yet the project is nowhere near the take-off stage! And this is being written on 8 Jun 2014, a fortnight after the swearing-in of the Modi Government.

As will be seen here, the whole project is a tangled skein of politics being paid by several vested interests, local tribals being pulled in different directions, and the UPA-II Government helpless as a mute witness (till 26 May 2014)!

But this is not the only project (even if this be the largest, most prominent and in the name of the most prominent business house, the Tatas, in the country) stuckup in political and procedural logjam!

The fortnightly which carries this detailed analysis is known to be Leftist by conviction, as its one-time long-serving editor N Ram, was once a card-carrying Communist, and even today, after giving up editorship, holds an influential executive position in this family- controlled publication of the Hindu Group of Channai. This bit of advisory was deemed necessary, before discussing the issue in detail, some of which are gleaned from the Frontline.

India's hinterland, densely forested and mineral rich is inhabited by poor and vulnerable tribal people. This region "is witnessing a saga of broken promises, dislocation, deprivation and disempowerment". Whether it is Niyamgiri in Odisha, Jhursuguda in Jharkhand, or any other place in India, "Tribal people are up in arms against policies that seek to dislodge them from their homes and their land".

The tenor and tone of this story is based on the premises that but for this fortnightly, represented by the correspondent, Tripathi, everyone in India – its political class, officialdom, all business houses, Central and State Governments, common intelligentsia *et al* – is bent upon decimating the tribal communities! The former do not understand that development is the only answer to the "deprivation" of tribals noted above. If the ilk of

Tripathi or Medhapatkar, helped and abetted, by the N Rams of India, had their way, there would be no Narmada projects, no steel plants, no schools, no roads, and no hospitals would have come up in India. They would like to preserve the 'tribal communities' as museum pieces for the benefit of the tourists, particularly of foreign vintage. Their masters and gods, the Chinese Communists have learnt their lessons, but not the N Rams, CPM's Karats, and Ganapattis of the CPI (Maoist). They are all stuck up in Marxist – Leninist – Maoist (MLM) quicksand of moribund thought of the mid - 20th century! It was the work of some foreign – funded NGOs that vigorously opposed the completion of the Kundankalam nuclear plant in Tamil Nadu after nearly 95 per cent work had been completed – surely they had the backing of N Rams and MLM brigade!

Next few lines are worth quoting in extension : "The Bastar region of Chhattisgarh is the latest on the list. After some delay, Tata Steel recently got the Centre's approval to divert a huge tract of forest land for its mega green field mega steel plant at Lohandiguda in Jadgdalpur in the region. Work in the region may begin anytime. Villagers, who face eviction, were unaware of the development until this correspondent broke the news to them. Immediate reaction was disbelief, followed by despair. Many residents ...affected by the project, said they would die fighting rather than part with their land."

This correspondent is rather taking too much credit about informing the villagers. Can one believe that despite repeated meetings, consultations at all levels, the concerned villagers waited for this correspondent to be aware of the impending "doom"! It is this type of exaggerated, biased reporting – we would die . . . rather than part with our Land - - that does disservice to a national cause!

The controversy is about the agricultural land belonging to the 1707 "account holders." The local administration says 80 per cent of this land stands acquired, while Tata officials say the entire compensation money has been deposited with the administration for the purpose of acquisition.

Even after all this, this correspondent's claim of villagers being unaware till her visit is rediculous, to put it mildly. She wrote this in Apr 2012. And work on the project has not started till date, Jun 2014!

The company and the local administration arranged a public meeting on environment impact assessment (EIA) for the project on 12 Oct 2009 at the proposed project site in Lohandiguda. It was attended by Varun Jha, Tata Steel Vice President in charge of the project. At the meeting, Tata officials promised to invest Rs 2,000 crore for environmental protection and conservation.

A year later, on 12 Oct 2010, the District Collector hold a public hearing on the Collectorate premises to sound out the villagers on the issue. Later, he claimed overwhelming support from the villagers. The villagers, however, claimed that both meetings were stage-managed, and people who were actually affected were prevented from attending them. Those who attended, they allege, were people from Jagdalpur, contractors, real estate agents and the others with vested interests. The villagers, in fact, organized a parallel public hearing in Nov 2009 at Badanjee village, where the project was unanimously shot down. They sent copies of the minutes to the then Minister for Environment and Forests, Jairam Ramesh. There was no response to their complaint, and on Oct 22, 2010, the Ministry of Enviornment gave clearance to the project. The clearance said the work could begin only after the Union Government gave approval for the diversion of forest land. This approval was granted in Mar 2012. It is obvious that this whole write-up is tendentious and overly biased as explained here.

1. The two meetings held by administration were stage – managed, and one held by villagers at Badanjee in Nov 2009 was authentic.
2. Out of 10 villages affected, the correspondent does not tell who all and how many attended. He gathers these details after two and half years after the meeting.
3. In this day and age, no administration can keep the affected villagers away from such a meeting.
4. If the Government did not respond to the minutes of Nov 2009 meeting, they could have gone to the courts. Why, even this correspondent's magazine, The Frontline could have dragged the Government to the court.
5. That a Minister like Jairam Ramesh would ignore the interests of the tribals is a bit too thick! (His emotions for the tribals and his devotion to their development would be clear when its details are mentioned elsewhere).
6. To say the least, this report is mischievous, to say the least. It is not only intentionally misleading, it is irresponsible. Perhaps; the parallel meeting was arranged due to political compulsions. Some vested elements goaded by N Rams, Leftists and Maoists arranged this meeting for ulterior motives.
7. The popular Chief Minister, Raman Singh, was re-elected 3rd time in Nov 2013, despite the ambush of the Congress leaders in May

that years. Analysts had pronounced his defeat because of that tragedy. But he won! This correspondent and his menders / handless are obviously barking up the wrong tree!

Now, some factual information on the Tata Project. Some 20,000 people in ten villages will be affected by the project. Nine of these are in Lohandiguda block : Badanjee, Belar, Takraguda, Kumhali, Chindgaon, Dhuragaon, Dabpal, Paroda and Beliapal. The tenth, Sirisguda, is in Tokapal block.

There are allegations "the police are bullying them to fall in line. 100 villagers have been booked under false charges" for the same aim, making them fall in line. Some villagers told the correspondent : "They can't scare us into giving up our land . . . Let them first kill us, but before they do that, we will kill them as well." Follow villagers Ramu Ram Maurya, an activist of the CPM and some others echoed these sentiments too. Some said they were forced into giving their signatures.

They were initially promised Rs 3.75 lakh to Rs 5 lakh a hectare. Now, administration has promised Rs 25 lakh a hectare. Hirmoram Mandavi, a farmer and the sarpanch of Takraguda village, a vocal opponent of the project: "we will not give up our land. We do not know what to do with money but even a small patch will ensure that we have something to eat". Surely these are orchestrated answers, "stage-managed" to use this correspondent's terminology. Rs 25 lakh, from initial after of Rs 5 lakh, is no no ! Not only that. He says, even if "we are offered a job each in a family, because lack of skills, we will only get lowest paid jobs." To sum it up : The negativity is drilled into this mindset. They have a problem to every possible solution! This is a political motivation, unvarnished and obvious! Some are dialogically opposed to any development plans of the Government. For them, there is no scope of any argument!

Interestingly, the Congress is backing the State's BJP Governments on the issue. It is again ideological divide: The villagers, backed by the CPI, are willing to undertake fast into death to stop the project.

Collector of Jagdalpur, Angalban P, says: "Despite the collateral damage, the returns are high. The fertility here is not very high and the project will bring in many related economic activities as a result of auxiliary and ancillary units coming up, which will benefit the villagers. The profile of this area will be transformed and it will become one of the richest townships, like Bhilai or Jamshedpur."

To counter this all, the typical arguments about degradation of environment were offered. "The 6.25 MW captive power plant will add to the pressure on environment. Trees on 42 ha of forest area will be cut down. The tribal population of the region depends on the forests for minor forest produce, such as tendu leaves, mahua, tamarind, and timber." Benefits accruing from the projects are simply ignored!

Are these local vested interests and some NGOs working on behalf of some foreign entities who want to block India's development for ulterior purpose? It is worth mentioning an IB report submitted to the new Modi Government on 6 Jun 2014. They have talked about some foreign (official) agencies and entities who are funding some Indian NGOs to block some Indian projects, ostensibly on human rights violations and environmental destruction bases. To seem credible, they used the data provided by the Indian NGOs to build a case against India and its Government. The hidden intent is to thwart India's economic march. These are hizards of people enjoying too many democratic rights and unwittingly providing ammunition to enemies of India to be used against our interests!

If and when the work on the Tata Project starts, the issue will be revisited again.

'Red' Road Blocks in developing Naxal areas

Even in normal times, undertaking the development works in Maoist-affected areas is an extremely hazardous job because of several ambushes sprung by the ultras, attacks on the work force and security forces guarding them, and explosions caused by IEDs planted on the roads tracks used by the security forces for their operational and administrative movements. An occasional abduction of police men at junior level was also considered par for the course.

But in 2012, there were cases when senior IAS officers were abducted by the ultras. This was obviously something the authorities could not accept with equanimity. The issue is discussed here in view of such abductions, and further affect it had on developmental activities.

The discussion here is essentially based on an article by Ashok Mishra, Om Prakash and the others (The Hindustan Times, 6 May 2012).

Abductions in the Red Corridor is not a new strategy, as mentioned earlier, but "recent two successive high profile abductions have deepened the hue of Red Terror." Even though the BJD MLA Jhina Hikaka and Sukma Collector Alex Paul Menon are back with their families, the fear among the political and official classes is obvious, and understandably so.Consequently, development and welfare (economic and social) could be seriously affected.

OP Chaudhary, 2005 – batch IAS officer, who took over as Dantewada Collector in Apr 2011, said, "Life is not the same. Free movement is restricted." He asked his officers to be more vigilant, as "such abductions dampen the spirit and efficiency." "It becomes more challenging for the Collector since he needs to move around with his team."

The life in other states is no different. In West Bengal dread of Maoists is not new. A former BDO, who had served in Belpahari, West Midnapore, said, on condition of anonymity, "It was like life in jail, for two years, there . . . I could not move out of the residential area without proper security." Life was no different for the Collector or SP of Odisha's Malkangiri district after abduction of its Collector RV Krishna in Feb 2011. Officials in Bihar too, are playing safe. The abductions have had the impact of pushing them into a cocoon, further reducing the government's already low direct contacts with the masses, especially in Maoist-hit regions. Consequently, acting on the government's directive, several district "have stopped visiting the remote area". The cascading impact of such avoidance, the officials said, could be gauged most tellingly in the Maoist – hit districts like Gaya, Aurangabad, Arwal, Rohtas, Kaimur, Jamui, Lakshisarai, Munger, Banka, Sitamarhi, Sheohar, and Muzaffarpur.

In Maharashtra's Gadchirauli district, Naxals "have already thrown an open challenge to the administration and the democracy. "A recent spate of political killings (four political leaders / workers in April 2012 alone) by Naxals, followed by mass resignations of office – bearers of local bodies owing to Red's threat, the people's representative too feld threatened".

There is definite aim in examining such analytical stories appearing in press, as this one in the Hindustan Times of 6 May 2012. The aim to see if the correspondent is able to maintain a balance in his analysis. It is obvious that this bunch of the reporters (this story is done by eight of them) have lost sight of broader picture. They want us to believe that the Maoists have overpowered the officials at district level, and even politicians too are frightened out of their wits. It is obvious these young reporters themselves suffer from excessive negativity, rather pessimism. They do not, obviously, know India's strength and vitality. They are ignorant and too young to know that India has waded through very difficult waters in the past, starting with the Srikakulam district, Hyderabad, Nagas, Mzos and other tribals in the North-East, through Khalistan turbulence to J and K. One has not even mentioned Tamil secessionist threats! The 'youngsters' get carried away with what little they come to hear from lower level bureaucracy! They lack the skills, maturity and knowledge of history for an objective analysis of such sensitive issues.

These reporters also see fear psychosis spread across politicians, officials and even teachers in Karnataka, just "because MLAs like CT Ravi,

DN Jeevaraj and others are taking extra care while travelling in such areas despite having armed security details provided by the State Intelligence Department". A simple answer to this simplistic formulation: can anyone be too careful with one's personal security in the areas under threat from barbarians like Maoists?

Then the report goes to talk about slow pace of development including housing for the poor and other welfare measures. Is it anything unexpected?

Luckily, these reporters finally talk of some brave hearts who are doing their duty consciously despite the adverse, and even dangerous, situations. "In Odisha's Malkangiri district, work continues because of personal courage of a few officials." The Chintalwada gram panchayat office was "blown up by the Maoists two years back" (in 2010), and has not been reconstructed. Yet, Panchayat Executive Officer "Bijay Kumar Sahu set up a table under a tree to register people for pensions for widows, old people and the disabled."

Then the report talks about something which is widely known and believed. Some of these things are briefly mentioned below:

1. "Every village under Chintalwada Gram Panchayat, some 750 km south-east of Bhubaneswar, has a village committee, of the rebels which virtually decides how the government sponsored welfare programmes would be implemented.
2. "It is the field level officials like the BDOs and tehsildars who have to implement government schemes. And they have come to terms with the Maoist diktats.
3. "But one officer who has served in the district for over 5 years said : 'I have never received any threatening calls from the Maoists'.
4. "Nonetheless, field officers get short and crisp notes from the rebels forwarding to them people's grievances relating to welfare schemes.
5. "Maoists want people to come to them with grievances rather than going to the administration. Later, they get the things done through the same administrative network."

This was in mid-2012. Undoubtedly, some of these things were true. It needs to be added that the local tribals are intelligent enough to know who is giving them the bread, even if the clever Maoists want them to believe that but for them, government would do for them what they are presently doing! But such a palpable nonsense is too clever to be misunderstood!

Today, two years down the line (June 2014) things have changed for the better. It is no one's case that Maoist menace has disappeared or defeated. But things are on the mend. Recent surrenders by the ultras, even if not in a torrent, are suggestive of a trend. Finally, one can say, "We shall over come." The new Modi Government has brought even bigger hope!

Some examples of Bravehearts

What follows is an account of work done by three brave souls in the Maoist-infested areas, their battle fields. The Nation can indeed be proud of such children of hers!

Balwant Singh, 34: Collector Malkangiri

This IAS officer, presently (mid-2012) District Collector of Gadchiroli, has only served in Maoist-infested districts of Odisha since he started as a probationer in Mayurbhanj in 2009.

His first posting was as sub-collector, Baliguda, in Kandhamal district in the very year Swami Laxmananda was killed 'allegedly' by the Maoists. In the aftermath of that killing, "my focus was rehabilitation of riot victims", says Balwant. In 2010, he moved to Malkangiri district as Project Director, District Rural Development Agency.

In Feb 2011, Malkangiri Collector R. Vinel Krishna was abducted by Maoists. During the 8-day hostage crisis, Balwant was the face of the district administration. After his release, Krishna was transferred out and Balwant elevated to be collector (Malkangiri).

After Krishna's abduction, the government issued instructions regarding movement of officers into Maoist-affected areas.

"Rs 1,000 Cr for roads in Naxal areas" New Delhi: 7 Feb 2009

"The UPA Government is allocating Rs 1,000 Cr for a complete overhaul of the road infrastructure notwork in the Naxal-hit areas of the country". It was reported by a daily in Feb 2009.[1]

The Government decided to execute these projects under the Engineering Procurement Contract (EPC) mode after realising that PPP model was not working due to reluctance of private sector in undertaking the work due to Naxal threat.

The Ministry of Road Transport and Shipping has already got assurance from the Planning Commission that Rs 500 Cr will be made available in the Vote-on-Account in the coming Parliament session to start work on the roads in these areas through the EPC mode.

The Government stepped up its efforts to build roads in Naxal – hit areas as the lack of development is cited main reasons for the appeal of the Maoists for the youth joining LWE.

A Planning Commission report makes an interesting if contradictory observation: "In matters of physical infrastructure like roads and school buildings, the Naxals on occasions did exert pressure on the government for improvement, but in many places, they acted cynically: thwarting government projects on the same assets and even killing contractors doing the job.

"Jairam seeks to modify flagship schemes for Maoist-hit districts": Raipur: 13 Nov 2011

Warning that delays in wage payements were crippling the MGNREGA in Maoist-hit districts of Chhattisgarh, Union Minister for Rural Development Jairam Ramesh outlined his Ministry's latest attempts to jumpstart development in such areas.[2]

In the part, Ramesh had spoken about prioritizing development in country's 60 LWE districts as a crucial prong in his Government's battle against guerilla army of the banned CPI (Maoist). But speaking after a 3-day visit to the state, he said: "Five districts in south Chhattisgarh will be allowed to disburse MGNREGA wages in Cash rather than through bank accounts of job-card holders…I am not happy about it, but we are compelled to do so in the absence of a banking sector in these areas."

Ramesh said each payment would be made in the presence of gram panchayat members and members of women's self help groups and each payment would be video recorded to ensure that money was paid to the right people.

Under the provisions of the Act, workers are to be paid no later than 15 days after the completion of the project. But recent studies illustrate that only 4 per cent of workers in Chhattisgarh get their wages in the stipulated 15 days.

Acknowledging the need to equip panchayats with the resources to conceptualize and demand work under MGNREGA, Ramesh announced the appointment of a Panchayat Development Officer (PDO) and a Junior Engineer (JE) in each gram panchayat of Bastar, Dantewada, Narayanpur and Bijapur.

He said 75 per cent of the funds for these appointees (for salaries) shall come from the Centre and the rest 25 per cent will be state's share.

"Red Corridor paved with corruption" A newspaper Finds out facts: 9 Dec 2011

A daily has done a good job, and its report is published under a loud, nay, thundering, headline. Its blurb is even direct: "Important national highways in Maoist-infested regions are disintegrating due to poor construction and maintenance". The correspondent has obviously, physically travelled on the road before producing this report for his daily. It is reproduced here in her own words.[3]

> "A charming drive through Keshkal Valley on NH-43 introduces a visitor to Chhattisgarh's many picturesque waterfalls and forests; traversing the State's southern part from the State capital of Raipur to Jagdalpur in Bastar. There is nothing to indicate that anything is amiss; if anything, the pleasurable drive conveys a sense of prosperity and development in this rural belt in India's hinterland. "Turning off the tourist circuit reveals a rather different picture. And the questions begin to tumble out: Why are few roads in Bastar well constructed and others are at their unbelievable worst? Why is the problem-undeveloped roads, still awaiting a solution i.e. construction of roads despite the availability of ample resources i.e. 5-year plan budgets? "The collective answer seems rather evident in its simplicity: Maoist presence. Labelled the stonghold of the guerrilla force of the banned CPI (Maoist), the Bastar region has always had development process lagging, with roads being the first target. Union Minister for Rural Development Jairam Ramesh, who, visiting the region last month, called for speedy completion of public welfare projects, primarily rural roads, within three to four years with a sense of urgency and with his characteristic 'Get-it-done attitude, would certainly believe so.
>
> "But there is more to the situation than meets the eye. For, a grave issue plagues Bastar, putting it at par with rest of the country, yet making the consequences for more disastrous here as compared to other more developed states: corruption. On the pretext of road construction, several contractors, bureacerats and politicians have, over the years, garnered massive benefits for themselves. If you will set out to find one such incident, you will stumble upon many. This, however, does not take away the sufferings caused to the region due to Maoist violence, for the road leading to this level of corruption was laid down by this extremist violence itself.
>
> "NH 43 has two partial bridges, whose construction had started several years ago. Over the years, accidents, traffic jams, diversions and other inconveniences are the only "benefits" the locals have received from

such development projects. The road from Kanker to Bhanupratapur in Kanker districts is similarly scattered with a number of bridges, some of which were completed after extension of two to three years, while others are still hanging in the balance.

"Poor maintenance of roads between Dantewada and Bijapur districts tell a similar tale. The difficult road journey from Bhairamgarh (or Bahramgarh) to Nimedh is dotted with several CRPF camps. It would be considerably easier to repair these roads if the labourers were allowed shelter in the camps, since they are vulnerable to Maoist attacks. Reports of Maoists setting ablaze road repair machinery ignore the fact that the rusting machines were doing little for the badly pot-holed roads, in any case. Such 'dramatic' incidents only whittle away some more hope among the locals of having the convenience of connectivity in the near future. "The better-constructed and maintained roads in the blocks of Bastar District disprove the belief that the Maoist violence is the cause of poor development in the region. The well-established transport nexus is dependent on the few well-constructed roads. From Narayanpur, there is no road connecting the 5 Km short distance to Dev-gaon, let alone Kondagaon further on. It is ironical that nothing bars the felling of trees in the name of road construction, but several factors seem to obstruct the provision of roads and electricity in the interiors. Undoubtedly, the region reflects the barriers crated by the deep-rooted Maoist presence but coupled with the even deeper-rooted malaise of corruption, the challenges appear insurmountable.

"Contractors are believed to face life threats by Maoists, even as terrified workers leave the work incomplete; yet budgets do not go unspent. The Keshkal Block's Bahigaon region, an entire is believed to exists on paper, though no such road exists in the village. In villages not affected by Maoist activity, corrupt contractors often dump poor quality material on the road side and get away with it in the name of Maoist terror.

"Dealing with such rampant corruption behind the pretext of Maoist fear needs streamlined planning. Before announcing new projects and road development, the Ministry must check the quality of roads built in the State since its birth in 2001. The contractors and bureaucrats, if found guity, should be dealt with severely. The security arrangements for development projects must be handed over to the CRPF, not the local police, in line with the suggestion made by Ramesh. "There should be greater snergy between security forces and the implementing agencies."

"Unemployed youth from the communities can play constructive role in the implementation of these initiatives, posting them to areas they do not hail from, thus preventing the creation of a locally-rooted nexus. Such a strategy was successfully implemented during recruitments in the education sector, where improvement have begun to show."

"CRPF Combat unit to help lay roads in Naxal-infested areas: New Delhi": 9 Apr 2012

A suggestion made by a daily, as dealt with in the preceding entry seems to be accepted as the title of this news story tells us. Its blurb clarifies the way it will be done. "Initiative on the lines of Border Roads Organization (BRO)". The very opening para tells it all " "The Government has cleared a proposal to raise a combatised unit under the CRPF on the lines of the BRO for construction of the roads in LWE areas."[4]

The reasons for this requirement are easy to understand: Contractors are reluctant to respond to road construction tenders in these areas for fear of extortions by the Maoist, and worse, even death threats by them; even if tenders are responded to, the progress is normally too slack; the roads that are not paved are more prone to be used by the ultras for planting land mines and IEDs as detection becomes tougher.

Well aware of the fact that road links are an important ingredient in the anti-Naxal operations, the efforts are on to source engineering manpower requirement from personnel on deputation from the Military Engineering Services (MES).

The MHA had sought the combatised engineering wing as it was vital to provide accessibility to the security forces for the anti-Naxal ops in deep forest areas that are presently dominated by the Maoists. The combatised engineering wing will help in building/supervising road construction in nine Naxal-hit states, in a major way as the security component will be used with the unit executing construction work.

CRPF DG K Vijay Kumar "has been advised to supervise anti-Naxal operations in these states by air, as on-site inspections by such a high ranking officer entails extreme risks."

Road construction in such areas in further constrained by the fact that as many as 2,300 ward members out of the 3,000 were elected unopposed in Odisha and similarly high number of Surpanchs/ Mukhiyas backed by the Maoists were elected in the State. In Jharkhand, a similar situation was observed during the local bodies elections two years back. Such elected representatives not only poses a threat to diversion of development funds for procurement of arms and ammunition or to further the Maoist agenda, but could also be helpful to the ultras in laying landmines will below the roads under construction. Significantly, the CRPF has been facing problems in identifying landmines and IEDs planted 12 feet under the surface.

Insiders believe Maoist violence represents the biggest threat to internal security with their writ running large even on political and development matters in certain parts and "the para-military leadership failing to meet the expectations due to apparent lack of leadership and visionary qualities". A rather harsh judgment on the CRPF leadership!

"It is a catch – 22 situation for high-ranking officials in Maoist areas": New Delhi: 23 Apr 2012

It is an interesting story that delineates the difficulties faced by the IAS and other senior officers posted in LWE states. The daily cites the examples of three officers posted in Maoist-hit districts: 20 Apr 2012, DC Bijapur Rajat Kumar (Chhattisgarh) was travelling when an IED planted by Maoist exploded under his convoy, his vehicle escaped the explosion three people including a Zilla panchayat member and BJP's district Vice President were killed; on 21 April, Maoist guerrillas abducted the DC of the adjoining district of Sukma Alex Menon and killed his security guards; and the abduction of DC Malkangiri R Vinel Krishna in 2011.[5]

Seen in the context of the three cases, the "recent attacks by Maoists on civil administration officials have revealed the difficulties in the State and Central governments' strategy of prioritizing development works in the Maoist-infested districts.

Kumar paints two sides of the dilemma faced by officers like him: "It is a catch – 22 situation. The only way to ensure that the projects are completed is to have high – ranking officers conduct regular inspections on the ground; yet, precisely such visits make it easier for them to be captured. Travel plans have to be broadcast to enable the villagers to convey their problems to the DC directly. Maoists take advantage of such information to plan their attacks . . . we can make our trips more random . . . . . but if we travel 100 km to an interior village without prior notice, there may be no villagers around to present their complaints".

More security a problem

Prior to Menon's abduction on the 21st, security officers disclosed that civil administration officials were wary of travelling with too much security as they felt Maoists would target the troops themselves. Vineel Krishna says: "It is a real dilemma. Rajat Kumar was travelling with full security when his convoy was attacked. The police had even laid out a road opening party."

Krishna who was abducted in 2011 feels the recent attacks seemed to be part of a deliberate strategy to target the civil administration. "After the 1987 case [in which 11 officers were kidnapped in Andhra Pradesh] they stopped targeting the civil administration. I was able to travel freely in Malkangiri, thinking they would not attack me. Now it would be hard to motivate officers to enter these areas," said Krishna.

"The Maoists are clearly threatened by bright young officers like Vineel, Alex and Rajat", said Union RD minister Jairam Ramesh. In 2010- 11, the Union government allocated Rs 30 Cr of discretionary funding for 78 Naxal – hit districts under a two – year Integrated Action Plan. The current attacks, Ramesh said, pointed to the need to begin a political process to accompany a surge in development and security-related projects.

There is a contrary view by the security experts, who question if development really is a way to tackle Maoist insurgency. Stressing that he is a supporter of expanding infrastructure for education, health and nutrition in principle, Ajai Sahni of the Institute of Conflict Management, is unconvinced by the premise of the current anti-Maoist strategy. "We do not have the manpower for a 'clear, hold and build' strategy", said Sahni, referring to a policy of deploying troops to provide security cover for development workers.

Noting that "it takes for less time to blow up a school than build one", Sahni said the government was also unable to safeguard those projects which have already been completed. One option, he said, could be to empower security forces to undertake certain kinds of development works while the special forces were used in high-impact intelligence – led operations aimed at the Maoist leadership.

The Maoists could not be contacted for their comment on this specific instance. In a pamphlet lasts year, the Maoists had maintained that officials like Krishna were abducted not because of their individual attributes, but because they were symbols of a state structure that the guerrillas were committed to overthrowing.

"Reds liberated zones to get face lift" New Delhi: 6 May 2012

A daily speaks about development plans across Jharkhand and Chhattisgarh to be launched soon.[6]

"Quiet baby steps are on to implement centrally coordinated and funded development operations in states to consolidate the gains of security forces in Maoist 'liberated zones', a breakthrough in the tricky debate over federalism that dogs the issue of terror". The Union RD Ministry would soon launch a development plan across Jharkhand Chhattisgarh to build on the police pressure in the tri-junction that is in Naxal grip. It would straddle across Latehar and Garhwa in Jharkhand and Balrampur in Chhattisgarh. The plan has been approved by the states and the Centre.

RD Minister Ramesh said Sukma – Malkangiri plan is also under way. Sukma, in the news for the recent abduction of its DC Paul Menon, and Malkangiri in Odisha are heavily Naxal-infested and have poor development record.

The inter-state initiatives overseen by the Centre appear to deepen the process of 'securitizing development', a move started in Saranda in Jharkhand's Singhbhum district in 2011 and then in Latehar's Sarju area recently. Both were long time 'liberated zone' lorded over by Naxals that were freed by security forces, and inter-state plan is seen as a step forward.

The development offensive aims to bring swift developments to these Red areas with focused implementation of the rural welfare schemes. It is aimed to win over poor tribals who gravitated towards Naxals because of government indifference.

The Latehar-Garhwa-Balrampur trijunctin plan (LGBT), comprising 98 villages in Garhwa, 155 in Latehar and 41 in Balrampur, may break fresh ground in the growing efforts to remove federal concerns as stumbling block in the way of reducing development deficit in Naxal strongholds.

The overcoming of sensitivities over the Centre dictating development across states is seen as a key to putting Naxals under pressure. Officials believe Maoists enjoy triple advantage in LGBT: It is remote, hilly and forested; a traditional Naxal area and on the border of Jharkhand and Chhattisgarh.

According to the government, the Naxal leadership in Jharkhand shifted south and south-west abutting Chhattisgarh after Operation Prahaar at Saryu, Kone and Oria pocket won the axis of control from Red outlaws. Now, the greater coordination between the Centre and States could dent the advantage enjoyed by Naxals, thanks to old sensitivities of turf – conscious governments.

It is believed the L G B T plan could be a bigger challenge than Saranda or Saryu. The area involved has a bigger geographical spread, multiple districts and inter-state implications. Given the high number of villages, it would mean involvement of a bigger populace and thus more Naxal sympathizers. "It may require greater intensity of development - - a bigger basket of schemes", says a paper on the L G B T initiative.

"Issue of civil administration officers under lens again" : New Delhi and LWE Districts: 6 May 2012: Fear Factor

The subject of problems faced by the civilian officers in Naxal-hit areas has just been critiqued. Here is one more on the same subject, with different take on it. The article also discusses the cases of four officers in Naxal-hit areas: three IAS and one IPS. The title of the news story is, "Red Road Block". Then, a longish blurb which reads: "LIMBO: Recent high – profile abductions have left officials in Maoist – hit states in a tough spot - - venture out and face Red reprisals or stay put behind security fences and neglect work at the cost of development."

This detailed assessment is penned by multiple scribes.[7]

The assessment opens with an observation that sums up the entire problem: "Abduction in the fast expending Red Corridor is not new as a strategy. However, two successive high-profile abductions have deepened the hue of Red terror. Though both BJD MLA Jhina Hikaka and Sukma DC Alex Paul Menon are black with their families, one thing is obvious - - the fear among the politicians and officials is palpable. Consequently, development and welfare (of tribals) could be seriously affected."

The fear seems certain in Chhattisgarh. Here is OP Chaudhary 2005 – batch IAS officer who took over as DC Dantewada in Apr 2011: "Life is not the same. Free movement is restricted." He goes on: "Such abductions dampen the spirit and efficiency. It becomes more challenging for the collector as he needs to move around with his team."

In West Bengal, the dread of the Maoist is not new. Wanting to speak anonymously, a former BDO who worked in Belpahari, West Midnapur, said: "It is like life in a jail for two years . . . . I was not allowed to move outside the residential area without proper security, forget visiting villages."

In Malkangiri, Odisha, officers like DC and SP stay put in their barb fire-fenced premises following government's guidelines after abduction of DC Vineel Krishna in Feb 2011.

Officials in Bihar too are playing safe, spending a cocooned life. "It has further reduced the government already low direct contact with the masses, especially in LWE-hits area of the state."

Following a government directive, the DMs posted in such areas "have virtually stopped touring remote areas." Cascading impact of this avoidance could be gauged more tellingly in Maoist-hit district like Gaya, Aurangabad, Arwal, Rohtas, Kaimur, Jamui, Lakhisarai, Munger, Banka, Sitamarhi, Sheohar and Muzaffarpur.

In Maharashtra's Gadchiroli district, "Naxals had already thrown an open challenge to the administration and the democracy". A recent spate of political killings (at least four political leaders/ workers in April 2012 alone) by Naxals, followed by mass resignations by office bearers of local bodies because of Reds' threat, the people's representatives too feel disenchanted.

In Karnataka, where Maoist threat is relatively new, the fear psychosis is spread across politicians, officials and even teachers. There is increased fear among politicians belonging to Naxal – hit areas in the Western Ghats. MLAs like C T Ravi, D N Jeevaraj and others area taking extra care while travelling in such areas despite having armed security details provided by the State Intelligence Department.

Fear Spreading

Fear has spread to other departments, like public works, rural development, and revenue. A village accountant, wanting anonymity, said, "We are working in the villages and conduct public work on a day-to-day basis. We have already sought police protection and written to the government."

Fear Stalling work

Development is likely to suffer as officials fearing Maoists refrain from visiting the interiors. DC Gumla Rahul Sharma is honest and direct: "If we stay back in our office fearing Maoist reprisals, villagers will be the biggest losers. The police asked us to take extraordinary precautions and keep them updated on our movement in such areas."

In Bihar too, Maoists are holding up development work in various districts. An official, aware of goings-on in north Bihar districts like Sheohar and Sitamarhi, tells the daily: "Monitoring of important welfare schemes like the Indira Awas Yojana (IAY), the housing scheme for the poor, has suffered a set-back as officers are reluctant to visit interior villages. This has increased the risk of IAY funds being cornered by unscrupulous persons."

In Gadchiroli, fear is achieving what Maoists want. Due to demoralization in the district and local administration, a posting in this district is treated as punishment and officials would lobby hard to get out of it.

There are laudable exceptions too. In Odisha's Malkangiri district, work continues essentially because of the personal courage of a few officials. The Chintalwala gram panchayat office was blown by the ultras two years back and had not been reconstructed; so the Panchayat Executive Officer Bijay Kumar Sahu set up a table under a tree to register people for pension for widows, old people and the disabled.

"This is not the right place to talk", said Sahu when asked about problems he was facing as a government official in Maoist-hit district like Malkangiri.

Every village under Chintalwada gram panchayat, some 750 km south – east of Bhubaneswar, has a village committee of the rebels which virtually decide how government sponsored welfare programmes would be implemented. It is the field level officers like BDOs and Tehsildars who have to implement government schemes. And they have come to terms with the Maoists' diktats.

Here is one more official's honest-speak if we are to believe his words: "I have never received any threatening call from the Maoist". He has served in the district (Malkangiri) for over five years.

Nonetheless, the field officers get short and crisp notes from the rebels, forwarding to them people's grievances on welfare schemes. Their modus oprendi is simple: They want people to come to them with their grievances rather than going to the administration. Subsequently, they just get the things done through the same administrative network.

State officials who are hard at work in Maoist-infested areas: Sincere

Large number of officers working in LWE-hit districts are indeed sincere hard-working and devoted to their duty. Some four of them are mentioned below, with some relevant details.

Balwant Singh, 34, Collector, Malkangiri

Balwant Singh, the Collector of Malkangiri has only served in Maoist – affected districts of Odisha since he started as a probationer in Mayurbhanj in 2009.

His first posting was as sub-collector of Baliguda in Kandhamal district, the same year as the aftermath of Swami Laxmananda's killing allegedly by Maoists. "My focus was rehabilitation of riot-affected people", he says.

In 2010, Singh moved to Malkangiri as project director, District Rural Development Agency. Collector Vineel Krishna was abducted by Maoists in Feb 2011 and during the 8-day hostage crisis, he was the face of the district administration. After his release, Krishna was transferred and the government elevated Singh to be Collector.

After Krishna's abduction, the government issued guidelines for officers' movement in Maoist-hit area. "The biggest challenge is restriction on movement", he admits. However, he called it an "occupational hazard" like any other job, adding, "without challenges, there is no administration."

Restrictinos have made Singh depend on electronic gadgets and a team of officials, civil society, panchayati Raj institutions and local youth to implement welfare programmes. The second challenge is the lack of quality human resource. "That is why we are not getting results", he says.

His most tough task is to win over people. There are two generations: one aged, illiterate and the other, children and youth. Different schemes are needed for different demographics.

Singh informs there are some 25,000 tribal children residing in tribal welfare hostels in the district. "In education, we are making strides; that is the only hope.

Pooja Singhal, 33, DC Palmu

A posting in Naxal – hit region demands that an officer go the extra mile. Nothing can be left to chance. Palamu DC Pooja Singhal, 33, makes that extra effort to keep government machinery going in a district that has been a battle ground for the LWE.

Babus in Maoist-hit Jharkhand work slow and prepare for excuses to run home for the weekend. But at Daltonganj, headquarters of Palamu, Singhal is preparing for a surprise operation. Without informing subordinates, she drives to Hurmur village deep in the forests. Palamu was one of the eight districts in the country selected by the Centre for its pilot anti-Maoist campaign in 2007. However, Maoist threats have never dissuaded this Chandigarh girl from travelling in their strongholds and reaching out to poor. She tries to take government's pro-poor schemes to its beneficiaries.

On reaching Hurmur, a village of tribe groups, she visits an anganwadi to inspect the mid-day meal scheme. She is disappointed by the *Sevika,* who has failed to take care of the children. She orders her removal.

The paradox of the trip is that security men escorting her left the moment her vehicle moved onto non-metal roads to reach the village. "They have bigger threats to their lives", she says, trying to play down their misconduct. "We have accepted that the Naxalites will not harm civil administration. But post-Malkangiri DC Vineel Krishna and Sukma DC Alex Menon's abduction, we are out of the misnomer."

The result? "Already wary field officers now have valid excuses to not visit the country side, thereby making neglected areas more vulnerable to neglect".

Abhishek Krishna, 32, Collector Gadchiroli

The Collector Gadchiroli, a Maoists-hit district, has his task - - to ensure that the administration reaches out to the last man in the society - - cut out for him.

Krishna, the IAS batchmate of Sukma DC Alex Paul Menon, who was kidnapped and released by the Maoists after 12 days in captivity 3 May 2012, has been working in tribal areas in Maharashtra since he joined the service in 2006.

The son of a university teacher, Krishna wanted to join civil service to work for the upliftment of the poor and always laid stress on the importance of education and healthcare.

Krishna says, "After Alex's kidnapping, my family and police prevent me to go to interior areas without proper security. His official residence now resembles a police Chhaoni (cantonment), given the presence of heavily – armed security following the Sukma kidnapping. The Maoist threat notwithstanding Krishna believes in doing his work, win the trust of tribals to ensure development.

During his two-year stint as Gondia Zilla Parishad CEO, Krishna was instrumental in ensuring that every school in the district has basic facilities such as clean drinking water, toilet, electricity and proper building.

When a contractor was reluctant to undertake the work of school buildings of Murkutdoh, Dingori and Murkutdoh (Khed) in Maoist-hit Saleksa region in Gondia, Krishna went there on motorcycle to persuade him and got the work completed before schedule.

Krishna wants to repeat his Gondia experience in Gadchiroli.

Alok Kumar, 43, Commander, Anti – Naxal Force, Karnataka

Alok Kumar, IPS officer belongs to 1994 batch and he is now IGP rank, serving as Commander ANF (Anti – Naxal Force), Karnataka. Famous for his investigative skills and heading the INF which comes under the Internal Security Division of the State, he camped at the ANF Headquarters based in the Forest Area of Karkala, in Udupi District.

It is known that the South – Western Regional Bureau (SWRB) of the CPI (Maoist) has decided to extend its activities from Western Ghats, Eastern Ghats through Karnataka, Kerala and Tamil Nadu to expand the Red Corridor.

Kumar, who busted the Bangaluru serial blasts case by arresting the kingpins along with the politically powerful Abdul Nasser Madani from Kerala, when he was Joint Commissioner of Police, Bangaluru, is now with a different job of curbing the Maoist menace in Karnataka, which steadily grew since 2000 in the State. Naxalites are presently confined to Shimoga, Chikmagalur, Udupi and Dakshina Kannada districts. Now they are extending their activities to three more districts: Hassan, Kadagu and Chamarajanagar.

Kumar told the daily about the High Power Committee created by the government to sort out the Maoist menace, that includes the Secretaries of home, Forest, Revenue and PWD departments. They will Chalk out plans to identify the problems in the Maoist-hit areas and suggest solutions. "But there are several glitches including the Forest Act of the State that does not allow roads and other facilities inside the forest areas. So, there is a scope of amendments in such acts, the rules and regulations."

Road Projects in Slow Motion: An over view

UPA-II government had ambitious plans to bring development to Maoist-dominated areas as a part of its strategy to wean away Naxalite supporters. But by mid-2012, it seemed to be going nowhere! The tardy pace has not only resulted in the extension of deadlines more than once, it has also resulted in an escalation of the project costs.

Two indicators of the dismal picture are given here.

- Length of the roads
  1. Approved by the cabinet in Feb 2009, 5,477 Km
  2. Completed till Mar 2012, 1,335 Km
- Total Project Cost
  1. Planned Rs 8,500 Cr.
  2. Spent by MHA till Mar 2012 Rs 1,891 Cr.

Progress of road projects under LWE Phase 1 till Mar 2012

State	Sanctioned	Completed	Districts	Sanctioned	Completed
Bihar	674 Km	417 Km	Aurangabad	115 Km	46 Km
Maharashtra	420 Km	177 Km	Gadchiroli	323 Km	103 Km
Odisha	614 Km	69 Km	Malkangiri	290 Km	0 Km
Chhattisgarh	1,947 Km	283 Km	Dantewada	354 Km	19 Km
Jharkhand	542 Km	22 Km	Palmu	72 Km	0 Km

"Dantewada Education City among top 100 infrastructure projects: Dantewada: 9 Jul 2012

"Global audit major KPMG has selected Dantewada Education City as one of the 100 urban infrastructure projects in the world. Coming up over 170 acres at Gidam on the Jagdalpur – Bijapur NH-30, the Education City will have around 15 institutes, including an engineering college, an IIT, a sports schools, a tribal girls school, a Kasturba Gandhi Vidyalaya, besides a residential school for children orphaned in Naxal violence.

The importance of the project lies in the fact that "Dantewada has seen maximum number of incidents of police-Maoist violence in the last decade (2001 – 2010) with educational institutions being the biggest casualties. As civic administration failed to provide even basic amenities, tribals suffered the most. This daily had earlier reported on this project that drew praise from CM Raman Singh.

The recognition acknowledges the efforts of DC Dantewada OP Chaudhary, who within a few months of assuming charge, conceived and laid foundation of Rs 100 Cr project. The entire campus is solar-powered, and a few of its institutions have already started functioning. "All institutes are set to get operational in 18 months from now".

Explaining the idea behind Infrastructure 100, KPMG report notes: with more than half of humanity condensed in cities, which collectively make up less than 2 per cent of planet's land cover, urban infrastructure has become one of the World's greatest Challenges. The Infrastructure 100 was created to share those leading edge developments among those in the industry as well as raise infrastructure's profile among those outside of the industry and clarify infrastructure's importance and impact on the society."

Besides the Dantewada Education City, four more projects are selected from India: Delhi – Mumbai Industrial Corridor; Chennai Solar Economic Zone; Sabarmati Riverfront Development Project; Gorai Dumping Ground Scientific Disclosure Project.

"Govt to link road projects with security cover in Naxal areas, New Delhi: 3 Sep 2012

This is another news story dealing with creation of infrastructure such as roads in the Naxal areas. Its essential difference is linking road projects with security cover. Considering the statistics in this article, it is obvious that it is based on the same hand out from the Road Ministry as the previous one. But this article has given it a different shade by bringing in the 'security cover' angle.

To push the road projects that have slowed down in the Naxal areas due to violence and lack of coordination between different government agencies, the Ministry out has chalked out a revised strategy to remove the road blocks. It plans to construct 5,477 Km stretch of two - lane roads in 34 districts across the eight Naxal-hit states. "But it has managed to construct just 1,811-Km stretch."[8] The Concept is clarified here:

> "The Ministry has now decided that road construction plans in 'Category III' areas (high risk zones) will have to be finalized in tandem with the deployment plan of security forces in these areas. The itinerary for shifting of camps for the security forces will have to be included in the Road Requirement Plan itself"

Depending on threat perception, the government had put the entire 5,477 – Km stretch in LWE areas in three categories of the total in such areas, 1800 Km fall in category III in which only 51 – Km stretch could be completed.

A Ministry official says: "Unlike in the past, when contactors could simultaneously start work at several points on a particular stretch without depending on the availability of the security forces, now they would have to make their construction plans along the route of security deployment."

The decision to work in close coordination with the security forces was necessitated as presently a sizeable number of ongoing road projects fall in Category III. "These areas are exposed to maximum violence and it is difficult to work there without the security cover", said an official. This decision was taken in Aug 2012 in a meeting held in Chhattisgarh which was headed by Road Secretary AK Upadhyaya.

Till now, the Ministry has spent Rs 2,132 Cr out of the Rs 7,300 Cr earmarked for the LWE areas.

Pushing Development: Worst Performers

Government has spent Rs 2,132 Cr out of Rs 7,300 Cr earmarked for LWE areas

State	Sanctioned Length (KM)	Completed (KM)	Worst hit districts	Sanctioned (KM)	Completed (KM)
Odisha	614	93	Malkangiri	290	0
Chhatisgarh	1,523	452	Dantewada	354	19
Jharkhand	645	35	Palamu	72	0

"Despite threats from Maoist, Centre to start work on Rowghat mines" New Delhi: 2 Nov 2012

Deciding to ignore Maoists' threats, the Union Government is going ahead with developing an iron ore mine in the LWE-hit districts of Kanker and Narayanpur in Chhattisgarh that would supply raw material to the iconic Bhilai steel plant. It has also decided to construct a 90-Km long railway track through Maoist strongholds to transport ore from Rowghat to the plant.[9]

At a meeting, senior officials of the MHA, Steel Ministry and senior management of SAIL, which runs the Bhilai plant, decided to go ahead with developing the mines that is crucial for the plant, as its current source of ore from Dalli – Rajhara will run out in the next four to five years.

A senior MHA official told the daily: "We have assured the Steel Ministry and SAIL officials that it would provide enough security men so that the work on the important project could go on smoothly. All statutory clearances for the project have been taken and work on the project would commence soon. Although Maoists have threatened to disrupt work at the new mine, which lies in a remote area, we are sure that our security men, along with local people, will ensure that the work is completed at the earliest, which will also help in the development and progress in the region."

To ensure smooth work at the Rowghat mines and other project areas, spread over 2,030 hectares, SAIL has sought five battalions of CPMF. SAIL plans to invest Rs 5,000 Cr in developing the Rowghat mines, which includes Rs 702 Cr for laying of railway track. As per SAIL's plan, work on laying the first 17 Km of the track will begin Dec 2012 while the remaining will be taken up in mid – 2013. Mining will commence once the track is laid.

"CRPF seeks construction of Vital roads in Chhattisgarh" New Delhi: 10 Dec 2012

Aiming to further boost anti-Naxal operations, particular in Chhattisgarh, CRPF DG Pranay Sahai has taken up the issue of non-construction of vital roads in operational areas with State CM Raman Singh reports a daily in Dec 2012.[10] Sahay pointed to the CM that CRPF formations are connected by *kacha* tracks which has made movement of paramilitary personnel risky as many jamans have lost their lives due to IED blast on these tracks.

Sahay also raised the issue of allotment of land for use by the paramilitary in New Raipur and adjoining districts for setting up various CRPF establishments. The CM assured him of early construction of roads and also allotment of land in New Raipur as well as in Rajnandgaon. Other points mentioned by Sahay are described here

- Construction of roads in operational areas pending since 2003 mainly because of reluctance of contractors to work in such fearing Maoist attacks. CRPF has now assured the State authorities that security cover could be provided to such contractors.

- The DG also raised concern with the CM over the failure of the State police in making arrests or filing charge sheets against the Naxal cadres who had inflicted major losses on the CRPF men. He also flagged concerns over acquittal of Naxal cadres in certain cases due to "weak investigation".
- Sahay also underlined before the CM that a vacuum has been created by the lack of political activities in many areas and Naxals have taken advantage of the situation in furthering their militant agenda. Singh told him that major political parties of the State are trying to fill the vacuum.
- The issue of conversion of forest land on which CRPF camps are located to revenue category also figured during the meet.
- On lack of mobile/ telephone connectivity in many of the CRPF camps in Bastar region, the CM agreed to take up the issue with BSNL and Sahay gave the assurance to pursue the matter with the MHA as well as with Department of Telecommunication.

"Development projects fail to take off in Naxal – hit areas: Raipur: 14 Dec 2012

This subject has been covered in more than one entry earlier. This one will also be critiqued for any new points. Its blurb reads: "only 2 of 30 roads planned have been completed. Contractors abandon work midway after threats."

The opening para is loud and clear: "If the completion of road projects is any indication of the success of government schemes to develop Naxal – hit districts, then such schemes have been a grand failure in Chhattisgarh. Only two of the 30 roads planned under the LWE eradication programme have been completed in the last three years. As per the July (2012) report of the Chhattisgarh PWD, in the last three years only 2 of the 30 roads have been completed under the MHA's LWE eradication programme. The situation has not changed over the last one year. 15 of the 30 projects approved in 2010 or earlier are stuck at various stages of receiving or awarding tenders. The execution of the remaining 13 projects have stopped, as in the most cases the contractors have simply disappeared in the middle of the work, presumably after being threatened by the Maoists. In some cases, the PWD's report has tried hard to sound optimistic - - "work is possible", it has said. The PWD has had to re-do some of the tenders as only one bid has been received. A PWD officer, working on the LWE projects, only confirms the well-known with some specific information: "Besides, companies bid online for projects in Bastar seeing the google map and then run away when they are challenged by the Maoists".

Sources in the MHA say in most cases, contractors disappear after taking advances, which are recovered only after years of court battles. A senior MHA official discloses details of contractors' cleaver and smart ways: "The contractors themselves burn their machinery in some case and fund renegade Maoist groups to do that after taking advance. If an interest free work advance of Rs 20 cr is returned after three years, without even a scratch on the road, imagine how much money the contractor is making by investing it in the market in the name of Maoists."

A project that did not take off, MHA sources say, is the 70 – Km – long Awapalli – Jagargunda road which has not started according to the July report even after the Pune-based construction company - - Patil Construction and Infrastructure - - took a hefty advance. While refusing to discuss the advance the company has received, an official of Patil Construction acknowledged that working in the stretch was "seriously difficult" job.

"One of our employees was killed there in March (2012) and cars burnt down. We suffered financially. No contactor sabotages his own work. The work has 'just started' in that stretch. The question, however, is why central paramilitaries are not engaged substantially to complete the road projects", argues Col Vivek Bhatnagar, GM (HR) of the company.

Here is counter argument from an official of the MHA: "We have managed to complete one patch between Palnar and Sameli in Dantewada, which is very difficult area, using CRPF, why the same cannot be done elsewhere?" The PWD officials deny any "nexus" between contractors, a section of the Maoists and the civilian administration that slows down LWE projects for "personal financial benefits."

In the last six months, top officials of the state government, the police and paramilitary forces met at least thrice in Kanker and Raipur to discuss the fate of the roads in south Chhattisgarh. "In last week's meeting, CM Raman Singh told PWD's managers that the construction "has to be completed" especially as it is the best time of the year after monsoon to wrap up the ongoing projects".

"However, the CM has not been pushy given the vulnerable security situation of the area", said N Baijendra, Principal Secretary to the CM. While acknowledging CM's concern, PWD officers told the daily that the job is nearly "impossible".[11]

"We got all the support from the forces but the question is if any number of forces is sufficient to protect men and machinery", says a PWD official.

But LWE's road projects of Chhattisgarh go on round the clock as the money, amounting to almost Rs 2,000 cr, is budgeted. "And being budgeted, the money arrives every year during monsoon, partly gets spent as "advance" and the rest goes back to Delhi to come back again in the following year only to get spent again as an advance" [This explanation should get an award for a situation going round and round MEANINGLESSLY]. A few more meetings are convened hurriedly in Central Raipur's Circuit House, a few more reports are submitted and the cumulative length of the road remains more or less the same!

"Infra push in Maoist – hit areas." New Delhi: 16 Dec 2012

Development and welfare seem to be the government's intent as conveyed in this news story pertaining to LWE area. "The Centre has lined up a series of plans and interventions to encourage infrastructure development in LWE-hit areas along with promoting economic inclusiveness. While the Planning Commission has agreed to fund setting up of ultra small bank branches in 60 such districts over the next five years, the Department of Posts would open 8,042 post offices in these areas by 2017."[12]

The MHA is also batting for cell phone connectivity for locals by the end of 2013.

To expedite a range of schemes and development initiatives, the Cabinet Secretary, who heads the Committee of Secretaries (CoS), "has called a meeting of over a dozen secretaries on 15 Dec 2012 (Tuesday). Army Chief Gen Bikram Singh will also attend the meeting, being held after all the wings of the Centre associated with tackling the LWE submitted their feed-back to the Secretariat. "At least 82 districts have been identified as affected by Maoist insurgency.

The Secretariat had swing into action after Union RD Minister Ramesh took up the issue of non-existent physical and social infrastructure in LWE districts in July (2012). Ramesh had cited that out of 28,037 gram panchayats only 15,139 have post offices, coupled with poor health facilities.

Opening of post offices and small bank branches are crucial considering the government plans to cover all areas under its game-changer direct cash transfer scheme. Highlighting how primary schools in these areas did not have children to study, Ramesh had pushed the proposal of setting up of big residential schools where 1,000 to 2,000 children could stay and study.

The CoS committee of Secrataries on the 15th "is scheduled to take up a range of issues, including the need to push cellphone connectivity and location of towers in these regions".

While the BSNL has submitted that they have planned for satellite phone facilities for security forces posted here, the MHA wants that the mobile connectivity should be provided not just to police but to people.

Summary: Important Issues

1. 8,042 more post offices to be opened during 2012 – 17.
2. Ultra small bank branches in 60 districts during 2012 – 17.
3. Mobile phone connectivity to people by Dec 2013.
4. MHA identified 2,199 locations for establishing mobile phone towers.
5. Mobile medical vans to deal with malaria cases.
6. Expedite forest clearance for laying power transmission lines.
7. Expedite road construction.
8. Setting up large residential schools, each catering for 1,000 to 2,000 children.

Notes

1. Priyadarshi Siddharta, Indian Express, 7 Feb. 2009.
2. Aman Sethi, The Hindu, 13 Nov. 2011.
3. Asha Shukla, The Pioneer, 9 Dec. 2011.
4. Rakesh K. Singh, The Pioneer, 9 Arp. 2012.
5. Aman Sethi, The Hindu, 23 Apr. 2012.
6. Subodh Ghildiyal, Times of India, 6 May, 2012.
7. Ashok Mishra, Om Prakash, Pradip Maitra, B. Vijay Murty, Naveen Ammembala, Snigdhendu Bhattacharya, Priyaranjan Sahu and Ejaz kaiser; Hindustan TImes, 6 May 2012.
8. Moushumi Das Gupta, Hindustan Times, 3 Sep. 2012.
9. Sandeep Joshi, The Hindu, 2 Nov. 2012.
10. Rakesh K. Singh, The Pioneer, 10 Dec. 2012.
11. Subojit Bagchi, The Hindu, 14 Dec 2012.
12. Dipak Kumar Dash, Times of India, 16 Dec 2012.

17

Forest Rights Act and Development

Law Secretary urged MoFE to move SC: 12 Jan 2013

This is an important article dealing with an important issue: "The blame game between the NHAI and the Ministry of Environment and Forests (MoFE) might have escalated after the former filed a writ petition against the latter in the Supreme Court but a document submitted by NHAI in its petition shows that an inter – ministerial committee headed by Law Secretary had in Nov 2012 urged the MoEF to move the apex court seeking modification of its guidelines for delinking Environment Clearance (EC) and Forest Clearance (FC) in the case road projects."[1]

The Law Secretary had recommended this after convening a meeting on the issue and after the Highways Ministry sought relaxations on the need to get approval of gram sabhas for road widening projects on 8 Nov 2012. The meeting was convened on the recommendation of the Committee of Secretaries (CoS) and was attended by officials from the Highways, Environment and Tribal Affairs Ministries.

The recommendation issued by the Law Secretary on 19 Nov 2012, said: "For making EC independent of FC in case of road projects, MoEF should modify its OM (Office Memorandum) and because now, there are guidelines issued by SC in Lafarge Judgement making prior FC mandatory for EC, MoEF should approach the SC through an appropriate application seeking modification of its guidelines to the said effect in case of road project."

But the MoEF circulated new guidelines to states easing clearance for road projects on 7 January(2013), the day infrastructure major GMR officially announced its exit from the largest highway project. The company had committed to pay Rs 9,000 Cr premium to NHAI in case it was successful in executing the project. GMR had cited delay in getting green clearance as the main reason for walking out.

Earlier, Highways Secretary AK Upadhyay, in his letter to the Law Secretary, had highlighted that the procedure of granting EC for road projects had changed radically after MoEF's OM issued on 23 Mar and 26 Apr in 2011. "Before these OMs, the letter of EC was issued subject to FC for the forest land, which meant that the work in the non-forest area could start. The work in forest area was taken up only after the FC, which used to take long time."

Upadhyay also mentioned that OMs of the MoEF predated Lafarge judgment. "SC took cognizance of guidelines and made them part of their order. But these are essentially MoEF guidelines. Now a way has to be found to resolve this problem which is created by the government", he had stated in his letter.

"Strike a balance between green concerns and infrastructural needs:" 14 Jan 2013

Another look on the subject just critiqued above. It appears in an editorial of a daily in Jan 2013. "Last Week, the PM cautioned against erecting a 'licence – permit – quota raj' over grant of environmental clearance (EC)." This was in the context of the National Highway Authority of India (NHAI) moving court regarding clearance norms of the MoEF, following infrastructure major GMR exiting an expressway project citing delayed approvals. NHAI seeks delinking of forest clearance (FC) and EC for highway projects. Reportedly, the Law Secretary had advised MoFE to itself approach the judiciary on this matter.[2]

Confronting NHAI, however, MoEF initially cited the rule-book on environmental needs requiring prior FC. But it later issued a guideline relaxing norms for linear projects like roads in non-forest areas. Why did not the tussle end there?

Clearly, the government should be more proactive on in-house disputes resolution. Formed to fast-track infrastructure projects, the Cabinet Committee on Investment must deliver on collective monitoring of clearance–linked time–lines. Else, we will remain big on rhetoric and short on performance. Recall the ambitious goal of building 20 km of highways her day. Contracts awarded this fiscal fall way short of the 8,800 km targeted for highway construction.

Overall, delayed clearances and land-related hurdles have blocked road, power and mining projects worth Rs 2,00,000 cr. Regulatory streamlining and transparency are urgent. Besides revisiting some Forest Conservation Act provisions, it is worth considering industry's proposal that a number of clearances be issued before projects are bid on. On easing Land acquisition, the related Bill's scope for retrospective application and consent clause for private players will disincentivise investors.

Finally, all arms of the government must realize that while green norms need strict enforcing, pushing growth mandates infrastructural support. It is not a case of either /or.

"Top surrendered Naxal says govt plan of development with crack-down working." Gadchiroli: 17 Jan 2013

A daily conceded the success of government's twin strategy of security with development.[3]

The daily's report was based upon what a surrendered Maoist Badarpu Mallaiyya alias Shekhar told it on 16 Jan 2013. Shekhar is in-charge of the South Gadchiroli Divisional Committee of the CPI (Maoist), who surrendered before the Andhra Pradesh police in November (2012). He said the government twin strategy [of security with development] "has begun to hurt the Maoists, leaving the morale of this cadre affected."

He explained: "The senior leadership of the party is worried over setbacks due to operation Greenhunt and the various developmental works undertaken by the government in remote areas of district like Gadchiroli."

Originally from Macchupetha village of Karimnagar district in Andhra, Shekhar, 48, was in Gadchiroli for questioning by the local police. He had been heading the Maoist operations in Bhamragarh, Perimili, Aheri and Sironcha from 2008 till his 'arrest'.

He tells the daily: "The morale of the party has been affected by the pressure created by Operation Green hunt. A lot of areas have been lost to the police…With people getting employment in government works like road construction, digging of wells, forest jobs etc as well as under the MGNREGS, fewer people were joining the Maoists".

He admitted that lucrative surrender offers had also enticed many to lay down arms, even as police had stepped their combing operations. "Barring parts of Chhattisgarh and Jharkhand, the situation elsewhere is more or less is equally bad for the party."

Shekhar specifically cited the loss of many parts of Aheri, Perimili and Sironcha in south Gadchiroli that he commanded, along with Bhamragarh and areas of Kurkheda and Korchi in the north.

Asked about the biggest concerns of the Maoists, his reply: That the party is not growing. Fresh recruitment has virtually stopped, and the Dalam strength has gone down from 15 to 10...Maoists are trying to counter this by exhorting cadre to enhance contact with people".

Shekhar, who was part of the encounter at Lahiri that killed 17 policemen, defended targeting police: "The pressure of police was growing and the party had suffered a lot of losses. So there was a directive from the top leadership for big action".

A veteran of many bloody encounters in Andhra and Maharashtra during his 24 years as a Maoist, Shekhar surrendered along with his wife Ponnam Saroj alias Vijaya, partly because he is suffering from "kidney and liver" ailments and also because of "disillusionment" following the suicide last year (2012) by senior Maoist Divakar. "Divakar moved around a lot in Civil (dress) and was doubted by senior leaders for possible links with police. I did not approve of the allegation against him and also questioned party leaders like Narmada about it. They objected to my raising questions and sidelined me", Shekhar said.

About the allegation that cadre from Andhra have an upper hand over tribals in the CPI (Maoist), he said: "The promotion in the party is generally according to seniority. But there is some discrimination against tribals. At least the tribals do complain about it."

He admitted handing down death to 12 alleged police informers in Gadchiroli but claimed he was asked to do so by the leadership. Asked if any evidence is sought before an "informer" is killed, Shekhar said: "People's opinion is considered as valid. If later it is found that someone has been wrongly killed, we go and apologies to the family."

Talking about funding, Shekhar said each divisional committee chief gets Rs 20 lakh annually for spending. "I used to collect Rs 2 Cr during tendu season in my division. The bamboo extraction charge is collected by the DKSZC, which is higher body."

Shekhar, who joined Manthni Dalam in Karimnagar district in 1988 at the age of 24, allegedly under pressure from landlords, claims that when he visited his village after his surrender, everyone, including the landlord families, came to see him "They were all very happy to see me. It is no more the kind of village it used to be."

"Centre's road plans in Red areas held up" New Delhi: 30 May 2013

A daily reports: "As violence in the Naxal belt escalates, one of the Centre's key strategies against Maoists… providing road connectivity to far flung areas passing through some of the worst-affected districts-seems to be floundering".[4]

Two key Union Ministries, Home and Road, are currently involved in tug of war after the Road Ministry citing paucity of funds decided to pull out of Phase II of building 5,624 km of roads in the Red Corridor. The MHA, on the other hand, is insistent that the Road Ministry does some "innovative dovetailing" with ongoing Central funded schemes of other ministries to fund Phase II of the road building project.

As against its requirement of Rs 16,000 Cr, the Finance Ministry has allocated just Rs 5,400 Cr to the Road Ministry believe this is just about enough to complete Phase I work. It has sought an additional Rs 9,400 Cr for Phase II.

To iron out the differences, Cabinet Secretary Ajit Seth held a high level meeting on 28 May where it was decided to give more monetary support to states to build roads in such areas.

"Apex Court notice to Centre, States on development policy in Naxal den" New Delhi: 10 Sep 2013

The Supreme Court wants to know from the Centre and nine States on the fate of the ongoing Integrated development Action Plan (IAP) for LWE areas. In a PIL, former MP MLA Kishore Samrite, raised the concern over the growing clout of Naxal outfits and sought a central policy to handle the menace.[5]

The Bench of CJI P Sathasivan and Justice Ranjana Desai directed States of Chhattisgarh, Odisha, Jharkhand, West Bengal, Bihar, Maharasthra, Andhra Pradesh, Karnataka and UP Governments to give response within four weeks.

The petition said that despite the IAP meant for development of Naxal areas, the scheme failed to take off due to differences between the MHA and the Ministry of Rural Development (MoRD) over its implementation.

"Road tender norms to be relaxed in Naxal belts" New Delhi: 17 Feb 2014

A daily reports: "In order to facilitate developmental works in rural areas in LWE districts, the government has decided to allow states to award tenders for construction of roads under the Pradhan Mantri Gram Sadak Yojana (PMGSY) on a nomination basis, as against the current norm of inviting bids. This relaxation comes weeks before the Central Election Commission (CEC) is expected to announce dates for the Lok Sabha (LS) polls, following which the Model Code of Conduct [MCC] will come into effect".[6]

These will be applicable in the 27 worst LWE districts across nine states, as per the circular issued by the Ministry of Rural Development (MoRD).

The MoRD says owing to Maoist threat, there is often no response to call for tenders issued by the state repeatedly. In order to "enhance government presence and improve programme of delivery in these areas and to provide access to social, economic, educational and health facilities to population of these areas", the MoRD says it has decided to allow these states to award tenders by nomination in cases where at least two calls inviting tenders have not elicited any response.

Such nominations will be decided by a committee headed by DM. The MoRD order says: "The Committee will look into every such work and decide on merit to award the same on nomination basis with full justification to be recorded in the file".

The MoRD official informs that "the CRPF has also expressed interest in taking over construction of some roads in Chhattisgarh and talks have already been initiated to take this forward." Under the new relaxation, CRPF will not have to bid for the tender and can simply be nominated by the state.

"A citizen writes to a daily on Maoists" Mumbai: 14 Mar 2014

The views of experts and scribes on a variety of issues concerning Maoist violence have been critiqued in this book. It is time the views of a common Indian is aired, as he expressed in a letter to the editor of a daily. These are reproduced here in toto.[7]

Not about ideology

"This refers to the editorial 'The Sukma Warning' (IE, 13 Mar 2014). The recent deadly strike on security personnel, who were reportedly protecting road construction work in Sukma, proves that the Maoists are bent on obstructing any development activity in the area.

"It is only in grossly under developed tribal areas that the insurgency is effective in sowing the seeds of discord/ discontent. That is primarily reason behind the targeting of educational institutions and hospitals.

"The government and right-minded people must realise that the so-called Maoists are not driven by ideology. They seem to be driven more by the lure of power and money.

"Official dialogues with the insurgents are doomed to fail, because it is in their interest to keep up the Churn. [Chandramohan, Mumbai)

"Arrest Dissent " (NGO against any development)

The Raman Singh-led BJP, Government has a good record of fixing 'bad tribals'. Rajesh Bhaskar, the head of a sarpanch body, said educated tribals and "tribals with posts" had become targets of recent intimidation. To be Naxal-proof, a sarpanch these days better be a police spy. "Ram Kumar Mandavi, sarpanch (Muragaon), Ganesh Kurgan, sarpanch (Timnor), Dhannu Ram Dhuru, sarpanch (Tadoki)," lists Bhaskar, showing a petition with names of those arrested on the charge of being "Naxal supporters." An ongoing study by Shalini Gera, Isha Khandelwal and Parijata Bhardwaj, of a Jagdalpur-based lawyers' collective, showed that sarpanch or no sarpanch, the state is not being choosy about its arrests.

"Three school boys were picked up from Tirathgarh in Bastar and presented before the media as hardcore Naxalites. Maoists in school dress make a great story I suppose", said Khandelwal. "There seem to be no thieves or drug traffickers in Chhattisgarh anymore; anyone up is slapped with 7 – 8 cases on an average. The first FIR may complain of an attack by unknown people; after a few months, when a statement is recorded, the complainant will remember all their names, the names of their villages and even the name of the Maoist commander who is said to have led the attack, and the divisions/he belongs to", she added. The groups' RTI on the disposal of cases in the Dantewada Session's Court between 2005 – 2012, for example, have revealed that complete acquittal in "majority of cases, including Naxal cases" in these years have been around 94 percent. "Most cases are bogus and they don't stand in court. But that is after the accused has spent two – to – three years in jail. That is enough to break a human being" she said. "Villagers claim police stations have also become extortion dens", said Bhardwaj.

Visits to some of the 35 villages to be affected by the Raoghat project revealed considerable BSF and CRPF presence. "They serve as forces of intimidation, to harass the local population even though the pretext is that they are here to protect them", said Samantha Agarwal, a member of the

Chhattisgarh Bachao Andolan, an alliance of 22 organisations that has been working with displaced people in the state.

Much like the FBI's counter-intelligence programme run for over a decade, in the 60s and 70s, against the Black Civil Rights movement in the USA, the security apparatus in Chhattisgarh, has been targeting people exercising the right of democratic dissent, in the name of development or public peace. To protest and to want to negotiate with power, as Gawde and others like him have done, is to be an impractical, anti-modern dreamer; a voice crying in the wilderness and, therefore, purportedly somebody else's mouth piece. The scale of arrests here is massive, and while the outrage around it is low-key, and of necessity, invisible, it points to the subterranean resistance and fight-back that is happening all over Chhattisgarh today.

"They caught Badri over Raoghat. But he was protesting with villagers, and had villages with him so they got scared," said Narendra Nag, a sarpanch of a village in Gawde's town. Gawde had snatched the roll of the opposition both from Congress and the Maoists. The extremes of neo-liberal policies are best carried out by the BJP but the spoils of mining in Chhattisgarh are shared by both the Congress and the BJP," pointed out Bijoy, a forest rights activist. "Gawde was turning out to be a problem for everybody."

Forced to 'develop'

The three tribal-dominated states of Chhattisgarh, Odisha and Jharkhand account for 80 per cent of India's high-grade iron ore. For India, that may be a key resource; for the tribal communities, it is a curse. Contrary to claims of the government and industry, mining does not usher in prosperity for the local population. Were that so, Dantewada, one of the richest districts in terms of iron ore deposits, would not rank 7th among the 150 most backward districts of the country shown by a 2008 Centre for Science and Environment (CSE) report. In Dalli-Rajhara, the local population suffers from longstanding respiratory anemia problems, said Dr. Saibal Jana of Shaheed Hospital. "When Raoghat came into focus the BSP started CSR initiatives like organising health camps in Antogarh, once the mine starts, the CSR will stop", he said.

What guarantee then that Dalli-Rajhara's state or Dantewada's plight will not be replicated in the area around Raoghat? If land is to be acquired for Raoghat who will ensure that all the land acquisition processes are duly followed? Consider these official versions, one cancelling the other. According to its own website on mines, there are 13 existing mines in Kanker; Raoghat will be its 14th. Kanker Collector Alarmel Mangai D, speaking over the phone, however, said. "There are no mines in Kanker. On being asked about Raoghat and rumbles around its land appropriation, she said, "There have been no challenges."

In 2013, the Chhattisgarh Peoples' Union for Civil Liberties (PUCL) said that in villages in and around the BSP's (Bhilai Steel Plant) proposed mining lease areas, such as Anjrel, Special Police Officers (SPOs) have been attacking villagers in contravention of the Supreme Court's order in *Nandini Sundar and Ors* Vs *State of Chhattisgarh,* 2011. Keshav Shori, who had been part of the PUCL fact-finding team, said, legally, the government cannot take over the land. "The gram sabha, not the sarpanch, has to pass two resolutions, one of consent for the take over of forest land, and second, a resolution saying all formalities regarding the Forest Rights Act have been completed. Instead, villagers have been hit by the police on their backs and stomachs. For Raman Singh's government — and why just his? — development is actually a euphemism for military solution. Gawde was raising question like these", he said.

Can a tribal speak?

"The Congress sidelined Arvind Netam and other tribal leaders, the BJP did that with Sohan Potai, the moment he started talking about tribals' rights", pointed out freelance journalist Kamal Shukla. Bottomline: A tribal leader as a pawn is a good role model. But he should not speak.

Netam, one of the most promising tribal politicians of India from Chhattisgarh till the mid-1990s, was suspended from the Congress in 2012 for backing PA Sangma's bid for Presidency. "1980 was a lesson for us. We realised that no party would allow a tribal Chief Minister", he said. "In the MP Assembly polls, which the congress won, voting for CM was between Arjun Singh and Shivbhanu Singh Solanki, a tribal. Solanki was winning, so the counting was stopped by Delhi. The person winning the elections was made DyCM, Singh, who was losing, was made the CM."

Badri Gawde was playing for much lower stakes. "Gawde was not even talking of an overhaul of the system, but his opposition to Raoghat and other issues of every day struggle was becoming visible", says Sukhranjan Usendi's a NGO, The Indian People's Liberation Group. Usendi, like Gawde, and the Salwa Judum leader Mahendra Karma, who locals called the BJP's "11th minister"...slain last year by the Maoists...is a product of trade unionist politics that peaked and waned in Chhattisgarh from the 60s to the 80s as India moved from a controlled economic model to a market – driven one.

The need for steel (iron ore is its raw material) the mainstay of a developing economy, is being fulfilled by land which, inconveniently, is populated by people. The rail line from Dalli-Rajhara is at present being laid on land acquired after evicting 115 families. They now stay in one of the run-down BSP labour hovels abandoned by sacked workers.

Santosh Kumar, a Dalit shop keeper at Antagarh, voiced doubts about a mine – driven development even as he said he is open to the idea. "I am not against Raoghat, but if the land goes, their (tribals') culture goes. Will a forest dwelling tribal adjust to living in a township even with compensation? Many local youths will, however, get jobs". The myth of employment is busted by CSE report, though. It shows that the formal mining industry employed just 6.6 lakh people, between 1991 and 2004, and that the number of workers employed since have come down by 30 per cent. The mining industry does not need people; it needs big machines and specialised operators to run them.

Jeet Guha Niyogi (his father Shankar Guha Niyogi, a BSP mine worker led a 14-year long labour movement around Dalli until he was murdered in 1991), who now heads the Jan Mukti Morcha outfit, claimed Raoghat will "not employ more than 900 workers." The opening of mine always carry an impact, a senior officer of one of the BSP mines said on condition of anonymity. "Raoghat will bring jobs. Trees may be cut but we have also planted trees… PSUs, need to look at the market, but we also serve society", he added.

Iron ore for India's development does not wash. So who is it really for? It is for China. China consumes more of Indian ore than do our own domestic industries. China's share in India's export of iron ore has increased from some 30 per cent in 2000 – 01 to 83 per cent in 2005 – 06. That is an ominous portent for Chhattisgarh, a situation that the predicted slump in Chinese demand for 2014 will or can change little. The iron ore reserves in the hills and forests of Baster seems to have become the iron heel for people who live in them.

In *Days of Destruction, Days of Revolt,* writer Chris Hedges and graphic journalist Joe Sacco talk of how white settlers displaced and destroyed Native American land and lives in their bid for power and control. It ends will the Occupy Movement where a new generation of Americans began their long protests against their nation's corporate elite and oligarchs. The government first sent their police with their batons to remove them. Then they sent their PR machinery to 'understand' the protesters and effect a compromise. They tailed. In Badri Gawde's case too, the government possibly feels that keeping one person in jail will scare the many behind them. Will it succeed? It will certainly try.

The Row Over Rowghat: Some specific details why Raoghat?

BSP produces some 5.3 MT per year (rated capacity 4.5 million tonnes) of hot metal. For this, it needs 9 MT of raw material per year. This was met by Rajhar mines which BSP says will be over in 6-7 years. Post-modernisation, BSP requires 14 MT iron ore by 2020 and this they want from Raoghat.

Ownership

BSP has acquired 2028.797 hectares to extract iron ore. Yet, forest clearance for this project was granted for a mere 883.22 hectares. BSP has the majority of ore, but private companies will develop and work the mine. In two years, small quantities of ore will be ferried by trucks from Raoghat to Rajhara.

Environment Impact

Findings by the National Environmental Research and Engineering Institute itself appointed by SAIL–BSP has been ignored by the project: there are at least 35 villages within 5–15 km radius of the site; tribal presence here is 60.07 per cent, more than the national average; most people are unaware of the project or their impending displacement. Mining waste dumps will dry up the Sarang Kohra Nala, the major tributary of the Mudiyaldodki River, the only semi–perennial river of the western valley and will affect the drainage pattern of the entire valley. The dense forest cover will be badly hit.

Wildlife hit

This is a migratory route for tigers to the Eastern Ghats. Even though government censuses say less than 2,000 tigers are left in India, the danger to tigers has not been mentioned in the company's Rapid Environmental Impact Assessment report, its public hearing proceedings or in its application of forest clearance. Raoghat will also affect the dwindling population (just 2,900) of the Asian wild Buffalo.

Land Taker over

According to Section 4 (5) of Scheduled Tribes and other Traditional Forest Dwellers (Recognition of Forest Rights) Act, 2006, there can be no eviction of people from forest land unless their rights have been recognised and the verification procedure is complete. Nine sarpanches were selected to receive official information about the project when there at least 35 tribal villages within 15 Km radius of the project. BSP has produced 6 No Objection Certificates (NOCs) in its application for forest clearances. Three of the six NOCs are partially illegible and/or lack key specifications (like village and designation of the signatories). Besides, the NOCs do not have any legal validity as it is the gram sabha and not the sarpanch who is the legal authority to give permission for land diversion.

Source: Chhattisgarh Bachao Andolan Objection Report.

"Centre may tweak forest laws in Naxal-hit areas" : New Delhi: 12 Jun 2014 (to encourage development)

The blurb of the news story explains its purpose: "To encourage development in Red Zone."

The daily reports that "as a part of its effort to stream line environment issues in a realistic manner to assist development in Naxal-hit areas, the Centre will change some rules in the Forest Rights Act and Forest Conservation Act to step up economic activity in worst affected states including Chhattisgarh, Odisha, Jharkhand, Maharashtra and West Bengal."[8]

Minister of Environment and Forest (MoEF) said, "LWE districts need to have separate criteria for development and environment protection". His remarks came after his meeting with Chhattisgarh CM Raman Singh on Tuesday (10.06.2014) during which he is believed to have assured the State to wait for a policy which will take care of development goals of Naxal-hit states. Official privy to the discussion hinted to some changes which will be different for Coastal states, Naxal region having rich forest cover, North-East states and the rest of the country.

The changes may include extending the limit of diversion of forest area in Naxal – hit IAP districts for development and providing exemptions to certain projects including restricted mining under the existing laws. Presently states in the Maoist belt have rights to give clearance to minor projects up to five hectares of forest land. BJP-ruled Chhattisgarh has long been demanding extending the limit up to 40 hectares under the Forest Conservation Act.

It is expected that other states may also get power to issue forest clearance for areas up to 10 hectares of forest land. "States with higher forest cover should not be penalised", said Javadekar.

Indicating the change in approach, the Minister had tweeted after meeting with the CM of Chhattisgarh on Tuesday (9 June): "We are not for 'we vs they' for Centre-State issues. We consider 'We are family' for development and environment protection."

It is learnt that the Minister may also move a proposal to release compensatory afforestation funds to states to increase forest cover.

"Naxal terror fails to kill zeal of foreign, domestic tourists: New Delhi: 23 Jul 2014

The terror of Naxals seem to have failed to dampen the zeal of the country's domestic tourists as well as foreigners to explore the tribal areas and eco-tourism in the Maoist-hit States. It was reported by a daily in Jul 2014.[9]

The latest data from the Union Tourism Ministry say while Domestic Tourist Visits (DTVs) in the Maoist belt states reported an increase in footfall to 62.43 Cr in 2013 from 59.23 Cr in 2012, for Foreign Tourist Visits (FTVs), it was 88 lakh against 66 lakh for the same period.

If the foreigners' favourites were hotspots in Jharkhand and Chhattisgarh, the Indians, preferred to venture mostly in Chhattisgarh, UP and MP which reported double digit growth.

In fact, it was the tourist-hotspots in Chhattisgarh in Naxal belt which topped the list in most preferred destinations as it witnessed 51 per cent growth rate in 2013 over the 2012, with 22 lakh against 15 lakh making visits to the State during the corresponding period.

Statistics say that Bihar, Odisha and Jharkhand just managed to stay in the positive bracket with not many domestic tourists visiting these states. But worst-hit was Andhra Pradesh which was avoided by the tourists, both domestic and foreign, during 2013. It reported a steep decline of 26 per cent and 23 per cent respectively in DTVs (15.21 Cr) and FTVs (22.35 lakh) footfalls in 2013 over the previous year.

During the 2013, besides Andhra Pradesh, foreigners gave a miss to Bihar and Chhattisgarh which reported negative growth.

Overall, the domestic tourist visits across the country also reported a rise, though marginally from 104.50 Cr in 2012 to 114.52 cr in the following year. (see table on the next page)

"Tribals halt mining activities of Adani group in Chhattisgarh Ambikapur (North Chhattisgarh): 2 Sep 2014

The tribals in Parsa and Kante Basin Coal mines area of Ambikapur, north Chhattisgarh, have brought mining activities of the Adani enterprises to a complete halt since Friday, (30 Aug 2014). All efforts by the officials of the company and the administration to seek a settlement were in vain, when some 250 tribals gathered on the 29 August.[10]

Foreign Tourists Vs Domestic Tourists

Andhra Pradesh	-26.6	23.7
Bihar	.7	-30.2
Chhattisgarh	51.6	-6.9
Jharkhand	.4	44.1
MP	18.6	1.6
Maharashtra	10.5	56.7
Odisha	8.3	3
UP	34.6	3
West Bengal	12.4	2.1
(Figures in percentage)		

The villagers told the SDM NS Bhagat and Adani officials that they would continue with the protests. They demanded action on the ground, and not mere words of assurances.

Adani group bagged the Parsa East and Kante Basin coal block contract for the entire operations from Rajasthan Rajiya Vidhyut Nigam Ltd, which get the block in Ambikapur district in 2007. According to the agreement, the Adani Enterprise will work as mine-developer – cum – operator through its subsidiary Adani Mining.

A villager, Bholenath Singharmo, cited that the forest in the area happened to be elephant corridor. "Before the mining, the rights of the tribals and forest dwellers in the area must be settled. We rely on tankers to get drinking water, there is no facility of school or dispensary that were promised", he told the daily.

But Adani officials hope to get the dispute settled soon. Anurag Tyagi, Liaison Manager, Adani Corporate Affairs, told the daily: "The school, dispensary and other demanded facilities will follow the due process and take time."

Tribal Activist Gangaram Paikara said that earlier this year (2014), the National Green Tribunal expressed surprise over the approval to the project carried out in an open cast coal mine as it was part of "no go" area classified by MoFE.

Adani officials said that the issue of any additional compensation demanded against the land needs to be handled by the state government. What they demand.

- Rehabilitate villagers whose lands were taken away.
- Jobs to unemployed as per eligibility (not outsource to contractors)
- Facility of school and dispensary.

- Drinking water and roads.
- Enhanced compensation and area development.

Adani to resume mining after pact with Chhattisgarh villagers, Raipur: 3 Sep 2014

The logjam over the coal blocks operated by Adani Mining Pvt Ltd in Ambikapur district ended on Tuesday (2 Sep 2014) after an agreement was signed between the affected villagers, company and local administration.

The company operates two coal blocks of Parsa East and Kante (Kete?) Basin in the area. Demanding Compensation, rehabilitation and jobs promised earlier, "local villagers began a *dharna* on the premises last week and forced the company to suspend all operations."[11]

In the agreement, the company agreed to begin rehabilitation work from 20 September (2014). It was also agreed that company and local administration will hold a monthly meeting with the villagers concerned to sort problems if any. "If the rehabilitation work does not begin by the given date, I will lock the company's premises", ADM EKKA told the gathering of villagers, who in turn said of their demands were not met, they would begin protest afresh.

"We welcome today's developments. We will follow the advice of administration in true spirit", said the aforesaid Anurag Tyagi.

The villagers of Parsa East and Kete lost their farmland and forest land consequent to their acquisition by the company. "They were to be rehabilitated in the first phase but the work is not yet over. As per the MoEF rules, individual and community forest rights were to be implemented before diverting land but it has not yet happened", Chhattisgarh Bachao Andolan's convener Alok Shukla said.

"Forest Rights Act diluted for projects": Amendment: Move to ease approval for new projects near green areas not recorded as forests by British, New Delhi: 30 Oct 2014.

Continuing with its business-friendly regulatory changes, the Narendra Modi government has brought in a key change diminishing applicability of watershed Forest Rights Act (FRA) for seeking statutory forest clearance (FC) for projects. The MoEF has exempted plantations, notified as forests within 75 years of the FRA coming into force on 13 Dec 2005 - - and not having tribal population as per 2001 and 2011 census - - from this Ministry's 2009 circular that made implementation of the Act mandatory for green approval of the projects.[12]

It would mean that FRA provision would not apply to a large chunk of forest areas such as the one the Odisha government acquired despite resistance from local for India's biggest foreign direct investment (FDI) projects …the POSCO steel plant in Jagatsinghpur. The move would ease approval process for projects coming up near green areas not recorded as forests by the British and not having tribal population since 2001. But it fails to recognise rights of other forest dwellers.

The change "notified by the Ministry through a circular on Tuesday (29 October) gives powers to the district collectors to notify whether FRA is applicable to the project site or not. And they will have to certify that the green area was not a notified forest in 1930 and that no tribals live in the villages as per the last two censuses.

That would be enough for the Ministry Forest Advisory Committee (FAC) to exempt FRA compliance for the project, government officials said. It's another benefit would be that the mandatory consent of the body of villagers in and around the project site called Gram Sabha will not be required.

The Ministry said the FRA does not apply for forest dwellers who have not been living in forests for more than 75 years since the applicability of the law. "Since the villages will not have any person belonging to both the categories scheduled tribes and forest dwellers . . . . question of recognitions of their rights does not arise," the Ministry's circular says.

Exemptions in the Forest Rights Act

- Acquisition of land not mandatory for seeking environment approval.
- Environment clearance can be sought without applying for wildlife approval.
- Linear projects exempted from mandatory consent of body of villagers called Gram Sabha.
- Relaxation given in allowing projects within 10 kms of the wildlife areas.

"Girl from Dandkaranya Naxal Camp may soon be a doctor from China" Hanamkonda (Warangal): 14 Dec 2014

"Tejaswi's father is highest – ranked Maoist to have ever surrendered, she is perhaps the only Naxal child to study abroad"

It is an extremely heartening story about a girl born in a Naxal camp in jungle and now awaiting her time to become a doctor. The story was brought to us by a daily, known for its investigations powers for a long time in the world of Indian journalism, in Dec 2014.[13]

The daily puts it as aptly and as sharply as it deserves: "Even her birth was an act of rebellion. Her parents belonged to a guerrilla outfit that 'prohibits procreation'." They have their reasons: "Having babies in the forest, its senior ideologues believed, thwarted the revolutionary ideal. Her father Lanka Papi Reddy was passionate about the revolution, but he wanted a baby."

When Saroja, his wife, gave birth to her in Oct 1994 in a guerrilla camp in Maoist citadel Abujh Maad, Reddy named her Tejaswi (= the girl with an aura).

"On Tuesday (12 Dec 2014) at 1 AM, on a flight from Hyderabad, Tejaswi left for China, to begin a five-year MBBS course at Hebei University in China's eastern Hebei province. Once of the very few babies to ever be born to Maoists in Dandakarnya (their number countable on fingers) is on her way to become perhaps the only offspring of a Naxal to have studied abroad."

"I fought with my friends for her. I could have never dreamt that one day she would fly to China", Reddy reminisces at his Hanamkonda home in Telengana's Warangal district.

For first few years after her birth, all that the Reddys could think of was how to raise her: By the time she was two, they had realised that a life in jungle ambushes was no place for a child to grow up. So one night Reddy quietly slipped out of the forest, crossed the Godavari and left her with his family in Warangal, unsure if they would ever meet her again.

The two guerrillas would eventually see Tejaswi over a decade later, in 2008, after Reddy, by then a Central Committee Member, CPI (Maoist), decided to surrender for "personal reasons". Saroja, a platoon commander, followed soon.

Reddy's mother who raised Tejaswi, did not tell her about her parents' past till they returned. "It was in the news. I remember", Tejaswi told the daily, before leaving for China. "Then, grand mother told me my papa is coming."

Reddy's homecoming was a major event. The only Central Committee member to have ever laid down arms, he had surrendered before the then Andhra Pradesh Home Minister K. Jana Reddy. Few in the family recognized him when he arrived home, laughs Reddy. "Even my other… I had to show her a mark on my leg."

Theirs is a rich landlord family with politics in its blood. Reddy's father, a Congress man, was a freedom fighter, while his uncle was a senior Communist leader.

Reddy joined the Naxal movement in the 1970s went underground in 1976 after his brother was shot dead in an encounter during emergency. In the early 1980, he was among the first batch of selected Naxals to march into Bastar, and helped establish a guerrilla zone that the Indian State I still unable to breach.

Reddy remembers the struggle that followed to "reclaim my daughter", by then 14. He told her about the Naxal struggle, and their belief in the cause. Tejaswi told him she was proud of his "fight for the people". Though happy about that, Reddy nurtures a regret. "Life was better inside (the forest). I was living for a just society, it gave me satisfaction. I am earning more now, but I participate in all evils. Earlier, I would beat up all those who took bribe, now I am forced to give bribe."

Interested in Cinema, Tejaswi first wanted to be a film maker. She chose to be a doctor to "serve people". With several students from Warangal already studying at Hebei University, she opted for it. Seeing her off at Hyderabad airport, Reddy told Tejaswi to study well, and to "not forget that you have to serve people."

Two days after reaching Hebei, she texted the scribe: "I love my dad sooo muchhh." She echoed what Aleida Guevara had written about his father: "The more I read (his life), the more in love I was with the boy my father had been."

The iconic Latin American revolutionary is also Tejaswi's WhatsApp display photograph. Reddy misses Tejaswi already, and they Skype at least twice a day. When she was in a Hyderabad hostel preparing for medical entrance, he would visit every Sunday, carrying homemade chicken. For the next five years now, she will visit only once annually.

All his wishes for his daughter met, the 52-year-old says he has a last remaining one. Secretly relieved that she did not follow her parents into the jungle, Reddy wishes that after Tejaswi becomes a doctor, she will be able to serve the tribals in forbidden Abujh Maad.

One day, he hopes, he will take her to her place of birth, a small village called Balibeda, near a river called Nai Berad. With a pause, Reddy adds, "I do not know if she would ever be able to go there."

An Evocative Journey: Raipur to Rajnandgaon

What follows is a journey in Chhattisgarh from Raipur to Rajnandgaon, totaling 286 km done in two days.

Raipur to Kanker 140 Km 23 Dec 2014

Kanker to Rajnandgaon 146 Km 24 Dec 2014

To maintain its integrity and smooth narration, it is told in the words of the reporter scribe.

"Raipur to Kanker": 140 Km : 23 Dec 2014

If you remember Ajit Chandila, the cricketer from the IPL scandal, you will know what Sandeep Rathi looks like - - even down to these wraparound shades. To know more about him, the shiny gold bracelet on his wrist and this opening line should be enough: "I don't usually drive these taxis, I have got employees to do that. Actually, I am into real estate."[14]

Raipur to Kanker, on the outside edge of Bastar, Chhattisgarh, begin with a blur of big city wanting to be bigger city: Blue signboards to the airport, the cricket stadium in New Raipur, some familiar destinations - - Dantewada, Champaran - - Mintu International School, and Yash Spoken English Class.

Rathi, meanwhile, has reached Bangkok. "I go there every two – three years. Do you know they drive 160 Kmph in Bangkok? *Kya gadi chalate hain wahan ke log* (What a way the people drive their vehicles there)!

Sensing an audience, Rathi now moves into top gear. "Have you ever heard of Acharnak Marg - - where anything can happen any time in the night all of a sudden? Nobody knows why, but it is a road near Bilaspur side, where a number of unnatural deaths are said to occur. Is it spooked"? I don't know but the dhabawallahs at the beginning of that stretch always warn drivers not to proceed there in the night."

Remind him of the other big Bilaspur story - - the sterilisations that went wrong, killing 13 women this years - - and he almost starts frothing at the mouth. After spitting out a bunch of expletives, directed at everyone allegedly involved - - the doctor, the medicine supplier, the politician - - he sums it all up in one terse sentence: "*Sab Chor hain, Saale* (All of them are thieves, these morous)."

Next topic? An alcohol-free state. "There are two Ms that people her can't live without - - *murgi* (chicken) and *mahua* (locally brewed liquor). And the government wants a *daru – mukt* Chhattisgarh," fumes Rathi. As his anger rises, his command over English slips. "Tell me, how can you do that possible?", he asks.

With Rathi in full flow, the milestones whiz part unnoticed till the car gets stuck in an unfamiliar situation almost half way through, traffic jam.

It is Dhamtari town, big enough to boast of a jam, with college girls in tights hanging out at the main junction, sharing a laugh.

The effort to get free drains Rathi and silence accompanies an empty stretch lined on both sides by what appears to be the outer edge of a forest. Then, everyone shakes awake. On the left, tied to a tree is a small, faded red flag. With a nervous laugh, Rathi say, *"Bhailog ka area shuru ho gaya, bas mudke mat dekhna, chalte raho.*" (The Maoists' area has started, now don't look back, keep going). Silence, a few boards go by - - Charama, Jhipatola - - and finally a bright sight that brings a smile back to Rathi's face. It is the "famous Mukri Dhaba", a Punjabi welcome to Kanker, a small trading outpost surrounded by hills, with its Doodh river, Garhiya hill, and yes, this name plate outside a house: Datta Roy Mansion.

"Kanker to Rajnandgaon": 146 Km : 24 Dec 2014

"The Raja, his daughter, and a book on birds"

The kick-off from Kanker, which is in the midst of a local fair with cock fights, colourful beads and more colourful language, happens at an unlikely site - - a palace. The Kanker Heritage Palace, as the property set in 1937 is now called, flaunts a sprawling compound that the two younger descendents of the local Rajah are trying to turn into a tourist destination, with four cottages on the lawns.[15]

The USP here is that the 37-year-old Suryapratap Deo, or simply and quite aptly "Jolly", and his younger brother Ashwini Pratap Deo personally take care of the guests. On their property, there are enough remnants of a distant past to capture anyone's imagination - - vintage vehicles, black and white photos, and a coat of arms. Yet, the take away image is that of smiling Jolly carefully wrapping up a book on "Birds of India" as a gift for his 5-year daughter, who is happily playing outside with her pet dogs, and a busy lunch of guinea fowls.

The drive to Rajnandgaon from where you can catch a bus to Nagpur en route to Khasgaon in Maharashtra, the next stop on Latitude 20^0 15', takes you back in time - - grass – thatched roofs, smoke curling up from a back yard - - till two tribal women cut into the road on their bright blue Kinetic Honda. And, as you turn left from Kurud, driver Chiranjeevi's "Top-a-top road" from Balodh to Lohara is a 20 km surface comparable to some of the best in the country.

"Road Construction: Govt to remove hurdles in the Red Zone", New Delhi: 13 Jan 2015 (Contractors in unvilling to work)

Struggling toward some 1,600 Km roads out of a total sanctioned 5,470

Km in LWE-hit districts in the past six years, the Centre is now reaching out to state governments to resolve bottlenecks for speedy implementation of this work.[16]

Road Transport Ministry informs that due to security constraints and Naxal threats, contractors are not coming forward to bid for the workre on certain stretches, since these fall in the high-risk Category III areas: Gadchiroli district in Maharashtra; Balaghat in MP, Bastar region in Chhattisgarh; Malkangiri district in Odisha; and Palamu, Garhwa, Dumka and Simdega districts in Jharkhand. A Government source tells the daily: "In such areas both men and machines face major threat as there are several threats of Maoist attacks. Recently, there was an incident in Khammam district at a place on Telengana – Chhattisgarh border where a plant and machinery were set ablaze. This impacted a 6 Km stretch nearing completion on the Hyderabad – Bhopalpatnam road.

Another official explains: "First, they tell the labour that they are fighting for their rights so that they get their dues, persuading them to leave the site. Subsequently, they set the entire machinery afire".

Bandhs and protests by the Maoists during working season range between a day and a fortnight. Several steps have been taken to address these issues. Road Transport Minister Nitin Gadkari "is meeting CMs of Chhattisgarh, Jharkhand and Bihar and PWD Ministers of other concerned states in Raipur on Tuesday (13 January)" to fine-tune the process further and to expedite construction.

Status of roads in LWE areas

- Length sanctioned 5,469 Km
- Length awarded 4,908 Km
- Length completed 3,308 Km
- Incomplete Work
  1. Chhattisgarh 689 Km
  2. Jharkhand 331 Km
  3. Odisha 229 Km
  4. Maharashtra 152 Km
  5. MP 99 Km
- Progress in Telengana, Bihar and UP 90 per cent

"Maoist-hit areas to get more banks, Post offices and ATMs" New Delhi: 19 Feb 2015

Three of the worst Naxal-hit districts in the country - - Sukma, Bijapur and Dantewada - -in Chhattisgarh have only 44 banks and regional rural bank branches in total.[17]

Sukma and Bijapur have only 10 ATMs. Over 100 post office branches are non-functional. In Sukma, 13 mobile towers are non-functional. It was revealed by a MHA data.

The data has been culled by the MHA after consulting the DMs of the three district - - considered the den of the Maoists and the stark reality was presented to all stakeholder ministries and state government "when Home Minister Rajnath Singh sat with them last week to review development projects of the region".

An MHA official further clarified : "To make the benefits of an innovative, financially inclusive scheme like Pradhan Mantri Jan Dhan Yojana reach the targeted people in these three districts, we need to have more bank branches there. All post offices need to be functional for their financial inclusion. Making them part of the communication revolution happening elsewhere in the country requires at least already installed telephone exchanges and mobile towers to be functional first. This is what we are going to focus on in the coming months."

The district-wise data follow: A sad picture

- **Sukma.** It has only four sub-post offices and all 61 branch post offices are non-functional. Out of five telephone exchanges, one is non-functional.
- **Bijapur.** It has five sub-post offices and 53 branch post offices but only two of them are functional. Its 14 mobile towers are functional but 14 new sanctioned one are yet to be installed.
- **Dantewada.** It has six sub-post offices and 59 branch post offices. Nine of these don't have single employee. In total, 50 per cent of post are lying vacant. Three out of twenty mobile towers are non-functional in the district.

"Stop work in the Maoist areas: forest staff tell the CM"

"Chhattisgarh: Seek release of guard, held in police informer's murder case, say rebels forced him."

Here is a telling story about forest employees of Chhattisgarh requesting CM Raman Singh, through a letter dated 21 March (2015), to stop all departmental work in the interior areas, citing the Maoist threat. The letter written by Chhattisgarh Forest Employees Union convener Umesh Singh, speaks of the foresters threatening to go on strike from the 25th if their demands were not met. A copy of the letter has also been sent to the Chief Secretary and Forest Secretary.[18]

This letter and demand there-in seem ironic midst the claims by the Centre and the State Government that Maoist activities are on the decline.

A section of the forest employees are already on strike since 12 March.

This is probably the first instance in Chhattisgarh when employees of any department have written to the CM, urging him to discontinue all works in Maoist areas.

Their main demand, of course, is the unconditional release of a Forest guard Ramsai Vadde, accused of the murder of a tribal Budhram Salam.

How did it all begin? On 24 Dec 2014, Maoist abducted Vadde and some labourers while working in Edka area of Narayanpur district of Bastar. Maoist made Vadde call Salam, a resident of his village and asked him to reach Edka on some pretext. As Salam arrived, Ultras released Vadde and others. Salam was found dead next day. Subsequently, police arrested Vadde and charged him with criminal conspiracy to commit the murder of Salam. Some labourers, who had been working with him were also arrested for murder.

Forest Union President Satish Mishra explains to the daily: "Vadde has no role in this. They put a gun on his head, forcing him to call Salam, a police informer. What do you do when threatened this way? Police thrashed Vadde badly. We demand his unconditional release."

Here are some other points from the letter of Umesh Singh: "Forest employees undertake development and departmental work in sensitive areas. They are bound to occasionally come across the Naxal cadres. Under these circumstances, they can be abducted any time or forced to do the Maoists' bidding. If we want to prevent Narayanpur – like incidents, then the entire work of the forest department will have to be stopped in the interiors. . . . If Naxals can kidnap senior officers like collectors and relatives of ministers, and negotiate terms for their release, then the forest employees can be abducted any time and carry out the Maoists' biddings. We are unhappy and sad at the indifference of administration in this case."

"We are also concerned about his arrest, and trying our best to resolve the issue", Principal Chief Conservator of Forest Ram Prakash told the daily.

"Govt commitment to bring development to Maoist-affected areas Raipur: 16 Aug 2015

CM Raman Singh stressed 15 Aug 2015 that his government will overcome the hindrances in development in LWE areas of the State while marching ahead in the path of inclusive growth and public participation.[19]

He said this at the Independence Day function at the police grounds in Raipur City.

Turning into a consummate politician which he indeed is, he noted that "it is the first time since formation of the State that the same political party has been elected both at the Centre and in State", and said, "Single motto of positive politics - - *"Sabka Sath Sabka Vikas"* with every one, and development for every one—is echoing across the State as well as the nation."

He mentioned several welfare schemes and other plans of his Government:

> His Government has sanctioned Rs 2,400 Cr to provide bonus to farmers for their paddy at the rate of Rs 300 per quintal.
>
> Farmers will be provided interest-free loans worth Rs 3,100 Cr and 100 new agricultural equipment service centres will be opened for the convenience of the farmers.
>
> As many as 15 Nagar Panchayats will be upgraded to the level of Municipal Councils while the two Municipal councils at Dhamtari and Birgan will be turned into Municipal Corporations.

Notes

1. Dipak Kumar Dash, Times of India, 12 Jan 2013.
2. Editorial, Times of India, 14 Jan 2013.
3. Vivek Deshpande, Indian Express, 17 Jan 2013.
4. Moushumi Das Gupta, Hindustan Times, 30 May 2013.
5. PNS, The Pioneer, 10 Sep 2013.
6. Ruhi Tewari, Indian Express, 17 Feb 2013.
7. Chandra Mohan, Mumbai. Indian Express, 14 Mar 2014.
8. Vishwa Mohan, Times of India, 12 Jun 2014.
9. Archana Jyoti, The Pioneer, 23 Jul 2014.
10. Ejaz Kaiser, Hindustan Times, 2 Sep 2014.
11. Indian Express, 3 Sep 2014.
12. Chetan Chauhan, Hindustan Times, 30 Oct 2014.
13. Ashutosh Bhardwaj, Indian Expess, 14 Dec 2014.
14. Indian Express, 3 Jan 2015.
15. *Ibid,* 4 Jan 2015.
16. Dipak Dash, Times of India, 13 Jan 2015.
17. Rajesh Ahuja, Hindustan Times, 19 Feb 2015.
18. Ashutosh Bhardwaj, Indian Express, 23 Mar 2015.
19. PTI, Indian Express, The Pioneer, 12 Aug 2015.

18

Left-Wing Extremism and National Security

It is of some import to stress Prime Minister's assertion made repeatedly since 2009 that "the Maoist insurgency is the gravest internal security threat facing the country." It is important to mention this fact at the very beginning of this book.

India is at War

It again is unfortunate that a majority of Indians, mostly well meaning and generally well-informed otherwise, have failed to understand and appreciate that India is at war and the enemy is undoubtedly more dangerous than any of our external enemies!

The enemy here is a section of our own people, infused by an alien ideology and aided and abetted by foreign countries and agents. It is more difficult to fight this internal enemy than an external aggressor, for the simple reason that helping the latter will be anti-national and even traitorous, but helping the Maoist is fashionable among the drawing room intellectuals to establish their liberal credentials, "at the cost of the national interest", as asserted by an exasperated security officer engaged in counter-Naxalite operations! They display such passion on the television debates that some of them can be dubbed as the overground arm of the underground Naxalites. They are so inanely irrational in their thinking that they truly believe that the Indian state and its security agencies are actual culprits who are responsible for creating this insurgency. How does one argue with this lot. They never understand, rather don't want to understand, that declared aim of the Maoist ultras is to overthrow the elected government of the country through an armed insurrection and establish the true Communist State—a utopian ideology which failed to deliver (in its homelands) during more than ten decades of its existence on the face of earth and caused untold miseries—torture, murders, starvations, public humiliations—to their subjects. Can the humanity forget the carnages ordered by Mao and Stalin on their hapless compatriots? Now that the experiment has failed and the Communist states have nearly disappeared, to try and resuscitate the dead can be termed as passion gone berserk! But their overground intellectual friends should know better. They cannot act like the morons. And the way some of these overground 'Maoist' and some Human Rights wallah speak on the television debates nearly convinces the innocent and the uninitiated listeners that it is, indeed, the security personnel who are responsible for the all round destruction and mayhem in the country and not the 'idealistic', violent Naxalites!

How the Maoist Insurrection is viewed?

Discourse on the "Maoist conflict is suffused with black and white images and interpretations." Some views on the nature of this movement– even if some analysts feed it is no more a movement, it is more of a terrorism-driven tyranny—are discussed here:

- It is a law and order problem. In initial stages, any such movement can be so described. If a stage arrives when it is no longer amendable to law enforcement agencies, it ceases to be so. That "It is a law and order problem" has become a cliché which is often employed by the opponents of the government to make the point that the latter does not understand the real nature of the Maoist revolt and its implications for the national security and it is treating it as a merely law and order problem. What is left unsaid by these critics is that the Government is not serious in tackling Naxalite/Maoist threat! It is a facetious view to, say the least. No one in the position of responsibility either in political or in security establishment has ever made a statement that Maoism can be settled through the application of the force. This stance is often attributed to the erstwhile Home Minister, P Chidambram – which is patently untrue. What is true is that without force of arms, these criminal elements—this is what these Maoist are in the eye of security forces——would never come to the negotiation table. It is only then that socio-economic development of the backward areas can be undertaken. It is well-known fact that these ultras will block this development work with all means at their disposal. If that is allowed to happen, the Maoists will lose their appeal to those poor and deprived people who have been fed all this while on the propaganda that the Government does not care for their well-being! Let it be understood by one and all that no truculent elements, terrorists and Maoists included—have never been convinced by Gandhian ways in any part of the world. It is only when the Maoists are convinced that the Indian state means business that the socio-economic development projects can be started. In some case, this can also be started during the Maoist violence if there are sufficient forces available to subdue these recalcitrant Maoists. Of Course, the Government must convince those poor people that their good is its prime concern and they must not fall prey to the machinations of the Maoists. Even when they come to the negotiation table, the Government must make doubly sure that the Maoists do not exploit the interregnum of cease fire to rearm and regroup their cadres.

- Some look upon the conflict as "a fight for social justice, equality, protection, security and local development." It is for note that these are a observations on the Maoists by a report commissioned by India's Planning Commission[1].

Realities on the ground

There are shades of grey between the two views mentioned above. Complexities of an issue like the Maoist insurrection lend themselves to be analysed in different ways by the scholars in the field. Here are diametrical opposite perceptions of this conflict: If some see the state as protector and the Maoists as terrorists, others view the state as oppressor and the Maoists as saviours. In this contrarian interpretations, the roles of the two entities, in a manner of speaking, are inter-changeable. If the Government is the evil one case, the Maoists are deemed as the culprits in the other.

The CPI (Maoists), the main Maoist formation, if not the only one, has caused death and destruction of the 'enemy', has been declared a terrorist organisation by the Government of India in June 2009[2]. "Undoubtedly, it perpetrate violence against civilians, meant to terrorise the larger population. But some analysts claim that similar tectics of resorting to violence have also been used by its opponents gainst it:

> In the form of counter-insurgency operations launched by the State, or by vigilante groups like the Salwa Judum created by it in Chhattisgarh." So some of these analysts have put the law breakers and law enforcers in the same category (Sudha Ramachandran, "The Maoist Conflict in Dandakaranya", in *The Naxal Threat,* VR Raghavan, Ed, 2011.). This perverse view of the two entities has been fostered by the Left intellectuals, some Human Rights Wallahs, foreign Human

Rights Organisations like the Human Rights Watch of the USA, and more vigorously by the overgrounds arms of the Maoists.

So some analysts have suggested that the Salwa Judum too has carried out similar attacks (as have the Maoists). The action by the Salwa Judum has been dealt with in detail in chapter[3].

Impact of Maoist Conflict

Maoist violence made a small beginning but fanned to large areas of the country.

Progressive spread of violence

Maoist violence can only be countered and defeated by the might of the state. At times, the insurgents claim they are compelled to use force against the security forces. It is an empirical observation that armed conflicts across the world indicates that violence that is employed to quell violence often intensify it. Attacks trigger counter-attacks, adding progressively to the quantum of violence.

Occasionally, security forces hunting the Maoists find some collaborators in the villages. If they impose collective punishment on the villages, there is strong reaction to it, giving an opportunity to the Maoists to exploit the situation to their advantage. If both sides engage in punishment and revenge, each is seeking to retaliate with deadlier violence.

The Maoists claimed that their ambush of CRPF personnel at Chintalnar in April 2010 was in response to the governments' bid to reclaim the areas that had controlled for years. This vicious ambush brought in a strong reaction from the security forces. Fearing police wrath, hundreds of tribals from the surrounding villages of Mukram, Tarmetla, Rehadgatta, Pamra, Karigundam, Kodapalli, Rengam, Murpalli, and Jadka fled to neighbouring Orissa and Andhra Pradesh. The village of Mukram was the worst affected. One of the Maoist commanders, Rukhmati, was from the village and it was in this very village that the CRPF men had rested the night before the Ambush. Suspecting some Maoist links, the CRPF carried out a search operation in Mukram and some men were punished. Aimala Rane, wife of Mukram's Sarpanch says that they spared no one in her village. "They beat every man, woman and child they could find, and they took away my husband Aimla Nanda." Even girls were not spared, she alleged. "Not surprisingly Mukram is turning into a ghost town.[4]"

Here is an unfortunate fact of life for people inhabiting the strife-torn areas. Above was a brief account of what Mukram's residents had to suffer over a few weeks. "But those living in zones of armed conflict like

Dantewala, this cycle of violence is a familiar experience. An attack or offensive by one side leads to reprisals by the other, which in turn prompts more intimidation, punishment and violence."

The Author wishes to clarify the reasons behind putting certain text in inverted commas:

1. Basically and usually, it is commonly understood that the text in inverted commas is by another writer/analyst.
2. More importantly, it also signifies that this Author per se does not agree with the averment made by the text.
3. Any analysis that compares, and also, puts the security forces and the lawless elements like the Maoists on equal footing, is distasteful to this Author, to put it mildly. Undoubtedly, the security forces do commit wrong and/or excesses, and they are taken to task as they operate within the laws of the land. The Maoists have no such obligations and are lawless, rogue elements.

Human Costs are High, indeed

The Left Wing Extremism has created havoc in the areas of its operations. Undoubtedly, at times, innocent civilians are caught in the cross-fire and suffer injuries, including fatal one. The Maoists, and also some fellow travellers, would believe and like the rest of us to believe that security forces are solely responsible for the miseries the civilians are subjected to as a result of this bloody conflict. Unfortunately, a few publications give the balanced picture of this horrendous tragedy —most others give a gory picture of atrocities committed by the security forces in lurid details, for whatever reasons. Here is one given by a weekly, generally purveying anti-security forces stuff. Here is the experience of Shyamal Pojamma, of village Koras in Chhattisgarh, "providing insights into the multiple implications that conflict has for people living in the conflict zone. They suffer the impact of loss of kin, trauma and unending pain of displacement."

Pojamma had fled to Andhra Pradesh to escape the Salwa Judum. "But the insecurity dogs her." Here is her account:

1. My 18-year old son, Shyamal Admaiya, was killed by the Salwa Judum and the police in a fake encounter in Singaram village on 8 January 2009. I saw his body. He was shot between the eyes. In addition to this, they had used a sickle to cut open his head. I can't erase the images from my mind. Admaiya was my youngest son.
2. For two months after this, we lived in the forest, terrified that Salwa Judum would come back and kill the rest of us. My two

elder sons and their families decided to walk to Andhra Pradesh since they were tired of constantly living in fear. I refused to leave. I wanted to die in my village.

3. Two weeks back, Salwa Judum returned to my village. My husband and I again escaped to the forest....Then we too went and joined them in Andhra Pradesh.
4. There is no food here. No lands to cultivate...Back home we were kings. Now all we can afford is one portion of rice gruel a day. The Naxal are safe, the Salwa Judum is safe. We are only one dying in the middle[5].

It is gruesome account by all means, and should have elements of truth also. But Indian security forces are not known to be so cruel as to "use a sickle to cut open his head." Salwa Judum might have been guilty of certain excesses, but is simply beyond belief that they, with police men, could have acted as gholes.

These have been several allegations of rape and disappearance of civilians in the conflict zone. These are generally inquired into and action taken as necessary.

The table below shows that the number of fatalities has almost doubled between 2002 and 2009

Number of Fatalities in the Maoist conflict 2002-2009

Year	2002	2003	2004	2005	2006	2007	2008	2009
No. of Fatalities	482	515	566	677	678	696	721	908

Source: Government of India, Ministry of Home Affairs, *Annual Reports,* 2005-06, 2008-09, 2009-10.

The number of injured is expectedly far higher, many are dealing with life-long physical disabilities. The Maoists are increasingly making use of the IEDs, consequently taking heavy toll on the security forces. Here are some telling statisties IEDs account for about 40 per cent of the 408 troop fatalities in Chhattisgarh since 2007 till 2010, and nearly 70 per cent of all injuries sustained by security forces from January 2008 to March 2010. IEDs cause death and injuries. Their psychological impact is devastating[6].

It is equally true that an increasing number of civilians are getting killed. It is an unfortunate fact that civilians do get caught in the crossfire between the security forces and the Maoists.

The impact of the conflict has been particularly harsh on the children. Children's education has been severely affected as many schools have been destroyed/ blown up by the Maoists. On the other hand, at times the security forces too are forced to occupy some schools[7].

Worse than the children's loss of educational facilities is the fact of Maoists recruiting them for fighting the security forces. The Maoists organise children in the 6-12 age group into *bal sanghams,* where they are indoctrinated on Maoist ideology and prepared for later *dalam* activity. Those above the age of 12 years are deployed as fighters to engage in hostilities against the security forces and Salwa Judum, to make and plant land-mines and bombs, to gather intelligence and for sentry duties. These facts are from HR Watch Report of 2008. But the same Reports further on says: "Children have recruited by the Salwa Judum for similar purposes. What is more, the state is recruiting children as SPOs. This Report also describes Tarrem Kosa's experience "as a child soldier with the Maoists and then as an SPO, lays bare the tragic lives of children living in the conflict zone." (Human Rights Watch, *Dangerous Duty: Children and Chhattisgarh Conflict* (New York: HRW 2008)

Tarrem Kosa was recruited into a Maoist *dalam* when he was a class eight student, trained with bows and arrows, and then bombs. He participated in several encounters. He often felt home sick but did not know the way out of his life in Maoist camps. He paid a heavy price when he left the Maoists: "They killed both his younger brothers, beat his mother and broke her arms; took all their belongings; and burnt their house." After his surrender, the police use him as an informer, and later was appointed an SPO. He now accompanies security forces on anti-Maoist. Combing operations. He is wanted by the Maoists. Posters with his photograph says he should be killed[8].

New Delhi often denies reports about child soldiers serving the security forces. But some official somewhere must have transgressed the laid-down guidelines. There must be some truth in such reports. In this case, the HR Watch has even supplied the name of a child soldier.

At the end, a painful truism: For many in the conflict zone—civilians or combatants…there appears to be no escape from a life of violence.

Rule of law: A casualty

It is an interesting aspect of Maoists revolt, which by itself is the main violator of rule of law of the country. Besides, in the large stretch of land under the influence—and in certain areas, even under control of Maoists, normal administration is weakened, if not altogether decimated/eliminated. If the Maoist violence and activities are cause of breakdown of rule of law, certain actions, and/or absence of these actions, by the State and its functionaries are also responsible for this breakdown.

In the Maoist areas, it is their 'laws' that govern the lives of people, and normal constitutional provisions fall by the wayside. In the districts like Malkangiri and contiguous areas, the Maoists and tribal mass organisations are known to be grabbing land illegally by taking the law into their hands. It is a fact that some such organisations have taken control of thousands of acres of agricultural land from non-tribals, possibly the latter being the original land-grabbers, or at the very least, they were squatters. Again, possibly these tribals are getting their land back, which belongs to them under Schedule Five. If so, the tribals are merely asserting their constitutional rights. The tribal activists assert that "with the police and courts supporting non-tribals, they have been pushed to take the law into their hands to enforce/claim what is due to them under the Constitution and various legislations." The following paras only corroborates this averment.

Non-tribals are helped by the unscrupulous officials to take possessions of the tribal lands. What is even worse, State itself is showing scant regards for the laws. Legislations like PESA " have been observed in their breach by the state governments that actually govern the Fifth Schedule areas[9]." The laws enacted by the state governments to implement PESA militate against its very spirit.

The acquisition of land by the State for development and mining activity is a contentious issue, since the tribal activists feel it is gross violation of laws that it itself has enacted. Under the PESA, the Government cannot acquire land or issue mining rights on tribal lands without the express permission of the *gram sabhas*. But the state officials are acquiring lands in the face of *gram sabhas's* opposition. Their consent is obtained through coercion and other dubious means. Some activists hold, this was the way the land was acquired by the Tata Group and Essar Steel in Chhattisgarh. In 2006, the villages of Sirisguda, Belar, Takraguda, Kumli, Dhuragaon, Chintagaon, Bhadeparoda and Dabpal in Bastar were pressurised to hand over their land to the Tata's steel plant in Bastar. Gram Sabha meetings were hold with tight security cordon around the venue. "Hundreds of police were deployed in the area to intimidate the tribals, while administration and company officials "persuaded" the gram sabha members to agree to part with their land[10]."

Same story of coercion and high-handedness is repeated in Andhra Pradesh! Work on the Polavaram dam project across the River Godavari has been going on in the face of the stiff opposition from the tribals. The site of the dam is located in the Fifth Schedule area which mandates that the consent of the *gram sabhas* be obtained. But not one of the nine mandal praja parishads—which are the "panchayat of the appropriate level" that is required to be consulted under PESA rules—has been consulted. Yet the project is steaming ahead. It will displace a minimum of 276 villages, all of them situated in the Fifth Schedule area[11]. This is the way India treats the poor, for the so-called common good of the country.

A bitter critic here has a point: 'The violation of the Constitution by the State, the intervention of the State on behalf of private business interests and its nurturing of vigilante groups have undermined the credibility of the Indian Constitution. The state can not absolve itself of responsibility for the breakdown of law and order in tribal areas as it is the 'principal violator of the very laws it is meant to uphold."

The new Land Acquisition Bill is under the active consideration of the Union Government, as it has already been placed before the Cabinet (Nov 2012). It is hoped the Parliament will discuss the same in its Budget Session 2013.

Maoist threat in India: Defining its nature

Prime Minister Manmohan Singh describes the Maoist insurrection as "the biggest internal security threat facing the Country", on 9 Jan 2010.

True to the traditions of an argumentative Indian, a maverick politician, Trinamool Congress MP Kabir Suman, faxed a letter 16 Jan 2010 to the Prime Minister, disagreeing with his formulation on the Naxalism, rather Maoist insurrection, being the "biggest internal security threat to the country." He said he "does not agree with this notion of the Prime Minister, and that the poverty, lack of education and medical treatment, lack of basic social and economic development and lack of opportunities pose the real threat to the national security.

Here is Kishanji's take on the issue: "The ultimate aim of the Maoists remains seizure of power at the Centre and establish new democracy. ...Without expansion, we can't retain our existing bases. So we want expansion of these presently existing bases and creation of new bases at the same time."

At the end of it all, he adds intriguingly: "We desire statehood for Telengana." This is a sinister demand, coming as it is from the Maoists! The analysts have been warning that a separate and smaller Telengana will prove to be a "feeding ground for the Maoists." (Now that the new State of Telengana has been created on 2 Jun 2014, Chief Minister KC Rao and his administration must be fully aware about the Maoist danger looming large on its horizon. They must ensure that the Maoism does not get revived, knowing well that the erstwhile composite State of Andhra Pradesh had achieved a singular success in eradicating and defeating Maoist insurrection two decades ago!)

An Expert: Implications for National Security (Ajai Sahni))

If the Maoist insurrection poses a direct threat to national security, its consequences indirectly threaten the same.

Geographical Expansion of Conflict

There has been phenomenon expansion in the area of Maoist (violent) movement since its Naxalite days of 1970s. Movements in different parts of India in different times have been covered briefly earlier in this chapter. Here are given the stages and areas of its expansion in the country as a whole.

In the early 1990s, 15 districts in four States were declared to be affected by Maoist violence. How the figures jumped in the subsequent years are mentioned here.

1. November 2003: 55 districts of nine States were described as 'Maoist-affected'.
2. September 2004: It is 156 districts in 13 districts. It is a huge jump in ten months.
3. September 2009: Home Minister Chidambram says that 223 districts across 20 states (of a total of 626 districts and 28 States) are hit by the Maoist violence.

Ajai Sahni, a specialist on the subject offers nuanced information. He argues that areas of 'Maoist activity' or those that are 'Maoist-affected' include not only areas hit by Maoist violence but also those that are in "the early stages of 'revolutionary mobilization' – the creation of basic networks, the establishment of underground and 'overground' organisations, and the opportunistic harnessing of local grievances for radical political activity." Thus, not all the 223 districts are convulsed in violence. However, the Home Minister also disclosed that "violence has been consistently witnessed in some 400 police station areas of about 90 districts in 13 states. Sahni makes a significant point: "90 districts experiencing consistence violence is far greater than the total of 55 variously affected districts in 2003[12]."

The first decade of the 2000th has witnessed not only an expansion in the area of Maoist influence in varying degrees but also in the area experiencing consistent violence.

Why and How did the Area of violence expand

Some interesting arguments for expansion of area of Maoist influence have been adduced. Some of the important ones are examined here. Where reasons reek of pro-Maoist bias, certain clarificatory note will be added, in particular, if there is an attempt to place security forces and Maoist rebels at equal footing—as the wont of some Left analyst and Maoist sympathisers.

1. "The expansion of areas of consistent violence is the result of both the Maoists' 'expansion strategy and the State's 'military' operations." It will be more honest to say that the rebels are solely responsible for expansion of this area. After all, it is their mission to take over the country, displacing the current polity. State's role is 'reactional', aiming to restrict the violent rebels within the current area of activity, or to thwart their expansion into additional, contiguous areas. If the Maoists keep on expending their areas of operations, the security forces are duty bound to expand theirs to checkmate them. If at all the State is to take a blame for expanding the area of Maoist influence, it is through governance deficit and inefficiency of counter-Maoist operations for a variety of reasons. If the government cannot eradicate poverty and destitution among the governed, it is inviting the Maoist in the area. The term 'military' operations is a misnomer. These counter-Maoist operations carried out by the police and paramilitary forces. India Army has not till date has been given the task.
2. Anti-Maoist operations by the Greyhounds, a special counter-Maoist police unit, in Andhra Pradesh since the 1990s forced hundreds of Maoist cadres to escape to safe havens in the Dandakaranya forests, spread over the border areas of Chhattisgarh, Orissa and Maharashtra. Chhattisgarh was an area of low-key Maoist violence in the 1990s. By the closing years of the decade, additional cadres from Andhra Pradesh increased Maoist attacks in the state. "Its emergence as epicentre of Maoist violence is also due to the Salwa Judum activities."
3. Demonisation of Salwa Judum in certain quarters has already been commented upon.

Is it civil war situation?

A democratic polity not only allows dissent but in fact encourages it. This is the strength of democracy, and also its weakness. An Arundhati Roy can disown India, and still flourish here among the intellectuals! In China, she would have disappeared in a version of the Cultural Revolution.

The Bhushans could take an anti-national stand without any harm coming their way! A Left and Maoist sympathiser can make any outlandish and irresponsible statement by adding an indemnifying "reportedly" or "allegedly." One might have some minor infraction of law to support his case, it can be magnified tremendously for effect. If any terrorist is arrested, there is immediate public chorus on his innocence, and any encounter death becomes 'death in fake encounter'. If these are great pluses for Indian democracy, then, these can also be its huge negatives. The text below is to be read not as gospel truth, a particular viewpoint nurtured and espoused by certain section of academics and analysts, of course keeping the preceding cautionary preamble in mind (contrarian view):

1. More disturbing is the use of extra-judicial violence by the state. Captured Maoists are executed instead of putting them through the due process of justice. They are eliminated in fake encounters, (Anuradha Raman and Saikat Datta, "shoot and shut up", Outlook, 13 Sep 2010.) (This academic says Maoist leader 'Azad' as reportedly shot at point-blank range indicating that he was executed rather than killed in an encounter.)
2. In Andhra Pradesh, the police armed surrendered Maoists not only to fight the Maoists but also eliminate civil society activists who were critical of the police. Killer gangs with names like Nallamalla Black Cobras, Kakatiya Cobras, Naxalite victims Association, and Narsa Cobras that targets dozens of human rights activists were nurtured by the police[13].
3. The State took its extra-legal violence to a new level through the setting up of the Salwa Judum and arming of tribals in the name of fighting Maoists. This has militarised society. It has divided tribal society into pro-Maoist and anti-Maoist villages. It has turned brother against brother. Salwa Judum has turned the conflict in Dantewada into a near civil war.
4. When it was set up, tribals were forced to attend Salwa Judum rallies. Many village heads, whose authority was usurped by sangham leaders, saw it as an opportunity to wrest back their lost power.
5. Villages that refused to join Salwa Judum were deemed "Maoist villages" and attacked. Entire villages were burnt down. Over 600 villages were thus emptied and the land then become Salwa Judum land, which was then sold to mining companies and other vested interests. Land which was not under Salwa Judum was looked upon as 'Maoist land' and blockaded.

6. Researcher Jason Miklian says...."Salwa Judum has altered the conflict landscape in Dantewada...Salwa Judum has resulted in 'warlordisation' of the region. Local Salwa Judum leaders control the relief camps set up for the displaced. They protect them from the Maoists and in return receive funding, food and weapons from the government. The leaders meet monthly to demarcate Dantewada territory among themselves, consolidate efforts to increase monetary and arms support from the State, and strategically plan to ensure that Salwa Judum continue to thrive. Increasingly Salwa Judum warlords seem to be functioning autonomously. It is the Salwa Judum warlords and camp leaders who 'police' roads in parts of Dantewada and stop and search vehicles plying on 'their territory'. It is the Salwa Judum, not the police—not even its higher echelons- that call the shots in places like Dornapal[14]."
7. Whatever authority the government exercised over the villages and small towns in Dantewada seem to have been ceded to the Salwa Judum.

This Author has already expressed his views on the demonisation of Salwa Judum. Anything further on the issue will be unnecessary. But brief comments in general are offered for the closure on the issue:

1. It must be accepted that the above arguments and averments/ assertions are rhetorical but not factual. Most of the views/statements are highly exaggerated bordering on the distortion of the reality; some are not even half truths; and the rest pure falsification to serve and vindicate preconceived notion of the things.
2. Para 5 above. "600 villages", not one less. The entire Para is an absurdity and should not be dignified through a rebuttal.
3. Para 1 above: "Azad was executed..." The dictum is simple: use the term 'reportedly' to write any irresponsibility, even absurdity! This academic should have quoted that great mediator, Agnivesh, to fortify his imagination. The Swami had publicly declared. "I was carrying a letter from the Maoist leader (Azad), and government killed him to thwart my mediation bid..." But what was the text of the letter, no one knows! The Swami chose to go silent on that all important Letter!
4. It is worth mentioning that there are some periodicals/dailies which are ever ready to glorify the Maoists and purvey anti-Government stuff in season or out. Some are named in the appropriate order: *The Tehelka, Frontline* and The Hindu (from the Hindu stable), and The Outlook. This author has a personal

lunch, nay near-conviction, that the great patriotic editors of these publications would feel greatly vindicated if the LWE/Maoists succeed in their mission and take over the country. One can even visualise the essence of their editorials in the wake of that tragic eventuality: "Politicians betray India...Ideology wins over venality!"

5. To give the other side of the picture, a detailed interview with the man who conceited the idea of Salwa Judum will be reproduced at the end of this very Chapter. It should restore some balance to the Salwa Judum idea.

"National security through redefinition" (Arun Shourie)

"In the first of a two part analysis of national security focusing on Naxalites...issue, Arun Shourie deals with increasing Naxalite terrorism across India and the Centre's inadequate response"

New Delhi: 1 Aug 2006

This is one of the earliest analysis of Naxalite threat to National Security by one of the foremost analysts of the country on the issue[15].

It was just a year before that the MCC and PWG were to join to create CPI (Maoist) or more popular term, 'Maoists', to displace the democratic polity of the country to take over its governance through violent uprisings. Excerpts from the article are given below.

Excerpts

"This has not happened in six months' time. In 2001, it was 131 districts, in 2003, it has gone up to 143, and in 2004, this number has goneup, but it has not up only in six month's time, it has gone up in three years' time. That has to be borne in mind."

That was Shivraj Patil, the Home Minister speaking in the Rajya Sabha in Nov 2004.

I had cited figures from official sources about the spread of the Naxalite violence. Could it be any consolation that the sway of these violent groups had been spreading for a longer period than just six months? Quite the contrary: Every year, year after year, the reach and lethality of Naxalites had continued to spread, showing that the rot in governance had continued to increase without let.

The situation continued to worse. By Oct 2005, open sources were reporting that the number of districts affected by Naxalite violence had risen to 165. The Rajya Sabha debated the issue again in Nov 2005. Shivraj

Patil improved on the reasoning. Though the figures I was citing are published by the MHA itself, he said that such figures give a misleading impression. If one village in a district is affected, the whole district is counted as affected, he said. Hence the figures gave an impression of large stretches of country being in the grip of extremist violence when that is not the case.

Why not disaggregate further, I had to inquire. After all, when the terrorists attack, they do not decimate the entire village. They just kill a handful from the village. They burn just a few houses. Why not publish figures by household? And divide the number of households that have been attacked by the total number of households in the region, and thereby do even more to keep people's morale up? Better still, why not disaggregate and count number of individuals who had been killed and divide that number by total population of the region or the country? Would not we even feel safer?

Home Minister's reasoning has prevailed. Faced with more lethal attacks over a wider area, his Ministry has just stopped giving figures of the total number of districts that are affected by Naxalite operations and activity. It now gives figures only of districts "badly affected" by Naxalite violence. This comes to 76 districts. Isn't that reassuring? National security through redefinition!

A truer index of the extent to which this virus is spreading is the fact that, after all, the MHA had been using the same criteria for decades. On that basis, in the early 1990s, 16 districts were affected. In 2003, it was 56 districts. In Oct 2005, the number had risen, as I said, to 165. Since then, the situation has become much, much worse.

The Naxalites are actually carrying out attacks on police stations, that they are actually executing people is not the index of their sway. Violence comes at a much later stage of their operations; in almost every case, years later. In an interview with the *Telegraph* daily (15 Jul, 2005), a member of the Maoists' Central Committee, "Comrade Dhruba", is reported as saying that, apart from Bankura, Purulia and Midnapur districts, "our mass base in Murshidabad, Malda, Burdwan and Nadia is ready." He adds, and this is what has a bearing on the Home Minister's way of measuring, "After five years, we will launch our strikes."

By the time violence is unleashed, the Naxalites have entrenched themselves firmly in the area. They commence with surveys—a 56-page survey that was recently recovered of "perspective areas" in a targeted state is so proficiently done that it would put some of our best institutions to shame: pattern of holdings; crops; problems of each crop; issues relating to wages and tenure; caste composition and tensions. Then front organisations are formed to instigate people on these issues. Experts instigate the demonstrations into violence. Reprisals fuel polarisation. Sympathisers and agents are steered into "voluntary organisations", local bodies, cooperatives. Only after years of such capture and coordination are the *dalams* and the like formed. Violence is unleashed thereafter.

By that time, the situation has gone so far beyond the reach of the State apparatus hat it can only do what the Home Minister is doing now.

The Proper Criteria

The criteria, therefore, is not whether the violence has actually been unleashed, nor whether the level of violence has become embarrassingly "bad". That entire area must be taken to be affected by terrorist activity in which that group—say, Naxalites——is able to prevent officials of the State from carrying out their primary functions: of governance, of dispensing justice, of executing development works. The relevant questions to be asked, therefore, are:

- Do the people of the area look to the police for protection from the Naxalites, or, are they now conducting themselves in suxh a way that Naxalites would spare them?
- Have the contractors of the area to pay Naxalites a cut for the works they execute, say, on construction involved in "development projects"?
- Who is dispensing "justice" in the area? The regular Courts, or the Naxalites' mobile courts.
- Are the government officials themselves not paying protection money to the Naxalites?

And remember, there are many types of insurgencies that are afoot in different parts of the country. The tests apply to the NS CN(IM) in Nagaland, to the score or so groups in Manipur, to the terrorists in Kashmir, as much as they apply to Naxalites.

Comprehensive Mechanism

In Nov 2005, in his reply, the Home Minister had gone further in providing comfort. The way he spoke, he seemed to have shared a great secret of the state. He said a comprehensive mechanism is already in place to tackle challenges to internal security: "This mechanism is already there. Probably, it is not known to the Hon. Members because it is an internal matter that we are doing." He shared this State Secret, the information about this mechanism: "We have a Special Security Secretary here. The responsibility given to him is to talk to the DIGs and other officers in the

Naxalism-hit states every month or two months or whenever it is necessary, and decide what has to be done. Then, there is a committee presided by the Home Secretary, who talks to the Chief Secretaries of the States and their DIGs and they decide as to how the policy should be evolved to deal with the Naxalites' or the terrorists' activities in J and K or the North-Eastern States. And then, there are regional committees of the Home Minister and the Chief Ministers who meet periodically to decide about the policies. And then, the CMs have been talking to the PM and the Home Minister every now and then, whenever they want. There is coordination. There is institution for coordination. You don't think that we are not talking."

So there is a mechanism. There is committee upon committee. There are meetings after meetings. All concerned are talking. The result is before you—in the increasingly lethal depredations wreaked by Naxalites—by now in 14 States; they must have been visible in the trains in Mumbai.

But as I mentioned, that is not even a partial index of state of affairs. Captured documents indicate that Naxalites have already put in place "Regional Bureaus" for two-thirds of the country: including one for Delhi, Punjab, Haryana, Bihar and UP—and a high authority on the LW violence tells me, the person who is believed to be heading this "Bureau" is one of the very best organisers among them; Further, barring the NE, J and K, Himachal and Rajasthan, "State Committees" are by now in place for every other state, "Special Area Committees" have been instituted for UP, Himachal, Bihar-Jharkhand, and Bengal.

An "Urban Perspective Document" sets outs out detailed strategy for extending operations into and unsettling urban areas. Governance is weakening in many cities even now, it notes. And this weakening can only accelerate: Urban population is expected to increase from 285 million to 540 million by 2020. A fertile field.

The point is that each such terrorist movement is proceeding systematically. Its programmes cover every aspect: land, caste-tensions, "Courts", targets for raising finances, recruitment, training, capture and production of arms, calibrated, unleashing of violence. And on our side?

The Home Minister's "Comprehensive mechanism." His "100 per cent implementation." His redefinitions of the area that is affected.

And yet, the inattention to LW violence is not the worst of the problems.

"Manipur PLA reaches out to Maoists and J and K separatists"
New Delhi: 8 Oct 2011

The strategy of the Maoists joining hands with some anti-India outfits in the North-East and J and K or the vice versa, enhances the potential of there insurrectionists to pose direct threat to India's national security.

This is the first such news story on combining of the anti-India forces against the nation's interests. Its implications need to be understood[16].

The analysis opens up with a worrisome possibility for India's security managers: "Banned People's Liberation Army (PLA) of Manipur is working hard to rope in Maoists and J and K-based terrorist groups for launching a concerted attack on Indian Government."

This startling revelation came from two high-ranking militants of PLA who were arrested by Delhi Police Special Cell on 1 Oct 2011. Special Commissioner of Police (SCP), Special cell, PN Aggarwal claimed on the 7th that the arrest helped in exposing the nexus between PLA and other enemies of the State. PLA aims to liberate Manipur through the armed struggle, just as the CPI (Maoist) does!

"The Delhi Police has arrested five hardcore members of the PLA from the capital in the last few days." Two senior PLA militants N Daleep Singh (51), Arun Kumar Singh Salam (36), and a self-styled captain of the PLA Arjun were arrested by a team Special Cell, from Paharganj area. The duo had reached Delhi on 28 September to meet some of their associate.

Aggarwal told the press: "Daleep and his deputy Arjun allegedy helped Maoists in training and procuring arms, ammunition and explosives in the national capital. With this, Delhi Police has arrested 13 Maoist cadres from the capital in the past three years.

Their interrogation revealed that Daleep was incharge of external operations of the Maoists. Investigations also revealed the PLA being in the forefront of providing logistics, training, weapons and communication system to the CPI (Maoist), and had twice trained their cadres in the jungles of Jharkhand and Odisha in 2009 and 2010. The PLA had also planned to conduct two more training camps for the Maoists in 2012. The investigations further revealed the plans of the outfit for another camp in the jungles of Myanmar for training of the banned LWE outfit and the Nepali Maoists.

Their subsequent interrogation led to the arrest of three more PLA militants by Manipur police in Imphal. Aggarwal said Daleep and Arun admitted they were sent to Delhi by their superiors to discuss the ways and means of providing logistics, training of weapons and communication training to Naxals. Special Cell even recovered a laptop from them, as also some incriminating documents exposing the nefarious nexus between the PLA and the Maoists. It was further found out that the two had agreed on a joint declaration "intending to form a 'strategic United Front' to extend full support to each other in their struggle to overthrow the Government of India."

Even more sinister were the plans of the PLA after the strategic United Front with the CPI (Maoist) was sealed. The PLA was working to rope in the militant outfits of the North-East and the terrorists and secessionist groups in Jammu and Kashmir to this Front. The duo told the police that the aim was to challenge the might of India through this "combined strategic tie-up."

It may be noted that the PLA was created in 1978 combining ethnic groups like the Nagas, Kukis, and Meiteis with the aim of liberating Manipur. PLA militants are equipped with sophisticated arms and are regularly involved in extortions and killings.

The Delhi Police had arrested 28-year old self-styled Lieutenant Oinam Ibomcha Singh of the banned outfit in Jan 2011. His interrogation had led to the busting of PLA's plans of troubling Indian Government.

Aggarwal disclosed that "investigations are going on to identify more PLA activists believed to be hiding in the capital and its peripheral regions."

"CRPF pats itself over job well done, trashes canards" Jhargram: 26 Nov 2011

This news story on the death of one of the top leaders of the CPI (Maoist) Kishanji, important though it is in itself, may not seem to belong to this chapter about the Maoist (violent) movement and its implications for the national security. But there is considered reason for its inclusion here.

The death of an important Maoist leader in an encounter with security forces is of course important for morale of the latter, as also an important indicator of success in a nation's fight against the LWE. But the real danger to the national security comes from 'Liberal-Left' lobby and over-gound sympathisers—nay 'members' of the LWE/Maoist who raise cain whenever some important Maoist is killed in an encounter. The usual twist is to dub it a 'fake' encounter. In the hell-raising cacophony of noise, bluster and shouting on the TV screens, the voice of moderation, balance and reason is lost. Something happened in this case too.

Kishanji was killed in the Burisole forest in Jangal Mahal area of West Midnapore district of West Bengal, on 23/24 Nov 2011[17].

"It was not easy to nab Kishanji", admitted K Vijay Kumar, speaking to the daily on 25 November in Burisole forest. He gave three reasons for it. Firstly, Kishanji had won the confidence of the locals out here which gave him great support and secure base to operate from. Secondly, he had well-trained security system all the time around him. Thirdly, Kishanji was always close to the border area, which meant that he had an escape plan if he thought things were going too hot for him.

He was addressing the press, after offering congratulations to his men who had achieved this landmark success. He had cautioned them against an retaliatory action from the Maoists.

Reacting to the allegations of a 'fake encounter' by Kishanji's family (read mother) and Telgu poet and Maoist sympathiser—rather ideologue––Varavara Rao, Kumar said Kishanji was killed in a "very clean and a successful operation by joint forces where even a minute was not wasted." It was joint operation by the CRPF and the West Bengal Police. "The Maoists here were under severe pressure and rather at a loss as they had lost the local support they had always enjoyed earlier."

A senior political analyst elucidates: "The support dwindled due to certain palpable efforts made by West Bengal CM Mamata Banerjee to bring peace to this area and also assure people of a better livelihood. In the past several years, no leader had actually visited these people or made any effort to ameliorate their lot. It is certain that development of the area and providing basic infrastructural facilities to the people of Jangal Mahal has been one of her top priorities since she took over as CM."

The surrounding villages near Burisole forest were deserted. "All this may change on Saturday (the 26th) with the Maoist calling a 2-day bandh in the State." There was some concern amongst the state-appointed interlocutors assigned to talk peace with the Maoists. They are apprehensive that this incident might have adverse repercussions on the future dialogue between two sides.

Now comes the more worrying part, the one that poses a threat to national security—the outpourings of the "sympathisers", whom this Author calls the 'closet Maoists'. Prasun Bhowmik, one of the members of this "Peace Coordinating Group", says: "This is an incident that may actually turn out to be a hurdle especially at a time when peace talks had been planned and about to started." A local Bengali TV Channel said on the 25th that they were informed by a Maoist leader that "the rebels were no longer interested in peace talks after Kishanji had been killed."

Some observations are in place on the issue of peace talks being derailed due to this death: How often have the Maoists been sincere in the peace talks held in the past; they have always utilised this 'peace talks' interregnum to regroup and rearm their cadres; it is a standard and a set pattern that whenever a Maoist leader is killed, you will have the Swami Agnivesh's of this world claiming that the deceased leader was carrying a peace proposal which is too pat to carry conviction. If carrying a message, or coming for peace talks, what was Kishanji doing scouring the forests of Jangal mahal? When he could not come out of the dragnet of the forces, then the nonsense about him being on a peace mission surfaces. With his contacts with the villagers/tribals in the area, he could have easily sent a word across to the forces, or even to the State Government about him coming for peace talks. None of such things happened and his over ground agents want to befool the world about his peace mission. It is time they stop speaking this convenient untruth, and the more honestly, stop spreading this piffle about the peace talks!

"Maoists are enemies of the people" (Chandan Mitra)

"The Maoists are waging war against the Indian State; it is war against democracy, against the rule of law and against freedom. The state must defeat them to preserve liberty and ensure development."

New Delhi: 8 Apr 2012

This is an article by a senior political analyst of the country, highlighting the threat to the nation posed by the Maoists[18]

Excerpts

"Maoists beheaded an intrepid police inspector and left his dismembered body on the Ranchi-Jamshedpur highway. Alongside they scattered a set of hand-written posters threatening more such gruesome killings. Two days later, they gunned down as many as 17 policemen in an ambush in Gadchiroli, Maharashtra. All 17 were local tribals in whose name the Naxalites are ostensibly conducting their liberation struggle—euphemism for mayhem, murder and terror. Media-savvy leaders of the blood-thirsty outfit are unapologetic: Kishanji has proudly asserted their intention to ramp up the campaign of violence. (Mercifully, he has been liquidated since).

"Yes, it is war. It is war against the lawfully constituted Indian State, it is war against democracy, war against the rule of law and judicial system; it is war against freedom itself. This is now being waged in the ever-extending area. It is one-third of the country in the so-called Red Corridor. They have audaciously announced their aim of violently overthrowing the state. Is there any other option other than to confront them head-on and eliminate this grievous threat to our value system.

"I should think not. But shockingly, there is a significant section of the effete urban middle class that demurs. Admittedly, it is a small section but wields a disproportionate influence as so-called intellectuals and opinion makers. I have been progressively appalled listening to their perverted logic on TV Channels, equating the state with the outlaws, demanding "State terror" end before any plaintive appeal goes out to Maoist blood hounds. Interestingly, these spokespersons of Naxalite terror are regarded with contempt by the very people whose cause they espouse! Marxists in general and Maoists in particular, have always treated the intelligentsia with ill-concealed disdain. Wherever their insane political philosophy had triumphed (Russia, China, Cuba etc), intellectuals were the first to be lined up before firing squads. Yet, like moths to a flame, a kind of fatal attraction draws rootless intellectuals masquerading as human rights activists to the Maoist 'prairie fire.'

"To my dismay, I find even the organised Communist parties, often the first targets of the ultra Leftist insurgents, nowadays spouting homilies about the democratic rights of these merchants of mass murder. The other day, I was accused of being a devotee of George W Bush by CPM leader Nilotpal Basu in a TV discussion for advocating a relentless war on terrorists; this despite the fact the scores of CPM cadres have been mercilessly gunned down by their estranged ideological cousins. Last week, CPI leader AB Bardhan glibly pronounced "certain failure" of the security forces offensive against the Naxalites, claiming violence was not the answer to the violence.

"Considering all communists (irrespective of the shade of red they adhere to) believe that force is the essential mechanism to bring about a proletarian revolution, Bardhan's new-found doctrine of pacifism and compassion towards terrorists seems amusingly out of place.

"The less said about the JNU variety of intellectuals the better. They have been arguing, in effect, that while the police must act according to every letter of the law, Maoists should be free to shoot, behead, maim, torch and destroy individuals and establishments that represent the state. Clearly taking a leaf out of Mao Zedong's dictum, "Revolution is not a dinner party and revolutionaries are not expected to follow table manners", Naxalite promoters in intellectual clothing brazenly argue that different sets of rules must apply to the state and non-state players (an euphemism for terrorists of every hue—Lashkar to Maoists).

"I must, however, admire their clarity of purpose and capacity for intrigue. They have swallowed up organisations like PUDR and PUCL, originally established to be genuine watchdogs of human rights, civil liberties and excesses by organs of the state. As a result, several such bodies have become de facto Maoist mouth pieces. For them, human rights of ordinary citizens are of no consequence. Even pre-teen children can be brutally killed on the charge that their parents are police 'informers'. This has been going on for years in Chhattisgarh's Bastar region as a recent report by a fact-finding team irrefutably establishes. For these selective peddlers of human rights only 'innocent' Maoists and equally 'innocent' LeT activists like Ishrat Jahen need to be defended against the 'predatory' Indian state. They fit perfectly into an uncharacteristically acerbic remark former Prime Minister PV Narasimha Rao once made: "From the hue and cry made by some people every time an encounter takes place, it would seem in India only terrorists have human rights and nobody else does."

"For too long, the rest of India watches in trepidation as all manner of Leftists ran riot over India's air waves and newspaper opinion columns. They bellowed all voices of sanity and balance into terrified silence. So much so that today it appears civil society comprises only those who can mount an assault on the state and the nation. It is time for those that refuse to be led on a leash by these intellectually dishonest and morally bankrupt advocates of spurious logic to stand up and be counted.

"But the ongoing war is not only about reclaiming civil society space for the majority of right-thinking Indians. It is also about the battle to bring development and prosperity to abjectly poor villagers, mostly tribals so woefully rejected by regimes in New Delhi and the States all these decades. Arguably, though, Maoists forcibly prevent any development activity from taking place in regions where they wield influence. No roads can be built, schools and public health centres are routinely torched and innocent villagers terrorised into becoming executors of a macabre philosophy. It is the state and civil society that must together lauch a war to liberate villagers living in abject poverty and under development from the clutches of Maoists. It is not just a war against Maoist terror; it is also a war against much earlier, but then it is never too late to dedicate oneself to a just cause."

"Dangerous nexus between Manipur rebels and the Maoists" :Evidence piling up."

The LWE/Maoists were called the biggest threat to India's internal security by a former PM. But things have changed qualitatively over the past few years. The nexus between the Maoists and other secessionist outfits in the North-East and the terrorist outfits of J and K have been posing a direct threat to India's national security. In fact, it has the potential to subvert and damage India's integrity and sovereignty.

Two stories on this dangerous nexus and collusion between the Manipuri rebels and the Maoists are examined in the succeeding pages. The two appeared in different dailies, dated 13 May 2012 and 19 Dec 2012.

"Mysterious outsiders stalk Jharkhand jungle"

Nearly 100 Manipuri rebels train, arm Maoist guerrillas" New Delhi: 13 May 2012 (one)

The sighting of a group had instantly aroused a strong suspicion. And it wasn't without reasons. For, the group comprised a large number of persons "with Mongolian features." To add to it, their movement was spotted deep in the jungle's of Jharkhand[19].

Surely, it was not a normal affair. It had much more to it than meets the eye. More so, since the group of the 100-odd "Mongolian-like" persons was moving around in areas where the Maoist writ ruled and in a state, which is now worst affected by Naxalism. A sustained trail followed thereafter. And what emerged is giving sleepless night to the security agencies.

It turned out that CPI (Maoist) has entered into a tactical alliance with the PLA of Manipur. Thus, the outlawed outfit of Manipur had joined hands with the banned CPI (Maoist). The alliance between the two was further corroborated after the interrogation of top Naxal commander Amit Bagchi presently under judicial custody in Vizag Jail. Bagchi was active in Jharkhand before his arrest.

CRPF insiders say the insurgents were seen moving deep in the jungles of Latehar and Palamu districts. They point out that as per the understanding, the CPI (Maoist) has agreed to respect the "sovereignty" of PLA in Manipur, and the latter will respect the Naxal outfit's "liberation" in the rest of India.

The sources informs the daily: "PLA's trainers from its camps in Myanmar have provided training to the Naxals at different places in the country, including in the forests of Saranda in Jharkhand. PLA has also been supplying sophisticated weapons to the Naxals against cash. Movement in such large numbers suggest that the PLA is taking part in the Naxal strategy against the state, they maintain. CPI (Maoist) is spreading violence across the host of states and is responsible for 95 per cent of the Naxal violence.

The alliance is aimed at furthering military training and consolidating supply of weapons, improving tactics and strategy to ensure Maoist outfit continued to hold sway over the so-called liberated zones.

The CPI (Maoist) has been looking at tactical alliance for the last few years with the twin agenda of spreading its areas far and wide and ensuring sanctuaries for its cadres.

"Manipur rebels supplying arms to Maoists, say NIA": New Delhi: 19 Dec 2012 (Two)

A supplementary charge sheet by the National Investigation Agency in the CPI (Maoist)-PLA nexus reveals: "LWE have been procuring Chinese arms and communication equipment from banned Manipuri outfit, PLA, via Myanmar and routing it to Kolkata through Guwahati between 2006 and 2011."

As per the chargesheet, all the communication equipment recovered from Maoists have made-in-China marks, while arms recovered from the PLA members too belonged to Chinese brands.

It is, however, yet to be established conclusively whether they came from China and were routed via Myanmar or were pilfered out of Myanmar or some other route.

The chargesheet has been filed against Maoist leaders Pallab Barborah, Indranil Chanda and PLA's External Affairs Chief Asem Ibotombi Singh alias Angou, who were all arrested this year from Assam, Kolkata and Odisha respectively. The accused allegedly played a significant role in training of Maoists by PLA in Jharkhand's Saranda forests, apart from procurement of arms and communication equipment.

Earlier, NIA had filed a chargesheet against three top PLA leaders: N Dalip Singh alias Wangba, Senjam Dhiren Singha alias Raghu and Kh Arnold Singh alias Bacon.

One of the main evidence against accused in the chargesheet is the email that PLA members had exchanged among themselves, and their Myanmar-based bosses. The emails exposed the nexus, helping agencies to sniff them out. An official privy to the probe says: "Maoists use very little modern technology. They rely on human couriers. But PLA members regularly wrote emails to their bosses in Myanmar. This exposed them."

The emails also mentioned aliases of Borborah and Chanda whose real identity was later established following statements of former PLA and Maoist activists and are part of the chargesheet.

"Naxals have forged ties with ISI with SIMI's help: Bengal: New Delhi: 19 Oct 2012

"Maoists may have been facing all-round reverses in West Bengal ever since CM Mamata Banerji took over, but they have forged a deadly alliance with Pakistan's spy agency ISI through overground radicals and remnants of the banned terrorists outfit SIMI during the period[20]."

It should be understood that it is even more dangerous development for India's national security than the CPI (Maoist) forging tie with the likes of Manipur's PLA and Kashmir's separatist groups, knowing as well as we do the resources of men, material and money the ISI has at its command.

The revelation about this dangerous liaison came when the DG, West Bengal Naparajit Mukherjee addressed a gathering of the Chief secretaries and DGsP of other Naxal-hit States on 18 October. He talked about the ominous, growing Maoist-ISI nexus in four districts of his state: Murshidabad, West Midnapore, Purulia, and Bankura.

Expressing his serious concern over it, he disclosed that nexus was reported after arrest of some Maoists who elaborated how overground sympathisers of the Red ultras acted as a 'link' for them.

In these four districts, State police had noticed actions that hinted at the Maoist-ISI linkages. The link is believed to be helping the ultras in getting arms and ammunition through the existing network of North-East insurgents. Even if the Union MHA did not react to the revelation, security and intelligence agencies spoke about the possibility through Maoists' sympathisers. They also revealed that the Maoists' support to the J and K terrorists for their cause in the border State had never been a secret.

The latest figures from the MHA on Naxal violence show that West Bengal——once a hot bed of Maoist violence—has, in fact, moved closer to what Andhra Pradesh had achieved by reporting zero casualties consistently over the last so many years.

The MHA statistics, based on the State's reports, show that none of the three highly Maoist-affected districts, viz West Midnapore, Purulia and Bankura, reported any killings in the last 10 months. What is even more significant is that the period, which coincides with the Banerjee rule in the state, has also witnessed the elimination of some senior Naxal leaders, including Politburo Member Kishanji and arrest of several others during the joint operations by the State Police and the CPMF like CRPF.

Now to some specifics. West Midnapore, which witnessed as amany as 360 fatalities in civilian and security men, in 2009-11 period, has reported zero deaths this year (2012).

Purulia, Bankura, Birbhum, Murshidabad and Malda have also not reported any casualty.

"Hizb threat impedes anti-Maoist operations." New Delhi: 11 Nov 2012

The blurb of this news story clarifies the issue in simple words: "Danger to J&K Panches stalls the shifting of CRPF troops to the LWE/Red areas[21]."

Hizbul Mujahideen (HuM) Chief Syed Salahuddin has unwittingly become an obstacle in India's plans for an early elimination of the Maoist menace from the Red Zone. He threatened more attacks on Panches and Sarpanches in the State, thereby thwarting India plans to shift 6,000 troopers from there to the Maoist-hit districts for a determined fight against the Reds.

This only proves in an indirect way the consequences of the 'unplanned' nexus between the two armed outfits working to destabilise the Indian polity.

The MHA had asked the CRPF to deploy 10,000 additional men for an intnsified operations in the coming months. These 10,000 were to come partly from the Kashmir Valley, some 6,000 and the rest through fresh recruitment. The redeployment was scheduled for completion by 2013. The pull out from the Valley was result of government decision on de-escalation of forces in the state due to a number of factors. This plan was put paid to by the violent threat to the local elected representatives of the people. Ironically, in view of 800 Panches announcing their resignations, the concerned Centre deemed it necessary to send 7,000 additional. CRPF troops to the valley to face the new situation. With 68,000 strong CRPF already in the State, the fresh induction would bring its total to 75,000.

This development has put the CRPF in a tight corner, scrounging for troops as it has only 4,000 fresh recruits ready for deployment in LWE areas. "Presently, CRPF, being the main CPMF entity assigned for the anti-Naxal fight, already has 75,000 personnel in the Red Corridor." A CRPF officer, in the know of things, explains: "This is the right and peak season for operations. If additional forces have to be deployed, it has to be done before March (2013) for any fruitful results. Once peak summer and rains set in, it becomes difficult to conduct operations in these jungles."

Sources in the security agencies said the situation in the Valley was such that a quick withdrawal of troops was no more an option. CRPF, consequently, is in a fix as to where the troops are to be withdrawn from. The officer paints a tough situation: "No troubled state, such as those in the North-East, will be willing to act go of the present deployments. We have to work out a way to cobble up the numbers. These troops, then, will have to be specially trained before re-deployment for anti-Naxal role. So, there is n't too much time. If we miss the deadline, we will have to look at the next year."

Oncoming polls in Gujarat, which has consumed a sizeable strength from the force, has further complicated the situation for it. Sources said things, perhaps, will be clear only by December (2012) when the Assembly polls are over.

It is better to remember what Salahuddin recently told a news magazine in an interview: "There would be more attacks on the panches in the valley...The militancy has not died."

"Pak markings on Naxal arms seized in Jharkhand" "Amid LOC row, India gets proof to turn heat on Pakistan" New Delhi: 11 Jan 2013

"Grenades and ammunition made in Pakistan were among the items recovered from the site of the Maoist attack in Jharkhand, sources said, adding a fresh twist to the ongoing India-Pakistan stand-off[22]."

A couple of grenades, pieces of blasted grenades and fired bullet cases recovered from Latehar, Jharkhand, have clear markings to show that these were manufactured in Pakistan. All ammunition contain details of the country of origin, so do all the recovered ammunition from Latehar, where 11 CRPF men were killed and their bodies booby trapped with explosives.

It is for the first time that ammunition with Pakistani markings was recovered from Maoists. In the past, though, some Chinese-manufactured ammunition has been recovered.

The attack was described by senior security officials as one of the most gruesome Maoist attack. After CRPF jawans, their bodies were tied with IEDs and when these were picked by the recovery times, they blew up injuring those men. Subsequently, it was found out that the Maoists had surgically planted the IEDs inside the (abdomen of) a dead body of a slain jawan.

The recovery of arms with Pakistani markings would add fresh pressure on the government in light of beheading and mutilation of Indian soldiers in Jammu's Mendhar sector by Pakistani troops. For the past some months, evidence has been mounting of Maoists securing ammunition supplies from Pakistan and China. But it is, still, not clear if there is any credible evidence of Maoists enjoying any direct contacts with the agencies of these two countries. It is on the cards that these supplies from the foreign countries are through third party.

But there are more worrisome questions on this sensitive but dangerous issue: "Has the Pakistani security establishment extended its reach beyond the Kashmiri groups to establish contacts with Maoists, enabling it to foment the low cost war into the very heart of India?" The country cannot, and should not, forget that the same Pakistan has created mayhem and murder in India only two decades back through Khalistani terrorists.

"Internal Maoist document targets 12 political leaders" New Delhi: 12 Mar 2014

This is another aspect of national security being threatened when the Maoists plan elimination of nation's political leadership through targeted attacks. They have already achieved a measure of success in this objective some two years back when they practically decimated the entire Congress leadership of Chhattisgarh in a May 2012 ambush. Maoist document on the issue must be taken seriously whenever recovered by the security forces. A daily has drawn our attention to one such document in a recent issue.[23]

"An internal document prepared by the Central Committee of the CPI(Maoist) and recovered recently by Indian security agencies, "has asked its cadres to boycott the oncoming General Elections 2014 for the Lok Sabha on two fronts: political and military. If the political strategy speaks about cornering the government on issue like corruption, displacement of tribals, flood, inflation and food security, the military strategy is foucused on attacking security forces as well as political leaders of BJP, Congress, and Jharkhand Vikas Morcha (JVM).

The MHA has already issued an alert to Bihar, Chhattisgarh, Jharkhand, Odisha and Andhra Pradesh on the basis of these documents seized from a Maoist Hide-out in Feb 2014.

About the 11 March (2014) attack in Chhattisgarh, a senior official said the failure of Maoists to carry out any spectacular attacks during Assembly polls in 2013 made them "desperate" and warned that there could be more such attacks in run-up to the elections.

The document mentions names of some political leaders in Hindi codes—"Nare Baba, Nunu, Ram, Ud, Ani, Binde, Prah, Jeev, Lal, Prem, Shai"—who are to be "eliminated at any cost despite them having security cover".

The document adds: "A special Committee to boycott the polls should be constituted and regional issues like corruption, drought, flood, displacement should be discussed with the people—"

"Raw to monitor ISI Alliance with Maoists" New Delhi : 12 Oct 2014

The pace of the ISI interacting with the Maoists has picked up, of late, as a weekly reported recently (Oct 2014)[24]. An MHA official said "the Ministry is dealing with the situation effectively. Concerned SPs in affected districts have been directed to be alert on the issue."

The first indication that the ISI was helping the Maoists came in 2009 when a fake currency racket, operating from Dubai, was busted. Late, one of the men, whose arrest revealed information about the network, told the police that a Dubai-based group at the behest of the ISI was financing the Maoists. He was arrested with Rs 25 lakh which was supposed to be delivered to a Maoist sympathiser. He also disclosed that the ISI tried to get in touch with Maoists through a Lashkar-e-Taiba operative.

Officials are certain that the ISI was now using members of the banned SIMI to help the Maoists. Using SIMI's network, it is sending arms and ammunition to the Maoists.

Recent intelligence inputs also disclose that "SIMI members are also helping Maoists in Bengal. An Official affirms: "We are keeping a watch on West Bengal, with local inputs suggesting increased activity among the SIMI elements and Maoist sympathisers."

In Oct 2012, the then West Bengal DGP Naparajit Mukherjee had informed the MHA about the nexus between the Maoists and ISI. In a meeting chaired by the then Home Secretary RK Singh and attended by other DGPs, Mukherjee had set the alarm bells ringing, saying the SIMI was helping Maoists in West Bengal

Notes

1. Government of India, Planning Commission, Development Challenges in Extremist Affected Areas, Report of an Expert Group to Planning Commission, 2008, 59-60.
2. Government of India, Press Information Bureau, "CPI (Maoist) included in the list of the terrorist organizations to avoid any ambiguity", June 22, 2009.
3. Sudha Ramachandra, The Maoist Conffict in Dandakaranya, Lence in The Naxal Threat, VR Raghavan, Ed, 2011.
4. The Hindu, 29 May 2010.
5. Shyamal Pojamma, "We are the only one dying", Tehelka, 7, No 6, 13 February 2010.
6. Aman Sethi, "Troop fatality figure show changing Maoist strategy', The Hindu, 5 April 2010.
7. Human Rights Watch, Sabotaged Schooling: Naxalite Attacks and Police Occupation of Schools in India's Bihar and Jharkhand States (New York: HRW 2009.
8. *Ibid.*
9. Mani Shankar Aiyar, "Government's sheathed weapon", Economic Times, 20 May 2010.
10. Aman Sethi, "New battle zones", Frontline, 24, No 18, 8-21 Sept 2007.
11. K. Balagopal, "Illegal Acquisition in the Tribal Areas", Economic and Political Weekly, 42, No 40, 6 Oct 2007.

12. Ajai Sahni, "The Dreamscape of 'Solutions' ", Seminar, 607, March 2010.
13. PC Vinod Kumar, "The Cobra Fields, Tehelka, 4 March 2006.
14. Jason Miklian, "The Purification Hunt", 449-50.
15. Arun Shourie, Indian Express, 1 Aug 2006.
16. Pramod Kumar Singh, The Pioneer, 8 Oct 2011.
17. Sutapa Mukerjee, The Pioneer, 26 Nov 2011.
18. Chandan Mitra, The Pioneer, 8 Apr 2012.
19. Rakesh K. Singh, The Pioneer, 13 May 2012.
20. Vishwa Mohan, Times of India, 19 Oct 2012.
21. Deeptiman Tiwari, Times of India, 11 Nov 2012.
22. Josy Joseph, Times of India, 11 Jan 2013.
23. Vijaita Singh, Indian Express, 12 Mar 2014.
24. The Sunday Guardian, 12 Oct 2014.

Index

B

D

T

NAXAL AND MAOIST TERROR IN INDIA

NAXAL AND MAOIST TERROR IN INDIA

VOLUME - IV

CHHATTISGARH AND JHARKHAND

Col. Ved Prakash

KALPAZ

ISBN : 978-93-5324-034-9 (Vol - IV)
978-93-5128-212-9 (Set)

First Published, 2019

Published by

Kalpaz Publications
C-30, Satyawati Nagar,
Delhi – 110052
Ph.: 011-47034999, 9811692060
www.kalpazpublications.com
E-mail: kalpaz@hotmail.com

Printed at: G. Print Process, Delhi

Cataloging in Publication Data—DK
Courtesy: D.K. Agencies (P) Ltd. <docinfo@dkagencies.com>

Prakash, Ved, *Col.*, **author.**
Naxal and Maoist terror in India / Col. Ved Prakash.
volumes cm
Contents: volume I. Expanding red corridor — volume II. Combating Maoism — volume III. Development of Naxal infected regions — volume IV. Chhattisgarh and Jharkhand — volume V. Odisha and West Bengal.
ISBN 9789351282129 (set)

1. Naxalite movement—India. 2. Communism—India. 3. Communist Party of India-Maoist. 4. India—Politics and government—1947- I. Title.

LCC HX393.5.P73 2019 | DDC 320.532093 23

Contents

Volume - IV

Chhattisgarh and Jharkhand

(*Series Page No. 915-1408 See Below*)

Volume - V

Odisha and West Bengal

(*Series Page No. 1409-1808 See Below*)

19

Closet Maoists

The Author of this book has coined this term, 'Closet Maoists', to describe and define a category of academics, commentariat, analysts, newspaper columnists, *et al,* who act, behave and speak as the overground arm of the underground Maoists.

Some of these 'sympathisers' are so loud, assertive and passionate during their participation in the TV discussions that a gullible viewer is likely to the convinced of their articulation! But certainly not the cognizant! The mere passion cannot conceal the reality from the people who know. One person who perfectly epitomises the specimen is Gautam Navlakha. He speaks in a manner that shows he is convinced it is the officers and soldiers of the security forces, constitutionally mandated to safeguard the sovereignty and integrity of the nation even at the cost of their supreme sacrifice, who are to blame for the Maoist insurrection in the country, not the ruthlessness of the Maoist cadres! They deliberately mix up the cause and its effect. If a member of a family takes up a gun and starts shooting and killing his kin, he must be restrained, at the very least, or killed, as a last resort. India is an extended family! When the Maoist start their game, creating mayhem and causing death and destruction, a nation must act determinedly. It is the political will of the ruling class that is the deciding factor between success, or its absence. When the war against Maoist insurrection is politicised, the nation suffers...especially so, India.

Then, these 'overground' Maoists argue that anti-Maoist action should not be termed a 'war', after all they are Indians struggling for a 'cause' they are fervently convinced of. The Government of India itself define the Maoists as Indians gone astray, and go all out to bring them back on the right track, initially through negotiations and through use of appropriate and proportionate use of force at its command. But when the violent Maoists refuse to see the reason, the harsher measure are resorted to. The example of a violent member of a family mentioned above becomes aptly relevant. The aim and objective of the Maoists are destruction of the state and replace it with their own rule. This is exactly what a foreign enemy/ invaders aim at achieving. So how do these 'closet' Maoists distinguish one from the other? At that stage, the Maoists deserve no soft-handling or mercy. A republican democracy may take longer for several reasons, but it cannot afford to go under. India is too proud and too big a nation to surrender before these blood-thirsty Red Devils — whatever the cost. India is not Nepal. It might have taken decades for us to eliminate and subdue various insurrection in its North-East, and some may be still simmering, but overcome we shall. This is the firm belief of an Indian, who as a soldier has, not only studied the subject extensively but also, more importantly, fought these insurrections in Nagaland (1957-59) and Mizoram (1975-78), as also in Jammu and Kashmir.

This entire chapter is devoted to study the view of the contributors/ scribes of the articles and Chapters in the book, "The Naxal Threat, 2011, Ed(Lt Gen. Retd), VR Raghavan", and their contents. Interestingly, if surprisingly, all the analysts in this look are pro-Maoists. They did not have a single word of praise for the security forces or the Government. For them, all Maoists, especially their leaders are heroes, undoubtedly and unquestioningly. If anything, security personnel is the villain of the piece. In one line, the outpourings of these worthies lack balance, even rationality. They will be name here, after a while.

Yet again, it is a telling commentary on their mentality and thinking that they cry foul whenever a senior Maoist, like Azad or Kishanji, is killed in an encounter. It is always and invariably a 'false' encounter. And they, in most cases, if not all, go right up to the Supreme Court, appealing for a Court-supervised inquiry. All their sympathese, emotions and compassion are reserved for the Maoist terrorists only. Even when a number of security personnel is killed, there is no question of condemnation of the perpetrators. At the most, on repeated urgings, the press may be able to extract a sympathy for the bereaved, which in their heart of heart, is a mere ritual, an empty and meaningless one, knowing their leanings and mental block on the subject.

Who are the types who suffer from this inability to see the things for what they are? One can include the Leftist intellectuals, the 'Liberals' some of whom found a perch in the Sonia Gandhi-led National Advisory Council and the traditional bleeding-hearts which each nation must have to contribute to its pool of tears for easy display. To hark back to a terminology of the not-so-distant past, some of them can be dubbed 'Jhola Wallahs'! One does not know about the depth and sincerity of their passion for and conviction about the cause of Maoists and their fight-to-finish for it! Why can't they, at least some of them, join the actual fight on the ground which their much-beloved comrades are waging against the much-despised Governments! If one is to believe their passion on the TV screens, they will make brave and reckless Commandos. One would like to see their derring-do on the ground in the actual fight, rather than on the TV screen! Why can't a vast country like India produce one, the French idealist, philosopher and thinker, who joined the fight with his heroes for his passion?

Some of the 'Closet' Maoists culled from Lt Gen(Retd) VR Raghavan's book named above are mentioned here.

- Sudha Ramachandran: A Bangalore-based analyst, with extensive work on South Asia, including Maoist insurrection.
- Jason Miklian: A foreigner who has made repeated visits to India for field work on subjects of his speciality, including Maoist rebellion.
- Arandhuti Roy: That some Indians painted her larger than life after she won the Booker Prize, was to have an unfortunate fall-out in consequence. She expressed her ultra-leflist views on our polity which were lapped up sans any critique, particularly by the left-leaning publications like the Hindu and the Frontline headed by one-time card-holding Communist, N Ram, and the Outlook, led by the RSS/BJP baiter Vinod Mehta. Till a couple of years back, she was more anti-American than the Communists of the yore. Of late, she has not appeared in press. May be, she is working on her second book.
- Gautam Navalakha: He has been mentioned above. His actions do not match his passions otherwise he should have been in the field with his heroes.
- Venkitesh Ramakrishnan: He is from the Frontline stable, headed by the Leftist N. Ram.
- Praveen Swami: From the Hindu stable, led yet again by N. Ram, mentioned above.
- Saikat Dutta: He works for the Outlook weekly, edited by Vinod Mehta, mentioned earlier.
- Nandini Sundar: An academic in a Delhi university. A confirmed pro-Maoist writer.

- Praful Bidwai: A congenital anti-India and anti-Government activist. The professor has never found anything right with India's position in nuclear, Maoism, labour policy and foreign policy fields.

It bears repetition that none of the worthies mentioned above has ever thought of joining their Maoist heroes in the jungle. In the interest of the fairness, Arundhati Roy must be mentioned as an exception: she did take the trouble of visiting the Maoists in their jungle habitat, spending a couple of days there studying their functioning, harsh living conditions, operational milieu and morale of the cadres. Unkind critics dismiss the visit as a publicity stunt, affording a photo-op with her heroes in their jungle hide-outs! Whatever way taken, the visit did give her a chance to spend time in the Jungle.

The above 'closet' Maoists are taken from the specific book mentioned above. More will be added in the next Chapter, adducing evidence from their actions and their writings.

Entities fighting the Maoism

In a manner of speaking, none of the parties to the conflict is a homogenous entity. Sharp differences on strategy are evident at the highest levels of government. There are, on the other hand, tensions and contradictions too between the largely urban, educated middle class Maoist leadership and the rank and file, which is tribal or low caste/ Dalit, on strategy and tactics as well as objectives. Lower level commanders and fighters are said to be keen on land reforms and livelihood rather than the overthrow of the State. The security agencies engaged in counter-insurgency duties are expected to factor in these nuances while planning their operations.

As for the differences at the highest levels of governments, the issues must be looked into at this early stages of discussions of the subject in two parts here.

1. Digvijay Singh vs Home Minister P Chidambram. There have been stories in the press about serious differences on ways to tackle the Maoist threat in the first half of the year 2010. In short, it was conveyed that there was considerable opposition to the Home Minister's focus on the military approach to dealing with the Maoists from others within the ruling party, especially from Congress General Secretary Digvijay Singh. Much was made of Singh's article, "Rethink Counter-Maoist Strategy: Digvijay Singh to P Chidambram," *Economic Times,* 14 April 2010. There is a

need to examine this issue. Digvijay is a loose cannon. How often one has seen his comments being disowned by the Congress spokespersons. At the other times, his views have been dismissed "as personal, nothing to do with the official line". At personal level Chidambram has intellectual acumen for superior to those like Digvijay. Taking pot shots at him is deemed one way to balance out that deficiency. Politics is the bane of the Indian polity and people like Digvijay don't even realise that they are serving the enemy cause through such irresponsible statement. If some people can dub Arundhati Roy's stance on Maoists' activities as anti-national, the crime of Digvijay, being a senior Congress-man, is worse. Such open opposition does not only cause confusion among the people, but also effects the morale of forces engaged in fighting the battle on the nation's behalf. Politics of irresponsibility on this issue with be discussed in more detail later in this Chapter.

2. Differences between the Centre and the States. Acceptedly, there are differences between these two entities on dealing with the Maoists. Indian politician's weakness for vote-bank is known to one and all. Mulayam Singh had asked for lifting of ban on the Indian Mujhahiden, knowing well that it was a terrorist outfit and had been banned by New Delhi. Same way, Bihar Chief Minister Nitish Kumar had publicly disagreed with the Centre's approach to eliminating the menace of Maoism. Such differences, publicly aired, also affects the security agencies engaged in mortal Combat with the Maoists. How one wishes the politicians like Digvijay. Mulayam and Nitish understand the harm they are causing to a national cause, through such irresponsible statements!

Is Maoists' an armed Conflict?

Here is an instance of a conflict which is viewed differently by a nation state and an international institute.

Some analysts consider "the Maoist conflict is an armed conflict, although the government has denied that it is the one under international law."[1] According to the Uppsala Conflict Data Program, "armed conflict is a contested incompatibility that concerns government and/or territory where the use of armed forces between two parties, of which at least one is the government of a state, results in at least 25 battle-related deaths in one calendar year"[2]. So the scholar asserts that by this definition, the Maoist conflict qualifies to be called an armed conflict, the fatalities having crossed the annual armed conflict benchmark of 25 every year over the past four decades. According to official data, the number of fatalities in 2009 was

908. Data collated by the South Asia Terrorism Portal puts the figure at 998, just short of the high-intensity conflict benchmark of 1000 fatalities per year. Thus, the conflict is not just an armed conflict but the one that is on the brink of becoming a high intensity conflict[3]. In fact, some analysts describe the conflict as a civil war[4].

Maoist operations 2000-2010: A summary

The latest escalation phase, and the last, started towards the late 1990s. The mergers, splits and re-mergers in various factions have been described in chapter 2. In this part, Maoists activities/ raids during the last decade, particularly in the post-2004 PWG-MCC merger period, are described.

To put the issues in perspective, the following table should be useful to understand the level of violence unleashed by the Maoists.

Number of Maoist-related incidents

Year	2002	2003	2004	2005	2006	2007	2008	2009
No. of Incident	1465	1597	1533	1608	1509	1565	1591	2258

In the previous escalatory phases, say in 1970s, 1980s, and even in early 1990, Naxalite operations were largely hit-and-run attacks, targeting 'class enemies' i.e. landlords, money lenders and police informers. In the current phase, late 1990s onwards, their attacks are far more sophisticated and deadly–successfully attacking several high-profile personalities. Andhra Pradesh Chief Minister Chandrababu Naidu, among the Z-category protected politicians, was attacked in 2003 near Tirupati and was lucky to have escaped the landmine explosions. Some examples of their daring are cited below:

- They have executed several meticulously planned jail breaks. The better-known among them is the 2005 one at Jehanabad in Bihar when they succeeded in freeing 350 of their jailed comrades.
- They have raided armouries and camps of the police and paramilitary forces. Obviously, they want to convey that they have the capacity to stand and fight the security forces. In 2009, they stormed the government-owned National Aluminium Company Ltd (NALCO) in Koraput and battled security forces for nine hours before retreating from the scene.
- In Apr 2010, Maoist killed 76 CRPF men in an ambush at Chintalnar in Dantewada. One among the deadliest of the Maoist attacks in terms of fatalities, they are believed to have massed some 600 cadres at the site. The following remarks[5] of an adoring

analyst about this ambush deserve some informed comments: "That they were able to mass such a large number of fighters in an area where the security forces were present, without arousing the suspicious of the latter signals their formidable capacity for planning and executing major operations today." The comments are:

1. The civilian scholars, academics and analysts generally take a pro-Maoist line in their writings. They easily marvel at their somewhat mundane achievements. May be people like Arundhati Roy and Gautam Navlakha have shaped their opinions— the two seldom having criticised the ultras but always ready to pounce at the security personnel's "wrong doings", mostly imaginary. When ever a terrorist or a Maoist is killed, there are any number of Swami Agniveshs to claim that an "innocent" has been killed", "that it was a fake encounter". But equally truly, they have no tears to shed when a soldier is killed performing his duty and defending his country and countrymen. A soldier can never understand the psyche of the Roys, the Navlakhas and the Agniveshs of India.
2. With the latest technology and devices available to the Maoists…often they are better equipped than the security forces personnel…it is not difficult to get 600 men at a spot. They can choose time and place of their raid/ambush and have ample time at their disposal for planning.
3. Maoists are highly motivated, with strong ideological underpinning. Compared to them, security forces are seldom fresh or adequately rested for a sudden operation. They have multitude of duty to perform…guarding their posts, patrolling duty, security of the visiting dignitaries, cleaning and maintaining there posts *et al.*
4. Laying ambush is not an act of bravery. You select a spot on a height and open out hell fire when you find your prey at the most vulnerable spot down below. Then blowing a vehicle carrying security men does not need a great degree of ingenuity. Infact it is an act of cowardice. In fact, the Left-wing insurrection is an unequal fight. The ultras have no laws or rules to observes, where as hit victims, men in uniform, are subject to the laws of the land.
5. Security forces seldom have adequate manpower for tasks assigned to them. Then again, nation has not provided them with anti-mine vehicles, equipment and bullet-proof vests and uniforms to come out triumphant against the Maoists' mine warfare.

6. Security forces are shorts of manpower, generally, whereas the Maoist can concentrate the required numbers from more than one place.
7. In the vast forests of Dandakaranya, or anywhere else, maintaining secrecy is not a problem. The security forces deployed on a post can't do patrolling beyond a certain distances. The Maoists are known to have their annual or periodic strategy sessions in the forest areas of Orissa, Jharkhand, Dandakaranya etc for a week long deliberations without being discovered/disturbed by the security men.
8. It is advisable that scholars do not put halos around the heads of the Maoists, some of them hardened criminals, for whatever reasons.

Counter-Maoist Operations

Considering the scale of Maoist attacks, security forces per force had to upscale their counter-deployment as also scale of operations. In the earlier escalatory phases, say till the late 1980s, it was the state police at the fore- front of the counter-Maoist operations. Given the then existing circumstances, there was little inter-state coordination, allowing the ultras to flit across the border when under hot pursuit.

Things are no longer the same, essentially because the sophistication achieved by the Maoists in their weaponry and operational capabilities displayed by them under a unified command ambience, matching encounter measures were called for. This resulted not only in greater coordination among the states and their security forces, but also improved means of fighting the Maoists viz authorising small air wings to the counter-Maoist forces, anti-mines vehicles and equipment, and of late, some number of UAFs to them. The best example of coordinated effort is simultaneous launch operations Green Hunt in more than one state. Paramilitary forces have been assigned for counter-Maoist operations in several states to augment the efforts of their police forces.

Counter-Maoist effort: An instance

"Magnitude of this operations (Green Hunt) is unprecedented". If a nation is at war, as India indeed is, even if some analysts and scribes do not understand, and others even don't want to, it must do anything it takes to win that war.

Here are the figures for Bastar Zone alone, an area of 40,000 square kilometres: 14 battalions of the CRPF, each of some 1,000 men, besides five battalions of the BSF. Then there some 5,000 police and seven battalions of the State Armed Police[6].

Request for deployment of Army

There has been calls for deployment of the Indian Army in counter-Maoism role. Luckily, the demand has been turned down for the time being. Such a call is an unhealthy trend in the country. As it is, the Army has been deployed on the internal security duties far too often, at the cost of its main role...the defence of the borders against external threat. That could be a legitimate call in certain pressing situations. But to do too often is not good for the country, neither for the image of the Army. It is worth recalling in this connection that sections of Indians in South wanted the Army to be assigned the task of capturing that sandalwood brigand Veerappan from his jungle hide out! But some limited role has been assigned to the Army in Counter-Maoist endeavour: (a) Army officers will be involved in strategizing the counter-Maoist operations; (b) Army will help the Para-military and State police forces to train their personnel in their counter-insurgency and jungle warfare schools. Some states have already established such schools; and (c) certain number of men from paramilitary and state police forces will be trained at similar schools run by the Army.

Helicopters of the Indian Air Force are providing logistical support in the counter-Maoist operations of the paramilitary forces. This mainly involves evacuation of the casualties, and at times, flying emergency supply missions. Some academics are apprehensive that "their use in combat against Maoists in the near future cannot be ruled out." Such an apprehension is not easy to understand. If natinal security interest demand it, why should that possibility create any apprehensions? One academic is on record that this may cause escalation:

> "Possibility of the use of IAF helicopters in combat against Maoists cannot be ruled out. Already they have been granted permission 'to fire in self-defence'. This has the potential of seriously escalating the conflict".

This academic feels that even the permission to fire in self-defence has the potential of seriously escalating the conflict. Is it suggested that because of this possibility of escalation, country should bar the IAF choppers not to fire even in self-defence? She further says "IAF choppers have come under fire twice so far, in Pedia in Bastar in November 2008 and then in Gadchiroli a few months later. Finally, she warned the nation about the implication of the permission to IAF "to fire in self-defence"[7].

Changes in ways of Maoist operations

In the earlier phases of conflict escalation too, Maoists did target civilians. Landlord and moneylenders who were deemed to be exploiting the poor were killed. Same way, villages believed to be informing the police on their activities were dubbed as traitors and executed. But the Maoists refrained from carrying out attacks that would cause high civilian casualties. This all was true till mid-1990s, particularly since the onset of the last phase of their operations in the late 1990s.

Attacks now on the 'soft targets' have escalated in frequency and magnitude. The May 2010 attack on a private passenger bus in Chhattisgarh is an opt example of this new 'heartless' attitude of the Maoists against the 'poor and deprived' tribals, whom till now they were vehemently claiming to be protecting against the rapacious landlords and cruel Greyhounds of India's security agencies. In this attack, Maoists blew up the bus at Chingawaram in Dantewada, killing 31 civilians. They sought to justify this horrendous carnage by claiming that 11 Special Police Officers (SPOs) were travelling in this bus and that the Government was using civilians as human shields. Not only that, their leadership mouthed the same cliché that the USA use in such cases, 'collateral damage' , though the words used were different. A senior Maoist leader in the south Dandakaranya region, Azad, said civilian deaths "could not be helped", signalling that the Maoists now see civilian casualties as inevitable and acceptable collateral damage in their war against the State[8].

When the Maoists raised the level of violence, the security forces per force had to enhance their response to counter this mindless killing of the civilians by them. How this counter-measure by the security forces was seen by certain civil society activists and NGOs is described below.

As for the State, in previous phases of escalation it did arrest or "kill" civilians thought to be Maoist sympathizers. Many villagers and students were killed in the course of anti-Maoist operations and many civilians in Maoist area were drawn into the battle as police informers. However, in recent years, the State has been arming civilian as part of a planned strategy to fight the Maoists. Here is what the People's Union of Civil Liberties (PUCL) has to say on this particular issue:

How PUCL saw it Group Heading

"In 1990, an anti-Naxal group called Jan Jagran Abhyan (JJA) was set up in Chhattisgarh by MLA Mahendra Karma. JJA threatened villagers to hand over *sangham* members (Maoists and Maoist sympathizers) or else face punishments, which involved beating, rape and killing of villagers, looting and burning of their homes. The JJA had the moral support of the BJP and the CPI"[9].

Yet again, there is another fellow traveller of the PUCL who supports the facetious arguments offered by the latter: "The JJA was morally supported by the BJP leadership, but there was no official funding or arms given from the State"[10].

The "liberals"[11] say that "in the recent years the State has been arming civilians as a part of planned strategy to fight the Maoits. This has taken the armed conflict to a new higher level. In June 2005, a supposedly spontaneous uprising against the Maoist called Salwa Jadum emerged in Baster and Dantewada". They continue in the same cynical tone:

> "Subsequent events revealed that there was little spontaneous about the Salwa Judum; it was a government-sponsored strategy that involved arming tribal youths, including children, and surrendered Maoists to fight the Maoists. Government forces and Salwa Judum activists jointly raided villages. They unleashed violence on an unprecedented scale, torturing, raping, and killing villagers, looting their homes and burning down entire villages". The above have been culled from three sources.

Which are detailed below (three sources)

1. "War in the Heart of India: Excerpts from the Report by the Independent citizens' Initiative", *Social Scientist,* 34, No. 7/8 (July-August 2006): 47-61. Six signatories to this report are:
    - Ramachandra Guha
    - Harivansh
    - Farah Naqvi
    - EAS Sarma
    - Nandini Sundar
    - BG Verghese
2. PUCL, "when the State makes war"
3. The purification Hunt", 441-59.

Comments from the Author on the Above

- The Author is a retired Army Officer who served the Army from 1957 to 1989 and participated in all the wars country fought during his service.
- He also fought counter-insurgency operations in Naga Hills and Mizo Hills when the insurgency inspired by Phizo and Laldenga was at its worst in both the areas at two different levels. In Naga

Hills, as a young officer leading patrols and laying ambushes, and raiding rebels' camp, commanding a platoon or a commando team. It was, so to speak, at a gut level when one experiences the things in the raw. Shooting rebels and getting shot at, handling a dead rebel or a bleeding comrade in uniform, seeing civilians getting killed or wound *et al.* In Mizo Hills, he was commanding an Infantry unit engaged in active anti-insurgency operations. Here his job involved planning and executing units' operations against the Mizo rebels through his subordinate officers, sometimes negotiating a surrender of rebels, sometimes rewarding a rebel for giving intelligence about his colleagues etc.

- His comments are based upon military knowledge and personal experience in active oprations, not only in Naga Hills and Mizo Hills but also in Goa and Jammu and Kashmir. If at times, a harsh comment is offered on certain individuals and situations, it should be deemed to be well-deserved.

Nature of this book

- It is not a rum-of-the-mill book on the Maoist problem of India. Let me emphasise the points made in the preface, at the cost of repetition: This book not only dilates upon the issues of insurgency and counter-insurgency, it also goes beyond and examine the outpourings of some academics, analysts and left and "Liberal" analysts who find nothing right with the governments and security agencies' actions in fighting the Maoists and treat the Maoists as heroes.
- No wonder this Author treats them as the overground arm of the underground rebels.
- It is worth mentioning here that the term 'Liberals' used in inverted commas ("Liberals") should be read as a pejorative, suggesting strong disapproval, even contempt, for them.

"Government forces and Salwa Judum activists jointly raided the villages. They unleashed violence on an unpreceded scale, torturing, raping and killing villagers, looting their homes and burning down entire village".

- These critics must realise that a hyperbole does not prove an allegation. In fact, it detracts from an argument.
- Democracies do not 'kill' their citizens. Mao's China and Stalin's Russia did it. Maoists are killing their fellow citizens. And ironically, the "liberals" have great admiration for them.

- Indian security forces do not go around looting and burning around “entire villages”. They are in battle to protecting Indian citizens against the marauders called Maoists. When the intention is to malign governments and official agencies, the truth is the casualty.

“The JJA had the moral support of BJP”

- It is an interesting argument. The BJP was a weapon so far in the hands of non-Congress parties. Whenever they wanted to support Congress or to join it, the crass and usual argument was: “we wanted to defeat the communal forces” So obviously, only BJP is the Communal party. The *mantra* has spread to the academic charlatans also. You want ot condemn or criticise anybody or anything, associate BJP with it, and the former gets automatically and comprehensively tarnished, and painted in black and lurid colours.

Salwa Judum

- If there is one entity that has been criticised ad nauseam without any convincing arguments, it is Salwa Judum. The man who conceived it, Mahendra Karma, had his reasons. He genuinely believed that the desperados mostly tribals read, Maoists — could be defeated at their own game by their fellow tribals. Why should the ordinary tribals prove a sitting duck to the armed devils, just because they had weapons with them. Has any of the arm-chair critics, writing ensconced in their luxurious drawing room comforts tried to find out the circumstances which goaded Karma to think of forming an outfit like Jan Jagran Abhyan, and subsequently Salwa Jadum? He lost his wife, two sons, some half a dozen close relatives to the Maoist marauders. It was then that he thought of creating an institution to counter the Maoists. Is there anything wrong in that?
- Even if we accept that certain excesses have been committed, is that reason enough condemn it or even disband it? Institution do develop flaws or commit some wrongs, do you just abolish it? Civil services, security forces, or even judiciary have been found wanting or even developed some structural shortcomings, do we abandon them, disband them or subject them to death penalty as we have done in the case of Salwa Judum? Has anyone suggested disbanding the IAS since several of its officers have indulged in horrendous acts of criminal import, or indulged in serious scams?

None! Same goes for judiciary. It is well known that judiciary at lower level and middle level has been infected by corruption bug. Has anyone thought of throwing it out of the window. Things do not stop here. A father and son due has publicly accused the majority of retired Supreme Court Chief Justices of corruption, why has not the highest Court in the land thought of proceeding against the accusers through much-feared "contempt of the Court" law? Just because Salwa Judum is not as highly regarded institution, and its critics (like RC Gupa) are too well-known a court has simply ordered its closure.

- The Indian courts are becoming too activist for country's over all good. They feel they can offer solutions to all problems — administrative, political, social, economic, religious — of the country. A cynic asks why can't courts find solution to the ills afflicting the judiciary, namely, mounting arrears, delivering reasonably timely judgements, rising corruption in its fraternity *et al.* Armed force too seem to be victims of all-knowing and activist judges. A judge in Jammu and Kashmir went to the extent of laying down quantity and quality of food to be served to a terrorist besieged within a house and surrounded by the Army personnel. How will judiciary act or react if a General was to advise it how to run the business of courts. After this "biryani to be served to the terrorist" judgement, will the judges be emboldened to tell the Army as to how to plan and execute its tactical operations?

Judiciary and Salwa Judum

- It is sad decision to have ordered the disbandment of the Salwa Judum. If the Maoists can turn into a murdering machine, should not the local tribals arm themselves to safeguard their homes and hearths? Should they offer themselves as sitting ducks at the altar of such judgement? Even individuals can pick up arms in self-defence. On the same principle, why can't they pick up arms and bind themselves in an organisation? If they have committed some wrongs, so have a lot of other organisations, as detailed above. Again, are the judges and the civil society activists who passionately argued against the Salwa Judum, aware that in some areas of Jammu and Kashmir women armed themselves with rifles and sten guns against the jihadi terrorists who would frequent their homes to loot, and sometime, rape them?

Stressful situations the forces work under

- It happened in 1958 in Naga Hills. A patrol was ambushed by the

Naga rebels near a village in Kohima district. Some soldiers were killed in that ambush. The dead included a Junior Commissioned Officer (JCO) who was to proceed on retirement the very next day after 31 years of services. Can the honourable judges and arm chair critics understand the agony, anger and the desire to avenge of the men who served under this JCO? In some such situations, there is possibility of excess being committed by men under extreme stress. Men in uniform, too, are human beings. This is not a plea to justify such excesses, but merely an appeal to understand.

How the two entities think alike

- **It is a case of the chips off the old block.** It is interesting to note that two separate entities have used the same phraseology.

PUCL: The JJA had the moral support of the BJP.

Jason Miklian: The JJA was morally supported by the BJP leadership. It seems to be an assembly line production. One think tank supply the goods.

BJP and CPI making a common cause

- BJP and CPI are the opposite poles of Indian politics — ideological enemies, so to say. Still the PUCL says: "The JJA had the moral support of the BJP and CPI". If that be so, something must be right about the Salwa Judum and its predecessor, JJA. It can't be all wrong!

Are the Indian Authors penning the essays for consumption of the foreigners and their subsequent approval? Are they hungry of and aspiring for accolades from the foreign eminences?

- Miklian's essay was published in the Dialectical Anthropology, December 2009. Its very title is suggestive: "The Purification Hunt: The Salwa Judum counter ininsurgency in Chhattisgarh, India".
- The very heading of the PUCL report is suspect: "When the State make war on its own people: A Report on the violation of people's rights during the Salwa Judum Campaign in Dantewada, Chhattisgarh". The "State making war on its own people" will draw the eye balls, more from the foreign lands than from within the country. The PUCL is bringing bad name to the Indian democracy; howsoever imperfect it may be, it is serving the nation very well. It is the same imperfect democracy that is permitting/ accepting the freedom of expression to all kinds of opinion- including the irresponsible ones, even anti-national ones.

Book published under foreign funding

- One is compelled to comment on a book published by an Indian Think Tank, Centre for Security Analysis, (CSA) Chennai, and funded by an American entity, Mac Arthur Foundation. One can not understand the rationale of an Indian Think Tank publishing books funded by the foreign institutions. But the tenor and tone of this book "The Naxal Threat: causes, state responses and Consequences", is troubling . It paints the Government of India as anti-people...particularly two of its essays which cover two-thirds of the pages of this 178 page book. The essay by Sudha Ramachandran is so pro-Maoist in its tone and import that it is not balanced, nor fair to all the parties in the dispute. A scholar must not lose sight of sobriety and balance. Likewise, the essay by Saranya Nayak and Malini Subramaniam is written more to depict the tribals' side of the argument forgetting the and prerequisites of a modern and globalised economy. In any case, why do these two joint authors admit that India did not treat its tribals the way the USA and Australia did theirs. It is shameful dishonesty to say that the USA treated its tribals decently. They were killed and their lands taken over with force of gun. India never did such a horrendous and despicable act. We can be proud of our country in this respect.

Combating Maoism

There cannot be one straight-jacketed response to Maoist ideology and the consequent violence it unleashes on its opponents. It has to be multi pronged approach to deal with the Maoist conflict: viz, to address the tribal grievances that underline their growing alienation from the State, and to respond with military force to their armed action against security agencies and the innocent civilians. The latter is meant to convince the Maoists to come to the negotiations table for face-to-face discussions with the authorities. The former course involves an array of poverty alleviation measure and legislation to protect tribal rights and interests.[12]

The Fifth Schedule of the Indian Constitution designates districts in nine states as tribal areas. The Schedule guarantees tribals rights over the land they live on. Governors of the states in question are bestowed extensive powers to prevent or amend any law enacted in the Parliament and/or the state assemblies that goes against the interest of the tribals. PESA, enacted in 1996, goes further in protection of tribal rights: provides tribal self-governance, recognize the traditional rights of tribal communities over their natural resources, it provides for the setting up of *gram sabhas* and *gram panchayats* to manage their community resources. It empower them to control social sector functionaries, own minor forest produce, manage water bodies, give recommendations for mining lease, be consulted for land acquisitions, enforce prohibition, identify beneficiaries for poverty alleviation and other government programmes, and more importantly, have a decisive say in all development projects in their villages[13].

Besides the above measures the government has adopted certain programmes to ensure livelihood security of tribals and other rural poor:

- Mahatma Gandhi National Rural Employment Guarantee Act (MGNREGA), 2005. It guarantees a minimum of a hundred days of wage employment in a year to a rural household. In November 2012, Lal Krishna Advani leading the Indian delegation to a committee of the UN General Assembly, hold up the MGNREGA as an effective poverty-alleviation legislation before the world.
- Scheduled Tribes and Other Traditional Forest Dwellers (Recognition of Forest Rights) Act, 2006, popularly known as the Forest Right Act (FRA). This landmark legislation recognises the forest rights of tribal communities, including the right to live in the forest, to self-cultivate, and to use miner forest produce … further strengthening these rights already mentioned/provided for under the PESA, mentioned earlier here.

Land Acquisition

If land acquisition is a major problem, it is also a part of the solution. Of late, there has been increasing protests over land acquisition…the best celebrated one being the one under Mamta Banarjee against the Tata's Nano project in West Bengal. It is only expected as the acquisition deprives the peasants not only of their livelihood but also results in their displacement. Consequently, the government has formulated the National Rehabilitation and Resettlement Policy, 2007. It is aimed at "striking....a balance between the need for land for development activities, and at the same time, protecting the interests of the land owners whose livelihood depends on the land involved".

The 2007 Act seeks to minimise displacement and to promote, "as far as possible, non-displacing or least-displacing alternatives, to ensure adequate rehabilitation package......" where tribals "are being displaced in sizeable numbers, a well thought-through Tribal Development Plan must be put in place", says the policy[14].

Some other Socio-economic measures

To contain the crushing impact of poverty, the government has implemented several programmes meant to reduce hunger and malnutrition, to improve literacy" and so on. These are:

1. Integrated Child Development Scheme (ICDS). Aims at ensuring food and health security of children under the age of six years.
2. Public Distribution System (PDS). Aims at providing those below the poverty line (popularly, BPL...a much-used acronym) with food grains at subsidized rates.
3. Sarva Shiksha Abhiyan (SSA), a popular scheme launched by the Vajpayee-led NDA. A literacy programme aimed at achieving universal elementary education.

Using underground treasures

An important point at issue is the use – and to employ a proper and relevant terminology, "exploit" – of mineral wealth the tribels are sitting on. There are two views on it. Left-Liberals feel it is the exclusive properly of the tribals who live in those jungles. The other view holds this underground treasures as the national property to be used for the common good of not only that tribal community but also of the entire nation. It is an accepted reality of life today that underground wealth – be it gold, platinum, coal, petroleum, minerals *et al.*—belongs to the nation that its government must extract, refine and utilize for the national interest. Same way, mineral wealth of the forests should be deemed to belong to the nation, but considering their poverty and state of general deprivation, weightage should be given to the overall well-being and betterment of the tribals in the area in the interest of the social equity. By all means, use the forest wealth to ameliorate the lot of the forest dwellers there, but there is and should be no question of the Liberals adumberating the pernicious theory that outsiders have nothing to do with such a forest wealth!

An important way for the government to ensure the development of the tribal areas is to encourage investment in the extractive and refining industry to make optimum gains from the immense mineral wealth there. This development will not only amebiorate the lot of the tribals by creating local jobs for them, it will also spur India's economic growth. As is well-known, upto the early 1990s, the government and its official enterprises, popularly called, Public Sector Undertakings (PSUs), were the main players in the field of extraction and refining of minerals. But in the post-Narasimha –Manmohan reforms period, a number of private companies, Indian as also MNCs, have entered the tribal areas.

Containing Maoist violence

If the government address tribal poverty and discontent through socio-economic and political measures to reduce their alienation with the State, as also to wean them away from the Maoist ideology and their propaganda, it also uses force to convince the Maoists that they can not, under any circumstances, undermine and defeat the idea of India through the use of mindless violence. If India is too big and mighty to fall to the machinations of some foreign enemies and states, it certainly is not amenable to be worsted by internal disruption, impelled by ideological forces of any hue.

The Maoists can be persuaded to find a peaceful solution to their ideological differences through use of arms or negotiations. But it must be quite clear to their sympathizers and over-ground arm, represented by the bleeding hearts, the Left and the liberals, per se, that they will not resort to the latter alternative till the former one compels them.

The Andhra Pradesh Government engaged the Maoists in talks during 2004, but the peace process collapsed within a few months. Reasons: The Maoists were being duplicious exploiting the interregnum to rearm and regroup their cadres or the government officials were not sincere in their intent, trying to achieve on the negotiations table what they could not in the field…depending upon the side of the divide you were speaking from! Here is a sympathiser's View on these talks' failure

1. Security analysts argued that the government has been compelled to use military means against the Maoists as the political and constitutional means have not worked with them. They often points to the failed talks in 2004-2005 to allege that the Maoists used this period to regroup rather than find a negotiated solutions.
2. But a close examination of how events unfolded during this period reveals that the negotiations failed because they were not pursued by either side seriously or in a way that would result in a constructive outcome[15].
3. Further more, while the government has put in place several projects to address poverty and hunger in tribal areas, implementation of these has been half-hearteds. Funds have benefitted contractors and middle men, rather than the tribals. Besides, the government's approach to economic developments of triabl areas, which consists of encouraging investment in mining and other extractive activity, is deepening structural violence and inequity.
4. Thus, while the main parties are using a range of political, legislative, developmental and military measures to pursue their goals, they have pursued the political and constitutional means less assiduously than they have the military ones.

COMMENTS

The above are the views of sympathisers who often speak and plead for the Maoist cause. Their views are slanted in favour of the Maoists, and have been reproduced above in the almost original words. What follows are the parawise comments of the Author on the preceding.

1. The security analysts “allege” that the Maoists used the period to regroup. The term ‘allege’ is a giveaway. A Maoists will use this terminology. Obviously, this academic’s sympathies are with them! Isn’t one reminded of the oft-used phrase ‘overground’ arm of the underground outfit?
2. So, “negotiations because they were not pursued by either side seriously.” Putting the government which represent the country on equal footing with rebels is an unfortunate stance. If one stands for security of the country and the other for jeopardizing it, and comparing the two is anamolous, indicative of a prejudiced mind! It needs to be mentioned that this academic/activist was the mediator between the Maoists and the Government during 2011 and 2012.
3. Implementation of the development projects “has been half-hearted”. Only a small part of half-heartedness is due to usual lethargy of the government machinery, but major blame lies with the destructive and disruptive ways of the Maoists…laying IED in the project areas, kidnapping the workers and labourers, killing the contractors, blocking the movement of necessary men and material in and out of the area, and inciting the local populace against the project citing the dubious and utterly wrong/false premises. That “funds have benefitted contractors and middle men…”, is not only half-truth but self-serving lie! Most of the money made by the contractors and middlemen goes into the large size pockets of the Maoist leaders. In fact, they are real middlemen–in term of obnoxious connotation usually attached to it! Yet again, it needs to be noted that it serves the purpose of the Maoists to block and disrupt the development of the tribal habitats, so that they continue to exploit their consequent poverty and deprivation for their ideological propaganda. A develop area with its contented tribes will put these so-called revolutionaries out of their lucrative profession! That investment in extractive activity “is deepening structural violence and inequity” is a self-serving falsehood. If it be so, the blame should lie with the violent Maoists. In fact, if they allow this extractive activity, it should decrease and finally

eliminate this much-condemned "structural violence and inequity." In the manner of their 'foreign' forefathers, viz the Communists, the Maoists deploy the worn-out-cliches – which have lost their significance due to excessive but repetitive use – to argue their case! It is a *bankruptsy* of thought. In fact, the continuing inequity will serve them and their ideology effectively...hence their determination to ensure its longevity, and if possible, its permance, to ensure their own life!

4. Para 4 above shows the perils of weariness affecting this academic/activist, working hard to create contrived reasoning! He, in fact, wants to blame the State/government for pursuing the political and constitutional means less assiduously than they have the military ones." But to sound even handed, he writes "the main parties – he obviously means government and Maoists – are using legislative, developmental, political and military measures to pursue their goals...." One did not know the Maoists too have "Legislative, developmental and political" measures in their armoury! It is ridiculous! Or, is this pro-Maoist academic making a desperate effort to equate the two inequatables – one responsible and peace-making and the other irresponsible destructive, law-breaking, violence-loving and illegal by birth! This author is certainly harsh in his comments, but knowing the passionate supporters...two of these named earlier[16]...of the Maoists, this severity is called for.

Using Excessive force?

An analyst says "the governments' approach to tackling the Maoists has leaned on coercive means. Right from the 1940s, it has used extreme force to suppress the Maoists. .....The scale and nature of anti-Maoist operations have escalated over the decades. Besides police and paramilitary forces, special commando units are being deployed in districts worst-hit by Maoist violence.

Use of extra legal groups like Salwa Judum has been an important part of the government's strategy". The views of the analysts like the above need a critical examination, and some kind of rebuttal to an attempt at suppressing the truth and pedal the half truths:

1. The world is yet to see a revolt being defeated by no-coercive mean. Some analysts do not seem to have understood or realised that country is at war! Maoism cancer has spread to one-fourth of India's district, and now it has a red corridor nearly under it,

running from Karnataka to Bihar-Nepal border. Do they really expect a kid-gloves treatment?

2. India is deemed to have used extreme force to suppress the Maoists. India can't afford to use less than the adequate force to deal with the hardened criminals which some of the Maoist cadres are, just to please some bleeding hearts!
3. If the scale and nature of anti-Maoist operations have escalated over the decades, so has the violent killings and disruption by these desperados! Some of these Limo Liberals do not know, or do not want to, that the Maoists are not only getting arms and financial help from some secessionist outfits like the ULFA of Assam and the PLA of Manipur within the country, certain foreign powers and NGOs, are doing the same.
4. No commando units of the Indian Army are deployed to counter the Maoists. Some assistance in training the paramilitary personnel indeed has been given by the Army – nothing beyond that.
5. The Salwa Judum was hardly extra legal entity. It is a pity that the judiciary deemed it fit to intervene in an operational matter, and to order its disbandment. As far its being an important part of government's strategy, it operated in just one district of one state!

The Counter-Maoist strategy

The development is essential as a measure to defeat the Maoists whose ideology attracts the poor and deprived to its ranks. But often the Maoists thwart the government projects to develop the area lest the movement loses its appeal, and its raison d'etre!

Since the year 2009, the Centre has been working on a two-pronged strategy that involves coordinated drive by the State police and paramilitary units to eliminate Maoists from the worst-affected districts, followed by development activity. Often the two proceed simultaneously, notwithstanding a determined drive by the Maoists to sabotage the development. It needs to be emphatically mentioned/stressed that there are no "coordinated military operations" against the Maoists anywhere in the country.

A senior Home Ministry official describes the reality: "It is a comprehensive operational strategy that would first seek to clear an area of Maoists, occupy it Militarily (he means by force) and follow it up with socio-economic development activity[17]". Home Minister P. Chidambram made his government's policy stand clear in his statement in the Parliament: "The two pillars of the policy are calibrated police action and development.

Central paramilitary forces have been provided to the affected states, including Chhattisgarh, to help the state governments carry out counter-insurgency operations, regain control of the area dominated by the Naxalites, restore the civil administration and restart development work[18]" Now we have a comment from Left/Maoist leaning activist, flourishing his flag-waving persona:

> "While the government has described its policy towards Maoists as one that is as much about development as it is about elimination of Maoists, it is clearly more pre-occupied with the latter at present. Some have drawn parallels between the violence of the Salwa Judum strategy and that of operation Green Hunt.[19]"

It is interesting to critique the views of scholars like the one in the preceding para. So the government is "more pre-occupied with the elimination of the Maoists". It seems to such scholars that the government is committing some sort of crime if the Maoists get killed in this war. They fail to understand that the Maoists are enemy of the State, who are holding the country to ransom. Again, police facing a violent mob is expected to fire with the aim of injuring, and not killing the demonstrators. They are dealing with their own countrymen. When we are facing the enemy of the State, the security forces open fire to kill. Are these Maoist sympathisers and/ or partisans even aware how many Indians, including security men, women, children, have been murdered by the Maoists? One can't understand why an Agnivesh feel so sad and passionate when a Maoist is killed? He is immediately certified an 'innocent', 'killed in a fake encounter'. The Agnivesh's of this world are overpowered by their ideological predilection, and see the death of a murderer through partisan blinkers. These bleeding hearts have no tears to shed when a soldier dies, just doing his duty in the defence of the country. It is this blinkered vision which is beyond the comprehension of men in uniform.

Here is another partisan who is drawing parallels between the violence of the Salwa Judum strategy and that of the Operation Green Hunt, "the only difference being that operation Green Hunt is being conducted under the official mandate of the State, rather than under the fig-leaf the so-called people's movement[20]". The bias and prejudice is obvious from the use of words "fig leaf" of a so-called people's movement. If the victims and likely targets of Maoist murderous violence band together to fight the desparados rather than becoming sitting ducks for their convenience, it is a mere "fig leaf". It is obvious that this academic/ activist/ analyst has not heard of some Gujjar women banding together, arming themselves with rifles and facing the Jihadi terrorists bravely when their husbands are out on work.

They thought it is better to die fighting than being slaughtered by the terrorists, unheard and unsung. In Assam, some ULFA militants were attacked and killed by unarmed villagers when the former were on extortion mission in the area. As for the parallels between the violence of the one versus the other, the very averment is uncalled for, even inane – considering the scale and size of the operations carried out by the two entities and the relevant areas in question. If one is spread to an entire state and often beyond it, the other is restricted to some areas of a district. It bears repetition to say that the Salwa Judum was conceived by a Congress leader whose six kin fell to the Maoists' violence, and he got the support of not only the people who had similarly suffered but also of the BJP.

Is India over-doing its counter-Maoist measures?

It is only natural that there can be more than one view on any issue of public interest, and particularly so if the issue is so important as to impinge upon a country's national security. Certain sections of the commentariat, essentially the Left-leaning and Maoist sympathizers, do feel New Delhi employs excessive force while dealing with the Maoist insurgents. They feel the government is making serious bid to suppress dissent, an essential part of a democratic polity. Finally, an extreme view holds that certain measures employed in eliminating the Maoists can be dubbed draconian!

It should be useful to examine views of some of the academics and analysts who feel on these lines about India's strategy and tactics to deal with the Left-wing extremist threat to Indian national security, defined as the most serious for India's integrity and sovereignty, by no less a person than her Prime Minister.

Are both sides undermining India's democratic Polity?

If dissent and its tolerance are the soul of a functional democracy which India claims to be, then it is only expected that the views of those who are opposed to those of the government are heard patiently, even respect fully. It is not necessary that the Government has to accept them all the time, but to dismiss them out of hand is also not the sign of a healthy democracy. It is with this consideration in mind that views of some of the harshest critics of Government's policy of dealing with the violent Maoism are given in the succeeding text. For most part, these views are in the near original language.

The State, says this critic, claims to be fighting the Maoists in defence of India's parliamentary democracy but the Maoist assert it is a sham democracy and they want to displace it with a genuine democracy, a people's democracy of their conception. "Yet experience on the ground shows that the actions of both the adversaries has weakened democracy".

The State is criminalising dissent. Critics of its counter-insurgency policy are dubbed as Maoists. It goes even further. In the conflict zone, any protest or criticism of government actions is labelled 'Maoist'. A sarpanch puts it rather expressly: "We protest about anything...the corruption in NREGA, the take-over of our land...and we are immediately dubbed Maoists. Basically, if we raise against something the government is doing, no matter how illegal or unfair we feel it might be to us, we become Naxals or Maoists.[21]"

Those who work amidst tribals are also labelled Maoists. This was the fate of Binayak Sen, a doctor cum civil rights activist, who was in custody for two years before he was let out on bail[22].

Here is another case of a health worker who used to visit villages of the Banda tribe in Malkangiri "where no government doctor, nurse or government official would go", received a Letter from the Collector ordering her to leave the district. The reason behind the order was rather simplistic: Since she was working in villages in Maoist zone, she must be a Maoist.[23]"

Are some Legislative Measures too to blame?

In May 2010, the Home Ministry warned civil society groups, NGOs, intellectuals and the general public that supporting the Maoist ideology would attract action under the UAPA.[24] It has drawn up a list of 57 organisations it says are working "for the cause of the Maoists". While some of the entities in the list do have Maoist link, many do not. PUCL and PUDR figure in the list, they are critical of human rights violations by the Maoists even if they have criticised the State's use of extra judicial methods.

Several of the listed organisations engage in democratic activity in the public domain, even contesting elections. Rights activists complain the government's definition of a rebel sympathiser is so "open ended" that "anyone working for tribal rights get branded as pro-Maoist[25].

Praful Bidwai dubs certain laws as draconian because they "aid the State in its undermining of democracy." He cites the examples of the UAPA and the Chhattisgarh Special Public Security Act (CSPSA), 2005, which empowers police to arrest anyone without hard evidence and "imprison him without due process". In the name of fighting Maoists, the CSPSA has led to increased repression and suppression of people rights. It criminalises even peaceful protest, declaring it a danger or menace to public order, peace and tranquility" because it might interfere with or "tends to interfere with the maintenance of public order (or) the administration of law."[26]

May be, to seem fair and neutral, the critics say the Maoist display a similar "if you are not for us, you are against us" perception of the World.

In response to a 2006 Letter by the Independent Citizens Initiative (ICI) calling on the Government and the Maoists to give up armed warfare and initiate dialogue, they described those like the ICI, which condemn the violence of both sides, as "apoligists for the oppressors, in spite of their good intentions and sincere attitude."[27]

Then some criticism of the rebels, who claim to be fighting for socio-economic betterment of the tribals. But they are uncomfortable with the NGOs, who are working among the tribals. The Maoists deeply resent the activists as they advocate a path different from theirs to achieve the same social-economic change. For the same reasons, they are equally uncomfortable with tribal organisations who conduct mass struggles to redress their grievance. They are known to undermine these struggle by infiltrating their ranks to sabotage these by inciting violence.

Here is a final proof that puts the law enforcers and law breakers on equal footing. The intolerance of both the parties is amply proved by the way they attacked, a Gandhian, Himanshu Kumar's Vanavasi Chetna Ashram. Kumar had been working in Dantewada through this Ashram, for over two decades, proving legal aid to the victims of violence. "The Ashram has experienced the wrath of the Salwa Judum, the security forces and Maoists." In 2009, "the headquarters of his NGO in Kanwalnar in Dantwada was destroyed by CRPF and Chhattisgarh police personnel."

The final conclusion by the critic: "It is evident that the State and the Maoists are demolishing the democratic middle ground."

Comments on the critic's dissenting views

Binayak Sen's case was widely discussed in the press. He might have been working for the tribals but police had enough proof for his complicity in Maoist activities. He was convicted by the court of law, as they too decided that there was adequate evidence to send him to court. If the Supreme Court bailed him out after two long years, it must have its reasons. He has not been cleared of the charges, nor his release on bail proves his innocence. The case is still on. In extreme cases, accused had been declared innocent after spending years in jail. It is the functioning of the judicial system that should be faulted. With this one example, case can't in any case, be made that all other cases too belong to this category. Even on Sen's case, last word has not yet been heard.

Most interesting, if astounding, observations come from Bidwai, and certainly not unexpectedly. So, the UAPA is draconian law. And, it has been passed by the Indian Parliament. The CSPSA has "given powers to police to arrest anyone and ....imprison him without due process of law!"

A greater absurdity could not have been imagined or invented. Can we imagine the police sending people to prison? He is only working his deep set prejudices. Could such a law be passed by any state assembly? We are living in the age of PILs! In any case, one is yet to read anything from Bidwai's pen supporting government or security forces. For him, nothing is right in the country. He indeed does not deserve any serious response.

It indeed is possible that at times an individual official, of police or civil, might have transgressed his limit in a moment of stress and strain, but there is no question of such a thing happening too often. Neither is one pronouncing that the criticism voiced above is motivated or wholly wrong. In human affairs, imperfection has a space. Critics aim should be to offer corrective and constructive ideas to improve the system.

There should be no effort to equate the law enforcer with law breakers, as mentioned above. It should be clear that it is a matter of cause and affect and two can't be put on equal footing. The dissent is welcome. But critics have no idea the pressure under which the security forces have to function in an insurgency environment. Here you do not know your enemy, as you do in the war situation. Here is a sincere plea to the critics to be understanding of the agonies of the security forces men who face fatal threats all the time.

State's Response to Maoist Revolt: An Overview

Most-quoted on the subject of Maoist insurrection in India is, of course, Prime Minister Manmohan Singh's: Naxalism is the biggest threat to India's internal security and integrity. The solution to this nearly-intractable problem lies in two fields, and possibly in simultaneous actions in the both. But it needs to be stressed that in the areas where Naxalites ('Maoists' is the current term) are effectively blocking the government's socio-economic projects to ameliorate the poverty and deprivation of the tribal communities, there State's might must precede any developmental endeavours. In this case, destructive resistance of the Maoists must be eliminated, or at the very least, brought within certain limits to enable the government to proceed with the projects Leftist academics, arm-chair ideologues and opposition parties and ill-informed politicians… that Maoist violence can not be defeated through use of arm sonly…must be put to rest: No government has ever said that they would eliminate rebels through sheer force of arms, and New Delhi has certainly never claimed so.

Maoist Aims

Seizure of political power or state power has remained consistent and ultimate objectives of the rebels. An analyst has put it more bluntly, in a nuanced clarity: "The real aim of the Naxalites is neither the domain of the economics nor state welfare. It is a political movement having its goal as the seizure of political power i.e. State power." It has been said by no less a person than the then Director of Sardar Vallabhbhai Patel National Police Academy, S. Subramanian[28]. It is time some self-serving ideologues and Left supporters of the murderous Maoists stop gushing about "their socio-economic projects in the tribal areas under their control." It is a power game, pure and simple. These is only one difference. Much-maligned politicians can be removed through ballot, these blood thirsty Maoists are not amenable to these peaceful tools of democratic polity. The language of the gun is the only one they understand, and if at times India talks to them in that language, the carping critics and the overground arm of the Maoist must understand, if not loudly applause it.

How powerful (if violent) Maoists came into being

Detailed progression of this violent movement from the Naxals of 1967 and Maoists of today has been described in another chapter of this work. Here it is mentioned briefly, to put the subject in context. It is safe to say the immediate ancestor of the Maoists was Charu Mazumdar of the 1967 Naxalbari revolt, armed one at that – even if there were some armed uprisings of earlier vintage. Following the series of mergers and splits in the Naxalite movement – which obviously is a naked power struggle for power, no different from power games Indian politicians play – two emerged as the largest and most powerful: Marxist-Leninist (People's War), or CPI-ML (PW), popularly known as the PWG (People's War Group), and the Maoist Communist Centre of India (MCCI), popularly MCC. These two groups merged on 21 September 2004 to found CPI (Maoist).

How did the Union Government respond – and when?

1967 Naxalbari armed uprising was rather a local affair, handled and suppressed…ruthlessly, if we are to believe the contemporaneous narratives, by the District Superintendent of Police…by Government of Bengal's coalitions ministry, in which Jyoti Basu was the Home Minister-ironically! Ironically again, even though it was suppressed and nearly decimated in West Bengal, it still spread and survived in other parts of India, particularly in Orissa, Bihar and and Andhra Pradesh.

When it spread to more than one state of the Union of India, then it became a subject and problem for the Union government. To be more specific, Naxalite – incidentally, the term spawned by the Naxalbari uprising, survived in its home of origin – challenge attracted the attention of the Union Government for the first time in 1998, when a Coordination Centre was constituted in the Ministry of Home Affairs (MHA) headed by the

Home Secretary, consequent to the heightened violence by the rebels in 1997. The members of the Coordination Centre included the DGSP of Maharashtra, MP, Andhra Pradesh and Orissa, originally. Over the time, the membership of this Centre kept getting enlarged to accommodate DGsP of the additional states to cater for the spatial spread of Maoist violence ." Their influence and violence has spread to, now, 16 States of the Union, holds one estimate."

Even in 1988, Naxal threat does not seem to have been taken with seriousness it certainly deserved by them. This is clear from the action (or lack of it) by the states afflicted by the Naxal contagion at that time. As is its wont in such situations, the MHA advised the states concerned to formulate a holistic security and development to deal with the Naxal threat comprehensively. While the states concerned procrastinated in formulating and submitting their action plans, the MHA too, surprisingly did not act any differently…taking a lighter view of this challenge.

In contrast, the Maoist were operating purposefully and were determined to expand their area of influence. In 2001, the then PWG conducted its third Congress and proceeded to declare some additional areas as guerrilla zones, which consequently led to the enhanced violence by the rebels. In a manner of speaking, the Naxalite movement entered the second, guerrilla phase[29] (presently, Maoists are in the Mobile Warfare phase in the Dandakaranya region of Chhattisgarh)[30]. Since then, i.e. 2001, the Maoists also began to penetrate virgin territories. Their lethal arsenal also began to acquire greater sophistication after they began to seize weapons from the Security Forces (SFs) in attacks on police stations, armouries, and in ambushes and raids on patrol parties.

Along with these two important trends (increasing militarisation and spatial expansion) that continued since 2001, the Naxalite outfits were splitting and merging at different stages. The important event of this period was the merger of CPI-ML(PW), popularly known as PWG and MCC which resulted in the founding of the CPI(Maoist) in 2004. It held its first Unity Ninth Congress in January 2007. The Unity congress was followed by an increasing violence as also number of attacks by the Maoists, touching alarming, new heights.

As the Maoists were increasing their war zones, so to say, the Union Government was seen to be hiding the facts from the public – or at the very minimum obfuscating the issues. More damaging was the fact of government authorities at various levels giving out contradictory information on the strength and spatial spread of the Maoists over a number of years, as will be seen in the next section here.

The Union Government held the view all along that its response would be development and security. Even the current Government has emphasised the same approach. Prime Minister Manmohan Singh's speech at the Chief Minister's Conference on the Internal Security on 20 December 2007 in New Delhi. But some analysts feel "the emphasis has been more on militarily dealing with the Maoist[31]."

Spread and Magnitude of Maoist Uprising: Inconsistency in Government's Estimates

What has been the spatial spread of the Maoist insurgency at different periods over the past few years? It is utterly amazing that various authorities at the official and ministerial levels have been giving divergent data over an important security issue – that has been threatening the national integrity on the ideological grounds. Some instances of these differing perceptions are given here.

We began with 22 May 2006 when the Home Minister told the Lok Sabha: "I have personally collected data…only 50 districts are affected."[32] Was he publicly differing with his Prime Minister who had given a vastly different data on this issue? He had told the Standing Committee of Chief Ministers of Naxalite-affected States that the Naxalite movement "has now spread to over-160 districts." It is the Home Minister 50 districts versus Prime Minister 160.

The incoherence continued the next year. On 21 November 2007, the Minister of State (MOS) for Home Affairs, replying to an unstarred question, said 91 districts in 11 states were affected by Maoist violence. Again, he obviously was not aware what Cabinet Secretary BK Chaturvedi had said on the same subject some months back. The latter, while speaking at the annual Conference of Chief Secretaries, had said on 20 April 2007 that a total of 182 districts in 16 States were Maoist affected. For such statistical divergence, glaring and unacceptable, especially on issues/ subjects of national importance, the officialdom must be held accountable.

More interestingly, the Maoists have their own updates on the subject. Mallojula Venugopal alias Sonu alias Bhupathi, incharge of the Dandakaranya Special Zone Committee (DKSZC) in the Central Committee of the Maoists, told. People's March a Maoist mouthpiece, in July 2007. "Our party has a presence in 17 States."

It was not only the Central Minister and the secretaries of the Union Government who, expected to be in the know of things, supply such information, but even some governors try to tread this difficult field. A former Governor of Chhattisgarh had perceived that the rebels had a far greater presence, compared to the one given in preceding paras. He said in an interview to a website in 2007: "I would like to share that currently from the figures I have been able to obtain, 256 districts have been declared as Naxalite affected districts....."

Now comes an interesting, if unexplained inexplicable, change in paradigms to determine the districts/areas under the Maoist influence/ control. So for the first time, in its Annual Report 2005-06, the MHA gave information on number of police stations from which Maoist, violent activities were reported but remained silent about the number of police stations where rebels had influence/presence. Ever since that year, the Government has maintained that parameter.

Why this changed paradigm for measuring the extent of spread of the Maoist violence in the Country? The Government/ MHA has not deigned to explain it. One could not be certain about its intention/reasons! But could it be an attempt at perception management? Things on this front may be clearer once we mention one more change in informing people about the areas affected by the Maoist violence.

In 2008, the Government introduced yet another change in paradigm for measuring the extent of territory under the Maoist influence/ control/ violence. The newer parameter was to give the statistics about the number of villages from which Maoist violence was reported, and that as a percentage of the total number of villages in the country. Accordingly, the Rajya Sabha was informed on 19 March 2008 that a mere 14000 villages out of a total of 650,000 villages "are Maoist affected, which accounts for just 2 percentage points." Moreover, the Rajya Sabha was also informed that "the number of Naxal violence related incidents at 700 accounts for a mere 1.1 per cent of the total extremist related incidents in the country."[33]

It is now fair to assume, after examining the two fresh/new parameters to determine the Maoist-afflicted...it is more apt term to express the menace and dangers posed by the Maoist terror than the comparatively insipid 'Maoist-affected...that Government of India/MHA are going the whole hog to 'manage people's perception' of the intensity and seriousness of the problem, rather than vigorously pursue the MHA's "Public Perception Management efforts, which constitutes an element of the triad of the Centre's response to the Maoist challenge. The remaining two elements of this triad are: issuing of advertisements[34] in newspapers at frequent intervals, approximately one every month and hosting tribal youth programmes involving hundreds of tribal youth in the Maoist affected areas[35].

Eventually, from under-200 figures in 2007, the violence-affected districts jumped to 223 (in 20 states) in 2009, as Home Minister

P. Chidambaram told the Conference of DGPs/IGPs, 2009, New Delhi on 14 September 2009.

Variety of Responses

As mentioned in the beginning of this section, there are generally two category of responses to counter the national threat posed by the Maoists: Developmental and counter-force or security response. But some analysts add a third one: Political Response.

Before any of the three responses, 14-point Policy spelt out by the MHA is re-produced below.

14-Point Policy to Deal with Maoist Challenge

The Union Government spelt out this 14- Point in March 2006 to tackle the Maoist challenge[36]. These are as follows:

1. The Government will deal sternly with the Naxalites indulging in violence.
2. Keeping in view that Naxalism is not merely a law and order problem, the policy of the Govt. is to address this menace simultaneously on political security, development and public perception management fronts in a holistic manner.
3. Naxalism being an inter-state problem, the states will adopt a collective approach and pursue a coordinated response to counter it.
4. The states will need to further improve police response and pursue effective and sustained police action against Naxalites and their infrastructure individually and jointly.
5. There will be no peace dialogue by the affected states with the Naxal groups unless the latter agrees to give up violence and arms.
6. Political parties must strengthen their cadre base in Naxal-affected areas so that the potential youth there can be weaned away from the path of Naxal ideology.
7. The states from where Naxal activity/ influence, and not Naxal violence, is reported should have a different approach with special focus on accelerated socio-economic development of the backward areas and regular interaction with NGOs, intelligentsia, civil liberties groups etc to minimise overground support for the Naxalite ideology and activity.
8. Efforts will continue to be made to promote local resistance groups against Naxalites but in a manner that the villagers are

provided adequate security cover and the area is effectively dominated by the security forces.

9. Mass media should also be extensively used to highlight the futility of Naxal violence and loss of life and property caused by it and developmental schemes of the government in the affected, areas so as to restore people's faith and confidence in the Government machinery.
10. The States should announce a suitable transfer policy for the Naxal affected districts. Willing, Committed and competent officers will need to be posted with a stable tenure in the Naxal affected districts. These officers will also need to be given greater delegation and flexibility to deliver better and step up Government presence in these areas.
11. The Government of Andhra Pradesh has an effective surrender and rehabilitation policy for Naxalites and has produced good results over the years. The other states should adopt a similar policy.
12. The State Governments will need to accord a higher priority in their annual plans to ensure faster socio-economic development of the Naxal affected areas. The focus area should be to distribute land to the landless poor as part of the speedy implementation of the land reforms, ensure development of physical infrastructure like the roads, communication, power etc. and provide employment opportunities to the youth in these areas.
13. Another related issue is that development activities are not undertaken is some of the Naxalite affected areas mainly due to extortion, threat or fear from the Naxalite cadres. In these areas, even contractors are not coming forward to take up developmental work. Adequate security and other measures would need to be taken to facilitate uninterrupted developmental activities in the Naxal-affected areas.
14. The Central Government will continue to supplement the efforts and resources of the affected areas on both security and development fronts and bring greater coordination between the states to successfully tackle the problem.

Development Response

Whatever the Left-Liberals, Maoist supporters and critics might say, the Government has accorded priority to the development approach to counter the Maoist challenge to its legitimacy. That is how it should be in any democratic polity. It also needs to be admitted in all honesty that plans and projects undertaken in the Maoist-affected areas have not achieved desired results because of the venal politicians and inefficient administrators. Corruption is the bane of any democracy, normally affecting the development works…leakage of money, tardy implementation etc. As bad, if not work, is the corruption indulged in by the Maoists. They extort money from the contractors, even from the poor labourers. Often, they delay and sometime even force the government to abandon, the projects through coercion and threats. Where the Maoists are powerful enough not to let even the project take off, the State resort to the security first approach. When conditions permit the workers and managers to assemble and start the work, development approach takes over. But to put it in perspective, usually two approaches happen simultaneously.

Anti-poverty schemes

Since India was a state with widely pervading poverty, all governments post-1947 have put into practice several development schemes targeting the poor. As of the present, there are several such schemes under execution. They also benefit the tribal communities, as the do the rest of the poor and deprived in the other parts of India. Some of these are mentioned here:

- **Pradhan Mantri Grameen Sadak Yojana.** The project means to build rural roads to improve connectivity. The Annual Report, 2007-08, MHA, P-22, says: "The State Governments have been requested to identify and prioritize unconnected habitations having population of 500 and above in plain areas and 250 and above in tribal areas for preparing detailed project reports as per PMGSY programme guidelines.
- **National Rural Employment Guarantee Programme (NREGA-A For Act).** Initially initiated in 200 districts, it was extended to 330 in April 2007. Presently, it covers all the districts in the country.
- **The earlier Backward Districts Initiative (BDI).** A component of Rashtriya Sam Vikas Yojana (RSVY)…now stands subsumed into the **Backward Regions Grant Fund (BRGF).** BDI scheme was launched during the financial year 2003-2004 with the main objective of putting in place programmes and policies with the joint effort of the Centre and States which would remove barriers of growth, accelerate the development process and improve the quality of life of the people. The scheme aims at focused development of backward areas which would help reduce imbalances and speed up development. So says the document

from the Planning Commission, MLP Division, "Backward District Initiative-Rashtriya Sam Vikas Yojana. The Scheme and Guidelines for preparation of District Plans. Also, BDI was intended to "address the problems of low agricultural productivity, unemployment and to fill critical gaps in physical and social infrastructure. The BDI was implemented in 147 districts, whereas the BRGF is being implemented in 250 districts.

- Indira Aawas Yojana.
- Grameen Vidyuti Karan Yojana.
- Bharat Nirman.
- National Rural Health Mission (NRHM).
- Sarva Shiksha Abhyan (SSA).
- Integrated Child Development Services (ICDS).

Naxal-hit Areas: Exclusive Pilot Project

The Union Government announced in October 2007 a comprehensive plan for speedy socio-economic development in eight districts in four States as a pilot Project (Aurangabad and Gaya in Bihar, Bijapur and Dantewada in Chhattisgarh, Chhatra and Palamu in Jharkhand: and Malkangiri and Raygada in Orissa). Subsequently, at the Conference of Chief Ministers on Internal Security, the Prime Minister extended the programme to 33 districts in eigth States.[37] The Inter Ministerial Group (IMG), which monitors, this project, at its 7th meeting on 16 April 2008, reviewing its progress, "clearly determined the course of action in respect of development measures envisaged in the integrated security and development action plants."[38]

Besides the IMG, a Task force under the chairmanship of the Cabinet Secretary was formed on 12 February 2008, as disclosed by the MHA Annual Reports 2007-08, "to promote coordinated efforts across a range of development and security activities so that problems in the Naxal-hit areas can be tackled in a comprehensive manner."

Two years after the Task Force came the programme known as Unified Action Plan (UAP), announced by the Union Cabinet on 24 November 2010. Originally known as Integrated Action Plan (IAP), the UAP was Rs 13,742 crore project meant to herald rapid socio-economic development in Naxal-hit districts. Initially, it was operational in 35 districts, was gradually expanded to cover 60 districts. It was a Planning Commission designed programme.

Implementation and Delivery: Same Sad Story

In spite of monitoring at multiple levels, delivery is deficient. As the

Panchayati Raj Minister informed the Parliament (LOK SABHA) in reply to Unstarred Question no 2240, on 23 April 2008: Nearly five years after the RSVY was launched, of the total Rs 6615 Crore earmarked, at the time it was "subsumed into the BRGF programme in August 2006, the districts concerned had claimed only Rs 2850 Crore." That means the districts concerned could utilise a mere 43 per cent of the allocated funds. The minister further informed that of the 147 districts under the RSVY, as on that date, a more 70 districts claimed their full entitlement of Rs 45 crore: 39 districts had to claim the last instalment, 30 districts two more instalments and eight had to claim three or more instalments.

Now for some lamentations from the supervisory monitoriing committees. The Parliamentary Standing Committee on Home Affairs in its 126th Report, tabled in the Lok Sabha on 26 April 2007 notes: "The Committee, however, feels that there is no perceptible change on the socio-economic front.. There needs to be an effective monitoring mechanism......" The reasons for deficient delivery are not far to see. What a Steering Group of the Planning Commission noted in 2001 is equally true today: "The Working Groups strongly felt that though the programme for poverty alleviation were well-designed, poor delivery was a major hurdle in eradicating poverty......It was felt that the government machinery at the cutting edge level was too thinly spread, poorly trained and ill equipped to implement programmes, which require not only commitment to poor....."

'Leakages' is the term academics use for corruption, which really means siphoning off funds by the influential. That is a major contributing factor in the benefits not reaching the target groups. This is starkly illustrated in a March 2008 personal communication from a Superintendent of Police (SP) of a district in the south Telengana region of Andhra Pradesh[39]. It is para-hrased here: "Under the NREGS some Rs 200 Crore has been allotted to each districts. In this (particular) district, not much money has been spent, on the ground that wheelers-dealers would siphon off funds. Thus a huge amount has been left unspent. The approximate figure for misappropriation is over Rs 50 lakh par mandal (taluq): and there are 66 mandals in the district. Besides, there is total mayhem in the villages at the meetings of the social audit parties, with the wheeler-dealers (local legislators henchmen) creating disorder. There have also been instances when members of the social audit parties were threatened and manhandled. So, we are back to 1985, when the then Prime Minister Rajiv Gandhi said at Kalahandi, Orissa: "Of every rupee spent by the Government, only 17 paise reached the intended beneficiary." On 17 January 2008, MP from UP, Rahul Gandhi echoed his father. speaking from Bundelkhand, UP, on the implementation of, and rampant misappropriation, in the NREGS, he said: "Now the situation is even worse......I have seen job cards of 50 people with the same serial number, and not even one card has the entry of work[40]."

But there are sign that things have, indeed, improved over the last 4-5 years. More on it later.

Security Response

A number of analysts have felt and asserted that response of the Centre and Naxalite-hit states has been military oriented, meaning thereby, the response mean crushing the Maoists/rebels through security force operations. Some feel that both security response and development response are weak even lacklustre.

At the best, this view could be a little misplaced. In fact, the liberals and Maoist supporters would only prefer the State should deal with such uprising through negotiations and development strategy. But that is idealism at the best and impracticable in reality. There is a reason why most analysts feel the way they do. To begin with, a democracy deals with any dissent, and even anti-national activities, through kid-gloves treatment – reasoning "they are brother-Indians, even if gone astray, misinformed, or misled by certain disinformation. But when the dissent become violent, or assumes anti-national dimensions, security response is the course of last resort. Yet again, even when the development response has been adopted, it might not produce desired results for a considerable period for a number of reasons: results may be downplayed by the vested interests, including and most likely by the rebels, the development process in itself is time-consuming, and will be visible in a small area of the total hit by violence/uprising, a road-building or bridge-construction does not make 'explosive' headlines for the press compared to injuries or fatalities caused in security force operations or rebel violence, and supporting rebels' cause and opposing state's policies establish one 'liberal' and humanitarian credentials – in any case, being anti-establishment is fashionable. Finally, it must be acknowledge that a democracy because of deficit governance or misgovernance fails to eradicate poverty and deprivation in a certain time frame, and offers ideologically motivated individuals/ outfits a fertile ground for anti-State activities.

More interestingly and certainly surprisingly, even paramilitary Chiefs go along the line taken by majority of analysts that "over the years, the state response has tended to remain largely police centric......"

The Centre helps the States

The Centre helps and guides the States in militarily dealing with the Maoists:

- It has advised the States to improve its intelligence gathering mechanism; improve the functioning of their police forces by augmenting their strength, fortify police stations and their beat systems, provide incentives, by professional training and create specialised police units by establishing jungle warfare schools.
- It provides units of central paramilitary forces like CRPF, BSF, CISF etc on demand to the states for their counter-Maoist operations.
- The Centre provides financial assistance for the Modernisation of the Police Forces (MPF) and 100 per cent financial assistance under the Security Related Expenditure (SRE) scheme for various expenses incurred by the affected States.

SRE Guidelines, 2005

The Guidelines for States and Districts are given here.

A. Criteria for inclusion of States under the SRE Scheme

1. Existence of and activities by one or more of the organisations (which have been declared unlawful associations, terrorist organisations either under the Unlawful Activities (Prevention Act, 1967 or any other Act in the State).
2. Enactment of legislation by the State to tackle activities of Naxal extremists or similar organisations.
3. Raising of India Reserve Battalions by the concerned states for curbing the activities of extremists.
4. Inadequate development of affected areas due to hindrances created by extremist activities.

B. Criteria for inclusion of districts under the SRE Scheme

1. Intensity of Naxal violence over a period of five years. Exceptions can be made in some cases where it is found that a particular district which was earlier not a particular district which was earlier not affected or marginally affected, has over the past two/ three years, been reporting a large number of cases of Naxal violence.
2. The organisational consolidation attained by the various Naxal outfits in the affected districts. Whether the districts are having

'liberated areas' or 'guerrilla zones' where the extremist outfits virtually run a parallel administration even though the over-all violence profile may not be vey high.

3. The presence of armed dalams, their free movement and their fire power which would determine the potentiality of an extremist outfit to commit violence acts and be serious threat to internal security. The sophistication in arms holding has to be a determining factor.
4. The spread of active mass front organisations of the Naxal groups that lend constant and effective support in terms of logistics and safe refuge to the armed cadres, needs to be taken into consideration to judge the extent to which particular districts are affected.
5. Extent of pro-active measures initiated by the police/administration to counter the Naxal extremist. *Source:* Parliamentary Standing Committee on Home Affairs 112th Report, Demands for Grants, 2005-2006, New Delhi, Rajya Sabha Secretariat, April 2005.

Did SRE Scheme work?

Here are some of the dilemmas the authorities faced in executing the scheme, and its effectiveness or otherwise to achieve its aims. The SRE scheme is implemented on a re-imbursement basis. What was the level of utilisation of the amounts earmarked? In one word: It had mixed record.

The record for the first year, 2005, was not creditable. The MHA informed the Parliamentary Standing Committee on Home Affairs that until 2005, that

(a) Only 50 per cent of the expenditure was reimbursed.

(b) States were always under financial constraints and were, thus, hesitant to commit funds[41].

Of the total funds budgeted for 2004-2005, Rs 29,20,000 crore, for SRE…in all the three insurgency-hit sectors, viz North-East, Jammu and Kashmir, and Maoist uprising – only Rs 14,97,529 crore was utilised by the States, and the balance Rs 14,22,471 crore was deemed as "saved". Considering this unhappy situation, the MHA decided on 100 per cent re-imbursement and revision of the guidelines. In view of these two major changes, the Committee hoped for better utilisation of funds. As the table below shows, the things have indeed, improved, even if there is scope for further improvement'.

SRE Reimbursement to Naxalite hit States 2006-2009

S. No.	States	2006-07	2007-08	2008-09
1.	Andhra Pradesh	6.1	5.00	308.79
2.	Bihar	0.04	2.30	305.18
3.	Chhattisgarh	9.68	6.50	1540.69
4.	Jharkhand	14.72	4.40	1876.25
5.	Madhya Pradesh	2.51	1.70	381.36
6.	Maharashtra	5.26	3.70	389.49
7.	Orissa	7.16	6.73	969.91
8.	Uttar Pradesh	-	.80	11.46
9.	West Bengal	1.50	2.80	100.19

Data: In crores of rupees.

Source: Adopted from the Annexture to the Reply to Lok Sabha Starred Question No. 276, answered on 4 December 2007, New Delhi: Lok Sabha Secretariat, cited PV Ramana, Note 31, p. 83.

MPF allocations: Analysis of utilisation of Funds

The funds allocated for Modernisation of Police Force (MPF) too were not fully utilised. To wit, of the Rs 1190.63 Crore (Budget Estimates –BE) for 2007-2008, as on 7 March 2008, only Rs 834.96 crore were utilised by the States, leaving Rs 355.67 crore unutilised.[42] The standing Committee on Home Affairs observed : "......The role of the Ministry is not confined to merely allocating funds to States..... but it should insist upon all the States to send utilisation certificates at the earliest in order to ensure that States spend the funds meant for modernisation of thier police forces in an efficient manner."[43]

Even DGPs feel the State prefer Security Response!

To any retired officer as this Author is, it is a big surprise...to be more honest, a revelation...that DGsP of some of the affected States, DG CRPF and top officials of the IB said so in so many words. They said that in a report submitted by the committed which was constituted by the MHA in 2005 and comprising of the above-mentioned officers[44].

> "While the mechanism constituted for countering Naxalism envisaged a multi-pronged approach, over the years the State response has tended to remain largely police centric, with the main effort being to counter the movement with superior force. The approach has often swung from one extreme – that of using overwhelming force...to the other, structured around 'ceasefires' and 'peace talks'. While it is recognised that the Naxal problem goes well beyond mere law and order

dimensions, the broader socio-economic issues have not attracted serious attention......"

Some analysts insist that there does not seem to be a radical change in the government orientation, even if 33 districts have been selected for rapid socio-economic development as a counter-strategy to Maoist ideological onslaught. The Prime Minister said in his 20 December 2007 at the Chief Minister's Conference on Internal Security at New Delhi: "......Affected States must set up Special Task Forces on the Andhra Pradesh pattern and the Centre will provide Assistance for this purpose. I would also urge the Home Ministry to also consider establishing a dedicated trained force at the Centre either as part of an existing force or as a separate one. In fact, an expert panel of the Planning Commission in its report of April 2008 was also of the view that the State response has largely been military oriented. For instance, at the first meeting of the Empowered Group of Ministers (EGoM), constituted to address the Naxalite-issue in a comprehensive manner, the focus was essentially on the 'Security response', while 'development response' was near totally ignored. Then this analyst quotes a daily, without naming it, supporting his views about security centric approach of the State.

A comment is called for on the above analyst's unbalanced views about government adopting security approach to counter the Maoists' mindless violent and murderous tactics. The development work undertaken by various States is ignored to 'suite' one's argument. One can quote dailies – in fact, any number of them – supporting government stand and also clearly asserting and approving its rightness and giving details of development projects undertaken by the State. But then such analysts will quote from obscure daily just to vindicate themselves. That is not being a good or reasonable journalist. If the Prime Minister of a country talks about need for security measures, he has his reason to do so.

Firstly, he was talking to the Chief Ministers on security counter-measures to thwart the Maoists advances using effective and modern weapons. Moreover, they have joined hands with the militants/insurrectionists of North-East, and even worse, with the Maoists of Nepal. When a country's executive head is concerned on the Maoists' increasing threat to India's sovereignty and integrity, he has to speak about more effective security measures! Time for offering peace talks will come when the rebels show some interest in them. Secondly, and more importantly, this analyst forgets that India is facing and battling for over 40 years (1960s-2007) and failed to convince Maoists to take a reasonable stance. In this situation, security measures are the only alternative... continuing with the development projects already in progress over the past couple of decades. Knowing the situation in the North-East and Jammu and Kashmir, the Government will be blamed of dereliction of duty if it does not press on with serious security operations against the enemies of the State, including the Maoists. The Maoists supporters like the one under the lens must understand, if not appreciate such balanced approach of New Delhi.

Some Specialist Units of CRPF and Training Institutions to counter the violent Maoism

The MHA had planned in 2007 some 20 counter insurgency and Anti-Terrorist (CIAT) Schools to impart specialised training to police forces engaged in counter-Maoist operations. They will be trained for counter-insurgency and anti-terrorism operations, as also for jungle warfare. The priority will be four Maoist –hit states, which have been sanctioned seven CIAT Schools: Chhattisgarh 2, Jharkhand 2, Orissa 2, and Bihar 1. An amount of Rs 10.50 crore was sanctioned by mid 2007 for these four States.

It needs to be mentioned in passing that Indian Army is running such a school, Counter-Insurgency and Jungle Warfare (CIJW) School in Mizoram. It has international reputation and besides training Indian Army Officers and men, it also trains personnel from a number of foreign countries. A Brigadier from CIJW school was loaned to the Maoist- hit States to advise and assist them to establish their CIAT schools.

In addition to these CIAT schools, the MHA decided in 2008, to raise 10 battalions of CRPF to create a specialised force to exclusively combat the Maoists. Roughly raising two battalions each year, the target is to be achieved by the end of 2013, even though the Ministry had planned to achieve by 2011. The total cost envisaged was Rs 1389 crore – Rs 898 crore for infrastructure and Rs 491.35 crore for their training. These units were to be designated as COBRA Battalions.

'Rationale', indeed! (Security-heavy Policy)

This scholar, who feels India is adopting security-heavy approach to defeat the Maoism quotes another like-minded analyst to justify his own. biased views on the issue of Maoist uprising. He says while analysing this tendency of security-centric view of the Naxalite issue, one analyst wrote in 2007 that the "...Militaristic approach adopted by the Centre and State govenments in assessing the field level situation, is perhaps extremely convenient to the ruling parties, since a military statistics-driven assessment would emphatically lead to planning on military plane. The execution of development oriented programmes is naturally place at a secondary level."[45] Here is the rationale behind this approach as the scholar sees it: "Thus, the successes of the government are assessed on the basis of number of rebels killed/arrested/surrendered, or incidents of violence or exchange of fire, or numbers of weapons looted from the security forces recovered from the guerrillas."

So, if we are to take these two scholars seriously, the government prefers the security approach against the depredations of the Maoist to win a 'statistical war'! Nothing could be more outlandish than this sort of specious scholarship and analysis! Even the flippancy must have its limits! Such inanity should be denied the dignity of any further comments!

Political Response

The Maoist problem is essentially a political one, even if some opposition parties, Leftist opinion and pro-Maoist intellectuals accuse the government of treating it and tackling it as a law and order problem. The latter group also adds in a self-congratulatory tone, thinking the change in government's perception of the issue is result of their doing, that "the Centre has subsequently, veered around to recognise that the movement has strong socio-economic underpinning." The government's view on the issue is best summed up by some relevant contents of the Report of the Planning Commission's Expert Group, of April 2008: "......The Naxalite movement has to be recognised as a political movement with a strong base among the landless and poor peasantry and Adivasis......Though its professed long-tern ideology is capturing state power by force, in its day-to-day manifestation it is to be looked upon as basically a fight for social justice, equality, protection and local development. The two have to be seen together without overplaying the former....Since the goals of the movement are political, it has to be addressed politically."[46]

Political approach/ response in this context essentially means ameliorating the socio-economic lot of the poor and the deprived tribal and other communities, and bringing the Maoists to negotiations table to end their so-called politically motivated violence. It might sound flippant, but even the Maoists would not interpret the meaning of political response to translate into the Government handing over the State power to them! Before we discuss the nuances of the political response, some pertinent observations are called for. The same follow:

> The apologists are fond of saying that "though its professed long term ideology is capturing state power, in its day to day manifestation it is to be looked upon as basically a fight for social justice, equality, protection and local development. The two have to be seen together without overplaying the former. Since the goals of the movements are

political, it has to be addressed politically."[47] Some comments and correctives are deemed necessary to some of the naive advice these apologists are giving to the government, and pro-Maoist and self-serving arguments they proffer to the other scholars and analysts:

1. "Since the goals of the movement are political, it has to be addressed politically." It seems and reads so reasonable, but, in fact, it is a sinister formulation. They do not expand the implications and ways to address the Maoist violence 'politically'. As one can make out, there are only two ways to do so – through negotiations and vigorous socio-economic development of the poverty-ridden tribal areas. The latter it is carrying on within it resource limitation and in spite of vigorous, violent efforts of the Maoists (to block and thwart this development)! Has any apologist asked the Maoists to shun their violent ways to let the development projects be completed expeditiously, which the apologists claim to be their objective too.
2. In fact, the apologists are being dishonest to themselves, knowing well that if they allow a peaceful environs to the government to complete the socio-economic development of the 'deprived and poor areas', the Maoists lose the very *raison d'être* of their ideology-driven movement.
3. Again, look at their one more ingenious advice: "though its long term ideology is capturing state power by force, in day-to-day manifestation... is to be looked upon as basically a fight for social justice, equality and local development." The nation must ignore their use of violence to capture state power, but it must only pay attention to their "fight for socal justice, equality and local development!" Pray, how do they fight for social justice and development? By killing tribal's, dubbing them as 'informer, murdering labour and contractors who are building roads and executing development projects, and ambushing and killing the security forces! The government should take such murderous activities as Maoist way of achieving equality and social justice, and accept all this with equanimity. To add insult to the injury, the government is advised not to overplay the Maoist use of force to capture state power. Here is the duplicitous advice.

   "The two – to capture state by force....and....to achieve social justice and equally – have to be seen together without overplaying the former." It is not clear as to whom the apologists are trying to fool?

4. In the same vein, some apologists have postulated that Maoists have done socio-economic development of the areas under their control/ influence. Nothing could be more preposterous than this claim. What resources they have to undertake such development? Precisely, 'zilch'! In fact, they thwart such work by looting material brought to the site by official agencies.

What was the record of their fathers (CPM, capturing power through democratic means) in West Bengal and forefathers Russia and China after capturing state power? CPM ruled for over three decades through the local commissars, *'dadas'* in local lingo, who ruled through high handed and repressive ways and got their local charges to vote the party back to power, election after election! No dissent was allowed and neither was real democracy. It needed a feisty Mamata Banerjee to dislodge them from their permanent perch in an election harshly supervised by an Election Commission which meant business. In China, Mao tse Tung unleashed 'cultural revolution' and Grest Leap Forward' to perpetuate oppressive Party rule and today his successor are ruling through capitalist ways under the facade of communism! As for Russia, no dictator can ever hope to better the record of Stalin in repression and genocidal practices. Can one ever forget or forgive the way Stalin and Mao put their own compatriots out of their way by killing en masse and condemning them to labour camps? Will the Indian Maoists be any different if, god forbid, they capture state power by force? Then the apologists might be wiser but that will be too late!

To talk or not to talk

Some analysts of a particular persuation, they can be designated as 'apologists' for Maoists and their excesses, can always trusted to find fault with any and everything the Government do or do note do! This book is an effort to look on both sides of the coin. Not the detailed views of pro-Maoist scholars and then show/discuss the alternative facts and views. As a rule, analysis of pro-Maoist partisans (this Author prefer to call them 'apologists') is given in the first instance, followed by corrective and a more balanced analysis.

Two streams on Talks within the Government

The Planning Commission hold that the government can not rule out the possibility of conducting negotiations with the rebels. But the declared policy of the Centre is that there can be no talks with the Maoists unless they abjure arms and violence.

From Charu to Ganapathy: Consistency on the aim

Charu Mazumdar said: "Militant struggles must be carried on not for land, crops, etc, but for the seizure of State power." The Maoists of today, too, are equally clear and emphatic on it. On the occasion of founding of CPI (Maoist) in October 2004, its two top leaders… Ganapatty and Kishan …made a similar assertion: "The immediate aim and programme of the Maoist party is to carry on and complete the already ongoing and advancing New Democratic Revolution. This revolution will be carried out and completed through protracted people's war with armed seizure of power remaining its central and principal task."

Vacillation and Inconsistency in Government's stand

The Centre categorically stated in its 14-point policy, announce on 13 March 2006 that "there can be no peace talk with Maoists unless they agree to abjure violence and arms." Here, the analyst sees Centre's lack of consistence because earlier at the sidelines of the Conference of Chief Ministers of Naxalite-hit States, the Home Minister had said on 19 September 2005: "If they drop arms, it is good. But if they want to carry arms and still talk .....we have no problem." The "vacillation continues even today", says the analyst, because the Home Minister in an interview told a news agency: "I have not used these words..... Besides, I am too practical to know that they will not lay down arms. They have to halt violence which means halt the wanton destruction of railway tracks, roads, telephone towers, school buildings and bridges."

Comments on the preceding para

One can always find fault if it is one's sole aim. The statement on the sidelines of a conference in 2005 is not a policy statement, which the 2006, 14-point adumberation certainly was one. India is not a dictatorship, as Maoist movement certainly is, and a democratic polity makes its policy changes in the interests of the people, which it represent. The point is valid if the 2009 statement is quoted as 'inconsistency' but only to a point. But in political parlance, as Churchill said once, consistency is characteristic of fools! Moreover, the 2009 statement is wisely nuanced. They may not lay down arms, but they must stop and shun wanton violence, says the Home Minister. It is really an about turn? Even more ironically, if the State is willing to adopt political approach, as its guiding line of action, the apologists, who want the government to avoid security-heavy approach, are still cribbing and critical of it! Obviously, the aim of the Maoist-supporters is to damn the Government, either way if it does or does not do!

Another interesting point is the certificate of consistency given to Maoists from Charu to Ganapathy. Yes, their ideological line and statements following from that are indeed consistence. But that is the way the Communists…CPM, CPI or CPI(ML)…speak, repeat 'speak'! The Central Committee lays down the "party position", and the same get repeated and nauseam down the line. But are they really consistent. In their doctrine and policy statements, the 'negotiations' are not even mentioned. So, they can never be blamed for inconsistency, irrespective of the fact that they engage in negotiations or they do not! So, "If the revolution will be....completed through protracted people's war with the armed seizure of power......", then why are sending missives to the Centre and the States for negotiations? Why do they send the Agniveshes and his ilk to New Delhi.

More on Maoists' Consistency

One does not understand the reasons or motives of the apologists for singing paeans of praise for the Maoists whom one sees as power hungry at ideological level, and murderous lot as human beings! The Maoist-supporters and apologists have spurious and faceous arguments in their praise while castigating the governments for adopting, or at the very least, preferring security approach to the political one – and in so many other aspects of counter-Maoist operations. Here they are singing about their consistency in achieving their goal through armed revolution. If that be so, why are they looking, often desparately, for negotiations with the government? Here is the latest "proof" of their much-touted consistency!

Letters seized from Maoist 'commander' Ghasi alias Chenda Bhushanam, who was arrested in April 2011, indicate that he was in touch with at least one MLA and one MP of the Biju Jantata Dal and one Congress MLA. The daily (Indian Express) of 7.01-13 carries their names also. The ostensible purpose of the Letters was to ask these law makers to attend the Koraput –Srikakulan Divisional Committee meeting at Narayanpatna Block to hear the complaints of the people against the government. Since 2009, this Block, which sits at the tri-junction of Orissa, Andhra Pradesh and Chhattisgarh, has been a Maoist strongh old. This letter was written by Daya, who is Secretary of this Divisional Committee. The real reason for such Letters would be clear once the antecedents of Ghasi, who is presently in Koraput jail, are mentioned. Ghasi, a top 'commander' of the Andhra-Orissa Border Special Zonal Committee, carries a ward of Rs 10 lakh on his head. The 46 year old Ghasi has over 100 cases against his name. This Maoist collected Rs 50-60 lakh a month from local politicians, traders and officials. "Such was his terror that youths were known to extort money in his name with or without his knowledge." This is the type of brigand the apologists extoll for their ideological consistency. Have the latter asked their 'ideological idols' how do they use such huge extortions?

More details on this case and other such related ones will be described in different State chapters.

Will the Maoists come to the Negotiations Table?

The Planning Commission and the Central Government are generally in favour of talks with the Maoists, even if they lay a conditionality of their laying down arms prior to the talks. The critics argue the Centre can not apply different standards for talks with different rebel groups. If the Centre can hold talks with the Naga and the United Liberation Front of Assam (ULFA) rebels with this pre-condition, why not with the Maoists, then? It must be admitted that the Government has not been rigid on this issue. They have shown their readiness for talks, even if the Maoists agree to abjure violence during the period of talks, as the Home Minister's statement, in the preceding paras, indicated. This should be a welcome sign even if when opinion within the MHA is that the Maoists use the period of talks for training and regrouping their cadres.

As for the Maoists, they too seem to be rhetorical on the issue of talks. Even when they periodically express their readiness for talks, they all the time keep maintaining their refrain of "continuing with their armed struggle to capture state power." No wonder the Union Home Minister said, "I regret to say that the response so for has been disappointing." Soon after came the declaration from Muppala Lakshmana Rao alias Ganapathy on 17 October 2009: "We shall confront the new offensive of the enemy by stepping up......heroic resistance and preparing the entire party, People's Liberation Guerrilla Army (PLGA), the various revolutionary parties and organisations and the entire people." It is not only a grand rhetoric, but also grandstanding from Ganapathy.

Now to the ultimate question: How will the Maoist Conundrum be sorted out? These are no easy answers, and certainly not in short term. But one thing is for sure: A country like India cannot be blackmailed into meek submission, and question of its giving in to an outfit like Maoists'. India is a resilient nation which has faced far more serious threat from Nagas, Mizos, ULFA, Manipur and Tripura rebels in the past and these have either resolved or nearing resolution. For the present, India is facing Jihadi terrorism besides the Maoism. Indian polity has...and should have...the confidence and credibility to resolve these two contentious issues too, without offering too much or too many concession! India can concede certain demands of the Maoist to convince them that India too is deeply convinced of socio-economic development of the tribal areas and justice for them in all matters.

In any case, this is the essence of the Maoist movement. But as for their ultimate aim about capturing state power through armed and violent means, they should have no expectations from the nation to receive any kid-gloves treatment. State's might in all its manifestations is, and should be the only response to the violent and murderous ways of the Maoists. This should be quite clear to them and their supporters/apologist.

Again, another point needs to be made about conceding their demands. If the Government does not fulfil their demands, consequent to the negotiations, for valid reasons, they have no business to go to town blaming it of being insincere, as was the experience in Andhra Pradesh in October 2004.

Response of Different States

One view is that, compared to the Centre's, the response of the various states, affected by the Maoist uprising, "has often, if not always, at the least, been found to be lagging and reactive" – with the sole exception of Andhra Pradesh. Some comments are called for the interesting, if somewhat one-sided, analysis of the situation.

- Such generalisation are meaningless in such situations. To dub the States' response as "lagging" and "reactionary", without adducing any evidence for such 'judgement' is indicative of a unilateralism… so often seen in the writings of some analysts of certain bent of mind! In their mind-set, governments can always be, and generally should be, found fault with

  "They are reactionary." In the prevailing situation governments have to 'react'…in fact, they can only react! Maoists' policy is not to negotiate: As and when they are ready for talks, a State Government becomes reactionary if its agrees to respond positively to the Maoists offer to talks. As for the governments, they keep inviting the rebels but to no avail. More ironically, such an initiative…inviting the rebels to talk…is taken sign of governments' weakness! Either way, governments are damned.
- Andhra Pradesh Government is held up as a shinning exception! But what has been the experience of the Government and conduct of the Maoists during the 2004 negotiations? It was the Government's disillusionment and Maoists' duplicity! What was the end result of Governments' sincere exertions to break the logjam? Prevarication, procrastination and evasiveness on the part of the Maoists! Did their supporters and the apologists criticise them for such a conduct, after coming forward for negotiations, much less condemn them?

Is the stance of various governments' uniform on the Maoist issue?

It will normally not be the case...uniformity of response...especially when different political parties are ruling in these states. More significantly, Maoist violence and influence may vary from state to state, and hence a different stance on the issue of negotiations. Not only their stance on this issue, even on the question of threat perception of Maoist insurgency may differ among the State governments. Consequently, different states differ on the question of banning the Maoists.

While the States like Chhattisgarh and Tamil Nadu have proscribed the CPI (Maoist), West Bengal decided against the proscription. Some observations should be appropriate about the decision of the West Bengal Government. Its CPM Government may not have banned it due to ideological reasons. How can a Communist government bana movement led by Communists, of what-so-ever persuation the latter might be! This, when they blamed their arch rival, Mamata Banerjee, of colluding with Maoists during the last two years of their long-running rule in the State. Ironically, by mid-2012 or so, Ms Banerjee as Chief Minister also started feeling the Maoist heat. But, may be, because of past relationship, she has refrained from banning the outfit.

Orissa initially held its hand, but subsequently banned the CPI(Maoist). On the contrary, Karnataka Government too prevaricated on the issue initially, issuing contradictory statements, but finally chose not to ban the CPI (Maoist).

Andhra's is an interest case study for dealing with the Maoist insurgency. It had banned the Maoists, but later, receiving an indication of their readiness for negotiations, the State allowed the ban to lapse. The State initiated talks with the Maoists, but after somewhat prolonged sessions, the talks failed essentially because of their duplicitous and contradictory stances in the end of 2004. The Government was forced to re-impose the ban consequent to the assassination of a sitting MLA in August 2005. Andhra Pradesh was not only the first State to engage the Maoists in negotiations, it was also the first to launch a well-planned offensive against them successfully, and pushing them into Dandakaranya region.

Some critics feel it is pertinent to point out in this context barring the CPI(Maoist), no other Naxalite groups in the country has been banned in any of the States or by the Centre, even when some of them are also committed to protracted arms struggle. This criticism might seem justified at its face value, but to be sure, it will be simplistic! CPI (Maoist) had to be banned since it was created by the merger of several potent outfits engaged in the mission of capturing State power by force of arms and violent means.

It was posing a positive threat to country's sovereignity and intergrity. There are sound reasons for not banning any other Naxalite-like entity. There are certain criteria for an all-India ban...essentially, it must be operating in more than one State, and must be a threat to nation's integrity. There is no such potent outfit on the horizon. The same rule is applicable for the states. There is no rebel outfit in any State that is amenable the required criteria. There may be some outfits known for their nuisance value but nothing more. Some of these may create law and order problem but nothing beyond that! Interestingly, the critics have refrained from naming any such group. One feels their aim was merely to blame the Centre and the States for adopting double standards——but that obviously is not only for fetched but also patently untrue.

Yes, a mention can be made to some civil organisations and individuals who are operating in the Maoist-hit areas as their overground arms, supporters, or apologists. Some of them, especially certain individuals, have in the past, even voiced anti-national sentiments and pronouncement, but the Centre chose to ignore them rather then bestow certain 'respectability' through a ban. Another point need to be made. Proscription of an organisation is the last step. Banning an outfit, without sufficient grounds, gets it prominence and national attention which governments defer till it becomes unavoidable.

Coordination among the States

In the early years of the 2000s, there was not much of coordination between/among the States to combat Naxalism. But the need to do so was accentuated by the 2004 emergence of CPI(Maoist) as a potent armed group with the merger of some prominent Naxalite outfit. But things stated moving by mid 2005 in the right direction as was witnessed with the seizure of 875 empty rockets shell in September 2006. A Little earlier, this trend could be discerned with every single state, hit by the Maoists, submitted its security and development plans for addressing the Naxalite issue towards end August 2006.

During the last couple of years 2010-2012, things have improved a lot by way of inter-state intelligence sharing, operational coordination, and finally setting up some supra-coordination bodies like the Committee of Chief Ministers of affected States. The assertion by the Home Minister/ MHA that the Maoist challenge would be dealth with in three years is overly unrealistic, but at the best it is a pointer to nation's resolve to act purposefully to counter the menace. The more realistic time frame should be 7 to 10 years. If the states like Chhattisgarh, Andhra Pradesh, Jharkhand are resolutely pursuing their counter-insurgency measures through security force operations, socio-economic development and stiffer laws on acquisition of land for industrial purposes, other affected States too are following suite …even if not that passionately.

There is certain measure of consensus among the affected States, and they are accordingly building up the capabilities of their police forces. In the same way, a large number of CPRF men/units are helping the concerned States in combating the insurgents. Specialist units and training schools too have been established for the same purpose. Once the Centre and the States get their act together and succeed in convincing the people (in need of good governance, socio-economic development and justice) of their sincerity and effectiveness, the Maoists will no longer get ready takers of their destructive and coercive ways. The state would reoccupy the space that it had vacated for consequent to depredations. Gradually but surely, the people would either be won over, or at the very least, weaned away from the rebels. Hopefully, that would be time when the Maoists would shut shop, or they would be unwelcome among the very people who were there constituency in the happier times.

"Politics of closet comrades and comrade Congressmen": June 2013

Left wing ideologues usually are a tough lot to tackle and the Indian Maoists of CPI (Maoist) variety are a specimen by themselves. Things become a lot more difficult to deal with these obstreperous outlaws if they get vociferous support from certain Left –Liberal lobby in this country. Unfortunately, some of them are safely ensconced in a Sonia-led NAC, which some commentators dub as India's Super Cabinet.

This Author finds an echo of his views in a letter published on 3 June 2013[47], reproduced here.

> "This is with reference to the editorial 'fight the war like a war' in your weekly of 9.6.2013. After gruesome killing of 27 Congress persons by the Maoists in Dantewada on 25 May, VVIPs of Delhi rushed to Raipur by air along with their bullet proof cars to visit the spot where this ghastly incident happened and to console the bereaved families. Sonia Gandhi looked very worried and nervous. Rahul Gandhi in his speech avoided the word 'Maoists'. Sonia Gandhi's NAC and Manmohan Singh always have difference of opinion and in approach towards this serious problem. Her NAC members and other associates like Aruna Roy, Harsh Mander, Fr John Dayal, Swami Agnivesh and other Leftists being groomed at the JNU, Jadavpur and Kolkata universities are sympathisers of Maoists.

"Top Congress leaders like Digvijay Singh and Manishankar Aiyar have been very vocal in favour of Maoists. After this incident, they have no word to speak. It appears they are still obsessed with imaginary saffron terror.

"The most shocking is that the congress in election rallies in Dantewada has been blatantly propagating about the police excesses. It even withdraw from all-party meeting called by CM Dr Raman Singh. How long can we ignore this monster-like problem? When will the UPA be serious?"

Individual Warriors helping the Maoists

There are a large number of civilians in India, some of them active in civil society movement, who are wittingly or unwittingly helping the Maoists in their violent, murderous insurrection, an armed struggle. Most of them are doing so wittingly out of conviction, ideological impelled or otherwise. Some may be doing so incidentally or accidentally.

Following pages have details of individuals, in a few cases of entities, who are/ can be legitimately dubbed sympathisers/ supporters of the Maoists. This Author has a name for them of his choice: Closet Maoists.

Some among them are well known: Soni Sori, Binayak Den and GN Saibaba. A detailed look at them and their careers in called for. Then there are academics who use the press to help the Maoists, justifying their own conduct and ways. They are called Pen Pusher or Pen warriors. Then there are others who got sucked into the current accidentally or otherwise.

"Activists arrested with Maoist Literature" Ranchi: 10 Sep 2013

Activists in Ranchi criticised Jharkhand police's arrest of two anti-displacement activists of Visthapat Virodhi Jan Vikas Andolan (VVJVA) on charges of being affiliated with the CPI(Maoist). Members of VVJVA, an umbrella organisation opposing forcible land acquisition in Jharkhand and other Ranchi-based activists announced a public meeting on 11 Sep 2013 to oppose the arrests.[48]

One of the arrested/accused, Vishvanath Singh Khairwar, has been working as a caretaker at the VVJVA office in Ranchi since 2009. The other, Utpal Vaske, a cultural activist had come to Ranchi to appear at the hearing by a district court in a 2011 case in which he was earlier accused of being a CPI(Maoist) cadre. The two were arrested at 4 AM on 31 Aug 2013 from the VVJVA office.

Intelligence reports

The FIR says the district armed police on the orders of the SSP Ranchi surrounded VVJVA's office at 3.30 AM on the 31st. He had received the intelligence inputs about the presence of Naxals there to plan an attack. FIR 289/13 at Bariatunates that the two men tried to flee on seeing the police. Varke took out the SIM from his mobile phone and began chewing it when he was ordered to split out on search of the house, Naxal literature was recovered.

Among Naxal literature, the FIR lists "receipts of membership fees of Krantikaari Kisan Samiti (KKS), a CPI(Maoist) publication *'Marxwad Leninwad ke Roshan Lal Jhande ko Uuncha Uthaaye',* and two copies of Ranchi Declaration, publication 'Jan Vikas Model' and the monthly magazine 'Lalkaar' published by VVJVA. The FIR says the two accused confessed to being members of Jharkhand Evan affiliated with the CPI(Maoist).

KN Pandit, 75, Convenor, VVJVA and a trade unionist explains the way it happened: " Our colleagues say that they were about to go for their morning ablutions at 4 AM when the police barged into the office and started harassing them. Vishvanath is from a very poor family from Garhwa handling phone calls and paper work for our meetings since 2009. Uptal had appeared in the Ranchi Court the same day. Our magazines focus on issues of agriculture and people-oriented development. Experts from several states and press have attended our events."

"Earlier they arrested cultural activist Jiten Marandi and his wife in the same manner without any evidence and now they are harassing these people. Displacement is the biggest public issue in Jharkhand and their work is very important", said VVJVA member academic BP Keshri, who retired from the Tribal and Regional Languages department at Ranchi University. "We have already returned some of the literature to their office after we found it was not related to Maoist activities. KKS and Jharkhand Evan are cultural organisations that work as front organisations for Maoist rebels involved in armed struggle and we are still investigating," said DSP(Silli) Anand Tigga.

SSP Ranchi did not respond to request for comment.

The accused have been sent to Birsa Munda Jail.

Kabir Kala artistes took part in arms training": Anti-Terrorism Squad (ATS): 'Culture Vultures' at work Mumbai: 1 Jul 2013

"Charge sheet against four members say they trained with 150 Naxals."[49]

A charge sheet filed against four members of the cultural group Kabir Kala Manch (KKM) on 29 Jun 2013, the Maharashtra ATS alleged that artistes Sheetal Sathe, her husband Sachil Mali and others had participated in three arms training camps between Nov 2011 and Apr 2012 along with 150 Naxals.

Sathe, Mali and two others, Sagar Gorke and Ramesh Gaichhor had courted arrest during Apr-May (2013) outside Vidhan Bhawan in Mumbai. While the group claims it is being targeted for openly criticising governments, the ATS in its charge sheet claims to have gathered witness statements from three surrendered Naxals to show these youths had Naxal links.

Sathe, eight months pregnant, was released on bail by the Bombay High Court (HC) on the 29th. The other three are in judicial custody in the Arthur Road prison. In 2010, six other members of the KKM were arrested but later released on bail by the HC. In granting bail, the Court had said: "sympathy for Maoist philosophy with a likelihood to indulge in various violent activities is not sufficient ground to conclude that the accused are presently active members."

Another member, Angella Sontakke, wife of Teltumbde and an alleged member of Maharashtra State Committee of CPI(Maoist) from Thane district, is still behind bars.

The three surrendered Naxal youths deposed that the four youths, all in their late 20s, along with other members of KKM and Milind Teltumbde, alleged secretary of CPI(Maoist), participated in several camp meetings and arms training. One of the three witnesses told the ATS: "These leaders had appealed to their cadres to follow armed revolt against the capitalists and democracy and to establish the ideology of Mao, Lenin and Marx. All the participants, including the leaders, were carrying rifles." This wintness says 'Korchi Dalam', he was member of, had hacked five persons between 2003-2012. He claimed he had not participated in the killing.

Two similar testimonies of surrendered Naxalites have been attached with the charge sheets along with the ones from other witnesses from among the accuseds colleagues, their relatives to establish their alliance with the KKM.

In the 131-page chare sheet, the ATS has attached 17 witness statements.

The ATS has also called the KKM a front for the Maoists, collecting money for their activities. While senior advocate Mihir Desai rubbished the claims of the ATS, Vijay Hiremath, appearing for the group, said "these testimonies do not invoke any trust." Hiremath noted the evidence gathered against the four pertains to the period only between Dec 2011 and 2012, while the FIR was registered on 25 Apr 2011.

"A Swiss 'tourist' held after he attends a Naxal event"

A foreigner gets involved: Thiruvananthapuram: 30 July 2014

A Swiss national, identified by the police as Jonathan Bord, was arrested in Kerala on 29 Jul 2014 on charges of violating visa regulations after he was found attending a public function held in the memory of a suspected Maoist leader Sinoj.[50]

Bord, 24, who had been on a tourist visa, was picked up from Thriprayar in Thrissur where an ultra-Left group had organised a meeting to commemorate Sinoj on the 28th. Sinoj, a native of Valappad near Thriprayar, was alleged killed while handling explosives.

A Thrissur magistrate Court remanded Bord in judicial custody for 14 days. Section 14(b) of Foreigners Act and Section 2(b) of Foreigners Amendment Act were slapped on him. The police told the press: "He says he is a research scholar on Communism. Malayalam and English literature on Communism were seized from his hotel room in Kannur." The police futher added: "Bord had come to the venue after reading about the incident in a local English daily. He had also attended the 'Save Gaza' meeting organised by CPI(M) in Kozhikode last week. He gave a short interview to CPI(M) daily. Deshabhimani, introducing himself as Mathews, a research scholar and a proud Communist."

The police sought the help of an interpreter after Board claimed he was not familiar with English. It suspected it to be a ploy as he sought to speak only after intervention of the Swiss Embassy. People who had attended the meeting said Bord had Communicated in English there.

Meanwhile, ultra-Left activists deplored the arrest of Swiss man.

"Swiss man held for attending 'Maoist event' in Kerala freed:"

Kochi: 10 Aug 2014

This is the second news story on the Swiss man held in Kerala. It deals with the event of his release on 9 Aug 2014, after 12 days in jail[51].

Some additional points will be included in this piece. Bord, "who plans to return to his country next week, has to face trial in the case registered for violation of visa conditions. A student of International Economic History in Geneva, Bord is yet to get back his passport." For that, the Swiss Embassy would have to furnish an undertaking that "it will produce him for further proceedings either in the Court or before the police whenever required." The Kerala High Court granted him bail on the Eighth.

The circumstances of his arrest had been mentioned above. A Left-Sympathiser, "he fell into the hands of the police, who saw a Maoist in the foreigner." As police could not establish Maoist links, he was charged under section 14(b) of the Foreigners Act, which pertains to any act in violation of the conditions of the valid visa issued for entry and stay in India.

Although police did not single out any specific violation of the Act, Thrissur District SP N Vijayakumaran says, " A tourist is here only for sightseeing. He should not have attended that meeting. We are not concerned whether he is a research scholar or not."

Bord's professors at Geneva University rushed letters to Kerala saying he is a genuine research scholar, who had shown interest in social movements there as well. His thesis guide Prof Mathieu Leimgruber said, " As a student representative of the faculty of social sciences, Boud had participated in a very committed way in several Committees and governing bodies of the University of Geneva."

Boud and his friend Valerie reached India on 1 July. After visiting various states/places, he landed in Kozhikode on 25 July, and attended an event organised by the CPI(M). He then moved on to Thriprayar in Thrissur, where he attended a function organised by the Sinoj Memorial Committee.

A police team detained him after the function as he wasn't carrying his passport and Id proof. However, the Valappad police got a copy of his passport that night. In the mean time, he was questioned by the IB. On 29 July, he was produced in the magistrate Court which remanded him in police custody for 14 days.

Boud's counsel in the HC P Ravindranath called the case a classic example of miscarriage of justice. He plans to file a fresh plea seeking quashing of the FIR.

"If I don't come back, means police have put fear into me"

Kochi: 13 Dec 2014

This is the third news story on the Swiss man Boud, on his ultimate release from jail on 2 Dec 2014[52].

The daily sums up the entire sad story of Jonathan Boud in the opening two paragraphs.

" On Friday (12 Dec 2014), a 24-year-old Swiss tourist left Kerala with unforgettable memories of nearly six months spent in 'God's own Country.' So unforgettable, that he now plans to file a case for compensation to make up for these six months."

"The story of Boud has to be read to be believed – jail, bail, Court, 28 Jul- 2 Dec (2014), and the release."

And all this for spending a few moments at a public meeting held near Thrissur in memory of a suspected Maoist who died in June (2014). On the insistence of organisers, for whom a foreign face was a novelty at the meeting, Boud also said a few words there: "Thank you for welcoming me, I appreciate the democracy in the Country." He was arrested a few minutes later, as he was walking to a bus stop.

The Kerala HC "observed last week" while quashing the charge sheet against Boud, "No doubt, continuance of this prosecution will be a sheer abuse of the legal process." And, here is what Boud said before boarding the flight to Geneva. "Hearing my case and other cases. I feel India's judiciary is fair. The questions the judge posed to the prosecution made me hopeful of a positive outcome." Contrary to what one could expect, Boud wants to return to India one day, "If I don't come back, that means police have succeeded in driving fear into me."

His advocate confirmed that Boud would seek compensation for losing out on a semester of his International Economic History course at Paul Bairoch Institute of Economic History in Geneva. Then, there is the mental trauma and financial loss due to a "baseless case", and a possible appeal to the National Human Rights Commission. The local police had tried to make a case by highlighting Boud's self-avowed Marxist leanings and some research papers found in his possession. They also played a video of him at the function. But at the HC, Justice Pubaid was firm. "The prosecution does not have a firm or clear case."

Ironically, the video ended up working in Boud's favour—while the police said he was at the function for 15 minutes, the clipping was of just two minutes. Bouds sums it all up: "I could not find any reason why I was jailed."

Boud arrived in India with his friend Valerie on 1 July with a visa valid till September. The two had reached Kerala 9 days later. He attended the Sinoj memorial meeting on the 28th, after which he was arrested, "which was sheer abuse of power by police", he says. He was taken to the Valappad police station in Thrissur, and grilled by officials of Kerala police, State intelligence and IB. He says: "I was taken into custody at 5 PM. The police continued to question me until 1 AM without allowing me to even contact my friend or anyone else. Some ten officials repeatedly questioned me, about my links with Maoists. I told them I was innocent and had nothing to do with the Maoist movement. They insisted I was a foreign agitator brought to Kerala by the organisers of the meet. I showed them my passport and bus tickets, but they would not believe me."

But soon he came to know that he was detained under section 14(b) of the Foreigners Act, as already explained above. He was remanded to police custody for 14 days. From a sub-jail in Irinjalakkuda, he was shifted to the Central Jail, Thrissur.

"I was in jail and refused to meet anyone including my friend", he recalls. Police questioned him again, this time with the help of a French translator. On 7 August, he was released on bail by the HC, with the condition that the Swiss Embassy would furnish an undertaking to produce him for further proceedings, either in court or before the police. But Baud's lawyers P Raveendranath and Sukumar Oommen claimed the Embassy failed to provide any such undertaking, telling them that such an act went against their country's Constitution.

The lawyers took care of Baud thereafter, helping him find a shelter in Kochi while their, petition for quashing the case was being heard there.

Meanwhile, Bauds friends back home started raising funds for his defence because his parents…his father is a social worker and mother a school teacher…could not shoulder the burden alone. Baud's mother even came to Kochi to support her son.

Ravendranath believes the following facts helped Baud in the Court: the meeting he attended had not been banned; there was no case against the organisers; they had caught only the Swiss tourist; and as evidence, police even produced the poster on the meeting, in Malayalam but did not book the person who wrote it. Even among the 61 objects, or documents, produced by the police to substantiate the case, there was little to link Baud to Maoism, since a major chunk comprised his personal belongings and literature on Marxism. Yet again, there was nothing to show that Baud was a radical or a member of any radical outfit in India or abroad.

Justice Ubaid ruled: "The DG, Prosecution repeatedly said that attending a meeting itself amounts to violation of visa conditions. I find no such rule prohibiting the alleged act of attending a meeting.....Tourists visiting Kerala can see different meetings organised by political or other groups. They can not identify whether a meeting is organised by political, or communal or radical groups. They, out of curiosity, may just step in and view such meetings. If that is understood as violation of Visa conditions, every tourist visiting Kerala will have to be prosecuted.

On video clipping, the Judge said "what is made available to me has nothing objectionable. I fail to understand on what material or on what basis police suspected that he is a radical."

At the end of it all, Baud flew out on a exit permit granted by the Bureau of Immigration. SP Thrissur Rural N Vijaya Kumar said: "We don't know why the court was not convinced of the case. The Maoist threat has to be tackled effectively. Police acted according to what we had learnt..... we would go by what the court says."

"128 Naxal fronts of CPI (Maoist) exposed"

New Delhi : 11 Oct 2013

"Intends to enlist support and prep for violent revolution." This is the blurb of the article that appeared in a daily in Oct 2013[53].

This is an important analytical article on the Maoist ways of spreading their tentacles in the country, and the need for India to be on the alert and be forewarned of the impending deluge and violent convulsions unless desired counter-measures are initiated in time.

It also shows how aware and normal citizens are converted into fellow-travellers through some of these fronts and finally into sympathisers and supporters. The Gautam Navlakhas are the finest examples of the success of the Maoists in creating their most passionate, aggressive and shouting clones for their cause. This Author's name for this species is "closet Maoists."

The article is so well-written and its examination of the Maoists' fronts so realistic that it is considered necessary not to change a word of it. Consequently, what follows is the full, unabridged text of the article that appeared in the daily.

Text of the Article

"The banned CPI(Maoist) has put in place as many as 128 front organisations across 16 states for carrying Naxal propaganda and bringing newer areas under its influence.

"Apart from the Naxal-hit states, there are as many as nine such outfits in Delhi, three in Gujarat, eight in Haryana, 10 in Punjab, 12 in Karnataka, four each in Kerala and Tamil Nadu and two in Uttarakhand.

"Among the Naxal-hit States, Jharkhand tops the list with 17 front organisations, followed by 13 in Andhra Pradesh, 10 each in Bihar, and Odisha, nine each in West Bengal and Maharashtra, six in Chhattisgarh and two in Uttar Pradesh.

"The propaganda stage is the first step by the Maoists before carrying out violence. The front outfits also mobilise people against the State when the Maoists suffer setbacks at the hand of security agencies.

"These outfits intend to create disenchantment among the masses against State apparatus with the twin objective of enlisting their support for *dharnas* and demonstrations and to prepare them for violent revolution later.

"The growth of these outfits in States like Delhi, Haryana, Punjab in the north, Gujarat in the West, and Karnataka, Kerala and Tamil Nadu in the south is an indication that Maoists aim to enlarge their area of operations and arc of violence. The expansion in these States also suggests that the ultras have plans to bring urban areas the ambit of Naxal violence, a senior security official explained.

"The active outfits in Delhi include Delhi General Mazdoor Front, Democratic Students' Union, Nari Mukti Sangh, Revolutionary Democratic Front, Vikalp (cultural front), Forum Against War on People, Committee for Release of Political Prisoners, People's Democratic Front of India, and Mehnatkash Mazdoor Morcha. Gujarat working Class Wing, Karatikari Kamdar Sangathan and Naujwan Bharat Sabha.

"The outfits under the scanner of security agencies in Haryana include Disha Sanskritik Manch, Jan Chetna Manch, Karantikari Mazdoor Sangathan, Mahila Mukti Morcha, Naujawan Dasta, Shaheed Bhagat Singh Kisan Manch and Shivalik Jan Sangharsh Manch. The outfits in Punjab include Jamhoori Adhikar Manch, Kirti Mazdoor Union, Lok Manch, Punjab Radical Student Union, operations Green Hunt Virodhi Jamhoori Manch."

Kabir Kala Manch: Also a Maoist Front

A daily had reported in Jun 2012 that "Kabir Kala Manch artistes had taken part in arms training in Maoist camp." In a charge sheet file against four members of this cultural group, the Maharashtra Anti-Terrorist Squad (ATS) alleged that artistes Sheetal Sathe, her husband Sachil Mali, Sagar Gorke, and Ramesh Gaichhor, had participated in three arms training camps between Nov 2011 and Apr 2012."

What a cruel irony: people using the name of an apostle of peace, harmony and communal brotherliness Saint, Kabir indulging in murderous violence.

168: Summary of Maoist Fronts (Number)

52: In Non-Maoist hit states		76: In Maoist hit states	
Delhi	9	Jharkhand	17
Gujarat	3	Andhra	13
Haryana	8	Bihar and Odisha (each)	10
Punjab	10	WB and Maharashtra (each)	9
Karnataka	12	Chhattisgarh	6
Kerala and Tamil Nadu each	4	UP	2
Uttarakhand	2		

Human Rights Wallahs (HRW)

A Dangerous species in India

Human Rights (HR) movement the world over must have started with noble aims and lofty purposes. HR activists wanted to secure the rights of the poor, the downtrodden and deprived sections of the society in every country. Its headquarters are located in the capitals of the richest countries of the world. HRw, obviously, convinced themselves that oppression against the poor and deprived was practised by the governments and rich classes of the third world countries of of the world. India was on the top of the last of such countries where their services were urgently required.

These West-based HRW easily got and coopted their local clones in every country they started their do-gooder operations. In India, they came to be known as Jholawallahs, because they all carried one strung over their shoulder. It is from this term that this Author has coined the term HR Wallahs. Today, most of them are supporters of LWE/Maoists. Presently, situation has reached where the HRW Brigade feel the only persons whose HRs are under threat are the 'poor' Maoists!

It was in this context that a senior journalist wrote in a moment of genuine pain and despair about the actions of these HRW:

"For these selective peddlers of human rights, only 'innocent' Maoists and equally 'innocent' LeT activists like Ishrat Jahan need to be defended against the predatory Indian State. They fit perfectly into an uncharacteristically acerbic remark former Prime Minister PV Narasimha Rao once made: 'From the hue and cry made by some people every time an encounter takes place, it would seem in India only terrorists have human rights and nobody else does."[54]

The above is a sort of preamble to the three entries on the following pages on the subject under discussion: Human Rights.

"Bullet for every bullet"

This is the heading of an editorial in a daily in May 2012. Its blurb: "That is the only way to exterminate Maoist terror."

This is about as blunt and scathing title of an editorial as any Indian daily could have chosen to express its strong feelings against the Maoists and their murderous ways.[55]

The editorial was occasioned by the Supreme Court "dismissing an absurd plea by a group of self-appointed activists ('HRW' is a better term as explained above) for an 'independent' inquiry into the death of Cherukuri Raj Kumar alias Azad, spokesperson and senior member of the CPI(Maoist)."

Raj Kumar was killed in an encounter with the police in Andhra Pradesh in Jul 2010, and few tears were shed over his death. Since then the Jholewallahs, who are obsessed with protecting the HRs of terrorists and mass murderers guilty of inhuman crimes, have been maligning Andhra Pradesh police by accusing it of killing Raj Kumar in a 'fake' encounter. Now that the apex Court has virtually repudiated their alleged version of events, born of their jaundiced, if fervent, imagination, the sanctimonious activists must desist from spreading their perverse canard any further.

Although it was neither necessary nor called for, the government the circumstances of Raj Kumar's death. It came to the conclusion that the ultra was killed in an encounter, and it was not a staged one. Ignoring the CBI findings, the activists went on to demand an inquiry by a SC-appointed SIT or a judicial Commission to ascertain the 'truth'. This was obviously a play to remain in the headlines. By rejecting their fresh plea, the SC has put these busy-bodies in their place. Will these HRW act gracefully and stop peddling their bunkum on their pet issue? Are we demanding too much from this Maoist Fan Club?

Now came the usual ploy from these HRW: The ultra was killed when he was engaged in seeking a cease-fire deal and was negotiating for it with Union Home minister P Chidambram. Obviously, no third person was privy to these 'talks'. If that was so, why would forces kill him, and again, what was he doing in the jungles? He should have used emissaries for the talks. Was he trying to reach New Delhi for one-on-one with Chidambram? If he really was engaged in 'talks', at least, he should have abandone his violent campaign and also told his comrades to stop their murderous assault on the Indian State. He did neither. He continued to live by gun and died by it when the police caught up with him in his playground, the jungles. He died the way a more reputed guerrilla of his ilk, Kishanji, did in the forests of West Bengal in Nov 2011. Some 'closet Maoist' had then too claimed that Kishanji was 'coming' for peace talks! These Maoists have a strange ways of 'talking' peace. "No sincere peace-maker needs to die such a violent death, no police man lusts for blood as the Maoists do."

It is time we accept that the Indian State and the Maoists are locked in a war which the former can't afford to lose and the latter are determined to win, no matter what the cost! Dealing with Maoists is unlike dealing with political rebels who may have a cause but not an ideology of hate. To that extent, the war on Maoists is integral to India's war on terror…if the Jihadis pose a threat to the nation, so do the Maoists. The only difference is the shade of their banner. In this asymmetrical war, security forces will suffer casualties, there will be collateral damage, but that should not deter the

State from inflicting overwhelming costs on those who wants to destroy the republic through armed means.

"It is a 'plain slaughter' in Bijapur": say Rights activists: Hyderabad: 28 July 2012

It is the other end of the spectrum, as for Indian press is concerned. This is a report in a daily, known for its Leftist leannings. The entire story is based on the report of HRW, and contents are on expected lines. Still it must be reported to see other side of the hill.

An all-India fact-finding team of HRW (the daily uses the term "rights activists") "has brought out graphic details of what it described as the 'plain slaughter' of tribals of Sarkeguda and Kottaguda in Bijapur district of Chhattisgarh as the CRPF gave no quarter even to those who survived its firing on the 28 June (2012) night. The 16-member team had visited Sarkeguda, Kottaguda and Rajpenta on 6 and 7 July.

The report claims villagers told it that "those who did not die from bullet wounds were killed by the police with axis they picked up from the village itself."

Eye witnesses, including the media persons who saw the bodies, said "the victims were brutalised with deep hacking cuts in the chest and foreheads."

"I have never seen such a butchery in my 25 years' work in human rights", said VS Krishna, General Secretary, Human Rights Forum, referring to the death of 17 Adivasis in the firing by CRPF and CoBRA men. Some 60 Adivasis had assembled around 8 PM on 28 June in an open area between Sarekeguda and Kottaguda. As the sowing reason was about to begin, they were to discuss *biju pondum*, the traditional seed sowing festival, distribution of land for tilling, lending help to families without cattle, deciding rent for a new tractor and arrears of Rs 10,000 due to them for tendu leaf collection."

"It was a cloudy night and visibility was poor. A contingent of CRPF and CoBRA commandos, numbering over a hundred, cordoned off the area. At about 10 PM, there was a burst of gunfire, that hit three Adivasis, killing them instantly. Firing followed from other directions, sending the terrified villagers running and screaming. It continued for some 30 minutes after which CRPF men fired two flares to light up the area and survey the scene."

"16, including six minors, died that night, and one of the next day. The 17th victim was Irpa Ramesh. After the firing began, he made it to the safely of his house, and stepped out at dawn to survey the area. He was fired upon immediately and, though hit, he managed to get back into his house."

The CRPF men followed and clobbered him to death with a brick in front of his wife and three children, and also took away Rs 5,000 from their house, the report said.

The CDRO sought to debunk the CRPF's attempts to portray of carnage as a result of an exchange of fire with dreaded Maoists and Union Home Minister Chidambram's repetition of this claim. Observing that the plea of self-defence was a favourite invocation by police to explain away extra judicial killings, the team said there was no exchange of fire, it was one-sided, unannounced and unprovoked. It was plausible that the injuries to six CRPF and Cobra men were caused by firing by their colleagues from the other side.

"Hear the silence of our human rights activists"

"Maoists plant explosives in the abdomen of CRPF jawans and put them to brutal death. But the regular band of bleeding hearts that cries out when the State targets the Red terrorists, has not squeaked a word in protest now."

New Delhi: 15 Jan 2013 (Silence of HRW)

This article in a daily deals with the silence of HRW and the bleeding-heart liberals over the inhuman and depraved atrocities committed by the Maoists over the bodies of the slain CRPF men. It also deals with the money the Maoists make by exploiting the forest wealth of the area under their influence/control.[56]

Above the sound of gunfire and IEDs was the deafening silence of the Human Rights Industry, Binayak Sen, Arundhati Roy and Mahasweta Devi *et al,* quick to berate Government over alleged atrocities against murderous Maoists, did not squeak when Maoists in Latehar, Jharkhand surgically planted IED/ explosives in the stomachs of two slain CRPF men on 10 Jun 2013, after 17 persons, including 12 CRPF jawans, lost their lives in operations in the Latehar forests. One, DGP Jharkhand has said that the Maoists are receiving support from outside India. Two, the connection between the mineral wealth of the forests and the Maoists operating there-in can no longer be ignored. In Latehar district alone, there are twenty coal blocks, eight of them in private sector.

The situation calls for deep introspection. In Africa, countries have been torn apart by rebel militias that have seized control of rich mines by terrorising the countryside, they are exceedingly well-armed and have links with international Corporations. In India, Maoists thrive in mineral-rich districts of Odisha (15), Jharkhand (14), Bihar (7), Andhra Pradesh (10),

Chhattisgarh (10), MP (8), Maharashtra (2), and West Bengal (1). Conservative estimates put at Rs 14 billion the Maoists make annually through extortion from these districts.

Human Rights activist Suhas Chakma warns that Maoists acquire huge amounts of explosive substances and detonators from mining companies and pose a major threat to the country. In a presentation to the Parliamentary Standing Committee on Coal and Steel in 2011, he said the security forces recovered 1,50,940 Kg of ammonium nitrate explosives, 60,511 detonators, 8000 rings for grenade making, and 1,964 kg of gelatin and 1,918 gelatine sticks from Maoists between Jan 2009 to Sep 2010. In the same period, security forces say Maoists snatched 54,500 Kg of explosives.

It is pertinent that explosives are issued from the government factories to various licensees. The easy access to explosives has enormously empowered the Maoists in recent years, they no longer need to confront the security forces, but simply cause casualties on them through ambushes and plant mines on the roads and explode them through detonators obtained from the mining industry. In large swathes of Maoist-hit districts, the writ of the Indian State is confined to the fortified camps of the security forces.

But in the same districts, mining companies operate successfully. May be, they are in league with the Maoists, obliging them with certain supply of explosives. Beyond that, the Maoists enable/force these companies to engage in illegal mining beyond the licensed areas and share the booty. That should be possible by keeping locals and snoopy officials at bay.

Knowing its potential for mischief, and even more sinister threat to internal security, the government must strictly monitor the procurement, stocking, and end use of all explosives issued to licensees. Strict punitive action must be take whenever a leakage is detected in any areas whether voluntarily or under Maoist threat. Even when the PM has described Maoists as biggest threat to India's internal security years back, his Government has displayed little seriousness in protecting tonnes of explosives held by the State-owned mining companies. Coal India Ltd for instance, buys explosives worth Rs 1,500 Cr annually for mining purposes, which constitute 30 per cent of the total explosives used in the country. The explosives, including gelatine and detonators, commonly used by Maoists in landmines, are stocked in 150 storehouses across eight states, seven of which are in the Maoist belt. "The security arrangements here are utterly inadequate, despite instances of Maoists looting the depots."

The lack of concern afflicts the political level as well. There has been no amendment to the Explosives Act, 1184 or the Explosives Rules (Revised 2008) to ensure that explosives sold or sanctioned to licencees are used only for the lawful activities or the purposes allowed under the Act and the Rules. Nor is there any provision for monitoring end use of explosives by physical inspection on-site, there is only banal rule 24 of the Explosives Rules, 2008 which calls for "maintenance of records and submission of returns." End-use monitoring could curb the menace of illegal mining, to a large extent.

As of now, explosives are sanctioned by the Petroleum and Explosive Safely Organisation (PESO) under the Ministry of Commerce and Industry. Thus, the anti-terror bodies like Multi-Agency Centre (MAC) under the MHA, or the State MAC are unaware of the explosives and other materials being sanctioned by PESO.

The human costs of easy access to detonators and explosives are devastating. As per the South Asia Terrorism Portal, from Jan 2005 to 14 Nov 2010, Maoists triggered 533 explosive devised bombs, of which 380 explosions were fatal and caused the death of 442 persons and injuries to 422 others. Between Jan and Dec 2011, Maoists triggered 72 bombs, damaging public property like bridges, school buildings, police stations, rail tracks and killing 50 persons including six civilians. The failure to regulate mining is putting India's security forces and civilian lives at grave risk.

Maoists operate in regions rich in iron ore, coal, bauxite, manganese, and other minerals with the potential to attract large investments (and provide handsome extractions). No one should be under the illusion that the Maoists are fighting on behalf of poor villagers and tribal communities whose resources are being exploited, they have killed more than 9,200 civilians and security persons since 1998.

At Latehar, the authorities hoped to nab Maoist Central Committee member Dev Kumar Singh alias Arvindji. But information of the raid by 300 CRPF and anti-Maoist Jharkhand Jaguars was leaked and the group ambushed. In a deadly surprise the Maoists booby-trapped the bodies of two jawans with IEDs. The body of Baidyanath Kisku exploded when moved, killing four villagers. Luckily, the body of Babulal Patel did not explode when airlifted to Ranchi District hospital. But the police who recovered a 2.75 Kg IED from the abdominal cavity. A search of the surrounding the jungles revealed that the Maoists had practised this ghastly tactic on innocent animals.

"IED supply to Maoists: CEO, 8 held" Hyderabad, Bhubaneswar: 17 Sep 2013: Innocent or helpless?

Nine employees of a Hyderabad-based construction firm, Lekcon Infrastructure Pvt Ltd, including its CEO A Bhupal, were arrested

14 Sep 2013 on charges of supplying explosives to Maoists in Malkangiri district.

District SP Akhilesh Singh said the nine were arrested with 50 Kg of IEDs, gelatine power, potassium nitrate and a lot of Maoist literature.

Threatened by Maoists and facing financial losses due to delay in completion of road projects, the firm allegedly agreed to supply explosives to Maoists on the Andhra Pradesh-Odisha border areas in exchange for letting work continue at its various sites.

It was sixth such incident this year (2013) of police intercepting vehicles of construction firms working in Odisha or Chhattisgarh and finding cash or goods meant for Maoists. In the past, Andhra police seized food, rations and medicines, besides cash from the employees of construction firms working in the two neighbouring states. The firms buckle in under threats by Maoists to kidnap or kill employees, and destroy their machinery.

An official of the firm Narendra Naidu denied the charges, saying the explosives were meant for construction and they were not connected to Naxalites in any way. The BSF and Odisha police seized the explosives from the SUV of Bhupal. The eight others travelling with him were also arrested. The nine were produced before a local court on the 15th.

Enjoying a good reputation, the Rs 200 crore Lekcon Infrastructure is involved in road construction in Balimela, Kalimela, and Padi areas of Malkangiri district, apart from roads and irrigation projects in other parts of the State and Chhattisgarh. It also has a small raw materials mixing plant near Potrel village.

The employees had left Hyderabad on the 13th and had crossed the border into Odisha from Khammam.

They were nearing Potrel in Malkangiri district where they allegedly were to hand over the explosives to Maoists when they were intercepted.

The SP said they had got suspicious of Bhupal's movements as he had travelled once earlier to Malkangiri allegedly to deliver explosives to an arms dealer of the Maoists. "We received information that vehicle carrying Bhupal and others was again on its way towards Potrel village and we intercepted it. Besides gelatine sticks, we also found nitric acid and 34 other types of explosives in various quantities in 12 gunny bags. Bhupal said he was going to deliver these to Karunakar Reddy, who we believe is the arms dealer working for Maoists and is currently absconding. Bhupal as well aware that the explosives would ultimately reach the Maoists…They had materials the construction firms normally don't require. The material is normally used for making Claymore mines. Some two weeks back too, they had brought about 80 Kg of such explosives for Maoists. Though we had intelligence inputs then, we could not catch them red-handed."

Police also found several new mobile phones and Maoist literature in Telugu in the vehicle which the firm had got translated on Maoists' demand. A couple of bags containing more explosives were allegedly found dumped behind a small factory owned by Lekcon Infro in Patrel village. A Tata Xenon vehicle and a Bolero pick-up vehicle were also seized.

Malkangiri police officials said apart from Karunakar Reddy, another arms dealer working for the Maoists in Chitrakonda are, Sudhakar Reddy, was to collect the consignment but fled when police intercepted the vehicle.

Officials of the anti-Maoist Special Intelligence Branch said Construction and infrastructure companies were major targets of Maoists and were forced to pay protection money or provide medicines, food and rations or arms and explosives to them in exchange for letting their project go smoothly. In April (2013), the General Manager of a Pune-based construction firm was arrested by the Khammam police with Rs 50 lakh in cash that he was carrying to be paid for alleged protection money to Maoists in Chhattisgarh.

Apart from Bhupal, the eight arrested were C Sudhakar Naidu, T Yogananda, Y Lingamaya, N B Ravi Kumar, K Sudhakar, Pradeep Biswas, G Ratnam, and Benu Madhab.

Comments on this article

The police did not catch Bhupal and others red-handed. It is a weak case, which the police officers are boasting as some kind of a great success. Throughout the narration, police is vainly patting itself on the back. The case would not stand in a court. One does not know why the daily was tongue-tied when police is going on and on. One simple question would have left the police gasping for breath: Why did not they wait till the actual transaction——Bhupal handing over the stuff to the Maoist arms dealer, —took place? That would have been "catching red-handed." The entire boast of police is 'foolish', and the daily's scribes even more foolish! To be generous towards the police: they were just being amateurish!

"The In-Betweeners" :7 May 2012 (Mediators Imediation)

"A Mediators tell their views. Whole history of mistrust and failed dialogue stalks this 'diplomacy.' "

This is a detailed article in a weekly about mediators and mediation history about the talks between the government and the Maoists. Its opening shot is well-aimed even if rhetorical[57]. It is mediator's version!

"What is the fuss all about?" It is a Maoist interlocutor asking, with just a hint of irritation, referring to the outrage caused by the abduction of Chhattisgarh's Sukma DC Alex Paul Menon. And what about the thousands of 'innocent' villagers detained by the state after being labelled Maoist, he asks rhetorically.

Significantly, the MHA annual report is silent on number of Maoist arrested and held in jails. The interlocutors believe the number would run into thousands, possibly as high as 20,000 or more in 9 States. The MHA says there have been 1,554 abductions by Maoists in the last four years (489 in Chhattisgarh, 463 in Jharkhand) with 328 of the kidnapped not returning alive.

The interlocutors (more popularly, mediators) under mention in this analytical story are: Dr BD Sharma, the administrator and one-time DM in Bastar; Swami Agnivesh, the activist; Prof G Hargopal, the academic, and Dandapani Mohanty, the trade unionist.

The interlocuters unanimously believe the high-value abduction, like that of DM Paul Menon, by Maoist will go on. Mohanty, who was involved in the negotiations for release of two Italians and BJD MLA Jhina Hikaka taken hostages in Odisha in Apr 2012, believes such abduction by Maoists are part of a counter-strategy to ease pressure on themselves and draw attention to their demands. The one not mentioned by Mohanty is that they grab prime-time head lines.

Maoists generally treat their hostages well, says another mediator, Dr Sharma. Paul's abductors did allow medicines to be brought in for him. On the day before Sharma was flown to Raipur to mediate, he was confident that no harm would come to Paul.

The mediators believe the governments, whether in the States or at the Centre, are not serious about a lasting solution. Once the DM is released, everything will go back to square one! "The security forces would resume operations, make their presence felt by destroying alleged Maoist hideouts, holding alleged sympathisers, and "unleash their own brand of terror." One of them is cynical: "Paul, meanwhile will go on leave, then seek a transfer to the capital on a central deputation to recover from the trauma." The weekly says, "he adds with a chuckle."

While governments are averse to holding dialogues with underground outfits, seeking to overthrow by violent means democratically elected power structures, they scarcely allow rebels to kidnap or kill civil servants, policemen or politicians.

Sharma was rather expansive on the issues involved: "Tribals who refuse to move out or resist the plunder of their resources are all described as the Maoists. In the US, some 200 years ago, the native Americans put up a resistance and subdued only at gun point. History is repeating itself in India with the State usurping minerals, water and forests for business and corporate interests.

The abduction of one DC here or one MLA there is of peripheral interest. Both the state and media refuse to address the real issues, which to my mind are ownership and distribution of natural resources, State oppression and injustice meted out to tribals....". A day before he is due to negotiate with the Maoists and the Chhattisgarh government for Paul's release, he maintains that unless the core issues are addressed, any peace overtures couldn't possibly last.

But not all mediators are convinced about the 'war over resources' theory. Swami Agnivesh feels that the issue is overblown, because it serves everyone's interest. The Maoists, he feels, enjoy disproportionate notoriety when one compares their strength and support base. His suspiciousness, perhaps surprisingly, find endorsement in a survey carried out by the Centre for Study of Developing Societies (CSDS) two years ago. CSDS fellow Sanjay recalls that survey in Maoist-hit areas indicated that the situation is not 'as bad as it is portrayed.' The discontent, the repression, the terror were all exaggerated. Agnivesh believes the embellished threat perception serves everyone's interest.

The civil servant and the policeman can get away with anything in such circumstances, he points out. He goes even beyond: "There is apparently a scramble among civil servants to secure a posting in Maoists – hit areas. They are said to be lured by prospect of a mandate of zero accountability, no responsibility and the chance to spend or appropriate public funds."

For the record, Rs 2,600 Cr has been spent in 78 Maoist-hit districts in the last two years under the Integrated Action Plan (IAP) by the Centre. And another Rs 18,000 Cr has been or is being spent under the Road Requirement Plan (RRP).

The interlocutors are, however, unanimous that governments at whatever level, do not mean business. They all claim to have been let down by the government at one time or the other.

Sujato Bhadra, an academic and human rights activist from Kolkata, quips, "It is a sad commentary that the State responds more readily to violence." He has own sad story to tell. He was handpicked by Ms Mamata Banerjee to broker talks between Maoists and the West Bengal Government. Bhadra recalls a meeting he was invited to attend in Kolkata before the 2009 General Elections, along with the representatives of the Left Front Government then in power and Election Commission (EC) officials. The EC and State Government wanted an undertaking that the Maoists would not disrupt the polls. In return, the Left Front Government promised to review cases against Maoists following the polls. But while the Maoists kept their word, and elections passed without an incident, the cases against Maoists were never reviewed.

A bitter Mohantly remembers the time in 2004 when he, Varavara Rao and others were invited by Odisha CM Naveen Patnaik for a dialogue in Bhubaneswar. A day after the talks were held, several of the participants were arrested by the police, who languished for years in prison.

Till 2004, all political leaders including Manmohan Singh, Patnaik and YSR had described Maoist issue as a socio-economic problem, but after 2004, it becomes most serious threat to internal security", Mohantly exclaims.

The Swami has his own tale of woes. He recalls former Union Home Secretary GK Pillai's offer of a preliminary dialogue with top Maoist ideologues like Narayan Sanyal, Kobad Ghandy as also others held in prison. "Pillai said the government would identify these leaders and put them together for talks. Thereafter, talks could be broadened," says Agnivesh, who met Sanyal and Ghandhy in jail to convey Pillai's message. Both had welcomed the move and said their party would be more than happy to respond. But the government back tracked and it never took off.

Agnivesh also remembers an out-of-the blue call from Maoists who offered to release five policemen they had abducted in Chhattisgarh and held captive for over a month. While Agnivesh secured their release, he recollects asking State CM Raman Singh to reciprocate by releasing five incarcerated Maoists. "There were at that time, at least 1,700 people held in prison for being Maoists or Maoist sympathisers in the State and the CM publicly welcomed the suggestion at a joint press conference and promised to respond positively", a bemused Agnivesh says. Despite repeated reminders, the State Government didn't honour its commitement. It wouldn't be the last time.

The four interlocutors: Some details

On the pages below are some details about the four interlocutors.

Dr BD Sharma: The administrator

A former DM in Bastar, he resigned from the IAS opposing a Rs 2,000 Cr project to promote pulp and paper industry in the area. Associated with Bharat Jan Andolan, he was named as an interlocuter by the Maoists to negotiate the release of abducted Sukma DC Paul Menon.

Swami Agnivesh: The activist

Once taught courses in business management, law at St Xavier's College, Kolkata (then Calcutta). Spearheaded a national movement against bonded labour. His services were sought by the MHA to initiate a dialogue with Maoists, but it never took over, following the killing of CPI (Maoist) spokesman, Azad.

Prof G. Hargopal: The academic

Political science professor and Professor emeritus at Central University, Hyderabad. He meditated the release of IAS officer Vineel Krishna, abducted by Maoist in Odisha in 2011. Was a negotiator in resolving the 1993 Andhra Pradesh hostage crisis, involving an IAS officer and a Congress MLA.

Dandapani Mohanty: The trade unionist

Founder President of the Odisha unit of the Indian People's Front (IPF), the overground outfit of the CPI (ML) in the 1980s, he has been spearheading agitation by forest workers and providing legal assistance to Maoists and suspects in jail. Continues to be an activists.

JNU and Leftist causes (It is pro-LWE?)

Ever since its establishment, this University has been linked to…or, deemed so…Left Wing activism, or even LWE. That sounds ironic, since it is the most pampered of the Central Universities. It is believed to be the resort of the rich. This could be the reason, since that class deems it *a la mode* to be so. More directly, that class afford it!

There are three entries on the JNU; first two dealing with the same issue, in two dailies with different perspectives and the third one speaks about the existence of a Maoist cell in this 'class' university.

"Ex-JNU student held for alleged Naxal links"

"Hem Mishra, who has a Master's Degree from JNU, was held in Maharashtra' Red hub of Gadchiroli where he acted as a courier, police said."

25 Aug 2013

A daily reports the arrest of a former student of the JNU Hem Mishra on Thursday (22 Aug 2013) from a forest area[58].

The police arrested Mishra along with two others—Pandu Narote, and Mahesh Teerki—in the Naxal hotbed of the Gandchiroli district for his alleged links with Naxalites. The trio was picked up in forests adjoining Morewada village in Aheri tehsil.

The police said the trio, from whom a microchip and crucial documents were recovered was working as Naxal couriers at the behest of a top cadre. The three were remanded to police custody for 10 days. The Facebook profile of Mishra shows him as a "believer in Leninist-Marxist and Maoists views."

The arrest of Mishra, who has a Master's Degree in Mass Communication from the prestigious JNU again stresses the reach of the Maoists in cities. Police disclosed that Mishra, a native of Almora, Uttarakhand, had the microchip and a letter meant to be delivered to a top woman cadre Narmada Akka. Police also found mobile phone memory cards which they say hold messages from Naxals to cadres in cities.

"Mishra said he was not a student of JNU, but stayed at the varsity hosteld," says Gadchiroli SP Mohd Suvez Haque. Bono, Mishra's colleague from JNU's Democratic Students' Union, said Mishra had a "problem in his hand" for which he was going to Prakash Amte's hospital in Hemal Kasa. The trio was picked up some 140 Km from Hemalkasa. Haque said: "The three revealed they worked for Narmada. We are also probing if Naxals have made inroads into the varsity."

"JNU student with 'Naxal links' sent to 10 days police custody"

- "Police claim to have recovered a microchip and some secret documents."
- 'Hem Mishra is a member of the Democratic Students Union (DSU) and a keen cultural activist.'
- 'He was planning to go inside the forest to meet some senior Naxal leader.'

25 Aug 2013

The Maharashtra police on Saturday (24 August) remanded Hem Mishra to ten days police custody for Naxal-related activities.[59]

Mishra, 30, was arrested with Pandu Pora Narote, 27 and Tirki, 24 at a bus station in Ahiri division, Gadchiroli, said DIG Gadchiroli Range Ravindra Kadam.

A police press release said the three were roaming around in Aheri suspiciously whey they were arrested, "Norote and Tirki also accepted that both of them were regular Couriers of Narmada and other senior leaders in Chhattisgarh and Maharashtra."

Implicated

Denying all this, Hem's father KD Mishra told this daily: "He has been studying in JNU for the last four years. He has serious problem in his left hand but he is extremely active in social and political circles of Uttarakhand and JNU. He is being implicated falsely."

Hem Mishra is a member of DSU, which called his arrest "absolutely ridiculous." Banajyotsna Lahiri, an executive member of the DSU said, "The entire University can testify for him. His friends at JNU say he is a member of the DSU and "a keen cultural activist ." Rona Wilson, his friend, adds her testimony: "He is quite keen on tribal issues and he was a part of many fact finding teams and would often visit conflict areas." Lahiri, after calling his arrest "absolutely ridiculous", goes further: "He is a well-known cultural activist in JNU circles. The entire varsity can testify for him. He was planning to go to Dr Prakash Amte hospital in Gadchiroli to get his hand treated."

But DIG Kadam refuted Lahiri's claims, arguing: "Are there no doctors in Delhi? What was the need for coming all the way to Gadchiroli? This is absolutely ridiculous. He was planning to go into the forests to meet some senior Naxal leaders."

Facebook

His Facebook page was abuzz with anti-police slogans, after his arrest, and "condemning the arrest of Comrade Hem on fake charges by the Maharashtra police."

"Resist the witch-hunt of students, intellectuals and activists who dare to stand up against systemic injustice, oppression and State repression", read one post, demanding that Mr Mishra be freed immediately.

"JNU Student's papers hint at Maoist cell in university"

Nagpur: 18 Sep 2013

Documents seized from alleged Naxal courier Hem Mishra, a student of JNU, "revealed that country's premier educational institute is becoming a hub of Left Wing Extremists, security agencies have claimed.[60]

Sources in the investigating team on Mishra, arrested from Aheri on 22 August, claim there was at least one active party cell of the banned CPI

(Maoist) in this institution with students as its cadres. A former PhD student of history from Assam, earlier an active member of party cell, is now a part of Naxal's core team based at Abujhmadh. Sources chaimed that the cadre had been christened by Naxals as Navin. "Navin was present on Facebook. He might have got some inkling about security agencies stalking him in cyber space. The Facebook account was soon deleted but we believe he would be present through pseudonyms in social networking systems to remain in touch with his colleagues", said a senior officer.

"Navin had already attained status of a professional revolutionary while studying at JNU. We believe there are a couple of more now enrolled as students but their identities are not clear right now", he said.

Though Mishra has denied being part of any party cell, the interrogators have learnt India's capital has a couple of more student-based cells outside JNU, while interrogating him in custody. Apart from students, cells also comprise faculty members. A senior member of the interrogation team claimed that each party cell comprised three to five members. He explained: "These cells recruit youngsters from metros for guerrilla squads".

Following searches at the home of DU professor GN Saibaba in New Delhi, the security agencies were trying to ascertain whether senior faculties members too were part of cells.

"Is judiciary interfering excessively in matters operational?"

This is a worrisome question that must be analysed in depth. It is fine that the judiciary is the final arbiter in the country. But is it right for judges to assume an all-knowing attitude? Certain issues must be left to the experts and professionals in their respective fields. They should be realists enough, if not humble, that operational matters are best left to the ones working in that field at great personal risks.

"Centre, Chhattisgarh pulled up on SPOs: Supreme Court

"We have serious doubts about the Constitutional validity of such appointments: Supreme Court (SC)

- Special Police officers (SPOs) are appointed under the colonial 1861 Police Act.
- Supreme Court seeks details as to how many SPOs are deployed.

26 Apr 2011

The SC on 24 Apr 2011 pulled up the Centre and the Chhattisgarh Governments for appointing SPOs taking shelter under the colonial 1861 Police Act which provides for such appointments for a short period.[61]

A bench of Justices B Sudershan Reddy and SS Nijjar questioned the Centre's rationale in giving financial support to the State Government for appointing these SPOs. The Bench was hearing petitions filed by social anthropologist Nandini Sunder and others.

Justice Reddy, expressing serious concern over the appointment of SPOs, told Solicitor General (SG) Gopal Subramaniam : "This is most disturbing and not acceptable. You are providing funds and legitimising what all they do. You rely on 1861 Act for appointing these SPSs for three months on a salary of Rs 3,000 a month, taking advantage of their poverty. What is their knowledge of law? Whether these SPOs are answerable. Do they know what the law on 'self-defence'? You are clothing them with firing power. How can you let loose such SPOs on the people of this county? It is a very serious issue, how can this be allowed to go on?" He said: "we have very serious doubts on the Constitutional validity of such appointments as it has serious implications for the people. Should you (Centre) be a party to this at all? You finance them."

The SG maintained that not only in Chhattisgarh but even in Jammu and Kashmir such appointments were made. Not convinced by the reply, Justice Reddy told the SG: "we are more concerned about what is happening to the SPOs. If something happens to the SPOs, who is responsible? Are you giving any pension to the families of the SPOs or leave them in lurch? It is very dangerous to give arms to SPOs in a conflict area. Can you appoint somebody as police officer merely because they know the local terrain and they know how to fire?"

Justice Nijjar questioned the rationale of appointing SPOs under the 1861 Act after Constitution came into force. He observed that this Act was used by the British rulers for colonial policing.

The Bench asked senior counsel Harish Salve to file an affidavit explaining how many SPOs had been appointed in Dantewada district and for how many months, how many SPOs had been killed or injured.

Justice Reddy made it clear to Salve that the state could not divide the people by letting loose the SPOs to fight the people.

When Justice Reddy asked salve why the Chhattisgarh Government should not order an independent pro be into the burning of 300 tribal houses in Dantewada district and enquire into the attack on Swami Agnivesh, the latter said the CM would write to the CJ of Chhattisgarh HC requesting him to spare the services of a sitting for the Commission of Inquiry. He said the Government would enlarge the terms of reference and include the two incidents also for a thorough probe.

Justice Reddy told Salve that the State's affidavit was "delightfully vague. You must tell us how many SPOs are deployed, where are they deployed"?

The Bench in a brief order recorded the submissions of the Mr Salve..... and made it clear that only a sitting judge should be appointed to head the Commission of Inquiry.

The Bench directed the Centre to clarify the position on appointment of SPOs and posted the matter for further hearing on 2 May (2011).

"Centre may challenge 'political prisoner' status for Maoists"

26 Sep 2012 (Judiciary goes over board)

- MHA : Such a status will affect the morale of security forces who fight Maoists.
- Agnivesh: Move will make the Maoists join the national mainstream.

The Union Government is likely to challenge a Kolkata Court's declaration that nine suspected Naxalites arrested by the NIA in an illegal arms manufacturing case as 'political prisoners."

The MHA seems to have no option but to challenge the verdict as more arrested Maoists would now seek the same status.

The Judgement was also a big let-down for the security forces, who live in difficult conditions and in an inhospitable terrain while fighting armed revolutionaries.

The Judges and Courts surely are aware of the implications of granting 'political prisoner' status to the murderous Maoists! This status entitles an inmate several privileges over other prisoners as he will get to live in a separate cell and enjoy greater freedom inside jail, besides getting access to home-made food, newspapers, books and other reading material. There will be relaxation allowed in meeting relatives and advocates[62].

Specifics of the case

In August (2012), the Kolkata HC had declared eight suspected Maoists, including CPI (Maoist) backed leader Chhatradhar Mahato, as "political prisoners."

MHA worries are genuine

The MHA is deeply worried over this decision of the said HC as the murderous rebels involved in killings or supplying arms, which includes CPI (Maoist) Technical Committee head Sadula Ramakrishna alias RK, will get this status.

Wrong precedent

A senior MHA official explains his concerns. "According such a status to hardened criminals waging war against the State is unacceptable.....it will set a wrong precedent. Already some suspected Maoists are on hunger strike in a Maharashtra jail, demanding they to be declared 'political prisoners'. It will also affect the morale of our security forces who, living in tough and hard conditions, fight these anti-national marauders." But the public opinion seems divided on this decision.. If social activist Swami Agnivesh, who in the past negotiated with the Maoists for the government, said it would help the government in its peace efforts, former DG BSF Prakash Singh wants the government to challenge it as it would only strengthen the LWE.

Agnivesh expands his argument

"Challenging the order will be a mistake...Here is an opportunity for the government to tell the Maoists that they too would be treated with dignity inside jails. This move will let Maoists trust the Constitution and Indian laws. They are also part of our society and all efforts should be made to bring them back to the national mainstream. The government should accord the same status to all Maoists lodged in various jails across India."

Prakash Singh's views: will encourage Maoism

He warned that if the government failed to stop the trend, it would be an invitation to other Maoists to take up arms and intensify situation.....those who support Maoists through their write-ups and peaceful protests can be treated as political prisoners, but how can a person responsible for killing security men and innocent people be given special status inside jails.....If the government did not challenge this 'theoretical order', it would be yet another step backwards in its fight against terrorism. We can not ignore harsh ground realities...Maoists are engaged in guerrilla warfare, in fighting the Indian State. Even the PM recently referred to the Maoists as the biggest threat to our internal security. The government needs to wake up before more Maoists demand the same status."

It is noteworthy that since the formation of the CPI (Maoist), over 5,291 security men and civilians have lost their lives to Maoist bullets/ IEDs/violence!

"Show-cause notice by Supreme Court to Chhattisgarh for flouting orders on Salwa Judum"

23 Aug 2013

The Supreme Court (SC) on 22 Aug 2013 asked the Chhattisgarh

Government to show cause why contempt proceedings should not be initiated against it for its failure to carry out the court directions, issued on 5 Jul 2011, banning Salwa Judum, and asking authorities to vacate all schools and ashrams occupied by security forces.

Acting on petitions filed by social anthropologists Nandini Sundar, Ram Guha, Swami Agnivesh, Kartam Joga and others, the Court on 5 Jul 2011 had given a series of directions to the Central and Chhattisgarh governments and sought a Compliance report. The petitioners complained that the State government had not complied with many of the directions.

A Bench of Justices SS Nijjar and Ibrahim Kalif-ul-la, after hearing senior counsel Ashok Desai, issued notice on the contempt petition and posted further hearing to 3 Oct (2013).

Prof Sundar and others said the State government had negated the Court order with impunity. The SPOs were not allowing the CBI to conduct a probe and as a result the investigating agency was now seeking protection from the SPOs.

Though a direction was issued to stop all support to Salwa Judum, the State Government never acknowledged or punish illegal acts committed by the civil militia. The court directed registration of FIRs for investigation of criminal cases but only negligible action was taken on cognisable offences cited by NHRC.

Further, nobody had been compensated for loss of properties, even in camps, leave alone villages, the petitions said. Nor were victims of Salwa Judum compensated even for loss of life. Only those who were victims of Naxal violence were compensated. The widespread property damage witnessed by an NHRC team was just dismissed by the Chhattisgarh government.

The petition said the State was patently false in claiming the SPOs were not being used for combating Maoists and that no erstwhile SPO was in possession of arms. "This claim was both perjury and contempt since all that has been done is to change their names from the SPOs to armed auxiliary forces and they remain erstwhile SPOs."

A Jharkhand Minister too helps Maoists (Ranchi and New Delhi: 6 Oct 2014)

Finally, we have a former minister of agriculture of Jharkhand arrested in the national capital Delhi on Saturday, 4 Oct 2014, nearly a month after he resigned and went absconding following allegations that he formed a criminal gang.

Because of its important implications for the political class, four dailies covered the news item in their issue dated 6 Oct 2014. All the reports are examined for their contents. Names of the dailies with their correspondents are given here:

- The Indian Express: Deepu Sebestian Edmond and Sarah Hafeez
- The Hindustan Times: HT Correspondent
- The Times of India: Raj Shekhar
- The Pioneer: Staff Reporter

Indian Express: "Ex-Jharkhand minister 'who set up criminal gangs' held'

Under this title, the daily says it was a joint operation by Jharkhand Police's CID and the Delhi Police that resulted in the arrest of Sao. A Delhi Court on the 5th granted the Jharkhand Police a transit remand of three days for Sao.

A debutant MLA of the Congress, who represents the mineral-rich Barkagaon in the Assembly, 50-year-old Sao resigned on 12 Sep (2014) following sustained pressure from within the party. A district court in Hazaribagh had issued a non-bailable warrant against him on 16 September.

The CID had been claiming that the former minister could not be found even though he gave a series of interviews to Jharkhand-based media outlets.

The State Police said in a statement Sao was arrested from the house of a Panna Lal Mahto in a JJ colony of Delhi Shakurpur. Delhi Police said Sao had been constantly changing locations to evade arrest. Delhi Additional CP (crime) Ashok Chand disclosed : "He hid in Assam and Bihar before coming to Delhi on 30 September. He was staying with an associate, also a resident of Jharkhand in Shakurpur's JJ colony. He was arrested on a tip-off."

The Jharkhand Police "had approached Delhi Police Crime Branch five days ago to track Sao."

The MLA claims to have been "trapped" by the police because of his opposition to various "police atrocities."

The case began with the arrest of five men from Giddi in Jharkhand on 1 September for illegal possession of firearms. On interrogation, their leader Raj Kumar Gupta told the police that he headed a banned criminal gang, Jharkhand Tiger, also classified as the LW Extremist outfit in the state.

In a statement recorded under Section 164 of the CrPC, Gupta told the police that it was Sao who had set-up the gang in early 2014 to carry out extortions, and that the MLA provided him guns, money, bikes and posters. Gupta claimed the initial payment to the gang was Rs 75,000, along with three bikes. Delhi Police said Sao also formed another criminal outfit with links to the LWE groups, the Jharkhand Bachao Andolan.

The only leader to have come out in Support of Sao has been of former Ranchi MP Subodh Kant Sahay, who had himself to resign as Union Minister in Oct 2012 following allegations of involvement in the coal block allocation scam.

Apart from facing extortion charges, the Jharkhand Tiger is suspect in at least two kidnappings. It was reportedly preparing to attack a project site of GVK Group when its members were arrested.

Hindustan Times

"Former Jharkhand minister arrested for helping extremists"

Sao, 45, was alleged by "harbouring and operating" two extremist outfits: Jharkhand Tiger Group (JTG) and Jharkhand Bachao Andolan (JBa) in Hazaribag. The MLA is an alleged accused in 13 other cases of murder, attempt to murder, rioting, criminal intimidation and extortion in Jharkhand.

Ashok Chand also said he was founder member of the JTG and JBA. Gupta told the police that Sao oprated the outfit and his personal assistant used to supply arms and ammunition to the extremists. Sao's official vehicle was used to ferry these weapons.

Based on Gupta's confessional statements, the police obtained warrants against Sao. Looking at the gravity of allegations, the "State government has recently handed over the case to CID.

Sao was a minister in the cabinet of CM Hemant Soren.

Times of India

"Jharkhand MLA with Maoist links held" Sao is suspected Maoist sympathiser and is accused to running two terror outfits, which carry out anti-social activities, police said. Sao was taken to Ranchi on the 5th.

Security agencies were baffled when Gupta, heading the JTG, told them that a Maoist training camp in Hazaribagh was being run by Sao. Pawan, Sao's cousin, was also held during CID operations, who confessed to be working on Sao's orders.

Police have evidence of Sao's involvement into the Beltu massacre of Hazaibagh in 2001. Maoists had beheaded 13 people and allegedly played football with the severed heads. The men arrested in the case had confessed that Sao was involved in the conspiracy.

The Pioneer

"Ex-Jharkhand Min Sao held in city for Maoist links"

He was arrested in connection will an FIR lodged under the Arms Act as well as for facilitating commission of crime. "Till now, some 11 members of the two outfits have been arrested on charges of committing heinous crimes."

Pen pushers: Tribal Rights Proponents (Four)

The 'closet Maoists' operate through multiple channels and ways. One of the more commonly used is the newspaper articles and columns. And more influential dailies are ready to give them space, for whatever reasons.

Their one-sided view are apparent. This part carry the stories of four activists. Two well-known and other too not that well known. The former category is represented by two articles each penned by the proponents themselves, viz Nandini Sundar and Harsh Mander.

Excerpts are reproduced from various articles on the four Pen Pushers, for whom the Maoists are always right and the governments, security forces always wrong.

Excerpts

Everywhere, a Maoist plot"

"Chhattisgarh government is unable to accept the right to protest and unwilling to hear the people's voice."

By Nandini Sunder: Indian Express: 3 Jan 2014

By going to town as the Chhattisgarh police and media have recently done on my alleged Maoists links, the real questions have been sidelined. As citizens of the country, do we have the right to protest democratically and constitutionally, and as journalists, researchers or human rights activists, are we free to pursue our vocation?

The police arrested one Badri Gawde on 23 January ...He revealed to the media that I was working on behalf of the Maoists to oppose the mines and railway line that are to come up in the Raoghat area of the state... These activities shown to be led by me even when I am taking classes in Delhi amazes me.

Like many youngmen in conflict areas, Gawde is a man of many parts. With political ambitions, he is active both with the Congress and is local Gond community politics. But being political in these parts also means perforce, keeping up with the Maoists.....In Nov 2013, soon after the Assembly polls, I visited Bastar as part of my research on 'counter-insurgency and democracy.' With me was a friend with ancestral roots in Narayanpur-Antagarh. Badri mentioned he was going to meet a Maoist leader and asked if we would like to come. Since it was a rare opportunity for us, we went along.

While the Maoists have often given access to embedded journalists, they have been deeply resentful of my criticism of them... If meeting Maoists is a crime, all these journalists should be arrested... There can't be different laws on meeting Maoists, one for the journalists and other for scholars.

Our meeting with the young Maoists, who had a child like face and giggled frequently, lasted an hour or so…we discussed Raoghat mines, also Godse versus Gandhi. I came away from that meeting with sense of sadness, after travelling through some of the most spectacular scenery.... This area deserves to be treated as a national biodiversity paradise rather than mined into waste land...Each hill top houses a clan god, and people come from far away places on Maharashtra and Andhra Pradesh to their clan festivals every few years.. And yet the fake gram sabha certificates, which the government has produced as evidence of popular consent...

Part of the sadness I felt is that while people thinks Maoists are saving the land, they are hardly the answer. The government, however feel insistent on stopping all peaceful protests....to ensure that the mines come up.

Sadly for democratic politics, the post-1947 governments has inherited among other things, a colonial theory of incitement. Unable to accept that people have a right to safeguard their lives, they are always looking for conspirators to explain resistance. In this case, aim is not only to target me, but to pre-emptively act against all democratic, peaceful and lawful opposition to the Raoghat mines by raising the Maoist bogey. It also helps the Chhattisgarh government to deflect attention from its deliberate refusal to act on the Supreme Court's orders. Schools are still occupied by security forces, putting girl students at risk....No one has been compensated for their houses being burnt.

The Chhattisgarh government has long tried to claim that our petition against the Salwa Judum in the Supreme Court has been filed at the behest of the Maoists....My co-petitioners, Ramchandra Guha and EAS Sarma, can hardly be accused of being Maoist dupes.

The incitement and urban network theory can only go so far. Till the day our Constitution says that the profits of the mining companies outweigh the right to life, affected villagers will continue to fight, and democratic people will continue to support them.

> Mandini Sundar is a professnor of Sociology, Delhi University, and co-petitioner in an ongoing PIL in the Supreme Court against the Chhattisgarh government on the Salwa Judum.

"A new kind of Slash and burn"

"The NDA government is pursuing a clear anti-Adivasi agenda in the name of countering the Maoists."

By Nandini Sundar, The Hindustan Times, 6 Sep 2014

Excerpts

One area is which the Modi Government's first 100 days has brought absolutely no surprises is the policy on the Naxalites. Everything is as predicted, from increased militarisation to the vitiation of environmental protections.

What is extraordinary is not the continuity in policy between the UPA and NDA, but how little the government has learnt from the past 10 years. Union Home Minister Rajnath Singh may think he can finish the Maoists in "3 years" by flooding Chhattisgarh with troops (one lakh by 2016), but he should recall that in Mar 2010, P Chidambram had with equal hubris had declared his government would solve the problem in "2-3 years". The MHA officials, who should have longer institutional memory than their ministers, have revived all the elements of a plan right down to the community policing and the use of the Naga India Reserve Battalions in Chhattisgarh. Their cruelty between 2005-07 is hardly likely to ensure that villagers will now welcome them with open arms and information.

Similarly, the invocation of single 1G/DIG command – with Punjab's KPS Gill as model – is an open invitation to unchecked authority, starting with the posting of SRP Kalluri as 16 Bastar range. Kalluri was posted out after a particularly egregious incident in 2011 – when 300 homes in Tadmetla and neighbouring villages were burnt, people killed and women raped by security forces. The fact that he is now being sent back suggests the state wants operations untrammelled by human rights, law and the Constitution.

On 15 Aug 2014, the CRPF claimed to have achieved a major success by hoisting the national at Tadmetla, which is close to the spot where 76 CRPF men and 8 Maoists were killed in an ambush in 2010 (5 Apr). They forget that in 2011, after the attack on villagers, CM Raman Singh had visited the village and promised to re-start the primary school. Three years later, there is no school, only a flag. The CBI has not submitted its findings on the incident to the SC despite being asked in 2011 to give preliminary report within 6 months.

Adivasi communities are people and not backward Hindus—with distinctive languages, spoken by millions and distinctive faiths.

Comment

Without dignifying this one-sided essay which speaks in clichés and over-use rhetoric, only one comment should suffice: It must have warmed the cockles of Maoist heart. They couldn't have done a better job of espousing their cause. One wouldn't be surprised if a cynic was to arrest that the articles were sent to her by the Comrade Maoists, and she affixed name to these!

"Violence and the State": By Harsh Mander

"Armed struggle is not the only way to respond to state violence. There are other ways of democratic dissent."

The Hindu: 28 Aug 2011

Excerpts

Those who defend violent resistance believe it is justified because of the unremitting scale and the hopelessness of the oppression to which the impoverished masses are subjected. They argue that the opponents of the Maoist violence ignore the 'structural violence' of the State and, by implication, equate it with emancipatory violence of the oppressed. The CPI (ML) People's War wrote to, Sankaran Committee which attempted to mediate and end Maoist violence and State repression in Andhra Pradesh that 'extremism (democratic struggle of the people) is inevitable in a situation of inadequately addressed social and economic problems', and felt that the Committee made 'wrong assessments' only by 'isolating the cruelty and violence from people's struggle, and wrongly equating police violence with the Naxalite violence.'

But, in fact, on the contrary in their reports and communications, the Committee headed by the humanist SR Sankaran did repeatedly acknowledge the structural violence built into the societal system, such as inequality, exploitation and lack of freedom or democratic space.

Transgressive State

I too have no doubt that ethically the most condemnable violence is by the State when it acts unjustly and law lessly, because the modern State assumes the monopoly of the legitimate exercise of violence with the pledge that it will protect all citizens with fairness and justice.... Especially when confronted with both violent and non-violent dissent, the State's practice is often abysmal.

We observed in my earlier column that violent killing of civilians by Maoists occasionally is followed by explanation that such deaths are inevitable as a kind of 'collateral damage', and expressions of regret. But even such rare regret is missing when those killed by Maoists are men in uniform.

Those who justify killing of security men ignore the fact that most of these are just poor, working classmen, often of peasant stock, who join the police or security forces as one of the few sources of livelihood available to them.

Legitimate Target

After the killing of 76 men of CRPF in one of the worst/biggest Naxalite attacks in Dantewada district of Chhattisgarh on 5 Apr 2010, a loose coalition called 'Citizens Initiative for Peace' tried to mobilise signatures from rights activists and writers who usually denounce State violence, to condemn this particular attack. One writer who refused to sign explained in an open email that: "Frankly speaking, I don't feel any anguish... Honestly, what happened at the CRPF camp was a part of Civil war where combatants get killed.... Though, as HR activist, I surely condemn the Maoists for killing non-combatants..I can't condemn them for targeting the CRPF, which is their military combatant. The CRPF is the most notorious arm of the Indian State."

I felt constrained to respond to him: "I do mourn the loss of lives of the CRPF jawans. I mourn the loss of innocent unarmed citizens' lives which has been killed in the conflict. I mourn the loss of lives of those who have picked up the guns. Human life is precious, and I cannot endorse a hierarchy of more or less legitimate killings."

"Alternative to the politics of hatred"

" A life-long believer in non-violence rebuts Modi's charge that he is a Maoist sympathiser."

By Harsh Mander:The Hindu: 26 Jun 2013

Excerpts

I am resolutely opposed to the politics represented by Narendra Modi, which I find deeply inimical to the pluralist and humane idea of India.

There are many…who are attracted by his muscular style of leadership and his focus on market-led economic growth.

In some recent statements, Mr Modi has described me repeatedly as a Maoist sympathiser. I am constrained to respond because his remarks are utterly false and contradict my life-long convictions. I have …since my college days, in my years in civil service and the decade since in my public life…always been passionately and publicly opposed to all forms of violence: violence which is communal, terrorist, anti-Dalit, anti-woman, anti-poor and also equally, Maoist violence.

No justification

I strongly disagree with these, among them my liberal friends, who in any way romanticise or even indirectly rationalise the resort to violence by Left militants, suggesting their violence is justified because of the structural violence of poverty, exploitation and state violence. I am convinced there is no such violence as altruistic violence.

As evidence of my Maoist sympathies, Mr Modi speaks of the employment in an orphanage run by a NGO with which I am associated, of a Maoist's wife. The relevant facts are as follows. As one part of our resistance to the politics of hatred, it is our conviction that we must also build an alternative politics and civic action based on love and caring. One such task we chose, was to reach out to as many homeless children as possible who are brutalised on city street. Over the past seven years, we helped establish and run 45 residential homes for the education and care of some 4,000 homeless street girls and boys. These employ some 500 staff, as child carers and teachers.

For running these homes, it is our policy to give preference to single women, women survivors of domestic violence, and homeless and destitute women as house mothers and home managers, so that the children's home also provides them a place of safety and healing. Under the name of Sirisha, a woman came to my colleagues in Hyderabad in 2008, saying she was estranged from her husband and only son, and was in severe depression, and she be given the chance to live among the children as a volunteer so that fit would help her to heal.

In time, when a position in the same home fell vacant, she was appointed as one of the home managers, because she performed her duties of child care well. No one had the faintest idea about her true identity. After more than two years with us, she applied for 10 days' long leave for the first time. A few days later, we learnt from the newspapers that she was Padma, second wife of a Maoist leader, and she was arrested by the police in Odisha. Apart from her, we learnt after several years about another former staff who also hid his Maoist antecedents.

I have consistently written about my resolute opposition to all forms of violence, including Maoist violence. Before he claimed I have 'Maoist sympathies', Modi's advisers could have undertaken a casual search on the internet about my numerous writings against violence, some of which are reproduce here.

Comment

He has not told us if subsequently the Maoists wife was removed from his employment.

"Jailed for Maoist links, journalist claim he was wrongly convicted" By Ashutosh Bhardwaj: Indian Express: 30 Sep 2014

Excerpts

The boy stopped short: Tightly clutching his school bag, he stretched his hand felt the old man's face. "You just look like my father", he said. Pragya Jha had returned home from school and met the man his grandmother had often told him about.

Pragya was just a year old when his grandfather Prafulla Jha was arrested in Jan 2008, and later convicted of sedition and having Maoist links, the first journalist in Chhattisgarh to be held guilty of the offence.

After completing seven years in jail, he was released on 28 Sep 2014 from Raipur jail He found his city's landscape changed almost beyond recognition. "Are these the same roads? he asked his wife Kavita, who told him that his release came a day after he turned 69.

Jha was among seven others, including his son Pratiek, arrested in Jan 2008 in what police termed as "the biggest case of urban network of Maoists." None of them, the Court said was a Maoist. There were alleged recoveries—a bag of weapons from Jha's house among others—mostly before police witnesses that formed the basis of their conviction. Among the convicted were two cloth merchants and a tailor who were held guilty of providing and stitching clothes for the Maoists.

Jha's case was curious. The court noted that he was not a Maoist and his interrogation report called him "a Gandhian who would never resort to or support violence." The police had admitted that he was not a Maoist and attributed the bag recovered from his home to his son, but added "his arrest was necessary to teach others a lesson." In a way, he was the victim of the fear psychosis created around the term "urban network."

Some Maoists lived in Raipur and Bhilai since the late 1980s and were friends with journalists. Their articles used to appear in newspapers and someone had to arrested, and it was Jha.

Seven years later, the "Gandhian" Jha does not hold a grudge. "yes, I was wrongly convicted and I will fight against it, but I utilised my time inside for reading. I read a lot," he said.

The first book he asked from jail library was Tulsidas' *Ramcharit Manas,* followed Balgangadhar Tilak's *Gita Rahasya* and Mahatma Gandhi's *My Experiment with Truth.* "I had read these books several times earlier. But behind bars, I found rare wisdom in their pages. Gandhi was the only Indian who blended *Ramayana* and *Gita* in his life."

He soon aroused curiosity among jail staff, wondering "how could an atheist Naxal read religious literature?" So he told them: "Neither I am a Naxal nor these books are religious. I suggested these books as compulsory reading to know Indian society and culture."

Due to his daily schedule as a devoted "Brahmin", involving early morning *pooja,* the jail staff soon began calling him 'Maharaj'. "I was treated very well in jail", he said, and also praised Raipur Jail Superintendent RK Gupta.

His release was due in January, but his sentence was remitted by a few months. Another convict Meena Chaudhary was also released with him and Jha's son Pratiek will be released in a few days.

"Muzzled in Jharkhand"

"Unable to deal with rising protests against land acquisition, the Jharkhand government is digging up old cases against activists to silence them."

Soumik Mukherjee, The Tehelka, 8 Dec 2012

Excerpts

In yet another case of witch-hunt against grass-roots activists, the Jharkhand government on 24 Nov 2012 arrested anti-mining activist Xavier Dias and five of his colleagues. The state was acting on the basis of a 21-year-old case for their alleged role in leading a protest against Tata's iron ore mine in Noamundi, in the West Singhhum district. This is the latest in a spate of arrests, which started with Dayamani Barla's detention amid a crackdown on the land rights movement in Nagri village near Ranchi.

Though Dias and his colleagues were granted bail on 26 November, the arrest raises about the intentions of the current BJP-led government in the State Jharkhand was formed in 2000, after a long movement for separation from Bihar, as a new state meant for the tribal-dominated population of the region.

Dias was part of the movement for a separate Jharkhand when the Bihar police filed a case against him in 1991. Ironically, when the State was formed, he was honoured by the state government for his role in the 'freedom movement', and assured that he and his colleagues would be acquitted of all the charges against them. "This is State ploy. They never close the old cases and use them whenever they want to", says Dias.

The arrest follows a long period of police harassment and intimidation. "The persons arrested with Dias are all mining labourers. They could it stand the police harassment and surrendered before the court along with Dias," says Gopinath Ghosh, Dias' colleague.

Dias has dealt serious blows to the pro-mining policies in Jharkhand infamous for its mining scams, and has vehemently opposed land acquisition for mining projects.

The current scenario of growing people's movements in the State explains why the BJP –led government is raking up old cases against these activists. Dias arrest came when he was preparing for a protest against the expansion of a mine owned by Tata in Noamundi.

The villagers of Noamundi have written a letter to the Central Pollution Control Board alleging that the expansion does not follow the norms set by the agency. "Even the public hearing for land acquisition was a fraud. It was held inside the Tata Iron and Steel Company (TISCO) facility, heavily guarded by the police. The villagers had no say in the entire process," says a protestor on condition of anonymity.

Dias believes that these efforts to silence dissenting voices will only increase in the future. "People's movement and dissent among the masses against land grabbing and other anti-Adivasi activities have reached their zenith in this State. The government fears a retaliation from the people, so they will keep detaining those who lead such movements", says Dias.

Earlier last month, Barla who leading a protest against land acquisition in Nagri, was detained in connection with a 6-year-old case. Since her arrest on 16 Oct (2012), he bail plea has been rejected thrice by the Ranchi High Court. "Barla is a person who can mobilise the people and the state fears such people. Look at what happened to Sunilam in MP", says Dias.

The arrest of Barla and Dias are indications that a state meant for tribals has strayed far away from the original vision with which it was formed. Not only are leaders being detained, criminal case are also being slapped on minors in Nagri for 'destroying peace'. All this seems to suggest that it will take a long time for the 'freedom fighters' of Jharkhand to achieve what they fought for.

"Questions over PMRDF Naxal Links": 28 June 2013

Any scheme started after due thought and with good intentions is likely to develop snags or flaws at a certain stage. Given human nature, such a situation must be expected, unless, of course, the humans can change to a state of perfection. The cracks, call them snags or flaws, are apparent in the opening paragraph of a report in a daily that appeared in Jun 2013:

> "At a time when simultaneous security operations and developmental works are continuing well in Gadchiroli, the issue of a Prime Minister's Rural Development Fellow (PMRDF) and his friend being scrutinised for suspected Naxal links has put cold water on the good coordination that had come to be established between the collector and top police officials."

Main points from the report are given hereafter.

Vivek Deshpande, Indian Express, 28 June 2013

The police claimed they registered cases against PM RDF Mahesh Raut from Chandrapur and his friend Harshali Potdar from Mumbai after two arrested "Naxalites" revealed that the couple was travelling with them to meet top Naxal leaders. Police also claimed Raut and Potdar had been under surveillance after they were found protesting against a proposed Jindal Steel iron are mining project "in the district last month" (May 2013).

Raut refutes the allegations with interesting if surprising statements and assertions. He tells the daily that his work involve routine visits to interior villages: "It was only coincidental that we were in Koinvarshi where the two (alleged Naxals) were caught." He goes beyond this defence of this coincidental happening and asserts that being at a protest was not a sign of Naxal links."

What made matters even more puzzling was the decision of police to invoke the Unlawful Activities (Prevention) Act [UPPA] against the two but not arresting them!

Now comes the other side of the story, unfortunate, if not disturbing, indicative of sheer lack of coordination, possibly distrust, between the civilian and police heads of the district. DC Abhishek Krishna said he was not (even) told by the police of any offence being registered against the two. Even more striking was Krishna's claim of Raut being the best of the three PMRDFs in the district. What is more intriguing is this daily silence, not expected of it knowing its reputation as a pioneer of investigation in the print media and its mast heading claiming every morning of it practicising a "Journalism of Courage!" The silence of its scribe not asking a simple question of DC: What does he thinks of Raut asserting that being at a protest was not a sign of Naxal link?

Even as the gap between the administration and the police was now in the open, the question being asked is if the police had evidence to register cases against the two, and that too under the UAPA, why did it not arrest them? DIGP Ravindra Kadam claimed it was not necessary as the two had been cooperating with the police and it did not fear the two absconding.

The daily claims its sources told it that "offence" against Raut was in the nature of his "connections with some Naxal sympathisers" while Potdar's was "a threshold case of initiation into Maoist propaganda machinery."

The daily's conclusion is a bit of worry: "Be that as it may, Gadchiroli can scarce afford this seemingly unnecessary controversy over a flagship anti-Naxal plan by the Centre."

"In defence of PMRD Fellow, Ramesh writes to CM Chavan

Nagpur: 1 Jul 2013

Union Minister for Rural Development Jairam Ramesh, wrote to Maharashtra CM Prithviraj Chavan, seeking his personal intervention in connection with the interrogation of PMRDF Mahesh Raut, detailed above. He felt "adverse media reports have caused incalculable damage to the goodwill fellowship."

The details have been given earlier. To put it briefly, Raut and Potdar were in the village (Koinvarshi) when the two Naxals were nabbed. The two had been seen protesting againt Jindal Steel's mining project in a public hearing in May (2013).

The letter date 28 June states, "As a minister in charge of PMRD fellowship, I am concerned with the prolonged interrogation of the PMRDF by the police." The police had registered case against him under UAPA, as explained already. But Ramesh seems to be giving a cleanchit to Raut, obviously on the say-so of the DC, who has called Raut as the best of the three fellow in his district. Ramesh's words: "I independently enquired into the allegation from reliable sources. I understand that Mahesh was working successfully with the district administration in helping the poor to access government programmes. He has generated significant goodwill among the locals. He fully participated in the camps organised jointly by the district administration and the police. He has been visiting remote villages unfrequented by officials and staying there to interact with the people......

It is quite possible that while doing such work, PMRD fellows will face suspicion and backlash particularly in IAP districts where there is a climate of distrust unless we are alert about who protect the poor and who exploits them, we will not be able to solve the problem of alienation that plagues these regions....156 young men and women with bright academic qualifications and commitment to serve the poor in these difficult areas and were selected in 2012 through a highly competitive selection and induction process by my Ministry with the help of TISS. The aim to develop a cadre of development professionals who are committed to working for the poor and disadvantaged.....I definitely do not want to second guess the local civil and police administration, who function in very difficult circumstances. So I seek your personal intervention to clear the air and bring the issue to an end so that the PMRDFs are able to work without fear. Mahesh Raut should be allowed to continue working in God chiroli and the Collector may be directed to provide all necessary support."

"A definite role for PMRD Fellow": 2 Jul 2013

> "A year after inducting the first batch of PMRD Fellows, the government addresses the teething trouble of scheme, including identity crisis of the new recruits."

A daily carries an article in Jul 2013 which attempts to assess the functioning of the scheme about deployment of PMRDFs in Naxal-hit areas. It opens with a current controversy.[63]

The controversy concerns the Gadchiroli police registering a case against one PMRDF (Raut) under the UAPA and Minister Ramesh defending him in a letter to the State CM, all this detailed earlier.

This controversy put the focus back on this ambitious one-year-old scheme. The PMRDF announced in Sep 2011, inducted its first batch in Apr 2012, who thus, completed one year recently. The scheme aims at inducting young professionals for short durations at the district administration level in LWE- hit areas to assist in improving programme delivery and also serving as an interface between the administration and the marginalised sections in these areas. On an average, two Fellows are posted in 82 such districts, spread across nine States, the maximum being in Jharkhand and Odisha. The RD Ministry officials disclose that recruitment for a fresh batch (second) is set to begin anytime now.

The over all implementation record of the programme over the one year of its functioning has been the proverbial mixed bag. Perhaps the biggest indicator of the relative success of this scheme has been the very low attrition level, surprising even the Ministry officials. Of the total 150 Fellows inducted last year, only seven dropped out, a less than five per cent drop-out rate. This, despite the youngsters being placed in fairly difficult conflict areas.

The fellows believe they learnt immensely being part of the programme, while contributing to policy and implementation work at the district level. They also found an outlet for sharing their experience with the PMRDF blog being updated regularly with posts from Fellows.

Here is what Priyanka Yadav, 26, posted at Kanker district, Chhattisgarh, says: "The programme has changed my perspective completely towards several issues and the government. I have been involved in the implementation and design of National Rural Livelihoods Mission (NRLM) and have worked closely on youth-livelihood issues."

Vamsi Krishna, a post graduate from Tata Institute of Social Sciences, had similar views: "There are broadly two mandates. One is working in research and evaluation projects at the state-government level and the other is district specific. I am working on looking at sustainable livelihood opportunities in IAP districts and am satisfied with my experience." Krishna is posted at Karimnagar in Andhra Pradesh.

But this is one side of story. The scheme has its share of teething problems, some of which are now being addressed. To start with, there has been a considerable confusion about the exact role of the Fellows and where they fit in the established structure of the district administration. Moreover, the absence of a well-settled and clearly understood institutionalised structure has meant transitional problems and resultant instability with any change of guard in the district. This is neither surprising nor unexpected as the institution of PMRDF is in existence for just one year.

PMRD Fellows, who are paid Rs 75,000 pm with a 10 per cent hike in subsequent years, are required to report directly to the DCs. A RD Ministry explains the glitches: "We have had a mixed response to the programme. In some districts, the administration has been very supportive, especially where there are young, tech savvy DCs. But since DCs assign work to Fellow, there are problems when ever an incumbent changes and new person comes in. We are giving the scheme a definite structure that should help transitional problems."

There was also an identity crisis: were the Fellows researchers or assistants to the DCs? In June 2013, the Ministry guidelines defined them as 'development facilitators.'

There were some reports of the misuse of the Fellows. A senior Ministry officials disclosed: "In one State, five Fellows were working in the Chief Secretary's office, merely assisting him, rather than working in the field.

To resolve the concern over instability in Fellow's work with a change in administration and also to standardise the work, the Ministry decided to allot them a defined work area. Fellows will now be linked with NRLM, to work on the livelihood issues.

Some Fellows voiced their views: the DCs change often, 70 per cent of the key functionaries in my district have been transferredd in the last year; there is lack of clarity on exact-position, ambiguously defined roles, we are not part of hierarchy and this often confuses the DCs, our role should be concretised at district level and put in writing, and there should be a "sensitisation process" about the programme for the DCs.

The programme originally was for two years, the new guidelines convert it into a three-year one, which cannot be extended. But retaining Fellows for three years may be a challenge.

Both Krishna and Yadav said they were not sure if they would continue beyond two years, reasoning that they would have got significant experience by them. The challenge becomes greater given that the Fellows are professionals who might have left attractive jobs to gain on-the-field experience.

Aditya Tyagi, a JNU post-graduate and a consultant by profession, however, said he wanted to continue for three years. Tyagi, who is posted at Jamui in Bihar, has been working on two areas…initiating educational and livelihood programmes as well as working on identifying crops that can withstand droughts but with high commercial value.

"Andhra University Professor held for helping Maoists"

Hyderabad: 7 Nov 2014

Vishakhapatnam rural police arrested an assistant professor, Dr Jarla Appa Rao, of Andhra University in the early hours of 4 Nov 2014 (2 AM) for allegedly facilitating procurement of explosives including 300 Kg of ammonium nitrate for the East Visakha Division of the CPI (Maoist)[64].

Dr Appa Rao, head of the varsity's Telugu Department and a tribal rights activist, was nabbed from staff quarters on campus. Vizag Rural SP Dr Koya Praveen told the daily that they had evidence that Rao mediated with mine owners on behalf of the Maoists. The SP said: "Dr Rao met mine owners and gave them list of things Maoist leaders demanded to allow mining operations to continue."

Here is details of what the SP told the press: "It was a quid pro quo arrangement that Dr Rao was involved in and he encouraged mine owners and contractors to fulfil the Maoist demands. In the past Rao had supplied cell phones, camera flashes, batteries, hearing aid to the rebels. This time he was involved in facilitating procurement of explosive material like ammonium nitrate, cordex wires, and detonators. He was using contacts within the mining industry who had licence to purchase explosives and the material was pilfered along the way. These materials reached the Maoists through several intermediates. Whether he did it under pressure or not, it is a serious offence for a professor and a government servant...Three others involved in procuring and transporting explosives were arrested two days ago. The cache of 500 electronic detonators and 300 kg of ammonium nitrate, a tablet and 300 cell phones were recovered from Narsipatnam."

Of the three persons arrested, two said Dr Rao knew how and where the explosives were procured from the SP said: "We also came to know that there was a godown at Kathipudi in East Godavari district from where explosives were pilfered. On the 3 November night, one police team went to raid the godown while another went to bring Dr Rao for interrogation. We could not wait till morning because Dr Rao was already aware that the explosives Cache had been caught by police and he may have escaped .. call records show that Rao was regularly in touch with the representatives of the Maoists."

Meanwhile, the sudden arrest of Dr Rao drew criticism from academicians, students tribal outfits. Hundreds of teachers and students of the varsity demonstrated outside the SPs office in Vizag, demanding his immediate release. The varsity's teacher and student outfits called for a university bandh for 5 November.

Prof Yohan Babu said Dr Rao inspired students from backward communities and was popular on the campus.

Student leader K Kanta Rao said Dr Rao helped poor students. "He is also a good guide and assists students in choosing research subjects", he added. Rao's colleague Prof DVR Murthy said: "He had a clean record. His arrest is a big surprise because we were not aware of his alleged Maoist connections."

The college teacher was also a tribal rights activist and regularly attended meetings of several outfits working in the field.

"Andhra University professor held on charges of aiding Maoists": 7 Nov 2014

Another daily covered the arrest of Prof Rao. Some points are called from its story[65].

Prof Rao's wife, Mynavathi, with their children Sai (6) and Charana (4) and relatives and students, sat on *dharna* in front of the SP's office from 11 AM protesting against his arrest on "false cases" and stayed there till late evening when her husband and others were produced at a press conference.

The police named Vasapari Prasad, a tribal man in Narsipatnam, and Ganapathiraju Subbaraju of Kakinada, who were caught at Narsipatnam while allegedly transporting, electrical detonators, 300 kg of ammonium intrate, a tablet and a mobile phone, as accused No. 1 and No. 2, respectively. Subbaraju's friend K Jagadeesh Reddy, also from Kakinada, and the professor are the third and fourth accused in the case booked by the Narsipatnam Town Police.

Under provisions of the Indian Penal Code, Explosives Act, unlawful assembly Act and Preventive Detention Act. While he was being taken to the press conference, Prof Rao shouted that he had been framed. He has been critical of the bauxite mining proposed in the Vishakapatnam Agency.

"Honest citizens punished, powerful traitors applauded as patriots," says PUCL convention

"Human rights activists accuse State of violations, stifling democratic voices; call for fair trial, addressing growing inequality."

Jaipur: 2 Dec 2012

Two-day 11th National convention of the People's Union for Civil Liberties (PUCL) was held at Jaipur on Saturday and Sunday, 1 and 2 Dec 2012. What follows is the verbatim report on the first days's proceedings as published in a daily.

Proceedings of 1 Dec 2012

Civil rights activists attending a national convention of the PUCL on Saturday at Jaipur expressed concern over state authorities resorting to violation of human rights of citizens for challenging the nature of development policies, police excesses, allocating of resources to private interests and brazen support for the rich and industrial elite.

The two-day convention is devoted to the theme, "People's insecurity in the name of national security: Citizens' rights, democracy and State terrorism". Nearly 300 delegate from 15 States are taking part in the event to deliberate on the challenges before democracy and rule of law in a complex and "violence ridden" context when protests and agitations are being crushed with force.

The PUCL members honoured former Delhi HC Chief Justice and the famous Sachar Committee chairman Rajinder Sachar for his distinguished work for protection of human rights of vulnerable sections. Noted Mumbai-based activist and Citizens for Justice and Peace (CJP) Secretary Teesta Seetalvad was also felicitated for her courageous work for justice, peace and harmony.

Activists pointed out that citizens who agitate as an expression of their fundamental right to live with dignity and freedom of speech are termed "traitors" by the State and beaten, killed, arrested and crushed. In contrast, those in power, who sell natural resources and mineral wealth to foreign capitals, are feted as "patriots" and rules are bent to favour them.

In her keynote address, Ms Satalvad said the immunity enjoyed by the police officers who unleash violence and brutality on common citizens warrants structural changes ensuring accountability.

"When the State honours are given to Shiv Sena supremo Bal Thackeray during his cremation, we need to seriously ponder over the question of impunity in the public domain."

Ms Setalvad said there was an urgent need to create a jurisprudence on the hate speeches and hate writings which evolve an atmosphere facilitating communal and caste violence, even as the majority of people are forced to remain silent. "The issue is also related to destruction of evidence, as witnessed in 1984 in Delhi and 2002 in Gujarat. There should be laws for prosecution of officers destroying evidence of communal violence", she said.

The CJP activist who has been in the forefront of the campaign to get justice for the Gujarat victims, noted that the recent Naroda Patiya case judgement…in which the BJP and VHP were awarded life imprisonment… was a tribute to the country's justice system. However, refusal of bails to the accused in Godhra train burning case for nine years and prompt release of the accused in the post-Godhra violence cases indicated "discriminatory justice".

Ms Setalvad suggested that closed-circuit TV camera be installed in the tribal courts to facilitate deposition by witnesses without intimidation and ensure free and fair trial. She also questioned the tendency of political parties to field candidates of dubious background in elections despite allegations of their involvement in violence and crime.

Justice Sachar said poverty of large section of population was the biggest violation of the human rights and noted that the gap between the rich and the poor was constantly widening.

Social activist Aruna Roy, who is also vice-president of PUCL—— Rajasthan, said the flaws in the democratic system should be addressed through honest efforts and human rights protected by evolving a positive mind-set.

The sessions on the convention's inaugural day dealt with subjects like "anti-democratic laws" such as the Armed Forces (Special Powers) Act (AF-SPA), Unlawful Activities (Prevention) Act (UAPA) and Information and Technology Act, combating State Terrorism, politics of communalism and terrorism, struggles for justice and humanity and the politics of resource grabbing on the pretext of development.

PUCL national president Prabhakar Sinha, PUCL Rajasthan president Prem Krishna Sharma and PUCL national General Secretary V Suresh threw light on strategies for maintaining the organisation's relevance in the context of "anti-people" policies of the government. Prof Sinha said the governments selected by the people have served a microscopic minority of the rich at the cost of the commonman.

Citing the latest instance of two young girls arrested in Palghar for posting Facebook remarks, activists the governments, both at the Centre and the States, were violating with impunity Constitutional protection to free speech and freedom of association and protest to oppose the State policies. The koodankulam agitation in Tamil Nadu was cited as one of the most inspiring acts of peaceful civil protest in recent years.

"PUCL Flays UAPA amendments" Jaipur: 3 Dec 2014

What follows is the verbatim respect of second day's proceedings (2 Dec 2014) of the PUCL convention at Jaipur, as published in a daily.

PUCL Proceedings of 2 Dec 2014 at Jaipur

Though Union Home Minister SK Shinde assured Parliament that the government would never allow misuse of UPAP, the PUCL has unanimously condemned the passage of amendments to to the Act in the Lok Sabha on 30 Nov 2012. At its 11th convention at Jaipur on 2 December, the PUCL alleged that the unlawful activities prevention (Amendment) Bill 2011 was "stealthily passed by the Lok Sabha without any discussion".

The PUCL has been campaigning for the repeal of the UAPA, claiming that there was enough evidence to show that it was being extensively abused in the name of combating LWE, forcing innocent citizens to languish in prisons.

"It is shocking to learnt that the new amends aim at changing the definition of person (Section 2) which is a direct attack on Article 19 (of the Constitution), as now the government can label any unregistered association of persons as unlawful", Kavita Srivastava told the daily. She continues: "It is also disturbing that the government, by amending Section 6, is planning to extend the ban on organisations from two to six years. These and other amendments go against the letter and spirit of the Constitution and represent one more step towards silencing people posing a challenge to the government."

The PUCL resolved to lobby against the passage of the amendments in the Rajya Sabha.

The PUCL Convention, which was inaugurated by activist Teesta Setalvad saw the new executive taking over. While Prabhakar Sinha continues to be president, V Suresh, senior advocate from Tamil Nadu, took over as general secretary. Ritu Priya, from the JNU took over as treasurer. While Dr Binayak Sen, Sanjay Parikh and PBD'sa continue to be vice presidents. Mahipal Singh, Chittranjan Singh and Ms Kavita Srivastava will continue as national secretaries.

Delhi University Professor's house searched: 12 Sep 2013

Prof GN Saibaba's house was searched on 12 Sep 2013 by Maharashtra's Gadchiroli District Police on the suspicion that he sent some secret information to the Maoist leadership hiding in the forests of Abujh Maad in Chhattisgarh.

The Professor teaches English at Ram Lal Anand College, in South Delhi, and it comes under the Delhi University.

The event has been covered extensively by the newspapers. If it turns out to be true, the Professor should be an eminent candidate to figure among the leading 'overground Maoists' or the 'closet Maoists' as that is this author's preferred term, which is so expressive and meaningful. More importantly, there will be cacaphanonous outcry by so-called 'activists and intellectuals' about the Professor being innocent and the 'vicious' police being hell-bent to frame him.

The dailies which covered the event and whose contents will be examined are listed below:

	Name	*Correspondent*	*Dated (2013)*
1.	Indian Express	Vijaita Singh and Aditi Vatsa	13 Sep
2.	Indian Express	ENS	14 Sep
3.	The Hindu	Shubhomoy Sikdar	15 Sep
4.	Indian Express	ENS	15 Sep

"DU Professor's house searched, police claim he had information for Maoist leaders": Indian Express: 13 Sep 2013

Gadchiroli police on the 12th searched Prof GN Saibaba's house, claiming he was aware of a big Maoist congregation to be held in the Abujh Maad area. But Saibaba told the daily that they had barged into the house, they were already inside when he reached into the afternoon, and they "could have planted the material in my house."

Police seized a lap top, three hard-disks, four pen drives, one microchip, a SIM card, mobile phones of Saibaba's daughter, two old phones and some booklets from the house.

He told the daily: "When I returned home around 3 PM, there were some 50 police persons at my house. Saying they had a search warrant, they barged into the house. Apart from my family, my wife and daughter, the driver too was locked in during the three-and-a-half-hour search."

Saibaba, who is chair-borne, is the Deputy Secretary, Revolutionary Democratic Front (RDF), an outfit which has been on the radar of intelligence agencies for suspected links to Maoists.

Police said they searched Saibaba's residence in Gwyer Hall area of North Campus based on disclosures made by former journalist Prashant Rahi "who was arrested by Gadchiroli police last week."

Police disclosed Rahi was arrested after questioning of JNU student Hem Mishra "who was held in Aheri area of Gadchiroli a fortnight ago."

Ravindra Kadam, DIG Gadchiroli Range, told the daily. "When Hem Mishra was arrested, we recovered a coded message. He told us he had been asked by Rahi to deliver the message to Maoists Chief Ganapathi. When we arrested Rahi, he told us that he had been sent by Saibaba to meet the Central Committee members. We also recovered some documents from Rahi which were prepared by Saibaba."

Saibaba also objected to the content of the search warrant and the objects which were seized from his house. He said: "The search warrant says my house was used as a place for deposit of property stolen from Aheri. None of the items which they took way has anything to do with Gadchiroli. I live on the university premises; they did not have permission from the University for the search."

"Delhi Prof got in touch with Maoist leaders on line: Police (Indian Express: 14 Sep 2013)

A day after the police raided the house of DU Prof Saibaba for his links with Maoists, the security agencies alleged that he had set up an internet group chat, which is being used to communicate with top leaders of the CPI (Maoist). The also would soon approach the DU Vice Chancellor for strict action against Saibaba who teaches English in Ram Lal Anand College.

He denied all allegations: "I am not part of any internet group chat. There is a great degree of imagination by the police who are coming up with fictitious stories."

He did acknowledge JNU student Hem Mishra who was arrested by Gadchiroli police for alleged links with Maoists but denied giving him any coded chip. Security agencies claim they have found evidence of Saibaba alleged communication with CPI (Maoist) General secretary Ganapathi. The agencies also claim to have strong evidence to suggest Saibaba alleged gave chip containing a coded message to Mishra so he could pass it to top Maoist leaders.

On the 12th, Maharashtra police had made a search of Saibaba house and carried away some items as already detailed above. Agencies claimed Saibaba had been associated with an outfit called Revolutionary Democratic Front, considered a front for the CPI(Maoist). The RDF has been proscribed by Andhra Pradesh. Sources said Saibaba's name had earlier surfaced during the interrogation of the jailed CPI (Maoist) Politburo member Kobad Ghandy. Ghandy had disclosed that Saibaba was the "All India Coordinator" for the mass organisations of the CPI(Maoist).

Saibaba still maintains: "he has no pseudonyms and the police earlier gave false evidence in the name of Ghandy before the Court. It was an attempt to frame me. Ghandy had also denied the statement quoted by the police."

"Voices of dissent being suppressed, says DU Prof raided for Maoist links" [The Hindu: 15 Sep 2013]

This daily has a longish article giving full details of the statements/ assertions/counter-points made by Prof Saibaba to a press conference he addressed at his residence. There is a large photo heading this article. Below the photo is description of the participants which reads: GN Saibaba (centre), DUTA President Nandita Narain (left), author and social activist Arundhati Roy (extreme right) along with teachers of DU during a press conference in New Delhi on Saturday (14 Sep 2013).

Reproduced Below is the Entire Text

He suspected that the raiding team had members from the NIA too. By targeting activists and public intellectuals, the State was trying to suppress voices of dissent that questioned its "so-called Development policies."

Maharashtra police say one of the several evidences purportedly linking Saibaba to several top Maoist leaders was the record of internet "chat sessions" between them. He said the very suggestion of Maoists using Internet for communication was laughable as they could trace easily.

At the conference, which was also addressed by the representatives from the DU Teachers' Association (DUTA) and other public intellectuals, copies of the search warrant issued by a Maharashtra court were circulated among journalists. The warrant was issued for recovery of stolen items. The speakers described the charge of harbouring "stolen property" as outrageous and feared that the raiding team had planted certain objects, which would later be used to frame charges against Saibaba.

Drawing a parallel between parliamentary attack case convict Afzal Guru and Saibaba, noted author Arundhati Roy said in that case, too, it all started with a raid and recoveries made were later used to incriminate Guru.

On the recovery of laptops, hard disks etc, he said that digit devices had his research material and other documents pertaining to the time table and roster of RLA college where he teaches, and had no Maoist literature as was being claimed. He alleged that raiding team had flouted rules. They entered the professor's house before its members were screened to ascertain if they were carrying anything, which would later go in the seizure record. Saibaba said: "Teachers from the varsity were not allowed in and instead two terrified local barbers were picked up by the police and brought in as "neutral observers" for some duration of the raid. They were also coerced into signing on the seizure sheet as witnesses."

Reacting to the allegation that Revolutionary Democratic Front, of which Saibaba is a functionary, was a front outfit of the CPI (Maoist), the speakers said that all groups, which oppose policies leading to displacement of poor people for setting up corporate projects, were targeted by the agencies and there was conspiracy to silence all dissenting voices by hounding them.

Prof Manoranjan Mohanty, a former faculty member of the Du, said: "with the police now targeting someone like Prof Saibaba, who has always voiced the cause of the poor and criticised violence of any kind, it seems as if "Operation Green hunt" is now knocking at the doors of the Capital."

Maoist sympathisers planning meet in Delhi": Police

Maoist sympathisers are planning to organise a 3-day meet in Delhi possibly to talk about operation Greenhunt, says a daily in Sep 2013[66].

The meet, International People's Tribunal, aims at highlighting the "impact of Operation Green Hunt on the tribals", according to the senior police officers in Nagpur.

They say the plan was revealed by one of the documents seized from Prashant Rahi, the alleged Maoist courier from Uttarakhand who was arrested at Deori in Gondia district.

Police claimed the document, like several other papers, originated from DU Prof Saibaba. The document(s) contain elaborate guidelines on how to prepare dossiers and compilation of "fact-finding" reports on the issue from various places, including Bastar, Saranda, Latehar and Gadchiroli. "The affected people should be brought from the areas to depose before the tribunal", the documents say.

Among those to be mobilised for the conclave, according to the documents, are advocates taking up the cases of encounter killings, political prisoners, journalists, activists, writers, artists, film makers, and academicians. The "Jury" of the proposed "Tribunal" consists names such as Arundhati Roy, Rajender Sachar, AP Shah, Sudarshan Reddy and M Suresh.

"DU Professor probe baseless" says DUTA Chief: New Delhi: 18 Sep 2013

DUTA President Nandita Narain wrote to Union Home Minister SK Shinde on 17 Sep 2013, apprising him of Maharashtra Police's raid on Saibaba's house on the 12th. In her letter, she claimed that "during the course of this wholly baseless investigation, the entire family was kept captive—sometimes individually, prevented from or making calls, or meeting anyone who sought to meet them[67]."

The letter claimed that the varsity community was deeply concerned that a pattern of police targeting, thrashing, molesting, and otherwise intimidating and bullying university students and teachers, including persons with disabilities, has developed. She continues: "We condemn the attempt by police to fabricate a specious case against Saibabad", while requesting the Minister to ensure that "no attempt should be made to arrest him... Saibaba suffers from 90 per cent disability and is wheel chair-bound. Given his condition, such unnecessary and excessive police action is especially traumatic not only for him but for his entire family."

"ABVP, Left members clash at venue of Saibaba meeting in Delhi University" [21 Sep 2013]

A meeting in the DU Faculty of Arts, called to protest the police raid at the house of Prof Saibaba, was disrupted by members of the Akhil Bharatiya Vidyarthi Parishad (ABVP) who clashed with students affiliated to the Left unions. The ABVP members tried to cross the barricades put up by the police to separate the two groups. Later, several ABVP members were detained[68].

Interestingly, the clash between the two groups comes day after they marched together to VC's office demanding accommodation for students.

"Last week, the police had searched Saibaba house for allege links with Maoists. "The meeting today was held under heavy police cover." It was attended, among others, by AAP member Prashant Bhushan, Arundhati Roy and Shabnam Hashmi.

DUTA President Nandita Narain said, "The university is a space where you give voice to the country's conscience....The varsity has been turned into a police garrison." Now comes Arundhati Roy, who, criticising the police action at the Saibaba house, said: "Fifty policemen entered his house. Even students and professors who had gathered outside were not allowed to enter."

The meeting was organised a day after historian Romila Thapar and economist Jayati Ghosh, among others, wrote an open letter backing Saibaba.

Professor Saibaba is arrested on 9 May 2014

The expected has happened. Prof GN Saibaba was arrested on 9 May 2014 when he was returning home from the college.

Chronology of Events: From questioning to arrest

12 Sep 2013

Saibaba questioned by Maharashtra police for five hours at his house in north Delhi for Maoist links.

9 June 2014

Questioned again for four hours, shown evidence.

9 May 2014

- Maharashtra police stops his car near Daulat Ram College around 2 PM.
- His driver alleges he was blind folded and taken to Civil Lines police station.
- Saibaba's wife learns about his arrest around 3 PM.
- Saibaba taken to airport around 4 PM, driver told to go back.

The event was covered by the following dailies:

Daily	Correspondent	Date (2014)
Indian Express	Aditi Vatsa and Vivek Deshpande	10 May
The Hindu	Vijetha SN	10 May
Times of India[I]	Raj Shekhar	10 May
Times of India[II]	Somreet Bhattacharya	10 May
The Pioneer	Rashmi Rajput	10 May

"DU Professor held for 'Maoist links" Indian Express

Months after he was questioned for suspected Maoist links, DU Prof GN Saibaba was arrested the Gadchiroli Police, Maharashtra on the 9th afternoon. Saibaba's family says he was returning home for lunch. Car drivers Prashant says: "while returning from college, we were stopped outside the School of Open Learning by 5-6 men in civilian clothing. I was blindfolded and taken to Civil Lines police station. After that I was not allowed to see him."

Saibaba's wife Vasantha said: "when he did not reach home, I called him and his driver. Both did not take my call. Around 3 PM, I got a call from someone who claimed to be from Gadchiroli police. He told me they have arrested him. When I asked why, the call was cut."

Vasantha went to Maurice Nagar police station, where she was told about a team from Godchiroli that arrived at 9 AM. They had arrested her husband.

Saibaba, who teaches at Ram Lal Anand College and is wheelchair-bound, is the Deputy Secretary, Revolutionary Democratic Front. IGP Nagpur Range Ravindra Kadam confirmed his arrest at 2 PM.

His arrest comes months after he was questioned at his house in Sep 2013. Police had searched his house and taken away pen drives and reading material. This was consequent to the disclosures made by journalist and activist Prashant Rahi who had been arrested by Gadchiroli police. Rahi was held after the police had arrested and questioned JNU students Hem Mishra for suspected Maoist links.

Saibabas was charged under various sections of the UAPA and will be produced before a Court in Aheri town of Gadchiroli where a charge sheet has been filed against the trio: Saibaba, Mishra and Rahi.

Kadam was confident: "We have established their Maoist connections on the basis of various material, including a hard disk recovered from Saibaba's house during a search in Sep 2013, and a microchip seized from

Rahi, apart from other literature. We got the material checked from government forensic authorities..... Saibaba was a single-point hub between underground and urban Maoist cadres."

"DU Professor arrested for alleged Maoist links" The Hindu

The way this daily has worded the opening is telling and indicative of its ideological leanings and prejudices.

"After spending the morning evaluating question papers, Prof Saibaba was on his way to lunch when he was way— laid by policemen in plain-clothes and bundled into a waiting car on the 9th. His drive was blind folded and sent to a nearby police station....His family said they were informed about his arrest, for alleged Maoist links several hours later by a police man on the airport."

Several of his colleagues along with social activists gathered at his house 9th evening to extend support to him. Here is DUTA President Nandita Narain: "He had cooperated wholly when the police interrogated him twice in the past. His medical condition is bad, and there is no way that he can be a flight risk that they have to remove him from Delhi in this clandestine manner."

Arundhati Roy adds her weighty, profound observations: "It wa an illegal abduction which amounted to a human rights violation" for the 90 per cent disabled and wheel chair-using professor. It was not a random act but consistent effort by those in power to show that they could do what they wanted, when they wanted and to whom they wanted and to people who spoke up for the rights of the downtrodden. And, that too, even in the time of election when the eyes of the public were on the people in power."

She continues: "Last time they raided Dr Saibaba's house, they took away his things and the seizure memo was not shown to any of the professors who were waiting outside, instead they go the memo signed by someone uneducated they found on road. They did not take his things for nothing, they had the opportunity to doctor whatever they want to. They can now do this to any of us, take away our cell-phones and implicate us.... Special cell of the police is a "genetically-modified cell."

But police denied all allegations. Deputy Commissioner of Police, North District Sindhu Pillai said: "He was taken to Civil Lines (police) station and his wife was informed that he is going to be sent to Maharashtra. All due procedure was followed."

"DU Professor arrested for Maoist links, flown to Mumbai": Times of India(I)

In an operation that lasted two hours, a Maharashtra police team picked up Saibaba from North campus, produced before a magistrate for transit remand, taken to the airport around 4 PM and flown to Mumbai, on charges of Maoist links. His family and activists at a press conference in the evening called it a case of abduction by plain clothes men.

Police claimed Saibab's name had come up during the interrogation of the said Hem Mishra who acted as a courier between the Professor and the banned Maoist cadre holed up in the Abujh Maad forests of Chhattisgarh. The probe showed that he was in direct touch with CPI (Maoist) Central Committee members through a series of couriers using two pseudonyms: Prashant and Chetan. He was found to be in touch with CPI (Maoist) General Secretary Ganapathi and carried out his directives, both at home and abroad.

Police believe Saibaba was a Maoist ideologue and motivator who ran a Maoist front outfit Revolutionary Democratic Front.

Saibaba last spoke to his wife around 1.50 PM when he was leaving Daulat Ram College, where he had gone to check exam papers.

During their interrogation in Sep 2013 and Jan 2014, police claim Saibaba had accepted that he knew Kobad Ghandy, a Doon School educated Maoist ideologue in jail for four years. He denied knowing Bachcha Singh, another arrested Maoist, or having sent a letter (in Telugu) to a CPI (Maoist) leader or to Ghandy.

Sources said apart from Hem Mishra, three other arrested Maoist leaders....Ghandy, Prashant Rahi and Bachcha Singh...have named Saibaba as their ontact in the Capital.

Hem Mishra was arrested with two others in Gadchiroli in Aug 2013. Mishra allegedly had a microchip and a letter meant to be delivered to Narmada Akka, a divisional commander of Maoists, who according to some reports which were later disputed, was killed in an encounter in Dec 2012. Mishra also had some mobile MMS messages from the Naxals to the cadres, police said.

"Saibaba family, friends call arrest a 'brazen act' "Times of India (II)

Full text: Fulminations from the Saibaba supporters

Hours after Saibaba was arrested, activists and professors from the DU led by author Arundhati Roy held a press conference at his house.

They demanded that he be released on health and professional grounds, or they be given the reasons for his arrest.

"This is a brazen flouting of the Constitutional rights of a citizen. Earlier, it was just confined to poor villagers where no one would question the rapes and abductions, but now it has reached cities, too", said an infuriated Roy. She added that the laws like UAPA were made to cater only to the interests of the political bosses of the country and Saibaba was a victim because he had questioned their activities.

Slamming Delhi Police's Special Cell, Roy said the unit had become special because it was a group of genetically modified cells known for illegal detentions or such abduction.

"They use the paramilitary against the poor men when they start questioning govt's move to acquire forest land and use police against urban intellectuals. There are more than 200 MOUs signed secretly between the government and corporate bodies and when people question them the government tags them as part of a banned organisation", Roy said.

Terming the arrest as nothing but the harassment and punishment without any ground, CPI(M-L) Liberation leader and a politburo Member Kavita Krishnan said that the membership of a banned organisation can not be a ground for arrest.

There will be a protest against the arrest outside the Maharashtra Sadan on 10 May (2014).

"DU suspends Professor Saibaba": "Maoist Links: College says suspension not punishment, can be revoked." New Delhi and Nagpur: 16 May 2014

Five days after he was arrested by Maharashtra Police for suspected Maoist links and remanded in Judicial custody, Delhi University on 15 May 2014 suspended Prof GN S Saibaba, the wheel chair-bound English teacher, till further orders[69].

Malay Neerav, Media coordinator, DU, said on the 15th the Professor has been suspended with immediate effect as the university "had accepted the recommendation for suspension received from Ram Lal Anand (RLA) College yesterday." Authorities from the College, however, said suspension was only a "procedural matter that should not be viewed as punishment." An official from the college told the daily: "It is a deemed suspension in accordance with the Central Government rules. Once cleared of his charges, he can request revocation of the suspension order."

Meanwhile, the arrest sparked protests, with the parties condemning and supporting the move in equal measure. While Delhi University Students Union (DUSU) and BJP student wing Akhil Bharatiya Vidyarthi Parishad (ABVP) held a protest march demanding Saibaba be arrested, PUCL condemned the arrest and demanded intervention by National Human Rights Commission (NHRC) to ensure his release. The Jamia Teachers' Solidarity Association too condemned the "gross violation of Saibaba's human rights in Judicial custody."

NHRC spokesperson Jaimini Kumar, however, said, he was not aware of any complaint being filed by PUCL regarding Saibaba's arrest, but assured that if such a complaint was lodged with Commission, it will take appropriate action.

Gadchiroli police claimed that documents in the external hard disk seized from Saibaba's house in 2013 contained "clinching evidence to establish his "Maoist identity."

"The charge sheet filed against Saibaba and alleged Maoists' couriers Prashant Rahi and Hem Mishra observed that a meeting of the Fraction Committee (FC)——one of the urban panels of CPI (Maoist)——referred to a residence eviction notice served by DU on Chetan. The meeting further noted that the issue was later resolved and Chetan was allowed to stay on. The charge sheet observed that since Saibaba has also been served an eviction notice by DU, but was subsequently allowed to stay on, Chetan was none other than Saibaba himself."

This para is not clear if the DU indeed had issued notice to Chetan in the first instance!

According to the charge sheet, a letter by Prakash to the Central Committee (CC) about organising the Anuradha Ghandy (late Maoist leader) memorial lecture and communication between Maoist leader late Azad and the CC was also found on Saibaba's external hard disk.

According to the police, Saibaba was communication hub between the urban and underground Maoist cadres and was operating with two main aliases…Prakash and Chetan…as one of the five members of the FC.

Police said a "clinching" letter to the CC was also found on the hard disk. The letter referred to the financial problems faced by the FC and requested it to send Rs/5 lakh for various activities. The charge sheet said the letter proved that Saibaba and others in the FC were receiving funds from CPI (Maoist).

"Dalit activist vows to fight for Saibaba's release": 1 June 2014 "Mumbai-based Sudhir Dhawale was released from prison after 40 months for his alleged links with Naxalities"

Mumbai-based Dalit activist, Sudhi Dhawale, who is out of jail after spending 40 months there on charges of being a Naxal-supporter, vowed to fight for the release of Saibaba, who is presently in Nagpur jail on similar charges[70].

Dhawale, 45, editor of the Marathi periodical *Virodhi,* says he met Saibaba five days before his own release on 16 May. He says: Saibab and I have been friends for over fifteen years. I am working for his release under the banner Panther Jati Antachi Chawal, a movement aimed towards the release of all those who have been branded Naxalites by the state governments."

He continues passionately: "Saibaba's health is too delicate and he needs immediate medical help. He suffers from blood pressure, has spondylitis and polio. He is immobile form waist down and always moves around in a wheel-chair. He needs someone to take care of him 24×7. I don't think his wife and daughter came to meet him during the time I was there. Having books and documents related to the Maoist thought is not a crime. An Internet search in 0.37 seconds throws up over 8.5 lakh links to Maoist activities which can be accessed by anybody. Sessions Court Judge RG Asmar has mentioned in my 121-page release order that it is not a crime to believe in the Naxal ideology, and on this basis alone Saibaba to needs to be released. Saibaba applied for bail in the Gadchiroi Sessions Court, which is yet to come through."

"Bombay High court quashes Professor Saibaba's bail plea": 26 Aug 2014

The Nagpur Bench of Bombay HC rejected the bail application of DU Prof Saibaba on 25 August. He is behind bars since May (2014) for alleged Maoists links.

Government pleader Bharti Dangre says a bench of Justice Sunil Shurke, while rejecting Saibaba's argument that he could not be branded a Maoist or a sympathiser only on the basis of resemblance between his social activism and Maoist ideology, said prime facie case existed against him for involvement in Maoist activities as a prominent leader.[71]

Saibaba also cited his physical disability as grounds for bail. His lawyer Surendra Gadling, on rejection of his ground, says the court accepted police argument that he was being provided adequate assistance facilities and medicines.

Gadling, on rejection of 'resemblance' argument says court felt a case existed against him. He had also argued police hadn't sufficient material to substantiate their claims. The judge obvious accepted police's claim that there was sufficient material including pen drives and hard disks that were recovered from Saibaba's house. They contain clear evidence of his involvement in Maoist activities as a prominent leader, coordinating urban and international activities of the banned CPI (Maoist).

Confined to wheel chair, Saibaba is currently loged in Nagpur's Central Jail.

Saibaba's arrest had followed interrogation of two alleged Maoists, Hem Mishra and Prashant Rahi who had been nabbed earlier. Police claim the duoled them to Saibaba.

Significantly, Rahi was granted bail on 25 August (2014).

Dr Binayak Sen: A supporter or a Naxal (arrested)

Sen was arrested 14 May 2007 from Bilaspur on the charges of carrying messages and letters from Maoist ideologue Narayan Sanyal [who was arrested on 3 Jan 2006 at Bhadrachalam, district Khammam, Andhra Pradesh], for underground Maoist leaders. A Kolkata-based businessman and his associate Piyush Guha was arrested on 6 May 2007 in Raipur. He was found to be in possession of Maoist publications and three letters purportedly written in jail by Sanyal and delivered to him by Sen. He was granted bail by the Supreme Court on 25 May 2009. The Raipur Sessions Court in Chhattisgarh held him guilty of sedition U/S 124 (a) of IPC, read with Section 20(b) of IPC, and had sentenced him to life imprisonment. He was granted bail by the Supreme Court on 15 Apr 2011, "saying he may be a sympathiser. That does not make him guilty of sedition." He was released on a personal bail bond of Rs 50,000, a surety of Rs 50,000 and on condition that he surrender his passport and attend court whenever summoned.

Binayak Sen's release on bail: Right or Wrong?

What follows is a detailed discussion on the issue of release granted to Binayak Sen, accused of being a Maoist or a Maoist sympathiser. It is an issue that involves not only an important question of personal liberty all Indians are entitled to, but even more importantly, it also impinges upon the national security of the nation.

"Binayak Sen released on bail"

"I know in my heart that I never betrayed the people of this country." Raipur: 19 Apr 2011

At 7 PM on a sultory Mondya (18 Aypr) evening, human rights activist and paediatrician Binayak Sen walked out of the Raipur Central Jail and into the arms of his daughters Aparajita and Pranhita. "I know in my heart that I never betrayed the people of this country", Dr Sen said soon after he was released on bail, pursuant to March 15 order of the Supreme Court[72].

Background of the case

On 24 Dec 2010, A Raipur District and Sessions Court sentenced Dr Sen, Kolkata businessman Piyush Guha and alleged Maoist activist Narayan Sanyal to life imprisonment on the charges of conspiring to commit sedition and aiding the banned CPI (Maoist).

Sen was released on a parronal bail bond of Rs 50,000, a surety for Rs 50,000 and on the condition that he surrender his passport and attend court whenever summoned.

At a news conference at his residence in Raipur later, Sen thanked the broad alliance of national and international activist who had campaigned for his release. Following his conviction, activists from across the country and 40 Nobel laureates issued statements of solidarity and support. "I am not alone. We are all in it together", Sen said.

In Mar 2011, Sen and Guha had appealed against their conviction and moved the Chhattisgarh High Court for bail. While the HC agreed to re-examine the sentence, Justices TP Sharma and RL Jhanwar refused to grant bail. Sen was finally released after his defence filed a special leave petition in the SC.

Sen was arrested in May 2007 on the suspicion that he had served as a courier for Narayan Sanyal. Prison records indicate that Sen had visited Sanyal several times in the Raipur jail, where Sanyal was lodged.

Sen had maintained that he had made the visits in his capacity as a doctor and the Chhattisgarh Secretary of the PUCL.

In his interaction with the media, Sen reflected on the "hundreds of prisoners fighting charges of sedition in Chhattisgarh and elsewhere in the country." Pointing to a recent statement in which Union Law Minister Veerappa Moily spoke of re-examining the sedition law. Sen said, "I hope we can break out of this colonial framework and work towards a free citizenry in a free country."

Reiterating his support for a peaceful and lawful solution to the Maoist insurgency in central India, Sen called for a dialogue between all parties in the conflict.

Reactions to Sen's Release

Reactions from public are recorded below to the release of Sen from different people, in brief.

"Binayak Sen is smiling" "So are Maoists who wage war on India[73]."

The Supreme Court, in its profound wisdom, has granted bail to doctor-turned Maoist activist Binayak Sen, who was sentenced to life imprisonment after being convicted of sedition by a trial court in Chhattisgarh last Dec (2010). Earlier the lower court and High court had refused bail to Sen, giving elaborate reasons to justify their rejection of his petition. As the highest court of appeal in the land, the SC has the right to set aside orders from lower courts. Hence, it would be incorrect to question Friday's (15 April) decision to set Sen free on bail.

However, the SC could have avoided the observations that were made while accepting Sen's plea, not the least because they were clearly uncalled for. The petition before the court was not about the merits of the trial court's judgement, hence to suggest, as the SC Judges have done, that no case of sedition is made out against Sen is unjustified. Let us not forget that Sen had moved a petition seeking bail, not the quashing of the judgement holding him guilty of sedition. There is more. The SC has strangely come to the conclusion that while Sen "can be said to be a sympathiser" of the Maoist cause, that "does not amount to sedition." The line dividing 'sympathy' and 'support' is difficult to locate; those who join Maoist ranks and participate in horrendous violence can also be described as 'sympathisers' of the cause espoused by the Red terrorists——to overthrow the Indian State and supplant it with Pol Pot like regime....

This is not the first time the SC has taken such a lenient view. In the past, persons found guilty of being associated with ULFA has been set free.... Nor should our judges, more so in the higher judiciary, feel compelled to be seen as being 'politically correct' and pander to the view made fashiable by the Left-Liberal intelligentsia. Sadly, the Supreme Court's sanctimonious and gratuitous observations while granting bail to Sen suggest otherwise.

Some letters to the Editor "Binayak Sen is guilty by association" By S. Shankar Singh (New Delhi): The Pioneer: 18 Apr 2011

Sir This refers to Editorial Binayak Sen is smiling, of 19 April. Sen and Maoists have every reason to smile. The highest court had overlooked the fact that Maoists have avowed to over throw a democracy through armed violence.

They destroy roads, bridges, schools, hospitals etc. They merciless behead innocent civilians and security men in Talibiani style .....should not an accomplice of killers and secessionists be held guilty?

"Flawed logic" By Sravana Ramachandra (Ooty): The Pioneer: 19 Apr 2011

Sir- This refers to the Editorial .....I find SC's argument, that mere possession of Maoist literature does not make Sen guilty, unconvincing. Borrowing the Judges' words ......Is that your logic ....that having....Maoist literature at Sen's house, puts him in breach of law....one would like to ask whether a person found carrying illegal arms would be designated a criminal or not?

The SC by granting bail to Sen has sent a wrong signal not just to Maoists but all secessionist groups. Why did not the Court question what prompted Sen to visit Narayan Sanyal, the jailed Maoist leader, 33 times?

"Bail for this (Maoist) activist will embolden Maoists" SC Panda (Bhubaneswar): The Pioneer: 18 Apr 2011

Sir- This refers to ......The Bench said Sen may be a sympathiser.....but not a Maoist....One wonders whether a sympathiser of an outfit waging war against the State should walk free.

Sen's counsel Ram Jethmalani opined that the verdict was an endorsement of the right to freedom of speech as a "principle of democracy." Will Jethmalani ask Maoists if they believe in democracy?

True, no case can be made by were possession of Maoist literature. I would like to point out that the Chhatisgarh Government has sought permission from the SC to file documents establishing close links between the PUCL and PUDR with the CPI (Maoist). The connection between the two outfits came to light during the Delhi Police's investigations of alleged Maoist activities of Kobad Ghandy.

Many like me are of the opinion that SC's granting bail to Sen will embolden Maoists and undermine the efforts of the security forces who are fighting against heavy odds.

"Sen is a Maoist publicist" by M Ratan (New Delhi), The Pioneer, 21 Apr 2011

Sir –This refers to the Letter headlined 'Binayak Sen is guilty by association" (19 Apr). Sen is also guilty of being silent on the atrocities committed by Maoists against humanity. Though he claims to be human rights activist, he has never been condemning Maoist violence on tribals and others. Knowing the violent ways of Maoists .....the SC has obviously overlooked these realities (of murderous Maoists) when granting bail to Sen.

Sen's first TV interview on 18 April, after his release on bail, indirectly brought to the fore his pro-Maoist leanings. At no stage in the interview, did he ask Maoist to shun the path of violence and opt for the ballot. His emphasis was on protecting 'poverty-ridden people' from 'structured state terror' —without doubt, he was mouthing the (well-rehearsed) jargon of the Maoists. But how about protecting people from the planned violence and terror unleashed by Maoists.

"Binayak not allowed to visit Kathmandu" Mumbai: 2012

Rights activist Sen has been denied permission to participate in an international seminar in Kathmandu by a Raipur court, saying. Sen sought permission for visit after confirming his participation to the seminar organisers, hence "the application is not bona fide[74]."

A book confirms that Sen indeed was helping Maoists

"The role of social activist and Planning Commission Steering Committee member Binayak Sen in allegedly helping the Maoists, has come under fresh scrutiny with revelations made in the book, *Let us call Him Vasu"*

30 June 2013

The publication of recent book *Let's call Him Vasu: With the Maoists in Chhattisgarh* by Shubhranshu Choudhary, has brought the focus on Binayak Sen and his links with the Maoists. The author was given access to their network.

It is fair to say that "Nowhere throughout the narrative the *Let's call him Vasu* does the impression come across a bipartisan reader that Choudhary has favoured the state or has gone out of his way to demonise the Maoists[74]."

One of the most important talking points of the book is reference to Dr Binayak Sen. The so-called civil rights activist is now a member of Planning Commission Steering Committee on Health for the 12th Plan (2012-17). The Congress-led UPA brought him on board despite the fact that he is facing a trial in a Chhattisgarh court for his alleged involvement in Maoist activities. Even if the SC criticised the prosecution for pressing charges of sedition against him and released him on bail (critiqued earlier on these pages, it did not clear him of various other charges of colluding with the banned Maoists.

Now to the book about his links to the banned CPI (Maoist)/ Maoists. The author opens up the issue with one of the Maoists who identifies himself as Anil, at a rendezvous, asks: "Did he [Sen] really help courier messages for you"? The answer is unhesitating and unambiguous, "ah yes, of course".

Anil then elaborates the way money meant for Maoist leader Narayan Sanyal was first collected from the Party's Odisha Secretary Sabyasachi Panda by Piyush Guha (who too was arrested along with Sen and who had been a courier for our leader Narayan Sanyal"), and then tried to pass it on to Sen for onward delivery.

It is a revelation that negates all the defence put forth by Sen and his sympathisers, who have been maintaining that he had no connection with the Maoists and that he was merely doing social service. When Choudhary contacted Sen for his version of Anil's claim, he did not answer. His lawyer Ram Jethmalani called back to rubbish Anil's claim as hearsay. It was a disconcerting situation for them. It is for the first time that Sen and friends are faced with a situation that has not been, as they would have said in usual manner, concocted by "class enemies' (a pet hate phrase of the Lefties and Commies) and government officials. It is not enough to brush it aside through a lawyer, they must answer this truly substantial revelation in some substantial measure! Even the Union Government/ MHA must take note of it. But they will not, having just appointed the 'suspect' to a Planning Commission Committee!

Returning to the narrative in the book, Anil hastens to add a kind of elucidation: "I will not say Binayakda worked for the party....He was an old friends of Narayanda (Maoist leader Narayan Sanyal) and only helped him at a personal level". This is a direct quote from the book. But two other conversations will make this "personal level" nonsensical). This piece of statement becomes even more interesting when it is seen in the context of another conversation that the author (of the book) has with a group of Maoist including one named Kosa and a young commander, Dev ji, in the jungles. When Choudhary confronts them with reports that Sen had blamed even Maoists for brutal violence and asked whether Sen had spoken similar language when he was with them. Dev ji called Sen as one of those "intellectuals who change their opinion according to their convenience."

"There is a clear feeling of betrayal among the Maoists, a feeling which can not come by the statement of just some 'personal' friend of a Maoist leader." It is a reaction to the turn around by some one who had once approved of the methods of violence that the Maoists regularly use in their confrontation with the State.

Here is the second conversation that would show the reality of this 'suspected' Maoist! In this context, it is pertinent and essential to record author's conversation with well-known human rights activist K Balagopal in Hyderabad. Balagopal is quoted as saying: "I tried to start a peace process in Chhattisgarh like in Andhra (Pradesh) but Binayak Sen opposed it. Our entire initiative was scuttled by his opposition." And, this is not hearsay, the author says he cross-checked this information and found it to be correct. "Thus, at the very least Sen appears to have been not just closely associated with the Maoist movement in one form or the other——as friend, courier or otherwise but had also been supportive one time of the violence struggle of the Red terrorists.

In the end, Choudhary can not resist a jibe, as he summarises the episode thus: "It appears that the time spent in jail had helped Dr Sen to revise his view on the subject of violence."

From the Balagopal conversation, it is reasonable to believe and conclude that he was not a mere courier that Sen once certainly was, he had a leadership role in the hierarchy. He blocked Balagopal's initiative, scuttling his move to start a peace process in Chhattisgarh. One wonder if someone can find a way to appraise the SC of Binayak Sen's position in the CPI (Maoist) outfit!

View of some eminent journalists on certain relevant issues concerning Maoist movement Shekhar Gupta on Binayak Sen and Maoists

Indian Express: Jun 2013

That is why we say that on the Naxal issue, the UPA's response would confuse George Bush himself. How would his simple maybe simplistic and uncluttered mind deal with a situation where a government is against an enemy, and also with it? Or, forget poor Bush. How would your mind deal with it? And mine? For nine years now, the UPA and its various elements, ranging From the PM and those considered close to Sonia and speaking for her from the Home Ministers (I use the plural deliberately, because even the three who ran that Ministry, Shivraj Patil, Chidambram and Shinde, spoke in different voices, with the first being a pure root-cause man) to NAC members spoke at cross-purposes. One set called them a grave threat, a bunch of bandits and so on, while the other romanticised them as merely misguided). Well-meaning people, fighting for the tribal victims of "extractive" industries. For a full nine years, the leadership of the Congress bought this unquestioningly. It followed, even welcomed, the embedding of the Maoist middle ground and sympathisers within its establishment, notably the NAC and Planning Commission.

Remember that one of these eight Maoists released in exchange for the abducted DC Malkangiri Vineel Krishna was A. Padma, wife of top Maoist Akkiraju Haragopal alias Ramakrishna (RK). And she managed Aman Vatika, an orphanage run by activist and then NAC members Harsh Mander ("At NAC members's NGO, they wait for Padma, wife of top Maoist", Indian Express, 24 Feb 2011, goo.gl/ckoia).

Many of us, including this paper, sympathised with Dr Binayak Sen for being charged and convicted under the obviously archaic sedition law. He is also a very likeable, soft-spoken, sincere paediatrician. But must you appoint him in a key planning committee (steering committee on health, drafting their 12th Five Year Plan)? Gentle, children's doctor, yes. But he is a convicted Maoist sympathiser. Bringing him inside the tent like this, what message are you sending out to the security forces, to the police and security agencies and people of India? Or, to twist the knife, and twist a popular Hindi heartland slogan as well, *Sainiko tum Sangharsh Karo, haemin pata nahin hum kiske saath hain* (fight on soldiers, just that we are not sure whose side we are on). And finally, what message are you sending out to the Maoists? They only let you know last week how they read your confuse minds, by wiping out the entire leadership of your party. (Indian Express, 1 June 2013)

Chandan Mitra on Human Rights wallahs, PUCL, PUDR and a variety of intellectuals vis-á-vis Maoists: The Pioneer: 8 Apr 2012

Murderous Maoists are on the rampage…beheading and killing innocent people.... They have declared was on Indian state. They are conducting their liberation struggle, an euphemism for mayhem and terror. Media savvy leaders of the blood thirsty outfit are unapologetic: Kishanji has proudly asserted their intention to ramp up the campaign of violence (mercifully, he has been liquidated since).

Yes, it is war......against Indian state, democracy, rule of law and judicial system. It is now being waged on an ever expanding are....by now nearly one-third of this country. Their aim violently overthrowing the state...is there any option other than to confront them head-on and eliminate this grievous threat to our value system?

I should think not. But shockingly, there is a significant section of the effete urban middle class, that demurs. Admittedly, it is a small section but wields a disproportionate influence as so-called intellectuals and opinion makers. I have been progressively appalled listening to their perverted logic on TV channels, equating the state with the outlaws, demanding "state terror" end before any plaintive appeal goes out to the Maoist blood hounds.

Interestingly, these spokespersons of the Naxalite terror are regarded with contempt by the very people whose cause they espouse. Marxists in general and Maoists in particular, have always treated the intelligentsia with ill-concealed disdain. Where ever their insane political philosophy had triumphed (Russia, China, Cuba etc), intellectuals were the first to be lined up before the firing squads. Yet like moths to a flame, a kinds of fatal attraction draws rootless intellectuals masquerading as human rights activists to the Maoist 'prairie fire.'

The less said about the JNU variety of intellectuals the better. They have been arguing, in effect, that while the police must act according to every letter of the law, Maoists should be free to shoot, behead, maim, torch and destroy individuals and establishments that represent the State. Clearly, taking a leaf out of Mao Zedong dictum, "Revolution is not a dinner party and revolutionaries are not expected to follow table manners", Naxalism's promoters in intellectual clothing brazently argue that different sets of rules must apply to the state and non-state players (an euphemism for terrorists of every hue...Lashkar to Maoist).

PUCL and PUDR not merely infiltrated, but actually absorbed in total

I must, however, admire their clarity of purpose and capacity for intrigue. They have swallowed up organisations like PUDR and PUCL, originally established to be genuine watchdogs of human rights, civil liberties and excesses by organs of the state. As a result, several such bodies have become de facto Maoist mouthpieces. For them human rights of ordinary citizens are of no cnsequence. Even pre-teen children can be brutally killed on the charge that their parents are police 'informers'. This has been going on for years in Chhattisgarh's Bastar region as a recent report by a fact-finding team irrefutably establishes. For these selective peddlers of human rights, only 'innocent' Maoists and equally 'innocent' LeT activists like Ishrat Jahan need to be defended against the 'predatory' Indian state. They fit perfectly into an uncharacteristically acerbic remark former PM PV Narasimha Rao once made: "From the hue and cry made by some people every time an encounter takes place, it would seem in India only terrorists have human rights and nobody else does."

For too long, the rest of India watched in mute trepidation as all manner of Leftists ran riot over India air waves and newspaper opinion columns. They bellowed all voices of sanity and balance into terrified silence. So much so that today it appears civil society comprises only those who can mount an assault on the state and the nation. It is time for those who refuse to be led on a leash by these intellectually dishonest and morally bankrupt advocates of spurious logic to stand up and be counted.

Arun Shourie: On Naxals: Indian Express: 1 Aug 2006

That the Naxalites are actually carrying out attacks on the police stations, that they are actually executing the people, is not the index of their sway violence comes at a much later stage of their operations: in almost every case, years later.

In an interview with the Telegraph (15 Jul 2005), a member of the Maoist Central Committee, "Comrade Dhruba", is reported as saying that apart from Bankura, Purulia and Midnapur districts, "our mass base in Murshidabad, Malda, Burdwan and Nadia is ready." He adds, and this is what has a bearing on the Home Minister's way of measuring (the spread of Naxalism in India): *"After five years, we will lunch our strikes"*.

By the time violence is unleashed, the Naxalites have entrenched themselves firmly in the area. They commence with surveys—a 56-page survey that was recently recovered of "Perspective Areas" in a targeted state is so proficiently done that it would put some of our best institutions to shame: pattern of holdings, crops, problems of each crop, issues related to wages and tenure, caste composition and tensions. Then front organisations are formed to instigate people on these issues. Experts instigate the demonstrations into violence. Reprisals fuel polarisation. Sympathisers and agents are steered into "voluntary organisations", local bodies, cooperatives. Only after years of such capture and consolidation are *dalams* and like formed. Violence is unleashed thereafter.

By that time, situation has gone so far beyond the reach of the state apparatus that it can only do what the Home Minister is doing now!

Notes

1. Sudha Ramachandran, "The Maoist Conflict in Dandakaranya", in VR Raghavan, Ed, The Naxal threat, 2011.
2. Uppsala University, "conflict definitions", available online at http://www.pcr.uu.se/research/ucdp/data.
3. South Asia Terrorism Portal (SATP), South Asia Assessment 2010.
4. Amalendu Misra, "Subaltern and the Civil War: An Assessment of left-wing Insurgency in South Asia," Civil wars, 5, No. 4 (winter 2002): 56-88.
5. Sudha Ramchandran, see note.
6. 'Praveen Swami, "the Seduction of Maximum Force", *The Hindu*, 31 May 2010 and Saikat Dutta, "On War Footing", Outlook, 26 October 2009.
7. See Sudha Ramachandran, "Chopper ruling raises Maoist tensions", *Asia Time online,* 17 August 2010.

8. Azad quoted in *The Telegraph*, 19 may 2010.
9. See PUCL, when the state makes war on its own people: A Report on the Violation of People's right during the Salwa Judum campaign in Dantewada, Chhattisgarh, (New Delhi, PUCL, 2006), 11-12.
10. Jason Miklian, "The purification Hunt: The Salwa Judum counter insurgency in Chhattisgarh, India," *Dialectical Anthropoloty,* 33, No. 3-4, (Dec 2009): 447.
11. When the Author uses the term 'liberals' in inverted commas ("liberal"), it is a pejorative, to denote that such views are disagreeable, even disgusting, to use a strong word. One would go even beyond that. The views of (Arundhati) Roys and (Gautam) Navlakhas on the Government of India's handling of Maoist insurgency can be deemed to be anti-national.
12. An overview of Constitutional and legislative safeguards and developmental programmes and measures adopted by the government can be found in Ram Babu Mallavarapu's "Development, Displacement and Rehabilitation: An action Anthropological study on Kovaddo Reservoir in West Godavari Agency of Andhra Pradesh, India", *International Journal of Social Sciences,* 1, No. 1 (Winter 2006).
13. Vidhya Das, "PESA: A reality check", Agragamee, cited Sudha Ramachandran, Note 1.
14. For the text of the policy, see Government of India, Ministry of Rural Development, National Rehabilitation and Resettlement Policy, 2007.
15. K. Balagopal,"Naxalites in Andhra Pradesh: have we heard the last of the Peace Talks? "Economic and Political Weekly, 40, No 13 (Mar 26-Aprl, 2005): 1323-9.
16. Arundhati Roy and Gautam Navlakha.
17. Venkitesh Ramakrishnan, "Flawed operation, *"Frontline,* 27, No. 9, 24.5.09.
18. *Ibid.*
19. Sudha Ramachandran: *The Naxal Threat,* VR Raghavan Ed, p. 45.
20. Nandini Sunder, "Pleading for Justice", Seminar, 607, March 2010.
21. It is from a 45-page Chapter tilled, "PESA, Left-Wing Extremism and Governance: Concerns and Challenges in India's Tribal Districts". It formed part of a larger Report Commissioned by the government and researched by Institute of Rural Management, Anand (IRMA). The chapter provides details of how PESA is being violated in Fifth Schedule Areas, providing/ creating room for the growth of Left-Wing Extremism. Interestingly, rather ironically, this chapter was excluded from the final publication of the Report. See Ajay Dandakar and Chitrangada Choudhury, "PESA, left-wing Extremism and Government: Concerns and Challenges in India's Tribal Districs".
22. Shoma Choudhury, "The Doctor, the State, and a Sinister case", *Tehelka,* 5, No. 7, 923 Feb. 2008.
23. See note 21.
24. Sudha Ramachandran, "Delhi targets rebels with a cause", *Asia Times Online,* 8 June 2010.
25. Sudha Ramachandra, "India's war on Maoists under attack," *Asia Times Online,* 26 May 2010.

26. Praful Bidwai, "Dealing with Naxalism in Chhattisgarh," Transnational Institute, October 2007.
27. V Ganapathi, Letter to ICI dated 10 Oct 2006.
28. S. Subramanian, "Naxalism: Fact, Fiction and future", Paper presented at the "Workshop on Naxalism: A distortion of Democratic Development," Rajaji International Institute for Public Affairs and Administration (RIIPPA), Hyderabad, 7 April 1990.
29. Revolutionary movement has three phases. Organisational Phase, Guerrilla Phase, and Mobile Warfare Phase.
30. See the details of three phases in K. Srinivas Reddy, "The Maoist challenge," *Seminar,* No 569, January 2007.
31. PV Ramana, "State response to the Maoist Challenge: An overview", in VR Raghavan, Ed,The Naxal Threat, (Vij Books, New Delhi) 2011, p. 73.
32. This must be the first time (and will possibly be the last) that a central minister has to collect such data 'personally'!
33. Most of the statistical data in this section in from PV Ramana, See note 31, and certain information also is from the sources cited by him.
34. Like some other well-intended official plans, this advertisement plan has not seen the light of the day. As someone who 'studies'half-a-dozen dailies and same number of periodicals, this author can vouchsafe that not to speak of monthly ones, there have not been any such advertisements in media ever since the Maoist uprising! May be the funds crunch killed it.
35. Ministry of Home Affairs, "Action Plan-III, Oct 2009 to Mar 2010," New Delhi, Ministry of Home Affairs.
36. Status Paper on the Naxal Problem, Internal Security Division, MHA, New Delhi, 13 Mar 2006.
37. These 33 districts are 10 in Jharkhand, seven in Chhattisgarh, six in Bihar, 5 in Orissa, two in Maharashtra and one each in Andhra Pradesh, Madhya Pradesh, and Uttar Pradesh.
38. PV Raman, See note 21, p. 78.
39. *Ibid,* p. 81.
40. Santosh K. Joy, "Rahul echoes Rajiv Gandhi's on Public Funds", Rediff News, 17-01-08.
41. Government of India, Parliamentary Standing Committee on Home Affairs, 112th report, Demands for Grants, 2005-2006, New Delhi: Rajya Sabha Secretariat, April 2005.
42. Parliamentary Standing Committee on Home Affairs, 132nd *Reports, Demands for Grants,* 2008-09, New Delhi: Rajya Sabha Secretariat, Apr 2008, see VR Raghav, p. 84.
43. *Ibid.*
44. Cited, from an internal report of the MHA, copy of which is available with PV Ramana, Note 31.
45. K Srinivas Reddy, "The Maoist Challenge," *Seminar,* New Delhi, January 2007.
46. See the Report of the Planning Commission Export Group, p. 51.

47. The letter in the Organiser, a weekly, is written by HS Mehtani, 89/7, East Punjabi Bagh, New Delhi-26.
48. Anumeha Yadav, The Hindu, 10 Sep 2013.
49. Sukanya Shantha, Indian Express, 1 Jul 2013.
50. Shaju Philip, Indian Express, 30 Jul 2014.
51. Shaju Philip, Indian Express, 10 Aug 2014.
52. Shaju Philip, Indian Express, 13 Dec 2014.
53. Rakesh K. Singh, The Pioneer, 11 Oct 2013.
54. Chandan Mitra, The Pioneer, 8 Apr 2012.
55. Editorial, The Pioneer, 4 May 2012.
56. Sandhya Jain, The Pioneer, 15 Jan 2013.
57. Uttam Sengupta, The Outlook. 7 May 2012.
58. Soumitra S Bose and Shreya Roy Chowdhury, Times of India, 25 Aug 2013.
59. Pavan Dahat, The Hindu, 25 Aug 2013.
60. Soumitra S. Bose, Times of India, 18 Sep 2013.
61. J. Venkatesan, The Hindu, 26 Apr 2011.
62. Sandeep Joshi, The Hindu, 26 Sep 2012.
63. Ruhi Tewari, Indian Express, 2 Jul 2013.
64. Sreenivas Janyala, Indian Express, 7 Nov 2014.
65. G Narasimha Rao, The Hindu, 7 Nov 2014.
66. Viviek Deshpande, Indian Express, 15 Sep 2013.
67. Times of India, 18 Sep 2013.
68. ENS, Indian Express, 21 Sep 2013.
69. ENS, Indian Express, 16 May 2014.
70. Mamta Sen, Sunday Guardian, 1 June 2014.
71. Vivek Deshpande, Nagpur, India Express, 26 Aug 2014.
72. Aman Sethi, The Hindu, 19 Apr 2011.
73. An Editorial in the Pioneer, 18 Apr 2011.
74. Suvojit Bagchi, The Hindu, 2012.

20

Andhra Pradesh and Telangana

Andhra Pradesh was the state to be hit in a big way by LWE, post-Naxal infection in North Bengal. Naxalism nearly died after initial flare-up due to the leadership of its founding father, brilliant but impetuous Charu Mazumdar.

Prairie fires lit in Andhra Pradesh in the 1970s was (nearly) extinguished in the province but was forced out and spread beyond its northern borders, its flames engulfing eastern Maharashtra region of Gadchiroli, southern region of MP, present Chhattisgarh and Odisha.

Andhra Pradesh is the only success story in India's country-Naxalite fight ("Naxalbari", of course, was a small area comprising some villages around Naxalbari in north Bengali's Darjeeling district, where the fires were put out in a couple of years in the 1960s). Presently, the LWE is spread in nearly one-third of the country as detailed in the earlier chapters.

As for Andhra Pradesh, a brief summary provides essential facts.

Origin

The movement started in the early 1970s. Peasants supported by Naxals revolted against landlords, moneylenders.

Bloody Era	:	1980 – 2000.
Key Issues	:	Exploitation of tribals and rural landless.
Status Check	:	The State has been free from Maoist Violence since 2006.

The Maoists are now trying to regain a foot hold.

Kiran Kumar Reddy, CM (Dec 2011) Cautions

"We should not remain, complacent. Naxalites, on the run, might try to re-enter the state."

Major events, incidents and developments are recorded on the following pages.

Long Last Success in 2006, Andhra Pradesh Cleared of LWE

In 2006, the state had won the battle against the Maoists.

Period leading to the success (History)

By 2003, all 23 districts were infested by Naxalism. On 1 Oct 2003, CM N Chandra Babu Naidu was nearly killed in a Maoist attack.

Andhra Pradesh (AP) has had decades – long experience, of dealing with the Naxalite violence. The state is reputed to have launched various initiatives to counter and defeat the CPI (Maoist) war machine, including the much-analyzed Oct 2004- Jan 2005 peace talks, which had generated a huge controversy.

First about how it all started. If a date is to be fixed for beginning of Naxalism in AP, it has to be 31 Oct 1967, when a huge meeting organized by the Jatapu and the Savara tribes in Srikakulam was disrupted by Medi Satyam of the Congress Party. In the ensuing violence, Satyam and two tribals were killed. That was the day it all began in AP. Incidentally, the revolutionary movement sprang in Darjeeling's Naxalbari in May 1967.

Now a word on the peace talks. The State Police admitted that in the manner of Assam's ULFA, the Naxals here also utilized the ceasefire to augment their strength and enhance its fighting capabilities. Post Ceasefire the number of the Maoist fighters grew from 700 to 1200. During the peace, the Naxalites succeeding in reclaiming their domination and evolving a comprehensive plan to make Telengana the beacon of revolutionary movement again.

Both the Maoists and State Police agree that "the Peace Talks are history" now! Even the writer and activist poet, P Varavara Rao, who was a member of the trio of Maoist delegates to participate in the talks, admits as much.

Even the top police officials of the SIB and the Greyhounds involved in the anti-Naxal operations admit that recruitment drive by the Reds went up as did the militant activity. No wonder that CM YSR Reddy was severely criticized for inviting ultra – Left Maoists to talks soon after winning the 2004 Assembly polls, without thinking through the issues involved. Criticism was possibly well founded: "His hasty step bestowed greater credibility on the Maoist leadership that had possibly been done by the years of work of the balladeer Ghadar. But it must be remembered that the CM felt obliged to hold talks to redeem his poll pledge.

Post – Peace talks scenario

DGP Swaranjit Sen seemed quite clear as to what his police should do: "Police offensive must continue to neutralize the Maoist threat. A many as 167 rebels were killed last year (2005) in encounters. At the same, the police cannot oppress the villagers in the name of getting information on the ultras, colouring them as sympathizers[1]."

Police action ensured that Maoists' stronghold in AP – the North Telengana Zonal Committee (NTZC) - - has weakened. Even, the earlier nucleus of Naxal movement, Warangal, is no more its stronghold. ASP Warrangal, again confirm it : "Our information network is much superior. It is now apparent that several NTZC members have retreated into Chhattisgarh."

But critics warn the government against sense of complacency, as "it has only won a battle". It was far from winning the war. But certain new potential signs of danger were surfacing. Firstly, such threat comes from CPI (Maoist) AP State Committee, based in the Nallawalla and Rayalaseema areas. The second comes from the Maoist Division of Andhra – Odisha Border Committee. In both the said areas, forest cover is dense and the terrain difficult, and to make the matters worse for the state and welcome for the ultras, the police information network is weak and sparse. Consquently, it should have come as no surprise to the State authorities and observers alike that the Maoists' "month – long 9th Congress" was convened at the Andhra – Odisha border area in a 'secured' enclave in early 2007.

Evaluating AP's anti-Naxal 'Success': 2007

Reddy was criticized for the peace talks to the Maoists, when they had been pushed into a corner by the previous Naidu government, and expectedly they agreed as they had needed a ceasefire urgently. The issue has been discussed above. It needs to be recorded that after completing full circle, the Reddy government itself launched a Naidu-like offensive against the Maoists in 2006, having realized the futility of 2004 Peace talks. And having completed three years in office early 2007, the Reddy government, claimed a victory over the Naxals, and a good number of analysts seemed to accept the tenability of this claim. What follows is a dominant opinion on this operation and consequent success:

> "The year – long exercise turned the tide completely in the battle against the LWE in AP. After spectacular success by the police in targeting and eliminating key leaders of the CPI (Maoist), the year ended with the Naxalite Army in a shambles.

"In the course of 2006, the killing of 42 senior leaders - - including AP Committee chief Burra Chinnaiah alias Madhav and at least one Central Committee member Wadkapur Chandramouli - - delivered such a blow to the outfit that it was forced to suspend it operations in the State[2]."

The Naxalite toll for the year 2006 is fatal and too grievous as detailed below:

1. State Committee Chief and at least one Central Committee member, as mentioned above.
2. Three State Committee members.
3. Four State Committee Secretaries.
4. 12 District Committee members.
5. 20 Squad Commanders.
6. 320 Maoists surrendered and 717 others arrested.
7. After 1999, when the police killed three senior Central Committee members (Nalla Adi Reddy, Seelam Naresh and Santosh Reddy) in a single incident, this (2006) was the most successful year for the anti-Maoist operations.

To demonstrate the supremacy the police had established, DGP Sen personally visited and marched through the thick forest of Nallahmallah, once the impregnable fortress of the Maoists and the Dandakaranya forests on the Andhra – Odisha border. "These were the names the policemen would tremble even while mentioning them".

The strategy was to target the top State and District leadership of the Maoists. The idea was that once the pillars fell, the edifice would crumble in a confused mass.

But depend upon Gaddar, the part poet and part ideologue, to see it differently:

"This is not an adept internal security (management), but a 'betrayal'. We have lost so many top leaders because of tactical mistakes and our failure to understand the enemy. The Government talked of peace but pursued violent methods. Police agents infiltrated the Maoist camps and the insurgents failed to identify them in time. Tech Madhu, one of the Maoists, expert on munition, is a good example of this. He had been 'won over' by the government during peace talks, when he was arrested and released by the (government)/Police. He provided information to the police on many leaders...Many of the deaths were not in battle, but in "false encounters". He insisted that each death has motivated cadres even more, and the revolution is not far away!

It is good parting shot by balladeer Ghaddar, a bravado. The fact is that the Maoists "have been left crippled." The most significant operation was the one that yielded 875 rockets and 27 rocket launchers supplied to the Maoists from the neighboring Tamil Nadu. So was the funds flow curtailed. The police seized Rs 1.38 crore from the Naxalites in various searches during 2006.

Some related events and circumstances

Before closing the "success story", it is worthwhile to mention some relevant information:

- The change, indeed, is dramatic. In the early 1990s, the Naxalites were reputedly running a parallel 'government' in the State. In 2003, they nearly killed CM Naidu. Each new attack turned to be more audacious than the previous one. Their fire power had been augmented with the add-ons like the AK 47 and IED. The Rs 50 – 60 crore extortion from the contractors, businessmen, officials and local politicians had transformed the pro-poor "proletarian Army" into a resource rich enemy!
- 2002 saw a first glimmer of hope for the hapless victims of their violence. The Naidu Regime and the People's War - - now part of the CPI (Maoist) - - agreed to hold talks. The PW nominated poet Varavara Rao and Balladeer Ghaddar to represent it at the talks, which soon collapsed, leaving the two sides blaming each other. A year later, Naidu escaped assassination attempt atop the Tirumala Hill near Tirupati. This marked the start of an intense confrontation.
- The second dramatic change came with YSR Reddy coming to power in May 2004 and inviting the Reds for talks as per his poll pledge. To facilitate the emergences of Maoist leadership from their jungle hideouts, the government allowed the 12 – year- long ban on the PW to lapse. Consequently, the rebel leaders, including the State Committee chief Ramakrishna, travelled to Hyderabad for 'peace talks' in Oct 2004. Ramkrishna was even allowed to address a public meeting in Guntur.

What vitiated the air just a day before the formal talks was the announcement of the CPI (M-L)-PW combine that it was merging with the Bihar-based MCC of India to create the CPI (Maoist). The PW chief Ganapathi was to lead the new supra-Maoist outfit, spread across 13 States.

If this raised suspicions, the Maoist demand that, despite the peace talks, they be permitted to carry arms and reserve their right to armed struggle, did not help. By Jan 2005, talks had broken down. The sound of gun fire was once again heard in the forest once again. When Congress leader C Narsi leader and 10 others were killed in Mahbubnagar district, the government was forced to reimpose the ban on CPI (Maoist) and its front organizations.

At the end, it is useful to note that some critics felt that effusive self-congratulations were uncalled for, and that the war was yet to be won. A sane advice, knowing as we do now that subsequently, the Maoists had been succeeding in reviving their outfit in AP.

1 Oct 2003

An attempt on the life of Andhra CM Chandra Babu Naidu at Alipiri near Tirupati, by the P.W.

A senior Maoist leader killed, 16 Jun 2006 (Ravi Kumar)

A top Maoist leader, Matkam Ravi Kumar alias Anil was killed on 16 Jun 2006 in an encounter with the police in the interior Nallamalla forest area. On a tip-off, the police started combing the forests, and spotted him along with two others at Pitchirajuthanda, some 25 km from Yarra-gondapalem. In the ensuing fire fight, he was killed. When they reached the spot, Ravikumar was found lying dead in a pool of blood. The other two had made good their escape.

Police say Ravikumar was a member of the State and Central Committees. Deemed an intellectual? He was actively engaged in policy-making and issuing directives and guidelines for the extremist movement. Some other details are mentioned here:

1. He drafted the documents for the State and Central Committees.
2. Technology savvy, he was the first among Maoists to use palm top computers.
3. He was also member of the Propaganda Committee.
4. He hailed from Tandur in Ranga Reddy district and was an engineering graduate.
5. He joined the rebels in 1986.
6. Penned several articles under the pen name Manjeera.
7. Being a Central Committee member, he carried a bounty of Rs 15 lakh on his head.

CPI (Maoist) State Secretary Madhav called some select news men to condemn the killing Paying glowing tribute to Ravikumar, he recalled his 30 years of service in the cause of the LWE movement, and termed his death as an irreparable loss to the Maoist movement. He squarely blamed

CM Reddy and DGP Sen for continuing repression of the movement and encounter killings. He vowed revenge.

Top Andhra Maoist killed, 24 Jul 2006 (Madhav)

The Andhra Pradesh police on 23 Jul 2006 gunned down eight Maoists, including top leader and CPI (Maoist) State Committee Secretary Madhav, in an encounter in Prakasham district. Though the encounter took place in the morning, the police could establish the identities of the slain ultras, including Madhav, only late in the evening[3].

CM YSR Reddy reviewed the situation with DGP Swaranjit Sen, and it was decided to alert the police against the reprisal attacks by the Maoist in the wake of Madhav's killing.

SP Prakasam district N Balasubramanyam confirmed Madhav's death. This was done after a surrendered Maoist from nearby Guntur district was brought to the site of the encounter and identified Madhav's body among others.

60 police teams from Prakasam, Guntur, Kurnool and other districts took part in the operations, surrounding the Nallamulla forest where the encounter took place.

The police force had surrounded an area in the forest following a tip off that a group of 20 – 30 Maoists were holding a meeting to discuss the move to bring back senior Maoist leader Akkiraju Haragopal aka Ramakrishna, as State Committee Secretary.

Madhav had replaced Ramakrishna as State Committee Secretary in 2005 after peace talks between the Maoists and the AP Government had failed in late 2004.

Two among the killed were identified as Burra Chinnaiah alias Madhav alias Ashok alias Malanna hailed from Mangapet hamlet of Srirampur village in Karimnagar district.

The police recovered eight weapons from the encounter site: one AK-47 rifle, two single-barreled guns, two 303 rifles, and three double-barreled guns besides eight kit bags.

Sudarshan and two others killed, 6 Oct 2006

Three Naxalites, including a top leader Sudarshan alias Satyam, Secretary, Nallamalla Forest Division Committee of the outlawed CPI (Maoist), were killed in an encounter with the Greyhound commandos in Anantpur district, when the latter were carrying out combing operations in Goonepalli forest area, near Bulakpatnam village. Rayalaseema Regional

Committee member Obuyleshu was also killed in the fierce gun battle while the third Naxalite was not identified.

A wanted Naxalite, Sudarshan carried a bounty of Rs 3 lakh on his head. He was responsible for killing of 8 villagers at Vempenta village of Kurnool district in 2005 and was involved in as many as 103 criminal cases, including 30 murders. He was involved in 20 criminal cases in Prakasam district alone. Again, he was one of the four Naxalites involved in a daring attack on SP Prakasam District Mahesh Kumar Ladda early 2007.

Hailing from Warrangal district, he had also worked as Nalgonda District Committee Secretary. DGP Sen remarked the killing of Sudarshan signified an end of the Maoist hold on the Nallamara forest area, and it was a blow to the CPI (Maoist).

A Deputy Commander of Gurtedu squad killed, 7 Oct 2006

The Deputy Commander was killed during the combing operations launched by the Greyhound commandos in GK Veedhi Mandal forest area in Vishakhapatnam district. This was a day after a police constable was injured in a landmine blast at Palkajeedi village in Koyyur Mandal. During the search operations, the police encountered the members of the Gurtedu Dalam when exchange of fire took place.

The incident comes a day after the police had gained a major success in killing Sudarshan, a senior Maoist, as already covered in the preceding entry.

Likely Naxalite attacks in AP worry CRPF, 24 Oct 2006

The CRPF on 24 Oct 2006 expressed concern on the possible intensification of attacks by Naxals in AP and its adjoining areas as some reports suggested that some rocket shells seized by security forces in the State might have already found their way to the LWE outfits. The Tamil Nadu and AP police forces in a joint operation had recently seized 875 rockets and other ammunitions from different places in Mahboobnagar and Prakasham districts.

Ahead of the 67th Raising Day of his force on 28 October, DG CRPF JK Sinha on the 24th expressed his concerns to the reporters: "Though a husband-wife duo has been arrested, some reports suggest some rocket shells have already reached the Maoists. They have only to fill in some explosive material and shells are ready for use against security forces. Precautionary measures are already in place and various state governments alerted.

When asked a question on the recommendations made by the Union Tribal Welfare Ministry to scrap the Salwa Judum movement, DG Sinha gave his considered view: "Such movements needed support from the government as it was people's voice against the Maoist depredations. One should not even think of scrapping the movement. If it was scrapped, people will never come forward and extend such whole hearted support . . . . For the tribals involved in the Salwa Judum, it would either be a meek surrender before the Naxal groups or fall prey to their bullets. There is no third way for them if the Government were to withdraw support to the Judum . . . . In turn, we should be at the forefront of the movement which has seen large number of the tribals, coming forward on a joint platform against the Maoists, especially in the worst-hit Dantewada district of Chhattisgarh".

AP Police hit on a Goldmine of information on Naxals, Jan 2007

Two raids by AP police on the key hideouts of the Maoists in the latter half of Jan 2007 in Bhopal and Rourkela led not only to the arrest of some senior cadres and recovery of arms and ammunitions but more significantly to the seizure of gold mine of information about the Naxalite outfit in the form of CDs, DVDs and hard discs.

Sources involved with the operations in two cities aver that CDs, DVDs and computer hard discs seized in the raids "contain so much information that it will take several months to analyse it all." The information concerns the details of Maoist network in different states as also their own analysis of the past failures and future strategies and plans. The importance of treasure trove could be measured from the fact that it also includes animation films on the assaults and counter-assaults on the police forces and other targets. Same way, there is also technological information on the arms manufacturing and presentation for the training camps of the Maoists.

It is obvious that the seizure and the information it affords to the security and intelligence agencies will have serious and far reaching implications for the organizational functioning and operating capabilities of the Maoists throughout the country.

The information yielded by the technical gadgetry has fully given out the present strength and location of the Maoist cadres in various parts of the country[4].

Besides the police officers from different states, the IB officers too are involved in analyzing the information contained in these CDs etc. Some analysts believe the CPI (Maoist) has suffered this blow when it is already on the run in AP where the police gained much success against it in 2006. In a related report, it has been confirmed that the Maoist leadership has been sending its cadres to new bases, yet to be consolidated, in the Western Ghats, Goa and Karnataka.

DGP Mohd Abdul Basit is happy that coordination with other states against the Maoists has yielded good results, and the recent encounters were the result of this strategy. On his first visit to the Maoist-hit Prakasam district after taking over as DGP, Basit is realistic: "It cannot be claimed that the Maoist problem has been completely contained, even if we have achieved a conspicuous success."

Maoists plan a corridor Ghats to Ghats: Feb 2007

The Maoists "are believed to be creating a corridor from Sesha Chalam Hills of Eastern Ghats to the Western Ghats via Jawadi Hills, Bennari and Satyamanglam. The Maoists are also trying to expand their activities in coffee plantations in Ooty and adjoining districts of Karnataka. They have been intervening in local labour disputes in these places."

To resist the growing Maoist influence, coffee growers in Malnad region formed an organization, Grameena Jagruti Sena, in end January.

Andhra Naxals find Shelter in Western Ghats, Feb 2007

Coming under relentless pressure consequent to combing operations by the AP police, Maoists in the lush Nallawalla and Bhadrachalam forest of Dandakaranya are moving to the harsh and rocky terrain of the Western Ghats, reports a daily[5], in Feb 2007.

It was only recently that State Special Intelligence Bureau (SIB) learnt that the Western Ghats had become the new refuge of the Maoists of AP. The State authorities had believed that their operations would drive the ultras to the neighbouring Chhattisgarh and MP. They, instead, seem to prefer Karnataka and parts of Western Ghats, including Goa areas.

A policeman says: "We learn that the Maoists are conducting special training camps to help their cadres survive in the terrain of these Ghats."

It is expected consequences of this movement that Naxal activities in Kerala, Karnataka and parts of Maharashtra will witness a spurt. These states are keeping a tab on the Naxal movement on their territories. The Karnataka police has intensified combing operations in Chikmaglur, Raichur and Malnad.

The Maoist presence in the Western Ghats was first noticed in 2001 when a tribal woman, Cheramma, suffered a bullet injury when she fired a gun accidentally at village Menasenahadya in Chikmaglur, Karnataka. Since then, Maoists have been trying to establish a hold over the Western Ghats.

But their plans were spoiled by the activities of sandalwood smuggler Veerappan and the special task force hunting him.

The things have quietened down after the death of Veerappan and the Maoists, who are on the run in the State, now consider Western Ghats their least refuge.

Naxals high on marijuana in AP, Mar 2007

Arrests by AP police show that the State's "ganja' farms are now used to provide funds for purchase of weapons for the Maoists from two persons: Shahad Bhai of Bokarpur in Munger district in Bihar and Anand in Satna, MP. So far, they have supplied 39 country made pistols and two carbines to Naxal groups operating in AP[6].

"In their latest run last week, the gang had gone to Jabalpur in MP with eight quintals of 'ganja' and sold it for Rs 7 lakh." The amount was used to purchase five 9 mm pistols, four 7.62 mm pistols and extra magazines from Bihar for Rs 1.22 lakh. The gang then did not take the train back to Jabalpur. They returned in modified vehicles. On a tip off, the police intercepted them at Annasagar crossroads on the outskirts of Warrangal city.

Besides the weapons, eleven bags of marijuana were also recovered from their house. Police believe this might not be the only gang engaged in this lucrative business in the state. DSP K Narayan feels while these smugglers may not be directly associated with the ultra groups, they had 'close relations' with many top commanders. Besides Goutham, police also arrested Sasarla Raman Reddy, Kothapalli Darshan, Naini Naveen Reddy and eight other from Warrangal.

Two transporters, whose Tata Sumo and DCM vans were modified to hide and transport the contraband under crates of fruit, were also arrested. Naik said Marijuana was grown in Sileru, near Vishakhapatnam, in Warrangal, near Karimnagar and Adilabad borders, and in Medak district.

The police disclosed the weapons procured in this manner were being sold at a premium to Naxal groups listed below [and possibly some others]:

1. CPI (ML) - - Pratighatana
2. CPI (ML) - - Praja Pratighatana
3. Communist Party of United States of India [CPUSI]

AP Police unearth Naxal Arms Dump, Mar 2007

Close on the heels of Naxal's major success in killing 55 police during their attack on Rani Bodla police camp in Chhattisgarh on 15 Mar 2007, the AP police found a large arms dump of the same outfit in Nallamalla forest. Significantly, it contained long range explosives which could be used to target police stations and camps.

The dump was also discovered on 15 Mar 2007 itself, only hours after the Rani Bodla massacre. Arms and explosives seized from the dump are detailed below:

1. Over 270 rockets and launchers, with adequate material to assemble another 100 rockets. The rockets were similar to the ones discovered by the police in Mahboobnagar in 2006, which first led the police to believe that the ultras had this type of fire power, SP Gunlur district B Shivadhar Reddy explains: "It appears as though this batch of rockets too was made in the same factory as the earlier one. The two are identical in nature".
2. These rockets were found at the Guntur – Prakasam border near Pullala Ghuruvu, and DGP Basit said the shoulder-fired rockets had a range of some 5 km.
3. Now for the material for making rockets: 112 rocket pipes, basic components of the rockets, and empty warheads. There were also large number of smaller parts like rocket propeller nuts, propeller caps and the fins.
4. Police also retrieved 47 Anti-personnel Claymore mines, mine springs and spare parts used in pressure mines.
5. There were also one double barrel gun, a country-made pistol and 0.30 rifle ammunition.
6. Some grenades, 380 grenade strikers, 360 detonator caps, etc.
7. Some walkie – talkies and camera flashes.

In Sep 2006, the AP police had found 875 rockets meant to be transported into Nallawalla forest for Naxalites. The rockets were believed to have been manufactured in factories war Chennai, and these were raided by the Tamil Nadu police. They later arrested the 'designer' of the rockets, Tech Madhu and his wife, who subsequently turned approvers.

AP : Top Naxal leaders surrender, 25 Mar 2007

Two top Naxal leaders, Durgam Ramanaiah alias Ravi and Merugu Sambaiah alias Ganesh Ueike, surrendered before the AP police in Warrangal on 25 Mar 2007. While the former surrendered due to ill health, 55 year – old Sambaiah gave up because he was "disillusioned with the outfit's ideology". Incidentally, Sambaiah is a contemporary of party founder Kondapalli Seetaramaiah[7].

Sambaiah's wife Ballamkonda Sarakka, who too was undergrounder over the last few years, has also surrendered. If he was involved in cases like the Koraput jail break of 2004 and attacks on police stations in Koraput and Etunagaram, She headed the Chaitanya Natya Manch in Dandakaranya.

Sambaiah explains his decision: "The group has failed to involve the masses and the leadership was unwilling to change with times. There was stark difference between the Nepal's Maoists and India's. I was among the pioneers of the movement in the region."

Ramanaiah was involved in cases like the murder of Yellandu Market Committee Chairman and an attack on Kothagudem Thermal power station. He joined the party in 1993 and was part of the Radical Students Union, said SP warrangal Saumya Mishra. He was also member of the North Telengana Special Committee, DK Zone and the Central Military Commission. He had been conducting military training camps till Jan 2007 for the State Committee members and the divisional committee secretaries of the group. These camps were held in West Bastar, and the Andhra – Odisha Border areas of Gaikonda, Gangaluru, Bairangadh and Made.

7 – 8 Sep 2007. Maoists exploded a landmine at Vakalu in Nellore district as former CM of Andhra Pradesh N. Janardhan Reddy along with his wife passed in a motorcade. He was targeted by the Maoists as he had cracked down on LWE in early 1990s. They hold him responsible for killing some 400 Naxalites.

AP to set up 13,000 - strong Anti-terror Force

6 Sep 2007

The AP Government decided to create an Anti – Terrorist Squad (ATS) of police, comprising 13,000 members, to deal with terrorist activities. Announcing this on 6 Sep 2007, State Home Minister K Jana Reddy said: "Efficient men with good performance record now working in different wings of police would be inducted into the proposed ATS. Its constitution will be completed in one and a half months."

Background

The plan for creation of the ATS was prepared by a committee headed by Chief Secretary J. Harinarayana. Its members were DGP MA Basit, ADGP (Intelligence) K Arvinda Rao and Hyderabad Police Commissioner Balwinder Singh. The Committee was tasked to make recommendations after studying the functioning of counter – intelligence wings of different countries.

CM had declared that the proposed ATS would be on the lines of highly successful anti-Maoist outfit Greyhounds, with a very high standards of fitness and efficiency for its men.

Ominous name for ATS: OCTOPUS, 7 Sep 2007

The elite intelligence-cum-combat force, created by the AP Government to fight terrorism, has been christened OCTOPUS, Organisation to counter terrorist operations. It will be headed by an ADGP and will have various wings, including special (Intelligence) Branches at city, district and state levels.

A press release issued by CM Reddy's office, after he reviewed the law and order situation in the state, in Hyderabad, says the OCTOPUS will have essentially three wings mentioned below:

1. **Intelligence and Analysis Wing.** To collect intelligence inputs at city, sub division, district and state levels.
2. **Technical Intelligence Wing.** To monitor communication, forensic and cyber – related activities.
3. **Research and Analysis Wing.** To undertake data interpretation, analysis, inter-agency coordination and planning.

The OCTOPUS would undertake surveillance operations by way of shadowing recording, interpretation; field operations through assault teams and bomb disposal squads and rescue operations equipped with ambulances and para-medical teams.

15 Feb 2008. Maoists attacked Nayagarh and Daspalla towers, killing 14 cops. They took away 11 × 47AKs, 75 × SLR rifles, 250 × INSAS rifles, 6 × LMGs, 69 × 9 mm pistols and many .303 rifles and muskets. They also circulated a 28-page booklet on "Operation Ropeway", terming the attack as historic and complete success.

15 Feb 2009. Secretary, State Committee of CPIC (Maoist) Konakuri Ilaich alias Simbaasivdu, who had planned the Oct 2003 blast to kill the then AP CM Chandrababu Naidu, surrendered before the Hyderabad Police (The Indian Express, 17.02.2009).

24 May 2009. Patel Sudhakar Reddy, (Chief of the intelligence unit of the Party, member of the Central committee and Central Military Commission) who carried a reward of Rs 12 lakh on his head as he was wanted in many serious cases, war killed in Prakasam district, Andhra Pradesh. K. Venkataiah, State Committee member, was also killed on 24 May in Tadvai forest in Warrangal districts. "Rights groups claimed that the encounter was stage – managed."

Act against bauxite mining: Minister Deo tells AP Governor, New Delhi: 8 Jul 2012

Three months after Union Tribal Affairs Minister (TAM) V Kishore Chandra Deo wrote to AP Governor ESL Narasimha, to exercise his constitutional powers to cancel the permission given for bauxite mining in Vishakhapatnam as it was fuelling LWE there, the latter has finally responded - - referring the issue to the State government which, had, in the first place, signed MoUs with several companies to permit bauxite mining[8].

Commenting on Governor's letter, Mr Deo told the daily he did not know why he referred the matter to the state government. He just had to verify the facts and take action.

In his 14-page letter of 7 Apr 2012, Mr. Deo pointed out that ever since the state government signed a series of MoUs (between 2005 and 2010) with several companies "neither owned nor controlled by people belonging to STs", and then went on to recommend 13 more applications in favour of AP Mining Development Corporation (APMDC) "for prior approval of mining leases, Maoists have begun to gain ground in Vishakhapatnam district "by gaining sympathy of the locals only due to the threat of boxing mining."

Mr. Dew, who is familiar with Vishakhapatnam as it is one of the four district, that fall in his Araku parliamentary constituency, had met PM Manmohan singh and Congress president Sonia Gandhi to explain the situation.

The MoUs signed with various companies as well as clearing of the applications of the APMDC, by the then YSR Reddy government, Mr. Deo write, "betray our commitment for the cause of the people who belong to the ST communities amount to flagrant violation and affront of our constitutional provisions."

In the letter, Mr. Deo says Governors are empowered by the constitution to make regulations for peace and good governance, including those relating to Land Alienation and Transfer Allotment of Land in Schedule V areas (designated tribal areas in the mainland, just as Schedule VI refers to the tribal areas in the North-East). For this purpose, the Governor can repeal or amend any Central or State law or any existing law applicable to such an area. Further, the Governor is not bound by the aid and advice of the Council of Ministers in performing of functions under Schedule V.

The impugned orders of the late CM, Mr. Deo adds, also negate the purpose for which the Forest Rights Act and the Panchayat Extension to Scheduled Areas Act (PESA) were enacted. If the first promised to give the tribals and forest dwellers rights over the land they give on, the PESA gave the people control over their own resources, with the gram sabhas approving plans related to a host of issues connected with land, including recommending prospecting licences and mining leases for minor minerals.

Bauxite mining in Vishakhapatnam, Mr. Deo says, will also destroy the sources of the three rivers which originate in the region - - the Gosthani, the Champavathi and the Sarada - - and which are the main sources of irrigation and drinking water in Vizianagaram and Vishakhapatnam districts.

"Officials fear Naxal resurgence", 26 Dec 2012: Nagpur

"Andhra police worried after arrest of infrastructure firm manager on mission to help Maoists"[9].

The arrest of three, including the manager of an infrastructure firm from AP, by Gadchiroli police on 25 Dec 2012 "has again sparked fears about a possible Naxal resurgence in this southern state.

Maoists were believed to have been wiped out in the AP districts bordering Maharashtra, Chhattisgarh and Odisha. But officials believe that in the wake of Telengana agitation, the Maoists may be regrouping and clandestinely resuming operations.

A senior Maharashtra police officer, who has worked closely with Andhra police for a long time, explains:

"After all these years of retreat, Naxals are trying to regain their hold once again. They are silently recruiting in districts like Adilabad, Warangal, and Karimnagar. Extortion and civilian murders are now showing an upward incline. A lot of Congress leaders from many villages have run away. Apparently, Telengana agitation and sentiment are in a way helping nobody is talking about it yet…I feel the long silence of Maoists in 2012 should not 2000 beaten . . . . They have concentrated on consolidation in 2012, hence not got into any major action. Resurgence in AP may well be one of their local activities this year."

The infrastructure company, whose manager was hold last week, is working on a canal of a proposed inter – state irrigation project, and the officials believe Venkatraman Reddy was on a 'clandestine' mission to help Maoists in Gadchiroli when he was arrested. The two hold along with him were Chinmaya Soyam, a former sarpanch of a village in neighbouring Adilabad district of Andhra, and a local NCP leader and former Chairman of Sironcha Panchayat Samiti-Suryanarayan Parpatwar.

DIG Gadchiroli Range Ravindra Kadam says Reddy is the manager – cum – supervisor for Sushee Infrastructure Pvt Ltd, a firm based in Hyderabad, which is working on the Pranhita – Chevella inter – state irrigation project which is expected to be a soother for the strife – affected Telengana region. But the company does not have, as yet, environmental and forest department clearance.

An official speaks to the daily on condition of anonymity: "It is an irony that a project which is coming up for Telengana should be used by Naxals for extracting logistical support from managers of companies working on the project".

The Telengana agitation is often seen as having Maoist support.

"Tribal women missing after 'raid'", Hyderabad: 22 Jan 2013

"Chhattisgarh : Andhra cops say they did not conduct raid; human rights forum moves High Court."

Two tribals, a pregnant woman and a young girl, have gone missing from Nimmalagudem village in Sukma, Chhattisgarh, after a team of Khammam police and Greyhound commandos of AP "raided" the village in search of Maoist informers. The village is tree km from AP border.

A fact finding team of AP Human Rights Forum (HRF) says: "The "raid" took place on 12 January. The police whisked away six persons, including the two missing women: Madhvi Parvathi, 21, and Kovasi Somidhi, 15.

The "raid" was apparently carried out after Maoists shot and injured two greyhound commandos the previous night in Korepalli in Khammam and escaped to Chhattisgarh.

HRF President V S Krishna said: "The police released four persons. But the women are missing, since 10 days. Khammam police say they did not even conduct the raid.

On 18 January, Madhvi's mother Punam Jogamma and Somidhi's mother Kovasi Aite, faxed a letter to the C J of the AP HC. Following this, Krishna filed a Habeas Corpus in the HC, seeking direction to the Khammam police to produce the two missing.

The fax from the mothers say their daughters, tribal civilians, were forcibly taken away by the police. They feel they were in police custody, and there was danger to their lives. They had informed Bhadrachalam Sub - Collector on 16 June at Cherla in Khamman but to no avail.

SP Khammam AV Ranganath said: "No cross-border raid took place on the 12th. Maoists fired and injured our commandos inside the AP borders. We have nothing to do with the raid in Nimmalagudem as it falls in Chhattisgarh. It must have been that State's police.

The report of the said fact finding team has details: "The village has 30 households and comes under the Konta block of Sukma districts. Residents, all farmers, said a police team, 100 – strong, including Greyhounds, came to the village at day break on the 12th. Seeing them, most men fled into the forest. The police began abusing and beating the residents, that included women and children. Among these beaten up were a 10-year-old girl Sodi Devi and a 12 – year old boy Madvi Venkatesh, who lost three teeth…The police then picked up five persons: Podium Chukkaiah, a former, and his son P Bhimaiah, 11, Madhvi, Somidhi, and Madkam Saramma. Their hands were tied, they were taken to a place near a hillock where there were signs of a camp set up by Maoists. The police accused the entire village of helping the Maoists and beat the four with hands and sticks. Several women including the two said mothers entreated the police not to harm their daughters. . . . The police beat and even kicked them…Soon after they almost disrobed the two women and forcibly took them away before letting go the other three.

"Police: Woman Maoist held, played role in Bastar attack", Hyderabad: 5 Jun 2013

"Madhavi is the wife of North Telengana Secretary of CPI Maoist"

A suspected woman, Maoist, allegedly involved in the 25 May attack on the Congress convoy in Bastar, was arrested by the police in Khammam district on 4 Jun 2013. Madhavi, 38, is the wife of P Shankaranna alias Chandaranna, CPI (Maoist) North Telengana Zone secretary, who was also allegedly involved in that attack, wherein the Congress leaders were killed.

Here arrest was a chance, as the Khammam police was checking the vehicles when the car in which Madhavi and two others were travelling, fled away. In the consequent chase, she was caught as her Maruti car overturned while negotiating a bend near Bhadrachalam. The police learnt about her identity only she herself disclosed her name.

"However, the police have not issued any official confirmation so far." Madhavi is believed to be going to Vijaywada to consult a doctor. A second year MA student of Hyderabad University and his father, who were in the car, were also detained by the police[10].

Maoists blame AP Government for Prasadam's death: 7 Jul 2013

The Dandakaranya Special Zone Committee (DKSZC) of the CPI (Maoist) condemned the death on 6 July 2013 of activist Ganti Prasada Rao alias Prasadam, 60, and blamed the Andhra Pradesh Government for what the ultras called an "organized assassination." Claiming that Prasadam was assassinated in a planned manner, the statement signed by DKSZC spokesperson Gudsa Usendi said: "…. The State (AP) was threatening all those forces who are raising their voices, agitating and fighting against its anti – people and oppressive policies[11]."

Prasadam was critically injured following an attack near a Nellore hospital on 4 July. He died of a deep knife wound early on the 6th morning. He joined the Srikakulam Girijan Armed Peasant Struggle and started working with the undivided CPI (ML) in his teens. Later, he joined the AP State Committee of the People's War. He was arrested and eventually released but continued with open mass organization. "He continued in the committee of relatives and friends of Martyr Heroes [Amaraveerula Bandhumitrula Committee] and participated in all legal and open democratic movements that have been going on in AP. He stood in support of the revolutionary literary movement also. He integrated with the ongoing mass movement for separate Telangana State," the CPI (Maoist) said.

The statement says the killing of Prasadam has to be seen in the back-drop of retaliatory attack by the State to avenge the 25 May ambush of the Congress convoy "In the pretext of this attack (25 May ambush), the rulers of the country have conspired to crush all democratic and revolutionary movements and to carry on their offensive with more severity. Comrade Ganti Prasadam's killing should also be seen as a part of this conspiracy."

"Maoists call for a week – long bandh from today" (15 Jul 2013) Jagdalpur: 15 Jul 2013

To protest the killing of their commander Ganti Prasada Rao in AP, the ultras called for a week long bandh in Chhattisgarh, Odisha and AP from 15 to 21 Jul 2013.

Waltair Division of the East Coast Railway on the 14th issued a circular to the station master of Jagdalpur, Bacheli, Kirandul stations regarding suspension of operations of the lone passenger train running on KK Line between Jagdalpur and Kirandul and also halting the services of goods train in night during this week.

Maoist commander Rao alias Prasadam was killed in Nallore of AP as some unidentified person shot him on 4 July and to protest against his death, the Maoist called for this bandh.

Andhra bifurcation dynamics will pose a new Naxal threat: New Delhi:11 Mar 2014

Ajit Seth, Cabinet Secretary, in a review note, delineates the implications of division of AP: "The dynamics arising out of bifurcation of AP will pose a new threat from Naxals as 'the new generation of officers is not exposed to a hardcore counter-' insurgency."

In a recent meeting to analyze countrywide Maoist threats ahead of the Lok Sabha polls, it was said Jharkhand, Chhattisgarh and Bihar were among worst-affected states and Maoists may disrupt elections by carrying out a "spectacular strike."

Intelligence agencies had earlier opposed the move to bifurcate AP on the ground that it could lead to a rise in Maoist activities. The review meeting last week by the Cabinet Secretary noted: "The influence of the outfit was noticed when it tried to disrupt panchayat elections in Jul 2013 and gave a call to boycott panchayat polls . . . .the polls could not be conducted in 18 panchayats in Vishakhapatnam district."

Based in the SWOT analysis of Naxal-hit states, the government review note said, "The geographical area of Naxal activity has shrunk substantially. In 2013, Naxal violence was witnessed under 330 police stations of 75 districts in 10 states, the corresponding figures for the previous (2012) year were 400, 85 and 11." The review further noted that the CPI (Maoist) retains its core strength in parts of Chhattisgarh, Jharkhand, Bihar and Odisha and they were still capable of resorting to spectacular strikes in these strongholds.

"Khammam Village gets forest rights deed" Hyderabad: 14 Jul 2014

"Telengana's First: Research fellow's efforts pay off, villagers auction bamboo to raise Rs 26 lakh"[12].

Sirasanapalli village of Bhadrachalam Division of Khammam district became the first village in Telengana and undivided AP to get a Community Forest Rights (CFR) title deed in the name of gram sabha for its forest boundary. After a 10-year struggle, Surasanapalli villagers were able to harvest and sell bamboo from the forest where they live in.

A Fellow of the Prime Minister's Rural Development Fellowship Scheme (PMRDF), Prathima Nalabolu, who has been working with the gram sabha since May 2012, played a key role in the village getting its title deed on 21 June.

On 19 May, the villages conducted their first auction in which 36 bidders participated. The gram sabha was apprehending that these bidders could form a syndicate to keep the prices low. But with the Forest Department Officials keeping a watch, the process was successful and the 41,400 harvested bamboo stalks were auctioned to raise Rs. 26.10 lakh. Till now, bamboo was handed over to the state forest department which auctioned it.

The villagers fight started a decade ago with a slogan "our bamboo, our right", when they opposed the control of the Forest Department over the sale of the bamboo cut by them. Besides the Department's they had also to overcome the stiff resistance from the bamboo transporters lobby. However, the Integrated Tribal Development Agency, Bhadrachalam, stepped in and asked the Department to fall in line and grant the Department their rights.

Prathima Nalabolu, who joined the villager's efforts after training for three months at the Dr. Marru Channa Reddy Human Resource Development Institute at Hyderabad, said: "I have been working as a facilitator for the gram sabha, helping them completing the documentation and GPS survey for filing Community Forest Rights claim and working with Bhadrachalam to ensure gram sabha receives a title deed. I held gram sabhas in the village on decision-making and gave on-job training for resolution writing ...My idea was to ensure that by the end of this process, their capacities are built so that they can manage the activities on their own from the next year."

The jubiliant village decided to spend half the income earned on forest regeneration activities including bamboo regeneration, irrigation via farm pond, canals far fields that are currently rain – fed and safe drinking water for all households.

Another 25 per cent would be divided among the 31 families as dividend while the remaining 25 per cent has been kept as the reserve fund towards the expenses for the next year's sale, according to Badisa Gangaiah, a village elder.

The gram sabha had elected a 10 – member forest management and protection committee which is now overseeing the process, writing resolutions, managing accounts and distributing the labour charges.

Madivi Kanna Rao, president of the village's CFR management committee, says: "To gain rights over the collection and sale of minor forest produce had been a daily struggle for us. We have overcome 10 years of struggle to access the bamboo in our forest. We will continue harvesting bamboo every year and use the income generated to convert our village into a model village."

"Andhra: Three Naxals lynched": Hyderabad: 2 Oct 2014

Three Maoist, including a commander of the Korukonda area committee of CPI (Maoist), were lynched by tribals in Chintapalli in Vishakhapatnam district on 1 Oct 2014 night while they were holding a 'praja court'.

The Maoists had last week shot village leader G Sanjiv Rao. When the Maoist arrived on the 1st to hold another 'praja court', tribals attacked and killed commander Sharat, police said. The two other Maoists who were lynched were yet to be identified.

"TDP MP raises Naxal issue, Seeks Centre aid: New Delhi: 5 Dec 2014

This news story concerns the consequences for the AP State (residual) after the formation of Telengana out of it!

An MP holds out a threat (People might turn to Naxals)

Lamenting serious financial crisis his state (AP) was facing after Telengana was carved out of it and also on account of vast damage due to cyclone Hudhud, TDP MP Muthamsetti Srinivasa Rao said on 3 Dec 2014 that if the Centre did not come to the State's rescue, its people might veer towards Naxalism[13].

He told the daily: "our state has got ruthlessly devastated. We are facing cyclone every year but little help is coming from the Centre. We have no capital . . . no money to build it . . . our people will have no option but to take extreme steps like committing suicide or taking to Naxalism."

Earlier in the day, speaking in the Lok Sabha in discussion on natural calamities, Rao said: "We have a deficit of Rs 15,000 cr. The Centre should adopt our state . . . . we have no educational institutions. There are no industries. Only the old name Andhra Pradesh remains. Everything else, including Hyderabad, has been given to Telengana by the previous UPA government…"

Later talking to the daily, he indicated that a "movement" was building up along the Andhra Pradesh – Odisha border that needed to be checked up…."

"Telengana fears resurgence of Maoists after over a decade", Hyderabad: 10 Jan 2015

More than a decade after lying low, the Maoists are now riding rural disputes and tribal issues in a bid to resurface in areas now under Telengana[14].

Officials read the signs after some 20 armed cadres of the banned CPI (Maoist) held a 'people's court' in Mukunur village in Telengana's Karimnagar district. They descended from nowhere to probe a fairly old clash between upper caste landlords and Dalits and thrashed some villagers for being police informers. On this incident, here is an IPS officer who had led Grey Hounds operations on the ground against the Maoists: "The Maoists moved beyond river Godavari to Chhattisgarh after their movement in the undivided AP declined by 2004. This incident is a disturbing signal that they are determined to regain hold in the Karimnagar-Warrangal-Khammam stretch. They could have been emboldened by slackening of the operations along the border with Chhattisgarh."

Apart from holding kangaroo courts, the Maoists struck in border areas of Khammam district "this week, setting trucks ablaze, exchanging fire with police and attempting to blow up a mobile tower.

The police, though, are more worried by the Maoists' bid to recruit the youth believed to have dumped their ideology years ago. SP Karimnagar V Shiva Kumar said: "They need the local issues and local cadres. So they are trying to make their presence felt and recruit, too,."

Officials are wary as most of the Maoist leaders hail from AP and Telengana, though the cadres are predominantly from Chhattisgarh, and are based and operating from there. The leadership has been calling upon Dalits to fight oppression and distributing pamphlets to the tribal people to occupy the lands of politicians and landlords.

A police officer in Hyderabad believes sociological factors make Telengana more vulnerable to a Maoist come back than AP.

But the Telengana movement headed by K. Chandrasekhra Rao - - he used to make pro-Maoist statements during the statehood movement – sees no immediate threat. A home department officials says: "We are apprised of their activities, and if there is a need, we will revise our strategy."

AP, where Maoists are active on the border with Odisha, perceives the Red threat. DGP JV Ramudu told the daily: "We are geared up to prevent them from spreading."

Interestingly, this news story in the daily has a picture of a pylon in ruins, with the description under it reading:

- The Maoists' Amaraveerula Stoopam (Martyrs' pylon) - - said to be Asia's second – largest - - once towered over Husnabad town and surroundings in Karimnagar district. The pylon was blasted, allegedly by the police, in the 1990s.

"Maoists claim credit for state's welfare tilt" Adilabad: 11 Jan 2015

Maoists will like to believe and also tell the tribals that government's benevolent and welfare programmes like food security, social pensions and employment generation are only due to the struggle waged by the Maoists in support of the poor. More specifically, a Maoist *dalam* currently engaged in an indoctrination campaign in villages on the fringes of the Mangi forest area in Tiryani and Rebbena mandals is said to be invoking enthusiasm among Adivasi youth by claiming to have influenced the government to address people's problem.

The aim obviously was to recruit fresh blood, opined a Police Department source who is involved in anti-Naxal operations in the eastern part of the district (of Adilabad).

It is believed that much-sighted armed *Dalam,* which was twice engaged in exchange of fire last year (2014) visited Sonapur, Parsa Nambala and Khairiguda in Rebbena mandal and Dorli village in Tiryani mandal in the first week of January (2015).[15]

The ultras conducted separate indoctrination classes attended by some 15 youths from each of these villages for 3 to 4 days, curiously hinging much of their talk on the performance of the first government in Telengana.

Sources further disclosed: "The Maoists are reportedly comparing the past and the present governments while driving home their point. The dalam leaders are known to have stoked passions among the gullible youngsters by exhibiting their sophisticated fire arms."

Police are puzzled

Meanwhile, the police are puzzled over the continued movement of the extremists in the district despite the heat generated by their pursuit of the underground cadres during the last few months.

Dalam truncated

The dalam seems to have been truncated to seven members with Atram Shobhan alias Charles, Adilabad Area Committee Secretary and Mylarapur Adellu alias Bhaskar and his wife Kanthi Lingavva, both Area Committee members, in the lead.

The police are also surprised over the facts that dalam members these days are more seen in the villages rather than the forests - - the latter being their expected habitat for operations as also for logistics.

The area of movement of the ultras span between Gangapur in Kadem Mandal and Rebbena.

"Maoists regaining foothold in Telengana", New Delhi: 2 Feb 2015 "Exploiting fault lines in Division of Andhra Pradesh to Bounce Back"

Maoists are slowly finding a fresh foothold in Telengana thanks to a botched up division of the erstwhile AP State asserts a daily in Feb 2015.

Intelligence inputs point at CPI (Maoist) re-entering the region from where they had been painstakingly pushed out by concerted efforts by state and CPMF towards the close of the 2000 decade[16].

Much of the Maoist activity seems to be initiated in districts bordering the new AP. A security officer disclosed: "CPI (Maoist) has even formed a Special Zonal Committee and movement of cadres has been spotted. Significant Maoist activity has been reported from districts such as Bhadrachalam in Telengana."

Some observers believe the haphazard division of the state led to many local issues cropping up in bordering districts which Maoists are leveraging. An officer elucidates: "Several villages in the bordering districts have been arbitrarily exchanged between the two states, without thorugh consultation with stake-holders and residents. This has led to suffering and discontent which Maoists are fishing into. They were, anyway, looking at the separation of the state as an opportunity to resurrect themselves in an uncertain administrative atmosphere. Such mistakes have given them a window."

Such fears had been expressed in the run-up to the division of the state as well. However, these were brushed aside on the ground that a small state would be easier to police and unlike Chhattisgarh, state administration in united Andhra had been able to reach the most remote corners of the state leaving little window for Maoists to stir up passions.

Beginning 2008, Maoists had hardly been able to mount attacks inside Andhra, with total casualty of security forces between 2008 and 2013 coming to just three. However, given that majority of CPI (Maoist) top leadership comprises of people from Telengana, the desire to resurrect Maoism in state has always been there with the outfit.

Giving details of the Maoist leadership during a press conference held at AP Bhavan in New Delhi on 18 November, then AP CM Kiran Kumar Reddy had said: "Of the 11 Central Committee leaders, nine are from Telengana, while two are from Andhra region; at the next rung [of leadership] of 18 members, 15 are from AP of which 14 are Telenganites and one is from Andhra [region]."

Sources, however, believe the situation is not alarming and an alert state administration along with Central assistance can nip the threat in the bud.

"Among shot 'Maoists', a 19 – year – old Univ dropout" Hyderabad: 15 Jun 2015

One of the three alleged Maoists shot dead in an 'encounter' by the police on the Telangana – Chhattisgarh border on 12 Jun 2015 was a

19-year-old Kodamagundla Vivek, a dropout from Osmania University who had played a major role during the students' agitation for Telengana during 2012-14.

Hundreds of people, Osmania University students and alumni attended Vivek's funeral and a meeting at Suryapet on the 14th to protest against the alleged encounter[17].

Soon after the killing, a CPI (Maoist) North Telangana spokesperson, Jagan, had issued a statement accusing the police of killing an unarmed Vivek and two others in cold blood.

A member of the Telangana Vidyarthi Vedika, the students political wing of Osmania University, Vivek had dropped out of a five-year integrated law course in Sep 2014, and with Telangana formed as a separate state, disappeared from the campus scene soon after. A fiery orator and a speaker at Osmania University, Vivek would often feature in news papers and social media in photos where he was being dragged away by police during protests.

"I cannot believe this 19 – year – old boy has been shot dead by police," said revolutionary writer and poet Vara Vara Rao, who met Vivek's family at Suryapet on the 14th afternoon.

Hailing from Nalgonda district, Vivek left home on 8 October (2014), telling his parents he wanted to work for the poor and told them about his resolve to join the Maoists. Vivek's father K Yoganand says: "We tried to reason with him but he did not listen. He was very active in students' agitation in Osmania and, during that period, he seemed to have drifted towards Maoists. After leaving, he called one day, and promised to return home soon".

A few days before he left, he had posted a leaflet on his Facebook page, issued by the Committee Against Operation Greenhunt, demanding that police operation against Maoists be stopped.

"He was very passionate about the rights of people, especially the poor. Although he used to talk about it a lot, few people know what was on his mind until he left Hyderabad to join the Maoists," his friend Tekula Kranti said.

Vivek's parents Yoganand and K Madhavi, are government teachers while his brother K Srinivas has done B Tech.

Notes

1. Madhavi Tata, The outlook, 15 May 2000.
2. Omer Farooq, The Pioneer, 28 Jan 2007.
3. Ashok Das, Hindustan Times, 24 Jul 2006.

4. Omer Farooq, The Pioneer, 4 Feb 2007.
5. SA Isaqui, Asian Age, 3 Feb 2007.
6. Karn Kowshik, Indian Express, 6 Mar 2007.
7. Karn Kowshik, Indian Express, 27 Mar 2007.
8. Smita Gupta, The Hindu, 8 Jul 2012.
9. Vivek Deshpande, India Express, 26 Dec 2012.
10. Sreenivaj Janyala, indian Express, 22 Jan. 2013.
11. ENS, Indian Express, 5 Jun 2013.
12. Suvojit Bagchi, 7 Jul 2013.
13. Sreenivas Janyala, Indian Express, 14 Jul 2014.
14. Raghvendra Rao, Indian Express, 5 Dec 2014.
15. Prasad Nichenametla, Hindustan Times, 10 Jan 2015.
16. S. Harpal Singh, Indian Express, 11 Jan 2015.
17. Deeptiman Tiwari, Times of India, 2 Feb 2012.

21

Bihar

Bihar has been among the three worst hit states of the union concerning the violence and spread of the Naxalism is concerned.

Background note

Origin: A movement against the oppression of the low caste tillers by the upper caste landlords in 1967.

Bloody Era: 1980s.

Key issues: Exploitation of tribals.

Status check: Maoists have spread their activities to at least 30 of the 38 districts.

CM Nitish Kumar speak (Jul 2010): "Naxal elements are a part of our society. Enforcement action alone lead to wider alienation, making heroes out of leaders of the extremist outfits."

If Andhra Pradesh was the first state in the south to nurture a fledgeling LWE, this distinction goes to Bihar in India's East! After all, Maoist Communist Centre (MCC) in Bihar was to unite with the People's War Group= PWG) of Andhra to create the monster called CPI (Maoist) in Sep. 2004.

The situation in Mar 2007 had reached a point where a Bihar police officer tells a daily that Maoists have established links with internal and external disruptive forces including Nepal Maoists so as to acquire arms and sophisticated communication equipment that can intercept police conversation. Kameshwar Baitha, a Maoist leader, disclosed during interrogation that Maoists in Bihar had "recently purchased eight AK-47 rifles from AP Rs 2 lakh a piece[1].

If needs to lee notes that after Bihar's MCC merged with the PWG of AP in sep 2004, and declared a unilateral ceasefire with CPI(ML) Liberation in Jan 2005, the Maoist movement, understandably gained huge momentum. DGP Bihar Ashish Ranjan Sinha had said, then: "The Nepali and Bihari Maoists have formed a Bihar-Nepal Border Coordination Committee to provide shelter to Each other's cadres. In view of this known fact, it is difficult to give credit to the Nepalese Maoist leader Prachandas statement — made during the time when he came to India in Nov. 2006 to participate in the Hindustan Times convened Leadership Conference at New Delhi — that there was no understanding between the Nepalese Maoists their Indian Counterparts.

To reiterate, if Naxalism sprang from eponymous movement in Darjeeling district of West Bengal in May 1967, it was born in Andhra Pradesh on 31 October of the same years (1967) when a huge meeting organized by the Jatapur and Savaratribes in Srikakulam was disrupted by Medi Satyam of Congress Party, and in the ensuring violence, satyam and two tribals were killed. Thence on, West Bengal in the east and AP in the south were set to develop into some kind of epicentre's of Naxalism, and inevitable violence related to it, in India.

Bihar comes early in the picture. The Naxalism in West Bengal was controlled and ruthlessly eliminated West Bengal by Naxalite cousin, CPI (M) under Jyoti Basu, in a short span of a couple of years. Consequently and inevitably, Naxalism crossed over into the bordering state of Bihar. As a result, Bihar, not West Bengal, become the epicenter of Naxal violence. To wit, the MCC was born in Bihar, whose merging with PWG, as explained above, created the monster CPI (Maoist).

"As of today (Mar 2007), there are 18 dalams in Vishakhapatnam, Vizianagaram, Srikakulam, Gangavaram, Koraput and Gajapati" The Moists had designaed this belt, including the Dandakaranya forest, as the Andhra-Odisha Border Zone.

They now hope to open a link with neighbouring Jharkhand. The larger plan is to create an uninterrupted North-South corridor, and Odisha's central and western regions are essential for this vision.

"Annual Report Oct 2005-Sep 2006: Maoist reveal their terror plan": Jun. 2006

The Naxal onslaught at Riga in Sitamarhi district of Bihar "has been seen as a first of the series of such attacks planned by the ultras in areas where large mining, irrigation or industrial projects are planned to be set up[2].

This is suggested by the fact that an annual reports of the Maoists , oct 2005-Sep 2006, seized by the security forces recently had listed several upcoming projects in Bihar, Chhattisgarh, Jharkhand, Odisha and AP for attacks, as reported by a daily in Mar 2007.

The Riga attack might just be a symbolic call for the battle to create a Red terror in the nearby region, where the proposed Kosi Irrigation Project is to come up. Incidentally, Kosi project is on the top of the Maoist hit list, with said Annual Report saying the region needed attention for not only repulsing the government machinery but also mobilising the mass support.

Thoughts on initial spread of Maoism

By Mar 2007, the Maoists had spread to 32 of Bihar's 38 districts. Major responsibility for it must rest with Lalu Prasad Yadav and his consort Rabri Devi who between them ruled the state for 15 years," 1990-2005, even if it was not among the most advanced of the the Indian States before they took over.

During the 15-year rule of Lalu Rabri combine, the Maoists won the heart of the people by constructing small scale irrigation projects in Gaya, Nawada and Kaimur districts.

5 Jan 2005 : Maoists attacked Bihar Kajra railway station in Munger (Bihar) – Jamalpur Rail Division.

5 Jan 2005 : They killed six policemen including local SP KC Surender Babu in Munger district.

"Maoist leader dies in custody": 8 Mar 2007 (Bhala Kahar)

Zonal commander of the Maoists Bhala Kahar died in police custody at Gaya, Bihar on this day Death of Kahar, arrested from Konch police station area of Gaya, was due to asthama on the 6th, said DIG Police, Magadh Range, Umed Singh.

Locals, however, alleged Kahar died of police torture during his interrogation.

"Maoists attack Railway Station to enforce Bandh"

In yet another dare-devil operation in Bihar some 100 armed Maoists raided Narganjo railway station in Asansol Division of the Eastern Railway 1 AM on 21, Apr 2007, to enforce the bandh call " to protest death of one of their leaders, Bal Govind Yadav in Jamui Jail recently" consequently, the movement of trains remained suspended for seven hours.

Maoists locked the station entrance, took away cabin master M Riwari and a porter as hostages, releasing them free after five hours. The ultras claimed planting mines on the tracks.

CPRO Eastern Railway S Mozumdar told the press that soon after the station was raided, an SOS was sent to the Asansol control room whence the movement of trains was suspended. It was only by day break that the Railways despatched a strong RPSF contingent from Jhajha at 6:30 AM. The security men checked the up and down tracks and found them safe. Consequently, the tracks were cleared for traffic at 7:50 AM.

DRM Asansol AK Rawat said the authorities have asked the DM Jamul and the Railway police superintendent to step up the security measures" DGP RPF MK Sinha said Eastern Railway's Chief Security Commissioner had been instructed to coordinate with the state police, including the GRP, to check such incidents.

This was the second time that the Naxals targeted Narganjo station in less than two weeks. On 8 April, they had gunned down two RPF Constables in a running train and looted one SLR and two pistols from them near this very railway station.

"Maoist Fighting capability in Bihar"

The Maoists in Bihar have, say intelligence inputs, 200 police rifles, over 100 SLR, 130 carbines, dozen of AK-47s, 8 rifles of. 315 bore, five LMGs and four semi-automatic rifles.

"Maoists behead two in Bihar"

Throwing a virtual challenge to the Natish Government claim, the Maoists beheaded two ruling party members (of JDU) from the Satgharma village in Munger district on 30 May 2007.

This obviously belies this self-serving claim of having contained the Maoist violence. Some 100 armed ultras swooped on the village, dragged out Ramchandra Yadav, Anil Yadav, Sambhu Yadav, and Ranjan Kumar of the same family from their home.

They slashed the throats of the former two, killing them on the spot. After the Maoists left the village subsequent to committing this inhuman, heinous crime, the beheaded bodies of the two were found at an isolated spot outside the village.

The Maoist alleged that the two were acting as police informers. Incidentally, Munger is among the 23 Nexalite-infested districts of Bihar's 38 total.

"They blow up a bridge in Bihar"

A group of 500 heavily armed Maoist rebels on 31 Mar 2007 blew up a bridge near Dhang, using dynamite, thus snapping road link to Riga.

Subsequently, they attacked BDO office and the police station in Riga in Sitamarhi district of Bihar. More details follow:

- They stormed the Central Bank of India at Raja and injured its manager and a homeguard while attempting to loot cash from the chest. But they failed to break it open.
- Thence, they laid virtual siege to the police station, Riga at 6:15 PM and exploded several bombs. Then followed exchange of fire with the men of the Bihar Militery Police (BMP) and special Auxiliary Police (SAP) for over 45 minutes. They failed to snatch arms from the police men.
- They looted several shops in the Riga bazaar.
- The Maoist fled when the reinforcements arrived from the district HQ.
- There were no casualties. There details were given by SP MRP Nair while briefing the journalists on the incident.

On the 31 March night, the authorities sealed the Indo-Nepal border in Sitamarhi district. The SSB Jawans conducted combing operations.

"Bihar Govt receives bizarre criticism"

What follows are parts of an editorial written by a national daily questioning the means and strategies adopted by the police and the government of the Bihar-state in its counter-Maoist fight:[3]

"India is presently in the midst of a serious crisis created by mindless, violent terrorism perpetrated by the banned CPI (Maoist) guerrillas, it calls its cadres, in a large swath of its territory. It bears repetition that PM Manmohan Singh not too long ago terned Naxalite extremist threat as biggest danger to India's internal security, intergrity and sovereignity. Given this reality, the extremism-affected states are adopting all kinds of strategies and means to defeat/control this violence.…As exposed by this newspaper, street dogs are to be sheltered in police stations for (an) instant alert against ultras. It is an oblique admission of an intelligence failure to come to grips with a daunting challenge. Dogs are expected to be more effective where the state endeavour have failed."

"India is a democratic polity and freedom of speech is a fundamental and valuable right its citizens enjoy, and most of the argumentative Indians make full use of it; for reasons right or wrong, is altogether on other matter. Enjoying this freedom of expression, it is no surprise that occasionally state governments face criticism for designing and adopting a particular anti-Naxal strategy to deter and control the murderous Maoist, from committing inhuman, egregious and heinous crimes."

"The most well-known instance of the above symptom was the passionate, vigorous criticism the Salwa Judum campaign, conceptualised and initiated by that braveheart tribal leader Mahendra Karma, was subjected to by the Human Rights 'busy-bodies' and 'elitist' campaigners like Arundhati Roy [it needs to be mentioned that the brave man paid with his life for his long, persistent and dedicated fight for eradicating the "Maoist scourge from his beloved Chhattisgarh]."

Coming to the editorial, couched in angry and furious language, it is 'fuelled' by the Bihar Government's decision to deploy dogs in and around the police stations to alert the policemen against the furtive arrival of the murderous Maoists. It is also obvious that Bihar was possibly emulating the fledgeling state of Jharkhand (carved out of it in 2000) by adopting this practice.

The 'innovation' if one is allowed to call it so, has been dismissed as "an awfully disingenuous method to cope with the Maoist challenge".

It is unexplicable that a daily of some standing and reputation has thought it worth its while to devote an editorial on this not-an-unusaul measure adopted by a Maoist-infested state, going all-out to control and eradicate this scourage from its territory. This daily says it all—as quoted above—in its editorial in a language sneering and disdainful, which is suggestively titled : "Bihar gets bizarre: A dogged determination against the Maoists."

The daily proudly says, "As exposed by this newspaper, stray dogs are…in police stations." The daily used the term "expored" as if it has brought out some highly guarded confidential state secret in the open. Stray dogs being sheltered in a police station was a common knowledge among the locals, and consequently, so must be the case among the Maoists! No great sleuthing was needed by this daily.

Because the dogs have been deployed by the police, the paper jumps to the conclusion that it was the result of intelligence failure! Possibly, the erudite editors of this daily have never heard or known that even birds are deployed for intelligence gathering.

As the daily unaware that Indian Army is using dogs in Kashmir in its anti-terrorist operations. As the daily unhappy that the SHO Gaya is keeping 'stray'dogs in his police station catch the high-minded, ideologically-inspired Maoists? Is the daily suggesting that keeping their exalted idealogy in mind, the SHO should deploy pedigreed dogs, say Labradors or German Shepherds!

To be rather kind to the daily, it is fair to say that entire editorial seems…rather reads…funny, even silly. The issue does not deserve to be elevated to such eminence and respectability, demanding an editorial scrutiny. The editorials are quintessential wisdom which a daily chooses to devote to an important incident or issue. These 36 stray dogs certain don't deserve a such an eminence! To be harsh, the editorial is cynical in its tone, slipshed in its arguments, shallow in its contents and over all, a 'cheap stuff'. To put it simply, the editorial is obviously inane, jejune and almost meaningless! One fails to understand how such a "preposterous"—to borrow a term from this editorial—editorial could find a place on the pages of this national daily, which was only one of the two dailies (other being the courageous Indian Express) who bravely defied Indira Gandhi and her Emergency!

11 May 2008 (a Maoist arrested)

Pramod Mishra, hailing from Aurangabad district, in-charge of Naxal operations in entire north India and a politburo member, was arrested from Dhanbad. His interrogation revealed that Nepal's Maoist Leader Prachanda had indeed visited and inauguarded the 9th Congress of CPI(Maoist) in the forest area of Bhimbandh in Jamui district, Bihar, in 2007. Earlier Prachanda had asserted the debate over links between the Maoists of the two countries was a "figment of imagination". The story headlined "arrested Maoist leader belies Prachanda's claim", by Amar Nath Tiwari from Patna appeared in the Pioneer of 14 May 2008. Pramod Mishra further added: "… the party is planning to expand its base to Punjab and Haryana with an aim to attack the Government's vital installations there." Mishra's Party colleague and a politburo member Misir Besra, arrested in 2007 near Khunti had also made similar statements about his outfit deciding to shift its operations from rural to urban areas in North India (Manoj Prasad, Indian Express, 15 May 2008). Vishwa Mohan wrote in The Times of India of 18 Feb 2008: "Pramod Mishra was made operational in-charge of New Delhi during the 9th Congress of the Maoists held in the forest of Bhimband in Bihar for ten days in 2007…Naxalites have 60 crore budget for their struggle."

9 Feb 2009

Eight cops killed in Maoist attack in Nawada village bordering Jharkhand. Naxals again killed ten policemen in Bihar's Mahuliland village.

20 May 2009

Maoist blew up a government building in Gaya.

13 Oct 2009

The panel cabin of Bansipur Railway station was ransacked by Maoists during the "bandh' they had called in Bihar.

"Tendu leaves, illegal mining, dictate game plan in Naxal heart land": Chenari (Bihar): 9 Aug 2011

- Illegal mining mafia makes Karbandia hills in Rohtas district Bihar's Bellari.
- Tendu leaf business is another thriving source of income for Maoists.

Here is a marked man

Sugreev Kharwar is a marked man. A week ago (on Sunday), three of his relatives including a brother, were gunned down by Naxals in Rohtas district of Bihar. Several houses of Kharwar tribals were torched that night in Banda village, perched high in the wooded Kaimur hills stretching along the twin districts of Rohtas and Kaimur.[4]

The hills, part of Vindhya mountain chain, facilitate a Red Corridor gateway starting from AP, extending through MP, Chhattisgarh and Jharkhand into Bihar via Kaimur and Rohtas.

The Banda killing were carried out by Yadav Naxals to avenge the slaying of Birendra Rana Yadav, a self-styled Zonal commander of Soneganga Vindhyachal Zone Committee (as this are a is known in Naxal parlance). Sugreev had played a key role in bringing about Rana Yadav's death, aiding COBRA commandos in the encounter that killed the latter. Since then, the rebels have unleashed a retaliatory wave of terror in Kharwar villages, summarily beating people and gutting their house. A swift panicky exodus from six villages has ensued with more than 300 Kharwar families seeking asylum in Chenari Block near the foothills.

Cramped in a flea- bitten inspection bungalow and bereft of belongings, livestock and their vocations, a hundred-odd Kharwar families subsist on salt, rice and daal in Chenari.

Inter-tribal killings

The Kharwars, along with tribes like Oraons and Cheros, constitute more than half of the population in these hills. While some of these tribes cast their lot with the Naxals in the early 1990s, the Kharwars of late have started resenting the increasing domination of the Yadavs within the Naxal hierarchy.

The 'Kaimuranchal Vikas Morcha' established by Sugreev in 2004, has been vocal against Naxal interference in the region, which it perceives primarily to be in Yadav hands.

But to dub the Yadav-Kharwar tussle as a simple case of caste antagonism is tempting but misleading, as both groups are part of an intricate economic game being played out against the sweeping background of the Vindhya ranges. This game is pivoted on two factors: Control of the tendu leaf business in the dense Kaimur forests and the illegal mining mafia along the Karbandia hills (lower Kaimur range) in Sasaram, Rohtas.

As per the government records, 36 settled mining leases, mainly for sandstone and shale, had been allotted in Rohtas till 2010 before the Bihar Government withheld grant of any further lease last year (2010) by amending the Bihar Minor Minerals Concession, 1972 in a bid to check illegal mining.

However, informed government told the daily that at least 20 of these kept operating even after the expiry of their term, making Karbandia Bihar's own Bellari of the eight valid leases operating today, six have encroached upon protected forest area. Sources said that contrary to these leases feeding 135 stone crushers, there are at least 400 stone crushers operating in the Karbandia hills in Rohtas. While levy extraction from mining works is rampant, tonnes of ammonium nitrate ostensibly meant for mining purposes, are used by Naxals against police men in this region.

The tendu leaf business is another thriving source of income for the Maoists, with illegal pickings flourishing on a massive scale inside the forbidden Kaimur wildlife sanctuary are spread across 1492 sq km in both districts. The Protected Forest Area (PFA) where tendu leaf plucking is legal constitute barely 314 sq km.

" It is hard to detect whether the leaves are picked inside the sanctuary, or on the peripheral PFA zone. This is an illegal business carried out with every legal permit under the sun", said a forest officer requesting anonymity. The Naxals and the contractors are thick as theives, he added, thanks mainly to the former's complete domination of the Kaimur plateau which encompasses the wildlife sanctuary.

The contractors value per bundle at an average Rs 60, say the tribals. While exact numbers are hard to ascertain, Forest Department sources say the Tendu Leaf business yields Rs 10-15 crore only in 85 mountain villages of Rohtas. The tribals are kept out of the profit cycle, being doled out labour charges. They are paid Rs 25 per kg, a paltry Re 1 for a pola or bundle (1 bundle equals approx. 60 leaves).

Maoist rakes in the profits

Extremist domination of these two businesses has been made easier in the absence of law and order machinery which does not make its presence felt for 2100 sq km in the Kaimur Plateau, with Adhaura in Kaimur being the last police outpost. Despite repeated letters from senior police officers posted in this region, there has been no government attempt to establish an outpost in the wilderness.

The inaccessibility of the Kaimur hills poses an extremely tougah challenge for policing", says Vikas Vaibhav, Ex-SP Rohtas and the man behind 'Sone Mahotsava', a unique community police initiative to win tribal hearts and minds.

The three ascents to the hills are usually landmined, which has claimed the lives of a number of security men during the last three years, adds Vaibhav. But the imitation of Sone Mahotsava in Nov 2008 aimed at promoting tribal identitly has paid off rich dividends by weaning the Kharwars away from Naxal ranks. The programme conducted in hitherto inaccessible parts of the district saw free distribution of the food, blankets and cycles among the tribals along with community sports being arranged.

A symbolic culmination saw the unfurling of the national Tricolour on Republic Day and Independence Day atop the Rohtasgarh Fort.

While the initial confidence building phase has paid off, the fate of tribals hinges on how the State Government crystallizes its gains, says Vaibhav, adding, "After this recent wave of violence , the Kharwars within the Naxal hierarchy will doubtlessly revolt. This is a golden opportunity to snap the back of extremist domination".

"Touched by cop's kindness, Maoists abjure violence": Patna : 16 Apr 2012

Dreaded Maoist Sudama Oraon and 21 fellow rebels have had a before and after transformation in jail, touched by the gesture of an IPS officer.

The power of kindness to reform—the kind shown in director V Shantaram's celebrated 1957 movie Do Aankhen Barah Haath—has played in real at Sasaram jail in Rohtas district of western Bihar bordering UP[5].

Oraon and his comrades have turned their back on violence after being deeply affected by the way SP Rohtas Manu Maharaj has embraced their families. In a recent letter to authorities, oraon and the others acknowledged they were deeply overwhelmed by the kindness with which Maharaj treated them in prison and their families outside.

The ultras also expressed their desire to abjure violence and rejoin the mainstream, disenchanted with double standards of top Maoist leaders.

Oraon, a Maoist sub-zonal commander of Sone-Ganga Vindhyachal Zone, had earned notoriety for his participation in numerous Maoist strikes, including his role in the 2002 murder of Rahtas district forest officer Sanjay Singh.

Oraon, in jail since 2006, said Maharaj, a 2005- batch IPS officer, offered financial assistance to the jailed Maoists' families and helped them lead a decent life. "Maharaj even took pains to sort out land disputes. He has also helped send our children to schools and colleges. The physically challenged ones were given tricycles, which gave them a new life."

Maharaj, who hails from Himachal Pradesh, said he did what he thought was right. He added: "The family members are being imparted driving lessons so that they can eke out a living. We have even provided books, laptops and computers."

"Maoist leaders exploit women"

Oraon and 21 other hardcore Maoists including state-level leaders Rajendra uraon, Jagdish Chhero and Sitaram Chhero formed the Adivasi Chetna Manch (ACM) in Sasaram jail in Sep 2011. Oraon took this step as he was disenchanted with the "high-flying" lifestyle of top Maoists.

He hinted at a caste war within the CPI(Maoist) between dominant Yadavs and cadre belonging to the depressed classes. He accused the Maoist leadership of sexually exploiting women. He said: "The Naxal ideology has been sacrificed. Naxal leaders use branded soaps and sends their kids to top-end schools".

"Gallantry medals for anti-Naxal op heroes": New Delhi: 26 Jan 2013

Personnel involved in anti-Naxal operations have cornered most of the President's police medals this year (2013). CRPF bagged the most medals, including the three for its men involved in the killing of senior Naxal leader Kishanji. S Sreenu, Birendra Kumar Singh and Deepak Kumar Xaxa, who were part of the special COBRA team that killed the CPI(Maoist) Central Committee member in the forests of Burisole in West Bengal on 24 Nov 2011, were among the 32 CRPF personnel named for the police medals.

Last year, CRPF Assistant Commandant Vinoj P Joseph and Nagendra Singh...both officers of the COBRA battalion— were decorated with the Shaury. Chakra for the same operation. Altogether, 875 police and parmilitary personnel have been decorated by the President for gallantry and outstanding services this year.

Constable Daler Singh (Posthumous) from J&K is the sole recipient of the President's Police Medal for gallantry this time. The other awardees were:

•	Police medal for gallantry	115
•	President's police medal for distinguished services	88
•	Police medal for meritorious services	671
•	President's police medal for gallantry	1
	Total	**875**

"Naxal abduct 8 workers (labourers) in a Bihar village" Patna: 28 Jan 2013

Suspected Naxals kidnapped eight construction workers from Badaldiah village in Khaira police station area in Jamui district of Bihar in the wee hours on Sunday (26 Jan 2013) presumably to extort money from their company for their safe release[6].

SP Jamui Upendra Sharma told the press that the police has established contacts with the company to check if they have received any ransom call. He said combing operations were on at the probable hide-outs of the extremists to ensure safe release of the workers.

Bihar State Bridge Construction Company had awarded the contract to a Munger-leased company for constructing the road bridge at the village Badaldiah. Ultras swooped at the camp of the labourers and took them away with themselves.

Jamui district, bordering Giridih district of Jharkhand is notorious for such kidnappings, and a good number of such incidents have been reported from various parts of the district since 2011. Number of the kidnapped might differ in such incidents.

Fortunately, all labourers were set free by the Maoists in all the past such incidents of kidnapping as private companies conceded the ultra's demand for money. Ultras had even damaged construction sites and burnt company's vehicles in a show of strength and to score their employees.

Maoist had also attacked a police team under Khaira police station a Iamui district in Sep 2012, killing an inspector and injuring other policemen.

More than three dozen armed Naxals had surrounded the camp, and took away eight workers engaged in building a bridge over Badalidih river. The ultras had objected to the resumption of work on the bridge a fortnight ago without a "levy" being paid to them.

Area commander of the Naxals in Jamui on the 26th issued a statement through the local media owning responsibility for the kidnapping the labourers and threatening to kill them if construction work on the bridge (under construction over the past five years) was not stopped immediately.

Naxal-infested Jamui has over a dozen road and bridge construction projects in progress.

Badaldiah village is 30 km from the district headquarters.

Those kidnapped hail from Badaldiah, Dalsinghsarai in Samastipur and Raghopur in Saran district.

"3 Bihar districts account for 60 per cent of Naxal violence" New Delhi: 6 Mar 2013

Raising concern over Bihar's efforts to tackle Naxalism, the Centre has revealed that three of its districts…Gaya, Jamui and Aurangabad … accounted for more than 60 per cent of Maoist violence in 2012. The MHA wrote to state's Chief Secretary Ashok Kumar Sinha to act immediately to counter the rebels[7].

Gaya, the MHA noted, was the worst affected. The rebels put up flags and banners in several villages declaring they have paddy fields and that common people are free to harvest them. It also noted that anti-Naxal operations did not yield desired results in 2012.

The contribution of anti-Naxal special forces was not visible in Bihar. This could have serious repercursions as the Maoists would attempt to regain the areas they have been driven out of over the years.

In its letter to Sinha, the MHA expressed concern that the Revolutionary Democratic Front, alleged to be a Maoist Front outfit, enjoyed a free rum in the state. It was allowed to hold a rally at Muzaffarpur in Dec 2011 though the centre was against it. The rally organised under the banner of Janata Par Yudh Virodhi Manch and attended by over 1000 people, has not gone down well with the central forces fighting the Maoists. A top CRPF officer claimed: "The event was meant to show case organisational capabilities of the north Bihar unit of the CPI (Maoist). It was aimed at conducting mass mobilisation, which needs to be viewed seriously by the state administration."

He said the Bihar police has all but stopped operations against the Maoists, and thus frittered away gains made over the past five years.

The rebels are exploiting this lull to consolidate, the MHA said, and suggested that Bihar immediately restart the operations and hold the SPs accountable for it.

"Maoist arrested in Bihar" Patna: 19 Jun 2013

The Bihar police on 17 June 2013 arrested a Maoist from a private nursing home in Patna.

Kapildeo Yadav alias Indrajeet, a resident of Dumariya in Bihar's Gaya district, was seeking treatment for injuries at the Ishwar Dayal Hospital in Patna. He had sustained injuries allegedly during an encounter in Jharkhand's Latehar on 12 Jun 2013.

On a tip-off, the police arrested him, DGP Abhayanand told a daily[8].

Kapildeo is the commander of Eastern Regional Bureau in Jharkhand. He is involved in over two dozen cases in Jharkhand. His are of activity is spread over Latehar, Palamu, Gumla and Lahardagga in Jharkhand, IG (Operations) Amit Kumar said. The Jharkhand Police "will be arriving in Bihar to take him in custody."

AIIMS training saved jawans shot by the Maoists" New Delhi: 13.7.13

"This might be a lesson for anyone who has ever donned a uniform, olive green or Khaki" Two CRPF Jawans…ambushed right in the middle of a jungle in Bihar's Dumariya, one of them even shot at on the chest by Naxals…decided to recall some basic lessons they had picked up in a medical training course in Delhi last year (2012) to try and survive another day[9].

On 10 Jul 2013, as one of them was being discharged from the AIIMS Trauma Centre almost one month after that encounter, hale and fine, all he could do was thank the doctors. But he did not thank them because they had successfully operated upon him." He thanked us because we taught them first hand how to deal with a situation when you had lost a lot of blood", said Nirmal Thakur, a PRO at the AIIMS Trauma Centre.

On 13 June (2013), CRPF recruits Ravi (31) and Birender along with others were on a routine anti-Naxal patrolling operations in Dumariya. The very day, the Reds had attacked a train further ahead at Jamui. Ravi said: "I was leading the advance party when suddenly they attacked us. I got shot at immediately. I decided along with Birender to try and roll back but

I was against allowing these men from getting my rifle. I left my carry bag and began rolling with the weapon. We carried out a 70 mts withdrawal, after which I decided to get myself some medical attention as taught to me at AIIMS."

As had been taught to them, Ravi managed to put a tough stitch and them used a pressure bandage. Both made their 14 Km retreat in good time and were admitted to Patna's Rajeswari Hospital before being airlifted to Delhi's AIIMS. Ravi, who lives in Bihar with his wife and a child, said he would like to return to action soon.

Both these CRPF men had undergone the training at the AIIMS between 31 Jul and 16 Aug 2012.

Three years after the AIIMS Trauma Centre began training Jawans from the Army, Air Force, Paramilitary forces and even the Border Road Organisation, the result of the effort was there for all to see.

The training — consisting of how to respond to snake bites, sudden loss of blood, stroke, electrocution or hypo thermia…consists of not only of tough theoretical courses, but also getting trained first hand at various departments of the hospital. "Each batch has 30 persons and the aim is to ensure that the training allows the participants to survive under all conditions", said Thakur.

A doctor at the hospital said: "We are thankful Ravi has survived the bullet by using the skills that we imparted. But we want more such personnel to become better trained so that they can guard us."

"Maoists loot 30 Fire arms" Patna : 19 Jul 2013

The Maoist attack in Aurangabad on 17 July 2013 proved costly. While six men died in it, the rebels looted 30 firearms belonging to the forces.

On the 18th, accepting responsibility for the attack, a Maoist spokesman said it was in retaliation to the State Governments Operation Greenhunt. He claimed they managed to take away 3 AK-47s, 11 SLR s and 16 INSAS rifles.

Two private security men and three Jawans of the Special Auxiliary Police (SAP) had been killed in the attack. A driver, 6th fatality, also succumbed to his injury.

" Close shave for Rajdhani: Naxals blow up Gaya track" Patna: 4 Aug 2013

Passengers of Howrah-Delhi Rajdhani Express had a providential escape when the railway tracks between Paraiya and Guraru stations in Gaya districts were blown up by Maoists late on the 2 Aug 2013 night, disrupt the movement of various important trains including two more Rajdhani Express.

The railway line on the down line measuring 3.5ft were blown in the blast. The outlaws triggered the blast at 10.52 PM while it was noticed by the driver of the advanced pilot engine of the said Express sometime later. The driver immediately informed the staff at the Railway Station Paraiya.

Two can bombs were placed on the railway tracks on the down line. The Maoists succeeded in triggering one, the second was found by security men during the search operation on the site.

Some Maoist literature, electricity wires and other incriminating objects were recovered from the site.

The train services on the up line resumed at 5.50 AM while on the down-line it was at 7.30 AM.

"Reds Kill 7 in Bihar revenge strike" Gaya : 18 Oct 2013

In a daring and well-planned attack on 17 Oct 2013, evening, the Maoists detonated a can-bomb…a trademark IED used by them to blow up vehicles…killing all seven occupants of a vehicle near Pothara village in Aurangabad district, some 130 km from Patna.

The victims included Sushil Pandey, suspected Ranbir Sena activist and husband of Zila Parishad member Usha Devi. The Maoists targeted his vehicle when he was on his way to his village Pisai.

The Maoists suspected Pandey's hand in killing of their cadres in Magadh region by the Sena.

The attack comes barely a week after the Patna HC acquitted all the accused in the Laxmanpur Bathe massacre case for lack of evidence. Maoists hold Ranbir Sena responsible for the massacre that claimed the lives of 58 Dalits on the 1 Dec 1997 night. Principal Secretary (Home) Amir Subhani said as per initial reports, six person including Pandey were killed in the incident.

They were travelling in Tata Safari, returning to their villaged Pishay from Obra market about 6 PM . A former Shiv Sena 'Commander', Pandey had a stint in jail in a murder case[10].

Police said Pandey was in war with Maoists in the area for over 17 years. In Patna, DGP Abhayananda said: "Additional reinforcements have been sent but the nature of the operation is still to be defined."

"In Aurangabad, Naxalism not an issue until after the polls" Aurangabad: 3 Apr 2014

Pitted against each other, these old time rivals from the Congress and BJP "have one thing in common in this Naxalism hit Lok Sabha Constituency, Aurangabad. Asked how they propose to tackle Naxalism, both say they would talk about it only after the polls."

In a constituency where Rajputs and Yadavs constitute the numerically dominant groups, with a substantial Muslim presence, Nikhil Kumar had reason to be confident and resign as governor of Kerala and contest as congress caudidate once the alliance with RJD was sealed. Asked about his solution for Naxalism, Kumar, also a former Delhi Police Commissioner, said: "I will talk about it only after the polls." Posters of Sonia Gandhi, Lalu Yadav and Rabri Devi are pasted on the walls of his house[11].

Though his close associates maintained he is opposed to Naxalism, the sitting JD(U) MP and now the BJP candidate from Aurangabad, Sushil Kumar Singh, also refused, to spell out his plans to tackle Naxalism: "Please ask me about it after the polls. All I can say is that the State government is indifferent to this issue and making no attempt to tackle it. Naxal violence has only gone. In the last six months, there have been three major incidents of violence, killing 20 people, including cops."

Once a member of the CPI student wing AISF, Nikhil cited his Gandhian belief against violence. "I approve the doctrine of Communism minus violence. In Bihar, there is no development. They (Maoist) have almost assumed the role of an alternative government step by step. I (accept) their grievances but not the way they are addressing it. I am influenced by Gandhian philosophy."

While Nikhil is banking on the Rajput-Yadav-Muslim combine to romp home, the BJP candidate counters all this saying he visits Aurangabad once in five years.

Nikhil a former governor of Nagaland besides Kerala, had won this seats in 2004, and describes how he helped his constituents: helping someone in surgery at AIIMS, or a youngster get his passport in Mumbai. The BJP is also making an issue of Nikhil Kumar drinking nothing but Bisleri water. This is simple and clear: A local, grounded, accessible next-door candidate versus the distant, urbane and inaccessible.

The political rivalry between the two hopefuls is, in fact, not new. It dates back to the 1960s when Sushil's father Ramnaresh Singh, had a falling out with Nikhil's father, SN Sinha. When Sinha Bihar CM in 1989, he fielded Nikhil's wife, Shyama Singh, from Aurangabad and she was defeated by Ramnaresh, almost known as Lutan Singh. In 1991, Ramnaresh defeated Sinha. And in 2009, Shushil defeated Nikhil.

Now in 2014, Shushil refrain is: " Nikhil Kumar is beyond the reach of the common man. I am here for them 24 hours."

While Nikhil's legacy and caste equations makes him a formidable candidate, the BJP (candidate's) campaign also seems to be getting resonance.

According to a retired jute mill manager, MK Singh, in Bharthauli village, "Nikhil Kumar is so good, so honest, but you have to come fact-to-fact with the people all the time, not just once in five years. I think he will get some Rajput votes."

"15 villages in Naxal belt voting for the first time" New Delhi: 10 Apr 2014

Here is an interesting if amazing revelation: "Many residents of 15 hill top villages in the Chakarbanda forest in Gaya district will see a polling booth near their homes after 30 years." No booth was set up during this period for fear of an attack by the Maoists, who had taken control of the area, declaring it a "liberated zone."

Two booths have been set up in the area which was declared free of LWE 15 months after the CRPF moved in. The CRPF with the state police claimed to have restricted the movement of the Reds, paving the way for the Election Commission and the district administration to set up booths for the 2014 Lok Sabha polls. In the 2009 Lok Sabha and 2010 Assembly polls, booths for these villagers had been set up 10 km away, and only 21.35 and 15.13 per cent voted, respectively.

CRPF officials claim to have been able to clear 200 sqkm area of Maoist–dominated Chakarbanda forest and they are certain of clearing the remaining 100 sq km in the next few months. Its population of some 8000 includes many first-time voters of Bhuiyan and Yadav communities.

DM Gaya Balamurgan D says: "During the last elections, only people living close to the foot hills came out and voted. The presence of the Maoists had forced us to relocate the booths but this time around, they will be set up right in the hills[12]."

The CRPF had seven major encounters with Maoists (in the first three months of) this year (2014), three of these in the Chakarbanda forest alone!

DIG CRPF (Bihar) ER Kumar claims: "We set up camps in the forests in Dec 2012. We have pushed the ultras back". A senior government further elucidates: "Until a few years ago, people here did not know what a government official looked like. A parallel government used to be run here by the Maoists. Since the CRPF set up base here, even local employment has gone up. Many villages here will be voting for the first time".

Some prominent candidates in Red Zone

Naxal-hit constituencies of Gaya, Jamui, Nawada, Aurangabad, Karakat and Sasaram vote on 9 Apr 2014.

Congress candidates Meira Kumar (Sasaram) and Nikhil Kumar (Aurangabad), RLSP's Upendra Khushwaha (Karakat), and LJP's Chirag Paswan (jamui) are among those contesting.

Sasa ram: Straight fight between Congress and BJP (Chhedi Paswan).

Jamui: Assembly speaker Uday Narayan Choudhary vs Chirag Paswan vs Sudhanshu Shekhar

Aurangabad: Bagi Kumar Verma (JDU) vs former Kerala Governor Nikhil Kumar.

Karakat: Upendra Khushwaha vs Mahabali Singh (BJP) vs Kanti Singh (RJD).

Nawada: Giriraj Singh (BJP) vs

Rajballabh Yadav (RJD) vs

Kaushal Yadav (JDU).

"Maoists strike poll-bound Bihar: Two CRPF men killed": Patna/ Bhagalpur: 11 Apr 2014

Two CRPF men were killed on 9 Apr 2014 in a Maoist attack when they were on their way to a polling station at Gangta village in Jamui Lok Sabha Constituency. SP Munger district Varun Kumar gave this information. Seven other jawans were injured in the cross fire between the ultras and forces. The attack meant to enforce a ballot boycott, left their mark on the elections for the six Lok Sabha for which polling took place the next day on the 10th.[13]

The Maoist imprint was evident in the low turn-out recorded in the constituencies of Sasaram, Karakat, Aurangabad, Gaya, Nawada and Jamui. Additional Chief Electoral Officer R Lakshaman said, an hour before the voting closed:" Around 45 per cent of the electorate voted."

Even though the area is part of Munger district, it falls within the geographical limits of Jamui Lok Sabha Constituency in south-eastern Bihar. The Jamui administration cancelled voting at 12 polling booths.

Officials said the ultras first triggered an IED planted under a bridge when some CRPF men—some on foot and others in a public vehicle—were passing through the Sawa Lakh Baba temple at the entrance of the Bhimbandh jungle. Experts did not rule out the procedural lapse on the part of jawans, who should have avoided using vehicles as a precaution against landmines.

Maoists also blew up the building of Narottampur High School under Kajra police station of Lakhisarai district. Blast occurred early in the day, luckily, just after security men, put up in the school building, had left for the polling duty.

There was a brighter side too. More than 50 landmines, can bombs and cylinder bombs planted by Maoists were recovered in Gaya.

SSP Gaya Nishant Kumar Tiwari said, "six can bombs weighed 30 kg each. They all were defused."

"Maoists blast railway track in Bihar" Patna : 24 Jul 2014

In yet another strike in Bihar, the Maoists triggered a blast at a railway track late on the 22 Jul 2014 night between Ismailpur and Rafiganj section in Aurangabad district of the state. The blast later led to the derailment of a pilot engine running ahead of the Bhubaneshwar New Delhi Rajdhani Express.

No casualty was reported in the incident. Chief PRO of East Central Railway (ECR) said: " The pilot engine jumped off the track due to the blast …nearly 3 mtr of the track was damaged. Electric wires overhead too were damaged. Due to blast, nearly one dozen mail and express trains, including three Rajdhani Express ones, were stranded at various places between Gaya and Mughalsarai stations in the ECR section.

The police said the blast was so powerful that it created a 4-ft deep crater on the stop[14].

Earlier, the Maoists had given a one-day bandh call to protest police firing in Aurangabad and Rohtas districts of Bihar. The Aurangabad firing was recently triggered during anti-Naxal operations by CRPF in which two people, a woman and a child, were killed.

The 24- hour bandh call was given by Maoists from the 22nd midnight to 23 Jul 2014.

Some sources believed the governer-designate of West Bengal, KN Tripathi, was among the stranded passengers.

Police in Gaya and Aurangabad cordoned off the area and stopped all train movements on the route between Dhanbad and Mughalsarai.

After some confusion over the jurisdiction of the accident site whether it fell in Gaya …or Aurangabad…an FIR was lodged with Rafiganj police station in Aurangabad, a police officer told the daily.[15]

The same stretch and train were targeted, as in 2001, when a Maoist blast left 57 passengers of the Howrah-New Delhi Rajdhani dead.

The police said the blast was triggered by the Maoists just before the beginning of their 24-hour Bihar band from the 22 Jul midnight to protest police firing at Madanpur on 21 July.

"Probe to find how Naxals get bullet proof jackets" Patna: 18 Sep 2014

The Gaya police on 17 Sep 2014 set up a team under a DSP to find possible links between serving or retired Army men and conduits of Maoist leaders in supplying bullet proof jackets to some top Naxals in Bihar.

A joint team of STF and Gaya police had arrested two persons, including an ex-Army-man, and seized a bullet proof jacket that was meant to be delivered to a local Maoist leader, Shivji Dhobi alias Tyagji.

The police had recovered an Army bullet proof vest from one Mohd Shams on the 15th, who told them he had procured the vest from Rajiv Kumar, a retired Army man from Ark Devaria village. Rajiv, who presently works as a guard at a bank in Aurangabad, was also arrested.

Shams was arrested when he was on his way to deliver the item to one Gautam Kumar, a Sherghati (Gaya) resident, who was to deliver it further to Maoist leader Tyagiji.

The police were now looking for a serving Armyman, Amresh Kumar, currently posted at Ranchi. Shams told the police that he was to deliver two more jackets to Sandeep ji, a top Maoist leader in Magadh Zone.

A senior STF officer told the daily: "On prima facie, it looks an Army bullet-proof jacket. We are trying to find out how it reached a retired Armyman, and if any serving Armymen are behind it."

Rampur police station SHO Gaurishankar Gupta says: "An FIR had been lodged against Shams and Rajiv Kumar as also against Gautam Kumar and Amresh Kumar under Unlawful Activities (Prevention) Act and some IPC Sections."

Gaya DSP Alok Kumar Singh was asked to probe the matter.

"Bihar STF had traced Maoist to Rampal ashram" Chandigarh: 18 Dec 2014

"3 months before siege : Trial of second Maoist in Sirsa dera went cold; HC says monitor Dera Sacha Sauda."

This news story reveals a very disturbing, nay dangerous, development concerning the 'deras' of the 'holy' men! It speaks about Maoists taking shelter in some of these *deras.*

The details follow

On 18 Aug 2014, three months before self-style godman Rampal was arrested from his Haryana ashram (*dera*), namely, Satlok Ashram in Barwala in Hissar, a joint team of the policemen from Patna and Hissar showed up at the doors of his Satlok ashram in Barwala. The Patna STF, using electronic surveillance, had homed in on a wanted Maoist who had sought refuge in the ashram.

Shown a photograph of CPI (Maoist) member Mahaveer Saklani alias Prithvi, the owner of a kiosk outside the ashram identified "Bhagat ji, who often charges his phone here." Prithvi was arrested, produced in a local court where transit remand was obtained and taken to Patna.[16]

Around that time, the STF also had information on another Maoist hiding in a Sirsa dera. "But after we arrested Prithivi, the trail went cold," a source in the STF said.

At the time of his arrest, Prithvi, who hails from East Champaran in Bihar, claimed he was a disciple of Rampal. But no investigation was conducted on his activities at the Ashram.

Now, a fortnight after the arrest of Rampal, police have started looking into his suspected links with Maoists. IG Hissar Range Anil Rao told the daily that he had written to intelligence chiefs of several states in this regard. On the basis of his disclosure statement, the police have, besides the other charges, also booked him under the UAPA.

Reached for his comments, IGP (Operations) Bihar Sushil M Khopde said: "We arrested Mahaveer Saklani in August (2014) from Haryana in connection with old cases against him in North Bihar districts including his home district Eastern Champaran. We completed our own interrogation and he has since been in judicial custody.

On Solanki's possible links to a dera, Khopde said the interrogation by STF did not look at this aspect since "it was much later Bihar Police heard about it, though not officially from Haryana Police and Punjab Police."

He continued: "If we are asked formally, a request can be made for Saklani's police remand and he can be interrogated on possible dera links."

The Haryana government has been reluctant to probe the activities of *deras* and religious institutions. Appearing before the Punjab and Haryana High Court on 28 November (2014), AG Baldev Mahajan argued that inquiring into affairs of religious institutions was not advisable as there were institutions of several persuations in the State.

Dera Sacha Sauda counsel SK Garg had said that expanding the ambit of probe against Rampal to the Dera Sacha Sauda in Sirsa was not only beyond the jurisdiction of the Court, but go beyond the scope of the contempt of court petition being heard against the Barwala sect leader. Incidentally, the Dera Sacha Sauda supported the BJP in the Haryana Assembly polls that swept the party to power.

But the court called for a search of the Dera Sacha Sauda premises in Sirsa, saying "monitor the activities of the dera on a periodic basis—to avoid future bloody confrontation and safeguard the interest of public at large and the state." It also issued notices to the governments of Punjab, Haryana and Chandigarh UT.

The Haryana government also drew flak from amicus curiae and senior advocate Anupam Gupta who told the Bench about "a conscious and wilful collusion between the state apparatus and Rampal to provide him a camouflage for not appearing in court."

After the Court issued a contempt notice on 29 September to Dr OP Hooda… a private practitioner, he had issued a medical certificate to support Rampal's plea for exemption from personal appearance in Court…the Hissar DC stepped in and nominated a team of doctors to assess Rampal's condition.

AG Mahajan told the Court that this was DC's own initiative to verify the "veracity of information passed on by one of Rampal's disciples that he was ill."

On 8 November, two days before he was to be produced in Court, three government doctors concurred with the opinion of Rampal's own physician, Dr Anant Ram, that he be advised bed-rest for 72 hours. The medical report was submitted by the government to explain its inability to produce him in court on 10 November.

But the Court rejected the medical opinion. After Rampal was arrested on 20 November, a fresh medical examination was conducted in Panchkula and he was declared fit and healthy.

"Ashrams run by 'Godmen' are centres of terror: BJP: New Delhi: 8 Dec 2014

In an ironic turn of events, the BJP has condemned " 'ashrams' (deras) run by 'Godmen'." It has just been said earlier that Dera Sacha Sauda had supported the party for the recently held Haryana Assembly polls and it had romped home "as a result". Now to the BJP's criticism of deras.

"The BJP sought a ban on ashrams run by 'godmen' like Rampal, saying they had become centres of 'terror' in the name of faith," reports a daily[17].

An editorial in the latest issue of party mouth piece 'Kamal Sandesh' said: "These ashrams which have become centres of terror in the name of faith should be deeply investigated. People like Rampal are not born in a day.

They spread their network of superstition gradually in the society— There should be a ban on these types of ashrams."

Questioning as to who should be called a saint or 'baba', the journal edited by BJP Vice President and Rajya Sabha member Prabhat Jha, did not name any "godman" except Rampal. The BJP's such strong criticism of such ashrams assumes significance because of their wide presence in several states and alleged proximity of some of these "godsmen" with the saffron party. One ashram, Dera Sacha Sauda, which is based in Sirsa and commands large following, had announced its support to BJP for the Assembly elections. The dera's head is facing several criminal cases.

"Arms haul from Maoist den in Gaya" New Delhi: 19 Feb 2015

"CRPF seizes large number of suitcase IEDs, can bombs weighing up to 40 kg, 25 petrol bombs, 90 kg explosives besides 9 kg of ammonium nitrate, detonators, cordex wire, gums, radio sets and 23 hand grenades among others."

The CRPF has busted a major arms dump of the banned CPI (Maoist) and seized huge cache of arms, ammunition and explosives from the Chakarbandh forest at Dumaria in Gaya district of Bihar.

The seizures include large number of suitcase IEDs, can bombs weighing up to 40 kg , 25 petrol bombs, 90 kg explosives besides ammonium nitrate (9 kg), detonators, cordex wire, guns, radio set and 23 hand grenades among others. The security forces also seized three 12 bore guns and other items related to fabrication of explosive devices.

The CRPF officials believe the explosives could have been used against the security forces as the CPI (Maoist) is conducting the Tactical Counter

Offensive Campaign (TCOC) against the police and par a military forces during this month but without any "success so far."

While the recovered can bombs were of different weights of 40, 25, 10 and 2 kg, the suitcase IEDs weighed 20 kg each. In an earlier operation on 2 February, the security forces had recovered another dump in the same area.

The CRPF said in a statement: "A credible intelligence input generated by a CRPF officer led to a recovery of major haul of arms, ammunition, explosives and IED dumped in the Chakarbandha forest under Dumaria Police station in Gaya district of Bihar on 17 February. The operation was jointly conducted by the CRPF and State police. The dump was found inside a deep cave located amidst deep forest."

Chakarbandha forest, which is spread in the Gaya and Aurangabad districts of Bihar and touching the fringes of neighbouring Jharkhand, was a stronghold of CPI (Maoist) till about two years back. However, the Maoist activities have been checked through the presence of security forces, especially the establishment of CRPF camps in the forest in 2013.

The dump is suspected to be owned by the Madya Zone of Bihar-Jharkhand Special Area Committee of the CPI (Maoist).

The sustained offensive by the security forces across the Maoist-hit States has in the recent led to surrender of large number of ultras, including their field commanders, have surrendered before the governments. The desparate Maoist leadership is seeking to regain foothold in the areas lost to the security forces by carrying out some major actions against the police and paramilitary forces in such areas.

"60 IEDs found in Munger": Munger (Bihar): 19 Feb 2015

In a joint CRPF, STF and Bihar Police, 60 IEDs were on 18 Feb 2015 found in Bhimbandh forest in Bihar's Munger district. SP Varun Kumar Sinha told the press that the police had received information about a training programme being held by Maoists in the forest when a joint operation was launched.

One suspected Maoist identified as Murmur Koda was arrested during the operation.

"Woman Maoist killed in Gaya" Patna: 18 May 2015

A woman commander was killed and 10 others, including a zonal secretary, were arrested in separate incidents in Gaya. The Police also recovered an INSAS rifle and walkie-talkie from the encounter spot at Teleatand village on 17 May 2015.

The commander killed in a joint operation by the CRPF and Gaya police was identified as Babita Bhokta, an area commander in Koteshwari sub zone of Madhya zone. That she was moving with an INSAS makes her an important operative of the Maoists. Babita was known to be one of 12 members of woman squad that moved with the Madhya Zone Chief, Indalji. CRPF IG (Bihar and Jharkhand) Arun Kumar told press in Gaya: "The joint spotted a 25-strong group of men and women in police uniform during a combing operation in area. We opened fire when they tried to escape …seven Maoists were injured but none could be arrested."

In a separate operation, the Gaya police on the 16th night arrested Magadh Zone Secretary Sanjeevan Baitha and nine of his associates, wanted in a dozen cases, including the 2003 attack on Goh unit of Special Auxiliary Police (SAP) in which three SAP men were killed.

Notes

1. The Statesman 27 Mar 2007.
2. Manoj Prasad, Indian Express, 6 march 2007.
3. The Statesman, 27 March 2007.
4. Shoumojit Banerjee, The Hindu, 9 Aug 2011.
5. Avinash Kumar, Hindustan Times, 16 Apr 2012)
6. Dheeraj Kumar, The Pioneer, Hindustan Times, Indian Express, all of 28 Jan. 2013.
7. Rahul Triparhi, Indian Express, 6 Mar 2013.
8. Staff Reporter, The Hindu, 19 Jun 2013.
9. Dwaipayan Ghosh, Times of India, 13 Jul 2013).
10. Abdul Qadir,Times of India, Staff Reporter, Hindustan Times, both 18 Oct 2013.
11. DK Singh, Indian Express, 3 Apr 2014.
12. Vijaita Singh, Indian Express, 10 Apr 2014.
13. Avinash Kumar and Avijit Biswas, Hindustan Times, 11 Apr 2014.
14. Amarnath Tewari, The Pioneer, 27 Jul 2014.
15. Anil Kumar Ojha and Avinash Kumar, Hindustan Times, 24 Jul 2014.
16. Chander Suta Dogra, Indian Express, 8 Dec 2014.
17. Indian Express, 8 Dec 2014.

22

Chhattisgarh - 1

Chhattisgarh is one of the two, or three, worst-hit states in the Maoist corridor running north to south; along with Jharkhand and Bihar. In the State, Bastar is the worst-hit region,where the Government is going all out to change the things for better.

To begin with, a brief BACKGROUNDER.

Chhattisgarh

Origin : Kondapalli Seetharamaiah formed the PWG in 1980 and brought Dandakaranya...comprising parts of Chhattisgarh, Odisha, Maharashtra and Andhra...under its control.

Bloody Era: 2000-12

Key issues : Exploitation of tribals, lack of development.

Status Check : 15 of 27 districts affected.

Raman Singh, CM: in 2012: "Naxals are on the backfoot. However, we cannot rule out their presence. It is a national issue and needs to be dealt with accordingly."

Ground Realities of Naxalite influence in Chhattisgarh Till 2010

As stated above, Chhattisgarh is one of the two worst-hit states regarding the spread of the Maoism.

Situation as of 2006

"The Naxalites dominate 9 of the 16 districts of the State and are rapidly spreading their influence in four other districts." This was reported by a weekly in its issue of 11 Jun 2006. Some other important observations from this weekly are given here:

- "The intelligence report makes a dark prediction: 'The Maoists could capture 60 per cent of the land in these areas by 2010"

[Interestingly, the deadline coincides with the Commonwealth Game period. Are they conveying a hidden, even a sinister message?]

- "In the State's Bastar division, the Naxals have forcibly occupied 20,000 hectares of forest land and are running a parallel government."
- "As many as 175 incidents were reported in the State during Jan-Apr 2006. On 29 Apr 2006, the 2089 Maoist killed 15 members of the Salwa Judum campaign, and earlier on 25 April, they had kidnapped 52 villagers from Bastar.
- "Between Nov 2005 and Apr 2006, they had killed at least 90 people, including 50 security men."

The above are direct quotes from the weekly's issue is Jun 2006. It needs to be noted that the number of districts in Chhattisgarh had risen to 27 by 2013.

At the end of this report in the weekly, the correspondent, in what can be classified as 'huge exaggeration', wrote: "In fact, almost all of Chhattisgarh's 16 districts are Naxal-infested, with over 700 women cadres in the guerrilla squads."

It bears repetition that above was penned in June 2006.

Important Events 2006-2007

Training Police to face Maoists: counter-Terrorism school: Mid 2006

A weekly was very critical about the preparedness of the State police to face the Maoists. Then it puts a positive side of the scene:

"Now meet Sub-Inspector Praveen Purseth, of the Chhattisgarh Armed Police (CAP), but now an instructor at the Counter-Terrorism and Jungle Warfare School (CTJWS) in Kanker. Fit and alert, he carries his AK 47 like a third arm and is product of the Indian Army's Counter-Insurgency and Jungle Warfare School (CIJWS) at Varangte in Mizoram."[1]

Presently, Purseth is one of the instructors at CJJWS, engaged in training State's policemen to acquit themselves better in Counter-Maoist battles. A school for training policemen for this task was urgently needed and it is a happy sign that one is already functioning under (Brig) 1GP BK Ponwar, a retired Brigadier from the Infantry arm of the Army.

What is Ponwar's mandate: "To transform the police not just in Chhattisgarh, but from neighbouring Maoist-hit states such as Odisha, and Jharkhand, into a fighting force Ponwar has several instructors like Purseth under him to achieve this transformation.

Brig Ponwar, a Counter-Insurgency expert, tells the weekly in detail about his hopes and aims: the Maoists are not just well-trained but their ability to merge with crowds introduces the surprise element, the goal is to train the police in guerrilla tactics and establish a Counter-Insurgency grid so that we can dominate areas where the strong arm of the state is missing today; along with the physical fitness and psychological preparedness, the men are being taught to make friends with the villagers and be sensitive, since without local intelligence, everything could fail; policemen trained by him will find it easier to worst the Maoists if they can befriend the local population; and hence the cliché that the real war is to win the heads and hearts of the civilians caught in the cross fire from the Maoists and forces."

UAV deployed for anti-Naxal Operations: Jan 2007

The Centre has long last deployed one UAV (Unarmed Aerial Vehicle) in Chhattisgarh for mapping the dense forests in Bastar region that are heavily infested by the Maoists. Dense Sal forests in the region provides a safe sanctuary to the ultras. They operate an illegal arms factory in the deep jungles of the state, hit by the LWE.

The demand for the UAV has a long history. Chhattisgarh had requested the Centre as far back as 2004 that the ISRO be approached to have the area mapped by its satellites. It has had a long pending demand to have this are a mapped by the UAVs to enable it to combat the Naxals effectively. It got a UAV by the end-2006.

A source in the MHA said: "The use of the UAVs in anti-Naxal operations has helped the security forces in containing the menace to a large extent."

The growing sophistication of the insurgent outfits is a matter of serious concern for the security agencies. The insurgents have moved for beyond the use of mobile phones in detonating IEDs and now using multiple detonators against the security forces.[2]

DG National Security and CRPF JK Dutt, acknowledges the use of sophisticated technology by the insurgents: "The security forces need to be extra cautious while defusing IEDs as there is no way to detect multiple detonators in a bomb. Technology for jamming such devices are being indigenously developed and also imported to counter the, new threat....In view of this sophistication, training aspects of the security forces need constant up gradation to face newer challenges."

Appointment of a Governor is Welcome: March 2007

It is not often that the state governments take kindly to the appointment of a Governor by the Centre, because they think he is essentially an agent of the Centre. But there seems to be a happy exception at the appointment of Mr ESL Narasimhan as Governor of Chhattisgarh.

What could be the possible reason behind this rare welcome by Raipur? State Home Minister Ravi Vichar Netam explains the reason: "Narasimhan can be of tremendous assistance to his Government in tackling the decade-old menace of Maoism. Our government would definitely seek his guidance and suggestions on the issue."

The Minister's keenness in this respect in understandable in view of the fact that the Maoist violence, in the year 2006 alone, claimed some 400 lives, including 320 civilians.

Question raised on police postings in Maoism-hit Chhattisgarh: Post-Rani Bodli 15: Mar 2007

The huge loss suffered in 15 Mar 2007 Rani Bodli attack by the state police has brought into focus the quality and fairness of police administration and particularly on the subject of police postings and transfers to and out of the worst LWE-hit districts/regions.

The conspicuous and obvious name that comes to mind, and understandably so, is that of Mohd Hussain, who, at 55, was in command at Rani Bodli police outpost in Dantewada when Maoists attacked it on 15 Mar 2007 and massacred 55 police on the spot. Ironically, after being suspended by the state government consequent to the attack, he has been restored and given command of two posts that are some 7.25 km apart!

The suspended officer has his own grievances and explanation: "I have been made a scapegoat, and made to serve in the Naxal-hit areas even when the government orders lay down that officers above 54 should not be posted to such areas. I was present at Polikhand, and the fact was known to my seniors and juniors when the attack came."

The allegation comes when the Chhattisgarh is busy explaining irregularities in such postings. "These posted in Naxal-hit areas have been burdened with many responsibilities."

Chhattisgarh, "which has worst record in fighting Naxals, has lost over 150 security men to Naxalite violence in the past three years." Yet again, the state does not have a full-time IG (Naxal Intelligence), it is held as an additional charge by the IG (CAP). Even worse, State's Intelligence unit is also operating without any DIG and SP rank officers. Only two Additional SPs have been posted to this all-important unit, mandated to function as the eyes and ears of the State Police in its anti-Maoists war.

As a measure to fight the Naxals affectively, the state government has created ranges for select Naxal-affected areas like Surguja, Rajnandgaon, Raigarh, Dantewada, and Kanker and two posts of DIGs in CAP. But the government-seems to have forgotten to post officers to these sensitive posts, especially created to combat the Naxal threat. Or, perhaps, more accurately, the Officers are shying away from shouldering such responsibilities for obvious and understandable reasons. Worse still, the government and the DGP are unable or unwilling to force the issue. Any which may, it is a sad reflection on the administration of the state facing most serious threat from the marauding Maoists.

As if all these facts were not bad enough, there are more to come. As many as three SPs—of Sarguja, Korea and Jashpurnagar—and eight commanding officers of the CAP battalions are non-cadre officers. They seem to have been posted flouting the cadre rules. What seems to be an apparent attempt to explain away this criticism, DGP OP Rathor claims there is a shortage of IPS Officers in the state, a claim immediately rubbished by the state police officers in the know.

To paraphrase the poet, the things are not OK in the state of Chhattisgarh!

CM Raman Singh demands unified command and unified Action to combat Maoists: Mar 2007

The man most concerned with the 4 Mar 2007 assassination of JMM MP Sunil Mahato in the neighbouring Jharkhand is Chief Minister Raman Singh of Chhattisgarh. A red alert was sounded all over the state after this assassination.

He demanded constitution of separate (dedicated) Central Para-Military Force (CPMF) to deal with Maoist menace in 155 affected districts in the country. He wants this CPMF to be deployed in Maoist-hit states and they should be trained on the lines of the Indian Army. More importantly, they must have all facilities at par with the Army. He feels Maoism was a threat to the Indian democracy.

In fact, Chhattisgarh, where more than 400 people have fallen to the Maoist violence in the last one year (2006), has again called for a unified action against the armed rebels. The state has all along been demanding a unified command from the Centre and stressed the need for a joint action— well-coordinated and thought-through in a profassional manner — by all the Maoism hit states under the Central direction, to combat the Red Terror.

Chhattisgarh shares the borders with other Maoist-hit states like Jharkhand, Odisha, AP and Maharashtra. Even they can at their level plan joint coordinated anti-Naxal operations to ensure that the ultras under pressure in one state do not go across to the neighbouring state. Eight of its 16 (number in 2007) districts are seriously affected by the LWE.

Delay in finding a new DGP for Chhattisgarh: Jun 2007

Even in normal times, the states must ensure that a new incumbent is positioned to take up his job the day after a DGP retires. It should not be a problem, even when we are aware of pulls and pressures by the likely candidates themselves in the race and their political backers above them, because the date of retirement of the serving DG is known months in advance. This is necessary not only because the new incumbent would have been chosen after due considerations of his merits but also because an all-important post like that of a DGP state could not be allowed to remain vacant for weeks on end.

The above observations are applicable in a normal situation, because law and order is an important subject. But low and order is not in a happy situation in most of the states of India, and urgency in putting a new incumbent in the chair is obvious and clear. But keeping such a post vacant even for a short time in a state which is worse-affected by Naxalism is an act of political irresponsibility, if not delinquency.

In fact, the practice should be to announce the new incumbent well before the incumbent retires. That will be very desirable as the new incumbent will have leant the ropes by the time he takes over. This is even more essential in a state facing serious LWE.

These thoughts cross one's mind when a daily of 19 Jun 2007 reports that Chhattisgarh has been without a DGP for a month. The post fell vacant on 21 May 2007 following the death of OP Rathore, who suffered a massive cardiac arrest while, ironically, delivering a lecture on tackling the Naxalite threat in the State. That it should lie vacant for a month is a poor reflection for the administration of state facing a serious threat. Accepting that it was not a normal retirement, even then the Chief Minister and Home Minister should have acted with certain despatch to find a replacement[3].

However, CM Raman Singh assured that the process of appointing a new DGP is under way:

"Presently we are talking to MHA regarding relieving Vishwa Ranjan, now on deputation as Additional Director, IB, for the position."

Four senior IPS Officers were reportedly in the running for the top job. Ranjan and Praveen Mahendru are the seniormost officers from the Chhattisgarh cadre. The two others are Rajeev Mathur (Director Prosecution) and Anil Nawani (DG Prisons).

Prisoners shifted to safer jails in Chhattisgarh: Jun 2007

Transnational Terrorism

After intelligence warned that Maoists might attack vulnerable prisons in an attempt to free their comrades, the State Government has shifted 60 hard core LWE to more secure areas of the state. It was reported by a daily on 8 Jun 2007.[4]

The Maoists were shifted form Dantewada subjail to Jagdalpur Central jail. Anil Nawani, DG (Prisons) confirmed the news: "The operation was conducted discreetly, amid tight security, as the ultras could have attacked the convoy."

The step to shift these high-risk inmates followed specific inputs from Central Intelligence agencies that prisons in Chhattisgarh were particularly vulnerable to Maoist attacks. "The central agencies cited the 14 Nov 2005 incident in Bihar when Naxalites stormed Jehanabad district jail, 45 km from Patna, killing at least 12 people." The attack was aimed at 'rescuing' the comrades lodged in jail, and led to the escape of half of jail's 650 inmates.

Intelligence agencies feel the threat had increased after the ultras blew up high tension power transmission tower on 31 May (2007), causing a black out in many Naxalite-hit areas.

Chhattisgarh seeks young IPS officers to combat Maoists: Jun 2007

14 Jun 2007, Chhattisgarh requested Centre to post young IPS officers to the State to deal affectively with the Maoist violence. The demand was made by the State officials during their discussions with the MHA officials in the State capital Raipur.

Presently, the state does not have even the sanctioned strength of 81 IPS officers, 11 shy of it. An officer who attended the discussions, explains: "We have requested for posting of more young IPS officers even if it called for an out-of-the-way arrangements. ....Given the gravity of situation and the fact that the state government has taken the Maoist problem as a challenge, we have requested the Centre to post more young IPS officers so that the State can fight Maoists with greater efficacy. In fact, the state needs more IPS officers than the sanctioned strength. But for now, we have demanded to fill at least the vacant posts."

The meeting also discussed development projects in the Maoism-hit areas as the development itself is considered anti-dote to the Maoist constant refrain of tribals suffering deprivation due to lack of any development in their areas. The state officials also informed the visiting team, that included Additional Secretary, MHA, Vijay Kumar and the head of the Anti-Maoist Cell, MHA, GK Sinha, about various development projects taken up in the affected areas.

After the launch of anti-Maoist Salwa Judum campaign, the Maoists have become more aggressive, and have been targeting both civilians and security men. One instance of it is Maoist strike at Errabore area on 9 Jul 2007.

Constable to SHO in one step: Bastar: Aug 2007

Faced with a serious shortage of officers in Naxal-hit Bastar region, the Chhattisgarh Police have decided to deploy lower-ranking personnel from other districts and post them as SHOs in hypersensitive police stations. "In fact, ten police constables have been selected as part of this process from Durg district. All of them would be posted as Sub-Inspectors in charge of police stations in Bastar, Dantewada, Kanker, Narayanpur, and Bijapur districts of Bastar Division and will have to serve for a tenure of five years in the Region." A daily reported it on 8 Aug 2007.[5]

They will be required to undergo a physical test and clear a written examination.

DGP Vishwa Ranjan said decision to promote senior constables was part of government policy to provide manpower to Naxal-affected police stations. "If we go in for fresh recruitment, the process could take up to two years. But the existing employees do not need to be given much training and can be deployed almost immediately." The DGP explained.

Constables seeking 'promotion' will need to be graduate and below 48 years of age. The selected candidates will have to go in for a two-month training in Jungle warfare and also learn about the basic responsibilities of a SHO. "As most of the selected candidates are expected to be familiar with the CrPC and IPC, we don't think there should be any problem in their handling of the higher responsibility", the DGP added.

While the process has been initiated in the Durg district, the special promotion drive will be started in other districts too where Naxalite pressure is comparatively less.

Officials indicated that the State Government is aiming to appoint some 100 SHOs through this process.

Maoists violence and incidents: 2006-2007

9 Feb 2006

Maoists raided main store of NMDC at Hirauli in Dantewada district, Chhattisgarh. Killed 18 CISF men and looted 14 tonnes of explosives and 14 SLR rifles.

28 Feb 2006

A landmine planted by Maoists at Eklagoda, near Errabore in Dantewada district killed 55 civilians and injured 14 more. They kidnepped 125.

17 Jul 2006

25 killed and 18 injured when over 800 armed Naxals attacked a village in Dantewada district, Chhattisgarh.

Oct 2006

Budhini Munda @ Shobha, wife of Prashant Bose @ Kishanda, No. 2 in CPI (Maoist) hierarchy, arrested by police near Ramjodi, near and under Lathikata Police station, along with her bodyguards.

11 Nov 2006

185 rifles looted from Home Guards Training Centre.

17 Jun 2006

Two Naxalites were killed in Bijapur district in a joint operation mounted by the police forces of Chhattisgarh and AP. The ultras had fired at the police column. In the ensuing shoot out, two of them were killed.

20-21 Jun 2006

Some 300 armed Maoist cadres raided Dantewada district and took away 25 villagers as hostages. Subsequently, they shot, beat and stabbed seven of them to death and injured three others on 20 June night. They also burnt 25 houses in the village. The police recovered the bodies on the 21st morning. Condemning the killing, CM Raman Singh said: "Massacre has ashamed humanity. CPI (Maoist) has become desperate ever since the Bastar tribals launched the Salwa Judum campaign. With the campaign reaching AP, the Naxalites were feeling more and more insecure. As they are losing ground, they are targeting innocent villagers."

Killings, Abduction and Economic Blockade by Maoists: Jun 2006

Maoists killed two villagers, including a surrendered comrade on 14 Jun 2006 and looted their belongings in the Bijapur district.

These attacks came a day after the abduction of seven villagers, including six women, by the rebels in Dantewada district (on the 13th).

Both the men killed in two separate incidents on the 14th in Tumnar village of Bijapur police station are named Kowaram Telam. Surrendered Naxalite Telam, 57, was picked up from his village past mid-night and axed to death by a group of Naxalites.

In a separate incident, they killed the village head (Patel) of Tumnar, Telam, 55, and looted his properties worth Rs 48,000.

Meanwhile, the economic blockade call given by CPI (Maoist) to protest the Salwa Judum in Dantewada district on 14 Jun 2006 passed off peacefully but its impact was witnessed in the tribal belt of Chhattisgarh, Jharkhand and Odisha.

In Chhattisgarh, majority of markets in Dantewada, Kankar, Bastar, and Sarguja districts remained closed and vehicles kept off the roads. The worst-affected areas were Geedam, Behramgarh (Bhairamgarh), Bhopalpatnam, Bhanupratap pur, Pakhanjor, Kisnar, Kondgaon, Narayanpur and Ambagarh Choki, as Maoist blocked roads[6].

In several parts of Odisha, life came to a near stand still, and buses and trucks remained off the roads. All the State Transport buses had been advised to remain away from the Maoist-hit areas. Overnight journeys were discouraged both by government and private vehicle owners. The impact of the blockade was mostly seen in the southern districts of Malkangiri, Gajapati and Rayagada.

Prior to the commencement of the blockade, Tumnar village, 10 km from Bijapur police district headquarters in Chhattisgarh, suffered a deparadation late on the 12 Jun night at the hands of Maoists. More than 100 armed cadres attacked the villagers who were seen as the Salwa Judum sympathisers, killing two of them, as already discussed above.

Did Andhra Maoists train Chhattisgarh Maoists? 2005-2006

"The upswing in the Naxal attacks on police camps and outposts in Chhattisgarh in recent times is surprising many analysts." One theory doing the rounds is that this upswing can be ascribed, many experts believe, to the training being imparted to them by the fugitive Maoists from AP. This is perfectly sustainable proposition knowing as we do the kinds of pressures and unceasing anti-Maoist operations mounted by the AP authorities during 2006. There may be another explanation for this upswing: some shortcoming within Chhattisgarh. The state intelligence admits and security experts agree that lack of proper training of the state police officers in the anti-Naxal combat is also aggravating the difficulties of the State in countering the Maoist activities[7].

Chhattisgarh is the only Naxal-hit state in the country with a dedicated UAV to survey and map the Maoist camps and their movement. But that does not seem to have enhanced the anti-Naxal capability of the state. Even if some analysts and AP police officers tend to blame Chhattisgarh police for this weakness, this may not be the whole truth. Even if we admit that the state police is not up to it to make full use of the UAV for operational successes, one can not ignore the fact that the state police is not adequately equipped due to variety of reasons to mount a quick attack/response even if a Naxal hideout is reported by the UAV in a distant hill/jungle area. It simply lacks the requisite mobility to reach the spot, unless it is a short distance from a police camp or post.

There is a war of words between the two neighbouring states. A Chhattisgarh police officer asserts AP Maoists were part of the group that attacked Rani Bodli. He counterpart from AP denies it: “It is not true. My information is that the attack group comprised Maoists from within the State.

13 Maoists killed and 13 held Dec 2006

The anti-Maoist campaign in the State achieved a major success with the arrest of 13 Maoists from Koeelibara area of Kanker district on 5 Dec 2006. Acting on tip off about the ultras planting mines in the area, the police rushed there and did the needful.

In a separate incident the same day, the police killed two ultras in an encounter in Abujh Maad forest area in the worst-hit Bastar district of the State.

Just a day before on the 4th, the police eliminated 13 rebels in a fierce encounter in Dantewada district, at Cherpal, some 450 km from Raipur. The encounter followed an attack by the armed cadres at a CRPF outpost of Cherpal. It was repulsed jointly by the State police and the CRPF, firing over 1,100 rounds.

Four Maoists were killed by the police on the 3rd.

Statistics

- Over 50,000 people in Maoist-hit areas in Bastar region have left their villages and taken shelter with government-run 27 relief camps. This is essentially the result of Maoists' vicious attacks on Salwa Judum camps.
- Some 350 people, including the police men and civilians have been killed this year (2006) at various places in Naxal violence in the state.

IED kills 7 in Bastar: Jan 2007

Seven security men were killed in an IED blast near Jharia village, 30 km from Kanker city in Bastar district, and some 350 km from Raipur. The impact of the explosion was so devastating that it created a huge crater in the ground. There was a brief exchange of firing. The seven killed are: an Assistant Commandant of CRPF, an ASI of police, and five constables. The injured were moved to district hospitals in Jagdalpur and Raipur.

IG Bastar RK Vij informs: "Explosion occurred when a 30-member patrol——comprising men from CRPF, Chhattisgarh police and Chhattisgarh Security Force——was trying to cross a narrow bridge over a rivulet at 5 PM on 16 Jan 2007. Naxal cadres, waiting in an ambush for this very moment set off the IED which killed seven men on the spot."

It needs to be emphasised that the Maoists stepped up violence in Bastar after the launch of Salwa Judum in South Bastar in Jun 2005. The NGOs believe the government is endangering the lives of the civilians by sponsoring the Salwa Judum and putting young men in the firing line.

79 Maoists surrender 3 Jan 2007

Chhattisgarh police achieved a major success in the ongoing anti-Maoist operations when 79 Left guerrillas surrendered before CM Raman Singh at the Police Headquarters in Raipur of the 79, 29 had a bounty on their heads, ranging from 1,500 to Rs 20,000. 32 others were wanted in some major case while 12 were members of the Sangham, an anciliary outfit of the rebels.

The surrenderees took oath of loyalty to the country and resolved to join the social mainstream. The surrenderees belonged to four dalam, viz, Keshkal, Gurghat, Barda and Kiskodo. These dalams are active in the Bastar region. A *dalam* is the basic operational region of the Maoists. It can be equated roughly to an Infantry 'section' of the Army and popularly called a 'squad.'

The Maoists who surrendered "last month (Dec 2006) were also brought to Raipur for the occasion from the worst-hit Bastar region.

DGP OP Rathor told the press: "This surrender was the result of community policing and welfare measures started by us. Efforts are on to in-still confidence in tribals."

8 Feb 2007

In a major strike, Nexalites on 8 Feb 2007 killed a civilian and four security men and injured 12 others by triggering an IED in Bijapur district. The blast took place between Bodli and Bhairamgarh villages on the National Highway 16, that connects Bastar Region with Nizamabad of AP.

Bhairamgarh police station sources gave details of the fatalities.

- An officer and a jawan of Nagaland Armed Force.
- An ASI of Chhattisgarh police.
- A Special Police Officer (SPO).
- A Civilian.

15 Mar 2007

Naxals killed 16 officers of Chhattisgarh Armed Force. They also killed 39 SPSs, and injured 12 at Salwa Judum Camp in Rani Bodli village—one of the biggest Naxal attacks in Bastar. They also looted 48 rifles. It was a strong message against Salwa Judum activists. Fatalities later rose to 68.

26 Mar 2007

Maoists once again attacked the Maraiagudem police outpost night 26 Mar 2007. Some 300 Maoists and Sangham members surrounded the outpost, hurled grenades at it and then opened fire.

There was heavy firing from both sides. Konda SDPO Prafulla Kumar Thakur said the firing went on for an hour or so. There were no casualties.

Maoist vacate Andhra Forests: Mar 2007

The 15 Mar 2007 Maoist attack in Chhattisgarh must have come as a surprise to AP, even if the strike was not totally unexpected. Sources disclosed that in the second week of March (2007), some 200 Maoist cadres had migrated from the forests of Nallamalla and North Telangana to the Andhra-Odisha border areas and Dandakaranya forest, so said a daily of 16 Mar 2007[8].

Reports on the subject suggest that over 40 senior leaders/cadres of the CPI (Maoists) were also in the group. Police officers claimed that most of the Maoists had been vacated from Nallamalla forest by mid-Mar 2007.

But senior AP police officers claim the exodus had nothing to do with the Rani Bodli attack, as the Naxals from AP who were part of exodus, do not know much about the terrain in these areas (of Rani Bodli). The Dandakaranya forest touches Chhattisgarh, Jharkhand, Odisha, and Andhra. Police presence in the area is limited due to the difficult terrain and dense forest cover.

Meanwhile, AP police have put on the high alert all police stations on Andhra-Odisha and Khammam district (AP)-Chhattisgarh borders, following the Rani Bodli. Anti-Naxal forces have also stepped up combing, as they expect weapons from the Rani Bodli attack will be used to equip other Maoist group.

Tabulated-Statistical Information

Fatalities

The MHA figures show that 551 people have been killed in Maoist attacks in Chhattisgarh state since 1 Jan 2006 to Mar 2007. Their break down:

- Civilians 316
- Maoists 88
- Security Forces 147

A daily says 676 people killed in Maoists violence over the last two years (Period dates not mentioned).

Rani Bodli massacre: 15 Mar 2007

1. • 2 AM. Heavily armed 400 Naxal terrorists raid the security forces (essentially Salwa Judum activists) camp at Rani Bodli and block all exists by surrounding it.
   - Hurl grenades and pistol bombs inside the camp. Ensure no one escapes by lighting up the area with portable gensets.
   - Taken by surprise, there is hardly any counter action by the inmates. The Reds set the camp afire after the 3-hour 'battle', before making away with weapons of the security forces.
2. Distances. Rani Bodli site is 525 km south-west of Raipur, and 50 km from the headquartere of Bijapur district.
3. Fatalities in action. 55 killed on the site. Of these 55, 38 were SPOs of Salwa Judum and 17 from Chhattisgarh Armed Police (CAP). Fatalities rose to 68 finally.

4. Strength. Collector KR Pisda, 60 SPOs and 23 from the CAP were stationed at the Rani Bodli Camp/Post in the Maoist-infested area of Dantewada district.

Why Dantewada?

- Government supported Salwa Judum campaign, an anti-Naxal movement by the local tribals, was sponsored, conceived and launched by that brave Congressman Mahendra Karma in Jun 2005, in this district.
- Dantewada has a huge forest cover: Dandakaranya Forest.
- It borders AP, Odisha, Maharashtra. Easy for rebels to escape after attacks.
- Its extensive landmass of 10,239 sq km has a population of just over six lakh. Its abundant forest cover coupled with hills and inhospitable terrain sans any roads made it ideal for the Maoists to spread their ideological tentacles. Their task turned out even easier as there were hardly any institutions of governance worth the name in the district.

Major Naxal strikes

- **Nov 2004.** Killed 17 policemen in an attack in Chandaulu district of AP.
- **3 Sep 2005.** 20 policemen in Bilaspur district of Chhattisgarh by a landmine.
- **Nov 2005.** Raided Jehanabad jail in Bihar. Killed 12 policemen and freed 305 inmates (Maoist cadres, mostly).
- **Nov 2005.** Looted 207 rifles and 25,000 rounds of ammunition from the Guard Training Centre at Giridih, Jharkhand.
- **28 Feb 2006.** 25 civilians killed in landmine blast at Errabore in Dantewada district, Chhattisgarh.
- **25 Mar 2006.** 13 civilians killed in landmine blast in Kanker district, Chattisgarh.
- **16 Apr 2006.** 10 policemen killed in an attack on a police outpost in Dantewada district, Chhattisgarh.
- **28 Apr 2006.** 13 of the 50 hostages executed in Dantewada district, Chhattisgarh.
- **16 Jul 2006.** 32 tribal inmates killed by the Naxals when they attacked Salwa Judum Relief Camp at Errabore in Dantewada district, Chhattisgarh. Some sources said "32 tribal participants in a Salwa Judum camp at Errabore killed in a Naxal attack."

Difference in categorization of victims in the same incidents is too glaring to be missed. If one source describes them as "innocent civilians" the other calls them the members/activists of Salwa Judum, an anti-Naxal movement.

- **2 Dec 2006.** 13 policemen killed in a landmine blast in Jharkhand.
- **4 Mar 2007.** JMM MP Sunil Mahato, watching a football match at a village near Jamshedpur, Jharkhand killed/shot dead.
- **15 Mar 2007.** Rani Bodli massacre. 55 killed on site. Figure rose to 68, as 13 others succumbed to their injuries in hospitals. Attack by 400 cadres. Dantewada district, Chhattisgarh. Details given earlier.

Maoist arms dump busted: 15 Mar 2007

In an uncanny coincidence, on the day of the Rani Bodli massacre, AP police unearthed a huge catche of rockets, rockets launchers, landmines and ammunition during a raid on a Maoist hide out in Nallawalla forest near Pullela Cheruvu in Prakasam district on 15 Mar 2007.

The police said the dump was a part of rocket launcher, rockets and other materials manufactured by Maoist Tech Madhu last year (2006) to target police stations, and other security installations in the state, AP.

The details of the seizure are given here:

- 272 fully-assembled rockets.
- 7 rocket launchers.
- 47 anti-personnel pressure mines.
- 1 SBBL gun.
- 112 rocket pipes, 111 rocket heads, 360 rocket propellant nuts, 30 rocket launcher stands, 271 propeller caps, 2200 propeller blades, all raw materials to manufacture rockets.
- 104 pressure mine springs and 360 detonator caps.
- 380 grenade springs.
- 360 rounds of .303 rifle ammunition

CRPF averts Naxalite attack: Mar 2007

An alert squad of the CRPF and the SPOs of Chhattisgarh police repulsed a major attack by 400-strong Maoist cadre at a Salwa Judum camp at Marriqudda in Dantewada district early on the night 24/25 Mar 2007. The Maoist escaped the scene taking advantage of the dense forest cover.

A senior CRPF official said on 26 March that the Naxalites opened fire at the camp covered by the CRPF personnel, when reinforcements were rushed to the spot and there was fire fight. The official further added: "During the search operations after the encounter, the troops noted fresh blood stains which indicated that 10 to 15 Maoists were either killed or seriously injured; one Naxal commander, Attu, is also believed to be either killed or seriously injured by our forces; and no casualty of the security forces has been reported in the incident."

The arms, ammunition and equipment recovered from the site during the combing operations: one gun, 15 bombs, 5 detonators, 17 rounds of rifle ammunition, 100 mtr electric wire, two camera flashes, 16 plastic water cans, three diaries, three search lights, 40 batteries (1.5 volt), 3 search lights and Rs 27,500 in cash.

The recoveries were handed over to the state police and an FIR has been lodged in this connection.[9]

A word on the claim by the security forces about the casualties suffered by the Maoists after the encounters. Some analysts feel the Naxal casualties as estimated/claimed by the officials after such operations may bear no relationship with the realities on the ground. Most of the times, these estimates could be an egregious exaggeration, and at the worst, a figment of someone's imagination. Some analysts believe all such tell tale estimates are self-serving. The fact of life is that it is seldom that the anti-Naxal operations yield a body of a dead Maoist. Let the case rest here for the present.

Chhattisgarh: 6 more districts to get Anti-Naxal Cells: Jun 2007

"Conceding that Maoists menace has spread to almost the entire State, the Chhattisgarh government has decided to establish the Anti-Naxalite (Operations) Cells in six more districts, which were till now free from the LWE." This was revealed by State Home Minister Ram Vichar Netan on 12 Jun 2007. These six districts are: Raipur, Kawardha, Rajnandgaon, Dhamtari, Durg and Mahasamund.

With the setting up of these six special units, of the State's 20 police districts, only four will remain without such units, meaning only four districts can deemed to be free of Maoist scourge. These four are: Bilaspur, Korba, Raigarh and Janjgir.

The ten districts already having functional Anti-Naxal Cells are: Bastar, Kanker, Bijapur, Dantewada, Narayanpur, Sarguja, Korea, Jashpur, Balrampur and Surajpur.

The decision to set up these six new cells comes after the intelligence inputs and interrogation of top arrested Naxalites revealed that after strengthening their base in tribal belt, the Maoists were now planning to further spread their tentacles in the plains of Chhattisgarh.

Explaining the decision Home Minister Netam disclosed the proposal was sent to the MHA during the tenure of the late DGP OP Rathore, who had feared that the Naxalites had started to extend their base to the non-tribal areas of the State as well. “It has now been approved by the Government, as we prepare to deal with the extremist”, said Netan[10].

Reinforcing the Minister’s averments, Acting DGP SK Paswan stated the interrogation of Dandakaranya Divisional Committee Chief Satyam Reddy also confirmed the Maoists’ plans to spread to these areas.

Reddy alias Gopanna was arrested in May 2007, along with his two accomplices Surendra and Suresh from Gariyaband area of Raipur district. Gopanna had a bounty of Rs 5 Lakh on his head.

Sources disclosed Naxalite cadres had been visiting these areas regularly and attempting to woo the locals with Maoist literature and tracts. “Naxal literature seized by the police also points to the direction the Maoists want to head into”, the sources said.

Once these new cells are in place, additional police strength will be allotted to these districts. The police in these districts will also get specialized training to confront the Maoist cadres.

The Anti-Naxal Cells be directly responsible to the SSPs and SPs of the respective districts.

Some observations on new districts

The above text about number and name of districts concern the period of 2007. Some changes as of the present (2014) are given here:

- Chhattisgarh has 27 districts presently: The eight new districts are: Sukma, Kodgaon, Gariband, Balouda-bazar, Baaloud, Bemetara, Mungeli, Surajpur, Balrampur.
- Korea is now spelt as Koriya.
- Janjgir is now Janjgir Champa.

Chhattisgarh emerges as worst Naxalism-hit state: Mar 2007

Chhattisgarh has surpassed Andhra Pradesh in terms of number of Naxal-related incidents and attack, and resulting casualties. This was reported by a daily in its 17 Mar 2007 issue. “Over the last two years, while Chhattisgarh registered a sharp increase with over 757 incidents that left 551 dead, AP had 192 fatalities from as many incidents.”[11]

A further break-down of the figures provides a rather grim picture. In case of Chhattisgarh, security forces are at receiving end, in contrast to southern states where most fatalities belong to the rebel camp. The following statistics make the point:

- In Chhattisgarh, 147 security men and 316 civilians have been killed by the Naxals in the last two years against 88 Naxalites' fatalities.
- In sharp contrast is the figure of Naxalite fatalities in AP during the same period: of the 192 killed, 141 are Naxalites.

The Naxalites are equipped with modern arms and ammunition, said Union MOS Home Sriprakash Jaiswal. In response to a Parliamentary question, he said on 16 Mar 2007 said the security forces had recovered 854 weapons such as SLR and .303 rifles, sten guns and DBBL guns besides grenades, land mines and detonators from Maoist outfets during 2006.

"Maoist Crimes: Will they ever get just deserts?" : May 2007

Chhattisgarh's, dubious reputation as the State worst by LWE violence got reconfirmed with the killing of nine of policemen on 28 May 2007 in the Bastar region.

The policemen on anti-Naxal patrolling in a remote area were killed in a serious of explosions and an unremitting gunfire when they were ambushed. The modus operandi reflects the growing capability of Maoist ultras in Chhattisgarh to execute coordinated operations[12].

The ambush is one of the series of deadly Maoist attacks this year (2007), the most lethal being the March attack on Salwa Judum camp at Rani Bodli that killed 68 policemen. Data compiled by the Institute of Conflict Management reveal that 2005, 2006 and 2007, Maoist have killed more security men in Chhattisgarh than in other Naxalism-hit states like Bihar and Jharkhand.

In all, the year 2006 saw over 500 people killed in Chhattisgarh as a result of the Maoist depredations. Most of the victims were civilians. Maoists are also involved in what are plain criminal activities such as abduction, hostage-taking, murders and beheadings[13] Chhattisgarh may have emerged as the worst-affected State, Maoists are also on the rampage in several other states such as Jharkhand, Bihar, Maharashtra, Odisha and MP. Consequently, the daily lives of citizens in large swathes of the country are severely disrupted.

The rapidity with which Maoist crimes are escalating and increasing scale of their activity can only suggest their gaining upperhand vis-à-vis the Security forces. The security establishment has a reason to be deeply concerned if the internal security situation is spinning out of control. It is not without significance that situation on the violent Maoist front has started inviting attention of the international media. This is happening not because of India's sudden and extraordinary newsworthiness but because of repeated and increasing massacres committed by the Maoists that shows country's soft under-belly, indicative of its unravelling internal situation.

Yet, this gravity of situation in Chhattisgarh and other LWE-hit states does not seem to have caught the attention of policy-makers in meaningful degree. Even if the centre grudgingly acknowledges its serious, all it does is to pass the buck to the states, because it is a law and order problem. More irksome is the fact that while doing so, it ritually and mechanically mouths a meaningless cliché, "offering all help to the states as and when requested." It is time the Centre understands that Maoist insurgency is far more than a mere law and order problem, in fact, it is biggest threat to country's internal security and integrity. In turn, states like Chhattisgarh, which adopt quick-fix methods, of ad hoc nature, to deal with this serious security threat, are extremely sensitive to anything that can remotely be perceived as criticism of their ways of handling this Maoist threat. To wit, services of the renowned terrorism expert and saviour of Punjab KPS Gill were requisitioned for one year but were not renewed in May 2007.

Analysts ascribe the marked increase in Maoist violence in Chhattisgarh over the past three years or so to the merger and consequent consolidation of the two major LWE outfits, MCC and PWG. "The most significant expansion of their destructive capabilities came during the 2004-2005 ceasefire agreement in the neighbouring AP between the State Congress Government and the Left ultras. The AP ceasefire, supported by the Centre was worth trying under the circumstances but failed in its objective of achieving de-escalation. Intelligence officials believe is actually led to an expansion of the theatre of the extremist violence."

Unfortunately, Maoist violence (terrorism, in fact, should be its proper appellation) has become a subject of political rhetoric in India, particularly in the hands of elitist libertines like Arundhati Roy. Obviously, there are more than one opinion on the subject. First, the ground realities. The situation in Central India is essentially that of asymmetrical warfare. On the one hand, there are the ideologically charged and politically motivated Maoists forces that have international links and employ terror tactics in an attempt to undermine and finally destabilize the Indian State. They indulge in politico-criminal activities in their operations, and also at individual levels Ultimate aim: overthrowing the Indian state, a la the neighbouring Nepal.

The activists and leadership are well-aware of the vastly different objective situation in Nepal and India, but aspiring high is a tactic and wanton practice of the revolutionaries the world over. Ranged against the determined desperadoes, on the other hand "are creaking security machinery and the calcified sporofic response of the Indian State." This mismatch of a feeble response to what is emerging as the most insidvous threat to the Republic is ominous, to say the least. It is easy to underestimate the strength of the guerrilla force and distance from New Delhi makes it easier for the policy-makers functioning from there to make unrealistic and sometimes even facile assumptions and analysis of the situation in the Maoism-hit states.

Some analysts are warning the security establishment to realize what can happen, citing example of neighbouring Nepal, if anti-national forces are not handled seriously and put down ruthlessly. It is no longer a secret that Maoists are running parallel 'administrations' in several deceptively peaceful districts of the country.

That is the reason serious enough for the Indian State to cease to be in denial mode about the dimensions of the Maoist problem. This, in fact, has to be the first step in crafting an effective policy framework to first contain and then eliminate the Maoists. What is required utmost is the political will. If AP was successful in putting the Maoists on the run, there is no reason why others can't do the same!

There is the third angle to the Maoist issue the Left Liberals and elites of various hues. They blame the governments for keeping the tribal areas undeveloped, deprived and out-of-the national mainstream, thus creating conditions where LWE thrive for right reasons. And these sections become sympathizers of the Maoists and their insurrectionary violence, some of them even overground Maoists, more dangerous than the underground cadres.

These elitists elements assert the worsening situation can be blamed ...as the opposition BJP-ruled states/governments tend to do...on the neighbouring states' and Central Governments. They assert there is nexus between the deepening crisis and the state governments' policies in tackling Naxalite challenge. "This is highlighted by the notorious Salwa Judum (Purification Hunt) campaign. This officially supported effort to mobilize tribal people against Maoists has caused enormous social damage. It has pitted tribal against the tribal, village against village, and resulted in the death and displacement of huge number of innocent people." Then again, it is alleged that the state government has failed to distinguish between the perpetrators of the violence and the voices of legitimate dissent and democratic dissent.

Some dismiss this criticism as motivated fuelled by the gumption of the state police to arrest a well-known civil rights activist Binayak Sen.

Be that as it may, the fact remains that Naxals remain a serious threat in Chhattisgarh, and consequently country at large. Thus, they need to be handled more effectively than hitherto fore. Kid gloves treatment would not do. The scourge must be stopped in its tracks, ruthlessly if unavoidable.

19 May 2007

Maoist violence claimed the lives of 10 policemen in the Bastar forests on 19 May 2007. This blow in Bastar comes shortly after blowing up of the railway track at two places at Bhansi and Bacheli villages effectively cutting off transport of iron ore from the Bailadilla mines in Chhattisgarh.

On 19 May, policemen riding motor cycles became sitting ducks for the terrorists, who lay in wait near Kudur village, blasted 20 mines and simultaneously opened fire. Nine of them, including a sub-inspector and two havildars, were killed in the operation that lasted an hour.

The other members of the police patrol escaped and reached the nearby police station some 20 km away. A police team rushed to the location on receiving the information.

About the movement of the ultras, IG of SIB, Chhattisgarh Giridhar Nayak told the press: Possibly the information was planted to lure the policemen to the heavily-mined area.

The same day some 30 civilians had miraculous escape in a landmine explosion triggered by militants in Malkangiri district of Odisha, abutting the strife-torn Bastar area.

A CRPF jawan lost his life in another exchange of fire in Gangalur Police Station area falling in the neighbouring Bijapur district.

Jun 2007

On 5 June, the Naxals began a week-long bandh against the Salwa Judum in Chhattisgarh. The rebels also resorted to civilian killings and attacks on policemen.

On the 6th, they killed a relative of the police officer at Mohangaon village in Kurkheda tehsil, who the Naxals suspected had killed a member of their woman cadre in an encounter last month (May 2007).

Senior Maoist leader arrested in Chhattisgarh: Jun 2007

The State police claimed 3 Jun 2007 to have arrested a senior Naxal Commander Subhash alias Aitu Kursa alias Vijay from Maoist-hit

Rajnandgaon district. Aitu is the commander of Darrekasa Dalam, operating in Rajnandgaon district of Chhattisgarh and Gondia district of Maharashtra.

The arrest was made from Dongagarh on the 2 June evening, and Aitu was shifted to Rajnandgaon for interrogation. SP of the district Amit Kumar said: "Aitu was involved in several offences, which includes an attack on police party in 2006 in which several policemen, including a DSP, were injured, and another attack in which a train engine was set on fire at Darrekasa station."

Aitu had sneaked into Dongagarh town for some medical treatment and on a tip-off, was arrested when police laid a trap.

After interrogation, Aitu led the police to a Naxalite ammunition dump which yielded the following items.

1.	AK-47 rifles	2
2.	SLRs	2
3.	.12 bore rifles	3
4.	Gelatin sticks	150
5.	Wireless sets	4
6.	Photography flashes	10
7.	Bundles of wire	10

Maoists kill 23 police in ambush in Dantewada district: Jul 2007

Carrying out another big strike in Chhattisgarh, Maoist cadres killed 23 security men and a civilian in the forests near Errabore in Dantewada district, some 550 km from Raipur.

The security force party, comprising 155, was ambushed 9 Jul 2007 evening by some 300 Maoists between Regergetta and Uppelmetta villages near Errabore. Of the 24 dead, the breakdown is: CRPF 15, SPOs 6, state police 2 and Civilian 1.

The attack took place after the security men, on being alerted about the presence of the Maoists in the area, headed for a hill top at Uppelmetta, 6 km from Gaganpalli.

Reports reaching Raipur said 60 SPOs, 10 CRPF men and one state policeman had managed to reach the Ellabore police post.

IG (Bastar) RK Vij gave details of security men who were despatched on search operation in the Errabore forests: a total of 155, comprising 25 CRPF, 84 SPOs and three from state police posted at Errabore camp. Vij added 44 men had gone missing after the attack ambush.

The Maoists took away over two dozen weapons, including AK-47s, SLRs and .303 rifles.

The ambush is the first major strike after the 15 Mar 2007 Rani Bodli attack that left a total of 68 security men dead.

After the launch of Salwa Judum, the Maoists have got more aggressive and have been targeting both civilians and security forces.

"Chhattisgarh to have its own Greyhounds": Sep 2007

Frustrated by repeated attacks on an ill-trained and ill-equipped police force, "Chhattisgarh is set to roll out the heavy artillery against Naxals."

These are the words from a daily of 6 Sep 2007. The State aims to set up a Special Task force on the lines of Andhra Pradesh's much vaunted Greyhounds, under the command of a colonel from the Army.

DGP Vishwaranjan said some 4,000 crack personnel will be deployed with the STF. They would be imparted commando training at the state's Jungle Warfare School at Kanker. They would also be trained in advance weaponry, enabling them to launch an offensive against the Maoists inside the dense jungles[14].

Col Rajnish Sharma, selected to lead the STF would shortly resign from the Army and join the state police in the rank of DIG. The STF men would be picked up from the existing police force. 1300 officers and men in the age group of 18-25 have already been selected.

The decision to create the STF is the latest measure by the Raman Singh Government to deal with the LWE, which of late have been hitting at the police and rag-tag civil defence unit called Salwa Judum almost at will.

29 Oct 2007

Five policemen killed after Naxals surrounded a police party in Bijapur district, Chhattisgarh.

2 Nov 2007

15 Policemen killed in Bijapur district.

16 Dec 2007

Chhattisgarh Dantewada prison break. 299 prisoners escaped, of which 105 were suspected Maoists.

20 Dec 2007

Yet again a prison break at Kistavam, Dantewara. It is a sad reflection on the functioning of the state police. Two prison breaks within a space of four days! 12 security men killed, this time, and 110 Maoists escaped from jail.

8 Feb 2008

Six policemen gunned down.

24 Apr 2008

DKSZC members set on fire 47 vehicles of Essar steels in their premises at Kadampal locality, Chhattisgarh. 100 Maoist woman cadres were involved in this attack. Wearing green uniforms, they claimed that the land, water and forest belong to Bastar tribes and they alone have the right to enjoy them.

19 Jun 2008

Three SPOs abducted by Maoists following an encounter on 18 June were killed in Banda Police station limits of Dantewada district. Five policemen, abducted along with the SPOs, were let off, warning them to keep off Salwa Judum and the police. SPOs shot dead were Gopal, Bhadru, and Lakshmaiah.

10 Oct 2008

12 CRPF men killed at Kongupelli in Bijapur.

7 Nov 2008

11 security personnel killed in Bijapur.

10 Nov 2008

10 Mizo Battalion soldiers killed in Chhattisgarh.

14 Nov 2008

Maoists shot dead Sgt Mustafa Ali when he was on a mission to evacuate three BSF men in Chhattisgarh.

Crucial phase in Bastar? May 2008 (Is the State Winning)

"Naxals short of manpower, as battle enters crucial phase in Bastar." This is the headline of an article in a weekly[15] examining the status of counter-Maoism battle in Chhattisgarh. It should be a worthwhile exercise to see if this analysis hold water, or is too early to be so optimistic on this issue.

Here is a youth in his teens, Koma Markam, with a doubting if inquisitive mind. In a Naxal meeting, his questioning mind sough to know the "relevance of armed struggle" (waged by them). Not used to such questioning, they chased him out of the meeting. Subsequently, he realised that they would rather eliminate him than answer his queries. The survival instinct led him to join the Chhattisgarh Police. Years later, when the same analyst meet him (in 2008), he found Markam neither a 'changed' nor a 'reformed' man. He was taking this visitor, riding pillion on his motorbike, to the forward police post of Polampalli in Dantewada. During this journey Marham is telling the latter over his shoulder: "Being a journalist, you must have met Naxals. Have you asked them why they are shedding blood? They say, they are fighting for us, tribals. Then why are they demolishing our schools and hospital and disrupting our mid-day meals and electric supply."

Markam did find his refuge in the police force but others had only two choices: Swallowing their doubts and joining the outlaws or joining the counter-Maoist Salwa Judum. Bastar is verily a war zone: 182 security men were killed in 2007 in Chhattisgarh's Naxal-hit areas where as the combined figure for the militancy hit North-East and J and K stood at 186. Nowhere else in the country in the battle against the Maoism as intense as in Bastar, a 39,114 sq km district, which is larger than some of the states like Kerala, Goa, and all states in the North-East barring Assam and Arunachal Pradesh. "Over 25,000 security personnel are deployed in Bastar." They are equipped with the latest guns, anti-land mine vehicles, UAVs and Choppers. Bastar has a dense and dangerous jungle, with 20,000 landmines. On their part, the Maoists have destroyed the roads, many buildings and power towers. Ironically, they are doing all this destruction to ameliorate the socio-economic condition of the tribals.

On way to Polampalli, shops selling multinational consumer goods/ durables are interspersed with commemoration pillars for the victims of mindless violence. In spite of threats to their lives, the businessmen are seemingly doing well. The reasons are obvious: Cozy relationship and understanding between them and the ultras, the former share their profits with the latter. Crudely known as extortion, or protection money in gentler terms, both sides are coexisting happily. DGP Vishwa Ranjan tells us, "Maoists prefer to term it as rent." Tendu leaf contractors are part of the system.

The potholed road to Golapalli was paved with mines. The security forces have the choice of moving their men and supplies by choppers, even if, at times, they per force move larger bodies of troopers by vehicles on this road. The traders have no such luxury of choice: They bring commodities on bullock carts from across the border of Andhra Pradesh and "sell them at double cost." One should not grudge them this "huge profit", since the rates include the rent money they pay to the Maoists. "They are doing brisk business thanks to the police, soldiers, some business thanks to the police, soldiers, some well-to-do locals, workers in mines and 23 government-run relief camps."

The prence of the Border Roads Organisation adds colour to the landscape, with their machinery, including diggers, earth moving equipment. All this adds to the warzone atmosphere. The BRO was called in as the contractors are unwilling to undertake road repair work, scared of the Maoists. The ultras have vested interest in thwarting the road work. Pucca roads facilitate the fast movement of troops and they make it difficult to lay landmines.

There was palpable fear in some areas. Due to this, Naxals have been able to paralyse some democratic institutions here. They had called for the poll boycott in 2004. Consequently, some 65,000 candidates had been elected unopposed to the panchayat in the seven districts of Bastar and Sarguja division[16]. Here is a bold, if well-known admission of some unpleasant facts of life in the area by none other than the DGP of the State, Vishwa Ranjan: "The writ of CPI (Maoist) runs in Bastar. People live under the shadow of Maoist guns. They have Maoist courts or *Jan Adalats*. The media dare not file any report not censored by the Maoists. Visits to this area have to be sponsored by the Maoists or their friends. The visitors hear and see only what the Maoists want them to."

Their sympathisers and zealous supporters are dime a dozen among the intellectual classes, for a variety of reasons. A best known celebrity, Arundhati Roy, paid a well-publicised visit to the Maoist dens years later, and the Outlook welcomed her subsequently by publishing a long-winded 14-page article, condemning the country, its governments, its security forces…all but paying high encomiums to the 'brave' Maoists. India can certainly do without frauds like Roy.

The Naxals and their informer network is omni-present in the area. Having lost some 2,000 men in a 10-year-long (1998-2008) operation, the police understandably cautious. The policemen are required to operate in plain clothes in sensitive situations. For the same reasons, the identifiable vehicle registration numbers and beacon lights are done away with. This is exactly what the Army practices in the battle-field situations. The situation that prevails in counter-Maoist war are worse than the soldiers face in battle. Here, the CRPF and police do not know their enemy, till the latter attack them. As a CRPF commandant puts it pithily, "It is a 360-degree war unlike the one in J and K or North-East."

The forces have their problems. The intelligence network is only being developed." The CRPF has to rely on the local police and the Salwa Judum members for operational support, especially the latter as they have knowledge of area and topography. Again, it needs to be noted that the Government insures each member of the operational team for Rs 10 lakh. All men (barring the CRPF personnel who have their own training institutions) have been trained at the Counter-Terrorism and Jungle Warfare College in North Bastar.

Fighting Maoists is a demanding task, as they are not only well-trained inhospital jungles but also are highly motivated by ideological brainwashing. Force only occasionally get to move in anti-landmine vehicles, which again are not yet foolproof. India is under attack, and it is most effective form of LWE-guerrilla warfare as the Naxals are trained to inflict maximum casualities while suffering minimum themselves. They generally attack security forces contingents and outposts after full preparations… thorough reconnaissance, repeated rehearsals, gaining thorough knowledge of the terrain etc. Yet again, they have in place fool proof plan of escape after inflicting heavy casualties. In most cases, when they attack after full preparations, they suffer almost nil casualty. Even if they do, they take the bodies with. They normally move in a group of 100-200, with proper line of command and control. (In April 2010, where they killed 75 CRPF troopers, their reported number was 500). To confuse the opponents, they often operate in battle fatigues. Consequently, some operations ended up with our people killing our own men.

At times, they achieve complete surprise once they attacked a police station from atop a bus, on which they had made a bunker. Again, what they often do in such cases, they made away with the police arms and ammunition.

Besides such looted arms, the Naxals have sources to buy weaponry from the international open market. Official estimates put the number of armed ultras operating in the area at 12,000—undoubtedly an exaggeration. But fair estimate can be some 2000 of them. The Number of Naxal sympathisers, supporters, overground zealots should come to 50,000—a clearly believable figure. As for arms, they have 900 AK-47s, 200 LMGs, 100×2 inch mortars, and thousands of the 303s, SLRs and 12-bore rifiles.

By this period (Mid-2008), Chhattisgarh had become the focal point of the Red corridor, even worse, the grooming ground, a kind of Nursery, for the Maoists. This was particularly so after mid-2010, when Andhra Pradesh had started achieving conspicuous success in its anti-Maoists operations, and consequently, the Maoists had abandoned the State and started fleeing across its northern borders into Chhattisgarh, Odisha and Gadchiroli in Maharashtra.

It is to be noted, as the table above shows, that since 2007, more security personnel have been killed in the Red Corridor than those killed in J&K and the North-East put together.

Interview: DGP Chhattisgarh Vishwa Ranjan: May 2008

A journalist from *The Week* talked to this senior police officer fresh from a visit to Gollampalli, the post where some 100 police men have died in the past five years. Ranjan "has been fighting Leftist extremism in various capacities for over two decades." He certainly seems to be a man of many talents. When not outfoxing the Naxals, he pens articles countering their ideological propaganda. He is equipped eminently for it, as he is a voracious reader of serious books. Besides this all, he is an amateur photographer, painter and poet.

Q: What makes Central Paramilitary Forces vulnerable in Bastar area?

A: We lose most men not during combat but while providing logistic support. Recently, Naxals ambushed a 12-member party sent to evacuate six malaria-affected jawans. Our men fought back and survived.

Q: What do the Naxals want in Bastar?

A: Not just Bastar, they want to replace Constitutional democracy with Maoist governance in whole of India. They have been in Bastar since 1982, and have been growing and Consolidating.

Q: You were the Superintendent of Bastar in 1982.

A: When I was the SP, they had just started on the southern fringes of the district. I pushed them back. But they were able to exploit tribal anger against the Forest Act.

Q: NGOs like People's Union for Civil Liberties are against you.

A: PUCL want to protect human rights. However, if you go through secret Naxal documents, you will see they aim to infiltrate such organisations and, eventually control them. If a PUCL member turns out to be a Maoist mole, it does not mean that the Organisation is Maoist. It just shows the extent of contamination.

Q: Do forest officials and entrepreneurs face problems?

A: The Forest Department is not doing anything. Many of the officers' quarters are uninhabited. Businessmen are milked because the Naxals need money for propaganda, litigation and cadre upkeep. They call it rent.

Q: Who pays the Rent?

A: Reportedly, big names like Ispat, Essar and Tata are indirectly paying rent. Their sub-contractors pay for them. There are even reports that these payoffs are in tainted money.

11 May 2009

Maoists blew up a police jeep in Dhamtari, Chhattisgarh, killing 13 and injuring 12. 25 people in a police jeep?

16 May 2009

A CRPF man abducted from a bus while proceeding.

7-19 Jun 2009

Two jawans of Chhattisgarh Armed Force, Ram Bhuwan Patel and Dhananjay Verma, were kidnapped by Maoists from a hilly stretch in Bijapur district on 17 June. The slit their throasts.

12 Jul 2009

Maoists killed 30 policemen, including one SP (BK Choubey), in three separate incidents in Rajnandgaon districts, Chhattisgarh.

Courts acquits ten in Tadmetla massacre

In a major set back in the country's worst-ever Naxal attack of Apr 2010, when 76 security personnel, 75 from CRPF, were massacred at Tadametla jungle, Dantewada, a court in the same district on 7 Jan 2013 ordered acquittal of 10 accused allegedly involved in that horror! Additional Sessions Judge Anita Deharia acquitted 10, asserting that the prosecution had failed to provide any substantial evidence of their involvement in the case. All the 10 accused had been charged under various sections of the IPC, the Arms Act and under certain provisions of the Explosive Act.

The prosecution obviously had produced witnesses to establish their case, but the judge thought that was not good enough for their conviction. The court ordered the released of Payami Ganga, Podiyami Hirma, Swayam Hirma, Kawasi Budra, Joro Jogga, Varse Ratna, Markam Ganga, Rajesh Naik, Ratan Joga, and Marvi Dula who had been arrested in this case.

Even if the police had named some other senior Maoist leaders, including key conspirator Papa Rao, but they had failed to arrest them.

It deserves to be stated that 75 CRPF men and a State Police Officer were killed in 6 Apr 2010 ambush in the forests of Tadmetla, an area dominated by the Maoists. They were attacked by CPI (Maoist) and People's

Liberation Guerrilla Army cadres numbering close to 350, along with 200-odd militia, attacked them by triggering a series of blasts and then shooting down from atop a hill.

Naxalite-related Incidents "Civil war-like situation in 3 Chhattisgarh villages": May 2011

SC Panel Report: Villagers live in fear of violence at hands of Koya Commandos, anti-Naxal forces.

The above is the headline of a news story in a daily of 1 May 2011. Produced below the headline is the blurb. It is undoubtedly a disturbing story and it has come from a panel appointed by the apex court of the country. Hence the need to examine its contents in full[17].

It opens up with these lines: "An undeclared Civil War-like situation prevails in the three villages of Chhattisgarh's Dantewada district, where hundreds of Koya commandos (local armed militia) and anti-Naxalite special forces alleged burnt houses, grain reserves and movably properties of tribal people on 11 March". These are the findings of the Supreme Court (SC) panel.

The SC's Special Commissioner on right to Food, Harsh Mander, was asked by the SC to visit the villages and submit a report, after the PUCL filed a petition alleging it feared that conditions of acute hunger and starvation were rampant in Morpalli, Timapuram and Tarmetla.

"According to the report which is likely to be considered by the SC next week—the villagers lived in unabated conditions of fear. "....their perceived Maoist support results in grave and exorable consequences for the villagers. Many are jailed as Maoist sympathisers and languished for long periods in prison, without even the succour of national and international support and human rights backing as surged for Dr Vinayak Sen."

Mander, who visited violence-hit Morapalli village along with Chhattisgarh's Principal Secretary Vivek Dhand, Bastar Divisonal Commissioner Srinivasulu and Dantewada DC Omprakash Choudhary on 6 April, however, ruled out any starvation deaths, as reported in a section of the media.

"The indigent tribal communities are trapped in unending cycle of brutal violence, unleashed consecutively by Maoists, security forces and vigilante armed civilian groups such as the Salwa Judum and its incarnations..." the report said, adding PDS grais were diverted to Salwa Judum camps.

"The government officially admits to around 50,000 people being housed in 20 Salwa Judum camps between 2005-08, and even during my visit to Morapalli it was clear that the subsidised grain for the village had been diverted to the Salwa Judum Camps," the report said.

On 25 April, the SC had taken strong objection to the Centre and State Government using a colonial law to arm the local tribal population to take on Naxals, but the Centre said it supported the law as it enabled the insurgency-hit states to recruit Special Police Officers (SPOs).

The report said: "Villagers informed the team that three deaths could have occurred because old and feeble persons who had fled into the forests had lost their way and were unable to procure adequate food."

Some Select Violent Assaults

What follows is a brief summary of certain depredations by the Maoists.

9 Policemen killed: 19 Aug 2011

Eleven people including nine policemen were killed and three others injured in a Maoist ambush on the 19th evening at Metalacheru, 4 km from Bhadrakali police station in Bijapur district, some 520 km from Raipur. A police team of 45 drawn from the District Police and Chhattisgarh Armed Police had gone that morning on a routine exercise towards Bhopalpatanam. Their brief, among other things was to provide cover to policemen returning from leave.

ADG (anti-Maoist operations) said two police team of some 150 men of the State Police were on a routine road-opening exercise on a stretch of 18 km. Besides, they had some administrative assignments like escorting rations. "The team which was going with a tractor laden with ration and other materials, was ambushed. The other team, moving ahead, returned soon and also engaged the ultras. Three to four of the Maoist seemed to have been killed", the ADG said.

In the recent times, Bijapur has been one of the worst Maoist-hit districts of the State. "More than 55 security men have been killed in various incidents of rebel attacks this year (till the instant one).

Three SSB men killed in Naxal blast: 7 Oct 2011

Three men of Sashatra Seema Bal (SSB) were killed and another injured in a landmine blast detonated by the Maoists on 7 Oct 2011 in Bastanar area on the National Highway in the insurgency-hit district of Dantewada, some 355 km from Raipur. The private vehicle carrying SSB men was tossed in the air and torn into pieces, creating six-feet crater in the ground.

ADG (Naxal Operations) Ram Nivas said SSB personnel of 41 battalion, who were deployed for the protection of Salwa Judum camp by the

Chhattisgarh Police. "Two battalions of the SSB have been deployed in the state since 2008 for protection of the Salwa Judum camps created by the State Government to house thousands of people who fled their villages to escape Maoist terror.

The three men killed at the site, near Geedam, were driver Vivek Kumar, Constables Dilip Chakrokli and Dharmesh Nath. The injured Praveen Kumar was brought to Raipur by Chopper.

Assessing Maoist problem in Chhattisgarh: Sep 2011

It is over a decade when the State was carved out of the then Madhya Pradesh. It is time to examine the 'progress' made by the 'permanent revolution' of Mao's concept. Mao's acolytes in India, CPI (Maoist) outfit, are right now engaged in replacing democratic dispensation with their version of 'People's Democracy'. A daily[18] has an analysts of the situation in some detail under the caption: "There is more to Chhattisgarh than Maoist lies." This analysis is put under the lens for its objectivity in the following pages, along with the inputs from various known sources. A balanced analysis should be the aim of all such exercises.

The enduring image of Chhattisgarh is of wide-spread violence prevailing in the State, particularly its southern parts defined by undivided Bastar. Maoist violence is maximum here, followed by Jharkhand. The tribal communities, in and around Bastar, are seemingly sandwiched between the Maoist cadres and security forces. Obviously, the tribals are leading compromised lives because of the given situation. But they have reasons to look up for a better future, seeing that the last ten years or so have made them hopeful. The State had been a part of a larger MP. From its capital, it was a distant entity, and in one word, a neglected one. Empirically speaking, a smaller states created out of larger ones, have done well for themselves. Chhattisgarh is no exception. Its tribal communities were living in one of the most heavily forested regions rich in mineral and natural resources. It was a tailor-made situation for the new state marching into prosperity with the new Government opting for development paradigm for its economic policy and results are showing.

Over the time, these issues have been addressed, keeping the tribal communities in focus. The new state was lucky, getting political leadership dedicated to all round development of the State, particularly its tribals. The *mantra* is efficient governance, underpinned by transparency, accountability and having an ear to the ground. Raman Singh was the man of the moment and he is in the middle of his second as Chief Minister. Here are the policy prescriptions his Government has ordained. For transparency, all the major schemes are being monitored through an online process. So, details of millions of ration card holders, the quality of food grains purchased for the fair price shops are all available online. Thus, all development programmes, including the ones aimed at helping the poorest like this ration distribution system, can be seen by every one...end-users, the community and authorities, all on the same page, so to say.

Next, the agriculture, which is predominant activity in the state, giving likelihood to millions and producing massive quantity of paddy, earning it the soubriquet of a 'Rice Bowl'. The Government took some innovative policy measure to ensure an enabling environment for promotion of agriculture: ensuring remunerative prices for the product, it is first state in the country where farmers are getting loans at a mere three per cent interest; cash is disbursed through 'Kisan Credit Card' while some loans also cover inputs and equipment, the farmers are given an insurance cover worth Rs 124 Crore under National Agriculture Insurance Scheme. The transparency mentioned earlier is ensured: the support price of paddy which is attuned to this need is available on line and so is the data related to over 1300 primary cooperative societies and more than 1,500 paddy procurement centres. The names of farmers, the quantity of paddy sold and the payment made, are all available information.

Irrigation system since the formation of the State has vastly improved. As part of MP, the region now in Chhattisgarh had only 13 per cent of the crop area under irrigation. Within first five years of State's formation, the figure rose to 23 per cent. It rose to 32 per cent in the year, 2010. During the last 6 years (2004-2010), irrigation facilities have covered 3.23 lakh hectares of crop area. Besides this, 2,783 medium and small projects have been initiated in there six years. There are ambitious plans to extend irrigation coverage to some 4,00,000 hectare of crop area using funds allocated under the five-year plan. It is to the credit of the Government that while combating violence unleashed by the blood-thirsty Maoists, it has taken concrete steps to improve the socio-economic condition of its people, and the positive results are there for all to see. In the year 2009-10, the Government purchased 44 lakh metric tonnes of paddy, the highest in the country for any state[19]. Farmers were paid a whopping Rs 4,700 crore, yet again, the highest payment by any state in the country. There are such other creditable achievements not to be mentioned here for reasons of space. One factual information deserves to be mentioned by way of exception. The States PDS has been rated as the best and most efficient in the country. Finally, the Tendu leaf plucking tribals had the best of it all. During 2010, the Government distributed Rs 108 Crore amongst the 14 lakh people engaged in this practice, along with an additional bonus worth Rs 94 Crore. At an individual level, the bonus per bag has been increased from Rs 300 in 2004 to Rs 700.

The Government has not forgotten to add human touch among the flurry of developmental activities. Footwear was distributed free of cost to the barefooted men and women, protecting them from the thorns, twigs and stones during plucking. Yet again, the State initiated another pro-poor scheme: distributing free raincoats and agricultural tools amongst the labourers.

There is no doubt that the conflict in the State has its roots in deprivation during the time when it was part of composite MP. And true to their ideological tactics, the Maoists exploited this deprivation to spread their practice of death and destruction. Not to lose their grip on "poor" tribals, they have put every hurdle, including killing of those very "poors" aud the contractors in the Government's determination to bring development to the deprived communities. Not only are they killing the tribals engaged in building roads, and economic projects, they are also killing tribal sports-men, panchayat members as also destroying schools, hospitals etc to spread panic.

It is obvious that they are not succeeding in their nefarious designs. One substantial proof of this failure is the third successive victory of the Raman Singh Government in the Nov 2013 Assembly elections, even when the Congress was widely expected to win because of the sympathy wave in its favour generated by the May killings of its entire state leadership by the Maoists. Is there any doubt that the tribals, whom the Maoists are claiming to be fighting for, have seen through their lies.

Raman Singh is believed to be among the half-a-dozen Chief Ministers who are sincere, efficient and effective, delivering their true to their people, especially the poor and the tribal.

"Fingerprint data base for surveillance on Maoists in Chhattisgarh soon": Nov 2011

A news story datelined Raipur, 12 Nov 2011 says: "If all goes as planned, district police stations in Chhattisgarh may soon maintain a data base of the fingerprints of every cook, waiter and helper in every hotel, restaurant and road side dhaba (eateries) across the state. The information, the police hope, will help security forces in their battle against the guerrilla army of the banned CPI (Maoist)[20].

"The fingerprints would be stored at the district level and shall aid the police", says Ram Niwas, State's ADGP (Naxal Operations), adding that the prints would not be recorded as biometric information, but as ink-impressions on paper. Mr Niwas said prints would be collected as part of a broader police strategy to improve surveillance across the State. "We issued an order to all the districts some months back to increase checking at hotels, *dhabas,* airports bus stands and shops selling electrical goods ....The exact implementation has been left to the SP of each district", he said.

In the district of Rajnandgaon, for instance, the police has ordered all shopkeepers to maintain a record of individuals who purchase more than 200 feet of electrical wire (=61 mtrs) as the wire could be used by the Maoists to trigger IED. IEDs accounted for the 40 per cent of all police deaths in the anti-Maoist operations in Chhattisgarh since mid-2007.

However, the district shopkeepers feel the idea is "ill-conceived and hard to implement." "It is hard for us to maintain records of every individual who buys wire from us", Raja Bojwani, the proprietor of a prominent electrical shop told this daily on phone. "Most of our customers buy more than 200 feat of wire, and customers go elsewhere when we ask for their name, address and mobile number."

Bojwani said the police orders came just a few weeks before Diwali, a time when business is hectic. "Last year, the police asked all grain merchants to report anyone who bought more than a certain amount of grain as he might be a Maoist supplier", he pointed out. But Rajnandgaon SP BS Meena disputed Bojwani's assertions. "All shopkeepers need to maintain records for the purpose of paying sale tax in any case" said the SP. "We are simply asking them to maintain a record of their customers and report any suspicious person."

Mr Meena said his department is still developing the surveillance apparatus in the district. "We were not working on any fixed formula at present."

District Collector Menon Abducted : 21.4.12 (First ever)

In a first-ever case of kidnapping of an IAS officer in Chhattisgarh, over a dozen Maoist cadres abducted Sukma District Collector Alex Paul Menon at gunpoint from Manjhipara village, killing his two bodyguards who tried to obstruct the ultras, at 4.30 PM on 21 Apr 2012. Menon was meeting a group of villagers for a government outreach programme, name 'Gram Suraj.'

The Raman Singh-led BJP Government in the State has been holding a mega rural contact drive since 18 April in all 27 districts of the State under which Government officials and people's representatives have been asked to hold meetings with villagers to assess performance of Government welfare schemes. The two-phase drive was scheduled to end on 27 April.

Manjhipara jungle is some 500 km from Raipur. The 32-year old 2006-batch officer is from Tamil Nadu cadre. Some 90 Maoists clad in tribal outfit waited for hours for the Collector at the function. A dozen of them kidnapped him in full public view, taking him into the neighbouring forest. The kidnapping incident happened just a day after Maoist carried out a deadly attack on the convoy of BJP legislator Mahesh Gagde and Bijapur District Collector Rajat Kumar in Bijapur District of Bastar Region, in which three persons (two BJP leaders and legislator's driver. Yet again the abduction came even uncertainty looms over the fate of BJD MLA Jhina Hikaka, who is being held captive by Odisha Maoists.

A top official says Menon defied instructions from police headquarters not to attend Gram Suraj in the area, which has been dominated by Maoists since the late 1980s. DGP Anil M. Navaney and top officials held a meeting at the headquarters and expressed surprise over how the Collector visited Maoist territory despite specific intelligence inputs[21].

Another first needs re-emphasis! This is the first time Maoists in Bastar, under the operational control of Dandakaranaya Special Zone Committee (DKSZC) abducted a senior (IAS) administrative official, although there have been, in the past, instances of abduction of police constables.

Stiff terms for DM's release by Maoists

Keeping the entire State administration at its wits' end throughout the day, the Maoist late on the 22nd evening' demanded release of eight top militants and ceasing all anti-Naxal operations for the safe return of Menon. These eight include some of the hard core rebels, viz, Marakam Gopannam, Nirmal Akka, Devpal Chandra Shekhar Reddy, Shanti Priya Reddy, Meena Choudhari, Korasa Sunny, Markan Sunny, and Asit Kumar Sen.

The abduction news were followed by top-level meetings. Late night cabinet meeting on the 22nd decided to set up a 5-member Committee to examine the Naxal demands. Meanwhile, red alert was sounded in the entire border areas of the State adjoining Odisha and Andhra Pradesh, following the reports of the abducted collector being taken to Odisha even as the Chhattisgarh DGP was in close contact with his counterparts in the neighbouring states.

The State Government discussed the issue at an all-party meeting on the 23rd. On the 22nd, people observed bandh in Sukma in protest against the abduction and staged peace marches demanding his safe release. Police failed to locate the abductees for a week after the date of incident, even when CRPF had mounted search operations soon after the abduction. Rumours were rife that Maoist leaders, Ramana and Bhima, were planning to move their VIP hostage to Chitragonda in Odisha to hand him over to their Odisha counterparts.

Requisite political meetings were held in Raipur as also in Delhi. Collector's wife, Asha Menon, who incidentally is expecting a child, made frantic appeals to the Maoists to release her husband as he was asthmatic, and was not carrying adequate medicines.

Details of militants Maoists want released

1. Three out of eight Maoists whose release has been demanded by the ultras are women: Nirmala @ Nirmalaka; Kavita alias Meena Chowdhary and Malati alias Shantipriya Reddy.
2. There is one couple in the list of eight. Nirmala alias Nirmalaka alias Vijay Lakshmi and her husband Chandrashekher Reddy alias Jaypal. Both are members of Dandakaranya Special Zone Committee of the CPI (Maoist).
3. Nirmala has maximum number of criminal cases (67) against her in the group, has been in Jagdalpur jail since Jul 2007.
4. Nirmala's husband, Chandrashekhar has 18 criminal cases against him in Jagdalpur jail since Jul 2007.
5. Gajela Satyam Reddy alias Madkam Gopanna (33 cases), in Jagdalpur jail since May 2007.
6. Asit Kumar Sengupta, in Raipur jail since Jan 2008.
7. Korsa Sanny.
8. Markam Sanny.

Other demands of the Maoists

1. Stop anti-Naxal operations.
2. Stop combing operations.
3. Move police into barracks.
4. Drop charges against innocent villagers, claiming these are fake charges.

The rebels spared the sub-divisional magistrate SK Vaidya who was also present in Manjhipara village with Collector Menon, when they took the latter away into the adjoining forest.

A word on Ramanna and Bhima who are believed to be the Maoists who ordered the abduction. Ramanana is a central committee member and Bhima is the Chief of Dornapal area committee.

It is worth a note that for the first time a Maoist group in Dandakaranya has targeted a senior administrative official, abductions were limited to constables so far.

Sukma District: It all happened here

Barely three months into its creation, the new district was in the news for all the wrong reasons! If Chief Minister Raman Singh was deeply concerned about the safety of his intrepid Collector Menon, he was equally unhappy about the affect this abduction would have on the morale of such other brave collectors who are required to go into the far-spread and remote areas to interact with the people under the aegis of an outreach programme for the welfare of his people, christened "Gram Suraj." At personal level, the parents and family of Menon, who had plunged into his job to ameliorate the lot of tribals under his charge with a missionary zeal, were naturally praying for his safety and security. It was deeply emotional moment for his wife, Asha Menon, who was expecting a child, and simultaneously concerned about her abducted husband, who was an asthmatic and did not have adequate medicines with him.

Here follows snapshot of the newly-created district, also the newest Maoist hotspot.

- **Beginning.** Sukma was carved out of insurgency hit Dantewada district in South Chhattisgarh on 16 January this year (2012).
- **People.** Tribals constitute 90 per cent of the district's population.
- **Green Cover.** The region is heavily forested and has one of India's best Sagwan (teak wood) forest.
- **Some Sundry Details.** The district has a total area of 5,635 sq km, 379 villages with a population density of 45 per sq km.
- **Not so good.** At 36 per cent, its literacy rate is worst among the State's 27 districts.
- **Female paradise.** With 1016 females for every 1000 males, its sex ratio is above/better than the national average[22].

To repeat, Sukma, carved out of Maoist-hit district of Dantewada, was the worst region known to be the Maoist hotbed. It was in this region that the rebels have unleashed major attacks against security forces after the anti-Naxal campaign, 'Salwa Judum', involving the local tribals in the respective areas, was launched in June 2005.

Alex Menon: A sincere and Conscious man

District Collector Alex Paul Menon was viewed by his peers as an enthusiastic officer who took his job in the country's worst-affected district as a mission. And to wit, he had gone to a place near Kerlapal on a motorcycle, along with others as a part of "Gram Swaraj Abhyan", aimed at improving basic services in Sukma district since it was felt it, being among the poorest and worst affected by Maoist violence, needed special administrative attention. It was an example of political outreach to the poorest of the poor.

Menon was not only a sincere, dedicated officer, driven by his missionary zeal to improve the lot of the poor under his administrative charge, there was also an ideological conviction behind all this zeal and enthusiasm. An analyst put it aptly: "Alex Paul Menon, the 32-year old District Collector of Sukma, may disagree with his captors' style of functioning, but (he) share a common hero with them: Che Guevara[23]."

Menon is believed to have reacted calmly when the Maoist shot dead two of his bodyguards and abducted him on the 21st. This did not surprise his friends, who know him as a dedicated IAS officer who loves the tribals. They say Tirunelveli native's concern for the tribals is inspired by his hero Che Guevara…the Latin American revolutionary's compassion for the cause of the exploited masses he fought for half a century ago is well-known.

A writer who has covered Maoist-affected areas in Chhattisgarh for long vouchsafes Menon being inspired by Che: "Che Guevara's memoir 'The Motorcycle Diaries' inspired Menon to go alone on visits to tribal villages on his motorbike even at night, despite knowing he was on the hitlist of the Reds in the Maoist-dominated area in Chhattisgarh. Unlike many other bureaucrats, Menon reads a lot and has a deep understanding of the socio-economic conditions of the country."

Menon's blog, Kuraigudam, discusses the problems created by rigid rules that delay the efforts to solve peoples issues in India. His father-in-law VR Venugopal, said the relatives had cautioned him against venturing into dangerous areas too frequently. He obviously was not listening. "He continued visiting tribal areas in the day and at night, unmindful of his personal safety…committed unbelievably as he was to the tribals and their welfare and progress."

An analyst who met his family learnt that the officer took his first name from former Defence Minister VK Krishna Menon, when he held in great admiration. At the personnel level, Menon loved popular culture, especially the Tamil movie 'Subramanyapuram' and in an obvious empathy for its protagonist, the book 'The Autobiography of a Sex Worker' by Nalini Jameela.

Searching for Menon: UAV deployed

Sukma District Collector was abducted on the evening of 21 Apr 2012 when he was surveying the implementation of the development schemes in the district in village Manjipara, amidst the villagers. It is the state's outreach programme, called "Gram Suraj", under which Alex Paul Menon was interacting with the villagers.

The Chhattisgarh Government the very next day asked security forces to scale down 'pro-active anti-Naxal operation' and stay 'low-key' in the region. But on the other hand, it was active on tracking the movement of the Maoist in and around the spot the Collector was abducted from, through UAV.

It is obviously determined not to act in a hurry, as it could jeopardise the life of Menon. Having learnt from the experience of Odisha Government which recently handles that twin abduction of two Italians and one MLA, the state want to move caustiously. Its first priority was send necessary medicines to the abductees who is a asthma patient. Having achieved that object in due course, it intensified the operations of the unmanned Aerial vehicle. Meanwhile contacts had been established with the mediators to contact the Abductors. It was obviously, a multi-pronged approach strategy Raipur was pursuing.

Within a day or so, the search was narrowed down to a forested stretch 15 km from Manjhipara, with an UAV relaying images of a group of Maoists suspecting to be holding the official near the Odisha border. In normal anti-Naxal operations, this information would have been acted upon within a short time to nab the ultras, but it could not be the case in this instance as the life of District Collector was at stake. The security forces have been instructed, for this very reason, to exercise extreme restraint. In fact, they have been asked to remain in camps at this juncture, lest any move in the area could be misconstrued by the ultras, leading to unfortunate results. This when the "latest imagery sent by the UAV' shows a gathering of 300-400 suspected Maoists in the area."

Security forces view this abduction as an attempt by the Maoists to compel the former to slow down, if not discontinue, their anti-Naxal operations, which, of late, seemed to have gained considerable success. And they, indeed, had a precedent to take recourse to this strategy. They had tasted certain success following such a strategy when they abducted the District Collector of Malkangiri, in Odisha Vineel Krishna in 2011. Not only this, the ultras repeated the strategy in Mar 2012, when they abducted two Italian tourists and BJD MLA Jhina Hakka.

The Odisha Government not only discontinued operations against them since 18 March, it also agreed to release 25 Maoists.

Ironic as it may seem, Chhattisgarh Chief Minister Raman Singh had talked about Naxal's new strategy a mere one week before Menon's abduction. Speaking at the Chief Ministers' meeting called by Prima Minister Manmohan Singh on 16 April to discuss the Internal Security Issues, Rama had said, reminding the participants about the ultras' strategy: "It is now clear that the Maoists are trying to gain control in the areas with abundant natural resources through their terror tactics.....Abduction seems to be their strategic weapon in the fight."

Meanwhile, on 23 Apr 2012, the Centre took stock of the Chhattisgarh situation in a high-level meeting chaired by Home Minister P. Chidambaram. Subsequently, the Ministry sent an advisory to the Naxal-infested states, asking them to frame Standard Operating Procedures (SOPs) for civil administration officials and politicians visiting Maoist-dominated zones. Such an advisory is a poor reflection on a country combating insurgency since the 1940s and Maoist menace over three decades. For the Ministry, it is always a fire-fighting exercise. Whenever there is fight, rush in the machines! It is pro-forma habit! Such SOPs should have been in place during the first few years of the Maoist violence. Any particular/ new Maoist ravages and ways could be recovered in subsequent instructions. Not only this inefficient way of dealing with a serious issue is condemnable, but also indicative of a casual and lacklustre way of confronting what country's Prime Minister described a decade ago as "the most serious threat to nation's internal security." What is even more condemnable is the supercilious may the centre/MHA officials view such unfortunate incidents in Maoist-affected States! Just examine what a central official told a daily about this abduction: "Since district collectors and senior officials have always been on Maoist hit list, it is advisable to move in the area with adequate forces after doing proper sanitization exercise and informing local police station, unlike what Menon did." This MHA official seems to suggest that Menon is somewhat "like a street urchin bent upon hurting himself while running about recklessly!"

The meeting was also attended by National Security Advisor Shivshankar Menon and IB Chief Nehschal Sandhu. At the end of the meeting, Union Home Secretary RK Singh made, yet again, a pro forma statement before the press: "We are in touch with the State government. Whatever support is needed by them is being given."

Officials were believed to have discussed exploring the option of having some guidelines "to deal with hostage situations in the Naxal-affected states as there is no set policy." Yet again, as is so typical in our country on dealing with such incidents, an official said: "This option will, however, be discussed with all the concerned states in due course. The guidelines, if any, will be framed with consent of all stakeholders." This again is typical of lackadaisical attitude of the Central towards a serious threat commonly faced by more than nine states of the Union. This is indicative of the government unwilling or unable to bring serious intent to confront the Naxal insurgency ravaging large of Swathes of regions running from Nepal-Bihar border down to south-eastern Kerala.

To sum it all up, nothing shows the inability of the ruling party at the Centre to build a consensus in the country to fight terrorism as its failure to bring the states on the same page on this issue which is threatening the very integrity of India.

Towards Menon's release

Undoubtedly, he was a popular man. As the news about his likely release trickled in, Jagdish, the owner of the tea stall outside the Collectorate has been all smiles. The work has obviously stalled in his absence. Menon's stenographer says it best: "Everyone has been affected. People have been praying and appealing (to the Maoists) for his release."

Sukma town (the district headquarters) has an area of just 3 sqkm. At one end is the transit bungalow-turned-Collectorate, across the road is Menon's official residence, and the forest is just 700 MTR away. But the current security arrangements belie the crisis. There are no security personel or CCTVs at the entrance, and visitors and media persons amble in and out freely.

Vijay Madkam, Secretary, South Bastar Divisional Committee (CPI-Maoist) sent an SMS to media houses late Tuesday (1 May): "We are ready to handover Mr Menon to our mediators in front of the people of Tadmetla on 3 May." The Maoists are masters of making best of such an occasion, a propaganda godsend. They were not expected to forego the advantage it offered them to impress the local tribals with their kindness in releasing their well-loved Collector. More importantly, the selection of site for Menon's release is important: A reminder of grim tragedy, the site of gruesome massacre of the security forces two years ago by the Maoists. Again, advance notice of the time and place will ensure media persons rushing to the spot in huge numbers. The event will be splashed live on the TV screens and the front pages of the dailies. Yet again, this is their way of not only drawing miles of propaganda for their cause, but also to prove that the outcome is the result of negotiations between the two equal entities, the

CPI (Maoist) and the State. As a matter of detail, Tadmetla in Dantewada district, is the place where the Maoists had achieved their biggest success against India, murdering 75 CRPF men on 6 Apr 2010.

As stated earlier, the Maoists, mixed up among the tribals, waited for him for over an hour at a function in Manjhipara village, which was part of the Government's "Gram Swaraj Abhyan"—a village contact programme. It was believed they took him deep inside the forests of Kerlapal, some of which are suspected to be heavily mined by them. Kerlapal forests are contiguous to the neighbourhood of the Manjipara village.

A police team under DSP Abhishek Shandilya launched a search operation soon after the abduction to try and rescue Menon. A special team was also constituted to join the effort after DGP AM Nawani held an emerging meeting with his top officials.

Raman Singh assured his state's best effort to secure Menon's release, even as the Home Ministe P Chidambaram spoke to him, with assurance of all help to sort this crisis out.

Kidnapping OK: says the mediator BD Sharma

Chhattisgarh Government had finally decided to begin negotiations for the release of Menon on 26 Apr 2012. Sharma, one of the too mediators hand-picked by the Maoists said on the 25th, "I do not condemn the abduction", which he claimed had happened in a war-like situation. Setting the tone for the gruelling job ahead, Sharma, a retired IAS Officer and former Commissioner of the National Commission for SC/ST, said it was important to note that the Maoists were not begging for some favours, implying it was the Government which was doing so.

On the 26th, Sharma was to be flown from New Delhi to Raipur, where he "will first contact the other Maoist-nominated interlocutor, G Hargopal, before meeting up the two Chhattisgarh Government nominated mediators—former chief secretaries of Madhya Pradesh and Chhattisgarh, Nirmala Buch and SK Mishra, respectively.

The stand taken by Sharma, while addressing a press conference at New Delhi a day before the beginning of the negotiations, was in sync with the Maoists' professed stand of justifying their violence in their cause. One can't be sanguine about the reason for a retired IAS taking up such a stance, aware as we are about his knowing all about Maoists and their brutal ways during his long service in the administration, and especially when he had served as Collector in Bastar. Is it that he as an administrator was convinced that the governments were not sincere to look into and address the problems/grievances of the tribals. Was he himself any different in treating these poor tribals, compared to the run-of-the-mill bureaucrat, or, was he trying to send the 'right' signals to the Maoists?

It is of some interest, as also of regret, that Mediator Sharma is speaking the logic and language of his 'employers', the Maoists! Evading all questions on killing of innocents by Maoists, he said all such things happened in "war-like" situation that must be corrected, taking in view the 'violence' committed by the other side (read security forces) against tribals. Here is what he said, arguing his case to support the Maoists ways: "Collector's abduction has become an issue of deep concern from countless perceptions. I refuse to condemn Menon's abduction, but abduction of two Italians in Odisha was not right. After all, foreigners are not harming tribals and villagers who are victims of existing system...Maoists are not begging for favours. They are of the opinion that hundreds of fake cases have been forced on innocent tribals who are unaware of them. They are being held in jails of Dantewada and Raipur without knowing what it was all about. They have also demanded that cases registered against an elderly journalist and Binayak Sen should be withdrawn."

Notes

1. Smita Gupta, The Outlook, 15 May 2006.
2. Asian Age, 29 Jan 2007.
3. *Ibid,* 19 Jun 2007.
4. *Ibid,* 8 Jun 2007.
5. Nitin Mahajan, Indian Express, 8 Aug 2007.
6. Shivam Vij, op cit.
7. Ch VM Krishna Rao, Asian Age, 16 Mar 2006.
8. The Editorial, The Pioneer, 16 Mar 2007.
9. Ralesh K Singh, Asian Age, 27 Mar 2007.
10. Nitin Mahajan, Indian Express, 16 Jun 2007.
11. Pradeep Thakur, Times of India, 17 Mar 2007.
12. Hindustan Times, 4 May 2007.
13. Editorial, The Hindu, 30 May 2007.
14. Amitabh Tiwari, Times of India, 6 Sep 2007.
15. Deepak Tiwari, The Week, 1.6.2008.
16. Op. cit.
17. Satya Prakash, Hindustan Times, 1 May 2011.
18. Jha, VK, Indian Express, 12.9.11.
19. Op. cit.

20. Aman Sethi, The Hindu, 13 Nov 2011.
21. Kumar, Sujit, The Pioneer, 22.4.12 and 23.4.12.
22. Kaiser, Ejaz, Hindustan Times, 2.5.12.
23. Janardhana, Arun, Times of India, 24.4.12.
    - Op. cit.,
    - Rakhi Chakrabarty, Times of India, 6 Jul 2002.
    - Rakhi Chakrabarty, Times of India, 9.7.12.

23

Chhattisgarh - 2

Deals Menon's Release: Implications

Because of the inherent compulsion the State Government faces in the given situation viz to ensure the release of its District Collector, the Maoists could be expected not only to maintain an upper hand during the negotiations, but also to ensure both short-term and long-term gains for their cause. In getting their own cause and aim furthered, they are also greatly lucky to have their mediators in synch with their thinking and ideology. Given these favourable situation, it is natural that the agreement on the release of the Collector may, nay will, end up serving the long-term interests of Maoists. This is said to be the feelings of people close to the developments[1].

The most important of the agreements between the two sets of mediators is the one that sets up a high-powered Committee to regularly review cases of arrest of Maoists. "It could start work within an hour of Menon's release. A senior officer, who closely observed the dialogue in Raipur told a daily that "rebels might gain an upper hand following Committee's formation." The mechanism of this Committee will be shown as a means to obtain justice for the tribals of the State. Any local who gets released as a result of decision by the Committee will be shown as a person who was wrongly done in by the government, and ultimately got justice as a result of exertions by the Maoists, the true friends of the tribals. Besides winning the confidence of the Chhattisgarh tribals, the Maoist leadership in the State would score a brownie point over its counterpart in Odisha, as a result of this Committee's functioning. The argument will be that unlike in Odisha, where Maoist leader Sabyasachi Panda was seen as a commander who was more interested in securing the release of his wife in exchange for two abducted Italians, the Chhattisgarh leadership will be depicted as saviours of the tribals and their interests. It is not that entire Odisha leadership was involved in ensuring the release of Panda's wife. In fact, two groups of Maoist leadership were dealing with the release of two different entities in two different dialogues, one for two Italian abductees and the other for an Odisha MLA. But it suited the Chhattisgarh comrades to paint all the Odisha Maoists with a broad brush.

The official sources say "the Maoist will produce a database of some 1,000 members who have been languishing in jail on 'trumped up' charges". Even if 100 among them are released as a result of deliberations at the Committee dialogues, the Maoist would not only earn the gratitude of their kith and kin, but also establish their credentials among the local populace. They are playing a long lasting game.

And Finally, the Release: 3 May 2012

The 12-day ordeal was over, for the Centre but more seriously for the BJP Government in Raipur, on 3 May 2012. If the Crisis tested the nerves of Raman Singh, it also brought anti-Maoist operations to a grinding halt. Finally, Menon's release brought relief to his family. Beaming faces of his father (A Varadhas), mother, wife and daughter in a photo in a daily said it all[2].

The Maoists handed the Collector over to their interlocutors Haragopal and sharma, who had flown in a government helicopter to Chintalnar and then ridden motorcycles deep inside the Bastar forests. Large media contingents, which had stationed themselves at Chintalnar and Sukma, were initially asked not to accompany the mediators. Not the ones to let go of such an opportunity for a huge publicity blitz, the Maoists later invited the journalists to Tadmetla, where the two mediators emerged with Menon. This was not the only move based upon a lot of thinking and calculations by the Maoists.

There was one more. Initially, the release was believed to be scheduled for the afternoon and accordingly, a chopper was positioned at Chintalnar to fly Menon and the mediators to Sukma. As the mediators did not appear till the late afternoon, there was palpable consternation in the air. The trio appeared late in the evening. It was a strategie move by the ultras to ensure that the impending dark would afford a cover for retreat of their cadres deep into safety of the woods. Consequently the chopper could not fly at night, Menon walked to Chintalnar and from there driven to Sukma, some 45 km away.

Making the forces position the Chopper at Chintalnar was a well-calculated move yet again by the ultras. It was a grim way to remind their 'enemies' about the macabre happening there two years ago when 75 CRPF troopers were massacred by the Maoists.

The four mediators had discussed the rebel demands for three days and hammered out an agreement. Significantly, the government did not immediately concede the demand for release of eight jailed Naxalite, even if the security forces had been confined to the barracks in Bastar. Meanwhile, a bail application was moved in a Raipur Court for the release of two Maoist leaders: Santipriya Reddy, wife of Gudra Usendi, a member of the DKSZC; and Malati Chowdhary. The two were amonge the eight whose release was demanded by the ultras in exchange for the abductee.

True to the terms of agreement the high-powered Committee headed by the former Chief Secretary Nirmala Buch, met within an hour of the release of Menon, to start regular review of all cases of undertrials, including the Maoist-related cases too. The other members of the Committee are Chief Secretary Sunil Kumar and DGP Anil Navaney.

"Maoists herded us to meeting, we were too scared to refuse": Jul 2012 (Sarkeguda village meeting)

This is another story about villagers who are accused of being Maoists by the security forces but the former vehemently denying the charge with a variety of reasons, or 'excuses' as the latter would wish to believe. Here are two opening paragraphs of the news story carried by a daily, datelined Raipur 6 Jul 2012:

- "After the 29 Jun encounter by joint forces in south Chhattisgarh's district, Kaka Senti and Markam Soma were flown to Raipur by CRPF for treatment with six injured jawans. They were suspected to be Maoists."
- "Lying in the state-run Dr Ambedkar Hospital in Raipur with bullet wounds, both denied they were Maoists. Soma, however, said the meeting at the neighbouring Sarkeguda village, the site of the gun battle that killed 17 people last Friday (29 Jun 2012), was called by Maoist."

Here are the facts as narrated by Soma, a resident of Bijapur's Kottaguda village in the Maoist liberated zone: "Three Maoists came to our village and herded all villagers together for a meeting around 10 PM. Two of them had guns. I sat in the meeting with the rest of the village but could not understand their language. We speak Dorla whild the three Maoists were speaking Muria."

Senti, also from Kottaguda, was at the meeting.

"The men wore shorts and were not from our village. They discussed various issues, including distribution of land for tilling", said Soma, adding, "usually, meetings are not held late. But me could not refuse to attend the meeting as the Maoists would kill us."

While the meeting was on, police came and circled the village, Senti said, "There was heavy firing. A bullet hit my leg and I fell unconscious." At the crack of the dawn, both were flown to hospital by helicopter. They had never ventured as far as Raipur before. "I don't like it", Senti said, pointing to a chain tied to his leg. He missed his children and wife who is pregnant.

In another Raipur hospital, six jawans lay with bullet wounds. Two COBRA commandos, Wahid-ul-Islam and Gyanendra Prakash were still in ICU but out of danger. Splinters pierced Islam's chest during the encounter. Prakash too had splinter injuries on his face. "Both narrowly escaped death", said Ashok Zargar, hospital's Chief of Medical services.

Another trooper, Havildar K Ranjan, relived the encounter: "We marched from Basaguda Camp in single line. We were supported to go to Silgar where there was information about Maoists' assembling". SS Rana, shot in his left thigh, was sixth in the line. "Barely 3-4 km from the camp, we heard voices screaming 'police, police'. This was followed by a burst of firing".

Islam and Prakash took the first hits and fell. Four others were also hit. "It was dark and we could see at least 30-40 men firing and retreating into the jungle when our force fired in retaliation and cordoned off the village", said A Ghosh, who had fractured his toes.

Chhattisgarh govt ordered judicial probe

The State Government 5 July ordered a judicial probe into "last week's encounter in Bijapur district where 17, including Maoists, were killed and six CRPF jawans were injured. The decision was taken at a Cabinet meeting. The government request the Chief Justice of the HC to appoint a sitting judge[3].

The probe will inquire into various aspects: was there an encounter, was any Maoist, security personnel or anyone else killed or injured, and could the firing had been avoitded? DG CRPF Vijay Kumar said, "we are open to any enquiry. Since the day of the encounter, we have been sharing all information."

"Khooni Raasta (road)" in Bijapur District

On the night of 28 Jun 2012, a joint operations team of CRPE, COBRA commandos and state police were fired at by the Maoists at Sarkeguda village, some 3km from Basaguda in Bijapur district. 17 people were killed and six CRPF men injured.

Sarkeguda village in south Chhattigarh's Bijapur district, lies off a road that locals call the "Khooni Raasta" (killer road). It is the 52-km road linking Bijapur district headquarters to Basaguda that is called so, and can be extended to include Sarke guda, where the said encounter took place on the 28th. Skeletons of several vehicles along the road cutting through the thick, sullen forests are reminder of the blood spilled on this rock since 2006. During the six year between 2006 and 2012 , the road was bloodied by more than a dozen blasts bay Maoists, and several gun battles between the ultras and the security forces.

Giving further details, police confirm the Maoists triggered at least six IED blasts blowing up the vehicles carrying villagers. They blew up several vehicles of security forces also, killing at least a dozen jawans. Maoists, at gun point, forced passengers out of the buses and looted rations meant for the troops. Presently, there are five CRPF camps along the road, the last one being at Basaguda from where the joint operations team had marched out on the 28th for 'Operation Silger'. When they reached Sarkeguda, they came under fire from the Maoists, as the police told a daily[4].

Sarkeguda village, part of Basaguda police limits, falls in the so-called "Maoist liberated zone", falls in the so-called "Maoist liberated zone" which lied across the Taalperu river which flows by Basaguda CRPF camp, and was dubbed the LOC (Line of Control). The area beyond the bridge on the Taalperu was the Liberated Zone between 2006 and 2009. After the 28th encounter, "villagers are haunted by memories of their lives in exile not so long ago. "The road and surrounding villages were ravaged by the scourge of Maoists, Salwa Judum and securuty forces." They fled their villages in 2006 "and with the help of some NGO, returned only in 2010."

The above is rather a sketchy account of what the police has dubbed the "biggest Naxal encounter" in Chhattisgarh. A detailed discussion is called for of this encounter.

"Villagers, Jawans battle distrust, Reds": Jul 2012

'Malaria, lack of facilities add to Misery'

The above headline, and its blurb, indicate the main contents and concerns of a news story carried by a daily of 11 Jul 2012. This article delineates the problems and difficulties faced by India's counter-Naxal forces while combating the LWE. This article is obviously based upon the interaction the correspondent of the daily had with the men of the CRPF which presently is the main force combating the Maoist menace in the country.

The news story is datelined Basaguda (Bijapur), 10 Jul 2012. The three opening paragraphs of the analytical story are reproduced:

- "Several CRPF men stood around tall polls with a black box mounted atop each at CRPF's Basaguda camp in south Chhattisgarh's Bijapur district. One of them tried to fix the position of the box, a wireless Local loop (WLL) transmitter, while the others gazed intently for a bar to appear in the receiver".
- "For them, the elusive bar means connecting with loved ones. "I can then hear the voice of my children and wife at home in Kanpur", said a jawan of CRPF's 168 battalion. He last spoke to his loved ones back home about two days ago".
- "We have various phones, including satellite ones. But, often the landline constantly gives out a busy tone and the mobile phone network goes off", said a commandant. The jawans are then taken in batches to villages closer to the district headquarters to call up their families".

The situation and difficulties of security men are clear from the above. These are added to by the Maoists, who often dig up roads and cut electric wires plunging the tents or pre-fabricated huts where jawans live in darkness for days.

Villagers, too, are cut off from the world. After the Sarkeguda encounter, villagers told the daily that Markam Soma and Kaka Senti were missing. Their wives feared that they had been killed by the police. Clutching her children, Senti's wife said, "I am pregnant. Where will I go looking for him?"

Nobody from the government had bothered to inform them that Soma and Senti were undergoing treatment at Raipur's Dr Ambedkar Hospital, their legs chained to bedposts. The CRPF's Basaguda camp is the last post signalling government presence. Beyond it stretches the Maoist liberated zone. Basaguda recently grabbled headlines after the encounter at Sarkeguda, some 3 km from the CRPF camp, in the liberated zone. About 400 CRPF, COBRA commandos and state policemen marched out of the Basaguda camp on 28 Jun (2012) night for operation Silger.

Villagers have suffered the police, Salwa Judum, and Maoists. "One night some 4-5 years ago, some '*andarwale'* (Maoists) came to our village and asked for food. We gave them. Next morning, the Salwa Judum and policemen came and asked why we gave them food", recounted an old man at Sarkeguda. When the villagers said they fed Maoists fearing their lives, the Salwa Judum and police beat them mercilessly. "After they left, we fled our homes and did not return for 3 to 4 years", he said.

Since the encounter, villagers at Sarkeguda are wary of any stranger. "We try to figure out if a stranger is from police, or sent by the Maoists"? said a girl, studying in class X.

Even earlier, men folk would run away when CRPF men patrol near the villages, said a CRPF jawan. Distrust, fear and malaria stalk villagers and jawans. "Battling malaria is as tough here as battling the Maoists", said an officer. Between January to June, 40 cases of malaria and 50 of typhoid were reported in 168 Battalion of CRPF, comprising some 1,100 men. "Last year (2011), 90 malaria cases were reported.

The jawans are treated by doctors or flown to a city hospital. "Villagers die like flies. There are no doctors for miles. By the time a serious patient is carried on bamboo poles to the nearest hospital, he is almost dead", said Markam Narayan of Sarkeguda. Getting supplies and ration to camp is akin to launching an operation. A road opening party precedes the vehicle carrying ration to check for explosives, landmines or ambushes by Maoists. "In 2010, 12 people were killed while bringing ration to the camp", said the commandant[5].

After that, private vehicles were used to ferry ration to the camps. "That increased risk of our lives", said a villager from neighbouring Murdonda.

One daily published some details of this encounter, which are discussed in the following pages. Subsequent to the two encounters on 28 Jun 2012, there were some tribals and NGOs who raised doubts about their genuineness[6].

On the night of the 28th, three joint teams of the CRPF, Special Task Force (STF) and the district police set off from three sites in Sukma and Bijapur districts of Chhattisgarh towards Silger—a forested area where top Maoists from Odisha were reported to be camping. Police said none of the three teams could make it to Silger as they met resistance on the way from Maoists. The situations facing the three columns follow:

- Chintalnar (in Sukma district) team had a brief encounter in which two alleged Naxals were killed.

- Jagargunda (in Sukma district) too met with some resistance, but there were no casualties.
- Basaguda (in Bijapur district) team led by Selango, DIG (Ops), CRPF, Bijapur, crossed Taalperu, a river beyond which the police/ security forces had hardly ventured earlier. 17 people were killed here in what police called "the biggest Maoist encounter."

Earlier here, Taalperu has been described as LOC. Across this river lies the Maoist 'Country'! It was in this area where 17 'alleged' Maoists were killed. It were these Maoists killed here which later the locals and some NGOs called 'innocent' tribals, implying they were killed in a fake encounter. As will be seen later here, the State was forced to order an inquiry into this 'fake' encounter.

Once among the most prosperous and picturesque regions of Bastar, the villagers here (Sarkeguda, Kottagudda and Rajpenta) were ordered to be evacuated by the forces during the days of the Salwa Judum. Forces and Moists often laid their sieges on either side of Taalperu till the villagers returned to their homes in 2009 (having been ousted in 2006). The recovery was gradual. The villagers (all tribal, BPL families who worked as marginal farmers) got a school, a ration Centre, and some shops. Then, even bus service resumed. Still, beyond the Taalperu lay the forest whose topography forces knew through the Google images.

What follows is the detailed account of things a daily collected in its investigation of the encounter. One should be honest here to say that the daily is biased against the services, as will be seen in some direct quotations.

"That night, the security forces took a route they have never been onto before, they say. A few minutes from the Basaguda thana, from where they had set off, they reached Sarkeguda village and chanced upon a 'Maoist meeting'. An 'encounter' followed, leaving 16 people dead (one person died in the hospital later). The alleged encounter took place in the middle of the night, yet all bodies were recovered (Naxals usally never leave behind bodies of their cadres). And despite 'heavy firing from the Naxals for hours', only three *bharmars* (country-made fire arms) were found".

The above paragraph is directly reproduced from this daily. Some comments are offered on certain parts/sentences hinting at wrong-doings by the men in uniform as also on certain factual information:

- The journalist makes no mention of the fact that six CRPF men were injured in the encounter. That shows the obvious bias, unless he wants to imply that these injuries were self-inflicted.

- "The forces took the route they have never been onto before." It is factually wrong. The CRPF/police did patrol the area between Basaguda and Sarkeguda periodically. Taalperu flows by the village Sarkeguda and it is across the river that the forces had not been before.
- "A few minutes from Basaguda.....they reached Sarkeguda village". The distance between the villages in 3 km. It is stretching "a few minutes" a little too much. In the area, it would take a minimum of 60 to 90 minutes to cover those 3 km, remember they are marching in a battle area, have to walk carefully and cautiously, and can't cover it in a "few minutes" as if troops are doing 'forced march' in a peace-time exercise!
- They…came upon a "Maoist meeting". Why in "....."? Why can't it be Maoist meeting? If it is not, what were the local tribals doing at that hour of midnight? One can understand tribal youth sitting and gossipping at a place during day-light hours, but at midnight?
- An 'encounter' followed. 'Encounter' in commas indicate from the very beginning that the journalist decided it was a fake encounter!
- "The alleged encounter…. in the middle of the night and yet all bodies were recovered. (Naxals never leave behind bodies of their cadres)." This is an incredulous way to look at things by an objective journalist and the daily he works for! Even if it is midnight, is it difficult to trace these bodies if they happened to be lying within a radius of 50, or 100, or even 150 yards. This should be an easy job, particularly when the Maoists have fled the site! Now to the bit "Naxals never leave the bodies". 'Never' can't be a gospel truth. It is possible for the desperados to take away the bodies from roadside hillocks from where they fire upon the troops who have been ambushed while moving over a booby trapped road or the road where the IED was buried under! In the instant case, they couldn't have removed 16 bodies. Obviously, there were more than 16, who fled the scene. There could be reasons for death of some innocent tribals, as explained below.
- Possibly, some Maoists had come down to Sarkeguda to talk to the locals. Obviously, they were not interesting to talk to the people from Sarkeguda only. The residents of Kottaguda and Rajpenta villages too had been called over. As the daily tells us, the 17 people who were killed on the 28th belonged to Kottaguda (9), Sarkeguda (6) and Rajpenta (2). Maybe, people from some

other villages were there too, who succeeded in running away to their villages. For obvious reasons, the villagers couldn't tell the whole truth, after all, they have to play both the sides, out of compulsion. Possibly, a large number of the locals were called over. Some Maoists have come down to be in the meeting. Apparently, a few who came made good their escape, post-haste.

- This whole story is written to put troops in poor light and with certain 'mischief' behind it. "And despite heavy firing from the Naxals for hours, only three 'bharmars' were found". "Only three"! How many 'bharmass' recovered would have convinced this cynical journalist, rather doubting Thomas, about the genuiness of the encounter. One wonders if this is a responsible attitude of an Indian daily to doubt everything that troops or government say! After all, it affects troops' morale.

Some more excerpts from this daily's story are reproduced hereafter, to be subsequently commented upon. "The next day, the police struggled with the crime records of the people they called 'hard core Naxals"….All except Madkam Suresh were residents of Sarkeguda, Kottaguda and Rajpenta, the villages that fall under Basaguda thana, from where the team set off for the 'operation'…Among those killed were two boys who studied and lived in a government hostel adjoining the *thana.* Many of the others who died that night routinely crossed the thana and several CRPF camps in between to visit the nearest town Amapalli. Even two days after the incident, the policemen in the Basaguda thana were clueless about the Naxal records of the dead".

Some of the comments on the above text are offered hereafter.

- Next day police "struggled" with the crime records of the people they called 'hardcore Naxals'. Why the word 'struggled', with certain 'pejorative' implications. So, this "parachute" journalist 'imperially' expected policemen at the local thana to supply entire information on the 17 Naxals killed less than 12 hours ago-around midnight 28/29 June. Are all the *thanas* equipped with the computers? Are those policemen trained in their use? Incidents taking place in cities like Delhi and Mumbai take days and weeks, if not months, to reach certain conclusion. He expects solutions in less than 12 hours in police stations in Naxal affected areas! Some hot-headed presumptuousness, this! He is obviously unaware of conditions the counter-Naxal forces are operating in Maoist-affected areas. He wants everything on a platter, this Journalist Highness, in less than 12 hours!

- "All the 17 were residents of the three villages named above, which falls under Basaguda thana, from where the team set off for the 'operation'." There is even more sinister suggestion here. If the encounter was fake, is the daily suggesting that 17 of them were taken to Sarkeguda and murdered there in coldblood? Yet again, what is this journalist suggesting by putting the word 'operation' in commas?
- There is more mischief further on. "The two boys killed among the 17 were living and studying in government hostel adjoining the Thana". What is he implying? The police took the two from hostel and killed them at Sarkagudda! If not so, did the journalist ask the hostel authorities why did the boys go missing? Indulging in wild suggestions and vile innuendoes is not responsible journalism.
- "Many of the others who died that night routinely crossed the *thana* and several CRPF camps in between to visit the nearest town Awapalli". What is the journalist trying to convey with these words? Did the police kill them when they were criss-crossing the area under this thana? And then took the bodies to Sarkeguda! But more importantly, why has not this journalist asked what were these villagers doing at mid-night at Sarkeguda? He does not inquire into such obvious, and keeps indulging into vicious innuendo.
- Here comes the final condemnation of the police. "Even two days after the incident, policemen.... in thana were clueless about the Naxal records of the dead". Again an example of magisterial loftiness. This has been dealt with earlier.

Then this daily gives the biographic sketches of the 17 killed. He gets the information from the locals. He mentions some names with Naxals background, but exculpates on the say-so of the local residents. The entire text is not edifying! It is not the best example of objective journalism!

A word on the Chintalnar team. They met Naxal resistance, where in two Naxals (Sodi Dulla and Madkam Lachcha) were killed. A .303 rifle and a *bharmar* were allegedly recovered from them. Interestingly, whatever the police says has to be qualified by "allegedly". On the other hand, whatever he is told by villagers, is accepted without demur, objectivity be damned!

He has met some injured person. Their account of that night is similar to that of the villagers: They had gathered to discuss Beej Pundum when the police attacked them. It wasn't a Naxal meeting. This journalist is bold, rather brazenly so, when it comes to putting the blame on security forces. For him, the forces can do nothing right, or even say nothing right. But he is tongue-tied while talking to the villagers. Some examples of this partiality and bias are given below. Such behaviour is paying in a democracy, especially in India. You are bold journalist if you abuse the government, and criticise/pillory the forces engaged in a life-and-death clashes with the murderous Maoists! Now some points that shows this journalists naevte:

- He seems to have talked only to some villagers, and some constables of the district police. Why didn't he talk to some senior police officers, say, like District SP, a DIG, or even DGP? He would have been able to produce a more balanced story for his newspaper. May be he was more interested in telling his editor that it was an out and out a fake encounter!
- Why didn't he ask the villagers—his main interlocutors—as to why were they holding their meeting at Sarkeguda while the majority of people were from other villages? Basaguda would have been a better choice, safer and central.
- Why were they holding a meeting so late in the night?
- This journalist is based in Chhattisgarh only, why was he in a hurry to rush back. In any case, his story was published full 10 days after the 28th incident!

The above comments upon the story are made with a serious intent. It is an attempt to tell this journalist and his daily not to trivialise such serious of Maoist insurgency, counter-Maoist operations and sufferings of the people unhabiting the regions affected by Maoist dance of death.

This another, who has fought the insurgency in its worst phases in Nagaland (1957-59), Mizoram (mid-1980s) and Jammu and Kashmir (late 1980s) is painfully aware of the miserable life of the common man during insurgency-fuelled violence. Undoubtedly, some innocents suffer, along with the confirmed Naxals. Often, it is unavoidable. It is understandable in the context of Jihadi Terrorism in India. So many Muslims have spent years in jails, and they are ultimately declared innocent. In either case innocent suffer. To go on the other extreme and assert that every 'Naxals' killed in the encounter was an innocent villager, is equally preposterous! All the same, there is the need for balance.

Judicial probe into Naxal encounter

The Chhattisgarh Government on 5 Jul 2012 decided to order a judicial inquiry, to be headed by a judge of Chhattisgarh High Court in Bilaspur, to ascertain the Chronology of events, the reasons behind the firing, the identity of those killed, circumstances under which the forces had to open fire, was firing avoidable, and was any person other than policemen or Naxals injured or killed in the incident?

A week after the 28th incident, government has been under pressure from the rights group as also the opposition parties to order an independent inquiry as the relatives of the victims claimed that the victims/deceased were innocent tribals. A magisterial inquiry, a mandatory requirement whenever an encounter takes place, is already on.

Chief Minister Raman Singh said the government was not succumbing to political pressure to hold the police accountable for their action, but to dispel confusion surrounding the counter-insurgency operations.

This is the second such probe ordered in so many years. The Government ordered a judicial inquiry in Mar 2011 after "the Hindu reported that the security forces had torched some 300 houses, killed three persons and sexually assaulted three women in Sukma district. "After passage of 15 months, Justice TP Sharma's report is yet to be made public".

The MHA officials, meanwhile, said on 6 Jul 2012 the nine Naxal-affected states and all Central paramilitary forces "have been called for a 13 July meeting in Delhi, specifically to discuss the issue of 'human shields' Naxals used against the security forces". The forces "have been asked to make an assessment of the cost and feasibility of providing sophisticated night vision devices to the personnel to enable them to see better in the darkness".

Encounter at Sarkeguda again : 5 Jul 12

A team of CRPF, including COBRA commandos on 5 July engaged in an encounter with the suspected Maoists at the same spot in Sarkeguda village where 19 people were killed a week ago on the 28th June.

Some 100 CRPF who were on patrolling duty, ahead of the day-long bandh called by the Maoists in the area for the 6th to protest against the 28th killings, came under fire from the Maoists. Pankaj Kumar Singh, IG (Operations), Delhi, said the encounter continued for about half an hour. But no one was injured/killed in the gun fight. The operation was planned to maintain continuous pressure on the Maoists and thwart their attempts for a come-back in the area. Security officials said the ultras held meetings with the villagers on the 4th urging to make the 6 July bandh a success.

Maoists Surrender

A woman Maoist guerrilla surrendered to the police on 20 Aug 2012. She accused the rebel leadership of using tribals for its own aims.

Ramdai Nareti alias Fulwa laid down arms to join the mainstream. She will be granted all benefits due to her under the State Government's rehabilitation scheme. Narayanpur SP briefed the press. Fulwa was wanted for her involvement in several cases.

Fulma was a member of the Keshkal Area Committee's Platoon No. 17 and had taken part in a number of operations in Kiskodo, Korad, Daula and Benur areas of Narayanpur district. Narayanpur is one of the seven districts in the Bastar Division, affected by Maoist insurgency. Fulwa told police she was from Gotiya village and was forcibly taken away to the forests by Keshkal Area Committee members three years ago.

Eight Naxals arrested in three Raids : Nov 2012

On the 26th, a joint team of Bijapore police and Chhattisgarh Armed Forces (CAF) nabbed Kulmumi Minoo alias Manoj near Ghudsakal village. Explosives and ten detonators were seized from Minoo, who was carrying a reward of Rs 28,000 over his head. In another combing operation, four Naxals (Chapa Narariyya, Vacham Ramaiyya, Talandi Pavarao and Matti Sukhram were arrested from the jungles of Kottaguda and Kamlapalli in Bijapur district.

In Etebalka village of Kanker district, police arrested three more Maosits (Santosh Kumar Anchala, 25; Birsingh Anchala, 38 and Baisakhu Ram, 35). Kanker SP said they were accused of ambushing a police team near Etebalka on 21 Jul 2010.

CRPF man killed : 19 Sep 2012

One CRPF was killed and two others injured when Maoist guerrillas, hidden in the nearby forest, attacked a team of security forces engaged in securing the area prepared for landing of a helicopter carrying ration for the CRPF camp based at Gorkha village, near Sukma, some 140 km from the divisional headquarters at Jagdalpur. The men engaged in area domination near the temporary airstrip were from the 2nd Battalion, CRPF.

The attack happened at 10.30 AM. Jawan Mahadev Minz was shot in his chest and died, while his comrade, B Suresh was shot in the leg. After a brief encounter, the ultras retreated into the jungle. Newly promoted DG (incharge Naxal operations) Ram Nivas, confirmed the incident. Injured men were taken to Raipur for further treatment.

Sukma, a new district carved out of Dantewada, has long been a hotbed of insurgency. In May itself, District Collector Alex Paul Menon was abducted by the Red rebels. A few years back, helicopter MI-17 was attacked by the Naxals in the same area.

Naxals kill two CISF men

Two jawans of the CISF were killed on 4 Nov 2012 when armed Maoists opened fire at a check post on a hilltop at Akash Nagar, which is close to iron ore Deposit No. 5 in Bailadila hills of Dantewad a district.

NDMC has several massive mines in this area, composed of Bacheli and Kirandul sectors. It was a well-planned attack, which perfectly exploited foggy weather. CISF Head Constable P N Chatterjee, from West Bengal, was killed on the spot, while Constable K R Arjun, from Maharashtra, succumbed to his injuries later in hospital. The rebels numbering some 25 also took away an AK-47 and a SLR which belonged to the two victims.

Moral degradation of Maoists

Humans being what they are, any movements launched on ideological tenets are bound to travel towards moral degradation, as the incidents of rape described below should indicate.

Two minor girls raped by Maoists

The State Police on 4 Nov 2012 booked three Naxals (Kudiam Gujja, Nagesh and Shivaji) on the complaint of two girls who were 'allegedly' raped by them in Muded area of the Bijapur district. It was disclosed by the SP. The three ultras subjected them to repeated sexual assaults after abducting them from their villages in this district. A CRPF team came across the girls (one of them is 12-years-old and the other is 11) during a combing operations on 1 November. They were rescued by the CRPF.

The girls alleged that the ultras forcibly picked them up from their houses and made them work as Bal Sangham (children wing of the Maoist outfit) members. They were forced into physical relations with the three cadres named above.

It is obvious that the Maoists are not only forcing the minors into insurgency and also raping them in confinement—depriving them of their right to education as also of their human rights. The victims also told the police that the practice of rape of minors in confinement was going on for long. The Naxals threaten their parents of dire consequences when they object. Thus, the Maoists forcibly take away minor girls and boys for ostensible purpose of recruiting them into Bal Sangham, but they are often exploited sexually. After months of exploitation, the Maoists later abandoned them into jungle.

The Union MHA sanctioned 6 November a compensation of Rs 5 lakh each to the two victims following a report from the district SP, suggesting reprisals from the Naxals if they return to their villages. The girls themselves wanted to stay in Balak Ashrams.

"Chhattisgarh leader (Mahendra Karma) escapes Naxal attack" Nov 2012

Mahendra Karma, the Congress leader who spearheaded the controversial anti-Naxalite campaign Salwa Judum survived an attack by the Maoists on 10 Nov 2012.

The landmine attack on his motorcade took place around 9.40 AM when Karma was going to Barsur in Dantewada district. As the landmine hit the front portion of the bullet proof vehicle, Karma escaped unhurt. But four people, including his security personnel, were injured in the blast.

The Maoists had specifically targeted the fourth vehicle in the convoy in which Karma was travelling. Police suspect the Maoists had prior information about his movement. Karma has "Z-Plus" security cover since past several years. "I am on the hit list of the Maoists. In the past also, the Maoists had attacked me. Despite threats, I will continue to fight Naxalites", Karma told reporters at the Dantewada district hospital where he underwent a medical checkup. Later, he was airlifted to Raipur for treatment as he complained of a mild chest pain.[7]

The 60-year old tribal leader was a former minister in the Ajit Jogi Cabinet. He had also served as leader of opposition in the State Assembly after the 2003 polls. The former Dantewada MLA lost the 2008 Assembly polls when BJP swept 10 of the 11 seats in Bastar Division.

"He was moving in a convoy of seven vehicles when the blast took place. The Maoists managed to target his vehicle (4th from front) in the entire convoy", Special D G Ramnivas said. He ruled any security lapse.

This is not the first time when Karma was attacked. "He has been in the hit-list of the Maoists as he had launched Salwa Judum in Bastar several years ago".

President visits Abujhmaad Forest area: First President to do so Nov 2012

Marking the first visit by any President to Abhujmaad forest in Chhattisgarh, Pranab Mukherjee visited the Ramakrishna Mission Ashram in Narayanpur district on 8 Nov 2012. He also inaugurated the new integrated terminal building of Raipur airport and the Secretariat in the new capital Naya Raipur.

Praising the Mission for providing education to tribals in this remote forests, the President said: Abujhmaad is home to one of the particularly vulnerable tribal groups of our country, the Abhujmariahs. It symbolizes the cultural legacy that we must preserve, as well as challenges of taking the fruits of development to the people in the most remote areas of the country".

Spanning over 6,000 sqkm, Abhujmaad was once described by former Home Secretary GK Pillai as the "liberated zone of Maoists" and has seen little development. Government officers rarely visit it as the 237 villages that lie inside the forest have just few schools…mostly on the periphery…and sub health centres[8].

During the visit, which also marked the 12th year of State's formation, he praised the state government for its overall efforts: "I am delighted to know that Naya Raipur is the first planned capital city of the 21st century in India and is being developed as a modern and green city. I single out rainwater harvesting and solar projects that would make it an eco-friendly capital. I compliment the leadership for developing Raipur with vision and a commitment to sustainable urban development."

During his two-hour visit to Ashram, in the far-off tribal area of Narayanpur district, the President said "it was a learning experience" for him as well. After an emotional address to the students and members of the Mission Ashram, he interacted with the tribal children enrolled in the school in Narayanpur[9].

It is the first visit, as stated above, of a President to Narayanpur district, one of the districts worst-affected by the LWE. "The Ramakrishna Mission Ashram is rendering yeoman service to the social-economic development of the people of Abujhmaad."

This daily writes: "Abujhmaad has a population of 34,000 tribals in 233 villages over a sprawling area of 4,000 sqkm. It is a tangled knot of hills with inaccessible terrain that remains cut off from the rest of civilized world for some six months in a year, even to this day. Due to inaccessibility and Naxal violence, there are no educational facilities, almost no communication and a complete lack of medical facilities that result in a high death rate and infant mortality."

New DGP to focus on Curbing Naxalism Nov 2012

Ram Niwas took over as new DGP of Chhattisgarh on 30 Nov 2012. He told the media that Maoist insurgency is the toughest problem facing the State and it is also a challenge to democratic values of the country.

The Maoist menace will be curbed under guidance of the State and Central Governments, and he sought the cooperation of all concerned to effectively tackle it. He asserted that his force was committed to protect human rights of the citizens. This was obviously meant for the consumption of the overzealous human rights NGOs. He made further averments given below:

- Youth living in the Naxal-hit areas must take the benefits of the Governments welfare schemes and join the national mainstream.
- Police personnel, both officers and men, posted in the Maoist-hit areas work under difficult circumstances and they should be provided with good facilities.
- The police would be continuously trained to upgrade their skills to face any situations. It would also be equipped to handle cyber crimes.

Naxals torch two trucks in Sukma

A group of Naxals 'allegedly' set on fire two tipper trucks used in road construction work in Tongpal area of Naxal-hit Sukma district on 4 Dec 2012.

When the trucks, belonging to private contractors, reached Jerum valley, some 60 Maoists, including 50 armed ones and dressed as villagers, stopped the tippers, asked the people to get down and set the vehicles ablaze. The vehicles were going from Jagdalpur Chhindgadh carrying the road construction equipment and material.

The irony of the situation must be obviously clear to the supporters and overground zealots of these murderous Maoists: The ultras are helping the poverty-stricken tribals whose areas have not been developed by the uncaring governments over the years!

Maoists back teachers' strike

The strike by the Chhattisgarh teachers entered second week on 14 Dec 2012, without an end in sight. It is snow baling into a major concern of the State, as also of the local intelligentsia. Another complicating entity has entered the field : while the teachers refuse to resume their work, the banned CPI (Maoist) has announced their support for their strike.

As the strike is growing by the day, the agitators are adopting newer methods to invite greater public sympathy for their cause—tonsuring each other's heads to embarrass the government, even while the Assembly is debating their demands. The government, meanwhile, refuses to meet the teachers' 'unreasonable' demands, and the stalemate continues.

Who are teachers involved in the agitation and what are their demands? The agitators are the teachers employed after 1998, and their primary demands are: one, the employment under the Education and Tribal Departments, rather than under the panchayats; two, a substantial hike in their salary. These teachers are employed by the gram panchayats or the Municipal Corporations in order to strengthen the Panchayati Raj system. These teachers are some 1,50,000 in number, and are on strike since 3 Dec 2012. Their starting salary is Rs 8,500 a month compared to Rs 20,000 earned by their counterparts under the Education Department. A seemingly agitated Sanjay Sharma, main coordinator of the Teachers Sangharsh Samiti, an umbrella organisation of nine panchayat teachers associations, says: "we should be given the same (Rs 20,000) salary rather than the panchayat one."

Sapre School Ground in Central Raipur has turned into the 'Tahrir Square' for the agitating teachers of the State. More than 50,000 teachers and their families, including one-year-old, are spending days and nights at the ground. If some spend their time under plastic sheets, the others do so under makeshift tents. Aggressive slogans can be heard, taking a dig at Raman Singh and his government says an angry teachers: "We have been seriously harmed by this government. Our salary is less than what the peons get, and we report to the Panchayat Department even when we are full scale teachers[10]."

Naxalite Scene: 2013 to 2015

This chapter deals with three years of Maoist depredations in Chhattisgarh: from 2013 to 2015; and necessary counter-action by the security forces consequently.

The year 2013 is marked by a successful ambush by the Maoist cadres that came to be known as Darbha (valley) massacre, which decimated practically the entire Congress leadership of the State. Equally significantly, the ambush came to be known for murder of that valiant Congress leader Mahendra Karma who fathered the Salwa Judum campaign which rattled the CPI (Maoist) leaders to such an extant that they made it the target of their vicious attacks. Not only that, their anti-Salwa Commie-liberal and Human Rights activists to appose it even more viciously. In any case, this four-some lobby does not need much persuation to get worked up and froth at the mouth to being pro-leftie and anti-establishment, even if it oceasconally implies anti-national sentiment.

If 2013 is marked by Darbha, 2014 should be marked by advent of the Modi-Government in May of the year. It is a paradigm shift in the Indian polity.

The year 2013

The year 2013 can be divided into three parts to deal and discuss major events and incidents of this year. The foremost, of course, is the Darbha massacre as emphasised in the proceeding paragraphs. So, this year is dealt with in three parts:

- Part I: Darbha Ambush
- Chintagufa fauxpas
- The other events.

Part I: Darbha Ambush

It is discussed in two main parts:

- NIA investigations and conspiracy theories
- Post-ambush events and developments

Congress leaders ambushed: May 2013

25 May 2013, heavily armed rebels ambushed a convoy, which also had most of the Congress leadership of the State, travelling in it. These leaders were returning after attending their party's 'Parivartan Yatra' in restive Sukma. They were ambushed in Jiram Valley of Bastar district, near Darbha.

Some 32 people were killed. The prominent Congress leaders among the fatalities were PCC chief Nand Kumar Patel, his son Dinesh, senior Congress leader Mahendra Karma and ex-MLA Uday Mudaliyar.

Admitting his government's failure, including some security lapses, that led to such a major tragedy, Chief Minister Raman Singh ordered a judicial probe into it. The Prime Minister also ordered immediate probe by the National Investigation Agency (NIA) into this Darbha Naxal attack.

NIA investigations and conspiracy theories

Darbha/Jiram valley attack rank among the worst outrages by the Maoists, especially as it involved decimation of entire Congress leadership of the State, viz PCC chief Nand Kumar Patel and his son Dinesh, Mahendra Karma, ex-MLA Udaya Mudaliyar and that old war horse of Emergency infamy VC Shukla. It was because of this serious blow to the State Government's anti-Naxal credentials that CM Raman Singh ordered a judicial probe into the tragedy. The PM, Manmohan Singh, also gave orders for an immediate probe by the National Investigation Agency (NIA).

NIA wants to question ex-Maoist for Darbha Attack

To put the issues in perspective, three incidents are mentioned here:

- **6 Apr 2010.** 76 jawans killed in landmine blast in Dantewada district.
- **25 May 2013.** 32 people including Congress leader killed in Maoist ambush in Darbha Valley, Bastar.
- **8 Jan 2014.** GVK Prasad alias Gudsa Usendi, alleged master mind of the attacks, surrenders before the police.

"The NIA has sought the custody of surrendered Maoist leader Gudsa Usendi to question him on the Darbha attack". The custody was sought after a special court set up in Bilaspur to hear the cases related to the attack, instructed the NIA officials to record Usendi's statement on a video within 30 days in the presence of a magistrate and a forensic expert.

The move assumes significance since many questions regarding circumstances and the motive of the attack remain unanswered, especially the killing of the state Congress President and his son.

Wavering Stand

The Maoists themselves have dilly-dallied on the attack. They released a statement, two days after the 25 May attack through Usendi, spokesman of the CPI (Maoist), Dandakaranya Special Zone Committee (DKSZE), which said Nand Kumar Patel was killed because of his "history of suppressing the people".

But in October (2013), Secretary of the same DKSZC and senior Maoist Commander Ravulu Srinivas alias Ramanna, called killing of the Patels "a big mistake". Detailed statement by Ramanna will be found at the end of this section.

In big post after the attack, Congress General Secretary Digvijay Singh raised questions about the attack: "The Maoists were not looking for Mahendra Karma (Congress leader and founder of the Salwa Judum, also killed in the attack) but were looking for Nand Kumar Patel. Why were they looking for him who was apparently not supporter of Salwa Judum and atrocities on the tribal people in Bastar? Why did they kill him and his son?[11]"

On 9 Apr 2014, Digvijay told the daily that he welcomed NIAs move to question Usendi: "Any effort that will bring out the truth in this case is welcome". Asked whether the questions raised in his blog still remained, he said he was unable to comment.

In Hyderabad, Usendi, who surrendered in Jan 2014, said he had no role in the attack: "I was not personally involved in the attack; in fact, I was far away when the attack took place".

The NIA had identified at least 100 Maoists who took part in the attack and was seeking the help of Central forces to track them down in Odisha, Maharashtra and Chhattisgarh.

A Word on the Conspiracy theories

In an interesting development, the Maoists themselves came out to reject the conspiracy theories, slamming the media coverage of their activities and expressed "weariness" at making it to the headlines only after such incidents. CPI (Maoist) Central Committee spokesman Abhay say: "what we really want to draw the attention of the people to is the perplexing way in which democracy comes up for discussion only when such attacks happen.... In fact, we are also wary of the manner in which we Maoists also makes headlines only during such incidents. So for a change, why don't we look up at what is happening as a routine in our daily lives to make democracy or Maoism a topic of everyday relevance?"

He pointed at the meeting on internal security and the all-party meet after the 25 May attack that described the Bastar incident as a "direct attack on democracy and freedom.[12]"

In a stinging riposte, Abhay asks rhetorically: "Democracy? Freedom? Whose and what for? Better ask the women who were raped/gang raped and/or killed and the children who have been witnessing and are even victims of atrocities/massacres that are being committed by vigilante gangs like SJ and armed forces on their families and villages?"

Rejecting the conspiracy theories behind the Bastar attacks, he said these are diversionary tactics to shift the onus. "There is no purpose to the conspiracy theories doing the rounds in the media about the reasons for this attack other that diverting the people's attention from the truth", he said.

Jogi under lens in Naxal massacre

Theories suggesting a political conspiracy in the Darbha Ghati (=valley) massacre have not yet been ruled out by the NIA.

The agency which is probing the attack, has even put under scanner a 'padyatra' that Amit Jogi, son of the former CM of the State Ajit Jogi, had embarked upon in Bastar some three years ago.

Since the attack, various theories have been doing the round: ranging from rivalry within the Congress state unit to the conspicuous role of MLA Kawasi Lakhma precipitating the massacre[13].

BJP leaders have gone on record to suggest Ajit Jogi's complicity as both Ajit and Lakhma are known to be close and survived the attack even as almost the entire state Leadership of the Congress was wiped out. While Lakhma was part of the convey, Jogi had taken a chopper ride.

Even though the agency has not as yet found any evidence to support any of these theories, it has kept the investigation open given the circumstances of the case. The agency is waiting for a big catch from among the Naxals to clear the air on the myriad theories. One NIA source only confirmed this all: "we have not ruled out anyone's involvement as yet. Be it Lakhma or anyone else from any party. We are even looking at Amit Jogi padyatra in Bastar. Either he was very fortunate or there were some arrangements that saved his life...We are concentrating on catching the culprits who led the attack...only a senior leader can unravel the truth..."

NIA recently questioned two alleged Naxals arrested by Odisha police in connection with this case. But they were junior cadres who only provided logistic support to Naxals who attacked the convey on 25 May. "They have no knowledge about any conspiracy."

NIA finds no inside hand in the attack

A weekly reports in Jun 2013 that the NIA has found no evidence of any kind of larger conspiracy or the involvement of any insider behind the 25 May attack. The sources say the investigations are complete and report could be handed over to the MHA any day. The NIA has examined many people, including Congress MLA Lakhma who was also in the convoy but he survived.

A senior official said "no conspiracy has come to light... but one thing can be said for certain. It is that the operation was meticulously planned and executed with precision."

However, officials familiar with the investigations stated that lapses in security of the slain Congress leaders have been found.

"The two Maoists arrested from Odisha and mentioned earlier, disclosed that 35 Maoists were called from Odisha to take part in the operation and after the operation was over, they fled to the different parts of Andhra Pradesh and Odisha. They also told the officials that the Maoists had conducted a mock operation just two days before Darbha Valley attack[14].

No SOP violation in attack on Congress leaders: Home Minister Rajnath Singh 7 Aug 2014

The Home Minister on 6 Aug 2014 told Congress leader Digvijay Singh in reply to his question that "there was no violation of SOP by security forces providing cover to the convoy…ambushed by the Maoist on 25 May 2013." More significantly, he also said that the Congress leaders were asked to avoid the route where the attack took place.

He also refuted Digvijay's allegation that proper security was not provided on the route and added "the Congress leaders were cautioned not to use the particular road in Sukma."

The Minister was fielding questions on security forces following SOP in Naxal hit areas. He replied these (SOP) were flexible, depending upon the situation on the ground and the commanding officer was the best judge to take a decision. He informed the Rajya Sabha that six complaints of SOP violations by security forces were received in various Naxal violence related cases. He further said: Government is committed to effectively tackle the LWE problem. The SOP for the security forces during the operations are dynamic in nature and are revised regularly, based on changing tactics adopted by the Maoists."

D Raja raised the issue of arrest of wheelchair-bound Prof G N Saibaba in the middle of the night from the Delhi University some months back for allegedly supporting LWE and asked what operating procedures are followed in such cases. Singh replied: "No SOP is required in (carrying out) arrests. No violation of SOP happened here (in case of Saibaba)", and assured Raja that the security forces are sensitized about human rights of tribals living in Naxal areas."

MOS Home Kiran Rijiju informed the House:

- 131 civilians and 61 security force were killed by Naxal in the current year, between Jan and 15 Jul 2014. 38 Naxals were also killed during this period.
- During this period, 630 people Maoist-related violent incidents were reported across the affected States.
- 809 Maoists were arrested during this period.

(PNS, The Pioneer, 7 Aug 2014)

Post-ambush events and incidents

The Congress Parivartan Yatra to resume

The Congress decided to revive the Parivartan Yatra from Keshlur itself to fulfil the desire of the slain leaders, as that was the place the Congress convoy was heading for on that fateful day, 25 May, before it was attacked by Maoists.

This decision was taken at the Pradesh Congress Committee (PCC) meeting held at the Congress Bhavan in Raipur on 2 Jun 2013. The meeting was also attended by the AICC Treasurer Motila Vora, Union Minister Charandas Mahant and Chhattisgarh in-charge BK Hariprasad. In the meeting, tributes were paid to the martyrs of Darbha attack. Other decisions taken were: Yatra will end in Raipur in which Congress President Sonia Gandhi and Vice-President Rahul Gandhi will be invited; meetings will be organized at all district headquarters on 6 June and block headquarters on 7 June to pay tributes to the martyrs of the 25 May attack.

Congress Converts Parivartan into Kalash Yatra: 4 Jul 2013

"The Congress Party's Kalash (ashes of the Martyrs' to be put in containers) Yatra begins on 4 Jul 2013 from Rajim to pay tributes to the martyrs". It will be under persistent terror shadow as the State "intelligence advisory to the security forces have sounded maximum alert during the movement of the convoy".

(PNS, The Pioneer, 3 Jun 2013)

Even while Rajim remains out of the 'Red Zone' swarmed by the Maoists during a typical attack like the one of 25 May, the threat perception remains as high as issued for any Maoist-infested zone in Bastar.

Intelligence inputs sent to the security forces have warned against threats which are 'non-conventional' and 'hard to predict' in non-combat territories. "Due precautions have been taken to look into every aspect of the threat as also on routes where there is no perceptible history of Maoist violence of any kind during the past decades," sources stated.

The 'Kalash Yatra' would have a posse of plain clothes security personnel to carry out surveillance at every stage while keeping tabs on every movement of those who move with the convoy, they informed.

This is also the first occasion after the Darbha/Jeeram Ghati massacre that security tasks are being totally in sync with minute-to-minute report from the spot as to be reported by the intelligence personnel who would be part of the convoy[15].

"Silence of the Scared'

"Darbha After Shock: More than poverty, it is uncertainty that rules the villagers"

"Chhattisgarh: With the Maoist-government battle set to escalate, life comes to a halt".

This is the title and the blurb, eye-catching but alarming, from a daily of 30 May 2013. Its four opening paragraphs are reproduced below, datelined Dantewada/New Delhi:

- Pusaosaran, a marginal farmer in Chhattisgarh's Dantewada districts, where Salwa Judum founder Mahendra Karma grew up as an anti-Maoists crusader, is a worried man these days. He has to keep both the bands of Maoists camping in nearby jungles and security forces in good humour".
- Since the villagers never escaped aftershock of the blood fight between security forces and Maoists, tension is quite palpable in villages around Darbha in Bastar where the rebels killed 18 Congressmen, including almost the entire state leadership, on 25 May.
- There are more CRPF jawans on the roads than villagers. The local bazaar in Kavalnar, next to Karma's native village Pharaspal, looks deserted. Ganpat Sau, a local trader, says: "Everybody is avoiding being seen in the open ever since the incident occurred".
- The fear of the uncertain is more intense now than ever before as there is a growing perception that the Maoists' guns are now trained on the political class. Even local politicians—friends, protectors, and also exploiters—seems to have lost their nerve. Napu Tula, a district level BJP leader, is thinking of quitting politics. "For me, security comes first".

One is not certain if this is an objective analysis and assessment of the situation vis-à-vis Maoist strategy and thinking on the political class and its elimination. The daily has rustled up this article/analysis based upon one incident of 25 May. In hindsight, we know there was second thoughts on the 25 May massacre of Congressmen within the Maoists' ranks, as will be seen in a subsequent news story. For the time being, it needs to be accepted and recognized that these are views of the two correspondents of the day, which are given in the succeeding paragraphs[16].

The daily further adds, there is no one to answer Pusao Saran's question; "Ware poor. Who will make us feel secure?" in fact, the security forces don't represent him. And the people he voted to power are scampering off to safer places. It is everyman for himself and the devil take the hindmost."

But why did the Chhattisgarh Maoists take such a violent step against the politicians when they had always targeted the security forces? Kumar Sanjay Singh, a Moaist strategy expert, explains: "The morale of the cadre was sinking with more than half the Central Committee members being either behind bars or eliminated. There was need to stage a spectacular strike." And the poorly guarded convoy of congressmen, including Karma and state Congress Chief Nand Kumar Patel, was only too tempting for the Maoists.

What is more, the movement of the convoy coincided with the rebels' annual tactical counter-offensive exercise from mid-March to June, they plan and carry out attacks.

This reason suites them. By the time security forces scramble to launch a counter-offensive, it is time for the monsoon. After the shoot-and-scoot operations, the rebels take shelter deeper in the jungles where the forces cannot enter till the rains are over.

The rains, however, may not bring respite for the villagers this time, as the massacre has made the rebels more blood thirsty and the forces may not wait out the monsoon at their barracks.

The fear is so widespread that even the local administration staff, most of whom are tribals and are at peace with the rebels, think even they would not be spared this time for doing government jobs.

A tehsildar in Dantewada told the daily that some lower-rung officials have already started avoiding field visits. Only doctors appear to be feeling safe. "We treat whoever comes to us and we don't bother about their identity", said Dr Sunil Kumar at Basaguda in Bijapur district.

Amid all this, the wedding session has just begun in Dantewada. But an eerie silence has replaced the Cherry drums and flutes. "We are no stranger to violence, but this uncertainty is killing us", said Phirat, a farmer whose son will get married on 31 May.

Brief Notes

This article carries brief observations which are reproduced here:

Changing Track

- Lately, Maoists suffered serious military reverses. Half its top leaders are either in jail or have been eliminated.
- Many top leaders were reportedly spotted in Sukma and Jagdalpur areas during the past few days.
- Intelligence reported on impeding strikes, 2010 Chintalnar ambush mastermind Ganesh VK warned both the Congress and BJP rallies.
- In change of strategy, top politicians targeted for the first time in Chhattisgarh.

Leaders in danger

- **Oct 2003.** TDP chief and then Andhra CM N Chandrababu Naidu attacked by a special team of Maoists on his way to Tirupati.
- **Nov 2008.** Then West Bengal CM Buddhadev Bhattacharya and Union Ministers Ramvilas Paswan and Jitin Prasade escape a landmine blast while returning to Kolkata from West Midnapore.

"Maoists' rejoicing tinged with disquiet"

Aftermath: Maoists, supporters feel such attacks will invite vicious state wrath.

This is the news story about the hard-headed Maoists being concerned about the consequences for them of their 25 May attack which killed a large number of politicians.

Amid the jubilation over this attack, there is certain disquiet in small section of Maoists and their supporters that such attack will invite vicious retaliation; but more significantly, it way prove counter-productive to the Maoist movement in the long run.

A top security officials tells the daily about disquiet among many Maoists, especially among overground workers and sympathisers… that such indiscriminate killings…harm the movement.

The daily brings in the usual 'suspects' to speak on the question of long term effects on the Maoist movement:

- Binayak Sen, leading rights activists: "Whether such attacks will harm the movement in the long run or not, the Maoists should sit back and assess. While we condemn the attack, it has to be seen in the context and atmosphere of violence…both by Maoists and the State…where non-combatants die."
- Varavara Rao, poet and Maoist ideologue: "As far as the long term impact of such strikes on the Maoist movement is concerned, the middle class may be having some problems with that as it sits over judgements….But there is no problem with people who live with realities on the ground level in Adivasi land who see their rights tramped every day."

The security official mentioned above adds that the possibilities of more such 'spectacular' attacks on soft targets like politicians are increasing in Bihar, Chhattisgarh, Odisha and Jharkhand. (He has given no empirical evidence of this).

Expansion to urban warfare

On their ability to stage attacks on large cities and wage urban Warfare, the security official felt it would be a sign of desperation: "Except in a few pockets of Maharashtra, their urban warfare ability stands destroyed." In the 1990s, the Maoists had erected notable urban warfare infrastructure in Hyderabad under Varanasi Subramaniam, a Central Committee member who was tasked to expand such infrastructure and create expertise. This official continues: "After Subramaniam's arrest in Bihar's Katihar in 2011, no replacement has been made. So their urban Warfare plans are in the back burner as of now....Most senior leaders too are not supportive of such a genre of warfare, and in the past, they have often termed it as 'left adventurism.' "

International Contacts

Recent written intercepts indicate that the Maoists are actively pursuing international contacts too. One such letter speaks of organisations in 27 countries supporting the Maoist movement in India. "They showed their solidarity towards Maoist movement in India, and opposed the Operation Green Hunt by the State", says this letter written in Telugu by one 'Gangur', suspected to be top leader Katakan Sudarshan alias Anand". The letter further reads: "On 12 May, a meeting is being organised in Germany on the problem of political prisoners all over the world. One TKPML (a Communist group of Turkey) is showing interest in organising such a programme."

New IG Bastar : Jun 2013

Newly appointed IGP Bastar Range Arun Dev Gautam took the charge of the office on 5 Jun 2013. Obviously, the State government affected these changes in police and district administration of Bastar in the background of 25 May massacre fiasco.

After receiving training at Jabalpur, the 1992 batch IPS officer Gautam was first appointed as ASP in Bhopal, the then capital of the undivided state of Madhya Pradesh.

It is sad commentary on the professionalism of the newspaper and the journalist behind this story that the name of the erstwhile IGP of Bastar is not even mentioned.

CRPF probe gives a clean chit to its men in Darbha massacre: Jun 2013

After concluding its internal inquiry into the Darbha Ghati massacre of 25 May, the CRPF sent its report to the MHA, absolving its men of any kind of negligence. The CRPF, which is the main anti-Naxal CAPF in the state, had instituted the inquiry following the direction from the MHA, conveyed by Home Secretary R K Singh.

The CRPF conveyed in its inquiry report that "the man deployed in the region did more than what they had been asked to and assisted the local police to sanitise the route of the Congress convoy." This was in reply to R K Singh's letter to DG CRPF Pranay Sahay a week after the attack, asking him to find out whether the CRPF companies deployed at Tongpal and Darbha failed to reach the venue of attack in time.

The report made some observations in reply to the Home Secretary's letter:

- The CRPF company from Darbha was the first responder to the attack and we were the ones to reach the venue on motor-cycles.
- Providing security to the convoy was the prime responsibility of the State police and the CRPF being a Central police provides assistance to them on receiving the request.
- Its inquiry has established that the road opening party (ROP) comprised three policemen from State police and 30 men from the CRPF. The ROP was done 5 km each from Tongpal and Darbha. the distance between the two places in 23 km. Thus, a good 12 km stretch was not sanitized at all. It was on this stretch that the attack took place.

Another point needs a notice sources disclose the Home Secretary had in his letter insisted that the two company commander be suspended immediately before commencement of any inquiry. The CRPF responded this would affect the morale of its men and insisted that they would take any steps only after an internal inquiry[17].

NIA starts interrogation: Jun 2013

A Team of NIA officials 27 Jun 2013 arrived Malkangiri to start their interrogation of two Maoists, "Who were arrested early this week" over their involvement in Darbha attack of 25 May.

The NIA team led by an officer of SP ranked started joint interrogation of the arrested Maoists kosa kunjam and ura Madhi with the Odisha policee.

The two Maoists, who were among the 35 people in the attack, were brought on police remand on 27 June.

New norms for VIP travels in Naxal areas: Jul 2013

In the backdrop of the 25 May attack on the Congress Convoy, the Centre has circulated a new set of SOPs for the Road Opening Parties

(ROPs) in the Naxal-hit areas. It asked the security forces to carry out intensive search operations using 'binoculars' and 'Jammers' during sanitization exercise ahead of any VIP visit.

The SOPs, circulated to all state police forces and CPMF, mandated all precautions during widely-known programmes such as VIP visits, elections and other public functions which politicians and other senior functionaries might be attending. Highest level of alertness was essential for all such occasions.

A committee of Bureau of Police Research and Development, a central body under the MHA, prepared the new guidelines after discussions and deliberations with Army and police experts.

The SOP document lays down: "During a VIP visit, ROPs should open up the area and pickets may be placed at vantage positions, if possible, with Binoculars."

Action against Bastar SP a blow to morale: Jul 2013

This was the view strongly expressed by a daily in its issue of 20 Jul 2013. It says: "Policemen is Chattisgarh are right to feel aggrieved in singling out of Bastar SP Mayank Srivastava over the Darbha attack."

This first IPS officer to be suspended in the state is considered among the state's young police officers, the youngest to win the Police Medal for Gallantry twice from the President within just six years of service.

Surprisingly, even when the NIA and judicial inquires are still on in the 25 May incident, the administration has found him guilty without waiting for the completion of these probes. His suspension order has fixed his guilt, "he committed negligence." A DIG then takes less than a week to complete his preliminary inquiry and find him guilty, without giving him a hearing, "for sending his force to other districts and ignoring providing security to the ill-fated Congress Convoy. Srivastava now faces a charge sheet from the Home Department.

Nobody seems to be pointing out that his force, as from several other districts, had been dispatched to Narayanpur and Bilaspur for providing security to CM Raman Singh's Vikas Yatra, that was due a day after the 25 May attack. The orders for sending the forces had come from Raipur. DGP Ramnivas is simply being disingenuous when he says " Srivastava should have said 'no'". Does he believe an SP can refuse his seniors and political bosses, especially when it comes to CM's rally? Even more importantly, his police bosses knew the date of the Congress Convoy and still sent orders to Srivastava for his force to be sent for the CM yatra!

It is obvious he is being made a scapegoat to deflect attention from the negligence of top police officers. In fact, had the Maoist struck just a few km before they did, within Sukma boundaries, then the very same top police officers would not have any excuse to blame the SP. Here is an important point for note: when the Congress held its rally there (in Sukma) earlier in the day, again with little protection, Sukma SP Ashok Shandilya had not been present. He had been away in the interior forests for a fortnight for an anti-Maoist operation on the orders of his bosses.

It is not unlikely that like Srivastava, Shandilya had little say in his district. At a time when the Centre is considering making district SP as front soldier in anti-Maoist operations, the action against a decorated officer who has spent almost his entire career in Naxalite zones sends the worst possible message. Chhattisgarh can bet it is not just its stressed police force that is matching but also the Maoists!

Maoists tender rare apology: Oct 2013 (for killing of Congress President)

Less than a month to go for the State Assembly, the outlawed CPI (Maoist) issued a rare apology for killing the State Congress President Nand Kumar Patel and his son Dinesh. The apoplogy has been issued by none other than the secretary of the most powerful state committee of the CPI (Maoist) DKSZC, Ramanna alias Ravulu Srinivas. He said this and a lot of other things in a customised interview where the scribe's name has not been disclosed. The unsigned seven-page interview was mailed on 15 Oct 2013 to a daily[18].

The recently-elected Secretary has made some important observations and statements that needs detailed scrutiny, which follows:

- We unambiguously regretted the killing of father and son by their military wing, calling the murder as a "big mistake."
- He also regretted the killing of journalist Nemichand Jain.
- It is an important document, first of its kind after he took over as the party chief. The elaborate document has measured the strengths and weaknesses of the party in south Chhattisgarh. While highlighting the demerits of various government policies, the Ramanna document has also denounced some of the actions of the follow comrades, as noted above.
- "While ten years back, as the Home Minister he tried to suppress our movement, Patel was not opposing us in any personal capacity. Moreover, Congress is out of power for ten years. The senior leader was raising his voice against tribal killing (by security

forces) in Sarkeguda and Edesmetta, the decision to terminate him was not right.

- Being more candid on Dinesh Patel, he says "killing Dinesh was a big mistake. He had not done anything against our party or movement. Fixing responsibility for death of Dinesh, he goes on, "The PLGA command that led the offensive was in haste and took a wrong decision." "Dinesh had no record of anti-party activity."
- Regretting that some innocent people, including some Congress leaders, were killed in exchange of fire…., some leaders were not our enemies…"
- A significant advice, possibly to his military wing, "We need to educate ourselves."
- Commenting on the death of journalist Jain, "the incident illustrate a need to educate cadres about class structure." He acknowledged that "a section of the cadre have surrendered before the enemy, as a result of continuous influx of imperialist culture, uninterrupted psychological warfare, and malicious propaganda using corporate media."
- Secretary Ramanna, who reports to the highest decision-making body of the party (=Politburo), criticised the government's welfare policies like distribution of subsided food or MGNREGA, but landed the role of one democratic institution, Supreme Court of India for empowering the voters to reject candidates. "Even the Court, being part of system, had to accept that people are losing interest in elections. Hence we feel boycotting the elections ought to be part of people's right….The party would boycott the election and resist government's plan to conduct the elections by force in south Chhattisgarh."
- "Allegations of molestation in Maoist camps made by surrendered cadres are fake and baseless. The cadres are tutored by the police once they surrender and allegation are clearly baseless…..In fact, exploitation of women reduced substantially once the Maoist cadres entered south Chhattisgarh.
- Several conspiracy theories were making rounds in the State floated by the two main political parties against each other, after the Jeeramghati, Darbha attack by the Maoists. Consequently, both the media and political parties publicly speculated about some involvement of these two parties or certain individuals. But Secretary Ramanna put such speculations to rest. "There is no

political conspiracy. People informed PLGA about the Congress' 'Parivartan Yatra' (Rally for Change), and offensive was planned accordingly. The Congress and BJP are merely scoring debating points against each on this sensitive issue during the election season. That shows political bankruptcy."

There are interesting observations culled from an important document issued by the newly appointed Secretary of the Maoists. Two comments are offered on it. He is harsh on the Military Wing of the CPI (Maoist). Is it indicative and suggestive of infighting in the Party? Is there intra-party factionalism? Possibility of new equations? A word on the nature and content of the rhetoric in the document. It is the same that started with Marx and Lenin, through Chou and Mao, to Indian Communist's of CPI-CPM variety!

Congress: Make NIA Report Public

Congress leaders injured in Darbha Naxal attack staged a 'dharna' (demonstration) in Raipur, protesting that the NIA report on the issue has not been yet made public. The Prime Minister had ordered NIA inquiry into the May Carnage, and consequently the people found guilty for dereliction of duty have not as yet been punished. Similarly, the probe report of the State Government-constituted judicial commission into the attack too is awaited.

In a memorandum to Governor Shekhar Dutt, they requested him to bring both the reports in public domain and to ensure that the culprits are brought to the book.

"Chhattisgarh Police and IAF in spat over injured cop": Jan 2013: Chintagufa (IAF in poor light)

This is the headline of a story in a daily about "how an injured policeman was left waiting for help by some IAF men",[19] for hours. This was an unfortunate case of disharmony…an extreme term could be, "Bad Blood"… between two wings of India's security forces. So, a detailed examination is called for in this incident of 18 Jan 2013.

To begin with, for some factual details. IAF officials said in Delhi that the helicopter, Mi-17, took off from Jagdalpur in Bastar, Chhattisgarh, at 4.45 PM after receiving a call from the CRPF to evacuate "two of its injured jawans." Around 5.20 PM, the chopper on its way to evacuate "an injured jawans and the body of another personnel from the Chhattisgarh Armed Force (CAF) in Timmilwada area of Sukma jungles, came under heavy fire from suspected Naxals, forcing it to crashland near Puswada village, some 2.5 km from Timmilwada. The chopper took 15 hits, busting its fuel tank and hydraulic system. None of the six IAF men was injured but the wireless operator from the State Police MK Sahu sustained bullet injuries in his stomach.

The pilot was able to land safely at a site in a field between Chintagupha and Timmilwada.

Another report said the copter was on its way to rescue Constable Besuram Mandawi and Assitant Plantoon Commander Nand Kishore who had been injured in a gun battle in the jungles of Sukma district. Unfortunately, Mandawi died before he could be evacuated, but Kishore is getting treatment at a police camp.

Now a brief description of the spat aforementioned: "While Chhattisgarh Police have expressed anguish at the fact that six IAF personnel left behind an injured policeman, choosing to run to the safety themselves, the IAF is furious that its courage and commitment to duty is being questioned."

A senior police officer said, "Our policemen could have died. I can't understand why the IAF men could not carry him (with them) to the Chintagupha camp for immediate medical help." Here is the IAF counter: "The policeman was immobilised. If we had moved him on foot, he could have died as it took us more than two-and-a-half hours to reach Chintagupha due to the dense jungle. The very fact that we came under fire shows that the police had failed to sanitize the area, a pre-requisite for our air assistance to them." The IAF spokesman said: "The crew reached CRPF camp at Chintagupha and informed them of the exact location (of crashland chopper, with the injured policeman inside)…An inquiry has been ordered." The IAF thus accused CRPF and State Police of failing in their duty of sanitizing the area before the arrival of the chopper, leading to its ambush.

It seems the IAF is petty fogging the issue. If the aim was to arrange/ organise help, where was the need for all six to set off, leaving behind a profusely bleeding Sahu. It is of interest to note that the six IAF personnel included two Garud Commandos! How are the two any different from the rest of them, asked an exasperated police officer.

The seriously injured Sahu lay inside the unguarded helicopter for at least two (another report says "three") hours until some 100 CRPF men reached the spot, secured the machine, gave first-aid to Sahu and moved him to a hospital in Chintagupha on a motorcycle.

Considering all the facts/information adduced above, there is no doubt that the IAF has a lot to answer for. Bravado can't help it. A balanced reply is called for, even an admission that somewhere its airmen fell short of high standards of dedication, commitment and camraderie expected of uniformed community of India. Even beyond this all, the higher moral values that inform the India's armed forces, seem to have been dented a bit by the actions of the six IAF personnel!

There was further criticism of the IAF 6. The special CRPF commando unit, that was sent to rescue the MI-17 that had crash landed in the Sukma district after being fired upon by the Maoists, could not locate the machine for two hours, as the 6 IAF men, who had abandoned it with injured Sahu sitting inside, could not provide its exact location. Here is some what "misreporting" by a respected daily[20].

Meanwhile the wireless operator, Constable MS Sahu, kept sending out SOS calls on his communication equipment. For at least five hours, he kept requesting his colleagues to have him evacuated, to just get him some water…Airlifted to Raipur finally on 20th afternoon, his condition is critical, said SP (Sukma) Abhishek Shandilya.

It needs to be said that waiting period of five hours is highly exaggerated. Coming from a police official, an interested party in this case where the IAF 6 are on the receiving end, it apparently is overdone! Calculating everything on the higher side, the total waiting time should be placed between 3.5 and 4 hours: IAF 6 covering 2.5 km to Chintagupha in 1.5 hours; CRPF 100 doing so to reach the spot 2 hours, given their effort to reach the site not known to them; and another cushion of half an hour.

Some additional information

A largely inaccessible forested Chintanlar terrain has been considered a Maoist hotbed since the late 1980s. They had carried the biggest ever attack on security forces in the same area in Apr 2010, where 75 CRPF (and one policeman) troopers were massacred.

The IAF "has deployed six MI-17 helicopters for the last four years" for ferrying troops and casualty evacuation. The chopper that crash landed had taken off from Jagdalpur. This incident comes nearly two years after a chopper was fired upon by the Naxals, and two IAF men were seriously injured[21].

Let this unfortunate incident end on a positive note. When asked if the State Police would take up with the IAF officials as to why their seriously injured Constable was left behind, Chhattisgarh DGP Ram Niwas said: "The IAF personnel did their best to save the situation and we are not going to lodge any protest. We have to work in close coordination."

Two more news story on the spat between State police and IAF are examined

Two other dailies covered this story in their issues dated 21 Jan 2013. Their analyses are detailed on the succeeding pages.

"Probe into why copter was not given Cover": New Delhi, 20 Jan 2013

The first three paragraphs from this daily's news story on the subject read:

- The Chintagupha police has launched an internal probe after it was found that the helipad adjacent to the Timliwad police camp was not sanitized for chopper landing.
- The Maoists had opened fire on the IAF MI-17 copter when it attemped to land there on 18 Jan 2013. After being fired upon for at least 14 times, the pilot landed the chopper 3 km away in the nearby dense jungle. A police constable in the chopper was injured in the attack.
- The six IAF personnel on board the chopper walked back to the Chintagupha camp of the CRPF. Officials said the Maoists used SLRs and. 12 bore rifles to attack the Chopper[22].

ADGP RK Vij tells the daily: "We have started an internal inquiry why the helipad was not sanitised. The Chopper came under attack when it was hovering above the helipad adjacent to the police camp. The Maoists had taken refuge in the nearby village.

A joint team of senior police officials and the CRPF had visited the site on Sunday, the 20th evening. After the attack, the IAF men had told the CRPF that they were not given adequate security cover.

"Earlier too, there have been attempts to attack the chopper. This time it was on a way to airlift junior policemen who had been attacked in an encounter earlier in the day. There was not enough security on the ground even though a hundred policemen were present in the adjacent camp", said a senior police officer in Chhattisgarh.

Officials said a technical team of the IAF, which was repairing the copter, would at least take two more days to make it flight ready.

"We have deployed enough security men to guard the helicopter. The police and CRPF commandos are being put on rotational duty", said the officer.

"Chintagupha faux pas exposes chinks in anti-Naxal mission": Raipur, 21 Jan 2013

This daily opens up with a very damaging paragraph about the functioning of the security forces in their anti-Naxal operations: "There has hardly been a faux pas in anti-Naxal operations in recent months as discomforting to the forces as Friday, 18 Jan 2013, night's tactless act in

Chintagupha area in South Chhattisgarh. Security officials unanimously agreed that there was a 'serious lack of coordination' between police, paramilitary and IAF personne[23].

On the 18th afternoon, during a road opening exercise, the 9 Battalion of Chhattisgarh Armed Forces (CAF) came under heavy firing from suspected Maoists in the Chintagupha area, resulting in the death of Head Constable Besuram Mandawi. To evacuate the injured including Platoon Commander Nand Kishore Bhadoriya and lift Mandawi's body, an IAF Chopper, MI-17, was called from Jagdalpur airbase by the State police. As it was about to land at Temilwara helipad, the Chopper was fired at from all sides by members of the PLGA.

Inordinately close

The close range of the attack has surprised senior security officers. "The proximity of the gunmen was 250-300 mtr from the sanitised zone, and was an inordinately close range", said a senior IAS official involved with the mission. In any conflict area, the security forces are supposed to undergo a 'sanitization exercise' (securing the copter's landing site by area domination) and the standard practice is to sanitize a 3-5 km radius in a forest, an area of 1.5-2 km is normally cleared. "But it is evident that copter was hort from a distance of 250 mtr", said the official.

However, Chintagupha police chief Ram Niwas refused to accept that sanitization, a responsibility of his force, was inadequate. "If there was no sanitization, how did the entire crew survive? Given that it is hostile area, the best possible sanitization was done, and hence velocity (of bullet) was reduced.

A police release said wireless operator of the district police M Sahu, who was inside the chopper, got shot and the pilot had to make an emergency. All six IAF men, including two of the Special Forces Unit, Garud Commandor Force, 'walked to the local police station (Chintagupha) and only at night informed the police of the incident', the release said. The injured Sahu was left alone in the Chopper for five hours, approximately between 5 and 10 PM, until a joint forces of the CRPF (150 Battalion) and CoBRA (201 Battalion) rescued him. The officers and men of the Chhatttisgarh police were left bewildered. "How can one leave an injured comrade in enemy-controlled areas and slip into a safer zone? Even Maoists can't do that," said a senior police officer.

The IAF official, however, said the allegation was a 'perception'. "The captain of the copter did what he thought was right at that point of time. Moreover, these are highly-trained manpower and high value helicopters.

We cannot waste those. So, we feel the gentleman did the right thing by coming out and informing the security personnel", he told the daily on phone on condition of anonymity. The question is why the IAF men left behind the 'high value helicoper' in the middle of the forest. As part of the IAF's SOP, an investigation into the incident has been initiated", said the official.

Ram Niwas said he did not want to involve in a 'blame game in a warlike situation'. That the Maoists had not taken the injured radio operator hostage also surprised the security officials. Questions have been raised about the role of state police as well. A senior CRPF officer said: "It is strange that the police did not go out of the Timilwara camp to rescue Mr Sahu, a member of their force, while being close to the spot where the copter landed".

The other Events of the year 2013; Naxals kill Sarpanch in Bijapur: 2 Jan 2013

Budhram, 45, sarpanch of Mankeli village in Bijapur district was stabbed to death on the 2nd, police said.

The ultras, dressed in school uniforms, attacked Budhram with sharp weapons in Nayapara locality of Bijapur when he was taking a walk outside his house. The site is some 350 km from Raipur. Budhram had shifted to Bijapur from Mankeli after the Salwa Judum, a movement aimed at countering the Maoists in the region, was launched, said Superintendent of Poilce Prashant Agrawal.

Maoists kill tribal Kabaddi Player: Jan 2013

Maoists killed a local tribal kabaddi player during an inter-village match in Umarpal, Rajnandgaon district on 27 Jan 2013 (Sunday). The match was to mark the Republic Day Celebrations. The ultras appeared suddenly and opened fire at the players. Parmeshwar, 30, was killed on the spot and Birbal was injured. Paremeshwar, a resident of Kanker district, was brother of Amrit, an auxiliary constable in Kanker—a direct cause for his being targeted from a short range.

Police was outraged. DGP Ram Niwas said: "This is against all human values. Killing a sportsman for no reason is spreading terror. What was his fault. They talk about anti-Capitalism, but kill only tribals. Have they ever touched any capitalist? SP Rajiv Shukla also reacted: "This is a Kasab-like incident. Local boys were playing in their village. Maoists came and opened fire with their AK-47s. It was a game between local teams, administration or the police had absolutely nothing to do with it. This is among the worst kind of terrorist acts Maoists have ever committed". General Secretary, Chhattisgarh Kabaddi Association Rambisal Sahu condemned the killing.

CRPF officer killed in Red Attack Raipur, 1 Jan 2013

An Assistant Commandant of the CRPF, SK Das, was killed on 31 May 2013 in a Maoist firing at village Khallari, 15 km from Nagri town in Dhamtari district of the State, in an encounter.

Following a tip-off about the presence of ultras in the area, 50 men from 211 Battalion, CRPF were on the combing operations when the Maoists opened fire indiscriminately, leading to the encounter. The attack comes a week after wowing down of the Congress leaders on the 25th.

Anti-insurgency operations in and around Darbha are getting hampered by booby traps laid by Maoists. "Every inch of the area gives an impression that there could be some sort of explosive that might take off if stepped on or even touched[24].

An example of a booby trap: an effigy of CM Raman Singh lay by a tree with a note, '*Hamari jan adalat Raman Singh ko phansi ki saza deti hai* (our people's court orders Raman Singh to be hanged till death).' This was near Narayanpur area. Before the effigy could be taken down, a cow began grazing the area and when it got close to it, the effigy exploded, wounding the cow severely.

"Cyber cops ask FB to remove Maoist page"

Cyber police in Chhattisgarh 1 Jun 2013 sent a request to Facebook authorities to Menlo Park, California, to shut down the account of 'Naxal Chattishgarh' going viral with Maoist propaganda.

The page contains pictures of the bodies of Congress leaders killed in the 25 May attack, and also of a few Maoists. The profile says, 'Hamar Chhattisgarh, Laal Salaam', with numerous 'likes'. There are also a few offers open to users for purchasing, selling, reselling and repairing of arms and weapons. It says, "contact Naxal Chhattisgarh, leave us a message with our Contact details (sic)".

ASP Shweta Sinha said she had received many complaints about the profile. "We are trying to trace the IP address to know who created it and is maintaining its profile", Sinha said.

"Slain Karma's PSO succumbs to injuries"

Senior leader Mahendra Karma's PSO Siyaram Singh who was critically injured in the 25 May ambush of the Congress convoy in Darbha Valley, Bastar, succumbed to his injuries at a hospital in Raipur on 31 May 2013, taking the death toll in the tragedy to 28. Dr. Sandeep Dave at Ramkrishna Care Hospital said: "PSO Siyaram Singh, who had received serious intestinal injuries in the gun fire, died of multiple organ failure in the wee hours." Singh had received bullet injuries which caused infection in several body parts. Ten other injured persons being treated in the hospital since the 25th ambush, are out of danger.

Chhattisgarh Armed Force (CAF) jawan Siyaram, a native of Bihar, was paid rich tributes at Raipur's 4th Battalion, Mana Camp. Maoists "had ambushed a Congress Convoy at Darbha last Saturday (25 May), killing 27 people[25]."

8 Convicted of spreading Naxalism in urban areas: Chhattisgarh: 9 Jul 2013, Raipur

"Prosecution presented 40 witnesses; major success for State Cops; 17 others absconding"

A Raipur Court 9 July 2013 convicted eight persons for spreading the Maoist network in urban areas. This is being seen by Chhattisgarh police as its biggest success so far in cracking Maoist cases.

Of the eight accused, the Court of Additional Sessions Judge ND Tigala found five of them guilty of conspiring to wage war against the government and sedition, and they were sentenced to seven years of religious imprisonment (RI). They are: KS Priya, Meena Chaudhary, senior journalist Prafulla Jha, his son Prateek Jha and Siddharth Sharma[26].

These five were also found guilty of charges that attracted provisions of IPC, Arms Act, Prevention of unlawful Activities Act, and the Chhattisgarh Public Security Act.

The other three—Ramesh Khubwani, his brother Naresh and Dayaram Sahu, were found guilty under the Chattisgarh Public Secruity Act and sentenced to three years of RI.

The police said Priya lived in Durg and is the wife of Gudra Usendi, spokesperson of DKSZC of the CPI (Maoist). Last year (2012), the Maoists had demanded the release of Priya and Meena in exchange for abducted Sukma Collector Alex Paul Menon. In Oct 2010, Priya was awarded 10 years jail for sending Maoist-related CDs to MLAs in the State.

In the latest case, the prosecution said on 21 Jan 2008, Priya and Prafulla were travelling in a car with some bags that contained arms, wireless sets, charges and other equipment. Another Maoist team was supposed to collect them. But when they did not turn up, the two dropped these items at Dangania, Raipur. These were later seized by the police. On the same night, the police raided Maharashtra Mandal in Raipur and arrested Priya and Meena. Based on their statements, the police arrested Prafulla, Prateek and Siddharth.

The prosecution said the Khubwanis have a cloth store in Bilaspur where they stitched uniforms for the Maoists, with the help of Raipur-based tailor Sahu. The police seized 634 mtr of military green cloth. 200 trousers, 107 shirts were also seized from them. The three got bail later.

The police had named 17 others, including Usendi, and some other senior Maoist leaders were also named in the Charge sheet filed on 23 Mar 2009. The prosecution presented some 40 witnesses.

Sadiq Ali, counsel for Priya and Meena, expressed satisfaction with the verdict. "The three have already served their term and should be released soon. The other five have already served five and a half years in prison", he said.

However, many say jail term was less when compared to the Charges. Priya was given 10 years' RI for sending CDs to MLAs, an offence far less serious when compared to present Charges.

They kill three policemen: 13 May 2013

There men of the Chhattisgarh Armed Force (CAF) were killed in an encounter with Maoists in Kauslanar area under Jhara police station of Narayanpur district on the 13th.

ADG (Naxal) RKVij said: "A joint team of CAF and district police had left the police station for an operation, when a group of Maoists in civilian dress suddenly opened fire at this team around 12.30 PM". The fire fighting continued an hour or so. The dead were identified as Head Constable Son Bahadur Thapa and Constables Mahendra Singh and Manoj Singh.

DGP Ram Niwas 'claimed' six ultras were also killed. Such claims should not be taken at their face value. In such cases, the bodies of the ultras, claimed to have been killed by the security forces, are seldom recovered. The police's defence is that the Maoists remove their dead comrades to their jungle hideouts! Maybe, such claims are made for public consumption and to convince their bosses (in police and government) about the brave counter-fight put up by the security forces. Additionally, one may says such claims are made to boost the morale of their own men: If me lost three, we killed six Naxals! As is the case in the instant case.

Tribals detained for Naxal Links: Raipur 15 Sep 2013

Nine tribal people, including two teen age girls, were detained on 15 Sep 2013 by the Dantewada police for the alleged links with the Naxals.

While eight of them were later released, a small farmer, Onga Pandu, and a local panchayat member, Sonuram Kunjam, who were arbitrating on behalf of the villagers, were not.

The police, meanwhile, denied the villagers' allegations, that some of the tribal people were severely beaten up in custody. The villagers, they said, were released by evening after "some interrogation."

A team of 200 police surrounded the Eroli village, 7 km south of the mining town of Kirandul. SP of Dantewada Narendra Khare says: "A meeting of the Maoist cadres took place in the village and our team was sent to investigate the incident." But Eroli villagers denied hosting any such meeting.

An eyewitness told the daily, on condition of anonymity, on phone: "Police entered houses and picked up Gond tribal people almost randomly. None of them had anything to do with the Maoists." He also alleged that those arrested were severely beaten up by the police in custody throughout the day. "Few hundred villagers went to the police station to get them released. After a 12-hour negotiations, they were released[27]."

Maoists set ablaze NMDC Conveyor belt

Dozens of armed Naxals carried out an attack at the NMDC Ltd, India's largest iron ore producer and exporter in public sector in violence-hit Dantewada district on 17 Sep 2013. They targeted Deposit-5 at Bacheli under Bailadila hills. Some 200 MTRS of Conveyor belt was set on fire, around 1 AM. The Maoists walked away free after executing the attack and arson.

After the news of the attack and gun shots in the air spread, NMDC officials, leaders of various trade unions and CISF men as also the fire brigade rushed to the spot. The blazing and wide-spread fire was brought under control after three hours. The officials termed the incident as one of the biggest attacks on the NMDC facilities in the State in recent years. They said production at Deposit-5 could not be started at least for next 15 days. The violent attack caused millions worth of loss to the NMDC. The Corporation has several iron ore mines at the sprawling Bailadila hills which is made up of Bacheli and Kirandul.

"Naxals may subvert Polls:" MHA

Ahead of the November Polls for the State Assembly, the Centre wrote to the State Government on 21 Oct 2013 about intelligence inputs that the Maoists "may have deployed small action teams to attack soft targets, particularly outside their core areas.... Including the helicopters, especially during landings and take-offs."

The Centre wanted strengthening anti-Naxal operations and an awareness campaign to encourage the people to vote, and expressed its concern over a lull in anti-Naxal operations by the State Police, CRPF and BSF. Post the 25-May attack on the Congress convoy, the Centre had drawn up a fresh strategy to counter the Maoist violence, but things had not moved on the ground. The IB inputs had indicated Maoist regrouping in the State and being joined by groups from Odisha and Maharashtra.

The Letter said: "Maoists have been threatening government employees, especially school teachers, not to undertake poll duties. They are preparing for fabrication of IEDs and Molotov cocktails and have already planted IEDs on the main highways and arterial roads." Such reports induced the MHA to mobilize 400 companies of paramilitary forces for poll duties in Chhattisgarh. The other points made by the Centre are as given below:

> "Maoists may target security forces, polling parties, political leaders, besides indulging in arson, abduction of candidates, and looting of EVMs. With a whole-hearted effort and well-planned strategy, their aim will be subvertion of elections."

This time too, they will adopt a well-planned and-practised two-pronged strategy of creating fear-psychosis among the people against voting and also poll boycott campaign[28].

Assembly Polls in Chhattisgarh: Maoist Policy (Voter turn-out higher)

Nov 2013 Assembly polls in the State showed a calibrated approach adopted by the Maoists on the issue. As the following treatment would show, total boycott of the polling by the electorate, as forcefully argued by them in the post, was modified for the November polls.

The districts of Chhattisgarh partially controlled by Maoists—voted overwhelmingly in the polls of 2013. Compared to 2008, voter turnout in 2013 increased by 9.67 percentage points in these 12 constituencies, while the State-wise polling was only 6.81 percentage points than the last one. It is obvious that the rebel-dominated areas embraced democratic process more avidly then the rest of the State. The rise in polling in south Chhattisgarh, where 600 companies of Central Paramilitary Forces were deploy for peaceful conduct of the elections (which was double 2008) was attributed to this huge deployment and also to the reduction in Maoist strength. The credit for the peaceful polls was mostly given to these forces, at least in the first few days after the elections. But subsequently the DGP put the record straight saying credit goes to all sections of the society, rather than the forces only. The DGP said: "We had requested the civil society—

including a few Gandhians — to ask Maoists to exercise restraint during polls." Here are some examples of the way some villages in Maoist-dominated areas, as culled from a daily's report[29].

- **Elengnar.** It is a tiny village 20 km east of road connecting Darbha to Sukma. It was on this road that the 25 May 2013 attack by Maoists had wiped out the entire State leadership of the Congress. Subsequently, the police, during the search operations, picked up several residents from the village, as it is considered a Maoists stronghold. On 11 November, however, 95 residents of this village marched 20 km to vote in the middle school of Tahakwada situated on the Darbak Sukma Road and thus registered 20 per cent polling. (This is in stark contrast to city dwellers who at times finds it difficult to go to polling both a few yards from their houses because it is their siesta time, or weather is too uncomfortable to stand in the queue.)
- **Dornapal.** It is among the villages located deep inside Maoist area. In both 1 to 4 of this village on the eastern fringe of the Sukma district, polling went from 15-30 per cent to 80 per cent.
- **Maraiguda and Puspal.** These villages, again deep inside Maoist areas, had significantly higher polling.
- **Modakpal area of Bijapur district.** This area, where four CRPF men were killed post-polls, too reached 80 percentaged figure.

Two important points, indicating two realities of life in most Naxal-affected states, and Chhattisgarh being no exception, are state here:

1. A senior police officer of Bastar tells a daily: "Like all of us, the villagers in conflict areas have two or more identities. They vote for development and keep quiet while rebels plant the mines." Perhaps a harsher truth has never been spoken so honestly and in a pithier manner.
2. It is an open secret and there is enough evidence to suggest that Maoists put up their preferred candidates in the Assembly polls. While the names of such candidates are withheld for security reasons, a scrutiny of booth-wise results in Maoist strongholds underscores the presence of strong support for a few candidates.

Are the Maoist losing grip? It is an interesting, even more relevant, question. If it is generally believed that Maoists are fading in Chhattisgarh, there must be certain factors and ground realities to strengthen such a belief. Some are suggested here: a decreasing number of ambushes conducted on the forces; contradictory statements from the rebel leaders—simultaneously supporting and condemning the killing's of politicians—indicating fissures in rank and file; killing of leaders and large scale desertion of cadres in some areas; increasing frequency and intensity of security operations in base areas hitherto unexplored by the forces; and the initiation of welfare programmes in Bastar Division. All these "have pushed the rebels to the brink, resulting in a record voter turn-out in the 2013 polls in Maoist 'Country'. But this is one side of this story. Some positives are mentioned in the next paragraph.

But the very officials, who believe that the rebels are losing grip, also concede that their military strength has grown massively over the last few years. Official documents illustrate that during the 2008 polls, Maoists had only three companies in south Chhattisgarh and 13 platoons. In the 2013 polls, the respective figures rose to twelve and 25, plus a few supply platoons. They were also in the process of raising a third battalion. Even more significantly, eight out of 12 political-cum-Administrative Divisions of Dandakaranya Special Zone Committee (DKSZC) are well in place even after a couple of divisions, like the North Telengana Special Zonal Committee, were wiped out in police encounters.

Here are some more interesting, if significant facts of life in Maoist-affected areas. As a result of well-established political and military network, the Maoists "still control half of at least four south Baster districts and one third of the rest. In Bijapur, most of the government-run welfare programmes are not allowed by the rebels in 36 of 147 gram panchayats; government officials never undertake any road construction projects without tacit approval from the local Commanders; tribal constables request the Maoist to protect their families in at least one-third of the district, and surprisingly, polling in the same Bijapur has gone up by 15.5 percentage points!

Did the Maoists ensure calibrated polling? The observers noted that given the facts above, even then, the Maoists did not allow uniform polling everywhere in Bastar Division. Here are some interesting examples: in Bijapur, 47 booths polled less than 10 votes in 2013, while the voting figure was same in 2008 for 58 booths, in Konta, same voting figure was seen in 32 of 193 booths in 2013, while it was so in 29 of 187 booths in 2008; likewise, less than 10 votes were polled again in 13 of 228 booths in 2013, while figure was 6 in 2008. Coming to Dantewada, if 12 booths polled less than 10 votes in 2013, it was 8 in 2008. There are even more surprisingly dismal figures for several booths in bordering areas between the States and the districts—less than one percentage point of the total votes. What could be the reason for this abismal figure? Maybe, the voters were under threat from two Naxal commanders of the neighbouring States/districts! Yet again, in Jagdalpur, while allowing villagers of Elengnar to vote, the rebels obstructed polling in Koleng, Chhindgar or Mundagarh in adjacent panchayats. Clearly, the ultras adopted differentiated for separate booths, rather than sticking to one overarching "official" policy to boycott the elections.

"While it could be argued that many of these booths were shifted out of the respective villages, their reducing the poll percentage, what is puzzling is that Maoists are adopting contradictory approachers"[30]. An analysis tells that while they asked the villagers to walk 15-20 km in some of the relocated booths to exercise their franchise, as in Elengnar, but they resisted polling in some other areas. Preliminary survey of 90 per cent of south Chhattisgarh, booths shows that "rebels have encouraged calibrated polling in some areas for the first times in several decades, while refusing to expose the villagers from robust base areas."

This analyst feels that in final analysis, it could be premature, or too presumptuous, to suggest that the rebels were forced to allow polling uniformly across Bastar. He cites CPI leader Manish Kunjam from Sukma in support of his thesis about Calibrated polling in Maoist areas. Kunjam warns against such "misplaced notions" in a press statement soon after the Nov 2013 polls. "No one would dare to vote despite the presence of a large number of forces, unless the Maoists approve of it", said he, warning against "provoking" the rebels. This analyst says perhaps Kunjam is right, and adds: "The Government certainly needs another round of cooperation from the rebels to conduct another election later in the year (2014) (It may be of some interest here to mention that at the day of this writing—8 May 2014—eight of the mine rounds of general elections for the 16th Lok Sabha stand completed as on 7 May 2014.)

A Journalist killed in Bastar

Maoist killed Sain Reddy, a senior reporter of a local daily, *Deshbandhu,* at a weekly market in Basaguda village of Bijapur district of Bastar Region on 6 Dec 2013. Reddy, in his early 50s, was a native of an interior village, working with this oldest daily of the State.

President of Bastar Patrakar Sangh S. Karimuddin expressed his organisation's outrage and called for Bastar Bandh on the 7th. He condemned the killing and said Reddy was caught in the police-Maoist conflict. Some seven years ago, police had arrested Reddy suspecting him to be a Maoist informer. He was set free later as police could not find any evidence against him. Ironically, a couple of years before this arrest, the Maoists had burnt down his village home, suspecting him to be an informer. He had then fled to Andhra Pradesh. He had returned after a while, and had been working for **Deshbandhu** ever since.

This was not the first killing of a journalist in Bastar, that 'distinction' belongs to Nemchand Jain. When Jain was killed in Sukma in February this year, it raised a huge outrage, compelling the Maoists in March to apologise. So two journalists were killed by the ultras in 2013, in Bastar.

In the instant case, Reddy was visiting his village for the weekly Friday market on the 6th. He was at his home around 1.30 PM when 3-4 youths attacked him with exes and other sharp weapons. Injured badly, he ran towards the nearby police station. The assailants chased him and attacked him again. He died on the way to hospital.

Karimuddin, who knew Reddy for decades on, said, "We owe allegiance to none, still both sides suspect us." Bijapur journalists termed it the "Most cowardly act" of Maoists so far.

A statement issued by the South Regional Committee of the Dandakarnya Special Zone Committee of Maoists, said, Reddy was working with police against our revolutionary people's programme in Basaguda and Usur block for over two decades. He was involved in the Jan Jagran of 1997 and actively participated in Salwa Judum during 2005." Having apologised earlier in the year for killing of another journalist, Nemichand Jain, the Maoists were at pains to explain their reasons for the elimination of Reddy. The statement signed by Secretary of the Committee Ganesh Uike further added: "Reddy was quite active in bringing people to Salwa Judum, making them SPOs and was involved in murder of innocent villagers and creating a network of informers.... Maoists are not against journalists in Bastar. It is not our Party's policy to kill journalists who write against us, neither do we attack their independence."

After his killing on the 6th, Maoists had been suspected for this crime. They issued this statement, trying to justify their heinous crime. While apologising for the killing of Sain in February, they had stated in March: "Our junior cadres had committed this act. The Central Committee is probing the case and would take action against the culprits." Of course, nothing were heard subsequently from the Maoists.

Notes

1. Op cit.
2. Reddy, K. Srinivas, The Hindu, 4.5.12.
3. Rakhi Chakrabarty, Times of India, 6 Jul 2012.
4. Rakhi Chakrabarty, Times of India, 9.7.12.
5. ibid, 10 Jul 2012.

6. Bhardwaj, Ashutosh, Indian Express, 8.7.12.
7. TNN, Times of India, 9 Nov 2012.
8. ENS, Indian Express, 9 Nov 2012.
9. Aarti Dhar, The Hindu, 9 Nov 2012.
10. Bagchi, Suvojit, The Hindu, 17.12.12.
11. Rahul Pandita, The Hindu, 10 Apr 2014.
12. ENS, Indian Express, 20 Jun 2013.
13. Deeptiman Tiwari, Times of India, 25 (?) Jun 2013.
14. Abhinanden Misha, Sunday Guardian, 30 Jun 2013.
15. *Ibid,* 5 Jul 2013.
16. Ejaz Kaiser and Sanjib K. Baruah, Hindustan Times, 30 May 2013.
17. Vijaita Singh, Indian Express, 28 Jun 2013.
18. Bagchi, Suvojit, The Hindu, 17.10.13.
19. Times of India, 20.1.2013.
20. The Indian Express, 20.1.13.
21. The Pioneer, 19.1.13.
22. Vijaita Singh, Indian Express, 21 Jan 2013.
23. Suvojit Bagchi, The Hindu, 21 Jan 2013.
24. TNS, Times of India, 2 Jun 2013.
25. *Ibid,* 2 Jun 2013.
26. Ashutosh Bhardwaj, Indian Express, 10 Jul 2013.
27. Suvojit Bagchi, The Hindu, 16 Sep 2013.
28. The Indian Express, 22.10.13.
29. Bagchi, Suvojit, The Hindu, 6.1.14.
30. Opcit.

24

Chhattisgarh - 3

The Year 2014

The year 2014 also proved fairly bloody for Chhattisgarh in relation to the Maoist strikes.

Two particularly deserves mention being among the worst strikes by the Maoist terrorists, namely, poll-related incidents of 11 Mar 2014 and 12 Apr 2014, and worse still 1 Dec 2014 strike in Chintagufa area. All these will be discussed in chronological order.

Two CRPF and three Naxals killed: Feb 2014

Two CRPF men, Dy Comdt Mohd Nihal Alam and Constable Raju Rawat, were killed and eight injured in a Maoist ambush in Bastar region on 8 Feb 2014, after a lull of nearly three months. They were lured into the ambush by a false lead. Consequently, a joint team of CRPF and State Police left in the morning from Bhejji police station in Sukma district for Bodrajpal village where large number of ultras was reported to be camping.

The ADG(Naxal) said: "They left Bhejji, covered some 10 km when they spotted a hut. They cordoned it off, when a blast, possibly inside the hut, took place.....Maoists also opened fire at our personnel."

The two deceased and seven injured belonged to 219 Battalion, CRPF, while one of the injured is from the State Police.

Bhejji Police Station is probably to most inaccessible in Chhattisgarh. Situated in the middle of an unpopulated forest, supplies and personnel are airlifted here monthly.

In a separate incident, the police claimed to have killed three 'alleged' Maoists in Bijapur district. The operation was carried out jointly by

Chhattisgarh and Maharashtra police forces. They encountered Maoists near Bada Kakler village on 8 Feb 2014. The spot is some 20 km from the nearest police post in Farsegarh. Bijapur SP said, "We had a successful operation. We recovered three bodies of Naxals and returned today." He was speaking on the 9th.

Farsegarh is the last administrative presence towards Abhujmaad forest in Bijapur district—beyond which the Maoists rule the territory. "Security forces have not crossed Farsegarh over the past 6 to 7 years. This is probly the first encounter in this zone." This is the SP of Bijapur speaking[1].

Maoists violence and 2014 Polls

What follows here are some incidents related to the Apr-May 2014 General Elections in India. The Maoists did unleash violence before and during the State Assembly polls. In the impending Lok Sabha elections, they should be expected to repeat their bloody practice during and before and long-running event.

Maoists kill 15 security personel (11 Mar 2014 attack)

Weeks before the poll in Bastar, Maoists launched their worst attack on the security forces in the three years on 11 Mar 2014, killing 15 of them (11 of CRPF and four from Sukma district police) and one civilian. The contingent was pursuing the intelligence inputs and looking for the ultras believed to be concentrated on the border of Bastar and Sukma districts. Some 100 Maoists were involved in the attack.

One security team was deployed for protection of road construction party working on the National Highway 30, connecting Raipur to Sukma. On receipt of intelligence inputs, a 45-member force left the Tongpal police station at 10 AM. They became the soft target in the hostile terrain. Maoists surrounded them and brought intense fire, inflicting heavy casualties, near Takabada village under Tongpal police station, Sukma district. The firing lasted for 15 minutes and the rebels managed to loot heavy ammunition from the dead, including six AK-47, some even fitted with UBGLs, 18 magazines of these rifles, one LMG with 10 magazines, nine INSAS rifles with 30 magazines, two SLRs with six magazines and two wireless sets.

Worryingly, the ambush took place barely 10 km south of the spot (near Darbha) where Maoists had attacked the Congress Convoy, killing 27 people. Days after the attack, the CRPF had set up a major camp at the site. Obviously, this new camp did not improve the security situation.

As is usual in such calamitous situations, intelligence claimed they had sent is accurate inputs, implying certain failure on the part of the security forces. Smart-aleck observations made by ADG (Intelligence) Mukesh Gupta to a daily are summed up here:

> "We knew about it. A road was under construction there. We knew Maoists had assembled there to attack the security detail at the construction site. We had been sending several alerts in this regard. This morning the CRPF company commander discussed it with the police. They decided to go into the jungle, but unfortunately they were caught.

This is not all! Gupta's deputy, DIG(Int) Dipanshu Kabra, adds further minutia, to pat his own back, which seems so silly and uncalled for in the wake of the grim tragedy:

> "Our branch sent at least six inputs from 5 to 9 March about Maoists assembling in the area and the possibility of an attack. A 6 March alert mentions the presence of a noted Maoist Gaganna in the area…and these Maoists can attack a police party deployed for road construction. A 9 March alert also mentioned the heavy presence of Maoists and warned they can launch a planned attack on the security forces deployed for the protection of road construction. Inspector Subhash of CRPF was leading a team of some 40 security personnel. He was also killed. We suspect that Maoists have escaped towards Odisha border. We have launched STF operations to trace them[2]."

One should note in these remarks of the DIG(Int) that not only is he giving day-by-day details of the Intelligence alerts, he is also telling the daily about launching of operations. Obviously, the Intelligence 'blokes' are also briefing the press about matters beyond their remit. May be, the officers concerned with the operational matters are either too traumatised after this tragedy or are too busy in their work. So, the Intelligence people have the entire field available to them to play around. Even beyond this, ADG(Int) Gupta can expand even on matters operational: "It was our bold, courageous step to go in their pursuit. But the terrain and dominant position it gives you has great role to play. If someone has a good weapon and holds a dominant position, he can wipe out an entire company."

A comment is called for on this Intelligence ADG's shallow observations/remarks. A rifleman positioned on a hill can bring down effective fire on the enemy troops on the road down below, but cause fatalities only if his victims are surrounded by the enemy. Otherwise, they can disperse to safety in the neighbourhood. But more importanty, the ADG(Int) does n't explain a paradoxical situation: If 15 of the 45 security men were killed, how did the remaining 30 allow the ultras to loot and take away large cache of arms and ammunitions? Why did not the 30 disengage and regroup to thwart the looters from taking away such a precious booty. Even if the civilian correspondent did not ask such inconvenient questions, the AIG must explain!

The spot has a hill on one side and a ditch on the other. The Maoists positioned in such situation could not be attacked by the troops caught on the road in between.

A Constable quits over 11 March Naxal attack: Mar 2014 (Criticise DGP)

We are living in interesting times! A constable of CRPF has criticised CRPF top brass, its DG, for mishandling Naxal threat to the country.

Constable Dileep Kumar Pandey, presently serving in 43 Bn CRPF in Srinagar, has faxed his resignation to his commandant, with a copy to the DG. Along with his resignation, he has sent a Letter in Hindi, saying, "he is very hurt over the manner in which department is being run and should be relieved from service."

Pande lives in Allahabad (Naini area) and has been on medical leave since Oct 2013, and said, "Itried sending it to Srinagar office of Commandant but could not get it across due to avalanche and bad weather, hence sent it to the DG on 13 Mar 2014." It is indeed interesting, surprising, and more significantly, instructive the way a CRPF constable is ticking off his own DG, as also the mighty Central Government about their inefficiency, smugness and failure to deal with the Naxal insurgency to date! Before reproducing extensive excerpts from his Hindi letter, should one ask if there is a hidden hand behind it? The excerpts:

> "What has happened to the government? In the past four to five years, so many personnel have been killed in Maoist violence. Why can't the Government take tough action and ensure such anti-national forces are wiped off? A personnel is supposed to be disciplined. But that does not mean that their family members do not feel the pain when they get butchered.
>
> "From Dantewada (Apr 2010), when 76 personnel were killed, we know they (Maoists) do not attack us unless they are over 200 in strength. What then is the point in sending troops with 40, 50, or even 75 personnel in those areas? If the government cannot order us to crush the Maoist completely, they should at least ensure the troops are in a position to put up a fight.

The daily tells us Pandey has three minor children and his wife, Seema is a homemaker. As of now, one can't say what action the CRPF would take against Pandey. Will he be allowed to continue in service, or dismissed immediately? Interesting possibilities, indeed!

"There were 400 Maoists in 3 groups": says CRPF

In a detailed presentation before Union Home Minister SK Shinde, the CRPF said days before the 11th attack, the force had acted on intelligence inputs from the State Police about Maoist assembling in three villages, 10-15 km from the site of the said attack, but nothing was found.

The attack by 400 Maoists, divided in three groups, came when they were making security arrangements for a road construction team. One of the groups, comprising mainly of women in black uniforms, fired from behind. "At least three men killed had bullet injuries on their backs. More than 1,000 rounds were fired by their men at Maoists." The CRPF is obviously telling the Minister that their men gave a good fight to the ultras. More comments would appear on this presentation later on.

The presentation goes on: "There were specific inputs on 5, 6 and 9 March that Maoists had assembled at Badegadam, Moranga and Elignar. A team of 300 CRPF and State police went to Badegadam and Moranga on 6 and 7 March but nothing was found. On the 6th and 9th, there was an input for Elignar village which was followed up, but nothing was found.[4]"

Now the telling part, the CRPF DG Dilip Trivedi says: "On the day of the attack, there were no specific alerts. The team was attacked by around 400 Maoists near Tongpal."

The above remarks by the DG at the presentation is point-by-point rebuttal of the so-called intelligence alerts by the State police! After any unpleasant events—be they terror strikes or Maoist violence, killing security personnel…one always hears the Intelligence claiming numerous well-time alerts, implying that, if anything, the security forces failing to act on their alerts! Such 'smartness' does not speak well of the intelligence agencies.

Again, as expected, the DG tells at the presentation that not only were the alerts acted upon, and that there was none on the day that mattered, his force also acted bravely in the face of overwhelming strength of the attacking Maoists. Here are the relevant excerpts from his presentation:

> "The (400) Maoists in three groups were spread over one kilometre. When the first group fired, the joint team of CRPF and State police retaliated. The second lot of the joint team trailing them fired at this group......gradually they retreated. There was firing from one more direction, and the first line of security personnel had to engage with them. While the encounter with the second group was on, there was firing from the third group comprising women commanders from behind."

This indeed is a good description of the battle details, 'proving' that his men acquitted themselves well against the heavy odds. One wonders if the Minister, or anyone else present at the presentation, asked the DG an all-important question about this 'tough' battle! This question was asked while discussing above tall claims made by the AIG (Int) about this attack. He left this question unanswered! Unexplained. When one-third of the CRPF men in battle were killed, why did not the remaining two-thirds prevent the Maoists from looting and taking away a large number of weapons and ammunition of the dead? DG also failed, or did not choose, to explain this discrepancy!

There was criticism of the CRPF on some other counts also from different quarters, that will be covered in the following pages.

Another senior CRPF officer told the press how its men acted prudently in the battle: "Eight IEDs along the road did not explode....They wanted to trap the team and placed IEDs. Had our team not spaced out, all of them would have been killed."

CRPF: Police stalled our plan (Blames Police)

Going beyond its presentation to the MHA, the CRPF in Chhattisgarh says if the State police had not stalled its major anti-Naxal operations in February, the 11 March disaster perpetrated by the Maoist could have been averted. This is the sum total of the statement 14 Mar 2014 by the senior most CRPF officer in the State, HS Siddhu.

The state police had its own reasons not to go along the CRPF. Citing "risky terrain, Maoist threat and unprovoked firing by new (CRPF) troops" that caused two major controversial killings of tribals that sullied the public image of forces, the State police allegedly shot down the CRPF plans for major anti-Naxal operations.

The CRPF's 1G, Chhattisgarh, HS Siddhu 14 Mar 2014 blamed the "senior police officers of the State at whose instance the plan was shelved at the last moment. The latest show down marked a new low in the already frayed relations between the central paramilitary forces and the State police. Siddhu claimed his force had planned a 40-day operation with 3,000 troops across the base zones of Maoists in Bastar. The state police was kept informed from the very start, forces had already left their camps after proper induction training in February but the State's top police officers asked "us to cancel it at the last moment for no reason."

As for the rules, the CRPF cannot launch any operation on its own without a prior approval from the State police. The State police personnel have to accompany the CRPF in all their operations. The CRPF wanted to launch these operations in the base zones of the Maoists in Bastar before the beginning the latter's Tactical Counter-Offensive Campaign in March. The CRPF perceived this as a window of opportunity to destabilise the Maoists and damage their offensive capability before the polls. It was to be a 30-40 day operation to cover entire areas of Bijapur, Dantewada, Sukma and Abujhmaad. Most of these are no-go areas for security forces. Keeping this in mind, we mustered our best men from all over the State to the total of 3000, trained and equipped them for the operation and even issued them necessary rations. They were all assembled at Jagdalpur. Finally troops were on way to Bijapur to be launched from these on 9 February. The plan was to move these troops simultaneously from 20 spots, batches of 150 from each of these. Unexplicably, they denied us the sanction at the last moment on the 9th. "We still waited for two days, asking reasons for the refusal of sanction. When we got no reply, we withdrew our men on 11 February." Siddhu gave these details to a daily[5].

Siddhu's claim seems to be reasonable. "The last leg of this operation was scheduled in Darbha and Tongpal zone around 10 March, If it would have been allowed, the massive entry of forces would have sanitised the entire area and the recent incident (of the 11th) would have been averted."

The daily learnt that no official communication was received from the state police to shelve the operation, and verbal instructions for cancellation were based up a 4-page letter of 8 Feb from Bijapur SP Prashant Agarwal. The confidential letter was addressed to senior officers including ADG (Naxal operations) RK Vij, ADG(Int) Mukesh Gupta and 1G Bastar AD Gautam. When the daily contacted them to seek some information on the issue, the State Officials response was on expected line. Agarwal said: "It being a confidential matter, I can't talk to the media." RK Vij says: "It is very unfortunate that the CRPF Officers are raising these issues of national security through the media. If they had any complaint, they should have raised it with us."

Agarwal's reasons were rather interesting, and some even unconvincing: he cautioned against military adventurism, he did not have enough police force to lend for the operations, and he noted CRPF plan was rather "risky" as "the area being addressed is one of the highly-affected." Significantly, he referred to the two incidents involving the CRPF in his district in June 2012 and May 2013, in which 19 and 8 persons were killed respectively in the CRPF firing. The SP added these incidents sullied the hard-earned image of the security forces, and even thought the "new forces (of CRPF) often open fire without provocation."

The CRPF had initially claimed the victims in both cases were Maoists, later it emerged they were tribals. Both the incidents, alleged to be fake encounters, "are presently under probe by a retired High Court Judge", and took place during Agarwal's tenure.

It is ridiculous that a SP is deciding major operations being risky, as "the risks far outweigh the benefit. The State police top brass confirms that officers of other districts also showed similar apprehensions about the operation and they also repeated Bijapur SP's reasoning—not having sufficient police forces to send with the CRPF in the planned operations.

This is the best example of "how not to fight the operations." May be, it is a question of ego clash among the police officers! The State police, and even the SP, might be feeling the 1G CRPF, also a police officer, was throwing his weight about. It also needs to be noted that there was no system of joint command for anti-Naxal operations in Chhattisgarh. There is no knowing why did not the CRPF discuss this major operation with the State DGP. Keeping them informed is not good enough. Finally, the State's political leadership is, obviously, missing.

Siddhu, 1G, CRPF, saying, "We had been informing the State police from the very beginning and if they had any objections, they could have informed us earlier", is not good enough. Did he inform the DG, CRPF at Delhi? He should have raised the level.

All in all, a sad commentary on our ways to fight the most serious threat to nation's internal security.

CRPF repeats: Police gave no specific inputs

In its first official report to the MHA on the Tongpal, Sukma, encounter of 11 March, the CRPF denied receiving any specific inputs from intelligence. In its report of the 17th, the CRPF did in detail what they had abready done in their presentation on the 12th. This was a direct contradiction of what the State police intelligence had claimed earlier...having sent repeated alerts to the CRPF about the impending Naxal attack.

This brought to the fore the clear rift between the State Police and the Central paramilitary force in Chhattisgarh, the CRPF, primarily responsible for anti-Naxal operations in the State.

Here is an interesting remark by DG, CRPF, "Some local newspapers reported that at least six Maoists were killed in the encounter. We are verifying the report and trying to ascertain the identity of persons named." Is not intriguing that the DG of CRPF quotes local newspapers about the fatalities in the encounter which involved his own force? The papers seem to have even named the Naxal cadres who died! And, pray what is their source of this information. The DG, of course, does not tell the press that the CRPF have seldom recovered the bodies of the cadres they claim to have killed.

NIA takes over probe: 12 Mar 2014

A day after the 11th attack, Home Minister Sushil Kumar Shinde ordered that the probe be transferred to the NIA. "NIA suspects the involvement of the 28 Maoist cadres…who formed the inner cordon during the May 2013 Maoist attack on the Congress convoy…in the 11 Mar 2014 attack also, which killed 15 security men.

A Home Ministry team that visited the State alongwith Shinde on the 12th said "there were lapses on part of the security forces in following the standard operating procedures (SoP). A senior Ministry official said there were specific inputs about the movement of Naxals in the area from State and Central intelligence agencies. The official further added: "After intelligence alerts, security forces conducted more than half a dozen operations but could not lay their hands on any of the cadres. These operations not yielding results made the forces think that it was either false alarm or Naxals have retreated." The State police and the Directors General of central paramilitary forces "have been asked to draw up a fresh strategy to counter Maoist ahead of the Lok Sabha polls. The officials suspect that "the Maoist have started Tactical Counter Offensive Campaign ahead of the polls to garner support, mobilise forces, kill policemen, harvest weapons and attack government installations. After all, it is well-known that "recently Naxals killed three civilians in Khammam, Gadchiroli and Bijapur, and left their bodies to trap policeman."

There were further speculations about identity of certain Naxal leaders by the NIA. It "suspects the role of Maoists who participated in the 2013 attack, who have since been promoted." Out of the 28 Maoists named by the Agency, one was Surinder, head of the Darbha Divisional Committee, and another was Jailal, who was incharge of second Regional Command Company of CPI (Maoist). There is more of the same stuff from the NIA. No suspect had been arrested. Zeroing in on names thrown up by the interrogation of the surrendered Maoists and statements of the witnesses. But the NIA, continuing to play its games, became even specific on details, when there were no means to verify such and other details. Here are its unverifiable 'conclusions':

> "The Naxal team that formed the inner cordon in the May 2013 attack is from Chhattisgarh. Their role has been established from the

documents seized during raids, according to investigators (who, of course, are from within the family).

"Nearly 250 cadres were trained by the Maoists for three days ahead of the May 2013 attack, that killed 27 people, including Nand Kumar Patel, his son Dinesh, Mahendra Karma, and octogenarian VC Shukla."

How one wishes the intelligence agencies like the NIA restrain their temptation to paint themselves to be all-knowing, super-efficient and always-on-the target demi-goods! In real life, they are nearly the opposite! Because of the very nature of the their charter, neither they need to tell too much, nor can people be allowed to ask too much from them. Certain balance and restraint are two traits that should inform their functioning.

As for the MHA, it demanded two IAF helicopters from the MoD to secure Naxal-dominated areas during the polls and sanctioned deployment of additional security forces to ensure their safe conduct.

Yet again, the politician in Home Minister Shinde reacted in a same stereotype 'bombast'. While assigning 11 March Naxal attack to the NIA for investigations, he "vowed to take 'revenge' for the attack! Asked how will he take revenge, he said: "As in the past, the central and state forces will jointly conduct anti-Naxal operations and hunt down the Maoist involved in the ambush....we know where they are." Ministers must resist such statements. To put it bluntly, such 'insane' statements after every terror or Naxalite aggressive, murderous depredations has become the staple of politicians! Let his Home Secretary or DG of the relevant force react to such an attack and they will speak in more realistic manner.

Yet again, he mouthed the oft-repeated and meaningless assertions: "There were reports that the CPI (Maoist) had been weakened....The cadres of the outfit are scared due to presence of security forces and continuous anti-Naxal operation." Notwithstanding these two 'facts' as mouthed by the Minister, the Maoists are still able to inflict heavy fatalities on the security forces and the innocent tribals at near regular intervals/ periods.

Finally, the Minister did utter one verity, against the oft-repeated self-serving statements by the Intelligence agencies: "Contrary to reports, there was no prior specific intelligence input about the Naxal attack in Sukma." One should, indeed, thank God for the small mercies!

Critique: Naxal attack of 11 Mar 2014

The 11 March attack was the biggest launched by the Maoists on the security forces since 26 CRPF men were killed in an ambush in Narayanpur district in June 2010. It is also the deadliest attack after May 2013 on the Congress convoy in the Darbha Valley that led to 27 deaths. The 11th attack occurred barely 10 Km from the spot where the Congress convoy was attacked in May 2013. Both attack polls were timed for elections: Lok Sabha polls were round the corner for the 11th one while the Darbha came amid the build-up to the 2013 Assembly elections.

Critics feel necessary lessons were not learnt from the previous attacks and the patterns to which they apparently hew. This is particularly worrying at a time when the intensity of Maoist violence had appeared to be steadily declining. More importantly that decline (arguably in the face of the twin strategy of wide-ranging joint security operations begun in 2009 by Central paramilitary and state police forces and developmental outreach) had been confirmed by an internal document of the CPI(Maoist) last year (2013) that acknowledged an erosion of manpower and munitions as well as ideological reach.

There can be no room for complacency. They all must reassess their operational planning and practices, and understand the inviolability of the SOPs. It must be clear that the Maoists will continue their guerrilla was as long as the State's writ is not firmly re-established in the affected districts. They will not sue for the peace unless they are convinced about the State's capability and willingness to defeat them in the field. The State should not relent from the project of reclaiming the physical space from the Maoists and restoring normally to the people's everyday lives.

There was criticism on some other score also. One, the force, which moved to the road construction site, unthinkingly moved on the road, instead of moving off it on the jungle trails, sideway route through the forest, as advisable in such situations. Two, former DG, BSF EN Rammohan, makes the same point in more scathing language: "The leader of the ROP (Road opening party) did not follow the SOP and that caused the attack. It is a major negligence they keep repeating." Incidentally, Rammohan had headed the one-man Commission to probe the Tadmetla ambush of Apr 2010 in which 75 CRPF personnel were killed.

A daily pointed out to the gaps between the official version and facts on the ground[6]. Blaming to "hostile terrain" for allowing the Maoists to ambush security personnel, the Chhattisgarh police had said the force targeted on the 11th fought "a very thick battle" but finally yielded to the "dominant position" of the rebels, resulting in the death of 15 men. But the facts on the ground contradict those claims.

There is no hill on the side of the road, or a deep ditch on the other side of the ambush site near Tahkawada village in Sukma district as claimed by the police. Clear fields stretch on both sides for a good distance before the hills begin. The Maoists obviously did not fire from the hill but took positions on the farmland, just metres off the national highway. Policemen engaged in the search operations at the site on the 12th confirmed this fact.

The ill-fated team of 45 men, from the CRPF and district police, has left that morning from Tongpal police station in the morning and headed north when it was attacked after covering some 3 km. While the police claimed that the area was regularly sanitised as road construction work was on and forces were deployed to protect the workers, the Maoists had laid several IEDs on the road, and wires of some were still seen.

The police claimed to have fought long battle. However while 15 policemen were killed, the ultras took away 18 rifles, some UBGL and 64 magazines. "Officers are tight-lipped about the number of rounds fired by the police. But forces present at the site said the resistance was minimum."

CRPF DG told the daily men were killed not because they did not follow the SOP but because "they were outnumbered by the groups of Maoists who could be somewhere around 400."

Another report suggested in Apr 2014 that usually soft-spoken CM Raman Singh almost screamed at the officers: "If you cannot fight even here, what can you do?[7]" The CM was annoyed because 15 men had been killed on an open road with fields on either side allowing clear lines of vision, in an areas that was supposed being sanitised regularly. Forensic examination showed the Maoists had fired from less than 50 MTRs away. Some of the unfortunate facts need to be emphasised, yet again:

- Three of the country's biggest Maoist attacks of the last 11 months have now taken place in Darbha Valley—the worst being the ambush of the Congress leaders in May 2013.
- Darbha is a 50 km stretch of NH 30, straddling the districts of Sukma and Bastar, a patch that has both hills and plain fields. It shares border with Odisha, western districts of which are now considerable Maoist base.
- The CRPF has opened several camps along the stretch, and the road has been repaired and rebuilt. Compared to the sites of other major attacks like Taadmetla (76 killed) and Rani Bodli (55 killed), Darbha is easily accessible and reinforcements can reach

in minutes. The site of the Tongp ambush of 11 March was a 5-minute drive from a CRPF camp. The Congress convoy was attacked 10 minutes from the camp. Yet, reinforcements took 3 hours to reach the site.

- The analyst asserts: "All three attacks happened because of fundamental operational errors.

It is a harsh judgement, passed in hindsight a month after the attacks. But all one knows it could have elements of truth. There is other side to it, too. The Maoists have the luxury of choice of time, date and place. Then, they are highly motivated. They can launch an operation after deliberate planning, launching fully equipped and well-rested cadres into the battles. Opposed to this, CRPF personnel could be out almost daily, at times tired, if not jaded, when countering an operation/ambush. This difference, indeed, is significant to understand as to why the security forces come second best, most of the times, in their encounters against the Maoists.

Maoists strike post-poll: 12 Apr 2014

In an audacious post-poll attack, at least 14 people, including polling officials and security men, were killed on 12 Apr 2014, when their vehicles were blown up in two separate Naxals strikes in Chhattisgarh. They struck two days after polling finished in the state's Bastar Lok Sabha seat.

Thus, relief over the relatively peaceful 10 April poll evaporated on the 12th as Maoists blew up a bus taken by polling officials and an ambulance used by the CRPF men, killing 14 and injuring several others. This was reported by another daily[8].

Some more details

In this first strike, seven polling officials were killed and three injured when the bus carrying them was blown up in the Ketunlar area, 22 km from the district headquarters of Bijapur "The polling officials were advised to walk and not to use any vehicle. But they were tired and boarded the bus, which was blown up in a landmine blast", said Arun Dev Gautam 1GP Bastar.

The second attack also took place around noon in Bastar district, targeting five CRPF men, part of 8^{0th} Battalaion's ROP and two ambulance technicians. Five CRPF men were injured. They were travelling in an ambulance in Darbha Valley, which was blown up in a landmine blast.

Reacting to the tragedy, Chief Election Commission VS Sampth said the Election Commission would stand by the families.

Summary of two attacks

Bijapur District·	Bastar District·
• Bus with people returning from poll duty attacked at 11 AM.	• 100 km away from the first attack.
• Landmine blast followed by firing	• CRPF men were travelling in a 108 Sanjeevani ambulance through Darbha.
• Six killed on the spot. One succumbs to injury later	• Blast kills seven including the two ambulance technicians.

"Did complacence of CRPF men cost lives?

Has the CRPF men acted upon "suspicious movement of two villagers before the ambulance carrying them was blown up by the Naxals in Bastar, the incident could have been averted, according to preliminary investigation.

Five men of the CRPF 80th Battalion were killed. "The preliminary investigation revealed that two villagers were spotted keeping an eye on the ROP, of the 80th Battalion during its operation in the restive Darbha stretch", a senior IB official told PTI on the 13th. He said the CRPF men too noted these two villagers but overlooked them and continued with their operation on Darbha-Jagdalpur road[9].

The official continues: "Apparently, both these suspects must have passed the information to their comrades positioned near Ketunlar village where the landmine blast was triggered."

More details from another daily are given in the nextentry.

Maoists negate their own Constitution

The Maoists seemed to have discarded their Constitution and also a fundamental tenet of their guerrilla war in Chhattisgarh: first by targeting teachers, and second, by attacking medical men. They killed 14 people in two attacks, seven in each, at places some 200 km apart, on 12 Apr 2014.

The first attack came near Ketulnar in Bijapur district around 11 AM. An IED ripped apart a mini bus, carrying poll officials returning from duty in Kutru to the district headquarters, with polling material. The attack killed five 'Shiksha Karmis' (the name used for teachers in Bastar) who had been on poll duty. A forest department employee travelling with the five, and the helper of the mini bus too were killed. Nearly 130 polling personnel were moving from Kutru to Godma, accompanied by security personnel. Later, the polling officials boarded four mini buses. While three of these passed safely, the last one got blown up over the IED.

This attack marks the biggest ever loss of teachers in an ambush by Maoists.

As the officials were grappling with this gruesome Maoist murders, within an hour came the news about another Maoist attack in Darbha, the second in that region in the space of a month. Here, a Sanjivani 108 ambulance was blown up, one of the fleet of specially equipped vehicles that have proved effective in reaching medical aid to the poor in remote areas.

Maoists have fired a Sanjivani 108 ambulances in isolated incidents earlier, but then quickly apologised for the "mistake". They have repeatedly claimed that it was against their constitution to attack medical professionals and teachers.

This outrage is the first instance of an IED blowing an ambulance to smithereens. Over ten people were injured in the attacks who were treated at a hospital in Raipur.

Five men of 80 Battalion, CRPF, taking a lift in the ambulance, were killed in the attack, as were the driver of the vehicle and a technician. These five CRPF personnel were part of a road opening party, returning from Darbha after ensuring safe passage for election party. Bastar SP Ajay Yadav said they had taken a lift in the ambulance because "they were tired." A few minutes later, just about a kilometre ahead, they were dead in the explosion, which left a crater several metres across on the National Highway 30. Police believed some 30 kg of explosives were used[10].

Now the usual critique, which seems well-argued. Some of it has been mentioned earlier too. The attack did raise questions because the area was claimed to be heavily guarded. After all, the very area had witnessed a major attack on a Congress convoy in May 2013 and ambush on a CRPF team this March (2014) itself, in which 27 and 16 people were killed respectively. Importantly, the road was built only some months ago, the IED is likely to have been placed at the time of construction. It might seem unlikely, but it obviously has unnoticed.

Bastar sees 52 per cent polling down from 70 per cent in Assembly polls

The Maoist-affected Bastar constituency registered a turnout of 52 per cent on 10 Apr 2014 despite the rebels' call for a poll boycott. Though the Assembly polls last November (2013) saw a 70 per cent turnout in the strife-torn region, the two previous Lok Sabha polls had lower voter participation: 2004 (47 per cent) and 2009 (48 per cent).

Election officers said many tribal villagers "who ignored the Maoist/ diktat threat during Assembly pools four months ago, did not turn up in this election.

State election commission officials said the threat perception from the Maoist was apparant this time. CRPF officials said the "aggressive and offensive" approach by the forces during the November Assembly polls was not witnessed this time. The official further explains: "During the Assembly polls the forces arrived at least a month in advance. We entered the Maoist strongholds and chased them away but the forces this time arrived very late, in March-end, from outside and in reduced numbers.... This did not give them enough time to get into an offensive action plan[11].

It needs to be noted here that 2014 Lok Sabha polling percentage of 52 may be lower than the November Assembly palls percentage of 70 but it is higher than the ones in two previous Lok Sabha polls of 2004 which was only 47 and for the 2009 which was 48. It is essential that comparison must be between two similar events.

Despite Naxal threat, Bastar registers 12 per cent higher turn-out

This is the headline of another daily covering the same subject as the one covered by the news story of the previous entry by a different daily. Obviously, the present story's headline is more accurate than that of the previous one.

The Paragraph one of this daily's story reads more accurate:

> "Despite the Maoists' call for a poll boycott and a terror threat looming large, there was 12 per cent more polling in Bastar this time round, compared to the last Lok Sabha elections."

This daily gives percentage of polling in each Assembly segments of the Lok Sabha Constituency for this 2014 polling on 10 April.

Bastar	78.86
Konta	31.10
Kondagaon	74.43
Jagdalpur	70.22
Narayanpur	66.25
Chitrakot	65.63
Dantewada	50.03
Bijapur	35.05

The Bastar Lok Sabha constituency comprising eight Assembly constituency segments is spread over six districts has an electorate of 12,98,971, including 6,65,290 women voters[12].

It needs to be noted that something credit worthy is indicated by these figures: The women out-number the male voters! It does not happen in non-tribal areas!

Congress worried over return of polling parties from Bastar: 2014 Lok Sabha polls: Apr 2014

"The State Congress has raised concerns over the inordinate delay in the return of polling parties from Bastar and demanded a probe on 12 Apr 2014. The polling was held on the 10th.

Bhupesh Baghel, President, Chhattisgarh Pradesh Congress Committee (CGPCC), also met with Chief Electoral Officer (CEO) Sunil Kujur and alleged that the State Government was not cooperating in bringing back the polling parties.

Baghel was addressing a press conference at the Congress Bhavan, party's State headquarters.

- He raised a question: Why it was taking more than 50 hours to arrive back at the respective district headquarters when they could reach the polling stations in 12 hours prior to the voting.
- Polling parties were forced to stay in the police camp along with the EVMs and a possibility of manipulation in voting machines during this period can be ruled out.
- Families of the polling parties were anxious to have them back at their homes, and appropriate arrangements must be made to ensure this.

Maoists kill three Commandos: Apr 2014

Less than 24 hours before the polling begins in Bastar constituency, Maoist attacked two places, 150 km apart, in Chhattisgarh, on 9 Apr 2014.

In the first incident, they attacked a CoBRA team of nearly 70 personnel, between Chitagufa and Burkapal, as they were returning after escorting a polling team to a polling booth. There CoBRA commandos were, killed, and three personnel, including the Deputy Commandant Rakesh Singh, were injured. RK Vij, ADG (Naxal Ops), said, on expected lines: "Three constables were killed when they were returning from poll duty. Our men fought well. We expect casualty of Maoists."

Among other weapons, Satellite phones and bullet proof jackets, the Maoists snatched an X-95 assault rifle, an Israeli-made and a highly sophisticated weapon used by CoBRA personnel.

In the second incident, three CRPF personnel were injured in an IED blast in Gangalur area of Bijapur district, some 150 km, away from the first.

Menwhile, Narayanpur police seized two tiffin bombs of 5-kg each.

Unfortunately, the State DGP AN Upadhyaya, did speak like a man who was not very sanguine about the capabilities of his own police! Asked about the possibility of recuring the elections, he said: "The problem has been going on for the last 40 years, no guarantee can be given for this." It is a lacklustre statement. Even a politician could have given better statement on the same subject. The DGP must understand such namby-pamby statement on the capabilities of his force would not have raised the morale of his own men! Earlier, the State Police and CRPF officers had made a different kind of statement: "The Maoists had conducted recce of certain police camps were likely to launch smaller attacks instead of a major ambush."

Soni Sori in polls: A supporter or a Maoist?

It is a problem in India, particularly, while combating Maoist murderers. A good number of 'intellectuals' deem it a badge of honour and distinction to sympathise/support the LWE on ideological grounds, even to act as their over ground arm! When the State acts against them for various infractions of the law, they go to town, crying 'Government's intolerance' of the dissent—a hallmark of a democratic country. This stance of such self-serving individuals, to have it both ways, posing as great liberal ideologues fighting for the liberty and freedom of even murderous Maoists and also unwilling to face the consequences of their anti-national activities, is not acceptable, it is in-fact condemnable.

Soni Sori is an apt example of one such overground Maoist. Here is the story of her arrest and subsequent transit remand of three days to be produced before a court in Chhattisgarh.

Soni Sori arrest and remand

A city Court, Additional Sessions Judge Yogesh Khanna, on Friday 7 Oct 2011, denied bail to a suspected woman Maoist, Soni Sori who was arrested on 4 October in Delhi, and referred the issue of transit remand to the court of Additional Chief Metropolitan Magistrate (ACMM) Naveen Aroa. The ACMM accepted Chhattisgarh Police's plea for taking 36-year-old Sori, charged with sedition for allegedly acting as a conduit between Maoists and private firm Essar, to Dantewada on a 3-day transit remand, but ordered that necessary protection be given to her.

Earlier, seeking bail Sori had said she was falsely implicated in the case and should not be handed over to Dantewada police as she feared for her life. Sori had told the Court that she was a primary school teacher and the police had forced her to make a call and demand Rs 15 lakh on behalf of the Naxals. The suspect claimed that she was let off after she made the call as directed by the police, and thence told to flee Chhattisgarh. That was how she came to Delhi, where she was arrested.

Chhattisgarh Police denied any threat to Sori, and asserted custodial interrogation of Sori was needed, as four cases were pending against her. She was arrested from South Delhi for reasons explained above. She hailed from Dantewada district of Chhattisgarh, a hot bed of Maoist activities.

Soni Sori stands for polls: Divide Maoists

AAP (Aam Admi Party) fields Soni Sori for general elections as its candidate from Bastar in Apr 2014 and the local Maoists get divided. While the North Regional Committee of DK SZC of the CPI (Maoist) "has officially issued a statement opposing the polls and has appealed to people to boycott AAP candidate Sori, Maoists in Darbha and Katekalyan has asked locals to vote for her[13].

Bastar IGP welcomed the development, as the Maoists supporting any candidate means they were taking part in country's democratic process. The issue of Maoist support "is crucial here as one of Sori's campaign managers is known to have close links with local Maoists in east Bastar. He reportedly mediates between contractors and Maoists.

In neighbouring Kanker constituency, sitting BJP MP Sohan Potai was named by an arrested contractor, Dharmendra Chopra, for his close links with the Maoists. Here is something that shows Chopra being on strong grounds for his assertion. Described as a Maoist conduit by the police, Chopra was arrested from Potai's vehicle when he was trying to flee to the Raipur airport. Consequently, BJP was forced to drop Potai in this (Apr-May 2014) poll. The leader who replaced him is the former forest minister, Vikram Usendi, "is yet again another leader named by Chopra as having sought Maoist's support."

Sori has own grouse, perhaps well-founded: "Many prominent people have links with Maoists, seek their active support but never have been arrested. Four were arrested in the Essar case for similar charges; while two influential persons of these four were released within months, I and Linga (her nephew Lingaram Kodapi) remained in jail for two and a half years."

Interestingly, AAP says more than 100 NGOs "recently visited Bastar to campaign for Sori." While candidates of other parties could not visit the interiors, these NGOs moved freely without any security. That helped the non-existent AAP to make inroads in forests AAP'S Bastar convener Anil Singh is exuberant: "We did not face any resistance from anyone." There should be no surprise if two main parties, the BJP and Congress, accuse the AAP of being in hand and gloves with the anti-national rebels like the Maoists and secessionist elements like the Hurryat in Jammu and Kashmir!

Besides other parties' candidates, Sori also faces a challenge from a family member, Vimla Sori, her nephew. She has been fielded by the CPI, which claims to be the sole custodian of the tribal rights. The two belong to the same village of Dantewada, and have huge families. The families and neighbourhood, however, support Vimla and not Sori. CPI fielding Vimla "has baffled many as the Party is known to have better candidates in Bastar, especially its old warhorse Manish Kunjam. Yet they chose relatively obscure candidate, Vimla, who, to the locals, is known as Sori's cousin. The calculations are obvious: Vimla will cut into Sori's vote share, spoiling her chances. Sori says she realised within just two months that politics is very dirty, full of lies and deceits: "you never reveal your true self but always put up a false face. It is also sad the first time I have realised that tribals have lost (their) self-respect. At many places where I went for campaigning, they asked for money. 'Hamein vote ke badle kiya dogi' (what will you give us for votes), they asked. It is so sad."

Martyrdom issue is employed here to play with people's emotion. In Congress posters, debutant candidate Deepak Karma stands with the party vice-President Rahul Gandhi. The background has the photos of their deceased fathers, Rajiv Gandhi and Mahendra Karma were killed violently in the same month of May, separated by 22 years.

Maoist support for the AAP candidate, Soni Sori, is not something entirely unexpected. A number of candidates in Parliamentory and Assembly elections have been receiving support, overt or covert, from the Maoists. BJP condidate Dinesh Kashyap did get Maoist support in 2009 Lok Sabha polls, as was confirmed by BJP's then Dantewada MLA Bheema Mandavi in 2013. Like Deepak, Kashyap too rides on his father's legacy. Kashyap's father Baliram established BJP in Bastar and won the Lok Sabha seat four times, consecutively until his death in 2011.

"Is Bastar, the valley of death" : May 2014

"A 40-km stretch has become the new hunting ground of Maoists"

This is an alarming assessment published by a daily of 29 May 2014, about the increased Maoist threat to the area that stood shocked by the Darbha valley massacre only one back. Here are three opening paragraphs from this news story:

- With Maoists inching closer to the key town of Jagdalpur, the new government at the centre is confronted with a mounting challenge in Bastar.
- "A simple law and order approach to the Naxalite will not work. I only hope the new government is briefed properly on these issue", EN Rammohan, former DG BSF, said on what PM Manmohan Singh termed the "biggest internal security threat."
- A 40-km stretch from the villages of Kamanar to Tahakwada on National Highway 221 has become the new hunting ground for the Maoists. In one year alone, over 60…including senior political leaders, security personnel and civilians…have been killed.

The daily then reminds the readers that the most recent Maoist attack, in which nine persons were killed, came two days after polling in the Bastar Lok Sabha constituency on 12 April, just 35 km from Jagdalpur. "The attack was unexpected and shocking. We were manning all the sensitive points of areas and this blast took place on the main road", said a CRPF official in the area.

A month before the polls, the Maoists targeted a joint team of the CRPF and police from Tongpal station near Tahakwada, killing 15 personnel and one civilian.

This area includes the dense valley of Jeram where 28 people were killed last year on 25 May.

New target (Jeeram Ghati)

"This area hardly witnessed any activity until two years ago. So police presence was less here. This is a thinly populated area with the hard terrain and the interstate boundary only makes the situation complicated, IG Bastar Range Arun Dev Gautam told the daily[14].

According to Kichhai Nanda, a former group leader of the SPOs, the Maoists often target the new area where their presence is hardly expected by the police. He tells the daily: "For over a year, Jeeram Ghati has become their new target, so the security forces will also focus on this area. But it gives time to the Maoists to regroup in their strongholds deep inside forests."

After the 25 May 2013 attack, a CRPF camp was set up near the site. But an officer from another camp says the anti-Naxal operations face several other hurdles.

"Until now, the State government would put the blame on the Centre for Maoist menace. Now that both the State and the Centre are being ruled by the BJP, it will be interesting to see how they tackle this problem, especially in Jiram area", Kewasi Lakhma, a Congress MLA, part of the 25 May convoy, which was attacked last year, said "The tribals must get their rights. Tribal advisory councils have to be set up, " Mr Rammohan, who inquired into 2010 Naxal attack in which 76 police personnel were killed in Chhattisgarh, stated.

In Naxal-hit Bastar, SP uses Whats App to connect with scribes: Aug 2014

It is an interesting story carried by a daily of 12 Aug 2014, indicating innovative use of technology by a police officer, the SP of Kanker (Bastar), to connect with the press on important issues of the day.

Kanker SP RN Dash "has resorted to technology to connect with the journalists. He formed two Whats App groups called "Police News Kanker" and "Police and Press" where he posts messages and photographs related to crime in the district. The groups comprising journalists remain abuzz with discussions as Dash posts nearly two dozen messages from his phone. Most of Dash's posts relates to Maoists, while others are press statements, including details of seizures and surrenders[15].

An average message posted by Dash on "Police News Kanker" invites participation of the members: "Anyone wants to cover a news what they (Maoists) normally do with children in Bastar?.....A NX (Naxal) commander Jani Islam, who was operating in Rawas area of Kanker and recently surrendered to AP police with his gunman—a child who was supposed to be in school—" Dash followed up this message posted on Sunday with a photograph from the police records in which a uniformed Maoist is seen with a child.

"Maoists of neighbouring states are using Chhattisgarh tribal kids as gun fodder. I hope people take up the issue and debate its implications", he told the daily. This is the first instance of an SP of a Maoist-hit district in Bastar using Whats App to connect with journalists.

One must mention what is not mentioned in the text of the message from the SP: The child in the photo is in uniform, with a gun on his lap (the child is sitting with a uniformed Maoist). Nothing could be more illustrative and explicit then this 'child soldier' being prepared to be used as a gun fodder whenever needed or unavoidable.

CRPF Convoy on way to hoist Tricolour in Tedmetla, Sukma face Red-triggered blasts and bullets: 15 Aug 2014

Maoists exploded a landmine and fired indiscriminately along the route of CRPF 1G (Operations) Chhattisgarh's convoy travelling to remote Tadmetla in Sukma district to hoist national flag on 15 Aug 2014. Two CRPF jawans suffered life-threatening injuries. Due to bad weather and unavailability of Dhruv choppers, it took some 10 hours to shift them to Raipur for treatment.

"After the CRPF opened retaliatory fire, Maoists retreated. Despite this, CRPF hoisted the national flag at Tadmetla and held a medical comp for villagers there," said CRPF IG (Operations) Zulfiquar Hasan.

Tedmetla, some 500km from Raipur, is where Maoists killed 75 CRPF men in Apr 2010. For the first time ever, the CRPF hoisted the national flag at Tedmetla in 2013 to signal their domination. Incidentally, the CRPF bagged 71 gallantry medals, highest among Central police forces awarded on the 68th Independence Day. Of the 71 medals, the CRPF got 52 for anti-Maoist operations[16].

CRPF takes action for 11 Mar 2014 Maoist attack at Tahakwada, Sukma district on the eve of 2014 Lok Sabha polls: Sep 2014

There were a total of 16 fatalities in this attack launched by the Maoists on 11 Mar 2014 at Tahakwada. Their breakdown: CRPF 11, Chhattisgarh State Police 4; and one Civilian.

This is an important subject, fixing responsibility for dereliction of duty, so the issue is examined in some detail, as covered by two dailies in their three issues.

"17 CRPF men suspended for Sukma ambush inaction"

This is the heading of a news story as explicit as possible in a daily of 7 Sep 2014. It opens up very meaningfully: "In a rare punitive action the CRPF has suspended 17 of its personnel, including four junior officers, for dereliction of duty and deserting martyred colleagues during a deadly ambush in Sukma earlier this year (2014), in which 11 paramilitary personnel (read CRPF), four from state police and a civilian were killed[17].

The moves comes after a Court of Inquiry (Col) instituted after the 11 March incident (read ambush) in Chhattisgarh stated in its preliminary findings that these personnel (who stands suspended now) displayed "lack of action and did not show satisfactory counter-action" to save their fellow troops as themselves ran for cover.

CRPF DG Dilip Trivedi told the daily, "They have been suspended by IGP (Operations) Chhattisgarh after the preliminary inquiry found them guilty on these charges." The final quantum of punishment will be decided after the inquiry is completed within the next three months.

There preliminary findings have come six months after the 11 March ambush.

It is a rare disciplinary action by the CRPF against its own men deployed in anti-Naxal theatre. CRPF is designated as the lead agency (among the CMPF) for anti-Naxal operations in the country and is assisting the State police forces in this combat for over a decade.

"Those suspended include 14 constables and four subordinate officers in the rank of Inspector and ASIs."

The inquiry was conducted by a Commandant-level officer and recommendations are now being processed by a DIG rank officer related to anti-Naxal operations. Preliminary findings hold "the incident reflected a clear-cut violation of SOPs and soldierly conduct expected from the members of the joint squad. The patrol was ambushed around 10 AM that day and the looted booted the weapons and ammunition from the slain men. "Their conduct during the ambush was sheer cowardice and casualties on the patrol squad could have been minimised had they acted in due manner. Retaliatory action could also have inflicted casualties on the Maoists."

The 11 March ambush brought back painful memories of the audacious 2010 Dantewada massacre in which 76 CRPF men were gunned down in the same area in a flawed operation planned and launched by the then DIG, CRPF and IPS officer Nalin Prabhat.

The 200-strong Naxal group attack the joint contingent of security forces personnel at Jeerum Nullah. The attack came during intelligence alert that ultras have planned a *Chunav bahishkar* (boycott the elections) during the Parliamentary polls (for the Lok Sabha) earlier this year. The area is notorious for the Naxal influence.

The attack was believed to be the handiwork of the Dandakaranya Special Zone Committee (DK SZC) of the banned CPI (Maoist). The committee carried out this (11 March) attack barely 5 km from the spot in which the entire Congress leadership of the State was wiped out.

"Its men dead, CRPF suspends 17 for not fighting Maoists in ambush"

The CRPF suspends 17 of its men for lack of...counter action during Maoist attack 6 months ago (on 11 March) at Tahakwada in Sukma district in which a total of 16 were killed.

This is the first instance of such an action in counter-Naxal operations[18].

The State police have also suspended a head constable (HC) an alleged "Maoist mole" in the force who informed the Maoists about the police movement before the ambush (on the 11th). Bastar IGP SRP Kalluri gave details: "....We have suspended HC Mahadev Nag. He informed one Manjhi Ram Kashyap that forces have left the thana. Kashyap later informed the Maoists about the force movement." Kashyap was arrested a fortnight ago.

Several of the CRPF suspended men have been sent on leave and sources indicated they might be dismissed after the departmental inquiry, likely to be completed within three months.

While Bastar has seen killings of several security men in Naxal ambushes, the Tahalwada incident is different. A joint team of 45 CRPF and state police had left Tongpal police station for a patrol on the National Highway around 9:30 AM. They had barely walked 3-4 km when they were ambushed in a plain area, where there were no hills or forests as in other ambushes. The Maoists fired from behind the small hedges in a field, just 40 to 50 mtr from the road and managed to kill 15 men of the front row in the first burst of fire itself.

It now emerges that the first section and personnel were behind this first section and instead of coming to their help, they stayed behind and later deserted their colleagues.

The Maoists easily managed to snatch the rifles of the slain men.

While Chhattisgarh police and CRPF DGP Dileep Trivedi had claimed after the ambush that the forces fought a brave battle and "the firing took place for over three hours, a report later prepared by Tongpal Thana noted that the encounter lasted for just 30 minutes. In fact the team of 45 personnel fired just 427 rounds in retaliation.

23 CRPF men, Cops 'left without a fight' as Naxals ambushed colleagues

The inquiry into the Tahalwada ambush has found that most of the survivors, who followed the first section that was ambushed instead of helping their trapped colleagues stayed behind and later deserted them.

The probe ordered by IG CRPF (Chhattisgarh) HS Siddhu found out that 23 of the 28 survivors prima facie guilty of "inaction and lack of satisfactory counter action". The CRPF has already suspended 17 of its men, and suggested the police act against six of its men for dereliction of duty.

The probe report also said the deceased men fought bravely and has recommended gallantry awards to 10 of the 11 killed in the counter.

Of the five survivors who were let-off in the probe, three could have been charged with "non-action", but then had suffered injuries in the gun battle.

The inquiry also noted "there was delay in sending reinforcements[18].

Tongpal police camp was only 3-5 minute drive from the ambush site but the reinforcement party, comprising 25 personnel (both CRPF and police) who were present in the camp, "did not arrive in time" "These 25 have not been suspended for now but will face a separate departmental inquiry.... The role of Tongpal Thana is also under scanner", said a CRPF officer.

Interestingly, while 15 security men had died in the ambush, the Maoists snatched 18 rifles, indicating that even some survivors...possibly three in number—could not manage to save their weapons! Did they throw them away to save their lives? It is a legitimate question.

Six AK-47s, some fitted with under barrel grenade launcher (UBGL), 18 magazines of same rifles, one LMG, nine INSAS rifles with 30 magazines, two SLRs with six magazines and two wireless sets were looted—sufficient to raise a company of the Maoists, says the daily.

"Maoists losing ground in Bastar": Sep 2014

"Tribal support waning, say surrendered cadre"

This is the headline of a news story that should give some comfort to the security experts on the Naxal front. But this is entirely based on the statements of some surrendered cadres of Bastar region. The former Maoists also said they, the Maoists are losing support of the tribal communities also.

Despite being the heartland of the Maoists, Bastar has witnessed a wave of surrenders—over 150 in the past three months, the police said usaru koram, alias sutte, former commander of the Maoist military company No. 6, told the daily that the exploitation and discrimination" of the local Chhattisgarh-cadre by the "outsider" Andhra cadre was one of the main reasons for the increase (in surrenders).

"Almost all senior leaders are from AP. In every incident, they ask us to lead and fight from the front, while they keep themselves in the back under security cover", said Usaru, who was involved in six major incidents, including the killing of the SP Rajnandgaon.

"Though tough and challenging life of the forest is driving many Maoists to lay down arms", said Chaitram Salam, former section commander of the Maoists' Central Regional Committee, who was also involved in the Jeeram Ghati attack on the Congress convoy last year that look the lives of senior Congress leaders like VC Shukla and Mahendra Karma.

"Indiscriminate Killing"

Chaitram's wife, Manjula, a member of the Maoists' military company, who was allegedly involved in the massacre of 76 CRPF men near Tedmetla village in 2010, said "indiscriminate killing" of many tribal people was eroding the party base. Manjula said women cadres faced problems from senior leaders.

"The discontinuation of the Salwa Judum campaign had a major effect on the party support base. Many tribal people from Bastar joined the party because of the excesses committed by the Judum mobs", said Sanjay Potam, alias Badru, former CPI (Maoist) Divisional Committee member in the Darbha area.

Maoists kill Chhattisgarh constable in bus said: Oct 2014

Maoists allegedly killed a constable, Shiv Kumar, of 9th Battalion of Chhattisgarh Armed Force, in Sukma district on 18 Oct 2014 morning. Kumar, a resident of Raigar, was travelling in a passenger bus when Maoists forced the driver to stop it near Temelwada. Kumar was asked to get down, and shot dead. The bus was travelling from Chintalnar to Dornapal.

Here are comments of ADG (Naxal) Ops RK Vij to a daily: "He was unwell and travelling in a bus to reach a health centre. The Maoists did not even spare a patient. It shows their cruel behaviour and disregard for human rights."

A police statement informed about the suspension of Kumar's company commander "for not following the SOPs as he allowed the constable to travel in a passenger bus[20].

The 18th incident was the third such incident in the region in the past fortnight.

"Maoists apologise for killing a policeman"

The CPI (Maoist) has apologised for killing Shiv Kumar Sidar, constable with the Chhattisgarh Armed Force in "Sukma district of Bastar last week."

The Maoist killed Sidar when he was travelling to reach a health centre for treatment on the 18th October, as detailed in the preceding entry, and threw his body on the Dornapal Jagargunda road.

The apology was issued by the South Bastar Divisional Committee of the Party: "one of our guerrilla squads killed him near Timilwada without the permission of CPI (Maoist) leadership. We apologize for his death. He was sick and travelling to Dornapal for treatment. He was not carrying any weapon. We consider it our mistake to have killed him in such a situation and we regret it.

The statement also warned policemen posted in the Timilwada and Chintagufa camps against "troubling and exploiting villagers."

In a press statement issued by the Kistaram Area Committee, the Maoists said a civilian of Mettaguda village in Sukma district was killed by the security forces on 20 October: "A joint operation by CRPF, CoBRA, Koya commandos and Grey Hounds in Kistaram area 19-21 October.... The forces killed Sodi Masa of Mellagua village who had come to Palachalma village to visit his relatives, and later on declared him a Maoist[21].

The CPI (Maoist) alleged that the security forces damaged properties of villagers in Goddigua, Kamalafaram, Palachalma, Ampetta, Senempetta, Mangelguda, Sesam, Kasaram and many other villages and demanded transfer of IGP, Bastar, SRP Kalluri.

Woman Maoist surrenders: Oct 2014

A news story headlined Raipur of 26 Oct 2014 "reported surrender of a dreaded woman Maoist, Sita alias Jagarbati, 23, in Dandewada district. The police reported she carried a bounty of Rs 8 lakh on her head.

Sita turned herself in before the police citing atrocities and exploitation of the female cadres by senior Maoist leaders, Dantewada SP Kamlochan Kashyap told the PTI.

Associated with the outlawed CPI (Maoist) since 2010, Sita was working as a member of 2nd Battalion of Mad Uttar Bastar Division in Naxal den Abujhmaad she had been involved in several crimes in the region.

3 Naxals surrender citing ill-treatment by seniors: Oct 2014

Three Naxals, including a couple and a Maoist Jan Militia commander Sukhram Kawde, carrying rewards ranging from Rs 1-8 lak for their arrest, surrendered in Bastar region on 28 Oct 2014, police said.

All three, Manku Kachlam, 31, his wife Anita, 30 and Kawde, 22, cited disillusionment with the functioning of the CPI (Maoist) and ill-treatment by senior cadres as the reason for their surrender.

While Manku and Anita surrendered in Kondagaon, Kawde did so in Dantewada district.

The couple cited ill-treatment by the senior cadres from Andhra. This was disclosed by ASP Surjit Atri of Kondagaon. Popularly known as 'shikshika' (teacher) among the ultras in the region, Anita was a prominent cadre in Kondagaon. The ASP further added: "She worked in Barda dalam of Maoists between 2006-09 and subsequently shifted to Pakhanjore and worked along with ultras of Maharashtra.

15 Maoists surrender: Nov 2014

15 Maoist cadres surrendered before the police and two were arrested by it in Bastar region on 3 Nov 2014.

Bastar Range IGP, SRP Kalluri, informs. "Fifteen Maoists surrendered in presence of senior police officers in Dantewada district.

The surrendered Maoists include Lakhma Vette, who was involved in Jiram Ghati attack on Congress convoy in May 2013."

Maoists fire at IAF Chopper, two injured: Nov 2014

An IAF flight gunner MK Tiwari and a CRPF man were injured when Maoists opened fire at Mi-17 chopper in Jagdalpur area on 21 Nov 2014. The Chopper was evacuating five other CRPF men who had been injured in an ambush by the Naxals in the Bastar region.

The aircraft later landed safely in Jagdalpur where the two were treated. An IAF officer explained: "The Mi-17 Chopper was pressed into action to evacuate five CRPF casualties. On its way back, the helicopter was fired at[22].

The other five the chopper was evacuating were injured during an encounter between a CoBRA team led by CRPF's Chhattisgarh IG HS Siddhu and Maoists in the Elmagunda forests near Chintagufa. The IG's gunman Rupak Rawat was among those injured.

CRPF and state police teams "have been conducting massive operations in the interior zones of Sukma district over the last week." Several teams, comprising over 5000 personnel, have been combing the Maoist hit areas. "Over a dozen operations are going on in Bastar. This was the first instance where we faced such resistance from the Maoists. Our 5,000 men are still present in various areas", IGP Bastar SRP Kalluri said.

Meanwhile, three men were injured while defusing a landmine in Bijapur district on the 22nd.

Earlier attacks

While elaborate security guidelines have been issued to ensure the safety of Mi-17s in Bastar, Maoists have often managed to hit these choppers:

2013: Maoists bring down an Mi-17 in Chintafuga. While IAF men managed to escape, the aircraft remained the forests for a few days before it was retrieved by engineers.

2011: Rebels fire at Mi-17 on operational sortie in Sukma. Chopper loses communication, was reported missing for some time.

2008: Maoists kill an election officer on board a chopper that was deployed on Assembly poll duty in Bastar.

CRPF's worst single day loss this year: 1 Dec 2014

It being the worst loss of this CPMF in 2014, it needs to be examined in detail as reported by several dailies.

14 men killed in Chhattisgarh by Maoists

Sukma: Dy Commandant, assistant commandant among those killed; Rajnath says "personally hurt."

In the CRPF's biggest single-day casualty in Chhattisgarh this year (2014), 14 of its men including two officers, were killed in a Maoist attack in Chintafufa area of Sukma district on 1 Dec 2014 afternoon. 15 other men have been injured, five being in serious condition.

The victims, including Dy Commandant DS Verma and Assistant Commandant Rajesh Kapuria, were from 223 Battalion, CRPF.

"Our parties were inside the forest for an operation when the Maoists ambushed them, fourteen were killed", confirmed ADG (Naxal Ops) RK Vij. The incident took place deep inside the forest, some 10 km south-west of the last police camp at Chintagufa[23].

A large team of over 550 CRPF and state police had left the police camps in Chintagufa and Kankerlanka for the operation on 29 Nov 2014. One party was led by CRPF IG (Chhattisgarh) HS Siddhu. Around 2 PM, 1 December, the security men faced Maoist resistance near Tondamarka village in Kasarpad. Maoists opened heavy fire, and ambush lasted for an hour.

The Maoists also looted a large number of weapons. The forces returned to the Chintagufa camp. The injured and fatalities could not the rescued due to low light.

This incident took place in the same region where seven men were injured in a Maoist attack just over a week back, when they had managed to hit the Mi-17 that was sent to evacuate the injured. "Considered a 'liberated zone', the forces have rarely been able to venture into this area."

Home Minister Rajnath Singh said: "It is a challenge for the country. I am personally hurt by this incident...I would reach Sukma district tomorrow."

The attack comes at a time when Chhattisgarh has been citing record Naxal surrenders in the last six months. "Just yesterday, 30 November, CM Raman Singh had said 'the Maoists would be finished from the state' soon." The CRPF has recently undertaken massive operations in the interiors of Sukma distrct.

Rajnath who was on a visit "curtailed it and is returning to the capital tonight. He will hold a meeting with the senior officers."

The attacks comes a day before the PLGA of the CPI (Maoist) is set to begin its foundation week from 2 to 8 December.

Significantly, a delegation of the National Security Advisory Board is in Chhattisgarh these days to review the Maoist situation there.

Biggest Maoist attacks in 2014

11 March: 11 CRPF men, 4 state police men and one civilian killed in Sukma.

12 Apr: Two attacks in Bastar and Bijapur districts. Total of 14 people, cops and civilians, killed.

1 Dec: 14 CRPF men killed in Sukma ambush.

Tribals used as human shields for carnage

This is the headline of a second daily, giving important information. Here is its assessment in the opening paragraph: "Naxals who are on the run for the past six months in their breeding ground in Chhattisgarh on 1 December used local tribals as human shields to attack a patrolling team of CRPF, killing 14...the team was conducting combing operations in the jungle.[24]

In the evening, PM Modi condemned ....the inhuman and brutal attack by anti-national elements."

A CRPF officer based at the Dornapal base camp claimed the Maoists used the tribals as human shield to attack massive CRPF contingent, who failed to retaliate in full intensity, adding: "The casualties are basically due to lack of solid intelligence inputs. We failed to know that Naxal has assembled in hundreds in the area with sophisticated weapons to take on the CRPF.....We must admit getting a specific intelligence in Left-insurgents-commanded jungle war zone is always a difficult task."

At least six ultras were reportedly gunned down by the forces in the jungle.

It would not be possible to evacuate the casualties till the 2nd morning. Chintagufa is always bracketed as the den of Naxals where they have several major hideouts since the early 1990s "and security forces were scared to carry out anti-Naxal operations in the area till recent times.

Another important observation made by this daily is: "The Bastar region is spread over an area of 40,000 sqkm, and in majority of entire forested interiors, rebels run a parallel government, but in the past six months, insurgents were put under heavy pressure by periodic attacks."

14 CRPF men die in Maoist strike, 13 more grievously injured, bodies still at the encounter site

This is the third daily, with necessary information in the headline. More importantly, it has three observations....blurbs may be a better term....on the top of the news story:

- "Maoists did not use villagers as human shield"
- 2nd attack in 10 days in Kasalpara village.
- The squad has not yet returned to the base camp[25].

The story open with: "Ending an eight-month calm, Maoists killed 14 CRPF…on 1 December"

The ambush took place near Kasalpara village.

"A joint team of more than 200 men had left for an area domination and combing exercise on 29 November. They ambushed on their back to the Base camp", said D Upadhay, DIG, CRPF, Dantewada Range.

Some recent strikes

- 16 November: CRPF launches large-scale operations in Sukma districts.
- 21 Nov.: CRPF contingent attacked, Mi-17 Chopper on rescue mission fired at.
- 29 Nov.: Squad leaves for area domination, combing exercise. CRPF men fire back. Encounter ends at 7 PM. Encounter half a km away from 21 November attack site.
- 1 December: Around 4 PM.

  Maoists open indiscriminate firing as squad returns to base camp, after operations.

14 CRPF men killed in Chhattisgarh Naxal ambush, toll may rise

Hospital 100 km away, injured stuck in jungle. This is news story in 3rd daily.

"A day after Chhattisgarh CM Raman Singh asserted that the state will become Naxal-free soon, Maoists struck in Sukma district killing 14 CRPF men…[26]"

The ambush took place deep inside a forest, some 6 km from Tadmetla, 76 CRPF jawans were mowed down in Apr 2010 in the deadliest single day insurgent attack on the Indian security forces.

The toll could rise as the wounded men will have to survive the night on first-aid at CRPF medical camps.

"The Maoists allegedly used villagers as human shields. Our troops could not retaliate with full force as that would have cost villagers lives", said a CRPF officer.

Red Targets in the past

- 1 Dec 2014: 13 CRPF men killed in Maoist ambush in Sukma district.
- 11 Mar 2014: 11 CRPF men, 4 state police and a civilian killed in Sukma.
- 25 May 2013: Front line Congress leaders in Chhattisgarh killed when their convoy was ambushed in Sukma. They included state Congress President Nand Kumar Patel and his son Dinesh, Salwa Judum founder Mahendra Karma and former Union Minister VC Shukla. Total fatalities: 28.
- 6 Apr 2010: 76 CRPF men, including 1 policeman killed in Darbha/Jeerak valley area, Dantewada district.
- 9 Feb 2006: 8 CISF men killed as a National Mineral Development Corporation warehouse attacked in Jagdalpur.

Paramilitary men killed in action will also be treated as martyr: Dec 2014

Paramilitary personnel killed in line of duty should get the same compensation as that granted to Army martyrs.

This long standing demand has been accepted by the Union Home Minister Rajnath Singh on 1 Dec 2014. The MHA has conveyed this to the Finance Ministry.

They should also get allowances at par with Army soldiers for deployment in 'hard' areas, it has been recommended.

Maoists use villagers as human shields, kill 14 CRPF men

This daily speaks of Maoists using villagers as human shields in the headline itself.

The exchange of fire took place in the jungle 10 km south of Chintagufa.

Maoists guerrillas, claiming to fight for the rights of tribal communities and landless farmers, often engage in gun fights with the government forces in the forested and hilly terrain of central and East India and have a presence in 16 of state's 27 districts, including Sukam[27].

The daily is unhappy: "The CRPF is also without a chief after former DG Dilip Trivedi retired on Sunday (30 Nov)." A counter-insurgency official joins the daily in criticising the government on this issue, requesting anonymity. "Why this ad hocism when daily operations are on against Maoists? The government could have appointed Trivedi's successor at least two weeks before his appointment so that he would have known where his men are fighting."

Last 2 years: Blood bath in Red Corridor

- 1 Dec 2014: covered in the earlier list.
- 11 Mar 2014: covered in the earlier list.
- 28 Feb 2014: Five policemen killed in Dantewada
- 27 Nov 2013: Four CRPF men killed in Bijapur.
- 17-18 Jul 2013: Six people, including three jawans killed in Goh.
- 2 Jul 2013: A SP and five policemen gunned down in Dumka.
- 25 May 2013: Congress convoy massacre, covered earlier.

IAF failed to send Choppers to Sukma

Maoist attack: Officials distressed that IAF Choppers didn't come to their aid on time.

The daily gives details of Chopper availability: "There are four IAF Mi-17 helicopters in Chhattisgarh at any given point of time to assist the security forces during the crisis. At least two Mi-17s always remain stationed at Jagdalpur, the district headquarters of Bastar[28].

However, none of the machines were pressed into service during the encounter that took place on 1 December at Chintagufa in Sukma around noon and left 14 CRPF jawans dead and about a dozen injured.

"There was no Mi-17 Chopper take-off till 6:30PM", one SP told the daily. Several officials deployed on the ground expressed their displeasure and distress at not finding an IAF Chopper flying during the crisis. During such a crisis, a chopper is expected to assist in big way and as a matter of course, but that did not happen. Reasons are known to them only.

Previously, when a number of jawans were injured near Chintagufa some months ago, the IAF did not fly to their rescue.

"And finally, the state government has sent its own chopper, Chetak, to air-lift the injured troopers" a senior officer, not authorised to speak to the media, told the daily.

Repeated attempts to contact the IAF officials based in Raipur for their comments failed to elicit any response.

Chhattisgarh also has indigenous Dhruv Chopper in Raipur, maintained by the BSF.

To put the issue in perspective, other dailies, as noted above, reported that chopper could not go due to 'poor light' conditions.

Naxal unit that killed 76 jawans of CRPF in 2010 was behind Sukma attack also

The 1 December massacre of 14 CRPF jawans in Sukma was carried out by Battalion one of the PLGA, the same CPI (Maoist) military unit that killed 76 CRPF men in Tadmetla in 2010.

The attack was led by PLGA commander Hidma, who along with a cadre of 100 Maoists is learnt to have opened fire on combing CRPF parties from three sides—a local village near Chintagufa, the jungles on the side and from atop trees in the area. As one of three parties of a CRPF company reached near a village in Chintagufa area, it received firing from the village. The CRPF men took position and began to fire, only to realize that Maoists were line up behind villagers. The troops had to thus restrain from firing to save civilian lines, says this daily[29].

Bullets, however, soon began flying from all directions, and the party realized it had been surrounded. A senior CRPF officer explained: "There were bullets coming from the village, the jungle on the side and from atop trees. PGLA had positioned its cadres on trees and they were firing down. Our men were severely outnumbered but fought hard." The officer added that forces too killed 15 Maoists, as per the information received from the region.

The Maoists, however, carried away all bodies from the encounter site, besides looting weapons, ammunition and grenades from the fallen CRPF jawans, said sources.

Preliminary investigations have not indicated any lapse on the part of forces so far, even though 14 lives have been lost and 15 suffered serious injuries. "The place where encounter took place is a Maoist stronghold. It is natural they would have prior information of force movement and would be better prepared to attack us. The operation, too, has been on for days now. We are wading deep into the jungles to register our presence and dominate the area. More such encounters may took place in future", said another CRPF officer.

However, effectiveness and utility of the strategy of swarming Maoist strongholds with large force to register dominance is being debated in the MHA. Many feel large force movements make the personnel noticeable and hence vulnerable to Maoist attacks.

IAF denies laxity in evacuation operation

The IAF has strongly denied any laxity in undertaking evacuation operation for injured paramilitary personnel from the encounter site in the Sukma district.

Even as several sorties by its Mi-17 V5 helicopters airlifted the injured men and bodies to Jagdalpur on 2 December morning, the IAF made it clear that its Choppers could not immediately swing into action since dusk was fast approaching by the time it go SOS alert. "There was no clarity on whether the landing area in the jungle had been sanitized. There is a joint Defence Ministry-MHA SOP in place for such contingencies," said an official.

"The Mi-17 V5s have night-flying capabilities but proper landing facility as well as sanitized zone around it is required to operate the helicopters safely. There is no disconnect between IAF and CRPF on the ground, he added. Incidentally, an IAF Chopper on another rescue mission to evacuate five injured paramilitary jawans in the same area had come under fire from Maoists on 21 November. It was the sixth time that IAF helicopters, which are providing logistical and reconnaissance support to the ongoing anti-Naxal operations, came under attack from the Maoists. The police forces are usually required to 'sanitize' a 1.5 km area around a helipad since the helicopters are the most vulnerable while taking-off and landing.

Surrenders behind Sukma ambush?

It is a known fact that there has been a spate of surrenders in the Bastar region during the last few months, starting Jan 2014. This obviously is the result of pro-active stance of the security forces in its anti-Naxal operations. The surrenderee Maoists give a member of reasons behind these surrenders. It is obvious that behind these surrenders can be seen low morale among the Maoist fighters, possibly consequent to the aggressive posture of the anti-Naxal forces.

Analysts see that attacks by the Maoists around Chintagufa area and inflicting serious damage to the anti-Naxal forces could be a means to boost the morale of their cadres.

Figures: Bastar Division in 2014(till 24 Nov)

Details of surrenders are given here

Jagdalpur	4
Narayanpur	28
Dantewada	54
Sukma	49
Bijapur	40
Kanker	60
Kondagaon	92

Maoist strike: CRPF Blames BSF pilots for 'misconduct', says fire them: 10 Dec 2014

This is an interesting news story that could have been headlined: "CRPF vs BSF." Here is the opening paragraph of the story as carried by a daily in its issue of 11 Dec 2014:

"In an unprecedented action, the CRPF has sought the 'immediate dismissal from service' of two BSF pilots, blaming their 'deliberate and intentional misconduct' for the Maoists attack in Kasalpad village of Sukma on 1 December, in which CRPF lost 14 of its men, its highest single-day casualty in the last four years."

In a 7 Dec 2014 letter to the BSF headquarters in New Delhi, Chhattisgarh's CRPF IG Siddhu has said that a day before the attack, he had repeatedly requested the pilot, Ajay Ramakrishnan, and Co-pilot, Bhupinder Kumar, to evacuate eight of his men suffering from malaria, but they did not comply.

Siddhu contented the attack could have been averted if the men had been evacuated on 30 November. On 1 December, CRPF men had to spend time sanitizing a new "helipad" in Kasalpad village, "exposing the entire party to a grave attack by Naxals", said the letter, which has been accessed by this daily.[30] "Their (pilots') inaction amounts to major failure and was unfortunate and deplorable", wrote Siddhu.

Main points from this letter follow:

- While kumar refused to offer any comment Krishnan could not be contacted despite repeated attempts.
- It is the first time that an officer of a paramilitary force in Chhattisgarh has blamed officers of another central armed police for a Maoist attack and sought their immediate dismissal.
- Krishnan was informed on 29 November that the men needed to be evacuated and was requested "to remain ready in the early morning of the 30th". On the 30th, CRPF officers made repeated efforts, but Krishnan did not attend his phone.
- The CRPF then contacted Kumar and asked him to keep the copter ready for the task. After sanitizing the area, the CRPF called up Kumar at 11:45 AM, and requested him to take off earliest as condition of the patients was serious. Kumar handed over phone to Krishnan who said he would "not be able to take off without clearance of fight plan."
- Siddhu noted that though the fight plan had already been communicated, Krishnan "stated that for new places, he required to first have a trial landing." This came as a shock to Siddhu, "since over many years of work, pilots have undertaken emergency casualty/medical evacuation from new helipads."
- Krishnan later flew the Chopper but "did not come over the prepare helipad" in the forest and "deliberately remained away from that areas" before "turning back towards Jagdalpur."
- "The radio operator of the copter stated that the pilot refused to land", wrote Siddhu, which caused disappointment to troops and exposed them to avoidable extra work of sanitization.
- The men had to move a distance of 20 km on foot, after the failed evacuation. Because of this, the whole exercise had to be repeated on 1 December, causing extreme inconvenience to troops and patients, apart from exposing the entire party to a very grave attack by Naxals on 1 December.
- Siddhu claimed they were forced to consider Kasalpad village for a fresh landing ground, and the attack could have been averted if the troops had not spent time in sanitizing a "helipad" around the village. Earlier, CRPF had said its Kasalpad unit had been "isolated" from the main party and spent considerable time in the village, making the forces vulnerable.

- The Maoists, who were trailing the CRPF for three days, encircled the troops on the outskirts of the village and killed 12 of them in the first burst of fire, besides looting a huge cached of weapons and ammunition, including several UBGLs.
- The BSF and IAF helicopters are stationed at Jagdalpur and make sorties at the request of forces for transporting rations, personnel or rescue purposes.

Comments on 1 December strike by Press

Here are comments on the Maoist attack on the CRPF combing party in Chintagufa area on 1 Dec 2014.

"No room for complacency"

This is the heading of an editorial in a daily that commented on the 1 December strike. Some of the observations are reproduced here[31].

- Maoists guerrillas struck again....killing 14 CRPF men. It came just a few days after CM Raman Singh of Chhattisgarh claimed that day was not far off when his state would become Naxal-free.
- While it is a fact that Naxals have been on the backfoot in the last few months, but even then, to dismiss their strike capability would be a mistake as this attack proved yet again.
- The sustained security operations may have shrunk their areas of influence, still the Maoists hold sway over large swathe of land where the presence of the State is next to zero. Also they are highly motivated and their knowledge of local topography is much better than that of the security forces.
- On the other hand, the CRPF personnel on the forefront of the anti-Naxal oprations, have to struggle agaust too many odds, thus becoming easy prey to such attacks.
- For years governments refused to acknowledge the fact that Naxalite problem has its roots in the socio-economic deprivation that has existed in the large parts of Central and eastern India.
- Even if the acknowledgement has reluctantly come, at least partially, on the ground it is very often being treated as a pure 'law and order problem.'
- As the recent sterilisation-related tragedy in Chhattisgarh showed, the poor and marginalised tribal population in the entire region has little to thank the administration for. Instead of bringing in development, the state has brought more violence into their lives.

- The Naxalites have also treated them as pawns in their fight against the state. As a result, people in the region are caught between the devil and the deep sea.

"NTRO delayed sending UAV on the Day of Maoist attack"

This is an interesting finding by a weekly on the 1 December strike by the Maoists by a weekly. Here is its blurb:

"The Unmanned Aerial Vehicles (UAVs) are needed by CRPF to keep an eye on the Maoists[32].

Opening paragraph of this weekly's analytical story reads:

> "National Technical Research Organisation (NTRO), which has the operational command of Heron UAVs that are needed by the CRPF to keep an eye on the Maoists, failed to send the UAV at the decided time on the day the ultras killed 14 CRPF men in an ambush at Kasalpada village in Sukma district. When it finally came, it left in less than two hours. Sources said the CRPF had asked for the deployment of the UAVs well in advance in view of the anti-Maoist operations that it has been carrying out for the last one month. The UAVs are based in Hyderabad."

A senior officer familiar with the operational situation tells the weekly: "Through proper channels, we had placed our requisition for the UAV to be used over Sukma on 1 December in the time period of 7 AM and 4 PM. The UAV reached Sukma around 12:15 PM, but was recalled by the NTRO at 1:30 PM. Since area domination exercises like these are planned well in advance, we could not ask our team to wait for the UAV. Hence the area domination exercise started at the given time in the morning. If the UAV had reached Sukma at the stipulated time, as we had requested our men would not have walked straight into the Maoist ambush.

The UAV, which transmits live images, if it had reached by 7AM, would have relayed the presence of the Maoists to the CRPF. The Maoists ambush the CRPF squad around 10:30 AM, some 8 km from its Chintagufa base camp.

This serious lapse on the part of the NTRO has caused a lot of resentment in the CRPF top brass, and the dispute has already reached the MHA.

As per the eye-witness accounts, a large number of Maoists, including women wearing Khakis, were waiting for a 200-strong CRPF contingent at Kasalpara village. An officer who was present at the base camp, explains: They caught us in a V-shaped ambush. Initially, we mistook them to be our men. By the time we realised the truth, many of us were caught in the sight of direct fire. After the initial firing, they stopped the firing, and resumed it again when we tried to rescue our injured colleagues. The whole operation was planned very carefully and the Maoists were in control of the situation for the entire ambush period. They fired at our men, killed them, took their weapons and left."

The CRPF 223 CoBRA Battalion, apart from 14 of its men, also lost 10 AK-47s, three UBGLs, one INSAS LMG with 300 rounds, an INSAS rifle with one magazine, 30 grenades of UBGL, four bullet proof jackets, a GPS device and two binoculars.

CRPF 1G Clarifies on his role through his lawyer (From the Hindu dated 14 Dec 2014)

A daily had published three reports written by Rahul Pandita, who was formerly with the daily, headlined respectively, "Jawans were left leaderless in Maoist bastion", "CRPF troops kept waiting while commander met 1G", and with officers killed, troops were in shock" on page 1 and an inside page, all in its issue of 13 Dec 2014. In addition, the same issue carried a fourth article, headlined "The Central Reserve Police Mess" published on 'Comment' page.

These articles made certain references to the sequence of events in the run up to an attack on CRPF men by Maoists in Sukma district of Chhattisgarh.

Responding to the account of the role there of the CRPF's IG (Operations) in Chhattisgarh, Mr HS SIddhu, his lawyer, Mr KK Arora, writes on his behalf, as excerpted:

- In the said news items imputations have been levelled against my client with an ulterior motive to the effect that my client was camping in close proximity of 400 mtr in Kasalpad (Chhattisgarh) with 250 CRPF troops and he chose not to support other CRPF personnel who were being attacked by the Maoists
- It has further been alleged in the said news item that though my client was camping at a distance of 400 mtr from the spot, he reached at the place of incident at 2:30 PM, allegedly about four hours after the incident occurred. The said news item is not based on facts, is plainly incorrect, is a work of fiction, a fabrication and concoction of lies and falsehood. The contents thereof have been deliberately twisted in an unfair and malicious manner to allege dereliction of duty on the part of my client, where as it is not so.

- The fact of the matter is that as and when the news of the incident was communicated to my client, he immediately turned all the parties back to the place of incident and he himself individually was the first to reach the spot with his party. It is notable that my client and his party reached there and provided support to the injured even before other personnel who were part of the party itself that was attacked did so.
- The reality is that my client along with his party including other officers and personnel immediately responded and reached the spot for the reinforcement of the concerned party in spite of being at a distance of about 2 km at the time of incident and exchanging firing with the Maoists who tied to stop their party. That due to this move, the Naxals took to their heels and fled the area. At notime was my client camping 400 mtrs from the spot of incident as reported and published by you noticees.
- It has further been alleged in the said new item on arrival my client merely said...the words "Bharat Mata Ki Jai" and then told his men "Jo Hua So Hua." It is correct that slogans of "Bharat Mata Ki Jai" were raised by personnel but to imply, mean and impute that instead of taking other required measures such as securing the place and attending to the injured etc, mouthing these words was the only action taken is a blatant lie. My client took proper action on reaching the spot, exhorted the troops to be steadfast and courageous and did not behave in the manner reported by you.
- By quoting an anonymous commando in this regard in the said news items, you noticees, have tried to convey a false message to the public as well as to the persons acquainted with my client, including his seniors that my client adopted a casual approach towards the incident itself as well as troops who were martyred/ injured in the Maoist attack.
- Where as my client has acted correctly and appropriately after reaching the incident spot. Further, since his posting as IG (Operations) CRPF in Chhattisgarh, has made strong efforts to curb the menace of Maoist terrorism in Chhattisgarh. He has personally led his troops from the front in various operations and encouraged his troops in the nation's fight against Maoists. My client always acted courageously in the fight against the Maoists and is the senior most officer in the CRPF to have ever personally led operations against Maoists at the ground level in the most risk-prone areas".

At the end of this letter from the IG's lawyer, the daily adds a bracketed remark and close the issue between the IG and his daily. The remarks follow.

(The Hindu regrets any inaccuracies that have crept into the reports. – Editor-in-Chief)

The year 2015

Some of the more important events and incidents related to the Maoist violence are detailed in the succeeding pages in the chronological order.

Villagers accuse forces of killing tribal in Chhattisgarh: Jan 2015

The death of a tribal, Nupo Bhima, in Dantewada district has stirred a controversy in the area. Bhima was shot dead 6 Jan 2015 in Revali village. While villagers alleged security forces killed him, the police said Maoists killed him. Consequently, the Maoists have pushed villagers to protest against the forces.

The FIR filed at Nakulnar police station says Bhima was killed by un-identified Maoists, but the villagers accuse police of fudging the FIR. Over a thousand villagers held a march from the village to the Nakulnar station on 17 January and demanded a fresh FIR.

Bhima's wife Nupo Budhri claimed she was present at the spot when forces killed her husband. Another villager supported her: "The police filed a wrong FIR. They blamed Maoists in the FIR. It should be security forces..."

Dantewada SP Kamlochan Kashyap admitted that "security forces patrolled the area that day, but it is Maoists who killed Bhima. The Maoist are now persuading villagers to blame the police." The SP further adds: "The FIR was duly written by Nakulnar police in the presence of villagers and the Deputy Sarpanch...villagers dictated the FIR in Gondi language and the Deputy Sarpanch translated it in Hindi. We duly narrated the text after filing it. Why would we change the FIR?"

Aam Admi Party leader Soni Sori has galvanized villagers and also participated in the protest march.

Naxals kill 7 of elite force in Sukma: Apr 2014

"Maoists ambush STP party, force personnel to retreat, leaving bodies in the jungle"

Seven men of Chhattisgarh's elite Special Task Force (STF) were killed and 10 injured in a Maoist ambush 11 Apr 2014 morning in Sukma district, in the biggest attack on security forces this year (2015) in the State. The bodies had not been recovered till the 11th night. The site of ambush, in forests near Pidmel village, is 11 km from the Kankerlanka police station.

This is the STF's biggest single-day casualty in several years. The contingent numbering 60, was attacked between 9 and 10 AM by cadres suspected to belong to the CPI (Maoist)'s South Bastar Battalion, headed by Hidma.

The STF men were forced to retreat, leaving their dead comrades behind. Maoists also looted several quality weapons and ammunition.

A massive contingent of forces is now being deployed to retrieve the bodies. But the exercise will have to wait till the 12th morning, nearly 24 hours after the incident. The delay is forced by the intervening night of 11 and 12 Apr.

Among the deceased is STF Platoon Commander Shankar Rao, popularly called 'Fighter Rao' by his colleagues. ADG (Naxal Ops) RK Vij said: "He was extremely courageous. We lost a brave man."

The others killed were Head Constables Rohit Sori, Mohan Vike, and Manoj Baghel, and Constables Rajman Tekam, Kiran Deshmukh and Rajkumar Markam.

Rao left the Polampalli police camp with his 60-strong team, at 2:30 AM on the 11th and headed into interior forests. If some police officers said the Platoon Commander was acting on a specific intelligence input, others questioned the wisdom of going into the forests at that time of the day with just 6o men.

After the first encounter in which most deaths happened, the "SRF men tried to retreat but continued to face Maoist fire for nearly an hour more. A couple of more men died in these encounters."

The injured men reached Kankerlanka in the afternoon and "were airlifted to Raipur hours later."

It was in the same area Sukma, that CRPF had lost 14 men in Dec 2013, while in 2010, Naxals had killed 76 CRPF men in the biggest ever attack and biggest ever fatalities.

"Forces retrieve bodies after long wait"

Pilmed (Sukma): 12 Apr 2014; Sukma Encounter 11 April: Maoists allowed CRPF to take back bodies only after five hours.

The security forces on the Maoist front had one of their most helpless moments on 12 April when nearly 300 heavily armed men of CRPF and

Chhattisgarh STF had to wait for hours before the Maoists allowed them to take the bodies away. The 300 men armed with top weapons like X-95 rifles, 51 MM mortars and Carl Gustav Grenade Launchers, reached the site between 10 and 11 AM, 12th April, but the Maoists denied them permission before they relented after a few hours.

The jawans could begin their return journey, with bodies on their shoulders, only around 3 PM.

"Permission hi nahin diya. Kai ghanta bithaya rakha" (They did not give us permission. Made us sit for hours), said Raju Nayak, who was the first to reach the spot with his tractor with a few journalists. Before the personnel reached Pilmed, senior police officers had requested journalists to ensure that bodies are safely recovered. Some journalists arranged two tractors and reached Pilmed but the Maoists refused to hand over the bodies. Dornapal-based journalist Raja Rathore, among those who first reached Pilmed, was told so.

A similar incident had taken place in Apr 2013, when the Andhra Pradesh Grey Hounds could not collect the body of their commando killed in a Maoist ambush. A Bijapur-based journalist had then gone, following the request of the AP police, and brought the body back on a tractor[33].

"Today, as was the case in Apr 2013, the Maoists were not at the spot, but stationed at least a few km away. Still, they controlled the scene through local villagers.

Sitting amid bushes and trees, the personnel talked about the possible options if they were eventually denied the permission.

The site was 60 km from district headquarters. Last night, several special contingents of the CRPF had reached Polampalli station in ambulances following Home Minister Rajnath Singh's directive.

It was around 1:30 PM that the rebels relented. The policemen started collecting the bodies, scattered over 4 sq km area, indicating the length and massiveness of the ambush.

An injured jawan confirmed that as they left Polampalli station around 12 AM on the 11th, they were trapped by the Maoists through a false input. "Around 1.40 AM, the Platoon Commander came to us and asked us to move immediately. We walked for a few hours before we came across some villagers who suddenly began running away from us. We chased them but they disappeared. We then decided to take some rest at a hillock, and suddenly firing began from all sides. We were trapped", said a constable admitted in a Raipur hospital.

At Pilmed, some jawans first thought of calling a Chopper for airlifting the bodies. But aircraft landing could be risky. So they decided to carry the deceased on their shoulders, on improvised stretchers made from tree branches. It was a long journey through forests and rivulets. They were cautious, entire contingent was spread across several sq km, with those carrying the bodies in the middle.

"Cops misread situation in hunt for top Maoists"

New Delhi, 12 April A day after the Sukma incident in which seven STF men were killed by the Maoists, a senior official said Chhattisgarh police probably misread the situation as only 49 men were put on the job to catch Hidma, one of the most wanted Maoist commander in the area[34].

Though the police did not inform the CRPF about the operation, as they were well within their rights to do, it was a well-known fact that Hidma always moved around with a large number of men, more than a hundred armed cadre, said the official.

"After STF suffered casualties, they sought CRPF help and a team of CoBRA commandos were rushed to the encounter site. The CRPF helped in taking the injured to the hospital and even retrieved the bodies of the STF jawans which were lying at the encounter site for more than 24 hours", said the official.

Hidma is also said to be involved in one of the worst attacks on forces in 2010 when 76 CRPF men were killed.

It is not only anti-Naxal operations, CRPF has been tasked with providing security for the construction of 246 km road in the dense jungles of Chhattisgarh that would expedite the movement of the security forces in the area. "Last year, we lost 42 men in encounters. How can I accept this? We have decided to go ahead with meticulously planned operations now. Since the December (2014) incident, when we lost 13 men in a Maoist encounter, we have carried out 63 big operations", said CRPF DG Prakash Mishra.

The final report in the Court of Inquiry held into the December 2014 encounter is yet to be tabled before the MHA. CRPF had come under fire for poor planning of the operation then, where around 300 personnel moved around in jungles looking for Maoists, giving the latter enough time to execute an attack on them. Mishra said, "If the roads are built, then half the battle is won. CRPF is providing security to at least five big road projects in Chhattisgarh.

Road construction under CRPF watch

		Km
1.	Bijapur-A wapalli-Sarki guda road	47
2.	Bhairamgarh-Bijapur Road	73
3.	Jeeram, Tongpal road	10
4.	Kirandul-Aranpur road	38
5.	Sukma-Konta road	78
	Total	**246**

Sukma ambush: We killed 20 Maoists, claim police: Dantewada, 13 Apr 2015

This is an interesting—some would also say, a self-serving—story essentially telling police version of 11 Apr 2015 ambush by the Maoists. Even then, its contents must be put on record. Since it is totally police version, it is reproduce below in its entirely, from a daily of 14 Apr 2015[35].

- "Terming the Pilmed ambush—in which the Chhattisgarh STF lost its seven men –among the "greatest battle" it ever fought, the police Monday (13 April) claimed to have "killed at least 20 Maoists in retaliation." The police also defended the action of Platoon Commander Shankar Rao, who had left at 2:30 AM on Saturday (11 April) with a team of 49 personnel from Polampalli police station in Sukma, and said he did what was needed at that moment."

"DGP AN Upadhyaya and ADG (Naxal Ops) RK Vij visited Polampalli and met the personnel who were part of the STF team. "They narrated us the entire incident. Rao had received intelligence input about the presence of 25 well-armed Maoists. Rao asked each of his men to keep 100 rounds extra. It shows the level of his preparation", Vij said in a statement. He continues: "They walked for hours before taking some rest at a hillock. Here, Maoists opened fire at them. Rao faced the first bullet in his chest. A constable, Rajesh Atre, told us that Rao collapsed, but asked others that *'aar paar ki ladai ladni hai.* Don't withdraw."

"Atre, according to Vij, then assumed leadership and the small STF team retaliated. "They killed at least 20 Maoists. When they realised reinforcement could not reach there, they began to retreat. A km later, the Maoists again opened fire. We lost a few personnel ", the ADG said. Claiming that the STF inflicted massive casualties on Maoists, Vij said, "It was among our greatest battles."

The force, however, could not recover any Maoist body. The STF team also retreated leaving the bodies of its men behind which could be recovered only 30 hour later.

"Chhattisgarh 'hostage': Maoists kill one tribal, others return home": Dantewada, 9 May 2015: "Ahead of PM Dantewada visit, rebels took away over 200 villagers"

The villagers who were forcibly taken away by the Maoists in State's Sukma district ahead of PM Modi's visit to neighbouring Dantewada on Saturday (9 May) have been asked to return home, but they are coming back with the body of one of the "hostages" who was killed in a Kangaroo Court, police said.

The villager Sadaram Nag refused to follow their diktat against working on any government project. "He was killed in a Jan Adalat by the Maoists. The Maoists had taken these people for a Jan Adalat. Others are returning home", said RK Vij, ADG (anti-Naxal ops).

Now, the daily makes an interesting observation about the government and police making contradictory statement: "Earlier, the Chhattisgarh government and the police had contradicted each other over the status of "villagers held hostage by the Maoists on Friday (8 May 2015) night. While CM Raman Singh said "around 200-250 men have been taken hostage" and "five people have gone to ensure their release", State Home Minister Ramsewak Paikre noted "the abducted villagers were BJP members and they were coming for the PM rally." Local Congress MLA Kawari Lakhma said around 1,000 armed Maoists forcibly look away residents of five villages with them on Friday night.

The State police, however, had maintained that the villagers, involved in construction work, were forcibly taken away the Maoists as they did not want them to work on government project[36].

Sukma SP DS Sravan said: "The Maoists asked them not to undertake any such work. They have taken their relatives and some villagers away." He stressed that "such situations are usual here. Naxals often take such villagers for indoctrination and release them soon."

The MHA had also asked for details about the situation, as PTI quoted Union Home Minister Rajnath Singh saying "efforts are on to rescue the villagers."

"3 cops, 2 Maoists killed in encounter" Raipur, 17 May 2015

Three policemen and two Maoists were killed in an encounter in Bijapur district on 17 May 2015. The encounter took place early in the morning near Ponjed at Mirjur in Gangalur police station area where a team of STF and state police were conducting anti-Naxal operation.

STF Constable Sitaram Kunjam and Assistant Constable of district force Moti Ram were killed on the spot. Another jawan Payku Ram Poyam succumbed to his injuries when he was being taken to Jagdalpur.

Among the Maoists killed was a senior guerrilla fighter Hemlata Masa alias Vijay, Commander of Company 2 of West Bastar Division of CPI (Maoist).

RK Vij, ADG (Naxal Ops), said: "Fifteen rounds of AK-47, nine shells of UBGL, a .12 bore rifle and a wireless set were recovered from him."

Speaking on rebels presence in the area, Vij said the area was "highly affected." "Our team had gone for an operation when the Maoists opened fire at them. Our jawans retaliated. We have recovered bodies of two uniformed Maoists", he said[37]

The STF, which is specially trained for anti-Maoist operations, has had its maximum casualties this year (2015). As many as 11 STF men have already been killed in 2015. Last month (April), the STF lost its seven men in Sukma's Pidmel area.

This year (2015) is turning out to be a difficult year for security forces fighting Maoists in Chhattisgarh, with 30 casualties so far (till mid-May 2015). The last three years have witnessed deaths of 62, 43, and 52 men respectively.

Considering that the death count this year does not include a single person from CRPF, precisely because it has stopped sending its men to distant areas for operations, the casualty list also becomes worrisom for the Chhattisgarh police.

ASP Bijapur district Indira Kalyan Elesela told a daily, "our operation will continue."

The encounter site happens to be the hot bed of the LWE who were engaged in their annual 'tactical counter offensive campaign' (TCOC) to regain their strength in south Bastar. Some 150 security men were on the operation on a specific tip-off regarding the movement of Maoists near Mirtur, ADG (Naxal Ops) RK vij said. Reinforcements were rushed to the area to assist the police[38].

Chhattisgarh police bring body of Maoist Commander" Raipur, 20 May 2015

A Chhattisgarh police team registered a major psychological win against Maoists Saturday 17 May 2015 when it managed to bring body' of a senior guerrilla fighter Hemla Masa alias Vijay, Commander of Company of West Bastar Division of CPI (Maoist) (Partly covered in the preceding two entries).

Police said Masa was the topmost cadre whose body they have recovered in the entire history of the Maoist conflict.

This daily has covered the event with more accurate details: "On 17 May 2015 (Saturday), a team of STF and District Reserve Guard travelled over 12 km through the forest after a long encounter and brought all the five bodies with them. Security forces are rarely able to recover the bodies of their fellow personnel immediately, let alone those of the Maoists."[39]

Last month, the STF had retreated, leaving the bodies of its seven men in Pilmed area of Sukma. The bodies were brought only 30 hours later.

DGP AN Upadhyaya said 17 May: "It was among our best battles. The Maoists were completely over powered by the police and left the body of even their commander."

ADG (Naxal ops) promised out-of-turn promotion for several men who were part of 17 May operation encounter.

Maoists Cite SC NOTA ruling to justify poll boycott: Raipur, 17 Oct 2015

To justify their poll boycott call, the Maoists have cited the recent Supreme Court (SC) ruling giving the electorate the option of not voting for any of the candidates in the fray by pressing the "None of the above (NOTA)" button[40].

In a set interview, sent in a Q and A format, emailed to this daily, Rammanna, Secretary Dandakaranya Special Zone Committee (DK SZC) denounced the election system and stated that even the SC had to intervene to give the voters alternative of 'none of the above', which he said was a negative voting.

"This means that the judiciary, which also is part of the present system, has admitted that the interests of the people in the present election process is consistently on the decline. So, we believe that boycotting polls is also a justified people's right", the Maoist leader said.

The rebels said if the government adopts repressive measures to make the poll boycott campaign unsuccessful, it would "certainly be opposed", thereby keeping open the possibility of a counter-offensive during the upcoming elections.

The Maoist leader described the killing of Congress tribal leader Mahendra Karma as a "historic success" but said killing Pradesh Congress Committee Chief Nand Kumar Patel and his son Dinesh had been big mistake. "To kill Patel and his son was a wrong decision taken in haste by the PLGA, who were in command", Ramanna said. The PLGA is a trained military outfit of the CPI (Maoist).

18 of the 27 districts in the Chhattisgarh are Maoist-affected. According to the Election Commission, 233 polling stations across these districts face a threat.

Number of casualties in Maoist-related violence in Chhattisgarh

2011	204
2012	109
2013	25 (till May)

Salwa Judum: A Curse or a boon

This is the last issue to be examined and discussed in this Chapter on Chhattisgarh. Salwa Judum was conceived and initiated by that brave, intrepid and activist politician of Chhattisgarh, Mahendra Karma. It was a campaign of Civil militia against the Maoists, initiated and led by Mahendra Karma.

There is a strong evidence to suggest that the Maoists were unnerved by the success of this campaign. They adopted two-pronged strategy to counter Salwa Judum: Intense attack on Salwa Juduon fighters: mainly the SPOs and building up a strong anti-Judum propaganda blast with the help of its Left-Commic lobby of overground 'Maoists' and Human Rights do-gooders. The latter did achieve better results with some well known public intellectuals like historian RC Guha condemning it in severe terms. Finally, the Supreme Court ordered its disbandment.

Even today, there are analysts who feel "Salwa Judum is desparately needed." One does wish the Apex Court had acted wisely! A brief discussion follows.

Is Salwa Judum maligned?

On the night of 28 Jun 2012, a joint team of CRPF, CoBRA Commandos and state police came under fire from the Maoists at Sarkeguda village in Bijapur district. 17 people were killed and six CRPF men were injured. This again revived the unhappy memories of the 52-km Bijapur-Basaguda road, known as the "Khooni Raasta" (Killer Road), which bloodied by more than a dozen blasts by Maoists and several gun battles between them and the security forces between 2006-12. There were at least six IED blasts blowing up vehicle carrying villagers, and others carrying security men. The site of the 28th encounter, Sarkeguda is 3 km away from Basaguda, from where the joint team had marched off on the 28th.

There are five CRPF camps along this Killer Road, the last being at Basaguda. The Taalperu flowing by this village is- rather, was- dubbed the LoC (Line of Control). From 2006 to 2008 the river divided the Maoist Liberated Zone (MLZ) from the territory held by the Government. Its security forces and Salwa Judum. CRPF admitted that till about 2009, they could not cross the bridge over Taalperu river (into the said Zone). Sarkeguda village, which is within the jurisdiction of Basaguda police station, falls in the MLZ. But after the 28th encounter, villagers are haunted by memories of their lives in exile "not so long ago"—till 2010, to be a little more accurate. "We left our homes when "our villagers were ravaged by scourge of Maoists, Salwa Judum, and security forces." It is bad enough that the villages are equating Maoists with the Security forces and Salwa Judum activists. But more unfortunately, Kamlakaka of neighbouring Kottaguda village is more direct, blaming the Salwa Judum directly: "We fled our homes in 2006 after Salwa Judum members looted and burnt our homes." It is obvious that some members of the organisation did indulge in such brutal excesses such abhorrence against the Judum, which otherwise earned a well-deserved encomiums in their anti-Maoist battles.

Across Dantewada and undivided Bastar, people from 644 villages were internally displaced following arson, loot, murder and rape by the Maoist desperadoes. Again a daily blames the Judum. "Some (as in Lingagiri village) fled homes after Salwa Judum accompanied by security forces attacked villagers and burnt their harvest and homes[41].

Markam Narayan, sarpanch of Sarkeguda, laments for the plight of Basaguda: "Soon, the once-bustling trade cadre at Basaguda turned into a ghost town. Earlier traders from Andhra Pradesh and Maharashtra came to Basaguda for business."

Two years ago, in 2010, with the help NGOs, villagers had returned to reclaim their land and rebuild their lives among rubble. Talking about the 28th encounter, Lakshmi Kaka, whose son, Kaka Rahul, 16, was killed in the same, said: "After the police killed our people, our children, villagers fear if they have to flee their homes again."

It is rather worrisome that in the encounter where security contingent is attacked by the Maoists, resulting in civilian deaths, locals blame police for these deaths. What could be the reason behind this unequivocal assertion? Is it fear of the outlaws? Blaming them is risky, and it cost them their lives.

On the other hand, blaming security is a safe choice! May be, such situations can't be seen in black and white. It will be discussed in greater detail in the following pages.

The Salwa Judum: Chhattisgarh

These are preliminary observations on the contentious subject of Salwa Judum. The issue will be dealt with in greater detail in subsequent pages. To put it in perspective, Bastar is home to the launching of the concept of Salwa Judum.

An analyst asserts that the issue of exploitation of the Adivasis of Bastar is a little different from the ones in Andhra Pradesh, West Bengal, Bihar, and even Maharashtra. The area affected—perhaps, afflicted —in Madhya Pradesh is roughly in Bastar and adjoining Dandakaranya, which now falls in Chhattisgarh, a state created in 2000. The area borders Telengana and Srikakulum, and also Koraput in Orissa. The Adivasis here, in Bastar, are a comparatively a simpler lot, compared to their counterparts in the other states mentioned. When Andhra Pradesh planned counter-insurgency operations against the Naxals it created a new force, Christened Greyhounds, in 1989 with the help and guidance of a retired Security Service Bureau Officer. The Greyhounds performed efficiently and the Leftist guerrillas found themselves on the receiving end. They were forced to retreat into the neighbouring area of Bastar and Koraput, where they found their brother adivasis much more meek and tolerant of the oppression by the caste Hindu landlords and the Banias.

The problem there, in Bastar area, was less to do with exploitation on land and more with the sole of the forest produce. The hardened cadres of guerrillas from Andhra found their hosts too timid to arouse and join forces with them against the oppressors. Making an error of judgement, the new comers tried to intimidate the hosts—coercing them to join their hard line against the exploiters. This 'Press Ganging' alienated many of the local adivasis which persuaded them to seek help from the local district authorities.

It was at this point in time that some adivasi political leaders, the local civil officials and police officers conceived the idea of resettling the forest dwelling adivasis in areas where their security could be ensured against the Naxalite cadres. Obviously, the latter would not have easy access to these newly-created settlements. "This meant forcing many forest dwellers to leave their huts and move to the settlements nearer the towns."

A civilian analyst, who toured the area to study the situation, was "a-ghast see the miserable conditions of these forest dwellers living in dist and squalor in miserable shanties. Some other observations of the scholar, Sudeep Chakravarthi, are adduced below:

- "In many cases, the police and civil bureaucracy had forced the forest dwelling families to burn their huts in forest glades and come to live in the settlements.
- "This concept of resettling forest dwelling adivasis is the worst step that a professional fighting an insurgency will take.
- "It is worse than the regrouping of villages done in the Naga Hills and Mizo Hills district. The Nagas and Mizos have not forgotten the scars of that terrible period.
- "There was one saving grace in that resettlement (because) no politicians were involved. In the Salwa Judum, the lead role is of the politician[42]."

Comments on Sudeep Chakravarty's views

The Author, as a retired Army man and having participated in counter-insurgency operations including grouping of villages in Nagaland and Mizoram, feels some comments are called for on the preceding paragraph's contents, which are Mr Chakravarty's views based upon what he saw and experienced during his visit to certain areas under insurgent activities. These comments are offered in the context of difficult and dangerous situations that the existed in insurgency-affected areas, and a civilian academic, scholars or civil society activists cannot understand and appreciate the same during a brief visit. This should by no means be misconstrued as disrespect to them. Here are brief comments by this Author:

- As for his seeing "these forest dwellers living in dirt and squalor in miserable shanties", one can bet that even today some city-bred, not exposed to the life of less fortunate Indians, would find dirt and squalor worse than what he saw, in some villages in Eastern UP and Bihar.
- This concept of resettlement of the adivasis near townships "seems to be worst step" in fighting the insurgency flows from ignorance of necessity to do so. It gives no pleasure to anyone to uproot the people from the hearth and home. But sometimes the bitterest of medicine must be administered to save the life of a patient. There are strong reasons for this regrouping: One, it is to ensure the safety and security of the tribals who live at the mercy of these desperadoes. Otherwise, they are sitting ducks for these ruthless Naxalites, two, far off villages are easy prey, who are forced contribute money and rations for these Naxalities. As the

regrouped villages are under security, access to them becomes difficult for these terrorists.

- It must be understood by some of these 'bleeding hearts' that these regrouped villages are not left to the mercy of the elements. A lot of thought goes into the site selection of these regrouped villages on matters like availability and supply of Virtuals, source of water in the neighbourhood, grazing ground, et al. Recreational and schooling facilities are catered for.
- If the houses at the old sites are destroyed, it ensures that the Naxalite do not take shelter there-in. They must be denied the use of those huts, hence the destruction.
- It needs to be understood that this resettlement of villages is resorted to as the last resort. It is important to save lives of these poor tribals, even if it entails certain inconveniences, and hardships, however extreme. There can be no two opinions that the life is precious. No security forces will ever be able to provide security to so many villages dispersed far and wide. This experiment was tried in the South-east Asia by Gen Templer viz Malayan campaign.
- As for "the Nagas and Mizos have not forgotten the scars of that terrible period," one wonders if this academic has visited these twin states in subsequent years. Mizoram is the most peaceful state in the North-east, if not the country. Yet again, it beat Kerala last decade in literacy ratings to emerge as No. 1 state in India. And it is being ruled by an erstwhile rebel. Same could be said about the Nagaland, more or less. The Negotiations with the Naga Rebels of NSC (I-M) are in final stages. Meanwhile, the Nagas themselves are ruling their land, through their politicians. It is time academics like Chakravarti understand that this country has remained united and vibrant because of these much-maligned politicians, even if some of them corrupt and venal.
- He is merely mouthing Cliches and being rhetorical when he says "…..one saving grace in that resettlement no politicians were involved. In the Salwa Judum, the lead role was that of the politicians." He possibly does not that Phizo and Laldenga were politicians, and they could outwit their interlocuting politicians. We may not be laudatory about our politicians, even then we need not be unduly condemnatory of them. He just needs to look around our neighbourhood, and realise the debt we owe to our politicians. In the post colonial period, no country of our size and

diversity has made such a successes in democratic governance as India. As for corruption, one is not supporting it by merely drawing attention to a much worse situation in China under a ruthless dictatorship! Moreover, does Chakravarty know which all criminal acts, besides the rampant corruption amongst their ranks, Maoists indulge in, including rape of minor girls, looting, killing the innocent civilians et al?

- As for the politician alluded to by the academic (Karma), he must rest assured that he is no devil or demon. He is a brave man. He has lost two brothers, a son, and half a dozen other relatives to the Naxalites and he has not given up his fight. Should such a man be demonised by the armchair critics from the comfort of their luxurious drawing rooms? More on Salwa Judum in a later chapter.

Notes

1. The Indian Express, 10.2.2014.
2. Bhardwaj, Ashutosh, Indian Express, 12.3.14.
3. Pandey, Prashant, Indian Express, 14.3.14.
4. Singh, Vijaita, Indian Express, 14.3.14.
5. Bhardwaj, Ashutosh, Indian Express, 15.3.14.
6. Bhardwaj, Ashutosh, Indian Express, 13.3.14.
7. Bhardwaj, Ashutosh, Indian Express, 13.4.14.
8. PNS, The pioneer, 13 Apr 2014, and Pavan Dahat, The Hindu, 13Apr 2014.
9. PTO,The Pioneer, 14 Apr 2014.
10. Bhardwaj, Ashutosh, Indian Express, 13.4.14.
11. Ejaz Kaiser, Hindustan Times, 11 Apr 2014.
12. Staff Reporter, The Pioneer, 14 Apr 2014.
13. Bhardwaj, Ashutosh, Indian Express, 8.4.14.
14. Pawan Dahat, The Hindu, 29 May 2014.
15. ENS, Indian Express, 11 Aug 2014.
16. Rakhi Chakrabarty, Times of India, 16 Aug 2014.
17. PNS, The Pioneer, 7 Sep 2014.
18. Ashutosh Bhardwaj, Indian Express, 7.9.2014.
19. *Ibid.,* 8.9.14.
20. ENS, Indian Express, 19 Oct 2014.

22\. Staff Reporter, The Hindu, 27 Oct 2014.

22\. ENS, Indian Express, 22 Nov 2014.

23\. Ashutosh Bhardwaj, Indian Express 2 Dec 2014.

24\. PNS, The Pioneer, 2 Dec 2014.

25. Pavan Dahat, The Hindu, 2 Dec 2014.
26. Joseph John, Times of India, 2 Dec 2014.
27. Ejay Kaiser and Rajesh Ahuja, Hindustan Times, 2 Dec 2014.
28. Ejaz Kaiser, Hindustan Times, 2 Dec 2014.
29. Deeptiman Tiwari, Times of India, 3 Dec 2014.
30. Ashutosh Bhardwaj, Indian Expres, 11 Dec 2014.
31. Editorial, The Hindu, 5 Dec 2014.
32. Abhinandan Mishra, Sunday Guardian, 7 Dec 2014.
33. Ashutosh Bhardwaj, Indian Express, 13 Apr 2014.
34. Vijaita Singh, Indian Express, 13 Apr 2014.
35. ENS, Indian Express, 14 Apr 2015.
36. ENS, Indian Express, 10 May 2015.
37. ENS, Indian Express, 18 May 2015.
38. Ejaz Kaiser, Hindustan Times, 18 May 2015.
39. ENS, Indian Express, 21 May 2015.
40. Ejaz Kaiser, Hindustan Times, 18 Oct 2015.
42. Rakhi Chakrabarty, Times of India, 9.7.12.
42. Sudeep Chakravarti, red Sun: Trivedi in Naxalite Country (New Delhi, Penguin, 2008.

25

Jharkhand - 1

Jharkhand is the second worst-hit State by Maoist insurrection after Chhattisgarh.

Status Report

Origin: Naxalites made their presence felt in 1996 (then it was part of the united Bihar)

Bloody era: 2005 -2009

Key issues: Illegal mining and forcible displacement of tribals from their land.

Status check: Death of Politburo member Kishanji and anti-Naxal operations have put the rebels on the back foot in all but 10 of the State's 24 districts.

CM Arjun Munda in Dec 2011: "Naxalism is a serious issue and there should be no politics in it. It requires participation of all people to find a solution."

Incidents: 2002 to 2005

19 Dec 2002: MCC Ultras killed 18 armed policemen and injured 38 others, in Singhbhoom district in western Jharkhand. The Naxals took away their weapons and ammunition.

16 Jan 2005: Mahendra Singh CPI (ML) murdered in Jharkhand, a day after he filed his nomination papers to seek re-election for a fourth consecutive term from Bagedar constituency in Girdih district.

22 Jan 2005: A former MP belonging to Lok Janshakti Party, Rajesh Kumar killed while campaigning for the Feb 2005 Assembly polls.

13 Nov 2005: Jehanabad Jail break by Maoists. Freed 375 prisoners, including Ajay Kanu and 130 Naxalites. They looted 185 rifles and 200 rounds of ammunition from Girdih armoury, Jharkhand.

13 Mar 2006: 50 Maoists hijacked a train going from Barmadi in Jharkhand to Mughalsari (UP). They stopped it in jungles of Jharkhand, held its passengers hostage. Police suspected it to be retaliation for the death of an area commander Jagannath Koiri in nearby Palamu, 10 days earlier.

Naxal related activities and violence

Incidents and Events: 2006: Rebel groups battle for supremacy, Oct 2006

The LWE in Jharkhand is split among various factions. This news story details the clash between the Revolutionary Communist Centre (Third Conference) and the CPI (Maoist) on the night 22 – 23 Oct 2006. The clash brought to the light the singular fact of a battle – to - the finish between them. It is a war for supremacy.

By now, the cadres of the third Conference, a break – away faction of the CPI (Maoist), are known to have made their presence felt in Latehar, Palamu and Chatra districts of the State. SP Chatra admits as much: "They are still spreading their tentacles despite our efforts to contain them".

After year of rivalry, the MCC and PWG merged 2004 to form CPI (Maoist). The creation of the Third Conference, rather its splitting from the main outfit, was attributed to two main factors:

- Desire of the cadres at the Ground Zero to make use of the levy money collected by them at their level rather than share it with the distant top brass located far away.
- Caste conflict among the cadres. A senior police officer, preferring anonymity told this daily; "Most of those who have parted ways with the Yadav – dominated CPI (Maoist) are Dalits. DGP JB Mahapatra was rather blunt, and uncommunicative, "We do not want to share with the media any information gathered by the intelligence[1].

The daily, however, has learnt that a minimum of 20 Naxalite cadre from these warring factions were killed in six clashes of attrition during the period 1 Aug till 24 Oct (2006). Consequently, there was no major incident of attack on the police during this period.

Interestingly, to cause damage to the other faction, each has planted a number of landmines in different areas. This also enables them to carve out their respective areas of influence.

Recovery of landmines in Chhatra district last month (Sep 2006) only confirms the above mentioned postulation.

"Red flags means fallow land", Oct 2006

More than 2,000 cultivable acres in Jharkhand's Palamu district lie fallow for fear of Maoist terror. Intelligence reports ascribe this to the ultras' high – handed treatment of landlords: "Red flags were planted on these fields ahead of the monsoons, prohibiting agricultural activity."

A source said: "Drought – affected Palamu counted upon good harvest this year as it had good rains after three dry years. But due to the Naxal fears, there was no cultivation. Consequently, the daily – wage labourers were badly hit - - surely not the aim of these Maoists, who claim to be working for the poor and the deprived tribals".

But this is not the worst loss. There is more of this because of oppressive LWE: "Ramgarh village in Chainpur has not had 800 acres of its fertile land worked on for the last nine years as some land owners refused to pay the Maoists in cash or kind." Uldanda, Nenuara khura, Karso, Hutar, Bedma, Panchlema and some other villages too have suffered the same fate over the past two years.

Police is not of much help either, as the landowners and villagers are too scared to even report to it. District SP Udayan Singh told the daily: "We have visited villages and deployed our men there. But this wasn't enough to eliminate the fear factor[2].

Maoists' fears: "Marriages are blessed in the Temple": Nov 2006

Hari Shankar Prasad got married on Nov 2006 morning in Harihardhan temple at Bagodhar in Giridih district, as he did not want to take his *baraat* deep into jungle for fear of the Maoist cadres. Like him, scores of families solemnize the marriages of their children at this temple, fearing the Maoist violence.

The temple is located on the Ranchi Giridih National highway, 190 km from Ranchi: During the marriage season, people have to book in advance the time and day as the priests have to manage a crowded schedule. No. body wants to go deep into the jungle which is known den of the guerrillas.

No wonder, this year - - Jan to Oct 2006 - - 1369 couples tied their knots in this temple, which has 65 – ft high Shiva lingam. The families of the brides and grooms belong to the villages in Maoist – hit areas, and Harihardhan temple is the safe bet. Going deep into the jungle can invite trouble, as the local put it: "Maoists simply kill the *baraatis*."

Giridih is one of the worst Maoist-hit district. People fear going into the jungle even during the broad day light: "The CPI (Maoist) run a parallel government here. The Jan Adaalat takes place here and people are executed in the adaalat (on the spot)[3].

Giridih, to repeat, is one of worst Maoist-hit district. To wit, it is the same district—

- Where Maoists butchered 15 villagers in Belumaghati in 2005, because they were opposing their activities.
- Where the ultras attacked a Home Guard Training Centre in 2005 and killed six security men.
- Where the lone CPI (ML) MLA Mahendra Singh was murdered by the Maoists in the jungle.

Maoist recruitment forms seized in Jharkhand: Dec 2006

Jharkhand police seized some recruitment forms from different parts of the State from the arrested Maoist cadres. 17 - point form also includes the endorsement of the members of the CPI (Maoist). The outfit seems to have adopted a new method of recruitment to preclude entry of informers into its ranks, as also to maintain the family profile of the members.

Some of the 17 points are: 1. Educational qualification; 2. Annual income; 3. Nationality; 4. Conjugal status; 5. Address; 6. Reasons for wanting to join the CPI (Maoist); 7. Oath of loyalty through filling a column to remain faithful to the outfit and to spread its ideology; 8. Ever sent to jail? If so, the reasons thereof.

The applicant's form will be accepted only if there is signature of one member of the outfit who must endorse the application. Police say the CPI (Maoist) also makes monthly payments to its cadres depending upon the position and post they hold.

A police officer involved in the anti-Naxal operations, told a daily[4].

- "It sems the Maoist leaders are concerned about the new entrants. Some of their cadres were involved in activities like loot and rape which got bad name for the outfit."
- "Such forms have been seized from the arrested cadres. They distribute such forms in the rural areas among its cadre and ask them to ensure entry of the people into the outfit by filling these forms."

"Maoists torch Bridge Construction material": Dec 2006

Maoists set afire equipment and makeshift camp of a construction company, engaged in bridge construction at Shyamsunderpur in East Singhbhum district on night 16 – 17 Dec 2006.

Some 30 armed Maoist cadres beat up some labourers of the Chaibasa-based company engaged in building of a road bridge over the Suvarnarekha river which linked Shyamsunderpur and Ghatsila in the interiors of Jharkhand. They also set on fire a motor cycle and a generator set, and looted Rs 1.25 lakh before decamping.

The incident comes three weeks after the ultras torched valuable equipment of another construction company engaged in laying a road under the Central Government Scheme in Patmda block of Ghatsila sub-division on 29 November.

Officials led by DSP, Ghatsila SP Burnmal reached Shyamsunderpur sometime after the Maoist depredation.

While blaming the government for keeping the tribal areas under developed, they go about meticulously destroying the bridges and roads under construction, also the ones already completed, in these under – developed areas. They thwart all efforts of the government to bring development to these areas. If they let that happen, that is, development to the underdeveloped regions, they lose the very raison d'être of their armed insurgency. To put it simply, for the Maoists all this strategy is necessary to ensure that they can ply their trade of murderous violence and destruction –all in the name of protest against the denial of development to the tribal areas, their favourite constituency to be exploited ad nauseam! Ironically, one does not find passionate human rights and enlightened Left-Libbar sections of India raising their voices even feebly against such murderous and destructive activities of their beloved Maoists.

Jharkhand: More security men killed in 2006 than the Maoists

Some security analysts believe that security agencies of Jharkhand are not receiving the logistical and weapons support from the State Government which the require to counter Maoists' violence. That should be on obvious inference from the fact that during the last six years, 2001 to 2006, the security forces suffered more fatalities than the Maoists. Fatality figures for these six year are given here:

1.	Security men (State police, CPM forces, put together.)	262
2.	Maoist cadres	256
3.	Innocent civilians killed by the Maoists	323

The figure of 256 for Maoist fatalities may even be over-stated, as the anti-Naxal forces have hardly managed to recover 50 bodies of the Maoists. The police and CPMF are wont to explain this discrepancy with a usual reply: The rebels take the bodies of their comrades with them while abandoning the site of encounter. But this facile explanation does not mash with the cognescenti: How come they always succeed in achieving a clean get away, without being pursued by the security forces! The only situation where they can carry the bodies of their comrades with them is when they ambush/encounter a small parts of security men and all of the latter are killed in the firefight.

Till date, the State has spent Rs 144 Cr on the police modernisation. What has this amount translated into vis-à-vis the state police?

- Of the total 323 police stations, more than half are in dilapidated condition.
- 20 per cent of its police stations are running from rented premises.
- Of the rented variety, "25 percent of the buildings can collapse any time.

"It is obvious from these facility data that the rebels have upper hand when confronted by the security forces. The following are natural consequences of this unequal fight[5].

1. When Jharkhand was carved out of Bihar in Nov 2000, Maoist rebels were active in only eight of its districts. In the last six years, it has double the number.
2. Due to fear of the Maoists, security men do not go for patrolling during the night to avoid ambush and landmines.

It is not that remedial measures are unknown to the senior police officers and their political superiors. Somehow things are not moving. Is it any surprise that a senior police officer is ready to pour out his frustrations to a journalist unmindful of all the restraints by his service regulations.

- One example should suffice to indicate the plight of the State Police in its fight against the Maoists. Over the last year (2001 – 2006), two helicopters, repeatedly promised by the State Government for anti-Naxals operations, have not materialized as of date.
- Yet again, "our wireless system and landmine detecting machinery are still the old ones...We continue to fight the rebels with traditional weapons and technologies." Obviously, this officer's frustrations are well – felt genuine ones. May be these are indicative of his anger, and not anything else!

If provided improved weaponry to match the one with the Maoists, and better technology for its counter-Naxal operations, the State Police will surely redeem itself.

Incidents and Events: 2007

Some of the more important incidents of the year: 2007 are recorded on the succeeding pages.

Fund crunch derails anti-Naxal operations in Jharkhand: Feb 2007

This story only confirms what was mentioned in the preceding one about the difficulties and shortcomings the State Police face in its anti-Naxal drive[6]!

This news analysis published by a daily on 23 Feb 2007 is a sad reflection of the ways Jharkhand Government and its nodal agency responsible for combating the Maoist menace perform the assigned task. The State police could not launch and sustain anti – Naxal operations for the first two months of the year 2007 as it had run out of the funds for the purchase of petrol and diesel for its vehicles required for the purpose. And to wit, Jharkhand with Chhattisgarh, is one of the two worst – hit states suffering the Maoist violence in India.

The funds were finally released on 22 Feb 2007 by diverting money from the police modernization account. The Police Headquarters had no money in the relevant account as the amount allotted in the budget 2006 – 07 for purchase of petrol and diesel for the purpose had been spent "as for back as 6 months and the Home Department had been approached to arrange this money through the first supplementary budget."

This was disclosed to the daily by a senior police officer, who further added: "But the department slept over the file, causing shortage of fuel. The first supplementary budget was passed in the Monsoon Session in Sep 2006, and the second one passed in the Winter Session in December. And the home Department never bothered to push the file to the Finance Department". This officer added more grim colours to the picture:

> "We had asked for Rs 10 Cr for petrol, food articles and other items for the personnel in patrol duty. But the Home Department did not find itself prudent enough to move the file. We are not able to send money to Maoist-infested districts in absence of the budgetary provisions."

Even DGP Jharkhand JB Mahapatra admitted that the money meant for the purchase of petrol and diesel had already been spent.

To wit, 16 of the State's 22 districts are Maoist – infested and the "district police chiefs have to fend for sources of funds to meet the requirement to fuel the anti-Naxal operations."

Another police officer, in the know of the things, talked about his difficult position: "According to one estimate, a sum of over Rs 3 Cr is due to different petrol pumps' owners but we are unable to pay them."

24 Mar 2007: MP Sunil Mahato killed

Naxalites kill JMM MP Sunil Mahato while he is watching a foot ball match. He was shot dead by the Maoist cadres including several women. Their anger and provocation: Mahato had conducted a vigorous campaign against the Maoists over the past some years, leading to the killing of some of their top leaders.

The match was being held at a village near Jamshedpur in East Singhbhum district, Jharkhand.

Anti-Naxal MP killed by Maoists on Holi: 4 Mar 2007

JMM MP from Jamshedpur Sunil Kumar Mahato, who was the chief guest at the function to celebrate Holi on 4 Mar 2007, was killed at the Naxal – infested village of Bakuria in Ghatsila block of East. Singhbhum district, while attending a foot ball match, by unidentified gunmen.

He wanted to leave after watching the women's football match, as he had some other engagement. But he was requested to stay a little longer to watch the boys' football match also. The organizers even promised to cut it short, to be played in two halves of 10 minutes each. It was during this period that Mahato was gunned down by 15 – 20 armed assailants who jumped from behind the dias and let loose a volley of shots on him at point blank range. Mahato becomes the first MP to be killed by the Maoists. Two of Mahato's bodyguards and a JMM activists were also killed[7].

It is surprising that even the name of the place Mahato was gunned down is mentioned differently. If one daily names it Barkuria village, as mentioned above, another says "the incident took place at Galudih, 28 km from Jamshedpur[8].

"Here comes a Conspiracy theory"

As in all things political, a conspiracy theory must creep up! Soon after Mahato was gunned down on 4 March, Jharkhand Government blamed the assassination on the Maoists. But the very day, the 5th, Nalini Dean, sister-in-law of the slain MP, said, "We are suspicious of the assailants were actually Maoists" Dy CM and senior JMM leader Sudhir Mahato also hinted at the conspiracy angle, saying, "We are probing the matter to find out the reason, political or personal."

CM Madhu Koda cited revenge as a possible reason for the assassination: "We cannot deny it. Naxals normally target MPs, MLAs and government officials. This is a pre-planned attacks."

A day after killing, MOS Home Sripraksh Jaiswal blamed the killings on the Maoists, but left enough room for a theory that it could be a revenge killing[9].

Central agencies suspect the killing of the MP to be a handiwork of the Maoists, who had reasons to be sore with the leader who had been conducting vigorous anti – Naxal compaign by mobilizing his constituents against the Red ultras, and even beyond his constituency. Though the Union Home Secretary, VK Duggal, on 5 March stopped short of making a categorical assertion about the Naxals being behind the killing, as that could spell trouble for the Madhu Koda Government[10].

But the Central agencies and the State Police had little doubt about the MP falling prey to the Maoist bullets.

It is indeed a sad commentary on the state of politics and its practitioners in the State of Jharkhand, and even across the country in general, that the assassination of an MP, passionately involved in anti-Maoist fight, is turned into a political foot ball, to be kicked around by various stake holders as it suites their political ends! These politicians can't rise above their partisan interests even while dealing with as serious in issue as Maoist armed insurgency that threatens the very sovereignty and integrity of India. The ramshackle Koda Government was installed after dislodging a reasonably stable BJP-led Government. The Congress Party at the State or even at the Centre will not accept publicly that the MP was killed by the Maoists. It will not only make Mahato a hero and a martyr, but also be an adverse reflection of their anti-Naxal strategy and its effectiveness in fighting the scourge of LWE!

Seen in this context, it should come as no surprise that the MOS Home and a senior bureaucrat and his Home Secretary are hedging their bets!

The rot goes deeper; far beyond the senior civilian bureaucracy. It has even infected the police officers, who should know better, they being not only the first ranks of defence against this armed rebellion but also leading the anti-Naxal war along with the CAPF. Obviously, if a senior bureaucrat like the Union Home Secretary can parrot the line of the MOS Home, why should me expect any better from the DGP and his minions in the State police? Just read what they have said on the issue:

- DGP JB Mahapatra acknowledged that there was some controversy and that a football match can never be over in 20 minutes! "The attempt was to make him stay back for a longer time."
- A police source, obviously a senior police officer, intones: "The organizers of the football tournament will soon be questioned.

It is also amazing that the driver of the MP's car, who never used to leave Mahato alone, had miraculous escape, as he had the dias a few seconds before the gunshots were fired at the MP."

- The police, which suspect that the killing could be the outcome of a feud between the local mafia and the slain MP, also said that the assailants had kicked the body of Mahato after he fell on the ground. Not to be left behind, CM Koda sought a CBI inquiry into the killing to determine if there was any conspiracy angle to it. He said the assailants might have sneaked into Purulia district of West Bengal that shares the border with East Singhbhum, after killing the MP. He added the areas bordering Odisha, Bihar and Chhattisgarh have also been sealed.

The killing points to a level of sophistication as well as motivation which only ideology driven Maoist cadres possess!

The dawn-to-dusk state-wide bandh called by the JMM supporters on 5 March was also near total and largely successful.

The last rites of the slain MP were performed at his native village in Saraikela Kharsawan district on 8 March.

Sunil Kumar Mahato: Brave anti-Naxal warrior

In his passionate fight against the Maoists, the only other person Mahato can be compared with is that brave congressman Mahendra Karma from Chhattisgarh. Both leaders fought bravely, incessantly and passionately against the Maoists without a care for their personal security and both paid for this fearless fight with their lives!

A word on the anti-Naxal fight Mahato put up in his entire life is called for.

Even when Home Secretary Duggal baulked at making a categorical assertion about Naxals being behind his killing for fear of a political fall – out, he still made certain significant remarks concerning the death of Mahato. His assertions indicated how the leader might have been killed in a "retaliatory action". He also mentioned that Mahato, being an MP, was part of the Nagrik Surakasha Samiti (NSS), a civilian organization which has been active in mobilizing people against the Maoists. He also mentioned the JMM's leader's involvement in raising a strong protest movement against the Maoists.

Sunil Mahato plunged into politics when the movement for a separate Jharkhand State was at its peak in 1986. Born into a family of farmers, Mahato hogged the lime light as one of the founder members of the All

Jharkhand Students Union (AJSU), spearheading the separate statehood agitation in Seraikela – Kharsawan and East Singhbhum region.

He was the first treasurer of the AJSU when it converted itself into a political party. He even unsuccessfully contested the Bihar Assembly polls as an AJSU candidate. Internal bickering compelled him to quit the AJSU and join the JMM in the early 1990s.

Soon, the Kurmi leader rose in the JMM ranks, helped by his mass base and close proximity to Shibu Soren - - the JMM supremo and much respected separate state agitation leader.

Known to have considerable influence among Santhals, he emerged as one of the popular faces in the JMM. He was elected to the 14th Lok Sabha from Jamshedpur in 2004, and become General Secretary of the party.

Born on 11 Jan 1966 at Chota Gamharia village in Saraikela – Kharsawan district, he graduated from the Cooperative College in Jamshedpur.[11]

If analysts believe Mahato's exertions against the Maoists may have brought his end, they may not be far off the mark. In fact he started this battle some years back and possibly paid for his actions and convictions. An example or two should be in order here.

On 9 Aug 2003, when cadres of the PWG raided Lango village, its residents led by Bhado Bandra, battling Naxalites under the banner of Nagrik Raksha Dal (NRD), fought back and lynched nine PWG raiders. The very next day, Sunil Mahato, the former AJSU activists who had by then become General Secretary of the JMM, praised the villagers and distributed sweets.

He was later elected MP in 2004. He always backed the NRD and was extremely critical of the Maoists and their murderous ways.

His assassination on 4 March brought his supporters to the streets, pelting stones and setting up road blocks to demand a high-level probe into his killing, which brought Jamshedpur and neighbouring towns to a complete halt on the 5th.

But Lango's Bandra talks about Sunil Mahato and discloses certain facets of his life as he observed them personally, summed up here:

- Mahato, unlike others in the party, had taken on Naxalites. Whenever anybody contacted him and sought help against the Naxals, he would respond.
- He would even show up alone on a motorcycle.
- In Dec 2006, when CPI (Maoist) cadres set off a landmines and killed 25 policemen at Kangiro in Bokaro, Mahato was among the

first to issue a statement, blaming Maoists. This may have PWG target him, echoing what many in the area believe to be the reason for the killing.

But SSP Jamshedpur Pankaj Darad, who took over last month, Feb 2007, as was Bandre: "There is no doubt he was against the Naxalites. But the evidence gathered so far is not sufficient conclude that this was the motive." This is in line with the police officers' take on the murder.

Surprisingly, some in the JMM too think it was not the Naxalites, basing their argument that no outfit has claimed responsibility for the killing. JMM's Jamshedpur based spokesman Ashoke Mahato was rather direct: "It was a pre-planned murder. The plan was hatched by some of his rivals who laid a trap by organizing a football match on Holi, inviting him as the chief guest."

Murder leaves uneasy posers for local administration

The killing of JMM MP may have thrown up some uncomfortable questions for the State administration.

"Mahato was a key functionary of the Nagrak Suraksha Samiti (NSS), a civil society movements against Naxalism. We are looking at the security provided to him during the sports function and the SOP." This was Union Home Secretary Duggal posing some such questions at New Delhi. Security arrangements for him became an even mored important issue when his death is seen as retaliation for his active anti-Naxal stance throughout his political career.

The MHA has also noted with concern that the incident occurred in the same belt where the outlawed CPI (Maoist) had held the month-long 9th congress past month (Feb 2007).

Taking the cue from the fatal incident, the Ministry has outlined the need for identifying sensitive areas as well as leaders who had taken a stand against the Maoist for a long period.

Jharkhand's inability to contain Naxal violence has made it an area of concern for the Centre. There is a general feeling that the State has not done enough on the Naxal front. Two points in this regard has been brought to the Centre's attention:

1. The high number of vacancies in the State police force. (Part of blame for the lacuna must lie with the Centre - - read the MHA)
2. Improper use of funds allotted to the State, especially for the anti-Naxal operations and other related issues.

Maoists Kill second leader in a week: 8 Mar 2007

Close on the heels of the killing of JMM MP, Sunil Kumar Mahato, the son of another JMM leader, Sukhdeo Hemberom, was shot dead on 8 Mar 2007 in Chakradharpur locality of Jamshedpur in West Singhbhum district.

Sukhdeo had gone to drop his son Lakshman in a bus where he spotted Ratan Tiu who was travelling in the same bus. Ratan snatched the rifle from Sukhdeo's security guard and shot dead the son.

Ratan had attempted killing Sukhdeo when he had fought unsuccessfully the 2005 Assembly polls against the former. Now he kills his son. Ratan was later arrested by the police.

Naxals threaten Deputy CM Sudhir Mahato: Apr 2007

More than a month after its cadres gunned down JMM MP Sunil Mahato in East Singhbhum district, CPI (Maoist) has come out with a letter dated 8 Apr 2007, threatening the Dy CM of dire consequences if he does not stop speaking against their party. The letter reads as given here.

- "You have been issuing false statements from time to time. Your aim and motive is clear to the people. However, we feel it right to challenge your statements and warn you against letting loose a barrage of lies.
- "To come to your false propaganda about your espousing the cause of the Jharkhandis, we make it loud and clear that you have betrayed them in every conceivable way. You and your party's corrupt leaders have proved traitors to the long cherished dream of a democratic Jharkhand. If you continue to support the anti – Naxal Nagrik Suraksha Samiti (NSS), you will meet Sunil's fate[12]".

Sudhir Mahato's answer to this threat was brief, to the point and sans any flourish and bravado: "We have discussed the matter with top brass in New Delhi, and sought 30 companies of paramilitary forces."

The JMM cadres are up in arms against the Maoists. Under the patronage of the Dy CM, 2000 Adivasis belonging to the NSS had recently gathered at the Bagudia football ground in East Singhbhum district and paid tributes to the slain leader, Sunil Mahato.

NSS Chief Shankar Chandra Hembrom, who was close to the slain leader, declared on the occasion that the Adivasis instead of bowing before the Naxals, would carry out a drive against them. "It is a matter of shame that a 3000 – odd Naxalites have begun to dominate over 2.69 Crore people of the State," said Hembrom.

CM Madhu Koda said "his Government will not enter into a dialogue with the Maoists till they give up arms."

How one wishes activists led by the likes of Arundhati Roy and sitting in Delhi, Visit Jharkhand, meet people like Sudhir Mahato and Shankar Hembrom who are putting up a brave fight against the Maoist marauders, instead of issuing anti-Salwa Judum statements from New Delhi.

Jharkhand plans jungle warfare training for its policemen: Apr 2007

It is learnt that Madhu Koda-led UPA Government had decided to set up a special school to its police in jungle warfare to effectively fight the Maoist ultras in this insurgency-infested state.

The Government seems to have finally realized the threat of growing Maoist violence to the state, sources said on 16 Apr 2007. The envisaged school is expected to give extra teeth to the police and the paramilitary forces against the Maoists.

Nearly 550 people, including 245 security forces men, have been killed in the last five years in Jharkhand alone. One indicator of fast spreading Naxal menace is the fact that when Jharkhand was carved out of Bihar in Nov 2000, Maoists were active only in eight out of its 22 districts, and presently the number of Maoist-hit districts stand at 16. It is thus obvious that the decision to set up a Jungle Warfare School has not come a day too early[13].

The proposed school to be set up in Hazaribagh district during the fiscal 2007 – 08, will be first of its kind in the State. The school is mooted to provide training to the police to combat Maoists in all possible scenarios, including, in particular jungle areas where they are often ambushed by the ultras.

After initial basic police training, policemen will be inducted into the (planned) School. Once the specialized training is over, they will be deployed in the Maoist-hit districts and on security for the VIPs.

Help from the Army and BSF will be requisitioned for training the police men in the School, certainly for the initial years.

Jharkhand is covered with forest and hills and the Maoists make use of the avenues provided by these two features to harass, attack and ambush the security forces. It is widely believed that the police are unable or unwilling to carry out night patrolling for fear of getting blown up in the Maoist-laid minefields or getting entrapped in their ambushes, as they are not trained to face such combat situations. The training at this School will fill up this lacuna.

Some 1200 of the 4564 panchayat areas (over 25 per cent of the total) in the State are said to be under the (partial) influence of the LWE, where they now virtually run a paralled government: collecting taxes, holding courts and delivering on the spot, 'rough and ready' Naxal justice, and at grassroots level, adjudicating in social/ personal disputes. Besides these measures, an eborate machinery for "levy and tax collection" from government contractors and industrial/ commercial establishments, is in place.

Maoists have made full use of State's rich forest and hill cover to establish camps and training schools for their cadres in several areas. Some of these locations are mentioned here:

- Jhumra Hilss of Bokaro.
- Saranda Forest in West Singhbhum district.
- Border region of Hazaribagh and Chatra districts.
- Baruhatu and Shilaghati Hills of Ranchi.
- Madhuban Hills of Giridih.
- Some places in the Latehar and Garhwa districts.

Muktanchal (= Liberated Zone/ belt) on Jharkhand – West Bengal Border: Apr 2007

This is 'liberated' territory in the Maoist lexicon. "Law does not live in the Naxal land", as an analyst puts it rather infelicitously. The reference is to the Muktanchal (= Liberated or free zone).

Muktanchal astride the Jharkhand – West Bengal boarder is a verdant hilly terrain dotted with springs and natural forests. "It is the bombed forest rest house and the guest house in the area that indicate that Naxalites run a parallel government here."

Where exactly is this 'free' land ? It has some 200 villages of the two States spread across the three border police station areas: Ghatsila in Jharkhand and Belpahari and Bandwan in West Bengal. This area constitutes the so-called Muklanchal, as designated and proclaimed by the ultras. Whose writ runs here? No prizes for the answer. If there is an iota of doubt on the question, the following two horrific incidents should suffice to clear it:

- Former MP, the late Sunil Mahato visited Huludboni, the remotest village of Ghatsila, in Feb 2007. A fortnight later, he was dead; killed by the Maoists in Baguria, one of their strongholds. Ever since, no politician has dared to travel to Huludboni. Given the Maoist terror in the region. Chances of a Jharkhand politician visiting that village is rare.

- Anil Mahato, Belpahari Circle Secretary of the ruling CPM of West Bengal, spoke against the Maoists at a couple of meetings. Some 50 armed Naxalites raided his house in 2006 and killed him and his wife as they were asleep. Most of the CPM leaders under Belpahari police station have fled, abandoning their homes, pledging never to return[14].

Now, the larger picture. 19 politicians belonging to this region astride the Jharkhand-West Bengal border and hailing from these two states have been killed here in the last four years. Most of them were from the JMM and CPM. The killings have practically driven the legislation (read, politicians) out of the region. Political activity is at low ebb. Even party flags are rare sight here.

The remaining two branches of the administration are only slightly better. The State police men seldom venture into the region without the company (and protection) of the CRPF or BSF. Even when they visit, it is during the day, either on foot or on motor cycles; and at times, in anti-landmine vehicles.

The judiciary exists, but not of the kind as seen in the rest of the country. Jan adalats, run by the Maoists, dispense justice here - - rough and ready. These can be compared to Kangaroo courts.

The Maoist writ is sacrosanct. People in Muktanchal has no option but to approach these courts, where the Maoists dispense justice as they see it. In any case, people have nowhere else to go for getting justice. NSS President and JMM leader Shankar Hembrom is on record, telling us what happens if they do: "A couple of Kesarpur Panchayat villagers were punished brutally for approaching the police for justice in a criminal case.

Unfortunately, and this is the worst aspect of the Naxal rule in Muktanchal: "The people may forget, or even reject under compulsion, the democratic tradition of this country. A press party visited Dwarsimi, a border village of West Bengal, to cover a rally, taken out by the Border Jungle Mahal Jan Jagran Samiti (BJM – JJS), allegedly a Maoist-sponsored outfit, to protest police atrocities. Samiti President Panchanan Singh, had a word of caution for the press party: 'Please to not write anything detrimental to the villagers' interest.' So, even reporting the proceedings of a rally can harm the people's interest!"

Ghatsila DSP Shailendra Burnwal rightly attributed the Maoist dominance in the area to sluggish development, and then honestly spoke about the facts of life in the region:

"Except police, nobody visits these villages. Commissioned to maintain law and order, we are also fighting Naxalites, besides carry out minor welfare work for the villagers. You will seldom see doctors, teachers or BDOs discharging their duties in the area. This has given the edge to the Naxalites, who are growing in power."

"Fight back the Naxals": Says Sibu Soren: May 2007

JMM Chief Sibu Soren, presently in prison has asked his party cadres to "be prepared to take the Naxalites head on." He sent his message through his lieutenants.

JMM Central Committee Suprio Bhattacharya told the press: "Guruji has given a call for direct confrontation with the Naxalites. He had not anticipated that the Naxalites would kill JMM MP Sunil Mahato".

But Soren's appeal has alarmed the State Police, which could lead to a blood bath between the die-hard JMM cadres and the Naxalites, killing many innocents in the cross firing.

Police vs Naxalites: Is it an unequal battle?

Some of the indicators are adumbrated here:

- Jharkhand Police have a clear brief these days: to locate and defuse the lethal landmines that Maoists had planted across their strongholds in the State during the monsoons. The problem? They do not have sufficient mine detectors.
- Police estimate there are more than 4,000 Maoist cadre in Jharkhand. Almost 500 of them, including 150 women, are hardcore elements.
- 18 of the 22 Jharkhand's 22 districts are Naxal-infested. 21 of these share borders with the neighbouring states. Poor coordination among them help Maoists to shift basis and avoid capture.
- Almost 250 police men have been killed in the anti-Naxal operations in the State till date.
- The ultras use modern weapons, including INSAS and SLRs AK series rifles (most of these looted from police) and even rocket launchers from Andhra Pradesh.
- Police estimate that Naxals in the State gather nearly Rs 100 crore as a levy each year.

Maoists can display compassion also : Apr 2007

Maoists killed six people, including two CISF men in Bermo, near Ranchi on 7 Apr 2007. But six other CISF men survived the attack courtesy a trait not common among the gun-toting Naxal, viz. compassion. These survivors owe their lives to a young women Maoist cadre, who pleaded and finally persuaded her comrades to let the injured CISF men live.

ADGP (Special Branch) Gauri Shankar Rath said: "When the Maoists barged into their barracks after hours of gun fire, the CISF men had no ammunition left. They were injured and expected to be killed. But the woman saved them".

The survivors told the press the cadres had raised their guns to shoot them, and had that women not intervened, they would have been killed. A police officer said in Bokaro, "It seems women cadres, despite donning Maoist uniform, still have some compassion."

But equally true is another fact of the female cadres. Recent Maoist attacks in Bihar and Jharkhand also show a launching of attacks on the forces. The ultras that attacked Bermo had many women leading their groups. Rath has the last word, "The woman are dangerous, but more trustworthy."

Minors working for Naxals in Jharkhand: Jun 2007

It is known for long that minors are working for the Maoists in the State. Periodic incidents of this fact keep coming to public notice. The latest example of this is from the 18 Jun 2007 issue of a daily.

> "Recently, a high speed chase down the dirt tracks of Nadwelva village of Latehar district resulted in the arrest of two motorcycle borne Maoist cadres. They were later identified as CPI (Maoist) Sub Zonal Commander Visheshwar Yadav and its Child Wing (= Baldasta) member Vimal, who was the pillion rider."
>
> "When asked why he joined the ultras, 9-year-old Vimal said he was playing cricket outside his house a year ago, when he was picked by Naxals. 'Lokeshi (a Maoist, still at large) caught and forced me to accompany him at gun-point', class III student told the police."

Vimal, obviously, is not the first minor to be arrested for Maoist links. On 15 Jun 2006, 15-year-old Vipul Kumar was nabbed after a night-long encounter between the Maoists and the forces in Domuhan forest.

In another similar case, a teenager was arrested on 17 May 2006 after an encounter near Simaria police station in Chatra district. Earlier, two Kherwar tribal boys were booked under POTA[15].

Police records show the Maoist have been abducting minors from their areas and training them to work as spies and cooks. Others are being trained to provide logistically support like carrying arms and ammunition during operations in remote areas.

Latehar District SP Diwakar Dhan told the daily that with the information provided by Vimal, the police was able to arrest two wanted Maoist cadres, including a Zonal Commander on 16 June.

Naxals have become Tech – Savvy: counter-measures required: Jun 2007

"Recent landmines blasts in Jharkhand carried out by the Maoists, have forced the security forces to realize that the rebels are neither far – removed from modern technology nor are they shy of using it." Thus, reports a daily in its issue of 16 Jun 2007[16].

A study conducted by forensic experts indicates that the Naxalites are discarding conventional methods of triggering the landmine blasts in favour of more technologically advanced ones. Consequently, instead of using fuse, gelatine and wire, they have graduated to using camera flash and cell phones. Some recent instances of the latter as counted below, on the authority of police information:

- 8 May 2007. A landmine blast in Bokaro was triggered with a micro-wave – operated high-frequency wireless set looted from the police earlier. An antenna was recovered from the site of the explosion.
- A little earlier, on 13 March, a landmine was exploded in Garhwa which was triggered by a camera flash.
- In yet another one in Giridih district, Jharkhand, a cell phone was employed to activate a landmine on 15 January.

Police are reportedly busy finding ways to counter this new-fangled technology – enabled threat. As a CRPF officer discloses: "The Naxals have managed to reduce the use of manpower to execute such explosions. This has only added to the problems of the security men engaged in counter – Maoist responsibilities." DGP Jharkhand JB Mahapatra explains how and why: "Earlier, we received tip-off from villagers who spotted them moving about or laying the mines. But now the informers find it difficult to smell a rat a one person can undertake to execute the entire operation helped by (the latest) technology."

26 – 27 Jun 2007: Economic Blockade

Power and transmission line were snapped, and rail and road traffic disrupted. Supply of minerals and ores in Jharkhand and Chhattisgarh came to a grinding halt during the 48 – hour blockade. No loss of life was reported but it had major impact on economic and industrial activities in the four

Naxal-hit states of Jharkhand and Chhattisgarh in a big way, and it also hit to an extent the two states of Bihar and Odisha.

The blockade was a result of the mobilization planned by the CPI (Maoist) at its month-long 8th congress, Jan-Feb 2007.

Maoists had added to Forces' troubles (with multiple factions)

Besides the above, factions within the Maoists have added to the security forces troubles. Several local leaders have set up outfits in the areas of their own influence like the Jharkhand Liberation Tigers (JLT) and the Tritya Prastuti Committee (TPC), which translates into 'Third Presentation Committee', which interestingly is represented by the same acronym (TPC).

A number of recent cases of extortion from corrupt officials, contractors and business men have underlined the multiple split which has virtually triggered a war of supremacy, leading to inter-faction/outfit violence in South Chotanagpur, North Chotanagpur and Palamu divisions. Some such incidents (in 2007) are noted here:

- **29 May.** Four comrades owing allegiance to the CPI (Maoist) kidnapped and killed in Latehar by the JLT.
- **30 May.** Two JLT cadres kidnapped and killed/shot by the TPC.
- **2 June.** Three TPC supporters abducted and killed in Garhwa district by CPI (Maoist) activists.
- **6 June.** Four villagers suspected to be the TPC supporters were shot by the CPI (Maoist) activists in Chhatra.
- **8 June.** Sanjay Singh, who reportedly patronized the JLT, was shot in Palamu.

The State too has responded with two-pronged strategy. "The acting Chief Secretary holds a meeting with the police brass every month to pave a way for the administration and the police to work in tandem to maintain law and order", says DGP Mahapatra.

26 -27 Oct 2007. Maoist posing as CRPF personnel massacred 17 people including former CM Babulal Marandi's son Arup Marandi in Chilkari village, Girdih district, Jharkhand.

13 Apr 2008. Maoists attacked Jha Railway Station as a part of wider plan of People's Revolution to target Government infrastructure, including railway stations, dams, roads etc all over the country. This plan was discovered when police recovered a hard disc from a laptop of Malti alias KS Priya, wife of DKSZC spokesperson Vijay Reddy alias Gudsa Usendi on 22 Jan 2008 from Durg. She was arrested along with Prafulla Jha, former journalist and Meena Chaudhury - - wife of a top Naxalite. The Hard Disc revealed that these Naxalites were highly trained and experts in their respective fields. CPI (Maoist) called for a 24-hour Jharkhand Bandh.

13 Apr 2008. Same day, they raided Fesar Railway Station in Aurangabad district, Bihar. To confirm this pattern, during the period 2005-08, daring attacks like Jharkhand Jail Break (2005), Rani Bodli Police Station attack (2007), Dantewada Jail Break (2007), killing of MP Sunil Mahato and Nayagarh attack, took place.

28 Aug 2008: Religion plays a part. A hard-core Maoist Shankar Bhuiyan alias Sanjay Ram arrested in Jharkhand. He was a Sub Zonal Commander. While searching his hidout, the police stumbled upon a 200 – page training manual of Maoists. Divided into two sections, the book contains details of planning and assault strategy in different terrains. It has political depiction and graphic details on how to use a particular weapon and adopt a different strategy for a variety of situations. Even a layman can easily understand its contents. Buiyan also revealed that Maoists in Jharkhand were being trained by retired Army men in guerrilla and Jungle warfare.

In Odisha, Sabyasachi Panda confirmed that they killed Swami Laxman Saraswati, as he was indulging in anti-Christian activities. He further added that most of the Naxalite cadres in Odisha are Christian, and "the Swami was working for revival of Brahmanism[17]. Maoist posters warned against Pariwar (BJP, VHP, RSS) activities in Odisha. The Maoists "have held Bengal to ransom", becoming strong in all its 17 districts. They threatened Government against employing CRPF to counter them: "Call CRPF, face bloody reprisals."

30 Aug 2008. 11 policemen killed in East Singhbhoom, Jharkhand.

11 Apr 2009. 5 CRPF men killed in Khunti, Jharkhand.

14 Apr 2009. Maoists abducted three Railway officials in Jharkhand.

15 Apr 2009. Two CRPF men, two civilians and five Maoists killed at Bidania Ghat in Latehar.

22 Apr 2009. A train hijacked at Hehegarha by 400 Maoists.

22 Apr 2009. They blow up Chiyanki Railway Station Palamau district.

24 Aug. 2009. Red rebels torched 7 dumpers and one ten-wheeler truck in Ranchi area.

7 Sep 2009. Commandos of Special Operations Group (SOG) arrested a hard-core Naxalite Mala Madakami, a member of Potturu Dalam, from Kaliamela Jungle. She is resident of Kangurkonda under Kalinda Police Station.

9 Sept 2009. (1) Maoists target Topadihi Station Master. (2) Blow up Kalta police outpost, mobile towers. (3) Railways employees abducted earlier are released on 18 Sep 2009.

30 Sep 2009. Francis Induwar, Policeman posted in Khunti district kidnapped. His decapitated body, a symbol of Talibani justice, was found on 6 October.

25 Oct 2009. Kundan Pahan of Platoon – 39, who had shot (decapitated) Francis Induwar, was shot by police.

23 Dec 2009. Pauush Surin, a Naxalite Zonal Commander of a breakaway CPI (Maoist) faction, won from Torpa in the State Assembly elections. He defeated Koche Munda of BJP from Torpa seat in Khunti district.

Incidents and Events: 2011

This was not as bad a year for the Naxal violence as the ones that followed it. Some of these events are recorded here.

"Wage a relentless war" 'Maoists deserve mercy nor forgiveness': May 2011

This is the clarion call for waging a relentless war against the LWE by a daily in its strongly worded editorial. It is reproduced in full here to convey its forceful pleading for the stance it takes against the Maoist violence.

- Violent clashes between Maoists and security forces are by all accounts the norm in areas commonly referred to as India's "Red corridor". Yet the recent surge in the number of encounters between the insurgents and jawans of our paramilitary forces, pointing towards the ruthlessness of the Maoists, has shocked the nation. On Tuesday (3 May 2011) morning, eight CRPF jawans and three belonging to the State police were killed while another 26 were injured in the Senha area of Lohardaga district in Jharkhand after the Maoists lured the security team to a hill top village and blasted some 50 landmines that they had planted around a two km radius.
- As per the reports, they demanded surrender of the security forces, which included two CRPF companies and two police team, but instead our brave men in fatigues and their Khaki – clad colleagues chose to take on the enemy in a headlong firefight. Eventually, after four hours of intense fighting, the security forces were abde to push back the Maoists who then retreated to their

jungle hideouts. In a sense, it was a moment of victory for the armed forces. Sadly, it was also one that cost us the lives of 11 brave men. Critics of the bullet – for – bullet policy would call this a setback for the Government is its war on Maoists. But it is in situations such as these that we must remind ourselves of the reality: Collateral damage and casualties are inevitable in the ongoing asymmetric war with the Red terrorists, enjoying a certain damage as they do not have to follow the rules of engagement or abide by the law of the land which, much as it may sound silly, the security forces and the state must follow.

- In association with the Governments of the States that have been badly hit by the Maoist insurgency, the union government has launched a concerted counter-offensive to eliminate what PM Manmohan Singh has repeatedly - - and rightly - - described as the greatest threat to our internal security. Hence, there will be collateral damage, there will be fatalities, there will be casualties, such as these in Jharkhand this week. But none of these should deter either the people or the Government from persisting with hunting down those who wage war on the state and dealing with them without any trace of either mercy or forgiveness.
- Maoists are killers and understand no other language but that of the gun.
- That a counter-offensive is integral to eliminating Maoist terror has been proven in recent months by the number of successes our security forces have stacked up. On Tuesday (3 May 2011) itself, for example, there was another fierce encounter at a Maoist transit camp in the Jhumra hillocks, some 65 km from the district headquarters of Bokaro. The four hour long fire fight ended with the Maoists fleeing their camp, while the police confiscated all that they had left behind. The Dy SP of Silly was shot in the wee hours of 3 May while leading a joint operation against a Maoist commander in Ranchi district. Terrorism, irrespective of the shade of the ideology of terrorists, cannot be countenanced in a democracy with a plural and open society. It is the responsibility of the state to deal with terrorists, whether home grown or from foreign shores, with an iron fist.
- The war against Maoists must be taken to its logical conclusion[18].

"Jharkhand shows how to fight hunger, poverty": Oct 2011

Development and socioeconomic progress in an area are the effective anti – dotes against the Maoists' ideology. The lack of former two are the main reasons the Maoists exploit in popularizing and spreading their ideology among under – or un-developed areas, mostly in the tribal belts of India. The news analysis in a daily under the above headline, in its issue of 13 Oct 2011, speaks about a populist mid-day-meal scheme "started by the Jharkhand State Government has changed lives without any great show over ensuring food security for the poor." Such socio-economic changes in the lives of the poor will go a long way in effectively defeating the Maoism.

> "Sukal Hansdak from Bhairavpur village, in the panchayat with the same name in Dumka district, Jharkhand, has been pulling a rickshaw for last 30 years, to keep him and his family going. Asked how much he earns in a day, he answers, "between Rs. 100-150". The next logical question: "Is this enough", He says: "I give Rs. 25 – 40 as rent to the rickshaw owner for the day. That leaves between Rs. 75 – 125. He spends Rs. 25 – 30 on – his own food which leaves precious little for other household expenses".

This is the opening paragraph of the news analysis under consideration. It continues with details of work others in the village engage in for their meager, if not stark, conditions of their lives and livelihood[19].

Handsak and many others like him in the village go to nearby towns to ply their rickshaws, to work on construction sites and sell wares on *thelas* to eke out a living. For all practical purposes, notwithstanding the definition of poverty, they are poor. Rising food expenses is a killer, and this is where innovative measures by the State Government have been a boon. People who live on edge are feeling a little less burdened since the Mukhyamantri Dal – Bhaat Yojana started operating from 15 Aug (2011). Now just for Rs 5, they can have a full mid-day meal. This frees up the money that they necessarily needed to use for their own food.

Hansdak's relief and joy finds echo across Jharkhand's villages, amongst a wide cross-section of people who struggle to earn a meager wage within the rural economy. The region falls within the Santhal belt that is predominantly tribal. The women also work on such sites to make both ends meet, mostly as agricultural labour and as domestic help in rich households.

While the ambitious Food Security Bill (at national level) is being thrashed out, in keeping with this essence, Jharkhand has taken steps to mitigate this scourge.

Village women Ms Mangal Turi, Phagu Besra and Santosh Harijan applaud the move. The 'Dal – Bhaat Yojna' is nothing less than a manna from heaven, helping them to not only stave off hunger but also save the precious amount being spent on food.

This is, indeed, the human face of poverty alleviation ignoring the terms defining poverty by various committees and the Planning Commission, the Government of Jharkhand has responded to a crying need of a large section of people who are obviously very poor. Agricultural labourers rickshaw pullers, hand cart pullers, people working in unorganized sector, those who go to towns and cities every day. These are the beneficiaries in Jharkhand.

The challenges of development in this relatively new state, carved out of Bihar in Nov 2000, have been immense. For a region full of mineral and natural resources, with a high percentage of tribal population, it was crucial to cater to the needs of the poor people - - tribal and non-tribal, both, with their own unique life styles and livelihood patterns.

Essentially run by the department of Food, Public Distribution and Consumer Affairs, these attract milling crowds at the centres which are typically housed in public institutions like hospitals, health care centres and a Public Welfare Council amongst others. Even if it is populist scheme, but what is important is that it is catering to the core need of the marginalized and the vulnerable amongst the rural society.

Still the scheme needs to be broadened, systematized in order to benefit the largest number of the deserving people. Presently, each centre cater to around 400 people, which is a drop in the ocean. A programme like this needs to have its scope wide open so that none who is deserving is turned away.

The justification, and indeed the *raison d'être* of such a scheme lies not in political expediency but in responding to the basic needs of a section of the rural population that lives on the margins. The response in Jharkhand has been humane, driven by the need felt on the ground and by taking steps to mitigate what is simply un acceptable. Yes, such an impetus needs a policy framework, not merely to function but to sustain. Hopefully, the State Government will continue to show sagacity and sensibility in overcoming hunger.

More importantly, other Maoism-hit states must follow the example of Jharkhand's and initiate such schemes for the poor and the deprived. It is this section in the tribal areas of states like Chhattisgarh, Bihar, Odisha and pokets of Assam and West Bengal that supplies foot-soldiers to the Maoist leadership, mostly from Andhra Pradesh. Even more than development, the schemes like Jharkhand's will play a role in defeating Maoist ideology by denying easy access to the vulnerable sections of the poor and deprived.

Maoists plan strategy to foil P. Chidambram and Ramesh Visit to Jharkhand: Nov 2011

The proposed visit of Union Rural Development (RD) Minister Jairam Ramesh and of Union Home Minister P. Chidambram (PC) to Jharkhand in connection with the anti-Naxal operations "has moved the Maoist into vigorous action[20]. A daily of 8 Nov 2011 reports this.

They have, in fact, renewed their offensive to protest the operations by the security forces. While a State –wide bandh was called by Maoists on 1 November to protest the proposed visit of Ramesh to their den in Saranda Forest, the Naxals made their presence felt in the State by killing two men subsequently, in Saranda area, reacting to the official announcement about Chidambram's itinerary.

Consequently, the tall claims about the security forces having cleared the Saranda Forest from the Maoist influence have proved to be hollow.

"Although PC is scheduled to visit the State on 9 November along with DG CRPF Vijay Kumar to review the status of the ongoing anti-Naxal operations in the State, Ramesh - - who had espoused the idea to initiate a counter-insurgency move by ensuring implementation of the Centre – sponsored development schemes in the Saranda area - - is believed to be unable to finalise the date of his visit after the discouraging feedback he received from the Central team that visited the area last month (October).

The Central team under the leadership of the Joint Secretary RD Ministry is believed to have cautioned the Government about a possible threat of reprisal if populist measures are introduced in the area without working out proper strategies.

The team had also witnessed the crash of a chopper near Ranchi that was en route to airlift team members from Chaibasa (headquarters of the West Singhbhum district) to the Saranda Forest.

Acting on the feedback from the Central team, the Union Government decided to make Cash payments to beneficiaries under Central schemes, including Old-Age Pension, NREGA and Indira Awas

However, district administration of West Singhbhum that had been entrusted with the task to distribute the amount among beneficiaries of the Saranda area under different schemes is unable to act on the Government decision. The district administration had to withold its proposal to make cash payments to the Old-Age Pensioners when Maoists killed two villagers engaged by it to coordinate with the co-villagers to avail the benefits on Friday last (4 November). Leaving a brief note on the site of occurrence, the Maoists warned villagers of dire consequences if they sland by the

Governments demagogic move the inflame public opinion against the ultra-left outfits.

Incidentally, the gruesome incident of killing took place when the officials were preparing a detailed map to introduce a road system inside the Saranda Forest to enable the Government machinery to implement developmental schemes. Subsequently, the officials had to suspend their action plan. More-over, the district administration failed to ensure construction of Indira Awas houses too for want of facilities to carry bricks and other material to the Saranda Area. Beyond kiribura area, situated along the Saranda Forest, there is poor visibility inside the dense forest and the administration had to face difficulties in carrying out the developmental schemes in a proper manner.

However, past bears testimony to the fact that when Chidambram had tried to be aggressive against Maoists in Jharkhand, West Bengal and Chhattisgarh, in particular, the ultras had reacted to his action with renewed vigour.

In the beginning of 2010, Chidambram had summoned officials of the then Sibu Soren Goernment thrice to Delhi and Kolkata within a span of one-and-a-half months to discuss strategies about exercising coercive measures against Maoists in Jharkhand and adjoining states of West Bengal and Chhattisgarh. He had turned down the proposal by Jharkhand Government to evolve an amicable solution to the tangle by initiating a dialogue with the Maoists.

But his proactive stance turned out to be a major disaster when the incidents like the worst ever Maoist attack at Dantewada in Chhattisgarh took place, claiming 75 lives of the policemen. The Dantewada attack was a sequel to the Maoist attack at a police station in West Bengal that left 25 policemen dead. That was not the end: The Howrah – Mumbai Gyaneshwari Express was derailed by the Maoists in which some 70 persons died. In addition, dozens of people in Jharkhand were killed in different Maoist attacks.

To top it all, if well placed sources in intelligence are to the believed, secret parleys are on among the ultra-left outfits across the country to combat the Chidambram-Ramesh Combine's strategic move to take on the Red Brigades in Jharkhand.

Police claim Maoist involvement in Nun murder: Nov 2011

The police 20 Nov 2011 claimed involvement of Maoists in the killing of Sister Valsa John and arrested seven persons in connection with the incident.

"In all, there were 45 people, who had surrounded her house. Of them, 30 were Maoists", IGP (Santhal Pargana) Arun Kumar Oraon told the press on the 20th. A daily tells this story, datelined Pakur (Jharkhand), 20 Nov 2011[21].

The 30 Maoists, including the area commander, Ramesh Soren, belonged to Ram Lal Rai's firing squad. All the seven persons arrested were detained on the 19th. Ms Valsa made three calls before she was hacked to death on 8 November. One of the calls was traced to her associate Sonia Deheri, Mr. Oraon said.

"Jharkhand launches well-timed offensive against Reds": Nov 2011 'Kishanji was in Parasnath Hills of Jharkhand last month' (Oct 2011)

This is the headline of a news story about the anti-Naxal offensive, with its blurb below it, carried by a daily dated 26 Nov 2011[22].

Maoist leader Koteshwar Rao alias Kishanji, killed by CoBRA forces in the jungles of Burisole in West Midnapur district on Thursday (24 November 2011) evening, was in Parasnath Hills of Giridih district in Jharkhand before leaving for Odisha last month (October).

Kishanji, the Central Committee Member of the CPI (Maoist) and head of its Central Military Commission (CMC) and also of the Eastern Regional Bureau (ERB), was killed along with other four Maoists in the fierce gun battle which went on for half-an-hour on the 24th evening.

On 24 October, Kishanji sneaked in to the forests of Parasnath Hills in Giridih district which share borders with West Bengal and Bihar, with some 25 of his close associates and held a high level meeting in the forests with leaders from Bihar, Jharkhand and even West Bengal. Intelligence officials claim they were precisely tracking kishanji for the past three months and a special team was dedicatedly working in West Bengal as well as in the Naxal Division of the MHA.

On 26 October, the high level meeting of Kishanji started with other leaders who included erstwhile Maoist Command Centre (MCC) leaders and the purpose was to restrengthen the outfit in Bihar – Jharkhand – Odisha belt. "The meeting focused on reducing the differences between the MCC and CPI (Maoist) as most of the leaders of the former outfit believed that they were neglected and their senior leaders were either killed or arrested due to mistrust between them and the PWG leaders," said an intelligence official.

"Several other issues like the effect of operation Monsoon in Saranda Forest, Kangaroo courts and matters related to collection and distribution of levy and purchase of fire arms from the North – East were also discussed at length in the day-long meeting." After the meeting, Kishanji and Suchitra had moved to Odisha through Saranda Forest. It was from Odisha that Kishanji and Suchitra along with some other leaders returned to West Bengal a Week ago. The information on their return had reached the security forces and finally they launched an intensive operation on Tuesday (22 November) evening in the Burisole forests.

After the death of Kishanji, Jharkhand police have gone on an all – out offensive against the Maoists in a well – planned strategy. Special operations were launched against the Maoists in Jhumra Hills of Bokaro district, Sataki jungle of Ranchi district, Saranda Forest of West Singhbhum and Saryu jungle of Latehar district.

"Forces are still in the jungle and the operation was launched after a specific input on Maoist movements in the forest," said Ranchi SSP Saket Kumar Singh. "Continuous operation has been launched in the area."

In Bokaro district, where the operation was launched in Jhumra Hills after specific inputs on the movement of the Navin – Manji led squad, it was called off late in the evening without any success. In Saryu jungles too, security forces did not have any success, and so was the case in Saranda Forest.

IG (Operations) SN Pradhan said the operations in the State are being launched after specific inputs and Maoists in different parts are being cornered. "With the Maoist leader Kishanji killed in police encounter, it is evident that Maoist movement in Jharkhand will also take a beating and security forces will try to take upper hand," said Pradhan.

Wanted Woman Maoist nabbed by Bermo Police: Nov 2011

A hardcore woman Maoist wanted in over a dozen cases was arrested late on 24 Nov 2011 evening, when she was coming to meet her associate in Tenughat Jail in Peterwar police station jurisdiction. Acting on a tip-off, a woman cadre Subhasani alias Anita had come to meet one of her associates at Tenughat jail.

Peterwar police raided the hide out and arrested the duo on the spot. According to Bermo DSP Santosh Pathak, Subhasani had joined the outfit at the tender age of 15 and has been with it for 20 years. Police says she become a dreaded name in Bokaro, Giridih and surrounding areas, and her influence was gradually growing.

She was wanted in some ten cases, including police encounters in Vasungarh and Hazaribagh. Pathak believes arrest of Subhasani was a good achievement for the police department. Belonging to Pirtard area of Giridih district, she was a direct link with almost all top Naxalite leaders in the State. Police have got vital information related to Maoist activities and are working on it, he said[23].

Incidents and Events: 2012

The year opens with Union Minister Jairam Ramesh visiting the State in January (2012).

Jairam Calls for tribal cooperation to combat Naxalism: Jan 2012

"The political endeavour under the Saranda Action Plan (SAP) - - not just to bring the government closer to the local tribal population but also to give them a stake in the democratic set up and unfetter the control of the Naxalites who infest the dense forests - - seems to have made some progress." It was the opening paragraph in a news analysis of the Naxal issue in its edition dated 31 Jan 2012[24].

Union RD Minister Jairam Ramesh and Jharkhand CM Arjun Munda had launched the Rs 250 Cr scheme some two months ago (in end Nov 2011) to benefit a population of 35,000 at Digha panchayat, 40 Km from Chotanagra Panchayat of Manoharpur block.

On 30 Jan 2012, the focus of the SAP was on Digha Panchayat again when Ramesh, along with Jharkhand Social Justice Minister Vimla Pradhan laid the foundation stone for the construction of two roads and an Integrated Development Centre (IDC), which will within the same premises, provide facilities such as health centre, school, public distribution system and payment of pension to the aged, widowed and disabled to name a few. Ramesh told the local people:

"The objective of the SAP is to get the government near you and correct the historical mistake of 50 years of neglect of the tribal and rural people. But without your cooperation, this battle against Naxalism cannot be won. You have to repose faith in the government and that your interests could be best taken care of by the government and not the Naxalites."

He made further points summed up here:

- "Please repose the responsibility of development with the government to ensure the development of the community. That will put pressure on the government. It is only if you have confidence and faith that the government will work for you and this new scheme will succeed."
- "The fight against Naxalism will be a long psychological battle. The success of the SAP is critical in taking forward the battle against the Naxalites across the country."

- "Without the cooperation of the people, deployment of any number of Central forces and helicopters would not yield the necessary result. There is need for the political parties to unite and come forward to make their presence felt in the Naxalite-hit areas."

People attended the function in large numbers and they aired problems ranging from lack of higher secondary school, health facility and check dams to migration of youth for want of job. They also alleged irregularities in the execution of the Mahatma Gandhi NREGS and refusal by forest officials to allow construction of roads.

Six Maoists and CoBRA Jawan killed in Jharkhand encounter: Apr 2012

"Security forces are believed to have gunned down around six Maoist cadres in a fierce gun battle in the deep forest of Karamdih under Barwadih police station in Latehar district on 5 Apr 2012[25].

The encounter started 12 PM in the afternoon when a joint team CRPF's CoBRA commandos, Jharkhand Jaguar commandos and Jharkhand Armed police men was conducting search operations in the area close to the Chhattisgarh border. The encounter lasted for three hours. During the operation, Maoists also fired at a BSF helicopter which was flying at low altitude at the time.

During the gun battle, one CoBRA jawan, Satyaprakash Jaiswal succumbed to the bullet injury while another jawan of Jharkhand Jaguar, Sanjay Kumar Paswan, was rushed to Apollo Hospital Ranchi.

A State police spokesperson RK Mallick told the daily: "Our men spotted the Maoists taking away the body of their guerrilla squad member . . . . The chopper returned safe to Ranchi.

Nawarnabhu was another site, some km away from Karamdih, where security forces engaged Maoists in another pitched battle.

It is learnt that a top Maoist leader, Sudhirji, who is a member of CPI (Maoist) Central Executive Committee, has been, of late, operating in this area.

While some additional forces have been summoned to this area, certain additional deployment has also been made by the Chhattisgarh police in its border area.

"Maoists losing grip on Saranda": Jul 2012

A daily opens up an interesting, and even handed manner, its analysis of situation in Saranda area. The story is datelined Ranchi, 5 Jul 2012:

"Whether it is security forces or ultra left outfits, none any longer enjoy the confidence of Saranda villagers. While the central forces are accused of killing innocent villagers, the Maoist stands condemned in their eyes for exploiting the situation by fanning public opinion against the government[26]."

The daily goes on: "The residents of 56 villages of Saranda have now dubbed the 'populist' measures floated by Union RD Minister Jairam Ramesh there as a subtle move to gain political mileage. They held a meeting on 4 Jul 2012 to elicit views on whether their brethren should stand by the Government action against Maoists".

The villager also sought clarification from the Government in the matter pertaining to the alleged killing of villagers Mangal Honhanga and Soma Guria by security forces in 2011 and death of 19 persons in Chhattisgarh. They also questioned the role of Ramesh who persuaded them to stand by the Government during his frequent visits to Saranda with the much – acclaimed action plan of Rs 248 Cr for the area.

The villagers complained that the report of the magisterial inquiry into the killing of Honhanga and Guria has not been made public. They alleged when the family members of the slain villagers sought the details of the magisterial inquiry were sought under the RTI Act, it was denied to them.

Sources in the NHRC told the daily that as per the Supreme Court guidelines, the Commission had conducted on inquiry on the alleged custody death and the security forces have been indicted in the magisterial inquiry report.

Maoist image suffer

Significantly, the pro-poor image of the Maoists is at stake. Villagers resolved in the meeting to defy Maoist diktats and oppose their gun battles (against the forces). Like their counterparts in Nandigram they now plan to fend for themselves without the support of ultras. They contended that if the Maoists were concerned with the plight of the villagers, they would allow the implementation of welfare schemes there.

"Jharkhand will map the Maoist mind: Jul 2012

The Jharkhand police will use the technique of brain mapping on the arrested Maoists to understand the LW rebels. This, the police hope, will help them reform the Maoists in general and stop young rebels from turning into hard core militants. The plan has been approved by the Jharkhand Government and the exercise will be conducted at the Ranchi Institute of Neuro-psychiatry and Allied Sciences (RINPAS) in Ranchi[27].

This is the first time that brain mapping will be used on the Maoists. RINPAS director Dr. Amool Ranjan Singh said: "Brain mapping will tell us why Maoists leave the mainstream and take up arms, why normal youngsters suddenly join the LWE…We hope to understand and possibly restructure their way of looking at issues so that they can come back to the mainstream."

The idea of brain mapping the Maoists was conceived in 2005 by the then DGP VD Ram. He told the weekly: "It (brain mapping) is part of the psychological operations that we undertook to counter the Maoists. The only offensive action that we used to take against them was through guns. But the Maoists are carrying out an ideological warfare, so we decided to do the same."

The psychological operations have yielded good results. Ram continues: "Many Maoists surrendered because of our psychological warfare. We were able to dissuade many arrested Maoists from returning to their old ways… Police also spread misinformation among the cadres to demoralize them, which led to many Maoists surrendering or leaving their outfit."

As part of the psyops, the police also sought help from the Indian Army. "Brigadier William of the Army came to Jharkhand and taught us how we could launch the psychological warfare against the ultras", Ram said.

Alert against Jharkhand Maoist top guns: Jul 2012

"Even as a major operation against the Maoists continues in the jungles of Jharkhand, the intelligence agencies have issued an alert to the State Government to ramp up troop levels given that some of the topmost Naxal leaders are slated to participate in a proposed congregation shortly and for whom the ultras surely might have put in place a very strong security cordon and kept a major offensive mechanism in readiness."

This was report of a daily of 19 Jul 2012[28].

The MHA had issued the alert. Some of the leading Maoist leaders who were noticed on the border between Manika Police Station under Latehar district and Panki Police Station under Palamu district are: Anup Thakur, member, Bihar – Jharkhand – North Chhattisgarh Special Area Committee; Nanho Mochi alias Prabhat and Chhotu Kharwar, both, members, Bihar Regional Committee; Nakul Yadav, Zonal commander, Koel – Sankh Zonal committee; Shyamlal Yadav, Yogeshwar Yadav and Umesh Yadav, all Sub-Zonal Commanders, Koel Sub – Zonal Committee.

"The extremists appear to have congregated for an important meeting scheduled to be hold shortly for reviewing organizational affairs, most probably of the BRC, as armed contingents have been requisitioned from else where", said the secret alert sent to Principal Secretary (Home), Jharkhand Government. The copy has also been endorsed to: DGP Jharkhand; Nodal Officer (Naxal Matters), Jharkhand Government, and DGP CRPF.

The alert seems to have conveyed further precise information about the individual movement of Naxal commander. Here it is:

- "Nakul Yadav has moved with his group into the area from his designated field of operations in Lohardaga district, while Anup Thakur and his armed group have come from Burha Pahar, located on the trijunction of Latehar – Garhwa (both in Jharkhand) and Balrampur (Chhattisgarh) districts, during the first week of July."
- Deo Kumar Singh, alias Arvind, Central Committee member, CPI (Maoist), Umesh Ganjhu alias Birsai, member BJNCSAC, and Inderjit, Company Commander, Eastern Regional Bureau (ERB), along with their armed teams are scheduled to move from their current location (Police Station Bhandaria, district Garhwa) near Burha Pahar towards Manika shortly."

Notably, an operation was launched on the night 14 July on Manika – Panki border by mobilizing personnel from CoBRA of CRPF and Jharkhand Jaguar to dismantle these groups. However, the security forces till so far have not been able to establish any contact with (these) Maoists.

Security forces have since launched a major operation in the jungles bordering Jharkhand and Chhattisgarh. The Centre further said: "In view of the large assembly of the extremists in the area, that is poised to grow even further, it is 'requested' ( ) to induct additional troops and carry out sustained search operations till either establishment of contact or disintegration of these groups."

Report meanwhile, said suspected Naxals have killed a trainee constable under Bhansi police station in Dantewada district of Chhattisgarh. Naxals reportedly have also killed six suspected police informers in the State during this month (Jul 2012).

Jharkhand's stunning seizure: USA Army rifle being sold to Maoists: Aug 2012

It was a stunning seizure. The Jharkhand Police caught two men in a jungle bordering Bihar in possession of a US Army issue assault rifle M16. It created a flutter in the State, with the police saying they would investigate if a network of suppliers of foreign-made weapons was reaching out to Maoists.

"An NIA team has already reached the state".

A M16 rifle, with markings which identify it as US army property was, thus, seized on 29 Aug 2012 by Hazaribagh district police from Praful Malakkar and Anil Yadav, who were held in Chouparavi[29].

Manufactured by Colt Defense, the M16 is the first American made weapon confiscated in Jharkhand, where security men have been battling Maoist cadres.

The M16 family, with 80 lakh manufactured piece, has been the primary service rifle of the US armed forces since the Vietnam war. Efforts are on to phase it out.

SP Hazaribagh Manoj Kaushak has the details:

"Malakkar and Yadav, both residents of Bihar, were arrested while transaction was underway. Apart from the M16, we found a bullet proof jacket, Rs 28 lakh in case, live cartridges for AK 56s and 47s, mobile phones and imported pistols. Yadav was to receive the supply and was carrying Rs 9 lakh. All except a lakh was the payment for the M16."

IG (Operations and Intelligence) SN Pradhan makes interesting and significant observations on the subject:

"It is not yet clear how the rifle came to the suppliers. It could be someone hoarding a few pieces and selling them at a premium. Maoists are always looking for the weapons that stay true and do not malfunction at critical times. There is an uninterrupted supply of crude weapons to them, but maintenance of locally-manufactured weapons is a big issue."

"Therefore, care is taken to ensure that at least 20 per cent of weapons in a Maoist platoon are always good arms."

"The M16 per se is not a huge threat. An AK-47 is always preferred by a Maoist. But we have to look into the supply of these weapons."

Naxals: Government wants NIA to probe US rifle seizure: Sep 2012

The recent seizure of a US Army assault rifle "from a senior Maoist cadre" has set the alarm bells ringing among the security agencies here. The MHA sought details of the seizure. The Centre wants the NIA to probe the matter as the inquiry so far has not gone beyond the arrest of two persons.

The Jharkhand seized a M16 assault rifle, on AK-56, four 9 mm pistols with live cartridges, cash, mobile phone and a bullet proof vest from senior

Maoist cadre Anil Yadav and arms supplier Praful Malakkar, as briefly mentioned in the preceding news story.

Details emerging from questioning of the duo have revealed that these weapons were procured through middle men. An official of the MHA adds: "There are some specific leads which needs to be probed by a Central agency as it will involve inter – state coordination. The probe by police has so far not been able to move beyond the local module."

The man suspected to be carrying out to trading of weapons has been identified as Dev Kumar Singh alias Arvindji, a Central Committee member and Secretary of Bihar – Jharkhand – North Chhattisgarh Special Area Committee (BJNCSAC). "From the details emerging so far, it is possible that Arvindji might have procured these weapons from North – East groups. Another senior Maoist leader, Prashanto Bose alias Kishanda, presently on the run, is among the prime suspects", said the official[30].

The questioning of arrested duo revealed that the small arms were being procured by the Maoists for the protection of their senior leaders. Central intelligence agencies suspect that such sophisticated weapons - - seized from the Maoists for the first time - - may have been supplied by the North – East insurgent groups.

The official explains: "We have recently unearthed a nexus between the PLA of Manipur and CPI (Maoist) where in the former was helping Naxals to procure sophisticated arms and also to impart training to their cadres".

There was a joint declaration by the PLA and Maoists to this effect in 2008 and the investigations consequently did show that Rs 33 lakh was paid by the Maoists towards the procurement of weapons and communication equipment. The deal between the PLA and Maoists was fixed at Rs 50 lakh. However, seizure of M16 Colt has taken the agencies by surprise. The MHA official concludes, "We want to unearth the entire network and identify supply chain. We have sought the opinion of local administration for a probe by the NIA."

"2 months on, CRPF revises slain Maoist list": Sep 2012

Bijapur Encounter: Had said 7 of 17 killed were rebels, now, claims 2 more had 'Naxal links.'

This is typical of the press to make a mountain of a mole hill! The headline and the blurb wants to tell its readers that the CRPF is whimsical, does not do its job diligently! It wants to convey that the paramilitary is guilty of some major faux pas! This daily often criticizes politicos for taking 'populist' decisions or measures. Ironically, the daily does not realize that it itself is indulging in 'populist' journalism by publishing such stories. If the CRPF, after further examination stories. If the CRPF, after further examination the encounter, came to determination that another two persons among the civilians, besides the seven found earlier, had Maoist links, what is so surprising about it? Why go to town on it? Is it the daily's case that initial investigations must find all details of the case, encounter here, and any subsequent findings and revelations are suspect? Be that as it may, what follows are the contents of the news story in this daily in its issue of 11 Sep 2012[31].

This is how the daily opens up the news story: "More than two months after the Bijapur encounter in Chhattisgarh, the security agencies have established that two more persons among those killed had Naxal links. Earlier, the police had said that seven out of the 17 people killed in an ambush in Basuguda area of Bijapur district had Naxal records, asserting that not all those who were killed were innocent villagers."

Amid allegations of human rights violation, the Chhattisgarh Government had ordered a judicial inquiry into the case.

The CRPF, which had conducted the operation along with the Chhattisgarh police on the night 28/29 June (2013), said that after that incident they have changed their SOPs. From now on, the CRPF will engage "more and more trackers before undertaking any operation. It has also requested the government to provide it with night vision devices of higher resolution. A senior CRPF officer elucidates the point in detail.

- "We are engaging more number of trackers before undertaking any kind of operation so that we have clear picture of the ground reality. The areas affected by the Maoist activity are quite complex in nature in terms of terrain and climate."
- "We have requested the MHA to expedite the process to procure the night vision devices."
- "There is a lot of anguish and resentment when adolescents and children are killed. We suspect they could have been used a human shields. A judicial inquiry is on, so we cannot give more details."

After Saranda, it is Latehar

"After clearning the Saranda forest area of Naxal presence last year, the next area of action would be Latehar district in Jharkhand, where police action and development would take place simultaneously." This is DG CRPF

K Vijay Kumar speaking on his future plans. The interstate border areas of Jharkhand, Chhattisgarh and Odisha are on priority list, too.

Reacting to the reports about a study conducted by the IIM, Ahmedabad, that a lot of CRPF men are leaving the force due to stress, here is Kumar's reply: "That is true. There is a lot of stress among the troops because of continuous deployment. We will have to give them rest and recuperation".

Jharkhand Reds kill two for stealing goats: Oct 2012

'Suspected' Maoists killed two 'alleged' goat thieves at Phattitarn in Gumla district after chopping off their hands in presence of villagers on 19 Oct 2012. Police Inspector Amish Hussein identified the two as Lachhan Lohra and Ramdeo Kharwar. He said another person, Jitra Oraon, managed to escape[32].

Reports said a Maoist squad had caught Lohra, Kharwar and Jitra while they were coming from nearby Ghaghra with a pair of goats, allegedly stolen from the village. After inquiring about the goats, the Moists abducted them. "The hands of the two were tied and chopped off. Then they were beaten to death by the rebels while Jitra escaped," a police officer said. One of the deceased had a criminal history while another had just come out of jail. Police have started probe into the incident.

Preliminary probe showed the cadres killed the two as they thought the two were close to Jharkhand Janmukti Morcha, a new splinter group of CPI (Maoist) in the State. The outfit has 70 members and all of them were active Maoists at one point.

Comments

It is of interest to make some comments on this news story carried by this daily.

- 'Suspected' word is used by the press in such cases to be on the right side of the law, after all when the story appeared in the press, there was no proof that the perpetrators indeed were the Maoist cadres. It is equally true that the scribe and the daily also want to be on the right side of the ultras, since they have the gun in their hands.
- Having said the above, it is also inexplicable that in the rest of the text of the news story, following the opening paragraph where the term 'suspected' is used, the daily is not squeamish about using the word 'Maoist' more than once.
- Same goes for the word 'alleged.'

- This incident is a good example of rough and ready justice handed out by the Maoists to the villagers. Equally true is the cruelty and inhumanity of the two Maoists: Chapping of their hands and then beating the two to death in the presence of the villagers, for demonstrative effect. This cruelty is also on display when the Maoist cleave the stomach of the slain policemen and stitch it after putting IEDs inside!

Two of eight fugitive Maoists found: Nov 2012

Two of the eight Maoists, who fled while being taken to jail after the ultras fired on a transit van in Giridih, have been found.

While Baijnath returned on his own, another Maoist Bipin Mandal was in a nursing him where police men injured in (Friday) 9 Nov 2012 attack were admitted.

This was disclosed by IGP SN Pradhan. The other six Maoists were still missing[33].

"Jharkhand Maoists ambush police vehicles and free cadres": Nov 2012

Another daily has covered the incident briefly dealt with in the preceding entry, in much greater detail which is described in this entry. First two paragraph of this news story are reproduced here:

- "Three policemen and a prisoner were killed when Maoists opened fire on a police van and a police escort vehicle carrying their cadres and other prisoners to Giridih Jail on 9 Nov 2012.
- "Senior officials put the number of constables injured in the attack at six though eye witnesses said 10 police personnel including three women constables, were being treated for injuries in local hospitals (in Giridih)."

The daily covered the incident in greater detail in its 10 Nov 2012 issue[34].

DSP Shatrughan Razzak offers some details: "A group of some 24 Maoists, including women, on 12 motor cycles, a Bolero and a Scorpio blocked the road at Udanabad Mod at 4:30 PM and threw bombs and opened fire at the police vehicles. Eight Maoists and 25 other prisoners who were being taken from the court to jail are absconding. We found the Bolero stuck in sand in a river on the Bihar – Jharkhand border near Bihar's Jamui district while searching the area."

DGP Jharkhand GS Rath said: "Three policemen - - ASI Prabhu Nath Singh, Constable Raj Kumar Das and Driver Gagrai - - lost their lives in the attack. There were 32 prisoners in the vehicles. Eight Maoists fled towards Bihar, 25 are absconding, one prisoner was injured."

The eight Maoists who fled were: Baijnath Tiwari; Ramesh Mandal; Mithlesh Mandal; Nimchand Mahato; Sahedeo Soren Manjhi; Bipin Mandal; Chotka Mirandi and Panstosh Hembram. Ramesh Mandal is an accused in the killing of Jharkhand MLA Mahendra Singh in 2006, and Manjhi is the Bihar – Jharkhand Special Area Committee member. Other accused include Maoists arrested for attacking under – construction police Bhavan in Giridih earlier this year (2012).

Among those injured, three are being treated at the Sadar Hospital in Giridih, five at a private hospital and two grievously injured have been referred to hospitals outside Giridih. The district which is located on Jharkhand's border with Bihar is known for its coal mines and mica deposits.

The attack took place in an industrial area about a kilometer from the Giridih jail.

A team of senior police officials - - IG (Operations) SN Pradhan, IG Bakaro Range Murarilal Meena, DIG Suman Gupta and CRPF spokesperson IG MV Rao - - visited the ambush site the next day, the 10th.

7 held for Giridih ambush: 10 Nov 2012

In a major breakthrough, the Giridih police on 10 Nov 2012 arrested seven persons in connection with the Naxal attack on the 9th where three policemen were killed while the Maoists succeeded in freeing eight of their cadres while they were being taken back to the jail after production before the different courts in Giridih.

The police have also recovered a Bolero jeep, a tractor and 12 motor cycles from the Devri and Bengabad area which were said to be used in the attack by the Maoists on the 9th.

Police say intensive search operation has been started in the adjoining areas and it succeeded in getting vital clues against the culprits who were involved in the attack. State police spokesperson SN Pradhan gave details: "It appears that the operation was conducted to free hard core Maoist Anuj ji and raid on the police van was conducted by one Chirag Dasta (= squad or group). The Maoists also took away six carbines and one 303 rifle with them. It was a deliberate mistake on the part of the police. Those found responsible for the incident will not be spared, and duly punished. There are bleak chances of their arresting those absconding Maoists as they might have escaped from the area[35]."

Raising concern on the incident, the Police Association has said that despite having intelligence input that the Maoists might resort to such an attack to free their cadres, police was negligent while ferrying the prisoners, resulting in the killing of the three policemen.

Sources disclosed that major part of police force on the 9th, the day incident took place, was deployed at former CM Babulal Marandi's programme in the area without any apprehensions about possibility of such an incident!

Chances of involvement of the local unions could not be neglected or ignored as there were substantial inputs that intensive reconnaissance was being carried out by the Maoists of the area for the last few days.

In the news again: 18 Nov 2012

The sensational November ambush in Giridih which resulted in the freeing of 32 prisoners, including six hardcore Maoists, was once again in the news on the 18th when the Giridih police arrested four persons in connection with the security disaster of the 9th.[36]

SP Giridih Honkar Amol Venukant disclosed: "They were arrested on the basis of a lead while security forces were on an operation in the jungles near Deori. Two motor cycles which were believed to have been used in the ambush, along with six bombs, have also been rcovered."

Of the four arrested, Babulal Besra is from Jamui, Ashok Chode from Munger, Chandar Marandi and Mukesh Yadav from Chaka of Jamui.

The SP says, "they have revealed quite a lot of information during interrogation."

"Naxal shadow looms large, tiger stripes blur": Nov 2012

That the Maoists have played havoe with men, materials and nation's image and to an extent, its sovereignty are well known. What is not so well-known is that a prised possession of Jharkhand, its tigers, too have suffered because of the Maoists' presence and consequent violence in that state. The article in a daily under the above caption brings to light this very uncomfortable fact of life.[37]

This is how the daily introduces the emotional subject: "Jharkhand, proud parent to acres of forests across its lolling countryside, seems to have nevertheless extinguished the 'tiger, tiger, burning bright' within. The fact that it is hardly the only state to have lost its way in tiger conservation is a small consolation. Jharkhand has a lone reserve dedicated to the striped cat and has let it down rather badly. Bizarrely enough, the strong Naxal presence has played a prime role in the entire drama taking place quietly behind the forest curtains."

The following text, paraphrased here and there, gives the details of this irreparable loss to the State, nay, the entire nation.

The forests of Palamu Tiger Reserve (PTR) and Betta National Park (BNP) fall smack within the fiery Red Zones. By quirk of geography, the deep jungles are home to both deadly and widely feared species - - the tiger and the Maoist.

Even the most zealous of forest officials find it tough to actually be at ground zero to save the tiger. Infrastructure is miserly within these areas, and the life tough for all but the most seasoned locals. As a result the administration seems literally in the dark on the wild cat. Though the Forest Department vehemently denies the Naxal link, it is the sorry truth that the reserve has a complete lack of officials, forest guards, camera traps and, unfortunately, tigers.

Authorities claim that they are sorely hampered by manpower crunch; they complain that villagers graze their cattle in the core area and refuse to budge and despise persuasion; the latest excuse is the ongoing anti-Naxal operations in the area. But no one can tell when was the last time a striped cat was sighted in the PTR. Some 40 years ago, Project Tiger roared on to the conservation stage, with ambitious plans. 46 reserves have come up across the country but have barely managed to shelter this magnificent creature. The numbers remain unchanged and dismal at a 1,700 – odd.

Jharkhand has not fared any better. The Project Tiger figures say that Palamu Reserve had a score or so tigers when this conservation effort began, and claim to have increased them by about 10 by 2002. It is a dubious notion, with figures between two census nearly doubling at times and then dipping round to the same base in course of several years. For all its lofty claims, to repeat, no one can tell when was the last time a stripped cat was sighted in the PTR.

Smuggling of Sal wood is rampant and trees are felled with impunity even in the core areas of the reserve.

There are many reasons handy for lack of action but no one can explain why everyone except forest officials enter and exit deep jungles with ease. No one names the Naxals or the locals' belief that the rebels are a lesser evil than Government officials. But villagers and tribals in Jharkhand, Chhattisgarh and Odisha do side with the Maoists. The rebels are a perennial presence even as officialdom comes and go.

Ironically, the authorities are bent on proving the locals the villain of the piece, despite the fact that there are much bigger fish in the water.

High alert in Jharkhand for Maoist 'Martyr Week': Nov 2012

"As State police headquarters sounds a high alert, Maoists have begun preparations to make their 'Martyr Week' a grand success from Saturday, 24 Nov. 2012, coinciding with Kishanji's death anniversary." A daily carries this report on the subject of Maoist 'Martyr Week' in its issue of 26 Nov 2012[38].

Other than nocturnal meetings in the rural segment in Topchanchi and Tundi Blocks of Dhanbad district, the ultras are reported to have grand plans for impressive flag marches as well, to openly display their arsenals. Sources revealed that at several villages coming under Topchanchi police station, Maoist cadre have been seen singing songs in honour of Kishanji on Saturday, 24 Nov 2012.

In covert meetings held a couple of days ago, a decision has also been taken to perpetrate some overt acts against the police in Bokaro, Giridih or Hazaribagh.

Earlier, the Centre had asked all Naxal-hit states, including Jharkhand, to step up operations as "the ultras were planning to intensify their offensive this week."

IG (Operations) SN Pradhan adds: "There were intelligence inputs suggesting that the Maoists, who observe Martya Week from 2 – 8 December, had decided to enforce it this week from 24 November to coincide with Kishanji's death anniversary".

House in session: Dec 2012 "Naxal hand in Panem Conflict"

"Marandi should clarify details of meeting with Panem officials" Simon Marandi.

While the JMM leveled serious allegations against the JVM chief Babulal Marandi for his alleged 'interest' in the Panem controversy, the Government on 3 Dec 2012 distanced itself from the said 2006 agreement, taking a stand for the first time since the Panem issue snowballed in Panchuwara of Pakur.

Outside the house, JMM's Simon Marandi even alleged a Naxal hand: "Babulal Marandi's dharna is a drama and being done with the help of the Naxals to frighten the management and local administration. Anti-social elements have become a part of it. He (Marandi) had met senior officials of Panem in Kolkata before the JVM launched its protests in the area. Marandi should make public details of his meeting with Panem officials, to avoid dubious link between the party and Panem."

Heated exchanges also saw BJP's Raghuwar Das charging the JVM of raking up the issue for the sake of money.

Earlier in the house, replying to the issue raised by Jharkhand Vikas Morcha's (JVM) Pradeep Yadav, Dy CM - cum – Mining Minister Hemant Soren said: "The 2006 agreement is not the Government's agreement but has been signed between Rajmahal Pahad Bachao Samiti and Panem. It is not the Government responsibility to make sure that the agreement is implemented. If someone had made some commitments, how can the Government fulfill those?"

Hemant instead blamed the JVM for misguiding tribals to get political mileage by aggravating the situation.

The agreement between the Samiti and Panem management was inked in Nov 2006, days before the scheduled hearing in the Supreme Court in December. Hemant pointed out: "The petition had been withdrawn from the Supreme Court a few days before the judgment. Stephen Marandi (then Dy CM) was also a witness. Now he is sitting on dharna." He continued, flaying the JVM's claims: "We should also take into consideration that it is slowly becoming inter-state dispute. The agitation is politically motivated. Programmes of dance, music and langar are taking place there by misguiding poor people."

Earlier, the JVM stalled proceedings of the Assembly for almost the entire day and demanded reply from the CM, alleging breach of the agreement by the coal mining company. The speaker adjourned the House three times and it finally met at 3.10 PM.

However, the Dy CM's reply could not pacify party legislators. Yadav said the land was acquired by the Government and given to Panem for mining and the agreement, disowned by the government-now, came into existence because of this. (The MLA) Yadav continued: "It was you who acquired the land and gave it to Panem. Tribals signed the agreement due to this. Now, when the management is not fulfilling the agreement, is it not your responsibility?"

The MLA also denounced the offer of departmental investigation into JVM's allegations of Panem dishonouring commitments and irregularities in coal mining. "We have no faith in your probe. We demand that a panel of three secretaries go there and investigate. We also demand a CBI probe into Sister Valsa's murder", said Yadav.

JVM seeks CBI probe into MP-Maoist link: Dec 2012

The battle between the JVM and JMM continued in the Assembly on 4 Dec 2012 as well. If it was Panem agreement earlier, on the 4th it was the link between the Maoists and an MP. Here are the details as given by a daily.

The JVM on the 4th demanded a CBI probe instead of the ongoing CID investigation into the conversation recorded on a CD between JVM MP Ajay Kumar and a Maoist to allegedly influence the result of the Lok Sabha by poll held on 1 Jul 2011.

Raising the issue in the Assembly during the zero hour, JVM's Legislature Party leader Pradip Yadav demanded a CBI probe to distinguish the voice on the CD and accused the State of conspiracy to malign its MP.

The Government had ordered a CID probe after BJP leader Saryu Roy made the CD available to the media on polling day in 2011. He had alleged that the conversation on the CD was between Kumar and Maoist leader Samarji.

Notes

1. Manoj Prasad, Indian Express, 25 Oct 2006.
2. Dipankar Bose, The Statesman, 27 Oct 2006.
3. Nityanand Shukla, The Pioneer, 15 Nov 2006.
4. *Ibid,* 5 Dec 2006.
5. *Ibid,* 8 Jan 2007.
6. *Ibid,* 23 Feb 2007.
7. Kumar Uttam, Asian Age, 6 Mar 2006.
8. Manoj Prasad, Indian Express, 6 Mar 2007.
9. Sonali Das, Times of India, 6 Mar 2007.
10. *Ibid.*
11. Jaideep Deogharia, Times of India, 6 Mar 2007.
12. Manoj Prasad, Indian Express, 10 Apr 2007.
13. Ambrish Dutta, The Tribune, 17 Apr 2007.
14. Vijay Murti, Hindustan Times, 12 Apr 2007.
15. Manoj Prasad, Indian Express, 19 Jun 2007.
16. Manoj Prasad, Indian Express, 16 Jun 2007.
17. The Pioneer, 6.12.2008.
18. The Editorial, The Pioneer, 5 May 2011.
19. Amrendra Suman, The Pioneer, 13 Oct 2011.
20. DP Sharan, The Pioneer, 8 Nov 2011.
21. PTI, The Hindu, 21 Nov 2011.
22. Manohar Lal, The Pioneer, 26 Nov 2011.
23. ENS, The Pioneer, 26 Nov 2011.
24. K Balchand, The Hindu, 31 Jan 2012.
25. PNS, The Pioneer, 6 Apr 2012.
26. DP Sharan, The Pioneer, 6 Jul 2012.
27. Abhinandan Mishra, Sunday Guardain, 15 Jul 2012.

28. Rakesh K. Singh, The Pioneer, 19 Jul 2012.
29. Deepu Sebestian Edmond, Indian Express, 1 Sep 2012.
30. ENS, Indian Express, 4 Sep 2012.
31. Vijaita Singh, Indian Express, 11 Sep 2012.
32. TNN, Times of India, 21 Oct 2012.
33. ENS, Indian Express, 11 Nov 2012.
34. Anumeha Yadav, The Hindu, 10 Nov 2012.
35. Mukesh Ranjan, The Pioneer, 11 Nov 2012.
36. PNS, The Pioneer, 19 Nov 2012.
37. Neha Prasad, The Pioneer, 19 Nov 2012.
38 Ashish Sinha, The Pioneer, 26 Nov 2012.

26

Jharkhand - 2

Jairam Ramesh lauds Jharkhand's MNREGA: Dec 2012

Union Rural Development Minister Ramesh 9 Dec 2012 suggested states replicate Jharkhand's performance in MNREGA under which it has constructed 78,000 wells in the last two years. It is a record and the Minister suggested the state put the construction details on the website. It would help other states to follow the Jharkhand's model of construction of wells under MGNREA[1].

Ramesh added details: "Development works in Saranda (forest areas) are going on with two of the nine roads set to be inaugurated within 15 days. The finished roads are the 2.5 km stretch from Domari to Salai and 3 km road between Iasiapecha and Jojobutu."

Ramesh expressed satisfaction after reviewing rural developmental works and said the State Government officials had told him that Rs 670 Cr was spent under the MGNREGA so far.

Anti – Naxal operations spread across Dalma: Dec 2012

With reports suggesting CPI (Maoist) cadres trying to regain their grip at Dalma, Bodam and Patamola where they have almost been eliminated in the anti-insurgency operations carried out during the past couple of years, a joint force of CRPF and district armed police engaged in flushing out ultras of CPI (Maoist), on 14 Dec 2012 launched an offensive operation at the Dalma area.

Acting on a tip–off, the security has been beefed up in Dalma hills and goes on with search operations to nab the ultras.

The district police confirmed launching of fresh anti-insurgency operation in the Bengal boarder area along the Dalma-Patamda and MGM area. A combing operation was started at Bota and Konkadasa villages deep into the sprawling Dalma (in Purab Singhbhum district). Though the police and CRPF did not come across any Maoists as such, in the initial stages they have found evidence of the armed Naxals roaming in a number of villages which till Dec 2009 used to be a stronghold area of the ultras[2].

Revealing the fresh movement of the ultras, the SP (Rural) Rajiv Ranjan Singh said they had information about an eight member armed squad of Maoists frequently visiting Konkadasa village since the past one month.

Police was not in a position to give any information about the operation due to security reasons but the fact is the operation was undertaken after getting authentic information on the movement of Naxals in the villages on the Damla Hills.

Maoists torch 14 vehicles of Railway project in Saranda: Dec 2012

During the ongoing anti-Naxal operation, Anaconda-2, in Saranda forests of West Singhbhum district, armed Maoist guerrillas torched 14 vehicles of a private company involved in a rail track and tunnel construction on the Howrah-Mumbai main line near Mahadevshal in Goelkera block of West Singhbhum district, 180 km from Jamshedpur 16 November night[3].

35-40 armed ultras reached the site near Derwa and torched dumpers, road rollers, earth digging JCB machines and a poke-lane vehicle after over powering the employees of the Triveni Construction Company to which the vehicles belonged.

The ultras also partially torched seven trucks there. The company was engaged in the construction of a third rail line on the route for the past one year.

Disclosing the incident SP West Singhbhum District Pankaj Kamboj said some 35 Maoists had swooped on a workers' camp nears Mahadevshal and torched the vehicles, which include 10 dumpers, two poclains and as many rollers.

The workers camp had been put up by a railway contractor for executing a railway line project. The ultras asked the workers to keep their mobile phones switched off. Once that was done, the Maoists torched all the vehicles within moments. Kamboj further added: "we had warned the contractor against working in such a badly hit Naxal area without proper security, but he did not listen to us."

Incidentally, there was no untoward incident at the railway project during the last one year. But the contractor had four days ago approached the office of the SP West Singhbhum, through the Chakradharpur railway divisional office, for permission to use explosives required to be used for making a tunnel for the third line project.

The SP, who is conducting the inquiry into the violence, wondered how could the ultras swoop over the construction site camp just four days after the divisional railway authority had approached for permission to use explosives at the third line project site and subsequent request to keep forces at the project site.

Meanwhile, the CRPF have been asked to be ready for launching a combing operation at the site of the latest Maoist violence.

"The security forces are presently engaged in the Operation Anaconda-2 which began last week to flush out the ultras from Saranda forests". The operation was undertaken to ensure the smooth running of the Centre-sponsored Rs 250 cr Saranda Action Plan, under which the development of that remote area was being carried out. This is the second incident of Maoist violence in West Singhbhum during the last three weeks. Earlier, on 26 November, the Maoists had torched six vehicles at a road construction site at Usaris village under the Kiriburu block of Saranda.

Maoist Insurgency: Kundan Pahan Zonal Commander: 8 Dec 2012

The Adivasi warlord who stirs Jharkhand's Maoist pot.

A major news story on the Naxal insurgency was published by a weekly in its 8 Dec 2012 issue. It has a drawing of a Zonal commander, named Kundan Pahan, spread across the page under the bold headlines, reproduced above. The story is the result of a prolonged research carried out by the scribe on the subject. It essentially deals with the life and deeds of this Maoist commander, along with details of fictions within the CPI (Maoist) in Jharkhand.

The contents of this story need a serious look, and are mentioned in detail in the pages that follow[4].

Incidentally, this is the last story on the Maoist insurrection for the year 2012, dealt with in this chapter.

The weekly says at the very start, rather meaningfully and rather matter-of-factly: "G Vishnu reports from Jharkhand's killing fields where Kundan Pahan, a 'most wanted' Maoist, has become a metaphor for the frightening chaos spawned by a plethora of armed groups at war with each other."

The above neatly sums up the two main aspects of this analysis, as mentioned earlier, namely, the doings or misdoings of this 'most wanted 'Maoist commander and the fact of internicive warfare among the various factions of the CPI (Maoist) in Jharkhand's theatre of LWE violence.

Kundan Pahan is perhaps only the second Adivasi from Jharkhand to become a member of the Bihar – Jharkhand – north Chhattisgarh Special Area Committee (BJNC SAC) of the CPI (Maoist). He had first grabbed the attention of the national media in Oct 2009 with the abduction and gruesome beheading of Francis Induwar, 37, an Adivasi police officer working with the intelligence wing of the Jharkhand Police. Induwar was picked up by Kundan's squad from Arki market in Khunti district, and taken to the forests near Bundu in Ranchi district. The Maoists demanded the release of three leaders, including politburo member Kokad Ghandy, currently lodged in Tihar Jail, Delhi. A week later, body of Induwar, along with his severed head, was found at Namkum, 12 km from Ranchi. This brutal murder sparked outrage in civil society and was even criticized by even the then CPI (Maoist) spokesperson Azad.

Paragraph 2 of this analysis conveys several home truths about the LWE situation in Jharkhand and its origin and consequences: "With a bounty of Rs 25 Lakh on his head, Kundan is today one of the 'most wanted' Maoists in Jharkhand –and a symbol of what is wrong with the state. With a section of the political establishment in Cahoots with crony business houses, the state has become a battle ground for a whole array of violent militant groups, promising nothing but a slow bloodbath in the coming decade. The shocking brutality of Indumar's beheading is just one strand of brutality of Indumar's life, which intermeshes the narrative of Kundan's life, with other threads of a sad yet significant tale of how young Adivasis in Jharkhand's impoverished hilly and forest tracts end up as Maoist outlaws, hunted by, and hunting, other Adivasis—not just members of the security forces, but also of rival armed groups (which are sometimes encouraged by the police to take on the Maoists and then disowned). The story of this Adivasi Maoist leader also shows how the CPI (Maoist), despite its claims to be fighting for the rights of Adivasis, seems to be operating like a brigand's gang in Jharkhand, with high stakes in the 'extortion economy' and involving a bloody turf war with other armed groups."

Now for some history of Kundan and his squad. More than two years before the infamous beheading of Induwar, Kundan's squad had been named in the Mar 2007 of JMM MP Sunil Mahato in Baguria. Another high-profile murder followed in Jul 2008, this time the victim was JD (U) MLA and former minister Ramesh Singh Munda. It is believed these killings were "punishment" for breaking the promises made to Kundan during the elections. This 'punishment theory' is tersely corroborated by a top cop, who has worked in the IB, on condition of anonymity: "Show me one politician in Jharkhand worth his salt who has not struck a deal with the Maoists or other militant groups during the polls. Without Maoist support, no politician can ever find a foothold in the hilly, forested constituencies."

In may 2008, Kundan's squad looted Rs 5.5 Cr from an ICICI Bank van (Sources say he sent Rs 1 cr of this to his party). Two months later, they triggered a landmine blast killing six cops, including DSP Bandu Promod Kumar.

Sources say his squad his killed over 100 people in the past four years – alleged police informers, SPOs, dissenting villagers and security personnel. While sympathizers speak of the dangers of having police informers in the villages, the police hold almost a personal grudge against him for what he has done to their colleagues.

Moreover, Kundan is known to have scant regards even for his party's diktats and has often charged its "Bihari and Bengali leadership" in this zone. So why did he join the Maoist party? Among several tales doing the rounds, the most cited related to a land dispute in which his father lost a plot to his uncle.

Kundan , now 35, was born to a family of Pahans (Adivasi priests). His childhood friend Mahadev Munda recalls that he was a slow learner at school. He first left his village Barigada (1989) when an engineer from Gaya, who was building a dam across the Kanchi River nearby, hired 12-year-old Kundan to look after his Jersey cow. When he returned after three years, the land dispute between his father and uncle had begun. Two years later, he joined the MCC which merged with the PWG to form the CPI (Maoist) in 2004. By 1997, he had become the MCC's Bandu-Tamar area commander.

Bikram Vohra , a rice mill worker from a neighbouring village, is believed to have inducted Kundan into the party. Bikram was shot dead by the Maoists after he became police informer and SPO around 2000. A former aide says Kundan never spoke out against Bikram.

Kundan Pahan becomes important

Kundan's silence on Bikram was attributed to "some strange feeling of servitude." But, 'gratitude' may perhaps be a better term instead of 'servitude'; after all he had got Kundan into the CPI (Maiost). Be that as it may, but nobody harboured any illusions about Dhananjay Munda, a close aide who surrendered and become an SPO. Today, Dhananjay[5] is said to be a major asset for the police force, helping in strategizing anti-Maoist operations.

Barigada is 18 km towards the forests from the Tamar block bus stand on the Ranchi- Jamshedpur highway. A village with a middle school, it has 75 houses and a population of 450 that depends on agriculture and MGNREGA work for livelihood. Village records show Kundan's father Narayan Pahan as a beneficiary of the MGNREGA. Narayan, 73, is still the village Pradhan. "I perform the puja in our village Sarna (a grove of sal tree and a place of worship) and for our Bonga Buru (tribal deity). That is why the tigers do not attack us. That is why family still lives with some dignity", says Narayan.

"We urged Kundan, the youngest of our six sons, not to join the party, but he was stubborn. Then he became a leader. Why will a leader listen to us? We kept hoping against hope that he will come back", rues Narayan, who last saw Kundan more than three years ago. His elder sons Dimba and Shyam, too, followed Kundan into the Maoist fold and are said to be part of the same squad, while Hari and Jungal became labourers in Ranchi. Only Lohar, the second youngest son, stays with his father. Kundan has an eight-year-old daughter who does not live with his father, and Narayan is happy that she is not part of the violent world that his father has come to make his.

Every villager here remembers what the security forces unleashed during the combing operations in the past decade. They recount in hushed tones those horrific nights when all the men would flee to the forest at any hints of the police Said. "Every one feared for the boys and the village would be empty for weeks. Fed up with being thrashed every time and fearing for my life, I left the village in 2002 and stayed away for seven years", says Eshwar Munda[6], a resident of the village. In 2004, Narayan was arrested and accused of murder. He still shudders remembering his 11 months in custody. It is suspected that his arrest was an attempt to force Kundan to surrender.

However, the police no longer seem interested in getting Kundan to surrender. "We will bump him off the moment we lay our hands on him. He has left us with no other option", says a senior cop, a veteran of three operations hunting for Kundan. Indeed, the forces have gone great lengths to find Kundan and neutralize him. Moreover, his former aides have publicly denounced his leadership and stories of sexual exploitation of women cadres have been highlighted.

"It is out of fear that the villagers feed him. He remains our biggest challenge since 2008 and we carry out at least four operations every month to get at him", says Naushed Alam, DSP Bundu. Part of the challenge is to take on the military strategy adopted by the Kundan squad. Two columns of 14-15 cadres are deployed at a distance from the core column of 40 to keep a look out for the police. Moreover, Kundan never camps anywhere for too long. "He is always on the run", says Ramesh, a former aide who is still underground.

Kundan: A prize catch

Many in the security and intelligence set-ups, including DGP GS Rath, deny it, still it is no secret that Kundan will surely make a prize catch for the security force today in the state! After all, he is the only Adivasi to have made it to the leadership ranks, after Special Area Committee (SAC) member Samar Ji, 45, an educated Adivasi of the Ho community. Given the Telugu-Bengali hegemony in the Maoist leadership, Kundan's Adivasi identity and Mundari mother tongue make him a necessary prop for the party in the region. Through levy collections and extortion, he has contributed massively to his party funds, and brought in new cadres even as the Maoists face attrition in their ranks in Jharkhands, with several cadres joining splinter groups that are easier on the discipline.

"Kundan and his party have gone into a spiral of violence. He can not stop and think why he is there, or why he is on the run. I am sure he can not speak fine cogent sentences on his party's ideology", says SN Pradhan, IG (special branch). "The way he perceives violence, he seems closer to the People's Liberation Front of India (PLFI), a violent extortionist outfit with neither ideological commiment nor discipline".

Pradhan, a 1998 batch IPS officer, quotes from WB Yeat's The Second Coming to describe the current violence: "The Centre can not hold and more anarchy is loosed upon the world......" He says, "There are so many groups, and they are all contributing to breaking up the Maoist movement. It is good in a way for us, but it is also a tough job to deal with the varied sets of problems posed by different militant groups".

Splinter groups

Another top cop, who has led several anti-Maoist operations, says Kundan will most likely meet his death at the hands of another Adivasi. Besides the splinter militant groups that moonlight for the security forces for money and mercy, nearly 100 Adivasi SPOs keep a constant watch on the movement of Maoists in the Bundu- Tamar region. Among those gunning for Kundan life is Pankaj Purty, a Munda Adivasi, who was earlier with the PLFI and now leads his own group, the Village Republic Guard of India (VRGI), of 50 boys all in the age group of 15-25, in the Arki block of

Khunti district. The group aims to protect villagers from the Maoists, and collects 'donations' from the traders, transport companies and villagers. Pankaj proudly claims that his group has managed to keep Kundan squad out of the area.

Speaking to the weekly, Pankaj revealed that the local police had initially provided "all kinds of support", but later backed off. "It has been six years since I left home. I can't go back and take up agriculture again until it is more peaceful, but I don't know when this conflict would end" 'he says.

All splinters are in it: "Rs 200cr 'Extortion Economy'

In fact, no stake holder in this conflict expects it to end any time soon. The mother outfit, CPI (Maoists) and all the splinters spawned by it are stake holders in an "extortion economy" worth over Rs 200 cr per annum, at a conservative estimate. Some of the prominent splinter Maoist factions are named here:

- PLFI
- Tritiya Sammelan Pragati Committee (TPC)
- TPC-1 (A Break- Away Group of (TPC)
- Jharkhand Liberation Tigers (JLT)
- Jharkhand Jan Mukti Parishad (JMP)
- Shastra Pratirodh Manch (SPM)
- Swatantra Jharkhand Prastuti Committee (SPC)
- Jharkhand Prastuti Committee (JPC).

In fact, the groups have long held each other as enemies, even exchanging fire, killing cadres as also civilians. Though recently they have made attempts to keep a certain distance from each other, the CPI (Maoist) still considers the splinter groups as "Counter- Revolutionary", going by their Central Committee's Jul 2012 bulletin. Even as the CPI (Maoist) faces attrition in its ranks, the other groups have thrived due to the initial benevolence of the state machinery and the mainstream political parties that nurtured them to serve their own interests.

DGP Jharkhand Rath denied any kind of cooperation between the state and the splinter groups. But another senior police officer admitted that district level officers have sometimes actively nurtured elements within these groups to target the Maoists. "Some SPs thought it would be beneficial for us to have these groups fight the battle on our behalf as they know the terrain and language better (than our men), but the groups went on to become very violent and also rich", he says on condition of anonymity. The weekly also spoke to two district- level officers who confirmed this stance-possibility.

On 6 Oct 2012, the DGP announced the starting of operations against the PLFI, the second largest of the ultras groups. For the first time, the operations would also include the CRPF—earlier used only in operations against the CPI (Maoist). Though only the TPC is, technically speaking, a splinter group of the CPI (Maoist), having broken away from the MCC citing "cultural differences" before its merger with the PWG, the State has clubbed all the groups under the rubric of LWE.

"We are very clear and determined that we will not tolerate any non-state actor indulging in violence" , Rathi told the weekly. Another police officer adds: "If we find Dinesh Gop, the leader of PLFI tomorrow, nothing will stop us from going for him. Though there is less political clarity on tackling Maoists in Jharkhand than in Chhattisgarh, even JMM Chief and former CM Shibu Soren never stopped us from doing what we had to do, though he said elsewhere that the Maoists are his brothers."

In this scenario, turning those who get caught in the vicious cycle of violence into SPOs is only a cynical 'solution', with devastating consequences, to what is otherwise a complex equation—though senior police officers may call it a "trick of the trade". But it is trick that plays havoc with the lives of the people, especially the poor and the deprived.

Take the case of Sanjay Purty, as an SPO he was close to some VRGI cadre and was short dead by PLFI cadres in Khunti on 25 September (2012). When asked about Sanjay, Rath says, "He was probably an SPO in the distant past, and had gone astray and developed illicit relationships with some militant groups". The weekly has in its possession a Bank of India cheque (No. 009324) dated 23 Mar 2012 for Rs 27,000 `issued by former Khunti SPM Tamil Vanan, to Sanjay as payment for his services.

If the DGP terms as "illicit" the hazy relationships that these foot soldiers of chaos maintain in their microcosms, the Maoists and other militant groups, too, see the SPOs as "enemy agents". Though it is not a declared state policy, surrendered Maoists and other militants have been turned into SPOs, spies and informers, thus pushing them into the same war they wanted to run away from.

The DGP himself admitted the lack of clarity on a surrender policy. Moreover, one of the seniormost cops in Jharkhand revealed that the establishment does not intend to make compromises with the "brains" of the Maoist movement. "In the case of Narayan Sanyal (alleged politburo member) and others in the CPI (Maoist) leadership, we are very clear that we can not afford to have them in the open. They will always try to strengthen the movement", says a police officer handling intelligence in the case of 78-year-old Sanyal. The State Police have tried everything in their hands to keep him in jail, despite a hunger strike by Maoist cadres inside Hazaribagh jail where he is currently lodged.

"They want to make examples out of Sanyal and Sushil Roy, another Maoist leader currently admitted in the AIIMS, Delhi, with a kidney ailment. They want both to breathe their last in prison", says a Ranchi-based Human Rights activist, explaining the difficulties in ensuring human rights for Maoist prisoners.

It is keeping in mind this dark canvas that one needs to reflect on the tale of Kundan Pahan. In this war of all-against – all, where the line between perpetrator and the victim is often blurred, the question of who is fighting whom and for what cause, becomes the least important factor shaping the fate of individuals. Indeed, Jharkhand's bloody quagmire is pregnant with many Kundans and Bikrams – people swept away by the circumstances of their homes and surroundings into a tunnel with no light at the end.

Statistics and data from this article

This analytical article has some useful data that should be of interest and use for future by scholars interested in the study of this subject. The same is given below.

The War within : Jharkhand

Rs 400 Crore

The annual cost of anti-Naxal operations to the exchequer, 40 per cent of which is contributed by the State.

100 Companies

Of CRPF, besides two battalions of COBRA forces.

90 Companies

Of Jharkhand Armed Police.

20 Units

Of Jharkhand Jaguar forces anti-Naxal Special Forces.

Efficient Intelligence Network

The State has invested heavily in building of a network of spies and informers, leading to the arrest of two Special Area Committee (SAC) members in 2012.

Effective Weaponisation Programme

The CRPF, Jaguar and COBRA forces have access to INSAS rifles, AK-47, Glock 17 and 19 pistols and 600 LMGs placed on vehicles used in combing operations, which include around 100 mine-protected vehicles, each worth over Rs 1 Cr.

The Maoists and their splinters: Jharkhand Prastuti Committee (JPC)

With many cadres becoming SPOs, the group is on the back foot but still has some 200 cadres.

Areas of Presence (Districts)

Palanu, Chatra, Hazaribagh, Khunti.

Jharkhand Liberation Tigers

A top leader, Masih Charan Purti, contested the 2009 Assembly polls from jail on a JMM ticket.

Area of Presence (Districts)

Khunti.

TPC

With 300 armed cadres and another 1,500 members, it makes Rs 15 cr in levies annually. Recently, its founder Bhikhan Ganju joined the All Jharkhand Students Union (AJSU) , a mainstream political party.

Area of Presence-Influence

Chatra, Hazaribagh, Giridih, Ranchi, Latehar.

PLFI

Founder in 2007 by Dinesh Gop, it has 500 armed cadres and another 800 members. It makes nearly Rs 20 cr annually from extortion. A former member, Polus Surin, joined the IMM and is currently an MLA. In Jan-Oct 2012, PLFI cadres killed 97 people in Khunti district.

Area of Influences (Districts)

Ranchi, Lohardaga, Gumla, Khunti, Simdega.

CPI (Maoist)

It has 2500-300 armed cadres making up eight companies and 16-18 platoons besides a 'jan militia' cadre strength of some 5,000. Sources close to the Maoists claim these figures are exaggerated. Several cadres have quit over the past decades, some of whom have joined PLFI and TPC.

Area of Operations (Districts)

Garhwa, Palamu, Chatra, Hazaribagh, Koderma, Giridih, Deogarh, Dumka, Godda, Sahib Ganj, Pakaur, Jamtara, Dhanbad, Bokaro, Ramgarh, Ranchi, Lohardaga, Latehar, Gumla, Khunti, Saraikela Kharsama, East Singhbhum, West Singhbhum, Simdega.

Incident and Events: 2013

The year 2013 might be marked by two happenings in its January: the Maoists rigged the bodies of slain policemen with the IEDs and explosives and a Union Minister unfurling the national flag in the Saranda Forest area, and senior police officer killed by the Maoists in July.

Events and Incidents: Jan 2013

7 CRPF men killed in Latehar ambush: 7 Jan 2013

At least seven CRPF men were killed and around 12 injured in a fierce encounter between the CRPF and CPI (Maoist) at Hehegarh under Barwadih police station in Latehar district on 7 Jan 2013. Several ultras were also reportedly killed in the incident[7].

It seems to be a story, heard several times earlier. The security was snared into a trap planned by the wily ultras. But why should the CRPF have 'rushed into it' is inexplicable. Be that as it may, the reported details follow.

On a tip-off that a large number of Maoists were assembling in the Katia jungle, four companies of CRPF rushed to check them but were ambushed by the reveals on the way. Intense firing took place between the two sides at Katia jungles of Arnuatiker for the whole day after the security forces were interrupted by the ribels in Katia Jungle who were present there, fortifying themselves.

A senior CRPF official Apoorva told the daily: "Till now, we have information of seven fatalities of our men in the encounter while 12 Jawans were injured seriously and they have reached Latehar.

Apoova also said the injured men who reached Latehar informedo us that several ultras (20) were also killed in the fire fight.

Three companies of 112 Battalion of CRPF were engaged in firing which continued from 12 to 4 PM on the 7th. The security forces had cornered over 100 cardres of the Maoists in the jungle. The areas was further surrounded by the 214 Battalion of the CRPF

Meanwhile, Palamau Zonal IG Deepak Verma along with IG CRPF DK Pandey, took an aerial view of the operation area to take stock of the situation but failed to bring back the injured to Latehar due to fierce firing from both sides.

Another daily reports Jharkhand DGP GS Rath as saying: " 9-10 injured men are from CRPF and Jharkhand Jaguars. The injured, most of who suffered bullet injuries on their arms and legs, were shifted to Daltonganj in a special train.

Sources said the Maoists squads comprised outsiders such as some Nepali faces.

"The first major encounter this year came close on the heels of Minister Ramesh's visit to the Naxal hit areas.

Another daily reported "the injured, including three critically wounded men, waited hours for medical attention as bad weather prevented an IAF helicopter from landing on the site".

The Maoist group involved in the encounter is believed to be headed by Arvind, an important leader thought to be holed up in the area for the past 25 days. The CRPF "has been camping there since 20 December (2012) to try and capture him[8]".

The encounter, named 'Operation Saamna', involved 220 CRPF and some Jharkhand police personnel. Armed with AK-47s, the Maoists fired incessantly at the raiding teams. "The men were gunned down when they were climbing the hills, the four men in the front line died instantly while eight others received bullet injuries", said Pamkaj Kumar Singh, IG (Operations), CRPF.

The CRPF depends on an IAF Mi-17 and a BSF Dhruv chopper for rescue operation in the maoist hit areas of Jharkhand and Bihar. The Mi-17 helicopter can't operate in low-visibility conditions.

Jharkhand Encounter: Bodies of 5 missing CRPF men found: Bodies were multilated as Maoists used 2 of the bodies as booby trap: 9 Jan 2013

After hours of fierce fighting/ gun battle with Maoists, security forces on the 9th finally able to retrieve the bodies of five CRPF personnel, who went missing during the 7th encounter in the Latehar district.

CRPF officials said the Maoists had mutilated the bodies of two of the personnel—one had his eye gouged out while other had been rigged with explosives. The ultras had also planted landmines around the bodies to inflict more casualties on the para military force. Three villagers who went to retrieve the bodies on the 8th were killed when they stepped on the landmines. The body of one of the CPRF men was blown to pieces in the explosion[9].

On the 9th, the CRPF revised the death toll to 13, ten security men and three civilians.

Earlier in the day, an 800-strong contingent, including COBRA commandos, marched to the remote area and recovered the bodies following the gun battle. The Maoists, numbering some 200 and led by Central Committee Member Arvindji, were armed with AK-47s, INSAS, LMGs and grenades. The Maoists had 13-14 women commandos and they were moving around the area mounted on horses.

Pankaj Kumar Singh, IG (Operations), CRPF spoke indignantly about the IAF. After talking about redrawing the CRPF strategy and plans to launch a major operation against the Maoists in the coming week, he said "we would also take up with the IAF the matter of delay in evacuation of at least five persons who died on the 7th night in a trench waiting for medical help….. This is an extremely serious incident and the injured persons kept pleading for help, hours after which five of them died… They kept waiting to be airlifted".

The IAF had alleged refused to land their helicopter owing to bad weather.

The CRPF, which has 18,000 personnel deployed in the fight against Maoists, does not have its own air-wing. It depends on IAF's Mi-17 choppers and BSF; Dhruv Choppers for evacuation. The officials said the CRPF had written to the MHA to hire two Pawan Hans helicopters to ferry their injured personnel in the inhospitable areas. The MHA is yet to take a decision on this proposal.

Reds placed injured jawan on landmines to kill more : 9 Mar 2013

Another daily gave a different version of the Maoist's brutal ways: "They placed injured jawan on the land mines", not his dead body as mentioned by other dailies as already discussed on the earlier pages. This is how this daily puts it in the opening paragraph of its report in its issue of 10 Jan 2013[10].

"In an action reminiscent of scene from Oscar-winning Bosnian war film *No Man's Land,* Naxalites in Latehar district put the body of critically injured and incapacitated jawan over a landmine following a fierce battle between the Maoists and the paramilitary on the 7th morning. On the 8th evening, security forces along with local villagers found the jawan's body deep in Karmatiya jungles. However, as soon as the body, was picked up, the mine exploded, killing three villagers and blasting the jawan to smithereens."

The film 'No Man's Land' had ended with an injured Bosnian soldier in the mine while still alive with no hope of rescue. Bosnian Serbs had put his body over a land mine while he was unconscious.

Source said, in all probability the Jawan bled to death while lying on the mine, adding that even if he had gained consciousness and tried to move, he would have died. Following the blasts, the forces retreated on the 8th night and the combing operation was re-started with reinforcement on the 9th.

On the trail of senior CPI (Maoist) leader Arvindji, some 300 soldiers from CRPF and Jharkhand Jaguars were combing Karmatiya forests when they were ambushed by a contingent some 200 Maoists—led by a woman – who were firing at them from hill top. The forces had taken the only narrow path that cut through the jungle and then opened into a plain with hills surrounding it. That the Maoists were in Army fatigues confounded matters. Some 600 Maoists cadres are suspected to be hiding in the jungles moving between Bihar and Jharkhand.

"The government, however, is not perturbed by the deaths as the operation is part of a "fight –to-finish" war to flush out Maoists from Latehar (of Jharkhand) and Chhattisgarh's Sukma districts. A MHA official says: "Maoists have been considerably weakened as is evident from constantly decreasing incidents of Naxal violence (from 2,258 in 2009 to 1,412 in 2012). This is the season (before the onset of monsoons) to strike and we want to considerably weakem then through continuous offensive.

Two events and incidents related to 7 January encounter

The following two incidents are discussed on the following pages :

- One hardcore Maoist nabbed.
- Fatalities and injuries a day after the 7 January encounter.

Operation Anaconda-2: Hardcore Maoists nabbed from West Singhbhum

In a major achievement for security forces engaged in flushing out the ultras, a hard core Maoists ultra Bimal Gudia was nabbed from Saranda forests under Manoharpur police station of West Singhbhum on 7 Jan 2013 during ongoing massive anti- Naxal combing operation 'Anaconda-2' operation[11].

In a joint operation of the CRPF and Jharkhand police team, Gudia, wanted in two dozen cases of Naxal violence, including landmine blasts, murders and extortion, was caught.

The late father of Gudia was also a notorious ring leader of Naxals who had played a role in the creation of CPI (Maoist) in 2004, consequent to the merger of the MCC and PWG. His sister was also arrested in the past for involvement in the Naxal activities.

Operation Anaconda-2 was launched early Dec 2012 to flush out Maoists from Saranda and pave way for speedy implementation of the Centre sponsored Rs 250 cr Saranda Action Plan (SAP).

As police could not give further details of ongoing operations due to security reasons, but "they have nabbed a hard-core cadre.

To ensure that the ultras do not hamper development projects under Rs 250 cr SAP, second phase of the operation—Anaconda-2-was launched to flush out the Maoists from the Saranda forests.

The SAP is the brain child of Union RD Minister Ramesh, who visited Saranda four times in the last one year. That was the prime reason for launching second phase of the operation.

"3 more Jawans, 2 civilians killed in Maoist Latehar rampage"

This is the news story in a daily, a day after the 7 Jan 2013 encounter. It says, "Maoist ambush in Latehar continues to claim lives on the 8th. Two civilians and three security men were killed and a local resident injured in a landmine blast in Arnutiker village[12]".

Latehar SP Karanti Kumar Garhdeshi gives details : " The Maoists had killed two of the four missing CRPF soldiers. They planted landmines under the bodies and waited for security personnel to come and retrieve them. As they approached, the ultras triggered the blast.. Till now, 14 personnel are injured and nine killed, seven of them security men. Still, two CRPF men are missing and we are searching for them.

The daily claims the security personnel casualty figures were much more than the official numbers: "The information with the daily is that 10 soldiers and two civilians were killed in the ambush by Tuesday, 8th evening. Sources said seven CRPF Jawans were killed on the 7th and four were missing. Out of these four, three were killed by the ultras on the 8th, along with two civilians (villagers) who died in the landmine blast".

Earlier on the 8th, the CRPF and Jharkhand Jaguar soldiers injured in the ambush were airlifted from Palamau to Apollo Hospital in Ranchi for better medical treatment.

DGP Rath visited the region to assess the situation for himself. CRPF IG D K Pandey, Palamau IG Deepak Verma and some other senior police officers are currently in Latehar. Rath had earlier made it clear that Operation Anaconda-II will go on without a break. There are reasons for that as explained by Garhdeshi : "Currently, several companies of CRPF, COBRA, Jharkhand Jaguar and district police have been deployed for combing operations. We are estimating that there are some 250 Maoist cadres still hiding in the forests."

7 CRPF men killed in Latehar district

DIG Palamu Range Praveen Singh confirmed the killing of seven CRPF Jawans in Karmatiya forests of Latehar district, 250 km from Ranchi on 7 Jan 2013.

The State intelligence had informed the district police about the presence of large number of Maoists in the Barwadih jungles. A contingent was dispatched to eliminate the ultras hiding there. As the CRPF and Jharkhand Jaguars were carrying out combing operations in the contiguous Karmatiya jungles, they were ambushed by the Maoists hiding on a hill. The men who took position immediately were caught in a taetiecally poor location. This resulted in the heavy casualties, including seven fatalities. To explain it further, the forest they were searching for the ultras in lead to a series of hills, which they had occupied after a due thought. The jawans paid heavily as a result.

Latehar is considered a Maoist hot bed. Maoists killed 24 people in the district in 2011, as per the police figures. Another figure, extremely chilling, needs to be told here. In the Chintalnar massacre in neighbouring Chhattisgarh on 16 Apr 2010, 75 men from 62 Battalion of CRPF (and a policemen) were wiped out during an "area-domination" operation.

Maoism : Brutality Personified

Maoists are known to be cruel and inhuman. But what they did to the body of a slain security man who was killed on 7 January 2013 beats their own record of brutality. If their icon Maotse Tung could starve, torture and kill millions of his countrymen to test his own ideas and ideology, one should expect no better from his Indian acolytes and disciples.

Let this act of barbarity be described in the words of a daily in its issue of 11 Jan 2012, under the headline: In a chilling first, Naxals insert bomb in the body of a slain CRPF trooper".

> "In the first incident of its kind, Maoists placed a 2-kg IED fitted with gelatin sticks, detonator and battery, packed in a plastic container, inside the stomach of a CRPF man killed in an encounter on the 7th.

"The body of Constable Babulal Patel, 29, was recovered along with four other bodies of security men on the 9th. It was kept in an isolation ward at the Rajindera Institute of Medical Sciences (RIMS), Ranchi, after doctors noticed stitches on the abdomen.

"Doctors found that abdomen had been cut open horizontally with "surgical precision" and sutured again. Vital organs like intestines and spleen had been removed to fit in the bomb.

On the 10th, the IED was defused with the help of the NSG bomb experts in Delhi, who coordinated with the CRPF's bomb disposal squad in Ranchi over the phone. An "electronic claw" and "water jet" were used to defuse the bomb[13]".

A doctor showed the bomb taken out of the constable's body to the media people, placed on a white cloth.

The body was possibly taken into the forest in the 7th night to perform the procedure. The incident indicated a "dramatic change" in Maoist strategy, as they now move with all necessary equipment. "They even have a compounder. They would have the medical equipment to open the body and suture it", said S N Pradhan, Jharkhand police spokesman, Pradhan, also IG (Operations and Special Branch), further added: "It was the NSG team that suggested we use water jet. They hoped the bomb would explode in the helicopter or during transit, inflicting massive casualties."

One of the injured persons told the officers that "the ultras came as close as 5 mtr from out position and asked us to surrender with arms and ammunition".

The officials believe the group of some 200 Maoists, led by Dev Kumar Singh alias Arvindji, was trying to cross over to Saranda forests, probably to attend a meeting of the CPI (Maoist) Eastern Regional Bureau.... The group was experimenting with explosives and was trying to make sophisticated IEDs".

Police records say Arvind ji is about 65 years old, has a limp, and moves around the hilly areas of Jharkhand on a horse. A former member of the PWG, he carries a reward of Rs 7 lakh on his head.

Constable Babulal Patel belonged to 112 Battalion, CRPF.

In an eight-minute audio clip sent to a daily on the 10th, CPI (Maoist) Special Area (Bihar - Jharkhand – North Chhattisgarh) Military Commission spokesperson Toofan claimed that the PLGA had killed 17 security men, seven on 7 January and 10 on the 8th, and seized sniper rifles, LMGs, INSAS rifles and other explosives. Toofan said: "The central forces beat local villagers and forced them to act as shields and carry corpses. This is against the norm of any war and we condemn it, and express regret for the death of five innocent villagers: Jogeshvar Bhuia, Manav Singh, Vijay Turi, Promod Sau of village Navadi, and one more. The Central forces have put rockets and grenades as booby traps, which are still around villages."

To stop post-mortem, Naxal plant bomb in Jawan's corpse: 11 Jan 2013

Another daily express strong feelings on the Maoist brutality in its issue of 11 Jan 2013:

"If any body can surpass the cowardice, brutality and inhumane acts of the Pakistan Army, it seems it is the deadly Maoists.

"In one of the most heinous act in the history of Naxalism in the country, their cadre implanted a 2.58 kg IED in the body of a martyred CRPF jawan Babulal Patel, 24, to inflict maximum casualty.

"The 'corpse bomb' was tactfully put in the uniform so that nobody would suspect their foul deeds.

"To ensure surety of the blast, the Maoists connected the bomb battery to a solar charger. The bomb would have exploded when some body tried to disturb stitches for autopsy.[14]"

"Before post-mortem, we noticed amateur stitches on the jawan's body. We called up CRPF Headquarters to check if he had undergone any operation of late.

Finding no such medical history, our suspicions solidified into serious doubts and we thought it prudent not to proceed with the post mortem". This is Dr. Binay Kumar, associate professor in the Department of Forensic Medicine at RIMS. The rest of the story has already been told above.

The CRPF martyr with the belly bomb hailed from Allahabad, joined the CRPF in 2006 and got married in Mar 2012.

At Latehar, the Naxal had beheaded a civilian and chopped of his hands. His identity remains unconfirmed. Obviously, the Maoist brutality that surfaced during the recent ambush has not ended there.

"Maoists stitched IEDs into slain jawans, bodies, confirm police" : 13.1.2013

Another daily confirms the fact that "Maoists had placed IEDs inside the bodies of two CRPF jawans and stitched them up. This confirmation came from the police officers on 12 January[15].

This daily in an even handedness', blamed both the sides: "civil society activists in Ranchi condemned use of such tactics by Maoists, as well as the use of civilians by police to recover bodies. It quotes social activist Shashi Bhushan Pathak of the Coordination of Democratic Rights Organizations: "Seizing bodies of those killed in battle and putting bombs inside bodies are against Human rights. Maoist must clarify their stand on it. The police must also explain why they put villagers in the front while an operation was on."

"Maoists gouged out eyes while CPRF man was still alive" : 12 Jan 2013

Here is one more daily telling things as they are! "The Maoists gouged out the eyes and chopped off the tongue of a CRPF man while he was probably still alive during an ambush at Ambatikar forest in Lateher area on 6 January[16]"

A police officer said 11 Jan 2013 that the basis of the suspicion was that the jawan, Shankar Lal, was "found with his hands tied behind his back". The Maoists had practiced planting light- sensitive IEDs on animals for six months before placing the bombs into the stomachs of two other CRPF men.

As security forces mounted an offensive against the Maoists, government officers in Delhi said Prabhat Mochi, the arrested General Secretary of the CPI (Maoist) Koel –Sankh Zonal Committee that covers Jharkhand, parts of Bihar and North – Chhattisgarh, gave details of how the method of planting bombs in the stomach was perfected.

One bomb had exploded while the body was being removed from the jungle. The CRPF officers believed it was pressure bomb Maoists use to booby-trap bodies of slain policemen.

The second body was flown to the RIMS in Ranchi for autopsy where doctors spotted [crude / amateur stitches] in the abdomen and called senior police officer. Subsequently, the bomb experts took out a 2.5 kg IED from his stomach and the story in detail has been told earlier.

7 Jan 2013 ENCOUNTER: Comments, Criticism and afterthoughts

The 7 January encounter has drawn a lot of criticism, comment and analysis from the press and the commentariat (if one can "invent" this English word) disproportionately large compared to any recent or past incident of similar kind. Some of there are included on the following pages, mostly in the original text.

"Latehar ambush boosts Red's morale"

The Maoists battling desertion and diseases, got a short in the arm after the Latehar encounter where 10 security men, including nine from the

CRPF, were killed. Veterans involved in anti-Maoist operations, however blamed it on flawed strategy and faulty planning.

"Maoists are a guerrilla force. We've got the best results in anti – Maoist operations when we, too, fought like guerrillas in small groups. The success of such operations depend heavily on quality intelligence inputs", said a senior officer at Delhi, handling anti-Maoist operations.

"Such incidents sag the morale of security forces, but can give the Maoists struggling to keep their flock together a fillip", said an officer. Maoists are finding it difficult to find fresh recruits even in their bastion of Chhattisgarh. Instead of appointing experienced guerrilla commanders, young cadres are being re-designated, say, as area commanders.

Insiders admitted educated youth are reluctant to join the rebels. Adding to their woes is the increase in desertions and surrenders—440 Maoists surrendered in 2012 and 394 in 2011 — across the country. Arrests, 1,882 in 2012 and 2,030 in 2011, have jolted them, too. Moreover, diseases like malaria, malnourishment and depression are taking a toll on the Maoists.

"Maoists use CRPF walkie-talkie to trap jawans"

The Latehar slaughter has exposed, in a single stunning blow, many fault- lines that riddle the government's offensive against Maoists.

The most significant of them is, perhaps, the widely –suspected fact that the police establishment denies – leakage of or the rebels' prior access to forces' strategic movement.

An analysis of lapses and lacunae during and before the operations indicates that Maoists were mall prepared. Forces walked right into a trap and leave easy picking for a Maoist contingent some 300 –strong, occupying high vintage points and armed with LMGs.

It couldn't be that nobody in the Arnuatiker locality knew of arrangements for murder on such a large scale. The price paid for poor ground intelligence was a casualty list totalling 13.

The modus operandi is strikingly similar to the 2010 Sukma episode in Chhattisgarh, where 76 CRPF personnel were butchered. Analysing both espisodes with recorded intra – group communications among security forces that day, 7 January, the Maoists had seized a walkie-talkie from a dead jawan. But IG (Operations) SN Pradhan insisted: "we lost one walkie-talkie but not during the operations. The Maoists were not able to track our movement."

Another top official confides that when forces were communicating over the walkie-talkie about their missing colleagues after the attack, the audio records exposed clear audible background noises, suggesting the rebels were coordinating and repositioning their armed groups for a chase.

"Charlie *hamare 17 log missing hain* (Charlie, 17 of our people are missing)", the forces were heard saying, while informing about their move in a certain direction. "force tumhare taraf ja raha hai. Udhar se ghero .... *gaajar mooli ki tarah kaat denge* (forces are moving towards you. Trap them from that side...we shall butcher them)", a Maoist directed their striking group[17].

In Sukma, too, forces had missed a walkie-talkie during a long range operation, not even noticing the loss then. The Maoists laid hands on the set and tracked and trapped forces a couple of days later.

A top Jharkhand police officer admitted as much to the daily: "It is result of poor ground intelligence of the police, CRPF, IB and others. What we get is often too little and too late, and also incorrect mostly. Latehar is a case of double-cross. Forces acted and marched in haste."

Prashan contradicted this: "We had information on the presence of Maoists in the hillocks. We were caught at the entry point."

However, forces had inputs about only 4-50 whereas there were 300 Naxals. "Using LMG, a long and a lethal striker, in itself indicates a plan for a bigger action. It makes no sense if frontline boys were sent without bullet- proof jackets", a security expert pointed out. Pradhan, though, blames it on a paucity of jackets.

Jharkhand DGP Rath adds his version to this sordid tale : "The difficult terrain and bad weather multiplied the tragedy". He also hinted at settling scores.

Most of Latehar forests are a great unknown wilderness that had now turned into the Maoist de facto headquarters, after being flushed out from Saranda. The problem is that forces are better monitored by the Maoists, than vice versa. The Maoists are insiders in more ways than one; the Government and forces remain outsiders.

"Maoists catch security set-up off-guard"

The security establishment sees the treatment meted out to bodies of security men in Latehar district by Maoists as a sign of their desperation to strike back and defend one of their strongholds.

A senior official of the MHA said the Maoists were slowly being confined to smaller areas and it has become now a matter of existence for them. And that for this, they were even resorting to brutality so as to demoralise the forces.

After the Latehar encounter, which took a tall 10 security men, the Maoists had rigged the bodies of jawan with IEDs and explosives and in a first, implanted a 2kg IED in the abdomen of one of them.

While the brutality may be a sign of desperation, what the incident has has also laid bare is that the officials were completely caught off-guard by the scale of the attack.

In the lack of a well-entrenched intelligence network, Central forces like the CRPF depend heavily on the information from the State police for any operation in any area affected by the LWE. The State machinery may or may not help. Former Home Minister P Chidambram had tried to plug this hole by creating a new intelligence wing for the force. But even after a year, it is yet to function on an independent basis. Many key positions are still vacant.

While the Naxal menace has been identified as India's biggest internal security challenge security agencies do not still have any fresh information on the top 10 leaders in the Maoist hierarchy, let alone their new photographs. All one can get hold of are grainy pictures, some as old as their college days or at least a decade old, others culled out from old records in government files. The Maoists, on the other hand, continue to be armed with the best of weapons and remain in strong numbers, a fact not assessed judiciously by the official network.

To intensify its anti-Naxal operations, the government has started using UAVs, interception machines and other sophisticated gadgets. But in the absence of an ear on the ground, technology can do only so much.

"Let us call spade a spade"

The grisly news that Maoists locked in a raging gun battle with CRPF men in Latehar cut open the belly of a CRPF jawan to plant a 2.75 kg bomb inside to wreak maximum mayhem, only further establishes the bruatality of these murderers. The ambush left 13 people dead, many among them (9) brave security personnel fighting against all odds to contain the Red menace and some local villagers, for whose rights the Maoists are ostensibly waging this bloody battle against the state. Even by the Maoists own ruthless and bloody standards, this is perhaps one of the most barbaric and audacious acts yet in recent times, the connotations of which make the blood run cold[18].

Ironically enough, the recent outrage which has left the families grieving and authorities ringing their hands in hopelessness, has failed to elicit any response from bleeding hearts and Jholawallahs who are quick to condemn even the smallest response of the state against the Maoists. Forget about condemnation or a platitude of sympathy being proffered, it is silence of the votaries of human rights that is deafening and inexplicable. Could it be that those why cry foul and always blame security men for violations and agitate over instances when the Maoists are killed, have found nothing horrific in the mutilation of a jawan, who was only doing his bounden duty? Surely, a soldier has as much right to dignity even in death as any one else. This selective silence on the part of activists over the issue of human right demonstrates their misplaced sympathy for the barbaric Maoists.

Even a cursory glance at the various instances of violence triggered by Maoists will show that for from fighting for the rights of the displaced or the under privileged, the Maoists have actually been targeting innocent citizens across the country. They are no better than the terrorists who cross over into India from other countries. The recent killing in Jharkhand, the Dantewada massacre in Chhattisgarh in which 77 security personnel were slaughtered a couple of years ago and the attack on Gyaneshwari Express in West Bengal in May 2010, in which 80 innocent people who could not have had any direct enmity with the Maoists, lost their lives, are just three incidents which highlights this stark reality.

The Latehar incident has only underlined what many in the country believe – that Maoists are a bunch of ruthless killers and hostage takers that hold the state and its people to ransom. It is true that several people who have joined the Maoists may have been victims of some injustice on the part of the state machinery, but that does give them the right to claim innocent lives in the garb of fighting for social justice. Though pseudo - liberals and rebel – sympathizers love to categorize them as 'misguided ideologues', to romantacise the violent movement is to shut ones eyes to reality.

"Anti- Naxal battle gets fiercer and bloodier": Red menace: 10,000 more security personnel to fight Maoists

The battle against the Maoists is going to fiercer and bloodier. Determined to get back at the Maoists that killed and booby – trapped bodies of CRPF men, the MHA has sent out orders to deploy another 10,000 men in the Maoist heartland within the next two months.[19]

Besides Odisha and Bihar, the new deployment plan would focus on raising presence of security personnel in Jharkhand where 18 CRPF battalions (each battalion has a sanctioned strength of 1,050) have been fighting pitched battles with the Maoists. "The operations will be intensified. We will take forward the strikes", DG CRPF Pranay Sahay said, referring to the continuous offensive to corner the 100-150 Maoists in Jharkhand's Latehar district.

The additional 10,000 will push the total number of security personnel in Maoist – infested districts to over 85,000.

Nine CRPF and one state police personnel have died in the latest round of encounters as security forces approached Maoists who controlled the hilltop.

It was a cost that security establishment was ready to pay. "There will be more casualties on both sides.... It is a battle for survival and preserving their stronghold in these forests", said government official at Delhi, who is associated with the operations.

And it is not going to be restricted to Jharkhand. Home Secretary RK Singh, who has a reputation of being a hard administrator, has ordered induction of 10 more battalions (5 of CRPF, 3 of Sashastra Seema Bal and 2 of BSF) into the Maoist heartland.

"Eye in sky: security forces push for UAVS closer to Maoist war zone"

Despite being a success in the fight against Naxals, UAVs are still not being deployed over the whole war theatre spread in the border districts of Chhattisgarh, Jharkhand and Odisha.

The demand to deploy the UAVs over the Naxal theatre is pending for nearly one year. "Air surveillance can be a game-changer in the Naxal theatre. We want these unarmed UAVs to be flown from somewhere in centre of the war theater. There are pre-independence air strips in Ambikapur (Chhattisgarh) and Palamu in Jharkhand where these UAVs can be based to cover the whole Naxal-infested area. But they are still being flown from Hyderabad from where these eyes in the sky can only reach lower districts of Chhattisgarh like Bijapur and Dantewada", said a senior security officer dealing with the subject[20].

According to sources, at a time only one UAV can be flown as they have been provided only with one ground control station in Hyderabad to central their flight.

These UAVs are piloted by the Air force personnel who have been sent on deputation to the National Technical Research Organisation (NTRO) that manages the operation and gathers the imagery gathered by them.

"Despite our repeated requests, the move to transfer the UAV operation to a centrally located base has not been acceded with. If we het an eye in the sky everywhere, it will be difficult for the Maoists to ambush security personnel like they did in Latehar. Besides, we can plan our operations in much better way", said an official in New Delhi.

Jawan cremated in home town

The mortal remains of Yashvir Singh Jadaun, a CRPF jawan who was killed in the Naxal attack in Latehar on 7 January, were cremated at his native town Bhattapura in Morena district of MP on 10 January.

The body of 38-year-old Yashvir was brought here and cremated with full state honours. In all, nine CRPF personnel, one from the state's special anti-Naxal force, 'Jharkhand Jaguars' and for civilians were killed in the encounter that took place on 7 January.

"Latehar Lessons: 'Tactical Lapses' mar CRPF Ops"

While the MHA is yet to grapple with the operational details of the encounter on the 7th in Latehar that cost 9 CRPF lives, fingers are being pointed at the leader of the platoon for engaging Maoists without anticipating their actual strength.

In an incident report to the MHA, the CRPF is believed to have admitted at least two "tactical lapses", including the role of an assistant commandant (AC) leading the raid party who became "over enthusiastic" during the encounter. But DG CRPF Pranay Sahay said, "We have not come across anything of such sort[21]."

At the same time, another CRPF officer said it was the AC who took the initiative to lead the operations against Maoists. "There were some verbal discussion on this subject and an analysis was done whether it was right to go ahead without anticipating the strength of the Maoists. But that would only be blame game", he added.

Clearly, there are two versions of incident as the opinion of the security hierarchy that deals with the Naxal violence is divided. A careful analysis of the SOP during such operations is also being carried out. In its report, CRPF is also learnt to have expressed "the need for a review of tactics" and exercise "more patience" at the time of operations.

It may be noted that after the 2010 Dantewada massacre, the security forces have been treading cautiously while carrying out operations. The security establishment has been mulling over the option of either launching offensive operations or continuing with area domination approach without being "over-adventurous.'"

The Latehar incident has sparked off a debate in the North Block (read 'MHA') on how to reflect the outcome of the present incident. Meanwhile, the Centre has asked the Maoist-hit states to be on the high alert in the wake of Maoists Tactical Counter Offensive Campaign (TCOC), which is likely to be held this summer.

TCOC is observed till the month of June while the Naxals begin their preparations around February. In order to divert the attention of the security forces, Naxals also sent small teams to different areas while large congregations are given intensive training.

"Latehar storm after Maoist lull": 'Maoists lay low in 2012 for a number of reasons; ambush dispels any notion that they have been contained'

The audacity of the Latehar ambush, which ended with Maoists implanting explosive devices inside the corpses of CRPF men, comes amid security forces' claim that rebels are a declining force. What was probably the cruelest ever assault on security forces came at a time police on several states were praising themselves for having contained Maoists.

Over the last 14 months, Maoists violence had declined partly because they had lost a number of their top cadres (detailed in the next entry below) to encounters – and road accidents, illness and even snake bites – and partly because forces had made significant advances in several region hither to considered 'liberated'. Rather than confront advancing forces, guerrillas preferred to retreat; CRPF men were lulled into a sense by near zero confrontation during their 10-day Abujhmaad march last year[22].

It now turns out the Maoists had been regrouping while recovering from these setbacks. Then Home Minister P. Chidambram had been cautious during his last visit to Chhattisgarh: "It can be considered that the Maoists' violence is going down, it could also mean that security forces and Naxals are not engaging with each other". On the other hand, several top officers of the police and security agencies, including Chhattisgarh DGP Ramniwas, had asserted the morale of the Maoists was down and the battle was in its last phase.

The Maoists themselves stress 2012 was a good year far them. "The various tactical counter-offensive campaigns and military actions by the PLGA in the past one year in various guerrilla zones had good political impact", Deoji of Central Military Commission said in a year- end statement. He listed a series of major ambushes in the year, including the one on the elite COBRA force in Gadchiroli that left 12 persons dead. Deoji said 114 cops were killed last year, several of them in audacious attacks.

The PLGA had been formed in 2000. The last two years have shown a drop in incidents involving Maoists – from 2,213 in 2010 to 1,760 in 2011 and 1,365 in 2012 – after the preceding few years had shown a successive increase – from 1,565 in 2007 to 1,591 in 2008 and 2,258 in 2009.

The regrouping phase saw Maoists devising new strategies, the planting of IEDs inside corpses being the latest. They have cited the Latehar attack as their response to the Saranda Development Plan (it is, in fact Saranda Action Plan, SAP), launched by RD Minister Ramesh after advancing CRPF troops had cleared these forests in West Singhbhum district. Maoists have a counter interpretation of the Ramesh's, SAP. They describe the SAP as a plan to hand over mining resources to the private companies: "The Central Government is trying to get control over natural resources through such tactics. Our killings are in response to their designs", Toofan, spokesperson of the Bihar – Jharkhand –North Chhattisgarh Special Area Committee of the CPI (Maoist), said in an audio statement to the daily.

Toofan said the explosives they had stitched in was their response to similar tactics by the CRPF in the area. "The CRPF laid booby traps in the form of rocket launchers and grenades across Latehar and Palamu districts. They are also using children and villagers as human shields. We regret the death of innocent villagers in the incident."

The CRPF refused to comment on "such madness". "Only saner comments and actions can be responded to", said Jharkhand IG CRPF M V Pradhan. Pankaj Kumar Singh, CRPF IG (Operations), said: "They are acting in desperation, trying to savage whatever they can. We should continue with greater force."

Maoist's losses in 2012

An estimated 70 Maoist cadres died in the year. This was one major reason, analysts believe, for the relative lull during the year some key deaths are listed here.

Key Maoist deaths during the year 2012

Harak alias Srikanth

Died of illness on 26 February. A Dandakaranya Special Zonal Committee member, he worked among Chhattisgarh activists and youths and was active culturally. He was an editorial board member in *Prabhat*, the outfit's mouthpiece in the zone. He joined Dandakaranya's Godchiroli Division in 1998 and was elected into the Special Zonal Committee in 2005.

Mangu Paddam Alias Sukku

Killed in an encounter in Raigarh on 27 January. A Divisional Committee member working for expansion of the movement in Central India as part of the Chhattisgarh-Odisha Border Area Group. Worked in North Bastar and PLGA for a long time.

Vijay Madkam, 45

Died in a tractor accident on 15 July. A member of the South Regional Committee (SRC) and Secretary, South Bastar Division of Dandakaranya. Born in Sukma, he joined the movement in 1988 and played a crucial role in developing Janata Sarkars to counter Salma Jndum forces. He was in Divisional Committee from 2000 and in Regional Committee since 2009[23].

Gundeti Sankar alias Seshanna

Died of snake bite on 18 March. The North Telengana Special Zone Committee member was working to revive the (North) Telengana movement. In a 30 year career, he rose from a squad member to a state level leadership. He wrote literary pieces, worked in political and military wings, and engaged in propaganda work.

Siddharth Buragohain

Killed in a May encounter in Assam, along with three other Maoist cadres. Was a member of the Assam Leading Committee. "These losses are severe for us due to the strategic significance of the revolutionary movement of the North-East…", said a Maoist release.

Ajay Ganju

Killed in Kundu forests Chhatra, Jharkhand, was a Bihar – Jharkhand –North Chhattisgarh Special Area Committee leader. He was involved in over 50 attacks on security forces.

Swaroopa Alias Sunita

Died of breast cancer in March. She served in the technical field under the AP State Committee and Central Committee for nearly three decades and also as a tailor in Dandakaranya in her last years.

Sameera

Killed in police encounter in Mainpur Division on 31 May. Worked in Chhattisgarh – Odisha Border Area. Born in Andhra Pradesh, she worked in the Protection platoon of the State Committee. Became part of the Dandakaranya in 2009 and worked among women in West Bastar, later worked in Gobra in Mainpur and became an Area Committee Secretary.

Ameela Aruna

Died in the encounter in which Sameera was killed. Ameela was a perming artiste who helped organize cultural troops (perhaps troope).

Other leaders...

1. Pramod, killed by the body guard of an assassination target, was West Bastar Action Team Commander. 2. Mitu, killed, in an encounter was an Area Committee member in Odisha Organizing (perhaps, Organization) Committee. 3. Ungal, killed in an accidental mine blast, was in Central Regional Company.

.... And cadres

Nearly 30 lower cadres of Bihar-Jharkhand-North Chhattisgarh Special Area were killed. Among those were Yogender Oraon, Pancham Paswan and Gulach Munda.

"Perched on tree tops along hillock, Naxals waited for CRPF soft targets"

This is the analysis of the 7 January encounter by a daily published by it in its issue of 17 January 2013, that is 10 days after the incident. The story is filed from Latehar[24].

An anecdote shared by villagers of Amwatikar, 40 km from Latehar, suggests that many of them anticipated one-sided encounter after CRPF troops had passed the village. "CRPF marched through the village around 11 on Monday (7 January) (last week)," said a villager who wished to remain unnamed. "One of the children in the school told the teacher, 'the party (Maoist) too went that side earlier. These people are going to be surprised."

Taken by surprise they indeed were. Some 300 troops – a company of 134 Battalion, two of 112 Battalion, CRPF and one of Jharkhand Jaguars—walked into an ambush. About 250 members of CPI (Maoist) military wing were waiting for them along a hillock, having built platforms on the tree tops. "Tree tops are not ideal positions for a sustained fight. Staying there makes one an easy targets", said an officer who did not wish to be named either. "However they are great to launch first volley of bullets. The Maoists climbed down immediately after firing the first shots, with their people on the ground providing the covering fire."

The 300-odd men were part of a larger operation that had been in progress for the past 21 days. Security forces had received inputs about the presence of the CPI (Maoist) Central Committee member Arvindji in the area. "We had encounters with the 250-member group accompanying Arvindji in the Chatra- Daltonganj border and near NH-75", said IG S N Pradhan, spokesman for the Jharkhand police, and in charge of 'Operations and Special Branch'. "They gave us slip both the times", said another officer.

"There was a suspicion that Arvindji was here for a Central Committee meeting in the Saranda forests, but now we suspect that he could have been going elsewhere, or missed the meeting."

Officers now admit their forces had been lured into the trap by PLGA cadres. "They were clearly waiting for our men", said one officer. "The group was supposed to go in another direction. Then someone emerged from the forest, waving his arms. He was indicating he was unarmed, and our scouts asked him to approach slowly, but he ran away. Those of the 134 Battalion, who we in front pursued him and the bullets hit them."

Shooting would go on for at least two-and–half hours starting 11.30 AM.

The wounds left on trees along the Damasdag hillock give a telling picture of how effectively the Maoists had used their tree top positions against the CRPF men at the bottom. As one walks down the slope, the number of trees with bullet marks on them increases, as does the number of hole in the topmost one. Lower down, some bullet marks are as high as seven feet. Then, on level ground, are abandoned socks, clotted blood behind tree where some one had tried to take a stand, and the crater left by a blast, half a boot and parts of an IED still inside.

The signs suggest the security men could never advance from their initial positions. Rather, they were retreating all the time they fought. This forced them to leave behind the first casualties, who possibly bled to death overnight. These bodies were located only the next morning by villagers—who have since alleged that security forces used them as human shields against possible booby traps. The first night, only five bodies of the ten dead had been recovered. "We are now thinking of evolving methods by which the injured and dead are not left behind before retreating", said IG Pradhan.

The Maoists had pursued the retreating troops all the way to opag village before going back into the forest. There they put into action their plans to surgically place IEDs inside two of the bodies.

Officers estimate they too killed eight or more PLGA cadres. "We saw drag marks. There were also reports of people wearing chappals—those are not the fighters, so there is an assumption that the Maoists have designated people to take away their injured and their dead. They must have been taken away on horses", said an officer who had inspected the ambush spot.

Since the encounter, the Maoists have appeared bolder than ever. Shots were heard in the Amwatikar area 'last Wednesday (9 January)' afternoon, barely 48 hours after the ambush. On 14 January, the Maoists successfully enforced a bandh in the region, even coming within a kilometer of Latehar's Garu police station at 10.30 PM on the 13th. They shouted anti-police slogans using a portable public address system, firing a few shots in the air.

"They wanted to provoke us, lure us into another ambush our forces refused to be provoked", said Latehar S P Kranti Kumar Garhdeshi.

On the 15th, eight days after the ambush, hundreds of CRPF jawans were transferred by road into the forests of Latehar.

"Panick-stricken villagers continue to flee": 24 Jan 2013

'Belly bomb was meant to maximize casualties among security forces, says note from Maoists'

This is the news story in a daily of 24 Jan 2013, about villagers fleeing their houses. If the headline spreads panick, its blurb gives the source of the news, Maoists' note. This daily also believes and practices the ideology of the Maoists. To wit, its owner, or controller or majority share holder, was – perhaps, still is – a card carrying communist. Though the gentleman – N Ram – ceded the editorship of this daily to his younger brother after a let of intra- family conflict, he still wields greater control on it than the latter. It must possibly be the only daily in India which publishes a note from the murderous Maoists under a eight-column headline, which gives Maoist version of the fact of two bodies of slain policemen getting IED explosives implanted in the stomachs, and justifying it[25].

The article is datelined Latehar, and its text follow more or less in original. "Panic- stricken villagers continue to flee Navadih and Amvatikar villages in Latehar district, where 11 security men were killed in an encounter with Maoists on 7 January. Four villagers were killed in a blast triggered the next day when they lifted the body of a CPRF trooper on police's instructions."

Now comes the handwritten note signed by Bihar-Jharkhand-North Chhattisgarh special Area Military Mission spokesman Toofan, sent to the daily on 21 January:

"The PLGA had sewn a time bomb with an ordinary circuit inside the jawan's belly, not a circuit connected to the stitches, as the government claim. The bomb was set to explode at the site to maximize casualties among the security forces but did not do so because fluids entered the circuit. We condemn the use of villagers to lift bodies."

On 23 January, the villagers alleged that the CRPF used a tractor to demolish a house allotted to Babulal Bhuian under the Indira Awaas Yojna, accusing his son Mrityunjay Bhuian of being a Platoon Commander in the PLGA. Later S P Kranti Kumar denied the allegation. "We had a property warrant against his son and only seized their movable property on the 21st," he said.

The CRPF, COBRA and Jharkhand Jaguar troopers camped in the deserted villages on the 20th night and 21 January as they carried out the combing operations in the Katiya forests along Jharkhand's western border with Chhattisgarh. Villagers made their way not of the area in the darkness.

"I sent my daughter to Barwadih with my neighbours on the 8th but I stayed back with the cattle. But now there is no option but to leave", said Rani Devi as she carried two plastic bags full of clothes and grain on a mud trail leading to Namadih on the 20th. Several other women and children walked behind cows in the darkness. "Eleven members of my family went out of fear when the police sent for us to look for their jawan's bodies last week. If the Maoists come there will be fight again. The wheat and vegetables we planted is here, everything we have is here. How will we go?" asked Anita Devi, the *Sahiya* (health worker) in Amvatikar.

A majority of households in both villages are Parhaiyas, categorized as Particularly Vulnerable Tribal Group (PTGs) i.e. tribes with less population which were dependent on pre-agricultural technologies at the time of census in the 1970s. "I have not been able to go into the forest since two weeks to get bamboo for my work because if the Maoists come, the police will fire indiscriminately. May be, the Maoist may kill us too", said Suresh Parhaiya who earns Rs150 a week making bamboo baskets, brooms and fans.

Parhaiya says CRPF troops hit him with rifles and boots when he tried to run after a blast was triggered when villagers tried to lift jawans' bodies after the encounter.

Nine km from Amvatikar, villagers in Kuku, on the other side of the Bhauluwahi hill, where the encounter took place, said the Maoists warned them to not enter the forest still strewn with landmines.

On 7 and 8 January, these three villages became the site of confrontation between the forces and PLGA in a chase that began near Gaya in Bihar in 9 December (2012), when companies of the PLGA's Military Commission, led by their leader Arvindji, started moving south of Gaya for Saranda forest in West Singhbhum district of Jharkhand. Senior police officials supervising the Opertation Saamna say the CRPF intercepted the PLGA on Jharkhand's border with Bengal and Odisha. The PLGA then headed north-west to reach Latehar in early January.

When CRPF and PLGA started exchanging fire a few 100 mtr from Amvatikar in the morning of 7 January, most villagers were at the *"bal samagam"* (children's fare/festival), where hockey matches and races were organized at the government school in Nawadih for children.

"We heard shots all day. Next day, Promod Sau from our village said I would have to bring my tractor to the police to carry bodies from Nawadih to Heregerha station. Some villagers were asked to sprinkle water on the school playground so that a helicopter could land there, other villagers, including women, were asked to walk to the forest to search the jawans' bodies", said Mithlesh Sau.

Five hours later, a blast occurred when villagers tried to lift a jawan's body, killing four. "After that CRPF men abused me and asked me to look for the villagers' bodies. I was scared to climb the hill. I spotted Pramod Sau lying with his face bleeding and carried him back", he added.

SP Kranti Kumar said the villagers were making statements blaming the police under pressure from Maoists.

"Slain CRPF man's kin on hunger strike" : 20 Jan 2013

"Parents of CRPF Constable Babulal Patel whose body was rigged with the IED explosives by the Maoists have gone on hunger strike against the state government for neglecting them." A daily in its news story datelined Lucknow gave this information in its issue of 20 January 2013.

Babulal's father Munni Ram, 75 and mother Jagpat Devi, 72 are staging dharna outside the village Shivlal ka Purva which is located on the Lucknow-Allahabad Highway. The dharna entered third day on the 19th.

The family feels grieved that even though Babulal died over a week ago, still no one from the state (UP) government has come to meet them. Babulal's cousin Madan Lal said: "We want that CM Akhilesh Yadav should come to our village and meet the family of Babulal who laid down his life for the country.

On the 19th, senior officers of the CRPF met the family and handed over cheques for Rs 16 lakh to them. Babulal's brother-in-law complained that the state government has not provided any financial help to the family.

Others who were sitting on dharna are Babulal's wife Rekha, 22, their relatives and local residents.

National General Secretary Apna Dal Anupriya Patel also joined the dharna, demanding compensation for the family. She wanted the State government to pay Rs 25 lakh to Babulal family, as such an amount was paid to the family of Slain LINK Hemraj in Mathura. Babulal was victim of Naxalite violence, laying his life for the nation.

They end strike

The parents ended their strike (dharna) on 20 January after the officials assured them the CM would visit them on the 25th. The officials also said the family would get a financial aid of Rs 20 lakh.

Anupriya Patel said the dharna had been called off because the state government agreed to give the same amount of financial aid to Babulal's family as was given to the family of slain Lance Naik Hemraj in Mathura.

"Naxal bomb leaves 8 CRPF men hurt, 3 critical, in Jharkhand" 'The CRPF forces mistakenly went over a powerful pressure bomb when they were returning to their base after patrolling'

It is a familiar story, repeatedly told in the anti-Naxal operations / campaing, about security forces suffering casualties from the Naxal-laid anti-personnel mines. Luckily this time around, there were no fatalities.

As said above, it is a familiar story: "Eight jawans of the 26 Battalion, CRPF were injured on 20 Jan 2013 afternoon by a pressure bomb planted by Naxals. The explosion took place at Jamiajara in Bokaro, bordering Ramgarh and Hazaribagh district, when a contingent of the CRPF was returning long range patrolling at Jhumra Hills.[26]"

DGP Jharkhand GS Rath told the daily: "Our men mistakenly went over a powerful pressure bomb. The condition of three men is serious." Anong the critically injured are Surendra Kumar, Santosh Kumar and Ghasi, who are scheduled to be taken to Ranchi, whereas a others were admitted to a Government Hospital at Ghato, in Ramgarh. The other injured jawans were Manoj Oraon (dog squad), Juneswar Kumar, Jeevlal, M Jatinsingh and D Singh, whose condition is stable.

The security forces had launched an intensive operation in the range of the Jhumra Hills, "which is a traditional Maoist stronghold. This comes in the wake of the Latehar encounter".

The area is a hotbed of Maoist violence. In Dec. 2012, four IEDs were recovered from a road frequently used by the force for combing operations at the Jhumra Hills. They would have caused serious damage had they gone undetected. More recently, of course, was the 7 January encounter where 11 men of forces were killed, and which has been covered extensively in the preceding pages.

"Emotions run high with Tricolour at Saranda" 'jairam unfurls Flag after a decade, inaugurates a Rs 1.37 cr road'

It was a historic moment as Union Minister for Rural Development Jairam Ramesh hoisted the Tricolour at the Digha village in Saranda forests of West Singhbhum district, erstwhile dreaded den of the Maoists, after more than a decade on the Republic Day (2013). The story is datelined Chaibasa[27].

Ramesh became quite emotional: *"main chahta hoon, mera antim sanskar Digha main hi ho. Marne ke bad mera nam Jairam Ramesh Munda rakh dena* (cemate me here when I die and call me Jairam Ramesh Munda).

It was the first National Flag hoisting ceremony at Digha in the last 12 years. The village was the epicenter of the Naxal activities as they would raise black flags all over the region during the Republic Day and Independence Day celebrations.

Hoisting the National Flag at the Digha Primary School, Ramesh also expressed concern over the tardy pace of the Saranda Development Plan. He said there was an urgent need in construction of infrastructure in contiguous areas of Maoist-hit States, claiming that the Centrally-funded work under State Governments was 'slow' and it should be speeded up.

'I have witnessed major changes as part of the Saranda Action Plan (SAP) but a lot still needs to be done. I am really happy to see National Flag being unfurled after more than a decade. The Tricolour gives us a sense of pride and security. The smiles on their faces are enough to tell they are satisfied with the progress being made," he noted while talking to the media. He added: "roads, bridges and other infrastructural development is being taken up within the State. Now, the role of the Central Government will be in building inter-state roads and bridges".

The minister had made five visits of Saranda forests including four to Digha so far and the multi-billion rupee Saranda Action Plan – meant for all-round development of 56 villages in this 850 sq km jungle area – was also his brain child.

As a part of the visit, Ramesh also inaugurated a solar drinking water pump set near the school and reviewed under construction PCC roads. He also went to Manoharpur Block office and unfurled the National Flag. He then visited the free cataract surgery camp at St Anthony High School in Manoharpur.

"Well on the path to democracy" : Ramesh

If the preceding news story was datelined Chaibasa /Jamshed, this one is from Ranchi. The Minister arrived here from Chaibasa. "The Minister was all positivity during his sixth visit to Saranda, despite reports suggesting the return of Maoists to reclaim their old bastion." He observed "the disturbed areas have been on the path of democracy since the Saranda Development Plan was initiated about two years ago[28]."

He told the media persons on the 29th that he had to face some protests this time when he went to Digha to hoist the National Flag. "People came protesting against the administration. They were demanding basic facilities and power. I am very happy the people are raising their voices. This is the sign of return of the democracy that was missing for so long", he said.

Saranda forests are rich reserves of iron ore and sal forests but has also been a Red rebel stronghold. Their heavy presence overpowered the voices of the poor tribals. Ramesh, who has shown intense interest in the area and toiled hard to bring it back to the mainstream, also pointed out that the state political parties had to fill the vacuum there. He continued: "Women of Saranda are now talking aggressively Lots of women self-help groups are coming up. I can see the light of democracy. People, women and youth are now with us. I have felt a great need for a political process at Saranda. The political parties would have to become active as the door has been opened." He was obviously cautioning against the return of the outlaws.

He counted the efforts made for skill upgrading, giving the example of 100 girls who would be trained as nurses at Tata Hospital and employed there, while two training centres would be opened at Chaibasa for skill development.

Exploring future strategies, he said after Saranda, Saryu was on his radar in Jharkhand. "Saranda can now be kept on autopilot. We have to focus on Saryu, comprising Latehar, Garhma, and Palamau."

He also called on Gram Sabhas to pass resolutions unanimously against Naxals and alcoholism: "I am in favour of panchayats being given rights but there should be accountability as well. There should not be just decentralisation of corruption.... I have talked to the Governor and his advisors", he said.

Advocating more rights for the tribals, the Minister held the Indian Forests Act and Forest Conservation Act responsible for breeding Naxalism. "There are forest officials who are responsible for Naxalism and distancing tribals from us. India has developed a lot in the last 60 years but one section (tribals) had to pay a heavy price. Forest officials should implement the Forest Right Act speedily", he said.

"Jairam wants his his last rites on ex-Red turf"

Another daily covered Ramesh's visit to the Saranda forest on the 26th under the headline given above. Ramesh said: "Now that Maoists have gone and development work has begun in your village, you have another big task to overcome. Giving up consumption of liquor and making your village a dry zone." Some other points he made[29].

- "Normally, ministers celebrate Republic Day in New Delhi or state capitals. But I chose to celebrate amidst you.
- "As I said in Digha that when I die, my last rites should be performed there. But before that, I have many things to do for you – provide roads, electricity, drinking water, sanitation and many other things.
- "I visited the area many times, though I am neither an MLA nor an MP from the region. I wanted a better life for the tribals.

  "I have seen women working here from dawn to dusk, while men away their time talking and taking liquor from noon. You have to pledge that you would make your village a dry zone.
- My next promise is to provide you electricity. During my next visit, I should see electric lamps in your households".

Digha village, in Manoharpur Block of the district (West Singhbhum) border Odisha, is cut off from the mainland because of the thick presence of the forest. Dotted with tall sal trees with a presence of rich fauna, Digha along with many other villages in the Saranda forests was a tourist hot spot during the British rule. With the discovery of iron ore in the region, the area later became a favourite destination of mining companies, but in the late 1980s the Maoists chose it as their destination because of the remoteness and absence of government agencies.

Referring to the prevailing political situation in Jharkhand, he said President's rule was not an alternative to an elected government, which was needed to achieve rapid growth.

"Jharkhand must vote for stability" 'the mineral-rich state is back to being politically volatile. The government has fallen, and there is no immediate replacement'

If the last paragraph of the preceding story wants an elected government in Jharkhand for achieving a rapid growth as President's rule cannot do that, the present article, under the above-mentioned headline, pleads for stability in the state. And this must come as a result of a fresh poll. What follows are the arguments of the academic for this denouement[30].

Jharkhand faced political instability once again following the resignation of BJP-led Government on 8 Jan 2013. The State, rich in natural resources, seems fated to suffer instability since its formation in 2000 (along with two other States, viz Chhattisgarh and Uttarakhand). During the last 12 years – that is since its creation—the State has seen eight CMs and has gone twice under the President's Rule. It seems to be heading for a third stint of President's Rule unless another party is willing to form a Government.

CM Arjun Munda recommended dissolution of the Assembly and fresh polls. Whether the Governor accepts his recommendations is yet to be seen. Arjun Munda seems to have taken a clue from Mayawati, who was CM of coalition government comprising her party, BSP, and the BJP. Breaking away from the BJP, Mayawati in 2003 recommended dissolution of the Assembly and a fresh poll (in UP). But to her chagrin, the then Governor of UP did not accept her recommendation and SP Chief Mulayam Singh Yadav formed the Government with the help of other parties.

Expectedly, the Congress adopted wait and watch approach. The JMM is a partner in UPA-2 while it supported the BJP in the State. Remember, it was JMM chief Shibu Soren's vote that saved UPA-2 in Parliament on the India – USA nuclear deal. More recently, the JMM voted with the UPA on the issue of the FDI and for Pranab Mukharjee in the Presidential Poll. All these patterns indicated that the two parties were cosying up. The JMM was waiting for an occasion to sever ties with BJP. Soren's reason – or excuse – was that Arjun Munda had failed to hand over power to him.

Now that Munda has resigned, Governor Syed Ahmed would explore the possibility of an alternative Government as per the norms in such a situation. He could invite the Congress or the JMM to form the Government, as these are the only two parties who have the double digit numbers in the 82 – member Assembly.

The number of seats in the Assembly: JMM -18, the Congress-13, RJD – 5. The first two are keen to form the Government, but presently are weighing their options.

It seems the President's Rule is more acceptable to all the parties, barring the Jharkhand Vikas Morcha (JVM). JVM Chief Babulal Marandi hopes to gain from early elections. President's Rule would benefit the Congress as it means Central Rule. For that very reason, it will be a set back for the BJP.

There are reports of Maoists having taken over parts of State, and running their Parallel government there. "it is also a fact that the State's bureaucrats and politicians have not shown any sincerity and honesty to implement welfare programmes. In all these 12 years, since its formation, the State Assembly has barely met for some 365 days to discuss the problems besieging the State."

Plagued by political and economic problems, is there a hope for this small state? Although the fact remains that some smaller states face political instability, but then there are other smaller states like Himachal Pradesh, Tripura and Chhattisgarh which have enjoyed stability despite the odds. So, Jharkhand should vote for stability and performance and only then there can be some hope.

"JMM, Congress talks on Government formation stuck up"

Even as Jharkhand languishes in the grip of political uncertainty, talks between the JMM and Congress remain stuck on the critical issue of who will lead the coalition government. The Congress has conveyed to the JMM that it has support of independents and smaller partieds, apart from the RJD, and therefore, should lead the coalition. But the JMM is keen too have its own Chief Minister, given that it would be the single largest party in the coalition.

Shibu Soren has urged the Congress to play the role of a "guardian" and help form the Government "as Jharkhand has suffered under the Presidents Rule twice already."

Soren's reputation for being a slippery customer has also divided the Congress on the issue of striking a deal with the JMM.

This was the situation on 11 Jan 2013, a week after the fall of the BJP led Government.

Incidents- Events of June 2013

This month should start with the 'war-within" in the CPI(Maoist). Some news on the faction – ridden Maoists in the State have already been included in the text early. The one below is the latest instance of it.

"Naxal outfit wiped out : Jharkhand police"

Joint operations by the Odisha and Jharkhand police contingents seem to have succeeded in eliminating Pahari Cheeta, a LWE group active in both the states. The biggest break came on 26 May 2013 when the police killed the Supreme Commander of the outfit, Dilip Sahu, 27, in Sundergarh, Odisha. Simdega SP Prabhat Kumar gives detail: "We had large team there, along with the Sundergrh police. The operation started the Jharkhand border. They got him about 2.30 – 3 AM."

After his killing, confirms DGP Rajiv Kumar, the incidents involving Pahari Cheetah have been negligible. "There are two – three members who are capable of rising to Sahu's position. We need to make a few arrests to ensure the outfit is finished off. As off now, they could hit back any time", said the SP.[31]

Sahu, who hailed from Jharkhand's Gumla after walking out of the PLFA, another splinter group of the CPI (Maoist). He has 31 cases against him and had expanded his outfit to Gumla and Simdega districts of Jharkhand and Rourkela and Sundergarh of Odisha. Prabhat Kumar said: "The outfit has cadres in Chhattisgarh, too, but they are not yet organized. All top members of the outfit are from Gumla."

The Pahari Cheeta is reportedly not a monolithic group but Sahu headed the largest and the most influential faction within this faction of the CPI (Maoist). The SP added: "I have seen that they became active in Simdega since 2009 when cases against them started getting registered."

The flipping point seems to have been the Pahari Cheetah's excesses in Sundergarh on the 16 April night, when they killed four people in Talsara. The outfit had made extortion and contract killing its main money-making activity. It hd taken contract from an individual to murder his detractors over a business deal. Among the dead was a 15-year –old boy. On 7 May, the police killed Arjun Sahu, Dilip's brother and second –in – command in Sundargarh, and picked some other of Dilip's associates.

"The other ultra- leftist faction TSP taking on the Maoist"

'Parallel outfit fights CPI (Maoist) in Jharkhand, questions its ideology and builds a support base in local communities, unchallenged despite being banned.'

The analysis in this story pertains to the Tritiya Sammelan Prastuti (TSP), the most influential and the largest of the factions in CPI (Maoist) in Jharkhand, carried by a daily of 24 Jan 2013[32].

"A parallel ultra-left outfit has been posing Maoists in Jharkhand a challenge with muscle as well as ideology." The TSP, itself a banned outfit, killed 10 Maoists in March (2013) and has wrested considerable territory from the CPI (Moist). It has gained some public acceptance, and "accused the CPI(Maoist) of indulging in mindless killings rather than striving towards man awakening." (This is a good sermon from one killer to a bigger killer against 'mindless killings'. Ironic, indeed!).

The TSP, mostly young outfit, comprises former MCC cadres. The CPI (Maoist) was formed in 2004 after the merger of the MCC and PWG.

The correspondent, who penned this analysis, claims to have recently travelled through the region where the TSP committee (TSPC, mostly known with its shortened acronym TSP) has wrested control, and met its cadres in forest camps. They remain like their former comrades in some ways and are different in other aspects. They follow the same Maoist ideology and are familiar with the strategies and combat skills of the CPI (Maoist) cadres.

They have, however, been refraining from violence against civilians including politicians. Unlike Maoists in, say, Bastar, they allow Government officers to work and also offer them protection against Maoists. And though it is a banned outfit, many of its members have contested elections and openly interacted with political leaders.

Rivalry and Differences

"By announcing war, Maoists are caught in quicksand", says the TSP's Jharkhand commander Akraman. "This is no time to fight, but to awaken and prepare masses. They have been weakened by concentrating their entire energy on launching attacks.

Akraman claims it was his platoon that killed 10 Maoists and held other 25 as hostages in Lakadmanda village of Chatra in March. He had joined the MCC in 1994, when he was just 12, and became CPI (Maoist) Zonal Commander before he left and joined the TSP in 2006.

"The Maoists had deviated from their path and come to indulge in plain violence without a mass movement", said TSP chief Brajesh Ganjhu. "There is little Lenin or Mao left in them."

The biggest complaint against the Maoists is that they kill "their own brothers and dissenters'. Around 2002, when PWG –MCC merger talks were at their peak, several comrades in Bihar and Jharkhand left the MCC on ideological grounds. Maoists began killing the deserters and then the 2004 merger with the PWG made them a stronger force.

Ganjhu says: "As we had left the MCC, Maoists killed over 200 of our people from 2002-04. Here the remaining ones decided to come together and form the TSP. soon, others from CPI (Maoist) joined us."

CPI (Maoists) literature justifies these attacks, calls TSP members "police pets" and describes Bharaiji , a former MCC leader under whom PSP was set up, as a "traitor." He later moved to Bengal. The outfit has been wresting parts of Chatra from Maoists, besides areas in Palamu, Latehar and a few other districts on the Bihar- Jharkhand border.

Development

Lawalong block in Chatra had no phone signals. Akraman is said to have asked private companies to install towers and assured protection from Maoists. Now major cell phone companies have set up towers. In most of interior Bastar, BSNL has been planning towers for years but the project gets stalled due to the Maoist threat. "Government officers consult us before implementing schemes. We ensure they work. Compare this with Maoist areas, no Block Development Officer here can give the excuse of not visiting interior areas", TSP spokesperson Sagar says.

A narrow lane branching off NH-99 in Latehar district was a stretch of mud until recently. TPS assured officers protection from Maoists in lieu of a commission, and today the road has been constructed, under PM GSY. Quality PM GSY roads have been contructed, or are under construction, through the forest that connects Palamu and Lawalong, two of their strongholds.

Chatra was among the first districts to have come under the MHA's pilot project for Maoist- hit areas over a decade ago. Yet Kunda and Lawalong in Chatra, where some of TSP's top men are based, remain Block HQ without power, "There is no grid", Chatra Collecter Manoj Kumar says.

Politics

Chif Brajesh is among the TSP men who, besides several of their relatives, contested and dominated the Chatra panchayats polls in 2010, the first ever in Jharkhand. Some have fought Assembly polls too. Today, members of all major parties – BJP, JMM, JVM RJD – interact with those of the banned outfit. Upendra Singh, BJP leader from Lawalong, praises TSP cadres for releasing 25 surrendered Maoists in Lakadmanda. "The TSP gave che supreme example of humanity by releasing them," Singh said, as he was moving around with Ganesh Ganjhu, Brajesh's elder brother, who contested the 2009 polls on JMM ticket and came second. "That is the strategy Says Sagar." "An armed revolution is the last resort. But if we can enter politics and use the system for our ends, nothing better."

Violence

Besides intergroup killing, the only criminal charges they face are of extortion and bullying, police concedes that violence in the TS P areas has gone down. Chatra, once considered among the most severely Maoist-hit districts of the country, does not figure in the MHA's list of 26 severely affected districts that accounted for 80 per cent of Naxal violence in the last three years. 'Why kill people? Yes, we want to change the system, but violence is the last resort', says Brajesh.

Alignments

Two allegations they face are that their battle with the Maoists is actually one between Yadavs and Ganjhus, an SC community, and that the police created them to fight Maoists. "We too have heard the police are using us. But one can look at it the other way too: We are using them. We are in our nascent stage, trying to spread across Bihar, Jharkhand and other states. To avoid a confrontation with police at this moment is our strategy", Sagar says. He does not deny "some understanding with the police."

"We have no connection with them. Our operations against them are going on and they will be arrested soon", asserts DGP Rajeev Kumar.

Akraman explains how Ganjhus do not dominate the outfit: "When we were leaving the MCC, Maoists killed five men of my squad – Ritesh Kharmar (tribal), Uttaran Sao (baniya), Jitendra Ravidas, Ishwari Yadav and Kalo Turi (tribal). None of them was a Ganjhu". He continues: "This Yadav versus Ganjhu is propaganda both by the police and Maoists. In fact, the first man to be killed in the Lakadmanda encounter was our cadre Amresh Pal, and he was not a Ganjhu".

Sagar insists the split from the MCC was on ideological and not on a caste basis. Maoist literature does not mention them as Ganjhu–dominated outfit either, and lists many non- Ganjhus among the TSP men killed.

Statistical Details: TSP Mostly Young

- 500 Armed cadres, thousands of supporters and members in Jharkhand and some borders of Bihar. No woman commander.
- 30. Nearly all cadres are below that age and possibly none has a class X certificate. The only man in his mid -30s is Chief Brijesh Ganjhu, already termed 'Bajurga' (the old man). He is also the moderate face of the outfit.
- 14. Age of the youngest cadre. He stands 4 ft 10 and is heavily armed, in fatigues, with a gun, magazine, walkie-talkie and bomb pouch. "I don't want to encourage a child army. But Baal Chhapaamaar have been in all revolutions—China, Vietnam, Peru", says TSP's Jharkhand commander Akraman. The boy does not go to school. "We tried but he wants to be with us. This too is learning."

"Saranda tribes angry with Centre for allowing mining by private firms" : 23 Jun 2013

'The Environment Ministry has allowed Jindal Steel and Power, and Jindal South West to carry out iron ore mining over 1,500 hectares of land in the area. Recently, it also gave permission to Rungta mines to start exploration work in the region.'

"Tribal groups have taken strong exception to the Centre giving clearances to the private companies to carry out mining activities in Jharkhand's Saranda forest despite assurances to the contrary by the Union R D Minister Ramesh". This is the report in a weekly of 23 Jun 2013[33].

The Environ Ministry's Forest Advisory Committee has allowed Jindal Steel and Power, Jindal South West to carry out iron ore mining over 1,500 hectares of land in the area.

Recently, it also gave permission to Rungta Mines to start exploration work in the region. Earlier, the government gave its clearance to SAIL.

Saranda is spread over an area of 81,901 hectares, out of which 9,351 hectares has already been leased out to different companies.

Chaibasa's District Mining officer (DMO) has sent to the Central Government a proposal to give mining lease to 85 companies. This will require 82,404 hectares of land, which is more than the total area of Saranda.

Tribal rights activist and convener of Adivasi Moolvasi Astitva Raksha Manch Dayamani Barla said she has got "feedback" about mining companies already starting work in the area. She intends to soon visit the area to take stock of the situation, "we will oppose mining activities in the region at any cost". Barla said the tribals do not have any objection to the government's efforts to bring some development to the region, "but if they are working for the companies, we will not allow that to happen."

A PIL has been filed at the Jharkhand High Court to check mining activities in Saranda.

The rich sal forest of Saranda is located at the tri-junction of Jharkhand, Odisha and Chhattisgarh and is of strategic importance. It also houses the rich iron ore mines of Chiria.

Ramesh has been visiting Saranda area frequently for development of the region. "The Maoists Eastern HQ and many training camps are located in Saranda. While launching the Saranda Action Plan (SAP) in 2012, Ramesh had said: "The Union Government was doing it for development of the area. It was not intended to create a conducive atmosphere for mining companies." He said he would roll back the SAP if any fresh mining leases were given to any companies.

The work under the SAP was welcomed by the locals.

"Villagers deny Maoists abducted six school children"

"Residents of Kuwari, a village in Jharkhand's Gumla district, denied reports that six children, of Class VI-X were forcibly taken away by Maoists last week for conscription."

This is the opening paragraph of a report in a daily, based on a Bishnupur datelined story, in its issue of 24 Jun 2013[34].

That is not all. The daily handily has Nakulji, Maoist commander of the East Koel Sankh Zonal Committee –spread over Gumla, Lahardaga, Latehar districts—too denying the allegation: "We do not forcibly recruit any one, especially children, and we cannot. If we did that, those who join will become a risk to the lives of other cadres by not following party discipline. There are some incidents in which adolescents join the party because they are drawn to what they see around them, even if their parents may not be supportive of their decision." This is Nakulji speaking to the daily's correspondent at the rebel's camp.

What followed is the Para-wise text of the story put out by the daily in its account of the said issue in its edition (24 Jun 2013) mentioned above.

- "People of Kuwari, 130 km from Ranchi, said that after reading the front-page reports in Hindu daily *Prabhat Khabar* on Friday (21 June) of Maoists abducting six children after holding a meeting in the village on Tuesday (18 June), they submitted a statement on Saturday to the Gunla police, denying the report.
- "Bihar's former DGP Anand Shankar, who was recently appointed adviser to the Jharkhand's Governor, expressed concern at the incident and ordered a police investigation.
- "It is true that a few children had accompanied the party cadre after they held a meeting in the village. They went with them to help them ferry their luggage and *pithoos* (back packs) to their camps. We cannot refuse the cadre if they make such a request. But the children came back', said Chandramuni Oraon.
- "Six men from the village went on bicycles to the Bishnupur thana this morning (Saturday morning) to inform the police that the children were back in the village. We have submitted a statement to the thana that no children had been abducted…. by the Maoists", said an elder Sukan Oraon.
- "A majority of the 60 families in the village are Oraon Adivasis and Khairwars, working as small farmers. A few families say they had only recently returned from brick kilns in Varanasi to cultivate their small plots of land.
- "While the villagers said six children had returned, most families said their children were not home when asked for the children's version of events. 'School gets over by noon, and they have left to play", said one parent. Others said children were away at relatives' houses
- "Based on preliminary investigation by the district police, it appears children are back in the village", said Jaharkhand DGP Rajeev Kumar.
- "Gumla SP Rakesh Bansal said investigations were under way."

At the end of the article, the daily says "names changed on request."

"Cops: 8 Naxals killed in Jharkhand" 'Security forces claim encounter took place in Latehar, but have not found bodies'

The Jharkhand Police claimed 27 Jun 2013 that about eight Maoists were killed in an ongoing encounter within the Kumandi forest of Latehar district. Senior Maoist leaders, including a Central Committee member, were suspected to be present in the region.[35]

No bodies have been recovered "so far"—as on 27 June by the forces. No security men were injured. "The encounter is part of an operation that began Tuesday (the 25th) evening. DGP Rajeev Kumar said they moved on specific intelligence inputs about the presence of top Maoist leaders in the area. He revealed no specifics. Senior police officers suspected the presence of Arvindji, alias Nishantji, a Central Committee member of the CPI (Maoist).

Latehar is the headquarters of Eastern Regional Bureau (ERB) of the Maoists, and therefore it is assumed that Birsai, the chief of ERB, is also present.

"The operation is on within the jurisdiction of the Manik police station. Intermittent firing is on since the 25th. The CRPF, its COBRA and the district police and its Jharkhand Jaguar teams are participating in the operation."

The encounter comes in the wake of a series of recent successes by the Latehar police, which have weakened the ERB hierarchy. On the 19th, the Patna police arrested Indrajit alias Kapil Yadav as he was under treatment for bullet injuries in a private clinic,. He is the operational commander of the ERB, essentially the man who carries out the orders of Birsai on ground. Hence, it is fair to assume that he was present when the IEDs were implanted in the bodies of the two slain security men in the Katiya forest on the night 7/8 January. He was injured near the Kumandi railway station in 12 June in an encounter with a team that included Latehar SP S Raj.

The 7 January incident/ambush where 10 of their men were killed and no Maoist bodies recovered had spurred a series of victories for the Government forces. Anup Thakur, a member of the CPI (Maoist) Military Commission, was arrested on 28 May from Bihar's Muzaffarpur. The police believes Thakur too was involved in the incident of IEDs being implanted in the bodies of the security men. Three bodies of Maoists were recovered on 29 April after an encounter when a CRPF- led operation went in search of Indrajit within the Barmadih police station area.

"Five top Maoists cornered in Jharkhand: cops"

"An ongoing operation launched jointly by the CRPF and state police in the Kumandi forest (partly covered in the preceding entry) of Latehar district "has cornered five top CPI (Maoist) leader", said the police sources on 29 Jun 2013[36].

These five could include: Central Committee member Arvindji; ERB's company commander and Bihar- Jharkhand-North Chhattisgarh Special Area Committee member Birsai, Platoon Commander Chhotu Kharmar; and two Zonal Commanders "Bada" Vikas (who operates in Latehar and Garhma) and Sylvester (who operates in Gumla and South Latehar). They are present within Kumandi forest.

DGP Rajiv Kumar says: "We estimate that there are some 200 Maoists. We have cut off their exit routes and supply lines." Around 500 personnel are involved in these joint operations. The security forces sources add: "The cadres of the PLGA, who accompany senior leaders, are highly motivated and capable of fighting on despite the odds. The ground is proving extremely inhospitable. The Maoists have surrounded themselves with landmines, slowing the advance of the security forces".

July 2013

The month was marked by the killing of Pakur District SP Amarjeet Balihar in an ambush on the 2 Jul 2013 afternoon. It is not too often that a senior police officer at the level of a district police Chief falls to Maoists' bullets. It was natural that the news made headlines in the national dailies too, and was covered widely.

So, it is only natural that the event is covered in this chapter at large. It will also examine the ways various dailies examined and commented on it.

"When Maoists caught IPS officers off guard" (details of five)

The killing of an IPS officer by Maoists has come four years after they eliminated an SP in Rajnandgaon district of Chhattisgarh on 12 July 2009. This time it is the SP of Pakur in Jharkhand. This daily has given details of five earlier instances where Maoists eliminated police officers[37].

Expressing concern at the deaths of senior (police) officers, Chhattisgarh ADG (Naxal Operation) R K Vij said: "Sacrifice of policemen are among the supreme sacrifices. This should strengthen our resolve to fight this insurgency". Former DGP Chhattisgarh has his own take on the issue: "These things will continue. We will have to fight for long. You have to put them under tremendous pressure then only will they either be terminated or come to the negotiating table. Unfortunately, we have been celebrating smaller success, relative decline in violence, which amounts to nothing".

Earlier similar killings

The daily pointed out above that last such death (of an IPS officer) was in 2009. Then it goes on to say that "while there are not many instances across the country when Maoists killed an IPS officer, the manner of attack has been strikingly innovative." Some assaults came at the most unexpected places like stadiums and traffic signals, even the ambushes were not the usual ones. In one instance, policemen were lured by false inputs, in another; it was an 'area ambush', a guerrilla warfare term roughly equivalent to 'carpet bombing'. Here is a look at some of attacks in the past.

DIG K S Vyas on 27 Jan 1993

In the first ever murder of an IPS officer, cadres of PWG killed Vyas when he was jogging at a stadium in Hyderabad. His wife, bodyguards and other officers were at the stadium for routine morning exercises when the rebels fired at him. Considered to be the founder of the anti-Naxal Grey Hound force, Vyas was instrumental in the creation of a Special Intelligence Wing in Andhra that eliminated several Maoists. His name topped the PWG hit list.

AIG (sports and welfare) C Umesh Chandra : Sep 1999

Killed in broad daylight at a traffic light in Hyderabad. He was included in the PWG hit list after the successful anti- Naxal operations in Warrangal and Karimnagar districts. Killing of this officer with an excellent academic record, gold medals in graduation and post-graduation, had become controversial as it came months after he was transferred, allegedly following an inter-departmental rivalry, to a rather sinecure post at the police headquarters after years of successful stint in the field. He was not provided adequate security and had only a driver and a gunman when the Maoists attacked him.

Lohardaga SP Ajay Kumar Singh : 4 Oct 2000

Killed by the MCC cadres in suspicious circumstances. He had left office in a vehicle with a few gun men for a designated place. But soon for the reasons that still remain inexplicable to the police, he asked them to change the destination and they took a different road than the one they were scheduled to do. Later, they first faced a blast and as he came out of the vehicle with his men, Maoists fired at them. A bullet killed him on the spot.

Munger SP KC Surendra Babu : 5 Jan 2005

He was returning from an operation with a few policemen when Maoist triggered a_landmine blast. It was so powerful that the vehicle was blown into smithereens and they all were killed on the spot. Maoists made away with their weapons. While the MCC and PWG had by then merged to form the CPI (Maoist), the attack was suspected to have been carried out by the cadres of the MCC, dominant in Bihar. Maoist document claimed Babu was lured into a false operation. A day earlier, the Maoists had attacked a railway station in the nearby district of Lakhisarai. The rebels expected that Babu, an officer of Andhra Cadre who was trained for anti-Naxal operations, would visit the site. He indeed did that and was ambushed during his return journey. A section of the police, however, saw an insider hand in the killing. Like Pakur, Munger was not among the Maoist-dominated districts.

Notes

1. PTI, The Hindu 10 DEc 2016.
2. Parvinder Bhatia, The Pirneer, 15 Dec 2012.
3. 18 Dec 2012.
4. G Vishnu, The Tehelka, 8 Dec 2012.
5. Some names Changed on request, Says the Weekly.
6. Op cit.
7. Mukesh Ranjan, The Pioneer, 8 Jan 2013.
8. Vijaita Singh, Indian Express, 8 Jan 2013.
9. *Ibid.,* 10 Jan 2013.
10. Deeptiman Tiwari, Times of India, 10 Jan 2013.
11. PNS, The Pioneer, 8 Jan 2013.
12. Vivek Punj, The Pioneer, 9 Jan 2013.
13. Vijaita Singh and Depu Sbestian Edmond, Indian Express, 11 Jan 2012.
14. Ajeet Tiwari, The Pioneer, 11 Jan 2013.
15. Anumeha Yadav, The Hindu, 13 Jan 2013.
16. Rajesh Ahuja and Aloke Tikku, Hindustan Times,12 Jan 2013.
17. Vijay Deo Jha, the Pioneer, 12 Jan 2013.
18. Vijita Singh, Indian Express, 12 Jan 2013.
19. The Editorial, The Sioneer, 12 Jan 2013.
20. Rajesh Ahuja, Hindustan Times, 12 Jan 2013.
21. Rahul Tripathi, Indian Express, 15 Jan 2013.
22. Ashutosh Bhardwaj, Indian Express, 14 Jan 2013.
23. *Ibid.*
24. Deepu Sebestin Edmond, Indian Express, 17 Jan 2013.
25. Anumeha Yadav, The Hindu 24 Jan 2013.
26. PNS, The Pioneer, 21 Jan 2013.

27. Parvinder Bhatia, The Pioneer, 28 Jan 2013.
28. Santosh Narayan, The Pioneer, 28 Jan 2013.
29. Jadeep Deogharia, The Times of India, 28 Jun 2013.
30. Kalyani Shankar, The Pioneer, 11 Jan 2013.
31. Deepu Sebetian Ednond, Indian Express, 10 Jun 2013.
32. Ashutosh Bhardwuaj, Indian Express, 24 Jun 2013.
33. Navtan Kumar, Sunday Guardian, 23 Jun 2013.
34. Anumeha Yadav, The Hindu, 24 Jun 2013.
35. Deepu Sebestion Edmond, Indian Express, 28 Jun 2013.
36. *Ibid,* 30 Jun 2013.
37. Ashutosh Bhardwaj, Indian Express, 3 Jul 2013.

27

Jharkhand - 3

Rajnand gaon SP Chaubey: 2 Jul 2009

Killed in an ambush Code – named 'Operation Vikas' by Maoists, their literature termed the attack as an "area ambush", as four ambushes were executed at a short distance within hours. The first was at Madan-wada police camp around 6 AM in which two policemen were killed. Soon SP Chaubey and Durg IG Mukesh Gupta rushed to the site with separate reinforcements. The second ambush was laid near village Korkotti, some 15-20 km from Madanwada. While Chaubey's party managed to cross the spot, another police party rushed into this ambush. 11 policemen were killed. Chaubey returned with additional force, only to be killed in the third ambush.

This article puts the 2 July ambush in perspective, the following one provides some details about it, the latest one.

"Naxals strike again, kill top cop, four others in Jharkhand". 2 July 2013 'RED TERROR: Ambush convoy in Dumka forest, kill SP Pakur district; strike in Odisha too'

Red terror struck again on 2 July 2013 afternoon, this times in Damini forest of Jharkhand's Dumka district, killing five policemen, including an IPS officer—Pakur SP—and maiming too others critically. The style of attack on police convay grimly resembles the 25 May attack in Chhattisgarh's Darbha Ghati in which 28 persons, including Congress leaders Mahendra Karma and VC Shukla were ambushed and killed.

On 2 July, some 60 armed Maoists hiding in the bushes along the unpaved road in Naxal-hit Kathikund block (some 415 km from Ranchi) ambushed the police convoy led by Pakur SP Balihar by triggering a land mine blast. Heavy gunfire followed. The SP and four others were killed. The other were Balihar's driver Ashok Shrivastav and his body guards Chandan Kumar Thapa, Manoj Kumar Hembron, and Rajeev Kumar Sharma. DGP Rajiv Kumar said: "our brave SP has been martyred"

Another encounter with the guerrillas in Odisha's Sonepur district left a Special Operations Group sergeant injured. His police team had raided a maoist camp in a forest. They recovered five rifles from the comp site.

The Jharkhand ambush followed a series of offensives launched by the forces against the Maoists, especially after the 25 May ambush of the Congress Convoy. The operation in the districts of Latehar, Gumla, West Singhhum and Palamu districts (of Jharkhand) had apparently led to major successes. The police claimed to have killed at least 35 Masist cadres in the last six months, and destroyed their training camps and hideouts. Some 26 security men also lost their lives in these clashes.

The SP had gone to Dumka, the divisional headquarters, to attend a meeting called by the DIG Priya Dubey on security. Post-lunch, the officers headed for their own headquarters.

Heavy rains, broken roads and poor communications delayed the rescue operations and counter attack. By the time reinforcements reached the site, the ultras had fled and the SP and his bodyguards were dead.

The injured were moved to the Dumka Sadar Hospital, 40 km away, where "doctors arrived only after the angry Constables created a ruckus."

Kathikund had been in the news for increased Naxal activity. In April, the ultras had torched eight vehicles of a road construction company working in a remote area deprived of any development for decades.

Balihar had joined as Pokur SP on 17 May. The tribal officer had an impeccable service record.

In the last years, the Jharkhand Police have lost 243 officers and constables in the war against the LWE.

The daily gives brief account of some major Maoist attacks in the recent past, which are reproduced here. This daily, besides the story covered here, also has two more news analyses on the same issue. These two are also examined in the following pages.

Major Strickes in the recent past

2 July 2013

Just Covered.

13 Jun 2013

Three persons killed as Maoists attack a train between Jamui and Bhalui stations in Bihar.

25 May 2013

28 leaders and workers of Congress killed in an ambush in Bastar, Chhattisgarh.

25 Feb 2010

24 policemen killed in an attack on a camp at silda in West Bengal.

7 Apr 2010

Maoists gun down 76 CRPF men at Dantewada in Chhattisgarh.

22 May 2009

Maoists ambush a patrol party in Gadchiroli, Maharashtra, killing 16 policemen.

16 Jul 2008

21 cops killed in a Maoist strike at Malkangiri in Odisha.

29 June 2008

Maoists attack a boat on Balimela reservoir in Odisha, kill 38 troops.

"SP ignored alert, fell into death trap"

Dead End: Maoists tracked police officer's movement, planned attack for days

"By all accounts, slain Pakur SP Balihar took lightly the headquarter's alert to police superintendents to remain extra vigilant because of the operation against the Maoists in the Palamu and Latehar districts."

This is how a daily opens its analysis on the death of the SP in its issue of 3 Jul 2013[1]. The daily has its reasons: "He travelled to Dumka with a lean force, comprising mostly his guards and an escort team."

The Maoists, closely following his movements for the past few days, laid a trap and ambushed him on his return journey.

Some 3,000 security officers and jawans of the Jharkhand Police and CRPF, have been carrying out an operation against a Maoist group in the jungles of Palamu since 25 June. According to several intelligence alerts sent to police headquarters, after having lost several cadres in the past one week – the police, however could not recover the bodies – the mere looking for an opportunity to strike at some other location to throw the police off the scent. Their targets are politicians and police men.

During the last weekend, following an intelligence alert, the police did not allow the convoy of for Deputy CM Sudesh Mahato to cross the Bundu Valley in Ranchi District and advised him to return to Jamshedpur. Mahato followed the advice. All political leaders have subsequently been advised to minimise their movements in the rural areas after the sunset.

"The Maoists have carried out the dastardly act to divert our attention from the ongoing operation in Palamu, where we are about to reach their strongest and safest hideouts", DGP Rajiv Kumar said before flying out to Dumka to assess the situation with senior officers of the state police and CRPF.

Dumka, Pakur, Sahebganj and Godda districts are among the poorest, remotest and predominantly underdeveloped districts of Jharkhand.

Sharing borders with Bihar in the north and West Bengal in the east, several parts of Dumka remain cut off from the mainstream and there is very poor road and telephone connectivity.

For more than two decades, the local Santhal tribes have successfully prevented the Maoists from spreading their lease in the region. But with increasing mining activites and consequent displacement, the ultras have gradually started getting acceptance.

"Attack Opportunistic ambush, says MHA"

2 July attack that killed Pokur SP appears to be an "opportunistic ambush" by the Maoists aimed at making their presence felt after suffering steady attritions, K Vijay Kumar, MHA adviser on anti-Naxal policy, said.

The MHA believes the attack could be aimed at helping the Maoists gain a toe hold in Pakur where they have a negligible presence. The intelligencies reported that the Maoists only had a small guerrilla squad in Pakur which may have carried out the attack[2].

That incidents of Maoist violence in this area being few and far between seem to have lulled the local police into a false sense of security. "The Maoist clearly exploited this situation", an MHA official said.

The Maoists have recently lost many cadres in Jharkhand in gun fights with the police and subsequent arrest of senior leaders like Anoop Thakur.

A recent MHA review held that the offensives had reduced the strength of the Maoists from 1,000 last year to 600. "This is the estimated strength of the hard core well-armed Maoist military company fighters and does not take local guerrilla squads into account," an MHA official told the daily.

Asked if the Pakur attack – soon after the 25 May Maoist attack on the Congress convoy in Jhiram Valley – was part of a centrally–planned retaliatory action by the ultras, Kumar said there was no information to indicate so. The attack could also be part of the Maoists' Tactical Counter Offensive Compaign carries out every year from February to June – July.

"Tribal Dalit officers are soft targets for Maoists"

"The death of Pakur SP in 2 Jul ambush in Dumka district has been a blow to the Maoist image among the tribals and Dalits of the State. The self-proclaimed Champions of these two marginalized sections, the people now feel, have turned their gun against them[3]."

"The Maoists have always singled out the tribal and Dalit officers and killed them. Tribal officers are soft targets", said a relative of Balihar on condition of anonymity.

In fact, the tribals and Dalits have been hit once too often. While hundreds of Jharkhand policemen – a majority of them tribals – die during anti-Naxal operations every year, Balihar was the third prominent police officer to be targeted.

In Oct 2006, Maoists beheaded Special Branch Inspector Francis Induwar. In Sep 2010, they killed Bihar Military Police Jawan Lucas Tete.

The caste war is rooted in the Maoist fold too, at least in Jharkhand. In 2001, a Chunk of Ganjhu Cadres—members of a Scheduled Caste—defected and formed a parallel outfit, Tritiya Prastuti Committee, which is the largest enemy of the Maoists.

"Safe haven turned bloody battle ground for Balihar"

Around 2 in the afternoon on 2 July, SP Balihar called up her wife to let her know that he would be joining the family at their Ranchi residence on the 3rd.

Less than two months ago, Balihar had got independent charge of Pakur and his family was thrilled as the new posting was not that notorious in terms of Maoist activities. But an hour after the 2 July call, Balihar was killed along with four other in an ambush in Damini forests in Dumka district.

He is survived by his wife, two daughters, a son, two younger brothers and parents. This year, his elder daughter appeared for the class 12 exams and the younger one for class 10[4].

Balihar, who had completed his schooling as well as college from Ranchi, was drafted in the Bihar Police Service as a DSP in 1986.

Promoted to the IPS from the State Police service in 2003, Balihar served at different places before being given independent charge of Pakur district as SP as recently as 17 May 2013.

"My brother was a role model for us. It is an irreparable loss for us," said a sobbing David Balihar, the slain SP's Younger brother, who served as Block Development Officer (BDO) with the Jharkhand Government.

Maoists knew of Cops meet in Dumka

The Maoist attack in Dumka on 2 July was perhaps the most "well-planned" ambush targeting cops, police sources said. The ultras had positioned themselves in the forests and were well-aware of the police convoy's movement[5].

SP's three SUV convoy was ambushed during his return journey from Dumka, resulting in the death of the SP and four other policemen, while two policemen were injured", said DGP Kumar, "who was directed to leave for the site along with Home Secretary NN Pandey to assess the ground situation." Jharkhand is under the President's Rule presently.

Police sources believe the ultras were trying to replicate the 25 May ambush of the Congress convoy in Bastar's Jhiram Valley, this time too. Maoists were obviously waiting for the Balihar convoy on his return journey from Dumka. They might have positioned themselves in the ambush site soon after the Balihar passed the site on its way to Dumka. "Since the road runs throught the dense forests and cuts through a hill, Maoists found it easier to hide behind the trees and fire at the SUVs of the Balihar Convoy. They hurled at least six crude bombs before the two escort vehicles and the SP's car before the victims could realize what was happening." This turn of events is as reconstructed by the police sources.

A police man told the daily: "We have seen several encounters in the State in which Maoists have killed policemen, but this was probably their most well-planned ambush. The policemen did not even get the time to move from their seats as the Maoists sprayed bullets indiscriminately."

Comments on the preceding paragraph.

- This is mere idle prattle: this being the most well-planned ambush. This is one of the ways a scribes adds a flourish to his analysis. To a layman, this may sound convincing. To those who know the realities of such ambushes, there is nothing extraordinary about this ambush. Given the topography of the site, the hills and the jungle, such an ambush needs no brains to plan. May be a police man has made a fool of this scribe by making this ambush as the most well-planned.
- There is another version which makes this scribe look foolish or gulible. Another daily says Balihar came out of his car and was killed by a direct hit of a bullet.

- Such silly assessments or views from police sources is a mere attempt to pretty-up his copy—in today's lingo, it is an attempt to sex-up his copy!

"Maoists kill SP, four cops in Jharkhand ambush"

It should be clarified in the beginning that this new story is penned by the same scribe who has done the preceding one. Obviously, the daily has split the same story in two, wanting to give the impression that it has done two stories on the same issue.

All the same, this story is being examined for any additional points this scribe might have added in this part.

Under the headline, the blurb in being reproduced here[6].

" First senior cop to be slain by Naxals after State formation".

"Around 100 armed Maoists ambushed and killed SP of Pakur district…..", in Jamia village of Dumka district, just 30 km, from West Bengal district. "The group was returning to Pakur around 3 PM after a review meeting in Dumka, and were attacked along 65 km stretch of hilly terrain which made it easy for the ultras to strike and disappear into jungle."

"This was the first Maoist killing of a top police officer since the State was carved out Bihar in Nov 2000, Lohardaga SP Ajay Kumar Singh was killed on 4 Oct 2000, just before Jharkhand was formed."

"In the last 13 years, more than 300 security personnel have been killed by the Maoists in State."

"Two injured constables were taken to hospital from Amrapara, around 250 km from Ranchi."

"SP among 6 killed in Maoist ambush"

This is the last report on the incident to be covered here. This is from its issue of 3 Jul 2013, as were all reports earlier. Only additional points from this daily will be taken note of here, as were not mentioned by other dailies. "In one of their most fierce strike…..[7]"

"The SP of Pakur was returning after attending an official meeting in Dumka, the adjoining district.

The review meeting had been called by DIG, Dumka Range, Priya Dubey in Dumka, 60 km away (from Pakur). "DIG Dumka had taken charge only three days back and called the meeting to take stock of the area". The meeting was attended by SPs from all six districts in the range…" More than 50 Maoists surrounded the vehicle…", said Jharkhand Police spokesperson DIG (Personnel) Shambhhu Thakur.

Three injured policemen were rushed first to Dumka Government Hospital and later referred to the Government Hospital in Dhanbad.

"An encounter was on between paramilitary forces and Maoist rebels for over five days last week in Latehar district along Jharkhand's western border with Chhattisgarh as CRPF personnel baricaded Kumandih railway station and carried out search operations in nearby villages. CPI (Maoist) spokesperson Gopal had issued a statement on Saturday (29 Jun 2013) threatening that attack will be intensified "if the government did not call off operation Greenhunt."

Before being posted to Pakur in may, Balihar served as a comandant Jharkhand Armed Police II last year. He had also worked as additional SP Special Branch and had several postings as sub-divisional police officer (SDPO) in Khunti and Latehar districts, and in Rajgir in then Bihar. Ranchi SSP Saket Kumar Singh reminiscences: "We interacted regularly when Balihar was posted at Ranchi. He had an excellent reputation among all officers and was highly regarded by all his colleagues."

His wife is a lecturer in a college in Hazaribagh, his two daughters and a son are students of class X II, X and VIII respectively in Ranchi.

Post-Balihar Ambush Events: July 2013

Here ara some incidents after the 2 July killing of the Pakur SP

Massive operation launched in Santhal Pargana

A massive operation was launched by the security forces in Pakur and Dumka to check cross-border movement of the Maoists involved in the 2 July attack, killing the SP and four policemen. Atleast 10 teams of security forces drawn from Jharkhand Armed Police (JAP) in Pakur and Dumka districts, were pressed into action to plug all possible escape routes of the insurgents[8].

Police suspect the Maoists might take advantage of thick vegetation, the hilly terrain and heavy rains to cross the Jharkhand-West Bengal border. Once considered a peaceful area, the Maoists are slowly catching up in Santhal Pargana due to the lack of development in the area. DGP Rajiv Kumar adds further: "Dumka had been a peaceful area till now……. we have sent in two battalions of Jharkhand Jaguar to Santhal Pargana. Operations will be conducted all over the state."

Reacting to the incident, Governor's Advisor Anand Shankar says: "The security forces are not discouraged and strict action against the Maoists will be taken. We are in constant touch with the security forces engaged in counter-Naxal operations. I am leaving for Dumka to review the situation.... Strategy is being prepared, keeping in mind all the points and we have also sought support from the Centre in this regard.... The operations in the state will be intensified further."

Intelligence sources believe over 100 armed Maoists were involved in the attack on the SP convoy.

Due to sheer neglect of Santhal Pargana in the past, the area is gradually turning into a Maoist stronghold, while the State government is yet to take measures to curb their movement.

More than 30 battalions of the CRPF, JAP, IRB and State Police are involved in anti-Naxal operations in North and South Chotanagpur, Palamau and Singhbhum-Kolhan divisions, but Santhal Pargana has been neglected so far.

Meanwhile, Advisor Anand Sharma, Home Secretary NN Pandey and DGP Rajiv Kumar visited Dumka to take stock of the situation in the area. They also talked to the officer incharge to the surrounding areas of Kathikund.

Pakur SP was last to die, says DGP

DGP Rajiv Kumar said 2 July that the Dumka incident was an ambush which was carried out by not more than 10-15 ultras. "As there was a culvert and the road was under construction, the SP's cavalcade automatically slowed down," he added.

Revealing details on return from Dumka and Pakur, he said the body-guards did not get time to retaliate as some of them died in the vehicle itself and the SP was last to die in the attack.

Comments

- One does not know what is the source of his revelation that the SP was last to die. Nobody in the car survived to tell the story.
- Again, what is it that the DGP is trying to convey by this 'revelation'? Is it of any consolation to any one?

Before being shot, SP called for help

Pakur SP Balihar managed to make a call to a subordinate as his two-car convey come under attack on 2 July, top police officers said on the next day. DGP Rajiv Kumar gives details : " The SP managed to get out of his car, move to the left side of the road and make a call to the officer in charge (OC) of Amrapara, 30 km away, in Pakur, at 2.30 PM. The OC told me that the SP had managed to pass on the information that he was ambushed. That the SP managed to make that call indicates that the Maoist squad was small.

It is suspected that a group of Maoist cadres led by Zonal Commander Pradeep Majhi alias Praveer carried out the attack.

Maoists had taken positions mostly on the right side of the road near a culvert on the Kathikund-Amrapara road, some two km into the forest. The attack began as the two vehicles—a Scorpio with the SP, gun man and driver and a Bolero with a driver and five gun men – slowed down to negotiate the culvert.

The Maoists clearly knew which car to target—all except the right near tyre of the Scorpio has been shot out, while the Bolero has all four intact. The SP's body was found in a gutter by the road, shot possibly around the time he had just finished calling for help[9].

Focus on Maoist who took Control in Feb (2013)

"The killing of Pakur SP and five other policemen has brought the focus on a previously little-known Maoist, who rapidly moved up the rebels' hierarchy to become the zonal ommander of the Santhal Pargana region only in Feb 2013…Pradeep Majhi alias Praveer has emerged as the main suspect who led the band of Maoist that attacked SP Balihar's convoy."

The above was told to the press by the officials on 3 July and published in a daily in its issue of 4 July 2013.[10]

Police says the previous Zonal Commander Ramlal Rai was arrested in February and his second-in-command Majhi took control days later. The 2 July attack is considered his major strike, to stamp his authority in the area.

"It is certainly a loss. But our forces are resilient and mature enough to respond to this," said K Vijay Kumar, senior adviser on Naxal issues at the MHA, who was till recently an adviser to the Jharkhand Governor. Earlier, he was the DG, CRPF.

Majhi hails from Giridih. He was instrumental in sneaking the CPI (Maoist) into the region, where the erstwhile MCC did not traditionally hold sway.

"There was a murder in 2001 within the Ramgarh police station area. A Paharia (tribal) leader was killed by the Mahajans (money lenders). The Maoists exploited that, and Badri Rai became their leader here", said an IPS officer, who has served in the region. Previous Zonal Commander Ramlal is Badri's son.

Shahdev Rai, Ramlal's elder brother, who works with Majhi, raising suspicious that attack could have been in retaliation to his arrest.

"They formed an armed squad in 2005, training local people. Most of the leaders were from Giridih and Bihar. I recknon there are 20-25 active members in Kathikund-Amrapara (the SP was killed along the road connecting these two areas), with 15 of them possessing police weapons", said the IPS officer.

The police had also arrested four Maosts in the Pakur – Godda border area in April, which may have weakened the outfit considerably. The attack on the SP is also seen as an operation to boost the Maoist morale.

"The Maoists were spotted in Pakur in April"

Although considered to be a district relatively free of Maoist presence, Pakur had seen movement of several rebel cadres in April this year (2013).[11]

Former CRPF DG K Vijay Kumar, "who served as adviser on Naxal operations to the Jharkhand Governor till last week and is presently advisor again to the MHA on Naxal issues", told the daily: "Pakur is not completely free of Maoist activities but it is certainly not a hot bed like Palamu and Dumka districts. In Apr. 2013, forces had spotted the movement of rebels around 30-40 km from the place of attack."

A police officer said: "It (ambush spot) was a carefully chosen site. The culvert was completed only three-four days ago. There was a road depression connecting this culvert. This depression has not yet been filled. So, the convoy has to slow while negotiating this depression and the culvert" that provided a great opportunity to the Maoists waiting at the ambush site to spray the (slowed down) convoy of the SP with bullets.

"Police intensify search operations in Latehar": 4 Jul. 2013 'Destroys a few Maoist camps, seize IEDs and detonators'

The Jharkhand Police on 4 July 2013 continued search operations in Dumka and Pakur disticts along the States border with West Bengal in the wake of 2 Jul ambush that killed the SP and five other policemen. Senior police officers told this to a daily.[12]

Meanwhile, 1,200 policemen and para-military forces were deployed in Latehar district in West Jharkhand along the border with Chhattisgarh. They were tasked to surround areas of the Kumandih forest in Manika block where 200 Maoist cadres are believed to have gathered for meetings.

"Continuing the operation for the 10th day (as of 4 Jul) in the area, State police and paramilitary troops, including from the CRPF's COBRA and Jharkhand Jaguar, destroyed some camps on 3 and 4 July and seized three IEDs, 13 detonators, several backpacks, mobile chargers and literature from a camp near Murhar hills near Kumandih. DGP Jharkhand, who visited the area on the 3rd, told the daily: "We have information that several top leaders of the Koel Sankh Zone were having meetings in the area. We are proceeding cautiously as Maoist had planted explosives in the entire area. In some parts of the thick forests, they have occupied hills terrain, where they will have an advantage."

Security forces surround 250 Maoists in Jharkhand

The preceding story has also been covered by another daily. Some additional observations from it are mentioned here.

The "Jaal Char" operation jointly launched by the state police and CRPF ten days ago in Latehar, "in a well-planned manner with some 2,000 security personnel now surrounding the hill. Gun battles took place at least on five days. We have cut the Maoist supply lines by deploying forces at Kumandih railway station." This is a police officer, who is engaged in the operation, speaking to the daily.[13] Police claim to have killed at least eight Maoist guerrillas.

The troops have laid siezo to a hill, which is spread around 17 sq km. With more than 15 villages located in the area, the forces are gradually closing upon the guerrillas.

The MHA was informed of the operation. On 5 July, DGP Rajiv Kumar, who is monitoring the operation, said Maoists should either surrender or face the bullets.

Latehar Operation: Jharkhand Cops Confident of nabbing Maoists soon:" 6 Jul 2013

As the game of hide and seek with the Maoists continues in Latehar, DGP Rajiv Kumar came back to the headquarters after spending the night with the security forces in the jungles of Kumandih. He termed the terrain of Kumandih as the most difficult one in Jharkhand. Notably, the operations are being carried out in Latehar exclusively by the state police. His other observations are summed up here.

- Kumandih Reserve Forest is the toughest of all the terrains in Jharkhand, as compared to Jhumra and other terrains. This is the reasons ultras have selected the place for their hiding. This time, we are right on track and hopeful of catching them.
- The operation is being carried out by the State Police without the involvement of the CRPF. It also means we have come of age and are capable of handling the situation. It also proves we are sufficient enough to tackle the Maoists in the State.

(Mukesh Ranjan, The Pioneer, 8 Jul 2013)

Over 50 assault groups of COBRA, and Jharkhand Jaguar jawans are engaged in the encounters. As per the police intelligence, the Maoists are running short of arms, ammunition and food supply as their supply lines have been cut off by the police.

DGP, alongwith the DIG Jharkhand Jaguars Praveen Kumar Singh, reached Kumandih with some of the other officials on the 6th to monitor the situation at ground zero.

The DGP climed around 5,000 feet atop and scaled Mur-har hills in the afternoon covering over 25 km on foot where the rebels are said to be hiding for the last few days.

"The Maoists are changing their base camps from one hill to another", he said.

Latehar woman losses leg stepping on Maoist-planted IED : 15 July 2013

A 45-year-old farmer, Jasmatiya Devi, lost her right foot as she stepped on IED, said to be planted by the Maoists, near her village in Latehar's Manika Block on 14 Jul 2013. "We will have to Amputate her right leg : Her left leg is also injured but we are hopeful it will recover," said Kartik Patro, resident doctor at the Rajendra Institute of Medical Sciences in Ranchi (RIMS).

The incident comes days after a massive paramilitary operation against the Maoists in Manika block.

At the RIMS, Devi's son Kamendra Singh Khair was said "his parents were on their way back from Bayan hill, a km away from their village, when the explosion occurred at 8 AM. My father carried her on his shoulders half way down the hill and then ran to the village for help."

"There is a sub-centre nearby in Kumandih but there were no medicines. So we put Devi on a cot and carried her up to the Kumandih railway station", said her neighbour Surajmani Devi. Villagers who gathered at the RIMs said they had received no warning about the possibility of IEDs having been planted by the Maoists.

Massive operation

In a long confrontation between the para-military forces and the Maoists, over 1,500 policemen and troopers of the COBRA and Jharkhand Jaguar had surrounded an area of 22 sq km in Kumandih from 20 June to 5 July. The police believe there were more than 250 Maoists in the area that time undergoing training. Maoist spokesperson Gopal said the meeting had been called to appoint Sameer alias Jayanto as a Politburo member.

On 27 June, DGP Rajiv Kumar, who visited Latehar, said eight Maoists had been killed in the operation but no bodies could be recovered. The police were unable to make any significant headway as the ultras had stationed themselves on the hills and planted several IEDs before escaping, said officials.

Hero of Chatra op gets Shaurya Chakra : 19Aug 2013

Deputy Commandant of CRPF Prakash Ranjan Mishra, one of the recepients of Shourya Chakra this year (2013, survived five bullet wounds during the anti-Maoist operation "Panther" in Jharkhand's Chatra district in Sep 2012. He bled for nearly six hours as an IAF helicopter could not land due to thick cloud cover. Hit by the bullets for the first time in his life, he continued to lead his team of 24 personnel and was successful in eliminating Sub Zonal commander of Naxals Rahuvanshi alias Maheshji[14].

"I was one among the first people who volunteered to join COBRA when it was formed in 2009," says 41-year-old, who has been serving in the areas affected by the LWE for the last eight-and-a-half years and not taken a leave in the last four years.

Mishra, who hails from Patna, joined the CRPF in 1997 as a Sub-Inspector. "It (CRPF) was a force that I had seen working in nearby areas", he says. Mishra became as Assistant Commandant in 2007. He was posted to Jharkhand in 2005.

Currently on deputation with Jharkhand Police as Chatra's Additional SP (Operations), Mishra has also been recommended for a Police Medal for Gallantry taking his tally of gallantry awards to six, which includes a President's Police Medal for gallantry in 2012.

For security reasons, Mishra, who has taken part in 20 encounters, does not give details of his acts that won him the other five awards. His first award came in Jun 2009 for a 2007 operation.

His medals have made him a prize catch for the Maoists, but the officer does not seem to be affected by it. "There is, of course, the chance of death. But thinking of it will only invite fear", he says with a smile.

No gallantry awards for Jharkhand's Cops this year: Aug 2013

With 21 deaths, Jharkhand Police lost a maximum number of its personnel in the LWE-related casualties last year (2012), but not a single of them figured in this year's (2013) list of gallantry awards. A delay in filing the applications seems to be the major reason. "We had a problem with documentation. Some applications were filed late. Some lacked requisite documents", said DGP Rajiv Kumar[15].

A senior police officer said the State had forwarded about ten names. "We will make up for this next year by applying on time. We will have at least 20 individuals on the gallantry list", said the officer.

However, a MHA source said a majority of anti-Naxal operations in Jharkhand were led by CRPF last year, and that could have affected the State Police's Chances. The CRPF took the honours in gallantry awards this year (2013). With 34 of its personnel awarded President's Police Medal for gallantry or Police Medal for Gallantry. Jammu and Kashmir came next, with a total of 22 awardees. Among the LWE-hit states, Odisha and Maharashtra bagged 17 and 21 medals respectively. Though it missed out on gallantry awards, Jharkhand police bagged two President's Police Medal for "distinguished services" and eight Police Medals for Meritorious Services.

Hemant Soren Invites Maoists for talks

Jhark CM Hemant Soren 13 Sep 2013 offered to hold talks with the Maoists and other extremists. This is the first offer from the JMM-led government after taking over the reins in July.

Soren said, "We are ready for a dialogue". It was on the occasion of his laying online foundations for welfare projects to the tune of Rs. 135 cr in Khunti districts. Expressing concern over the historic district's image being tarnished following extremism, Soren appealed to the misguided youth to join the mainstream and participate in the development of the State[16].

Jharkhand's digital leap : 15 Sep 2013

From Naxal cadres to maps of Red zones, and police weapons looted to FIR's filed, the State police's award-winning IT Wing has information of their finger tips.

This is the story of Jharkhand's leap into the field of information technology. It is an achievement any state can be truly proud of, not to speak of a State in the backwards of economic indicators but also a State wracked by Maoist violence.

This is a story that needs detailed telling. Its beginning was rather small : "It began in an anteroom adjacent to the office of the DGP in Ranchi, expanded to an abandoned garage and then to a canteen." Details follow:

- The first team of 5-10 people attempting to draw up a rudimentary seniority list has grown in eight years into an Information

Technology Wing that has since then uploaded information about 2,759 Naxal cadre along with details of 4,227 individuals considered supporters or sympathisers to the Maoist, and even data on the 810 police weapons looted by them.

- The efforts of the Jharkhand Police's IT Wing helped it win independently in the categories of Naxal Information Systems, Crime and Criminal information in Policing Use of information and communication in Policing and Web Portal of Jharkhand Police at the Skock Digital Inclusion Awards (for government entries) for a single entity of a State police.
- As of Jul 2013, 31,454 police personnel have undergone basic IT training at this Data Centre, while 7,218 have taken an advanced course to manage Common Application Software. That covers more than half the State police strength of 55,000 (against sanctioned 70,000).
- An impressed state government, which has long been planning a data centre for itself, is now using the servers at the police HQ to upload certain data such as on commercial taxes and UID.
- The state police first saw the opportunity in IT in 2007-08 when the MHA proposed a modernisation programme for intelligence. "We were one of the few states to receive the whole Rs. 18.5 cr after they were impressedwith our proposal and approved critical components like a GIS (Geographic Information System) and Server Room", says ADGP (Modernization) SN Pradhan.
- The driving force behind the Jharkhand Police IT upgrade, Pradhan recalls that the idea came about when he was DIG (Modernisation), in 2004-05. "a simple thing like a digitized seniority list of police officers was not available at the HQ. Then. I requested for an ante-room attached to the then-DG's office, set up computers and made five-ten boys sit there, typing out the list," he says.
- The Server Room came up where once a garage and Canteen existed, and has now become the heart of the modernisation.
- Pradhan and Debrabrata Naik, a scientist at Ranchi's Informatics Centre Office, together founded what is called the 'Open Group of E-governance (OGE)' when they started the development centre using open sources software in 2009, says Naik, there were only four members. "Now there are 131 individuals in IT support, training and development."

- The OGE works in modules, with each team taking up a project. The *jhpolice.gov.in* Website has since come to host most of these projects.
- Apart from impressive data, the portal houses an online complaint support centre called e-samadhan, e-schools that train personnel to comply with the MHA's requirement for Crime and Criminal Tracking Network and Systems (CCTNS), and an e-learning Academy for the public as part of an outreach programme. Away from the public eye, there is a Naxal Information System, the Crime and Criminal Information System to be integrated with the (CCTNS) and a GIS that supplies customised maps that are vital to operations against Maoist groups.
- For its Naxal Information System, each input—even if seemingly trivial—is fed in. Therefore, as of July 2013, there were 19,790 inputs about 19-and-growing LWE outfits in the state. The system tracks data from 46,237 mobile towers. There are details of 4,896 LWE-related incidents. The data on police weapons looted by LWE outfits has helped track down 262 of them.
- Pradhan admits that it was tough to familiarise officials who had not even operated a computer before with IT. "It was a challenge to even take out the apprehension aspect. There were those who had never even touched a computer before", he says.
- "We started a year late with the CCTNS work, but because of what we had been doing, we are already among the top five states," says Pradhan.
- The OGE has helped start a pilot project in Dhanbad's Jharia to monitor attendance and mid-day real stock through SMSes, as well as helped digitise records of the past ten years, including four lakh FIRs. An Enterprise Management software will feature the records of all purchases in the past 12 years.
- "We have not outsourced a single job of data entry. It has been done by our own trained personnel", says Pradhan.
- An OGE member is now working on software that will help mine data that will be thrown up as records go online. The trends that emerge can be a building block in the predictive policing project that the state police want to try. Another group is working on a mobile application for officers that will throw up profiles once a name is keyed in. The OGE will also animate 50 major LWE incidents in Jharkhand and make it accessible to police personnel for training purposes.

- The idea is to have ultimately a Unified Command and Control Centre—a war room, if you like—located within the police HQ. It is ambitious programme, involving state-of-the-art Land Mobile Radio System, helping integrate multiple platforms.
- "We plan to connect 816 sites, establishing 1,200 links. All devices, even radios, will be, will be integrated. This will go hand-in-hand with the GIS centre we are proposing to establish with the Jharkhand Space Application Centre. All SPs have laptops pre-loaded with the customised GIS maps. Hand-helds with the same will be distributed. That will pave the way for a first-of-its-kind GIS and Ops Centre", Pradhan says[17].

Jharkhand Maoists deny abduction plan : Sep 2013

Two days after the Jharkhand police said they had discovered pamphlets that allegedly dwelt on a plan by the CPI (Maoist) to abduct Latehar Collector Aradhana Patnaik, the Naxals in a radio-statement to the daily, rubbished what they said was a "police conspiracy".

The Palamu police on 13 Sep 2013 claimed to have recovered a country-made revolver, pamphlets and Maoist literature from a room during a raid on a Medninagar hotel following a tip-off. No one was arrested.

A senior police officer based in Ranchi, Ranchi, however, said on the 13th that state police were yet to establish the authenticity of the pamphlet that detailed the abduction plan.

In his denial on the 15th . Maoist spokesperson Gopal, in a 15- minute audio clip, said the police were "spreading rumours to turn ordinary people and intellectuals against Maoists" by claiming that they had planned to abduct a woman official. No one from our Cadre had gone to town or hotel. We are focused on class struggle. I request Ms. Patnaik to consider our ideology and not believe the police version. We guarantee her and all women officials and people's representatives security if they work for people.[18]"

"Maoists abduct Jharkhand kids for bomb lessons, one dead" : 19 Sep 2013

'A 10-year-old boy was killed in an explosion while planting an IED. The Reds threatened his family into silence'

This is the true nature of Maoists and their ideology, based on the theory of class struggle. This news story by a daily exposes their cruelty as also the hypocrisy attached to all they do and preach—both miles apart!

"Maoists in Jharkhand are kidnapping children in the 10-16 age group and teaching them to assemble and plant bombs, police sources said. A 10-year old boy died in an explosion on 18 Sep 2013 during one such training session, blowing the led off the rebels' sinister plan[19]".

Now the full details of this cruel, despicable and horrendous practice of Maoists. Pardeshi Lohra was among 7-8 children forcibly taken from their homes in Latehar district by CPI (Maoist) a few days ago. He was killed while planting a bomb. The other children are still in captivity.

"The Maoists handed over Pardeshi's body to his parents on the 16th morning and threatened them into performing the last rites without letting anyone know the cause of death," said Latehar SP Michael Raj.

However, the police got wind of the incident on the 17th , exhumed the body and sent it for post mortem. SP Raj said: "This has exposed the real face of the CPI (Maoist) who claims to be champions of the poor."

Maoists have been indoctrinating children and using them for propaganda for decades. But this is probably the first report of them being used as foot soldiers—a trend associated with the Talibans or the insurgent groups in several African countries.

Earlier this year (2013) in Latehar, the Reds had planted bombs in the bodies of CRPF jawans they had killed. "The Maoists are getting more inhuman by the day", said ADGP SN Pradhan.

Jharkhand accounts for nearby a third of the Maoist violence in India with 163 people killed last year (2012). Till 1 Aug 2013, Maoists have killed 97 people.

Incident and Events: 2014

Jharkhand to phase out CRPF deployment: 13 Jan 2014

To reduce the burden on its State exchequer, the Jharkhand Government decid to phase out the deployment of CRPF in its anti-Naxal role during the next five years. To achieve this goal, the SPs have been asked to minimise the dependence on the CRPF and take help of the State police in carrying anti-Naxal operations. This was reported by a daily on 13 Jan 2014.[20]

The issue was also discussed by Home Secretary NN Pandey with the Finance Commission during its recent visit to Ranchi. He was advised to take steps to raise a parallel force on the lines of the CRPF so that the latter could be progressively phase out from the State.

In his presentation to the Commission, Pandey mentained the local force will be more suitable in achieving coordination with the local police and the villagers, as they understand the both better than an outside force.

What is more important is that the State already has dedicated anti-Naxal force, viz. the Jharkhand Jaguar. The state should add to its numbers and make it more affective with better training and weaponry.

Now, Maoists want poll boycott to be legal: 22 Mar 2014

The CPI (Maoist) has asked the Election, Commission to legalise the right to boycott the polls. They have issued a call for boycott of 2014 General Elections, nonetheless! It was reported on 22 Mar 2014.

The daily met the Maoist leaders at one of their training camps in Gumla district on the Jharkhand-Chhattisgarh border. The gun-toting rebels, the most dressed in black robes, spoke at length on the plans to sabotage these polls and other issues[21].

Some of the observations made by them are noted here.

- "We do not intend to disturb or harm any process", said Ashish, 35, a State Committee leader, wiping his SLR, looted from police. "If the forces try to thrust polls on the people, we will retaliate as we did on 11 March in Chhattisgarh, by killing 15 of them." It should not be a surprise that fear and anxiety grip some of the polling staff sent to the Maoist-hit areas. 'In the recent Assembly polls in the state, at least four election officers died of heart attack after being sent to sensitive polling booths. Maoists have a word of caution for them. "Do n't risk your lives. accompany police to the polling booths Protest and walk out if you are forced to do so. We do not harm civilians", said Sylvestor, 55, another commander of the Bihar-Jharkhand. North Chhattisgarh Special Area Committee.
- The leaders argued the present system could never end corruption. "Sting operations and the Charades of Lok Adalat and Lokpal Bill are stupid. Over the past 66 years, several governments came and went, but the class divide between the rich and the poor has only widened", said Deenbandhu, Regional Secretary of the banned outfit.
- "Unfortunately, any one disagreeing with the poll system is declared a Maoist", he added. " 'None of the Above' (NOTA) or the 'scratch vote' option was meaningless as those in disapproval of all the candidates did not bother to go to the polling booths.... Bogus Voters cast their ballots instead."
- They are clever at making seemingly convincing arguments to make their view points : "Election boycott is a fundamental right and strength of people and hence they could be permitted to

exercise this right without any hindrance," said another top Maoist leader. So for them, the elections are a farce.

Moists have strong influence in at least 60 districts spread over eight states. Police have a major challenge at their hands, holding polls in these districts.

Meanwhile, fresh banners, posters and pamphlets are out and being clandestinely distributed among villagers. One such pamphlet shown to the daily asked people to boycott the 2014 polls and instead, work towards bringing in a government for, off and by the famers and the working class.

This story is datelined Gumla.

Comments

Some editorial comments are called for.

- It is amusing to see the Maoists talking of a faulty democracy in India. One wonders if they even know the meaning of this term.
- As for the class differences, it exists among the Maoists in its worst form. The majority of their leaders are from rich and educated families, and that too mostly from Andhra. The foot soldiers are from Bihar, Jharkhand and Chhattisgarh. Are the two classes equal, or treated so?
- Worst form of government may be a democracy, even then, it is the best among the alternatives. Look at the Maoists ? Why are factions killing each other's cadres?
- As for the corruption, it exists among the CPI (Maoist) in worst from, and cadres can't even talk about it! There is no accountability of money collected by its leaders through extortions and levies. How much a leader at junior and middle keep it with him for personal use out of total collection only he knows. The details come to the police only when a surrendered leader or a cadre spills the beans. Are we unaware of luxurious living style senior leaders of the banned outfit? Yet again, the sexual exploitation of their female cadres by the Maoist leaders is rampant. This is disclosed not only by victims of this exploitation, viz, the female cadres, but also by their male colleagues.
- It is even more amusing to see a banned out demanding that poll boycott be made legal!
- Yet again, it is the strength of the Indian democratic set up, imperfect as it is, according the murderous Maoists, that the threats of dire consequences including the death, do not stop the

common voters from venturing to the polling booths and exercising their franchise. To wit, notwithstanding the threats of murder and mayhem by the terrorists in J & K, Maoists in LWE states, and insurgents in the North-East, percentage of voting polled in these three Regions is higher than it is in some other states of the union and much higher than those in most of the metro cities. It simply means one thing : The poor and deprived, the constituency claimed by these LWE, understand the value of the vote better than their richer counterparts. Incidentally, emergency was undone by the former classes than the latter, who chose to crawl when asked to bend, to borrow the unforgettable quote from LK Advani.

- A word about such interviews. The interviewer doses not….dare not….. ask any inconvenient questions. Partly because he is overwhelmed by the favour granted to him by the mighty Maoists, and partly because the interviewee has his gun in his hand, even if it is for the ostensible reason of cleaning it (the SLR). The clever Maoists use such interviews and interviewers as a propaganda conduits for their name and failed ideology: Left-Commie Nonsence! One does not why the dailies are compelled to do their bidding? They can get the same silly, repetitive nonsense from their tracts and handouts available in all LWE-hit areas; and better still from the closet-Maoists in well-heeled areas of metropolitans like Delhi, Mumbai or Kolkata, and they mouth this familiar jargon from there air conditioned rooms, and better still, these loud-mouths are often sighted in the TV studios!

Three cops injured in PLFI attack in Jharkhand

Three policemen were injured after an IED allegedly planted by PLFI cadres went off while they were travelling. The explosion took place at Murhu in Khunti districts on 25 Mar 2014. Here is an interesting claim made by Aditional DGP (CID) SN Pradhan : "They have fired back during operations. They have also used IEDs against civilians to threaten them during extortion beds. However, using an IED against the police 'without provocation' is a first.[22]"

The attack comes at a time when, police claim, the PLFI has taken over the CPI (Maoist) to become the largest LWE outfit in the State in terms of incidents. "The PLFI is now responsible for 36 per cent of LWE violence; while the CPI (Maoist) figure stands at some 34 per cent", says Pradhan.

The three injured policemen—SHO of Murhu police station, a Jharkand Armed Police Constable and a driver—were out of danger. Some individuals were detained by police for questioning.

IGP (Operations) ML Meena was rather concerned. "This is a very worrying development and comes at a (bad) time when the elections are on. The movement of troops will have to be planned very carefully." Pradhan had his own take : "The incident is a follow-up on the press statement issued by the PLF a few months back, saying they will now start targeting police."

"Take up ploughs, drop gun: Modi to Maoists"

'Arousing Interest : Supporters throng his rallies in Jharkhand, defying rebels' 'bandh calls; in Gaya crowd goes wild, groups clash, police resort to lathi charge'.

BJP Prime Ministerial candidate on 27 Mar 2014 advised Maoists to drop their guns and pick ploughs, instead. He said this at his Bharat Vijay Rallies in Jharkhand's LWE-hit districts of Gumla and Chhatra, where supporters thronged the venues despite a shut down call given by the Maoists[23].

In these districts, Modi appealed to the Maoists to embrace non-violence and end the spilling of the innocent's blood in the Country. "Don't arm the gullible youth with guns. Instead, pick up the plough and distribute it among youngsters, since you need to feed scores of people who sleep hungry in this Country...Also ensure the youth picks up the pen as only education can lead to progress and development in the villages."

In the morning, state BJP leaders were worried lot as the Maoist Bandh call had adversely impacted the movement of public transport, leaving supporters stranded in their districts.

Housewife with 'Maoist link' : 9 Apr 2014

A whisper campaign threatens to derail Chatra's first-ever 'local' candidate fielded for Lok Sabha by Babulal Marandi's Jharkhand Vikas Manch (Prajatantrik). Her opponent say in private that Neelam Devi, a 37-year-old housewife who was previously not known as a leader, has the support of CPI (Maoist). A top police officer says "there are rumours that CPI (Maoist)' Regional Committee member Nakul Yadav is supporting her". The officer, who spoke on condition of anonymity, further clarified : "We cannot prove it, but I have come to know that her family is close to Nakul Yadav and that he has declared support for her[24]."

However, another officer differed, saying, "I heard about the allegation through informal conversations. We have no information on her". For the record, Neelam's affidavit lists no criminal cases.

The JVM(P) has ticked several bones by fielding Neelam. Along with Geeta Kora—the Jai Bharat Samanta Party from Singhbhoom—she is one of the two women candidates from the 14 Jharkhand seats with a realistic chance of victory. Congress, BJP and JMM have not nominated any women. Neelam is the only one in JVM's list and is going the extra mile to appeal directly to women voters.

What adds to Neelam's appeal is that she is among the select few candidates who reside in the constituency. No resident has ever won from Chatra. "Even when we were part of Bihar, when we had Gaya and Latehar and Chatra in the Constituency, no one from here won", said Mohd Ehsan, the JVM(P)'s Constituency incharge. The BJP and Congress have never fielded a local candidate/leader. That trend continues with the BJP fielding Bihar's Sunil Singh and the Congress, Lohardaga's Dhiraj Prasad Sahu.

Neelam Devi's Yadav identity may help her in Dalit-stronghold of Chatra, with Sunil Singh being a Rajput and Dhiraj Prasad Sahu, a Teli. However, the BJP is expecting a victory. "A large number of Telis could end up voting for us as Narendra Modi is from the caste", said Amit Choubey, Lamta panchayat president and a BJP supporter.

Babulal Marandi's presence and Neelam's resident status in Latehar could also attract Adivasi votes. "Recently, there was a meeting organised for Adivasi voters of the constituency, I could see a lot of support for her," said Surendra Lakra, from Latehar's Babumath block. The BJP is worried about the influence of friend-turned-foe, sitting Chatra MP and Independent Inder Singh Namdhari, who is working to defeat its candidate in both Chatra and Palamu as he was denied a ticket.

Muslims could hold the key. "Muslim voters are still undecided. Their primary aim is to defeat BJP, so they might vote for the candidate they think is BJP's nearest rival. The JVM(P) is trying to get them to vote for us", said Mohd Ehsan.

Jharkhand on alert as police fear Maoist attacks : 13 Apr 2014

Jharkhand is on high alert in light of the Lok Sabha polls as police believe security forces in the state could come under Maoist attacks. "Advisories have been issued to State Police to stay alert as Maoist guerrillas could target the trains carrying security forces," a police officer said 12 Apr 2014[25].

This officer believes Maoist guerrillas are upset because the Phase-I of the polls in the state was peaceful. In Phase-I on 10 April, polling took place for four seats where Maoists have strong presence. The second phase too is in Maoist-affected areas. The official further added : "The Maoists are deperate to execute a big attack on the forces... The roads and railway routes are vulnerable is both pass through jungle areas."

The polling percentage in Phase – I was 58.03—an increase of eight per cent over the previous poll's – despite a boycott call from the Maoists.

Tharkh and police along with the paramilitary contingents combed the area before phase I polls. In phase II, six of the 14 Lok Sabha constituencies—Ranchi, Giridih, Hazaribagh, Dhanbad, Khunti and Chaibasa – will go to polls.

As a precautionary, security forces and polling staff were airlifted to the polling booths.

In Khunti Constituency, AAP candidates Dayamani Barla complained to the police that Maoist outfit PLFI is threatening its party supporters. Maoist cadres are active 18 of the State's 24 districts.

Rising illegal mining emerges as main poll plank in Singhbhum : 13 Apr 2014

For long West Singhbhum district of Jharkhand was known for its abundant forest resources and rich tribal culture. Abundant with iron ore and other minerals, there was nothing that set it apart from other tribal-dominated patches of the region.

"However, things have changed quicker with passage of time. The region is now a throbbing ground of mining operators who have simply revolutionised West Singhbhum way beyond recognition. The transformation, however, gave rise to illegal mining that led to environment imbalance in the process and many of the ore mafias turned into millionaires.

No wonder, the candidates in fray have made the rising illegal mining as main poll plank in the Singhbhum constituency, that goes to polls on 17 April.

Taking the lead, BJP candidate Laxman Gilua is targeting his arch rival sitting MP Madhu Koda's wife Geeta Koda of Jai Bharat Samanta Party for their involvement in the illegal mining. As per the local poll pundits, Gilua is in attack mode on Koda family for the allocation of lease to several mining companies during 2006-2008 in the State[26].

The fraud involving allocation of the iron ore lease was a part of multi-crore money laundering case involving former CM Madhu Koda. Social worker Binil Purty said that the vested interests in the mining sector are bent to destroy the world famous Saranda forest and adjoining forest areas.

They just want to mine every inch of the area at the cost of ecology, environment, biodiversity, wild life for which Saranda is known the world wide. "People have been worst hit due to illegal mining and Gilua Jee has promised the local people if voted to power he will work to curb the illegal mining activites", said Purty.

Not only Geeta Koda, BJP is also targeting Congress Party's Chiktrasen Sinku for Union Government's failure in taking initiative in maintaining the ecological balance of the area.

Singhbhum Lok Sabha Constituency comprise the six Legislative Assembly segments, including Seraikela, Chaibasa, Majghaon, Jaganathpur, Manoharpur and Chakradharpur.

In Khunti, AAP candidate battles 'extremist threats' : 15 Apr 2014

Rather than corruption, AAP in Jharkhand has found itself tackling a new enemy : LWE outfit ! Its Khunti candidate Dayamani Barla has registered two FIRs and written to the Election Commission after alleged cadres of the PLFI threatened and attacked her supporters. She alleges the PLFI men asked her cadre to campaign for former minister Anosh Ekka, who faces cases on disproportionate assets[27].

The PLFI, which has its origins in Khunti district's Torpa block, is the most dangerous outfit in the state in terms of incidents : it accounts for 36 per cent of them, ahead of the CPI (Maoist)'s 34 per cent. Barla said, "At 4 PM on 9 April, my supporters were campaigning at Biguadag village. Six armed people on two moter cycles beat the driver with the butt of a rifle and snatched everyone's mobiles. One among these men claimed he was a Zonal Commander of the PLFI. Barla faces seven-time BJP MP Kariya Munda and Jharkhand Party's Ekka.

She disclosed one women was forced to stay back, go around the village touching the feet of people and requesting them to vote for Ekka.

She turned down the security offered to her by the police, and said : "The PLFI men clicked my supporter's pictures on their mobiles, so we are worried about what happens after the polls."

SP Khunti Anis Gupta said they were investigating the FIRs. There were no names in the 6 April case but they were trying to identify six men involved in the 9 April attack.

Barla, a former journalist, operates a tea shop in Ranchi. She led two key agitations in Khunti. One was against the Koel-Karodam during which eight Adivasis were shot dead on 2 Feb 2001. The other was against Arcelor Mittal steel plant.

Maoist eye mining pie, keep gun silent in Jharkhand : 22 Apr 2014

The guns are quieter in Jharkhand this election. The troubled eastern state has hardly had elections without bloodshed. Maoists and their splinter groups killed eleven persons in the 2009 Lok Sabha polls and 12 in the Assembly polls that years. The two phases of the General Elections have been peaceful barring a landmine blast in Bokaro that injured four CRPF troopers.

Other Maoist-hit states has been far more violent. Chhattisgarh and Bihar have so far reported 12 and two deaths respectively[28].

So what happened in Jharkhand that witnessed 383 Maoist-related incidents compared to 353 in Chhattisgarh? Senior police officers and activists here feel that the ultra groups are refraining from big-bang attacks for share of the lucrative iron ore mining trade.

An SP heading a sensitive district told the daily : " Several rebel groups have been tacitly supporting a number of candidates to gain control over the mineral-rich constituencies and this could be one of the reasons behind fewever violent incidents this election." A prominent anti-mining activist Xavier Dias seems to agree with the SP's take on the issue : "Many candidates in the Red terror zones of Chatra, Palamu, and Khunti districts have reached an understanding with Maoists and their offshoots. All the major groups including the CPI (Maoist), PLFI, TPC, have supported one candidate or the other". He did not take names but locals know who are backing whom. Besides, rebels have voiced their choices.

CPI (Maoist) Regional Committee member Nakul Yadav announced support for Neelam Devi, JVM candidate from Chatra. Its rival outfit TPC is widely believed to be supporting the BJP in the same constituency. In Khunti, the PLFI is actively helping Jharkhand Party candidate Anosh Ekka.

Many believe the iron trade is too lucrative for the Maoists to stay away from. In West Singhbhum's Saranda Region alone, 19 mining projects are in different phases of approval . Here is Dias's analysis: "Once a powerful force, the Maoists have not only been divided into various splinter groups but have also come under severe attack from the state. They are on the backfoot, and so they want to control the area politically."

This possibly explains why Maoists have checked their habit of boycotting polls.

DGP Rajiv Kumar did not rule out any Maoist –candidate understanding but insisted the rebels have lost steam because of heavy deployment of security forces and intense combing operations. He says: "We are better prepared this time with 90,000 security personnel deployed in the two phases. Also, we began search operations on a massive scale in Nov 2013."

With elections in four less sensitive constituencies - - Dumka, Dhanbad, Godda and Rajmahal - -due on 24 Apr, the people of Jharkhand hope the guns remain quieter.

Polling staff falls victim to Maoist attack

The Maoist strike on an election party claiming eight lives on 25 Apr 2014 in Dumka shattered a brief lull in Jharkhand which otherwise witnessed a relatively peaceful phase polling.

The polling officials and Jharkhand Police personel were part of a team that was returning in a minibus to the district HQ Dumka after polling in the Shikaripara Assembly segment. The vehicle hit a Maoist planted IED on the Sarsajor Palasi road and was damaged, killing five policemen and three polling staff[29].

Poll officials were advised not to take buses in a Maoist –hit areas and walk back with the EVMs to the district HQ. DGP Rajiv Kumar said: "We have ensured peaceful polling by adhering to the SOP. We will have to examine what went wrong here."

Maoists kill Assistant Commandant of CRPF : 4 Jul 2014

A CRPF Assistant Commandant, Hira Kumar Jha, was killed and two other security men injured in an encounter on 4 Jul 2014 between joint forces of the state police and CRPF and Maoist rebels in Jharkhand Giridih district.

Following the directive from the Centre (MHA), Jharkhand police along with the CRPF launched massive operations against the LWE "during the last three day"—starting 2 Jul 2014. "This is the first time the forces are foraying into the jungle seven during the difficult monsoon months."

The encounter took place when forces were conducting a search operation in the Kauwakol-Khaira forest in the Giridih district of the State, which borders Bihar's Jamui district. This jungle is located across the Jharkhand-Bihar border. The forces arrested three Maoists, including a woman identified as Sabita, when the trio was trying to escape this jungle.

This fierce encounter took place in Tisri location of this jungle, 80 km from Giridih district headquarters[30].

Giridih SP Kranti Kumar Garhdesi disclosed police also "recovered a huge cache of arms and ammunitions, including a sniper rifle and live cartridges from their possession." He said "the forces were faced with intermittent firing from thick foliage on the hillocks". The DGP office ordered rushing the reinforcements to the site. " A manhunt was launched with the help of these reinforcements in the area", said IGP Bokaro Range Laxman Prasad.

"Slain Jha's body has been recovered and is likely to be brought to Dhanbad by the late evening (4 July). His family (wife and two minor children) was flown in to Ranchi from New Delhi."

Jharkhand : CBI Must Probe 'fake'Naxal Surrenders : 19 Jul 2014

The Jharkhand Government " has asked for a CBI inquiry into reports that a former Military Intelligence (MI) official, Ravi Bodra, and some CRPF officers falsely projected some 150 Adivasi youths as members of various LWE outfits in 2011-12, in a bid to boost their surrender statistics[31]."

The youths were lured into the act with a promise of jobs in the CAPF. They were, obviously, told that these jobs to surrendered members of the LWE outfits. "Some of them were even made to pay as much as Rs 2 lakh", the reports said. The scam was the result of an ambitious MHA project that went wrong. The MHA had brought in former MI officer Ravi Bodra after his work in Assam where he had convinced some Bodo militants to surrender. Now the same Bodra is accused of being the 'lynchpin' of this "false surrender scam". Ranchi SP Anup Birthare has some additional details: "Bodra was in the Army and served in Nagaland. He later joined the MI and proved effective in getting a number of extremists surrender in Assam. He wanted to replicate that 'succes' in Jharkhand and was indeed successful for a while in the Khunti district." But the SP refused to divulge which specific agency had given Bodra the Jharkhand mission.

Incidentaly, Ravi Bodra was also known as Ravi Barla.

It should come as no surprise that the MHA decided to use his 'expertise' to boost the surrenders in Jharkhand. "The CRPF as also the police were kept in the loop on Bodra's activities. He also maintained good relations with Maoist leaders,"a source tells this daily. There were even a plan to present the youth en masse a Minister of the MHA.

After their "surrender" in late 2011, the youths were kept in the Old Ranchi Jail for upto a year, guarded by the personnel of the 203 Battalion of the CRPF's COBRA. This Jail had not been in use since 2006, after a new jail was built on the outskirts of Ranchi.

An FIR registered at the Lower Bazaar police station on 3 March 2014 lists Bodra, Dinesh Prajapati, Caroline Kerketta and another individual as accused. Prajapati was Director, Dighdarshan Coaching Institute and Kerketta acted as an agent. "We have recorded statements of 18 students claiming that Prajapati and Bodra took Rs. 55,000 – 1.5 lakh from each of them, promising jabs in the Army and paramilitary forces and then made them pose as Maoists ", said the Ranchi SP.

However, it was not clear whether those responsible for this scam also claimed the benefits due to the surrenderces under the MHA Surrender Policy : one, Rs. 1.5 – 2.5 lakh cash on surrender, depending on his/her rank in the outfit; two, Rs 4,000 monthly stipend to each surrenderee for first 36 months.

The daily met 14 such youths who claimed that 500-550 others hailing from Ranchi, Khunti, Gumla and Lohardaga districts were in jail with them. None of them had any criminal record.

Here are specifics

- "A man named Vijay Bara came to our village Gutia-Jamgai in Namkum Block of Ranchi district, in Nov 2012 and said CRPF was conducting direct recruitment. At first, he said, we would have to pay 30,000. It was increased later. A total of 13 youths, aged 19-31, paid Rs 30,000 – 60,000, and surrendered as Maoists from this village". This is Sundra Kujur of the named village speaking to the daily (read its scribe). "I went with Ramesh Tudu, (another youth) to Bara's house in Chalangi village in Khunti's Torpa block to pay the money. In the evening, three Boleros with 'Bharat Sarkar' written on them, came to Chalangi. There were others inside. Once we got inside the car Ravi Bodra gave each of us a pistol and a bullet. He then explained we would have to surrender."

Though it was the first time he was holding a fire arm, Sundra knew what "surrender" meant. "I would have to pretend to be a Maoist. Anything for a job, " I thought," he said.

- Bodra also instructed the youths on what to say to their interrogators. Sundra would later claim he was part of Area Commander Ranjit Bodra's armed squad. Fellow villager Alok Tidu claimed he was part of Nageshwar Pahari's squad.

- Most of us did not even know whether these area commanders were of the CPI (Maoist) or the PLFI. I was told Pahan was a PLFI leader and that I was supposed to have been a porter in his squad for about a year-and-a-half", said Alok Tidu.

In the jail, both Bodra and Bara did not enter the room in which the CRPF officials stood. The youths, who were made to surrender in small groups over a month, were asked to sign a register. They were sent to cells which were kept unlocked through out the duration of their stay and allowed to keep their cellphones.

The youths said they were given two hours of physical training each morning and were expected to clean the jail premises later. A senior government official said those responsible for the "scam" paid COBRA personnel for food provided to the youths.

They were allowed to leave the premises two-three days every three months or so, after making prior request. When they finally realised it was all a "scam", they went on "leave" and never returned.

"Two senior officers named Lakhinder and Chetan were responsible for us. When ever a senior officer came, we were asked to stay out of sight and keep quiet", said Sundra, who stayed in the jail for nine months. When contacted, the officer named Chetan did not give his second name and refused to comment.

Despite recording the most LWE incidents in the country in 2012 and 2013, the number of those who surrendered in Jharkhand was just six and 15 respectively. In 2014, the figure stands at four (upto 31 May). In contrast, Andhra recorded 301 surrenders in 2012, while Odisha had 101 in 2013.

Key aide of Jharkhand Maoist shot dead after gun battle: 22 Jul 2014

A Sub Zonal Commander of CPI (Maoist), Tulsi Das alias Vishal, 33, believed to be the right-hand man of Jharkhand's most-wanted Maoist leader Kundan Pahan, was shot dead 22 Jul 2014 at Lembo village in Arki block of the Khunti district.

Vishal was a member of the Maoists' Bihar-Jharkhand-North Chhattisgarh Special Area Committee (BJNC – SAC). He was killed after a two-and-a-half hour gun battle, that began around 2.30 AM.

The state government had declared a bounty of Rs 2 lakh on his head. After his death, DGP Rajiv Kumar distributed the amount among the memebers of the team that eliminated him[32].

Vishal was close to Maoist Zonal Commander Kundan Pahan of BJNC Zone. Vishal had recently started working again under Pahan after spending three years in a different Zone. He hails from Bundu area in Ranchi. The items found on him included on AK-47 rifle that belonged to security forces and was missing sinc killing of five CRPF men at a village in Khunti in Apr 2009.

Maoists gun down a Congress leader in Jharkhand : 30 Aug 2014

A Congress leader Kishan Sau was killed on 29 Aug 2014 by the Maoists, who branded him a police informer, in a bustling local market in Jharkhand's Gudabandha area, under Ghatsila Sub-division.

Sau was gunned down at point blank range and died on the spot. The ultras left a poster branding him an informer and left the body overnight in the market. Police reached the spot in the morning. Mosabani DSP B Kujur defended the delay : "We avoided visiting the spot as there were intelligent inputs that the ultras might use Saw's body as a booby trap to attack the police." He added forces "have been sent out into the jungles nearby to seach for the ultras[33]."

The killing of a political leader is bound to become a political issue. So it was in this case. The killing of the young Congress leader led to severe protests in the area. Saw's family refused to take the body away after the autopsy demanding adequate compensation.

Senior Congress leader Manoj Kumar Yadav and District Congress president Vijay Khan, who visited Ghatsila, condemned the callous approach of the authorities, saying . We will try to meet the CM and demand security for our party workers, who are being targeted and killed. State Congress President Sukhdeo Bhagat said the Party had lost a good party worker. Saw was a fire brand leader in his area."

Secretary Nagrik Surakhsha Samity Sailen Barkey said that an after the incident he had informed the police about the armed militants in Gurabandha (earlier spelt as Gudabandha) but "they did nothing to arrest the advance of the Maoist faction."

Operation on in Jharkhand to flush out Maoists : 3 Sep 2014

"Joint forces comprising state police and CRPF on Wednesday are combing suspected hideouts of the Maoists in States Latehar district, one of India's highly LWE-hit districts," reported a daily on Thursday, 4 Sep 2014. "The operation launched last week is in full spring despite late monsoon showeres in the area[34]."

The police said the operation is part of the security forces' strategy for setting up Forward Camping Sites (FCS) or base camp at the strategic locations in highly Maoist-infested areas of the district.

The operation is essentially meant to flush out Maoists from the Latehar district.

"On motor Cycle in Naxal hot bed" : 23 Sep 2014

This photo of Union Home Minister riding, rather driving, a motor cycle at the Thalkobad CRPF camp at Saranda forest in the West Singhbhum district of Jharkhand on 23 Sep 2014 finds a place in this Chapter / book for two reasons.

One, it is good for ministers to visit the camps of CRPF, presently the main paramilitary force deployed against the Maoist insurgency. They not only get a chance to receive a briefing from the CRPF's field commanders directly involved in the anti-Maoist operations but also has a chance to meet CRPF men first hand, that is good for their morale[35].

Two, it is noteworthy that the Home Minister Rajnath Singh is driving the bike bare-headed, and the CRPF officer riding pillion behind the Minister has a beret on his head, not helmet. They should have been more attentive and avoid presenting such wrong images to public. But then, who will dare tell a ministere to wear helment before trying his hand at driving a bike!.

CRPF man killed, officer injured in Naxal encounter : 16 Sep 2014

A CRPF man of specialised COBRA unit was killed and a Deputy Commandant injured in an encounter with the Maoists at Chiklam village in Naxal-hit Ghatsila sub-division on 17 Sep 2014. DIG (Kolhan Range, Jharkhand) Mohd Nehal disclosed that police had received information that a huge Maoist squad had entered the village from the dense Dalma forest on the night 16 September[36].

A joint operation was launched by the personnel from the CRPF, District Armed Police (DAP) of Jharkhand, a COBRA unit, 69 Bn CRPF, SISF, and police officials from Jhargram in West Bengal early morning on the 17th, cordoning off the village. This was disclosed to the press by DIG Kolhan Range and SDPO of Jhargram.

The encounter lasted from 5 AM to 8 AM in the morning, with security forces firing nearly 200 rounds. The intermittent firing continued even afterwards. Area had been cordoned off but the 'flushing out' operation was started till the late evening the 17th, "as the Maoists were still holed up in the village."

SSP East Singhbhum Amol V Homkar informed that the injured Deputy Commandant of the COBRA, Alok Kumar, was airlifted to a hospital in Ranchi.

Maoist leader involved in major attacks arrested in Jharkhand: 27 Sep 2014

A Maoist leader, allegedly involved in either planning or executing three major attacks in the last four years in Jharkhand's Santhal Pargana region was arrested from Dumka district on 28 Sep 2014.

Sukhlal Murmu, 39, known as Prabirda in the party, hails from Giridih district's Pirtand and was arrested from Dumka's Ramgarh police station area. He is listed as the accused in the murder of Catholic nun Valsa John in 2011, killing of Pakur SP Amarjit Balihar in 2013 and the attack on officials returning after conducting the 2014 Lok Sabha polls. Dumka SP Anoop Mathew says : "He has accepted that CPI (Maoist) was involved in the murder of Sister John, and that he led the attack on SP Balihar. Further interrogation will yield additional details," said SP Dumka Anoop Mathew.

It is believed the CPI (Maoist) was so impressed by Prabirda's work that in July-Aug 2014, it accept his request to form a special Area Committee (SAC) for Purvi Bihar-Purvother Jharkhand Zone, and made him a member of this SAC. This Zone covers parts of Jamui, Bhagalpur and Patna districts of Bihar and Koderma, Giridih and the six districts of Santhal Pargana Division of Jharkhand. In fact, he was arrested while returning from a meeting of this SAC[37].

Prabirda's interrogation also revealed the importance the Maoist have accorded to the Santhal Pargana division/region, once considered impenetrable due to strong influence of the JMM. A senior police officer told the daily: "He has told us that he was given the responsibility of the region in 2003. This, after the party had conducted a survey and failed to move into the region under a different leader in 2001." Pralbir used frontal organisations to expand the party and in 2006, formed an armed squad. The Maoists targeted money lenders, moved on issues of displacement and farmers' woes to gain the trust of the people. Since then, his team has carried out a major attack almost each year—the attack on the police parties in Shikaripara and Kathikund in 2008 and 2010, and the killing of two BSF jawans in 2009, among them.

Maoist faction kills 7 in Gumla

Suspected terrorists belonging to the PLFI, a breakaway faction of the CPI (Maoist), gunned down seven people in Gumla district on 3 Nov 2014.

The victims were reportedly members of the Shanti Sena, a local outfit formed to maintain peace and brotherhood. Jharkhand police's spokesperson Anurag Gupta confirmed the deaths.

The polic had no information on the Shanti Sena. They could not find any immediate reason, political or otherwise, for the killings. Assembly polls are scheduled in Gumla district in the first phase of the elections on 25 November (2014).

The PLFI cadres opened indiscriminate firing on a SUV carrying several members of the Shanti Sena between Harup and Rerwa villages under Kamdara police station area around 6.30 PM. "The spot is surrounded by dense forests and the rebels were hiding", said a police officer[38].

A Maoist leader admits ground lost in stronghold : 6 Nov 2014

A Platoon Commander of the CPI (Maoist)'s PLGA has confessed that the outfit is not in a healthy state in its former stronghold of Porahat Sub-Zone, blaming its absence at the grassroot level. "We had to hurriedly celebrate the Martyr's Week (in July). The Foundation Week celebrations too were held hurriedly. Police were swarming here," said Jeevan Kandulna, 36, speaking to the daily in the Porhat forest of West Singhbhum in a rare interview[39]. The story is datelined Porhat.

Maoists in the area have not been able to even plan their Tactical Counter Offensive Campaign (TCOC) for executing major attacks "on the security forces this year (2014). And they are yet to make their stand clear on the Assembly polls due later this month (Nov 2014)."

Kandulna, or Gajendra Singh, admitted that the response to their efforts to draw mass support for the protests too has been mild. "When a school teacher was arrested for being a supporter of ours, we tried to conduct a mass agitation demanding his replacement be posted immediately. People did not turn up", he dregretted. Villagers have also remained cold to Maoist effortt to mobilise alleged victims of sexual harassment by the security forces.

Kandhulna blamed it on the outfit not making its presence felt at the ground level. "The party works through its Committees. We do not have the Nari (Mukti Sangh) and the Krantikare Kisan Committee is non-existent. I am the only person running the party here, there should be at least three."

As a result, the CPI (Maoist) is becoming an overtly militaristic outfit, with overground work by frontal organisations shrinking. He agreed that their militia remained strong. He says, "Recruitment is still healthy. Our cadres could do with more training though. Also, a number of them don't stay long."

Most of the 10-15 members of Kandulna's squad look well under 18 years of age. Another Platoon Commander Suresh (Real name Dimba Pahan), who was present with Kandulna, said, "The two of us are the only seniors. Every one else is gone."

A full platoon of the PLGA comprises 30 fighters. There are at least two other platoons in the Porahat Sub-Zone. Kundan Pahan, Suresh's brother and the second most wanted Maoist leader in the state, more around with one of them.

Kandulna got de facto charge of the Porahat Sub-Zone following the arrest of Krishan Ahir alias Pradji by the Ranchi police on 13 August (2014). He notes that the Central Committee has neither sent the replacement, nor even talked to him since Kundan's arrest. "I am supposed to Coordinate with Bundu Sub-Zonal commander Dheeraj da, but that has not been easy," said Kandulna.

A Munda tribal hailing from Khunti districts's Torpa block, Kandulna joined the PLGA in 2009, after a neighbour who was with the splinter group PLFI, killed one of his sisters.

Kandulna also cites reasons other than personal for becoming a Maoist. "I was there when the Koel-Karo firing (Feb 2001, in Khunti) took place. I saw people die because they had nothing to fight back with," he said.

The life can get lonely. For a long time recently, he was unwell, having contracted brain malia in June. He hasn't yet not seen his daughter, born seven months ago, while his wife was arrested in July. It has been a while since he met his mother, who suffers from mouth cancer.

Poll-related News stories

Now follow some poll-related news caused by Maoists or because of their involvement.

Hurt BJP candidate uses ambulance for Latehar Compaign : 20 Nov 2014

The sight of an injured candidate with his hand in a plaster, going around in an ambulance, asking the people to vote for him, has given the BJP a boost ahead of this months's (Nov 2014) polls in Jharkhand's Latehar district. Braj Mohan, 56, escaped death "when a dumper truck hit his car last week, killing his driver and an associate. Ram was admitted in a hospital, but he persuaded doctors to let him go and booked an ambulance for the Campaign[40].

Ram claims to be a victim of conspiracy to kill him.

The BJP won the Latehar seat in 2009, but did not repeat sitting MLA Baidyanath Ram, choosing instead to field a new entrant Narayan Bhokta, because of former's alleged association with the LWE TPC.

JVM(P)'s Prakash Ram calls it a publicity stunt. Ram brushed off the criticism, lobbing the ball back in Prakash's Court. "Will my opponent be willing to get hit by a speeding dumper just for the sake of sympathy vote?," he quipped.

"Jharkhand MLA hopefuls campaign in absentia"

'Maoist Mischief: Fearing attack by rebels, parties reach out to voters through posters and pamphlets posted in schools.': 20 Nov 2014

For villagers living in Jharkhand's Maoist – hit areas, the pomp and show of seeing a political rally and hope of being heard by an MLA hopeful are but dreams[41].

Here is a contrast with the way the candidates run their poll campaigns in villages and cities not affected by Naxalism.. "My son who works at a shop in Bundu Touwn of Ranchi district told me that the leaders visit villages asking for votes and hear people's problems. They move in cars and on bikes and play loud music", said Joba Munda, 63, resident of Mundatola village, 70 km from Ranchi. Bhuduram Munda, resident of another village, Jobitola, said : "I only know about the contestants through the posters. We have several problems here but not a single leader has ever come to listen to our problems."

The team of this daily visited some of the villages near Hesu hills under Tamar Constituency, a safe haven for Maoist leader Kundan Pahan and his Pratoon – 29, and discovered that fearing attacks by Maoists, no political leader has ever visited certain forest villages in the area. The difficult terrain also makes these villages inaccessible. The only means for candidates to reach out to people here are through word of mouth and pamphlets. Hopefulls usually use pictorial posters and pamplets to acquaint themselves to the voters without visiting them. This years too the candidates have printed posters containing large picures and a few, short sentences. These posters also carry the picture of the symbol and EVM highlighting the button to press.

The candidate hand over the posters to the villagers, requesting them to paste these on the walls of school or panchayat bhavan.

Mukhilala Oraon, 42, of Juboria village, says: "Our children who attend the school, read these posters and explain us their contents."

Jharkhand polls peaceful with 61.92 per cent turn out: 25 Nov 2014

The first round of Assembly polls in 13 segments across the six Maoist-hit districts in Jharkhand passed off peacefully on 25 Nov 2014, setting the tone for the remaining four phases of polling in the State. These six districts recorded 61.92 per cent voting despite the Maoist poll boycott call[42].

These polls witnessed an increase of 3.07 per cent and 5.89 per cent in voter turnout compared to the Lok Sabha and Assembly polls in 2009. The lowest turn out of 53.85 per cent was recorded in Chatra while the highest of 69.60 per cent was in Bhawnathpur.

The Maoist presence is believed to be in all the 24 districts of the state, but the six districts which went to the polls on the 25th are the worst-hit. Some 40,000 security personnel were deployed at 3,961polling stations. In Hariharpur, forces found four bombs but they turned out to be fake (filled up with sand and mud).

Phase II peaceful: 66 per cent turnout (Dec 2014)

Conforming to the upward swing in voter turnout in the first phase of Assembly polling on 25 November, the Second Phase in 20 constituencies across seven Maoist-hit districts, too recorded a highter voting percentage of 65.72 per cent on 2 Dec. 2014[43].

Defying the Maoist call for boycotting the polls, people came out in large numbers when the voting began at 7 AM. In the Saranda forest area of West Singhbhum, tribal men and women trudged long distances to polling booths, and this included villages which had n't voted for years before the 2014 Lok Sabha polls.

2 Naxals killed, 8 give slip to cops in Jharkhand jail break: 9 Dec 2014

Two Maoist prisoners in Chaibasa jail were killed and three others injured when police opened fire on the inmates who tried to flee the jail. However, 15 inmates, including eight Maoists, managed to flec. All exit points in the district were sealed and a manhunt launched to nab them[44].

The incident took place when the prisoners, who had been brought back after being produced in the local courts, were disembarking from the police vans. Some of the prisoners tried to running towards the main exit, which drew firing from the guards.

DIG Kolhan Range Mohd Nehal identified the two killed Maoist as "hard core Naxals Tipa Das and Ramvilas Tanti, both hailing from Chotanagra."

The police van had 54 prisoners on board at the time of the incident.

Police ruled out the involvement of the Maoists in the jail break as the van was safely inside the jail campus when the accident occurred.

Earlier, three hardcore Maoist cadres—Motilal Soren, Raghunath Hembrom and Mangru Mahato – who were undergoing trial for the massacre of dozens of security men in Saranda, had escaped from the Chaibasa Divisional Jail in Jan 2011.

"ASI hurt as 'Maoists' open fire in Pakur district" : 18 Dec 2014

A police officer, an ASI, was injured as three suspected Maoists opened fire on policemen in Pakur district on 18 Dec 2014. The district goes to polls in the fifth and final phase of Assembly election on the 20th. Later, the alleged Maoists fled with three rifles, the police said. The injured ASI was rushed to the local hospital, whence he was referred to the Rajindera Institute of Medical Sciences, Ranchi.

The polls in this Maoist-hit state began on 25 November with the First Phase. This attack is the second case of firing on the police men during the extended five-phase polls in the state. On 14 December, at least five alleged ultras opened fire at the security personnel at Pirtand in Giridih district but there were no casualities.

Notes

1. B Vijay Murti, Hindustan Times, 3 July 2013.
2. Alok Tikku, Hindustan Times, 3 Jul 2013.
3. B Vijay Murti, Hindustan Times, 3 Jul 2013.
4. HT Correspondent, Hindustan Times, 3 July 2013.
5. Sanjay Ojha, Times of India, 3 July 2013.
6. Op cit.
7. Anumeha Yadav, The Hindu, 3 July 2013.
8. Mukesh Ranjan, The Pioneer, 3 Jul 2013.
9. Deepu Sebestian Edmond, Indian Express, 4 July 2013.
10. Op cit.
11. Vijaita Singh, Indian Express, 4 July 2013.
12. Anumeha Yadav, The Hindu, 5 Jul 2013.
13. IANS, The Pioneer, 6 Jul 2013.
14. Mukesh Ranjan, The Pioneer, 8 July, 293.
15. Deepu Sebestian Edimond, Indian Express, 19 Aug 2013.
16. Op cit.
17. PTI, The Hindu, 14 Sep 2013.
18. Deepu Sebestian Edmond, Indian Express, 15 Sep 2013.

19. Anumeha Yadav, The Hindu, 16 Sep 2013.
20. Vishal Sharma and Deepak Mahato, Hindustan Times, 19 Sep 2013.
21. Mukesh Ranjan, The Pioneer, 13 Jan 2014.
22. B Vijay Murti, Hindustan Times, 22 Mar 2014.
23. Deepu Sebestian Edmond, Indian Express, 26 Mar 2014.
24. B Vijay Murti, Vishal Sharma, and Srinand Jha, Hindustan Times, 28 Mar 2014.
25. Deepu Sebestian Edmond, Indian Express, 9 Apr 2014.
26. IANS, The Pioneer, 13 Apr 2014.
27. Parvinder Bhatia, The Pioneer, 13 Apr 2014.
28. Deepu Sebestian Edmond, Indian Express, 15 Apr 2014.
29. Rajesh Kumar, Hindustan Times, 22 Apr 2014.
30. Deepu Sebestian Edmond, Indian Express, 26 Apr 2014.
31. HT Correspondent, Hindustan Times, 5 Jul 2014.
32. Deepu Sebestian Edmond, Indian Express, 20 Jul 2013.
33. *Ibid,* 24 July 2014.
34. Probal Sanatani, Hindustan Times, 31 Aug 2014.
35. Hindustan Times, 4 Sep 2014.
36. The photo is carried by The Hindu and The Pioneer in their 24 Sep 2014 issue.
37. Press Trust of India, Indian Express, 18 Sep 2014.
38. Deepu Sebestian Edmond, Indian Express, 4 Nov 2014.
39. Alok Kumar Mishra, Times of India, 4 Nov. 2014.
40. Deepu Sebestian Edmond, Indian Express, 6 Nov 2014.
41. B Vijay Murty, Hindustan Times, 21 Nov 2014.
42. Deepak Mahato, Hindustan Times, 21 Nov 2014.
43. Sonali Das, Times of India, 26 Nov. 2014.
44. *Ibid,* 3 Dec 2014.

Index

B

D

E

F

G

N

O

P

NAXAL AND MAOIST TERROR IN INDIA

NAXAL AND MAOIST TERROR IN INDIA

VOLUME - V

ODISHA AND WEST BENGAL

Col. Ved Prakash

KALPAZ

ISBN : 978-93-5324-035-6 (Vol - V)
978-93-5128-212-9 (Set)

First Published, 2019

Published by

Kalpaz Publications
C-30, Satyawati Nagar,
Delhi – 110052
Ph.: 011-47034999, 9811692060
www.kalpazpublications.com
E-mail: kalpaz@hotmail.com

Printed at: G. Print Process, Delhi

Cataloging in Publication Data—DK
Courtesy: D.K. Agencies (P) Ltd. <docinfo@dkagencies.com>

Prakash, Ved, *Col.*, author.
Naxal and Maoist terror in India / Col. Ved Prakash.
volumes cm
Contents: volume I. Expanding red corridor — volume II. Combating Maoism — volume III. Development of Naxal infected regions — volume IV. Chhattisgarh and Jharkhand — volume V. Odisha and West Bengal.
ISBN 9789351282129 (set)

1. Naxalite movement—India. 2. Communism—India. 3. Communist Party of India-Maoist. 4. India—Politics and government—1947- I. Title.

LCC HX393.5.P73 2019 | DDC 320.532093 23

Contents

VOLUME - IV

CHHATTISGARH AND JHARKHAND

(*Series Page No. 915-1408 See Below*)

VOLUME - V

ODISHA AND WEST BENGAL

(*Series Page No. 1409-1808 See Below*)

28

Karnataka, Kerala and Tamil Nadu and The Press on the Maoists

Karnataka

A Back grounder to the LWE in the State

Origin

The Naxalite movement started when a group of rebels from West Bengal entered the districts adjoining Andhra Pradesh in the mid-1990s.

Bloody Era

2003-05

Key issues

Lack of basic amenities.

Status Check

Naxalites area confined to just four of the 30 districts.

DV Sadananda Gowda, CM : in Mar 2012

"Action will be taken against Naxals. Steps will also be taken to provide basic amenities in the affected areas."

13 May 2009

Shimoga Police arrested two Maoists, A.S. and H.S., in Chitradurga. They were 'wanted' in Malad region, Karnataka.

Maoists getting active in Karnataka: Early 2007

At the Sep 2006 CMs conference on internal security in New Delhi, Karnataka CM HD Kumaraswami admitted that 13 districts in his state were affected by the LWE. There were some 200 Maoist cadres active in the state, 60 of that number were operating in two to three armed groups each in the Malnad and Western Ghat regions alone.

During Jan-Jun 2007, these two regions, comprising Karnataka's districts of Shimoga, Chakamagalur, Dakshina Kannada and Udipi witnessed what the state police described as "heightened Naxal activity." The region has witnessed a series of police encounters and counter-offensives that has claimed the lives of eight alleged Maoists or sympathisers and four policemen or police informers.

The Maoists were left leaderless after the death of Saketh Rajan on 6 Feb 2005 in police encounter. He was a post graduate in mass communication. In the recent months, the Naxals began being assertive, dictating terms especially over the issue of forest economy in the said region. Police disclosed that after Rajan's death, the LWE movement in the State was revived with the leadership outsourced from Andhra Pradesh.

In the face of increased Naxalite violence in the Malnad region, CM Kumaraswamy expressed his readiness to talk to the ultras. They responded, asking the Government to withdraw the ANF (Anti-Naxal Forces) from the region as a precondition.

The ultras had gained popularity and following in the region because of the state government's policy to shift the tribesmen out of the Malnad forest area. The victims of this high handed policy proved easy prey to the recruiters for the Maoist movement. Consequently, the government discontinued the eviction of the tribals from these forests. As a result, the locals are no mood to swell the ranks of the ultras.

Karnataka Maoist movement splits : Feb 2007

Sharp differences are over Maoist strategy of area-wise seizure of power – "intensifying the revolution in rural areas first and thence spreading it to the urban area"—led to the split in the outfit leading LWE in Karnataka, reported a daily on 14 Feb 2007[1].

There were purists who did not want to move away from Mao's teachings : overpower and take over the rural areas first, and then overwhelm the urban areas. This has been mentioned briefly earlier, too. But the ideologues who disagreed with the Mao's techings went their own way and floated a new party Maoist coordination committee (MCC for short)

This is, in a way, a major split. It has come at a time when the Central leadership of the CPI (Maoist) was intensifying its efforts to unite smaller LWE groups/parties in the country under its ruleric. It is an obvious set back for the central leadrship. It is even a bigger set back and a shock for it when majority of the cadres quit the parent body and joined the MCC.

The name of the main leader who engineered the split has not been made public. He is believed to be busy contacting LWE leaders of the other states, wooing them to join the new outfit.

Alarmed over the development, CPI (Maoist) Politburo wrote to all party members in the country to expose the opportunistic and disruptionist activites of the dissenting and splitting leaders and ideologues.

The split was believed to have been discussed at the last Politburo meeting held, 6-24 Nov 2006. The meeting, attended by the CPI (Maoist) Chief Ganapathi, decided to step up efforts to convince, their cadres on the 'futility' of the 'new line'. It is believed the Central Committee failed to initiate steps to stem ideological dissent, which in fact seem to have accentuated following the killing of Saketh Rajn on 6 Feb 2005.

Maoist activity is witnessed with varying degree of intensity in the state's districts named here : Bidar, Gulbarga, Bellary, Raichur, Shimoga, Chikmagalur, Uduppi, Dakshina kannada, Hassan, Kodagu, Tumkur and Kolar.

The split is bound to adversely affect its further spread in the State.

Bhopal 'manufacturing unit' of the CPI (Maoist) brings in a police raid

The MP Police informed the press on 19 Jan 2007 that five hard-core Maoist cadres "were arrested last week when a Maoist weapons workshop was busted in Bhopal.

More importantly, they disclosed that the Maoists have an active *dalam* (an operational unit of the Maoists) in Surat, the textile city of Gujarat. As a large number of Andhra migrants are working in that industry in Surat, it is easy for the Telugu-speaking Maoist cadres (from Andhra) to set up a dalam there (in Surat)[2].

This is how Mao and Karnataka Unit of the CPI (Maoist) enter the picture, as explained hereafter. The idea of setting up a base in Surat is yet another indication that the Maoists are choosing urban areas and cities where they are least likely to arouse suspicions. So far in this book, we have mentioned about the CPI (Maoist) having set up their presence/ bases in Bhopal, Rourkela and 'now, Surat, major cities in India. But this very idea goes against Mao's teaching of overpowering and taking over the rural areas completely before (the Communists) turning to the urban areas and larger cities.

This Mao-speak is the reason behind the split in the ranks of the cadres of the CPI (Maoist) unit in Karnataka. The ultra-loyals did not want to go against the teachings of the Great Oarsman, even to a minor degree. This minor, if practically paying, infringement is explained here.

The Maoists, as a matter of policy and demands of practical wisdom, do not strike where they are operating in such urban centres. Instead, they use these centres for manufacturing parts of weapons or assembling them. By now, police is in the know of two such towns at least, viz Surat and Bhopal. Therefore, it is natural that the IB has already cautioned the states to keep an eye on those workers and joints who are operating lathe-machine units in their towns.

Andhra Police raid on Maoist hideouts yield rich cache of CDs and DVDs : Jan 2007

Two raids on the key hideouts of the Maoists by the AP Police in the latter half of Jan 2007 in Bhopal and Rourkela led to the recovery of arms and ammunition, and more significantly, the seizure of "gold mine of information about the outfit in the form of CD's, DVDs and hard discs."

Police sources believe that this gadgetry contains so much information that it could take months to analyse it. This treasure trove also has animation films on assaults and counter-assaults on the Police forces. All this information with the police will have serious for organisational functioning and operational capabilities of the CPI (Maoists)[3].

It is a serious blow to the Outfit at a time when it is already on the run in Andhra, where several of its leaders were eliminated by the police in 2006. It has has been confired that the Maoists have been sending their cadres to new bases, yet to be consolidated, in the Western Ghats, Karnataka and Goa.

Maoists spread to Southern States (Karnataka, Kerala and Tamil Nadu): MHA Report: Apr 2007

Maoists are attempting to increase their activities and influence in Karnataka, Kerala and Tamil Nadu, where they did not have a strong presence earlier. Tamil Nadu has been a threshhold state, but of late, they are wanting to expand base in the southern states. These are the findings, recorded in the MHA Report 2006, quoted by a daily of 2 Apr 2007[4].

The Report says the new areas are mostly in the said states. In Karnataka and Kerala, the Maoist violence has only been on the fringes. Andhra Pradesh has been the epicentre of Maoist violence in the recent past. It has now shifted to Chhattisgarh. The attacks on railway and other property had been more prominent in Andhra Pradesh, Bihar and Jharkhand, where the ultras were also targeting mines and mining-related activities.

The Government has also appointed an Empowered Group of Ministers (E GoM) to closely monitor the Naxal situation and evolve strategies to deal with the problem.

The Maoists have also been attempting to intensify their efforts at social mobilisation. The Revolutionary Democratic Front (RDF), set up in May 2005 for this purpose, has enlarged itself into Revolutionary Democratic Front of India (RDFI).

Jan adalats (Kangaroo Courts) are being Convened by the Naxalites to dispense crude and instant justice, supplant the state apparatus and assert their hegemony over the rural tracts.

"Caught in a Vortex, Malekudiyas of Kuthlur year for freedom"

Besides the fear of eviction, they have to contend with both Maoists and ANF (Anti-Naxal Forces : 6 Apr 2012

"With threats from the Maoists, alleged suspicion and ill-treatement from the ANF, and the fear of being evicted from their forest homes, the Malekudiyas of Kuthlur village in Belthangady taluk find themselves in an unenviable situation. Residents of Kuthlur, a Naxal-hit village, expressed these fears during a meeting organised by the Adivasi Hakkugala Samanvaya Samiti, affiliated to the CPI (Marxist) [CPI(M)], in Alamba area of the forest village on 6 Apr 2012[5]."

This (above) is the opening paragraph of a news analysis by a daily, datelined Kuthlur (Dakshina Kannada District), 6 Apr 2012, about the plight of a village caught in the cross fire between the ideologically- driven LWE and the law-enforcement agencies fighting the rebels.

There is a backdrop to this meeting organised by the CPI (M). On 3 March (2012), two residents of the village, viz, Linganna and his son Vithala, a journalism student, were arrested from their house on the charge of aiding Maoists.

'No' to package

Shashidhar, a Malekudiya, said in the meeting that several of them had applied to the Integrated Tribal Development Officer (ITDO), seeking right to remain in the forest under the Scheduled Tribes and Other Traditional Forest Dwellers (Recognition of Forest Rights) Act, 2006, but "heard nothing" from the department in this regard.

The village was included within the Kudremukh National Park (KNP) when it was notified under the Indian Wildlife Protection Act, 1972 in Jun 2001. The law does not allow the presence of human beings inside the national park, and this has raised fear of eviction among over 2000 families living in the KNP area.

Scared of police

Poovappa, 35, said that the "Rs. 10 lakh package should go". He said that none of the villagers wanted to leave their forest homes and that they wanted that Compensation package be scrapped. Shashidhar said, "We are scared of the police. They are here even now. How can we speak freely? They speak nicely to us in public.... Can't they go after the Naxals instead of bothering us?" He said he wanted to tell the IGP about the "harassment" they faced from the police.

Taluk Secretary of the CPI(M) Shiv Kumar SM said General Secretary of the Samiti GC Bayya Reddy would speak to the IGP.

The meeting decided to pursue the demands to construct and repair of roads in the village under the MGNREGA, provide power supply to the houses of Malekudiyas and retain the Malekudiyas' right to remain in their forest houses, during a 24-hour *dharna* to be staged in front of the tahsildar's office on 13 April.

Fear of Naxals

Hukra, 60, of the Baringady area of the village, told the daily that Malekudiyas in the forest had three problems: The Naxals, the ANF and fear of eviction. "While Maoists turn up with guns, the ANF men too point their guns at us and question us about food supplies", he said. He continued: "We buy provisions (tea, sugar, Salt and Chilli) to last a week.... ANF personnel picked up my brother Chinkra the other day (2 March) and let him off a few hours later."

Expressing fears of being forced to leave her forest home, Puttamma of Baringady said : "The thought of what we will do if we are forced to move out (of the forest) disturbs me."

Puttamma and other women in the past applied to the panchayat for funds to construct a toilet, but lilttle came of it.

Karnataka Anti-Naxal Force (ANF) shot youth dead when he fled: probe : 28 Apr 2014

A 23-year old Muslim Youth (Mohd Kabeer) who was shot dead by a constable of Karnataka Police's ANF at a forest check-post on the Sringeri-Karkala route on 19 April (2014) was hit thrice from the back from a distance of over five feet, a preliminary probe into the controversial shooting incident has revealed[6].

The bullet entry wounds at the back of the body and the estimated distance from which the AK-47 rifle was fired seem to establish that Mohd Kabeer was shot down while trying to flee, and not at the chest at point blank range as suggested initially by some reports from the spot of the shooting at the Thanikodu check-post in the Chikmagalur district. Kabeer and four associates were travelling in a pick-up truck transporting cattle when they were stopped at a forest check-post for a routine check around 3.30 AM on 19 April by a police also comprising members of the ANF which operates in the Western Ghats region.

Kabeer was shot by ANF constable G Naik after he allegedly tried to run away. Two of his associates who managed to run away have provided contradictory statements and alleged the ANF personnel fired without provocation. The ANF claimed its men mistook Kabeer for a Naxalite because he tried to flee when confronted. Constable Naik, a 2012 President's Gallantry Medal Winner for a Naxal encounter, fired around nine rounds from his AK – 47 including the three that hit Kabeer. He was arrested on 25 April after Umar Farooq, who was in the truck with him, filed a complaint.

The investigation of the controversial case has been handed over to the CID of the State Police amid demands, even from within the ruling Congress, for a CBI probe. The killing has taken a political and communal turn with the opposition BJP questioning the arrest of Naik and Kabeer's kin being paid a compensation of Rs 10 without investigation being completed.

Sources said that initial investigations revealed the ANF Constable first fired in the air when he saw the youths abruptly fleeing the pick-up truck and later in their direction, resulting in Kabeer being hit. While Kabeer had a large wound on the front of his body as documented in the postmortem, he had two on his back and third on the back of his arm. Sources said the large wound on the front was caused by the exit of two bullets.

It is suspected that Kabeer, who had four cases of illegal cattle smuggling against him in the Mangalore region, took to his heels along with two associates after seeing the armed ANF personnel and feared he would be arrested for cattle smuggling.

The issue of cattle smuggling has been a source of tension in the region with Right Wing Hindu groups setting up vigilante units to target transporters, illegally moving cattle to slaughter houses. "There does not seem to have been any provocation for those in the pick–up truck to run away when the ANF men walked around to check the contents of the truck. The firing seems to have been a reflexaction to the running away", sources familiar with the case said.

Kerala

Story of Naxalism – its beginning and spread – seem to be like the ones in West Bengal's northern district of Darjeeling and in Andhra Pradesh in the 1960s.

How it all began

In the 1960s, around the time Naxalbari village in Darjeeling district of West Bengal lent its name to a potent far-left ideology, viz 'Naxalism', the hills of Wayanad and other north Kerala districts became the hotbeds of LWE. A Verghese, a CPI (M) leader who later turned to Naxalism, and K Ajitha, now a prominent activist, were part of what came to be known as 'Spring Thunder', a powerful Maoist campaign in Wayanad against the alleged exploitation of tribals by landlords[7].

Weakening and Revival

But the death of Verghese, followed by a few high-profile arrests in the 1970s, blunted the LWE. For decades, Naxalism was dormant in the districts of north Kerala, before its revival in the late 2000s. But some more details, relevant to the issue.

As mentioned in the beginning, certain northern districts of north Kerala, viz Wayanad, Kozhikode Kannur, were hot beds of LWE in 1960s. The movement saw violent Naxal attacks at police stations at Thirunelli and Thalassery.

Verghese, who led the Naxal campaign in Wayanad, was alleged involved in the murder of a few landlords. On 18 Feb 1970, he was shot dead by the CRPF in a forest tract in Wayanad. Police had then called it an encounter death. But 40 years later, the CRPF constable who pulled the trigger, confessed that Verghese had been shot dead after he surrendered. Retired CRPF IG K Lakshmana, who ordered the Verghese's killing was sentenced to life imprisonment.

Revival of LWE in Kerala

If a date had to be assigned to the revival of the LWE in the State, it could be towards the end of the 2000s. Subsequently, a pattern emerged: Naxals visiting a village, followed by the police. It all started with an article.

Maoist leader Roopesh writes an article

An article in the *Mathrubhumi* weekly in 2014, purportedly written by underground Maoist leader Roopesh, said that Maoist cadres had set up the Western Ghats Special Zone Committee in the forested tri-juntion of Kerala,

Karnataka and Tamil Nadu and that members of the PLGA had visited villages in Kannur district. He wrote about villagers receiving them warmly and serving them rice and curry. The threat of Naxalism rearing its head once again in Kerala looked more real than ever before. So the tinge of the Red was just getting darker. But what is not real in how the police see the problem. Their exaggerated response to peceived Naxal threats has put the entire force and the hills of northern Kerala on the edge, the operation often bordering on the comical.

Naxalism is now Kerala's latest bogey, an issue that gets talked about everywhere – in the media, as the bulk of FM jokes and in Assembly. For a government tottering on wafer-thin majority, this is a welcome distraction. Before any details of Naxal violence in the recent years (essentially post-2010) is mentioned, a brief description of an encounter.

7 Dec 2014 police-Maoist encounter

On the evening of 7 Dec 2014, KR Raman, a Kurichiya tribal living on the fringes of Periya Reserve Forest in Wayanad district, heard deafening blasts. Farmers in the region routinely burst high decible crackers to drive away herds of wild elephants from their fields. He had even seen the smoke rising above the trees from that area of the forest, a mere 10-minute walk from his dwelling, but he understandably ignored it.

That evening, after watching the TV, he was wiser. The blasts he had heard were not of fire crackers but of big guns. The forests close to his Chappa settlement had been the site of an encounter between police and alleged Maoists.

The police says the exchange of fire was between eight Maoists and a Thunderbolt team of 20 security men. The police claimed to have recovered 'parts' of AK-47 rifles and shreds of clothes worn by the Naxals. The police kept the tribals and the media out of the site of the alleged encounter. There were niggling questions, but none were entertained. The following day, when the media raised these doubts, State Home Minister Ramesh Chennithala shot back: "You write, what I say."

A pattern during the last three years

For three years now, Kerala police's Maoist chase has had a pattern:

A few outsiders – men and women both – in military fatigues or in black clothes would turn up at tribal hamlets in north Kerala, not after 9 PM, spend sometime talking to villagers about the benefits they get from the governments, and at times, instigate them to fight against the establishment. Then they would demand some rice and groceries from the villagers and slip back into the forests. Hours later, police teams would troop in and raid villages for 'Maoists'. They would flash a few grainy photographs at tribals and ask them, 'is this the person you saw yesterday?' If one of the tribals as much as nodded his head in affirmation, the following day there would be media reports, quating the police, which said that "the gang that visited the colony, included Maoist Roopesh and other Maoists who face a look out notice". The only deviation from this line would be the count of Maoists – it is usually five-member band with two women; but sometimes, it is an eight-member gang.

Almost everybody in these parts has a Naxal-sighting story.

K Dasan of Vendekkumpetty near Nilambur says,"Five people came by from the nearby forests. They said they were Maoists and asked for rice. Soon after they left for the forest, police came to conduct a search".

At Edakkara near Nilambur, farmer Govindan Nair said that in Jun 2014, a five – member group with guns had come to his house. "When we asked them who they were, they laughed and said we needn't worry. When we begged of them to leave, they agreed. Next evening, the police came with a bunch of photographs. We could not identify any of them, as there was only a dim light in the house."

Kerala's Maoist story has stuck to this script. It is a story that gets repeated across villages in Malappuram, Kozhikode, Wayanad, Kannur, and Palakkad districts, who have reported Maoist sightings. Any stranger is now a suspected Maoist. Two weeks ago, a group of Pilgrims from Wayanad who were on their way to the shrine of Sabarimala, were mistaken for Maoists. Like some of the most devout Sabarimala pilgrims, this three-member team, dressed in ritualistic black dhotis, had chosen to rough it out and walk through forests. At Munderi in Malappuram, they deviated from the forest path to stop at an eatery. They got talking to the villagers and asked them the most accessible forest treks. But soon after the pilgrims left, the villagers got suspicious and alerted the police. A crack unit of the force swung into action and conducted a search operation, but later admitted that the outsiders were not Maoists.

A few months ago, a migrant worker from Odisha got stranded in a village in Kozhikode and turned up at some house, asking for some food. The family, aware of stories of Maoists demanding food, prompltly alerted the police who grilled the man for several hours before letting him off.

The Kerala Police's anti-Naxal narrative has one glaring hole : so far, the police has not come across any Naxals, save the Chappa case which is riddled with inconsistencies. There have been about half-a-dozen attacks on private ventures like KFC and McDonald's, and on houses and government offices towards the fag end of 2014 that have been attributed to Naxals, but there is little evidence.

A police officer has this to say : It is confirmed that there is Maoist presence in Kerala. But so far, police has not directly seen any Maoist. Tribals and villagers claim to have noticed the movement of certain people, some toting guns. They are either in military fatigues or in black clothes. When people alert us, we conduct searches".

The police don't think much of the fact that they have not come across any Naxal so far. A senior police intelligence officer says : "Think of forest brigand Veerappan. He gave police the slip for three decades. Forests make for a completely different terrain and crime here can't be tackled like other conventional crime."

Other officers clarified that Maoist belt of northern Kerala is part of a larger forest region that runs through the states of Kerala. Tamil Nadu and Karnataka. "Gangs can slip through jurisdictions with ease. They may be 50 or 100 mtr. away from us and still give us the slip," says the officer.

For now, the police operation is strictly hinged on these 'sightings'. Kannur DIG Dinendra Kashyap, who is in charge of the anti-Maoist drive in the state, says: "The terrain is tough, with some dense forests where Naxals slip into. So, in most cases, we are inclined to believe what villagers say."

So police is so high-strung that almost any activist worth his name is branded a Maoist. In 2014, police had issued look-outs against CPI leader Baby Thomas, anti-endosulfan agitation committee leader N Subramanian and PUCL General Secretary PA Pauran. Tribal leader Chathan from Wayanad too figured in the look-out notice when he was already in jail in a criminal case.

Early January (2015), police raided the office of *Keraleceyam,* a magazine on tribal issues, detained three people and sealed the building. But the police could build no case and the office was de-sealed.

But it was Swiss national Jonathan Baud's arrest and detention in police custody for 11 days that exposed the police's paranoia. In Jul 2014, Baud was arrested after he attended a public meeting held in memory of a Maoist leader. He was initially branded a Maoist but when police could not establish that, Baud was slapped with charges relating to flouting visa rules. On 2 Dec 2014, the high court quashed the case against him.

The media, meanwhile, is involved in another chase. Almost every 'Naxal' sighting and attacks gets reported and the police plays along. Two weeks ago, a long iron bar was found along a railway attack at kozhikode. The police cried sabotage and media promptly reported it as one. Days later, the real story spilled out : a thief had stolen the rod, figured it could be a useful tool but found it too long and hoped it would break under a running train.

Not every one is amused at this hide-and-seek game between police and the Moists. M Geethanandan, convenor of Adivasi Gothra Maha Sabha, says anti-Maoist operation is a "desparate attempt" by the police to blow the issue out of proportion. "This way, they are only contributing to building up tension in tribal areas. Police have been hunting down activists in the name of acting against Maoists," he says: Geethanandan continue: "The socio-economic profile of today's Kerala is very different from that of the 1960s when the Naxal movement had a foothold in the tribal belts of Wayanad. Those days, the Naxal movement was a war against feudalism. The tribal community in Kerala has evolved a lot since those days."

An intelligence officer of the state justifies the police's methods : "We didn't want tribals to get caught in the middle. We don't want to go in for violent means to nab Maoists. With the support of various government agencies, police are trying to build a good rapport with the tribal community and the public. These are just combing operations."

Extent of spread of the LWE in Kerala

Though Kerala does not figure anywhere in data compiled by the MHA's LWE Division for mine months till Sep 2015, the State Police have identified 16 police stations in North Kerala as being vulnerable to Maoist attacks. Some of these police stations have been fortified with sand bags and four all-terrain vehicles have been allottted to North Kerala region for anti-Maoist operations. Under a Central scheme to tackle insurgency, police stations in Naxal-hit areas get Rs 2 cr, of which 80 per cent is funded by the centre. Critics allege that the state police's Naxal-drive is just a means to corner funds from the Centre.

[It is anti-police report for reasons known to the scribe]

"Cynicism and absurd remarks follow"

While the polilce fumble on, the people have figured out that a 'Naxal' visit need not be such a bad thing—a Naxal sighting catches the administration's attention and bring them a bit of fame too.

On 24 April 2014, a four-member 'Maoist' gang reportedly attacked the house of Police Constable AB Pramod at Mattilayam in Wayanad. His mother, Palamattamkunnu Janaki says, "A four member gang—three women and a man—came home at night and pointed a gun at us. One of them said he was Roopesh. The women were carrying guns. They said Pramod was helping the Thunderbolt. The gang wanted Pramod to quit his police job. They left after torching a bike parked outside the house."

After she has enthusiastically narrated the events of that night, Janaki pipes down somewhat. She now has her doubts, informing us about a longstanding dispute with one of the relatives in the same locality. "They used to repeatedly threaten Pramod, saying they will ensure that he was without a job. The Maoists said the same thing, Now I suspect our relatives hired the Maoists to attack our house."

Did she report her suspicion to the police? "No. If we had complained against our relatives, they would have attacked our house again."

But thanks to the 'Maoist attack', Pramod's family now enjoys police protection and their colony is under regular surveillance, which, Janaki says, has ensured less trouble from their relatives.

Profile of the Roopesh Couple

Roopesh, hailing from Thrissur district, is a Maoist leader who figures high on the police's wanted list. A former State Secretary of the CPI (Maoist), Roopesh had been accused of sheltering Malla Raja Reddy, a top Maoist leader from Andhra Pradesh. After the AP police arrested Reddy in 2007, Roopesh and his wife Shyna went underground. It is widely believed that Roopesh, a law graduate, and Shyna, who worked as a clerk in the Kerala High Court, are leading the present Maoist Operation in the forests of North Kerala.

In 2008, Shyna in a letter to the then CM V S Achuthanandan, said, "your police made me a Maoist." The couple's two daughters live at Valappad in Thrissur with their grand mother. Sinoj, another wanted Maoist from Kerala, was reportedly killed in Jun 2014, while making explosives. Police suspect that most of the Maoists operating in Kerala belong to other states.

Intelligence agencies sense Maoist infiltration: Apr 2012

"A series of incidents involving the banned CPI(Maoist) in recent weeks, including the abduction of Alex Paul Menon, DC Sukma in Chhattisgarh on Saturday, are a wake-up call for the State Government to the threat posed by LWE infiltrating from neighbouring states, say the intelligence agencies."

The above is reported by a daily in its news story datelined Kozhikhode in its issue dated 23 Apr 2012[8].

Sources in the intelligence agencies told the daily on the 22nd that Maoists from Andhra Pradesh, Odisha and Tamil Nadu had been using the border areas of Kerala and Karnataka as a hideout eversince the CRPF launched what is called "operation Green Hunt" against the Naxalites. Most of these fugitives had slowly moved to the jungles of the Western Ghats.

The sources said the tri-junction of Kerala, Karnataka and Tamil Nadu, comprising Gudalur, Wayanad, Nilambur, Kodaikanal, Udupi and Dakshina Kannada, had already developed into a "perspective area" for CPI (Maoist) cadres for building its operational base. Plans were afoot to set up a *dalam* in Mananthavady after infiltrating the local populace and subsequently organising training camps.

The South India Regional Committee of the CPI (Maoist) started functioning at this tri-junction following the disbandment of its state units of Tamil Nadu, Kerala and Karnataka. Now several camps operated in Dakshina Kannada, Udupi and Chikmagalur districts in Karnataka. In Mar 2012, the anti-Naxal force of the Karnataka Police recovered a large cache of arms and ammunition in Dakshina Kannada. Maoist literature in Malayalam, Kannada, Tamil and Telugu was recovered from some of the abandoned camps.

Officials engaged in counter-insurgency operations said that Kerala was yet to constitute an elite police force led by an officer of the rank of DIGP, especially to tackle any Naxalite problem. The commando wing of the State Police could be used only in clandestine and destructive raiding.

Maoist-type operations required specific long term solutions.

Sensing this, the Karnataka government has mooted that its anti-Naxal unit get similar training given to CoBRA, a para-military unit of the CRPF, for tackling Maoist group.

Kerala needs to train a special police force in guerrilla warfare to be ready if at all the Dalams will develop and engage in a hit-and-run offensive against the law-enforcing agencies and government officials.

The State Police had cut a sorry figure when activists of the Ayyankkali Pada stormed the Palakkad Collectorate and held District Collector WR Reddy hostage for ten hours in Oct 1996.

Such incidents cannot be ruled out as the Maoists' strategy is to build its activities slowly from jungles to villages and urban areas, the sources said.

24 Apr 2014

A four-member gang threatens a woman and her son, a police constable, at their house at Vellamunda in Wayanad.

A mother's wait ends, with news of the death of her Maoist son Jul 2014

'PLGA 'political head' went missing three years ago, cadres tell mother he died handling explosives'.

After her son went missing three years ago, Velakkattil Indira will never go to bed without checking TV Channels for late-night crime bulletins.

When the news finally came, the 64-year-old least expected it. On 8 Jul 2014, Mundur Ravunni, the leader of the radical outfit Porattam, knocked at her house in Thalikkulam in Thrissur district. Without any ado, she was told that her 38-year-old son VS Sinoj, a prominent Maoist leader in Kerala, was dead.

A day earlier, on the 7th , Sinoj's former friends had visited her and told her to be home the next day as Ravunni might visit. "I thought they had come to talk about his marriage or discuss cases. I have heard about women cadres being among them (Maoists). May be, I thought, Sinoj had developed a relationship with one of them. I thought Sinoj had sent her friends to get my consent for the marriage", says Indira, a CP (M) worker.

Sinoj died handling explosives in a forest on 16 June (2014) and was buried nearby with full "official honours", according to *Kattu thee* a Maoist bulletin published in Malayalam. He had been the political head of the Kabani faction of the PLGA, the armed wing of the CPI(Maoist). Ravunni said he found the bulletin in his letter box in Kochi, with a separate message to inform the family about Sinoj's death.

As Sinoj's family planned the rituals held after person's death, Indira has not given up the hope that he might still be alive. "I want evidence of his death. Where is his dress? He had a unique collection of ink pens, which would have definitely be on him", she says.

Hailing from a family of CP(M) supporters, Sinoj got attracted to ultra Left movement during his school days. In 1990, he became a full time revolutionary activist after dropping out in the final year of his graduation. Initially, he was associated with the CPI (ML-Naxalbari). Later, he joined the PWG, which became the CPI(Maoist) after merger with the MCC. Sinoj is believed to have identified many persons in the Maoist movement.

Some two decades ago, Sinjoj started staying away from home, making only occasional, unexpected visits. Indira had got used to him missing for days together. "He did not come even when his father died eight years back", she says.

As the Maoists extended their operations to the Western Ghats of Kerala, Tamil Nadu and Karnataka, Sinoj is believed to have received training in guerrilla warfare and armed struggle. The Maoist bulletin announcing his death said Sinoj led a guerrilla life against heavy odds[9].

In 2009, he was arrested from a tribal colony in Wayanad district on charges of propagating Maoist ideology and instigating tribals to wage war against the State. After being released on bail, he returned home and started living as an autorikshaw driver.

In 2011, he vanished for the last time, after living with the family for five months at a stretch. "He left without informing anybody, after setting on fire all his ID proofs", says Sinoj's brother VS Manoj, a CP(M) local Committee member.

Just before going into hiding, Sinoj had been active in the agitation against highway development in Kerala, under a build, operate, transfer scheme. He is believed to have narrowly escaped the anti-Naxal force of the Karnataka police several times, including in 2012, when Maoist Yellappa died in a battle with the police near Hassan.

Since he had always come back earlier, the family kept hoping Sinoj would return this time too. "Every time, he left the family in the same manner. Pointing out the peaceful life led by the ex-Naxalites, I used to advise him to abandon the radical way. He never answered, standing silently instead", says Indira.

Hunt on for Maoist leader on CD: Sep 2014

"Various agencies have started investigating the surfacing of video CD showing Kerala Maoist leader Rupesh (or Roopesh) calling for armed revolution against the state. The effort is to find out the origin of the video, the hideout of the Maoist leader and how serious the contents of the CD are. A massive hunt has already been launched for the Maoist leader himself."

"The video clipping on the CD showed Rupesh, with face blurred, speaking about the urgency of launching an armed struggle against the State which has allegedly been militarised. A statement attached to the copies of the CD distributed to the media said this was being issued on the occasion of the tenth anniversary of the CPI(Maoist)."

The above two paragraphs are from a daily of 24 Sep 2014[10].

The agencies looking into the matter are : the Central agencies like the IB; Kerala's Internal Security Investigation Team; its Special Branch and the Anti-Naxal squad of the Kerala Police. The first effort is to find out whether the person seen in the video is Rupesh himself and the place of recording of video.

Despite the probe, senior state police officials feel that the CD can be merely part of a campaign strategy of the Maoists since the State did not have the circumstances and the conditions that are conducive to launching and nourishing a LWE movement. A top official believes that most probably, it is a bid to catch attention of the people and the State following their failure to get support in the society. Home Minister Ramesh Chennithala said there was Maoist presence in Kerala "but it has not assumed the shape of a threat. The Government is viewing with seriousness the reports that extremist activities are taking place in the State and the police has been instructed to take stringent action against this."

Personnel of the Kerala Police and its specialist commando wing, Thunderbold have already started combing certain areas of Malappuram, Kozhikode, Kannur and Wayanad districts to identify the place where the recording had been done. Since the background in the Video resembles a jungle, the Police presume that it was shot somewhere in this forest region.

The face of Rupesh, absconding for the past several years, as seen in the video has been blurred in order to avoid identification. The agencies are trying to reconstruct the face from the video using digital technology and the assistance of the Kerala Police's Cyber Cell has already been called for.

According to the CD, believed to be issued by the Western Ghats Zonal Committee of the CPI(Maoist), the organisation has reached a stage where armed struggle has become inevitable. The state has already been militarised and even democratic struggle were being suppressed using brute force, says Rupesh in an interview grabbed on the CD.

The ultra leader claims that Adivasis' life has become terrible, farmers are unable to carry on with their work and even the middle class is in debt trap. In this situation, the CPI (Maoist) is planning to launch people's struggle bringing all these sections together and more and more people are joining the Maoist movement, he says.

Anti-Naxal Squad of the Kerala Police had launched its hunt for the Maoists in the forests of Kannur and Wayanad in Feb 2013 after Adivasis in these areas reportedly spotted armed unidentified persons near their colonies. The Thunderbolt Commandos took over the search later on but so far, the forces have not been able to find even a single Maoist.

The failure of the police in their mission had given rise to allegations that the entire operation was based on lies and hearsays and that they were terrorising the Adivasis in their colonies in the name of the reported presence of Maoists. Allegations of funds misappropriation have also been levelled against the anti-Maoist operation.

10 Nov 2014 : Gelatine firm office attacked

A nine-member gang vandalises the corporate office of Netta Gelatine India Ltd. in Kochi's Panambilli Nagar. The suspected LWE damaged glass walls, computers and vehicles.

The group of masked men allegedly raising Maoist slogans carried out the attack 8 AM on 10 Nov 2014, according to the police and the office's security guard.

IGP Ernakulam Range MR Ajit Kumar said that the attack was perhaps carried out by the Left extremists (read LWE) and they left behind a two-page note in Malayalam. The security guard said that one of the group was speaking in Malayalam while the others were using Hindi. They raised Maoist slogans during the attack.

The men wore jeans and shirts and all of them had covered their faces with handkerchiefs. The entire attack was recorded on the CCTV system at the office. The group carrying iron rods smashed the glass windowpanes and damaged some computers at the office and some vehicles parked in the office compound[11].

The letter left behind by them spoke about the need to take action against the company which was causing pollution from its factory at Kathikudam in Thrissur district.

'Maoist' attack on Kerala tourist resort : 18 Nov 2014

Suspected Maoists attacked a private tourist resort in Thirunelli, a pilgrimage centre among the forests of Kerala's Wayanad district, early 18 Nov 2014 morning. Maoist presence had been suspected in Wayanad district a long time ago. This is the second incident of alleged Maoist attack in Kerala within a span of eight days.

The tourist resort employees informed that a four-member gang carried out the attack 3 AM on the 18th. The employees did not come out of their quarters even after hearing the commotion as they initially thought it was an invasion by the wild elephants into the resort compound, a not an uncommon event. But then they heard slogans being shouted, they said[12].

The ultras carried out the attack possibly in the light of mobile phones, or some alternative source, after switching off the power of the entire resort. They smashed the glass panes of the resort's reception and restaurant and damaged telephones computer monitors and printer at the resort's office.

Posters of the CPI (Maoist) were found stuck on the walls of the resort, calling upon the people to join the tenth anniversary celebrations of the formation of the CPI (Maoist). There were only six employees and three families, including the one from Germany, at the resort at the time of the 'Maoist' attack.

The Wayanad SP came on the preliminary inspection of the resort, post-attack. "A huge police posse and a team of the Kerala Police's specially-trained anti-Naxal commandos, Thunderbolts, were deployed at the resort and its surroundings. A detailed investigation would be carried out into the attack.

A local resident spoke about the talks of the Maoists' presence in the area in the recent times. The entire Wayanad district has been under the observation of the Kerala Police and its Thunderbolt guerrillas since Feb 2013 when presence of the Maoists in the forest areas of north Kerala was reported for the first time.

There were reports of Maoist posters on the walls of the Government College and near the post office in Mananthawady in the district some days ago. There were also report of armed seven-member Maoist squad visiting the Kurichya colony at Thalappuzha recently and talking to the Adivasis on the Maoist ideology for a long time.

As detailed in the preceding entry, the suspected Maoists had vandalised the corporate office of the private Nitta Gelatine company in Kochi on 10 November (2014) as a warning to it against the pollution its factory had been causing in the village of Kathikudam in the Thrissur district. Several computers, cars and furniture had been damaged in the attack. Three days after this incident, a letter was issued in the name of the Western Ghats Zonal Committee of the CPI(Maoist), claiming responsibility for this attack on the Gelatine Firm's office. The letter said the attack was just a symbolic response to the company's atrocities, warning that further responses would not be merely symbolic.

Maoists claimed responsibility for 18 November attack

The CPI (Maoist) claimed responsibility on 29 Nov 2014 for the attack on a private resort at north Kerala's hill district Wayanad. The resort named Agraharam, located in Thirunelli, was ransacked on 18 November by a four-member gang.[13]

The resort is owned by Sebestian Joseph, a senior journalist with Kerala's leading daily Malayala Manorama. The gang entered the resort early morning of the 18th and smashed the windows and furniture. They left behind pro-Maoist pamphlets.

On the 29th, media offices in Palakkad district got a press release believed to be from the Western Ghat Zonal Committee of the CPI(Maoist) saying that its cadres had attacked the resort. It said the attack was a warning against unbridled encroachment of the real estate-tourism mafia in Wayanad district, which was once a land of paddy fields. Police was probing the case.

Kerala Police, Maoist exchange fire : 7 Dec 2014

Kerala police men and suspected Maoists exchanged fire in the jungles of Wayanad district on 7 Dec 2014. The firing lasted 20 minutes, preliminary reports saying that nobody had been hurt. Home Minister Ramesh Chennithala confirmed the incident. "This was probably the first direct encounter between the police and Maoists in Kerala.

The firing between the Commandos of Thunderbolt, Kerala Police battalion of specially trained personnel for anti-Naxal operations, and Maoists took place in the forest near an Adivasi colony coming in the Vellamunda police station areas in Wayanad district. The police reportedly fired 30 rounds at the Maoists, who replied with eight [another daily, Indian Express of 11 Jan 2015, reported the firing "on the outskirts of Periya Reserve Forest at Chappa (village) in Wayanad."[14]

However, the ultras escaped into the dense jungles. Additional Thunderbolts had been deployed in the particular forest area and the police stations in the region had been put on high alert.

The incident occurred when the Commandos arrived in the area on specific intelligence inputs about the Maoists' appearance near the Adivasi Colony.

Anti –Maoist operations had started in the jungles of Kannur, Wayanad, Kozhikode and Malappuram districts long back. Sources in the police said the incident confirmed the presence of armed Maoist cadres in the State.

Maoists strike again in Kerala Forest offices: KFC outlet attacked 22 Dec 2014

Suspected Maoists 22 Dec 2014 executed three attacks at three different places in the State. Two of these attacks were on the offices of the Forest Department while the third was on a KFC-McDonald's outlet in Palakkad at 7.50 AM. Police arrested two persons in connection with the third incident.

The Forest Range office at Mukkali in the Silent Valley National Park in Palakkad district came under attack at 1.20 AM on the 22nd, while the exact time of the attack on the Forest Section Office at Kunjom near Vellamunda in Wayanad district was not known.

A strange statement from the State Home Minister

Sources in State's Intelligence and the collectors fo the Palakkad and Wayanad districts said the attacks on the forest offices had all the characteristics of typical Maoist actions but State Home Minister Ramesh Chennithala said : "I do not consider the incidents currently taking place as Maoist operations. These are attacks to gain cheap popularity[15].

In the attack on the Forest Range Office at Attapadi, a department vehicle was torched, window panes were broken and four computers, a camera, several files destroyed. There was also an attempt to break open the door of the weapons store, but it did not succeed. The attackers were a 15-member group. A woman staying near the Forest Office thought there could be more than 15 men in that group. She said : " We came out of the house hearing commotion and sound of the breaking glass. A person standing outside asked us to go back inside, saying that they were Maoists and had no intention of harming us. The commotion had lasted for half an hour."

The posters stuck in the area in the name of CPI(Maoist) asked the people to join the Maoist struggle and to get ready for the armed struggle. Accusing the forest officials of being the informers of the police, the posters said the Adivasis and other marginalised people need not expect anything from the Government.

The remaining two attacks

The Forest Section Office that came under attack on the 22nd at Kunjom, Vellamunda, was just two kilometres away from the spot where the Maoists and the Thunderbolt commandos of the Kerala police, had exchanged fire on 7 December. Some window panes of the outpost were found broken and several files burnt.

Posters in the name of Maoist publication *Kattuthee* (=wild fire) were found on the walls in the area. "Though 15 days are gone by since the reported firing incident at Kunjom, the police have not been able to nab any Maoist or to produce any evidence of Maoist presence though they claim to have found some caps and pieces of clothes used by the ultras."

Now for the KFC-McDonald outlet. A group of eight masked men attacked at Chandra Nagar in Palakkad town at 7.50 AM on the 22nd. Maoist posters found on the walls in the area had anti-US slogans on them, proclaiming multinational food joints were not needed in a country where the poor people are still starving. Police arrested two people connected with this incident and confirmed their Maoist links. They were charged under the provisions of the Unlawful Activities (Prevention) Act, UAPA. The police suspected the duo had been involved in another attack the Maoists had carried out in Kochi in Nov 2014.

Another daily gave some details of the two arrested within hours of the attack. They are : a journalism student and a B.Ed student[16].

To repeat, what has already been covered earlier in details : "Suspected Maoists had vandalised the corporate office of gelatin manufacturing company, Nitta Gelatin, in Kochi city on the morning of 10 November 2014. A similar attack had been carried out on a private tourist resort, Agraharam, at Thirunelli, a temple town in Wayanad district on 18 November 2014."

Recovery of pro-Maoist literature and pamphlets from all the three targets raised suspicions that the CPI (Maoist) were behind these attacks.

"In Wayanad, a forest outpost at Kunjom near Periya Reserve Forest was attached."

"In the past few months, there have been several stray incidents of attacks, attributed to Maoists. But, police have failed to prove the cases. Two weeks back, Police and Maoists reportedly exchanged fire at Vellamunda in Wayanad[17]."

"Maoists in a bid to establish base in north Kerala": Dec 2014

This is an analytical piece about the Maoists' exertions to establish their base and presence in north Kerala.

This indeed is an interesting fact that the Naxalism had registered its presence in Kerala in the mid-1960s, along with other two states of West Bengal and Andhra Pradesh. But curiously, for decades after the initial foot-prints, it went dormant for decades. It was only towards the end of the first decade of this 21st century that there were some signs of its revival in Kerala.

For the last three years, starting 2012, there have been incidents of violence, which analysts believe resemble the pattern akin to the Maoists'. But till date, no Maoist cadre has fallen in the hands of the police. For this reason, few want to assert that it is Naxalism behind the recent violent incidents. It is for this reason that to examine the news story appearing under the above-mentioned headline in an issue of daily dated 27 Dec 2014 becomes important[18].

The daily opens its analysis with these words: "the banned CPI (Maoist) is eyeing fertile ground for building its presence in at least three district of northern Kerala—Malappuram, Palakkad and Wayanad."

They plan to exploit the popular sentiment against environmental pollution, caused by mining and quarrying activities, exploitations of natural resources, alleged high handedness and misdeeds of forest and police officials and displacement of tribals due to tourism projects and wild life sanctuaries.

Recently, the CPI (Maoist), through its mouth piece, highlighted the miserable condition of tribals in Manjeri in Malappuram district and blamed it on the attitude of forest and tribal welfare departments. It claimed to have forced the state government to address the problems of the affected people, including tribals. The extremist outfit has already formed an armed squad in Malappuram district.

Recent actions undertaken by the Western Ghats Special Zonal Committee of the CPI (Maoist) in Pallakkad and Wayanad have left the Central security agencies worried over Kerala being the latest entrant to the list of the LWE-hit states. For instance, suspected Maoists vandalised a forest outpost in Wayanad and a forest range office in Palakkad on 21 and 22 Dec 2014. Another group targeted two fast food restaurants in Palakkad on 22 December. Pamphlets issued by the outfit were recovered from the attack sight, giving the call for intensification of class struggle and asserting people's right overland, water and forest resources.

On 10 November, Maoists belonging to "Urban action team" damaged an industrial unit office in Kochi, alleging that it was polluting a local water resource. Another group vandalized a tourist resort in Wayanad on 18 November. Meanwhile, the Government is discussing including Malappuram, Wayanad and Kannur districts of Kerala among the 106 districts covered under the Security Related Expenditure re-imbursement scheme.

Maoists attack Crusher unit: 2 Jan 2015

Suspected Maoists armed with guns attacked the office of the stone quarry-crusher unit in Kannur district and set it on fire early morning 2 Jan 2015. The Maoist attack, 8th in the past two months in the State, occurred hours after Home Minister Ramesh Chennithala celebrated the New Year with Adivasis in the colonies of the nearby forest region on 1 January.

The attack on the office of the New Bharat Stone Crushers at the Twenty-Fourth Mile in Nedumpoil near forest areas with Adivasi colonies in Kannur district took place at 2.20 AM on the 2nd, and the action lasted only 10 to 15 minutes, according to the police officers who confirmed that Maoists were behind the altacks. However, no one was hurt in the attacks.[19]

This was the eighth major attack the Maoists had carried out in the State since 10 Nov 2014, the day when the ultras attacked the corporate office of a gelatin company in Kochi city. Since then, they have struck at a private tourist resort, forest department offices and multinational eateries, and have eaten exchanged fire with the police in northern Kerala.

Before leaving the crusher unit, the ultras stuck posters on the office walls. The posters, in the name of the Western Ghats Special Zonal Committee of the CPI (Maoist), demanded cessation of "attacks" by the police and forest officials on the Adivasis and other people. The posters also asked the people to use armed struggle to establish their rights over resources.

Confirming that the attack was carried out by Maoist sympathisers, the Home Minister said the State would counter the extremist designs with the support of the Adivasis and other people. "Those who carried out such nightly attacks are cowards. Their attention is to grab attention", he said.

Security staff at the crusher unit office said the gang, that encluded two women, had reached the spot shouting Maoist slogans keeping the unit's employees at gun point, they asked for the keys of the office, and broke open the door when the keys were denied to them, said Gopinathan, a security guard at the unit.

The Maoists broke window-panes, destroyed two CCTV cameras, two computers, and took away the computer hard disks in which CCTV recordgins could have been stored. They also burnt down most of the furniture of the office. Gopinathan said, ".... But they did not hurt us."

The gang was most probably led by Keralite Maoist leader Rupesh, said sources. "There were reports of Rupesh visiting the Adivasi colonies a few days ago. It is said the police failed to take action even after they were informed about this visit".

A woman in a nearby colony told the daily : "Four persons, including Rupesh and two women, came to our village. They took rice, sugar, other provisions and vegetables from us. Two of them spoke in Malayalam. I know Rupesh well....Rupesh knew everything about the colony."

The local police headed by the SP, PN unniraja, the Thunderbolt commando wing of the State Police and the Forest Department have started investigating the incident. However, what is worrying the security forces is the fact that this was the 4th attack the Maoists had carried out in the region since 18 November 2014.

A Forest Department camp shed at Anavay near Silent Valley National Park in Palakkad district was burned down on 1 January. Forest Department officials have concluded Maoists were behind this attack also. The camp shed was a few kilometres away from the Forest Range Office at Mukkali in the Silent Valley National Park which had come under Maoist attack on 22 December 2014.

This is the second attack by suspected Maoists on a stone quarrying unit in the Western Ghats region of north Kerala. In 2013, a quarry unit in Kozhikode district was attacked and an earth mover was torched. Recently, Maoist pamphlets recovered from various places had warnings against illegal quarrying units operating in the Western Ghats.

Tale of Attacks and Destruction

10 Nov 2014	Attack on corporate office of Nitta Gelatin Company in Kochi City.
18 Nov 2014	Private tourist resort Agraharam at Thirunelli, Wayanad comes under attack.
7 Dec 2014	Left ultras and police exchange fire in Vellamunda, Wayanad.
22 Dec 2014	Forest office at Mukkali, Silent Valley, Palakkad district, vandalised.
22 Dec 2014	Forest outpost at Vellamunda, Wayanad vandalised
22 Dec 2014	KFC, McDonald's Outlets in Palakkad town come under attack.
1 Jan 2015	Forest camp shed at Anavay near Mukkali torched.
2 Jan 2015	Attack on stone crusher unit office at Nedumpoil, Kannur.

Eight attacks in 52 days, but where are the Maoists: An Analysis: Jan 2015

Here is one more analytical story on the LWE attacks in Kerala. The one earlier was by a different daily (The Hindu).

"Suspected Maoists carried out eight surprise attacks in Kerala in 52 days (the last being on 2 Jan 2015) but the Kerala Police, its intelligence wing and Thunderbolt, the specialised anti-Naxal unit of the police, are still groping in the dark in their hunt for the LWE, despite the crores of rupees spent so far in the name of anti-Maoist operations." This was carried in a daily of 4 Jan 2015[20].

Police officials admit that the six-member ultras gang headed by Maoist leader Rupesh which had attacked a stone quarry – Crusher unit at Nedumpoil in Kannur district early morning 2 January had escaped after collecting provisions from a nearby Adivasi colony but the cops have so far not been able to form even a rough idea as to the direction in which they could have escaped.

Similarly, the reported incident of Maoists exchanging fire with Thunderbolt Commandos at Kunjom, Vellamunda in Wayanad district had taken place on 7 December but the police are yet to find out even its basic aspects like how many extremists had taken part in the action, what kind of weapons had been used, etc.

Despite all these attacks and the obvious support the extremists are getting from the Adivasis in the colonies in northern Kerala forests, State's Congress Home Minister Ramesh Chennithala is saying that the trouble makers are not proper Maoists but their sympathisers and that they are just anti-social elements showing cowardic by conducting attacks under the cover of darkness.

"In short what we are witnessing in the Maoist scene in the State is a combined failure of the Government and the police. The people should now be beginning either to suspect that the entire Maoist stories are just lies or our police force is just a bunch of amateurs standing stunned at the extremists' prowers," said a former officer of Kerala's Police Intelligence Wing. He continues : "The Home Minister keeps on saying that there is Maoist presence in the State but they have not grown to be a threat even when frequent attacks are taking place. He is also saying that the ultras are an isolated lot while his own police are sure that they are getting immense support from the Adivasis. What kind of an amateur system is this?" he says.

Even top police officials admit that the recent incidents have proved the futility of the two-year, multi-crore rupee project of anti-Maoist combing operations by Thunderbolt commandos in the forests of Wayanad, Kannur, Kozhikode, Palakkad and Malappuram. Such a situation may prompt the people to suspect the intent and sincerity of the police operation, they warn.

The Thunderbolt commandos had started the combing operations in Feb 2013 in the northern jungles with the help of the Forest Department and Adivasi trackers but they have not been able to find any extremists or their hide-outs though there have been frequest reports about their sighting at Adivasi colony and even in the same forests being combed by the cops.

Police officials say that shortage of properly trained personnel and lack of sophisticated surveillance and communication equipment and rough terrain vehicles are some of the reasons for the failure of the operations. Sources in the Home Department allege that the Finance Department is refusing to release funds for crucial programmes citing Treasury constraints.

It is all over for Roopesh Kerala's most-wanted: May 2015

It is a calm afternoon at Shyna Manzil, a day after the Kerala Government confirmed the arrest on Friday (5 May 2015) of the State's most wanted Maoist couple by Andhra police outside a bakery in Tamil Nadu.

But behind the calm, inside the Thrissur home of Roopesh and Shyna, is their 17-year-old daughter who says her struggle has just begun. "I will bring them out. My parents are not meant to be locked up, in a room somewhere," says Ami TR[21].

Daughter Vows: "will get parents out"

The arrest of her parents hit headlines across the country. But Ami, who has completed class XII and wants to pursue a career in law, is engaged in a serious discussion with a group of youngsters with the next edition of Padantharam, a monthly magazine launched in March (2015) that focuses on the education sector. She is one of its sub-editors.

"I have grown hearing more slogans than lullabies", says Ami, adding that her mother had carried her along when she was just 50 days old to a protest venue, placing her inside a makeshift cradle nearby. Then again, Ami and her younger sister Savera were caught by the police when they were attending a meeting to discuss a new political movement – they were later made witnesses by the National Investigation Agency (NIA) that took over the case, Ami says.

"Police wanted to know if I had sexual relations with the others arrested in the case. They even tried to force me to undergo a virginity test. But I stood firm. I have a right to go where ever I want and do whatever I want", she says. Apart from Ami and Savera the third member of this family is 70-year-old Nafeeza, a widow and mother of Shyna. For her, the arrest of Roopesh and her daughter has come as a bit of relief. "Every day, we used to scan the newspapers for reports of a fake encounter", says Nafeeza, a former employee of the State government's health service.

But Savera, a class VII student, collapsed after hearing the news of the arrest. "She feared that police would torture our parents. But she regained her composure after I talked to her".

Ami recalled that Savera was five years old when Shyna handed over two children over to Nafeeza in Jan 2008, along with a power of attorney. Shyna, then a clerk at Kerala High Court, went on to write a letter to the then Kerala CM VS Achuthanandan about the alleged atrocities committed by security forces, saying, "your police made me a Maoist."

Ami says Roopesh has been "a rare visitor to our house" ever since he left the family to activity join the Maoist movement in 2003. "He has not returned to the house after 2007", she says, adding that the two sisters have travelled to different parts of Kerala to meet their father there. Yet it has not been easy for Ami and Savera.

Their home in the coastal village of Valappad has always been under police watch, says Ami. "My school mates were afraid to mingle with me. Many parents have prevented their children from speaking to me. The police had even come to the school where I studied to inquire about me," she adds. So what now after her parents' arrest? Her reply : "New leaders will emerge. I have an attachment towards the ideology. But I cannot predict whether the impression will stay with me as I grow up".

Her grand mother is not so sure about the path her daughter took, though. "Shyna met Roopesh at college during their early college days. Then, activists of ultra-left outfits started visiting our house. I did not like it. So I sent her to Kollam to study pharmacy. But she continued her relations with Roopesh and the agitations", says Nafeeza. "Couple studied law after marriage. After practising in Kerala High Court for a while, Shyna got a job as a court clerk," she says.

Roopesh, meanwhile, got involved in a case related to providing shelter to a leader of the eastwhile PWG, just when he was about to enroll as an advocate.

Since then, things have never been the same for this family of five.

"Kerala Minister tells daughters of Maoists not to follow their parents": 4 Jul 2015

Kerala Home Minister Ramesh Chennithala has advised the daughters of Maoist couple Roopesh and Shyna not to follow in their parents foot steps. Maoist couple, facing a slew of cases in Kerala, was arrested from

Tamil Nadu two months back. Daughters Ami and Savera had greeted the parents with slogans when they were produced in a Kochi court. Elder daughter Ami, 17, had openly stated that she was proud of her parents, who, according to her, fought for future generations[22].

Chennithala, in a letter published in his blog, said he was pained about the two daughters who have been deprived of parental care in their teen days. He wanted them to focus on studies. "Do not opt for the path treaded by your parents. There will be many persons who will glorify the approach of your parents. The path of violence and weapons do not take persons anywhere".

Recently, a letter purportedly written by the Maoists, had claimed that the arrest of the couple was not the end of the Maoist plan in Kerala.

Referring to the letter, the Minister refuted their claim. "The Maoists' activities in Kerala are nearing an end due to the steps initiated by the government", he said.

Kerala Maoist held in Pune is son of a ex-diplomat: 8 May 2015

The Maharashtra Anti-Terrorism Squad (ATS) arrested top Maoist leader Murali Kannampalli alias Ajitha, 62, and an aide from a hospital 30 km away from Pune on 8 May 2015, with police sources in Kerala labelling him as the "backbone" of the movement in the State.

Officers identified the aide as 29-yuear-old CP Ismail and said Murali was receiving treatment for various ailments. A court letter remanded the two to the custody of ATS for seven days. Murali's arrestcomes over a week after the Andhra Police arrested Kerala's most wanted Maoist couple, Roopesh and Shyna, from outside a bakery in Tamil Nadu[23].

Murali is the son of Konnampalli Karunakara(n) Menon, who had worked as a diplomat in Indian missions in several European countries.

When Emergency was declared in 1975, Murali had been a final-year Engineering student at Regional Engineering College, Kozhikode (now NIT-C). He then went underground.

K Venu, a prominent Naxal leader of the 70s, said Murali had played a crucial role in building the movement in the college at the time. "He had initiated P Rajan and several others into LWE", he said.

Rajan had later died a victim of police torture during the Emergency in a controversial case that finally led to the resignation of former Kerala CM K Karunakaran.

"Murali had wide contacts with Maoist movements across the world and had even acted as a mediator in Nepal where Maoism was hit by dissidence", Venu said. He added that Murali was the "true" Maoist leader from Kerala, who maintained close links with national leadership—he remained elusive, was reluntant to be photographed and never interacted with the media. Venu said he had last met Murali six years ago. "He has been moving freely every where as none could recognise him. He has authored books and several articles under the name Ajith, and has always been an efficient organiser and ideologue of Marxist-Leninist politics", said Venu.

Murli had been brain behind the incident in which Maoist held a District Collector in Kerala hostage for several hours in 1996 to highlight the tribal issues. "But his name never figured in the list of the accused as the arrested did not divulge his name", said police sources.

Many pro-Maoists in Kerala attribute the arrest of Murali to the failed merger of CPI(ML-Naxalbari), of which he was the Secretary, with CPI (Maoist) in 2014. "He might have been trapped by some one in the Maoist camp", sources said. Murali had married a Dalit women, but later separated. Their only son is living with Murali's brother.

Police identified Murali's arrested aide as Ismail, the leader of the frontal Maoist outfit in Kerala, called Porattam.

PM Modi's advice to Maoists: Listen to your Victims : 9 May 2015

Assuring people that the "drama of death" being played out in the Maoist-hit areas (of Chhattisgarh) will end, PM Narendra Modi on 9 May 2015 appealed to the ultras to spend just "five days" with a child who has lost its parents to the violence to realise that "if there is any future, it is in peace." Addressing a public gathering in Dantewada on his first visit to the region since becoming PM (May 2014), he said, "wear tribal clothes and visit a child who has lost his parents. Spend five days with him. Talk to him, don't reveal who you are. I can tell you with certainty that the boy….. will force you to reconsider. You will be shattered by the grave sin you had committed…intoxicated by violence[24]."

Modi added, "embrace humanity once and meet the aggrieved families. You will never take that path again. You will feel that you have committed something wrong. Much more than any government or any law can change you, you will be transformed by a boy who suffered by your bullets."

Speaking hours after interacting at the Education City project in Jawanga village, 22 km away, with some 800 children affected by extremist violence. Modi said, "violence has no future. If there is any future, it is in peace, and I have experienced it today."

Saying that "a plough, not a gun on the shoulder" was the way forward. He cited the examples of the Naxalbari movement in West Bengal and the insurgency in Punjab. "I want to tell you that there is no need to lose hope. This (Maoism) too will end. When bloody battles were on in Punjab, did anybody think that it could end? I am sure the people who have taken the wrong path on this land will also sooner or later see humanity emerge from within them," he added. "Will this drama of death end here or not? There is no need to despair. Even here, it will stop."

The PM added that "development was the only road to solve your problems" and asked Maoists "to sit together" with the government. "If Chhattisgarh is freed from this problem, it has the potential to rise to No. 1 in India. It can change the future of youth here, and the future of India," he said.

Stressing that providing employment is his first priority, he said that no parents want their sons to travel thousands of kilometres to cities and live in a slum. "It is the responsibility of the government that development reaches every corner of the country, remote areas and the hut of the poor", he said.

Kerala's democratic revolution, or why Maoism is a non-starter An analysis: May 2015

This is an important analysis on Maoism in Kerala, and the author is certain it has no future in this 'most literate' state of India.

This analytical article by Amrith Lal was published in the Indian Express issue of 7 May 2015.

It is reproduced below

- "After Roopesh, alleged Chief of the Western Ghats Zonal Committee of CPI (Maoist), his wife Shyna, and three others were arrested this week, a former Naxal leader from Kerala remarked that the State had no Naxalites, "Only Exalites" (ex-Naxalites). There is some truth in the witticism. Maoist activity in Kerala has been limited mostly to distributing leaflets and pasting poster in isolated Adivasi hamlets. An active Maoist movement is absent and is unlikely to emerge in the near future.
- "Maoism had its moment in Kerala in the late 1960s and 1970s. Naxalbari had resonance in the State, which was home to a vibrant Communist movement with a history of agrarian and working class mobilisation. Radicalised sections of the CP(M), unhappy with the parliamentary path to political change, agreed with Charu Mazumdar.

- "Internationally, the 1960s was a heady decade for radical rebellions. The first phase of Naxalism in Kerala drew in people who were associated with the Communist Parties and had a record of political activism. A thousnd political lines and groups bloomed with action focussed on "annihilation of class enemies". Police killed Verghese, arguably the only mass leader to emerge from the Naxalite movment, in a fake encounter, and arrested most of the leaders.
- "The second spurt came in the months before the emergency, when a young K Venu rallied around various groups to form a party. But this too was short-lived, as the police arrested most of them.
- "The third phase was just after the Emergency, when the Naxalites resorted to mass action. Interventions like putting corrupt doctors on public trial and cultural activities under the banner of Janakeeya Samaskarika Vedi helped them gain influence.
- "This was also the phase when many talented youth, writers, theatre activists were drawn to the movement. But the internal dissensions and inability to sustain a political activism in an open and dialogic framework led to disintegration of the movement in the 1980s. Venu disbanded his party and politically active "Exalites" went on to re-invent themselves as public activists, championing causes that mainstream politics had ignored – gender, environment, etc.
- "Activists like Roopesh, shaped by the politics of the CPI (Maoist), recall the first generation of Naxalites in their rhetoric—apparently ignoring the radical changes Kerala has undergone since then. Social and economic oppression do exist, but the most oppressed groups, including the Adivasis, have found agency—and are no longer waiting for political saviours to "educate" them or to fight their causes. *Adivasis* – favoured by the Naxalites in the 1960s and Maoists in this century—have, for instance, produced fine leaders such as CK Janu in Kerala, who express political concerns within a rights-based framework.
- "Numerous struggles, on issues from land to environment, dot Kerala's landscape. Blue collar employees ignored by trade unions, such as textile shop floor workers and nurses, electorally small segments like the landless, raise their voice within the democratic space. Their concerns are specific, demands precise, and their language is of rights. A vibrant media, especially the noisy TV

channels, ensure that the political class is forced to confront the agitations. In a highly competitive electoral space, where narrow margins decide elections, no political party can afford to ignore any protest for long. The campuses prefer to organise and protest on social media, and have succeeded in making their concerns heard—the 'kiss of Love' protest against social conservatism was an example. The presence of a vibrant civil society that keeps constant watch on the political mainstream—which is mostly responsive – is one reason why movements such as Anna Hazare's fail to gain traction in Kerala.

- "The Maoist political thought and plan is a clear misfit in Kerala. Their revolutionary rhetoric and pretensions have no constituency. They have not initiated a single popular struggle in Kerala, nor can they join any. They do not even recognise that their political moment is past – or that it never perhaps existed. Their impact has been mostly negative, such as exposing unsuspecting and vulnerable sympathisers to police harassment. What is true, though, is that their fleeting appearances in the Western Ghats have forced the political mainstream to engage with issues like usury in Adivasi hamlets and indiscriminate quarrying.
- "Most of the first generation communists in Kerala cut their teeth in the social reform or freedom movement, and recognized the local context and their lineage early. They abandoned the adventurist line in the 1940s, opting for mass action and electoral demorcracy. That helped to build up a democratic revolution in Kerala over the decades, now reflected in the State's development indices.
- "Kerala will surely debate the Maoist arrests in the coming days. A rainbow coalition of various anti-Maoist voices could emerge to voice the right of the arrested people to be treated as political prisoners and to get a fair trial, and to guard against police harassment of genuine citizen activists. But that is a kind of democratic morality that the Maoists are unlikely to recognise or understand."

Tamil Nadu

There has been reports of Maoist efforts to extend their presence to Tamil Nadu. It has not succeeded so far, or so it seems.

It had LWE presence once

Tamil Nadu, indeed, was one of the states that had Naxal presence in the past, but "the movement is claimed to be dead." But it is still active in its Dharmapuri area, once the cradle of LWE.

But Venkatesan, leader of the Farmers Liberation Front, a constituent – more correctly, a 'front' – of the CPI (ML), says the Maoists here are more concerned with solving the problems of the people, settling communal disputes and encouraging inter-caste marriages.

There are laudable objectives, and are unexceptionable. But these are mere façade to endear themselves to the people. The real aim obviously is to spread the Maoist ideology in the area, that supports LWE, which is presently engaged in an armed insurgency to displace the democratically elected.

The concern for the moment is that the Maoist violence may not spread beyong the Dharmapuri area.

Special staff to monitor Naxal Movement: Feb 2007

"Policemen in the rank of Head Constables will be deployed in the nine police stations along the Tamil Nadu-Andhra Pradesh border to track information on the activities or presence of those attracted by the Naxalite movement." This was disclosed by DIG P Kancheepuram Range Mohd Shakeel Akhter on 20 Feb 2007.

These Head Constable, assigned special duty, will also be interacting with their counterparts attached to the AP police stations along the border and exchanging information or data with regards to suspected movements of Naxalites. The nine police stations in question are : Arambakkam, Pathiri Vedu, Uthukottai, Kannurpet, K K Chatram, Tirutani, Pothatturpet, Pallipattu and RK Pet.

Besides this, there is a plan to revamp and infuse fresh blood into the Village Defence Committees (VDCs) to deploy them in law and order maintenance, night patrolling and itraffic management, where ever required.

Three nabbed by villagers in Tamil Nadu: Are the Maoists advancing South ? June 2007

It has been widely believed since the 2002 Uthangarai operation in Tamil Nadu that Naxalite presence in the State was negligible. But that perception seems to have changed on 5 Jun 2007 when residents of a backward village in Theni district in South Tamil Nadu helped nab three youths, said to be members of the CPI (Maoist), with a pile of arms and ammunition. Seven others, most of them prominent activists, are believed to have escaped the scene[25].

The three nabbed by the villagers were found with a significant quantity of arms and ammunition, leading police to believe they were in the process of recruiting sympathizers and building a Maoist base in the State.

The incident spurred the state government to launch a drive to flush out Naxals from the forest ranges. The responsibility for this operation is being assigned to ADG P K. Vijay Kumar – the police officer who led Operation Cocoon which resulted in the elimination of the outlawed brigand and much-wanted teakwood smuggler Veerappan.

A senior Q Branch official, wanting not to alarm the public at the incident, said confidently : "we are sure there are only a handful of activists in Tamil Nadu". The police seem certain that the incident was only a Naxal "spurt" and not a revival, or even an attempt at it. Fairly worried and unwilling to take chances, the state government ordered the police to mount a major combing operation in the forest ranges of Coimbatore, Teni, Periya(r) kulam, Salem, Dharmapuri and Krishnagiri districts.

That the state government was cautious post-incident was only to be expected. It could not have been unaware of the decisions taken at the 9th Congress of the CPI (Maoist) held Jan-Feb 2007 on the Jharkhand-Odisha border. One among the decisions was to extend the presence of the Naxalism across the borders of Tamil Nadu and Karnataka. The cadres involved in the incident were possibly tasked to make the fresh recruitment for the outfit, and then initiate the novices into basic arms training and guerrilla tactics.

So, the Naxals have already started the recruitment drive, first step to concretise the expansion plans decided upon by their leadership at the said 9th Congress.

Tamil Nadu: Will it relapse into LWE ?: Jul 2007

It is, rather, was, widely believed that Tamil Nadu had successfully quelled the Naxalite threat by the end of 2002. There was a reason for the belief. After all, the last Naxal-related incident in the state had taken place way back in Nov 2002. What was that incident all about?

Following a tip-off from the villagers, Q Branch swooped down on a group of some 35 youths, including six women, claiming to be members of the Radical Youth League (RYL), being trained in guerrilla warfare in the dense mangroves of Jalajothipatty, some 30 km from Dharmapuri. Operation Uthangarai (a village close to Jalajothipatty) lasted a week, resulting in the police nabbing 28 of the youths. One Person, Parthipan alias Shiva, was killed in the operation.

If the last anti-Naxal operation was the result of a tip-off from villagers, a village couple's chance 'discovery' on 6 Jun 2007 is suggestive of Naxal attempts to revive the 'nearby' defunct Naxalism in Tamil Nadu. Now on to some details about this chance discovery.

On the morning of the fateful 6 June, Subramani and his wife Pushpa went on their usual trek up Murugamalai, a bald hillock just outside their village in Kakkanji Nagar, close to Theni, to collect firewood, their daily chore. They saw a bundle covered with plastic and *dhoti* on the slope, and raised an alarm fearing it to be a dead body.

By evening, a group of men armed with sickles and wooden clubs arrived at the hill, and found three persons guarding the bundle, claiming to be students on a hike. The said bundle contained ration for their trek. But when the suspicious villagers uncovered it, they found to their surprise and shock a neat pile of guns, grenades and cartridges[26].

The villagers tied up the three, one of whom hailed from the nearby E Pudukkottai village, and informed the Theni police. The three confessed they were members of the CPI (Maoist) and pleaded with the villagers to either kill them or let them escape. Villagers also learnt that seven others escaped, including V Sundaramurthy, who was later nabbed, and Kalidas, key Maoist leader, attempting to revive Maoism in Tamil Nadu, had escaped.

This incident sent panic waves across the state administration, which until this incident had believed that any significant Naxal activity in the State had been guelled. A deeply concerned government pulled out ADG P K. Vijay Kumar, the former STF chief popular for heading the operation that killed Veerappan, from an inconsequential post, and handed him the brief to flush out the Maoists hiding inside the State's forests.

Six special police teams were formed to comb the forest ranges in the districts of Chennai, Madurai, Salem, Coimbatore, Dharmapuri and Krishnagiri, where the Maoists wre believed to be hiding. Q Branch sources disclosed : "Seven people are still absconding. We believe there are only a handful of these, who now call themselves CPI (Maoist) memebrs, fashioning themselves after the Naxalites of Andhra Pradesh."

SP Theni R Sudhakar clarifies : "If you take a look at the guns, you can see that many of them are rusted and not in operating condition. The arms were meant only for imparting training and not for operations."

Q Branch sources dismissed reports that arms were being sourced from Karnataka for Tamil Nadu by AP Maoists. "The group engaged in reviving the movement is very small. Moreover, they are far from even being in a position to recruit for starting any major operation," said an officer.

Meanwhile, police stepped up their hunt for Kalidas, said to be the key person behind the renewed attempt to recruit villagers for training. He has been on the run since the Nov 2002 Uthangarei operation, detailed above. He has seven cases registered against him, including one under TADA and two attempts to murder cases. Police are also on the look-out for Chandra, wife of Sundaramurthy, who was nabbed in a house in Tiruppur near Comboitore on 13 Jul 2006.

A senior police officer, part of the present anti-Naxal operations, explains : "The *modus operandi* of the Maoists is simple. Villagers, gullible enough to join the group, are made accomplices in the incidents of dacoities and murders. They then go underground and have little option but to join the ultras. We believe the handful of the active Maoists were in the process of recruiting villagers and have not been very successful in the act."

But back in E. Pudukkottai, it is a different story. S Bhaskaran, senior DMK leader in the village, whose wife Latha is a Panchayat President, pointed out that Velmurugan, a law student, and one of those nabbed by the villagers in Murgugamalai and hailing from E. Pudokkottai, had successfully formed a Committee and roped in some 50 village youths as members. But before he could initiate them into the movement, Velmurugan was arrested.

There seems to be a certain sense of complacence about the success or otherwise of the Naxal attempt at reviving their movement in Tamil Nadu. This could mean a serious error of judgement, on the part of authorities and persons concerned, especially, the state police. While dealing with the Maoists, it is better to be prepared than to be surprised or sorry. They would always be looking for new avenues to spread their movement and its ideoloqy. They have surreptitiously been spreading their movement in Madhya Pradesh and even made an attempt at the same in Gujarat, then why should Tamil Nadu be an exception ?

Naxal Special Division (NSD) strengthens ties with people of remote hamlets bordering Kerala: 5 Mar 2015

The NSD which consists of two teams in Coimbatore and Nilgiris districts, has been successful in building cordial relationship with people in tribal villages and hamlets bordering Kerala. IGP West Zone K Shankar said that the teams have met the primary target of building ties with the villagers.

The teams are operational from 1 Feb 2015 followiong the attacks on a forest office and a few other places in Palakkad district of Kerala in Dec 2014. The dedicated teams were formed in addition to the combing operations by the Special Wings of the police and tightening vigil at the border by the local police[27].

During the last one month, the teams, have visited each village at least a couple of times and interacted with the residents there, creationg awareness on government schemes, enquiring about their needs, and also requesting them to share information with the police on movement of strangers in their areas.

Recruitment

Stating that there is no Naxal movement in this part of the State, Mr. Shankar added that the police had also targeted recruitment of 75 Home Guards in bordering hamlets in Ooty and around 30 in similar areas in Coimbatore district by the end of March (2015).

Efforts were also underway to identify and induct more youth in bordering areas as Home Guards and for honorary positions as 'friends of police' or 'community police'. It is learnt that involving youth in these activities would give them confidence that they two mere part of the system (active policing).

The NSD personnel in Coimbatore are also trying to identify places such as blue metal manufacturing units that use explosives.

Stating that though such hazardous units were at a safe distance from the border, efforts are under way to identify those located at secluded places. The unit oweners would be advised to keep the hazardous material in a safe and secure place in the premises and also to have alarm systems.

Print Media on the Maoist Insurrection

The following pages would describe the stance of some newspapers on the issue of Maoist violence. The pattern would be same as we adopted in case of articles by some academics and specialists.

"Fallen heroes forgotten: The Pioneer : 20.9.2011

Men fighting Maoists are ignored

Here are some excerpts from an editorial in this daily.

- "On 18 Sep 2009 when Assistant Commandants Manoranjan Singh and Rakesh Kumar Chaurasia of the 201 Combat Battalion for Resolute Action (COBRA) let their elite team of six security personnel into the heart of Dantewada in Chhattisgarh where they eliminated some 30 Maoists and destroyed a vital arms factory, their brave expedition marked the successful initiation of the Union Government's five-State paramilitary counter-offensive against Red insurgents. Believed to be a part of the Operation Green Hunt, the massive two-day offensive was one of the earliest successes registered by the Government in its long battle against the Maoists. It proved that it indeed was feasible for the Para-military Forces to infiltrate into the territory held by the Reds and launch an offensive against them. The State's DGP Vishwa Ranjan had said at that time : "For the first time, Maoists were worried about their losses. They were forced to retreat."

- "While the team was returning from this success, they were ambushed by the heavily-armed insurgents. A Court of Inquiry report filed in Dec 2009 that in violent battle that ensued, Manoranjan and Chaurasia led their men bravely as the sadly outnumbered team caved in against heavy odds. The entire team perished. The names of the other four martyrs were: Sub-Inspector Sushil Kumar Verma, Head Constable Lalit Kumar and Constables Uday Kumar Yadav and Manoharlal.
- "Two years later, as the battle against the Maoists continues, the brave Six who laid down their lives for the country have already been forgotten—not just by the people and media, but also by the Government that ideally should have given them gallantry awards. Yet, officers supervising anti-terror operations have been duly acknowledged for their contributions. While this newspaper does not be grudge the five IPS officers who have been decorated with at least six gallantry awards in the past few years for monitoring anti-terror operations in J & K, it does regret the manner in which foot-soldiers fighting India's most significant threat to internal security have been wholly ignored—not only by the Government but by the people of this Country too."

The above is a sad story of the Government neglecting the martyrs from the Para-military forces who are laying down their lives for the country. Is the Central Government only to be blamed for this neglect? Did the CRPF top bosses recommend the cases of these Six Braves ? Did the State Government did its bit? These facts are not available. Still, this newspaper taking up their case is welcome. The Press too has its responsibility.

"No end to Red terror" : The Pioneer : 10 Oct 2011 Maoists continue to strike at will

Excerpts

- The killing of the three security personnel in a landmine blast triggered by the Maoists in Chhattisgarh is a chilling reminder that the Red terrorists continues to flourish and attack at will, and that they do not deserve kid-gloves treatment which many human rights activists and some Congress and UPA leaders continue to advocate for them.

- The UPA Government have extended them an olive branch time and again, offering them talks if they suspended the violence. They were not even asked to surrender their arms. They not only ignored Home Minister P. Chidambram's call, but also responded with last week's attack.
- "That there were no major attacks during the last couple of months until the 7 October landmine explosion suggests the Maoists were busy regrouping, rearming and recalibrating their tactics. There are reports that they have equipped themselves with advanced weaponry to shoot down helicopters ferrying security personnel to the Red-infested regions, as also carrying supplies and evacuating casualties. If they are able to sabotage such logistics exercise, it will be a serious blow to anti-Maoist operations. The Government simply cannot ignore this threat since the information is based on intercepted conversations among senior Maoist leaders. Since the fresh Maoist offensive has come after Chidambram acknowledge that battle against the Red extremism has been less than successful so far, it is incumbent the Central Government to step up its counter-campaign in collaboration with the affected State Governments and stop sniping at them for their supposed failure in curbing the menace.
- "What is required is the need for the Government to improve its real-time intelligence, spread development to areas which are the recruiting ground for Maoist cadres. More importantly, Maoists have to be convinced that they cannot defeat India. For that it is necessary that the Government stop limp-writed approach to the Maoist intransigence and proceed resolutely to defeat them on the ground."

"A good step forward: The Pioneer: 9.4.2012

It has to be an all-out war on Maoists

Excerpts

- "In a welcome move, the Cabinet Secretariat has cleared proposal to position Rashtriya Rifles personnel in Maoist-infested States to help the local police force in matters of deployment and training. The Union Government must now ensure that the decision is turned into a ground reality rather than staying in files. [For a long time, issue of involving the Armed Forces in combating the Maoists has been in public domain. Some within the Government and political system are opposed to the idea the former should directly wage war against the Maoists, the people of the country. Those who are for it also don't want direct involvement of Army, but only it helping in logistics and training to paramilitary forces directly confronting the Maoists.

- The Maoists are expanding their strongholds while cocking a snook at the elected governments, largely due to pusillanimity of those in power—Odisha being a good recent example of it. The Maoists are terrorists and nation must fight them with all its might, it being the biggest threat to its integrity. Not only Army's services, even the Air Force must be pressed into serving/helping the anti-Maoist operations, for the purpose of reconnaissance and ferrying of forces involved in fighting the Reds. As the Maoists are getting more technology savvy, the Armed Forces can help the Paramilitary forces in securing the best available de-mining equipment and anti-nines vehicles for faster and safer movement in the Maoist-dominated areas.
- "The immediate task before the Union Government is to secure the consent of various Governments for deployment of Rashtriya Rifles in their respective states for anti-Maoist operations. Knowing the recent face-off between the UPA Government and Non-UPA State Governments over the creation of anti-terrorist entity, the task would not be easy. The latter must be assured that the Rashtriya Rifles would function within the parameters of the powers they enjoy."

"Whose journalism is it anyway?" 28.1.201: Suvojit Bagchi

Blurb

- "Journalists of Bastar are often exposed to serious security threats by Maoists who want to release a statement or by the police who want to gather information.

Excerpts

- "Summer 2013, this correspondent was preparing for a motorbike ride in the forests of Bastar, when he got a request from the State Government to mediate with the Maoists to recover the body of a Greyhound soldier killed in an encounter with the rebels. A journalist from Bijapur, some traders and this scribe took a 100-km bike ride in search of the body. The events that transpired inter alia this journey form a curious interpretation of the pressure on journalists in the hostile region of south Chhattisgarh (Bastar division).

- "Once the police were informed of the location of the body, another set of requests emerged: 'take a tractor to recover the body, don't touch it yourself as it may have been mined by the rebels, the villagers accompanying you will recover it.' So instructed a police officer who was overseeing the recovery operation from Bhadrachalam in Andhra Pradesh.
- "Editorial trainers and journalists have spoken in unison : 'If you are working with a media organisation you cannot help any side in a conflict. In this case recovery of a body make no sense as a person is already dead…you are not saving lives…you may lose credibility and risk your own life.' This line of advice and averments came from Elva Narcia, former BBC man and adviser with Internews, the international media development NGO in Afghanistan and Jason Burke, *The Guardian's* South Asia Correspondence.
- "But the local journalist from Bijapur had to oblige, did go in and returned with the body, raising a few questions in the process. Can a journalist in the conflict area, whose security and career depends on his relationship with the local police, afford to turn down such a request on the basis of journalistic ethics? With little risk assessment, the journalists in Bastar are exposed to serious security threats by national and international standards. For example, they are often summoned into forest area to receive a press statement. At times, they are called in for a casual conversation with the intention of gathering intelligence. The police also try to gather some information from them about a village or individuals. By obliging any one or both, journalists subject themselves to several risks, including threats to their lives. Besides, it is an open secret that journalists raise money from big industrialists, local traders and the local administration in parts of India, and south Chhattisgarh is no exception. PROs of mining companies, DCs and SPs routinely pay local journalists and media houses. Such practices in rural India raise risks as these very entities are working against the Maoists. If we do not divulge information or take money, we will be suspected of taking favours from the Maoists,' says a journalist from Narayanpur."

- "Journalists in these rural areas are either paid poorly or not paid fixed salaries. Most Hindi media journalists receive a 15 per cent commission on advertising sales, a small commission on circulation but bizarrely no fixed salary for reporting. Sometimes, journalists become, out of financial compulsions, mouth piece of some local mafia, corrupt politicians, or some local agency who are appointed by a channel or a local daily, to look after its ad-sales, circulation or reporting. This agency pays 'fifty thousand and above' for these services, and sometime journalists buy these agencies (franchises of well-known papers or news channels) with a hefty loan from local mafia or politicians, becoming willy-nilly partners inunhealthy practices.
- "The distinction between editorial and ad-sales is waning in the conflict zones of Bastar and is also severely threatening the existence of journalists. A former reporter in Sukma district explains how he was threatened by the Maoists for working both as a salesman and a reporter for the same paper. He says : 'If a journalists recovers revenue from the market, it is unethical but not risky in an urban set up. In Bastar, one could be killed for that. The Maoists once summoned him to explain paper's revenue model. The Maoist said, 'your paper is funded by the mining mafia of Jaggalpur, you raise advertisements from the local administration and work as on hawker-cum-reporter. How can we expect any neutral reporting from you?" The middle-aged journalist's reply : "They should not", and decided to quit the job.
- "No journalists' organisation or even the Press Council of India seems to be seeking any understanding of how the distinction between editorial line and marketing policies is increasingly getting blurred in Bastar. Perhaps, it is quite late to clarify this demarcation to protect the interests of journalists and journalism in the confluct areas of south Chhattisgarh."

The above article appeared in *The Hindu* of 28 Jan 2014. It faithfully reflects the problems of journalists working in Maoist-infested areas of Bastar (and by extension, in the entire Red corridor of the country) and serious threats they face to their very lives. It simply proves the Maoists pose serious threats to all sections of our population.

"Maoists on Rampage." The Pioneer : 13 Mar 2014 But Congress-led UPA has no counter-strategy

- "The horrific Maoist attack on security personnel in Chhattisgarh on 11 March that claims 16 lives adds to the high price the nation continues to pay for the Congress-led UPA Government's inability to fight the radicals. Over a decade, the regime has failed to come up with a coherent anti-Maoist policy. This attack was staged in the same area where 27 people, including nearly all the state Congress leaders, were killed by the Maoists last May. If the last attack happened while the politicos were engaged in the Assembly polls, this one was timed for the Lok Sabha electioneering. Spectacular attacks have been the Red's standard response to nation's electoral exercises, reflecting their disdain for India's democratic values.

- "Between 5 and 9 March, the intelligence is believed to have sent six inputs to the local security forces about Maoists assembling in the area, and additional insurgents trooping in from the neighbouring states. Yet, the Union Home Minister claimed there was no 'specific' intelligence. Was his Ministry really in the dark? Or, is he reluctant to concede that despite these alerts, the Ministry could not prevent the attack. One hopes the Government will get its act together, as the general elections approach, even if its past record belie this hope. Take Dantewada attack that killed 76 policemen in 2010. It steeled the then Home Minister Chidambram" will to prioritise the Maoist threat, which had fallen off the Union Government's radar during his predecessor Shivraj Patil's tenure. But the initiative lost its tempo progressively. Two years later, when Shinde replaced Chidambaram, even the semblance of an offensive was lost.
- "The UPA's counter-insurgency efforts have suffered because of Congress's ideological infirmity towards the Maoists. If there is an occasional leader like Chidambaram who sought a strong line against the rebels, you have (a perennial saboteur like) Digvijay Singh portraying the terrorists as 'misguided ideologues,' publicly criticising Chidambram/other colleagues for advocating harsh line on the insurrection, and even scuttling bipartisan political response by bad-mouthing non-Congress State Governments. To make the matters worse, there is National Advisory Council, Sonia Gandhi's personal think-tank, a number of whose members often empathises with the Maoists and their ideology (They will be included in the last of 'over ground Maoists,' in a later chapter).
- "As a result of the Congress's fickle-minded approach, even the country's occasional successes in the fight against the Maoists—such as the ones by the Grey Hounds in Andhra Pradesh—could not be scaled-up into a national strategy."

This article from the *Pioneer* reflects its strong views on the Maoists insurrection. Unlike several other newspapers, this daily comes out to be more nationalistic in its approach to deal with this anti-national LWE. No wonder it is extremely critical of lackadaisical approach of the Congress in dealing with this national threat to India's integrity and sovereignty.

"Tripping on old mistakes:" *The Hindu* : 13 Mar 2014

This article deals with the same issue, the Maoist attack of 11 March, as was the subject discussed in an editorial of *The Pioneer* of 13 Mar 2014, in the last entry.

Excerpts

- "The killing of 15 Central and State police officers in Chhattisgarh on 11 March is just the latest in the string of hideous losses India's anti-Maoist counter-insurgency has suffered at regular intervals. India has generally accepted these as inevitable costs of a war inflicted by insurgents whom Prime Minister Manmohan Singh once described as most serious threat to country's internal security. The sacrifice, if that is what it is, appears to be paying off. The Maoist insurgency has been in steady decline since 2010. From a peak of 1180 lives lost that year, the authoritative South Asia Terror Portal date base records, fatalities fell to 421 in 2013. The slow choking of the Maoists is evident. Key leaders in Chhattisgarh and Odisha have left the party and its efforts did nothing to stop a large turnout in the Assembly polls held in Chhattisgarh last year. The Maoists' efforts to expand into small towns and cities have yielded little success. The Fourth Central Committee meeting of the CPI (Maoists) issued a resolution admitting to the stark fact of declining public support, even in the Party's heartland regions.
- "Yet the truth is that much of the loss of life in these anti-Maoist war were avoidable—even inexcusable. The succession of the tactical errors which enabled this latest attack is depressingly similar: near–identical mistakes were made in disaster after disaster, from annihilation of an entire CRPF Company in Chintalner to last year slaughter of Congress leaders. The ill-fated patrol, as the Hindu has revealed, headed blithely into the area where State and Central intelligence services had warned Maoists were preparing an ambush. It used vehicular transport and tranversed a fixed route repeatedly, both lethal areas where ambushes using IEDs are common. Little efforts seems to have been made to initiate regular offensive patrols along the routes being used by the CRPF and the

police, a standard means of making ambushes more difficult. Just as worrying, India's multi-million dollar fleet of surveillance drones, not for the first time, failed to pick up any signs of an attack that involved over 200 insurgents.

- "These errors all point ot the fact that, many years into a counter-insurgency campaign that has been billed as country's most important, deficit of training, technology, leadership remain endemic. As in the past cases, New Delhi and Raipur has busied themselves criticising each other for the loss of lives. It is time for both to step forward and admit that they are accountable for mistakes made, and lay out a blueprint to make amends.

Comments

This editorial from *The Hindu* deserves a detailed examination since it is a Leftist publication. Its editor, N. Ram, was once a Card-holding Communist. This daily reflects his dogma in all its implications.

"15 ...police officers" were killed. It is a common fallacy among the Indian publication : 'Every one in the police is an officer'. There are no constables, no head constables. A sub-inspector may be deemed to be an officer, even though he is not one. But all ranks below him are not officers. But the Indian press insists on designating them as such. This ignorance is crass, and annoying to most congnoscenti.

"It is the latest in the string of hideous losses which India has accepted as the inevitable Costs of war inflicted by insurgents whom Prime Minister Manmohan Singh once described as the most serious threat to country's internal security. The sacrifices, if that is what it is, seem to be paying off as Maoist insurgency has been in steady decline since 2010-from 1180 lives lost that year to 421 in 2013. Choking of Maoists is evident : the key leaders have left the Party in Chhattisgarh and Odisha and its efforts failed to stop large turn-out in the 2013 Assembly polls in Chhattisgarh. Most of the arguments are either self-serving or misplaced."

- As for the Manmohan Singh's oft-quoted remark on the Maoist's violence, that seem to be the only contribution of the then Prime Minister to the debate. He singularly failed to check, much less reprimand, some Congress leaders like Digvijay Singh for their utterly irresponsible statements on the rebels, "our own misguided countrymen." Such statements affect the morale of lower ranks bearing the brunt of the Maoist attacks, and sow seeds of doubt in the mind of their commanders.

- "The sacrifice, if that is what it is", is indicative of the mind of Leftists and liberals in the country. They fight shy of calling it sacrifice when the country's braves lose their lives in anti-Maoist operations. It is reflective of the sick mind of such overground Maoists, whether they are in the NAC, owning a daily newspaper or esconced in the NGOs.
- The daily says the costs are inevitable, but they are worth it as the insurgency is on the decline. It is wrong on many counts. One, no leader of any importance has surrendered. Killed, they surely have been. If the voting turn-out was high, it is no thanks to the Maoists, as they did all they could to thwart the voters coming to the booths, but it is because of effective security forces actions, and even more importantly, the locals who trooped to the booth ignoring the Maoist's threat. It indeed is a tribute to indian electorate which is ready to face the bullets to reach the ballot box. Didn't they bravely reached the ballot boxes in Jammu and Kashmir ignoring the bullets of the Jihadists, to set a record of highest turn out in the 2014 Assembly polls?
- Again, the editorial makes a self-serving averment that the Maoists have failed to expand to small towns and cities. In fact, they have indeed, as will be seen in the next article, "Waiting for Maoists to encircle Delhi."
- If indeed, the security forces have succeeded in bringing down their losses between 2010 and 2013, then why is the paper blaming them for making repeated mistakes and incurring loss of lives?
- The paper lists a succession of tactical errors. "near-identical mistakes were made in disaster after disaster from Chintalnar to 2013 Congress leaders' slaughter". "The patrol headed blithely into the area where Maoists were preparing an ambush as per intelligence reports." It is a pity the civilians writing such editorials are either ignorant of matters military or wilfully write half truths to turn out a 'smart' copy! The Press, and Hindu in particular, should know that human beings do not blithely march into jaws of death—even if they wore the Army fatigues. They care for their lives, but willingly offer supreme sacrifice if needed to uphold the *izzat* of their unit and interests of the nation. If they understand the military ethos and requirements of a particular combat situation, the armchair specialists will not talk and speak so flippantly. As for the reports of prior intelligence inputs being available, less said the better! Have we known any tragedy, inflicted by the

terrorists, Maoist or Jihadist, when 'sources' reveal post-explosion that there were intelligence reports on the explosion that were not made use of! The intelligence people are clever, often too clever, to be credible. They always seem to be in the know of an attack by Maoists after it has happened.! If there were actionable intelligence, why would not a unit act on it? Mostly, the intelligence report are not specific e.g. "Maoists may attack a post in district 'A' of Jharkhand in Apr 2015. "Maoist may ambush a patrol on road B-D, a distance of over 85 km, in the first fortnight of July 2015. Maoists were seen assembling on Andhra-Odisha border first week of (last) May month." Another ploy of the sleuths: Renew a warning every year, every month or every fortnight! Press will always say: "Inspite of such intelligence reports, the troops marched on blithely. So, that is that!"

- Multi-million dollar fleet of surveillance drones failed, not for the first time, failed to pick up any signs of the attack that involved over 200 insurgents. Where is the fleet of drones? Perhaps, it is a reference to the IAF drones. They have agreed to place one or two of such machines at the disposal of the security forces for anti-Maoist operations. And it is not easy to pick up the Maoists in thick jungles. And they do not expose themselves to drones, well-trained as they are but who is interested in such realities and facts on ground. The press, like the Hindu, is interested in turning out a smart copy!

"Waiting for the Maoists to encircle Delhi : 3.7.2013

This article by Maj Gen Ashok Mehta appeared in the Pioneer.

Excerpts

- "The ambush by Maoists on 2 July (2013) in Jharkhand reflects total ill-preparedness of the country to deal with the insurgents. The Maoist threat will not be resolved any time soon. Like the monsoon's invasion of India's pride, the Delhi international airport, the Maoists will shortly migrate from rural to urban areas.
- "The recent Darbha ambush in Chhattisgarh, which wiped out the entire State Congress leadership, was meant to be a wake-up call for the sleepaholic establishment. Nothing, it seem, will shake the Government from its slumber till the Maoists arrive in Delhi, which is their political objective, with a war cry: "Dilli ghere lebo, ghere lebo" (we will besiege Delhi).

- "The British decided in 1925 to preserve the social fabric and culture of the tribals in the forested Dandakaranya belt, some 1,23,000 sq km bordering seven of the nine Maoist-affected states. Like in the Federally Administered Tribal Area in Pakistan, the British did not extend civil administration to Dandakaranya. The Maoists have fully secured 40,000 sq km of this area, where they run a parallel administration, calling it a liberated zone. Abujhmad in Chhattisgarh, which the security forces tried to penetrate recently, was found impregnable—covered with three lines of mines and defences—much like the departed Prabhakaran's *sanctum* sanctorum in Wanni in Sri Lanka. Colombo displayed political will and national unity to reclaim the liberated zone.
- "By contrast, New Delhi shied away from mounting a surgical operation in Chhattisgarh in 2005 following a drone detecting a big, hot maiost camp. The camp was not removed even after the Prime Minister and Home Minister showed extreme enthusiasm. The Maoist wound will become cancerous. There are varied and many reasons for this diagnosis. The Maoists are waging a full-blown insurgency to capture political power. It is not, and never was, a law and order problem, a preserve of a State Government under the Constitution. Internal security issue subsumes considerations of federal autonomy, and needs to be placed on the concurrent list.
- "It is apparent that State intelligence and police forces do not have requisite capability and motivation to subdue the Maoists. Neither do, at present, the Central police forces. Without a political consensus between the Central Government and Maoist-affected states, without putting aside the differences the ruling party at the Centre and those in the States and breaking the nexus between the States and the Maoists, no headway can be made. Clearly there are constitutional, political and capability problems which include the lack of unified counter-Maoist grid and strategy, backed by a unified command. Special Forces are required as also a more creative employment of the Army and IAF, for a break through. The Army, indeed, was used in West Bengal in 1969—a full Infantry Division and the Parachute Brigade — to form the outer cordon for the police to defeat the Naxals in the Birbhum (district) forest areas.
- "The big myth surrounding the Maoists is that they are fighting for the rights of tribals. They are doing nothing of the sort ; they

are only promoting their own political interests. When the Maoists in Nepal with whom they have fraternal links, abandoned the bullet for the ballot and urged their Indian counter-parts to join the political mainstream, the former were chastised by the latter for betraying the people's armed struggle. This is a load of gibberish. Maoists are anti-development and have excelled in depriving the tribals of what little development the State and Union Governments are able and willing to provide. They have demolished schools, health and welfare facilities, roads and culverts, bombed drinking water and sanitation projects…The list is endless.

- "The pro-tribal mirage of the Maoists is backed by a platoon of intellectuals who glibly talk of the 'alternate narrative': The Maoist understanding of democracy and development etc, and being Gandhians with guns. These 'Gandhians' have stuck grenades and IEDs in the skulls and abdomens of dead soldiers. This variety of barbarity was excelled only by Attila, the Hun. The misguided 'intellectuals' have put an undeserved halo around their heroes.
- "The recent Consensus in the all-party resolution on dealing with the Maoists was impressive, but it cannot hid the intrinsic institutional handicaps which continue to debilitate State and Central responsis. Neither in Jammu and Kashmir nor in the North-East did the Union of India allow the creation of a liberated zone. Sopore in Kashmir briefly enjoyed this status, but it was promptly cleared by the Army and the BSF. Freeing the 40,000 sq km, which is equal to the Chinese territorial claim in Ladakh, from the Maoists must be a priority task to re-integrate the tribals. You do not need an all-party resolutions like the ones against Pakistan and China to reclaim every inch of the territory lost.

Comments

This is an article by a senior retired Army officer, Maj Gen Mehta. He has made some pertinent observation as on Dandakaranya forest belt and suggestions like the one to put internal security on concurrent list of the Constitution. He is pleading for use of Army and IAF to fight Maoists, something publicly opposed by both the services. The solution possibly lies in finding a KPS Gill from the armed forces.

The General has mentioned Prime Minister Manmohan Singh's oft – quoted declaration that "Maoist insurrection is the most serious threat to India's internal security." To be generous to the Prime Minister, this Author feels that this is the only contribution he has made to the anti-Maoist campaign of the nation. Otherwise, his failure to gag irresponsible senior Congress leaders like Digvijay Singh against making misleading statements about the nature of Maoist insurrection is condemnable. One just can't understand, much less appreciate, his inability, or unwillingness, to control anti-national averments from such Congress leaders. When Digvijay publicly chastises Home Minister for allowing strict anti-Maoist strategy, Prime Minister's silence and his failure to back P. Chidambram are inexplicable. Even if Digvijay is deemed to be speaking for Rahul Gandhi, or at least, deemed to be close to him, the Prime Minister must publicly rebuke him. His silence emboldens some other leaders to follow Digvijay. A divided Government, unable to put its own house in order, can certainly not fight the hardened criminals which the Maoists are. More so, When the Maoists, have the tacit support of the 'intellectuals' of the Left –Liberal variety.

Notes

1. Mukesh Ranjan, the Pioneer, 10 Dec 2014.
2. K Srinivas Reddy, The Hindu, 14 Feb 2007.
3. Milind Ghatwai, Indian Expressing, 20 Jan 2007.
4. Omer Farooq, The Pioneer, 4 Feb 2007.
5. Staff Reporter, Asian Age, 4 Apr 2007.
6. Anisha Sheth, The Hindu, 7 Apr 2012.
7. Johnson TA, The Hindu, 29 Apr 2014.
8. Shaju Philip, Indian Express, 11 Jan 2015.
9. Biju Govind, The Hindu, 23 Apr 2012.
10. Shaju Philip, Indian Express, 25 Jul 2014.
11. VR Jayaraj, The Pioneer, 24 Sep 2014.
12. PNS, The Pioneer, 11 Nov 2014.
13. PNS, The Pioneer, 19 Nov 2014.
14. Shaju Philip, Indian Express, 30 Nov 2014.
15. PNS, The Pioneer, 8 Dec 2014.
16. VR Jayaraj, The Pioneer, 23 Dec. 2014.
17. Shaju Philip, Indian Express, 11 Jan 2015.
18. Shaju Philip, Indian Express, 23 Dec 2014.
19. TNS, Times of India, 27 Dec 2014.
20. VR Jayaraj, The Pioneer, 3 Jan 2015.
21. *Ibid,* 4 Jan 2015.
22. Shaju Philip, Indian Express, 6 May 2015.
23. *Ibid,* 5 Jul 2015.

24. *Ibid,* 10 May 2015.
25. Ashutosh Bhardwaj and Sagnik Chowdhary, Indian Express, 10 May 2015.
26. Anubhuti Vishnoi, Indian Express, 6 Jun 2007.
27. PNS, The Pioneer, 11 Jun 2007.

29

Central and Western India

This chapter will cover four states for Maoist activities:

1. Madhya Pradesh (MP)
2. Uttar Pradesh (UP)
3. Maharashtra
4. Gujarat.

Maharashtra is seriously affected

Of the four states, the three are marginally affected, or may be termed even lightly affected. Only Maharashtra among the four can be termed as seriously affected by the Maoist violence. The Gadchiroli area is the one worst-hit by Naxalism. To initiate Naxalism in Maharashtra, K Seetharammaiya sent his cadres from Andhra Pradesh into the Gadchiroli area in 1970s.

Presently, all the Naxal-hit districts of Maharashtra border three contiguous stated of MP, AP and Karnataka. Further details will be found in Maharashtra section of this chapter.

Madhya Pradesh

Backgrounder to the LWE in the State

Origin

It started in the late 1980s' when Chhattisgarh was still a part of Madhya Pradesh.

Bloody Era

1994-95 and 2004-05.

Key issues

Corruption, lack of development.

Status check

Naxalites occasionally target development works in Balaghat district.

CM Shivraj S Chouhan: In Jul 2010

"Those talking of bullets cannot be termed revolutionaries. Their aim is to capture power in Delhi."

Madhya Pradesh worried: Maoists reach Bhopal: 13 Jan 2007

It was a shock and surprise for the state Government when its police discovered a Naxal arms factory right in its capital town of Bhopal. Five suspected Maoist cadres were arrested from Satnami Nagar, a residential locality adjacent to an industrial area of Bhopal. Parts of weapons and ideological literature were seized from the premises on 11 and 12 Jan 2007.

The presence of LWE and running an arms manufacturing factory in Bhopal must make the MP Government sit up and take note of the growing threat. If all this while the State has been pressing the Centre for long to declare Sidhi district, which shares borders with UP and Chhattisgarh, Naxal-hit, it was caught unaware about this arms factory in its own capital, its front yard, so to say.

Balaghat, Mandla and Dindori districts have already been declared Naxal –affected. It needs a notice that since 1990, the State has recorded 360 cases of Maoist violence, though most of them minor ones, certainly not the type and intensity of those occurring in Chhattisgarh and AP.

CM Shivraj Singh Chouhan was honest enough to admit that it (discovery) was a warning signal and his Government needed to be alert[1].

The daily says the States inexperience to deal with a fall-out of such stunning discovery and huge seizures was admitted rather honestly: "We are not even sure if the names given by the five arrested suspects are true. So, it was only on 12 January the MP got in touch with their counterparts in Maharashtra, Andhra and Karnataka, the states the five say they hail from. He continues: "All of them speak good Hindi, but are not divulging anything. The teams from other states will help the MP Police in establishing the identity of the five, which include a woman. They may turn out to be some senior leaders, but at the moment there was confusion about their identity. We are finding it difficult to crack them".

This officer is speaking on the 12th to the press. This is where his 'inexperience' indeed shows up. The initial arrests were made a day earlier, and some seizures were made on the 12th. Where is the tearing hurry for this officer to share all this information with the press – so early in the day, so to say? May be, he was carried away by his circumstance and the occasion. Maybe, 'smart' journalists coaxed or provoked him into such unnecessary and avoidable speak. Worse still, this police officer was too young, too inexperienced to be allowed to face an aggressive press. May be, he was overwhelmed by the occasion, as suggested above.

One of the suspects displayed an aggressive stance, an apparent bravado, daring his interrogator to kill him: "I know you will kill us. Do it now!"

At their unit (arms factory), they maintained a low profile. Neighbours thought they ran a lathe machine behind the closed shutters and since they were South Indians, did not know Hindi. They worked for fixed hours, leaving the unit at 5 pm. They either walked to the unit, or used bicycles. The police were surprised to find posters of Hindu gods and goddesses at the unit. ADGP (intelligence) SK Rout explained it: "They did this to mislead others."

A team from the Andhra police was on its way to Bhopal on the 12th, to interrogate Madhukumar, who claimed to be a resident of Guntur. Other's arrested were : Madhukar's wife Rajlaxmi alias Sonam, Ashok alias Rajshekhar, Srinivas alias Anna alias Balamurli. The name of the fifth was not disclosed.

An interesting comment can be added here, with an advantage from hindsight! In an issue of a daily of 20 Jan 2007, there are details of five Maoist cadres' names and their career profile in the party. None of the four names disclosed by the suspects on the 11th matches with any given in the issue of the 20th. Obviously, they gave false names on the 11th. Possibly, Andhra police cracked the correct names of the five cadres. These are to be found under Gujarat coverage of the Maoist activities. The raid on the 11th in Satnami Nagar was followed by searched in Siddaharth Enclave, Bijli Nagar and Krishna Nagar, the meighbourhoods the suspects had lived. No further arrests were made from these locations, but the searches there did yield another cache of weapons and literature.

So Madhya Pradesh is too in it, well and proper this time. All this flowed from a functional Maoist arms factory.

Naxal arms factory unearthed in Bhopal: Jan 2007

The above story is also covered by another daily in its 16 Jan 2007 issue, which is examined here. Only additional details and information from this daily will be included in this narrative[2].

The opening paragraph on the news story in this daily is rather disparaging for the name and reputation of the MP Police.

> "The unearthing of an illegal Naxal arms factory, which is clandestinely supplying weapons to their cadres in states like Gujarat, Karnataka, Chhattisgarh etc, in the heart of the State Capital, seems to have made the MP Police extremely wary and cautious. "Never famed for their valour or daredevilry like their counterparts in Punjab or Jammu and Kashmir, officers of the rank of SP and above have promptly had their name plates removed from their staff cars, and a few even from their bungalows. Public appearances in uniform too are being curtailed[3]".

The factory, functioning for three years, was a key point in the Maoist weapons trail. The 11-13 January interrogation of the six inmates arrested earlier, revealed: "Their job was to train new recruits in the neighbouring states, especially Gujarat where an arms-making had been planned."

None of the six arrested was a common criminal. "They are intelligent and well-educated, and speak English, Hindi and Telugu fluently". That the ultras might have been planning something big was evident from size-able quantity of gunpowder seized. What is publicly known or disclosed seems to be only a tip of the iceberg, IB sources told the press. The ground reality could possibly be much worse.

The daily says with a certain concern that 'their (IBs) hands were tied due to the system – built restrictions". The bust-up in Bhopal, in fact, had already resulted in unearthing of another Naxal arms workshop in what was a joint operation of the Andhra and Odisha police forces.

When asked if the powers- that –be were aware of the magnitude of the threat the Maoists posed to the nation's security and the crisis it could be plunged into by their fanatical creed, violent Naxalism, the (official) sources said with an air of finality and certitude: "Eurything was known, even the finer details. "But the political will to tackle the Naxalism was lacking. Much of it has to do with the disproportionate influence wielded by the Communists in the current dispensation at the Centre. But the things were neither vastly better under previous regimes".

It is time that the nation, its leaders and intelligentsia realised that the danger posed to the nation's unity was in no way less than from terrorists. The two, Maoists and terrorists, had commonality of interest which was being overlooked, even ignored. This internal threat, gnawing at the vitals of the nation, should be taken seriously before it is too late.

The next entry also pertains to this very event of unearthing an arms factory in Bhopal on 11 Jan 2007, by a daily in its issue of 20 January, which gives more accurate details about the arrested cadres.

Bhopal (MP) : Hub of manufacturing for the CPI (Maoist) : Jan 2007

The MP police informed the press on 19 Jan 2007 that five hard-core Maoist cadres "were arrested last week after a Maoist weapons workshop was busted in Bhopal's Satnami Nagar area".

More importantly, they disclosed that they (Maoist) have an active *dalam* (an operational unit of the Maoists) in Surat, the textile city of Gujarat. As a large number of Andhra migrants are working in that industry in Surat, it is easy for Telugu-speaking cadres (from Andhra) to set up a *dalam* there.

What should worry the MP Government and its police is the fact of type of weaponry the maoist 'manufacturing unit' at Bhopal is capable of producing. Here are some related details. These five have been 'working' for six years in Bhopal. Before this, they had worked for two years at Jabalpur and another four years in Indore[4].

DIG Anuradha Shankar talked about their manufacturing capabilities. The Bhopal 'unit' yielded arms, components, literature and a huge stock of books on weaponry. The police claims it was the biggest Maoist library so far discovered. Shankar disclosed the Maoists, from making crude bombs, have come close to making rocket launchers like the RPG 7. Even more worrying is the fact of the military intelligence informing the MP police that "even the Indian Army has not as yet acquired the plastic grenades of the type recently recovered from the Maoists !"

Andhra police raid maoist hideouts in Bhopal and Rourkela: Jan 2007

Two raids by AP police on the key hideouts of Maoists in the latter half of Jan 2007 in Bhopal and Rourkela led not only to the arrest of senior cadres and recovery of arms and ammunition but more significantly to the seizure of a gold mine of information about the ultra outfit in the form of CDs, DVDs and hard discs. The sources in the state police say that all this material seized "contain so much information that it could take months to analyse it." the information could yield details about:

- Maoist network in different states, as also their own analysis of the past failures and future plans and strategies.
- The importance of this treasure trove could be measured from the fact that it also includes animation films on the assaults and counter-assaults against the police forces of different states and other targets.

- There is also technological information on the arms manufacturing and presentations for the training camps of the Maoists. some other points on the issue are summed up here.
- It is obvious that the seizure and information it affords to the security and the intelligence agencies will have serious and far-reaching implications for the organisational functioning and operating capabilities of the Maoists through out the country.
- The information yielded by the technical gadgetry has fully given out the present strength and location of the Maoist cadres in various parts of the country[5].

Besides the police officers from different states, the IB officials are also involved in analyzing the information contained in this gadgetry. Some analysts assert that the CPI(Maoists) has suffered this debilitating blow at a time when it is already on the run in AP, where several of its top leaders were eliminated by the police during 2006, curtailing the level of violence perpetrated by it. In a related report, it has been confirmed that Maoist leadership has been sending its cadres to new bases, yet to be consolidated, in the Western Ghats and Goa.

Maoists create R and D cells with experts : Mar 2007

Madhya Pradesh

The Maoists may have hundreds of weapons in their armoury, almost all looted from the police, and they certainly form the backbone of their fire power, but their far-sighted leadership looks far beyond this impressive treasure.

Preparing to take a high-tech route, they have set up a full-fledged R and D wing, tapping into growing network among scientists, “extending upto sensitive institutions like the Bhaba Atomic Research Centre (BARC)”. The BARC link might read incredible, but this and other information in this entry was revealed by the Government that the ultras used “an improved version of petrol bombs at the Rani Bodli police camp, massacering 55 of them”.

Now, the specifics of the *Barc* link. A married couple, found to have been working at it till recently, was discovered by the police to have ultra-Red background. When confronted by the authorities, the two did not conceal their ideological leanings.

The two might have, since, left the facility, but the case has put the security establishment on tenterhooks, shaken and deeply concerned over the network of the activists and sympathizers that the Naxals (might) have built among the scientific community.

Now comes Madhya Pradesh links to this disturbing story. "Security agencies recenty unearthed an R and D unit of the CPI(Maoist) near the capital of the State, Bhupal." A greater cause of concern was that they "found a number of such wings running in different parts of India[6]".

Even though Naxals are known to have used such petrol bombs earlier, the preliminary reports of the 15 March Rani Bodli attack revealed their more potent use, suggesting Maoist expertise in improving and making conventional bombs more lethal.

Uttar Pradesh

Uttar Pradesh can be deemed to be among the least Naxalism-affected states of India. The tables at the initial pages of this book indicate there were three Naxal-hit districts –Chandauli, Mirzapur and Sonbhadra—in UP, as per the Panchayat Raj ministry figures for 2006-07, on its website. The total for India was 55.

As many as 749 people were killed in the Naxalite conflict in India in 2006, says the Asian Centre for Human Rights Report for 2006, release on 10 Jan 2007 in New Delhi[7]. Among the 749 fatalities, two were in UP.

A bit surprisingly, the Planning Commission figures for the Naxal-hit districts stand at 125, as per the Times of India of 22 Sep 2007. UP contributes 6 to these 125.

Some incidents of Maoist relevance are detailed below.

UP claims success against Maoist violence : June 2006

The UP Government on 22 Jun 2006 claimed that the two pronged strategy to counter Naxalite insurgency has paid off as this year, 2006 (till mid-June) there had been no incidents in the State.

State Home Secretary RM Srivatava told the press that the success of the Government's strategy was evident from intelligence reports that most Naxal leaders in the three most affected districts of Chandauli, Mirzapur and Sonebhadra, had moved to neighbouring Bihar, MP, Jharkhand Chhattisgarh. Some of the ring leaders also migrated to AP.

As per the survey by the State Home Department and police, 680 villages in eight districts of Mirzapur, Chandauli, Sonebhadra, Ghazipur, Ballia, Mau, Deoria, and Kushinangr, were identified as centres of Naxalite presence in the State, with the problem being more acute in 23 police stations of Chandauli, Mirzapur and Sonebhadra districts, on the border with Bihar or near it.

The official esxplained the two-pronged strategy involved economic development of the identified areas under the Samagar Gram Vikas Yojna

(SGVY) and strict surveillence of the unlawful avtivities. He said the Union Government also wanted that State Government focuses more on development of the backward regions in a bid to find a permanent solution to the problem and root out the menace.

The CM had constituted a high-powered panel headed by Agriculture Minister Ashok Bajpai. It met on 20 Jun 2006 and decided to form a long-term plan for integrated development of these 680 villages under the SGVY.

Disclosing that Rs 114 cr was spent during the 2005-06 financial year under the scheme, the Home Secretary said Rs 180 cr was planned to be spent during 2006-07 on education, health facilities, rural roads and power generation.

Major Arms Haul in Varanasi: Apr 2007

The police on 20 Apr 2007 seized 6,000 detonators and 400 highly-explosive gelatin rods from the Ramnagar area of Varanasi, suspected to have been transported there by Naxals to disrupt the ongoing Assembly polls in UP.

Ramnagar police station incharge KD Tripathi told the journalists a police team on patrolling duty near the Vishwasunderi bridge on the border of Chandauli- Varanasi districts found the explosive materials lying abandoned in a jungle area late on the night 2012, April.

The seizure in the area prone to Naxalite activities, pointed to the possibility of the consignment having been brought for carrying out subversive acts to vitiate the electoral process in the region.

Another reason could be the plans of the MCC to avenge the killing of its self-styled Zonal Commander Sanjay Kol in Chandauli district earlier in the week in a gun battle. Luckily, the consignment did not reach the insurgents.

7 Feb 2010

UP police STF arrested 8 activists of CPI(Maoist) in Kanpur. Half a truckload of printed material, CDs and pen drives, and Rs 8.16 lakh in cash, were recovered from them. The arrested persons were:

1. Balraj @ BR @ Arvind @ Baccha Prasad, head of Northern Regional Bureau of CPI (Maoist). A close associate of Kobad Ghandhy.
2. Bansidhar alias Chintan da, a politburo member. Holds M.Phil degree from JL Nehru University, Delhi, was in jail for 3 years. Hails from Champaran district, Bihar.

3. Six cadres.

(The Pioneer, 2.2.2010 and the Times of India, 9.2.2010)

Maoist commander arrested for multiple murders has a ticket from jailed don's party: "out of jail, contest the poll": Mar 2014

It is an interesting aspect of Indian electoral democracy that one charged with serious crimes can contest a poll till he is convicted on these charges. There is one consequence that flows from this anamolous provision: A person of dubious character could sit as a legistatoe and law maker for years, given the gap between filing of on FIR and final conviction by a court of law. Be that as it may, here is an interesting news story on Maoist commander Lalvrat Kol, carried by a daily on 31 Mar 2014[8].

Kol, a Naxal commander jailed on charges of killing several policemen in UP, Bihar and Jharkhand is contesting the Sonbhadra seat for the Quami Ekta Dal, the party of jailed mafia don Mukhtar Ansari, for May 2014 Lok Sabha polls.

Hailing from Sonbhadra's Jhariyava village, Kol, as per police records, was the pioneer of the Naxal movement in UP, launching it in districts like Sonbhadra, Mirzapur and Chandauli.

Expectedly, his seat is Sonbhadra, the district he hails from, and from where he was arrested in 2012. Kol, 42, is lodged in Varanasi central jail.

Afzal Ansari, Mukhtar's brother and national president of Quami Ekta Dal, confirmed that the party has fielded Kol from Sonbhadra, and gave the reason, the party wants to bring "people who have lost hteir way", into the mainstream. Quami Ekta Dal workers have started campaigning for Kol in the constituency, party Vice President Athar Jamal Lari said. Sonbhadra goes to polls on 12 May, 2014.

"Two sisters of Lalvrat Kol, Pushpa and Kiran, too are lodged in jail for being associated with the Naxals groups", conceded Basmati Kol, cousin of Lalvrat and a member of the UP State Women's Commission. She said Kol and his wife Gyan Devi, have three children, the youngest a boy of nine. The family lives at Machigava village in Sonbhadra district. Basmati says : "All relatives are in the campaign. Meetings are being held seeking support for him."

Kol, who carried a bounty of Rs 1 lakh on his head, was arrested by Sonbhadra police following an encounter in Chopan area on 29 May 2012. Police claimed then that he was associated with the Songanga Vindhya Zonal Committee, which operates in the border areas of UP, Bihar and Jharkhand.

Kol, who was initially sent to Mirzapur jail, was shifted to Varanasi jail in 2013 on aadministrative grounds. Kol's lawyer Roshan Yadav said some 40 criminal cases are pending against him in districts such as Chandauli, Mirzapur and Sonbhadra, as also in Jharkhand and Bihar.

He admitted that Kol is accused of masterminding the attack on PAC truck in Chandauli district in 2004, in which 16 policemen were killed. He is also accused of leading the Naxal group that had attacked a PAC camp in Mirzapur and looted over a dozen SL rifles. Another case he faces is for leading a Naxal group that had triggered explosion at a forest office in Chandauli, killing three employees.

So, this is the story of journey from bullet to ballot.

Arundhati's picture on anti-Red banners triggers protests; Dec 2014

Police in UP's Maoist-affected Sonbhadra district have used a picture, supposedly of a Naxal group, in which noted writer Arundhati Roy is shown sitting with them in hoardings warning people against "falling in the Red trap".

Rights groups have raised the issue but police denied using Roy's image for publicity material. It appears the agency that made the hoardings sourced the picture from the website of a news magazine for which Roy had written a cover story on Naxals.

They were apparently unaware that the woman shown in the picture is the Man Booker Winner. But when the hoardings appeared on the Sonbhadra streets, there was an outcry and led to protests. The picture on the hoardings went viral on the social media.

SP Shiv Shankar Yadav told the daily: "I have made it clear that the woman shown in the hoardings put up by the police is not Arundhati Roy. If people are not ready accept our clarifications, they should consider the woman referred to as Arundhati is shown convincing the misguided youths to return to mainstream."

The SP said police use many fictitious characters and also real ones after seeking their consent in publicity material. Though the design of publicity material was given to local printers and advertising agencies three years back, print orders were not given.

The SP offers his clinching argument: "I ordered for the printing of publicity materials for a noble cause. No objectionable comments or remarks have been made against any one in any poster."[9]

Maharashtra

Backgrounder to the LWE in the State

Origin

The naxalites infiltrated Gadchiroli, one of Maharashtra's most backward districts, from Andhra Pradesh in the late 1980s.

Bloody era

1990 to 2010.

Key issues

Exploitation of tribal bamboo and tendu leaf collectors by contractors.

Status check

The movement is active in Gadchiroli.

CM Prithviraj Chavan : in Apr 2012

"We will do everything to stop the menace. Police are studying the Andhra strategy, which has been effective."

Maoists presence in Mahaashtra, some useful information: Early 2000s

In Maharashtra, the Naxals dominate the forests and mountainous tracts of the Gadchiroli and Gonda districts, and of late, have extended their influence to Chandrapur, and Yavatmal districts.

Compared to 2003, Naxal violence in the State increased by 15 per cent in 2004. The Maharashtra Government, which has chalked out a Rs 733 cr anti-Naxal programme for two districts of Gadchiroli and Chandrapur, has urged the Centre to set up a helicopter base in Nagpur, with a medical support team and station CRPF men there.

Besides the four districts mentioned above, two others –Bhandara and Nanded—have been designated as 'Naxalite-prone'. There six districts of Maharashtra, significantly border the Naxalism-affected districts of three neighbouring States:

- Districts of Adilabad, Karimnagar, and Nizamabad of Andhra Pradesh.
- Rajnandgaon, Bastar, Kanker and Dantewada of Chhattisgarh.
- Balaghat district of Madhya Pradesh.

"Dalits to be Maoists' Driving Force": Documents of Dec 2006

"Khair Lanji sparked a debate on the link between Naxals and the protests by Dalits in Maharashtra. This need not remain a speculation or a hypothetical proposition if we are to go by the policy documents of the CPI (Maoists) seized during the past two years, 2004 to 2006, and the recent letters believed to be written by CPI (Maoist) Secretary Chandra Kant to some newspapers. These documents show without any reasonable doubt that the Maoist plan to absorb Dalits in their fold already appears to be in full swing,"

Thus, wrote a daily on 18 Dec 2006[10].

A lucid document on strategy and tactics on Dalits

"Strategy and Tactics", a Naxal policy document issued by the Maharashtra State Committee to its cadres and seized immediately after the formation of the CPI (Maoist) in 2004 with the merger of the MCC and PWG, is a lucid articulation of their plans on the issue. The Maoist leadership must be congratulated on clarity of thought and deep strategic insight that mark this document. Maoist leaders are never short of thinking new ideas in crafting their new strategy to expand the LWE. The felicity of expansion and the linguistic skills that distinguish this document compel praise. The excerpts from the document as quoted by the daily follow.

- The document "Strategy and Tactics" say the "Dalits are treated as a special social section that is peculiar to the obnoxious caste-ridden Indian society. Though a vast majority among them belongs to poor and landless peasantry and to the proletariat and other wage-earning sections, they are also the victims of social oppression and upper caste atrocities."
- "While mobilizing the vast masses of Dalits, who constitute 17.5 per cent of Indian population, into the agrarian revolution, we must also lay special emphasis on the task of fighting all forms of social oppression and caste discrimination practised by upper castes against them."
- "Appropriate organisational forms should be evolved at various levels to fight the evils of untouchability, upper caste atrocities and other forms of discrimination. At the same time, we must desist from forming exclusively caste based organisation for the Dallits, which will only lead to their further segregation.
- "We must expose the hollowness of the politics of the ruling class and opportunist Dalit leaders who build their own electoral fortunes in the name of taking up Dalit issues."

Another document seized from arrested Maharashtra State Committee member Madan Lal, however, tries to distinguish between Prakash Ambedkar and other Republican party faction leaders:

"Athavale (Ramdas), Gavai (RS) and Dhasal (Namdeo) have lost their independent public base and have become puppets in the hands of main ruling parties. By taking up a broad socio-economic programme, Prakash Ambedkar tries to break ahead of the exclusive Dalit cordon, but it has not been able to gather momentum as, because of semi-capitalist class, Dalits remained within the political framework."

While decrying the "petty bourgeoisie" exclusive Dalit organisations, the 2005 document, as a matter of strategy, advises to "sometimes work jointly with these bourgeoisie organizations while exposing the reformism and opportunism of the leadership".

Interestingly, the 2005 document also eulogizes efforts to establish a separate Maratha region called Shiv Dharma by Purushottam Khedekar, a State PWD engineer. "It has come up to counter Hindutva politics and Brahmanism", says the document.

The 2004 document also refers to the murder of goon Akku Yadav in a Nagpur court two years ago, seeing in it the revival of the dormant women's movement. This only shows how 'ideological blinkers' enable the dyed-in –wool ideologues to put whole meanings and implications into a single such incidents.

Now comes an official of the State Government with his own takes, perhaps well thought-through, on the issue: "The linking of the Naxalites to the post-Khairlanji struggle attracted ridicule and criticism, but documents clearly show how Maoists have been taking keen interest in Dalit struggle since the past two years. The attempt here is to exploit the Dalits' ire to swell their ranks."

Prakash Ambedkar vs other Dalit leaders, Maoist document of 2005

Another documents seized from arrested Maharashtra State Committee member Madan Lal shows the Maoists keep a sharp eye on the political equations in the State. They feel the Dalits have not been able to make much of their legacy here: "Athavale (Ramdas), Gavai (RS) and Dhasal (Namdeo) have lost their independent public base and become puppets in the hands of main ruling parties."

By taking up a broad socio-economic programme, Prakash Ambedkar tries to break ahead of the exclusive Dalit cordon, but it has not been able to gather momentum as, because of semi-capitalist class, Dalits remained within the political framework.

While decrying the "petty bourgeoisie" exclusive Dalit organisations, the 2005 document, as a matter of strategy, advises to "sometimes work jointly with these bourgeoisie organisations while exposing the reformism and opportunism of the leadership".

Interestingly, the 2005 document also eulogizes effort to establish a separate Maratha region called Shiv Dharma by Purushottam Khedekara, a state PWD engineer. "It has come up to counter Hindutva politics and Brahmanism", says the document.

The 2005 document also refers to the murder of goon Akku Yadav in Nagpur court two years ago, seeing in it the revival of the dormant women's movement. This only shows how ideological blinkers' enable the dyed-in-wool ideologiues to put whole meanings and implications into a single such incident.

Now comes an official of the State Government with his own take, perhaps well thought through, on the issue: "The linking of the Naxalites to the post-Khairlanji struggle attracted ridicule and criticism, but the documents clearly show how Naxalites have been taking keen interest in Dalit struggle since the past two years. The attempt here is to exploit the Dalits ire to swell their ranks."

Maharashtra State Committee Documents: Dalits to be Maoists' driving force :Dec 2006

Khair Lanji sparked a debate on the link between Naxals and the protests by Dalits in Maharashtra. This need no longer remain a speculative postulation or hypothetical proposition if we are to go by the policy documents of the CPI (Maoist) seized during the past two years, 2004 to 2006, and the recent three letters believed to have been written by Maharashtra CPI (Maoist) Secretary Chandra Kant to some newspapers.

These documents show beyond any reasonable doubt that the Maoists' plan to absorb Dalits in their fold already appears to be in full swing.

"Strategy and Tactics", a Maoist policy document issued by the Maharashtra State Committee to its cadres and seized immediately after the formation of the CPI (Maoist) in 2004 with the merger of erstwhile MCC and PWG, is a lucid document. The Maoist leadership deserves to be felicitated for clarity of thought and deep strategic insight that mark this document. The Maoist leadership is seldom short of ideas in crafting its new strategic plans. The felicity of expansion and linguistic skills that mark this document demands prise.

The excerpts from the document, as quoted by a daily dated 18 Dec 2006, are given here[11].

- Though a vast majority among them belong to poor and landless peasentry and to the proletariat and other wage-earning sections, they are also the victims of social oppression and upper caste atrocities.

- While mobilizating the vast majority of Dalits who constitute around 17.5 per cent of the Indian population into the agrarian revolution, we must also lay special emphasis on the task of fighting all forms of social oppression and caste discrimination practised by upper castes against them.
- Appropriate organisational forms should be evolved at various levels to fight the evils of untouchability, upper caste atrocities and other forms of discrimination. At the same time, we must desist from forming an exclusively caste- based organization for the Dalits, which will only lead to their further segregation.
- "We must expose the hollowness of the politics of the ruling classes and opportunistic Dalit leaders who build their own electoral fortunes in the name of taking up Dalit issues".

Naxal- Timber Mafia Links Maharashtra : Jan 2007

The arrest on 14 Jan 2007 of seven Naxals of the Pratighatana faction and 16 timber smugglers by the Gadchiroli police in the area beyond Asarali, in the southern part of Gadchiroli district on the Andhra Pradesh border has for the first time established a Naxal- timber mafia link.

Special IGP (Anti- Naxal Operations) Pankaj Gupta told a daily that seven Naxalites were arrested after an encounter. Further details: "they were in the process of transporting wooden logs, 150 of which have been seized from them. We had made smaller seizures earlier and knew there was a link. But this is the first time that we caught the smugglers along with the ultras. This clearly establishes an organized Naxal-timber mafia link..... Rs 50,000 too were recovered from them."

The press was told that "the police will produce the arrested lot before a magistrate in Karimnagar district where the arrests were technically affected after a hot pursuit, and seek their transfer to Gadchiroli."

Naxalites target the vehicles during local polls: Mar 2007

Naxalites set ablaze two vehicles on 8 Mar 2007 in Gadchiroli district and one a day earlier on the 7th at Kondamahi, belonging to an NCP candidate.

In another incident, 25-30 Naxalites from the Tipagarh *dalam* captured a vehicle at Karwafa and later set it afire.

These incidents were staged on the eve of the Zila Parishad polls scheduled for 11 Mar 2007.

Maoists face cadre crunch in Eastern Maharashtra : Jul 2007

Police sources said 3 Jul 2007 that the Maoist movement in the most-affected Gadchiroli and Gonda districts in Eastern Maharashtra "has weakened with some of the *dalams* operating in the area virtually winding up following a cadre crunch'.

The shrinking number of cadres has forced the Nazal leaders in Vidharbha region of the State to wind up four of their *dalams* : Gamini, Kotagaon, Dhanora and Jimmalghatta.

The Naxal quartet led by Murli alias Mahesh Reddy, arrested by Nagpur police on 8 May (2007), have also confirmed the intelligence inputs of the police that there has been no fresh recruitment for quite a long time.

Additional DGP (anti-Naxal Operations) Pankaj Gupta, confirming the depletion in the Naxal cadre, said : "In a desparate move, Naxals are shifting some of their cadres from the adjoining Chhattisgarh". Citing reasons for weakening of the LWE movement in Vidharbha, Gupta said the 'gaonbandi' (barring entry into the villages) scheme of the Maharashtra Government proved very effective as villagers are putting up a stiff resistance to their movements.

Besides, a member of Naxals and their supporters have already surrendered to avail certain benefits, including cash money, while some of their cadres are on way to abandon the Naxalism.

Filling up vacancies : A contrast : Government versus Maoists : Jun 2007

Analysts have noted a curious mismatch when it comes to the question of filling up sensitive posts by the government and the Naxalites.

Even a month after Shirish Jain's transfer from the post of SP Gadchiroli, the Government has still not announced a replacement for the crucial position in the State's crucial Naxal heartland.

In an obvious contrast, the Maoists are quick to replace Divisional Secretary of North Gadchiroli- Gondia Divisional Committee, Muralee, by sending Anand, a senior cadre from AP. Muralee was arrested last month (May 2007) by Nagpur Police along with Arun Ferrier of Mumbai and two others from Deekshabhoomi Nagpur[12].

Anand joined within five days of Murali's arrest. In contrast, the Government has been making do with Gonda SP Cherring Dorje who is holding additional charge of Gadchiroli since 6 May (2007).

Meanwhile, DGP P S Pasricha told the daily that he "will issue the order for the new incumbent either today or tomorrow". But we refused to divulge the name of the new officer being sent.

A month after Jain's exit, Naxals staged a bandh against the arrest of Murali and Ferrier, and they followed it up with an economic blockade.

A senior official talks honestly to the daily: "It is widely known that nobody wants to take up the Godchiroli post for obvious reasons. That, unfortunately, also highlights the motivational difference between the Naxalites and police". Another reason why nobody wants to go there is that the promise to shift an officer from there is rarely kept.

The daily in question has headlined its news story rather suggestively if, also, meaningfully, "Godchiroli gets a new Naxal boss...."

- **2005.** 14 policemen killed in two Naxal attacks in Gondia and Gadchiroli districts.
- **15 Jun 2008.** Maoists behead Anand Ram Koram, former member of their party who had earlier surrendered to the police. They also warned another former cadre who had surrendered with Koram. They are very sensitive towards the police informers, especially so towards their surrendered erstwhile colleagues! The two had surrendered in Dhanora Tehsil, North Gadchiroli[13].
- **16 Jun 2008.** Naxalites slit the throat of Laxman Parlipal.
- **26 Aug 2008.** A Divisional Committee member Suresh Harami surrenders before Godchiroli police, along with Dalam Commander and a Deputy Dalam Commander.
- **26 Oct 2008.** 80 Maoists killed four policemen in Godchiroli.
- **1 Feb 2009.** Ultras gunned down a team of 15 Maharashtra policemen of Chhattisgarh-Maharashtra border. A woman leader Narmada, reportedly led the attack.
- **21 May 2009.** 16 cops killed by Maoists in Godchiroli district.
- **8 Oct 2009.** A 40-man police patrol was ambushed by a 300 Maoist guerrilla band, killing 17 policemen in the jungles of Godchiroli. Tarakka, wife of Central Committee member and Maharashtra In-charge Mullajhola Venugopal alias Bhupati, was involved in planning the operation in her capacity as South Gadchiroli Division committee member. Apart from Tarakka, Eaitu, the dreaded local commander-in-chief of Maoists and member of DK SZC, was the other instrument of planning the ambush (The Times of India), 10 Oct 2009.

- **4 Oct 2009.** Naxals killed six police men in an encounter at Tadgaon, in Gadchiroli district. Kishanji, No. 2 of CPI (Maoist), said Gadchiroli killing was meant to avenge the murder of senior Maoist military strategist Marang by alleged CPI (M) cadres and the police. He further added, "Gadchiroli was only an exercise to warn the police against such misadventures".

Ominous Feb 2009 for Maharashtra

Feb 2009 was marked by the killing of 15 policemen in an ambush spring by the Maoists on Sunday 1 February. The police team that get ambushed was headed for site of the 30 January Maoist attack.

The succeeding pages cover the grievous incident and consequent actions and events in great detail.

Maoists kill 15 State policemen in jungle ambush: 1 Feb 2009

In one of the worst Maoist attack on security forces in Maharashtra, 15 policemen including a sub-inspector (SI) were killed in the jungles of Markegaon village in Dhanora tehsil of Gadchiroli district, some 300 km from Nagpur, on 1 Feb 2009 morning. No casualties were reported among the ultras[14].

Police believe some 40 Maoists of the newly created Border-platoon Dalam sprung the ambush.

Markegaon is close to the Gyrapatti – Sawargaon road and Gyrapatti police assistance centre, which is near the Maharashtra – Chhattisgarh border.

The last time the State suffered police fatalities in similar large number was in 1992 when nine of the policemen were gunned down in the Gondia district.

The police SI killed was identified as Bhupendra Gudgekar of Amravati. A number of cops took bullet injuries. "The police party was heading towards Markegaon, some 45 km from Dhanora, to investigate the 30 January arson committed by the Maoists, when the ultras attacked them. "The police party was ambushed in such a manner that all the members, including the SI, were killed on the spot".

The ambush took place at 11 AM. When a relief team reached the site to help the ambushed, they too came under fire, preventing any rescue effort. That was possible only in the late afternoon of that day when 3,000 –strong reinforcement made it to the site. This strength was obviouslsy aimed at conducting combing operations in the jungles near the site of the ambush.

This ambush, obviously, resulted from an incident when some 40 Maoist cadres of Tippagarh Dalam torched a road roller and tractor deplayed for building a bridge near Markegaon village on Sawargaon- Kotgul road on 30 January. The policemen were on their way to investigate the incident of arson when they were ambushed.

Now the politician speak ! State MoS Home Nitin Raut, condemned the attack and said : "Not satisfied with killing the cops, the Maoists also placed explosives on their dead bodies. They also took away the weapons". He admitted that State's anti- Naxal operations helicopter was not flight worthy for the last few months. But another chopper flew to Dhanora from Nagpur for rescue work. The bodies of the policemen were airlifted to Gadchiroli by the 1st evening.

One fails to understand why do ministers can't resist the temptation to address the press on such incidents of Maoist violence. Why the MoS Home here has to pass 'SILLY' remarks. The IGP or DGP should be the man to brief the press after such incidents.

The daily publishes a list of some recent Naxal attacks.

Recent Naxal Attacks

- **10 Nov 2008:** 10 Mizo battalion soldiers killed in Chhattsgarh.
- **7 Nov 2008:** 11 security personnel killed in Chhattisgarh's Bijapur district.
- **10 Oct 2008:** 12 CRPF troopers killed at Kongupelli in Bijapur.
- **30 Aug 2008:** 11 policemen killed in Jharkhand's East Singhbhum.
- **29 Aug 2008:** 15 policemen killed in Bijapur, Chhattisgarh.
- **29 Jul 2008:** 36 elite Greyhound commandos killed in Odisha's Malkangiri bordering Andhra after Maoist attack, and sink their motorboat.
- **16 Jul 2008:** At least 20 policemen killed in Malkangiri, Odisha.
- **15 Feb 2008:** 13 policemen killed in Odisha.
- **20 Dec 2007:** 12 security personnel killed at Kistavam in Dantewada, Chhattisgarh.
- **15 Mar 2007:** 55 cops killed at Rani Bodli, Bijapur, Chhattisgarh.

"Women led attack" Informer lured police into Naxalite trap in Maharashtra: 3 Feb 2009

A woman named Narmada led the deadly Maoist attack that killed 15 policemen in Gadchiroli on 1 Feb 2009. Her deputy too was a woman, named Taraka alias Vimlaa. That is what intelligence sources speaking on the customary condition of anonymity told a daily[15].

The attack in the jungles of Marke village was a joint operation of the North Bastar and Gadchiroli units of the CPI (Maoist). Narmada, 44, a college drop-out from Andhra, has been leading the Maoists' Gadchiroli unit since shortly after the death of its last leader, Shivanna, who was killed in a police encounter in Chhattisgarh in 2008. She is married to Maoist leader Sudhakar alias Kiran who works for outfit's publicity wing.

Her deputy, Taraka, a tribal girl from Gadchiroli, is also the wife of a senior Maoist leader, Bhupathi. He is a member of the Group's Central Committee.

Since she took charge, Narmada has entrusted key posts to women. Most of her local organisational squads, which consists of 10-15 Maoist cadres each, are headed by women.

The State police lunched a massive search to find the group. Over 2,000 heavily armed personnel have been deployed for combing operations in the area, which is 80 km by road from the district headquarters, Gadchiroli town.

70 policemen have been killed by Maoists in Gadchiroli and Gondia districts of Vidarbha since 2002, says the Anti-Naxal Operations unit of the State police. Naxalites of PWG, and later of the CPI (Maoist) have been active in this area since 1980.

DGP Maharashtra A N Roy denied media reports that bodies of the policemen who died in the attack had been mutilated, saying this is absolutely.

Agencies investigating the attack say the Maoists used a police informer to draw the policemen to their deaths. The ultras knew about the movement of the police team, who were on their way to investigate the burning down of a road roller and a tractor by the Maoists on 30 January.

Maharashtra, Chhattisgarh launch operation against Maoists : 2 Feb 2009

The police forces of the two states launched joint operations against the Naxals who killed 15 policemen on the first February. Fresh report said the ambush was spring by 100-strong ultras, divided into five squads, of 20 each. When the police team reached Marke village, they were fired upon from all sides.

The policemen, armed with 8 × AK-47, 2 × INSAS rifles, 6 × SLRs one 2" Martar and one pistol, retaliated and a heavy exchange of fire ensued. The battle lasted for over an hour, in which 15 policemen lost their lives. This information was given by Vijay Chafle, Dy SP (Headquarters), at Godchiroli.

Godchiroli Collector Niranjan Kumar Sudhanshu said the encounter ended at 12 PM, having started at 11.15 AM. "Combing operation by a police team is continuing at Dhanora, bordering Chhattisgarh", says Sudhanshu. SDPO Godchiroli Sandeep Bhaji Bhakare chips in: "Forces have been mobilized to track the attackers".

Political side of it

CM Ashok Chavan visited the district next day, on the 2nd, to offer his condolences. He said at a recent cabinet meeting at Delhi, it was perceived that Naxalism in Maharashtra was on the decline. However, this incident was a sad development, "the state would now intensify anti-Naxal operations".

"Sunday attack is believed to be in retaliation to the arrest of 15 Naxals last week by the Anti- Naxal squad at Ettapalli Taluka in Godchiroli district. The district is a Naxal stronghold, bordering Chhattisgarh. It has seen many a deadly attack. In 2008, four police 'officers' were killed in the Rajaram Khanla region of south Godchirol. In 2006, seven police 'officers' were killed in a landmine blast at Bewartola in Gondia district. In 2005, blasts in Godchiroli and Gondia districts killed 14 police 'officers'. In 2003, a landmine blast killed five police 'officers' near Hemalkasa village of Godchiroli".

Comment

It is sad to know that the scribe and this daily believe and convey that Maharashtra police have ONLY officers in its RANKS.

Maharashtra wants Air Force base in Godchiroli after Naxal ambush : 6 Feb 2009

"Following the Naxal ambush in Godchiroli last Sunday (1 Feb 2009) that claimed the lines of 15 policemen, the State Government will request the Centre to let the IAF set up an operational base in the region". This was a daily speaking in its issue of 6 Feb 2009[16].

The government's desire for an air base, officials said, was needless. There is a functional air strip in Gondia (20 minutes flying time from the Godchiroli forests) and Nagpur (half an hour's flight away).

Home Department officials believe that the idea of setting up an AF station in Godchiroli is not advisable given the dense forest cover in this Naxal-hit region: "Helicopters are not bullet proof. They are sitting ducks for any bullets shot from an unseen tree – top."

Moreover, Chavan's statement flies in the face of State's own inadequate response to combating Naxal attacks in Godchiroli/ Maharashtra.

Sources said though Maharashtra is among the worst Naxalism – hit states, it has not only shown little initiative in facing the problem but has also failed to respond to the Centre's overtures.

Chavan said A P, Chhattisgarh and Maharashtra were planning to pool their resources for a joint strategy, but an anti – Naxal plan, put in place by the Centre, is yet to take off in Maharashtra due to government's inertia on the issue. In fact, the State, has not even responded to a year-old plan to set up an elite anti-Naxal unit in the state, called COBRA. It is learnt that government has yet not allotted any land for this proposed unit. "If put into place, this unit will anyway build an airstrip for its operations," said an officer.

Chavan said: "if necessary, the state was ready to pay for the AF station in Godchiroli. We need a larger air base which will accommodate bigger helicopters like Mi-8 for conducting Naxal operations." The regular helicopters are not good enough.

The cabinet has also decided to set up an airport with the help of Maharashtra Airport Development Corporation for quick deployment of troops.

The government decided to award the same terms of compensation to the families of policemen who died in the 1 February ambush.

In reply to a question whether poor weaponry did the police team in, Chavan said: "There is no need to believe that. The policemen had AK-47s and pistols. The naxals were just too many to be overpowered".

The Cabinet has also approved a Rs 13,86.51 Cr package for speedy development of six Naxal – hit districts such as Godchiroli, Chandrapur, Gondia, Yavatmal, Nanded and Bhandara over three years, starting 2009-10.

13 arrested for Gadchiroli carnage : 7 Feb 2009

The police arrested 13 persons from four villages in north Godchiroli for their suspected involvement in 1 February massacre of 15 policemen near Markegaon.

Of the 13 arrested, six are from Markegaon, three from Bandur, three from Katezari and one from Gurekasa village, all closely located. They were produced before a court in Kurkheda, and were remanded to police custody for 12 days.

S P Gadchiroli Rajesh Pradhan tells the daily : "All the arrested were present at the scene of action when the accident occurred and have a criminal record. Some of the villages in the vicinity of Markegaon have long been supporting Naxals. At least, 10 Dalam members from various Dalams are known to belong to Markegaon and Kosmi[17]".

Some years ago, when Rajvardhan was Godchiroli S P, a police team that had gone for search operations to Kosmi village was attacked. The village women had provided shelter to the attackers, forcing the police to call women cops and arrest the people wanted in various cases of arson.

Early 2008, some Kosmi residents had demolished the house of police commando Arvind Madavi in nearby Harange village and attacked his parents who were later evacuated by police. A 120- strong police team had conducted an operation in the village which had put up stiff resistance. "Our force was fired at from inside the village and we later recovered some 15 fire arms", Pradhan said.

45-year old Maina Pandi Naitam was among the arrested. Her Condition suddenly deteriorated and she was administered treatment on the spot. Later she was taken to Godchiroli but she died before getting any further treatment. The case, being an instance of custodial death, was handed over to the CID and post-mortem was conducted by a panel of four senior doctors at Nagpur Government College. The report had cited cardiac arrest as cause of death.

"The woman was the president of Naxal Range Commiittee that controlled five to six nearby villages and was suspected to be involved in the killing of PSI Dharmaji Surjagade from Gyarapatti police station two years ago. Her husband and son are active Naxal Dalam members", Pradhan said. That she was a Naxal cadre later became clear when the Naxal mouth piece *Prabhat* paid glowing tributes to her in its July- December issue.

"But later we decided to reach out to the villagers and I personally visited Kosmi and asked them what their demands were. They listed many of them. So, we conducted Operation Sarvodaya Camp in Jul 2008 and provide land extracts, caste certificates and such other documents to many villagers. We also organised a medical camp at the village. The villagers had then taken a pledge that they would not indulge in Naxal activities. But that apparently was not to be", the SP said.

Red terror in Maharashtra

A maoist attack on 15 policemen in Maharashtra gives the lie to the claim that the Naxalites have been controlled, writes T N Raghunatha, and exposes the Chief Minister's lack of understanding of the Naxal situation in the State

It is an analytical article in a daily on the ambush incident that resulted in 15 fatalities, in its issue of 8 Feb 2009, and it is the last one on that tragic incident. More significantly, it is obvious from its blurb, as reproduced above, that the article is critical not only of Maharashtra State and its police, but also of Chief Minister Ashok Chavan[18].

It is reproduced blow word for word

- Apart from sending a chill down the spines of the Anti-Naxal Squad in the State, the gruesome killing of 15 policemen in a Naxalite ambush in Markegaon of Gadchiroli district on 1 Feb 2009, has come as an embarrassment for CM Ashok Chavan.
- For, on 7 Jan 2009, Chavan had – while addressing a high – level meeting of C Ms from Naxal-hit states convened by PM Manmohan Singh in New Delhi – claimed that the Maharashtra Government had succeeded in reining in the Naxalites operating in the eastern districts of the State like Gadchiroli, Chandrapur, and Gondia. Chavan had made this claim while presenting a Rs 1,350 Cr Special Action Plan (SAP) for 38 talukas in six Naxalite-infested districts - - Gadchiroli, Chandrapur, Gondia, Bhandara, Yavatmal and Nanded – in the Vidarbha region and was seeking a 50 per cent assistance from the centre to implement the plan.
- The 1 February events exposed the CM's lack of understanding of the Naxal situation in the State Second, the attack laid bare the hoplessness of the Maharashtra police in combating the Naxal groups operating in the Maharashtra districts bordering Chhattisgarh and Andhra Pradesh.
- It is instructive to look at the sequences of events leading to the massacre. Of the 17 police personnel present at the Gyarapatti police station, located 10 km away from the Chhattisgarh border, 15 policemen, led by Sub Inspector Bhupend Ugdekar, left for Markegaon, a tiny village with a population of 400. Their mission was to inquire into the burning down of two tractor trolleys by a group of Naxalites in the village, a few days prior to the ambush.
- Little did the ill – armed policemen know what was in store for them at Markegaon, where 200- odd armed Maoist cadres were laying an ambush for them. Immediately after reaching, the policemen were waylaid by the Naxalites, who fired at them with AK -47s, SLRs and LMGs. The police party returned fire for a brief period. Before long, all the 15 policemen were felled.
- Not satisfied by killing the policemen, the ultras dismembered their bodies, and tied hand grenades to the body parts in a bid to inflict more casualties on police search parties. Their play did not

work since the Special C – 60 Anti – Naxal Squad that visited the site after the incident had foreseen such a mischief by the Naxalite attackers.

- Though ADGP (Anti – Naxal Operations) Pankaj Gupta claimed the police team had killed "7 to 18" Naxalites in what he described as an "encounter" between the two sides, the police did not manage to lay down their hands on the body of even one Naxalite – a development that suggested that the police men had completely been overpowered by the 200 – strong Naxalite group.
- The 1 February ambush has brought to the fore the shortcomings faced by the Maharashtra police in general and the Anti – Naxal Squad in particular, in combating Naxalites operating in the eastern parts of Maharashtra.
- Sadly enough, the visiting police party had no intelligence whatsoever that 200 Naxals would be lying in wait for them at Markegaon. Nor did they have the cover in the form of trained C – 60 Anti – Naxal Squad members.
- From the look of it, Markegaon villagers had kept the visiting police team in the dark – either deliberately or out of fear – about the presence of so many armed Naxalites in their village. How else can one explain the manner in which the police walked into the trap laid by the ultras on the outskirts of Markegaon?
- Retired IPS officer M N Singh, who was instrumental in setting up a jungle warfare centre for lthe Anti – Naxal squad at Nagpur, sympathises with the police personnel killed in the "Naxal ambush when he says : "You must realize that the police personnel in the Naxal – infested areas are operating in a difficult terrain and hostile environment. They do not receive the necessary cooperation from villagers who most of the time refuse to open their mouth, fearing threat to their lives from the Naxalites. The intelligence failure in the Markegaon incident seems to have more to do in the apparent lack of cooperation from the villagers concerned, than anything else."
- "Let us face it, the police cannot take on the Naxalites in such remote areas unless they have the support of the local people. It is the responsibility of the concrned State Government to take measure to build confidence among the people in Naxal infested villages so that the police bebefit from their imputs," Singh adds.
- CM Ashok Chavan may have erred in thinking that the Naxalites in eastern Maharashtra had been reined in, but his new SAP

scheme for 38 *talukas* in six Naxalite-infested districts in Vidarbha region, though it comes late, seems to be a step in the right direction. The State Government has said that it would utilise a part of the Rs 1,350 cr package for purchasing Mi-17 helicopters and weapons like grenade launchers for use in Naxal infested areas. It remains to be seen, though, how much of the money would be used for purchasing arms, ammunition and other material required for the Anti – Naxal operations, even while taking care of the tribals in the Naxal - belt of the Maharashtra.

- As expected, the State Government has announced that its police personnel would work in close coordination with their counter – pasts in the States of Chhattisgarh, Andhra Pradesh and MP to fight the growing Naxal threat. Even in the past, the Maharashtra government had made similar statements, but not backed them up with action. The absolute lack of coordination among the Naxalite – hit States becomes evident from Chavan's statement that Maoists behind the 1 February incident had come from a neighbouring State.
- Let alone arresting the insurgents behind the Markegaon ambush, the Maharashtra police have so far not been able to pinpoint which Naxal outfit or group the Naxals belonged to. The police suspected two to three Naxal groups had – under the leadership of Dandakaranya Zonal Committee functionary Diwakar alias Mangal Singh and his wife Jyoti – jointly organised the attack on the police personnel. There are no answers yet from the police top brass to questions like how the 200 –odd Naxalites escaped after the ambush or whether they were still holed up in the Maharashtra jungles. And if they have indeed fled the State, them which neighbouring State they have taken shelter in?

Medha Lekha to be the first village to harvest bamboo after 150 Years: 23 Apr 2011

Over 150 years after a traditional right of poor tribals – to harvest bamboo – was snatched by British Government, it will be restored next Wednesday (28 Apr 2011) in a small tribal village of Naxal – infested Gadchiroli district of Maharashtra.

Medha Lekha in the district will become the first village in India where harvesting bamboo will be recognised as a community right of tribals and other forest dwellers.

Since 1857, bamboo has remained under the grip of India's forest bureaucracy, which has refused to let go of this money spinning forest produce. It finally became a legal right for forest bureaucracy when the British enacted the Indian Forest Act in 1927, which categorized bamboo as a tree, thereby preventing local forest dwellers from harvesting them without requisite permission from the forest department. The regime had been followed in the independent India.

The change became possible after Environment Minister Jairam Ramesh in March (2011) informed the state governments that bamboo will not be treated as a tree under the Indian Forest Act anymore and will be considered a minor forest produce like tendu leaf.

Congress-ruled Maharashtra was the first state to leap on the opportunity provided by Ramesh, a Congress minister in the Centre. The right will be granted to Mendha Lekha village in presence of Maharashtra CM Ashok Chavan and Ramesh Next Wednesday (28 Apr 2011).

"In slain Maoist's, village, nothing to back up government claims"

31 Jan 2012

"A week ago, six militants of the CPI (*Maoist*) were shot dead by commandos of Maharashtra's anti – Naxal C-60 force at Govindgaon, a village in Godchiroli district. Shankar Anna alias Munneshwar Jagatu Lakada, 43, was leading the Maoist squad that organized the meeting on the 19 January (2012) night at Govindgaon, villagers say."

"Gadchiroli police say Shankar Anna was secretary of the CPI (Maoist) Aheri Area Committee and Divisional Committee member of the South Godchiroli Division. He hailed from Raman tola village in Etapalli tehsil. The village of this slain Maoist stands testimony to the government's efforts at developing the Naxal – hit areas."[19]

These are two opening paragraphs of a report on the issue of development of Maoist – affected areas in a daily of 31 Jan 2012.

A small village with 60 households, Ramantola straddles the borders of Chhattisgarh and Maharashtra. It has no road connectivity. A Maoist sympathizer says the village is almost part of the Naxal liberated zone, but it has no Naxal Jantana Sarkar.

Some police sources say the Maoists have never been able to establish a *Jantana Sarkar* in Godchiroli. "An attempt was made, but swift police action put paid to their plans". But the Central and State Governments have no presence in village either.

Ramantola is 30 km from Kasansur, a town with road connectivity. From Kasansur, one has to walk down to Sewari, a village seven km away which can be reached by a two – wheeler. From Sewari, one has to walk the next 23 km to reach Ramantola.

On 26 January, when some reporters asked Maharashtra Home Minister R R Patil, the guardian minister for the district, about the bad condition of the road to Sewari, he said: "So what? There are villages in Godchiroli where people have to walk 40 km." For him, the lack of proper roads is no big deal.

The scribe of this article was "advised" against visiting the village on the next day of the encounter and was told to come by the other route" next time.

The other route is Ramantola is from Chhattisgarh's Kanker district. From Pakhnjore town, Ramantola is 35 km. A road runs to Lrapnar village; but from there, one has to walk 14 km to Ranantola.

A government school building and three hand – pumps (which yields polluted water when it rains) are the only proof in Ramantola of the fact that the government has not forgotten this village. As there is no electricity, the villagers depend upon three transistors for links to the outside world.

Some youngsters do have mobile phones, but they are used only for listening to music, in the absence of network. Shankar Anna's body was claimed by his father Jagtu Lakada, but villagers are not keen on speaking about his funeral details. "We got to know about his death a full three days after the incident", says a villager.

Jivi Kavadu, a temporary teacher in the Ramantola school, "advised this reporter not to ask questions about Shankar Anna, since villagers are in shock after his death." But the village is not hostile to the visitors. Asked about their problems, almost all villagers spoke up. "It is all in the open you can see how this village is", says Chandra.

The full –time school teacher is hardly present in the school, which is looked after by Jivi Kavadu, explains a villager. Nor is there a health centre. In the past five years, even the Primary Health Centre's flying squads have not visited Ramantola. The nearby health centre is 7 km away, at Mendhri, but Mendhri residents say their centre has been a shambles for the past three years.

The district health office of Godchiroli informs there were six deliveries in 2011 and three in 2012. But the condition of the health centre building tells a different story. "We have to go either to Pakhanjore in Kanker or to Kasansur for treatment", says 22-year old Shanti Kalvadu.

Even to goto the weekly market, Ramantola villagers have to walk 14 km, to Irapanar. "This is the condition of every village in this area.

Even the people of neighbouring village Viketola have to go to a hospital in Chhattisgarh's Kanker district," says Laxman Uike, a temporary teacher at Uike.

Almost 90 per cent of the families at Ramantola hails from the Madia tribe and the rest are the OBCs. Some Bengalis (Bangladesh refugees) are found in the nearby villages.

Very few have landholdings, which employ villagers, but only during the rainy season.

It is futile to ask whether the Central Government's NREGA works here. Besides the school teacher, the only other government representatives to visit Ramantola are security force men, villagers say. "There have been regular search operations by the CRPF after every two months in this area", says Chandra. "But they do not enter the village".

Some villagers remember Shanker Anna, as "a well built and a handsome youngman". He lost his mother when he was five. His father married again but Shankar could not get along well with his step mother and left the village at the age of 15.

The house of Shankar Anna was locked. His step mother refused to speak, and his father had gone to Godchiroli to claim his body.

"This is the situation, and we can't do much….", says Shanti, 22, who wants to open an electrical shop at Etapalli for which she is studying in an ITI in the town.

The government claims that it has been trying to tackle the "Naxal menace by carrying out the security operations and bringing development to these areas", but Ramantola tells a different story. SP Godchiroli Suvez Huque says the administration is doing a "wonderful job."

"Godchiroli blast death toll goes up to 13" : 6 Apr 2012

"The death toll in the landmine blast triggered by suspected Maoists 10 days ago in Godchiroli district went up to 13 on 5 Apr 2012 after a CRPF jawan died in a private hospital in Nagpur. "Nayan Jyoti, a constable from the 192 Battalion CRPF, did on the 5th night", SP Godchiroli Viresh Prabhu told a daily on 5 Apr 2012."[20]

Nayan Jyoti hails from Assam and his body would be flown to his native place.

In the landmine blast on 27 March, 28 CRPF jawans were injured and 12 killed. The jawans belonged to 191 and 192 Battalions of the CRPF. The troops were engaged in the area domination and road opening when the landmine went off.

The police have so far arrested five persons. "We have arrested five militia members who were involved in planning and execution of the blast", Prabhu said. They hail from Pushtola and Bhapda villages in Godchiroli.

Guns and No Roses in Gadchiroli": 13 April 2012

"While it is the first district in Maharashtra to implement the Forest Right Act, development has not come easy"

Aarda village near Saroncha in Gadchiroli district has seen few VIPs. As the helicopter with Union Minister Jairam Ramesh landed, there was much hysteria. The last time a union visited this place was when Shantaram Potdukha, who was an MP from Chandrapur and MOS Finance came here.

The Ramesh's meeting is held near a newly constructed road under the MGNREGA. Some 47 people work on this 1.5 km road. The rural employment scheme is not very popular here as people have agriculture and harvest crops in two seasons, say a PWD engineer. Sironcha is 285 km from Gadchiroli district headquarters, and there is no hospital close by Of the 41 gram panchayats in Sironcha taluka, nearly 12 don't have drinking water[21].

The BSNL building lie unused, and was burnt down a while ago by unidentified miscreants. Women outnumber men in Aarda gram panchayat and this village claims it is Maoist-free since 2008. To put it simply, no Maoists are allowed to enter the village limits.

But development has come to Sironcha in the form of bridges, the construction of which has been pending since a decade. Rajni Lohare, PWD engineer, is jubilant about the activity and says that the bridge across Godavari costing Rs 185.82 cr will link Andhra Pradesh for the first time, while a second bridge will span the Indravati river at a cost of Rs 156.36 cr. A third one will connect Sironcha to Jagdalpur across Pranhita river. For the people of this remote area, these bridges are a lifeline to the outside world, says a local resident.

Gadchiroli district has the lowest HDI in Maharashtra at 0.21 and is one of the districts in the Maoist's Dandakaranya Special Zone Committee. There are 468 gram panchayats in Gadchiroli district and 200 of these are under the Maoists. Minister Ramesh has been talking of empowering Advisis using the Forest Rights Act and motivating the youth in the Maoist dominated regions to take part in the political process instead of joining ranks with the Maoists.

In Mendha Lekha, the first village to receive rights to out and transport bamboo, Ramesh advocated gram subhas pass resolutions against the

Maoists and not allow them to enter villages. Forest rights have been granted to 27, 810 individuals and community forest rights were given to 777 villages in Gadchiroli. The district is number one in the State in the implementation of the Forest Rights Act.

In a bid to boast development in the district, Ramesh inaugurated a solar energy pump project in Rampur under which 288 villages will get drinking water. Many places in this district don't have power and recently State Home Minister RR Patil mentioned in the State Assembly that there were 52 villages which did not have power for nine years. People have to walk long distances, at least 30 km to 40 km to reach primary healthcare or rations. Gadchiroli had the lowest per capita income in the State and 35 per cent of government posts are vacant.

Road development under the Prime Minister's Gram Yojana (PM GSY) was an indicator of the intensity of Maoist problem.

Minister Ramesh says programme was doing badly in the district. The Maoists were targeting PMGSY and in the district were 108 habitations with a populations of more than 250 which had to be connected and of these only 78 were connected and works on roads for 30 habitations was slow or not happening with instances of contractors being killed. He was considering handing over road works to gram sabhas in the Maoist dominated areas. In the rest of the 20 districts in other States like Chhattisgarh, Odisha and Jharkhand, where the Maoists had stranglehold, of 1097 km of roadwork, on 430 km there was little progress for three years.

There are flaws too in the Integrated Action Plan (IAP) for the Maoist-dominated district. For instance, in Gadchiroli, it was used to build a public stand.

A committee of Collector, the Zila Parishad head and forest officials will now decide on how to spend the funds of Rs 30 Crore each in 78 districts. Of this, the hard core elements were in 20 districts and these were in the tri-junction areas of three States[22], for example, Sironcha which was on the border of AP, Chhattisgarh and Maharashtra. A major problem was the lack of infrastructure in these places which has to be addressed.

Maoists behead two branding them police informers and abduct 12: 27 April 2012

Maoists beheaded two tribals in public and abducted at least 12 others from Markegaon village in Maharashtra's Gadchiroli district on 26 Apr 2012. A rebel group killed Ramu Narote, 31 and Deosai Usendi, 34, after branding them police informers.

The killings take the death toll of villagers branded "police informers" to eight in the troubled district this year (2012 – till April). Since Jan 2010, Maoists have killed 85 civilians, including three women and two school students, in Gadchiroli.

Cops bust three extortion gangs in Gadchiroli: 8 July 2012

Posed as Naxalites; 10 held, including education baron; extorted over 50 lakh

"Over the past two weeks, the police have busted three gangs that posed as Maoists and extorted lakhs of rupees in Gadchiroli. Ten persons, including Srinivas Ganmukulwar, who runs a chain of schools and colleges in the district, have been arrested, the police said."

It was reported by a daily of 8 July 2012, Ganmukulwar, who was arrested on 7 July 2012, was part of a 4-member gang that extorted money from contractors, traders and companies in Gadchiroli and Gondia districts.

The first racket was busted on 26 June after a chilli trader from AP was waylaid by a gang and robbed of valuables worth Rs 70,000. Aheri SDPO Suhas Bawche informs: "The incident occurred on 13 June but the trader approached us on 26 June. On his inputs, we arrested six persons on the 27th. They have been operating for 2 to 3 years."[23]

Soon after, the police detained a couple after a contractor complained that they tried to extort money from him, posing as Maoists. "We are questioning them before can arrest them". Bawche said. The husband is a government malaria squad worker.

"The main gang, of which Ganmukulwar was part, was Led by Somayya Mallayya Durgum from Aheri. Durgam was working for Ganmukulwar's Manav Dayal Mandir educational institute. His main activity, however, was extortion. We have so far found extortion money of Rs 50 lakh collected by them. There may be more", said Bawche.

Two members of the gang, Jagar Pirla and Venkati Kothari, were operating out of Asarali, a Maoist stronghold. "They have confessed to the crime", Bawche said.

"The extortion rackets have been operating since 2004", said the police officer.

"Maharashtra urges Maoists to surrender": 25 Aug 2012

"The Maharashtra police have appealed to Maoist cadre to surrender and assured them of all possible help. The appeal was made in a statement issued by the SP, Gadchiroli on 24 August 2012. Police disclosed that seven Maoist cadres had surrendered during the last eight months in the district".

This was reported by a daily in its issue, datelined Nagpur, 25 August 2012.

The surrendered cadres are: Nirmala Kulmethe, Sukhram Madavi and Mangesh Atram of the Kohakameta LOS Dalam of Maoists; Damaji Dugga and Kishor Madavi of the Perimili Dalam's and Chanda Uike and Ranuka Dhannuti of Platoon 14[24].

"Sarpanchs quit in Gadchiroli, alarm bells ring in Delhi": 25 November 2012

"More than 100 elected local leaders at the panchayat and district levels have resigned in the past few months following a Maoist diktat. Not just that, no nominations were filed in 172 of the 225 gram panchayats that went in far recent by-polls, setting off alarm bells in Delhi".

This was reported by a daily in its issue dated 25 November 2012[25].

While district authorities were asked to negotiate with Sarpanchs and panchs to persuade them to retract their resignations, sources believe there is unease in the Centre that government may be losing ground in the district, where plans were underway for a major political push.

Until October 2011, 127 public representatives belonging to various panchayat raj institutions had tendered their resignations. Of these, 99 were either sarpanchs or panchs while 18 were from Tanta Mukti Samitis and nine from other local bodies.

Elections in Gadchiroli were held earlier this year (2012) and the first spate of resignations happened in June, following which there were concerted efforts to get them to retract their resignations, but without much success.

Official estimates put 30 per cent of the Gadchiroli district under Maoist control, and panchayati raj institutions were meant to counter their influence. Since the polls, there have been diktats and individual threats to the elected members, asking them to give up their posts to avoid persecution.

"Last week, the daily reported the killing of Narayan Shrirange, 35, a deputy Sarpanch, Motla – Tekda village. Shrirange was dragged out of his house and shot alleged by a Maoist group on 22 November night. It was the 24th civilian killing in Gadchiroli by the Maoists this year (till November 2012).

The issue is being closely examined at the highest levels, with senior leadership in the Maharashtra Government even paying a visit to the place.

However, the progress has been slow, with the Centre now weighing the option of increasing paramilitary presence. The assessment is that may be, there is a need to first fill the security void by undertaking more operations against the Maoists, particularly given the slow down in recent months.

"Woman Naxalite killed in encounter": 26 November 2012

A woman Maoist cadre was killed in an encounter with police 25 November 2011 morning in the forest area of Abapur village near Ghot in Chamorshi Taluka, Gadchiroli district, police told a daily on 25 Nov 2012.

While the police were patrolling the forest area of Abapur, some ultras who were hiding there, opened fire at the police team at 9.30 AM. Retaliatory fire by the police killed one woman cadre. The body was yet to be identified.

A 12 – bore rifle and some Naxalite literature were recovered from the spot. "A search operation continued in the area."

Prakash Amte performed Vasectomies on Maoists in Gadchiroli: 3 December 2012

Magasaysay award winner Dr. Prakash Amte, son of legendary social activist Baba Amte has conducted vasectomy surgery in his community centre in Gadchiroli district. But he says he only did his duty as a doctor and never helped or intended to help extremists through the procedure that has become controversial."

"Surrendered Maoists have often said that they were forced to undergo sterilization by their leaders but top Maoists have denied this and termed it as police propaganda. Chhattisgarh police have termed this operation as the "greatest violation of human rights."[26]

This was reported by a daily on 3 December 2012. The daily had reported in October 2012 that three ex-Maoists underwent reverse Vasectomy surgeries as they wanted to become fathers and lead a normal life. They said some 40 Maoists have undergone vasectomy at Amte's Lok Biradari Prakalap in Hemalkasa village so far. These include some senior leaders and even a member of the Central Committee of the CPI (Maoist). The daily claimed to have the details of some of these Maoists but withheld their names to protect their identity.

Amte admitted conducting the operations, explaining that it was his duty as a doctor. He asserted it was less risky than abortion, adding that at times he was not aware of the identity of those who came for surgery. He said to the daily: "Several tribal's in the area approached me for vasectomy or tubectomy. It is a problem to ascertain their identity. I opt for vasectomy as it is safer. Again, Maoists came to me for abortion of their wives and vasectomy of their cadres. Abortion is risky for women, as it endangered their life. There was also a possibility that if we conduct abortion once, they may come for another operation of the same woman. It involved great health risk for her, so I opted for a lesser evil - - vasectomy. More over, I know vasectomy was reversible."

He asserts: "By conducting vasectomy, at no point in time I helped Maoists or their movement. I only performed my duty as a doctor on purely humanitarian grounds. I have provided Medicare to thousands of tribals in the area."

Hemalkasa, just a few kilometers outside the Abujhmadh forest is a remote tribal village bordering Chhattisgarh and Andhra Pradesh, 175 km from Gadchiroli district headquarters. Baba Amte set up a community project, Lok Biradari Sankalap in the village in 1973. A year later, Prakash quit his masters in surgery course, opened a medical centre in a hut and settled down there with his doctor wife Mandakini.

Starting in the 1980s, the region became stronghold of the Maoists. The ultras would visit the Prakalap for Medicare and at times they also sought vasectomy surgery for their cadres. Some Maoists said the operation was conducted by Amte himself. The cadres who underwent surgery included even teenagers. One of them told the daily he was only eighteen "when I was sterilised".

Amte's clinic is the first and only choice for tribals living in an area spread over hundreds of square kilometers and until a few decades ago, there was no government health centre in the vicinity. Besides his wife, Amite's two sons and daughters-in-law also live in the Prakalap, a small community the family has formed and the one which is highly respected by the locals.

While Baba Amte won the Magsaysay in 1985, Prakash and his wife won it in 2008 for "enhancing the capacity of the Madia Gonds through healing and teaching and other compassionate interventions." It is the only instance in India where two relatives of a family have won the 'Nobel of Asia'.

When Amte came to Hemalkasa, it did not have reads, electricity and schools. Today, the Prakalap treats 50,000 patients every year, a third of them from neighbouring Chhattisgarh and 5,000 from AP, almost all of them from tribal communities.

Besides this, it also has a residential school with 650 children and an animal rescue centre.

A woman Naxalite killed in an encounter: 6 December 2012

A woman Naxalite was killed in an encounter near the Hikker forests in the Etapalli Division of the Gadchiroli district on December 2012.

The Gadchiroli police say the Naxals opened fire on a police team that was conducting a combing operation in the jungle along the Maharashtra – Chhattisgarh border. The woman was killed when the police returned the fire. The firing continued for some half an hour.[27]

The Naxals escaped into the forest with the body of the woman. The police recovered one rifle, two back packs and some Maoist literature from the encounter spot.

This is the second casualty of a woman on the Maoist side in the district in the last 10 days.

Dreaded Naxal leader active in Gadchiroli: 10 January 2013

"Dreaded Naxal leader Thakapalli Vasudev Rao alias Assanna alias Satish alias Sujit has entered Gadchiroli", according to the Gadchiroli police. SP Suvez Haque tells a daily: "Assanna, a resident of Warangal district of Andhra Pradesh, was a member of Dandakaranya Special Zonal committee of the CPI (Maoist) and military instructor of its armed living."

It was disclosed by a daily of 10 Jan 201[28]

Assanna is believed to be the mastermind behind an assassination bid on the then CM of AP, N Chandrababu Naidu, near Tirupati in 2003. He is wanted in cases related to the killing of DIG K S Vyas near the Lal Bahadur Shastri Stadium in Hyderabad, the murder of Karimnagar SP Umesh Chandra and the murder of Karnul MLA Budda Vengal Reddy and many other cases, said Haque.

Assanna is currently a member of Central Committee's Action Team of CPI (Maoist). Police suspect he might be in Gadchiroli to plan a major operation.

The police have declared Rs 1 lakh as a reward for any one who provides information about him.

The police are also not sure about the death of one of the senior-most woman Naxal leader Narmada Akka. As per the police sources, on 4 December 2012, a woman Naxalite was killed in an encounter in the Bhamragad Division of Gadchiroli and her body was dragged inside the forest by the Maoists. Post-encounter, there were rumours that 57- year-old Narmada Akka, Divisional Secretary of South Gadchiroli, CPI (Maoist), was the one killed.

It is believed by the police that Narmada Akka's funeral was carried out at a village in Chhattisgarh but the ultras did not issue any statement regarding her death.

Narmada Akka has 53 cases registered against her in Maharashtra.

"Naxals set 26 vehicles on fire in Gadchiroli": 14 January 2013

Suspected Maoists 12 January 2013 set on fire 26 vehicles deployed in north Gadchiroli for road construction work. The incident occurred between Lekha and Dodalmahi villages in Dhonora tehsil around 2 PM. The spot is 10 km from Dhanora police station. The act was carried out by 50 Naxals. The vehicles set afire included 19 tractors, two JCB machines, a road roller, two water tankers, and two motor cycles[29].

The vehicles belonged to a Ingole – Patil Construction Company of Pune, according to DIGP (Gadchiroli Rane) Ravindra Kadam.

This follows close on the heels of a similar incident in Shamragarh tehsil two days ago, when three vehicle were set afire. Kadam said, "This is unprecedented, but it also shows how Naxals are opposed to development works being undertaken in Gadchiroli in a big way". Sources said: "Road works in Gadchiroli have been given to many big companies, a reason why small local contractors get antagonized. Such incidents should be seen in the context of this resentment."

Gadchiroli policemen learn the rules of engagement: 14 January 2013

Encounters: Peaked at 42 in 2012 but not many Naxals were killed in them; one reason being cited is that security men lost their nerve when bullets were flying around them.

Gadchiroli police are training how to hold their nerve when they get into an encounter with the Maoists. The district saw 42 encounters in 2012, its highest for a single year, but the casualties were lopsided: four Naxals to 14 security men (13 of them in a mine blast).

Among the many factors as responsible for the poor success of operations is the loss of nerve when bullets start flying all around. Anti-Naxal Operations (ANO) command as are now undergoing intensive "battle in-oculation" training in Gadchiroli and at Nagpur's Unconventional Operations Training Centre (UOTC). The training involves crawling under, and in a direction perpendicular to, continuous crossfire.

"The idea is for the commandos to get accustomed to the sound of heavy fire, which often has a suppressive effect as far as the ability to hold one's nerve is concerned", DIGP (Gadchiroli Range) Ravindra Kadam said[30].

ANO commandos rarely manage to capture or kill Naxals, and even if they do kill some, Naxals often flee with the dead on their shoulders. The last major security strike was in 2008, when the bodies of four Naxals were recovered from Dobur. The previous day, platoon commander Chaitu was killed in an encounter in Sironcha, with other three Naxals believed to have been killed.

"In the thickly wooded and hilly terrain of Gadchiroli, when our men trace a Naxal hideout or camp, it becomes actually very difficult to get very close to them, and then pounce upon them since they have their scouting parties and even sentries who engage us to facilitate camp inmates' escape", said Kadam. "The same goes for Naxals, who manage to strike at us only when they blast a landmine, not otherwise."

Police engagements with Naxals in encounters has gone up substantially over the past few months, with December (2012) registering 10, the highest for any month in the district. The previous two years had seen 16 in 2010 and 18 in 2011, encounters. "It is very significant and encouraging. It must have had a dampening effect on the Naxal morale," said Rajesh Pradhan who was Gadchiroli SP during the Dobur encounter. During his tenure, the district counted 10 Naxal deaths and 143 surrenders in 2008. Yet Pradhan, now Solapur SP, agrees it is difficult to get to the Naxals during the encounters.

Pradhan's predecessor, Shirish Jain, during whose tenure the Naxals suffered their highest casualties - - more than 30 in three years, including 20 in 2006 – says: "Engaging Naxals more and more should be the strategy. That not only increases the chances of getting them alive or dead but also brings them out of their hideouts for retaliatory attacks and leaves them no time to consolidate."

He admits Naxals have an advantage in being acclimatized to the forests and terrain, and in the ability to mix with locals whenever they see police threat. But he says: "Encounters have another advantage. Locals tend to support the side that dominates. The police must be seen to dominate."

In 2009, 52 policemen were killed in encounters in Gadchiroli. The next two years saw Naxals attacking police stations with 10 police casualties in 2010 and 9 in 2011, besides 32 and 40 civilian deaths (this came down to 24 in 2012).

Asked how much are the police have managed to "clear", as envisaged in Operation Green Hunt, Kadam said: "We do not claim that as yet, but the north Gadchiroli and the Gondia division movement has been considerably weakened, as borne out, by the Naxals' own internal assessment.

"Police gun down six Naxals in Gadchiroli": 21 January 2013

"The Gadchiroli Police in an anti – Naxal operation gunned down at least six Maoists near Jimalgatta in Aheri tehsil around 1.30 AM on 18 January 2013. The operation is said to have achieved biggest success for the police in the district. The ambush was carried out by two commando groups totaling 50 near Govindgaon village and was based on precise intelligence inputs."

The above was reported by a daily of 21 January 2013.[31]

DIG, Gadchiroli Range Ravindra Kadam explains: "We had information that Naxals were holding a meeting in the village. We sent two parties that laid an ambush at a vantage position from where they could see a meeting being conducted with villagers participating". When the meeting ended, 10 – 15 Naxals started walking away from the village. Police men opened fire. Six of them were killed on the spot and possibly two others injured. The rest managed to flee. The Maoists tried to retaliate, but were badly exposed to police firing. "They could not hold the ground as probably the six of them died in the first burst of firing itself", said Kadam.

The deceased ultras were identified as Shankar alias Muneshwar Ladka, 43, member, South Gadchiroli Division of CPI (Maoist); Vinod alias Chandrayya Kodape, 30, Aheri, local organisational squad commander, Vinod's wife Geeta, 25 Deputy Commander, Platoon 14, Zuru Mattami, 20; Mohan Kowase, 25 and Sunita alias Pale Bandy Kodape, 18.

Two SLRs and two .303 rifles were also recovered. "They did not have shoulder bags as they were probably heading for their nearby camp site where we suspect a platoon was camping", Kadam said.

In 2008, the police had killed five Maoists in an encounter at Dobur in Bhamragarh. Jimalgatta is one of the most sensitive places in south Gadchiroli where Naxals are known to have a free run. It was near hear that they held their Jana Adalat last year.

Here is the opening paragraph on the same incident in another daily, giving some additional facts: 'Police shot dead six Maoists in Gadchiroli district in an "encounter" early on Sunday. A statement from the office of the SP Gadchiroli says the "Maoists attacked a Special Operations Squad of Gadchiroli Police and the Anti-Naxal C-60 Force, which was carrying out a search operation near the forest of Govindgaon under the Gimmal-gutta police post in Aheri tehsil at 1.30 AM'.[32]

When the police team retaliated, six ultras, including two women were killed on the spot.

The six killed are mentioned with a different descriptions of their position – posts, and even the names. They are as per this daily: Secretary, Aheri Area Committee of the CPI (Maoist) Shankar alias Munneshwar Jaktu Lakada, 43; Aheri Dalam Commander Vinod alias Chandrayya Kodape, 30; Deputy Commander of Aheri Dalam Mohan Kowase, 25; Jhurru Mattami, 20; member, Aheri Dalam Gita Usendi, 28 (wife of Vinod Kodape); and Sunita alias Pale Bandu Kodape, 18, a member of Sironcha Local Operating Squad (LOS).

However, this daily, significantly, adds a brief para, typical of it and its ideological pedigree and stance:

> "However, the police version of the encounter was contradicted by the villagers and local sources."

Yet again, the daily does not care or feel the need of identifying the particulars of "local sources" besides the villagers!

Back to the daily's text] Eleven Maoists of the Aheri Area Committee and Aheri LOS came to Govindgaon under Gimmalgutta sub-division in Aheri of Gadchiroli on 17 January around 8 PM for a meeting, villagers said. The villagers were called to the village centre.

The meeting lasted for same four hours. The Maoists warned the villagers against consumption of liquor and cutting of trees from nearby forests, a villager said. The meeting concluded 12.30 AM after which the Maoists asked the villagers to go home. The Maoists they went to a house in the village for dinner. After finishing dinner, they were planning to leave when around 400 – 500 police personnel attacked them.

"However, when a team of journalists visited the "encounter" site, it appeared to be right at the centre of the village."

According to some sources, it was a well planned "raid" by the police. The villagers said it was the police who opened fire on the Maoists, killing six of them on the spot[33].

A press conference was called at the Aheri police headquarters at 11 AM, on 18 January to give information about the "encounter". Police suspect that two more Maoists might have been badly injured.

Now, some observations from a third daily on the same incidents.

All the (six) bodies were brought to the Aheri Police Headquarters for postmortem. Coming under immediate fire, the police team retaliated which led to the deaths of six Maoists on the spot, no policemen were injured in the encounter[34].

The tribal district of Gadchiroli, the most backward region of the State, has been under Maoist influence since 1980s. It was first noticed when Peddy Shankar, a young Maoist of the then CPI PWG, died in an encounter near Sironcha in 1980.

Naxal couple slip away from the ambush site to surrender: 14 June 2013

"Even as the Gadchiroli Police felicitated rehabilitated 27 Maoists who surrendered earlier this week under Nav Jeevan scheme, a couple slipped out of their group immediately after a failed ambush and walked for over three days through the forests before laying down their arms."

"They eventually surrendered two days after the other members of their group, a senior police officer told the daily."

The daily reported the matter in its issue of 17 June 2013[35].

Manku Pada, 30, a commander of Platoon A of Company 10 of CPI (Maoist) and his wife Sushila, 27, gave their group the slip immediately after the Nargunda encounter on 31 May (2013) to walk for three days through the forest to reach Punnur village in Kasansur area of the district before coming to Gadchiroli. One more couple is expected to surrender soon.

The Gadchiroli police had publicly feted the 27 Naxals who surrendered under the Nav Jeevan scheme at a function recently. The cadres had responded to the calls made by the police through their kin when senior officials visited them in their villages. The highly successful campaign saw over 17 surrenders in just one month of April. Most of these are *'dalam member'* rank, though there are some seniors too.

At the felicitation function, most of them who had surrendered spoke of the futility of being part of the Naxal movement and of the desire to lead normal life.

Many families of the Naxals still active in the ranks were also invited for the programme. The police also solemnised the marriage of two former cadres…dalam commander Jeevan Narote and member Janaki Timma.

Two senior Maoist leaders convicted: 26 June 2013

A Nagpur Sessions Court 25 June 2013 convicted senior Naxalites Vernon Gonsalves and Sridhar Srinivasan – both Central Committee members of the CPI (Maoist) - - under the Arms Act, Explosives Act and Unlawful Activities (Prevention) Act (UAPA).

This is first time in the State that Naxals have been convicted in a UAPA case.

Angela Sontakke, a CPI (Maoist) State Committee member, who was arrested from Thane in 2011, was acquitted but her trial will continue in cases registered in Thane, said special public prosecutor Prashant Sathianathan.

Gonsalves and Srinivasan were found guilty of possessing arms and sentenced to three years in Jail, under the Arms Act. Under the UAPA, Srinivasan was sentenced to six years and Gonsalves to five years in Jail. Under the Explosives Act, Srinivasan was awarded six years imprisonment, while Gonsalves was absolved of the charge[36].

Gonsalves and Srinivasan were arrested by Mumbai ATS in June 2007. Nine detonators, 20 gelatin sticks, a walkie – talkie set, a computer, Naxal literature were also seized from the duo in a raid in a Chawl in Govindi, Mumbai, according to the prosecution.

The two had been living there for five months and were introduced to the landlord by a women called Sharda, who identified herself as Srinivasan's wife. The landlord was one of the witnesses.

Sathiananathan said, "Sharda had told the landlord that Srinivasan was employed in Gujarat."

Suspected Naxals kill cop: 28 June 2013

Four suspected Naxals killed a police constable in Gadchiroli district on 27 June 2013. Raj Reddy Pocham Gaddewar was fired at close range by four unidentified persons when he was returning home from a hospital in Assarali town around 2.30 PM. He died of serious injuries in the neck and chest, the police said[37].

According to some eye witnesses, attackers pushed away Reddy's wife and two children, and fired three rounds at him.

The 'Urban' Maoist front: September 2013

A daily known for its analytical and investigative skills, carried two articles in its issue of 16 September 2013. It hints at the Maoist leadership's endeavour to build and expand its movement to urban areas. Both article's are well – reasoned and provide ample evidence of the daily's belief about the Maoist plans to go to the urban centre's and areas. The two articles are carried in the succeeding pages.

Significantly, the blurb reads: "Both from Uttarakhand and champions of people's causes."

"Gadchiroli police say twin arrests are a pointer to new leadership being built, link these to raids on Delhi Professor's home": Nagpur: 15 September 2013

An emerging thrust area in the Maoist movement is the building of a second-rung leadership in urban areas, says DIGP Gadchiroli Range Ravindra Kadam, who cites as an example visits by Hem Mishra and Prashant Rahi, both arrested for alleged Maoist links. Their visits should be viewed in that context, he says[38].

It was the information police got from the duo that led it to raid the house of Delhi University professor GN Saibaba. "On Saturday, 14 September 2013, Saibaba denied being a Naxal sympathiser while conceding that he had met Mishra.

Mishra and Rahi, both hailing from Uttarakhand, were arrested at Aheri in Gadchiroli and Deori in Gondia along with alleged couriers for two senior Naxals, Narmada and Ramdev. DIGP Kadam has the details:

> "An eroding tribal cadre base due to depleting recruitment, as also difficulty of intellectually equipping tribal cadre well enough to take the movement forward, are the reasons why CPI (Maoist) leaders are looking up to the urban cadres to be ready to take over.
>
> - "The urban cadres have of late been discussing this subject with the Central Committee and have been seeking financial help to run urban activities and guidance on how to develop better coordination among the urban frontal organisation of the party.
> - "One of the main sub-texts of this programme is to cultivate urban cadre to lead militant activities that are facing leadership crisis due to depleting recruitment, elimination of existing cadres due to security operations and large – scale surrenders by senior cadres.
> - "The urban front comprise organisations in 'revolutionary democratic' activities, opposition to 'war on people' displacement and 'violence on women' and in 'cultural activities'.
> - "They are, however, finding it difficult since urban cadres find life in the forests too difficult to sustain. The visits by couriers such as Mishra and Rahi are basically to help coordinate and streamline these activities."

With Mishra, police allegedly found an encrypted microchip embedded inside a visiting card, along with some "sensitive" documents. Police say that is what led the searches at Saibaba's home. The two told the police they had been handed over the material sized from them by Saibaba. That is why the police searched Saibaba's Delhi residence and seized the hard dises, pen drives etc. The police "sealed it all and will have them forensically checked."

In New Delhi on 14 September 2013, Saibaba told reporters: "My pen drives, hard disks, laptops were confiscated without proper seal, which leaves open the possibility of planting fake evidence later".

Sources say two Gadchiroli arrests are a culmination of infighting between Rahi and the core faction that implements the urban activities. An officer says: "Rahi worked independently without following the core faction system, incurring the wrath of the faction's members. He would interact directly with State Committees."

Among other tasks before the CPI (Maoist), according to a document police claim to have seized, is to raise in each state a chapter of Front Against War on People to counter Operation Green Hunt.

Comment

Going over the above, it is obvious that this is an analysis by the police brass carried by this daily in its said issue.

The duo and their histories: 15 September 2013

The two alleged Maoist couriers arrested in Gadchiroli are both activists who have taken up various social causes in Uttarakhand.

Prashant Rahi, 54, is an engineer turned journalist who hails from Maharashtra and whose daughter Shikha is a film maker, an assistent director for *Taare Zameen Par.* He was arrested in 2007, too, for alleged Maoist links, and got bail three years later. He participated in labour and other movements in Maharashtra and UP in the 1990s before settling in what is now Uttarakhand, where he worked as a journalist. He was working on providing legal aid to suspected Maoists - - political prisoners – when he was arrested, allegedly while organizing a Maoist training camp.

Hem Mishra, 30, cut his teeth as a student – activist in Almora before moving four years ago to the JNU to study Chinese. The causes he took up included water, forest and land, and a shift of the capital from Dehradun to Gairsain. Every year, he would join a programme to pay tribute to those killed in the Rampur Tiraha firing incident in 1994 during the statehood agitation, say people who know him.[39]

Mishra was arrested in August (2013) while allegedly couriering material on behalf of Maoists. The arrest of Rahi came days later, in September (2013).

"As part of the Progressive Students Front, Hem used to participate in street plays and recite poems written by Girish Tiwari Girda", says Shamsher

Singh Bishta, himself an activist in Almora. He participated in a *padyatra* in support of shifting the capital."

Retired teacher Keshavdutta Mishra describes Hem, the youngest of his three sons, as "an intelligent boy who loves to participate in cultural activities." Hem graduated from the SSJ campus of Kumaon University. "Four years ago, he was selected for MSc in Mathematics and also for Chinese in JNU," says his father. "He chose the JNU course ... yes, he is very social and a lover of music. But he has never carried home any literature that would suggest he is involved in Maoist activities."

He says it is normal practice in Gadchiroli to describe any person after his arrest, as a Naxal.

Rahi, 54, or Prashant Sangalikar - - police also calls him Navin and Mahesh – hails from Nashik. He won a B tech from Banaras Hindu University in 1982, followed by an M Tech, and worked in a power company in UP's Sonbhadra district, a LWE – hit area.

Intelligence sources in Uttarakhand cite a long history with movements – a labour movement in Maharashtra in the 1990s, work with youth organisation Purvanchal Naujwan Sabha in UP, and a movement for rehabilitation of people affected by Tehri Dam project in what is now Uttarakhand. He had arrived in this region in 1993 and worked till 2000 as a journalist with a local newspaper. What raised suspicion that he was a Maoist sympathizer were his efforts to provide legal help to people arrested for spreading the Maoist ideology.

"Police got information in 2004 about the presence of Maoists in the forest area near Saufutia. They found evidence suggesting training camp", an intelligence officer said. This led to a match on suspected sympathizers and Rahi was arrested from Nanakmata in December 2007. He was charged under IPC Sections for waging or abetting war against the state, sedition and other offences, and under UAPA for being a member of a terrorist organisation or gang.

Police claimed to have recovered copies of a magazine Aamukh, with articles related to CPI (Maoist)'s expansion to Uttarakhand and suggesting that it had set up a zonal committee.

His daughter Shikha, then 24, had fought a long legal battle for his relase. In 2011, after his release on bail, she had told this daily that the police had accused her father of having conducted training camps in villages.

How Gadchiroli is policed: S Pinvited by the MHA: 18 September 2013

"Higher cop morale, local trust and welfare schemes help encounter Naxals"

In July 2013, Gadchiroli SP Suvez Haque, 34, was invited by the MHA to make a presentation before polices officers of 27 LWE – affected states on the "Gadchiroli Model", which had led to a record 23 Maoists being killed in the year since he joined. Police attribute the success to a more confident force and the trust of the locals on account of various schemes. Some of the important events and observations are noted here[40].

- In August and September 2013 came the arrests of Hem Mishra and Prashant Rahi, the alleged Maoist couriers. Their mission the police now describe as a pointer to the district's strategic importance. Mishra was allegedly planning to enter Abhujmaad in Chhattisgarh through Lahiri, the last motorable point on the Maharashtra side.
- Roads are central to the police's plans for helping the district to shed the tag of being the gateway to Abhujmaad; Maoists find it easy to dodge security forces, who managed to enter Abhujmaad for the first time only in March 2012. A 500 km road network (the existing networks is 12,383 km) has been pending for the 32 years since Gadchiroli was carved out of Chandrapur district. With road contractors unwilling to associate themselves with administration, they are now being provided security "clandestinely", district administration sources say.
- The district has 268 villages that remain to be electrified. And 211 habitations bordering Chhattisgarh remain cut off. The Centre has now approved a plan for 37 mobile towers, which will come up in the next one year.
- SP Haque elucidates: "It is not just a police problem. Policing and development have to go hand in hand. The next one year will be a watershed in the history of Gadchiroli. Police have won the trust of locals in a systematic manner. We have started a Gram Bhet scheme where policemen visit every village and note local problems. It could be about a bore-well, absent teachers or the electricity pole. The civic action team sends these complaints to the concerned authorities."

Till 15 August 2013, the police had visited 2800 villages; in the entire previous year (2012), they had visited 2,678. "Where we were going once a year earlier, we are going ten times now," says Haque. District Magistrate

Abhishek Krishna adds: "We are going to areas where we earlier did not. One of our tehsildar is so popular that he can win an election."

The State administration has started the Nav Jeevan Yojana under which the officers visit the families of Naxal leaders. The administration and police also organise vocational training and many locals have got jobs at urban coffee outlets, and as guards. Posters countering Maoist propaganda are drawing villagers to schemes, and Maoists to surrender before police. Police estimate the district has 300 Maoists.

Krishan says development work has to be sustained for the next 10 years. "Our focus is on forest products as these will sustain generations. We have done away with middle men. Earlier they were getting Rs 20, say, for 10 kg *mahua* flowers; now they get Rs 10 a kg. We have 22 branches of various banks and now to reach remote locations, we are trying to open ultra-small branches."

One task Haque had to handle early was to lift the force's moralc after the killing of 52 Maharashtra policemen in 2009 alone, which had led to the CRPF being deployed in 19 of the 50 police posts in border areas. "Whenever I hold a meeting, I ask about their problems, note these down, and make it a point to solve them within seven days. We have also opened a helpline called Samadhaan, which I monitor", says Haque "Today, my men fight over going for operations. Earlier, there would seldom be volunteers."

The CRPF has 5,000 men deployed and the district police said in a recent meetings that they would like them phased out. This has upset CRPF officers, one of whom says: "We are not claiming any credit but since our coming here, the number of deaths of security personnel has considerably dropped. Earlier, these men were too scared to even get out of their security posts. Our force is deployed in all the difficult posts. The fact that the police have been able to carry out operations is because we have held fort on the border. All the police operations are along the middle action."

Life after Maoist camps: 18 September 2013

Raghu Saolmake, 40, alias Jalamsai, is keen to adopt a baby girl. The former Maoist commander, who hails from Lahiri, had to undergo a vasectomy, while his wife Bharati, who was commanding a women's wing, is recovering from a uterine surgery. "Since two of us are more or less settled now, I would love to adopt a baby girl, says Raghu, who has been engaging in agriculture since he surrendered four years ago.

Raghu was leading a group of 70 cadres since 1990 and met Bharati, who is from Chhattisgarh, in 1998. "I can count the number of times I met her in the first 10 years since we married", he says. "We were not allowed to stay together. One day she wrote to me that she was suffering from a terrible pain in the abdomen. Our seniors tried to treat her but the pain kept increasing."

He wrote to her one day and they fled and surrendered. They now live in a small house on the outskirts of Gadchiroli town, built with Rs 3 lakh granted to her by the government as surrender money. "We have five rooms", says Bharati, whose surrender money has gone into fixed deposit. She can barely walk after operation to remove a tumour from the uterus.

"I don't know how many time I might have opened fire on the security forces. But not many people in the neighborhood know about my past", says Raghu, who grows maize in his backyard and shares it with locals, for whom it is an unfamiliar crap. "I was inducted as an SPO as an incentive for surrendering. Neighbours think I do something for the police."

A small flat next to the SP's office in Gadchiroli town has been designated as 'surrender cell'. Before the money and other dues for the surrender are granted, cadres are required to stay under police watch for a minimum of six months. If convinced, the District Magistrate decides on the compensation.

Another surrendered couple is Mahesh Dev Mattami, 30, and Sumitra Lalu Wadde of Chhattisgarh. He joined a Maoist dalam in 2004 and rose to become a divisional commander. He was sent to Bastar in 2008. "We were shown various movies featuring Bhagat Singh and Mahatma Gandhi. There were videos of war in Vietnam, Russia, China and Sri Lanka, too, shown to us. I met Sumitra on the Job in 2008", says Mahesh. "Some one else wanted to marry her but she chose me. She had joined the *dalam* as she was fascinated by the song and dance."[41]

He adds : "Once I fell into a ditch during an operation. I badly hurt my left – leg. There was nobody to take care of me as my wife was not allowed to stay with me for more than a week. The pain was too much for me to bear, and one night, the two of us ran away. We had to hide for 6- 7 months till we came here."[40]

Village in Gadchiroli gets power 66 years after independence : 4 October 2013

Pandurang Hichami of Garanji village is a delighted man these days. He has just bought a small Hilton TV. His mud – and brick house is among the four in the village to have one. He bought the TV set in July 2013 when this village in Maharashtra's Naxal belt of Gadchiroli finally got electricity - - 66 years after Independence.

The above in reported by a daily of 4 Oct 2013[42].

"We were accustomed to this darkness. Our kids studied under kerosene lamps, some of them opting to go to the nearby town to study. No government official, including the primary school teacher, stayed in our village as there was no power", he says. 13 other villages in Gadchiroli are on their way to getting electricity for the first time. They are in different phases of electrification, the first such effort by the State. Bizarrely, several other villages here had power connections but could not get supply because of equipment damage. The electricity department did not make an effort to restore connections because of the tough terrain and Naxal presence.

As we have seen earlier, the Naxals also comes in the way of tribal areas getting modern facilities, besides the financial and other constraints faced by the government.

But the district administration finally decided to move the matters. The former Collector, Abhishek Krishna, asked the Maharashtra State Electricity Distribution Company (MSEDCL) to prepare a list of such villages. "Initially the company told us there were only 30 such villages in Gadchiroli. But a survey should there were 268 such villages, in the district sans power," said Krishna. Out of the total, 62 were never electrified and the remaining got a connection some 35 years ago. "But the people stayed without light as the power lines had snapped", Krishna added.

Garanji was selected to be the first village to be electrified but the path to power was not easy. "Being a Naxal area, no contractor came forward to lay the power lines on the 12 – km stretch from Vikaspalli to Garanji. After some persuasion, a contractor agreed but then the Forest Department refused permission since some trees would have to be cut to lay the power line. We sought permission in 2011 but got the go ahead only two years later," said Dilip Kumbhare, an MSEDCL official who led the team which electrified Garanji.

Forest Department sanction granted, the people of Garanji came forward to help Kumbhare's team. "Villagers helped us in cutting some of the trees and branches that lay in the way of the power line. But in their enthusiasm, they ended up dismantling 40 poles", recollected Kumbhare. It took another two months to re-install the poles. Power came to Garanji on 14 July (2013), but went off in just four days after a key transmission line snapped. Heavy rains and dense forest delayed the repair work. The connection was only restored a month later.

Officials say the pending work in 13 villages like Garanji, which are being electrified for the first time, will be completed by December (2013).

Today, most of the houses in Garanji have CFL bulbs and table fans. A TV set tops the priority list of many in the village. "Who wants to line in dark? It was just that we had no other option. Wait for the paddy season to finish and you will see a TV set in every house", says Ratan Haldar.

3 Jawans die in Naxal attack in Gadchiroli: 18 October 2013

Three special action group Jawans were killed in a landmine blast triggered by Maoists inside a school in Gadchiroli district on Thursday, 16 October 2013, marking a return to the bloody ways after lull. The ultras are back to the violence.

"But incensed by the attack, the cops turned on the villagers, with sources telling the daily that they beat up many of them suspecting them to be Maoist sympathizers. The blast at 11 PM on the 15th ripped through the floor of two class rooms of the Zila Parishad School at Motazeila village, where the Jawans were resting after dinner. The location is 85 km from Gadchiroli and 4 km off the main road in thick forests[43]".

However, instead of chasing the rebels, policemen hit out against the people of Motazeila, leaving several tribals injured. "One among the injured was a 12 – year – old, while the oldest among them was 80. Men and women showed their bare, bruised backs and swollen limbs from the merciless beating."

Motzeila has 26 houses, with 150 residents. A villager, Samari Pulsingh Puro, said she was turned away by Primary Health Centre staff and denied medicine and treatment. "Not a single villager could get treatment after the police beat us up. Some of us can't even lift ourselves from the Bed", she told the daily.

However, DIG Gadchiroli Range Ravindra Kadam denied the allegations.

Maoists gun down 3 cops in Gadchiroli: 18 October 2013

Another daily has covered this incident even more briefly. Its text is reproduced here[44].

"Three jawans of the C – 60 Commando Force were killed by Maoists in a forest area in Gadchiroli district on Chhattisgarh border in Maharashtra. Acting on a tip-off about Maoists hiding in the area, the Anti-Naxal Force launched combing operations in the Bada Zariya forest area under Gyarapatti police station late Wednesday (15 October 2013) night when the Naxals triggered a landmine blast."[44]

How different the two reports are on the same single incident in content and even tone is too obvious to be dilated upon! The second daily obviously has not gone to the village, nor talked to any villagers. It has simply taken the police version and condensed it to a skeletonized version.

The first daily's reports cannot be too much off the mark, as its news story of the Naxal – triggered blast and consequent beating of the villagers by the 'incensed' policemen carry a photograph of two villagers, with their bare backs showing all the tell tale marks of beatings, without any doubts of their authenticity.

7 'Maoists' killed in Gadchiroli encounter : 19 February 2014

Seven alleged Maoists were killed in an encounter with police in Gondia late Monday, 16 February 2014 night. Among the dead that included two women, were some senior Maoist leaders, police said.

The encounter took place when the ultra were returning on foot from Khursipaar village after burning a gram panchayat building there on the 15th. IGP Nagpur Range Ravindra Kadam told a daily : "Around 10.30 PM on 16 February night, a police team spotted the Naxals a few km from the village. An encounter ensued in which all the seven members of the group were killed."

Police identified the dead as : Lalsu alias Bidal, 42, from Bastar who was a member of the North Gadchiroli – Gondia Division of the CPI (Maoist); Sunil Tadami, 28; Navin alias Durrusing Sattarsingh Tofa, 28; Veeru alias Vinay Dulesh Kanjilal Naitam, 40; Rajesh Lalsu Soneray Tofa, 27; and the two women were Lalsu's 26- year- old wife Shamko alias Shanta Korcha and Veeru's wife Punni Ratti Narote, 36. Police said both were members of the outfit.

The number of offenses ranging between 26 and 48 were pending against the seven.

Police also recovered two AK-47s, two SLRs, one carbine, one .303, one 12-bore gun, a pistol, and a walkie-talkie from the spot.

This has been the biggest success for the security forces in Gadchiroli area in the recent years.

Poll Battle 2014 is on Stance of political leaders: Mar-Apr 2014

The battle for Lok Sabha elections – better known as General Elections – has been on since the last year, 2013. Presently, March - May 2014, it is in full swing, with all the heat and dust connected with the Indian elections. As the polls are moving towards the final phases, it has gained even greater vigour and momentum. The following pages would cover the electioneering by senior leaders and some others dealing with brave voters converging on to the polling booths, the Maoist threats notwithstanding.

In Naxal hub, Modi appeals : "Make earth green not red": 29 March 2014

Addressing his second rally in Bastar, BJP's Prime Ministerial candidate Narendra Modi made his first statement on the Maoist issue, and urged the rebels to "accept democracy", which has the "best solution for all the problems" Campaigning for the party's Bastar candidate Dinesh Kashyap in Kondagaon district on 28 March 2014, Modi also blamed the Maoist for "misleading youths for selfish interests[45].

The PM candidate continues: "The Maoism has turned this earth red with blood. It is the call of the time, Maoists must accept the power of democracy. Democracy has the best solutions for problems. Bombs, guns and pistols can cause bloodshed but cannot give a new life. We have to shed sweat, not blood. We have to make this earth green, not red, we have to hold pen, instead of bomb, guns and pistols, and participate in the democratic process. Maoism is not going to lead us anywhere."

Modi saluted those who voted in large numbers amid Maoist threat in the lass Assembly polls and slammed the Congress for its "sins." "This is the first election that being contested not by any party but the country. Crores of people are themselves contesting this election. People are no longer voting only for mere change, but to remove Congress and bring BJP", he said.

This story is datelined Kondagaon.

"In Gadchiroli, Rahul steer clear of the issue": 29 March 2014

"It was supposedly a bid to allure people living in Naxal strongholds towards Congress, but this did not turn out well for party Vice-President Rahul Gandhi who was on 28 March 2014 forced to abruptly end his speech amid a protest and people walking off the rally[46]."

This was reported by a daily in a news story datelined Wadsa (Gadchiroli) 28 March 2014.

Rahul's appeal. "Arre Bhai, zara ruko" failed to step sizeable crowd, which had waited for him for three hours but chose to leave when he started making his speech.

During his speech, Rahul refrained from making any remark on Maoism. Gadchiroli is one of the backward districts in the State, with high poverty and Maoist activities.

This time, a campaign in Naxal belt : 7 April 2014

"At Kotgul, a remote village in Gadchiroli troulled Korchi tehsil, Congress workers, visibly tired after a day of campaigning for party candidate Namdeo Usendi, stop for tea at a local shop. It is dark but the village is still bustling with political activity."

"At Korchi, over 2,000 people wait for state BJP leader Vinod Tawde to arrive in a helicopter to address a poll gathering. Tomorrow, they will have another opportunity to see the helicopter when congress leader Harsh Wardhan Patil visits them".

These are poll-related activities as reported by a daily of 7 April 2014. The report is datelined Kotgul, Bhamragarh in Gadchiroli district[47].

At his wooden- hut office at Bhamragarh, BJP functionary Sunil Vishwas shifts through a heap of papers to check the progress of the campaign and expresses satisfaction with the administration's preparations for the elections.

For once, politicians in Gadchiroli and remote Maoist – hit area of this Maharashtra district are confident this time, thanks to police crack downs and breakthroughs. Security forces have shot dead over 36 Naxals since January 2013, including seven at Betkathi near Kotgul in February 2014. Only last year, 2013, the Naxals had forced some 27 sarpanchs of Korchi tehsil to resign. Since then, they all have taken back their resignations and are back in the saddle.

In the past, Naxal posters calling for a boycott of the polls would appear all over the district. This time, they have been restricted to a few places and even the movement of the Maoists have been limited, claim security forces. It is not as if the boycott calls work. Gadchiroli has always registered high turnouts, largely because security personnel have been escorting voters to the booths. What has changed this time is the campaigning where there used to be little.

"In 2009, we had to go on bikes, hiding campaign materials. This time around, it has been easier. The two police camps that have come up in the close vicinity have helped. We are sure the voter turn out will go up substantially in our area", says a Congress worker in Kotgul.

"The forces have been moving in the interiors for over a month now. The atmosphere is much more relaxed. However, we are still leaving the campaigning to our workers in the villages. No vehicles, no loudspeakers yet," Vishwas of the BJP.

Politcal workers feel development is now the keyword even in remote villages. "They want development. They understand that development is suffering because of insurgency", an activist said. "Candidates either feared to venture out into the open areas, or they are not allowed by the police, but we do go inside", says Namdeo Usendi of the Congress.

Ashok Nete of the BJP says. "Since the 2009 poll defeat, I have travelled to several interior villages and have met people. I have no problem." Workers, however, say Usendi and Nete have not been to many places, yet. A local journalist says, "The constituency is large. They better go to places where it matters the most".

Polling stations in the district have gone up from 839 to 872, and the number of hyper – sensitive booths dropped from 234 in 2009 to 209 (in 2014). This time only 27 polling stations have been shifted due to security concerns, as against 49 in 2009. "We have found no traces of Naxals, but we are alert," say IGP (Nagpur Range) Ravindra Kadam.

Gadchiroli braves Maoist threat; says it has to vote: 11 April 2014

This is a heartening story of a 64- year-old woman walking more than 10 km and six hours to caste her vote. This is the Indian democracy we can all be proud of!

Frail and wrinkled Kutake Gota walked from her village Ekra Khurd to a booth 5 km away. There, they realized their booth had changed. Angry but determined, her family trudged another seven km and finally got their fingers inked in the village of Peth.

This story is about the Chukalus, a family of four, including the said Gota, carried in a daily of 11April 2014, datelined Yetapalli, Gadchiroli[48].

Defying the diktat issued by the Maoists to boycott the general elections, more than 70 per cent of the voters in the Gadchiroli – Chimur Lok Sabha constituency showed up on 10 April 2014. In 2009, the turnout here was 65 per cent. The scribe saw long queues at the booths he visited during the polling. The polling officers were confident the villagers "would continue to come to vote till the close".

It needs to be emphasized that the turn out here in 2014 as also 2009 was far higher than in the metropolitans such as Delhi, Mumbai, Kolkata or Chennai. This only shows the vote has great value for the poor and common man than the spolt elite, pampered middle classes and the proverbial 'educated' Indian!

At 3.30 PM, some insurgents opened fire at a polling party on its way back from work near Jambia Gatta in the Yetapalli taluka. The skirmish lasted for a few minutes, and then the rebels melted into the dense forests. But the incident was as exception. The polling was largely peaceful.

Like Gota and the Chukalu family, most said they feared the Maoists and their unexpected attacks, but not voting was out of the question. "Several booths recorded turnouts as high as 80 per cent", said DC of Gadchiroli Ranjeet Kumar.

Suresh Barsagade of the Janhit Mahiti Seva Kendra : "The lack of development in this area is crippling. Even though they (voters) might want to sympathise with the Maoists or are forced to do so, they desperately want the fruits of development to reach them. That is why they are willing to stick their neck out and vote for governance." Seva Kendra is an organisation that seeks to create awareness about government plans among the backward communities.

This news story is accompanied by a picture of security men on either side of a man in civilian clothing, and its subtitle reads:

> Maoist – turned policeman Raoji Naitam (Centre) accompanies a 100 – strong security posse around a polling party heading to Kulbhatti, a village in Gadchiroli, to set up a polling booth – Raoji, who spent seven years as a Maoist, was offered the post of a Special Police Officer (SPO) after his surrender in January 2013.

Cop shot by Naxals in Gadchiroli: 29 April 2014

Naxals shot dead a police constable, Lalsu Pungati, 25, at the weekly market of Gyarapatti village in Kurkheda tehsil of Gadchiroli district on 27 April 2014. He was shot seven times by an "action team of Naxals" comprising six to seven members around 3 PM when Pungati was on an intelligence mission.

SDPO Kurkheda Sachin Pandkar told the daily : "He was talking to his personal informer when he was taken away by the latter on the pretext of giving some information. An action team of Naxalites came to the spot and shot Pungati seven times. The Naxals also took away his AK-47 and 200 rounds."[49]

7 cops killed in Gadchiroli Naxal attack : 12 May 2014

Blast: Strike at unlikely spot, two days after the arrests of Prof G N Saibaba

Two days after the Gadchiroli police arrested Delhi University Prof G N Saibaba for alleged Maoist link, Naxalites triggered a powerful landmine blast on 11 May 2014 in an unlikely area of the district, killing seven policemen and leaving two grievously injured.

IGP (Nagpur Range) Ravindra Kadam gives details: "The blast took place between 9 to 10 AM when a police van passing by Murmuri village of the district was hit by a powerful IED…while seven died on the spot, the two injured policemen were flown to Nagpur in a chopper."[50]

The police vehicle was part of a convoy of eight carrying 48 troops, returning from a routine anti-Naxal operation in Kasansur. Two vehicles had passed over the spot when the landmine went off.

A CPI (Maoist) statement admitted responsibility, but said the attack had "nothing to with the arrest of Saibaba." A man claiming to be Comrade Shrinivas, the "CPI (Maoist) PRO", called up the daily to give their "statement." Asked about Saibaba's arrest, Shrinivas said, "Everyone knows he is a professor in Delhi, he is not a Maoist party member. His arrest is an example of *Janata Ka daman* (suppression of people) by the government."

Shrinivas said: "The attack on the 11th was against the government, for targeting innocent people. The arrest of Saibaba is a similar one. Saibaba was remanded in magisterial custody for 14 days by a Gadchiroli court on 10 May 2014.

On the 11th, Naxals struck at a spot in the plains, with no forests along the road. They rarely conduct attacks in such open area. IGP Kadam admitted that they were surprised as "no Naxal activity was known previously at the attack site.

He also added it was too early to links the attack to Saibaba's arrest.

A Sunday shocker for Gadchiroli police : 12 May 2014

60 Maoists had surrendered ; Lok Sabha polls have been largely peaceful.

The same incident of the killing of seven policemen has been covered by another daily, under the above – mentioned headline, the blurb explaining the reason for this headline[51].

This daily, known for its accurate reporting and giving full details of the events covered by it, gives all necessary information in the two opening para's of the news story:

> "After two days of combing in the Maoist-hit areas of the Dhinora Division of Gadchiroli, commandos of C-60 force, the Maharashtra Police's Special Anti-Naxal unit, arrived Yedunar in the Chamorshi Division and called for the vehicles to reach the Gadchiroli police headquarters, hardly 30 km away, on 11 May 2014. But a Maoist – triggered blast would soon take away the lives of seven of them and leave two seriously injured." Not even in our dreams had we imagined that such a blast could take place in Chamorshi", a police officer posted in the area told the daily after the deadly landmine blast.

The tribal district, once a Maoist stronghold, witnessed a spate of encounters in the past two years, resulting in the elimination of 40 Maoists.

The Maharashtra Police launched "Campaign Nav Jeevan" in 2013, appealing to Maoists to surrender. In fact, a police officer visited the families of senior Naxal cadres in the district, promising them assistance under this campaign.

The Gadchiroli police claim the campaign was a "success", and it resulted in the surrender of over 60 Maoists. The Gadchiroli district witnessed a comparatively peaceful polling on 10 April. Two incidents of firing were reported in which one policeman was killed and five were injured.

"If some senior police officers posted in Gadchiroli are to be believed, Maoists were on the "back foot" in the district.

The daily accessed telephone conversation of DIG (Anti-Naxal Range) Ravindra Kadam[52] with a police informer in which Kadam claimed the way "things" are happening in Gadchiroli, the district will be "Maoist-free" within a year and a half.

The daily wanted to contact DIG Kadam for his comments on the said assertion and claim, perhaps overly optimistic and necessarily self-serving, but he did not respond to the repeated calls from the daily.

Intelligence failure

But the landmine attack has shocked the authorities. Sources have an interesting take on the issue. Pappu Gupta, who helped the police nab seven Maoists in February 2014, turned hostile subsequently because of "police indifference".

"Pappu Gupta was used and dumped by the police and it has sent a wrong message to the police informers", a surrendered Maoist told the daily. This attack, of 11 May, was a "big" failure of police intelligence, he said, adding the police needed to address the concerns of informers immediately.

The State Assembly polls are due in October (2014) and after almost peaceful Lok Sabha elections, the State Police are trying hard to maintain a "tight – grip" on Gadchiroli, at least till the Assembly elections.

Some local journalists believe the Maoists will not miss the opportunity provided by a "troubled network of informers" and may carry out some big strikes.

Over 50 policemen were killed in Gadchiroli in violence during the 2009 Assembly polls.

"Home Ministry failed miserably": BJP

In all such serious incidents concerning India's security, politics can't be found lagging far behind.

The BJP on 11 May 2014, demanded a high-level inquiry into the Naxal attack in Gadchiroli, that killed seven policemen and injured two. Opposition leader in the State Legislative Council Vinod Tawade slammed the intelligence agencies for failing to prevent the attack. He said the MHA failed miserably by not anticipating retaliation for the arrest of Prof Saibaba for suspeated Maoist links.

The BJP leader demanded that a permanent framework to prevent Naxal attacks be put in place[53].

"Dr Saibaba to go on hunger strike" : His family : 15 May 2014

"Delhi University Prof GN Saibaba, who was arrested by the Maharashtra police for his suspected Maoist links and taken to the State, will go on a hunger strike from 15 May 2014 if conditions of his confinement do not improve".

This was the story carried by a daily in its issue of 15 May 2014[54].

This decision of Saibaba was announced by his family, colleagues and social activists at a press conference in New Delhi on 14 May.

His wife Vasantha informed: "When his brother visited him on the 12th, he heard that they were keeping him in unsanitary, solitary cell without any helpers and convenient toilet facilities. His medicines, also prescribed and provided by the police doctor, were leaving denied to him. He is 90 per cent disabled, he was inflicted with polio when he was five, and is a wheelchair user and cannot move properly without assistance. He is also a heart patient, suffers from high blood pressure and has chronic and severe pain in his lower back."

She made further points summed up here

- "Dr Saibaba, who comes from a poor family, was the sole bread winner of the family and they were now apprehensive that the university would suspend him and cut off their income.
- "They have been trying to evict us for a long time. In the middle of summer last year, the vice chancellor who talks about globalising the university and bringing in world-class facilities and standards, got our water and electricity supply cut. The police have questioned us twice in our own house. When they came for the search last time, there was one man in the police uniform and some others in plain-clothes and they pushed their was into our house. Many among those present questioned Delhi University's silence on the matter, when the professor was allowed to be abducted, and the manner in which the authorities sought his

eviction last year (2013). They said dissenting voices were sought to be crushed."

Documentary film-maker Sanjay Kak said, "He was someone who brought voices from the other end to city dwellers like us. I first met him when he was organising a protest against Operation Greenhunt."

Sumit Chakravarti, an activist who was present along with representatives of the Delhi University Students Union, said, "He even spoke up against the new four-year undergraduate programme. The government has brought about a new law regarding the manner in which the disabled people should be treated, but here it is violating everything about it."

University teacher Karen Gabrielle said: "The Delhi University Community against Police Repression stands in solidarity with Dr Saibaba and his family and opposes the systematic targeting of democratic voices by the police force."

G N Saibaba to challenge bail denial in Supreme Court: 25 December 2015

Delhi Univeristy Prof G N Saibaba on 24 December 2015 said "he will surrender as directed by the court but will challenge his bail cancellation in the Supreme Court[55]."

This was reported by a daily on 25 December 2015.[55]

The Nagpur Bench of the Bombay High Court had on 23 December cancelled the bail of Saibaba, a wheel chair – bound professor with 90 per cent disability, was arrested in 2014 by the Maharashtra police for alleged Maoist links. He was then lodged in the Anda cell of the Nagpur Jail.

As his health started deteriorating in June 2015, he was granted bail for three months which was later extended for another three months, up to 31 December 2015. But on 23 December 2015, the Bombay High Court concelled his bail application and asked him to surrender within 48 hours. "I am being prosecuted on false charges. It appears that I am a victim of a witch hunt. But I am confident that I will prove my innocence during trial. I am extremely disappointed but I will abide by the order and surrender", said Saibaba, who is not keeping well even now.

The Committee for the Defence and Release of Saibaba too had said that the denial of bail to him was an attack on his democratic rights. The Committee also expressed concern on the criminal contempt against Arundhati Roy for her article about the professor.

The Committee said in a press statement: "The timing of the order has left us puzzled as it robs us of taking any legal recourse. The order came a day before the Supreme Court closes for Christmas."

Will it be Gujarat, Too? 20 January 2007

"Gujarat obviously seems to have been lucky as it has been saved from the ravages of the LWE virus!

"But of late, some evidence is turning up to show that the Naxalites are attempting to spread their tentacles in this State also. One instance of recent vintage is cited here."

This worrisome news was carried by a daily, known for its investigative reputation and skills, in great detail in its issue of 20 January 2007. This extensive coverage is educative for the students of LWE in India to understand as to how serious the Maoists are to spread their ideological thought in practice to all corner of the counry[56].

It has Bhopal connection

The Madhya Pradesh informed the press on 19 January 2007 that five hard-core Maoist cadres, "arrested last week after a Maoist weapons workshop was busted in Bhopal's Satnami Nagar area, have told their interrogators that they have an active Dalam (= a section of infantry or squad, that is, an operational unit of Maoists, at the lowest level, then comes their platoons companies, and battalions, all these designations are borrowed from the Army) in Surat, the textile city of Gujarat, as it has a large migrant population, including a large Chunk from Andhra Pradesh working in its processing units." But the police, understandably, refused to identify the part of Surat the arrested cadres had visited recently.

It is clear that the LWE could be spreading their wings to Gujarat. A police officer points out that it is easy for the Telegu-speaking Maoists to operate there as thousands of workers from Andhra Pradesh are employed in the textile industry.

A Gujarat police team was among the first to interrogate the arrested five with the teams from six other Naxal-hit states, the BSF and Military Intelligence MI Directorate, Army Headquarters. It needs to be noted that Gujarat has been considered relatively insulated from the LWE activities, even if the presence of activists in its southern parts has always been expected and talked about and discussed among the cognoscenti.

The idea of setting up a base in Surat is another indication that the ultras are choosing urban areas and cities to expand their presence as they are least likely to raise suspicions. But the idea itself goes against Mao's teaching of overpowering and taking over the rural areas completely before turning attention to the cities and urban areas. (Significantly, this Mao-speak is the reason behind the split in the Maoist unit of Karnataka). But it needs notice that this departure from Maoist tenet is of minor nature : It is a matter of policy and practical wisdom that they do not plan or run any aggressive operations in such urban centres. Instead, they use such centres for manufacturing parts of weapons or assembling them. In this context, police have discovered two such towns by now where this activity goes on — these are Bhopal and Surat. Therefore, it is no surprise that the IB has already alerted the states to keep an eye on (these workers and) joints who are operating lathe machines in their various towns.

The five cadres arrested in Bhopal in January 2007 had earlier operated for two years in Jabalpur 1996 onwards, and thence shifted their base to Indore for nearly four years before moving finally to the state capital Bhopal in 2001. Thus, they had been working and operating for some six years in Bhopal before being detected and arrested. DIG Anuradha Shankar gave these details to the daily.

SP Bhopal Anant Kumar gave details about the smooth operations at their 'lathe units' in such urban centres. The Maoists operating in cities always have a female member, which enabled them to rent a house without any undue difficulty. They hardly mix with the locals but pay their bills in time. The units are set up with lathe machines as a front and their location is usually close to the industrial units from where they can easily source raw material for their 'manufactures'.

The Bhopal 'units' yielded arms, components, literature and a huge stock of books on weaponry. The police claim it was the biggest Maoist library so far discovered. Shankar disclosed the Maoists, from making crude weapons, have come close to making rocket launchers like the RPG 7. Even more worrying is the fact of the MI informing the MP Police that "even the Indian Army has not as yet acquired plastic grenades of the type recently confiscated from the Maoists!"

Initially, as it turned out later, these five misled their local interrogators by faking their identities and addresses. But then, the MP Police sought the help of their Andhra counterparts to establish their real identities, and to ascertain their standing in the Maoist hierarchy. The five were apparently in touch with the central leadership, and the arms assembled or manufactured at Bhopal 'unit' were being sent to Jharkhand and Chhattisgarh.

The Big Five

The five arrested from Bhopal were obviously among the top leadership bracket of the CPI (Maoist). Here are their brief sketches.

Chakkakrushna, 47

A resident of Kajipetha mandal in Guntur, he is a member of the Central Technical Committee (CTC) of the CPI (Maoist) and also a member of the Andhra Pradesh State Committee. He is believed to be the chief of the R and D Wing of the party. He carries a bounty of Rs 10 Lakh on his head.

Yalwarthy Lilakrishna, 35

Resident of Kathlaru, Swaliyapuram in Guntur district, he is a District Committee Secretary, CPI (Maoist).

He carries a bounty of Rs 5 lakh on his head.

Ramesh Siddhi, 40

Resident of Brahman Kodru, Punni mandal in Guntur district, he is a District Committee Member of the CPI (Maoist). Reward on his head: Rs 3 lakh.

Gandrakota Pentaiyya, 57

Resident of Intikanne, Keshmudram, Warangal district, he is a member of the Area Committee. Reward on his head: Rs 2 lakh.

Lanjupalli Rani, 25

Hailing from Julapalli Piduguralla, she is a member of the Area Committee. Reward on her head: Rs 2 lakh.

Cabinet clears Nagpur Metro. Mobile towers in Naxal belts: 21 August 2014

The Union Cabinet on 20 August 2014 approved the Rs 8,600 – crore Nagpur Metro Rail Project and long-pending proposal to install mobile towers at 2199 locations in the Naxal-hit districts by BSNL at a cost of Rs 3,216 crore that will be borne by the Government.

The latter project is relevant to the subject matter of this book. The news item was carried in a daily on 21 August 2014[57].

On the mobile services in the Naxal-hit areas, Telecom Minister Ravi Shankar Prasad told the press after the Cabinet meeting: "The Cabinet has approved setting up of 1,836 Baste Transmission Towers (BTT) in LWE-affected districts. People in these areas and security forces have asked to improve the mobile connectivity in these districts."

These mobile services will be provided in AP, Bihar, Chhattisgarh, Jharkhand, Maharashta, MP, Odisha, Telangana, UP and West Bengal.

The establishment of Mobile services would augment public communication facilities in backward regions besides providing a platform for mobile – based information dissemination and easy access to governance and policing. 363 towers under the programme have already been set up for which subsidy will be given from the Universal Services Obligation Fund.

The project implementation cost through the open tendering process is approximately Rs 3,568 Cr against the revised estimate of Rs 3,216 Cr.

Notes

1. Milind Ghatwai, Indian Express, 13 Jan 2007.
2. Sudhir K. Singh, Asian Age, 16 Jan 2007.
3. *Op Cit.*
4. Milind Ghatwai, Indian Experss, 20 Jan 2007.
5. Omer Farooq, The Pioneer, 4 Feb 2007.
6. Vishma Mohan, Times of India, 16 Mar 2007.
7. The Hindu, 12 Jan 2007.
8. Manish Sahu, Indian Express, 31 Mar 2014.
9. TNS, Times of India, 11 DEc 2014.
10. Vivek Deshpande, Indian Experss, 18 Dec 2006.
11. Vivek Dedhponde, Indian Express, 18 Dec 2006.
12. Vivek Deshpande, Indian Express, 8 Jun 2007.
13. The Pioneer, 16.6 2008.
14. TNS, Times of Indian, 2 Feb 2009.
15. Pradip Kumar Maitra, Hindustan Times, 3 Feb 2009.
16. Seema Kamdar, Mail Today, 6 Feb 2009.
17. Vivek Deshande, Indian Express, 7 Feb 2009.
18. TN Raghunatha, The Pioneer, 8 Feb 2009.
19. Pavan Dahat, The Hindu, 31 Jan 2012.
20. Staff Reporter, The Hindu, 6 Apr 2012.
21. Meena Menon, The Hindu, 13 April 2012.
22. HT Correspondent, Hindustan Times, 27 April 2012.
23. Vivek Deshpande, Indian Express, 8 July 2012.
24. Staf Reporter, The Hindu, 25 Aug 2012.
25. Pranab Dhal Samanta, Indian Express, 25 November 2012.
26. Ashutosh Bhardwaj, Indian Express, 3 Dec 2012.
27. Staff Repoter, The Hindu, 6 Dec 2012.
28. Staff Repoter, The Hindu, 10 Dec 2012.
29. ENS, Indian Express, 14 Jan 2013.
30. Vivek Deshpande, Indian Express, 14 Jan 2013.

31. ENS, Indian Express, 21 Jan 2013.
32. Staff Reporter, The Hindu, 21 Jan 2013.
33. Staff Reporter, The Hindu, 21 Jan 2013.
34. Pradip Kumar Maitra, Hindustan Times, 21 Jan 2013.
35. Vivek Deshpande, 17 Indian Express, Jan 2013.
36. ENS, Indian Express, 26 Jun 2013.
37. Staff Reporter, The Hindu, 28 Jun 2013.
38. Vivek Deshpande, Indian Express, dateline Nagpur 16 Sep 2013.
39. Sanjay Singh, *ibid,* dateline Dehradun.
40. Vivek Deshpande, Indian Express,18 Sep 2013.
41. *Ibid.*
42. Pavan Dahat, The Hindu, 4 Oct 2013.
43. Soumittra S Bore, Times of India, 18 Oct 2013.
44. HTC, Hinustan Times, 18 Oct 2013.
45. Sashutosh Bhardwaj, Indian Express, 29 Mar 2014.
46. Vivek Deshpande, Indian Express, 29 Mar 2014.
47. Vivek Deshpande, Indian Express, 7 Apr 2014.
48. Kunal Purohit, Hindustan Times, 11 Apr 2014.
49. ENS, Indian Express, 29 Apr 2014.
50. ENS, Indian Express, 12 May 2014.
51. Pavan Dahat, The Hindu, 12 May 2014.
52. Ravindra Kadam's appointment needs clarification. The earlier report said he was IGP (Nagpur Range). This one says he is DIG (Anti-Naxal Range). In fact, he could be IGP (Anti-Naxal Operations). But if he were holding double charge, which is a possibility, he could be IGP (Nagpur Range and Anti-Naxal operations.
53. Staff Reporter, *ibid.*
54. Vijetha SN, The HIndu, 15 May 2014.
55. HT Correspondent, Hindustan Times, 25 Dec 2015.
56. Milind Ghatwa(n)i, Indian Express, 2 Jan 2007.
57. PNS, The Pioneer, 21 Ang 2014.

30

Odisha

Backgrounder to LWE in the State

Origin

The Naxal movement gained momentum from 1968 onwards with unarmed groups raising issues such as rights over bamboo and forest produce, and mining.

Bloody Era

2004-12.

Key issues

Livelihood of tribals.

Status check

More than 20 of 30 districts are affected by Maoist violence.

CM Navin Patnaik : In Aug 2011

"Development can not be achieved through violence… I appeal to the extremists to shun violence and join the mainstream."

Naxalism in Odisha : Early 2000s

"The Maoists have been consolidating their base in Odisha, too. CM Naveen Patnaik has admitted that 10 of his state's 30 districts were affected by Naxalite violence."

The Maoists are employing well-known and tested methods to draw the youth into their fold. They are mobilizing unemployed young men for Rs 2,000 a month.

They have successfully launched some major attacks in Odisha. In 2002, they attacked Golpada police station in Rayagada district. In 2005, the Kalimela police station in Malkangiri district was the target. It was a planned escalation of violence, with over 200 armed CPI (Maoist) cadre attacking the Ramagiri – Udaigiri sub-jail in Gajapati district and freeing 40 prisoners, including Ghirsingha Majhi, a senior Maoist leader. They also attacked the police station, the camp of the 3rd Battalion, Odisha State Armed Police, and treasury.

Analysts feel they are the "blooding" operations where-in cadres are exposed to military operations to prepare them to undertake a wider mobilisation across the entire Maoist Corridor along India's eastern board.

6 Feb 2004. 180 Maoists besieged Odisha police station, district jail and the Treasury, killing four policemen. They looted 500 rifles from District Police Armoury in Koraput, Odisha.

24 Mar 2006. Some 500 armed Maoists attacked Odisha State Armed Police Camp in Udaigiri. They killed three policemen, freed 40 prisoners, and looted arms. Raided police station, barracks, sub-jail and Treasury. Blasted jail compound.

26 Apr. 2006. 200 Maoists attacked the villagers of Manikonta, abducted and thrashed 95; of these they killed 13, lynched two, and released the rest.

Odisha outlaws Maoists and announces Surrender Package: Jun 2006

In a significant decision, the Naveen Patnaik Government has outlawed the CPI (Maoist) and its seven front organisations – 'overground arms' of the Maoists', as this author likes to dub them—under the Criminal Law Amendment Act (CLA), 1908[1].

State Chief Secretary explained : "The organisations were banned under Section 16 of the CLA. The front organisations have been providing a platform to the Naxalites to propagate their ideology. Their activities have been affecting administration and law and order. The government gave the Naxals an opportunity to reform and provided maximum support to bring them back to mainstream but they did not heed the government's proposals and continued with violence. Finally, there was no other way and we were forced to declare them unlawful. The State government has promised rehabilitation package to militants who surrender to help them join the mainstream.

Home Secretary Santosh Kumar offers further details : "Unlike in other states, no special law has been enacted in Odisha. There is a technical difference between imposing a ban on organizations and declaring them unlawful. A ban would empower the police to arrest the office bearers, while declaring them unlawful would mean that they would be liable for punishment if they continued with their activities. But the state government has maintained that they are open to negotiations with the Maoists without any pre-conditions."

Daman Pratirodh Manch (DPM), one of the seven front outfits, challenged the ban in the Odisha High Court (HC). It convenor Dandapani Mohant Said : "DPM is a democratic organisation and the ban on it is an undemocratic move. We have no links with the Maoists and DPM is tackling grassroots problems concerning the downtrodden and the tribals of the State. This ban would be a stumbling block in the path of any possibility of talks among the Naxals, the pro-people leaders and the government."

Some parties have also opposed the ban on the Maoists. Odish Gana Parishad leaders believe that banning the Naxalites would create more problems. CPI leader Judhistir Rout said the ban had come at an "inopportune" time.

Besides outlawing CPI (Maoist), the state government has also come up with a "relief package" for surrendering Maoist cadres. The main points of this relief package are mentioned here.

1. Goodies on surrender.
   - Immediate payment of upto Rs 10,000.
   - Allotment of a plot for a house.
   - Housing grant upto Rs 25,000.
   - Bank loans upto Rs 200,000, with a subsidy component of Rs 50,000 after repayment of 75 per cent of the loan.
2. The state Cabinet decided to give surrendered cadres Rs 15,000 if they marry.
3. Free treatment in a government hospital.
4. Withdrawal of minor cases against them.
5. The reward money if he had a bounty on his head.
6. They would be paid for each weapon they surrender. Amount due for each weapon is mentioned here
   - Rocket launcher Rs 15,000.
   - AK – 47 and Assault rifle Rs 10,000.
   - 303 rifle or pistol Rs 5,000.

It is, indeed, an attractive surrender package. How many ultras would be induced to give in to there liberal terms will be known only after a while.

Maoists want parts of Odisha to join two parts of the Red Corridor Mid June 2006

As of today, Jun 2006, there are 18 *dolams* in Visakhapatnam, Vizianagram, Srikakulam, Gangavaram, Koraput and Gajapati. "This belt, including the Dandakaranya, has been designated, by the Maoists, as the Andhra-Odisha border."[2]

They now want to open a link with the neighbouring Jharkhand. The larger plan is to create an uninterrupted north-south corridor, and Odisha' Central and Western regions are a must for that to fructify.

Significantly, Maoists are known to be active in 10 of Odisha's 30 districts, but the State Government denies any Maoist problem in its territory. This must seen surprising when on 24 Mar 2006, some 200 armed Maoists had attacked the Ramagiri-Udaygiri subjail in Gajapati district, freeing 40 prisoners, including Ghersinga Majhi, a senior Maoist leader.

They had also attacked the police station, 3rd Battalion, Odisha State Armed Police Camp, the treasury, the Tehsildar's office and a telecom tower. Officer-in-charge, Police Station Ranjan Kumar Mallick, and Jailor Rabinarayan Sethi were abducted.

CM Naveen Patnaik told the Assembly that the Ultras had come from Andhra's Vizianagram district.

A year earlier (in 2005), the Maoists had targeted the Kalimela police station in Malkangiri district of the State. The Golpadar police station in Rayagada district was attacked by them in 2002.

The pattern of these attacks should be carefully studied. It seems to be reflecting a strategic design going for beyond freeing the Maoist prisoners, looting arms and demoralisation of the police and paralysis of the administration. It possibly could be a determined bid to infiltrate central and western regions of Odisha to create north-south Corridor, as suggested above. Even more sinisterly, these could be "blooding" operations aimed at exposing cadres to serious combat against the state forces and law-enforcing agencies of the Centre to prepare them for a wider mobilisation across the entire Maoist corridor along India'a Eastern Board.

Origins in West Bengal and AP and expansion into Odisha: Links across the states : Jun 2006

A Bihar police officer says the Maoists have established links with internal and external agencies and the Communist Party of Nepal (Maoist), CPN (M), to acquire arms and sophisticated communication equipment that can intercept police conversation.

Kameshwar Baitha, a Maoist leader, disclosed during interrogation that Naxalites in Bihar had "recently purchased eight AK – 47s from Andhra Pradesh at Rs 2 lakh a piece.

After the MCC merged with the PWG in Sep 2004 and declared a unilateral ceasefire with the CPI (ML) Liberation in Jan 2005, the Maoist movement has understandably gained momentum. DGP Bihar Ashish Ranjan Sinha say, "The Nepali and Bihari Maoists had formed a Bihar-Nepal Border Coordination Committee to give shelter to each other's cadres. In view of this fact, it is difficult to give credit to the Nepalese Maoist leader Prachanda's statement – during his Nov 2006 visit to India to participate in the Hindustan Times convened Leadership Conference – that there was no understanding between the Nepalese Maoists and their Indian counterparts.

If Naxalism sprang from an eponymous village in West Bengal Darjeeling district in May 1967, it was born in Andhra Pradesh on the last day of Oct 1967 when a huge meeting organised by the Jatapur and Savara tribes in Srikakulam district was disrupted by Medi Satyam of the Congress and in the ensuing violence Satyam and two tribals were killed. From then on, West Bengal in the east and Andhra Pradesh in the south were set to develop into some kind of epicentres for LWE, and violence related to it, in India.

"As of today, there are 18 *dalams* in Visakhapatnam, Vizianagram, Srikakulam, Gangavaram, Koraput and Gajapati." More importantly, "The Maoists have declared this belt, including the Dandakaranya forest, as Andhra Pradesh – Odisha Border Zone[3].

They now hope to open link with the neighbouring Jharkhand. The larger plan is to create an uninterrupted north-south corridor, Odisha's Central and Western regions are required to be a part of this "uninterrupted Corridor."

Maoists in Odisha

Interestingly, Maoists are known to be active in 10 of the 30 districts of Odisha, but the State Government denies any Naxalite problem. On 24 Mar 2006, some 200 armed Maoists attacked the Ramagiri Udaigiri Sub-Jail in Gajapati district and freed 40 prisoners, including Ghirsing Majhi, a senior Maoist leader. They also attacked the police station, 3 Battalion of the Odisha State Armed Police, the treasury, the tehsildar's office and a telecom tower. The officer-in-charge of the police station, Ranjan Kumar Mallick, and the jailor, Rabinarayan Sethi, were abducted.

CM Navin Patnaik told the Assembly that the Ultras had come from Vizianagram district of AP. A year earlier (in 2005), the Kalimela police station in Malkangiri district was targeted. The Golpadar police station in Rayagada district was attacked in 2002.

The pattern of these attacks should be studied carefully. It seems to be reflecting a strategic design going for beyond freeing the Maoist prisoners, looting Maoists and demoralisation of the police and paralysis of the administration. It possibly could be a determined bid to infiltrate the Central and Western regions of Odisha to create an uninterrupted north-south corridor.

Even more sinisterly, these could be the "blooding" operations aimed at exposing the cadres to serious combat against the state forces and law enforcing agencies of the Centre to prepare them for a wider mobilisation across the entire Maoist corridor along India's eastern board.

Odisha : Is it ready to counter Naxalism: Oct 2006

Odisha may not be one of the worst-hit states on the Naxalite stakes, as are Jharkhand and Chhattisgarh, but it should never be seen complacent in its fight against the ultras' and their violence. It is time that this violence is brought under an analytical focus as also its preparedness to face the threat. Recent killing of its DIG Jaswinder Singh (23 Oct 2006) is not the only reason for this critical review.

Eversince the Naxalite infiltration began in the state in the early 1990s, the system of policing to counter their presence and activities has not been found to be effective. Some analysts believe it "to have been a big mess". In statistical terms, it is an extremely worrying situation. As many as 20 of the State's 30 districts are presently (Oct 2006) plagued by the presence – or is it virus? – of the Naxals[4].

The recent killing of its DIG by the Naxals brought the states unpreparedness to face the LWE under sharp focus (This his gunning down was later attributed to his security guard raised facile questions about managing information). But the real question for the State is this : How capable are the armed rebels to strike at its security apparatus and how well-prepared is its police to counter it? It needs to be understood that southern Odisha is particularly vulnerable to Naxal depradations.

Broad areas of concern in the counter-Naxalite campaign are mentioned here:

- The gulf between the field commanders and their seniors sitting in the headquarters.
- Inadequate training in anti-Naxal operations.
- Poor equipment, and even weaponry, held by the police compared to the ones with the Naxals.

- Equally important, failure of the state to counter Maoist propaganda among the tribals.

The administrative machinery is reported to be ineffective. Even worse, a sense of insecurity is evident among the police personnel posted for duty in the southern districts of Odisha, and consequently, many among police—right from Top level officers to the constable down the line—deem a posting in these districts on anti-Naxal duties as punishment rather than a challenge. They may have reasons, at least in some cases, for such sinking feelings but it is certainly unfortunate.

There are certain attributing factors for such a mindset : difficult terrain; lack of essential equipment; and an indifferent top administration. It is, thus, understandable that the security personnel assigned to combat the Maoists are neither motivated enough nor in the best of their morale. Perhaps, some of them may be in a highly demoralized state of mind.

Reasons for such unhappy and undesirable situation are not for to sec. Often, their essential requirements are not provided to them. The Armed Police Force, assigned the combing operation task in the deep forests, to search and arrest the ultras, are authorised jungle boots for the job. But they are given canvas shoes instead, which do not work even in the plains. Yet again, instead of getting a light weight rain coat, they are often walking in the rains in heavy tarpaulin overcoats. Now comes the most disconcerting of the factors that adversely affects the combat efficiency: The disconnect between the top officers who do not have much experience of anti-Naxal combat and those actually involved in the job on the ground who keeps complaining that the former keep issuing orders "without caring to know the ground realities." This mutual 'grouse' and recrimination between the headquarters and the 'field' is not unknown in such situations but it seems to be more pronounced in Odisha.

Given the factors enumerated above, which are bound to create difficulties in the way of efficient and effective performance of State's Counter-Naxal campaign, if not make it dysfunctional, it should come as no surprise that the ultras carried out violent attacks, at times with worrying regularity, in the past few years. Some major ones are mentioned here.

1. The Left Extremists targeted the police at will in Malkangiri, Koraput, and Gajapati districts.
2. They laid siege to Koraput district headquarters town, and noless, in 2004 and looted arms.
3. In 2002, more than half-a-dozen policemen were blown up in a land mine blast.

4. Then there was Ramagiri-Udaigiri jail- break in mid – 2006. This was an example of clear dereliction of duty as the security in the prison located in the highly vulnerable area had not been reinforced as it should have been as it had been subjected to a similar raid in 1998 by the same ultras.

Effective anti-Naxal strategy and policy needed

It is obvious from the preceding narrative that the State has not been able to put in place an effective anti-Naxal strategy to confront the present, serious challenge. It is beyond doubt that the political executive is doing a commendable job by executing development projects in the State's backward areas, which is the long-terms anti-dote to the spread of the LWE. But it is equally essential that it does not ignore the need to defeat the Naxal violence in its present strongholds. It is, indeed the far-sighted political leadership that should guide the police top brass in this serious situation. The two must get their act together and draw up an effective anti-Naxal strategy. Analysts feel merely asking for financial help and some additional paramilitary forces every time there is a Naxal strike, as a reflex action, can at the best to the news for the media, but certainly not a substitute for an effective counter-Naxal action plan.

An urgent action is called for from the State on this issue in view of the fact that the Centre has made it clear that combating Maoist challenge is the responsibility of the individual states, even though it was ready to provide all necessary help to them to defeat the LWE. The Centre has also advised the affected states to work out plans for inter-state cooperation and coordination to defeat this terror outfit. The states can expect from the Centre financial packages, additional security forces, intelligence inputs and over-all guidance as and when required. For the last mentioned, the Centre (read MHA) has set up various mechanisms mentioned here.

1. Empowered Group of Ministers (E GoM) to deliberate upon the policy issues concerning the Maoist terror and insurrection.
2. Anti-Naxalite Task Force, set up by the MHA composed of ministers, senior civil and police officers from the Naxal-hit states and concerned ministries at the Centre, which periodically discuss issues of mutual interest on anti-Naxal plans formulated by various states.
3. National Coordination Centre on Naxalism (NCCN), composed of the Home Secretaries and DGPs of the affected states and presided over by the Union Home Secretary, is charged with the task of coordination of counter-Naxalite strategies of various states at the level of officials.

But there is one urgent task that must be the primary necessity to shore up Odisha's anti-Naxal capabilities in the form of a committed cadre of trained officers and men, equipped in all aspects to take on the ultras under extremely harsh and hostile conditions. They should not only be provided with requisite weaponry, technologically sound communication equipment and intelligence back-up but also imbued with self-confidence which comes only with the full knowledge that the political and police leaderships will back them to the hilt. This is an extremely essential requirement in the current political milieu. Security forces are not unaware of the fact that after any serious anti-terrorist or anti-Maoist actions, particularly those which result in some fatalities, ruling party in the state comes under serious pressure to institute inquiries against their men for either killing the 'innocents' or 'excessive' use of force. And not unoften, the Chief Ministers end up conceding the inquiry, or at the very least, sacking senior police officers.

Some believe the most important task for the administration is the training of police personnel for anti-Naxal operations, including guerrilla and jungle warfare training. It is an unexceptionable fact and a beginning has been made by Jharkhand, setting up a Jungle Warfare School at Hazaribagh to conduct anti-Naxal training courses for its police. It is certainly not suggested that each Naxal-hit state must set up its own school to train for anti – Naxal operations. What can strongly be recommended is that one or two more such schools be set up and all Naxal-hit states – currently, the number stands at nine—must train requisite number of their police personnel at any of these school after certain coordination among the states, or by the MHA.

At the end, the need for a counter-Naxalite is unquestionable.

Dreaded Sobha's arrest brings relief : 8 Oct 2006

The arrest of Sobha, a dreaded Maoist Area Commander, has brought a sigh of relief for the police administrations of four states: Jharkhand, Chhattisgarh, Bihar and Odisha.

Sobha, arrested with two others from Lathikata market in Sundargarh district of Odisha on 7 Oct 2006, is said to be a member of the CPI (Maoist) Central Committee. The other two arrested with her, Rajan Munda and Bijoy Munda, are members of the No. 39 Platoon of the Maoists.

Along with her husband, Prasant Bose, a West Bengal-based active Maoist leader, Sobha was instrumental in planning attacks in these four states, said SP Sundargarh, Dhirendara S Kutte.

Andhra Police raid Maoist hideouts in Bhopal and Rourkela: Jan 2007

Two raids on the key hideouts of Maoists by the AP Police in the latter half of Jan 2007 in Bhopal and Rourkela led to the arrest of senior cadres and recovery of a lot of arms and ammunition. More significant is the seizure of "gold mine of information about the outfit in the form of CDs, DVDs and hard discs."

Police sources feel that all the gadgetry seized "contain so much information that it could take months to analyse it". It yields information on the Maoist network in different states. This treasure trove also has animation films on assaults and counter-assaults against the police forces[5].

With all this information available to the security and intelligence agencies it is not difficult to imagine as to what serious implications it will have for organisational functioning and operational capabilities of the CPI (Maoist) throughout the country.

Maoist Deputy Area Commander Killed : Feb 2007

On the eve of the state panchayat polls, scheduled for 13 Feb 2007, Special Operations Group (SOG) of the State Police and the CRPF personnel on 12 Feb 2007 gunned down two Maoist cadres, including a Deputy Area Commander and injured two others after a gun battle in the southern district of Malkangiri. The incident occurred 9.30 AM when the SOG was heading for the Radigata polling booth under Kalimela police station, while the polling party was expected to follow the police team.

When the extremists opened fire on the policemen from inside the Kurup forest, the latter returned fire. The casualties mentioned above occurred as a result of the half-an-hour fire fight that ensued.

Police recovered grenades, explosives, kit bags, some literature/ pamphlets and polythene sheets from the spot. Later, a detailed search of their jungle hideout yielded a solar phone, electronic detonators and some fuse wire. It is to be noted that the Maoists had earlier warned the people and wanted them to boycott these panchayat polls in the area of South-West police Range. The incident created certain 'panic' among the polling parties charged with the responsibility of conducting polls at different polling booths in the LWE-hit area on 13 February. The ultras had earlier killed a Havildar of the CRPF on 26 January in this very area.

This incident led to an intensified combing operations and arrest of several suspects by the police. On 30 January, the forces had arrested three Maoist cadres following a gun battle between the two sides in the forest near Karamguda village under Chitrakonda police station, Malkangiri district.

Fire fight in Sambalpur Forest: Mar 2007

There was a heavy exchange of fire on 26 Mar 2007 evening between the SOG and CRPF men and the Maoists in the Kutab Forest area between Gariakhaman and Budhi Khaman villages under the Kisinda police station in the northern district of Sambalpur.

Fire fighting took place when security men came across some rebels during combing operations of the said forest area. If the former fired some 95 rounds, the rebels replied with some 50 bullets before escaping from the scene. SP Sambalpur S Debadutta Singh told the press : "We have alerted all entry points bordering Andhra Pradesh and Chhattisgarh and intensive combing operations have also been carried out to nab the Ultras. Security forces suspected that some 30 ultras are active in Kisinda area. The ultras are painting the State's development initiatives as anti-people and we are countering it."

Earlier on 13 March, district police had arrested an employee of the Odisha Forest Development Corporation (OFDC) for his alleged role in providing arms and ammunition to the Maoist outfit. Police had then recovered three rifles and some bullets on the spot.

To trace the ultras who had disappeared into the jungle on 26 March, Kisinda and Jujumara police stations were alerted and police parties were sent out to launch a massive combing operations.

Maoists protest Nandigram deaths : Odisha's Response Mar: 2007

The Naxalites called for a *bandh* across four states – Odisha, Bihar, Jharkhand and West Bengal—to protest the police shooting 15 villagers in Nandigram in West Bengal.

Barring some stray incidents in the South-Western Police Range of Odisha, the 20 Mar 2007 *bandh* by the CPI (Maoist) evoked a mixed response. DGP Amarananda Pattanayak said : "We have reports of violence in Malkangiri while the *bandh* was partial success and there were no reports of any major untoward incident during it." On the other hand, the Maoists in a statement issued by one Sunil, said : "The people must come to terms with the fact that the governments in these states are agents of imperialist forces and should rise to fight their anti-people agenda."

The ultras have been opposing the Special Economic Zone (SEZ) and the consequent tribal displacement.

Meanwhile the SOG and CRPF arrested a Maoist leader near Orkelguda village under Malkangiri police station close to Chhattisgarh border. He was identified as Laxaman, an expert in laying landmines. His arrest followed a heavy exchange of fire between forces and ultras near Kalimela. No bodies were recovered while police claimed the death of three Maoists.

But the *bandh* affected normal life in Malkangiri, Gajapati, Rayagada and Koraput while the districts of Sambalpur, Angul, Jajpur, Dhenkanal and Rourkela, were those among the Maoist-hit regions which were not affected by the bandh, said police sources.

Thus, the *bandh* call by the LWE evoked a "partial response" in Odisha, by now, a standard reply of any ruling party to describe the affect of a strike.

7 Southern Towns under Maoist threat : Jun 2007

"At least seven major towns under the Southern Police Range have come under serious Maoist threat while more than 500 Maoist cadres have been coming along the Odisha-Andhra Pradesh border in the Southern and south-western Police Ranges of Odisha." This was reported by a daily in a news story datelined Parla Khemundi, 11 Jun 2007.

Latest intelligence inputs suggest the ultras have been camping in the ditricts of Gajapati, Ganjam, Rayagada, Koraput, Nawrangpur, Malkangiri and several other places, with a view to implementing the decisions taken during the 9th Congress of the CPI (Maoist).

Meanwhile, Maoists have also been conducting camps in which they are attempting to convince the people against the development schemes of the state. Ultras are conducting camps in the dense forest areas of South Odisha, where the security forces often failed to locate the Maoist bases located there-in.

Forces are suspecting that the top Maoist leader, Sudhakar, is camping there to work out the future plans and programmes for South Odisha. The cadres are also believed to be moving along the Odisha-Chhattisgarh border.

Considering these developments and the said movement of the Maoist cadres, the SOGs of the police and CRPF have intensified their combing operations along the areas of the state bordering Andhra Pradesh and Chhattisgarh. In additions, a high alert has been put in place at all the sensitive junctions under the Southern Police Range.

Road re-routed to bring Naxal heartland on Map : Jun 2007

Odisha Government has long dreamt of a road through its 12 insurgency-hit districts, bringing these tribal areas closer to the rest of the State, and hopefully to the development, as well! It sees a solution to its Maoist insurgency in this dreamroad.

A 5 Jun 2007 report in a daily datelined New Delhi speaks of a recent Cabinet meeting chaired by PM Manmohan Singh where the Ministry of Shipping, Road Transport and Highways was asked to expedite the finalisation of the DPR (Detailed Project Report) for the Vijayawada (AP)-Ranchi (Jharkhand) Corridor cutting through Odisha, and take it up on priority basis. The two-lane road demanded by Odisha will be part of this Corridor. The alignment of this road follows : Vijayawada (AP) – Malkangiri-Koraput-Rayagada-Gajapati-Ganjam-Kandhamal-Angul-Sambalpur-Deogarh-Keonjhar-Mayurbhanj-Ranchi (Jharkhand)-Bolangir (Boudh). Of the 1,729 km long corridor, 2-lane 1219 km portion will be in Odisha, linking its 12 district towns named above. The State has requested the Centre that its state highways, district and rural roads running along the alignment be incorporated in the corridor and special assistance be given to it for the purpose. This way, 235.8 km of National Highway section, 875 km of state highways and 104.5 km rural roads will be part of the Corridor.

The road from Vijaywada enters Odisha at Motu in Malkangiri district and leaves it at Tiring in Mayurbhanj district on the north.

Odisha has long sought as security corridor through the 'Red' tribal belts. The State, in fact, wanted that the entire stretch through its territory be declared a National Highway (NH) or at least, be developed on par with NHs. While the Ministry may not call the stretch NH as yet, with the PM taking a keen interest, it is set to be developed as per NH standards.

What is means is that tribal area of the 12 districts named above—Koraput, Malkangiri, Rayagada, Gajapati, Ganjam, Kandhamal, Angul, Sambalpur, Deogarh, Keojhar, Mayurbhanj and Boudh, currently insurgency - hot beds, may emerge out of the hinterlands.

Confirming that the project has been put on the fast track, a senior official of the Ministry said: " The DPR of the corridor is underway and should be ready in six-seven months."

Joint Command achieves a success: Jun 2007

The Joint Command set up by the State Government to track down the Maoists in the industrial hubs on 10 Jun 2007 achieved a success when the security forces after 5-day – long combing operations in the dense forests of Kankadhada [Kankadahad?] Forest Beat area under the North-Central Police Range in Dhenkanal district, gunned down two Maoists, demolished a camp and recovered a heavy cache of arms and ammunition.

Informing a daily about the first success of the Joint Command, DIG North-Central Range Arun Sarangi said[6].

- "The security forces have managed to bring the whole area under their control, while the combing operation has been further intensified to crack down on more ultras.
- "We are suspecting that two are dead, though their bodies are yet to be recovered. The amount of arms and ammunition seized point to a major future plan of the ultras in the Kankandahad forest.
- "In all, 75 rounds of live ammunition, one SLR, a revolver, a land-mine, five detonators, six gelatine sticks, and a large quantity of personal belongings from the camp was recovered, after the Maoist retreated into the jungle.
- "The 17-member Joint Command team led by SP Dhenkanal Sanjay Kousal strongly fought against the rebels for four hours. The encounter took place in the Kanarapathara Kata jungle close to the area where the Maoists had abducted and killed three Forest Department employees, including a forester and two forest guards recently. The killing was indicative of the fact that the ultras have recently penetrated into the area".

DIG Sarangi, who heads the Joint Command added: "Every precaution has been taken to negate possible Maoist strikes and security forces have been working overtime in close coordination with the security system put in place by different industrial houses in four districts : Jajpur, Dhenkanal, Angul and Keonjhar."

Alerts have also been sounded to intelligence networks in the wake of the incident and the Maoist movement, which was so far confined to most of the northern districts, was recently notices in Angul and Dhenkanal districts.

The Jharkhand – bordering Keonjhar district, the mining belt of the State, is on top of the agenda of the ultras. Admitting that the LWE belonging to the CPI (Janashakti) group have strengthened their base in the three districts of Jajpur, Dhenkanal and Keonjhar, the State Home Department inducted four SOGs—two in Dhenkanal and one each in Jajpur and Keonjhar districts.

However, sources claimed that mainline ultras have already made a corridor from Sundargarh to Ravagada via Sambalpur, Deogarh and Phulbani, from where they are stated to carry out their depradations. The area from where the new outfit is operating from is about 10,000 sq km, covering these three districts.

The problems confronting the police in combating and routing out the ultras from this large area are both logistic and administrative in nature. Though for the Maoists, the area constitute a single operational unit, on which they can manage to bear all their fighting cadres and support resources, for the police it falls within the jurisdictions of three districts, and making it even worse, coming under the three different police ranges. Yet again, while the ultras are well-conversant with the roads and passes, the police from the three districts are just picking up the pieces, being unfamiliar with the road communications and Maoist hideouts to begin with, anyway.

Meanwhile, in the wake of poster campaign carried out by Left ultras in Sambalgarh and Deogarh districts under the Northern Police Range, security forces have intensified their combing operations while an alert has also been sounded at all the sensitive points.

"A close watch has been maintained on the National Highways and railway lines passing through the Sambalpur and Deogarh areas", said the police sources.

Jul 2007. Sriramulu Srinivasulu arrested from Bariguda forest in Kalimela area of Malkangiri district, Odisha. Released on bail by Odisha High Court on 21 Apr 2011 and ordered to leave the State within 24 hours. His release was one of the demands of the CPI (Maoist) in Malkangiri Collector RV Krishna's abduction case on 24 Feb 2011.

Maoist hideout in Malkangiri destroyed : Aug 2007

The SOG and District volunteers Force on 14 Aug 2007 jointly destroyed a Maoist hideout in Prajaguda and Kurup villages, near Rajurkonta area of Kalimela block of southern district of Malkangiri under the South-Western police Range in Odisha. The incident assumes significance as the LWEs had called for a Black Day on the Independence Day, Wednesday, 15 Aug 2007.

Malkangiri SP Satish Gajbhiye spoke to the daily on phone : "The combing operations team raided a Maoist hideout at Rajurkonta and Kurup areas where 12 cadres including some women cadres, had gathered for a meeting ahead of the Independence Day. We recovered one landmine, a detonator, 'huge' quantities of explosives and large quantity of medicines which was required to be used for the injured cadres was also recovered after an hour-long exchange for fire."

Security forces destroyed the Shahid Pillar (Martyrs Column) recently erected by the ultras and search operation was intensified at Kalimela.

Posters and banners had been put up in Kurmnur, Papulur, Vejangiwada Panchayat areas on Andhra-Odisha border. The ultras were on a whirlwind tour of Chitrakonda, Kalimela, Motu and MV-79 Villages, urging their residents to boycott the Independence Day Celebrations. The ultras had decided to hoist black flags on the offices and school buildings, protesting against the government inaction, alleging it had done nothing for the tribals during the last 60 years. Schools in the interior villages were reportedly closed since the afternoon of 14 Aug 2007.

On the other hand, the ultra cadres in Rayagada, Gajapati, Koraput and several other insurgency-hit districts had geared up to observe Independence Day as 'Black Day'. DIG South-Western Range SK Nath added, "The security has been tightened while combing operations have also been intensified." SP Gajapati AN Singh spoke on elaborate security arrangements against any disruption by the ultras, in his district also.

To check any cross-border infiltration, a red alert had been sounded along the State's borders with Chhattisgarh, Andhra Pradesh and Jharkhand.

To ensure peace during the 15 August celebrations, the police forces under the South-Western, North – Central, Southern, Northern and Western Police Ranges were put on high alert.

A senior Home Department official also Chimes in, "We have also made elaborate security arrangements in all LWE-hit districts, where some ministers are stated to hoist the Tricolour."

There were rumours of Maoists' plan of launching operations to capture Barapahar forest region skirting the Hirakud Dam reservoir, extending into both the Sambalpur and Baragarh districts. This would enable them to establish a Corridor to Koraput and Kalahandi. When contacted on this potential threat, Bargarh SP Sanjiv Panda ruled out any possibility of materialising of Maoist threat in his district, assuring that ample security measures are in place for 15 August celebrations being celebrated peacefully.

Aug 2007. Padma @ Padmakka, wife of Bhaskar Rao@Balakrishna, a senior member of the Maoist Andhra-Odisha Border Zonal Committee was arrested in Bijapur, Chhattisgarh, and booked u/s 302, 149 of IPC and 27 (1) Arms Act. She was acquitted in Aug 2009, but re-arrested. She hails from Hyderabad. Her release was demanded by CPI (Maoist) for releasing Malkangiri Collector R Vinod Krishna, IAS, who was abducted on 24 Feb 2011.

29 Jun 2008. Maoists attacked a launch (a large motor boat) carrying 60 Grey – Hound Commandos of Andhra Pradesh in Balimela reservoir located in Odisha's Malkangiri disctrict. The boat sank and 38 commandos lost their lives.

16 Jul 2008. Maoists below up an anti-land mine vehicle on Kaliamela-Motu Road near Malkangiri village, killing 17 SOG men.

29 Jul 2008. 36 Grey-Hound commandos killed in Malkangiri by Maoists.

29 Aug 2008. Maoists admit to have killed Swami Lakshmananda Saraswati on 23 Aug 2008 for his "fascist activities".

28 Feb 2009. A group of 60 Maoists blow up Bhalulata railway track near Rourkela.

19 Mar 2009. Prabhat Kumar Panigrahi, a homeopath doctor with RSS links, gunned down by Maoists in Rudiguma village in Kandhamal district. The assailants left behind Maoist posters, stating : "All those who misuse religion to incite communal riots and interfere in the dietary habits (e.g. opposing beef eating) of the local people will meet the fate of Swami Saraswati[7].

24 Mar 2009. Some 100 armed Maoists destroyed a police outpost and nearby Rest House in Malkangiri district's Podia Block.

9 Apr 2009. Maoists slit the throat of Somnath Madkami of Samruddha Odisha candidate from Malkangiri Assembly seat. His body was found near Arshaguda village (*The Hindu,* 10.4.2009).

12 Apr 2009. 200 Maoists target NALCO mine and a CISF post in Damanjodi, Odisha, killing 11 CRPF men.

24 Apr 2009. Maoists gunned down village head of Talkonde, Kasha Madhi under Malkangiri police station.

7 Jun 2009. A police station at Baipariguda in Koraput district was demolished, and its vehicles set ablaze.

27 Oct 2009. Maoists laid siege to Bhubaneshwar-New Delhi Rajdhani Express at Banstala, 8 km from Jhargram, and abducted its driver. Kishanji denied Maoist participation in detaining the train but, all the same, justified the action of supporters of the Police Santrosh Birodhi Janasadharan Committee (PSBJC).

4 Nov 2009. Maoists attacked Essar Group Guest House in Malkangiri district in South Odisha.

20 Dec 2009. Some dozen Maoists attacked power generation plant at Baliamela Hydro-electricity Project in Malkangiri.

100 Maoists blew up a double-storey school building in development Block under Dhibra Police Station. In this very month, December (2009), Maoists targeted more than 20 school buildings.

"ASI killing frustrate Odisha policemen" : 7 May 2012

The brutal murder of ASI Kruparam Majhi in Nuapada district days after the twin hostage drama has shocked the Odish police. Some reactions proved that feeling in an ample measure. The frustration with the state police is marked, as is obvious from this reaction of police in general, says a journalist : "While it was ready to release in exchange for the two abducted Italians and a BJD MLA, it was not doing enough for the forces who are charged to fight and defeat the Maoists but are unable to persuade the government to provide them the where withals to do so successfully."[8]

The mood was amply reflected in the statement of the DGP, Odisha on 8 May: "The Maoists brutally killed Majhi, while he was on a routine duty". One of his policemen was more direct : "Shooting down Majhi, who had his hands and feet tied, was barbaric. It was done just to send a message to policemen across the state." Here are some other instances :

- Citing the example of Ajit Bardhan, a sub-inspector brutally murdered in Sundergarh in 2009, a policeman said Maoists deploy savage methods to instil fear in forces.
- In 2008, they killed special operations group assistant commandant Pramod Satpathy during the attack on Nayagarh armoury.
- On 21 March 2012, the government started negotiations with the rebel-backed mediators for the release of the Italians, Maoists shot dead a policeman in Malkangiri districts.

There were some other indicators of unease, even anger, among the police ranks on certain decisions of the government. The police was up in arms. The state police association warned they would boycott duty in the Maoist areas if the government released hardcore Maoists. Said a policeman posted in Nuapada, "There are certain do's and don'ts which prevent policemen from going aggressively against the Maoists." They are of the opinion that if the government does not give them some leeway in this direction, it would be rather difficult to work in the Maoist infested areas.

The Punjab police was in somewhat similar predicament – perhaps even worse – when they got a redeemer called KPS Gill. Will they get one in Odihsa?

A tribal from Nuapada's Beltukuri village, Kruparam had joined the police at the age of 27. He is survived by his parents, wife and four daughters. The state government announced an ex-gratia of Rs 8 lakh and job for a member of the family.

Abduction of two Italians and one MLA Testing times for the Chief Minister

The twin abductions had brought a lot of much-needed publicity to the Maoist cause during March and April 2012. Summary details of these abductions are adduced hereafter.

- Italians, Tour operator Paolo Bosusco, 55, and tourist Claudio Colangelo, 60, are abducted from Kandhamal district on 14 March 2012. The latter is released after 11 days (25 March) but the former gets lucky only after 29 days on 12 Apr 2012. They were abducted by the Odisha State Organising Committee led by Sabyasachi Panda.
- Laxmipur MLA Jhina Hikaka is abducted on 24 Mar 2012 by the Andhra-Odisha Border Special Zone Committee (AOBSZC) of Maoists. Aruna is its spokesman. The MLA was released on 26 April.

Games played during negotiations

In the background of negotiations between the Maoist mediators Dandapani Mohanti and BD Sharma and the state government officials, Chief Minister Naveen Patnaik announced 5 Apr 2012 the names of 27 persons whose release the government would facilitate through legal steps to ensure the release of BJD ML Hikaka and tour operator Paolo from the hands of Maoists.

Of these 27 persons, 15 were to be members of Chasi Mulia Adivasi Sangha (CMAS) and eight Maoists from different jails for the release of the MLA and four others for the release of the Italian. These four would include Subhashree Das, wife of Panda, secretary of the Odisha Maoists Committee. The CM made this statement, meaning the 27, in the State Assembly, claiming that his government's gesture was based on humane grounds. He hoped that the abductees would be freed immediately. It is to be noted that Mr Patnaik announced 4 April his government's decision to facilitate the release of 27 persons after the abductors of the MLA had fixed 5 April as the deadline for the government to fulfil their demands, and the abductors of the Italian asked it to meet the demands instead of playing delaying tactics.

To be specific, the MLA had been kidnapped by the Maoists belonging to the Srikakulam-Koraput Division of the Andhra. Odisha Border Special Zone Committee of the Maoists on 24 March, while Paolo had been kidnapped on the 14th of March. But the Maoists had released Colangelo on 25 March, as mentioned above, as a good will gesture. Details of the 27 to be released by the state are given hereafter.

- The eight Maoists are Narsi Kendruka, Joruka Kendruka, Deba Madhi, Ganga Sodi, Bhima Padiami, Mangaraj Darua, and a married couple from Andhra Pradesh, Murla Neelam Reddy and Setu Pangi.
- The 15 members of the CMAS are Rupuni Sirika, Miniaka Sandal, Miniaka Jama, Saura Kartasia, Nachika Suba, Wade ka Diba, Rabi Tadingi, Dhana Hantal, Dora Hantal, Ramesh Nachika, Hulukukesaba, Ina Tadingi, Rupana Huluku, Argu Sirika and Bijay Tadingi.
- The four to be released for the Italian's freedom are Ms. Panda (mentioned above), Arati Majhi, Suka Nachika, and Chakra Tadingi[9].

Meanwhile, Italian Ambassador to India Giacomo Sangfelice di Monteforte and Italian Consul General Joel Melchiory met with the Chief Minister at Bhubaneswar on 5 April to discuss the release of the Italian (Paolo).

Belying hopes that the Puri-based Italian, Paolo, would be freed following the CM's 5 April announcement, Panda on the 6th refused to free the Italian and set 96-hour deadline to the government. Panda said in a fresh audio tape released on the 6th that they can't release Paolo since the government had not signed any agreement with the mediators despite talks to free the hostage. He wanted that this tape must be treated as a press release. The main points from his taped statement are detailed here.

> He accused the government of failing to meet their demands for release of Paolo which he termed "democratic demands"– an interesting if ironic terminology used by a Maoist. These demands included release of prisoners held under fabricated charges, legal action against police officials involved in corruption and rape of innocents and fake encounters and lifting of ban on political and mass organisations. When the talks resumed, they had demanded that the government provide detailed information regarding the number of persons to be released immediately and other prisoners to be freed later and to conclude an agreement with the mediators participating in the dialogue on our behalf.... There was no other way for the government but to sign the agreement with the mediators for fulfilment of the demands to secure the release of the Italian.

Panda then averred that they had sent names of seven Maoists languishing in various jails in Koraput and Malkangiri for their release in exchange for Paolo but the CM on the 5th announced only four names and even there exists some ambiguity over the name of the fourth person. The three names they recognise are Ms Panda, Arati Majhi and Suka Nachika.

The statement is drafted appropriately, showing Panda's adroitness in dealing with the government, drawing propaganda dividends from this audio and posing himself to be a true democrat by deploying terms like 'rue' and 'lamenting'. Panda 'rues' that "the government has turned the talks into a farce and was stabbing the democratic process from the back as it was not taking the mediators into confidence while announcing steps relating to the fulfilment of the demands…. Besides, the government was taking half-hearted approach in the entire process, even suspending the dialogue midway despite his organisation's goodwill gesture in releasing one of the two Italians (refers to the release of Colangelo on 25 March) to create a conducive atmosphere for solution of the problems." He again deploys two terms for effect (as he has often done in this statement) : "This amounted to nothing but stabbing the democratic talks from the back," Sabyasachi 'lamented'; and the Maoist leader 'rued' that the government "was compelling the organisation to take extreme steps."

Now Panda deals with the factionalism within his outfit in a clever if contrived logic. He imputes motive behind the abduction of MLA Hikaka. He says : "The government joined hands with a "discarded member of the CMAS" to capture the Zilla Parishad in Koraput. It was now trying to expose us after the kidnap of the MLA and hence was ignoring democratic talks." Warning the government of dire consequences, Panda stated that the Maoists would be compelled to take extreme steps unless the government concluded an agreement within 96 hours regarding the release of seven persons as per their demand. Being a 'true' Indian, he is concerned with India's image in the world, warning that "the Government will be held responsible if it is condemned at the international level!"

The meaning of the words "discarded member of the CMAS" should be clear to us, as also their implication. CMAS is not merely an activist outfit working for the interests of the tribals, in fact, they are more than the overground sympathisers of the Maoists. They are actively working for one faction of the Maoist outfit or the others in their violent operations! The passionate Human Rights Wallahs need not be so credulous, or 'innocent'. In India, it is in fashion to be seen on the side of 'Maoist ideology', as it indeed helps to establish one's 'liberal' credentials, forgetting the depredations, the cruelty and hardships inflicted on the poor whom they want to help! Ironically, the Maoists feed off the misery and economic deprivation of the poor but will kill the people who are engaged in improving their lot by building roads, schools and health centres in their areas.

The Maoists are never short of funds, running into thousands of crores. Their sources? Drug money, extortions from contractors, traders, even the labourers, businessmen (protection money), donations/contributions from foreign entities. Some one has coined a term for these 'liberals' who are not only sympathisers of the Maoists but also their overground arm – "paid ideologies". A cynic, rather a critic has gone beyond this term – he feels the 'liberals' are suffering from a disease that can be called 'liberalitis'!

Returning to the narrative, Panda had already released two audio tapes concerning his demands through the media.

However, a day after the CM announced the swap offer of 27 prisoners on the 5th, talks continued between the three Government negotiators and the two Maoist mediators named above, for about half an hour at the State Guesthouse in Bhubaneshwar. While the Home Secretary UN Bahera, who led the Government side, said they apprised the mediators about the official announcement, both the Maoist interlocuters sought to know what they meant by "steps to facilitate release" of the prisoners.

It is worth examining the stance and mindset of the (so-called) mediators while talking to the press persons on 6 Apr 2012. "We do not have any suggestions or objections at this moment, we are examining the Government's swapping offer. It is the Maoists who have to respond", Dandapani Mohanty said, putting a question, "when 'we' had given names of nine persons, how could the Government announce four names". Mohanty, of the two mediators, comes out as someone speaking only for the Maoists, as the term 'we' makes it obvious. This is the term lawyers use while addressing a court on behalf of their clients. Mohanty is more of a spokesman for the Maoists than a mediator between the two sides. Dr. BD Sharma, a retired IAS Officer, maintains a balance while speaking to the press : "They would take the next step only after the response of the Maoists was available. We are concerned about the release of the Italian[10]." But the next averment was like the two being mediators indeed : "However, the mediators made a fresh appeal to both the factions of Maoists to release the Italian national and the MLA as well.

Fight is for the Land: Maoists sought release mostly of tribal activists

The last of the two Italians, Paolo, having been released on 12 April, now it was for AOBSZC to bargain for the release of the MLA. On 8 April, it has demanded release of 30 prisoners. But on the 15th, they had reduced the figure to 29. But the rebels brought down the number by one as the State refused point-blank to release Chenda Bhushanam alias Ghasi. They had a reason : Ghasi was believed to be involved in the killing of 55 policemen in Odisha and Andhra Pradesh. Consequently, Maoists had struck Ghasi's name off their list.

It must be, and is, well-known to the analysts and students of the LWE that land—tribal and jungle—is at its core. Even people within the government (ministers and officials) are aware that the land taken over by the governments and private entities/individuals through means fair and foul is the cause of tribal unrest, and even violence at times. The consequent dispossession, causing deprivation and hardships, propel them into violent reaction – which is understandable, and even inevitable after a time.

It should, therefore, be no surprise that the AOBSZC claimed that the people on the list, 29 in all, were mostly members of the Leftist tribal organisation, CMAS, or just "apolitical people". Obviously, they are merely fighting for their lands. To be more precise, 24 of these 29 are tribals and they have nothing to do with the Naxal operations in their region in Orissa. "It may sound strange but it is true", says an analyst.

Of the remaining, only two are Maoists, says Dandapani Mohanty, convener of the Jan Adhikar manch, who was acting as an interlocutor for the talks with the government. The two Maoists are Murla Neelam Reddy and Setu Pangi, both hailing from neighbouring Andhra Pradesh. Another is Subhashree Das, wife of Sabyasachi Panda, whose outfit had abducted Paolo from Kandhamal district on 14 March. Mrs. Das (read Panda) was released from the jail after a fast track Court at Gunupur in Koraput district acquitted her on 10 April.

Land rights activists

Mohanty told The Hindu (13.4.12) that the 24 tribals, whose release was demanded by the two different groups of Maoists who had kidnapped Paolo and Hikaka, were activists of the CMAS, a local outfit fighting for land rights for tribals for nearly two decades. Tracing the reasons behind the cases against these activists, Mohanty said these can be attributed to an attack on the Narayanpatna police station in Koraput district ; taking over possession of their land that had been in the custody of non-tribal families for long; and a quarrel between the two factions of the CMAS. 89 other CMAS activists, who faced similar charges, were already acquitted by different courts, Mohanty claimed. But many were still facing trials.

As for the fresh demand by the AOBSZC, which had abducted Hikaka on 24 March, for release of five more persons, only one of them, Ghasi was a Maoist, said Mohanty. Among the other four was CMAS advisor and social activist Gananath Patra. The remaining three were also activists of the CMAS that was fighting for land rights for tribal people as well as opposing liquor trade in their region.

Interestingly, both groups of the Maoists had demanded the release of Patra, who was acquitted by a court in Koraput district "during the day", 12 April, in a case of atrocities on SC people, for want of evidence. In the recent past, he was acquitted in an abduction case. But two more cases are still pending against him.

Release of Paolo Bosusco

This Italian, who ran a tour and travel agency in Puri (the temple town of Odisha), took foreigners, mainly Italians, on trekking expeditions to tribal districts such as Kandhamal, Rayagada and Koraput in south Odisha. He talked to the press, three hours after his arrival at the state guest house in Bhubaneswar. Earlier on 12 April, he was released in south Odisha's Kandhamal district, and reached the capital accompanied by the Maoist-nominated mediator Dandapani Mohanty.

Nearly a mouth in Maoist Custody has not dimmed Paolo's "special love for Odisha" he told the press. Here is a summary of the main points made by him[11].

> "I am happy being a free man now. I am tired and need some rest, will go to Italy to meet my father and sister who is in hospital.... I am fine. I was treated well. I have spent some 22 years in Odisha and got the love, kindness and friendship of the people".

The 55-year old was heading to his country for rest, and was undecided on returning. Paolo said during his captivity he learnt about the case of tribal girl Arati Majhi, whose release was demanded by his abductors. "I felt bad after hearing about Majhi's plight. I will be happy if she is released. A few hours earlier, a court in Gajapati district had rejected Majhi's bail plea. Policemen had allegedly raped Majhi before arresting her. Maoists maintain Majhi—who has spent more than two years in jail—is not involved in their activities. Paolo said he had heard about injustice meted out to poor tribals. "I am not a political person. But I hope no one faces injustice."

Conspiracy Theories

When the atmosphere is so charged, such theories are the natural currency. Here is a look at some of these doing the rounds since the twin abductions.

- Italian Paolo was believed to be supplying weapons to the Maoists and also training them. He stage-managed the hostage crisis, trapping unsuspecting countryman Colangelo. Was it aimed at helping the Maoists to compel the State to release some of their leaders and cadres? Interesting possibilities (or conjectures?), indeed!

- Paolo, who had been staying in Puri for some 25 years till then, and the Maoist leader Sabyasachi Panda, a native of Puri himself, knew each other. Did Panda exploited this fact by staging this abduction to achieve his ends, which he indeed did.
- Interestingly, Panda himself adumberates a theory, imputing motives behind the abduction of Hikaka: "The government joined hands with a discarded (discredited) member of the CMAS to capture Zila Parishad in Koraput. It was now trying to expose (defame) us after the kidnap of the MLA (by us)."
- BJD MLA offered to be abducted since he wanted jailed Maoist supporters and activists of an Adivasi body (CMAS?) freed. Hikaka was an activist with this body till he became MLA (with its help?).
- Both abductions were planned by a section of the BJD to deflect attention from major issues during assembly session.
- Panda will surrender soon and be projected as a leader by the BJD in the 2014 General Elections. (This one can be discarded right away as the election is on at the time of the writing, Apr 2014, and Panda is still busy leading his Maoists).

Some of the conspiracies are rather fanciful, others too imaginative and still others too outlandish. Consequently, one is free to make one's pick, depending on his own lights.

Government moves in National Investigation Agency

About the time the Italian hostage Paolo walked free on 12 Apr 2012, a key Ministry of Home Affairs meeting in Delhi decided to give an important assignment to the NIA: to probe and dismantle the trail of the weapons supply and communication devices of the Maoists. Thus it ordered the NIA to take over its first anti-Naxal case when it decided to transfer investigation into the arrest of Sadanala Ramakrishna, the Warrangal Engineering College alumnus who headed the technical Committee of the CPI (Maoist).

Ramakrishna, who had gone underground 34 years ago, was arrested in Kolkata on 29 Feb 2012 by a joint team of Kolkata Police and Grey Hounds from Andhra Pradesh.

The 12 April meeting was convened to vet this decision. It was chaired by the Union Home Secretary, RK Singh and attended by the heads of the central police forces deployed in the anti-Naxal operations and the IB.

The meeting decided to transfer two more recent cases of seizure of weapons and communications equipment, once the states concerned give their concurrence. Argument was since the logistics chain extends beyond state boundaries, it was felt that inter-state investigation was called for to ascertain the supply linkages and dismantle them. Hence the NIA being called in.

The security officials, expectedly, conducted an in-depth assessment of the recent Naxal violence, including the twin high-profile abductions in Odisha, and five-tuned the tactics to defeat the LWE.

The meeting felt that the two high-profile abductions of 14 and 24 Mar 2012 did indicate that the Maoists in Odisha, as in Jharkhand, were operating independent of the Maoist Central leadership.

Have Maoists scored a political point?

What led to BJD MLA's: release? Behind-the-scene operations, rather manoeuvres, hushed deals, or just the government succumbing to Maoist pressure? Some analysts say: None of these.

Even if government stood firm, refusing to release just 30 people against a demand of more than 300 initially, whittled down to 150 by AOBSZC, the Maoists still scored a political point : putting in sharp focus the tribal rights and alienation. A large section of media discussed the related issues. Analysts assert even the Maoists knew that the government would not yield anymore. But they wanted to put maximum pressure on the Government. They are adept at the game of one-up-manship. "The Maoist have become media-savvy; they know how to garner public sympathy for their cause", commented a police officer. They know that their cause for the marginalised and the down-trodden has in the past invited popularity and sympathy from the Left-Liberal elite and the Common man and would do so in future too. They are well aware that once the government engages them in structured negotiations, it establishes ipso facto an equation between the two sides. During the talks, focus is more on them, which they enjoy and exploit to the helt!

This was visible on local news channels, "where panellists across party lines agreed that more needed to be done for the tribals." A senior ruling BJD leader, Damodar Rout, who had debated the issue on a channel, told a daily[12]: "The problems of the tribals can't be ignored any further. Efforts should be made to bridge the gap between the government and the tribals."

Hikaka had been abducted by the AOBSZC, who simply did not agree to the negotiations, inspite of the best efforts of the BJD leaders at the back channels. The State then agreed to facilitate the release of 25 people (tribals) mostly working with the CMAS, and withdraw prosecution against 13 of them. Being realists, the Maoists fell in line, government having stood firm at certain point. On the other side, officials conceded, that many of the cases were fabricated.

Playing with personal emotions

Abductors of MLA Hikaka on 8 April sent a Letter to a section of the media, asking his wife Kaushalya to reach Balipeta Village in Narayanpur district. This letter reportedly was written to Kaushalya personally. She was told to reach the place near the village along with 30 persons, including 23 people, whose release the State Government had promised/decided to facilitate. The outfit wanted her to be accompanied by BD Sharma and Dandapani Mohanty, who were interlocuters for the release of Italian Paolo. The MLA would be released if the team reached the village without any police or intelligence officials on 10 April. It is worth a note that Panda too had set the same date, 10 April, for the release of Paolo.

After postponing his release three times, which added to his wife's agony on daily basis, the MLA was set free on 26 April. As demanded by the AOBSZC, NR Patnaik, a lawyer for the CMAS, had accompanied her to the release site.

It should be interesting, even instructive, to note as to how the Maoists kept to the timings precisely as announced by them a day earlier. The scheduled time for release was 10 AM, but the stage was set around 8.30 AM, when Maoists and CMAS members started blocking the paths to the village with logs. At 9, rebels scoured the area and reviewed the arrangements at 9.30 AM. Kaushalya and Patnaik reached a mango grove near the village at 9.45. At 10, the rebels freed Hikaka outside the village. Accompanied by tribals, he walked towards the grove and found himself surrounded by jostling media. Wiping the sweat off his clean-shaven face, he (wearing green khadi Kurta) hugged Patnaik before putting a hand on his wife's shoulder. Amid the reunion, villagers kept looking curiously at the outdoor broadcasting (OBC) vans of news channels and journalist. The media, both visual and print, could not have asked for better occasion to flash their cameras at all comers! It is not without a reason that the Maoists stage such ceremonies with such meticulous timings and punctuality. It is such publicity they hanker after and make use of it for propaganda purposes, and they revel in it.

After 33 days of separation Kaushalya credited god foremost for the release of her husband from Maoist captivity. She said amidst sobs, holding her husband's hand : "He has come back due to god's grace. These 33 days have been like 33 years". She, however, did not forget to thank her husband's captors and activists of the leftist tribal outfit Chasi Mulia Adivasi Sangha (CMAS) for his release. Was it a coincidence or an induced forgetfulness that like her husband, she too was silent on the State Governments role?[13]

Around 11 AM, Hikaka, Kaushalya and Patnaik left for Koraput district headquarters, where hundreds of people accorded him a rousing welcome at the government circuit house. He left with his wife for his village, Dumripadar, in Laxmipur constituency and reached home about 4 PM. Hikaka broke down as his ailing mother and two sons held.

MLA's abduction: a high-profile case

It being the first such case where a politician was involved, it drew a lot of attention from the press as also the public. Expectedly, the AOBSZC initially demanded the release of activist of the CMAS and Maoists in Koraput and Malkangiri jail, more than 150 in all. But when the government agreed to release only 22 detainees, including eight Maoists for Hikaka's release, the AOBSZC demanded the release of five more Maoists. Reason : they claimed that only two of the original eight were Maoists. But in a letter to the media on 11 Apr, AOBSZC spokes person Jagabandhu had sought the release of 30 Maoists in all in exchange for Hikaka.

It deserves a mention that the AOBSZC that was behind the abduction of Hikaka refused to talk to the state authorities through mediators for release of their hostage throughout the period of 33 days it was under their charge, even when two mediators (Sharma and Mohanty) were engaged in prolonged talks with the authorities on behalf of the rival Maoist faction led by Sabyasachi Panda, leader of the Odisha Maoists, which had abducted two Italians on 24 March, the same day the AOBSZC had taken away the MLA. The latter announced their demands throughout those 33 days via the audio tapes and press releases.

MLA returns to his home and Constituency: 5 months after

After spending five months in the State capital under the protection of the CM and away from his home and constituency since his 'conditional' release by the Maoists following a month long captivity and negotiations, Laxmipur MLA Hikaka on 3.10.12 "strategically dared to pay his first visit" to the Koraput district and his constituency, being convinced that he had to re-establish his links with the people or he would be treated locally as a trailor.[14] It was not a happenstance that his mentor and protector, the CM, was scheduled to pay an official visit to Koraput and Malkangiri districts, the bastions of the red rebels, on the 5th where Hikaka would accompany him to different programmes. The conjunction of Patnaik and Hikaka is seen as a well-planned move to normalise the strain created out of fear of the 'condition' set by his captors that Hikaka would have to resign in case he failed to fulfil their demands within a certain timeframe.

The district police was in a tizzy, worried about providing security cover to the MLA, perceived to be still under threat by the Maoists, and at Koraput and his village Podapadar, Hikaka was seen surrounded by policemen in plain clothes. The security cover was bound to be reinforced on the eve of and during the visit of the CM to the two Maoist-infested districts on 5 October.

Wife denounces and disagrees with husband : Both Maoist

Despite describing her husband and Maoist leader Sabyasachi Panda as her friend, philosopher and guide," wife Sibhashree Das (Ms Panda) alias Mili on 12 Apr denounced the act of taking a foreign national (Paolo) hostage and showed willingness to become to mediator. "It is not right to keep anyone hostage for fulfilment of certain demands. One should not put pressure on the government in this manner", Das told the media.

This couple must be a rare exception : wife not only disagreeing with her husband but going beyond that in publicly denouncing his actions/ decisions. One never saw such disagreement between A K Gopalan and his wife in the long past, nor would one see it between varinda Karat and her husband today. In the international Communism, a member could not openly disagree with a Stalin or a Mao, and if they did, they paid with their lives. But the Communists seem to have changed today, seeing what is happening in West Bengal and Kerala. Does it all mean Maoists believe in unfettered democracy?

To end on meaningful specifics : Das was acquitted by a court only on 10 April and the Italian Paolo himself was released on the 12th itself – the day she was offering her mediatory services! All the same, this does not take away anything from her bold statement!

Italy welcomes hostage release

Rome on 12 Apr welcomed the release of its national, Paolo, after being held a hostage for 29 days, hailing India and its own diplomats "for the freeing of tour operator seized while trekking nearly a month ago".

Its Foreign Minister Giulio Terzi said, inter alia: "It is an end to a risky and very complicated affair in which we were constantly engaged on all levels with the aim of guaranteeing the lives of our compatriots.

Mediators

The details are given below:

- **On the government side.** Home Secretary UN Behera, Panchayat Raj Secretary PK Jena, and SC/ST Development Secretary SK Sarangi.
- **On Maoists side.** Former IAS officer and tribal rights activist. BD Sharma and social activist and chief of the Jan Adhikar Samiti Dandapani Mohanti. The above five are for the case of Italian abductees.
- **Mediators for Hikaka.** Maoists were not willing to talk, hence there were no mediators.

"Shameful Capitulation"

Naveen Patnaik surrenders to Maoist terror: Editorial in a daily of 6 Apr 2012

- To the abiding shame of this nation of more than a billion people, CM of Odisha Naveen Patnaik has once again capitulated in the face of Maoist terror and, instead of refusing to negotiate a deal with the marauders, succumbed to their patently unacceptable tactics. To argue, as Mr. Patnaik and his effete regive will no doubt do, that there was no other option but to agree to the terms set by the Maoists to secure the release of two hostages – an Italian national and a BJD legislator – help captive by them would be the least convincing.
- This is not the first time that CM Patnaik has chosen to give in without a fight. Last year (2011), he agreed to set free Maoism-spouting hard core criminals who had been captured after a great effort by the police to secure the release of a District Collector who had been taken hostage by Red terrorists. That surrender is turning out an annual ritual of the State Government genuflecting at the altar of Maoism and paying obeisance by way of setting free thugs guilty of mass murder and worse.
- It is absurd to suggest that the State Government was left with no choice—if Mr. Patnaik had the courge which is expected of a head of Government, he would have dared the Maoists to do their worse and thereby exposed them for what they are: Remorseless killers whose lust for blood can never be satiated. That he chose the easy way out speaks volumes about his ability to withstand pressure from those who are waging war. On the state; having

tasted blood twice over, the Maoists will now be bath to either fear or respect the authority Mr. Patnaik notationally represents.

- This tragic story of abject capitulation should not be allowed to end with the two captives being released by the Maoists. Mr. Patnaik and the weak administration he heads must be confronted with some tough questions; they have to be answered because explanation is owed not only to the people of Odisha but also that of the country. First, why were the Italians allowed to venture forth in an area where the Maoists are locked in a battle with security forces ? Do foreigners, especially Europeans, have a free run of Patnaik's Odisha? Was the first Italian to be freed interrogated by the police? If yes, the details must be made public. Similarly, the BJD MLA who was abducted must be made to explain what was he doing in an area where Maoists are known to be present. Second, why is Mr. Patnaik reluctant to pursue a tough policy while dealing with criminals who mock at the Constitution of India and are ideologically committed to the demise of the Indian state?
- Why does he insist on breaking ranks with other States fighting the Maoist menace? Should his desire to be seen as a liberal politician who is different from others be allowed to over-ride national security? Third, Odisha cannot have everything its own way. It can not demand Central assistance to deal with Maoist terror and yet be seen to be doing nothing to terminate the Red terrorists. It can't take refuge in federalism to cover up its gross failure to fulfil its constitutional obligation of upholding law and order. There is no percentage in standing by a State Government that is not fully committed to taking the battle against the Maoists to its logical conclusion."[15]

Blow to Maoist chief as bodyguard surrenders in Odisha: 5 May 2012

The Maoists in the State appeared to have received a body blow on Friday, 4 May 2012, following the surrender of a loyal bodyguard of a top Maoist leader Sabyasachi Panda in Gajapati district and the arrest of a senior woman militant in Jajpur district on 2 May. Panda himself had a close shave on 30 April when the police and SOG men exchanged fire with his group in Paniamba Jungle under Sorada police station limits in Ganjam district and he had to flee camp.

The above was reported by a daily story lined Parlakhemundi (Jaipur) 4 May 2012.[16]

Sushant alias Prashant Majhi, 20, who was bodyguard of Panda, the Secretary of the Odisha State Organising Committee of the CPI (Maoist) surrendered 4 May 2012 before SP Gajapati Sarthak Sarangi alleging gross misbehaviour by the Chhattisgarh Cadre on the (Odisha) State cadre. He was one of the very few faithful lieutenants of Panda and was involved in major operations.

Sushant, hailing from Tudupanka village in Gajapati district, had joined the Maoists when he was a high school students and was involved in seven cases of violent incidents including Paniganda BT house explosion, Katama violence, attack on contractor at Jhanjiriguda and torching of wood laden truck at Gajalbadi. After these cases, he had become one of the most wanted Maoists on police record.

Since his surrender before the police, Majhi has revealed details about several secret Maoist's activities and trends : the Maoist leaders are derailed from their ideology; most of them are working for their self interest; the Odisha Maoists are being tortured by the Chhattisgarh cadre; even the female cadres are subjected to mental and physical torture.

"I wanted to live like a common man, so I left the Maoist outfit," says Sushant.

In Jajpur, a district known for mining activities and the Kalinganagar industrial hub, a woman Maoist and former Sarpanch of Gobarghati gram panchayat under Kalinganagar police station limits, and allegedly involved in the killing of security men and several other crimes, was arrested on 3 May 2012 from the dense forests bordering Jaipur and Keonjhar. Giving some details, Aloka Ray of Jajpur Town Police Station says : "Sini Sai, 50, of village Gobaraghati was arrested in a joint combing operation by the Jajpur and the Keonjhar police. Sini had been once elected Sarpanch of the Gobarghati gram panchayat in the past."

Incidentally, her son was one among the 13 killed in the 2006 Kalinganagar firing in a violent resistance to industrialisation without proper compensation and resettlement.

Police feel the arrest of the senior woman Maoist would weaken their group in the region. She was involved in the attack on the Daitari police station, abduction of a police officer, Umesh Marandi, other crimes and violent incidents in Jajpur and Keonjhar districts.

Summary of Violent Incident by Maoists

There were three high profile abductions in three months of 2012, which are summarised here.

- **14 Mar 2012.** Italian nationals abducted in Kandhamal district. Claudio Colangelo released 25 March and Paolo Bosusco on

12 April. Odisha State Organising Committee led by Sabyasachi Panda was the faction behind it. Five Maoists released including Mrs. Panda.

- **24 Mar 2012.** BJD MLA Jhina Hikaka abducted from Koraput district. He was released on 26 April by the AOBSZC faction of the Maoists Release of 25 promised.
- **21 Apr 2012.** Sukma Collector Alex Menon was abducted from eponymous district of Chhattisgarh and was released on 3 May. The outfit concerned was South Bastar Divisional Committee of Maoists. CM Raman Singh denied any deal. Maoists started with demands to free 17, but ended without a single release. The State set up a high-powered panel to review cases of Maoists undertrials in Chhattisgarh.

It may be worth mentioning another high-profile abduction in Odisha in 2011. It is summarised here.

- **16 Feb 2011.** Malkangiri District Collector R Vineel Krishna and two junior engineers, Pabitra Majhi and Damodar Suchet, were abducted from a village in the district. Suchet was released the sameday, Majhi after 6 days and Krishna after seven days. AOBSZC was behind it. There are some interesting facts about their demands. Their 14-point demand, including release of 700 'Maoists', scrapping Polavaram project and MoUs with MNCs; cancellation of bauxite mining lease; judicial inquiry into alleged rape of tribal girl Arati Majhi in Gajapati district (Andhra Pradesh) by policemen. Subsequently, Maoist leader Ganti Prasadam was granted bail by the Odisha High Court, but he refused to leave the jail unless the State takes steps to release 600 other comrades.

Maoists kill BJD leader's son: 12 Jul 2012

Suspected Maoists 11 Jul 2012 killed Sushiram Bhoi, son of Khaprakhol block chairman Ganeshram Bhoi at village Saangurjee Bhata under the Khaprakhol Police station in Balangir district.

The ultras came to the village and inquired about Sushiram, who was a contractor executing road projects in Nuapada district. The family members denied his presence in the house. Letting the matter rest at the denial, they blocked all exists from the village. Having ensured this, the ultras barged into his house and killed Sushiram with bayonet attacks.

SP Balangir R Prakash told the daily's correspondent : "The main reason for killing Sushiram was a dispute over payment of money to the Maoists, the former obviously not meeting the demands of the latter in full."[17]

Ganeshram had also received threats from the Maoists before this fatal attack on his son, Sushiram.

Study: 70 per cent Maoists in Odisha outsiders

In perhaps the first-ever study of armed Maoists in the state, the Odisha police found that between 70 and 80 percent of them do not belong to the state. The result of the study were revealed in a daily dated 11.9.12.[18]

Some 50 per cent of the armed cadres belong to the Andhra-Odisha Border Special Zone Committee (AOBSZC), operating Koraput and Malkangiri districts.

The study puts the total number of armed Maoist cadre at a little over 500 in Odisha. While many of them joined the outfit as recently as six months ago, some have been members for 30 years. The number could be higher as there was a lot of movement from other states to Odisha, particularly from Andhra Pradesh and Chhattisgarh. There may be other Maoists offering cover to actual armed cadre whose number has not been calculated.

The firearms they use range from single barrel muzzle loader to AK-47 and 9 MM pistol, says an officer, "It is the first we could build a complete profile of Maoist cadres operating inside Odisha, and the kind of firearms they use, their sociological background, their aliases, how long they have been operating in Odisha etc." Only Andhra Pradesh has done such a profile of its Maoists so far. "We plan to keep the list updated, taking into account the cadres who are killed or offer surrenders."

The AOBSZC is the largest, with an estimated 240-250 cadres. Then comes the Dandakaranya Zonal Committee, with some 100 armed cadres mostly from Chhattisgarh. The third largest is Odisha State Organising Committee, with 80 armed cadres. Officials believe the Odisha Maovadi Party formed by the recently expelled Sabyasachi Panda may not have more than 20 armed cadres.

5 Maoists killed, one arrested in Odisha encounter: 15 Nov 2012

In a major success in anti-Naxal drive, security forces 14 Nov 2012 gunned down at least five Maoists in a gunbattle and seized arms and explosives in a forest on the border of Odisha's Ganjan and Gajapati districts.

This was disclosed to the press by the police on 14 Nov 2012.[19] The news story is datelined Berhampur/Bhubaneswar.

A Maoist was captured after the encounter in which two security men were also injured in Bhaligada jungle under Mohana police station.

DGP Prakash Mishra told reporters in Bhubaneswar : "Five Maoists were killed in the exchange of fire that took place after the ultras fired at combing team and forced the jawans to retaliate in self-defence."

Acting on an intelligence input about the presence of a Maoist camp, a joint team of Special Operations Group (SOG) and District Voluntary Forces of Ganjam and Gajapati districts, was conducting a combing operation in the said forest, when the ultras opened fire.

Five ultras were killed in the gunbattle while the rest ran away, disappearing in the forest.

Bodies of the five dead were recovered and identified. All of them were residents of Kandhamal district. (That means the Maoists operate with a cohesive group, where the cadres are intimately known to each other. Such a grouping are bound to yield better results in any engagement with the security forces).

Some arms, ammunition and explosives were seized/recovered from the site and the security team continued its search operations to nab the ultras who had fled the skirmish, the DGP said.

Police killed villagers, not Maoists: Sabyasachi Panda: 20 Nov. 2012

The killing of five Maoists was given a fresh and understandable twist when the State's top Maoist asserted on Sunday, 19 Nov 2012 that the five (so-called Maoists) killed by the security men were innocent villagers, and not the Maoist cadres as claimed by the Odisha Police and its boss, DGP Prakash Mishra.

Here is the news story carried by a daily in its issue of 20 Nov 2012:

- The encounter killing of five Maoists in Odisha four days ago took a fresh turn on Sunday, 19 Nov 2012, after the State's top rebel leader Sabyasachi Panda said those killed were innocent civilians and not his loyalists, as the police were claiming.
- "The police killed ordinary villagers and then put Maoist uniforms on the bodies", said Panda in an audiotape released to the media[20].

Police did not react to his statement, which was backed by social activist Dandapani Mohanty, one of the two mediators who had negotiated the release of two Italians abducted by Panda in March (2012).

Mohanty added his bit : "The so-called encounter is nothing but cold-blooded murder, which requires an inquiry by a sitting high court judge. The state government should pay a compensation of Rs. 10 lakh to the families of each of the dead."

Police had claimed to have killed at least five Maoists in an encounter with a group of rebels led by Panda in Gajapati district in southern Odisha on 14 Nov 2012.

Pand, who was expelled by the CPI (Maoist) in August for criticising General Secretary and Supreme Commander Mupala Laxmana Rao alias Ganapathi, has floated the Odisha Maoist Party.

Five Maoists killed in an encounter on 14 Nov 2012

Odisha police killed at least five Maoists following an encounter with a Naxal group led by rebel leader Sabyasachi Panda in Gajapati district. Panda, who had floated the outfit Odisha Maoist Party, after falling out with the CPI (Maoists), however managed to escape.

The encounter took place at 10.30 AM in a forest areas of the district, some 200 km south-west of Bhubaneshwar, following an overnight combing operations.

Two Maoists held in Koraput

The Koraput police arrested two hardcore Maoists from the Dumbaguda area of the district, and produced them in the court on 25 Nov 2012. The duo, Habika Lingama and Habika Tamaya, were involved in various crimes, including murder.

The district SP Avinash Kumar said : "They were the key strategists in the abduction of Laxmipur MLA Jhina Hikaka on 24 March this year. While 12 cases have been pending against Lingama, nine are registered against Tamaya in different police stations in the district."

35 Gram Rakhis quit job after Maoist threat

35 Gram Rakhis (members of Panchayati Raj Institutions: PRI) resigned from their job to the Boipariguda police station officials, in consequence of the killing of two Gram Rakhis in this police station limits. While 12 left the job on 2 Dec. 2012, 23 had resigned a week earlier. A total of 40 Rakhis had been working in the jurisdiction of this police station, and Ramgiri outpost. While two of these were killed, the rest were told to quit, accusing them of being police informers. Some of those who quit the service include Dukhu Khillo, Gurunath Santa, Dhanpati Durua, Rama Durua, Sadan Pujari, Pitambar Achary, Harsanand Christian and Panchanan Achary.

The Maoists are observing PLGA Week from 2 Dec 2012, and have given fresh warning to the SPOs to quit their service. As a result, the SPOs are also gripped by certain fear. This has caused consternation for the Koraput district police and Odisha's Home Department authorities because if the SPOs quit, the law and order situation was bound to worsen further in the district[21].

Some background information on these resignations is deemed necessary. On 5 July, pressured by the Maoist-backed CMAS, 35 PRI members of the Kalimela block, which falls in the Maoist-infested Malkangiri district, threatened to resign from their posts. It sent shockwaves in Odisha administration. This was the result of a meeting of the tribal villagers in the remote forested area of Kalimela, called by the CMAS. They asked the Kalimela Panchayat Samiti Chairperson Debe Madhi, Zila Parishad member Sahadeb Matam and 33 others to quit their posts, as the State Government had failed to build the Kartamballi-Manyamkonda Canal that would have irrigated the tribal farmlands.

Madhi, a Congressman, explained : "It is not enough for us to win the elections. If we can't give basic facilities to our villagers, there is no point continuing as elected panchayat members." Congress leader and Zila Parishad member decried the government negligence in building roads to the villages and said "we have decided to resign." State Home Department officials admitted that the resignations would send a message that the Maoists were calling the shots.

All the 35 PRI members who attended the CMAS meeting on the 5th, later called on the Kalimela BDO and reiterated their threat. On 2 December they turned their threat into reality, as detailed in the preceding paras.

They surrender and Shun arms

Here are two instances of the Maoists seeing the light of the day for whatever reasons.

Two hardcores surrender

Fed up with the ideology of the Maoist outfits two hardened armed cadres—Bijoy Honhaga alias Rakesh, 30 and Jadurai Soy alias Chamara, 36—surrendered before the Rourkela SP on 2 Dec 2012. They were highly active in the Saranda forest in Jharkhand-Odisha border area. Honhaga was secretary Jan Militia Squad and President, Krantikari Kissan Committee. Police say they confessed during the interrogation on the 4th about their involvement in various incidents of Maoist activities in the Jharkhand-Odisha border areas since 2005 and revealed they joined the Maoists in 2005 on being threatened by Anmol Hembram alias Samarj, the then secretary of the Dakhin Chhotanagpur Zonal Committee of the CPI (Maoist). They also revealed that the Maoist of Saranda forest under the leadership of Samarji were involved in the killing of the innocent Adivasis in the name of police informers.

They collected heavy cash from the industrialists businessmen and contractors for personal enrichment. The women contingents were sexually and mentally harassed by the senior cadres, and the minors and innocent tribal people were exploited. Police sources revealed that the duo was most wanted for their involvement in many heinous crimes under the Bolanga, Koira, Chandiposh and Bisra police stations. They will be rehabilitated under the surrender policy of the State.

The development carries significance in the background of the fact that they had been observing PLGA week beginning from 2 December which had prompted the CRPF to beef up security in the Naxal-prone areas of the State including Andhra-Odisha border area.

Notes

1. Bibhuti Pati, The Tehelka, 24 Jun 2006.
2. Lalita Aiyer, The Week, 11 Jun 2006.
3. Lalita Iyer, The Week, 11 Jun 2006.
4. Siba Mohanty, Indian Express, 26 Oct 2006.
5. Omer Farooq, The Pioneer, 4 Feb 2007.
6. Tarini Prasad Panda, The Pioneer 11 Jun 2007.
7. Hindustan Times, 20.3.2009.
8. Priya Ranjan Sahu, The Hindustan Times, 9.5.12.
9. The Hindu, 6.4.12.
10. The Pioneer, 7.4.12.
11. The Hindustan Times, 13.4.12.
12. Priya Ranjan Sahu, The Hindustan Times, 27.4.12.
13. The Hindustan Times, 27.4.12.
14. Lalmohan Patnaik, The Pioneer, 4.10.12.
15. The Pioneer, 6 Apr 2012.
16. PNS, The Pioneer, 5 May 2012.
17. Sudhir Mishra, The Pioneer, 12 Jul 2012.
18. Mohanty, Debabrata, The Indian Express, 11.9.12.
19. PTI, The Pioneer, 15 Nov 2012.
20. HT Correspondent, Hindustan Times, 20 Nov 2012.
21. The Pioneer, 4.12.12.

31

Odisha - 2

Mining Issues: State and Centre to talk

The issue of mining in several states is a contentious one. There are political pressures as also exertions by some lobbies for and against certain projects relating to mining and allied fields. Some activist minister for forests and environment at times blocks projects already cleared, and a harassed Prime Minister replaces him to get things moving. The most recent such case is appointment of V Moily to this critical Ministry. The case discussed here pertain to the year 2012.

In mid-Dec 2012, the Odisha Government and the Centre began discussing mining issues after a 9-month stand off. It came when State Chief Secretary BK Patnaik met Union Steel Secretary DRS Chaudhary in Bhubaneswar. The last time the two sides discussed a related issue was in March 2012 when the officials met to examine POSCO's 12 million tonne steel plant/project. That meeting had come just before Prime Minister Manmohan Singh left on a tour of South Korea, where the POSCO naturally figured[1].

Since that March, there has hardly been any movement, with POSCO waiting for the Odisha government to renew its MoU that had expired in June 2010, and restart the land requisition process stalled since June 2011. During this interregnum, the State had served a notice on several companies, alleging illegal mining. To regularise this illegality, it demanded payment of additional royalty. Matters stood further complicated as the MB Shah Commission on illegal mining had pulled up the State on the issue too.

Meanwhile not only POSCO, even some public sector projects too have not made much forward movement. An example of this statemate is an RINL application for mining lease, which is stuck up with the state government for some three years. The State insisted that there should be value addition within the state borders, meaning the company had to set up at least something like a pelletization plant for the ore to be processed. This mid-December meeting was important not only for POSCO but also for several other big-ticket steel and mining industries. Some of the major potential investors in the state are Arcellor Mittal, Steel Authority of India Ltd, Rashtriya Ispat Nigam Ltd, Total Steel, Jindal Steel and National Mineral. Development Corporation. It was expected that under CM Patnaik the State's agro-based economy would become more driversified. But after 9 years and several MoUs, it has not happened. It is obvious from the fact that by the end of 2012, Odisha achieved steel production capacity of only 12.66 million tonnes per annum out of India's 69.5 million tonnes (2011-12).

Naxal transit camp destroyed in Balangir: 8 Jan 2013

A transit camp of the Maoists was destroyed in a joint operation by the Special Operation Group (SOG) and CRPF jawans on 7 Jan 2013 in the Gandhamardarn Reserve Forest area near Saapmund and Beherapani villages in Khaprakhol block, SP Balangir R Prakash told the media in Balangir on 6 January.

Prakash gave details: "As the security forces approached the camp, the Maoists, who were busy in some activity there, opened fire and the police retaliated. After the exchanged of fire, the ultras moved to the camp on the top (of the hill) and opened fire again, resulting in a jawan being injured. The injured jawan was shifted to the Burla hospital for further treatment."[2]

The police seized some leaflets and other publicity material from the Maoists' first camp.

Three Maoists held in Odisha: 24 Jun 2013

The police in Maoist-hit Malkangiri district 23 Jun 2013 arrested three Maoist rebels and seized five IEDs during a combing operation.

The District Volunteer Force (DVF) and the Special Operation Group (SOG) of the State Police during a joint combing operation in a forest near Gamphokonda arrested Padiya Podiami, 23, Debendra Madkami, 26, Rama Madhi, 45, and Pandra Sodhi, 25. All of them belong to Patakonda and Tumkimadka villages in the district. These details were disclosed by SP Malkangiri Akhileswar Singh[3].

Singh continued: "These three are key people in Maoist set-up of Malkangiri as they are the people who know the location of the IEDs buried underground. They are the persons who triggered blast during ambush. We seized five tiffin bombs, two bundles of electric wire of about 100 mtrs.from them."

Locked land of POSCO

Tangled: Fear of losing betel vines rallied Odisha farmers against (POSCO) steel project: 24 Jun 2013

"It has been an eight-year long uneven battle between betel vines and a steel plant. And steel has not won yet."

"For, eight villages in costal Odisha'a Dinkia, Nuagaon and Gadaku Janga gram panchayats in Jagatsinghpur district, some 150 km east of State Capital Bhubaneswar, have put up a stiff resistance against South Korean steel major POSCO's proposed Rs 52,000 cr project."

"The reason : It will take away their traditional sources of income, viz, betel vines."

The above are three opening paras of a news story that simply but clearly explains the problems faced by the POSCO's steel plant in the area. This was reported in a daily of 24 Jun 2013.[4]

POSCO had signed a deal with the State Government in 2005 for acquiring 4004 acres (one acre = 43,560 sq feet or 4,840 sq yards) for the project. But the site of the project— backed by the single-largest foreign investment in India – virtually has nothing except some pre-fabricated site offices in a hurriedly fenced-off piece of vacant land.

The tell-tale signs of the battle are strewn every where in the area earmarked for the project: felled trees, destroyed betel vines and hostile villagers who have been fighting with the State to protect their vines.

Popular resistance and environmental clearance have made it difficult for the State to push through the 12 – million-tonnes a year green-field project which should have gone on stream by 2011.

Of the 4004 acres, some 3,000 acres is forest land. And more than 5,000 betel vines dot the sandy landscape in this forest land, each generating an average assured income of Rs 20,000 a month.

Two years ago (in 2011), the administration had to suspend land acquisition after hundreds of women and children blocked the entry point to the vines near the Gobindpur-Nuagaon border in scorching summer.

In Feb 2013, the administration took a step forward by resuming the process in Gobindpur. Though the state considers dismantling about

300 betel vines in three months to be some success, the drive seems to have lost stream by the end of May (2013). A villager, Tuna Baral, explains the 'awkward' situation: "They are coming like thieves ion the wee hours and trying to dismantle vines before we wake up and protest. We have re-erected several vines dismantled by them."

But DC Jagatsinghpur SK Mallick tells other side of the story : "But the administration is being careful. Land acquisition continues peacefully. We are trying to convince people to part with their vines and accept compensation.

'The project has split the village community, with a group called the United Action Committee (UAC) – having some influence in Nauagaon—supporting POSCO. But that has not helped matters. "Today, Nuagaon is a picture of despair, with villagers having exhausted their compensation money and are left with no means to sustain themselves.

Kabindra Rout, a betel farmer, said: "The administration dismantled my betel vine in 2011 and I got a compensation of Rs. 2.28 lakh. But now I am jobless." Many who earlier used to own betel vines and could employ others have now been reduced to daily wage-earners in the vines in Dhinkia, the stronghold of the anti-POSCO movement, which the police have not been able to enter during the past eight years.

On 7 Jun 2013, after meeting CM Naveen Patnaik, POSCO India Chairman and Managing Director Young-Won Yoon said, "We are hopeful the land will be handed over to us soon."

But 'soon' may prove to be far off—or even a delusion – as the 20,000 – odd residents of the eight villages are showing no sign of retreating from their betel vines.

The Project: Some details

4,004 acre area needed for the project.

2,700 acres : Project area scaled down to.

1,704 acres : Land handed over so far $ 12 billion investment

12 million tonne : Expected annual production of steel.

5,000 vines in three gram panchayats.

900 vines dismantled since 2011.

Rs. 15,000 monthly incomes from a 10-decimal betel vine.

Project: Present status

2005 : Odisha signs MoU with POSCO to set up a 12-million

steel plant in Jagatsinghpur. MoU expires in 2010 but State government continues work on the project.

2007 : The project gets an environment clearance for five years. Later, a panel backs the villagers' claims advising the Ministry of Environment and Forests to withdraw clearance.

2011 : The then Minister of Environment and Forest allows the project with riders, conditions and assurance from the government that forest rights laws will be safeguarded. Land acquisition starts.

2013 : After two years, it resumes acquisition in February in Gobindpur. In May, the National Green Tribunal asks the government to stop cutting trees.

Anti – POSCO outfit threatens massive stir ahead: 24 Jun2013

This is another news story on the same subject, POSCO steel project, carried in another daily of 24 Jun 2013, incidentally the same date as the earlier one. If this is datelined Paradip, the earlier one was datelined Gobindpur. Only new points covered in this daily will be examined and included in the pages below.

The opening para of this analysis is rather ominous for the project management as well as for the Odisha Government : "On the completion of the eight years of the signing of a MoU with POSCO India by the State Government to start the steel mill here, the anti-project outfit POSCO Pratirodh Sangram Samiti (PPSS) observed the Black Day on 22 Jun 2013."[5]

The rest of the news story gives details the resistance put up by the PPSS to block any further progress of the construction of the steel plant.

Notably, on 22 Jun 2005, the State Government had entered into an agreement with the POSCO for their biggest ever investment in India in terms of the establishment of a steel plant in Jagatsinghpur district.

However, controversies have been dogging land acquisition for the South Korean firm for the last eight years with the State Government having failed to provide the required land as yet. The PPSS has been waging a struggle against the illegal land acquisition for the steel plant thus putting a spoke in the taking off of the project.

A large procession had started on 24 June from Dhinkia and Govindpur villages and culminated in Patana village where a huge protest meeting was held by the PPSS activists. CPM MP from West Bengal Prabodh Panda, Lok Janasakti Abhyan President Prafulla Samantara, CPI leader Ashish

Kanungo, Forward Block leader Santosh Mitra and Congress leader Jayanti Biswal led the procession.

The meeting was presided over by PPSS Secretary Sisir Mohapatra in absence of its President Abhaya Sahoo, who is now cooling his heels in jail after being arrested in connection with several cases against him. The speakers lambasted the State and Central Governments for their honeymoon with the POSCO and for forcing the local inhabitants to leave their fertile land and the betel vines for the steel plant.

The company and State Governments have violated all norms, which may cause catastrophe in future like Uttarakhands' as many strong and old trees have been cut in the areas making the villages vulnerable to the sea water, alleged the leaders.

They also warned that the struggle would continue till the Government cancels the project.

Land acquisition for POSCO complete: 5 Jul 2013

This story coming days – 11 days, to be exact—after the somber picture painted by the previous entry is unexpected and most surprising, to put it mildly!

First three paras of the news story that appeared in a daily of 5 Jul 2013 are so positive about the POSCO project.[6]

- The Naveen Patnaik Government completed land acquisition of the proposed POSCO steel plant in Odisha's Jagatsinghpur district on Thursday, 4 Jul 2013, despite continued protests by the locals.
- POSCO – India required 2,700 acres of land to establish an eight-million tonne per annum-capacity plant. As many as 28 betel vines were demolished during the day.
- "The land acquisition process is now complete and we will start construction of the boundary wall and felling of trees on the land once the National Green Tribunal vacates its stay", DC Jagatsinghpur Satya Kumar Mallick told the daily.

Thereafter follow other details of the project-related information. POSCO-India has already been given 1,703 acres by the Odisha State Industrial Infrastructure Development Corporation. The remaining land will be transferred to the company in due course, Mr. Mallick added.

The State government acquired about 2,000 acres by May 2012 and it took a little over one year to acquire the rest. The police resorted to lathi-charge several times when the villagers tried to stop the demolition of their betel vines. This led to sharp criticism from rights activists from time to time.

POSCO – India informed the Odisha government in 2012 that it required 2,700 acres to establish an eight-million tonne capacity plant instead of 4,004 acres it sought for a 12-million tonne capacity plant while signing the MoU in Jun 2005. This made the task somewhat easy for the government, which reduced the project area by excluding private land belonging to locals, particular residents of the Dhankia gram panchayat, the nerve centre of the anti-POSCO agitation. The Moll for the project, which expired in 2010, has not been renewed so far.

The 2,700 acres required for project was forest and revenue land. Though the entire land belonged to the government, the local used it to cultivate the betel vines.

Meanwhile, the People's Pratirodh Sangram Samiti, which has been leading protests against the proposed projects since 2005, said agitation would continue. "The villagers will re-occupy the land and reconstruct the betel vines soon. We will continue our opposition to the setting – up of the plant in the locality, "its spokesperson Prashant Paikray said.

Samiti president Abhay Sahoo was arrested in May 2013 in a case pertaining to the death of three persons in a bomb blast at the site.

Niyamgiri : First of the 12-village vote rejects Vedanta mining: 19 Jul 2013

"Vedanta Aluminium's controversial plan to mine the Niyamgiri hills for bauxite received a major jolt Thursday, 18 Jul 2013, after local tribal people unanimously rejected the proposal, claiming religious and cultural rights over the entire hills after 200 minutes of high drama and suspense. In the first of the 12 pallisabhas or village meetings held in Serkapadi on the hills of Rayagada district, 36 registered voters of the village present at the meeting voted against Vedanta's proposal to mine Niyamgiri hill top."

The above was reported by a daily in its issue of 19 July 2013.[7]

On 18 Apr 2013, the Supreme Court (SC) had ordered that the Union Environment Ministry would take a final decision on the grant of Stage II clearance for the bauxite mining project within two months of the decisions of the pallisabhas.

Following the SC order, the Odisha government had notified that pallisabhas would be held in 12 villages in Rayadada and Kalahandi districts between 18 Jul and 19 Aug 2013.

"Niyamgiri is our God, Our parent. It means everything to us. We have been worshipping it for years...our forefathers too. If we are thrown out of Niyamgiri, we would die like fish without water. Does the government was us to die like insects," asked an emotional Govind Sikaka of Serkapadi, in Kui and Oriya language, echoing the emotions of the Niyamgiri tribal people present the meeting.

"We can give our head, our blood, but not Niyamgiri. It has given us everything, fruit, water, air," said Rupu Jakesika, a woman of Serkapadi, who signed two resolutions—one rejecting the proposal to mine Niyamgiri and the second staking a community rights claim over the Niyamgiri mountain.

Tempers soared high when Dongria Kondh tribal men and women insisted that an earlier resolution prepared by the State Tribal Affairs Department restricting their community rights under the Forest Rights Act be scrapped. The earlier resolution on community rights limited the rights of Serkapadi to a few acres. When the tribals of the village refused to sign the resolution, Rayagada District Judge Sarat Chandra Mishra appointed an independent observer and threatened to end the proceedings.

The judge was further miffed when a Dongria Kondh asked for making changes in the resolution and wanted a copy for the village. "How can you be given community right for the entire Niyamgiri range," the judge asked.

The first resolution rejected Vedanta's proposal to mine Niyamgiri would be sent to the OoEF after pallisabhas are held in the remaining 11 villages of Rayagada and Kalahandi. The second resolution, staking community rights under FRA would be sent to a sub-divisional committee of the district. In the last three years, only 20 individual claims under FRA have been settled in Serkapadi, but no community right, which is still to be settled.

The Serkapadi vote does not come as good news for Vedanta Aluminia whose 1 million tonne per annum refinery in Lanjigarh has been faciong a tough time. After it was closed on 5 Dec 2012 due to pancity of bauxite, it reopened on 11 Jul. 2013 following supplies from Gujarat.

The refinery has been facing massive bauxite ore supply crisis after the MoEF withdrew in Aug 2010 the Stage II forest clearance for the diversion of 660.749 hectares of forest land for mining bauxite from the Niyamgiri hills.

The MoEF order came after the NC Saxena Panel recommended that mining in Niyamgiri would affect the area's ecology as well as the primitive tribal group of Dongria Kondhs living on Niyamgiri.

Nine Maoists shun arms in Malkangiri : 10.9.13

Nine Maoists, including three women, surrendered before Malkangiri, SP Akhleshwar Singh on the 10th. Of these nine, eight are from the Chitrakonda area and the remaining one from Malkangiri area. They wanted to join the mainstream since their life was always under threat. One of the Maoists said: "I wanted to live with my family as I was distressed with the activities of the outfit. We were always living under a constant threat, posed by frequent combing operations mounted by the police. Wanting to join the mainstream, we surrendered."

Earlier, on 4 September, four Maoist cadre, including a woman, had surrendered in the district.

These ultras disclosed they had joined the Maoists after they were told about the police atrocities on the innocent tribals. They were rather disillusioned when they found out that their leaders were deviating from the Maoist path and ideology.

The SP said the surrenderees would be suitably rehabilitated as per the Government package.

13 Maoist killed in encounter in Odisha : 15 Sep 2013

At least 13 Maoists, including a women, were killed in an exchange of fire with the police in the Salaikota Reserve Forest, 11 km from Padia and 35 km from Malkangiri, in South Odisha on 14 Sep 2013.

Police said a huge cache of ammunition was recovered from the site where 30-40 Maoist cadres were conducting a training camp. A senior IPS officer told the daily: "13 bodies were shifted to the district headquarters town of Malkangiri. Search operations for the dead and injured are continuing. An inquest is being conducted."

A gun fire took place in the early hours after the Maoists fired at a group of the District Volunteer Force, mostly comprising ex-servicemen and personnel of the Special Operation Group of the Odisha police late night on 13 September[8].

On the 14th morning, we found 13 bodies along with two big Claymore mines, several IEDs, AK-47s, countrymade pistols and magazines", the official said.

Odisha DGP Prakash Mishra told the press in Bhubaneswar before flying to Malkangiri that the operation led by SP Malkangiri Akhileswar Singh, was well-planned and – executed. Mr. Prakash set an ultimatum for the militants to leave Odisha or face sever consequences. This is the first major operation the Odisha police conducted without involving the CRPF and Andhra Pradesh police.

The site is close to Darbha in Chhattisgarh, where Maoists had killed Salma Judum founder and tribal leader Mahendra Karma and 18 others in the deadly attack on the convoy of the Chhattisgarh Congress leaders on 25 May.

The police suspect the dead belonged to the Local Operational Squad (LOS) of the Padia area and the Dandakaranya Special Zone Committee (DKSZC). The two groups were part of the Kalemala squad, which is active in the Dandakaranya region of Odisha and Chhattisgarh. Maoists increased their activities in the Dandakaranya region after they were flushed out of North Telangana of Andhra Pradesh. The feature has a picture of Ramulamma, mother of Nalgonda, Promeela, carrying/displaying a photo of her daughter killed in the encounter, at Kazipet in Warangal.

Maoists scaring away foreigners, staff : HAL to Odisha: 3 Oct 2013

The 27 Aug 2013 landmine blast triggered by Maoists in Koraput, in which four BSF men were killed, has cast its shadow on Navratna PSU Hindustan Aeronautics Limited's factory in the district with foreign nationals, mainly Russian engineers, reluctant to visit there fearing similar attacks.

In two separate letters to Odisha Chief Secretary Jugal Mohapatra in Sep 2013, HAL Executive Director Anirudh Kumar said that apart from the Russians, vendors and suppliers from the different parts of the country are reluctant to come to Sunabeda—where the factory is located – to provide necessary supply and support for machineries and other equipment.[9]

"Our employees and their family members are also worried in view of the deteriorating law and order situation. Officials from other divisions of HAL located in Bangaluru, Nashik, Kanpur, Lucknow and Hyderabad are reluctant to visit Sunabeda on official work or being posted on transfer. The transfer requests to move out of Sunabeda is increasing", Kumar wrote. He continues : "Such an incident not only affects the operations of the factory, but also puts expansion and the new projects in jeopardy. It is requested to take appropriate steps to mitigate the situation for the sake of the defence requirements of the country, smooth operation of a vital installation in Odisha and in the interests of around 25,000 direct and 1 lakh indirect beneficiaries."

The HAL factory in Sunabeda, set up in 1995, manufactures engines for the MiG series and Su-30 MK 1 fighter aircraft for the IAF, Navy, Coast Guard and BSF.

Although the district has seen Maoist presence for several years now, the 27 August attack on NH 26 in Pottangi area of Koraput has triggered the fears. The blast spot is just 35 km from the HAL facility. The HAL official said that since Visakhapatnam in AP is the nearest point from where they can get rail and air connectivity to other parts of the country, they have no other option but to travel on the Pottangi route. HAL Koraput also uses the same route to send aircraft engines direct to the IAF bases.

The PSU has also demanded revival of the Jeypore airport, about a km away from its factory for better air connectivity and landing of Avro and AN-32 Carrier aircrafts. The Jeypore runway was in use till 1987.

In the letter, HAL has also raised the issue of encroachment, saying three hamlets in its land pose a risk to its township. HAL complained that people of these hamlets are making unreasonable demands like return of their land by state government, employment, free medical and education facilities and resorting to agitational methods.

Fear on highway

- Visakhapatnam, which is 180 km from Sunabeda, is a vital travel point for HAL employees as well as the facility's vendors and engineers.
- National Highway 26 is important as it connects Sunabeda with the Andhra port city, which has the nearest rail junction and international airport.
- The 27 August landmine blast, targeting the BSF convoy, took place in Pottangi area on NH – 26, which is just 35 km from Sunabeda and is one of the points the HAL employees regularly cross.

Small force (DVF) that provides the cutting edge : 16 Sep 2013

"Young men from a small constabulary unit in the Odisha Police, the District Voluntary Force (DVF) not more than 500 strong, played a key role in the operation that saw the killing of 13 Maoists in Malkangiri Saturday, 14 Sep 2013. SP Akhileshwar Singh had led the team of DVF and Special Operations Group (SOG) men on foot through the Sialkota forests until they spotted the Maoist camp."

This is the opening para of an analytical article in a daily of 16 Sep 2013 about the good work done by a small unit of DVF, created out of the State Police.[10]

The DVF works in small sub-units of 8-10 in an operation, and on a familiar terrain. An official explains its composition: "Around 40 per cent of them are former SOG jawans, as no one can continue in the SOG beyond the age of 35. The rest are local boys picked on the basis of their skills by the district SP. Since they know the local terrain and speak the local dialect, they have a head start on other groups/forces who came from other districts."

Their basic pay is 30 per cent higher than the rest, but in all other aspects, they look like any other policemen, with no additional lapels or badges. Headed by district SPs, the force was raised in 2009 and has since been involved in a number of successful operations (given at the end of this entry). Odisha DGP Prakash Mishra confirms : "It has proved a very effective force against Maoists. A force is as good as its strike rate and DVF has ensured we stay ahead of Maoists."

Though there are eight BSF battalions, eight CRPF battalions, a COBRA battalion and 5 SOG teams in Odisha, officials say it is the DVF that provides the cutting edge. It was raised because senior officials found it took too long to initiate a purely SOG-based operation as orders have to come from Bhubaneswar. A DVF operations involved no such formality, as the SP at the district headquarters can launch the operation.

An official adds: "In DVF, some constables would collect intelligence, while others are strictly meant for the operation. When the CM visits Maoist areas, the innermost security cordon comprises DVF personnel."

Though the SOG gets anti-extremist training at Police Special School at Chandaka and tactical training at the Army base in Jabalpur, it is not always familiar with the local terrain. But the DVF, too, has its limitations. "When the number of Maoists is high, we have to send SOG forces to prevent casualties on our side.

Track Record of the DVF

- **23 Aug 2013:** DVF-SOG team kills Madhav alias Golla Ramulla, a senior Maoist.
- **20 Jul 2013:** Three Maoists are gunned down by DVF-SOG team at Turei Ghati.
- **Jan 2012:** Maoist leader Chitrakam Reddy alias Sitru and his Maoist wife killed in an exchange of fire with DVF in Koraput.
- **Jan 2011:** 9 Maoist cadres, including 4 women, killed in an encounter in Rayagada district.

'Big Success': 13 Maoists killed : Sep 2013

At least 13 Maoists, including a women, were killed in an exchange of fire with the police in the Salackota reserve forest, some 11 km from Padia and 35 km from Malkangiri, in South Odisha on 14 Sep 2013. The gun fight had started late prevous night after the Maoists fired at the group of the District Voluntary Force (DVF), mostly comprising ex-servicemen and personnel of the Special Operations Group (SOG) of the Odisha police. On the 14th morning, the police found 13 bodies along with two big Claymore mines, several IED, AK-47s, country-made pistols and magazines. The bodies were shifted to Malkangiri. A huge Cache of ammunition was recovered from the site where 30 to 40 Maoists were conducting a camp.

Odisha DGP Prakash Mishra said the operation led by Malkangiri SP Akihleswar Singh, was well-planned and – executed. The DGP issued an ultimatum to the Maoists to leave his State or face severe consequences. The site is close to Darbha in Chhattisgarh where the ultras had killed Salma Judum founder and the brave tribal leader Mahendra Karma and 18 others in a deadly attack on the convoy of Chattisgarh Congress leaders on 25 May.

The police believe the dead belonged to the Local Operations Squad (LOS) of the Padia area and the Dandakaranya Special Zone Committee. The two groups were part of the Kalimela squad, which is active in the Dandakaranya region of Odisha and Chhattisgarh. Maoist had increased their activity in the Dandakaranya region after they were flushed out of North Telengana of Andhra Pradesh. The 30 Maoists were led by Rakesh, the Divisional commander, and they were planning to attack the security forces.

Rakesh was among the dead. Their camp was located some 20 km from the Chhattisgarh border and 70 km from Malkangiri. An NIA team arrived Malkangiri to probe if these Maoists had any link to the 25 May Darbha Ghati attack in Chhattisgarh which wiped off the entire congress leadership of that State, including its president and his son.

Besides the 13 dead, the SOG captured one Maoist in the encounter. DGP Prakash Mishra said they had information about infiltration of Maoists from Chhattisgarh to Padia area of Malkangiri districts.

Importantly, this is the first major operation the Odisha police conducted without involving Central Armed Police Forces and the Andhra Pradesh police. This is claimed to be the biggest success in the anti-Naxal drive of the State police, and will prove a morale booster.

A daily claimed it was a mole—a Koya tribal—within the rebel camp that helped police carry out Odisha's biggest ever encounter. The mole and his interlocutor were part of a small team of 40 policemen led by the district

SP. Seniormost of the rebel leaders present, however, escaped in the attack. Rain also helped the police, as the rebels were all forced under the three tents. "We had precise information...They were in a small clearing, 1000 metres in length and breadth, surrounded by Phoosa hills and thick forests," the SP told the daily[11]. He further added: "The downpour also drowned out the sound of police movement. Confident of the precise nature of information, we did not feel the need to call additional men or Central Forces. A small team is always handy in such cases."

Odisha has two prominent Special Zone Committees of the CPI (Maoist): AOB (Andhra Odisha Border) and COB (Chhattisgarh Odisha Border. Malkangiri falls under the former, that has seen major setbacks this year (2013).

Maoist among 8 jailed for VHP man's (Swami Laxmananda Saraswati) murder

A court in Odisha on 3 Oct 2013 sentenced eight people to life imprisonment for the murder of the VHP activist Swami Laxmananda Saraswati and four others in 2008. Those sentenced are Bjaya Kumar Sanaseth, Buddhadev Naik, Sanatan Bada Majhi, Duryodhan Sunamajhi, Bhaskar Sunamajhi, Munda Badamajhi, Gadanath Chalanseth and Maoist Pulari Rama Rao alias Udaya. The court acquitted Somanath Dandasena for insufficient evidence.

The charge sheet filed by the Crime Branch on 5 Sep 2011 said the Maoist leaders had formed a "militia group" to execute the plan to gun down the Swami. Maoist leader Sabyasachi Panda had given TV interviews he and other Maoists had killed Laxmananda for spreading hatred in the name of religion. Laxmikant Dash, Secretary, Swami Laxmananda Saraswati Shradhanjali Samiti, hailed the verdict but slammed the state government for its failure to nab the "conspirators" even five years after the murders, and punishing the foot soldiers only.

Santosh Padhi, counsel for seven of the convicts, said : "There was no evidence against my clients and I would advise them to move the High Court." Udaya's lawyer Bijoy Mishra said he too would go to the High Court in appeal. The state government had handed over the case to the Crime Branch and also ordered a judicial probe into the murder and the communal strife in its aftermath. The judicial panel was yet to submit its report.

It is to be noted that the violence was described as ethno-communal riots because the Kandhas, identified as Hindus, had attacked another tribal group, the Panas, who are mostly converts to Christianity.

Why Odisha's mining order lacks steel: Analytical piece in a daily: 17 Nov 2013

- From being a soporific department under which miners had a free run in the State's ore-rich hinterland, the Odisha Steel and Mines Department has suddenly changed tack and showing a fresh burst of energy. The biggest example of this was the Rs 76,000 – odd Crore penalty levied recently on companies for extracting ore in excess of set limits and violating environmental laws over the past ten years.
- Last months, Oct 2013, the Department also ordered that those waiting for their mining lease to be renewed should restrict production to their captive requirement, and that areas which had not been leased out would be given to state-run Odisha Mining Corporation (OMC).
- To give an idea of the staggering penalty, consider that it would wipe off Odisha's Rs 40,000, crore debt, allow the State to have a tax-free budget for the next few years and still leave enough to run several populist schemes. What the Naveen Patnaik Government also hopes is that the figure would blind every one to how the mining mess came to this in the first place. It may not just be a coincidence that the penalty was imposed just days before the MB Shah Commission landed in Odisha for the mining probe.
- Activists seeking a CBI inquiry say the government has deliberately left loopholes in the penalty order to let the violators go scot free. For example, they point out, it has not cancelled the lease of miners who violated their lease conditions, which it could have done, and instead levied fines, which it may not have the authority to do under environment laws.
- Besides, the government is silent on the role played by the officials of the Odisha Pollution Control Board, the Deputy Directors of Mines, Indian Bureau of Mines and Forest and Environment Department in the excess mining.
- The decision to let the Odisha Mining Corporation become the default miner may not be good idea either as the Corporation is barely able to run three of its 35 mines, and is itself accused of illegal mining worth over Rs 2,000 Crore.
- Over the past three years, mining has become a major source of revenue for the State, earning it Rs 4,517 Crore in 2012 alone. It is time Odissa treated this asset as an asset.[12]

Surrounded, Panda plans to surrender : 17 Nov 2013

"With five of his associates killed in an encounter, Maoist leader Sabyasachi Panda seems to be readying for a deal with the police for a possible surrender."

The above was reported by a daily in its issue of 17 Nov 2013.[13]

During the 14 Nov 2013 encounter at Bhalipada village in Gajapati district, five of Panda's men—all from Kandhamal—were killed by the joint team of the SOG and District Volunteer Force men. A resurgent police combed Panda's base in Kandhamal and recovered landmines, gelatin sticks and tiffin bombs.

Panda formed the Odisha Maovadi Party after being expelled from the CPI (Maoist) in Aug 2013 over "betraying the party and revolution and the great cause of the toiling masses, particularly of the oppressed masses of Odisha."

With Panda cornered and surrounded by police from one side and Maoists from Koraput side, the police sources said Panda was using his official contacts for a safe exit. His wife Mili was supposed to meet DGP Mishra at his official residence on 15 Nov 2013 but the talks were cancelled. The DGP said he was unaware of any talks of surrender by Panda, and that if he wanted to surrender, it would be as per "surrender policy." He was non-committal when asked if the government would withdraw cases against Panda. Mili downplayed the meeting. "I wanted to register my protest over the way the police killed youth terming them as Maoists. There was no plan to discuss Sabyasachi's surrender", she said, adding that Panda can surrender if cases against him are withdrawn.

Panda has over 50 criminal cases against him apart from the murder of Laxamananda.

"Maoist activities on decline in Odisha"

Some stories in the press carried news about the declining trend of Maoist activities in Odisha. One excerpt from a newspaper that appeared towards the end of 2013 is reproduced below.[14]

> Even as the Maoist menace continues to be a major internal security challenge affecting almost one-third of total districts in the country, activities of the Left Wing Extremists (LWE) in Odisha, parts of which were once hotbeds of the ultras' violence, have shown remarkable improvement with atleast seven to eight affected districts almost reporting as the 'Maoist-free zones'.

The Odisha police headed by DGP Prakash Mishra, were reportedly making all efforts to come at par with the "neighbouring Andhra Pradesh which has been reporting Zero Maoist activities in the entire state for the past so many years."

Odisha's central region districts like Mayurbhanj, Keonjhar, Jajpur, Dhenkanal, Sambalpur, Deogarh and Nayagarh are now seen as ultra-free zones, said a top police officer. "There is hardly any Maoist violence in these districts." DGP Mishra seems up beat over the positive developments in controlling the Maoist menace as these areas are reporting zero casualities, the sources said.

While the Unified Command meeting chaired by Chief Secretary BK Patnaik recently took stock of situation on the ground, the anti-Maoist operations were being planned for the Maoist hotbed of western Odisha, bordering Chhattigarh, one of the worst-affected states in the country.

With proper coordination the Central Forces and the Special Operations Group (SOG) of the State Police, positive results have started coming even from the Red Zones. The CRPF is coordinating with state police on day-to-day basis. The BSF authorities too are not left out of the net. There are 14 battalions of the CRPF and BSF deployed in these so-called Red Zones. Two more battalions are on their way to Odisha, said DGP Mishra.

The information and consequent conclusions drawn there after are essentially based upon the averments made by the Odisha DGP Mishra and his senior officers. Hence the need to be cautious while assessing the value of such "handouts", which indeed they are. While one needs not be totally cynical about the veracity of such assertions made by the State police, there is no wisdom in taking these as gospel truths. There can be an element of truth (even if very small) in these "facts", handed out to the always-hungry-for-the-news press men. Still the case to be overcautious cannot be overstated. It needs to be noted that the districts in the central Odisha were the ones where LWE was least intense. Achieving success in that region, obviously, was not too difficult. To replicate the same in the worst-affected western districts of the State will not be that easy. In one word, it is essential that such self-serving, may be, even motivated, assertions and averments are examined critically to assess their veracity.

Maoists blow up block office building in Odisha : 26 Dec 2013

Maoists blew up a block office building at Padia in Malkangiri district in the early hours of Wednesday, 24 Dec 2013 using powerful explosives, police said. Armed ultras, including women stormed the block office building in Padia, SP Akhileshwar Singh said.

They set the building on fire before triggering a powerful blast causing extensive damage to the structure. No one was injured in the attack. Four of the five rooms of the building that had asbestos roofs were completely destroyed and important documents and records were damaged, gram panchayat officer Basant Behera said.

The SP felt the attack was desparate attempt by Maoists to counter the stepped-up anti-Naxal operations by security forces in the region.

Maoist kill village leader : 30 Dec 2013

Maoists killed Kosa Madhi, 38, of Sangel village under the Kalimela police station, suspecting him to be a police informer. He was secretary of the local Pani panchayat and had been abducted by the ultras on 27 December when they triggered a blast with explosives and destroyed the bridge over the river Poteru to stop movement of security forces between Kalimela and Padia.

Madhi was produced before a Maoist "Kangaroo Court", sentenced to death and thereafter killed. The villagers, who informed the police of this murder, spotted the body of Majhi in the neighbourhood, on the same day, the 27th, the Maoist had also looted the house of SPO Lacha Madkami, one of Madhi's relatives, of the same village.

Malkangiri SP Akhleshwar Singh said : "The inquiry in the murder is on…The Maoists have become vengeful and are creating terror among the people in the face of heightened action against them by the security forces through raids and vigorous combing operations in the district…. Besides, they are also deeply concerned due to the increasing surrender of their cadres to the police." Meanwhile, ADG (Intelligence) Sunil Roy, IG (Operations) Soumendra Priyadarshi and IG South-West Range Jaswan Jethwa visited 30 December the blast site in the Padia area of the district where the Maoists had blown up the (portions of) bridge two days ago, as mentioned above. The three senior officers also held discussions with the BSF DIG on the incident.

In the meantime, the 4-day bandh call given by the Maoists in Malkangiri and adjoining district of Koraput demanding a halt to the operations against them and alleged atrocities against the tribals entered third day on the 30th. It did affect, expectedly normal life in Maoist hinterlands including the Padia, Kalimela and Motu areas of Malkangiri, but hardly had any effect in Koraput district.[15]

Odisha: The year 2014

The year 2014 in Maoist-hit Odisha will be marked by the arrest of its most prominent face, Sabyasachi Panda!

This part of the chapter opens up with a news story on Panda, which will culminate in his arrest after some incidents of Maoist violence. The part will end up with some other incidents of Maoist attacks post-Panda's arrest. Obviously, Panda's arrest does not signal the end of LWE in the State.

Maoist killed in Malkangiri District

In a fierce battle on 12.1.14, the security forces gunned down a Maoist and seized four rifles from the spot in Chikatpali forest near Ralegada in Chitrakonda cut-off area of Malkangiri district. The rest of the Maoists succeeded in fleeing the clash.

Receiving information about the movement of some 30 red rebels in the cut-off area, the BSF men reached Chikatpali village and started a combing operation to locate the hide-out of the ultras in the forest near the village. As they were closing in their hide-out, the ultras opened fire which was immediately returned. In the ensuing exchange of fire lasting an hour, one Maoist cadre was killed, the rest making good their escape, said the district police chief, Akhileshwar Singh.

Nine Naxals in net in Narayanpur District

In a major success, a combined force of Chhattisgarh Armed Force (CAF) and the district police arrested nine hardcore Maoist ultras from a dense forest under Jhara police station, informed district SP Amit Kamble on 12.1.14. They were nabbed from the jungles of Badenghol-Kaushapara village, some 9 km from Jhara police station, from where the joint party had started from for area domination/search operation. The force, based on intelligence inputs came across the group of suspected Naxals in these jungles, and they were arrested.

Some of those arrested are members of the Jan Militia, a banned outfit of the Maoists. Those arrested were identified as Sarju Korram, Jairam Salam, Maniram Salam, Sudren Salam, Ratu alias Burka Rati, Lekhan alias Lakah Banju, Aytu Lohar – all seven are residents of Jharaghati area—and the last two carried cash awards of Rs 10,000 each on their arrest : Mangtu alias Manglau and Sona Der.

Ousted Maoist commander looks for exit from Odisha forest hide-out : 8 Mar 2014

Injured Sabyasachi Panda trapped near Ganjam-Kandhamal border.

"He was once a darling of the CPI (Maoist) leadership. From his bastion in the Kandhamal forests of Odisha, Top Maoist Commander Sabyasachi Panda planned and executed many daring operations for his party. But two years after being forsaken by the Party leadership, 45-years-old Panda is trapped now somewhere along the Ganjam-Kandhamal border with a bullet injury in the thigh. The police are closing in on his hideout."

The above was reported by a daily in its issue dated 8 Mar 2014.[16]

SP Ganjam District Ashish Singh confirms: "We are very close to him and we will get him very soon."

Panda is believed to have been injured in an encounter with the police on 15 Feb 2014. While he took one bullet in the thigh, another shattered his laptop. This was revealed to the police by his bodyguard Nikita, who was arrested with two other women rebels on the night of 28 Feb 2014. One of Panda's close associates told the daily that he was trapped with only three rebels, one a woman. Other 24 associates have either been killed in police action or arrested. The four, the associate believe, have no food left. "They are in possession of very few weapons and hardly any cash," he said. There are indications that in the past two weeks, Panda has been desparate to secure an exit for himself.

The Odisha police say he is in touch with Aam Aadmi Party to save his life and secure his "political career". However, one of the Executive Member of the AAP, who the police believe is in touch with Panda, has denied it. "I have never met Sabyasachi Panda, and he has never contacted me about joining the AAP or anything else", he said in an e-mail response.

Panda, a mathematics graduate, was the mastermind of the Nayagarh raid in Feb 2008, in which 14 policemen were killed and a huge cache of arms and ammunition was looted. He faces over 30 charges of murder, including that of VHP leader Laxmananda Saraswati. The killing triggered off the 2008 Kandhamal riots.

In a 16-page letter addressed to the Maoist Supreme Commander Ganapathi in Jul 2012, Panda accused the party's Telugu leadership of "superiority complex". Two days later, the CPI (Maoist) expelled him. Panda then went on to create his own outfit. But in the absence of party support, he got isolated along with a handful of rebels.

The feature carries a picture of three people sitting, engaged in conversation : Its subtitle reads: "A 2012 file picture of Sabyasachi Panda (with him wrapped in a cloth and his back to the camera) in the middle, speaking to mediapersons at a camp in Kandhamal." This group is surrounded by the security guards of Panda and some armed Maoist cadres.

Stage set for 'surrender', Odisha Maoist stays away: 12 Mar 2014

Nachika Linga, who formed the Maoist frontal outfit Chasi Mulia Adivasi Sangh that was instrumental in abduction of BJD MLA Jhina Hikaka in Koraput district two years ago, on Tuesday, 11 Mar 2014, did not make the much-awaited surrender before the police in a village in Koraput.

The 42-year-old Linga, tribal leader from Narayanpatna block of Maoist-hit koraput district with over 50 cases of violence against him, shot to prominence in Apr 2012 when he helped Maoist abduct Hikaka when he was returning home. He has been under ground since he allegedly led an attack on police in 2009.[17]

He was supposed to surrender at Balipeta village before his supporters at 11 AM, 11 Mar 2014. But with large number of BSF and policemen lurking in the background, he did not turn up. IG South-Western Range said police welcome anyone who wants to leave the party of violence, but only courts can take a decision on Linga's future.

Now behind him, promise he made his Maoist captors : 3 Apr 2014

Two years ago, before Maoists released him from captivity that had lasted a month, Jhina Hikaka, then a youthful MLA of BJD from Laxmipur, wanted to leave politics. At a Praja Court organised by Maoists, two days before his release, Hikaka was reportedly made to promise to bid good bye to politics.

The above was reported by a daily in its issue of 3 Apr 2014.[18]

Hikaka, 39, was taken hostage by members of Andhra-Odisha Border Special Zonal Committee at Tayaput village on Laxmipur-Koraput Road in Mar 2012, when he was returning to Laxmipur after attending a party meeting. His release came after the State government acceded to the Maoist demand to release 25 ultra prisoners.

Now, during CM Naveen Patnaik's whistle stop tour to Koraput, Hiraka says he has put the 2012 incident behind him—he is the BJD candidate from the Koraput Lok Sabha seat. "That is the past. Why do you keep raking it up?" he asks, after attending two rallies addressed by the CM on 2 April. "I never feared anyone till the abduction. My movements have been restricted since."

Hikaka was asked to shift to the seat after party workers revolted against the sitting MP Jayram Pangi. He is confident : "Everything has been achieved under the Patnaik Government. As an MP, I will focus on livelihood programmes, skill development and technical education of tribal youths as well as eco-tourism.

Dissidence within BJD over the nomination of Pangi's son and nephew from two Assembly segments of the Koraput (Lok Sabha) seat could work against him. Hikaka's main opponent is Giridhar Gomang of the Congress who was elected from here (Koraput) for a record nine times before losing to Pangi in 2009. Gamang insists he has not lost touch with the people.

"Koraput has been a Congress bastion. 2009 result was just a set back", says Gomng, after the Semiliguda rally addressed by Rahul Gandhi. "I have kept in touch with the people through my music troupe. Thousands attend my musical evenings." But Gomang has no new promise to make except speak of his past. "In 1993, when I was the Union Minister for Planning, I identified an irrigation project in Koraput under Special category assistance. I was the first tribal development minister. I was also telecom and mining minister, but he never made money illegally", he says.

In Maoist-affected Narayanpatna and Laxmipur in Koraput, however, people are not impressed with either Gamang or Hikaka. "I never saw Gamang until he become CM in 1999. He was in Delhi while Koraput suffered", says a paan-shop owner in Laxmipur. In Naraynpur, people wonder whether Hikaka will visit them after becoming an MP as he has not come since he shifted to Bhubaneshwar two years ago.

Close shave for BSF men as 'Maoists' trigger IED blasts: 7 Apr 2014

A group of BSF personnel had a narrow escape after two explosives, allegedly planted by Maoists, went off within short interval in Kalimela area of Malkangiri district.

The BSF men had gone to the area to remove posters put up by Maoists asking people to boycott the Lok Sabha polls, SP Akhileshwar Singh said. While no BSF men were hurt, two cows were killed. The police and security personnel are now maintaining strict vigil.

The news story is datelined Malkangiri (Odisha), 6 Apr 2014.[19]

Policeman who fought Maoists is a candidate in Malkangiri: 7 Apr 2014

"In his 20-year career as a police officer, he has seen the rise of Maoists in the Red Zone of Malkangiri district and thrice he came close to death. A landmine blast by the ultras almost blew up his father, a Congress leader of Malkangiri district. But he, too, survived. As the threats became more severe and his name appeared on the hit list of Maoists in 2002, he had to be posted out of Malkangiri to Koraput police station as the officer-in-charge."

The above is the opening para of a news story about a policeman published in a daily in its issue dated 7 Apr 2014.[20]

In the 2014 General Elections, former police officer Sarat Chandra Buruda was back to fight as a politician in the same area where he and the Maoist rebels once played the cat-and-mouse game. Buruda, a Koya tribal from Sherpalli village of Malkangiri, resigned the job in Feb 2014 to contest from Chitrakonda Assembly constituency on a BJP ticket. Here is Buruda, talking from his temporary election office in Chitrakonda town: "There is a dearth of leadership in Malkangiri. Several politicians have become MLA from Chitrakonda but never came back to stay after their victory. But I want to change this. My goal was to change the image of Chitrakonda from a Maoist-dominated area to a development zone. In 2009, I offered my resignation but it was not accepted. But this time I was determined to quit my job and fight the polls."

Few have experienced the violent history of Chitrakonda more closely than the 44-year-old former police officer. In 2000, when he was the Officer-in-charge of the Chitrakonda police station, Maoists had accosted him for his police revolver. But Buruda says he craftily hid his revolver, and the rebels, failing to find it, let him go. The second time he gave death a miss was in 2001 when a Maoist landmine blast's timing went awry. The third time he says he survived Maoists was on 6 Feb 2004, just a month before the General Elections, when over 200 Maoists attacked significant police establishments such as Koraput arrmoury, five police stations, Koraput jail, an SP's office and the OSAP battalion, killing four policemen, including three CRPF men, and injuring six others. After the attack, he was shifted to the Special Intelligence Wing, the anti-Maoist intelligence force of Odisha police.

Buruda believes Maoists have now become dacoits : "The corrupt officers and Maoists are sharing the funds that come for development of Malkangiri. The Maoists are no longer friends of tribals. I want to help the area make a fresh start and bring in real development."

According to local residents of Chitrakonda, Buruda has a good chance of winning as the Bengalis in the district should vote for him; they are unhappy with the BJD for not giving an assembly ticket to former minister Arabinda Dhali, a Bengali.

Top Maoist get 10 years RI: 11 Jun 2014

A Sessions Court in Koraput district on 10 Jun 2014 sentenced hard core Maoist Chenda Bhusanam alias Ghasi to 10 years of rigorous imprisonment for keeping fire arms and attacking police personnel on duty.

The court also imposed a fine of Rs. 35,000 on him, and if he fails to pay the fine, he would undergo another two years' RI.

The above news were published by a daily of 11 Jun 2014.[21]

Koraput Additional District Judge Pradip Kumar Mahanta had on 9 June convicted Ghasi under Section 27 of Arms Act, Section 17 Criminal Law Amendment Act and Section 20 of Unlawful Activities (Prevention) Act. He is the first top Maoist to be convicted in the last five 5-6 years, police officials said.

Hailing from Vishakhapatnam district of AP, Ghasi was one of the top commanders of the Andhra-Odisha Border Special Zonal Committee of the CPI (Maoist). He was arrested in Apr 2011 with a cash reward of Rs 10 lakh on his head. Now lodged in Koraput Jail, Ghasi was said to be involved in almost all the major Maoist-related operations in Odisha and Andhra. He has 63 cases filed against him in Vishakhapatnam alone between 1991 and 1996.

In Odisha, he was involved in the Alampanka incident, in which 38 Greyhounds drowned in the Balimela Reservoir in Jun 2008. He was also involved in the MPV blast in Kalimela in which 17 policemen were killed.

Ghasi strengths lay in ambushing police parties, setting landmine blasts, and shooting down informers or policemen. He would allegedly extort Rs 10-20 lakh a month from local traders, contractors, corporate houses and politicians. In Jan 2013, Ghasi was acquitted in a double murder case due to lack of evidence. Ghasi is still accused in a dozen more Maoist-related cases in Odisha.

Army proposes ecotask force, Odisha differs on role : 7 Jul 2014

Citing the POSCO project "that would lead to increase in pollution levels", the Army has proposed an environmental task force for Odisha but the State government differs on what its role should be. The Army suggests the Eco Task Force (ETF) help plant 1 lakh trees per year. The Odisha Forest Department, however, would rather have the ETF protect forest officials from the Maoists.

The ETF scheme, initiated by the MOD in 1982, has led to such battalions in Uttarakhand, J and K, Himachal Pradesh, Assam, Nagaland, Rajasthan and Delhi. Brig DS Chahal, of the Adjutant General (AG) Branch, proposed an ecological battalion for Odisha early 2014. Brig Chahal wrote to Army Central Command, in whose jurisdiction Odisha falls into: "POSCO project... provides us an excellent opportunity to explore inclusion of our veterans in projects dealing with preservation of environment."[22] In Jun

2014, Sub-Area (Chhattisgarh-Odisha) commander Brig Balraj Mehta wrote to the Odisha Government, "Raising of ETF would help in maintenance of ecological balance…." He proposed the ETF help plant 1 lakh tree a year with the help of NCC cadets, scouts and NGOs. "Taking 50 per cent as survival rate will amount to 50,000 trees a year, it will actually be possible to achieve the target."

In the last week of Jun 2014, the officials of Home and Forest Departments met over the proposal. Principal Chief Conservator of Forests JD Sharma says he made it clear his department needs EFT to protect forest guards in some 30 locations rather than go for afforestation activities. "Our teams are unable to man Maoist-hit areas like Sunabeda in Nuapada district and Simlipal in Mayurbhanj district due to presence of Maoists. Most of my men don't have arms," Sharma tells the daily.

Forest officials said they hoped the ETF would help guard forests the way CRPF has been guarding the Barbara forest in Khurda district.

Sharma says adding one lakh trees is not an issue with Odisha as the latest Forest Survey of India Report showed that between 2009 and 2011, more than 48 sq km green cover was added.

A State government official said that the Army has proposed that 70 per cent of the total cost of Rs 5.5 Cr for ETF's operations be funded by the Centre, 25 per cent by the State ad 5 per cent by the corporates in the districts.

The Army suggested the legal authority be vested with the ETF to prosecute anyone found cutting trees planted by the forces.

Though POSCO signed its MoU for a 12-million-tonne steel plant in Jagatsinghpur in 2005, the project has struggled to take off due to regulatory hurdles as well as popular protests on the ground. Environmental clearance for the first phase was renewed in Jan 2014 with the condition that the country spend 5 per cent of its total investment on corporate social responsibility.

Top Odisha Maoist Sabyasachi Panda held : 19 Jul 2014

Odisha's most-wanted Maoist leader Sabyasachi Panda, who allegedly masterminded the murder of VHP leader Laxmananda Saraswati that triggered the 2008 Kandhamal anti-Christian riots, has been arrested after 15 years on the run, police said Friday, 18 Jul 2014.

Panda, facing more than 100 cases including those of attacks on security forces, and the 2012 abduction of two Italians, was arrested following a raid at a three-storied house in the South Odish town of Behrampur late

17 July night after "accurate intelligence inputs." Panda, who was suffering from diabetes and an eye ailment, had been staying at the house for the past fortnight, the police said. Several SIM cards that Panda used helped track his movements, but the confirmation of his exact location came from informers. DIG South Range Amitabh Thakur said at a press conference : "The Special Intelligence Wing of Odisha Police identified his location using technological inputs as well as human resource who shadowed him."[23]

A Ruger revolver, about 800 gram of gold jewellery, 10 cell phones, several SIM cards, Rs 2 lakh cash, two external hard drives, several pen drives and a laptop were recovered from him. A driving licence issued in West Bengal in 2004 in the name of Prabir Das and carrying his photo was also seized from him.

Berhampur SP Anirudh Singh, who led the operation to arrest Panda, said his team spotted Panda at the house with two women 11 PM. "Panda sensed danger and locked up the main door of the house. Some of our men climbed to the first floor, but could not get in as Panda locked the other entrance. He then managed to get out of that house, probably through the toilet window", said the SP Anirudh Singh.

As a desperate Panda tried to slip out, the police team saw his shadow. Singh sneaked from behind and arrested him. Though Panda had the revolver and four rounds of bullets in it, he did not fire a single shot. But the police were not sure if he was Panda as they had never seen him and all that they had with them was a decade-old photograph. "We asked him if he was the same Sabyasachi, and he nodded", Singh said. Panda was produced in the court of sub-divisional judicial magistrate in the evening and was remanded in the police custody for 10 days for interrogation.

The police believe Panda, who once carried a bounty of Rs 20 lakh on his, had lost his prominence over the past couple of years as several of his associates were either killed, arrested or deserted him after his expulsion from the CPI (Maoist). The police too had brought down the reward money on him to Rs 5 lakh. "Most of his associates left him as he sexually exploited the women cadres and tortured innocent tribal youths. He used to exploit money from corporates, contractors and businessmen", said DIG Thakur.

Panda, in his 50s, had formed his own Maoist outfit, viz Odisha Maovadi Party, after his expulsion from the CPI (Maoist). "Last month (Jun 2014), he changed his party's name to CPI (Marxist-Leninist-Maoist). As per police records, he has around 100 cases, including half-a-dozen attacks on security men, against him since 1999 when he first came on police radar after attacking a temporary police post in Rayagada district." He had looted all material kept in the camp, including VHF sets.

Mathematics Graduate who turned a rebel

The daily had given some important information on Panda in the news story, reproduced here.

Left Leaning

Born to Ramesh Panda, a freedom fighter from Ranapur area of Nayagarh district who later joined the CPM and then BJD, Sabyasachi did his graduation in Mathematics from a Puri College. He was deeply inspired by CPI (M-L) leader Nagbhushan Patnaik, and joined the Naxal movement in 1991. In 1995, he gave the call for an armed struggle and formed Kui Lewang Sangha, which later became a front organisation for the PWG.

Major Attacks

24 Mar 2006: Panda masterminded the attack on a subjail and a police station in Udayagiri town of Gajapati and freed prisoners after killing two policemen. The rebels, some 80 of them, also took hostage the officer-in-charge of the police tation and jailor before releasing them a few days later.

Feb 2008: He planned and executed the attack on police armoury in Nayagarh district, which claimed 18 lives. The attack gave the ultras truckloads of weapons such as AK-47s, SLRs, INSAS and hand grenades.

Aug 2008: He masterminded the killing of VHP leader Laxmananda Saraswati and five of his accomplices, which led to riots in Kandhamal district. More than 40 people were killed in the riots.

Mar 2012: He abducted two Italian tourists from the jungles of Ganjam-Kandhamal districts and kept them hostage for 29 days.

Area of operation

In 2001, PWG formed Andhra-Odisha Border Special Zone Committee and made Panda its Odisha head. After the PWG merged with MCC to form CPI (Maoist), he was appointed a secretary of Basdhara Division that looked after northern and Central districts of Odisha. Panda then focus on the southern Odisha districts of Kandhamal, Rayagada, Gajapati and Ganjam.

Another daily covers the arrest of Panda

Another daily covered this important incident of Panda's arrest in greater detail in two analytical articles. Both are covered below.

From revolution's postor boy to 'old dog'

Sabyasachi Panda once most sought after by political parties : 19 Jul 2014

"Odisha's Deputy leader of the Opposition once called him the "voice of 57 per cent in Odisha, who have only Rs 12 per day to spend". Before he fell out with the CPI (Maoist), Maoist Commander Sabyasachi Panda was so popular that political parties in Odisha offered him ticket to fight elections. But he said he was wedded to "revolution". The son of a freedom fighter, Panda is a mathematics graduate and was with two mainstrean Left parties before he went underground." Thus, wrote a daily of 19 Jul 2014.

In 1998, the Maoist organisation Party Unity merged with the bigger party, CPI (ML)-People's War to form the People's War Group (PWG). Panda, who was close to the former, joined the PWG in the same year. He rose to prominence soon afterwards in 1999 when he attacked a police post in Rayagada district. But his high point would come almost a decade later in Feb 2008 when under his command, a group of 160 Maoist rebels attacked a police armoury in Nayagada district. The attack lasted for several hours, and the Maoists were able to loot a cache of arms and ammunition so huge that they had to leave behind some of the less sophisticated ones[24].

Six months later, Maoists struck in Kandhamal when they killed the popular Hindu leader Swami Laxmananda Saraswati. Police say Panda was the mastermind of the killing that triggered off anti-Christian riot. Investigations revealed that Panda and Maoist leadership hoped that the ensuing violence would result in many riot-affected persons joining their ranks. In fact, as police investigation would later reveal, many had signed up to join the CPI(Maoist). But due to timely intervention by the then Collector Krishan Kumar (who announced training and jobs for those the Maoists had approached), most of them ditched Panda.

The Maoist leadership was not happy with the outcome and relationship with Panda soured. Somehow, he survived in the Party till the senior Maoist leader Kishenji, who had taken a liking to him, was alive. In Nov 2011, after Kishenji was killed in an encounter, Panda was left to fend for himself. A month later, he severed communication with leadership.

In Mar 2012, Panda took two Italians (tourists) hostage. Then he declared a ceasefire with the Odisha government. To embarrass him, the CPI(Maoist) abducted a local politician.

In Aug 2012, finally, Panda wrote a 16-page letter to Maoist Supreme Commander Muppalla Laxman Rao alias Ganapathi, accusing him and other

Telugu cadres of "superiority complex". He also came heavily on the practice of "unnecessary class annihilations". He elucidated further :

> "In doubt and due to lack of proper class education, our forces killed as many as 14 common policemen (in Nayagda/Nayagarh); those who were not retaliating and mostly had sympathies with our movement.... In spite of having worked with tribals for 30 years, the Maoists had failed to develop a concrete model for development of tribal zones."

The party retaliated by expelling him. From there, Panda floated his own party, Odisha Maovadi Party. He feared that Maoist leadership had intentions of eliminating him. "kill the old dog after it becomes old – that is the CPI (Maoist)'s ideology", he said.

Since Feb 2014, the police was closing in on him. Five months later, the "old dog", tired and injured, fell into their trap, when he was nabbed from his aide's house in Berhampur on 18 Jul 2014.

Some other points need to be noted :

- Sabyasachi Panda, 48, picked up after a tip-off from his hideout.
- Aliases : Sunil, Sarat, Che Guevara of Odisha.
- He had turned down Odisha State's Olive branch in 2013.
- CM Naveen Patnaik says : "State will reward police personnel for this spectacular achievement."

Panda was in Berhampur to woo youngsters to his outfit: Police : 19 Jul 2014

Maoist leader Sabyasachi Panda had reached Berhampur to recruit cadres for his newly formed outfit CPI (Maxist-Leninist-Maoist), where he was nabbed by police on 1 AM 18 Jul 2014. Addressing a press conference, on 18 Jul 2014 at Berhampur, DIG Southern Range Amitabh Thakur said : "As per initial findings, Panda had arrived Berhampur some 12 days back. As his support base had declined drastically since past two years and he had formed the new outfit in 2014, he was camping in the city to woo youngsters into his organisation."[25]

On the 17th night, the police on a tip off about Panda's presence in a house in the Badabazar area, identified three houses where they believed he could be hiding. Led by SP Beerhampur Annirudha Singh, three police teams surrounded the suspected three houses. But the information was not absolutely accurate. The police parties realised Panda had been hiding in a house two houses away from one of the marked houses, said Mr. Singh. The police team then surrounded the house and entered it through the terrace.

By that time, Panda had sensed their presence and had jumped into an adjacent house. But his moving shadow was spotted by the policemen who finally arrested him.

Panda, as per police, did not resist arrest even as he was carrying a revolver. Pointing to the recovery of gold and cash from his hideout, the DIG said Panda "may have been continuing with the practice of extortion."

Panda was later produced in front of the Sub-Divisional Judicial Magistrate (SDJM) of Berhampur amid tight security on the 18th evening where he was ordered to be sent on 10-day police remand.

Allow him to rejoin mainstream : Wife 19 Jul 2014

"Subhashree Panda, wife of Sabyasachi Panda, who was caught by the police, made an appeal to give her husband an opportunity to return to the mainsteam."

This was reported by a daily in its issue datelined Bhubaneswar, 18 Jul 2014.[26]

Expressing apprehensions about Maoist leader's safety in police custody on the 18th, Ms Panda said Bhubaneswar, "my husband should not be treated like a petty Criminal. He was fighting for a public interest cause although his medium of struggle was wrong. Police should immediately provide him proper treatment." She claimed that Sabyasachi himself was not involved in killing of innocent people.

Odisha's top Maoist leader in police net: 19 Jul 2014

It must be noted that this daily produced four analytical stories on the arrest of Panda, this being the 4th one. It is datelined Bhubaneswar/New Delhi, 19 Jul 2014.[27]

Sabyasachi Panda, Odisha'a most wanted Maoist leader and main accused in the murder of the VHP leader Laxmananda Saraswati was arrested in the early hours of the 18th. The police had been close on his heels since Feb 2014 after he received a bullet injury during an encounter in the forest area on the Ganjam-Gajapati border with just three other rebels.

"He was arrested in an intelligence-based operation", said State DGP Sanjeev Marik. Recoveries from his hideouts has already been maintioned /detailed above. Once dubbed as Odisha's "Che Guavara", Panda fell out with the CPI (Maoist) in Aug 2012 after he accused its Supremo Ganapathi, of being "feudal" in an open letter. The rest of the story has been told above.

"Crucial breakthrough"

Maoist leader Panda nabbed. Now, punish him: Editorial: 22 Jul 2014

- The arrest of one of the country's most prominent and ruthless Maoist leaders, Sabyasachi Panda, is certainly a feather in the cap of Odisha Police and a setback to the Maoist movement in the country. He is wanted in over five dozen criminal cases, including the killing of Swami Laxmananda Saraswati and abduction of two Italian tourists in 2012.
- But the arrest is only a beginning. The road to ensuring justice for the victims or the nabbed Maoist leader is long and arduous. The prosecution has to present a strong case if it hopes for a court verdict in its favour. For that to happen, Odisha Police has to gather water-tight evidence. We have seen in many past instances how culprits have got away either because the prosecution failed to convince the court or the investigating agency blundered in its job. Panda will have a lot to tell the Police, and if the interrogation is handled efficiently, the police should have enough material to put the Maoist leader in the dock.
- Since there have been instances where political will sagged during investigation and inversely affected the outcome of the probe, it is hoped such a catastrophe will not strike the Panda case. Of course, there is no reason yet to believe that Mr. Naveen Patnaik's Government will go soft; the CM's appeal to Maoists to give uparms and join the democratic mainstream, if they are serious about improving the lot of lesser privileged sections of society, should not be seen as appeasement.
- Meanwhile, extraneous issues are already being raised by certain quarters to present Panda in less negative light. It is being said that Panda has been for sometime now seeking an 'exit' route. In other words, he was exploring the possibility of leaving behind the big, bad Maoist world, and join the mainstream. Unconfirmed reports have even suggested that he had been in touch with certain Aam Aadmi Party leaders. There is no confirmation of all this, but what is known from police accounts is that he was nabbed while on an assignment to rope in new recruits to his outfit. If he has been having a change of heart, there is no evidence of that. Moreover, facts relating to his sinister past cannot be brushed aside; they have to be addressed to have effective closure. For instance, let us not forget that the killing of Swami Laxmananda had triggered

massive communal unrest in the Kandhamal region of Odisha in which at least 40 persons lost their lives and more than 25,000 were displaced. It also had political repercussions.[28]

- Panda's arrest need not, however lead to unbridled celebration, although the nabbed Maoist leader is an important catch—he had, after all, survived and flourished after breaking ranks with the Supreme Commander of CPI (Maoist), Ganapathi, whom he accused of being "feudal". Since a significant section of the Maoist movement in Odisha is managed by the Andhra/Telangana-dominated cadre, the Maoists in the State may not have received a body blow as of now. Also, the ruthless Red movement is still strong in several part of the country, and must be snuffed out. Odisha Police and security forces across the country need to be on their toes since the Maoists will seek to strike back to avenge Panda's arrest.[28]

Odisha Maoist who helped abduct BJP MLA 'surrenders' : 29 Oct 2014

Prominent Maoist leader Nachika Linga, who in 2006 formed Maoist frontal outfit Chasi Mulia Adivasi Sangh (CMAS), surrendered before the police on 28 Oct 2014 in his native village Bhaliaput in Koraput district.

Linga, 42, a tribal leader from Narayanpatna block of rebel-hit district of Koraput with 49 cases of violence including abduction and murder against him, shot to prominence in Apr 2012 when he helped the Maoists abduct BJD MLA Jhina Hikaka, two years ago. He had gone underground after allegedly leading at attack on police in 2009.[29]

IGP South-Western Y K Jethwa said the police had persuaded Linga through intermediaries to surrender. "During negotiation, we had told him he would be produced before court as he had 33 non-bailable warrants pending against him", said Jethwa. Of the 49 cases against him, Linga has been charge-sheeted in 43.

Social activist Prafulla Samantara, however, claimed that Linga was arrested from Bhaliaput and police's story about surrender is false. He urged the State government to withdraw "false" cases against Linga as he was not a member of any banned outfit.

In Mar 2014, Linga was supposed to surrender in Narayanpatna block in presence of social activists, but he did not surface due to presence of police and paramilitary police in large numbers.

Sources said that though Linga helped the Maoists in Hikaka's abduction, differences between him and the rebels cropped up soon over his plans of joining electoral politics.

In Mar 2014, the Srikakulam-Koraput Divisional Committee and Narayanpatna Anchalika Committee of the CPI(Maoist) had publicly denounced him. The Maoists then had termed Nachika's surrender move as "drama" that would serve his own interests at the cost of interests of the tribals. Maoists had also accused Linga of weakening the tribal agitation by joining hands with the BJD.

Odisha: 11 abducted villagers released, cops suspect Naxal ploy to 'terrorise' tribals: 17 Apr 2015

Eleven people, abducted by Maoists from Odisha's Malkangiri district, were released on 16 Apr 2015 evening. Though initial reported suggested only seven people were abducted on the 14th night, later it was found four more were picked up by the ultras from the neighbouring Chhattisgarh.

Over 20 Maoists, from Darbha Ghati, led by one Vinod Kashyap, had abducted the villagers from Karlanpalli, Barha and a few other villages under Malhili panchayat Samiti of Malkangiri district. Among those abducted was former Chairman of panchayat Samiti Trinath Bhumia, a Paraja tribal. No villager had come forward to lodge a police complaint in connection with the abduction.

The villages from where the ultras took away 11 people are located near Darbha Ghati in Chhattisgarh's Sukma district, the worst LWE-affected in the country.

Nine of the abductees had to face Kangaroo court of the Maoists, where three including a sarpanch, were thrashed for "helping the police". They were also threatened of dire consequences if they were found giving information to the police.[30]

Odisha DGP Sanjiv Marik, however, said: "It is hard to say if these people were abducted as they are Maoist sympathisers. A few of them are former militias of the Maoists. We would interrogate the 11 to find out the truth."

Police officials said the "abduction" could be a Maoist tactic to terrorise the tribals. Since Mar 2015, the police and the paramilitary officials have started a poster campaign in Mathili and other interior areas of Malkangiri. The security forces are putting up posters of wanted top Maoist leaders such as Ramakrishna, Katakam Sudarshan and Jinugu Narsimha Reddy, urging people to contact their nearest police station to give inputs on the whereabouts of the Maoist leaders.

Maoist Politburo member Katakam Sudarshan has a cash reward of Rs. 2.47 Crore on his head as announced by different states. Ramakrishna and Reddy carry a cash reward of Rs 1.52 Crore each on their head.

After the abduction on the 14th night, posters against Maoists had come up in several areas of Malkangiri district by a local tribal organisation, Malkangiri Adivasi Sangh. In these posters, the tribal body threatened to take up arms against Maoists, if the abducted persons were not released.

In the posters, the tribal body threatened to unite tribals of Malkangiri for a major movement against the Maoists, if non-tribal Naxal leaders from Andhra Pradesh and Chhattisgarh do not stop their violent activities against them.

Three women Maoist cadres surrender in Odisha : 19 May 2015

Three women Maoist cadres with a bounty of Rs 1 lakh each on their heads surrendered before the police in Odisha's Koraput district on 18 May 2015.

Lachhmi Praska, 22; Sapai Maniaka, 21; and Talasa Wateka, 20 are armed cadres of the Andhra Odisha Border Special Zone Committee of the CPI (Maoist).[31]

The above information was given to the media by IGP South-Western Range Yashwant Jethwa.

Naxalite who led attack on VC Shukla and Mahendra Karma killed: 20 Sep 2015

In a major breakthrough in the fight against Maoists, security men 19 Sep 2015 gunned down three ultras, one of whom, Sunadhar, was in the forefront of the 2013 Darbha Ghati massacre in which senior Congress leaders of Chhattisgarh, CV Shukla, Mahendra Karma and Nand Kumar Patel were killed.[32]

Odisha police sources said a joint team of District Voluntary Force (DVF) and SOG killed the rebels in an encounter in Bhejaguda forest, 30 km from Malkangiri in the jurisdiction of Mathili police station on the 19th morning. DIG South-Western Range S Shyni told the daily : "We were tipped – off about the movement of a group of 10-12 Maoists in the forest area and launched an operation. The gun battle lasted for half-an-hour."

"While coming across the crime spot, we recovered the three bodies. Others managed to flee", said SP Malkangiri Mitralchanu Mohapatra.

Besides the attack on Congress Convoy, Sunadhar alias Kishor Korram, a member of Darbha Divisional Committee, was involved in killing over

100 security men and carried a bounty of Rs 5 lakh and Rs 8 lakh in Odisha and Chhattisgarh, respectively. His accomplice Kunjami was an area committee member of the same Division while the third ultra could not be identified.

27 people were killed in the Darbha Ghati attack which virtually wiped out the Congress leadership in Chhatisgarh. The Darbha Division of the CPI (Maoist) operates in the Darbha valley of Sukma district of Chhattisgarh and Mathili block of Malkangiri in Odisha.

"We are in touch of our counterparts in Chhattisgarh to get more details about Sunadhar", added the DIG.

Police seized three walkie-talkie, one 9 mm pistol, two bags, few sharp-edged weapons and Maoist literature from the spot.

Notes

1. Mohanty, Debabrata, The Indian Express, 15.12.12.
2. PNS, The Pioneer, 8 Jan 2013.
3. ENS, Indian express, 24 June 2013.
4. Priya Ranjan Sahu, Hindustan Times, 24 Jun 2013.
5. PNS, The Pioneer, 24 Jun 2013.
6. Prafulla Das, The Hindu, 5 Jul 2013.
7. Debabrata Mohanty, Indian Express, 19 Jul 2013.
8. Santosh Patnaik, The Hindu, 15 Sep 2013.
9. Debabrata Mohanty, Indian Express, 3 Oct 2013.
10. Debabrata Mohanty, Indian Express, 16 Sep 2013.
11. Ashutosh Bhardwaj, The Indian Express, 16.9.13.
12. Deleaerata Mohanty, Indian Express, 17 Nov 2013.
13. Debabrata Mohanty, Indian Express, 17 Nov 2013.
14. The Pioneer, 30 Nov (?) 2013.
15. The Pioneer, 31.12.13.
16. Rahul Pandita, The Hindu, 8 Mar 2014.
17. Debabrata Mohanti, Indian Express, 12 Mar 2014.
18. *Ibid,* 3 Apr 2014.
19. Indian Express, 7 Apr 2014.
20. *Ibid,* 7 Apr 2014.
21. ENS, Indian Express, 11 Jun 2014.
22. Debabrata Mohanty, Indian Express, 7 Jul 2014.
23. Debabrata Mohanty, Indian Express, 19 Jul 2014.
24. Rahul Pandita, The Hindu, 19 Jul 2014.
25. Sib Kumar Das, The Hindu, 19 Jul 2014.
26. Prafulla Das, The Hindu, 19 Jul 2014.

27. Prafulla Das and Rahul Pandita, The Hindu, 19 Jul 2014.
28. Editorial, The Pioneer, 22 Jul 2014.
29. Debabrata Mohanty, Indian Express, 29 Oct 2014.
30. *Ibid,* 17 Apr 2015.
31. Hindustan Times, 19 May 2015.
32. Satyanarayan Pattnaik, Time of India, 20 Sep 2015.

32

West Bengal - 1

West Bengal

Backgrounder to the LWE in the state.

Origin

The movement had its origin in Naxalbari village of the Darjeeling district where a section of CPI (Marxist) initiated a violent uprising in 1967. The second phase started in the late 1990s under Kishan ji.

Bloody era

1967-72 and 2008-11.

Key issues

Exploitation of the poor by landlords, industrialists and traders.

Status Check

No major attack since Feb 2010.

CM Mamata Banerjee

"We want Maoists to return to mainstream. We still believe development is a key issue in Jangalmahal.

West Bengal

The history of Naxalism-Maoism in the mercurial state of West Bengal can be divided into two neat parts, named after the ruling dispensation.

- Communist Era or Pre-Mamata Period.
- Post Communist or Mamata Era.

Communist Period

The beginning of it all

The beginning of the present day LWE in India can be dated from the Naxalbari uprising in this village of Darjeeling district of West Bengal. The village lent its name to the LWE in India, Naxalism. Later, in terminological context, it was supplanted by Maoist insurrection. All this has been discussed and delineated in detail in the preceding chapters.

Situation of LWE in West Bengal Mid-2000s

It may seem ironic, but still a fact that the Naxals did not spare the State long ruled by their ideological fraternity, a coalition of the four Left parties, so to say. This Left combine comprised Communist Party of India (Marxist), Communist Party of India, Revolutionary Socialist Party and Forward Block.

Starting with the Naxalbari armed uprising of 1960s, which, of course, was extinguished by the Jyoti Basu-led State Police with a heavy hand, the revived LWE has made inroads into the State's 19 districts. The worst-affected districts are Purulia, West Midnapur, and Bankura, followed by Nadia, Hooghly and 24 Parganas.

Active in Jadavpur, Behala and Bagmari areas of Kolkata, the Naxalites have infiltrated the two universities of Kolkata and Jadavpur.

The West Bengal Government of Buddhadeb Bhattacharjee honestly admits it has failed to provide basic facilities to the people.

CRPF-Maoist clash: Dec 2006

"After hailing the Bagduli Talab area encounter as a major boost to the morale of men in uniform the Bankura police failed to locate any rebel despite intensive combing operations in border areas of West Midnapur, Bankura and Purulia."

The reference is to the clash in Bagduli Talab area under Barikul police station in Bankura district of West Bengal on the 15 Dec 2006 night between the CRPF and Maoists. Two Maoists cadres and one jawan of CRPF were killed in the counter. Two men of the CRPF were injured who were admitted into SSKM Hospital, Kolkata. The slain cadres remained unidentified.

SP Bankura Rajesh Singh informed the combing operations "are also on in the West Bengal-Jharkhand border areas along with Jharkhand police." On the 17th, the police said it was highly probable that the two women squad cadres who fought with the 171 Bn, CRPF men are Jagori

Baski and Sulekha Mahato, the two much sought-after guerrilla from the outlawed outfit.

The CRPF "hailing" a clash where it lost one of its own against two rebels killed, is rather unnecessary, and even misplaced hype, which is avoidable, to say the least. This is an honest comment from someone who should know!

Naxal made a come back in West Bengal in 2006: Dec 2006

Naxals made a come back in West Bengal in 2006 after a lull in 2005. "Their activities have spread to at least four districts of West Mednipur, Jalpaiguri, Purulia and Bankura. Their subversive activities during the year (2006) include IED explosion at a CRPF camp in January, and another in a general compartment of Haldibari-New Delhi passenger train in November."

Besides these, the Naxals also burnt down eight vehicles and also planted tiffin box bombs in support of a bandh call by CP (M) on 13 December and tried to abduct a local leader of the CPI from Bagduli. Talab in Bankura district on 15 December, detailed in the preceding entry.

Start of the Movement in West Bengal

The Maoist movement in the State started in 1988 and continued till 1994, following a complete lull in 1995, as mentioned above. However, sporadic incidents started in 1996 and continued till 2000. The year 2001 did not witness any untoward incident, but Maoist activities revived in 2002 and continued till 2004, followed by a peaceful 2005, said the MHA sources.[1]

This 2006 comeback may pose a serious threat in the coming years, with the networking of the insurgents with the ISI-backed terrorist outfits, operating from Bangladesh and Nepal.

At the IB-organised conference in Nov 2006 in New Delhi, DGP West Bengal had expressed concern regarding illegal migration from Bangladesh. He also expressed his reluctance/inability of the state police to take illegal Bangladeshi migrants into custody due to shortage of space in state's jails that remain crowed with such migrants. One MHA official sounded a note of warning:

> "Indo-Bangladesh border currently poses a great difficulty due to the high-level of infiltration and illegal immigration. India's economic progress vis-á-vis other nations in the Sub-continent made it an attractive destination for migrants, which was affecting the territorial and physical integrity of the nation."

Are the Maoist behind Nandigram?: Jan 2007

The meticulously planned resistance "being put up by Nandigram farmers and the violence that has ensued have surprise the people and the analysts alike. Consequently, the question every one is asking is: who is actually leading the movement?"

Ostensibly, the Bhumi Uchhed Pratirodh Committee, a platform of several organisations, is running the show as champion of the farmers' causes. It has the active support of the Trinamool Congress (TMC) and Congress parties.

But a daily claims on 18 July 2007 that investigations revealed that Maoists are playing the key role by training the people on how to fight the police and armed CP (M) cadres. Cutting off approach roads and destroying bridges are well known guerrilla tactics Maoists have often employed to a great effect.[2]

The Maoists first entered Nandigram in Oct 2006, a time when Singur was coming to a boil.

They sent a 7-member team to find out the people's opinion on state acquisition for Salim groups' SEZ project. "We hoped that at least a few people would agree to speak with us. To our surprise, where ever we went, hundreds gathered to say they are not willing to give up their land. It was an eye-opener", said Chhoton Das of the Gana Unnayan Jana Adhikar Samity (GUJAS), an umbrella group of 22 parties, including Maoists and Jamayat-ulema-e-Hind, which began the struggle in Nandigram.

GUJAS decided to send another team to Nandigram between 22 and 25 Nov 2006.

"Last is yet to be heard of Nandigram and issues thrown by it", says the daily. At one time, CM Buddhadeb Bhattacharjee did feel uncomfortable, but later, he was able to get over the difficult situation.

"At the end, suffice it to say that there is Maoist stamp on Nandigram siege.

Roles Reversed: Nandigram Saga: West Bengal CPM are oppressors, say Maoists Jun 2007

It is a succinct case of ironic role reversal: The CPM ascended to power 30 years ago, mouthing Marxist slogans of the then ruling Congress being the oppressors of poor farmers, is at the receiving end of exactly the same charges by CPI (Maoists) —the present self-proclaimed champions of the farmers, landless and unorganised workers, labourers, tribal et al.

The obvious question then is: Are the CPI (Maoist) biggest threat to West Bengal's ruling CPI (M)? Is the Naxal Chief, CM Bhattacharjee's enemy No.1? Considering the going-on in and around Nandigram today in West Bengal and beyond it in the Red Corridor post-Jan 2007 9th Unity Congress of the CPI (Maoist), that indeed seems to be the case. The issue deserves a critical analysis, says the daily.

The Maoists seem to be all over in anti-CP (M) agitation in West Bengal. They played a leading role in protests against violence that erupted on 3 Jan 2007 at Nandigram and in protests against the fencing at Singur. They were present when land acquisition for a SEZ was underway. They are at the forefront of organising the Abandoned Labour in West Bengal's close tea gardens, and even more portentously, they — not the mainstream unions...are mobilizing workers in Hindustan Motors' Uttar opara factory.

Thus, Maoists have emerged as Bhattacharjee's strongest threat, working among the dispossessed, the landless labour and marginal farmers to spread their message: Bhattacharjee and CPI (M) are the enemies of the poor. It bears repetition: This is very charge CPI (M) constantly laid at the door of (the then) ruling Congress till they supplanted it in 1977! Will the history repeat itself? More accurately, is it already repeating itself?

A book in the recent past is useful to understand the present stand-off. Even before the police firing on 14 Mar 2007 at Nandigram leading to the death of 14 villagers, the State police had warned the authorities that they had set up bases in the area with arms and ammunition. In fact, following the raids the first outbreak of violence in January, the police had arrested three Maoists, all students of Jadavpur University, equipped with a laptop from a remote village in Nandigram.[3]

Earlier, in Dec 2006, the CPI-ML (Liberation) sent two state committee members with 22 students from Jadavpur University and other institutions to resist the fencing of the land meant for Tata small car project in Singur. Police arrest all of them.

Here is one more ironic event. At Hind Motor, the CITU, the CPI (M)'s labour wing, found its union at the backfoot, when a breakaway faction led by the Naxals forced the management to declare a suspension of work. The CITU, known as the source/root of all strikes, found itself criticising the breakaway faction's tactics, and horror of it all, supporting the management! Can one imagine a bigger irony? Surrealist indeed, all this!

Even more interesting things have been happening in the land of Marxism in India, West Bengal. The solidarity of the Left Front seems to have been breached. The Naxals were able to subvert the loyalty of some partners of the CPI (M) in the Left Front at all these troubled spots at different times, of course. So, at Nandigram, the Naxals were able to initially muster the support of the local CPI leaders for their cause. At the North Bengal's tea gardens, the Naxals got the support of the local leaders of the RSP. At Hind Motor, Naxal leader Anitava Bhattacharya got the support of CPI leader and MP Gurudas Dasgupta.[4]

CM Bhattacharjee and the ruling CPI (M) would be making a serious mistake if they think that Nandigram and Singur are its success stories for their plans for industrialisation of West Bengal. Dipankar Bhattacharya, All India General Secretary of the CPI-ML (Liberation) warns the CPI (M). "If they think their actions represent the Red Flag, they are making a mistake and we will give a befitting reply." Bhattacharya says his party has already developed extensive contacts with the people at the lowest level, and its effort at explaining to them that CPI (M) Government's actions are against small and landless farmers. There is an obvious truth about these assertions because the CP (M) district level leaders themselves have confirmed so.

CP(M) sources say their district report have indeed confirmed that the Naxalites are spreading a campaign against the government among the people and also among the CP (M)'s lower levels. At Dhaniakhali in Hoogly district, the Naxals have been using a former CP (M) leader Mahadeb Murmu, to campaign against the CP (M). Sometime back, the tension reached a flash point and the local CP (M) cadres attacked Murmu's people, leaving six persons seriously injured.

Kartick Pal, state secretary, CPI-ML (Liberation) claims that a large number of CP(M) Cadres are conlacting them to voice their protest against Buddhadeb Bhattacharjee's policies.[5]

The claims, like the ones just made above, of the CPI-ML (Liberation) or CPI (Maoist) leaders may have an element of exaggeration, but their essential truth cannot be faulted. If these two parties are attacking the ruling CP(M) on the ideological front, the TMC and Congress are doing so even more passionately at the polical front. No one can be envious of CP (M) in its given predicament.

What is even worse for CM Bhattacharjee is the innuendo among some senior leaders of his own party: Is he and will he prove the Gorbachev of India, with all its sinister, if unmentioned, implications! One more thought could be even more dangerous for the CP(M): Islam and Communism are two fundamentalist ideologies, and in the former, empirical evidence shows, the hardliners always supplant the moderates!

10 Dec 2006

Some 25 Maoist boarded a train from Tea Nagar to Kharagpur, snatched rifles from railway guards, took away Walkie-Talkie of the engine driver and looted Rs 1,00,000 which was the salary of the railway staff.

2 Nov 2008

Maoist made an attempt on West Bengal Chief Minister Bhattacharjee's life at Kalaichand near forested Lalgarh area.

25 Dec 2008

They torched a CPM leader's house at Madhupur under Shalboni police station in West Medinipore district. Maoist had rival group called M2 whose complete nomenclature was idealistic: Democratic Guarrilla Army. Hindu (Maobadi), according to Odisha police, formed his Hindu Maoist Army[6].

22 June 2009

Maoists detonated a remote controlled device on an anti-land mine vehicle at Chakulia on the West Bengal-Jharkhand border.

26 June 2009

Security forces reclaimed control of Kadosole village located to the north of Lalgarh in West Midnapore, from the Maoists.

19 Sep 2009

Asit Sarkar, a senior district leader, was shot dead by unidentified persons in Bin Garbeta, West Bengal.

9 Oct 2009: Maoists thwart development

Maoist-backed (or a Maoist-creation, as some others would like to believe) People's Comittee Against Police Atrocities (PCAPA) chief Chhatradhar Mahato and the Party Treasurer (arrested some days back) revealed that Maoists were giving arms training to some 200 teenagers in the interior wooden regions of Lalgarh-Ramgarh area. More specifically, the training were being run in the dense forests of Bhalukbasara, Barapelia, Adharia, Kumarbandh and Salboni (The Pioneer, 9.10.2009).

In order to establish "their (Maoist) rule, absolute and total, they went to make sure that government's attempts at developing Naxal-infested areas are effectively thwarted." The under-developed, undeveloped areas are their argument favouring their ideology. They effectively exploit the poverty and social backwardness of the villages/tribals to spread their ideology among those downtrodden. Hence their determination to prevent development of any variety in such areas in order to assure that no such threat comes to their influence from such 'development'. So it is fully understandable they should determinedly start uprooting the electric poles, digging up roads, blowing up bridges and railway tracks/school buildings etc.

They achieve their above-mentioned missions in such a well-practised surprise attacks that police is often unable to track and arrest these ultras. Interestingly, such destructive 'achievements' do not draw the attention of the human-rights warriors or pro-Maoist NGOs, who are quick to shout anti-police slogans when ever an ultra falls to the police bullets in consequence of a well-publicised encounter/confrontation. But same whomever is missing when a security force member is killed by the Maoists. In that case, not only shrieks are missing, there is not even a whimper of protest! Some odd one like Swami Agnivesh will still claim after the even, or when his silence is questioned in such cases, "but I condemned it." May be this condemnation is so 'silent' that no one heard it! Less said the better about these over ground voices of the Maoists, or more honestly, these over-ground (intellectual) Maoists, or better still, human rights fakes/pseudo-human rights traders!

20 Oct 2009

30 Maoists abducted officer-in-charge, Sankrail Police station, Atindra Nath Dutta. Kishanji declared that the government assurance on meeting our demands would result in Dutta's release. Maoists killed two of Dutta's colleagues (Dipankar Bhattacharya and Swapan Roy) inside the police station. Maoists took away 6×rifles, 3×Revolvers, a 9MM pistol and large number of cartridges from the police station. They also looted Rs 9.23 lakh from local SBI branch.

Succumbing to Maoist pressure, the Government freed 23 Maoist prisoners for release of Dutta on 22 October. He joined duty on 10 November at Midnapore Headquarters.

Bengal PWD Minister Kshiti Goswami admitted his speaking to Maoist leader Kishanji, who had been surrounded by police on all four sides on 21 October night near Puranpani. Obviously, the ruling party of West Bengal chose Atindranath Dutta's life over Kishanji arrest.

7 Nov 2009

Maoists gun down a former legislator of the CPI (M) Subhas Soren at Gopiballabhpur in the Lalgarh region. Two other bodies found at the site were of Lakshman Das Manoranjan Mahali and Jayaram Hansda. They were killed as they were alleged spies working for police.

27 Dec 2009

The State Police arrested CPI (Maoist) Mohd Khalek@Gautam Das, with a cache of arms while he was en route to Lalgarh, West Midnapore. He got these arms from Sentu, an arms dealer working out of Suri Birbhum (The Hindustan Times, 28.12.2099).

Jangalmahal and Chief Minister Mamata Banerjee

It was the end of cold peace between the Chief Minister and the Maoist, with the former giving 7-day ultimatum to the Maoists on 15 Oct 2011: "Shun violence, come for talks, or government knows how to bring peace through democratic means."

Has she finally decided to catch the Red Bull by its horns? Refusing to be cowed down by Maoists' strong arms tactics, she gave an open challenge to the outlaws—whom she dubbed '*supari* killers'——to block her development initiatives. She was addressing an impressive rally at Jhargram stadium, from where she declared a plethora of projects: upgradation of a civil hospital to a district hospital; laying foundation of bridge and seventeen girls hostel, four mini indoor stadia; giving away land *pattas*; and declaring the issuance of 6.5 lakh new ration cards.

Despite Maoists' threat warning people against attending the rally, a large crowd mustered courage to attend the same, nevertheless. In her trade-mark defiant ways, Mamata even dared them to "come and murder me if you have the courage to do so." Come and fight with us face to face to see whether democracy is a strong force or anarchy. Come and confront us in Jhargram itself. I promise you the police will not be present. You shall stand with your comrades and I with the public." But as a cynical journalist note, "the irony of her remarks was striking as there was a huge security deployment at the grounds where the rally was held."[6]

She then talked about the respective promises made by the two sides: "We had said if peace is restored to Jangalmahal there will be no need for joint security operations. I have kept my word, you have not. There have been no joint operations in jangalmahal for the past four-and-a-half months (that her government has been in power in the State). You have indulged in killings, you have intimidated the people. You are regularly roaming the region brandishing your guns." She said all this without naming the Maoists. In fact, she did not name them even once in her long address, while most of the time she was talking about them and throwing challenges at them; even condemning the cowardice of "the killers who come in the groups of 20 on motorbikes under the cover of darkness, commit a murder and scamper off."

She said some people fear development, so they are hindering peace process. "They would certainly lose ground in Jangalmahal if we are able to develop the area." She asserted one-week ultimatum is not a hollow one, adding, "we are determined to bring peace in the area through democratic process and no guns and bullets can stop us." She reiterated the government would not pull out Central Forces, and would act tough if they continued with their acts of bloodshed. She asked the Maoists to follow in the footsteps of the Darjeeling Hills, ending with a rhetoric, "If the Hills can, why can't Jangalmahal?" Continuing with the tough stance, she said: "This is my challenge visit to Jangalmahal—to usher in a new era of development and the government knows how to deal with those who come in our way." Some other issues she mentioned are summed up hereafter:

1. She and her party have worked on human rights issues for a long time and the Maoists had no right to speak to her on their violation when the police go to arrest suspected murderers in Jangalmahal, they are accused of human rights violation and of outraging the modesty of the women of the family of the accused.
2. No other state has done this, only the West Bengal Government has set up 13 human rights courts. "If you have genuine cases, approach these courts.
3. "There is no 'isms' involved. It is neither Marxism nor Maoism nor the politics of Congress or nationalism. It is only the politics of killing....They are misusing names."
4. Outlining a new three-point programme for the region, she said the Maoists must give up their arms, people must be allowed to return to mainstream, and her government wants work with the people to ensure development.

Interestingly again, she made no reference to the month-long "conditional ceasefire" from the State leadership of the CPI (Maoist) while offering them "negotiations if you give up your arms." It is noteworthy that Banerjee's tough talk comes close on the heels of a ultimatum issued by Maoists to people not to join the Jangalmahal specific police force comprising locals as mooted by the CM. In fact response to the government advertisement inviting applications for police jobs has been dismal due to the threat of the Maoists. Her hardening of stance also comes against the background of some frightening reports from the police brass which reportedly told her how the ultras had taken advantage of the ceasefire to spread their network as far as Chamkaitala bordering Hoogly, Bankura and West Midnapore. Banerjee was also told how hundreds of acres in Jangalmahal had been mined by the Maoists[8].

During her address, she held aloft the child of Lalmohan Mahato, a supporter of the TMC, who was killed by (suspected) Maoists recently. The families of Lalmohan Mahato and Babu Bose, a leader of Jharkhand Samanoy Manch, who was also killed by the Maoists, were on the dais during the function.

"How many jobs do you want? I will provide as many as you demand. Do you need food? We will provide it. Do you need schools, colleges, hospitals, roads? We will give them all, within our limitations', she said, even as she announced a host of projects for the region, as detailed earlier. She promised that the rate of procurement of Kendu leaves, that are used in bidi manufacture and are one of the main sources of livelihood in the tribal areas, would be increased from the present Rs 46.25 to Rs 75 per kg.

In June 20011, she had visited Lalgarh, becoming the second Chief Minister to visit Jangalmahal, the first one to travel by road. This was her second visit to the areas as CM.

Mamata Banerjee prior to Polls: Post-poll, volta-face

Ahead of the polls that brought her to power, Mamata had asserted that resolving the issues that were causing unrest in the Darjeeling Hills and Jangalmahal region "within three months of coming to power" was her key election promise.

During the time when she was engaged in 'mortal' combat against the Communists, she had made some intriguing, even outlandish, statements of which she would be embarrassed if reminded today. But then she was engaged in rhetoric battles with the ruling Left, more interested in scoring debating points than appreciating and analysing the ground realities and issues in perspective. Some of these statements are mentioned here.

In that past, TMC Chief Banarjee had maintained "that there are no Maoists in West Bengla" and the situation in Jangalmahal region was the result of infighting between the Marxists. The politicians in opposition are often prone to making off-the-cuff remarks and at times, even irresponsible statements. And Mamata Banderjee can't be an exception. The Mamata, who made these remarks while in opposition, saw the realities differently within less than six months of coming to power. No wonder that on 15 October she lashed out at the rebels without naming them outright, labelling them as "supari killers, "Jungle mafia", and "cowardly goons" hiding in the forests. Here is one more statement that is even more embarrassing, and Ms Banerjee would run the most! Sometime in Sep 2010, she addressed a rally at Lalgarh and stirred a controversy when she offered her respects to the soul of comrade Azad', CPI (Maoist) Central committee spokesperson who was controversially killed in an encounter. The Maoists later claimed he was preparing for peace talks and consulting other members of the CC on the issue. A year later, on 15 Oct 2012, the same Mamata condemns them for killing innocent tribals, and acting like goons! She now asserts that the Maoists "do not have any ideology".

Ms Banderjee, as Chief Minister, had seldom talked so tough against the rebels. In fact, she had initiated a peace process by setting up a team of civil society led by Professor Sujata Bhadra and Chhotan Das as interlocutors, who had been talking with the Maoists on her Government's behalf. The Maoists had acquainted the intermediaries with their demands: withdrawal of central forces, and release of political prisoners including top Maoist leaders. Even Mamata's former allies, like writer Mahasweta Devi, who had joined her in her war against the Left Front, had early Oct 2011 demanded withdrawal of forces and release of prisoners.

Is Chief Minister Mamata Banerjee losing her patience?

Ms Banerji had seen CPM members being targeted and killed during the last years of the Left front rule. In her private moments, she even might have felt elated! Now that the Maoists have started killing TMC workers, within a few months of her assuming power, she must be feeling the heat. So, it should be no surprise that a furious Mamata on 4 Nov 2011 said she was seriously thingking of beginning afresh CRPF operations in Jangalmahal.

Soon after her statement, a posse of Central forces swooped down in villages neighbouring Jhargram and picked up Joydev Mahato, a senior leader of PCAPA and a key Maoist link man along with two of his cronics.

The chain of events on the 4th detailed above took place within hours of TMC worker Jitu Singh Sardar being gunned down by the Maoists at Balrampur, Purulia district.

The Chief Minister stated after coming to power "we had stopped the police operations hoping the talks would bear fruits. But these killers are not willing to take the dialogue route." She disclosed the Government was planning to resume joint operations, as the common men could not be allowed to be killed that way.

Mahato was key functionary who was acting as the linkman between the Maoists and the other political Committees active both in Jangalmahal and Kolkata, said police, indicating more such arrests would follow that of Mahato's as the government had given a green signal.

Taking a dig at the intellectuals who on the 4th condemned the arrest of Mahato, wondering why the Chief Minister was ignoring the presence of her "masked party men taking motorcycle rallies armed to the teeth" and targeting PCAPA leaders, an angry Banerjee dismissed them with, "Those who backed Maoists are not intellectuals." She added: "some foreign powers who do not want India to thrive and grow are behind the rise of the Maoists."

Kin of Maoist leader to join Police: An Irony

In Oct 2011, a few months after coming into power, she had announced her Governments' decision that to reduce unemployment in the LWE-affected region, the youth from the Jangalmahal would be given jobs as police constables, home guards and in National Volunteer Force. Accordingly, a massive recruitment drive was on, after this announcement, in the region to recruit 10,000 youth for this Jangalmahal-specific force. At a rally in Purulia district on 11 Nov 2011, Ms Banerji announced that this figure is just for the first phase of recruitment.

The drive gave rise to interesting situations. Jayanto Mahato is the squad Commander active in the Maoist depredations in Janalmahal. Three brothers of Jayanto submitted their forms to be enrolled as junior constables in the police force on 13 November. Jayanto's sister-in-law has also taken an application form and might be submitting it soon, Jhargram SP Gaurav Sharma told a daily on the phone.[9] Consequently, its correspondent depicted the intra-family situation rather pithily: "The family of Maoist squad Commander Jayanto Mahato is a house divided along the fault lines that separate the rebels in the forests of the Jangalmahal region from the State that has launched joint security operations against them."

Now that irony of the situation——synics may choose to describe this situation as 'delicious' in somewhat insensitive terms—where the brothers, if they are selected, they in Khaki would be pitched against their own brother in his (Maoist) battle fatigues. Jayanto Mahato "is wanted in several cases of kidnapping and murder and has probably been involved in every major Maoist attack in the area." His success as a local area commander had been such that the squad itself was name after him, "the Jayant Mahato squad." The family of Jayanto live in Amtalia, a village near the State's border with Jharkhand in the Binpur police thana area.

Police outsourced security to CPM men: Maoists killed them: June 2009 [CPM in/ out of power] [Lalgarh violence]

Moaist attack on 17 June 2009 unfortunately prove that during the long Communist rule int the state, the Party systematically subverted the institutions, encouraging, if not officially authorising, its cadres to act on behalf of the State.

It was generally believed by mid-2009 that the Congress-ruled Centre had been mulling over deploying of security forces in West Bengal to confront the Maoist menace. The situation had also deteriorated because of the then Chief Minister Bhattachargee had taken a policy decision to help the industrialists to set up their units in the State, forcibly taking over the land from the farmers. Its best-known example is Mamata Banerjee putting up an aggressive fight against the Tata's anti-Nano factory at Singur, and succeeding.

Reverting back to 2009, Maoists too were well-aware of the Centre's plans to dispatch Central armed police forces to the state. Realising that this deployment was only a matter time, armed squads of the Maoist Brigade went on the rampage in Lalgarh with a sense of urgency, hounding out the CPM cadres and their leaders, targeting their party offices and digging roads and setting up barricades to block the access of security forces "whose arrival then was deemed to be imminent then." To wit, the Maoists began with killing three men at Banksole village early morning of 17 June 2009. Two of those shot dead were local CPM supporters, and the third a CPM branch committee secretary of Banksole[10].

These murders underline how administrative institutions, systematically subverted over the years by the Party in power, CPM, collapse when there is a threat of power shift, reducing party cadres to sitting ducks. Nothing illustrates this letter than the story of those who were killed: Tinku Mahao, 27, Anil Mahato, 48, the branch committee secretary of the CPM; and Abhijit Mahato, a college student, 23.

Tinku, an MA in Sanskrit from Vidyasagar University, was recently employed as a "para-teacher" in the village primary school. But Tinku was also the secretary of a "security syndiacate" that employed nearly 200 youths of the village as security guards.

The other two killed, Anil and Abhijit, were also key members of this syndicate. Their job: to provide security cover to the vehicles on the National Highway 6 as they passed the vulnerable Lodhasuli forest stretch where armed robbery is common.

This was and should have been the job of the Jhargram police, but they had, in effect, outsourced this responsibility to this syndicate, largely comprising CPM supporters. Routinely, armed robbers deflate tyres of vehicles on this stretch by littering the road with "improvised nails", and loot the passengers. The police had asked Tinku Mahato's team to take over. What were the terms of agreement between the police and the "syndicate"? Mahato would employe his cadres from 6 PM to 6 AM and, in return, free to collect "taxes" from the vehicles. The money, ranging between Rs 50 and Rs 500, thus collected would be shared among the syndicate.

A fortnight before this attack, the Maoists had asked Tinku through posters to "dissolve the syndicate" and quit. Tinku's father, Ajoy Mahato, had lodged an FIR with Jhargram police station about this threat and also submitted them the poster also. "I knew he was facing danger. Today my worst fears have come true. Police took no action, did not even visit the village once", he said. The motor-cycle-borne assailants shouted Maoist slogans, and waved guns at the villagers. Anil, the branch secretary of the CPM, was a "bigger target" than Tinku. They chased him inside a fairly crowded morning village *haat* for quite some distence before gunning him down. Tinku and Abhijit were killed at the haat as well. It was obviously an insiders' job, thought Dileshwar Mahato, a CITU member of Mohanpur, the village next to Banksole, also suggesting that the CPM cadres, sensing power shift, have switched over to the opposition.

Later in the day, several CPM party offices in Belatikri were attacked. They torched the houses of three more leaders in the Lalgarh area, houses they claimed were symbols of "wealth and influence" among the region's poverty. The CPM had called for a 12-hour West Midnapore bandh for the 18th.

There was no explaining the fact that the central security forces, having already arrived, (16th) were still on stand-by. When asked, DIG (Law and Order) Raj Konojia said: "These forces are at the disposal of the State Government, but when and where they will be deployed are details that cannot be divulged."

There are, perhaps, reasons for the delay. They seem to be working on a strategy, given the fact that barricades have come up around the village, and they are new to the area. They seem to be working on one plan: sealing the Jharkhand-West Bengal border before launching an operation in Lalgarh in coordination with the state police. This elaborate planning and preparedness is dictated by some intelligence reports suggesting that a large armed squad had succeeded in sneaking into the Lalgarh-Bankura-Purulia belt bordering Jharkhand.

DGP Surjit Sarkar and the Home Secretary reached the district headquarters in Midnapore later in the day for consultation with district officials but no one visited Lalgarh, the epicentre of the violence.

"Ironically, Central Forces are doubling up as guards of the Lalgarh police station." Here is something more telling and instructive about the police under the CPM rule in West Bengal. The visiting journalist (referred to in the preceding note) reporting about the 17 June 2009 violence in Lalgarh area, informs his readers: "The police station itself is under lock and key through the day. No villager comes to lodge any complaint to the police or seek any help. In fact, policemen are facing a village 'boycott', accused as they are of 'torturing' those who are not with the CPM." Here is one more "truth" about this very police. Asked if they had received any instructions since the violence began, a police official, wanting/demanding anonymity, says: "We have heard nothing, no one has told us what we need to do."

Before the end of this text on the Lalgarh violence, a word about the CPM rule in West Bengal should be in place. It was unique in the history of the world, as also of the Communism itself, that Communists 'captured' power through democratic process. Yet again, it was possibly only in India, a predominantly Hindu country. They certainly did a fine job of administering the State and even gained wide acceptability, and even huge popularity, especially through genuine land reforms. It was essentially because of their giving land to the landless and the tenants. Yet again, being young and new, they must have studied for long years the ills and shortcoming of long years of Congress rule, put in place corrective measures. Given this, it is understandable that stayed as long as 33 long years.

All this must be truce for some initial years of their rule, when they were able to maintain "purity" of their creed. May be after first 5-year term, or certainly during the second, corrosive effects of power must have started corroding the great principled beliefs of the Communist rulers. This notwithstanding, CM Jyoti Basu achieved an iconic status as an administrator. He received kudos and felicitatory messages when he became the longest-serving Chief Minister of a state in India. Still, it must be accepted that the rot and consequent disillusionment with the Communists and their rule must have set in during the middle years of his long tenure. To use a popular term of the present times, the "Congressisation" of the CPM and other three smaller Left parties must have started long before he hung his shoes. The power must have corrupted ruler down the life, and highhandedness of the cadre, often violent, must have completed the root.

The entire blame could not belong to B. Bhattacharjee for Communists losing out to Mamata's TMC. Besides the rot at its worst, Bhattacharjee was in a hurry to revive the economy of his State, which had been ruined by his party, pushing it down amongst the last five or six in the table, and he adopted capitalist ideology to achieve his aim. It was really during his time in 2009 that the Government adopted highhandedness to forcibly acquire the land for industrialisation. That also provided an opportunity to Mamata Banerjee to display her combative mettle at Singur, which made her a household name in West Bengal. The forcible acquisition also made the Communists unpopular, besides giving up a fillip to the Maoist ideology.

While on the subject, it should be in place to make a couple of other points. Majority of Communist leaders came from rich *Bhadralok* class, and some of them persisted with "their capitalist" ways. Throughout his tenure as Chief Minister. Jyoti Basu continued to go on his annual pilgrimage to the capitalist London, hub of the much-hated ideology, for a comfortable holiday. Another interesting fact need to be mentioned about the great patriarch Basu. He had apparently retired due to old age, being unable to perform onerous duties of a state Chief Minister. But years later he was willing to take over as country's Prime Minister, even though his younger colleagues in the Politbureau denied him the permission and honour! Subsequently, he rued his colleague's decision as a historic mistake, more than once!

CoBRAs sent to West Bengal

In view of the wide-spread gloom in the state due to inability or unwillingness of the Left-rule administration to squarely face the Maoist terror, the Centre had been mulling over the option of despatching Central Police Forces to West Bengal. The possibility of the Maoists striking their targets had been seen by the intelligence agencies early 2009.

Five companies of the CRPF had been sent to the state on 16 June 2009, amid the reports that the Maoists had been planting landmines to block out central forces from the area. The intelligence reports were not far off the mark. On the 17th, the Maoists struck in the Lalgarh area, as detailed earlier here. It again is a matter of coincidence, and more so of urgency perceived by the Centre (MHA: Ministry of Home Affairs) that on this very day, 17 June, the CoBRA units were ordered to move into West Bengal. The Centre pulled up the West Bengal government for failing to act effectively against the Maoists, and on the 17th it ordered the move of four units of the CoBRA Commandos, each comprising 30-40 men trained extensively in jungle warfare and counter-Naxal operations.

The CoBRA units would add sting to five companies of the CRPF ordered into WB a day earlier. The CoBRAs are newly-raised anti-Naxal elite units. These four units had completed their only a couple of months ago, and Lalgarh would be their first real test. They were airlifted into West Bengal from Orissa.

Here is another coincidence. The decision to order CoBRA into West Bengal came on a day Union Home Minister P. Chidambram said the Centre was "getting an impression that a section of the (state) government wants to act while the rest does not, fearing the consequences."[10] Chidambram was not entirely off the mark in his observations. As armed Maoists went on the rampage on the 17th, the state police, ordered to not fire, deserted their posts. The CPM government had their political compulsions. It feared that firing on the mob might lead to the repeat of the Nandigram situation, offering another opportunity to Mamata's TMC to exploit it politically.

While despatching the CRPF/CoBRAs, the MHA, being mindful of the fact that maintenance of law and order is primarily the responsibility of the states under constitutional scheme of things, made it clear that the CRPF would be deployed only to assist the state police in fighting the Maoists. The Centre is believed to have advised the state government that besides its regular police force, it must also deploy the East Frontier Rifles and Special Armed Police in its counter-Naxal operations. But being realists and well-aware of the situation in the Lalgarh area, they know that the state police was not equal to the job and in all likelihood it would be the CRPF taking up the frontal position against the Maoists and the tribals.

The five CRPF companies which reached west Midnapore on the 16th, were engaged in consultation with the state police leadership regarding their deploy till the 17th evening. Such consultations are only natural, because the new arrivals must familiarise themselves with the current situation and environment they would be required to operate in immediate future. More importantly, they had to decide how they would coordinate with the state police in the counter-Naxal operations. These units came from the CRPFs' group centre in Sindri, Bihar and are believed to be experienced in handling mob violence. Many of the men now called in for Lalgarh had been deployed in Nandigram during the violent agitation against land acquisition earlier.

Watershed Elections in West Bengal: May 2011: Mamata is CM

May 2011 elections in the state were a landmark in its history. It was preceded by a two-year struggle—'campaign' may be a more suitable term—by that spirited lady, Mamata Banerjee, to displace the 33-year Communist rule there. It was not only a bitter struggle, but also the one which occasionally lapsed into violence. Mamata, as she is popularly known, won the polls and became CM, as her party, Trinamool Congress (TMC) received the mandate (majority) from her people.

In a manner of speaking, the history of Naxal movement in West Bengal can be studied in two parts: Pre-Mamata Banerjee (Communist) period and Mamata Banerjee (post-Communist) period. To understand and appreciate the tempo of electioneering in the State, it should be helpful to view the ambience preceding the last phase of polling on 10 May 2011.

Scene on the eve of last phase (Jangalmahal)

Limelight will be on Jangalmahal when parts of the thre Naxal-hit districts of the State– West Midanpore, Bankura and Purulia—go to polls in the sixth and last phase of the state poll on 10 May 2011.

But West Midnapore's Jhargram constituency would invite maximum attention of the press as also of the common people. And there is reason behind this extraordinary interest here. This is because the Trinamool would context against Chhatradhar Mahato, the jailed spokesman of the Maoist-backed People's Committee against Police atrocities (PCAPA).

Mahato, booked under Unlawful Activities (Prevention) Act (UAPA), has been under trial. The Left alleged that the TMC is hand-in-glove with both the PCAPA and Maoists. They have point here. It was widely believed that Mamata had taken help of the Maoists, or at the very least, the elements allied to them, in her struggles against ruling Communists prior to this poll. After all, the fact that TMC chief Mamata had shared the dais with the very same Mahato in 2009 does go so distance to show some truth in this belief. But it is also an undeniable fact that since the attack on the Jnaneswari Express in May 2010, in which the PCAPA was alleged to be involved, she distanced herself from the group.

Jhargram had been in the headlines for the last three years, in particular, as the Maoists had made an attempt on the life of the (then) CM, Buddhadeb Bhattacharjee on 2 Nov 2008 in a landmine blast. Following this assassination attempt, the area suffered under police repression. It was ironic that the LWE target a communist CM. Importantly, the core area of Lalgarh movement had been under complete Maoist Control (they call it a Free Zone) for over seven months till the security forces reclaimed it. Thereafter, it saw the deaths of over a hundred 'police informers'. "Over the last couple of years (end 2008-mid 2011), the CPM cadres set up armed camps" which confronted the Maoists bent upon avenging their Lalgarh discomfiture The mutual 'warfare' resulted in the Netai Carnage, in which nine villagers were killed, and many more were injured[12].

It is officially a triangular fight for Jhargram constituency: the CPM, TMC and the PCAPA. In fact, it is a dual. This will be clear once you went past the Jhargram town, the CPM flags and graffiti disappear. The entire area is wrapped in the saffron-while green of the TMC and the green and white of Mahato's PCAPA. Manoj Mahato, former secretary-spokesperson of the PCAPA, asserted that "the fight is mainly between usand the TMC, the CPM is no factor." Released recently on bail, he took charge of Chhatradhar's campaign. On 8 May, he led a rally of some 1,000 locals at Manikpara, also attended by Chhatradhar's wife, Niyoti.

On 10 May, both parties, TMC and PCAPA, held hectic rallies. CM Bhattacharya had done his bit earlier on 7 May, seeking votes for the CPM candidate and sitting MLA Amar Basu. Now we have two locals speaking about the outcome of the poll in the constituency. Says Radharaman Mahato, one of the PCAPA strongholds: The parties involved have waged war for two long years in their efforts to capture political ground, now is the time to know which side of the people are on." A labourer in Lodhashuli area, Dilip Hansda says: "Nobody has any idea what is going to happen, all holding their breath." All this one day before the poll date! This daily had headlined this story, as given here:

> In the shadow of Naxal terror
> In red fort Jhargram, Trianmool
> Battles jailed 'Maoist' Mahato

"Disruptions, attacks and forces can shoot."

This is another headline in the same daily, giving details about the security forces deployed for the last phase of polling on 10 May 2011[13]. The men of the Central Forces had been authorised to shoot even without orders in case of an armed attack aimed at disrupting the 10 May poll in the ultra-red belt of Lalgarh (Jhargram), West Bengal. "The final phase of the poll is most crucial and we are not taking chances", said TB Rao, 1G, CRPF. "In case of an armed attack, even the constables have been empowered to shoot. They will not used to seek orders from their superiors for self-defence or to protect government property." This indeed is an unprecedented situation, but unavoidable given the apprehension about the level of potential violence on or before 10 May. In contrast, the Central Forces were under strict orders to show utmost restraint in the first five phases of poll. May be, it is an unprecedented solution for an equally unprecedented possibility.

West Midnapur district, comprising of seven volatile constituencies of Gopiballavpur, Midnapur, Shalboni, Garbeta, Jhargram, Nayagram and Binpur, going to polls, is the epicentre of the high-level security arrangements. Here is a telling statement from Rao: "Never in the history of elections in India has this been done. West Midnapore alone will have 360 companies, totalling 36,000 armed personnel, which is a record." To wit, the entire poll process in Assam needed 360 companies! Altogether, 1 lakh security men will be present in these three districts (Bankura, Purulia and West Midnapore) for the last Phase of polling on 10 May.

The number of security men deployed at each polling station will be six times larger. Instead of just four armed personnel as in the past, each polling station will have a platoon— a minimum of 24 armed men.

The security had to extend beyond the polling stations. Eighteen companies from CoBRA (Combat Battalion for Resolute Action) units, specialised in combating Maoists, had been deployed in the forest areas of Jhargram and Lalgarh. In addition, two helicopters from Kalaikunda airbase would keep vigil from the skies.

Finally, it is understandable that the security forces were ordered to show restraint in the five phases of elections and they did a commendable job. "But now that facing the marauding Maoists, it was necessary to change the rules."

Killing machine Kishanji killed at Last: 24.11.11

This was the headline of a story carried by a daily dated 25.11.11. K.Koteswar Rao, alias Kishanji was one of the main architects of the PWG-MCC merger and believed to be a big military brain.

A big blow indeed to the Maoists

It was a major blow to the CPI (Maoist), when the security forces gunned down its politburo member Kishanji. This was claimed by senior officials who conducted the precise two-hour operation, and added, "things would be made public officially after eliminating all doubts about the identity of the slain Maoists."

The corpse of the 58-year-old Maoist leader Molajula Koteswara Rao, popularly known by his alias Kishanji, was found and identified soon after the encounter. The body was extensively damaged, possibly in the mortar attack. Some documents and his AK-47 rifle were found by the slain leader's side.

It was the biggest ever anti-Maoist operation in the past one year, mounted by the 184 unit of 207 CoBRA Battalion, in coordination with the

CRPF and CIF, deep inside Burasholi forest near Kushabani village, said police chief of West Midnapore (now Paschim Medinipur) district. The joint team comprised 200 commandos and achieved success in the wake of coordinated operation from Jharkhand and Odisha sides. The police of these two states had deployed their units on the border to block any exit routes.

A large posse of security forces, some 1,000 armed men, had raided the are a on 22/23rd night. Working on a specific tip-off, they surrounded Kushaboni but Kishanji managed to escape from the area after a heavy gun fire. CIF SP Manoj Verma disclosed this, further adding the forces had to break through the four-tier security cordon planned by the ultras led by Kishanji and Suchitra Mahato, the widow of Sasadhar Mahato, elder sibling of jailed PCAPA leader Chhatradhar Mahato.

The forces got information of his presence after they recovered some letters to one Chandan by Kishanji and Suchitra dated 21.11.11 from a house in Gosainbandh village from where some people were picked up, said Verma, explaining why they did not pull out of the area even after botched operation of the 23rd.

Undoubtedly, it is a major success for the security forces, eliminating a leader who was No. 3 in the hierarchy of the CPI (Maoist), and obviously, it is a huge set back for the Maoist for that very reason, as averred by the Union Home Secretary RK Singh[14]. He says security forces "were following Kishanji for a time on specific information and today's operation was the result of that."

The death of Kishanji not only affords a major success for the CM who was unable to concentrate on industrialisation and other developmental works in Jangalmahal but also could help the anti-Naxal operations in Chhattisgarh, Jharkhand and Orissa. Another analyst says: "Politically, the 24th's success would enable the TMC to strike its organisational roots firmly in the wooded boondocks in absence of the fleeing Marxists and Subjugated Maoists", says a senior police officer recently brought back by Mamata in anti-Maoists operations. It was also believed that with the death of the top leader, incarceration of other senior Maoists like Somen, Sudip Chongdar, and Telugu Dipak, and surrender of second rung operatives like Jagori Baskey, the LWE are left with only a few operatives like Jayanta, State Secretary Akash and Ranjit Pal leading some stray armed squads who would be left without a Central Command at least for sometime to come.

This seems and read a too rosy a picture for the security forces, and conversely, too gloomy one for the Maoists. Such assessments need to be informed by some balance and certain balance, which would be found in the later pages.

If the security forces are too effusive in claiming credit for just one death of a Maoist, even if it happens to be of a person no less than Kishanji, the CPM does not wish to lag behind. Its senior leader in the State, Shyamal Chakrabarty pleads that "the Government should now concentrate on rebuilding the area and allow all political parties a level playing field, pointing to the "sacrifices the CPM made" in fighting against Maoist rebels. "We lost more than 300 comrades to Maoist attacks", he said, adding it was the Left Government that had broken the backbone of the Maoists. Some claim, this! On the contrary, this success was a boost for their nemesis, Mamata Banerjee who had taken a political risk by ignoring advice from her erstwhile allies—in her struggle against the Left Front Government—in the civil society and boldly went ahead against the Red Rebels. It will be obvious when we discuss her determined drive against them in the Jangal Mahal.

It needs to be said about Kishanji that he was the top operational commander of the Maoists, who was active in Chhattisgarh, Odisha, Jharkhand and West Bengal. He had given the security forces a slip in 2009, when he was reportedly wounded after a gun fight inside the Metala forests. He had since fled to Chhattisgarh. His inexplicable return to West Bengal early October (2011) remains a mystery. He was too shrewd a strategist to be unaware of ground realities there!

This decision by that sharp mind deserves some explanation, some examination!

Searching for Suchitra Mahato

"Day after, fear stalks Burisole's dusty path", was bold headline of a daily, describing the atmospherics in the area where the Maoist leader was killed after a firy encounter. Prolonged gun fight had been heard and 'seen' by the population in and around Burisole. It was not unexpected that wild apprehension hung in the air. By 10 AM, after scouring the area around the village, the security force personnel had gathered in large number in the village. With some holding on to the lashes of sniffer dogs, they went inside each of the 60 thatched houses of the village in search of a woman. The questions asked were simple: Have you seen anyone? Have you seen a village?

They were searching for a Maoist leader, Suchitra Mahato, widow of slain Maoist Sasadhar Mahato, who was suspected to have been with Kishanji when he died. Like in Burisole, the houses in adjoining villages of Sarkata and Barsole too were subjected to search, to locate Suchitra.

Meanwhile, the DG, BSF cautioned his men to be on guard against retaliation by the 'wounded' Maoists.

They say: It was a fake encounter

As was only expected, Maoist sympathisers——read, overground unarmed Maoists—the day after the gunning down of Kishanji, in a chorus, said he was killed in a fake encounter. They were, equally expectedly, led by the so-called revolutionary poet and Maoist ideologue Varavara Rao, who addressed a rally of activists of the Association for Protection of Democratic Rights (APDR) at Kolkata on 25 Nov 2011. He said the Maoist had been taken into custody the 23rd itself, tortured and later killed. All this seem so incredible. All this will be discussed in detail in a separate chapter. For now, some statements by DGP CRPF K.Vijay Kumar follow: "It was an absolutely clean operation.....It is the habit of such people to accuse the security forces of fake encounter...It is a custom to accuse the police, but that is part of our job....when we die in large numbers, it is always a very fair deal, and when we are able to take them on, this is what they say!"

Deepa Rao, niece of Kishanji, was present at the rally in Kolkata, and during the march of APDR volunteers to the state secretariat, she was shown crying for her dead uncle. One wishes we could have spared this agony scene. It may be uncharitable to speak this language, still, she should tell us if she ever cried when that Killing Machine, who happend to be her uncle, tortured, beheaded and cruelly killed her innocent, unarmed victims mostly the very tribals he had taken to arms for! One is not mentioning the security forces men here, who are meant to be killed in any case, if we are to believe some state politicians!

A pall of gloom was reported to have descended on the village of Peddapally in Karimnagar district (Andhra Pradesh) on hearing about his death. Some in the villages demanded that his body be handed over to his family for his last rites.

The Association for Protection of Democratic Rights was reported to have been assigned by Kishanji's mother to file a writ in Calcutta High Court, demanding a probe into the alleged fake encounter in which the rebel top gun was killed on 24 November.

"Maoists may be down, but not out"

This was a realistic and telling headline of a story about the post-Kishanji scene in the Maoist camp, a month after his elimination[15].

Maoist top gun Kishanji's death has dealt a body blow to the rebel leadership in West Bengal but they still have men and firepower for retaliatory strikes, says an intelligence report sent to the MHA. This daily claims to have a copy of it.

The report prepared by the Subsidiary Intelligence Bureau (SIB) details the status of Maoist squads active in Jangalmahal (forest areas of Paschim Mednipur, Bankura and Purulia) and other districts after Kishanji's death in an encounter on 24 November. Some of the more important points called from the SIB report are mentioned hereafter.

1. Nine Maoist squads with more than 100 members are active in Paschim Medinipur and Purulia districts. All members are being fire arms.
2. The biggest of these nine squads is Ayodhya Squad in Purulia, with nearly 40 members.
3. They have 30 sophisticated firm arms, including five AK-47, and five INSAS rifles, apart from a host of other weapons.
4. Maoist squads in Belpahari, Jhargram East, Jhargram West, Jamboni, Binpur, Nayagram and Lalgarh are active in Paschim Medinipur district. Among these, Belpahari is the biggest, with more than 20 members under the leadership of Madam Mahato.
5. Maoist action squad members are present outside Jangalmahal region too, in Birbhum, Nadia, and Murshidabad districts.
6. Maoists do not have any indigenous squad in Bankura. Their Belpahari squad covers Bankura specifically Barikul and Ranibandh areas.

Uneasy calm in Jangalmahal

Jangalmahal had been in the news for long years before Mamata came to power in West Bengal as the nerve centre of Maoist depredations and death dance. Their morbid violence peaked in the last years of the Communist rule in the State, starting from 2009. With the killing of Kishanji, it suddenly earned a huge salience, and that was six months after the Lady assumed power. Post Kishanji's death, an apprehensive ambience prevailed in the area, a kind of "uneasy calm", as a daily put it.[15]

The situation immediately after this death is discussed here, as also certain issued connected with this death. Two excerpts aptly describing the scene and things are reproduced here (datelined 25 Nov 2011):[16]

- It could be psychological yet one could feel a nauseating reek of blood and gunpowder. More than 20 hours have elapsed since his death but the ground beneath is still soaked in blood, dried up and darkened; flies hovering around.

- By a mound lay the blown up body of Kishanji who terrorised Jangalmahal and neighbouring Jharkhand—nay, even the security forces for his uncanny ability to slip in and out of the wooded villages at will—for more than half-a-decade before dying by the gun as he lived by.

A CRPF Officer, who was guarding a hard disc, some documents, a ladies' purse reportedly belonging to Suchitra Mahato, a close accomplice of Kishanji, all recovered from the site, describes the scene surrounded his death: "He was firing with venom from behind this mound. He did not give up even when asked to surrender. Then we fired mortar which neutralised him, after which our boys rained bullets."

It was comparatively clear: some few hundred metres, and 500 metres away from the main roads. Another senior officer wondered, unclear as to why a master strategist like Kishanji entered West Bengal at a time when the CPI (Maoist) was losing the organisational glue, indicated by recovery of hundreds of KGs of explosives and arms from the forests. Sources disclosed he slipped into the state on 22 November. Before this he had a meeting with party colleague Sabyasachi Panda in Odisha discussing the latter's entry into the Politburo.

Even the security forces were at loss to explain or understand his re-entry into West Bengal at a time when the Party was fast losing its grip among the people. PCPA leader Nemai Mahato feels he came on a peace mission with Mamata Banerjee government but his military commanders like Jayanta and Ranjit Pal played spoil sport by bumping off TMC workers. Such a conflict between political and military wings of a rebel movement and insurrectionary campaign is not unknown, in fact fairly common. The ULFA is an outstanding example of this conflict (in Assam). The second theory holds that it was a deliberate decision to reach the State and boost the organisational set up there to raise the morale of the Maoists cadre, even if it involves "great personal risk." Being Kishanji, he was not a stranger to such great risks, as he had shown in the past by slipping in and out of elaborate cordons created by the security forces for his capture. It is just that this time his luck ran out. There is a third explanation too, which blames his towering ambition to retain his supremacy in the party hierarchy. He had reasons for this apprehension. He had been under pressure to explain the loss of support in West Bengal. It seems series of mindless killings in Jangalmahal for the last few years had not been appreciated by the Central Committee. Besides, it had alienated not only the common man in the State but also the tribals themselves in the area, who were supposed to be the recruiting base for the Maoists. The tribals had regularly been targeted after dubbing them the police informers.

Here is a CRPF officer making an honest statement: "It is still not sinking in, that finally we have hit the target. We are still wondering how the Maoist top gun led the security forces to a merry dance in the region for the past half-a-decade. He could well have repeated his feat (this time too) had it not been for a chance interruption of a call purportedly made by Kishanji to his Jharkhand comrades demanding 'urgent reinforcements' in order to break through the cordon thrown around by the CRPF."

The call led to the house of Dharmendra Mahato alias Chander, a college student at Gosainbandh. CRPF recovered a laptop, some letters dated as late as 22 November, making them sure of his presence.

A day after Kishanji was shot deal inside the Bursole forest, a "blood curdling calm prevailed over a dozen of hamlets nestled in 10 km radius. In view of this 'calm', the call by CPI (Maoist) State secretary for a 48 hour bandh in West Bengal seems to uncalled for! More so, considering what Sona Tudu, a retired teacher who regularly shuttles between Gidhni and Jhumuria, asserts while talking to a journalist: "We have seldom seen a deadly calm as this." Mouthing similar views, the journalist who personally visited the area and experienced the atmospherics, says: "The Jangalmahal would, however, not utter a word. Not a bird would chatter, let alone a man. Though quiet descends fast in winter over the woody land of Jangalmahal, such a deadly calm is absolutely unusual."

Post-Kishanji: Maoist central committee (CC) is concerned

After the death of the leading Maoist, No. 3 in the hierarchy, the CPI (Maoist) had reasons to be deeply concerned. What should worry them even more seriously is what has happened in the recent past, and what could, in the near future, as the intelligence agencies in the different LWE-affected states "have been striking gold in either arresting or killing the top leadership."[17]

The Maoist movement suffered a series of setbacks in 2011 as the security forces succeeded to arrest four CC members earlier, and fifth and the most serious blow was dealt in the killing of Kishanji, who single handedly nurtured the Marxist-Leninist-Maoist movement in West Bengal, Jharkhand and Bihar.

The series of killings or arrests of members of the Maoist CC, the all-powerful body of the most secretive organisation, is an indication that the core principle of counter-insurgency strategy is to hit the leadership.

More worrying should be the fact that the arrest of these four CC members was based on the highly accurate inputs provided by the intelligence agencies of different states. The four arrested earlier this year are: Jhantu Mukherjee alias Sahebda; Vijay Arya alias Jaspal ji; Varanasi Subramaniam; and Akhilesh Yadav alias Bhupesh. The fifth and the latest stike is in West Bengal, which again is backed by 'actionable' intelligence inputs. The latest strike, indeed, must be morale-shattering.

Even if the Maoists managed to pull some spectacular attacks on security forces in different States, notwithstanding these set-backs, they too began bleeding in all States, save for Chhattisgarh. In a way, security forces backed by fully functional intelligence units in Bihar, West Bengal, Jharkhand and Odisha managed to turn the tide, even if these States continue to face intensified rebel activity. However, the qualitative change that is obvious is that the concerted efforts in these States led the counter-insurgency operations from a stage of 'strategic defensive' to 'strategic equilibrium.' The only exception in this change is Chhattisgarh, where the Maoist movement is in a 'strategic offensive' stage.

As seen above, the security forces are targeting the top leadership of the Maoists, the intellectual persuaders/ enticers/gurus of the foot soldiers of the LWE. Consequently, their targets are the members of the CC (CCM) and of the Politburo (PBM). So, the pattern is obvious. Besides the five mentioned above, the CCMs and PBMs killed earlier included: Patel Sudhakar Reddy, Chief, Maoist Intelligence Wing, May 2009, and Cherukuri Raj Kumar alias Azad, CCM/PBM and spokesperson, Jul 2010.

CPI (Maoist) Central Committee

1. Mupala Laxaman Rao @ Ganapathi (Secretary)
2. Prashanth Bose @ Kishanda
3. Namballa Keshava Rao @ Baswaraj
4. Misir Besra @ Sunirmal
5. Mallojula Venugopal @ Abhay
6. Katakam Sudershan @ Anand
7. Mallaraji Reddy @ Sathenna
8. Tippiri Tirupati @ Deoji
9. Dev Kumar Singh @ Nishanth
10. Jiniugu Narismiha Reddy @ Jampanna
11. Akkiraju Haragopal @ Ramakrishna
12. Kuppuswamy Devaraj @ Ramesh
13. Kadari Satyanarayan Reddy @ Kosa

14. Gajanand @ Parush
15. Chenderi Yadav @ Paryag
16. Mohan @ Mahesh
17. Ranjith Bose @ Kanchan
18. Manoj @ Rajesh
19. Pulluri Prasada Rao @ Chandranna
20. Ramchandra Reddy Pratap Reddy @ Chalapathi
21. Modem Balakrishna @ Bhaskar.

Birbhum violence : November 2012

If the Jangalmahal was CM Mamata's most challenging problem, Birbhum and Singur proved only a little less challenging, even if the scale and spread of the former was much daunting. The trouble started on 6 Nov 2012 at Loba and some other villages of Birbhum district when the police allegedly fired at villagers who were demanding a better deal from the firm Bengal EMTA following their displacement. The villagers had attacked a team of some 150 policemen, including the district SP, additional SP and the officer-in-charge who had gone to recover the earth-moving equipment the locals had seized from the firm. A company executive said: "we had offered the amount decided by the state government——but they did not allows us to start work." 30 people, including six villagers were injured in the firing.

The genesis of the land problem was the granting of mining rights to Bengal EMTA and DVC, which had acquired 3500 acres spread over 16 villages. The land was required for lifting coal for the thermal power plant run by the DVC. The villagers formed the Krishi Jomi Raksh Committee (KJRC) and began demanding more compensation and rehabilitation.

Some 40 days before their violent confrontation with the police over rehabilitation issues, the locals of Loba village in Birbhum had written to CM Mamata Banerjee on 27 Sep 2012, apprising her of the problem surrounding the purchase of land by mining company Bengal EMTA. It is understandable that the Loba farmers wrote to the CM; after all it was Mamata herself as leader of the opposition who had spearheaded the struggle against land acquisition when the Left Front was in power in West Bengal. Equally noteworthy is the fact that before writing to the CM, Loba farmers had communicated with the state Commerce and Industries Minister, Partha Chatterjee, local MP Shatabdi Roy, the district magistrate and the district SP.

In their Letters, the KJRC leadership alleged the Bengal EMTA had not spoken to the villagers. "They started buying land through touts. However, they could not start their project unless they bought all the land", the Letter read. "We are an apolitical platform formed to preserve the interests of the working class and farmers. We are not obstructing the development of the coal industry in Birbhum. We simply want proper rehabilitation package. However, by influencing certain sections of the administration, Bengal EMTA is unleashing terror in the area." The letters establish that all wings of the state government, the CM included, had been forewarned by the agitators. This is the background to the 6 November violence as describe earlier here.

In such situations, where the farmers agitate for their rights and rehabilitation, the politics looms large in the backstage. Now it was the turn of the Congress to jump in the fray, the very party which had been pushed off the centre stage by the communists 33 years ago. Expectedly, Union Minister of State for Urban Development Deepa Darmunshi came to the state and addressed residents of the violence-hit Loba village at a rally in Birbhum in the last week of Nov 2012. The ruling party at the Centre was only expected to help its state unit to start reviving its fortunes, however tentatively, after its decades of slumber when the Communists rule the state.

Mamata visits troubled Loba village

Four weeks after 30 people including six villagers were injured at Loba village in the Dubrajpur area of the State's Birbhum district over land requisition issue, CM Banerjee visited the area on 4 Dec 2012. She assured the villagers that the TMC government will not acquire their lands forcibly, and they could be at peace and sleep peacefully.

She was only the second, Chief Minister to visit the area, but the first by road.

The CM had made a sudden deviation in her on going tour of Bankura and Purulia to visit the village. Violence had erupted at Loba on 6 November, as detailed above, when a huge police contingent tried to take possession of earth-moving equipments of DVC EMTA Coal Mines Pvt Ltd, which the villagers had seized in Dec 2011. The dispute between the parties was over the compensation offered for the land, which the company was trying to acquire for an opencast mining project.

Referring to the protests against forcible land acquisition, which she had led at Singur and Nandigram, Ms Banerjee said that unlike the previous Left government, her government would not forcibly occupy (their) land.

She asked people to trust her to keep her word. "I can sacrifice my life for it", she said, adding that her government would award a compensation of Rs 25,000 each to six villagers injured in the violence. The villagers were asked to directly sell their land to the company, and not to allow the land agents to trade off their land. She said the problem of land acquisition started in the area in 2009 during the rule of the previous government.

She admitted that "what happened that day (6 November) was a mistake and all the police officers responsible for the incident have been removed." Though the State is waiting for the Centre to finalise its policy on land acquisition, she said "we have decided in principle that there will be no forcible land acquisition here."

Earlier in the day, she had addressed a public meeting in Bankura district, and pledged to proved basic amenities like drinking water, schools and health facilities to the people.

An analyst felt "Mamata ignored smoke signals on Birbhum row", and reached the area a month after the violence, whereas Loba residents had written to her on rehabilitation issues 40 days before the violence."[18]

Sangur Saga: The Aftermath: Movement turns a full circle

The anti-Nano movement at Singur, which earned Mamata wide-spread support and a lot of publicity, seems to have turned a full circle, as Becharam Manna, the new Minister of State for agriculture, was gheraoed by the local farmers of Singur in BDO office at Singur on 28 Nov 2012.

Besides inter-faction fights within the TMC, the dissatisfaction of Singur villagers with the tardy pace of supply of subsidised rice to farmers as promised by CM Banerjee, can be described as major reason for the disillusionment.

The incident is viewed by the critics as the beginning of end of the TMC's bonhomie with Singur. Manna, a Banerjee confident and prominent face in the anti-Nano movement at Singur had "only last week replaced another local senior leader and former Agriculture Minister Rabindranath Bhattacharya, prompting the latter to launch a frontal attack on the party leadership." After the ouster of Bhattacharya, the mud slinging between the two TMC factions in Sangur had intensified. Manna had come to the Sangur BDO office to supervise the distribution of the subsidies. The Minister faced the ire of the farmers who had gathered there to collect the slips for subsidised rice. The farmers were unwilling to give away their land over the issue of non-availability of Rs 2,000 and 8 Kg of rice per month to each family of such farmer, as had been promised by the CM.

A farmer said: "We have repeated told our leaders that we are not getting the money and ration as promised by the CM. We are yet to give our land back. The government is not keeping the promises it made. Today, when we saw the Minister, we expressed our anger."

Bhattacharya, an octogenarian leader, was earlier shifted (from Agriculture) to a low key ministry (Programme Implementation), prompting him to tender his resignation from the Mamata Cabinet. He said extortionists and corrupt elements "have swelled the Trinamool rank and file, adding to the discomfort of the State government which was already reeling pressure on account of rising law and order problem.

In fact, Minister Manna had gone to the village (Sangur) to distribute free rice and arrears of grants announced by the CM a few months ago. The irate villagers gheraoed him, questioning him "as to why the leaders have dumped them after winning the polls."

Surrenders in West Bengal

Maoist couple surrenders: Mamata's success

Jagori Baskey, one of the most dreaded names among West Bengal's Maoist, "called" on (or surrendered before) the CM Mamata Bannerji on 17 Nov 2011, along with her rebel husband Rajaram Soren, at the writers Building. The couple have brought their child (Bahadur) with them.

While the duo had first discussed their surrender with the district police in Purulia, they surrendered before the 1G (Intelligence Branch), and desired to meet the CM. Their surrender has put the stamp of success on the CM's Jangal Mahal policy of carrot and stick[19]. Congratulating the due, he stated that her government would examine the legal case against the couple while supporting their rehabilitation in every possible way. The Ramakrishna Mission would be approached to admit the child in one of their school and the state would provide for his education till high school, and his parents would get the government would get the government package.

Their history of crimes

Jagori was mentored by Kishanji, and was feared throughout Jangalmahal as also the border areas of the Jharkhand state for her spiteful acts. She had been a founder member of the Maoists' woman strike squad from 1999-2000 and led a host of blood-curdling strikes—including the one of Shilda Camp——and abduction of Sankrail police station's officer in-charge. In 15 Feb 2010 attack on Shilda Camp, 24 men of Eastern Rifles were killed. She had also murdered a police officer in Purulia and a host of CPM leaders, including a district committee member.

Jagori Baskey, who became the first Maoist to surrender/call on the CM at Writers Building, poured venom against her mentors, who allegedly caught her young when she was barely 16 and trained her in handling sophisticated weaponry and planting explosives. She confessed to crimes committed over the past decade and asserted, "Maoists are bad people who are misleading the poor like us and sucking them into doing all kind of acts like killing and looting."

Soren, alias Sagen Santhal, 34, is also involved in a host of cases of murder and subversive activities. Their son Bahadur is 4-year old. Soren said he was led into the Maoist fold a decade ago, but felt betrayed when the rebels started killing the very tribals, whose lot they had sought to change.

The both said they had realised they had chosen wrong path and were keen to return to society's mainstream.

Is Mamata Bannerji succeeding?

The surrender comes at a time when CM Banerjee efforts to restore peace in the Jangalmahal is at the cross roads with the interlocutors backing out of the negotiations process and the government mounting a fresh offensive against the Naxals.

"The duo's compass of action covered a fairly large area from three Jangalmahal districts of West Bengal to areas inside Jharkhand", said a senior police officer, adding Jagori's surrender would not only demoralise the Maoist cadre but also help them derive crucial information on the rebels' plans and strategies.

Following the officials line of treating the LWE as misled youth enticed into violent ways by the vily Maoists, the CM said: "The surrender of Jagori should be a lesson to all those brothers and sisters who were misguided and deviated from the mainstream. They should shun violence and come to the normal life as violence leads nowhere to, take advantage of the Government's economic package."

The surrendered Maoists are likely to receive Rs 2,000 per month and Rs 1.5 lakh as deposits fixed in their names to be paid to them if they showed good conduct over three years. The Government also promised payments on differentiated basis for a variety of weapons to be surrendered by the ultras: Rs 25,000 for machine gun: Rs 15,000 for an AK-47, Rs 10,000 for a satellite phone; Rs 3,000 each for a revolver and a landmine and Rs 1,000 per Kg of explosives.

The Chief Minister, however, launched a scathing attack of those acting as the brains behind the Maoists and conspiring. She said they do not love their country. She further added: Let the fight be one of ideologies, not one through guns and bloodshed. Please return to civil life... The areas in Jangalmahal are also among the poorest in the State, where such a bloodshed is totally unwarranted—unrest can't bring peace which is a continuous process."

36 Surrenders in a year

Before Jagori and Soren's surrender in Nov 2011, another Maoist couple, Duryodhan Raj Kowar alias Sujan and his wife Akri Sahis, had surrendered before the Purulia police.

Three members of the CPI (Maoist) laid down their arms before the Bankura police on 22 Dec 2012. The most important among the three who surrendered was Besanti Tadu alias Malti, a member of the banned outfit for 11 years. She had shifted her base a number of times across various districts in the State. Having been associated with the squad of Maoists leaders Bikash and Tara for quite sometime, Malti surrendered with an Insas rifle, informed Bankura SP Mukesh Kumar.

In the expected language, Malti told the journalists that she became disillusioned with the Maoists after they committed atrocities on the people, especially women and the infirm. The same language was used by Jagory, as seen in the earlier pages here. Is it disillusionment and change in ideological and thinking or merely enough-is-enough tiredness and inability to continue to horrendous depredations after youthful enthusiasm has yielded to do the 'wisdom' dictated by the age.

The other two of three were Buddhadeb Mandi alias Mantri and Sukhdeb Singh Sardar alias Damu. Both had been associates of Arjun Munda's squad operating in the Belpahari-Ranibandh area of Paschim Medinipur district. The two surrendered a single-barrel gun and a muzzle-loading rifle.

With these three, the number of those who had surrendered over the past one year since the death of Politburo member K.Koteswara Rao alias Kishanji, "have gone upto 36".

Large arms haul in Maoist zone: Nov 2011

Security forces recovered a huge cache of weapons during anti-Maoist operations in Paschim Medinipur district. It included nine guns that were seized by the LWE in an attack on the Sildha camp of the East Frontier Rifles on 15 Feb 2010, the police said on 18 Nov 2011. Operations were conducted in Kotwali, Lalgarh and Salboni police thana areas. "During the last week, police recovered 11 sophisticated weapons, 250 detonators, 786 rounds of ammunition, 200 Kg of explosives and 32 landmines."

In the Sildha attack, in which 24 EFR men were killed, the Maoists had taken away 46 weapons.

Jairam praises Mamata role in Jangalmahal: 9 Nov. 2012

Union Rural Development Minister Jairam Ramesh 9 Nov 2012 praised West Bengal Chief Minister Mamata Banerjee and TMC MP Suvendu Adhikari for their "political mobilisation" to counter the Naxal threat/menace in Jangalmahal region of the state. What Ramesh told West Bengal Rural Development Minister Subrata Mukherjee is reproduced here:

"The kind of political mobilisation that happened in Jangalmahal during the last two years is worth mentioning and one should not take away the credit due to her. While Banerjee has been an overarching figure behind this political mobilisation, Suvendu Adhikari has been instrumental in organising it on the ground. Both of them should be praised for playing an instrumental role in changing the ground situation in Jangalmahal."

The analysts tend to agree with Ramesh about an improvement on the Jangalmahal front. There, indeed, has been considerable drop in incidents of violence in that area with the number of casualities coming down to 26 so far this year (till 31 Oct 2012) from 125 civilians in West Midnapore district in 2009.

Notes

1. Jaya Menon, Indian Express, 22 July, 2007.
2. *Ibid,* 18 Jul 2007.
3. Rakesh K Singh, Asian Age, 21 Dec 2006.
4. Alok Banerjee, Hindustan Times, 11 Jun 2007.
5. Bidyut Roy, Indian Express, 12 Jun 2007.
6. The Times of India, 6.1.2009.
7. Dutta, Ananya, The Hindu, 16.10.11.
7. Sengupta, Sauger, The Pioneer, 16.10.11.
9. Ananya Dutta, The Hindu, 14.11.11.
10. Nagchoudhury, Subrata, The Indian Express, 18.6.2009.
11. Amitabh Sinha, The Indian Express, 18.6.2009.
12. Bhattacharya, Snigdhendu, The Hindustan Times, 9.5.11.
13. Bhattacharya, Ravik, The Hindustan Times, 9.5.11.
14. Sengupta, Sangar, The Pioneer, 25 Nov 2011.
15. Biswas, Surbek, The Hindustan Times, 20.12.11.
16. Sengupta, Saugar, The Pioneer, 26.11.11.

17. Reddy, K.Srinivas, The Hindu, 26.11.11.
18. Hazra, Surojit Ghosh, The Hindustan Times.
19. Sengupta, Saugar, The Pioneer, 18.11.11.

33

West Bengal 2 and the North-East

Post Mamata Banerjee take over: 20 May 2011

This is the last part of this Chapter on the Maoist insurrection in West Bengal, deals exclusively with the period after Mamata Banerjee takes over as the Chief Minister.

It is essentially divided in three parts:

- Analysis of Banerjee's handling of Maoist violence within first two months of her Chief Ministership.
- Her successes in dealing with Jungalmahal stronghold of the Maists.
- Some other incidents.

Jungalmahal was the main battle ground for the intrepid Mamata Banerjee: Some salient facts

The Jungalmahal region 8,000 sq km spread in three districts of West Bengal, viz West Midnapore, Purulia and Bankura.

It was once the worst-affected area in West Bengal and in three years, after Mamata taking over as CM in May 2011, it was to become one of the Trinamool Congress (TMC) regime's few success story.

Not many saw it turning that way when she rode it power in 2011, joining hands with several outfits with close links to the Maoists, particularly the People's Committee Against Police Atrocities PCAPA.

During he Assembly polls campaign in 2010-11, she had denied the presence of Maoists in Jungalmahal, and repeatedly sought the removal of Central paramilitary forces from there.

An olive branch full of thorns: 30 Jul 2011

Mamata Banerjee had promised to solve the Jungalmahal riddle by talking to the Maoists. But her subsequent actions have kept every one guessing.

The above is an analysis of political situation about Jungalmahal imbroglio, under this heading of a new story. The blurb under the title of the analytical article in a weekly news magazine in its issue of 30 Jul 2011 indicates the line of argument the scribe is set to follow. The article is penned, it needs to be noted, just two months after CM Banerjee took over on 20 May 2011.[1]

The opening three paragraphs of this somewhat longish article are reproduced below:

- On the evening of 17 Jul (2011), as the sun disappeared into the Jhargram's Lodhasuli forests, a cavalcadre of uniform men sped down National Highway 6. They stopped down near a busy truck stop in Gajasimul, some four hours away from Kolkata and barely a few kilometres from where a dense canopy of green begins. Men of 167 Battalion of the CRPF walked towards a Tata truck laden with onions. In the backseat at scrawny man lay sleeping on a thin sheet. They asked his name, matched his face with a photo recently seen, and hauled him out. Underneath the sheet, they found a country made pistol and two rounds of ammunition.
- The man later identified himself as Biren Mahato, Jhargram Sub-Divisional Commander of the CPI (Maoist). According to the CRPF sources, Mahato is the first Maoist arrested in West Bengal after the Assembly Polls that ended 34-year Left rule and brought TMC's Mamata Banerjee to power.
- Only a week ago, on the sweltering after of 12 July, another convoy had sped down the highway, past Jhargram and into Nayagram, a village that was once considered a Maoist stronghold. Along with an entourage of ministers, Mamata became only the second CM to visit these parts of West Midnapore district, the first to go by road.

In the run up to the Assembly polls, Mamata had vociferously argued against an outgoing joint operation launched in 2009 to combat the spreading influence of the Maoists. If voted to power, she had promised peace in Jungalmahal an area spanning 69 development blocks in three of the State's poorest districts mentioned above, declared by the Centre as affected by LWE.

It bears repetition that during the election campaign, she had not only denied the presence of the Maoists in Jungalmahal, but even demanded the withdrawal of the CRPF from the Region. At presents, there 6,000 paramilitary forces deployed in the State, 31 companies of CRPF in west Midnapore, and two each in Purulia and Bankura districts. Post-elections, CM Banerjee has kept mum on the withdrawal of troops and focussed instead on a kind of "bread-bombing."

On 12 July, Mamata had stood on a stage in Nayagram and announced a mega development package: Rs 112 Crore for drinking water, rice at Rs 2 per Kg for anyone with an annual income of less than Rs 42,000, pattas of forest rights, land rights, 900 primary schools in the tribal Santhali language, free sfor the girls studying in class 9-12, colleges, hostels, nursing training centre, and agricultural marketing centres. She delivered the key message: the state has not forgotten you. *Esho, amar ghore esho* (come back home to me)", she said.

In the end, loudest applause came for a bridge. "what do you want?" She screamed into the mike. "Bridge, bridge, bridge", the crowd chanted. Four kilometres of concrete across what is now water would cut daily commute by hours.

The bridge alone may not be enough. In the weeks preceding her Jungalmahal visit, in order to keep her pre-election promises, she had appointed two key committees.

One to review the cases of political prisoners in the state and the other comprising professors and civil liberties activists as interlocuters to negotiate with the Maoists. Extending an offer for peace talks, she signed an agreement that the State government would be willing to talk to any group that lays down arms.

Maoists reject Mamata's offer

This has split public opinion in West Bengal. Many groups that had earlier supported Mamata, sees this as her going back on her poll promise. The two main points of contention are the unconditional withdrawal of forces and release of all political prisoners. Maoists rejected the offer and dubbed the development package as "lollipop".

Post-polls, Jungalmahal is a ship-wreck: says the weekly

Travelling through Jungalmahal after the polls is like navigating a ship wreck. The faultlines between the CPM and TMC run deep. And then there are new power equations, new battles fought under new acronyms, the Maoists have returned, the PCAPA is holding meetings, their earlier leader

Chhatradhar Mahato has contested the polls under a new banner (Santrash Durniti Manch SDM), the TMC is holding meetings and rallies, some CPM leaders remain, Harwad Vohini has fled or joined any of the previous groups, and sometimes it is hard to tell which new heroes are old villains in disguise.

There is also a Gunda vahini: armed and masked men on bikes. "Dead bodies will fall if you don't go to Mamata's rallies", some villagers say they heard as this vahini zoomed through the forest darkness. The weekly could not verify this independently, it is possible that these are TMC opponents.

Just as it is possible that any of these above groups could have burned Prashanto Das' house and look shop on the night of 16 July. Immediately after the incident, two trucks of villagers, assisted by local TMC leaders, drove to SDO office to demand a CRPF camp in their area. This how the Naxal conflict in West Bengal is in extricably complicated by local politics. This is why Jungalmahal continues to simmer.

To understand the fault lines, follow the story of Pallabh Das, now a daily labourer at a CRPF camp in Lalgarh. On the 16 July evening, a few days after the CM's call for peace, five policemen came to his two-room hut in the bylanes of Lalgarh. Das was not home, message was delivered to his grandmother instead: "Tell him to leave Chhatradhar's party or his life will be in danger. We will arrest him if we spot him." Das says: "They searched my room, seized blank CDs and took way my motor bike." No FIR has yet been registered, and no seizure list produced.

Das says this threat is linked not to grand war between people and the state, but to local school elections. Later in July, 18 candidates will contest for six seats in the Lalgarh Education Board. TMC and Jharkhand Party have fielded six candidates each. For the first time, Chhatradhar's new party, SDM, has fielded six. The CPM has fielded none. TMC does not want us to contest. Hence the threat. Das' logic: "Everyone has right to participate in politics. If we don't how will there be an opposition party."

It is a strange cross roads. CM's development package could render Maoists and PCPA irrelevant. CPM is not in a position to prove effective opposition, which a democracy needs. Who will provide that if not the SDM?

To understand the development challenge, zoom into Jhargram, a block that is slowly becoming the epicentre of the conflict, with the Maoist shifting base from Lalgarh. The Jhargram Development Block is one of the largest of the 29 blocks in West Midnapore district. Officials at the BDO told the weekly that until "this year (2011) polls, seven of the 13 gram panchayat's that make up the block, were deemed 'closed'. Citing the Naxal conflict as the reason, seven GP offices had shut shop, most turning into armed camps housing paramilitary forces and the Harmad. All civil administration had, ceased to function and panchayat members had fled or forced to flee.

Tapan Rana is one of them. On 13 June, following orders of the new government, Jhargram BDO ordered all closed GP offices to open. Despite the orders, Rana has not been able to return to work. His Lodhasuli Gram Panchayat office has been turned into India Reserve Battalion (IRB) camp. The weekly visited the place and found the barracks occupied by men in green fatigues. Rana could not enter the area even when he showed the BDO's letter. Jawans told him they "have been instructed to stay here in case another Silda-type attack happens", referring to the Maoist raid on an Eastern Rifles camp that killed 27 cops. Rana says: "I was not given even one room. Villagers are suffering. I can not plan roads and bridges sitting far away." Other GPs too continue to be dysfunctional. The Radhanagar GP office is also a CRPF camp. The Aduibone GP pradhan has been untraceable for the past one year.

The deputy pradhan resigned a month ago. The Salboni pradhan was murdered and all other panchayat members fled. While no official figures are available'. CRPF confirmed that GP offices continue to serve as camps. Even a meeting room at the BDO in Jhargram is home to the 2nd Battalion of the IRB. It houses 17 constables and an officer. "I don't know what to do", says BDO Sudeep Narayan Ojha.

The predicament of the pradhan and the BDO indicates the problems to be faced by the new government as it tries to usher peace in Jungalmahal: "How to balance the development and security? Can development erase the old fault lines in a place where the personal and political are so deeply intertwined?

Meanwhile, construction for a permanent CRPF base in Jungalmahal has begun. IG CRPF Alok Kumar says 143 acres have been acquired in Salboni for the base that will house the 207 CoBRA Battalion of the CRPF and a training Centre. 2000 personnel will be based here. Commandant Shyamchand Dey of the 167 Battalion speaks about the operation which is on since 2008: "We have not received any instructions for the state Government to call off operations. Operations are on because we are focussing on intelligence based ones. We are not arresting people unless we have proper proof we are organising sports events, giving free medicines, identifying blood donors, planting guava and coconut trees and repairing bridges. We want people to believe we are there for their security. But our strategy remains the same. If we find a Maoist, we will arrest him. If we are fired upon, we will fire in self-defence."

What has come as surprise in Mamata's dealing with the Naxal riddle is this appeal in the heart of Jungalmahal: "If you want to pick up a gun, do it for your country. Take the state's gun, not a private gun. I announce that 10,000 people from this area will be given police jobs, recruited in the National Volunteer Force (NVF), Home Guards and as Special Police Constables."

"This is the equivalent of making the naughtiest student the class monitor", says a TMC source. "By taking Jungalmahal youth in the police force, we are ensuring they would not join the Naxals." CRPF's Raj speaks in the same vein: "Development is needed but also need massive recruitment drive. The CRPF also recruited 456 constables from Jungalmahal in 2010, but we need more. There boys will assist us. As they know the area, they will be better placed to guide the forces."

While the government has not yet spelled out its recruitment policy, it appears dangerously similar to what the Supreme Court has recently ruled as unconstitutional— the arming of tribals as special police officers (SPOs) in anti-Naxal operations in Chhattisgarh and elsewhere in the country.

The NVF positions too temporary posts for three months. The NVF——unique to the state—— was constituted under the West Bengal National Volunteer Act, 1949, "for the protection of border districts and also to give training to some citizens in the use of fire arms so that their services could be used during an emergency." Since then, amendments to the Act have altered the duration of recruitment from 10 years to mere three months.

Even a 2002 SC order hearing a petition (West Bengal vs Jiban Krishna Das) on the NVF has ruled: "The whole concept of the National volunteer Force is different from that of the police force...It can be said that it is a standby force…to aid and help the regular police force or members of the other services. It is clear that the provision of the Act never intended to give permanency to the members of the NVF. Merely because the members have to be treated as public servants and their duties regulated by some prescribed code of conduct, it can not be said that they will have to be treated as constables of the police force."

In its order, the SC squashed the Kolkata High Court ruling that put NVF cadre at par with the police. "The direction of the division bench to give status and other benefits (to NVF) as employees of the state government was not legal. It is also not correct to say that the members of the West Bengal NVF are entitled to get permanency. According to us, they form two different classes in public service. In this background, the High Court was in error in treating them at par with the Constables of the states police force."

This SC order…itself an admission of how the NVF mirrors SPOs in Chhattisgarh…accepts and legalises the impermanent nature of NVF cadres. But perhaps in the current context of Jungalmahal, what is legal can not be the only yardstick to evaluate what is judicious and wise.

Chotton Das, one of the government appointed interlocutors, says: "Any state will have a legal police force that must function within the law. If the intention is to kill tribals and destroy people's movement, we will oppose this. We will have to wait and see what the intention is." Das is secretary, Bandi Mukti Committee.

The above is analysis of CM Mamata Banerjee's handling of Maoists within two months of her ascendance to power. To put it in brief: It is premature and a job in hurry. The weekly should have done this analysis when Mamata was 4-6 months in the Chair. It is unsatisfactory analysis, if not shoddy.

It also has unnecessary and avoidable comment on the issue of the SC verdict on NVC. What is worse, the scribe has further made his own interpretations based on very brief comments by the SC as quoted by him.

This Author feels strongly on the judiciary, including the Supreme Court, pronouncing on matters military and strategic which should not lie in its domain. It should not assume the omniscience to advise the armed forces as to how they should do their job of defending the nation. The SC must curb its temptation to pronounce themselves on such matters just because it is the last court of the land.

CM Mamata Banerjee wins her Jungalmahal battle (Achievement)

This is a success story any politician, especially a Chief Minister, can be proud of! This part narrates it from the beginning till its culmination into freeing the lawless Jungalmahal from the murderous Maoists.

She achieved this success with lots of boldness and certain degree of élan.

Full details of incidents and events leading to the final act are discussed in the following pages.

Peace talks elusive in Jungalmahal: 13 Sep 2011

As the Red ultras are cool to Mamata Banerjee's overtures

"The West Bengal Maoists seen to be gradually reverting to their old ways. Despite all out efforts by CM Mamata Banerjee to bring the rebel groups to table, the Red ultras seem to be gradually backing out of their peace promise."

The above was written by a daily in its issue dated 13 Sep 2013.[2]

Further contents of the news story gives details about the Maoists' reluctance to walk their earlier talk.

Bengal CPI (Maoist) Secretary Akash on 12 Sep 2011 aired his "doubts over the real intentions of the new government to bring peace in Jangalmahal."[3]

The main bone of contention seems to be the CM's plans to raise a 10,000-strong NVF from Jangalmahal. Terming Banerjee initiative a ploy to "set a brother against a brother", the senior rebel leader said: "Before coming to power, the CM had demanded withdrawal of CRPF from the state (Jangalmahal). She had also promised unconditional release of political prisoners but now her Government is going back on her promise.

The Maoist have already warned the villagers across the state against joining the proposed NVF. Akash added: "The Government could as well have generated employment by creating jobs in other fields, but this (NVF) move clearly vitiated the current peace and is a clear instigation by the state which is trying to walk the path taken by the Left Front Government."

The Maoists are also peeved by the Government efforts to set up a CoBRA base in Jangalmahl at Salboni in West Midnapore district. According to IG (Operations) CRPF Alok Raj the facility will spread over a 143-acre area and the "land has already been finalised for the purpose." Besides, the talks have also reached the final stage for setting up the headquarters of 165 Battalion, CRPF.

Reluctant to slacken their stranglehood on Jangalmahal, which is strategic in terms of connectivity between South India and Nepal, the Maoists would do everything to retain their writ on this stronghold.

Bengal Maoists offer one-months ceasefire

Rider: Ask Government to rein in forces; experts believe it is a ploy to regroup: 5 Oct 2011

For the first time in West Bengal, Maoist 4 Oct 2011 declared they would observed cease-fire for a month if the state government reined in the CRPF and the state police forces.

In a statement, Asham Mandal alia Akash, State Secretary, CPI (Maoist) said: "We are in favour of peace. If the state government promises to halt joint operations for a month and adhere to it in letter and spirit, we will also restrain arms for the same duration." Historian Sujato Bhadra and social activist Chotton Das, two of the six interlocutors engaged by CM Banerjee on 7 July to initiate dialogue with the rebels, have also signed the statement.

The statement further added: "It is also incumbent upon the government to seize illegal arms from vigilante groups. If we come under attack from such groups, we will bring it to the notice of the government through the mediators." Bhadra said: "We are yet to discuss the proposal with the CM. Such a meeting may take place after the Puja on 11 October." (Hindustan Times, 5.10.2011.

"I have no comment to make", said DGP Naparajit Mukherjee, who visited West Midnapur last week to meet CRPF and district officials to fine-tune the resumption of anti-Maoist operations. The Union MHA also did not comment. But sources in the security establishment were suspicious about the development. One officer wondered as to how the CPI (Maoist) could go on ceasefire in one state and fight security forces in another. He went further: "Our assessment is that the Maoists are going to use this time to plant more landmines, organise large-scale mobilization of frontal organisations and recruit cadres....This is what they did in Andhra Pradesh in 2004."

The forces had killed a Maoist for the last time in Mar 2011. After coming to power in May 2011, Banerjee had suspended anti-Maoist operations. But a series of killings by the rebels, including two TMC leaders, forced her to warn them of action on 25 Sep 2011.

Some relevant information

Bloody Corriodor

Calm after the polls: Three days after Banerjee took oath as CM on 20 May 2011, Maoist State Committee spokesman Vikram welcomed her government.

Violence resumes: End-Angust, a West Midnapore TMC leader, Rabindranath Mishra, was murdered for forming a "vigilance gang". Two more murders took place in September.

Banerjee's threat: On 26 September, she said dialogue and killing could not go together. She threatened action against Maoists.

Death toll so far in 2011 (till Sep) in clashes with the Maoists

	West Bengal	*All India*
Civilians	38	214
Security forces	1	101
Maoists	4	185
Total	**43**	**500**

"The government is earnest for talks, but Maoists should also realise that it would not sit tight if they keep on killing common people and leaders." Mamata Banerjee, West Bengal CM.

Interlocutors can continue talks with Maoists: Mamata: 19 Oct 2011

- **Mamata: Maoists must shun violence**
- **Month-long truce offer by rebels conveyed to the CM.**

"By asking the State-appointed interlocutors here (Kolkata) on Tuesday, 18 Nov 2011, to continue talks with the Maoists, to broker peace in the Jangalmahal region, West Bengal CM Mamata Banerjee may have indicated some flexibility in regard to the seven-day deadline she had given the extremists three days ago to lay down their arms and sit for negotiations."

This was the opening para of a news story on the CM meeting the negotiations, carried in a daily of 19 Oct 2011.[4]

"The dialogue process is on and will be continuing", said Sujato Bhadra, speaking to the press shortly after a strategy session held by CM Banerjee with a team of five interlocutors. Bhadra was among the five. Three senior ministers were among those present. Chotton Das, another interlocutor, told the daily: "The CM asking us to continue the dialogue process could mean that she has an open mind regarding the (7-day) deadline given to the Maoists."

The meeting was held against the back drop of fresh violence in the Bankishole area in Paschim Medinipur district where joint security forces team and a group of rebels were engaged in a gun battle earlier in the day (18 October). There was, however, no report of any casualty.

The CM reportedly told the interlocutor that Maoists will have to make a public commitment not to brandish weapons, shun violence and stop intimidating the people in Jangal Mahal. She asked them to get back to her earliest after speaking to the Maoists. Bhadra's choosing not to elaborated further on the outcome of the meeting and take any questions from journalists did not come as a surprise, considering the pressure the interlocutors are under.

The meeting came in the wake of developments that have contributed to complicating the situation. The rebels' offer of a month-long cease-fire on the condition that security operations against them were suspended has given a new twist to search for peace in Jangalmahal. The offer was formally conveyed to the CM during the meeting by the interlocutors.

There are also reports of the government seeking two additional battalions of CRPF for deployment in the Jangalmahal area——a precursor to a fresh offensive against the Maoists.

What has emerged is that Ms Banerjee would not like to call off in a hurry the dialogue process the interlocutors are engaged in, but will not hesitate to intensify security operations against the Maoists if they resort to any act of violence.

Peace initiative with Maoists salvaged after meeting with Mamata: 20 Nov 2011

"The peace initiative launched by Mamata Banerjee government after it came to power six months ago will continue. This ends, at least for now, the uncertainty that the entire process was plunged into after the team of interlocutors appointed by Ms Banerjee requested to be relieved of their assignment earlier this week."

The above was decided after a two-hour meeting held at the state-secretariat on Saturday (19 Nov 2011) between the CM and six-member team of interlocutors led by Sujato Bhadra. "Peace process will continue he told the journalists, after the meeting[5].

Bhadra said holding parleys of this sort was time-consuming. "Getting in touch with them, getting their views across to the government....going back and forth.. these things take time", he said even as he expressed anguish over the role played by a section of the media.

Another team member said the CM has asked the interlocutors to carry on with the task assigned to them. "People want place...we all want peace", he said. Asked if any discussions were held on the issue of suspension of joint operations during the peace process, the team member said that he was not in a position to share with the media everything that transpired during the long interaction.

Amid the escalating violence in the Jangalmahal area, the interlocutors, in a letter sent on 16 November to the CM had expressed desire to be relieved of their responsibilities. The positive "news" comes at the end of a rapid-fire round of developments when Ms Banerjee shifted her earlier stand to blame the Maoists for the 2010 Janeswari Express incident.

The surrender by a hard-core Maoist couple and their meeting with the CM brought some cheer which was dampened a day after a "discovery" of Maoist leaflets crying for the scalp of Ministers in the Mamata Banerjee government near a Minister's Chamber.

All but one interlocutors pull out of peace process: 29 Nov 2011

"We had taken up the issues with hope; the issue is now dead."

"The West Bengal Government's initiative to broker peace with the Maoists suffered a major set-back on 28 Nov 2011 with all but one of the six interlocutors appointed by it in July to explore the possibility of talks with the LWE informing CM Banerjee of their decision to pull out of the excercise."

The above was reported by a daily in its issue of 29 Nov 2011.[6]

The decision comes on the fourth day after the killing of CPI (Maoist) Polit Bureau member Koteswar Rao alias Kishan ji by joint security forces team in the Burisole forest of Jangalmahal region in the state's Paschim Medinipur district. One of the main interlocutors told the daily. "Our role come to an end. We had taken up the issue with hope. The issue is now dead. The suspension of the joint security operations in the Jangalmahal area was a requisite for the dialogue. While it is true that murder, violence and dialogue cannot go together, neither can military operations and dialogue."

He was obviously alluding to the most-recent security operations in which Kishanji was killed. "One can not have dialogue at gun point." He continues: "None of the two sides involved seem to be listening, and the government is more responsible [for this situation] as it failed to take advantage of the month-long truce offer by the Maoists from 30 Sep (2011)."

"The prevailing situation in Jangalmahal does not allow us to carry forward the peace talk. We have expressed our helplessness and inability to the CM", said a statement signed by Sujato Bhadra on behalf of the five of the six interlocutors, adding that one of the interlocutor had "differed on the issue." Bhadra and his associates had intimated the CM their desire to withdraw from the peace process earlier this month (Nov 2011), but decided to carry on with their efforts after the later prevailed on them to reconsider their move on 19 Nov 2011.

But this time round, the situation has undergone a qualitative change. The entire dimension of the issue and its complexity is altered. It is worst than the last time. One of the stakeholders [the Maoists] has reportedly said that it will not sit for discussions anywhere else in the country. It must be understood that Kishanji was not a simple cadre of the CPI (Maoist). He was one of their most important leaders", the interlocutor told the daily.

The interlocutor continues: "under the changed circumstances, if we carry on as interlocutors it will only create confusion and could be ascribed as a design [of the government]. We do not want to be accused of being part of such a design."

Maoist activities across Jangalmahal brought undr control: 19 Feb 2012

'Stating that Maoist activity in the state's Jangalmahal region has been considerably brought under control after the new government came to power in West Bengal, Union Home Minister P. Chidambaram (PC) said [at Kolkata] on 18 Feb 2012 that both the Central and the State Governments will work together to eliminate the LWE from the State."

"I think after the new government took over, the people of West Bengal should readily appreciate and acknowledge that the Naxal problem that was affecting the Jangalmahal region of the State has been controlled to a substantial extent", he said, at the inauguration of the Regional Hub of the NSG at Badu in state's North 24 Parganas district.

The above two paras are from a daily of 19 Feb 2012.[7]

This news story also deals with certain aspects of functioning of the NSG Hub, besides the LWE problem. For sake of integrity of the contents of this story, details of both the subjects will be included in its narration in this book.

To continue with the news story, this is what PC says further: "The success in combating Maoist problem can be attributed to cooperation between the Centre and the State government. I want to take the opportunity to warmly compliment the West Bengal government that they have accepted our advice. They have used our security forces, taken the help of central agencies and used their own intelligence to bring about considerable improvement in the situation in West Bengal... working together, I can assure that we can fully put down the Naxal menace and rid West Bengal of Naxalism."

The Home Minister who inspected the permanent infrastructure of the Regional Hub of NSG said the Hub will serve as a mini-regional centre for the region. "We want the Kolkata Hub to become a mini-regional centre.

The Hub will not only serve the states in the eastern part of India but also those in the North-East", he said.

Announcing that the State government has allocated 34 acres of land for the NSG Hub at Rajarhat in the same district, he said the facilities would be augmented there and the Hub will have double the facility than is available in Mumbai and Chennai.

He urged the state government to widen and concretise the road linking the airport to the Hub to help NSG commandos reach the airport quicker.

Ramesh pats Didi on Jangalmahal; 9 Nov 2012

Union Rural Development Minister Jairam Ramesh on 8 Nov 2012 showered wholesome praise on West Bengal CM Mamata Banerjee, terming her approach to tackle Naxalism, as the "right approach" and for showing political courage in developing Jangalmahal.

The comments hold significance because just a year ago, to be precise, on 19 Nov 2011, Ramesh after his visit to the area had expressed serious concern over the poor development performance in the former Maoist hotbed and called the situation "gloomy."[9]

Jangalmahal forest, spread over parts of three districts of the state [Paschim Medinipur, Bankura and Purulia] was the worst Naxal-affected zone in the state during CPM rule.

After meeting West Bengal Rural Development Minister Subrato Mukherjee in New Delhi, Ramesh appreciated the state government's efforts in developing Jangalmahal zone.

Ramesh was effusive in his tone and expression: "The kind of political mobilisation that happened in Jangal mahal during the last two years is worth mentioning and one should not take away the credit due to her..Mamata's approach is the right approach [for tackling Naxal problem]. She may not be our ally now but I must say that she has transformed the scenario in Jangalmahal. She had shown the political Courage required for the changes in the Naxal-hit areas."

Expressing his gratitude to Mr Ramesh, Subroto Mukherjee said: "We are getting full cooperation from him in speedy execution of projects. For Jangalmahal, we will be constructing 2000 km road under PM GSY. The state Government is on the job to introduce biometric system for NREGA. That will help the entire process become transparent and we want to introduce it in the state."

Mamata-led TMC had withdrawn support to the UPA Government over the reforms measures, including FDI in retail. The Minister also appreciated Bengal Government's role in speedy execution of MGNREGA for the rural poor. Ramesh said: "The state has ascended to Number 3 position from Number 21 in NREGA. There were about 13,000 km-long road sanctioned under Pradhan Mantri Gram Sadak Yojana (PMGYY) in 2012-13."

Jangalmahal residents vote fearlessly: 14 Jul 2013

The above is a title of an editorial in a weekly dated 14 Jul 2013, which is reproduced below verbatim[9].

- The residents of Jangalmahal, till recently a Maoist-infested region, voted in large numbers in West Bengal's Panchayat elections on 11 July. Even in former violence-prone areas like Lalgarh, Amlashole, Bagmundi, Nayagram and Ayodhya Hills, the voter turn-out was between 75-81 per cent. The tribal population in these areas could not vote in the last Assembly and Lok Sabha elections because of Maoist threats. The Jangalmahal region comprises Paschim Medinipur, Purulia and Bankura districts.

- According to several families of Amlashole, where starvation claimed several lives in 2004, vote this time was a "penance" for leaning towards the Maoists in the wake of the Left Government's apathy. Along with many surrendered Maoists, many leaders of the former People's Committee against Police Atrocities (PCPA), frontal outfit of the Maoists in Jangalmahal, contested on TMC ticket.
- Running for a Bankura district panchayat seat for the TMC, Probir Gorai, husband of Suchitra Mahato, a close aide of the slain Maoist leader Kishanji, and who had publicly surrendered to the government at the State Secretariat, said: "I will work under TMC to press for development of the region as no other CM visited this area in the past as Mamata Banerjee did."
- In West Midnapore's former CPI (Maoist) bastions of Kashpur and Garbota, where opposition political party supporters were not allowed to come out of their homes or were told in no uncertain terms on polling days that their votes were already cast, headed for palling booths in droves for the first time since 1998.

Law in the Jungle: 13 Apr 2014

"Mamata's threat to quit if the West Midnapore SP was removed on the EC's orders may have been just the kind of muscle flexing the CM is known to indulge in, but she was right in her claims about Jangalmahal. Madhuparna Das finds a region and its women thriving in peace."

This is an article on detailed assessment about the situation in Jangalmahal in Apr 2014—three years after Ms Banerji took over as CM and three weeks before the Lok Sabha polls in the area on 7 May 2014. This article appeared in a daily on 13 Apr 2014[10].

It is worth a recall that a similar assessment has been recorded in the earlier pages, that appeared in a weekly within less than two months of Ms Banerjee's ascendance to power. For obvious reasons, the preset analysis (of Apr 2014) more realistic, given its time frame.

Some relevant information

- Jangalmahal votes on 7 May (2014)
- Area of Jangalmahal: 8,000 sq km
- **Districts in Jangalmahal:** West Midnapore, Purulia and Bankura
- **Parliamentary Constituencies:** Bankura, Bishnupur, Purulia, Jhargram, Midnapur, and Ghatal, Polling is on 7 May, All the six constituencies were won by the Left in 2009.
- **Maoist violence**

  125 civilians killed in West Midnapore in 2009, 311 in 2010, 26 in 2011, and not one instance of murder or abduction in 2012-14 (till Mar 2014).
- **Panchayat participation**

  168 of the 290 panchayat pradhans in West Midnapore are women, a majority of newcomers. Over 1,100 of its total 2115 panchayat members are women. They make up around 400 of the 798 panchayat samiti members, and over 30 of the 67 zilla parishad members.

The contents of the analytical article

The article opens with an interesting paragraph commenting upon 'mercurial Mamata's' characteric style: Her defiant response when the Election Commission ordered the transfer of SP West Midnapore Bharati Ghosh on the eve of General Elections. She threatened resignation if Ghosh was shifted out. Mamata turned this confrontation with the EC into "her versus the other" debate and about "peace in Jangalmahal versus the Region going up in flames again."

If her stance that moving out Ghosh will hurt peace in Jangal is debatable, at the best, few dispute that the region spread over 8000 sqkm area and three districts, once the Worst-hit by the Maoist violence in the state, is one of the TMC regime's success story. But few saw this success coming when she rode to power in 2011, Joining hands with several outfits with close links to the Maists, in particular the PCPA. Worse than this, she had surprised her critics by denying the presence of Maoists in Jangalmahal and demanding the withdrawal of the CPMF from the state.

These two things could be a part an expected pre-poll rhetoric, and result of her not being fully aware of ground realities. She was obviously wiser after coming into power. As CM, she slowed down the pace of counter-Naxal operations initially, and then declared a ceasefire, expecting reciprocity. When the Maoists launched some violence, the tenuous cease-fire snapped.

A major turning point was the killing of Kishanji in Nov 2011. Five of the six interlocutors appointed by her to talk to the Maoists quit after Kishanji's killing. While the government ascribed his death to a well-planned encounter, the Maoists asserted he was called for a dialogue and killed. All this has been covered in the earlier pages.

In a manner of speaking, Kishanji's death paved the way for Mamata to reclaim Jangalmahal.

Mamata's 'spectacular' success

The objective 'spectacular' may indicate a bit of 'hyper' description, but it is absolutely well deserved. The simple fact is that Mamata achieved a 'peaceful' Jangalmahal within two years of assuming power—not to forget that the region was a stronghold of Maoists for years and no go area for security forces and most politicians. To put it in perspective, the operations to clear the region had been on since 2009 and some work had also been done by the Left Government in its last couple of years of a long stint of power. Even then, to achieve what she did in Jangalmahal within those two years is nothing short of spectacular! How did she achieve it?

It was her tenacity employed with certain practical wisdom that yielded results for her! With a combination of political measures and strong administrative action, including her decision against rescuing jailed PCPA (or, also PCAPA) leader Chhatradhar Mahato, she succeeded in managing to bring Maoists and their supporters into the mainstream and restore peace. To wit, in the last two years, 2012-2014 (till March), the police has not recorded a single case of murder or abduction by Maoist utras in Jangalmahal. There is more positives. In 2011, 26 Civilians had been killed by the ultras in Jangalmahal. On the other hand, 43 senior Maoist leaders have surrendered in the last three years, while several senior leaders have been arrested. In the Amlashol village middle school, one of the Jangalmahal's remotest, the student count went up to 78 in 2013, from 13 earlier.

Even voting figures make a point

One instance should suffice to indicate the change in the winds. Jhargrame Lok Sabha constituency, one of the seven in Jangalmahal region, has been won by the CPM 10 consecutive times, including the last one in 2009. In that year, a Maoist threat ensured that constituents did not venture out of their houses to cast their franchise. It is a sea change in 2014. The residents are visibly enthused about the polling. That is the measure of success wrought in by Mamata since May 2011.

Befitting the times and giving their due to the long-forgotten, or at least long-ignored, tribals, Mamata's TMC has fielded tribal Uma Soren for Jhargram seat. The TMC has fielded three star-turned politicians Sandhya Roy, Dev Adhikari, Moon Moon Sen—from three other constituencies from the Jangalmahal region. Polling in all of six constituencies of Jangalmahal is due on 7 May. All six were won by the Left in 2009.

Women to the fore

Mamata has consciously promoted women's participation in public sphere. No where is this transformation more visible than in the growing number of women in Jangalmahal's public offices. Some telling instances should make the point.

Ilabati Mahato can still remember the painful last three months of 2010 "when her densely-forested village of Sapdhara in Jhargram district—considered one of the worst Naxal-hit panchayat areas of West Bengal—witnessed 17 murders by Maoists. One of them was of school teacher Dibakar Hansda, who was killed in front of his students, a case that made national headlines. Ilabati painfully remembers that women like her would n't dare venture out of their mud homes in those days.

Here is the change, if not a revolution: In 2013, TMC approached her husband to ask her to contest for the post of pradhan of Sapdhara gram panchayat. The same year, 30 Maoist cadres became TMC candidates and won in the panchayat elections. During those polls (in 2013), Jangalmahal voted in large numbers and through the night!

Having studied up a class X, Ilabati, a housewife, was adequately qualified for the job. But she remembers: "I was nervous and in a dilemma." Not only did she win, but five of the nine members of the panchayat are women. The Sapdhara panchayat is among the 1000 in the state that recently received a grant from the World Bank for "exemplary work in project implementation", says a proud Ilabati.

Ilabati, who had never been associated with a political party till the 2013 polls, still finds it difficult to believe the change in her fortunes. She speaks up: "In 2010-2011, every day we would see a bullet-ridden body on the Sapdhara-Jamboni link road. At night, they would come to our villages with sophisticated weapons and order us to give them food and shelter. Security forces too would hold the maximun raids in our area. Six men from our village abducted in 2011 are still missing."

These are painful memories not easy to leave one's mind nor in a hurry to do so!

Now to another instance of a woman, who saw a change in her life, even if not of same magnitude as that of Ilabati's.

Lakshmirani Mandi's 'achievement' may be minor compared to Ilabati's, but for this 18-year-old, no less remarkable. The daughter of a landless agricultural labourer from Tentutala village—located in remote corner of West Midnapore——was for four years an active member of the PCPA, a frontal organisation of CPI (Maoist). She joined in 2010 [obviously, at the age of 14) soon after her brother Gopinath Mandi was dragged out of their home, charged under sections dealing with sedition and criminal conspiracy, and branded a Maoist. [It is a very normal way of people joining LWE after certain excesses committed on a member of their family by the police, for reasons valid or otherwise].

As an activist of PCPA, Laxmirani was arrested several times for blocking roads and gheraoing police camps. "Earlier this year (2014), Lakshmirani returned home." In Jan 2014, she was among a dozen teenage girls from Jangalmahal chosen and trained for a fashion show in Kolkata. The rest of the story is best told in her own words:

- "Announcements regarding the beauty pageant were made in all the villages of Dahijuri. All our friends queued up when a madam with her team came to take auditions in nearby Barro Jhuria-murrah village. Nine of us were selected from Jangalmahal. For the first time, I went out of Jhargram. For the first time, I boarded a train. We were put up at Netaji Indoor Stadium in Kolkata and stayed a week there", Lakshmirani recalls, giggling.

Now she has gone back to school to improve her educational qualifications. It is never too late in the field of education or self-improvement. Here is her further story in her own words.

- "I will perhaps never become a model, but now I want to do something. Maoist terror and repression no longer exist. Police do not visit our villages as they used to Maoists squads too do not hold meetings at night for which they used together villagers at gun point. We want to live. I want to study and want to be a teacher", Lakshmirani says, smiling.

Now to the case of a third woman, Sakolmoni Hansda, a class IX students. Like Lakshmirani, she too is enthusiastic about school. Daily, she travels at least 8 km to Dahijuri High School from her village Gosainbandh. "Earlier, I used to walk. But now I have a cycle that government gave me last year," says Sakolmoni. At 13, she was among the youngest participants at the fashion show.

There are reasons for Mamata's success

Another major decision by CM Banerjee that made big difference in the lives of the tribals was to make all tribal families as BPL to enable them to get rice at Rs 2 per kg. Sakolmoni does not remember ever having two full meals a day before that decision of the CM.

While Maoist held sway in Jangalmahal during the CPM rule —— with the Left doing nothing to make a dent in their support base among the tribals—Mamata made the first crack in that bastion by, making some Maoists join her party. TMC Salboni MLA Srikanta Mahato and its Gopiballavpur MLA Churamoni Hansda, are both former Maoist cadres. "During the Left rule, youth of Jangalmahal was forced to join the Maoists to fight the repression and torture of the CPM. But Didi has changed everything and now these youths want to join mainstream politics. So we are giving them a chance," says Srikanta Mahato.

TMC MP and Mamata's pointman in Jangalmahal, Subhendu Adhikary, says: "Didi has established a link between tribal population in Jangalmahal and the administration and politics here. If you can't involve people in the system, you can not win their trust. Didi has involved them. We could make cadres come back to mainstream politics. To increase women participation in the three-tier system, Didi told us to get more and more women panchayat candidates here."

Deepak Sarkar, CPM district secretary of West Midnapore, does not have convincing explanation of why Mamata succeeded where the Left did not. He argues: "Maoists cadres joining the TMC proves that the TMC had joined hands with them when the Left government was trying to fight the Maoists politically. Now the same political party is against the Maoists. But by joining hands with them earlier, the ruling party has been able to track the network of Maoists."

Another TMC scheme that made a difference is recruitment of 10,000 special police constables from tribal villages. Apart from providing job opportunities in a region with few avenues, it helped the administration build a vast intelligence network at the grass-roots level, keeping them abreast of any Maoist presence or fresh arrivals. There are 4-5 constables in every affected village in Jangalmahal. The network is believed to have been instrumental in recent arrest of Maoist leaders.

After Kishanji's death, the state government speeded up the recruitment of constables and home guards to ensure that the Maoist who were trying to boost their numbers did not poach Jangalmahal youth. Not only tribal men but 13,000 tribal women from three districts of Jangalmahal submitted applications for the post of junior constables in Jan 2012. Official records speak of 93, 285 tribal men and women applying for post of special police constable in 28 police stations across the three districts. About 8,000 constables have been appointed from the tribal villages.

To keep the youth away from the Maoists, the government also promoted sporting activities. It announced a Jangalmahal Cup, an annual football tournament in which 22 teams of tribal girls participated in the first year. Malti Manid, who is now in class VII, is part of the team in Jamboni where Kishanji was killed in an encounter. Malati gives details: "I started playing when I was in class V. The local clubs selected us after physical tests. I remember two years, my parents used to send me to my maternal uncle's house is Midnapur town, as our village was not safe. My father and brother were forced to join the meetings held by Maoists. But now my brother is a constable and he is posted at the Jamboni police station."

Now every block in Jangalmahal has at least a couple of girl football teams", says Durgesh Malladev, TMC president of the Jhargram sub-division.

In Nov 2012, in a rare praise, Jairam Ramesh, a Congress Minister at the Centre, applauted CM Mamata of the TMC for achieving peace in Jangalmahal— details recorded earlier in this chapter.

Sources say "the reason Mamata objected to Bharati Ghosh's transfer as SP Midnapore by the EC last week was because of the rapport she enjoys with the officer. Jangalmahal is the show-piece of the Mamata regime and she has taken care to ensure that she has officers here who meet her requirements, apart from making several visits here personally to announce schemes.

Ghosh joined the post in Aug 2013, much after peace had already returned to Jangalmahal. A police officer of the district talks about Ghosh. "She has always been seen as an official on good terms with the ruling party. She made several Maoist cadres to return to the mainstream politics and join the TMC. During her tenure, a dozen cadres became panchayat candidates. Political activities in the Maoist stronghold villages increased too."

Purnima Mandi is pradhan of the Barojhoriamurrah gram panchayat. Her husband is a teacher. "A couple of years ago, we could never think of coming out of our houses. Men and young boys used to stay out due to police raids as security men would pick any youth they saw, and we would stay inside with our children and elderly members", the 28-year-old says. "The TMC leaders convinced me that Didi wants women participation in the area to strengthen the peace process in Jangalmahal. And now, I am the panchayat pradhan."

The TMC candidate for the Jhargram parliamentary seat, Uma Soren, is a 30-year old tribal doctor. She is pursuing her MD degree.

There are other signs of change. Like the beauty parlour run by a woman entrepreneur at Belpahadi, a Maoist hot bed that was once Kishanji's favourite shelter. "Many tribal women are lining up to have their shaped or to get a facial. They all want to look beautiful," says Mala Adhikari, the owner. "We conducted a programme in which 30 tribal women were trained. A group of beauticians came and trained them. Now they can start their own beauty parlours in their homes", says sarbody Saha, BDO, Binpur II, adding that they had found a high demand for such courses.

According to Sukumar Hansda, Minister for Development of Western Region: "Bringing woman to the mainstream is an indicator of normalcy in the region. Didi always told us to get more and more tribal region into politics and other professional fields. Didi believes if women starts resisting Maoists in their villages, it would be tougher for them to recapture the area and regroup", says Hansda.

Fear of Maoist return

However, the fear that Maoists may make up a come back remains. Uma Soren campaigns with a platoon of 30 security guards armed with weapons. In the last one-and-a-half years, no senior Maoist leader has surrendered, or been arrested, while some of the dreaded leaders like Akash and Bikash are still at large.

With reports from some villages of Maoist squads issuing calls to boycott polls, Mamata asked people in her public meeting a couple of days ago to lodge FIRs if threatened.

Not that she would be unduly worried. The TMC is set for big gains in Jangalmahal's six.

They came from all over for a film festival: 13 Apr 2014

This is a story of a film festival in Jangalmahal, a far cry from the Maoist domination in that zone, carried in daily of 13 Apr 2014 and reproduced below[11].

- When film maker Pradipta Bhattacharya came to Haripada Sahitya Mandir in Purulia in February (2014) to attend the first edition of the Jangalmahal International Film Festival, he had done his homework on the political scenario of the place and thought he knew what to expect.

- "I had visited Jhargram, which falls in the area, and knew there was n't any Maoist-related violence there any more, "says Bhattacharya, who screened his debut feature film *Baakita Byaktigyato* at the festival. What he was not prepared for was the audience participation. "The hall where my film was screened was filled to capacity. It is a three-hour long film and to my surprise not a single person left during the screening. Most of them stayed back after the screening for the audience interaction and asked some pertinent questions too. I was wondering where are these people coming form"? says Bhattacharya.
- They came from Bankura, Purulia, Bokaro and even Jamshedpur to attend the festival from 7-9 February. The festival was a matter of pride for Jangalmahal, they said.
- For years we have been in the news for all the long reasons. People knew Jangalmahal as a Maoist stronghold. They assume that it is violence-ridden and has no cultural significance. We want to change that notion, says Siddharatha Roy Bhandari, a theatre artistie from the area and a member of Cine dot Manbhum, which organised the film festival.
- "We are culturally inclined youths of the area and we want this festival to go from strength to strength", adds Anirban Bandopadhyay, a member of the organising committee.
- The festival was attended by TMC leader Shantiram Mahato, Minister, Self-Help Group and Self-Employment. Stressing that, their organisation is completely apolitical, Bandopadhyay says: "He wanted to help us with the festival but unfortunately he was busy with the Rajya Sabha elections happening them".
- Eleven movies were screened at the festival, including an Iranian and a Bangladeshi film. "I was amazed at the way people reacted to the Iranian film *My Tribe.* Since the people of this area are not exposed to world cinema, I was apprehensive about their ability to grasp a sensitive film like that", says film scholar and Head of the department (Editing) of Satya jit Ray Film and Television Institute, Shyamal Karmakar.
- A festival such as this can go a long way towards benefitting the economy of a place like Jangalmahal, feels Karmakar. "This is a beautiful place and there is no reason why should shy away from it." Tourism will help develop the area and if we manage to promote this festival properly, there is no reason why it can not be a destination festival", he says.

The above text is accompanied by a picture of group of men and a couple of children standing against a cinema hall.

Its sub-title reads:

"Cabinet Minister Shantiram Mahato (Centre) at the festival."

Story through pictures

The news story recorded above also had some telling pictures accompanying it. These picture are described through their sub-titles. First will be a brief description of the pictures, then will follow the subtitle.

- 6 young girls standing in a file, with a girl shown with a measuring tape, taking sizes of their clothes.

  "Tribal girls who participated in a fashion show in Kolkata in their village in Jhargram, West Midnapore."
- A woman is shown in her office, with some other men and women sitting in front of her in a semi-circle.

  "Ilabati Mahato, the first woman gram panchayat pradhan of Sapdhara in Jhargram."
- Six young girls shown walking abreast, with one of them holding a football in her hands.

  "Girls foot ballers of the Nao Sagel Haryal Gaonta Club at Jhargram."
- A group of girls in school uniform shown riding on their bicycles.

  "Students going to school on cycles provided by the TMC government."
- A group of villagers on their cycle carrying loads of brushwood, branch of trees etc meant as a fuel for their *chulhas* are shown emerging out of a jungle clearance.

  "Recruitment of 10,000 special constables from among the tribal has made a difference."

Mamata cements Jangalmahal peace: 15 Jul 2014

Development: Rs 615 cr cement plant inaugurated in former heartland of Maoists in West Bengal, Viz Salboni.

CM Mamata Banerjee inaugurated a cement manufacturing plant at the once-Maoist hotspot of Jangalmahal on 14 Jul 2014. The Rs 615 Crore Bengal Cement Works factory at Godapisal is 8 km away from the spot where former WB CM Buddhadeb Bhattacharjee's motorcade was targeted in bomb blast in 2008. The unit is spread over 154 acres.

The above information by a daily was contained in its issue of 15 Jul 2014.[12]

The factory has been commissioned by OCL India, a Dalmia cement Bharat Company who get the land for the unit in 2012. Speaking at the inauguration, Puneet Dalmia, director, OCL India, Promised to undertake "community development works in terms of roads, bridges, health and education facilities", in the region. "We plan to scale up our presence in the West Bengal market by completing the first of investment in the plant", he said.

OCL is a major cement player in eastern India and has two factories in Rajgangpur and Cuttack in Odisha. This is the first project that has been set up in the troubled Maoist zone ever since the TMC surged to power in the state in 2011. The CM used the occasion to highlight her government's achievements.

CM Mamata Banerjee said at the inauguration:

- "During our time, Bengal has witnessed about Rs 35,000 crore in investment, the highest in the country...Jangalmahal has potential for further industrialisation.
- My Government has already drawn up an IT and industry policy and was in the process of formulating a tourism and jute policy.

Jindals warned: start work or you will lose land: 15 July 2014

West Bengal CM Mamata Banerjee has asked Jindal Steel Works to start work on the 4,000 acre land allocated to the company in 2007 at Salboni in West Midnapore, for a steel plant by the then CM Buddhadeb Bhattacharjee.

"The land can't be left unutilised for long", Mamata thundered at a rally on 14 Jul 2014 not for from the project site.[13]

Biswadip Gupta, MD of the project, preferred not to comment. In the past, JSW has sited the economy and lack of iron ore linkage as reasons for not taking the Rs 35,000 crore project forward.

Mamata, however, did not look in a mood for any further excuses. "If they do not build their plant at the earliest, we will give the land to others." She threatened.

She also demanded that the company pay Rs 5,000 per month to the families who gave up their land for the project.

Maoists make a come back in Jangalmahal villages: 5 Oct 2014

Maoists are fanning out to remote areas, urging the youth to join their squads

Maoists are attempting to replenish their cadres by covertly visiting villages in Purulia district, urging the youth from the forested village homes to join their squads. They are coming down from Ayodhya Hills in Jangalmahal region of the district in the dead of the night and moving from door to door.

The above was reported by a weekly in its issue dated 5 Oct 2014.[15]

Small groups are fanning out to remote areas to interact and empathise with villagers "to share their pain", an activity not witnessed since the death of Maoist senior leader Kishanji in an encounter with joint team of CRPF and the state police in Nov 2011 in West Midnapore's Burishole Forest.

Masquerading as Rahul, Maoist squad leader Ranjit pal, formerly active in Jharkhand, was seen doing the rounds with 50-odd men and women cadres by the residents of Purulia's Bandwan administration division. Police have confiscated posters and banners from the roads and walls of buildings in Belpahari and Balrampur, in which villagers were asked to take up arms as part of the 10-year foundation week commemorating the merger of the PWG and MCC to form the CPI (Maoist).

Local TMC Panchayat and block level leaders spearheading resistance movements against Maoist activities in Jangalmahal are coming under attack.

Aghore Hembram and Dipak Paharia managed to escape when the Maoists knocked on their doors. Paharia's elder brother Sriram, a civic volunteer recruited by the State Home Department for monitoring law and order in a Balrampur village, stays away from home in fear.

The movement of Maoist inside Jangalmahal forest also coincided with the death of a CRPF CoBRA jawan and the wounding of a commander last month in a gun battle at Jharkhand's Chekam, bordering West Midnapur.

Polcie are tight-lipped about the resurgence of Maoist activities in Jangalmahal, but the West Midnapur TMC Youth Wing President, Joy Roy, told the weekly, "yes, Maoists are trying to come back to Jangalmahal covertly, but the Central Forces and the State administration are very alert."

Roy did not rule out attacks on the local TMC leaders, but said, "they were minor incidents to create disturbances and stop governments' development activities in Jangalmahal." Disappointment against the government is rife in Jangalmahal, where a large amount of Ponzi firm

Saradha's money mobilisation took place. Some pro-TMC villagers were recruited as civic policemen after Kishanji's death and the traditional metal *dokra* craft for making crockery is fast facing extinction.

Maoist Shadow lingers on Jangalmahal

This news story is about eletioneering in Jangalmahal area for the Lok Sabha polls due in the area on 7 May 2014.

Uma Soren, 28, doctor-turned-TMC candidate from Jhargram, campaigns with 12 vehicles and 30 commandos around her, and refuses to come out of her SUV to interact with voters at Nayagram, a rocky, forested area at the tri junction of three states, viz Odisha, Jharkhand and Bengal, that is frequently visited by the Maoist cadres. "I have nothing to say; speak to my party leaders", Soren responds when asked about her experience as a first-time candidate, hand-picked by Mamata Banerjee.

While CM Mamata Banerjee hopes that her party will do extremely well in Jangalmahal, with rebel leaders Kishanji killed within six months after she assumed power, there is a fear of retaliation. Jangalmahal has five constituencies: Jhargram, Midnapur, Bankura, Bishnupur, and Purulia.[15]

The district and police administration officials say they have to be ready to fight an "invisible enemy." A police officer give more details in clarification. "CPI (Maoist) leader Akash, Bikash, Ranjit Paul, Jayanta often come here (Jhargram), we have proof of that. Our Special operations Group, SOG, missed Bikash, at least, thrice during the last one year which shows they are not sitting idle....Maoist posters calling for a poll boycott have been found in Purulia."

Vara Vara Rao, a Maoist ideologue, says: "The boycott call is valid for the entire country and Bengal is not out of that[16]."

Going by the results of the last panchayat polls in which the TMC won 80 per cent of the seats and all the three zila parishads, Mamata may be eying for a rich haul of LS seats.

Swarup Bhattacharya, TMC leader in charge of Soren's campaign, says: "Soren is part of a 35-member team of doctors and nurses working in tribal areas of Andhra Pradesh, Odisha, Jharkhand and Bengal. That is how she caught Didi's attention." The party website says that "if she is elected...she will be the first Santhal woman MP of India."

Dulal Murmu, MLA from Nayagram, defend's Soren's reclusive behaviour: "She is young, new to politics, and has been fielded from Jhargram, once a Maoist hot bed. Her fear is justified." Murmu, Soren's father, was a group D employee in the Indian Railways.

Her closest rival is CPM's Dr Pulin Behari Baskey, the sitting MP. In 2009, Baskey had won by 3.5 lakh votes, the highest for any Left candidate. Baskey say: "Tribals are our traditional voters. In 2009, amid Maoist violence and boycott calls, the tribal turn out was 90 per cent. And they had to pay for supporting us. At least, 250 of our supporters have been killed. Now we see violence by the ruling party, as all Maoist leaders have joined the TMC. We fear booth capturing."

Congress candidate Anita Hansda is daughter-in-law of Subodh Hansda, a former central minister. Anita claims, "our family has remained loyal to Congress. Her brother-in-law Dr Sukumar Hansda is a TMC minister. It is an 'interesting' case and example of family loyalty to the Congress Party when the once former Central Minister's son is a TMC Minister in Bengal!

In Bankura, nine-time MP and senior CPM leader Basudeb Acharya is dismissive of the Congress and his TMC rival, actor Moon Moon Sen. "We will win comfortably", he says.

In Purulia, Congress MLA Nepal Mahato is seen as the strongest contender after sitting Left MP Narahari Mahato.

Some other important incidents and events in West Bengal

After covering Jangalmahal extensively, now it is on to certain other events in the West Bengal State.

Security forces, Maoists exchange fire in Paschim Medinipur district: 19 Oct 2011

"Amid a deadline set by CM Banerjee to Maoist to disarm themselves and come for negotiations, there was an exchange of fire on 18 Oct 2011 between security forces and LWE at a village in the Banskisol- Alluberia area in Paschim Medinipur district. There were reports that Akash, Secretary, State Committee of the CPI (Maoist), was among the ultras who escaped."

The above was reported by a daily of 19 Oct 2011[17].

A police officer tells the daily over telephone: "We received a tip-off about the presence of Maoists and conducted a raid. The Maoists attacked the police and we returned fire." The police chased the ultras and they managed to escape. However, a detonator, a .303 rifle, 10 rounds of ammunition, Maoist literature and some were recovered from the site.

At a public rally in Jhargram on 15 Oct 2011, Ms Banerjee said she had "fulfilled her promise" to Maoists and "there was no joint operation in Jangalmahal for the last four-and-a-half months [that her Government has been in power]". She said she is giving Maoists another seven days to agree for "negotiations if you give up arms."

The raid was conducted on a day when a meeting the CM and a team of interlocutors, appointed by the State Government to bring Maoists to the negotiations table, was scheduled (18 Oct 2011) to be held.

Maoist poster found outside Minister's office: 19 Nov 2011

State Food and Supply Minister Jyoti Priya Mallick said in Kolkata 18 Nov 2011 that Maoist posters threatening his life had been found in the lobby outside his office. "They could not paste the posters. So they scattered them in the lobby and ran away....Eleven posters were found. The posters demanded head of the Food Minister", he said.

Mr Mallick said the Maoists were opposed to the development initiatives of the TMC-led government.

He said 53 outlets had been set up in the Maoist-affected Jangalmahal region and another 47 will soon be opened to provide subsidised food grains to the people in the region.

CM Mamata Banerjee reacted to the incident in an "interview to a local television channel during the day (18 November)."[18]

Mamata's 'Maoist' attends BJP rally: 2 Dec 2012

Shiladitya had told Mamata not to make empty promises as farmers we dying

Shiladitya Choudhury, a marginal farmer from Jangalmahal, who was arrested after being dubbed a Maoist by Mamata Banerjee for questioning her commitment to farmers was present at a BJP rally in Kolkata[19].

Shiladitya's arrest from a Belpahari rally, presided over by Mamata Banerjee in July 2011, sparked wide-spread protests and a probe was ordered by the State Human Rights Commission. Surprising every body present, Shiladitya was brought on stage by BJP State President Rahul Sinha. Holding Shiladitya's hand, Sinha said: "He is attracted to the BJP Party, but not a member as yet."

Shiladitya had told Mamata not to make empty promises as farmers were dying in the state for lack of money and asked what she was doing for them.

Didi claims Left, Congress, media and Maoists want to eliminate her 20 June 2013

"CM Mamata Banerjee now has many 'assassins' to worry about. They include the Central government and its agencies, the usual suspect, CPI(M), the Congress, Maoist and even a section of the media."

"Banerjee on 19 June 2013 kicked off her panchayat poll campaign from Gaighata in North 24 Parganas, 60 km from Kolkata, accusing almost everyone of conspiring to kill her."

The above scary scenario was reported by a daily in its issue of 20 June 2013[20].

"I have information and even the police told me that the CPM, Congress, Maoists and a section of the media are conspiring to kill me. Day before yesterday, when I went there (village of a college student raped and murdered on 8 June), I was not aware a (pro-Maoist) outfit was entrenched there", she said in a meeting. She was booed for her belated sympathy when she visited the family of the victim at Kamdani village on 17 June. A day before her visit, representatives of five ultra-Left outfits including Matangini Mahila Samiti carried out a rally in the area.

But she did not explain why and how her opponents were plotting to eliminate her.

Panchayat Polls may be postponed

With the State and Central governments in a legal battle over security forces, the panchayat poll may not take place in July (2013). The State Election Commission says it needs 1.49 lakh security men for the first phase due on 2 July but the State has only 48,000 personnel.

"It is increasingly becoming unlikely that the polls could be held on time. We are all waiting to hear what the court decides on Monday [22 June]," said an official of the poll panel.

Last of the IM's local leadership in net: 26 Mar 2014

After Wagas, Tehseen Akhtar alias Monu is arrested in Naxalbari

The news story appearing in a daily of 26 Mar 2014, under the above-mentioned headline and also its sub-title are indicative of, at first sight, an interesting interpretation of the two facts: arrest of an IM terrorist, and of greater interest, is the venue of arrest, the Naxalbari region of Darjeeling district of West Bengal. An IM terrorist taking shelter in one-time epicentre of LWE in India: is it a matter of chance and convenience or is there something more sinister to it[21]?

The special cell of the Delhi Police on 25 Mar 2014 said it had arrested a suspected key Indian Mujahideen (IM) operative and the terrorist group's operational chief in the country, Tehseen Akhtar alias Monu, from Naxalbari.

The announcement came three days after the arrest of another alleged top IM operative, Pakistani national Zia-ur-Rehman alias waqas, from

Ajmer, Rajasthan. Security agencies believe the two arrests are a huge set back to the IM as most of its senior members across the country are now in custody.

24-year-old Tehseen was hiding near the India-Nepal border in the Pani Tankhi area of Naxalbari and the Union MHA arranged for a chartered aircraft to bring him to the capital from Bagdogra airport in West Bengal. Tehseen, whose name has figured in several bomb attacks in recent years, including blasts in Mumbai, Hyderabad and Varanasi, is believed to have taken over the reins of IM after the arrest of co-founder Yasin Bhatkal last August.

SN Srivastava, Special Commissioner of Police (special cell) said Tehseen was arrested after Waqas' interrogation. Waqas was arrested 22 March morning from outside the Ajmer railway station while he was on his way to meet three associates in Rajasthan.

Shrivastava told the daily. "Tehseen is being brought to Delhi by our men. It is too early to divulge what he was planning. As of now, we can say he was running the operations in India and was the Key link between the IM and several splinter groups of SIMI. Since he was the head of IM, we will now verify the claims made by the four operatives arrested recently".

Police claimed Tehseen had fled to Jaipur after Bhatkal's arrests and stayed in the house of three operatives arrested a few days back. He is later believed to have stayed with Waqas in Munnar in Kerala. He is also said to have fled to Nepal for a month, before returning to the country a few days ago. Police suspect he was trying to flee either to Bangladesh or Nepal and had asked Waqas and three operatives to meet in Rajasthan for a terror strick. The three operatives told the police that Waqas and Tehseen had discussed avenging the 2011 Gopalgarh riot in Bharatpur district of Rajasthan.

Tehseen, carrying a bounty of Rs 50 lakh on his head, hails from Darbhanga, Bihar. He was introduced to Bhatkal by Gayur Jamali and learnt to make bombs from IM operative Qoated Siddique.

He had received Waqas and Asadullah Akhtar, who was arrested with Yasin Bhatkal in Khatmandu in 2013. He had planned bomb blasts in Varanasi, Mumbai and Hyderabad since 2010. Waqas and other suspects told interrogators that although Tehseen had not been in IM for too long, he had made it to the top fast and impressed the Bhatkal brothers in Pakistan. He was managing all modules in India after Bhatkal was arrested.

During his preliminary interrogation, Tehseen is believed to have claimed that two LeT operatives from Pakistan had joined recently and had infiltrated into UP to carry out fidayeen attacks. Sources said the claim would be verified and the UP ATS alerted.

North-East India

It should be expected that having reached West Bengal, the Maoists would surely try to go further east of the country to establish their presence in Inida's North-East.

The last parts of this chapter examine this possibility.

"Maoists look at the North-East"

With the collapse of insurgencies in the North-Eastern States, the Maoists are trying to secure a toe-hold in the region by striking deals with rump outfits.

The above is the title of an article on the issue, with its blurb that appeared in a daily of 5 Nov 2012.[22]

Its opening two paragraphs are reproduced here:

- "It is time when the conflict profile in the North-East is improving gradually, with fatalities recording a steep decline, and the insurgent groups are being progressively marginalised, the CPI (Maoist) is making determined moves to fill the void, raising grave concerns within the country's security establishment. If recent reports are any indication, the Maoists, who far long have been forging connections with the insurgents in this troubled region, have now created a strong presence and are in the process of further consolidating their base."
- "The Union MHA recently asked the police and security forces across the Norht-East to remain alert and vigilant, as the entire region has of late been facing an upsurge of disquiet on different issues, and the Maoists are known to capitalise on mass movements to establish their roots. The Maoists are specially targeting victims of ethnic riots, floods and erosion, besides olienated sections in tribal communities, for recruitment and to expand their 'ideological support base.' As a result, largely peaceful Arunachal Pradesh has emerged as a hotbed of Maoist activity, with people in the Dibang valley region of the state protesting against the 3,000 MW Dibang Multipurpose Project at New Anaya."

The above is as clear an opening of Maoist exertions to spread their footprints in the North-East as any. The author of the article is a well-known scholar on the issue, presently with the prestigious Delhi-based think-tank Institute of Conflict Management.

The remaining arguments in his article are recorded below, with few changes.

Reports indicate that the Eastern Region Bureau (ERB) of CPI (Maoist), under Koteshwara Rao alias Kishanji, national chief of People's Liberation Guerrila Army (PLGA) and Politburo member, has been entrusted with the task of establishing a foot-hold in the North-East. Trends indicate that the Maoists are engaged in a bid to set up a corridor through north Bengal, particularly Siliguri, linking their primary Red Corridor strongholds with the North-East to access the predominant route for the weapon smuggling into the country. With the Maoists regaining some of their foot-holds in the Jangalmahal area of West Bengal, it has become easier for them to penetrate deeper into the North-East.

There are reports suggesting Maoists already have 'arrangements' with some insurgent outfits in place, besides their decision to set up their own units in the region, especially in Assam. Certain modules of theirs are believed to be already operative. A news story, citing an unidentified source, says: "There are specific intelligence inputs indicating that youth from Assam are veering towards the Maoist philosophy. We have been exchanging information with all intelligence agencies and it seems that the Maoists are trying to establish their base in Assam."

Here is more concrete evidence of initial success achieved by the Maoists in this region.

> "The arrests of the President of Assam Students Youth Organisation (ASYO) Aditya Bora, General Secretary, Assam Chah Janajati Suraksha Samiti (ACJSS) Tingrai Orang aud another North-East militant at a Maoist camp in the Saranda Forest bordering Odisha and Jharkhand in early 2012 invited attention to the fact that Maoist 'Upper Assam Leading Committee, (UALC) was already active in Assam. The UALC, floated by the Maoists has received Rs 3,00,000 in 2011 and Rs 5,00,000 in 2010 from the CPI (Maoist) towards "organisational expenses."

Meanwhile media reports tell us that some 18 Maoist cadres were arrested in Assam's Tinsukia and Sivsagar districts during Sep-Oct 2012. A police officer in Tinsukia district tells the daily: "What is worrying is that most of there arrested persons are ethnic Assamese youth. A few of them have received training in Jharkhand and Manipur." Earlier on 29 Jan 2011, the police had arrested six Brihat Nadibandh Pratirudh Manch (Mega Dam Project Forum or BN PM) activists, including two women from various locations in Dhemaji district of Assam. All admitted to their Maoist links.

Maoists are also trying to extend their base into the Goalpara, Kokrajhar, Dhubri, Kamrup, Sonitpur, and Darrang districts of Assam. As per the disclosures by Tarjan Majhi, Sonitpur District Commander of the Adivasi People's Army (APA), who was arrested along with five others in the late 2011, at Bhairabguri in Sonitpur district, 'Sergeant-Major Das' of ULFA had provided arms training to APA cadre at Majbat in Udalguri district, and helped them establish contacts with other Maoists.

The Maoists are known to have forged links with ULFA, APA, Krishak Mukti Sangram Samiti (KMSS), National Democratic Front of Bodoland (NDFB) and All-Adivasi National Liberation Army (AANLA) in Assam. State CM Tarun Gogoi said on 2 Sep 2012: "Maoists have infiltrated into the State. ULFA is helping them to grow. Some youth from the State took training in Maoist camps outside the state." Mr Gogoi disclosed that Maoists "have two 'overground' or cover organisations in Assam, viz ASYO and ACJSS".

Earlier, the CM had asserted that several organisations in Assam had links with the Maoists. He particularly mentioned two of them: KMSS and AANLA. He was emphatic: "I am speaking on the basis of intelligence inputs and evidence. There are several organisations which has links with Maoists. I don't want to name all. The KMSS and AANLA have links with Maoists. Their members had gone to take training (at Maoist camps)". Significantly, way back on 30 Jul 2008, two AANLA cadres viz, Mikhail Bina and Raju Gaur, were arrested at Golaghat.

They had confessed that a large number of outfits were being trained by the Maoists at their Jharkhand Camps.

The Maoists' links with ULFA have a long history and have once again been admitted by Kishan ji in a media interview published in January (2011): "We unconditionally support ULFA's struggle for self-determination in Assam. We only want them to stop attack the Indian proletariat. We will continue to engage with ULFA on this issue...ULFA can not ignore the revolutionary struggle of Indians and our enormous goodwill for their struggle…They have trust us… I sincerely want ULFA, the PLA and other such groups fighting for separate home lands or self-determination to fight the exploitative Indian State alongside us."

The NDFB has also declared their support for the Maoists. Its 'chairman' DR Nabla, in a statement e-mailed to the media, had said a couple of years ago: "I would like to agree and congratulate the Maoists who are fighting for their legitimate rights and also extend all help to them in their fight against the ruling cliques".

Notably, a 21 Jun 2012 report stated that militants of the anti-talks faction of the NDFB [NDFB-ATF] had taken refuge in the northern areas of West Bengal. Similarly, in Manipur the Maoists have already signed an agreement with the PLA. Incidentally, the PLA has signed three joint resolutions with the Maoists to carry on their respective 'struggles'. These links came to the fore during the month long operation Monsoon in the Saranda Forest of Jharkhand's West Singhbhum District.

A picture speaks loudly

This analysis (article) has a large picture in its centre. It shows an old women crying, flanked by two young girls. At the end of the article, there is a subtitle for this picture. "The accompanying visual shows the grieving grand mother of Manipur CRPF jawan IM Singha killed by the Maoists."

Editorial Comment on the article

As a practice, analytical articles from the newspapers and periodicals are mostly accepted and included in this work in their original text. Certain changes are made only if the text or its grammar are found wanting.

But if there is factual error, then an editorial comment is added, as this one. The text mentions Kishanji as chief of the ERB in Nov 2012 [the date of publication of this article] and his media interview published in Jan 2012. These are major faux pas. Kishanji was killed in an encounter in Nov 2011!

Four Maoists killed in Assam shoot out: 10 May 2012

Four Maoists, including a local commander, were killed in an encounter with police at Sadiya in Assam's Tinsukia district on 9 May 2012, the state police said.

A police commando was injured in the shoot out, the first involving Maoists in the State. It is deemed a major blow...killing of four Maoists...to Maoists' who are trying to extend their base into Assam.

"About 10.45 AM 9 May, police killed four Maoists at Borgora. The dead include top Maoists leader Siddharatha Borgohain, while police commando Achinta Das received a bullet injury in his leg", said State Home Secretary GD Tripathi. The other three slain was identified as Rajib Gogoi, Arup Chetia, and Kamala Burhagohain.

Three AK-47s, two grenades, and a huge cache of ammunition were recovered from their possession. A source disclosed the AK-47s were among the weapons the Maoists had snatched from the police in Rajobari in Tinsukia district in 2011. Several documents, including letters seeking money contributions, were also recovered.

A police officer said: "Last year, the first military commander of the Maoists in Assam, Paul Gogoi was killed by security forces[23].

Naxal threat, Assam violence, top security Review Agenda: 3 Sep 2012

"Prime Minister Manmohan Singh will next week review the security situation in the country with top police officers at a high-level conference in the backdrop of fresh statistics that indicate the number of districts under Naxal influence had increased over the last one year."

This was reported by a daily on 3 Sep 2012[24].

The issues high on the agenda during the three-day conference starting on 6 Sep 2012 will be: recent violence in Assam and subsequent exodus of North-Eastern people from different parts of the country; threats posed by activities in the cyber world; increased infiltration attempts from across the Indo-Pak border, and ongoing operations against the Maoists.

But the conference, the first to be attended by Home Minister Sushil Kumar Shinde, will be an opportunity for the new minister to articulate his position on the key internal security challenges. This is particularly true of the government policy on Naxal insurrection, something that had undergone a muanced shift during P Chidambram's stint as the Home Minister who recognized that security had to precede development in these [Naxal-hit] areas.

The conference also comes at a time when fresh statistics indicate the governments' success in reducing the number of districts under Naxal control might have been too optimistic. The MHA hold that the number of Naxal-hit districts had declined from a high of 223 in 2008 to a little over 180 in 2011. The government, however, recently revised its assessment and declared that 203 districts were under the influence of Maoists. This list includes three North-Eastern States of Arunachal Pradesh, Assam and Tripura.

[It needs to be mentioned here that the two most-affected districts of Arunachal under Maoist influence are Changlang and Tirap, touching or neighbouring Nagaland/Naga Hills. Earlier these two districts provided transit route to the Naga militants of the 'K' faction to cross over to their strongholds in Myanmar (then Burma)]

"Two Assam districts may be declared Maoist-hit": Ramesh 2 Dec 2012

Union Minister for Rural Developement Jairam Ramesh said 1 Dec 2012 that two districts of Assam might soon be included in the list of Maoist-insurgency or the LWE hit districts of the country. The two are Tinsukia and Dibrugarh.

This was reported by a daily in its issue of 2 Dec 2012.

Ramesh said this while addressing a press conference in Guwahati on the 1st, adding that his Ministry has moved the proposal in this regard to the Planning Commission as there are reports that the Maoist activity is on the rise in these two districts. The minister said: "Two districts of Assam might join the list of LWE-hit districts in the country as his Ministry has moved a proposal to the Planning Commission in this regard." The two, if included in the list of LWE-hit districts, will receive a special package of Rs 30 Cr each annually for development activities. At present, there are 82 such districts across the country included in the list under the Integrated Action Plan (IAP), which is implemented by the Planning Commission.

Earlier, the Assam Government had taken up the matter several times with the PMO. During PM Manmohan Singh's visit to Assam in April (2012), state CM Gogoi had appealed to him to include seven districts of Assam under the IAP. The Assam Government had already identified seven such districts of the state where the Maoist activities are growing and asked the DCs of the concerned districts to implement more development schemes in the areas.

The Union Minister has also said that about 13,000 km of road is being built in Assam with maximum unacceptable quality of 5 per cent in the last 11 years. He also said the proposal by the Assam Government for setting up of an academy of construction in the state has been agreed in principle by the Central Government, while the latter is considering the state's proposal to have an equipment bank, which will be useful for the construction agencies in the region.

Declare Tinsukia and Dibrugarh as LWE affected districts: Jairam 2 Dec 2012

This is the second daily covering the same issue, which has been included in the text and already discussed in the previous entry. Only additional points from this news story will be taken up, avoiding any repetition[26].

"Couple of months ago, I had visited Tinsukia and Dibrugarh and one of the suggestions that I made to the PM was that Tinsukia particularly and Dibrugarh also should be declared as LWE-affected districts" Union Rural Development Minister Jairam Ramesh said 1 Dec 2012.

As per intelligence, there is evidence about the presence of Maoist in both these districts, he said. "The PM has reacted positively. And, we are expecting the Planning Commission to make a formal announcement. Special PM Gram Sadak Yojana would be extended to Tinsukia and Dibrugarh. These areas are very remote. They require infrastructure, roads and bridges particularly.

"Under-attack Adivasis might look up to Maoists, fret security agencies": 27 Dec 2014[27]

"Security agencies engaged in counter-insurgency operations in Assam are concerned about the possibility of Adivasis moving closer to Maoists because of frequent attack on them".

This was reported by a daily in its issue of 27 Dec 2014.

In recent years, Maoists have stepped up their activities in Assam's tea belt dominated by Adivasis. Similar fears raised by security forces about Muslims, after the frequent Bodo attacks against them in 2013 and in the past, have now turned true as elements from Bangladesh have infiltrated into the minority community.

"After being at the receiving end, each community will tend to look for ways to defend itself", said a police officer. Significantly, every community in Assam has more than one outfit. The ULFA represented the majority Assamese community, while there have been more than three Bodo outfits.

There are five Adivasi militant outfits, all of which were engaged in peace process during P Chidambram's time as Home Minister.

"They have already made their presence known in Lakhimpur, Golaghat, Dhemaji and Tinsukia districts in Assam", a security source said.

Notes

1. Tusha Mittal, The Tehelka, 30 July 2011.
2. Saugar Sengupta, The Pioneer, 13 Sep 2011.
3. This Author prefers this 'pure' spelling of Jangalmahal than the hybrid Junglemahal.
4. Marcus Dam, the Hindu, 19 Oct 2011.
5. Indrani Dutta, The Hindu(?), 20 Nov 2011.
6. Marcus Dam, ibid, 29 Nov 2011.
7. Shiv Sahay Singh, The Hindu, 19 Feb 2012.
8. PNS, The Pioneer, 9 Nov 2012.
9. Susenjit Guha, Sunday Guardian, 14 Jul 2013.
10. Madhuparna Das, Indian Express, 13 Apr 2014.
11. Prem Kumar Biswas, ibid, 13 Apr 2014.

12. Kaushik Dutta, Hindustan Times, 15 July 2014.
13. HT Correspondent, *ibid.*
14. Susenjit Guha, Sunday Guardian, 5 Oct 2014.
15. It needs to be noted as per a daily, quoted in the earlier pages, there are six constituencies in the Region.
16. Madhuparna Das, Indian Expres, 7 May 2015.
17. Anansya Dutta, The Hindu, 19 Oct 2011.
18. Ananya Dutta, The Hindu, 19 Nov 2011.
19. Susenjit Guha, Sunday Guardian, 2 Dec 2012.
20. HT Correspondent, Hindustan Times, 20 Jun 2013.
21. Pravesh Lama and Ananya Bhardwaj, Indian Express, 26 Mar 2014.
22. Ajit Kumar Singh, The Pioneer, 5 Nov 2012.
23. TNS, Times of India, 10 May 2012.
24. HT Correspondent, Hindustan Times, 3 Sep 2012.
25. Anup Sharma, The Pioneer, 2 Dec 2012.
26. PTI, Indian Express, 2 Dec 2012.
27. Prabin Kalita, Times of India, 27 Dec 2014.

34

Chhattisgarh update 1

Chhattisgarh

Finger print data base for surveillance on Maoists in Chhattisgarh soon: 13 Nov. 2011

"If all goes as planned, district police stations in the state may soon maintain a data base of the fingerprints of every cook, waiter and helper in every hotel, restaurant and road side Dhaba (eatery) across the state. The information, the police hope, will help security forces in their battle against the guerrilla army of the CPI (Maoist)".

This was reported by a daily in its 13 Nov 2011 issue.[1] State's ADG (Naxal Operations) Ram Niwas explained to the daily: "The fingerprints will be stored at the district level and shall aid the police. The prints will not be recorded as biometric information but as ink-impressions on paper…..The prints will be collected as part of a broader police strategy to improve surveillance across the states. We issued an order to all districts a few months ago to improve checking at hotels, dhabas, airports, bus stands and shops selling electrical goods. The exact implementation has been left to the SPs of the districts".

In the Rajnandgaon district, for instance, the police have ordered all shopkeepers to maintain a record of all persons who purchase more than 200 feet of electrical wire, as the wire could be used by Maoist cadres to trigger IEDs. The IEDs account for 40 per cent of all police deaths in anti-Maoist operations in the state since mid-2007. But the district shopkeepers feel the idea is ill conceived and hard to implement: "It is hard for us to maintain records for every person who buys wire from us…. Most of our customers buy more than 200 feet of wire, and they go elsewhere when we ask for their name, address and mobile numbers", said a prominent electrical shop owner Raja Bojwani to the daily. Bojwani further said: "The police order came just a few weeks before Diwali, a time when business is hectic....Last year, the police asked all grain merchants to report anyone who bought more than a certain amount of grain, as he might be a Maoist supplier".

SP Rajnandgaon BN Meena disputed Bojwani's assertions:" All shopkeepers need to maintain records for the purpose of paying sales tax in any case. We are simply asking them to maintain records of their customers and report any suspicious person. My department is still developing the surveillance apparatus in the district. We are not working on any fixed formula at present".

Methodology

- Prints would be collected as a part of a broader police strategy to improve surveillance.
- Increase security at hotels, dhabas, airports, bus stand, and shops selling electrical goods.

Maoists master skill of making weapons: 2 Apr 2012

List includes hand grenades rockets, launchers, rifles, booby traps

- Technique involves making weapons parts in workshops and assembling them in Bastar.
- Maoist started such unit's way back in 1989.

"Technical wizards among Maoist rebels have apparently mastered the art of reverse engineering".

"Working in nondescript workshops in industrial areas of various cities, Maoist techies made grenades, rifles, booby traps, rockets and rocket launchers, pressure activated mines and even carbine, sub-machines guns, using volumes of technical diagrams".

"These weapons were made using the commonly available mechanical equipmenta such as lathe machines".

These opening paragraphs under the above mentioned headline are illustrative of the skills Maoist techies have in developing a variety of weaponry that can be deployed effectively against the security forces during their anti-Maoist operations. The news analysis appeared in a daily in its issue of 2 Apr 2012.[2]

Other details from the article are given in the succeeding pages.

These weapons provided a tactical advantage to Maoists in successfully preventing the Advance of security forces into their strongholds in Bastar or Saranda forests of Jharkhand.

It is believed such units have been set up in Tamil Nadu, Karnataka, Bihar, Jharkhand, Chhattisgarh, Odisha, Maharashtra and Andhra Pradesh.

The recent arrest of a top Maoist leader, Sadanala Ramakrishna alias Dokra, has thrown more light on the vast network of these units. Dokra, who holds a Mechanical Engineering degree from the Regional Engineering College (renamed as National Institute of Technology, NIT) in Warangal, was the chief of the Technical Research and Arms Manufacturing (TRAM) units. He is said to be an exceptionally intelligent engineer.

Eluded intelligence

The methods adopted by TRAM units were so ingenious that they escaped the attention of intelligence agencies as well as local police.

Parts of these weapons were made in cities such as Bhopal, Rourkela, Chennai, Kolkata, Bangaluru and Mumbai and sent to Bastar where 'mobile assembly units' assembled them to make weapons.

Informed sources say Maoists started such units way back in 1989. They set up a 'technical unit' led by Dokra in Basavanagudi area of Bangalore. It was later shifted to Sholapur and to Pune for a variety of reasons.

At that time their focus was more on making double barrel weapons. But soon they laid emphasis on producing bombs and weapons such as rockets and rocket launchers. This came to light only in Sep 2006, when the police seized a huge contingent of rocket launchers in Mahabubnagar and Prakasam districts of Andhra Pradesh.

Within a fornight, Maoist techie Thota Kumara Swamy alias 'Tech Madhu' was arrested. His interrogation led to the busting of weapon parts making units in Ambattur industrial area of Chennai and in Bhopal and Rourkela.

- 'Tech Madhu' told police that he had manufactured 1550 rockets and 40 shoulder-fired rocket launchers.
- "Police believe that Dokra manufactured thousands of rockets and hundreds of launchers in addition to thousands of pressure-activated mines.

Congress leadership ambushed Chhattisgarh: 25 May 2013

A critique by various persons and newspapers

The Maoists achieved a major success on 25 May 2013, when they ambushed a convoy of Congress leaders and practically wiped out its entire leadership in the State in one lethal blow.

As it was an important event in the history of LWE movement in the country, it is discussed in details from various angles in the succeeding pages.

Insider hand in ambush: Karma's son: "Raman used my dad and then dumped him"

It is a news story datelined Allahabad, 31 May 2013. It is entirely based on what the son of the slain leader Mahendra Karma told the press on 31 May 2013 at Allahabad where he had gone to immense the ashes of his father at the Sangam.

It appeared in the issue of 1 June 2013 of a national daily[3].

"Maoist's meticulous planning for the 25 May attack on the Congress convey in Bastar indicated that they had 'targeted a particular line of the congress leadership." This was Deepak Karma speaking, virtually giving credence to conspiracy theories on alleged involvement of an insider (belonging to the rival faction of the Congress), resulting in the killing of his father Mahendra Karma, along with other Congress leaders.

Deepak told the daily at Sangam, "Maosits are well organized and armed to the teeth. But they cannot carry out such a major operation successfully without inputs on the Congress leader's movement. This information was provided by someone who was privy to the movement plan".

Besides blaming a Congress faction for the death of his father, he also accused CM Ram Singh of "betraying" his father by disbanding Salma Judum: "After coming to power in 2004, Raman Singh used my father and later dumped him. My father used the outfit (Salma Judum) to destroy Maoist network. However his dream was shattered after the Chhattisgarh government withdrawn support to the movement".

Being an astute politician, Deepak would not say, not to speak of 'admit', that the Judum was disbanded under the orders of country's highest Court!

No conspiracy, it is an act of terror: says Shinde: 1 Jun 2013

Terming the 25 Amy Maoist attack in Chhattisgarh as an "act of terror", Union Home Minister Sushil Kumar Shinde on 31 May 2013 said security lapses could have led to the ambush that virtually wiped out the state's Congress leadership[4].

"Whether there was an intelligence failure or any other conspiracy will be revealed after the probe", Shinde said, after reviewing the security situation in the wake of the 25th attack. He adds:

"We have asked the probe agencies to get to the truth without being influenced by anything. The Centre and the State Government have decided on a joint action to deal with the Maoists. We have assured the State of all possible assistance. A commando force on the lines of Andhra Pradesh elite anti-Maoist force, the Greyhounds, needs to be raised in all the Maoist-hit states".

He, however, dismissed the conspiracy theories, linking Congress insiders to the plot.

30 Kg of high-grade ammonium nitrate used in Bastar attack

The same issue carries the details of explosives and materials used by the ultras to trigger blasts that intercepted the convey. "Maoists used nearly 30 Kg of high grade ammonium nitrate and military grade Chinese hand grenades to trigger blasts that intercepted the convoy of Congress leaders at Darbha Ghati in Bastar during the 25 May attack that killed 25 people."[5]

Samples of the explosive materials have been sent to forensic laboratories in Kolkata and Hyderabad. A senior forensic expert offered that explosive materials might have been mixed with ammonium nitrate to trigger the deadly blast.

War of complexities: 2 Jun 2013

- **Clash:** The audatious attack by Naxalites on 25 May which took the lives of the 28 people have brought the spotlight back on three-decade old internal conflict. Between the Naxals and the state, it is the local tribals who suffer.
- This is the title of an analytical article on the issue of Maoist insurrection that appeared in a daily on 2 Jun 2013. The article that follows is also on the same subject by different scribes. Both analyzed are recorded here in extenso: First the "War of Complexties."[6]
- The talk of thousands of crores of development programmes and legislations to improve their lot puzzles Pitam Mukka, 51, a tribal hailing from Kavalnar, near Pharaspal in Dantewada (Pharaspal is the native village of senior Congress leader Mahendra Karma who was killed by Maoists in 25 May attack). Mukka used to farm on his small piece of land and collected minor forest produce– a life line for thousands like him in the Bastar forests. Life was simple".

- But that was during the 1990s. Now I work as a daily wage contract worker. If there is no work, I have to struggle to feed my family of six", he says.
- Mukka's story is typical to Bastar where thousands of tribals feel deprived in their own land, often attributed to the excesses by private money lenders or junior government functionaries and officials in the revenue and forest departments.
- It was those years, the 1990s, when the Naxals set up their activities in Chhattisgarh, then a part of MP. The Maoists capitalised on the lopsided governance structures and exploited the growing discontent to organise the people against the government of the day.
- Government intervention through the laws like the Forest Laws Act 2006 ensuring rights over land to the tribals came at least 10 years too late for people like Mukka who were by then had been separated from their routes and resources.
- It was three years later—in the summer of 2009— that the government woke up to the crisis at hand. Union Home minister P. Chidambram realised that the Maoists just could not be wished away. Maoists had killed 900 people that year (2009). The states did not have the money, resources or even political will to take on the LWE. That laid the foundation for centrally coordinated anti-Maoist offensive, underway during the last three years (2010-13) and grounded in the common sense that the government could not develop the land it could not entre. The rule: enter, hold and develop.
- Around the time of 25 May attack, there were 82,000 CAPF personnel in the Red Corridor. It was double the number of the Central forces fighting the Maoists before the Centre launched the all out offensive.

At least for Mukka there is some government interventions, even if not fully sufficient, like the monthly ration under the public distribution system (PDS) and NREGA wages. But lakhs of his counterparts in the interiors of Chhattisgarh Dandakaranya there was no government earlier nor it is there now, at least not an elected one. It is the ultras who hold sway of such areas—large swathes of forests in Central India and established 'liberated zones' like Abujhmad—completely inaccessible to the government machinery or security forces.

LWE was termed the biggest internal security threat to India's security, and Chhattisgarh has become its citadel. The States police budget rose four fold to Rs 1019 cr in 2010-11, compared to a decade earlier, when the State was created in 2001. The State has also the highest deployments of CAPF in the country. Even then, its security structure is awry. The ultras have consistently; with strategic lulls in between, executed attacks, which are essentially targeting the security forces "Violence remains the political philosophy of Maoists", say PC Hota, a scholar Maoist strategy and history.

The Salwa Judum, brain child of Karma who was killed in the 25 May attack, enlisted and armed tribals miffed by the Maoists till the SC termed it illegal and unconstitutional, disbanding it two years back, (in 2011). In several cases, innocent tribals were caught in the cross fire resulting in the diminution of the humane face the Maoists had assumed, the do-gooders fighting for the rights of the tribals. Of late and understandably, there are voices against the Maoists influence. "Naxals are no well wishers of the locals and have, in fact destroyed their culture", says BK Manish, a tribal rights activists. But the problem, Manish says, is the government "punishing its concept of development without asking the tribals villagers exactly what they need".

An example cited to substantiate his averment is the Integrated Action Plan (IAP), the Centre's initiative in the LWE-hit districts, ten of which are in Chhattisgarh. The Planning Commission of India scheme provided block grants to each district for projects like school buildings, crèches; health centers, drinking water, roads and street lights. The project has been criticized for it having been decided, not by the gram sabhas (Village councils), but by the trio of district collector, SP and the forest officer.

The IAP is supposed to plug development deficits in these districts, but after three years of implementation, several gaps still persist-depriving forest communities the fruits of the UPA growth story. Data shows that against 105 anganwadi buildings taken up in Bastar, only 62 were completed by May 2013. Several drinking water projects are incomplete as are school projects and most importantly, 142 road projects that connect these remote Bastar habitations with the outside world.

Some 20 per cent of the IAP projects are still under way in the state—many in the most-affected regions.

A district IAP official explains it all: "The problem here is accessibility, given the strong presence of Maoists which blocks major schemes from reaching these poor tribals". "We need 37-30 more battalions to fill the security vacuum that exists in several areas like Darbha, the attack spot, that hardly has security presence", says a senior CRPF official. No. wonder, it took the police over two hours to reach the site when the news of the 25th ambush first came in.

The MHA officials concede that there are no quick-fix solutions. Regaining Control of thousands of Kms of territory—where Maoists often have the last words– was never expected to be easy.

"Maoists have built their bases in Bastar and elsewhere over a period of 25 years. Give us atleast 5 years to flush them out for good", appeals a senior MHA official.

Naxalism in India: thriving or surviving ? 2 Jun 2013

"The attack in southern Chhattisgarh on the 25th has again raised questions– and some bogeys—about India's internal conflicts and the place Maoist rebels occupy in this universe. What is the solution? And what is likely to happen?"

This is the opening para of second analytical article in the same daily on the same day, 2 Jun 2013[7].

The short answer is that over the past 3-4 years, Left wing rebels led primilarly by the CPI (Maoist) have been severely depleted by the surrender, arrest or death of leaders and cadres. Pressured by the onslaught, often kneejerk, of both Central and various state governments, the Maoist's effective area of combat has shrunk to southern Chhattisgarh and adjacent areas of eastern Maharashtra and south-west Odisha (known as Dandakaranya to a common man, and Dandakaranya Special Zone, in Maoist parlances), Bihar, a few pockets in Jharkhand, a silver of Andhra Pradesh. While it is an emphatic weakening, the area is still vast, and cadre numbers and abilities enough to inflict severe damage in areas of strength.

The Dandakaranya zone, where the 25 May attack took place, is both major Maoist sanctuary and a core laboratory in administration, education, healthcare and way of community living and economic activity run by the Janatana Sarkar, or people's government. This remains among the most inaccessible and forbidding policing and combat terrains in the country. This is where top Maoist leadership shelters. This is where some of the most battle-hardened cadres are!

Naturally, this is also where most government forces combating Maoists are located. For Maoists, this region is also quite different from the rough and tumble in Bihar and Jharkhand where Maoist cadres for long have been less concerned with trying to provide an alternate grass roots model; because of what can be called 'objective conditions' of rebellion, more engaged in retribution and survival.

The Maoist duress is manifold. Among other things, they appear to be hard-pressed to communicate issues. There is a core hard-left-leaning pool in urban India that will continue to provide recruits for on-ground action and eventual, ideological leadership. As ever, this core is driven by angry intellectualism, and can move easily, generationally from farmers rights-related land issues prevalent in the 1960s and 1970s to, say, land-related issues of tribal rights, and callous, often corrupt land acquisition for various projects. Given the enormity of such ongoing government and business-led misdemeanour, it may be of some prise that the intensity of Maoist recruitment has waned. But tools of protest and redress increasingly available in India's imperfect but dodgy democracy– Right to Information, protests by local communities and civil society, judicial and media activism, investor watch dogs– are showing ways to negotiate solutions that do not require the gun. The Forest Rights Act is not perfect – indeed, several critics feel it does little to protect the interests of tribal folk. PESA (Panchayat (Extension to Scheduled Areas) Act] is also known for lack of true application. And the Land Acquisition, Resettlement and Rehabilitation Bill, 2011 is floundering in Parliament as it takes hits from political and corporate interests seeking to weaken it; give less to project affected. Yet, these are entirely democratic and non-violent moves to strengthen such ostensibly people friendly legislation.

In this respect, in their strategic measurement the Maoists appear to be focusing more on the negative aspects and failure of India than calculating the aspirational, positive aspects and strengths of India.

Scribe's belief

I believe this, as much as great force applied by central and state governments by using vast numbers of Para militaries and police against Maoist rebels, will ensure that LWE remains in pocket. Nobody with rational expectations expects LWE to disappear, because the root causes that feed it are unlikely to disappear for the next few decades. Anybody disagreeing with this assertion need only to look at the internal conflict map since 1967, when the so called Naxalbari phase exploded into play, and contributed the terms, 'Naxal' and 'Naxali' to India's tragically robust vocabulary of conflict.

This initial movement which I term Mark I, was physically demolished but the early 1970s. But successive movements –factions and large groups coalescing and breaking rapidly with rebel ego and expediency—worked through the 1980s and 1990s to emerge as Mark IV in 2004 with the formation of CPI (Maoist) after merger of two major factions.

As India grew, prospered and evolved, so did rebellion, spreading from one district to nearly a third of India's 600 –odd districts, from basic to intense.

Now, with massive state domination and internal party contradictions, it has already morphed into mark V. With such pressure, it is not unrealistic to expect CPI (Maoist) to further fracture along geographic and organisational fault lines, though there are already desperate efforts to knit and evolve this organisation, extend limits of indocrination and maintain routes of resupply.

One future is clear: Whatever the formation, Left wing rebellion is here to stay. (Note on the scribe: Sudeep Chakravarti is the author of Red Sun: Travels in Naxalite Country and Highway 39: Journeys through a fractured land. He addresses conflict situations in south Asia).

The dark side of a very Red Moon (one-sided article)

- **The Bastar tragedy proves that our paramilitary forces and our Adivasis are both hunters and the hunted.**

3 June 2013

This article appeared in a daily of 3 June 2013.[8]

An editorial comment needs to be added here. Many paras in this article are repeated, word for word, in this scribe's news story dated 13 Mar 2014 already included in this book. Paras which have already been included in the 13 Mar 2014 articel have been excluded here.

The state got the best intelligence it could have hoped to get through Alex Paul Menon, one of its district collectors who was taken hostage by the Naxal to the year ago (2012). In the 13 days he spent in custody, menon had long conversations with his Naxal kidnappers. Of the over 100 armed rebels he had a chance to interact with, as many as 70 per cent told him they had taken to arms in reaction to Salwa Judum. That was a year ago, but lesson was not put to any use, for Chhattisgarh, instead of undoing the damage, is still continuing arming civilians. It is just not using the Salwa Judum nomenclature.

Now we are hearing of plans to take the war into Naxal camp. We are also hearing of surgical strikes and enhanced air force missions, but let us come back to the plain truth– the Naxals live amidst the tribals. What have the state and central governments done to wean the tribals from the Naxals? What indeed have the Governments done to craft a policy around the basic principle of making the tribal the shareholder? The tribal's have only been divided into the hunter and the hunted. It is imperative now for the state to reflect and not demand another offensive, another war.

If that is what they will do because fire fight is all they can do— I suggest they leave their air conditioned rooms in Raipur and New Delhi, and talk to the Para paramilitary forces. They will tell you they are living a dog's life and are being hunted by day and night because they have been forced into an inhospitable war where they do not know who they battling and who they have been forced to declare war against. Be fair and just by the tribals that is the only starting point for the present and future.

We will uproot Naxals from Bastar: Interview CM Raman Singh: 3 Jun 2013

Q: There are allegations that the state government did not provide adequate security to the Congress Parivartan Yatra while your Vikas Yatra was duly secured. Is it true that intelligence inputs were also ignored?

A: Ample force was deployed for Parivartan Yatra and for road opening, both in Sukma and Bastar districts. Of course, there were some security lapses that resulted in 25 May tragedy. We have instituted a judicial probe. But saying the Congress' yatra did not have enough security is absolutely wrong.

Q: What about the charge that your government is visible in Bastar only during elections or after a major attack.

A: It is completely wrong to suggest that government is missing in action. The Bastar development authority is quite active and the zone has benefitted a lot. A single district in 1998, Bastar has been divided into seven districts to bring administration closer to the people. But the region has been facing Naxal violence from even before the creation of Chhattisgarh.

Q: Your former security advisor KPS Gill says your government completely ignored his recommendations and advised him to enjoy his stay in Chhattisgarh.

A: He has the experience of dealing with terrorism in Punjab but there is a huge difference between terrorism and Naxalism. Maoists adopt guerrilla warfare strategies. Besides, the topography of Punjab and south Chhattisgarh are different. So his role as security advisor was not very effective. If what he says now is correct, how come his conscience allowed him to enjoy his salary and perks without doing any work?

Q: In the wake of conspiracy theories what about the demand from the relatives of Mahendra Karma and Nand Kumar Patel for a CBI probe?

A: We too want a thorugh inquiry and have set up a judicial commission. The NIA is investigating. We want to get to the truth and punish the guilty.

Q: How do you see this issue panning out in the elections?

A: Chhattisgarh has been suffering from the Naxal problems for a few decades now. I strongly feel this is not the time to think about the political gains or the losses. Saving our democracy which Naxals oppose, is the need of the hour. All political parties must fight the Naxal scourge unitedly.

Q: Maoists now seem to be striking soft targets? How do you plan to counter his challenge?

A: The state has adopted a 'zero tolerance' policy on Naxalism. Whatever the challenge, we will fight and uproot the Maoists from Bastar. We are increasingly posting competent young officers who have brought about positive changes.

Q: Maoists express regret immediately after killing innocents but security forces justify killing of the civilians. How can you condone this?

A: Maoists neither follow the rule of law nor respect the human rights. Their regret is nothing but lip service. We are responsive to the people's sentiments and don't defend unjustified action People's trust and support are important to us in our fight against Naxals.

Q: What is on the state government's agenda now?

A: Our aim is to defeat the Maoists convincingly and wipe them off Bastar. We will focus more on reworking security aspects, besides boosting infrastructure, social indicators and human resource development.[9]

Winning battle of Bastar (Story of Success)

- Inch by inch:- Despite recent Naxal attacks, military action backed by development is undoing years of neglect, atrocities on tribals. But will India overcome corruption, build roads, and bridges of mind? Abhijit Mazumdar reports from Bastar, iconic heart of Maoist insurgency: 23 Jun 2013

"Every day, the punishment for missing the target changes. Today's penance: Applying the rain wet, red earth of Bastar all over your face. At the Karnpur headquarters of the CoBRA, the elite jungle commandos of the CRPF, AK-47 bullets missing the cardboard target during practice means humiliation outside the camp, it could means death."

The above is the opening paragraph of an analysis of Naxal situation in Bastar in a daily of 23 Jun 2013[10],

The rest of the analysis follows. In Bastar, the iconic heart of the Maoist insurgency in India, the paramilitary and the state police can't afford to miss targets in the war against one of the most wiliy and ruthless guerrilla force outfits in the world.

While the forces fight to recover the territory still under the Maoist control, other wings of the government struggle to reclaim every inch of tribal mind space lost over years of neglect, arrogance and atrocities.

The good news is– it is difficult to believe—democracy is winning. The progress is painfully slow, the path savagely slippery and peperred with land mines. Snipers lie in wait on both sides, claiming in their latest road kill, 28 people at the misty Darbha Ghat, some high profile Congress leaders among the victims. Where there is no road, there is corruption involving government officials and contractors, who take money but don't take the tar to the remote, cut off villages.

There are massive problems of inter-state coordination between agencies fighting an insurgency spread across 10 states at the heart of India Equipments like UAV is dated Political will to exterminate Red terror wildly fluctuates.

But since 2010, somethings having gone right. The LWE killed 908 and 1005 people in 2009 and 2010, while the toll slid to 600 and 415 in 2011 and 2012. There were 2,259 attacks in 2009 compared to 1415 in 2012. Till 30 Apr 2012, there were 162 deaths, while it is 120 in the same period in 2013.

Dantewada, once a dreaded 'liberated zone' of the Maoists, is now an educational town. A hive of schools, colleges, hostels and a market place dotted with ATMs buzz below hoardings of actress Katrina Kaif seductively sipping coda.

The muddy Dankani river gurgles nearby, as the small town, like many that post-liberalised India has spawned, goes about its business A huge educational hub is coming nearby.

Dantewada is one of the victories in this long battle. While the interiors are still prone to Naxal activity, the town and surroundings areas stand as an example of how military action followed by determined developmental work can reclaim spaces that democracy had lost.

"The insurgency is fuelled by the Maoist leadership from the neighbouring Andhra Pradesh. We are slowly winning over our tribals whom these leaders intimidate and indoctrinate", says Chhattisgarh CM Raman

Singh, "We are coming up with social, health and educational schemes for the tribal's and have got clear results on the ground".

The CRPF organises more than 100 telemedicine camps each on Mondays and Thursdays connecting locals to the AIIMS branch in Raipur over Skype. The troops distribute footballs, solar panels, medicines and other stuff among the tribal's– mainly Gonds and Halbas– who comprise 69 per cent of the region's population. The state's biggest medical college is coming up on the outskirts of Jagdalpur, biggest town on the Bastar region.

In the last one year, access of forces in 'liberated zone' has increased dramatically, says Zulfiquar Hasan, IG,CRPF Chhattisgarh. Encounters with Maoist guerrillas used to happened at an average 4-5 km from CRPF camp. These exchanges have been happening at an average 12-13 km from the camps nowaday's, indicating the troops' greater capacity to engage the enemy in its own territory, continues Hasan.

In south Odisha's Malkangiri called the 'cut –off' area, a place the Maoist Supremo Ganapathy is believed to be hiding in, the BSF has managed to break into some places and the CoBRA has conducted operations.

In Sarkaguda where 12 villagers along with half a dozen Maoists were killed a couple of years ago, the CRPF has managed to build a camp nearby and keep in touch with villagers, mainly because of community work, say officials.

The highway beyond Sarkaguda, however bears scars of thc raging war. More than 200 ditches have been dug up, some up to 6 feet deep, and the stretch is carpeted with land mines.

In Basaguda, where a few years ago, a board used to hang on a blasted bridge proclaiming 'Forces not allowed', the Pota Cabin residential school has come up.

As one enters the Sukma district from Dantewada, the forests thicken. This is still a hunting ground of the Naxals. The Maoist core group visits the remote villages, holds enrollment drives (annual membership fee is Rs 10, instruct villages on issues to agitate on, organize medical camps, and even run schools.

But even parts of Sukma seems to be changing. Lalu Mada, 21, says he does not want to be a Maoist. He takes three much younger siblings back home from a tribal fair. Celebrating Ban Durga (the Goddess of Forests). Although, he never went to school, he says almost all the children in the nearby villages are school going. "There is lots of school now. The National Mineral Development Corporation (NMDC) has built these", he says: Rahul

Sheikh, a postal employee in Sukma, says his post office deals with a fair volume of fixed deposits, pension and NREGA money.

The Maoists are bitterly opposed to NREGA, the country's largest rural job scheme, but wouldn't keep their hands off the juice, either. A PWD contractor in Sukma, requesting anonymity says 10 to 20 per cent of NREGA money the contractors distribute among their workers is taken away by the Maoists. "No road or development work in this area happens without their permission and a part of the money going to them", he says.

Of late, the Maoists have raised two army-like battalions and 10 companies of fighters, says an intelligence source. The desperation of being hunted in their own territory has made them opt for unusual, high-visibility attacks on politicians and civilians.

People in Bastar feel the 25th attack on Congress politicians could be a turning point. Maoist assault on former West Bengal CM Buddhadev Bhattacharyya and ex-Andhra CM Chandrababu Naidu had invited massive state reprisals. "They are desperate. The government should not show its panic. That is what they want. We are winning this. We should coordinate better and stay detenmined', should coordinate better and stay determined", says a paramilitary officer.

Maoists' recent pamphlets point to an acute shortage of arms, which possibly prompted this attempt to rob arms on 14 June 2013. There is stiff resistance to mining in Kanker, Raoghat and other areas because jobs will mean the tribal youth away from Maoists.

Maoists carry out Tactical Counter Offensive Campaign (TCOC) after the winter harvest and till just before monsoon– between mid-March and mid June when they can co-opt the tribal agricultural work force in their blood sport. But the community policing by both the state and paramilitary is making them nervous. "Boycot civic action by the forces", a pamphlet cautions villagers. It bitterly opposes the massive educational city at Geedam.

Also, they are hounding leaders of the disbanded Salwa Judum, a government supported outfit of the local tribals, after killing its most prominent leader and founder Mahendra Karma on 25 May 2013. "In their pamphlets, at their meetings, they talk about killing me and other Salwa Judum leaders", says Soyam Mukka, who lives in fear in Konta." The locals have no complaint and situation has vastly improved. It is only through guns that Maoists control them, make them join their meetings, serve food, dug uproars send daughters and sons for terror training".

The biggest challenge for democracy is that the Maoists reach where government cannot: hundreds of nameless or little known places where there are no roads or communication.

In Chhattisgarh and Jharkhand, two worst Naxal-affected states, teledensity (number of phones per 100 people) was below 10 per cent in 2010. India's current mobile density is more than 80 per cent.

There are allegations of wanton corruption and nexus between state engineers and private contractors. The contractor gets a hefty advance running into crores which he can keep for 10 years without paying any interest. Often after getting the advance, contractors burn their own vehicles or destroy their own site, presenting it as a Maoist attack. This helps them wriggle out of the rest of the work, citing lack of protection.

In most cases, they complete WBM and earth work in which profit margins are very high. "The so-called Maoist attack happens only at the bitumen or pitch work stage because there is very little money in black tar carpeting", says a district officer, requesting anonymity.

"Roads are the life line of a democracy. Which is why Maoist do not want them to be built in the remote interiors", says Ajay Yadav, Jagdalpur SP. He took over "last month (May 2013) after the last SP was suspended following the 20 May attack".

"Even if we suffer casualties, we are willing to provide security for road building", he says. The roads will have to be built, but buildings bridges are perhaps more crucial. Anger against the government still simmers.

After the 25th May attack, a note released by Gudsa Usendi, spokesman, Dandakaranya Special Zone Committee, CPI (Maoist) said on May 17, eight people including three innocent children" were killed by police and paramilitary forces in Edsametta village of Bijapur district.

But forces say the direction of the wind is slowly changing. "Earlier there was near-total hostility from the local population. The real achievement on the ground today is that in most places, we know that given a chance, the local people are with us," says Uday Divyanshu, 38, commander, 38 CoBRA battalion, and among the most highly regarded young officer on the frontline of the war against Red Terror.

Officers say that more than bullets, a football lobbed at the swarm of tribal children makes a big difference here.

Red riding wolves of the angry forest: Bastar's deadly women guerrillas : 23 Jun 2013

"On 25 May, Mahendra Karma, the leader and founder of now disbanded anti-Maoist militia Salwa Judum, was stabbed 78 times by a dozen Maoist women cadres in forest fatigues who then sang and danced around his body. This grim, primeval spectacle put a blood seal on what many had suspected for long: Women play a major role in the Maoist guerrilla ranks. Not very different from Sandanistas of Nicaragua, Zapatistas of Mexico, the Kurdish insurgency in Turkey, and the deadly women warriors of LTTE in Sri Lanka."

The above are the opening paras of an analysis of Maoist women cadres in a daily of 23 June 2013.[10]

Bastar, tribal dominated district where the sex ratio is 1,023 females per 1000 males (the national average is 940), has been prime recruiting ground. A long history of the state atrocities against tribal women only makes the Maoist head hunters' job easier. "In Bastar, the state has used international warfare methods o targeting women to threaten the community and break morale. It has used rape as a tool to undermine dignity", says Himanshu Kumar, a Gandhian activist who has worked in the region for 18 years. He had prepared 522 cases of state atrocities between 2005 and 2009 of which 99 were of rape.

Prominent guerrillas include Meenakka, Sharda, Kamla, Basanti, Ganga. Each one has four or five aliases. If one of them is killed, somebody else takes her identity to keep the legend of the revolution alive.

Maoists usually sends their women for recce. She will come close to the enemy sometimes with a goat herd, sometimes to pick *mahua*. But all the time, she is watching you. In Bijapur, a woman came to a mobile CRPF camp and said she needed medicines for her child. The Jawans gave her the medicines. But something about her felt suspicious, so they moved the camp 4-5 km further into the forest. after a few days, the women appeared again, making an arduous track through the jungle. This time she had a large bowl of local meat curry for the soldiers to thank them.

Long after she was gone, they realised that the food was exquisitely laced with poison. Women are traced as pharmacists, signal and wireless operations. A seized text book is titled Mahila Sawaal Par-drishtikon, published by the Central committee, CPI (Maoist). It spouts progressive ideals about women, attacks patriarchy and religion.

But the reality is often quite different, say police and paramilitary officials. Maoists take away tribal boys and girls when they are very young, indoctrinate them, and there have been reports of sexual exploitation by Maoist commanders.

Shanty Salam, a social worker and former Sarpanch from Kangoli, Bastar, says there are no securities for tribal women at all. "Either Maoists take them away forcibly or they are trafficked as labourers to Bangalore and Hyderabad by agents. Government job schemes often do not reach them, and most girls aged 11-15 were found to be severely anemic", she says.

Salam says CRPF and BSF are a lot more disciplined now. Earlier, tribal women had predatory men from both sides, the Maoists and the forces.

Forces admit there had been rapes, especially when the SPO units were operating [The scribe obviously means Salwa Judum personnel]. But not now, they say. "Huge protests will break out, especially in the politically vibrant north Bastar", says a police official. "Forget rape, even echo of a slap finds its way to the next day's local paper".

Intelligence alerts, on Naxal build up, possible spot of attack

Sent to police, CRPF: (Games the Intelligence plays)

- **Darbha attack:**

Express has copies of alerts; CRPF, Bastar IG say no specific inputs: 1 Jul 2013.

"Over a fortnight before the Darbha ambush, nearly two dozen specific alerts were reportedly faxed from the office of ADG (Intelligence) Mukesh Gupta about Maoists camping and training in the area, and the possibility of a major attack at Jeeram Ghati. A section of the forces, however, said they did not get the alerts. Alerts reportedly did not even reach the Subsidiary Multiagency Centre (SMAC) which acts as the central pool for all intelligence sharing". The above was reported in a daily on 1 Jul 2013.[12]

The daily claims it has copies of these alerts that, among others, were worked to the DGP, CRPF IG (Ops), ADG (Naxal) and IG (Bastar). The CRPF and IG Bastar have denied receiving the alerts.

But ADG (Naxal) RK Vij said he received them. Asked why his forces had not acted on the specific inputs vij replied: "IGs and SPs are primarily responsible for operations in the ranges as we have given them forces according to their requirements. If some coordination is required across ranges or they need more forces, then I step in as the ADG (Naxal)". At the heart of the security alerts on a gradual build up by Maoist in the area is a fax reportedly sent on 9 May which notes that around 50-60 armed and uniformed Maoists are camping at Badhanpal village and can commit an incident in Jeeram Ghati— the spot of the ambush of 25 May 2013. The CRPF, Bastar police and SMAC did not receive this alert. A CRPF officer says plainly: "why wouldn't he act if there was such a specific inputs? Also if situation was so alarming, would you waste time in writing and send a fax or make a phone call? We do receive inputs from them, but did not receive anything specific to Jeeram Ghati".

Some officials alleged that the alerts were created with back dates to absolve certain officers. Other alerts were reportedly sent after 8 May. However, the daily could not verify whether they reached the various departments or not.

- An alert sent on 11 May notes the presence of 10-12 Maoists and 30-35 members of Jan Militia with Maoist leader Sukhram Marjum village of Tongpal.
- An input reportedly sent on 12 May notes Special Zone Committee member Ayatu's presence near a pond at Marjum village. It says he has put up a tarpaulin shed and is camping with 30 cadres to give them training.
- Another alert reportedly sent on 13 May mentions Ayatu's presence at Marjum village, with 25-30 armed members, for the last three days.

Jeeram Ghati lies between Jongpal and Darbha police stations of Sukma and Bastar district, respectively with the NIA and a judicial commission probing the security and intelligence failure behind the Darbha attack, these alerts may be the important in establishing the negligence of some officers. While Bastar SP Mayank Srivastava was suspended after the incident, Bastar IG Himanshu Gupta was shunted out. The CRPF meanwhile, has given itself a clean chit.

Incidentally ADG (Intelligence) Gupta was also in charge of VIP security. Two alerts issued from his office earlier noted the threat to former leader of opposition Mahendra Karma and other Congress leaders. A 10 April input mentions that during their "tactical counter-offensive campaign 2013", Maoists had formed three action team to kill Karma and Congressman Vikram Mandavi and Ajay Singh. Each team compressed four members armed with 9 mem pistols and shot guns". Direct their security guards to take special precautions and ensure them proper security according to their status", the alert said. A week later, an alert sent on 17 April, again emphasized the threat and noted that the Maoist team was headed by Rakesh, a member of the Maoist military company platoon 2".

All the three Congress leaders mentioned in the alert– Karma, Mandevi and Singh– were travelling in the same vehicle at the time of the 25 may attack. While Karma was killed the other two survived.

Asked why he did not deploy extra security forces or stop the Congress convoy taking the Jeeram route despite such specific inputs, Gupta replied: "The security aspect should be seen in a holistic manner, considering availability of forces and vialoility of set upin such movements. Whether it was a security lapse should be probed".

Most of the security forces were deployed for CM Raman Singh's 26 May Vikas Yatra at Bijapur and Narayanpur in Bastar. In fact, then Bastar IG Himanshu Gupta was in Bijapur on 25 May to oversee the security operations for the CM's visit.

Chhattisgarh govt shows the way to handle tragedy: 2 Jul 2013

This is the last article on 25 May ambush subject in this section. Its first two paragraphs follow:

- "It is more than a month when people of Chhattisgarh and its political fraternity was shaken up by a deadly ambush of a Congress convey in a jungle pocket of restive Bastar region".
- "The State is yet to recover from this ambush that claimed the life of 30 people, including State Congress chief Nand Kumar Patel, architect of Salwa Judum movement Mahendra Karma and nine time Congress MP and former Union Minister VC Shukla". The news story appeared in a daily of 2 Jul 2013.[13]

The stunned BJP regime in Chhattisgarh was found in complete isolation when the news about the killing of Congress leaders broke out. At that time, CM Raman Singh was at Arang in Raipur district as part of his ongoing 6000 km long Vikas Yatra. The State Government suddenly found itself amidst severe criticism and public anger for alleged security let up at the Congress Parivartan Yatra. The CM and his coterie had never expected such a country wide outrage across the country over the killing of the state's entire Congress leadership. Even the threat of imposition of the President's rule in the state loomed large when a team of trusted officials of the CM showed real calibure and potential and proved how good and sensible governance can make a difference.

The Ayurvedic doctor-turned-politician Raman Singh literally broke down when he first heard the news about Darbha valley ambush and killing of high profile Congress leaders the put off the Vikas Yatra and rushed to Raipur. He held an emergency meeting with his senior officers at 9 PM. Thence he briefed the prime minister and the Governer on the situation.

Finally, the grieved CM convened a cabinet meeting at 10 PM, which ended at mid night, 25-26 May 2013.

"Raman Singh and his trusted officials did not sleep for several days and nights as they were put under Himalayan task to prove mettle and put the government out of 'nervous phase' on the basis of a genuine display of good governance."

The CM and his officials worked nonstop the 25th night and arranged air ambulances to airlift VC Shukla from Raipur to Delhi and 11 injured people from Bastar to Raipur for advanced medical treatment. Singh held another meeting with his officials at 1 AM that night and visited a private hospital in Raipur at 3:30 AM to see Shukla and the other injured. He held another meeting with his officials at 5 AM on 26 May and two hours later visited a government hospital at Jagdalpur, headquarters of Bastar region, where he met injured people and paid his last respects to Mahendra Karma and the other martyrs.

The CM had witnessed one of the tought test spells of his life in the post-25 May attack as he returned to Raipur at 11:10 AM directly from Jagdalpur to receive PM and Congress president Sonia Gandhi a day after the attack. The CM held a meeting with the PM at Rajbhawan at 12 noon and around 1 PM paid last respect to state Congress chief Patel and his son at Raipur airport and then visited Patel's house at 2 PM. Singh had another meeting with his officials at 5:30 PM on 26 May, followed by a cabinet meeting at 6:30 PM. The nonstop schedule of the CM went on for several days and he was looking quite nervous about image of his government as the BJP regime had not committed any blunders since Dec 2003 when saffron regime came to power for the first time in the state.

The CM sustained the toughest and nerve shattering phase of his Government because of committed team of officers who we always around him. Even his public relations department secretary Aman Kumar Singh who was with the CM every moment after 25 May attack, persuaded him to face media, mainly the bigger channels which rushed to Raipur from all over the country to grill BJP government over the incident. Aman Singh personally handled the entire situation.

State's intellectuals and even IAS and IPS officers were eager to see how the CM would face media but he defused media outrage in one stroke by admitting 'security lapse' and ordered judicial inquiry by a sitting high court judge. He even placed SP Bastar under suspension and shifted out IGP Bastar and Bastar Collector that convinced people Raman Singh can't be held accountable directly as he can't held gun in his hand to defend politicians of the state from Maoist attacks. After more than one month of that cowardly Maoist attack, the anger against the Raman Singh government has fully receded in public and now he gets ready to resume Vikas Yatra from August.

Even at the internal security meet convened by the MHA and inaugurated by the PM on 5 Jun in new Delhi in the backdrop of the 25 May attack, all participant CMs hailed the presentation of Raman Singh titled 'Response of the government of Chhattisgarh' in which he unfolded efforts of his government in post-25 May period. The Congress-led government at the Centre and CMs of Bihar and Gujarat and other states were on the same page and were all appreciation at the said meet regarding approach of the Chhattisgarh government to the tragedy.

A senior congress leader of the state sums up the whole incident: "People in Chhattisgarh have now exonerated BJP government from 25 May attack stigma and you can give credit to governance wonder in the state and its sensitive approach towards the whole issue till date, the other states can learn from Chhattisgarh how to counter sudden massive crisis".

He cited a recent crisis of Congress-ruled Uttarakhand where governance was exposed after it was hit by a flash flood. In Chhattisgarh where killings took place the state government imposed a ban on publishing advertisements while the flood ravaged Uttarakhand government put up advertisements with smiling pictures of Sonia Gandhi and other leaders about its efforts to handle the tragedy it shows the real difference in the style of governance.

An editorial comment is called for on the above news story. To put it bluntly. It is a PR job for the Chhattisgarh, done poorly in bad English.

15 security men killed in an ambush in Sukma district on 11 March 2014:Tongpal ambush

It was a major loss suffered by the security forces. There were a number of comments and critiques on this incident of ambush, which are mentioned and examined in the succeeding pages.

Improvising on SOPs saved majority of men: 14 March 2014

"Questions have been raised whether the 15 security men who were killed in the 11 March 2014 Naxal ambush in Sukma district of Chhattisgarh ignored the SoPs. But sources say if the troops had followed the SOPs strictly, all would have perished[14].

This is a contrarian view taken by a daily in its issue of 14 Mar 2014, against those who feel if the troops had followed the SOPs, loss would have been much less. This daily's reasoning is stated here.

A 45-member Road Opening Party (ROP) with men from the CRPF and state police had been clearing the road for the movement of a senior officer when they came under attack from some 300 Maoist cadres in Takbada area. According to SOPs, the troops should have been divided into three groups with one group marching in the middle and the remaining two flanking it on either side while avoiding the road. The company commander, however, decided against it and made the troops walk in straight line with 50 feet distance between two jawans.

This stretched the company to 1.5 km and when Naxals opened fire, only 21 men came in the line of direct fire. Those behind stopped after hearing gun fire and tried to surround the Naxals from behind, sources said. "Had they strictly stuck to the SPOs, all would have perished as the Naxals had lined the road with IEDs and waited for the entire contingent to walk into the trap. SOPs are only guidelines. Ultimately, it is the field commander who has to make the decisions, looking at the terrain and situation", said DG CRPF Dilip Trivedi.

CRPF seeks surveillance nod for intelligence: 14 Mar 2016 Wants power for Anti-Red ops

"The CRPF, nodal agency for anti-Maoist operations- has an intelligence wing but no power to intercept messages necessary for technical intelligence. After the Tongpal ambush in Sukma which killed 15 troops on 11 March, the force wants power to conduct electronic surveillance".

A month before the Maoists killed 26 people, including almost the entire leadership of the Chhattisgarh Congress on 25 May 2013 in Darbha Ghati, the CRPF had written to the MHA seeking powers to intercept".

The above two paras show our lackadaisical– even criminally neglectful– ways of dealing with issues that impinge on the national security. Even if it is accepted that the MHA has to examine carefully such requests and proposals from paramilitary forces even then its inability to reply to accept or reject these proposals is unthinkable and unpardonable. In fact, it is a case of dereliction of duty, as we say in the Army. Of course, one does not know if the CRPF ever thought of sending a remainder to the MHA, once, twice or thrice. Anyway, it is a poor reflection on the way two entities function, even on the issues that impinge on the national security. Back to the narrative after this editorial comment. The opening two paras appear in a daily of 14 Mar 2014[15].

Electronic surveillance is conventionally allowed to agencies with powers to investigate such as the police, IB and CBI. The Centre is not keen on expanding the list for fear of possible misuse.

The CRPF had its reasons. If the Indian Army can intercept in J and K for their counter-insurgency operations, it should have same power for its counter-insurgency operations in Maoist zone. The MHA is yet to decide on the proposal!

Currently, the CRPF depends on the IB and respective state police for intelligence inputs.

Focus on quality, not quantity of troops on ground: 13.3.14

- **The MHA is in the process of deploying more than 1 lakh additional central security personnel (essentially paramilitary) in the LWE-hit states**

A month before the 11 March Red strike, the MHA had written to the nine LWE– hit states, making such interesting observations on the way these states demand paramilitary forces for their counter-Maoist operations. Excerpts from the MHA letter are reproduced here:

- "The states should focus on quality and not on number of boots on the ground in Maoist-hit areas."
- "It was seen during the Chhattisgarh Assembly polls that demand or availability of the security forces appeared to be more than actually required in some places. Consequently, security forces of states with no LWE orientation were deployed which resulted in problems of ensuring their own safety."

The MHA is in the process of deploying more than one lakh additional CRPF men in the LWE-hit states. In the 2004 general elections, 109 LWE-related incidents took place, claiming nine lives. During the 2009 edition of these polls, respective figures increased to 125 and 25 (lives).

The MHA has categorized all LWE-hit districts into 'A' (hyper-sensitive), 'B' (moderately sensitive) and 'C' (less sensitive) on the basis of violence profile, past history and geographical locations. The ministry wants an emphasis on quality and not on quantity of numbers, especially in 'A' category districts[16].

In Chhattisgarh, the MHA has put the Sukma, Kanker, Dantewada, Narayanpur, Kondagaon, Rajnandgaon, Bijapur and Bastar districts in hypersensitive 'A' category.

The ministry has also told the states to scale up operations against Maoists in 'A' category districts with simultaneous exercises aimed at detecting 1ED and anti-personnel mines.

Only guns, No solution: 13 Mar 2014

Battling Maoists: Policy of relying on military might against the rebels need to be reviewed.

This is an article that appeared in a daily on 13 Mar 2014[17].

This is the type of article in where the journalist is trying to be clever, foolish and cynical all at once! For this very reason, it is reproduced word for word.

- The description of Jhiram (also Jiram) valley or Darbha Ghati in Chhattisgarh—where 15 troopers were killed on 11 March and where state Congress leaders got butchered in May 2013—as Ambush point, took me back to a journey I had made last year (2013) to another part of the state. I had hit ground zero in Bijapur, neighbouring Sukma – also a part of Bastar- and I was being driven by CRPF men along a slim metallic road. The 21 Km stretch had just been constructed under the supervision of gun-wielding security men and had its own milestones.
- "This is what we call ambush point. This is where we lost seven men to a Maoist attack", said a voice in the dark as we drove down the road where turning on headlights was equal to committing harakiri. A little further is where 12 men had been killed.
- Most security personnel don't want to be part of 'war'- the same war Home Minister Sushil Kumar Shinde on 12 March vowed to fight with renewed vigor. On a day's trip to Chhattisgarh Shinde said, "so many jawans have lost their lives in the attack, we will take revenge".
- What Shinde did not address are questions often asked by these jawans. "We do not know who is Maoist and who is an Adivasis", said one. In the jungles of Bijapur and Sukma and even in the thick foliage of Saranda in the neighbouring Jharkhand, the state is almost absent and the Centre has one response– pump in more troops. Already; there is clamour for more troops.
- But are more boots on the ground the answer? Will the additional troops be able to distinguish a Maoist from a tribal? Will it help them understand who the enemy is, who they need to train their guns at? A senior MHA official conceded there was a divide on how to tackle the Maoist menace. As he said, "The problem is that the hunters have become the hunted".
- 38 per cent of CRPF's 2862 companies of about 286200 men are deployed in the Red Corridor in nine states, and reveals a senior

officer, "the number of men seeking premature retirement is growing."

- As for the Adivasis, they have been deprived of their due: their minerals and land rights are being signed off in MoUs with mining companies and the state has already made the costly mistake of dividing the tribals through vigilante groups such as the Salma Judum.
- Shinde has once again declared the government intentions of taking the war right into the Maoist camp through enhanced intelligentled operations. His successors too, had scripted the 'enter, hold and develop' policy but said the MHA officials, "we need to relook our approach and focus on ways to win the hearts and minds of the tribals". Clearly, that is the only starting point for the present and the future.

Security men's dilemma

- The men khaki, parachuted into the nine Maoist-hit states are trained and equipped with automatic weapons.
- But these men drawn from distant Haryana and UP and Tamil Nadu know neither the terrains nor the language.
- The Centre's paramilitary forces are doing what the local police should be doing, but the latter are demotivated, scared of Maoist reprisals and their sympathies often lie with the tribals.
- Many local police officers have families in the villages of Sukma and Bijapur and know that if the locals veer towards the Maoits, it is because they want education, healthcare and rights over the land that is theirs.
- This is what the states and the Centre need to understand and craft into their anti-Maoist policy.

Maoists tried to lure security men into ambush thrice earlier: 13 March 2014

Initial investigations into the 11 March 2014 deadly ambush revealed that the ultras tried to lure security men into an ambush at three places– Bijapur in Chhattisgarh, Khammam in Andhra and Gadchiroli in Maharashtra– where they first killed three civilians by slitting their throats and left the bodies in jungles[18].

The strategy was to attack security men when they came to retrieve the bodies but the Maoist could manage to fire on the retrieval party only in

Bijapur where the encounter did not last long. An officials said: "once the conspiracy to trap the security personnel became clear, the information was shared. There was specific information about movement of Maoists in the area where the 11 March attack took place but sending road opening parties (ROPs) are vital part of the strategy to deal with Maoists".

The CRPF and state police party ambushed by the ultras on the 11th had mounted a road opening exercise for the visit of a senior CRPF official, said an MHA source. He continued: "To ensure secure movement of civilians security forces and officials, the ROPs are sent regularly and on the 11th also, an ROP was sent to clear way for a CRPF officials visit when it was ambushed."

"Maoists have launched what they call Tactical Counter Offensive Campaign (TCOC) to disrupt upcoming Lok Sabha polls in the area. During the TCOC they scale up violence. It is generally launched twice a year", said an officer.

The MHA has decided to send more CoBRA teams to the state for mounting precision attacks on the Maoists on a larger scale.

Sticking to their deadly plan: 12 March 2014

The latest killings of CRPF men suggest that

This is the title and blurb of an editorial in the Hindustan Times of 12 March. It is reproduced here word for word. Let it be said by way of editorial comment that this editorial is as simplistic and as flippant as the article by Harinder Baweja that is preceding it immediately and which too was published in this very daily. One expects more serious editorial from a so called national daily as the Hindustan Times.

- The Maoist attack in Chhattisgarh on 11 March was just a reply of many that have taken place since the most deadly ambush in April four years ago. For the past few years it is direct attack that has been resorted to in targeting the security forces. This is particularly worrying because it shows an increase in the number of guerrilla fighters who are ready to take up the cause of bringing about a revolution through violent means. This has been evident particularly since June 2008, when the Red Brigade attacked a boat on Balimera reservoir on the Andhra-Odisha border and killed 38 elite grey hound troopers. 12 CRPF jawans died in land mines blast in Gadchiroli, Maharashtra, in Mar 2012.
- The fact that the 11 Mar attack took place barely 15 km from the spot where Congress leaders were killed in May 2013 shows not

just a lapse of intelligence but also a measure of foolhardiness and collective amnesia. It cannot be that the entire paraphernalia of the police and insurgency strategists was not aware of the terrain that the Maoists could use to their advantage. The IB has responded by saying the team ignored alerts that the ultras were coming in from Odisha. Next comes the question of coordination among the police, CPMF and intelligence agencies. After 27 CRPF jawans were killed in Narayanpur in June 2010, the DGP Chhattisgarh almost blamed the CRPF by saying since they left early in the morning, they should have gathered intelligence inputs the night before. The CRPF's reply to this was that intelligence was not available to them in a 'proper manner'. Regardless of who was right, such a lapse is deplorable when it could cause a loss of human lives.

- Union Home Minister Shinde has vowed to take 'revenge' for the Maoist attack which is just a symptom of what PM Manmohan Singh has called the gravest "security threat" to India. The question is: why can't there be a political solution to the problem? When the district collectors of Malkangiri in Odisha and Sukma in Chhattisgarh were abducted, there were negotiations by the people whom both the state and the Maoists trusted to secure their release. There is ample opportunity to broaden the scope of this approach. The insurgencies in Punjab and Assam could be solved through a measure of diplomacy. In this case also, a beginning can be made through engaging people who have credibility, are competent and are unbiased.

Priya: Jawan's widow to lieutenant: 16 Mar 2014

After hubby's death in anti-Red op, 26-year old braves odds to become an officer

"Scripting history, 26-year old Priya Semwal, who, lost her husband in a counter insurgency operation two years ago, was on 15 Mar 2014 inducted into the technical wing of the armed forces as an officer".

This exhilarating news story was given by daily on 16 Mar 2014[18].

From a college going woman married to an Army jawan in 2006 to an officer commissioned into the corps of the Electrical and Mechanical Engineering (EME) of Army on 15 March, Semwal's life has come a full circle. She is one of the 62 women, besides 194 men, who were commissioned into the Indian Army as short service officers at the ceremonial passing out parade at the Officers Training Academy in Chennai.

The mother of the then four years old Khwahish Sharma, Semwal's future looked bleak when she heard the news about the death of her husband Naik Amit Sharma serving with 14 Rajput battalion in a counter-insurgency operation in Arunachal Pradesh in 2012. Col Arun Aggarwal, commanding Officer, 14 Rajput, tells the daily:" Her husband was serving in my unit. In that operation, he lost his life while others suffered injuries. When I learnt Amit had encouraged her to complete her degree and then PG, I thought she should become an officer".

Aggarwal's word of advice, however, was not received readily. "Her brother initially asked what was I saying? She just lost her husband and how can I ask them now. But eventually they all agreed", said the Colonel, who came all the way from the border to witness Semwal become an officer.

"Priya was qualified and I felt that she will do it. Initially, she had some apprehensions but once she was convinced, there was no turning back. Probably, this is the first that an Army Jawan's wife has become an officer in India," the Colonel said.

There might be instances where wives of Army officers would have joined the forces after their death, but this is probably the first time the wife of a Non-commissioned Officer (NCO) has become an officer, he pointed out.

General Elections: 2014

This section exclusively deals with the Lok Sabha polls of 2014, whose results would install a new government at the Centre. It could be UPA-III or NDA-II, knowing as we do that the good AB Vajpayee headed NDA-I in the early years of 2000 decade.

Various news stories on these polls are being examined in the succeeding pages.

Hold first-Phase polls in Maoist areas: Govt to the EC: 27 Feb. 2014

"The MHA has written to the Election Commission (EC) to hold the first phase of the forthcoming Lok Sabhas polls in the Maoist-infected 'hyper sensitive' districts. The ministry admitted that the anti-Maoist operations have not yielded any results 'in terms of attrition among the ultras in the last four months".

The above honest admission by the all-important ministry chiefly responsible for Control and elimination of the LWE in the country was reported by a daily on 27-Feb 2014[20].

The MHA said the additional deployments in 'hypersensitive' districts should largely comprise central paramilitary forces rather than state forces from non-LWE affected states "Who do not have the requisite tactical orientation", documents accessed by the daily reveal. The MHA note has categorized the Maoist-hit districts into three groups: 'A' (hypersensitive), 'B' (moderately sensitive) and 'C' (less sensitive).

(This categorisation has been discussed elsewhere. Various LWE-hit districts will be distributed in three categories in the succeeding news story).

The MHA note said anti-Maoist operations should be scaled up in the 'A' category districts as the 'window of opportunity' is available only in the remaining days of February and the first fortnight of March, " failing which, there can be major problems during the elections".

The MHA wants state governments to declare rewards for information on IEDs. EC was requested to set up polling booths around a large number of security forces camps.

Revelations to the police by Gudsa Usenda, spokesman of a Maoist formation, Dandakaranya Special Zonal Committee, has indicated that insurgents plan to take advantage of the rather thin deployments of the security forces during the parliamentary polls. Some 38 per cent of the total CPMF are deployed in Maoist– hit areas across Central India which is largely a tribal belt.

Traditionally, tribal communities across Central India have been the usual mainstray of the Maoists for support, shelter and cadres, with inaccessibility and remoteness of such areas facilitating construction of bases for weapons training and ideological indoctrination. The movement also found fertile ground among the tribals, whose angst due to a strong sense of being wronged and exploited, got largely channelised into the Maoist movement.

Bid for fair elections in Red corridor: 27 Feb 2014

The categorisation of Maoist-hit districts in nine states into three groups has been described in the news story just preceding this one:

'A' Hypersensitive

'B' Moderately sensitive

'C' Less sensitive

The categorisation into these three groups is based on Maoist violence, past history and geographic location. There are 33 districts in 'A' category, 29 in 'B'and 17 in 'C'.

The daily carries a graph which gives information about these districts from the nine affected states distributed into three categories.

The state-wise distribution of the districts in three categories is given hereafter

Bihar

'A' 5	Aurangabad, Gaya, Jamui, Muzaffarpur, Lakhisarai.
'B' 10	Munger, Gopalganj, Vaishali, East Champaran, Patna, Sitamarhi, Armal, Jihanabad, Kaimur, Rohtas.
'C' 3	Begusarai, Sheohar, West Champaran.
Total 18	

Chhattisgarh

'A' 8	Bastar, Bijapur, Sukma. Dantewada, Kanker, Narayanpur, Kondagaon, Rajnandgaon
'B' 4	Dhamtari, Gariyabandh, Balod, Balrampur
'C' 4	Raigarh, Jaspur, Mahasamund, Surguja
Total 16	

Jharkhand

'A' 12	Khunti, Gumla, Latehar, Simdegha, West Singhbhum, Ranchi, Dumka, Giridih, palamu, Garhwa, Lohardaga, Bokaro
'B' 8	Saraikhela, Kharswan, East Singhbhum, Hazaribagh, Ramgarh, Dhanbad, Godda, Koderma
'C' 2	Jamtara, Pakur
Total 22	

Odisha

'A' 4	Malkangiri, Koraput, Nuapada, Bolangiri
'B' 5	Baragarh, Rayagada, Gajapati, Kalahandi, Navrangpur
'C' 3	Kandhamal, Ganjam, Mayurbhanj
Total 12	

West Bengal

'A' -	Nil
'B' 1	Midnapore (Medinipur)
'C' 3	Bankura, Purulia, Birbhum
Total 4	

Maharashtra

'A' 1	Gadchiroli
'B' 1	Gonda
Total 2	

MP

Balaghat

'B' 1

Total 1

UP

Sonebhadra

'C' 1

Total 1

Andhra Pradesh

'A' 2	Vishakapatnam, Khamman
'C' 1	Adilabad
Total 3	

Ex- DGP, former Naxal in flight for BJP ticket: 2 Mar 2014

Both want to stand from Jharkhand's Palamu

A former Maosit leader and a retired DGP are lobbyting for a ticket from the same paramilitary constituency Palamu in Jharkhand. They are: Palamu MP Kameshwar Baitha a former Maoist who faces 17 murders cases, has quit JMM and wants a BJP ticket to retain his seat and former state DGP VD Ram, whose unique ways of tackling crime were the inspiration behind Ajay Devgan's lead role in the flim Ganga Jal.

That was reported by a daily in its issue of 2 Mar 2014.[21]

Baitha, who had been chased by Bihar, Jharkhand and UP Police was finally arrested by Bihar Police in May 2005. Ram took over as DGP Jharkhand in July 2005 and with him at the helm, Jharkhand police had taken Baitha on remand for interrogation. He was wanted in several cases in Palamu, Latehaar and Garhwa districts.

In the run up to the Lok Sabha polls the JMM got inputs from its party organisation that the Palamu MP had lost his popularity and was no longer a winning horse. Sensing trouble, Baitha started looking at alternatives. Fancying his chances of retaining his seat riding the Modi wave, he offered to join the BJP and requested for Palamu seat, the party, trying to project a clean image is reluctant to accommodate him. Meanwhile Ram went to Delhi to convince the saffron leadership that he was their man for Palamu. But he is a political green horn and lacks a strong support base. Ram tells the daily: "I am the man for this seat." Baitha too is unwilling to take no for an answer. He tells the daily: "I am planning to go to Delhi on 12 March to convince the BJP leadership".

A meeting of the BJP Central Election Committee on the 13th is likely to seal the fate of Baitha and Ram.

There is no room for violence

Maoists can serve their people better by taking the democratic path

This is an editorial in the Hindustan Times of 4 Apr 2014. Its contents are summarized here.

The Maoists are determined to disrupt the polls by all means, the latest of which are the bulk SMSes they are sending to the Bihar electorate. They have already told the Election Commission to make 'not voting' in the polls a right. They have threatened voters of dire consequences if they come to the booths under police protection. This only shows how out of line the ultras are with the world Communist movements or whatever is left of it! Even in India people who took to armed struggle in the wake of Spring Thunder in Naxalbari have repudiated the bloody ways of revolution. Everywhere the move is towards the unarmed mass movements and mass organizations which can ensure the empowerment of the dispossessed and win their due rights from the privileged classes.

The Red corridor in India may be long but the states where they are likely to strike are Chhattisgarh, Jharkhand, Bihar and Odisha. Serious preparations are afoot to thwart their disruptive tactics in these states. In Jharkhand, 8 of its 14 constituencies have been declared 'very sensitive' and adequate forces are being inducted there to defeat the disruption. In Odisha, 8 of the 21 constituencies have been declared prone to Maoist violence. In Bihar, the respective figures are 10 and 40. Similar security measures are planned for Chhattisgarh where memories are not too old of Congress leadership unified out in May 2013 and 15 troopers killed in Mar 2014. There is an interesting if worrying case of MLA Jhina Hikaka, who had been abducted in 2012 by the ultras. He was released on the condition that he would resign from the Assembly but subsequently he reneged on his promise.

One thing must be understand by the Maoists: whatever success they might have achieved, they can't bend the Indian State which has managed worse insurgencies in Nagaland and Mizoram. India is too strong for any such violent movement. For a variety of reasons, India has not deployed its potential against the Maoists.

The 2009 Lok Sabha elections were virtually violence free, and so were the Assembly elections in Jharkhand, Bihar and Chhattisgarh between 2009 and 2013. It is time the Maoist ponder what they have achieved for the people they profess to be fighting for. Indian state too hasten the pace of providing bare essentials to the tribal's such as schools, hospitals and their rights over their resources.

A war we cannot afford to lose: 14 apr 2014

The voter turn out in Maoist hit Bastar was average. This should be a cause for concern

The above is the title of an editorial in the Hindustan Times of 14 April 2014, which is briefly summed up hereafter.

It is tough to hold elections in the Maoist-hit areas, which include parts of Andhra Pradesh, Bihar, Chhattisgarh, Jharkhand, MP, Maharashtra, Odisha, UP and West Bengal. In these areas, holding polls is just one part of the challenge and perhaps easier one; the bigger challenge lies in getting ballot boxes, polling staff and security men safely out of the Maoist strongholds once the polling is over. While the 2013 Assembly polls in the Maoist strong hold of Bastar were virtually violence-free, the same is not true of General Elections held their on 10 Apr 2014.

In the run up to the polls, there were occasional skirmishes between the Maoists and the forces but first major report of the death came after the polls were over. 14 people including civilians, security men and polling officials were killed in multiple attacks by ultras in the Bastar region in the period 11-13 April.

What is of some concern is that turn out in Bastar this time was low at 52 per cent vis-à-vis the Assembly polls 70 per cent on the other hand, turn out in the Maoist-hit areas of Bihar was 53 per cent, 9 Percentage points higher than in 2009. In Jharkhand, the polling in the four constituencies in the Maoist strongholds held on 10 April, were peaceful. But advisories are out for second phase due on 17 April as the ultras are reported to be planning attacks on the security force.

But why did the polling percentage drop so drastically in Bastar? It seems there were not adequate security personnel on duty this time, and even they arrived late. For the 2013 polls, troops had infiltrated the Maoist areas a month in advance while this time around, they arrived only in March end, barely 10 days before the polls. It is desirable that the troops arrive well in time, not only to familiarize themselves with the topography of the area but also to undertake anti-Maoist operations to flush then out from the neighbourhood. Beides the above, 11 March attack that killed 12 troopers too might have affected the turn out.

The low turn out in Bastar, a region that suffers from development deficit should not be taken lightly because here the state is fighting a low-intensity seesaw battle against the Maoists. In such a scenario, it is important for the state to stamp its authority in a positive fashion.

Voters defy terror: 3 Dec 2014: High Turn-out

71 per cent turnout in J and K, 66 per cent in Jharkhand.

Inclement whether and a boycott call by separatists and Maoists did not deter voters from turning out in large numbers for the second phase of polling in J and K and Jharkhand respectively.

The above was good news carried out by a daily on 3 Dec 2014[22].

While polling for 18 Assembly constituencies in J and K saw 71 per cent turn out, some 66 per cent voters exercised their franchise for 20 seats in Jharkhand. A total number of 175 candidates were in the fray in the second phase in J and K. The Election Commission had set up 2,186 polling stations for over 15.42 lakh voters to ensure free and fair polling amid tight security arrangements.

In Jammu division district Reasi recorded the highest voter turnout of 80.73 per cent. The three Assembly seats in Udhampur district recorded over 75 per cent. The frontier Pooch district where National Conference, Congress and People's Democratic Party (PDP) are locked in a triangular context on all three Assembly seats recorded over 70 per cent polling.

Barring a comparatively low turnout in Homeshalibagh segment in South Kashmir, voters again turned up in large numbers in Kupwara and Kulgam districts of Kashmir Valley. They defied separatists call for boycott and braved chilly weather to cast their vote. Nine constituencies went to polls on 1 Dec 2014 in Kashmir Valley with Noorabad segment in Kulgan continued its record of high voter turnout, with 77.6 per cent. The frontier karnah segment in Kupwara district polled 75 per cent votes while Handwara and Langate recorded identical figures of 71 per cent each.

While the NCP is fighting a tough battle to retain its traditional constituencies of Handwara, Karnah and Kupwara, the PDP's nerve would be tested in Noorabad, Homeshalibaugh and Devsar constituencies. Surprisingly, Homeshalibagh recorded the lowest turnout of 36.5 per cent votes. A journalist from the area Farooq Rather told daily that this constituency has a sizeable influence of Jamaat-e-islami, a Politico-religious organisation that quit electoral politics after eruption of militancy in Kashmir. "The Jamaat-e-Islami voters did not turn up in compliance of the boycott call by the separatists", he said.

The most interesting contest would be witnessed in Kulgam segment where three time legislature My Trigami of the CPM is seeking re-election.

Jharkhand scene

Reports from Ranchi suggested that Phase II of the Assembly polls held in 20 constituencies, including 16 reserved for tribals, spread across Kolhan and South Chotanagpur registered higher turn out at 65.66 per cent with impressive figures for Jamshedpur (West) compared to the 2009 polls. The office of the Chief Electorial Officer of Jharkhand cited reasons for higher polling percentages in the two Jamshedpur seats: Voter awareness drive, continued efforts at updating voters list to eliminate ghost voters and a host of other measures. Here are comparative figures for 2009 and 2014.

	2009	2014
Jamshedpur (East)	45.14	58
Jamshedpur (West)	42.15	60

Nonetheless, the encouraging aspect of the elections was that there was no report of violence despite 262 extremely sensitive and 196 sensitive looths in 20 constituencies that went to polls in Phase II. Heavy deployment was made at booths in dense forests of Arki,Tamar, Khunti, Kolebira and ultra dominated Lapung under Mandar constituency.

Maoist strategy: From bullets to ballots through proxies: Khunti: 3 Dec 2014

"This poll season, the Maoists and other rebel groups in Jharkhand have come out all guns blazing not to scuttle polls but to prop candidate of their choice".

This scribe has given a different take, almost a twist, to the Jharkhand polls. If earlier reports talk about the Maoists' efforts to enforce boycott of the polls, this news story speak of the ultras pushing the candidates of their choice. The story was published in a daily of 3 Dec 2014.[23]

There was no call from the top rebel groups to boycott polls, which otherwise is the stage for fierce battle with security forces.

The CPI Maoist and half-a-dozen other rebel outfits are suspected of backing different candidates. Officials in the police headquarters in Ranchi talk about intelligence reports that point to this covert relationship. A senior IPS officer says: "Some of the candidates are blood relatives of Maoist leaders who here either surrended or are still active".

In Maoist-hit Chatra that went to polls in Phase I, the candidate of a national party is alleged to have links with rebels Tritya Prastuti Committee (TPC)– a breakaway faction of the CPI (Maoist) allegedly patronised by the Jharkhand police– has canvassed for particular candidates in Latehar and Chatra Districts. One of the candidates in Chatra is wife of a Maoist commander. The constituency saw a contest between Girija Singh and Vinod Sharma, both former Maoist cadres. An intelligence officer intones. "We have reports of Maoist visiting people to seek votes for a particular candidate."

Jharkhand police headquarters also has reports about Maoist and other insurgent groups supporting candidates in Ghatshila, Torpa and Kolebira Assembly constituencies that went to poll in Phase II on 1 December. In Tamar, JMM candidates Salomi Turi, the wife of jailed Maoist, took on notorious CPI (Maoist) sub-zonal commander Kundan Pahan's cousins Ravinath, a JVM candidate.

SP West Singhbhum Narendra Kumar Singh claims insurgents have given the customary boycott call in some pockets of Saranda forest, but are not in a position to enforce it. Singh explains: "The one major reason is that they have been flushed out of most parts of the forest". Incidentally, the polling percentage in Saranda forest in the recent General Elections jumped to 70 per cent almost double of the 2009 figures.

In Bengal, many former Maoists in fray as Trinamool candidates: Jhargram: 1 Jul 2013

"Hamlet Mandi, 26 used to be a Maoist squad member whose name evoked fear in Jangalmahal. He is now a Trinamool Congress (TMC) panchayat samiti candidate from Kanko *anchal* in Binpur, West Midnapore. He has five cases pending against him, including two murder charges.

Hamlets is one of the many former Maoists in the fray for the panchayat elections, scheduled to be held in Jul 2013. Some have already been elected unopposed. Most are fighting as TMC candidates. Hamlet was recruited by Maoist area commander Subodh Hansda in 2009.

"When I was 22, I left home. In 2010 end I was arrested. After 10 months I was granted bail", said Hamlet who joined the TMC after his release[24].

Two of his former squad members, Lakshikanta Mahto accused in six murder cases, and Yuvaraj Murmu accused in five murder cases, now campaign for him. Mahato says: "We went underground after joining the Maoists. We were ordered to recruit teenagers and given the task of raising funds from the government employees in the area by making them pay 25 per cent of their salaries. We were told to prepare a list of corrupt persons in the area who would then be killed by the squad".

Hamlet and his comrades often face threats from the Maoists now. "We are scared, if they manage to regroup, they will kill us. But the administration is helping us a lot", said Hamlet.

In Kharbandhu anchal in Gopiballavpur area of West Midnapur district, once the Maoists core area, the TMC has won 9 of the 10 seats uncontested. Most of the candidates are former Maoists.

There is Dulal Mandi, accused in three murder cases, who has won from Balipal. "I used to be a TMC worker earlier. We once caught a Maoist Sushil Mahato, who was extorting money in our village. We called the police, but got no help. After that Maoist would threaten us every day. Finally, I joined the squad to save my family", said Dulal who was arrested in Jan 3011. Prabir Jana, another Maoist and accused in two murder cases, has also won a gram panchayat seat. "After Mamata Banerjee came to power, we met TMC MP Subhendu Adhikari and told him that we want to join TMC. He gave us shelter. We even campaigned for the TMC in the Assembly polls", he claimed.

Subhas Baskey is another former Maoist who is a TMC candidate from Ergoda anchal in Silda, West Midnapur. "A group of 10-12 Maoists would knock at my door every evening and order me to cook for them and collect rations. They killed seven villagers, branding them as police informers. We did not have the courage to go to the police, so we went underground," he said. He faces charges of sedition, conspiracy and waging war against the state".

There are others in the neighbouring district of Bankura as well. Prabir Garai who married Suchitra Mahato said to be former Maoist leader Kishanji's trusted lieutenant, is contesting the zila parishad seat from kotalpur. Gorai used to be PCAPA activist. A local TMC leader is contesting against him as an independent.

Justifying the induction of former Maoists, Churamoni Jansda, TMC MLA from Gopiballavpur said: "they were forced to join the Maoists at gunpoint. If they remain alert, we believe Maoists will not be able to regroup in the area. Our leadership will also ensure that cases slapped against them are withdrawn– a promise we made before the assembly polls".

Srikanta Mahato, TMC MLA from Binapur, added: "During the CPM rule, Jungal Mahal youth was forced to join Maoist squads and PCAPA. But now they want to return to mainstream politics, leaving their life in the jungle. It is our moral duty to give them a chance".

Meanwhile, CPM has criticised the TMC for fielding former Maoists. Dipak Sarkar, CPM district secretary in West Midnapur said: "The TMC has a single point agenda. By fielding such candidates, they have spread the message of fear, ensuring that villagers do not put up other candidates. The Maoists have joined the TMC because they were assured that their cases would be withdrawn."

Target Red after saffron surge": 11 Jun 2014

A look at where the offensive against the Naxals stands in Chhattisgarh, which has sought more fire power.

The Chhattisgarh has demanded additional fire power against Maoists from the Centre and the latter has assured it on the same. The analysts are curious about this development as it has come at a time when the Maoists have consolidated themselves in certain key pockets, the BJP leaders are facing allegations of an understanding with the ultras and when the party has just won most of the Lok Sabha seats in Naxal dominated districts across the states.

The above critique appeared in a daily of 11 Jun 2014[24].

It was a fast track decision by the MHA as CM Raman Singh had presented his demands to the Minister, rajnath Singh, only on the 9th and the state government expressed satisfaction in a statement on the 10th itself for the Centre's approval for 12 battalions and its promise of additional choppers.

A coincidence

The new government (led by Narendra Modi) at the Centre was sworn in a year almost to the date after the attack on a Congress convey in Darbha valley on 25 May 2013. The critics note that since then, there has been little progress in the follow up offensive against the Naxals. Two further observations are equally apt: the NIA is yet to file a charge sheet on the attack and Darbha saw two more attacks during the recent polls, leading to 23 fatalities.

Decisions on the police stations

The Centre had sanctioned Rs 150 crore for 75 police stations in Maoist-hit areas of Chhattisgarh years ago but not one has yet been completed. A police officer adds: "56 are under construction and a proposal for change of location for 15 is pending with the Centre. For some existing police stations, such as Bhadrakali in Bijapur, one needs to boat across a river. Others, like the one in Farsegarh look like hutments."

Gains and losses

In May 2014, CPI (Maoist) brought on board the CPI (ML) Naxalbari, a group which operates in Kerala and Karnataka. The merger statement issued by CPI (Maoist) General Secretary Ganapathy and CPI (ML) Naxalbari secretary Ajith, exulted: "The recent expansion in the southern part of the Western Ghats is proof that the flames of revolution will continue…"

The MHA in a letter of 22 Jan 2014 addressed to top police officers of Naxal hit states, had noted that "Ganapathy had managed various factions well in difficult times". The acknowledgement came after the Maoists too had been admitting setbacks.

In 2013, the daily had reported a CPI (Maoist) Central Committee resolution in which top leaders admitted having lost their base, weaponry and address across zones. In 2014, the Maoists have noted some recovery amid the setbacks. Another resolution, accessed again by this daily from the annual meeting of the Dandakaranya Special Zone Committee held in Feb. 2014, reads:

"The recruitment target was achieved in south region (Sukma, Bijapur, Dantewada). Tactical counter offensive compaign was also achieved in south region".

The resolution goes on to describe the set backs:" TCOC failed in north and west regions. We failed to stop deserters…. The desertions are attributed to enhanced LIC of the enemy, our lacks of confidence, non-proletariat inclinations and our moral mistakes, the degradation of Communist ideals…. non-resolution of issues of cadres. Several cadres promoted too quickly later deserted. We had set up unified commands (Unicom) in all three regions of Dandakarnaya in 2013. It must be noted that the southern Unicom worked well and northern and western ones did not. It is acknowledged that the killing of journalists Sai Reddy and Nemichand Jain was a mistake. If media persons were found to be involved in anti party activities, then it should be thoroughly probed…They should be warned more than once and elimination should be only the last resort".

BJP in Red Zone

Of the 19 Lok Sabha seats in the 26 districts nationwide that the MHA identifies as severely hit by the Maoists, the BJP has won 13 and its ally the LJP one. "If police investigations have often hinted at a BJP understanding with Maoists, the electoral performance has revived such allegations". This is the way this Left-leaning daily puts it. Then it quotes at length an open letter written by veteran journalist Sumanta Banerjee, once associated with the naxal movement in Bengal, to Maoist supremo Ganapathy:

> "Curiously enough again, during polls your party has never targeted the BJP candidates in Chhattisgarh who have continued to get elected all these years even from constituencies which are your base areas. Can you please explain this intriguing phenomenon? Again, curiously enough, your landmines have never targeted any top brass of the Sangh Parivar and its gangster. Why? Is there any tacit understanding between your armed squads and the local BJP politicians and corporate houses in your areas of control? Can you please ask your cadres to preserve their fire power and keep dry whatever little gun power is still left in your armoury? To be able to fight the agents of Hindu fascism"?

The Lok Sabha Polls: May 2014

State	Seats	BJP won
Chhattisgarh	3	3
Jharkhand	6	6
Bihar	3	2+1(LJP)
Odisha	3	0
AP undivided	2	1
Maharashtra	1	1
West Bengal	1	0
Total	**19**	**13+1**

Monitoring the situation in Chhattisgarh: 3 Dec 2014

Security personnel deployed in the Red corridor are not dying in Maoist attacks.They are dying because the state does not care about them.

Most news stories in this book are detailed without any editorial comment. Even if the author of this book disagrees with the contents and presentation of a news story, it is taken in this book as it is. An editorial comment is added to this story because it is from a Left-leaning daily, the Hindu, which is invariably against the policy of Government of India, be it run by the UPA or the NDA in dealing with the LWE. Having clarified this, the contents that follow are as it appeared in the daily of 3 Dec 2014[26].

"I can only think of holiday." The soldier of the CRPF's 223 Battalion said this to one of his colleagues as they stepped out of their camp on 1 Dec 2014 in Chhattisgarh's Sukma district. The soldier died on 2 Dec at 3 AM, 16 hours after getting injured in a Maoist ambush that killed 13 of his colleagues. The injured were brought back to the camp where they spent the night and the next morning, struggling between life and death. The soldier who had holiday on his mind could not make it. The rest of the injured were evacuated the next afternoon, 24 hours after the ambush. "At least, three more will die", said a CRPF soldier to me. "Their organs are damaged, and they just waited and waited, hoping to hear the sound of the chopper".

It is safe to guess that most of the CRPF jawans who had been patrolling the same area of some 10 km radius in the last 15 days had holidays on their mind. As a CRPF officer in the area says, Every morning the soldiers put their coordinates in his GPS! And then he just wants to somehow be done with it". The CRPF men who were caught in the ambush followed the same pattern every day. It is not clear what they were asked to achieve. The Maoist guerrilla had been waiting for them in the area where there are hillocks in a U-shape formation. They could only exit from the point they had entered. The Maoist knew this and had set up their ambush accordingly. After the kill, they took away a huge cache of weapons, 10 AK47s, and 30 magazines, three UBGLs and 30 grenade rounds, one LMG and 300 rounds, four jackets bullet proof, GPS and night vision devices and a high frequency VHF Manpack radio. They left nothing or no one of their own behind.

No memory of the living: "Negative all the way"

Remembering the dead, the newly dead, is a performance art in India. There is a classical conditioning to it, especially when it comes to remembering those who die of the state's own weakness', of its inadequacies. Right after the ambush, PM Narendra Modi tweeted that his thoughts were with the families of those who lost their loved ones. Those thoughts would remain till he wears some other traditional headgear at this next public event which would have happened by the time you read this.

A few days ago, Union Home Minister Rajnath Singh spoke about setting up a national police memorial at a cost of Rs 50 cr. Like all his predecessors, the memory of the fallen concerns him in a way those who may be prevented from falling never will. If it did he would not have been required to pay a non-consequential visit to Chhattisgarh, later tweeting with the same inertia that he had asked the state authorities to "monitor the situation."

How does one "monitor the situation?" How does a state fighting a war against what it calls "India's biggest internal security threat" not ensure that there are a couple of helipads with waiting helicopters in an area like Sukma so that injured soldiers are evacuated immediately? A few days ago, a soldier from CRPF's 150 Battalion was hit by a bullet on his hand as he stood inside his camp in Chintagufa. He could have easily been saved but the injury opened up one of his arteries and he died of excessive bleeding. "Imagine, it was just a matter of clamping an artery", says one of his colleagues.

There is a camp of CRPF's elite anti-Naxal CoBRA force in Darbha where in 2013 where the Maoists wiped out almost the entire Congress leadership of the Chhattisgarh state. A commando living there tells me there are five toilets for 150 personnel there. "I am so sick of eating potatoes, soya been, nuggets and one type of dal", he said, "How am I supposed to fight for a state that cannot even ensure a supply of vegetables for me?" Such a supply he says is dependent on civilian transport. More than often, the driver arrives without supplies claiming the Naxals waylaid him and booted it away. More than often, he is lying. But what can we do!" the commando says Every fortnight, his men offer liquor to bus drivers as bribe, hoping to get their supply of vegetables and eggs. But there is no guarantee, the commando says.

Malaria is rampart. Hundreds of CRPF and other police forces on active anti-Naxal duty suffer from it. A few have died. "The soldiers fighting in the Second World War would have had better medicines than us", a CRPF officer says, adding: "Most of his men suffer from various skin diseases. The sanitary conditions are so pathetic that half my men can be seen holding their stomachs."

Justic unlikely: "CRPF's sad picture"

On 5 Nov 2014, a CoBRA commando Sujoy Mandal, sent a registered letter to the Home Minister, among others. He is currently attached to his battalion headquarters in Bhandara, Maharashtra, cursing the day he joined the CRPF. His officers have put him under suspension for putting up a brave fight against Maoist and for raising a flag against his superior who did not and who also violated several SOPs. His wife Tithe has been running around showing documents, showing picture of her husband with Pranab Mukherjee after he won a karate championship. She has kept all the receipts of the registered posts her husband has sent, explaining what went wrong in an operation, how he fought bravely and how the CRPF did not pay a penny for treatment of his injuries incurred during the Naxal attack.

In October (2014), a CRPF commandant is believed to have thrashed one of his commandos in Gadchiroli after he refused to accept a petty order from his wife. In November the commando was summoned to the CRPF headquarters. It is very unlikely that he would get justice.

"The salute is done; the cameras are gone" the CoBRA commando tells me. He has climbed on a hillock on a small patch where his cell phone catches a little signal. "It is tough to ask my men to fight", he says. They want to go on a holiday". The signal is faltering. "I want to go home too", he says and the signal is lost.

4 months old beaten to death by Reds: Raiput: 13 Dec 2015: Barbarity

"A group of Maoists beat a 4-month old baby to death in Chhattisgarh Bijapur recently and then buried him in front of his wailing mother", police said on 12 Dec 2014. The baby was repeatedly hit with a rod, IDP Bastar range, SRP Kalluri said.

The above was reported by a daily on 13 Dec 2014.[26]

The incident took place in Bijapur's Todka village. Infant's father, Tati Aaytu told the police that the Maoists had recently abducted him, his wife and his sister, as well as the infant, Somaru and beaten them up during a 'Jan adalat' (kangaroo court).

When Aaytu managed to escape, the abductors avenged his escape by killing the baby in the presence of his mother who was later freed. The police have booked the rebels Dulao Yam, Masa Tati and Mangu Tati.

Double jeopardy for journalists caught between a rock and a hard place: Bastar: 14 dec 2014

Ground reality: truth has two versions in Chhattisgarh's Bastar: one that fits the official narrative and the other that suits the Maoists

The above is the title of an article in a daily with its longish blurb on the issue of difficult problems faced by the journalists including the risk to their lives while doing their job in the Maoists-hit areas in various states of the Union. This appeared in a daily dated 14 Dec 2015.[25]

The opening para quotes the greatest British playwright:

"The one who brings unwelcome news holds a losing office", Shakespeare had written in Henry IV. Journalist who bear bad news face a similar situation in Chhattisgarh Bastar region that lies at the heart of a festering conflict between Maoist's rebels and government forces. "Each side shoots the messenger when the news is not to its liking?"

This times the messengers are journalists Santosh Yadav and Samaru Nag who have been jailed for allegedly providing information to the Maoists. Here are details, Yadav, who reports for the Dainik Chhattisgarh and Dainik Navbharat was picked up by the police on 29 Sept 2015 and slapped with the charges under the UAPA and Chhattisgarh Special Public Security Act (CSPA). Nag who ran a news agency for the Jaipur headquartered Hindi daily Rajasthan Patrika and wrote for them as well, was arrested on 16 July 2015 from Raipur. He is accused of keeping a watch on the movements of police while Maoists burnt down a crusher plant used for road construction.

The detention of Yadav and Nag which their supporters see as unlawful and an act of intimidation is snowballing into face off between journalists and authorities, as violation of human rights and free speech have come under the spot light in the insurgency-hit state. Journalists across the State "are planning a jail bharo andolan on 21 December". "If the state considers both the journalist as Naxals, they should come and arrest us all for supporting Naxals", said Kamal Shukla who heads the newly formed Patrakar Suraksha Kanoon Sanyukt Sangharsh Samiti that is demanding a law to protect journalists. Maoists are often called Naxals as their ideology and politics are rooted in a left wing peasant uprising in Naxalbari, West Bengal from the late 1960s.

On 10 October soon after Yadav was arrested, the Samiti held a protest outside CM Raman Singhs residence, asking the administration to provide proof of allegations against the duo in a month or set them free. Neither happened, "The usual system of law, that we are used to, stops short of conflict areas", said Anil Mishra, a Raipur-based journalist with Hindi daily Nai Duniya.

Mishra spent ten years in Bastar before he moved to Raipur for his safety. He recalls an incident when he and a collegue from Delhi met the state's police chief for a story on Binayak Sen. He says: "I was shocked by his first reaction when I introduced myself. He said, "were n't you Naxals…" and then he stopped. So clearly he had an impression that I was a Naxalite".

Nag, 24, whose father is a farmer and who has been behind bars for over four months along with two others accused of the attack on the crusher plant appeared clueless about his crime when he was brought to the Jagdalpur district court on 3 December. Nags tells the story when he was whisked away: "I was at my shop when the policemen come up and asked me to go with them. I fail to understand why they arrested me. I don't even know the other two accused".

In contrast, Yadav, 28, says he has been a victim of police harassment for sometime. It started in 2013 when he was the first to reach the spot of a Maost attack at Jiram Ghati in Bastar. The police presumed Yadav had prior information from the rebels which meant he worked for them.The allegations against him, however, are that he used to supply materials and shared information with Maoists. He was arrested and his name added to a case where 18 others from Darbha villages were arrested a month earlier for their alleged involvement in a police-rebel encounter during which a policemen was killed. On an earlier occasion, Yadav, a matriculate and now a father of three, "was detained at a local Thana tortured and even offered money to become a police informer which he refused", said Isha Khandelwal, a lawyer with a Tagdalpur-based all women legal aid group called Jag-LAG.

Intimidation by government forces is not new to journalists in Bastar. They understand that getting threats and harassed are occupational hazards. The first situation they faced was when Salwa Judum— a campaign under which the state armed tribal youths to fight the Maoists— was at its peak. It was time when journalists reported on wide spread human rights abuses and the immunity with which the forces operated. It was also a period when several journalists were harassed some even receiving death threats.

Salwa Judum meaning 'peace march' in the local Gondi dialect was later declared illegal and unconstitutional by the SC. Truth has two versions in Bastar: one that fits the official narrative and the other that suites the Maoists. In the war that is raging here and has claimed close to 1,000 lives in the past five years, neither side can afford to upset the media, but they would not let it report fairly. "A press conference in Bastar is usually a quiet affair. Journalists just record what is said or take the handout and regurgitate it on the paper. No one dares ask a question", said Prabhat Singh, a journalist for Rajasthan Patrika in Dantewada, a Maoist stronghold bordering Telangana.

Singh was allegedly singled out by Bastar IG SRP Kalluri when he asked about a missing person in one such conference. Kalluri's removal featured among demands journalists submitted to CM Rawan Singh during their protest in October (2015). He has been accused of creating an environment where journalists can't work freely. Kalluri declined to comment on the charges. His senior ADGP RK Vij who heads anti-Maoist operations in the state, said: "Personal behavior of any officer is beyond his control."

Vij also denied there was any infringement of journalists' rights though he wouldn't comment on Yadav and Nag as the matter was sub-judice. However it is not just the fear of police or arrest. In 2013, killings if two senior journalists Sai Reddy and Nemichand Jain by the Maoists terrified local journalists. They refused to cover any Maoist statement, prompting the rebels to issue an apology and admit that the killings were a mistake. More recently, two young journalists were interrogated at gun point by the rebels while on field visit for a story.

Paying the price: list of journalists

2006: Kamlesh Painkra, an adivasi journalist was targeted for writing on human rights violations by the Salwa Judum. His brother was jailed and was threatened into writing an apology. Painkara later quit the profession.

2008: Sai Reddy, who wrote for Hindi newspaper Desbandhu, was arrested under the CSPSA for having links with the Maoists.

2010: Pamphlets with death threats to three journalists, NRK Pillai, Anil Mishra, and Yashwant Yadav, were circulated in Dantewada reportedly issued by the Adivasis Swabhimaani Manch Mangal Kunjam, a young adivasi journalist in Bailadila. Dantewada was threatened with a staged encounter by the police after he reported the death threats on the three journalists on the CGNet Swara.

2013: In Februarys Sukma-based journalits Nemi Chand Jain was murdered by Maosits claiming that he was a police informer. In December Sai Reddy was hacked to death by Maoist in a market in Bilaspur.

2015: Somaru Nag and Santosh Yadav arrested for alleged links with Maoists.

The above is the text of the article as mentioned above, included in this book almost word-for-word. This anuthor should end this piece with one comment.

"It is one sided article, harsh on the security forces and that is understandable because they work within the law. A Kalluri or a Vij cannot order shooting of any inconvenient journalist. At the most they can take a recourse to the courts. Even that is resented by the scribe of this article. They dare not treat the Maoists same way, harshly, because they would not be there to tell their story. Deaths of journalist the world over is a professional hazard and they must learn to take as it is without crying too much about it. they can learn a little bit from army men in this respect."

Journalists in Bastar defer persecution stir: 22 Dec 2015

"Journalists in south Chhattisgarh strike-torn Bastar deferred their Jail Bharo Andolan ('court arrest' agitation) after CM Raman Singh assured them that a committee would be appointed to look into the issues troubling them".

This was reported in a daily dated 22 dec 2015.[29]

Over 250 journalists had assembled at Jagdalpur in Bastar on 21 Dec 2015 to draw attention towards the challenges faced by the journalists working in the zone affected by the LWE and urged the government to protect the freedom of the press. Government spokesman Rajesh Toppo said the CM had taken a decision to form a secretary level special committee that would include senior editors from other divisions of the state, besides government officials. CM Singh spoke to the representatives of Patrakar suraksha Kanoon Sanyukta Sangharsh Samiti, the umbrella organisation of the journalists created to safeguard the rights of those working in the conflict areas, over phone.

After the CM's assurance, they took out a symbolic protest rally and handed over a memorandum to the Bastar collector. Their demands include release of two scribes arrested on fake charges, enabling a conducive environment for journalists and removing controversial IGP SRP Kalluri from Bastar.

A press release issued by thc Bastar zonc PRO says "any complaint lodged with the committee regarding the arrest of the journalists would be probed on the basis of evidence available with the government and if necessary an appropriate decision would be taken in the interest of the affected journalist.

Notes

1. Aman Sethi, The Hindu, 13 Nov 2011.
2. K. Srinivas Reddy, the Hindu, 2 Apr 2012.
3. Mrigank Tiwari, Times of India, 1 Jun 2013.
4. *Ibid.*
5. *Ibid,* Anuja Jaiswal.
6. Ejaz Kaiser, Alok Tikku and Prasad Nichenametla, Hindustan Times, 2 Jun 2013.
7. Sudeep Chakravarti, *Ibid.*
8. Harinder Baweja, Hindustan Times, 3 June 2013.
9. *Ibid.*
10. Abhijit Majumdar, Hindustan Times, 23 Jun 2013.
11. *Ibid.*

12. *Ibid.*
13. Sujeet Kumar, the pioneer, 2 Jul 2013
14. Deeptiman Tiwari, Times India, 14 March 2014
15. *Ibid,* Rakhi Chakravarti.
16. Rajesh Ahuja, Hindustan Times, 13 Mar 2014
17. Harinder Baweja, Hindustan Times, 13 Mar 2014
18. Rajesh Ahuja, Hindustan Times, 13 Mar 2014.
19. Times of India, Agencies, 16 Mar 2014.
20. Sanjib Vr Baruah, Hindustan Times, 27 Feb 2014.
21. Alok KN Mishra, Times of India, 2 Mar 2014
22. PNS the pioneer, 3 Dec 2014.
23. *Ibid.*
24. Madhuparna das, Indian Express, 1 Jul 2013.
25. Ashutosh Bhardwaj, Indian Express, 11 Jun 2014.
26. Rahul Pandita, The Hindu, 3 Dec 2014.
27. Rashmi darolia, Times of India, 13 dec 2014.
28. Furquan Amen Siddiqui, Hindustan Times 14 dec 2015.
29. Ejaz Kaisar, Hindustan times, and 22 dec 2015.

35

Chhattisgarh update 2

Raman Singh, CM, must speak up on Rapes: 18 Dec 2015

"When I read the two-part report on the alleged gang rapes in Bijapur by security forces, I was aghast but not surprised. It did not surprise me either when I read that no one has been arrested till now. According to the reports, several women were allegedly gang raped, assaulted and looted by security personnel in this remote, Maoist-dominated area of Chhatisgarh for over 50 days. Intimidation and physical attacks on tribal's by security forces has happened before and unfortunately will continue to take place even though a new provision in the IPC provides for prosecution of rape crime by armed forces".

This unfortunately is the way the scribe opens his report on this subject in a daily of 18 Dec 2015.[1] It is being included in the book without any major change in the scribe's words:

- The story took me back to 2009 when I visited the same district. after crossing several security barricades and a run-in with a very angry young CRPF jawan who nearly broke my camera, I reached Lingagiri village in Bijapur's Basaguda block. "It is a ghost village", a local contact had earlier told me. It was indeed ghost village: There were several burnt down houses—many of them by then had been taken over by bats, a rice mill, a completely run down school and a health centre.
- But within 20 minutes of reaching there, at least 70 people surfaced from somewhere. They said they wanted to tell me their story of how security forces plundered "This is not only a case of their villages, physically assaulted them, forcing them to run away to the surroundings jungles and to Andhra Pradesh. Pregnant

women gave birth inside jungles, old people who could not walk fast enough were left behind and children went days without food. I followed the story for several months and then lost track. I have been to Chhattisgarh several times after that but never managed to go back to Bijapur. But to the best of my knowledge, no one was ever arrested. Former bureaucrat Harsh Mander tells me: gang rape of tribal girls and women the crimes are perpetrated by men in uniform in a militancy affected area. The Armed Forces Special Powers Act does not apply here, but even without it what enormous impunity men in uniform enjoy for rapes and killings in areas torn by uprisings! How much worse would be areas where there is legal impunity assured by AFSPA?"

- The security forces can continue to harass people because of the support they get from the democratically elected political class. Recently in Nagaland when security forces sent a notification to editors, the civil administrations refused to speak up. The same has again happened in Chhattisgarh. CM Raman Singh is yet to give a statement. Aren't the Bijapur rapes a big enough issue to warrant his attention?

"We have won the confidence of people in Maoist affected areas": 18 dec 2015

CM Raman Singh: An interview

Raman Singh is the only BJP CM after Narendra Modi to have completed 12 years in office. While he may not have any critics in his own party, Singh is yet to build a strong political team. What has also helped him all these years is the infighting within the opposition Congress. Raman Singh spoke to HT correspondent Eijaz Kaiser.

HT: Even after 12 years as CM, LWE continues to be your major challenge. Are you rethinking your counter-Maoist strategy?

CM: Winning the confidence of the people in the affected areas was our biggest achievement. Due to this, vast Sarguja region in north Chhattisgarh is now free from Maoist problem. In Bastar too rebels are confined to a limited area. Massive surrender of their cadres and simultaneous development with area domination has eroded the morale of the Maoists. Greater connectivity and infrastructure have made a difference. It is difficult terrain and porous interstate borders work to their advantage. This year, (2015) alone, 268 km of roads have been built in the interior areas and our target for next year is 500 km.

HT : What about the allegations of human rights violations in the Maoist infested areas? Two journalists are also in jail.

CM: We remain concerned with the rights of those affected by any atrocity or violence. The schools, aanganwadi centres, roads, bridges, health centres were destroyed by whom? What about the rights of hapless poor tribals? Almost 40 lakh of them are virtually living life as hostage, we should be sensitive to all. Why ignore the brutal punishments in Maoist' Jana adalat? If someone's rights get, infringed, the court is there to ensure justice. Bastar journalists too have distanced themselves from the issue.

HT: What are your major achievements and failures, if any?

CM: Our food security scheme has emerged as a model; infrastructure development turning north Chhattisgarh free from Maoist influence, creation of capital city Naya Raipur, all there have given us national recognition. The only wish remaining is ensuring total peace in Bastar. Effort are on and we will succeed.

HT: Do controversial statements by Sangh Parivar members threaten the image of BJP governments?

CM: Why are such statements needlessly attributed to the BJP? Any remark by leaders of some frontal organisations might not necessarily be the stand of the BJP. I believe any one should be on guard to avoid statements that hurt the sentiments of others.

HT: Is intolerance growing in the country after the formation of the Modi government?

CM: Some people are trying to create such an impression. But the spirit of tolerance is very much rooted in the DNA of Indians. States ruled by BJP and NDA alliance partners have a better record of religious and communal harmony.

In Chhattisgarh, 70 Maoists give up arms: 25 Dec 2015

Second big surrender in a fortnight: some record this

70 Maoists, including 15 women cadres surrendered to police and CRPF in Chintalnar in Sukma district on 24 Dec 2015. It was the second big surrender of rebels in the past fortnight. 26 Maoists had surrendered in Sukma in Bastar region on 9 December.

This was reported by a daily on 25 Dec 2015[2].

IGP Bastar range SRP Kalluri gives details: "Several factors have triggered the surrenders. Security forces have turned on the heat on

Maoists, persuaded people not to join the banned outfit and encouraged Maoists to surrender under state police. Rebels surrendered with two muzzle loading guns, a pipe bomb, an LED and Maoist literature. Some of the rebels have been involved in crimes such as arson, loot, extortion and even major attacks including the 2010 Tadmetla attack in which 76 CRPF personel were killed.

The surrendees admitted they were under pressure since the security forces were in hot pursuits and were also frustrated with the Maoist ideology that promoted violence. Most of them were from lower rungs of the guerrilla force.

ASP Irfan Khan tells the daily: "The villagers played a majr role in the surrenders. During our campaigns police found that communication was a major hurdle. We told people about state guarantees to Maoists. They were told that lower-rung rebels suffer during anti-Maoist operations and should join the mainstream and avail benefits of state policy." During a series of meetings, villagers provided the police a list of those willing to surrender. When the villagers were convinced about the state guarantees, they presented 70 Maoists before the police.

The Maoists surrendered at Jagargunda police station in Chintalnar. They are all residents of Chintalnar, Jagargunda, Tedmetla, Murkam and nearby areas of Sukma district a cash reward of Rs 10,000 each was given to all those who surrendered. In 2014, the police in Bastar region had drawn flak from activists for allegedly staging surrenders of rebels. Villagers had allegedly been forced to surrender posing as 'Maoists'.

In Chhattisgarh, children face Maoist threat for speaking up: 15 Feb. 2016

"School children are caught in the firing line between the government and the Maoists in the LWE-hit Chhattisgarh. Students are often seen marching under police security through streets of small towns and hamlets in Bastar region holding banners and placards, demanding peace and asking Maoists to end killing of innocent people, allegedly at the behest of the state authorities.[3]" This is from a daily of 15 Feb. 2016.

The above despite the SC in 2011 declaring as illegal the Chhattisgarh governments, anti-insurgency militia of young tribal's, called Salwa Judum.

But this passive aggressive campaign has not gone well with the Maoists. They sent out an advisory to parents and teachers this week and also distributed pamphlets in the area asking them to desist from allowing children to participate in such 'anti-people' rallies. "We appeal to the parents of the students to ensure their children are not used in anti-people (against the Maoist) events and rallies. We ask the school management and teachers too do not allow the students to be part of anti-people activisties that are based on lies", said the statement issued by Vikalp, the spokesperson of Dandakaranya Special Zonal Committee, the most powerful unit of the CPI (Maoist) in central India—covering the entire Bastar region along with Malkangiri, Koraput areas of Odisha and Gadchiroli in Maharashtra.

The Chhattisgarh police dismissed the appeal as 'ridiculous'. "Are the Maoists not using the children in their movement and destroying their lives? By issuing such statement, the Maoists are trying to create a threat perception among the masses and gain media hype", an ADGP told the daily. Nevertheless, this propaganda war has left the parents auxious. "There is a lot of fear and uncertainty here", said Idpa Ramvilas, a businessman in geedam. Another parent said, "their children were the most vulnerable as the school could act against them if they refused to participate in the marches and the Maoists could strike if they did. Maoists are known to forcibly pick up to induct as combatants and also urge villagers to willingly offer their children to be trained as rebel warriors".

"Madkami Hunga, 14 and Puja Markam, 16, from Aranpur in Dantewada were forced to join the Maoist outfit some three years ago Puja was traced by Malkangiri police in Odisha on 26 Jan 2016 after she fled", ASP Sukma Santosh Singh told the daily, adding that Puja was sent to a residential ashram in Dantewada for studies. Though the administration claims the student marches were voluntary and an attempt to counter the growing support for LWE among the youth, teachers admitted that the marches were conducted on the directive of the police and the district administration. "We comply with the orders given and ensure the participation of the students as directed," said senior teacher of Bijapur Government High School, requesting anonymity.

Another teacher in Sukma, who did not want to be named, said "It is believed that when you rope in students to hold meetings or rallies, it might garner support from people but this will not win the hearts and minds of Maoists".

But not everyone is against the involvement of students in the anti-insurgency operations and say the children's participation to create a terror free environment was largely restricted to safer areas. "Such activities might help build confidence in remote areas where people's trust in authorities remain abys-mally low", said Alok Shukla, a human rights activist. Anti-terrorist experts are not worried and see the advisory as a reflection of the Maoists frustration.

"With the local tribal population understanding the futility of the ideology of LWE, they are now increasingly going against the rebels whose statements clearly show their desperation. The people in the affected areas yearn for peace", said brig (retd) BK Ponwar, Director of Kanker-based Counter-terrorism and Jungle Warfare College.

Soni Sori in Delhi after attack in Chhattisgarh: 22 Feb 2016

Aam Admi Party (AAP) leader Soni Sori landed in Delhi 21 Feb 2016 even as Delhi CM Arvind Kejriwal condemned the attack on her in Dantewada on the 13th and demanded prompt arrest of the culprits. Swati Maliwal of the AAP said Sori was admitted to the Apollo Hospital in the city. This was disclosed by a daily in its issue of 22 Fb 2016.[4]

It was on a day when human rights lawyers were "Evicted" from Jagdalpur, Soni was attacked by an unidentified men who smeared a black chemical on her face. The incident took place at Geedam when the tribal leader was returning to Dantewada with her party associates from Jagdalpur.

Demanding action, Kejriwal tweeted "V painful. What happening every where? Hope she recovers fast. Chhattisgarh govt should nab culprits immediately". AAP state convenor Sanket Thakur said Sori, who is socially active in the tribal community was returning from jagdalpur after bidding farewell to human rights lawyers Isha kandelwal and Shalini Gera who were forced to pack up from Bastar.

The "shocked" Chhattisgarh unit of AAP said the situation in Bastar had turned "alarming". Thakur said: "This is an attempt to terrorise and force her (Soni) to leave Bastar. She has raised the issue of fake encounters and the high-handedness of the forces". Sanket Thakur continues "she has inflammation on her face and is in extreme pain. We can't trust the state administration anymore and are thus shifting her to Delhi for treatment".

As per the Dantewada police, three unidentified men on a motorcycle chased Sori, intercepted her near Geedam and fled after smearing some black chemical ink on her face. SP Dantewada Kamal Lochan Kashyap said: "An FIR has been lodged against unidentified persons. It was not an acid attack".

The year 2016

This part covers the events during 2016.

Troopers freed from Maoists: 5 Jan 2016

"The toll in Maoist ambush on security forces on 2 January in dense jungles just 10 km away from the fortified Kistaram CRPF camp in Sukma district of Bastar region, has gone upto three on 3 Jan 2016. 14 injured jawans were rescued on the 3rd after a 24-hour gun battle and the bodies of the three slain CoBRA commandos were brought to the camp in the afternoon".

The above was reported by a daily on 5 Jan 2016.[5]

The Maoists ambushed a team of 200 in the forests bordering Telangana on the 2nd, just two days after a joint operation was launched by CoBRA and District Reserve Guards. The operations was launched after eight rebels were killed in Chhattisgarh-Telangana border by a Greyhounds team. A reinforcement of 300 security men was rushed to the region which is controlled by Maoist women commanders Savitri and Hidma. On the 3rd 50-60 cadres resorted to the indiscriminate firing at several places to prevent security forces from rescuing their trapped collegues.

Talking to the daily, 208 CoBRA battalion commandant PS Yadav who had suffered bullet injuries on his foot, said: "We shot 12 Maosits but while we were trying to drag their bodies out, the guerrillas ambushed us. The rebels were sitting on the tree tops".

This news story carries a picture of "jawans returning to their camp after reinforcements extracted them from a maoist ambush in Sukma district on Friday (3 Jan 2016)".

23 Naxals surrender: 29 Feb. 2016

As many as 23 Naxals including two women, surrendered on 28 Feb. 2016 in Bastar district's headquarters citing "ill-treatment" by senior cadres, police said.[6]

The ultras turned themselves in before senior police officers saying they were "frustrated" with the ill-treatment meted out to them, SP Bastar RN Dash told the PTI. Of these , three cadres—Katku (Kudur Janatana Sarkar head), Lali Mandavi and Raju Mandavi (area committee members)—were carrying a reward of Rs 3 lakh each on their heads. Similarly, Kawasi Gore, 35, head of the Chetna Natya Manch (CNM) culture wing of the CPI (Maoist) carried a bounty of one Lakh on his head. Rest of the surrenders was lower-rung members.

An encouragement amount of Rs 10,000 was given to each of them and will later on get all entitlements, financial and other, due under Surrender and Rehabilitations policy.

Bastar villagers forced to surrender as Maoists: A Maoist leader: 1 Mar 2016

"The CPI (Maoist) has said that "goons and anti-social elements" are creating havoc in the Bastar region in the name of anti-Maoist operations[7].

A recent press statement issued by Mohan, the new secretary of south Bastar Divisional Committee of CPI (Maoist), also claimed that the recent attacks on human rights activists and journalists in Bastar were orchestrated at the behest of right wing groups. The statement by Mohan who recently replaced senior leader ganesh Uike as secretary of south Bastar divisional committee adds: "The atrocities on Bastar tribals are at their peak due to the BJP government's policy to loot minerals and land of Bastar tribals. It is all a part of bigger conspiracy to render the indigenous tribals landless. Tribal women are being gang-raped. There is no such things as administration in Sukma, Dantewada and Bijapur districts of Bastar. Innocent civilians are being killed and branded as Maoists and propaganda is being carried out in the media. Villagers from interior areas are being threatened with arrests and being made to surrender as maosists".

The Maoist leader also claimed that the police killed an eight-year-old child in Hurra village of Bastar on 19 February. While appealing to the people of Bastar to condemn attacks on the human rights activists and journalists, Mohan asked the government to dissolve the District Reserve Guard (DRG), a recently formed special anti-Maoist unit of Bastar police, consisting largely of local tribal youth but including some former dreaded Maoist leaders.

NHRC team to probe rights violation in Bastar: 1 Mar 2016

A six-member National Human Rights Commission team will visit Chhattisgarh on 1 Mar 2016 to probe into recent cases of atrocities on tribal women in the restive Bastar region of the state and attacks on and eviction of human rights lawyers and activists.[8]

Gemini Kumar Srivastava the NHRC spokesman told the daily: A team comprising six NHRC members will visit Raipur, Bijapur, Sukma, Dantewada and Jagdalpur district headquarters of Bastar from March 1. The team will look into the cases of alleged gangrapes of tribal women in Bijapur district. We have received a complaint from Indrani Chakravarti from Jagdalpur Legal Aid Group on the eviction of her collegues from Bastar. The team will look into it.

23 Maoists surrender in Chhattisgarh Raipur: 3 Mar 2016

The Chhattisgarh Police claimed to have busted a local Maoist network created by leaders from outside in Kumakuleng area of Jagdalpur, with the surrender of 23 cadres. Three of the Maoists carried a reward of Rs 1 Lakh each.[9]

Senior police officers said each of the surrendered Naxals had ration cards and aadhar cards. Most of them had electoral cards as well. A statement issued by the police said: "The police have been working towards getting local Naxals to surrender to break the back of the Naxal outfit. We want that local Naxals surrender and work with the police against those from outside. The Maoist leadership allows local cadres to get official documents so that "they can take cover as poor villagers, adivasis or labourers".

The release Maoists entered the Kumakoleng area in 2004.

Maoists kill 16 villagers in reprisal attacks: 3 Mar 2016

"Maoists allegedly killed 16 villagers in Narayanpur district after a Kangaroo Court accused the 16 of being police informers". This was reported by a daily on 3 Mar 2016.[10]

The incident took place on 29 February when the ultras called the villagers for a meeting during which the court was held.

The bodies of the three of the slain villagers have been recovered so far, "While thirteen are still with the Maoists". The locals belonged to Gram, Netanar, Albeda, Parpa, Kindula and Matbeda villagers, Bastar IGP SRP Kalluri said fewer villagers cooperated with Maoists these days, due to which they have murdered the locals.

Narayanpur's SP said he was aware of the situation and claimed that police personnel were deployed in the villagers to evaluate the situation and ensure the safety of the villages.

2 CRPF commandos killed, 14 hurt in anti-Naxal operations: 4 Mar 2016

Two CRPF commandos were killed and over a dozen injured in multiple encounters between security forces and Maoist cadres on 3 Mar 2016 in Chhattisgarh worst Maoist violence hit Sukma district, officials said while the two commandos succumbed to bullet injuries, 14 others, including team leader and commandant PS Yadav, were injured. The others who sustained bullet and splinter injuries include Assistant Commandant Rajveer Singh, Head Constable Santosh and Constable Sona Ram.[11]

The patrol team encountered multiple ambushes and fire fights beginning 12:30 PM and some teams of the patrol were still engaging in intermittent fire fight with Naxals in the area". The incident involving CoBRA commando of the CRPF first occurred in the jungles of Dabbanarka of Sukma district. While Singh was hit in this first fire exchange, the others were injured in the subsequent operations. The troopers belonged to 208 CoBRA battalion and were evacuated to a hospital in Raipur.

"All our injured men were evacuated by 2 PM [on 4 March]. The withdrawal has been tactical and orderly and after accomplishing a thorough search. The Maoists have sustained heavy losses (in the operations)" said CRPF IG Chhattisgarh sector Sadanand Date.[12]

One more died late in the evening of the 3rd. The three killed were Fateh Singh, NS Lanju and Laxman Kurti. The gun battle had lasted 24 hours.

On the delay in evacuating the injured jawans to Kistaram police station, ASP Sukma district Santosh Singh, who led the rescue, said: "The operation was launched some 16 km from Kistaram". He also claimed that CoBRA team was fired at from inside the houses of Dabbarmarka village. The second ambush was near Pottakapalli village.

Chase of top Maoist leaders led to Sukma encounter of 3 Mar 2016 analysis: 6 March 2016

"The encounter in Sukma last week, in which 208 CoBRA battalion of CRPF lost three commandos, was part of a planned security operation following information received about movement of senior Maoist cadres such as Ramanna. Secretary of Dandakaranya Special Zone Committee, his wife Savitri and Hidwa, commander of PLGA battalion 1.

The operation which lasted over a day also left 13 CRPF men injured. Senior officers involved in it claim there were 15 Maoist fatalities but they could not recover the bodies, given the heavy fire. The operation was based on the input that PLGA battalion 1 commandeered by Hidma had shifted base to Tondamarka and Bade Kedwal. On 27 February, there was further input that Ramanna and Savitri would be campaign near Tondamarka 2 March onwards. A senior CRPF officers tells daily: "After a lull of three months we had credible information about hidma. The teams were mobilized on 27 February and the plan was to hit Hidma at Dabbamarka on 3 March and Hidma at Bade Kedwal on the 4th as there was information that Ramanna was moving in that direction. The team had 159 CoBRA men and 30 members of the state police DRG accomplished them.

On 3 March while the team was stationed in Dabbamarka, a sentry noticed the Maoist movement at 10:30 AM. Half an hour later, more movement was spotted and sub inspector Rajveer Singh designated to check movement, was shot in the chest. As his condition was serious, it was decided to evacuate him to Kishtaram, the nearest camp 14 km away. The movement started with the ultras trailing the team. When it reached potakpalli, the Maoists fired from the huts and one trooper was injured[13].

As they moved towards Kishtaram they were ambushed, 700 meter away. "There was heavy gunfire, and our injured were put in a nallah towards the left flank. Subsequently, led by Commandant PS Yadav himself shot in the foot, CoBRA teams began attacking the right flank, forcing the ultras back. In the attempt to recover their bodies, Fateh Singh was shot at when Leju NS tried to pull Singh's body back, he too was shot at. Yadav then told his team to let the bodies be. As night fell they found they were o n high ground, so they dug in. But the number of injured meant reinforcements had to be sent in, while Maoists retreated a UAV monitored their movement.

The daily had reported on 4 March that 290 personnel were sent as reinforcement to Potakpalli while 300 others remained on standby. "The next morning, Maoists teams began to encircle the CRPF party again but there were orders to "not open fire till the Maoists reach within 25 yards in an open field. Under cover from reinforcements, the teams successfully made their way to Kishtaram".

Commandant Yadav tells the daily: "Ordinarily making our way back to Kishtaram would not have been a problem. But given our injuries, coming back was a herculean task. But we were immensely successful in protecting our injured. Even in hospital, all of them are doing fine".

Bastar: A Maoist stronghold anti-Naxal operations: An analysis: 6 Mar 2016

- As the Chhattisgarh police launches a strong push into this Naxal stronghold there have been other casualities: journalists and activists told to leave and a spike in alleged police excesses. Dipanker Ghose on the new lines in Bastar including between "outsiders" and patriotic voices".

This is an interesting analysis on the LWE-situation in Bastar region. It has routine and expected phrases about police excesses even if qualified by the term 'alleged'. It is produced below verbatim.

- Chhattisgarh home secretary BVR Subrahmayam sees the police renewed push in Bastar as "constantly" breaking records: IGP (Bastar Range) SR Kalluri describes it as "a turning point." For NGOs, activists and journalists on the other side of this all out operation though it is an open drive against "outsiders" with differentiation made between them and that now-familiar qualifier-"patriotic voices".
- One of the most steadfast bastions of Naxalism in the country and one of the few remaining places where Leftist insurgency continues

to hold sway, Bastar is seeing an upswing in police operations involving not just more boots on the ground but the deployment of surrendered Naxals in greater numbers than ever before. If in 2015, 46 bodies of alleged Maoists were recovered by the state police the number has already 21 by 20 February this year (2016). "In the last six months since the rains ended there have been 56 Naxals deaths in encounters. It is a record in itself. We begin to count these numbers from 1 Sep 2015, since, in the rains, operations are slow given the conditions in the forests. Since we started again in earnest, we are breaking our own records all the time and pushing them back. In November there was a record and then in January (27 ultras killed) the record was broken," says subrahmanyam.

- At present over 600 personnel of the District Reserve Group (DRG) which comprises surrendered Maoists are deployed in districts across Bastar. Nearly every recent operation has had DRG teams accompanying the state police or CRPF. In the 2015 budget, the state government had accounted for 600 more DRG posts and in February this year (2016), these posts were sanctioned. At the centre of it all is the controversial Kalluri, accused of being involved in attacks by security forces on three villages in Dantewada when he was SSP Bastar, during which security forces allegedly burnt homes and killed five persons.
- If that tenure was volatile, his term as IGP of Bastar Range only seems to have taken it up a notch. Weeks before a corrosive grease-like liquid was rubbed on her face in an attack, AAP leader and tribal activist Soni Suri had attempted to file a complaint against the IG accusing him of instigaling people against her, but no FIR was registered. Soni now alleges that even when she was attacked by three unknown men near her home town of Geedam, she was warned "Not to speak against the IG and let the issue of the Modum encounter go." In the days leading up to her attack, Soni had raised the issue of an alleged encounter in Sulenga village in the Modum area of Bastar district where the police had claimed they had killed a 40-year old Naxal identified as Hidma, who had Rs 1 Lakh bounty on his head. Hidma's family by her side, Sori alleged that Hidma was innocent farmer, a father of seven who was asked by the force to show them the way into the jungle.
- Newly appointed special DG (Anti-Naxal operations) DM Awasthi says he personally does not feel Bastar has become a police state.

"SPs have been asked to rein in anti-social elements and ensure safety and security of all citizens in the light of recent events", he says. While his emphasis on "Security of all citizens" followed Jagdalpur Legal Aid Group members and a journalist leaving Bastar allegedly under police pressure and attack on Sori, Awasthi is unequivocal about operational successes. "It is very clear that we are doing very well and the force is being used efficentky. In large pockets we have pushed the Naxals back. On the encounter in Modum we enquired and our forces have said that allegations of it being are not true. We are still looking into it, but there is a set precedent for a magisterial inquiry and any body can go to court," he says.

- Much of this confidence stems from shrinking over the past few years of the area dominated by Naxals. In Chhattisgarh's bloody history, districts such as Rajnandgaon, Kondagaon and Kanker were considered dens, but the Resistance there is much weaker "By 2017, save for small incidents we want to bring an end to Naxal violence in districts such as Kanker, Kondagaon and even Jagdalpur", says a senior officer. Officers such as Subrahmanyam talk of advances made in north and east Bastar, effect of which are now seen in south Bastar". One of the reasons for these 'successes' is better road connectivity and increased telecom connectivity—73 New mobile towers have been erected in Bastar connecting areas deep inside the forests. Each of these towers is either inside or next to the police or CRPF camp.
- Close attention is also being paid to the building of specific roads crucial to anti-Naxal operations. 29 of these projects have been identified by the civil administration, nine of them in Sukma. Of the 29, four have been completed, 13 are in progress while three are yet to be tendered of the 1218 km roads in the most difficult terrain, so far 481 km have been built.
- However, opinion is uniform on the primary reason, in terms of operations for the success: the DRG . "The turning point has been our use of the DRG. The surrendered Naxals know the jungles, it is in their DNA. They never lose that and we are using it to our advantages", says Kalluri. Many of the members who are part of the DRG have had stints at military training schools in the north-east. Three batches of DRG personnel, 300 to a batch, were sent to the counter insurgency and Jungle Warfare School (CIJW), where they underwent training for four weeks each.

- Officials say these cadres are often bigger assets in the jungle than the paramilitary forces. "A CRPF jawans comes to the Chhattisgarh for three years and treats this as a 'punishment' posting and will go away after that. These cadres hail from here, come from these villages themselves. They have commitment and want to end Naxalism, so they can return to their villages", Kalluri says. Another senior officer talks about their flexibility when it comes to combat situation. "Well-trained forces follow SOPs. These surrendered cadres don't follow rules and thus are better equipped for the jungle combat. For example, if a CRPF team has mapped out a way going in and coming out and if they get ambushed somewhere, it is the DRG that can tell them what jungle path to take. They speak the local language too. Apart from this is their local intelligence in identify Naxal networks in the villages".
- Critics of a the police point out that the concept of using surrendered Naxals as instruments of the state is modeled on the now banned Salwa Judum. In 2011, the Supreme Court while holding the Judum illegal had indicted the state for arming civilians to fight Maoists. But the administration argues that the DRG are not vigilantes but surrendered Naxals subsumed in the police system through formal channels and training. "The state has to incentivise surrenders by promising jobs and one of those avenues is the police. When they are brought into the system, it is undeniable that they are assets in operations. Unlike the SPOs those in the DRG are full police officers with the same accountability as anyone else, and thus the state is fully responsible for their actions", says an officer. However, for most surrendered Maoists, working with the police is not really a matter of choice. Kiran, who was once the Malangir area committee commander of the CPI (Maoists) , says: "When I left I was tired of life in the jungles and wanted normalcy. So now I have a roof over my head on most days. But in terms of a job, the only option was to join the police. I help them with my knowledge of terrain. *Penchanta hoon logon ko andar se* (I know the people inside). There are several operations in a month"?
- But many of these operations have been followed by police excesses with NGOs accusing DRG cadres often being at the centre of these acts. In Nov 2015, women in villages around Pedagellur in Bijapur who alleged sexual assault by security forces said the men spoke in Gondi and were surrendered cadres.

Many of the surrender numbers in fact don't stand up to official scrutiny. The State Intelligence Bureau have rejected many of these cases because they do not qualify under "The surrender policy of the state government". The real story, however, lies in the comparison from 2014 onwards, when the present police dispensation in Bastar took over. In 2013, out of 39 applications, 28 were cleared while in 212, 23 out of 39 were cleared. Cut to 2014 when the present IG took over and the year saw the police claiming 421 surrenders, 316 of which were rejected by the panel. In 2015, out of which 327 cases, 91 have been rejected, 36 approved, rest still pending clearance. In late Jan (2016), RK Vij, former ADG (Anti-Naxal Operations) who rejected the surrender applications, was transferred.

- For the first time, however, the allegations of assault in rural areas by forces or their men have been accompanied by hounding out of activists from urban centres Late one night of 27 February, Isha Khandelwal and Shalini Gera were told that they could no longer live and work out of a flat in Jagdalpur, the Bastar district head-quarters that had served as their home for two and a half years. The both worked for Jagdalpur Legal Aid Group. Given that their work involved fighting cases for tribal's in south Chhattisgarh and they routinely faced accusations of being involved with Maoists, it had never been easy. Khandelwal says: "we stayed through all that but this time they attacked those close to us. Our landlord (Pravin Baghel) was asked to come to police station late at night and sent home at 2 in the morning. Police seized his vehicles, his only source of income as a cab driver and told him to evict us. We understand he had no options so we had to leave." The same day they were told to clear out. Scroll in contributor malini Subramaniam was handed an eviction letter. The modus operandi was the same : her landlord had been called to police station and she was given a notice. She left the same day, the Legal Aid Group followed two days later.
- DC Bastar Amit kataria said the "check on landlords" was carried out on his orders. This was a routine check that happens everywhere in the country. My office issued orders that all papers and identity of tenants across Jagdalpur must be checked. A routine form had to be filled by landlords. When the legal aid team came to meet me, this is exactly what I told them. I conveyed to them that this was not about them personally and there is no question about intimidation", he says.

- SP RN Das denies seizing the vehicles of Baghel, the landlord of the flat that housed the Legal Aid Group. "Nowadays, police get dragged into everything. Police have no role in this. More than 200 cars are seized every day. How can I be expected to keep track of all", he says, Yet the allegations of intimidation go beyond eviction notices. On 7 Feb. a group called the Samajik Ekta Manch held a demonstration outside Subrahmaniam's home where she lived with her daughter shouting slogans of "Naxal samarthak murdabad", Naxal samarthak Bastar chodo", and Bharat mata ki jai". They took objections to my reports and warned me not to tarnish the image of the police Hours later at 2:30 AM, I heard a motorcycle enter my neighborhood. Stones were thrown and the rear window of my car was shattered", says Subrahmaniam. It took two days for the police to register a report and Subramaniam alleges that women in her neighbourhood gave witness statements against her complaint. Kalluri says he visited Subramaniam and the Legal Aid Group, assuring them of fair investigations and their safety, "after he got a call from someone he respects greatly". Subramaniam claims that despite these assurances the pressure continued with the police allegedly detaining her domestic help, putting her through several hours of interrogations and accusing her of throwing stones at her house.
- Critics of the police administration in Bastar speak of the Samajik Ekta Manch being part of the process of intimidation with the link between the Manch and police undeniable, they say. The two have been known to jointly organise the wedding of at least one surrendered couple. Manish Parikh, local BJP leader and member of the manch says intent is what matters "We are not from one organisation or party. There are lawyers, journalists, political people from different parties who believe that Bastar has had enough of Naxal violence. Naxals destroy schools, roads all sources of employment, our job is to tell people of their activisties in a peaceful democratic manner. We do not and have not indulged in violence. We even met Malini Subramaniam, may be, she should correct her work a little but there was no violence. Now tell me if I am holding a *Jan Jagran* in a colony and shouting slogans against Naxalism, why should anyone have a problem? We did not throw any stones but we have been attacked needlessly," Says Parikh.
- Asked about their links with the police he says, "I want you to write this: we believe the police, Mr. Kalluri, Raman Singh and

Narendra Modi are doing a great job, and that in 2016, we will rid the area of Naxals. *Bastar ka admi jag gaya* (The people of Bastar have woken up), but we don't need anyone from outside telling us what to do".

- It is this narrative of insiders versus outsiders that is playing out across Bastar, often aided and abetted by the police leadership. At a press conference in Raipur on 20 Feb 2016, Kalluri facing a volley of questions on the eviction of Subrahmaniam and the Jagdalpur Legal Aid Group said there was great anger within the Jagdalpur Bar Association which had passed a resolution against "these lawyers from outside", and that there was even a possibility of a "law and order problem". The president of the Jagdalpur Bar Association, Ashutosh Dwivedi says there was no fresh notice, but a reiteration of earlier directions issued by them. "Nothing personal against whom you are talking about was passed. We received complaints in August, September that lawyers from outside were arguing cases and even telling clients that local lawyers don't know their law which is against professional ethics. Put that aside, a lawyers who practice here must either be registered with the local bar or Chhattisgarh High Court. They can only argue through a local lawyer. Now when I get to know that we are unsure of credentials of these lawyers, the bar only issued a notice to its own lawyers who are working with those from outside that either you take responsibility for their eligibility to practice law or withdraw your names from their cases within ten days. The Legal Aid Group challenged this in the Bar Council and said that we had personally stopped them from arguing. In February, the Bar was notified through a petition by 150 lawyers that the earlier notice was not being followed and we issued directions again", he said. Journalists are also under watch as admitted by the administration itself. At the same 20 February press conference, Kalluri repeatedly said that in Raipur 300 km from Bastar journalists gave him "negative vibes" and went on to say, "We don't care about the national media. You have a different way of looking at things, we work with the media in Bastar that sits with us, eats with us, and come in helicopters with us".
- Days later BBC Hindi correspondant Alok Putul wrote a piece detailing how he was told by both IG and SP in Bastar that they only had time for "patriotic journalists". Kamal Shukla, president, Patrakar Suraksha Kanoon Sanyukta Samiti and a vocal police critics says, "All of this is happening because of this declared

Mission 2016, where they want to rid the area of Naxals. Under that there are fake encounters, fake surrenders of innocent tribals and any journalist speaking out is either being bought or silenced. Two journalists, Santosh Yadav and Somaru Nag are in jail on false cases and those who report independently are being threatened. Anybody with them is called a patriot. This same pattern is playing out with lawyers, too."

- The Bastar police had arrested Yadav and Nag late 2015 on allegations of being involved with Maoists. Yadav's arrest came on a day when villagers of Badrimau had travelled to the nearest police station of Darbha after being told that doing so would result in the police freeing five men picked up from the village. They however walked into an event that was painted as a village "giving up Maoism and asking for police protection", Yadav who was known to the villagers, allegedly took up issue with the senior police officers, including Kalluri. Within hours he was arrested. The arrest had caused an uproar among the journalists.
- The larger worry is that this may go beyond intimidation and be an attempt to cut lines of communication to Baster. Journalists Yadav, Subramaniam, and Jagdalpur Legal Aid Group were liaison points for most people from "outside" who sought to critically examine the work of the administration in Bastar. That door is slowly, forcibly being shut. For away from Bastar, in the quiet halls of the police headquarters in Raipur, there is much dissent and dissatisfaction. A senior police officer tells the daily: "their numbers of encounters, surrenders and arrests may be high but there is grave doubt about their veracity. Look at what weapons they recover with each encounter. It is always a country made weapons or something minor. There is also a little understanding of Maoism as a political problem. If you pick up a villager and label him a Maoist, the Maoists then use it for their own propaganda through their political wing. We are giving them the right to say 'look at how police are mistreating you.' If anybody believes that these high numbers show that the Naxalism is weakening they are fooling themselves and most importantly, young police officers are being taught the wrong things".

The article is accompanied by a table giving important information. It is produced here

"Mission 2016, in numbers: Data between 1 Sep 2015-29 Feb 2016

Encounters between police and Maoists	117
Surrendered Maoists	420
Maoist bodies recovered	56
Arrested Maoists	522
IEDs recovered	180
Weapons recovered	165
Force troopers killed	11
Civilians killed	23

Chhattisgarh budget focuses on irrigation and Bastar development: 10 Mar 2016

Chhattisgarh CM Raman Singh who also holds the finance portfolio presented the state budget for the 2016-2017 fiscal for Rs 73,996 crore adding "the state has had to overcome many challenges in the past year, including the drought and LWE.[13]

The CM announced four new battalions for anti-maoist operations and the creation of 4000 new posts for fighting LWE[14]

50 Maoists surrender in Bastar: 12 Mar 2016

The state police on 11 Mar 2016 announced the surrender of 56 Maoist from different parts of the rebel-hit Bastar. With this, the police said, 182 suspected Maoists have surrendered since Dec 2015. Senior police officers claimed that several Maoist cadres from Odisha had surrendered to Chhattisgarh police, indicating that state's surrender policy was attractive to them.[15]

Those who surrendered on the 11th include one area committee member (Mase, alias Shabnam, who was gunman for Central Committee member kadiri Satyanarayan Reddy) three Jan Militia commanders, One Jan Militia deputy commander, one DKMS leader, 12 DKMS members, 19 Jan militia members and 18 sanghatam members; 8 of the 56 suspected Maoists who surrendered are from Kumakoleng village. This comes after a similar mass surrender of 29 people from the area on 2 March.

A press note issued by the Bastar police said: "the most important part of this surrender is that in the village of Tulsi of the Tushi Dongri area, 17 people have surrendered. These Naxals had been trained by senior cadres Sonadhar, Vinod and Shankar who have been neutralized. Because of this even those who live far away in hills and even from across Odisha border have surrendered before the Bastar police....these surrenders are a part of a non-violent revolution against the Maoists".

Greyhounds helping Chhattisgarh police, CRPF in anti-Maoist operations: 13 Mar 2016

As many as eight top Maoists who ran operations in Chhattisgarh and Telangana were killed in an encounter on 1 Mar 2016

In one of the biggest counter-insurgency offensives in recent times, the Grey hounds wing of the Telangana police is coordinating with Chattisgarh police and the CRPF in fighting Maoists in the Dandakaranya forest in a strategic move cleared by the MHA.[16]

Due to this strategy as many as eight top Maoists who ran operations in Chhattisgarh and Telangana were killed in an encounter in Botetong forest in Bijapur district of Chhattisgarh on 1 March. The fact that the encounter took place when the ultras were holding a state committee meeting amid high vigil is considered to be a victory for the Greyhounds, CRPF and the state police. The eight top Maoists who were killed were capable of individually launching operations against the security forces. Gottimukkala Ramesh alias Latchanna, 53, was a technical expert who dealt with the landmines and weapons division of the Maoists in the Sukma division area. However, the key Maoists leader Jagan alias Haribhushan escaped the encounter.

The eight-hour operation, close to the area where the ultras were holding the state committee meeting in the border area of Chhattisgarh and Telangana, came as a blow to the extremists who had put in place a three, layered sentry system. This is perhaps the first time in recent times that the cops could strike at the Maoists while they were holding the state committee meeting with over 50 tops leader. PM Narendra Modi and home minister Rajnath Singh has particularly congratulated the Telangana police and the Greyhounds for the joint offensive. Enthused by the pat, DGP Telangana Anurag Sharma held a meeting with officials last week to tackle the possible maoist retaliation along the Telangana-Chhattisgarh border.

The Greyhounds, wing of Telangana is an elite force of some 2000 commandos trained to fight Maoists in their forest strongholds. Formed in 1989, this anti-Maoist force is developed mostly on the guerrilla tactics of Maoists in jungle and urban warfare. After the division of Andhra Pradesh, the Centre had decided to allow the Telangana Government to retain the Greyhounds as its headquarters has strategically been located in Hyderabad and would help counter Maoist threat from Maharashtra, Karnataka, MP and Chhattisgarh and even Andhra Pradesh and Odisha. The Telangana government had accorded top priority to the Greyhounds and enhanced the salary and special perks by 40 per cent making it one of the highly-paid police units in the country. Equipped with ultras-modern automatic weapons this anti-insurgency wing has been led by several officials including present CRPF DGK Durga Prasad once.

As part of its drive to clear Chhattisgarh forests of Maoists who gained control over hundreds of villagers and tribal hamlets since the late 1990s, the Centre has decided to adopt a multi-pronged strategy whereby overt and covert police moves would be utilized, according to some senior officials involved in the operations who spoke to the weekly.

Officials said the 1 March encounter named Operation Botetong, came after detailed homework for over six months after a series of disastrous set-backs to the CRPF and Chhattisgarh police since 2012. In three years, the Central and state forces have lost around 300 men and another 90 civilians in the hands of Maoists. "The situation is turning worse and the Centre is worried over the growing spread of Maoists in the hinterland of Chhattisgarh forests. The CRPF jawans who are posted on rotation are clueless about the forests and the local cops cannot match the Maoists in guerrilla tactics", a Telangana police official said explaining the need to involve Greyhounds in the operations. At a series of anti-insurgency operation meetings held in Delhi since they BJP-led NDA government came to power two years ago, the focus has been on containing damage to security forces in Chhattisgarh and tackling Maoists in an intelligent manner. It was then decided to involve Grey hounds in the anti-Maoist operations in the central India. Chhattisgarh is the headquarters for the Maoists who want to expand their activities all over the country. Of the four regional bureaus Chhattisgarh is the centre of the Central Regional Bureaus (CRB) that include three committees Dandakaranya Special Zonal Committee (DK SZC); Telangana State Committee and Andhra odisha border committee.

Excepting the northern regional bureau (NRB) that takes care of Bengal, Jharkhand and Bihar, the other two-southern regional bureaus (SRB) and the western regional bureau (WRB)—are nominal with limited squads. The police hold that the striking force of the Maoists is essentially dependent on their strength in the CRB. If the Maoists are weakened in the CRB, they stand weakened in the entire country. This is the assessment of the MHA as also of the Greyhounds. The present strength of the ultras in Chhattisgarh forests range 500-750, including the squad members and the couriers while some 2000 CRPF and local police are earmarked to fight them.

Still the security forces are unable to take them on effectively. The Greyhounds are now acting on the inputs received from 25 former Maoist cadres who had surrendered to the police since 2012. After that 1 March encounter, Telangana police have shared with Chhattisgarh police the details of 22 top leaders of Maoists moving on the border of both the state's. Overall, the police have details of some 50 top Maoist leaders who are behind every offensive against the security forces. "After the failure of the Salwa Judum. a state-run drive against the ultras the present phase is crucial," said a senior officer.

There has been a backlash from Maoist sympathizers and civil rights group in Telangana over the Botetong encounter. The Maoist gave a bandh call on 6 March that evoked poor response.

Telangana home minister Naini Narasimha Reddy told this weekly on 9 March: "We have not done anything, we just joined a joint operation in our neighbouring state".

Two BSF men killed fighting Maoists: 13 March 2016

Two BSF personel were killed and four others injured in an encounter with Maoists in Kanker district in the early hours of 12 Mar 2016. The encounter took place near the Chhotebethiya Pakhanjor jungle axis of the district[17].

A joint operation was launched by 117 and 122 battalions of CRPF as well as state police from the Chhote betoya camp, deep in the jungles of the Bandeh area in Kanker. "The exchange of fire took place at 2:30 AM when the troops reached a river in the dense forest near Beecha village. The ultras opened discriminate fire in which two BSF men were killed and four others killed.

The deceased were identified as Vijay Kumar and Rakesh Nehra. They joined in 2011-12. The injured are Manoj Kumar, S Thomson, Jagdish K and Bappa D.

"Six security force men died in three separate attacks in the past week." This was sign of advances security forces were making into Maoist strongholds. "The deaths are unfortunate and our hearts bleed for every soldier. If you analyse how these deaths occurred; one was during the building of crucial road in Sukma, three in an encounter in a maoist stronghold in Sukma and now in Kanker. Police are advancing and rebels are being pushed back," said an officer.

We are committed to protecting Soni Sori and minorities: we are winning against Naxals now: 16 Mar 2016

Interview: CM Raman Singh

Raman Singh is CM of Chhattisgarh speaking with Rohit E David,

Singh discussed the recent attack on a local church, fighting Naxals and protecting Soni Sori[18].

Q: Why is there silence on the attack that targeted Soni Sori?

A. This is incorrect, what happened to Sori is deplorable. I am very concerned about such incidents, while problems are created by Naxals who have become vicious in their attack on civilians as they are being pushed back, the state is committed to the rule of law. The moment the unfortunate incident with the Sori took place, an FIR was filed and considering the gravity of the matter, a special team under an IPS officer was constituted to investigate.

I personally directed our resident commissioner in Delhi to visit her in hospital to enquire about her welfare. The principal secretary (Home) along with the DC and SP also visited her house to meet her family members and reassure them about their safety. Security was provided at her home. Sori was given Y-category surprisingly, she refused it, which is perplexing.

Sori contested the last Vidhan Sabha elections from the AAP. Politics and elections have their own dynamics hence we provide security to politicians whenever necessary, but she refushed. I would like to reiterate that we are committed to provide Sori all the security she needs.

Q: A journalist was recently threatened in Raipur. Is the state unsafe for the press now?

A: I am not aware of the Raipur episode. My government believes in the freedom of the press. To provide a sense of security to journalists, we have set up a committee of senior officers with journalist representatives and Directro pubic relations, as member secretary to improve coordination between security forces and the media.

Q: What is the status now of fight against Maoists in Dantewada, etc?

A: We are moving ahead slowly and systematically, there is no silver bullet. Naxalism would be wiped out through a two pronged effort: development and security measures. Our approach is holistic development in tribal areas with a special focus on education, health, nutrition and agriculture. We provide nutrition security. We have established livelihood colleges in Naxal-hit districts where tribal youth avail vocational training. Recently, many surrendered Naxal youth also underwent training in these colleges.

Chhattisgarh spends 86 per cent of its budget on tribal populated areas which constitute 32 per cent of state's population. In other words, the state spends a greater part of the budget on the tribal areas compared to their population ratio.

On the security front forces have been systematically pushing Maoist back. We are gaining an upper hand. The figures speak for themselves: over 50 Naxals eliminated in a few months, over 400 surrenders. Their cadres is thinking. I am confident that inch by inch, we will progress and win the battle.

Q: Why do so many armed forces get killed in these operations? Does not it show lack of intelligence?

A: Our forces are fighting in one of the most difficult theatres anywhere is the world. But this battle has provided tremendous learning and the forces show extraordinary courage. The intelligence has been strengthened and in the past few months. Maoists have suffered major reverses.

Q: With Naxals recently surrendering, will they all be rehabilitated?

A: Well, Naxals are losing not only military war but also the ideological one. Today, tribals in Bastar are fed up with Naxals who systematically denied them development by keeping them in the dark ages under the garb of the so-called Maoist ideology. Stories are emerging about various kinds of exploitation of villager and low rung of Maoist cadres. As a result of our own policies, we are winning the heart and minds of tribal population, including the Naxal cadres. This, coupled with the surrender policy, ensures many maoist cadres are rehabilitated and joining the mainstream.

Q: Meanwhile, what do you feel about the attack on a local church?

A: The recent incident in Raipur was condemned unequivocally by me. Police acted swiftly and nine persons were arrested. This is a random incident. Too much should not be read into it.

Q: There is growing feelings of insecurity among the minorities, though.

A: In Chhattisgarh, there is no such feelings of insecurity. The law provides equal protection to all. India is a unity in diversity. Our culture is based on communal and social harmony. In my opinion, there is no religious intolerance in our country. A few incidents cannot affect national unity.

122 Naxals give up arms in Sukma: 10 Apr 2016

In a major achievement for the Chhattisgarh police, a record 122 Naxals, including their supporters, surrendered on 9 Apr 2016 with their arms in insurgency-riddled Sukma. The surrenderees include several hard core Naxals whom police was trying to apprehend for years for their involvement in major attacks on police and civilians in sprawling Bastar region, ASP Sukma Santosh Singh said 9 Apr 2016.[19]

"They surrendered Maoists were strongly disappointed with Maoist ideology which propagates terror and wanted to return to mainstream of the society", he added, out of these 122 surrenderees, 10 carried a bounty of Rs 1 Lakh each on their heads.

Golapalli LOS member Ramesh, Polampalli LOS member Raja, Kistaram LGS member Badru, Dandakaranya, Kisan Mazdoor Adivasi Sangh (DKAMS), president of Kanger Ghati Pitvas alias Guddu, KMS member Raje Jan Militia commanders Kosa and Hunga, Chetna Natya Mandali president Undam Bheema and Undam Joga carried cash reward of Rs 1 lakh each on their heads. Likewise, DKAMS president of Katekalyam area committee Mahadev carrying a bounty of Rs 1.05 lakh on head also surrendered before the police.

Apart from the Maoists carrying a bounty of Rs 1 Lakh or more, 52 DKAMS members, 33 KMS members, one CNM member, 12 GRD members, one Adivasi Balak Saugathan member, 3 militia deputy commanders, one from New Democratic Party (Telangana) and four naxal supporters have left the path of violence.

A Naxal school teacher, a militia member, a Jantana Sarkar member's a president of Naxal Agriculture Committee and a Militia Platoon member were also among the surrenderees.

The surrendering ultras were residents of various Maoist stronghold villages like Kistaram, Jagaruda, Chintagufa, Tongpal, Dornapal, Maraiguda and Konta.

They were provided with financial assistance of Rs 10,000 each. They all will be rehabilitated according to the state government policy.

Maoists in India: A miscellany

This section deals with Maoist issue in India, not connected with violent incidents. A variety of news stories are covered in this part.

Maoist in India: A USA assessment: 14 Mar 2016

US study lists Indian Maoists as world's fifth most dreaded perpetrators of violence

As many as 53 people were executed by Maoists after 'kangaroo courts' found them guility in the five worst Naxal hit states of the country in the last three years as per the MHA statistics. Highest of such killings were executed in the kangaroo courts known as the Jan Adalats of Maoists are in Chhattisgarh and Jharkhand.

Meanwhile, the recent studies by the US-based National Consortium for the Study of Terrorism and Responses to Terrorism, known as START had listed Indian Maoists as the fifth most dreaded perpetrators of violence.

The US study group listed ISIS as the first most dreaded perpetrators of violence in the world. Second terrorist organisation in the list is Boko Haram, followed by Taliban and al-Qaeda.

The MHA statistics hold that 18 people were killed following the directives of kangaroo courts in 2015 for being alleged police informers or for not believing in Maoist ideology. During the year, 41 'Jan adalat' were held by Naxal cadres in five LWE-affected states: AP (1). Bihar (6), Chhattisgarh (14), Jharkhand (14) and Odisha (6).

Altogether, 15 people were executed in 2014 following orders of 54 Jan adalats and 20 people were killed in 2013 under the directives of 63 Jan adalat.[20]

"To create terror among civilians in the LWE-hit areas, the Maoist cadres in their 'kangaroo courts', also called 'praja courts' execute the sentence against the civilians who do not subscribe to their ideology in the areas under their domain or labeling them as police informers", a home ministry official told PTI.

In 2006 (till 15 February) two 'jan adalats' have been held in Chhattisgarh while nearly one lakh paramilitary personnel continue to be deployed in LWE-hit areas, the 10 Naxal-hit states [AP, Bihar, Chhattisgarh, Jharkhand, MP, Maharashtra, Odisha, Telangana, West Bengal and UP] saw 226 deaths in 1088 incidents of violence perpetrated by Maoists in 2015.

In 2015, of the 226 deaths, 168 were civilians and 58 were security forces men. As many as 89 Maoists were also killed and 1668 were arrested and 570 cadres surrendered before the authorities during the year.

The START's study reveals that during 2000 to 2014, the Indian Maoists had conducted 337 coordinated terrorist attacks. The top ranking terrorist outfit ISIS conducted 757 and African jihadi outfit BOKO Haram executed 558 coordinated terrorist attacks. Taliban conducted 444 and Al Qaeda conducted 400 terror strikes. ULFA is listed as 18th in the list of the US study for coordinated terror attack during 2000 to 2014, ULFA has conducted 60 coordinated terror attacks.

Al Qaeda's Somalian affiliate al Shabaab is 6th in the list by executing 244 terror strikes during the past 14 years. Pakistan-based Tehriki-e-Taliban Pakistan (TTP) is 7th in the list with 175 terror strikes.

Fringe Maoist outfit takes centre stage after JNU row: 21 Feb 2016

"It has a fringe significance in the student politics of Jawahar Lal Nehru university. But because of its Maoist ideology and perhaps because it has to work extra hard to make itself heard on the campus, the Democratic Students Union (DSU) often tries to be provocative in its actions. It was in character, therefore, when some members planned to observe the third anniversary of Afzal Guru's hanging on 9 Feb 2016. But the tiny Leftist organisation possibly did not gauge the impact this would have DSU's sudden prominence may not enthuse the few subscribers to its agenda with the police out to nab some purported members, among them Umar Khalid and Banajyotsna Lahiri for sedition".

The above is the opening paragraph of an assessment of a little known Leftie outfit DSU in a daily of 21 Feb 2016.[21]

What is of interest and mild surprise is the fact that the brave Leftie leaders, Khalid and Lahiri, are now scared to their wit's ends since sedition charge has been filed against them. They had free run in the past as the Congress-led UPA let some such anti-national activities pass for vote-bank politics. This is Nehruvian legacy, which brough nation to the 1962 humiliation and 1991 bankruptcy! What a memorial to Nehru, this JNU who was a fake Leftie for garnering Brownie points in the international field to the detriment of nation's interest! His true successors Khalid and Lahiri are hiding from the police, instead of boldly handling themselves over to the police to face the consequences of their convictions and consequent action! It is so tempting to brave on the JNU campus and then turn coward outside its protection!

The rest of the analysis is reproduced here verbatim: "DSU has been around for three decades, and remains alive only on the margins of JNU's politics. It once was active in Jamia Millia Islamia and Delhi University (DU), but has lost its moral and intelliectual weight among students. Anand Kumar, a retired professor who has been associated with the JNU for 45 years, explained the raison d'etre of the student body: DSU is treated with benign neglect by rest of the student groups. It has its own ideas about extreme democratic transformation and follows certain ideologies of underground Maoist groups." Not many DSU members (and they number very few even in JNU) are prepared to speak about their organisation at the moment, fearing what they claim is a withc-hunt following allegations of anti-india, pro-Kashmir sloganeering at the 9 Febrauary event. "DSU is not a new oraganisation and it has never been banned by the government as reported in a section of the media", said one member as she sat near the JNU's administrative block, helping to make banners and posters for the Save JNU campaign. "DSU is 30-year old, older than AISA and yes, we hold completely different view on the Maoist issue different even from that of other Left groups".

- According to Sandeep Singh, president of JNU SU in 2007-08 who is on the campus extending his support to the students' protest against the police action against the participants of the Afzal Guru event and the arrest of JNU SU president Kanaiya Kumar, said, "DSU is a very small organisation that hardly manages 100-odd Votes in JNU's union elections. It is a Leftist union but it is opposed even to other left groups. The focus right now, however, is not on the organisation as much as it is on Umar Khalid. The reason why DSU is in the news at the moment is because the organisers of the controversial event were once members of the groups".
- Along with Khalid, the police are also looking for Lahiri who is a faculty member at the Ambedkar University Delhi (AUD). The university officials there said that she was newly appointed to the faculty and they were not sure how many classes she had taken. The AUD administration claimed that neither she has been seen on the campus since the day of the JNU event nor have they received an intimation about her absence from her.

Ignored by the media and politicians, Geelani family suffers in silence: 28 Feb 2016

Daughter asks why no protests have been organised in Delhi; son says father being targeted as he is a Kashmiri.

Syed Abdul Rahman Geelani, professor at Delhi University and some others organised an event on 10 Feb, 2016 at the Press Club of India, New Delhi on Parliament attack convict Afzal Guru. This after police action on organisers of a similar event a day earlier in the JNU campus where anti-india slogans were raised. A day later, on the 11th the Delhi Police registered on FIR against Geelani on the basis of a Zee News footage claiming anti-India slogans were raised at the event and he did nothing to stop that. His daughter, 23 years old Nusrat Geelani argues: but such events have been taking place since 2013. Last year, people marched on the streets against Afzal Guru's hanging. So why now?"

On 15 February, Geelani left for the college around 4 PM. His son, Atif says they had an apprehension as JNU SU president Kanaiya had been arrested from campus. At 8.30 PM Geelani called Atif and told him the police have detained him. "At 3 AM, the police formally arrested him", says Atif[22],

Unlike the JNU case where all the organizers of the Afzal Guru event are named in the police complaint, in the Press Club event only Geelani is named in the FIR. Atif is convinced his father has been targeted for being a Kashmiri, as he has been wrongly charged with the terror links in the past too. Geelani was named as one of the conspirators in the 2001 Parliament attack case, but was acquitted by the High Court in 2003.

Nusrat has her own list of grudes against many entities against her father's arrest:

1. "My father has been violated in the past and the state is after him again", says Nusrat as he too has been charged with sedition and put behind bars, like the JNU students. Geelani has been in custody "for the last two weeks for organizing an event in the Press Club.
2. However, unlike the furore over the arrest of JNU students Kanaiya Kumar, Umar Khalid and Anirban Bhattacharya, Geelani's case has failed to draw the attention of either the media or the politicians. "Not a single protest has taken place in Delhi for my father. No one wants to talk about him. why?" asks Nusrat.
3. In Kashmir, a strike was called on 27 Feb 2016 by separatist groups against the arrest of Geelani and JNU students.

Geelani, who is the one of the vice presidents of Committee for Release of Political Prisoners, was one of the organisers of the 10 February events, which was attended by many guests, including academics and journalists.

A native of Baramula, Srinagar, geelani teaches Arabic at a college in Delhi University. Ever since 2001, the first time he was arrested, his family have seen several ups and down. He escaped death a second time on the night of 8 Feb 2005, when he was shot at five times outside his lawyers residence. "That time his collegues and students stood with us, financially and emotionally. But this time, people and particularly the media have shut the door on us."

The family has met Geelani twice after his arrest. "They said they were scared for his safety after TV reports claimed Kanaiya was thrashed in custody. But when we met him, we were relieved. No such thing happened to him", says Nusrat.

Geelani's family resides in a non-descript south-east Delhi society. His two children, Nusrat and Atif, are pursuing law, conscious choice they made after his arrest in 2001. "Sometimes, circumstances force you to make some coreer choices. The only hope for justice is through the courts and we are preparing for it. My father has always fought for human rights, but today he is a victim."

Police trying to implicate us in Soni Sori attack: Relatives: 3 March 2016

"Tribal activist and AAP leader Soni Sori's relatives have alleged that they were being "intimidated and harassed" by Bastar police in the name of investigation. Sori's nephew Lingaram Kodopi went on to allege that the police were also trying to implicate her relatives in the case."

The above was reported in daily on 3 Mar 2016.[23]

Kodopi told the daily: "We fear that police might implicate me or Sori's cousin Ajay Markam in the case of an attack on her. Since the formation of the SIT, I have been askd to come to the police station thrice. Every time, they ask us the same questions and we are being given disrespectful treatment. Ajay Markam was also called to the police station for inquiry. Ajay Markam was told that he along with me and Sanjay Pant, were involved in the attack.

This was not the first time Kodopi, the only tribal journalist in Bastar, was being targeted by the authorities. A few years ago, Kodopi was implicated along with Soni Sori in an alleged case of a corporate house pay off to the Maoists.

Accordingly to him, he was inhumanly tortured in the custody and a petro chemical liquid was put in his rectum for which he is still undergoing treatment.

Despite poor health, Kodopi has been the main support for Soni Sori who has been emerged the face of tribal protest in Bastar in the past few years.

The nephew of Soni Sori also accused the police of pressurizing AAP leader Arvind gupta to take back the police complaint which he filed against unknown person after 19 Feb 2016 attack on Soni Sori. IGP Bastar range SRP Kalluri was not available for comments.

Child soliders reveal horrors of Red zone : 4 Mar 2016

There are two articles on this issue in a daily both are recorded here. Kidnapped from homes, kids trained to handle fire arms

"Eleven years old Golu, the native of a village in the Luggu forest of Jharkhand's Bokaro district, was trained to handle guns when he should have been using a brush to put his imagination to paper. But some exceptional presence of mind has now helped the child, a member of the notorious children's squad of the CPI (Maoist), the *bal dasta,* to extricate himself from the spiral of naxal violence. Seeing his apprehension by police as a Chance to escape, Golu refused to run away from the site of the 3 Mar

2016 encounter at Luggu. And, now his account has joined those of several before him to paint a grim picture of childhood sacrificed at the altar of extremism. The members of *bal dasta,* Golu told the police, are made to handle guns, apart from carrying equipment and cook".

The above explains the pernicious practice adopted by the maoists to get children in their ranks. This appeared in a daily on 4 Mar 2016[24].

Maoists have for long inducted the children of their cadres in the *bal dasta.* But of late, amid increasing pressure from the security forces and losses in encounters, they have shifted their focus to children who live in villages that fall within the Red corridor.

In Jharkhand alone, for example, a joint raid by police and CRPF led to the rescue of 16 children from a rebel den. In 2013, six Latehar children managed to escape from the clutches of Maoists.

In Apr 2015, the Jharkhand High Court had issued notices to the Union Home Secretary and the police in Jharkhand and Chhattisgarh, seeking a report after the local media reported kidnapping of over three dozen children from Gumla and Lohardaga by Maoists. At the time, some of the children came back following police intervention.

Former Latehar DC Aradhana Patnaik, now the secretary of school education, has interacted with a few members of the Bal Dasta. But of late, Amid increasing pressure from the security forces, and losses in encounters, they have shifted their focus to children who live in villages that fall within the Red Corridor.

In Jharkhand alone, for example, a joint raid by police and CRPF led to the rescue of 16 children from a rebel den. In 2013, six Latehar children managed to escape from the clutches of Maoists.

In Apr 2015, the Jharkhand High Court had issued notices to the Union Home Secretary and the police in Jharkhand and Chhattisgarh, seeking a report after the local media reported kidnapping of over three dozen children from Gumla and Lohardaga by Maoists. At the time, some of the children came back following police intervention.

Former Latehar DC Aradhana Patnaik, now the secretary of school education has interacted with a few members of the *bal dasta.* She says various government schemes have been initiated to bring children back to school. "Our *'school chalen, chalayen abhyan'* and the decision to distributes uniforms shows, school bags and text books, has attracted many childrens to schools", she added.

Jharkhand has also set up, Ashram schools, to ensure education for children in Maoist-Dominated pockets.

Talking to the daily, a Maoist ideologue however dismissed as government propaganda the reports that children were being used as soldiers, adding that those in police custody were coerced into propagating these stories. "Government schools distributes uniforms and mid day meals on paper, but most of these go the officers, and when we try to import education to the children, they are branded as members of the *bal dasta*". said the member who has done much to spread education in Latehar, Palamu and Garhwa between 2005 and 2009.

They worned I would be killed if I tried to flee: 4 Mar 2016

Eight-year-old Gappu, one of the two minors apprehended by police during an anti-Maoist operation at Luggu Hill under Gomia block on 3 Mar 2016, was a class 1 student at a government school when he was recruited by Maoists. Narrating his ordeal to police, Gappu said he "suffered in the Gomia jungles for three months". Talking about his induction, he added: I was alone at home when Maoist cadres knocked at my door. Pakaj Da (one of the guests) asked me about my parents. When they realized no one was around, they asked me to join them. I could not turn down their offer because I was scared in the jungle, I was given boiled rice and uniform of black T-shirt and trousers to wear. I did not like being in the jungle but I was afraid of Santosh Da (a senior Maoist). He threatened he would kill me if I made an attempt to escape. I missed my parents and brother but I could not do much. Later, I made friends with the other children in the squad".

This news story was datelined Bokaro 4 Mar 2016.[25]

Gappu went on to add that he was asked to carry items on his back and would help cook. "The commander asked me to guard the camp at night. Though I was not given a gun, I was told Birsen Da in the squad carried an AK-47, commander Santosh Da carried an INSAS rifle, and some women cadres carried carbines and rifles", he said.

Gappu said the squad was always moving through the jungles. "We would cover severa kiliometers. There were 20 members in the squad, including two girls," he added.

During the encounter on 3 March night Santosh Da asked Gappu to stay in the front while he opened fire at security men.

PM for rural electrification, net-connected panchayats: A counter-Naxal step: 6 Mar 2016

PM Narendra Modi on 5 Mar 2016 stressed upon speeding up the pace of development work ranging from rural electrification to bringing broad band internal connectivity to gram panchayats. At an infrastructure review meeting, NITI Ayog CEO Amitabh Kant made presentation about the physical performance achieved against the target set for the infrastructure sector.[26]

The PM was informed that 6000 villages have already been electrified out of 18,500 unelectrified villages and the renewable energy capacity had reached 39.5 GW against the target of 175 GW. While the PM called for the acceleration to provide broad band connectivity to all Gran panchayats, he was informed that 1,371 towers have been installed to provide mobile connectivity to villages affected by LWE and work has been expedited in the north-east and other hilly areas.

India tops IED blasts global list: 7 Mar 2016

Bombing by terrorists may be a routine features across trouble-torn countries worldwide but India tops the list globally in bearing the brunt of IED explosions. As many as 268 IED explosions were reported in the country in 2015, leaving 117 people dead and another 457 injured. India accontered for some 20.5 per cent of all the IED explosions reported in 68 countries in 2015.[27]

In fact, 2015 saw 441 per cent increase in IED blasts in India compared to 2014 and the resultant causalities increased by 55 per cent. Between 2006 and 2015, there have been an average of 28 blasts yearly with 270 fatalities and 850 non-fatal causalities.

Pakistan follows India with 208 IED blasts; the neighbouring country however, had 1308 blasts in 2015. Iraq (170), Bangladesh (167), Afghanistan (121), Nigeria (91) and Egypt (87) were the other nations most hit by the IED blasts [India is obviously topping the list in the sense that the pak blasts mostly are terrorism related while India's are mostly LWE related].

Syria hit by ISIS violence, reported 41 explosions in 2015, according to data compiled by National Bomb Data Centre of the elite counter-terror force National Security Guard (NSG). Philippines reported 39 IED blasts followed by 37 on Yemen, 32 in turkey, 30 in Thailand, 28 in Somalia and 22 in Ukraine

Israel had 11 blasts, Lebanon 7 and Saudi Arabia 9

In 2015, the most preferred targets in India were public areas and security forces. There was a 17 per cent increase in targeting of public areas in 2015 in contrast to 2014, likewise there was a 16 per cent decrease in targeting of security forces. This shift to soft targets is an indication of better handling of IED threats by security forces", the NSG pointed out.

While 268 blasts were reported in 2015, the number was 190 in 2014, 212 in 2013, 241 in 2012 and 172 in 2011. The number of causalities in 2014 was 75, 130 in 2013, 113 in 2012 and 157 in 2011.

Naxal-hit areas reported the most number of IED blasts with 131 explosions in 2015, followed by the north-east with 72 blasts, 14 in J and K and 51 in rest of the country. The figures in 2014 were 98 in Naxal-affected states, 61 in north-east, 19 in J and K and 12 in other parts of the country.

The naxal-hit states accounted for 49 per cent of the total IED incidents in 2015. West Bengal (39), Chhattisgarh (39), Jharkhand (15) and Odisha (15) were the worst hit states in 2015 with these number of blasts. However, fatalities in north-east were higher with 52 fatalities (42 per cent of the total causalities) as against 46 deaths in Naxal areas in 2015.

The higher fatality ratio in north-east states is indicative of better training and resolutions of the terror outfits operating there. There is need to impart more training and better equipping of the security forces engaged there", a senior officer said.

The assessment of the National Bomb Data Centre suggests the higher casuality ratio in the Naxal is an indication of an increasing expertise of the Maoists as regard IEDs.

The IED menace is spreading to the rest of the country and is not restricted to Naxal areas, north-east and J and K only.

80 per cent of the IEDs exploded in 2015 were made from the high explosives aimed at causing mass casualities. High explosives are preferred by terrorist groups but the easy availability of such material is a matter of grave concern and a strict control regime has to be put in place. It was highlighted by the NBDC in its annual journal.

GN Saibaba detention: A Naxal Sympathizer

He was arrested in May 2014, there have been various attempts for his release ever since.

Shifting Saibaba may be risky: Maharashtra government: 27 Feb. 2016

The Devendra Fadnavis government has opposed the ideas of shifting wheel chair bound Delhi university professor Saibaba from Nagpur jail to Gadchiroli district on the ground that the area was infested with the Maoists who may attempt to rescue him. The Supreme Court on 23 Feb 2016 questioned Saibaba's solitary confinement, asking Maharashtra government to make alternate arrangements at Gadchiroli for detaining him for criminal case, accusing him of having links with banned CPI (Maoist) was pending there[28].

Saibaba had moved the Supreme Court for bail on medical grounds, pleading he had to travel 170 km every time to attend his Case proceedings in Gadchiroli. In its affidavit before the top Court, Maharashtra deposed that it had received intelligence inputs about Maoist campaign to free him attacking the police when they are taking him to the court in order to free him.

"We want you (state) to make him comfortable. Tell us how you will make him comfortable. You cannot have him in solitary confinement", a bench had told the state counsel Nishant Katneshwarkar.

Shift Saibaba out of jail: SC tells Maharashtra: 23 Mar 2016

The Supreme Court on 22 Mar 2016 questioned the state government for putting Saibaba in solitary confinement in Nagpur Central Jail, and asked it to move him out of jail. A bench of justices JS Khehar and CN Nagappan said "No purpose will be served if the professor was confined to jail and it is not good for his health as he is 90 per cent disabled due to polio and suffering from various ailments. Why do you need to put him in solitary confinement? And you can make him stay in some other places outside jail premises, where his medical needs can be taken care of. You can put him in a guest house where he feels comfortable.[29]

The case was posted for 29 February. Senior advocate RS Cheema, appearing for Saibaba, told the court that his client was suffering from various life threatening ailments and he should be granted bail. The state opposed the bail plea, arguing that the professor would go underground if granted bail. It told the court that trial against him had begun and it would be finished within two months. The court was assured that jail authorities were taking care of his health and two jail inmates had been deployed to help him.

Saibaba released: 7 Apr 2016: An interview[30]

DU professor GN Saibaba was released from Nagpur jail on 7 Apr 2016 on Supreme Court orders. He spoke to a daily after his release.

Q: After JNU there have been protests in other campuses, do you know Kanaiya Kumar and plan to meet him?

A: A student's movement is developing against suppression. This may soon end up in anarchy. All the youths of JNU are like my students, including Kanhaiya Kumar, Anirban Bhattacharya or Umar Khalid. I am proud of my students they really love the people of this country. So did

Rohit Vemula. I have been an activist for 20 years and I know all of them. In fact, Kumar was in the defense committee when I was first arrested, we may meet again.

Q: There are sedition charges against Kumar and you had said that law should be scrapped. Why?

A: In the Supreme Court even the Maharashtra government argued that I would carry out anti-national activities if released. But a country is defined by its people and not the soil. What else can be better than serving the downtrodden like dalits and tribals. I believe sedition law should be done away with. Working against the government does not mean working against the nation. State is machinery and can be changed. Working for people's rights is no sedition.

Q: If there is Kanhaiya Kumar on one side, another youth leader Hardik Patel had emerged in Gujarat. Your views on the Patidar agitation?

A: Upper caste reservation demand reflects the fact that even the landed gentry are unable to make ends meet. There are no jobs and agriculture has been rendered unviable, however, an illusion has been created by ruling party that reservation will solve their problems. The upper casted like Jats, Patels, Marathas or Kapus do not deserve reservation. If granted, it will dilute the whole idea of affirmative action. Reservation should be limited to SC/ STs and to a certain extent OBCs.

Q: You call yourself a defender of rights. What rights are you defending?

A: The rights of the tribals that are being trampled upon. Right to organize, to rebel to establish an egalitarian order and all other basic rights. The tribal land is being gabbled up by corporates. They should have rights over the jungle and other natural resources. Even if you create a Silicon Valley in a place like Gadchiroli the tribal would not benefit. Their needs are different. They should first get two meals and education.

Q: But do you know farmers are happy to sell their land as farming is not very profitable?

A: I have seen in Gurgaon where locals are now begging after having sold their land for crores.

Police questions one more journalist: 14 Apr 2016

One more local journalist based in Dantewada district of Bastar region was questioned by the police for alleged Maoist links on 13 Apr 2016. Ajay Patel, a resident of Bade Gudra village of Dantewada and a "distributor and contributor" of a local Hindi daily, was asked to come to Dantewada police HQ on the 13th. Dantewada SP Kamlochan Kashyap told the daily:

"A Maoist leader was arrested for a case of an IED blast from Bade Gudra area recently. He confessed that the ultras bought wire from Patel's shop, we called him only to cross check Maoist leader's version. There is nothing much in the case and he is not a journalist. The police have a right to cross check if something comes out as part of our investigation. He was let off after questioning.

The above was reported in daily news story datelined Nagpur 13 Apr 2016[30].

Sceening committee

The president of south Bastar Press Union Bappi Roy said that the case has been referred to the screening committee which has been formed by the government of Chhattisgarh after journalists across the State protested against the back-to-back arrests of journalists based in Bastar.

Mr Roy said: "It seems they have not registered any case against Patel. The screening committee in Raipur has been asked to look into it. If he has any kind of involvement with the Maoists, then the police have full rights to act against him, if they are targeting him, then we will make sure we stand by him".

Four journalists from different parts of Bastar are in jail under various offenses and one journalist was forced to leave Bastar in last six months.

Despite facing continuous criticism and questions over the veracity of large numbers of alleged Maoist surrenders in Bastar, the police on the 13th claimed that 61 Maoists surrendered before them to join the mainstream.

"13 March surrendered Maoists include the Maoists' military wing the PLGA's supply member Fulo from Jiram village of Darbha and four Bal Sangham (Maoists' wing for teenagers), members. We will make sure that they get proper education now", said Bastar ASP Vijay Pande.

Naxals torch 4 vehicles and open fire on Chhattisgarh police: 16 Apr 2016

Naxals set ablaze four vehicles, including two engaged in a road constructions work, in Madanwada area of Rajnandgaon district of Chhattisgarh and exchanged fire with police on 15 Apr 2016, who were on their trail. SP of the district Sundarraj P said: "A group of 15-20 armed ultras torched these vehicles parked at an under construction bridge between Basely and Sahpal villages under Sitagaon police station limits late on the 15th." The vehicles included a truck, a poclain machine, a SUV and a motor cycle[32].

The Maoists also threatened the contractors and workers to stop construction work. In the wake of the torching incident, a joint team of security forces launched a search operation in the Madanwada and Kohka region, some 200 Km from Raipur, to trace the ultras during which a gun battle ensued on the 15th. There were no casualities on either side.

The joint team comprised men from STF, ITBP and district force, got a tip off on the presence of some cadres between Kaneli and Belgaon villages under Kohka police station. The ultras fled the stop, seeing the troops zeroing on them.

Police found a wireless set, a radio, a camera flash, besides a huge cache of maoist literature from the spot.

Anti-Maoist outfit (Samajik Ekta Manch) that hounded activists, journalists disbanded: 16 Apr 2016

"The Samajik Ekta Manch (SEM) a group working out of Bastar's Jagdalpur that had come under fire for its alleged role in hounding out activists, journalists and lawyers, announced its own "disbandment" with immediate effect on 15 Apr 2016" This was reported by a daily in its issue datelined Raipur, 16 Apr 2016[33].

The Manch organised rallies against the Maoists but drew flak for its close ties with the district police and for branding journalist Malini Subramaniam, lawyers Isha Khandelwal and Shalini Gera of Jagdalpur Legal Aid Group, activist Bela Bhati and economist Jean Dreze as Maoist sympathizers. These activists have called the Manch a "front for the police" and an attempt to intimidate "any voice critical of police excesses" in the rebel-hit region.

The Manch said in a release: "The residents of Bastar had created the SEM to support the central government, state government, district administration and police administration in their fight against Naxals. To this end, we had protested peacefully and democratically against Naxalism. But it is now being felt that in the guise of SEM, some people are trying to defame government, Police and administration. In these circumstances, the members of the SEM have unanimously decided to disband the organisation with immediate effect".

The Manch has been part of "several surrender ceremonies" with top police officials. Last week, the Manch's off shoot, Mahila Ekta Manch organised the burning of an effigy of Nandini Sundar, who had hit out at its activities in connection with an ongoing case on Salwa Judum in Supreme Court. Among members of the Manch are former members of Salwa Judum.

A senior government official admitted that the move to disband the Manch may not have been voluntary and might have been initiated by the state itself. "The state government was being criticized for what was happening in Bastar and it was felt that something had to be done. One of the points for which the state government drew flak was activities of groups like the Manch", he said.

On 28 Feb 2016, the daily had reported about a letter by DM Awasthi, special DG (Anti-Naxal Operation), to all seven SPs and Bastar IG, which said, "Anti-social elements were tarnishing the image of the police".

The move for the Manch to disband itself also comes after a wake of media pressure against its alleged role in hounding out activists.

Isha Khandelwal of Jagdalpur legal aid group said: "the fact that this action has been taken shows that the Manch was created to support the illegal activities of police in Bastar. But there are several other groups like this. There is Mahila Ekta Manch, Adivasi Ekta Manch and Naxal Peedit Sangharsh Samiti in Bijapur. The state must stop these groups harassing people".

Notes

1. Kumkum Dasgupta, Hindustan Times, 18 Dec. 2015.
2. Rashmi Drolia, Times of India, 25 dec 2015.
3. Ejaz Kaiser, Hindustan Times, 15 Feb. 2016.
4. Ejaz kaisar, hindustan times, 22 feb 2016.
5. Rashmi Drolia, Times of India, 5 Jan 2016.
6. PTI, The Hindu, 29 Feb. 2016.
7. Pavan Dahat, The Hindu, 1 Mar 2016.
8. *Ibid.*
9. ENS, Indian Express, 3.3.2016.
10. Agencies, Hindustan Times, 3 Mar 2016.
11. PTI, The Pioneer, 4 Mar 2016.
12. Pavan Dahat, The Hindu, 5 Mar 2016.
13. Dipanker Ghose, Indian Express, 7 Mar 2016.
14. ENS, Indian Express, 10 Mar 2016
15. ENS, Indian Express, 12 March 2016.
16. S. Ramakrishnan Sunday Guardian, 13 Mar 2016.
17. ENS, Indian Express, 13 March 2016.
18. Indian Express, 16 Mar 2016.
19. Staff reporter, the pioneer, 10 Apr 2016.
20. PNS, PTI, the Pioneer, 14 Mar 2016.
21. Manash gohain, times of India, 21 Feb 2016.

22. Maria akram, the hindu , 28 Feb 2016.
23. Pavan dahat, 3, Mar 2016.
24. Jaideep deo gharia, times of india, 4 Mar 2016.
25. Diva Khare, *Ibid.*
26. Mahendra Singh, Times of India, 6 Mar 2016.
27. Rakesh K Singh, The Pioneer, 7 Mar 2016.
28. Bhadra Sinha, Hindustan Times, 27 Feb. 2016.
29. Amit Anand Chaudhary, 23 Feb 2016, Times of India.
30. Shishir Arya, Times of India, 8 Apr. 2016.
31. Pawan Dahat, The Hindu, 14 Apr 2016.
32. PTI, The Pioneer, 16 Apr 2016.
33. Dipanker Ghose, Indian Express, 16 Apr 2016.

36

Jharkhand update (including Bihar, Odisha and West Bengal)

Hardcore Maoist nabbed from West Singhbhum: 8 Jan 2013

In a major achievement for the security forces engaged in flushing out the ultras, a hardcore maoist rebel Bimal Gudia was nabbed from Saranda forest, under Manoharpur police station of West Singhbhum district on 7 Jan 2013 during the ongoing massive anti-naxal combing operations 'Anaconda-2', police said.

In a joint operation of the CRPF and Jharkhan police team, Gudia wanted in some two dozen cases of Naxal violence including landmine blasts, murders and extortion, was caught.

The late father of the nabbed ultra was also a ring leader of Naxals who played a role in the formation of the CPI (Moist) in the Saranda in 2004 by merger of the then PWG and MCC. He father had also been arrested in the past for involvement in the Maoist violence.[1]

"Operation Anaconda-2 was launched early last month, Dec 2012 to completely flush out maoist from Saranda and pave way for speedy implementation of the Centre-sponsored Saranda Action Plan (SAP) a Rs 250 crore development project.

A district police officer talking to the daily said: "we cannot reveal on the status of the operation due to security reasons but yes, we have nabbed a Maoist...The forces are targeting the different areas under the Saranda forest Sources said the Maoist activities in the area may hamper the development works being carried under the ambitious Rs 250 cr SAP, a brain child of the rural development minister Jairam Ramesh "who had visited Saranda four times in the last one year".

This was the prime reason for undertaking Anaconda-2 operation.

Jharkhand voters defy Maoists

"Defying boycott call given by Maoist's about 65 per cent of the electorate cast their vote in the second phase of the polling in Jharkhand on 2 Dec 2014.

The above was reported by a daily on 3 Dec 2014.[2]

Of the 20 constituencies that went to the polls, 70 per cent are in the Maoist affected areas. Long queues of the voters could be seen at various polling stations especially in maoist-hit constituencies. In the first phase of polling on 25 November too the state witnessed an impressive turnout of 62 per cent voters.

Over 44 lakh voters decided the fate of 223 candidates in the fray including former CMs Arjun Munda and Madhu Koda.

Barring some cases of defective EVM machines at some places, polling was by and large incident-free polls officials said.

2 December turn out was an improvement from the 58.26 per cent recorded in 2009. The Election Commission seized Rs 1,12,83,479 in cash, 1.27 lakh litre liquor worth Rs 1.03 crore and drugs worth Rs 10.24 lakh.

The news story carries a photo of a beaming young tribal women with her baby and flaunting her Election Identity Card and its sub-title reads:

"A woman shows her identity card after casting her vote at Huttar in Jharkhand on Tuesday (2 Dec 2014)."

"Maoists kill 20-year-old girl who choose school over guns": Sick Mind: 8 Oct 2015

This is an expressive, evocative and telling headlines of a news report in a daily which is indicative of the mind and mental sickness of maoist murderous gangs! The story is datelined Ranchi/Gumla, 8 Oct 2015[3].

It opens up with an evocative para: She could have been India's Malala Yousafzai leaving behind a life of Maoist violence she was lured into as a child to start afresh, enrolling herself in school for studies and a bright future".

But Sanjeeta Kumari's dream of returning to the mainstream was shattered this week when Maoist insurgents killed her for allegedly spying on behalf of the police. Her blood-stained body was found near the hills of Gumla in Jharkhand on 6 Oct 2015.

Kumari who also went by the name of Guddi was lured into the outlaw group when she was eleven by a neighbour and transformed from a cook into crack shot serving under the Maoist banner for eight years before she decided to turn over a new leaf.

The 20-year old ran away from the rebels and went into hiding in Gumla where she rented a house and enrolled herself in a local school, but the outlaws continued to threatened her regularly.

When the daily met her on 28 July (2015) Guddi recounted chilling tales of the looming threat to her life but said she was committed to her studies and would not return to the extremist told under any condition. "I cannot surrender because the moment my leaders come to know they will kill my parents and siblings", she told the daily on the condition that her story would not be published. She continued: "I will be able to study as long as I am not identified and captured or my bosses in the jungle do not take me away forcibly."

But her dream wasn't to be! When she went home to see her parents and siblings in the maoist-infested village of Sibil on 4 October, she was abducted by the Maoists who left a hand written note behind saying Guddi had to die because she did not mend her ways despite several warnings.

Her body was brought to the hospital by local villagers, not police men "who live in constant fear of Maoist attacks." SP Gumla Bhimsen Tuti said, "she was not our spy, and we do not know any Maoist-related case against her so far."

Guddi had said she was bured into the group by her neighbour Savita Didi who was Maoist leader. Guddi served as a cook for a year before undergoing arms training. She became an expert at handling INSAS rifles and carbines.

Once fighting the forces in Latehar jungles, a bullet pierced her foot. "With the injured foot, I ran and walked for four days and nights till we reached a safer place", she said.

She fell in love with zonal commander Kanchan and wanted to marry him but he died in an encounter with the police.

Guddi also said Maoist commanders regularly exploit women sexually even if that was projected as consensual sex. She had disclosed other details:

> "Abortions are routine affair as women commanders cannot become mothers. When I left the camp in April (2015), there were 23 minor girls in zonal commanders Nakul ji's camp. Some of them as young as 10 years."

"The manufactured Maoists" cover story in India Today of 4 May 2015

- The story of 514 hapless Jharkhand men who were lured into surrender as Naxals.
- Double spread cover page carry photos of some 25 youngmen who were made victims of the fake Naxal surrender scam near Ranchi.
- The story is written by Amitabh Srivastava and photographs it carries are by Chandradeep Kumar.

A complaint unravels the scam

Pamesh Prasad, 21, a second year B.Com student and resident of Khunti district in Jharkhand files a complaint at the lower bazaar police station in Ranchi, accusing Dinesh Prajapati, owner of a local coaching centre named Digdarshan Institute, of cheating him after promising to get him recruited into a paramilitary force.

Prasad claims that Prajapati took Rs 2 Lakh from him in May 2012 and connected him to his friend Ravi Bodra, said to be former military intelligence informer.

Bodra, Prasad alleged, informed him about jobs being available in the CRPF under the "surrender policy". All he had to do was to claim to be a Naxalite, surrender before the CRPF with weapons supplied by Bodra, spend some months in jail and then get recruited in CRPF as a reformed extremist. Prasad took the bait and was lodged in the CRPF elite CoBRA battalion camp in Ranchi's old jail campus.

There were hundreds of other wide-eyed, young, mostly tribal men like him in the "open jail" aspiring to wear uniform and rise above their impoverished existence. But with the promised recruitment nowhere in sight, he fled much before a top cop in the CRPF smelt a rat and pulled down the curtains on a diabolic scam. His efforts to pursue the men who took him for a ride succeeded only some two years later when a tribal chief minister managed to push an apparently reluctant state police to investigate the complaints.

6 April 2014: Bodra picked up

When picked up by Jharkhand police, Bodra makes a "confessional statement" in the same lower bazaar police station. He claims to have facilitated surrenders and that he was acting under the guidance of senior police and CRPF officers he had known. Bodra is arrested and Prajapati surrenders in court and a charge sheet is filed in the case in May 2014.

Jharkhand CM Hemant Soren demands a CBI probe into the case. And then there is a silence. No policeman or CRPF officer is questioned. There is no investigation into how Bodra managed to arrange weapons as the surrendered men claimed and into the money trail. The demand for a CBI probe remains just that a demand.

Bodra is picked up in Apr 2014 and the weekly published the story a year later in May 2015.

And the Silence continues!

This silence is the story of 514 hapless Jharkhand men, most of them poor with no history of breaking the law, who begged borrowed or pledged their family wealth to raise the money to pay Bodra. Risk the tag of a Naxalite and spend nearly two years in the old Ranchi jail campus, all in the hope of getting a low paying job of constable in the CRPF, of donning a uniform and escaping the drudgery of life in some of Jharkhand's most backward regions. It is also the story of fly-by-night operators joining hands with unscrupulous elements in the establishment to exploit a national security imperative for gain or fame.

For Hope and Glory

The brick kiln furnace on the outskirts of Ghazipur district in eastern UP where in sundara Kujur works is some 400 km from the CoBRA battalion camp in Ranchi where he lived for more than a year as a" surrendered Maoist". But it is variance in the two places and not the distance that captures how much his life has turned upside down in the last three years.

Until Jan 2013, Kujur was a young man his villagers looked upto. From the non descript Jamgai village in Ranchi's Namkum block, Kujur had reached the CRPF's elite CoBRA battalion camp and was waiting to be recruited as a paramilitary constable. In the camp he discovered there were 500 other men like him, mostly from Ranchi and its neighbouring district of Khunti and Gumla. Each of them had paid Bodra anything up to Rs 2.5 Lakh after they were sold a lemon that the CRPF and possibly even the Jharkhand police would launch a "direct recruitment scheme" and these jobs would be given only to surrendered Maoists.

Over an l8-month period starting in Apr 2011, 514 men fell for it. Each of them was given a rifle or a pistol or bombs before they surrendered. They were then moved to CRPF camp. Life in the camp was good for the surrendered comrades. They only needed to do fitness drills besides running errands for the officers. They could visit their villages whenever they wanted, and sometimes a CRPF vehicle would even drop them home. The OG jacket they got at the camp inspired awe in the neighbourhood when they went visiting. It also drew more young men towards the camp. The only condition was to surrender as Maoists and few had any problem with that. It was a small price for a permanent government job.

Kuldip Bara, 24, from Palko in Gumla district paid 1 Lakh, which his parents borrowed from local money lenders, to Bodra. He claimed to be a cadre of the People's Liberation Front of India (PLFI) and surrendered with a double barreled gun which was given to him. He too stayed in the old Ranchi jail like Kujur. Devdutt Gope of ratu in Ranchi paid Rs 1 Lakh, Sukhdev Manda of Khatga paid Rs 1.5 lakh, Nathniyel Tirkey of torpa paid Rs 1.8 lakh, Roshan Gudiya of Loljimi paid Rs 55000 and Vilson Horro of Karra paid Rs 2 lakh. The list would possibly have continued to grow but for arrival of MV Rao as 1G of CRPF in Ranchi. Within a month of taking over, Rao wrote to the then DGP Jharkhand, GS Rath, questioning the reason for housing the 514 men in the old Ranchi jail which served as a CRPF camp. Rao wrote in the 3 Oct 2012 letter: "It has come to my notice when I visited the jail premises that only a few among these 514 so called surrendered Naxals have actual cases against them. Others it seems were brought without verifying their associations/participation in Naxal activities, hence the questioning of their involvement with Naxal activities has to be examined on a case-to-case basis. Otherwise, there is every possibility of unscrupulous elements exploiting the situation by making innocent me were criminals stage managing surrenders and claims benefits under the surrender policies". Rao also mentioned that surrender policy was the domain of the state government and not of a paramilitary force like the CRPF, which should be left alone to concentrate on anti-Maoist operations.

The letter indicated a possible nexus between CRPF and the state police in the surrender saga of fake Naxalites and not just a racket that involved Bodra and CRPF. Was this fake Naxal surrender racket a job scam scripted by elements in CRPF and state police that went wrong?

End of a dream

A senior state police officer thinks so: "They wanted to improve surrender statistics to earn brownie points from their MHA seniors. It was clearly a fraud committed on the innocent youth. CPMF cannot offer jobs to surrendered Naxals".

Rao could have driven these men out of his COBRA battalion camp the moment he wanted, but he shared his concern with the state police chief. He needed a go ahead from the latter to evict the boys.

The timing of the scam coincided with the tenures of UPA Home Ministers P Chidambaram (Dec 2008-Aug 2012) and Sushil Kumar Shinde

(Aug 2012-May 2014). Both were keen to fight LWE problem and had shown particular interest in Jharkhand, asking the state to push the extremists to surrender. "We believe senior officers in CRPF and state police had planned a big event for the Union Home Minister's visit: surrender of over 500 Maoist before him. Since they could not have arraged real Maoists, they made up the number luring the innocent to surrender as ultras, after giving them weapons". Alleges Shashi Bhushan Pathak of PUCL, Jharkhand. Kujur, the "surrendered Naxal" backs that claim.

Rao's letter had the obvious impact. The Jharkhand home department ordered a check of records of the 514 men in the camp only six of them had some links with Maoist activities, who could be considered eligible for benefits under surrender policy. The remaining 508 men were asked to leave the camp.

The state government accepted in assembly that 514 youths had been cheated on. As CM Soren had asked for CBI probe in May 2014. Soren tells the weekly in April 2015 that the CBI is reluctant to take up the investigation. He is no more the CM. Rajiv Kumar, a senior lawyer who had filed a PIL in the state High Court seeking a judicial order to the CBI to probe the case, accused the Jharkhand police of interested only in a cover up, as some senior officers are involved in the crime.

Besides the claim that each of the 514 youths were given arms and ammunition to make their surrenders look genuine raises another disturbing question: "This means at least 514 guns and a few thousand cartridges were planted. Are the CRPF and the state police into gun running?"

The blame Game

When the weekly, after investigating the case for weeks got in touch with senior CRPF and state police officers for their comments on the sordid saga, they were interested in distancing themselves from the scam, if not shifting blame. MV Rao, now posted in Hyderabad, refused to discuss the contents of the letter that blew the lid off the scams. The then DGP Jharkhand, whom the letter was addressed to feigned ignorance: "I don't recall anything now. I am a retired man now".

Kujur had more pressing concerns. He needs to earns Rs 40,000 as early as possible to get back the farmland his family had pawned to raise the money.

Kuldip Bara is among the few who are willing to forget the loss. Having studied up to class XII and also holding a degree from an ITI, he is confident of getting a job and returning the money he borrowed. "I don't want anything from the government neither justice nor punishment to those who hoodwinked us. I have a life to live and parents to support. Just wipe the Naxal tag off my name, arrange a character certificate for me from the local police station without which nobody would give us a job", he almost pleads.

It is a plea few are hopeful will be heard, unless there is judicial intervention or the Central Government steps in, more so the state is also now ruled by a BJP government. With needle of suspicion pointing towards both state and central police forces, only a neutral federal investigation agency is seen as capable of delivering justice to the victims.

Jharkhand police wield sedition stick to hunt down Maoist rebels: 3 Mar 2016

A wave of protests may have rocked the capital over the sedition charges against JNU student Kanhaiya Kumar but thousands of miles away, the Maoist violence-hit Jharkhand has the highest number of such cases.

The state registered 18 such cases in 2014. Most of them were against Maoist rebels, their front outfits and sympathizers, who have a presence in 16 of the state's 24 districts. Extremist violence has killed 499 civilians and 1689 policemen in the past 15 years.

Top officials say lower rung police officers use the 156-year-old sedition provision liberally against Maoist rebels when they attack forces, hoist black flags during national festivals or are found carrying pamphalets against India's unity and integrity but many of these cases collapse and embarrass the force." IPC section 124-A (sedition) is very loosely worded and open to varied interpretations", said state police ADGP (special branch) Anurag Gupta.

But do cases end up in convictions? "Unfortunately no, because evidences are scanty and procedures are not followed completely", Gupta said.

It was conceded that there was a severe lack of knowledge about sedition laws among lower-rung officers. In some cases, charge sheets were filed without seeking governments' permission mandatory for framing sedition charges, resulting in major embarrassment for the police in courts, said ADGP Anil Palta. "The cops blatantly use sedition against most of us. The idea was to prevent us from getting bail sooner whenever we got caught or surrendered", said Yugal Pal, once a senior Maoist commander and now a social activist in Palamu. Pal said as newer laws came into force, police switched from section 124-A to 17 Criminal Law Amendment Act (CLAA) and the Unlawful Assembly Prevention Act (UAPA), as these laws were tougher and required lesser intervention by the state.

But state secretary of the PUCL Shashi Bhushan Pathak said it was easy to frame Maoists for sedition as they were locals fighting forcible usurping of their land and minerals by corporates. Economist Harishwar Dayal, Director, Institute for Human Development (IHD) eastern Regional Centre, said until non state players shun violence and provide alternative growth plans, they will remain enemies in the eyes of law.[4]"

"India of 21st century does not require a law used by the colonial government to suppress India's voice", said Maoist turned activist Satishji. Slain CPI (Maoist) politburo member Kishanji had argued with this daily months before his death in an encounter with forces that Maoists were the biggest patriots "If Pakistan attacks India, we would be happy to form first line of defense against them, unfortunately the state considers us bigger enemies". Antother Maoist spokesperson, Bablooji had said they take 7 per cent levy for running their revolutionary force and carrying out the development programmes in villages. The government officers take 20-30 per cent cut in allocating welfare schemes. "Who is anti-national?"

They had asked. The news story carries some useful information, commentary on sedition law. It is reproduced here.

Colonial-era law

Enacted by the British rulers in 1860, sedition continues to be involked by successive governments.

What is sedition?

Sedition is a law which makes it illegal to incite hatred against the nation or bring the nation in disrepute by way of words or visual representations (pictures, banners).

When was it brought into Indian law?

- Sedition was introduced to Indian criminal law by the British in 1860 (section 124-A) nearly 10 years after the Indian Penal Code (IPC) was enacted.
- The law was called "highly objectionable and obnoxious "by JL Nehru, however, no government ever attempted to repeal the section.

What are the limits of their law?

- A sedition speech and expression may be punished only if the speech is an incitement to violence or public disorder (Kedar Nath vs. Bigar, 1962).

- A conviction under sedition requires incitement of immediate violence and simply debating revolution or calling for a violent overthrow of the state, won't amount to sedition (Balwant Singh vs. State of Punjab, 1995).

Penality for sedition

From three years to a lifetime in jail. A fine can also be imposed on the accused.

Most cases filed in states

Jharkhand	18
Bihar	16
Kerala	5
West Bengal	2
Odisha	2

Andhra Pradesh, Assam, Chhattisgarh and Himachal Pradesh 1 each.

Recent cases

Oct 2015:	Kovan, a singer for making internet posts "defamatory" to Tamil Nadu CM J Jayalalithaa.
Oct 2015:	Hardik Patel, Patel quota agitation leader in Gujarat for asking his supporters to allegedly assault police personnel during the Patidar compaign.
Sep 2012:	Aseem Trivedi, a Kanpur-based cartoonist for his cartoons attacking Indian politicians over corruption. Charges were dropped after he spent two weeks in jail.
Dec 2010:	Binayak Sen, a public health specialist working in Chhattisgarh was convicted of sedition for allegedly supporting Maoists. Supreme Court dismissed charge.
Nov 2010:	Arundhati Roy, a writer and a political activist, charged for advocating independence for Kashmir at a seminar along with Hurriyat Leader Syed Ali Shah Geelani.

Andhra Pradesh and Telangana court denies nod to Telangana police for taking Kobad Gandhi to state: 13 Jan 2016

A Delhi court dismissed a plea by Telangana police seeking its permission to take Maoist ideologue Kobad Ghandy, facing trial in Delhi, for allegedly trying to set up a base for the banned CPI (maoist), to produce him before a court in Telangana in some other cases.[5]

8 Maoists shot near Telangana-Chhattisgarh border: 2 Mar 2016

Outlawed CPI (Maoist) suffered a major blow in Telangana as eight of its members including the state committee secretary hari Bhushan, were killed in an encounter early on 1 Mar 2016.

Apart from anti-Maoist Greyhound force of Telangana and Chhattisgarh police, the central paramilitary force (read CRPF) also took part in the operation near cherla in khammam district of Telangana and Sukma district of Chhattisgarh.[6]

Divisional commander Lachchanna and three women were also among the fatalities. Recoveries from the scene of encounter in the forest area include an AK-47, believed to be of Hari Bhushan, semi-automatic rifles and .303 rifles.

DGP Telangana Anurag Sharma said the encounter took place around 7:30 AM when the Maoists and the police came face to face. Police are trying to identifying all the Maoists killed in the encounter.

Police had information about the ultras planning attacks in the region. Consequently, Telangana police and central forces had been carrying out combing operation for the last two days in the area leading to the encounter. Subsequently, police rushed in forces by choppers to take part in the operation.

This was one of the biggest operations in the Khammam district in a decade. Police believe 30 Maoists were involved in the encounter, however, the police did not suffer any losses in the operation.

As the incident had taken place deep in the jungle area, not accessible to the vehicles, authorities faced problems in retrieving the bodies to a hospital. Services of the local labour were hired to manually shift the bodies.

The combing/search operation was result of a tip off about a Maoist meeting in the area. Another daily gave some additional/ specific information on the encounter.

Eight fatalities included five women cadres. Those killed are suspected to be members of the venkatapuram Area Committee of CPI (Maoists) which operates in Bhadrachlam area in Khammam district.

Secretary Venkatapuram area committee Lachchanna and Telangana state secretary Haribhushan are believed to be among the dead but the Greyhounds could not confirm it[7].

The encounter took place near Sakler, 30 km from the Chhattisgarh Telangana border.

"The operation was planned and executed by the Telangana greyhounds since they were entering our territory, they had asked for some personnel with knowledge of the terrain", said ASP-anti-naxal operations). Sukma district, Chhattisgarh santosh said.

Despite encounter Naxals attract young recruits in Telangana: 6 Mar 2016

The killing of two women Naxalites of Wrangal, Anitha and Navatha, on the Telangana Chhattisgarh border on 1 Mar 2016 amply proves that though insurgency has come down drastically compared to the past, it has not been eliminated as claimed by the Telangana government.

As per the intelligence sources, as many as 36 persons in the district joined the Maoists since the separate state of Telangana were formed. The promise of more jobs and social justice does not seem to have impressed the youth who are attracted to the extremist ideology. The Telangana Rashtra Samiti (TRS) sympathised with the Naxals for quite some time also appears to have emboldened some youth to join the armed squads.[8]

A senior police officer says "although there is no organised movement as in the past, there are many Naxalites around. "A banner was placed by the Naxals on the Kakatiya University campus, where a condolence meeting of Vivek, a slain Naxal, was held. There were posters in Parkal and Bhupalpalli threatening the Speaker and Minister A Chandulal", he said. The police dismissed the possibility of the posters being put up by the miscreants. However, they are not sure who were behind them.

The killing a few month ago of Sruthi and Vidyasagar Reddy, who also hailed from Warangal, sent a strong signal to the rebels that the TRS government would not treat armed insurgency lightly. Both had joined the Maoist party after the formation of the Telangana state. Navatha and Anitha were recent recruits.

What surprises the police is the reason the youth, mostly educated, get attracted to the armed movement and the growing number of sympathizers. It has become difficult for them to identify Naxal sympathizers in the villages despite their best efforts, the police said

Senior Maosit leader dead: 10 Apr 2016

A top leader of the CPI (Maoist) Kudumula Venkata Ramana, alias Ravi, died of jaundice at a city (Visakhapatnam) hospital on 9 Apr 2016.

Ravi was member of the Andhra-Odisha Border Special Zonal Committee (AOBSZC) and commander of first company of the Central Regional Committee (CRC) of the CPI (Maoist), which was responsible for many operations in the area. He had planned several attacks on the police and destructions of property. Ravi carried a bounty of Rs 20 Lakh on his head.[9]

According to the police, Ravi was brought to the city from a place beyond Sapparla to the Chintapalli mandal in the morning but he was already dead. His relatives took the body back to the village. The police had learnt two months ago that he was suffering from severe jaundice.

Unconfirmed reports say that Ravi was brought to the sapparla PHC on 8 April and was shifted to King George Hospital (Visakhapatnam) since his condition was critical. From KGH, he was shifted to a corporate hospital but he was declared dead on arrival.

Amaravati in the cross hairs of Maoists: 14 Apr 2016

Alarm as the outfit seeks to cash in on resentment among section of farmers.

The CPI (maoist), which had a strong presence in united Andhra Pradesh until a few years ago, is trying to arrive on the scene in Amaravati, the upcoming capital of Andhra Pradesh.[10]

The party is studying among other things, the implementation of the Land Pooling Scheme, assurances given to farmers and unemployment in the capital region. The Maoist leaders discussed the situation in Thullur mandal in Guntur district. They enquired about the benefits announced by the AP government and actual situation in the capital's villages, intelligence sources said.

Action team

According to reliable sources, the party has formed an action team with Visakha East Division Committee members Gammela Keshava Rao alias Binsu and Jagamudi Venkateswara Rao alias Anand and Rajesh, an active member in Chhattisgarh unit.The committee members visited the capital's villages. They interacted with the landowners who are agitating against land pooling and those who could not get any benefits announced by the government.

It is learnt that the action team members are taking the help of a few committees which are fighting for the cause of the farmers.

The extremists are also tracking the movement of some people's representatives and officials visiting the region, the sources said.

The government took about 33,000 acres from farmers one years ago.

Farmers who parted with patta land were promised 1000 square feet per acre and those who parted with assigned lands were promised 450 square feet per acres.

Maoist burn mobile tower: 3 Mar 2016

A BSNL mobile tower was allegedly burnt by Maoists in a village in Gumla district late on 2 Mar 2016.

They also left posters on the spot claiming the act was a retaliation of killing of Maoist Sanjay Yadav in an encounter recently.

Forest guest house, jeep torched in Telangana: 17 Apr 2016

Attack could indicate resurgence of Naxalite movement in the state. A forest guest house and a jeep were torched allegedly by Naxalite at the Tadvai mandal headquarters between Warangal and Eturunagaram in Telagana on the night 15/16 Apr 2016. The guest house was recently renovated and some huts were constructed by the forest department to encourage tourism and attract visitors to the state[11].

The facility had remained defunct for many decades, fearing Naxal attacks in the thick forests. However, as the Naxal movement seemed to have declined, forest department recently renovated it.

Note from rebels

A note written in red ink, purportedly by Karimnagar-Khammam-Warangal party committee secretary Damodar said, the Telangana state government should stop taking away podulands of Adivasis, which are acquired in the name of development, end open-cast mining and stop arresting people leading the "people's movement".

SP (rural) AK Jha rushed to the spot to assess the situation. He told the daily the incident was investigated from all angles to determine whether it was an act by miscreants and disgruntled elements or was really carried out by the Maoist cadres. One version was that the attack could be the handiwork of the people who migrated from Chhattisgarh in the recent past. The forest officials were trying to evict them from the occupied forest lands. Those supporting them could have struck at the guest house.

Case registered

However, the SP said Maoist leader Damodar had been named as accused in the incident and cases under sections 147 and 436 of the IPC, read with sections 149 and sections 3 and 4 of the Prevention of Damage to Public Property (PDPP) Act, and section 13 of the Unlawful Activities (Prevention) Act, registered.

The incident created commotion among the people as it indicated that Naxalites were perhaps staging a come back after a lull of many years.

Down but not out

Even as the police and the Telangana government are trying to play down the presence of Naxalites in the state, the extremists have been trying to make their presence felt by resorting to periodic violence. The torching of the forest guest house and a jeep is an indication of their intent.

The sympathetic statements made by the Telangana Rashtra Samiti (TRS) before and after the general elections came in handy for the naxal leaders to bure the youth and the fence sitters. They embarked on a fresh recruitments drive in the newly formed Telangana state and succeeded to some extent at a time when the movement was thought to be waning due to intensified repression in neighboring Chhattisgarh, which was haven for extremists for many decades[12].

The Naxal movement was losing steam in Warangal district which was once the hot bed of Leftist insurgency, but it was never totally decimated as claimed by the authorities. While a section of the police officers point out that as many as 36 persons from Warangal have gone underground since the formation of the Telangana state, others claim that the number could be for the entire state.

Bihar

Jehanabad battles the bottle, not Maoist insurgency: 7 Oct 2015

In Aug 2015, seven girls belonging to Mahadalit families were raped in villages under Mukhdumpur Assembly constituency. Police recorded only four cases.

This was reported by a daily in its 7 Oct 2015 issue[13], Mukhdumpur is in Jehanabad district, once troubled by LWE. It is the home turf of former Bihar CM Jitan Ram Manjhi.

The NDA has blamed the Nitish Kumar government's liquor policy in the 2005 for the worsening law and order situation. Ironically the architect of this excise policy was former finance minister Sushil Kumar Modi. The policy had worked. Bihar's excise revenue jumped to a record Rs 2,765 crore in 2012-13 from Rs 535 crore in 2007-08.

While the BJP leaders are quiet on the liquor front, Manjhi's Hindustan Awam Mahaz (HAM) leaders have accussed Nitish Kumar of pushing rural people into excessive alcoholism, ruining scores of families and risking the lives of women. Chunnu Lal, HAM national committee secretary, said: "It is a deliberate attempts to incapacitate the dalits and mahadalits by making liquor easily available to them. Since Mahadalits support Manjhi, the police seem to be following nitish government's diktat not to listen to their please".

Jehanabad SP Aditya Kumar defended his men: "It is difficult to track the culprits since FIRs in all cases are against unknown persons. We have nevertheless made an arrest besides destroying many illegal hoochdens".

Bihar state women commission ex-chairperson Manju Prakash had criticized the government for promoting uncontrolled alcoholism, following which Nitish Kumar promised to ban liquor if his government retains power.

Maoists kill and get killed in Bihar: 31 Jan 2016

Interestingly, two incidents on maoist violence were reported in a daily in its issue of 31 Jan 2016.

Top Maoist killed in Bihar

A Special Area Committee (SAC) member of the CPI (Maoist) Chirag Das, with a Rs 30 lakh bounty on his head, was killed in a gun fight with security forces in jamui district on 29 Jan 2016. The body was recovered on the 30th along with a rifle, and two pistols.

Maoists shoot dead SI in Munger district on 30 Jan 2016

A police sub-inspector, Bhavesh Kumar, 42, was shot dead by Maoist cadres on 30 Jan 2016.[14]

Kumar was posted at the Dharahara police station in munger district. Munger (Sadar) SDPO Lalit Mohan Sharma said a police team led by SI Kumar was engaged in anti-Naxal operations on the 30th.

Reds blow up BDO office in Bihar kidnap 21 Rly workers: 16 Feb 2016

"On the first night of the 48-hour bandh called by the CPI (Maoist) in Bihar, the suspected rebels blew up the Barhat BDO office in Jamui and abducted two railway staff from Urain railway station".

The above was reported by a daily in its issue datelined Patna/Jamui/ Aurangabad of 16 Feb 2016[15].

The Bihar bandh was called protest the killing of Chirag Das alias Jodhan alias Ramchander Mahato, a member of Purvi Bihar Purvottar Jharkhand Special Area Committee and in charge of the outfits military wing, on 29 Jan 2016.

Besides, train movement between kiul and Jamalpur remained completely paralyzed for at least five hours from 14 Feb. midnight to 5 AM on the 15th, following kidnapping of two single men from Urain railway station. Superintendent railway police, Jamalpur, Umashankar Prasad said: "The railway staff were released after sometime with a warning that no train be allowed to run on this line [Kiul-Jamalpur section] until sunrise, or else be ready to face the consequences".

The Maoists had owned up the incident, said a CRPF official.

Odisha

Two tribals allegedly abducted by Maoists: 29 Feb 2016

Two Dongria tribal's of Kalyansinghpur police station area in Rayagada district are suspected to be abducted by maoists. At wee hours of 27 Feb. 2026, a major Maoist camp in Niyamgiri Hills region inhabited by Dongria tribal's in same police station area of Rayagada district had been busted by security forces. This Maoist camp existed on a hillock near Dangamati village. One Maoist had been killed in the exchange of fire which also led to seizure of large quantity of arms, ammunition explosives and other materials of Maoist use.[16]

The two missing Dongria tribals were residents of Dangamati village and the adjoining Khamberi which hints at their abduction by Naxalites who alleged them to be police informers. It is believed the abducted tribals were Shyam Sikaka and Ludu Wadeka hailing from Dangamati and Khambesi villages respectively.

Locals say Shyam was allegedly abducted from his home at Dangamati at wee hours by a group of persons suspected to be Maoists. Ludu was among the Dongria tribals who had gone to a hill top for annual 3-day worship of Niyamgiri hills that ended on the 28th. It is alleged that he was abducted while he was returning back after the worship.

Rayagada district police is yet to confirm these alleged abductions but investigation has been started with ample caution as these are chances that it may be part of some ambush plan of ultras.

Niyamgiri tribals oppose government move to hold fresh Gram Sabha: 9 Mar 2016

Insisting that the 2013 Gram Sabha decision denying Vedanta a chance to mine bauxite in Niyamgiri was still valid, Dongria Kondh tribals on 7 Mar 2016 said if the Odisha government did not back down from its idea of holding another Gram Sabha, it would lead to violence. "We Dongria Kondh tribals would never leave Niyamgiri.

If the government conspires to held another Gram Sabha, we would oppose it tooth and nail. If it leads to violence we are ready for it", said

Lado Sikaka president of Niyamgiri Suraksha Samiti, referring to the state government's petition in Supreme Court (SC) for holding a second Gram Sabha second time in Niyamgiri.[16]

In Apr 2013, a two-member SC bench while disposing of petition by Odisha mining corporation had ordered that the gram sabhas will take a final decision on whether mining would affect their religious, cultural or other rights or not.

The gram sabhas held in 12 villages in Niyamgiri in 2013 rejected the mining proposal, throwing a spanner in Vedanta plans of mining the hills.

Sikaka who along with other fellow Dongari Kondhs had come to Bhubaneswar to petition Governor SC Jamir against the state government move of holding a second gram sabhas, demanded that the government withdraw the petition immediately. "A public apology should be sent to all the 12 villages. The undemocratic attitude of approaching the SC for subvisiting the grassroots democracy should be rejected by the Governor", he said.

West Bengal

"Polls leave Bengal's Maoland cold": 15 Mar 2014

"Strange it may sound, but the ruling TMC which credits itself with bringing peace in Jangalmahal, the Maoist heartland of Bengal is fighting shy of campaigning in the area. And its bitter enemy, the CPI (M), is following its example, leaving the locals sorely perplexed", a daily reported the above in its issue of 15 Mar 2014[18].

The team of the daily, which covered large part of Midnapore district's Belpahari and Lalgarh could not spot a single wall graffiti in the name of Uma Saren, the TMC nominee in the Jhargram Lok Sabha seat.

Lalgarh was the cradle for the People's Committee Against Police atrocities (PCAPA or PCPA), the Maoist front that led the movement in 2008-10. But after coming to power in 2011, the Mamata Banerjee government dealt a body blow to the Maoists.

Of late, Jangalmahal has been an oasis of peace and the TMC has won high praise for its welfare projects and development work in the region. The party not only fared well in the last Assembly polls, but also had a near clean sweep in the 2013 panchayat elections.

Given the above positive scenario, why is the campaign this time a non-starter? The TMC district leaders conceded certain "organizational problems". The candidate, Uma Saren, a doctor, is a little known face and party sources disclosed a section of supporters, the TMC workers were not witting to campaign for her, citing her apparent lack of experience. The seniors are willing to wait. "There is enough time in hand. A meeting of the workers will be held next week, after which we will step up the campaign", said Nirmala Ghosh, working president of the local unit.

Quizzed on the CPM's inactivity, a party leader in Belpahari said: "we all know how the TMC is stepping up torture on our party leaders and cadres. But we are determined to mobilize campaign here".

Top Maoist leader arrested in Kolkata: 3 Apr 2016

The STF of Kolkata police arrested top Maoist leader Vikas alias Manasharam Henbram and his wife Tara alias Thakurmani Hembram at Kolkata on 2 Apr. 2016. Addressing the media, joint commissioner of police (STF) Vishal Garg said they were arrested near the Brigade Parade Ground under the Maiden police station in central Kolkata after receiving inputs from reliable sources.[19]

"Vikas is the state committee member of the Maoists as well as secretary of their state military commission. His wife Tara is the leader of their Salboni Squad. They were involved in several Maoist-related incidents, including those in Silda and goaltore" said Mr. Garg

24 paramilitary men were killed in a Maoist operation in Silda in Paschim Medinipur in 2010.

Change in Jangal Mahal, suddenly, new jobs and social mobility: 10 Apr 2016

Taralata Mahato, 25, draws awed whispers from women of Jhambeda village in West Midnapur Jhargram block as the only women from the village in police. Taralata lives in pucca two storey house with white washed walls and a huge cowshed a palatial home by Jhambeda's standards. Her family is among the more monied in the village. "My father and brother are in the West Bengal police service, so it was not difficult for me to get into the police when all women police station opened in 2012" says she. This was reported in 10 Apr 2016 daily[20].

Soon after Maoist leader Kishanji was killed by the police in 2011, West Bengal government Created 33,000 police jobs—including 300 post of women constables— in the Adivasi dominated Jangal Mahal districts of West Midnapore Bankura and Puruba. Three years on, an expanding Service class— a new rural middle class/is visible in the socio-economic profile of Jangalmahal but the benefits have been corned almost entirely by monied and socially powerful families like Taralata's.

"You get into these services only after paying local TMC bosses and police bribes ranging from thousands to lakhs, depending upon the posts", alleged a 28-year-old farmer who gave his name as Deb. "You should apply on if you have that kind of money", he says.

The new opportunities have seen many youths who had migrated to neighbouring states in search of jobs return. "I was a driver in Bhubneshwar since 2009. Three years ago a friend from Nedabohara, my village, told me that posts in civic police were open. I returned applied and got a job", said Manoj Mahato (30) a civic police volunteer in Jhargram. He says he makes Rs 200 a day.

Even as people return, a steady outmigration especially of agricultural labour and farmers, continues from the region that has seen poor rain for years now.

"Nearly 30 per cent of Jangalmahal populations has moved out to neighbouring districts for work. The Centre is not releasing funds for 100-day work scheme because the state has been misusing it", alleged Amiya Patra, CPM candidate from Taldangra

TMC leader Shivendra Bijay Malla Deb, however disagreed: "jobs in factories, contractual labour engaged in development work have all gone to villages and daily wages have also shot up since the left front days.[21]"

'Naxals have links in Philippines and Turkey: 27 April 2016

"The government said on 20 Apr 2016 that Naxals have close links with Maoist organisations in Philippines and Turkey and get support from several organisations in Europe".

This was reported in a daily on 27 Apr 2016.[22]

MOS for Home Kiren Rijiju said in the Lok Sabha on the 26th: "The CPI (Maoist) has close links with foreign Maoist organisations in Philippines, Turkey, etc. The outfit is also member of the Coordination Committee of Maoist Parties and Organisations of South Asia (CCOMPOSA)."

The Maoist parties of South Asian countries are members of this conglomerate Besides, LWE groups have participated in conferences/ seminars conducted in Belgium and Germany. Recovery of arms and ammunition of foreign origin from LWE in different countries is an indication of the fact that they are procuring weapons from different sources.

The minister further added:

- "The so-called: People's War, being waged by the CPI (Maoist)

against the Indian state has also drawn support from several Maoist fringe outfits located in Germany, France, Turkey, Italy etc.

- "Inputs indicate that some senior cadres of the communist party of Philippines imparted training to the cadres of CPI (maoist) in 2005 and 2011."

Notes

1. PNS, The Pioneer, 8 Jan 2013.
2. Amarnath tiwari, The hindu, 3 dec 2014.
3. B Vijay Murthy, Hindustan Times, 8 Oct 2015.
4. B Vijay Murty, Hindustan Times, 3 Mar 2016.
5. The Pioneer, 13 Jan 2016.
6. Omer Farooq, The Pioneer, 2 Mar 2016.
7. ENS Indian Express, 3 Mar 2016.
8. Gollapudi srinivasa Rao, The Hindu, 6 Mar 2016.
9. G. Narasimha Rao, The Hindu, 10 Apr 2016.
10. Rajulapudi Srinivas, The Hindu, 14 Apr 2016.
11. Goolaudi Srinivasa Rao, The Hindu, 17 Apr 2016.
12. Special Correspondent, *ibid.*
13. B Vijay Murty, Hindustan Times, 7 Oct 2015.
14. Times of India, 31 Jan 2016.
15. Kashi Prasad and Sayantanee Chaudhary, Times of India, 16 Feb 2016.
16. Staff Reporter, The Hindu, 20 Feb 2016.
17. Debabrata Mohanty, The Hindu, 9 March 2016.
18. Koushik Dutta, Hindustan Times, 15 Mar 2014.
19. Staff Reporter, The Hindu, 3 Apr 2016.
20. Sarah Hafeez, Indian express, 10 Apr 2016.
21. This series is being written under the aeges of the inclusive Media UNDP Fellowship, 2015.
22. TNS, Times of India, 27 Apr 2016.

Index

B

C

L

M

Q

R

S

V

W